סידור עבודת הלב
נוסח אשכנז

SIDDUR AVODAT HALEV
NUSAḤ ASHKENAZ

סידור עבודת הלב

איזו היא
עבודה
שבלב
הוי אומר
זו תפלה

THE RABBINICAL COUNCIL OF AMERICA

RABBI BASIL HERRING

Editor-in-Chief

RABBI LEONARD A. MATANKY

RABBI HESHIE BILLET

Associate Editors

THE RABBINICAL COUNCIL OF AMERICA

סידור

תפילות לחול, שבת, שלש רגלים, וימים מיוחדים
הלכות, תרגום, ביאורים ומאמרים נוספים על התפילה

Editor-in-Chief
Rabbi Basil Herring

Associate Editors
Rabbi Leonard A. Matanky
Rabbi Heshie Billet

Assistant Editors
Rabbi Arie Folger
Rabbi Aton Holzer
Rabbi Joshua Flug

Contributing Editor
Rabbi David Mescheloff

איזו היא
עבודה
שבלב
הוי אומר
זו תפלה

Weekday, Shabbat and Yom Tov prayers
including
laws and customs, special services,
additional texts, and explanatory essays.
With a new translation as well as commentary utilizing
classic as well as contemporary rabbinic and academic sources.

Nusaḥ Ashkenaz

The RCA Avodat HaLev Siddur
Nusaḥ Ashkenaz
Second Hebrew/English Edition, 2019

Distributed by The Toby Press Ltd.
POB 4044, Jerusalem 91040, ISRAEL
POB 8531, New Milford, CT 06776, USA

Printed in the PRC

Standard Size, Hardcover, ISBN 978 965 301 936 2

RCAA2

סידור עבודת הלב

IN MEMORY OF

Leslie Goldstein ז"ל
יהודה אריה ליב בן משה ז"ל

He lived with integrity, acted righteously and honestly.
He was compassionate, considerate, kindhearted, and constant.
He respected the faithful and kept his word consistently.
Generous with his time and resources,
the world he changed and the lives he influenced
are his living monument.
(Inspired by Psalms 15)

This Siddur is dedicated to the memory of Leslie Goldstein, loved husband, father, grandfather, leader, advisor and friend. Les was an honorable man of integrity and character, intelligence and wisdom, passion and compassion. From his modest beginnings in the Bronx, Les grew to be a man of stature and influence in the business and Jewish worlds. With his soft voice and mild manner he guided and influenced the Jewish community, the business community, the medical community, his family and friends. He was a proud Jew, heart and soul, and served in leadership capacities in local, national and international spheres.

Les and his wife and life-partner, Roslyn Goldstein, herself an inimitable powerhouse of compassion, leadership, and influence, established the Leslie and Roslyn Goldstein Foundation, through which they substantially advance the causes of medical research, Jewish agencies and synagogues, and health care and other philanthropic organizations.

TABLE OF CONTENTS

Prayer Thoughts and Tributes from the RCA President
xix

Preface
xxi

Editor's Introduction
xxiii

A Guide to Users
xxx

Declaration of the Uniqueness of God as the Essence of Prayer
R. JOSEPH B. SOLOVEITCHIK
XXXII

שער התפילה		SHA'AR HATEFILLA
שחרית לחול	2	*SHAHARIT* FOR WEEKDAYS
השכמת הבוקר	2	On Waking
טלית ותפילין	8	*Tallit* and *Tefillin*
הכנה לתפילה	16	Preparation for Prayer
ברכות השחר	20	Morning Blessings
קדיש דרבנן	52	The Rabbis' Kaddish
קדיש יתום	56	Mourner's Kaddish
פסוקי דזמרה	58	*Pesukei DeZimra*
ברכו	88	*Barekhu*
קריאת שמע	96	The *Shema*
עמידה	106	The *Amida*
וידוי	136	*Viduy*
אבינו מלכנו	138	*Avinu Malkenu*
סדר תחנון	144	*Taḥanun*
סדר קריאת התורה	158	Reading of the Torah
אשרי	172	*Ashrei*
עלינו	180	*Aleinu*
שיר של יום	184	The Daily Psalm
אמירות לאחר התפילה	202	Readings after the Service
בקשות אישיות	212	Personal Supplications

BERAKHOT	**216**	**ברכות**
Grace after Meals	216	ברכת המזון
The Traveler's Prayer	236	תפילת הדרך
Additional Blessings	240	ברכות נוספות
Blessings on *Mitzvot*	248	ברכות המצוות
***MINḤA* FOR WEEKDAYS**	**256**	**מנחה לחול**
***MA'ARIV* FOR WEEKDAYS**	**290**	**מעריב לחול**
Counting of the *Omer*	326	סדר ספירת העומר
The Bedtime *Shema*	338	קריאת שמע על המיטה
SHABBAT (AND YOM TOV)		**שבת (ויום טוב)**
Eiruvin	348	עירובין
Candle Lighting	350	הדלקת נרות
Teḥinot	350	תחינות
Welcoming Shabbat	360	קבלת שבת
Ma'ariv for Shabbat and Yom Tov	384	מעריב לשבת וליום טוב
Kiddush and *Zemirot* for Shabbat Evening	418	קידוש וזמירות לליל שבת
Shaharit for Shabbat and Yom Tov	444	שחרית לשבת וליום טוב
Pesukei DeZimra	446	פסוקי דזמרה
Nishmat	480	נשמת
Barekhu	488	ברכו
The *Shema*	498	קריאת שמע
The *Amida* for Shabbat	506	עמידה לשבת
Reading of the Torah	524	סדר קריאת התורה
Mi Sheberakh Prayers	534	מי שבירך
Prayer for the Welfare of the Government	554	תפילה לשלום המלכות
Prayer for the State of Israel	554	תפילה לשלום מדינת ישראל
Yizkor	1098	סדר הזכרת נשמות
Blessing the New Month	558	ברכת החודש
Kel Maleh Raḥamim	560	אל מלא רחמים
Musaf for Shabbat	568	מוסף לשבת
Kiddush and *Zemirot* for Shabbat Morning	610	קידוש וזמירות ליום שבת
Minḥa For Shabbat and Yom Tov	626	מנחה לשבת וליום טוב

תהלים למנחה של שבת	658	Psalms for Shabbat *Minḥa*
פרקי אבות	674	Ethics of the Fathers
סעודה שלישית	726	*Se'uda Shelishit*
מעריב למוצאי שבת	730	*Ma'ariv* for the Conclusion of Shabbat
קידוש לבנה	750	Sanctifying the New Moon
סדר הבדלה בבית	756	*Havdala* at Home
ראש חודש ויום טוב		**ROSH ḤODESH AND YOM TOV**
סדר נטילת לולב	764	Taking the Four Species
סדר הלל	766	*Hallel*
מוסף לראש חודש	780	*Musaf* for Rosh Ḥodesh
בדיקת וביעור חמץ	792	*Bedikat* and *Biur Ḥametz*
עירוב תבשילין	349	*Eiruv Tavshilin*
קידוש לליל יום טוב	794	*Kiddush* for Yom Tov Evening
תפילה כשנכנסין לסוכה אושפיזין	798	On Entering the Sukka and *Ushpizin*
תפילה כשיוצאין מן הסוכה	798	On Leaving the Sukka
ברח דודי ויום ליבשה	802	*Beraḥ Dodi* and *Yom LeYabasha*
עמידה לשחרית, מנחה ומעריב של יום טוב	810	*Amida* for *Shaḥarit, Minḥa* and *Ma'ariv* of Yom Tov
מוסף ליום טוב	828	*Musaf* for Yom Tov
ברכת כהנים	852	*Birkat Kohanim*
תפילת טל	862	Prayer for Dew
תפילת גשם	866	Prayer for Rain
אקדמות	872	*Akdamut*
הושענות לסוכות	880	*Hoshanot* for Sukkot
הקפות לשמחת תורה	920	*Hakafot* for Simḥat Torah
סדר הזכרת נשמות	1098	*Yizkor*
ימים נוראים		**YAMIM NORA'IM**
התרת נדרים	926	Release from Vows
קידוש לליל ראש השנה	930	*Kiddush* for Rosh HaShana Evening
סימנים לראש השנה	932	Symbolic Foods for Rosh HaShana
קידושא רבא לראש השנה	934	*Kiddush* for Rosh HaShana Day
סדר תשליך	936	*Tashlikh*
סדר כפרות	938	*Kapparot*
וידוי למנחה ערב יום הכיפורים	942	*Viduy* for *Minḥa* of *Erev* Yom Kippur
סדר הזכרת נשמות	1098	*Yizkor*

ḤANUKKA AND PURIM חנוכה ופורים

950 Ḥanukka חנוכה
954 Purim פורים

SELIḤOT סליחות

960 For the Tenth of Tevet לעשרה בטבת
974 For the Fast of Esther לתענית אסתר
986 For the Seventeenth of Tammuz לשבעה עשר בתמוז
1008 For the First Monday לשני קמא (בה"ב)
1013 For Thursday לחמישי (בה"ב)
1019 For the Second Monday לשני תנינא (בה"ב)

SHA'AR YISRAEL שער ישראל

1024 Remembrance Service for Holocaust Victims יום הזיכרון לחללי חורבן אירופה
1034 *Yom HaZikaron* for the Fallen of *Tzahal* יום הזיכרון לחללי צה"ל
1036 *Yom HaAtzma'ut* Service יום העצמאות
1046 *Yom Yerushalayim* Service יום ירושלים

SHA'AR HAḤAYYIM שער החיים

1048 Weddings and *Sheva Berakhot* נישואין ושבע ברכות
1058 Thanksgiving Prayer after Childbirth תפילת הודיה לאחר הלידה
1062 *Brit Mila* סדר ברית מילה
1074 *Pidyon HaBen* פדיון הבן
1076 On the Birth of a Daughter לידת בת
1080 Meal of Personal Thanksgiving סעודת הודיה
1080 Dedication of a New Home חנוכת הבית
1086 Prayers for the Sick תפילה לחולה
1088 Changing the Name שינוי השם
1092 The End of Life שכיב מרע
1096 Grace after Meals in a *Shiva* House ברכת המזון בבית האבל
1098 *Yizkor* סדר הזכרת נשמות

SHA'AR HAKERIA שער הקריאה

TORAH AND MEGILLA READINGS

1108 Mondays, Thursdays and Shabbat Minḥa לימי שני וחמישי ומנחה בשבת
1133 Rosh Ḥodesh, Fast Days לראש חודש, לתענית ציבור
1136 Ḥanukka and Purim חנוכה ופורים
1141 Pesaḥ, Shavuot, Sukkot לשלוש רגלים

Megillat Shir HaShirim	1168	מגילת שיר השירים
Megillat Rut	1170	מגילת רות
Megillat Eikha	1173	מגילת איכה
Megillat Kohelet	1176	מגילת קהלת
Megillat Esther	1183	מגילת אסתר

SHA'AR HATEHILLIM / שער התהלים

Reciting Psalms for Special Needs and Occasions	1190	אמירת תהלים לזמנים ולמאורעות מיוחדים
Prayers Prior to Reciting Psalms	1192	תפילה לפני אמירת תהלים
The Book of Psalms (with a complete English Translation)	1194	ספר תהלים
Prayers Following the Recital of Psalms	1328	תפילות לאחר אמירת תהלים
Additional Prayers	1336	תפילות נוספות
Yedid Nefesh (Alternate Text)	1342	ידיד נפש
Rabbis' Kaddish (Transliterated)	1344	קדיש דרבנן באותיות לועזיות
Mourner's Kaddish (Transliterated)	1345	קדיש יתום באותיות לועזיות
Table of Old and New Page Numbers for Key Prayers	1346	טבלת מספרי העמודים של התפילות בסידור הישן לעומת הסידור החדש

ESSAY SECTION

The Essay Section starts at the back with its own pagination ("E"), and proceeds from left to right.

SHA'AR YISRAEL

HISTORICAL AND HALAKHIC BACKGROUND

Commemorating the Holocaust: A Historical and Halakhic Review

R. JACOB J. SCHACTER

E7

Prayer on Israel's Days of Remembrance and Celebration

PROF. DAVID BERGER

E12

SHA'AR HAHALAKHA

Nusaḥ and *Nigunim* in *Tefilla*
R. GEDALIA DOV SCHWARTZ
E15

Lesser-Known Laws of Torah Reading
R. HERSHEL SCHACHTER
E17

Prayer and Interpersonal Halakha
R. DANIEL FELDMAN
E33

SHA'AR HAKAVANA

ON THE NATURE AND IMPORTANCE OF *KAVANA* IN PRAYER

Why Prayer Requires a Fixed Place and Fixed Texts
R. YECHIEL YAAKOV WEINBERG
E48

The Efficacy of Prayer
R. AHARON LICHTENSTEIN
E49

Fundamentals of Prayer
R. YEHUDAH AMITAL
E53

The Ultimate Goal of our Prayers
R. CHAIM YAAKOV GOLDVICHT
E64

Praying with *Kavana*: Hasidic Perspectives
R. NORMAN LAMM
E66

Berakhot – The Gateway to Prayer
R. PINCHAS PELI
E70

Understanding the Term *Tefilla*
R. HESHIE BILLET
E77

THE *KAVANA* OF SPECIFIC PRAYERS

The Correct *Kavana* When Reciting the *Shema* and Its Blessings According to R. Joseph B. Soloveitchik

R. *BASIL HERRING*

*E*80

The Shabbat Prayers as Explained by R. Joseph B. Soloveitchik

R. *ATON HOLZER*

*E*88

Introduction to *Yigdal* and the *Ani Ma'amin* Principles

PROF. DAVID SHATZ

*E*93

Sacrifices and Prayer: Past, Present, and Future

R. SHALOM CARMY

*E*95

Achieving *Kavana*: Praying from the Heart

RABBANIT ROOKIE BILLET

*E*97

A More Meaningful Prayer Experience

R. DAVID MESCHELOFF

*E*105

Prayer Thoughts and Tributes from the RCA President

Before the invention of the printing press and the mass production of siddurim, there was a concern that a person holding a precious and expensive siddur would be distracted from their prayers while holding this unique commodity and therefore wouldn't be permitted to pray with a prayer book (*Terumat HaDeshen* 17). The legal conclusion to this issue was that the siddur, like holding a *lulav* during *Tefilla* (Ritva, *Sukka* 41b), would not distract one from prayers but would serve as an instrument that would intensify one's focus and encounter with God.

A siddur today, though not a rare product, can still be a precious commodity in enhancing our prayer experience. The new RCA Siddur is a new and significant instrument in reinforcing our community's prayerful personalities, aligning ourselves with the classic *tefillot* of our *Mesora*, connecting us to the reality of *Medinat Yisrael*, and being inspired by articles from leading scholars of our community.

While the siddur is an important instrument for *tefilla*, it can and should be more. The Gemara (*Berakhot* 32b) describes how the pious ones would delay their exit from the synagogue for a period of contemplation, as stated in Psalms (140), "The upright will dwell in Your presence." In fact the Meiri (*Berakhot* 32b) explains that the addition of some of the *tefillot* following the *Amida* were for this specific purpose. As opposed to immediately exiting the synagogue after praying we evaluate the impact that the prayer service had on us. The Baḥ (*Oraḥ Ḥayyim* 133:1) suggests that this period of planned delay allows us to "fix in our hearts" what we accomplished during the service and, as importantly, sets the stage for our living with a sanctified existence when we leave the synagogue. This includes the respect that we must show to other people outside of our religious epicenters and our ethical behavior at our workplaces. The siddur is not only a means for prayer but it serves as a catalyst for our spiritual existence in our busy lives. This new Siddur will be such a tool and I am grateful to have played a role in its production and dissemination.

As you will see on almost every page of this Siddur, this work was a collaborative effort. R. Herring, the editor, has appropriately identified the leaders in the process of this production and R. Dratch has offered tribute to our generous donor. On a personal note, I offer gratitude to a few individuals who assisted me in the important concluding steps in the culmination of this Siddur. R. Leonard Matanky worked tirelessly to ensure the aesthetic and readable quality of this production and his standards of quality are present throughout this Siddur. R. Efrem Goldberg joined me in reviewing some important halakhic issues with Rav Hershel Schachter and I thank both for their dedication to the RCA. R. Matanky, R. Hershel Billet, and R. Goldberg played essential roles in bringing this project to fruition. I also thank all the Officers of the RCA for their leadership and support.

R. Shalom Baum

May 2017 / Iyar 5777

Preface

"ולעבדו בכל לבבכם" –
איזו היא עבודה שהיא בלב, הוי אומר זו תפילה
(תענית ב.)

In describing a Jew's obligation to pray, our sages of the Talmud point to a well-known phrase in the Torah: "To serve Him with all your heart" (Deut. 11:13). "What is *avoda shebalev* – the service of the heart?" they ask. "You must say it is prayer" (*Ta'anit* 2a).

For many, this Talmudic teaching leads to the conclusion that prayer is something that primarily demands an emotional investment as we serve God with our hearts. In the twenty-first century this has led many to focus on the music, the meditations, the motions, and the emotions of prayer. Yet, in the Torah the word "heart" means much more than that, for it also refers to the seat of knowledge and wisdom as we find in the phrase "a knowing heart" (Deut. 29:3).

As such, a real and comprehensive "service of the heart" requires one to be inspired not only by the sounds and rhythms of prayer, but also by the words and the meaning of prayer. We must both *shokel* and *shteig* in prayer, sing and study our *tefillot*.

It is for this reason that the Rabbinical Council of America is so proud to present our new siddur for the twenty-first century, Siddur Avodat HaLev. This Siddur includes all the traditional prayers in an accurate and attractive format, offering a new translation as well as prayers for life-cycle events and the modern observances of Yom HaShoah, Yom HaAtzma'ut and Yom Yerushalayim. But most importantly our Siddur Avodat HaLev presents a commentary that touches both the heart and the mind of a community as it stands before God and engages with His world.

In a lecture delivered at the 1963 Convention of the Rabbinical Council of America, the "Rav," R. Joseph B. Soloveitchik, **זצ"ל**, spoke of the famous dispute between Maimonides and Nahmanides regarding prayer. According to Maimonides, prayer is a biblical imperative, while Nahmanides maintains that prayer is a rabbinic imperative, and only rises to biblical imperative at times of crisis.

It was at that event that the Rav made the daring suggestion that Maimonides fundamentally agreed with Nahmanides. Maimonides, he posited, perceived humanity as living in a state of perpetual crisis, aware that without God one could not exist and fearful that one's connection to God would cease to exist. The Rav taught that only through prayer do we maintain our connection to God. Only through prayer can we achieve His mercy and the ability to live another day.

Is it any wonder then that our sages described prayer with the all-encompassing phrase of "*avoda shebalev* – the service of the heart"? Because prayer is at the center of our existence, and therefore we must use all our inner strengths, from our emotions to our intellect, to pray before the Almighty.

On behalf of the members of the Rabbinical Council of America and all those who will benefit from this Siddur, I extend sincere gratitude to R. Basil Herring, Editor-in-Chief of the RCA Press and this volume's editor. This project would never have seen the light of day without his energy, scholarship, and dedication. Our thanks are due to the siddur's most dedicated Associate Editor, R. Heshie Billet, to Assistant Editors, R. Arie Folger, R. Aton Holzer, and R. Joshua Flug, as well as the Contributing Editor, R. David Mescheloff. To RCA President R. Shalom Baum who tenaciously has guided the project to completion, to my predecessors R. Shmuel Goldin and R. Moshe Kletenik who initiated this project, to incoming RCA President R. Elazar Muskin who will shepherd this project forward, and to RCA Executive Vice President, R. Mark Dratch, whose wisdom has served us so well. May the prayers that emanate from this Siddur be a merit to your service of God and the Jewish people.

It is our sincere hope that this new RCA Siddur, its prayers, commentaries, essays, and insights will help us draw closer to God "*belevav shalem*," with a perfect and full heart dedicated to goodness, kindness, wisdom and the appreciation of God's creations great and small.

R. Leonard A. Matanky, Ph.D.
Honorary President, Rabbinical Council of America
May 2017 / Iyar 5777

Editor's Introduction

It has been thirty-four years since the widely used Rabbinical Council of America edition of the ArtScroll Siddur first saw the light of day. That siddur deservedly became a staple of the Orthodox community, both in its Hebrew-English and Hebrew-only formats, used in thousands of congregations and by hundreds of thousands of individuals over the course of a generation.

Much has changed since that siddur appeared in 1984. Firstly, the Orthodox community has been blessed with men and women of all ages who are committed to advanced Torah study as well as communal and personal prayer on a daily basis. For them it is important to have the benefit of ever-renewed and expanded perspectives on the words and ideas embedded in our prayer texts, beyond the familiar ones found in existing siddurim. Secondly, our communities include those who may have only a limited familiarity with the texts and protocols of the siddur, and who therefore desire a siddur that incorporates a translation and commentary that are lucid and accessible to those with limited Torah background or education. Thirdly, there has been a remarkable efflorescence over the past several decades of siddur commentaries, new perspectives on the Psalms, academic research on the history of siddur texts, and Torah literature in general, all of which have provided valuable insights into many traditional prayer texts. Fourthly, while it is certainly true that traditional prayer texts are timeless and for the most part unchanging, it is also true that the needs, sensitivities, and circumstances of the Jewish people and individuals are not static but dynamic. Hence, wherever possible and halakhically appropriate, a siddur should strive to reflect such changing realities.

This new RCA Siddur attempts to address these needs and realities. To this end, it incorporates the following features, among others:

TEFILLA TEXTS

- Tefilla texts sometimes vary from siddur to siddur, even within *Nusaḥ Ashkenaz*. This Siddur balances current sanctioned usage with historically and halakhically accurate variants as found in Siddur Tefillat Jeschurun (edited by R. Schlomo Hofmeister), and the Siddur Ezor Eliyahu, as well as related research by scholars in the field. In addition we have carefully reviewed the texts, including their punctuations, found in current widely used siddurim, with an eye to eliminating common occasional errors that have accrued over time.
- The current edition of this Siddur, with its English translation, is intended to be used primarily in Jewish communities outside of Israel. For this reason, we have omitted prayers, textual variants, Torah Readings, and halakhic instructions that are generally practiced only in Israel. God-willing, other future editions will reflect Israeli practice.
- This Siddur seeks to reflect a sensitivity to women's prayer experiences, providing appropriate female textual and grammatical formulations where needed (such as women's *Zimmun* or *Birkat HaGomel*). There are also additional texts intended to enhance women's prayer (such as candle-lighting *Teḥinot*).
- Given the centrality of so many psalms to both formal and informal prayer, the Siddur incorporates the entire book of Psalms, in Hebrew as well as in the English translation, at the back of the Siddur.
- Tefilla texts are provided for a range of special occasions, whether communal (such as Yom HaAtzma'ut or Holocaust Remembrance) or of a personal nature (such as when facing serious illness and death, or personal meals of thanksgiving).
- Correct formulations of texts commonly used by Leaders and *Gabba'im* are provided (such as for *Yizkor*, various *Misheberakh* formulations, as well as Prayers for Governments and their various leaders, male or female, and military personnel).

TRANSLATIONS

- Siddur translations commonly suffer from one of two diametrically opposed deficiencies. In their search to accurately translate the Hebrew or Aramaic texts, some siddurim employ a word-for-word approach that, while accurate, often does not reflect common English usage. Other siddurim, aiming to render the translation user-friendly or colloquially fashionable, misrepresent the precise intent or meaning of the Hebrew text. The translation found in this Siddur seeks to avoid both pitfalls by striking a careful balance between rendering the intent of the original Hebrew and Aramaic texts with the help of careful study and expert input, while also employing commonly used English words and sentence structures wherever possible. Notable exceptions occur in those parts of the Siddur that incorporate poetic structures, in which cases we have allowed ourselves to use more free-flowing poetic translations, some of them found in the RCA's Traditional Prayer Book for Sabbath and Festivals, published in 1960.

- Scriptural translations are largely based on the widely used 1917 JPS translation of the Bible. The exception is the book of Psalms, for which we have utilized the excellent Daat Mikra Koschitzky Hebrew-English edition of Psalms, published by Mosad HaRav Kook.

PRAYER INSTRUCTIONS

- Wherever needed, all prayer texts are preceded by carefully vetted halakhic directions. Here too, a balance has been sought: on the one hand to reflect current widespread practice in communities that identify with mainstream *Minhag Ashkenaz* whether in North America or elsewhere, but on the other hand to ensure that the Siddur follows only those practices that are approved by our halakhic authority.
- We have sought to place all prayer instructions on the same page that the prayers themselves occur, rather than burden the reader with having to turn to the back of the Siddur for halakhic instructions.

COMMENTARY

- The siddur is not just a repository of prayers. It is also an important vehicle for Torah study, reflecting and embodying ancient, medieval and modern Torah texts of many genres. The great teachers over the course of Jewish history have produced innumerable Torah insights based on the siddur, and conversely their insights on other Torah texts shed light on texts found in the siddur itself. From this perspective the siddur should be seen as an integral part of **תּוֹרָה שֶׁבְּעַל פֶּה** (the Oral Torah), worthy of serious study in its own right. We have thus sought to compile a commentary that incorporates, in summary form, a wide-ranging and (at least for the English-language reader) unprecedented range of rabbinic teachers and sources, spanning the generations, to enrich the prayer experience of every user, and stimulate further study. These selections cover the full gamut of rabbinic literature (including early *Midrash Halakha*, the Tannaitic literature, the Talmud Bavli and Yerushalmi, Kabbalistic literature, Geonic texts, a broad spectrum of comments by early medieval *Rishonim* and later *Aḥaronim* (both Ashkenazic and Sephardic in origin), as well as the thoughts and analyses of many great rabbinic leaders of recent generations, up to and including our own time.

- Among these, as would be expected of an RCA Siddur, pride of place is accorded to a selection of insights into the siddur by Maran HaGaon R. Joseph B. Soloveitchik, ז"ל, the leader and inspiration par excellence of the Rabbinical Council of America, and through it of the Jewish community at large.
- In parallel with such purely rabbinic sources, the commentary also incorporates valuable insights by numerous academic scholars, past and present, reflecting a variety of literary, historical, ethical, and philosophic methodologies and perspectives.
- In presenting our summaries of all this material we have sought wherever possible to keep them both brief and lucid, to avoid undue interruption or distraction from the main purpose of prayer, which, needless to say, is prayer addressed to God with understanding, intensity, and passion. For the same reason, and insofar as it is intended for use by both scholars and laymen, the commentary does not provide detailed source-references, but only the names of authors or their works.
- Thus, to avoid overwhelming the prayer text with excessive commentary on any given page, we have sometimes placed commentaries to repeated prayers at later points in the Siddur rather than concentrate them at the point of the prayer's first appearance. The reader is thus encouraged to read the commentary with such parallelisms in mind.
- Where the commentary or rubric refers to the Essay section the page references are preceded by E.

OTHER SUPPLEMENTARY MATERIAL

- Being mindful of the difficulties inherent in praying every day with *kavana* (concentration), we have included a variety of supplementary essays to facilitate such prayer. These include the following:
- The introduction of the Siddur includes a powerful, newly translated essay by R. Soloveitchik explaining the essential message and importance of the opening verses of the *Shema*.
- In the back of the Siddur there are a number of essays intended to help the user achieve *kavana*. Some are of a halakhic nature, others deal with philosophical or ethical dimensions of prayer, while yet others provide practical guidance in the search for ever more meaningful prayer experiences. The essays read from left to right and page references are preceded by E to denote the Essay section.

ACKNOWLEDGMENTS

Hundreds of people have contributed to the creation of this Siddur, both within and beyond the Rabbinical Council of America. Many of them are mentioned by name in the pages of the Siddur. There are, however, a number of individuals who deserve particular recognition for their contributions to one or another aspect of this multi-faceted endeavor. They include the following:

- R. Leonard Matanky provided crucial organizational leadership at every step of the way, while giving valuable input in carefully reviewing the finished product. R. Heshie Billet provided much-appreciated input and leadership, especially in the early stages of the Siddur. R. Aton Holzer MD and R. Arie Folger invested vast amounts of time in preparing many of the source materials used in the commentary. In particular R. Holzer demonstrated remarkable commitment, while sharing his extensive knowledge related to many aspects of siddur-commentary. The detailed halakhic instructions accompanying the prayer text were most ably written and coordinated by R. Joshua Flug. R. David Mescheloff was instrumental in formulating various texts used for tefillot to be used on special occasions.
- Time-consuming halakhic review and approval was provided by our eminent *posek* (halakhic authority) R. Hershel Schachter. In addition,

valuable halakhic guidance was provided by R. Gedalia Dov Schwartz and R. Mordechai Willig.

- Expert scholarly and academic guidance and counsel were provided by Professors David Berger (who graciously devoted countless hours to the project, reviewing much of the commentary with abiding care and expertise) and Shnayer Leiman. Other help was provided by Professors Alan Brill, Yaakov Elman ז"ל, Ephraim Kanarfogel, Devra Kay, Reuven Kimelman, Yosef Ofer, Jacob J. Schacter, Shai Secunda, Lawrence Schiffman, Bernard Septimus, Marc Shapiro, David Shatz, Richard Steiner, and Amram Tropper. Assistance in Bible Studies was provided by Rabbis Ronald Benun, Yoel Bin Nun, Shalom Carmy, Yitzchak Etshalom, Eric Levy, and Elchanan Samet.
- Reprint permissions were granted by:
  - Dr. Tovah Lichtenstein and Rabbanit Atarah Twersky, as well as R. Julius Berman, Esq., to utilize the introductory essay by R. Joseph B. Soloveitchik, as translated by Prof. David E. Fishman.
  - The family of R. Yehuda Amital, and Ktav Publishing, for his essay on prayer.
  - Mosad Harav Kook for the extensive use of the translation of the Psalms as found in the Daat Mikra Koschitzky Edition of Psalms.
  - The Cantorial Council of America to reprint the essay by R. Herschel Schachter that was originally published in the *Journal of Jewish Music and Liturgy* Vol 7 (1984–1985).
- Expert legal counsel was provided by Emanuel Adler, Esq.
- Others who graciously participated in a variety of ways include:
  - Commentary: Rabbis Avi Baumol, Micha Berger, Jack Bieler, Akiva Blum, Michael Broyde, Sol Cohen, Zvi Doron, Binyamin Ehrenkranz, Ephraim Goldstein, Shlomo Grafstein, Yaakov Hillel, Jacob Jaffe, Yechezkel Kaminsky ז"ל, Abraham Katz, Barry Kornblau, Doniel Kramer, Seth Mandel, Chaim Marder, Yaakov Nagen, Asher Oser, Yaron Raab Ed.D, Imanuel Ravad, Gidon Rothstein, Natan Slifkin, Avraham Steinberg, Elazar M. Teitz, Eliyahu Teitz, and Avraham Walfish.
  - Pastoral Care: Rabbis Moshe Abramowitz, Aaron Glatt MD, Doniel Kramer, Ira Kronenberg, Gary Lavit, Joseph Ozarowski, Bennet Rackman, Zev Schostak, and Charles Sheer.

- Thanks are also due to The Center for the Jewish Future at Yeshiva University, as well as Rabbis Elchanan Adler, Yaakov Leib Altein, Shlomo Appel, Hanan Balk, Cantor Bernard Beer, Gedalyah Berger, Ephraim Z. Buchwald, Rafi Cashman, Judah Dardik, Ephraim Epstein, Dov Fischer, Yossi Friedman, Cantor Sherwood Goffin, Jeffrey Goldman, Avrohom Gordimer, Shalom Aryeh Greenfield, Shmuel Jablon, Jacob Jaffe, Jay Kelman, Tzvi Klugerman, Lawrence Kobrin Esq., Maurice Lamm ז״ל, Yossi Posner, Fabian Schonfeld, Jonathan Schwartz, Chaim Strauchler, R. Abraham J. Twersky MD, Mark Weiner, Jeffrey Woolf, Michael Whitman, Reuven Ziegler, and Michoel Zylberman.
- The publication of this long-awaited Siddur is the fruit of a most felicitous partnership between the RCA and our publishers. In particular, it has been a delight and privilege to work with Matthew Miller, Rachel Meghnagi, Esther Be'er, Avishai Magence, Eliyahu Misgav, Yehudit Singer, Shlomo Peterseil, Yossi Pollak and Shari Fisch. I thank them for their expertise and patience in bringing the project to a successful conclusion.
- Four individuals were particularly helpful when it came to reviewing and providing corrections to the final text of the Siddur: Rabbis Reuven Bulka, Aton Holzer MD, Leonard Matanky, and Dr. Jordan Pollack. They each deserve special gratitude.
- *Aḥaron aḥaron ḥaviv*: without the unflagging encouragement, patience, and understanding of my dear wife Sherri, I could never have devoted the countless hours invested in this project over the course of multiple years since it was first envisaged. *Sheli veshelakhem, shela*.

The Torah teaches, and the Siddur text itself reflects, the principle that Divine providence can oft-times be seen only in hindsight. In that light, the many detours and delays on the path to publication of this Siddur, are testament to God's guiding hand in rendering the end result so much the better than it might otherwise have been. Hence we can assuredly declare **בָּרוּךְ אֵל הַהוֹדָאוֹת** (Blessed is the God of all thanksgiving,) in gratitude to Him on the occasion of its completion.

R. Basil Herring, Ph.D.
Editor
Shvat 5779 / February 2019

A Guide to Users

In the preparation of this Siddur, much care has been taken to facilitate correct prayer practices, the use of accurate Hebrew words and their pronunciations, as well as proper procedures by prayer leaders.

To this end users should take note of the following:

- When the name of God appears as יְ־הֹ־וָ־ה, it is pronounced as *ah-do-noy* (rhymes with "boy") for those who use Ashkenazic pronunciation, and *ah-do-nai* (rhymes with "tie") for those who use Sephardic pronunciation, in both cases with the emphasis on the final syllable. Those who are unable to recite the prayers in Hebrew should pronounce God's name in the original, as God's name does not have a perfect translation in other languages (R. Soloveitchik cited in *Nefesh HaRav* p. 118).
- Throughout the Siddur, whether in translations, instructions, or the commentary, references to "wine" also refer to grape juice, which according to many authorities is a suitable replacement for wine, especially for those who should not drink wine.
- Traditionally, Ashkenazi Jews did not recite prayers prior to performance of *mitzvot*. One simply recited the *berakha* and then performed the *mitzva*. In the eighteenth century, under Hasidic influence, some siddurim started to include various statements, including *LeShem Yiḥud*, to be recited before performing selected – but not all – *mitzvot* that are fulfilled during prayer. R. Yechezkel Landau (*Noda BeYehuda* Vol. I, *YD* no. 93) and other authorities, including at least one Hasidic one, opposed the recital of *LeShem Yiḥud* by the masses, for they would not understand its highly esoteric nature. Others, however, favored its recital. The matter has remained in dispute. In this Siddur we provide the text for those whose custom is to recite it. See pages 1336–1341.
- In the halakhic instructions, the abbreviations OḤ refers to Shulḥan Arukh Oraḥ Ḥayyim, while MB refers to the Mishna Berura.
- The following marks in the prayer texts are utilized to aid the user (and in some cases the prayer leader):
  - ▲ Upward arrow: indicates rising on the front of the feet

- ◂ Left arrow: indicates the starting point for the leader to recite aloud (on the Hebrew side)
- ▸ Right arrow: indicates the starting point for the leader to recite aloud (on the English side)
- ▸◂ Left and right arrows bracketing verses of Scripture: indicate verses that are said aloud by the congregation
- ▾ Downward arrow: indicates bowing

- Diacritical marks in the Hebrew text that facilitate correct pronunciation:
  - *Sheva na/sheva naḥ*: The *sheva na* (a pronounced vowel) is presented as a larger and bolder form of the *sheva naḥ* (an unpronounced vowel). See *nafshekha* (נַפְשְׁךָ).
  - *Kamatz katan/gadol*: The *kamatz katan* (an *oh* sound) is presented as a larger and bolder form of the *kamatz gadol* (an *ah* sound in Sepharadi pronunciation). See for example *ḥokhma* (חָכְמָה).
  - *Meteg*: Most Hebrew words are pronounced with a stress on the last syllable. For words where the stress is placed on the penultimate syllable, a short vertical line (the *meteg*) appears next to the vowel of that syllable. See for example *melekh* (מֶֽלֶךְ) – the stress is on the first syllable.

- Transliteration: Throughout the Siddur (prayer instructions, commentary) the transliteration of Hebrew words follows Modern Israeli Sepharadi pronunciation. We have transliterated the Hebrew ח with *Ḥ* or *ḥ*, and the כ with *kh*. The *sheva na* is represented by the letter *e* (for example, *Barekhu*), and the *tzere-yud* is represented by *ei* (for example, Tishrei). Whilst striving to maintain conventions we have found it necessary to compromise on consistency in favor of clarity and user-friendliness. For example, although we have generally omitted the *h* at the end of words with the suffix *kamatz-heh* (*havdala*, *kedusha*), we have retained it in words like "Torah" that are so widely recognized in the common spelling.

- We are aware that some who will use this Siddur have become accustomed over the years to finding (or announcing) key prayers with the help of familiar page numbers in the original RCA ArtScroll Siddur. While we were unable, for various reasons, to follow the same pagination, we have provided a table in the back of the Siddur listing corresponding page numbers for many such prayers as found in this Siddur. (See page 1346.)

Declaration of the Uniqueness of God as the Essence of Prayer

R. Joseph B. Soloveitchik

The following selection from the Rav's essay, "Di etish-moralishe zayt fun religyezer Yidishkeit" ("The Ethical-Moral Aspect of Religious Judaism"), was published in *Tog-Morgn Zhurnal*, January 3, 1955, p. 5, and was included in Joseph B. Soloveitchik, *Droshes un Ksovim/Yiddish Drashos and Writings*, ed. David E. Fishman, Toras Horav Foundation/Ktav Publishing, 2009, pp. 301–305. It was translated from Yiddish for this Siddur by Prof. David E. Fishman.

Prayer is intimately tied to the recitation of *Keriat Shema* (the recitation of the *Shema*). During *Shaḥarit* and *Ma'ariv*, Jews are obligated to recite *Keriat Shema* with its blessings that precede it and follow it, and immediately afterwards recite the *Amida*. The unified recitation of the *Shema* and the *Amida* is called in halakhic terminology *"semikhat geula letefilla"* (to join the blessing for redemption, *ga'al Yisrael*, which follows *Keriat Shema*, to the prayer, that is, to the *Amida*). We also know that the central theme of *Keriat Shema* and its blessings, is the declaration of the uniqueness of God, which is expressed in the first verse, "Hear, O Israel, the Lord is our God, the Lord is One."

The conclusion that one must draw from these two facts is quite simple: that the idea of the uniqueness of God is also a central theme in the prayer, in the *Amida*. The *Amida* is directly attached to *Keriat Shema* because they have something in common: the declaration of the uniqueness of God. Consequently, *halakha* required that they be melded into a single religious act.

What is declaration of the uniqueness of God? What is the message of the verse "*Shema Yisrael*" which became the motto of our faith, the definition of that which is unique and remarkable in Judaism? If we understand "*Shema Yisrael*" and the principle of the unity of God, then we will be able to fathom the content and essence of prayer.

Declaration of the uniqueness of God signifies, first of all, faith in the existence of God, blessed be He, as the only enduring living being, the Creator and Guide of the universe. Maimonides formulated the principle of the uniqueness of God at the very beginning of his *Mishneh Torah*:

> "The basic principle of all basic principles and the pillar of all sciences is to realize that there is a First Being Who brought every existing thing into being. All existing things, whether celestial, terrestrial or belonging to an intermediate class, exist only through His true existence… This Being is the God of the universe, the Lord of all the earth… This God is one and not two." [*Mishneh Torah, Hil. Yesodei HaTorah*, Chapter 1, *halakhot* 1, 5, and 7]

A Jew must believe, and also strive to understand and feel with all his soul, that all natural phenomena, both non-organic and organic, are realizations of the First Will, the will of the Creator. His infinite, all-powerful, and eternal First Will is manifested in the mathematical regularity and necessity that rules everywhere, and which we call the law of nature. When light flows, the wind blows, the sea storms, the rivers run, the birds fly, the insects buzz, the trees bloom and fade, blood circulates, the nervous system functions, the planets rotate, stars explode in the most distant corners of the universe, and so on and so forth – in all these wondrous natural processes the word of God resonates, the word which once split the unformed void, and brought into being a well-ordered, strictly arranged world: the word "*Yehi* – Let there be." This "One" rules in everything, over everything, and through everything. He poured His will into inanimate, vegetative, and animate beings, all of which carry out His command "*Yehi*" blindly and mechanically.

But the same Divine Will is also active in Man's spiritual personality, in his conscience and moral consciousness, in his longing for splendor and beauty, in his dreams of sanctity and of a loftier and better world. The First Will, which expresses itself in such everyday mechanical phenomena as the ebb and flow of the ocean waters, also reveals itself to Man in his moments of ethical elevation, and torments him in his hours of ethical descent. The *"Yehi"* of creation and the *"Anokhi"* ("I am the Lord your God") of Sinai are revelations of the same infinite Will.

When a Jew knocks on the gates of heaven during the fall daybreak *Seliḥot* prayers, or during the mysteriously holy and grace-enveloped night of *Kol Nidrei*, he is proclaiming, first of all, his belief in the uniqueness of God – the uniqueness of His Will in the cosmic-natural and spiritual-ethical realms. The congregation lovingly rustles, and the cantor festively proclaims:

> The heavens are Yours; the earth, too, is Yours. The world and the fullness thereof, You have founded them. You set all the borders of the earth. You made summer and winter. You tore the sea with Your strength. You broke the heads of the sea monsters in the waters… You split open springs and streams… You rule over the swelling of the sea. When its waves rise up, You still them.[1]

The *Seliḥot* Jew looks through the window, and sees the eastern sky gradually brightening and lighting up with the red flames of the rising sun; he sees the landscape flooded with purple and gold colors. The *Kol Nidrei* Jew looks through the window into the darkness of a holy evening, and sees the moon pour pale light onto the trees of the synagogue, which have been shaking for so many years along with the Jews in prayer. He sees the moon weave a silver web over the houses and gardens that are resting on this "Sabbath of Sabbaths." The Jew, at the daybreak of *Seliḥot* or in the nightfall of *Kol Nidrei*, thinks to himself: these rays of golden sunlight and of silver moonlight fulfill the same Will that I and all Jews seek to fulfill – the Will of the Infinite One, which seethes and rages inside each one of us. And he begins to declare fervently:

> *Lekhu neranena* – Come, let us sing to the Lord, let us shout joyfully to the Rock of our salvation… Righteousness and judgment are the base of Your throne. Loving-kindness and truth go before You. We kept sweet company together. We walked in the house of God in the crowd.[2]

1 From the first seliḥa of the Seliḥot service, citing Psalms 89:12, 74:17, 74:13, 74:15, 89:10 (ed.).
2 From the same seliḥa prayer (ed.).

The emphasis in these words is on "You": "Your throne," "Your strength," "Yours." There is only You, eternally You, everywhere You – You reveal Yourself in all natural phenomena and in all human aspirations. Only after the declaration of the uniqueness of the First Will in the world of nature and in the human personality does the Jew begin to recite the *Seliḥot*, the thirteen divine attributes, the *viduy*-confession, and begin to request and cling to the Creator of the universe.

The blessings of *Keriat Shema* and the *Amida* express this theme clearly and explicitly. What is the essence of the blessing "*Yotzer or* – Who forms light," if not the exquisite poem "Bless O Lord, O my soul. O Lord, my God, You are very great" (Ps. 104:1), if not amazement with God's revelation in nature, with its minutely small and infinitely large dimensions – "How great are Your works, O Lord! You have made them all in wisdom" (Ps. 104:24) – and with His revelation in the ethical-moral universal order. "*Zore'a tzedakot* – Sowing victory and reaping triumph. He creates healing."[1] What does the blessing of *gevurot* in the *Amida* mean? It declares the fact that His will is engraved in stone and in metal, in the animals and insects, in rays of light and in the blossoming rose, "You are eternally mighty, my Master." And at the same time, His will is embedded in ethical conscience and command: "*Mekhalkel ḥayyim beḥesed* – Sustaining the living with loving-kindness… You uphold the falling, You heal the sick, You free the bound."

Yes, *Keriat Shema* and the *Amida* are based on the ancient Jewish article of faith that being honorable and living in accordance with moral precepts is just as natural and simple as it is for the cherry tree to be covered with blossoms in the springtime, as it is for a bird to jump from one tree branch to another. His will was crystallized in both nature's mechanical blossoming impulse, and in man's conscious quest for the good and elevated.

But declaration of the Uniqueness of God, both in its positive expression, faith in the Uniqueness of His will, and in its negative expression, the prohibition against idolatry, consists of more than just a positive commandment: "*Anokhi* – I am the Lord Your God," or a negative commandment: "*Lo yihiye* – You shall have no other gods." It is more than a subjective faith in a theoretical-philosophical view of nature and man. Proclamation of the uniqueness of God

1 From the blessing that precedes the *Shema*: "*Yotzer hameorot*" (ed.).

consists of a practical program, a *Shulḥan Arukh*, which embraces all aspects of our life, both in the private-intimate sphere and in the social-public sphere. If only modern man, both Jew and non-Jew, apprehended this extremely beneficial world-view, he would spare himself many of his anxieties and neuroses.

Declaring the uniqueness of God requires that one approach all phenomena, objects, and persons, as being of relative value, that one assess them only from a social-historical perspective. They are not absolute, eternal, or totally true. Only One is absolute, eternal, uninfluenced by other forces, totally true, just, and kind. Only One is first and last, the source and the purpose – and that One is God, the Master of the universe. Everything else is temporary and fleeting. Regardless of how long an object has existed – it is insignificant and worthless compared to Him. If a Jew fails to understand this principle, and his enthusiasm and admiration lead him to exaggerate the worth of a created object, he is an idolater. Even if that Jew recites Rambam's thirteen articles of faith daily, studies the *Zohar* and observes both light *mitzvot* and stringent ones equally – as long as he puts all of his faith in a created object, and professes total loyalty to it, loyalty which should be given only to the Creator , he violates "*Anokhi* – I am the Lord Your God," and "*Lo yihiye lekha* – You shall have no other gods before Me."

סידור עבודת הלב

SIDDUR AVODAT HALEV

שחרית

The following order of prayers and blessings, which departs from that of most prayer books, is based on the consensus of recent halakhic authorities.

השכמת הבוקר

On waking, our first thought should be that we are in the presence of God. Since we are forbidden to speak God's name until we have washed our hands, the following prayer is said, which, without mentioning God's name, acknowledges His presence and gives thanks for a new day and for the gift of life.

מוֹדֶה /*women* מוֹדָה/ אֲנִי לְפָנֶיךָ מֶלֶךְ חַי וְקַיָּם, שֶׁהֶחֱזַרְתָּ בִּי נִשְׁמָתִי בְּחֶמְלָה, רַבָּה אֱמוּנָתֶךָ.

בָּרוּךְ אַתָּה יהוה אֱלֹהֵינוּ מֶלֶךְ הָעוֹלָם, אֲשֶׁר קִדְּשָׁנוּ בְּמִצְוֹתָיו וְצִוָּנוּ עַל נְטִילַת יָדָיִם.

בָּרוּךְ אַתָּה יהוה אֱלֹהֵינוּ מֶלֶךְ הָעוֹלָם, אֲשֶׁר יָצַר אֶת הָאָדָם בְּחָכְמָה, וּבָרָא בוֹ נְקָבִים נְקָבִים, חֲלוּלִים חֲלוּלִים. גָּלוּי וְיָדוּעַ לִפְנֵי כִסֵּא כְבוֹדֶךָ, שֶׁאִם יִפָּתֵחַ אֶחָד מֵהֶם אוֹ יִסָּתֵם אֶחָד מֵהֶם, אִי אֶפְשָׁר לְהִתְקַיֵּם וְלַעֲמֹד לְפָנֶיךָ. בָּרוּךְ אַתָּה יהוה, רוֹפֵא כָל בָּשָׂר וּמַפְלִיא לַעֲשׂוֹת.

הַשְׁכָּמַת הַבֹּקֶר / UPON ARISING

מוֹדֶה אֲנִי לְפָנֶיךָ – *I thank You.* Our very first act upon awakening is to thank God for restoring our faculties. The key words, רַבָּה אֱמוּנָתֶךָ, "You are abundantly faithful," stem from Lamentations 3:23: "Surely God's mercies are not consumed, surely His compassions fail not; they are new every morning; great is Your faithfulness." In this verse, the individual's awakening is cast as a metaphor for the future renewal of the Jewish nation.

THE LURIANIC PARADIGM FOR THE MORNING SERVICE

Lurianic Kabbalists (those who follow *Arizal*) ascribe a mystical dimension to the four stages in the morning prayers: the *Korbanot* (sacrifices), *Pesukei DeZimra* (Psalms of Praise), the *Shema* with its blessings, and the *Amida*. These stages reflect the four realms of divine creation that bring about the physical world we encounter each morning: *asiya* ("completion" which is the lowest realm of divine emanation), *yetzira* ("formation"), *beria* ("creation"), and *atzilut* ("emanation"), respectively.

בִּרְכוֹת הַשַּׁחַר / MORNING BLESSINGS

עַל נְטִילַת יָדָיִם – *To wash our hands.* The washing of the hands upon awakening is patterned after the requirement for a *Kohen* to wash his hands and feet prior to performing the Temple service. So too, as members of a "kingdom of

SHAḤARIT

The following order of prayers and blessings, which departs from that of most prayer books, is based on the consensus of recent halakhic authorities.

ON WAKING

On waking, our first thought should be that we are in the presence of God. Since we are forbidden to speak God's name until we have washed our hands, the following prayer is said, which, without mentioning God's name, acknowledges His presence and gives thanks for a new day and for the gift of life.

מוֹדֶה I THANK YOU, living and eternal King, for You have restored to me my soul in compassion. You are abundantly faithful.

בָּרוּךְ BLESSED ARE YOU, Lord, our God, King of the universe, Who has sanctified us with His commandments and commanded us to wash our hands.

בָּרוּךְ BLESSED ARE YOU, Lord, our God, King of the universe, Who in Your wisdom have formed man with a body made up of countless channels and conduits. It is revealed and known before the throne of Your glory that if these are torn or obstructed we would be unable to survive and stand before You. Blessed are You, Lord, Who heals all flesh and works miracles.

---

priests and holy nation" (Ex. 19:6), we wash our hands upon arising in preparation for serving God throughout the day (R. Shlomo Ganzfried).

אֲשֶׁר יָצַר אֶת הָאָדָם בְּחָכְמָה – *Who in Your wisdom have formed man.* Divine wisdom is manifest in the anatomy and physiology of the human body. For many Jewish thinkers of the Middle Ages, studying the human body was a source of profound faith, reflecting the biblical phrase, "from my flesh I behold God" (Job 19:26).

רוֹפֵא כָל בָּשָׂר – *Who heals all flesh.* God is "the healer of all flesh" not only in that He restores us to good health, but even more fundamentally in that He maintains our bodies in good health in the first place through "wondrous

NETILLAT YADAYIM

Before the *Shaḥarit* prayer, one washes one's hands and recites the *berakha* of *Al netillat yadayim*. Ideally, one should wash one's hands when one wakes up and then again immediately before prayers and recite the *berakha* after the second time one washes (*MB* 6:9). Regardless of whether one washes once or twice, the *berakha* should only be recited immediately after washing one's hands, not later when one is reciting the other morning blessings (*OC* 6:2 and *MB* 6:9).

אֱלֹהַי, נְשָׁמָה שֶׁנָּתַתָּ בִּי טְהוֹרָה הִיא. אַתָּה בְרָאתָהּ, אַתָּה יְצַרְתָּהּ, אַתָּה נְפַחְתָּהּ בִּי, וְאַתָּה מְשַׁמְּרָהּ בְּקִרְבִּי, וְאַתָּה עָתִיד לִטְּלָהּ מִמֶּנִּי, וּלְהַחֲזִירָהּ בִּי לֶעָתִיד לָבוֹא. כָּל זְמַן שֶׁהַנְּשָׁמָה בְקִרְבִּי, מוֹדֶה/*women* מוֹדָה/ אֲנִי לְפָנֶיךָ, יהוה אֱלֹהַי וֵאלֹהֵי אֲבוֹתַי, רִבּוֹן כָּל הַמַּעֲשִׂים, אֲדוֹן כָּל הַנְּשָׁמוֹת. בָּרוּךְ אַתָּה יהוה, הַמַּחֲזִיר נְשָׁמוֹת לִפְגָרִים מֵתִים.

לבישת ציצית

The following blessing is said before putting on a טלית קטן.

בָּרוּךְ אַתָּה יהוה אֱלֹהֵינוּ מֶלֶךְ הָעוֹלָם, אֲשֶׁר קִדְּשָׁנוּ בְּמִצְוֹתָיו וְצִוָּנוּ עַל מִצְוַת צִיצִית.

After putting on the טלית קטן*, say:*

יְהִי רָצוֹן מִלְּפָנֶיךָ, יהוה אֱלֹהַי וֵאלֹהֵי אֲבוֹתַי, שֶׁתְּהֵא חֲשׁוּבָה מִצְוַת צִיצִית לְפָנֶיךָ, כְּאִלּוּ קִיַּמְתִּיהָ בְּכָל פְּרָטֶיהָ וְדִקְדּוּקֶיהָ וְכַוָּנוֹתֶיהָ, וְתַרְיַ״ג מִצְוֹת הַתְּלוּיוֹת בָּהּ, אָמֵן סֶלָה.

---

actions" that allow our bodies to function in all of their complexity. In this respect He is the ultimate רוֹפֵא (physician) Who, by forming our bodies in the way that He does, minimizes sickness and disease in the first place (R. Basil Herring).

אֱלֹהַי נְשָׁמָה – *My God, the soul.* Unlike most *berakhot* that express gratitude for God's kindness in the present, this one also relates to both past and present, affirming that from the beginning of Creation God has created pure and holy souls for mankind. This affirms the Jewish belief that we are created without sin. We reject any notion that the soul may be tainted at birth because of the sins of Adam and Eve (R. Samson Raphael Hirsch).

It is preferable that this *berakha* follow immediately after the *Asher Yatzar berakha*, for such proximity eliminates the need for opening the *berakha* with the usual "Blessed are You" formulation (*Baḥ, Magen Avraham*). Furthermore, when we start out every day by reciting these two *berakhot* in this order we affirm that both body and soul were created and are sustained by God; that throughout the day we must act to care not just for our physical well-being but for our spiritual health as well.

בְּרָאתָהּ...יְצַרְתָּהּ...נְפַחְתָּהּ – *Created it... formed it... breathed it.* These three repetitive phrases allude to the three facets of the human spirit: *nefesh*, *ru'aḥ*, and *neshama*, that God has bestowed upon man (R. Yaakov Emden).

הַמַּחֲזִיר נְשָׁמוֹת לִפְגָרִים מֵתִים – *Who restores souls to the dead.* There are two interpretations of this phrase: Abudarham understands it to refer to the restoration of the soul upon awakening from sleep, while Ri ben Yakar takes

אֱלֹהַי MY GOD, the soul with which You have endowed me is pure. You created it. You formed it. You breathed it into me. You preserve it within me, and in due course You will reclaim it, and then will restore it to me in the life-to-come. So long as there is a soul within me, I will express my gratitude to You, Lord my God and God of my fathers, Ruler of all creation, Master of all souls. Blessed are You, Lord, Who restores souls to the dead.

TZITZIT

The following blessing is said before putting on tzitzit.

בָּרוּךְ BLESSED ARE YOU, Lord, our God, King of the universe, Who has sanctified us with His commandments and commanded us regarding the commandment of *tzitzit.*

After putting on tzitzit, say:

May it be Your will, Lord my God and God of my fathers, that the commandment of *tzitzit* be considered before You as if I had fulfilled it in all its specifics, details and intentions, as well as the six hundred and thirteen commandments dependent on it, Amen, Selah.

---

it to refer to the future Resurrection of the Dead.

לְבִישַׁת צִיצִית / PUTTING ON *TZITZIT*
Although strictly speaking one should recite the appropriate blessings when putting on each of the two garments, the prevalent custom for those who will wear a *tallit* during prayer is to omit the first blessing over the *tzitzit*, and keep in mind that the blessing לְהִתְעַטֵּף בַּצִּיצִת (to wrap ourselves in *tzitzit)* recited over the *tallit*, should apply to both garments. Since *tzitzit* need not be worn at night, the commandment of *tzitzit* (Num. 15:38) is classified as a time-bound positive commandment and as such is not required of women. Wearing a four-cornered garment without valid *tzitzit* is a transgression of a positive commandment; thus it is important to check that the *tzitzit* are in fact kosher prior to wearing them.

TALLIT KATAN
One who is going to wear a *tallit gadol* should not recite a *berakha* on the *tallit katan*. Rather, he should have in mind that the *berakha* on the *tallit gadol* covers the *tallit katan* (*MB* 8:24).

Before reciting the *berakha* on the *tallit katan*, one should check the *tzitzit* for any ripped strings (*OH* 8:9). The *berakha* should be recited while holding the (unfolded) *tallit katan* to ensure that the placement of the *tallit katan* takes place immediately after reciting the *berakha* (*MB* 8:2).

ברכות התורה

בָּרוּךְ אַתָּה יהוה אֱלֹהֵינוּ מֶלֶךְ הָעוֹלָם, אֲשֶׁר קִדְּשָׁנוּ בְּמִצְוֹתָיו,
וְצִוָּנוּ לַעֲסֹק בְּדִבְרֵי תוֹרָה.

וְהַעֲרֶב נָא יהוה אֱלֹהֵינוּ אֶת דִּבְרֵי תוֹרָתְךָ בְּפִינוּ וּבְפִי עַמְּךָ בֵּית
יִשְׂרָאֵל, וְנִהְיֶה אֲנַחְנוּ וְצֶאֱצָאֵינוּ (וְצֶאֱצָאֵי צֶאֱצָאֵינוּ), וְצֶאֱצָאֵי
עַמְּךָ בֵּית יִשְׂרָאֵל, כֻּלָּנוּ יוֹדְעֵי שְׁמֶךָ וְלוֹמְדֵי תוֹרָתְךָ לִשְׁמָהּ. בָּרוּךְ
אַתָּה יהוה, הַמְלַמֵּד תּוֹרָה לְעַמּוֹ יִשְׂרָאֵל.

בָּרוּךְ אַתָּה יהוה אֱלֹהֵינוּ מֶלֶךְ הָעוֹלָם, אֲשֶׁר בָּחַר בָּנוּ מִכָּל
הָעַמִּים, וְנָתַן לָנוּ אֶת תּוֹרָתוֹ. בָּרוּךְ אַתָּה יהוה, נוֹתֵן הַתּוֹרָה.

במדבר ו **יְבָרֶכְךָ** יהוה וְיִשְׁמְרֶךָ: יָאֵר יהוה פָּנָיו אֵלֶיךָ וִיחֻנֶּךָּ: יִשָּׂא יהוה
פָּנָיו אֵלֶיךָ וְיָשֵׂם לְךָ שָׁלוֹם:

משנה, פאה א:א **אֵלּוּ** דְבָרִים שֶׁאֵין לָהֶם שִׁעוּר, הַפֵּאָה וְהַבִּכּוּרִים וְהָרֵאָיוֹן, וּגְמִילוּת
חֲסָדִים וְתַלְמוּד תּוֹרָה.

בִּרְכוֹת הַתּוֹרָה / BLESSINGS OF THE TORAH
There are various views regarding these three *berakhot* over the Torah. R. Yona correlates them (in reverse order) with the ensuing quotations from (1) the Torah that deal with the sacrifices, (2) the Mishna – אֵיזֶהוּ מְקוֹמָן – that elaborates on details of the sacrifices, and (3) the *Midrash Halakha* – ר׳ יִשְׁמָעֵאל אוֹמֵר – that lays out the rules of interpretation. Hence there are three separate *berakhot*. R. Yaakov ben Asher (Tur), however, considers the second *berakha* to be a continuation of the first.

The study of Torah has two aspects. The first fulfills our obligation to study Torah and master its wisdom to the best of one's ability. The second is to be spiritually enriched by its study. This *berakha* in its two parts reflects these facets: (a) לַעֲסֹק בְּדִבְרֵי תוֹרָה (to be occupied in the words of the Torah), and (b) וְהַעֲרֶב נָא (may we experience the sweetness of the words of Torah). The first refers to the study of Torah per se. The second refers to the impact of that study on us: that through it we hope to be uplifted, purified, and worthy

BIRKHOT HATORAH
It is prohibited to study or recite words of Torah before one recites these blessings (*OḤ* 47:2). Therefore, it is preferable to recite *Birkhot HaTorah* before putting on one's *tallit* and *tefillin* because one recites verses of the Torah upon putting on *tallit* and *tefillin* (R. Hershel Schachter).

BLESSINGS OVER THE TORAH

בָּרוּךְ BLESSED ARE YOU, Lord, our God, King of the universe, Who has sanctified us with His commandments and ordered us to study Torah diligently.

Lord our God, make the teachings of the Torah pleasant on our lips and on the lips of all Your people, the house of Israel. Enable us, and our children and our children's children, to know Your name and to learn Your Torah for its own sake. Blessed are You, Lord, Who teaches Torah to His people Israel.

בָּרוּךְ BLESSED ARE YOU, Lord, our God, King of the universe, Who has chosen us from among all the other peoples and has given us His Torah. Blessed are You, Lord, Giver of the Torah.

Num. 6 יְבָרֶכְךָ MAY THE LORD bless you and keep you. May the Lord make His countenance shine upon you and be gracious to you. May the Lord lift up His countenance toward you and grant you peace.

Mishna Pe'ah 1:1 אֵלּוּ THESE OBLIGATIONS are unlimited: the corner of the field to be gathered by the poor, the gift of the first fruits, the pilgrimage offering, acts of mercy, and Torah study.

---

of bearing the name of God in the world (R. Joseph B. Soloveitchik).

לִשְׁמָהּ – *For its own sake.* May we study Torah for its own sake – for no other reason than to know it and become imbued with its wisdom (R. Ḥayyim of Volozhin). A different approach understands לִשְׁמָהּ as requiring study "for God's sake," i.e., to come ever closer to clinging to God, by uniting with His thought (R. Shneuer Zalman of Liadi).

הַמְלַמֵּד תּוֹרָה לְעַמּוֹ יִשְׂרָאֵל – *Who teaches Torah to His people Israel.* Every teacher of Torah should be proud to be called a *melamed*, as God Himself is so described in this *berakha* (R. Joseph B. Soloveitchik).

SELECTIONS FROM THE WRITTEN AND ORAL TORAH

Whether we view the *Birkhot HaTorah* as *birkhot hamitzva* or as thanking God for the Torah per se, it is appropriate to demonstrate our sincere commitment to the Torah by immediately engaging in its study. To this end, there follow selections from the Torah (Num. 6:24–26), the Mishna (*Pe'ah* 1:1), and the Gemara (*Shabbat* 127a).

אֵלּוּ דְבָרִים – *These obligations.* Most of these commandments have neither a minimum nor a maximum measure (Yerushalmi). *Pe'ah* (leaving a corner of the field for the poor) does have a rabbinically prescribed

שבת קכז. **אֵלּוּ** דְבָרִים שֶׁאָדָם אוֹכֵל פֵּרוֹתֵיהֶם בָּעוֹלָם הַזֶּה, וְהַקֶּרֶן קַיֶּמֶת לוֹ לָעוֹלָם הַבָּא, וְאֵלּוּ הֵן, כִּבּוּד אָב וָאֵם, וּגְמִילוּת חֲסָדִים, וְהַשְׁכָּמַת בֵּית הַמִּדְרָשׁ שַׁחֲרִית וְעַרְבִית, וְהַכְנָסַת אוֹרְחִים, וּבִקּוּר חוֹלִים, וְהַכְנָסַת כַּלָּה, וּלְוָיַת הַמֵּת, וְעִיּוּן תְּפִלָּה, וַהֲבָאַת שָׁלוֹם בֵּין אָדָם לַחֲבֵרוֹ, וְתַלְמוּד תּוֹרָה כְּנֶגֶד כֻּלָּם.

Some say:

דברים לג
תהלים קיא **רֵאשִׁית חָכְמָה** יִרְאַת יהוה, שֵׂכֶל טוֹב לְכָל־עֹשֵׂיהֶם, תְּהִלָּתוֹ עֹמֶדֶת לָעַד: תּוֹרָה
משלי א צִוָּה־לָנוּ מֹשֶׁה, מוֹרָשָׁה קְהִלַּת יַעֲקֹב: שְׁמַע בְּנִי מוּסַר אָבִיךָ
וְאַל־תִּטֹּשׁ תּוֹרַת אִמֶּךָ: תּוֹרָה תְּהֵא אֱמוּנָתִי, וְאֵל שַׁדַּי בְּעֶזְרָתִי. בָּרוּךְ שֵׁם כְּבוֹד מַלְכוּתוֹ לְעוֹלָם וָעֶד.

עטיפת טלית

At this point some follow the Hasidic custom of reciting additional prayers, which can be found on page 1336.

תהלים קד **בָּרְכִי** נַפְשִׁי אֶת־יהוה, יהוה אֱלֹהַי גָּדַלְתָּ מְּאֹד, הוֹד וְהָדָר לָבָשְׁתָּ: עֹטֶה־אוֹר כַּשַּׂלְמָה, נוֹטֶה שָׁמַיִם כַּיְרִיעָה:

minimum measure (1/60th of the total field), but no maximum – even if a person chose to dedicate the vast majority of his field as *pe'ah*, this would be a valid and meritorious performance of the commandment. These commandments, which emphasize the importance of human initiative and commitment in fulfilling divinely ordained precepts, represent the three pillars on which the spiritual world stands, according to the Mishna *Avot* 1:2, i.e., Torah study, service of God, and acts of kindness.

וְהָרֵאָיוֹן – *The pilgrimage offering* (previous page). There are two aspects to this commandment: the pilgrimage to the Temple and the elevation-offering (עוֹלַת רְאִיָּה) which the pilgrim is required to bring. The Torah does mandate a minimum number of annual pilgrimages, requiring visiting the Temple on each of the three pilgrimage festivals (Pesaḥ, Shavuot, and Sukkot), but there is no maximum – a Jew may visit the Temple as often as he or she wishes. Regarding the required elevation-offering, there is neither a minimum nor maximum (R. Avraham Walfish).

אֵלּוּ דְבָרִים – *These things*. Rambam (*Hil. Avel* 14:1) places these obligations into the following framework: "It is a positive rabbinic commandment to visit the sick, to comfort mourners, to accompany the dead, to provide for a bride, to host guests, to provide for all that is needed for burial including carrying the casket, walking before it, eulogizing, digging and burying. So too we are to facilitate the rejoicing of a groom and bride, and assist with all their needs. These are all in the category of **גְּמִילוּת חֲסָדִים שֶׁבְּגוּפוֹ**

Shabbat 127a אֵלּוּ THESE THINGS you will enjoy in this life and they will continue as your abiding riches in the life-to-come, and they are: honoring father and mother, acts of mercy, hastening early to the house of study morning and evening, hospitality to guests and strangers, visiting the sick, providing brides with a dowry, attending funerals, praying with devotion, and making peace between man and his fellow. But Torah study is equal to them all.

Some say:

Ps. 111 רֵאשִׁית חָכְמָה THE fear of the Lord is the beginning of wisdom, good prosperity
Deut. 33 for all who do them [His commandments]. His praise endures forever. The Torah
Prov. 1 Moses commanded us is the heritage of the congregation of Jacob. Listen, my son, to your father's instruction, and do not forsake your mother's teaching. May the Torah be my faith and Almighty God my help. Blessed is the name of His glorious kingdom forever and ever.

TALLIT

At this point some follow the Hasidic custom of reciting additional prayers, which can be found on page 1337.

Ps. 104 בָּרְכִי BLESS O LORD, O my soul. O Lord, my God, You are very great. You are clothed with splendor and majesty. He covers Himself with light as a garment. He spreads the heavens like a curtain.

(acts of kindness to be physically performed), which have no prescribed minimum. Even though these commandments are of rabbinic origin, they are also included in the Torah commandment to 'love your fellow like yourself.'"

וְתַלְמוּד תּוֹרָה כְּנֶגֶד כֻּלָּם – *But Torah study is equal to them all.* Rambam explains this to mean that Torah study in particular leads us to fulfill all of the other *mitzvot*. On the other hand, R. Ovadia of Bartenura understands it to be teaching that the reward for Torah study is the equal of all of the other *mitzvot*.

עֲטִיפַת טַלִּית / PUTTING ON *TALLIT*

בָּרְכִי נַפְשִׁי – *Bless...my soul.* Since the function of the *tzitzit* is to remind us of the command-

TALLIT GADOL

Before reciting the *berakha* on the *tallit gadol*, one should check the *tzitzit* for any ripped strings (*OḤ* 8:9). The *berakha* should be recited while holding the (unfolded) *tallit gadol* to ensure that the placement of the *tallit gadol* takes place immediately after reciting the *berakha* (*MB* 8:2). After the *berakha*, one should perform *atifa* (wrapping) which is the wrapping of one's head, body and face with the *tallit gadol* (*MB* 8:4).

Before wrapping oneself in the טלית*, say:*

בָּרוּךְ אַתָּה יהוה אֱלֹהֵינוּ מֶלֶךְ הָעוֹלָם, אֲשֶׁר קִדְּשָׁנוּ בְּמִצְוֹתָיו
וְצִוָּנוּ לְהִתְעַטֵּף בַּצִּיצִית.

According to the Shela (R. Isaiah Horowitz), one should say these verses after wrapping oneself in the טלית*:*

מַה־יָּקָר חַסְדְּךָ אֱלֹהִים, וּבְנֵי אָדָם בְּצֵל כְּנָפֶיךָ יֶחֱסָיוּן: יִרְוְיֻן תהלים לו
מִדֶּשֶׁן בֵּיתֶךָ, וְנַחַל עֲדָנֶיךָ תַשְׁקֵם: כִּי־עִמְּךָ מְקוֹר חַיִּים,
בְּאוֹרְךָ נִרְאֶה־אוֹר: מְשֹׁךְ חַסְדְּךָ לְיֹדְעֶיךָ, וְצִדְקָתְךָ לְיִשְׁרֵי־לֵב:

הנחת תפילין

At this point some follow the Hasidic custom of reciting additional prayers, which can be found on page 1336.

Stand and place the תפילין של יד *on the biceps of the left arm (or right arm if you are left-handed), angled toward the heart, and before tightening the strap, say:*

בָּרוּךְ אַתָּה יהוה אֱלֹהֵינוּ מֶלֶךְ הָעוֹלָם, אֲשֶׁר קִדְּשָׁנוּ בְּמִצְוֹתָיו,
וְצִוָּנוּ לְהָנִיחַ תְּפִלִּין.

---

ments (Num. 15:40), which are the ultimate manifestation of God's will, wrapping ourselves in the *tallit* is the equivalent of wrapping ourselves in God's glory.

הֲנָחַת תְּפִלִּין / PUTTING ON TEFILLIN
Four separate scriptural passages command Israel to put on *tefillin*; all are contained on the parchments inserted into the *tefillin*, and these are all mentioned in this prayer. Along with Shabbat and circumcision, *tefillin* are described as an אות, *a sign* of the covenant between God and Israel (Ex. 13:9, 16; Deut. 4:8, 11:18) – a measure of their profound significance.

HANAḤAT TEFILLIN
While one is placing *tefillin*, one may not interrupt at all or even communicate through facial or bodily expressions (*OḤ* 25:9 and *MB* 25:29). The *shel yad* is placed on one's left arm (or right arm if one is left-handed) on the lower portion of the bicep slightly angled toward one's heart (*OḤ* 27:1). The *berakha* is recited when the *shel yad* is in the correct place and one's right hand is holding the strap ready to tighten it on one's arm (*OḤ* 25:8).

The *shel rosh* is placed centered between one's eyes with the front of the *shel rosh* resting on top of one's head behind one's hairline (or where it used to be if one's hairline has receded). Before the *berakha*, the straps and the knot should be loose. One recites the *berakha* and then pulls down on the straps and the knot to secure it to one's head. The knot should rest where the skull meets the back of the neck (*OḤ* 27:9–10 and 25:8).

Before wrapping oneself in the tallit, say:

בָּרוּךְ BLESSED ARE YOU, Lord, our God, King of the universe, Who has sanctified us with His commandments and commanded us to wrap ourselves with the fringed tallit.

According to the Shela (R. Isaiah Horowitz), one should say these verses after wrapping oneself in the Tallit:

Ps. 36 מַה־יָּקָר HOW DEAR is Your loving-kindness, O God, and the children of man seek refuge in the shadow of Your wings. They are satisfied by the fatness of Your house, and You make them drink the river of Your pleasures. For with You is the fountain of life. In Your light we see light. Draw Your loving-kindness to those who know You, and Your righteousness to the upright in heart.

PUTTING ON TEFILLIN

At this point some follow the Hasidic custom of reciting additional prayers, which can be found on page 1337.

Stand and place the hand-tefillin on the biceps of the left arm (or right arm if you are left-handed), angled toward the heart, and before tightening the strap, say:

בָּרוּךְ BLESSED ARE YOU, Lord, our God, King of the universe, Who has sanctified us with His commandments, and has commanded us to put on *tefillin*.

According to Rabbeinu Tam, who in this regard is followed by Ashkenazim, the reason we make two separate *berakhot* on the *tefillin*, even though according to most authorities it is only one *mitzva*, is that in putting on *tefillin* we perform two separate fulfillments corresponding to the two aspects of the *mitzva* derived from the first paragraph of the *Shema*. Regarding the arm-*tefillin* we are commanded וּקְשַׁרְתָּם, i.e., to place/tie them to our arms, through a specific act, and that act is preceded by the first *berakha*, i.e., "to put on *tefillin*." As regards the head-*tefillin*, however, the command is וְהָיוּ, i.e., "they shall be (on your head)," with no mention of a specific action. For this we recite the *berakha* "regarding the *mitzva* of *tefillin*," without mention of any specific act. When the *tefillin* are on our head we fulfill the Torah's obligation in this verse to be "crowned" with a special sanctity that sets us recognizably apart from other nations. Accordingly this second *berakha* is not over a *mitzva* performance, but rather over our sanctified status that results each time we fulfill this *mitzva* (R. Joseph B. Soloveitchik).

Women are exempt from *tefillin* since they are not worn on Shabbat or Yom Tov, and hence they constitute a time-related positive commandment, from which women are exempt.

Wrap the strap of the hand-tefillin seven times around the arm. Place the head-tefillin above the hairline, centered between the eyes, and say quietly:

בָּרוּךְ אַתָּה יהוה אֱלֹהֵינוּ מֶלֶךְ הָעוֹלָם, אֲשֶׁר קִדְּשָׁנוּ בְּמִצְוֹתָיו, וְצִוָּנוּ עַל מִצְוַת תְּפִלִּין.

Adjust the תפילין של ראש *and say:*

בָּרוּךְ שֵׁם כְּבוֹד מַלְכוּתוֹ לְעוֹלָם וָעֶד

Some say:

וּמֵחָכְמָתְךָ אֵל עֶלְיוֹן תַּאֲצִיל עָלַי, וּמִבִּינָתְךָ תְּבִינֵנִי, וּבְחַסְדְּךָ
תַּגְדִּיל עָלַי, וּבִגְבוּרָתְךָ תַּצְמִית אוֹיְבַי וְקָמַי. וְשֶׁמֶן הַטּוֹב תָּרִיק
עַל שִׁבְעָה קְנֵי הַמְּנוֹרָה, לְהַשְׁפִּיעַ טוּבְךָ לִבְרִיּוֹתֶיךָ. פּוֹתֵחַ אֶת־יָדֶךָ תהלים קמה
וּמַשְׂבִּיעַ לְכָל־חַי רָצוֹן:

Wind the strap of the תפילין של יד *three times around the middle finger, saying:*

וְאֵרַשְׂתִּיךְ לִי לְעוֹלָם, וְאֵרַשְׂתִּיךְ לִי בְּצֶדֶק וּבְמִשְׁפָּט וּבְחֶסֶד הושע ב
וּבְרַחֲמִים: וְאֵרַשְׂתִּיךְ לִי בֶּאֱמוּנָה, וְיָדַעַתְּ אֶת־יהוה:

After putting on the תפילין*, say the following:*

וַיְדַבֵּר יהוה אֶל־מֹשֶׁה לֵּאמֹר: קַדֶּשׁ־לִי כָל־בְּכוֹר, פֶּטֶר כָּל־רֶחֶם בִּבְנֵי שמות יג
יִשְׂרָאֵל, בָּאָדָם וּבַבְּהֵמָה, לִי הוּא: וַיֹּאמֶר מֹשֶׁה אֶל־הָעָם, זָכוֹר
אֶת־הַיּוֹם הַזֶּה, אֲשֶׁר יְצָאתֶם מִמִּצְרַיִם מִבֵּית עֲבָדִים, כִּי בְּחֹזֶק יָד הוֹצִיא
יהוה אֶתְכֶם מִזֶּה, וְלֹא יֵאָכֵל חָמֵץ: הַיּוֹם אַתֶּם יֹצְאִים, בְּחֹדֶשׁ הָאָבִיב:

The Torah designates the purpose of *tefillin* as לְמַעַן תִּהְיֶה תּוֹרַת ה׳ בְּפִיךָ – "So that the Torah of the Lord will be in your mouth" (Ex. 13:9). The parallels between *tefillin*, God, and the Torah are many: *tefillin* symbolize the study of Torah (*Tosafot Rosh HaShana* 17a); they symbolize observance of the *mitzvot* of the Torah (*Kiddushin* 35a), as well as the Torah scroll itself (*Makkot* 11a). They also are a physical expression of the name of God (*Menaḥot* 35b), as seen in the letters שַׁדַּי formed by the *tefillin* (Rashi), as well as the many occurrences of God's name in the *parshiyot* inside the *tefillin* boxes (*Menaḥot* 36b). Furthermore, the Talmud teaches that God Himself, as it were, wears *tefillin*, thereby proclaiming His dedication to His people (*Berakhot* 6a), while they also testify to God's revealed presence (*Tosafot Menaḥot* 44b). In short, through the *tefillin* we bind ourselves to God and His Torah (R. Yaakov Nagen).

וְאֵרַשְׂתִּיךְ לִי – *I will betroth you to Me.* In these verses the prophet asserts that although a

Wrap the strap of the hand-tefillin seven times around the arm.
Place the head-tefillin above the hairline, centered between the eyes, and say quietly:

בָּרוּךְ BLESSED ARE YOU, Lord, our God, King of the universe, Who has sanctified us with His commandments, and has commanded us about the commandment of *tefillin.*

Adjust the head-tefillin and say:

BLESSED is the name of His glorious kingdom forever and ever.

Some say:

SUPREME GOD GRANT me some of Your wisdom. Give some of Your understanding. Enlarge me with your kindness. Employ Your strength to subdue my enemies. Pour good oil upon the seven branches of the menorah, to bring down Your goodness upon Your creatures. You open Your hand, and You satisfy the desire of every living thing.

Wind the strap of the hand-tefillin three times around the middle finger, saying:

Hos. 2 וְאֵרַשְׂתִּיךְ לִי I WILL BETROTH YOU to Me for ever; I will betroth you to Me in righteousness and justice, loving-kindness and compassion; I will betroth you to Me in faithfulness; and you shall know the Lord.

After putting on the tefillin, say the following:

Ex. 13 וַיְדַבֵּר THE LORD SPOKE to Moses, saying: Sanctify to Me every firstborn; the first issue of every womb among the children of Israel, of both man and beast, is Mine. Moses said to the people: Remember this day on which you departed from Egypt, from the house of bondage, for the Lord removed you from here with a strong hand, and therefore no leaven may be eaten. Today you are leaving in the month of springtime. And it will be that, when the Lord

---

human marriage may be dissolved, since it embraces only the social, externalized, aspect of the human personality, our betrothal unto God is eternal and unbreakable because the union of man and the "lonely," unique God penetrates to the core of the lonely, unique human personality (R. Joseph B. Soloveitchik).

בְּצֶדֶק וּבְמִשְׁפָּט – *In righteousness and justice.* When we embrace "righteousness and justice," God responds by blessing us with "loving-kindness and compassion" (Rashi).

קַדֶּשׁ לִי כָל בְּכוֹר – *Consecrate to Me every firstborn male.* The sanctification of the firstborn to God is the result of God's having spared the Israelite firstborn at the Exodus from Egypt. God thus has first claim, as it were, on Israel's first fruits, in every realm of human activity,

וְהָיָה כִּי־יְבִאֲךָ יהוה אֶל־אֶרֶץ הַכְּנַעֲנִי וְהַחִתִּי וְהָאֱמֹרִי וְהַחִוִּי וְהַיְבוּסִי, אֲשֶׁר נִשְׁבַּע לַאֲבֹתֶיךָ לָתֶת לָךְ, אֶרֶץ זָבַת חָלָב וּדְבָשׁ, וְעָבַדְתָּ אֶת־הָעֲבֹדָה הַזֹּאת בַּחֹדֶשׁ הַזֶּה: שִׁבְעַת יָמִים תֹּאכַל מַצֹּת, וּבַיּוֹם הַשְּׁבִיעִי חַג לַיהוה: מַצּוֹת יֵאָכֵל אֵת שִׁבְעַת הַיָּמִים, וְלֹא־יֵרָאֶה לְךָ חָמֵץ וְלֹא־יֵרָאֶה לְךָ שְׂאֹר, בְּכָל־גְּבֻלֶךָ: וְהִגַּדְתָּ לְבִנְךָ בַּיּוֹם הַהוּא לֵאמֹר, בַּעֲבוּר זֶה עָשָׂה יהוה לִי בְּצֵאתִי מִמִּצְרָיִם: וְהָיָה לְךָ לְאוֹת עַל־יָדְךָ וּלְזִכָּרוֹן בֵּין עֵינֶיךָ, לְמַעַן תִּהְיֶה תּוֹרַת יהוה בְּפִיךָ, כִּי בְּיָד חֲזָקָה הוֹצִאֲךָ יהוה מִמִּצְרָיִם: וְשָׁמַרְתָּ אֶת־הַחֻקָּה הַזֹּאת לְמוֹעֲדָהּ, מִיָּמִים יָמִימָה:

וְהָיָה כִּי־יְבִאֲךָ יהוה אֶל־אֶרֶץ הַכְּנַעֲנִי כַּאֲשֶׁר נִשְׁבַּע לְךָ וְלַאֲבֹתֶיךָ, וּנְתָנָהּ לָךְ: וְהַעֲבַרְתָּ כָל־פֶּטֶר־רֶחֶם לַיהוה, וְכָל־פֶּטֶר שֶׁגֶר בְּהֵמָה אֲשֶׁר יִהְיֶה לְךָ הַזְּכָרִים, לַיהוה: וְכָל־פֶּטֶר חֲמֹר תִּפְדֶּה בְשֶׂה, וְאִם־לֹא תִפְדֶּה וַעֲרַפְתּוֹ, וְכֹל בְּכוֹר אָדָם בְּבָנֶיךָ תִּפְדֶּה: וְהָיָה כִּי־יִשְׁאָלְךָ בִנְךָ מָחָר, לֵאמֹר מַה־זֹּאת, וְאָמַרְתָּ אֵלָיו, בְּחֹזֶק יָד הוֹצִיאָנוּ יהוה מִמִּצְרַיִם מִבֵּית עֲבָדִים: וַיְהִי כִּי־הִקְשָׁה פַרְעֹה לְשַׁלְּחֵנוּ, וַיַּהֲרֹג יהוה כָּל־בְּכוֹר בְּאֶרֶץ מִצְרַיִם, מִבְּכֹר אָדָם וְעַד־בְּכוֹר בְּהֵמָה, עַל־כֵּן אֲנִי זֹבֵחַ לַיהוה כָּל־פֶּטֶר רֶחֶם הַזְּכָרִים, וְכָל־בְּכוֹר בָּנַי אֶפְדֶּה: וְהָיָה לְאוֹת עַל־יָדְכָה וּלְטוֹטָפֹת בֵּין עֵינֶיךָ, כִּי בְּחֹזֶק יָד הוֹצִיאָנוּ יהוה מִמִּצְרָיִם:

be it first domestic animals, first fruits, first crops, and the various tithes, which are all consecrated to God.

וְכָל פֶּטֶר חֲמֹר תִּפְדֶּה בְשֶׂה – *Every firstling donkey you shall redeem with a lamb*. The donkey is the only non-kosher animal that enjoys the privileged status of the firstborn. The Gemara (*Bekhorot* 5b) suggests that this is a memorial to the Exodus, when the Jews left Egypt with countless donkeys laden with riches of the land. A donkey cannot be consecrated as an offering; if dedicated it must be redeemed with a lamb or kid, which become the private property of a *Kohen*. Should the Israelite owner refuse to redeem his donkey, he is denied its use: he must put it to death.

טוֹטָפֹת – *An emblem*. R. Akiva taught that the Hebrew word *totefet* means "four." He derived this from the Coptic word *tot* (meaning "two") combined with *fot* in African or Phrygian (with the sense of "two"). A number of nineteenth- and early twentieth-century scholars criticized this derivation from Indo-European languages to explain Semitic etymologies. Today with our knowledge of ancient southern Mesopotamian languages we know that the Sumerian "*tab*" means "two." Hence *tab-tab* connotes four. On the basis of Sumerian and Semitic phonetic changes *tab-tab* becomes *tap-tap*, which eventually becomes *totaf*, with the feminine ending "*-at*." It is possible that since Sumerian was already a dead language,

will bring you to the land of the Canaanites, Hittites, Emorites, Hivvites, and Jebusites, which He swore to your forefathers to give you – a land flowing with milk and honey – you shall perform this service in this month. Seven days you shall eat matzot, and on the seventh day there shall be a festival to the Lord. Matzot shall be eaten throughout the seven days; no leaven may be seen in your possession, nor may leaven be seen in your possession in all your borders. And you shall tell your son on that day, saying: "It is because of this that the Lord acted for me when I left Egypt." And it shall be for you a sign on your arm and a reminder between your eyes – so that the Lord's Torah may be in your mouth; for with a strong hand did the Lord remove you from Egypt. And you shall observe this ordinance at its designated time from year to year.

וְהָיָה AND IT SHALL be that when the Lord will bring you to the land of the Canaanites as He swore to you and your forefathers, and will have given it to you, then you shall set apart every first issue of the womb to the Lord — and of every first issue that is dropped by cattle that belong to you, the males shall belong to the Lord. Every first issue of a donkey you shall redeem with a lamb or kid; if you do not redeem it, then you must axe the back of its neck. And you must redeem every human firstborn among your sons. And it shall be when your son asks you in the future, "What is this?" you shall answer him, "With a strong hand the Lord removed us from Egypt, from the house of bondage. And it happened, when Pharaoh stubbornly refused to let us go, that the Lord killed all the firstborn in the land of Egypt, from the firstborn of man to the firstborn of beast. Therefore, I sacrifice to the Lord all first male issue of the womb, and redeem all the firstborn of my sons." And it shall be a sign upon your arm and a symbol between your eyes, for with a strong hand the Lord removed us from Egypt.

R. Akiva utilized contemporary foreign languages, a practice started by the earlier Alexandrians (R. Sol Cohen).

כִּי בְּיָד חֲזָקָה הוֹצִאֲךָ ה' מִמִּצְרָיִם – *That with a mighty hand the Lord brought us out of Egypt.* This verse explains that we are to place the *tefillin* on our arm to remind us every day that God had to take us forcibly from Egypt "with His strong arm." That is, our ancestors in Egypt did not deserve to be redeemed from Egyptian bondage on their merits. It was only because God interceded providentially that they were able to emerge from servitude. This is why the Torah refers to *tefillin* as a sign, i.e., an ongoing reminder of this important but easily forgotten truth (*Ḥatam Sofer*).

הכנה לתפילה

On entering the בית כנסת*:*

מַה־טֹּבוּ אֹהָלֶיךָ יַעֲקֹב, במדבר כד
מִשְׁכְּנֹתֶיךָ יִשְׂרָאֵל:
וַאֲנִי בְּרֹב חַסְדְּךָ אָבוֹא בֵיתֶךָ תהלים ה
אֶשְׁתַּחֲוֶה אֶל־הֵיכַל־קָדְשְׁךָ, בְּיִרְאָתֶךָ:
יהוה אָהַבְתִּי מְעוֹן בֵּיתֶךָ תהלים כו
וּמְקוֹם מִשְׁכַּן כְּבוֹדֶךָ:
וַאֲנִי אֶשְׁתַּחֲוֶה
וְאֶכְרָעָה, אֶבְרְכָה לִפְנֵי יהוה עֹשִׂי.
וַאֲנִי תְפִלָּתִי־לְךָ יהוה, עֵת רָצוֹן, תהלים סט
אֱלֹהִים בְּרָב־חַסְדֶּךָ, עֲנֵנִי בֶּאֱמֶת יִשְׁעֶךָ:

The following poems, on this page and the next, both from the Middle Ages, are summary statements of Jewish faith, orienting us to the spiritual contours of the world that we actualize in the mind by the act of prayer.

אֲדוֹן עוֹלָם אֲשֶׁר מָלַךְ בְּטֶרֶם כָּל־יְצִיר נִבְרָא.
לְעֵת נַעֲשָׂה בְחֶפְצוֹ כֹּל אֲזַי מֶלֶךְ שְׁמוֹ נִקְרָא.
וְאַחֲרֵי כִּכְלוֹת הַכֹּל לְבַדּוֹ יִמְלֹךְ נוֹרָא.
וְהוּא הָיָה וְהוּא הֹוֶה וְהוּא יִהְיֶה בְּתִפְאָרָה.
וְהוּא אֶחָד וְאֵין שֵׁנִי לְהַמְשִׁיל לוֹ לְהַחְבִּירָה.
בְּלִי רֵאשִׁית בְּלִי תַכְלִית וְלוֹ הָעֹז וְהַמִּשְׂרָה.

מַה טֹּבוּ אֹהָלֶיךָ – *How goodly are your tents.* The sages understand this praise of Israel as referring to Israel's "tents of learning and prayer." The term "tent" that usually refers to a home or dwelling place, underscores the similarities between a spiritual sanctuary (such as the Temple) and a Jewish home. The Jewish home incorporates and reflects the values of the Tabernacle and the Holy Temple, and by extension the values of the

PREPARATION FOR PRAYER

On entering the Synagogue:

Num. 24 מַה־טֹּבוּ HOW GOOD are your tents, O Jacob,
your dwelling places, O Israel.

Ps. 5 But as for me, I will come into Your house
in the abundance of Your loving-kindness.
I will bow down toward Your holy Temple in the fear of You.

Ps. 26 O Lord, I love the habitation of Your house,
and the place where Your glory dwells.

I will worship and bow down,
I will bend my knee before the Lord Who made me.

Ps. 69 But I pray to You, O Lord, for a time of favor. O God, in the greatness
of Your loving-kindness, answer me, in the truth of Your salvation.

The following poems, on this page and the next, both from the Middle Ages, are summary statements of Jewish faith, orienting us to the spiritual contours of the world that we actualize in the mind by the act of prayer.

אֲדוֹן עוֹלָם ETERNAL MASTER,
Who reigned before anything was created –

when by His will all things were brought into being,
then as King was His name proclaimed.

After all things have ceased to be,
He will reign alone in awesome majesty.

He was. He is. He will always be;
His eternal glory can never fade.

He is One. There is no other;
beyond compare, or any metaphor.

He had no beginning, will have no end.
He above all others has strength and power.

---

synagogue and study hall, that have replaced the Temple. This collection of verses expresses love and reverence for the synagogue that, in the absence of the Holy Temple, is the place of the residence of God's glory among Israel (R. Joseph B. Soloveitchik).

וְהוּא אֵלִי וְחַי גּוֹאֲלִי וְצוּר חֶבְלִי בְּעֵת צָרָה.
וְהוּא נִסִּי וּמָנוֹס לִי מְנָת כּוֹסִי בְּיוֹם אֶקְרָא.
בְּיָדוֹ אַפְקִיד רוּחִי בְּעֵת אִישַׁן וְאָעִירָה.
וְעִם רוּחִי גְּוִיָּתִי יהוה לִי וְלֹא אִירָא.

יִגְדַּל אֱלֹהִים חַי וְיִשְׁתַּבַּח, נִמְצָא וְאֵין עֵת אֶל מְצִיאוּתוֹ.
אֶחָד וְאֵין יָחִיד כְּיִחוּדוֹ, נֶעְלָם וְגַם אֵין סוֹף לְאַחְדּוּתוֹ.
אֵין לוֹ דְּמוּת הַגּוּף וְאֵינוֹ גוּף, לֹא נַעֲרֹךְ אֵלָיו קְדֻשָּׁתוֹ.
קַדְמוֹן לְכָל דָּבָר אֲשֶׁר נִבְרָא, רִאשׁוֹן וְאֵין רֵאשִׁית לְרֵאשִׁיתוֹ.
הִנּוֹ אֲדוֹן עוֹלָם, וְכָל נוֹצָר יוֹרֶה גְדֻלָּתוֹ וּמַלְכוּתוֹ.
שֶׁפַע נְבוּאָתוֹ נְתָנוֹ אֶל־אַנְשֵׁי סְגֻלָּתוֹ וְתִפְאַרְתּוֹ.
לֹא קָם בְּיִשְׂרָאֵל כְּמֹשֶׁה עוֹד נָבִיא, וּמַבִּיט אֶת תְּמוּנָתוֹ.
תּוֹרַת אֱמֶת נָתַן לְעַמּוֹ אֵל עַל יַד נְבִיאוֹ נֶאֱמַן בֵּיתוֹ.
לֹא יַחֲלִיף הָאֵל וְלֹא יָמִיר דָּתוֹ לְעוֹלָמִים לְזוּלָתוֹ.
צוֹפֶה וְיוֹדֵעַ סְתָרֵינוּ, מַבִּיט לְסוֹף דָּבָר בְּקַדְמָתוֹ.
גּוֹמֵל לְאִישׁ חֶסֶד כְּמִפְעָלוֹ, נוֹתֵן לְרָשָׁע רָע כְּרִשְׁעָתוֹ.
יִשְׁלַח לְקֵץ יָמִין מְשִׁיחֵנוּ לִפְדּוֹת מְחַכֵּי קֵץ יְשׁוּעָתוֹ.
מֵתִים יְחַיֶּה אֵל בְּרֹב חַסְדּוֹ, בָּרוּךְ עֲדֵי עַד שֵׁם תְּהִלָּתוֹ.

אֲדוֹן עוֹלָם / ADON OLAM

בְּיָדוֹ אַפְקִיד רוּחִי – *I entrust my spirit to His hand.* When we go to sleep we engage in an act of faith in which we entrust our souls to God, for which we are rewarded when He restores our souls the next morning. In the future each of us will entrust both our soul and our body to God on our deathbed, facing the great unknown. The experience of awakening each morning gives us confidence and renewed faith that after we will be laid to final rest, we shall again awaken to life, in the World to Come (R. David Fohrman).

יִגְדַּל / YIGDAL

יִגְדַּל אֱלֹהִים חַי – *Glorify... the living God*. The *Yigdal*, as well as the *Ani Ma'amin* which appears after *Shaharit*, are both modeled after the list of principles formulated by Rambam. Scholars generally attribute *Yigdal* to Daniei ben Yehuda HaKohen of Rome, who lived around the year 1300. For a fuller

He is my God, my living Redeemer,
a Rock when I am in pain in troubled times.
My banner and my refuge,
to Whom I will raise a cup on the day I proclaim my salvation.
I entrust my spirit to His hand,
when sleeping and when awake.
With my body my soul will stay;
the Lord is with me, I need not fear.

יִגְדַּל THE LIVING GOD will be exalted and praised;
He exists, and His existence endures beyond time.
He is One and His oneness is like that of no other;
He is beyond our comprehension, for His unity is infinite.
He has no physical image, neither does He have a body;
nothing can be compared to Him in His Holiness.
He preceded everything that was created;
He was the first, and His primordial existence had no beginning.
Behold He is the eternal Master,
and every creature shall make His greatness and sovereignty known.
He bestowed His prophetic overflow
upon those individuals who were His treasured and glorious ones.
Never did there arise in Israel another prophet like Moses,
who alone was able to view God's image.
God gave His people the Torah of truth
by the hand of His prophet who was the most trusted in all His house.
God will not exchange or replace His law;
never will He alter it to become something else.
He sees and knows all that we conceal;
He discerns the end result of all that happens before it.
He rewards the compassionate person in accordance with his deeds;
He imposes punishment on the wicked person
in accordance with his evil.
He will send our Messiah at the end of days
to redeem with His salvation those who await the end of days.
God in His great kindness will resurrect the dead;
blessed is His illustrious name for ever and ever.

ברכות השחר

The following blessings are recited aloud by the שליח ציבור *and quietly by the congregation (MB 46:13). It is our custom to say them standing.*

בָּרוּךְ אַתָּה יהוה אֱלֹהֵינוּ מֶלֶךְ הָעוֹלָם, אֲשֶׁר נָתַן לַשֶּׂכְוִי בִינָה, לְהַבְחִין בֵּין יוֹם וּבֵין לָיְלָה.

בָּרוּךְ אַתָּה יהוה אֱלֹהֵינוּ מֶלֶךְ הָעוֹלָם, שֶׁלֹּא עָשַׂנִי גּוֹי.

בָּרוּךְ אַתָּה יהוה אֱלֹהֵינוּ מֶלֶךְ הָעוֹלָם, שֶׁלֹּא עָשַׂנִי עָבֶד.

בָּרוּךְ אַתָּה יהוה אֱלֹהֵינוּ מֶלֶךְ הָעוֹלָם,
men שֶׁלֹּא עָשַׂנִי אִשָּׁה. / *women* שֶׁעָשַׂנִי כִּרְצוֹנוֹ.

בָּרוּךְ אַתָּה יהוה אֱלֹהֵינוּ מֶלֶךְ הָעוֹלָם, פּוֹקֵחַ עִוְרִים.

בָּרוּךְ אַתָּה יהוה אֱלֹהֵינוּ מֶלֶךְ הָעוֹלָם, מַלְבִּישׁ עֲרֻמִּים.

---

discussion of these prayers and Rambam, see page E93.

בִּרְכוֹת הַשַּׁחַר / BLESSINGS OF THANKSGIVING

אֲשֶׁר נָתַן לַשֶּׂכְוִי בִינָה – *Who gave the heart understanding.* According to most commentators, the word שֶׂכְוִי, based on Job 38:36, refers to the human heart or intellect (Ralbag). In Mishnaic times the word also referred to a rooster. In the context of this blessing, both meanings are implied: The rooster crows, announcing dawn, and the human heart understands (Rosh).

This first blessing with its focus on the rooster which crows at the beginning of the farmer's workday highlights the fundamental unity of all of creation, the single divine spirit that animates all of reality. When we fulfill our divine mission in the world, we elevate not merely ourselves and our immediate surroundings, but ultimately also the entire cosmos (R. Avraham Yitzḥak HaKohen Kook).

שֶׁלֹּא עָשַׂנִי גּוֹי...עָבֶד...אִשָּׁה – Most *berakhot* are positive affirmations. These three are unusual, being framed in a negative form. The *Tosefta* and Talmud Yerushalmi explain that this was intended to emphasize the centrality of *mitzvot* as fully equal to affirmations of faith and belief. Thus we thank God for not diminishing our *mitzva* obligations, which would be the case were He to have created us as Gentiles, or slaves or (in the case of men) as women, each of whom has specific *mitzva* exemptions: Gentiles are subject to only the Seven Noahide Laws, while slaves and women are exempted from time-bound positive *mitzvot* (*Beit Yosef*).

These three blessings pointedly separate the Jew from the affirmations of other faiths in these matters, such as the Gospels that declare that there is no distinction between Jew or Greek, freeman or slave, male or female. As far as Judaism is concerned, there are indeed fundamental distinctions between them in regard to their religious obligations. Their roles, functions, and responsibilities are not interchangeable,

BLESSINGS OF THANKSGIVING

The following blessings are recited aloud by the Leader and quietly by the congregation (MB 46:13). It is our custom to say them standing.

בָּרוּךְ BLESSED are You, Lord, our God, King of the universe, Who gave the heart the understanding to help us distinguish between day and night.

BLESSED ARE YOU, Lord, our God, King of the universe, Who has not made me a Gentile.

BLESSED ARE YOU, Lord, our God, King of the universe, Who has not made me a slave.

BLESSED ARE YOU, Lord, our God, King of the universe,
Men: Who has not made me a woman.
Women: Who has made me according to His will.

BLESSED ARE YOU, Lord, our God, King of the universe, Who opens the eyes of the blind.

BLESSED ARE YOU, Lord, our God, King of the universe, Who clothes the naked.

---

even though every human being is created equally in God's image, and the life of each human being is of equal value before Him.

The daily emphasis on *mitzva* obligations, in conjunction with the preceding *berakhot* that relate to the duty to study Torah, reflect the *halakha*-centric life of the Jew. While it is certain that every Jew is duty-bound to subscribe to fundamental principles of belief, what truly sets us apart from other faiths is our adherence to the *mitzvot* of the Torah in every aspect of our lives, as defined and delineated in the Oral Law.

שֶׁלֹּא עָשַׂנִי גּוֹי – *Who has not made me a Gentile.* According to many halakhic authorities converts as well should recite this blessing, even though they were not born as Jews. Some halakhic authorities are of the view that converts – who have become Jewish through their own active choice – should omit this blessing altogether (Abudarham). Others suggest that a convert should recognize the divine guidance that led to his or her choice, and thus they recommend a variety of alternative formulations, such as שֶׁהִכְנִיסַנִי תַּחַת כַּנְפֵי הַשְּׁכִינָה ("Who has brought me under the wings of the Divine Presence"), or שֶׁעָשַׂנִי גֵּר ("Who has made me into a convert"). This matter has not been settled in the halakhic literature.

שֶׁעָשַׂנִי כִּרְצוֹנוֹ – *Who has made me according to His will.* Some authorities see this *berakha* as an affirmation of the unique spiritual sensibilities of women, often more attuned to רְצוֹן ה׳ (the will of God). As such, when compared to her male counterpart, she is less in need of the constant discipline of *mitzvot* in pursuit of a

בָּרוּךְ אַתָּה יהוה אֱלֹהֵינוּ מֶלֶךְ הָעוֹלָם, מַתִּיר אֲסוּרִים.

בָּרוּךְ אַתָּה יהוה אֱלֹהֵינוּ מֶלֶךְ הָעוֹלָם, זוֹקֵף כְּפוּפִים.

בָּרוּךְ אַתָּה יהוה אֱלֹהֵינוּ מֶלֶךְ הָעוֹלָם, רוֹקַע הָאָרֶץ עַל הַמָּיִם.

בָּרוּךְ אַתָּה יהוה אֱלֹהֵינוּ מֶלֶךְ הָעוֹלָם, שֶׁעָשָׂה לִי כָּל צָרְכִּי.

בָּרוּךְ אַתָּה יהוה אֱלֹהֵינוּ מֶלֶךְ הָעוֹלָם, הַמֵּכִין מִצְעֲדֵי גָבֶר.

בָּרוּךְ אַתָּה יהוה אֱלֹהֵינוּ מֶלֶךְ הָעוֹלָם, אוֹזֵר יִשְׂרָאֵל בִּגְבוּרָה.

בָּרוּךְ אַתָּה יהוה אֱלֹהֵינוּ מֶלֶךְ הָעוֹלָם, עוֹטֵר יִשְׂרָאֵל בְּתִפְאָרָה.

בָּרוּךְ אַתָּה יהוה אֱלֹהֵינוּ מֶלֶךְ הָעוֹלָם, הַנּוֹתֵן לַיָּעֵף כֹּחַ.

בָּרוּךְ אַתָּה יהוה אֱלֹהֵינוּ מֶלֶךְ הָעוֹלָם, הַמַּעֲבִיר שֵׁנָה מֵעֵינַי וּתְנוּמָה מֵעַפְעַפָּי. וִיהִי רָצוֹן מִלְּפָנֶיךָ יהוה אֱלֹהֵינוּ וֵאלֹהֵי אֲבוֹתֵינוּ, שֶׁתַּרְגִּילֵנוּ בְּתוֹרָתֶךָ, וְדַבְּקֵנוּ בְּמִצְוֹתֶיךָ, וְאַל תְּבִיאֵנוּ לֹא לִידֵי חֵטְא, וְלֹא לִידֵי עֲבֵרָה וְעָוֹן, וְלֹא לִידֵי נִסָּיוֹן וְלֹא לִידֵי בִזָּיוֹן, וְאַל תַּשְׁלֶט בָּנוּ יֵצֶר הָרָע, וְהַרְחִיקֵנוּ מֵאָדָם רָע וּמֵחָבֵר רָע, וְדַבְּקֵנוּ בְּיֵצֶר הַטּוֹב וּבְמַעֲשִׂים טוֹבִים, וְכֹף אֶת יִצְרֵנוּ לְהִשְׁתַּעְבֶּד לָךְ, וּתְנֵנוּ הַיּוֹם וּבְכָל יוֹם לְחֵן וּלְחֶסֶד וּלְרַחֲמִים, בְּעֵינֶיךָ, וּבְעֵינֵי כָל רוֹאֵינוּ, וְתִגְמְלֵנוּ חֲסָדִים טוֹבִים. בָּרוּךְ אַתָּה יהוה, גּוֹמֵל חֲסָדִים טוֹבִים לְעַמּוֹ יִשְׂרָאֵל.

---

life of genuine sanctity and closeness to God (R. Shimon Schwab).

רוֹקַע הָאָרֶץ עַל הַמָּיִם – *Who stretches forth the earth over the waters*. Whatever model of the world may underlie the original formulation of this *berakha*, contemporary worshipers can see it as an expression of the fact that the exquisite design of our planet is ideal for human habitation. Underground water reserves are found beneath the planet's shallow subsurface, which is "spread out" upon them. The water drawn from these aquifers is protected from surface-water contamination, and provides a steady source of sustenance even when there is little rain, and is thus crucial for the maintenance of life on earth.

הַנּוֹתֵן לַיָּעֵף כֹּחַ – *Who gives strength to the weary*. This is one of several *berakhot* that are not found in the Talmud. The *Shulḥan Arukh* omits it, while R. Moshe Isserles (the Rema)

BLESSED ARE YOU, Lord, our God, King of the universe, Who releases those who are bound.

BLESSED ARE YOU, Lord, our God, King of the universe, Who raises up those who are bowed down.

BLESSED ARE YOU, Lord, our God, King of the universe, Who stretches forth the earth over the waters.

BLESSED ARE YOU, Lord, our God, King of the universe, Who provides for my every need.

BLESSED ARE YOU, Lord, our God, King of the universe, Who guides man's steps.

BLESSED ARE YOU, Lord, our God, King of the universe, Who girds Israel with might.

BLESSED ARE YOU, Lord, our God, King of the universe Who crowns Israel with glory.

BLESSED ARE YOU, Lord, our God, King of the universe, Who gives strength to the weary.

בָּרוּךְ BLESSED ARE YOU, Lord, our God, King of the universe, Who removes sleep from my eyes and slumber from my eyelids. And may it be Your will, Lord our God and God of our fathers, to enable me always to walk in the way of Your Torah and adhere to Your precepts. Lead us not into temptation, sin, transgression, or disgrace. Do not let the evil impulse control us. Keep us far from evil people, and reinforce our attachment to the good inclination and to good deeds. Guide our instincts to submit to You. Today and every day, grant us grace, kindness, and mercy in Your sight and in the sight of all, and bestow Your loving-kindness on us. Blessed are You, Lord, Who bestows authentic kindnesses upon His people Israel.

---

includes it. As Ashkenazim, we follow the latter.

שֵׁנָה מֵעֵינַי וּתְנוּמָה מֵעַפְעַפָּי – *Sleep from my eyes and slumber from my eyelids.* This blessing thanks God for the benefits of sleep which provides respite and rejuvenation from the travails of daily life (*Orḥot Ḥayyim*). The terms שֵׁינָה and תְּנוּמָה refer to different stages of sleep. First

יְהִי רָצוֹן מִלְּפָנֶיךָ יהוה אֱלֹהַי וֵאלֹהֵי אֲבוֹתַי, שֶׁתַּצִּילֵנִי הַיּוֹם וּבְכָל יוֹם מֵעַזֵּי פָנִים וּמֵעַזּוּת פָּנִים, מֵאָדָם רָע, וּמֵחָבֵר רָע, וּמִשָּׁכֵן רָע, וּמִפֶּגַע רָע, וּמִשָּׂטָן הַמַּשְׁחִית, מִדִּין קָשֶׁה, וּמִבַּעַל דִּין קָשֶׁה בֵּין שֶׁהוּא בֶן בְּרִית וּבֵין שֶׁאֵינוֹ בֶּן בְּרִית. ברכות טז:

פרשת העקדה

On the basis of Jewish mystical tradition, some have the custom of saying daily the biblical passage recounting the Binding of Isaac, the supreme trial of faith in which Abraham demonstrated his love of God above all other loves. On שבת *and* יום טוב*, most omit the introductory and concluding prayers,* אֱלֹהֵינוּ וֵאלֹהֵי אֲבוֹתֵינוּ *and* רִבּוֹנוֹ שֶׁל עוֹלָם*. Others skip to* לְעוֹלָם יְהֵא אָדָם *on page 28.*

אֱלֹהֵינוּ וֵאלֹהֵי אֲבוֹתֵינוּ, זָכְרֵנוּ בְּזִכָּרוֹן טוֹב לְפָנֶיךָ, וּפָקְדֵנוּ בִּפְקֻדַּת יְשׁוּעָה וְרַחֲמִים מִשְּׁמֵי שְׁמֵי קֶדֶם, וּזְכָר לָנוּ יהוה אֱלֹהֵינוּ, אַהֲבַת הַקַּדְמוֹנִים אַבְרָהָם יִצְחָק וְיִשְׂרָאֵל עֲבָדֶיךָ, אֶת הַבְּרִית וְאֶת הַחֶסֶד וְאֶת הַשְּׁבוּעָה שֶׁנִּשְׁבַּעְתָּ לְאַבְרָהָם אָבִינוּ בְּהַר הַמּוֹרִיָּה, וְאֶת הָעֲקֵדָה שֶׁעָקַד אֶת יִצְחָק בְּנוֹ עַל גַּבֵּי הַמִּזְבֵּחַ, כַּכָּתוּב בְּתוֹרָתֶךָ:

וַיְהִי אַחַר הַדְּבָרִים הָאֵלֶּה, וְהָאֱלֹהִים נִסָּה אֶת־אַבְרָהָם, וַיֹּאמֶר אֵלָיו אַבְרָהָם, וַיֹּאמֶר הִנֵּנִי: וַיֹּאמֶר קַח־נָא אֶת־בִּנְךָ אֶת־יְחִידְךָ אֲשֶׁר־אָהַבְתָּ, אֶת־יִצְחָק, וְלֶךְ־לְךָ אֶל־אֶרֶץ הַמֹּרִיָּה, וְהַעֲלֵהוּ שָׁם לְעֹלָה עַל אַחַד הֶהָרִים אֲשֶׁר אֹמַר אֵלֶיךָ: וַיַּשְׁכֵּם אַבְרָהָם בַּבֹּקֶר, וַיַּחֲבֹשׁ אֶת־חֲמֹרוֹ, וַיִּקַּח אֶת־שְׁנֵי נְעָרָיו אִתּוֹ וְאֵת יִצְחָק בְּנוֹ, וַיְבַקַּע עֲצֵי עֹלָה, וַיָּקָם וַיֵּלֶךְ אֶל־הַמָּקוֹם אֲשֶׁר־אָמַר־לוֹ הָאֱלֹהִים: בַּיּוֹם בראשית כב

---

we awake from שֵׁינָה, which is a deep sleep in which our thought processes are distorted, to enter the stage of תְנוּמָה in which we can think more clearly, even if our eyes are still closed. Finally, we awake completely as we open our eyelids to engage with the world around us (Vilna Gaon).

וִיהִי רָצוֹן – *And may it be Your will* (previous page). We do not recite Amen after hearing the preceding *berakha*, as what follows is a continuation of the *berakha* linked with the letter ו ("and").

יְהִי רָצוֹן – *May it be Your will.* The Gemara (*Berakhot* 16b) records this as the prayer of R. Yehuda HaNasi, which he recited after completing the *Amida*.

אֲבוֹתֵינוּ – *Our fathers.* We call upon God as *the God of our fathers,* because we wish to identify with the merit of our righteous forebears (*Etz Yosef*). The phrase אֱלֹהֵינוּ וֵאלֹהֵי אֲבוֹתֵינוּ, "our God and the God of our fathers," occurs frequently in prayer. It may be a reference to the same phrase at the beginning of the *Amida*, where the phrase stresses God's covenant with the patriarchs, Abraham, Isaac and Jacob (as it says in *Berakhot* 16b: "Only three are called patriarchs"), but it may at other times also stress God's personal relationship with all of our ancestors, with each of our fathers and mothers, their parents and their parents' parents through all generations since the founding of the Jewish family (Ramban).

Berakhot 16b Lord my God, God of my fathers, may it be Your will to rescue me today and every day from those who are shameless and insolent, from the wicked, from evil associates and evil neighbors, from accidents and the corrupting Satan, from harsh judgments and uncompromising opponents, whether or not they are members of the covenant.

THE BINDING OF ISAAC

On the basis of Jewish mystical tradition, some have the custom of saying daily the biblical passage recounting the Binding of Isaac, the supreme trial of faith in which Abraham demonstrated his love of God above all other loves. On Shabbat and Yom Tov, most omit the introductory and concluding prayers, "Our God and God of our fathers" and "Ruler of the universe." Others skip to "A person should" on page 29.

Our God and God of our fathers, think benevolently of us. From Your everlasting supreme heights, remember us with thoughts of mercy and deliverance. Lord our God, recall in our favor the love of the patriarchs, Your servants Abraham, Isaac, and Israel. Recall in our favor the loving-kindness of Your covenant-oath sworn to our forefather Abraham on Mount Moriah, when he bound his son Isaac upon the altar, as we are told in Your Torah.

Gen. 22 וַיְהִי IT CAME TO PASS after these things that God tested Abraham, and said to him, "Abraham," and he answered, "Here I am." And He said, "Take now your son, your only son, the one you love, Isaac, and go to the land of Moriah, and offer him there for a burnt-offering on one of the mountains of which I will tell you." So Abraham rose up early in the morning, saddled his ass, and took two of his young men with him, and Isaac his son; he cut the wood for the burnt-offering and rose up and went to the place of which God had told him.

When coming before God in prayer, we present ourselves not just as individuals in our merit, but also as members of the covenanted Jewish people that transcends place and time, united in the mission to bring God's world to ultimate perfection (R. Joseph B. Soloveitchik).

Having thanked God for giving us renewed life, health, and vigor at the start of a new day, in this paragraph we ask Him to provide the conditions that will allow us to serve Him without any obstacle (*Siaḥ Yitzḥak*).

פָּרָשַׁת הָעֲקֵדָה / THE AKEDA
The *Akeda* (Binding of Isaac) is the story of the most difficult challenge to Abraham's faith, as recorded in Genesis 22:1–19. At its conclusion (vv. 16–18) God swears that in the merit of this heroic act, Abraham's descendants will be blessed, multiplied and victorious in all their endeavors. Just as Abraham arose early in the morning (as the narrative relates) to do the will of God, we too invoke the memory of this epochal event when we arise to serve

הַשְּׁלִישִׁי וַיִּשָּׂא אַבְרָהָם אֶת־עֵינָיו וַיַּרְא אֶת־הַמָּקוֹם מֵרָחֹק: וַיֹּאמֶר אַבְרָהָם אֶל־נְעָרָיו, שְׁבוּ־לָכֶם פֹּה עִם־הַחֲמוֹר, וַאֲנִי וְהַנַּעַר נֵלְכָה עַד־כֹּה, וְנִשְׁתַּחֲוֶה וְנָשׁוּבָה אֲלֵיכֶם: וַיִּקַּח אַבְרָהָם אֶת־עֲצֵי הָעֹלָה וַיָּשֶׂם עַל־יִצְחָק בְּנוֹ, וַיִּקַּח בְּיָדוֹ אֶת־הָאֵשׁ וְאֶת־הַמַּאֲכֶלֶת, וַיֵּלְכוּ שְׁנֵיהֶם יַחְדָּו: וַיֹּאמֶר יִצְחָק אֶל־אַבְרָהָם אָבִיו, וַיֹּאמֶר אָבִי, וַיֹּאמֶר הִנֶּנִּי בְנִי, וַיֹּאמֶר, הִנֵּה הָאֵשׁ וְהָעֵצִים, וְאַיֵּה הַשֶּׂה לְעֹלָה: וַיֹּאמֶר אַבְרָהָם, אֱלֹהִים יִרְאֶה־לּוֹ הַשֶּׂה לְעֹלָה, בְּנִי, וַיֵּלְכוּ שְׁנֵיהֶם יַחְדָּו: וַיָּבֹאוּ אֶל־הַמָּקוֹם אֲשֶׁר אָמַר־לוֹ הָאֱלֹהִים, וַיִּבֶן שָׁם אַבְרָהָם אֶת־הַמִּזְבֵּחַ וַיַּעֲרֹךְ אֶת־הָעֵצִים, וַיַּעֲקֹד אֶת־יִצְחָק בְּנוֹ, וַיָּשֶׂם אֹתוֹ עַל־הַמִּזְבֵּחַ מִמַּעַל לָעֵצִים: וַיִּשְׁלַח אַבְרָהָם אֶת־יָדוֹ, וַיִּקַּח אֶת־הַמַּאֲכֶלֶת, לִשְׁחֹט אֶת־בְּנוֹ: וַיִּקְרָא אֵלָיו מַלְאַךְ יהוה מִן־הַשָּׁמַיִם, וַיֹּאמֶר אַבְרָהָם אַבְרָהָם, וַיֹּאמֶר הִנֵּנִי: וַיֹּאמֶר אַל־תִּשְׁלַח יָדְךָ אֶל־הַנַּעַר, וְאַל־תַּעַשׂ לוֹ מְאוּמָה, כִּי עַתָּה יָדַעְתִּי כִּי־יְרֵא אֱלֹהִים אַתָּה, וְלֹא חָשַׂכְתָּ אֶת־בִּנְךָ אֶת־יְחִידְךָ מִמֶּנִּי: וַיִּשָּׂא אַבְרָהָם אֶת־עֵינָיו, וַיַּרְא וְהִנֵּה־אַיִל, אַחַר נֶאֱחַז בַּסְּבַךְ בְּקַרְנָיו, וַיֵּלֶךְ אַבְרָהָם וַיִּקַּח אֶת־הָאַיִל, וַיַּעֲלֵהוּ לְעֹלָה תַּחַת בְּנוֹ: וַיִּקְרָא אַבְרָהָם שֵׁם־הַמָּקוֹם הַהוּא יהוה יִרְאֶה, אֲשֶׁר יֵאָמֵר הַיּוֹם בְּהַר יהוה יֵרָאֶה: וַיִּקְרָא מַלְאַךְ יהוה אֶל־אַבְרָהָם שֵׁנִית מִן־הַשָּׁמָיִם: וַיֹּאמֶר, בִּי נִשְׁבַּעְתִּי נְאֻם־יהוה, כִּי יַעַן אֲשֶׁר עָשִׂיתָ אֶת־הַדָּבָר הַזֶּה, וְלֹא חָשַׂכְתָּ אֶת־בִּנְךָ אֶת־יְחִידֶךָ: כִּי־בָרֵךְ אֲבָרֶכְךָ, וְהַרְבָּה אַרְבֶּה אֶת־זַרְעֲךָ כְּכוֹכְבֵי הַשָּׁמַיִם, וְכַחוֹל אֲשֶׁר עַל־שְׂפַת הַיָּם, וְיִרַשׁ זַרְעֲךָ אֵת שַׁעַר אֹיְבָיו: וְהִתְבָּרְכוּ בְזַרְעֲךָ כֹּל גּוֹיֵי הָאָרֶץ, עֵקֶב אֲשֶׁר שָׁמַעְתָּ בְּקֹלִי: וַיָּשָׁב אַבְרָהָם אֶל־נְעָרָיו, וַיָּקֻמוּ וַיֵּלְכוּ יַחְדָּו אֶל־בְּאֵר שָׁבַע, וַיֵּשֶׁב אַבְרָהָם בִּבְאֵר שָׁבַע:

---

our Creator, in the hope that we will merit the rewards promised his descendants in the merit of the *Akeda*.

There is also a profound lesson for the Jew in reciting this story at the beginning of each day. Abraham, who was dedicated to his daily pursuits as a shepherd and a trader, who accumulated wealth, was ready to sacrifice everything in the service of God, including his beloved only child. Covenantal man knows when to act like a warrior – majestic, dignified, and proud – and when to part with everything he has (R. Joseph B. Soloveitchik).

אֱלֹהִים יִרְאֶה־לּוֹ הַשֶּׂה לְעֹלָה, בְּנִי – *God will*

On the third day Abraham lifted up his eyes and saw the place far off. Then Abraham said to his young men, "Stay here with the ass; as for me and the lad, we will go yonder and worship and come back to you." So Abraham took the wood of the burnt-offering and loaded it on Isaac his son, and he took in his hand the fire and the knife; and they went both of them together.

Then Isaac spoke to Abraham his father, and said, "My father," and he answered, "Here am I, my son." And Isaac said, "Behold the fire and the wood, but where is the lamb for a burnt-offering?" Abraham said, "God will provide the lamb for a burnt-offering, my son"; and they went, both of them, together. And they came to the place of which God had told them, and Abraham built the altar and arranged the wood, bound Isaac his son, and laid him on the altar upon the wood. Then Abraham extended his hand and took the knife to slay his son. But the angel of the Lord called to him out of the heavens and said, "Abraham, Abraham," and he answered, "Here I am." And He said, "Do not extend your hand against the lad or do anything to him; for now I know that you are God-fearing, seeing that you have not withheld from Me your son, your only son." Then Abraham lifted up his eyes and looked, and behold, behind him a ram was caught in the thicket by its horns. So Abraham went and took the ram and offered it for a burnt-offering instead of his son. Then Abraham called the name of that place "The Lord will see," as it is said to this day, "The mount where the Lord is seen."

The angel of the Lord called to Abraham a second time out of the heavens, and said, "By Myself I swear, says the Lord, that because you have done this thing and have not withheld your son, your only son, I will surely bless you and will multiply your seed as the stars of heaven and as the sand on the seashore; your seed shall possess the gate of their enemies, and through your seed shall all the nations of the earth be blessed, because you have hearkened to My voice." So Abraham returned to his young men, and they rose up and went together to Beersheba; and Abraham dwelt at Beersheba.

---

provide the lamb for a burnt-offering, my son. The *Midrash* teaches that by placing "my son" after "lamb," rather than at the beginning of his response, Abraham conveyed, and Isaac understood, that he would be the sacrificial "lamb." Nevertheless, "*the two of them went*

Most omit this passage on שבת *and* יום טוב.

רִבּוֹנוֹ שֶׁל עוֹלָם, כְּמוֹ שֶׁכָּבַשׁ אַבְרָהָם אָבִינוּ אֶת רַחֲמָיו לַעֲשׂוֹת רְצוֹנְךָ בְּלֵבָב שָׁלֵם, כֵּן יִכְבְּשׁוּ רַחֲמֶיךָ אֶת כַּעַסְךָ מֵעָלֵינוּ וְיִגֹּלּוּ רַחֲמֶיךָ עַל מִדּוֹתֶיךָ. וְתִתְנַהֵג עִמָּנוּ יהוה אֱלֹהֵינוּ בְּמִדַּת הַחֶסֶד וּבְמִדַּת הָרַחֲמִים, וּבְטוּבְךָ הַגָּדוֹל יָשׁוּב חֲרוֹן אַפְּךָ מֵעַמְּךָ וּמֵעִירְךָ וּמֵאַרְצְךָ וּמִנַּחֲלָתֶךָ. וְקַיֶּם לָנוּ יהוה אֱלֹהֵינוּ אֶת הַדָּבָר שֶׁהִבְטַחְתָּנוּ בְּתוֹרָתֶךָ עַל יְדֵי מֹשֶׁה עַבְדֶּךָ,
ויקרא כו כָּאָמוּר: וְזָכַרְתִּי אֶת־בְּרִיתִי יַעֲקוֹב וְאַף אֶת־בְּרִיתִי יִצְחָק, וְאַף אֶת־בְּרִיתִי אַבְרָהָם אֶזְכֹּר, וְהָאָרֶץ אֶזְכֹּר:

קבלת עול מלכות שמים

תנא דבי אליהו, פרק כא **לְעוֹלָם** יְהֵא אָדָם יְרֵא שָׁמַיִם בְּסֵתֶר וּבְגָלוּי, וּמוֹדֶה עַל הָאֱמֶת, וְדוֹבֵר אֱמֶת בִּלְבָבוֹ, וְיַשְׁכֵּם וְיֹאמַר

דניאל ט **רִבּוֹן** כָּל הָעוֹלָמִים, לֹא עַל־צִדְקוֹתֵינוּ אֲנַחְנוּ מַפִּילִים תַּחֲנוּנֵינוּ לְפָנֶיךָ, כִּי עַל־רַחֲמֶיךָ הָרַבִּים: מָה אָנוּ, מֶה חַיֵּינוּ, מֶה חַסְדֵּנוּ, מַה צִּדְקוֹתֵינוּ, מַה יְּשׁוּעָתֵנוּ, מַה כֹּחֵנוּ, מַה גְּבוּרָתֵנוּ, מַה נֹּאמַר לְפָנֶיךָ, יהוה אֱלֹהֵינוּ וֵאלֹהֵי אֲבוֹתֵינוּ, הֲלֹא כָּל הַגִּבּוֹרִים כְּאַיִן לְפָנֶיךָ, וְאַנְשֵׁי הַשֵּׁם כְּלֹא הָיוּ, וַחֲכָמִים כִּבְלִי מַדָּע, וּנְבוֹנִים כִּבְלִי הַשְׂכֵּל, כִּי

---

together," joined in father-son collaboration, just as when they had set out earlier when "the two of them went together." Thus the *Akeda* was not a test just of Abraham, but of Isaac too.

קַבָּלַת עֹל מַלְכוּת שָׁמַיִם / ACCEPTING THE SOVEREIGNTY OF HEAVEN

לְעוֹלָם – *Should always*. The section beginning here and extending until the recitation of the opening verse of the *Shema* comes from the early *Midrash Seder Eliyahu Raba*, and is a succinct statement of Jewish faith and loyalty to God. It was likely introduced during a period of persecution as a substitute for the full recitation of the *Shema* (*Shibbolei HaLeket*). The ninth-century Gaon Mar Sar Shalom records that in the year 456 CE the Persian king Yezdegerd II forbade the observance of Shabbat as well as the *Shema*. An adherent of the Zoroastrian religion that proclaimed the existence of two gods (one of light/goodness and one of darkness/evil), Yezdegerd sought to eradicate the belief in one God. In response, the sages of the time instituted two recitations of the first verse of *Shema:* the one here, which was to be recited at home, and another one as part of the Shabbat *Musaf Kedusha*. Although both contain only the first verse of the *Shema*, this sufficed to fulfill the *Shema* obligation.

יְרֵא שָׁמַיִם בְּסֵתֶר וּבְגָלוּי – *Be God-fearing, whether in private or in public.* As this prayer was originally composed for a time of persecution, worshipers were urged to at least recite the *Shema* in private, hence the word וּבְגָלוּי is missing from older *siddurim*. In *Seder Eliyahu Raba*, the word בְּסֵתֶר, "privately," is missing, too. Rashi urged the omission of the entire phrase, lest one think that religious observance is only necessary in private (*Shibbolei HaLeket*). Indeed, this

Most omit this passage on Shabbat and Yom Tov.

Ruler of the universe, Lord our God and God of our fathers, in judging us, please count in our favor Your covenant with our fathers. Just as Abraham our father overcame his natural compassion for his only son in order to do as You willed, so let mercy prevail over justice in dealing with us. Let mercy temper justice. Display Your attributes of mercy and kindness in dealing with us, Lord our God, rather than the strict measure of what we deserve. In Your great goodness, turn the flame of Your displeasure away from Your people, from Zion Your city, from Your land, Your heritage. Instead, Lord our God, fulfill the promise given us in Your Torah
Lev. 26 when You said to Your servant Moses: "I will remember My covenant with Jacob and My covenant with Isaac; and also My covenant with Abraham will I remember, and the land will I remember."

ACCEPTING THE SOVEREIGNTY OF HEAVEN

Tanna DeVei Eliyahu, ch. 21 לְעוֹלָם A PERSON should always be God-fearing, whether in private or in public, acknowledging the truth, speaking the truth in his heart, arising early to proclaim:

Dan. 9 רִבּוֹן RULER of the entire universe! It is not because of our righteousness that we dare bring our requests to You, but because of Your great mercy. What are we? What is our life? What our goodness? What our righteousness? What our help? What our strength? What our power? What can we say in Your presence, Lord our God and God of our fathers? The most powerful humans are nothing before You, renowned people are nonentities, the learned are illiterates, the wise know nothing. For most of their deeds are pointless, the days of their

---

whole first sentence is not part of the prayer, but an instruction. The prevalent custom is to recite it, though some instead begin with "Master of all the Worlds" (R. Hershel Schachter).

וְדוֹבֵר אֱמֶת בִּלְבָבוֹ – *Speaking the truth in his heart*. The sages were very critical of those whose outward actions were not consistent with their innermost thoughts or convictions. The Gemara (*Makkot* 24a and *Bava Batra* 88a) spoke of R. Safra who would never mislead others, no matter the consequences to himself. Thus once, while reciting the *Shema*, someone approached him and offered to purchase an item for sale. While he was unable to respond, R. Safra made a mental note accepting the offer. The buyer, unaware of the real reason for R. Safra's silence, raised his offer. Later R. Safra refused to accept anything more than the original, lower, amount, clearly an act of punctilious adherence to the truth. A similar anecdote involving R. Safra is recorded in the Gemara *Ḥullin* 94b.

רִבּוֹן כָּל הָעוֹלָמִים – *Ruler of the entire universe*. This prayer, composed by R. Yoḥanan for the

קהלת ג רֹב מַעֲשֵׂיהֶם תֹּהוּ, וִימֵי חַיֵּיהֶם הֶבֶל לְפָנֶיךָ, וּמוֹתַר הָאָדָם מִן־הַבְּהֵמָה אָיִן, כִּי הַכֹּל הָבֶל:

אֲבָל אֲנַחְנוּ עַמְּךָ בְּנֵי בְרִיתֶךָ, בְּנֵי אַבְרָהָם אֹהַבְךָ שֶׁנִּשְׁבַּעְתָּ לּוֹ בְּהַר הַמּוֹרִיָּה, זֶרַע יִצְחָק יְחִידוֹ שֶׁנֶּעֱקַד עַל גַּבֵּי הַמִּזְבֵּחַ, עֲדַת יַעֲקֹב בִּנְךָ בְכוֹרֶךָ, שֶׁמֵּאַהֲבָתְךָ שֶׁאָהַבְתָּ אוֹתוֹ, וּמִשִּׂמְחָתְךָ שֶׁשָּׂמַחְתָּ בּוֹ, קָרָאתָ אֶת שְׁמוֹ יִשְׂרָאֵל וִישֻׁרוּן.

לְפִיכָךְ אֲנַחְנוּ חַיָּבִים, לְהוֹדוֹת לְךָ וּלְשַׁבֵּחֲךָ וּלְפָאֶרְךָ, וּלְבָרֵךְ וּלְקַדֵּשׁ וְלָתֵת שֶׁבַח וְהוֹדָיָה לִשְׁמֶךָ. אַשְׁרֵינוּ, מַה טּוֹב חֶלְקֵנוּ, וּמַה נָּעִים גּוֹרָלֵנוּ, וּמַה יָּפָה יְרֻשָּׁתֵנוּ. ◂ אַשְׁרֵינוּ, שֶׁאֲנַחְנוּ מַשְׁכִּימִים וּמַעֲרִיבִים עֶרֶב וָבֹקֶר, וְאוֹמְרִים פַּעֲמַיִם בְּכָל יוֹם

דברים ו **שְׁמַע** יִשְׂרָאֵל, יהוה אֱלֹהֵינוּ, יהוה אֶחָד:

Quietly בָּרוּךְ שֵׁם כְּבוֹד מַלְכוּתוֹ לְעוֹלָם וָעֶד.

Some congregations say the entire first paragraph of the שמע *(below) at this point.*

וְאָהַבְתָּ אֵת יהוה אֱלֹהֶיךָ, בְּכָל־לְבָבְךָ, וּבְכָל־נַפְשְׁךָ, וּבְכָל־מְאֹדֶךָ: וְהָיוּ הַדְּבָרִים הָאֵלֶּה, אֲשֶׁר אָנֹכִי מְצַוְּךָ הַיּוֹם, עַל־לְבָבֶךָ: וְשִׁנַּנְתָּם לְבָנֶיךָ, וְדִבַּרְתָּ בָּם, בְּשִׁבְתְּךָ בְּבֵיתֶךָ, וּבְלֶכְתְּךָ בַדֶּרֶךְ, וּבְשָׁכְבְּךָ וּבְקוּמֶךָ: וּקְשַׁרְתָּם לְאוֹת עַל־יָדֶךָ וְהָיוּ לְטֹטָפֹת בֵּין עֵינֶיךָ: וּכְתַבְתָּם עַל־מְזֻזוֹת בֵּיתֶךָ וּבִשְׁעָרֶיךָ:

Yom Kippur וִדּוּי (confessional) service, describes the kindness of God, Who in spite of His infinite majesty desires a personal relationship with us. He selected Israel as the vehicle for this relationship, and thus enabled us to reach up to Him in prayer, and achieve a life of holiness (R. Joseph B. Soloveitchik).

יִשְׂרָאֵל וִישֻׁרוּן – *Israel and Jeshurun*. These two names reflect Jacob's dual spiritual nature. The name יִשְׂרָאֵל (from שְׂרָרָה, *mastery*) refers to Jacob's triumph over the angel (Gen. 35:10), while יְשֻׁרוּן (from יָשָׁר, *upright, fair*) refers to his dedication to justice in accordance with God's will. Alternately, the name Israel reflects the holy nature of Jews' relationships with each other, while *Yeshurun* reflects the projection of our moral light upon the nations of the world via the Torah's moral teachings that the Jewish

SHEMA BEFORE KORBANOT

When one recites this paragraph, one should specifically have in mind not to fulfill the *mitzva* of reciting *Shema* unless one is concerned that he will not be able to recite *Shema* in its proper time (*MB* 46:31).

Eccl. 3 lives are empty in Your eyes. The pre-eminence of man over beast amounts to nothing, for all is vanity.

Yet we are Your people, the members of Your covenant. We are the children of Abraham, who loved You, and to whom You gave Your promise on Mount Moriah. We are the descendants of his only son, Isaac, who was bound on the altar. We are the community of Your firstborn, Jacob, whom You called Israel and Jeshurun because of Your love for him and Your rejoicing in him.

לְפִיכָךְ THEREFORE we must give thanks to You, we glorify and extol You, bless and sanctify Your name, and voice our gratitude to You. We are happy! We enjoy a goodly portion, a pleasant lot, a beautiful heritage! ▸ Happy are we who twice each day, in the morning and in the evening, declare:

Deut. 6 HEAR, O ISRAEL, the LORD is our God, the LORD is One.

Quietly: Blessed is the name of His glorious kingdom forever and ever.

Some congregations say the entire first paragraph of the Shema (below) at this point.

YOU SHALL LOVE the Lord your God with all your heart, and with all your soul, and with all your might. And these words which I command you this day shall be upon your heart. You shall teach them diligently to your children, speaking of them when you sit in your house and when you walk by the way, when you lie down and when you rise up. You shall bind them for a sign on your hand, and they shall be as *tefillin* between your eyes. And you shall write them upon the doorposts of your house and upon your gates.

---

nation has brought to the world (R. Avraham Yitzḥak HaKohen Kook).

שְׁמַע יִשְׂרָאֵל – *Hear, O Israel.* Since the *Shema* must be recited during the first quarter of daylight, and the congregation may not reach that part of the service in time (especially on Shabbat or Yom Tov), some authorities adopted the custom of reciting not just the first verse but the first paragraph of the *Shema* at this point to fulfill that obligation in timely fashion. This was the custom of the Maharshal (*Magen Avraham*). The *Mishna Berura* and *Arukh HaShulḥan* recommend that one who is concerned about missing the deadline for reciting the *Shema* should recite all three paragraphs at this point.

אֶחָד – *One.* What distinguishes God is not merely that He is one and not many, but that (as Rambam in particular explained at length, with all of its consequences for what we are to believe about Him) His unity is absolute, indivisible, and unlike any other unity. Thus He is one of a kind, incomparable, and in every respect utterly unlike anything else that has

אַתָּה הוּא עַד שֶׁלֹּא נִבְרָא הָעוֹלָם, אַתָּה הוּא מִשֶּׁנִּבְרָא הָעוֹלָם.
אַתָּה הוּא בָּעוֹלָם הַזֶּה, וְאַתָּה הוּא לָעוֹלָם הַבָּא. ◄ קַדֵּשׁ
אֶת שִׁמְךָ עַל מַקְדִּישֵׁי שְׁמֶךָ, וְקַדֵּשׁ אֶת שִׁמְךָ בְּעוֹלָמֶךָ, וּבִישׁוּעָתְךָ
תָּרוּם וְתַגְבִּיהַּ קַרְנֵנוּ. בָּרוּךְ אַתָּה יהוה מְקַדֵּשׁ אֶת שִׁמְךָ בָּרַבִּים.

אַתָּה הוּא יהוה אֱלֹהֵינוּ, בַּשָּׁמַיִם וּבָאָרֶץ, וּבִשְׁמֵי הַשָּׁמַיִם הָעֶלְיוֹנִים.
אֱמֶת, אַתָּה הוּא רִאשׁוֹן, וְאַתָּה הוּא אַחֲרוֹן, וּמִבַּלְעָדֶיךָ אֵין
אֱלֹהִים. קַבֵּץ קוֶֹיךָ מֵאַרְבַּע כַּנְפוֹת הָאָרֶץ. יַכִּירוּ וְיֵדְעוּ כָּל בָּאֵי
עוֹלָם, כִּי אַתָּה הוּא הָאֱלֹהִים לְבַדְּךָ לְכֹל מַמְלְכוֹת הָאָרֶץ.

אַתָּה עָשִׂיתָ אֶת הַשָּׁמַיִם וְאֶת הָאָרֶץ, אֶת הַיָּם וְאֶת כָּל אֲשֶׁר בָּם,
וּמִי בְּכָל מַעֲשֵׂי יָדֶיךָ בָּעֶלְיוֹנִים אוֹ בַתַּחְתּוֹנִים, שֶׁיֹּאמַר לְךָ
מַה תַּעֲשֶׂה.

אָבִינוּ שֶׁבַּשָּׁמַיִם, עֲשֵׂה עִמָּנוּ חֶסֶד, בַּעֲבוּר שִׁמְךָ הַגָּדוֹל שֶׁנִּקְרָא
עָלֵינוּ, וְקַיֶּם לָנוּ יהוה אֱלֹהֵינוּ, מַה שֶּׁכָּתוּב:
בָּעֵת הַהִיא אָבִיא אֶתְכֶם, וּבָעֵת קַבְּצִי אֶתְכֶם, כִּי־אֶתֵּן אֶתְכֶם צפניה ג
לְשֵׁם וְלִתְהִלָּה בְּכֹל עַמֵּי הָאָרֶץ, בְּשׁוּבִי אֶת־שְׁבוּתֵיכֶם לְעֵינֵיכֶם,
אָמַר יהוה:

---

or ever will exist, i.e., He is Unique (R. Joseph B. Soloveitchik).

אַתָּה הוּא – *You are.* After Yezdegerd's decrees forbidding the recital of *Shema* lapsed, this blessing was added to thank God for once again being able to sanctify and proclaim His name in public (*Levush*).

The phrase "אַתָּה הוּא" expresses two themes: divine closeness (אַתָּה – You, in the second person, conveying direct communication) and divine transcendence (הוּא – He, in the third person, conveys distance). The two words thus capture the tension between two seemingly contradictory aspects of God's relationship to the Jewish people (R. Avraham Yitzhak HaKohen Kook).

קַדֵּשׁ אֶת שִׁמְךָ עַל מַקְדִּישֵׁי שְׁמֶךָ – *Sanctify Your name through us who sanctify Your name.* When originally composed, this referred to the Jewish martyrs who had sanctified the name through their unyielding loyalty to Him, even if it resulted in death.

מְקַדֵּשׁ אֶת שִׁמְךָ בָּרַבִּים – *Who sanctifies Your name among the multitudes.* The *mitzva* of

אַתָּה YOU EXISTED before the world was created; You have existed ever since the world was created; You exist in this world; You will exist in the World to Come. ▸ Sanctify Your name through those who sanctify Your name, and sanctify Your name throughout Your world. Apply Your saving power to raise us up and strengthen us. Blessed are You, Lord, Who sanctifies Your name among the multitudes.

אַתָּה YOU ARE the Lord our God in every sphere of the heavens above and here on the earth below. In truth, You are the first and You are the last, and there is no God except You. From the four corners of the earth, gather in those who hope in You. Then all mankind will know and acknowledge that You are God, You alone, over all the kingdoms of the earth.

אַתָּה THAT YOU have made the heavens, the earth, the sea, and everything that is in them. Who among all the works of Your hands, celestial or terrestrial, would dare to question You?

אָבִינוּ שֶׁבַּשָּׁמַיִם OUR FATHER in heaven, deal graciously with us for the sake of Your great name by which we are called. Fulfill for us, Lord our God, the promise You gave us through Your prophet
Zeph. 3 Zephaniah: "At that time will I bring you in, and at that time will I gather you and single you out for renown and praise among all the peoples of the earth, when I bring back your captivity before your eyes, says the Lord."

קדוש ה' (sanctification of God's name) extends to the point of sacrificing one's life under specific circumstances. Needless to say, Jewish history is replete with instances of such martyrdom. This *berakha* is to be seen in that context. A notable, and inspirational, instance of such sanctification is provided by the following anecdote: During World War II in the Bochnia ghetto a number of young Jewish women were rounded up to be shot. As a last wish they requested that the *mikveh* of the ghetto be opened for them to immerse themselves. After their immersion, the German officer asked the young lady who spoke for them why they had done such a thing. She replied, "Cleanliness and purity of body and mind are part of our tradition and way of life. God has brought our pure souls into this world in the pure homes of our parents, and we wish to return in purity to our Father in heaven." The German officer took his pistol and at close range shot the woman between the eyes. Most of the other women were also killed that day (Prof. Yaffa Eliach).

סדר הקרבנות

חז״ל held that, in the absence of the Temple, studying the laws of sacrifices is the equivalent of offering them. Hence the following texts. There are different customs as to how many passages are to be said, and one should follow the custom of one's congregation. The minimum requirement is to say the verses relating to the קרבן תמיד on the next page.

פרשת הכיור

שמות ל **וַיְדַבֵּר** יהוה אֶל־מֹשֶׁה לֵּאמֹר: וְעָשִׂיתָ כִּיּוֹר נְחֹשֶׁת וְכַנּוֹ נְחֹשֶׁת לְרָחְצָה, וְנָתַתָּ אֹתוֹ בֵּין־אֹהֶל מוֹעֵד וּבֵין הַמִּזְבֵּחַ, וְנָתַתָּ שָׁמָּה מָיִם: וְרָחֲצוּ אַהֲרֹן וּבָנָיו מִמֶּנּוּ אֶת־יְדֵיהֶם וְאֶת־רַגְלֵיהֶם: בְּבֹאָם אֶל־אֹהֶל מוֹעֵד יִרְחֲצוּ־מַיִם, וְלֹא יָמֻתוּ, אוֹ בְגִשְׁתָּם אֶל־הַמִּזְבֵּחַ לְשָׁרֵת, לְהַקְטִיר אִשֶּׁה לַיהוה: וְרָחֲצוּ יְדֵיהֶם וְרַגְלֵיהֶם וְלֹא יָמֻתוּ, וְהָיְתָה לָהֶם חָק־עוֹלָם, לוֹ וּלְזַרְעוֹ לְדֹרֹתָם:

פרשת תרומת הדשן

ויקרא ו **וַיְדַבֵּר** יהוה אֶל־מֹשֶׁה לֵּאמֹר: צַו אֶת־אַהֲרֹן וְאֶת־בָּנָיו לֵאמֹר, זֹאת תּוֹרַת הָעֹלָה, הִוא הָעֹלָה עַל מוֹקְדָה עַל־הַמִּזְבֵּחַ כָּל־הַלַּיְלָה עַד־הַבֹּקֶר, וְאֵשׁ הַמִּזְבֵּחַ תּוּקַד בּוֹ: וְלָבַשׁ הַכֹּהֵן מִדּוֹ בַד, וּמִכְנְסֵי־בַד יִלְבַּשׁ עַל־בְּשָׂרוֹ, וְהֵרִים אֶת־הַדֶּשֶׁן אֲשֶׁר תֹּאכַל הָאֵשׁ אֶת־הָעֹלָה, עַל־הַמִּזְבֵּחַ, וְשָׂמוֹ אֵצֶל הַמִּזְבֵּחַ: וּפָשַׁט אֶת־בְּגָדָיו, וְלָבַשׁ בְּגָדִים אֲחֵרִים, וְהוֹצִיא אֶת־הַדֶּשֶׁן אֶל־מִחוּץ לַמַּחֲנֶה, אֶל־מָקוֹם טָהוֹר: וְהָאֵשׁ עַל־הַמִּזְבֵּחַ תּוּקַד־בּוֹ, לֹא תִכְבֶּה, וּבִעֵר עָלֶיהָ הַכֹּהֵן עֵצִים בַּבֹּקֶר בַּבֹּקֶר, וְעָרַךְ עָלֶיהָ הָעֹלָה, וְהִקְטִיר עָלֶיהָ חֶלְבֵי הַשְּׁלָמִים: אֵשׁ, תָּמִיד תּוּקַד עַל־הַמִּזְבֵּחַ, לֹא תִכְבֶּה:

קָרְבָּנוֹת / OFFERINGS
Two reasons are given for reciting the laws of sacrifices at this point. The first, in accordance with *Kiddushin* 30a, is that in so doing we are studying Torah (i.e., Scripture, Mishna, and Gemara), and thus following up on the earlier-recited *Birkhot HaTorah*.

The second reason echoes the words of the prophet Hosea (14:3) that proclaim וּנְשַׁלְּמָה פָרִים שְׂפָתֵינוּ, *"the words of our lips will compensate for [the absence of] the sacrificial animals."* Thus by quoting selected written Torah verses regarding sacrifices and studying their laws we temporarily substitute for the sacrifices until such time as the Temple will be rebuilt.

SACRIFICES

The sages held that, in the absence of the Temple, studying the laws of sacrifices is the equivalent of offering them. Hence the following texts. There are different customs as to how many passages are to be said, and one should follow the custom of one's congregation. The minimum requirement is to say the verses relating to The Daily Sacrifice on the next page.

THE BASIN

Ex. 30 וַיְדַבֵּר THE LORD SPOKE to Moses, saying, "You shall make a bronze laver with its base of bronze, for washing, and you shall set it between the Tent of Meeting and the altar, and in it you shall put water. From it Aaron and his sons shall wash their hands and their feet. When they go into the Tent of Meeting or when they approach the altar to minister, to cause to smoke an offering made by fire to the Lord, they shall wash in water so that they die not. They shall wash their hands and their feet so that they die not, and it shall be an everlasting statute for them, for Aaron and for his seed throughout their generations."

TAKING OF THE ASHES

Lev. 6 וַיְדַבֵּר THE LORD SPOKE to Moses, saying: Instruct Aaron and his sons, saying, This is the law of the burnt-offering. The burnt-offering shall remain on the altar hearth throughout the night until morning, and the altar fire shall be kept burning on it. The priest shall then put on his linen tunic, and linen breeches next to his body, and shall remove the ashes of the burnt-offering that the fire has consumed on the altar and place them beside the altar. Then he shall take off these clothes and put on others, and carry the ashes outside the camp to a clean place. The fire on the altar must be kept burning; it must not go out. Each morning the priest shall burn wood on it, and prepare on it the burnt-offering and burn the fat of the peace-offerings. A perpetual fire must be kept burning on the altar; it must not go out.

הַכִּיּוֹר / THE BASIN

In Exodus 38:8 we are told that the basin was made of brass from "the mirrors of the serving women who served at the entrance to the Tabernacle." *Targum Onkelos* translates this as "the mirrors of the women who came to pray at set times at the entrance to the Tabernacle." The reason that these righteous women donated their mirrors is related to Miriam's well, from which the Israelites drew all their water. The *Tosefta Sukkot* (3:3) explains that when the people encamped, the well would settle at the entrance to the Tabernacle, ready to pour forth its water. The women, including Miriam, would

יְהִי רָצוֹן מִלְּפָנֶיךָ יהוה אֱלֹהֵינוּ וֵאלֹהֵי אֲבוֹתֵינוּ, שֶׁתְּרַחֵם עָלֵינוּ, וְתִמְחֹל לָנוּ עַל כָּל חַטֹּאתֵינוּ וּתְכַפֵּר לָנוּ עַל כָּל עֲוֹנוֹתֵינוּ וְתִסְלַח לָנוּ עַל כָּל פְּשָׁעֵינוּ, וְתִבְנֶה בֵּית הַמִּקְדָּשׁ בִּמְהֵרָה בְיָמֵינוּ, וְנַקְרִיב לְפָנֶיךָ קָרְבַּן הַתָּמִיד שֶׁיְּכַפֵּר בַּעֲדֵנוּ, כְּמוֹ שֶׁכָּתַבְתָּ עָלֵינוּ בְּתוֹרָתֶךָ עַל יְדֵי מֹשֶׁה עַבְדֶּךָ מִפִּי כְבוֹדֶךָ, כָּאָמוּר

פרשת קרבן התמיד

במדבר כח **וַיְדַבֵּר** יהוה אֶל־מֹשֶׁה לֵּאמֹר: צַו אֶת־בְּנֵי יִשְׂרָאֵל וְאָמַרְתָּ אֲלֵהֶם,
אֶת־קָרְבָּנִי לַחְמִי לְאִשַּׁי, רֵיחַ נִיחֹחִי, תִּשְׁמְרוּ לְהַקְרִיב לִי
בְּמוֹעֲדוֹ: וְאָמַרְתָּ לָהֶם, זֶה הָאִשֶּׁה אֲשֶׁר תַּקְרִיבוּ לַיהוה, כְּבָשִׂים
בְּנֵי־שָׁנָה תְמִימִם שְׁנַיִם לַיּוֹם, עֹלָה תָמִיד: אֶת־הַכֶּבֶשׂ אֶחָד תַּעֲשֶׂה
בַבֹּקֶר, וְאֵת הַכֶּבֶשׂ הַשֵּׁנִי תַּעֲשֶׂה בֵּין הָעַרְבָּיִם: וַעֲשִׂירִית הָאֵיפָה
סֹלֶת לְמִנְחָה, בְּלוּלָה בְּשֶׁמֶן כָּתִית רְבִיעִת הַהִין: עֹלַת תָּמִיד,
הָעֲשֻׂיָה בְּהַר סִינַי, לְרֵיחַ נִיחֹחַ אִשֶּׁה לַיהוה: וְנִסְכּוֹ רְבִיעִת הַהִין
לַכֶּבֶשׂ הָאֶחָד, בַּקֹּדֶשׁ הַסֵּךְ נֶסֶךְ שֵׁכָר לַיהוה: וְאֵת הַכֶּבֶשׂ הַשֵּׁנִי
תַּעֲשֶׂה בֵּין הָעַרְבָּיִם, כְּמִנְחַת הַבֹּקֶר וּכְנִסְכּוֹ תַּעֲשֶׂה, אִשֵּׁה רֵיחַ
נִיחֹחַ לַיהוה:

ויקרא א וְשָׁחַט אֹתוֹ עַל יֶרֶךְ הַמִּזְבֵּחַ צָפֹנָה לִפְנֵי יהוה, וְזָרְקוּ בְּנֵי אַהֲרֹן
הַכֹּהֲנִים אֶת־דָּמוֹ עַל־הַמִּזְבֵּחַ, סָבִיב:

יְהִי רָצוֹן מִלְּפָנֶיךָ, יהוה אֱלֹהֵינוּ וֵאלֹהֵי אֲבוֹתֵינוּ, שֶׁתְּהֵא אֲמִירָה זוֹ חֲשׁוּבָה וּמְקֻבֶּלֶת וּמְרֻצָּה לְפָנֶיךָ, כְּאִלּוּ הִקְרַבְנוּ קָרְבַּן הַתָּמִיד בְּמוֹעֲדוֹ וּבִמְקוֹמוֹ וּכְהִלְכָתוֹ.

אַתָּה הוּא יהוה אֱלֹהֵינוּ שֶׁהִקְטִירוּ אֲבוֹתֵינוּ לְפָנֶיךָ אֶת קְטֹרֶת הַסַּמִּים בִּזְמַן שֶׁבֵּית הַמִּקְדָּשׁ הָיָה קַיָּם, כַּאֲשֶׁר צִוִּיתָ אוֹתָם עַל יְדֵי מֹשֶׁה נְבִיאֶךָ, כַּכָּתוּב בְּתוֹרָתֶךָ:

---

gather at that spot early each day to collect their share. Sometimes, however, the water did not come forth, and (as stated in Num. 21:17) special prayers had to be offered. On such occasions, being the first ones at the entrance, the women initiated the prayers before the men arrived. When informed that Miriam's well water would maintain and purify the basin, these women offered their mirrors for its construction, to ensure that all the water in the camp and Tabernacle would depend completely on the merit of righteous women (R. Zalman Sorotzkin).

May it be Your will, Lord our God and God of our fathers, to deal with us in mercy, to forgive all our wrongdoing, to make us atone for all our transgressions, and to pardon all our sins. May You rebuild the holy Temple speedily, so that we may atone before You by bringing our daily offering, in the spirit You prescribed for us in Your Torah through Moses Your servant, in these words:

THE DAILY SACRIFICE

Num. 28 **וַיְדַבֵּר** THE LORD SPOKE to Moses, saying, "Command the children of Israel and say to them, My offering, My bread for My offerings made by fire, you shall take care to offer to Me for a sweet savor in its due season. Say also to them, This is the fire-offering which you shall bring to the Lord: unblemished male lambs of the first year, two each day as a regular daily burnt-offering. One lamb you shall prepare in the morning, and the other lamb you shall prepare toward evening, with a tenth of an ephah of fine flour for a grain-offering, mixed with a fourth of a hin of pure oil. This is the regular daily burnt-offering as it was prepared at Mount Sinai, a fire-offering for a sweet fragrance to the Lord. And the libation that accompanies it shall be a fourth of a hin for the first lamb. You shall pour out the strong wine in the holy place as a libation to the Lord. The second lamb you shall offer toward evening, preparing it as the morning grain-offering and as its drink-offering, an offering made by fire, of a sweet fragrance to the Lord."

Lev. 1 One shall slay the sacrifice on the north side of the altar before the Lord, and the sons of Aaron, the priests, shall dash its blood against the altar all around it.

May it be Your will, Lord our God and God of our fathers, that this recitation be considered accepted and favored before You as if we had offered the daily sacrifice at its appointed time and place, according to its laws.

You are the Lord our God before Whom, in the days of the holy Temple, our ancestors burned the offerings of incense. For this is what You commanded them, through Moses Your prophet, in the words of Your Torah:

פרשת הקטורת

שמות ל **וַיֹּאמֶר** יהוה אֶל־מֹשֶׁה, קַח־לְךָ סַמִּים נָטָף וּשְׁחֵלֶת וְחֶלְבְּנָה, סַמִּים וּלְבֹנָה זַכָּה, בַּד בְּבַד יִהְיֶה: וְעָשִׂיתָ אֹתָהּ קְטֹרֶת, רֹקַח מַעֲשֵׂה רוֹקֵחַ, מְמֻלָּח, טָהוֹר קֹדֶשׁ: וְשָׁחַקְתָּ מִמֶּנָּה הָדֵק, וְנָתַתָּה מִמֶּנָּה לִפְנֵי הָעֵדֻת בְּאֹהֶל מוֹעֵד אֲשֶׁר אִוָּעֵד לְךָ שָׁמָּה, קֹדֶשׁ קָדָשִׁים תִּהְיֶה לָכֶם: וְנֶאֱמַר, וְהִקְטִיר עָלָיו אַהֲרֹן קְטֹרֶת סַמִּים, בַּבֹּקֶר בַּבֹּקֶר בְּהֵיטִיבוֹ אֶת־הַנֵּרֹת יַקְטִירֶנָּה: וּבְהַעֲלֹת אַהֲרֹן אֶת־הַנֵּרֹת בֵּין הָעַרְבַּיִם יַקְטִירֶנָּה, קְטֹרֶת תָּמִיד לִפְנֵי יהוה לְדֹרֹתֵיכֶם:

כריתות ו. **תָּנוּ רַבָּנָן:** פִּטּוּם הַקְּטֹרֶת כֵּיצַד, שְׁלֹשׁ מֵאוֹת וְשִׁשִּׁים וּשְׁמוֹנָה מָנִים הָיוּ בָהּ. שְׁלֹשׁ מֵאוֹת וְשִׁשִּׁים וַחֲמִשָּׁה כְּמִנְיַן יְמוֹת הַחַמָּה, מָנֶה לְכָל יוֹם, פְּרָס בְּשַׁחֲרִית וּפְרָס בֵּין הָעַרְבַּיִם, וּשְׁלֹשָׁה מָנִים יְתֵרִים שֶׁמֵּהֶם מַכְנִיס כֹּהֵן גָּדוֹל מְלֹא חָפְנָיו בְּיוֹם הַכִּפּוּרִים, וּמַחֲזִירָן לְמַכְתֶּשֶׁת בְּעֶרֶב יוֹם הַכִּפּוּרִים וְשׁוֹחֲקָן יָפֶה יָפֶה, כְּדֵי שֶׁתְּהֵא דַקָּה מִן הַדַּקָּה. וְאַחַד עָשָׂר סַמָּנִים הָיוּ בָהּ, וְאֵלּוּ הֵן: א הַצֳּרִי, ב וְהַצִּפֹּרֶן, ג וְהַחֶלְבְּנָה, ד וְהַלְּבוֹנָה מִשְׁקַל שִׁבְעִים שִׁבְעִים מָנֶה, ה מֹר, ו וּקְצִיעָה, ז שִׁבֹּלֶת נֵרְדְּ, ח וְכַרְכֹּם מִשְׁקַל שִׁשָּׁה עָשָׂר שִׁשָּׁה עָשָׂר מָנֶה, ט הַקֹּשְׁטְ שְׁנֵים עָשָׂר, י קִלּוּפָה שְׁלֹשָׁה, יא קִנָּמוֹן תִּשְׁעָה, בֹּרִית כַּרְשִׁינָה תִּשְׁעָה קַבִּין, יֵין קַפְרִיסִין סְאִין תְּלָתָא וְקַבִּין תְּלָתָא, וְאִם לֹא מָצָא יֵין קַפְרִיסִין, מֵבִיא חֲמַר חִוַּרְיָן עַתִּיק. מֶלַח סְדוֹמִית רֹבַע, מַעֲלֶה עָשָׁן כָּל שֶׁהוּא. רַבִּי נָתָן הַבַּבְלִי אוֹמֵר: אַף כִּפַּת הַיַּרְדֵּן כָּל שֶׁהוּא, וְאִם נָתַן בָּהּ דְּבַשׁ פְּסָלָהּ, וְאִם חִסַּר אֶחָד מִכָּל סַמָּנֶיהָ, חַיָּב מִיתָה.

פָּרָשַׁת הַקְּטֹרֶת / THE INCENSE

The incense offering (*ketoret*) plays an especially prominent role in the daily prayer service. During the Middle Ages, some communities incorporated the passages regarding the incense at the conclusion of the morning service (*Tur*, Rema), while others recited it here (*Eliyahu Raba* in the name of *Piskei Tosafot*). *Nusaḥ Sepharad* has adopted both customs, and includes this recitation here and also at the end of the service (in addition to reciting certain sacrifice-related verses before the daily *Minḥa* service). Interestingly, Siddur Rashi records a custom to also recite these passages after the *Ma'ariv* service. However, Rema notes the custom to refrain from reciting these passages every day at the end of the daily service, out of fear that worshipers hurrying to leave for work would imprecisely recite the list of ingredients and their quantities, thus invalidating the verbal offering. Some sources mention the heavenly capital punishment for offering improperly mixed incense (*Or HaḤayyim*). Hence, *Nusaḥ Ashkenaz* excludes this recitation from the conclusion of the weekday service.

וַיֹּאמֶר ה' ... קַח־לְךָ סַמִּים – *The Lord said... Take as sweet spices.* The requirement for eleven spices is derived from this verse in the following man-

THE INCENSE

Ex. 30 וַיֹּאמֶר THE LORD SAID to Moses, "Take as sweet spices, oil of myrrh, onycha, and galbanum, together with clear frankincense, the same weight of each of these sweet spices. And you shall make it into incense, a perfume pure and holy blended by the perfumer, mixed with salt. And you shall crush some of it very fine, and put some of it before the Ark of Testimony in the Tent of Meeting where I will meet with you; most holy shall it be to you." It also says in the Torah: "Aaron shall burn the incense of sweet spices on the altar of incense; every morning, when he prepares the lambs, he shall burn it. And toward evening, when Aaron lights the lamps, he shall again burn incense, a perpetual incense before the Lord in every generation."

Keritot 6a תָּנוּ רַבָּנָן THE RABBIS TAUGHT how the incense was blended. The total measure of the incense was 368 manehs: one maneh for each day of the solar year, half a maneh brought in the morning and another half-maneh toward evening. The remaining three were for the High Priest to bring both his handfuls on Yom Kippur. The last three manehs were ground again, very fine, in a mortar on the eve of Yom Kippur so as to fulfill the command, "Take of the finest beaten incense." The incense was compounded of eleven different spices: seventy manehs each of [1] balm, [2] onycha, [3] galbanum, and [4] frankincense; sixteen manehs each of [5] myrrh, [6] cassia, [7] spikenard, and [8] saffron; twelve manehs of [9] costus; three manehs of [10] aromatic bark; nine manehs of [11] cinnamon; nine kabs of lye of Carsina; three seahs and three kabs of Cyprus wine, although if Cyprus wine was not available, strong white wine might be substituted for it; a fourth of a kab of salt of Sodom, and a small quantity of an herb that caused the smoke to ascend straight upward. R. Nathan said that a small quantity of kippah of the Jordan was also added. Adding honey made the incense unfit for sacred use. One who omitted any of the specified ingredients was deemed guilty of a capital offense.

---

ner: סַמִּים, *spices*, is plural, yielding two kinds; then three spices are named, for a total of five; the word סַמִּים appears again implying the addition of another group of five (equivalent to the five given above). Finally frankincense is added, for a total of eleven. The identity of the spices is not known with certainty, and is the subject of considerable debate among contemporary archaeologists and botanists. Some suggest that they are balsam (or gum sap), a part of a sea snail traditionally identified as clove, galbanum, frankincense, myrrh, cassia, spikenard, saffron, costus (a plant related to ginger), muskat nut bark, and cinnamon (Prof. Zohar Amar).

וְאִם חִסַּר – *Who omitted.* If he used either more

רַבָּן שִׁמְעוֹן בֶּן גַּמְלִיאֵל אוֹמֵר: הַצֳּרִי אֵינוֹ אֶלָּא שְׂרָף הַנּוֹטֵף מֵעֲצֵי הַקְּטָף. בֹּרִית כַּרְשִׁינָה שֶׁשָּׁפִין בָּהּ אֶת הַצִּפֹּרֶן כְּדֵי שֶׁתְּהֵא נָאָה, יֵין קַפְרִיסִין שֶׁשּׁוֹרִין בּוֹ אֶת הַצִּפֹּרֶן כְּדֵי שֶׁתְּהֵא עַזָּה, וַהֲלֹא מֵי רַגְלַיִם יָפִין לָהּ, אֶלָּא שֶׁאֵין מַכְנִיסִין מֵי רַגְלַיִם בַּמִּקְדָּשׁ מִפְּנֵי הַכָּבוֹד.

תַּנְיָא, רַבִּי נָתָן אוֹמֵר: כְּשֶׁהוּא שׁוֹחֵק אוֹמֵר, הָדֵק הֵיטֵב הֵיטֵב הָדֵק, מִפְּנֵי שֶׁהַקּוֹל יָפֶה לַבְּשָׂמִים. פִּטְּמָהּ לַחֲצָאִין כְּשֵׁרָה, לִשְׁלִישׁ וְלִרְבִיעַ לֹא שָׁמַעְנוּ. אָמַר רַבִּי יְהוּדָה: זֶה הַכְּלָל, אִם כְּמִדָּתָהּ כְּשֵׁרָה לַחֲצָאִין, וְאִם חִסַּר אֶחָד מִכָּל סַמָּנֶיהָ חַיָּב מִיתָה.

ירושלמי יומא ד, הלכה ה

תַּנְיָא, בַּר קַפָּרָא אוֹמֵר: אַחַת לְשִׁשִּׁים אוֹ לְשִׁבְעִים שָׁנָה הָיְתָה בָאָה שֶׁל שִׁירַיִם לַחֲצָאִין. וְעוֹד תָּנֵי בַּר קַפָּרָא: אִלּוּ הָיָה נוֹתֵן בָּהּ קָרְטוֹב שֶׁל דְּבַשׁ אֵין אָדָם יָכוֹל לַעֲמֹד מִפְּנֵי רֵיחָהּ, וְלָמָּה אֵין מְעָרְבִין בָּהּ דְּבַשׁ, מִפְּנֵי שֶׁהַתּוֹרָה אָמְרָה: כִּי כָל־שְׂאֹר וְכָל־דְּבַשׁ לֹא־תַקְטִירוּ מִמֶּנּוּ אִשֶּׁה לַיהוה: ויקרא ב

Each of the three following verses is said three times.

תהלים מו — יהוה צְבָאוֹת עִמָּנוּ, מִשְׂגָּב לָנוּ אֱלֹהֵי יַעֲקֹב סֶלָה:

תהלים פד — יהוה צְבָאוֹת, אַשְׁרֵי אָדָם בֹּטֵחַ בָּךְ:

תהלים כ — יהוה הוֹשִׁיעָה, הַמֶּלֶךְ יַעֲנֵנוּ בְיוֹם־קָרְאֵנוּ:

תהלים לב, מלאכי ג — אַתָּה סֵתֶר לִי, מִצַּר תִּצְּרֵנִי, רָנֵּי פַלֵּט תְּסוֹבְבֵנִי סֶלָה: וְעָרְבָה לַיהוה מִנְחַת יְהוּדָה וִירוּשָׁלָםִ, כִּימֵי עוֹלָם וּכְשָׁנִים קַדְמֹנִיּוֹת:

---

or less than the prescribed amount of any ingredient, he is liable to the heavenly death penalty (*Etz Yosef*). According to Rashi (*Keritot* 6b) this applies only to the Yom Kippur service in the Holy of Holies. Rambam, however, applies this ruling to the whole year, because an improper mixture is regarded as קְטֹרֶת זָרָה (a strange, i.e., unauthorized *incense*).

פִּטְּמָהּ לַחֲצָאִין – *Incense maker*. Instead of mixing 368 *maneh* as was customarily done, someone mixed only 184 *maneh*. Since the manner of compounding was transmitted orally, the question arose whether it was forbidden to prepare spice-mixtures totaling *less* than the usual 368 *maneh*. R. Natan stated that he had learned that it *was* permitted to make mixtures containing exactly half the normal amount, but he did not know whether smaller mixtures, too, were permitted. To this, R. Yehuda replied that any amount, even a one-day supply, was acceptable, provided the ingredients were in the correct proportion.

רַבָּן R. SIMEON son of Gamliel said that balsam resin was the balm required for the incense. The lye of Carsina was rubbed on the onycha to refine its appearance. The onycha was steeped in the Cyprus wine to make it more pungent. Urine would have achieved the same purpose, but was not used because it would have been unseemly to bring it into the Temple.

תַּנְיָא IT IS TAUGHT: R. Nathan said that when the priest ground the incense the overseer would say, "Grind it very fine, very fine grind it," because the sound of the voice is encouraging in making spices. If the incense maker only compounded 184 manehs (half the required quantity), it would be valid, but there is no tradition sanctioning a third- or a quarter-proportion of the required quantity. The general principle, according to R. Judah, is that a half-quantity of the incense was permissible if all the ingredients were in their correct proportions, but if one omitted any of the ingredients he was deemed guilty of a capital offense.

Keritot 6a תַּנְיָא IT IS TAUGHT: Bar Kappara said that some of the three manehs of incense from which the high priest took his handfuls on Yom Kippur was often left over; every sixty or seventy years, enough of this had accumulated to make up half the required amount of incense for the year. Bar Kappara also taught that if the smallest quantity of honey had been mixed into the incense, its aroma would have been unbearable. Why didn't they mix honey
Lev. 2 with the incense? Because the Torah states: "No leaven, nor any honey, shall you make smoke as an offering made by fire to the Lord."

Each of the three following verses is said three times.

Ps. 46 The Lord of hosts is with us. The God of Jacob is our refuge. Selah.
Ps. 84 O Lord of hosts, happy is the man who trusts in You.
Ps. 20 Lord, save! The King will answer us on the day that we call.

Ps. 32 You are my hiding-place. You will protect me from the enemy. You will surround me
Mal. 3 with songs of deliverance. Selah. May the offerings of Judah and Jerusalem please the Lord as they did in days of old and times long past.

ה׳ צְבָאוֹת עִמָּנוּ – *Lord of hosts, be with us.* The incense represents divine mastery over all, particularly the intermixing of disparate ingredients into one fragrant unity. This unifying principle is reflected in this name of God that conveys that His power encompasses every distinct phenomenon in creation, including our own souls (R. Abraham Yitzḥak HaKohen Kook).

סדר המערכה

יומא לג. **אַבַּיֵי** הֲוָה מְסַדֵּר סֵדֶר הַמַּעֲרָכָה מִשְּׁמָא דִגְמָרָא, וְאַלִּבָּא דְאַבָּא שָׁאוּל: מַעֲרָכָה גְדוֹלָה קוֹדֶמֶת לְמַעֲרָכָה שְׁנִיָּה שֶׁל קְטֹרֶת, וּמַעֲרָכָה שְׁנִיָּה שֶׁל קְטֹרֶת קוֹדֶמֶת לְסִדּוּר שְׁנֵי גִזְרֵי עֵצִים, וְסִדּוּר שְׁנֵי גִזְרֵי עֵצִים קוֹדֵם לְדִשּׁוּן מִזְבֵּחַ הַפְּנִימִי, וְדִשּׁוּן מִזְבֵּחַ הַפְּנִימִי קוֹדֵם לַהֲטָבַת חָמֵשׁ נֵרוֹת, וַהֲטָבַת חָמֵשׁ נֵרוֹת קוֹדֶמֶת לְדַם הַתָּמִיד, וְדַם הַתָּמִיד קוֹדֵם לַהֲטָבַת שְׁתֵּי נֵרוֹת, וַהֲטָבַת שְׁתֵּי נֵרוֹת קוֹדֶמֶת לִקְטֹרֶת, וּקְטֹרֶת קוֹדֶמֶת לְאֵבָרִים, וְאֵבָרִים לְמִנְחָה, וּמִנְחָה לַחֲבִתִּין, וַחֲבִתִּין לִנְסָכִין, וּנְסָכִין לְמוּסָפִין, וּמוּסָפִין לְבָזִיכִין, וּבָזִיכִין קוֹדְמִין לְתָמִיד שֶׁל בֵּין הָעַרְבַּיִם. שֶׁנֶּאֱמַר: וְעָרַךְ עָלֶיהָ ויקרא ו הָעֹלָה, וְהִקְטִיר עָלֶיהָ חֶלְבֵי הַשְּׁלָמִים: עָלֶיהָ הַשְׁלֵם כָּל הַקָּרְבָּנוֹת כֻּלָּם.

אָנָּא, בְּכֹחַ גְּדֻלַּת יְמִינְךָ, תַּתִּיר צְרוּרָה.
קַבֵּל רִנַּת עַמְּךָ, שַׂגְּבֵנוּ, טַהֲרֵנוּ, נוֹרָא.
נָא גִבּוֹר, דּוֹרְשֵׁי יִחוּדְךָ כְּבָבַת שָׁמְרֵם.
בָּרְכֵם, טַהֲרֵם, רַחֲמֵם, צִדְקָתְךָ תָּמִיד גָּמְלֵם.
חֲסִין קָדוֹשׁ, בְּרֹב טוּבְךָ נַהֵל עֲדָתֶךָ.
יָחִיד גֵּאֶה, לְעַמְּךָ פְּנֵה, זוֹכְרֵי קְדֻשָּׁתֶךָ.
שַׁוְעָתֵנוּ קַבֵּל וּשְׁמַע צַעֲקָתֵנוּ, יוֹדֵעַ תַּעֲלוּמוֹת.
בָּרוּךְ שֵׁם כְּבוֹד מַלְכוּתוֹ לְעוֹלָם וָעֶד.

רִבּוֹן הָעוֹלָמִים, אַתָּה צִוִּיתָנוּ לְהַקְרִיב קָרְבַּן הַתָּמִיד בְּמוֹעֲדוֹ וְלִהְיוֹת כֹּהֲנִים בַּעֲבוֹדָתָם וּלְוִיִּם בְּדוּכָנָם וְיִשְׂרָאֵל בְּמַעֲמָדָם, וְעַתָּה בַּעֲוֹנוֹתֵינוּ חָרַב בֵּית הַמִּקְדָּשׁ וּבֻטַּל הַתָּמִיד וְאֵין לָנוּ לֹא כֹהֵן בַּעֲבוֹדָתוֹ וְלֹא לֵוִי בְּדוּכָנוֹ הושע יד וְלֹא יִשְׂרָאֵל בְּמַעֲמָדוֹ, וְאַתָּה אָמַרְתָּ: וּנְשַׁלְּמָה פָרִים שְׂפָתֵינוּ: לָכֵן יְהִי רָצוֹן מִלְּפָנֶיךָ יהוה אֱלֹהֵינוּ וֵאלֹהֵי אֲבוֹתֵינוּ, שֶׁיְּהֵא שִׂיחַ שִׂפְתוֹתֵינוּ חָשׁוּב וּמְקֻבָּל וּמְרֻצֶּה לְפָנֶיךָ, כְּאִלּוּ הִקְרַבְנוּ קָרְבַּן הַתָּמִיד בְּמוֹעֲדוֹ וְעָמַדְנוּ עַל מַעֲמָדוֹ.

אָנָּא, בְּכֹחַ – *We pray, through the awesome power*. This prayer – ascribed by Rashba to the *Tanna* R. Neḥunia ben HaKana – is inserted at this point because, in Lurianic terminology, now that we have gathered the sacred kernels (through the recitation of the *Ketoret*) that were mixed in with the chaff ("*kelipot*"), the "roots" of evil, we want to establish the relationship between the "entry realm" of prayer – that of *asiya*, represented by the sacrifice section of prayer – to the contemplative realm of *yetzira* ("fashioning") that constitutes the next section,

THE ORDER OF THE PRIESTLY FUNCTIONS

Yoma 33a אַבַּיֵּי ABBAYE set down the sequence of the ordained daily ritual in the Temple in keeping with the accepted tradition and on the authority of Abba Saul. The wood was first set in order on the altar for the sacrifice, then for the incense, and then two pieces of wood were arranged. Next the ashes were removed from the inner altar, the five lamps were prepared, the blood of the daily offering was sprinkled, and the remaining two lamps were prepared. After this came the burning of the morning incense, the offering of the parts of the sacrifice, the grain-offering, the baked grain-offering, the libations, the additional offerings on Shabbat and festivals, the two spoonfuls of frankincense, and finally the
Lev. 6 daily burnt-offering toward evening, as it is said: "The priest shall lay the burnt-offering in order upon the altar, and offer on it the fat of the peace-offerings"; in other words, this completes the whole sacrificial ritual of the day.

אָנָּא WE PRAY, through the awesome power of Your right hand, that You set captive Israel free.
Receive Your people's prayer; uplift us, make us pure, God of awe.
Almighty God, we pray You guard as the apple of Your eye those who seek Your unity.
Bless us, cleanse us, and please, mitigate Your justice for us with Your mercy.
Almighty Holy One, lead us, Your flock, in Your bountiful goodness.
Supreme and Only God, turn to Your people who are mindful of Your holiness.
Accept our prayer, give ear to our cry, You Who know our most private thoughts.
Blessed is the name of His glorious kingdom forever and ever.

רִבּוֹן RULER of the universe! You required us to enact the daily offering at its appointed time, with the priests officiating, the Levites at their posts, and all Israel represented through their delegations. Now, for our sins, our Temple has been laid waste, its daily offerings are abolished, and we have neither officiating priest nor Levites at their posts nor Israelite delegations. But You have declared through Your prophet Hosea that we may substitute the prayer of our lips for the
Hos. 14 sacrifice of bulls. Therefore, Lord our God and God of our fathers, if it be Your will, please accept the prayer of our lips just as favorably as if we were offering the daily Temple sacrifice at its appointed time and we had stood at its station.

---

the *Pesukei DeZimra*. This forty-two word prayer is an acronym formed out of God's forty-two letter name that He invoked when creating the physical world of *asiya*.

On שבת *add:*

במדבר כח **וּבְיוֹם הַשַּׁבָּת** שְׁנֵי־כְבָשִׂים בְּנֵי־שָׁנָה תְּמִימִם, וּשְׁנֵי עֶשְׂרֹנִים סֹלֶת מִנְחָה בְּלוּלָה בַשֶּׁמֶן, וְנִסְכּוֹ: עֹלַת שַׁבַּת בְּשַׁבַּתּוֹ, עַל־עֹלַת הַתָּמִיד וְנִסְכָּהּ:

On ראש חודש *add:*

במדבר כח **וּבְרָאשֵׁי חָדְשֵׁיכֶם** תַּקְרִיבוּ עֹלָה לַיהוה, פָּרִים בְּנֵי־בָקָר שְׁנַיִם, וְאַיִל אֶחָד, כְּבָשִׂים בְּנֵי־שָׁנָה שִׁבְעָה, תְּמִימִם: וּשְׁלֹשָׁה עֶשְׂרֹנִים סֹלֶת מִנְחָה בְּלוּלָה בַשֶּׁמֶן לַפָּר הָאֶחָד, וּשְׁנֵי עֶשְׂרֹנִים סֹלֶת מִנְחָה בְּלוּלָה בַשֶּׁמֶן לָאַיִל הָאֶחָד: וְעִשָּׂרֹן עִשָּׂרוֹן סֹלֶת מִנְחָה בְּלוּלָה בַשֶּׁמֶן לַכֶּבֶשׂ הָאֶחָד, עֹלָה רֵיחַ נִיחֹחַ, אִשֶּׁה לַיהוה: וְנִסְכֵּיהֶם, חֲצִי הַהִין יִהְיֶה לַפָּר, וּשְׁלִישִׁת הַהִין לָאַיִל, וּרְבִיעִת הַהִין לַכֶּבֶשׂ, יָיִן, זֹאת עֹלַת חֹדֶשׁ בְּחָדְשׁוֹ לְחָדְשֵׁי הַשָּׁנָה: וּשְׂעִיר עִזִּים אֶחָד לְחַטָּאת לַיהוה, עַל־עֹלַת הַתָּמִיד יֵעָשֶׂה, וְנִסְכּוֹ:

דיני זבחים

זבחים פרק ה א. **אֵיזֶהוּ** מְקוֹמָן שֶׁל זְבָחִים. קָדְשֵׁי קָדָשִׁים שְׁחִיטָתָן בַּצָּפוֹן. פַּר וְשָׂעִיר שֶׁל יוֹם הַכִּפּוּרִים, שְׁחִיטָתָן בַּצָּפוֹן, וְקִבּוּל דָּמָן בִּכְלִי שָׁרֵת בַּצָּפוֹן, וְדָמָן טָעוּן הַזָּיָה עַל בֵּין הַבַּדִּים, וְעַל הַפָּרֹכֶת, וְעַל מִזְבַּח הַזָּהָב. מַתָּנָה אַחַת מֵהֶן מְעַכָּבֶת. שְׁיָרֵי הַדָּם הָיָה שׁוֹפֵךְ עַל יְסוֹד מַעֲרָבִי שֶׁל מִזְבֵּחַ הַחִיצוֹן, אִם לֹא נָתַן לֹא עִכֵּב.

ב. פָּרִים הַנִּשְׂרָפִים וּשְׂעִירִים הַנִּשְׂרָפִים, שְׁחִיטָתָן בַּצָּפוֹן, וְקִבּוּל דָּמָן בִּכְלִי שָׁרֵת בַּצָּפוֹן, וְדָמָן טָעוּן הַזָּיָה עַל הַפָּרֹכֶת וְעַל מִזְבַּח הַזָּהָב. מַתָּנָה אַחַת מֵהֶן מְעַכָּבֶת. שְׁיָרֵי הַדָּם הָיָה שׁוֹפֵךְ עַל יְסוֹד מַעֲרָבִי שֶׁל מִזְבֵּחַ הַחִיצוֹן, אִם לֹא נָתַן לֹא עִכֵּב. אֵלּוּ וָאֵלּוּ נִשְׂרָפִין בְּבֵית הַדָּשֶׁן.

דִּינֵי זְבָחִים / LAWS OF OFFERINGS, MISHNA ZEVAḤIM

According to R. Safra, the reason that this section and the following one (the Thirteen Principles of R. Yishmael) were inserted here following the sacrifices is that we are to study the three components of Torah equally each day – i.e., Scripture, Mishna, and Talmud – and studying *Midrash Halakha* is equivalent to studying Talmud. This section consists of the *mishnayot*

On Shabbat add:

Num. 28 **וּבְיוֹם הַשַּׁבָּת** ON SHABBAT you shall bring two unblemished male lambs of the first year, a grain-offering of two-tenths of an ephah of fine flour mixed with oil, and its libation. This is the burnt-offering for every Shabbat, in addition to the regular daily burnt-offering and its libation.

On Rosh Ḥodesh add:

Num. 28 **וּבְרָאשֵׁי חָדְשֵׁיכֶם** AT THE BEGINNINGS of your months you shall bring as a burnt-offering to the Lord two young bullocks, one ram, and seven unblemished male lambs of the first year. And a grain-offering of three-tenths of an ephah of fine flour mixed with oil for each bullock, and a grain-offering of two-tenths of an ephah of fine flour mixed with oil for the one ram, and a grain-offering of one-tenth of an ephah of fine flour mixed with oil for each male lamb, a burnt-offering of a sweet savor, an offering made by fire to the Lord. And the libations with them shall be wine: half a hin for each bullock, a third of a hin for the ram, and a fourth of a hin for each male lamb. This shall be the burnt-offering for the beginning of each month for the months of the year. In addition, one he-goat shall be offered to the Lord as a sin-offering, along with the regular burnt-offering and its libation.

LAWS OF OFFERINGS, MISHNA ZEVAḤIM

Zevaḥim Ch. 5

1. **אֵיזֶהוּ** WHICH were the places of sacrifice in the Temple? The most sacred offerings were slaughtered on the north side of the altar, including the bull and the he-goat for Yom Kippur. Their blood was there received in a ritual vessel to be sprinkled between the staves of the Ark, before the veil of the Holy of Holies, and upon the golden altar. Omission of the sprinkling invalidated the atonement ceremonial. The priest poured out the remaining blood on the western base of the outer altar, but if he failed to do so, the atonement ceremony was not invalidated.

2. THE BULLS and the he-goats that were to be totally burned were slaughtered on the north side of the altar, and their blood was there received in a ritual vessel to be sprinkled before the veil and upon the golden altar. The omission of even one sprinkling invalidated the atonement ceremonial. The priest poured out the remaining blood at the western base of the outer altar; but if he failed to do so, the atonement ceremonial was not invalidated. These as well as the preceding offerings were burned in the repository of ashes.

---

of *Zevaḥim* chapter 5, related to the foregoing sacrifices. The passage of R. Yishmael is found in the *Midrash Halakha* at the beginning of *Torat Kohanim,* introducing the sacrifices (*Tur*).

This chapter was also chosen insofar as it

ג. חַטֹּאת הַצִּבּוּר וְהַיָּחִיד. אֵלּוּ הֵן חַטֹּאת הַצִּבּוּר: שְׂעִירֵי רָאשֵׁי חֳדָשִׁים וְשֶׁל מוֹעֲדוֹת. שְׁחִיטָתָן בַּצָּפוֹן, וְקִבּוּל דָּמָן בִּכְלִי שָׁרֵת בַּצָּפוֹן, וְדָמָן טָעוּן אַרְבַּע מַתָּנוֹת עַל אַרְבַּע קְרָנוֹת. כֵּיצַד, עָלָה בַכֶּבֶשׁ, וּפָנָה לַסּוֹבֵב, וּבָא לוֹ לְקֶרֶן דְּרוֹמִית מִזְרָחִית, מִזְרָחִית צְפוֹנִית, צְפוֹנִית מַעֲרָבִית, מַעֲרָבִית דְּרוֹמִית. שְׁיָרֵי הַדָּם הָיָה שׁוֹפֵךְ עַל יְסוֹד דְּרוֹמִי. וְנֶאֱכָלִין לִפְנִים מִן הַקְּלָעִים, לְזִכְרֵי כְהֻנָּה, בְּכָל מַאֲכָל, לְיוֹם וָלַיְלָה עַד חֲצוֹת.

ד. הָעוֹלָה קֹדֶשׁ קָדָשִׁים. שְׁחִיטָתָהּ בַּצָּפוֹן, וְקִבּוּל דָּמָהּ בִּכְלִי שָׁרֵת בַּצָּפוֹן, וְדָמָהּ טָעוּן שְׁתֵּי מַתָּנוֹת שֶׁהֵן אַרְבַּע, וּטְעוּנָה הֶפְשֵׁט וְנִתּוּחַ, וְכָלִיל לָאִשִּׁים.

ה. זִבְחֵי שַׁלְמֵי צִבּוּר וַאֲשָׁמוֹת. אֵלּוּ הֵן אֲשָׁמוֹת: אֲשַׁם גְּזֵלוֹת, אֲשַׁם מְעִילוֹת, אֲשַׁם שִׁפְחָה חֲרוּפָה, אֲשַׁם נָזִיר, אֲשַׁם מְצֹרָע, אָשָׁם תָּלוּי. שְׁחִיטָתָן בַּצָּפוֹן, וְקִבּוּל דָּמָן בִּכְלִי שָׁרֵת בַּצָּפוֹן, וְדָמָן טָעוּן שְׁתֵּי מַתָּנוֹת שֶׁהֵן אַרְבַּע. וְנֶאֱכָלִין לִפְנִים מִן הַקְּלָעִים, לְזִכְרֵי כְהֻנָּה, בְּכָל מַאֲכָל, לְיוֹם וָלַיְלָה עַד חֲצוֹת.

ו. הַתּוֹדָה וְאֵיל נָזִיר קָדָשִׁים קַלִּים. שְׁחִיטָתָן בְּכָל מָקוֹם בָּעֲזָרָה, וְדָמָן טָעוּן שְׁתֵּי מַתָּנוֹת שֶׁהֵן אַרְבַּע, וְנֶאֱכָלִין בְּכָל הָעִיר, לְכָל אָדָם, בְּכָל מַאֲכָל, לְיוֹם וָלַיְלָה עַד חֲצוֹת. הַמּוּרָם מֵהֶם כַּיּוֹצֵא בָהֶם, אֶלָּא שֶׁהַמּוּרָם נֶאֱכָל לַכֹּהֲנִים, לִנְשֵׁיהֶם, וְלִבְנֵיהֶם וּלְעַבְדֵיהֶם.

ז. שְׁלָמִים קָדָשִׁים קַלִּים. שְׁחִיטָתָן בְּכָל מָקוֹם בָּעֲזָרָה, וְדָמָן טָעוּן שְׁתֵּי מַתָּנוֹת שֶׁהֵן אַרְבַּע, וְנֶאֱכָלִין בְּכָל הָעִיר, לְכָל אָדָם, בְּכָל מַאֲכָל, לִשְׁנֵי

---

contains no differences of opinion among the sages, because its contents are a מִשְׁנָה בְּרוּרָה לְמֹשֶׁה מִסִּינַי (unambiguous teaching from Moses at Sinai) (*Ra'ah*).

This chapter surveys the various kinds of animal sacrifices, highlighting the main characteristics of each, and arranging them in order from the holiest to the least holy. The opening question focuses attention on the main (though not the only) feature which confers upon each sacrifice its unique character and degree of sanctity, i.e., its location. The first five *mishnayot* discuss "most holy" offerings (the term appears in *mishnayot* 1 and 4): sin-offerings of various kinds (*mishnayot* 1–3), elevation-offerings (*mishna* 4), communal peace-offerings (*mishna* 5), and guilt-offerings (*mishna* 5). These are all marked by the special

3. THE SIN-OFFERINGS of the whole congregation (namely, the he-goats offered on Rosh Ḥodesh and on festivals) and those of individuals were slaughtered on the north side of the altar, and their blood was there received in a ritual vessel. Four sprinklings of the blood were required, one on each of the four corners of the altar. How was this done? The priest went up the ramp to the altar and around its edge, successively, to its southeast, northeast, northwest, and southwest corners. He poured out the remaining blood at the southern side of the base of the outer altar. These sacrifices, prepared for food in whatever way was desired, were eaten within the Temple court by the males of the priesthood over the course of that day and evening until midnight.

4. THE BURNT-OFFERING was one of the most sacred of the offerings. It was slaughtered on the north side of the altar, and its blood was there received in a ritual vessel. Two double sprinklings of that blood were required, altogether constituting four sprinklings. This offering had to be flayed and dismembered and wholly consumed by fire.

5. AS FOR the peace-offerings of the whole congregation and the trespass-offerings: Trespass-offerings are required for robbery, for profane misappropriation of sanctified things, and for violating a betrothed handmaid; such offerings also are brought by a Nazirite defiled by a dead body, by a leper at his cleansing, and by anyone who is uncertain whether an act he has committed is a sin that needs atonement. All of these were slaughtered on the north side of the altar, and the blood was received there in a ritual vessel. Two double sprinklings of that blood were required, altogether constituting four sprinklings. These sacrifices, prepared for food in any way desired, were eaten within the Temple court by the males of the priesthood over the course of that day and evening until midnight.

6. THE THANKSGIVING-OFFERINGS of individuals and the ram offered by a Nazirite on the conclusion of his vow period were sacred in a minor degree. They could be slaughtered in any part of the Temple court and, prepared for food in whatever way was desired, could be eaten by anyone anywhere in the city until midnight. The same rules pertained to the portions of these sacrifices belonging to the priests, except that they could be eaten only by the priests, their wives, their children, and their servants.

7. THE PEACE-OFFERINGS also were sacred in a minor degree. They could be slaughtered in any part of the Temple court. Two double sprinklings of their blood were required, altogether constituting four sprinklings. Prepared for food in any way desired, they could be eaten by anyone anywhere in the city

יָמִים וְלַיְלָה אֶחָד. הַמּוּרָם מֵהֶם כַּיּוֹצֵא בָהֶם, אֶלָּא שֶׁהַמּוּרָם נֶאֱכָל לַכֹּהֲנִים, לִנְשֵׁיהֶם, וְלִבְנֵיהֶם וּלְעַבְדֵיהֶם.

ח. הַבְּכוֹר וְהַמַּעֲשֵׂר וְהַפֶּסַח קָדָשִׁים קַלִּים. שְׁחִיטָתָן בְּכָל מָקוֹם בָּעֲזָרָה, וְדָמָן טָעוּן מַתָּנָה אַחַת, וּבִלְבָד שֶׁיִּתֵּן כְּנֶגֶד הַיְסוֹד. שִׁנָּה בַאֲכִילָתָן, הַבְּכוֹר נֶאֱכָל לַכֹּהֲנִים וְהַמַּעֲשֵׂר לְכָל אָדָם, וְנֶאֱכָלִין בְּכָל הָעִיר, בְּכָל מַאֲכָל, לִשְׁנֵי יָמִים וְלַיְלָה אֶחָד. הַפֶּסַח אֵינוֹ נֶאֱכָל אֶלָּא בַלַּיְלָה, וְאֵינוֹ נֶאֱכָל אֶלָּא עַד חֲצוֹת, וְאֵינוֹ נֶאֱכָל אֶלָּא לִמְנוּיָו, וְאֵינוֹ נֶאֱכָל אֶלָּא צָלִי.

ברייתא דרבי ישמעאל

רַבִּי יִשְׁמָעֵאל אוֹמֵר: בִּשְׁלֹשׁ עֶשְׂרֵה מִדּוֹת הַתּוֹרָה נִדְרֶשֶׁת:

א מִקַּל וָחֹמֶר;

ב וּמִגְּזֵרָה שָׁוָה;

ג מִבִּנְיַן אָב מִכָּתוּב אֶחָד, וּמִבִּנְיַן אָב מִשְּׁנֵי כְתוּבִים;

ד מִכְּלָל וּפְרָט;

ה מִפְּרָט וּכְלָל;

ו כְּלָל וּפְרָט וּכְלָל, אִי אַתָּה דָן אֶלָּא כְּעֵין הַפְּרָט;

---

location, in the northern part of the courtyard, where they must be slaughtered. Additionally, none of these most holy offerings may be consumed outside of the Temple courtyard: the burnt-offering is consumed by the fire on the altar (*mishna* 4), and sacrifices described in *mishnayot* 3 and 5 are consumed by priests in the courtyard; the sacrifices in *mishnayot* 1–2 are not consumed, but are removed to the place of ashes, where they are burnt. In contradistinction to these "most holy" offerings, the offerings of "lesser holiness" in *mishnayot* 6–8 may be slaughtered anywhere in the courtyard, and they may be consumed by anyone throughout the city of Jerusalem. The blood of most of these sacrifices is applied, like that of the sacrifices in *mishnayot* 4–5, on two corners of the altar, but the blood of the least holy of these offerings – the firstborn, the tithe of animals, and the Pesaḥ offering (*mishna* 8) – is applied in one location only, a part of the altar wall above its base. By ranking the sacrifices in order of sanctity in accordance with location, the *mishna* expresses the main function of animal sacrifices – to draw man nearer to the presence of God (R. Avraham Walfish).

over the course of two days and the intervening night. The same rules applied to the portions belonging to the priests, except that these could be eaten only by the priests, their wives, their children, and their servants.

8. THE FIRSTBORN, the tithe of cattle, and the paschal lamb were also sacred in a minor degree. These could be killed in any part of the Temple court. Only one sprinkling of their blood was required, but it had to be done at the base of the altar. Several distinctions applied to the eating of these offerings, however: Only priests could eat the firstborn animal, but anyone could eat the tithe. Both the firstborn animal and the tithe could be prepared for food in any way desired, in any part of the city, over the course of two days and the intervening night, whereas the paschal lamb had to be eaten on the night of Passover only, and not later than midnight. Moreover, it could only be eaten by members of a group organized prior to the offering, and it could only be roasted.

THE INTERPRETIVE PRINCIPLES OF R. YISHMAEL

רַבִּי יִשְׁמָעֵאל R. YISHMAEL says that the Torah may be expounded by the following thirteen principles of logic:

[1] Inference from minor to major, or from major to minor.

[2] Inference from similarity of phrases in texts.

[3] A comprehensive principle derived from one text, or from two related texts.

[4] A general proposition followed by a specifying particular.

[5] A particular term followed by a general proposition.

[6] A general law limited by a specific application and then treated again in general terms must be interpreted according to the sense of the specific limitation.

בְּרַיְתָא דְּרַבִּי יִשְׁמָעֵאל / THE INTERPRETIVE PRINCIPLES OF R. YISHMAEL

THE ORAL LAW

God intended the Torah to be understood according to interpretive principles, which would teach how the תּוֹרָה שֶׁבְּעַל פֶּה (Oral Law) ultimately flows from the תּוֹרָה שֶׁבִּכְתָב (Written Law), both of which were revealed at Sinai. The Oral Law is the "sacred culture" of Judaism, a corpus that preserves and expounds upon the linguistic, historical and organic context of the Written Law. It was originally learned by heart, with melody, while manuscripts, which individual teachers

ז מִכְּלָל שֶׁהוּא צָרִיךְ לִפְרָט, וּמִפְּרָט שֶׁהוּא צָרִיךְ לִכְלָל;

ח כָּל דָּבָר שֶׁהָיָה בִּכְלָל, וְיָצָא מִן הַכְּלָל לְלַמֵּד, לֹא לְלַמֵּד עַל עַצְמוֹ יָצָא, אֶלָּא לְלַמֵּד עַל הַכְּלָל כֻּלּוֹ יָצָא;

ט כָּל דָּבָר שֶׁהָיָה בִּכְלָל, וְיָצָא לִטְעֹן טְעַן אֶחָד (נ״א אַחֵר) שֶׁהוּא כְעִנְיָנוֹ, יָצָא לְהָקֵל וְלֹא לְהַחֲמִיר;

י כָּל דָּבָר שֶׁהָיָה בִּכְלָל, וְיָצָא לִטְעֹן טְעַן אַחֵר שֶׁלֹּא כְעִנְיָנוֹ, יָצָא לְהָקֵל וּלְהַחֲמִיר;

יא כָּל דָּבָר שֶׁהָיָה בִּכְלָל, וְיָצָא לִדּוֹן בַּדָּבָר הֶחָדָשׁ, אִי אַתָּה יָכוֹל לְהַחֲזִירוֹ לִכְלָלוֹ, עַד שֶׁיַּחֲזִירֶנּוּ הַכָּתוּב לִכְלָלוֹ בְּפֵרוּשׁ;

יב דָּבָר הַלָּמֵד מֵעִנְיָנוֹ, וְדָבָר הַלָּמֵד מִסּוֹפוֹ;

◄ יג וְכֵן שְׁנֵי כְתוּבִים הַמַּכְחִישִׁים זֶה אֶת זֶה, עַד שֶׁיָּבוֹא הַכָּתוּב הַשְּׁלִישִׁי וְיַכְרִיעַ בֵּינֵיהֶם.

יְהִי רָצוֹן מִלְּפָנֶיךָ, יהוה אֱלֹהֵינוּ וֵאלֹהֵי אֲבוֹתֵינוּ, שֶׁיִּבָּנֶה בֵּית הַמִּקְדָּשׁ בִּמְהֵרָה בְיָמֵינוּ, וְתֵן חֶלְקֵנוּ בְּתוֹרָתֶךָ, וְשָׁם נַעֲבָדְךָ בְּיִרְאָה כִּימֵי עוֹלָם וּכְשָׁנִים קַדְמוֹנִיּוֹת.

---

and students may have kept, served only as private notes of their learning experiences. As noted above, the sages prefaced *Shaḥarit* with selections from Scripture, Mishna, and Gemara, the latter two embodying the Oral Law.

Implicit within the oral tradition are the specific contexts in which these principles may be applied; this sort of exegesis may not be applied in ad hoc fashion, but must follow clearly established rules. Normative halakhic decision-making generally considers Mishnaic and Talmudic conclusions based upon these rules to be closed to revision in post-Talmudic times. R. Zvi Hirsch Chajes explains that the redaction of the Mishna included a gathering of the sages of the time, whose consensus established the authoritative nature of the majority of the laws recorded therein. This consensus "closed the canon" regarding dispute on traditions laid out in the Mishna, with the exceptions of select traditions that were known (by R. Yehuda HaNasi's foremost disciples, Rav and R. Ḥiya) or determined, by comparison to contemporaneous Tannaitic sources, to represent the views of individual sages, not those of the consensus. While R. Sa'adia Gaon asserts that the principles represent a method for the recovery of textual allusions to support practices known since Sinai, Ramban and R. Yosef Albo write that they are really the principles as originally outlined at Sinai, but

[7] A general proposition requiring a particular or specific term to explain it, and conversely, a particular term requiring a general one to complement it.

[8] When a subject included in a general proposition is afterwards specifically excepted to give information about it, the exception is made not just for that one instance, but applies to the general proposition as a whole.

[9] Whenever anything is first included in a general proposition and then excepted to prove another, similar proposition, this specifying alleviates and does not aggravate the law's restriction.

[10] But when anything is first included in a general proposition and is then excepted to state a case that is not a similar proposition, such specifying alleviates the law's restriction in some respects, and in others aggravates it.

[11] Anything included in a general proposition and afterwards excepted to determine a new matter cannot be applied to the general proposition unless this is expressly done in the text.

[12] An interpretation may be deduced from the text or from subsequent terms in the text.

▸ [13] Similarly, when two texts contradict each other, we follow the second, until a third text is found that reconciles the contradiction.

May it be Your will, Lord our God and God of our fathers, that the holy Temple be rebuilt, speedily and in our own time, and grant us a portion in Your Torah. And may we worship You there with due reverence, as in days of old and times long past.

---

whose applications were derived by the בַּעֲלֵי מְסוֹרָה (transmitters of the oral tradition).

Each of these thirteen principles also functions as an allegory for the way in which God is manifested in the world. Thus, for example, כְּלָל וּפְרָט (the generality and the detail) corresponds to the enlightenment of the general light of Torah, which informs the detailed affairs of man, and פְּרָט וּכְלָל (the detail and the generality) corresponds to the enlightenment that individual *mitzvot* shed upon life in general (R. Avraham Yitzḥak HaKohen Kook).

קדיש דרבנן

The following prayer, said by mourners, requires the presence of a מנין.
A transliteration can be found on page 1344.

אבל: **יִתְגַּדַּל** וְיִתְקַדַּשׁ שְׁמֵהּ רַבָּא (קהל: אָמֵן). בְּעָלְמָא דִּי בְרָא כִּרְעוּתֵהּ. וְיַמְלִיךְ מַלְכוּתֵהּ בְּחַיֵּיכוֹן וּבְיוֹמֵיכוֹן וּבְחַיֵּי דְכָל בֵּית יִשְׂרָאֵל, בַּעֲגָלָא וּבִזְמַן קָרִיב, וְאִמְרוּ אָמֵן. (קהל: אָמֵן)

קהל ואבל: יְהֵא שְׁמֵהּ רַבָּא מְבָרַךְ לְעָלַם וּלְעָלְמֵי עָלְמַיָּא.

אבל: יִתְבָּרַךְ וְיִשְׁתַּבַּח וְיִתְפָּאַר וְיִתְרוֹמַם וְיִתְנַשֵּׂא, וְיִתְהַדָּר וְיִתְעַלֶּה וְיִתְהַלָּל שְׁמֵהּ דְּקֻדְשָׁא בְּרִיךְ הוּא (קהל: בְּרִיךְ הוּא), לְעֵלָּא מִן כָּל בִּרְכָתָא / בעשרת ימי תשובה: לְעֵלָּא (וּ)לְעֵלָּא מִכָּל בִּרְכָתָא/ וְשִׁירָתָא, תֻּשְׁבְּחָתָא וְנֶחֱמָתָא דַּאֲמִירָן בְּעָלְמָא, וְאִמְרוּ אָמֵן. (קהל: אָמֵן)

עַל יִשְׂרָאֵל וְעַל רַבָּנָן, וְעַל תַּלְמִידֵיהוֹן וְעַל כָּל תַּלְמִידֵי תַלְמִידֵיהוֹן, וְעַל כָּל מָאן דְּעָסְקִין בְּאוֹרַיְתָא, דִּי בְּאַתְרָא הָדֵין, וְדִי בְּכָל אֲתַר וַאֲתַר, יְהֵא לְהוֹן וּלְכוֹן שְׁלָמָא רַבָּא, חִנָּא וְחִסְדָּא, וְרַחֲמֵי, וְחַיֵּי אֲרִיכֵי, וּמְזוֹנֵי רְוִיחֵי, וּפֻרְקָנָא מִן קֳדָם אֲבוּהוֹן דִּי בִשְׁמַיָּא, וְאִמְרוּ אָמֵן. (קהל: אָמֵן)

יְהֵא שְׁלָמָא רַבָּא מִן שְׁמַיָּא וְחַיִּים, עָלֵינוּ וְעַל כָּל יִשְׂרָאֵל, וְאִמְרוּ אָמֵן. (קהל: אָמֵן)

קַדִּישׁ דְּרַבָּנָן / THE RABBIS' KADDISH
For the eleven months following the death of a parent and on the annual *yahrzeit*, a son must recite *Kaddish* as a source of merit for the soul of the departed. Daughters may recite *Kaddish*, too, in merit of the deceased, though customs vary regarding whether she should recite it in an undertone or out loud and whether or not she may recite it if she is the only mourner present.

In addition, whenever ten or more men engage in the study of the Oral Law – for example, Mishna, *Halakha*, or even *Midrash* or *Aggada* – one of them should recite קַדִּישׁ דְּרַבָּנָן (the Rabbis' *Kaddish)* upon conclusion of the study (Rambam). *Magen Avraham* rules that this *Kaddish* is recited only after an Aggadic passage was studied, and he would consequently not consent to the recitation of the Rabbis' *Kaddish* here. The *halakha* is in accordance with Rambam; however, most communities generally respect the view of the *Magen Avraham*, by reciting a brief Aggadic passage at the conclusion of an Oral Torah study session. The notable exception is here, where *Kaddish* is

THE RABBIS' KADDISH

The following prayer, said by mourners, requires the presence of a minyan. A transliteration can be found on page 1344.

Mourner: יִתְגַּדַּל EXALTED AND HALLOWED may God's great name be, in the world He created as He willed. May He reign in your lifetimes and in your days, and in the lifetime of the whole house of Israel, speedily and soon, and say, Amen.

All: May His great name be blessed forever and all time.

Mourner: Blessed and praised, honored, extolled, glorified, adored and exalted above all be the name of the Holy One, blessed is He, (*Between Rosh Hashana & Yom Kippur:* above and) beyond any blessing, hymn, praise, or expressions of consolation that may be uttered in this world, and say, Amen.

May the Jewish people, and our teachers, together with their students and all their students' students, as well as all who engage in Torah study here and in every other place, have abundant peace, grace, kindness, mercy, length of days, abundant food, and deliverance at the hands of their heavenly Father, and say, Amen.

May abundant peace descend from heaven, as well as life, for us and for all Israel, and say, Amen.

---

recited despite the lack of study of any Aggadic passage (R. Hershel Schachter).

אָמֵן – *Amen*. This word is used to accept an oath or covenant. With it, the listener affirms agreement with what the speaker has just proclaimed. It is derived from the same root as אֱמוּנָה, "faithfulness" (*Tur*) and אֱמֶת, "truth." Additionally, it is understood as an acronym for אֵל מֶלֶךְ נֶאֱמָן, "God, the King Who is faithful" (*Shabbat* 119b).

בְּעָלְמָא דִּי בְרָא כִרְעוּתֵהּ – *In the world He created as He willed*. God intended to create a perfect world, and He proceeded to implement that idea (*Ran*). R. Yehuda ben Yakar explains the phrase to mean that the perfect world of God will only be realized when all of mankind acts properly. According to the Vilna Gaon the passage should be translated as "May His great name be exalted and sanctified – as He wills it – in the world He created."

יְהֵא שְׁמֵהּ רַבָּא – *May His great name*. The Gemara (*Berakhot* 3a) explains that the response יְהֵא שְׁמֵהּ רַבָּא (*"May His great Name"*) is so significant that upon hearing it, God prides Himself with His nation of Israel and regrets, as it were, having exiled them. Though it is preferable to raise one's voice when saying it, one should not say it so loudly that one invites ridicule (*R. Yona*).

לְעֵלָּא (וּ)לְעֵלָּא – *Above all*. During עֲשֶׂרֶת יְמֵי תְּשׁוּבָה, *the Ten Days of Repentance* when the

Bow, take three steps back, as if taking leave of the Divine Presence, then bow, first left, then right, then center, while saying:

עֹשֶׂה שָׁלוֹם/ בעשרת ימי תשובה: הַשָּׁלוֹם/ בִּמְרוֹמָיו, הוּא יַעֲשֶׂה
שָׁלוֹם עָלֵינוּ, וְעַל כָּל יִשְׂרָאֵל, וְאִמְרוּ אָמֵן. (קהל: אָמֵן)

On שבת *and* יום טוב *continue* שחרית *on page 444.*

שחרית ליום חול

מזמור לפני פסוקי דזמרה

תהלים ל **מִזְמוֹר** שִׁיר־חֲנֻכַּת הַבַּיִת לְדָוִד: אֲרוֹמִמְךָ יהוה כִּי דִלִּיתָנִי, וְלֹא־
שִׂמַּחְתָּ אֹיְבַי לִי: יהוה אֱלֹהָי, שִׁוַּעְתִּי אֵלֶיךָ וַתִּרְפָּאֵנִי: יהוה,
הֶעֱלִיתָ מִן־שְׁאוֹל נַפְשִׁי, חִיִּיתַנִי מִיָּרְדִי־בוֹר: זַמְּרוּ לַיהוה חֲסִידָיו,
וְהוֹדוּ לְזֵכֶר קָדְשׁוֹ: כִּי רֶגַע בְּאַפּוֹ, חַיִּים בִּרְצוֹנוֹ, בָּעֶרֶב יָלִין בֶּכִי
וְלַבֹּקֶר רִנָּה: וַאֲנִי אָמַרְתִּי בְשַׁלְוִי, בַּל־אֶמּוֹט לְעוֹלָם: יהוה, בִּרְצוֹנְךָ
הֶעֱמַדְתָּה לְהַרְרִי עֹז, הִסְתַּרְתָּ פָנֶיךָ הָיִיתִי נִבְהָל: אֵלֶיךָ יהוה אֶקְרָא,
וְאֶל־אֲדֹנָי אֶתְחַנָּן: מַה־בֶּצַע בְּדָמִי, בְּרִדְתִּי אֶל שָׁחַת, הֲיוֹדְךָ עָפָר,

second לְעֵלָּא is inserted, the prevalent custom is to contract the two words מִן כָּל into the single word מִכָּל, in accordance with those Kabbalists who teach that there should be twenty-eight words in this section of *Kaddish*. There are varying customs as to whether there should be a *vav* preceding the second word. In this Siddur we follow the view of *Teshuva MeAhava* that omits it, based on early *siddurim* that omit the *vav*.

PSALM 30

This psalm, commemorating the dedication of the First Temple, teaches the benefits of frequenting the synagogue and study hall, for they facilitate spiritually fulfilled lives. The psalm stresses that we can escape the allure of "our enemy" (i.e., the evil inclination) with the help of these places, for they remind us that a life of Torah and *mitzvot* is the ultimate blessing. The psalm also emphasizes that all that we enjoy, including good health, material prosperity, and spiritual strength, are fully dependent on God's providence. This leads us to rejoice every morning in prayer, in contrast to other times of the day when we are fearful in His apparent absence (R. Moshe Feinstein).

חֲנֻכַּת הַבַּיִת – *The dedication of the house.* The classical commentators disagree as to what "the dedication of the house" refers to, since the psalm is introduced by לְדָוִד (by, or to, David), who did not live to see the Temple. It may have been read posthumously by Solomon when inaugurating the Temple, David having composed it in joyous anticipation of the

Bow, take three steps back, as if taking leave of the Divine Presence, then bow, first left, then right, then center, while saying:

May He Who makes peace in the highest heaven, make peace for us, and for all Israel, and say, Amen.

On Shabbat and Yom Tov continue Shaharit on page 445.

SHAHARIT FOR WEEKDAYS

A PSALM BEFORE VERSES OF PRAISE

Psalm 30 **מִזְמוֹר** A PSALM. A song at the dedication of the house. Of David. I will extol You, O Lord, for You have lifted me up, and You have not made my enemies rejoice over me. O Lord, my God, I cried out to You, and You healed me. O Lord, You brought me up from the underworld. You kept me alive, that I should not go down into the pit. Sing praise to the Lord, O you His pious ones, and give thanks to the remembrance of His holiness. For He remains a moment in His anger, a lifetime in His favor. In the evening one goes to sleep weeping, but in the morning there is joy. But I said in my prosperity: I will never stumble. O Lord, by Your favor You made my mountain stand strong. You hid Your face, and I was dismayed. I cried to You, O Lord, and to my Master I made supplication. What profit is there in my blood, when I go down into the pit? Shall the dust give thanks

---

Temple's construction (Radak). It may even have been intended for the future dedication of the Second or Third Temples. In that case the mention of enemies and illness would be a reference to the travails of the Jews' subsequent intervening exiles (Ibn Ezra).

If we understand לְדָוִד as "to David" or "for the sake of David," as Radak interprets the term in his commentary on Psalms 110:1 ("One of the poets said this [Psalm] about David, and the *lamed* of לְדָוִד means 'for the sake of'"), then this psalm may have been recited at the dedication of the Temple in honor of David, who had first proposed that it be built (Prof. David Berger).

כִּי רֶגַע בְּאַפּוֹ – *A moment in His anger*. The realization that when God is angry with us, even momentarily, our very physical existence is endangered – reveals to us that we owe Him every breath, every moment (R. Aton Holzer).

וַאֲנִי אָמַרְתִּי בְשַׁלְוִי, בַּל־אֶמּוֹט לְעוֹלָם... הִסְתַּרְתָּ פָנֶיךָ הָיִיתִי נִבְהָל – *But I said in my prosperity: I will never stumble... You hid Your face, and I was dismayed*. When we feel secure we are

הַגִּיד אֲמִתֶּךָ: שְׁמַע־יהוה וְחָנֵּנִי, יהוה הֱיֵה־עֹזֵר לִי: ‹ הָפַכְתָּ מִסְפְּדִי לְמָחוֹל לִי, פִּתַּחְתָּ שַׂקִּי, וַתְּאַזְּרֵנִי שִׂמְחָה: לְמַעַן יְזַמֶּרְךָ כָבוֹד וְלֹא יִדֹּם, יהוה אֱלֹהַי, לְעוֹלָם אוֹדֶךָּ:

קדיש יתום

The following prayer, said by mourners, requires the presence of a מנין.
A transliteration can be found on page 1345.

אבל: **יִתְגַּדַּל** וְיִתְקַדַּשׁ שְׁמֵהּ רַבָּא (קהל: אָמֵן), בְּעָלְמָא דִּי בְרָא כִרְעוּתֵהּ.
וְיַמְלִיךְ מַלְכוּתֵהּ בְּחַיֵּיכוֹן וּבְיוֹמֵיכוֹן וּבְחַיֵּי דְכָל בֵּית
יִשְׂרָאֵל, בַּעֲגָלָא וּבִזְמַן קָרִיב, וְאִמְרוּ אָמֵן. (קהל: אָמֵן)

קהל ואבל: יְהֵא שְׁמֵהּ רַבָּא מְבָרַךְ לְעָלַם וּלְעָלְמֵי עָלְמַיָּא.

אבל: יִתְבָּרַךְ וְיִשְׁתַּבַּח וְיִתְפָּאַר, וְיִתְרוֹמַם וְיִתְנַשֵּׂא וְיִתְהַדָּר וְיִתְעַלֶּה
וְיִתְהַלָּל שְׁמֵהּ דְּקֻדְשָׁא בְּרִיךְ הוּא (קהל: בְּרִיךְ הוּא), לְעֵלָּא מִן כָּל
בִּרְכָתָא / בעשרת ימי תשובה: לְעֵלָּא (וּ)לְעֵלָּא מִכָּל בִּרְכָתָא / וְשִׁירָתָא,
תֻּשְׁבְּחָתָא וְנֶחֱמָתָא דַּאֲמִירָן בְּעָלְמָא, וְאִמְרוּ אָמֵן. (קהל: אָמֵן)

יְהֵא שְׁלָמָא רַבָּא מִן שְׁמַיָּא וְחַיִּים, עָלֵינוּ וְעַל כָּל יִשְׂרָאֵל, וְאִמְרוּ
אָמֵן. (קהל: אָמֵן)

Bow, take three steps back, as if taking leave of the Divine Presence, then bow, first left, then right, then center, while saying:

עֹשֶׂה שָׁלוֹם/ בעשרת ימי תשובה: הַשָּׁלוֹם/ בִּמְרוֹמָיו, הוּא יַעֲשֶׂה שָׁלוֹם
עָלֵינוּ, וְעַל כָּל יִשְׂרָאֵל, וְאִמְרוּ אָמֵן. (קהל: אָמֵן)

---

convinced that our good fortune will continue forever, but when He hides His face, we are terrified (Rashi). History and personal experience teach us that at the moments of our greatest success or triumph we are most vulnerable to setback and failure. Our very existence, not to speak of our accomplishments, can end in unforeseen and unanticipated ways. So it is as well in reverse, for at moments of failure or crisis we ought never to despair of God's ability to transform and redeem our lives, in spite of everything. This is a fundamental teaching of our daily blessings and prayers. In this regard, the power of this particular psalm is well illustrated by the autobiographical story told by Natan Sharansky, the prisoner of Zion cruelly incarcerated in the Siberian Gulag of the Soviet Union. At the very moment of his liberation he refused to go free without his treasured copy of the book of Psalms. As he describes the

to You? Shall it declare Your truth? Hear, O Lord, and be gracious to me. O Lord, be my helper. ▸ You turned for me my mourning into dancing. You loosened my sackcloth and girded me with gladness. Therefore glory will sing praise to You, and will not be silent. O Lord, my God, I will give thanks to You forever.

MOURNER'S KADDISH

The following prayer, said by mourners, requires the presence of a minyan. A transliteration can be found on page 1345.

Mourner: יִתְגַּדַּל EXALTED AND HALLOWED may God's great name be, in the world He created as He willed. May He reign in your lifetimes and in your days, and in the lifetime of the whole house of Israel, speedily and soon, and say, Amen.

All: May His great name be blessed forever and all time.

Mourner: Blessed and praised, honored, extolled, glorified, adored and exalted above all be the name of the Holy One, blessed is He, (*Between Rosh Hashana & Yom Kippur:* above and) beyond any blessing, hymn, praise, or expressions of consolation that may be uttered in this world, and say, Amen.

May abundant peace descend from heaven, as well as life, for us and for all Israel, and say, Amen.

Bow, take three steps back, as if taking leave of the Divine Presence, then bow, first left, then right, then center, while saying:

May He Who makes peace in the highest heaven, make peace for us, and for all Israel, and say, Amen.

---

occasion, "I took that book and turned to Psalm 30, which I had long ago decided to recite at the moment of my release."

וְנֶחֱמָתָא – *Expressions of consolation.* The straightforward meaning of וְנֶחֱמָתָא is consolation. This understanding appears problematic in our context, where one would expect a synonym for praise. One suggestion validating the standard translation proposes that the reference here is to words of solace that praise God as the ultimate source of consolation. We thus translate the phrase throughout the Siddur as "expressions of consolation." Prof. Moshe bar Asher has suggested that in certain linguistic usages *ayin* and *ḥet* could have been interchanged. Thus, וְנֶחֱמָתָא could be the equivalent of נְעִימָתָא in the sense of pleasing tribute.

פסוקי דזמרה

At this point some follow the Hasidic custom of reciting additional prayers, which can be found on page 1338.

The introductory blessing to the פסוקי דזמרה *is said standing, while holding the two front* ציציות *of the* טלית*. They are kissed and released at the end of the blessing at* בַּתִּשְׁבָּחוֹת *(on next page). From the beginning of this prayer to the end of the* עמידה*, conversation is forbidden. See "Interruptions during Pesukei DeZimra" below.*

בָּרוּךְ שֶׁאָמַר וְהָיָה הָעוֹלָם, בָּרוּךְ הוּא. בָּרוּךְ עוֹשֶׂה בְרֵאשִׁית, בָּרוּךְ אוֹמֵר וְעוֹשֶׂה, בָּרוּךְ גּוֹזֵר וּמְקַיֵּם, בָּרוּךְ מְרַחֵם עַל הָאָרֶץ, בָּרוּךְ מְרַחֵם עַל הַבְּרִיּוֹת, בָּרוּךְ מְשַׁלֵּם שָׂכָר טוֹב לִירֵאָיו, בָּרוּךְ חַי לָעַד וְקַיָּם לָנֶצַח, בָּרוּךְ פּוֹדֶה וּמַצִּיל, בָּרוּךְ שְׁמוֹ. בָּרוּךְ אַתָּה יהוה אֱלֹהֵינוּ מֶלֶךְ הָעוֹלָם, הָאֵל הָאָב הָרַחֲמָן הַמְהֻלָּל בְּפִי עַמּוֹ, מְשֻׁבָּח וּמְפֹאָר בִּלְשׁוֹן חֲסִידָיו וַעֲבָדָיו. וּבְשִׁירֵי דָוִד

פְּסוּקֵי דְזִמְרָה / PESUKEI DEZIMRA

The *Pesukei DeZimra* consist of psalms and related readings preceded and followed by the two *berakhot*: *Barukh She'amar* and *Yishtabaḥ*. In this, they resemble the *Hallel* (which the sages refer to as the "Egyptian *Hallel*," as it refers prominently to the Exodus) which also consists of psalms that are preceded and followed by two *berakhot*. Yet the Talmud (*Shabbat* 118a) regards these two prayers very differently. Regarding the Egyptian *Hallel* they declare that "one who recites it every day is like a blasphemer," while R. Yose declared, "May my portion be among those who recite the *Hallel* [of *Pesukei DeZimra*] every day." If they both praise God for His wonders, why is one objectionable and the other welcomed? The answer is that they refer to different categories of miracles. The Egyptian *Hallel* celebrates those rare occasions when God suspends the laws of nature to deliver His people from trouble. Such events include the poor man becoming wealthy, and the childless mother who gives birth (Psalm 113), the Sea of Reeds that parts (Psalm 114), various miraculous interventions (Psalm 115), and the inexplicable salvation of the righteous from sickness (Psalm 116) or their enemies (Psalm 118). In contrast, the *Pesukei*

LAWS FOR ONE WHO HAS FALLEN BEHIND THE CONGREGATION

If one cannot keep up with the congregation or one came late to synagogue, certain portions of *Pesukei DeZimra* can be skipped so that one can recite the *berakhot* of *Keriat Shema* with the congregation. The core of *Pesukei DeZimra*, which is *Barukh She'amar*, *Ashrei* and *Yishtabaḥ* cannot be skipped. The other portions may be skipped, but if time allows, certain portions are given priority over others (*OḤ* 52:1 and *MB* 52:1–5). The order of priority is:

1. Psalms 148 and 150
2. Psalms 146, 147, and 148
3. *Vayevarech David* until *Leshem Tifartekha*
4. *Hodu* until *Vehu Raḥum*

PESUKEI DEZIMRA

At this point some follow the Hasidic custom of reciting additional prayers, which can be found on page 1339.

The introductory blessing to the Pesukei DeZimra (Verses of Praise) is said standing, while holding the two front tzitziot of the tallit. They are kissed and released at the end of the blessing at "songs of praise" (on next page). From the beginning of this prayer to the end of the Amida, conversation is forbidden. See "Interruptions during Pesukei DeZimra" below.

בָּרוּךְ שֶׁאָמַר BLESSED IS HE Who spoke and the world came into being, blessed is He. Blessed is He Who creates the universe. Blessed is He Who speaks and it is done. Blessed is He Whose decrees are always fulfilled. Blessed is He Who has compassion for the world. Blessed is He Who has compassion for those He created. Blessed is He Who rewards those who revere Him. Blessed is He, ever living, existent forever. Blessed is He Who redeems and saves, blessed is His name. Blessed are You, Lord, our God, King of the universe, God the merciful Father, exalted on the lips on Your people, praised and glorified on the tongues of Your pious servants. We too, Lord our God, will sing Your praises with the psalms of Your servant David.

DeZimra celebrate the hand of God in the routine rhythms of life and nature. Its psalms describe God Who controls the stars, clouds, rain, snow, frost, and the grass. The ceaseless motions of the heavenly bodies, the cyclical seasons and climate changes, the landscape,

INTERRUPTIONS DURING PESUKEI DEZIMRA

The following are generally permitted interruptions. As a general rule, from the time one recites *Barukh She'amar* until the conclusion of *Taḥanun* one should not speak (*OḤ* 51:4 and *MB* 51:6–11). However, there are certain interruptions that are permissible during *Pesukei DeZimra*:

- One may answer *amen* to a *berakha* that one heard (but not *barukh Hu uvarukh shemo*).
- One may recite *Asher Yatzar*.
- If one was called for an *aliya*, one may accept the *aliya* (ideally the *gabbai* should not call someone for an *aliya* who is in the middle of *Pesukei DeZimra*).
- If one is concerned about missing the final time to recite *Shema*, one may recite it during *Pesukei DeZimra*.
- If one forgot to recite *Birkhot HaTorah*, one may recite them with the accompanying verses during *Pesukei DeZimra*.
- If one did not yet place *tallit* and *tefillin* (such as in a case where the congregation starts *Pesukei DeZimra* before the time for *tallit* and *tefillin*), it is preferable to place them after reciting *Yishtabaḥ* before *Kaddish* and recite the *berakhot* as usual. The Leader, however, should place his *tallit* and *tefillin* before reciting *Yishtabaḥ* (*OḤ* 53:3).

עַבְדֶּךָ, נְהַלֶּלְךָ יהוה אֱלֹהֵינוּ. בִּשְׁבָחוֹת וּבִזְמִירוֹת, נְגַדֶּלְךָ וּנְשַׁבֵּחֲךָ וּנְפָאֶרְךָ. וְנַזְכִּיר שִׁמְךָ וְנַמְלִיכְךָ, מַלְכֵּנוּ אֱלֹהֵינוּ, ◂ יָחִיד חֵי הָעוֹלָמִים מֶלֶךְ, מְשֻׁבָּח וּמְפֹאָר עֲדֵי עַד שְׁמוֹ הַגָּדוֹל, בָּרוּךְ אַתָּה יהוה, מֶלֶךְ מְהֻלָּל בַּתִּשְׁבָּחוֹת.

הודו

דברי הימים א, טז

הוֹדוּ לַיהוה קִרְאוּ בִשְׁמוֹ, הוֹדִיעוּ בָעַמִּים עֲלִילֹתָיו: שִׁירוּ לוֹ, זַמְּרוּ־לוֹ, שִׂיחוּ בְּכָל־נִפְלְאוֹתָיו: הִתְהַלְלוּ בְּשֵׁם קָדְשׁוֹ, יִשְׂמַח לֵב מְבַקְשֵׁי יהוה: דִּרְשׁוּ יהוה וְעֻזּוֹ, בַּקְּשׁוּ פָנָיו תָּמִיד: זִכְרוּ נִפְלְאֹתָיו אֲשֶׁר עָשָׂה, מֹפְתָיו וּמִשְׁפְּטֵי־פִיהוּ: זֶרַע יִשְׂרָאֵל עַבְדּוֹ, בְּנֵי יַעֲקֹב בְּחִירָיו: הוּא יהוה אֱלֹהֵינוּ בְּכָל־הָאָרֶץ מִשְׁפָּטָיו: זִכְרוּ לְעוֹלָם בְּרִיתוֹ, דָּבָר צִוָּה לְאֶלֶף דּוֹר: אֲשֶׁר כָּרַת אֶת־אַבְרָהָם, וּשְׁבוּעָתוֹ לְיִצְחָק: וַיַּעֲמִידֶהָ לְיַעֲקֹב לְחֹק, לְיִשְׂרָאֵל בְּרִית עוֹלָם: לֵאמֹר, לְךָ אֶתֵּן אֶרֶץ־כְּנָעַן, חֶבֶל נַחֲלַתְכֶם: בִּהְיוֹתְכֶם מְתֵי מִסְפָּר, כִּמְעַט

plants, animals and human society all testify to God's power. Between these two categories of miracles it is much more difficult – but also more important – to perceive God's power in the everyday events surrounding us. That is why for the Gemara those who base their faith on overt miracles (as described in *Hallel*) can eventually lose their faith, given the rarity of such events, unlike those who see God's hand in everyday nature. In this respect, Abraham is a greater role model for us than Moses, for Abraham discovered God by examining the world around him, whereas Moses knew God only via miraculous divine revelation (such as at the burning bush). Only subsequently did Moses discover God's providential ways in nature. For us as individuals it is Abraham's steadfast search for the hidden God over many years that should inform and inspire our faith, and the daily regimen of our prayers. Hence we recite the *Pesukei DeZimra* every morning (R. Joseph B. Soloveitchik).

It is a prerequisite to proper prayer that we understand the meaning of God's name as used in prayer and blessings. R. David Tzvi Hoffman explains that this is why *Barukh She'amar*, the opening blessing of *Pesukei DeZimra*, does not open with the standard formula of בָּרוּךְ אַתָּה ה׳ אֱלֹקֵינוּ מֶלֶךְ הָעוֹלָם, but rather begins by listing, and blessing, all the ways in which the proper name of God is understood by our sages, and only then proceeds to the standard blessing formula (R. Isaiah Wohlgemuth).

וְנַמְלִיכְךָ, מַלְכֵּנוּ – *And Your sovereignty, our King.* The main purpose of this paragraph is קַבָּלַת עֹל מַלְכוּת שָׁמַיִם, i.e., to prepare ourselves to accept God's sovereignty through the recital of the psalms of David that follow and then the *Shema* thereafter (R. Yissachar Jacobson).

With praises and hymns will we declare Your greatness, Your praise, and Your glory. We will acclaim Your name and Your sovereignty, our King and our God, ▸ Only One, Who gives life to the worlds. O King, lauded and praised be Your great name forever and ever. Blessed are You, Lord, the King Who is extolled with songs of praise.

HODU

I Chr. 16 הוֹדוּ GIVE THANKS to the Lord, call on His name. Proclaim His deeds among the peoples. Sing to Him, chant His praise, recite His wondrous works. Glorify His holiness. Let your hearts rejoice, you who seek the Lord. Seek out the Lord and His might. Seek His presence continually. Recall the wonders He has brought about, His many acts of providence and guidance. Seed of Israel His servant, children of Jacob His chosen one, never forget that He is the Lord our God; His judgments are in all the earth. Always remember His covenant, the words He ordained for a thousand generations, the covenant He made with Abraham, and His oath to Isaac, which He confirmed as a statute with Jacob, an everlasting covenant for Israel, saying: "To you will I give the land of Canaan as the portion of your inheritance." When you were but few in number, very few

---

הודו / GIVE THANKS

This section of the *Pesukei DeZimra* contains forty-nine verses: the first twenty-eight in their entirety are taken from I Chronicles 16:8–36, while the remaining twenty-one are taken from Psalms. Those from Chronicles form what the sages referred to as the שִׁיר שֶׁל תָּמִיד ("the Song to Accompany the Daily Sacrifice"). As described there (and in II Samuel 6,) when King David established the City of David as the capital of the kingdom, he brought the Ark to the city from Givon, with great celebration and sacrifices, accompanied by the Levites who recited these verses composed for the occasion. The *Seder Olam* records that at David's instruction they continued to be sung at the daily sacrifice (the first fifteen at the morning sacrifice, and the last thirteen at the afternoon sacrifice) for the next forty-three years until Solomon's Temple was finally built. Thus recital of these verses invokes the memory of the daily sacrifice as the basis of our morning prayers, and the centrality of Jerusalem in Jewish history. It also facilitates our recognition of God's providential hand in the affairs of the Jewish people and in our own lives (R. Yehuda Kiel).

קִרְאוּ בִשְׁמוֹ – *Call on His name.* We do not all necessarily accomplish this "calling out in God's name" in the same way. "There is one who sings the song of his soul, and he finds

וְגָרִים בָּהּ: וַיִּתְהַלְּכוּ מִגּוֹי אֶל־גּוֹי, וּמִמַּמְלָכָה אֶל־עַם אַחֵר: לֹא־
הִנִּיחַ לְאִישׁ לְעָשְׁקָם, וַיּוֹכַח עֲלֵיהֶם מְלָכִים: אַל־תִּגְּעוּ בִּמְשִׁיחָי,
וּבִנְבִיאַי אַל־תָּרֵעוּ: שִׁירוּ לַיהוה כָּל־הָאָרֶץ, בַּשְּׂרוּ מִיּוֹם־אֶל־יוֹם
יְשׁוּעָתוֹ: סַפְּרוּ בַגּוֹיִם אֶת־כְּבוֹדוֹ, בְּכָל־הָעַמִּים נִפְלְאֹתָיו: כִּי גָדוֹל
יהוה וּמְהֻלָּל מְאֹד, וְנוֹרָא הוּא עַל־כָּל־אֱלֹהִים: ◄ כִּי כָּל־אֱלֹהֵי
הָעַמִּים אֱלִילִים (*pause*), וַיהוה שָׁמַיִם עָשָׂה:

הוֹד וְהָדָר לְפָנָיו, עֹז וְחֶדְוָה בִּמְקֹמוֹ: הָבוּ לַיהוה מִשְׁפְּחוֹת עַמִּים,
הָבוּ לַיהוה כָּבוֹד וָעֹז: הָבוּ לַיהוה כְּבוֹד שְׁמוֹ, שְׂאוּ מִנְחָה וּבֹאוּ
לְפָנָיו, הִשְׁתַּחֲווּ לַיהוה בְּהַדְרַת־קֹדֶשׁ: חִילוּ מִלְּפָנָיו כָּל־הָאָרֶץ,
אַף־תִּכּוֹן תֵּבֵל בַּל־תִּמּוֹט: יִשְׂמְחוּ הַשָּׁמַיִם וְתָגֵל הָאָרֶץ, וְיֹאמְרוּ
בַגּוֹיִם יהוה מָלָךְ: יִרְעַם הַיָּם וּמְלוֹאוֹ, יַעֲלֹץ הַשָּׂדֶה וְכָל־אֲשֶׁר־
בּוֹ: אָז יְרַנְּנוּ עֲצֵי הַיָּעַר, מִלִּפְנֵי יהוה, כִּי־בָא לִשְׁפּוֹט אֶת־הָאָרֶץ:
הוֹדוּ לַיהוה כִּי טוֹב, כִּי לְעוֹלָם חַסְדּוֹ: וְאִמְרוּ, הוֹשִׁיעֵנוּ אֱלֹהֵי
יִשְׁעֵנוּ, וְקַבְּצֵנוּ וְהַצִּילֵנוּ מִן־הַגּוֹיִם, לְהֹדוֹת לְשֵׁם קָדְשֶׁךָ, לְהִשְׁתַּבֵּחַ
בִּתְהִלָּתֶךָ: בָּרוּךְ יהוה אֱלֹהֵי יִשְׂרָאֵל מִן־הָעוֹלָם וְעַד־הָעֹלָם, וַיֹּאמְרוּ
כָל־הָעָם אָמֵן, וְהַלֵּל לַיהוה:

◄ רוֹמְמוּ יהוה אֱלֹהֵינוּ וְהִשְׁתַּחֲווּ לַהֲדֹם רַגְלָיו, קָדוֹשׁ הוּא: רוֹמְמוּ תהלים צט
יהוה אֱלֹהֵינוּ וְהִשְׁתַּחֲווּ לְהַר קָדְשׁוֹ, כִּי־קָדוֹשׁ יהוה אֱלֹהֵינוּ:

וְהוּא רַחוּם, יְכַפֵּר עָוֹן וְלֹא־יַשְׁחִית, וְהִרְבָּה לְהָשִׁיב אַפּוֹ, וְלֹא־יָעִיר תהלים עח
כָּל־חֲמָתוֹ: אַתָּה יהוה לֹא־תִכְלָא רַחֲמֶיךָ מִמֶּנִּי, חַסְדְּךָ וַאֲמִתְּךָ תהלים מ

all within his soul, his complete fill of spiritual satisfaction. Then there is one who sings the song of the nation... and there is one whose soul broadens until it emerges and spreads beyond the borders of Israel, to sing the song of mankind... And there is one who... transcends more broadly, until he unites with the entirety of existence, with all the creatures, and with all the worlds, and with all of them he recites the praises of God" (R. Avraham Yitzḥak HaKohen Kook).

רוֹמְמוּ ה׳ אֱלֹהֵינוּ – *Exalt the Lord our God.* From this point until its end, these verses are taken from Psalms, which R. Profiat Duran, a refugee

and sojourners in the land, and when you wandered from nation to nation, and from one realm to another, He permitted no one to oppress you. Truly, on your account He castigates kings: "Do not touch My anointed ones or harm My prophets." Therefore sing to the Lord, let the whole earth, from day to day, proclaim His saving power. Declare His glory among the nations, His wonders among all the peoples. For the Lord's greatness extends beyond any human praise; He stands above every other god, ▸ because the gods of the heathens are no more than idols (*pause*), whereas the Lord made the heavens.

His very presence is the essence of majesty and grandeur, of strength and gladness in His omnipresence. Ascribe to the Lord, you families of nations, ascribe to the Lord glory and might, ascribe to the Lord the glory due His name. Bring an offering and come before Him, worship the Lord in the beauty of holiness; the whole earth trembles before Him, though the world is fixed and cannot be moved. Let the heavens rejoice and the earth be glad, and let it be declared among the nations that the Lord reigns. Let the ocean and its fullness roar, the fields and all that is in them rejoice. The trees of the forest will sing for joy before the Lord when He comes to judge the earth. Give thanks to the Lord because He is good, because His mercy endures forever, and say, "Save us, God of our deliverance; gather us together and free us from the nations to laud Your holy name and triumph in Your praise." Blessed is the Lord God of Israel from everlasting to everlasting. And all the people said Amen and praised the Lord.

Ps. 99 ▸ Exalt the Lord our God, and bow down before His footstool. He is holy. Exalt the Lord our God, and bow down before His holy mountain. Indeed, the Lord our God is holy.

Ps. 78 But He, the compassionate one, forgave iniquity, and did not destroy
them, and He often turned away His anger and did not stir up all His
Ps. 40 wrath. You, O Lord, withhold not Your mercies from me. May Your

---

from the Spanish massacres of 1391, describes as פְּסוּקֵי דְרַחֲמֵי (verses of mercy). Their unifying theme is a petition to end our exile and dispersion (*Tzelota DeAvraham*).

תהלים כה תהלים סח תָּמִיד יִצְּרוּנִי: זְכֹר־רַחֲמֶיךָ יהוה וַחֲסָדֶיךָ, כִּי מֵעוֹלָם הֵמָּה: תְּנוּ
עֹז לֵאלֹהִים, עַל־יִשְׂרָאֵל גַּאֲוָתוֹ, וְעֻזּוֹ בַּשְּׁחָקִים: נוֹרָא אֱלֹהִים
מִמִּקְדָּשֶׁיךָ, אֵל יִשְׂרָאֵל הוּא נֹתֵן עֹז וְתַעֲצֻמוֹת לָעָם, בָּרוּךְ אֱלֹהִים:
תהלים צד אֵל־נְקָמוֹת יהוה, אֵל נְקָמוֹת הוֹפִיעַ: הִנָּשֵׂא שֹׁפֵט הָאָרֶץ, הָשֵׁב
תהלים ג תהלים מו גְּמוּל עַל־גֵּאִים: לַיהוה הַיְשׁוּעָה, עַל־עַמְּךָ בִרְכָתֶךָ סֶּלָה: ◄ יהוה
תהלים פד צְבָאוֹת עִמָּנוּ, מִשְׂגָּב לָנוּ אֱלֹהֵי יַעֲקֹב סֶלָה: יהוה צְבָאוֹת, אַשְׁרֵי
תהלים כ אָדָם בֹּטֵחַ בָּךְ: יהוה הוֹשִׁיעָה, הַמֶּלֶךְ יַעֲנֵנוּ בְיוֹם־קָרְאֵנוּ:

תהלים כח הוֹשִׁיעָה אֶת־עַמֶּךָ, וּבָרֵךְ אֶת־נַחֲלָתֶךָ, וּרְעֵם וְנַשְּׂאֵם עַד־הָעוֹלָם:
תהלים לג נַפְשֵׁנוּ חִכְּתָה לַיהוה, עֶזְרֵנוּ וּמָגִנֵּנוּ הוּא: כִּי־בוֹ יִשְׂמַח לִבֵּנוּ, כִּי בְשֵׁם
תהלים פה קָדְשׁוֹ בָטָחְנוּ: יְהִי־חַסְדְּךָ יהוה עָלֵינוּ, כַּאֲשֶׁר יִחַלְנוּ לָךְ: הַרְאֵנוּ יהוה
חַסְדֶּךָ, וְיֶשְׁעֲךָ תִּתֶּן־לָנוּ: קוּמָה עֶזְרָתָה לָּנוּ, וּפְדֵנוּ לְמַעַן חַסְדֶּךָ:
תהלים מד
תהלים פא אָנֹכִי יהוה אֱלֹהֶיךָ הַמַּעַלְךָ מֵאֶרֶץ מִצְרָיִם, הַרְחֶב־פִּיךָ וַאֲמַלְאֵהוּ:
תהלים קמד תהלים יג אַשְׁרֵי הָעָם שֶׁכָּכָה לּוֹ, אַשְׁרֵי הָעָם שֶׁיהוה אֱלֹהָיו: ◄ וַאֲנִי בְּחַסְדְּךָ
בָטַחְתִּי, יָגֵל לִבִּי בִּישׁוּעָתֶךָ, אָשִׁירָה לַיהוה, כִּי גָמַל עָלָי:

The following psalm is not said on חול המועד פסח, ערב פסח *or* ערב יום כיפור. *The custom is to say it standing.*

תהלים ק **מִזְמוֹר לְתוֹדָה,** הָרִיעוּ לַיהוה כָּל־הָאָרֶץ: עִבְדוּ אֶת־יהוה
בְּשִׂמְחָה, בֹּאוּ לְפָנָיו בִּרְנָנָה: דְּעוּ כִּי־יהוה
הוּא אֱלֹהִים, הוּא עָשָׂנוּ וְלוֹ אֲנַחְנוּ, עַמּוֹ וְצֹאן מַרְעִיתוֹ:
בֹּאוּ שְׁעָרָיו בְּתוֹדָה, חֲצֵרֹתָיו בִּתְהִלָּה, הוֹדוּ לוֹ, בָּרְכוּ שְׁמוֹ:
◄ כִּי־טוֹב יהוה, לְעוֹלָם חַסְדּוֹ, וְעַד־דֹּר וָדֹר אֱמוּנָתוֹ:

On הושענא רבה *continue with* לַמְנַצֵּחַ *on page 452.*

מִזְמוֹר לְתוֹדָה / A PSALM OF THANKSGIVING
This psalm was recited by an individual prior to offering the קָרְבַּן תּוֹדָה (thanksgiving sacrifice) expressing gratitude to God for a particular act of salvation. It calls on all present to share in the thanksgiving, by recognizing and celebrating God's benevolence. The five verses reflect three stages (feelings, thoughts, and actions) in the service of God: joy and gladness in our heart (vv. 1–2), knowledge that God is our faithful shepherd (v. 3), and finally concrete steps to demonstrate our resulting loyalty to Him (vv. 4–5) (R. Amos Ḥakham).

Ps. 25 loving-kindness and Your truth always preserve me. Remember Your
Ps. 68 mercy, O Lord, and Your loving-kindnesses, which are of old. Give
God a melody. His majesty is over Israel, and His strength is in the
skies. O God, You are awesome from Your Temple. The God of Israel,
Ps. 94 He gives strength and might to the people. Blessed be God. God of
vengeance, O Lord, God of vengeance, reveal Yourself. Rise up, O
Ps. 3 Judge of the earth, render to the proud their recompense. Deliverance
Ps. 46 is the Lord's. May Your blessing be upon Your people. Selah. ▸ The
Ps. 84 Lord of hosts is with us. The God of Jacob is our refuge. Selah. O Lord
Ps. 20 of hosts, happy is the man who trusts in You. Lord, save! The King
will answer us on the day that we call.

Ps. 28 Save Your people and bless Your inheritance, and tend them and
Ps. 33 carry them forever. Our soul waits for the Lord. He is our help and
our shield. Indeed, in Him does our heart rejoice. Indeed, in His holy
name we trust. May Your loving-kindness, O Lord, be upon us, as we
Ps. 85 hope for You. Show us Your loving-kindness, O Lord, and grant us
Ps. 44 Your salvation. Arise and help us, and redeem us for the sake of Your
Ps. 81 loving-kindness. I am the Lord your God Who brought you up from
the land of Egypt. Open your mouth wide, and I will fill it. Happy is
Ps. 144 the people that has this. Happy is the people whose God is the Lord.
Ps. 13 ▸ But as for me, I trust in Your loving-kindness. May my heart rejoice in
Your salvation. I will sing to the Lord, because He has dealt bountifully
with me.

The following psalm is not said on Erev Pesaḥ, on Ḥol HaMo'ed Pesaḥ, or Erev Yom Kippur. The custom is to say it standing.

Ps. 100 **מִזְמוֹר לְתוֹדָה** A PSALM OF THANKSGIVING. Make a joyful noise to the Lord, all the earth. Serve the Lord with gladness, come before Him with singing. Know that the Lord is God. He made us, and we belong to Him. We are His people, and the sheep of His pasture. Enter His gates with thanksgiving, His courtyards with praise. Give thanks to Him, and bless His name. ▸ For the Lord is good, His loving-kindness is forever, and His faithfulness is for all generations.

On Hoshana Raba continue with Psalm 19 on page 453.

תהלים קד / תהלים קיג **יְהִי כְבוֹד** יהוה לְעוֹלָם, יִשְׂמַח יהוה בְּמַעֲשָׂיו: יְהִי שֵׁם יהוה
מְבֹרָךְ, מֵעַתָּה וְעַד־עוֹלָם: מִמִּזְרַח־שֶׁמֶשׁ עַד־מְבוֹאוֹ,
תהלים קלה מְהֻלָּל שֵׁם יהוה: רָם עַל־כָּל־גּוֹיִם יהוה, עַל הַשָּׁמַיִם כְּבוֹדוֹ: יהוה
תהלים קג שִׁמְךָ לְעוֹלָם, יהוה זִכְרְךָ לְדֹר־וָדֹר: יהוה בַּשָּׁמַיִם הֵכִין כִּסְאוֹ,
דברי הימים א׳ טז וּמַלְכוּתוֹ בַּכֹּל מָשָׁלָה: יִשְׂמְחוּ הַשָּׁמַיִם וְתָגֵל הָאָרֶץ, וְיֹאמְרוּ
בַגּוֹיִם יהוה מָלָךְ: יהוה מֶלֶךְ, יהוה מָלָךְ, יהוה יִמְלֹךְ לְעוֹלָם
תהלים י / תהלים לג וָעֶד. יהוה מֶלֶךְ עוֹלָם וָעֶד, אָבְדוּ גוֹיִם מֵאַרְצוֹ: יהוה הֵפִיר עֲצַת־
משלי יט גּוֹיִם, הֵנִיא מַחְשְׁבוֹת עַמִּים: רַבּוֹת מַחֲשָׁבוֹת בְּלֶב־אִישׁ, וַעֲצַת
תהלים לג יהוה הִיא תָקוּם: עֲצַת יהוה לְעוֹלָם תַּעֲמֹד, מַחְשְׁבוֹת לִבּוֹ לְדֹר
תהלים קלב וָדֹר: כִּי הוּא אָמַר וַיֶּהִי, הוּא־צִוָּה וַיַּעֲמֹד: כִּי־בָחַר יהוה בְּצִיּוֹן, אִוָּהּ
תהלים קלה / תהלים צד לְמוֹשָׁב לוֹ: כִּי־יַעֲקֹב בָּחַר לוֹ יָהּ, יִשְׂרָאֵל לִסְגֻלָּתוֹ: כִּי לֹא־יִטֹּשׁ
תהלים עח יהוה עַמּוֹ, וְנַחֲלָתוֹ לֹא יַעֲזֹב: › וְהוּא רַחוּם, יְכַפֵּר עָוֹן וְלֹא־יַשְׁחִית,
תהלים כ וְהִרְבָּה לְהָשִׁיב אַפּוֹ, וְלֹא־יָעִיר כָּל־חֲמָתוֹ: יהוה הוֹשִׁיעָה, הַמֶּלֶךְ
יַעֲנֵנוּ בְיוֹם־קָרְאֵנוּ:

חֲצֵרֹתָיו בִּתְהִלָּה – *His courtyards with praise* (previous page). This phrase reflects the procedure following the offering of the thanksgiving sacrifice (as explained by the *Netziv* - see the comment on page 772,) during which the public was invited to a סְעוּדַת הוֹדָאָה (thanksgiving meal) to occur within the confines (or "courtyards") of Jerusalem. There they would partake of the sacrificial meat while being told why the sacrifice had been brought, and consequently all would "praise, give thanks..., and bless His name." (R. Basil Herring).

The psalm is in chiasmus format (i.e., arranged in a mirror structure: A-B-C-B-A) with seven calls to praise God: הָרִיעוּ, עִבְדוּ, בֹּאוּ, דְּעוּ, בֹּאוּ, הוֹדוּ, בָּרְכוּ. First, the Psalmist calls upon the "entire earth" to sing before God (v. 1), and concludes with a parallel statement that God's kindness lasts forever (v. 5). The second verse summons the assemblage to worship in gladness and song. This call is matched in the fourth verse, where it picks up on the word בֹּאוּ and encourages the listeners to come to His gates ("come" – because the psalm is sung in the courtyard of the Temple) with thanksgiving. At the center of the structure (v. 3) there is a declaration of faith regarding three essential beliefs: (1) The Lord is God, (2) He is the Creator, and (3) we, as a nation, belong to Him (R. Yitzchak Etshalom).

יְהִי כְבוֹד ה׳ – *May the glory of the Lord*. The eighteen verses of this prayer are selected from various psalms, plus one verse from Proverbs. Together they function as a succinct summary of the six psalms that form the core of the *Pesukei DeZimra* (*Tzelota DeAvraham*).

Ps. 104 **יְהִי כְבוֹד** MAY THE GLORY of the Lord be forever, may the Lord
Ps. 113 rejoice in His works. Blessed be the name of the Lord from now
and forevermore. From the rising of the sun to its going down
the Lord's name is praised. The Lord is high above all nations. His
Ps. 135 glory is above the heavens. O Lord, Your name is forever. O Lord,
Ps. 103 Your renown is for all generations. The Lord has established His
I Chr. 16 throne in the heavens, and His kingdom rules over everything. Let
the heavens rejoice and the earth be glad, let the nations declare
Ps. 10 that the Lord reigns! The Lord reigns; the Lord reigned; the Lord
shall reign forever and ever. The Lord is King forever and ever. The
Ps. 33 nations have perished from His land. The Lord confounds the plan
of the nations. He makes the thoughts of the people of no effect.
Prov. 19 Many are the thoughts in the heart of man, but the Lord's wise
Ps. 33 guidance shall stand. The plan of the Lord will stand forever, the
thoughts of His heart for all generations. For He spoke, and it was.
Ps. 132 He commanded, and it stood. Indeed, the Lord has chosen Zion,
Ps. 135 He had desired it for His habitation. For the Lord has chosen Jacob
Ps. 94 for Himself, Israel for His special possession. For the Lord will
not abandon His people, and He will not forsake His inheritance.
Ps. 78 ▸ But He, the compassionate one, forgave iniquity, and did not
destroy them, and He often turned away His anger and did not
Ps. 20 stir up all His wrath. Lord, save! The King will answer us on the day
that we call.

כְּבוֹד ה׳ – *May the glory of the Lord.* The opening verse, from Psalms 104:31, contains the angels' proclamation upon witnessing the creation of the plant world in accordance with God's decrees (*Hullin* 60a). The last five verses celebrate the election of the Chosen People and plead for God's mercy and attentiveness to their prayers (R. Elie Munk).

יִשְׂמְחוּ הַשָּׁמַיִם וְתָגֵל הָאָרֶץ – *Let the heavens rejoice and the earth be glad.* When mankind recognizes God's all-encompassing sovereignty, nature will in turn also reveal God's hidden glory. The first letters of this phrase form the divine name י־ה־ו־ה (*Tikkunei Zohar*).

ה׳ מֶלֶךְ... מָלָךְ... יִמְלֹךְ – *The Lord reigns... reigned... shall reign.* This familiar expression is not found anywhere in Scripture. Rather, each phrase comes from a different verse (Psalms 10:16, 97:1, and Ex. 15:18). In combination, it expresses the timelessness of God's sovereignty (R. Yissakhar Jacobson).

אשרי

The line beginning with פּוֹתֵחַ אֶת יָדֶךָ *should be said with special concentration, representing as it does the key idea of this psalm, and of* פסוקי דזמרה *as a whole, that God is the Creator and Sustainer of all. Some have the custom to touch the* תפילין של יד *at °, and the* תפילין של ראש *at °°.*

אַשְׁרֵי יוֹשְׁבֵי בֵיתֶךָ, עוֹד יְהַלְלְוּךָ סֶּלָה: תהלים פד
אַשְׁרֵי הָעָם שֶׁכָּכָה לּוֹ, אַשְׁרֵי הָעָם שֶׁיהוה אֱלֹהָיו: תהלים קמד
תְּהִלָּה לְדָוִד תהלים קמה
אֲרוֹמִמְךָ אֱלוֹהַי הַמֶּלֶךְ, וַאֲבָרְכָה שִׁמְךָ לְעוֹלָם וָעֶד:
בְּכָל־יוֹם אֲבָרְכֶךָּ, וַאֲהַלְלָה שִׁמְךָ לְעוֹלָם וָעֶד:
גָּדוֹל יהוה וּמְהֻלָּל מְאֹד, וְלִגְדֻלָּתוֹ אֵין חֵקֶר:
דּוֹר לְדוֹר יְשַׁבַּח מַעֲשֶׂיךָ, וּגְבוּרֹתֶיךָ יַגִּידוּ:
הֲדַר כְּבוֹד הוֹדֶךָ, וְדִבְרֵי נִפְלְאֹתֶיךָ אָשִׂיחָה:
וֶעֱזוּז נוֹרְאֹתֶיךָ יֹאמֵרוּ, וּגְדוּלָּתְךָ אֲסַפְּרֶנָּה:

אַשְׁרֵי / PSALM 145

Ashrei consists of Psalm 145, preceded by two verses. The first of these is Psalm 84:5, and the second is Psalm 144:15 (i.e., it is the final verse of the preceding chapter). These verses were used to introduce *Ashrei* because historically these two psalms were recited when leaving the house of God, whether at the conclusion of the three pilgrimage festivals when pilgrims would return to their homes (Psalm 84), or when scholars would leave the study hall, bidding farewell to their teachers and colleagues quoting the words of Psalm 144 (*Berakhot* 17a). These two psalms were particularly suited to such occasions. Psalm 84 describes how just as every creature craves a home and place of respite in a hostile world, so for the Jew the "house of God" is the place where the Jew feels most at home. Thus *yoshvei* rather than *yoshvim* is used, as *yoshvei bayit* refers to those who are regular dwellers of a house, rather than those who happen to be sitting there. Such dwellers offer ongoing rather than occasional praises, hence the verse concludes *od yehalelukha*, i.e., "as steady attendees in Your house they praise You regularly." So too in Psalm 144 David describes his having to lead his armies against deceptive enemies and untrustworthy allies, while longingly anticipating returning home to the presence of God in the company of his fellow Israelites (R. Joseph B. Soloveitchik).

Ashrei is arguably the most significant psalm; it seems that the name *Tehillim*, was taken from this psalm, the only one which begins – and ends – with the word *Tehilla*, framing it as the archetype of "*Tehillim*." It is also fair to assume that this psalm played a central role in the Levites' service in the Temple (R. Yitzchak Etshalom).

תְּהִלָּה ... אֲרוֹמִמְךָ – *A praise... I exalt You.* The Gemara (*Berakhot* 4b) teaches that the sages

ASHREI

The line beginning with "You open Your hand" should be said with special concentration, representing as it does the key idea of this psalm, and of Pesukei DeZimra as a whole, that God is the Creator and Sustainer of all. Some have the custom to touch the hand-tefillin at °, and the head-tefillin at °°.

Ps. 84 אַשְׁרֵי HAPPY are those who dwell in Your house.
They will forever praise You. Selah.

Ps. 144 HAPPY is the people that has this.
Happy is the people whose God is the Lord.

Ps. 145 A PRAISE OF DAVID.

א I exalt You, my God, the King,
and I will bless Your name forever and ever.

ב Every day I will bless You,
and I will praise Your name forever and ever.

ג Great is the Lord, and very praiseworthy,
and His greatness is boundless.

ד One generation lauds Your works to another,
and they declare Your mighty deeds.

ה I speak of the splendid glory of Your majesty
and of Your wondrous works,

ו And they speak of the might of Your awesome deeds,
and I declare Your greatness.

---

assured a share in the World to Come to those who recite *Ashrei* three times a day. It explains that this is because it uniquely follows the alphabet, as well as containing the pivotal verse "You open Your hand, and You satisfy the desire of every living thing." It further explains that while the verse beginning with the letter נ (as it appears in Amos 5:2) is missing on account of the negative connotation of the "fall of Israel," King David compensated for this in the ensuing verse of *Ashrei* which, while indeed mentioning those who fall, also describes God as the One Who supports them. By wholeheartedly making this thrice-daily affirmation of trust in God, no matter the circumstance, one merits eternal life.

Early manuscripts of the Psalms (some dating to the period of the Dead Sea Scrolls) incorporate a verse beginning with *nun*: נֶאֱמָן אֱלֹקִים בִּדְבָרָיו וְחָסִיד בְּכָל מַעֲשָׂיו (God's word is trustworthy, all His actions are righteous). However, the Masoretic texts, transmitted faithfully from generation to generation, do not contain any such verse, and it is entirely plausible that a scribe would have added a verse to compensate for one that appeared to

זֵכֶר רַב־טוּבְךָ יַבִּיעוּ, וְצִדְקָתְךָ יְרַנֵּנוּ:
חַנּוּן וְרַחוּם יהוה, אֶרֶךְ אַפַּיִם וּגְדָל־חָסֶד:
טוֹב־יהוה לַכֹּל, וְרַחֲמָיו עַל־כָּל־מַעֲשָׂיו:
יוֹדוּךָ יהוה כָּל־מַעֲשֶׂיךָ, וַחֲסִידֶיךָ יְבָרְכוּכָה:
כְּבוֹד מַלְכוּתְךָ יֹאמֵרוּ, וּגְבוּרָתְךָ יְדַבֵּרוּ:
לְהוֹדִיעַ לִבְנֵי הָאָדָם גְּבוּרֹתָיו, וּכְבוֹד הֲדַר מַלְכוּתוֹ:
מַלְכוּתְךָ מַלְכוּת כָּל־עֹלָמִים, וּמֶמְשַׁלְתְּךָ בְּכָל־דּוֹר וָדֹר:
סוֹמֵךְ יהוה לְכָל־הַנֹּפְלִים, וְזוֹקֵף לְכָל־הַכְּפוּפִים:
עֵינֵי־כֹל אֵלֶיךָ יְשַׂבֵּרוּ, וְאַתָּה נוֹתֵן־לָהֶם אֶת־אָכְלָם בְּעִתּוֹ:
°פּוֹתֵחַ אֶת־יָדֶךָ, °°וּמַשְׂבִּיעַ לְכָל־חַי רָצוֹן:
צַדִּיק יהוה בְּכָל־דְּרָכָיו, וְחָסִיד בְּכָל־מַעֲשָׂיו:
קָרוֹב יהוה לְכָל־קֹרְאָיו, לְכֹל אֲשֶׁר יִקְרָאֻהוּ בֶאֱמֶת:
רְצוֹן־יְרֵאָיו יַעֲשֶׂה, וְאֶת־שַׁוְעָתָם יִשְׁמַע וְיוֹשִׁיעֵם:
שׁוֹמֵר יהוה אֶת־כָּל־אֹהֲבָיו, וְאֵת כָּל־הָרְשָׁעִים יַשְׁמִיד:
◂ תְּהִלַּת יהוה יְדַבֶּר פִּי, וִיבָרֵךְ כָּל־בָּשָׂר שֵׁם קָדְשׁוֹ לְעוֹלָם וָעֶד:
תהלים קטו וַאֲנַחְנוּ נְבָרֵךְ יָהּ מֵעַתָּה וְעַד־עוֹלָם, הַלְלוּיָהּ:

---

be missing, and it is highly improbable that a verse in such an oft-used psalm was simply lost. Indeed, we find precedent in Psalms for "imperfect" acrostics, such as Psalms 9–10, 25, 34, and 37, in which the alphabetical disruptions mark important thematic transitions (R. Ronald Benun). Moreover, there is a thematic shift between the verses preceding and those following this break. The מ verse concludes a lengthy section dealing with divine grandeur, and ס begins to describe divine intervention in the lower realms – hence the structure intentionally teaches that God "skips" down from glorious transcendence to involve Himself immanently in the details of nature (R. Aton Holzer).

זֵכֶר רַב – *The renown.* Some *siddurim* follow the Vilna Gaon in placing a *segol* vowel under the *zayin* of this word. Insofar as the text of Psalms found in the authoritative Aleppo Codex has a *tzerei*, we too use a *tzerei* for this verse throughout the Siddur.

רְצוֹן – *The will.* In light of the prevalence of the word כל ("all") in this psalm, it is noteworthy that the word is absent from "He performs the will of those who fear Him," indicating that while God is responsive to those who fear Him, this is not automatically and not all the time. While we pray for God to respond to us, we must be prepared for God to not respond, no matter how sincere or heartfelt

ז They express the renown of Your great goodness,
and sing of Your righteousness.
ח Gracious and merciful is the Lord,
slow to anger and great in loving-kindness.
ט The Lord is good to all,
and His mercies are upon all His works.
י All Your works thank You,
O Lord, and Your pious ones bless You.
כ They describe the glory of Your kingdom,
and speak of Your might,
ל To make known to the sons of man His mighty deeds,
and the glorious splendor of His kingdom.
מ Your kingdom is a kingdom for all times,
and Your dominion is for every generation.
ס The Lord supports all who fall
and raises up all who are bowed down.
ע The eyes of all await You,
and You give them their food in its time.
פ °You open Your hand,
°°and You satisfy the desire of every living thing.
צ The Lord is righteous in all His ways
and kind in all His works.
ק The Lord is near to all who address Him,
to all who address Him in truth.
ר He does the will of those who fear Him,
and He hears their cry and saves them.
ש The Lord preserves all who love Him,
but all the wicked He destroys.
ת ▸ May my mouth speak the praise of the Lord,
and may all flesh bless His holy name forever and ever.

Ps. 115 But we will bless the Lord from now and forevermore. Praise the Lord.

---

our prayers. After all, not everything that we ask for is in our best interests. It is God alone Who can make that determination (R. Avraham Walfish).

תהלים קמו **הַלְלוּיָהּ,** הַלְלִי נַפְשִׁי אֶת־יהוה: אֲהַלְלָה יהוה בְּחַיָּי, אֲזַמְּרָה לֵאלֹהַי בְּעוֹדִי: אַל־תִּבְטְחוּ בִנְדִיבִים, בְּבֶן־אָדָם שֶׁאֵין לוֹ תְשׁוּעָה: תֵּצֵא רוּחוֹ, יָשֻׁב לְאַדְמָתוֹ, בַּיּוֹם הַהוּא אָבְדוּ עֶשְׁתֹּנֹתָיו: אַשְׁרֵי שֶׁאֵל יַעֲקֹב בְּעֶזְרוֹ, שִׂבְרוֹ עַל־יהוה אֱלֹהָיו: עֹשֶׂה שָׁמַיִם וָאָרֶץ, אֶת־הַיָּם וְאֶת־כׇּל־אֲשֶׁר־בָּם, הַשֹּׁמֵר אֱמֶת לְעוֹלָם: עֹשֶׂה מִשְׁפָּט לָעֲשׁוּקִים, נֹתֵן לֶחֶם לָרְעֵבִים, יהוה מַתִּיר אֲסוּרִים: יהוה פֹּקֵחַ עִוְרִים, יהוה זֹקֵף כְּפוּפִים, יהוה אֹהֵב צַדִּיקִים: יהוה שֹׁמֵר אֶת־גֵּרִים, יָתוֹם וְאַלְמָנָה יְעוֹדֵד, וְדֶרֶךְ רְשָׁעִים יְעַוֵּת: ▸ יִמְלֹךְ יהוה לְעוֹלָם, אֱלֹהַיִךְ צִיּוֹן לְדֹר וָדֹר, הַלְלוּיָהּ:

תהלים קמז **הַלְלוּיָהּ,** כִּי־טוֹב זַמְּרָה אֱלֹהֵינוּ, כִּי־נָעִים נָאוָה תְהִלָּה: בּוֹנֵה יְרוּשָׁלַםִ יהוה, נִדְחֵי יִשְׂרָאֵל יְכַנֵּס: הָרוֹפֵא לִשְׁבוּרֵי לֵב, וּמְחַבֵּשׁ לְעַצְּבוֹתָם: מוֹנֶה מִסְפָּר לַכּוֹכָבִים, לְכֻלָּם שֵׁמוֹת יִקְרָא: גָּדוֹל אֲדוֹנֵינוּ וְרַב־כֹּחַ, לִתְבוּנָתוֹ אֵין מִסְפָּר: מְעוֹדֵד עֲנָוִים יהוה, מַשְׁפִּיל רְשָׁעִים עֲדֵי־אָרֶץ: עֱנוּ לַיהוה בְּתוֹדָה, זַמְּרוּ לֵאלֹהֵינוּ בְכִנּוֹר: הַמְכַסֶּה שָׁמַיִם בְּעָבִים, הַמֵּכִין לָאָרֶץ מָטָר, הַמַּצְמִיחַ הָרִים חָצִיר: נוֹתֵן לִבְהֵמָה לַחְמָהּ, לִבְנֵי עֹרֵב אֲשֶׁר יִקְרָאוּ: לֹא בִגְבוּרַת

הַלְלוּיָהּ, הַלְלִי נַפְשִׁי אֶת־ה׳ / PSALM 146
This psalm develops the theme of God's constant providence first set out in the previous psalm, and picks up on its call to those who are "close to God." In the central section of this psalm (vv.5–9) the Psalmist declares that unlike one who trusts in man and will ultimately be disillusioned, one who trusts in God will be happy. The subsequent verses stress that God can be relied on to honor His promises and commitments: He saves the downtrodden, and helps those in dire straits, including the innocent and the disenfranchised, while He disrupts the path of the wicked (R. Yitzchak Etshalom).

אֲהַלְלָה ה׳ בְּחַיָּי, אֲזַמְּרָה לֵאלֹהַי בְּעוֹדִי – *I will praise the Lord while I live. I will sing praises to my God while I exist.* This verse teaches that we should first praise God for the very fact that we are alive. Thereafter, as the second half of the verse states, we must thank Him for the untold additional kindnesses bestowed upon us. As the *Yalkut Shimoni* explains the final phrase of the last Psalm (150:6), כֹּל הַנְּשָׁמָה means "for each and every נְשִׁימָה (breath), תְּהַלֵּל יָהּ, you must thank God" (*Ktav Sofer*).

יִמְלֹךְ ה׳ לְעוֹלָם – *The Lord will reign forever.* This verse constitutes the response of the assembled crowds to the preceding call of the Psalmist to praise God, i.e., "We take God's kingship upon ourselves forever, and in accordance with what you have told us, we will not put our trust in princes, but in God alone." This

Ps. 146 הַלְלוּיָהּ PRAISE THE LORD. Praise the Lord, O my soul. I will praise the Lord while I live. I will sing praises to my God while I exist. Do not put your trust in princes, in a son of man in whom there is no help. His breath will leave, he will return to his earth. On that day his thoughts will perish. Happy is he who has the God of Jacob as his helper, whose hope is in the Lord his God, Who makes heaven and earth, the sea, and all that is in them, Who keeps truth forever, Who executes judgment for the oppressed, Who gives bread to the hungry, the Lord sets the prisoners free. The Lord opens the eyes of the blind, the Lord raises up those who are bowed down, the Lord loves the righteous. The Lord preserves the strangers, He strengthens the fatherless and the widow, and He makes crooked the way of the wicked. ▸ The Lord will reign forever, your God, O Zion, to all generations. Praise the Lord.

Ps. 147 הַלְלוּיָהּ PRAISE THE LORD. Indeed, it is good to sing to our God. Indeed, it is pleasant. Praise is seemly. The Lord is the builder of Jerusalem. He gathers the outcasts of Israel. He heals the broken-hearted, and binds their wounds. He counts the number of the stars. He calls them all by names. Great is our Master, and of great power. His understanding has no measure. The Lord lifts up the humble. He casts the wicked down to the ground. Sing to the Lord with thanksgiving, play the lyre to our God, Who covers heaven with clouds, Who prepares rain for the earth, Who makes grass grow upon the mountains. He gives to the beast its food, to the ravens that cry. He

---

verse was used by the sages in formulating the *kedusha* of the *Amida* because it mentions Zion, which is the fulcrum of God's kingdom on earth (R. Amos Ḥakham).

הַלְלוּיָהּ, כִּי־טוֹב / PSALM 147
The psalm has an elegant structure, with three stanzas – vv. 1–6; 7–11; 12–20. Each begins (v. 1, 7, 12) with a call to praise God; followed by a description of God as He Who strengthens the city and blesses the people (vv. 2–3; 13–14 – this component is missing in the middle stanza), a description of the divine wisdom of creation (vv. 4–5; 8–9; 15–18); and a conclusion stating that God favors not the mighty but the humble (vv. 6, 10, 19–20). Each stanza grows in intensity (R. Yitzchak Etshalom).

בּוֹנֵה יְרוּשָׁלַםִ – *The builder of Jerusalem*. The word בּוֹנֵה can also be translated as a present-tense verb: "He builds." God not only built it from the ground up, He is also the One Who continues to build it as it continues to grow and expand throughout history (R. Amos Ḥakham).

הַסּוּס יֶחְפָּץ, לֹא־בְשׁוֹקֵי הָאִישׁ יִרְצֶה: רוֹצֶה יהוה אֶת־יְרֵאָיו, אֶת־
הַמְיַחֲלִים לְחַסְדּוֹ: שַׁבְּחִי יְרוּשָׁלַםִ אֶת־יהוה, הַלְלִי אֱלֹהַיִךְ צִיּוֹן:
כִּי־חִזַּק בְּרִיחֵי שְׁעָרָיִךְ, בֵּרַךְ בָּנַיִךְ בְּקִרְבֵּךְ: הַשָּׂם־גְּבוּלֵךְ שָׁלוֹם,
חֵלֶב חִטִּים יַשְׂבִּיעֵךְ: הַשֹּׁלֵחַ אִמְרָתוֹ אָרֶץ, עַד־מְהֵרָה יָרוּץ דְּבָרוֹ:
הַנֹּתֵן שֶׁלֶג כַּצָּמֶר, כְּפוֹר כָּאֵפֶר יְפַזֵּר: מַשְׁלִיךְ קַרְחוֹ כְפִתִּים, לִפְנֵי
קָרָתוֹ מִי יַעֲמֹד: יִשְׁלַח דְּבָרוֹ וְיַמְסֵם, יַשֵּׁב רוּחוֹ יִזְּלוּ־מָיִם: ◂ מַגִּיד
דְּבָרָו לְיַעֲקֹב, חֻקָּיו וּמִשְׁפָּטָיו לְיִשְׂרָאֵל: לֹא עָשָׂה כֵן לְכָל־גּוֹי,
וּמִשְׁפָּטִים בַּל־יְדָעוּם, הַלְלוּיָהּ:

תהלים קמח

הַלְלוּיָהּ, הַלְלוּ אֶת־יהוה מִן־הַשָּׁמַיִם, הַלְלוּהוּ בַּמְּרוֹמִים: הַלְלוּהוּ
כָל־מַלְאָכָיו, הַלְלוּהוּ כָּל־צְבָאָו: הַלְלוּהוּ שֶׁמֶשׁ וְיָרֵחַ,
הַלְלוּהוּ כָּל־כּוֹכְבֵי אוֹר: הַלְלוּהוּ שְׁמֵי הַשָּׁמָיִם, וְהַמַּיִם אֲשֶׁר מֵעַל
הַשָּׁמָיִם: יְהַלְלוּ אֶת־שֵׁם יהוה, כִּי הוּא צִוָּה וְנִבְרָאוּ: וַיַּעֲמִידֵם לָעַד
לְעוֹלָם, חָק־נָתַן וְלֹא יַעֲבוֹר: הַלְלוּ אֶת־יהוה מִן־הָאָרֶץ, תַּנִּינִים
וְכָל־תְּהֹמוֹת: אֵשׁ וּבָרָד שֶׁלֶג וְקִיטוֹר, רוּחַ סְעָרָה עֹשָׂה דְבָרוֹ:
הֶהָרִים וְכָל־גְּבָעוֹת, עֵץ פְּרִי וְכָל־אֲרָזִים: הַחַיָּה וְכָל־בְּהֵמָה, רֶמֶשׂ
וְצִפּוֹר כָּנָף: מַלְכֵי־אֶרֶץ וְכָל־לְאֻמִּים, שָׂרִים וְכָל־שֹׁפְטֵי אָרֶץ:

מַגִּיד דְּבָרָו לְיַעֲקֹב – *He proclaimed His words to Jacob.* The term מַגִּיד always signifies detailed exposition of the matter at hand. Here the Psalmist intentionally did not formulate the more common terms אוֹמֵר (speak) or מְדַבֵּר (say), for he wishes to convey that while it is indeed true that God gave the Written Law to Israel to be shared with the nations of the world, He gave the Oral Law only to Israel, for it contains all of the detailed explanations and applications of the Torah's statutes and laws (R. Elazar Figo).

לֹא עָשָׂה כֵן לְכָל־גּוֹי – *He has not done so for any other nation.* Rashi explains Songs of Songs 1:2 ("Let Him kiss me with the kisses of His mouth, for Your love is better than wine") to be referring to the request of the Jewish people that God reveal to them that which is hidden in the Torah. This is to be explained in light of the *Midrash Raba* that understands the second half of that verse to refer to the seventy nations of the world (as the numerical value of the word יַיִן equals 70). Together, they affirm that whereas the תּוֹרָה שֶׁבִּכְתָב (written Scripture) is to be shared with all of humanity, the תּוֹרָה שֶׁבְּעַל פֶּה (Oral Law) is the exclusive possession of the Jewish people. The very term "kiss" connotes an oral transmission from God's mouth to ours, as in "The Lord gives wisdom; out of His mouth come knowledge and understanding" (Prov. 2:6). Note that this verse

does not desire the strength of the horse. He does not want the thighs of man. The Lord wants those who fear Him, those who hope for His loving-kindness. Praise the Lord, O Jerusalem. Extol your God, O Zion. For He has strengthened the bars of your gates, He has blessed your sons in your midst. He places peace in your border. He satisfies you with the finest of wheat. He sends His command to the earth. His word runs very swiftly. He gives snow like wool. He scatters frost like ashes. He casts His ice like crumbs. Who can stand before His cold? He sends His word and melts them. He makes His wind blow, and the waters flow. ▸ He proclaimed His words to Jacob, His statutes and judgments to Israel. He has not done so for any other nation, and as for judgments, they do not know them. Praise the Lord.

Ps. 148 הַלְלוּיָהּ PRAISE THE LORD. Praise the Lord from the heavens, praise Him in the heights. Praise Him, all you His angels. Praise Him, all you His hosts. Praise Him, sun and moon. Praise Him, all you stars of light. Praise Him, heavens of the heavens, and the waters that are above the heavens. Let them praise the name of the Lord, that He commanded and they were created. And He established them forever and ever. He gave a command and it will not be annulled. Praise the Lord from the earth, O sea creatures and all depths. Fire and hail, snow and vapors, stormy wind fulfilling His word. The mountains and all hills, fruit trees and all cedars. Beasts and all cattle, creeping things, and winged birds. Kings of the earth and all peoples, princes,

---

says God "gives," not "gave" – for it refers to the Oral Law given by God to us continually, as we interpret the Torah in accordance with divinely revealed guidelines. This knowledge is given to the Jewish people alone. As the *Midrash Raba* explains, the written Torah is to be shared with all of humanity; the oral Torah is the legacy of the Jewish people alone (*Beit HaLevi*).

הַלְלוּיָהּ, הַלְלוּ אֶת־ה׳ / PSALM 148

הַלְלוּיָהּ, הַלְלוּ אֶת־ה׳ מִן־הַשָּׁמַיִם, הַלְלוּהוּ בַּמְּרוֹמִים – *Praise the Lord. Praise the Lord from the heavens, praise Him in the heights.* It is said in the name of R. Yona that this verse is the key to prayer with כַּוָּנָה (proper intent). It requires that we imagine that we have transcended our physical state, to ascend to the heavens, bereft of every physical pleasure or dimension, intent only on serving God in imitation of the angels who are pure spiritual beings. When we pray in this manner our main concern is to connect our souls to their source in heaven. Hence the verse declares that we must "praise the Lord from the heavens and in the heights" (R. Ḥayyim of Volozhin).

בַּחוּרִים וְגַם־בְּתוּלוֹת, זְקֵנִים עִם־נְעָרִים: ‹ יְהַלְלוּ אֶת־שֵׁם יהוה,
כִּי־נִשְׂגָּב שְׁמוֹ לְבַדּוֹ, הוֹדוֹ עַל־אֶרֶץ וְשָׁמָיִם: וַיָּרֶם קֶרֶן לְעַמּוֹ,
תְּהִלָּה לְכָל־חֲסִידָיו, לִבְנֵי יִשְׂרָאֵל עַם קְרֹבוֹ, הַלְלוּיָהּ:

הַלְלוּיָהּ, שִׁירוּ לַיהוה שִׁיר חָדָשׁ, תְּהִלָּתוֹ בִּקְהַל חֲסִידִים: יִשְׂמַח תהלים קמט
יִשְׂרָאֵל בְּעֹשָׂיו, בְּנֵי־צִיּוֹן יָגִילוּ בְמַלְכָּם: יְהַלְלוּ שְׁמוֹ
בְמָחוֹל, בְּתֹף וְכִנּוֹר יְזַמְּרוּ־לוֹ: כִּי־רוֹצֶה יהוה בְּעַמּוֹ, יְפָאֵר עֲנָוִים
בִּישׁוּעָה: יַעְלְזוּ חֲסִידִים בְּכָבוֹד, יְרַנְּנוּ עַל־מִשְׁכְּבוֹתָם: רוֹמְמוֹת
אֵל בִּגְרוֹנָם, וְחֶרֶב פִּיפִיּוֹת בְּיָדָם: לַעֲשׂוֹת נְקָמָה בַּגּוֹיִם, תּוֹכֵחוֹת
בַּלְאֻמִּים: ‹ לֶאְסֹר מַלְכֵיהֶם בְּזִקִּים, וְנִכְבְּדֵיהֶם בְּכַבְלֵי בַרְזֶל:
לַעֲשׂוֹת בָּהֶם מִשְׁפָּט כָּתוּב, הָדָר הוּא לְכָל־חֲסִידָיו, הַלְלוּיָהּ:

הַלְלוּיָהּ, הַלְלוּ־אֵל בְּקָדְשׁוֹ, הַלְלוּהוּ בִּרְקִיעַ עֻזּוֹ: הַלְלוּהוּ תהלים קנ
בִגְבוּרֹתָיו, הַלְלוּהוּ כְּרֹב גֻּדְלוֹ: הַלְלוּהוּ בְּתֵקַע שׁוֹפָר,
הַלְלוּהוּ בְּנֵבֶל וְכִנּוֹר: הַלְלוּהוּ בְתֹף וּמָחוֹל, הַלְלוּהוּ בְּמִנִּים וְעֻגָב:
הַלְלוּהוּ בְצִלְצְלֵי־שָׁמַע, הַלְלוּהוּ בְּצִלְצְלֵי תְרוּעָה: ‹ כֹּל הַנְּשָׁמָה
תְּהַלֵּל יָהּ, הַלְלוּיָהּ: כֹּל הַנְּשָׁמָה תְּהַלֵּל יָהּ, הַלְלוּיָהּ:

בַּחוּרִים וְגַם־בְּתוּלוֹת – *Both young men and virgins*. The Psalmist upholds clear distinction between the genders, reflecting their diverse psyches and their unique respective approaches to prayer, praise, and the service of God. Before God male and female are equal, but at the same time they are created with diverse and inherent differences, allowing each to approach and serve Him in their respective fashions.

הַלְלוּיָהּ, שִׁירוּ לַה׳ / PSALM 149
This psalm follows a clear chiastic structure (A-B-C-B-A), with its nine verses all revolving around verse 5, the mid-point. Verses 1, 5, and 9 (the beginning, middle, and end) all make mention of the "loyalists" of God – חֲסִידָיו and verses 2 and 8 (adjacent to the middle one) both mention royalty (R. Yitzchak Etshalom).

יִשְׂמַח יִשְׂרָאֵל בְּעֹשָׂיו – *Let Israel rejoice in Him Who made him*. Everything that exists in the cosmos is an expression of God's will, and thus everything possesses a unique purpose. It is He Who brought it into being and He Who maintains its existence to that end. When we understand that our own lives fulfill God's purpose, and thus cannot be meaningless, we are filled with joy, strength, and tranquility – aware that God has chosen to reveal His will through the lens of our own lives. Then we can banish any shadow of sadness or suffering that may afflict us, and replace them with pure joy at being alive. Hence "let Israel rejoice in

and all judges of the earth. Both young men and virgins, old men and boys. ▸ Let them praise the name of the Lord, that His name alone is exalted. His glory is over the earth and the heavens. And He has raised the horn of His people, praise for all His pious ones, for the children of Israel, the people near to Him. Praise the Lord.

Ps. 149 הַלְלוּיָהּ PRAISE THE LORD. Sing to the Lord a new song, His praise in the congregation of the pious. Let Israel rejoice in Him Who made him. Let the children of Zion be joyful in their King. Let them praise His name in dance. Let them play to Him on the timbrel and the lyre, That the Lord takes pleasure in His people, He honors the oppressed with salvation. Let the pious be joyful in glory, let them sing upon their beds. The praises of God are in their throat, and a two-edged sword in their hand, to execute vengeance upon the nations, chastisements upon the peoples, ▸ to bind their kings with chains, and their nobles with fetters of iron, to execute upon them the written judgment. He is an honor to all His pious ones. Praise the Lord.

Ps. 150 הַלְלוּיָהּ PRAISE THE LORD. Praise God for His sanctity, praise Him for His power in the firmament. Praise Him for His mighty acts, praise Him in accordance with His exceeding greatness. Praise Him with the sounding of the shofar, praise Him with the harp and lyre. Praise Him with the timbrel and the dance, praise Him with flutes and the pipe. Praise Him with sounding cymbals, praise Him with loud clashing cymbals. ▸ Let everything that has breath praise the Lord. Praise the Lord. Let everything that has breath praise the Lord. Praise the Lord.

---

being one of God's creations" (R. Yaakov Moshe Charlap).

הַלְלוּיָהּ, הַלְלוּ־אֵל / PSALM 150

This is the final psalm. The central stanza, comprising verses 3–5, lists nine instruments including wind, string and percussion. Such an ensemble has the power to reach the deepest human emotions in response to musical chords, rhythms, and harmonies, when set to spiritual themes. This effect was further heightened when these instruments were complemented by the melodious voices of the Levites, together creating a glorious symphonic song of praise to God.

For Natronai Gaon this chapter is the high point of the *Pesukei DeZimra*. The Arizal explained that the highest service of God occurs when we transcend our usual worries

תהלים פט
תהלים קלה
תהלים עב

בָּרוּךְ יהוה לְעוֹלָם, אָמֵן וְאָמֵן: בָּרוּךְ יהוה מִצִּיּוֹן, שֹׁכֵן יְרוּשָׁלָםִ, הַלְלוּיָהּ: בָּרוּךְ יהוה אֱלֹהִים אֱלֹהֵי יִשְׂרָאֵל, עֹשֵׂה נִפְלָאוֹת לְבַדּוֹ: ◂ וּבָרוּךְ שֵׁם כְּבוֹדוֹ לְעוֹלָם, וְיִמָּלֵא כְבוֹדוֹ אֶת־כָּל־הָאָרֶץ, אָמֵן וְאָמֵן:

Stand (see commentary) until after בָּרְכוּ *on page 88.*
It is customary to give money to charity while reciting ואתה מושל בכל.

דברי הימים א, כט

וַיְבָרֶךְ דָּוִיד אֶת־יהוה לְעֵינֵי כָּל־הַקָּהָל, וַיֹּאמֶר דָּוִיד, בָּרוּךְ אַתָּה יהוה, אֱלֹהֵי יִשְׂרָאֵל אָבִינוּ, מֵעוֹלָם וְעַד־עוֹלָם: לְךָ יהוה הַגְּדֻלָּה וְהַגְּבוּרָה וְהַתִּפְאֶרֶת וְהַנֵּצַח וְהַהוֹד, כִּי־כֹל בַּשָּׁמַיִם וּבָאָרֶץ, לְךָ יהוה הַמַּמְלָכָה וְהַמִּתְנַשֵּׂא לְכֹל לְרֹאשׁ: וְהָעֹשֶׁר וְהַכָּבוֹד מִלְּפָנֶיךָ, וְאַתָּה מוֹשֵׁל בַּכֹּל, וּבְיָדְךָ כֹּחַ וּגְבוּרָה, וּבְיָדְךָ לְגַדֵּל וּלְחַזֵּק לַכֹּל: וְעַתָּה אֱלֹהֵינוּ מוֹדִים אֲנַחְנוּ לָךְ, וּמְהַלְלִים לְשֵׁם תִּפְאַרְתֶּךָ:

נחמיה ט

אַתָּה־הוּא יהוה לְבַדֶּךָ, אַתְּ עָשִׂיתָ אֶת־הַשָּׁמַיִם, שְׁמֵי הַשָּׁמַיִם וְכָל־צְבָאָם, הָאָרֶץ וְכָל־אֲשֶׁר עָלֶיהָ, הַיַּמִּים וְכָל־אֲשֶׁר בָּהֶם, וְאַתָּה מְחַיֶּה אֶת־כֻּלָּם, וּצְבָא הַשָּׁמַיִם לְךָ מִשְׁתַּחֲוִים: ◂ אַתָּה הוּא יהוה הָאֱלֹהִים אֲשֶׁר בָּחַרְתָּ בְּאַבְרָם, וְהוֹצֵאתוֹ מֵאוּר כַּשְׂדִּים,

---

and distractions, to reach an elevated state of mental and spiritual tranquility (R. Reuven Melamed).

כֹּל הַנְּשָׁמָה תְּהַלֵּל יָהּ – *Let everything that has breath praise the Lord* (previous page). Every soul, even that of sinners, will in due course be recognized as having contributed in one way or another to the fulfillment of God's will and the redemption of the world, irrespective of their intentions at the time. We see this in the biblical story of Ruth, for it was through the selfish actions of Elimelekh, Mahlon and Kilyon that the Davidic dynasty eventually arose, leading ultimately to Messianic redemption. This is the deeper meaning of "On that day the sins of Israel will be sought but not found… for I will forgive the remaining sins" (Jer. 50:20). It teaches that at the end of days there will be a full recognition that all past transgressions will have ultimately contributed to the fulfillment of God's will. Even the heavenly accusers will thus be silenced, and God will be "free" to forgive and destroy the sins of the past (R. Moshe Feinstein).

וַיְבָרֶךְ דָּוִיד / THEN DAVID BLESSED

This passage is taken from I Chronicles 29, where King David, at the end of his life, publicly acknowledges that all of his accomplishments – spiritual and intellectual leadership, military victories, material and economic successes in strengthening the Israelite kingdom – were not of his own doing, but directly attributable to God's power, benevolence, and mercies.

We rise for this paragraph because, as the

Ps. 89 Ps. 135 **בָּרוּךְ** BLESSED is the Lord forever. Amen and amen. Blessed is the Lord from Zion, He Who dwells in Jerusalem. Praise the Lord.
Ps. 72 Blessed is the Lord God, the God of Israel, Who does wondrous things alone. ▸ And blessed is His glorious name forever, and may the whole earth be filled with His glory. Amen and amen.

Stand (see commentary) until after "Bless the Lord" on page 89.
It is customary to give money to charity while reciting "And You rule over all."

I Chr. 29 **וַיְבָרֶךְ דָּוִיד** THEN DAVID BLESSED the Lord in the sight of all the congregation. David said, "Blessed are You, Lord, God of our father Israel, forever and ever. Yours, O Lord, are greatness, and power, and glory, and victory, and majesty; yes, all that is in the heavens and on the earth. Yours, O Lord, is the dominion, and You are supreme over all. Riches and honor come from You, and You rule over all. In Your hand are power and might, it is in Your hand to make great and give strength to all. Now therefore we thank You, our God, and we praise Your glorious name."

Neh. 9 You are the Lord, You alone. You have made the heavens, the heaven of heavens and all their host, the earth and all that is on it, the seas and all that is therein. You give life to them all, and the hosts of heaven worship You. ▸ You are the Lord, the God Who chose Abram, and brought him forth from Ur of the Chaldees and gave him the name Abraham.

Mishna *Bikkurim* 3:3 states, when people would bring their first fruits to Jerusalem, workers on the side of the road would rise to honor them for performing that *mitzva*. Here too, because at this point in the service it was customary to collect *tzedaka* from those present, we stand in honor of those who facilitate this *mitzva* (R. Joseph B. Soloveitchik).

כִּי־כֹל בַּשָּׁמַיִם – *Yes, all that is in the heavens.* David's life embodies the widest spectrum of human experience, overcoming multiple obstacles to rise to the heights of human accomplishment. He struggled with sin and then repented; he suffered discrimination on account of his ancestor Ruth who was a Moabite; he was doubted by his own family members due to the questionable circumstances of his birth. Throughout it all he was able to retain a profound and lasting relationship with God, as expressed in the psalms, reflecting a life of the most exalted spiritual heights. Hence he can declare – כִּי־כֹל בַּשָּׁמַיִם וּבָאָרֶץ, "for all that is in the heaven and in the earth is Yours" (R. Shimshon David Pinkus).

לְךָ מִשְׁתַּחֲוִים – *Worship You.* With these words they declare that the timing of our prayers,

וְשַׂמְתָּ שְׁמוֹ אַבְרָהָם: וּמָצָאתָ אֶת־לְבָבוֹ נֶאֱמָן לְפָנֶיךָ,
וְכָרוֹת עִמּוֹ
הַבְּרִית לָתֵת אֶת־אֶרֶץ הַכְּנַעֲנִי הַחִתִּי הָאֱמֹרִי וְהַפְּרִזִּי וְהַיְבוּסִי
וְהַגִּרְגָּשִׁי, לָתֵת לְזַרְעוֹ, וַתָּקֶם אֶת־דְּבָרֶיךָ, כִּי צַדִּיק אָתָּה: וַתֵּרֶא
אֶת־עֳנִי אֲבֹתֵינוּ בְּמִצְרָיִם, וְאֶת־זַעֲקָתָם שָׁמַעְתָּ עַל־יַם־סוּף: וַתִּתֵּן
אֹתֹת וּמֹפְתִים בְּפַרְעֹה וּבְכָל־עֲבָדָיו וּבְכָל־עַם אַרְצוֹ, כִּי יָדַעְתָּ כִּי
הֵזִידוּ עֲלֵיהֶם, וַתַּעַשׂ־לְךָ שֵׁם כְּהַיּוֹם הַזֶּה: ◂ וְהַיָּם בָּקַעְתָּ לִפְנֵיהֶם,
וַיַּעַבְרוּ בְתוֹךְ־הַיָּם בַּיַּבָּשָׁה, וְאֶת־רֹדְפֵיהֶם הִשְׁלַכְתָּ בִמְצוֹלֹת, כְּמוֹ־
אֶבֶן בְּמַיִם עַזִּים:

שירת הים

שמות יד **וַיּוֹשַׁע** יהוה בַּיּוֹם הַהוּא אֶת־יִשְׂרָאֵל מִיַּד מִצְרָיִם וַיַּרְא יִשְׂרָאֵל
אֶת־מִצְרַיִם מֵת עַל־שְׂפַת הַיָּם: ◂ וַיַּרְא יִשְׂרָאֵל אֶת־הַיָּד
הַגְּדֹלָה אֲשֶׁר עָשָׂה יהוה בְּמִצְרַיִם וַיִּירְאוּ הָעָם אֶת־יהוה וַיַּאֲמִינוּ
בַּיהוה וּבְמֹשֶׁה עַבְדּוֹ:

---

and the orientation of the Temple toward the east ensure that the rising sun itself join us in the service of God, its rays streaming through its doors from the east to "bow before God," in accordance with the verse יִירָאוּךָ עִם־שָׁמֶשׁ וְלִפְנֵי יָרֵחַ דּוֹר דּוֹרִים (Ps. 72:5) (R. Yoel Bin Nun).

וּמָצָאתָ – *Finding.* This phrase is not the end of a verse, but its beginning, which continues with וְכָרוֹת, even though the word is arranged so as to begin a new paragraph. One explanation for this break is that it reflects the dramatically transformed status of the founder of the Jewish people once he entered into this covenant with God. This is highlighted by the juxtaposition in these verses of the names Abram and Abraham, signifying his becoming the patriarch of the Jewish nation, which would in the course of history transform all of humanity.

When a circumcision is to be performed in the synagogue, it is a widespread custom that the *mohel* or rabbi lead the congregation in chanting the section beginning with וְכָרוֹת, because Abraham's circumcision sealed the covenant. In some congregations, all the verses from וְכָרוֹת until (but not including) יִשְׁתַּבַּח are recited responsively, while in other congregations, the *mohel* recites the verses from וְכָרוֹת until בְּמַיִם עַזִּים.

THE SONG AT THE SEA/שִׁירַת הַיָּם

וַיִּירְאוּ ... וַיַּאֲמִינוּ – *Revered... believed.* Why did seeing the miracle induce fear of God, and why did this miracle induce more fear in the Israelites than all of the preceding miracles of the Exodus? The answer is that what induced the fear of God at that moment was not simply that Israel was saved, but that the Egyptians were punished precisely in accordance with each Egyptian's treatment of the Israelites. Those who acted with greater cruelty died with greater suffering, while those who were less guilty were spared excessive agony. When the Israelites saw God's knowing precision in this

Finding his heart faithful to You,

You made the covenant with him to give his seed the land of the Canaanite, the Hittite, the Amorite, the Perizzite, the Jebusite, and the Girgashite. You have fulfilled Your words, because You are true. You saw the affliction of our fathers in Egypt, and hearkened to their cry by the Sea of Reeds. There You performed signs and wonders on Pharaoh and all his servants and all the people of his land, because You knew that they had dealt tyrannously with our fathers. And in so doing You made a glorious name for Yourself known even to this day. ▸ The sea You divided before them, so that they went through the midst of the sea on dry ground, but their pursuers You cast into the depths like a stone in the mighty waters.

THE SONG AT THE SEA

Ex. 14 **וַיּוֹשַׁע** THUS THE LORD saved Israel that day from the power of the Egyptians, and Israel saw the Egyptians dead upon the seashore. ▸ Israel beheld the great power that the Lord had displayed against Egypt, and the people revered the Lord and believed in the Lord and in His servant Moses.

---

regard, they experienced heightened "fear of God" at the prospect of their own future punishment for any violations of God's will. This explains why in *Ma'ariv* following the *Shema* we say, "He drowned their pursuers and haters," that is, the punishment at the Sea of Reeds distinguished between those who pursued the Israelites only because they were ordered to do so, and those who acted out of hatred for them, and punished them accordingly (*Netziv*).

THE STRUCTURE OF AZ YASHIR

This paean of praise to God divides neatly into two sections. The first celebrates God for having smitten the Egyptian army and saved Israel. The second turns to the broader repercussions of that miracle on the nations in their path en route to the Promised Land, for whom these events proved to be a source of fear and trepidation. Just as God was careful not to lead the people on a direct route to Israel lest the people encounter their enemies and – being fearful of battle – choose to return to Egypt, so too, by these events God instilled the fear of Israel in their potential enemies, and in so doing facilitated the eventual inheritance of the land by the children of Israel.

This event became the very embodiment of God's intervention in history and nature on our behalf, and bears witness to the promised completion of the Jewish mission, when all the nations will come to accept and worship the God proclaimed by the Jews. For this reason it forms the ideal introduction to the next section of *Shaḥarit*: the blessings of the *Shema* as well as the *Shema* itself, which together affirm the acceptance of God's sovereignty over the universe (R. Aton Holzer).

שמות טו

אָז יָשִׁיר־מֹשֶׁה וּבְנֵי יִשְׂרָאֵל אֶת־הַשִּׁירָה הַזֹּאת לַיהוה, וַיֹּאמְרוּ
לֵאמֹר, אָשִׁירָה לַּיהוה כִּי־גָאֹה גָּאָה, סוּס
וְרֹכְבוֹ רָמָה בַיָּם: עָזִּי וְזִמְרָת יָהּ וַיְהִי־לִי
לִישׁוּעָה, זֶה אֵלִי וְאַנְוֵהוּ, אֱלֹהֵי
אָבִי וַאֲרֹמְמֶנְהוּ: יהוה אִישׁ מִלְחָמָה, יהוה
שְׁמוֹ: מַרְכְּבֹת פַּרְעֹה וְחֵילוֹ יָרָה בַיָּם, וּמִבְחַר
שָׁלִשָׁיו טֻבְּעוּ בְיַם־סוּף: תְּהֹמֹת יְכַסְיֻמוּ, יָרְדוּ בִמְצוֹלֹת כְּמוֹ־
אָבֶן: יְמִינְךָ יהוה נֶאְדָּרִי בַּכֹּחַ, יְמִינְךָ
יהוה תִּרְעַץ אוֹיֵב: וּבְרֹב גְּאוֹנְךָ תַּהֲרֹס
קָמֶיךָ, תְּשַׁלַּח חֲרֹנְךָ יֹאכְלֵמוֹ כַּקַּשׁ: וּבְרוּחַ
אַפֶּיךָ נֶעֶרְמוּ מַיִם, נִצְּבוּ כְמוֹ־נֵד
נֹזְלִים, קָפְאוּ תְהֹמֹת בְּלֶב־יָם: אָמַר
אוֹיֵב אֶרְדֹּף, אַשִּׂיג, אֲחַלֵּק שָׁלָל, תִּמְלָאֵמוֹ
נַפְשִׁי, אָרִיק חַרְבִּי תּוֹרִישֵׁמוֹ יָדִי: נָשַׁפְתָּ
בְרוּחֲךָ כִּסָּמוֹ יָם, צָלְלוּ כַּעוֹפֶרֶת בְּמַיִם
אַדִּירִים: מִי־כָמֹכָה בָּאֵלִם יהוה, מִי

אָז יָשִׁיר – *Then... sang.* The correct response to witnessing the saving hand of God is to sing His praises. For this reason the *Midrash Shir HaShirim Raba* explains that the righteous King Hezekiah lost the opportunity to become the Messiah because he failed to lead the people in singing God's praises after God saved Jerusalem from the hand of the Assyrian army.

The unexpected future tense verb יָשִׁיר ("will sing") instead of the more usual past tense שָׁר ("sang") teaches that those same Israelites will one day be resurrected to sing the song yet again, thus pointing to the belief in the future Resurrection of the Dead (Rashi).

ה' שְׁמוֹ – *The Lord is His name*. Whereas the power of kings of flesh and blood is seen in their armies, God's might is manifest by the very nature of His divine name, which, when invoked, brings victory over His enemies. Alternatively, this verse attests to the ever present Divine mercy – implied by the four-letter name of God as it appears here, which usually is associated with compassion and forgiveness – even when He strikes the wicked (Rashi).

זֶה אֵלִי וְאַנְוֵהוּ, אֱלֹהֵי אָבִי וַאֲרֹמְמֶנְהוּ – *This is my God and I will glorify Him, my father's God and I will extol Him. Targum Onkelos* translates the first three words of this phrase as "this is my God and I will build a tabernacle for Him." We can understand the *Targum* as follows: God instructed us to build a tabernacle so that, as the Torah teaches, He would dwell in our midst. From this we learn that when we violate God's

Ex. 15 **אָז** **THEN MOSES** and the children of Israel sang this song to the Lord, and thus did they say:

I will sing to the Lord, for He has triumphed gloriously;
the horse and his rider He has thrown into the sea.
The Lord is my strength and song,
and He has become my liberation.
This is my God and I will glorify Him,
my father's God and I will extol Him.
The Lord victorious, the Lord is His name.
Pharaoh's chariots and his host He has cast into the sea,
and in the Sea of Reeds are sunk his chosen captains.
The deeps cover them; they went down in the depths like a stone.
Your right hand, O Lord, glorious in power,
Your right hand, O Lord, crushes the enemy.
In the greatness of Your majesty You overthrow them
who rise against You.
You send forth Your wrath; it consumes them like stubble.
At the blast of Your wind the waters piled up;
the tides stood upright as a heap,
the deeps congealed in the heart of the sea.
The enemy said, "I will pursue, overtake,
divide the spoil, my lust shall be glutted with them;
I will unsheathe my sword, my hand shall destroy them."
You did blow with Your wind, the sea covered them;
they sank like lead in the mighty waters.
Who is like You, Lord, among the mighty?

---

will the result is that He is less present in our midst, that is, He figuratively "stays in the heavens." This is the deeper meaning of this phrase: when we act in accordance with His will, God remains in our midst and He is אֵלִי (my God), as if וְאַנְוֵהוּ (I have built a tabernacle for Him to dwell in our midst). But when we transgress His will we forfeit any personal relationship with Him, and then He is only אֱלֹהֵי אָבִי (the God of our fathers who preceded us,) and as a result וַאֲרֹמְמֶנְהוּ (I am the cause of Him rising to His heavenly abode) and He no longer resides in our midst (*Ḥatam Sofer*).

בְּמַיִם אַדִּירִים – *Mighty waters*. There are two ways to translate this phrase, each of which gives a different understanding of the verse. Conventionally it can be understood as "they sank in the *mighty waters* like lead." The *Mishna Berura* prefers the alternative "the mighty sank

כָּמֹכָה נֶאְדָּר בַּקֹּדֶשׁ, נוֹרָא תְהִלֹּת עֹשֵׂה
פֶלֶא: נָטִיתָ יְמִינְךָ תִּבְלָעֵמוֹ אָרֶץ: נָחִיתָ
בְחַסְדְּךָ עַם־זוּ גָּאָלְתָּ, נֵהַלְתָּ בְעָזְּךָ אֶל־נְוֵה
קָדְשֶׁךָ: שָׁמְעוּ עַמִּים יִרְגָּזוּן, חִיל
אָחַז יֹשְׁבֵי פְּלָשֶׁת: אָז נִבְהֲלוּ אַלּוּפֵי
אֱדוֹם, אֵילֵי מוֹאָב יֹאחֲזֵמוֹ רָעַד, נָמֹגוּ
כֹּל יֹשְׁבֵי כְנָעַן: תִּפֹּל עֲלֵיהֶם אֵימָתָה
וָפַחַד, בִּגְדֹל זְרוֹעֲךָ יִדְּמוּ כָּאָבֶן, עַד־
יַעֲבֹר עַמְּךָ יהוה, עַד־יַעֲבֹר עַם־זוּ
קָנִיתָ: תְּבִאֵמוֹ וְתִטָּעֵמוֹ בְּהַר נַחֲלָתְךָ, מָכוֹן
לְשִׁבְתְּךָ פָּעַלְתָּ יהוה, מִקְּדָשׁ אֲדֹנָי כּוֹנְנוּ
יָדֶיךָ: יהוה יִמְלֹךְ לְעֹלָם וָעֶד:

יהוה יִמְלֹךְ לְעֹלָם וָעֶד. יהוה מַלְכוּתֵהּ קָאֵם לְעָלַם וּלְעָלְמֵי עָלְמַיָּא.

כִּי
בָא סוּס פַּרְעֹה בְּרִכְבּוֹ וּבְפָרָשָׁיו בַּיָּם, וַיָּשֶׁב יהוה עֲלֵהֶם אֶת־מֵי
הַיָּם, וּבְנֵי יִשְׂרָאֵל הָלְכוּ בַיַּבָּשָׁה בְּתוֹךְ הַיָּם:

---

like lead in the waters." This latter approach is more in accord with the cantillation notation which separates the two words. This is preferable, even though ocean waves are described in the Psalms as אַדִּירִים מִשְׁבְּרֵי־יָם – "mighty are the waves of the sea" (R. Mosheh Lichtenstein).

שָׁמְעוּ עַמִּים יִרְגָּזוּן – *Peoples heard, they tremble.* The sages inform us that this refers to the surrounding nations who were shaken by these events, to the point that many among them sought to convert to Judaism, as explained by Rashi to Song of Songs 1:3 ("the maidens love You") in reference to the conversions of Yitro and Raḥav. But when Amalek attacked Israel shortly thereafter, and cooled their conversionary ardor, Moses understood that most would not in fact convert or join the people as they entered the Promised Land. He foresaw that in due course Israel would have to go into exile where they would encounter the descendants of those peoples and finally be able to facilitate their becoming righteous converts. Only thereafter would they all return to the land of Israel. This is the meaning of Moses' prayer that God "bring them and plant them on the mountain of your heritage" (*Beit HaLevi*).

תִּפֹּל עֲלֵיהֶם אֵימָתָה וָפַחַד – *Terror and dread fall upon them.* Just as King David was disqualified from building the Temple because he had shed blood in war, so too Moses understood that if

Who is like You, glorious in holiness,
inspiring in praises, working wonders?
You did stretch out Your right hand, the earth swallows them.
In Your love You guide the people You have redeemed;
You will lead them by Your strength to Your holy dwelling.
Peoples heard, they tremble;
pangs seized the inhabitants of Philistia.
Then were the chieftains of Edom frightened,
the mighty men of Moab, trembling takes hold of them,
all the inhabitants of Canaan melted away.
Terror and dread fall upon them;
by the greatness of Your arm they are still as stone –
until Your people pass over, O Lord,
until the people whom You have acquired pass over.
Bring them and settle them in the mountain of Your inheritance,
the shrine, O Lord, that You make for Your dwelling,
the sanctuary, my Master, that Your own hands establish.
The Lord shall reign forever and ever.

The Lord shall reign forever and ever.
The sovereignty of the Lord is established forever.

When the horses of Pharaoh went into the sea
with his chariots and his horsemen,
the Lord turned the waters of the sea back upon them,
while the children of Israel walked on dry ground in the midst of the sea.

---

his generation of Israelites would have blood on its hands as a result of having to fight wars against the Canaanite nations, it too would be disqualified from building the Temple after defeating them. For this reason Moses here pleads with God to instill sufficient fear of the Israelites in the hearts of the Canaanite nations so that they would either preemptively abandon the land, or surrender without a fight; as a result the Israelites would be immediately able to proceed to בְּהַר נַחֲלָתְךָ (i.e., the Temple Mount,) and there build מִקְּדָשׁ ה׳ כּוֹנְנוּ יָדֶיךָ (the Temple of God for which God would have prepared the way). Moses argues that if this were to happen the course of history would change, the world would be permanently redeemed, and ה׳ יִמְלֹךְ לְעֹלָם וָעֶד (God's sovereignty would be established forever). Sadly, Moses' request was denied, for the Israelites did not merit such a divine dispensation (*Ḥatam Sofer*).

‹ **כִּי** לַיהוה הַמְּלוּכָה וּמֹשֵׁל בַּגּוֹיִם: וְעָלוּ מוֹשִׁעִים בְּהַר צִיּוֹן לִשְׁפֹּט אֶת־הַר עֵשָׂו, וְהָיְתָה לַיהוה הַמְּלוּכָה: וְהָיָה יהוה לְמֶלֶךְ עַל־כָּל־הָאָרֶץ, בַּיּוֹם הַהוּא יִהְיֶה יהוה אֶחָד וּשְׁמוֹ אֶחָד: תהלים כב / עובדיה א / זכריה יד

(וּבְתוֹרָתְךָ כָּתוּב לֵאמֹר, שְׁמַע יִשְׂרָאֵל, יהוה אֱלֹהֵינוּ יהוה אֶחָד:) דברים ו

יִשְׁתַּבַּח שִׁמְךָ לָעַד, מַלְכֵּנוּ, הָאֵל הַמֶּלֶךְ הַגָּדוֹל וְהַקָּדוֹשׁ בַּשָּׁמַיִם וּבָאָרֶץ. כִּי לְךָ נָאֶה, יהוה אֱלֹהֵינוּ וֵאלֹהֵי אֲבוֹתֵינוּ, שִׁיר וּשְׁבָחָה, הַלֵּל וְזִמְרָה, עֹז וּמֶמְשָׁלָה, נֶצַח, גְּדֻלָּה וּגְבוּרָה, תְּהִלָּה וְתִפְאֶרֶת, קְדֻשָּׁה וּמַלְכוּת, ‹ בְּרָכוֹת וְהוֹדָאוֹת, מֵעַתָּה וְעַד עוֹלָם. בָּרוּךְ אַתָּה יהוה, אֵל מֶלֶךְ גָּדוֹל בַּתִּשְׁבָּחוֹת, אֵל הַהוֹדָאוֹת, אֲדוֹן הַנִּפְלָאוֹת, הַבּוֹחֵר בְּשִׁירֵי זִמְרָה, מֶלֶךְ, אֵל, חֵי הָעוֹלָמִים.

During the עשרת ימי תשובה*, and on* הושענא רבה*, many congregations open the* ארון קודש *and say this psalm responsively, verse by verse.*

שִׁיר הַמַּעֲלוֹת, מִמַּעֲמַקִּים קְרָאתִיךָ יהוה: אֲדֹנָי שִׁמְעָה בְקוֹלִי, תִּהְיֶינָה אָזְנֶיךָ קַשֻּׁבוֹת לְקוֹל תַּחֲנוּנָי: אִם־עֲוֹנוֹת תִּשְׁמָר־יָהּ, אֲדֹנָי מִי יַעֲמֹד: כִּי־עִמְּךָ הַסְּלִיחָה, לְמַעַן תִּוָּרֵא: קִוִּיתִי יהוה קִוְּתָה נַפְשִׁי, וְלִדְבָרוֹ הוֹחָלְתִּי: נַפְשִׁי לַאדֹנָי, מִשֹּׁמְרִים לַבֹּקֶר, שֹׁמְרִים לַבֹּקֶר: יַחֵל יִשְׂרָאֵל אֶל יהוה, כִּי־עִם־יהוה הַחֶסֶד, וְהַרְבֵּה עִמּוֹ פְדוּת: וְהוּא יִפְדֶּה אֶת־יִשְׂרָאֵל, מִכֹּל עֲוֹנוֹתָיו: תהלים קל

ה׳ אֶחָד וּשְׁמוֹ אֶחָד – *The Lord shall be One and His name One.* Since we fail to perceive God's nature as it is expressed in the true pronunciation of His name, we may not say it out loud. Instead we pronounce it *Adonai* ("my Master"), a pronunciation that conveys God's mastery over the physical world. We cannot grasp or understand God's nature in itself – all we can hope to understand is how God deals with His creation. In the future, however, the true nature, and name, of God will become clear (R. Ḥayyim of Volozhin).

יִשְׁתַּבַּח / YISHTABACH

הַבּוֹחֵר בְּשִׁירֵי זִמְרָה – *Who delights in songs of praise.* Music has an unparalleled ability to help us express our deepest feelings. When words fail us we can often give expression to our thoughts or emotions through song or dance. Through this phrase the *Yishtabaḥ* prayer declares that God favors ("chooses") such expression, for He surely knows that we are not always able to sufficiently articulate our spiritual feelings and aspirations in words alone. This is especially the case when music and poetry are joined together as שִׁירֵי זִמְרָה (songs of praise). So too, the words of the Torah are not simply read out loud during services but recited according to their traditional musical cantillations, and the Psalms were put to music to be sung by the Levites as melodic accompaniment

Ps. 22 ▸ כִּי FOR the kingdom is the Lord's, and He is the ruler over the nations.
Ob. 1 Deliverers shall go up to Mount Zion to rule the hill country of Esau,
Zech. 14 and sovereignty shall be the Lord's. And the Lord shall be King over all
the earth; in that day shall the Lord be One, and His name One.

Deut. 6 (As it is written in Your Torah, saying: "Hear, O Israel, the Lord is our God, the Lord is One.")

יִשְׁתַּבַּח MAY YOUR NAME be praised forever, God our King, great and holy in heaven and on earth. For to You, Lord, our God and God of our fathers, are due song and praise, acclaim and hymn. Yours are strength and dominion, eternity, greatness and might, praise and glory, holiness and sovereignty, ▸ blessing and thanksgiving henceforth and evermore. Blessed are You, Lord, God and King, great in praises, God of thanksgivings, Master of wonders, Who chooses songs of praise, King, God, Who gives life to the worlds.

Between Rosh HaShana and Yom Kippur, and on Hoshana Raba, many congregations open the Ark and say this psalm responsively, verse by verse.

Ps. 130 שִׁיר הַמַּעֲלוֹת A SONG OF ASCENTS. From the depths I call out to you, O Lord. My Master, hear my voice. Let Your ears be attentive to the sound of my supplications. If You, Lord, pay heed to iniquities, who, my Master, will stand? Indeed, forgiveness is with You, so that You may be feared. I wait for the Lord, my soul waits, and I hope for His word. My soul waits for my Master, among those who watch for the morning, who watch for the morning. Israel, hope for the Lord, for with the Lord is loving-kindness, and with Him is abundant redemption. And He will redeem Israel from all his iniquities.

---

to the Temple service. Similarly our comprehension of the Talmud is best accomplished by way of correct tonal (i.e., musical) inflection. That said, when set prayers are put to notes or music the goal should always be to clarify their meaning and augment participatory כַּוָּנָה (concentration), rather than to provide passive entertainment (R. Basil Herring).

שִׁיר הַמַּעֲלוֹת / A SONG OF ASCENTS

מִמַּעֲמַקִּים קְרָאתִיךָ ה' – *From the depths I call out to you.* "The depths" in this verse does not simply refer to the external circumstances in which we find ourselves. In pleading for God's mercies we declare that our transgressions do not express our innermost, deepest, being. Rather, they are an expression of our surface-personality, a pseudo-self that has overshadowed our true selves. Our innermost being, our soul, remains pure and untainted, even if our actions are those of a despicable sinner. Thus, we plead "O God, the real me is crying out to You מִמַּעֲמַקִּים (from the depths of my being), to beseech You to not despair of me, but to give me another chance" (R. Joseph B. Soloveitchik).

חצי קדיש

ש״ץ: **יִתְגַּדַּל** וְיִתְקַדַּשׁ שְׁמֵהּ רַבָּא (קהל: אָמֵן). בְּעָלְמָא דִּי בְרָא כִרְעוּתֵהּ. וְיַמְלִיךְ מַלְכוּתֵהּ בְּחַיֵּיכוֹן וּבְיוֹמֵיכוֹן וּבְחַיֵּי דְכָל בֵּית יִשְׂרָאֵל, בַּעֲגָלָא וּבִזְמַן קָרִיב, וְאִמְרוּ אָמֵן. (קהל: אָמֵן)

קהל וש״ץ: יְהֵא שְׁמֵהּ רַבָּא מְבָרַךְ לְעָלַם וּלְעָלְמֵי עָלְמַיָּא.

ש״ץ: יִתְבָּרַךְ וְיִשְׁתַּבַּח וְיִתְפָּאַר וְיִתְרוֹמַם וְיִתְנַשֵּׂא, וְיִתְהַדָּר וְיִתְעַלֶּה וְיִתְהַלָּל שְׁמֵהּ דְּקֻדְשָׁא בְּרִיךְ הוּא (קהל: בְּרִיךְ הוּא), לְעֵלָּא מִן כָּל בִּרְכָתָא / בעשרת ימי תשובה: לְעֵלָּא (וּ)לְעֵלָּא מִכָּל בִּרְכָתָא/ וְשִׁירָתָא, תֻּשְׁבְּחָתָא וְנֶחֱמָתָא דַּאֲמִירָן בְּעָלְמָא, וְאִמְרוּ אָמֵן. (קהל: אָמֵן)

ברכות קריאת שמע

The following blessing and response are said only in the presence of a מנין.
The שליח ציבור *says the following (while bowing at* בָּרְכוּ *and straightening at Hashem).*
The קהל *followed by the* שליח ציבור *responds by bowing at* בָּרוּךְ *and standing straight at Hashem.*

ש״ץ: **בָּרְכוּ** אֶת יהוה הַמְבֹרָךְ.

קהל: בָּרוּךְ יהוה הַמְבֹרָךְ לְעוֹלָם וָעֶד.

ש״ץ: בָּרוּךְ יהוה הַמְבֹרָךְ לְעוֹלָם וָעֶד.

בָּרְכוּ / BAREKHU

Both *Kaddish* and *Barekhu* are examples of a דָּבָר שֶׁבִּקְדֻשָּׁה, prayers of such special sanctity that they can only be recited with a *minyan*. In fact, it is their very recital at this point of the service that creates the *minyan*, and thereby transforms the prayer experience entirely. The prayers up to this point are those of individuals, but from here on there is true communal prayer – תְּפִלָּה בְּצִבּוּר. This is not merely a quantitive change, but a qualitative one. There are the prayers of individuals and there are prayers of the collective, or *minyan*, and the latter are much more powerful and transformative.

This transition is effected via the recital of *Kaddish* and *Barekhu*. The latter specifically "elevates" the *Shema*, and the former does this for the *Amida*, but it must be recited at this point, for if said immediately preceding the *Amida* it would constitute an interruption (R. Joseph B. Soloveitchik).

What exactly is the nature and power of such communal prayer? It is the fact that God's kingship is strengthened when His people accepts and embraces His sovereignty. Thus Rambam writes that "communal prayer is always heard by God." This is because God's sovereignty can only be complete when there is a people that submits to His authority. Thus

HALF KADDISH

Leader: יִתְגַּדַּל EXALTED AND HALLOWED may God's great name be, in the world He created as He willed. May He reign in your lifetimes and in your days, and in the lifetime of the whole house of Israel, speedily and soon, and say, Amen.

All: May His great name be blessed forever and all time.

Leader: Blessed and praised, honored, extolled, glorified, adored and exalted above all be the name of the Holy One, blessed is He, (*Between Rosh Hashana & Yom Kippur:* above and) beyond any blessing, hymn, praise, or expressions of consolation that may be uttered in this world, and say, Amen.

BLESSINGS OF THE SHEMA

The following blessing and response are said only in the presence of a minyan. The Leader says the following (while bowing at "Barekhu" and straightening at Hashem). The congregation followed by the Leader responds by bowing at "Barukh" and standing straight at Hashem.

Leader: בָּרְכוּ BLESS THE LORD, the blessed One.

Cong: Blessed is the Lord Who is blessed for all eternity.

Leader: Blessed is the Lord Who is blessed for all eternity.

INTERRUPTIONS DURING SHEMA AND ITS BLESSINGS

As a general rule, one may not interrupt Shema and its blessings. There are certain "permitted responses" which should ideally be recited when one is "between paragraphs." Those four places are:

- Between the first blessing and the second blessing.
- Between the second blessing and *Shema*.
- Between the first and second paragraphs of *Shema*.
- Between the second and third paragraphs of *Shema*.

The following are common situations where interruptions are permissible.

- Answering *Barekhu* (by the Leader or by someone receiving an *aliya*); *Kedusha* (just the two verses "*Kadosh kadosh*" and "*Barukh kevod*"); the first three words of *Modim*; "*Amen yeheh shemeh raba*" etc."; or *Amen* to *da'amiran be'alema*, *HaKel HaKadosh* and *Shome'a tefilla* (*OḤ* 66:3 and *MB* 66:17).
- Between paragraphs, one may put on *tallit* and *tefillin*. The *berakhot* on the *tefillin* may be recited as well, but one should wait until the end of one's prayers to recite the *berakha* on the *tallit* (*OḤ* 66:2).

Some authorities permit answering *Amen* to all *berakhot* (*MB* 66:22). It should be noted that between the *berakha* of *Ga'al Yisrael* and the *Amida*, one may not interrupt at all, even for the responses listed above.

ישעיה מה

בָּרוּךְ אַתָּה יהוה אֱלֹהֵינוּ מֶלֶךְ הָעוֹלָם, יוֹצֵר אוֹר וּבוֹרֵא חֹשֶׁךְ, עֹשֶׂה שָׁלוֹם וּבוֹרֵא אֶת הַכֹּל.

הַמֵּאִיר לָאָרֶץ וְלַדָּרִים עָלֶיהָ בְּרַחֲמִים, וּבְטוּבוֹ מְחַדֵּשׁ בְּכָל יוֹם
תָּמִיד מַעֲשֵׂה בְרֵאשִׁית. מָה־רַבּוּ מַעֲשֶׂיךָ יהוה, כֻּלָּם תהלים קד
בְּחָכְמָה עָשִׂיתָ, מָלְאָה הָאָרֶץ קִנְיָנֶךָ: הַמֶּלֶךְ הַמְרוֹמָם לְבַדּוֹ מֵאָז, הַמְשֻׁבָּח וְהַמְפֹאָר וְהַמִּתְנַשֵּׂא מִימוֹת עוֹלָם. אֱלֹהֵי עוֹלָם, בְּרַחֲמֶיךָ הָרַבִּים רַחֵם עָלֵינוּ, אֲדוֹן עֻזֵּנוּ, צוּר מִשְׂגַּבֵּנוּ, מָגֵן יִשְׁעֵנוּ, מִשְׂגָּב בַּעֲדֵנוּ. אֵל בָּרוּךְ גְּדוֹל דֵּעָה, הֵכִין וּפָעַל זָהֳרֵי חַמָּה, טוֹב יָצַר כָּבוֹד לִשְׁמוֹ, מְאוֹרוֹת נָתַן סְבִיבוֹת עֻזּוֹ, פִּנּוֹת צְבָאָיו קְדוֹשִׁים, רוֹמְמֵי שַׁדַּי, תָּמִיד מְסַפְּרִים כְּבוֹד אֵל וּקְדֻשָּׁתוֹ. תִּתְבָּרַךְ יהוה אֱלֹהֵינוּ, עַל שֶׁבַח מַעֲשֵׂה יָדֶיךָ. וְעַל מְאוֹרֵי אוֹר שֶׁעָשִׂיתָ, יְפָאֲרוּךָ סֶּלָה.

יוֹצֵר אוֹר וּבוֹרֵא חֹשֶׁךְ – *Who forms light and creates darkness.* This opening phrase is an almost verbatim quote from Isaiah 45:7, containing a prophecy regarding Cyrus who would rule over the Persian empire some 170 years after Isaiah lived. Confronted with a world in which good and evil were intertwined, where there appeared to be a constant war between forces of good and evil, pleasure and pain, suffering and joy, the contemporary Zoroastrian faith (as represented by Cyrus) believed that the cosmos and all that occurred in it were the product of two competing forces or "gods," a god of light (or good) and a god of darkness (or evil), with one or the other in the ascendancy at any given time. Isaiah rejects this dichotomy of faith, and declares unambiguously, "I am the Lord, there is none other; I form light and I create darkness, I make peace and create evil, I am the Lord Who makes all of these" (Is. 45:6–7). As the Gemara (*Berakhot* 10b) explains, when

when a community (that is, a minimum of ten adult males) proclaims God's greatness (in the *Kaddish*) or blessedness (in *Barekhu*), it becomes a vehicle which enhances God's sovereignty in the world.

בִּרְכוֹת קְרִיאַת שְׁמַע / BLESSINGS OF THE SHEMA
These three *berakhot*, two of which precede and one of which follows the *Shema*, echo and enlarge upon the main theme of each of the three paragraphs of the *Shema*. These are that (1) God's will permeates and animates all of His creation at every moment; (2) God's will is equally expressed in the commandments of the Torah (both written and oral) that He revealed to His people Israel; and (3) we must recall the Exodus as the archetype of God's revelation, as well as the redemption of His people. In affirming these three foundations of faith, we take upon ourselves the yoke of God's sovereignty (R. Joseph B. Soloveitchik).

Is. 45 **בָּרוּךְ** BLESSED ARE YOU, Lord, our God, King of the universe, Who forms light and creates darkness, Who makes peace and creates all things.

הַמֵּאִיר HE GIVES LIGHT to the earth and on all who dwell on it, with compassion; and in His goodness ever renews each day the work
Ps. 104 of creation. "How great are Your works, O Lord! You have made
them all in wisdom. The earth is full of Your creatures." King, exalted uniquely since the beginning, extolled, praised sublimely from days of old, God of all time, abounding in pity, have mercy on us, Master of our strength, our sheltering Rock, our saving Shield, our protecting Fortress. God, blessed and all-knowing, planned and created the brilliance of the sun. The Beneficent One made glory for the sake of His name. He placed luminaries round about His majesty. The chiefs of His hosts are holy beings that extol the Almighty. They constantly describe the glory and holiness of God. Lord our God, may You be blessed in praise of the work of Your hands and for the light-emitting luminaries You created, may they praise You, Selah.

---

composing this blessing, the sages substituted the more gentle word הַכֹּל ("everything") for Isaiah's רָע (evil).

Isaiah's message is timeless, no matter the passage of the centuries, or the changing of surrounding faiths. Even today, the Jew must thank and bless God no matter the circumstances, whether good or evil, whether or not we can comprehend His ways. We must affirm, with Isaiah, that God in His wisdom and omnipotence created evil to achieve a goal consistent with His goodness. We believe that it is because evil exists that we can choose the good, and thereby contribute to the ultimate triumph of good over evil, in a future redeemed world. Our mission in life is to live in this beautiful, but still imperfect world, and do all we can to perfect it and spread the knowledge of God. This is the central affirmation of the first verses and paragraph of the *Shema* (R. Micha Berger and R. Arie Folger).

הַמֵּאִיר לָאָרֶץ וְלַדָּרִים / HE GIVES LIGHT

מָה רַבּוּ מַעֲשֶׂיךָ – *How great are Your works*. The Gemara (*Hullin* 127a) understands the term רַבּוּ to mean "diverse," that is, God's creations are found on land, in the air, and under the sea. Another meaning of the word רַבּוּ is "maturity" (Ezek. 16:7). Thus we can understand this phrase as saying "how well developed and intricate are God's creatures" (R. Joseph B. Soloveitchik).

אֵל בָּרוּךְ – *God, blessed*. The words of this paragraph are arranged in alphabetical order.

תִּתְבָּרַךְ צוּרֵנוּ מַלְכֵּנוּ וְגוֹאֲלֵנוּ, בּוֹרֵא קְדוֹשִׁים, יִשְׁתַּבַּח שִׁמְךָ לָעַד, מַלְכֵּנוּ, יוֹצֵר מְשָׁרְתִים, וַאֲשֶׁר מְשָׁרְתָיו כֻּלָּם עוֹמְדִים בְּרוּם עוֹלָם, וּמַשְׁמִיעִים בְּיִרְאָה יַחַד בְּקוֹל, דִּבְרֵי אֱלֹהִים חַיִּים וּמֶלֶךְ עוֹלָם. כֻּלָּם אֲהוּבִים, כֻּלָּם בְּרוּרִים, כֻּלָּם גִּבּוֹרִים, וְכֻלָּם עוֹשִׂים בְּאֵימָה וּבְיִרְאָה רְצוֹן קוֹנָם, ◂ וְכֻלָּם פּוֹתְחִים אֶת פִּיהֶם בִּקְדֻשָּׁה וּבְטָהֳרָה, בְּשִׁירָה וּבְזִמְרָה, וּמְבָרְכִים וּמְשַׁבְּחִים וּמְפָאֲרִים, וּמַעֲרִיצִים וּמַקְדִּישִׁים וּמַמְלִיכִים,

אֶת שֵׁם הָאֵל הַמֶּלֶךְ הַגָּדוֹל, הַגִּבּוֹר וְהַנּוֹרָא, קָדוֹשׁ הוּא. ◂ וְכֻלָּם מְקַבְּלִים עֲלֵיהֶם עֹל מַלְכוּת שָׁמַיִם זֶה מִזֶּה, וְנוֹתְנִים רְשׁוּת זֶה לָזֶה, לְהַקְדִּישׁ לְיוֹצְרָם בְּנַחַת רוּחַ, בְּשָׂפָה בְרוּרָה וּבִנְעִימָה, קְדֻשָּׁה כֻּלָּם כְּאֶחָד עוֹנִים, וְאוֹמְרִים בְּיִרְאָה

All say aloud:

ישעיה ו קָדוֹשׁ, קָדוֹשׁ, קָדוֹשׁ יהוה צְבָאוֹת, מְלֹא כָל־הָאָרֶץ כְּבוֹדוֹ:

◂ **וְהָאוֹפַנִּים** וְחַיּוֹת הַקֹּדֶשׁ, בְּרַעַשׁ גָּדוֹל מִתְנַשְּׂאִים לְעֻמַּת שְׂרָפִים, לְעֻמָּתָם מְשַׁבְּחִים, וְאוֹמְרִים

All say aloud:

יחזקאל ג בָּרוּךְ כְּבוֹד־יהוה מִמְּקוֹמוֹ:

As finite beings we are incapable of providing a comprehensive or even adequate accounting of God's glory. All we can do is make use of every sound in our limited human repertoire (R. Joseph B. Soloveitchik). By formulating the praises of God in the precise order of the letters of the alphabet, this paragraph conveys the ordered and structured nature of God's creation (R. Meir Simḥa of Dvinsk).

קָדוֹשׁ קָדוֹשׁ קָדוֹשׁ – *Holy, holy, holy*. *Targum Yonatan* to Isaiah 6:3 (whence this verse is taken) explains that the triple exclamation of "holy" refers to the three dimensions of God's holiness: in heaven, on earth, and throughout time. Alternatively this triplicate conveys the unlimited nature of God's holiness. Finally, the repetition may represent the speech of the angels calling and responding to each other, to summon their colleagues to declare in unison קָדוֹשׁ ה׳ צְבָאוֹת (R. Yehuda ben Yakar).

Kedusha was inserted at this point so as to rebut those who contended that after God created the heavenly bodies He left the governance of the world to them. By proclaiming "the entire world is filled with His glory," we affirm that His providence continues unabated in our midst even though He is hidden from view (Abudarham).

תִּתְבָּרַךְ MAY YOU BE BLESSED, our Rock, our King, our Redeemer, Creator of holy beings. May You be forever extolled, our King, Creator of the ministering angels who stand in the firmament on high, who reverently proclaim in unison, aloud, the words of the living God, the eternal King. All are beloved, all pure, all powerful, all performing in reverent awe the will of their Maker. ▸ Opening their mouths in holiness and purity, with song and hymn, they all bless and praise and glorify and revere and sanctify and declare the sovereignty of

God's name, the great, mighty and awe-inspiring King, holy is He. ▸ All accept upon themselves the yoke of the heavenly kingdom, from one to another, and grant permission, one to another, to sanctify their Maker in serenity, in clear and sweet utterance, all proclaiming His holiness in unison, and declaring in awe:

All say aloud:

Is. 6 "HOLY, HOLY, HOLY, is the Lord of hosts, the whole world is filled with His glory."

▸ וְהָאוֹפַנִּים THEN THE OPHANIM and holy Ḥayyot rise up toward the Seraphim with great noise and respond by praising and proclaiming:

All say aloud:

Ezek. 3 "BLESSED is the glory of the Lord from His place."

ה׳ צְבָאוֹת – *The Lord of hosts.* This name of God emphasizes the particular relationship between God and Israel, as the term צְבָאוֹת is shorthand for אֱלֹהֵי צִבְאוֹת יִשְׂרָאֵל ("God of the legions of Israel") (Vilna Gaon).

There is a tension between the two central verses of the *Kedusha*, both here and in the *Amida*. Isaiah proclaimed קָדוֹשׁ קָדוֹשׁ קָדוֹשׁ during the glorious era of the First Temple, when God's presence was palpable and self-evident. Thus Isaiah experienced the angels as praising God "Whose glory fills the entire world." On the other hand Ezekiel proclaimed בָּרוּךְ ... מִמְּקוֹמוֹ ("Blessed Lord's glory from His abode") when the destruction of the Temple and exile were imminent. His vision of the divine chariot at the River Chebar in Babylonian exile reflects a time of הֶסְתֵּר פָּנִים (the hiding of God's face). For Ezekiel, therefore, the angels proclaim a divine glory that has withdrawn to מְקוֹמוֹ ("His abode") rather than being diffused throughout the cosmos. This hidden aspect of God's being is reflected in His name הַמָּקוֹם (lit. "the Place"), perhaps derived from this very verse. Appropriately, this name is invoked when we console mourners to convey that even though there are times that He is hidden from us, and we are intensely aware that His ways are ultimately

לָאֵל בָּרוּךְ נְעִימוֹת יִתֵּנוּ, לְמֶלֶךְ אֵל חַי וְקַיָּם, זְמִירוֹת יֹאמֵרוּ וְתִשְׁבָּחוֹת יַשְׁמִיעוּ, כִּי הוּא לְבַדּוֹ, פּוֹעֵל גְּבוּרוֹת, עוֹשֶׂה חֲדָשׁוֹת, בַּעַל מִלְחָמוֹת, זוֹרֵעַ צְדָקוֹת, מַצְמִיחַ יְשׁוּעוֹת, בּוֹרֵא רְפוּאוֹת, נוֹרָא תְהִלּוֹת, אֲדוֹן הַנִּפְלָאוֹת, הַמְחַדֵּשׁ בְּטוּבוֹ בְּכָל יוֹם תָּמִיד מַעֲשֵׂה בְרֵאשִׁית, כָּאָמוּר, לְעֹשֵׂה אוֹרִים גְּדֹלִים, כִּי לְעוֹלָם חַסְדּוֹ: תהלים קלו ‹ אוֹר חָדָשׁ עַל צִיּוֹן תָּאִיר וְנִזְכֶּה כֻלָּנוּ מְהֵרָה לְאוֹרוֹ. בָּרוּךְ אַתָּה יהוה, יוֹצֵר הַמְּאוֹרוֹת.

אַהֲבָה רַבָּה אֲהַבְתָּנוּ, יהוה אֱלֹהֵינוּ, חֶמְלָה גְדוֹלָה וִיתֵרָה חָמַלְתָּ עָלֵינוּ. אָבִינוּ מַלְכֵּנוּ, בַּעֲבוּר אֲבוֹתֵינוּ שֶׁבָּטְחוּ בְךָ, וַתְּלַמְּדֵם חֻקֵּי חַיִּים, כֵּן תְּחָנֵּנוּ וּתְלַמְּדֵנוּ. אָבִינוּ, הָאָב הָרַחֲמָן, הַמְרַחֵם, רַחֵם עָלֵינוּ, וְתֵן בְּלִבֵּנוּ לְהָבִין וּלְהַשְׂכִּיל, לִשְׁמֹעַ, לִלְמֹד וּלְלַמֵּד, לִשְׁמֹר וְלַעֲשׂוֹת, וּלְקַיֵּם, אֶת כָּל דִּבְרֵי תַלְמוּד תּוֹרָתֶךָ בְּאַהֲבָה. וְהָאֵר עֵינֵינוּ בְּתוֹרָתֶךָ, וְדַבֵּק לִבֵּנוּ בְּמִצְוֹתֶיךָ, וְיַחֵד לְבָבֵנוּ לְאַהֲבָה וּלְיִרְאָה אֶת שְׁמֶךָ, וְלֹא נֵבוֹשׁ לְעוֹלָם וָעֶד. כִּי בְשֵׁם קָדְשְׁךָ הַגָּדוֹל וְהַנּוֹרָא בָּטָחְנוּ, נָגִילָה וְנִשְׂמְחָה בִּישׁוּעָתֶךָ. ° וַהֲבִיאֵנוּ לְשָׁלוֹם (*At this point, one should gather the* ציצית *strands. See below.*)

---

inscrutable, we still affirm our faith in Him by our unconditional acceptance of His will (R. Joseph B. Soloveitchik).

אַהֲבָה רַבָּה – *With great love.* This is the second of the *Shema* blessings. It corresponds to the second paragraph of the *Shema*, in that they both focus on the study of the Torah and the observance of the 613 commandments. Just as that paragraph commands us to "listen diligently to My commandments" and "teach them to your children," this *berakha* implores God to help us study, understand, observe, and fulfill "all the words of Your Torah's teaching." Even more than the sacrifices, it is the sustained study of the Torah and in particular the study of the Talmud that binds the Jew to God, as the *Zohar* states: "Torah, God, and Israel are one." For this reason this paragraph frames the gift of תַּלְמוּד תּוֹרָתֶךָ ("the study of Your Torah") to the Jewish people as an act of surpassing divine love (*Netziv*).

Our own generation is witness to the stark reality that the most effective mechanism for Jewish continuity, and antidote to Jewish assimilation and loss of identity, is the sustained study of the Torah. The more men and women of all ages engage in Torah study, making it an integral part of their everyday life, the more they and their communities can withstand and overcome the ravages of estrangement from Jewish life in its totality. Every other strategy seeking to strengthen Jewish life, no matter

לָאֵל בָּרוּךְ TO THE BLESSED GOD they offer sweet melodies; to the King, Who is God and Who lives forever, they pronounce hymns and proclaim praises. For He alone performs mighty deeds, initiates unprecedented events, determines the outcome of wars, sows the seeds of just outcomes, makes salvations sprout forth, creates healing, is the awesome object of praise, and controls miracles. In His goodness He every day constantly renews the work of Creation, as it says, "He makes great lights, for His loving-kindness is forever." ▸ May You shine a new light on Zion, and all of us soon merit its illumination. Blessed are You, Lord, Maker of the heavenly lights.

אַהֲבָה רַבָּה WITH GREAT LOVE You have loved us, Lord our God; with great and overflowing compassion You have pitied us. Our Father, our King, for the sake of our fathers who trusted in You, and whom You taught the statutes of life, please also be gracious to us and teach us. Our Father, merciful Father, always compassionate, have mercy on us. Give us understanding and discernment, so that we can grasp all the words of Your Torah's teaching – learning and transmitting them by lovingly observing, practicing, and fulfilling them. Open our eyes through Your Torah so that our hearts can cleave to Your commandments. Make our hearts a harmony of love and reverence for Your name, so that we will never feel shame. And insofar as we have trusted in Your holy, great, and awesome name, let us rejoice and be happy in Your saving power. (*At this point, one should gather the tzitziyot strands. See below.*) °Bring us in peace from the four corners of the earth

---

how seemingly attractive in the short run, has never compensated over the long run for the absence of Torah study, which is and has always been the primary driver of Jewish continuity.

וְהָאֵר עֵינֵינוּ – *Open our eyes.* One of the purposes of the disclosure of the hidden secrets of the Torah is to view the secular from within the perspective of the holy Torah, to realize that there is not, in truth, anything completely secular in the world (R. Avraham Yitzḥak HaKohen Kook).

מֵאַרְבַּע כַּנְפוֹת הָאָרֶץ – *From the four corners of the*

GATHERING OF TZITZIT

At this point, one should gather the four (some have the tradition of only gathering the front two) *tzitzit* strands (*Arukh HaShulḥan* 60:9). The *tzitzit* strands should be held in one's left hand between the pinky and ring-finger (*MB* 24:4).

מֵאַרְבַּע כַּנְפוֹת הָאָרֶץ, וְתוֹלִיכֵנוּ קוֹמְמִיּוּת לְאַרְצֵנוּ. ◂ כִּי אֵל פּוֹעֵל
יְשׁוּעוֹת אָתָּה, וּבָנוּ בָחַרְתָּ מִכָּל עַם וְלָשׁוֹן, וְקֵרַבְתָּנוּ לְשִׁמְךָ הַגָּדוֹל
סֶלָה, בֶּאֱמֶת, לְהוֹדוֹת לְךָ וּלְיַחֶדְךָ בְּאַהֲבָה. בָּרוּךְ אַתָּה יהוה, הַבּוֹחֵר
בְּעַמּוֹ יִשְׂרָאֵל בְּאַהֲבָה.

שמע

The שמע *must be said with intense concentration. In the first paragraph one should accept, with love, the sovereignty of God; in the second, accept the* מצוות *as the will of God. The end of the third paragraph constitutes fulfillment of the* מצווה *to remember, morning and evening, the Exodus from Egypt.*

When not praying with a מנין*, some say:*

אֵל מֶלֶךְ נֶאֱמָן

The following verse should be said aloud, while covering the eyes with the right hand:

דברים ו **שְׁמַע** יִשְׂרָאֵל, יהוה אֱלֹהֵינוּ, יהוה ׀ **אֶחָד**:

Quietly בָּרוּךְ שֵׁם כְּבוֹד מַלְכוּתוֹ לְעוֹלָם וָעֶד.

Touch the תפילין של יד *at* ° *and the* תפילין של ראש *at* °°.

דברים ו **וְאָהַבְתָּ** אֵת יהוה אֱלֹהֶיךָ, בְּכָל־לְבָבְךָ וּבְכָל־נַפְשְׁךָ וּבְכָל־מְאֹדֶךָ:
וְהָיוּ הַדְּבָרִים הָאֵלֶּה, אֲשֶׁר אָנֹכִי מְצַוְּךָ הַיּוֹם, עַל־לְבָבֶךָ:

הַבּוֹחֵר בְּעַמּוֹ יִשְׂרָאֵל בְּאַהֲבָה / HABOḤER BE'AMO YISRAEL

According to the *Mishna Berura*, it is preferable for the congregation to recite this blessing in an undertone simultaneously with the Leader so as to avoid having to answer *Amen* to the *berakha* (*MB* 59:25). However, those who follow the practice of reciting *Amen* to the *berakha* should complete the *berakha* before the Leader does, and then answer *Amen* to his *berakha*. The Leader should make sure to recite the *berakha* out loud.

earth. At this point many follow the custom to take the four *tzitziyot* in our hands. The parallel is striking: just as we gather the *tzitziyot* that are symbols of our aspiration to heed God's will (as will be expressed in the third paragraph of the *Shema*) from the four corners of our garment, so (as the *berakha* continues to state) may God reciprocate by gathering us from the four corners of the compass to return to Zion (R. Basil Herring).

שְׁמַע / THE SHEMA

Recital of the three paragraphs of the *Shema* twice a day, morning and evening, fulfills a positive commandment of the Torah. When reciting it, one should have in mind that

and lead us, standing upright, to our land, ▸ for You are the God Who brings salvation. You have chosen us from among every other people and tongue, and have brought us near in truth to Your great name so that we can give thanks to You and lovingly proclaim Your unity. Blessed are You, Lord, Who so lovingly chooses His people Israel.

SHEMA

The Shema must be said with intense concentration. In the first paragraph one should accept, with love, the sovereignty of God; in the second, accept the mitzvot as the will of God. The end of the third paragraph constitutes fulfillment of the mitzva to remember, morning and evening, the Exodus from Egypt.

When not praying with a minyan, some say:

God, the King Who is faithful.

The following verse should be said aloud, while covering the eyes with the right hand:

Deut. 6 HEAR, O ISRAEL, the LORD is our God, the LORD is One.

Quietly: Blessed is the name of His glorious kingdom forever and ever.

Touch the hand-tefillin at ° and the head-tefillin at °°.

Deut. 6 וְאָהַבְתָּ YOU SHALL LOVE the LORD your God with all your heart, and with all your soul, and with all your might. And these words which I command you this day shall be upon your heart. You shall

---

we accept עֹל מַלְכוּת שָׁמַיִם (the yoke of the Kingdom of heaven) that is, to recognize and accept God's will, to love Him unconditionally, to study His Torah, to live in accordance with His commandments, and to remember the Exodus from Egypt. One should take care to recite each word carefully and deliberately. For a more detailed exposition of the correct intent in reciting the *Shema*, as understood by R. Joseph B. Soloveitchik, see the introductory essay to this Siddur, page xxxii, as well the further analysis found on page E80.

שְׁמַע יִשְׂרָאֵל – *Hear, O Israel.* It is not enough to simply believe in the uniqueness of God; it is also necessary to bring our fellow Jews to believe in it as well. That is why this cardinal verse begins with "Hear, O Israel." It teaches us to implore our fellow Jews to listen carefully to our proclamation of faith, so as to make it their own. Only in that way can there be a realization of "You are One, Your name is one, 'and who is like Your people Israel, a unified people on earth'" (II Samuel 7:23) (R. Menachem B. Sacks)

וְאָהַבְתָּ ... בְּכָל־נַפְשְׁךָ – *You shall love... with all your soul.* In the biblical context, the term אַהֲבָה also bears the connotation of loyalty and faithfulness to a covenant (Prof. Ḥayyim Tawil).

וְשִׁנַּנְתָּם לְבָנֶיךָ וְדִבַּרְתָּ בָּם, בְּשִׁבְתְּךָ בְּבֵיתֶךָ וּבְלֶכְתְּךָ בַדֶּרֶךְ, וּבְשָׁכְבְּךָ וּבְקוּמֶךָ: °וּקְשַׁרְתָּם לְאוֹת עַל־יָדֶךָ °°וְהָיוּ לְטֹטָפֹת בֵּין עֵינֶיךָ: וּכְתַבְתָּם עַל־מְזֻזוֹת בֵּיתֶךָ וּבִשְׁעָרֶיךָ:

Touch the תפילין של יד *at* ° *and the* תפילין של ראש *at* °°.

דברים יא

וְהָיָה אִם־שָׁמֹעַ תִּשְׁמְעוּ אֶל־מִצְוֹתַי אֲשֶׁר אָנֹכִי מְצַוֶּה אֶתְכֶם הַיּוֹם, לְאַהֲבָה אֶת־יהוה אֱלֹהֵיכֶם וּלְעָבְדוֹ, בְּכָל־לְבַבְכֶם וּבְכָל־נַפְשְׁכֶם: וְנָתַתִּי מְטַר־אַרְצְכֶם בְּעִתּוֹ, יוֹרֶה וּמַלְקוֹשׁ, וְאָסַפְתָּ דְגָנֶךָ וְתִירֹשְׁךָ וְיִצְהָרֶךָ: וְנָתַתִּי עֵשֶׂב בְּשָׂדְךָ לִבְהֶמְתֶּךָ, וְאָכַלְתָּ וְשָׂבָעְתָּ: הִשָּׁמְרוּ לָכֶם פֶּן־יִפְתֶּה לְבַבְכֶם, וְסַרְתֶּם וַעֲבַדְתֶּם אֱלֹהִים אֲחֵרִים וְהִשְׁתַּחֲוִיתֶם לָהֶם: וְחָרָה אַף־יהוה בָּכֶם, וְעָצַר אֶת־הַשָּׁמַיִם וְלֹא־יִהְיֶה מָטָר, וְהָאֲדָמָה לֹא תִתֵּן אֶת־יְבוּלָהּ, וַאֲבַדְתֶּם מְהֵרָה מֵעַל הָאָרֶץ הַטֹּבָה אֲשֶׁר יהוה נֹתֵן לָכֶם: וְשַׂמְתֶּם אֶת־

וְדִבַּרְתָּ בָּם – *Speaking of them*. The Gemara (*Yoma* 19b) comments that "we are to speak of them, but not of the *Amida*." This can be understood in the context of the next phrase "when you sit in your house and when you walk by the way." The entire verse refers to the *mitzva* of continuous Torah study, all day and all night, of which the *Shema* itself is a partial fulfillment. The *Amida*, however, may be recited only three times a day, as the Gemara derives from the story of Daniel. The lesson is that we should not strive to spend our days in prayer, but rather in Torah study (R. Barukh HaLevi Epstein).

עַל־יָדֶךָ... בֵּין עֵינֶיךָ – *On your hand... between your eyes*. The Gemara (*Menaḥot* 36a) derives from here that we are to put on the hand *tefillin* first, opposite the heart, and thereafter the head *tefillin*. The educational lesson for parents and teachers is that first we must teach our children and students to subordinate the emotions of their hearts to God and the Torah, and only thereafter teach them how to use their minds to serve Him (R. Menachem B. Sacks).

וּלְעָבְדוֹ, בְּכָל לְבַבְכֶם – *To serve Him with all your heart*. The Gemara (*Ta'anit* 2a), based on the *Sifrei*, understands this phrase to be referring specifically to prayer, by which we serve God "in our hearts." Based on this and other verses, Rambam (*Hil. Tefilla* 1, *Sefer HaMitzvot* 5) considers prayer once a day to be a Torah obligation for both men and women (the latter insofar as there is no stipulated time involved) Ramban disagrees, arguing that the phrase does not directly require prayer, and thus there is no daily Torah obligation to pray – all that is required (see Numbers 10:9) is that we implore and petition God for help in times of צָרָה (trouble or crisis.) The *Sefer HaḤinukh*, following Rambam, explains that the *mitzva* reflects God's desire to benefit us by providing a mechanism to acquire what is in our best interest.

teach them diligently to your children, speaking of them when you sit in your house and when you walk by the way, when you lie down and when you rise up. °You shall bind them for a sign on your hand, °°and they shall be as *tefillin* between your eyes. And you shall write them upon the doorposts of your house and upon your gates.

Touch the hand-tefillin at ° and the head-tefillin at °°.

Deut. 11 **וְהָיָה** IT SHALL COME TO PASS that if you will listen diligently to My commandments with which I charge you this day, to love the LORD your God and to serve Him with all your heart and with all your soul, then will I send the rain for your land in its due season, the autumn rain and the spring rain, that you may gather in your corn, your wine, and your oil. And I will give grass in your field for your cattle, and you shall eat and be satisfied. Be careful lest your heart be deceived, and you turn aside and serve other gods and worship them. For then the LORD's wrath will be kindled against you, and He will shut the heavens so that there will be no rain, the land will not yield her produce, and you shall perish quickly from the good land which the LORD gives you. Therefore place these words of Mine

---

וְנָתַתִּי מְטַר־אַרְצְכֶם בְּעִתּוֹ – *Then will I send the rain for your land in its due season.* Rambam questions why this paragraph starts by commanding us to serve God unconditionally, and out of love, with all of our hearts, but then goes on to promise earthly rewards as a material incentive to fulfilling God's commandments. He answers that the Torah is not only intended for sages and intellectuals, but also for ordinary people who need to be motivated on their level. He provides the analogy of an effective teacher or loving parent who motivate a child or student with age-appropriate rewards and incentives. Only in due course will the child reach the stage in which good behavior can be appreciated for its own sake, or in this case "for the love of God." So too, the Torah chooses "level-appropriate" incentives.

הִשָּׁמְרוּ לָכֶם – *Be careful. "You shall eat and be satisfied… be careful lest your heart be tempted":* Herein lies a paradox insofar as the very rewards that God bestows upon us for observing His commandments can also result in our "going astray to worship other gods." For when we feel secure and satisfied, we can, if we are not careful, become self-satisfied or dismissive of the very God Who bestowed these rewards on us. Precisely at the moment of our success and well-being we must take care to remain humble, loyal, and appreciative to God for all we have (Rashi).

דְּבָרַי אֵלֶּה עַל־לְבַבְכֶם וְעַל־נַפְשְׁכֶם, °וּקְשַׁרְתֶּם אֹתָם לְאוֹת עַל־
יֶדְכֶם, °°וְהָיוּ לְטוֹטָפֹת בֵּין עֵינֵיכֶם: וְלִמַּדְתֶּם אֹתָם אֶת־בְּנֵיכֶם
לְדַבֵּר בָּם, בְּשִׁבְתְּךָ בְּבֵיתֶךָ וּבְלֶכְתְּךָ בַדֶּרֶךְ, וּבְשָׁכְבְּךָ וּבְקוּמֶךָ:
וּכְתַבְתָּם עַל־מְזוּזוֹת בֵּיתֶךָ וּבִשְׁעָרֶיךָ: לְמַעַן יִרְבּוּ יְמֵיכֶם וִימֵי
בְנֵיכֶם עַל הָאֲדָמָה אֲשֶׁר נִשְׁבַּע יהוה לַאֲבֹתֵיכֶם לָתֵת לָהֶם, כִּימֵי
הַשָּׁמַיִם עַל־הָאָרֶץ:

Hold the ציציות *in both hands, kissing them at °.*

במדבר טו
וַיֹּאמֶר יהוה אֶל־מֹשֶׁה לֵּאמֹר: דַּבֵּר אֶל־בְּנֵי יִשְׂרָאֵל וְאָמַרְתָּ
אֲלֵהֶם, וְעָשׂוּ לָהֶם °צִיצִת עַל־כַּנְפֵי בִגְדֵיהֶם לְדֹרֹתָם,
וְנָתְנוּ °עַל־צִיצִת הַכָּנָף פְּתִיל תְּכֵלֶת: וְהָיָה לָכֶם °לְצִיצִת, וּרְאִיתֶם
אֹתוֹ וּזְכַרְתֶּם אֶת־כָּל־מִצְוֹת יהוה וַעֲשִׂיתֶם אֹתָם, וְלֹא תָתוּרוּ
אַחֲרֵי לְבַבְכֶם וְאַחֲרֵי עֵינֵיכֶם, אֲשֶׁר־אַתֶּם זֹנִים אַחֲרֵיהֶם: לְמַעַן
תִּזְכְּרוּ וַעֲשִׂיתֶם אֶת־כָּל־מִצְוֹתָי, וִהְיִיתֶם קְדֹשִׁים לֵאלֹהֵיכֶם: אֲנִי
יהוה אֱלֹהֵיכֶם, אֲשֶׁר הוֹצֵאתִי אֶתְכֶם מֵאֶרֶץ מִצְרַיִם, לִהְיוֹת לָכֶם
לֵאלֹהִים, אֲנִי יהוה אֱלֹהֵיכֶם: °**אֱמֶת**

The שליח ציבור *repeats:*

◂ יהוה אֱלֹהֵיכֶם אֱמֶת

וַיֹּאמֶר ה׳ – *The Lord spoke.* When we recite the third paragraph of *Shema* we fulfill the commandment to recall the Exodus every day. This is important in that it reminds us that (1) we must be eternally grateful to God for having redeemed our ancestors, and by extension, ourselves, hence we serve Him exclusively; (2) God continues to be involved in human history, even if not always via miraculous intervention or Revelation, as He was at the Exodus; and (3) as former slaves who suffered the indignities of a murderous regime, we have a special responsibility to show supreme sensitivity toward the vulnerable and disadvantaged members of society.

פְּתִיל תְּכֵלֶת – *A thread of blue. Tekhelet* is the color of wool that has been dyed with the secretion of the *ḥilazon* snail. While many authorities continue to regard the exact identification of the *ḥilazon* as unknown, in the late twentieth century some scholars have identified it as the mollusk Murex Trunculus, found on the shores of the Eastern Mediterranean. Even in the absence of the *tekhelet* thread,

upon your heart and upon your soul, °and you shall bind them for a sign on your hand °°and they shall be as *tefillin* between your eyes. And you shall teach them to your children, speaking of them when you sit in your house and when you walk on the way, when you lie down and when you rise up. And you shall write them upon the doorposts of your house and upon your gates. That long as the days of the heavens above the earth may be your days and the days of your children in the land which the Lord promised your fathers to give to them.

Hold the tzitziyot in both hands, kissing them at °.

Num. 15 **וַיֹּאמֶר** THE LORD SPOKE to Moses, saying: "Speak to the children of Israel and tell them to make for themselves °*tzitzit* on the corners of their garments, throughout their generations, putting a thread of blue upon the °*tzitzit* of each corner. It shall be to you a °*tzitzit* which you may look upon and remember all the commandments of the Lord and do them, that you shall not stray after your heart and your eyes, after which you sinfully follow. So may you remember and do all My commandments and be holy for your God. I am the Lord your God Who brought you out of the land of Egypt to be your God; I am the Lord your God." °TRUE IT IS –

The Leader repeats:

▸ The Lord your God. True it is –

---

the commandment of *tzitzit* remains binding (*Menahot* 38a).

וִהְיִיתֶם קְדֹשִׁים לֵאלֹהֵיכֶם – *Be holy for your God.* In these few words the Torah encapsulates the purpose of the 613 Commandments, which is to facilitate a life of holiness dedicated to God. It is human nature to seek reasons behind specific commandments, in the form of some benefit that will follow from keeping them. While we can sometimes identify such benefits, in the end we do not observe the *mitzvot* for the sake of such outcomes. Ultimately we cannot know the reasons behind individual *mitzvot*, even those that seem logical to us. All we can know is the general purpose of the *mitzvot* in their totality, which is to attain a life of holiness in the service of God (R. Samuel Belkin).

אֱמֶת – *True it is.* The prophet Jeremiah (Jer. 10:10) declared, וַה׳ אֱלֹהִים אֱמֶת – "The Lord God is the truth." Jeremiah was asserting the truth of God's existence, and prophesying

וְיַצִּיב, וְנָכוֹן וְקַיָּם, וְיָשָׁר וְנֶאֱמָן, וְאָהוּב וְחָבִיב, וְנֶחְמָד וְנָעִים, וְנוֹרָא וְאַדִּיר, וּמְתֻקָּן וּמְקֻבָּל, וְטוֹב וְיָפֶה, הַדָּבָר הַזֶּה עָלֵינוּ לְעוֹלָם וָעֶד. אֱמֶת אֱלֹהֵי עוֹלָם מַלְכֵּנוּ, צוּר יַעֲקֹב מָגֵן יִשְׁעֵנוּ, ◂ לְדוֹר וָדוֹר הוּא קַיָּם וּשְׁמוֹ קַיָּם, וְכִסְאוֹ נָכוֹן, וּמַלְכוּתוֹ וֶאֱמוּנָתוֹ לָעַד קַיֶּמֶת. ◂ וּדְבָרָיו חָיִים וְקַיָּמִים, נֶאֱמָנִים וְנֶחֱמָדִים, לָעַד (*kiss the* ציצית *and release them.*) וּלְעוֹלְמֵי עוֹלָמִים, עַל אֲבוֹתֵינוּ וְעָלֵינוּ, עַל בָּנֵינוּ וְעַל דּוֹרוֹתֵינוּ, וְעַל כָּל דּוֹרוֹת זֶרַע יִשְׂרָאֵל עֲבָדֶיךָ.

עַל הָרִאשׁוֹנִים וְעַל הָאַחֲרוֹנִים, דָּבָר טוֹב וְקַיָּם לְעוֹלָם וָעֶד. אֱמֶת וֶאֱמוּנָה, חֹק וְלֹא יַעֲבֹר. אֱמֶת שָׁאַתָּה הוּא יהוה אֱלֹהֵינוּ וֵאלֹהֵי אֲבוֹתֵינוּ, ◂ מַלְכֵּנוּ מֶלֶךְ אֲבוֹתֵינוּ, גּוֹאֲלֵנוּ גּוֹאֵל אֲבוֹתֵינוּ, יוֹצְרֵנוּ צוּר יְשׁוּעָתֵנוּ, פּוֹדֵנוּ וּמַצִּילֵנוּ מֵעוֹלָם שְׁמֶךָ, אֵין אֱלֹהִים זוּלָתֶךָ.

עֶזְרַת אֲבוֹתֵינוּ אַתָּה הוּא מֵעוֹלָם, מָגֵן וּמוֹשִׁיעַ לִבְנֵיהֶם אַחֲרֵיהֶם בְּכָל דּוֹר וָדוֹר. בְּרוּם עוֹלָם מוֹשָׁבֶךָ, וּמִשְׁפָּטֶיךָ וְצִדְקָתְךָ עַד אַפְסֵי אָרֶץ. אַשְׁרֵי אִישׁ שֶׁיִּשְׁמַע לְמִצְוֹתֶיךָ, וְתוֹרָתְךָ וּדְבָרְךָ יָשִׂים עַל לִבּוֹ. אֱמֶת אַתָּה הוּא אָדוֹן לְעַמֶּךָ, וּמֶלֶךְ גִּבּוֹר לָרִיב רִיבָם. אֱמֶת אַתָּה הוּא רִאשׁוֹן וְאַתָּה הוּא אַחֲרוֹן, וּמִבַּלְעָדֶיךָ

---

that all peoples will come to recognize that truth. Thematically, the expression bridges between our past, private redemptions – the main theme of our blessing – and the future redemption which is included shortly before the conclusion of the blessing.

אֱמֶת ... וְיַצִּיב – *True it is... And firmly grounded.* Rashi and Tosafot explain that the morning blessing, אֱמֶת וְיַצִּיב recited in the light of day, focuses on God's kindness in having redeemed us from Egypt, while אֱמֶת וֶאֱמוּנָה that is recited at night, emphasizes our faith that God will redeem us in the future, just as He did at the time of the Exodus. So too, in the psalm for Shabbat the Psalmist writes that "in the morning we declare Your kindness, while at night we affirm Your faithfulness."

וְיַצִּיב AND FIRMLY GROUNDED, ordered and established, right and permanent, lovely and precious, pleasant and sweet, solemn and revered, accepted as well as good and beautiful, is this matter for us for all time. The eternal God is truly our King, the Rock of Jacob, our protecting shield. ▸ He endures, as does His name, to all generations. His throne is established, and His sovereignty and faithfulness endure forever. ◂ His words live and endure, faithful and precious, forever (*kiss the tzitziot and release them*) and for all eternity. They were incumbent upon our forefathers, and so they are and will be for us, for our children and our descendants, and for every generation of the seed of Israel, Your servants.

For the early and the later generations, these words are a doctrine that is good and enduring forever; true and faithful, a law that shall not pass away. In truth, You are the Lord, our God and the God of our fathers; ▸ our King and the King of our fathers; our Redeemer and the Redeemer of our fathers; our Maker, the Rock of our salvation; our Savior and Deliverer – this has ever been Your name; there is no other god besides You.

עֶזְרַת אֲבוֹתֵינוּ FROM OF OLD You have been the help of our fathers, a shield and a savior for their children after them in every generation. Although Your dwelling is in the heights above the cosmos, Your works of righteousness and justice extend to the ends of the earth. Happy is the man who hearkens to Your commandments, who sets Your Torah and Your word in his heart. True it is that You are the Master of Your people, their mighty King to champion their cause. True it is that You are the first and You are the last, and besides You

---

The third of the *Shema berakhot* begins at this point and concludes with the ending *berakha* גָּאַל יִשְׂרָאֵל ("Who redeemed Israel"). As explained earlier, this lengthy passage corresponds to the third paragraph of the *Shema*, and echoes its themes of miraculous

אֵין לָנוּ מֶלֶךְ גּוֹאֵל וּמוֹשִׁיעַ. מִמִּצְרַיִם גְּאַלְתָּנוּ, יהוה אֱלֹהֵינוּ, וּמִבֵּית עֲבָדִים פְּדִיתָנוּ, כָּל בְּכוֹרֵיהֶם הָרַגְתָּ, וּבְכוֹרְךָ גָּאָלְתָּ, וְיַם סוּף בָּקַעְתָּ, וְזֵדִים טִבַּעְתָּ, וִידִידִים הֶעֱבַרְתָּ, וַיְכַסּוּ־מַיִם צָרֵיהֶם, אֶחָד מֵהֶם לֹא נוֹתָר: עַל זֹאת שִׁבְּחוּ אֲהוּבִים, וְרוֹמְמוּ אֵל, וְנָתְנוּ יְדִידִים זְמִירוֹת, שִׁירוֹת וְתִשְׁבָּחוֹת, בְּרָכוֹת וְהוֹדָאוֹת לַמֶּלֶךְ אֵל חַי וְקַיָּם, רָם וְנִשָּׂא, גָּדוֹל וְנוֹרָא, מַשְׁפִּיל גֵּאִים וּמַגְבִּיהַּ שְׁפָלִים, מוֹצִיא אֲסִירִים, וּפוֹדֶה עֲנָוִים וְעוֹזֵר דַּלִּים, וְעוֹנֶה לְעַמּוֹ בְּעֵת שַׁוְּעָם אֵלָיו. תהלים קו

Stand in preparation for the עמידה*.*
Some take three steps back at this point. Others do so before צוּר יִשְׂרָאֵל*.*

◂ תְּהִלּוֹת לְאֵל עֶלְיוֹן, בָּרוּךְ הוּא וּמְבֹרָךְ, מֹשֶׁה וּבְנֵי יִשְׂרָאֵל, לְךָ עָנוּ שִׁירָה בְּשִׂמְחָה רַבָּה, וְאָמְרוּ כֻלָּם,

מִי־כָמֹכָה בָּאֵלִם, יהוה, מִי כָּמֹכָה נֶאְדָּר בַּקֹּדֶשׁ, נוֹרָא תְהִלֹּת, עֹשֵׂה פֶלֶא: שמות טו

◂ שִׁירָה חֲדָשָׁה שִׁבְּחוּ גְאוּלִים, לְשִׁמְךָ עַל שְׂפַת הַיָּם, יַחַד כֻּלָּם הוֹדוּ וְהִמְלִיכוּ, וְאָמְרוּ,

יהוה יִמְלֹךְ לְעֹלָם וָעֶד: שמות טו

◂ צוּר יִשְׂרָאֵל, קוּמָה בְּעֶזְרַת יִשְׂרָאֵל, וּפְדֵה כִנְאֻמֶךָ יְהוּדָה וְיִשְׂרָאֵל. גֹּאֲלֵנוּ יהוה צְבָאוֹת שְׁמוֹ, קְדוֹשׁ יִשְׂרָאֵל: בָּרוּךְ אַתָּה יהוה, גָּאַל יִשְׂרָאֵל. ישעיה מז

submission to the yoke of God's kingdom, by proclaiming that "other than You we have no King or Redeemer."

deliverance from the afflictions of Egyptian bondage, as well as the salvation at the Sea of Reeds. Here again, the *berakha* asserts our

we have no king who saves and redeems. From Egypt You redeemed us, Lord, our God, and from the house of bondage You delivered us; all their firstborn You slayed, but Your firstborn, You redeemed. You divided the Sea of Reeds and drowned those who had oppressed us.
Ps. 106 The people You loved You brought across the sea, "And the waters covered their adversaries, not one of them was left." For this, the beloved ones praised and exalted God; the cherished ones sang hymns, songs and praises, blessings and thanksgivings to the King, the ever-living and enduring God. Supremely exalted, all-powerful and awe-inspiring, He brings low the arrogant and raises the meek, sets free those who are bound, rescues the lowly, helps the needy, and answers His people when they cry to Him.

Stand in preparation for the Amida.
Some take three steps back at this point. Others do so before "Rock of Israel."

▸ Praises to the supreme God, ever blessed be He. To You Moses and all the children of Israel chanted songs with great joy, all proclaiming:

Ex. 15 WHO IS LIKE YOU, Lord, among the mighty? Who is like You, glorious in holiness, inspiring in praises, working wonders?

▸ By the shore of the sea the rescued people sang to Your name a new song of praise. Together they all acknowledged and proclaimed Your sovereignty, saying:

Ex. 15 THE LORD shall reign forever and ever.

▸ Rock of Israel, rise up to the aid of Israel, and fulfill Your promised
Is. 47 word to deliver Judah and Israel. Our Redeemer, Whose name is the Lord of hosts, is the Holy One of Israel. Blessed are You, Lord, Who redeemed Israel.

גָּאַל יִשְׂרָאֵל / GA'AL YISRAEL

It is preferable for the congregation to recite this blessing in an undertone simultaneously with the Leader (*MB* 66:35). The Leader should make sure to recite the *berakha* out loud (R. Yosef Eliyahu Henkin, *Edut LeYisrael*, p. 161).

עמידה

One begins the עמידה *by taking three steps forward (OḤ 95:1). According to some traditions, one should first take three steps back before moving forward (MB 95:3). The* עמידה *is recited with one's feet together. One should try to concentrate on the simple meaning of the words of the* עמידה *with the awareness throughout that one is standing in the presence of the Almighty (OḤ 98:1 and MB 98:1). At the points indicated by* ▾*, bend the knees at the first word, bow at the second, and stand straight before saying God's name.*

תהלים נא אֲדֹנָי, שְׂפָתַי תִּפְתָּח, וּפִי יַגִּיד תְּהִלָּתֶךָ:

אבות

▾בָּרוּךְ אַתָּה יהוה, אֱלֹהֵינוּ וֵאלֹהֵי אֲבוֹתֵינוּ, אֱלֹהֵי אַבְרָהָם, אֱלֹהֵי יִצְחָק, וֵאלֹהֵי יַעֲקֹב, הָאֵל הַגָּדוֹל הַגִּבּוֹר וְהַנּוֹרָא, אֵל עֶלְיוֹן, גּוֹמֵל חֲסָדִים טוֹבִים, וְקוֹנֵה הַכֹּל, וְזוֹכֵר חַסְדֵי אָבוֹת, וּמֵבִיא גוֹאֵל לִבְנֵי בְנֵיהֶם לְמַעַן שְׁמוֹ בְּאַהֲבָה.

בעשרת ימי תשובה: זָכְרֵנוּ לְחַיִּים, מֶלֶךְ חָפֵץ בַּחַיִּים, וְכָתְבֵנוּ בְּסֵפֶר הַחַיִּים, לְמַעַנְךָ אֱלֹהִים חַיִּים.

(If forgotten, no corrective action is necessary.)

מֶלֶךְ עוֹזֵר וּמוֹשִׁיעַ וּמָגֵן. ▾בָּרוּךְ אַתָּה יהוה, מָגֵן אַבְרָהָם.

עֲמִידָה / AMIDA

אֲדֹנָי, שְׂפָתַי תִּפְתָּח – *O my Master, open my lips.* We declare from the very outset that we are incapable by ourselves of adequately expressing God's praises – hence we implore Him to help us find the right words to express our prayers in His presence (Abudarham).

The Gemara (*Berakhot* 4b) regards this verse as an intrinsic part of prayer, that is, it is a prayer to be able to pray meaningfully. Accordingly we can conclude that reciting this verse does not constitute an impermissible interruption between the preceding *berakha* for redemption and the *Amida* itself. Therefore, just like the rest of the *Amida* repetition, the Leader should say it aloud when repeating the *Amida* (R. Joseph B. Soloveitchik).

The first section of the *Amida* contains three *berakhot*, each corresponding to one of the three patriarchs. The first refers to God as a גּוֹמֵל חֲסָדִים (One Who bestows kindnesses), corresponding to Abraham who was the very embodiment of kindness. The second refers to God as the גִּבּוֹר (mighty One), corresponding to Isaac, whose near self-sacrifice was emblematic of his quality of heroic self-discipline, for which he experienced rebirth and resurrection as reflected in the *berakha*. The third *berakha* highlights God's קְדֻשָּׁה (sanctity), the virtue that is particularly associated with Jacob, and which he bequeathed to his descendants the people of Israel, who, like Jacob, sanctify God in their lives – as Isaiah 29:23 states: וְהִקְדִּישׁוּ אֶת קְדוֹשׁ יַעֲקֹב – "They shall sanctify the Holy One of Jacob" (Rashba).

AMIDA

One begins the Amida by taking three steps forward (OḤ 95:1). According to some traditions, one should first take three steps back before moving forward (MB 95:3). The Amida is recited with one's feet together. One should try to concentrate on the simple meaning of the words of the Amida with the awareness throughout that one is standing in the presence of the Almighty (OḤ 98:1 and MB 98:1). At the points indicated by ▾, bend the knees at the first word, bow at the second, and stand straight before saying God's name.

Ps. 51 "O MY MASTER, open my lips, and my mouth will relate Your praise."

PATRIARCHS

▾בָּרוּךְ BLESSED ARE YOU, LORD, our God and the God of our fathers, the God of Abraham, the God of Isaac, and the God of Jacob, the God Who is great, mighty, and awesome, God most exalted, Who bestows rewards of benevolent kindness, Who is the Creator of everything, Who remembers all the kind acts of the fathers, and Who brings a redeemer to their children's children, for the sake of His name, with love.

Between Rosh HaShana & Yom Kippur: Remember us for life, King Who desires life, and inscribe us in the book of life for Your sake, Living God.

(If forgotten, no corrective action is necessary.)

King Who helps, saves, and shields, ▾blessed are You, LORD, Shield of Abraham.

אָבוֹת / PATRIARCHS

The Gemara (*Berakhot* 40b) records the view of R. Yoḥanan that every *berakha* must include מֶלֶךְ הָעוֹלָם ("King of the universe"), a requirement that is codified by the major authorities. Yet none of the nineteen *berakhot* of the *Amida* includes that phrase. The reason is that because the first *berakha* of the *Amida* opens and closes by referring to Abraham, this "is the equivalent of declaring His kingship insofar

REPETITION OF THE AMIDA

When repeating the *Amida* the Leader should recite the verse "*Hashem sefatai*" quietly (*MB* 111:10). R. Joseph B. Soloveitchik maintained that it should be recited aloud. Throughout the repetition, the congregation should pay attention to the words of the Leader and should not engage in other activities, not even Torah learning (*OḤ* 124:4 and *MB* 124:16). Certainly it is forbidden to engage in idle conversation during the repetition (*OḤ* 124:7). It is preferable to stand during the repetition of the *Amida* (*OḤ* 124:4).

גבורות

אַתָּה גִּבּוֹר לְעוֹלָם, אֲדֹנָי, מְחַיֵּה מֵתִים אַתָּה, רַב לְהוֹשִׁיעַ.

בחורף: מַשִּׁיב הָרְוּחַ וּמוֹרִיד הַגֶּשֶׁם

מְכַלְכֵּל חַיִּים בְּחֶסֶד, מְחַיֵּה מֵתִים בְּרַחֲמִים רַבִּים, סוֹמֵךְ נוֹפְלִים, וְרוֹפֵא חוֹלִים, וּמַתִּיר אֲסוּרִים, וּמְקַיֵּם אֱמוּנָתוֹ לִישֵׁנֵי עָפָר. מִי כָמְוֹךָ, בַּעַל גְּבוּרוֹת, וּמִי דּוֹמֶה לָּךְ, מֶלֶךְ, מֵמִית וּמְחַיֶּה וּמַצְמִיחַ יְשׁוּעָה.

בעשרת ימי תשובה: מִי כָמְוֹךָ אַב הָרַחֲמִים, זוֹכֵר יְצוּרָיו לְחַיִּים בְּרַחֲמִים.

(*If forgotten, no corrective action is necessary.*)

וְנֶאֱמָן אַתָּה לְהַחֲיוֹת מֵתִים. בָּרוּךְ אַתָּה יהוה, מְחַיֵּה הַמֵּתִים.

When saying the עמידה *silently, continue with* אַתָּה קָדוֹשׁ *on page 112.*

as Abraham promulgated God's universal sovereignty" (Tosafot).

Ramban (Ex. 15:26), while apparently accepting the view of Tosafot (as explained by R. Charles B. Chavel), provides an additional reason for not mentioning God's universal sovereignty during the *Amida*. He explains that *birkhot mitzva* begin in the second person ("Blessed are You") and continue in the third person ("Who has commanded us with His *mitzvot*") because the third person usage expresses awe and respect for the "King of the universe" Who, like all kings, demands obedience to His command. By contrast, in the *Amida* we come into God's presence, speaking directly to Him, in heightened intimacy, experiencing Him not as the King but as our Father.

The Gemara (*Megilla* 17b) records that at the direction of R. Shimon ben Gamliel of Yavneh in the second century, R. Shimon HaPakuli and his colleagues formulated a precise text of the *Amida*. At this historical moment, shortly after the destruction of the Temple, the Jewish people needed a vehicle to strengthen their special relationship with God. The text of the *Amida* was formulated to serve this purpose. Thus the first *berakha* of the *Amida* deliberately emphasizes that He is "our God" and "the God of our fathers," omitting reference to "the King of the universe," while the rest of the *berakhot* simply refer to Him as "our God," the One with Whom we have a special relationship as a people. Moreover, given this pressing need to reassert the special nature of the Jewish people, R. Shimon ben Gamliel saw to it that the *Amida* was formulated so as to express the prayers of the entire Jewish nation, rather than merely those of its individuals. So too, as recorded in the *Tosefta* and Gemara *Rosh HaShana* 34b, he viewed the vocal repetition of the *Amida* by the Leader as taking precedence over silent individual recitations in discharging our prayer duties, for it represents the all-important *Amida* of the Jewish nation as a collective (Prof. Ezra Fleischer).

גְּבוּרוֹת / GOD'S MIGHT

אַתָּה גִּבּוֹר לְעוֹלָם, אֲדֹנָי – *You are eternally mighty, my Master*. The most powerful manifestation of God's power is in His unique ability to overcome

GOD'S MIGHT

אַתָּה YOU, my Master, are forever mighty, You are the Resurrector of the dead, with great power to save.

In winter: He makes the wind blow and the rain fall

He sustains the living with kindness, He resurrects the dead with great compassion, He supports those who are falling, He heals the sick, He sets the incarcerated free, and He fulfills what He has promised to those who sleep in the dust. Who is like You, O mighty One, and who can be compared to You, O King Who causes death and resurrects, and Who causes salvation to sprout?

Between Rosh HaShana & Yom Kippur: Who is like You, merciful Father, Who in compassion remembers for life those He has created.

(*If forgotten, no corrective action is necessary.*)

Trustworthy are You to resurrect the dead. Blessed are YOU, LORD, Resurrector of the dead.

When saying the Amida silently, continue with "You are holy" on page 113.

---

death, via the Resurrection of the Dead, in both body and soul. Given that the sages saw the need to emphasize the belief in bodily resurrection, they included it both at the beginning and end of this *berakha*. (Prof. Ephraim Urbach).

The reason that this line is inserted in the same paragraph as the future Resurrection of the Dead, is that it contains a double meaning. In addition to the simple meaning, it praises God Who will one day be the מַשִּׁיב הָרוּחַ (the One Who will restore the spirit, i.e., the soul) and the מוֹרִיד הַגֶּשֶׁם (the One Who will restore our גַּשְׁמִיּוּת, i.e., our material bodies to earthly existence) (R. Ephraim Lunshitz).

הַגֶּשֶׁם – *The rain.* The text of almost all prayer books appearing prior to the end of

OMISSION/INSERTION OF MASHIV HARU'AH

Mashiv haru'ah is inserted only in the period from Shemini Atzeret until the first day of Pesah. If it was erroneously omitted or inserted, then:

- If one erroneously inserted it *but* did not yet complete the *berakha*, one returns to "*Ata gibor*." If one already completed the *berakha*, one must return to the beginning of the *Amida* (*OH* 114:4).
- If one erroneously omitted it, but did not yet complete the *berakha*, or if one completed the *berakha* and did not yet start the next *berakha*, one may insert the phrase and continue. If one already started the next *berakha*, one must return to the beginning of the *Amida* (*OH* 114:5–6).
- If one recited *morid hatal* instead of *mashiv haru'ah* there is no need for any repetition (*OH* 114:5).

קדושה

During חזרת הש"ץ*, the following is said standing with feet together, rising on the toes at the words indicated by* ▲.

קהל *then* ש"ץ: **נְקַדֵּשׁ** אֶת שִׁמְךָ בָּעוֹלָם, כְּשֵׁם שֶׁמַּקְדִּישִׁים אוֹתוֹ בִּשְׁמֵי מָרוֹם, כַּכָּתוּב עַל יַד נְבִיאֶךָ, וְקָרָא זֶה אֶל־זֶה וְאָמַר ישעיה ו

קהל *then* ש"ץ: ▲קָדוֹשׁ, ▲קָדוֹשׁ, ▲קָדוֹשׁ יהוה צְבָאוֹת, מְלֹא כָל־הָאָרֶץ כְּבוֹדוֹ:

ש"ץ: לְעֻמָּתָם בָּרוּךְ יֹאמֵרוּ

קהל *then* ש"ץ: ▲בָּרוּךְ כְּבוֹד־יהוה מִמְּקוֹמוֹ: יחזקאל ג

ש"ץ: וּבְדִבְרֵי קָדְשְׁךָ כָּתוּב לֵאמֹר

קהל *then* ש"ץ: ▲יִמְלֹךְ יהוה לְעוֹלָם, אֱלֹהַיִךְ צִיּוֹן לְדֹר וָדֹר, הַלְלוּיָהּ: תהלים קמו

ש"ץ: לְדוֹר וָדוֹר נַגִּיד גָּדְלֶךָ, וּלְנֵצַח נְצָחִים קְדֻשָּׁתְךָ נַקְדִּישׁ, וְשִׁבְחֲךָ אֱלֹהֵינוּ מִפִּינוּ לֹא יָמוּשׁ לְעוֹלָם וָעֶד, כִּי אֵל מֶלֶךְ גָּדוֹל וְקָדוֹשׁ אָתָּה. בָּרוּךְ אַתָּה יהוה, הָאֵל הַקָּדוֹשׁ./ בעשרת ימי תשובה: הַמֶּלֶךְ הַקָּדוֹשׁ./

The שליח ציבור *continues with* אַתָּה חוֹנֵן *on the next page.*

---

the eighteenth century, as documented by R. Ḥayyim Kraus, vocalized this word with a *segol*, so that it was read as *geshem*. Accordingly, most authorities (including R. Yaakov Emden, R. Shlomo Zalman Auerbach, and R. Joseph B. Soloveitchik) agree that it should be read *geshem*. The generally quoted source for the alternative *gashem* reading is the *VaYe'etar Yitzḥak Siddur*, whose editor assumed that the word ends the line, and thus should read *gashem*. In many subsequent prayer books and communities in America and elsewhere this became the default reading. This reading was indeed endorsed by R. Moshe Feinstein. The majority view, however, is that, as the Rosh and the *Tur* stated, the word is connected to what follows, that is, God "causes the rain to fall" and in so doing "He sustains the living, etc." We thus omit an end-of-line punctuation after the word *geshem*, so that there is no pause before beginning the next paragraph.

קדושה – *Kedusha.* As Rashi and the *Maḥzor Vitri* both note, the Talmud does not consider the *Kedusha* prayer as we know it to be an obligatory prayer. Its absence from the original *Amida* is likely the result of the sages' desire to avoid the kind of mystical speculation regarding מַעֲשֶׂה מֶרְכָּבָה (celestial matters) that was popular in certain separatist circles at the time. It is likely, however, that the verses from Isaiah ("Holy, holy, holy…) and Ezekiel (Blessed is the glory…) were originally part of the third *berakha* of the *Amida*, recited by individuals in their silent *Amida*, and by the Leader alone in the repetition. However, as the *Tosefta Berakhot* 1:9 records, this changed over time, as reflected in the apparently innovative practice of R. Yehuda to enthusiastically recite

For laws regarding *"Responding to the Leader during Kedusha,"* see page 510.

KEDUSHA

During the Leader's Repetition, the following is said standing with feet together, rising on the toes at the words indicated by ▴.

Cong. then Leader: נְקַדֵּשׁ WE WILL SANCTIFY Your name in this world, as they sanctify
Is. 6 it in the heavenly heights, as is written by Your prophet: "They called to one another, saying":

Cong. then Leader: ▴"Holy, ▴holy, ▴holy is the LORD of hosts; the whole world is filled with His glory."

Leader: Those who face them declare, "Blessed –"

Ezek. 3 *Cong. then Leader:* ▴"Blessed is the glory of the LORD from His place."

Leader: And in Your holy Writings it is written as follows:

Ps. 146 *Cong. then Leader:* ▴"The LORD will reign forever, Your God, O Zion, to all generations. Praise the LORD."

Leader: To all generations we will proclaim Your greatness, and forever declare Your holiness, and the praise of You, our God, will never leave our mouth, for You are God and King, great and holy; blessed are You, LORD, the holy God. / *Between Rosh HaShana and Yom Kippur:* the holy King. /

The Leader continues with "Graciously You grant" on the next page.

these verses responsively with the Leader. In due course such participatory practices spread and slowly took hold, with additional introductory phrasing as well as other verses being added, eventually developing into the *Kedusha* as a responsive prayer to be recited only with a *minyan* quorum, in which even ordinary Jews could join with the angels in singing the nation's praises of "the God of Zion" (Prof. Ezra Fleischer).

Achieving holiness requires us to move beyond our narrow personal and material existence, so as to identify fully with the Jewish people in its covenantal relationship with God. Hence we only recite the *Kedusha* with a *minyan*, which is a microcosm of the larger Jewish people (R. Avraham Yitzḥak HaKohen Kook).

The public repetition of the *Amida*, and the *Kedusha* in particular, is not merely a "public prayer" (תְּפִלָּה בְּצִבּוּר), but the "prayer of the congregation" (תְּפִלַּת הַצִּבּוּר) that carries special significance in its own right, and hence qualifies as a דָּבָר שֶׁבִּקְדֻשָּׁה (a matter of special sanctity), which by definition can only take place by virtue of being recited with a *minyan*. This is also the case with *Barekhu, Kaddish*, and the Reading of the Torah (R. Joseph B. Soloveitchik).

הָאֵל הַקָּדוֹשׁ – This third *berakha* of the *Amida* naturally succeeds the preceding *berakha* that praised God's power as manifested in the physical universe. Here the focus is on praising Him for all that He does in the celestial universe, the world of the angels. Taken together, the three opening *berakhot* thus affirm that God is the Creator and the Sustainer of both realms, the spiritual and physical alike. This affirmation was particularly important during the time of R. Gamliel and R. Shimon HaPakuli, when Gnostic Dualism and other sectarian

קדושת השם

אַתָּה קָדוֹשׁ וְשִׁמְךָ קָדוֹשׁ. וּקְדוֹשִׁים בְּכָל יוֹם יְהַלְלוּךָ סֶּלָה. בָּרוּךְ אַתָּה יהוה, הָאֵל הַקָּדוֹשׁ. / בעשרת ימי תשובה: הַמֶּלֶךְ הַקָּדוֹשׁ./

(*If forgotten, repeat the* עמידה.)

בינה

אַתָּה חוֹנֵן לְאָדָם דַּעַת, וּמְלַמֵּד לֶאֱנוֹשׁ בִּינָה. חָנֵּנוּ מֵאִתְּךָ דֵּעָה בִּינָה וְהַשְׂכֵּל. בָּרוּךְ אַתָּה יהוה, חוֹנֵן הַדָּעַת.

תשובה

הֲשִׁיבֵנוּ אָבִינוּ לְתוֹרָתֶךָ, וְקָרְבֵנוּ מַלְכֵּנוּ לַעֲבוֹדָתֶךָ, וְהַחֲזִירֵנוּ בִּתְשׁוּבָה שְׁלֵמָה לְפָנֶיךָ. בָּרוּךְ אַתָּה יהוה, הָרוֹצֶה בִּתְשׁוּבָה.

movements promoted opposing views. It can also be noted that this affirmation accords with the first *berakha* preceding the *Shema*, which likewise emphasizes that God is the Creator "of all," for which He is praised above and below, by the angels as well as by man (Prof. Ezra Fleischer).

THE MIDDLE בקשה (PETITIONARY) SECTION

As explained earlier, the *Amida* was intended, and formulated, primarily to express the prayer of the Jewish people as a collective, following the destruction of the Temple, rather than as a petition to God for our individual needs. Accordingly, even the middle section that begins at this point, which is formulated in the plural, can be understood as our petitioning God to bring about, in logical and chronological order, the Messianic redemption of our people. In this understanding, the *berakhot* asking for knowledge, repentance, forgiveness, relief from trouble, and healing request the fulfillment of conditions leading to national redemption (Prof. Ezra Fleisher). This approach also accounts for the various contemporaneous tannaitic views recorded in *Avoda Zara* 7b–8a, as to where individuals may insert personal petitions – whether before, after, or in specific locations during the *Amida*, in order to maximize the intensity of the prayer experience. These *tanna'im* recognized that the fixed *Amida* text is not directed toward our personal needs, but those of the nation as a whole, even while it recognizes the essential role of the prayers of the individual in bringing about our national restoration, and the importance of a personal motive to focus our prayers (Prof. Yaakov Blidstein).

OMISSION OF HAMELEKH HAKADOSH

Between Rosh HaShana and Yom Kippur, if one recited *HaKel HaKadosh* instead of *HaMelekh HaKadosh* or one is not sure if one did, one must return to the beginning of the *Amida* (*OH* 582:1). If one corrected oneself immediately after reciting *HaKel HaKadosh*, no corrective action is necessary (*OH* 582:2).

HOLINESS

אַתָּה YOU ARE HOLY and Your name is holy, and holy ones will praise You every day, forever. Blessed are You, LORD, the holy God. /*Between Rosh HaShana & Yom Kippur:* the holy King./

(*If forgotten, repeat the Amida.*)

INSIGHT

אַתָּה GRACIOUSLY You grant man wisdom, and teach understanding to mortal man. Grant us, with grace, the wisdom, insight, and discernment that come from You. Blessed are You, LORD, Granter of knowledge.

REPENTANCE

הֲשִׁיבֵנוּ BRING US BACK, our Father, to Your Torah, and draw us near, our King, to Your service. Facilitate our return to You in complete repentance. Blessed are You, LORD, Who desires repentance.

The sages formulated the petitions of the *Amida* to teach us that even if we are blessed to enjoy good health, financial security, material blessing, spiritual wholeness, social cohesion, or political stability, we must always remember that any of these can change in a moment. We can never know the future, and we must recognize the frailty of our lives and our condition. Thus we must always be aware that even if now we are not habitual sinners, we might at any point in the future succumb to temptation; even if we are currently healthy we must always pray sincerely for continued good health; even if we are today financially secure we must ask God to keep it that way; and certainly if in any given historical period we are blessed to enjoy a secure political environment, we should constantly petition Him to preserve that status quo. None of God's blessings can be taken for granted (R. Moshe Feinstein).

In biblical depictions physical salvation always precedes spiritual revival. In our own time as well we have seen the beginnings of the physical process of the ingathering of the exiles. We yearn for the restoration in due course of justice, and a subsequent progression that will culminate in the restoration of the Davidic throne over the Jewish people, who in turn will serve as a universal model of social justice, morality, and spiritual redemption (R. Avraham Yitzḥak HaKohen Kook).

תְּשׁוּבָה / REPENTANCE

הֲשִׁיבֵנוּ אָבִינוּ לְתוֹרָתֶךָ – *Bring us back, our Father, to Your Torah*. This *berakha* specifically asks God "our Father" to bring us back to the Torah because a father has the obligation to teach Torah to his children (*Tur Oraḥ Ḥayyim* 115).

This phrase asks God to help us to once again embrace the Torah in its original form prior to the breaking of the first tablets. The second tablets were granted us as an act of extraordinary compassion, reflecting God's Thirteen Attributes of Mercy. This *berakha* pleads with God to bring us back fully to His

סליחה

Strike the left side of the chest at °.

סְלַח לָנוּ אָבִינוּ כִּי °חָטָאנוּ, מְחַל לָנוּ מַלְכֵּנוּ כִּי °פָשָׁעְנוּ, כִּי מוֹחֵל וְסוֹלֵחַ אָתָּה. בָּרוּךְ אַתָּה יהוה, חַנּוּן הַמַּרְבֶּה לִסְלֹחַ.

גאולה

רְאֵה בְעָנְיֵנוּ, וְרִיבָה רִיבֵנוּ, וּגְאָלֵנוּ מְהֵרָה לְמַעַן שְׁמֶךָ, כִּי גּוֹאֵל חָזָק אָתָּה. בָּרוּךְ אַתָּה יהוה, גּוֹאֵל יִשְׂרָאֵל.

On Fast Days the שליח ציבור *adds:*

עֲנֵנוּ יהוה עֲנֵנוּ בְּיוֹם צוֹם תַּעֲנִיתֵנוּ, כִּי בְצָרָה גְדוֹלָה אֲנָחְנוּ. אַל תֵּפֶן אֶל רִשְׁעֵנוּ, וְאַל תַּסְתֵּר פָּנֶיךָ מִמֶּנּוּ, וְאַל תִּתְעַלַּם מִתְּחִנָּתֵנוּ. הֱיֵה נָא קָרוֹב לְשַׁוְעָתֵנוּ, יְהִי נָא חַסְדְּךָ לְנַחֲמֵנוּ, טֶרֶם נִקְרָא אֵלֶיךָ עֲנֵנוּ, כַּדָּבָר שֶׁנֶּאֱמַר: וְהָיָה טֶרֶם יִקְרָאוּ וַאֲנִי אֶעֱנֶה, עוֹד הֵם מְדַבְּרִים וַאֲנִי אֶשְׁמָע: כִּי אַתָּה יהוה הָעוֹנֶה בְּעֵת צָרָה, פּוֹדֶה וּמַצִּיל בְּכָל עֵת צָרָה וְצוּקָה. בָּרוּךְ אַתָּה יהוה, הָעוֹנֶה בְּעֵת צָרָה. ישעיה סה

(*If forgotten, see* LEADER'S ANEINU *below.*)

רפואה

רְפָאֵנוּ יהוה וְנֵרָפֵא, הוֹשִׁיעֵנוּ וְנִוָּשֵׁעָה, כִּי תְהִלָּתֵנוּ אָתָּה, וְהַעֲלֵה רְפוּאָה שְׁלֵמָה לְכָל מַכּוֹתֵינוּ

Torah, as we were before the Golden Calf episode. In so doing we acknowledge our present shortcomings as a people in dire need of His help in completing the *teshuva* process, so that we can once again taken full possession of the Torah (R. Yitzchok Hutner).

גְּאֻלָּה / REDEMPTION

This is not a prayer for redemption from exile, but rather a plea to help us deal with the everyday challenges that burden us (Rashi, *Megilla* 17b).

רְאֵה בְעָנְיֵנוּ – *See our suffering.* Though the Jewish people may sin, and God sometimes inflicts our punishment in the form of cruel suffering at the hands of other nations, our enemies cannot justifiably claim that they are doing God's work, since – as happened with Pharaoh – as a rule our enemies afflict us beyond what God intended (*Etz Yosef*). As the prophet Zechariah proclaimed, "Thus says the Lord of Hosts… 'I am very displeased with the nations

LEADER'S ANEINU

If forgotten, then (1) If God's name has not yet been pronounced at the end of the next blessing, *Aneinu* should be recited, followed by *Refa'enu*. (2) If God's name was already recited, the text of the individual's *Aneinu* of *Minḥa* (page 272) should be inserted into *Shema Kolenu* (page 122). (3) If *Shema Kolenu* was completed, no further corrective action is necessary (*SA* 119:4, *MB* 16; 19).

FORGIVENESS

Strike the left side of the chest at °.

סְלַח FORGIVE US, our Father, for we have °sinned. Pardon us, our King, for we have °transgressed. For You are the One Who pardons and forgives. Blessed are You, LORD, gracious and abundantly forgiving.

REDEMPTION

רְאֵה SEE OUR SUFFERING and advocate for us. Speed our redemption for the sake of Your name, for You are a mighty Redeemer. Blessed are You, LORD, Redeemer of Israel.

On Fast Days the Leader adds:

עֲנֵנוּ ANSWER US, dear God, please answer us, on this day of our fasting. For we are in great distress. Do not invoke our wickedness, and do not hide Your face from us, nor turn away from our pleading. Rather be responsive to our cry, and comfort us with your kindness. Answer
Is. 65 us even before we cry out, as it says "I will answer them even before they call out, I will hear them even while they speak." For You are the LORD Who answers in a time of trouble, Who redeems and saves in every instance of trouble and suffering. Blessed are You, LORD, Who answers in times of trouble. (*If forgotten, see* LEADER'S ANEINU *below.*)

HEALTH AND HEALING

רְפָאֵנוּ HEAL US, LORD, and we shall be healed; save us and we shall be saved; for You are our praise. Bring complete healing from all our afflictions,

---

that are at ease, for I was but a little displeased, and they helped for evil'" (Zech. 1:14–15).

גּוֹאֵל יִשְׂרָאֵל – *Redeemer of Israel.* This verb takes the form of the present tense, unlike the past-tense גָּאַל יִשְׂרָאֵל (Who redeemed Israel) *berakha* that precedes the *Amida*. The earlier blessing refers to the Exodus from Egypt, whereas here the *berakha* refers to God Who constantly redeems us from assimilation into the surrounding nations (R. Yaakov Emden).

רְפוּאָה / HEALTH AND HEALING

רְפָאֵנוּ ה' וְנֵרָפֵא – *Heal us, Lord, and we shall be healed.* God has granted man the wherewithal to combat illness, and has commanded him to vanquish human suffering. But we must also recognize that health providers in all of their activities are agents of divine providence, experts at facilitating the natural processes that God has put in place in His world. And while their efforts are not always completely successful, when God *Himself* undertakes to cure the

The following prayer for a sick person may be said here:

יְהִי רָצוֹן מִלְּפָנֶיךָ יהוה אֱלֹהַי וֵאלֹהֵי אֲבוֹתַי, שֶׁתִּשְׁלַח מְהֵרָה רְפוּאָה שְׁלֵמָה מִן הַשָּׁמַיִם רְפוּאַת הַנֶּפֶשׁ וּרְפוּאַת הַגּוּף לַחוֹלֶה/לַחוֹלָה *name of patient* בֶּן/בַּת *mother's name* בְּתוֹךְ שְׁאָר חוֹלֵי יִשְׂרָאֵל.

כִּי אֵל מֶלֶךְ רוֹפֵא נֶאֱמָן וְרַחֲמָן אָתָּה. בָּרוּךְ אַתָּה יהוה, רוֹפֵא חוֹלֵי עַמּוֹ יִשְׂרָאֵל.

ברכת השנים

בָּרֵךְ עָלֵינוּ יהוה אֱלֹהֵינוּ אֶת הַשָּׁנָה הַזֹּאת, וְאֶת כָּל מִינֵי תְבוּאָתָהּ לְטוֹבָה

Beginning in springtime, from the intermediate days of Pesaḥ to the evening preceding December 5 (in some years December 6), say:

וְתֵן בְּרָכָה

Beginning with the winter season, from the evening preceding December 5 (in some years December 6) to Pesaḥ, say:

וְתֵן טַל וּמָטָר לִבְרָכָה

עַל פְּנֵי הָאֲדָמָה, וְשַׂבְּעֵנוּ מִטּוּבֶךָ, וּבָרֵךְ שְׁנָתֵנוּ כַּשָּׁנִים הַטּוֹבוֹת. בָּרוּךְ אַתָּה יהוה, מְבָרֵךְ הַשָּׁנִים.

קבוץ גלויות

תְּקַע בְּשׁוֹפָר גָּדוֹל לְחֵרוּתֵנוּ, וְשָׂא נֵס לְקַבֵּץ גָּלֻיּוֹתֵינוּ, וְקַבְּצֵנוּ יַחַד מֵאַרְבַּע כַּנְפוֹת הָאָרֶץ. בָּרוּךְ אַתָּה יהוה, מְקַבֵּץ נִדְחֵי עַמּוֹ יִשְׂרָאֵל.

---

patient directly, we can be confident that it will not be a temporary or partial measure, hence we say "Heal us, Lord, and *we shall be healed*" (*Etz Yosef*).

The twenty-seven words of this *berakha* for good health correspond to the twenty-seven words in Exodus 15:26 by which God promises Israel that if they will fulfill His commandments, He in turn will heal them (*Tur*).

This *berakha* is to be distinguished from the אֲשֶׁר יָצַר *berakha* (recited at the outset of our prayers and after relieving ourselves). For while that *berakha* also refers to God as a healer, it is a more generic formulation in that it refers to God as the רוֹפֵא כָל בָּשָׂר (healer of *all*

The following prayer for a sick person may be said here:

יְהִי MAY IT BE Your will, LORD my God and God of my fathers, that you send speedily a complete healing from heaven, a healing of the soul and a healing of the body, to the sick person (*name* son/daughter of *mother's name*), among the other sick people of Israel.

for You, God, King, are a faithful and compassionate Healer. Blessed are You, LORD, Who heals the sick of His people Israel.

PROSPERITY

בָּרֵךְ BLESS THIS YEAR for us, LORD our God, along with all its many kinds of produce for good.

Beginning in springtime, from the intermediate days of Pesaḥ to the evening preceding December 5 (in some years December 6), say:

Send blessing

Beginning with the winter season, from the evening preceding December 5 (in some years December 6) to Pesaḥ, say:

Send dew and rain for a blessing

on the face of the earth, and satisfy us with Your benevolence, and bless our year as the best of years. Blessed are You, LORD, Who blesses the years.

INGATHERING OF THE EXILES

תְּקַע SOUND the great shofar of our freedom; hoist the banner to gather our exiles and bring us together from the four corners of the earth. Blessed are You, LORD, Who gathers the scattered of His people Israel.

וְתֵן טַל וּמָטָר / VETEN TAL UMATAR

Veten berakha is recited from Ḥol HaMo'ed Pesaḥ until *Minḥa* of December 4th (or 5th in the year before a civil leap year). *Veten tal umatar* is recited from *Ma'ariv* of December 4th (or 5th) until Pesaḥ. If one recited *veten tal umatar* during the summer months, one must return to the beginning of the *Barekh aleinu* blessing. If one already completed the *Amida* by taking three steps back, one must repeat the *Amida* (*OḤ* 117:3 and *MB* 117:14). If one omitted *veten tal umatar* (or just the word *matar*) during the winter months, if one did not yet recite *Shema koleinu*, it can be recited in that *berakha* immediately before "*ki ata shome'a.*" If one began reciting *Retzeh*, one must return to the beginning of the *Barekh aleinu* blessing. If one already completed the *Amida* by taking three steps back, one must repeat the *Amida* (*OḤ* 117:4–5 and *MB* 117:15–19).

השבת המשפט

הָשִֽׁיבָה שׁוֹפְטֵֽינוּ כְּבָרִאשׁוֹנָה וְיוֹעֲצֵֽינוּ כְּבַתְּחִלָּה, וְהָסֵר מִמֶּֽנּוּ יָגוֹן וַאֲנָחָה, וּמְלֹךְ עָלֵֽינוּ אַתָּה יהוה לְבַדְּךָ בְּחֶֽסֶד וּבְרַחֲמִים, וְצַדְּקֵֽנוּ בַּמִּשְׁפָּט. בָּרוּךְ אַתָּה יהוה, מֶֽלֶךְ אוֹהֵב צְדָקָה וּמִשְׁפָּט. / בעשרת ימי תשובה: הַמֶּֽלֶךְ הַמִּשְׁפָּט./

(*If forgotten, no corrective action is necessary.*)

ברכת המינים

וְלַמַּלְשִׁינִים אַל תְּהִי תִקְוָה, וְכָל הָרִשְׁעָה כְּרֶֽגַע תֹּאבֵד, וְכָל אוֹיְבֶֽיךָ מְהֵרָה יִכָּרֵֽתוּ, וְהַזֵּדִים מְהֵרָה תְעַקֵּר וּתְשַׁבֵּר וּתְמַגֵּר וְתַכְנִֽיעַ בִּמְהֵרָה בְיָמֵֽינוּ. בָּרוּךְ אַתָּה יהוה, שׁוֹבֵר אוֹיְבִים וּמַכְנִֽיעַ זֵדִים.

צדיקים

עַל הַצַּדִּיקִים וְעַל הַחֲסִידִים, וְעַל זִקְנֵי עַמְּךָ בֵּית יִשְׂרָאֵל, וְעַל פְּלֵיטַת סוֹפְרֵיהֶם, וְעַל גֵּרֵי הַצֶּֽדֶק, וְעָלֵֽינוּ, יֶהֱמוּ

---

flesh) by means of natural processes. This one, on the other hand, is much more case-specific: it asks God to specifically heal חוֹלֵי עַמּוֹ יִשְׂרָאֵל ("the sick of His people Israel"), if necessary by supernatural intervention (R. Ḥayyim Berlin).

In reciting this *berakha* we should also have our spiritual health in mind, for that too is a form of sickness that requires healing. This is why the *berakha* uses a double phrase הוֹשִׁיעֵנוּ וְנִוָּשֵׁעָה ("save us and we shall be saved") for it refers to both types of healing. This is also the case in the next *berakha* which is also concerned with our spiritual needs (R. Tzadok HaKohen of Lublin).

בִּרְכַּת הַמִּינִים / AGAINST SLANDERERS

According to the Gemara (*Berakhot* 28b), Shmuel HaKatan was commissioned by the sages of Yavneh shortly after the destruction of the Second Temple to compose this *berakha* as an addition to the *Amida*, when the actions of certain disloyal Jews posed a substantial threat. The precise identity of these groups remains subject to scholarly debate. In the Middle Ages beleaguered Jews certainly had their contemporary persecutors in mind when they recited this *berakha*. When medieval Christians became aware of this text, they added it to the litany of their attacks against Jews and Judaism. Consequently, through a combination of Christian pressure or censorship, and internal Jewish sensitivities, the text of the *berakha* was modified to refer to informers or slanderers without specific reference, at least in *Nusaḥ Ashkenaz*, to "heretics." In reciting this

JUSTICE

הָשִׁיבָה RESTORE our judges as in the beginning, and our counselors as they were to begin with, and relieve our sorrows and our troubles. Reign over us, LORD, You alone, lovingly and mercifully, and vindicate us in judgment. Blessed are You, LORD, King Who loves righteousness and justice. / *Between Rosh HaShana & Yom Kippur:* the King of justice. (*If forgotten, no corrective action is necessary.*)

AGAINST SLANDERERS

וְלַמַּלְשִׁינִים AND LET THERE BE no hope for slanderers, and may all evil instantly disappear. May all Your enemies be swiftly cut down, and the wicked be uprooted, broken, overthrown, and subdued – speedily, and in our day. Blessed are You, LORD, Who crushes enemies and subdues the wicked.

THE RIGHTEOUS

עַל הַצַּדִּיקִים MAY YOUR COMPASSION be upon the righteous, and the pious, and the elders of Your people the house of Israel, and the remnants of their scholars, and the righteous converts, and upon us,

---

text today, even Jews who retain the word מִינִים along with מַלְשִׁינִים (as some versions render it) generally think not of other religions but of renegade Jews who seek to undermine the Jewish community, as well as non-Jews who are אוֹיְבִים (active enemies) of the Jewish people.

The same Shmuel HaKatan is quoted in the Ethics of the Fathers (4:24) as habitually citing the verses: "When your enemy falls, do not rejoice, and when he stumbles, do not let your heart be glad, lest the Lord see and it be evil in His eyes, and He turn away His anger from him [to you]" (Proverbs 24:17–18). It is likely that this is precisely why he was chosen for this task: that in composing this *berakha* the author would not be motivated by any personal agenda to undermine individuals with whom he might be at odds. So too, when we recite the *berakha*, our motive should be purely to see the destruction of the enemies of the Jewish people (R. Avraham Yitzḥak HaKohen Kook).

צַדִּיקִים / THE RIGHTEOUS

פְּלֵיטַת סוֹפְרֵיהֶם – *The remnants of their scholars.* It was necessary to include a reference to "the remnant of scholars" of preceding generations, for they are the essential link between the current generation of rabbinic leaders and those of preceding generation. While it is wonderful that each generation has its scholars who are able to uncover new Torah insights in response to the realities and challenges of the day, while providing informed leadership for their contemporaries, it is also crucial that

רַחֲמֶיךָ יהוה אֱלֹהֵינוּ, וְתֵן שָׂכָר טוֹב לְכָל הַבּוֹטְחִים בְּשִׁמְךָ בֶּאֱמֶת, וְשִׂים חֶלְקֵנוּ עִמָּהֶם, וּלְעוֹלָם לֹא נֵבוֹשׁ כִּי בְךָ בָּטָחְנוּ. בָּרוּךְ אַתָּה יהוה, מִשְׁעָן וּמִבְטָח לַצַּדִּיקִים.

בניין ירושלים

וְלִירוּשָׁלַיִם עִירְךָ בְּרַחֲמִים תָּשׁוּב, וְתִשְׁכֹּן בְּתוֹכָהּ כַּאֲשֶׁר דִּבַּרְתָּ, וּבְנֵה אוֹתָהּ בְּקָרוֹב בְּיָמֵינוּ בִּנְיַן עוֹלָם, וְכִסֵּא דָוִד מְהֵרָה לְתוֹכָהּ תָּכִין. בָּרוּךְ אַתָּה יהוה, בּוֹנֵה יְרוּשָׁלָיִם.

מלכות בית דוד

אֶת צֶמַח דָּוִד עַבְדְּךָ מְהֵרָה תַצְמִיחַ, וְקַרְנוֹ תָּרוּם בִּישׁוּעָתֶךָ, כִּי לִישׁוּעָתְךָ קִוִּינוּ כָּל הַיּוֹם. בָּרוּךְ אַתָּה יהוה, מַצְמִיחַ קֶרֶן יְשׁוּעָה.

among them there are those who by their very personae and historical perspective provide continuity in the chain of the *Mesora*. Without having them in our midst as a living link to the past, the teachings of the Torah can easily be misinterpreted or distorted (R. Joseph B. Soloveitchik).

וְעַל גֵּרֵי הַצֶּדֶק – *The righteous converts* (previous page). Rambam (*Sefer HaMitzvot* 207) explains that we need a special obligation in the Torah to love the convert even though one might have thought it redundant insofar as converts are fully fledged Jews included in the *mitzva* to love our fellow Jews. The reason, he explains, is that having voluntarily embraced our faith and people, the convert is entitled to a special measure of our love and concern. One can add further justification for this supplementary Torah obligation in view of the difficulties sometimes experienced by righteous converts in being welcomed into the Jewish community, Sadly, there are Jews who, instead of facilitating acceptance of converts, fail to live up to this requirement. Hence this *berakha* reflects the personal and communal obligation to treat all righteous converts with proper sensitivity.

The story of a Lithuanian convert known as Avraham ben Avraham, as told by R. Joseph B. Soloveitchik, graphically illustrates the consequences of failure to observe this *mitzva*. The son of an aristocratic Polish family, he secretly converted to Judaism even though doing so was punishable by death at the hands of the authorities. Eventually his conversion became known in the Jewish community. It once happened that, while studying Torah, he incurred the wrath of a member of the Jewish community who accused him of not really being a Jew, and then proceeded to inform the authorities

Lord our God. Give good reward to all those who sincerely trust in Your name, and place our portion with them, and may we never be shamed, for in You we trust. Blessed are You, Lord, Who is the Support and Trustee of the righteous.

REBUILDING JERUSALEM

וְלִירוּשָׁלַיִם AND MAY YOU RETURN to Jerusalem Your city in compassion, and may You dwell within it, as You promised. Rebuild it speedily in our days, such that it will remain built up forever, and establish within it soon the throne of David. Blessed are You, Lord, Builder of Jerusalem.

KINGDOM OF DAVID

אֶת צֶמַח MAY THE OFFSPRING of David, Your servant, soon flourish, and may his glory be exalted by Your salvation – for we hope for Your salvation all day long. Blessed are You, Lord, Who causes the glory of salvation to flourish.

---

that he had renounced Christianity. Avraham was sentenced to death. While in prison he was visited and comforted by the Vilna Gaon. When his well-connected family secured amnesty for him on condition that he renounce his Jewish faith, he refused their entreaties. Consequently on the second day of Shavuot 1749 he was executed in Vilna's Cathedral Square, and his body cremated. A few Jews disguised as Gentiles gathered his ashes and buried them. R. Soloveitchik indicated that he had personally visited the grave of the martyr in the 1930s.

מַלְכוּת בֵּית דָּוִד / KINGDOM OF DAVID

אֶת צֶמַח דָּוִד – *May the offspring of David.* The *Amida* of the Jews in Israel originally had only seventeen blessings; וְלִירוּשָׁלַיִם עִירְךָ and אֶת צֶמַח דָּוִד formed one blessing ending with the formula בָּרוּךְ אַתָּה ה׳ אֱלֹקֵי דָוִד וּבוֹנֵה יְרוּשָׁלָיִם. The addition of בִּרְכַּת הַמִּינִים completed the *Amida* to eighteen blessings. It is for this reason that poetry from the land of Israel that was added to the blessings of the *Amida* – such as the *Krovetz* for Purim by R. Elazar HaKalir – does not contain verses for the blessing of אֶת צֶמַח דָּוִד. In Babylonia, however, the blessing was split into two. R. Soloveitchik explained that the Jews in exile felt more ideological pressure from Christians around them, and felt the need for a separate blessing to emphasize that the Messiah had not yet arrived. Early exilic Jewish communities needed more strength and stamina to maintain their identity, endure hardships, and survive to see that great era (R. Isaiah Wohlgemuth).

On fast days, if the שליח ציבור *did not add* עֲנֵנוּ *in the* חזרת הש״ץ *(page 114) he may add it here at the asterisk, without the concluding blessing.*

When saying the עמידה *silently, one may add a personal prayer for forgiveness and for livelihood (below) at the asterisk.*

שומע תפלה

שְׁמַע קוֹלֵנוּ יהוה אֱלֹהֵינוּ, חוּס וְרַחֵם עָלֵינוּ, וְקַבֵּל בְּרַחֲמִים וּבְרָצוֹן אֶת תְּפִלָּתֵנוּ, כִּי אֵל שׁוֹמֵעַ תְּפִלּוֹת וְתַחֲנוּנִים אָתָּה, וּמִלְּפָנֶיךָ מַלְכֵּנוּ רֵיקָם אַל תְּשִׁיבֵנוּ,*

A personal prayer for forgiveness:

אָנָּא יהוה, חָטָאתִי עָוִיתִי וּפָשַׁעְתִּי לְפָנֶיךָ, מִיּוֹם הֱיוֹתִי עַל הָאֲדָמָה עַד הַיּוֹם הַזֶּה (וּבִפְרַט בַּחֵטְא...). אָנָּא יהוה, עֲשֵׂה לְמַעַן שִׁמְךָ הַגָּדוֹל, וּתְכַפֶּר לִי עַל חֲטָאַי וַעֲוֹנַי וּפְשָׁעַי שֶׁחָטָאתִי וְשֶׁעָוִיתִי וְשֶׁפָּשַׁעְתִּי לְפָנֶיךָ, מִנְּעוּרַי עַד הַיּוֹם הַזֶּה. וּתְמַלֵּא כָּל הַשֵּׁמוֹת שֶׁפָּגַמְתִּי בְּשִׁמְךָ הַגָּדוֹל.

Continue with כִּי אַתָּה שׁוֹמֵעַ *below.*

A personal prayer for livelihood:

אַתָּה הוּא יהוה הָאֱלֹהִים, הַזָּן וּמְפַרְנֵס וּמְכַלְכֵּל מִקַּרְנֵי רְאֵמִים עַד בֵּיצֵי כִנִּים. הַטְרִיפֵנִי לֶחֶם חֻקִּי, וְהַמְצֵא לִי וּלְכָל בְּנֵי בֵיתִי מְזוֹנוֹתַי קֹדֶם שֶׁאֶצְטָרֵךְ לָהֶם, בְּנַחַת וְלֹא בְצַעַר, בְּהֶתֵּר וְלֹא בְאִסּוּר, בְּכָבוֹד וְלֹא בְבִזָּיוֹן, לְחַיִּים וּלְשָׁלוֹם, מִשֶּׁפַע בְּרָכָה וְהַצְלָחָה, וּמִשֶּׁפַע בְּרֵכָה עֶלְיוֹנָה, כְּדֵי שֶׁאוּכַל לַעֲשׂוֹת רְצוֹנֶךָ וְלַעֲסֹק בְּתוֹרָתֶךָ וּלְקַיֵּם מִצְוֹתֶיךָ. וְאַל תַּצְרִיכֵנִי לִידֵי מַתְּנַת בָּשָׂר וָדָם. וִיקֻיַּם בִּי מִקְרָא שֶׁכָּתוּב: פּוֹתֵחַ אֶת יָדֶךָ, וּמַשְׂבִּיעַ לְכָל חַי רָצוֹן. וְכָתוּב: הַשְׁלֵךְ עַל יהוה יְהָבְךָ וְהוּא יְכַלְכְּלֶךָ.

Continue with כִּי אַתָּה שׁוֹמֵעַ *below.*

כִּי אַתָּה שׁוֹמֵעַ תְּפִלַּת עַמְּךָ יִשְׂרָאֵל בְּרַחֲמִים. בָּרוּךְ אַתָּה יהוה, שׁוֹמֵעַ תְּפִלָּה.

שׁוֹמֵעַ תְּפִלָּה / RESPONSE TO PRAYER

שְׁמַע קוֹלֵנוּ – *Hear our voice.* The final *berakha* of the middle section of the *Amida* makes a general plea to hear the preceding prayers and petitions. Both the opening and closing phrases of the *berakha* refer to God as *hearing* our prayers, rather than *answering* them. This is because we should never assume that God will fulfill our requests, for it could well be that what we have asked God to grant us is in fact not in our best interest, and therefore God in His infinite wisdom does not "answer" that prayer. We therefore need to understand that the essence of prayer is to petition God, to know that He has heard us, but then to accept His judgment as to what is in our best interest (R. Joseph B. Soloveitchik).

Similarly, the blessing of the New Moon,

On fast days, if the Leader did not add "Answer us" in the Repetition of the Amida (page 115) he may add it here at the asterisk, without the concluding blessing.
When saying the Amida silently, one may add a personal prayer for forgiveness and for livelihood (below) at the asterisk.

RESPONSE TO PRAYER

שְׁמַע קוֹלֵנוּ HEAR OUR VOICE, LORD our God, have pity and compassion for us, and accept our prayer in compassion and favor, for You are God Who hears prayers and pleas. Do not turn us away empty-handed, our King, from Your presence,*

A personal prayer for forgiveness:

אָנָּא PLEASE, LORD, I have sinned, been iniquitous, and transgressed before You, from the day I came into being on this earth until this day (in particular with the sin of…). Please, LORD, act for the sake of Your great name and grant me atonement for my sins, my iniquities and my transgressions committed in Your presence, from my youth until this day. May You make whole all the names I have damaged in Your great name. *Continue with "for You hear" below.*

A personal prayer for livelihood:

אַתָּה YOU are the LORD, the God, Who nourishes, sustains, and supports, from the oryxes' horns to the eggs of lice. Provide me with my due portion of bread, and bring forth for me and all members of my household, my food before I have need for it: in satisfaction and not in pain, in a permissible manner and not a forbidden one, in honor and not in disgrace, for life and for peace, from the flow of blessing and success, and from the flow of the heavenly spring, so that I may be able to do Your will and engage in Your Torah and fulfill Your commandments. Let me not become needy of human charity, and may there be fulfilled in me the verse as it is written: "You open Your hand, and You satisfy the desire of every living thing." And it is written: "Cast your burden upon the LORD, and He will sustain you."

Continue with "for You hear" below.

---

for You hear the prayer of Your people Israel with compassion. Blessed are You, LORD, Who hears prayer.

---

as well as the final phrase of the *berikh shemeh*, ask God to fulfill the requests of our hearts "for good," that is, only if He deems the fulfillment of our request to be to our benefit.

כִּי אַתָּה שׁוֹמֵעַ – *For You hear.* As discussed in the commentary to the first of the middle *berakhot*, the Gemara (*Avoda Zara* 7b–8a) teaches that it is customary to insert personal prayers at this

עבודה

רְצֵה יהוה אֱלֹהֵינוּ בְּעַמְּךָ יִשְׂרָאֵל, וּבִתְפִלָּתָם, וְהָשֵׁב אֶת הָעֲבוֹדָה לִדְבִיר בֵּיתֶךָ, וְאִשֵּׁי יִשְׂרָאֵל וּתְפִלָּתָם בְּאַהֲבָה תְקַבֵּל בְּרָצוֹן, וּתְהִי לְרָצוֹן תָּמִיד עֲבוֹדַת יִשְׂרָאֵל עַמֶּךָ.

On ראש חודש *and* חול המועד*, say:*

אֱלֹהֵינוּ וֵאלֹהֵי אֲבוֹתֵינוּ, יַעֲלֶה וְיָבוֹא וְיַגִּיעַ, וְיֵרָאֶה וְיֵרָצֶה וְיִשָּׁמַע, וְיִפָּקֵד וְיִזָּכֵר זִכְרוֹנֵנוּ וּפִקְדּוֹנֵנוּ וְזִכְרוֹן אֲבוֹתֵינוּ, וְזִכְרוֹן מָשִׁיחַ בֶּן דָּוִד עַבְדֶּךָ, וְזִכְרוֹן יְרוּשָׁלַיִם עִיר קָדְשֶׁךָ, וְזִכְרוֹן כָּל עַמְּךָ בֵּית יִשְׂרָאֵל, לְפָנֶיךָ, לִפְלֵיטָה לְטוֹבָה, לְחֵן וּלְחֶסֶד וּלְרַחֲמִים, לְחַיִּים וּלְשָׁלוֹם בְּיוֹם

בראש חודש: רֹאשׁ הַחֹדֶשׁ / בפסח: חַג הַמַּצּוֹת / בסוכות: חַג הַסֻּכּוֹת

הַזֶּה. זָכְרֵנוּ יהוה אֱלֹהֵינוּ בּוֹ לְטוֹבָה, וּפָקְדֵנוּ בוֹ לִבְרָכָה, וְהוֹשִׁיעֵנוּ בוֹ לְחַיִּים. וּבִדְבַר יְשׁוּעָה וְרַחֲמִים, חוּס וְחָנֵּנוּ וְרַחֵם עָלֵינוּ וְהוֹשִׁיעֵנוּ, כִּי אֵלֶיךָ עֵינֵינוּ, כִּי אֵל מֶלֶךְ חַנּוּן וְרַחוּם אָתָּה.

וְתֶחֱזֶינָה עֵינֵינוּ בְּשׁוּבְךָ לְצִיּוֹן בְּרַחֲמִים. בָּרוּךְ אַתָּה יהוה, הַמַּחֲזִיר שְׁכִינָתוֹ לְצִיּוֹן.

point. This is based on Psalms 142:3 – "I pour out my prayer before Him, I declare my trouble before Him," that is to say, first there is (fixed) prayer, followed by one's personal concerns. The Gemara quotes other views permitting personal prayers at the conclusion of each *berakha* of the middle section, reflecting the theme of the *berakha*.

In general the sages taught that personal prayers are more effective when they are inserted as additions to the *Amida*, rather than as spontaneous expressions of the heart at other times, insofar as the times of fixed prayer are עֵת רָצוֹן (a propitious time) to be heard. This was derived from Psalms 102:1 – "A prayer of the afflicted when he is faint, when he pours out his prayer before the Lord," in which the second half of the verse is taken as referring to the *Amida* (*Netziv*).

THE HODA'A (THANKSGIVING) SECTION OF THE *AMIDA*

עֲבוֹדָה / TEMPLE SERVICE

The third and final section of the *Amida* starts here. Like the first section, it consists of three *berakhot*. Only the middle *berakha* explicitly expresses thanksgiving. It is preceded by a petition that the Temple be rebuilt, so that the sacrifices will once more be offered as in the days of old. It would have made sense to place this *berakha* immediately after אֶת צֶמַח דָּוִד as the fitting culmination of Messianic

TEMPLE SERVICE

רְצֵה LOOK FAVORABLY, LORD our God, upon Your people Israel and their prayer, and restore the service to the Holy of Holies of Your House. Accept with love and favor the fire-offerings of Israel and their prayer. May the service of Israel Your people Israel always find favor with You.

On Rosh Ḥodesh and Ḥol HaMo'ed, say:

אֱלֹהֵינוּ וֵאלֹהֵי אֲבוֹתֵינוּ OUR GOD and God of our fathers, may there arise, arrive, reach, appear, be favored, heard, considered and remembered, our remembrance and recollection, Your remembrance of our fathers, of the Messiah son of David Your servant, of Jerusalem Your holy city and of all Your people the house of Israel. May they come before You for deliverance and benefit, for grace, kindness and mercy, for life and peace, on this day of:

On Rosh Ḥodesh: Rosh Ḥodesh.
On Pesaḥ: the Festival of Matzot.
On Sukkot: the Festival of Sukkot.

LORD our God, remember us this day for good. Be mindful of us this day for blessing, preserve us this day for life. Regarding redemption and mercy show us compassion and grace, and have pity on us and save us. For our eyes are lifted toward You, for You are a gracious and merciful God and King.

May our eyes witness Your return to Zion in compassion. Blessed are You, LORD, Who will restore His Divine Presence to Zion.

redemption. But placing it here makes sense insofar as there are days (Shabbat and Yom Tov) when the entire middle section is omitted, and it was seen as important that every day of the

יַעֲלֶה וְיָבוֹא / YA'ALEH VEYAVO

On Rosh Ḥodesh or Ḥol HaMo'ed, if one omitted *Ya'aleh VeYavo* and did not yet begin *Modim*, one should recite *Ya'aleh VeYavo* and continue. If one already began *Modim*, and did not yet complete the *Amida* by taking three steps back, one should return to the beginning of *Retzeh* and insert *Ya'aleh VeYavo* in its proper place. If one already completed the *Amida*, one must repeat the *Amida* (*OḤ* 422:1). If *Ya'aleh VeYavo* of Rosh Ḥodesh was omitted at *Ma'ariv*, no corrective action is necessary. It should be noted that according to R. Ḥayyim HaLevi Soloveitchik, if one omitted *Ya'aleh VeYavo* at *Shaḥarit* and is planning on reciting *Musaf* in the morning hours, one should not repeat the *Amida* for *Shaḥarit* (*Nefesh HaRav*, p.174).

הודאה

Bow during the first five words.

ˈ**מוֹדִים** אֲנַחְנוּ לָךְ, שָׁאַתָּה הוּא
יהוה אֱלֹהֵינוּ וֵאלֹהֵי
אֲבוֹתֵינוּ לְעוֹלָם וָעֶד. צוּר חַיֵּינוּ, מָגֵן
יִשְׁעֵנוּ, אַתָּה הוּא. לְדוֹר וָדוֹר נוֹדֶה לְּךָ
וּנְסַפֵּר תְּהִלָּתֶךָ, עַל חַיֵּינוּ הַמְּסוּרִים
בְּיָדֶךָ, וְעַל נִשְׁמוֹתֵינוּ הַפְּקוּדוֹת לָךְ,
וְעַל נִסֶּיךָ שֶׁבְּכָל יוֹם עִמָּנוּ, וְעַל
נִפְלְאוֹתֶיךָ וְטוֹבוֹתֶיךָ, שֶׁבְּכָל עֵת,
עֶרֶב וָבֹקֶר וְצָהֳרָיִם. הַטּוֹב, כִּי לֹא כָלוּ
רַחֲמֶיךָ וְהַמְרַחֵם, כִּי לֹא תַמּוּ חֲסָדֶיךָ,
מֵעוֹלָם קִוִּינוּ לָךְ.

During חזרת הש"ץ, the קהל says quietly:

ˈ**מוֹדִים** אֲנַחְנוּ לָךְ, שָׁאַתָּה
הוּא יהוה אֱלֹהֵינוּ
וֵאלֹהֵי אֲבוֹתֵינוּ, אֱלֹהֵי כָל
בָּשָׂר, יוֹצְרֵנוּ, יוֹצֵר בְּרֵאשִׁית.
בְּרָכוֹת וְהוֹדָאוֹת לְשִׁמְךָ הַגָּדוֹל
וְהַקָּדוֹשׁ, עַל שֶׁהֶחֱיִיתָנוּ
וְקִיַּמְתָּנוּ. כֵּן תְּחַיֵּנוּ וּתְקַיְּמֵנוּ,
וְתֶאֱסֹף גָּלֻיּוֹתֵינוּ לְחַצְרוֹת
קָדְשֶׁךָ, לִשְׁמֹר חֻקֶּיךָ וְלַעֲשׂוֹת
רְצוֹנֶךָ וּלְעָבְדְּךָ בְּלֵבָב שָׁלֵם,
עַל שֶׁאֲנַחְנוּ מוֹדִים לָךְ. בָּרוּךְ
אֵל הַהוֹדָאוֹת.

On חנוכה *and* פורים *continue with* עַל הַנִּסִּים *on the next page.*
On all other days continue with וְעַל כֻּלָּם *on page 130.*

---

year feature a petition for the restoration of the Temple service. Hence it was moved to this location, where it would never be omitted (Prof. Ezra Fleischer).

These two *berakhot* are linked by the Gemara *Megilla* 18a, which says that *avoda* (serving God) and *hoda'a* (thanking God) are one and the same. In other words, it is not enough to utter words of gratitude. Our sentiments must be accompanied by a sincere commitment to serve God (R. Elie Munk).

Whereas the preceding שְׁמַע קוֹלֵנוּ *berakha* asks God to hear our prayers, רְצֵה (which evokes the phrase וְנִרְצָה לוֹ in the context of sacrifice) asks God to regard our prayers as veritable sacrifices, literally עֲבוֹדָה שֶׁבַּלֵּב (a sacrificial service of the heart) which instead of offering an external object, becomes an act of self-sacrifice (R. Joseph B. Soloveitchik).

הוֹדָאָה / THANKSGIVING

מוֹדִים – *We thank You.* The Talmud (*Berakhot* 20b) declares that the essence of prayer is רַחֲמֵי (petitioning). This refers to the central section of the weekly *Amida*. Yet, that segment cannot stand alone. It must be preceded by praise and followed by gratitude. To that end, the final part of the *Amida* thanks God for His constant gifts, including the very fact of our continued existence, morning, noon, and night. It declares that God's gifts confirm His boundless compassion and unending kindness, without which we could not live for even a moment. Being reminded three times a day of our countless blessings, we are strengthened to withstand whatever difficulties we might encounter in the course of our daily lives.

נִסֶּיךָ ... נִפְלְאוֹתֶיךָ – *Your miracles... Your constant*

THANKSGIVING

Bow during the first seven words.

מוֹדִים WE THANK YOU, for You are the LORD our God and the God of our fathers for all eternity. You are the Rock of our life and Shield of our deliverance. From generation to generation we will thank You and recount Your praise for our lives that are in Your hands, for our souls that are given over to You, for Your miracles that are with us every day, and for Your constant wonders and favors, evening, morning and noon. You are good, for Your compassion does not cease, and You are compassionate, for Your kindness never ends. We have placed our hope in You forever and ever.

During the Leader's Repetition, the congregation says quietly:

מוֹדִים WE THANK YOU, for You are the LORD our God, the God of our fathers and God of all flesh. You are our Maker, the Maker of Creation. Blessings and thanks are due Your great and holy name for You have given us life and preserved us in life. May You continue to keep us in life and preserve us. Gather our exiles to the courtyards of Your Temple so that we may fulfill Your commandments and do Your will, serving You with a perfect heart, in the merit of our giving thanks to You now. Blessed is the God of all thanksgiving.

On Ḥanukka and Purim continue with "We thank you" on the next page.
On all other days continue with "For all this" on page 131.

---

wonders. The word נֵס, in the biblical context, always means pole or "banner" (Rashi). Miracles such as those of the Exodus are "banners" or "flags" which afford us the ability to reflect upon the entire natural order, so as to recognize their truly miraculous, God-given origin (R. Yonason Sacks).

מודים דרבנן – *The Rabbi's Thanksgiving*. In the rest of the repetition of the *Amida* it suffices to answer *Amen* to the *berakhot* recited by the Leader, but in this paragraph, we must ourselves articulate gratitude. The reason is that it is not appropriate to delegate to a third party our expression of appreciation for gifts received from a benefactor (Abudarham).

The Gemara (*Sota* 9a) records that various sages had their own preferred texts for this *berakha*. Rather than choosing among them, it was decided to combine all of them into one integrated format. Hence it is referred to as the מוֹדִים דְּרַבָּנָן (the Sages' Expressions of Gratitude) bringing together formulations by numerous sages (*Beit Yosef*).

עַל שֶׁאֲנַחְנוּ מוֹדִים לָךְ – *In the merit of our giving thanks to You now*. There are various translations and commentaries regarding this ambiguous phrase. Our translation follows that of the *Beit Yosef* to *Tur Oraḥ Ḥayyim* 127, and the *Ma'adanei Yom Tov* (found at *Rosh Berakhot* 3:20) (Prof. Mark Steiner).

בחנוכה ובפורים:

עַל הַנִּסִּים וְעַל הַפֻּרְקָן וְעַל הַגְּבוּרוֹת וְעַל הַתְּשׁוּעוֹת וְעַל הַמִּלְחָמוֹת
שֶׁעָשִׂיתָ לַאֲבוֹתֵינוּ בַּיָּמִים הָהֵם בַּזְּמַן הַזֶּה.

בחנוכה:

בִּימֵי מַתִּתְיָהוּ בֶּן יוֹחָנָן כֹּהֵן גָּדוֹל חַשְׁמוֹנַאי וּבָנָיו, כְּשֶׁעָמְדָה מַלְכוּת יָוָן הָרְשָׁעָה עַל עַמְּךָ יִשְׂרָאֵל לְהַשְׁכִּיחָם תּוֹרָתֶךָ וּלְהַעֲבִירָם מֵחֻקֵּי רְצוֹנֶךָ, וְאַתָּה בְּרַחֲמֶיךָ הָרַבִּים עָמַדְתָּ לָהֶם בְּעֵת צָרָתָם, רַבְתָּ אֶת רִיבָם, דַּנְתָּ אֶת דִּינָם, נָקַמְתָּ אֶת נִקְמָתָם, מָסַרְתָּ גִבּוֹרִים בְּיַד חַלָּשִׁים, וְרַבִּים בְּיַד מְעַטִּים, וּטְמֵאִים בְּיַד טְהוֹרִים, וּרְשָׁעִים בְּיַד צַדִּיקִים, וְזֵדִים בְּיַד עוֹסְקֵי תוֹרָתֶךָ, וּלְךָ עָשִׂיתָ שֵׁם גָּדוֹל וְקָדוֹשׁ בְּעוֹלָמֶךָ, וּלְעַמְּךָ יִשְׂרָאֵל עָשִׂיתָ תְּשׁוּעָה גְדוֹלָה וּפֻרְקָן כְּהַיּוֹם הַזֶּה. וְאַחַר כֵּן בָּאוּ בָנֶיךָ לִדְבִיר בֵּיתֶךָ, וּפִנּוּ אֶת הֵיכָלֶךָ, וְטִהֲרוּ אֶת מִקְדָּשֶׁךָ, וְהִדְלִיקוּ נֵרוֹת בְּחַצְרוֹת קָדְשֶׁךָ, וְקָבְעוּ שְׁמוֹנַת יְמֵי חֲנֻכָּה אֵלּוּ, לְהוֹדוֹת וּלְהַלֵּל לְשִׁמְךָ הַגָּדוֹל.

Continue with וְעַל כֻּלָּם.

בפורים:

בִּימֵי מָרְדְּכַי וְאֶסְתֵּר בְּשׁוּשַׁן הַבִּירָה, כְּשֶׁעָמַד עֲלֵיהֶם הָמָן הָרָשָׁע,
בִּקֵּשׁ לְהַשְׁמִיד לַהֲרֹג וּלְאַבֵּד אֶת־כָּל־הַיְּהוּדִים מִנַּעַר וְעַד־זָקֵן טַף אסתר ג
וְנָשִׁים בְּיוֹם אֶחָד, בִּשְׁלוֹשָׁה עָשָׂר לְחֹדֶשׁ שְׁנֵים־עָשָׂר, הוּא־חֹדֶשׁ
אֲדָר, וּשְׁלָלָם לָבוֹז: וְאַתָּה בְּרַחֲמֶיךָ הָרַבִּים הֵפַרְתָּ אֶת עֲצָתוֹ, וְקִלְקַלְתָּ
אֶת מַחֲשַׁבְתּוֹ, וַהֲשֵׁבוֹתָ לּוֹ גְּמוּלוֹ בְּרֹאשׁוֹ, וְתָלוּ אוֹתוֹ וְאֶת בָּנָיו עַל
הָעֵץ.

Continue with וְעַל כֻּלָּם.

עַל הַנִּסִּים / AL HANISSIM

If one forgot *Al HaNissim* and didn't yet recite Hashem's name at the conclusion of the *berakha*, one may recite *Al HaNissim*. If Hashem's name was already recited, one should continue and no corrective action is required. One may recite *Al HaNissim* in the *Elokai Netzor* paragraph (before the second *Yiheyu leratzon*) using the following alternate text: הָרַחֲמָן יַעֲשֶׂה לָנוּ נִסִּים וְנִפְלָאוֹת כְּשֵׁם שֶׁעָשִׂיתָ לַאֲבוֹתֵינוּ בַּיָּמִים הָהֵם בַּזְּמַן הַזֶּה. בִּימֵי וכו׳ (*OH* 682:1).

בִּימֵי מַתִּתְיָהוּ – *In the days of Mattathias.* This paragraph emphasizes the goal of the persecutors "to force them to forget Your Torah," and the perseverance of the "devotees of Your Torah." This also explains why we continue to light the *menora*: in the Second Temple the *menora* came to represent the power of Torah, both written and oral, and the centrality of its

On Ḥanukka and Purim add:

עַל הַנִּסִּים [WE THANK YOU] for the miracles, the deliverance, and the triumphant victories and salvation, as well as wars which You wrought for our ancestors in those days at this season.

On Ḥanukka:

IT HAPPENED in the days of Mattathias son of Johanan, the Hasmonean high priest, and his sons. Then the cruel Hellenist power rose up to force Your people Israel to forget Your Torah and transgress the commands of Your will. In that hour of their distress, You in Your great mercy rose to take up their cause and defend their rights. Meting out retribution You delivered the strong into the hand of the weak, the many into the hand of the few, the impure into the hand of the pure, the evil ones into the hand of the righteous, and the wicked into the hand of devotees of Your Torah. You thereby made for Yourself a great and holy name throughout Your world, as well as bringing about great deliverance and salvation for Your people Israel (known) to this day. Then Your children came to the Holy of Holies in Your house, cleared Your Temple, purified Your holy place, kindled lights in Your holy courts, and instituted these eight days of Ḥanukka to give thanks and sing praise to Your great name. *Continue with "For all this."*

On Purim:

IN THE DAYS of Mordechai and Esther, in Shushan the capital, when
Esther 3 the wicked Haman rose up against them, he sought to destroy, to kill, and to annihilate all the Jews, young and old, women and infants, in one day, the thirteenth day of the twelfth month, Adar, and plunder their possessions. In Your great mercy You nullified his counsel and subverted his designs, causing them to recoil on his own head so that he and his sons were hanged on the gallows.

Continue with "For all this."

sustained study. It was this Torah that gave the Jews light and wisdom in a dark and ignorant world. The Torah gave us the strength and the power to flourish as a separate nation with our own identity over the millennia. In our own time as well we can see how the study of Torah is a powerful force that ensures a commitment to Jewish life (R. Yaakov Ariel).

וְעַל כֻּלָּם יִתְבָּרַךְ וְיִתְרוֹמַם שִׁמְךָ מַלְכֵּנוּ תָּמִיד לְעוֹלָם וָעֶד.

בעשרת ימי תשובה: וּכְתֹב לְחַיִּים טוֹבִים כָּל בְּנֵי בְרִיתֶךָ.

(*If forgotten, no corrective action is necessary.*)

וְכֹל הַחַיִּים יוֹדְוּךָ סֶּלָה, וִיהַלְלוּ אֶת שִׁמְךָ בֶּאֱמֶת, הָאֵל יְשׁוּעָתֵנוּ וְעֶזְרָתֵנוּ סֶלָה. ׳בָּרוּךְ אַתָּה יהוה, הַטּוֹב שִׁמְךָ וּלְךָ נָאֶה לְהוֹדוֹת.

ברכת כהנים

The following is said by the שליח ציבור *during* חזרת הש״ץ *except in a* בית אבל *house and on* תשעה באב.

אֱלֹהֵינוּ וֵאלֹהֵי אֲבוֹתֵינוּ, בָּרְכֵנוּ בַּבְּרָכָה הַמְשֻׁלֶּשֶׁת, בַּתּוֹרָה, הַכְּתוּבָה עַל יְדֵי מֹשֶׁה עַבְדֶּךָ, הָאֲמוּרָה מִפִּי אַהֲרֹן וּבָנָיו כֹּהֲנִים עַם קְדוֹשֶׁיךָ, כָּאָמוּר

במדבר ו

יְבָרֶכְךָ יהוה וְיִשְׁמְרֶךָ: קהל: כֵּן יְהִי רָצוֹן

יָאֵר יהוה פָּנָיו אֵלֶיךָ וִיחֻנֶּךָּ: קהל: כֵּן יְהִי רָצוֹן

יִשָּׂא יהוה פָּנָיו אֵלֶיךָ וְיָשֵׂם לְךָ שָׁלוֹם: קהל: כֵּן יְהִי רָצוֹן

שלום

שִׂים שָׁלוֹם טוֹבָה וּבְרָכָה, חֵן וָחֶסֶד וְרַחֲמִים עָלֵינוּ וְעַל כָּל יִשְׂרָאֵל עַמֶּךָ. בָּרְכֵנוּ אָבִינוּ כֻּלָּנוּ כְּאֶחָד בְּאוֹר פָּנֶיךָ,

בִּרְכַּת כֹּהֲנִים / THE PRIESTLY BLESSING

בַּבְּרָכָה הַמְשֻׁלֶּשֶׁת, בַּתּוֹרָה, הַכְּתוּבָה – *With the threefold blessing, in the Torah, written.* This phrase is correctly read with a brief pause after the word הַמְשֻׁלֶּשֶׁת (threefold), as well as a pause after the word בַּתּוֹרָה (in the Torah) The first pause, strongly recommended by R. Joseph B. Soloveitchik, aims to prevent the misunderstanding that the blessing appears three times in the Torah. In fact, it is a threefold blessing because it consists of three verses. As to the second pause, its presence or absence determines the meaning of the continuation. Without the pause, הַכְּתוּבָה must be understood as modifying תּוֹרָה, and the meaning would have to be that the blessing is found in the Torah that was written by Moses and is said by Aaron and his sons. However, the fact that this passage is about בִּרְכַּת כֹּהֲנִים should lead us to expect characterizations of the blessing, not of the Torah, and on stylistic grounds It appears highly likely that הַכְּתוּבָה and הָאֲמוּרָה are parallel and refer to the same noun. Thus, the blessing was (a) written by Moses Your servant, and (b) said by Aaron and his descendants. To yield this meaning, the sentence must be read with a pause after בַּתּוֹרָה (Prof. David Berger).

יְבָרֶכְךָ – *Bless you.* Rashi explains that the first verse refers to material blessings, asking God

For all this, our King, may Your name be blessed and exalted continually, forever and ever.

Between Rosh HaShana & Yom Kippur: Inscribe all the children of Your covenant for a life of goodness. (*If forgotten, no corrective action is necessary.*)

All that lives will give thanks to You forever and praise Your name in truth, God, our salvation and our help forever. ˚Blessed are You, Lord, for Your name is "The Good One" and it is appropriate to give thanks to You.

THE PRIESTLY BLESSING

The following is said by the Leader during the Repetition of the Amida, except in a shiva house and on Tisha B'Av.

אֱלֹהֵינוּ OUR GOD, God of our fathers, bless us with the threefold blessing, in the Torah, written by Your servant Moses and spoken by Aaron and his descendants, being priests, Your holy people, as it is said:

Num. 6 "May the Lord bless you and keep you." *Cong:* May this be His will.
"May the Lord make His countenance shine upon you and be gracious to you." *Cong:* May this be His will.
"May the Lord lift up His countenance toward you and grant you peace." *Cong:* May this be His will.

PEACE

שִׂים שָׁלוֹם GRANT PEACE with welfare and blessing, and grace with loving-kindness and mercy on us and all Israel Your people. Bless us, our Father, all together, with the light of Your presence. For in

---

to provide them, and then יִשְׁמְרֶךָ (safeguard them) once given. The second verse refers to the spiritual blessing of Torah knowledge, as the *Midrash Raba* states "the 'light of God's countenance' is the light of Torah," for the verse states תּוֹרָה אוֹר (Torah is light), that is, it brings חֵן (good will and respect) to those who study it. And as Seforno explains, "May your eyes be illuminated by the light of His face to see wonders in His Torah and His works, after you obtain your needs through His first blessing."

The third verse asks God to combine the preceding material and spiritual blessing into a seamless, harmonious and serene whole. This ascending order and increasing surge of blessing is reflected in the language and rhythm of the verses, growing from three, to five, then seven words, spreading the blessing out like an ever-flowing spring (Prof. Nehama Leibowitz).

שָׁלוֹם / PEACE

שִׂים שָׁלוֹם – *Grant peace.* The reason for concluding all of our prayers with a request for

כִּי בְאוֹר פָּנֶיךָ נָתַתָּ לָּנוּ יהוה אֱלֹהֵינוּ, תּוֹרַת חַיִּים וְאַהֲבַת חֶסֶד, וּצְדָקָה וּבְרָכָה וְרַחֲמִים וְחַיִּים וְשָׁלוֹם. וְטוֹב בְּעֵינֶיךָ לְבָרֵךְ אֶת עַמְּךָ יִשְׂרָאֵל, בְּכָל עֵת וּבְכָל שָׁעָה בִּשְׁלוֹמֶךָ.

בעשרת ימי תשובה: בְּסֵפֶר חַיִּים, בְּרָכָה וְשָׁלוֹם, וּפַרְנָסָה טוֹבָה, נִזָּכֵר וְנִכָּתֵב לְפָנֶיךָ, אֲנַחְנוּ וְכָל עַמְּךָ בֵּית יִשְׂרָאֵל, לְחַיִּים טוֹבִים וּלְשָׁלוֹם.*

בָּרוּךְ אַתָּה יהוה, הַמְבָרֵךְ אֶת עַמּוֹ יִשְׂרָאֵל בַּשָּׁלוֹם.

**During the* עשרת ימי תשובה*, many end the blessing:*

בָּרוּךְ אַתָּה יהוה, עוֹשֶׂה הַשָּׁלוֹם.

At this point when the שליח ציבור *repeats the* עמידה *he should complete the repetition by saying the verse beginning "*יִהְיוּ לְרָצוֹן*" out loud.*

תהלים יט יִהְיוּ לְרָצוֹן אִמְרֵי־פִי וְהֶגְיוֹן לִבִּי לְפָנֶיךָ, יהוה צוּרִי וְגֹאֲלִי:

ברכות יז. **אֱלֹהַי**, נְצֹר לְשׁוֹנִי מֵרָע וּשְׂפָתַי מִדַּבֵּר מִרְמָה, וְלִמְקַלְלַי נַפְשִׁי תִדֹּם, וְנַפְשִׁי כֶּעָפָר לַכֹּל תִּהְיֶה. פְּתַח לִבִּי בְּתוֹרָתֶךָ, וּבְמִצְוֹתֶיךָ תִּרְדֹּף נַפְשִׁי. וְכָל הַחוֹשְׁבִים עָלַי רָעָה, מְהֵרָה הָפֵר עֲצָתָם וְקַלְקֵל מַחֲשַׁבְתָּם. עֲשֵׂה לְמַעַן שְׁמֶךָ, עֲשֵׂה לְמַעַן יְמִינֶךָ,

peace is that our prayers correspond to the sacrifices, and at the conclusion of every sacrificial ritual the priests would bless the people, as it says, "Aaron raised his hands toward the people, and blessed them" (Lev. 9:22) (Abudarham). So too, it is appropriate to immediately follow the closing but brief priestly blessing of peace with this more extended prayer for peace, goodness, and blessing.

One should conclude one's prayer by asking for peace, for nothing portends blessing more than peace. Peace is the precious jewel that binds Jews together. When saying this prayer one should have in mind that there should be no dissension, envy or hatred among us, but only a love to bind us together, in brotherhood and fellowship. One should also have in mind the fulfillment of the obligation of "you shall love your fellow as yourself." To that end one should also pray to be spared feelings of anger, for where there is antagonism there can be no peace (*Ya'arot Devash*).

אֱלֹהַי, נְצֹר – *My God, guard my tongue*. This concluding paragraph by Mar b. Ravina is one of a number of similar petitions by various sages recorded in *Berakhot* 16b–17a. It asks God to help us cultivate a life of quiet moral virtue, not distracted or dismayed by the contrary behaviors of our fellows. This is a fine example of a prayer that serves to educate and sensitize us in the right path of life.

In the rest of the *Amida* we do not pray for ourselves but rather for all of Israel, by asking that all Jews be completely whole and at one with God (as the Gemara *Berakhot* 85a says, "that they direct their hearts to their Father in heaven"). Here, however, it is proper to pray for one's own needs (Vilna Gaon).

that light, LORD our God, You have given us the Torah of life, and love of kindness with justice, blessing, tenderness, life and peace. May it be good in Your eyes to bless Your people Israel at all times, at every hour, with Your peace.

Between Rosh HaShana & Yom Kippur: In the book of life and blessing, peace and prosperity, may we and all the house of Israel Your people be remembered before You and inscribed for a life of goodness and peace.*

Blessed are You, LORD, Who blesses His people Israel with peace.

**Between Rosh HaShana and Yom Kippur many end the blessing:*
Blessed are You, LORD, Who makes peace.

At this point when the Leader repeats the Amida he should complete the repetition by saying the verse beginning "May the words" out loud.

Ps. 19 MAY THE WORDS of my mouth and the meditation of my heart be acceptable before You, LORD, my Rock and my Redeemer.

Berakhot 17a אֱלֹהַי MY GOD, guard my tongue from evil, and my lips from speaking deceit. Let my soul be silent to those who curse me; let my soul be humble toward everyone like the dust. Open my heart to Your Torah that my soul may follow Your commandments. As for all those who contemplate evil against me, speedily nullify their plans and spoil their schemes. Do so for the sake of Your name. Do so for Your right hand.

נְצֹר לְשׁוֹנִי מֵרָע וּשְׂפָתַי מִדַּבֵּר מִרְמָה – *Guard my tongue from evil, and my lips from speaking deceit.* These two phrases refer to different consequences of evil speech: (a) The tongue that is within our mouth can harm our own moral and spiritual fiber, while (b) the lips that

INTERRUPTIONS DURING ELOKAI NETZOR

During *Elokai Netzor*, one may respond to the following: *Barekhu* (by the Leader or by someone receiving an *aliya*); *Kedusha* (just the two verses "*Kadosh kadosh*" and "*Barukh kevod*"); *Amen* to *da'amiran be'alema*, *HaKel HaKadosh* and *Shome'a tefilla* (*OḤ* 122:1 and *MB* 122:1). If one completed the paragraph but is waiting for the person behind him to take three steps back, all responses are permissible (*MB* 122:4). If one is still reciting the *Amida* and senses that the congregation is short one person for the necessary quorum to begin the repetition, or is waiting for the rabbi, the principle of *tirḥa detzibura* (improper imposition on the congregation) permits that individual to abbreviate the *Amida* as follows: Say the final blessing (i.e., *Hamevarekh et amo*), then omit the *Elokai Netzor* paragraph, recite the verse *yiheyu leratzon*, then take three steps back.

עֲשֵׂה לְמַעַן קְדֻשָּׁתֶךָ, עֲשֵׂה לְמַעַן תּוֹרָתֶךָ. לְמַעַן יֵחָלְצוּן יְדִידֶיךָ, תהלים ס
הוֹשִׁיעָה יְמִינְךָ וַעֲנֵנִי: יִהְיוּ לְרָצוֹן אִמְרֵי־פִי וְהֶגְיוֹן לִבִּי לְפָנֶיךָ, יהוה תהלים יט
צוּרִי וְגוֹאֲלִי:

Bow, take three steps back, then bow, first left, then right, then center, while saying:

עֹשֶׂה שָׁלוֹם/ בעשרת ימי תשובה: הַשָּׁלוֹם/ בִּמְרוֹמָיו, הוּא יַעֲשֶׂה שָׁלוֹם
עָלֵינוּ, וְעַל כָּל יִשְׂרָאֵל, וְאִמְרוּ אָמֵן.

יְהִי רָצוֹן מִלְּפָנֶיךָ יהוה אֱלֹהֵינוּ וֵאלֹהֵי אֲבוֹתֵינוּ, שֶׁיִּבָּנֶה בֵּית הַמִּקְדָּשׁ
בִּמְהֵרָה בְיָמֵינוּ, וְתֵן חֶלְקֵנוּ בְּתוֹרָתֶךָ, וְשָׁם נַעֲבָדְךָ בְּיִרְאָה כִּימֵי
עוֹלָם וּכְשָׁנִים קַדְמֹנִיּוֹת. וְעָרְבָה לַיהוה מִנְחַת יְהוּדָה וִירוּשָׁלָםִ כִּימֵי עוֹלָם מלאכי ג
וּכְשָׁנִים קַדְמֹנִיּוֹת:

When praying with a מנין*, the* עמידה *is repeated aloud by the* שליח ציבור*.*

On days when תחנון *is said (see page 144), start* תחנון *on page 152.*
On Mondays and Thursdays start תחנון *on page 144.*
On fast days (except תשעה באב*) most congregations say* סליחות *on page 960 before* אבינו מלכנו *on page 138.*
During the עשרת ימי תשובה *(but not on* ערב יום כפור*, unless it falls on Friday), say* אבינו מלכנו *on page 138.*
On ראש חודש*,* חנוכה*,* חול המועד*,* יום העצמאות *and* יום ירושלים*, say* הלל *on page 766.*
On other days when תחנון *is not said (see page 144), the* שליח ציבור *says* חצי קדיש *on page 156.*

---

face the external world can by mere utterance cause inestimable harm to others (R. Avraham Yitzḥak HaKohen Kook).

Similarly, Rambam (Sefer HaMitzvot Negative #317) explains that the Torah (Lev. 19:14) forbids us to curse the deaf – because the very act of cursing another harms ourselves and stains our own character by making it more likely that we will ourselves be affected by debilitating emotions such as revenge and anger towards those whom we curse.

וְנַפְשִׁי כֶּעָפָר לַכֹּל תִּהְיֶה – *Let my soul be humble toward everyone like the dust* (previous page). As noted, these words were composed by the prominent sage Mar b. Ravina. It reflects his awareness, and concern as a leader, that even a *tzaddik* can to succumb to pride when elevated to a position of prominence, leading one to transgression. This lesson is taught by the Torah when it says that God blessed Abraham בַּכֹּל. The *Midrash* explains this to mean that even though he was greatly admired and honored by his contemporaries, Abraham resisted every impulse to consider himself superior to them (hence בַּכֹּל means "in regard to all others"). In this prayer we ask God to help us see ourselves "like dust" in relation to others, no matter our social standing or material and spiritual success (*Netziv*).

עֹשֶׂה שָׁלוֹם בִּמְרוֹמָיו – *He Who makes peace in His heights*. This refers to God's unique ability to reconcile the opposing principles of truth and peace. *Midrash Raba* 8:5 records that when man was about to be created the angel of truth opposed God's intention on the grounds that

Ps. 60 Do so for Your holiness. Do so for Your Torah, that Your loved ones may
Ps. 19 be delivered. Save with Your right hand, and answer me. May the words of my mouth and the meditation of my heart be acceptable before You, Lord, my Rock and my Redeemer.

Bow, take three steps back, then bow, first left, then right, then center, while saying:

He Who makes peace in His heights, may He create peace for us and for all Israel. Amen.

יְהִי רָצוֹן May it be Your will, Lord our God and God of our fathers, that the Temple be rebuilt speedily in our days and may You grant our portion in Your Torah. We will serve You there in reverence as in the days of antiquity and in
Mal. 3 years gone by. "And may the offering of Judah and Jerusalem be pleasant to the Lord as in the days of antiquity and in years gone by."

When praying with a minyan, the Amida is repeated aloud by the Leader.

On days when Taḥanun is said (see page 145), start Taḥanun on page 153.
On Mondays and Thursdays start Taḥanun on page 145.

On fast days (except Tisha B'Av) most congregations say Seliḥot on page 961 before Avinu Malkenu on page 139.

Between Rosh HaShana and Yom Kippur (but not on Erev Yom Kippur, unless it falls on Friday), say Avinu Malkenu on page 139.

On Rosh Ḥodesh, Ḥanukka, Ḥol HaMo'ed, Yom HaAtzma'ut and Yom Yerushalayim, say Hallel on page 767.

On other days when Taḥanun is not said (see page 145), the Leader says Half Kaddish on page 157.

---

man would violate the truth, while the angel of peace was in favor, for man would perform acts of charity. In response God cast the angel of truth to the ground, and proceeded to create man. There is a deeper meaning to this *midrash*, for in fact none of the angels opposed man's creation. Rather they foresaw that by his very nature man could not be both entirely truthful and completely peace-loving, for an uncompromising adherence to the truth generally leads to conflict between competing views of the truth. Faced with this argument, God found a way to reconcile the opposites. He commanded man that in most instances he should seek peace and harmony, even if in so doing his version of the truth would be compromised, while God also told man that in a minority of cases he should insist on his view of the truth, even if it would undermine peace and harmony. The question then arises: how can we in any given situation know when to favor peace, and when to insist on our view? The answer is always to be found in the Torah which epitomizes truth, and which (as the *Midrash* goes on to say) God brought down to earth. By mastering it through careful and sustained study we can learn the proper balance between truth and peace, when to invoke the one, and when the other. This is the meaning of עֹשֶׂה שָׁלוֹם בִּמְרוֹמָיו, "He Who makes peace in His heights, may He create peace for us and for all Israel" (R. Joseph B. Soloveitchik).

וידוי

Some congregations say וידוי *before reciting* תחנון*.*
It is said while standing, and is omitted when תחנון *is omitted.*

אֱלֹהֵינוּ וֵאלֹהֵי אֲבוֹתֵינוּ, תָּבוֹא לְפָנֶיךָ תְּפִלָּתֵנוּ, וְאַל תִּתְעַלַּם מִתְּחִנָּתֵנוּ, שֶׁאֵין אֲנַחְנוּ עַזֵּי פָנִים וּקְשֵׁי עֹרֶף לוֹמַר לְפָנֶיךָ, יהוה אֱלֹהֵינוּ וֵאלֹהֵי אֲבוֹתֵינוּ, צַדִּיקִים אֲנַחְנוּ וְלֹא חָטָאנוּ, אֲבָל אֲנַחְנוּ וַאֲבוֹתֵינוּ חָטָאנוּ.

At each expression, strike the chest on the left side:

אָשַׁמְנוּ, בָּגַדְנוּ, גָּזַלְנוּ, דִּבַּרְנוּ דֹפִי, הֶעֱוִינוּ, וְהִרְשַׁעְנוּ, זַדְנוּ, חָמַסְנוּ, טָפַלְנוּ שֶׁקֶר, יָעַצְנוּ רָע, כִּזַּבְנוּ, לַצְנוּ, מָרַדְנוּ, נִאַצְנוּ, סָרַרְנוּ, עָוִינוּ, פָּשַׁעְנוּ, צָרַרְנוּ, קִשִּׁינוּ עֹרֶף, רָשַׁעְנוּ, שִׁחַתְנוּ, תִּעַבְנוּ, תָּעִינוּ, תִּעְתָּעְנוּ.

סַרְנוּ מִמִּצְוֹתֶיךָ וּמִמִּשְׁפָּטֶיךָ הַטּוֹבִים, וְלֹא שָׁוָה לָנוּ. וְאַתָּה צַדִּיק עַל כָּל־הַבָּא נחמיה ט
עָלֵינוּ, כִּי־אֱמֶת עָשִׂיתָ, וַאֲנַחְנוּ הִרְשָׁעְנוּ:

When praying without a מנין *continue with* וְהוּא רַחוּם *on page 144.*

י״ג מדות

אֵל אֶרֶךְ אַפַּיִם אַתָּה, וּבַעַל הָרַחֲמִים נִקְרֵאתָ, וְדֶרֶךְ תְּשׁוּבָה הוֹרֵיתָ. גְּדֻלַּת רַחֲמֶיךָ וַחֲסָדֶיךָ, תִּזְכֹּר הַיּוֹם וּבְכָל יוֹם לְזֶרַע יְדִידֶיךָ. תֵּפֶן אֵלֵינוּ בְּרַחֲמִים, כִּי אַתָּה הוּא בַּעַל הָרַחֲמִים. בְּתַחֲנוּן וּבִתְפִלָּה פָּנֶיךָ נְקַדֵּם, כְּהוֹדַעְתָּ לֶעָנָו מִקֶּדֶם. מֵחֲרוֹן אַפְּךָ שׁוּב, כְּמוֹ בְּתוֹרָתְךָ כָּתוּב. וּבְצֵל כְּנָפֶיךָ נֶחֱסֶה וְנִתְלוֹנָן, כְּיוֹם וַיֵּרֶד יהוה בֶּעָנָן. ‹ תַּעֲבֹר עַל פֶּשַׁע וְתִמְחֶה אָשָׁם, כְּיוֹם וַיִּתְיַצֵּב עִמּוֹ שָׁם. תַּאֲזִין שַׁוְעָתֵנוּ וְתַקְשִׁיב מֶנּוּ מַאֲמָר, כְּיוֹם וַיִּקְרָא בְשֵׁם יהוה, וְשָׁם נֶאֱמַר:

All say aloud:

וַיַּעֲבֹר יהוה עַל־פָּנָיו וַיִּקְרָא שמות לד

יהוה, יהוה, אֵל רַחוּם וְחַנּוּן, אֶרֶךְ אַפַּיִם וְרַב־חֶסֶד וֶאֱמֶת: נֹצֵר חֶסֶד לָאֲלָפִים, נֹשֵׂא עָוֹן וָפֶשַׁע וְחַטָּאָה, וְנַקֵּה: וְסָלַחְתָּ לַעֲוֹנֵנוּ וּלְחַטָּאתֵנוּ, וּנְחַלְתָּנוּ: סְלַח לָנוּ אָבִינוּ כִּי חָטָאנוּ, מְחַל לָנוּ מַלְכֵּנוּ כִּי פָשָׁעְנוּ, כִּי־אַתָּה אֲדֹנָי טוֹב וְסַלָּח וְרַב־חֶסֶד לְכָל־קֹרְאֶיךָ: תהלים פו

On Mondays and Thursdays continue with וְהוּא רַחוּם *on page 144; on other days with* וַיֹּאמֶר דָּוִד *on page 152.*

VIDUY

Some congregations say Viduy before reciting Taḥanun.
It is said while standing, and is omitted when Taḥanun is omitted.

אֱלֹהֵינוּ OUR GOD and God of our fathers, Let our prayer come before you, and do not ignore our plea, for we are not so brazen or obstinate as to say before You, Lord our God and God of our fathers, "Righteous are we and we have not sinned;" but rather, "We and our fathers have sinned."

At each expression, strike the chest on the left side:

אָשַׁמְנוּ WE HAVE BEEN GUILTY, we have betrayed, we have stolen, we have spoken ill, we have been perverse, we have been wicked, we have been wanton, we have been violent, we have dealt in lies, we have advised evil, we have deceived, we have mocked, we have rebelled, we have cast aside, we have strayed, we have done wrong, we have transgressed, we have oppressed, we have been obstinate, we have been wicked, we have destroyed, we have been disgusting, and misled, and had led others astray.

Neh. 9 We have gone aside from Your commandments and from Your good laws, and it was not worth our while, for You are righteous in all that has happened to us – for You have acted in truth, and we have been wicked.

When praying without a minyan continue with "But He, the Compassionate One" on page 145.

THIRTEEN ATTRIBUTES OF DIVINE COMPASSION

אֵל אֶרֶךְ YOU ARE A GOD full of forbearance, and You have been called the Master of mercy, and You have taught the way of repentance: now remember today and every day the greatness of Your mercy and kindness for the children of You beloved one. Turn to us in mercy, for You are the Master of mercy. We come to meet You with pleading and prayer, as You showed a humble one long ago. From Your burning rage, turn back, as is written in Your Torah. And in the shade of Your wings we shall take cover and rest, as on the day when the Lord came down in a cloud. Pass over our transgressions and wipe away our guilt, as on the day when He stood with him [Moses] there. Hear our plea and listen to our speech, as on the day when He cried out the name of the Lord – and there it is said:

All say aloud:

Ex. 34 וַיַּעֲבֹר THE LORD passed by before him and pronounced:

THE LORD, the Lord, God of mercy and grace, full of forbearance and much kindness and truth, Who guards His kindness through thousands of generations, bearing with wrongs and transgressions and sins, and absolving – forgive us our wrongs and our sins, and bring us into Your inheritance. Forgive us, our Father, for
Ps. 86 we have sinned; pardon us, our King, for we have transgressed. Indeed, You, my Master, are good and forgiving, and of bountiful loving-kindness to all who call upon You.

On Mondays and Thursdays continue with "But He, the Compassionate One" on page 145;
on other days with "David said" on page 153.

אבינו מלכנו

On fast days (except תשעה באב*) most congregations say* סליחות *on page 960 before* אבינו מלכנו.
During the עשרת ימי תשובה *(but not on* ערב יום כיפור, *unless it falls on Friday), say* אבינו מלכנו *below.*

The ארון קודש *is opened.*

אָבִינוּ מַלְכֵּנוּ, חָטָאנוּ לְפָנֶיךָ.

אָבִינוּ מַלְכֵּנוּ, אֵין לָנוּ מֶלֶךְ אֶלָּא אָתָּה.

אָבִינוּ מַלְכֵּנוּ, עֲשֵׂה עִמָּנוּ לְמַעַן שְׁמֶךָ.

אָבִינוּ מַלְכֵּנוּ, בָּרֵךְ/ בעשרת ימי תשובה: חַדֵּשׁ/ עָלֵינוּ שָׁנָה טוֹבָה.

אָבִינוּ מַלְכֵּנוּ, בַּטֵּל מֵעָלֵינוּ כָּל גְּזֵרוֹת קָשׁוֹת.

אָבִינוּ מַלְכֵּנוּ, בַּטֵּל מַחְשְׁבוֹת שׂוֹנְאֵינוּ.

אָבִינוּ מַלְכֵּנוּ, הָפֵר עֲצַת אוֹיְבֵינוּ.

אָבִינוּ מַלְכֵּנוּ, כַּלֵּה כָּל צַר וּמַשְׂטִין מֵעָלֵינוּ.

אָבִינוּ מַלְכֵּנוּ, סְתֹם פִּיּוֹת מַשְׂטִינֵנוּ וּמְקַטְרְגֵנוּ.

אָבִינוּ מַלְכֵּנוּ, כַּלֵּה דֶּבֶר וְחֶרֶב וְרָעָב וּשְׁבִי וּמַשְׁחִית וְעָוֹן וּשְׁמַד מִבְּנֵי בְרִיתֶךָ.

אָבִינוּ מַלְכֵּנוּ, מְנַע מַגֵּפָה מִנַּחֲלָתֶךָ.

אָבִינוּ מַלְכֵּנוּ, סְלַח וּמְחַל לְכָל עֲוֹנוֹתֵינוּ.

אָבִינוּ מַלְכֵּנוּ, מְחֵה וְהַעֲבֵר פְּשָׁעֵינוּ וְחַטֹּאתֵינוּ מִנֶּגֶד עֵינֶיךָ.

אָבִינוּ מַלְכֵּנוּ, מְחֹק בְּרַחֲמֶיךָ הָרַבִּים כָּל שִׁטְרֵי חוֹבוֹתֵינוּ.

אָבִינוּ מַלְכֵּנוּ / AVINU MALKENU
The Gemara (*Ta'anit* 25b) attributes the core of this prayer to R. Akiva who composed and recited several stanzas at a time of intense drought, and was immediately answered. The opening phrase in each line conveys our

AVINU MALKENU

On fast days (except Tisha B'Av) most congregations say Seliḥot on page 961 before Avinu Malkenu. Between Rosh HaShana and Yom Kippur (but not on Erev Yom Kippur, unless it falls on Friday), say Avinu Malkenu below.

The Ark is opened.

אָבִינוּ מַלְכֵּנוּ OUR FATHER, our King, we have sinned in Your presence.

OUR FATHER, our King, we have no other king but You.

OUR FATHER, our King, act kindly with us for Your name's sake.

OUR FATHER, our King, /*bless / for us a good year.

/ **Between Rosh HaShana & Yom Kippur:* renew/

OUR FATHER, our King, cancel all harsh edicts against us.

OUR FATHER, our King, cancel the plots of our enemies.

OUR FATHER, our King, overturn the plans of our foes.

OUR FATHER, our King, put an end to every oppressor, antagonist and accuser who threatens us.

OUR FATHER, our King, cover the mouths of those who accuse and denounce us.

OUR FATHER, our King, put an end to the epidemics and violence and hunger and captivity and destruction and iniquity and persecution that threaten the children of Your covenant.

OUR FATHER, our King, keep contagion away from Your inheritance.

OUR FATHER, our King, pardon and forgive all our wrongs.

OUR FATHER, our King, wipe out and sweep away our transgressions and sins from before Your eyes.

OUR FATHER, our King, erase, by your great mercy, all the accounts of our sins.

---

dual relationship to God: He is our loving and merciful Father, but He is also the all-powerful King Who sits in judgment and punishes us when necessary.

The following nine sentences are said responsively, first by the שליח ציבור*, then by the* קהל*:*

אָבִינוּ מַלְכֵּנוּ, הַחֲזִירֵנוּ בִּתְשׁוּבָה שְׁלֵמָה לְפָנֶיךָ.

אָבִינוּ מַלְכֵּנוּ, שְׁלַח רְפוּאָה שְׁלֵמָה לְחוֹלֵי עַמֶּךָ.

אָבִינוּ מַלְכֵּנוּ, קְרַע רֹעַ גְּזַר דִּינֵנוּ.

אָבִינוּ מַלְכֵּנוּ, זָכְרֵנוּ בְּזִכָּרוֹן טוֹב לְפָנֶיךָ.

During the עשרת ימי תשובה*:*

אָבִינוּ מַלְכֵּנוּ, כָּתְבֵנוּ בְּסֵפֶר חַיִּים טוֹבִים.

אָבִינוּ מַלְכֵּנוּ, כָּתְבֵנוּ בְּסֵפֶר גְּאֻלָּה וִישׁוּעָה.

אָבִינוּ מַלְכֵּנוּ, כָּתְבֵנוּ בְּסֵפֶר פַּרְנָסָה וְכַלְכָּלָה.

אָבִינוּ מַלְכֵּנוּ, כָּתְבֵנוּ בְּסֵפֶר זְכֻיּוֹת.

אָבִינוּ מַלְכֵּנוּ, כָּתְבֵנוּ בְּסֵפֶר סְלִיחָה וּמְחִילָה.

On Fast Days:

אָבִינוּ מַלְכֵּנוּ, זָכְרֵנוּ לְחַיִּים טוֹבִים.

אָבִינוּ מַלְכֵּנוּ, זָכְרֵנוּ לִגְאֻלָּה וִישׁוּעָה.

אָבִינוּ מַלְכֵּנוּ, זָכְרֵנוּ לְפַרְנָסָה וְכַלְכָּלָה.

אָבִינוּ מַלְכֵּנוּ, זָכְרֵנוּ לִזְכֻיּוֹת.

אָבִינוּ מַלְכֵּנוּ, זָכְרֵנוּ לִסְלִיחָה וּמְחִילָה.

End of responsive reading.

אָבִינוּ מַלְכֵּנוּ, הַצְמַח לָנוּ יְשׁוּעָה בְּקָרוֹב.

אָבִינוּ מַלְכֵּנוּ, הָרֵם קֶרֶן יִשְׂרָאֵל עַמֶּךָ.

אָבִינוּ מַלְכֵּנוּ, הָרֵם קֶרֶן מְשִׁיחֶךָ.

אָבִינוּ מַלְכֵּנוּ, מַלֵּא יָדֵינוּ מִבִּרְכוֹתֶיךָ.

The following nine sentences are said responsively, first by the Leader, then by the congregation:

OUR FATHER, our King, bring us back in complete repentance before You.

OUR FATHER, our King, send complete recovery to those ill among Your people.

OUR FATHER, our King, tear up our sentence.

OUR FATHER, our King, remember us with a good remembrance before You.

Between Rosh HaShana and Yom Kippur:

OUR FATHER, our King, write us in the book of good life.

OUR FATHER, our King, write us in the book of redemption and salvation.

OUR FATHER, our King, write us in the book of livelihood and sustenance.

OUR FATHER, our King, write us in the book of merits.

OUR FATHER, our King, write us in the book of forgiveness and pardon.

On Fast Days:

OUR FATHER, our King, remember us for good life.

OUR FATHER, our King, remember us for redemption and salvation.

OUR FATHER, our King, remember us for livelihood and sustenance.

OUR FATHER, our King, remember us for merit.

OUR FATHER, our King, remember us for forgiveness and pardon.

End of responsive reading.

OUR FATHER, our King, make salvation sprout forth for us soon.

OUR FATHER, our King, raise the proud horn of Your people, Israel.

OUR FATHER, our King, raise the proud horn of Your Messiah.

OUR FATHER, our King, fill our hands with Your blessings.

אָבִינוּ מַלְכֵּנוּ, מַלֵּא אֲסָמֵינוּ שָׂבָע.

אָבִינוּ מַלְכֵּנוּ, שְׁמַע קוֹלֵנוּ, חוּס וְרַחֵם עָלֵינוּ.

אָבִינוּ מַלְכֵּנוּ, קַבֵּל בְּרַחֲמִים וּבְרָצוֹן אֶת תְּפִלָּתֵנוּ.

אָבִינוּ מַלְכֵּנוּ, פְּתַח שַׁעֲרֵי שָׁמַיִם לִתְפִלָּתֵנוּ.

אָבִינוּ מַלְכֵּנוּ, זְכֹר (נ״א זָכוּר) כִּי עָפָר אֲנָחְנוּ.

אָבִינוּ מַלְכֵּנוּ, נָא אַל תְּשִׁיבֵנוּ רֵיקָם מִלְּפָנֶיךָ.

אָבִינוּ מַלְכֵּנוּ, תְּהֵא הַשָּׁעָה הַזֹּאת שְׁעַת (נ״א שַׁעַת) רַחֲמִים וְעֵת רָצוֹן מִלְּפָנֶיךָ.

אָבִינוּ מַלְכֵּנוּ, חֲמֹל עָלֵינוּ וְעַל עוֹלָלֵינוּ וְטַפֵּנוּ.

אָבִינוּ מַלְכֵּנוּ, עֲשֵׂה לְמַעַן הֲרוּגִים עַל שֵׁם קָדְשֶׁךָ.

אָבִינוּ מַלְכֵּנוּ, עֲשֵׂה לְמַעַן טְבוּחִים עַל יִחוּדֶךָ.

אָבִינוּ מַלְכֵּנוּ, עֲשֵׂה לְמַעַן בָּאֵי בָאֵשׁ וּבַמַּיִם עַל קִדּוּשׁ שְׁמֶךָ.

אָבִינוּ מַלְכֵּנוּ, נְקֹם לְעֵינֵינוּ נִקְמַת דַּם עֲבָדֶיךָ הַשָּׁפוּךְ.

אָבִינוּ מַלְכֵּנוּ, עֲשֵׂה לְמַעַנְךָ אִם לֹא לְמַעֲנֵנוּ.

אָבִינוּ מַלְכֵּנוּ, עֲשֵׂה לְמַעַנְךָ וְהוֹשִׁיעֵנוּ.

אָבִינוּ מַלְכֵּנוּ, עֲשֵׂה לְמַעַן רַחֲמֶיךָ הָרַבִּים.

אָבִינוּ מַלְכֵּנוּ, עֲשֵׂה לְמַעַן שִׁמְךָ הַגָּדוֹל הַגִּבּוֹר וְהַנּוֹרָא, שֶׁנִּקְרָא עָלֵינוּ.

◂ אָבִינוּ מַלְכֵּנוּ, חָנֵּנוּ וַעֲנֵנוּ, כִּי אֵין בָּנוּ מַעֲשִׂים, עֲשֵׂה עִמָּנוּ צְדָקָה וָחֶסֶד וְהוֹשִׁיעֵנוּ.

The ארון קודש *is closed.*

During מנחה *continue with* תחנון *on page 282.*

OUR FATHER, our King, fill our granaries with plenty.

OUR FATHER, our King, hear our voice; shelter and have mercy on us.

OUR FATHER, our King, accept, with mercy and favor, our prayer.

OUR FATHER, our King, open the gates of heaven to our prayer.

OUR FATHER, our King, remember that we are dust.

OUR FATHER, our King, please do not turn us away empty-handed from Your presence.

OUR FATHER, our King, may this time be a time of mercy, a moment of favor in Your presence.

OUR FATHER, our King, show compassion to us and to our little ones and children.

OUR FATHER, our King, act for the sake of those who have passed through fire and water to sanctify Your name.

OUR FATHER, our King, avenge, before our eyes, the spilt blood of Your servants.

OUR FATHER, our King, act for Your own sake, if not for ours.

OUR FATHER, our King, act for Your own sake and save us.

OUR FATHER, our King, act for the sake of Your great mercy.

OUR FATHER, our King, act for the sake of Your great, mighty and awesome name, by which we are known.

▸ OUR FATHER, our King, deal graciously with us and answer us,
for we have no deeds to recommend us.
Do with us what is righteous and kind –
and save us.

The Ark is closed.

During Minḥa continue with Taḥanun on page 283.

סדר תחנון

On Mondays and Thursdays, when תחנון *is said, begin with* וְהוּא רַחוּם *below.*
On other days when תחנון *is said, begin with* וַיֹּאמֶר דָּוִד *on page 152.*

The following until וַיֹּאמֶר דָּוִד *on page 152* *is said standing.*

תהלים עח **וְהוּא רַחוּם**, יְכַפֵּר עָוֹן וְלֹא־יַשְׁחִית, וְהִרְבָּה לְהָשִׁיב אַפּוֹ וְלֹא־יָעִיר
כָּל־חֲמָתוֹ: אַתָּה יהוה לֹא־תִכְלָא רַחֲמֶיךָ מִמֶּנּוּ, חַסְדְּךָ
תהלים קו וַאֲמִתְּךָ תָּמִיד יִצְּרוּנוּ. הוֹשִׁיעֵנוּ יהוה אֱלֹהֵינוּ וְקַבְּצֵנוּ מִן־הַגּוֹיִם, לְהוֹדוֹת
תהלים קל לְשֵׁם קָדְשֶׁךָ, לְהִשְׁתַּבֵּחַ בִּתְהִלָּתֶךָ: אִם־עֲוֹנוֹת תִּשְׁמָר־יָהּ, אֲדֹנָי מִי
יַעֲמֹד: כִּי־עִמְּךָ הַסְּלִיחָה לְמַעַן תִּוָּרֵא: לֹא כַחֲטָאֵינוּ תַּעֲשֶׂה לָּנוּ, וְלֹא
ירמיה יד כַּעֲוֹנוֹתֵינוּ תִּגְמֹל עָלֵינוּ. אִם־עֲוֹנֵינוּ עָנוּ בָנוּ, יהוה עֲשֵׂה לְמַעַן שְׁמֶךָ:
תהלים כה זְכֹר־רַחֲמֶיךָ יהוה וַחֲסָדֶיךָ, כִּי מֵעוֹלָם הֵמָּה: יַעֲנֵנוּ יהוה בְּיוֹם צָרָה,
תהלים כ יְשַׂגְּבֵנוּ שֵׁם אֱלֹהֵי יַעֲקֹב. יהוה הוֹשִׁיעָה, הַמֶּלֶךְ יַעֲנֵנוּ בְיוֹם־קָרְאֵנוּ:
אָבִינוּ מַלְכֵּנוּ, חָנֵּנוּ וַעֲנֵנוּ, כִּי אֵין בָּנוּ מַעֲשִׂים, צְדָקָה עֲשֵׂה עִמָּנוּ לְמַעַן
שְׁמֶךָ. אֲדוֹנֵינוּ אֱלֹהֵינוּ, שְׁמַע קוֹל תַּחֲנוּנֵינוּ, וּזְכָר לָנוּ אֶת בְּרִית אֲבוֹתֵינוּ
וְהוֹשִׁיעֵנוּ לְמַעַן שְׁמֶךָ.

TAḤANUN IS OMITTED ON CERTAIN DAYS OR WHEN CERTAIN EVENTS OCCUR.

These include the following:

1. In a *shiva* house (*OḤ* 131:4)
2. In the presence of a groom or bride celebrating *sheva berakhot* (*MB* 131:21). Some omit *Taḥanun* if there is a groom or bride present who is going to be married later that day (*ibid.*)
3. If a *brit mila* is taking place in the synagogue that day or either the father of the baby, the *mohel* or the *sandak* is present at the *minyan* (*OḤ* 131:4 and *MB* 131:22)
4. Tu B'Av, Tu BiShvat, Rosh Ḥodesh, Ḥanukka, Purim, Shushan Purim, Lag BaOmer (*OḤ* 131:6), Tisha B'Av (*OḤ* 131:7), Purim Katan (the 14th and 15th of Adar I during a leap year, *MB* 131:33), Yom HaAtzma'ut and Yom Yerushalayim.
5. On the days listed in #4, Tahanun is also omitted at Minha on the previous day (MB 131:33)
6. The entire month of *Nisan* (*OḤ* 131:7)
7. Between Yom Kippur and Sukkot (*OḤ* 131:7). Many congregations extend this until the end of Tishrei (*Sha'arei Teshuva* 131:19)
8. The first five days of the month of Sivan (*OḤ* 131:7). Some congregations extend this until the 12th or 13th of Sivan (*MB* 131:36 and *Sha'arei Teshuva* 131:19)
9. The day prior to Rosh Hashana and prior to Yom Kippur (OH 131:6)
10. Some congregations omit *Taḥanun* on the 14th of Iyar (Pesaḥ Sheni) (*Sha'arei Teshuva* 131:19)

TAḤANUN

On Mondays and Thursdays, when Taḥanun is said,
begin with "But he, the Compassionate" below.
On other days when Taḥanun is said,
begin with "David said" on page 153.

The following until "David said" on page 153 is said standing.

Ps. 78 **וְהוּא רַחוּם** BUT HE, the Compassionate One, forgives iniquity, and does
not completely destroy; and He often turns away His anger, and He
does not stir up all His wrath. You, O Lord, withhold not Your mercies
from us. May Your loving-kindness and Your truth always preserve us.
Ps. 106 Save us, O Lord our God, and gather us from among the nations, to give
Ps. 130 thanks to Your holy name, to triumph in Your praise. If You, O Lord,
pay heed to iniquities, who, my Master, will stand? Indeed, forgiveness
is with You, so that You may be feared. Do not treat us as befits our sins;
Jer. 14 do not give us back what our iniquities deserve. If our iniquities bear
Ps. 25 witness against us – Lord, act for the sake of Your name. Remember
Your mercy, O Lord, and Your loving-kindnesses, which are of old. May
the Lord answer us in the day of trouble. May the name of the God of
Ps. 20 Jacob exalt us. O Lord, save us! The King will answer us on the day
that we call. Father, King, grant us grace, grant us response, for we have
no deeds to defend us; perform charity with us, for the sake of Your
name. Lord, God, hear the sound of our supplications, and remember
the covenant of our forefathers for us, and save us, for the sake of
Your name.

סֵדֶר תַּחֲנוּן / TAḤANUN
According to Rambam, *Taḥanun* is part of the *Amida*; the *Kaddish Titkabal* that concludes the *Amida* unit is recited only after it. During prayer, we follow the precedent of Abraham and stand erect before God while arguing with Him regarding our fate and that of our people. When we reach the end of the *Amida*, we suddenly recognize the audacity of what we have done, and fall to the ground in embarrassment and surrender ourselves to Him. In the *Amida* we stress the potential greatness of humanity as a partner to God in Creation. In *Taḥanun* we reveal the reality, that we are completely dependent on God's mercy and grace (R. Isaiah Wohlgemuth).

There are various accounts of the historical origins of this lengthy supplication. Some scholars trace them to the seventh-century persecutions by the Franks and Goths. The Roke'aḥ records a tradition that it was authored by refugees from the destruction of the Second

דניאל ט **וְעַתָּה** אֲדֹנָי אֱלֹהֵינוּ, אֲשֶׁר הוֹצֵאתָ אֶת־עַמְּךָ מֵאֶרֶץ מִצְרַיִם בְּיָד חֲזָקָה
וַתַּעַשׂ־לְךָ שֵׁם כַּיּוֹם הַזֶּה, חָטָאנוּ רָשָׁעְנוּ: אֲדֹנָי, כְּכָל־צִדְקֹתֶךָ
יָשָׁב־נָא אַפְּךָ וַחֲמָתְךָ, מֵעִירְךָ יְרוּשָׁלַםִ הַר־קָדְשֶׁךָ, כִּי בַחֲטָאֵינוּ וּבַעֲוֹנוֹת
אֲבֹתֵינוּ, יְרוּשָׁלַםִ וְעַמְּךָ לְחֶרְפָּה לְכָל־סְבִיבֹתֵינוּ: וְעַתָּה שְׁמַע אֱלֹהֵינוּ
אֶל־תְּפִלַּת עַבְדְּךָ וְאֶל־תַּחֲנוּנָיו, וְהָאֵר פָּנֶיךָ עַל־מִקְדָּשְׁךָ הַשָּׁמֵם,
לְמַעַן אֲדֹנָי: הַטֵּה אֱלֹהַי אָזְנְךָ וּשֲׁמָע, פְּקַח עֵינֶיךָ וּרְאֵה שֹׁמְמֹתֵינוּ
וְהָעִיר אֲשֶׁר־נִקְרָא שִׁמְךָ עָלֶיהָ, כִּי לֹא עַל־צִדְקֹתֵינוּ אֲנַחְנוּ מַפִּילִים
תַּחֲנוּנֵינוּ לְפָנֶיךָ, כִּי עַל־רַחֲמֶיךָ הָרַבִּים: אֲדֹנָי שְׁמָעָה, אֲדֹנָי סְלָחָה, אֲדֹנָי
הַקְשִׁיבָה וַעֲשֵׂה אַל־תְּאַחַר, לְמַעַנְךָ אֱלֹהַי, כִּי־שִׁמְךָ נִקְרָא עַל־עִירְךָ
וְעַל־עַמֶּךָ:

אָבִינוּ הָאָב הָרַחֲמָן, הַרְאֵנוּ אוֹת לְטוֹבָה וְקַבֵּץ נְפוּצוֹתֵינוּ מֵאַרְבַּע
ישעיה סד כַּנְפוֹת הָאָרֶץ. יַכִּירוּ וְיֵדְעוּ כָּל הַגּוֹיִם כִּי אַתָּה יהוה אֱלֹהֵינוּ: וְעַתָּה
יהוה אָבִינוּ אָתָּה, אֲנַחְנוּ הַחֹמֶר וְאַתָּה יֹצְרֵנוּ וּמַעֲשֵׂה יָדְךָ כֻּלָּנוּ. הוֹשִׁיעֵנוּ
יואל ב לְמַעַן שְׁמֶךָ, צוּרֵנוּ מַלְכֵּנוּ וְגוֹאֲלֵנוּ. חוּסָה יהוה עַל־עַמֶּךָ, וְאַל־תִּתֵּן
נַחֲלָתְךָ לְחֶרְפָּה לִמְשָׁל־בָּם גּוֹיִם, לָמָּה יֹאמְרוּ בָעַמִּים אַיֵּה אֱלֹהֵיהֶם:
יָדַעְנוּ כִּי חָטָאנוּ וְאֵין מִי יַעֲמֹד בַּעֲדֵנוּ, שִׁמְךָ הַגָּדוֹל יַעֲמָד לָנוּ בְּעֵת
צָרָה. יָדַעְנוּ כִּי אֵין בָּנוּ מַעֲשִׂים, צְדָקָה עֲשֵׂה עִמָּנוּ לְמַעַן שְׁמֶךָ. כְּרַחֵם
אָב עַל בָּנִים כֵּן תְּרַחֵם יהוה עָלֵינוּ, וְהוֹשִׁיעֵנוּ לְמַעַן שְׁמֶךָ. חֲמֹל עַל
עַמֶּךָ, רַחֵם עַל נַחֲלָתֶךָ, חוּסָה נָּא כְּרֹב רַחֲמֶיךָ, חָנֵּנוּ וַעֲנֵנוּ. כִּי לְךָ יהוה
הַצְּדָקָה, עֹשֵׂה נִפְלָאוֹת בְּכָל עֵת.

Temple. In his account, the Romans set groups of refugees adrift on rudderless boats. One of those groups landed on a distant shore where they encountered persecution, whereupon two brothers, R. Yosef and R. Binyamin, together with their cousin, R. Shmuel, led the people in prayer and fasting, leading to their salvation upon the unexpected death of the local king. Seeing this as confirmation of the efficacy of their prayers, they combined them into a single composition and distributed copies to other Jewish communities, which in due course became the core of the *Taḥanun* service for Mondays and Thursdays.

More recently, Professor Yaakov Gartner traced the origins of the *VeHu Raḥum* supplications to early customs of communal fasting on Mondays and Thursdays, which were already days of communal gathering for market and court sessions. *Seliḥot* prayers on

Dan. 9 וְעַתָּה AND NOW, my Master, our God, You Who brought Your people out of the Land of Egypt with a mighty hand, spreading Your fame to this day – we have sinned, we have been wicked. My Master, reach to the full height of Your righteousness and turn back Your rage and Your fury; away from Jerusalem, Your city, Your holy mount – for in our sins, in the iniquities of our forefathers, Jerusalem and Your people have become the mockery of all our neighbors. And so now, listen, God, to the prayer of Your servant, to his pleading – and have Your face shine out upon Your desolate Temple – for the sake of my Master. Turn Your ear, my God, to hear; open Your eyes to see our ruins, the city that bears Your name; for it is not by our righteousness that we throw our supplications down at Your feet – but by Your endless compassion. Master, listen; Master, forgive; Master, hear us and act and do not come too late – for Your sake, my God, for Your city and Your people bear Your name.

אָבִינוּ OUR FATHER, compassionate Father, show us a sign of good tidings; bring our scattered ones together from the four corners of the world. And
Is. 64 all nations will realize and know, that You are the Lord our God. Now, Lord, You are our Father; we are the clay and You are the Potter – and all of us are the work of Your hands. Save us, for the sake of Your name – our
Joel 2 Rock, our King, our Redeemer. Have mercy, Lord, on Your people; do not give Your people over to be disgraced; to be ruled over by nations. Why should it be said among the nations – "Where is their God now?" I know that we have sinned, and that none can stand to defend us; but let Your great name rise up to defend us at every time of trouble. We know that we have no deeds to defend us; perform charity with us, for the sake of Your name. As a father has mercy upon his children, just so, Lord, have mercy upon us – and save us, for the sake of Your name. Have mercy on Your people; show compassion for Your inheritance; spare us, please, as fully as Your compassion is great. Grant us grace; grant us response – for it is Yours, Lord, to perform charity – You Who perform wonders at every moment.

---

those days, seeking divine forgiveness, were appended to the end of the Leader's repetition of the *Amida*, and only those verses appear in the Geonic prayer books. When the practice made its way from Babylonia to Ashkenaz, these prayers were reinterpreted as more

הַבֵּט נָא, רַחֶם נָא עַל עַמְּךָ מְהֵרָה לְמַעַן שְׁמֶךָ בְּרַחֲמֶיךָ הָרַבִּים יהוה אֱלֹהֵינוּ. חוּס וְרַחֵם וְהוֹשִׁיעָה צֹאן מַרְעִיתֶךָ, וְאַל יִמְשָׁל בָּנוּ קֶצֶף, כִּי לְךָ עֵינֵינוּ תְלוּיוֹת. הוֹשִׁיעֵנוּ לְמַעַן שְׁמֶךָ. רַחֵם עָלֵינוּ לְמַעַן בְּרִיתֶךָ. הַבִּיטָה וַעֲנֵנוּ בְּעֵת צָרָה, כִּי לְךָ יהוה הַיְשׁוּעָה. בְּךָ תוֹחַלְתֵּנוּ אֱלוֹהַּ סְלִיחוֹת, אָנָּא סְלַח נָא אֵל טוֹב וְסַלָּח, כִּי אֵל מֶלֶךְ חַנּוּן וְרַחוּם אָתָּה.

אָנָּא מֶלֶךְ חַנּוּן וְרַחוּם, זְכֹר וְהַבֵּט לִבְרִית בֵּין הַבְּתָרִים, וְתֵרָאֶה לְפָנֶיךָ עֲקֵדַת יָחִיד לְמַעַן יִשְׂרָאֵל. אָבִינוּ מַלְכֵּנוּ, חָנֵּנוּ וַעֲנֵנוּ, כִּי שִׁמְךָ הַגָּדוֹל נִקְרָא עָלֵינוּ. עֹשֵׂה נִפְלָאוֹת בְּכָל עֵת, עֲשֵׂה עִמָּנוּ כְּחַסְדֶּךָ. חַנּוּן וְרַחוּם, הַבִּיטָה וַעֲנֵנוּ בְּעֵת צָרָה, כִּי לְךָ יהוה הַיְשׁוּעָה. אָבִינוּ מַלְכֵּנוּ מַחֲסֵנוּ, אַל תַּעַשׂ עִמָּנוּ כְּרֹעַ מַעֲלָלֵינוּ. זְכֹר רַחֲמֶיךָ יהוה וַחֲסָדֶיךָ, וּכְרֹב טוּבְךָ הוֹשִׁיעֵנוּ, וַחֲמָל נָא עָלֵינוּ, כִּי אֵין לָנוּ אֱלוֹהַּ אַחֵר מִבַּלְעָדֶיךָ צוּרֵנוּ. אַל תַּעַזְבֵנוּ יהוה אֱלֹהֵינוּ אַל תִּרְחַק מִמֶּנּוּ. כִּי נַפְשֵׁנוּ קְצָרָה, מֵחֶרֶב וּמִשְּׁבִי וּמִדֶּבֶר וּמִמַּגֵּפָה. וּמִכָּל צָרָה וְיָגוֹן הַצִּילֵנוּ, כִּי לְךָ קִוִּינוּ. וְאַל תַּכְלִימֵנוּ יהוה אֱלֹהֵינוּ, וְהָאֵר פָּנֶיךָ בָּנוּ, וּזְכָר לָנוּ אֶת בְּרִית אֲבוֹתֵינוּ וְהוֹשִׁיעֵנוּ לְמַעַן שְׁמֶךָ. רְאֵה בְצָרוֹתֵינוּ, וּשְׁמַע קוֹל תְּפִלָּתֵנוּ, כִּי אַתָּה שׁוֹמֵעַ תְּפִלַּת כָּל פֶּה.

אֵל רַחוּם וְחַנּוּן, רַחֵם עָלֵינוּ וְעַל כָּל מַעֲשֶׂיךָ, כִּי אֵין כָּמוֹךָ יהוה אֱלֹהֵינוּ. אָנָּא שָׂא נָא פְשָׁעֵינוּ, אָבִינוּ מַלְכֵּנוּ צוּרֵנוּ וְגוֹאֲלֵנוּ, אֵל חַי וְקַיָּם הַחֲסִין בַּכֹּחַ, חָסִיד וָטוֹב עַל כָּל מַעֲשֶׂיךָ, כִּי אַתָּה הוּא יהוה אֱלֹהֵינוּ. אֵל אֶרֶךְ אַפַּיִם וּמָלֵא רַחֲמִים, עֲשֵׂה עִמָּנוּ כְּרֹב רַחֲמֶיךָ, וְהוֹשִׁיעֵנוּ לְמַעַן שְׁמֶךָ. שְׁמַע מַלְכֵּנוּ תְּפִלָּתֵנוּ, וּמִיַּד אוֹיְבֵינוּ הַצִּילֵנוּ. שְׁמַע מַלְכֵּנוּ תְּפִלָּתֵנוּ, וּמִכָּל צָרָה וְיָגוֹן הַצִּילֵנוּ. אָבִינוּ מַלְכֵּנוּ אָתָּה, וְשִׁמְךָ עָלֵינוּ נִקְרָא. אַל תַּנִּחֵנוּ, אַל תַּעַזְבֵנוּ אָבִינוּ וְאַל תִּטְּשֵׁנוּ בּוֹרְאֵנוּ וְאַל תִּשְׁכָּחֵנוּ יוֹצְרֵנוּ, כִּי אֵל מֶלֶךְ חַנּוּן וְרַחוּם אָתָּה.

---

general supplications, together with additional prayers for redemption and the restoration of the Temple. Included among these are Daniel's supplication (9:15–17) that was intended to

הַבֵּט נָא LOOK DOWN, please; have mercy, please – for Your people – quickly – for the sake of Your name, and by Your endless compassion, Lord our God. Have mercy, show compassion, and save the flock You pasture. Let no fury oppress us – for our eyes look only to You. Save us, for Your name's sake. Have mercy on us, for the sake of Your covenant. Look down and answer us at our time of trouble; for rescue, Lord, is in Your hands. It is only You we long for, God of forgiveness; please – forgive us, please – good and forgiving God, for You are God and King in grace and compassion.

אָנָּא PLEASE, gracious and merciful King – remember and regard the Covenant between the Pieces; and let the vision of the binding of the only son be present before You, for the sake of Israel. Father, King, grant us grace, grant us response, for we bear Your great name. You Who perform wonders at every moment – act among us as befits Your loving-kindness. Gracious and merciful, Look upon us and answer us at our time of trouble – for rescue, Lord, is in Your hands. Father, King, our Shelter – do not treat us as befits our worst offenses; remember Your compassion, Lord, and Your kindness, and great as Your goodness is – save us, show us mercy, please, for there is no other God for us: none but You, our Rock. Do not leave us, Lord our God, and do not be distant from us. For our endurance is brief, with violence and captivity, epidemics and contagion. Save us from every trouble and sadness – for it is You alone that we are waiting for. Do not shame us, Lord our God; let Your face shine out to us, and remember, in our favor, the covenant of our forefathers – and save us, for Your name's sake. Look upon our troubles, and hear the sound of our prayer, for it is You Who hears the prayers spoken by every mouth.

אֵל COMPASSIONATE, gracious God, have compassion for us and for all You have created, for there is none like You, our Lord, our God. Please, bear our transgressions, Father, King, our Rock, our Redeemer – living, enduring God, power and strength, kind and beneficent to all Your creations – for it is You: You are the Lord our God. Patient God, full of mercy – act among us with the greatness of Your compassion; save us, for the sake of Your name. Listen, King, to our prayer, and save us from the hands of our enemies. Listen, King, to our prayer, and save us from every trouble and sadness. You are our Father, our King, and we bear Your name. Do not let us go and do not leave us, Father; do not abandon us, Creator, and do not forget us, You Who formed us – for You are a gracious and merciful King.

אֵין כָּמְוֹךָ חַנּוּן וְרַחוּם יהוה אֱלֹהֵינוּ, אֵין כָּמְוֹךָ אֵל אֶרֶךְ אַפַּיִם וְרַב
חֶסֶד וֶאֱמֶת. הוֹשִׁיעֵנוּ בְּרַחֲמֶיךָ הָרַבִּים, מֵרַעַשׁ וּמֵרֹגֶז
הַצִּילֵנוּ. זְכֹר לַעֲבָדֶיךָ לְאַבְרָהָם לְיִצְחָק וּלְיַעֲקֹב, אַל תֵּפֶן אֶל קְשְׁיֵנוּ
שמות לב וְאֶל רִשְׁעֵנוּ וְאֶל חַטָּאתֵנוּ. שׁוּב מֵחֲרוֹן אַפֶּךָ, וְהִנָּחֵם עַל־הָרָעָה לְעַמֶּךָ:
וְהָסֵר מִמֶּנּוּ מַכַּת הַמָּוֶת כִּי רַחוּם אָתָּה, כִּי כֵן דַּרְכֶּךָ, עֹשֶׂה חֶסֶד חִנָּם
בְּכָל דּוֹר וָדוֹר. חוּסָה יהוה עַל עַמֶּךָ וְהַצִּילֵנוּ מִזַּעְמֶךָ, וְהָסֵר מִמֶּנּוּ מַכַּת
דניאל ט הַמַּגֵּפָה וּגְזֵרָה קָשָׁה, כִּי אַתָּה שׁוֹמֵר יִשְׂרָאֵל. לְךָ אֲדֹנָי הַצְּדָקָה וְלָנוּ
בֹּשֶׁת הַפָּנִים: מַה נִּתְאוֹנֵן, מַה נֹּאמַר, מַה נְּדַבֵּר וּמַה נִּצְטַדָּק. נַחְפְּשָׂה
תהלים קיח דְרָכֵינוּ וְנַחְקֹרָה וְנָשׁוּבָה אֵלֶיךָ, כִּי יְמִינְךָ פְשׁוּטָה לְקַבֵּל שָׁבִים. אָנָּא
יהוה הוֹשִׁיעָה נָּא, אָנָּא יהוה הַצְלִיחָה נָא: אָנָּא יהוה עֲנֵנוּ בְּיוֹם קָרְאֵנוּ.
לְךָ יהוה חִכִּינוּ, לְךָ יהוה קִוִּינוּ, לְךָ יהוה נְיַחֵל. אַל תֶּחֱשֶׁה וּתְעַנֵּנוּ, כִּי
נָאֲמוּ גוֹיִם, אָבְדָה תִקְוָתָם. כָּל בֶּרֶךְ וְכָל קוֹמָה, לְךָ לְבַד תִּשְׁתַּחֲוֶה.

הַפּוֹתֵחַ יָד בִּתְשׁוּבָה לְקַבֵּל פּוֹשְׁעִים וְחַטָּאִים, נִבְהֲלָה נַפְשֵׁנוּ מֵרֹב
עִצְּבוֹנֵנוּ. אַל תִּשְׁכָּחֵנוּ נֶצַח, קוּמָה וְהוֹשִׁיעֵנוּ כִּי חָסִינוּ
בָךְ. אָבִינוּ מַלְכֵּנוּ, אִם אֵין בָּנוּ צְדָקָה וּמַעֲשִׂים טוֹבִים, זְכָר לָנוּ אֶת
בְּרִית אֲבוֹתֵינוּ וְעֵדוֹתֵינוּ בְּכָל יוֹם יהוה אֶחָד. הַבִּיטָה בְעָנְיֵנוּ, כִּי רַבּוּ
מַכְאוֹבֵינוּ וְצָרוֹת לְבָבֵנוּ. חוּסָה יהוה עָלֵינוּ בְּאֶרֶץ שִׁבְיֵנוּ, וְאַל תִּשְׁפֹּךְ
חֲרוֹנְךָ עָלֵינוּ, כִּי אֲנַחְנוּ עַמְּךָ בְּנֵי בְרִיתֶךָ. אֵל, הַבִּיטָה, דַּל כְּבוֹדֵנוּ בַּגּוֹיִם
וְשִׁקְּצוּנוּ כְּטֻמְאַת הַנִּדָּה. עַד מָתַי עֻזְּךָ בַּשְּׁבִי, וְתִפְאַרְתְּךָ בְּיַד צָר. עוֹרְרָה
גְבוּרָתְךָ וְקִנְאָתְךָ עַל אוֹיְבֶיךָ. הֵם יֵבוֹשׁוּ וְיֵחַתּוּ מִגְּבוּרָתָם. וְאַל יִמְעֲטוּ
לְפָנֶיךָ תְּלָאוֹתֵינוּ, מַהֵר יְקַדְּמוּנוּ רַחֲמֶיךָ בְּיוֹם צָרָתֵנוּ. וְאִם לֹא לְמַעֲנֵנוּ,
לְמַעַנְךָ פְעַל, וְאַל תַּשְׁחִית זֵכֶר שְׁאֵרִיתֵנוּ, וְחֹן אֹם הַמְיַחֲדִים שִׁמְךָ
דברים ו פַּעֲמַיִם בְּכָל יוֹם תָּמִיד בְּאַהֲבָה, וְאוֹמְרִים, שְׁמַע יִשְׂרָאֵל, יהוה אֱלֹהֵינוּ,
יהוה אֶחָד:

---

bring about the end of the Babylonian exile at its prophetically ordained terminus, i.e., the seventieth year of exile. This request was deemed so important that it was recited despite the life-threatening danger thus incurred (R. Yaakov Medan).

אֵין כָּמוֹךָ THERE IS NO ONE so gracious, so merciful as You, Lord our God – none so patient, or so abounding in loving-kindness and truth. Save us, in Your great mercy, save us from thunder and fury. Remember, for the sake of Your servants: of Abraham, Isaac and Jacob – and do not look too closely at our
Ex. 32 stubbornness, our wickedness, our sin. Turn back from Your burning rage, and relent of the evil You have planned for Your people. Make its mortal wound fade away, for You are merciful, for such is Your way, You Who act with unquestioning kindness, in every generation that comes. Spare Your people, Lord, and save us from Your rage; remove from us the effects of contagion and
Dan. 9 harsh decrees – for You are Israel's Protector. Charity is Yours, my Master, and ours is the shame. How can we complain, what would we say? What words could we speak and how try to absolve ourselves? We will look to our own ways, seek them out, and we will come back to You – for Your right hand is
Ps. 118 held out to receive the penitent back. We beseech You, O Lord, please save us. We beseech You, O Lord, please give us success. We beseech You, Lord, answer us on the day when we call. It is You, Lord, we hope for; You, Lord, we long for – You, Lord we still await. Do not keep silence: answer us, for the nations have boasted, "Their hope is lost." Every knee and every high demeanor should bend only to You.

הַפּוֹתֵחַ YOU WHO OPEN Your hand for repentance, receiving transgressors and sinners – our spirits are overcome with all our sorrows. Do not forever forget us; rise up again, and save us, for it is in You that we seek shelter. Father, King, if we have no righteousness and good deeds to our name, remember the covenant of our forefathers in our favor, and the testimony we bear every day: "The Lord is One." Look upon our oppression – for our pain, and the anguish of our heart, grows very great. Spare us, Lord, in the land of our captivity, and do not pour Your rage out upon us, for we are Your people, part of Your covenant. God, look and see – our honor has grown thin among the nations; we are despised – outcasts, impure to them. How long will Your power remain captive, Your glory in the hands of the enemy? Awaken Your might and Your passion against Your foes. And let them be filled with shame and terror, and lose all their power. Do not think our hardships slight – quickly bring Your mercy forth to greet us on the day of our anguish. If not for our own sake, do this for Yours; and do not let the memory of our remnant be destroyed. Grant grace to the people who declare the Oneness of Your name, twice
Deut. 6 every day, with love, saying, Hear, O Israel, the Lord is our God, the Lord is One.

נפילת אפיים

On Sundays, Tuesdays, Wednesdays and Fridays, begin תחנון *here.*
The following, until וַאֲנַחְנוּ לֹא נֵדַע *on page 156, is said sitting. When praying in a place where there is a* ספר תורה*, one should lean forward, resting one's head on the left arm (unless one is wearing* תפילין *on the left arm, in which case rest on the right arm out of respect for the* תפילין*), until* יֵבֹשׁוּ רָגַע*.*
R. Soloveitchik would rest his head on his arm even absent a ספר תורה*.*

וַיֹּאמֶר דָּוִד אֶל־גָּד, צַר־לִי מְאֹד, נִפְּלָה־נָּא בְיַד־יהוה, כִּי רַבִּים רַחֲמָו, וּבְיַד־אָדָם אַל־אֶפֹּלָה: שמואל ב, כד

רַחוּם וְחַנּוּן, חָטָאתִי לְפָנֶיךָ. יהוה מָלֵא רַחֲמִים, רַחֵם עָלַי וְקַבֵּל תַּחֲנוּנָי.

יהוה, אַל־בְּאַפְּךָ תוֹכִיחֵנִי, וְאַל־בַּחֲמָתְךָ תְיַסְּרֵנִי: חָנֵּנִי יהוה, כִּי אֻמְלַל אָנִי, רְפָאֵנִי יהוה, כִּי נִבְהֲלוּ עֲצָמָי: וְנַפְשִׁי נִבְהֲלָה מְאֹד, וְאַתָּה יהוה, עַד־מָתָי: שׁוּבָה יהוה, חַלְּצָה נַפְשִׁי, הוֹשִׁיעֵנִי לְמַעַן חַסְדֶּךָ: כִּי אֵין בַּמָּוֶת זִכְרֶךָ, בִּשְׁאוֹל מִי יוֹדֶה־לָּךְ: יָגַעְתִּי בְּאַנְחָתִי, אַשְׂחֶה בְכָל־לַיְלָה מִטָּתִי, בְּדִמְעָתִי עַרְשִׂי אַמְסֶה: עָשְׁשָׁה מִכַּעַס עֵינִי, עָתְקָה בְּכָל־צוֹרְרָי: סוּרוּ מִמֶּנִּי כָּל־פֹּעֲלֵי אָוֶן, כִּי שָׁמַע יהוה קוֹל בִּכְיִי: שָׁמַע יהוה תְּחִנָּתִי, יהוה תְּפִלָּתִי יִקָּח: יֵבֹשׁוּ וְיִבָּהֲלוּ מְאֹד כָּל־אֹיְבָי, יָשֻׁבוּ יֵבֹשׁוּ רָגַע: תהלים ו

Sit upright.

נְפִילַת אַפַּיִם / FALLING ON ONE'S FOREHEAD To fall upon one's face (i.e., to bury one's forehead in one's arm, which in turn rests on a physical support) is to convey a sense of hopelessness. Thus, for instance, in Numbers 14:5 in the incident of the twelve spies, Moses and Aaron fall on their faces after the people rebel, leaving Moses and Aaron without any hope for saving the people (Rashi). The Gemara (*Ta'anit* 14b) points out that on that occasion Joshua and Caleb also tore their garments in anguish. We however express our remorse without tearing our garments, as in the *Taḥanun* we are seeking forgiveness only for our own transgressions, not those of the entire people, and for this private purpose it is sufficient to fall on one's arm (R. Barukh HaLevi Epstein).

Doubling over in this fashion symbolizes our loss of human dignity as a result of our sins, to the point that we feel reduced to an animal-like state in which we cannot sit or stand erect in God's presence (R. Joseph B. Soloveitchik).

Taḥanun originally was said in the pose of "falling on the face," in a bowing position. In late Geonic times the practice developed to recite *Taḥanun* lying on the left side, and in Ashkenaz, where most synagogues had stone floors, on which prostration is forbidden, the stance of *Taḥanun* assumed that familiar to us today, bending over the left arm from a seated position (Prof. Yaakov Gartner).

ה׳ אַל־בְּאַפְּךָ – *Lord... in Your anger.* This entire section comes from Psalm 6 (with the exception of the first verse). It is divided into

FALLING ON ONE'S FOREHEAD

On Sundays, Tuesdays, Wednesdays and Fridays, begin Tahanun here. The following, until "And we do not know" on page 157, is said sitting. When praying in a place where there is a Torah scroll, one should lean forward, resting one's head on the left arm (unless one is wearing tefillin on the left arm, in which case rest on the right arm out of respect for the tefillin), until "suddenly frustrated." R. Soloveitchik would rest his head on his arm even absent a Sefer Torah.

II Sam. 24 וַיֹּאמֶר דָּוִד DAVID SAID to Gad, "My anguish is great. Let us fall into the hand of the Lord, for He is full of mercy; and let me not fall into the hands of man."

COMPASSIONATE and Gracious One, I have sinned before You. Lord Who is full of mercy, have mercy on me and accept my pleas.

Ps. 6 יהוה LORD, do not punish in Your anger, and do not chastise me in Your wrath. Favor me, Lord, for I am broken. Heal me, Lord, for my limbs are dismayed. And my soul is greatly dismayed, but You, Lord, how long? Turn, Lord, rescue my soul. Save me for the sake of Your loving-kindness. For in death there is no remembrance of You. In the underworld, who will give You thanks? Every night I make my bed swim. I melt my couch with my tears. My eye is dimmed because of grief. It has become old because of all my adversaries. Depart from me, all you workers of iniquity, for the Lord has heard the voice of my weeping. The Lord has heard my supplication. The Lord will accept my prayer. May all my enemies be frustrated and greatly dismayed. May they turn back, may they be suddenly frustrated.

Sit upright.

---

two sections. The first (verses 2–8) expresses David's despair at the realization that he has failed God, as he implores God to forgive him. In the second half, verses 9–10 describe the transformation that occurs when David senses that his prayers have been heard, and that he has been pardoned, while his enemies have been consigned to defeat. Such is the power of repentance: at one moment there is the agony of guilt and shame, at the next moment there is cleansing and exhilaration. A similar transformation is found in Psalm 30, at the outset of the *Pesukei DeZimra*.

This immense power of prayer to completely transform the life of the sinner is uniquely described by Rambam in *Hilkhot Teshuva* 2:4, where he writes, "It is the way of repentance for the penitent to cry out constantly to God in tears and supplications, giving charity, distancing himself from his erroneous ways, changing his name as if to say 'I am a different person, I am not the one who did those things,' and thus to change all of his habits in pursuit of good and righteous ways." From Rambam we learn that we are indeed capable not just of repentance but of actual self-transformation, by which we can become an entirely new person (R. Joseph B. Soloveitchik).

On Mondays and Thursdays, say the following.
On other days, continue with שׁוֹמֵר יִשְׂרָאֵל *on the next page.*

יהוה אֱלֹהֵי יִשְׂרָאֵל, שׁוּב מֵחֲרוֹן אַפֶּךָ וְהִנָּחֵם עַל הָרָעָה לְעַמֶּךָ.

הַבֵּט מִשָּׁמַיִם וּרְאֵה כִּי הָיִינוּ לַעַג וָקֶלֶס בַּגּוֹיִם, נֶחְשַׁבְנוּ כַּצֹּאן לַטֶּבַח יוּבָל, לַהֲרֹג וּלְאַבֵּד וּלְמַכָּה וּלְחֶרְפָּה. וּבְכָל זֹאת שִׁמְךָ לֹא שָׁכָחְנוּ, נָא אַל תִּשְׁכָּחֵנוּ.

יהוה אֱלֹהֵי יִשְׂרָאֵל, שׁוּב מֵחֲרוֹן אַפֶּךָ וְהִנָּחֵם עַל הָרָעָה לְעַמֶּךָ.

זָרִים אוֹמְרִים אֵין תּוֹחֶלֶת וְתִקְוָה, חֹן אֹם לְשִׁמְךָ מְקַוֶּה, טָהוֹר יְשׁוּעָתֵנוּ קָרְבָה, יָגַעְנוּ וְלֹא הוּנַח לָנוּ, רַחֲמֶיךָ יִכְבְּשׁוּ אֶת כַּעַסְךָ מֵעָלֵינוּ. אָנָּא שׁוּב מֵחֲרוֹנְךָ וְרַחֵם סְגֻלָּה אֲשֶׁר בָּחָרְתָּ.

יהוה אֱלֹהֵי יִשְׂרָאֵל, שׁוּב מֵחֲרוֹן אַפֶּךָ וְהִנָּחֵם עַל הָרָעָה לְעַמֶּךָ.

חוּסָה יהוה עָלֵינוּ בְּרַחֲמֶיךָ, וְאַל תִּתְּנֵנוּ בִּידֵי אַכְזָרִים. לָמָּה יֹאמְרוּ הַגּוֹיִם אַיֵּה נָא אֱלֹהֵיהֶם, לְמַעַנְךָ עֲשֵׂה עִמָּנוּ חֶסֶד וְאַל תְּאַחַר. אָנָּא שׁוּב מֵחֲרוֹנְךָ וְרַחֵם סְגֻלָּה אֲשֶׁר בָּחָרְתָּ.

יהוה אֱלֹהֵי יִשְׂרָאֵל, שׁוּב מֵחֲרוֹן אַפֶּךָ וְהִנָּחֵם עַל הָרָעָה לְעַמֶּךָ.

קוֹלֵנוּ תִשְׁמַע וְתָחֹן, וְאַל תִּטְּשֵׁנוּ בְּיַד אֹיְבֵינוּ לִמְחוֹת אֶת שְׁמֵנוּ. זְכֹר אֲשֶׁר נִשְׁבַּעְתָּ לַאֲבוֹתֵינוּ כְּכוֹכְבֵי הַשָּׁמַיִם אַרְבֶּה אֶת זַרְעֲכֶם, וְעַתָּה נִשְׁאַרְנוּ מְעַט מֵהַרְבֵּה. וּבְכָל זֹאת שִׁמְךָ לֹא שָׁכָחְנוּ, נָא אַל תִּשְׁכָּחֵנוּ.

יהוה אֱלֹהֵי יִשְׂרָאֵל, שׁוּב מֵחֲרוֹן אַפֶּךָ וְהִנָּחֵם עַל הָרָעָה לְעַמֶּךָ.

עָזְרֵנוּ אֱלֹהֵי יִשְׁעֵנוּ עַל־דְּבַר כְּבוֹד־שְׁמֶךָ, וְהַצִּילֵנוּ וְכַפֵּר עַל־חַטֹּאתֵינוּ לְמַעַן שְׁמֶךָ׃ תהלים עט

יהוה אֱלֹהֵי יִשְׂרָאֵל, שׁוּב מֵחֲרוֹן אַפֶּךָ וְהִנָּחֵם עַל הָרָעָה לְעַמֶּךָ.

רְפָאֵנִי ה׳ – *Heal me, Lord* (previous page). "If a sick person recites this prayer with proper concentration and a broken heart he can be sure that God will answer his prayer" (Shela).

While some commentators understand this entire psalm to be the prayer of a seriously ill person, others see it as referring to one confronted by war and the prospect of violent death. How can we reconcile these seemingly contradictory foci of the psalm? Perhaps both are correct, in that the extreme stress of imminent war and death at the hands of one's enemies can sometimes lead to serious physical breakdown and illness, whereas a renewed faith and awareness of God's saving grace can dispel physical illness too (R. Amos Hakham).

The fact that the congregation omits *Taḥanun* whenever an individual in attendance

On Mondays and Thursdays, say the following.
On other days, continue with "Protector of Israel" on the next page.

יהוה LORD, God of Israel, turn back from Your burning rage, and relent of the evil You have planned for Your people.

LOOK DOWN from heaven – see that we have become the mockery, the curse of all the nations; we are regarded as sheep to be led to slaughter, to be killed, destroyed, beaten and insulted. And for all that, we have not forgotten Your name – please, do not forget us.

LORD, God of Israel, turn back from Your burning rage, and relent of the evil You have planned for Your people.

STRANGERS say that our situation is hopeless. Grant grace to the people whose hope is in Your name. Bring close our rescue, Pure One; we labor and are granted no rest; let Your mercy wrest Your anger from us. Please – turn back from Your anger and have mercy on the treasured people You chose.

LORD, God of Israel, turn back from Your burning rage, and relent of the evil You have planned for Your people.

PROTECT US, Lord, in Your mercy, and do not surrender us to the hands of the ruthless. Why should the nations say: "Where, pray, is their God?" Show us kindness, for Your sake, and do not act too late. Please – turn back from Your anger, and have mercy on the treasured people You chose.

LORD, God of Israel, turn back from Your burning rage, and relent of the evil You have planned for Your people.

LISTEN to our voice, and grant us grace. Do not abandon us to the hands of our enemies, for our name to be erased. Remember what You swore to our forefathers: "I shall make Your children as many as there are stars in the sky;" and yet now we have been left but few of many. And for all that, we have not forgotten Your name – please, do not forget us.

LORD, God of Israel, turn back from Your burning rage, and relent of the evil You have planned for Your people.

Ps. 79 HELP US, O God of our salvation, because of the glory of Your name, and deliver us and pardon our sins for Your name's sake.

LORD, God of Israel, turn back from Your burning rage, and relent of the evil You have planned for Your people.

---

is celebrating a personal *simḥa* (such as a wedding or *brit mila*) or marking a sad occasion (such as *shiva*) is a remarkable and concrete halakhic manifestation of the importance of sharing in our fellow Jews' occasions of joy or sadness (R. Avraham Berliner).

On all days continue here:

שׁוֹמֵר יִשְׂרָאֵל, שְׁמֹר שְׁאֵרִית יִשְׂרָאֵל, וְאַל יֹאבַד יִשְׂרָאֵל, הָאוֹמְרִים שְׁמַע יִשְׂרָאֵל.

שׁוֹמֵר גּוֹי אֶחָד, שְׁמֹר שְׁאֵרִית עַם אֶחָד, וְאַל יֹאבַד גּוֹי אֶחָד, הַמְיַחֲדִים שִׁמְךָ, יהוה אֱלֹהֵינוּ יהוה אֶחָד.

שׁוֹמֵר גּוֹי קָדוֹשׁ, שְׁמֹר שְׁאֵרִית עַם קָדוֹשׁ, וְאַל יֹאבַד גּוֹי קָדוֹשׁ, הַמְשַׁלְּשִׁים בְּשָׁלֹשׁ קְדֻשּׁוֹת לְקָדוֹשׁ.

מִתְרַצֶּה בְּרַחֲמִים וּמִתְפַּיֵּס בְּתַחֲנוּנִים, הִתְרַצֵּה וְהִתְפַּיֵּס לְדוֹר עָנִי, כִּי אֵין עוֹזֵר.

אָבִינוּ מַלְכֵּנוּ, חָנֵּנוּ וַעֲנֵנוּ, כִּי אֵין בָּנוּ מַעֲשִׂים, עֲשֵׂה עִמָּנוּ צְדָקָה וָחֶסֶד וְהוֹשִׁיעֵנוּ.

Stand at ▲.

וַאֲנַחְנוּ לֹא נֵדַע ▲מַה־נַּעֲשֶׂה, כִּי עָלֶיךָ עֵינֵינוּ: זְכֹר־רַחֲמֶיךָ יהוה וַחֲסָדֶיךָ, דברי הימים ב׳ כ / תהלים כה
כִּי מֵעוֹלָם הֵמָּה: יְהִי־חַסְדְּךָ יהוה עָלֵינוּ, כַּאֲשֶׁר יִחַלְנוּ לָךְ: תהלים לג
אַל־תִּזְכָּר־לָנוּ עֲוֹנֹת רִאשֹׁנִים, מַהֵר יְקַדְּמוּנוּ רַחֲמֶיךָ, כִּי דַלּוֹנוּ מְאֹד: תהלים עט
חָנֵּנוּ יהוה חָנֵּנוּ, כִּי־רַב שָׂבַעְנוּ בוּז: בְּרֹגֶז רַחֵם תִּזְכּוֹר: כִּי־הוּא יָדַע תהלים קכג / חבקוק ג / תהלים קג
יִצְרֵנוּ, זָכוּר כִּי־עָפָר אֲנָחְנוּ: ▸ עָזְרֵנוּ אֱלֹהֵי יִשְׁעֵנוּ עַל־דְּבַר כְּבוֹד־שְׁמֶךָ, תהלים עט
וְהַצִּילֵנוּ וְכַפֵּר עַל־חַטֹּאתֵינוּ לְמַעַן שְׁמֶךָ:

חצי קדיש

ש״ץ: **יִתְגַּדַּל** וְיִתְקַדַּשׁ שְׁמֵהּ רַבָּא (קהל: אָמֵן) בְּעָלְמָא דִּי בְרָא כִרְעוּתֵהּ וְיַמְלִיךְ מַלְכוּתֵהּ בְּחַיֵּיכוֹן וּבְיוֹמֵיכוֹן וּבְחַיֵּי דְכָל בֵּית יִשְׂרָאֵל, בַּעֲגָלָא וּבִזְמַן קָרִיב, וְאִמְרוּ אָמֵן. (קהל: אָמֵן)

קהל וש״ץ: יְהֵא שְׁמֵהּ רַבָּא מְבָרַךְ לְעָלַם וּלְעָלְמֵי עָלְמַיָּא.

ש״ץ: יִתְבָּרַךְ וְיִשְׁתַּבַּח וְיִתְפָּאַר וְיִתְרוֹמַם וְיִתְנַשֵּׂא וְיִתְהַדָּר וְיִתְעַלֶּה וְיִתְהַלָּל שְׁמֵהּ דְּקֻדְשָׁא בְּרִיךְ הוּא (קהל: בְּרִיךְ הוּא) לְעֵלָּא מִן כָּל בִּרְכָתָא / בעשרת ימי תשובה: לְעֵלָּא (וּ)לְעֵלָּא מִכָּל בִּרְכָתָא/ וְשִׁירָתָא, תֻּשְׁבְּחָתָא וְנֶחֱמָתָא דַּאֲמִירָן בְּעָלְמָא, וְאִמְרוּ אָמֵן. (קהל: אָמֵן)

שׁוֹמֵר יִשְׂרָאֵל ... הָאוֹמְרִים שְׁמַע יִשְׂרָאֵל – *Protector of Israel...they who say, "Hear, O Israel."* This is to be understood in light of the Gemara (*Sota* 42a) referring to Deuteronomy 20:3 that instructs the priest to tell the people as they prepare to go to war "Hear, O Israel... let your

On all days continue here:

שׁוֹמֵר יִשְׂרָאֵל PROTECTOR of Israel, protect the remnant of Israel, and let Israel not be lost – they who say, "Hear, O Israel."

PROTECTOR of a unique nation, protect the remnant of a unique nation, and do not let the unique nation be lost – they who declare the Oneness of Your name, proclaiming: "The Lord is our God, the Lord is One."

PROTECTOR of a holy nation, protect the remnant of a holy nation, and do not let a holy nation be lost – they who repeat three times the three-fold declaration of the sanctity of the Holy One.

YOU WHO ARE appeased by mercy, and won over by prayers – be appeased and won over by this impoverished generation, for there is none to help us.

FATHER, King, grant us grace, grant us response, for we have no deeds to defend us; perform charity, deal kindly with us, and save us.

Stand at ▲.

II Chr. 12 **וַאֲנַחְנוּ** AND WE do not know ▲what we can do – for our eyes are on You.
Ps. 25 Remember Your mercy, O Lord, and Your loving-kindnesses, which are of
Ps. 79 *Ps. 33* old. May Your loving-kindness, O Lord, be upon us, as we hope for You. Do not
remember against us former iniquities. Let Your mercies quickly go ahead of
Ps. 123 us, for we are brought very low. Be gracious unto us, O Lord, be gracious unto
Hab. 3 us, for we have suffered our fill of contempt. In the midst of fury – remember
Ps. 103 compassion. Indeed, He knows our desires, He remembers that we are dust.
Ps. 79 ▸ Help us, O God of our salvation, because of the glory of Your name, and
deliver us and pardon our sins for Your name's sake.

HALF KADDISH

Leader: **יִתְגַּדַּל** EXALTED AND HALLOWED may God's great name be, in the world He created as He willed. May He reign in your lifetimes and in your days, and in the lifetime of the whole house of Israel, speedily and soon, and say, Amen.

All: May His great name be blessed forever and all time.

Leader: Blessed and praised, honored, extolled, glorified, adored and exalted above all be the name of the Holy One, blessed is He, (*Between Rosh Hashana & Yom Kippur:* above and) beyond any blessing, hymn, praise, or expressions of consolation that may be uttered in this world, and say, Amen.

---

hearts not be fearful..." R. Shimon b. Yoḥai takes this to mean "even if you have only recited *Shema Yisrael* ('Hear, O Israel') twice a day, that will suffice so that you will not be defeated by your enemies." Accordingly, we here petition God by saying, "Protect the remnant of Israel even if our only saving grace is the fact that as a people we recite *Shema Yisrael* twice a day" (R. Yitzchak Elchanan Spektor of Kovno).

הוצאת ספר תורה

A detailed description of many הלכות *relating to* קריאת התורה *can be found on page E17.*

The following paragraph is said before taking out the תורה *on Monday and Thursday. It is omitted on* תשעה באב, ערב פסח, ראש חודש, חול המועד *(and in some congregations* טו באב, ערב יום כיפור, חנוכה, פורים, שושן פורים*), the 14th and 15th of* אדר א*, and in a* שבעה *house. It is also omitted on* יום העצמאות *and* יום ירושלים*.*

There are varying customs regarding which textual variant (Version א *or Version* ב*) of the prayer is recited. Congregations that have no specific tradition should consult a rabbinic authority.*

א. **אֵל** אֶרֶךְ אַפַּיִם וְרַב חֶסֶד וֶאֱמֶת, אַל בְּאַפְּךָ תוֹכִיחֵנוּ. חוּסָה יהוה עַל עַמֶּךָ, וְהוֹשִׁיעֵנוּ מִכָּל רָע. חָטָאנוּ לְךָ אָדוֹן, סְלַח נָא כְּרֹב רַחֲמֶיךָ אֵל.

ב. **אֵל** אֶרֶךְ אַפַּיִם וּמָלֵא רַחֲמִים, אַל תַּסְתֵּר פָּנֶיךָ מִמֶּנּוּ. חוּסָה יהוה עַל יִשְׂרָאֵל עַמֶּךָ, וְהַצִּילֵנוּ מִכָּל רָע. חָטָאנוּ לְךָ אָדוֹן, סְלַח נָא כְּרֹב רַחֲמֶיךָ אֵל.

The ארון קודש *is opened and the* קהל *stands. All say:*

במדבר י **וַיְהִי בִּנְסֹעַ** הָאָרֹן וַיֹּאמֶר מֹשֶׁה, קוּמָה יהוה וְיָפֻצוּ אֹיְבֶיךָ וְיָנֻסוּ
ישעיה ב מְשַׂנְאֶיךָ מִפָּנֶיךָ: כִּי מִצִּיּוֹן תֵּצֵא תוֹרָה וּדְבַר־יהוה
מִירוּשָׁלָםִ: בָּרוּךְ שֶׁנָּתַן תּוֹרָה לְעַמּוֹ יִשְׂרָאֵל בִּקְדֻשָּׁתוֹ.

The ספר תורה *is removed from the* ארון קודש *before the recitation of* בְּרִיךְ שְׁמֵהּ *(Iggerot Moshe, OḤ 4:70:9).*

זוהר ויקהל **בְּרִיךְ שְׁמֵהּ** דְּמָרֵא עָלְמָא, בְּרִיךְ כִּתְרָךְ וְאַתְרָךְ. יְהֵא רְעוּתָךְ עִם עַמָּךְ יִשְׂרָאֵל לְעָלַם, וּפֻרְקַן יְמִינָךְ אַחֲזִי לְעַמָּךְ בְּבֵית מַקְדְּשָׁךְ, וּלְאַמְטוּיֵי לַנָא מִטּוּב נְהוֹרָךְ, וּלְקַבֵּל צְלוֹתַנָא בְּרַחֲמֵי. יְהֵא רַעֲוָא קֳדָמָךְ דְּתוֹרִיךְ לַן חַיִּין בְּטִיבוּ, וְלֶהֱוֵי אֲנָא פְקִידָא בְּגוֹ צַדִּיקַיָּא, לְמִרְחַם עֲלַי וּלְמִנְטַר יָתִי וְיַת כָּל דִּי לִי וְדִי לְעַמָּךְ יִשְׂרָאֵל. אַנְתְּ הוּא זָן לְכֹלָּא וּמְפַרְנֵס לְכֹלָּא, אַנְתְּ הוּא שַׁלִּיט עַל כֹּלָּא, אַנְתְּ הוּא דְּשַׁלִּיט עַל מַלְכַיָּא, וּמַלְכוּתָא דִּילָךְ הִיא. אֲנָא עַבְדָּא דְקֻדְשָׁא בְּרִיךְ הוּא, דְּסָגֵדְנָא קַמֵּהּ וּמִקַּמֵּי דִּיקַר אוֹרַיְתֵהּ בְּכָל עִדָּן וְעִדָּן. לָא עַל אֱנָשׁ רָחִיצְנָא וְלָא עַל בַּר אֱלָהִין סָמִיכְנָא, אֶלָּא בֶּאֱלָהָא דִשְׁמַיָּא, דְּהוּא אֱלָהָא קְשׁוֹט, וְאוֹרַיְתֵהּ קְשׁוֹט, וּנְבִיאוֹהִי קְשׁוֹט, וּמַסְגֵּא לְמֶעְבַּד טַבְוָן וּקְשׁוֹט. ◂ בֵּהּ אֲנָא רָחִיץ, וְלִשְׁמֵהּ קַדִּישָׁא יַקִּירָא אֲנָא אֵמַר תֻּשְׁבְּחָן. יְהֵא רַעֲוָא קֳדָמָךְ דְּתִפְתַּח לִבַּאי בְּאוֹרַיְתָא, וְתַשְׁלִים מִשְׁאֲלִין דְּלִבַּאי וְלִבָּא דְכָל עַמָּךְ יִשְׂרָאֵל לְטָב וּלְחַיִּין וְלִשְׁלָם. (אָמֵן.)

קְרִיאַת הַתּוֹרָה / THE READING OF THE TORAH

The Gemara (*Bava Kama* 82a) considers Exodus 15:22 ("They went for three days in the wilderness and did not find water") to be referring to the absence of Torah study and the terrible consequences that result. Thus Moses instituted the practice of reading the Torah in public not only on Shabbat but on Mondays and Thursdays as well, so that the people not go three full days without hearing the words of the Torah (Rambam).

The public Torah reading reenacts the Revelation of the Torah. In addition, those who hear the reading fulfill the *mitzva* of Torah study.

REMOVING THE TORAH FROM THE ARK

A detailed description of many halakhot relating to the Reading of the Torah can be found on page E17.

The following paragraph is said before taking out the Torah on Monday and Thursday. It is omitted on Hol Hamo'ed, Rosh Ḥodesh, Erev Pesah, Tisha BeAv (and in some congregations 15 Av), Erev Yom Kippur, Hannukah, Purim, Shushan Purim, the 14th and 15th of Adar 1, and in a shiva house. It is also omitted on Yom HaAtzma'ut and Yom Yerushalayim.

There are varying customs regarding which textual variant (Version A or Version B) of the prayer is recited. Congregations that have no specific tradition should consult a rabbinic authority.

A. אֵל GOD, slow to anger and full of kindness and truth, do not punish us in Your anger. Have pity, Lord, on Your people and save us from all evil. We have sinned against You, Master; forgive us, we beg You, in accordance with Your great compassion, God.

B. אֵל GOD, slow to anger and full of kindness and truth, do not conceal Your face from us. Have pity, Lord, on Your people Israel, and rescue us from all evil. We have sinned against You, Master; forgive us, we beg You, in accordance with Your great compassion, God.

The Ark is opened and the congregation stands. All say:

Num. 10 וַיְהִי בִּנְסֹעַ WHEN THE ARK moved forward, Moses would say, "Arise, O Lord, and may Your enemies be dispersed, and they who hate You
Is. 2 flee from You." For from Zion shall go forth Torah, and the word of the Lord from Jerusalem. Blessed is He Who, in His holiness, has given the Torah to His people Israel.

The Torah is removed from the Ark before the recitation of Berikh Shemeh (Iggerot Moshe, OḤ 4:70:9).

Zohar, Vayak-hel בְּרִיךְ שְׁמֵהּ BLESSED IS YOUR NAME, Master of the universe; blessed is Your crown; blessed Your place. May You always favor Your people Israel. In Your Temple, reveal to Your people the redeeming power of Your right hand. Grant us of Your beneficent light and mercifully accept our prayer. May it be Your will to prolong our lives in goodness. Count me among the righteous to whom You show love, protecting me and all that is mine, as well as all that belongs to Your people Israel. You are He Who provides food for all and sustains all. You are He Who rules over all. You are He Who rules over monarchs, for the dominion is Yours. I am the servant of the Holy One, blessed is He, before Whom, and before Whose glorious Torah, I bow at all times. Not on man do I rely, nor do I trust in any angel, but only on the God of the heavens Who is the God of truth, Whose Torah is truth and Whose prophets are true, and Who acts with abundant love and truth. ▸ In Him alone is my trust, and it is to His holy and glorious name that I utter praises. May it be Your will to open my heart to Your Torah, and to fulfill the desires of my heart and the hearts of all Your people Israel for good, for life, and for peace. (Amen.)

Hence it is preceded by *Barekhu* and a *berakha* over *Talmud Torah*, which together constitute a communal declaration of acceptance of God's sovereignty (R. Joseph B. Soloveitchik).

The שליח ציבור *bows toward the* ארון קודש*, raises the* ספר תורה *and says:*

תהלים לד
גַּדְּלוּ לַיהוה אִתִּי וּנְרוֹמְמָה שְׁמוֹ יַחְדָּו:

The ארון קודש *is closed. The* שליח ציבור *turns to his right and carries the* ספר תורה *to the* בימה *and the* קהל *says:*

דברי הימים א, כט
לְךָ יהוה הַגְּדֻלָּה וְהַגְּבוּרָה וְהַתִּפְאֶרֶת וְהַנֵּצַח וְהַהוֹד, כִּי־כֹל בַּשָּׁמַיִם וּבָאָרֶץ, לְךָ יהוה הַמַּמְלָכָה וְהַמִּתְנַשֵּׂא לְכֹל לְרֹאשׁ:

תהלים צט
רוֹמְמוּ יהוה אֱלֹהֵינוּ וְהִשְׁתַּחֲווּ לַהֲדֹם רַגְלָיו, קָדוֹשׁ הוּא: רוֹמְמוּ יהוה אֱלֹהֵינוּ וְהִשְׁתַּחֲווּ לְהַר קָדְשׁוֹ, כִּי־קָדוֹשׁ יהוה אֱלֹהֵינוּ:

אַב הָרַחֲמִים הוּא יְרַחֵם עַם עֲמוּסִים, וְיִזְכֹּר בְּרִית אֵיתָנִים, וְיַצִּיל נַפְשׁוֹתֵינוּ מִן הַשָּׁעוֹת הָרָעוֹת, וְיִגְעַר בְּיֵצֶר הָרָע מִן הַנְּשׂוּאִים, וְיָחֹן אוֹתָנוּ לִפְלֵיטַת עוֹלָמִים, וִימַלֵּא מִשְׁאֲלוֹתֵינוּ בְּמִדָּה טוֹבָה יְשׁוּעָה וְרַחֲמִים.

The ספר תורה *is placed on the* שולחן *and the* גבאי *calls a* כהן *to the* תורה.

וְתִגָּלֶה וְתֵרָאֶה מַלְכוּתוֹ עָלֵינוּ בִּזְמַן קָרוֹב, וְיָחֹן פְּלֵיטָתֵנוּ וּפְלֵיטַת עַמּוֹ בֵּית יִשְׂרָאֵל לְחֵן וּלְחֶסֶד וּלְרַחֲמִים וּלְרָצוֹן וְנֹאמַר אָמֵן. הַכֹּל הָבוּ גֹדֶל לֵאלֹהֵינוּ וּתְנוּ כָבוֹד לַתּוֹרָה. *כֹּהֵן קְרַב, יַעֲמֹד (פלוני בֶּן פלוני) הַכֹּהֵן.

**If no* כהן *is present, a* לוי *or* ישראל *is called up as follows:*

/אֵין כַּאן כֹּהֵן, יַעֲמֹד (פלוני בֶּן פלוני) בִּמְקוֹם כֹּהֵן./

בָּרוּךְ שֶׁנָּתַן תּוֹרָה לְעַמּוֹ יִשְׂרָאֵל בִּקְדֻשָּׁתוֹ.

The קהל *followed by the* גבאי*:*

דברים ד
וְאַתֶּם הַדְּבֵקִים בַּיהוה אֱלֹהֵיכֶם חַיִּים כֻּלְּכֶם הַיּוֹם:

בָּרוּךְ שֶׁנָּתַן תּוֹרָה – *Blessed is He Who... gave the Torah.* This paragraph consists of two obviously relevant verses (וַיְהִי בִּנְסֹעַ, כִּי מִצִּיּוֹן) plus this *berakha*-like pronouncement praising God for "having given the Torah to His people Israel." We can account for this declaration by recalling the very similar statement at the Pesah *Seder* made prior to studying the *Maggid* section of the *Haggada* (בָּרוּךְ הַמָּקוֹם... בָּרוּךְ שֶׁנָּתַן תּוֹרָה לְעַמּוֹ יִשְׂרָאֵל), which R. Soloveitchik considered a derivative form of *berakha* to precede the study of the *Midrash Halakha* at the core of the *Seder*. Thus this declaration preceding the Torah reading accomplishes for the congregation what the individual called to the Torah does when reciting his *berakha*, i.e., blessing God prior to performing the *mitzva* of Torah study via hearing the Torah reading (R. Basil Herring).

The Leader bows toward the Ark, raises the Sefer Torah and says:

Ps. 34 גַּדְּלוּ MAGNIFY the Lord with me,
and let us exalt His name together.

The Ark is closed. The Leader turns to his right
and carries the Torah scroll to the bima and the congregation says:

I Chr. 29 לְךָ YOURS, O LORD, are greatness, power, glory, victory, and majesty;
indeed, everything that is in the heavens and on earth. Yours, O Lord,
Ps. 99 is the dominion, and You are supreme over all. Exalt the Lord our
God, and bow down before His footstool. He is holy. Exalt the Lord
our God, and bow down before His holy mountain. Indeed, the Lord
our God is holy.

MAY THE FATHER of mercy have compassion on the people borne by Him. May He remember the covenant with the mighty (patriarchs), and deliver us from evil times. May He reproach the evil impulse in the people He carries, and graciously grant us eternal survival. May He fulfill in good measure our requests for salvation and mercy.

The Torah scroll is placed on the bima and the Gabbai calls a Kohen to the Torah.

וְתִגָּלֶה AND MAY His sovereignty over us soon be revealed and made apparent. May He be gracious to our surviving remnant and the surviving remnant of His people, the house of Israel, in grace, loving-kindness, compassion, and favor, and let us say: Amen. Let us all declare greatness to our God and give honor to the Torah. Let the *Kohen* come forward. Arise (*name* son of *father's name*), the *Kohen*.

**If no Kohen is present, a Levi or Yisrael is called up as follows:*

Since there is no *Kohen*, arise (*name* son of *father's name*) in place of a *Kohen*.

Blessed is He Who, in His holiness, gave the Torah to His people Israel.

Congregation followed by the Gabbai:

Deut. 4 And you who cleave to the Lord your God, all of you are alive this day.

כֹּהֵן קְרַב – *Kohen come forward.* Rambam in *Sefer HaMitzvot* 32 explains that a *Kohen* is the first to be called to the Torah because of the verse "You shall sanctify him because he offers the food of your God" (Lev. 21:8), which requires us to honor the descendants of Aaron, raising them on high even if they refuse the honor, for in so doing we give honor to God Who chose them to serve Him. So, too, the *Kohen* should be the first to recite a *berakha* and have the finest portion.

ברכות התורה

The קורא *shows the* עולה *the section to be read. The* עולה *touches the* ספר תורה*, but not the letters themselves, with his* ציצית *or the Torah belt or cover, which he then kisses. Holding the handles of the* ספר תורה*, he says:*

עולה: **בָּרְכוּ** אֶת יהוה הַמְבֹרָךְ.

קהל: בָּרוּךְ יהוה הַמְבֹרָךְ לְעוֹלָם וָעֶד.

עולה: בָּרוּךְ יהוה הַמְבֹרָךְ לְעוֹלָם וָעֶד.
בָּרוּךְ אַתָּה יהוה, אֱלֹהֵינוּ מֶלֶךְ הָעוֹלָם, אֲשֶׁר בָּחַר בָּנוּ מִכָּל הָעַמִּים
וְנָתַן לָנוּ אֶת תּוֹרָתוֹ. בָּרוּךְ אַתָּה יהוה, נוֹתֵן הַתּוֹרָה.

The appropriate Torah portion is read.

At the conclusion of each portion, the עולה *recites this concluding* ברכה*:*

עולה: בָּרוּךְ אַתָּה יהוה אֱלֹהֵינוּ מֶלֶךְ הָעוֹלָם, אֲשֶׁר נָתַן לָנוּ תּוֹרַת אֱמֶת וְחַיֵּי
עוֹלָם נָטַע בְּתוֹכֵנוּ. בָּרוּךְ אַתָּה יהוה, נוֹתֵן הַתּוֹרָה.

ברכת הגומל

One who has been delivered from danger recites this blessing.

בָּרוּךְ אַתָּה יהוה אֱלֹהֵינוּ מֶלֶךְ הָעוֹלָם הַגּוֹמֵל לְחַיָּבִים טוֹבוֹת, שֶׁגְּמָלַנִי
כָּל טוֹב.

If a man recites the ברכה*, the* קהל *responds:*

אָמֵן. מִי שֶׁגְּמָלְךָ כָּל טוֹב הוּא יִגְמָלְךָ כָּל טוֹב, סֶלָה.

If a woman recites the ברכה*, the* קהל *responds:*

אָמֵן. מִי שֶׁגְּמָלֵךְ כָּל טוֹב הוּא יִגְמָלֵךְ כָּל טוֹב, סֶלָה.

Special מִי שֶׁבֵּרַךְ *prayers may be said at this point.* *See pages 534–540.*

אֲשֶׁר בָּחַר בָּנוּ...וְנָתַן לָנוּ אֶת תּוֹרָתוֹ – *Who selected us... and gave us His Torah.* This *berakha* teaches that God did not give us His Torah as a result of our innate intellectual abilities, or our ability to reach unique spiritual refinement. Rather, it came solely as a result of a choice made by God, dependent solely on His initiative, and not because of any quality inhering in those who were chosen (R. Menaḥem Mendel Schneerson).

אֲשֶׁר נָתַן לָנוּ תּוֹרַת אֱמֶת... נוֹתֵן הַתּוֹרָה – *Who gave us the Torah of truth... Giver of the Torah.* This *berakha* first declares in the past tense that God "gave" us the Torah but then goes on to conclude with the present tense that He "gives" the Torah. This first phrase refers to the written Torah that was given in its entirety at Sinai, while the second one refers to the oral Torah which, with God's help, the scholars of each generation further develop and teach, allowing the people to receive the Torah anew. So, too, the Torah commands us to "ask your fathers and they will instruct you" (Deut. 32:7), meaning, heed the words of earlier authorities, while also following the instruction of the sages of your own generation as delineated in Deuteronomy 17:11. Hence, God "gave" us His

BLESSINGS OF THE TORAH

The Reader shows the oleh the section to be read. The oleh touches the scroll, but not the letters themselves, with his tzitzit or the Torah belt or cover, which he then kisses. Holding the handles of the scroll, he says:

Oleh: בָּרְכוּ BLESS the Lord, the blessed One.

Cong: BLESSED is the Lord Who is blessed for all eternity.

Oleh: BLESSED is the Lord Who is blessed for all eternity.
BLESSED are You, Lord, our God, King of the universe, Who has chosen us from all peoples and has given us His Torah. Blessed are You, Lord, Giver of the Torah.

The appropriate Torah portion is read.

At the conclusion of each portion, the oleh recites this concluding blessing:

Oleh: BLESSED are You, Lord, our God, King of the universe, Who has given us the Torah of truth, planting eternal life among us. Blessed are You, Lord, Giver of the Torah.

BLESSING OF GRATITUDE

One who has been delivered from danger recites this blessing.

בָּרוּךְ BLESSED are You, Lord, our God, King of the universe, Who bestows favors on the undeserving, and Who has bestowed every good thing on me.

Congregation responds:

Amen. May He Who has bestowed every good thing on you continue to grant you every good thing, forever.

Special Mi Sheberakh prayers may be said at this point. See pages 535–541.

Torah at Sinai, but He also "gives" it to us anew in each generation (*Benei Yisaskhar*).

וְחַיֵּי עוֹלָם – *Eternal life.* The Rambam (Guide 3:54) explains that we acquire eternal life to the extent to which we have studied and acquired truth and intellectual virtue in our lifetime. Thus when we study the Torah properly and internalize its truth we are blessed with immortality in the next world.

בִּרְכַּת הַגּוֹמֵל / BLESSING OF GRATITUDE

(See further commentary on page 542.)

The Gemara (*Berakhot* 54b) lists four instances when one must thank God: after crossing a desert, after crossing the ocean, after a serious illness, and when freed from imprisonment. We can only feel complete gratitude for God's gifts after we have been denied them in a way that has threatened our lives (R. Baḥya).

ברוך שפטרני

After a בר מצווה *has concluded the* תורה *blessings, his father says aloud:*

בָּרוּךְ (*Some say* אַתָּה יהוה אֱלֹהֵינוּ מֶלֶךְ הָעוֹלָם) שֶׁפְּטָרַנִי מֵעָנְשׁוֹ שֶׁלָּזֶה.

אזכרה

In some congregations, on days of or preceding a yahrzeit,
אֵל מָלֵא רַחֲמִים *for a relative is said.*

אֵל מָלֵא רַחֲמִים, שׁוֹכֵן בַּמְּרוֹמִים, הַמְצֵא מְנוּחָה נְכוֹנָה תַּחַת (נ״א עַל) כַּנְפֵי הַשְּׁכִינָה, בְּמַעֲלוֹת קְדוֹשִׁים וּטְהוֹרִים, כְּזֹהַר הָרָקִיעַ מַזְהִירִים, לְנִשְׁמַת

For a man:

(פלוני בֶּן פלוני) שֶׁהָלַךְ לְעוֹלָמוֹ, בַּעֲבוּר שֶׁ(פלוני בֶּן פלוני) יִתֵּן / שֶׁ(פלונית בַּת פלוני) תִּתֵּן / צְדָקָה בְּעַד הַזְכָּרַת נִשְׁמָתוֹ, בְּגַן עֵדֶן תְּהֵא מְנוּחָתוֹ. לָכֵן, בַּעַל הָרַחֲמִים יַסְתִּירֵהוּ בְּסֵתֶר כְּנָפָיו לְעוֹלָמִים, וְיִצְרֹר בִּצְרוֹר הַחַיִּים אֶת נִשְׁמָתוֹ, יהוה הוּא נַחֲלָתוֹ, וְיָנוּחַ בְּשָׁלוֹם עַל מִשְׁכָּבוֹ, וְנֹאמַר אָמֵן.

For a woman:

(פלונית בַּת פלוני) שֶׁהָלְכָה לְעוֹלָמָהּ, בַּעֲבוּר שֶׁ(פלוני בֶּן פלוני) יִתֵּן / שֶׁ(פלונית בַּת פלוני) תִּתֵּן / צְדָקָה בְּעַד הַזְכָּרַת נִשְׁמָתָהּ, בְּגַן עֵדֶן תְּהֵא מְנוּחָתָהּ. לָכֵן, בַּעַל הָרַחֲמִים יַסְתִּירֶהָ בְּסֵתֶר כְּנָפָיו לְעוֹלָמִים, וְיִצְרֹר בִּצְרוֹר הַחַיִּים אֶת נִשְׁמָתָהּ, יהוה הוּא נַחֲלָתָהּ, וְתָנוּחַ בְּשָׁלוֹם עַל מִשְׁכָּבָהּ, וְנֹאמַר אָמֵן.

There are various opinions regarding the need to recite the blessing after completing international air travel. In many communities it is customary for women who have faced life-threatening situations (including childbirth) to recite this blessing. It is preferable that they do so in the presence of a *minyan* of ten men.

When we thank God we should not restrict ourselves to the particular matter at hand, but must refer to His many blessings. Hence this *berakha* and its response both refer to כָּל טוֹב ("every good thing"); the מוֹדִים paragraph of the *Amida* lists many kindnesses one after another; and the בִּרְכַּת הַמָּזוֹן (Grace after Meals) does not thank God only for the food He has given us, but for numerous other kindnesses as well. We should never be selective in expressing our gratitude to Him when everything that we possess is entirely thanks to Him (R. Joseph B. Soloveitchik).

בָּרוּךְ שֶׁפְּטָרַנִי / BAR MITZVA BLESSING
In the *Midrash Raba* R. Elazar teaches that this is to be said by a father when his son becomes a

BAR MITZVA BLESSING

After a bar mitzva has concluded the Torah blessings, his father recites:

בָּרוּךְ BLESSED be (*Some say:* You, Lord, our God, King of the universe,) He Who has released me from further responsibility for this youth.

AZKARA

In some congregations, on days of or preceding a yahrzeit, "God, full of mercy" for a relative is said.

אֵל מָלֵא רַחֲמִים O GOD, FULL OF MERCY, Who dwells on high, grant fitting rest beneath (*Some say:* above) the protective wings of the Divine Presence, where the souls of the holy and pure ones – whose radiance is like that of the heavens – reside, to the soul of

For a man:

(*name of the deceased*) the son of (*father of the deceased*), who has gone to his eternal reward. May the Garden of Eden be his resting place, insofar as (*name of supplicant*) will make a charitable gift in memory of his soul. For this reason may the ever-merciful One shelter the deceased under His protective wings forever, and may He join his soul to lasting life. For the Lord will surely be his benefactor, so that he can rest in peace in his allotted place. And let us say, Amen.

For a woman:

(*name of the deceased*) the daughter of (*father of the deceased*), who has gone to her eternal reward. May the Garden of Eden be her resting place, insofar as (*name of supplicant*) will make a charitable gift in memory of her soul. For this reason may the ever-merciful One shelter the deceased under His protective wings forever, and may He join her soul to lasting life. For the Lord will surely be her benefactor, so that she can rest in peace in her allotted place. And let us say, Amen.

---

bar mitzva. The reason is that until a boy reaches age thirteen his father is obligated to teach him Torah. Up to that point if the child sins it is because the father did not discharge his paternal responsibility sufficiently. Therefore, the father is held accountable for his son's behavior until the *bar mitzva.* Thereafter the son is considered sufficiently mature to take responsibility for his own actions (*Magen Avraham*).

The *Tashbetz Katan*, Maharil, and Vilna Gaon are of the opinion that this is a regular *berakha*, and thus should be recited using God's name. The Rema prefers that we not invoke God's name in this case, since the Talmud does not mention this *berakha.* Ashkenazic communities of Eastern Europe mostly follow the Rema, while German-Jewish communities and followers of the Vilna Gaon tend to recite the blessing in full.

חצי קדיש

After the קריאת התורה, *the* קורא *says* חצי קדיש:

הקורא: **יִתְגַּדַּל** וְיִתְקַדַּשׁ שְׁמֵהּ רַבָּא (קהל: אָמֵן) בְּעָלְמָא דִּי בְרָא כִרְעוּתֵהּ. וְיַמְלִיךְ מַלְכוּתֵהּ בְּחַיֵּיכוֹן וּבְיוֹמֵיכוֹן וּבְחַיֵּי דְכָל בֵּית יִשְׂרָאֵל, בַּעֲגָלָא וּבִזְמַן קָרִיב, וְאִמְרוּ אָמֵן. (קהל: אָמֵן)

הקהל והקורא: יְהֵא שְׁמֵהּ רַבָּא מְבָרַךְ לְעָלַם וּלְעָלְמֵי עָלְמַיָּא.

הקורא: יִתְבָּרַךְ וְיִשְׁתַּבַּח וְיִתְפָּאַר וְיִתְרוֹמַם וְיִתְנַשֵּׂא, וְיִתְהַדָּר וְיִתְעַלֶּה וְיִתְהַלָּל שְׁמֵהּ דְּקֻדְשָׁא בְּרִיךְ הוּא (קהל: בְּרִיךְ הוּא), לְעֵלָּא מִן כָּל בִּרְכָתָא / בעשרת ימי תשובה: לְעֵלָּא (וּ)לְעֵלָּא מִכָּל בִּרְכָתָא/ וְשִׁירָתָא, תֻּשְׁבְּחָתָא וְנֶחֱמָתָא דַּאֲמִירָן בְּעָלְמָא, וְאִמְרוּ אָמֵן. (קהל: אָמֵן)

הגבהה וגלילה

The ספר תורה *is lifted and the* קהל *says:*

דברים ד **וְזֹאת הַתּוֹרָה** אֲשֶׁר־שָׂם מֹשֶׁה לִפְנֵי בְּנֵי יִשְׂרָאֵל: עַל־פִּי יהוה בְּיַד־מֹשֶׁה:

Some add:

משלי ג עֵץ־חַיִּים הִיא לַמַּחֲזִיקִים בָּהּ וְתֹמְכֶיהָ מְאֻשָּׁר: דְּרָכֶיהָ דַרְכֵי־נֹעַם וְכָל־
ישעיה מב נְתִיבֹתֶיהָ שָׁלוֹם: אֹרֶךְ יָמִים בִּימִינָהּ, בִּשְׂמֹאולָהּ עֹשֶׁר וְכָבוֹד: יהוה חָפֵץ
לְמַעַן צִדְקוֹ יַגְדִּיל תּוֹרָה וְיַאְדִּיר:

יהי רצון ליום שני ויום חמישי

On those Mondays and Thursdays when תחנון *is said, the* שליח ציבור *says the following while the* ספר תורה *is being bound:*

יְהִי רָצוֹן מִלִּפְנֵי אָבִינוּ שֶׁבַּשָּׁמַיִם, לְכוֹנֵן אֶת בֵּית חַיֵּינוּ, וּלְהָשִׁיב אֶת שְׁכִינָתוֹ בְּתוֹכֵנוּ, בִּמְהֵרָה בְיָמֵינוּ, וְנֹאמַר אָמֵן.

יְהִי רָצוֹן מִלִּפְנֵי אָבִינוּ שֶׁבַּשָּׁמַיִם, לְרַחֵם עָלֵינוּ וְעַל פְּלֵיטָתֵנוּ, וְלִמְנֹעַ מַשְׁחִית וּמַגֵּפָה מֵעָלֵינוּ, וּמֵעַל כָּל עַמּוֹ בֵּית יִשְׂרָאֵל, וְנֹאמַר אָמֵן.

HALF KADDISH

After the reading of the Torah, the Reader says Half Kaddish:

Reader: יִתְגַּדַּל EXALTED AND HALLOWED may God's great name be, in the world He created as He willed. May He reign in your lifetimes and in your days, and in the lifetime of the whole house of Israel, speedily and soon, and say, Amen.

All: May His great name be blessed forever and all time.

Reader: Blessed and praised, honored, extolled, glorified, adored and exalted above all be the name of the Holy One, blessed is He, (*Between Rosh Hashana & Yom Kippur:* above and) beyond any blessing, hymn, praise, or expressions of consolation that may be uttered in this world, and say, Amen.

HAGBAHA AND GELILA

The Torah scroll is lifted and the congregations says:

Deut. 4 וְזֹאת הַתּוֹרָה THIS IS THE TORAH that Moses set before the children of Israel. It was according to the Lord's command, at the hand of Moses.

Some add:

Prov. 3 It is a tree of life for those who grasp it, and they who uphold it are made happy. Its ways are ways of pleasantness, and all its paths are peace. Length
Is. 42 of days is in its right hand, and wealth and honor in its left hand. The Lord was pleased, for the sake of [Israel's] righteousness, to magnify the Torah and glorify it.

YEHI RATZON FOR MONDAYS AND THURSDAYS

On those Mondays and Thursdays when Tahanun is said,
the Leader says the following while the Torah scroll is being bound:

יְהִי רָצוֹן MAY IT BE the will of our Father in heaven to prepare the home of our [national] existence, and to return His Presence amongst us, speedily in our days – and let us say: Amen.

MAY IT BE the will of our Father in heaven to have compassion for us and upon our surviving remnant, and to keep destruction and contagion away from us and from all His people, the house of Israel – and let us say: Amen.

יְהִי רָצוֹן מִלִּפְנֵי אָבִינוּ שֶׁבַּשָּׁמַיִם, לְקַיֵּם בָּנוּ חַכְמֵי יִשְׂרָאֵל, הֵם וּנְשֵׁיהֶם וּבְנֵיהֶם וּבְנוֹתֵיהֶם, וְתַלְמִידֵיהֶם וְתַלְמִידֵי תַלְמִידֵיהֶם, בְּכָל מְקוֹמוֹת מוֹשְׁבוֹתֵיהֶם, וְנֹאמַר אָמֵן.

יְהִי רָצוֹן מִלִּפְנֵי אָבִינוּ שֶׁבַּשָּׁמַיִם, שֶׁנִּשְׁמַע וְנִתְבַּשֵּׂר בְּשׂוֹרוֹת טוֹבוֹת, יְשׁוּעוֹת וְנֶחָמוֹת, וִיקַבֵּץ נִדָּחֵינוּ מֵאַרְבַּע כַּנְפוֹת הָאָרֶץ, וְנֹאמַר אָמֵן.

All:

אַחֵינוּ כָּל בֵּית יִשְׂרָאֵל, הַנְּתוּנִים בְּצָרָה וּבְשִׁבְיָה, הָעוֹמְדִים בֵּין בַּיָּם וּבֵין בַּיַּבָּשָׁה, הַמָּקוֹם יְרַחֵם עֲלֵיהֶם וְיוֹצִיאֵם מִצָּרָה לִרְוָחָה, וּמֵאֲפֵלָה לְאוֹרָה, וּמִשִּׁעְבּוּד לִגְאֻלָּה, הַשְׁתָּא בַּעֲגָלָא וּבִזְמַן קָרִיב, וְנֹאמַר אָמֵן.

הכנסת ספר תורה

The ארון קודש *is opened. The* שליח ציבור *takes the* ספר תורה *and says:*

יְהַלְלוּ אֶת־שֵׁם יהוה, כִּי נִשְׂגָּב־שְׁמוֹ לְבַדּוֹ תהלים קמח

The קהל *responds:*

הוֹדוֹ עַל־אֶרֶץ וְשָׁמָיִם: וַיָּרֶם קֶרֶן לְעַמּוֹ, תְּהִלָּה לְכָל־חֲסִידָיו, לִבְנֵי יִשְׂרָאֵל עַם קְרֹבוֹ, הַלְלוּיָהּ:

As the ספר תורה *is returned to the* ארון קודש, *say:*

לְדָוִד מִזְמוֹר, לַיהוה הָאָרֶץ וּמְלוֹאָהּ, תֵּבֵל וְיֹשְׁבֵי בָהּ: כִּי־הוּא עַל־יַמִּים יְסָדָהּ, וְעַל־נְהָרוֹת יְכוֹנְנֶהָ: מִי־יַעֲלֶה תהלים כד

אַחֵינוּ כָּל בֵּית יִשְׂרָאֵל – *Our brethren the whole House of Israel*. When we pray for the well-being of our fellow Jews, as we do in reciting this paragraph, we are to consider all Jews as being "our brothers," members of the "house of Israel," that is, like one household, the members of which are like a single family. The corollary of this attitude is that while we may disagree or argue from time to time, we must do so lovingly, as family members. The paragraph in its totality epitomizes the imperative of Jewish co-responsibility. The Gemara (*Sanhedrin* 27b and *Shevuot* 39a) refers to this principle as עֲרֵבוּת (mutual responsibility), based on Leviticus 26:37, to be expressed in two ways. First, we are responsible for other Jews' fulfillment of

MAY IT BE the will of our Father in heaven to preserve among us sages of Israel: them, their wives, their sons and daughters, their students and their students' students, in all their dwelling places – and let us say: Amen.

MAY IT BE the will of our Father in heaven that we may hear and be given good tidings of salvation and consolation, and that He gather our dispersed from the four corners of the earth – and let us say: Amen.

All:

MAY THE OMNIPRESENT ONE have mercy on our brethren the whole House of Israel who are in distress or captivity, whether on sea or land. May He lead them from distress to relief, from darkness to light, and from oppression to redemption, now, swiftly and soon – and let us say: Amen.

RETURNING THE TORAH TO THE ARK

The Ark is opened. The Leader takes the Torah scroll and says:

Ps. 148 **יְהַלְלוּ** LET THEM PRAISE the name of the Lord, that His name alone is exalted.

The congregation responds:

His glory is over the earth and the heavens. And He has raised the horn of His people, praise for all His pious ones, for the children of Israel, the people near to Him. Praise the Lord.

As the Torah scroll is returned to the Ark, say:

Ps. 24 **לְדָוִד מִזְמוֹר** OF DAVID. A psalm. The earth is the Lord's and the fullness thereof, the world and those who dwell in it. For He has

---

mitzvot. Thus – in the specific context of prayer – we can, through our recital of prayers and *berakhot* fulfill their prayer obligations under certain circumstances. Secondly, as R. Yona explains, we are obligated to protect them and save their lives. In short, if one Jew suffers, we should all share that pain; if one Jew transgresses we are all diminished; and if one Jew is morally culpable we are all held responsible by our enemies (R. Basil Herring).

לְדָוִד מִזְמוֹר – *Of David. A psalm.* This psalm is

בְהַר־יהוה, וּמִי־יָקוּם בִּמְקוֹם קָדְשׁוֹ: נְקִי כַפַּיִם וּבַר־לֵבָב, אֲשֶׁר
לֹא־נָשָׂא לַשָּׁוְא נַפְשִׁי וְלֹא נִשְׁבַּע לְמִרְמָה: יִשָּׂא בְרָכָה מֵאֵת יהוה,
וּצְדָקָה מֵאֱלֹהֵי יִשְׁעוֹ: זֶה דּוֹר דֹּרְשָׁו, מְבַקְשֵׁי פָנֶיךָ, יַעֲקֹב, סֶלָה:
שְׂאוּ שְׁעָרִים רָאשֵׁיכֶם, וְהִנָּשְׂאוּ פִּתְחֵי עוֹלָם, וְיָבוֹא מֶלֶךְ הַכָּבוֹד:
מִי זֶה מֶלֶךְ הַכָּבוֹד, יהוה עִזּוּז וְגִבּוֹר, יהוה גִּבּוֹר מִלְחָמָה: שְׂאוּ
שְׁעָרִים רָאשֵׁיכֶם, וּשְׂאוּ פִּתְחֵי עוֹלָם, וְיָבֹא מֶלֶךְ הַכָּבוֹד: מִי הוּא
זֶה מֶלֶךְ הַכָּבוֹד, יהוה צְבָאוֹת הוּא מֶלֶךְ הַכָּבוֹד, סֶלָה:

As the ספר תורה *is placed into the* ארון קודש, *say:*

וּבְנֻחֹה יֹאמַר, שׁוּבָה יהוה רִבְבוֹת אַלְפֵי יִשְׂרָאֵל: קוּמָה יהוה במדבר י / תהלים קלב
לִמְנוּחָתֶךָ, אַתָּה וַאֲרוֹן עֻזֶּךָ: כֹּהֲנֶיךָ יִלְבְּשׁוּ־צֶדֶק, וַחֲסִידֶיךָ
יְרַנֵּנוּ: בַּעֲבוּר דָּוִד עַבְדֶּךָ אַל־תָּשֵׁב פְּנֵי מְשִׁיחֶךָ: כִּי לֶקַח טוֹב נָתַתִּי משלי ד
לָכֶם, תּוֹרָתִי אַל־תַּעֲזֹבוּ: עֵץ־חַיִּים הִיא לַמַּחֲזִיקִים בָּהּ, וְתֹמְכֶיהָ משלי ג
מְאֻשָּׁר: דְּרָכֶיהָ דַרְכֵי־נֹעַם וְכָל־נְתִיבוֹתֶיהָ שָׁלוֹם: ◂ הֲשִׁיבֵנוּ יהוה איכה ה
אֵלֶיךָ וְנָשׁוּבָה, חַדֵּשׁ יָמֵינוּ כְּקֶדֶם:

The ארון קודש *is closed.*

---

recited when the Torah is returned to the Ark just as was done in antiquity whenever the Ark of the Covenant was brought back to the Temple. Appropriate to such an occasion, it affirms that (1) even though God dwells in His holy place, He can be encountered throughout the universe; (2) in addition to those who actually offer sacrifices others can qualify to enter the Temple by dedicating themselves to purity of thought and action; and finally (3) God, and no other, should be considered the King of glory (R. Amos Ḥakham).

The Gemara (*Shabbat* 30a) explains that this psalm relates to the first occasion on which Solomon brought the Ark into the Temple. In spite of his entreaties, the gates refused to open, until he invoked the merit of his father David. This event is alluded to in the subsequent paragraph quoting Psalm 132:10, "For the sake of David Your servant, do not turn away the face of Your anointed." While David was not privileged to build the Temple it was only in his merit that the Temple could be inaugurated. We learn from this that it is not always given to us to see the success of our labors in our own lifetime. Sometimes we must experience failure, only to have our efforts bear fruit long after we are gone. Ultimately we are not measured by our immediate successes or victories, but by our determination and effort

founded it upon the seas, and has established it upon the floods. Who shall ascend the mountain of the Lord, and who shall stand in His holy place? He who has clean hands and a pure heart, who has not sworn in vain "by my soul," and has not sworn deceitfully, he shall receive the blessing from the Lord, and righteousness from the God of his salvation. This is the company of those who seek Him, who seek Your face, Jacob. Selah. Lift up your heads, O gates, and be lifted up, O everlasting doors, so that the King of glory may come in. Who is this King of glory? The Lord strong and mighty, the Lord mighty in battle. Lift up your heads, O gates, and lift them up, O everlasting doors, so that the King of glory may come in. Who is He, this King of glory? The Lord of hosts, He is the King of glory. Selah.

As the Torah scroll is placed into the Ark, say:

Num. 10 **וּבְנֻחֹה** AND WHEN the Ark rested, Moses would say: "Return, O
Ps. 132 Lord, to the myriad thousands of Israel." Arise, O Lord, to Your
resting place, You and the Ark of Your strength. May Your priests
be clothed in righteousness, and may Your pious ones shout for joy.
For the sake of David Your servant, do not turn away the face of
Prov. 4 Your anointed. I have given you a good doctrine, My Torah, do not
Prov. 3 forsake it. It is a tree of life for those who grasp it, and they who
uphold it are made happy. Its ways are ways of pleasantness, and all
Lam. 5 its paths are peace. ▸ Lord, turn us to You once again, for we wish to
return; renew our days as of old.

The Ark is closed.

---

toward the goal of furthering God's name in His world (R. Basil Herring).

חַדֵּשׁ יָמֵינוּ כְּקֶדֶם – *Renew our days as of old.* We do not seek a redemption that will depart radically from the patterns of the past, but rather one that will reconstitute the glory, both moral and spiritual, that once was ours. The future utopia for which we pray will not involve a rejection of the past, but rather a fulfillment of the values and aspirations of the Jewish people since time immemorial. The old will be renewed, and the new will be sanctified (R. Avraham Yitzḥak HaKohen Kook).

סיום התפילה

Some have the custom to touch the תפילין של יד *at* °, *and the* תפילין של ראש *at* °°.

תהלים פד **אַשְׁרֵי** יוֹשְׁבֵי בֵיתֶךָ, עוֹד יְהַלְלוּךָ סֶּלָה:

תהלים קמד אַשְׁרֵי הָעָם שֶׁכָּכָה לּוֹ, אַשְׁרֵי הָעָם שֶׁיהוה אֱלֹהָיו:

תהלים קמה תְּהִלָּה לְדָוִד

אֲרוֹמִמְךָ אֱלוֹהַי הַמֶּלֶךְ, וַאֲבָרְכָה שִׁמְךָ לְעוֹלָם וָעֶד:

בְּכָל־יוֹם אֲבָרְכֶךָּ, וַאֲהַלְלָה שִׁמְךָ לְעוֹלָם וָעֶד:

גָּדוֹל יהוה וּמְהֻלָּל מְאֹד, וְלִגְדֻלָּתוֹ אֵין חֵקֶר:

דּוֹר לְדוֹר יְשַׁבַּח מַעֲשֶׂיךָ, וּגְבוּרֹתֶיךָ יַגִּידוּ:

הֲדַר כְּבוֹד הוֹדֶךָ, וְדִבְרֵי נִפְלְאֹתֶיךָ אָשִֽׂיחָה:

וֶעֱזוּז נוֹרְאֹתֶיךָ יֹאמֵרוּ, וּגְדוּלָּתְךָ אֲסַפְּרֶנָּה:

זֵכֶר רַב־טוּבְךָ יַבִּיעוּ, וְצִדְקָתְךָ יְרַנֵּנוּ:

חַנּוּן וְרַחוּם יהוה, אֶרֶךְ אַפַּיִם וּגְדָל־חָסֶד:

טוֹב־יהוה לַכֹּל, וְרַחֲמָיו עַל־כָּל־מַעֲשָׂיו:

יוֹדוּךָ יהוה כָּל־מַעֲשֶׂיךָ, וַחֲסִידֶיךָ יְבָרְכוּכָה:

כְּבוֹד מַלְכוּתְךָ יֹאמֵרוּ, וּגְבוּרָתְךָ יְדַבֵּרוּ:

לְהוֹדִיעַ לִבְנֵי הָאָדָם גְּבוּרֹתָיו, וּכְבוֹד הֲדַר מַלְכוּתוֹ:

מַלְכוּתְךָ מַלְכוּת כָּל־עֹלָמִים, וּמֶמְשַׁלְתְּךָ בְּכָל־דּוֹר וָדֹר:

סוֹמֵךְ יהוה לְכָל־הַנֹּפְלִים, וְזוֹקֵף לְכָל־הַכְּפוּפִים:

עֵינֵי־כֹל אֵלֶיךָ יְשַׂבֵּרוּ, וְאַתָּה נוֹתֵן־לָהֶם אֶת־אָכְלָם בְּעִתּוֹ:

°**פּ**וֹתֵחַ אֶת־יָדֶךָ, °°וּמַשְׂבִּיעַ לְכָל־חַי רָצוֹן:

צַדִּיק יהוה בְּכָל־דְּרָכָיו, וְחָסִיד בְּכָל־מַעֲשָׂיו:

קָרוֹב יהוה לְכָל־קֹרְאָיו, לְכֹל אֲשֶׁר יִקְרָאֻהוּ בֶאֱמֶת:

אַשְׁרֵי / ASHREI

In accordance with the Gemara *Berakhot* 4b in the name of R. Avina, that reciting *Ashrei* three times daily merits life in the World to Come, this constitutes the second recital, while the third initiates the *Minḥa* service.

CONCLUSION OF THE SERVICE

Some have the custom to touch the hand-tefillin at °, and the head-tefillin at °°.

Ps. 84 **אַשְׁרֵי** HAPPY are those who dwell in Your house.
They will forever praise You. Selah.

Ps. 144 HAPPY is the people that has this.
Happy is the people whose God is the Lord.

Ps. 145 A PRAISE OF DAVID.

א I exalt You, my God, the King,
and I will bless Your name forever and ever.
ב Every day I will bless You, and I will praise Your name forever and ever.
ג Great is the Lord, and very praiseworthy,
and His greatness is boundless.
ד One generation lauds Your works to another,
and they declare Your mighty deeds.
ה I speak of the splendid glory of Your majesty
and of Your wondrous works,
ו And they speak of the might of Your awesome deeds,
and I declare Your greatness.
ז They express the renown of Your great goodness,
and sing of Your righteousness.
ח Gracious and merciful is the Lord,
slow to anger and great in loving-kindness.
ט The Lord is good to all, and His mercies are upon all His works.
י All Your works thank You, O Lord, and Your pious ones bless You.
כ They describe the glory of Your kingdom, and speak of Your might,
ל To make known to the sons of man His mighty deeds,
and the glorious splendor of His kingdom.
מ Your kingdom is a kingdom for all times,
and Your dominion is for every generation.
ס The Lord supports all who fall and raises up all who are bowed down.
ע The eyes of all await You, and You give them their food in its time.
פ °You open Your hand, °°and You satisfy the desire of every living thing.
צ The Lord is righteous in all His ways and kind in all His works.
ק The Lord is near to all who address Him,
to all who address Him in truth.

רְצוֹן־יְרֵאָיו יַעֲשֶׂה, וְאֶת־שַׁוְעָתָם יִשְׁמַע וְיוֹשִׁיעֵם:
שׁוֹמֵר יהוה אֶת־כָּל־אֹהֲבָיו, וְאֵת כָּל־הָרְשָׁעִים יַשְׁמִיד:
◂ תְּהִלַּת יהוה יְדַבֶּר פִּי, וִיבָרֵךְ כָּל־בָּשָׂר שֵׁם קָדְשׁוֹ לְעוֹלָם וָעֶד:
תהלים קטו וַאֲנַחְנוּ נְבָרֵךְ יָהּ מֵעַתָּה וְעַד־עוֹלָם, הַלְלוּיָהּ:

Omit on ראש חודש, ערב פסח, חול המועד, תשעה באב, ערב יום כיפור,
חנוכה, פורים, שושן פורים, *the 14th and 15th of* אדר א׳ (פורים קטן),
יום העצמאות, יום ירושלים, *and in a* שבעה *house.*

תהלים כ **לַמְנַצֵּחַ** מִזְמוֹר לְדָוִד: יַעַנְךָ יהוה בְּיוֹם צָרָה, יְשַׂגֶּבְךָ שֵׁם אֱלֹהֵי
יַעֲקֹב: יִשְׁלַח־עֶזְרְךָ מִקֹּדֶשׁ, וּמִצִּיּוֹן יִסְעָדֶךָּ: יִזְכֹּר כָּל־
מִנְחֹתֶךָ, וְעוֹלָתְךָ יְדַשְּׁנֶה סֶלָה: יִתֶּן־לְךָ כִלְבָבֶךָ וְכָל־עֲצָתְךָ יְמַלֵּא:
נְרַנְּנָה בִּישׁוּעָתֶךָ, וּבְשֵׁם־אֱלֹהֵינוּ נִדְגֹּל, יְמַלֵּא יהוה כָּל־מִשְׁאֲלוֹתֶיךָ:
עַתָּה יָדַעְתִּי כִּי הוֹשִׁיעַ יהוה מְשִׁיחוֹ, יַעֲנֵהוּ מִשְּׁמֵי קָדְשׁוֹ, בִּגְבֻרוֹת
יֵשַׁע יְמִינוֹ: אֵלֶּה בָרֶכֶב וְאֵלֶּה בַסּוּסִים, וַאֲנַחְנוּ בְּשֵׁם־יהוה אֱלֹהֵינוּ
נַזְכִּיר: הֵמָּה כָּרְעוּ וְנָפָלוּ, וַאֲנַחְנוּ קַּמְנוּ וַנִּתְעוֹדָד: ◂ יהוה הוֹשִׁיעָה,
הַמֶּלֶךְ יַעֲנֵנוּ בְיוֹם־קָרְאֵנוּ:

וַאֲנַחְנוּ נְבָרֵךְ יָהּ – *But we will bless the Lord*. This verse from Psalm 115 was added to the end of *Ashrei* (i.e., Ps. 145). The reason is that the last verse of Psalm 145 declares the praise of י־ק־ו־ק (the Lord), i.e., God's four-lettered name, adding, "May all flesh bless His holy name forever and ever." The verse from Psalm 115 refers to ק־ה (His two-lettered name) which "we will bless... from now and forevermore." Thus the verse in Psalm 145 declares that in the Messianic era all mankind will come to know God in the fullness of His name, that is, when He will be revealed in all of His glory. By contrast, the verse from Psalm 115 declares that "we (i.e., the Jewish people) will bless ק־ה (God) now," that is, even in this pre-Messianic era when His glory is only partially revealed (as symbolized by His two-lettered name). This is in spite of the tribulations of הֶסְתֵּר פָּנִים (His hiddenness from us) – still we faithfully bless Him, now and forevermore (R. Joseph B. Soloveitchik).

יַעַנְךָ ה׳ בְּיוֹם צָרָה – *May the Lord answer you in the day of trouble*. The *Midrash Shoḥer Tov* explains this verse by the following analogy. A father and his son set out on an inter-city journey. After a long time passes the son asks, "Father, when will we reach our destination?" To which the father replies, "when you see a cemetery you will know we are almost there, for cemeteries are located right outside cities." So too, God declares to his people: "If you experience suffering or loss know that soon God will answer you to redeem you." The verse can also be understood in light of the statement of Ben Hei Hei (*Pirkei Avot* 5:26) that our reward will be in accordance with our צַעַר, that is, God rewards us as a result of, and in accordance with, our pain.

ר He does the will of those who fear Him,
and He hears their cry and saves them.
ש The Lord preserves all who love Him,
but all the wicked He destroys.
ת ▸ May my mouth speak the praise of the Lord,
and may all flesh bless His holy name forever and ever.

Ps. 115 But we will bless the Lord from now and forevermore. Praise the Lord.

Omit on Rosh Ḥodesh, Erev Pesaḥ, Ḥol HaMo'ed, Tisha B'Av, Erev Yom Kippur, Hanukka, Purim, Shushan Purim, the 14th and 15th of Adar I (Purim Katan,) Yom HaAtzma'ut, Yom Yerushalayim, and in a shiva house.

Ps. 20 **לַמְנַצֵּחַ** TO THE DIRECTOR of music. A psalm of David. May the Lord answer you in the day of trouble. May the name of the God of Jacob exalt you. May He send you help from the sanctuary, and may He support you from Zion. May He remember all your offerings, and may He accept the ashes of your burnt-offerings. Selah. May He grant to you according to your heart, and may He fulfill all your counsel. May we shout for joy in your salvation, and may we gather in the name of our God. May the Lord fulfill all your petitions. Now I know that the Lord will deliver His anointed one. He will answer him from His sanctuary in heaven, with the mighty acts of His right hand which delivers. Some trust in chariots, and some in horses, but we will proclaim the name of the Lord our God. They have knelt down and fallen, but we have risen and overcome. ▸ O Lord, save us! The King will answer us on the day that we call.

הֵמָּה כָּרְעוּ וְנָפָלוּ, וַאֲנַחְנוּ קַמְנוּ וַנִּתְעוֹדָד – *They have knelt down and fallen, but we have risen and overcome.* In the closing days of the Second World War, R. Yeḥezkel Ruttner was deported from Auschwitz to the ruins of the Warsaw Ghetto to clean up the debris. As the surrounding Soviet army shelled the city, some German soldiers sought refuge with their Jewish prisoners, in the belief that the Russians would avoid killing the remaining Jews. One night, with cannon-fire falling all around them, a fearful SS officer instructed the rabbi to pray for them all. He replied, "I will pray, but the prayers of a group are more effective. In Judaism unity of the people is essential. A quorum of ten is needed for prayer." The officer agreed, and thus, in the ruins of the Warsaw Ghetto, under SS orders, a *minyan* of Jews recited Psalm 20, with special attention to the verse: "They have knelt down and fallen, but we have risen and over-

In a שבעה *house and on* תשעה באב *omit the verse beginning* וְאַתָּה קָדוֹשׁ *and continue with* וַאֲנִי זֹאת בְּרִיתִי.

ישעיה נט **וּבָא לְצִיּוֹן** גּוֹאֵל, וּלְשָׁבֵי פֶשַׁע בְּיַעֲקֹב, נְאֻם יהוה: וַאֲנִי זֹאת בְּרִיתִי אוֹתָם, אָמַר יהוה, רוּחִי אֲשֶׁר עָלֶיךָ וּדְבָרַי אֲשֶׁר־שַׂמְתִּי בְּפִיךָ, לֹא־יָמְוּשׁוּ מִפִּיךָ וּמִפִּי זַרְעֲךָ וּמִפִּי זֶרַע זַרְעֲךָ, אָמַר יהוה, מֵעַתָּה וְעַד־עוֹלָם:

תהלים כב ◄ **וְאַתָּה קָדוֹשׁ** יוֹשֵׁב תְּהִלּוֹת יִשְׂרָאֵל: וְקָרָא זֶה אֶל־זֶה וְאָמַר,
ישעיה ו
קָדוֹשׁ, קָדוֹשׁ, קָדוֹשׁ יהוה צְבָאוֹת, מְלֹא כָל־הָאָרֶץ כְּבוֹדוֹ:

תרגום יונתן ישעיה ו
וּמְקַבְּלִין דֵּין מִן דֵּין וְאָמְרִין, קַדִּישׁ בִּשְׁמֵי מְרוֹמָא עִלָּאָה בֵּית שְׁכִינְתֵּהּ, קַדִּישׁ עַל אַרְעָא עוֹבַד גְּבוּרְתֵּהּ, קַדִּישׁ לְעָלַם וּלְעָלְמֵי עָלְמַיָּא, יהוה צְבָאוֹת, מַלְיָא כָל אַרְעָא זִיו יְקָרֵהּ.

יחזקאל ג ◄ וַתִּשָּׂאֵנִי רוּחַ, וָאֶשְׁמַע אַחֲרַי קוֹל רַעַשׁ גָּדוֹל, בָּרוּךְ כְּבוֹד־יהוה מִמְּקוֹמוֹ:

תרגום יונתן יחזקאל ג
וּנְטָלַתְנִי רוּחָא, וּשְׁמָעִית בַּתְרַי קָל זִיעַ סַגִּיא, דִּמְשַׁבְּחִין וְאָמְרִין בְּרִיךְ יְקָרָא דַיהוה מֵאֲתַר בֵּית שְׁכִינְתֵּהּ.

שמות טו
יהוה יִמְלֹךְ לְעֹלָם וָעֶד:

תרגום אונקלוס שמות טו
יהוה מַלְכוּתֵהּ קָאֵם לְעָלַם וּלְעָלְמֵי עָלְמַיָּא.

---

come." No bomb fell on them that night, and R. Ruttner survived the war (Prof. Yaffa Eliach).

וּבָא לְצִיּוֹן / UVA LETZIYON

This is the only "*Kedusha*" mentioned in the Talmud, as found in *Sota* 49a. There Rava states that the continued existence of the world depends on "the recital of *Kedusha deSidra* and *Yeheh shemeh raba* following study of *Aggadeta*." Rashi explains this as referring to the widespread custom in Babylonia to study Torah at the conclusion of morning services, and thus by reciting the scriptural verses found in the *Amida Kedusha*, the congregation accomplished Torah study as well as 'קְדֻשַּׁת ה (the declaration of the sanctity of God). This, says Rashi, makes this a particularly desirable prayer. Clearly the unusual inclusion of the vernacular Aramaic translation and detailed commentary surrounding the quoted verses confirms that it was intended as Torah study by the untutored masses, followed in the prayer itself by a variation on the *Birkhot HaTorah*. Indeed, a responsum of R. Natronai

In a shiva house and on Tisha B'Av omit the verse beginning "As for Me" and continue with "In truth, You are holy."

Is. 59 וּבָא לְצִיּוֹן A REDEEMER shall come to Zion and to those in Jacob who turn away from sin – the Lord has said so. As for me, the Lord has said, "This is My covenant with them. My spirit which is upon you, and My words which I have put in your mouth, shall not depart out of your mouth, nor out of the mouths of your children, nor out of the mouths of your children's children, not now and not ever," so the Lord has said.

Ps. 22 ▸ וְאַתָּה קָדוֹשׁ BUT YOU ARE HOLY. You sit among the praises of Israel.
Is. 6 The angels called to one another and said, Holy, holy, holy is the Lord of hosts, the whole world is filled with His glory.

Targum Yonatan Is. 6 And they receive word from each other and say, Holy in the highest heaven, the abode of His Divine Presence, holy upon earth, the work of His mighty power, holy forever and to all eternity is the Lord of hosts. The whole earth is full of His glorious splendor.

Ezek. 3 ▸ Then a spirit uplifted me, and I heard behind me a powerful moving sound, Blessed is the glory of the Lord from His place.

Targum Yonatan Ezek. 3 Then a spirit lifted me up and I heard behind me the powerful moving sound of those who uttered His praise, proclaiming, "Blessed be the glory of the Lord from the abode of His Divine Presence."

Ex. 15 The Lord shall reign forever and ever.
Targum Onkelos Ex. 15 The sovereignty of the Lord is established forever and ever.

Gaon describes it similarly; it was not so much inserted as a prayer but as an act of daily Torah study, originally part of a lengthy סִדְרָא (study session) which over time was shortened to the study of only these few verses. It is likely that Rava was not referring primarily to the words of the *Kedusha* quoted in the prayer but rather to the *Kaddish* (and its associated *Yeheh shemeh raba*) that follows it, as is customary with all Torah study. Thus what upholds the world is not the recital of this derivative *Kedusha* but the all-important study of Torah that preceded it. The verses from the regular *Kedusha* were chosen for such study, in addition to the other selected verses, to also allow those who might have missed the *Amida Kedusha* (or who were praying without a *minyan*) to recite the *Kedusha* in an attenuated form (Prof. Ezra Fleischer).

The Kabbalists understood the three *Kedusha* prayers of *Shaharit* to reflect a spiritual

דברי הימים א׳ כט
יהוה אֱלֹהֵי אַבְרָהָם יִצְחָק וְיִשְׂרָאֵל אֲבֹתֵינוּ, שָׁמְרָה־זֹּאת לְעוֹלָם
תהלים עח
לְיֵצֶר מַחְשְׁבוֹת לְבַב עַמֶּךָ, וְהָכֵן לְבָבָם אֵלֶיךָ: וְהוּא רַחוּם
יְכַפֵּר עָוֹן וְלֹא־יַשְׁחִית, וְהִרְבָּה לְהָשִׁיב אַפּוֹ, וְלֹא־יָעִיר כָּל־חֲמָתוֹ:
תהלים פו
כִּי־אַתָּה אֲדֹנָי טוֹב וְסַלָּח, וְרַב־חֶסֶד לְכָל־קֹרְאֶיךָ: צִדְקָתְךָ צֶדֶק
תהלים קיט
לְעוֹלָם וְתוֹרָתְךָ אֱמֶת: תִּתֵּן אֱמֶת לְיַעֲקֹב, חֶסֶד לְאַבְרָהָם, אֲשֶׁר־
מיכה ז
נִשְׁבַּעְתָּ לַאֲבֹתֵינוּ מִימֵי קֶדֶם: בָּרוּךְ אֲדֹנָי יוֹם יוֹם יַעֲמָס־לָנוּ, הָאֵל
תהלים סח
יְשׁוּעָתֵנוּ סֶלָה: יהוה צְבָאוֹת עִמָּנוּ, מִשְׂגָּב לָנוּ אֱלֹהֵי יַעֲקֹב סֶלָה:
תהלים מו
יהוה צְבָאוֹת, אַשְׁרֵי אָדָם בֹּטֵחַ בָּךְ: יהוה הוֹשִׁיעָה, הַמֶּלֶךְ יַעֲנֵנוּ
תהלים פד
תהלים כ
בְיוֹם־קָרְאֵנוּ:

בָּרוּךְ הוּא אֱלֹהֵינוּ שֶׁבְּרָאָנוּ לִכְבוֹדוֹ, וְהִבְדִּילָנוּ מִן הַתּוֹעִים, וְנָתַן לָנוּ תּוֹרַת אֱמֶת, וְחַיֵּי עוֹלָם נָטַע בְּתוֹכֵנוּ. הוּא יִפְתַּח לִבֵּנוּ בְּתוֹרָתוֹ, וְיָשֵׂם בְּלִבֵּנוּ אַהֲבָתוֹ וְיִרְאָתוֹ וְלַעֲשׂוֹת רְצוֹנוֹ וּלְעָבְדוֹ בְּלֵבָב שָׁלֵם, לְמַעַן לֹא נִיגַע לָרִיק וְלֹא נֵלֵד לַבֶּהָלָה.

יְהִי רָצוֹן מִלְּפָנֶיךָ יהוה אֱלֹהֵינוּ וֵאלֹהֵי אֲבוֹתֵינוּ, שֶׁנִּשְׁמֹר חֻקֶּיךָ
בָּעוֹלָם הַזֶּה, וְנִזְכֶּה וְנִחְיֶה וְנִרְאֶה וְנִירַשׁ טוֹבָה וּבְרָכָה,
תהלים ל
לִשְׁנֵי יְמוֹת הַמָּשִׁיחַ וּלְחַיֵּי הָעוֹלָם הַבָּא. לְמַעַן יְזַמֶּרְךָ כָבוֹד וְלֹא
ירמיה יז
יִדֹּם, יהוה אֱלֹהַי, לְעוֹלָם אוֹדֶךָּ: בָּרוּךְ הַגֶּבֶר אֲשֶׁר יִבְטַח בַּיהוה,
ישעיה כו
וְהָיָה יהוה מִבְטַחוֹ: בִּטְחוּ בַיהוה עֲדֵי־עַד, כִּי בְּיָהּ יהוה צוּר
תהלים ט
עוֹלָמִים: ◂ וְיִבְטְחוּ בְךָ יוֹדְעֵי שְׁמֶךָ, כִּי לֹא־עָזַבְתָּ דֹרְשֶׁיךָ, יהוה:
ישעיה מב
יהוה חָפֵץ לְמַעַן צִדְקוֹ, יַגְדִּיל תּוֹרָה וְיַאְדִּיר:

On ראש חודש *and* חול המועד*, the* שליח ציבור *says* חצי קדיש*, page 166. The service then continues with* מוסף *for* ראש חודש *on page 780, for* חול המועד *on page 828.*

On other days the שליח ציבור *continues with* קדיש שלם *on the next page.*

---

progression: (1) In the *Kedusha* preceding the *Shema* we describe angelic praise; (2) in the *Kedusha* of the *Amida* repetition we adopt the angelic praises as our own; and (3) as we prepare to leave the synagogue for the world of mundane activity, we make clear our determination to bring the life of the spirit into our daily activities.

אֲשֶׁר יִבְטַח בַּה׳ – *Who trusts in the Lord.* Our security will be in direct proportion to the

I Chr. 29 יהוה LORD GOD of our fathers Abraham, Isaac, and Israel, forever
forming the thoughts in Your people's heart, and directing their hearts
Ps. 78 toward You. But He, the compassionate one, forgave iniquity, and did
not destroy them, and He often turned away His anger and did not stir
Ps. 86 up all His wrath. Indeed, You, O Lord, are good and forgiving, and of
Ps. 119 bountiful loving-kindness to all who call upon You. Your righteousness is
Mic. 7 an everlasting righteousness, and Your law is truth. Grant truth to Jacob,
loving-kindness to Abraham, as You have sworn to our fathers from days
Ps. 68 of old. Blessed is the Lord day by day. The God of our salvation will load
Ps. 46 us generously. The Lord of hosts is with us. The God of Jacob is our
Ps. 84 *Ps. 20* refuge. Selah. O Lord of hosts, happy is the man who trusts in You. Lord,
save! The King will answer us on the day that we call.

בָּרוּךְ BLESSED BE our God, Who created us for His glory, separated us from those who stray, gave us the Torah of truth, and implanted in us eternal life. May He open our hearts through His Torah and arouse in us such love and reverence for Him that we shall perform His will and serve Him with perfect hearts, rather than labor in vain or bring forth disaster.

יְהִי רָצוֹן MAY IT BE Your will, Lord our God and God of our fathers,
that we keep Your statutes in this world, and thus be worthy to inherit
a life of goodness and blessing in the days of the Messiah and in the
Ps. 30 life of the World to Come. Grant that I sing Your praises and not be
Jer. 17 silent; O Lord, my God, I will give thanks to You forever. Blessed is the
person who trusts in the Lord, for then the Lord will be his security.
Is. 26 Trust always in the Lord, for the Lord is God, an everlasting Rock.
Ps. 9 ▸ And those who know Your name will trust in You, for You, Lord, have
Is. 42 not abandoned those who seek You. The Lord desired, for the sake of its
[Israel's] righteousness, to magnify the Torah and glorify it.

On Rosh Ḥodesh and Ḥol HaMo'ed, the Leader says Half Kaddish, page 167. The service then continues with Musaf for Rosh Ḥodesh on page 781, for Ḥol HaMo'ed on page 829.

On other days, the Leader continues with Full Kaddish on the next page.

TEFILLIN REMOVAL ON ROSH ḤODESH
Tefillin are removed before the *Musaf Amida* (*OḤ* 25:13). There are different views regarding whether to remove them before or after the *Kaddish* that precedes the *Amida* (*MB* 25:59). R. Joseph B. Soloveitchik recommended their removal prior to *Kaddish* (*Nefesh HaRav* p. 116).

קדיש שלם

ש״ץ: **יִתְגַּדַּל** וְיִתְקַדַּשׁ שְׁמֵהּ רַבָּא (קהל: אָמֵן), בְּעָלְמָא דִּי בְרָא כִרְעוּתֵהּ.
וְיַמְלִיךְ מַלְכוּתֵהּ בְּחַיֵּיכוֹן וּבְיוֹמֵיכוֹן וּבְחַיֵּי דְכָל בֵּית
יִשְׂרָאֵל, בַּעֲגָלָא וּבִזְמַן קָרִיב, וְאִמְרוּ אָמֵן. (קהל: אָמֵן)

קהל וש״ץ: יְהֵא שְׁמֵהּ רַבָּא מְבָרַךְ לְעָלַם וּלְעָלְמֵי עָלְמַיָּא.

ש״ץ: יִתְבָּרַךְ וְיִשְׁתַּבַּח וְיִתְפָּאַר, וְיִתְרוֹמַם וְיִתְנַשֵּׂא וְיִתְהַדָּר וְיִתְעַלֶּה
וְיִתְהַלָּל שְׁמֵהּ דְּקֻדְשָׁא בְּרִיךְ הוּא (קהל: בְּרִיךְ הוּא), לְעֵלָּא מִן כָּל
בִּרְכָתָא / בעשרת ימי תשובה: לְעֵלָּא (וּ)לְעֵלָּא מִכָּל בִּרְכָתָא / וְשִׁירָתָא,
תֻּשְׁבְּחָתָא וְנֶחֱמָתָא דַּאֲמִירָן בְּעָלְמָא, וְאִמְרוּ אָמֵן. (קהל: אָמֵן)

On תשעה באב*, omit the next verse and continue with* יְהֵא שְׁלָמָא.

תִּתְקַבַּל צְלוֹתְהוֹן וּבָעוּתְהוֹן דְּכָל יִשְׂרָאֵל, קֳדָם אֲבוּהוֹן דִּי
בִשְׁמַיָּא, וְאִמְרוּ אָמֵן. (קהל: אָמֵן)

יְהֵא שְׁלָמָא רַבָּא מִן שְׁמַיָּא וְחַיִּים, עָלֵינוּ וְעַל כָּל יִשְׂרָאֵל, וְאִמְרוּ
אָמֵן. (קהל: אָמֵן)

Bow, take three steps back, as if taking leave of the Divine Presence, then bow, first left, then right, then center, while saying:

עֹשֶׂה שָׁלוֹם / בעשרת ימי תשובה: הַשָּׁלוֹם/ בִּמְרוֹמָיו, הוּא יַעֲשֶׂה שָׁלוֹם
עָלֵינוּ, וְעַל כָּל יִשְׂרָאֵל, וְאִמְרוּ אָמֵן. (קהל: אָמֵן)

Stand while saying עָלֵינוּ*. Bow at* ▾.

עָלֵינוּ לְשַׁבֵּחַ לַאֲדוֹן הַכֹּל, לָתֵת גְּדֻלָּה לְיוֹצֵר בְּרֵאשִׁית, שֶׁלֹּא
עָשָׂנוּ כְּגוֹיֵי הָאֲרָצוֹת, וְלֹא שָׂמָנוּ כְּמִשְׁפְּחוֹת הָאֲדָמָה,
שֶׁלֹּא שָׂם חֶלְקֵנוּ כָּהֶם וְגוֹרָלֵנוּ כְּכָל הֲמוֹנָם. (שֶׁהֵם מִשְׁתַּחֲוִים
לְהֶבֶל וָרִיק וּמִתְפַּלְלִים אֶל אֵל לֹא יוֹשִׁיעַ.) ▾וַאֲנַחְנוּ כּוֹרְעִים

---

extent that we put our trust in God (*Ḥiddushei HaRim*).

עָלֵינוּ / ALEINU

The authorship of this prayer is a matter of dispute. *Roke'aḥ* and *Kol Bo* attribute it to Joshua, who would have recited it upon leading Israel across the Jordan. However, as *Iyun Tefilla* argues, there are reasons to question the attribution of this prayer to Joshua. He suggests, instead, that it was authored by

FULL KADDISH

Leader: יִתְגַּדַּל EXALTED AND HALLOWED may God's great name be, in the world He created as He willed. May He reign in your lifetimes and in your days, and in the lifetime of the whole house of Israel, speedily and soon, and say, Amen.

All: May His great name be blessed forever and all time.

Leader: Blessed and praised, honored, extolled, glorified, adored and exalted above all be the name of the Holy One, blessed is He, (*Between Rosh Hashana & Yom Kippur:* above and) beyond any blessing, hymn, praise, or expressions of consolation that may be uttered in this world, and say, Amen.

On Tisha B'Av, omit the next verse and continue with "May abundant peace."

May the prayers and pleas of all Israel be accepted before their Father Who is in heaven – and say, Amen.

May abundant peace descend from heaven, as well as life, for us and for all Israel, and say, Amen.

Bow, take three steps back, as if taking leave of the Divine Presence, then bow, first left, then right, then center, while saying:

May He Who makes peace in the highest heaven, make peace for us, and for all Israel, and say, Amen.

Stand while saying Aleinu. Bow at ▾.

עָלֵינוּ WE MUST, all of us, praise the Master of all, and ascribe greatness to He Who formed creation, for He did not make us like the nations of the world, nor render us like the families of the earth. He did not make our portion to be as theirs, nor our destiny like that of their masses. (For idolaters bow to vanity and emptiness and pray to a god who cannot save.) ▾We, however, bend our knees, bow, and

---

Rav (third-century *amora*), as an introduction to the core texts of the Rosh HaShana *Musaf* service, which he composed. Another view attributes it to the Men of the Great Assembly (R. Manasseh Ben Israel). However, as the *Tur* points out, *Aleinu* is found – in the singular עָלַי לְשַׁבֵּחַ – in the mystical, so-called *Heikhalot* literature, where it is taught that R. Akiva would recite this prayer as he embarked on his meditative heavenly journeys to stand before

וּמִשְׁתַּחֲוִים וּמוֹדִים, לִפְנֵי מֶלֶךְ מַלְכֵי הַמְּלָכִים, הַקָּדוֹשׁ בָּרוּךְ
הוּא, שֶׁהוּא נוֹטֶה שָׁמַיִם וְיוֹסֵד אָרֶץ, וּמוֹשַׁב יְקָרוֹ בַּשָּׁמַיִם מִמַּעַל,
וּשְׁכִינַת עֻזּוֹ בְּגָבְהֵי מְרוֹמִים. הוּא אֱלֹהֵינוּ, אֵין עוֹד. אֱמֶת מַלְכֵּנוּ,
דברים ד אֶפֶס זוּלָתוֹ, כַּכָּתוּב בְּתוֹרָתוֹ, וְיָדַעְתָּ הַיּוֹם וַהֲשֵׁבֹתָ אֶל־לְבָבֶךָ, כִּי
יהוה הוּא הָאֱלֹהִים בַּשָּׁמַיִם מִמַּעַל וְעַל־הָאָרֶץ מִתָּחַת, אֵין עוֹד:

עַל כֵּן נְקַוֶּה לְּךָ יהוה אֱלֹהֵינוּ, לִרְאוֹת מְהֵרָה בְּתִפְאֶרֶת עֻזֶּךָ,
לְהַעֲבִיר גִּלּוּלִים מִן הָאָרֶץ, וְהָאֱלִילִים כָּרוֹת יִכָּרֵתוּן, לְתַקֵּן עוֹלָם
בְּמַלְכוּת שַׁדַּי. וְכָל בְּנֵי בָשָׂר יִקְרְאוּ בִשְׁמֶךָ לְהַפְנוֹת אֵלֶיךָ כָּל רִשְׁעֵי
אָרֶץ. יַכִּירוּ וְיֵדְעוּ כָּל יוֹשְׁבֵי תֵבֵל, כִּי לְךָ תִּכְרַע כָּל בֶּרֶךְ, תִּשָּׁבַע כָּל
לָשׁוֹן. לְפָנֶיךָ יהוה אֱלֹהֵינוּ יִכְרְעוּ וְיִפֹּלוּ, וְלִכְבוֹד שִׁמְךָ יְקָר יִתֵּנוּ,
וִיקַבְּלוּ כֻלָּם אֶת עֹל מַלְכוּתֶךָ, וְתִמְלֹךְ עֲלֵיהֶם מְהֵרָה לְעוֹלָם וָעֶד.
כִּי הַמַּלְכוּת שֶׁלְּךָ הִיא וּלְעוֹלְמֵי עַד תִּמְלֹךְ בְּכָבוֹד, כַּכָּתוּב בְּתוֹרָתֶךָ,
שמות טו יהוה יִמְלֹךְ לְעֹלָם וָעֶד: ◄ וְנֶאֱמַר, וְהָיָה יהוה לְמֶלֶךְ עַל־כָּל־הָאָרֶץ,
זכריה יד בַּיּוֹם הַהוּא יִהְיֶה יהוה אֶחָד וּשְׁמוֹ אֶחָד:

Some add:

משלי ג **אַל־תִּירָא** מִפַּחַד פִּתְאֹם וּמִשֹּׁאַת רְשָׁעִים כִּי תָבֹא: עֻצוּ עֵצָה וְתֻפָר, דַּבְּרוּ דָבָר וְלֹא יָקוּם,
ישעיה ח כִּי עִמָּנוּ אֵל: וְעַד־זִקְנָה אֲנִי הוּא, וְעַד־שֵׂיבָה אֲנִי אֶסְבֹּל, אֲנִי עָשִׂיתִי וַאֲנִי אֶשָּׂא
ישעיה מו וַאֲנִי אֶסְבֹּל וַאֲמַלֵּט:

The reason that we conclude every service with *Aleinu* and its affirmation of God's sovereignty that will one day be universally recognized, is to prepare us as we go out to interact with non-believers. In this way we will not be tempted to follow them or engage in sinful thoughts (Baḥ).

The first paragraph of *Aleinu* refers to God in the third person, because He is described therein as "the King of the most exalted of kings," conveying His cosmic commanding sovereignty; hence we cannot experience Him in this context in the familiar second person

the Throne of Glory and sing God's praises with the angels. As he recited this prayer the heavens opened before him and he could see them in their glory. The earliest source for reciting *Aleinu* at the conclusion of prayer is found in the *Sefer Roke'aḥ*, in the early thirteenth century. Baḥ explains that *Aleinu* was added to the daily prayers to instill faith in the uniqueness of God's kingship, and the conviction that He will one day "remove detestable idolatry from the earth" and thus prevent Jews from following the beliefs and ways of the nations (*Iyun Tefilla* and *Emek Berakha*).

give thanks before the King of the most exalted of kings, the Holy One, blessed is He. He is the One Who spreads out the heavens and establishes the earth. The seat of His glory is in the heavens above, and His Presence in all its strength is found in its highest abode. He is our God – there is no other. In truth He is our King; there is none
Deut. 4 but Him; as is written in His Torah: "On this day you should know, and take to heart, that the Lord is God in the heavens above and on the earth below – there is no other."

We therefore hope in You, Lord our God, that we may soon see the glory of Your might when You will remove abominations from the earth and the idols shall be utterly destroyed, when the world shall be perfected under the rule of the Almighty. Then all mankind shall invoke Your name, to turn all the wicked on earth toward You. All dwellers on earth will perceive and understand that to You every knee must bend, every tongue vow fealty. Before You, Lord our God, all will kneel and bow down, and give honor to Your glorious name. They will all accept the rule of Your dominion, and You will speedily rule over them forevermore. For the kingdom is Yours, and to all
Ex. 15 eternity You shall reign in glory, as it is written in Your Torah, "The
Zech. 14 Lord shall reign forever and ever." ▸ And it is said, "And the Lord shall be King over all the earth; in that day shall the Lord be One, and His name One."

Some add:

Prov. 3 **אַל־תִּירָא** DO NOT FEAR sudden terror or the destruction when it comes to
Is. 8 the wicked. Devise a plan, and it will be thwarted; state a case and it will not
Is. 46 stand, for God is with us. And when you are old, I will remain; when you are aged, I will endure. I created you, I will carry you, I will endure, and I will rescue you.

---

form, as we do when reciting the *Amida* (Ramban).

The second paragraph addresses God directly in the second person. This reflects the transition between the two paragraphs: the first relates to the condition of the Jewish people in relationship to God and the nations throughout conventional history when God is not fully revealed, but rather is experienced in His hiddenness; the second paragraph deals exclusively with the hoped-for era of redemption when we will experience God

קדיש יתום

The following prayer, said by mourners, requires the presence of a מנין.
A transliteration can be found on page 1345.

אבל: **יִתְגַּדַּל** וְיִתְקַדַּשׁ שְׁמֵהּ רַבָּא (קהל: אָמֵן) בְּעָלְמָא דִּי בְרָא כִרְעוּתֵהּ
וְיַמְלִיךְ מַלְכוּתֵהּ בְּחַיֵּיכוֹן וּבְיוֹמֵיכוֹן וּבְחַיֵּי דְכָל בֵּית
יִשְׂרָאֵל, בַּעֲגָלָא וּבִזְמַן קָרִיב, וְאִמְרוּ אָמֵן. (קהל: אָמֵן)

קהל ואבל: יְהֵא שְׁמֵהּ רַבָּא מְבָרַךְ לְעָלַם וּלְעָלְמֵי עָלְמַיָּא.

אבל: יִתְבָּרַךְ וְיִשְׁתַּבַּח וְיִתְפָּאַר וְיִתְרוֹמַם וְיִתְנַשֵּׂא וְיִתְהַדָּר וְיִתְעַלֶּה
וְיִתְהַלָּל שְׁמֵהּ דְּקֻדְשָׁא בְּרִיךְ הוּא (קהל: בְּרִיךְ הוּא) לְעֵלָּא מִן כָּל
בִּרְכָתָא / בעשרת ימי תשובה: לְעֵלָּא (וּ)לְעֵלָּא מִכָּל בִּרְכָתָא / וְשִׁירָתָא,
תֻּשְׁבְּחָתָא וְנֶחֱמָתָא דַּאֲמִירָן בְּעָלְמָא, וְאִמְרוּ אָמֵן. (קהל: אָמֵן)

יְהֵא שְׁלָמָא רַבָּא מִן שְׁמַיָּא וְחַיִּים, עָלֵינוּ וְעַל כָּל יִשְׂרָאֵל, וְאִמְרוּ
אָמֵן. (קהל: אָמֵן)

Bow, take three steps back, as if taking leave of the Divine Presence,
then bow, first left, then right, then center, while saying:

עֹשֶׂה שָׁלוֹם / בעשרת ימי תשובה: הַשָּׁלוֹם / בִּמְרוֹמָיו, הוּא יַעֲשֶׂה שָׁלוֹם
עָלֵינוּ, וְעַל כָּל יִשְׂרָאֵל, וְאִמְרוּ אָמֵן. (קהל: אָמֵן)

שיר של יום

One of the following psalms is said on the appropriate day of the week as indicated.
After the psalm, קדיש יתום *above is said.*

After שיר של יום*, on* ראש חודש*, add* בָּרְכִי נַפְשִׁי*, page 194. On* חנוכה*, add* מִזְמוֹר שִׁיר־חֲנֻכַּת הַבַּיִת*, page 54 followed by* קדיש יתום*. From the second day of* ראש חודש אלול *through* שמיני עצרת*, add* לְדָוִד, יהוה אוֹרִי *on page 196. In a* שבעה *house the service concludes on page 198.*

Sunday הַיּוֹם יוֹם רִאשׁוֹן בְּשַׁבָּת, שֶׁבּוֹ הָיוּ הַלְוִיִּם אוֹמְרִים בְּבֵית הַמִּקְדָּשׁ:

תהלים כד **לְדָוִד מִזְמוֹר**, לַיהוה הָאָרֶץ וּמְלוֹאָהּ, תֵּבֵל וְיֹשְׁבֵי בָהּ: כִּי־הוּא
עַל־יַמִּים יְסָדָהּ, וְעַל־נְהָרוֹת יְכוֹנְנֶהָ: מִי־יַעֲלֶה

---

in the fullness, and closeness, of His revealed glory, hence it addresses God in more direct and intimate form (R. Basil Herring).

שִׁיר שֶׁל יוֹם / SONG OF THE DAY
The Mishna (*Tamid* 7:4) records that on each day of the week the Levites would

MOURNER'S KADDISH

The following prayer, said by mourners, requires the presence of a minyan. A transliteration can be found on page 1345.

Mourner: יִתְגַּדַּל EXALTED AND HALLOWED may God's great name be, in the world He created as He willed. May He reign in your lifetimes and in your days, and in the lifetime of the whole house of Israel, speedily and soon, and say, Amen.

All: May His great name be blessed forever and all time.

Mourner: Blessed and praised, honored, extolled, glorified, adored and exalted above all be the name of the Holy One, blessed is He, (*Between Rosh Hashana & Yom Kippur:* above and) beyond any blessing, hymn, praise, or expressions of consolation that may be uttered in this world, and say, Amen.

May abundant peace descend from heaven, as well as life, for us and for all Israel, and say, Amen.

Bow, take three steps back, as if taking leave of the Divine Presence, then bow, first left, then right, then center, while saying:

May He Who makes peace in the highest heaven, make peace for us, and for all Israel, and say, Amen.

THE PSALM OF THE DAY

One of the following psalms is said on the appropriate day of the week as indicated. After the psalm, the Mourner's Kaddish above is said.

After the Daily Psalm, on Rosh Ḥodesh, add Barekhi Nafshi, page 195. On Ḥanukka, add Psalm 30, page 55 followed by Mourner's Kaddish. From the second day of Rosh Ḥodesh Elul through Shemini Atzeret, add Psalm 27 on page 197. In a shiva house the service concludes on page 199.

Sunday: Today is the first day since the Sabbath, when the Levites in the Temple would say:

Ps. 24 לְדָוִד מִזְמוֹר OF DAVID. A psalm. The earth is the Lord's and the fullness thereof, the world and those who dwell in it. For He has founded it upon the seas, and has established it upon the floods. Who shall ascend the

---

sing a different psalm in honor of that day (known as *Shir shel Yom*). After the Temple was destroyed, the view of R. Yoḥanan that the recitation should continue became

בְּהַר־יהוה, וּמִי־יָקוּם בִּמְקוֹם קָדְשׁוֹ: נְקִי כַפַּיִם וּבַר־לֵבָב, אֲשֶׁר
לֹא־נָשָׂא לַשָּׁוְא נַפְשִׁי, וְלֹא נִשְׁבַּע לְמִרְמָה: יִשָּׂא בְרָכָה מֵאֵת יהוה,
וּצְדָקָה מֵאֱלֹהֵי יִשְׁעוֹ: זֶה דּוֹר דֹּרְשָׁו, מְבַקְשֵׁי פָנֶיךָ יַעֲקֹב סֶלָה:
שְׂאוּ שְׁעָרִים רָאשֵׁיכֶם, וְהִנָּשְׂאוּ פִּתְחֵי עוֹלָם, וְיָבוֹא מֶלֶךְ הַכָּבוֹד:
מִי זֶה מֶלֶךְ הַכָּבוֹד, יהוה עִזּוּז וְגִבּוֹר, יהוה גִּבּוֹר מִלְחָמָה: שְׂאוּ
שְׁעָרִים רָאשֵׁיכֶם, וּשְׂאוּ פִּתְחֵי עוֹלָם, וְיָבֹא מֶלֶךְ הַכָּבוֹד: ◂ מִי הוּא
זֶה מֶלֶךְ הַכָּבוֹד, יהוה צְבָאוֹת הוּא מֶלֶךְ הַכָּבוֹד סֶלָה:

קדיש יתום (*page 184*)

Monday הַיּוֹם יוֹם שֵׁנִי בְּשַׁבָּת, שֶׁבּוֹ הָיוּ הַלְוִיִּם אוֹמְרִים בְּבֵית הַמִּקְדָּשׁ:

תהלים מח
שִׁיר מִזְמוֹר לִבְנֵי־קֹרַח: גָּדוֹל יהוה וּמְהֻלָּל מְאֹד, בְּעִיר אֱלֹהֵינוּ,
הַר־קָדְשׁוֹ: יְפֵה נוֹף מְשׂוֹשׂ כָּל־הָאָרֶץ, הַר־צִיּוֹן
יַרְכְּתֵי צָפוֹן, קִרְיַת מֶלֶךְ רָב: אֱלֹהִים בְּאַרְמְנוֹתֶיהָ נוֹדַע לְמִשְׂגָּב:
כִּי־הִנֵּה הַמְּלָכִים נוֹעֲדוּ, עָבְרוּ יַחְדָּו: הֵמָּה רָאוּ כֵּן תָּמָהוּ, נִבְהֲלוּ
נֶחְפָּזוּ: רְעָדָה אֲחָזָתַם שָׁם, חִיל כַּיּוֹלֵדָה: בְּרוּחַ קָדִים תְּשַׁבֵּר
אֳנִיּוֹת תַּרְשִׁישׁ: כַּאֲשֶׁר שָׁמַעְנוּ כֵּן רָאִינוּ, בְּעִיר־יהוה צְבָאוֹת,

יום ראשון / THE FIRST DAY (previous page) The *Gemara (Rosh HaShana* 31a) explains the reasons for the choice of psalm for each day of the week. Thus for the first day it states: "They recited, 'The Lord's is the earth and its fullness' (Psalms 24:1) in reference to the fact that on the first day of Creation He created the cosmos to give it to mankind, while ruling over His world by Himself."

כִּי־הוּא עַל־יַמִּים יְסָדָהּ – *For He has founded it upon the seas.* The reference to the continents that are established upon the waters found below can be understood as a metaphor for the workings of the human mind; thus, our rational thoughts occur above a "sea" of irrational urges and thought processes. Our

normative. Mishna *Sofrim* (18:2) declares that "reciting a psalm at its appointed time is the equivalent of rebuilding the altar and making a sacrifice."

When we say the *Shir shel Yom* each day, prefacing each psalm with the words "Today is the first (or second, etc.) day of Shabbat" we fulfill the positive commandment to remember (זָכוֹר) Shabbat, while on Shabbat itself we fulfill the obligation to "keep" (שָׁמוֹר) the day. This follows the view of R. Yitzḥak in the *Mekhilta* who says, "Do not count the days of the week as others do, but rather count them in relation to Shabbat." In so doing we are reminded every day of the cardinal principle that God created, and continues to maintain, the cosmos (*Ramban*).

mountain of the Lord, and who shall stand in His holy place? He who has clean hands and a pure heart, who has not sworn in vain "by my soul," and has not sworn deceitfully, he shall receive the blessing from the Lord, and righteousness from the God of his salvation. This is the company of those who seek Him, who seek Your face, Jacob. Selah. Lift up your heads, O gates, and be lifted up, O everlasting doors, so that the King of glory may come in. Who is this King of glory? The Lord strong and mighty, the Lord mighty in battle. Lift up your heads, O gates, and lift them up, O everlasting doors, so that the King of glory may come in. ▸ Who is He, this King of glory? The Lord of hosts, He is the King of glory. Selah.

Mourner's Kaddish (page 185)

Monday: Today is the second day since the Sabbath, when the Levites in the Temple would say:

Ps. 48 שִׁיר מִזְמוֹר A SONG. A psalm for the sons of Korah. The Lord is great and exceedingly praised in the city of our God, His holy mountain. Beautiful in height, the joy of the whole earth, Mount Zion, the sides of the north, the city of a great king. In her palaces God is known as her fortress. For, behold, the kings were assembled, they passed together. They saw and they were astounded. They were frightened and they became confused. Trembling took hold of them there, anguish like a woman in travail, Like an east wind that breaks the ships of Tarshish. As we have heard, so have we seen in the city of the Lord of hosts, in the city of our God. God

---

task is to bring order and discipline to the chaos of our subconscious thought processes by developing and deploying our God-given intellect (R. Yitzchok Hutner). This insight may have been inspired by the thought of R. Yisrael Salanter, the founder of the *Musar* movement, but R. Hutner does not mention him in this discussion (Prof. Yaakov Elman).

יוֹם שֵׁנִי / THE SECOND DAY

"On the second day of the week the Levites recited, 'The Lord is great and much praised' (Psalms 48:2) because on that day He subdivided the world and reigned over them" (*Rosh HaShana* 31a).

אֱלֹהִים בְּאַרְמְנוֹתֶיהָ נוֹדַע לְמִשְׂגָּב – *In her palaces God is known as her fortress.* On the one hand the psalm depicts Jerusalem as an impregnable fortress, resulting from God's dwelling there in the midst of a righteous people. On the other hand the people are to realize that God's protective presence depends on their moral and spiritual righteousness, which if violated could lead to the destruction of the city and the exile of its people. The psalm thus emphasizes that the inviolability of Jerusalem is bound up with its status as the city of God, so that the joy and prosperity of Jerusalem can continue only so long as it remains the center for justice on earth (R. Aton Holzer).

בְּעִיר אֱלֹהֵינוּ, אֱלֹהִים יְכוֹנְנֶהָ עַד־עוֹלָם סֶלָה: דִּמִּינוּ אֱלֹהִים חַסְדֶּךָ, בְּקֶרֶב הֵיכָלֶךָ: כְּשִׁמְךָ אֱלֹהִים כֵּן תְּהִלָּתְךָ עַל־קַצְוֵי־אֶרֶץ, צֶדֶק מָלְאָה יְמִינֶךָ: יִשְׂמַח הַר־צִיּוֹן, תָּגֵלְנָה בְּנוֹת יְהוּדָה, לְמַעַן מִשְׁפָּטֶיךָ: סֹבּוּ צִיּוֹן וְהַקִּיפוּהָ, סִפְרוּ מִגְדָּלֶיהָ: שִׁיתוּ לִבְּכֶם לְחֵילָה, פַּסְּגוּ אַרְמְנוֹתֶיהָ, לְמַעַן תְּסַפְּרוּ לְדוֹר אַחֲרוֹן: ◂ כִּי זֶה אֱלֹהִים אֱלֹהֵינוּ עוֹלָם וָעֶד, הוּא יְנַהֲגֵנוּ עַל־מוּת:

קדיש יתום (*page 184*)

Tuesday הַיּוֹם יוֹם שְׁלִישִׁי בְּשַׁבָּת, שֶׁבּוֹ הָיוּ הַלְוִיִּם אוֹמְרִים בְּבֵית הַמִּקְדָּשׁ:

תהלים פב

מִזְמוֹר לְאָסָף, אֱלֹהִים נִצָּב בַּעֲדַת־אֵל, בְּקֶרֶב אֱלֹהִים יִשְׁפֹּט: עַד־מָתַי תִּשְׁפְּטוּ־עָוֶל, וּפְנֵי רְשָׁעִים תִּשְׂאוּ־סֶלָה: שִׁפְטוּ־דַל וְיָתוֹם, עָנִי וָרָשׁ הַצְדִּיקוּ: פַּלְּטוּ־דַל וְאֶבְיוֹן, מִיַּד רְשָׁעִים הַצִּילוּ: לֹא יָדְעוּ וְלֹא יָבִינוּ, בַּחֲשֵׁכָה יִתְהַלָּכוּ, יִמּוֹטוּ כָּל־מוֹסְדֵי אָרֶץ: אֲנִי־אָמַרְתִּי אֱלֹהִים אַתֶּם, וּבְנֵי עֶלְיוֹן כֻּלְּכֶם: אָכֵן כְּאָדָם תְּמוּתוּן, וּכְאַחַד הַשָּׂרִים תִּפֹּלוּ: ◂ קוּמָה אֱלֹהִים שָׁפְטָה הָאָרֶץ, כִּי־אַתָּה תִנְחַל בְּכָל־הַגּוֹיִם:

קדיש יתום (*page 184*)

Wednesday הַיּוֹם יוֹם רְבִיעִי בְּשַׁבָּת, שֶׁבּוֹ הָיוּ הַלְוִיִּם אוֹמְרִים בְּבֵית הַמִּקְדָּשׁ:

תהלים צד

אֵל־נְקָמוֹת יהוה, אֵל נְקָמוֹת הוֹפִיעַ: הִנָּשֵׂא שֹׁפֵט הָאָרֶץ, הָשֵׁב גְּמוּל עַל־גֵּאִים: עַד־מָתַי רְשָׁעִים, יהוה, עַד־מָתַי

יוֹם שְׁלִישִׁי / THE THIRD DAY

"On the third day of the week the Levites recited, 'God stands in the divine assembly' (Psalms 82:1) because on that day He exposed the cosmos to His wisdom, preparing it for His people" (*Rosh HaShana* 31a).

Psalm 82 describes a period in which the judges had become thoroughly corrupt, favoring the wicked while overlooking the weak and the orphaned. According to Radak this likely describes the era preceding the rule of Yehoshafat (II Chr. 19) who upon assuming power replaced the entire judicial system on account of its evil ways. The psalm portrays his charge to the new judges to act righteously at all times, being especially careful to treat the vulnerable with fairness and justice, and being aware that God too is present in the court. In light of this psalm that is recited before going out to our worldly occupations, we are reminded of our responsibility to implement the prophetic call to ensure justice and equity for all.

establishes it forever. Selah. We think, O God, about Your loving-kindness in the midst of Your temple. Like Your name, O God, so is Your praise to the ends of the earth. Your right hand is full of righteousness. Mount Zion should rejoice, the daughters of Judah should be glad, on account of Your judgments. Walk around Zion and encircle her. Count her towers. Consider her rampart, pass through her palaces, so that you may tell it to the next generation. ▸ For such is God, our God, forever and ever. He leads us *al-mut*.

Mourner's Kaddish (page 185)

Tuesday: Today is the third day since the Sabbath, when the Levites in the Temple would say:

Ps. 82 מִזְמוֹר לְאָסָף A PSALM of Asaph. God is standing in the congregation of God. He will judge in the midst of the congregation of God. How long will you judge unjustly and favor the wicked? Selah. Judge the poor and the fatherless. Judge fairly the afflicted and the needy. Deliver the poor and the destitute. Save them from the hand of the wicked. They do not know and they do not understand. They walk in darkness. All the foundations of the earth will collapse. I said: "You are angels, and all of you are sons of the Most High. Nevertheless you will die like a man, and you will fall like one of the princes." ▸ Arise, O God! Judge the earth. For You possess all the nations.

Mourner's Kaddish (page 185)

Wednesday: Today is the fourth day since the Sabbath, when the Levites in the Temple would say:

Ps. 94 אֵל־נְקָמוֹת GOD OF VENGEANCE, O Lord, God of vengeance, reveal Yourself. Rise up, O judge of the earth, render to the proud their

---

Judaism has never accepted the idea of one person judging another. How can a human being, who is just as imperfect as the person in the dock, render judgment on him? Yet the Torah allows human judgment, because without courts of law anarchy would prevail. How then should one function as a judge? By always remembering that when we act as judges we are mere agents of God, the true Judge. For this reason the verse states: "God stands in the congregation of God, in the midst of judges He judges," meaning it is God Who is the Master and the ultimate Judge standing over all, while human judges are mere guests invited to "take a seat in court" at God's pleasure (R. Joseph B. Soloveitchik).

רְשָׁעִים יַעֲלֹזוּ: יַבִּיעוּ יְדַבְּרוּ עָתָק, יִתְאַמְּרוּ כָּל־פֹּעֲלֵי אָוֶן: עַמְּךָ יהוה יְדַכְּאוּ, וְנַחֲלָתְךָ יְעַנּוּ: אַלְמָנָה וְגֵר יַהֲרֹגוּ, וִיתוֹמִים יְרַצֵּחוּ: וַיֹּאמְרוּ לֹא יִרְאֶה־יָּהּ, וְלֹא־יָבִין אֱלֹהֵי יַעֲקֹב: בִּינוּ בֹּעֲרִים בָּעָם, וּכְסִילִים מָתַי תַּשְׂכִּילוּ: הֲנֹטַע אֹזֶן הֲלֹא יִשְׁמָע, אִם־יֹצֵר עַיִן הֲלֹא יַבִּיט: הֲיֹסֵר גּוֹיִם הֲלֹא יוֹכִיחַ, הַמְלַמֵּד אָדָם דָּעַת: יהוה יֹדֵעַ מַחְשְׁבוֹת אָדָם, כִּי־הֵמָּה הָבֶל: אַשְׁרֵי הַגֶּבֶר אֲשֶׁר־תְּיַסְּרֶנּוּ יָּהּ, וּמִתּוֹרָתְךָ תְלַמְּדֶנּוּ: לְהַשְׁקִיט לוֹ מִימֵי רָע, עַד יִכָּרֶה לָרָשָׁע שָׁחַת: כִּי לֹא־יִטֹּשׁ יהוה עַמּוֹ, וְנַחֲלָתוֹ לֹא יַעֲזֹב: כִּי־עַד־צֶדֶק יָשׁוּב מִשְׁפָּט, וְאַחֲרָיו כָּל־יִשְׁרֵי־לֵב: מִי־יָקוּם לִי עִם־מְרֵעִים, מִי־יִתְיַצֵּב לִי עִם־פֹּעֲלֵי אָוֶן: לוּלֵי יהוה עֶזְרָתָה לִּי, כִּמְעַט שָׁכְנָה דוּמָה נַפְשִׁי: אִם־אָמַרְתִּי מָטָה רַגְלִי, חַסְדְּךָ יהוה יִסְעָדֵנִי: בְּרֹב שַׂרְעַפַּי בְּקִרְבִּי, תַּנְחוּמֶיךָ יְשַׁעַשְׁעוּ נַפְשִׁי: הַיְחָבְרְךָ כִּסֵּא הַוּוֹת, יֹצֵר עָמָל עֲלֵי־חֹק: יָגוֹדּוּ עַל־נֶפֶשׁ צַדִּיק, וְדָם נָקִי יַרְשִׁיעוּ: וַיְהִי יהוה לִי לְמִשְׂגָּב, וֵאלֹהַי לְצוּר מַחְסִי: וַיָּשֶׁב עֲלֵיהֶם אֶת־אוֹנָם, וּבְרָעָתָם יַצְמִיתֵם, יַצְמִיתֵם יהוה אֱלֹהֵינוּ:

תהלים צה ◂ לְכוּ נְרַנְּנָה לַיהוה, נָרִיעָה לְצוּר יִשְׁעֵנוּ: נְקַדְּמָה פָנָיו בְּתוֹדָה, בִּזְמִרוֹת נָרִיעַ לוֹ: כִּי אֵל גָּדוֹל יהוה, וּמֶלֶךְ גָּדוֹל עַל־כָּל־אֱלֹהִים:

קדיש יתום (*page 184*)

יום רביעי / THE FOURTH DAY

"On the fourth day of the week the Levites recited, 'A God of vengeance is the Lord' (Psalms 94:1) because on that day He created the sun and the moon, and He will exact punishment from those who worship them" (*Rosh HaShana* 31a).

אַשְׁרֵי הַגֶּבֶר אֲשֶׁר־תְּיַסְּרֶנּוּ יָּהּ – *Happy is the man whom You chasten, O Lord.* Some of our enemies professing other faiths point to our sufferings in exile as proof that God has rejected us. They say, "If your beliefs are correct, why does your God permit others to bring such misery on you?" To this accusation the Psalmist answers: "Happy is the man whom God afflicts," that is to say, our suffering reflects God's special concern for us, as the Torah says: "As a father disciplines his son, so I discipline you" (Deut. 8:5). Like a loving father, God subjects us to the whims of the nations to increase our eventual reward. Furthermore, we accept our travails in the belief that they will make us better human beings. So too the final phrase "and whom You teach from Your law"

recompense. How long will the wicked, O Lord, how long will the wicked rejoice? They utter and speak arrogance. All the workers of iniquity speak conceit. They oppress Your people, O Lords, and they afflict Your inheritance. They slay the widow and the stranger, and they murder the fatherless. And they say: the Lord does not see and the God of Jacob does not discern. Understand, you brutes among the people. And you fools, when will you become wise? He Who planted the ear, will He not hear? He Who formed the eye, will He not see? He Who instructs nations, will He not rebuke? It is He Who teaches man knowledge. The Lord knows the thoughts of man, for they are vanity. Happy is the man whom You chasten, O Lord, and whom You teach from Your law, to quiet him from evil days, until the pit is dug for the wicked. For the Lord will not abandon His people, and He will not forsake His inheritance. For judgment will return to righteousness, and all the upright in heart will follow it. Who rose up for me against the evildoers? Who stood up for me against the workers of iniquity? If the Lord had not been my help, my soul would actually have dwelt in the underworld. Whenever I said, My foot slips, Your loving-kindness, O Lord, would support me. When my thoughts within me were many, Your consolations would occupy my soul. Will the seat of wickedness join to You? Will he who performs mischief based on the law? They had gathered bands against the soul of the righteous, and they have condemned innocent blood. But the Lord has been my fortress, and my God has been the rock of my refuge. And He has brought upon them their own iniquity, and He has cut them off because of their wickedness, the Lord our God has cut them off.

Ps. 95 ▸ COME, let us sing to the Lord, let us shout joyfully to the Rock of our salvation. Let us come before Him with thanksgiving, let us raise our voice in song. For the Lord is a great God, and a great king above all gods.

Mourner's Kaddish (page 185)

---

teaches us that we can only acquire Torah on its highest level through self-discipline, hardship, and self-deprivation (Radak).

This psalm, with its repeated references to the fate of the Jew in a hostile world, served to fortify the Jew as he finished his morning prayers and prepared to go forth into a harsh, and often discriminatory setting.

Thursday הַיּוֹם יוֹם חֲמִישִׁי בְּשַׁבָּת, שֶׁבּוֹ הָיוּ הַלְוִיִּם אוֹמְרִים בְּבֵית הַמִּקְדָּשׁ:

לַמְנַצֵּחַ עַל־הַגִּתִּית לְאָסָף: הַרְנִינוּ לֵאלֹהִים עוּזֵּנוּ, הָרִיעוּ לֵאלֹהֵי תהלים פא
יַעֲקֹב: שְׂאוּ־זִמְרָה וּתְנוּ־תֹף, כִּנּוֹר נָעִים עִם־נָבֶל: תִּקְעוּ
בַחֹדֶשׁ שׁוֹפָר, בַּכֵּסֶה לְיוֹם חַגֵּנוּ: כִּי חֹק לְיִשְׂרָאֵל הוּא, מִשְׁפָּט
לֵאלֹהֵי יַעֲקֹב: עֵדוּת בִּיהוֹסֵף שָׂמוֹ, בְּצֵאתוֹ עַל־אֶרֶץ מִצְרָיִם, שְׂפַת
לֹא־יָדַעְתִּי אֶשְׁמָע: הֲסִירוֹתִי מִסֵּבֶל שִׁכְמוֹ, כַּפָּיו מִדּוּד תַּעֲבֹרְנָה:
בַּצָּרָה קָרָאתָ וָאֲחַלְּצֶךָּ, אֶעֶנְךָ בְּסֵתֶר רַעַם, אֶבְחָנְךָ עַל־מֵי מְרִיבָה
סֶלָה: שְׁמַע עַמִּי וְאָעִידָה בָּךְ, יִשְׂרָאֵל אִם־תִּשְׁמַע־לִי: לֹא־יִהְיֶה בְךָ
אֵל זָר, וְלֹא תִשְׁתַּחֲוֶה לְאֵל נֵכָר: אָנֹכִי יהוה אֱלֹהֶיךָ, הַמַּעַלְךָ מֵאֶרֶץ
מִצְרָיִם, הַרְחֶב־פִּיךָ וַאֲמַלְאֵהוּ: וְלֹא־שָׁמַע עַמִּי לְקוֹלִי, וְיִשְׂרָאֵל
לֹא־אָבָה לִי: וָאֲשַׁלְּחֵהוּ בִּשְׁרִירוּת לִבָּם, יֵלְכוּ בְּמוֹעֲצוֹתֵיהֶם: לוּ
עַמִּי שֹׁמֵעַ לִי, יִשְׂרָאֵל בִּדְרָכַי יְהַלֵּכוּ: כִּמְעַט אוֹיְבֵיהֶם אַכְנִיעַ,
וְעַל־צָרֵיהֶם אָשִׁיב יָדִי: מְשַׂנְאֵי יהוה יְכַחֲשׁוּ־לוֹ, וִיהִי עִתָּם לְעוֹלָם:
‹ וַיַּאֲכִילֵהוּ מֵחֵלֶב חִטָּה, וּמִצּוּר, דְּבַשׁ אַשְׂבִּיעֶךָ:

קדיש יתום (*page 184*)

Friday הַיּוֹם יוֹם שִׁשִּׁי בְּשַׁבָּת, שֶׁבּוֹ הָיוּ הַלְוִיִּם אוֹמְרִים בְּבֵית הַמִּקְדָּשׁ

יהוה מָלָךְ, גֵּאוּת לָבֵשׁ, לָבֵשׁ יהוה עֹז הִתְאַזָּר, אַף־תִּכּוֹן תֵּבֵל בַּל־ תהלים צג
תִּמּוֹט: נָכוֹן כִּסְאֲךָ מֵאָז, מֵעוֹלָם אָתָּה: נָשְׂאוּ נְהָרוֹת
יהוה, נָשְׂאוּ נְהָרוֹת קוֹלָם, יִשְׂאוּ נְהָרוֹת דָּכְיָם: מִקֹּלוֹת מַיִם רַבִּים,
אַדִּירִים מִשְׁבְּרֵי־יָם, אַדִּיר בַּמָּרוֹם יהוה: ‹ עֵדֹתֶיךָ נֶאֶמְנוּ מְאֹד,
לְבֵיתְךָ נַאֲוָה־קֹדֶשׁ, יהוה לְאֹרֶךְ יָמִים:

קדיש יתום (*page 184*)

יוֹם חֲמִישִׁי / THE FIFTH DAY

"On the fifth day of the week the Levites recited, 'Sing joyously to the God of our might' (Psalms 81:2) because on that day He created the birds and the fish to give praise to His name" (*Rosh HaShana* 31a).

יוֹם שִׁשִּׁי / THE SIXTH DAY

"On the sixth day the Levites recited, 'The Lord reigns, He is clothed in majesty' (Psalms 93:1) for on that day He completed His work and reigned over His creation" (*Rosh HaShana* 31a).

Thursday: Today is the fifth day since the Sabbath, when the Levites in the Temple would say:

Ps. 81 **יהוה מָלָךְ** TO THE DIRECTOR of music *al-HaGittit*, of Asaph. Sing for joy to God our strength. Make a joyful noise for the God of Jacob. Raise a song, sound the timbrel, the sweet lyre and the harp. Sound a shofar on the new moon, on the day of covering for our feast day. For this is a statute for Israel, an ordinance of the God of Jacob. He ordained this in Joseph for a testimony, when He went out over the land of Egypt. I hear a language that I did not know: I removed his shoulder from the burden. His hands were freed from the basket. You called in trouble and I rescued you. I answered you with thunder in the secret place. I tested you at the waters of Meribah. Selah. Hear, My people, and I will testify against you, O Israel, if you will hearken to Me. There shall be no strange god among you, and you shall not worship any foreign deity. I am the Lord your God Who brought you up from the land of Egypt. Open your mouth wide, and I will fill it. But My people did not hearken to My voice, and Israel did not desire Me. So I let them go after the stubbornness of their heart. Let them follow their own counsels! Oh that My people had hearkened to Me, that Israel had walked in My ways! I would have subdued their enemies in a moment and turned My hand against their adversaries. The haters of the Lord feign obedience to Him, and their time of punishment will last forever. ▸ But He will feed him from the finest of the wheat, and from the rock I will satisfy you with honey.

Mourner's Kaddish (page 185)

Friday: Today is the sixth day since the Sabbath, when the Levites in the Temple would say:

Ps. 93 **יהוה מָלָךְ** THE LORD REIGNS, He is clothed in majesty, the Lord is clothed, He has girded Himself with strength. The world, too, is established so that it cannot be moved. You throne is established from of old. You are from everlasting. The floodwaters have lifted up, O Lord, the floodwaters have lifted up their voice, the floodwaters have lifted up their pounding. Mightier than the voices of great, mighty waters, breakers of the sea, is the Lord on high. ▸ Your testimonies are very true, in Your house, Your holy habitation, O Lord, for length of days.

Mourner's Kaddish (page 185)

The Gemara (*Bava Batra* 74b) describes how when God separated the dry land from the oceans at Creation, the angel of the sea rebelled by directing the powerful waters

On ראש חודש*, the following psalm is said:*

תהלים קד **בָּרְכִי נַפְשִׁי** אֶת־יהוה, יהוה אֱלֹהַי גָּדַלְתָּ מְּאֹד, הוֹד וְהָדָר לָבָשְׁתָּ:
עֹטֶה־אוֹר כַּשַּׂלְמָה, נוֹטֶה שָׁמַיִם כַּיְרִיעָה: הַמְקָרֶה
בַמַּיִם עֲלִיּוֹתָיו, הַשָּׂם־עָבִים רְכוּבוֹ, הַמְהַלֵּךְ עַל־כַּנְפֵי־רוּחַ: עֹשֶׂה
מַלְאָכָיו רוּחוֹת, מְשָׁרְתָיו אֵשׁ לֹהֵט: יָסַד־אֶרֶץ עַל־מְכוֹנֶיהָ, בַּל־
תִּמּוֹט עוֹלָם וָעֶד: תְּהוֹם כַּלְּבוּשׁ כִּסִּיתוֹ, עַל־הָרִים יַעַמְדוּ־מָיִם:
מִן־גַּעֲרָתְךָ יְנוּסוּן, מִן־קוֹל רַעַמְךָ יֵחָפֵזוּן: יַעֲלוּ הָרִים, יֵרְדוּ בְקָעוֹת,
אֶל־מְקוֹם זֶה יָסַדְתָּ לָהֶם: גְּבוּל־שַׂמְתָּ בַּל־יַעֲבֹרוּן, בַּל־יְשׁוּבוּן
לְכַסּוֹת הָאָרֶץ: הַמְשַׁלֵּחַ מַעְיָנִים בַּנְּחָלִים, בֵּין הָרִים יְהַלֵּכוּן:
יַשְׁקוּ כָּל־חַיְתוֹ שָׂדָי, יִשְׁבְּרוּ פְרָאִים צְמָאָם: עֲלֵיהֶם עוֹף־הַשָּׁמַיִם
יִשְׁכּוֹן, מִבֵּין עֳפָאיִם יִתְּנוּ־קוֹל: מַשְׁקֶה הָרִים מֵעֲלִיּוֹתָיו, מִפְּרִי
מַעֲשֶׂיךָ תִּשְׂבַּע הָאָרֶץ: מַצְמִיחַ חָצִיר לַבְּהֵמָה, וְעֵשֶׂב לַעֲבֹדַת
הָאָדָם, לְהוֹצִיא לֶחֶם מִן־הָאָרֶץ: וְיַיִן יְשַׂמַּח לְבַב־אֱנוֹשׁ, לְהַצְהִיל
פָּנִים מִשָּׁמֶן, וְלֶחֶם לְבַב־אֱנוֹשׁ יִסְעָד: יִשְׂבְּעוּ עֲצֵי יהוה, אַרְזֵי
לְבָנוֹן אֲשֶׁר נָטָע: אֲשֶׁר־שָׁם צִפֳּרִים יְקַנֵּנוּ, חֲסִידָה בְּרוֹשִׁים
בֵּיתָהּ: הָרִים הַגְּבֹהִים לַיְּעֵלִים, סְלָעִים מַחְסֶה לַשְׁפַנִּים: עָשָׂה
יָרֵחַ לְמוֹעֲדִים, שֶׁמֶשׁ יָדַע מְבוֹאוֹ: תָּשֶׁת־חֹשֶׁךְ וִיהִי לָיְלָה, בּוֹ־
תִרְמֹשׂ כָּל־חַיְתוֹ־יָעַר: הַכְּפִירִים שֹׁאֲגִים לַטָּרֶף, וּלְבַקֵּשׁ מֵאֵל
אָכְלָם: תִּזְרַח הַשֶּׁמֶשׁ יֵאָסֵפוּן, וְאֶל־מְעוֹנֹתָם יִרְבָּצוּן: יֵצֵא אָדָם
לְפָעֳלוֹ, וְלַעֲבֹדָתוֹ עֲדֵי־עָרֶב: מָה־רַבּוּ מַעֲשֶׂיךָ יהוה, כֻּלָּם בְּחָכְמָה

---

to overcome their boundaries. This psalm portrays the defeat of the angel, as God robed Himself with strength to overcome the waves threatening to inundate the world. A number of the phrases found here echo the triumphant song of the Israelites at the Sea of Reeds, when once again God held back the powerful waves. These divine actions are emblematic of the wars that God has waged against His enemies in every generation, thereby repelling the tsunamis of hatred and violence directed against His people (R. Amos Ḥakham).

בָּרְכִי נַפְשִׁי / PSALM 104

This psalm recapitulates God's creation of the earth, in chronological order, starting with the creation of light, then the heavens, the earth,

On Rosh Ḥodesh, the following psalm is said:

Ps. 104 בָּרְכִי נַפְשִׁי BLESS O LORD, O my soul. O Lord, my God, You are very great. You are clothed with splendor and majesty. He covers Himself with light as a garment. He spreads the heavens like a curtain. Who roofs His chambers with water, Who makes the clouds His chariot, Who walks upon the wings of the wind. He makes His angels winds, His ministers flaming fire. He established the earth on its foundations, so that it should never collapse. You covered it with great waters as with a garment. The water stood above the mountains. At Your rebuke they fled. At the sound of Your thunder they hastened away. They went up the mountains, they went down the valleys, to the place that You prepared for them. You set a boundary that they could not pass over, that they would not return to cover the earth. He sends the springs into the streams. They go between the mountains. They water every beast of the field. The wild asses quench their thirst. Beside them dwell the birds of the sky. From among the branches they give voice. He waters the mountains from His upper chambers. The earth is satisfied with the fruit of Your works. He causes the grass to grow for the cattle, and plants for the service of man, and He brings forth food from the earth. And wine gladdens the heart of man, to brighten his face with oil, and bread sustains the heart of man. The trees of the Lord are satisfied, the cedars of Lebanon that He planted, where the birds make their nests. As for the stork, the cypress trees are her house. The high hills are for the wild goats, the rocks are a refuge for the badgers. He made the moon for the seasons. The sun knows its setting place. You put down darkness, and it is night, when all the forest beasts creep out. The young lions roar for their prey, and seek their food from God. The sun rises, they gather together, and lie within their dens. Man goes forth to his work, and to his labor until evening. How great are Your works, O Lord! You have made them all in

---

the vegetation, the sun, moon, stars, the fish of the sea, the animals of the field, and finally man (Ibn Ezra).

Taken as a whole, the psalm captures the beauty, power, rhythms, wisdom, and esthetics imbedded in God's mighty work of creation. More specifically, and tantalizingly, the phrase נוֹטֶה שָׁמַיִם כַּיְרִיעָה ("He spreads the heavens like a curtain") bears special consideration in light of recent scientific confirmation of Albert Einstein's 1916 Theory of General Relativity. According to that theory the cosmos is to be understood not as an empty void, but as an ethereal fabric, woven out of the warp and woof of time and space, which like a garment is subject to wave-like movements

עָשִׂיתָ, מָלְאָה הָאָרֶץ קִנְיָנֶךָ: זֶה הַיָּם גָּדוֹל וּרְחַב יָדָיִם, שָׁם־רֶמֶשׂ
וְאֵין מִסְפָּר, חַיּוֹת קְטַנּוֹת עִם־גְּדֹלוֹת: שָׁם אֳנִיּוֹת יְהַלֵּכוּן, לִוְיָתָן
זֶה־יָצַרְתָּ לְשַׂחֶק־בּוֹ: כֻּלָּם אֵלֶיךָ יְשַׂבֵּרוּן, לָתֵת אָכְלָם בְּעִתּוֹ: תִּתֵּן
לָהֶם יִלְקֹטוּן, תִּפְתַּח יָדְךָ יִשְׂבְּעוּן טוֹב: תַּסְתִּיר פָּנֶיךָ יִבָּהֵלוּן, תֹּסֵף
רוּחָם יִגְוָעוּן, וְאֶל־עֲפָרָם יְשׁוּבוּן: תְּשַׁלַּח רוּחֲךָ יִבָּרֵאוּן, וּתְחַדֵּשׁ פְּנֵי
אֲדָמָה: יְהִי כְבוֹד יהוה לְעוֹלָם, יִשְׂמַח יהוה בְּמַעֲשָׂיו: הַמַּבִּיט לָאָרֶץ
וַתִּרְעָד, יִגַּע בֶּהָרִים וְיֶעֱשָׁנוּ: אָשִׁירָה לַיהוה בְּחַיָּי, אֲזַמְּרָה לֵאלֹהַי
בְּעוֹדִי: ◂ יֶעֱרַב עָלָיו שִׂיחִי, אָנֹכִי אֶשְׂמַח בַּיהוה: יִתַּמּוּ חַטָּאִים מִן־
הָאָרֶץ, וּרְשָׁעִים עוֹד אֵינָם, בָּרְכִי נַפְשִׁי אֶת־יהוה, הַלְלוּיָהּ:

קדיש יתום (*page 184*)

During the month of אלול *(except* ערב ראש השנה*), the* שופר *is sounded (some sound the* שופר *after the psalm below). From the second day of* ראש חודש אלול *through* שמיני עצרת*, the following psalm is said:*

תהלים כז **לְדָוִד,** יהוה אוֹרִי וְיִשְׁעִי, מִמִּי אִירָא, יהוה מָעוֹז־חַיַּי, מִמִּי אֶפְחָד:
בִּקְרֹב עָלַי מְרֵעִים לֶאֱכֹל אֶת־בְּשָׂרִי, צָרַי וְאֹיְבַי לִי, הֵמָּה
כָּשְׁלוּ וְנָפָלוּ: אִם־תַּחֲנֶה עָלַי מַחֲנֶה, לֹא־יִירָא לִבִּי, אִם־תָּקוּם

or ripples that result from massive primordial cataclysms, movements which scientists are now able to observe. The Psalmist's formulation resonates with renewed meaning in light of these scientific developments regarding the fabric (or "curtain") of God's cosmos (R. Basil Herring).

There is specific reference to Rosh Ḥodesh in the phrase עָשָׂה יָרֵחַ לְמוֹעֲדִים, "He made the moon for the seasons" (Ps. 104:19). Pointedly, the term for "seasons" in this verse is precisely that which the Torah uses for the festivals whose dates are determined by the birth of the moon.

There is a deep connection between this psalm and Rosh Ḥodesh. The penultimate phrase, יִתַּמּוּ חַטָּאִים מִן־הָאָרֶץ , refers to our own potential to achieve spiritual renewal, as symbolized by the moon. For just as the light of the moon grows after having been diminished (what the sages refer to as פְּגַם הַלְּבָנָה) and comes to full radiance by mid-month, so too can we overcome our spiritual deficiencies (caused by our evil inclination) to achieve our own spiritual radiance. By harnessing the powers of our lower urges, each of us and the Jewish people as a whole can bring ourselves and all of creation to a state in which we can overcome and eliminate all sin. Accordingly, this phrase is to be understood as saying that "like the phases of the moon, earthly sins – חַטָּאִים מִן־הָאָרֶץ – can be harnessed to bring ourselves and our world closer to perfection" (R. Levi Yitzḥak of Berditchev).

wisdom. The earth is full of Your creatures. Behold, the great and wide sea, where creeping things are innumerable, small beasts and big ones. There go the ships, the leviathan that You made to play with. All of them wait upon You, to give them their food in its season. You give them, they gather it. You open Your hand, they are filled with good. You hide Your face, they are terrified. You take away their breath, they die and return to their dust. You send forth Your breath, they are created, and You renew the face of the earth. May the glory of the Lord be forever, may the Lord rejoice in His works. He looks upon the earth, and it trembles. He touches the hills, and they smoke. I will sing to the Lord while I live. I will sing praises to my God while I exist. ▸ My meditation will be sweet to Him. I will rejoice in the Lord. May the sinners be removed from the earth, and may the wicked be no more. Bless the Lord, O my soul. Praise the Lord.

Mourner's Kaddish (page 185)

During the month of Elul (except Erev Rosh HaShana), the shofar is sounded (some sound the shofar after the psalm below). From the second day of Rosh Ḥodesh Elul through Shemini Atzeret, the following psalm is said:

Ps. 27 לְדָוִד OF DAVID. The Lord is my light and my salvation. Whom shall I fear? The Lord is the refuge of my life. Whom shall I dread? When the evildoers came close to me to eat my flesh, those who were to me my adversaries and my enemies, it was they who stumbled and fell. If a host should encamp against me, my heart will not fear. If a war should rise

---

לְדָוִד, ה' אוֹרִי / PSALM 27

According to *Midrash Vayikra Raba* there are several references in this psalm to the successive festivals of Tishrei. Thus, on Rosh HaShana, when the moon and night sky are dark at the beginning of the month, "The Lord is my light"; on Yom Kippur when our lives are in the balance He is "my salvation"; on Sukkot when we leave our secure homes to enter the frail *sukka*, He "will hide me in His tabernacle (*sukka*)." Starting on Rosh Ḥodesh Elul we are summoned to "come home" to God, just as during that period God Himself, so to speak, comes to meet us. The psalm successively entreats God to not hide His face from us, but rather to show us the right path "home." In the final verses we declare our hope that we might yet witness God's goodness in the land of the living, that we may be sealed in the book of life.

Many have noted a contradiction at the core of the psalm, in that it announces that it will request "one thing" of God, but then goes on to list not one but seven items. The answer, however, is that all seven are merely multiple facets of the first, all-encompassing request "to dwell in the house of God." For each of the subsequent items refers to God's House, that is the Temple, by another name, and each reference is to the direct consequence of being "at home" with God (R. Amos Ḥakham).

עָלַי מִלְחָמָה, בְּזֹאת אֲנִי בוֹטֵחַ: אַחַת שָׁאַלְתִּי מֵאֵת־יהוה, אוֹתָהּ אֲבַקֵּשׁ, שִׁבְתִּי בְּבֵית־יהוה כָּל־יְמֵי חַיַּי, לַחֲזוֹת בְּנֹעַם־יהוה, וּלְבַקֵּר בְּהֵיכָלוֹ: כִּי יִצְפְּנֵנִי בְּסֻכֹּה בְּיוֹם רָעָה, יַסְתִּרֵנִי בְּסֵתֶר אָהֳלוֹ, בְּצוּר יְרוֹמְמֵנִי: וְעַתָּה יָרוּם רֹאשִׁי עַל אֹיְבַי סְבִיבוֹתַי, וְאֶזְבְּחָה בְאָהֳלוֹ זִבְחֵי תְרוּעָה, אָשִׁירָה וַאֲזַמְּרָה לַיהוה: שְׁמַע־יהוה קוֹלִי אֶקְרָא, וְחָנֵּנִי וַעֲנֵנִי: לְךָ אָמַר לִבִּי בַּקְּשׁוּ פָנָי, אֶת־פָּנֶיךָ יהוה אֲבַקֵּשׁ: אַל־תַּסְתֵּר פָּנֶיךָ מִמֶּנִּי, אַל תַּט־בְּאַף עַבְדֶּךָ, עֶזְרָתִי הָיִיתָ, אַל־תִּטְּשֵׁנִי וְאַל־תַּעַזְבֵנִי, אֱלֹהֵי יִשְׁעִי: כִּי־אָבִי וְאִמִּי עֲזָבוּנִי, וַיהוה יַאַסְפֵנִי: הוֹרֵנִי יהוה דַּרְכֶּךָ, וּנְחֵנִי בְּאֹרַח מִישׁוֹר, לְמַעַן שׁוֹרְרָי: אַל־תִּתְּנֵנִי בְּנֶפֶשׁ צָרָי, כִּי קָמוּ־בִי עֵדֵי־שֶׁקֶר, וִיפֵחַ חָמָס: ‹ לוּלֵא הֶאֱמַנְתִּי לִרְאוֹת בְּטוּב־יהוה בְּאֶרֶץ חַיִּים: קַוֵּה אֶל־יהוה, חֲזַק וְיַאֲמֵץ לִבֶּךָ, וְקַוֵּה אֶל־יהוה:

קדיש יתום (*page 184*)

תפילה בבית האבל

After the regular service, the following psalm is read in a שבעה *house during the* שבעה *week. On those days on which* תחנון *is not said,* תהלים טז (*on the next page*) *is substituted.*

תהלים מט

לַמְנַצֵּחַ לִבְנֵי־קֹרַח מִזְמוֹר: שִׁמְעוּ־זֹאת כָּל־הָעַמִּים, הַאֲזִינוּ כָּל־יֹשְׁבֵי חָלֶד: גַּם־בְּנֵי אָדָם, גַּם־בְּנֵי־אִישׁ, יַחַד עָשִׁיר וְאֶבְיוֹן: פִּי יְדַבֵּר חָכְמוֹת, וְהָגוּת לִבִּי תְבוּנוֹת: אַטֶּה לְמָשָׁל אָזְנִי, אֶפְתַּח בְּכִנּוֹר חִידָתִי: לָמָּה אִירָא בִּימֵי רָע, עֲוֹן עֲקֵבַי יְסֻבֵּנִי: הַבֹּטְחִים

אַחַת שָׁאַלְתִּי – *One thing have I asked*. King David seems to ask for many things in this psalm. And yet he declares that he seeks only "one thing." The answer is that the sundry items he requests in the verses that follow have but one goal, i.e., to have all that he needs so that he will not be distracted or prevented from his ultimate goal, which is to spend his days and nights in calm contemplation and sustained study in "the house of God." So too, as explained by the Rebbe of Karlin, all of our requests during the Ten Days of Repentance have only one goal: to receive from God all of the physical, emotional, and financial blessings necessary to live a life of tranquility and spiritual fulfillment devoted to the service of God throughout the year. In similar fashion when the Psalmist asks God to shelter him in "His tabernacle (*sukka*)," he is asking for our homes to be filled all year long with God's presence, spiritual havens that extend the aura of the *sukka*, in the face of the difficulties encountered in the mundane demands of daily life. Of course we should not ask God to free us of our responsibility to provide

against me, in this I trust. One thing have I asked of the Lord, that will I seek: That I may dwell in the house of the Lord all the days of my life, to behold the beauty of the Lord, and to contemplate His Temple, that He will hide me in His tabernacle on the day of evil, He will hide me in the shelter of His tent, He will lift me up upon a rock. And now my head will be lifted up above my enemies round about me, and I will offer in His tent sacrifices accompanied by the sound of trumpets. I will sing, and I will sing praises to the Lord. Hear, O Lord, my voice when I call, and show me favor and answer me. Of You my heart has said: Seek My face. Your face, O Lord, will I seek. Do not hide Your face from me. Do not turn Your servant away in anger. You have been my help, do not abandon me and do not forsake me, O God of my salvation. For my father and my mother have forsaken me, but the Lord will gather me in. Teach me Your way, O Lord, and lead me on an even path, because of my enemies. Do not deliver me to the desire of my enemies, for false witnesses have risen up against me, and a wicked witness. ▸ Were it not that I believed I would see the goodness of the Lord in the land of the living. Wait for the Lord, be strong and let your heart be encouraged, and wait for the Lord.

Mourner's Kaddish (page 185)

A SHIVA HOUSE

After the regular service, the following psalm is read in a shiva house during the shiva week. On those days on which Taḥanun is not said, Psalm 16 (on the next page) is substituted.

Ps. 49 לַמְנַצֵּחַ TO THE DIRECTOR of music. A psalm for the sons of Korah. Hear this, all the peoples. Listen, all the inhabitants of the world, Both the sons of the low and the sons of the high, all the rich and the poor. My mouth will speak wisdom, and the meditation of my heart will be understanding. I will incline my ear to the spirit of the poem. I will propound my riddle with the lyre. Why should I fear in the days of evil,

---

for our families and carry out our communal obligations, however we can surely ask Him, as this psalm does, to "show and lead us in the way" of making our homes into places where God is to be found "all the days of our lives," and where our families can experience spiritual tranquility and growth. In this, the psalm fully reflects the essence of our prayers during Elul and Tishrei (*Netivot Shalom*).

תְּפִלָּה בְּבֵית הָאָבֵל / A SHIVA HOUSE

לַמְנַצֵּחַ – *To the director.* The sons of Koraḥ did not die. The *Midrash* teaches that they separated themselves from their father at the last moment before he was swallowed up by the earth. As such they were witnesses to the mortal consequences of hubris, strife, and anger. Perhaps this was the impetus for their solemn words regarding life and

עַל־חֵילָם, וּבְרֹב עָשְׁרָם יִתְהַלָּלוּ: אָח לֹא־פָדֹה יִפְדֶּה אִישׁ, לֹא־יִתֵּן
לֵאלֹהִים כָּפְרוֹ: וְיֵקַר פִּדְיוֹן נַפְשָׁם, וְחָדַל לְעוֹלָם: וִיחִי־עוֹד לָנֶצַח,
לֹא יִרְאֶה הַשָּׁחַת: כִּי יִרְאֶה חֲכָמִים יָמוּתוּ, יַחַד כְּסִיל וָבַעַר יֹאבֵדוּ,
וְעָזְבוּ לַאֲחֵרִים חֵילָם: קִרְבָּם בָּתֵּימוֹ לְעוֹלָם, מִשְׁכְּנֹתָם לְדֹר וָדֹר,
קָרְאוּ בִשְׁמוֹתָם עֲלֵי אֲדָמוֹת: וְאָדָם בִּיקָר בַּל־יָלִין, נִמְשַׁל כַּבְּהֵמוֹת
נִדְמוּ: זֶה דַרְכָּם, כֵּסֶל לָמוֹ, וְאַחֲרֵיהֶם בְּפִיהֶם יִרְצוּ סֶלָה: כַּצֹּאן
לִשְׁאוֹל שַׁתּוּ, מָוֶת יִרְעֵם, וַיִּרְדּוּ בָם יְשָׁרִים לַבֹּקֶר, וְצוּרָם לְבַלּוֹת
שְׁאוֹל מִזְּבֻל לוֹ: אַךְ־אֱלֹהִים יִפְדֶּה נַפְשִׁי מִיַּד שְׁאוֹל, כִּי יִקָּחֵנִי סֶלָה:
אַל־תִּירָא כִּי־יַעֲשִׁר אִישׁ, כִּי־יִרְבֶּה כְּבוֹד בֵּיתוֹ: כִּי לֹא בְמוֹתוֹ יִקַּח
הַכֹּל, לֹא־יֵרֵד אַחֲרָיו כְּבוֹדוֹ: כִּי־נַפְשׁוֹ בְּחַיָּיו יְבָרֵךְ, וְיוֹדֻךָ כִּי־תֵיטִיב
לָךְ: תָּבוֹא עַד־דּוֹר אֲבוֹתָיו, עַד־נֵצַח לֹא יִרְאוּ־אוֹר: אָדָם בִּיקָר וְלֹא
יָבִין, נִמְשַׁל כַּבְּהֵמוֹת נִדְמוּ:

On those days on which תחנון *is not said, substitute:*

תהלים טז

מִכְתָּם לְדָוִד, שָׁמְרֵנִי אֵל כִּי־חָסִיתִי בָךְ: אָמַרְתְּ לַיהוה, אֲדֹנָי אָתָּה,
טוֹבָתִי בַּל־עָלֶיךָ: לִקְדוֹשִׁים אֲשֶׁר־בָּאָרֶץ הֵמָּה,
וְאַדִּירֵי כָּל־חֶפְצִי־בָם: יִרְבּוּ עַצְּבוֹתָם אַחֵר מָהָרוּ, בַּל־אַסִּיךְ נִסְכֵּיהֶם
מִדָּם, וּבַל־אֶשָּׂא אֶת־שְׁמוֹתָם עַל־שְׂפָתָי: יהוה, מְנָת־חֶלְקִי וְכוֹסִי,
אַתָּה תּוֹמִיךְ גּוֹרָלִי: חֲבָלִים נָפְלוּ־לִי בַּנְּעִמִים, אַף־נַחֲלָת שָׁפְרָה
עָלָי: אֲבָרֵךְ אֶת־יהוה אֲשֶׁר יְעָצָנִי, אַף־לֵילוֹת יִסְּרוּנִי כִלְיוֹתָי:
שִׁוִּיתִי יהוה לְנֶגְדִּי תָמִיד, כִּי מִימִינִי בַּל־אֶמּוֹט: לָכֵן שָׂמַח לִבִּי
וַיָּגֶל כְּבוֹדִי, אַף־בְּשָׂרִי יִשְׁכֹּן לָבֶטַח: כִּי לֹא־תַעֲזֹב נַפְשִׁי לִשְׁאוֹל,
לֹא־תִתֵּן חֲסִידְךָ לִרְאוֹת שָׁחַת: תּוֹדִיעֵנִי אֹרַח חַיִּים, שֹׂבַע שְׂמָחוֹת
אֶת־פָּנֶיךָ, נְעִמוֹת בִּימִינְךָ נֶצַח:

---

death in this psalm, which is recited in a *shiva* house. Eternal reward is the result of fortifying our spirit, following in the ways of God, seeking kindness toward our fellow man, and living a truly spiritual and moral life. This sobering but ultimately comforting psalm enhances our prayers in a *shiva* house (R. Avi Baumol).

when iniquity encompasses my heels? Those who trust in their wealth, and who boast about the multitude of their riches. No man can redeem his brother, nor give to God his ransom. And even if they pay dearly for the redemption of their soul, it will be unattained forever. Will he still live forever? Will he not see the pit? When he sees that wise men die, that all fools and boors perish, and leave their wealth to others. Inwardly their houses will stand for ever, their dwelling-places for all generations. Those on earth call them by their names. But man does not lie in honor. He is like the beasts that perish. This is their way. It is folly for them. And their posterity praise them with their mouths. Selah. Like sheep they descend to the underworld. Death is their shepherd, and the upright strike them in the morning. And their image goes from its dwelling to the horrors of the underworld. But God will redeem my soul from the hand of the underworld, for He will take me. Selah. Do not stand in awe when a man becomes rich, when the glory of his house becomes great. For when he dies he will not take anything. His glory will not descend after him. For while he is alive he should bless his soul, and they will praise you if you do well to yourself. It will go to the generation of his fathers. They will never see light. A man who is in honor but does not understand is like the beasts that perish.

On those days on which Taḥanun is not said, substitute:

Ps. 16 **מִכְתָּם לְדָוִד** A *MIKHTAM* OF DAVID. Preserve me, O God, for I seek refuge in You. You have said to the Lord: "You are my Master. My good is from none but You." To the holy that are in the land, and the mighty in whom is all my desire: "Let their idols multiply, those who cling to another god. I will not offer their libations of blood, nor will I take their names upon my lips." The Lord is the portion of my inheritance and of my cup. You maintain my lot. Portions have fallen to me in pleasant places, and my inheritance is pleasing to me. I bless the Lord Who has given me counsel. Even at night my kidneys admonish me. I have set the Lord always before me. Indeed He is at my right hand, so that I will not stumble. Therefore my heart is glad, and my honor rejoices. My flesh, too, dwells in safety. For You will not abandon my soul to the underworld. You will not allow Your pious one to see the pit. You will make known to me the path of life. In Your presence is fullness of joy. At Your right hand are pleasures forevermore.

אמירות לאחר התפילה

Some say the following daily after morning prayers:

שש זכירות

יציאת מצרים

דברים טז לְמַעַן תִּזְכֹּר אֶת־יוֹם צֵאתְךָ מֵאֶרֶץ מִצְרַיִם כֹּל יְמֵי חַיֶּיךָ׃

מעמד הר סיני

דברים ד רַק הִשָּׁמֶר לְךָ וּשְׁמֹר נַפְשְׁךָ מְאֹד פֶּן־תִּשְׁכַּח אֶת־הַדְּבָרִים אֲשֶׁר־
רָאוּ עֵינֶיךָ וּפֶן־יָסוּרוּ מִלְּבָבְךָ כֹּל יְמֵי חַיֶּיךָ וְהוֹדַעְתָּם לְבָנֶיךָ וְלִבְנֵי
בָנֶיךָ׃ יוֹם אֲשֶׁר עָמַדְתָּ לִפְנֵי יהוה אֱלֹהֶיךָ בְּחֹרֵב בֶּאֱמֹר יהוה אֵלַי
הַקְהֶל־לִי אֶת־הָעָם וְאַשְׁמִעֵם אֶת־דְּבָרָי אֲשֶׁר יִלְמְדוּן לְיִרְאָה אֹתִי
כָּל־הַיָּמִים אֲשֶׁר הֵם חַיִּים עַל־הָאֲדָמָה וְאֶת־בְּנֵיהֶם יְלַמֵּדוּן׃

מעשה עמלק ומחייתו

דברים כה זָכוֹר אֵת אֲשֶׁר־עָשָׂה לְךָ עֲמָלֵק בַּדֶּרֶךְ בְּצֵאתְכֶם מִמִּצְרָיִם׃ אֲשֶׁר
קָרְךָ בַּדֶּרֶךְ וַיְזַנֵּב בְּךָ כָּל־הַנֶּחֱשָׁלִים אַחֲרֶיךָ וְאַתָּה עָיֵף וְיָגֵעַ וְלֹא
יָרֵא אֱלֹהִים׃ וְהָיָה בְּהָנִיחַ יהוה אֱלֹהֶיךָ ׀ לְךָ מִכָּל־אֹיְבֶיךָ מִסָּבִיב
בָּאָרֶץ אֲשֶׁר־יהוה אֱלֹהֶיךָ נֹתֵן לְךָ נַחֲלָה לְרִשְׁתָּהּ תִּמְחֶה אֶת־זֵכֶר
עֲמָלֵק מִתַּחַת הַשָּׁמָיִם לֹא תִּשְׁכָּח׃

מעשי אבותינו במדבר

דברים ט זְכֹר אַל־תִּשְׁכַּח אֵת אֲשֶׁר־הִקְצַפְתָּ אֶת־יהוה אֱלֹהֶיךָ בַּמִּדְבָּר

מעשה מרים

דברים כד זָכוֹר אֵת אֲשֶׁר־עָשָׂה יהוה אֱלֹהֶיךָ לְמִרְיָם בַּדֶּרֶךְ בְּצֵאתְכֶם מִמִּצְרָיִם׃

שבת

שמות כ זָכוֹר אֶת־יוֹם הַשַּׁבָּת לְקַדְּשׁוֹ׃

READINGS AFTER THE SERVICE

Some say the following daily after morning prayers:

THE SIX REMEMBRANCES

The Exodus from Egypt

Deut. 16 THAT YOU may remember the day you left the land of Egypt all the days of your life.

The Revelation at Mount Sinai

Deut. 4 ONLY TAKE HEED of yourself, and keep your soul diligently, lest you forget the things which your eyes saw, and lest they depart from your heart all the days of your life; but make them known to your children and your children's children; the day that you stood before the Lord your God in Horeb, when the Lord said to me: "Assemble the people before Me, and I will make them hear My words that they may learn to fear Me all the days that they live upon the earth, and that they may teach their children."

Amalek

Deut. 25 REMEMBER what Amalek did to you on the way as you came out of Egypt; how he met you on the way, and smote all those that were enfeebled, lagging behind, when you were faint and weary; and he feared not God. Therefore, when the Lord your God gives you rest from all your enemies round about, in the land which the Lord your God gives you for an inheritance to possess it, you shall blot out the remembrance of Amalek from under heaven; you shall not forget.

The Golden Calf

Deut. 9 REMEMBER, and do not forget, how you provoked the Lord your God in the wilderness.

Miriam

Deut. 24 REMEMBER what the Lord your God did to Miriam on the way when you came out of Egypt.

The Sabbath

Ex. 20 REMEMBER the Sabbath day to hallow it.

עשרת הדיברות

שמות כ **וַיְדַבֵּר** אֱלֹהִים אֵת כָּל־הַדְּבָרִים הָאֵלֶּה לֵאמֹר:

א. אָנֹכִי יהוה אֱלֹהֶיךָ אֲשֶׁר הוֹצֵאתִיךָ מֵאֶרֶץ מִצְרַיִם מִבֵּית עֲבָדִים:

ב. לֹא־יִהְיֶה לְךָ אֱלֹהִים אֲחֵרִים עַל־פָּנָי: לֹא־תַעֲשֶׂה לְךָ פֶסֶל וְכָל־תְּמוּנָה אֲשֶׁר בַּשָּׁמַיִם מִמַּעַל וַאֲשֶׁר בָּאָרֶץ מִתָּחַת וַאֲשֶׁר בַּמַּיִם מִתַּחַת לָאָרֶץ: לֹא־תִשְׁתַּחֲוֶה לָהֶם וְלֹא תָעָבְדֵם כִּי אָנֹכִי יהוה אֱלֹהֶיךָ אֵל קַנָּא פֹּקֵד עֲוֹן אָבֹת עַל־בָּנִים עַל־שִׁלֵּשִׁים וְעַל־רִבֵּעִים לְשֹׂנְאָי: וְעֹשֶׂה חֶסֶד לַאֲלָפִים לְאֹהֲבַי וּלְשֹׁמְרֵי מִצְוֹתָי:

ג. לֹא תִשָּׂא אֶת־שֵׁם־יהוה אֱלֹהֶיךָ לַשָּׁוְא כִּי לֹא יְנַקֶּה יהוה אֵת אֲשֶׁר־יִשָּׂא אֶת־שְׁמוֹ לַשָּׁוְא:

ד. זָכוֹר אֶת־יוֹם הַשַּׁבָּת לְקַדְּשׁוֹ: שֵׁשֶׁת יָמִים תַּעֲבֹד וְעָשִׂיתָ כָּל־מְלַאכְתֶּךָ: וְיוֹם הַשְּׁבִיעִי שַׁבָּת לַיהוה אֱלֹהֶיךָ לֹא־תַעֲשֶׂה כָל־מְלָאכָה אַתָּה | וּבִנְךָ וּבִתֶּךָ עַבְדְּךָ וַאֲמָתְךָ וּבְהֶמְתֶּךָ וְגֵרְךָ אֲשֶׁר בִּשְׁעָרֶיךָ: כִּי שֵׁשֶׁת־יָמִים עָשָׂה יהוה אֶת־הַשָּׁמַיִם וְאֶת־הָאָרֶץ אֶת־הַיָּם וְאֶת־כָּל־אֲשֶׁר־בָּם וַיָּנַח בַּיּוֹם הַשְּׁבִיעִי עַל־כֵּן בֵּרַךְ יהוה אֶת־יוֹם הַשַּׁבָּת וַיְקַדְּשֵׁהוּ:

ה. כַּבֵּד אֶת־אָבִיךָ וְאֶת־אִמֶּךָ לְמַעַן יַאֲרִכוּן יָמֶיךָ עַל הָאֲדָמָה אֲשֶׁר־יהוה אֱלֹהֶיךָ נֹתֵן לָךְ:

ו. לֹא תִרְצָח

ז. לֹא תִנְאָף

ח. לֹא תִגְנֹב

ט. לֹא־תַעֲנֶה בְרֵעֲךָ עֵד שָׁקֶר:

י. לֹא תַחְמֹד בֵּית רֵעֶךָ לֹא־תַחְמֹד אֵשֶׁת רֵעֶךָ וְעַבְדּוֹ וַאֲמָתוֹ וְשׁוֹרוֹ וַחֲמֹרוֹ וְכֹל אֲשֶׁר לְרֵעֶךָ:

THE TEN COMMANDMENTS

Ex. 20 וַיְדַבֵּר AND GOD SPOKE all these words, saying:

1. אָנֹכִי I AM the Lord your God, Who brought you out of the land of Egypt, out of the house of bondage.

2. לֹא־יִהְיֶה YOU SHALL have no other gods before Me. You shall not make for yourself a graven image, nor any manner of likeness, of any thing that is in heaven above, or that is in the earth beneath, or that is in the water under the earth; you shall not bow down to them, nor serve them; for I the Lord your God am a jealous God, visiting the iniquity of the fathers upon the children to the third and fourth generation of them that hate Me; and showing mercy to the thousandth generation of them that love Me and keep My commandments.

3. לֹא תִשָּׂא YOU SHALL NOT take the name of the Lord your God in vain; for the Lord will not hold him guiltless that takes His name in vain.

4. זָכוֹר REMEMBER the Sabbath day, to keep it holy. Six days you shall labor, and do all your work; but the seventh day is a Sabbath to the Lord your God, in it you shall not do any manner of work, you, nor your son, nor your daughter, nor your man-servant, nor your maid-servant, nor your cattle, nor your stranger that is within your gates; for in six days the Lord made heaven and earth, the sea, and all that is in them, and rested on the seventh day; therefore the Lord blessed the Sabbath day, and hallowed it.

5. כַּבֵּד HONOR your father and your mother, that your days may be long upon the land which the Lord your God gives you.

6. לֹא תִרְצַח YOU SHALL NOT murder.

7. לֹא תִנְאָף YOU SHALL NOT commit adultery.

8. לֹא תִגְנֹב YOU SHALL NOT steal.

9. לֹא־תַעֲנֶה YOU SHALL NOT bear false witness against your neighbor.

10. לֹא תַחְמֹד YOU SHALL NOT covet your neighbor's house; you shall not covet your neighbor's wife, nor his man-servant, nor his maid-servant, nor his ox, nor his ass, nor any thing that is your neighbor's.

שלושה עשר עיקרים

א. **אֲנִי מַאֲמִין** בֶּאֱמוּנָה שְׁלֵמָה, שֶׁהַבּוֹרֵא יִתְבָּרַךְ שְׁמוֹ הוּא בּוֹרֵא וּמַנְהִיג לְכָל הַבְּרוּאִים וְהוּא לְבַדּוֹ עָשָׂה וְעוֹשֶׂה וְיַעֲשֶׂה לְכָל הַמַּעֲשִׂים.

ב. אֲנִי מַאֲמִין בֶּאֱמוּנָה שְׁלֵמָה, שֶׁהַבּוֹרֵא יִתְבָּרַךְ שְׁמוֹ הוּא יָחִיד, וְאֵין יְחִידוּת כָּמוֹהוּ בְּשׁוּם פָּנִים, וְהוּא לְבַדּוֹ אֱלֹהֵינוּ, הָיָה הֹוֶה וְיִהְיֶה.

ג. אֲנִי מַאֲמִין בֶּאֱמוּנָה שְׁלֵמָה, שֶׁהַבּוֹרֵא יִתְבָּרַךְ שְׁמוֹ אֵינוֹ גוּף, וְלֹא יַשִּׂיגוּהוּ מַשִּׂיגֵי הַגּוּף, וְאֵין לוֹ שׁוּם דִּמְיוֹן כְּלָל.

ד. אֲנִי מַאֲמִין בֶּאֱמוּנָה שְׁלֵמָה, שֶׁהַבּוֹרֵא יִתְבָּרַךְ שְׁמוֹ הוּא רִאשׁוֹן וְהוּא אַחֲרוֹן.

ה. אֲנִי מַאֲמִין בֶּאֱמוּנָה שְׁלֵמָה, שֶׁהַבּוֹרֵא יִתְבָּרַךְ שְׁמוֹ לוֹ לְבַדּוֹ רָאוּי לְהִתְפַּלֵּל, וְאֵין רָאוּי לְהִתְפַּלֵּל לְזוּלָתוֹ.

ו. אֲנִי מַאֲמִין בֶּאֱמוּנָה שְׁלֵמָה, שֶׁכָּל דִּבְרֵי נְבִיאִים אֱמֶת.

ז. אֲנִי מַאֲמִין בֶּאֱמוּנָה שְׁלֵמָה, שֶׁנְּבוּאַת מֹשֶׁה רַבֵּנוּ עָלָיו הַשָּׁלוֹם הָיְתָה אֲמִתִּית, וְשֶׁהוּא הָיָה אָב לַנְּבִיאִים, לַקּוֹדְמִים לְפָנָיו וְלַבָּאִים אַחֲרָיו.

ח. אֲנִי מַאֲמִין בֶּאֱמוּנָה שְׁלֵמָה, שֶׁכָּל הַתּוֹרָה הַמְּצוּיָה עַתָּה בְּיָדֵינוּ, הִיא הַנְּתוּנָה לְמֹשֶׁה רַבֵּנוּ עָלָיו הַשָּׁלוֹם.

ט. אֲנִי מַאֲמִין בֶּאֱמוּנָה שְׁלֵמָה, שֶׁזֹּאת הַתּוֹרָה לֹא תְהֵא מֻחְלֶפֶת, וְלֹא תְהֵא תּוֹרָה אַחֶרֶת מֵאֵת הַבּוֹרֵא יִתְבָּרַךְ שְׁמוֹ.

י. אֲנִי מַאֲמִין בֶּאֱמוּנָה שְׁלֵמָה, שֶׁהַבּוֹרֵא יִתְבָּרַךְ שְׁמוֹ, יוֹדֵעַ כָּל מַעֲשֵׂה בְנֵי אָדָם וְכָל מַחְשְׁבוֹתָם. שֶׁנֶּאֱמַר: הַיֹּצֵר יַחַד לִבָּם, הַמֵּבִין אֶל־כָּל־מַעֲשֵׂיהֶם: תהלים לג

יא. אֲנִי מַאֲמִין בֶּאֱמוּנָה שְׁלֵמָה, שֶׁהַבּוֹרֵא יִתְבָּרַךְ שְׁמוֹ גּוֹמֵל טוֹב לְשׁוֹמְרֵי מִצְוֹתָיו, וּמַעֲנִישׁ לְעוֹבְרֵי מִצְוֹתָיו.

יב. אֲנִי מַאֲמִין בֶּאֱמוּנָה שְׁלֵמָה, בְּבִיאַת הַמָּשִׁיחַ, וְאַף עַל פִּי שֶׁיִּתְמַהְמֵהַּ עִם כָּל זֶה אֲחַכֶּה לּוֹ בְּכָל יוֹם שֶׁיָּבוֹא.

יג. אֲנִי מַאֲמִין בֶּאֱמוּנָה שְׁלֵמָה, שֶׁתִּהְיֶה תְּחִיַּת הַמֵּתִים בְּעֵת שֶׁיַּעֲלֶה רָצוֹן מֵאֵת הַבּוֹרֵא יִתְבָּרַךְ שְׁמוֹ, וְיִתְעַלֶּה זִכְרוֹ לָעַד וּלְנֵצַח נְצָחִים.

THE THIRTEEN PRINCIPLES OF JEWISH FAITH

1. אֲנִי מַאֲמִין I BELIEVE with complete faith that the Creator, blessed be His name, creates and rules all creatures, and that He alone made, makes, and will make, all things.
2. I BELIEVE with complete faith that the Creator, blessed be His name, is One; that there is no oneness like His in any way; and that He alone is our God who was, is, and ever will be.
3. I BELIEVE with complete faith that the Creator, blessed be His name, is not physical, that no physical attributes can apply to Him, and that there is nothing whatsoever to compare to Him.
4. I BELIEVE with complete faith that the Creator, blessed be His name, is first and last.
5. I BELIEVE with complete faith that the Creator, blessed be His name, is the only one to whom it is proper to pray, and that it is improper to pray to anyone else.
6. I BELIEVE with complete faith that all the words of the prophets are true.
7. I BELIEVE with complete faith that the prophecy of Moses our teacher, peace be to him, was true, and that he was the father of the prophets – those who preceded him and those who followed him.
8. I BELIEVE with complete faith that the entire Torah now in our hands is the same one that was given to Moses our teacher, peace be upon him.
9. I BELIEVE with complete faith that this Torah will not be changed, nor will there be any other Torah from the Creator, blessed be His name.
10. I BELIEVE with complete faith that the Creator, blessed be His name, knows
Ps. 33 all the deeds and thoughts of humanity, as it is said, "It is He Who creates all their hearts, Who discerns all their deeds."
11. I BELIEVE with complete faith that the Creator, blessed be His name, rewards those who keep His commandments, and punishes those who transgress them.
12. I BELIEVE with complete faith in the coming of the Messiah, and though he may delay I wait daily for his coming.
13. I BELIEVE with complete faith that the dead will live again at a time of the Creator's choosing: blessed be His name and exalted be His mention for ever and all time.

שְׁלוֹשָׁה עָשָׂר עִקָּרִים / THE THIRTEEN PRINCIPLES

For an in-depth analysis of the Thirteen Principles see page E93.

The following is said after morning and evening prayers:

יְהִי יהוה אֱלֹהֵינוּ עִמָּנוּ כַּאֲשֶׁר הָיָה עִם־אֲבֹתֵינוּ, אַל־יַעַזְבֵנוּ וְאַל־יִטְּשֵׁנוּ: מלכים א׳ ח
לְהַטּוֹת לְבָבֵנוּ אֵלָיו, לָלֶכֶת בְּכָל־דְּרָכָיו וְלִשְׁמֹר מִצְוֹתָיו וְחֻקָּיו
וּמִשְׁפָּטָיו אֲשֶׁר צִוָּה אֶת־אֲבֹתֵינוּ: וְיִהְיוּ דְבָרַי אֵלֶּה אֲשֶׁר הִתְחַנַּנְתִּי לִפְנֵי
יהוה, קְרֹבִים אֶל־יהוה אֱלֹהֵינוּ יוֹמָם וָלָיְלָה, לַעֲשׂוֹת מִשְׁפַּט עַבְדּוֹ וּמִשְׁפַּט
עַמּוֹ יִשְׂרָאֵל דְּבַר־יוֹם בְּיוֹמוֹ: לְמַעַן דַּעַת כָּל־עַמֵּי הָאָרֶץ כִּי יהוה הוּא
הָאֱלֹהִים, אֵין עוֹד:

יהוה נְחֵנִי בְצִדְקָתֶךָ לְמַעַן שׁוֹרְרָי, הַיְשַׁר לְפָנַי דַּרְכֶּךָ: וַאֲנִי בְּתֻמִּי אֵלֵךְ, תהלים ה תהלים כו
פְּדֵנִי וְחָנֵּנִי: פְּנֵה־אֵלַי וְחָנֵּנִי כִּי־יָחִיד וְעָנִי אָנִי: רַגְלִי עָמְדָה בְמִישׁוֹר, תהלים כה תהלים כו
בְּמַקְהֵלִים אֲבָרֵךְ יהוה: יהוה שֹׁמְרִי, יהוה צִלִּי עַל יַד יְמִינִי. עֶזְרִי מֵעִם יהוה, תהלים קכא
עֹשֵׂה שָׁמַיִם וָאָרֶץ: יהוה יִשְׁמָר צֵאתִי וּבוֹאִי לְחַיִּים וּלְשָׁלוֹם, מֵעַתָּה וְעַד
עוֹלָם. הַשְׁקִיפָה מִמְּעוֹן קָדְשְׁךָ מִן־הַשָּׁמַיִם, וּבָרֵךְ אֶת־עַמְּךָ, אֶת־יִשְׂרָאֵל, דברים כו
וְאֵת הָאֲדָמָה אֲשֶׁר נָתַתָּה לָנוּ כַּאֲשֶׁר נִשְׁבַּעְתָּ לַאֲבֹתֵינוּ, אֶרֶץ זָבַת חָלָב
וּדְבָשׁ:

אֵל הַכָּבוֹד, אֶתֵּן לְךָ שִׁיר וְהַלֵּל וְאֶעֱבָד לְךָ יוֹם וָלֵיל. בָּרוּךְ יָחִיד וּמְיֻחָד,
הָיָה הֹוֶה וְיִהְיֶה, יהוה אֱלֹהִים אֱלֹהֵי יִשְׂרָאֵל, מֶלֶךְ מַלְכֵי הַמְּלָכִים,
הַקָּדוֹשׁ בָּרוּךְ הוּא. הוּא אֱלֹהִים חַיִּים, מֶלֶךְ חַי וְקַיָּם לָעַד וּלְעוֹלְמֵי עַד.
בָּרוּךְ שֵׁם כְּבוֹד מַלְכוּתוֹ לְעוֹלָם וָעֶד. לִישׁוּעָתְךָ קִוִּיתִי יהוה: כִּי כָּל הָעַמִּים בראשית מט
יֵלְכוּ אִישׁ בְּשֵׁם אֱלֹהָיו, וַאֲנִי אֵלֵךְ בְּשֵׁם יהוה אֱלֹהִים חַיִּים וּמֶלֶךְ עוֹלָם.
עֶזְרִי מֵעִם יהוה, עֹשֵׂה שָׁמַיִם וָאָרֶץ: יהוה יִמְלֹךְ לְעֹלָם וָעֶד: תהלים קכא שמות טו

לַמְנַצֵּחַ בִּנְגִינֹת, מִזְמוֹר שִׁיר: אֱלֹהִים יְחָנֵּנוּ וִיבָרְכֵנוּ, יָאֵר פָּנָיו אִתָּנוּ סֶלָה: תהלים סז
לָדַעַת בָּאָרֶץ דַּרְכֶּךָ, בְּכָל־גּוֹיִם יְשׁוּעָתֶךָ: יוֹדוּךָ עַמִּים
אֱלֹהִים, יוֹדוּךָ עַמִּים כֻּלָּם: יִשְׂמְחוּ וִירַנְּנוּ לְאֻמִּים, כִּי־תִשְׁפֹּט עַמִּים מִישֹׁר,
וּלְאֻמִּים בָּאָרֶץ תַּנְחֵם סֶלָה: יוֹדוּךָ עַמִּים אֱלֹהִים, יוֹדוּךָ עַמִּים כֻּלָּם: אֶרֶץ
נָתְנָה יְבוּלָהּ, יְבָרְכֵנוּ אֱלֹהִים אֱלֹהֵינוּ: יְבָרְכֵנוּ אֱלֹהִים, וְיִירְאוּ אוֹתוֹ כָּל־
אַפְסֵי־אָרֶץ:

Some say אדון עולם *(page 16) at this point.*

The following is said after morning and evening prayers:

I Kings 8 **יְהִי** MAY the Lord our God be with us, as He was with our fathers; let Him not leave us, nor forsake us; that He may incline our hearts toward Him, to walk in all His ways, and to keep His commandments, and His statutes, and His ordinances, which He commanded our fathers. And let these my words, with which I have made supplication before the Lord, be close to the Lord our God day and night, that He maintain the cause of His servant, and the cause of His people Israel, as every day shall require. So that all the peoples of the earth may know that the Lord is God; there is none else.

Ps. 5 **יהוה** LORD, lead me in Your righteousness because of my enemies. Make Your
Ps. 26 way straight before me. But as for me, I will walk in my integrity. Redeem me
Ps. 25 and be gracious to me. Turn to me and favor me, for I am alone and oppressed.
Ps. 26 My foot stands on an even place. In the congregations I bless the Lord. The Lord
Ps. 121 is my guardian. The Lord is my shade upon my right hand. My help is from the
Lord, the Maker of heaven and earth. The Lord will guard my going out and my
Deut. 26 coming in, for life and for peace, from now and forever. Look forth from Your holy
habitation, from heaven, and bless Your people Israel, and the land which You
have given us, as you promised our fathers, a land flowing with milk and honey.

אֵל GLORIOUS GOD, I bring before You song and praise; I shall worship You day and night. Blessed be the One and Only One – Who was, Who is and Who will always be. Lord God, God of Israel, King of the most exalted of kings, the Holy One, blessed is He. He is the living God, the living and ever, forever enduring King. Blessed is the name of His glorious kingdom forever and ever.
Gen. 49 I long for Your salvation, Lord. All the nations will walk, each in the name of its
god; and I will walk in the name of the Lord, the living God and eternal King.
Ps. 121 My help is from the Lord, the Maker of heaven and earth. The Lord shall reign
forever and ever.

Ps. 67 **לַמְנַצֵּחַ** TO THE DIRECTOR of music for instruments. A psalm. A song. May God be gracious to us and bless us. May He cause His face to shine upon us. Selah. That Your way may become known upon the earth, Your salvation among all nations. The peoples will praise You, O God. All the peoples will praise You. The nations will rejoice and sing. For You judge the peoples equitably and govern the nations upon the earth. Selah. The peoples will praise You, O God. All the peoples will praise You. The earth has yielded its produce. God, our God, will bless us. God will bless us, and all the ends of the earth will fear Him.

Some say Adon Olam (page 17) at this point.

תפילה כשיוצא מבית הכנסת

Say while seated:

תהלים קמ **אַךְ** צַדִּיקִים יוֹדוּ לִשְׁמֶךָ, יֵשְׁבוּ יְשָׁרִים אֶת־פָּנֶיךָ:

Stand and say:

כִּי כָּל הָעַמִּים יֵלְכוּ אִישׁ בְּשֵׁם אֱלֹהָיו, וַאֲנִי אֵלֵךְ בְּשֵׁם יהוה אֱלֹהִים חַיִּים
תהלים קכא שמות טו וּמֶלֶךְ עוֹלָם. עֶזְרִי מֵעִם יהוה, עֹשֵׂה שָׁמַיִם וָאָרֶץ: יהוה יִמְלֹךְ לְעֹלָם
וָעֶד:

Walk toward the door of the בית כנסת*, respectfully, without turning one's back, as one taking leave of the Divine Presence. At the door, bow toward the* ארון קדש *and say:*

תהלים ה **יהוה** נְחֵנִי בְצִדְקָתֶךָ לְמַעַן שׁוֹרְרָי, הַיְשַׁר לְפָנַי דַּרְכֶּךָ:

While leaving, say the following three verses:

בראשית מט שמואל א׳ יח **גָּד** גְּדוּד יְגוּדֶנּוּ, וְהוּא יָגֻד עָקֵב: וַיְהִי דָוִד לְכָל־דְּרָכָו מַשְׂכִּיל, וַיהוה עִמּוֹ:
בראשית ו וְנֹחַ מָצָא חֵן בְּעֵינֵי יהוה:

One who will conduct business says:

תהלים קכא תהלים נה **עֶזְרִי** מֵעִם יהוה, עֹשֵׂה שָׁמַיִם וָאָרֶץ: הַשְׁלֵךְ עַל־יהוה יְהָבְךָ וְהוּא יְכַלְכְּלֶךָ:
תהלים לז שם שְׁמָר־תָּם וּרְאֵה יָשָׁר, כִּי־אַחֲרִית לְאִישׁ שָׁלוֹם: בְּטַח בַּיהוה וַעֲשֵׂה־
ישעיה יב טוֹב, שְׁכָן־אֶרֶץ וּרְעֵה אֱמוּנָה: הִנֵּה אֵל יְשׁוּעָתִי אֶבְטַח וְלֹא אֶפְחָד, כִּי־עָזִּי
וְזִמְרָת יָהּ יהוה וַיְהִי־לִי לִישׁוּעָה: אֲנִי רוֹצֶה לֵילֵךְ הַיּוֹם לַעֲשׂוֹת מַשָּׂא וּמַתָּן
בִּרְשׁוּת הַשֵּׁם יִתְבָּרַךְ וּלְמַעַן שְׁמוֹ וְלִשָּׂא וְלִתֵּן בֶּאֱמוּנָה. רִבּוֹנוֹ שֶׁל עוֹלָם,
תהלים לב נחמיה ט בְּדִבְרֵי קָדְשְׁךָ כָּתוּב לֵאמֹר, הַבּוֹטֵחַ בַּיהוה חֶסֶד יְסוֹבְבֶנּוּ: וּכְתִיב, וְאַתָּה
מְחַיֶּה אֶת־כֻּלָּם: יהוה אֱלֹהִים אֱמֶת, תֵּן בְּרָכָה וְהַצְלָחָה בְּכָל מַעֲשֵׂה יָדַי,
כִּי בָטַחְתִּי בְךָ שֶׁעַל יְדֵי מַשָּׂא וּמַתָּן וַעֲסָקִים שֶׁלִּי תִּשְׁלַח לִי בְּרָכָה, כְּדֵי
שֶׁאוּכַל לְפַרְנֵס אֶת עַצְמִי וּבְנֵי בֵיתִי בְּנַחַת וְלֹא בְצַעַר, בְּהֶתֵּר וְלֹא בְאִסּוּר,
תהלים נה לְחַיִּים וּלְשָׁלוֹם. וִיקֻיַּם בִּי מִקְרָא שֶׁכָּתוּב: הַשְׁלֵךְ עַל־יהוה יְהָבְךָ וְהוּא
יְכַלְכְּלֶךָ, אָמֵן.

PRAYER UPON LEAVING THE SYNAGOGUE

Say while seated:

Ps. 140 אַךְ BUT the righteous will give thanks to Your name. The upright will dwell in Your presence.

Stand and say:

כִּי FOR ALL the nations will walk, each in the name of its god; and I will walk
Ps. 121 in the name of the LORD, the living God and eternal King. My help is from the
Ex. 15 Lord, the Maker of heaven and earth. The Lord shall reign forever and ever.

Walk toward the door of the synagogue, respectfully, without turning one's back, as one taking leave of the Divine Presence. At the door, bow toward the Ark and say:

Ps. 5 יהוה LORD, lead me in Your righteousness because of my enemies. Make Your way straight before me.

While leaving, say the following three verses:

Gen. 49
1 Sam. 18 גד GAD will recruit a regiment and it will retreat in its tracks. David was
Gen. 6 successful in all his ways; and the Lord was with him. And Noah found favor in the eyes of the Lord.

One who will conduct business says:

Ps. 121
Ps. 55 עֶזְרִי MY HELP is from the Lord, Maker of heaven and earth. Cast your burden
Ps. 37 upon the Lord, and He will sustain you. Preserve innocence and behold
Ibid. uprightness, for there is a future for the man of peace. Trust in the Lord and do
Is. 12 good, so that you may dwell in the land and always sustain yourself. Behold! God is my salvation, I shall trust and not fear, for God is my might and my praise – the Lord – and He was a salvation for me. Today I wish to go and engage in commerce, with the permission of the Lord, may He be blessed, and for His name's sake, and to trade and deal faithfully. Ruler of the universe, in
Ps. 32 Your holy writings is written: He who trusts in the Lord – He will surround
Neh. 9 him with loving-kindness; and it is written: You give them all life. The Lord, God of truth, grant blessing and success in all my handiwork, for I trust in You that through my commerce and activities, You will send me a blessing so that I can support myself and the members of my household in tranquility and not in pain, through permissible but not forbidden means, for life and for peace.
Ps. 55 May there be fulfilled in me the verse that says: Cast your burden upon the Lord, and He will sustain you. Amen.

בקשות אישיות

A prayer to God to help us avoid speaking or hearing לשון הרע*,*
composed by the חפץ חיים *(R. Yisrael Meir HaKohen):*

רִבּוֹנוֹ שֶׁל עוֹלָם, יְהִי רָצוֹן מִלְּפָנֶיךָ אֵל רַחוּם וְחַנּוּן, שֶׁתְּזַכֵּנִי הַיּוֹם וּבְכָל יוֹם לִשְׁמֹר פִּי וּלְשׁוֹנִי לְבִלְתִּי לְהִלָּכֵד בְּדִבּוּרִים אֲסוּרִים, דְּהַיְנוּ, מֵעֲוֹן לָשׁוֹן הָרָע, וְגַם מֵעֲוֹן רְכִילוּת. וְאֶהְיֶה זָהִיר מִלְּדַבֵּר אֲפִלּוּ עַל אִישׁ יְחִידִי, וְכָל שֶׁכֵּן מִלְּדַבֵּר דֶּלָטוֹרְיָא עַל כְּלַל יִשְׂרָאֵל, שֶׁעֲוֹנוֹ חָמוּר מְאֹד. וְכָל שֶׁכֵּן לְהִזָּהֵר מִלְּהִתְרַעֵם עַל מִדּוֹתָיו שֶׁל הַקָּדוֹשׁ בָּרוּךְ הוּא, שֶׁהוּא עָוֹן חָמוּר יוֹתֵר מִן הַכֹּל. וּמִלְּדַבֵּר דִּבְרֵי שֶׁקֶר, וּמִלְּדַבֵּר דִּבְרֵי חֲנֻפָּה, שֶׁמְּיַפֶּה לְאִישׁ עַל עֲוֹלוֹתָיו בְּפָנָיו, וּמִלְּדַבֵּר דִּבְרֵי לֵיצָנוּת, וּמִלֵּישֵׁב בֵּין לֵיצָנִים, וְלִהְיוֹת זָהִיר מֵאוֹנָאַת דְּבָרִים, וְלִהְיוֹת זָהִיר מֵהַלְבָּנַת פָּנִים, אֲפִלּוּ בִּשְׁעַת תּוֹכָחָה, וְלִהְיוֹת זָהִיר מִלְּדַבֵּר דִּבְרֵי גַאֲוָה, וְכֵן מִלְּדַבֵּר דִּבְרֵי מַחֲלֹקֶת, וְכֵן מִלְּדַבֵּר דִּבְרֵי כַעַס, וְזַכֵּנִי שֶׁלֹּא לְדַבֵּר, כִּי אִם דָּבָר הַצָּרִיךְ לְעִנְיְנֵי גּוּפִי אוֹ לְנַפְשִׁי, וְשֶׁיִּהְיוּ כָּל מַעֲשַׂי וְדִבּוּרַי לְשֵׁם שָׁמַיִם.

A prayer for the unity and love of Israel by the חיד״א *(R. Ḥayyim Yosef David Azulai):*

הֲרֵינִי מְקַבֵּל/מְקַבֶּלֶת עָלַי מִצְוַת עֲשֵׂה שֶׁל וְאָהַבְתָּ לְרֵעֲךָ כָּמוֹךָ, וַהֲרֵינִי אוֹהֵב/אוֹהֶבֶת כָּל אֶחָד מִבְּנֵי יִשְׂרָאֵל כְּנַפְשִׁי וּמְאוֹדִי וַהֲרֵינִי מְזַמֵּן/מְזַמֶּנֶת אֶת פִּי לְהִתְפַּלֵּל לִפְנֵי מֶלֶךְ מַלְכֵי הַמְּלָכִים, הַקָּדוֹשׁ בָּרוּךְ
דברים ד הוּא: הֲרֵינִי זוֹכֵר/זוֹכֶרֶת מַעֲמַד הַר סִינַי, כְּמוֹ שֶׁנֶּאֱמַר: רַק הִשָּׁמֶר לְךָ וּשְׁמֹר נַפְשְׁךָ מְאֹד פֶּן־תִּשְׁכַּח אֶת־הַדְּבָרִים אֲשֶׁר־רָאוּ עֵינֶיךָ וּפֶן־יָסוּרוּ מִלְּבָבְךָ כֹּל יְמֵי חַיֶּיךָ וְהוֹדַעְתָּם לְבָנֶיךָ וְלִבְנֵי בָנֶיךָ: יוֹם אֲשֶׁר עָמַדְתָּ לִפְנֵי יְהֹוָה אֱלֹהֶיךָ בְּחֹרֵב בֶּאֱמֹר יְהֹוָה אֵלַי הַקְהֶל־לִי אֶת־הָעָם וְאַשְׁמִעֵם אֶת־דְּבָרָי, אֲשֶׁר יִלְמְדוּן לְיִרְאָה אֹתִי כָּל־הַיָּמִים אֲשֶׁר הֵם חַיִּים עַל־הָאֲדָמָה וְאֶת־בְּנֵיהֶם יְלַמֵּדוּן:

וִיהִי רָצוֹן מִלְּפָנֶיךָ יְהֹוָה אֱלֹהֵינוּ וֵאלֹהֵי אֲבוֹתֵינוּ, שֶׁתִּתְמַלֵּא רַחֲמִים עָלֵינוּ, וְתִטַּע אַהֲבָה וְאַחֲוָה שָׁלוֹם וְרֵעוּת בֵּינֵינוּ וּבֵין כָּל יִשְׂרָאֵל וְנִהְיֶה כַּאֲחָדִים
שמות יט כְּשֵׁם שֶׁבְּהַר סִינַי הָיָה שָׁלוֹם בֵּינֵינוּ, כְּדִכְתִיב: וַיִּחַן־שָׁם יִשְׂרָאֵל נֶגֶד הָהָר: כְּאִישׁ אֶחָד בְּאַחְדוּת גְּמוּרָה.

כֵּן בְּרַחֲמֶיךָ הָרַבִּים תְּזַכֵּנוּ לְהַעֲבִיר מִמֶּנּוּ שִׂנְאָה וְקִנְאָה וְתַחֲרוּת, וְנִהְיֶה אוֹהֲבִים זֶה לָזֶה, וְתָשִׂים שָׁלוֹם בֵּינֵינוּ. וּכְשֵׁם שֶׁבְּמַעֲמַד הַר

PERSONAL SUPPLICATIONS

A prayer to God to help us avoid speaking or hearing Lashon Hara,
composed by the Ḥafetz Ḥayyim (R. Yisrael Meir HaKohen):

רִבּוֹנוֹ שֶׁל עוֹלָם RULER OF THE UNIVERSE, may it be Your will, gracious and merciful God, to grant me the merit today and every day to guard my mouth and my tongue so that I not be ensnared into forbidden speech, specifically the sins of gossip and slander. May I be careful not to speak against an individual and even more so to not speak deleteriously against the Jewish people as a whole which is an extremely grave sin. Even more so, may I not complain regarding the actions of the Holy One, blessed is He, which is the worst sin of all. May I avoid falsehood, obsequiousness, to make acceptable the burden of another's transgressions while in their presence, as well as scoffing and the company of scoffers. May I be careful to not hurt anyone with my words, to not embarrass people even while reproving them, careful to not speak arrogantly, careful to not speak words of discord; and not speak words of anger. Grant me the merit to speak only what is essential to my person and my soul, and that all my deeds and speech should be for the sake of heaven.

A prayer for the unity and love of Israel by the Ḥida (R. Ḥayyim Yosef David Azulai):

הֲרֵינִי BEHOLD, I accept upon myself the positive commandment of "loving your neighbor as yourself," and behold I love every Jew with all my soul and all my might, and I prepare my speech to pray before the King of kings, the Holy One, blessed is He: Behold, I remember the revelation at Sinai, as it is
Deut. 4 written, "But take utmost care and watch yourselves scrupulously, so that you do not forget that which you saw with your very eyes and so that they do not depart from your mind as long as you live. And make them known to your children and to your children's children. The day you stood before the Lord your God at Horeb, when the Lord said to me, 'Gather the people to Me that I may let them hear My words, in order that they may learn to revere Me as long as they live on earth, and may so teach their children.'"

May it be Your will, Lord our God, and God of our fathers, that You will be filled with mercy for us, and implant love, kinship, peace and camaraderie, among us and among all of Israel, and we should be united as at Mount Sinai
Ex. 19 when there was peace among us, as it is written, "And Israel encamped there facing the mountain, as one person in complete unity."

So too in Your abundant mercy, may You grant us the merit to remove from us hatred, jealousy and competition, so that we will love each other and make peace between us. And as it was at the revelation at Mount Sinai when the

סִינַי פָּסְקָה זֻהֲמָא מִמֶּנּוּ, וְזִכַּכְתָּ אוֹתָנוּ וְטִהַרְתָּנוּ מִכָּל טֻמְאָה וְחֶלְאָה
וְזֻהֲמָא, וְקִדַּשְׁתָּנוּ בִּקְדֻשָּׁתֶךָ, כֵּן בְּרַחֲמֶיךָ הָרַבִּים תְּטַהֲרֵנוּ מִטֻּמְאוֹתֵינוּ
וּמִזֻּהֲמָתֵנוּ, וּתְקַדְּשֵׁנוּ בְּמִצְווֹתֶיךָ וּתְטַהֵר רַעְיוֹנֵנוּ וְלִבֵּנוּ לַעֲבוֹדָתֶךָ
וּלְיִרְאָתֶךָ, וְתִטַּע תּוֹרָתְךָ בְּלִבֵּנוּ, וְתִהְיֶה יִרְאָתְךָ עַל פָּנֵינוּ לְבִלְתִּי נֶחֱטָא,
וּתְעוֹרֵר לִבֵּנוּ לְאַהֲבַת תּוֹרָתֶךָ, וּבְכָל יוֹם יִהְיֶה בְּעֵינֵינוּ כְּאִלּוּ אָנוּ מְקַבְּלִים
תּוֹרָתְךָ בִּדְבֵקוּת וּתְשׁוּקָה וּבְחֵפֶץ, וְהָאֵר עֵינֵינוּ בְּתוֹרָתֶךָ, וּתְדַבֵּק לִבֵּנוּ
בְּמִצְווֹתֶיךָ, וּתְיַחֵד לְבָבֵנוּ לְאַהֲבָה וּלְיִרְאָה אֶת שִׁמְךָ הַגָּדוֹל הַגִּבּוֹר
וְהַנּוֹרָא. וְתִגְאָלֵנוּ לְמַעַן רַחֲמֶיךָ, וּתְזַכֵּנוּ לְקַבֵּל וְלִשְׁמֹעַ תּוֹרָה מִפִּיךָ, כְּמוֹ
שֶׁנֶּאֱמַר: וְכָל־בָּנַיִךְ לִמּוּדֵי יְהוָה, וְרַב שְׁלוֹם בָּנָיִךְ: בִּמְהֵרָה בְיָמֵינוּ, אָמֵן ישעיה נד
כֵּן יְהִי רָצוֹן.

A prayer for livelihood:

אַתָּה־הוּא יהוה לְבַדֶּךָ, אַתָּ עָשִׂיתָ אֶת־הַשָּׁמַיִם, שְׁמֵי הַשָּׁמַיִם וְכָל־ נחמיה ט
צְבָאָם, הָאָרֶץ וְכָל־אֲשֶׁר עָלֶיהָ, הַיַּמִּים וְכָל־אֲשֶׁר בָּהֶם,
וְאַתָּה מְחַיֶּה אֶת־כֻּלָּם. וְאַתָּה הוּא שֶׁעָשִׂיתָ נִסִּים וְנִפְלָאוֹת גְּדוֹלוֹת
תָּמִיד עִם אֲבוֹתֵינוּ. גַּם בַּמִּדְבָּר הִמְטַרְתָּ לָהֶם לֶחֶם מִן הַשָּׁמַיִם, וּמִצּוּר
הַחַלָּמִישׁ הוֹצֵאתָ לָהֶם מַיִם, וְגַם נָתַתָּ לָהֶם כָּל צָרְכֵיהֶם, וְשִׂמְלָתָם לֹא
בָלְתָה מֵעֲלֵיהֶם. כֵּן בְּרַחֲמֶיךָ הָרַבִּים וּבַחֲסָדֶיךָ הָעֲצוּמִים, תְּזוּנֵנוּ וּתְפַרְנְסֵנוּ
וּתְכַלְכְּלֵנוּ וְתַסְפִּיק כָּל צָרְכֵנוּ וְצָרְכֵי עַמְּךָ בֵּית יִשְׂרָאֵל הַמְרֻבִּים, בְּמִלּוּי
וּבְרֶוַח בְּלִי טֹרַח וְעָמָל גָּדוֹל, מִתַּחַת יָדְךָ הַנְּקִיָּה, וְלֹא מִתַּחַת יְדֵי בָשָׂר
וָדָם.

יְהִי רָצוֹן מִלְּפָנֶיךָ, יהוה אֱלֹהֵינוּ וֵאלֹהֵי אֲבוֹתֵינוּ, שֶׁתָּכִין לִי וּלְאַנְשֵׁי בֵיתִי
כָּל מַחְסוֹרֵנוּ, וְתַזְמִין לָנוּ כָּל צָרְכֵנוּ, לְכָל יוֹם וָיוֹם מֵחַיֵּינוּ דֵּי מַחְסוֹרֵנוּ,
וּלְכָל שָׁעָה וְשָׁעָה מִשְּׁעוֹתֵינוּ דֵּי סִפּוּקֵנוּ, וּלְכָל עֶצֶם מֵעֲצָמֵינוּ דֵּי מִחְיָתֵנוּ,
כְּיָדְךָ הַטּוֹבָה וְהָרְחָבָה, וְלֹא כְּמִעוּט מִפְעָלֵינוּ, וְקֹצֶר חֲסָדֵינוּ, וּמִזְעֵיר
גְּמוּלוֹתֵינוּ. וְיִהְיוּ מְזוֹנוֹתַי וּמְזוֹנוֹת אַנְשֵׁי בֵיתִי וְזַרְעִי וְזֶרַע זַרְעִי מְסוּרִים
בְּיָדְךָ, וְלֹא בְּיַד בָּשָׂר וָדָם.

stain of impurity was removed from us, and You cleansed and purified us from all impurity, contagion and stain, and sanctified us in Your sanctity; so too in Your great mercy shall You purify us from our impurity and from the stain of impurity, and sanctify us in Your commandments and purify our thoughts and our hearts to serve You and be in awe of You. And implant Your Torah in our hearts, and Your awe upon our faces so that we will not sin, and arouse our hearts to love Your Torah, and may we view every day as one on which we receive Your Torah with devotion, passion and desire. And enlighten our eyes with Your Torah, and our hearts should cleave to Your commandments, and may our hearts be united to love and be in awe of Your great and mighty name. And may You redeem us for the sake of Your mercy, and grant us the
Is. 94 merit to receive and to hear the Torah from Your mouth, as it is written, "And all your children shall be taught of the Lord," soon in our days, Amen. May it be Your will.

A prayer for livelihood:

Neh. 9 **אַתָּה־הוּא** YOU ARE THE LORD, You alone; You made heaven, the heaven above the heavens, the earth and all that is on it, the seas and all that is in them, and You give life to them all. You are the One Who always performed miracles and great wonders for our forefathers. Also in the wilderness You rained down for them food from heaven, You drew water for them from the rock, You provided for all their needs, neither did their clothing wear out. So too in Your abundant mercy and overwhelming kindness, may You nourish us, sustain us, support us, and supply all our needs as well as the many needs of Your people the house of Israel, with fullness and abundance, without toil and great effort, provided by Your sublime hand rather than by the hands of people of flesh and blood.

MAY IT BE Your will, Lord, my God and the God of my fathers, that You prepare for me and for the members of my household all that we require, providing each day of our lives whatever we need, satisfying every single hour's necessities, sufficient nourishment for every bone of our bodies, in accordance with Your benevolent and generous hand, rather than according to the little that we deserve, or the inadequacy of our good deeds, or the little that we have earned. May my sustenance and that of my household, as well as that of my offspring depend on Your generosity, and not on the handouts of people of flesh and blood.

סדר סעודה וברכותיה

ברכת המזון

Before ברכת המזון *on weekdays, many have the custom to say* עַל־נַהֲרוֹת בָּבֶל (*Psalm 137*) *in memory of the Temple's destruction. On* שבת *and* ימים טובים, *and on such occasions as the meals celebrating a marriage,* ברית, *or* פדיון הבן, *or a festive meal celebrating* יום העצמאות *or* יום ירושלים, *it is improper to intrude upon the joy with memories of tragedy. At such times,* שִׁיר הַמַּעֲלוֹת (*Psalm 126*), *which describes the joy of redemption, is said instead.*

תהלים קלז

עַל־נַהֲרוֹת בָּבֶל, שָׁם יָשַׁבְנוּ גַּם־בָּכִינוּ, בְּזָכְרֵנוּ אֶת־צִיּוֹן: עַל־עֲרָבִים בְּתוֹכָהּ תָּלִינוּ כִּנֹּרוֹתֵינוּ: כִּי שָׁם שְׁאֵלוּנוּ שׁוֹבֵינוּ דִּבְרֵי־שִׁיר וְתוֹלָלֵינוּ שִׂמְחָה, שִׁירוּ לָנוּ מִשִּׁיר צִיּוֹן:

בִּרְכַּת הַמָּזוֹן / GRACE AFTER MEALS

The Torah (Deut. 8:10) commands us to bless God after we have eaten enough food so that we are not hungry, as it says "you shall eat and be satisfied, and bless the Lord your God." The same verse continues, "for the good land which He has given to you," that is, bless Him not just for the food that you have eaten, but for the land He has given to you, too. Hence, as the Gemara (*Berakhot* 48b) explains, the structure of בִּרְכַּת הַמָּזוֹן (Grace after Meals) includes four *berakhot*. The first one relates to the food we have eaten, while the next three relate to our possession of the land of Israel in varying degrees at different points in our history.

More specifically, that Gemara teaches that the first *berakha* that ends with "He feeds all" was composed by Moses when witnessing the manna that sustained Israel in the desert. The second one, which concludes with "for the land and for the food," was formulated by Joshua in appreciation of the conquest of the land of Israel, as commanded by the Torah in the above-quoted verse. The third *berakha* ("He is the builder of Jerusalem") was enacted in part by David ("on Israel Your people, on Jerusalem Your city"), reflecting his conquest of Jerusalem, and in part by Solomon ("on the

בְּרָכוֹת / BLESSINGS

For a fuller background introduction to the recital of *berakhot* on various occasions, see the comprehensive essay by R. Pinchas Peli in the back of the Siddur, page E70.

"The two names of God that are used in every *berakha* convey the essence of the entire Torah and its commandments. This is because even though God in His essence is hidden, He is also revealed via His actions. Therefore in every *berakha* we use the four-letter name which refers to His being hidden from us, as well as *Elokim* (God) which refers to His providence through which He is known to His creatures. This is why throughout the chapter of Creation He is referred to exclusively as *Elokim*. As to His providence itself, it has two separate facets. The first is a general providence over all creatures and the world at large. The second is a specific providence over Israel alone. Accordingly, *Elokim* refers to the former while *Elokeinu* refers to the latter. Thus in every *berakha* we say *Hashem Elokeinu Melekh ha'olam*, He is *Hashem* (the hidden God) Who is also *Elokeinu* (the God Who exercises providence over us in particular) while also being *Melekh ha'olam* (the King over the entire world)" (Vilna Gaon).

THE MEAL AND ITS BLESSINGS

GRACE AFTER MEALS

Before Grace After Meals on weekdays, many have the custom to say "By the rivers of Babylon" (Psalm 137) in memory of the Temple's destruction. On Shabbat and Festivals, and on such occasions as the meals celebrating a marriage, Brit, or Pidyon HaBen, or a festive meal celebrating Yom HaAtzma'ut or Yom Yerushalayim, it is improper to intrude upon the joy with memories of tragedy. At such times, A Song of Ascents (Psalm 126), which describes the joy of redemption, is said instead.

Ps. 137 **עַל־נַהֲרוֹת** BY THE RIVERS OF BABYLON, there we sat and wept, as we remembered Zion. On the willows in its midst we hung our lyres. For there our captors required of us words of song, and our mockers music, Sing to us

---

great and holy Temple"), reflecting his having built the First Temple. The fourth and final *berakha*, ending with "may He never deprive us of all good things," was authored centuries later by the sages of Yavneh after the destruction of the Second Temple and the failure of the Bar Kokhba revolt in 136 CE, in gratitude for the dignified burial they were able to provide for the dead martyrs of the time.

This fourth *berakha* is unusual in that the sages saw fit to institute a *berakha* to be recited by all future generations of Jews on a daily basis, because of a relatively obscure one-time event in our history. The reason they did so is that the preceding *berakhot* were intended to celebrate the way in which Providence transformed the Jews from an oppressed people in Egypt into a strong, independent nation-state. Those *berakhot* highlight how the forty years of manna in the desert purified their souls; how God helped them establish self-rule in the land of Israel; and finally how they conquered Jerusalem and built the Temple. But with the failure of the Bar Kokhba revolt following the destruction of the Temple, the nation was devastated. They were not even able to bury their dead. The sages of Yavneh feared for the very survival of the nation at the hands of rulers who would oppress and slaughter them, like a lamb at the mercy of seventy wolves. At that moment of despair they received miraculous permission from their oppressors to bury their dead. They took this as a sign that God had not abandoned them and that if in future generations their continued existence would be in doubt, He would again send rulers who would act compassionately toward them. This was when they instituted this *berakha*, to give us the faith and strength to survive during our years of bitter exile, and to not despair of our return to Israel and Jerusalem (R. Meir Simḥa of Dvinsk).

In any case, the first three blessings are unanimously considered biblically required, and indeed key phrases of the Grace after Meals are attested in very ancient Second Temple documents, including the one extra-canonical book which is cited explicitly in the Talmud, the Book of Ben Sira (36:17–19). As to the fourth, while according to R. Yishmael in the Talmud Yerushalmi (*Berakhot* 7:1) it is biblically prescribed, we follow the view that it is of rabbinic origin.

Following these four *berakhot*, there are nine הָרַחֲמָן petitions that expand on the themes of the fourth *berakha*. Three relate to divine sovereignty (majesty, blessing, and praise), three to the good He bestows upon us (sustenance in dignity, liberty, and abundance) and three to the final redemption (Elijah, the

אֵיךְ נָשִׁיר אֶת־שִׁיר־יהוה עַל אַדְמַת נֵכָר: אִם־אֶשְׁכָּחֵךְ יְרוּשָׁלָֽםִ, תִּשְׁכַּח יְמִינִי: תִּדְבַּק לְשׁוֹנִי לְחִכִּי אִם־לֹא אֶזְכְּרֵכִי, אִם־לֹא אַעֲלֶה אֶת־יְרוּשָׁלַםִ עַל רֹאשׁ שִׂמְחָתִי: זְכֹר יהוה לִבְנֵי אֱדוֹם אֵת יוֹם יְרוּשָׁלָםִ, הָאֹמְרִים עָרוּ עָרוּ עַד הַיְסוֹד בָּהּ: בַּת־בָּבֶל הַשְּׁדוּדָה, אַשְׁרֵי שֶׁיְשַׁלֶּם־לָךְ אֶת־גְּמוּלֵךְ שֶׁגָּמַלְתְּ לָנוּ: אַשְׁרֵי שֶׁיֹּאחֵז, וְנִפֵּץ אֶת־עֹלָלַיִךְ אֶל־הַסָּלַע:

תהלים קכו
שִׁיר הַמַּעֲלוֹת, בְּשׁוּב יהוה אֶת־שִׁיבַת צִיּוֹן, הָיִינוּ כְּחֹלְמִים: אָז יִמָּלֵא שְׂחוֹק פִּינוּ וּלְשׁוֹנֵנוּ רִנָּה, אָז יֹאמְרוּ בַגּוֹיִם הִגְדִּיל יהוה לַעֲשׂוֹת עִם־אֵלֶּה: הִגְדִּיל יהוה לַעֲשׂוֹת עִמָּנוּ, הָיִינוּ שְׂמֵחִים: שׁוּבָה יהוה אֶת־שְׁבִיתֵנוּ, כַּאֲפִיקִים בַּנֶּגֶב: הַזֹּרְעִים בְּדִמְעָה בְּרִנָּה יִקְצֹרוּ: הָלוֹךְ יֵלֵךְ וּבָכֹה נֹשֵׂא מֶשֶׁךְ־הַזָּרַע, בֹּא־יָבֹא בְרִנָּה נֹשֵׂא אֲלֻמֹּתָיו:

Some add:

תהלים קמה **תְּהִלַּת** יהוה יְדַבֶּר פִּי, וִיבָרֵךְ כָּל־בָּשָׂר שֵׁם קָדְשׁוֹ לְעוֹלָם וָעֶד:
תהלים קטו תהלים קלו וַאֲנַחְנוּ נְבָרֵךְ יָהּ מֵעַתָּה וְעַד־עוֹלָם, הַלְלוּיָהּ: הוֹדוּ לַיהוה
תהלים קו כִּי־טוֹב, כִּי לְעוֹלָם חַסְדּוֹ: מִי יְמַלֵּל גְּבוּרוֹת יהוה, יַשְׁמִיעַ כָּל־
תְּהִלָּתוֹ:

Patriarch's blessings for the Jewish people, and the Messianic fulfillment). These are followed by nine scriptural verses.

It is human nature that after we have eaten our fill we can easily become insensitive to the source of our food and our well-being, and thus forget to thank God Who gave all of this to us, as the Torah says in the ensuing verses, "lest you eat and be sated…and then forget the Lord your God" (Deut. 8:12, 14). Thus the Torah explicitly commands us that when we have eaten and are satisfied we are to bless and thank God for all that we have received from Him (R. Meir Simḥa of Dvinsk).

עַל־נַהֲרוֹת בָּבֶל / PSALM 137 (previous page)
It is proper to recall every day the destruction of the Temple (*Shulḥan Arukh OḤ* 1:4), and in this spirit, it is customary to recite Psalm 137 before *Birkat HaMazon*. On Shabbat, Yom Tov, and other days when *Taḥanun* is omitted, *Shir HaMa'alot* (Psalm 126), which describes the joys of the return to Zion is recited instead (Shela). Nowadays, this recitation of Psalm 126 on joyous days also evokes the newly restored Jewish sovereignty over the land of Israel – the subject of the second blessing of *Birkat HaMazon*.

עַל־נַהֲרוֹת בָּבֶל – *By the rivers of Babylon*. The

of the songs of Zion. How shall we sing the Lord's song in a foreign land? If I forget you, O Jerusalem, may my right hand forget. May my tongue cleave to the roof of my mouth, if I do not make mention of you, if I do not raise Jerusalem to the head of my joy. Remember, O Lord, against the children of Edom the day of Jerusalem, those who said, Raze it, raze it, to its very foundations. O daughter of Babylon, marked for devastation, happy is he who will repay you your recompense for what you have done to us. Happy is he who will seize and dash your infants against the rock.

Ps. 126 **שִׁיר הַמַּעֲלוֹת** A SONG OF ASCENTS. When the Lord brought back the return of Zion, we were like those who dream. Then our mouth was filled with laughter and our tongue with joy. Then they said among the nations: "the Lord did great things for these." The Lord did great things for us. We were glad. Bring back our return, O Lord, like the streams in the south. Those that sow in tears will reap in joy. May he who goes out weeping, bearing the sack of seed, come home in joy, bearing his sheaves.

Some add:

Ps. 145 **תְּהִלַּת** MAY MY MOUTH speak the praise of the Lord, and may all flesh bless
Ps. 115 His holy name forever and ever. But we will bless the Lord from now and
Ps. 136 forevermore. Praise the Lord. Give thanks to the Lord, for He is good, for
Ps. 106 His loving-kindness is forever. Who can relate the mighty deeds of the Lord?
Who can express all His praise?

Gemara (*Gittin* 57b) understood this psalm to be a Davidic prophecy regarding the destruction of both the First Temple at the hands of Babylon and the Second Temple at the hands of Edom/Rome. The Malbim regards it as having been composed in exile to describe the Levites in Babylon whose captors requested that they perform the music and songs of the Temple.

אִם־לֹא אַעֲלֶה... עַל רֹאשׁ שִׂמְחָתִי – *If I do not raise Jerusalem to the head of my joy.* No matter the occasion of personal joy, the sober memory of Jerusalem must take precedence (Ibn Ezra). This phrase is the basis of the customs by which a bridegroom places ashes on his head (עַל רֹאשׁ) prior to the marriage ceremony, and breaks a glass at the conclusion of the *Ḥuppa* ceremony in memory of Jerusalem (Rema).

בַּת־בָּבֶל הַשְּׁדוּדָה – *Daughter of Babylon, marked for devastation.* Babylon's regime was soon overthrown and it was absorbed into the Persian empire a mere half century after the destruction of the First Temple (Malbim).

The Jewish faith is not pacifist; we indeed hope to see divine justice done, and irredeemable evil uprooted from the world. However, we leave the task of vengeance in the hands of God, and trust Him to bring history to its appropriate conclusion, in accordance with the prophecy, "Thus said God, 'Behold, I will raise up against Babylon...and with you will I shatter (וְנִפַּצְתִּי) man and woman...the old man and the youth...the young man and the maid'" (Jer. 51:1, 22) (R. Yonatan Grossman).

סדר הזימון

For the זימון *said at a wedding or during the week of* שבע ברכות*, see page 1054. At a* ברית*, see page 1070. In a* בית אבל *when there are three or more men, see page 1096.*

Traditionally, the terms אבי מורי *("my father and teacher") and* בעל הבית *("the head of the household") were understood to include "mother and teacher" as well as the female head of the household, respectively. However, for those who prefer to be more explicit, the feminine versions are included in parentheses below.*

The זימון *when three or more men are present:*

Leader רַבּוֹתַי, נְבָרֵךְ.

תהלים קיג *Others* יְהִי שֵׁם יהוה מְבֹרָךְ מֵעַתָּה וְעַד־עוֹלָם:

Leader יְהִי שֵׁם יהוה מְבֹרָךְ מֵעַתָּה וְעַד־עוֹלָם:

בִּרְשׁוּת (אָבִי מוֹרִי / אִמִּי מוֹרָתִי / כֹּהֲנִים / מוֹרֵנוּ הָרַב / בַּעַל הַבַּיִת הַזֶּה / בַּעֲלַת הַבַּיִת הַזֶּה) מָרָנָן וְרַבָּנָן וְרַבּוֹתַי, נְבָרֵךְ (במנין: אֱלֹהֵינוּ) שֶׁאָכַלְנוּ מִשֶּׁלּוֹ.

Others בָּרוּךְ (במנין: אֱלֹהֵינוּ) שֶׁאָכַלְנוּ מִשֶּׁלּוֹ וּבְטוּבוֹ חָיִינוּ.

**People present who have not taken part in the meal say:*

*בָּרוּךְ (במנין: אֱלֹהֵינוּ) וּמְבֹרָךְ שְׁמוֹ תָּמִיד לְעוֹלָם וָעֶד.

Leader בָּרוּךְ (במנין: אֱלֹהֵינוּ) שֶׁאָכַלְנוּ מִשֶּׁלּוֹ וּבְטוּבוֹ חָיִינוּ. בָּרוּךְ הוּא וּבָרוּךְ שְׁמוֹ.

The זימון *for three or more women.*

Leader חֲבֵרוֹתַי, נְבָרֵךְ.

תהלים קיג *Others* יְהִי שֵׁם יהוה מְבֹרָךְ מֵעַתָּה וְעַד־עוֹלָם:

Leader יְהִי שֵׁם יהוה מְבֹרָךְ מֵעַתָּה וְעַד־עוֹלָם:

בִּרְשׁוּת (אָבִי מוֹרִי / אִמִּי מוֹרָתִי / כֹּהֲנִים / מוֹרֵנוּ הָרַב / בַּעַל הַבַּיִת הַזֶּה / בַּעֲלַת הַבַּיִת הַזֶּה) מָרָנָן וְרַבָּנָן וְרַבּוֹתַי, נְבָרֵךְ שֶׁאָכַלְנוּ מִשֶּׁלּוֹ.

Others בָּרוּךְ שֶׁאָכַלְנוּ מִשֶּׁלּוֹ וּבְטוּבוֹ חָיִינוּ.

Leader בָּרוּךְ שֶׁאָכַלְנוּ מִשֶּׁלּוֹ וּבְטוּבוֹ חָיִינוּ. בָּרוּךְ הוּא וּבָרוּךְ שְׁמוֹ.

רַבּוֹתַי, נְבָרֵךְ – *Esteemed companions, let us say grace.* R. Joseph B. Soloveitchik explained that in the view of Rambam and Tosafot (*Sukka* 38a), while a woman cannot join with two

LAWS OF זימון, ZIMMUN / INVITATION

If three or more males aged thirteen or older participate in a meal, a leader is appointed to formally invite the others to join him in the recitation of בִּרְכַּת הַמָּזוֹן – Grace after Meals. This formal invitation is called *zimmun*.

When three women and fewer than three men are at a meal, the women may (Tosafot), or must (Rosh), make a *zimmun*. The men present should respond to the women's *zimmun* (R. Shlomo Zalman Auerbach as quoted by R. David Auerbach in *Halikhot Beita*). The text used for the women's *zimmun* is below the line.

ZIMMUN / INVITATION

For the zimmun said at a wedding or during the week of Sheva Berakhot, see page 1055. At a Brit, see page 1071. In the house of a mourner when there are three or more men, see page 1097.

Traditionally, the terms "my father and teacher" and "the head of the household" were understood to include "mother and teacher" as well as the female head of the household, respectively. However, for those who prefer to be more explicit, the feminine versions are included in parentheses below.

The zimmun when three or more men are present:

Leader: רַבּוֹתַי ESTEEMED COMPANIONS, let us say grace.

Ps. 113 *Others:* BLESSED be the name of the Lord from now and forevermore.

Leader: BLESSED be the name of the Lord from now and forevermore. With your permission, (my father and teacher / my mother and teacher / the *Kohanim* / our teacher the rabbi / the head of this household) my masters and teachers, let us bless (*in a minyan:* our God,) the One of Whose bounty we have partaken.

Others: BLESSED be (*in a minyan:* our God,) the One of Whose bounty we have partaken and through Whose goodness we live.

**People present who have not taken part in the meal say:*

*BLESSED be (*in a minyan:* our God,) the One Whose name is blessed continually, forever and ever.

Leader: BLESSED be (*in a minyan:* our God,) the One of Whose bounty we have partaken and through Whose goodness we live. Blessed be He, and blessed be His name.

The zimmun for three or more women.

Leader: חֲבֵרוֹתַי MY FRIENDS, let us say grace.

Ps. 113 *Others:* BLESSED be the name of the Lord from now and forevermore.

Leader: BLESSED be the name of the Lord from now and forevermore. With your permission (my father and teacher / my mother and teacher / the *Kohanim* / our teacher the rabbi / the head of this household) my masters and teachers, let us bless the One of Whose bounty we have partaken.

Others: BLESSED be the One of Whose bounty we have partaken and through Whose goodness we live.

Leader: BLESSED be the One of Whose bounty we have partaken and through Whose goodness we live. Blessed be He, and blessed be His name.

---

men to form a *zimmun* (quorum) of three, if three men form a *zimmun* then a woman who participates in the meal is an integral part of the *ḥaburat hazimmun* (group reciting grace.)

ברכת הזן

בָּרוּךְ אַתָּה יהוה אֱלֹהֵינוּ מֶלֶךְ הָעוֹלָם, הַזָּן אֶת הָעוֹלָם כֻּלּוֹ בְּטוּבוֹ, בְּחֵן בְּחֶסֶד וּבְרַחֲמִים, הוּא נוֹתֵן לֶחֶם לְכָל בָּשָׂר, כִּי לְעוֹלָם חַסְדּוֹ. וּבְטוּבוֹ הַגָּדוֹל, תָּמִיד לֹא חָסַר לָנוּ, וְאַל יֶחְסַר לָנוּ מָזוֹן לְעוֹלָם וָעֶד, בַּעֲבוּר שְׁמוֹ הַגָּדוֹל. כִּי הוּא אֵל זָן וּמְפַרְנֵס לַכֹּל, וּמֵטִיב לַכֹּל, וּמֵכִין מָזוֹן לְכָל בְּרִיּוֹתָיו אֲשֶׁר בָּרָא. בָּרוּךְ אַתָּה יהוה, הַזָּן אֶת הַכֹּל.

ברכת הארץ

נוֹדֶה לְּךָ, יהוה אֱלֹהֵינוּ, עַל שֶׁהִנְחַלְתָּ לַאֲבוֹתֵינוּ אֶרֶץ חֶמְדָּה טוֹבָה וּרְחָבָה, וְעַל שֶׁהוֹצֵאתָנוּ יהוה אֱלֹהֵינוּ מֵאֶרֶץ מִצְרַיִם, וּפְדִיתָנוּ מִבֵּית עֲבָדִים, וְעַל בְּרִיתְךָ שֶׁחָתַמְתָּ בִּבְשָׂרֵנוּ, וְעַל תּוֹרָתְךָ שֶׁלִּמַּדְתָּנוּ, וְעַל חֻקֶּיךָ שֶׁהוֹדַעְתָּנוּ, וְעַל חַיִּים חֵן וָחֶסֶד שֶׁחוֹנַנְתָּנוּ, וְעַל אֲכִילַת מָזוֹן שָׁאַתָּה זָן וּמְפַרְנֵס אוֹתָנוּ תָּמִיד, בְּכָל יוֹם וּבְכָל עֵת וּבְכָל שָׁעָה.

בחנוכה ובפורים:

עַל הַנִּסִּים וְעַל הַפֻּרְקָן וְעַל הַגְּבוּרוֹת וְעַל הַתְּשׁוּעוֹת וְעַל הַמִּלְחָמוֹת שֶׁעָשִׂיתָ לַאֲבוֹתֵינוּ בַּיָּמִים הָהֵם בַּזְּמַן הַזֶּה.

בחנוכה:

בִּימֵי מַתִּתְיָהוּ בֶּן יוֹחָנָן כֹּהֵן גָּדוֹל חַשְׁמוֹנַאי וּבָנָיו, כְּשֶׁעָמְדָה מַלְכוּת יָוָן הָרְשָׁעָה עַל עַמְּךָ יִשְׂרָאֵל לְהַשְׁכִּיחָם תּוֹרָתֶךָ וּלְהַעֲבִירָם מֵחֻקֵּי

Continued on the top of the next page.

Thus, as with a male, the *zimmun* leader can invite her participation in the group, and then discharge her obligation if she merely responds "*amen*" to his blessings. This is similar to a *minyan*, i.e., while a woman cannot be one of the ten who make the *minyan*, she is certainly part of *tefilat hatzibbur* (public prayer group) and her obligation can be discharged by responding "*amen*" to the leader (R. Hershel Reichman).

For this reason, we inclusively translate רַבּוֹתַי נְבָרֵךְ in the gender neutral form "Esteemed companions," rather than "Gentlemen," insofar as the women who are at the table can be members of the *ḥabura* (group) reciting grace, and thus are invited, so as to respond, as part of the *zimmun*.

בִּרְכַּת הָאָרֶץ / SECOND BLESSING: BLESSING FOR THE LAND

While prayer in general emerges from a sense of personal or communal crisis, desolation, worthlessness or self-negation, *Birkat HaMazon*

BLESSING OF NOURISHMENT

בָּרוּךְ BLESSED ARE YOU, Lord our God, King of the universe, Who feeds the whole world in His goodness, with grace, kindness and mercy. He gives food to all flesh, for His mercy endures forever. Thanks to His great goodness we have never lacked what to eat. For the sake of His great name may we never be short of food, for He is the God Who feeds and sustains all, is good to all, and provides food for all His creatures as created by Him. Blessed are You, Lord, Who provides food for all.

BLESSING FOR THE LAND

נוֹדֶה WE THANK YOU, Lord our God, for the beloved, good and spacious land that You gave our fathers as an inheritance. We thank You, Lord our God, for bringing us out of the land of Egypt and redeeming us from the house of bondage. We thank You for Your covenant sealed in our flesh, for Your Torah which You have taught us, and for Your precepts that You made known to us. We thank You also for the life, grace, and kindness that You have graciously bestowed on us, and for the food we eat, with which You nourish and sustain us continually, every day, in every season, and at every hour.

On Ḥanukka and Purim add:

עַל הַנִּסִּים [WE THANK YOU] for the miracles, the deliverance, and the triumphant victories and salvation, as well as wars which You wrought for our ancestors in those days at this season.

On Ḥanukka:

IT HAPPENED in the days of Mattathias son of Johanan, the Hasmonean high priest, and his sons. Then the cruel Hellenist power rose up to force Your people Israel to forget Your Torah and transgress the commands of

Continued on the top of the next page.

---

reflects a sense of abundance and self-esteem. The blessing of בִּרְכַּת הָאָרֶץ in particular expresses courage, joy, hope and contentment. It best reflects the biblical vision of a sovereign nation living a secure life, inhabiting a fertile land flowing with milk and honey (Deut. 8:7–10). On a personal level, it conveys confidence in our destiny and awareness of our significance, as magnificent, regal beings before God (R. Joseph B. Soloveitchik).

חֶמְדָּה טוֹבָה וּרְחָבָה – *Beloved, good and spacious.* The Gemara (*Berakhot* 48b) considers this phrase essential to fulfilling the duty to recite *Birkat HaMazon,* because the verse that expresses the obligation specifically mentions "the good land" (Talmidei R. Yona).

רְצוֹנֶךָ, וְאַתָּה בְּרַחֲמֶיךָ הָרַבִּים עָמַדְתָּ לָהֶם בְּעֵת צָרָתָם, רַבְתָּ אֶת רִיבָם, דַּנְתָּ אֶת דִּינָם, נָקַמְתָּ אֶת נִקְמָתָם, מָסַרְתָּ גִבּוֹרִים בְּיַד חַלָּשִׁים, וְרַבִּים בְּיַד מְעַטִּים, וּטְמֵאִים בְּיַד טְהוֹרִים, וּרְשָׁעִים בְּיַד צַדִּיקִים, וְזֵדִים בְּיַד עוֹסְקֵי תוֹרָתֶךָ, וּלְךָ עָשִׂיתָ שֵׁם גָּדוֹל וְקָדוֹשׁ בְּעוֹלָמֶךָ, וּלְעַמְּךָ יִשְׂרָאֵל עָשִׂיתָ תְּשׁוּעָה גְדוֹלָה וּפֻרְקָן כְּהַיּוֹם הַזֶּה. וְאַחַר כֵּן בָּאוּ בָנֶיךָ לִדְבִיר בֵּיתֶךָ, וּפִנּוּ אֶת הֵיכָלֶךָ, וְטִהֲרוּ אֶת מִקְדָּשֶׁךָ, וְהִדְלִיקוּ נֵרוֹת בְּחַצְרוֹת קָדְשֶׁךָ, וְקָבְעוּ שְׁמוֹנַת יְמֵי חֲנֻכָּה אֵלּוּ, לְהוֹדוֹת וּלְהַלֵּל לְשִׁמְךָ הַגָּדוֹל.

Continue with וְעַל הַכֹּל.

בפורים:

בִּימֵי מָרְדְּכַי וְאֶסְתֵּר בְּשׁוּשַׁן הַבִּירָה, כְּשֶׁעָמַד עֲלֵיהֶם הָמָן הָרָשָׁע, בִּקֵּשׁ לְהַשְׁמִיד לַהֲרֹג וּלְאַבֵּד אֶת־כָּל־הַיְּהוּדִים מִנַּעַר וְעַד־זָקֵן טַף וְנָשִׁים בְּיוֹם אֶחָד, בִּשְׁלוֹשָׁה עָשָׂר לְחֹדֶשׁ שְׁנֵים־עָשָׂר, הוּא־חֹדֶשׁ אֲדָר, וּשְׁלָלָם לָבוֹז: וְאַתָּה בְּרַחֲמֶיךָ הָרַבִּים הֵפַרְתָּ אֶת עֲצָתוֹ, וְקִלְקַלְתָּ אֶת מַחֲשַׁבְתּוֹ, וַהֲשֵׁבוֹתָ לּוֹ גְּמוּלוֹ בְּרֹאשׁוֹ, וְתָלוּ אוֹתוֹ וְאֶת בָּנָיו עַל הָעֵץ. אסתר ג

Continue with וְעַל הַכֹּל.

וְעַל הַכֹּל יהוה אֱלֹהֵינוּ, אֲנַחְנוּ מוֹדִים לָךְ וּמְבָרְכִים אוֹתָךְ, יִתְבָּרַךְ שִׁמְךָ בְּפִי כָּל חַי תָּמִיד לְעוֹלָם וָעֶד, כַּכָּתוּב: וְאָכַלְתָּ וְשָׂבָעְתָּ, וּבֵרַכְתָּ אֶת־יהוה אֱלֹהֶיךָ, עַל־הָאָרֶץ הַטֹּבָה אֲשֶׁר נָתַן־לָךְ: בָּרוּךְ אַתָּה יהוה, עַל הָאָרֶץ וְעַל הַמָּזוֹן. דברים ח

ברכת ירושלים

רַחֶם (נָא) יהוה אֱלֹהֵינוּ עַל יִשְׂרָאֵל עַמֶּךָ, וְעַל יְרוּשָׁלַיִם עִירֶךָ, וְעַל צִיּוֹן מִשְׁכַּן כְּבוֹדֶךָ, וְעַל מַלְכוּת בֵּית דָּוִד מְשִׁיחֶךָ, וְעַל הַבַּיִת הַגָּדוֹל וְהַקָּדוֹשׁ שֶׁנִּקְרָא שִׁמְךָ עָלָיו. אֱלֹהֵינוּ, אָבִינוּ, רְעֵנוּ, זוּנֵנוּ, פַּרְנְסֵנוּ וְכַלְכְּלֵנוּ, וְהַרְוִיחֵנוּ, וְהַרְוַח לָנוּ יהוה אֱלֹהֵינוּ מְהֵרָה

בִּרְכַּת יְרוּשָׁלַיִם / THIRD BLESSING: BLESSING FOR JERUSALEM

וְעַל מַלְכוּת בֵּית דָּוִד מְשִׁיחֶךָ – *On the royal house of David Your anointed.* We are required to mention David's kingship in this *berakha* (*Berakhot* 49a). David recognized that his sovereignty was a mere extension of divine majesty, justice and righteousness. The construction

Your will. In that hour of their distress, You in Your great mercy rose to take up their cause and defend their rights. Meting out retribution You delivered the strong into the hand of the weak, the many into the hand of the few, the impure into the hand of the pure, the evil ones into the hand of the righteous, and the wicked into the hand of devotees of Your Torah. You thereby made for Yourself a great and holy name throughout Your world, as well as bringing about great deliverance and salvation for Your people Israel (known) to this day. Then Your children came to the Holy of Holies in Your house, cleared Your Temple, purified Your holy place, kindled lights in Your holy courts, and instituted these eight days of Ḥanukka to give thanks and sing praise to Your great name.

Continue with "For all these."

On Purim:

IN THE DAYS of Mordechai and Esther, in Shushan the capital, when
Esther 3 the wicked Haman rose up against them, he sought to destroy, to kill, and to annihilate all the Jews, young and old, women and infants, in one day, the thirteenth day of the twelfth month, Adar, and plunder their possessions. In Your great mercy You nullified his counsel and subverted his designs, causing them to recoil on his own head so that he and his sons were hanged on the gallows.

Continue with "For all these."

וְעַל הַכֹּל FOR ALL THESE blessings, Lord our God, we thank You and bless You. May Your name be blessed, in the mouths of all living beings,
Deut. 8 continually, forever and ever. As it is written, "You shall eat and be satisfied, and bless the Lord your God for the good land which He has given you." Blessed are You, Lord, for the land and for the sustenance.

BLESSING FOR JERUSALEM

רַחֵם (נָא) HAVE PITY (PLEASE,) Lord our God, on Israel Your people, on Jerusalem Your city and Zion the dwelling place of Your glory, on the royal house of David Your anointed, and on the great and holy Temple with which Your name is associated. Our God, our Father, shepherd us, sustain us, support us, provide for all our needs, maintain us, and, Lord our God, give us immediate relief from all our troubles.

---

of a permanent Temple, the center for divine service and the high court of justice – the ultimate purpose of Jerusalem – was fully the result of the military, political and spiritual accomplishments of David, even though he did not live to see it built.

מִכׇּל צָרוֹתֵינוּ. וְנָא אַל תַּצְרִיכֵנוּ, יהוה אֱלֹהֵינוּ, לֹא לִידֵי מַתְּנַת בָּשָׂר וָדָם, וְלֹא לִידֵי הַלְוָאָתָם, כִּי אִם לְיָדְךָ הַמְּלֵאָה, הַפְּתוּחָה, הַקְּדוֹשָׁה וְהָרְחָבָה, שֶׁלֹּא נֵבוֹשׁ וְלֹא נִכָּלֵם לְעוֹלָם וָעֶד.

On שבת*, say:*

רְצֵה וְהַחֲלִיצֵנוּ, יהוה אֱלֹהֵינוּ, בְּמִצְוֹתֶיךָ, וּבְמִצְוַת יוֹם הַשְּׁבִיעִי הַשַּׁבָּת הַגָּדוֹל וְהַקָּדוֹשׁ הַזֶּה, כִּי יוֹם זֶה גָּדוֹל וְקָדוֹשׁ הוּא לְפָנֶיךָ, לִשְׁבׇּת בּוֹ, וְלָנוּחַ בּוֹ בְּאַהֲבָה כְּמִצְוַת רְצוֹנֶךָ, וּבִרְצוֹנְךָ הָנִיחַ לָנוּ, יהוה אֱלֹהֵינוּ, שֶׁלֹּא תְהֵא צָרָה וְיָגוֹן וַאֲנָחָה בְּיוֹם מְנוּחָתֵנוּ, וְהַרְאֵנוּ, יהוה אֱלֹהֵינוּ, בְּנֶחָמַת צִיּוֹן עִירֶךָ, וּבְבִנְיַן יְרוּשָׁלַיִם עִיר קׇדְשֶׁךָ, כִּי אַתָּה הוּא בַּעַל הַיְשׁוּעוֹת וּבַעַל הַנֶּחָמוֹת.

On ראש חודש *and* חגים*, say:*

אֱלֹהֵינוּ וֵאלֹהֵי אֲבוֹתֵינוּ, יַעֲלֶה וְיָבוֹא וְיַגִּיעַ, וְיֵרָאֶה וְיֵרָצֶה וְיִשָּׁמַע, וְיִפָּקֵד וְיִזָּכֵר זִכְרוֹנֵנוּ וּפִקְדוֹנֵנוּ, וְזִכְרוֹן אֲבוֹתֵינוּ, וְזִכְרוֹן מָשִׁיחַ בֶּן דָּוִד עַבְדֶּךָ, וְזִכְרוֹן יְרוּשָׁלַיִם עִיר קׇדְשֶׁךָ, וְזִכְרוֹן כׇּל עַמְּךָ בֵּית יִשְׂרָאֵל, לְפָנֶיךָ, לִפְלֵיטָה לְטוֹבָה, לְחֵן וּלְחֶסֶד וּלְרַחֲמִים, לְחַיִּים וּלְשָׁלוֹם בְּיוֹם

בראש חודש: רֹאשׁ הַחֹדֶשׁ הַזֶּה.

בראש השנה: הַזִּכָּרוֹן הַזֶּה.

בפסח: חַג הַמַּצּוֹת הַזֶּה.

בשבועות: חַג הַשָּׁבוּעוֹת הַזֶּה.

בסוכות: חַג הַסֻּכּוֹת הַזֶּה.

בשמיני עצרת ושמחת תורה: הַשְּׁמִינִי חַג הָעֲצֶרֶת הַזֶּה.

זׇכְרֵנוּ יהוה אֱלֹהֵינוּ בּוֹ לְטוֹבָה, וּפׇקְדֵנוּ בוֹ לִבְרָכָה, וְהוֹשִׁיעֵנוּ בוֹ לְחַיִּים. וּבִדְבַר יְשׁוּעָה וְרַחֲמִים, חוּס וְחׇנֵּנוּ וְרַחֵם עָלֵינוּ, וְהוֹשִׁיעֵנוּ, כִּי אֵלֶיךָ עֵינֵינוּ, כִּי אֵל (בראש השנה: מֶלֶךְ) חַנּוּן וְרַחוּם אָתָּה.

OMISSION OF RETZEH OR YA'ALEH VEYAVO

If one omits *Retzeh* or *Ya'aleh VeYavo* from the *Birkat HaMazon* of the first two meals of Shabbat or Yom Tov, respectively, *Birkat HaMazon* must be repeated. If one omits *Ya'aleh VeYavo* from the *Birkat HaMazon* of Rosh Ḥodesh however, one is not required to repeat *Birkat HaMazon*. If one realizes the mistake after completing the *berakha* of *Uv'nei Yerushalayim* but prior to reciting *HaTov VeHaMeitiv*, one can recite a compensatory *berakha* at that point and there is no need to return to the beginning of *Birkat HaMazon* (*Shulḥan Arukh*, *OḤ* 188:5–8). For the various texts of the compensatory *berakhot*, see page 250.

Lord our God, do not make us dependent on the gifts of people of flesh and blood, or in need of their loans. Rather let us depend only on Your full, open, sacred, and bountiful hand, so that we need never be embarrassed or humiliated.

On Shabbat, say:

רְצֵה FAVOR and invigorate us, Lord our God, with Your commandments, and with the commandment of the seventh day, this great and holy Sabbath. For this day is great and holy before You, for us to desist from work on it, and lovingly rest on it in accordance with the commandment You have willed. May it be Your will, Lord our God, to grant us a rest during which there will be no sorrow, trouble, or sighing. And, Lord our God, may You show us Zion Your city comforted and the building of Jerusalem Your holy city, for You are the Master of salvation, and the Master of consolation.

On Rosh Ḥodesh and Festivals, say:

אֱלֹהֵינוּ OUR GOD and God of our fathers, may there arise, arrive, reach, appear, be favored, heard, considered and remembered, our remembrance and recollection, Your remembrance of our fathers, of the Messiah son of David Your servant, of Jerusalem Your holy city and of all Your people the house of Israel. May they come before You for deliverance and benefit, for grace, kindness and mercy, for life and peace, on this day of:

On Rosh Ḥodesh: Rosh Ḥodesh.
On Rosh HaShana: Zikaron.
On Pesaḥ: the Festival of Matzot.
On Shavuot: the Festival of Shavuot.
On Sukkot: the Festival of Sukkot.
On Shemini Atzeret & Simḥat Torah: the eighth day, this Festival of Atzeret.

Lord our God, remember us this day for good. Be mindful of us this day for blessing, preserve us this day for life. Regarding redemption and mercy show us compassion and grace, and have pity on us and save us. For our eyes are lifted toward You, for You are a gracious and merciful God (*on Rosh HaShana:* King).

רְצֵה – *Favor.*
The word רְצֵה is a technical term borrowed from the Temple service (cf. Lev. 1:4; *Yoma* 7b); we ask God to accept our remembrance and sanctification of Shabbat as He would a sacrifice.

In the house of a mourner, נַחֵם *on page 1096 is substituted for the next two paragraphs.*

וּבְנֵה יְרוּשָׁלַיִם עִיר הַקֹּדֶשׁ בִּמְהֵרָה בְיָמֵינוּ. בָּרוּךְ אַתָּה יהוה, בּוֹנֶה בְרַחֲמָיו יְרוּשָׁלָיִם, אָמֵן.

ברכת הטוב והמטיב

בָּרוּךְ אַתָּה יהוה אֱלֹהֵינוּ מֶלֶךְ הָעוֹלָם, הָאֵל אָבִינוּ, מַלְכֵּנוּ, אַדִּירֵנוּ, בּוֹרְאֵנוּ, גּוֹאֲלֵנוּ, יוֹצְרֵנוּ, קְדוֹשֵׁנוּ, קְדוֹשׁ יַעֲקֹב, רוֹעֵנוּ, רוֹעֵה יִשְׂרָאֵל, הַמֶּלֶךְ הַטּוֹב וְהַמֵּיטִיב לַכֹּל, שֶׁבְּכָל יוֹם וָיוֹם, הוּא הֵיטִיב, הוּא מֵיטִיב, הוּא יֵיטִיב לָנוּ, הוּא גְמָלָנוּ, הוּא גוֹמְלֵנוּ, הוּא יִגְמְלֵנוּ לָעַד, לְחֵן וּלְחֶסֶד וּלְרַחֲמִים, וּלְרֶוַח, הַצָּלָה וְהַצְלָחָה, בְּרָכָה וִישׁוּעָה, נֶחָמָה, פַּרְנָסָה וְכַלְכָּלָה, וְרַחֲמִים וְחַיִּים וְשָׁלוֹם וְכָל טוֹב, וּמִכָּל טוּב לְעוֹלָם אַל יְחַסְּרֵנוּ.

בקשות נוספות

הָרַחֲמָן הוּא יִמְלֹךְ עָלֵינוּ לְעוֹלָם וָעֶד. הָרַחֲמָן הוּא יִתְבָּרַךְ בַּשָּׁמַיִם וּבָאָרֶץ. הָרַחֲמָן הוּא יִשְׁתַּבַּח לְדוֹר דּוֹרִים, וְיִתְפָּאַר בָּנוּ לָעַד וּלְנֵצַח נְצָחִים, וְיִתְהַדַּר בָּנוּ לָעַד וּלְעוֹלְמֵי עוֹלָמִים. הָרַחֲמָן הוּא יְפַרְנְסֵנוּ בְּכָבוֹד. הָרַחֲמָן הוּא יִשְׁבֹּר עֻלֵּנוּ מֵעַל צַוָּארֵנוּ, וְהוּא יוֹלִיכֵנוּ קוֹמְמִיּוּת לְאַרְצֵנוּ. הָרַחֲמָן הוּא יִשְׁלַח לָנוּ בְּרָכָה מְרֻבָּה בַּבַּיִת הַזֶּה, וְעַל שֻׁלְחָן זֶה שֶׁאָכַלְנוּ עָלָיו. הָרַחֲמָן הוּא יִשְׁלַח לָנוּ אֶת אֵלִיָּהוּ הַנָּבִיא זָכוּר לַטּוֹב, וִיבַשֶּׂר לָנוּ בְּשׂוֹרוֹת טוֹבוֹת יְשׁוּעוֹת וְנֶחָמוֹת. הָרַחֲמָן הוּא יְבָרֵךְ אֶת מְדִינַת יִשְׂרָאֵל, רֵאשִׁית צְמִיחַת גְּאֻלָּתֵנוּ. הָרַחֲמָן הוּא יְבָרֵךְ אֶת חַיָּלֵי צְבָא הַהֲגָנָה לְיִשְׂרָאֵל, הָעוֹמְדִים עַל מִשְׁמַר אַרְצֵנוּ.

בְּרַחֲמָיו – *In His compassion*. Based on the verse "Zion will be redeemed through justice" (Isaiah 1:27), the Vilna Gaon deleted the word בְּרַחֲמָיו ("with mercy") from this *berakha*. That is to say, the return of the Jewish people to its ancient homeland and capital city will be a matter of justice, not simply mercy, in light of all that will have transpired in the interim (R. Mark Dratch).

אָמֵן – *Amen*. This *berakha* is unusual in that one responds *Amen* to one's own *berakha*. The reason for this anomaly is that the conclusion of the *berakha* separates the first three blessings which, according to the majority view, as

In the house of a mourner, "Comfort" on page 1097 is substituted for the next two paragraphs.

וּבְנֵה PLEASE REBUILD JERUSALEM the holy city soon in our own days. Blessed are You, Lord, Who in His mercy rebuilds Jerusalem. Amen.

BLESSING OF GOD'S GOODNESS

בָּרוּךְ BLESSED ARE YOU, Lord our God, King of the universe, God our Father, our King, our Sovereign, our Creator, our Redeemer, our Maker, our Holy One, Holy One of Jacob. You are our Shepherd, Shepherd of Israel, You are the King Who is good and Who does good to all. For every single day He has done good, continues to do good, and will do good for us. Just as He has bestowed that upon us, and continues to bestow it upon us, so may He forever bestow upon us grace, kindness, mercy, relief, salvation and success, blessing and redemption, consolation, livelihood, sustenance, compassion, life, peace, and all manner of good things. And may He never deprive us of any good thing.

ADDITIONAL REQUESTS

הָרַחֲמָן MAY THE COMPASSIONATE ONE reign over us forevermore. May the Compassionate One be blessed in the heavens and on earth. May the Compassionate One be praised in every generation, and glorified and honored among us for all time, eternally. May the Compassionate One maintain us with honor. May the Compassionate One break the yoke from our neck and lead us upright to our land. May the Compassionate One send us great blessing on this household and on this table at which we have eaten. May the Compassionate One send us the prophet Elijah – may he be remembered for good – to herald good tidings of redemption and consolation. May the Compassionate One bless the State of Israel, first flowering of our redemption. May the Compassionate One bless the members of Israel's Defense Forces, who stand guard over our land.

---

we have explained, are ordained by the Torah, and the next *berakha* which is rabbinic in origin (*Berakhot* 45b; Rambam; Tur). Since the word *Amen* is not part of the actual *berakha*, there should be a slight pause before it is said.

בַּקָּשׁוֹת נוֹסָפוֹת / ADDITIONAL REQUESTS

זָכוּר לַטּוֹב – *May he be remembered for good.* The sages use this generic term to refer to people who have rendered great and unforgettable service to the entire Jewish nation (*Berakhot* 3a, *Shabbat* 13b, *Bava Batra* 21a, *Avoda Zara* 8b). In addition to the service he rendered during his years on earth, Elijah will bring the news of the arrival of the Messiah (Malachi 3:23) (*Iyun Tefilla*).

רֵאשִׁית צְמִיחַת גְּאֻלָּתֵנוּ – *First flowering of our redemption.* For further discussion of this phrase,

The גמרא (ברכות מו.) *as well as the* שולחן ערוך אורח חיים *201:1,) record the following prayer to be recited by a guest for the well-being of a male host.*

יְהִי רָצוֹן שֶׁלֹּא יֵבוֹשׁ בַּעַל הַבַּיִת בָּעוֹלָם הַזֶּה, וְלֹא יִכָּלֵם לָעוֹלָם הַבָּא, וְיִצְלַח מְאֹד בְּכָל נְכָסָיו, וְיִהְיוּ נְכָסָיו וּנְכָסֵינוּ מֻצְלָחִים וּקְרוֹבִים לָעִיר, וְאַל יִשְׁלֹט שָׂטָן לֹא בְּמַעֲשֵׂה יָדָיו וְלֹא בְּמַעֲשֵׂה יָדֵינוּ. וְאַל יִזְדַּקֵּק לֹא לְפָנָיו וְלֹא לְפָנֵינוּ שׁוּם דְּבַר הִרְהוּר חֵטְא, עֲבֵרָה וְעָוֹן, מֵעַתָּה וְעַד עוֹלָם.

When a woman hosts a meal a guest says:

יְהִי רָצוֹן שֶׁלֹּא תֵּבוֹשׁ בַּעֲלַת הַבַּיִת בָּעוֹלָם הַזֶּה, וְלֹא תִכָּלֵם לָעוֹלָם הַבָּא, וְתִצְלַח מְאֹד בְּכָל נְכָסֶיהָ, וְיִהְיוּ נְכָסֶיהָ וּנְכָסֵינוּ מֻצְלָחִים וּקְרוֹבִים לָעִיר, וְאַל יִשְׁלֹט שָׂטָן לֹא בְּמַעֲשֵׂה יָדֶיהָ וְלֹא בְּמַעֲשֵׂה יָדֵינוּ. וְאַל יִזְדַּקֵּק לֹא לְפָנֶיהָ וְלֹא לְפָנֵינוּ שׁוּם דְּבַר הִרְהוּר חֵטְא, עֲבֵרָה וְעָוֹן, מֵעַתָּה וְעַד עוֹלָם.

הָרַחֲמָן הוּא יְבָרֵךְ

When eating at one's own table, say (include the words in parentheses that apply):

אוֹתִי (וְאֶת אִשְׁתִּי / וְאֶת בַּעֲלִי / וְאֶת אָבִי מוֹרִי / וְאֶת אִמִּי מוֹרָתִי / וְאֶת זַרְעִי) וְאֶת כָּל אֲשֶׁר לִי.

A guest at someone else's table says (include the words in parentheses that apply):

אֶת בַּעַל הַבַּיִת הַזֶּה (וְאֶת אִשְׁתּוֹ בַּעֲלַת הַבַּיִת הַזֶּה / וְאֶת זַרְעוֹ) וְאֶת כָּל אֲשֶׁר לוֹ.

Where the head of the household is a woman, a guest says:

אֶת בַּעֲלַת הַבַּיִת הַזֶּה (וְאֶת זַרְעָהּ) וְאֶת כָּל אֲשֶׁר לָהּ.

Children at their parents' table say (include the words in parentheses that apply):

אֶת אָבִי מוֹרִי (בַּעַל הַבַּיִת הַזֶּה), וְאֶת אִמִּי מוֹרָתִי (בַּעֲלַת הַבַּיִת הַזֶּה), אוֹתָם וְאֶת בֵּיתָם וְאֶת זַרְעָם וְאֶת כָּל אֲשֶׁר לָהֶם

For all other guests, add:

וְאֶת כָּל הַמְּסֻבִּין כָּאן

אוֹתָנוּ וְאֶת כָּל אֲשֶׁר לָנוּ, כְּמוֹ שֶׁנִּתְבָּרְכוּ אֲבוֹתֵינוּ, אַבְרָהָם יִצְחָק וְיַעֲקֹב, בַּכֹּל, מִכֹּל, כֹּל, כֵּן יְבָרֵךְ אוֹתָנוּ כֻּלָּנוּ יַחַד בִּבְרָכָה שְׁלֵמָה, וְנֹאמַר אָמֵן.

The Gemara (Berakhot 46a as well as the Shulḥan Arukh, OḤ 201:1,) record the following prayer to be recited by a guest for the well-being of a male host.

יְהִי רָצוֹן MAY IT BE Your will that the head of the household shall not suffer shame in this world, nor humiliation in the World to Come. May all he owns prosper greatly, and may his and our possessions be successful and close to hand. Let not Satan hold sway over his deeds or ours, and may no thought of sin, iniquity or transgression enter him or us from now and for evermore.

When a woman hosts a meal a guest says:

יְהִי רָצוֹן MAY IT BE Your will that the head of the household shall not suffer shame in this world, nor humiliation in the World to Come. May all she owns prosper greatly, and may her and our possessions be successful and close to hand. Let not Satan hold sway over her deeds or ours, and may no thought of sin, iniquity or transgression enter her or us from now and for evermore.

הָרַחֲמָן MAY THE COMPASSIONATE ONE bless –

When eating at one's own table, say (include the words in parentheses that apply):

me, (my wife/husband, / my father, my teacher / my mother, my teacher/ my children,) and all that is mine,

A guest at someone else's table says (include the words in parentheses that apply):

the head of this household, him (and his wife, the head of this household / and his children,) and all that is his,

Where the head of the household is a woman, a guest says:

the head of this household, her (and her children) and all that is hers.

Children at their parents' table say (include the words in parentheses that apply):

my father, my teacher, (head of this household,) and my mother, my teacher, (head of this household,) them, their household, their children, and all that is theirs.

For all other guests, add:

and all the diners here,

together with us and all that is ours. Just as our forefathers Abraham, Isaac and Jacob were blessed in all, from all, with all, so may He bless all of us together with a complete blessing, and let us say: Amen.

---

and these lines in general, see the commentary on pages 555–557.

בַּכֹּל, מִכֹּל, כֹּל – *In all, from all, with all.* According to the Gemara (*Bava Batra* 17a) the threefold repetition is a reference to the blessings granted to Abraham, Isaac, and Jacob, each of

בַּמָּרוֹם יְלַמְּדוּ עֲלֵיהֶם וְעָלֵינוּ זְכוּת שֶׁתְּהֵא לְמִשְׁמֶרֶת שָׁלוֹם, וְנִשָּׂא בְרָכָה מֵאֵת יהוה וּצְדָקָה מֵאֱלֹהֵי יִשְׁעֵנוּ, וְנִמְצָא חֵן וְשֵׂכֶל טוֹב בְּעֵינֵי אֱלֹהִים וְאָדָם.

At a meal after a ברית *add here* הָרַחֲמָן הוּא יְבָרֵךְ אֲבִי הַיֶּלֶד *on page 1072.*

בשבת: הָרַחֲמָן הוּא יַנְחִילֵנוּ יוֹם שֶׁכֻּלּוֹ שַׁבָּת וּמְנוּחָה לְחַיֵּי הָעוֹלָמִים.

בראש חודש: הָרַחֲמָן הוּא יְחַדֵּשׁ עָלֵינוּ אֶת הַחֹדֶשׁ הַזֶּה לְטוֹבָה וְלִבְרָכָה.

בראש השנה: הָרַחֲמָן הוּא יְחַדֵּשׁ עָלֵינוּ אֶת הַשָּׁנָה הַזֹּאת לְטוֹבָה וְלִבְרָכָה.

ביום טוב: הָרַחֲמָן הוּא יַנְחִילֵנוּ יוֹם שֶׁכֻּלּוֹ טוֹב.

בסוכות: הָרַחֲמָן הוּא יָקִים לָנוּ אֶת סֻכַּת דָּוִד הַנּוֹפָלֶת.

הָרַחֲמָן הוּא יְזַכֵּנוּ לִימוֹת הַמָּשִׁיחַ וּלְחַיֵּי הָעוֹלָם הַבָּא, מַגְדִּיל / שמואל ב׳ כב

On ראש חודש *,*חגים *,*שבת *and* מִגְדּוֹל / יְשׁוּעוֹת מַלְכּוֹ, וְעֹשֶׂה־חֶסֶד

לִמְשִׁיחוֹ, לְדָוִד וּלְזַרְעוֹ עַד־עוֹלָם: עֹשֶׂה שָׁלוֹם בִּמְרוֹמָיו, הוּא יַעֲשֶׂה שָׁלוֹם עָלֵינוּ, וְעַל כָּל יִשְׂרָאֵל, וְאִמְרוּ אָמֵן.

יְראוּ אֶת־יהוה קְדֹשָׁיו, כִּי־אֵין מַחְסוֹר לִירֵאָיו: כְּפִירִים רָשׁוּ תהלים לד

וְרָעֵבוּ, וְדֹרְשֵׁי יהוה לֹא־יַחְסְרוּ כָל־טוֹב: הוֹדוּ לַיהוה כִּי־ תהלים קיח

טוֹב, כִּי לְעוֹלָם חַסְדּוֹ: פּוֹתֵחַ אֶת־יָדֶךָ, וּמַשְׂבִּיעַ לְכָל־חַי רָצוֹן: תהלים קמה

בָּרוּךְ הַגֶּבֶר אֲשֶׁר יִבְטַח בַּיהוה, וְהָיָה יהוה מִבְטַחוֹ: נַעַר הָיִיתִי ירמיה יז תהלים לז

גַּם־זָקַנְתִּי, וְלֹא־רָאִיתִי צַדִּיק נֶעֱזָב וְזַרְעוֹ מְבַקֶּשׁ־לָחֶם: יהוה עֹז תהלים כט

לְעַמּוֹ יִתֵּן, יהוה יְבָרֵךְ אֶת־עַמּוֹ בַשָּׁלוֹם:

If ברכת המזון *was made on a cup of wine, then* בּוֹרֵא פְּרִי הַגָּפֶן *is said and the majority of the cup is drunk, after which* ברכה מעין שלוש*, on the next page, is said.*

At a wedding or שבע ברכות*, turn to page 1056.*

---

whom was given "all" in one form or another, as seen in Genesis 24, 27, 33.

וְנִמְצָא חֵן וְשֵׂכֶל טוֹב בְּעֵינֵי אֱלֹהִים וְאָדָם – *And may we find grace and good favor in the eyes of God and man*. The righteous do not only act to please God. They also strive to please their fair-minded fellow human beings, so as to sanctify God's name. R. Yehuda HaNasi states in *Pirkei Avot* 2:1 that wherever possible we should choose to act in a way that is inherently good (תִּפְאֶרֶת לְעוֹשֶׂיהָ), while also being תִּפְאֶרֶת לוֹ מִן הָאָדָם that is, praiseworthy in the eyes of our fellow human beings. Thus a truly "religious Jew" is not one who is what some refer to as "*frum*" (i.e., one who observes the *mitzvot* "between man and God"), but rather one who strives to observe

בַּמָּרוֹם IN HEAVEN may they invoke upon these people and ourselves sufficient merit to ensure peace, to bring blessing from the Lord, and to have the God of our salvation treat us charitably. May we find grace and good sense in the eyes of God and man.

At a circumcision feast add here "May the Compassionate One bless the father" on page 1073.

On Shabbat: MAY THE COMPASSIONATE ONE cause us to inherit the time that is entirely Sabbath with repose in eternal life.

On Rosh Ḥodesh: MAY THE COMPASSIONATE ONE renew for us this month for good and for blessing.

On Rosh HaShana: MAY THE COMPASSIONATE ONE renew for us this year for good and for blessing.

On Yom Tov: MAY THE COMPASSIONATE ONE cause us to inherit a day that is entirely good.

On Sukkot: MAY THE COMPASSIONATE ONE reestablish for us the fallen Tabernacle of David.

הָרַחֲמָן MAY THE COMPASSIONATE ONE make us worthy of the Messianic
II Sam. 22 Age and the life of the World to Come. *On weekdays:* He Who gives great salvation / *On Shabbat, Festivals and Rosh Ḥodesh:* He Who is a tower of salvation / to His king and shows kindness to His anointed, to David and his descendants forever. May He Who makes peace in the highest heaven make peace for us and for all Israel, and say, Amen.

Ps. 34 יְראוּ FEAR THE LORD, you His holy ones, for those who fear Him have no
lack. The young lions are poor and hungry, but those who seek the Lord
Ps. 118 will not lack any good thing. Give thanks to the Lord, for He is good, for
Ps. 145 His loving-kindness is forever. You open Your hand, and You satisfy the
Jer. 17 desire of every living thing. Blessed is the person who trusts in the Lord,
Ps. 37 whose trust is in the Lord alone. I was a young man and I have also grown
old, but I have not seen a righteous man forsaken and his seed begging
Ps. 29 bread. The Lord will give strength to His people. The Lord will bless His
people with peace.

If Birkat HaMazon was made on a cup of wine, then the blessing over wine is made and the majority of the cup is drunk, after which Al HaGefen, on the next page, is said.

At a wedding or Sheva Berakhot, *turn to page 1057.*

---

both the ritual and moral ("between man and man") *mitzvot*. Traditionally such a person was a called a "*kosher* Jew" (R. Joseph B. Soloveitchik).

צַדִּיק נֶעֱזָב וְזַרְעוֹ מְבַקֶּשׁ־לָחֶם – *A righteous man forsaken and his seed begging bread.* Many have struggled to explain this verse. R. Joseph

ברכה מעין שלוש

Grace after eating from the "seven species" of produce with which ארץ ישראל *is blessed: food made from the five grains (but not bread); wine or grape juice; grapes, figs, pomegranates, olives, or dates.*

בָּרוּךְ אַתָּה יהוה אֱלֹהֵינוּ מֶלֶךְ הָעוֹלָם, עַל

After grain products (but not bread or מצה*):*	*After wine or grape juice:*	*After grapes, figs, olives, pomegranates or dates:*
הַמִּחְיָה וְעַל הַכַּלְכָּלָה	הַגֶּפֶן וְעַל פְּרִי הַגֶּפֶן	הָעֵץ וְעַל פְּרִי הָעֵץ

After grain products (but not bread or מצה*), and wine or grape juice:*

הַמִּחְיָה וְעַל הַכַּלְכָּלָה וְעַל הַגֶּפֶן וְעַל פְּרִי הַגֶּפֶן

וְעַל תְּנוּבַת הַשָּׂדֶה וְעַל אֶרֶץ חֶמְדָּה טוֹבָה וּרְחָבָה, שֶׁרָצִיתָ וְהִנְחַלְתָּ לַאֲבוֹתֵינוּ לֶאֱכֹל מִפִּרְיָהּ וְלִשְׂבֹּעַ מִטּוּבָהּ. רַחֵם (נָא) יהוה אֱלֹהֵינוּ עַל יִשְׂרָאֵל עַמֶּךָ וְעַל יְרוּשָׁלַיִם עִירֶךָ וְעַל צִיּוֹן מִשְׁכַּן כְּבוֹדֶךָ וְעַל מִזְבְּחֶךָ וְעַל הֵיכָלֶךָ. וּבְנֵה יְרוּשָׁלַיִם עִיר הַקֹּדֶשׁ בִּמְהֵרָה בְיָמֵינוּ, וְהַעֲלֵנוּ לְתוֹכָהּ וְשַׂמְּחֵנוּ בְּבִנְיָנָהּ וְנֹאכַל מִפִּרְיָהּ וְנִשְׂבַּע מִטּוּבָהּ, וּנְבָרֶכְךָ עָלֶיהָ בִּקְדֻשָּׁה וּבְטָהֳרָה.

בשבת: וּרְצֵה וְהַחֲלִיצֵנוּ בְּיוֹם הַשַּׁבָּת הַזֶּה
בראש חודש: וְזָכְרֵנוּ לְטוֹבָה בְּיוֹם רֹאשׁ הַחֹדֶשׁ הַזֶּה
בראש השנה: וְזָכְרֵנוּ לְטוֹבָה בְּיוֹם הַזִּכָּרוֹן הַזֶּה
בפסח: וְשַׂמְּחֵנוּ בְּיוֹם חַג הַמַּצּוֹת הַזֶּה
בשבועות: וְשַׂמְּחֵנוּ בְּיוֹם חַג הַשָּׁבוּעוֹת הַזֶּה
בסוכות: וְשַׂמְּחֵנוּ בְּיוֹם חַג הַסֻּכּוֹת הַזֶּה
בשמיני עצרת ושמחת תורה: וְשַׂמְּחֵנוּ בְּיוֹם הַשְּׁמִינִי חַג הָעֲצֶרֶת הַזֶּה

כִּי אַתָּה יהוה טוֹב וּמֵטִיב לַכֹּל, וְנוֹדֶה לְּךָ עַל הָאָרֶץ

B. Soloveitchik taught that we learn from the punishments meted out to the Egyptians many years after enslaving the Israelites, that while divine justice is sometimes delayed, eventually justice is done – not just in the next world, but in this one too, and if not in our lifetimes then for our descendants. While the Rav himself did not link this perspective to our verse, the Psalmist here might be proclaiming a similar idea. Thus in his old age, having witnessed the passage of generations, he affirms that even if the righteous do not always receive what they deserve in their lifetimes, the rewards earned by them are bestowed on their descendants, for instance, being spared from having to beg for food (R. Basil Herring).

In its original context in Psalm 37, the "righteous person" appears to refer specifically to someone who lends his or her money and provides generously of his or her means to others. It is such righteous people who are assured that they will not be utterly abandoned –

BLESSING AFTER FOOD – AL HAMIḤYA

Grace after eating from the "seven species" of produce with which Israel is blessed: food made from the five grains (but not bread); wine or grape juice; grapes, figs, pomegranates, olives, or dates.

בָּרוּךְ BLESSED ARE YOU, Lord, our God, King of the universe,

After grain products (but not bread or matza):	*After wine or grape juice:*	*After grapes, figs, olives, pomegranates or dates:*
for the nourishment and sustenance,	for the vine and the fruit of the vine,	for the tree and the fruit of the tree,

After grain products (but not bread or matza), and wine or grape juice:
for the nourishment and sustenance and for the vine and the fruit of the vine,

and for the produce of the field; for the beloved, good and spacious land that You gave our fathers as an inheritance, that they might eat of its fruit and be satisfied with its goodness. Have pity (please,) Lord our God, on Israel Your people, on Jerusalem Your city and Zion the dwelling place of Your glory, and on Your altar and Your Temple. May You rebuild Jerusalem, the holy city swiftly in our time, and may You bring us back there, rejoicing in its rebuilding, eating from its fruit, satisfied by its goodness, and blessing You for it in holiness and purity.

On Shabbat:	Favor and invigorate us on this Sabbath Day.
On Rosh Ḥodesh:	Remember us for good on this day of Rosh Ḥodesh.
On Rosh HaShana:	Remember us for good on this Day of Zikaron.
On Pesaḥ:	Grant us joy on this Festival of Matzot.
On Shavuot:	Grant us joy on this Festival of Shavuot.
On Sukkot:	Grant us joy on this Festival of Sukkot.
On Shemini Atzeret & Simḥat Torah:	Grant us joy on the eighth day, this Festival of Atzeret.

For You, Lord, are good and do good to all and we thank You for the land

---

whether by God or by those who have been the beneficiaries of their generosity if they will themselves fall on hard times (R. Eric Levy).

בְּרָכָה מֵעֵין שָׁלֹשׁ / THE *AL HAMIḤYA BERAKHA*
After eating an olive-sized amount of grain-based food that is not in bread form, or after eating that amount of any of the five fruits that the Torah associates with the land of Israel, we recite an abbreviated Grace that contains the core ideas of the *berakhot* of the full *Birkat HaMazon*. Hence it is known as the "*Berakha* that is analogous to the Three (*Berakhot*)." Some consider it to be, like the full Grace, biblically required (Deut. 8:10), while others regard it as of rabbinic provenance, arguing that only bread is mentioned in the preceding verse.

וְעַל אֶרֶץ חֶמְדָּה – *For the desirable... land.* While

After grain products (but not bread or מצה):

וְעַל הַמִּחְיָה.
בָּרוּךְ אַתָּה יהוה, עַל
הָאָרֶץ וְעַל הַמִּחְיָה.

After wine or grape juice:

וְעַל פְּרִי הַגֶּפֶן.*
בָּרוּךְ אַתָּה יהוה, עַל
הָאָרֶץ וְעַל פְּרִי הַגֶּפֶן.*

After grapes, figs, olives, pomegranates or dates:

וְעַל הַפֵּרוֹת.**
בָּרוּךְ אַתָּה יהוה, עַל
הָאָרֶץ וְעַל הַפֵּרוֹת.**

After grain products (but not bread or מצה), and wine or grape juice:

וְעַל הַמִּחְיָה וְעַל פְּרִי הַגֶּפֶן.*
בָּרוּךְ אַתָּה יהוה, עַל הָאָרֶץ וְעַל הַמִּחְיָה וְעַל פְּרִי הַגֶּפֶן.*

**If the wine is from ארץ ישראל, then substitute גַּפְנָהּ for הַגֶּפֶן.*
***If the fruit is from ארץ ישראל, then substitute פֵּרוֹתֶיהָ for הַפֵּרוֹת.*

בורא נפשות

After food or drink that does not require ברכת המזון or ברכה מעין שלוש – such as meat, fish, dairy products, vegetables, beverages, or fruit other than grapes, figs, pomegranates, olives or dates – say:

בָּרוּךְ אַתָּה יהוה אֱלֹהֵינוּ מֶלֶךְ הָעוֹלָם, בּוֹרֵא נְפָשׁוֹת רַבּוֹת וְחֶסְרוֹנָן עַל כָּל מַה שֶּׁבָּרָאתָ (נ״א שֶׁבָּרָא) לְהַחֲיוֹת בָּהֶם נֶפֶשׁ כָּל חָי. בָּרוּךְ חֵי הָעוֹלָמִים.

תפילת הדרך

If one intends to return home on the same day, add the words in parentheses:

יְהִי רָצוֹן מִלְּפָנֶיךָ, יהוה אֱלֹהֵינוּ וֵאלֹהֵי אֲבוֹתֵינוּ, שֶׁתּוֹלִיכֵנוּ לְשָׁלוֹם, וְתַצְעִידֵנוּ לְשָׁלוֹם, וְתַדְרִיכֵנוּ לְשָׁלוֹם, וְתַגִּיעֵנוּ

LAWS OF PRAYER WHEN TRAVELING

Travelers are obligated to pray. But under certain circumstances special practices are appropriate. Thus, if standing during prayer or facing Jerusalem are impractical (e.g., where space is lacking, or the direction of the vehicle or train/airplane changes) one may face whatever direction is feasible, while directing one's mind to Jerusalem. If wearing *tefillin* is not possible, one should pray at the correct time even without *tefillin*, but then later repeat the *Shema* while wearing *tefillin*. One must take care to find a place that avoids foul smells, sights, or immodestly dressed people. While men and women should pray separately en route, a *meḥitza* is not required. When traveling overnight on an airplane one should not pray *Shaharit* until light is visible on the horizon. More generally, special care should be taken to avoid disturbing or alarming fellow travelers or crew members, even if it means that one must pray without a *minyan*, or say the *Amida* while seated.

After grain products (but not bread or matza):
and for the nourishment. Blessed are You, Lord, for the land and for the nourishment.

After wine or grape juice:
and for the fruit of the vine.* Blessed are You, Lord, for the land and for the fruit of the vine.*

After grapes, figs, olives, pomegranates or dates:
and for the fruit.** Blessed are You, Lord, for the land and for the fruit.**

After grain products (but not bread or matza), and wine or grape juice:
and for the nourishment and for the fruit of the vine.* Blessed are You, Lord, for the land and for the nourishment and the fruit of the vine.*

* *If the wine is from Israel, then substitute "her vine" for "the vine."*
** *If the fruit is from Israel, then substitute "her fruit" for "the fruit."*

BLESSING AFTER FOOD – BOREI NEFASHOT

After food or drink that does not require Birkat HaMazon or Al HaMiḥya – such as meat, fish, dairy products, vegetables, beverages, or fruit other than grapes, figs, pomegranates, olives or dates – say:

בָּרוּךְ BLESSED ARE YOU, Lord, our God, King of the universe, Who creates the many forms of life and their needs. For all You have (*Some say:* He) created to sustain the life of all that lives, blessed be the Giver of life to the worlds.

THE TRAVELER'S PRAYER

If one intends to return home on the same day, add the words in parentheses:

יְהִי רָצוֹן MAY IT BE Your will, Lord our God and God of our fathers, to lead us to peace, direct our steps to peace, guide us to peace, and

---

the *Al HaMiḥya* is a précis of the full *Birkat HaMazon*, it also very briefly mentions several additional themes that are particularly relevant to the seven species of the land of Israel. These include the Temple altar before which the first-fruits of those species were consecrated to God and given to the *Kohanim*, and the second tithe and fourth-year fruits of trees that had to be eaten in a state of personal holiness and purity within the area surrounded by the walls of Jerusalem. The text petitions God to bring about these activities in the rebuilt Temple, thus allowing us to consecrate and enjoy the bounty of God's blessings in every way (R. Yitzḥak Ze'ev Soloveitchik).

תְּפִלַּת הַדֶּרֶךְ / THE TRAVELER'S PRAYER
The Gemara (*Berakhot* 29b) states that when setting out on a journey one should pray to arrive safely. This prayer is not only a prayer for protection from roadside dangers, but a request for divine permission to travel, and as such applies even if one does not expect any danger (Meiri).

לִמְחוֹז חֶפְצֵנוּ לְחַיִּים וּלְשִׂמְחָה וּלְשָׁלוֹם, (וְתַחֲזִירֵנוּ לְבֵיתֵנוּ לְשָׁלוֹם) וְתַצִּילֵנוּ מִכַּף כָּל אוֹיֵב וְאוֹרֵב בַּדֶּרֶךְ, וּמִכָּל מִינֵי פֻּרְעָנִיּוֹת הַמִּתְרַגְּשׁוֹת לָבוֹא לָעוֹלָם, וְתִשְׁלַח בְּרָכָה בְּמַעֲשֵׂה יָדֵינוּ, וְתִתְּנֵנוּ לְחֵן וּלְחֶסֶד וּלְרַחֲמִים בְּעֵינֶיךָ וּבְעֵינֵי כָל רוֹאֵינוּ, וְתִשְׁמַע קוֹל תַּחֲנוּנֵינוּ, כִּי אֵל שׁוֹמֵעַ תְּפִלָּה וְתַחֲנוּן אָתָּה. בָּרוּךְ אַתָּה יהוה, שׁוֹמֵעַ תְּפִלָּה.

תהלים קכא **יהוה** יִשְׁמָר־צֵאתְךָ וּבוֹאֶךָ, מֵעַתָּה וְעַד־עוֹלָם:

Repeat three times:

בראשית לב **וְיַעֲקֹב** הָלַךְ לְדַרְכּוֹ, וַיִּפְגְּעוּ־בוֹ מַלְאֲכֵי אֱלֹהִים: וַיֹּאמֶר יַעֲקֹב כַּאֲשֶׁר רָאָם, מַחֲנֵה אֱלֹהִים זֶה, וַיִּקְרָא שֵׁם־הַמָּקוֹם הַהוּא מַחֲנָיִם:

Repeat three times:

במדבר ו **יְבָרֶכְךָ** יהוה וְיִשְׁמְרֶךָ: יָאֵר יהוה פָּנָיו אֵלֶיךָ וִיחֻנֶּךָּ: יִשָּׂא יהוה פָּנָיו אֵלֶיךָ וְיָשֵׂם לְךָ שָׁלוֹם:

תהלים קכא **שִׁיר לַמַּעֲלוֹת,** אֶשָּׂא עֵינַי אֶל־הֶהָרִים, מֵאַיִן יָבֹא עֶזְרִי: עֶזְרִי מֵעִם יהוה, עֹשֵׂה שָׁמַיִם וָאָרֶץ: אַל־יִתֵּן לַמּוֹט רַגְלֶךָ, אַל־יָנוּם שֹׁמְרֶךָ: הִנֵּה לֹא־יָנוּם וְלֹא יִישָׁן, שׁוֹמֵר יִשְׂרָאֵל: יהוה שֹׁמְרֶךָ, יהוה צִלְּךָ עַל־יַד יְמִינֶךָ: יוֹמָם הַשֶּׁמֶשׁ לֹא־יַכֶּכָּה, וְיָרֵחַ בַּלָּיְלָה: יהוה יִשְׁמָרְךָ מִכָּל־רָע, יִשְׁמֹר אֶת־נַפְשֶׁךָ: יהוה יִשְׁמָר־צֵאתְךָ וּבוֹאֶךָ, מֵעַתָּה וְעַד־עוֹלָם:

אשר יצר

After relieving oneself and washing one's hands, say:

בָּרוּךְ אַתָּה יהוה אֱלֹהֵינוּ מֶלֶךְ הָעוֹלָם, אֲשֶׁר יָצַר אֶת הָאָדָם בְּחָכְמָה, וּבָרָא בוֹ נְקָבִים נְקָבִים, חֲלוּלִים חֲלוּלִים. גָּלוּי וְיָדוּעַ לִפְנֵי כִסֵּא כְבוֹדֶךָ, שֶׁאִם יִפָּתֵחַ אֶחָד מֵהֶם אוֹ יִסָּתֵם אֶחָד מֵהֶם, אִי אֶפְשַׁר לְהִתְקַיֵּם וְלַעֲמֹד לְפָנֶיךָ. בָּרוּךְ אַתָּה יהוה, רוֹפֵא כָל בָּשָׂר וּמַפְלִיא לַעֲשׂוֹת.

Tefillat HaDerekh is based on the principle that prayer is essentially a response to an עֵת צָרָה (a time of perceived stress and danger). Therefore, the prayer is only recited if there is some element of potential danger leading to a concern for one's personal safety (R. Joseph B. Soloveitchik).

מַחֲנָיִם – *Mahanaim*. Ramban explains that

bring us to our desired destination in life, joy and peace (and bring us back to our home in peace). Rescue us from any enemy or ambush on the way, and from all kinds of disasters that sometimes happen in the world. Send blessing to the work of our hands, and grant us grace, kindness and compassion from You and from all who see us. Hear our pleas, for You are a God Who hears prayer and pleas. Blessed are You, Lord, Who hears prayer.

Ps. 121 יהוה THE LORD will guard your going out and your coming in from now and forever.

Repeat three times:

Gen. 32 וְיַעֲקֹב AND JACOB went on his way, and the angels of God met him. And Jacob said when he saw them: "This is God's camp." And he called the name of that place Mahanaim.

Repeat three times:

Num. 6 יְבָרֶכְךָ MAY THE LORD bless you and protect you. May the Lord make His face shine on you and be gracious to you. May the Lord turn His face toward you and grant you peace.

Ps. 121 שִׁיר לַמַּעֲלוֹת A SONG FOR ASCENTS. I lift up my eyes to the hills. From where will my help come? My help is from the Lord, the Maker of heaven and earth. May He not suffer your foot to slip. May He Who guards you not slumber. Behold, He Who guards Israel neither slumbers nor sleeps. The Lord is your guardian. The Lord is your shade upon your right hand. The sun will not smite you by day, nor the moon by night. The Lord will guard you from all evil. He will guard your soul. The Lord will guard your going out and your coming in from now and forever.

ASHER YATZAR

After relieving oneself and washing one's hands, say:

בָּרוּךְ BLESSED ARE YOU, Lord, our God, King of the universe, Who formed man in wisdom and created in him many orifices and cavities. It is revealed and known before the throne of Your glory that were one of them to be ruptured or blocked, it would be impossible to survive and stand before You. Blessed are You, Lord, Healer of all flesh Who does wondrous deeds.

Jacob named the place "Two Camps," when he realized that there was a heavenly camp of angels that had accompanied him on his earthly journeys. Reflecting this duality, Jacob's life journeys each had a dual aspect – a mundane one and a spiritual one (R. Elchanan Samet). So too, our own physical journeys should incorporate spiritual purposes (R. Aton Holzer).

ברכות נוספות

ברכות הנהנין

On washing hands before eating bread:

בָּרוּךְ אַתָּה יהוה אֱלֹהֵינוּ מֶלֶךְ הָעוֹלָם, אֲשֶׁר קִדְּשָׁנוּ בְּמִצְוֹתָיו וְצִוָּנוּ עַל נְטִילַת יָדָיִם.

Before eating bread:

בָּרוּךְ אַתָּה יהוה אֱלֹהֵינוּ מֶלֶךְ הָעוֹלָם, הַמּוֹצִיא לֶחֶם מִן הָאָרֶץ.

Before eating food, other than bread or מצה*,*
made from the five species of grain (wheat, barley, rye, oats and spelt), or rice:

בָּרוּךְ אַתָּה יהוה אֱלֹהֵינוּ מֶלֶךְ הָעוֹלָם, בּוֹרֵא מִינֵי מְזוֹנוֹת.

Before drinking wine or grape juice:

בָּרוּךְ אַתָּה יהוה אֱלֹהֵינוּ מֶלֶךְ הָעוֹלָם, בּוֹרֵא פְּרִי הַגָּפֶן.

Before eating fruit that grows on trees:

בָּרוּךְ אַתָּה יהוה אֱלֹהֵינוּ מֶלֶךְ הָעוֹלָם, בּוֹרֵא פְּרִי הָעֵץ.

Before eating vegetables, or fruit that does not grow on trees:

בָּרוּךְ אַתָּה יהוה אֱלֹהֵינוּ מֶלֶךְ הָעוֹלָם, בּוֹרֵא פְּרִי הָאֲדָמָה.

Before eating other food or drinking other liquids:

בָּרוּךְ אַתָּה יהוה אֱלֹהֵינוּ מֶלֶךְ הָעוֹלָם, שֶׁהַכֹּל נִהְיָה בִּדְבָרוֹ.

Before eating fruit for the first time in a season, the following שֶׁהֶחֱיָנוּ *is said.*
This blessing is also said when buying or wearing a new garment of significant value (e.g. a dress or suit); entering a new home for the first time; or hearing personal good news.

בָּרוּךְ אַתָּה יהוה אֱלֹהֵינוּ מֶלֶךְ הָעוֹלָם, שֶׁהֶחֱיָנוּ וְקִיְּמָנוּ וְהִגִּיעָנוּ לַזְּמַן הַזֶּה.

On wearing new clothes:

בָּרוּךְ אַתָּה יהוה אֱלֹהֵינוּ מֶלֶךְ הָעוֹלָם, מַלְבִּישׁ עֲרֻמִּים.

בִּרְכוֹת הַנֶּהֱנִין / BLESSINGS ON PLEASURES God does not need us to bless Him. He is beyond any and all needs. As R. Ḥayyim of Volozhin explains in the *Nefesh HaḤayyim*, the purpose of every *berakha* is to make clear God's role in the existence of every object and event in our world. For God wants man to be His agent to reveal His actions in the world. For instance, when we recite the *berakha* שֶׁהַכֹּל נִהְיָה בִּדְבָרוֹ ("by Whose word all things come to be") over a cup of water, we are proclaiming that "it is the hidden hand of God that created this water and that enables us to drink it - may His glory be recognized throughout His cosmos." The *berakha* thus declares that without the God Who hides Himself in His world, neither this water nor anything else would exist. In this fashion, every *berakha* that

ADDITIONAL OCCASIONAL BLESSINGS

BLESSINGS ON PLEASURES

On washing hands before eating bread:

בָּרוּךְ BLESSED ARE YOU, Lord, our God, King of the universe, Who has sanctified us with His commandments, and has commanded us about washing hands.

Before eating bread:

בָּרוּךְ BLESSED ARE YOU, Lord, our God, King of the universe, Who brings forth bread from the earth.

Before eating food, other than bread or matza,
made from the five species of grain (wheat, barley, rye, oats and spelt), or rice:

בָּרוּךְ BLESSED ARE YOU, Lord, our God, King of the universe, Who creates the various kinds of nourishment.

Before drinking wine or grape juice:

בָּרוּךְ BLESSED ARE YOU, Lord, our God, King of the universe, Who creates the fruit of the vine.

Before eating fruit that grows on trees:

בָּרוּךְ BLESSED ARE YOU, Lord, our God, King of the universe, Who creates the fruit of the tree.

Before eating vegetables, or fruit that does not grow on trees:

בָּרוּךְ BLESSED ARE YOU, Lord, our God, King of the universe, Who creates the fruit of the ground.

Before eating other food or drinking other liquids:

בָּרוּךְ BLESSED ARE YOU, Lord, our God, King of the universe, by Whose word all things come to be.

Before eating fruit for the first time in a season, the following is said.
This blessing is also said when buying or wearing a new garment of significant value
(e.g. a dress or suit); entering a new home for the first time; or hearing personal good news.

בָּרוּךְ BLESSED ARE YOU, Lord, our God, King of the universe, Who has given us life, sustained us, and brought us to this time.

On wearing new clothes:

בָּרוּךְ BLESSED ARE YOU, Lord, our God, King of the universe, Who clothes the naked.

---

we recite before or after an event is a partial fulfillment of our lifelong task to promote the recognition of God's role in all things (R. Joseph B. Soloveitchik).

ברכת הגומל

One delivered from danger recites this blessing in the presence of a minyan.

בָּרוּךְ אַתָּה יהוה אֱלֹהֵינוּ מֶלֶךְ הָעוֹלָם הַגּוֹמֵל לְחַיָּבִים טוֹבוֹת, שֶׁגְּמָלַנִי כָּל טוֹב.

If a man recites the ברכה, *the* קהל *responds:*

אָמֵן. מִי שֶׁגְּמָלְךָ כָּל טוֹב הוּא יִגְמָלְךָ כָּל טוֹב, סֶלָה.

If a woman recites the ברכה, *the* קהל *responds:*

אָמֵן. מִי שֶׁגְּמָלֵךְ כָּל טוֹב הוּא יִגְמְלֵךְ כָּל טוֹב, סֶלָה.

ברכות הריח

Upon entering a perfumery or upon smelling fragrances of (a) non-vegetable origin (e.g., Musk); (b) undetermined origin; or (c) a blend of spices of different origins:

בָּרוּךְ אַתָּה יהוה אֱלֹהֵינוּ מֶלֶךְ הָעוֹלָם, בּוֹרֵא מִינֵי בְשָׂמִים.

On smelling fragrant shrubs or trees:

בָּרוּךְ אַתָּה יהוה אֱלֹהֵינוּ מֶלֶךְ הָעוֹלָם, בּוֹרֵא עֲצֵי בְשָׂמִים.

On smelling fragrant herbs, grasses or flowers:

בָּרוּךְ אַתָּה יהוה אֱלֹהֵינוּ מֶלֶךְ הָעוֹלָם, בּוֹרֵא עִשְׂבֵי בְשָׂמִים.

On smelling fragrant fruit:

בָּרוּךְ אַתָּה יהוה אֱלֹהֵינוּ מֶלֶךְ הָעוֹלָם, הַנּוֹתֵן רֵיחַ טוֹב בַּפֵּרוֹת.

On smelling persimmon oil:

בָּרוּךְ אַתָּה יהוה אֱלֹהֵינוּ מֶלֶךְ הָעוֹלָם, בּוֹרֵא שֶׁמֶן עָרֵב.

ברכות הראייה

On seeing the wonders of nature, such as lightning, and for ברכת החמה*:*

בָּרוּךְ אַתָּה יהוה אֱלֹהֵינוּ מֶלֶךְ הָעוֹלָם, עוֹשֶׂה מַעֲשֵׂה בְרֵאשִׁית.

On hearing thunder or experiencing a hurricane:

בָּרוּךְ אַתָּה יהוה אֱלֹהֵינוּ מֶלֶךְ הָעוֹלָם, שֶׁכֹּחוֹ וּגְבוּרָתוֹ מָלֵא עוֹלָם.

The Gemara (*Berakhot* 35a) records the following: "Said R. Yehuda in the name of Shmuel: 'Whoever enjoys the benefits of this world without first pronouncing a *berakha* has taken improper advantage of that which belongs to heaven, as it says, 'the earth is the Lord's and the fullness thereof' [Psalms 24:1]. R. Levi asked: 'Does this not contradict the verse, 'The heavens are the heavens of the Lord, but He gave the earth to man' [Psalms 115:16]? The answer is that there is no contradiction – the first verse refers to what we take from the

BLESSING OF GRATITUDE

One delivered from danger recites this blessing in the presence of a מנין.

בָּרוּךְ BLESSED ARE YOU, Lord, our God, King of the universe, Who bestows favors on the undeserving, and Who has bestowed every good thing on me.

Congregation responds:

Amen. May He Who has bestowed every good thing on you continue to grant you every good thing, forever.

BLESSINGS ON FRAGRANCE

Upon entering a perfumery or upon smelling fragrances of (a) non-vegetable origin (e.g., Musk); (b) undetermined origin; or (c) a blend of spices of different origins:

בָּרוּךְ BLESSED ARE YOU, Lord, our God, King of the universe, Who creates the various spices.

On smelling fragrant shrubs or trees:

בָּרוּךְ BLESSED ARE YOU, Lord, our God, King of the universe, Who creates fragrant trees.

On smelling fragrant herbs, grasses or flowers:

בָּרוּךְ BLESSED ARE YOU, Lord, our God, King of the universe, Who creates fragrant plants.

On smelling fragrant fruit:

בָּרוּךְ BLESSED ARE YOU, Lord, our God, King of the universe, Who gives pleasant fragrance to fruits.

On smelling persimmon oil:

בָּרוּךְ BLESSED ARE YOU, Lord, our God, King of the universe, Who creates pleasing perfume.

BLESSINGS ON WITNESSING UNACCUSTOMED EVENTS

On seeing the wonders of nature, such as lightning, and on the 28-year solar cycle:

בָּרוּךְ BLESSED ARE YOU, Lord, our God, King of the universe, Who makes the phenomena of creation.

On hearing thunder or experiencing a hurricane:

בָּרוּךְ BLESSED ARE YOU, Lord, our God, King of the universe, Whose power and might fill the world.

---

world without making a *berakha,* while the second refers to what we take after we have made a *berakha.*" Therefore, reciting a *berakha* is the halakhic equivalent of a *kinyan,* meaning an act by which one acquires something from another person. The only difference is that rather than "paying" with a physical object, we use a *berakha* to effect the transfer.

בִּרְכַּת הַגּוֹמֵל / BLESSING OF GRATITUDE

See commentary on page 163 and page 542.

בִּרְכַּת הָרֵיחַ / BLESSINGS ON FRAGRANCE

The source for making a *berakha* over a pleasant smell is found in *Berakhot* 43b: "'Every soul will praise God' (Psalms 150:6) – what is it that brings pleasure to the soul but not to the body? It is a pleasant smell."

On seeing a rainbow:

בָּרוּךְ אַתָּה יהוה אֱלֹהֵינוּ מֶלֶךְ הָעוֹלָם, זוֹכֵר הַבְּרִית וְנֶאֱמָן בִּבְרִיתוֹ וְקַיָּם בְּמַאֲמָרוֹ.

On seeing the ocean or the Mediterranean Sea for the first time in thirty days:

בָּרוּךְ אַתָּה יהוה אֱלֹהֵינוּ מֶלֶךְ הָעוֹלָם, שֶׁעָשָׂה אֶת הַיָּם הַגָּדוֹל.

On seeing beautiful scenes of nature:

בָּרוּךְ אַתָּה יהוה אֱלֹהֵינוּ מֶלֶךְ הָעוֹלָם, שֶׁכָּכָה לּוֹ בְּעוֹלָמוֹ.

On seeing unusual people or animals:

בָּרוּךְ אַתָּה יהוה אֱלֹהֵינוּ מֶלֶךְ הָעוֹלָם, מְשַׁנֶּה הַבְּרִיּוֹת.

On seeing trees blossoming for the first time in the year:

בָּרוּךְ אַתָּה יהוה אֱלֹהֵינוּ מֶלֶךְ הָעוֹלָם, שֶׁלֹּא חִסַּר בְּעוֹלָמוֹ כְּלוּם, וּבָרָא בוֹ בְּרִיּוֹת טוֹבוֹת וְאִילָנוֹת טוֹבִים לְהַנּוֹת בָּהֶם בְּנֵי אָדָם.

On seeing an outstanding Torah scholar:

בָּרוּךְ אַתָּה יהוה אֱלֹהֵינוּ מֶלֶךְ הָעוֹלָם, שֶׁחָלַק מֵחָכְמָתוֹ לִירֵאָיו.

On seeing an outstanding secular scholar:

בָּרוּךְ אַתָּה יהוה אֱלֹהֵינוּ מֶלֶךְ הָעוֹלָם, שֶׁנָּתַן מֵחָכְמָתוֹ לְבָשָׂר וָדָם.

On seeing a Monarch or Head of State:

בָּרוּךְ אַתָּה יהוה אֱלֹהֵינוּ מֶלֶךְ הָעוֹלָם, שֶׁנָּתַן מִכְּבוֹדוֹ לְבָשָׂר וָדָם.

On seeing 600,000 Jews together in ארץ ישראל*:*

בָּרוּךְ אַתָּה יהוה אֱלֹהֵינוּ מֶלֶךְ הָעוֹלָם, חֲכַם הָרָזִים.

Upon meeting a friend who has recovered from a life-threatening illness.

בְּרִיךְ רַחֲמָנָא מַלְכָּא דְעָלְמָא, דִּי יַהֲבָךְ לָן, וְלָא יַהֲבָךְ לְעַפְרָא.

On hearing bad news, and said by a mourner before the ritual tearing of the garment:

בָּרוּךְ אַתָּה יהוה אֱלֹהֵינוּ מֶלֶךְ הָעוֹלָם, דַּיַּן הָאֱמֶת.

On seeing a once-destroyed synagogue that has been restored:

בָּרוּךְ אַתָּה יהוה אֱלֹהֵינוּ מֶלֶךְ הָעוֹלָם, מַצִּיב גְּבוּל אַלְמָנָה.

On seeing a place where miracles occurred to the Jewish people:

בָּרוּךְ אַתָּה יהוה אֱלֹהֵינוּ מֶלֶךְ הָעוֹלָם, שֶׁעָשָׂה נִסִּים לַאֲבוֹתֵינוּ בַּמָּקוֹם הַזֶּה.

On seeing a rainbow:

בָּרוּךְ BLESSED ARE YOU, Lord, our God, King of the universe, Who remembers the covenant, and is faithful to the covenant, which endures according to His word.

On seeing the ocean or the Mediterranean Sea for the first time in thirty days:

בָּרוּךְ BLESSED ARE YOU, Lord, our God, King of the universe, Who has made the great sea.

On seeing beautiful scenes of nature:

בָּרוּךְ BLESSED ARE YOU, Lord, our God, King of the universe, Who has [created] such things in His world.

On seeing unusual people or animals:

בָּרוּךְ BLESSED ARE YOU, Lord, our God, King of the universe, Who makes [all] creatures different.

On seeing trees blossoming for the first time in the year:

בָּרוּךְ BLESSED ARE YOU, Lord, our God, King of the universe, Who has withheld nothing from His world, but has created in it beautiful creatures and good trees for human beings to enjoy.

On seeing an outstanding Torah scholar:

בָּרוּךְ BLESSED ARE YOU, Lord, our God, King of the universe, Who has shared some of His wisdom with those who revere Him.

On seeing an outstanding secular scholar:

בָּרוּךְ BLESSED ARE YOU, Lord, our God, King of the universe, Who has given some of His wisdom to people of flesh and blood.

On seeing a Monarch or Head of State:

בָּרוּךְ BLESSED ARE YOU, Lord, our God, King of the universe, Who has given some of His glory to people of flesh and blood.

On seeing 600,000 Jews together in Israel:

בָּרוּךְ BLESSED ARE YOU, Lord, our God, King of the universe, Who is wise regarding hidden matters.

Upon meeting a friend who has recovered from a life-threatening illness.

בְּרִיךְ BLESSED IS the Merciful One, King of the universe, Who has returned you to us, and has not consigned you to the dust.

On hearing bad news, and said by a mourner before the ritual tearing of the garment:

בָּרוּךְ BLESSED ARE YOU, Lord, our God, King of the universe, the true Judge.

On seeing a once-destroyed synagogue that has been restored:

בָּרוּךְ BLESSED ARE YOU, Lord, our God, King of the universe, Who establishes limits for [the grieving of] a widow.

On seeing a place where miracles occurred to the Jewish people:

בָּרוּךְ BLESSED ARE YOU, Lord, our God, King of the universe, Who performed miracles for our ancestors in this place.

On seeing a place where miracles occurred to oneself or one's family (insert the relevant words):

בָּרוּךְ אַתָּה יהוה אֱלֹהֵינוּ מֶלֶךְ הָעוֹלָם, שֶׁעָשָׂה לִי (לְאָבִי/לְאִמִּי/לַאֲבוֹתַי) נֵס בַּמָּקוֹם הַזֶּה.

בביקור בבית הקברות

On visiting a cemetery, or seeing a Jewish grave, for the first time in thirty days:

בָּרוּךְ אַתָּה יהוה אֱלֹהֵינוּ מֶלֶךְ הָעוֹלָם, אֲשֶׁר יָצַר אֶתְכֶם בַּדִּין, וְזָן וְכִלְכֵּל אֶתְכֶם בַּדִּין, וְהֵמִית אֶתְכֶם בַּדִּין, וְיוֹדֵעַ מִסְפַּר כֻּלְּכֶם בַּדִּין, וְהוּא עָתִיד לְהַחֲיוֹתְכֶם וּלְקַיֵּם אֶתְכֶם בַּדִּין. בָּרוּךְ אַתָּה יהוה, מְחַיֵּה הַמֵּתִים.

אַתָּה גִּבּוֹר לְעוֹלָם אֲדֹנָי, מְחַיֵּה מֵתִים אַתָּה, רַב לְהוֹשִׁיעַ, מְכַלְכֵּל חַיִּים בְּחֶסֶד, מְחַיֵּה מֵתִים בְּרַחֲמִים רַבִּים, סוֹמֵךְ נוֹפְלִים, וְרוֹפֵא חוֹלִים, וּמַתִּיר אֲסוּרִים, וּמְקַיֵּם אֱמוּנָתוֹ לִישֵׁנֵי עָפָר. מִי כָמוֹךָ בַּעַל גְּבוּרוֹת וּמִי דּוֹמֶה לָּךְ, מֶלֶךְ מֵמִית וּמְחַיֶּה וּמַצְמִיחַ יְשׁוּעָה, וְנֶאֱמָן אַתָּה לְהַחֲיוֹת מֵתִים.

Upon reaching the grave, it is customary to place one's left hand on the monument and recite the following verses:

ישעיה נח

וְנָחֲךָ יהוה תָּמִיד וְהִשְׂבִּיעַ בְּצַחְצָחוֹת נַפְשֶׁךָ, וְעַצְמֹתֶיךָ יַחֲלִיץ, וְהָיִיתָ כְּגַן רָוֶה וּכְמוֹצָא מַיִם אֲשֶׁר לֹא־יְכַזְּבוּ מֵימָיו: וּבָנוּ מִמְּךָ חָרְבוֹת עוֹלָם, מוֹסְדֵי דוֹר־וָדוֹר תְּקוֹמֵם, וְקֹרָא לְךָ גֹּדֵר פֶּרֶץ מְשֹׁבֵב נְתִיבוֹת לָשָׁבֶת:

One then adds:

On a man's grave תִּשְׁכַּב בְּשָׁלוֹם וְתִישַׁן בְּשָׁלוֹם עַד בֹּא מְנַחֵם מַשְׁמִיעַ שָׁלוֹם.

On a woman's grave תִּשְׁכְּבִי בְשָׁלוֹם וְתִישְׁנִי בְּשָׁלוֹם עַד בֹּא מְנַחֵם מַשְׁמִיעַ שָׁלוֹם.

ברכות השמיעה

On hearing good news from which others as well as oneself will benefit:

בָּרוּךְ אַתָּה יהוה אֱלֹהֵינוּ מֶלֶךְ הָעוֹלָם, הַטּוֹב וְהַמֵּטִיב.

On hearing bad news, and said by a mourner before the ritual tearing of the garment:

בָּרוּךְ אַתָּה יהוה אֱלֹהֵינוּ מֶלֶךְ הָעוֹלָם, דַּיַּן הָאֱמֶת.

On hearing personal good news.

בָּרוּךְ אַתָּה יהוה אֱלֹהֵינוּ מֶלֶךְ הָעוֹלָם, שֶׁהֶחֱיָנוּ וְקִיְּמָנוּ וְהִגִּיעָנוּ לַזְּמַן הַזֶּה.

On seeing a place where miracles occurred to oneself or one's family (insert the relevant words):

בָּרוּךְ BLESSED ARE YOU, Lord, our God, King of the universe, Who performed a miracle for me (my father / my mother / my ancestors) in this place.

ON VISITING A CEMETERY

On visiting a cemetery, or seeing a Jewish grave, for the first time in thirty days:

בָּרוּךְ BLESSED ARE YOU, Lord, our God, King of the universe, Who formed you in judgment, Who nourished and sustained you in judgment, Who brought death on you in judgment, Who knows the number of you all in judgment, and Who in the future will restore you to life and maintain you in judgment. Blessed are You, Lord, Reviver of the dead.

אַתָּה YOU, my Master, are forever mighty, You are the Resurrector of the dead, with great power to save. He sustains the living with kindness, He resurrects the dead with great compassion, He supports those who are falling, He heals the sick, He sets the incarcerated free, and He fulfills what He has promised to those who sleep in the dust. Who is like You, O mighty One, and who can be compared to You, O King Who causes death and resurrects, and Who causes salvation to sprout? Trustworthy are You to resurrect the dead.

Upon reaching the grave, it is customary to place one's left hand on the monument and recite the following verses:

ישעיה נח וְנָחֲךָ THE LORD will guide you always, satisfying your thirsty soul, and rescuing your bones. You shall be like a watered garden and like a spring whose water never fails. The ruins of the world will be rebuilt from you, the structures of the generations will be reestablished, and they will call you "the one who repairs the breach and resettles the ways of civilization."

One then adds:

Lie in peace and rest in peace, until the coming of the consoler who will announce peace.

BLESSINGS ON HEARING UNACCUSTOMED NEWS

On hearing good news from which others as well as oneself will benefit:

בָּרוּךְ BLESSED ARE YOU, Lord, our God, King of the universe, Who is good and does good.

On hearing bad news, and said by a mourner before the ritual tearing of the garment:

בָּרוּךְ BLESSED ARE YOU, Lord, our God, King of the universe, the true Judge.

On hearing personal good news.

בָּרוּךְ BLESSED ARE YOU, Lord, our God, King of the universe, Who has given us life, sustained us, and brought us to this time.

ברכות המצוות

On fixing a מזוזה *to the doorpost:*

בָּרוּךְ אַתָּה יהוה אֱלֹהֵינוּ מֶלֶךְ הָעוֹלָם, אֲשֶׁר קִדְּשָׁנוּ בְּמִצְוֹתָיו, וְצִוָּנוּ לִקְבֹּעַ מְזוּזָה.

On making a protective railing around one's roof, or a fence around a pit:

בָּרוּךְ אַתָּה יהוה אֱלֹהֵינוּ מֶלֶךְ הָעוֹלָם, אֲשֶׁר קִדְּשָׁנוּ בְּמִצְוֹתָיו, וְצִוָּנוּ לַעֲשׂוֹת מַעֲקֶה.

On immersing utensils made by or bought from a Gentile:

בָּרוּךְ אַתָּה יהוה אֱלֹהֵינוּ מֶלֶךְ הָעוֹלָם, אֲשֶׁר קִדְּשָׁנוּ בְּמִצְוֹתָיו, וְצִוָּנוּ עַל טְבִילַת כְּלִי (כֵּלִים).

A woman on ritual immersion:

בָּרוּךְ אַתָּה יהוה אֱלֹהֵינוּ מֶלֶךְ הָעוֹלָם, אֲשֶׁר קִדְּשָׁנוּ בְּמִצְוֹתָיו, וְצִוָּנוּ עַל הַטְּבִילָה.

הפרשת חלה

On taking חלה*:*

בָּרוּךְ אַתָּה יהוה אֱלֹהֵינוּ מֶלֶךְ הָעוֹלָם, אֲשֶׁר קִדְּשָׁנוּ בְּמִצְוֹתָיו, וְצִוָּנוּ לְהַפְרִישׁ חַלָּה מִן הָעִסָּה.

*Separate the "*חלה*" dough and say:*

הֲרֵי זוֹ חַלָּה.

Some say:

יְהִי רָצוֹן מִלְּפָנֶיךָ יהוה אֱלֹהֵינוּ וֵאלֹהֵי אֲבוֹתֵינוּ, שֶׁיִּבָּנֶה בֵּית הַמִּקְדָּשׁ בִּמְהֵרָה בְיָמֵינוּ, וְתֵן חֶלְקֵנוּ בְּתוֹרָתֶךָ, וְשָׁם נַעֲבָדְךָ בְּיִרְאָה כִּימֵי
עוֹלָם וּכְשָׁנִים קַדְמֹנִיּוֹת. וְעָרְבָה לַיהוה מִנְחַת יְהוּדָה וִירוּשָׁלָםִ כִּימֵי עוֹלָם מלאכי ג
וּכְשָׁנִים קַדְמֹנִיּוֹת:

The following supplication is recited by married women.

יְהִי רָצוֹן מִלְּפָנֶיךָ יהוה אֱלֹהֵינוּ וֵאלֹהֵי אֲבוֹתֵינוּ, שֶׁהַמִּצְוָה שֶׁל הַפְרָשַׁת חַלָּה תֵּחָשֵׁב כְּאִלּוּ קִיַּמְתִּיהָ בְּכָל פְּרָטֶיהָ וְדִקְדּוּקֶיהָ, וְתֵחָשֵׁב הֲרָמַת הַחַלָּה שֶׁאֲנִי מְרִימָה, כְּמוֹ הַקָּרְבָּן שֶׁהֻקְרַב עַל הַמִּזְבֵּחַ, שֶׁנִּתְקַבֵּל בְּרָצוֹן. וּכְמוֹ

בִּרְכוֹת הַמִּצְוֹת / BLESSINGS ON MITZVOT The obligation to recite a *berakha* over *mitzvot* is of rabbinic origin (*Berakhot* 15a). The sages associated the obligation with the verse, "I have not violated Your commandments or forgotten them" (Deut. 26:13), as if to say, "I

BLESSINGS ON MITZVOT

On fixing a mezuza to the doorpost:

בָּרוּךְ BLESSED ARE YOU, Lord, our God, King of the universe, Who has sanctified us with His commandments, and has commanded us to affix the *mezuza.*

On making a protective railing around one's roof, or a fence around a pit:

בָּרוּךְ BLESSED ARE YOU, Lord, our God, King of the universe, Who has sanctified us with His commandments, and has commanded us to to affix a guard-rail.

On immersing utensils made by or bought from a Gentile:

בָּרוּךְ BLESSED ARE YOU, Lord, our God, King of the universe, Who has sanctified us with His commandments, and has commanded us about immersing a vessel (vessels).

A woman on ritual immersion:

בָּרוּךְ BLESSED ARE YOU, Lord, our God, King of the universe, Who has sanctified us with His commandments, and has commanded us about ritual immersion.

ON TAKING ḤALLA

On taking ḥalla:

בָּרוּךְ BLESSED ARE YOU, Lord, our God, King of the universe, Who has sanctified us with His commandments, and has commanded us to set aside *ḥalla* from the dough.

Separate the ḥalla dough and say:

This is the *ḥalla.*

Some say:

יְהִי רָצוֹן MAY IT BE Your will, Lord our God and God of our fathers, that the Temple be rebuilt speedily in our days and may You grant our portion in Your Torah. We will serve You there in reverence as in the days of antiquity and in years
Mal. 3 gone by. "And may the offering of Judah and Jerusalem be pleasant to the Lord as in the days of antiquity and in years gone by."

The following supplication is recited by married women.

יְהִי רָצוֹן MAY IT BE Your will, Lord our God and God of our fathers, that this commandment of separating *ḥalla* be considered as if I had fulfilled it in all its details and specifics. And let the raising of the *ḥalla,* as I raise it now, be considered as a sacrifice, sacrificed on the altar, received with favor. And just as

---

have not forgotten to bless You or invoke Your name over the commandments" (*Sifrei, Berakhot* 40b.) Even as regards *mitzvot* of rabbinic origin (such as Ḥanukka lights), which are not found in the Torah, we recite a *berakha* praising Him as the One "Who has commanded us" insofar as He has in fact commanded us to follow the decrees of the sages, as the Torah (Deut. 17:11) states (*Shabbat* 23a).

שֶׁלְּפָנִים הָיְתָה הַחַלָּה נְתוּנָה לַכֹּהֵן וְהָיְתָה זוֹ לְכַפָּרַת עֲוֹנוֹת, כָּךְ תִּהְיֶה לְכַפָּרָה לַעֲוֹנוֹתַי, וְאָז אֶהְיֶה כְּאִלּוּ נוֹלַדְתִּי מֵחָדָשׁ, נְקִיָּה מֵחֵטְא וְעָוֹן. וְאוּכַל לְקַיֵּם מִצְוַת שַׁבַּת קֹדֶשׁ וְהַיָּמִים הַטּוֹבִים עִם בַּעְלִי (וִילָדֵינוּ), לִהְיוֹת נִזּוֹנִים מִקְּדֻשַּׁת הַיָּמִים הָאֵלֶּה. וּמֵהַשְׁפָּעָתָהּ שֶׁל מִצְוַת חַלָּה, יִהְיוּ יְלָדֵינוּ נִזּוֹנִים תָּמִיד מִיָּדָיו שֶׁל הַקָּדוֹשׁ בָּרוּךְ הוּא, בְּרֹב רַחֲמָיו וַחֲסָדָיו, וּבְרֹב אַהֲבָה, וְשֶׁתִּתְקַבֵּל מִצְוַת חַלָּה כְּאִלּוּ נָתַתִּי מַעֲשֵׂר. וּכְשֵׁם שֶׁהִנְנִי מְקַיֶּמֶת מִצְוַת חַלָּה בְּכָל לֵב, כָּךְ יִתְעוֹרְרוּ רַחֲמָיו שֶׁל הַקָּדוֹשׁ בָּרוּךְ הוּא לְשָׁמְרֵנִי מִצַּעַר וּמִמַּכְאוֹבִים כָּל הַיָּמִים, אָמֵן.

ברכות למי ששכח

As indicated in detail on page 226, if one accidentally omitted the special שבת *or* יום טוב *insertions in* ברכת המזון*, compensatory blessings must be said. In all cases, the conclusion of the blessing* (בָּרוּךְ אַתָּה יהוה, מְקַדֵּשׁ...) *is said only at the first two meals of* שבת *and/or* ימים טובים (*except* חול המועד)*. After the appropriate blessing continue with* ברכת הטוב והמטיב (*page 228*).

If one forgot רְצֵה *on* שבת*:*

בָּרוּךְ אַתָּה יהוה אֱלֹהֵינוּ מֶלֶךְ הָעוֹלָם, אֲשֶׁר נָתַן שַׁבָּתוֹת לִמְנוּחָה לְעַמּוֹ יִשְׂרָאֵל בְּאַהֲבָה, לְאוֹת וְלִבְרִית. בָּרוּךְ אַתָּה יהוה, מְקַדֵּשׁ הַשַּׁבָּת.

If one forgot יַעֲלֶה וְיָבוֹא *on* ראש חודש*:*

בָּרוּךְ אַתָּה יהוה אֱלֹהֵינוּ מֶלֶךְ הָעוֹלָם, אֲשֶׁר נָתַן רָאשֵׁי חֳדָשִׁים לְעַמּוֹ יִשְׂרָאֵל לְזִכָּרוֹן.

If one forgot רְצֵה *and* יַעֲלֶה וְיָבוֹא *on* ראש חודש *that falls on* שבת*:*

בָּרוּךְ אַתָּה יהוה אֱלֹהֵינוּ מֶלֶךְ הָעוֹלָם, אֲשֶׁר נָתַן שַׁבָּתוֹת לִמְנוּחָה לְעַמּוֹ יִשְׂרָאֵל בְּאַהֲבָה, לְאוֹת וְלִבְרִית, וְרָאשֵׁי חֳדָשִׁים לְזִכָּרוֹן. בָּרוּךְ אַתָּה יהוה, מְקַדֵּשׁ הַשַּׁבָּת וְיִשְׂרָאֵל וְרָאשֵׁי חֳדָשִׁים.

If one forgot יַעֲלֶה וְיָבוֹא *on a* יום טוב*:*

בָּרוּךְ אַתָּה יהוה אֱלֹהֵינוּ מֶלֶךְ הָעוֹלָם, אֲשֶׁר נָתַן יָמִים טוֹבִים לְעַמּוֹ יִשְׂרָאֵל לְשָׂשׂוֹן וּלְשִׂמְחָה, אֶת יוֹם

בפסח: חַג הַמַּצּוֹת הַזֶּה. / בשבועות: חַג הַשָּׁבוּעוֹת הַזֶּה. / בסוכות: חַג הַסֻּכּוֹת הַזֶּה. / בשמיני עצרת ושמחת תורה: הַשְּׁמִינִי חַג הָעֲצֶרֶת הַזֶּה.

בָּרוּךְ אַתָּה יהוה, מְקַדֵּשׁ יִשְׂרָאֵל וְהַזְּמַנִּים.

in the past the *ḥalla* would be given to the priest, and this was for the atonement of iniquities, so may this now be for the atonement of my iniquities, and then I shall be as if I had been born afresh, clean of all sin and iniquity. And I will be able to fulfill the commandment of the holy Sabbath and the festivals with my husband (and our children), and be nourished by these days. And under the influence of the commandment of *ḥalla*, may our children be nourished at all times from the hands of the Holy One, blessed is He, in all His great mercy and loving-kindness, with great love, and may this commandment of *ḥalla* be received as if I had given a tithe. And just as I now fulfill the commandment to take *ḥalla* with all my heart, so may the mercy of the Holy One, blessed is He, be roused to guard me from trouble and pain at all times, Amen.

COMPENSATORY BLESSINGS

As indicated in detail on page 227, if one accidentally omitted the special Shabbat or Yom Tov insertions in Birkat HaMazon, compensatory blessings must be said. In all cases, the conclusion of the blessing (Blessed are You...Who sanctifies...) is said only at the first two meals of Shabbat and/or Yamim Tovim (except Ḥol HaMo'ed). After the appropriate blessing continue with the Blessing of God's Goodness (page 229).

If one forgot Retzeh on Shabbat:

בָּרוּךְ BLESSED ARE YOU, Lord, our God, King of the universe, Who gave Sabbaths for contentment to His people, Israel, with love, as a sign and a convenant. Blessed are You, Lord, Who sanctifies the Sabbath.

If one forgot Ya'aleh VeYavo on Rosh Ḥodesh:

בָּרוּךְ BLESSED ARE YOU, Lord, our God, King of the universe, Who gave days of Rosh Ḥodesh to His people, Israel, as a remembrance.

If one forgot Retzeh and Ya'aleh VeYavo on Rosh Ḥodesh that falls on Shabbat:

בָּרוּךְ BLESSED ARE YOU, Lord, our God, King of the universe, Who gave Sabbaths for contentment to His people, Israel, with love, as a sign and a convenant and days of Rosh Ḥodesh for a remembrance. Blessed are You, Lord, Who sanctifies the Sabbath, Israel, and days of Rosh Ḥodesh.

If one forgot Ya'aleh VeYavo on a Yom Tov:

בָּרוּךְ BLESSED ARE YOU, Lord, our God, King of the universe, Who gave festivals to His people, Israel, for happiness and gladness, this Festival of

On Pesaḥ: Matzot. / *On Shavuot:* Shavuot. / *On Sukkot:* Sukkot.

On Shemini Atzeret & Simḥat Torah: the eighth day, this Festival of Atzeret.

Blessed are You, Lord, Who sanctifies Israel, and the seasons.

If one forgot יַעֲלֶה וְיָבוֹא *and* רְצֵה *on a* יום טוב *that falls on* שבת*:*

בָּרוּךְ אַתָּה יהוה אֱלֹהֵינוּ מֶלֶךְ הָעוֹלָם, אֲשֶׁר נָתַן שַׁבָּתוֹת לִמְנוּחָה לְעַמּוֹ יִשְׂרָאֵל בְּאַהֲבָה, לְאוֹת וְלִבְרִית, וְיָמִים טוֹבִים לְשָׂשׂוֹן וּלְשִׂמְחָה, אֶת יוֹם

בפסח: חַג הַמַּצּוֹת הַזֶּה. / בשבועות: חַג הַשָּׁבוּעוֹת הַזֶּה. / בסוכות: חַג הַסֻּכּוֹת הַזֶּה. / בשמיני עצרת ושמחת תורה: הַשְּׁמִינִי חַג הָעֲצֶרֶת הַזֶּה.

בָּרוּךְ אַתָּה יהוה, מְקַדֵּשׁ הַשַּׁבָּת וְיִשְׂרָאֵל וְהַזְּמַנִּים.

If one forgot יַעֲלֶה וְיָבוֹא *on* חול המועד*:*

בָּרוּךְ אַתָּה יהוה אֱלֹהֵינוּ מֶלֶךְ הָעוֹלָם, אֲשֶׁר נָתַן מוֹעֲדִים לְעַמּוֹ יִשְׂרָאֵל לְשָׂשׂוֹן וּלְשִׂמְחָה, אֶת יוֹם

בפסח: חַג הַמַּצּוֹת הַזֶּה. / בסוכות: חַג הַסֻּכּוֹת הַזֶּה.

If one forgot יַעֲלֶה וְיָבוֹא *and* רְצֵה *on* חול המועד *that falls on* שבת*:*

בָּרוּךְ אַתָּה יהוה אֱלֹהֵינוּ מֶלֶךְ הָעוֹלָם, אֲשֶׁר נָתַן שַׁבָּתוֹת לִמְנוּחָה לְעַמּוֹ יִשְׂרָאֵל בְּאַהֲבָה, לְאוֹת וְלִבְרִית, וּמוֹעֲדִים לְשָׂשׂוֹן וּלְשִׂמְחָה, אֶת יוֹם

בפסח: חַג הַמַּצּוֹת הַזֶּה. / בסוכות: חַג הַסֻּכּוֹת הַזֶּה.

בָּרוּךְ אַתָּה יהוה, מְקַדֵּשׁ יִשְׂרָאֵל וְהַזְּמַנִּים.

If one forgot יַעֲלֶה וְיָבוֹא *on* ראש השנה*:*

בָּרוּךְ אַתָּה יהוה אֱלֹהֵינוּ מֶלֶךְ הָעוֹלָם, אֲשֶׁר נָתַן יָמִים טוֹבִים לְעַמּוֹ יִשְׂרָאֵל אֶת יוֹם הַזִּכָּרוֹן הַזֶּה. בָּרוּךְ אַתָּה יהוה, מְקַדֵּשׁ יִשְׂרָאֵל וְיוֹם הַזִּכָּרוֹן.

If one forgot יַעֲלֶה וְיָבוֹא *and* רְצֵה *on* ראש השנה *that falls on* שבת*:*

בָּרוּךְ אַתָּה יהוה אֱלֹהֵינוּ מֶלֶךְ הָעוֹלָם, אֲשֶׁר נָתַן שַׁבָּתוֹת לִמְנוּחָה לְעַמּוֹ יִשְׂרָאֵל בְּאַהֲבָה, לְאוֹת וְלִבְרִית, וְיָמִים טוֹבִים לְיִשְׂרָאֵל, אֶת יוֹם הַזִּכָּרוֹן הַזֶּה. בָּרוּךְ אַתָּה יהוה, מְקַדֵּשׁ הַשַּׁבָּת וְיִשְׂרָאֵל וְיוֹם הַזִּכָּרוֹן.

עירובין

The procedures and blessings for עירובין *can be found on page 348.*

If one forgot Retzeh and Ya'aleh VeYavo on a Yom Tov that falls on Shabbat:

בָּרוּךְ BLESSED ARE YOU, Lord, our God, King of the universe, Who gave Sabbaths for contentment to His people, Israel, with love, as a sign and a convenant, and festivals for happiness and gladness, this Festival of

On Pesaḥ: Matzot. / *On Shavuot:* Shavuot. / *On Sukkot:* Sukkot.
On Shemini Atzeret & Simḥat Torah: the eighth day, this Festival of Atzeret.

Blessed are You, Lord, Who sanctifies the Sabbath, Israel, and the seasons.

If one forgot Ya'aleh VeYavo on Ḥol HaMo'ed:

בָּרוּךְ BLESSED ARE YOU, Lord, our God, King of the universe, Who appointed festivals to His people, Israel, for happiness and gladness, this Festival day of

On Pesaḥ: Matzot. / *On Sukkot:* Sukkot.

If one forgot Retzeh and Ya'aleh VeYavo on Ḥol HaMo'ed that falls on Shabbat:

בָּרוּךְ BLESSED ARE YOU, Lord, our God, King of the universe, Who gave Sabbaths for contentment to His people, Israel, with love, as a sign and a convenant, and appointed festivals for happiness and gladness, this Festival day of

On Pesaḥ: Matzot. / *On Sukkot:* Sukkot.

Blessed are You, Lord, Who sanctifies the Sabbath, Israel, and the seasons.

If one forgot Ya'aleh VeYavo on Rosh HaShana:

בָּרוּךְ BLESSED ARE YOU, Lord, our God, King of the universe, Who gave appointed festivals to His people, Israel, this Day of Rememberance. Blessed are You, Lord, Who sanctifies Israel and the Day of Rememberance.

If one forgot Retzeh and Ya'aleh VeYavo on Rosh HaShana that falls on Shabbat:

בָּרוּךְ BLESSED ARE YOU, Lord, our God, King of the universe, Who gave Sabbaths for contentment to His people, Israel, with love, as a sign and a convenant, and appointed festivals to Israel, this Day of Rememberance. Blessed are You, Lord, Who sanctifies the Sabbath, Israel, and the Day of Rememberance.

EIRUVIN

The procedures and blessings for Eiruvin can be found on page 349.

עמידה בעת צרה – הבינני

In special cases of urgency only, the following short form of the עמידה *may be said. First say the first three* ברכות *of the* עמידה *from* אֲדֹנָי, שְׂפָתַי תִּפְתָּח *on page 106 until* הַקָּדוֹשׁ *on page 112, then say:*

הֲבִינֵנוּ יהוה אֱלֹהֵינוּ לָדַעַת דְּרָכֶיךָ, וּמוֹל אֶת לְבָבֵנוּ לְיִרְאָתֶךָ, וְתִסְלַח לָנוּ לִהְיוֹת גְּאוּלִים, וְרַחֲקֵנוּ מִמַּכְאוֹב, וְדַשְּׁנֵנוּ בִּנְאוֹת אַרְצֶךָ, וּנְפוּצוֹתֵינוּ מֵאַרְבַּע תְּקַבֵּץ, וְהַתּוֹעִים עַל דַּעְתְּךָ יִשָּׁפֵטוּ, וְעַל הָרְשָׁעִים תָּנִיף יָדֶךָ, וְיִשְׂמְחוּ צַדִּיקִים בְּבִנְיַן עִירֶךָ וּבְתִקּוּן הֵיכָלֶךָ, וּבִצְמִיחַת קֶרֶן לְדָוִד עַבְדֶּךָ וּבַעֲרִיכַת נֵר לְבֶן יִשַׁי מְשִׁיחֶךָ, טֶרֶם נִקְרָא אַתָּה תַעֲנֶה. בָּרוּךְ אַתָּה יהוה, שׁוֹמֵעַ תְּפִלָּה.

Continue with the final three ברכות*, from* רְצֵה *on page 124 until the end of the* עמידה*.*

תפילה בזמן בצורת בישראל

In times of drought in ארץ ישראל*, add prior to* רְפָאֵנוּ *on page 114:*

וַעֲנֵנוּ בּוֹרֵא עוֹלָם בְּמִדַּת הָרַחֲמִים, בּוֹחֵר בְּעַמּוֹ יִשְׂרָאֵל לְהוֹדִיעַ גָּדְלוֹ וְהַדְרַת כְּבוֹדוֹ. שׁוֹמֵעַ תְּפִלָּה, תֵּן טַל וּמָטָר עַל פְּנֵי הָאֲדָמָה, וְתַשְׂבִּיעַ אֶת הָעוֹלָם כֻּלּוֹ מִטּוּבֶךָ, וּמַלֵּא יָדֵינוּ מִבִּרְכוֹתֶיךָ וּמֵעֹשֶׁר מַתְּנַת יָדֶךָ. שְׁמֹר וְהַצֵּל שָׁנָה זוֹ מִכָּל דָּבָר רָע, וּמִכָּל מִינֵי מַשְׁחִית וּמִכָּל מִינֵי פֻרְעָנִיּוֹת, וַעֲשֵׂה לָהּ תִּקְוָה וְאַחֲרִית שָׁלוֹם. חוּס וְרַחֵם עָלֵינוּ וְעַל כָּל תְּבוּאָתֵנוּ וּפֵרוֹתֵינוּ, וּבָרְכֵנוּ בְּגִשְׁמֵי בְרָכָה, וְנִזְכֶּה לְחַיִּים וְשֹׂבַע וְשָׁלוֹם כַּשָּׁנִים הַטּוֹבוֹת. וְהָסֵר מִמֶּנּוּ דֶּבֶר וְחֶרֶב וְרָעָב, וְחַיָּה רָעָה וּשְׁבִי וּבִזָּה, וְיֵצֶר הָרָע וָחֳלָיִים רָעִים וְקָשִׁים וּמְאֹרָעוֹת רָעִים וְקָשִׁים. וּגְזֹר עָלֵינוּ גְּזֵרוֹת טוֹבוֹת מִלְּפָנֶיךָ, וְיִגֹּלוּ רַחֲמֶיךָ עַל מִדּוֹתֶיךָ, וְתִתְנַהֵג עִם בָּנֶיךָ בְּמִדַּת הָרַחֲמִים, וְקַבֵּל בְּרַחֲמִים וּבְרָצוֹן אֶת תְּפִלָּתֵנוּ.

AMIDA IN CASES OF URGENCY – HAVINEINU

In special cases of urgency only, the following short form of the Amida may be said. First say the first three blessings of the Amida from "O Lord" on page 107 until "the holy God" page 113, then say:

הֲבִינֵנוּ GRANT US understanding, LORD our God, to know Your ways. Sensitize our hearts so that we may revere You, and forgive us so that we may be redeemed. Keep us far from suffering and satisfy us with the pastures of Your land. Gather our scattered people from the four quarters of the earth. May those who go astray be judged according to Your will: raise Your hand against the wicked. May the righteous rejoice in the rebuilding of Your city, the restoration of Your Temple, the flowering of Your servant David's glory, and the radiant light of the son of Jesse, Your anointed. May You answer us even before we call. Blessed are You, LORD, who hears prayer.

Continue with the final three blessings from "Look favorably" on page 125 until the end of the Amida.

PRAYER IN TIMES OF DROUGHT IN ISRAEL

In times of drought in Israel, add prior to "Heal us, Lord" on page 115:

וַעֲנֵנוּ AND ANSWER US Creator of the universe, with the attribute of mercy, He Who chooses His people Israel to make known His greatness and the splendor of His glory. He Who hears prayer, grant dew and rain upon the face of the earth and satisfy the entire universe from Your bounty. Fill our hands from Your blessings and from the richness of the gift of Your hands. Protect and rescue this year from every evil thing, and from all manner of destruction and punishment, and create for it hope and a peaceful end. Have pity and compassion on us and on all our crops and our fruits, and bless us with rain of blessing. And may we merit life, satisfaction, and peace, as in the good years. Remove from us epidemics, violence, and hunger, harmful animals, captivity and plundering, the Evil Inclination, severe and harsh diseases, and severe and harsh events. Decree upon us goodly decrees before You, and may Your mercy prevail over Your other Attributes, so that You conduct Yourself with Your children with the attribute of mercy, and accept our prayers with compassion and favor.

מנחה לחול

The line beginning with פּוֹתֵחַ אֶת־יָדֶךָ *should be said with special concentration.*

אַשְׁרֵי יוֹשְׁבֵי בֵיתֶךָ, עוֹד יְהַלְלוּךָ סֶּלָה: תהלים פד

אַשְׁרֵי הָעָם שֶׁכָּכָה לּוֹ, אַשְׁרֵי הָעָם שֶׁיהוה אֱלֹהָיו: תהלים קמד

תְּהִלָּה לְדָוִד תהלים קמה

אֲרוֹמִמְךָ אֱלוֹהַי הַמֶּלֶךְ, וַאֲבָרְכָה שִׁמְךָ לְעוֹלָם וָעֶד:

בְּכָל־יוֹם אֲבָרְכֶךָּ, וַאֲהַלְלָה שִׁמְךָ לְעוֹלָם וָעֶד:

גָּדוֹל יהוה וּמְהֻלָּל מְאֹד, וְלִגְדֻלָּתוֹ אֵין חֵקֶר:

דּוֹר לְדוֹר יְשַׁבַּח מַעֲשֶׂיךָ, וּגְבוּרֹתֶיךָ יַגִּידוּ:

הֲדַר כְּבוֹד הוֹדֶךָ, וְדִבְרֵי נִפְלְאֹתֶיךָ אָשִׂיחָה:

וֶעֱזוּז נוֹרְאֹתֶיךָ יֹאמֵרוּ, וּגְדוּלָּתְךָ אֲסַפְּרֶנָּה:

זֵכֶר רַב־טוּבְךָ יַבִּיעוּ, וְצִדְקָתְךָ יְרַנֵּנוּ:

חַנּוּן וְרַחוּם יהוה, אֶרֶךְ אַפַּיִם וּגְדָל־חָסֶד:

טוֹב־יהוה לַכֹּל, וְרַחֲמָיו עַל־כָּל־מַעֲשָׂיו:

יוֹדוּךָ יהוה כָּל־מַעֲשֶׂיךָ, וַחֲסִידֶיךָ יְבָרְכוּכָה:

כְּבוֹד מַלְכוּתְךָ יֹאמֵרוּ, וּגְבוּרָתְךָ יְדַבֵּרוּ:

לְהוֹדִיעַ לִבְנֵי הָאָדָם גְּבוּרֹתָיו, וּכְבוֹד הֲדַר מַלְכוּתוֹ:

מנחה לחול / MINHA FOR WEEKDAYS

The *Minḥa* service was instituted in place of the daily Temple afternoon sacrifice. The name *Minḥa* is the biblical term for the meal-offering that accompanied most Temple sacrifices. In Rambam's view the Torah obligates us to pray only once a day, thus the addition by rabbinic decree of a second daily service is a "gift" (*minḥa*) to God (*Be'urei HaTefilla*).

When we interrupt our workday to recognize God's role in our life, we demonstrate a profound degree of submission before Him. When we engage in midday *Minḥa* services with a minyan, we enjoy numerous benefits, including spiritual comradeship with like-minded fellow Jews.

R. Yehuda Halevi (Kuzari 3:5) explains that praying three times a day is analogous to eating three meals each day. Just as our bodies need and look forward to the physical sustenance that food provides, so do our souls depend on the spiritual nourishment and stimulation provided by the thrice-daily prayer experience.

אַשְׁרֵי יוֹשְׁבֵי בֵיתֶךָ – *Happy are they who dwell in Your house.* As explained in the *Pesukei DeZimra*, the opening verse of *Ashrei* was added to Psalm 145 to teach us that

MINḤA FOR WEEKDAYS

The line beginning with "You open Your hand" should be said with special concentration.

Ps. 84 אַשְׁרֵי HAPPY are those who dwell in Your house.
They will forever praise You. Selah.

Ps. 144 HAPPY is the people that has this.
Happy is the people whose God is the Lord.

Ps. 145 A PRAISE OF DAVID.

א I exalt You, my God, the King,
and I will bless Your name forever and ever.

ב Every day I will bless You,
and I will praise Your name forever and ever.

ג Great is the Lord, and very praiseworthy,
and His greatness is boundless.

ד One generation lauds Your works to another,
and they declare Your mighty deeds.

ה I speak of the splendid glory of Your majesty
and of Your wondrous works,

ו And they speak of the might of Your awesome deeds,
and I declare Your greatness.

ז They express the renown of Your great goodness,
and sing of Your righteousness.

ח Gracious and merciful is the Lord,
slow to anger and great in loving-kindness.

ט The Lord is good to all,
and His mercies are upon all His works.

י All Your works thank You,
O Lord, and Your pious ones bless You.

כ They describe the glory of Your kingdom,
and speak of Your might,

ל To make known to the sons of man His mighty deeds,
and the glorious splendor of His kingdom.

---

meaningful prayer requires proper mental preparation. This is particularly true of *Minḥa* which generally occurs in the midst of our busy schedules, and in which the *Amida*

מַלְכוּתְךָ מַלְכוּת כָּל־עֹלָמִים, וּמֶמְשַׁלְתְּךָ בְּכָל־דּוֹר וָדֹר:
סוֹמֵךְ יהוה לְכָל־הַנֹּפְלִים, וְזוֹקֵף לְכָל־הַכְּפוּפִים:
עֵינֵי־כֹל אֵלֶיךָ יְשַׂבֵּרוּ, וְאַתָּה נוֹתֵן־לָהֶם אֶת־אָכְלָם בְּעִתּוֹ:
פּוֹתֵחַ אֶת־יָדֶךָ, וּמַשְׂבִּיעַ לְכָל־חַי רָצוֹן:
צַדִּיק יהוה בְּכָל־דְּרָכָיו, וְחָסִיד בְּכָל־מַעֲשָׂיו:
קָרוֹב יהוה לְכָל־קֹרְאָיו, לְכֹל אֲשֶׁר יִקְרָאֻהוּ בֶאֱמֶת:
רְצוֹן־יְרֵאָיו יַעֲשֶׂה, וְאֶת־שַׁוְעָתָם יִשְׁמַע וְיוֹשִׁיעֵם:
שׁוֹמֵר יהוה אֶת־כָּל־אֹהֲבָיו, וְאֵת כָּל־הָרְשָׁעִים יַשְׁמִיד:
◄ תְּהִלַּת יהוה יְדַבֶּר פִּי, וִיבָרֵךְ כָּל־בָּשָׂר שֵׁם קָדְשׁוֹ לְעוֹלָם וָעֶד:
וַאֲנַחְנוּ נְבָרֵךְ יָהּ מֵעַתָּה וְעַד־עוֹלָם, הַלְלוּיָהּ: תהלים קטו

חצי קדיש

ש״ץ: **יִתְגַּדַּל** וְיִתְקַדַּשׁ שְׁמֵהּ רַבָּא (קהל: אָמֵן) בְּעָלְמָא דִּי בְרָא כִרְעוּתֵהּ, וְיַמְלִיךְ מַלְכוּתֵהּ בְּחַיֵּיכוֹן וּבְיוֹמֵיכוֹן וּבְחַיֵּי דְכָל בֵּית יִשְׂרָאֵל, בַּעֲגָלָא וּבִזְמַן קָרִיב, וְאִמְרוּ אָמֵן. (קהל: אָמֵן)

קהל וש״ץ: יְהֵא שְׁמֵהּ רַבָּא מְבָרַךְ לְעָלַם וּלְעָלְמֵי עָלְמַיָּא.

ש״ץ: יִתְבָּרַךְ וְיִשְׁתַּבַּח וְיִתְפָּאַר וְיִתְרוֹמַם וְיִתְנַשֵּׂא, וְיִתְהַדָּר וְיִתְעַלֶּה וְיִתְהַלָּל שְׁמֵהּ דְּקֻדְשָׁא בְּרִיךְ הוּא (קהל: בְּרִיךְ הוּא) לְעֵלָּא מִן כָּל בִּרְכָתָא / בעשרת ימי תשובה: לְעֵלָּא (וּ)לְעֵלָּא מִכָּל בִּרְכָתָא/ וְשִׁירָתָא, תֻּשְׁבְּחָתָא וְנֶחֱמָתָא דַּאֲמִירָן בְּעָלְמָא, וְאִמְרוּ אָמֵן. (קהל: אָמֵן)

On fast days, go to הוצאת ספר תורה *on page 158. The* קריאת התורה *and* הפטרה *for fast days are on pages 1133–1134. After the* תורה *is returned to the* ארון קודש, *the* שליח ציבור *says* חצי קדיש.

---

occurs within moments of the beginning of the service. Reciting *Ashrei* at the outset of *Minḥa* helps us establish the correct state of mind to enter into God's presence in the *Amida*. Thus one should recite it slowly and carefully, optimally while seated, so as to be mentally prepared for the *Amida* that follows (R. Joseph B. Soloveitchik).

מ Your kingdom is a kingdom for all times,
and Your dominion is for every generation.
ס The Lord supports all who fall
and raises up all who are bowed down.
ע The eyes of all await You,
and You give them their food in its time.
פ You open Your hand,
and You satisfy the desire of every living thing.
צ The Lord is righteous in all His ways
and kind in all His works.
ק The Lord is near to all who address Him,
to all who address Him in truth.
ר He does the will of those who fear Him,
and He hears their cry and saves them.
ש The Lord preserves all who love Him,
but all the wicked He destroys.
ת ▸ May my mouth speak the praise of the Lord,
and may all flesh bless His holy name forever and ever.

Ps. 115 But we will bless the Lord from now and forevermore. Praise the Lord.

HALF KADDISH

Leader: **יִתְגַּדַּל** EXALTED AND HALLOWED may God's great name be, in the world He created as He willed. May He reign in your lifetimes and in your days, and in the lifetime of the whole house of Israel, speedily and soon, and say, Amen.

All: May His great name be blessed forever and all time.

Leader: Blessed and praised, honored, extolled, glorified, adored and exalted above all be the name of the Holy One, blessed is He, (*Between Rosh Hashana & Yom Kippur:* above and) beyond any blessing, hymn, praise, or expressions of consolation that may be uttered in this world, and say, Amen.

On fast days, turn to the Reading of the Torah on page 159. The Torah Reading and Haftara for fast days are on pages 1133–1134. *After the Torah is returned to the Ark, the Leader says Half Kaddish.*

עמידה

One begins the עמידה *by taking three steps forward (OḤ 95:1). According to some traditions, one should first take three steps back before moving forward (MB 95:3). The* עמידה *is recited with one's feet together. One should try to concentrate on the simple meaning of the words of the* עמידה *with the awareness throughout that one is standing in the presence of the Almighty (OḤ 98:1 and MB 98:1). At the points indicated by* ˅*, bend the knees at the first word, bow at the second, and stand straight before saying God's name.*

כִּי שֵׁם יהוה אֶקְרָא, הָבוּ גֹדֶל לֵאלֹהֵינוּ: דברים לב
אֲדֹנָי, שְׂפָתַי תִּפְתָּח, וּפִי יַגִּיד תְּהִלָּתֶךָ: תהלים נא

אבות

˅בָּרוּךְ אַתָּה יהוה, אֱלֹהֵינוּ וֵאלֹהֵי אֲבוֹתֵינוּ, אֱלֹהֵי אַבְרָהָם, אֱלֹהֵי יִצְחָק, וֵאלֹהֵי יַעֲקֹב, הָאֵל הַגָּדוֹל הַגִּבּוֹר וְהַנּוֹרָא, אֵל עֶלְיוֹן, גּוֹמֵל חֲסָדִים טוֹבִים, וְקוֹנֵה הַכֹּל, וְזוֹכֵר חַסְדֵי אָבוֹת, וּמֵבִיא גוֹאֵל לִבְנֵי בְנֵיהֶם לְמַעַן שְׁמוֹ בְּאַהֲבָה.

עֲמִידָה / AMIDA

While we can certainly pray to God to petition Him for our needs, it is best when praying to focus on His praises. For God knows very well what we need and what we deserve. Thus the *Amida* starts by focusing us on His greatness, compassion, and infinite ability to help us in ways that are beyond our comprehension. This realization can in itself cause God's will to change for the good. It is similar to a child who expresses appreciation to a parent for all that the parent has done, and as a result the parent is moved to help the child even more (*Sefat Emet*).

אָבוֹת / PATRIARCHS

In *Hilkhot Tefilla* 4:15, Rambam rules that one who recites the *Amida* without כַּוָּנָה (concentration) must repeat it. This implies that concentration is required for the entire *Amida*. Yet in *Hilkhot Tefilla* 10:1 he also rules that as long as there was proper concentration during the first *berakha* of the *Amida*, repetition is unnecessary. We can reconcile these two rulings as follows: for Rambam there are two kinds of *kavana* when praying: the first is to be intensely aware that one is (a) fulfilling the commandment to pray, and (b) standing in God's presence. Absent this awareness, one is not praying but simply mouthing words, hence repetition is necessary. The second refers to concentrating on the specific meaning of the words of prayer. In the first *berakha* of the *Amida* we are required to focus on both kinds of *kavana*. Failing that, we must repeat the *Amida*. But in the rest of the *Amida*, as long as we are fully aware that we are engaging in prayer before God, whether or not we concentrate on the meaning of the words, we have fulfilled the minimal requirement of prayer, hence no repetition is called for (R. Hayyim Halevi Soloveitchik).

As a practical matter, however, subsequent authorities recognized that while earlier generations were fully capable of such sustained concentration, later generations were not so endowed. Thus in fourteenth-century Provence, the Meiri commented (on *Berakhot* 30b) that "in these generations when such כַּוָּנָה is less prevalent one need not repeat the *Amida*, as long as one honestly tries to have כַּוָּנָה to the best of one's ability, in a God-fearing spirit." So too, the Rema (*OḤ* 101:1) in the sixteenth century saw no need to repeat the *Amida* in such circumstances, while the Ḥazon Ish (*Ma'aseh Ish*

AMIDA

One begins the Amida by taking three steps forward (OḤ 95:1). According to some traditions, one should first take three steps back before moving forward (MB 95:3). The Amida is recited with one's feet together. One should try to concentrate on the simple meaning of the words of the Amida with the awareness throughout that one is standing in the presence of the Almighty (OḤ 98:1 and MB 98:1). At the points indicated by ▾, bend the knees at the first word, bow at the second, and stand straight before saying God's name.

Deut. 32 WHEN I proclaim the name of the LORD, ascribe greatness to our God.

Ps. 51 "O my Master, open my lips, and my mouth will relate Your praise."

PATRIARCHS

▾ בָּרוּךְ BLESSED ARE YOU, LORD, our God and the God of our fathers, the God of Abraham, the God of Isaac, and the God of Jacob, the God Who is great, mighty, and awesome, God most exalted, Who bestows rewards of benevolent kindness, Who is the Creator of everything, Who remembers all the kind acts of the fathers, and Who brings a redeemer to their children's children, for the sake of His name, with love.

7:84) in the twentieth century similarly wrote that "unlike in earlier times, in more recent generations God hears our prayers even if they are not as focused they should be" (R. Shalom Baum).

אֱלֹהֵינוּ וֵאלֹהֵי אֲבוֹתֵינוּ – *Our God and God of our fathers.* The *Amida* refers to Him first as "our God," and only thereafter as "the God of our fathers," even though chronologically He was the God of our fathers before He became our own God. The reason is that it is human nature to place greater value on having a direct and personal connection to Him, rather than to have to depend on relationships experienced by others who preceded us. When there is a personal linkage we naturally invest greater energies in sustaining that relationship. Therefore the *Amida* focuses us immediately on "*our* God," the One with Whom we have a personal relationship, and the One with Whom our patriarchs had their own personal relationships (R. Menaḥem Mendel Schneerson).

הַגָּדוֹל הַגִּבּוֹר וְהַנּוֹרָא – *Who is great, mighty and awesome.* These three terms correspond to the qualities of Abraham (חֶסֶד or loving-kindness), Isaac (גְבוּרָה or strength) and Jacob (תִּפְאֶרֶת or splendor) respectively (Ya'avetz).

לְמַעַן שְׁמוֹ – *For the sake of His name.* We

For laws regarding "The repetition of the *Amida*," see page 107.

HEICHE KEDUSHA ("ABBREVIATED AMIDA REPETITION")

When there is not enough time to complete the *Amida* repetition and *Taḥanun* before sunset, opinions vary. The *Shulḥan Arukh* favors the Leader immediately reciting the *Amida* through *Kedusha*, then continuing silently. When the Leader begins immediately, the *Mishna Berura* favors the congregation starting the silent *Amida* only after reciting *Kedusha*, while R. Joseph B. Soloveitchik favors starting the *Amida* together with the Leader.

בעשרת ימי תשובה: זָכְרֵנוּ לְחַיִּים, מֶלֶךְ חָפֵץ בַּחַיִּים, וְכָתְבֵנוּ בְּסֵפֶר הַחַיִּים, לְמַעַנְךָ אֱלֹהִים חַיִּים.

(*If forgotten, no corrective action is necessary.*)

מֶלֶךְ עוֹזֵר וּמוֹשִׁיעַ וּמָגֵן. ▾בָּרוּךְ אַתָּה יהוה, מָגֵן אַבְרָהָם.

גבורות

אַתָּה גִּבּוֹר לְעוֹלָם, אֲדֹנָי, מְחַיֵּה מֵתִים אַתָּה, רַב לְהוֹשִׁיעַ.

בחורף: מַשִּׁיב הָרְוּחַ וּמוֹרִיד הַגֶּשֶׁם

מְכַלְכֵּל חַיִּים בְּחֶסֶד, מְחַיֵּה מֵתִים בְּרַחֲמִים רַבִּים, סוֹמֵךְ נוֹפְלִים, וְרוֹפֵא חוֹלִים, וּמַתִּיר אֲסוּרִים, וּמְקַיֵּם אֱמוּנָתוֹ לִישֵׁנֵי עָפָר. מִי כָמְוֹךָ, בַּעַל גְּבוּרוֹת, וּמִי דּוֹמֶה לָּךְ, מֶלֶךְ, מֵמִית וּמְחַיֶּה וּמַצְמִיחַ יְשׁוּעָה.

בעשרת ימי תשובה: מִי כָמְוֹךָ אַב הָרַחֲמִים, זוֹכֵר יְצוּרָיו לְחַיִּים בְּרַחֲמִים.

(*If forgotten, no corrective action is necessary.*)

וְנֶאֱמָן אַתָּה לְהַחֲיוֹת מֵתִים. בָּרוּךְ אַתָּה יהוה, מְחַיֵּה הַמֵּתִים.

When saying the עמידה *silently, continue with* אַתָּה קָדוֹשׁ *on the next page.*

קדושה

During חזרת הש״ץ, *the following is said standing with feet together, rising on the toes at the words indicated by* ▴.

קהל *then* ש״ץ: **נְקַדֵּשׁ** אֶת שִׁמְךָ בָּעוֹלָם, כְּשֵׁם שֶׁמַּקְדִּישִׁים אוֹתוֹ בִּשְׁמֵי מָרוֹם, כַּכָּתוּב עַל יַד נְבִיאֶךָ, וְקָרָא זֶה אֶל־זֶה וְאָמַר — ישעיה ו

קהל *then* ש״ץ: ▴קָדוֹשׁ, ▴קָדוֹשׁ, ▴קָדוֹשׁ יהוה צְבָאוֹת, מְלֹא כָל־הָאָרֶץ כְּבוֹדוֹ:

ש״ץ: לְעֻמָּתָם בָּרוּךְ יֹאמֵרוּ

קהל *then* ש״ץ: ▴בָּרוּךְ כְּבוֹד־יהוה מִמְּקוֹמוֹ: — יחזקאל ג

ש״ץ: וּבְדִבְרֵי קָדְשְׁךָ כָּתוּב לֵאמֹר

קהל *then* ש״ץ: ▴יִמְלֹךְ יהוה לְעוֹלָם, אֱלֹהַיִךְ צִיּוֹן לְדֹר וָדֹר, הַלְלוּיָהּ: — תהלים קמו

---

praise God for His compassion, so that even if the aforementioned merits of our patriarchs no longer apply for whatever reason, He will still redeem us "for the sake of His name" which exists forever, and thus cannot be exhausted (*Tur*).

For laws regarding "Omission/Insertion of *Mashiv Haru'ah,*" see page 109.

Between Rosh HaShana & Yom Kippur: Remember us for life, King Who desires life, and inscribe us in the book of life for Your sake, Living God.

(*If forgotten, no corrective action is necessary.*)

King Who helps, saves, and shields, ▼blessed are You, LORD, Shield of Abraham.

GOD'S MIGHT

אַתָּה YOU, my Master, are forever mighty, You are the Resurrector of the dead, with great power to save.

In winter: He makes the wind blow and the rain fall

He sustains the living with kindness, He resurrects the dead with great compassion, He supports those who are falling, He heals the sick, He sets the incarcerated free, and He fulfills what He has promised to those who sleep in the dust. Who is like You, O mighty One, and who can be compared to You, O King Who causes death and resurrects, and Who causes salvation to sprout?

Between Rosh HaShana & Yom Kippur: Who is like You, merciful Father, Who in compassion remembers for life those He has created.

(*If forgotten, no corrective action is necessary.*)

Trustworthy are You to resurrect the dead. Blessed are YOU, LORD, Resurrector of the dead.

When saying the Amida silently, continue with "You are holy" on the next page.

KEDUSHA *During the Leader's Repetition, the following is said standing with feet together, rising on the toes at the words indicated by* ▲.

Cong. then Leader: נְקַדֵּשׁ WE WILL SANCTIFY Your name in this world, as they sanctify it in the heavenly heights, as is written by Your prophet: "They called to one another, saying":

Is. 6 *Cong. then Leader:* "▲Holy, ▲holy, ▲holy is the LORD of hosts; the whole world is filled with His glory."

Leader: Those who face them declare, "Blessed –"

Ezek. 3 *Cong. then Leader:* ▲"Blessed is the glory of the LORD from His place."

Leader: And in Your holy Writings it is written as follows:

Ps. 146 *Cong. then Leader:* ▲"The LORD will reign forever, Your God, O Zion, to all generations. Praise the LORD."

For laws regarding "*Responding to the Leader during Kedusha,*" see page 510.

ש״ץ: לְדוֹר וָדוֹר נַגִּיד גָּדְלֶךָ, וּלְנֵצַח נְצָחִים קְדֻשָּׁתְךָ נַקְדִּישׁ, וְשִׁבְחֲךָ אֱלֹהֵינוּ מִפִּינוּ לֹא יָמוּשׁ לְעוֹלָם וָעֶד, כִּי אֵל מֶלֶךְ גָּדוֹל וְקָדוֹשׁ אָתָּה. בָּרוּךְ אַתָּה יהוה, הָאֵל הַקָּדוֹשׁ./ בעשרת ימי תשובה: הַמֶּלֶךְ הַקָּדוֹשׁ./

The שליח ציבור *continues with* אַתָּה חוֹנֵן *below.*

קדושת השם

אַתָּה קָדוֹשׁ וְשִׁמְךָ קָדוֹשׁ. וּקְדוֹשִׁים בְּכָל יוֹם יְהַלְלוּךָ סֶּלָה. בָּרוּךְ אַתָּה יהוה, הָאֵל הַקָּדוֹשׁ./ בעשרת ימי תשובה: הַמֶּלֶךְ הַקָּדוֹשׁ./

(*If forgotten, repeat the* עמידה.)

בינה

אַתָּה חוֹנֵן לְאָדָם דַּעַת, וּמְלַמֵּד לֶאֱנוֹשׁ בִּינָה. חָנֵּנוּ מֵאִתְּךָ דֵּעָה בִּינָה וְהַשְׂכֵּל. בָּרוּךְ אַתָּה יהוה, חוֹנֵן הַדָּעַת.

תשובה

הֲשִׁיבֵנוּ אָבִינוּ לְתוֹרָתֶךָ, וְקָרְבֵנוּ מַלְכֵּנוּ לַעֲבוֹדָתֶךָ, וְהַחֲזִירֵנוּ בִּתְשׁוּבָה שְׁלֵמָה לְפָנֶיךָ. בָּרוּךְ אַתָּה יהוה, הָרוֹצֶה בִּתְשׁוּבָה.

סליחה

Strike the left side of the chest at °.

סְלַח לָנוּ אָבִינוּ כִּי °חָטָאנוּ, מְחַל לָנוּ מַלְכֵּנוּ כִּי °פָשָׁעְנוּ, כִּי מוֹחֵל וְסוֹלֵחַ אָתָּה. בָּרוּךְ אַתָּה יהוה, חַנּוּן הַמַּרְבֶּה לִסְלֹחַ.

THE MIDDLE PETITIONARY SECTION

The Gemara (*Berakhot* 28b) and the Mishna (*Pirkei Avot* 2:18) teach that the prayers of one who prays by קֶבַע (rote) do not achieve the higher level of תַּחֲנוּנִים (supplications). This teaches that while we can pray merely so as to fulfill our obligation to serve and praise God, it is much better to engage in prayer by way of beseeching Him to fulfill our desires and needs "with all our heart and soul." For this reason, while the first three *berakhot* of the *Amida* indeed serve and praise God, it is the middle section consisting of the תַּחֲנוּנִים (supplications) that achieves this higher modality of prayer. This is reflected in the ruling of the *Ba'al Halakhot Gedolot* that the biblical source of the obligation to pray is "you shall fear the Lord your God and serve Him… הוּא תְהִלָּתְךָ וְהוּא אֱלֹקֶיךָ, He is the One Whom you praise, thereby making Him your own God" (Deut. 10:20–21). If we merely pray to fulfill an obligation we miss this entire dimension of prayer, together with its powerful consequences and rewards (Vilna Gaon).

For laws regarding "Omission of *HaMelekh HaKadosh*," see page 112.

Leader: To all generations we will proclaim Your greatness, and forever declare Your holiness, and the praise of You, our God, will never leave our mouth, for You are God and King, great and holy; blessed are You, LORD, the holy God. / *Between Rosh HaShana and Yom Kippur:* the holy King. /

The Leader continues with "Graciously You grant" below.

HOLINESS

אַתָּה YOU ARE HOLY and Your name is holy, and holy ones will praise You every day, forever. Blessed are You, LORD, the holy God. /*Between Rosh HaShana and Yom Kippur:* the holy King./

(*If forgotten, repeat the Amida.*)

INSIGHT

אַתָּה GRACIOUSLY You grant man wisdom, and teach understanding to mortal man. Grant us, with grace, the wisdom, insight, and discernment that come from You. Blessed are You, LORD, Granter of knowledge.

REPENTANCE

הֲשִׁיבֵנוּ BRING US BACK, our Father, to Your Torah, and draw us near, our King, to Your service. Facilitate our return to You in complete repentance. Blessed are You, LORD, Who desires repentance.

FORGIVENESS

Strike the left side of the chest at °.

סְלַח FORGIVE US, our Father, for we have °sinned. Pardon us, our King, for we have °transgressed. For You are the One Who pardons and forgives. Blessed are You, LORD, gracious and abundantly forgiving.

וְהַחֲזִירֵנוּ בִּתְשׁוּבָה שְׁלֵמָה לְפָנֶיךָ – *Facilitate our return to You in complete repentance.* R. Avraham Yitzḥak HaKohen Kook explains that the impetus to repentance can take various forms. On its simplest level, we might feel remorse for having failed to live fully in accordance with Torah and *mitzvot*. But there is a more subtle context in which we have a general sense that God and genuine spirituality are missing from our lives, that we are lacking the sense of purpose that occurs when we feel His presence. This *berakha* can be seen as encompassing both frameworks. First it asks God to help us as would a father and king so we can return to His Torah to serve Him by keeping His commandments. Then it asks God to facilitate תְּשׁוּבָה שְׁלֵמָה לְפָנֶיךָ (a complete return to Your presence) so that we can once again feel at one with Him, our lives filled with purpose and sanctity (R. Basil Herring).

גאולה

רְאֵה בְעָנְיֵנוּ, וְרִיבָה רִיבֵנוּ, וּגְאָלֵנוּ מְהֵרָה לְמַעַן שְׁמֶךָ, כִּי גּוֹאֵל חָזָק אָתָּה. בָּרוּךְ אַתָּה יהוה, גּוֹאֵל יִשְׂרָאֵל.

On Fast Days the שליח ציבור *adds:*

עֲנֵנוּ יהוה עֲנֵנוּ בְּיוֹם צוֹם תַּעֲנִיתֵנוּ, כִּי בְצָרָה גְדוֹלָה אֲנָחְנוּ. אַל תֵּפֶן אֶל רִשְׁעֵנוּ, וְאַל תַּסְתֵּר פָּנֶיךָ מִמֶּנּוּ, וְאַל תִּתְעַלַּם מִתְּחִנָּתֵנוּ. הֱיֵה נָא קָרוֹב לְשַׁוְעָתֵנוּ, יְהִי נָא חַסְדְּךָ לְנַחֲמֵנוּ, טֶרֶם נִקְרָא אֵלֶיךָ עֲנֵנוּ, כַּדָּבָר שֶׁנֶּאֱמַר: וְהָיָה טֶרֶם יִקְרָאוּ ישעיה סה
וַאֲנִי אֶעֱנֶה, עוֹד הֵם מְדַבְּרִים וַאֲנִי אֶשְׁמָע: כִּי אַתָּה יהוה הָעוֹנֶה בְּעֵת צָרָה, פּוֹדֶה וּמַצִּיל בְּכָל עֵת צָרָה וְצוּקָה. בָּרוּךְ אַתָּה יהוה, הָעוֹנֶה בְּעֵת צָרָה.

(*If forgotten, no corrective action is necessary.*)

רפואה

רְפָאֵנוּ יהוה וְנֵרָפֵא, הוֹשִׁיעֵנוּ וְנִוָּשֵׁעָה, כִּי תְהִלָּתֵנוּ אָתָּה, וְהַעֲלֵה רְפוּאָה שְׁלֵמָה לְכָל מַכּוֹתֵינוּ

The following prayer for a sick person may be said here:

יְהִי רָצוֹן מִלְּפָנֶיךָ יהוה אֱלֹהַי וֵאלֹהֵי אֲבוֹתַי, שֶׁתִּשְׁלַח מְהֵרָה רְפוּאָה שְׁלֵמָה מִן הַשָּׁמַיִם רְפוּאַת הַנֶּפֶשׁ וּרְפוּאַת הַגּוּף לַחוֹלֶה/לַחוֹלָה *name of patient* בֶּן/בַּת *mother's name* בְּתוֹךְ שְׁאָר חוֹלֵי יִשְׂרָאֵל.

כִּי אֵל מֶלֶךְ רוֹפֵא נֶאֱמָן וְרַחֲמָן אָתָּה. בָּרוּךְ אַתָּה יהוה, רוֹפֵא חוֹלֵי עַמּוֹ יִשְׂרָאֵל.

ברכת השנים

בָּרֵךְ עָלֵינוּ יהוה אֱלֹהֵינוּ אֶת הַשָּׁנָה הַזֹּאת, וְאֶת כָּל מִינֵי תְבוּאָתָהּ לְטוֹבָה

Beginning in springtime, from the intermediate days of Pesaḥ to the evening preceding December 5 (in some years December 6), say:

וְתֵן בְּרָכָה

Beginning with the winter season, from the evening preceding December 5 (in some years December 6) to Pesaḥ, say:

וְתֵן טַל וּמָטָר לִבְרָכָה

עַל פְּנֵי הָאֲדָמָה, וְשַׂבְּעֵנוּ מִטּוּבֶךָ, וּבָרֵךְ שְׁנָתֵנוּ כַּשָּׁנִים הַטּוֹבוֹת. בָּרוּךְ אַתָּה יהוה, מְבָרֵךְ הַשָּׁנִים.

For laws regarding "וְתֵן טַל וּמָטָר / *Veten tal umatar*," see page 117.

REDEMPTION

רְאֵה SEE OUR SUFFERING and advocate for us. Speed our redemption for the sake of Your name, for You are a mighty Redeemer. Blessed are You, LORD, Redeemer of Israel.

On Fast Days the Leader adds:

עֲנֵנוּ ANSWER US, dear LORD, please answer us, on this day of our fasting. For we are in great distress. Do not invoke our wickedness, and do not hide Your face from us, nor turn away from our pleading. Rather be responsive to our cry, and comfort us with your kindness. Answer us even before we cry
Is. 65 out, as it says "I will answer them even before they call out, I will hear them even while they speak." For You are the LORD Who answers in a time of trouble, Who redeems and saves in every instance of trouble and suffering. Blessed are You, LORD, Who answers in times of trouble.

(*If forgotten, no corrective action is necessary.*)

HEALTH AND HEALING

רְפָאֵנוּ HEAL US, LORD, and we shall be healed; save us and we shall be saved; for You are our praise. Bring complete healing from all our afflictions,

The following prayer for a sick person may be said here:

יְהִי MAY IT BE Your will, LORD my God and God of my fathers, that you send speedily a complete healing from heaven, a healing of the soul and a healing of the body, to the sick person (*name* son/daughter of *mother's name*), among the other sick people of Israel.

for You, God, King, are a faithful and compassionate Healer. Blessed are You, LORD, Who heals the sick of His people Israel.

PROSPERITY

בָּרֵךְ BLESS THIS YEAR for us, LORD our God, along with all its many kinds of produce for good.

Beginning in springtime, from the intermediate days of Pesaḥ to the evening preceding December 5 (in some years December 6), say:

Send blessing

Beginning with the winter season, from the evening preceding December 5 (in some years December 6) to Pesaḥ, say:

Send dew and rain for a blessing

on the face of the earth, and satisfy us with Your benevolence, and bless our year as the best of years. Blessed are You, LORD, Who blesses the years.

קבוץ גלויות

תְּקַע בְּשׁוֹפָר גָּדוֹל לְחֵרוּתֵנוּ, וְשָׂא נֵס לְקַבֵּץ גָּלֻיּוֹתֵינוּ, וְקַבְּצֵנוּ יַחַד מֵאַרְבַּע כַּנְפוֹת הָאָרֶץ. בָּרוּךְ אַתָּה יהוה, מְקַבֵּץ נִדְחֵי עַמּוֹ יִשְׂרָאֵל.

השבת המשפט

הָשִׁיבָה שׁוֹפְטֵינוּ כְּבָרִאשׁוֹנָה וְיוֹעֲצֵינוּ כְּבַתְּחִלָּה, וְהָסֵר מִמֶּנּוּ יָגוֹן וַאֲנָחָה, וּמְלֹךְ עָלֵינוּ אַתָּה יהוה לְבַדְּךָ בְּחֶסֶד וּבְרַחֲמִים, וְצַדְּקֵנוּ בַּמִּשְׁפָּט. בָּרוּךְ אַתָּה יהוה, מֶלֶךְ אוֹהֵב צְדָקָה וּמִשְׁפָּט. / בעשרת ימי תשובה: הַמֶּלֶךְ הַמִּשְׁפָּט./

(*If forgotten, no corrective action is necessary.*)

ברכת המינים

וְלַמַּלְשִׁינִים אַל תְּהִי תִקְוָה, וְכָל הָרִשְׁעָה כְּרֶגַע תֹּאבֵד, וְכָל אוֹיְבֶיךָ מְהֵרָה יִכָּרֵתוּ, וְהַזֵּדִים מְהֵרָה תְעַקֵּר וּתְשַׁבֵּר וּתְמַגֵּר וְתַכְנִיעַ בִּמְהֵרָה בְיָמֵינוּ. בָּרוּךְ אַתָּה יהוה, שׁוֹבֵר אוֹיְבִים וּמַכְנִיעַ זֵדִים.

צדיקים

עַל הַצַּדִּיקִים וְעַל הַחֲסִידִים, וְעַל זִקְנֵי עַמְּךָ בֵּית יִשְׂרָאֵל, וְעַל פְּלֵיטַת סוֹפְרֵיהֶם, וְעַל גֵּרֵי הַצֶּדֶק, וְעָלֵינוּ, יֶהֱמוּ רַחֲמֶיךָ יהוה אֱלֹהֵינוּ, וְתֵן שָׂכָר טוֹב לְכָל הַבּוֹטְחִים בְּשִׁמְךָ בֶּאֱמֶת, וְשִׂים חֶלְקֵנוּ עִמָּהֶם, וּלְעוֹלָם לֹא נֵבוֹשׁ כִּי בְךָ בָּטָחְנוּ. בָּרוּךְ אַתָּה יהוה, מִשְׁעָן וּמִבְטָח לַצַּדִּיקִים.

בניין ירושלים

וְלִירוּשָׁלַיִם עִירְךָ בְּרַחֲמִים תָּשׁוּב, וְתִשְׁכֹּן בְּתוֹכָהּ כַּאֲשֶׁר דִּבַּרְתָּ, וּבְנֵה אוֹתָהּ בְּקָרוֹב בְּיָמֵינוּ בִּנְיַן עוֹלָם, וְכִסֵּא דָוִד מְהֵרָה לְתוֹכָהּ תָּכִין. *בָּרוּךְ אַתָּה יהוה, בּוֹנֵה יְרוּשָׁלָיִם.

**At this point on* תשעה באב*, add* נַחֵם *on the next page.*

וְכִסֵּא דָוִד – *The throne of David.* Jerusalem cannot be considered fully rebuilt unless a worthy descendant of David is seated on the throne (R. Yitzḥak Ze'ev Soloveitchik).

INGATHERING OF THE EXILES

תְּקַע SOUND the great shofar of our freedom; hoist the banner to gather our exiles and bring us together from the four corners of the earth. Blessed are You, LORD, Who gathers the scattered of His people Israel.

JUSTICE

הָשִׁיבָה RESTORE our judges as in the beginning, and our counselors as they were to begin with, and relieve our sorrows and our troubles. Reign over us, LORD, You alone, lovingly and mercifully, and vindicate us in judgment. Blessed are You, LORD, / King Who loves righteousness and justice. / *Between Rosh HaShana & Yom Kippur:* the King of justice.

(*If forgotten, no corrective action is necessary.*)

AGAINST SLANDERERS

וְלַמַּלְשִׁינִים AND LET THERE BE no hope for slanderers, and may all evil instantly disappear. May all Your enemies be swiftly cut down, and the wicked be uprooted, broken, overthrown, and subdued – speedily, and in our day. Blessed are You, LORD, Who crushes enemies and subdues the wicked.

THE RIGHTEOUS

עַל הַצַּדִּיקִים MAY YOUR COMPASSION be upon the righteous, and the pious, and the elders of Your people the house of Israel, and the remnants of their scholars, and the righteous converts, and upon us, LORD our God. Give good reward to all those who sincerely trust in Your name, and place our portion with them, and may we never be shamed, for in You we trust. Blessed are You, LORD, Who is the Support and Trustee of the righteous.

REBUILDING JERUSALEM

וְלִירוּשָׁלַיִם AND MAY YOU RETURN to Jerusalem Your city in compassion, and may You dwell within it, as You promised. Rebuild it speedily in our days, such that it will remain built up forever, and establish within it soon the throne of David. *Blessed are You, LORD, Builder of Jerusalem.

**At this point on Tisha B'Av, add "LORD our God" on the next page.*

**At this point on* תשעה באב*, the following is inserted:*

נַחֵם יהוה אֱלֹהֵינוּ אֶת אֲבֵלֵי צִיּוֹן וְאֶת אֲבֵלֵי יְרוּשָׁלַיִם, וְאֶת הָעִיר הָאֲבֵלָה וְהֶחֳרֵבָה וְהַבְּזוּיָה וְהַשּׁוֹמֵמָה. הָאֲבֵלָה מִבְּלִי בָנֶיהָ, וְהֶחֳרֵבָה מִמְּעוֹנוֹתֶיהָ, וְהַבְּזוּיָה מִכְּבוֹדָהּ, וְהַשּׁוֹמֵמָה מֵאֵין יוֹשֵׁב. וְהִיא יוֹשֶׁבֶת וְרֹאשָׁהּ חָפוּי, כְּאִשָּׁה עֲקָרָה שֶׁלֹּא יָלָדָה. וַיְבַלְּעוּהָ לִגְיוֹנוֹת, וַיִּירָשׁוּהָ עוֹבְדֵי פְסִילִים, וַיָּטִילוּ אֶת עַמְּךָ יִשְׂרָאֵל לֶחָרֶב, וַיַּהַרְגוּ בְזָדוֹן חֲסִידֵי עֶלְיוֹן. עַל כֵּן צִיּוֹן בְּמַר תִּבְכֶּה, וִירוּשָׁלַיִם תִּתֵּן קוֹלָהּ. לִבִּי לִבִּי עַל חַלְלֵיהֶם, מֵעַי מֵעַי עַל חַלְלֵיהֶם, כִּי אַתָּה יהוה בָּאֵשׁ הִצַּתָּהּ, וּבָאֵשׁ אַתָּה עָתִיד לִבְנוֹתָהּ. כָּאָמוּר: וַאֲנִי אֶהְיֶה־לָּהּ, נְאֻם־יהוה, חוֹמַת אֵשׁ סָבִיב, זכריה ב
וּלְכָבוֹד אֶהְיֶה בְתוֹכָהּ: בָּרוּךְ אַתָּה יהוה, מְנַחֵם צִיּוֹן וּבוֹנֵה יְרוּשָׁלָיִם.

(If forgotten, no corrective action is necessary.)

Continue with את צמח *below.*

מלכות בית דוד

אֶת צֶמַח דָּוִד עַבְדְּךָ מְהֵרָה תַצְמִיחַ, וְקַרְנוֹ תָּרוּם בִּישׁוּעָתֶךָ, כִּי לִישׁוּעָתְךָ קִוִּינוּ כָּל הַיּוֹם. בָּרוּךְ אַתָּה יהוה, מַצְמִיחַ קֶרֶן יְשׁוּעָה.

שומע תפלה

שְׁמַע קוֹלֵנוּ יהוה אֱלֹהֵינוּ, חוּס וְרַחֵם עָלֵינוּ, וְקַבֵּל בְּרַחֲמִים וּבְרָצוֹן אֶת תְּפִלָּתֵנוּ, כִּי אֵל שׁוֹמֵעַ תְּפִלּוֹת וְתַחֲנוּנִים אָתָּה, וּמִלְּפָנֶיךָ מַלְכֵּנוּ רֵיקָם אַל תְּשִׁיבֵנוּ,*

**At this point on fast days, the* קהל *adds* עֲנֵנוּ *(on the next page).*

**When saying the* עמידה *silently, one may add a personal prayer for forgiveness and for livelihood (on the next page).*

נַחֵם / NAHEM

The earliest reference to this Tisha B'Av insertion is in the Talmud Yerushalmi (*Berakhot* 4:3, *Ta'anit* 2:2) and it is quoted in one form or another in early Geonic *siddurim*, and later in various medieval sources. Many early authorities favored its recital during all the *Amida* prayers of Tisha B'Av, but in due course it became the accepted practice (see the Rema) to recite it only at *Minḥa*. To understand this practice, R. Joseph B. Soloveitchik, following the *Midrash Eikha*, would point to the Gemara (*Ta'anit* 29a) which states that it was precisely on Tisha B'Av afternoon that the First Temple was set afire and continued to burn through the next day. This sequence, far from being a source of despair, was in fact one of consolation and strength, for up to that point the fear was that God would destroy the people of Israel. When, however, they saw that instead the wood and stones of the Temple were bearing the brunt of His anger, and the people as a whole would be allowed to survive into the future (even though many individual Jews were certainly killed) to be given a second chance, they were relieved and comforted. Hence נֶחָמָה (consolation) is in order for us at *Minḥa* time too,

**At this point on Tisha B'Av, the following is inserted:*

נַחֵם LORD OUR GOD, console the mourners of Zion and the mourners of Jerusalem, and the city that is bereaved, destroyed, scorned and desolate. Bereft of her children, destroyed of her buildings, scorned of her glory, and desolate of her inhabitants. She sits with her head covered, like a woman barren and childless. Legions have devoured her, idolaters have plundered her; they have cast Your people Israel to the sword, and purposefully killed the devoted ones of the Most High. Therefore Zion weeps in bitterness and Jerusalem raises her voice. My heart, my heart [breaks] for those they killed; my insides, my insides [ache] for those they killed. For You, LORD, with fire consumed her,
Zech. 2 and with fire You will someday rebuild her. As it is said: "And I Myself, says the LORD, will be a wall of fire surrounding, and I will be the glory in her midst." Blessed are You, LORD, Consoler of Zion and Builder of Jerusalem. *(If forgotten, no corrective action is necessary.)*

Continue with "May the offspring" below.

KINGDOM OF DAVID

אֶת צֶמַח MAY THE OFFSPRING of David, Your servant, soon flourish, and may his glory be exalted by Your salvation – for we hope for Your salvation all day long. Blessed are You, LORD, Who causes the glory of salvation to flourish.

RESPONSE TO PRAYER

שְׁמַע קוֹלֵנוּ HEAR OUR VOICE, LORD our God, have pity and compassion for us, and accept our prayer in compassion and favor, for You are God Who hears prayers and pleas. Do not turn us away empty-handed, our King, from Your presence,*

**At this point on fast days, the congregation adds "Answer us" (on the next page).*

**When saying the Amida silently, one may add a personal prayer for forgiveness and for livelihood (on the next page).*

and so we recite the paragraph then, and not before (R. Jacob J. Schacter).

הָאֲבֵלָה מִבְּלִי בָנֶיהָ – *Bereft of her children.* Given the current state of Jerusalem there is ongoing debate among contemporary authorities regarding the recital of *Naḥem*. One solution was proposed by R. Aharon Lichtenstein, who omitted this sentence on the grounds that in prayer we should strive for truthfulness, and thus while these words were certainly accurate in the past, that is no longer the case (R. Chaim Navon).

On fast days, the קהל *adds* עֲנֵנוּ.

עֲנֵנוּ יהוה עֲנֵנוּ בְּיוֹם צוֹם תַּעֲנִיתֵנוּ, כִּי בְצָרָה גְדוֹלָה אֲנָחְנוּ. אַל תֵּפֶן אֶל רִשְׁעֵנוּ,
וְאַל תַּסְתֵּר פָּנֶיךָ מִמֶּנּוּ, וְאַל תִּתְעַלַּם מִתְּחִנָּתֵנוּ. הֱיֵה נָא קָרוֹב לְשַׁוְעָתֵנוּ,
יְהִי נָא חַסְדְּךָ לְנַחֲמֵנוּ, טֶרֶם נִקְרָא אֵלֶיךָ עֲנֵנוּ, כַּדָּבָר שֶׁנֶּאֱמַר: וְהָיָה טֶרֶם יִקְרָאוּ ישעיה סה
וַאֲנִי אֶעֱנֶה, עוֹד הֵם מְדַבְּרִים וַאֲנִי אֶשְׁמָע: כִּי אַתָּה יהוה הָעוֹנֶה בְּעֵת צָרָה, פּוֹדֶה
וּמַצִּיל בְּכָל עֵת צָרָה וְצוּקָה.

Continue with כִּי אַתָּה שׁוֹמֵעַ *below.*

A personal prayer for forgiveness:

אָנָּא יהוה, חָטָאתִי עָוִיתִי וּפָשַׁעְתִּי לְפָנֶיךָ, מִיּוֹם הֱיוֹתִי עַל הָאֲדָמָה עַד הַיּוֹם הַזֶּה (וּבִפְרַט בַּחֵטְא...). אָנָּא יהוה, עֲשֵׂה לְמַעַן שִׁמְךָ הַגָּדוֹל, וּתְכַפֶּר לִי עַל חֲטָאַי וַעֲוֹנַי וּפְשָׁעַי שֶׁחָטָאתִי וְשֶׁעָוִיתִי וְשֶׁפָּשַׁעְתִּי לְפָנֶיךָ, מִנְּעוּרַי עַד הַיּוֹם הַזֶּה. וּתְמַלֵּא כָּל הַשֵּׁמוֹת שֶׁפָּגַמְתִּי בְּשִׁמְךָ הַגָּדוֹל.

Continue with כִּי אַתָּה שׁוֹמֵעַ *below.*

A personal prayer for livelihood:

אַתָּה הוּא יהוה הָאֱלֹהִים, הַזָּן וּמְפַרְנֵס וּמְכַלְכֵּל מִקַּרְנֵי רְאֵמִים עַד בֵּיצֵי כִנִּים. הַטְרִיפֵנִי לֶחֶם חֻקִּי, וְהַמְצֵא לִי וּלְכָל בְּנֵי בֵיתִי מְזוֹנוֹתַי קֹדֶם שֶׁאֶצְטָרֵךְ לָהֶם, בְּנַחַת וְלֹא בְצַעַר, בְּהֶתֵּר וְלֹא בְאִסּוּר, בְּכָבוֹד וְלֹא בְבִזָּיוֹן, לְחַיִּים וּלְשָׁלוֹם, מִשֶּׁפַע בְּרָכָה וְהַצְלָחָה, וּמִשֶּׁפַע בְּרֵכָה עֶלְיוֹנָה, כְּדֵי שֶׁאוּכַל לַעֲשׂוֹת רְצוֹנֶךָ וְלַעֲסֹק בְּתוֹרָתֶךָ וּלְקַיֵּם מִצְוֹתֶיךָ. וְאַל תַּצְרִיכֵנִי לִידֵי מַתְּנַת בָּשָׂר וָדָם. וִיקֻיַּם בִּי מִקְרָא שֶׁכָּתוּב: פּוֹתֵחַ אֶת יָדֶךָ, וּמַשְׂבִּיעַ לְכָל חַי רָצוֹן. וְכָתוּב: הַשְׁלֵךְ עַל יהוה יְהָבְךָ וְהוּא יְכַלְכְּלֶךָ.

Continue with כִּי אַתָּה שׁוֹמֵעַ *below.*

כִּי אַתָּה שׁוֹמֵעַ תְּפִלַּת עַמְּךָ יִשְׂרָאֵל בְּרַחֲמִים. בָּרוּךְ אַתָּה יהוה, שׁוֹמֵעַ תְּפִלָּה.

עבודה

רְצֵה יהוה אֱלֹהֵינוּ בְּעַמְּךָ יִשְׂרָאֵל, וּבִתְפִלָּתָם, וְהָשֵׁב אֶת הָעֲבוֹדָה לִדְבִיר בֵּיתֶךָ, וְאִשֵּׁי יִשְׂרָאֵל וּתְפִלָּתָם בְּאַהֲבָה תְקַבֵּל בְּרָצוֹן, וּתְהִי לְרָצוֹן תָּמִיד עֲבוֹדַת יִשְׂרָאֵל עַמֶּךָ.

שׁוֹמֵעַ תְּפִלָּה / RESPONSE TO PRAYER

טֶרֶם יִקְרָאוּ וַאֲנִי אֶעֱנֶה – *Before they call, I will answer.* This verse first says that God answers us even before we petition Him, but then it says the opposite, that "while we are reciting" our prayers He hears us and responds, and not before. The resolution is that there is a difference between those things that we need in order to stay alive, which God provides whether or not (i.e., "before") we pray for them, and those which relatively speaking are not essential for our survival, and hence can depend upon our requesting them first (R. Shlomo Zalman Auerbach).

On fast days, the congregation adds "Answer us."

עֲנֵנוּ ANSWER US, dear LORD, please answer us, on this day of our fasting. For we are in great distress. Do not invoke our wickedness, and do not hide Your face from us, nor turn away from our pleading. Rather be responsive to our cry, and comfort us with your kindness. Answer us even before we cry out, as it says "I will answer them even before they call out, I will hear them even while they speak." For You are the LORD Who answers in a time of trouble, Who redeems and saves in every instance of trouble and suffering.

Continue with "for You hear" below.

A personal prayer for forgiveness:

אָנָּא PLEASE, LORD, I have sinned, been iniquitous, and transgressed before You, from the day I came into being on this earth until this day (in particular with the sin of…). Please, LORD, act for the sake of Your great name and grant me atonement for my sins, my iniquities and my transgressions committed in Your presence, from my youth until this day. May You make whole all the names I have damaged in Your great name.

Continue with "for You hear" below.

A personal prayer for livelihood:

אַתָּה YOU are the LORD, the God, Who nourishes, sustains, and supports, from the oryxes' horns to the eggs of lice. Provide me with my due portion of bread, and bring forth for me and all members of my household, my food before I have need for it: in satisfaction and not in pain, in a permissible manner and not a forbidden one, in honor and not in disgrace, for life and for peace, from the flow of blessing and success, and from the flow of the heavenly spring, so that I may be able to do Your will and engage in Your Torah and fulfill Your commandments. Let me not become needy of human charity, and may there be fulfilled in me the verse as it is written: "You open Your hand, and You satisfy the desire of every living thing." And it is written: "Cast your burden upon the LORD, and He will sustain you."

Continue with "for You hear" below.

for You hear the prayer of Your people Israel with compassion. Blessed are You, LORD, Who hears prayer.

TEMPLE SERVICE

רְצֵה LOOK FAVORABLY, LORD our God, upon Your people Israel and their prayer, and restore the service to the Holy of Holies of Your House. Accept with love and favor the fire-offerings of Israel and their prayer. May the service of Israel Your people Israel always find favor with You.

כִּי אַתָּה שׁוֹמֵעַ – *For You hear.* It is correct and proper to pray every day for one's needs. This includes praying for financial security as well as children who will serve God

On חול המועד *and* ראש חודש*, say:*

אֱלֹהֵינוּ וֵאלֹהֵי אֲבוֹתֵינוּ, יַעֲלֶה וְיָבוֹא וְיַגִּיעַ, וְיֵרָאֶה וְיֵרָצֶה וְיִשָּׁמַע, וְיִפָּקֵד וְיִזָּכֵר זִכְרוֹנֵנוּ וּפִקְדוֹנֵנוּ וְזִכְרוֹן אֲבוֹתֵינוּ, וְזִכְרוֹן מָשִׁיחַ בֶּן דָּוִד עַבְדֶּךָ, וְזִכְרוֹן יְרוּשָׁלַיִם עִיר קָדְשֶׁךָ, וְזִכְרוֹן כָּל עַמְּךָ בֵּית יִשְׂרָאֵל, לְפָנֶיךָ, לִפְלֵיטָה לְטוֹבָה, לְחֵן וּלְחֶסֶד וּלְרַחֲמִים, לְחַיִּים וּלְשָׁלוֹם בְּיוֹם

בראש חודש: רֹאשׁ הַחֹדֶשׁ / בפסח: חַג הַמַּצּוֹת / בסוכות: חַג הַסֻּכּוֹת

הַזֶּה. זָכְרֵנוּ יהוה אֱלֹהֵינוּ בּוֹ לְטוֹבָה, וּפָקְדֵנוּ בוֹ לִבְרָכָה, וְהוֹשִׁיעֵנוּ בוֹ לְחַיִּים. וּבִדְבַר יְשׁוּעָה וְרַחֲמִים, חוּס וְחָנֵּנוּ וְרַחֵם עָלֵינוּ וְהוֹשִׁיעֵנוּ, כִּי אֵלֶיךָ עֵינֵינוּ, כִּי אֵל מֶלֶךְ חַנּוּן וְרַחוּם אָתָּה.

וְתֶחֱזֶינָה עֵינֵינוּ בְּשׁוּבְךָ לְצִיּוֹן בְּרַחֲמִים. בָּרוּךְ אַתָּה יהוה, הַמַּחֲזִיר שְׁכִינָתוֹ לְצִיּוֹן.

הודאה

Bow during the first five words.

ימוֹדִים אֲנַחְנוּ לָךְ, שָׁאַתָּה הוּא יהוה אֱלֹהֵינוּ וֵאלֹהֵי אֲבוֹתֵינוּ לְעוֹלָם וָעֶד. צוּר חַיֵּינוּ, מָגֵן יִשְׁעֵנוּ, אַתָּה הוּא. לְדוֹר וָדוֹר נוֹדֶה לְּךָ וּנְסַפֵּר תְּהִלָּתֶךָ, עַל חַיֵּינוּ הַמְּסוּרִים בְּיָדֶךָ, וְעַל נִשְׁמוֹתֵינוּ הַפְּקוּדוֹת לָךְ, וְעַל נִסֶּיךָ שֶׁבְּכָל יוֹם עִמָּנוּ, וְעַל נִפְלְאוֹתֶיךָ וְטוֹבוֹתֶיךָ, שֶׁבְּכָל עֵת, עֶרֶב וָבֹקֶר וְצָהֳרָיִם. הַטּוֹב, כִּי לֹא כָלוּ רַחֲמֶיךָ וְהַמְרַחֵם, כִּי לֹא תַמּוּ חֲסָדֶיךָ, מֵעוֹלָם קִוִּינוּ לָךְ.

During חזרת הש"ץ*, the* קהל *says quietly:*

ימוֹדִים אֲנַחְנוּ לָךְ, שָׁאַתָּה הוּא יהוה אֱלֹהֵינוּ וֵאלֹהֵי אֲבוֹתֵינוּ, אֱלֹהֵי כָל בָּשָׂר, יוֹצְרֵנוּ, יוֹצֵר בְּרֵאשִׁית. בְּרָכוֹת וְהוֹדָאוֹת לְשִׁמְךָ הַגָּדוֹל וְהַקָּדוֹשׁ, עַל שֶׁהֶחֱיִיתָנוּ וְקִיַּמְתָּנוּ. כֵּן תְּחַיֵּנוּ וּתְקַיְּמֵנוּ, וְתֶאֱסֹף גָּלֻיּוֹתֵינוּ לְחַצְרוֹת קָדְשֶׁךָ, לִשְׁמֹר חֻקֶּיךָ וְלַעֲשׂוֹת רְצוֹנֶךָ וּלְעָבְדְּךָ בְּלֵבָב שָׁלֵם, עַל שֶׁאֲנַחְנוּ מוֹדִים לָךְ. בָּרוּךְ אֵל הַהוֹדָאוֹת.

---

faithfully. While it is preferable to pray in Hebrew, one can also pray in whichever language one understands, as long as it is heartfelt (*Ḥayyei Adam*).

For laws regarding "יַעֲלֶה וְיָבוֹא / *Ya'aleh VeYavo,*" see page 125.

On Rosh Hodesh and Hol HaMo'ed, say:

אֱלֹהֵינוּ וֵאלֹהֵי אֲבוֹתֵינוּ OUR GOD and God of our fathers, may there arise, arrive, reach, appear, be favored, heard, considered and remembered, our remembrance and recollection, Your remembrance of our fathers, of the Messiah son of David Your servant, of Jerusalem Your holy city and of all Your people the house of Israel. May they come before You for deliverance and benefit, for grace, kindness and mercy, for life and peace, on this day of:

On Rosh Hodesh: Rosh Hodesh.

On Pesah: the Festival of Matzot. / *On Sukkot:* the Festival of Sukkot.

LORD our God, remember us this day for good. Be mindful of us this day for blessing, preserve us this day for life. Regarding redemption and mercy show us compassion and grace, and have pity on us and save us. For our eyes are lifted toward You, for You are a gracious and merciful God and King.

May our eyes witness Your return to Zion in compassion. Blessed are You, LORD, Who will restore His Divine Presence to Zion.

THANKSGIVING

Bow during the first seven words.

מוֹדִים WE THANK YOU, for You are the LORD our God and the God of our fathers for all eternity. You are the Rock of our life and Shield of our deliverance. From generation to generation we will thank You and recount Your praise for our lives that are in Your hands, for our souls that are given over to You, for Your miracles that are with us every day, and for Your constant wonders and favors, evening, morning and noon. You are good, for Your compassion does not cease, and You are compassionate, for Your kindness never ends. We have placed our hope in You forever and ever.

During the Leader's Repetition, the congregation says quietly:

מוֹדִים WE THANK YOU, for You are the LORD our God, the God of our fathers and God of all flesh. You are our Maker, the Maker of Creation. Blessings and thanks are due Your great and holy name for You have given us life and preserved us in life. May You continue to keep us in life and preserve us. Gather our exiles to the courtyards of Your Temple so that we may fulfill Your commandments and do Your will, serving You with a perfect heart, in the merit of our giving thanks to You now. Blessed is the God of all thanksgiving.

בחנוכה ובפורים:

עַל הַנִּסִּים וְעַל הַפֻּרְקָן וְעַל הַגְּבוּרוֹת וְעַל הַתְּשׁוּעוֹת וְעַל הַמִּלְחָמוֹת שֶׁעָשִׂיתָ לַאֲבוֹתֵינוּ בַּיָּמִים הָהֵם בַּזְּמַן הַזֶּה.

בחנוכה:

בִּימֵי מַתִּתְיָהוּ בֶּן יוֹחָנָן כֹּהֵן גָּדוֹל חַשְׁמוֹנַאי וּבָנָיו, כְּשֶׁעָמְדָה מַלְכוּת יָוָן הָרְשָׁעָה עַל עַמְּךָ יִשְׂרָאֵל לְהַשְׁכִּיחָם תּוֹרָתֶךָ וּלְהַעֲבִירָם מֵחֻקֵּי רְצוֹנֶךָ, וְאַתָּה בְּרַחֲמֶיךָ הָרַבִּים עָמַדְתָּ לָהֶם בְּעֵת צָרָתָם, רַבְתָּ אֶת רִיבָם, דַּנְתָּ אֶת דִּינָם, נָקַמְתָּ אֶת נִקְמָתָם, מָסַרְתָּ גִבּוֹרִים בְּיַד חַלָּשִׁים, וְרַבִּים בְּיַד מְעַטִּים, וּטְמֵאִים בְּיַד טְהוֹרִים, וּרְשָׁעִים בְּיַד צַדִּיקִים, וְזֵדִים בְּיַד עוֹסְקֵי תוֹרָתֶךָ, וּלְךָ עָשִׂיתָ שֵׁם גָּדוֹל וְקָדוֹשׁ בְּעוֹלָמֶךָ, וּלְעַמְּךָ יִשְׂרָאֵל עָשִׂיתָ תְּשׁוּעָה גְדוֹלָה וּפֻרְקָן כְּהַיּוֹם הַזֶּה. וְאַחַר כֵּן בָּאוּ בָנֶיךָ לִדְבִיר בֵּיתֶךָ, וּפִנּוּ אֶת הֵיכָלֶךָ, וְטִהֲרוּ אֶת מִקְדָּשֶׁךָ, וְהִדְלִיקוּ נֵרוֹת בְּחַצְרוֹת קָדְשֶׁךָ, וְקָבְעוּ שְׁמוֹנַת יְמֵי חֲנֻכָּה אֵלּוּ, לְהוֹדוֹת וּלְהַלֵּל לְשִׁמְךָ הַגָּדוֹל.

Continue with וְעַל כֻּלָּם.

בפורים:

בִּימֵי מָרְדְּכַי וְאֶסְתֵּר בְּשׁוּשַׁן הַבִּירָה, כְּשֶׁעָמַד עֲלֵיהֶם הָמָן הָרָשָׁע, בִּקֵּשׁ לְהַשְׁמִיד לַהֲרֹג וּלְאַבֵּד אֶת־כָּל־הַיְּהוּדִים מִנַּעַר וְעַד־זָקֵן טַף וְנָשִׁים בְּיוֹם אֶחָד, בִּשְׁלוֹשָׁה עָשָׂר לְחֹדֶשׁ שְׁנֵים־עָשָׂר, הוּא־חֹדֶשׁ אֲדָר, וּשְׁלָלָם לָבוֹז: וְאַתָּה בְּרַחֲמֶיךָ הָרַבִּים הֵפַרְתָּ אֶת עֲצָתוֹ, וְקִלְקַלְתָּ אֶת מַחֲשַׁבְתּוֹ, וַהֲשֵׁבוֹתָ לּוֹ גְּמוּלוֹ בְּרֹאשׁוֹ, וְתָלוּ אוֹתוֹ וְאֶת בָּנָיו עַל הָעֵץ. אסתר ג

Continue with וְעַל כֻּלָּם.

וְעַל כֻּלָּם יִתְבָּרַךְ וְיִתְרוֹמַם שִׁמְךָ מַלְכֵּנוּ תָּמִיד לְעוֹלָם וָעֶד.

בעשרת ימי תשובה: וּכְתֹב לְחַיִּים טוֹבִים כָּל בְּנֵי בְרִיתֶךָ.

(*If forgotten, no corrective action is necessary.*)

וְכֹל הַחַיִּים יוֹדוּךָ סֶּלָה, וִיהַלְלוּ אֶת שִׁמְךָ בֶּאֱמֶת, הָאֵל יְשׁוּעָתֵנוּ וְעֶזְרָתֵנוּ סֶלָה. ׳בָּרוּךְ אַתָּה יהוה, הַטּוֹב שִׁמְךָ וּלְךָ נָאֶה לְהוֹדוֹת.

For laws regarding "עַל הַנִּסִּים / *Al HaNissim*," see page 128.

On Ḥanukka and Purim add:

עַל הַנִּסִּים [WE THANK YOU] for the miracles, the deliverance, and the triumphant victories and salvation, as well as wars which You wrought for our ancestors in those days at this season.

On Ḥanukka:

IT HAPPENED in the days of Mattathias son of Johanan, the Hasmonean high priest, and his sons. Then the cruel Hellenist power rose up to force Your people Israel to forget Your Torah and transgress the commands of Your will. In that hour of their distress, You in Your great mercy rose to take up their cause and defend their rights. Meting out retribution You delivered the strong into the hand of the weak, the many into the hand of the few, the impure into the hand of the pure, the evil ones into the hand of the righteous, and the wicked into the hand of devotees of Your Torah. You thereby made for Yourself a great and holy name throughout Your world, as well as bringing about great deliverance and salvation for Your people Israel (known) to this day. Then Your children came to the Holy of Holies in Your house, cleared Your Temple, purified Your holy place, kindled lights in Your holy courts, and instituted these eight days of Ḥanukka to give thanks and sing praise to Your great name. *Continue with "For all this."*

On Purim:

IN THE DAYS of Mordechai and Esther, in Shushan the capital, when the
Esther 3 wicked Haman rose up against them, he sought to destroy, to kill, and to annihilate all the Jews, young and old, women and infants, in one day, the thirteenth day of the twelfth month, Adar, and plunder their possessions. In Your great mercy You nullified his counsel and subverted his designs, causing them to recoil on his own head so that he and his sons were hanged on the gallows. *Continue with "For all this."*

For all this, our King, may Your name be blessed and exalted continually, forever and ever.

Between Rosh HaShana & Yom Kippur: Inscribe all the children of Your covenant for a life of goodness.

(*If forgotten, no corrective action is necessary.*)

All that lives will give thanks to You forever and praise Your name in truth, God, our salvation and our help forever. ▾Blessed are You, LORD, for Your name is "The Good One" and it is appropriate to give thanks to You.

ברכת כוהנים בתעניות ציבור

On public fast days only, the following is said by the שליח ציבור *during* חזרת הש"ץ *except in a* שבעה *house and on* תשעה באב*.*

אֱלֹהֵינוּ וֵאלֹהֵי אֲבוֹתֵינוּ, בָּרְכֵנוּ בַּבְּרָכָה הַמְשֻׁלֶּשֶׁת, בַּתּוֹרָה, הַכְּתוּבָה עַל יְדֵי מֹשֶׁה עַבְדֶּךָ, הָאֲמוּרָה מִפִּי אַהֲרֹן וּבָנָיו כֹּהֲנִים עַם קְדוֹשֶׁיךָ, כָּאָמוּר

יְבָרֶכְךָ יהוה וְיִשְׁמְרֶךָ: קהל: כֵּן יְהִי רָצוֹן במדבר ו

יָאֵר יהוה פָּנָיו אֵלֶיךָ וִיחֻנֶּךָּ: קהל: כֵּן יְהִי רָצוֹן

יִשָּׂא יהוה פָּנָיו אֵלֶיךָ וְיָשֵׂם לְךָ שָׁלוֹם: קהל: כֵּן יְהִי רָצוֹן

ברכת שלום

שָׁלוֹם רָב עַל יִשְׂרָאֵל עַמְּךָ תָּשִׂים לְעוֹלָם, כִּי אַתָּה הוּא מֶלֶךְ אָדוֹן לְכָל הַשָּׁלוֹם. וְטוֹב בְּעֵינֶיךָ לְבָרֵךְ אֶת עַמְּךָ יִשְׂרָאֵל, בְּכָל עֵת וּבְכָל שָׁעָה בִּשְׁלוֹמֶךָ.

On fast days:

שִׂים שָׁלוֹם טוֹבָה וּבְרָכָה, חֵן וָחֶסֶד וְרַחֲמִים עָלֵינוּ וְעַל כָּל יִשְׂרָאֵל עַמֶּךָ. בָּרְכֵנוּ אָבִינוּ כֻּלָּנוּ כְּאֶחָד בְּאוֹר פָּנֶיךָ, כִּי בְאוֹר פָּנֶיךָ נָתַתָּ לָּנוּ יהוה אֱלֹהֵינוּ, תּוֹרַת חַיִּים וְאַהֲבַת חֶסֶד, וּצְדָקָה וּבְרָכָה וְרַחֲמִים וְחַיִּים וְשָׁלוֹם. וְטוֹב בְּעֵינֶיךָ לְבָרֵךְ אֶת עַמְּךָ יִשְׂרָאֵל, בְּכָל עֵת וּבְכָל שָׁעָה בִּשְׁלוֹמֶךָ.

בעשרת ימי תשובה: בְּסֵפֶר חַיִּים, בְּרָכָה וְשָׁלוֹם, וּפַרְנָסָה טוֹבָה, נִזָּכֵר וְנִכָּתֵב לְפָנֶיךָ, אֲנַחְנוּ וְכָל עַמְּךָ בֵּית יִשְׂרָאֵל, לְחַיִּים טוֹבִים וּלְשָׁלוֹם.*

בָּרוּךְ אַתָּה יהוה, הַמְבָרֵךְ אֶת עַמּוֹ יִשְׂרָאֵל בַּשָּׁלוֹם.

**During the* עשרת ימי תשובה *many end the blessing:*

בָּרוּךְ אַתָּה יהוה, עוֹשֵׂה הַשָּׁלוֹם.

At this point when the שליח ציבור *repeats the* עמידה *he should complete the repetition by saying the verse beginning "*יהיו לרצון*" out loud.*

יִהְיוּ לְרָצוֹן אִמְרֵי־פִי וְהֶגְיוֹן לִבִּי לְפָנֶיךָ, יהוה צוּרִי וְגֹאֲלִי: תהלים יט

THE PRIESTLY BLESSING ON FAST DAYS

On public fast days only, the following is said by the Leader during the Repetition of the Amida, except in a shiva house and on Tisha B'Av.

אֱלֹהֵינוּ OUR GOD, God of our fathers, bless us with the threefold blessing, in the Torah, written by Your servant Moses and spoken by Aaron and his descendants, being priests, Your holy people, as it is said:

Num. 6 "May the LORD bless you and keep you." *Cong:* May this be His will.
"May the LORD make His countenance shine upon you and be gracious to you." *Cong:* May this be His will.
"May the LORD lift up His countenance toward you and grant you peace." *Cong:* May this be His will.

PEACE

שָׁלוֹם רָב ESTABLISH ABUNDANT PEACE for Your people Israel forever, for You are the sovereign Master of all peace; and may it be good in Your eyes to bless Your people Israel at all times, at every hour, with Your peace.

On fast days:
שִׂים שָׁלוֹם GRANT PEACE with welfare and blessing, and grace with loving-kindness and mercy on us and all Israel Your people. Bless us, our Father, all together, with the light of Your presence. For in that light, LORD our God, You have given us the Torah of life, and love of kindness with justice, blessing, tenderness, life and peace. May it be good in Your eyes to bless Your people Israel at all times, at every hour, with Your peace.

Between Rosh HaShana & Yom Kippur: In the book of life and blessing, peace and prosperity, may we and all the house of Israel Your people be remembered before You and inscribed for a life of goodness and peace.*

Blessed are You, LORD, Who blesses His people Israel with peace.

**Between Rosh HaShana and Yom Kippur many end the blessing:*
Blessed are You, LORD, Who makes peace.

At this point when the Leader repeats the Amida he should complete the repetition by saying the verse beginning "May the words" out loud.

Ps. 19 MAY THE WORDS of my mouth and the meditation of my heart be acceptable before You, LORD, my Rock and my Redeemer.

ברכות יז. **אֱלֹהַי,** נְצֹר לְשׁוֹנִי מֵרָע וּשְׂפָתַי מִדַּבֵּר מִרְמָה, וְלִמְקַלְלַי נַפְשִׁי
תִדֹּם, וְנַפְשִׁי כֶּעָפָר לַכֹּל תִּהְיֶה. פְּתַח לִבִּי בְּתוֹרָתֶךָ,
וּבְמִצְוֹתֶיךָ תִּרְדֹּף נַפְשִׁי. וְכָל הַחוֹשְׁבִים עָלַי רָעָה, מְהֵרָה הָפֵר
עֲצָתָם וְקַלְקֵל מַחֲשַׁבְתָּם. עֲשֵׂה לְמַעַן שְׁמֶךָ, עֲשֵׂה לְמַעַן יְמִינֶךָ,
תהלים ס עֲשֵׂה לְמַעַן קְדֻשָּׁתֶךָ, עֲשֵׂה לְמַעַן תּוֹרָתֶךָ. לְמַעַן יֵחָלְצוּן יְדִידֶיךָ,
תהלים יט הוֹשִׁיעָה יְמִינְךָ וַעֲנֵנִי: *יִהְיוּ לְרָצוֹן אִמְרֵי־פִי וְהֶגְיוֹן לִבִּי לְפָנֶיךָ,
יהוה צוּרִי וְגֹאֲלִי:

Bow, take three steps back, then bow, first left, then right, then center, while saying:

עֹשֶׂה שָׁלוֹם/ בעשרת ימי תשובה: הַשָּׁלוֹם/ בִּמְרוֹמָיו, הוּא יַעֲשֶׂה שָׁלוֹם
עָלֵינוּ, וְעַל כָּל יִשְׂרָאֵל, וְאִמְרוּ אָמֵן.

יְהִי רָצוֹן מִלְּפָנֶיךָ יהוה אֱלֹהֵינוּ וֵאלֹהֵי אֲבוֹתֵינוּ, שֶׁיִּבָּנֶה בֵּית הַמִּקְדָּשׁ
בִּמְהֵרָה בְיָמֵינוּ, וְתֵן חֶלְקֵנוּ בְּתוֹרָתֶךָ, וְשָׁם נַעֲבָדְךָ בְּיִרְאָה כִּימֵי
מלאכי ג עוֹלָם וּכְשָׁנִים קַדְמוֹנִיּוֹת. וְעָרְבָה לַיהוה מִנְחַת יְהוּדָה וִירוּשָׁלָיִם כִּימֵי עוֹלָם
וּכְשָׁנִים קַדְמוֹנִיּוֹת:

On days when תחנון *is not said, the* שליח ציבור *says* קדיש שלם *on page 284.*

**A person undertaking a personal fast says the following at* מנחה *before the fast:*

רִבּוֹן כָּל הָעוֹלָמִים, הֲרֵי אֲנִי לְפָנֶיךָ בְּתַעֲנִית נְדָבָה לְמָחָר. יְהִי רָצוֹן מִלְּפָנֶיךָ יהוה אֱלֹהַי וֵאלֹהֵי אֲבוֹתַי, שֶׁתְּקַבְּלֵנִי בְּאַהֲבָה וּבְרָצוֹן, וְתָבֹא לְפָנֶיךָ תְּפִלָּתִי, וְתַעֲנֶה עֲתִירָתִי בְּרַחֲמֶיךָ הָרַבִּים, כִּי אַתָּה שׁוֹמֵעַ תְּפִלַּת כָּל־פֶּה.

On the afternoon of the fast, the following is said:

רִבּוֹן כָּל הָעוֹלָמִים, גָּלוּי וְיָדוּעַ לְפָנֶיךָ, בִּזְמַן שֶׁבֵּית הַמִּקְדָּשׁ קַיָּם, אָדָם חוֹטֵא וּמַקְרִיב קָרְבָּן, וְאֵין מַקְרִיבִין מִמֶּנּוּ אֶלָּא חֶלְבּוֹ וְדָמוֹ, וְאַתָּה בְּרַחֲמֶיךָ הָרַבִּים מְכַפֵּר. וְעַכְשָׁו יָשַׁבְתִּי בְתַעֲנִית, וְנִתְמַעֵט חֶלְבִּי וְדָמִי. יְהִי רָצוֹן מִלְּפָנֶיךָ, שֶׁיְּהֵא מִעוּט חֶלְבִּי וְדָמִי שֶׁנִּתְמַעֵט הַיּוֹם, כְּאִלּוּ הִקְרַבְתִּיו עַל־גַּבֵּי הַמִּזְבֵּחַ, וְתִרְצֵנִי.

וְתֵן חֶלְקֵנוּ בְּתוֹרָתֶךָ – *And may You grant our portion in Your Torah.* The thrust of this final paragraph of the *Amida* is to petition God to speedily rebuild the Temple. This single phrase ("and may You grant our portion in Your Torah"), however, seems out of place in a prayer for the rebuilding of the Temple. The answer can be found in light of a comment by R. Zalman Sorotzkin. In commanding the construction of the Tabernacle and its contents, God gives

Berakhot 17a אֱלֹהַי MY GOD, guard my tongue from evil, and my lips from speaking deceit. Let my soul be silent to those who curse me; let my soul be humble toward everyone like the dust. Open my heart to Your Torah that my soul may follow Your commandments. As for all those who contemplate evil against me, speedily nullify their plans and spoil their schemes. Do so for the sake of Your name. Do so for Your right hand.
Ps. 60 Do so for Your holiness. Do so for Your Torah, that Your loved ones
Ps. 19 may be delivered. Save with Your right hand, and answer me. *May the words of my mouth and the meditation of my heart be acceptable before You, LORD, my Rock and my Redeemer.

Bow, take three steps back, then bow, first left, then right, then center, while saying:

He Who makes peace in His heights, may He create peace for us and for all Israel. Amen.

יְהִי רָצוֹן MAY IT BE Your will, LORD our God and God of our fathers, that the Temple be rebuilt speedily in our days and may You grant our portion in Your Torah. We will serve You there in reverence as in the days of antiquity and in
Mal. 3 years gone by. "And may the offering of Judah and Jerusalem be pleasant to the LORD as in the days of antiquity and in years gone by."

On days when Taḥanun is not said, the Leader says Full Kaddish on page 285.

**A person undertaking a personal fast says the following at Minha before the fast:*

רִבּוֹן כָּל הָעוֹלָמִים RULER OF ALL worlds, I hereby undertake before You (without a vow or an oath) a voluntary fast tomorrow. May it be Your will, LORD my God and God of my fathers, that You accept me in love and favor, that my prayer may come before You, and that You answer my entreaty in Your abundant compassion, for You hear the prayer of every mouth.

On the afternoon of the fast the following is said:

רִבּוֹן כָּל הָעוֹלָמִים RULER OF ALL worlds, it is revealed and known before You that when the Temple stood a sinner would offer a sacrifice, yet nothing was offered except the fat and the blood, yet You in Your abundant compassion granted atonement. And now I have fasted, and my fat and my blood have been diminished. May it be Your will that this diminution of my fat and my blood, diminished today, be as though I had offered them on the altar, and may You show me favor.

For laws regarding "Interruptions during *Elokai Netzor*," see page 133.

During the עשרת ימי תשובה *and on fast days, except days when* תחנון *is not said,* אבינו מלכנו *(on page 138) is said here.*

סדר תחנון

תחנון *is omitted on various days.* *See page 144.*

נפילת אפיים

Say while sitting; in the presence of a ספר תורה *say until* יֵבֹשׁוּ רָגַע*, leaning forward and resting one's head on the left arm. R. Soloveitchik would rest his head on his arm, even absent a* ספר תורה.

וַיֹּאמֶר דָּוִד אֶל־גָּד, צַר־לִי מְאֹד, נִפְּלָה־נָּא בְיַד־יהוה, כִּי רַבִּים רַחֲמָו, וּבְיַד־אָדָם אַל־אֶפֹּלָה׃ שמואל ב, כד

רַחוּם וְחַנּוּן, חָטָאתִי לְפָנֶיךָ. יהוה מָלֵא רַחֲמִים, רַחֵם עָלַי וְקַבֵּל תַּחֲנוּנָי.

יהוה, אַל־בְּאַפְּךָ תוֹכִיחֵנִי, וְאַל־בַּחֲמָתְךָ תְיַסְּרֵנִי: חָנֵּנִי יהוה, כִּי אֻמְלַל אָנִי, רְפָאֵנִי יהוה, כִּי נִבְהֲלוּ עֲצָמָי: וְנַפְשִׁי נִבְהֲלָה מְאֹד, וְאַתָּה יהוה, עַד־מָתָי: שׁוּבָה יהוה, חַלְּצָה נַפְשִׁי, הוֹשִׁיעֵנִי לְמַעַן חַסְדֶּךָ: כִּי אֵין בַּמָּוֶת זִכְרֶךָ, בִּשְׁאוֹל מִי יוֹדֶה־לָּךְ: יָגַעְתִּי בְּאַנְחָתִי, אַשְׂחֶה בְכָל־לַיְלָה מִטָּתִי, בְּדִמְעָתִי עַרְשִׂי אַמְסֶה: עָשְׁשָׁה מִכַּעַס עֵינִי, עָתְקָה בְּכָל־צוֹרְרָי: סוּרוּ מִמֶּנִּי כָּל־פֹּעֲלֵי אָוֶן, כִּי שָׁמַע יהוה קוֹל בִּכְיִי: שָׁמַע יהוה תְּחִנָּתִי, יהוה תְּפִלָּתִי יִקָּח: יֵבֹשׁוּ וְיִבָּהֲלוּ מְאֹד כָּל־אֹיְבָי, יָשֻׁבוּ יֵבֹשׁוּ רָגַע: תהלים ו

Sit upright.

שׁוֹמֵר יִשְׂרָאֵל, שְׁמֹר שְׁאֵרִית יִשְׂרָאֵל, וְאַל יֹאבַד יִשְׂרָאֵל, הָאוֹמְרִים שְׁמַע יִשְׂרָאֵל.

שׁוֹמֵר גּוֹי אֶחָד, שְׁמֹר שְׁאֵרִית עַם אֶחָד, וְאַל יֹאבַד גּוֹי אֶחָד, הַמְיַחֲדִים שִׁמְךָ, יהוה אֱלֹהֵינוּ יהוה אֶחָד.

---

priority to the Ark, even though, as the *Midrash* teaches, Moses subsequently accepted Betzalel's contention that he should first build the Tabernacle infrastructure. R. Sorotzkin explains that the Ark was commanded first, and not the exterior of the Tabernacle housing, to teach us that the primary purpose of the Tabernacle was to place the study of Torah at the center of the life of the nation, whether physically (in the desert and the Promised Land) or spiritually in the priorities of the individual and nation. Thus this paragraph asks God to restore the Temple and everything associated with it, most particularly the centrality of Torah that is symbolized by the Ark at its very epicenter. A similar juxtaposition occurs in *Pirkei Avot* 5:23 where R. Yehuda b. Teima expresses the identical prayer (R. Basil Herring).

סֵדֶר תַּחֲנוּן / TAHANUN

As evident from the *Ne'ila* service of Yom Kippur, the waning moments of the day are a time of particular divine favor. However the first part of the night (from sunset till halakhic midnight)

Between Rosh HaShana and Yom Kippur and on fast days, except days when Taḥanun is not said, Avinu Malkenu (on page 139) is said here.

TAHANUN

Taḥanun is omitted on various days. See page 145.

FALLING ON ONE'S FOREHEAD

Say while sitting; in the presence of a Torah scroll say until "suddenly frustrated," leaning forward and resting one's head on the left arm. R. Soloveitchik would rest his head on his arm, even absent a Sefer Torah.

II Sam. 24 וַיֹּאמֶר דָּוִד DAVID SAID to Gad, "My anguish is great. Let us fall into the hand of the Lord, for He is full of mercy; and let me not fall into the hands of man."

COMPASSIONATE and Gracious One, I have sinned before You. Lord Who is full of mercy, have mercy on me and accept my pleas.

Ps. 6 יהוה LORD, do not punish in Your anger, and do not chastise me in Your wrath. Favor me, Lord, for I am broken. Heal me, Lord, for my limbs are dismayed. And my soul is greatly dismayed, but You, Lord, how long? Turn, Lord, rescue my soul. Save me for the sake of Your loving-kindness. For in death there is no remembrance of You. In the underworld, who will give You thanks? Every night I make my bed swim. I melt my couch with my tears. My eye is dimmed because of grief. It has become old because of all my adversaries. Depart from me, all you workers of iniquity, for the Lord has heard the voice of my weeping. The Lord has heard my supplication. The Lord will accept my prayer. May all my enemies be frustrated and greatly dismayed. May they turn back, may they be suddenly frustrated.

Sit upright.

שׁוֹמֵר יִשְׂרָאֵל PROTECTOR of Israel, protect the remnant of Israel, and let Israel not be lost – they who say, "Hear, O Israel."

PROTECTOR of a unique nation, protect the remnant of a unique nation, and do not let the unique nation be lost – they who declare the Oneness of Your name, proclaiming: "The Lord is our God, the Lord is One."

---

is a time of divine judgment. Therefore many communities omit *Taḥanun* should the Leader's repetition extend beyond sunset.

וַיֹּאמֶר דָּוִד – *David said.* This verse is taken from II Samuel 24:14, where King David expresses deep remorse at having carried out an improper census of the people. Given a choice of punishments, he prefers to suffer at God's hand "which is most merciful," rather than be at the doubtful mercies of his mortal enemies. This sets the tone for the rest of *Taḥanun*: we acknowledge that our failings are indefensible and thus we can only throw ourselves upon God's tender mercies. The line that follows this verse (beginning with רַחוּם וְחַנּוּן) is not a scriptural verse, but a separate prayer.

שׁוֹמֵר גּוֹי קָדוֹשׁ, שְׁמֹר שְׁאֵרִית עַם קָדוֹשׁ, וְאַל יֹאבַד גּוֹי קָדוֹשׁ, הַמְשַׁלְּשִׁים בְּשָׁלֹשׁ קְדֻשּׁוֹת לְקָדוֹשׁ.

מִתְרַצֶּה בְרַחֲמִים וּמִתְפַּיֵּס בְּתַחֲנוּנִים, הִתְרַצֵּה וְהִתְפַּיֵּס לְדוֹר עָנִי, כִּי אֵין עוֹזֵר.

אָבִינוּ מַלְכֵּנוּ, חָנֵּנוּ וַעֲנֵנוּ, כִּי אֵין בָּנוּ מַעֲשִׂים, עֲשֵׂה עִמָּנוּ צְדָקָה וָחֶסֶד וְהוֹשִׁיעֵנוּ.

Stand at ^.

וַאֲנַחְנוּ לֹא נֵדַע ^מַה־נַּעֲשֶׂה, כִּי עָלֶיךָ עֵינֵינוּ: זְכֹר־רַחֲמֶיךָ יהוה וַחֲסָדֶיךָ, כִּי מֵעוֹלָם הֵמָּה: יְהִי־חַסְדְּךָ יהוה עָלֵינוּ, כַּאֲשֶׁר יִחַלְנוּ לָךְ: אַל־תִּזְכָּר־לָנוּ עֲוֹנֹת רִאשֹׁנִים, מַהֵר יְקַדְּמוּנוּ רַחֲמֶיךָ, כִּי דַלּוֹנוּ מְאֹד: חָנֵּנוּ יהוה חָנֵּנוּ, כִּי־רַב שָׂבַעְנוּ בוּז: בְּרֹגֶז רַחֵם תִּזְכּוֹר: כִּי־הוּא יָדַע יִצְרֵנוּ, זָכוּר כִּי־עָפָר אֲנָחְנוּ: ◂ עָזְרֵנוּ אֱלֹהֵי יִשְׁעֵנוּ עַל־דְּבַר כְּבוֹד־שְׁמֶךָ, וְהַצִּילֵנוּ וְכַפֵּר עַל־חַטֹּאתֵינוּ לְמַעַן שְׁמֶךָ:

דברי הימים ב׳ כ, יב · תהלים כה · תהלים לג · תהלים עט · תהלים קכג · חבקוק ג · תהלים קג · תהלים עט

קדיש שלם

ש״ץ: **יִתְגַּדַּל** וְיִתְקַדַּשׁ שְׁמֵהּ רַבָּא (קהל: אָמֵן) בְּעָלְמָא דִּי בְרָא כִרְעוּתֵהּ וְיַמְלִיךְ מַלְכוּתֵהּ בְּחַיֵּיכוֹן וּבְיוֹמֵיכוֹן וּבְחַיֵּי דְכָל בֵּית יִשְׂרָאֵל, בַּעֲגָלָא וּבִזְמַן קָרִיב, וְאִמְרוּ אָמֵן. (קהל: אָמֵן)

קהל וש״ץ: יְהֵא שְׁמֵהּ רַבָּא מְבָרַךְ לְעָלַם וּלְעָלְמֵי עָלְמַיָּא.

ש״ץ: יִתְבָּרַךְ וְיִשְׁתַּבַּח וְיִתְפָּאַר, וְיִתְרוֹמַם וְיִתְנַשֵּׂא וְיִתְהַדָּר וְיִתְעַלֶּה וְיִתְהַלָּל שְׁמֵהּ דְּקֻדְשָׁא בְּרִיךְ הוּא (קהל: בְּרִיךְ הוּא) לְעֵלָּא מִן כָּל בִּרְכָתָא / בעשרת ימי תשובה: לְעֵלָּא (וּ)לְעֵלָּא מִכָּל בִּרְכָתָא/ וְשִׁירָתָא, תֻּשְׁבְּחָתָא וְנֶחֱמָתָא דַּאֲמִירָן בְּעָלְמָא, וְאִמְרוּ אָמֵן. (קהל: אָמֵן)

תִּתְקַבַּל צְלוֹתְהוֹן וּבָעוּתְהוֹן דְּכָל יִשְׂרָאֵל, קֳדָם אֲבוּהוֹן דִּי בִשְׁמַיָּא, וְאִמְרוּ אָמֵן. (קהל: אָמֵן)

יְהֵא שְׁלָמָא רַבָּא מִן שְׁמַיָּא וְחַיִּים, עָלֵינוּ וְעַל כָּל יִשְׂרָאֵל, וְאִמְרוּ אָמֵן. (קהל: אָמֵן)

Bow, take three steps back, as if taking leave of the Divine Presence, then bow, first left, then right, then center, while saying:

עֹשֶׂה שָׁלוֹם / בעשרת ימי תשובה: הַשָּׁלוֹם/ בִּמְרוֹמָיו, הוּא יַעֲשֶׂה שָׁלוֹם עָלֵינוּ, וְעַל כָּל יִשְׂרָאֵל, וְאִמְרוּ אָמֵן. (קהל: אָמֵן)

PROTECTOR of a holy nation, protect the remnant of a holy nation, and do not let a holy nation be lost – they who repeat three times the three-fold declaration of the sanctity of the Holy One.

YOU WHO ARE appeased by mercy, and won over by prayers – be appeased and won over by this impoverished generation, for there is none to help us.

FATHER, King, grant us grace, grant us response, for we have no deeds to defend us; perform charity, deal kindly with us, and save us.

Stand at ▴.

II Chr. 12 Ps. 25 וַאֲנַחְנוּ AND WE do not know ▴what we can do – for our eyes are on You.
Remember Your mercy, O Lord, and Your loving-kindnesses, which are of
Ps. 33 old. May Your loving-kindness, O Lord, be upon us, as we hope for You.
Ps. 79 Do not remember against us former iniquities. Let Your mercies quickly go
Ps. 123 ahead of us, for we are brought very low. Be gracious unto us, O Lord, be
Hab. 3 gracious unto us, for we have suffered our fill of contempt. In the midst of
Ps. 103 fury – remember compassion. Indeed, He knows our desires, He remembers
Ps. 79 that we are dust. ▸ Help us, O God of our salvation, because of the glory of
Your name, and deliver us and pardon our sins for Your name's sake.

FULL KADDISH

Leader: יִתְגַּדַּל EXALTED AND HALLOWED may God's great name be, in the world He created as He willed. May He reign in your lifetimes and in your days, and in the lifetime of the whole house of Israel, speedily and soon, and say, Amen.

All: May His great name be blessed forever and all time.

Leader: Blessed and praised, honored, extolled, glorified, adored and exalted above all be the name of the Holy One, blessed is He, (*Between Rosh Hashana & Yom Kippur:* above and) beyond any blessing, hymn, praise, or expressions of consolation that may be uttered in this world, and say, Amen.

May the prayers and pleas of all Israel be accepted before their Father Who is in heaven – and say, Amen.

May abundant peace descend from heaven, as well as life, for us and for all Israel, and say, Amen.

Bow, take three steps back, as if taking leave of the Divine Presence, then bow, first left, then right, then center, while saying:

May He Who makes peace in the highest heaven, make peace for us, and for all Israel, and say, Amen.

Stand while saying עָלֵינוּ*. Bow at* ▼.

עָלֵינוּ לְשַׁבֵּחַ לַאֲדוֹן הַכֹּל, לָתֵת גְּדֻלָּה לְיוֹצֵר בְּרֵאשִׁית, שֶׁלֹּא עָשָׂנוּ כְּגוֹיֵי הָאֲרָצוֹת, וְלֹא שָׂמָנוּ כְּמִשְׁפְּחוֹת הָאֲדָמָה, שֶׁלֹּא שָׂם חֶלְקֵנוּ כָּהֶם וְגוֹרָלֵנוּ כְּכָל הֲמוֹנָם. (שֶׁהֵם מִשְׁתַּחֲוִים לְהֶבֶל וָרִיק וּמִתְפַּלְלִים אֶל אֵל לֹא יוֹשִׁיעַ.) ▼וַאֲנַחְנוּ כּוֹרְעִים וּמִשְׁתַּחֲוִים וּמוֹדִים, לִפְנֵי מֶלֶךְ מַלְכֵי הַמְּלָכִים, הַקָּדוֹשׁ בָּרוּךְ הוּא, שֶׁהוּא נוֹטֶה שָׁמַיִם וְיוֹסֵד אָרֶץ, וּמוֹשַׁב יְקָרוֹ בַּשָּׁמַיִם מִמַּעַל, וּשְׁכִינַת עֻזּוֹ בְּגָבְהֵי מְרוֹמִים. הוּא אֱלֹהֵינוּ, אֵין עוֹד. אֱמֶת
דברים ד מַלְכֵּנוּ, אֶפֶס זוּלָתוֹ, כַּכָּתוּב בְּתוֹרָתוֹ, וְיָדַעְתָּ הַיּוֹם וַהֲשֵׁבֹתָ אֶל־לְבָבֶךָ, כִּי יהוה הוּא הָאֱלֹהִים בַּשָּׁמַיִם מִמַּעַל וְעַל־הָאָרֶץ מִתָּחַת, אֵין עוֹד:

עַל כֵּן נְקַוֶּה לְּךָ יהוה אֱלֹהֵינוּ, לִרְאוֹת מְהֵרָה בְּתִפְאֶרֶת עֻזֶּךָ, לְהַעֲבִיר גִּלּוּלִים מִן הָאָרֶץ, וְהָאֱלִילִים כָּרוֹת יִכָּרֵתוּן, לְתַקֵּן עוֹלָם בְּמַלְכוּת שַׁדַּי. וְכָל בְּנֵי בָשָׂר יִקְרְאוּ בִשְׁמֶךָ לְהַפְנוֹת אֵלֶיךָ כָּל רִשְׁעֵי אָרֶץ. יַכִּירוּ וְיֵדְעוּ כָּל יוֹשְׁבֵי תֵבֵל, כִּי לְךָ תִּכְרַע כָּל בֶּרֶךְ, תִּשָּׁבַע כָּל לָשׁוֹן. לְפָנֶיךָ יהוה אֱלֹהֵינוּ יִכְרְעוּ וְיִפֹּלוּ, וְלִכְבוֹד שִׁמְךָ יְקָר יִתֵּנוּ, וִיקַבְּלוּ כֻלָּם אֶת עֹל מַלְכוּתֶךָ, וְתִמְלֹךְ עֲלֵיהֶם מְהֵרָה לְעוֹלָם וָעֶד. כִּי הַמַּלְכוּת שֶׁלְּךָ הִיא וּלְעוֹלְמֵי עַד תִּמְלֹךְ
שמות טו בְּכָבוֹד, כַּכָּתוּב בְּתוֹרָתֶךָ, יהוה יִמְלֹךְ לְעֹלָם וָעֶד: ◄ וְנֶאֱמַר,
זכריה יד וְהָיָה יהוה לְמֶלֶךְ עַל־כָּל־הָאָרֶץ, בַּיּוֹם הַהוּא יִהְיֶה יהוה אֶחָד וּשְׁמוֹ אֶחָד:

Some add:

משלי ג **אַל־תִּירָא** מִפַּחַד פִּתְאֹם וּמִשֹּׁאַת רְשָׁעִים כִּי תָבֹא: עֻצוּ עֵצָה וְתֻפָר, דַּבְּרוּ דָבָר וְלֹא
ישעיה ח יָקוּם, כִּי עִמָּנוּ אֵל: וְעַד־זִקְנָה אֲנִי הוּא, וְעַד־שֵׂיבָה אֲנִי אֶסְבֹּל, אֲנִי עָשִׂיתִי
ישעיה מו וַאֲנִי אֶשָּׂא וַאֲנִי אֶסְבֹּל וַאֲמַלֵּט:

Stand while saying Aleinu. Bow at ▼.

עָלֵינוּ WE MUST, all of us, praise the Master of all, and ascribe greatness to He Who formed creation, for He did not make us like the nations of the world, nor render us like the families of the earth. He did not make our portion to be as theirs, nor our destiny like that of their masses. (For idolaters bow to vanity and emptiness and pray to a god who cannot save.) ▼We, however, bend our knees, bow, and give thanks before the King of the most exalted of kings, the Holy One, blessed is He. He is the One Who spreads out the heavens and establishes the earth. The seat of His glory is in the heavens above, and His Presence in all its strength is found in its highest abode. He is our God – there is no other. In truth
Deut. 4 He is our King; there is none but Him; as is written in His Torah: "On this day you should know, and take to heart, that the Lord is God in the heavens above and on the earth below – there is no other."

We therefore hope in You, Lord our God, that we may soon see the glory of Your might when You will remove abominations from the earth and the idols shall be utterly destroyed, when the world shall be perfected under the rule of the Almighty. Then all mankind shall invoke Your name, to turn all the wicked on earth toward You. All dwellers on earth will perceive and understand that to You every knee must bend, every tongue vow fealty. Before You, Lord our God, all will kneel and bow down, and give honor to Your glorious name. They will all accept the rule of Your dominion, and You will speedily rule over them forevermore. For the kingdom is Yours, and to all eternity You
Ex. 15 shall reign in glory, as it is written in Your Torah, "The Lord shall reign
Zech. 14 forever and ever." ▸ And it is said, "And the Lord shall be King over all the earth; in that day shall the Lord be One, and His name One."

Some add:

Prov. 3 **אַל־תִּירָא** DO NOT FEAR sudden terror or the destruction when it comes to the
Is. 8 wicked. Devise a plan, and it will be thwarted; state a case and it will not stand,
Is. 46 for God is with us. And when you are old, I will remain; when you are aged, I will endure. I created you, I will carry you, I will endure, and I will rescue you.

קדיש יתום

The following prayer, said by mourners, requires the presence of a מנין.
A transliteration can be found on page 1345.

אבל: **יִתְגַּדַּל** וְיִתְקַדַּשׁ שְׁמֵהּ רַבָּא (קהל: אָמֵן), בְּעָלְמָא דִּי בְרָא כִרְעוּתֵהּ. וְיַמְלִיךְ מַלְכוּתֵהּ, בְּחַיֵּיכוֹן וּבְיוֹמֵיכוֹן וּבְחַיֵּי דְכָל בֵּית יִשְׂרָאֵל, בַּעֲגָלָא וּבִזְמַן קָרִיב, וְאִמְרוּ אָמֵן. (קהל: אָמֵן)

קהל ואבל: יְהֵא שְׁמֵהּ רַבָּא מְבָרַךְ לְעָלַם וּלְעָלְמֵי עָלְמַיָּא.

אבל: יִתְבָּרַךְ וְיִשְׁתַּבַּח וְיִתְפָּאַר, וְיִתְרוֹמַם וְיִתְנַשֵּׂא וְיִתְהַדָּר וְיִתְעַלֶּה וְיִתְהַלָּל שְׁמֵהּ דְּקֻדְשָׁא בְּרִיךְ הוּא (קהל: בְּרִיךְ הוּא), לְעֵלָּא מִן כָּל בִּרְכָתָא / בעשרת ימי תשובה: לְעֵלָּא (וּ)לְעֵלָּא מִכָּל בִּרְכָתָא / וְשִׁירָתָא, תֻּשְׁבְּחָתָא וְנֶחֱמָתָא דַּאֲמִירָן בְּעָלְמָא, וְאִמְרוּ אָמֵן. (קהל: אָמֵן)

יְהֵא שְׁלָמָא רַבָּא מִן שְׁמַיָּא וְחַיִּים, עָלֵינוּ וְעַל כָּל יִשְׂרָאֵל, וְאִמְרוּ אָמֵן. (קהל: אָמֵן)

Bow, take three steps back, as if taking leave of the Divine Presence, then bow, first left, then right, then center, while saying:

עֹשֶׂה שָׁלוֹם / בעשרת ימי תשובה: הַשָּׁלוֹם / בִּמְרוֹמָיו, הוּא יַעֲשֶׂה שָׁלוֹם עָלֵינוּ, וְעַל כָּל יִשְׂרָאֵל, וְאִמְרוּ אָמֵן. (קהל: אָמֵן)

On חנוכה*, the lights are lit in the synagogue between* מנחה *and* מעריב *(page 950).*

MOURNER'S KADDISH

The following prayer, said by mourners, requires the presence of a minyan.
A transliteration can be found on page 1345.

Mourner: יִתְגַּדַּל EXALTED AND HALLOWED may God's great name be, in the world He created as He willed. May He reign in your lifetimes and in your days, and in the lifetime of the whole house of Israel, speedily and soon, and say, Amen.

All: May His great name be blessed forever and all time.

Mourner: Blessed and praised, honored, extolled, glorified, adored and exalted above all be the name of the Holy One, blessed is He, (*Between Rosh Hashana & Yom Kippur:* above and) beyond any blessing, hymn, praise, or expressions of consolation that may be uttered in this world, and say, Amen.

May abundant peace descend from heaven, as well as life, for us and for all Israel, and say, Amen.

Bow, take three steps back, as if taking leave of the Divine Presence, then bow, first left, then right, then center, while saying:

May He Who makes peace in the highest heaven, make peace for us, and for all Israel, and say, Amen.

On Ḥanukka, the lights are lit in the synagogue between Minḥa and Ma'ariv (page 951).

מעריב לחול ולמוצאי שבת

On מוצאי שבת *some have the custom to sing* לְדָוִד, בָּרוּךְ יהוה צוּרִי *and* לַמְנַצֵּחַ בִּנְגִינֹת מִזְמוֹר שִׁיר *before* תפילת מעריב (*page 730*).

וְהוּא רַחוּם, יְכַפֵּר עָוֹן וְלֹא־יַשְׁחִית, וְהִרְבָּה לְהָשִׁיב אַפּוֹ, וְלֹא־ תהלים עח
יָעִיר כָּל־חֲמָתוֹ: יהוה הוֹשִׁיעָה, הַמֶּלֶךְ יַעֲנֵנוּ בְיוֹם־ תהלים כ
קָרְאֵנוּ:

קריאת שמע וברכותיה

The following blessing and response are said only in the presence of a מנין.
The שליח ציבור *says the following (while bowing at* בָּרְכוּ *and straightening at Hashem).*
The קהל *followed by the* שליח ציבור *responds by bowing at* בָּרוּךְ *and standing straight at Hashem.*

ש״ץ: **בָּרְכוּ** אֶת יהוה הַמְבֹרָךְ.

קהל: בָּרוּךְ יהוה הַמְבֹרָךְ לְעוֹלָם וָעֶד.

ש״ץ: בָּרוּךְ יהוה הַמְבֹרָךְ לְעוֹלָם וָעֶד.

מַעֲרִיב / THE EVENING SERVICE
As the Gemara (*Berakhot* 27b) explains, while *Shaḥarit* and *Minḥa* are obligatory services that correspond to the daily morning and afternoon *Tamid* sacrifices, there was no daily evening sacrifice, and thus *Ma'ariv* was originally instituted as רְשׁוּת (a voluntary service). Rambam writes that in due course the Jewish people accepted *Ma'ariv* as an obligation, albeit with certain leniencies (e.g., it can be recited before dark and there is no repetition of the *Ma'ariv Amida*). According to Tosafot, *Ma'ariv* is considered to be voluntary only in the sense that it can be deferred in the face of other required obligations. This illustrates the general rule that we do not revise or disregard accepted prayer practices and customs. They are to be respected as fully obligatory, and thus maintained wherever possible (R. Asher Weiss).

וְהוּא רַחוּם – Before beginning to pray, we apologize for deigning to approach God despite our human weaknesses and at times

ONE WHO COMES LATE TO MA'ARIV
If one comes late to *Ma'ariv*, the highest priority is to recite the *Amida* together with the congregation, even if one must skip *Keriat Shema* and its blessings and recite them after the prayers (*OḤ* 326:3). If one can catch up to the congregation by skipping *Barukh HaShem LeOlam*, one should do so (*MB* 236:11). After the *Amida*, when one recites *Keriat Shema* and its blessings, one should omit *Barukh HaShem LeOlam*, or at least the *berakha* at the end (*ibid.*).

MA'ARIV FOR WEEKDAYS & THE CONCLUSION OF SHABBAT

On Motza'ei Shabbat some have the custom to sing Psalm 144 and Psalm 67 before the Ma'ariv Service (page 731).

Ps. 78 וְהוּא רַחוּם BUT HE, the Compassionate One, forgives iniquity and
does not destroy; often He has turned away His anger and not stirred
Ps. 20 up all His wrath. Lord, save! The King will answer us on the day that
we call.

BLESSINGS OF THE SHEMA

The following blessing and response are said only in the presence of a minyan. The Leader says the following (while bowing at "Barekhu" and straightening at Hashem). The congregation followed by the Leader responds by bowing at "Barukh" and standing straight at Hashem.

Leader: בָּרְכוּ BLESS THE LORD, the blessed One.

Cong: Blessed is the Lord Who is blessed for all eternity.

Leader: Blessed is the Lord Who is blessed for all eternity.

---

insincerity (see Psalms 78:36–37, *Ta'anit* 8a) and invoke His mercy. At a later time, this recitation became limited to *Ma'ariv* for various reasons: because at that time of the day there is no nighttime sacrifice to effect atonement (*Sefer HaPardes, Maḥzor Vitri*); the courts would administer corporal punishment around that time of day (*Sefer HaPardes*); and that nighttime during the week is the time of administration of punishment in Gehenna (R. Moshe De Leon) (Prof. Yaakov Gartner).

בִּרְכוֹת קְרִיאַת שְׁמַע / BLESSINGS OF THE SHEMA

As pointed out in the commentary on the blessings surrounding the *Shema* of *Shaḥarit*, there are many parallels between the three paragraphs of the *Shema* and the three *berakhot* that precede and follow them. The same is true for *Ma'ariv*, even though the precise formulations differ from their counterparts in *Shaḥarit*, so as to correspond to nighttime prayer (R. Joseph B. Soloveitchik).

INTERRUPTIONS DURING THE BLESSINGS OF SHEMA

As a general rule during *Ma'ariv* one should not speak from *Barekhu* until after the *Amida*. As in *Shaḥarit* (see page 89), there are certain exceptions (*MB* 236:1). At *Ma'ariv* the *Gabbai* is permitted to announce the insertions of *Ya'aleh VeYavo, Tal uMatar* or *Al HaNissim* before the *Amida* (*OḤ* 236:2 and *MB* 236:7).

בָּרוּךְ אַתָּה יהוה אֱלֹהֵינוּ מֶלֶךְ הָעוֹלָם, אֲשֶׁר בִּדְבָרוֹ מַעֲרִיב עֲרָבִים, בְּחָכְמָה פּוֹתֵחַ שְׁעָרִים, וּבִתְבוּנָה מְשַׁנֶּה עִתִּים וּמַחֲלִיף אֶת הַזְּמַנִּים, וּמְסַדֵּר אֶת הַכּוֹכָבִים בְּמִשְׁמְרוֹתֵיהֶם בָּרָקִיעַ כִּרְצוֹנוֹ. בּוֹרֵא יוֹם וָלָיְלָה, גּוֹלֵל אוֹר מִפְּנֵי חֹשֶׁךְ וְחֹשֶׁךְ מִפְּנֵי אוֹר, ‹ וּמַעֲבִיר יוֹם וּמֵבִיא לָיְלָה, וּמַבְדִּיל בֵּין יוֹם וּבֵין לָיְלָה, יהוה צְבָאוֹת שְׁמוֹ. אֵל חַי וְקַיָּם, תָּמִיד יִמְלֹךְ עָלֵינוּ לְעוֹלָם וָעֶד. בָּרוּךְ אַתָּה יהוה, הַמַּעֲרִיב עֲרָבִים.

אַהֲבַת עוֹלָם בֵּית יִשְׂרָאֵל עַמְּךָ אָהָבְתָּ, תּוֹרָה וּמִצְוֹת, חֻקִּים וּמִשְׁפָּטִים, אוֹתָנוּ לִמַּדְתָּ, עַל כֵּן יהוה אֱלֹהֵינוּ בְּשָׁכְבֵנוּ וּבְקוּמֵנוּ נָשִׂיחַ בְּחֻקֶּיךָ, וְנִשְׂמַח בְּדִבְרֵי תוֹרָתֶךָ וּבְמִצְוֹתֶיךָ לְעוֹלָם וָעֶד, ‹ כִּי הֵם חַיֵּינוּ וְאֹרֶךְ יָמֵינוּ, וּבָהֶם נֶהְגֶּה יוֹמָם וָלָיְלָה. וְאַהֲבָתְךָ אַל תָּסִיר מִמֶּנּוּ לְעוֹלָמִים. בָּרוּךְ אַתָּה יהוה, אוֹהֵב עַמּוֹ יִשְׂרָאֵל.

The שמע must be said with intense concentration. In the first paragraph one should accept, with love, the sovereignty of God; in the second, accept the מצוות as the will of God. The end of the third paragraph constitutes fulfillment of the מצווה to remember, morning and evening, the Exodus from Egypt.

When not praying with a מנין, some say:

אֵל מֶלֶךְ נֶאֱמָן

The following verse should be said aloud, while covering the eyes with the right hand:

דברים ו **שְׁמַע** יִשְׂרָאֵל, יהוה אֱלֹהֵינוּ, יהוה | **אֶחָד**:

Quietly בָּרוּךְ שֵׁם כְּבוֹד מַלְכוּתוֹ לְעוֹלָם וָעֶד.

כִּי הֵם חַיֵּינוּ וְאֹרֶךְ יָמֵינוּ – These two phrases complement each other. The first refers to the words of the Torah that connect us to God Who is our life-giving source. The second phrase highlights the words of the Torah as the essential modality for the refinement of our souls (R. Avraham Yitzḥak HaKohen Kook).

אֵל מֶלֶךְ נֶאֱמָן – *God, the King Who is faithful.* The *Midrash Tanḥuma* explains that the 245 words of the *Shema*, together with these three words, correspond to the 248 positive commandments of the Torah. This teaches us that God blesses our bodies when we observe His commandments.

שְׁמַע / THE SHEMA

For a more detailed exposition of the correct intent in reciting the *Shema*, as explained by R. Joseph B. Soloveitchik, see the introductory

בָּרוּךְ BLESSED ARE YOU, Lord, our God, King of the universe, at Whose command evening occurs, Who opens gates with wisdom, Who alters time periods and changes seasons with understanding, and Who places the stars in order according to their respective duties in heaven, in accordance with His will. He creates both day and night, making light give way to darkness, and darkness to light. ▸ He causes day to pass away and brings night, and separates day from night – Lord of hosts is His name. He is the living and enduring God, Who will always rule over us, forever and ever. Blessed are You, Lord, Who makes evening occur.

אַהֲבַת עוֹלָם WITH EVERLASTING LOVE have You loved the house of Israel Your people. You have taught us Torah and commandments, statutes and laws. Therefore, Lord our God, whenever we lie down to sleep, and whenever we arise, we will discuss Your statutes, and rejoice in the words of Your Torah and Your commandments forever and ever. ▸ For they are our life and our length of days, and we will meditate on them day and night. May You never deprive us of Your love. Blessed are You, Lord, Who loves His people Israel.

The Shema must be said with intense concentration. In the first paragraph one should accept, with love, the sovereignty of God; in the second, accept the mitzvot as the will of God. The end of the third paragraph constitutes fulfillment of the mitzva to remember, morning and evening, the Exodus from Egypt.

When not praying with a minyan, some say:

God, the King Who is faithful.

The following verse should be said aloud, while covering the eyes with the right hand:

Deut. 6 HEAR, O ISRAEL, the LORD is our God, the LORD is One.

Quietly: Blessed is the name of His glorious kingdom forever and ever.

---

essay on page xxxii, as well the further analysis found on page E80.

שְׁמַע יִשְׂרָאֵל – *Hear, O Israel.* This verse summons the Jewish people to join as one, to serve the One God. It is only to the extent that we are unified that we can experience God's Oneness. Conversely, we can achieve unity as a people only when we submit to God's sovereignty. This is why God precedes His revelation at Sinai by telling Moses to "Gather the people together so they can hear My words" (Deut. 4:10). So too, as the Gemara (*Pesaḥim* 56a) records, Jacob gathered his twelve sons together so they could recite the *Shema*. Moreover, as

דברים ו
וְאָהַבְתָּ אֵת יהוה אֱלֹהֶיךָ, בְּכׇל־לְבָבְךָ וּבְכׇל־נַפְשְׁךָ וּבְכׇל־מְאֹדֶךָ:
וְהָיוּ הַדְּבָרִים הָאֵלֶּה, אֲשֶׁר אָנֹכִי מְצַוְּךָ הַיּוֹם, עַל־לְבָבֶךָ:
וְשִׁנַּנְתָּם לְבָנֶיךָ וְדִבַּרְתָּ בָּם, בְּשִׁבְתְּךָ בְּבֵיתֶךָ וּבְלֶכְתְּךָ בַדֶּרֶךְ, וּבְשׇׁכְבְּךָ
וּבְקוּמֶךָ: וּקְשַׁרְתָּם לְאוֹת עַל־יָדֶךָ וְהָיוּ לְטֹטָפֹת בֵּין עֵינֶיךָ: וּכְתַבְתָּם
עַל־מְזֻזוֹת בֵּיתֶךָ וּבִשְׁעָרֶיךָ:

דברים יא
וְהָיָה אִם־שָׁמֹעַ תִּשְׁמְעוּ אֶל־מִצְוֺתַי אֲשֶׁר אָנֹכִי מְצַוֶּה אֶתְכֶם
הַיּוֹם, לְאַהֲבָה אֶת־יהוה אֱלֹהֵיכֶם וּלְעׇבְדוֹ, בְּכׇל־לְבַבְכֶם
וּבְכׇל־נַפְשְׁכֶם: וְנָתַתִּי מְטַר־אַרְצְכֶם בְּעִתּוֹ, יוֹרֶה וּמַלְקוֹשׁ, וְאָסַפְתָּ
דְגָנֶךָ וְתִירֹשְׁךָ וְיִצְהָרֶךָ: וְנָתַתִּי עֵשֶׂב בְּשָׂדְךָ לִבְהֶמְתֶּךָ, וְאָכַלְתָּ
וְשָׂבָעְתָּ: הִשָּׁמְרוּ לָכֶם פֶּן־יִפְתֶּה לְבַבְכֶם, וְסַרְתֶּם וַעֲבַדְתֶּם אֱלֹהִים
אֲחֵרִים וְהִשְׁתַּחֲוִיתֶם לָהֶם: וְחָרָה אַף־יהוה בָּכֶם, וְעָצַר אֶת־
הַשָּׁמַיִם וְלֹא־יִהְיֶה מָטָר, וְהָאֲדָמָה לֹא תִתֵּן אֶת־יְבוּלָהּ, וַאֲבַדְתֶּם
מְהֵרָה מֵעַל הָאָרֶץ הַטֹּבָה אֲשֶׁר יהוה נֹתֵן לָכֶם: וְשַׂמְתֶּם אֶת־דְּבָרַי
אֵלֶּה עַל־לְבַבְכֶם וְעַל־נַפְשְׁכֶם, וּקְשַׁרְתֶּם אֹתָם לְאוֹת עַל־יֶדְכֶם,
וְהָיוּ לְטוֹטָפֹת בֵּין עֵינֵיכֶם: וְלִמַּדְתֶּם אֹתָם אֶת־בְּנֵיכֶם לְדַבֵּר בָּם,
בְּשִׁבְתְּךָ בְּבֵיתֶךָ וּבְלֶכְתְּךָ בַדֶּרֶךְ, וּבְשׇׁכְבְּךָ וּבְקוּמֶךָ: וּכְתַבְתָּם עַל־
מְזוּזוֹת בֵּיתֶךָ וּבִשְׁעָרֶיךָ: לְמַעַן יִרְבּוּ יְמֵיכֶם וִימֵי בְנֵיכֶם עַל הָאֲדָמָה
אֲשֶׁר נִשְׁבַּע יהוה לַאֲבֹתֵיכֶם לָתֵת לָהֶם, כִּימֵי הַשָּׁמַיִם עַל־הָאָרֶץ:

Rashi explains, the verse asserts that there will come a time when all the nations will also recognize God's uniqueness. This is why in the Torah the letters ע and ד (that spell עֵד – "witness"), are enlarged. The letter ע signifies seventy, which is the symbolic number of the nations of the world, while the ד signifies four, representing the four points of the compass. Thus when the Jews who are scattered among the nations recite the *Shema* it will lead to the eventual redemption of humanity. Finally, this testimony facilitates our own acquisition of wisdom, as it says: "עֵדוּת ה׳ נֶאֱמָנָה, מַחְכִּימַת פֶּתִי – The testimony of the Lord is faithful, making the simple wise" (Psalms 19:8) (*Sefat Emet*).

וְאָהַבְתָּ – *You shall love.* Rambam in *Hilkhot Yesodei HaTorah* 2:2 explains how we can achieve love of God: The moment we reflect on God's deeds and creatures, which are wondrous and great, perceiving through them His immeasurable and infinite wisdom, we cannot but love, praise, and glorify Him, with an overwhelming desire to know His great name.

וְאָהַבְתָּ ... בְּכׇל־נַפְשְׁךָ – *You shall love... with all your soul.* Rambam, in his Introduction to *Pirkei*

Deut. 6 **וְאָהַבְתָּ** YOU SHALL LOVE the LORD your God with all your heart, and with all your soul, and with all your might. And these words which I command you this day shall be upon your heart. You shall teach them diligently to your children, speaking of them when you sit in your house and when you walk by the way, when you lie down and when you rise up. You shall bind them for a sign on your hand, and they shall be as *tefillin* between your eyes. And you shall write them upon the doorposts of your house and upon your gates.

Deut. 11 **וְהָיָה** IT SHALL COME to PASS that if you will listen diligently to My commandments with which I charge you this day, to love the LORD your God and to serve Him with all your heart and with all your soul, then will I send the rain for your land in its due season, the autumn rain and the spring rain, that you may gather in your corn, your wine, and your oil. And I will give grass in your field for your cattle, and you shall eat and be satisfied. Be careful lest your heart be deceived, and you turn aside and serve other gods and worship them. For then the LORD's wrath will be kindled against you, and He will shut the heavens so that there will be no rain, the land will not yield her produce, and you shall perish quickly from the good land which the LORD gives you. Therefore place these words of Mine upon your heart and upon your soul, and you shall bind them for a sign on your hand and they shall be as *tefillin* between your eyes. And you shall teach them to your children, speaking of them when you sit in your house and when you walk on the way, when you lie down and when you rise up. And you shall write them upon the doorposts of your house and upon your gates. That long as the days of the heavens above the earth may be your days and the days of your children in the land which the LORD promised your fathers to give to them.

Avot, explains that this obligates us to ensure that every activity in our lives contributes in some way to the ultimate goal of knowing and thereby loving Him. As proof, Rambam quotes Proverbs 3:6 ("know Him in all your ways"), which is understood by the Gemara (*Berakhot* 63a) to be referring even to acts that in some respect might be sinful. As Rashi explains, בְּכָל־לְבָבְךָ ("with all your heart") refers to both the good inclination and the evil one. As the Mishna *Avot* 2:11 states, "let all of your actions be for the sake of Heaven."

וַיֹּאמֶר יהוה אֶל־מֹשֶׁה לֵּאמֹר: דַּבֵּר אֶל־בְּנֵי יִשְׂרָאֵל וְאָמַרְתָּ במדבר טו
אֲלֵהֶם, וְעָשׂוּ לָהֶם צִיצִת עַל־כַּנְפֵי בִגְדֵיהֶם לְדֹרֹתָם,
וְנָתְנוּ עַל־צִיצִת הַכָּנָף פְּתִיל תְּכֵלֶת: וְהָיָה לָכֶם לְצִיצִת, וּרְאִיתֶם
אֹתוֹ וּזְכַרְתֶּם אֶת־כָּל־מִצְוֹת יהוה וַעֲשִׂיתֶם אֹתָם, וְלֹא תָתֻרוּ
אַחֲרֵי לְבַבְכֶם וְאַחֲרֵי עֵינֵיכֶם, אֲשֶׁר־אַתֶּם זֹנִים אַחֲרֵיהֶם: לְמַעַן
תִּזְכְּרוּ וַעֲשִׂיתֶם אֶת־כָּל־מִצְוֹתָי, וִהְיִיתֶם קְדֹשִׁים לֵאלֹהֵיכֶם: אֲנִי
יהוה אֱלֹהֵיכֶם, אֲשֶׁר הוֹצֵאתִי אֶתְכֶם מֵאֶרֶץ מִצְרַיִם, לִהְיוֹת לָכֶם
לֵאלֹהִים, אֲנִי יהוה אֱלֹהֵיכֶם: **אֱמֶת**

The שליח ציבור *repeats:*

► יהוה אֱלֹהֵיכֶם אֱמֶת

וֶאֱמוּנָה כָּל זֹאת וְקַיָּם עָלֵינוּ, כִּי הוּא יהוה אֱלֹהֵינוּ וְאֵין זוּלָתוֹ,
וַאֲנַחְנוּ יִשְׂרָאֵל עַמּוֹ. הַפּוֹדֵנוּ מִיַּד מְלָכִים, מַלְכֵּנוּ
הַגּוֹאֲלֵנוּ מִכַּף כָּל הֶעָרִיצִים. הָאֵל הַנִּפְרָע לָנוּ מִצָּרֵינוּ, וְהַמְשַׁלֵּם
גְּמוּל לְכָל אֹיְבֵי נַפְשֵׁנוּ. הָעוֹשֶׂה גְדוֹלוֹת עַד אֵין חֵקֶר, וְנִפְלָאוֹת עַד
אֵין מִסְפָּר, הַשָּׂם נַפְשֵׁנוּ בַּחַיִּים, וְלֹא־נָתַן לַמּוֹט רַגְלֵנוּ: הַמַּדְרִיכֵנוּ תהלים סו
עַל בָּמוֹת אוֹיְבֵינוּ, וַיָּרֶם קַרְנֵנוּ עַל כָּל שׂוֹנְאֵינוּ. הָעוֹשֶׂה לָּנוּ נִסִּים
וּנְקָמָה בְּפַרְעֹה, אוֹתוֹת וּמוֹפְתִים בְּאַדְמַת בְּנֵי חָם. הַמַּכֶּה בְעֶבְרָתוֹ
כָּל בְּכוֹרֵי מִצְרַיִם, וַיּוֹצֵא אֶת עַמּוֹ יִשְׂרָאֵל מִתּוֹכָם לְחֵרוּת עוֹלָם.
הַמַּעֲבִיר בָּנָיו בֵּין גִּזְרֵי יַם סוּף, אֶת רוֹדְפֵיהֶם וְאֶת שׂוֹנְאֵיהֶם

אֱמֶת וֶאֱמוּנָה – *True it is and unchanging*. The words כָּל זֹאת (all this) evoke Nehemiah 10:1 who said, "And yet for all of this we make a true covenant and transcribe it." So too, the word וֶאֱמוּנָה evokes the Second Temple period when the nation sealed an אֲמָנָה (covenant) to accept God's kingship and uphold Torah observance despite their dismal circumstances. The Jewish homeland was reduced to being a province of Persia, Jerusalem was desolate, and the Jews saw themselves as enslaved (Prof. Stefan Reif).

Emet and the related *emuna* are used in ancient documents to refer to loyalty to a covenant. The term *kayam* also meant accepting a covenant (see Esther 9:21). Thus they convey that our covenant with God is forever binding; if our circumstances in exile are dark as night it is only because "You are righteous and we have sinned" (Nehemiah 9:33). God has lived up to His commitment and we have not. In the remainder of the paragraph we enumerate God's past interventions on our behalf, and

Num. 15 וַיֹּאמֶר THE LORD SPOKE to Moses, saying: "Speak to the children of Israel and tell them to make for themselves *tzitzit* on the corners of their garments, throughout their generations, putting a thread of blue upon the *tzitzit* of each corner. It shall be to you a *tzitzit* which you may look upon and remember all the commandments of the LORD and do them, that you shall not stray after your heart and your eyes, after which you sinfully follow. So may you remember and do all My commandments and be holy for your God. I am the LORD your God Who brought you out of the land of Egypt to be your God; I am the LORD your God." TRUE IT IS –

The Leader repeats:

▸ The LORD your God. True it is –

וֶאֱמוּנָה AND UNCHANGING IN its entirety, and binding on us, that He is the Lord our God and there is none beside Him, and we Israel are His people. He redeems us from the might of kings, our King Who saves us from the hand of all oppressors. He is the God Who delivers us from our foes, Who brings retribution on all our mortal enemies. Who does great things beyond our understanding, and
Ps. 66 innumerable wonders. Who has put our soul among the living, and has not given over our foot to stumble. He has led us to surmount our enemies, and has raised our strength above all who hate us. He performed miracles on our behalf, while bringing vengeance upon Pharaoh; with signs and wonders in the land of the children of Ham. In His wrath He struck down all the firstborn of Egypt, and brought out His people Israel from amongst them to everlasting freedom. He led His children through the divided Sea of Reeds, and drowned their pursuers and those who hated them, in its depths. When His

---

express our confidence that our firm commitment to His covenant will bring our ultimate redemption (R. Aton Holzer).

אֱמֶת, *truth,* refers to something that we know to be true, either because our senses tell us so or because we have conclusive evidence. אֱמוּנָה, *faith,* in medieval Hebrew refers to something that we *believe,* even though we have no proof that it happened. We know the Exodus to be *true*, because our ancestors, who witnessed it in the millions, testify to its veracity, but the future redemption is not yet an accomplished fact. Nevertheless we have a perfect *faith* that God will bring it about, as

בִּתְהוֹמוֹת טִבַּע, וְרָאוּ בָנָיו גְּבוּרָתוֹ, שִׁבְּחוּ וְהוֹדוּ לִשְׁמוֹ, ‹ וּמַלְכוּתוֹ בְּרָצוֹן קִבְּלוּ עֲלֵיהֶם. מֹשֶׁה וּבְנֵי יִשְׂרָאֵל, לְךָ עָנוּ שִׁירָה בְּשִׂמְחָה רַבָּה, וְאָמְרוּ כֻלָּם,

שמות טו מִי־כָמֹכָה בָּאֵלִם יהוה, מִי כָּמֹכָה נֶאְדָּר בַּקֹּדֶשׁ, נוֹרָא תְהִלֹּת עֹשֵׂה פֶלֶא:

‹ מַלְכוּתְךָ רָאוּ בָנֶיךָ, בּוֹקֵעַ יָם לִפְנֵי מֹשֶׁה, זֶה אֵלִי עָנוּ, וְאָמְרוּ,

שמות טו יהוה יִמְלֹךְ לְעֹלָם וָעֶד:

ירמיהו לא ‹ וְנֶאֱמַר, כִּי־פָדָה יהוה אֶת־יַעֲקֹב, וּגְאָלוֹ מִיַּד חָזָק מִמֶּנּוּ: בָּרוּךְ אַתָּה יהוה, גָּאַל יִשְׂרָאֵל.

הַשְׁכִּיבֵנוּ יהוה אֱלֹהֵינוּ לְשָׁלוֹם, וְהַעֲמִידֵנוּ מַלְכֵּנוּ לְחַיִּים, וּפְרֹשׂ עָלֵינוּ סֻכַּת שְׁלוֹמֶךָ, וְתַקְּנֵנוּ בְּעֵצָה טוֹבָה מִלְּפָנֶיךָ, וְהוֹשִׁיעֵנוּ לְמַעַן שְׁמֶךָ. וְהָגֵן בַּעֲדֵנוּ, וְהָסֵר מֵעָלֵינוּ אוֹיֵב, דֶּבֶר וְחֶרֶב וְרָעָב וְיָגוֹן, וְהָסֵר שָׂטָן מִלְּפָנֵינוּ וּמֵאַחֲרֵינוּ, וּבְצֵל כְּנָפֶיךָ תַּסְתִּירֵנוּ, כִּי אֵל שׁוֹמְרֵנוּ וּמַצִּילֵנוּ אָתָּה, כִּי אֵל מֶלֶךְ חַנּוּן וְרַחוּם אָתָּה. ‹ וּשְׁמֹר צֵאתֵנוּ וּבוֹאֵנוּ לְחַיִּים וּלְשָׁלוֹם מֵעַתָּה וְעַד עוֹלָם. בָּרוּךְ אַתָּה יהוה, שׁוֹמֵר עַמּוֹ יִשְׂרָאֵל לָעַד.

He promised through the prophets (*Ḥiddushei HaRim*).

גָּאַל יִשְׂרָאֵל ... הַשְׁכִּיבֵנוּ – *Who redeemed Israel... Lay us down.* In *Shaḥarit* we follow the Talmudic principle (*Berakhot* 4b) of סְמִיכַת גְּאֻלָּה לִתְפִלָּה (the *Amida* must immediately follow the third *berakha* of the *Shema*) by avoiding any insertion. Yet in *Ma'ariv*, there are several insertions between the third *berakha*'s גָּאַל יִשְׂרָאֵל ("Who redeemed Israel") and the *Amida*. The reason for this distinction is alluded to in the familiar verse "לְהַגִּיד בַּבֹּקֶר חַסְדֶּךָ, וֶאֱמוּנָתְךָ בַּלֵּילוֹת – to speak of Your loving-kindness in the morning and Your faithfulness at night" (Psalms 92:3). In the bright light of day we celebrate God's *ḥesed* (loving-kindness) with confidence in His promised redemption, whereas in the darkness of night it is our faith that sustains us in spite of the blackness. Thus in *Shaḥarit* there is a direct connection between the celebration of past redemptions and the anticipation of a quick and positive response to our *Amida* supplications. In *Ma'ariv* we are less able to see a direct link between the glorious redemptions of time past and the promises of a future one, hence the *halakha* permits these insertions that reflect the distance and delay between these events (R. Joseph B. Soloveitchik).

children beheld His power, they gave praise and thanks to His name. ▸ It was then that they enthusiastically accepted His sovereignty over them. Then Moses and the children of Israel sang to You with great joy, all proclaiming:

Ex. 15 WHO IS LIKE YOU, Lord, among the mighty? Who is like You, glorious in holiness, awesome beyond praise, working wonders?

▸ Your children beheld Your sovereignty when You split the sea apart before Moses. "This is my God," they proclaimed, and then declared,

Ex. 15 "THE LORD shall reign forever and ever."

Jer. 31 ▸ And it is said: "For the Lord redeemed Jacob, and rescued him from the hand of one stronger than he." Blessed are You, Lord, Who redeemed Israel.

הַשְׁכִּיבֵנוּ LAY US DOWN in peace, Lord our God, and raise us up, our King, to life. Spread over us the canopy of Your peace, and direct us with Your wise guidance. Save us for the sake of Your name. Shield us and ward off from us enemies, epidemics, violence, hunger, and sorrow. Remove Satan from before us and from behind us. Shelter us in the shadow of Your wings, for You, God, are our Guardian and Deliverer, insofar as You are a gracious and merciful God and King. ▸ Guard our going out and our coming in, for the sake of life and peace now and forever. Blessed are You, Lord, Who guards His people Israel forever.

הַשְׁכִּיבֵנוּ – *Lay us down.* In the evening we affirm our faith in divine stewardship and majesty not merely in our request that He rule over the world, but in the fact that each night we place our souls in His care when we go to sleep. This is the theme of both הַשְׁכִּיבֵנוּ and the הַמַּפִּיל blessing before retiring. These two themes – God's universal majesty and His particular concern for our lives – are intertwined in the final blessing of בָּרוּךְ ה׳ לְעוֹלָם (R. Joseph B. Soloveitchik).

וְהָסֵר שָׂטָן מִלְּפָנֵינוּ וּמֵאַחֲרֵינוּ – *Remove Satan from before us and from behind us.* The name "Satan" that appears here as well as in the morning blessings and the Grace after Meals can be understood in light of the Gemara (*Bava Batra* 16a) in the name of Reish Lakish who declared that "Satan is the *yetzer hara* (the evil inclination), and also the angel of death." Accordingly, this prayer asks God to remove both manifestations of Satan from our lives: the one that is "in front of us" – the angel of death that seeks to entrap us in the future, as well as the one that is "behind us" – the *yetzer*

תהלים פט / תהלים קלה **בָּרוּךְ** יהוה לְעוֹלָם, אָמֵן וְאָמֵן: בָּרוּךְ יהוה מִצִּיּוֹן, שֹׁכֵן יְרוּשָׁלָםִ,
תהלים עב הַלְלוּיָהּ: בָּרוּךְ יהוה אֱלֹהִים אֱלֹהֵי יִשְׂרָאֵל, עֹשֵׂה נִפְלָאוֹת
לְבַדּוֹ: וּבָרוּךְ שֵׁם כְּבוֹדוֹ לְעוֹלָם, וְיִמָּלֵא כְבוֹדוֹ אֶת־כָּל־הָאָרֶץ,
תהלים קד / תהלים קיג אָמֵן וְאָמֵן: יְהִי כְבוֹד יהוה לְעוֹלָם, יִשְׂמַח יהוה בְּמַעֲשָׂיו: יְהִי שֵׁם
שמואל א, יב יהוה מְבֹרָךְ מֵעַתָּה וְעַד־עוֹלָם: כִּי לֹא־יִטֹּשׁ יהוה אֶת־עַמּוֹ בַּעֲבוּר
מלכים א, יח שְׁמוֹ הַגָּדוֹל, כִּי הוֹאִיל יהוה לַעֲשׂוֹת אֶתְכֶם לוֹ לְעָם: וַיַּרְא כָּל־הָעָם
וַיִּפְּלוּ עַל־פְּנֵיהֶם, וַיֹּאמְרוּ, יהוה הוּא הָאֱלֹהִים, יהוה הוּא הָאֱלֹהִים:
זכריה יד וְהָיָה יהוה לְמֶלֶךְ עַל־כָּל־הָאָרֶץ, בַּיּוֹם הַהוּא יִהְיֶה יהוה אֶחָד וּשְׁמוֹ
תהלים לג אֶחָד: יְהִי־חַסְדְּךָ יהוה עָלֵינוּ, כַּאֲשֶׁר יִחַלְנוּ לָךְ:

תהלים קו **הוֹשִׁיעֵנוּ** יהוה אֱלֹהֵינוּ, וְקַבְּצֵנוּ מִן־הַגּוֹיִם, לְהוֹדוֹת לְשֵׁם קָדְשֶׁךָ,
תהלים פו לְהִשְׁתַּבֵּחַ בִּתְהִלָּתֶךָ: כָּל־גּוֹיִם אֲשֶׁר עָשִׂיתָ, יָבוֹאוּ
וְיִשְׁתַּחֲווּ לְפָנֶיךָ, אֲדֹנָי, וִיכַבְּדוּ לִשְׁמֶךָ: כִּי־גָדוֹל אַתָּה וְעֹשֵׂה
תהלים עט נִפְלָאוֹת, אַתָּה אֱלֹהִים לְבַדֶּךָ: וַאֲנַחְנוּ עַמְּךָ וְצֹאן מַרְעִיתֶךָ, נוֹדֶה
לְּךָ לְעוֹלָם, לְדוֹר וָדֹר נְסַפֵּר תְּהִלָּתֶךָ:

בָּרוּךְ יהוה בַּיּוֹם, בָּרוּךְ יהוה בַּלָּיְלָה, בָּרוּךְ יהוה בְּשָׁכְבֵנוּ, בָּרוּךְ
איוב יב יהוה בְּקוּמֵנוּ. כִּי בְיָדְךָ נַפְשׁוֹת הַחַיִּים וְהַמֵּתִים. אֲשֶׁר בְּיָדוֹ
תהלים לא נֶפֶשׁ כָּל־חָי, וְרוּחַ כָּל־בְּשַׂר־אִישׁ: בְּיָדְךָ אַפְקִיד רוּחִי, פָּדִיתָה אוֹתִי
יהוה אֵל אֱמֶת: אֱלֹהֵינוּ שֶׁבַּשָּׁמַיִם, יַחֵד שִׁמְךָ וְקַיֵּם מַלְכוּתְךָ תָּמִיד,
וּמְלֹךְ עָלֵינוּ לְעוֹלָם וָעֶד.

יִרְאוּ עֵינֵינוּ וְיִשְׂמַח לִבֵּנוּ, וְתָגֵל נַפְשֵׁנוּ בִּישׁוּעָתְךָ בֶּאֱמֶת, בֶּאֱמֹר
לְצִיּוֹן מָלַךְ אֱלֹהָיִךְ. יהוה מֶלֶךְ, יהוה מָלָךְ, יהוה יִמְלֹךְ לְעֹלָם

---

hara in our nature that pushes us to succumb to illicit temptation (R. Basil Herring).

בָּרוּךְ ה׳ לְעוֹלָם – *Blessed is the Lord forever.* This prayer was instituted in Geonic times (*Maḥzor Vitri*). It consists of nineteen verses, and mentions God's name nineteen times. It thus parallels the nineteen *berakhot* of the *Amida*. Various explanations are given for its insertion in the *Ma'ariv* service at this point: (1) As *Ma'ariv* is not obligatory, it replaces the *Amida* if the full *Amida* cannot be recited (R. Natronai Gaon); (2) it was added to allow latecomers to catch up so everyone could go home

Ps. 89 / Ps. 135 — בָּרוּךְ BLESSED is the Lord forever. Amen and Amen. Blessed is the Lord
Ps. 72 — from Zion, He Who dwells in Jerusalem. Praise the Lord. Blessed is the
Lord God, the God of Israel, He Who alone works wonders. And blessed
is His glorious name forever, and may the whole earth be filled with His
Ps. 104 — glory. Amen and Amen. May the glory of the Lord be forever; may the
Ps. 113 — Lord rejoice in His works. Blessed is the name of the Lord from now and
I Sam. 12 — for evermore. For His great name's sake the Lord will surely not forsake
His people, because it pleased the Lord to make you His own people.
I Kings 18 — And all the people saw, and they fell on their faces and said, "The Lord,
Zech. 14 — He is God; the Lord, He is God." And the Lord shall be King over all the
Ps. 33 — earth; in that day shall the Lord be One, and His name One. May Your
loving-kindness, O Lord, be upon us, as we hope for You.

Ps. 106 — הוֹשִׁיעֵנוּ SAVE US, O Lord our God, and gather us from among the
nations, to give thanks to Your holy name, to triumph in Your praise.
Ps. 86 — All nations whom You have made will come and prostrate themselves
before You, my Master, and they will glorify Your name. Indeed, You
Ps. 79 — are great and You do wondrous things. You are God alone. But we, Your
people and the sheep of Your pasture, will thank You forever. We will
relate Your praise for all generations.

בָּרוּךְ BLESSED is the Lord by day; blessed is the Lord by night. Blessed
is the Lord when we lie down; blessed is the Lord when we arise. For
Job 12 — in Your hand are the souls of the living and the dead, "for in His hand is
Ps. 31 — the soul of all the living and the spirit of every human being." Into Your
hand I entrust my spirit. Redeem me, O Lord, God of truth. Our God
in heaven, establish the oneness of Your name with Your sovereignty
forever, and reign over us forever and ever.

יִרְאוּ MAY OUR EYES behold, our hearts rejoice, and our souls delight in the truth of Your saving power when it shall be said in Zion: "Your God reigns. The Lord reigns, the Lord reigned, the Lord shall reign forever

---

safely together (Tosafot *Berakhot* 2a); (3) after a full day's labor some might be too tired to recite the full *Amida*, hence this could serve as a worthy substitute (Abudarham, Ra'avad); (4) during periods of oppression when Jews were forbidden to recite the *Amida*, they would quietly substitute these nineteen verses (Rashba, *Ba'al HaMinhagot*); even though we may no longer have these concerns, we maintain the earlier custom to recite it out of respect for past practice (Rosh *Berakhot* 1:5; Abudarham); (5) it replaces the repetition

וָעֶד. ׳ כִּי הַמַּלְכוּת שֶׁלְּךָ הִיא, וּלְעוֹלְמֵי עַד תִּמְלֹךְ בְּכָבוֹד, כִּי אֵין לָנוּ מֶלֶךְ אֶלָּא אָתָּה. בָּרוּךְ אַתָּה יהוה, הַמֶּלֶךְ בִּכְבוֹדוֹ, תָּמִיד יִמְלֹךְ עָלֵינוּ לְעוֹלָם וָעֶד, וְעַל כָּל מַעֲשָׂיו.

חצי קדיש

ש״ץ: **יִתְגַּדַּל** וְיִתְקַדַּשׁ שְׁמֵהּ רַבָּא (קהל: אָמֵן). בְּעָלְמָא דִּי בְרָא כִרְעוּתֵהּ. וְיַמְלִיךְ מַלְכוּתֵהּ בְּחַיֵּיכוֹן וּבְיוֹמֵיכוֹן וּבְחַיֵּי דְכָל בֵּית יִשְׂרָאֵל, בַּעֲגָלָא וּבִזְמַן קָרִיב, וְאִמְרוּ אָמֵן. (קהל: אָמֵן)

קהל וש״ץ: יְהֵא שְׁמֵהּ רַבָּא מְבָרַךְ לְעָלַם וּלְעָלְמֵי עָלְמַיָּא.

ש״ץ: יִתְבָּרַךְ וְיִשְׁתַּבַּח וְיִתְפָּאַר וְיִתְרוֹמַם וְיִתְנַשֵּׂא, וְיִתְהַדָּר וְיִתְעַלֶּה וְיִתְהַלָּל שְׁמֵהּ דְּקֻדְשָׁא בְּרִיךְ הוּא (קהל: בְּרִיךְ הוּא), לְעֵלָּא מִן כָּל בִּרְכָתָא / בעשרת ימי תשובה: לְעֵלָּא (וּ)לְעֵלָּא מִכָּל בִּרְכָתָא/ וְשִׁירָתָא, תֻּשְׁבְּחָתָא וְנֶחֱמָתָא דַּאֲמִירָן בְּעָלְמָא, וְאִמְרוּ אָמֵן. (קהל: אָמֵן)

עמידה

One begins the עמידה *by taking three steps forward (OḤ 95:1). According to some traditions, one should first take three steps back before moving forward (MB 95:3). The* עמידה *is recited with one's feet together. One should try to concentrate on the simple meaning of the words of the* עמידה *with the awareness throughout that one is standing in the presence of the Almighty (OḤ 98:1 and MB 98:1). At the points indicated by* ׳*, bend the knees at the first word, bow at the second, and stand straight before saying God's name.*

אֲדֹנָי, שְׂפָתַי תִּפְתָּח, וּפִי יַגִּיד תְּהִלָּתֶךָ: תהלים נא

אבות

׳**בָּרוּךְ** אַתָּה יהוה, אֱלֹהֵינוּ וֵאלֹהֵי אֲבוֹתֵינוּ, אֱלֹהֵי אַבְרָהָם, אֱלֹהֵי יִצְחָק, וֵאלֹהֵי יַעֲקֹב, הָאֵל הַגָּדוֹל הַגִּבּוֹר וְהַנּוֹרָא, אֵל עֶלְיוֹן, גּוֹמֵל חֲסָדִים טוֹבִים, וְקוֹנֵה הַכֹּל, וְזוֹכֵר חַסְדֵי אָבוֹת, וּמֵבִיא גוֹאֵל לִבְנֵי בְנֵיהֶם לְמַעַן שְׁמוֹ בְּאַהֲבָה.

and ever." ▸ Yours is the kingdom, and to all eternity You will reign in glory, for we have no king but You. Blessed are You, Lord, the King Who in His glory will always and forever reign over us and over all His works.

HALF KADDISH

Leader: יִתְגַּדַּל EXALTED AND HALLOWED may God's great name be, in the world He created as He willed. May He reign in your lifetimes and in your days, and in the lifetime of the whole house of Israel, speedily and soon, and say, Amen.

All: May His great name be blessed forever and all time.

Leader: Blessed and praised, honored, extolled, glorified, adored and exalted above all be the name of the Holy One, blessed is He, (*Between Rosh Hashana & Yom Kippur:* above and) beyond any blessing, hymn, praise, or expressions of consolation that may be uttered in this world, and say, Amen.

AMIDA

One begins the Amida by taking three steps forward (OḤ 95:1). According to some traditions, one should first take three steps back before moving forward (MB 95:3). The Amida is recited with one's feet together. One should try to concentrate on the simple meaning of the words of the Amida with the awareness throughout that one is standing in the presence of the Almighty (OḤ 98:1 and MB 98:1). At the points indicated by ▾, bend the knees at the first word, bow at the second, and stand straight before saying God's name.

Ps. 51 "O MY MASTER, open my lips, and my mouth will relate Your praise."

PATRIARCHS

▾ בָּרוּךְ BLESSED ARE YOU, LORD, our God and the God of our fathers, the God of Abraham, the God of Isaac, and the God of Jacob, the God Who is great, mighty, and awesome, God most exalted, Who bestows rewards of benevolent kindness, Who is the Creator of everything, Who remembers all the kind acts of the fathers, and Who brings a redeemer to their children's children, for the sake of His name, with love.

---

of the *Amida* which is omitted in *Ma'ariv* (Abudarham, Ri ben Shushan).

הָאֵל הַגָּדוֹל הַגִּבּוֹר וְהַנּוֹרָא – *The God Who is great, mighty, and awesome.* These are the terms of praise spoken by Moses in Deuteronomy 10:17. The Gemara (*Megilla* 25a) derives from this that since the Men of the Great Assembly, the composers of the *Amida*, allowed themselves

בעשרת ימי תשובה: זָכְרֵנוּ לְחַיִּים, מֶלֶךְ חָפֵץ בַּחַיִּים, וְכָתְבֵנוּ בְּסֵפֶר הַחַיִּים, לְמַעַנְךָ אֱלֹהִים חַיִּים.

(*If forgotten, no corrective action is necessary.*)

מֶלֶךְ עוֹזֵר וּמוֹשִׁיעַ וּמָגֵן. ׳בָּרוּךְ אַתָּה יהוה, מָגֵן אַבְרָהָם.

גבורות

אַתָּה גִּבּוֹר לְעוֹלָם, אֲדֹנָי, מְחַיֵּה מֵתִים אַתָּה, רַב לְהוֹשִׁיעַ.

בחורף: מַשִּׁיב הָרְוּחַ וּמוֹרִיד הַגֶּשֶׁם

מְכַלְכֵּל חַיִּים בְּחֶסֶד, מְחַיֵּה מֵתִים בְּרַחֲמִים רַבִּים, סוֹמֵךְ נוֹפְלִים, וְרוֹפֵא חוֹלִים, וּמַתִּיר אֲסוּרִים, וּמְקַיֵּם אֱמוּנָתוֹ לִישֵׁנֵי עָפָר. מִי כָמְוֹךָ, בַּעַל גְּבוּרוֹת, וּמִי דּוֹמֶה לָּךְ, מֶלֶךְ, מֵמִית וּמְחַיֶּה וּמַצְמִיחַ יְשׁוּעָה.

בעשרת ימי תשובה: מִי כָמְוֹךָ אַב הָרַחֲמִים, זוֹכֵר יְצוּרָיו לְחַיִּים בְּרַחֲמִים.

(*If forgotten, no corrective action is necessary.*)

וְנֶאֱמָן אַתָּה לְהַחֲיוֹת מֵתִים. בָּרוּךְ אַתָּה יהוה, מְחַיֵּה הַמֵּתִים.

קדושת השם

אַתָּה קָדוֹשׁ וְשִׁמְךָ קָדוֹשׁ. וּקְדוֹשִׁים בְּכָל יוֹם יְהַלְלְוּךָ סֶּלָה. בָּרוּךְ אַתָּה יהוה, הָאֵל הַקָּדוֹשׁ./ בעשרת ימי תשובה: הַמֶּלֶךְ הַקָּדוֹשׁ./

(*If forgotten, repeat the* עמידה.)

---

to praise God in these terms only, based on a precedent in the Torah – so, too, we are not permitted to create our own praises of God and may only use the language utilized by those who preceded us. As the Talmud puts it, even our most lavish description of God's grandeur is inadequate, the equivalent of praising a king for his silver collection, when he has unlimited stores of gold.

The name of God is repeated in conjunction with each of the patriarchs to emphasize that each one had a different, personal approach to, and relationship with, God. By implication this encourages us to develop our own relationship with God, but one that is at all times consistent with the preceding words, "the God of our fathers," that is, what we learn from the Patriarchs as the models of faith (R. Joseph B. Soloveitchik).

גְּבוּרוֹת / GOD'S MIGHT

אַתָּה גִּבּוֹר לְעוֹלָם, אֲדֹנָי – *"You are eternally mighty, my Master:"* In this phrase God is not referred to by the name י-ה-ו-ה (usually translated as "Lord") as would be expected, but by the name אֲדֹנָי that means "my Master." This name

Between Rosh HaShana & Yom Kippur: Remember us for life, King Who desires life, and inscribe us in the book of life for Your sake, Living God.

(If forgotten, no corrective action is necessary.)

King Who helps, saves, and shields, 'blessed are You, LORD, Shield of Abraham.

GOD'S MIGHT

אַתָּה YOU, my Master, are forever mighty, You are the Resurrector of the dead, with great power to save.

In winter: He makes the wind blow and the rain fall

He sustains the living with kindness, He resurrects the dead with great compassion, He supports those who are falling, He heals the sick, He sets the incarcerated free, and He fulfills what He has promised to those who sleep in the dust. Who is like You, O mighty One, and who can be compared to You, O King Who causes death and resurrects, and Who causes salvation to sprout?

Between Rosh HaShana & Yom Kippur: Who is like You, merciful Father, Who in compassion remembers for life those He has created.

(If forgotten, no corrective action is necessary.)

Trustworthy are You to resurrect the dead. Blessed are YOU, LORD, Resurrector of the dead.

HOLINESS

אַתָּה YOU ARE HOLY and Your name is holy, and holy ones will praise You every day, forever. Blessed are You, LORD, the holy God.

/*Between Rosh HaShana & Yom Kippur:* the holy King./

(If forgotten, repeat the Amida.)

---

signifies God's power to overrule the laws of nature, as found in Exodus 34:9, and similarly His ability to suspend the strict laws (דִּין) by which He established the cosmos, in favor of compassion (רַחֲמִים) and forgiveness of sin. Moses invoked this name in pleading for divine forgiveness in the episode of the spies (see Numbers 14:17), and so, too, we invoke it at the outset of every *Amida* in speaking of God's might (*Netziv*).

For laws regarding "Omission/Insertion of *Mashiv Haru'aḥ*," see page 109.

For laws regarding "Omission of *HaMelekh HaKadosh*," see page 112.

בינה

אַתָּה חוֹנֵן לְאָדָם דַּעַת, וּמְלַמֵּד לֶאֱנוֹשׁ בִּינָה.

On מוצאי שבת *and* מוצאי יום טוב *add:*

אַתָּה חוֹנַנְתָּנוּ לְמַדַּע תּוֹרָתֶךָ, וַתְּלַמְּדֵנוּ לַעֲשׂוֹת חֻקֵּי רְצוֹנֶךָ, וַתַּבְדֵּל יהוה אֱלֹהֵינוּ בֵּין קֹדֶשׁ לְחֹל, בֵּין אוֹר לְחֹשֶׁךְ, בֵּין יִשְׂרָאֵל לָעַמִּים, בֵּין יוֹם הַשְּׁבִיעִי לְשֵׁשֶׁת יְמֵי הַמַּעֲשֶׂה. אָבִינוּ מַלְכֵּנוּ, הָחֵל עָלֵינוּ הַיָּמִים הַבָּאִים לִקְרָאתֵנוּ לְשָׁלוֹם, חֲשׂוּכִים מִכָּל חֵטְא וּמְנֻקִּים מִכָּל עָוֹן וּמְדֻבָּקִים בְּיִרְאָתֶךָ. וְ

חָנֵּנוּ מֵאִתְּךָ דֵּעָה בִּינָה וְהַשְׂכֵּל. בָּרוּךְ אַתָּה יהוה, חוֹנֵן הַדָּעַת.

תשובה

הֲשִׁיבֵנוּ אָבִינוּ לְתוֹרָתֶךָ, וְקָרְבֵנוּ מַלְכֵּנוּ לַעֲבוֹדָתֶךָ, וְהַחֲזִירֵנוּ בִּתְשׁוּבָה שְׁלֵמָה לְפָנֶיךָ. בָּרוּךְ אַתָּה יהוה, הָרוֹצֶה בִּתְשׁוּבָה.

סליחה

Strike the left side of the chest at °.

סְלַח לָנוּ אָבִינוּ כִּי °חָטָאנוּ, מְחַל לָנוּ מַלְכֵּנוּ כִּי °פָשָׁעְנוּ, כִּי מוֹחֵל וְסוֹלֵחַ אָתָּה. בָּרוּךְ אַתָּה יהוה, חַנּוּן הַמַּרְבֶּה לִסְלֹחַ.

Furthermore, whereas human strength is expressed as the ability to overcome and defeat other powers, this *berakha* describes God's power very differently. It is expressed in His compassionate ways, in which He supports those who fall, heals the sick, and frees the imprisoned (*Otzar HaTefillot*).

אַתָּה חוֹנַנְתָּנוּ – *You have graced us.* We recite this *Havdala* paragraph at the conclusion of Shabbat or Yom Tov following the first sentence of this *berakha* for two reasons. The first is that we need wisdom in order to make distinctions (הַבְדָּלָה) between similar but not identical things, and so we first affirm that God grants such knowledge to man, and then we immediately proceed to make such a *Havdala*. Secondly, because we cannot petition God for our needs while it is still Shabbat or Yom Tov,

אַתָּה חוֹנַנְתָּנוּ / ATA ḤONANTANU

If one forgot to recite *Ata ḥonantanu*, no corrective action is necessary. However, if one omitted *Ata ḥonantanu* and also ate before making *Havdala*, one must repeat the *Amida* with the *Ata ḥonantanu* insertion (*OḤ* 294:1).

INSIGHT

אַתָּה GRACIOUSLY You grant man wisdom, and teach understanding to mortal man.

On Motza'ei Shabbat and Motza'ei Yom Tov add:

אַתָּה חוֹנַנְתָּנוּ YOU HAVE GRACED US with the ability to study Your Torah, and You have taught us to perform the statutes of Your will. You have distinguished, LORD our God, between the sacred and the secular, between light and darkness, between Israel and the nations, between the seventh day and the six days of labor. Our Father, our King, may You begin for us the coming days in peace, free from all sin, removed from all iniquity, and embracing reverence for You. And –

Grant us, with grace, the wisdom, insight, and discernment that come from You. Blessed are You, LORD, Granter of knowledge.

REPENTANCE

הֲשִׁיבֵנוּ BRING US BACK, our Father, to Your Torah, and draw us near, our King, to Your service. Facilitate our return to You in complete repentance. Blessed are You, LORD, Who desires repentance.

FORGIVENESS

Strike the left side of the chest at °.

סְלַח FORGIVE US, our Father, for we have °sinned. Pardon us, our King, for we have °transgressed. For You are the One Who pardons and forgives. Blessed are You, LORD, gracious and abundantly forgiving.

---

we must begin the weekday middle section of the *Amida*, thereby terminating Shabbat, and only thereafter do we recite the abbreviated *Havdala* (Vilna Gaon).

Some ask why this insertion needlessly rephrases the opening "אַתָּה חוֹנֵן – Graciously You grant man knowledge" by using the similar words אַתָּה חוֹנַנְתָּנוּ ("You have graced us…"). The answer is that the first line of this *berakha* refers to wisdom that is attainable by all of mankind (and thus it refers to אָדָם, אֱנוֹשׁ, i.e., generic man), whereas the subsequent *Havdala* insertion refers only to the knowledge of Torah and its statutes, and the ability to discern between the holy and the profane. This knowledge is unique to the Jew, as Psalm 147

גאולה

רְאֵה בְעָנְיֵנוּ, וְרִיבָה רִיבֵנוּ, וּגְאָלֵנוּ מְהֵרָה לְמַעַן שְׁמֶךָ, כִּי גוֹאֵל חָזָק אָתָּה. בָּרוּךְ אַתָּה יהוה, גּוֹאֵל יִשְׂרָאֵל.

רפואה

רְפָאֵנוּ יהוה וְנֵרָפֵא, הוֹשִׁיעֵנוּ וְנִוָּשֵׁעָה, כִּי תְהִלָּתֵנוּ אָתָּה, וְהַעֲלֵה רְפוּאָה שְׁלֵמָה לְכָל מַכּוֹתֵינוּ

The following prayer for a sick person may be said here:

יְהִי רָצוֹן מִלְּפָנֶיךָ יהוה אֱלֹהַי וֵאלֹהֵי אֲבוֹתַי, שֶׁתִּשְׁלַח מְהֵרָה רְפוּאָה שְׁלֵמָה מִן הַשָּׁמַיִם רְפוּאַת הַנֶּפֶשׁ וּרְפוּאַת הַגּוּף לַחוֹלֶה/לַחוֹלָה *name of patient* בֶּן/בַּת *mother's name* בְּתוֹךְ שְׁאָר חוֹלֵי יִשְׂרָאֵל.

כִּי אֵל מֶלֶךְ רוֹפֵא נֶאֱמָן וְרַחֲמָן אָתָּה. בָּרוּךְ אַתָּה יהוה, רוֹפֵא חוֹלֵי עַמּוֹ יִשְׂרָאֵל.

ברכת השנים

בָּרֵךְ עָלֵינוּ יהוה אֱלֹהֵינוּ אֶת הַשָּׁנָה הַזֹּאת, וְאֶת כָּל מִינֵי תְבוּאָתָהּ לְטוֹבָה

Beginning in springtime, from the intermediate days of Pesaḥ to the evening preceding December 5 (in some years December 6), say:

וְתֵן בְּרָכָה

Beginning with the winter season, from the evening preceding December 5 (in some years December 6) to Pesaḥ, say:

וְתֵן טַל וּמָטָר לִבְרָכָה

עַל פְּנֵי הָאֲדָמָה, וְשַׂבְּעֵנוּ מִטּוּבֶךָ, וּבָרֵךְ שְׁנָתֵנוּ כַּשָּׁנִים הַטּוֹבוֹת. בָּרוּךְ אַתָּה יהוה, מְבָרֵךְ הַשָּׁנִים.

To expand on the Baḥ, the language of this prayer teaches that the ability to acquire all forms of wisdom is a gift from God, whether it is of the genre attainable by all people (in the realm of science, technology, social science, the arts, *et al.*), or that which is specific to the

declares, "He proclaimed His words to Jacob, His statutes and judgments to Israel. He has not done so for any other nation…" Thus the insertion makes it clear that God has granted the ability to acquire this type of knowledge "to us," and not "to them" (Baḥ).

REDEMPTION

רְאֵה SEE OUR SUFFERING and advocate for us. Speed our redemption for the sake of Your name, for You are a mighty Redeemer. Blessed are You, LORD, Redeemer of Israel.

HEALTH AND HEALING

רְפָאֵנוּ HEAL US, LORD, and we shall be healed; save us and we shall be saved; for You are our praise. Bring complete healing from all our afflictions,

---

The following prayer for a sick person may be said here:

יְהִי MAY IT BE Your will, LORD my God and God of my fathers, that you send speedily a complete healing from heaven, a healing of the soul and a healing of the body, to the sick person (*name* son/daughter of *mother's name*), among the other sick people of Israel.

---

for You, God, King, are a faithful and compassionate Healer. Blessed are You, LORD, Who heals the sick of His people Israel.

PROSPERITY

בָּרֵךְ BLESS THIS YEAR for us, LORD our God, along with all its many kinds of produce for good.

Beginning in springtime, from the intermediate days of Pesaḥ to the evening preceding December 5 (in some years December 6), say:

Send blessing

Beginning with the winter season, from the evening preceding December 5 (in some years December 6) to Pesaḥ, say:

Send dew and rain for a blessing

on the face of the earth, and satisfy us with Your benevolence, and bless our year as the best of years. Blessed are You, LORD, Who blesses the years.

Jewish people (i.e., Torah knowledge in all of its dimensions). The *berakha* in its totality asks God to enable us to acquire knowledge, understanding, and discernment in both the worldly and spiritual dimensions in the "coming days," so that we not be tempted to engage in any "sin and transgression" that might result from ignorance (R. Basil Herring).

For laws regarding "וְתֵן טַל וּמָטָר / *Veten tal umatar,*" see page 117.

קיבוץ גלויות

תְּקַע בְּשׁוֹפָר גָּדוֹל לְחֵרוּתֵנוּ, וְשָׂא נֵס לְקַבֵּץ גָּלֻיּוֹתֵינוּ, וְקַבְּצֵנוּ יַחַד מֵאַרְבַּע כַּנְפוֹת הָאָרֶץ. בָּרוּךְ אַתָּה יהוה, מְקַבֵּץ נִדְחֵי עַמּוֹ יִשְׂרָאֵל.

השבת המשפט

הָשִׁיבָה שׁוֹפְטֵינוּ כְּבָרִאשׁוֹנָה וְיוֹעֲצֵינוּ כְּבַתְּחִלָּה, וְהָסֵר מִמֶּנּוּ יָגוֹן וַאֲנָחָה, וּמְלֹךְ עָלֵינוּ אַתָּה יהוה לְבַדְּךָ בְּחֶסֶד וּבְרַחֲמִים, וְצַדְּקֵנוּ בַּמִּשְׁפָּט. בָּרוּךְ אַתָּה יהוה, מֶלֶךְ אוֹהֵב צְדָקָה וּמִשְׁפָּט. / בעשרת ימי תשובה: הַמֶּלֶךְ הַמִּשְׁפָּט./

(*If forgotten, no corrective action is necessary.*)

ברכת המינים

וְלַמַּלְשִׁינִים אַל תְּהִי תִקְוָה, וְכָל הָרִשְׁעָה כְּרֶגַע תֹּאבֵד, וְכָל אוֹיְבֶיךָ מְהֵרָה יִכָּרֵתוּ, וְהַזֵּדִים מְהֵרָה תְעַקֵּר וּתְשַׁבֵּר וּתְמַגֵּר וְתַכְנִיעַ בִּמְהֵרָה בְיָמֵינוּ. בָּרוּךְ אַתָּה יהוה, שׁוֹבֵר אוֹיְבִים וּמַכְנִיעַ זֵדִים.

צדיקים

עַל הַצַּדִּיקִים וְעַל הַחֲסִידִים, וְעַל זִקְנֵי עַמְּךָ בֵּית יִשְׂרָאֵל, וְעַל פְּלֵיטַת סוֹפְרֵיהֶם, וְעַל גֵּרֵי הַצֶּדֶק, וְעָלֵינוּ, יֶהֱמוּ רַחֲמֶיךָ יהוה אֱלֹהֵינוּ, וְתֵן שָׂכָר טוֹב לְכָל הַבּוֹטְחִים בְּשִׁמְךָ בֶּאֱמֶת,

---

קִבּוּץ גָּלֻיּוֹת / INGATHERING OF THE EXILES
This *berakha*, using language from Isaiah 27:13, pleads with God not to despair of any Jew, no matter how far removed in body or spirit from the Jewish people or the land of Israel.

וְקַבְּצֵנוּ יַחַד – *And bring us together*. A critical element of the tragedy of exile is the inability of the Jewish people to come together in spirit, as a result of being dispersed among the nations. The sages taught that internal dissension and hatred were themselves the cause of the destruction of the Second Temple and the subsequent exile. The reason is that sanctity cannot exist unless there is national unity, as we learn from the verse, "Speak to the entire congregation of Israel and say to them: 'You shall be holy'" (Lev. 19:2). Thus the exile was not *per se* a punishment but the natural consequence of this objectionable behavior, while our future redemption will be the result of overcoming our divisions (*Sefat Emet*). Perhaps this is why in this *berakha* we ask God to gather us יַחַד (together), to unify

INGATHERING OF THE EXILES

תְּקַע SOUND the great shofar of our freedom; hoist the banner to gather our exiles and bring us together from the four corners of the earth. Blessed are You, LORD, Who gathers the scattered of His people Israel.

JUSTICE

הָשִׁיבָה RESTORE our judges as in the beginning, and our counselors as they were to begin with, and relieve our sorrows and our troubles. Reign over us, LORD, You alone, lovingly and mercifully, and vindicate us in judgment. Blessed are You, LORD, / King Who loves righteousness and justice. / *Between Rosh HaShana & Yom Kippur:* the King of justice. (*If forgotten, no corrective action is necessary.*)

AGAINST SLANDERERS

וְלַמַּלְשִׁינִים AND LET THERE BE no hope for slanderers, and may all evil instantly disappear. May all Your enemies be swiftly cut down, and the wicked be uprooted, broken, overthrown, and subdued – speedily, and in our day. Blessed are You, LORD, Who crushes enemies and subdues the wicked.

THE RIGHTEOUS

עַל הַצַּדִּיקִים MAY YOUR COMPASSION be upon the righteous, and the pious, and the elders of Your people the house of Israel, and the remnants of their scholars, and the righteous converts, and upon us, LORD our God. Give good reward to all those who sincerely trust

---

us so that, with our sanctity restored, we will be able to overcome our exile and return from the four corners of the earth (R. Basil Herring).

הָשָׁבַת הַמִּשְׁפָּט / JUSTICE

הָשִׁיבָה שׁוֹפְטֵינוּ – *Restore our judges.* The *Midrash* to Deuteronomy 16:20 ("Justice, justice you shall pursue so that you may live and inherit the land") connects the two halves of the verse to teach that the appointment of righteous judges is necessary if we are to maintain ourselves in the land of Israel. Without social justice there cannot be strength and security in the land. To this end impartial judges and counselors are needed. The language of this *berakha* is derived from מֶלֶךְ בְּמִשְׁפָּט יַעֲמִיד אָרֶץ – "A king establishes society on justice" (Proverbs 29:4) (*Maḥzor Vitri*).

צַדִּיקִים / THE RIGHTEOUS

This *berakha* asks God to assure the success of

וְשִׂים חֶלְקֵנוּ עִמָּהֶם, וּלְעוֹלָם לֹא נֵבוֹשׁ כִּי בְךָ בָטָחְנוּ. בָּרוּךְ אַתָּה יהוה, מִשְׁעָן וּמִבְטָח לַצַּדִּיקִים.

בניין ירושלים

וְלִירוּשָׁלַיִם עִירְךָ בְּרַחֲמִים תָּשׁוּב, וְתִשְׁכֹּן בְּתוֹכָהּ כַּאֲשֶׁר דִּבַּרְתָּ, וּבְנֵה אוֹתָהּ בְּקָרוֹב בְּיָמֵינוּ בִּנְיַן עוֹלָם, וְכִסֵּא דָוִד מְהֵרָה לְתוֹכָהּ תָּכִין. בָּרוּךְ אַתָּה יהוה, בּוֹנֵה יְרוּשָׁלָיִם.

מלכות בית דוד

אֶת צֶמַח דָּוִד עַבְדְּךָ מְהֵרָה תַצְמִיחַ, וְקַרְנוֹ תָּרוּם בִּישׁוּעָתֶךָ, כִּי לִישׁוּעָתְךָ קִוִּינוּ כָּל הַיּוֹם. בָּרוּךְ אַתָּה יהוה, מַצְמִיחַ קֶרֶן יְשׁוּעָה.

שומע תפלה

שְׁמַע קוֹלֵנוּ יהוה אֱלֹהֵינוּ, חוּס וְרַחֵם עָלֵינוּ, וְקַבֵּל בְּרַחֲמִים וּבְרָצוֹן אֶת תְּפִלָּתֵנוּ, כִּי אֵל שׁוֹמֵעַ תְּפִלּוֹת וְתַחֲנוּנִים אָתָּה, וּמִלְּפָנֶיךָ מַלְכֵּנוּ רֵיקָם אַל תְּשִׁיבֵנוּ,*

**When saying the עמידה silently, one may add a personal prayer for forgiveness and for livelihood (below).*

A personal prayer for forgiveness:

אָנָּא יהוה, חָטָאתִי עָוִיתִי וּפָשַׁעְתִּי לְפָנֶיךָ, מִיּוֹם הֱיוֹתִי עַל הָאֲדָמָה עַד הַיּוֹם הַזֶּה (וּבִפְרָט בַּחֵטְא...). אָנָּא יהוה, עֲשֵׂה לְמַעַן שִׁמְךָ הַגָּדוֹל, וּתְכַפֶּר לִי עַל חֲטָאַי וַעֲוֹנַי וּפְשָׁעַי שֶׁחָטָאתִי וְשֶׁעָוִיתִי וְשֶׁפָּשַׁעְתִּי לְפָנֶיךָ, מִנְּעוּרַי עַד הַיּוֹם הַזֶּה. וּתְמַלֵּא כָּל הַשֵּׁמוֹת שֶׁפָּגַמְתִּי בְּשִׁמְךָ הַגָּדוֹל.

Continue with כִּי אַתָּה שׁוֹמֵעַ *on the next page.*

A personal prayer for livelihood:

אַתָּה הוּא יהוה הָאֱלֹהִים, הַזָּן וּמְפַרְנֵס וּמְכַלְכֵּל מִקַּרְנֵי רְאֵמִים עַד בֵּיצֵי כִנִּים. הַטְרִיפֵנִי לֶחֶם חֻקִּי, וְהַמְצֵא לִי וּלְכָל בְּנֵי בֵיתִי מְזוֹנוֹתַי קֹדֶם שֶׁאֶצְטָרֵךְ

Continued on the top of the next page.

---

those who have assumed active responsibility to implement God's will in His world. Among these are not merely appointed leaders, but also those who are moral and spiritual role

in Your name, and place our portion with them, and may we never be shamed, for in You we trust. Blessed are You, LORD, Who is the Support and Trustee of the righteous.

REBUILDING JERUSALEM

וְלִירוּשָׁלַיִם AND MAY YOU RETURN to Jerusalem Your city in compassion, and may You dwell within it, as You promised. Rebuild it speedily in our days, such that it will remain built up forever, and establish within it soon the throne of David. Blessed are You, LORD, Builder of Jerusalem.

KINGDOM OF DAVID

אֶת צֶמַח MAY THE OFFSPRING of David, Your servant, soon flourish, and may his glory be exalted by Your salvation – for we hope for Your salvation all day long. Blessed are You, LORD, Who causes the glory of salvation to flourish.

RESPONSE TO PRAYER

שְׁמַע קוֹלֵנוּ HEAR OUR VOICE, LORD our God, have pity and compassion for us, and accept our prayer in compassion and favor, for You are God Who hears prayers and pleas. Do not turn us away empty-handed, our King, from Your presence,*

**When saying the Amida silently, one may add a personal prayer for forgiveness and for livelihood (below).*

A personal prayer for forgiveness:

אָנָּא PLEASE, LORD, I have sinned, been iniquitous, and transgressed before You, from the day I came into being on this earth until this day (in particular with the sin of...). Please, LORD, act for the sake of Your great name and grant me atonement for my sins, my iniquities and my transgressions committed in Your presence, from my youth until this day. May You make whole all the names I have damaged in Your great name. *Continue with "for You hear" on the next page.*

A personal prayer for livelihood:

אַתָּה YOU are the LORD, the God, Who nourishes, sustains, and supports, from the oryxes' horns to the eggs of lice. Provide me with my due portion of bread,

Continued on the top of the next page.

---

models for the people – including righteous converts, and *ḥasidim*, which R. Yehuda ben Yakar takes to refer to penitents returning to the faith (R. Ezra Bick).

לָהֶם, בְּנַחַת וְלֹא בְצַעַר, בְּהֶתֵּר וְלֹא בְאִסּוּר, בְּכָבוֹד וְלֹא בְבִזָּיוֹן, לְחַיִּים וּלְשָׁלוֹם, מִשֶּׁפַע בְּרָכָה וְהַצְלָחָה, וּמִשֶּׁפַע בְּרֵכָה עֶלְיוֹנָה, כְּדֵי שֶׁאוּכַל לַעֲשׂוֹת רְצוֹנֶךָ וְלַעֲסֹק בְּתוֹרָתֶךָ וּלְקַיֵּם מִצְוֹתֶיךָ. וְאַל תַּצְרִיכֵנִי לִידֵי מַתְּנַת בָּשָׂר וָדָם. וִיקֻיַּם בִּי מִקְרָא שֶׁכָּתוּב: פּוֹתֵחַ אֶת יָדֶךָ, וּמַשְׂבִּיעַ לְכָל חַי רָצוֹן. וְכָתוּב: הַשְׁלֵךְ עַל יהוה יְהָבְךָ וְהוּא יְכַלְכְּלֶךָ.

Continue with כִּי אַתָּה שׁוֹמֵעַ *below.*

כִּי אַתָּה שׁוֹמֵעַ תְּפִלַּת עַמְּךָ יִשְׂרָאֵל בְּרַחֲמִים. בָּרוּךְ אַתָּה יהוה, שׁוֹמֵעַ תְּפִלָּה.

עבודה

רְצֵה יהוה אֱלֹהֵינוּ בְּעַמְּךָ יִשְׂרָאֵל, וּבִתְפִלָּתָם, וְהָשֵׁב אֶת הָעֲבוֹדָה לִדְבִיר בֵּיתֶךָ, וְאִשֵּׁי יִשְׂרָאֵל וּתְפִלָּתָם בְּאַהֲבָה תְקַבֵּל בְּרָצוֹן, וּתְהִי לְרָצוֹן תָּמִיד עֲבוֹדַת יִשְׂרָאֵל עַמֶּךָ.

On ראש חודש *and* חול המועד*, say:*

אֱלֹהֵינוּ וֵאלֹהֵי אֲבוֹתֵינוּ, יַעֲלֶה וְיָבוֹא וְיַגִּיעַ, וְיֵרָאֶה וְיֵרָצֶה וְיִשָּׁמַע, וְיִפָּקֵד וְיִזָּכֵר זִכְרוֹנֵנוּ וּפִקְדוֹנֵנוּ וְזִכְרוֹן אֲבוֹתֵינוּ, וְזִכְרוֹן מָשִׁיחַ בֶּן דָּוִד עַבְדֶּךָ, וְזִכְרוֹן יְרוּשָׁלַיִם עִיר קָדְשֶׁךָ, וְזִכְרוֹן כָּל עַמְּךָ בֵּית יִשְׂרָאֵל, לְפָנֶיךָ, לִפְלֵיטָה לְטוֹבָה, לְחֵן וּלְחֶסֶד וּלְרַחֲמִים, לְחַיִּים וּלְשָׁלוֹם בְּיוֹם

בראש חודש: רֹאשׁ הַחֹדֶשׁ / בפסח: חַג הַמַּצּוֹת / בסוכות: חַג הַסֻּכּוֹת

הַזֶּה. זָכְרֵנוּ יהוה אֱלֹהֵינוּ בּוֹ לְטוֹבָה, וּפָקְדֵנוּ בוֹ לִבְרָכָה, וְהוֹשִׁיעֵנוּ בוֹ לְחַיִּים. וּבִדְבַר יְשׁוּעָה וְרַחֲמִים, חוּס וְחָנֵּנוּ וְרַחֵם עָלֵינוּ וְהוֹשִׁיעֵנוּ, כִּי אֵלֶיךָ עֵינֵינוּ, כִּי אֵל מֶלֶךְ חַנּוּן וְרַחוּם אָתָּה.

כִּי אַתָּה שׁוֹמֵעַ תְּפִלַּת עַמְּךָ יִשְׂרָאֵל – *For You hear the prayer of Your people Israel.* It is significant that this refers in the singular to the "prayer" of Israel, and not, as one might have thought, to the "prayers" (plural) of the people of Israel. For in addition to the prayer of individuals, there is also the prayer of the צִבּוּר (congregation) that reflects the supplications of the Jewish people as an entity. This phrase in the *berakha* refers to the latter, and affirms that God is particularly attentive to it. Similarly, as noted earlier, R. Joseph B. Soloveitchik distinguishes between תְּפִלָּה בְּצִבּוּר (prayer *with* a congregation) and תְּפִלַּת הַצִּבּוּר (the prayer *of* the congregation), the former referring to the silent *Amida* recited by individuals, and the latter to the Leader's repetition as a communal act. Fittingly, Rambam (*Hil. Teshuva* 2:6) emphasizes this distinction by noting that whereas the prayers of individuals have special

and bring forth for me and all members of my household, my food before I have need for it: in satisfaction and not in pain, in a permissible manner and not a forbidden one, in honor and not in disgrace, for life and for peace, from the flow of blessing and success, and from the flow of the heavenly spring, so that I may be able to do Your will and engage in Your Torah and fulfill Your commandments. Let me not become needy of human charity, and may there be fulfilled in me the verse as it is written: "You open Your hand, and You satisfy the desire of every living thing." And it is written: "Cast your burden upon the LORD, and He will sustain you."

Continue with "for You hear" below.

---

for You hear the prayer of Your people Israel with compassion. Blessed are You, LORD, Who hears prayer.

TEMPLE SERVICE

רְצֵה LOOK FAVORABLY, LORD our God, upon Your people Israel and their prayer, and restore the service to the Holy of Holies of Your House. Accept with love and favor the fire-offerings of Israel and their prayer. May the service of Israel Your people Israel always find favor with You.

On Rosh Ḥodesh and Ḥol HaMo'ed, say:

אֱלֹהֵינוּ וֵאלֹהֵי אֲבוֹתֵינוּ OUR GOD and God of our fathers, may there arise, arrive, reach, appear, be favored, heard, considered and remembered, our remembrance and recollection, Your remembrance of our fathers, of the Messiah son of David Your servant, of Jerusalem Your holy city and of all Your people the house of Israel. May they come before You for deliverance and benefit, for grace, kindness and mercy, for life and peace, on this day of:

On Rosh Ḥodesh: Rosh Ḥodesh.

On Pesaḥ: the Festival of Matzot. / *On Sukkot:* the Festival of Sukkot.

LORD our God, remember us this day for good. Be mindful of us this day for blessing, preserve us this day for life. Regarding redemption and mercy show us compassion and grace, and have pity on us and save us. For our eyes are lifted toward You, for You are a gracious and merciful God and King.

---

impact when recited during the Ten Days of Repentance, the collective prayer of a צבור (congregation) is answered "whenever they repent and cry out to God sincerely, as it says, 'Who is like the Lord *our* God whenever *we* call out to Him'" (Deut. 4:7) (R. Basil Herring).

For laws regarding "יַעֲלֶה וְיָבוֹא / *Ya'aleh VeYavo,*" see page 125.

וְתֶחֱזֶינָה עֵינֵינוּ בְּשׁוּבְךָ לְצִיּוֹן בְּרַחֲמִים. בָּרוּךְ אַתָּה יהוה, הַמַּחֲזִיר שְׁכִינָתוֹ לְצִיּוֹן.

הודאה

Bow during the first five words.

מוֹדִים אֲנַחְנוּ לָךְ, שָׁאַתָּה הוּא יהוה אֱלֹהֵינוּ וֵאלֹהֵי אֲבוֹתֵינוּ לְעוֹלָם וָעֶד. צוּר חַיֵּינוּ, מָגֵן יִשְׁעֵנוּ, אַתָּה הוּא. לְדוֹר וָדוֹר נוֹדֶה לְּךָ וּנְסַפֵּר תְּהִלָּתֶךָ, עַל חַיֵּינוּ הַמְּסוּרִים בְּיָדֶךָ, וְעַל נִשְׁמוֹתֵינוּ הַפְּקוּדוֹת לָךְ, וְעַל נִסֶּיךָ שֶׁבְּכָל יוֹם עִמָּנוּ, וְעַל נִפְלְאוֹתֶיךָ וְטוֹבוֹתֶיךָ שֶׁבְּכָל עֵת, עֶרֶב וָבֹקֶר וְצָהֳרָיִם. הַטּוֹב, כִּי לֹא כָלוּ רַחֲמֶיךָ, וְהַמְרַחֵם, כִּי לֹא תַמּוּ חֲסָדֶיךָ, מֵעוֹלָם קִוִּינוּ לָךְ.

בחנוכה ובפורים:

עַל הַנִּסִּים וְעַל הַפֻּרְקָן וְעַל הַגְּבוּרוֹת וְעַל הַתְּשׁוּעוֹת וְעַל הַמִּלְחָמוֹת שֶׁעָשִׂיתָ לַאֲבוֹתֵינוּ בַּיָּמִים הָהֵם בַּזְּמַן הַזֶּה.

בחנוכה:

בִּימֵי מַתִּתְיָהוּ בֶּן יוֹחָנָן כֹּהֵן גָּדוֹל חַשְׁמוֹנַאי וּבָנָיו, כְּשֶׁעָמְדָה מַלְכוּת יָוָן הָרְשָׁעָה עַל עַמְּךָ יִשְׂרָאֵל לְהַשְׁכִּיחָם תּוֹרָתֶךָ וּלְהַעֲבִירָם מֵחֻקֵּי רְצוֹנֶךָ, וְאַתָּה בְּרַחֲמֶיךָ הָרַבִּים עָמַדְתָּ לָהֶם בְּעֵת צָרָתָם, רַבְתָּ אֶת רִיבָם, דַּנְתָּ אֶת דִּינָם, נָקַמְתָּ אֶת נִקְמָתָם, מָסַרְתָּ גִבּוֹרִים בְּיַד חַלָּשִׁים, וְרַבִּים בְּיַד מְעַטִּים, וּטְמֵאִים בְּיַד טְהוֹרִים, וּרְשָׁעִים בְּיַד צַדִּיקִים, וְזֵדִים בְּיַד עוֹסְקֵי תוֹרָתֶךָ, וּלְךָ עָשִׂיתָ שֵׁם גָּדוֹל וְקָדוֹשׁ בְּעוֹלָמֶךָ, וּלְעַמְּךָ יִשְׂרָאֵל עָשִׂיתָ תְּשׁוּעָה גְדוֹלָה וּפֻרְקָן כְּהַיּוֹם הַזֶּה. וְאַחַר כֵּן בָּאוּ בָנֶיךָ לִדְבִיר בֵּיתֶךָ, וּפִנּוּ אֶת הֵיכָלֶךָ, וְטִהֲרוּ אֶת מִקְדָּשֶׁךָ, וְהִדְלִיקוּ נֵרוֹת בְּחַצְרוֹת קָדְשֶׁךָ, וְקָבְעוּ שְׁמוֹנַת יְמֵי חֲנֻכָּה אֵלּוּ, לְהוֹדוֹת וּלְהַלֵּל לְשִׁמְךָ הַגָּדוֹל.

Continue with וְעַל כֻּלָּם.

בפורים:

בִּימֵי מָרְדְּכַי וְאֶסְתֵּר בְּשׁוּשַׁן הַבִּירָה, כְּשֶׁעָמַד עֲלֵיהֶם הָמָן הָרָשָׁע,
בִּקֵּשׁ לְהַשְׁמִיד לַהֲרֹג וּלְאַבֵּד אֶת־כָּל־הַיְּהוּדִים מִנַּעַר וְעַד־זָקֵן טַף אסתר ג

Continued on the top of the next page.

For laws regarding "עַל הַנִּסִּים / Al HaNissim," see page 128.

May our eyes witness Your return to Zion in compassion. Blessed are You, LORD, Who will restore His Divine Presence to Zion.

MODIM

Bow during the first seven words.

מוֹדִים WE THANK YOU, for You are the LORD our God and the God of our fathers for all eternity. You are the Rock of our life and Shield of our deliverance. From generation to generation we will thank You and recount Your praise for our lives that are in Your hands, for our souls that are given over to You, for Your miracles that are with us every day, and for Your constant wonders and favors, evening, morning and noon. You are good, for Your compassion does not cease, and You are compassionate, for Your kindness never ends. We have placed our hope in You forever and ever.

On Ḥanukka and Purim add:

עַל הַנִּסִּים [WE THANK YOU] for the miracles, the deliverance, and the triumphant victories and salvation, as well as wars which You wrought for our ancestors in those days at this season.

On Ḥanukka:

IT HAPPENED in the days of Mattathias son of Johanan, the Hasmonean high priest, and his sons. Then the cruel Hellenist power rose up to force Your people Israel to forget Your Torah and transgress the commands of Your will. In that hour of their distress, You in Your great mercy rose to take up their cause and defend their rights. Meting out retribution You delivered the strong into the hand of the weak, the many into the hand of the few, the impure into the hand of the pure, the evil ones into the hand of the righteous, and the wicked into the hand of devotees of Your Torah. You thereby made for Yourself a great and holy name throughout Your world, as well as bringing about great deliverance and salvation for Your people Israel (known) to this day. Then Your children came to the Holy of Holies in Your house, cleared Your Temple, purified Your holy place, kindled lights in Your holy courts, and instituted these eight days of Ḥanukka to give thanks and sing praise to Your great name. *Continue with "For all this."*

On Purim:

IN THE DAYS of Mordechai and Esther, in Shushan the capital, when the wicked Haman rose up against them, he sought to destroy, to kill, and to annihilate all the Jews, young and old, women and infants, in one day, the *(Esther 3)*

Continued on the top of the next page.

וְנָשִׁים בְּיוֹם אֶחָד, בִּשְׁלוֹשָׁה עָשָׂר לְחֹדֶשׁ שְׁנֵים־עָשָׂר, הוּא־חֹדֶשׁ אֲדָר, וּשְׁלָלָם לָבוֹז: וְאַתָּה בְּרַחֲמֶיךָ הָרַבִּים הֵפַרְתָּ אֶת עֲצָתוֹ, וְקִלְקַלְתָּ אֶת מַחֲשַׁבְתּוֹ, וַהֲשֵׁבוֹתָ לּוֹ גְּמוּלוֹ בְּרֹאשׁוֹ, וְתָלוּ אוֹתוֹ וְאֶת בָּנָיו עַל הָעֵץ.

Continue with וְעַל כֻּלָּם.

וְעַל כֻּלָּם יִתְבָּרַךְ וְיִתְרוֹמַם שִׁמְךָ מַלְכֵּנוּ תָּמִיד לְעוֹלָם וָעֶד.

בעשרת ימי תשובה: וּכְתֹב לְחַיִּים טוֹבִים כָּל בְּנֵי בְרִיתֶךָ.

(*If forgotten, no corrective action is necessary.*)

וְכֹל הַחַיִּים יוֹדוּךָ סֶּלָה, וִיהַלְלוּ אֶת שִׁמְךָ בֶּאֱמֶת, הָאֵל יְשׁוּעָתֵנוּ וְעֶזְרָתֵנוּ סֶלָה. ׳בָּרוּךְ אַתָּה יהוה, הַטּוֹב שִׁמְךָ וּלְךָ נָאֶה לְהוֹדוֹת.

ברכת שלום

שָׁלוֹם רָב עַל יִשְׂרָאֵל עַמְּךָ תָּשִׂים לְעוֹלָם, כִּי אַתָּה הוּא מֶלֶךְ אָדוֹן לְכָל הַשָּׁלוֹם. וְטוֹב בְּעֵינֶיךָ לְבָרֵךְ אֶת עַמְּךָ יִשְׂרָאֵל, בְּכָל עֵת וּבְכָל שָׁעָה בִּשְׁלוֹמֶךָ.

בעשרת ימי תשובה: בְּסֵפֶר חַיִּים, בְּרָכָה וְשָׁלוֹם, וּפַרְנָסָה טוֹבָה, נִזָּכֵר וְנִכָּתֵב לְפָנֶיךָ, אֲנַחְנוּ וְכָל עַמְּךָ בֵּית יִשְׂרָאֵל, לְחַיִּים טוֹבִים וּלְשָׁלוֹם.*

בָּרוּךְ אַתָּה יהוה, הַמְבָרֵךְ אֶת עַמּוֹ יִשְׂרָאֵל בַּשָּׁלוֹם.

**During the* עשרת ימי תשובה *many end the blessing:*

בָּרוּךְ אַתָּה יהוה, עוֹשֵׂה הַשָּׁלוֹם.

Some say the following verse:

תהלים יט יִהְיוּ לְרָצוֹן אִמְרֵי־פִי וְהֶגְיוֹן לִבִּי לְפָנֶיךָ, יהוה צוּרִי וְגֹאֲלִי:

וּכְתֹב לְחַיִּים טוֹבִים – *Inscribe... for a life of goodness*. During the Ten days of Repentance there are four insertions in the *Amida*. The first two, occurring in the opening section, both plead for חַיִּים (life). The last two, as they appear in the closing segment, both ask for חַיִּים טוֹבִים (*good* life). The reason is that at the beginning of the *Amida* we request only what is essential,

thirteenth day of the twelfth month, Adar, and plunder their possessions. In Your great mercy You nullified his counsel and subverted his designs, causing them to recoil on his own head so that he and his sons were hanged on the gallows.

Continue with "For all this."

For all this, our King, may Your name be blessed and exalted continually, forever and ever.

Between Rosh HaShana & Yom Kippur: Inscribe all the children of Your covenant for a life of goodness.

(*If forgotten, no corrective action is necessary.*)

All that lives will give thanks to You forever and praise Your name in truth, God, our salvation and our help forever. ▾Blessed are You, LORD, for Your name is "The Good One" and it is appropriate to give thanks to You.

PEACE

שָׁלוֹם רָב ESTABLISH ABUNDANT PEACE for Your people Israel forever, for You are the sovereign Master of all peace; and may it be good in Your eyes to bless Your people Israel at all times, at every hour, with Your peace.

Between Rosh HaShana & Yom Kippur: In the book of life and blessing, peace and prosperity, may we and all the house of Israel Your people be remembered before You and inscribed for a life of goodness and peace.*

Blessed are You, LORD, Who blesses His people Israel with peace.

**Between Rosh HaShana and Yom Kippur many end the blessing:*
Blessed are You, LORD, Who makes peace.

Some say the following verse:

Ps. 19 MAY THE WORDS of my mouth and the meditation of my heart be acceptable before You, LORD, my Rock and my Redeemer.

---

whereas at the end of our prayers, in the merit of the sincere prayers that we have just offered, we dare to ask for even more: that God should grant us both length of years, as well as quality time, without suffering, hardship, or poor health (*Tur* in the name of Maharam Rotenberg).

ברכות יז. **אֱלֹהַי**, נְצֹר לְשׁוֹנִי מֵרָע וּשְׂפָתַי מִדַּבֵּר מִרְמָה, וְלִמְקַלְלַי נַפְשִׁי
תִדֹּם, וְנַפְשִׁי כֶּעָפָר לַכֹּל תִּהְיֶה. פְּתַח לִבִּי בְּתוֹרָתֶךָ,
וּבְמִצְוֹתֶיךָ תִּרְדֹּף נַפְשִׁי. וְכָל הַחוֹשְׁבִים עָלַי רָעָה, מְהֵרָה הָפֵר
עֲצָתָם וְקַלְקֵל מַחֲשַׁבְתָּם. עֲשֵׂה לְמַעַן שְׁמֶךָ, עֲשֵׂה לְמַעַן יְמִינֶךָ,
תהלים ס עֲשֵׂה לְמַעַן קְדֻשָּׁתֶךָ, עֲשֵׂה לְמַעַן תּוֹרָתֶךָ. לְמַעַן יֵחָלְצוּן יְדִידֶיךָ,
תהלים יט הוֹשִׁיעָה יְמִינְךָ וַעֲנֵנִי: יִהְיוּ לְרָצוֹן אִמְרֵי־פִי וְהֶגְיוֹן לִבִּי לְפָנֶיךָ, יהוה
צוּרִי וְגֹאֲלִי:

Bow, take three steps back, then bow, first left, then right, then center, while saying:

עֹשֶׂה שָׁלוֹם / בעשרת ימי תשובה: הַשָּׁלוֹם/ בִּמְרוֹמָיו, הוּא יַעֲשֶׂה שָׁלוֹם
עָלֵינוּ, וְעַל כָּל יִשְׂרָאֵל, וְאִמְרוּ אָמֵן.

יְהִי רָצוֹן מִלְּפָנֶיךָ יהוה אֱלֹהֵינוּ וֵאלֹהֵי אֲבוֹתֵינוּ, שֶׁיִּבָּנֶה בֵּית הַמִּקְדָּשׁ
בִּמְהֵרָה בְיָמֵינוּ, וְתֵן חֶלְקֵנוּ בְּתוֹרָתֶךָ, וְשָׁם נַעֲבָדְךָ בְּיִרְאָה כִּימֵי
מלאכי ג עוֹלָם וּכְשָׁנִים קַדְמוֹנִיּוֹת. וְעָרְבָה לַיהוה מִנְחַת יְהוּדָה וִירוּשָׁלָםִ כִּימֵי עוֹלָם
וּכְשָׁנִים קַדְמוֹנִיּוֹת:

On מוצאי שבת *(except when* יום טוב *or* ערב פסח *falls in the following week),*
the שליח ציבור *continues with* חצי קדיש *on page 302, then* וִיהִי נֹעַם *on page 732.*

On מוצאי שבת *when* יום טוב *falls in the following week,*
the service continues with קדיש שלם *on page 736.*

On other evenings the שליח ציבור *says* קדיש שלם*:*

קדיש שלם

ש״ץ: **יִתְגַּדַּל** וְיִתְקַדַּשׁ שְׁמֵהּ רַבָּא (קהל: אָמֵן), בְּעָלְמָא דִּי בְרָא כִרְעוּתֵהּ.
וְיַמְלִיךְ מַלְכוּתֵהּ, בְּחַיֵּיכוֹן וּבְיוֹמֵיכוֹן וּבְחַיֵּי דְכָל בֵּית
יִשְׂרָאֵל, בַּעֲגָלָא וּבִזְמַן קָרִיב, וְאִמְרוּ אָמֵן. (קהל: אָמֵן)

קהל וש״ץ: יְהֵא שְׁמֵהּ רַבָּא מְבָרַךְ לְעָלַם וּלְעָלְמֵי עָלְמַיָּא.

ש״ץ: יִתְבָּרַךְ וְיִשְׁתַּבַּח וְיִתְפָּאַר, וְיִתְרוֹמַם וְיִתְנַשֵּׂא וְיִתְהַדָּר וְיִתְעַלֶּה
וְיִתְהַלָּל שְׁמֵהּ דְּקֻדְשָׁא בְּרִיךְ הוּא (קהל: בְּרִיךְ הוּא), לְעֵלָּא מִן כָּל
בִּרְכָתָא / בעשרת ימי תשובה: לְעֵלָּא (וּ)לְעֵלָּא מִכָּל בִּרְכָתָא / וְשִׁירָתָא,
תֻּשְׁבְּחָתָא וְנֶחֱמָתָא דַּאֲמִירָן בְּעָלְמָא, וְאִמְרוּ אָמֵן. (קהל: אָמֵן)

For laws regarding "Interruptions during *Elokai Netzor,*" see page 133.

Berakhot 17a אֱלֹהַי MY GOD, guard my tongue from evil, and my lips from speaking deceit. Let my soul be silent to those who curse me; let my soul be humble toward everyone like the dust. Open my heart to Your Torah that my soul may follow Your commandments. As for all those who contemplate evil against me, speedily nullify their plans and spoil their schemes. Do so for the sake of Your name. Do so for Your
Ps. 60 right hand. Do so for Your holiness. Do so for Your Torah, that Your loved ones may be delivered. Save with Your right hand, and answer
Ps. 19 me. May the words of my mouth and the meditation of my heart be acceptable before You, LORD, my Rock and my Redeemer.

Bow, take three steps back, then bow, first left, then right, then center, while saying:

He Who makes peace in His heights, may He create peace for us and for all Israel. Amen.

יְהִי רָצוֹן MAY IT BE Your will, LORD our God and God of our fathers, that the Temple be rebuilt speedily in our days and may You grant our portion in Your Torah. We will serve You there in reverence as in the days of antiquity and in
Mal. 3 years gone by. "And may the offering of Judah and Jerusalem be pleasant to the LORD as in the days of antiquity and in years gone by."

On Motza'ei Shabbat (except when Yom Tov or Erev Pesaḥ falls in the following week), the Leader continues with Half Kaddish on page 303, then "Vihi No'am" on page 733.

On Motza'ei Shabbat when Yom Tov falls in the following week, the service continues with Full Kaddish on page 737.

On other evenings the Leader says Full Kaddish:

FULL KADDISH

Leader: יִתְגַּדַּל EXALTED AND HALLOWED may God's great name be, in the world He created as He willed. May He reign in your lifetimes and in your days, and in the lifetime of the whole house of Israel, speedily and soon, and say, Amen.

All: May His great name be blessed forever and all time.

Leader: Blessed and praised, honored, extolled, glorified, adored and exalted above all be the name of the Holy One, blessed is He, (*Between Rosh Hashana & Yom Kippur:* above and) beyond any blessing, hymn, praise, or expressions of consolation that may be uttered in this world, and say, Amen.

תִּתְקַבַּל צְלוֹתְהוֹן וּבָעוּתְהוֹן דְּכָל יִשְׂרָאֵל, קֳדָם אֲבוּהוֹן דִּי בִשְׁמַיָּא, וְאִמְרוּ אָמֵן. (קהל: אָמֵן)

יְהֵא שְׁלָמָא רַבָּא מִן שְׁמַיָּא וְחַיִּים, עָלֵינוּ וְעַל כָּל יִשְׂרָאֵל, וְאִמְרוּ אָמֵן. (קהל: אָמֵן)

Bow, take three steps back, as if taking leave of the Divine Presence, then bow, first left, then right, then center, while saying:

עֹשֶׂה שָׁלוֹם / בעשרת ימי תשובה: הַשָּׁלוֹם/ בִּמְרוֹמָיו, הוּא יַעֲשֶׂה שָׁלוֹם עָלֵינוּ, וְעַל כָּל יִשְׂרָאֵל, וְאִמְרוּ אָמֵן. (קהל: אָמֵן)

From the second night of פסח *until the night before* שבועות*, the* עומר *is counted here (**page 326**). Some count the* עומר *after* עָלֵינוּ*.*

On פורים*,* מגילת אסתר *is read; on* תשעה באב*,* מגילת איכה *is read.*

On weeknights, the service continues with וְאַתָּה קָדוֹשׁ *on* *page 734**.*

When פורים *falls on* מוצאי שבת*, continue with "*וִיהִי נֹעַם*" (**page 732**).*

Stand while saying עָלֵינוּ*. Bow at* ▾*.*

עָלֵינוּ לְשַׁבֵּחַ לַאֲדוֹן הַכֹּל, לָתֵת גְּדֻלָּה לְיוֹצֵר בְּרֵאשִׁית, שֶׁלֹּא עָשָׂנוּ כְּגוֹיֵי הָאֲרָצוֹת, וְלֹא שָׂמָנוּ כְּמִשְׁפְּחוֹת הָאֲדָמָה, שֶׁלֹּא שָׂם חֶלְקֵנוּ כָּהֶם וְגוֹרָלֵנוּ כְּכָל הֲמוֹנָם. (שֶׁהֵם מִשְׁתַּחֲוִים לְהֶבֶל וָרִיק וּמִתְפַּלְלִים אֶל אֵל לֹא יוֹשִׁיעַ.) ▾וַאֲנַחְנוּ כּוֹרְעִים וּמִשְׁתַּחֲוִים וּמוֹדִים, לִפְנֵי מֶלֶךְ מַלְכֵי הַמְּלָכִים, הַקָּדוֹשׁ בָּרוּךְ הוּא, שֶׁהוּא נוֹטֶה שָׁמַיִם וְיוֹסֵד אָרֶץ, וּמוֹשַׁב יְקָרוֹ בַּשָּׁמַיִם מִמַּעַל, וּשְׁכִינַת עֻזּוֹ בְּגָבְהֵי מְרוֹמִים. הוּא אֱלֹהֵינוּ, אֵין עוֹד. אֱמֶת מַלְכֵּנוּ, אֶפֶס זוּלָתוֹ, כַּכָּתוּב בְּתוֹרָתוֹ, וְיָדַעְתָּ הַיּוֹם וַהֲשֵׁבֹתָ אֶל־ לְבָבֶךָ, כִּי יהוה הוּא הָאֱלֹהִים בַּשָּׁמַיִם מִמַּעַל וְעַל־הָאָרֶץ מִתָּחַת, אֵין עוֹד: דברים ד

עַל כֵּן נְקַוֶּה לְּךָ יהוה אֱלֹהֵינוּ, לִרְאוֹת מְהֵרָה בְּתִפְאֶרֶת עֻזֶּךָ, לְהַעֲבִיר גִּלּוּלִים מִן הָאָרֶץ, וְהָאֱלִילִים כָּרוֹת יִכָּרֵתוּן, לְתַקֵּן עוֹלָם בְּמַלְכוּת שַׁדַּי. וְכָל בְּנֵי בָשָׂר יִקְרְאוּ בִשְׁמֶךָ לְהַפְנוֹת אֵלֶיךָ כָּל

May the prayers and pleas of all Israel be accepted before their Father Who is in heaven – and say, Amen.

May abundant peace descend from heaven, as well as life, for us and for all Israel, and say, Amen.

Bow, take three steps back, as if taking leave of the Divine Presence, then bow, first left, then right, then center, while saying:

May He Who makes peace in the highest heaven, make peace for us, and for all Israel, and say, Amen.

From the second night of Pesaḥ until the night before Shavuot, the Omer is counted here (page 327). Some count the Omer after Aleinu.

On Purim, Megillat Esther is read; on Tisha B'Av, Megillat Eikha is read. On weeknights, the service continues with "But You are holy" on page 735. When Purim falls on Motza'ei Shabbat, continue with "Vihi No'am" (page 733).

Stand while saying Aleinu. Bow at ▼.

עָלֵינוּ WE MUST, all of us, praise the Master of all, and ascribe greatness to He Who formed creation, for He did not make us like the nations of the world, nor render us like the families of the earth. He did not make our portion to be as theirs, nor our destiny like that of their masses. (For idolaters bow to vanity and emptiness and pray to a god who cannot save.) ▼We, however, bend our knees, bow, and give thanks before the King of the most exalted of kings, the Holy One, blessed is He. He is the One Who spreads out the heavens and establishes the earth. The seat of His glory is in the heavens above, and His Presence in all its strength is found in its highest abode. He is our God – there is no other. In truth He is our King; there is none but Him; as is written
Deut. 4 in His Torah: "On this day you should know, and take to heart, that the Lord is God in the heavens above and on the earth below – there is no other."

We therefore hope in You, Lord our God, that we may soon see the glory of Your might when You will remove abominations from the earth and the idols shall be utterly destroyed, when the world shall be perfected under the rule of the Almighty. Then all mankind shall

רִשְׁעֵי אָרֶץ. יַכִּירוּ וְיֵדְעוּ כָּל יוֹשְׁבֵי תֵבֵל, כִּי לְךָ תִּכְרַע כָּל בֶּרֶךְ, תִּשָּׁבַע כָּל לָשׁוֹן. לְפָנֶיךָ יהוה אֱלֹהֵינוּ יִכְרְעוּ וְיִפֹּלוּ, וְלִכְבוֹד שִׁמְךָ יְקָר יִתֵּנוּ, וִיקַבְּלוּ כֻלָּם אֶת עֹל מַלְכוּתֶךָ, וְתִמְלֹךְ עֲלֵיהֶם מְהֵרָה לְעוֹלָם וָעֶד. כִּי הַמַּלְכוּת שֶׁלְּךָ הִיא וּלְעוֹלְמֵי עַד תִּמְלֹךְ בְּכָבוֹד,
שמות טו כַּכָּתוּב בְּתוֹרָתֶךָ, יהוה יִמְלֹךְ לְעֹלָם וָעֶד: ◄ וְנֶאֱמַר, וְהָיָה יהוה לְמֶלֶךְ
זכריה יד עַל־כָּל־הָאָרֶץ, בַּיּוֹם הַהוּא יִהְיֶה יהוה אֶחָד וּשְׁמוֹ אֶחָד:

Some add:

משלי ג **אַל־תִּירָא** מִפַּחַד פִּתְאֹם וּמִשֹּׁאַת רְשָׁעִים כִּי תָבֹא: עֻצוּ עֵצָה וְתֻפָר, דַּבְּרוּ דָבָר וְלֹא יָקוּם,
ישעיה ח כִּי עִמָּנוּ אֵל: וְעַד־זִקְנָה אֲנִי הוּא, וְעַד־שֵׂיבָה אֲנִי אֶסְבֹּל, אֲנִי עָשִׂיתִי וַאֲנִי אֶשָּׂא
ישעיה מו וַאֲנִי אֶסְבֹּל וַאֲמַלֵּט:

קדיש יתום

The following prayer, said by mourners, requires the presence of a מנין*.*
A transliteration can be found on page 1345.

אבל: **יִתְגַּדַּל** וְיִתְקַדַּשׁ שְׁמֵהּ רַבָּא (קהל: אָמֵן), בְּעָלְמָא דִּי בְרָא כִרְעוּתֵהּ. וְיַמְלִיךְ מַלְכוּתֵהּ, בְּחַיֵּיכוֹן וּבְיוֹמֵיכוֹן וּבְחַיֵּי דְכָל בֵּית יִשְׂרָאֵל, בַּעֲגָלָא וּבִזְמַן קָרִיב, וְאִמְרוּ אָמֵן. (קהל: אָמֵן)

קהל ואבל: יְהֵא שְׁמֵהּ רַבָּא מְבָרַךְ לְעָלַם וּלְעָלְמֵי עָלְמַיָּא.

אבל: יִתְבָּרַךְ וְיִשְׁתַּבַּח וְיִתְפָּאַר, וְיִתְרוֹמַם וְיִתְנַשֵּׂא וְיִתְהַדָּר וְיִתְעַלֶּה וְיִתְהַלָּל שְׁמֵהּ דְּקֻדְשָׁא בְּרִיךְ הוּא (קהל: בְּרִיךְ הוּא), לְעֵלָּא מִן כָּל בִּרְכָתָא / בעשרת ימי תשובה: לְעֵלָּא (וּ)לְעֵלָּא מִכָּל בִּרְכָתָא / וְשִׁירָתָא, תֻּשְׁבְּחָתָא וְנֶחֱמָתָא דַּאֲמִירָן בְּעָלְמָא, וְאִמְרוּ אָמֵן. (קהל: אָמֵן)

יְהֵא שְׁלָמָא רַבָּא מִן שְׁמַיָּא וְחַיִּים, עָלֵינוּ וְעַל כָּל יִשְׂרָאֵל, וְאִמְרוּ אָמֵן. (קהל: אָמֵן)

Bow, take three steps back, as if taking leave of the Divine Presence, then bow, first left, then right, then center, while saying:

עֹשֶׂה שָׁלוֹם / בעשרת ימי תשובה: הַשָּׁלוֹם/ בִּמְרוֹמָיו, הוּא יַעֲשֶׂה שָׁלוֹם עָלֵינוּ, וְעַל כָּל יִשְׂרָאֵל, וְאִמְרוּ אָמֵן. (קהל: אָמֵן)

invoke Your name, to turn all the wicked on earth toward You. All dwellers on earth will perceive and understand that to You every knee must bend, every tongue vow fealty. Before You, Lord our God, all will kneel and bow down, and give honor to Your glorious name. They will all accept the rule of Your dominion, and You will speedily rule over them forevermore. For the kingdom is Yours, and to all eternity You
Ex. 15 shall reign in glory, as it is written in Your Torah, "The Lord shall reign
Zech. 14 forever and ever." ▸ And it is said, "And the Lord shall be King over
all the earth; in that day shall the Lord be One, and His name One."

Some add:

Prov. 3 **אַל־תִּירָא** DO NOT FEAR sudden terror or the destruction when it comes to the
Is. 8 wicked. Devise a plan, and it will be thwarted; state a case and it will not stand,
Is. 46 for God is with us. And when you are old, I will remain; when you are aged, I
will endure. I created you, I will carry you, I will endure, and I will rescue you.

MOURNER'S KADDISH

The following prayer, said by mourners, requires the presence of a minyan. A transliteration can be found on page 1345.

Mourner: **יִתְגַּדַּל** EXALTED AND HALLOWED may God's great name be, in the world He created as He willed. May He reign in your lifetimes and in your days, and in the lifetime of the whole house of Israel, speedily and soon, and say, Amen.

All: May His great name be blessed forever and all time.

Mourner: Blessed and praised, honored, extolled, glorified, adored and exalted above all be the name of the Holy One, blessed is He, (*Between Rosh Hashana & Yom Kippur:* above and) beyond any blessing, hymn, praise, or expressions of consolation that may be uttered in this world, and say, Amen.

May abundant peace descend from heaven, as well as life, for us and for all Israel, and say, Amen.

Bow, take three steps back, as if taking leave of the Divine Presence, then bow, first left, then right, then center, while saying:

May He Who makes peace in the highest heaven, make peace for us, and for all Israel, and say, Amen.

From the second day of ראש חודש אלול *through* שמיני עצרת *the following psalm is said:*

תהלים כז **לְדָוִד,** יהוה אוֹרִי וְיִשְׁעִי, מִמִּי אִירָא, יהוה מָעוֹז־חַיַּי, מִמִּי אֶפְחָד: בִּקְרֹב
עָלַי מְרֵעִים לֶאֱכֹל אֶת־בְּשָׂרִי, צָרַי וְאֹיְבַי לִי, הֵמָּה כָשְׁלוּ וְנָפָלוּ:
אִם־תַּחֲנֶה עָלַי מַחֲנֶה, לֹא־יִירָא לִבִּי, אִם־תָּקוּם עָלַי מִלְחָמָה, בְּזֹאת
אֲנִי בוֹטֵחַ: אַחַת שָׁאַלְתִּי מֵאֵת־יהוה, אוֹתָהּ אֲבַקֵּשׁ, שִׁבְתִּי בְּבֵית־יהוה
כָּל־יְמֵי חַיַּי, לַחֲזוֹת בְּנֹעַם־יהוה, וּלְבַקֵּר בְּהֵיכָלוֹ: כִּי יִצְפְּנֵנִי בְּסֻכֹּה
בְּיוֹם רָעָה, יַסְתִּרֵנִי בְּסֵתֶר אָהֳלוֹ, בְּצוּר יְרוֹמְמֵנִי: וְעַתָּה יָרוּם רֹאשִׁי
עַל אֹיְבַי סְבִיבוֹתַי, וְאֶזְבְּחָה בְאָהֳלוֹ זִבְחֵי תְרוּעָה, אָשִׁירָה וַאֲזַמְּרָה
לַיהוה: שְׁמַע־יהוה קוֹלִי אֶקְרָא, וְחָנֵּנִי וַעֲנֵנִי: לְךָ אָמַר לִבִּי בַּקְּשׁוּ פָנָי,
אֶת־פָּנֶיךָ יהוה אֲבַקֵּשׁ: אַל־תַּסְתֵּר פָּנֶיךָ מִמֶּנִּי, אַל תַּט־בְּאַף עַבְדֶּךָ,
עֶזְרָתִי הָיִיתָ, אַל־תִּטְּשֵׁנִי וְאַל־תַּעַזְבֵנִי, אֱלֹהֵי יִשְׁעִי: כִּי־אָבִי וְאִמִּי
עֲזָבוּנִי, וַיהוה יַאַסְפֵנִי: הוֹרֵנִי יהוה דַּרְכֶּךָ, וּנְחֵנִי בְּאֹרַח מִישׁוֹר, לְמַעַן
שׁוֹרְרָי: אַל־תִּתְּנֵנִי בְּנֶפֶשׁ צָרָי, כִּי קָמוּ־בִי עֵדֵי־שֶׁקֶר, וִיפֵחַ חָמָס: ‣ לוּלֵא
הֶאֱמַנְתִּי לִרְאוֹת בְּטוּב־יהוה בְּאֶרֶץ חַיִּים: קַוֵּה אֶל־יהוה, חֲזַק וְיַאֲמֵץ
לִבֶּךָ, וְקַוֵּה אֶל־יהוה:

קדיש יתום *(previous page)*

In a שבעה *house the service continues on page 198.*

סדר ספירת העומר

The עומר *is counted each night from the second night of* פסח *until the night before* שבועות*. At this point some follow the Hasidic custom of reciting additional prayers, which can be found on page 1338.*

בָּרוּךְ אַתָּה יהוה אֱלֹהֵינוּ מֶלֶךְ הָעוֹלָם, אֲשֶׁר קִדְּשָׁנוּ בְּמִצְוֹתָיו
וְצִוָּנוּ עַל סְפִירַת הָעֹמֶר.

Select the appropriate day's count (below till page 334).

טז בניסן

1. הַיּוֹם יוֹם אֶחָד בָּעֹמֶר. — חסד שבחסד

יז בניסן

2. הַיּוֹם שְׁנֵי יָמִים בָּעֹמֶר. — גבורה שבחסד

סֵדֶר סְפִירַת הָעֹמֶר / COUNTING OF THE OMER
The Torah commands us to count each of the forty-nine days between the second day of Pesaḥ and Shavuot, with the עֹמֶר הַתְּנוּפָה

From the second day of Rosh Ḥodesh Elul through Shemini Atzeret the following psalm is said:

Ps. 27 לְדָוִד OF DAVID. The Lord is my light and my salvation. Whom shall I fear? The Lord is the refuge of my life. Whom shall I dread? When the evildoers came close to me to eat my flesh, those who were to me my adversaries and my enemies, it was they who stumbled and fell. If a host should encamp against me, my heart will not fear. If a war should rise against me, in this I trust. One thing have I asked of the Lord, that will I seek: That I may dwell in the house of the Lord all the days of my life, to behold the beauty of the Lord, and to contemplate His Temple, That He will hide me in His tabernacle on the day of evil, He will hide me in the shelter of His tent, He will lift me up upon a rock. And now my head will be lifted up above my enemies round about me, and I will offer in His tent sacrifices accompanied by the sound of trumpets. I will sing, and I will sing praises to the Lord. Hear, O Lord, my voice when I call, and show me favor and answer me. Of You my heart has said: Seek My face. Your face, O Lord, will I seek. Do not hide Your face from me. Do not turn Your servant away in anger. You have been my help, do not abandon me and do not forsake me, O God of my salvation. For my father and my mother have forsaken me, but the Lord will gather me in. Teach me Your way, O Lord, and lead me on an even path, because of my enemies. Do not deliver me to the desire of my enemies, for false witnesses have risen up against me, and a wicked witness. ▸ Were it not that I believed I would see the goodness of the Lord in the land of the living. Wait for the Lord, be strong and let your heart be encouraged, and wait for the Lord.

Mourner's Kaddish (previous page)

In a shiva house the service continues on page 199.

COUNTING OF THE OMER

The Omer is counted each night from the second night of Pesaḥ until the night before Shavuot. At this point some follow the Hasidic custom of reciting additional prayers, which can be found on page 1339.

בָּרוּךְ BLESSED ARE YOU, Lord, our God, King of the universe, Who has sanctified us with His commandments and has commanded us about the counting of the Omer.

Select the appropriate day's count (below till page 335).

16 Nisan

1. TODAY is the first day of the Omer.

17 Nisan

2. TODAY is the second day of the Omer.

יח בניסן

3. הַיּוֹם שְׁלֹשָׁה יָמִים בָּעֹמֶר. תפארת שבחסד

יט בניסן

4. הַיּוֹם אַרְבָּעָה יָמִים בָּעֹמֶר. נצח שבחסד

כ בניסן

5. הַיּוֹם חֲמִשָּׁה יָמִים בָּעֹמֶר. הוד שבחסד

כא בניסן

6. הַיּוֹם שִׁשָּׁה יָמִים בָּעֹמֶר. יסוד שבחסד

כב בניסן

7. הַיּוֹם שִׁבְעָה יָמִים, שֶׁהֵם שָׁבְוּעַ אֶחָד בָּעֹמֶר. מלכות שבחסד

כג בניסן

8. הַיּוֹם שְׁמוֹנָה יָמִים, שֶׁהֵם שָׁבְוּעַ אֶחָד וְיוֹם אֶחָד בָּעֹמֶר. חסד שבגבורה

כד בניסן

9. הַיּוֹם תִּשְׁעָה יָמִים, שֶׁהֵם שָׁבְוּעַ אֶחָד וּשְׁנֵי יָמִים בָּעֹמֶר. גבורה שבגבורה

כה בניסן

10. הַיּוֹם עֲשָׂרָה יָמִים, שֶׁהֵם שָׁבְוּעַ אֶחָד וּשְׁלֹשָׁה יָמִים בָּעֹמֶר. תפארת שבגבורה

כו בניסן

11. הַיּוֹם אַחַד עָשָׂר יוֹם, שֶׁהֵם שָׁבְוּעַ אֶחָד וְאַרְבָּעָה יָמִים בָּעֹמֶר. נצח שבגבורה

(barley-offering) at the beginning and the מִנְחָה חֲדָשָׁה (meal-offering) at the end, coinciding with the festival of Shavuot, hence the name סְפִירַת הָעֹמֶר (Counting the Omer).

But these days represent much more than the mere technical passage of time between two sacrifices and two festivals. In subsequent eras several crucial events occurred during these forty-nine days of the calendar. In the first place, during the weeks following the Exodus, our ancestors prepared themselves for receiving the Torah at Mount Sinai. Additionally the tragic deaths of R. Akiva's twenty-four thousand students occurred during this period (Yevamot 62b), perhaps during the Bar Kokhba revolt (*Iggeret Rav Sherira Gaon*, according to some scholars). In the Middle Ages, this period saw a string of bloody massacres of Jewish communities in the Rhineland during the Crusades starting in 1096. Finally the brutal massacres of Jews by Cossacks and Poles during the Chmielnicki uprising of 1648–1649 also began between Pesaḥ and Shavuot. Given the association of all these events with this seven-week period, the days of *Sefirat HaOmer* are a time of deep spiritual introspection and self-examination. We mourn (following various customs and practices) the deaths of R. Akiva's students and grieve over the destruction of important medieval and early-modern Jewish communities, and most significantly we use the time to prepare for

18 Nisan
3. TODAY is the third day of the Omer.

19 Nisan
4. TODAY is the fourth day of the Omer.

20 Nisan
5. TODAY is the fifth day of the Omer.

21 Nisan
6. TODAY is the sixth day of the Omer.

22 Nisan
7. TODAY is the seventh day of the Omer, totaling one week.

23 Nisan
8. TODAY is the eighth day of the Omer, totaling one week and one day.

24 Nisan
9. TODAY is the ninth day of the Omer, totaling one week and two days.

25 Nisan
10. TODAY is the tenth day of the Omer, totaling one week and three days.

26 Nisan
11. TODAY is the eleventh day of the Omer, totaling one week and four days.

---

our own renewed commitment to the Torah on Shavuot, on the fiftieth day of the count.

בָּעֹמֶר – *Of the Omer*. The *Shulḥan Arukh* states that the proper text is *ba'omer* (in the *omer*) while the *Mishna Berura* (489:8) prefers *la'omer* (to the *omer*). R. Joseph B. Soloveitchik explained the difference by pointing out that *ba'omer* is to be understood as "in the *omer* period between Pesaḥ and Shavuot," whereas *la'omer* means "relating to the *omer* sacrifice." Since there is no longer an *omer* sacrifice, the authorities are divided as to which formulation is preferred. Rambam (*Hil. Temidim uMusafim* 7:24) considers counting the days of the *omer* to be independent of the *omer* sacrifice, and so we remain biblically obligated to count the forty-nine days from Pesaḥ to Shavuot, and thus say *ba'omer*. Other early authorities disagree, as they understand the obligation to be directly linked to the *omer* sacrifice, hence not required by the Torah when there is no longer a Temple. In their view we should say *la'omer*, which conveys that counting the *omer* is linked to the *omer* sacrifice, and thus in our time a rabbinic, but not biblical, obligation. R. Soloveitchik sought to satisfy both views by reciting *ba'omer* out loud and then *la'omer* quietly, immediately followed by the prayer for the rebuilding of the Temple and the reinstitution of the *omer* sacrifice (R. Hershel Schachter).

כז בניסן

12. הַיּוֹם שְׁנֵים עָשָׂר יוֹם, שֶׁהֵם שָׁבְוּעַ אֶחָד וַחֲמִשָּׁה יָמִים בָּעְמֶר. הוד שבגבורה

כח בניסן

13. הַיּוֹם שְׁלֹשָׁה עָשָׂר יוֹם, שֶׁהֵם שָׁבְוּעַ אֶחָד וְשִׁשָּׁה יָמִים בָּעְמֶר. יסוד שבגבורה

כט בניסן

14. הַיּוֹם אַרְבָּעָה עָשָׂר יוֹם, שֶׁהֵם שְׁנֵי שָׁבוּעוֹת בָּעְמֶר. מלכות שבגבורה

ל בניסן, א׳ דראש חודש

15. הַיּוֹם חֲמִשָּׁה עָשָׂר יוֹם, שֶׁהֵם שְׁנֵי שָׁבוּעוֹת וְיוֹם אֶחָד בָּעְמֶר. חסד שבתפארת

א באייר, ב׳ דראש חודש

16. הַיּוֹם שִׁשָּׁה עָשָׂר יוֹם, שֶׁהֵם שְׁנֵי שָׁבוּעוֹת וּשְׁנֵי יָמִים בָּעְמֶר. גבורה שבתפארת

ב באייר

17. הַיּוֹם שִׁבְעָה עָשָׂר יוֹם, שֶׁהֵם שְׁנֵי שָׁבוּעוֹת וּשְׁלֹשָׁה יָמִים בָּעְמֶר.
תפארת שבתפארת

ג באייר

18. הַיּוֹם שְׁמוֹנָה עָשָׂר יוֹם, שֶׁהֵם שְׁנֵי שָׁבוּעוֹת וְאַרְבָּעָה יָמִים בָּעְמֶר.
נצח שבתפארת

ד באייר

19. הַיּוֹם תִּשְׁעָה עָשָׂר יוֹם, שֶׁהֵם שְׁנֵי שָׁבוּעוֹת וַחֲמִשָּׁה יָמִים בָּעְמֶר.
הוד שבתפארת

ה באייר, יום העצמאות

20. הַיּוֹם עֶשְׂרִים יוֹם, שֶׁהֵם שְׁנֵי שָׁבוּעוֹת וְשִׁשָּׁה יָמִים בָּעְמֶר. יסוד שבתפארת

ו באייר

21. הַיּוֹם אֶחָד וְעֶשְׂרִים יוֹם, שֶׁהֵם שְׁלֹשָׁה שָׁבוּעוֹת בָּעְמֶר. מלכות שבתפארת

ז באייר

22. הַיּוֹם שְׁנַיִם וְעֶשְׂרִים יוֹם, שֶׁהֵם שְׁלֹשָׁה שָׁבוּעוֹת וְיוֹם אֶחָד בָּעְמֶר.
חסד שבנצח

ח באייר

23. הַיּוֹם שְׁלֹשָׁה וְעֶשְׂרִים יוֹם, שֶׁהֵם שְׁלֹשָׁה שָׁבוּעוֹת וּשְׁנֵי יָמִים בָּעְמֶר.
גבורה שבנצח

ט באייר

24. הַיּוֹם אַרְבָּעָה וְעֶשְׂרִים יוֹם, שֶׁהֵם שְׁלֹשָׁה שָׁבוּעוֹת וּשְׁלֹשָׁה יָמִים בָּעְמֶר.
תפארת שבנצח

י באייר

25. הַיּוֹם חֲמִשָּׁה וְעֶשְׂרִים יוֹם, שֶׁהֵם שְׁלֹשָׁה שָׁבוּעוֹת וְאַרְבָּעָה יָמִים בָּעְמֶר.
נצח שבנצח

27 Nisan

12. TODAY is the twelfth day of the Omer, totaling one week and five days.

28 Nisan

13. TODAY is the thirteenth day of the Omer, totaling one week and six days.

29 Nisan

14. TODAY is the fourteenth day of the Omer, totaling two weeks.

30 Nisan, 1st day Rosh Ḥodesh

15. TODAY is the fifteenth day of the Omer, totaling two weeks and one day.

1 Iyar, 2nd day Rosh Ḥodesh

16. TODAY is the sixteenth day of the Omer, totaling two weeks and two days.

2 Iyar

17. TODAY is the seventeenth day of the Omer, totaling two weeks and three days.

3 Iyar

18. TODAY is the eighteenth day of the Omer, totaling two weeks and four days.

4 Iyar

19. TODAY is the nineteenth day of the Omer, totaling two weeks and five days.

5 Iyar, Yom HaAtzma'ut

20. TODAY is the twentieth day of the Omer, totaling two weeks and six days.

6 Iyar

21. TODAY is the twenty-first day of the Omer, totaling three weeks.

7 Iyar

22. TODAY is the twenty-second day of the Omer, totaling three weeks and one day.

8 Iyar

23. TODAY is the twenty-third day of the Omer, totaling three weeks and two days.

9 Iyar

24. TODAY is the twenty-fourth day of the Omer, totaling three weeks and three days.

10 Iyar

25. TODAY is the twenty-fifth day of the Omer, totaling three weeks and four days.

יא באייר

26. הַיּוֹם שִׁשָּׁה וְעֶשְׂרִים יוֹם, שֶׁהֵם שְׁלֹשָׁה שָׁבוּעוֹת וַחֲמִשָּׁה יָמִים בָּעֹמֶר.

הוד שבנצח

יב באייר

27. הַיּוֹם שִׁבְעָה וְעֶשְׂרִים יוֹם, שֶׁהֵם שְׁלֹשָׁה שָׁבוּעוֹת וְשִׁשָּׁה יָמִים בָּעֹמֶר.

יסוד שבנצח

יג באייר

28. הַיּוֹם שְׁמוֹנָה וְעֶשְׂרִים יוֹם, שֶׁהֵם אַרְבָּעָה שָׁבוּעוֹת בָּעֹמֶר. מלכות שבנצח

יד באייר, פסח שני

29. הַיּוֹם תִּשְׁעָה וְעֶשְׂרִים יוֹם, שֶׁהֵם אַרְבָּעָה שָׁבוּעוֹת וְיוֹם אֶחָד בָּעֹמֶר.

חסד שבהוד

טו באייר

30. הַיּוֹם שְׁלֹשִׁים יוֹם, שֶׁהֵם אַרְבָּעָה שָׁבוּעוֹת וּשְׁנֵי יָמִים בָּעֹמֶר. גבורה שבהוד

טז באייר

31. הַיּוֹם אֶחָד וּשְׁלֹשִׁים יוֹם, שֶׁהֵם אַרְבָּעָה שָׁבוּעוֹת וּשְׁלֹשָׁה יָמִים בָּעֹמֶר.

תפארת שבהוד

יז באייר

32. הַיּוֹם שְׁנַיִם וּשְׁלֹשִׁים יוֹם, שֶׁהֵם אַרְבָּעָה שָׁבוּעוֹת וְאַרְבָּעָה יָמִים בָּעֹמֶר.

נצח שבהוד

יח באייר, לג בעומר

33. הַיּוֹם שְׁלֹשָׁה וּשְׁלֹשִׁים יוֹם, שֶׁהֵם אַרְבָּעָה שָׁבוּעוֹת וַחֲמִשָּׁה יָמִים בָּעֹמֶר.

הוד שבהוד

יט באייר

34. הַיּוֹם אַרְבָּעָה וּשְׁלֹשִׁים יוֹם, שֶׁהֵם אַרְבָּעָה שָׁבוּעוֹת וְשִׁשָּׁה יָמִים בָּעֹמֶר.

יסוד שבהוד

כ באייר

35. הַיּוֹם חֲמִשָּׁה וּשְׁלֹשִׁים יוֹם, שֶׁהֵם חֲמִשָּׁה שָׁבוּעוֹת בָּעֹמֶר. מלכות שבהוד

כא באייר

36. הַיּוֹם שִׁשָּׁה וּשְׁלֹשִׁים יוֹם, שֶׁהֵם חֲמִשָּׁה שָׁבוּעוֹת וְיוֹם אֶחָד בָּעֹמֶר.

חסד שביסוד

כב באייר

37. הַיּוֹם שִׁבְעָה וּשְׁלֹשִׁים יוֹם, שֶׁהֵם חֲמִשָּׁה שָׁבוּעוֹת וּשְׁנֵי יָמִים בָּעֹמֶר.

גבורה שביסוד

11 Iyar

26. TODAY is the twenty-sixth day of the Omer, totaling three weeks and five days.

12 Iyar

27. TODAY is the twenty-seventh day of the Omer, totaling three weeks and six days.

13 Iyar

28. TODAY is the twenty-eighth day of the Omer, totaling four weeks.

14 Iyar

29. TODAY is the twenty-ninth day of the Omer, totaling four weeks and one day.

15 Iyar

30. TODAY is the thirtieth day of the Omer, totaling four weeks and two days.

16 Iyar

31. TODAY is the thirty-first day of the Omer, totaling four weeks and three days.

17 Iyar

32. TODAY is the thirty-second day of the Omer, totaling four weeks and four days.

18 Iyar, Lag BaOmer

33. TODAY is the thirty-third day of the Omer, totaling four weeks and five days.

19 Iyar

34. TODAY is the thirty-fourth day of the Omer, totaling four weeks and six days.

20 Iyar

35. TODAY is the thirty-fifth day of the Omer, totaling five weeks.

21 Iyar

36. TODAY is the thirty-sixth day of the Omer, totaling five weeks and one day.

22 Iyar

37. TODAY is the thirty-seventh day of the Omer, totaling five weeks and two days.

כג באייר

38. הַיּוֹם שְׁמוֹנָה וּשְׁלֹשִׁים יוֹם, שֶׁהֵם חֲמִשָּׁה שָׁבוּעוֹת וּשְׁלֹשָׁה יָמִים בָּעֹמֶר.

תפארת שביסוד

כד באייר

39. הַיּוֹם תִּשְׁעָה וּשְׁלֹשִׁים יוֹם, שֶׁהֵם חֲמִשָּׁה שָׁבוּעוֹת וְאַרְבָּעָה יָמִים בָּעֹמֶר.

נצח שביסוד

כה באייר

40. הַיּוֹם אַרְבָּעִים יוֹם, שֶׁהֵם חֲמִשָּׁה שָׁבוּעוֹת וַחֲמִשָּׁה יָמִים בָּעֹמֶר. הוד שביסוד

כו באייר

41. הַיּוֹם אֶחָד וְאַרְבָּעִים יוֹם, שֶׁהֵם חֲמִשָּׁה שָׁבוּעוֹת וְשִׁשָּׁה יָמִים בָּעֹמֶר.

יסוד שביסוד

כז באייר

42. הַיּוֹם שְׁנַיִם וְאַרְבָּעִים יוֹם, שֶׁהֵם שִׁשָּׁה שָׁבוּעוֹת בָּעֹמֶר. מלכות שביסוד

כח באייר, יום ירושלים

43. הַיּוֹם שְׁלֹשָׁה וְאַרְבָּעִים יוֹם, שֶׁהֵם שִׁשָּׁה שָׁבוּעוֹת וְיוֹם אֶחָד בָּעֹמֶר.

חסד שבמלכות

כט באייר

44. הַיּוֹם אַרְבָּעָה וְאַרְבָּעִים יוֹם, שֶׁהֵם שִׁשָּׁה שָׁבוּעוֹת וּשְׁנֵי יָמִים בָּעֹמֶר.

גבורה שבמלכות

א בסיון, ראש חודש

45. הַיּוֹם חֲמִשָּׁה וְאַרְבָּעִים יוֹם, שֶׁהֵם שִׁשָּׁה שָׁבוּעוֹת וּשְׁלֹשָׁה יָמִים בָּעֹמֶר.

תפארת שבמלכות

ב בסיון

46. הַיּוֹם שִׁשָּׁה וְאַרְבָּעִים יוֹם, שֶׁהֵם שִׁשָּׁה שָׁבוּעוֹת וְאַרְבָּעָה יָמִים בָּעֹמֶר.

נצח שבמלכות

ג בסיון

47. הַיּוֹם שִׁבְעָה וְאַרְבָּעִים יוֹם, שֶׁהֵם שִׁשָּׁה שָׁבוּעוֹת וַחֲמִשָּׁה יָמִים בָּעֹמֶר.

הוד שבמלכות

ד בסיון

48. הַיּוֹם שְׁמוֹנָה וְאַרְבָּעִים יוֹם, שֶׁהֵם שִׁשָּׁה שָׁבוּעוֹת וְשִׁשָּׁה יָמִים בָּעֹמֶר.

יסוד שבמלכות

ה בסיון, ערב שבועות

49. הַיּוֹם תִּשְׁעָה וְאַרְבָּעִים יוֹם, שֶׁהֵם שִׁבְעָה שָׁבוּעוֹת בָּעֹמֶר. מלכות שבמלכות

23 Iyar

38. TODAY is the thirty-eighth day of the Omer, totaling five weeks and three days.

24 Iyar

39. TODAY is the thirty-ninth day of the Omer, totaling five weeks and four days.

25 Iyar

40. TODAY is the fortieth day of the Omer, totaling five weeks and five days.

26 Iyar

41. TODAY is the forty-first day of the Omer, totaling five weeks and six days.

27 Iyar

42. TODAY is the forty-second day of the Omer, totaling six weeks.

28 Iyar, Yom Yerushalayim

43. TODAY is the forty-third day of the Omer, totaling six weeks and one day.

29 Iyar

44. TODAY is the forty-fourth day of the Omer, totaling six weeks and two days.

1 Sivan, Rosh Ḥodesh

45. TODAY is the forty-fifth day of the Omer, totaling six weeks and three days.

2 Sivan

46. TODAY is the forty-sixth day of the Omer, totaling six weeks and four days.

3 Sivan

47. TODAY is the forty-seventh day of the Omer, totaling six weeks and five days.

4 Sivan

48. TODAY is the forty-eighth day of the Omer, totaling six weeks and six days.

5 Sivan, Erev Shavuot

49. TODAY is the forty-ninth day of the Omer, totaling seven weeks.

הָרַחֲמָן הוּא יַחֲזִיר לָנוּ עֲבוֹדַת בֵּית הַמִּקְדָּשׁ לִמְקוֹמָהּ בִּמְהֵרָה בְיָמֵינוּ, אָמֵן סֶלָה.

Some add:

תהלים סז **לַמְנַצֵּחַ** בִּנְגִינֹת, מִזְמוֹר שִׁיר: אֱלֹהִים יְחָנֵּנוּ וִיבָרְכֵנוּ, יָאֵר פָּנָיו אִתָּנוּ סֶלָה: לָדַעַת בָּאָרֶץ דַּרְכֶּךָ, בְּכָל־גּוֹיִם יְשׁוּעָתֶךָ: יוֹדוּךָ עַמִּים אֱלֹהִים, יוֹדוּךָ עַמִּים כֻּלָּם: יִשְׂמְחוּ וִירַנְּנוּ לְאֻמִּים, כִּי־תִשְׁפֹּט עַמִּים מִישֹׁר, וּלְאֻמִּים בָּאָרֶץ תַּנְחֵם סֶלָה: יוֹדוּךָ עַמִּים אֱלֹהִים, יוֹדוּךָ עַמִּים כֻּלָּם: אֶרֶץ נָתְנָה יְבוּלָהּ, יְבָרְכֵנוּ אֱלֹהִים אֱלֹהֵינוּ: יְבָרְכֵנוּ אֱלֹהִים, וְיִירְאוּ אוֹתוֹ כָּל־אַפְסֵי־אָרֶץ:

אָנָּא, בְּכֹחַ גְּדֻלַּת יְמִינְךָ, תַּתִּיר צְרוּרָה.
קַבֵּל רִנַּת עַמְּךָ, שַׂגְּבֵנוּ, טַהֲרֵנוּ, נוֹרָא.
נָא גִבּוֹר, דּוֹרְשֵׁי יִחוּדְךָ כְּבָבַת שָׁמְרֵם.
בָּרְכֵם, טַהֲרֵם, רַחֲמֵם, צִדְקָתְךָ תָּמִיד גָּמְלֵם.
חֲסִין קָדוֹשׁ, בְּרֹב טוּבְךָ נַהֵל עֲדָתֶךָ.
יָחִיד גֵּאֶה, לְעַמְּךָ פְּנֵה, זוֹכְרֵי קְדֻשָּׁתֶךָ.
שַׁוְעָתֵנוּ קַבֵּל וּשְׁמַע צַעֲקָתֵנוּ, יוֹדֵעַ תַּעֲלוּמוֹת.
בָּרוּךְ שֵׁם כְּבוֹד מַלְכוּתוֹ לְעוֹלָם וָעֶד.

רִבּוֹנוֹ שֶׁל עוֹלָם, אַתָּה צִוִּיתָנוּ עַל יְדֵי מֹשֶׁה עַבְדְּךָ לִסְפֹּר סְפִירַת הָעֹמֶר, כְּדֵי לְטַהֲרֵנוּ מִקְּלִפּוֹתֵינוּ וּמִטֻּמְאוֹתֵינוּ. כְּמוֹ שֶׁכָּתַבְתָּ
ויקרא כג בְּתוֹרָתֶךָ: וּסְפַרְתֶּם לָכֶם מִמָּחֳרַת הַשַּׁבָּת, מִיּוֹם הֲבִיאֲכֶם אֶת־עֹמֶר הַתְּנוּפָה, שֶׁבַע שַׁבָּתוֹת תְּמִימֹת תִּהְיֶינָה: עַד מִמָּחֳרַת הַשַּׁבָּת הַשְּׁבִיעִת תִּסְפְּרוּ חֲמִשִּׁים יוֹם: כְּדֵי שֶׁיִּטָּהֲרוּ נַפְשׁוֹת עַמְּךָ יִשְׂרָאֵל מִזֻּהֲמָתָם. וּבְכֵן יְהִי רָצוֹן מִלְּפָנֶיךָ יהוה אֱלֹהֵינוּ וֵאלֹהֵי אֲבוֹתֵינוּ, שֶׁבִּזְכוּת סְפִירַת הָעֹמֶר שֶׁסָּפַרְתִּי הַיּוֹם, יְתֻקַּן מַה שֶּׁפָּגַמְתִּי בִּסְפִירָה (*insert appropriate* ספירה *for each day*) וְאֶטָּהֵר וְאֶתְקַדֵּשׁ בִּקְדֻשָּׁה שֶׁל מַעְלָה, וְעַל יְדֵי זֶה יֻשְׁפַּע שֶׁפַע רַב בְּכָל הָעוֹלָמוֹת, לְתַקֵּן אֶת נַפְשׁוֹתֵינוּ וְרוּחוֹתֵינוּ וְנִשְׁמוֹתֵינוּ מִכָּל סִיג וּפְגָם, וּלְטַהֲרֵנוּ וּלְקַדְּשֵׁנוּ בִּקְדֻשָּׁתְךָ הָעֶלְיוֹנָה, אָמֵן סֶלָה.

In some congregations, mourners recite the Mourner's Kaddish (*page 324*).
The service continues with עָלֵינוּ (*page 322*).

הָרַחֲמָן MAY THE COMPASSIONATE One restore for us the service of the Temple to its place, speedily and in our days, Amen, Selah.

Some add:

Ps. 67 לַמְנַצֵּחַ TO THE DIRECTOR of music for instruments. A Psalm. A song. May God be gracious to us and bless us. May He cause His face to shine upon us. Selah. That Your way may become known upon the earth, Your salvation among all nations. The peoples will praise You, O God. All the peoples will praise You. The nations will rejoice and sing. For You judge the peoples equitably and govern the nations upon the earth. Selah. The peoples will praise You, O God. All the peoples will praise You. The earth has yielded its produce. God, our God, will bless us. God will bless us, and all the ends of the earth will fear Him.

אָנָּא WE BESEECH YOU, by the strength of Your great right hand, release the captive ones. Accept Your people's prayer. Strengthen us, purify us, You Who are revered. Please, Mighty One, guard like the pupil of the eye those who seek Your unity. Bless them, purify them, have compassion on them, grant them Your righteousness always. Powerful One, Holy One, in Your abundant goodness guide Your congregation. Only One, Exalted One, turn to Your people, who proclaim Your holiness. Accept our plea and heed our cry. You Who know all mysteries. Blessed is the name of His glorious kingdom forever and ever.

רִבּוֹנוֹ שֶׁל עוֹלָם RULER OF THE UNIVERSE, through Moses Your servant You have commanded us to count the Omer so as to purify us from our enveloping
Lev. 23 uncleanness and our impurities. As You have written in Your Torah: "And you shall count, from the morrow after the day of rest, starting on the day that you bring the sheaf (omer) of the wave-offering, seven complete weeks. Until the morrow of the seventh week you shall have counted fifty days," in order to purify the souls of Your people Israel from their contamination. Therefore may it be Your will, Lord our God and God of our fathers, that in the merit of the Counting of the Omer that I have counted today, may you repair any damage on my part in the counting of (*insert the appropriate day's counting*). May I be purified and sanctified with heavenly holiness, and through this may there flow rich abundance in all the worlds, to repair our lives, spirits and souls from all dross and corruption. May it purify us and sanctify us with Your sublime holiness. Amen, Selah.

In some congregations, mourners recite the Mourner's Kaddish (page 325).
The service concludes with Aleinu (page 323).

קריאת שמע על המיטה

רִבּוֹנוֹ שֶׁל עוֹלָם, הֲרֵינִי מוֹחֵל/*women* מוֹחֶלֶת/ לְכָל מִי שֶׁהִכְעִיס וְהִקְנִיט אוֹתִי אוֹ שֶׁחָטָא כְּנֶגְדִּי, בֵּין בְּגוּפִי בֵּין בְּמָמוֹנִי בֵּין בִּכְבוֹדִי בֵּין בְּכָל אֲשֶׁר לִי, בֵּין בְּאֹנֶס בֵּין בְּרָצוֹן, בֵּין בְּשׁוֹגֵג בֵּין בְּמֵזִיד, בֵּין בְּדִבּוּר בֵּין בְּמַעֲשֶׂה, בֵּין בְּמַחֲשָׁבָה בֵּין בְּהִרְהוּר, בֵּין בְּגִלְגּוּל זֶה, בֵּין בְּגִלְגּוּל אַחֵר. וְלֹא יֵעָנֵשׁ שׁוּם אָדָם בְּסִבָּתִי. יְהִי רָצוֹן מִלְּפָנֶיךָ, יְהוָה אֱלֹהַי וֵאלֹהֵי אֲבוֹתַי שֶׁלֹּא אֶחֱטָא עוֹד, וּמַה שֶּׁחָטָאתִי לְפָנֶיךָ מְחֹק בְּרַחֲמֶיךָ הָרַבִּים אֲבָל לֹא עַל יְדֵי
יִסּוּרִין וָחֳלָאִים רָעִים. יִהְיוּ לְרָצוֹן אִמְרֵי־פִי וְהֶגְיוֹן לִבִּי לְפָנֶיךָ, יְהוָה צוּרִי וְגֹאֲלִי: תהלים יט

בָּרוּךְ אַתָּה יהוה אֱלֹהֵינוּ מֶלֶךְ הָעוֹלָם, הַמַּפִּיל חֶבְלֵי שֵׁנָה עַל עֵינַי וּתְנוּמָה עַל עַפְעַפָּי. וִיהִי רָצוֹן מִלְּפָנֶיךָ, יהוה אֱלֹהַי וֵאלֹהֵי אֲבוֹתַי, שֶׁתַּשְׁכִּיבֵנִי לְשָׁלוֹם וְתַעֲמִידֵנִי לְשָׁלוֹם, וְאַל יְבַהֲלוּנִי רַעְיוֹנַי וַחֲלוֹמוֹת רָעִים וְהִרְהוּרִים רָעִים, וּתְהֵא מִטָּתִי שְׁלֵמָה

קְרִיאַת שְׁמַע עַל הַמִּטָּה / THE BEDTIME SHEMA
We recite the *Shema* when retiring to strengthen our resolve against sin and to fall asleep while engaged in the study of Torah (Rashi, *Berakhot* 4b). The words of the prayer invoke divine protection against the perils of the night. The Arizal explains that the מַזִּיקִין that it refers to are mental phenomena that result from nocturnal arousal. They can be minimized by reciting or studying sacred texts at bedtime. Meiri understands them to be false or corrupt thoughts that enter our minds while we lie in bed before falling asleep (*Sheiruta deTzlota*).

רִבּוֹנוֹ שֶׁל עוֹלָם / RULER OF THE UNIVERSE
Late Kabbalistic sources introduced this particular prayer. See the Kabbalistic Siddur Kol Yaakov for some of this text. The Gemara (*Megilla* 28a) reports that R. Neḥunya ben HaKana attributed his remarkable longevity to several traits, among them his lifelong nightly practice to forgive anyone who may have angered him during the course of the day, and thus he was able to avoid bearing any debilitating grudges. More generally we learn from his nightly practice that we can accrue significant physical and psychological benefits by clearing away any residual sources of anger or conflict before we retire for the night. As his long life demonstrates, such forgiveness not only facilitates a good night's sleep and a more tranquil state of mind when awake, it also improves our health (R. Basil Herring).

בֵּין בְּגִלְגּוּל זֶה, בֵּין בְּגִלְגּוּל אַחֵר – *Whether in this incarnation or in another incarnation*. *Gilgul* refers to the doctrine of גִלְגּוּל נְשָׁמוֹת, transmigration of souls, otherwise known as reincarnation. It is a controversial concept in Jewish literature. R. Sa'adia Gaon and R. Joseph Albo explicitly deny the validity of the doctrine. The concept does

THE BEDTIME SHEMA

רִבּוֹנוֹ שֶׁל עוֹלָם RULER OF THE UNIVERSE, I hereby forgive anyone who has angered or provoked me or sinned against me, whether it be physically, financially, against my dignity, or against anything of mine; whether accidentally, deliberately, inadvertently or purposefully; whether in speech, in deed, in thought, or in reflection; whether in this incarnation or in another incarnation. May no person be punished on my account. May it be Your will, Lord my God and God of my fathers, that I may sin no more. And those sins I have committed before You, may You erase in Your abundant compassion,
Ps. 19 but not through suffering or grave illnesses. May the words of my mouth and the meditation of my heart be acceptable before You, O Lord, my Rock and my Redeemer.

בָּרוּךְ BLESSED ARE YOU, Lord, our God, King of the universe, Who casts the bonds of sleep upon my eyes, and slumber upon my eyelids. May it be Your will, Lord my God and God of my fathers, that You make me lie down in peace and arise in peace. Let not my imagination, bad dreams or bad thoughts trouble me. May my offspring be perfect before You. Enlighten my eyes lest I sleep the sleep of death, for it is

---

appear frequently in Kabbalistic literature, with its fullest development in the *Zohar* and by the Arizal. Ramban (Gen. 3:8) finds reference to it in the Torah in the commandment of levirate marriage, in which the soul of the departed husband is seen to inhabit the son born of that marriage. For some, such as *Sefer HaBahir*, reincarnation permits justice to be meted out over the course of generations, so that every soul is justly rewarded. For the Arizal, transmigration allows a soul to fulfill its mission over the course of several generations to achieve *tikkun* (repair) over time.

הַמַּפִּיל – *Who casts.* As with other *berakhot* where the act must follow the blessing without interruption, here too one should not eat, drink or talk after reciting the הַמַּפִּיל *berakha*, although it is permitted to interrupt for an urgent matter, since the preponderance of halakhic authorities agree that the blessing is

KERIAT SHEMA AL HAMITA

There are different traditions as to whether the *berakha* of *HaMapil* is recited at the beginning of *Keriat Shema al HaMita* or at the conclusion (*MB* 239:1). R. Joseph B. Soloveitchik noted that some omit the *berakha* of *HaMapil* altogether because the other prayers recited after *Shema* fulfill the same purpose as *HaMapil* (*Nefesh HaRav* p. 153).

לְפָנֶיךָ, וְהָאֵר עֵינַי פֶּן אִישַׁן הַמָּוֶת, כִּי אַתָּה הַמֵּאִיר לְאִישׁוֹן בַּת עָיִן. בָּרוּךְ אַתָּה יהוה, הַמֵּאִיר לָעוֹלָם כֻּלּוֹ בִּכְבוֹדוֹ.

When saying all three paragraphs of שמע*, say:*

אֵל מֶלֶךְ נֶאֱמָן

The following verse should be said aloud, while covering the eyes with the right hand:

דברים ו
שְׁמַע יִשְׂרָאֵל, יהוה אֱלֹהֵינוּ, יהוה | אֶחָד:

Quietly בָּרוּךְ שֵׁם כְּבוֹד מַלְכוּתוֹ לְעוֹלָם וָעֶד.

דברים ו
וְאָהַבְתָּ אֵת יהוה אֱלֹהֶיךָ, בְּכָל־לְבָבְךָ וּבְכָל־נַפְשְׁךָ וּבְכָל־מְאֹדֶךָ: וְהָיוּ הַדְּבָרִים הָאֵלֶּה, אֲשֶׁר אָנֹכִי מְצַוְּךָ הַיּוֹם, עַל־לְבָבֶךָ: וְשִׁנַּנְתָּם לְבָנֶיךָ וְדִבַּרְתָּ בָּם, בְּשִׁבְתְּךָ בְּבֵיתֶךָ וּבְלֶכְתְּךָ בַדֶּרֶךְ, וּבְשָׁכְבְּךָ וּבְקוּמֶךָ: וּקְשַׁרְתָּם לְאוֹת עַל־יָדֶךָ וְהָיוּ לְטֹטָפֹת בֵּין עֵינֶיךָ: וּכְתַבְתָּם עַל־מְזֻזוֹת בֵּיתֶךָ וּבִשְׁעָרֶיךָ:

תהלים צ
וִיהִי נֹעַם אֲדֹנָי אֱלֹהֵינוּ עָלֵינוּ וּמַעֲשֵׂה יָדֵינוּ כּוֹנְנָה עָלֵינוּ וּמַעֲשֵׂה יָדֵינוּ כּוֹנְנֵהוּ:

תהלים צא
יֹשֵׁב בְּסֵתֶר עֶלְיוֹן, בְּצֵל שַׁדַּי יִתְלוֹנָן: אֹמַר לַיהוה מַחְסִי וּמְצוּדָתִי, אֱלֹהַי אֶבְטַח־בּוֹ: כִּי הוּא יַצִּילְךָ מִפַּח יָקוּשׁ, מִדֶּבֶר הַוּוֹת: בְּאֶבְרָתוֹ יָסֶךְ לָךְ, וְתַחַת־כְּנָפָיו תֶּחְסֶה, צִנָּה וְסֹחֵרָה אֲמִתּוֹ: לֹא־תִירָא מִפַּחַד לָיְלָה, מֵחֵץ יָעוּף יוֹמָם: מִדֶּבֶר בָּאֹפֶל יַהֲלֹךְ, מִקֶּטֶב יָשׁוּד צָהֳרָיִם: יִפֹּל מִצִּדְּךָ אֶלֶף, וּרְבָבָה מִימִינֶךָ, אֵלֶיךָ לֹא יִגָּשׁ: רַק בְּעֵינֶיךָ תַבִּיט, וְשִׁלֻּמַת רְשָׁעִים תִּרְאֶה: כִּי־אַתָּה יהוה מַחְסִי, עֶלְיוֹן שַׂמְתָּ מְעוֹנֶךָ: לֹא־תְאֻנֶּה אֵלֶיךָ רָעָה, וְנֶגַע לֹא־יִקְרַב בְּאָהֳלֶךָ: כִּי

---

primarily a בִּרְכַּת הוֹדָאָה (blessing of thanksgiving) for sleep (*Ḥayyei Adam*).

שְׁמַע / SHEMA

Only the first paragraph of the *Shema* is said at bedtime. However one who said *Ma'ariv* before halakhic nightfall says all three paragraphs. *Magen Avraham* notes that it is desirable to say all three paragraphs in any case.

You Who illuminates the pupil of the eye. Blessed are You, Lord, Who enlightens the whole world with His glory.

When saying all three paragraphs of שמע*, say:*
God, the King Who is faithful.

The following verse should be said aloud, while covering the eyes with the right hand:

Deut. 6 HEAR, O ISRAEL, the LORD is our God, the LORD is One.

Quietly: Blessed is the name of His glorious kingdom forever and ever.

Deut. 6 וְאָהַבְתָּ YOU SHALL LOVE the LORD your God with all your heart, and with all your soul, and with all your might. And these words which I command you this day shall be upon your heart. You shall teach them diligently to your children, speaking of them when you sit in your house and when you walk by the way, when you lie down and when you rise up. You shall bind them for a sign on your hand, and they shall be as *tefillin* between your eyes. And you shall write them upon the doorposts of your house and upon your gates.

Ps. 90 וִיהִי נֹעַם AND LET the pleasantness of my Master our God be upon us, and establish the work of our hands upon us, and establish it, the work of our hands.

Ps. 91 יֹשֵׁב HE WHO DWELLS in the secret place of the Most High abides in the shadow of the Almighty. I say to the Lord, my refuge and my fortress, my God, I trust in Him. Indeed, He will deliver you from the baited trap, from the deadly pestilence. He will cover you with His pinions, and under His wings you will find refuge. His truth will be your shield and buckler. You will not be afraid of the terror by night, of the arrow that flies by day, of the pestilence that walks in the darkness, of the destruction that wastes at noonday. A thousand will fall at your side and ten thousand at your right hand. It will not come near to you. Only with your eyes will you behold, and you will see the destruction of the wicked. Indeed, You, O Lord, are my refuge. You have made the Most High Your habitation. No evil will befall you, and plague will not come near to your tent. Indeed, He will give His angels charge over you,

מַלְאָכָיו יְצַוֶּה־לָּךְ, לִשְׁמָרְךָ בְּכָל־דְּרָכֶיךָ: עַל־כַּפַּיִם יִשָּׂאוּנְךָ, פֶּן־תִּגֹּף בָּאֶבֶן רַגְלֶךָ: עַל־שַׁחַל וָפֶתֶן תִּדְרֹךְ, תִּרְמֹס כְּפִיר וְתַנִּין: כִּי בִי חָשַׁק וַאֲפַלְּטֵהוּ, אֲשַׂגְּבֵהוּ כִּי־יָדַע שְׁמִי: יִקְרָאֵנִי וְאֶעֱנֵהוּ, עִמּוֹ־אָנֹכִי בְצָרָה, אֲחַלְּצֵהוּ וַאֲכַבְּדֵהוּ: אֹרֶךְ יָמִים אַשְׂבִּיעֵהוּ, וְאַרְאֵהוּ בִּישׁוּעָתִי: אֹרֶךְ יָמִים אַשְׂבִּיעֵהוּ, וְאַרְאֵהוּ בִּישׁוּעָתִי:

תהלים ג **יהוה** מָה־רַבּוּ צָרָי, רַבִּים קָמִים עָלָי: רַבִּים אֹמְרִים לְנַפְשִׁי, אֵין יְשׁוּעָתָה לּוֹ בֵאלֹהִים, סֶלָה: וְאַתָּה יהוה מָגֵן בַּעֲדִי, כְּבוֹדִי וּמֵרִים רֹאשִׁי: קוֹלִי אֶל־יהוה אֶקְרָא, וַיַּעֲנֵנִי מֵהַר קָדְשׁוֹ, סֶלָה: אֲנִי שָׁכַבְתִּי וָאִישָׁנָה, הֱקִיצוֹתִי כִּי יהוה יִסְמְכֵנִי: לֹא־אִירָא מֵרִבְבוֹת עָם, אֲשֶׁר סָבִיב שָׁתוּ עָלָי: קוּמָה יהוה, הוֹשִׁיעֵנִי אֱלֹהַי, כִּי־הִכִּיתָ אֶת־כָּל־אֹיְבַי לֶחִי, שִׁנֵּי רְשָׁעִים שִׁבַּרְתָּ: לַיהוה הַיְשׁוּעָה, עַל־עַמְּךָ בִרְכָתֶךָ סֶּלָה:

הַשְׁכִּיבֵנוּ, יהוה אֱלֹהֵינוּ, לְשָׁלוֹם. וְהַעֲמִידֵנוּ, מַלְכֵּנוּ, לְחַיִּים. וּפְרֹשׂ עָלֵינוּ סֻכַּת שְׁלוֹמֶךָ, וְתַקְּנֵנוּ בְּעֵצָה טוֹבָה מִלְּפָנֶיךָ, וְהוֹשִׁיעֵנוּ לְמַעַן שְׁמֶךָ. וְהָגֵן בַּעֲדֵנוּ, וְהָסֵר מֵעָלֵינוּ אוֹיֵב, דֶּבֶר וְחֶרֶב וְרָעָב וְיָגוֹן. וְהָסֵר שָׂטָן מִלְּפָנֵינוּ וּמֵאַחֲרֵינוּ, וּבְצֵל כְּנָפֶיךָ תַּסְתִּירֵנוּ, כִּי אֵל שׁוֹמְרֵנוּ וּמַצִּילֵנוּ אָתָּה, כִּי אֵל מֶלֶךְ חַנּוּן וְרַחוּם אָתָּה. וּשְׁמֹר צֵאתֵנוּ וּבוֹאֵנוּ לְחַיִּים וּלְשָׁלוֹם מֵעַתָּה וְעַד עוֹלָם.

בָּרוּךְ יהוה בַּיּוֹם, בָּרוּךְ יהוה בַּלָּיְלָה, בָּרוּךְ יהוה בְּשָׁכְבֵנוּ, בָּרוּךְ
איוב יב יהוה בְּקוּמֵנוּ. כִּי בְיָדְךָ נַפְשׁוֹת הַחַיִּים וְהַמֵּתִים. אֲשֶׁר בְּיָדוֹ
תהלים לא נֶפֶשׁ כָּל־חָי, וְרוּחַ כָּל־בְּשַׂר־אִישׁ: בְּיָדְךָ אַפְקִיד רוּחִי, פָּדִיתָה אוֹתִי
יהוה אֵל אֱמֶת: אֱלֹהֵינוּ שֶׁבַּשָּׁמַיִם, יַחֵד שִׁמְךָ וְקַיֵּם מַלְכוּתְךָ תָּמִיד,
וּמְלֹךְ עָלֵינוּ לְעוֹלָם וָעֶד.

ה׳ מָה־רַבּוּ צָרָי / PSALM 3
Even though I fall asleep filled with worry I awake triumphantly in the morning filled with faith that God will help me (Rashi).

to keep you in all your ways. They will bear you up on their hands, lest you dash your foot against a stone. You will tread upon the lion and the adder. You will trample the young lion and the crocodile underfoot. Because he has clung to Me, I will deliver him. I will make him safe, because he has known My name. When he calls upon Me, I answer him. I am with him in trouble. I deliver him and I will honor him. I will satisfy him with long life, and I will show him of My salvation. I will satisfy him with long life, and I will show him of My salvation.

Ps. 3 **יהוה** THE LORD, how many are they that trouble me! Many are they that rise up against me. Many are they that say of my soul: There is no deliverance for him in God. Selah. But You, Lord, are a shield for me, my glory and the raiser of my head. With my voice, I call on unto the Lord, and He answers me from His holy mountain. Selah. I lay down and I slept. I awakened, for the Lord would sustain me. I am not afraid of ten thousands of people, who have arrayed themselves against me round about. Rise up, Lord. Save me, O my God. Smite all my enemies on the cheek bone. Smash the teeth of the wicked. Deliverance is the Lord's. May Your blessing be upon Your people. Selah.

הַשְׁכִּיבֵנוּ LAY US DOWN in peace, Lord our God, and raise us up, our King, to life. Spread over us the canopy of Your peace, and direct us with Your wise guidance. Save us for the sake of Your name. Shield us and ward off from us enemies, epidemics, violence, hunger, and sorrow. Remove Satan from before us and from behind us. Shelter us in the shadow of Your wings, for You, God, are our Guardian and Deliverer, insofar as You are a gracious and merciful God and King. Guard our going out and our coming in, for the sake of life and peace now and forever.

בָּרוּךְ BLESSED is the Lord by day; blessed is the Lord by night. Blessed is the Lord when we lie down; blessed is the Lord when we arise. For
Job 12 in Your hand are the souls of the living and the dead, "for in His hand is
Ps. 31 the soul of all the living and the spirit of every human being." Into Your hand I entrust my spirit. Redeem me, O Lord, God of truth. Our God in heaven, establish the oneness of Your name with Your sovereignty forever, and reign over us forever and ever.

יִרְאוּ עֵינֵינוּ וְיִשְׂמַח לִבֵּנוּ, וְתָגֵל נַפְשֵׁנוּ בִּישׁוּעָתְךָ בֶּאֱמֶת, בֶּאֱמֹר לְצִיּוֹן מָלַךְ אֱלֹהָיִךְ. יהוה מֶלֶךְ, יהוה מָלָךְ, יהוה יִמְלֹךְ לְעוֹלָם וָעֶד. כִּי הַמַּלְכוּת שֶׁלְּךָ הִיא, וּלְעוֹלְמֵי עַד תִּמְלֹךְ בְּכָבוֹד, כִּי אֵין לָנוּ מֶלֶךְ אֶלָּא אָתָּה.

בראשית מח **הַמַּלְאָךְ** הַגֹּאֵל אֹתִי מִכָּל־רָע יְבָרֵךְ אֶת־הַנְּעָרִים, וְיִקָּרֵא בָהֶם שְׁמִי וְשֵׁם אֲבֹתַי אַבְרָהָם וְיִצְחָק, וְיִדְגּוּ לָרֹב בְּקֶרֶב הָאָרֶץ:

שמות טו **וַיֹּאמֶר** אִם־שָׁמוֹעַ תִּשְׁמַע לְקוֹל יהוה אֱלֹהֶיךָ, וְהַיָּשָׁר בְּעֵינָיו תַּעֲשֶׂה, וְהַאֲזַנְתָּ לְמִצְוֹתָיו וְשָׁמַרְתָּ כָּל־חֻקָּיו, כָּל־הַמַּחֲלָה

זכריה ג אֲשֶׁר־שַׂמְתִּי בְמִצְרַיִם לֹא־אָשִׂים עָלֶיךָ, כִּי אֲנִי יהוה רֹפְאֶךָ: וַיֹּאמֶר יהוה אֶל־הַשָּׂטָן, יִגְעַר יהוה בְּךָ הַשָּׂטָן, וְיִגְעַר יהוה בְּךָ הַבֹּחֵר בִּירוּשָׁלָםִ, הֲלוֹא זֶה אוּד מֻצָּל מֵאֵשׁ: הִנֵּה מִטָּתוֹ שֶׁלִּשְׁלֹמֹה, שִׁשִּׁים

שיר השירים ג גִּבֹּרִים סָבִיב לָהּ, מִגִּבֹּרֵי יִשְׂרָאֵל: כֻּלָּם אֲחֻזֵי חֶרֶב, מְלֻמְּדֵי מִלְחָמָה, אִישׁ חַרְבּוֹ עַל־יְרֵכוֹ מִפַּחַד בַּלֵּילוֹת:

Say three times:

במדבר ו **יְבָרֶכְךָ** יהוה וְיִשְׁמְרֶךָ: יָאֵר יהוה פָּנָיו אֵלֶיךָ וִיחֻנֶּךָּ: יִשָּׂא יהוה פָּנָיו אֵלֶיךָ וְיָשֵׂם לְךָ שָׁלוֹם:

Say three times:

תהלים קכא **הִנֵּה** לֹא־יָנוּם וְלֹא יִישָׁן שׁוֹמֵר יִשְׂרָאֵל:

Say three times:

בראשית מט **לִישׁוּעָתְךָ** קִוִּיתִי יהוה: קִוִּיתִי יהוה לִישׁוּעָתְךָ, יהוה לִישׁוּעָתְךָ קִוִּיתִי

כָּל־הַמַּחֲלָה אֲשֶׁר־שַׂמְתִּי בְמִצְרַיִם – *All the disease I brought upon Egypt I will not bring upon you.* This verse's concise assertion that safety and success are contingent upon our adherence to the covenant continues the theme of acceptance of the yoke of heaven, and is most appropriate to the bedtime *Shema*.

יִרְאוּ MAY OUR EYES behold, our hearts rejoice, and our souls delight in the truth of Your saving power when it shall be said in Zion: "Your God reigns. The Lord reigns, the Lord reigned, the Lord shall reign forever and ever." Yours is the kingdom, and to all eternity You will reign in glory, for we have no king but You.

Gen. 48 הַמַּלְאָךְ MAY THE ANGEL who redeemed me from all evil, bless these youths. May they be called by my name and the names of my fathers Abraham and Isaac, and may they increase abundantly within the land.

Ex. 15 וַיֹּאמֶר HE SAID, "If you listen carefully to the voice of the Lord your God, and do what is upright in His eyes; if you attend to His commandments and observe all His statutes, all the disease I brought upon Egypt I will not bring upon you, for I am the Lord your Healer."
Zech. 3 And the Lord said to Satan, "The Lord shall renounce you, Satan!
The Lord Who has chosen Jerusalem shall denounce you! Is not
Song. 3 this a firebrand rescued from fire?" Here stands Solomon's bed, sixty soldiers all around it, heroes of Israel. Each carrying his sword, each learned in war, each with his sword at his thigh for very fear at night.

Say three times:

Num. 6 יְבָרֶכְךָ MAY THE LORD bless you and keep you. May the Lord make His countenance shine upon you and be gracious to you. May the Lord lift up His countenance toward you and grant you peace.

Say three times:

Ps. 121 הִנֵּה BEHOLD, He Who guards Israel neither slumbers nor sleeps.

Say three times:

Gen. 49 לִישׁוּעָתְךָ FOR YOUR SALVATION I hope, Lord. I hope, Lord, for Your salvation. Lord, for Your salvation, I hope.

הִנֵּה מִטָּתוֹ – *Here stands Solomon's bed.* Even Solomon, the most successful Israelite king, whose influence extended well beyond the borders of Israel, was helpless before God on his bed at night, despite his guards.

Say three times:

בְּשֵׁם יהוה אֱלֹהֵי יִשְׂרָאֵל, מִימִינִי מִיכָאֵל, וּמִשְּׂמֹאלִי גַּבְרִיאֵל, וּמִלְּפָנַי אוּרִיאֵל, וּמֵאֲחוֹרַי רְפָאֵל, וְעַל רֹאשִׁי שְׁכִינַת אֵל.

תהלים קכח **שִׁיר הַמַּעֲלוֹת,** אַשְׁרֵי כָּל־יְרֵא יהוה, הַהֹלֵךְ בִּדְרָכָיו: יְגִיעַ כַּפֶּיךָ כִּי תֹאכֵל, אַשְׁרֶיךָ וְטוֹב לָךְ: אֶשְׁתְּךָ כְּגֶפֶן פֹּרִיָּה בְּיַרְכְּתֵי בֵיתֶךָ, בָּנֶיךָ כִּשְׁתִלֵי זֵיתִים, סָבִיב לְשֻׁלְחָנֶךָ: הִנֵּה כִי־כֵן יְבֹרַךְ גָּבֶר יְרֵא יהוה: יְבָרֶכְךָ יהוה מִצִּיּוֹן, וּרְאֵה בְּטוּב יְרוּשָׁלָםִ, כֹּל יְמֵי חַיֶּיךָ: וּרְאֵה־בָנִים לְבָנֶיךָ, שָׁלוֹם עַל־יִשְׂרָאֵל:

Say three times:

תהלים ד **רִגְזוּ** וְאַל־תֶּחֱטָאוּ, אִמְרוּ בִלְבַבְכֶם עַל־מִשְׁכַּבְכֶם, וְדֹמּוּ סֶלָה:

אֲדוֹן עוֹלָם אֲשֶׁר מָלַךְ בְּטֶרֶם כָּל־יְצִיר נִבְרָא.\
לְעֵת נַעֲשָׂה בְחֶפְצוֹ כֹּל אֲזַי מֶלֶךְ שְׁמוֹ נִקְרָא.\
וְאַחֲרֵי כִּכְלוֹת הַכֹּל לְבַדּוֹ יִמְלֹךְ נוֹרָא.\
וְהוּא הָיָה וְהוּא הֹוֶה וְהוּא יִהְיֶה בְּתִפְאָרָה.\
וְהוּא אֶחָד וְאֵין שֵׁנִי לְהַמְשִׁיל לוֹ לְהַחְבִּירָה.\
בְּלִי רֵאשִׁית בְּלִי תַכְלִית וְלוֹ הָעֹז וְהַמִּשְׂרָה.\
וְהוּא אֵלִי וְחַי גּוֹאֲלִי וְצוּר חֶבְלִי בְּעֵת צָרָה.\
וְהוּא נִסִּי וּמָנוֹס לִי מְנָת כּוֹסִי בְּיוֹם אֶקְרָא.\
בְּיָדוֹ אַפְקִיד רוּחִי בְּעֵת אִישַׁן וְאָעִירָה.\
וְעִם רוּחִי גְּוִיָּתִי יהוה לִי וְלֹא אִירָא.

בְּשֵׁם ה' – *In the name of the Lord.* This enumeration of the angelic commanders of divine forces appears in *Pirkei deR. Eliezer*. The opening statement, "In the name of the Lord, the God of Israel," is appended here to make clear that we pray only to God Himself, not any angels, as prescribed in Yerushalmi *Berakhot* 9:1 (*Sheiruta deTzlota*).

וְעִם רוּחִי גְּוִיָּתִי – *With my body my soul will stay.* As previously explained (see commentary to *Adon Olam*, page 18), this stanza affirms that there is life after death, just as there is an awakening after sleep. With these words we calmly entrust our lives and our souls to God as we retire for the night, in the full anticipation of arising the next morning to serve God with all of our faculties.

Say three times:

בְּשֵׁם IN THE NAME of the Lord, the God of Israel: May Michael be at my right; at my left, Gabriel; before me, Uriel; behind me, Raphael; and above my head the Presence of God.

Ps. 128 שִׁיר הַמַּעֲלוֹת A SONG OF ASCENTS. Happy is everyone who fears the Lord, who walks in His ways. If you eat the labor of your hands, you will be happy and it will be well with you. Your wife will be like a fruitful vine in the innermost parts of your house, your children like olive plants around your table. Behold, truly the man who fears the Lord will be blessed. May the Lord bless you from Zion, and may you see the good of Jerusalem all the days of your life. And may you see your children's children. Peace be upon Israel.

Say three times:

Ps. 4 רִגְזוּ TREMBLE and do not sin. Commune with your heart upon your bed and be silent. Selah.

אֲדוֹן עוֹלָם ETERNAL MASTER,
Who reigned before anything was created –
when by His will all things were brought into being,
then as King was His name proclaimed.
After all things have ceased to be,
He will reign alone in awesome majesty.
He was. He is. He will always be;
His eternal glory can never fade.
He is One. There is no other;
beyond compare, or any metaphor.
He had no beginning, will have no end.
He above all others has strength and power.
He is my God, my living Redeemer,
a Rock when I am in pain in troubled times.
My banner and my refuge,
to Whom I will raise a cup on the day I proclaim my salvation.
I entrust my spirit to His hand,
when sleeping and when awake.
With my body my soul will stay;
the Lord is with me, I need not fear.

ערב שבת ויום טוב

עירוב תחומין

בָּרוּךְ אַתָּה יהוה אֱלֹהֵינוּ מֶלֶךְ הָעוֹלָם, אֲשֶׁר קִדְּשָׁנוּ בְּמִצְוֹתָיו וְצִוָּנוּ עַל מִצְוַת עֵרוּב.

בְּזֶה הָעֵרוּב יְהֵא מֻתָּר (לִי/לָנוּ) לֵילֵךְ מִמָּקוֹם זֶה אַלְפַּיִם אַמָּה לְכָל רוּחַ (בְּשַׁבָּת זוֹ/ בְּיוֹם טוֹב זֶה/ בְּיוֹם כִּפּוּר זֶה).

עירוב חצרות

בָּרוּךְ אַתָּה יהוה אֱלֹהֵינוּ מֶלֶךְ הָעוֹלָם, אֲשֶׁר קִדְּשָׁנוּ בְּמִצְוֹתָיו וְצִוָּנוּ עַל מִצְוַת עֵרוּב.

בַּהֲדֵין עֵרוּבָא יְהֵא שָׁרֵא לָנָא לְאַפּוֹקֵי וּלְעַיּוֹלֵי מִן הַבָּתִּים לֶחָצֵר, וּמִן הֶחָצֵר לַבָּתִּים, וּמִבַּיִת לְבַיִת, וּמֵחָצֵר לְחָצֵר, וּמִגַּג לְגַג, כָּל מַאי דִּצְרִיךְ לָן, וּלְכָל יִשְׂרָאֵל הַדָּרִים בָּעִיר הַזֹּאת (וּלְכָל מִי שֶׁיִּתּוֹסֵף בָּהּ, לְכָל שַׁבְּתוֹת הַשָּׁנָה, וּלְכָל יָמִים טוֹבִים).

עירוב תבשילין

בָּרוּךְ אַתָּה יהוה אֱלֹהֵינוּ מֶלֶךְ הָעוֹלָם, אֲשֶׁר קִדְּשָׁנוּ בְּמִצְוֹתָיו וְצִוָּנוּ עַל מִצְוַת עֵרוּב.

בַּהֲדֵין עֵרוּבָא יְהֵא שָׁרֵא לָנָא לַאֲפוּיֵי וּלְבַשּׁוּלֵי וּלְאַטְמוּנֵי וּלְאַדְלוּקֵי שְׁרָגָא, וּלְתַקָּנָא וּלְמֶעְבַּד כָּל צָרְכָּנָא, מִיּוֹמָא טָבָא לְשַׁבְּתָא (לָנוּ וּלְכָל יִשְׂרָאֵל הַדָּרִים בָּעִיר הַזֹּאת).

EIRUV TEḤUMIN

On Shabbat and Yom Tov, it is forbidden to walk more than 2,000 cubits (about 3,500 feet) outside of the *teḥum* (city boundaries). In order to allow someone to walk another 2,000 cubits, the rabbis required one to place food that is sufficient for two meals before Shabbat within the 2,000 cubit limit and that would allow the individual to walk another 2,000 cubits in that direction. The laws of *teḥum* and *eiruv teḥumin* are complex and should be discussed with a rabbi before establishing an *eiruv teḥumin*. If the rabbi determines that an *eiruv teḥumin* is appropriate, the above text is used.

EIRUV ḤATZEIROT

An *eiruv ḥatzerot* is required whenever one wants to carry objects from a private domain to someone else's private domain or a shared space. The laws of *eiruv* and *eiruv ḥatzerot* are complex and should be discussed with a rabbi before establishing an *eiruv ḥatzerot*. If the rabbi determines that an *eiruv ḥatzerot* is appropriate, the above text is used.

SHABBAT AND YOM TOV EVE

EIRUV TEḤUMIN

בָּרוּךְ BLESSED ARE YOU, Lord, our God, King of the universe, Who has sanctified us with His commandments, and has commanded us about the mitzva of Eiruv.

THROUGH THIS EIRUV may (I/we) be permitted to walk two thousand cubits in every direction from this place (during this Sabbath/Festival/Yom Kippur).

EIRUV ḤATZEROT

בָּרוּךְ BLESSED ARE YOU, Lord, our God, King of the universe, Who has sanctified us with His commandments, and has commanded us about the mitzva of Eiruv.

THROUGH THIS EIRUV may we be permitted to carry out or to carry in from the houses to the courtyard, and from the courtyard to the houses, from house to house, from courtyard to courtyard, and from roof to roof, all that we require, for ourselves and for all Jews living in this city (and to all who will move into this city, for all the Sabbaths and Festivals of the year).

EIRUV TAVSHILIN

בָּרוּךְ BLESSED ARE YOU, Lord, our God, King of the universe, Who has sanctified us with His commandments, and has commanded us about the mitzva of Eiruv.

THROUGH THIS EIRUV may we be permitted to bake, cook, insulate food, light a flame and do everything necessary on the festival for the sake of Shabbat (for us and for all Jews living in this city).

EIRUV TAVSHILIN

When Yom Tov occurs on a Friday, whether it is the first day of Yom Tov or the second day, there is an obligation to establish an *eiruv tavshilin* prior to Yom Tov. This allows one to prepare food on Yom Tov that is going to be served on Shabbat. The *eiruv tavshilin* consists of one cooked item and one baked item. If one wants to include others – beyond immediate family – in the *eiruv*, one should give the food items to an adult to lift the food items more than a *tefaḥ* (approximately four inches) for the purpose of acquiring the *eiruv* on behalf of the others. The individual establishing the *eiruv* then retrieves the items and while holding both items, recites the above *berakha* and then the declaration. If one included the entire community in the *eiruv*, one should recite the portion in brackets: לָנוּ וּלְכָל יִשְׂרָאֵל הַדָּרִים בָּעִיר הַזֹּאת.

הדלקת נרות

On ערב שבת *that is not a* יום טוב*, cover the eyes with the hands after lighting the candles, and say:*

בָּרוּךְ אַתָּה יהוה אֱלֹהֵינוּ מֶלֶךְ הָעוֹלָם, אֲשֶׁר קִדְּשָׁנוּ בְּמִצְוֹתָיו
וְצִוָּנוּ לְהַדְלִיק נֵר שֶׁל שַׁבָּת.

On יום טוב *and* יום כיפור *(if also* שבת *add the words in parentheses):*

בָּרוּךְ אַתָּה יהוה אֱלֹהֵינוּ מֶלֶךְ הָעוֹלָם, אֲשֶׁר קִדְּשָׁנוּ בְּמִצְוֹתָיו וְצִוָּנוּ
לְהַדְלִיק נֵר שֶׁל (שַׁבָּת וְשֶׁל) ביום טוב: יוֹם טוֹב / ביום הכיפורים:
יוֹם הַכִּפּוּרִים.

The following blessing is omitted on the seventh and eighth nights of פסח*:*

בָּרוּךְ אַתָּה יהוה אֱלֹהֵינוּ מֶלֶךְ הָעוֹלָם, שֶׁהֶחֱיָנוּ וְקִיְּמָנוּ, וְהִגִּיעָנוּ
לַזְּמַן הַזֶּה.

תחינות

Prayer after candlelighting (add the words in parentheses as appropriate):

יְהִי רָצוֹן מִלְּפָנֶיךָ יהוה אֱלֹהִים, אֱלֹהֵי יִשְׂרָאֵל שֶׁתְּחוֹנֵן לִי (לְאִישִׁי, וּלְאָבִי, וּלְאִמִּי, וּלְבָנַי וּלְבְנוֹתַי וּלְכָל קְרוֹבַי) וּלְכָל יִשְׂרָאֵל חַיִּים טוֹבִים וַאֲרוּכִים בִּבְרִיאוּת שְׁלֵמָה בְּהַצָּלָה מִכָּל רָע. וּבְהַצְלָחָה בְּכָל טוּב וְזָכְרֵנוּ בְּזִכְרוֹן טוֹבָה וּפָקְדֵנוּ בִּפְקֻדַּת יְשׁוּעָה וְרַחֲמִים וּתְבָרְכֵנוּ בְּרָכוֹת גְּדוֹלוֹת וְתַשְׁלִים בָּתֵּינוּ בְּטוֹבוֹת רַבּוֹת עֲצוּמוֹת, וְשַׁכֵּן שְׁכִינָתְךָ בֵּינֵינוּ וְלֹא יִהְיֶה בָּנוּ לֹא עָקָר וְלֹא

הַדְלָקַת נֵרוֹת / CANDLE LIGHTING

A brightly lit festive table represents a partial fulfillment of Isaiah's instructions to "proclaim the Sabbath a delight and the holy of the Lord honorable by honoring it…" (Is. 58:13–14). The lights honor Shabbat by brightening one's home, and thereby imparting dignity and importance to the Shabbat table (Rashi). The candles are

CANDLE LIGHTING FOR YOM TOV

It is the common practice that for Shabbat candle lighting one recites the *berakha* after lighting the candles and covering one's eyes. On Yom Tov, however, there are two traditions. One is to follow the same procedure as for Shabbat. The other is to recite the *berakha* before lighting (MB 263:27). If one is lighting for Shabbat and Yom Tov, all agree that one should follow Shabbat procedures. According to many poskim, the Yom Tov candles on the first night of Yom Tov should be lit before Yom Tov starts even though one may light candles on Yom Tov *(Shemirat Shabbat KeHilkhata* 44:2).

There is no requirement to recite *Sheheḥeyanu* at candle lighting on Yom Tov and it is preferable to fulfill the obligation to recite *Sheheḥeyanu* during Kiddush (MB 263:23). Yet some women have the practice to recite *Sheheḥeyanu* at candle lighting. *Sheheḥeyanu* is not recited on the last two night of Pesaḥ.

CANDLE LIGHTING

On Erev Shabbat that is not a Yom Tov, cover the eyes with the hands after lighting the candles, and say:

בָּרוּךְ BLESSED ARE YOU, Lord, our God, King of the universe, Who has sanctified us with His commandments and commanded us to light the Sabbath light.

On Yom Tov and Yom Kippur (if also Shabbat add the words in parentheses):

בָּרוּךְ BLESSED ARE YOU, Lord, our God, King of the universe, Who has sanctified us with His commandments and commanded us to light the (Sabbath light and the) *On Yom Tov:* festival light. / *On Yom Kippur:* light of Yom Kippur.

The following blessing is omitted on the seventh and eighth nights of Pesaḥ:

בָּרוּךְ BLESSED ARE YOU, Lord, our God, King of the universe, Who has kept us alive, sustained us, and brought us to this season.

SUPPLICATIONS

Prayer after candlelighting (add the words in parentheses as appropriate):

יְהִי רָצוֹן MAY IT BE Your will, Lord God, God of Israel, that You favor me, (*my husband, my father, my mother, my children and all my relations*) and all of Israel with good, long lives – in good health, and preserved from all evil, and with success and all good things. Remember us favorably, and bring upon us salvation and compassion. Bless us with great blessings, complete our household with many kindnesses, causing Your Shekhina to dwell in our midst and make peace

---

therefore a fulfillment of the rabbinic prescription of עֹנֶג, enjoyment of the Shabbat experience.

נֵר – *Light.* The prevalent custom calls for at least two candles. According to *Eliyahu Raba* the two candles symbolize husband and wife. Some follow a custom to add additional candles corresponding to the number of children in the household. Nevertheless, since one can fulfill the *mitzva* with a single candle, the *berakha* is couched in the singular form נֵר (light) and not נֵרוֹת (lights).

נֵר שֶׁל (שַׁבָּת וְשֶׁל) יוֹם טוֹב – *(Sabbath light and the) festival light.* Shabbat is mentioned before Yom Tov following the talmudic rule that we give priority to *mitzvot* that occur more frequently over those that are less frequent.

יְהִי רָצוֹן – *May it be Your will.* It is customary to recite this prayer after the candles are kindled. It reflects the Talmudic statement (*Shabbat* 23b) that those who are scrupulous in lighting Shabbat candles will be blessed to have children who are Torah scholars.

תְּחִנּוֹת / TEḤINOT

Teḥinot (supplications) recited by women first appeared in printed form in the middle of the seventeenth century. An example of a *teḥina* that was widely accepted and reprinted in various *siddurim* is "*Gott fun Avrohom,*" recited after the Havdala service. *Teḥinot* were part of a religious, ethical and liturgical Yiddish literature for women. It included translations of the Torah, the *Tzena Urena* Aggadic

עֲקָרָה לֹא שַׁכּוּל וְלֹא שַׁכּוּלָה לֹא אַלְמוֹן וְלֹא אַלְמָנָה וְלֹא יִהְיֶה בָּנוּ דְּבָרִים רָעִים כְּלַל וּתְזַכֵּנִי לְהוֹלִיד בָּנִים וּבְנֵי בָנִים חֲכָמִים וּנְבוֹנִים וִידוּעִים אוֹהֲבֵי יהוה יִרְאֵי אֱלֹהִים אַנְשֵׁי אֱמֶת זֶרַע קֹדֶשׁ בַּיהוה דְּבֵקִים שֶׁיָּאִירוּ עוֹלָמִים בְּתוֹרָה וּבְמַעֲשִׂים טוֹבִים וּבְכָל מְלֶאכֶת עֲבוֹדַת הַבּוֹרֵא וּשְׁמַע נָא אֶת תְּחִנָּתִי בָּעֵת וּבָעוֹנָה הַזֹּאת בִּזְכוּת שָׂרָה וְרִבְקָה רָחֵל וְלֵאָה אִמּוֹתֵינוּ וְהָאֵר נֵרֵנוּ שֶׁלֹּא יִדְעַךְ וְלֹא יִכְבֶּה לְעוֹלָם וָעֶד וְהָאֵר פָּנֶיךָ וְנִוָּשֵׁעָה וּלְכָל עַמְּךָ יִשְׂרָאֵל בִּמְהֵרָה בְיָמֵינוּ, אָמֵן סֶלָה וָעֶד.

For conceiving a child:

יוֹצֵר כָּל הָעוֹלָמוֹת אֲדוֹן כָּל הַנְּשָׁמוֹת, יוֹשֵׁב בְּגָבְהֵי מְרוֹמִים, וְשׁוֹכֵן בֵּין בְּחִירָיו שֶׁבָּחַר בָּהֶם, עַמּוֹ יִשְׂרָאֵל אֲשֶׁר אָהַב, וּמִתּוֹךְ אַהֲבָתוֹ הַגְּדוֹלָה צִוָּם שֶׁיִּהְיוּ טְהוֹרִים וְשֶׁיִּטָּהֲרוּ מִכָּל טֻמְאָה, אַתָּה טָהוֹר וּמְשָׁרְתֶיךָ טְהוֹרִים וְאֵין בֵּינֵיהֶם שׁוּם טֻמְאָה.

אֲדֹנָי אֱלֹהַי, אֲנִי (*name*) אֲמָתְךָ בַּת (*mother's name*) אֲמָתֶךָ, שָׁמַרְתִּי מִצְוָתְךָ הַיּוֹם בְּאַהֲבָה וְטִהַרְתִּי אֶת עַצְמִי מִכָּל טֻמְאָתִי, לָבוֹא טְהוֹרָה, לְהִדָּבֵק בְּבַעְלִי, בִּכְנִיעָה וּבְמַחֲשָׁבוֹת טְהוֹרוֹת, לְעוֹרֵר בַּעְלִי לְקַיֵּם מִצְוָתְךָ בְּתִפְאֶרֶת לְהָבִיא כָּבוֹד לָעוֹלָם וּלְמַלְאוֹ.

אֵל מָלֵא רַחֲמִים, שְׁלַח לִי מַלְאָכֶיךָ שֶׁיְּלַוּוּנִי בְּבוֹאִי אֶל בַּעְלִי, וְשֶׁלֹּא תִּפְגְּשֵׁנִי שׁוּם טֻמְאָה, וְטַהֵר לִבִּי וּמַחְשְׁבוֹתַי שֶׁלֹּא אֶזְכֹּר שׁוּם דָּבָר רָע. וְתֵן רוּחַ טָהוֹר בְּבַעְלִי שֶׁיִּהְיוּ לוֹ מַחֲשָׁבוֹת טוֹבוֹת וּטְהוֹרוֹת, בְּלִי שׁוּם פֶּגַע, בְּהִזְדַּוְּגוֹ בִי, וְשֶׁכָּל מַעֲשָׂיו יִהְיוּ בְּהַכְנָעָה גְדוֹלָה, בְּלִי שׁוּם עַזּוּת.

וּשְׁלַח לִי הַמַּלְאָךְ הַטּוֹב הַמְמֻנֶּה עַל הַהֵרָיוֹן, לְהָבִיא אֶת הַזֶּרַע לִפְנֵי כִּסֵּא כְבוֹדֶךָ וּלְהִתְחַנֵּן, בַּהֲבִיאוֹ אֶת הַזֶּרַע לְפָנֶיךָ, שֶׁאַתָּה אֲדֹנָי אֱלֹהַי, תִּגְזֹר שֶׁמֵּהַזֶּרַע הַזֶּה יֵצֵא צַדִּיק וְחָסִיד אֲשֶׁר יִירָא אֶת שִׁמְךָ הַקָּדוֹשׁ, יִשְׁמֹר מִצְוֹתֶיךָ וְיִמְצָא חֵן בְּעֵינֶיךָ וּבְעֵינֵי כָל בְּנֵי אָדָם.

---

compilation, *siddurim*, Psalms, Proverbs, moral tales, sermons, as well as manuals on leading a good Jewish life, the latter dealing in particular with the three responsibilities entrusted to women, i.e., the laws of family purity, baking *ḥalla*, and kindling Shabbat and Yom Tov candles. These books were inexpensive and mass-produced, unlike Hebrew books that were made to last. They were circulated all over Europe, from Amsterdam in the west, to Prague and beyond in the east, and proved to be immensely popular. During this period, while both boys and girls learned the *alef-beit*, only men learned Hebrew while women learned to read Yiddish. As a result women constituted the main readership of Yiddish literature. Some women became printers, editors, typesetters, and translators. Some authored new prayers,

between us. Let no man or woman among us suffer infertility, child-loss or widowhood; let no disasters at all befall us. Grant me the merit to bear wise, understanding, learned children, and grandchildren who love the Lord and fear God, who are people of truth, holy offspring, attached to the Lord, who light up worlds with Torah and good deeds and with every labor in the service of the Creator. Please, hear my plea at this time, in the merit of Sarah and Rebecca, Rachel and Leah our mothers, and cause our candle to shine and never darken nor be extinguished, ever, and let Your countenance shine so that we are saved – so may it be for all Your people Israel, speedily in our days and forever, Amen, Selah.

For conceiving a child:

יוֹצֵר כָּל הָעוֹלָמוֹת CREATOR OF ALL the world, Master of all souls, who sits on high and dwells among His chosen people Israel, and who with great love commanded us to be pure and to cleanse ourselves from all impurities; You are pure, and all Your servants are pure, and among them is no impurity.

My master, my God, I, Your devoted maidservant, (*name*), daughter of Your devoted maidservant (*mother's name*), have lovingly kept Your commandment today and cleansed myself of my impurity so that I may come purified to unite with my husband, with humility and pure thoughts. And may I bring him blissfully to the fulfillment of Your commandment, so we may honor and sustain the world.

Merciful God, send Your angel to meet me when I come to my husband so we may encounter no impurity. Cleanse my heart and my thoughts so I may think no evil. Give my husband a pure mind so he may have good, pure thoughts, not unseemly thoughts, when he unites with me, and may he act with great humility and no brazenness whatsoever.

Send me the good angel who is appointed over the womb, to bring the seed before the throne of Your glory, and that he may petition You, when he brings the seed before You, that You, my Master, my God, may decree that from this seed should arise a righteous, pious child, who will revere Your holy name, and who will keep Your commandments and find grace in Your eyes, and in the eyes of all people.

---

songs and devotional sermons that were intended for use by women as well as men. This literature was firmly rooted in traditional Jewish law and liturgy, and for this reason enjoyed the full approval and encouragement of the rabbinic authorities of the time (Dr. Devra Kay).

The *teḥinot* found here are excerpted from various manuscript sources, as will be explained.

יְהִי רָצוֹן – *May it be Your will* (previous page). This *teḥina* that asks God to bless one's family was printed in Venice in 1835, and is part of the Valmadonna Library Broadside Collection.

For a son:

וְכֵן יִלְמַד תּוֹרָה יוֹמָם וָלַיְלָה, וְאַל יִתְבַּיֵּשׁ בִּישִׁיבָה וְאַל יִכָּשֵׁל בִּדְבַר הֲלָכָה.

For a daughter:

זַכֵּה לִי בַּת, שֶׁתִּהְיֶה מְלֵאָה אוֹרָה בְּלִי עַזּוּת, וְתִלְמַד הַדֶּרֶךְ הַיָּשָׁר מִכָּל מְלַמְּדֶיהָ.

Continue:

אֵל מָלֵא רַחֲמִים, רַחֵם עָלַי, וְאַל תִּתֵּן לְהֶרְיוֹנִי לְהַכְבִּיד עָלַי, וְשֶׁלֹּא אֶתְאַב שׁוּם מַאֲכָל טָמֵא, מָאוּס אוֹ מַזִּיק לִבְרִיאוּת גּוּפִי וְעֻבָּרִי. חַדְּשֵׁנִי דַּשְּׁנֵנִי וְחַזְּקֵנִי לְעָבְדְּךָ תָּמִיד דְּשֵׁנָה וּבְשִׂמְחָה רַבָּה. יְהִי כֵן בְּשֵׁם יי, אָמֵן.

For the success of children:

רִבּוֹנוֹ שֶׁל עוֹלָם, זַכֵּנוּ שֶׁיִּהְיוּ בָּנֵינוּ מְאִירִים בַּתּוֹרָה, וְיִהְיוּ בְּרִיאִים בְּגוּפָם וְשִׂכְלָם, בַּעֲלֵי מִדּוֹת טוֹבוֹת, עוֹסְקִים בַּתּוֹרָה לִשְׁמָהּ. וְתֵן לָהֶם חַיִּים אֲרֻכִּים וְטוֹבִים, וְיִהְיוּ מְמֻלָּאִים בַּתּוֹרָה וּבְחָכְמָה וּבְיִרְאַת שָׁמַיִם, וְיִהְיוּ אֲהוּבִים לְמַעְלָה וְנֶחְמָדִים לְמַטָּה. וְתַצִּילֵם מֵעַיִן הָרָע וּמִיֵּצֶר הָרָע וּמִכָּל מִינֵי פֻּרְעָנִיּוֹת. וְיִהְיוּ לָהֶם חוּשִׁים בְּרִיאִים לַעֲבוֹדָתֶךָ. וְזַכֵּנוּ בְּרַחֲמֶיךָ הָרַבִּים שֶׁתְּמַלֵּא מִסְפַּר יָמֵינוּ בַּאֲרִיכוּת יָמִים וְשָׁנִים בְּטוֹב וּבַנְּעִימִים, וְאַהֲבָה וְשָׁלוֹם, וְנִזְכֶּה לְגַדֵּל כָּל אֶחָד מִבָּנֵינוּ וְכָל אַחַת מִבְּנוֹתֵינוּ לְתוֹרָה וּלְחֻפָּה וּלְמַעֲשִׂים טוֹבִים.

וְתַזְמִין לְכָל אֶחָד מִבָּנֵינוּ אֶת בַּת זוּגוֹ, וּלְכָל אַחַת מִבְּנוֹתֵינוּ אֶת בֶּן זוּגָהּ, וְלֹא יִדְחוּ לִפְנֵי אֲחֵרִים, חַס וְשָׁלוֹם, וּבָרֵךְ מַעֲשֵׂה יָדֵינוּ לִתֵּן לָהֶם מֹהַר וּמַתָּן בְּעַיִן יָפָה, וְנוּכַל לְקַיֵּם מַה שֶּׁאָנוּ מַבְטִיחִים לִתֵּן לָהֶם בְּלִי נֶדֶר, וּלְהַשִּׂיאָם עִם זוּגָם בִּימֵי הַנְּעוּרִים בְּנַחַת וּבְרֶוַח וּבְשִׂמְחָה, וּמֵהֶם יֵצְאוּ פֵּרוֹת טוֹבִים וּבָנִים צַדִּיקִים, זוֹכִים וּמְזַכִּים לְכָל יִשְׂרָאֵל.

וְלֹא יִתְחַלֵּל שִׁמְךָ הַגָּדוֹל עַל יָדֵינוּ, וְלֹא עַל יְדֵי זַרְעֵנוּ, חַס וְשָׁלוֹם. וּמַלֵּא כָּל מִשְׁאֲלוֹת לִבֵּנוּ לְטוֹבָה בִּבְרִיאוּת בְּהַצְלָחָה וְכָל טוֹב, וְיִתְגַּדֵּל כְּבוֹד שִׁמְךָ הַגָּדוֹל וּכְבוֹד תּוֹרָתְךָ עַל יָדֵינוּ, וְעַל יְדֵי זַרְעֵנוּ וְזֶרַע זַרְעֵנוּ, אָמֵן כֵּן יְהִי רָצוֹן.

יִהְיוּ לְרָצוֹן אִמְרֵי פִי וְהֶגְיוֹן לִבִּי לְפָנֶיךָ, יהוה צוּרִי וְגֹאֲלִי: תהלים יט

רִבּוֹנוֹ שֶׁל עוֹלָם – *Ruler of the universe*. This *teḥina* asking God to protect one's children originally appeared in the *Sefer Teḥinot uBakashot* manuscript collection of the Bodleian library.

For a son:

May he study Torah day and night, and never be shamed in the yeshiva and may he never err in a matter of law.

For a daughter:

Grant me a daughter to be a guiding light and not brazen, so she may learn to accept the guidance of all those who teach her.

Continue:

Merciful God, be merciful to me. Let me not have a difficult pregnancy and let me not desire that which is unclean, or inappropriate, or that which is unhealthy for me or for my child. Restore me, refreshed, strong and in good health, to serve You at all times, with freshness and in great happiness. May it be thus in God's name. Amen.

For the success of children:

רִבּוֹנוֹ שֶׁל עוֹלָם RULER OF THE UNIVERSE: Grant us the privilege that our children be illuminated with Torah, and be healthy in body and in mind, possess good character traits, and be occupied in Torah for its own sake. Grant them a long and good life, and may they be filled with Torah, wisdom, and fear of heaven. May they be beloved above and desired below. Rescue them from the evil eye, the evil inclination, and from all manner of punishments, and may they have healthy senses for Your service. In Your abundant mercy, make us worthy that You fill the number of our days with many good and pleasant days and years, with love and peace. May we be privileged to raise each of our sons and each of our daughters to Torah, the wedding canopy, and good deeds.

Prepare for each of our sons the girl who will be his mate, and for each of our daughters the boy who will be her mate, and may they not be pushed away for others, heaven forbid. Bless our handiwork to give them generous dowries and gifts, and may we be able to fulfill what we have obligated ourselves to give (without a vow), and to marry them off in their youth to their mates with ease, satisfaction, and happiness. May good fruit emerge from them – righteous children who earn merit and give merit to all Israel.

May Your great name not be desecrated through our actions, nor through those of our offspring, heaven forbid. Fulfill all our heartfelt requests for good with health, success, and all good things. May the glory of Your great name and the glory of the Torah be exalted through our efforts, and through the efforts of our offspring and of our offspring's offspring. Amen, may this be Your will.

Ps. 19 May the words of my mouth and the meditation of my heart find grace before You, Lord, my Rock and my Redeemer.

For a woman seeking a husband:

יְהִי רָצוֹן מִלְּפָנֶיךָ, יהוה אֱלֹהַי וֵאלֹהֵי אֲבוֹתַי, שֶׁתַּמְצִיא לִי בְּרַחֲמֶיךָ הָרַבִּים וּבַחֲסָדֶיךָ הַגְּדוֹלִים אֶת זִוּוּגִי הָרָאוּי לִי בִּזְמַנּוֹ, זִוּוּג הָגוּן הָרָאוּי לְהוֹלִיד, תַּלְמִיד חָכָם, גָּדוֹל בְּתוֹרָה וּבְיִרְאָה, מִזֶּרַע צַדִּיקִים וְאַנְשֵׁי אֱמֶת וְיִרְאַת חֵטְא, כְּמוֹ שֶׁהִמְצֵאתָ זִוּוּגוֹ לְאָדָם הָרִאשׁוֹן, לְאַבְרָהָם וְיִצְחָק וְיַעֲקֹב וּמֹשֶׁה, כָּל אֶחָד זִוּוּגוֹ בְּעִתּוֹ וּבִזְמַנּוֹ. וְאוֹתוֹ אִישׁ שֶׁתַּמְצִיא לִי לְזִוּוּגִי יְהֵא אִישׁ טוֹב, אִישׁ נָאֶה בְּמַעֲשָׂיו בַּעַל מַעֲשִׂים טוֹבִים, בַּעַל חֵן, אִישׁ מַשְׂכִּיל וִירֵא אֱלֹהִים, רוֹדֵף צְדָקָה וְגוֹמֵל חֶסֶד. וְלֹא יְהֵא בּוֹ שֶׁמֶץ פְּסוּל, מוּם אוֹ פְּגַם, וְלֹא יְהֵא כַּעֲסָן וְרַגְזָן, רַק בַּעַל עֲנָוָה וּנְמִיכוּת רוּחַ, בָּרִיא וּבַעַל כֹּחַ. וְאַל יְעַכְּבוּ אַכְזָרִיּוּת הַבְּרִיּוֹת וְשׂוֹנְאִים וּמַחְשְׁבוֹתֵיהֶם וְתַחְבּוּלוֹתֵיהֶם אֶת בֶּן זוּגִי שֶׁהוּכַן לִי.

יִהְיוּ לְרָצוֹן אִמְרֵי פִי וְהֶגְיוֹן לִבִּי לְפָנֶיךָ, יהוה צוּרִי וְגֹאֲלִי: תהלים יט

For a man seeking a wife (when there is no woman of the household to light candles):

רִבּוֹנוֹ שֶׁל עוֹלָם, בְּחַסְדְּךָ עוֹלָמֶךָ, וּבָרָאתָ אָדָם, וְעָשִׂיתָ לוֹ עֵזֶר, וְצִוִּיתָנוּ לִישָּׂא אִשָּׁה וּלְהוֹלִיד בָּנִים, וְהֶחְמִירוּ עֲבָדֶיךָ רַבּוֹתֵינוּ זִכְרוֹנָם לִבְרָכָה שֶׁלֹּא לְאַחֵר מִצְוָה זוֹ, וְיַעַן חַיֵּי הָאָדָם בָּעוֹלָם הַזֶּה וּבָעוֹלָם הַבָּא תְּלוּיִים כִּמְעַט בָּאִשָּׁה, וּבַעֲוֹנוֹתֵינוּ הָרַבִּים אֵין עוֹד נָבִיא וְלֹא בַּעֲלֵי רוּחַ הַקֹּדֶשׁ, לָדַעַת אֵיזוֹ רְאוּיָה כְּדֵי לְקַיֵּם מִצְוֹתֶיךָ. לָכֵן בְּלֵב נִשְׁבָּר בָּאתִי לְהַפִּיל תְּחִנָּתִי לְפָנֶיךָ אָב הָרַחֲמָן, וִיהִי רָצוֹן מִלְּפָנֶיךָ אֲדֹנָי אֱלֹהַי וֵאלֹהֵי אֲבוֹתַי שֶׁתִּתְמַלֵּא רַחֲמִים עָלַי וְתַזְמִין לִי בַּת זוּג נָאָה, יִרְאַת יהוה וּבַעֲלַת מִדּוֹת טוֹבוֹת וּבַעֲלַת מַזָּל טוֹב, וְטוֹבַת שֵׂכֶל וּמַצְלַחַת וּמְבֹרֶכֶת, כִּי בָּזֶה אוּכַל לַעֲבֹד עֲבוֹדַת הַקֹּדֶשׁ בְּלִי טִרְדָּה, וְהָיָה הַנַּעֲרָה אֲשֶׁר יְדַבְּרוּ לִי עָלֶיהָ וְהִיא רְאוּיָה, וְיֵשׁ לָהּ יִרְאַת יהוה וּמִדּוֹת טוֹבוֹת וּמַזָּל טוֹב וְהוֹגֶנֶת לִי, בְּרַחֲמֶיךָ הָרַבִּים תָּחֹן עָלַי וְתַטֶּה לִבִּי לִגְמֹר הַדָּבָר בְּאֹפֶן שֶׁאוּכַל לְקַיֵּם מִצְוֹתֶיךָ וְטוֹב לִי בָּעוֹלָם הַזֶּה וּבָעוֹלָם הַבָּא.

יְהִי רָצוֹן – *May it be Your will.* This *teḥina* was composed in the seventeenth century by the Shela (R. Isaiah Horowitz). It petitions God's help in finding a suitable husband.

רִבּוֹנוֹ שֶׁל עוֹלָם – *Ruler of the universe.* This *teḥina* was composed in the eighteenth century by the Ḥida (R. Ḥayyim Yosef David Azulai) and asks for God's assistance in finding a suitable wife.

For a woman seeking a husband:

יְהִי רָצוֹן MAY IT BE Your will, Lord, my God and the God of my fathers, that in Your great mercy, You provide for me, at the right time, my fitting soul mate. May he be a decent man, capable of fathering children, a Torah scholar, great in Torah and the fear of God, a descendant of righteous, sincere people, who fears sin — just as You found soul mates for Adam, Abraham, Isaac, Jacob, and Moses, to each his soul mate at the proper season and time. May the man whom you find for me be a good man whose deeds are good and beautiful. May he be gracious, intelligent, God-fearing, pursuing charity and performing deeds of loving-kindness. May he be without the slightest fault [of character and piety], may he not be quick to anger, but be humble and of modest spirit, healthy and strong. May the cruelty of people and the scheming of enemies not hold back the soul mate who has been prepared for me.

Ps. 19 May the words of my mouth and the meditation of my heart find grace before You, Lord, my Rock and my Redeemer.

For a man seeking a wife (when there is no woman of the household to light candles):

רִבּוֹנוֹ שֶׁל עוֹלָם RULER OF THE UNIVERSE, with Your loving-kindness You created Your world. You created man, and made a helpmate for him, and You commanded him to marry a woman and have children. And behold, our sages of blessed memory strongly insisted on not delaying fulfillment of this commandment. Considering that one's existence, both in this world and in the World to Come, depends almost entirely on one's wife, and considering that given our numerous sins we no longer have any prophets nor people inspired by the holy spirit through whom we might know who is a fitting wife with whom to fulfill Your commandments – therefore, with a broken heart I cast my supplication before You, merciful Father. May it be Your will, my Master, my God and the God of my fathers, that You will be all-merciful with me and provide for me a fitting, God-fearing soul mate of noble character, who is guided by Providence, is insightful, successful, and blessed, for with such a soul mate I shall be able to serve God in holy servitude without worry. And when it shall pass that the appropriate God-fearing woman of noble character will be presented to me, please, in Your abundant mercy, be gracious to me and incline my heart to bring the matter to a conclusion in a fashion that will allow me to fulfill Your commandments that it will be well with me both in this world and in the World to Come.

The service starts with מנחה לחול *on page 256. In some congregations individuals recite* שיר השירים *(page 1168) on Friday afternoon prior to* מנחה*. Most congregations sing* יְדִיד נֶפֶשׁ *at this point before* קבלת שבת*. On* מוצאי יום טוב *or* יום טוב *falling on* שבת*, or on* שבת חול המועד*, the service begins with* מִזְמוֹר שִׁיר *on page 374.*

On יום טוב *falling on a weekday, the service begins with* בָּרְכוּ *on page 384.*

An alternative version of ידיד נפש *can be found on page 1342.*

ידיד נפש

יְדִיד נֶפֶשׁ, אָב הָרַחֲמָן, מְשֹׁךְ עַבְדְּךָ אֶל רְצוֹנֶךָ
יָרוּץ עַבְדְּךָ כְּמוֹ אַיָּל, יִשְׁתַּחֲוֶה אֶל מוּל הֲדָרֶךָ
יֶעֱרַב לוֹ יְדִידוּתֶיךָ, מִנֹּפֶת צוּף וְכָל טָעַם.

הָדוּר, נָאֶה, זִיו הָעוֹלָם, נַפְשִׁי חוֹלַת אַהֲבָתֶךָ
אָנָּא, אֵל נָא, רְפָא נָא לָהּ, בְּהַרְאוֹת לָהּ נֹעַם זִיוֶךָ
אָז תִּתְחַזֵּק וְתִתְרַפֵּא, וְהָיְתָה לָהּ שִׂמְחַת עוֹלָם.

וָתִיק, יֶהֱמוּ נָא רַחֲמֶיךָ, וְחוּסָה נָא עַל בֵּן אֲהוּבֶךָ
כִּי זֶה כַּמָּה נִכְסֹף נִכְסַפְתִּי לִרְאוֹת מְהֵרָה בְּתִפְאֶרֶת עֻזֶּךָ,
אֵלֶּה חָמְדָה לִבִּי, וְחוּסָה נָּא, וְאַל תִּתְעַלָּם.

הִגָּלֶה נָא וּפְרֹשׂ, חֲבִיבִי, עָלַי אֶת סֻכַּת שְׁלוֹמֶךָ
תָּאִיר אֶרֶץ מִכְּבוֹדֶךָ, נָגִילָה וְנִשְׂמְחָה בָּךְ.
מַהֵר, אֱהֹב, כִּי בָא מוֹעֵד, וְחָנֵּנוּ כִּימֵי עוֹלָם.

יְדִיד נֶפֶשׁ – *Beloved of the soul.* The composition of this devotional poem is traditionally ascribed to R. Eliezer Azikri (1533–1600), one of the great kabbalists and halakhists of sixteenth-century Safed. He was a prominent member of the movement known as סֻכַּת שָׁלוֹם (The Canopy of Peace) which was dedicated to bringing Jews together in joyous repentance and service of God. The poem was quickly incorporated into Sephardic prayer books, to be recited prior to daily prayers, as well as *Kabbalat Shabbat* and the third Shabbat meal. R. Yaakov Emden introduced its recitation to the communities of Ashkenaz. A central theme of Azikri's writings is the cultivation of an intense love of God. This is reflected in the original superscription to the poem that proclaimed בַּקָּשָׁה עַל הַיִּחוּד וְחֵשֶׁק הָאַהֲבָה (a petition to achieve unity with, and love of, God) (Dr. Beni Gesundheit).

The combination of the first letter of each stanza spells the four letters of God's name, which by tradition is the name by which He is uniquely known to the Jewish people. This reinforces and reflects the notion that we are to seek a special closeness to God, as the poem lovingly portrays it.

The service starts with Minḥa for Weekdays on page 257. In some congregations individuals recite Shir HaShirim (page 1168) on Friday afternoon prior to Minḥa. Most congregations sing "Beloved of the soul" before the Kabbalat Shabbat service. On Yom Tov or Motza'ei Yom Tov falling on Shabbat, or on Shabbat Ḥol HaMo'ed, the service begins with Psalm 92 on page 375. On Yom Tov falling on a weekday, the service begins with "Bless" on page 385.

An alternative version of Yedid Nefesh can be found on page 1343.

YEDID NEFESH

יְדִיד נֶפֶשׁ BELOVED of the soul, compassionate Father, help me, Your servant, to do Your will.
May I, Your servant, run like a deer, and bow down before Your glory.
For the sweetness of your love will be better than a honeycomb or any other taste.

MY SOUL is love-sick for You Who are the glorious, pleasant, splendor of the universe.
Please dear God, heal her by revealing the pleasantness of Your splendor,
thus strengthening and healing her, to enjoy everlasting happiness.

ANCIENT ONE – may Your mercy be aroused. Take pity, please, on Your beloved son.
For I have long and passionately yearned to behold the splendor of Your might without delay.
This alone my heart desires, so please, take pity and do not hide from me.

PLEASE REVEAL Yourself, my Beloved, by spreading over me the canopy of Your peace.
Light up the world with Your glory so that we may be gladdened by rejoicing in You.
Hasten to show Your love, for the time has come to grace us just as in the days of yore.

There are two versions of *Yedid Nefesh*. It appears here in the form that has been accepted in many communities. It differs substantially from the text in R. Azikri's work known as *Sefer Ḥaredim*, although some of its textual variations accord with other very early manuscripts (Ezra Chwat). The text of the poem as preserved in manuscript in R. Azikri's own hand, as well as its translation, can be found on pages 1342–1343.

קבלת שבת

Mourners during the week of שבעה *leave the* בית כנסת *at this point, returning after* לְכָה דוֹדִי *on page 372.*

תהלים צה **לְכוּ נְרַנְּנָה** לַיהוה, נָרִיעָה לְצוּר יִשְׁעֵנוּ: נְקַדְּמָה פָנָיו בְּתוֹדָה,
בִּזְמִרוֹת נָרִיעַ לוֹ: כִּי אֵל גָּדוֹל יהוה, וּמֶלֶךְ גָּדוֹל עַל־
כָּל־אֱלֹהִים: אֲשֶׁר בְּיָדוֹ מֶחְקְרֵי־אָרֶץ, וְתוֹעֲפוֹת הָרִים לוֹ: אֲשֶׁר־לוֹ
הַיָּם וְהוּא עָשָׂהוּ, וְיַבֶּשֶׁת יָדָיו יָצָרוּ: בֹּאוּ נִשְׁתַּחֲוֶה וְנִכְרָעָה, נִבְרְכָה
לִפְנֵי־יהוה עֹשֵׂנוּ: כִּי הוּא אֱלֹהֵינוּ, וַאֲנַחְנוּ עַם מַרְעִיתוֹ וְצֹאן יָדוֹ,
הַיּוֹם אִם־בְּקֹלוֹ תִשְׁמָעוּ: אַל־תַּקְשׁוּ לְבַבְכֶם כִּמְרִיבָה, כְּיוֹם מַסָּה
בַּמִּדְבָּר: אֲשֶׁר נִסּוּנִי אֲבוֹתֵיכֶם, בְּחָנוּנִי גַּם רָאוּ פָעֳלִי: ◂ אַרְבָּעִים
שָׁנָה אָקוּט בְּדוֹר, וָאֹמַר עַם תֹּעֵי לֵבָב הֵם, וְהֵם לֹא־יָדְעוּ דְרָכָי:
אֲשֶׁר־נִשְׁבַּעְתִּי בְאַפִּי, אִם־יְבֹאוּן אֶל־מְנוּחָתִי:

תהלים צו **שִׁירוּ** לַיהוה שִׁיר חָדָשׁ, שִׁירוּ לַיהוה כָּל־הָאָרֶץ: שִׁירוּ לַיהוה,
בָּרְכוּ שְׁמוֹ, בַּשְּׂרוּ מִיּוֹם־לְיוֹם יְשׁוּעָתוֹ: סַפְּרוּ בַגּוֹיִם כְּבוֹדוֹ,

---

קַבָּלַת שַׁבָּת / KABBALAT SHABBAT

The Gemara *Shabbat* 119a records that as Shabbat approached R. Ḥanina would put on special clothing and call out, "Let us go out to welcome the Shabbat queen." Rambam refers to this Gemara in explaining that the obligation of כִּבּוּד שַׁבָּת (to honor the Shabbat) is fulfilled prior to the onset of the day by bathing in warm water, wearing festive clothing, and with due concentration awaiting the onset of the day, as one would do in going forth to greet a king. In the seventeenth century the Safed Kabbalists expanded on this practice by going out to the surrounding fields, where they would recite six psalms followed by *Lekha Dodi* that was composed by their contemporary R. Shlomo Alkabetz. Various explanations have been offered as to the number and choice of these psalms. The Kabbalistic *Tikkunei Shabbat* explains that the six psalms correspond to six of the *Sefirot* (divine emanations) by which God created the world over the course of the six days of Creation, followed by *Lekha Dodi* and then the psalm for the Shabbat day itself.

These psalms reflect our state of mind with the arrival of Shabbat, when we experience a heightened anticipation of the future redemption – of which Shabbat is a pale reflection – when all of the nations will happily recognize God's greatness. At that future time the holy sparks implanted by God throughout Creation will finally be lifted up and returned to their divine source, and all of Creation will reach its ultimate fulfillment (R. Naḥman of Breslov).

Psalms 95–99 form a single unit. It is likely that in their original Temple setting they were recited by the people at the outset of the three pilgrim festivals, as they drew closer to the Temple courtyard, reaching their crescendo with Psalm 29 (R. Amos Ḥakham).

WELCOMING SHABBAT

Mourners during the week of Shiva leave the synagogue at this point, returning after "Come my Beloved" on page 373.

Ps. 95 **לְכוּ נְרַנְּנָה** COME, let us sing to the Lord, let us shout joyfully to the Rock of our salvation. Let us come before Him with thanksgiving, let us raise our voice in song. For the Lord is a great God, and a great King above all gods, in Whose hand are the deep places of the earth, and the mountain peaks belong to Him. To whom the sea belongs, and He made it, and His hands formed the dry land. Come, let us bow down and bend the knee, let us kneel before the Lord our Maker. For He is our God, and we are the people of His pasture and the flock of His hand. O that today you would hearken to His voice. Do not harden your heart as at Meribah, as on the day of Massah in the wilderness, When your fathers tried Me, tested Me, although they saw My deeds. ▸ Forty years, I loathed that generation, and I said, They are a people who stray in their heart, and they do not know My ways. Therefore, I swore in My anger that they would not enter My resting place.

Ps. 96 **שִׁירוּ** SING a new song to the Lord. Sing to the Lord, all the earth. Sing to the Lord, bless His name, announce His salvation from day to day.

Similarly these psalms accompany our own spiritual journey "into Shabbat," joyously leaving behind our mundane weekday activities, rising higher and higher with each succeeding psalm.

לְכוּ נְרַנְּנָה / PSALM 95

The opening call to "come and sing for joy to greet God" serves as a summons to welcome the approaching Shabbat. The psalm refers to the incident of the spies in the Sinai desert that resulted in the forty-year forfeiture of God's "place of rest" (מְנוּחָתִי) in the Holy Land. We, however, are afforded the opportunity to experience מְנוּחַת שַׁבָּת (Shabbat rest) every week (R. Basil Herring).

אֲשֶׁר־נִשְׁבַּעְתִּי בְאַפִּי – *Therefore, I swore in My anger*. The Gemara *Ḥagiga* 10a quotes this verse to teach that after Israel sinned in the incident of the spies and God swore to punish them, God subsequently declared that because the oath had been uttered in anger rather than with due consideration, it could in retrospect be voided. This lesson should serve as a source of joy and spiritual strength for us as we begin our Shabbat, knowing that even if during the days of the week we might have angered God by our faithlessness we can still hope to be forgiven, and thus to achieve genuine closeness to Him (R. Aryeh Levine).

שִׁירוּ לַה' שִׁיר חָדָשׁ / PSALM 96

It is not just the Jewish people, but all of humanity, and indeed all of Creation, that sings

בְּכָל־הָעַמִּים נִפְלְאוֹתָיו: כִּי גָדוֹל יהוה וּמְהֻלָּל מְאֹד, נוֹרָא הוּא
עַל־כָּל־אֱלֹהִים: כִּי כָּל־אֱלֹהֵי הָעַמִּים אֱלִילִים, וַיהוה שָׁמַיִם עָשָׂה:
הוֹד־וְהָדָר לְפָנָיו, עֹז וְתִפְאֶרֶת בְּמִקְדָּשׁוֹ: הָבוּ לַיהוה מִשְׁפְּחוֹת
עַמִּים, הָבוּ לַיהוה כָּבוֹד וָעֹז: הָבוּ לַיהוה כְּבוֹד שְׁמוֹ, שְׂאוּ־מִנְחָה
וּבֹאוּ לְחַצְרוֹתָיו: הִשְׁתַּחֲווּ לַיהוה בְּהַדְרַת־קֹדֶשׁ, חִילוּ מִפָּנָיו כָּל־
הָאָרֶץ: אִמְרוּ בַגּוֹיִם יהוה מָלָךְ, אַף־תִּכּוֹן תֵּבֵל בַּל־תִּמּוֹט, יָדִין עַמִּים
בְּמֵישָׁרִים: ◂ יִשְׂמְחוּ הַשָּׁמַיִם וְתָגֵל הָאָרֶץ, יִרְעַם הַיָּם וּמְלֹאוֹ: יַעֲלֹז
שָׂדַי וְכָל־אֲשֶׁר־בּוֹ, אָז יְרַנְּנוּ כָּל־עֲצֵי־יָעַר: לִפְנֵי יהוה כִּי בָא, כִּי בָא
לִשְׁפֹּט הָאָרֶץ, יִשְׁפֹּט־תֵּבֵל בְּצֶדֶק, וְעַמִּים בֶּאֱמוּנָתוֹ:

יהוה מָלָךְ תָּגֵל הָאָרֶץ, יִשְׂמְחוּ אִיִּים רַבִּים: עָנָן וַעֲרָפֶל סְבִיבָיו, תהלים צז
צֶדֶק וּמִשְׁפָּט מְכוֹן כִּסְאוֹ: אֵשׁ לְפָנָיו תֵּלֵךְ, וּתְלַהֵט
סָבִיב צָרָיו: הֵאִירוּ בְרָקָיו תֵּבֵל, רָאֲתָה וַתָּחֵל הָאָרֶץ: הָרִים כַּדּוֹנַג
נָמַסּוּ מִלִּפְנֵי יהוה, מִלִּפְנֵי אֲדוֹן כָּל־הָאָרֶץ: הִגִּידוּ הַשָּׁמַיִם צִדְקוֹ,
וְרָאוּ כָל־הָעַמִּים כְּבוֹדוֹ: יֵבֹשׁוּ כָּל־עֹבְדֵי פֶסֶל הַמִּתְהַלְלִים
בָּאֱלִילִים, הִשְׁתַּחֲווּ־לוֹ כָּל־אֱלֹהִים: שָׁמְעָה וַתִּשְׂמַח צִיּוֹן, וַתָּגֵלְנָה

"a new song" to God, in the recognition that "before Him are majesty and splendor, strength and beauty in His מִקְדָּשׁ (holy place)." Just as the Temple was the spatial fulcrum of God's sanctity in the world, so is Shabbat the "pivot in time" around which we bring a heightened measure of sanctity not only to the Jewish people but to all of Creation. For that very reason, as we enter into the spirit of Shabbat, the psalm calls on all of the nations, and all of nature, to join in a new chorus of praise to God.

ה' מָלָךְ / PSALM 97

The unifying theme of this psalm is that those who serve God enjoy true joy in celebration of life under His sovereignty. Thus it successively describes in diminishing concentric circles the happiness of the "many nations," the exultation of Zion, the celebration of the daughters of Judea, the happiness of the upright, and the festivities of the righteous. This, we are told, is the opposite of the shame and misery that are the destiny of idolaters (R. Amos Ḥakham).

This psalm bids us to enter into the Shabbat spirit by casting aside the material and worldly concerns that serve to distract us during the week from focusing on more fundamental priorities. Shabbat observance helps us to put aside our many distractions, which in our own time include technological interruption, superficial social networking, and exposure to what is often a morally desensitizing culture. The Shabbat-observer is freed from such interruptions, and better positioned to engage in more spiritually-satisfying activities, deeper personal relationships with family and

Declare His glory among the nations, His wonders among all the peoples. That the Lord is great and greatly to be praised. He is to be feared above all gods. For all the gods of the peoples are idols, but the Lord made the heavens. Splendor and majesty are before Him, strength and glory are in His sanctuary. Give the Lord, O you families of the peoples, give the Lord glory and strength. Give the Lord of the glory due to His name; bring an offering, and enter His courts. Bow down before the Lord in the splendor of holiness; tremble before Him, all the earth. Say among the nations that the Lord reigns; the world, too, is established so that it shall not be moved. He will judge the people with equity. ▸ Let the heavens rejoice, and let the earth be glad. Let the sea roar, and its fullness. Let the field be joyful, and all that is in it. Then let all the trees of the forest sing, Before the Lord Who is coming, for He is coming to judge the earth. He will judge the world in righteousness, and the peoples in His faithfulness.

Ps. 97 **יהוה מָלָךְ** THE LORD is King, may the earth rejoice. May the many islands be happy. Cloud and mist are about Him. Justice and law are the foundation of His throne. Fire walks before Him, and it burns His enemies on every side. His lightnings illuminate the world. The earth sees and shudders. The mountains melt like wax before the Lord, before the Lord of all the earth. The heavens proclaim His righteousness, and all the peoples see His glory. Let all those who worship statues be ashamed, those who exult in false gods. All gods bow down to Him. Zion has heard and is glad, and the daughters of

---

friends, and extended time in transformative communal prayer and Torah study.

ה' מָלָךְ תָּגֵל הָאָרֶץ – *The Lord is King, may the earth rejoice.* The opening verse proclaims that when they will be judged – יִשְׂמְחוּ אִיִּים רַבִּים ("May the many islands [i.e., nations all over the world] be happy"). Yet two chapters later, at Psalm 99:1, the Psalmist contradicts this by saying that when they will be judged יִרְגְּזוּ עַמִּים (nations will tremble in fear). We can resolve this by noting the preceding contexts of these respective phrases. The final verse of Psalm 96 that precedes our verse refers to God judging each nation בֶּאֱמוּנָתוֹ (on matters of faith). Being judged on those grounds they will not need to fear excessive punishment, for doctrinal error can be understood as resulting from their intellectual weakness, and thus be more easily forgiven. On the other hand, the final verse of Psalm 98 preceding 99:1 says that the nations will be judged בְּמֵישָׁרִים, i.e., for their moral behavior. Thus judged, they will have good reason to be fearful, having

בְּנוֹת יְהוּדָה, לְמַעַן מִשְׁפָּטֶיךָ יהוה: כִּי־אַתָּה יהוה עֶלְיוֹן עַל־כָּל־הָאָרֶץ, מְאֹד נַעֲלֵיתָ עַל־כָּל־אֱלֹהִים: › אֹהֲבֵי יהוה שִׂנְאוּ רָע, שֹׁמֵר נַפְשׁוֹת חֲסִידָיו, מִיַּד רְשָׁעִים יַצִּילֵם: אוֹר זָרֻעַ לַצַּדִּיק, וּלְיִשְׁרֵי־לֵב שִׂמְחָה: שִׂמְחוּ צַדִּיקִים בַּיהוה, וְהוֹדוּ לְזֵכֶר קָדְשׁוֹ:

תהלים צח **מִזְמוֹר,** שִׁירוּ לַיהוה שִׁיר חָדָשׁ כִּי־נִפְלָאוֹת עָשָׂה, הוֹשִׁיעָה־לּוֹ יְמִינוֹ וּזְרוֹעַ קָדְשׁוֹ: הוֹדִיעַ יהוה יְשׁוּעָתוֹ, לְעֵינֵי הַגּוֹיִם גִּלָּה צִדְקָתוֹ: זָכַר חַסְדּוֹ וֶאֱמוּנָתוֹ לְבֵית יִשְׂרָאֵל, רָאוּ כָל־אַפְסֵי־אָרֶץ אֵת יְשׁוּעַת אֱלֹהֵינוּ: הָרִיעוּ לַיהוה כָּל־הָאָרֶץ, פִּצְחוּ וְרַנְּנוּ וְזַמֵּרוּ: זַמְּרוּ לַיהוה בְּכִנּוֹר, בְּכִנּוֹר וְקוֹל זִמְרָה: בַּחֲצֹצְרוֹת וְקוֹל שׁוֹפָר, הָרִיעוּ לִפְנֵי הַמֶּלֶךְ יהוה: › יִרְעַם הַיָּם וּמְלֹאוֹ, תֵּבֵל וְיֹשְׁבֵי בָהּ: נְהָרוֹת יִמְחֲאוּ־כָף, יַחַד הָרִים יְרַנֵּנוּ: לִפְנֵי יהוה כִּי בָא לִשְׁפֹּט הָאָרֶץ, יִשְׁפֹּט־תֵּבֵל בְּצֶדֶק, וְעַמִּים בְּמֵישָׁרִים:

תהלים צט **יהוה מָלָךְ** יִרְגְּזוּ עַמִּים, יֹשֵׁב כְּרוּבִים תָּנוּט הָאָרֶץ: יהוה בְּצִיּוֹן גָּדוֹל, וְרָם הוּא עַל־כָּל־הָעַמִּים: יוֹדוּ שִׁמְךָ גָּדוֹל וְנוֹרָא קָדוֹשׁ הוּא: וְעֹז מֶלֶךְ מִשְׁפָּט אָהֵב, אַתָּה כּוֹנַנְתָּ מֵישָׁרִים, מִשְׁפָּט

---

treated God's people with inexcusable hatred and cruelty (R. Yehezkel Abramsky).

מִזְמוֹר, שִׁירוּ לַה׳ שִׁיר חָדָשׁ / PSALM 98
This is the "new song" that the entire world was called on to sing in the preceding Psalm 96. It consists of three stanzas: In the first – the two and a half verses beginning with הוֹשִׁיעָה־לּוֹ – God has effectively lifted a veil from the eyes of humanity, and they have come to recognize God in the repeated salvation of Israel. The following three verses call upon them to echo the new ode of joy to Him. Facing an ever more intense revelation they will come to accept God's sovereignty. The final three verses call upon every created being to join with humanity in song (*Metzudot*).

הָרִיעוּ לַה׳ כָּל־הָאָרֶץ – *Make a joyful noise to the Lord, all the earth*. The Arizal explains that the first letters of these four words spell הֲלָכָה (*halakha*). The Ba'al Shem Tov explained that all of the disagreements in the Talmud were motivated by one desire: to identify the optimal approach by which to come ever closer to God. In their debates there were no selfish motives whatsoever. They were like engineers and builders who were invited to submit plans to provide optimal access routes to reach the royal palace, which in their case consisted of providing spiritual routes to reach God in His

Judah rejoice, on account of Your judgments, O Lord. Indeed, You, O Lord, are high above all the earth. You are exalted far above all gods. ▸ Those who love the Lord, hate evil. He preserves the souls of His pious ones. He saves them from the hand of the wicked. Light is sown for the righteous, and gladness for the upright in heart. Rejoice, O righteous, in the Lord, and give thanks to the memory of His holiness.

Ps. 98 **מִזְמוֹר** A PSALM. Sing to the Lord a new song, for He has done marvels. His right hand and His holy arm have gained Him the victory. The Lord has made known His salvation. He has revealed His righteousness in the sight of the nations. He has remembered His loving-kindness in His faithfulness to the house of Israel. All the ends of the earth have seen the salvation of our God. Make a joyful noise to the Lord, all the earth. Make a loud noise, and sing, and sing praise. Sing praise to the Lord with the lyre, with the lyre and the sound of song. With trumpets and the sound of a shofar, make a joyful noise before the Lord, the King. ▸ May the sea roar and the fullness of it, the world and those who dwell in it. May the rivers clap hands. May the mountains sing for joy together, Before the Lord Who is coming to judge the earth. He will judge the world in righteousness, and the peoples with equity.

Ps. 99 **יהוה מָלָךְ** THE LORD is King, let the peoples tremble. He is enthroned upon the cherubim, let the earth move. The Lord is great in Zion, and He is high above all the peoples. Let them praise Your name, O Great and Awesome One. He is holy. And the strength of the King loves justice. You have established equity, You have performed justice and

---

glory. This is the reason they were considered בּוֹנַיִךְ – builders. For this reason too the Gemara (*Megilla* 28b) describes their teachings by saying "do not call them *halikhot* but *halakhot*," i.e., the laws are really numerous paths to finding God. Through observing the *halakha* we approach ever closer to God's palace (*Razin DeOraita*).

So too on Shabbat we seek to reach God's palace, and to experience a higher order of spiritual living. This is accomplished by following faithfully in the spiritual path laid out for us by the *halakhot* of Shabbat, as derived and taught by the sages, which taken together transform the day into a joyous journey to transcendence.

ה׳ מָלָךְ / PSALM 99

This psalm describes how God's holiness is revealed in three concentric circles. In the first

וּצְדָקָה בְּיַעֲקֹב אַתָּה עָשִׂיתָ: רוֹמְמוּ יהוה אֱלֹהֵינוּ, וְהִשְׁתַּחֲווּ לַהֲדֹם
רַגְלָיו, קָדוֹשׁ הוּא: מֹשֶׁה וְאַהֲרֹן בְּכֹהֲנָיו, וּשְׁמוּאֵל בְּקֹרְאֵי שְׁמוֹ,
קֹרְאִים אֶל־יהוה וְהוּא יַעֲנֵם: › בְּעַמּוּד עָנָן יְדַבֵּר אֲלֵיהֶם, שָׁמְרוּ
עֵדֹתָיו וְחֹק נָתַן־לָמוֹ: יהוה אֱלֹהֵינוּ אַתָּה עֲנִיתָם, אֵל נֹשֵׂא הָיִיתָ
לָהֶם, וְנֹקֵם עַל־עֲלִילוֹתָם: רוֹמְמוּ יהוה אֱלֹהֵינוּ, וְהִשְׁתַּחֲווּ לְהַר
קָדְשׁוֹ, כִּי־קָדוֹשׁ יהוה אֱלֹהֵינוּ:

The following psalm is said standing:

תהלים כט **מִזְמוֹר לְדָוִד,** הָבוּ לַיהוה בְּנֵי אֵלִים, הָבוּ לַיהוה כָּבוֹד וָעֹז: הָבוּ
לַיהוה כְּבוֹד שְׁמוֹ, הִשְׁתַּחֲווּ לַיהוה בְּהַדְרַת־קֹדֶשׁ:
קוֹל יהוה עַל הַמָּיִם, אֵל־הַכָּבוֹד הִרְעִים, יהוה עַל־מַיִם רַבִּים: קוֹל־
יהוה בַּכֹּחַ, קוֹל יהוה בֶּהָדָר: קוֹל יהוה שֹׁבֵר אֲרָזִים, וַיְשַׁבֵּר יהוה
אֶת־אַרְזֵי הַלְּבָנוֹן: וַיַּרְקִידֵם כְּמוֹ־עֵגֶל, לְבָנוֹן וְשִׂרְיוֹן כְּמוֹ בֶן־רְאֵמִים:
קוֹל־יהוה חֹצֵב לַהֲבוֹת אֵשׁ: קוֹל יהוה יָחִיל מִדְבָּר, יָחִיל יהוה
מִדְבַּר קָדֵשׁ: › קוֹל יהוה יְחוֹלֵל אַיָּלוֹת וַיֶּחֱשֹׂף יְעָרוֹת, וּבְהֵיכָלוֹ,
כֻּלּוֹ אֹמֵר כָּבוֹד: יהוה לַמַּבּוּל יָשָׁב, וַיֵּשֶׁב יהוה מֶלֶךְ לְעוֹלָם: יהוה
עֹז לְעַמּוֹ יִתֵּן, יהוה יְבָרֵךְ אֶת־עַמּוֹ בַשָּׁלוֹם:

---

and outermost one (verses 1–3) God's holiness is seen as He rules over all the nations; in the second (verses 4–5) it is manifest in the direct relationship between God and His people Israel, over whom He rules with righteousness and justice; in the third circle, which is the smallest of all (verses 6–9) His sanctity stands revealed in His relations with the righteous such as Moses, Aaron, and Samuel. The relationship with this last group is particularly telling, insofar as they reflect His holiness in their own lives. For this reason, the Psalmist says, if they err in any way they are held to a particularly high standard, and punished accordingly (R. Amos Ḥakham).

מִזְמוֹר לְדָוִד / PSALM 29

While the preceding psalms follow their scriptural order this one stands on its own. It repeats קוֹל (God's voice) seven times, corresponding to the seven *berakhot* of each Shabbat *Amida* (Yerushalmi, *Berakhot* 4:3).

בְּנֵי אֵלִים – *Divine beings*. The phrase appears only one other time in the Bible, in Psalm 89, where it refers to angels (Ibn Ezra).

While the first stanza is a call to praise Him from heaven, the second (verses 3–9) describes events on earth, where God›s voice is heard "on the waters," via great storms and floodwaters (Malbim). God's voice destroys the mighty cedar trees of Lebanon (a symbol of might and

righteousness in Jacob. Exalt the Lord our God, and bow down before His footstool. He is holy. Moses and Aaron were among His priests, and Samuel was among those who would call upon His name. They would call upon the Lord, and He would answer them. ▸ He would speak to them in a pillar of cloud. They kept His testimonies and the statute that He gave them. O Lord our God, You answered them. You were a favoring God to them, and You took vengeance for the wicked deeds performed against them. Exalt the Lord our God, and bow down before His holy mountain. Indeed, the Lord our God is holy.

The following psalm is said standing:

Ps. 29 **מִזְמוֹר לְדָוִד** A PSALM of David. Ascribe to the Lord, O you divine beings, ascribe to the Lord glory and strength. Ascribe to the Lord the glory of His name. Bow down to the Lord in the splendor of holiness. The voice of the Lord is upon the waters. The God of glory thunders. The Lord is upon many waters. The voice of the Lord is powerful. The voice of the Lord is majestic. The voice of the Lord breaks cedars, and the Lord breaks the cedars of Lebanon. And He makes them skip like a calf, Lebanon and Sirion like a young wild ox. The voice of the Lord hews out flames of fire. The voice of the Lord shakes the wilderness. The Lord shakes the wilderness of Kadesh. ▸ The voice of the Lord causes the hinds to tremble, and strips the forests bare, and in His Temple all say: Glory. The Lord sat for a flood, but the Lord sits as King forever. The Lord will give strength to His people. The Lord will bless His people with peace.

---

stability – see Amos 2:9). It makes the two parallel mountain ranges of the north, *Levanon* and *Sirion,* dance like young animals, a metaphor that may refer to an ancient earthquake. God's voice is also manifested by fire, which could refer to lightning in a forest, felling trees by setting them ablaze. It is also manifest in sandstorms that engulf desert dwellers or travelers, leaving no escape (Ibn Ezra).

These manifestations of God's voice are experienced in awesome events within nature. The list of God's powers at first focuses on His ability to bring destruction and punishment. But in the final manifestation of God's power the Psalmist declares that "in His Temple all proclaim 'Glory!'" The true voice of God is witnessed, not by its destructive power but rather in His revealed Presence. After all of the earth-shattering power, we are left with the quiet glory (Malbim).

The following is said in some congregations:

אָנָּא, בְּכֹחַ גְּדֻלַּת יְמִינְךָ, תַּתִּיר צְרוּרָה.
קַבֵּל רִנַּת עַמְּךָ, שַׂגְּבֵנוּ, טַהֲרֵנוּ, נוֹרָא.
נָא גִבּוֹר, דּוֹרְשֵׁי יִחוּדְךָ כְּבָבַת שָׁמְרֵם.
בָּרְכֵם, טַהֲרֵם, רַחֲמֵם, צִדְקָתְךָ תָּמִיד גָּמְלֵם.
חֲסִין קָדוֹשׁ, בְּרֹב טוּבְךָ נַהֵל עֲדָתֶךָ.
יָחִיד גֵּאֶה, לְעַמְּךָ פְּנֵה, זוֹכְרֵי קְדֻשָּׁתֶךָ.
שַׁוְעָתֵנוּ קַבֵּל וּשְׁמַע צַעֲקָתֵנוּ, יוֹדֵעַ תַּעֲלוּמוֹת.
בָּרוּךְ שֵׁם כְּבוֹד מַלְכוּתוֹ לְעוֹלָם וָעֶד.

לְכָה דוֹדִי לִקְרַאת כַּלָּה, פְּנֵי שַׁבָּת נְקַבְּלָה.
לְכָה דוֹדִי לִקְרַאת כַּלָּה, פְּנֵי שַׁבָּת נְקַבְּלָה.

שָׁמוֹר וְזָכוֹר בְּדִבּוּר אֶחָד
הִשְׁמִיעָנוּ אֵל הַמְיֻחָד
יהוה אֶחָד וּשְׁמוֹ אֶחָד
לְשֵׁם וּלְתִפְאֶרֶת וְלִתְהִלָּה.
לְכָה דוֹדִי לִקְרַאת כַּלָּה, פְּנֵי שַׁבָּת נְקַבְּלָה.

לְכָה דוֹדִי / LEKHA DODI

This poem, composed by the sixteenth-century Safed Kabbalist R. Shlomo HaLevi Alkabetz, is based on the Gemara (*Shabbat* 119a) which records that as Shabbat drew near R. Yannai would clothe himself in special finery and declare, "Welcome O Bride, welcome O Bride." This reflects the midrashic statement that at Creation when the seventh day protested that – unlike the preceding six days that consisted of three pairs of two days each – it had no counterpart, God promised that the Jewish people would one day be joined with it. Fittingly, when God gave the Torah to Israel at Sinai, it was on Shabbat. Thus every Shabbat the bride and groom are reunited, their relationship renewed. On this level, the refrain "Come my Beloved" refers to God as the One Who ordained this union, joining us as we welcome our Shabbat bride.

On a deeper level, however, the refrain "Come my Beloved" refers to the Beloved Who appears repeatedly in the Song of Songs. There, God is דודי, the beloved One Whom the Jewish nation embraces, but sometimes forsakes, over the complex course of its history. On this level, Shabbat is only the sacred means by which the Jewish people renews its bond to its beloved God after six days of separation, and He in turn reciprocates by drawing closer to us as Shabbat arrives, echoing Shabbat at Sinai. Stylistically, this love is reflected in the refrain consisting of twenty-six letters, i.e., the numerical value of God's four-letter name, to which the

The following is said in some congregations:

אָנָּא WE BESEECH YOU, by the strength of Your great right hand, release the captive nation. Accept Your people's prayer. Uplift us, purify us, O Awesome One. Please, Mighty One, guard like the apple of the eye those who embrace Your unity. Bless them, purify them, have compassion on them; may Your righteousness always grant them reward. Powerful One, Holy One, in Your abundant goodness guide Your congregation. O One Who is exalted, turn to Your people who proclaim Your holiness. Accept our plea and heed our cry, for You know our innermost thoughts. Blessed is the name of His glorious kingdom forever and ever.

לְכָה דוֹדִי COME, my beloved, the bride to greet;
together the Sabbath we shall meet.

Come, my beloved, the bride to greet; together the Sabbath we shall meet.

THE GOD Who is Himself uniquely One,
made us hear "Keep" and "Remember" spoken as one.
The Lord is One and His name is One,
for the sake of His name, its splendor and its praise.

Come, my beloved, the bride to greet; together the Sabbath we shall meet.

Jewish people has a special relationship. So too the mystical *Ana beKo'aḥ* petition that immediately precedes *Lekha Dodi*, ascribed to the Tanna R. Neḥunia ben HaKana, consists of forty-two words alluding to God's forty-two-letter name, followed by בָּרוּךְ שֵׁם כְּבוֹד וכו׳, that blesses His name. It is similarly expressed in the contemporaneously composed *Yedid Nefesh*, the poem that bespeaks the intense love of God, and that sets the tone for *Kabbalat Shabbat* by spelling out the four letters of His name via the first letter of each of its stanzas (R. Basil Herring).

שָׁמוֹר וְזָכוֹר בְּדִבּוּר אֶחָד, הִשְׁמִיעָנוּ אֵל הַמְיֻחָד – *The God Who is Himself uniquely One, made us hear "Keep" and "Remember" spoken as one.* This refers to the Gemara (*Shavuot* 20b) stating that "Remember the Sabbath day" (Ex. 20:8) and "Safeguard the Sabbath day" (Deut. 5:12) are not contradictory reports of the divine utterance. Rather they reflect the fact that the Israelites were commanded simultaneously to heed both aspects of Shabbat, one positive and the other negative. On a yet deeper level, Ramban explains that this reflects the very nature of Shabbat, in that it brings God in His celestial abode together with His *Shekhina* that is manifested on earth. This stanza proclaims that on Shabbat "The Lord is One and His name is One," where "His name" refers to the *Shekhina* by which He makes Himself known in the world. So too when the final stanza proclaims "Come O Bride," it is referring to the *Shekhina* that is joined to God Himself on Shabbat. This is a foretaste of the end of time when God and His *Shekhina* will be joined forever (R. Tzadok HaKohen of Lublin).

לִקְרַאת שַׁבָּת לְכוּ וְנֵלְכָה
כִּי הִיא מְקוֹר הַבְּרָכָה
מֵרֹאשׁ מִקֶּדֶם נְסוּכָה
סוֹף מַעֲשֶׂה בְּמַחֲשָׁבָה תְּחִלָּה.
לְכָה דוֹדִי לִקְרַאת כַּלָּה, פְּנֵי שַׁבָּת נְקַבְּלָה.

מִקְדַּשׁ מֶלֶךְ עִיר מְלוּכָה
קוּמִי צְאִי מִתּוֹךְ הַהֲפֵכָה
רַב לָךְ שֶׁבֶת בְּעֵמֶק הַבָּכָא
וְהוּא יַחֲמֹל עָלַיִךְ חֶמְלָה.
לְכָה דוֹדִי לִקְרַאת כַּלָּה, פְּנֵי שַׁבָּת נְקַבְּלָה.

הִתְנַעֲרִי מֵעָפָר, קוּמִי
לִבְשִׁי בִּגְדֵי תִפְאַרְתֵּךְ עַמִּי
עַל יַד בֶּן יִשַׁי בֵּית הַלַּחְמִי
קָרְבָה אֶל נַפְשִׁי, גְּאָלָהּ.
לְכָה דוֹדִי לִקְרַאת כַּלָּה, פְּנֵי שַׁבָּת נְקַבְּלָה.

הִתְעוֹרְרִי הִתְעוֹרְרִי
כִּי בָא אוֹרֵךְ קוּמִי אוֹרִי
עוּרִי עוּרִי, שִׁיר דַּבֵּרִי
כְּבוֹד יהוה עָלַיִךְ נִגְלָה.
לְכָה דוֹדִי לִקְרַאת כַּלָּה, פְּנֵי שַׁבָּת נְקַבְּלָה.

מִקְדַּשׁ מֶלֶךְ – *The Sanctuary of the King*. The next six stanzas shift from Shabbat to Israel's longing for redemption, to be realized in particular through our Shabbat observance (*Shabbat* 118b). The majestic aspect of Jerusalem – the earthly center of God's presence – is stressed here in parallel with that of Shabbat, which is a microcosm of what will prevail in the World to Come. Both symbolize the divine attribute of מַלְכוּת (majesty), the unique repository of all divine attributes of action.

הַהֲפֵכָה ... בְּעֵמֶק הַבָּכָא – *State of destruction ... valley of tears*. The Valley of Baka is referenced in Psalms 84:7, referring to a dry valley located on the pilgrims' route to the Temple. This phrase implies that in the absence of the Temple, and the suspension of the thrice

LET US go out to welcome the Sabbath
for it is the source of all blessing.
It was designated from the outset at the very beginning;
it was the last thing created, but the first in intent.

Come, my beloved, the bride to greet; together the Sabbath we shall meet.

ARISE and go forth from your state of destruction,
O royal city that housed the Sanctuary of the King.
Enough of your dwelling in a valley of tears,
for in His compassion He will have mercy upon you.

Come, my beloved, the bride to greet; together the Sabbath we shall meet.

MY PEOPLE, arise from the dust, and stand erect.
Put on your garments of glory
in the company of the descendant of Jesse of Beit Leḥem
whose redemption will soon be with us.

Come, my beloved, the bride to greet; together the Sabbath we shall meet.

GET UP, get up, for your light has come, so rise and shine.
Arise, arise, call out in song,
for the glory of the Lord
has been revealed upon you.

Come, my beloved, the bride to greet; together the Sabbath we shall meet.

---

yearly pilgrimages, we yearn for the divine command to arise and reclaim the land of our heritage. The result will be a complete reversal of Jeremiah's pessimistic prophecy that said, "מִי יַחְמֹל – Who shall have pity upon you, O Jerusalem?" (15:5), so that instead God will shower "עָלַיִךְ חֶמְלָה – compassion upon you."

לִבְשִׁי בִּגְדֵי תִפְאַרְתֵּךְ עַמִּי – *My people... put on your garments of glory*. The priestly garments for the Temple service, which have languished in disuse throughout our long exile, are said to embody כָבוֹד וּתִפְאָרֶת – honor and splendor (Exodus 28:2). The Kabbalists teach that the *sefira* of תִּפְאֶרֶת (splendor) represents the "masculine" or active emanation from God, which unites on Shabbat with the feminine Divine Presence, the *Shekhina*, which resides with His people. In this stanza, the *Shekhina* becomes cloaked in "garments of splendor," that is, it unites with *tiferet* on Shabbat.

הִתְעוֹרְרִי – *Get up*. This central stanza, the fifth of this nine-stanza composition, captures the essence of the entire song, particularly with the words כִּי בָא אוֹרֵךְ קוּמִי אוֹרִי ("Wake up, wake up, for your light has come") which are offset sixty-five words (which is the numerical value of the Divine Name א־ד־נ־י) from both the beginning and the end of the song (not

לֹא תֵבֹשִׁי וְלֹא תִכָּלְמִי
מַה תִּשְׁתּוֹחֲחִי וּמַה תֶּהֱמִי
בָּךְ יֶחֱסוּ עֲנִיֵּי עַמִּי
וְנִבְנְתָה עִיר עַל תִּלָּהּ.
לְכָה דוֹדִי לִקְרַאת כַּלָּה, פְּנֵי שַׁבָּת נְקַבְּלָה.

וְהָיוּ לִמְשִׁסָּה שֹׁאסָיִךְ
וְרָחֲקוּ כָּל מְבַלְּעָיִךְ
יָשִׂישׂ עָלַיִךְ אֱלֹהָיִךְ
כִּמְשׂוֹשׂ חָתָן עַל כַּלָּה.
לְכָה דוֹדִי לִקְרַאת כַּלָּה, פְּנֵי שַׁבָּת נְקַבְּלָה.

יָמִין וּשְׂמֹאל תִּפְרֹצִי
וְאֶת יהוה תַּעֲרִיצִי
עַל יַד אִישׁ בֶּן פַּרְצִי
וְנִשְׂמְחָה וְנָגִילָה.
לְכָה דוֹדִי לִקְרַאת כַּלָּה, פְּנֵי שַׁבָּת נְקַבְּלָה.

Stand and turn to face the door or the rear (usually western side) of the בית כנסת*, as if to greet the incoming bride, bowing at the words* בּוֹאִי כַלָּה*, then turn back.*

בּוֹאִי בְשָׁלוֹם עֲטֶרֶת בַּעְלָהּ
גַּם בְּשִׂמְחָה וּבְצָהֳלָה
תּוֹךְ אֱמוּנֵי עַם סְגֻלָּה
בּוֹאִי כַלָּה, בּוֹאִי כַלָּה.
לְכָה דוֹדִי לִקְרַאת כַּלָּה, פְּנֵי שַׁבָּת נְקַבְּלָה.

Mourners during the week of שבעה *return to the* בית כנסת *at this point. They are greeted with the following words of consolation:*

הַמָּקוֹם יְנַחֵם אֶתְכֶם בְּתוֹךְ שְׁאָר אֲבֵלֵי צִיּוֹן וִירוּשָׁלָיִם.

including the refrain). Jerusalem's light has arrived, that is, God wills her – now, on the Sabbath – to shine forth, out of the ashes of exile, to return to her glory.

NO LONGER will you be embarrassed or humiliated;
why are you depressed and why are you distraught?
For in you will the impoverished of My people take shelter,
and soon will the city be rebuilt over its ruins.
Come, my beloved, the bride to greet; together the Sabbath we shall meet.

THOSE who have devastated you will themselves be destroyed.
All who consumed you will be banished far away.
And your God will rejoice over you
as a groom rejoices on account of his bride.
Come, my beloved, the bride to greet; together the Sabbath we shall meet.

YOU will break out to the right and to the left
and you will praise the Lord,
together with the descendant of Peretz
we will rejoice and sing out in exultation.
Come, my beloved, the bride to greet; together the Sabbath we shall meet.

Stand and turn to face the door or the rear (usually western side) of the synagogue, as if to greet the incoming bride, bowing at the words "come, O come," then turn back.

COME in peace O crown of her husband,
in joy and in exuberance
into the midst of the faithful of the treasured people.
Come O bride, come O bride.
Come, my beloved, the bride to greet; together the Sabbath we shall meet.

Mourners during the week of Shiva return to the synagogue at this point. They are greeted with the following words of consolation:

MAY God Who is ever-present comfort you among the other mourners of Zion and Jerusalem.

בֶּן פַּרְצִי – *Descendant of Peretz.* This refers to the Messiah, referencing Gen. 38:29 where Tamar names her firstborn son Peretz, and he in turn is listed in Ruth 4:18–22 as the forebear of David, whose lineage will include the Messiah, to be known as a descendant of Peretz.

NIḤUM AVEILIM

We comfort mourners immediately prior to accepting Shabbat because it is inappropriate to comfort mourners on Shabbat or to publicly display signs of mourning.

On יום טוב, שבת חול המועד *or* מוצאי יום טוב, קבלת שבת *begins here.*

תהלים צב

מִזְמוֹר שִׁיר לְיוֹם הַשַּׁבָּת: טוֹב לְהֹדוֹת לַיהוה, וּלְזַמֵּר לְשִׁמְךָ
עֶלְיוֹן: לְהַגִּיד בַּבֹּקֶר חַסְדֶּךָ, וֶאֱמוּנָתְךָ בַּלֵּילוֹת:
עֲלֵי־עָשׂוֹר וַעֲלֵי־נָבֶל, עֲלֵי הִגָּיוֹן בְּכִנּוֹר: כִּי שִׂמַּחְתַּנִי יהוה בְּפָעֳלֶךָ,
בְּמַעֲשֵׂי יָדֶיךָ אֲרַנֵּן: מַה־גָּדְלוּ מַעֲשֶׂיךָ יהוה, מְאֹד עָמְקוּ מַחְשְׁבֹתֶיךָ:
אִישׁ־בַּעַר לֹא יֵדָע, וּכְסִיל לֹא־יָבִין אֶת־זֹאת: בִּפְרֹחַ רְשָׁעִים כְּמוֹ
עֵשֶׂב, וַיָּצִיצוּ כָּל־פֹּעֲלֵי אָוֶן, לְהִשָּׁמְדָם עֲדֵי־עַד: וְאַתָּה מָרוֹם לְעֹלָם
יהוה: כִּי הִנֵּה אֹיְבֶיךָ יהוה, כִּי־הִנֵּה אֹיְבֶיךָ יֹאבֵדוּ, יִתְפָּרְדוּ כָּל־פֹּעֲלֵי
אָוֶן: וַתָּרֶם כִּרְאֵים קַרְנִי, בַּלֹּתִי בְּשֶׁמֶן רַעֲנָן: וַתַּבֵּט עֵינִי בְּשׁוּרָי,

---

מִזְמוֹר שִׁיר לְיוֹם הַשַּׁבָּת / PSALM 92

The Levites recited this psalm every Shabbat in the Temple. Having completed the six psalms corresponding to the six days of Creation, followed by the transitional *Lekha Dodi* by which we escort Shabbat into our midst, we now recite the psalm for Shabbat in Her presence.

The *Midrash Shoḥer Tov* relates that when man was created on the sixth day of Creation, in the ninth hour he was told to abstain from the fruit of the tree, he transgressed in the tenth, was judged in the eleventh, and sentenced in the twelfth as the sun set and Shabbat began. Thus the punishment was to begin on Shabbat itself. With that prospect at hand, Shabbat itself argued before God that it was unfair to diminish the sanctity of the day by inflicting punishment on a day intended to be filled with rest and sanctity. The result was that God temporarily suspended His decree, at which point Adam and Eve started to praise Shabbat, whereupon Shabbat proclaimed, "Do not praise me, rather let us both give thanks to God." Thus they sang together טוב להדות לה' – "It is good to give thanks to God."

וּכְסִיל לֹא־יָבִין אֶת־זֹאת – *A fool does not understand this*. What is the "this" that the fool does not understand? It is to be explained by way of the following parable. A peasant once rebelled against his king. To the amazement of the king's advisers, instead of exacting immediate punishment, the king elevated the commoner to a position of prominence and honor. In due course the king brought about the public disgrace and removal of the erstwhile rebel. At that point the King summoned his advisers and said, "Had I punished him when he was obscure and unknown, no one would have noticed or learned the consequences of not obeying me. That is why, even though you fools did not understand me at the time, I raised him to a position of honor. You thought that allowing a disobedient person to flourish

KABBALAT SHABBAT FOR YOM TOV AND ḤOL HAMOED

Many Ashkenazi congregations begin Kabbalat Shabbat on Yom Tov and Ḥol HaMoed with *Mizmor Shir*, skipping the six paragraphs of Psalms as well as *Lekha Dodi*. R. Yeḥiel Mikhel HaLevi Epstein, *Arukh HaShulḥan*, *Oraḥ Ḥayyim* 270:3, explains that it would a denigration of Yom Tov to have an elaborate acceptance of Shabbat that doesn't reference Yom Tov.

On Yom Tov, Motza'ei Yom Tov or Shabbat Ḥol HaMo'ed, Kabbalat Shabbat begins here.

Ps. 92 **מִזְמוֹר שִׁיר** A PSALM. A song for the Sabbath day. It is good to give thanks to the Lord, and to sing praise to Your name, O Most High, to relate Your loving-kindness in the morning and Your faithfulness in the nights. Upon an instrument of ten strings and upon the harp, to the melody of the lyre. For You, O Lord, make me glad through Your work. I rejoice in the works of Your hands. How great are Your works, O Lord! Your thoughts are very deep. A brutish man does not know, and a fool does not understand this. When the wicked spring forth, they are like grass, and when all the workers of iniquity flourish, it is only that they may be destroyed forever. But You, O Lord, are most high forever. Indeed, behold Your enemies, O Lord! Indeed, behold, Your enemies are perishing. All the workers of iniquity are being scattered. But You have exalted my horn like that of a wild ox. I have anointed myself with fresh oil. My eye has seen the downfall of my enemies,

---

would undermine my authority. Now, however, you can see that I raised him up – so that in due course my subjects would know my power to punish even one so powerful as him, and they will henceforth obey my every command." This is the meaning of the words "a brutish man does not know, and a fool does not understand this. When the wicked spring forth they are like grass…only to be destroyed forever." On Shabbat, in the perspective of eternity, we too are able to see clearly that the flourishing of the wicked who have rebelled against God our King is but a "flash in the pan," which He permits in the short term in order to eventually demonstrate His power, as well as the benefits we will reap from being faithful to Him (R. Ephraim Lunshitz).

The central theme of the psalm is to answer the perennial question of why the wicked prosper while the righteous suffer. The psalm answers in the perspective of eternity: "But You God remain exalted forever." This statement is placed at the epicenter of the psalm, with fifty-two words on either side of it (excluding the title verse). In its first half, the psalm is a jubilant expression of joy, having finally understood the principle of divine justice. While for the ignorant injustice appears to triumph, in the long run it is clear that justice ultimately prevails. The wicked prosper so as *to destroy them for eternity*, while by contrast the righteous will flourish, like date palms and cedars, which are symbols of strength and vitality (R. Ronald Benun).

לְהִשָּׁמְדָם עֲדֵי־עַד – *They may be destroyed forever.* God gives temporal success and happiness to the wicked as reward for whatever good deeds they may have done. Thereafter they will sink to destruction, while the righteous gain eternal reward (*Rashi*).

וַתָּרֶם כִּרְאֵים קַרְנִי – *But You have exalted my horn like that of a wild ox.* Some identify the *re'em* as the oryx, a white antelope with magnificent straight horns. Others identify it as the aurochs, the extinct giant ancestor of domestic cattle (R. Natan Slifkin).

בְּקָמִים עָלַי מְרֵעִים תִּשְׁמַעְנָה אָזְנָי: ▸ צַדִּיק כַּתָּמָר יִפְרָח, כְּאֶרֶז בַּלְּבָנוֹן יִשְׂגֶּה: שְׁתוּלִים בְּבֵית יהוה, בְּחַצְרוֹת אֱלֹהֵינוּ יַפְרִיחוּ: עוֹד יְנוּבוּן בְּשֵׂיבָה, דְּשֵׁנִים וְרַעֲנַנִּים יִהְיוּ: לְהַגִּיד כִּי־יָשָׁר יהוה, צוּרִי, וְלֹא־עַוְלָֽתָה בּוֹ:

תהלים צג

יהוה מָלָךְ, גֵּאוּת לָבֵשׁ, לָבֵשׁ יהוה עֹז הִתְאַזָּר, אַף־תִּכּוֹן תֵּבֵל בַּל־תִּמּוֹט: נָכוֹן כִּסְאֲךָ מֵאָז, מֵעוֹלָם אָתָּה: נָשְׂאוּ נְהָרוֹת יהוה, נָשְׂאוּ נְהָרוֹת קוֹלָם, יִשְׂאוּ נְהָרוֹת דָּכְיָם: ▸ מִקֹּלוֹת מַיִם רַבִּים, אַדִּירִים מִשְׁבְּרֵי־יָם, אַדִּיר בַּמָּרוֹם יהוה: עֵדֹתֶיךָ נֶאֶמְנוּ מְאֹד, לְבֵיתְךָ נַאֲוָה־קֹדֶשׁ, יהוה לְאֹרֶךְ יָמִים:

קדיש יתום

The following prayer, said by mourners, requires the presence of a מנין.
A transliteration can be found on page 1345.

אבל: **יִתְגַּדַּל** וְיִתְקַדַּשׁ שְׁמֵהּ רַבָּא (קהל: אָמֵן), בְּעָלְמָא דִּי בְרָא כִרְעוּתֵהּ. וְיַמְלִיךְ מַלְכוּתֵהּ, בְּחַיֵּיכוֹן וּבְיוֹמֵיכוֹן וּבְחַיֵּי דְכָל בֵּית יִשְׂרָאֵל, בַּעֲגָלָא וּבִזְמַן קָרִיב, וְאִמְרוּ אָמֵן. (קהל: אָמֵן)

קהל ואבל: יְהֵא שְׁמֵהּ רַבָּא מְבָרַךְ לְעָלַם וּלְעָלְמֵי עָלְמַיָּא.

אבל: יִתְבָּרַךְ וְיִשְׁתַּבַּח וְיִתְפָּאַר, וְיִתְרוֹמַם וְיִתְנַשֵּׂא וְיִתְהַדָּר וְיִתְעַלֶּה וְיִתְהַלָּל שְׁמֵהּ דְּקֻדְשָׁא בְּרִיךְ הוּא (קהל: בְּרִיךְ הוּא), לְעֵלָּא מִן כָּל בִּרְכָתָא / בשבת שובה: לְעֵלָּא (וּ)לְעֵלָּא מִכָּל בִּרְכָתָא/ וְשִׁירָתָא, תֻּשְׁבְּחָתָא וְנֶחֱמָתָא דַּאֲמִירָן בְּעָלְמָא, וְאִמְרוּ אָמֵן. (קהל: אָמֵן)

יְהֵא שְׁלָמָא רַבָּא מִן שְׁמַיָּא וְחַיִּים, עָלֵינוּ וְעַל כָּל יִשְׂרָאֵל, וְאִמְרוּ אָמֵן. (קהל: אָמֵן)

ה׳ מָלָךְ / PSALM 93
The psalm states that "גֵּאוּת לָבֵשׁ – He is clothed in majesty," because having completed the work of Creation He "wrapped" Himself in garments of glory. For this reason Psalm 93 is recited directly after the preceding Psalm 92 that celebrates Shabbat and God's acts of Creation (*Levush*).

This psalm is a continuation of Psalm 92 that has just been completed, and echoes its main theme that at the end of history God's justice will prevail and be recognized by all. They will see that God is "girded with strength," that His will cannot be thwarted forever, for even the greatest forces of nature,

and my ears have heard the doom of the wicked who rise against me. ▸ The righteous man flourishes like the palm tree. He grows like a cedar in Lebanon. They are planted in the house of the Lord. They will flourish in the courts of our God. They will still bring forth fruit in old age. They will be fat and flourishing. To declare that the Lord is upright, that He is my Rock, and there is no unrighteousness in Him.

Ps. 93 **יהוה מָלָךְ** THE LORD REIGNS, He is clothed in majesty, the Lord is clothed, He has girded Himself with strength. The world, too, is established so that it cannot be moved. You throne is established from of old. You are from everlasting. The floodwaters have lifted up, O Lord, the floodwaters have lifted up their voice, the floodwaters have lifted up their pounding. ▸ Mightier than the voices of great, mighty waters, breakers of the sea, is the Lord on high. Your testimonies are very true, in Your house, Your holy habitation, O Lord, for length of days.

MOURNER'S KADDISH

The following prayer, said by mourners, requires the presence of a minyan. A transliteration can be found on page 1345.

Mourner: **יִתְגַּדַּל** EXALTED AND HALLOWED may God's great name be, in the world He created as He willed. May He reign in your lifetimes and in your days, and in the lifetime of the whole house of Israel, speedily and soon, and say, Amen.

All: May His great name be blessed forever and all time.

Mourner: Blessed and praised, honored, extolled, glorified, adored and exalted above all be the name of the Holy One, blessed is He, (*Between Rosh Hashana & Yom Kippur:* above and) beyond any blessing, hymn, praise, or expressions of consolation that may be uttered in this world, and say, Amen.

May abundant peace descend from heaven, as well as life, for us and for all Israel, and say, Amen.

---

including mighty tides, irresistible floodwaters, or devastating tsunamis, cannot stand before God, Whose will is אַדִּיר בַּמָּרוֹם – mighty and above all (R. Samson Raphael Hirsch).

ה' לְאֹרֶךְ יָמִים – *O Lord, for length of days.* The psalm closes with a plea that when the Third Temple is finally rebuilt, it will stand for the full expanse of time, unlike the earlier two Temples that were destroyed in the course of time (R. David Kimchi).

Bow, take three steps back, as if taking leave of the Divine Presence, then bow, first left, then right, then center, while saying:

עֹשֶׂה שָׁלוֹם /בשבת שובה: הַשָּׁלוֹם/ בִּמְרוֹמָיו, הוּא יַעֲשֶׂה שָׁלוֹם עָלֵינוּ, וְעַל כָּל יִשְׂרָאֵל, וְאִמְרוּ אָמֵן. (קהל: אָמֵן)

במה מדליקין

The following is not said on שבת חול המועד *or* מוצאי יום טוב, יום טוב.

משנה שבת פרק שני

א **בַּמֶּה מַדְלִיקִין** וּבַמָּה אֵין מַדְלִיקִין. אֵין מַדְלִיקִין לֹא בְלֶכֶשׁ, וְלֹא בְחֹסֶן, וְלֹא בְכַלָּךְ, וְלֹא בִפְתִילַת הָאִידָן, וְלֹא בִפְתִילַת הַמִּדְבָּר, וְלֹא בִירוֹקָה שֶׁעַל פְּנֵי הַמָּיִם. וְלֹא בְזֶפֶת וְלֹא בְשַׁעֲוָה וְלֹא בְשֶׁמֶן קִיק וְלֹא בְשֶׁמֶן שְׂרֵפָה וְלֹא בְאַלְיָה וְלֹא בְחֵלֶב. נַחוּם הַמָּדִי אוֹמֵר: מַדְלִיקִין בְּחֵלֶב מְבֻשָּׁל, וַחֲכָמִים אוֹמְרִים: אֶחָד מְבֻשָּׁל וְאֶחָד שֶׁאֵינוֹ מְבֻשָּׁל, אֵין מַדְלִיקִין בּוֹ.

ב אֵין מַדְלִיקִין בְּשֶׁמֶן שְׂרֵפָה בְּיוֹם טוֹב. רַבִּי יִשְׁמָעֵאל אוֹמֵר: אֵין מַדְלִיקִין בְּעִטְרָן מִפְּנֵי כְּבוֹד הַשַּׁבָּת. וַחֲכָמִים מַתִּירִין בְּכָל הַשְּׁמָנִים, בְּשֶׁמֶן שֻׁמְשְׁמִין, בְּשֶׁמֶן אֱגוֹזִים, בְּשֶׁמֶן צְנוֹנוֹת, בְּשֶׁמֶן דָּגִים, בְּשֶׁמֶן פַּקּוּעוֹת, בְּעִטְרָן וּבְנֵפְט. רַבִּי טַרְפוֹן אוֹמֵר: אֵין מַדְלִיקִין אֶלָּא בְּשֶׁמֶן זַיִת בִּלְבָד.

ג כָּל הַיּוֹצֵא מִן הָעֵץ אֵין מַדְלִיקִין בּוֹ, אֶלָּא פִשְׁתָּן. וְכָל הַיּוֹצֵא מִן הָעֵץ אֵינוֹ מִטַּמֵּא טֻמְאַת אֹהָלִים, אֶלָּא פִשְׁתָּן. פְּתִילַת הַבֶּגֶד שֶׁקִּפְּלָהּ וְלֹא הִבְהֲבָהּ, רַבִּי אֱלִיעֶזֶר אוֹמֵר: טְמֵאָה הִיא, וְאֵין מַדְלִיקִין בָּהּ. רַבִּי עֲקִיבָא אוֹמֵר: טְהוֹרָה הִיא, וּמַדְלִיקִין בָּהּ.

ד לֹא יִקֹּב אָדָם שְׁפוֹפֶרֶת שֶׁל בֵּיצָה וִימַלְּאֶנָּה שֶׁמֶן וְיִתְּנֶנָּה עַל פִּי הַנֵּר, בִּשְׁבִיל שֶׁתְּהֵא מְנַטֶּפֶת, וַאֲפִילוּ הִיא שֶׁל חֶרֶס. וְרַבִּי יְהוּדָה מַתִּיר. אֲבָל

בַּמֶּה מַדְלִיקִין / BAMEH MADLIKIN
This selection of Mishna, and this particular chapter, had special resonance during Geonic times, in which traditional Judaism found itself under assault by the Karaites, a heretical sect which rejected the Oral Law and interpreted the written Torah in a manner incompatible with accepted rabbinic tradition. Among their assertions was that the Torah forbids maintaining a burning flame on Shabbat, based on a hyper-literal, nontraditional reading of Exodus 35:3 ("You shall not burn fire on Shabbat"). In their view, this verse prohibited all fire, including Shabbat candles, and as a result they spent Shabbat in cold, dark homes, eating only cold food. The present chapter

Bow, take three steps back, as if taking leave of the Divine Presence, then bow, first left, then right, then center, while saying:

May He Who makes peace in the highest heaven, make peace for us, and for all Israel, and say, Amen.

BAMEH MADLIKIN

The following is not said on Yom Tov, Motza'ei Yom Tov or Shabbat Ḥol HaMo'ed.

Mishna Shabbat, chapter 2

1. בַּמֶּה מַדְלִיקִין WITH WHAT materials may the Sabbath lamp be kindled, and with what may it not be kindled? Not with a wick made of cedar fiber, uncombed coiled flax, or floss-silk, nor with a wick made of willow fiber or wild grass, nor with aquatic reeds. Not with tree resin, liquid wax, castor oil, or consecrated oil that has become defiled and therefore has been set apart to be burned, nor with the tail fat of a sheep, nor with tallow. Naḥum the Mede declares that boiled tallow is acceptable, but the other rabbis say that tallow may not be used, whether boiled or not boiled.

2. ON A festival, too, the lights may not be kindled with defiled oil that has been set apart to be burned. R. Yishmael says that out of respect for the Sabbath, the lamp may not be lighted with resin. But the other rabbis allow all kinds of oil, including sesame oil, nut oil, radish seed oil, fish oil, colocynth seed oil, as well as resin and naphtha. R. Tarfon holds that it must be lighted only with olive oil.

3. NOTHING PRODUCED from a plant is appropriate for use as a wick except flax, because it cannot acquire tent pollution, whereas other plant products can. As for a slip of cloth that has been twisted together but not singed, R. Eliezer says it is subject to the law of pollution and must not be used for lighting, but R. Akiva declares that it remains clean and may be used.

4. ONE MAY not perforate an egg shell, fill it with oil, and place it so that the oil drips into the opening of the Shabbat lamp, nor may an earthenware vessel be used in this way. R. Yehuda allows it. But if the potter had originally

---

of Mishna thus highlights the perpetuation of the Mishnaic Oral tradition, as illustrated by the laws of Shabbat candle lighting (Prof. Naftali Wieder).

בְּעִטְרָן מִפְּנֵי כְּבוֹד הַשַּׁבָּת – *With defiled oil ... out of respect for the Sabbath.* The Shabbat candles bring "honor" to Shabbat by helping us to eat and engage in other activities in a well-lit

אִם חִבְּרָהּ הַיּוֹצֵר מִתְּחִלָּה מֻתָּר, מִפְּנֵי שֶׁהוּא כְּלִי אֶחָד. לֹא יְמַלֵּא אָדָם אֶת הַקְּעָרָה שֶׁמֶן וְיִתְּנֶנָּה בְּצַד הַנֵּר וְיִתֵּן רֹאשׁ הַפְּתִילָה בְּתוֹכָהּ, בִּשְׁבִיל שֶׁתְּהֵא שׁוֹאֶבֶת. וְרַבִּי יְהוּדָה מַתִּיר.

ה הַמְכַבֶּה אֶת הַנֵּר מִפְּנֵי שֶׁהוּא מִתְיָרֵא מִפְּנֵי גוֹיִם, מִפְּנֵי לִסְטִים, מִפְּנֵי רְוּחַ רָעָה, אוֹ בִּשְׁבִיל הַחוֹלֶה שֶׁיִּישַׁן, פָּטוּר. כְּחָס עַל הַנֵּר, כְּחָס עַל הַשֶּׁמֶן, כְּחָס עַל הַפְּתִילָה, חַיָּב. רַבִּי יוֹסֵי פּוֹטֵר בְּכֻלָּן חוּץ מִן הַפְּתִילָה, מִפְּנֵי שֶׁהוּא עוֹשָׂהּ פֶּחָם.

ו עַל שָׁלֹשׁ עֲבֵרוֹת נָשִׁים מֵתוֹת בִּשְׁעַת לֵדָתָן, עַל שֶׁאֵינָן זְהִירוֹת בַּנִּדָּה, בְּחַלָּה וּבְהַדְלָקַת הַנֵּר.

ז שְׁלֹשָׁה דְבָרִים צָרִיךְ אָדָם לוֹמַר בְּתוֹךְ בֵּיתוֹ עֶרֶב שַׁבָּת עִם חֲשֵׁכָה: עִשַּׂרְתֶּם, עֵרַבְתֶּם, הַדְלִיקוּ אֶת הַנֵּר. סָפֵק חֲשֵׁכָה סָפֵק אֵינָהּ חֲשֵׁכָה, אֵין מְעַשְּׂרִין אֶת הַוַּדַּאי, וְאֵין מַטְבִּילִין אֶת הַכֵּלִים, וְאֵין מַדְלִיקִין אֶת הַנֵּרוֹת. אֲבָל מְעַשְּׂרִין אֶת הַדְּמַאי, וּמְעָרְבִין וְטוֹמְנִין אֶת הַחַמִּין.

תַּנְיָא, אָמַר רַבִּי חֲנִינָא: חַיָּב אָדָם לְמַשְׁמֵשׁ בְּגָדָיו בְּעֶרֶב שַׁבָּת עִם חֲשֵׁכָה, שֶׁמָּא יִשְׁכַּח וְיֵצֵא. אָמַר רַב יוֹסֵף: הִלְכְתָא רַבְּתָא לְשַׁבְּתָא. שבת יב.

אָמַר רַבִּי אֶלְעָזָר, אָמַר רַבִּי חֲנִינָא: תַּלְמִידֵי חֲכָמִים מַרְבִּים שָׁלוֹם בָּעוֹלָם, ברכות סד.
שֶׁנֶּאֱמַר: וְכָל־בָּנַיִךְ לִמּוּדֵי יהוה, וְרַב שְׁלוֹם בָּנָיִךְ: אַל תִּקְרֵי בָּנָיִךְ, ישעיה נד

home. For this reason R. Yishmael prohibits use of foul-smelling materials, such as tar. Those who permit the use of tar gauge only whether a candle fuel is a reliable source of a clear light, not whether there are extraneous factors such as odor (R. Avraham Walfish).

עַל שָׁלֹשׁ עֲבֵרוֹת – *For three transgressions*. Of these three *mitzvot*, only the laws regarding family purity relate exclusively to women. The laws of separating dough and of kindling Shabbat candles apply to the household as a whole; however, inasmuch as women traditionally manage the affairs of the household, primary responsibility for these *mitzvot* is assigned to them (Rambam, *Hil. Shabbat* 5:3). The importance that the mishna ascribes to these activities, to the point of endangering a woman's life if she fails to fulfill them properly, stems from their essential role in determining the character and values of the household. The laws of family purity sanctify the relations between husband and wife; tithing sanctifies the family food; and Shabbat candles are essential for bringing peace and sanctity to the family home. The three *mitzvot* assigned to women are closely associated with three unique qualities which, according to the *Midrash*, characterized the homes of Sarah and Rebecca: their lamps

joined the two parts together, it is allowable, because then they form one vessel. Similarly, one may not fill a dish with oil, place it by the side of the Sabbath lamp, and put the end of the wick into it to draw up the oil, although R. Yehuda permits this also.

5. PUTTING OUT the Sabbath lamp is excused if it was because of fear of hostile heathen or robbers, or of an evil spirit, or so that a sick person would be able to sleep. But if done in order to save lamp, oil, or wick, it is a desecration of the Sabbath. R. Yose allows it, except in the case of saving the wick, because putting out the lamp causes tinder to form.

6. WOMEN may die in childbirth for three transgressions: failing to strictly observe the laws pertaining to menstruation, not setting aside the ḥalla portion of the dough when baking, and not kindling the Sabbath lamp.

7. ON THE EVE of the Sabbath near to dusk, a man must say three things in his home: "Have you separated the tithe? Have you prepared the *eiruv*? Light the Sabbath lamp!" If it is uncertain whether or not it is already dark, produce that has definitely not been tithed may no longer be tithed, nor may vessels be immersed for ritual cleansing, nor may Sabbath lamps be kindled. But it is still permitted to tithe something whose tithing status is uncertain, to make an eiruv, and insulate hot food.

Shabbat 12a תַּנְיָא IT HAS BEEN TAUGHT that according to R. Ḥananya, a man should search his clothing toward dusk on Sabbath eve lest he carelessly go outside carrying something. Said R. Joseph, This is an important Sabbath regulation.

Berakhot 64a אָמַר R. ELEAZAR quoted R. Ḥananya as saying that students of Torah increase peace in the world. This is in keeping with the words of the prophet Isaiah:
Is. 54 "When all your children shall be taught of the Lord, and great shall be the peace of your children." This can be said not only of your children, but of everyone who has been taught of the Lord to help build a future of peace.

---

burned from one Shabbat to the next, their dough was blessed, and a cloud – symbolizing the Divine Presence – hovered constantly over their homes (R. Avraham Walfish).

תַּלְמִידֵי חֲכָמִים מַרְבִּים שָׁלוֹם בָּעוֹלָם – *Students of Torah increase peace in the world.* Following study of a halakhic text, we usually recite an Aggadic text in order to hear *Kaddish de-Rabbanan*. Here, instead of the usual Aggadic Ḥanania ben Akashia passage, this text is recited because it mentions peace six times. This echoes a central theme of Shabbat, insofar as the Shabbat candles bring שְׁלוֹם בַּיִת (a peaceful home), a Shabbat *Eiruv* brings peace to the

אֶלָּא בּוֹנַיִךְ. שָׁלוֹם רָב לְאֹהֲבֵי תוֹרָתֶךָ, וְאֵין־לָמוֹ מִכְשׁוֹל: יְהִי־שָׁלוֹם בְּחֵילֵךְ, תהלים קיט
שַׁלְוָה בְּאַרְמְנוֹתָיִךְ. לְמַעַן אַחַי וְרֵעָי אֲדַבְּרָה־נָּא שָׁלוֹם בָּךְ: לְמַעַן בֵּית־יהוה תהלים קכב
אֱלֹהֵינוּ אֲבַקְשָׁה טוֹב לָךְ: ◂ יהוה עֹז לְעַמּוֹ יִתֵּן, יהוה יְבָרֵךְ אֶת־עַמּוֹ בַשָּׁלוֹם: תהלים כט

קדיש דרבנן

The following prayer, said by mourners, requires the presence of a מנין*.*
A transliteration can be found on page 1344.

אבל: **יִתְגַּדַּל** וְיִתְקַדַּשׁ שְׁמֵהּ רַבָּא (קהל: אָמֵן). בְּעָלְמָא דִּי בְרָא כִרְעוּתֵהּ.
וְיַמְלִיךְ מַלְכוּתֵהּ בְּחַיֵּיכוֹן וּבְיוֹמֵיכוֹן וּבְחַיֵּי דְכָל בֵּית יִשְׂרָאֵל,
בַּעֲגָלָא וּבִזְמַן קָרִיב, וְאִמְרוּ אָמֵן. (קהל: אָמֵן)

קהל ואבל: יְהֵא שְׁמֵהּ רַבָּא מְבָרַךְ לְעָלַם וּלְעָלְמֵי עָלְמַיָּא.

אבל: יִתְבָּרַךְ וְיִשְׁתַּבַּח וְיִתְפָּאַר וְיִתְרוֹמַם וְיִתְנַשֵּׂא, וְיִתְהַדָּר וְיִתְעַלֶּה
וְיִתְהַלָּל שְׁמֵהּ דְּקֻדְשָׁא בְּרִיךְ הוּא (קהל: בְּרִיךְ הוּא), לְעֵלָּא מִן כָּל בִּרְכָתָא
/בשבת שובה: לְעֵלָּא (וּ)לְעֵלָּא מִכָּל בִּרְכָתָא/ וְשִׁירָתָא, תֻּשְׁבְּחָתָא וְנֶחֱמָתָא
דַּאֲמִירָן בְּעָלְמָא, וְאִמְרוּ אָמֵן. (קהל: אָמֵן)

עַל יִשְׂרָאֵל וְעַל רַבָּנָן, וְעַל תַּלְמִידֵיהוֹן וְעַל כָּל תַּלְמִידֵי תַלְמִידֵיהוֹן,
וְעַל כָּל מָאן דְּעָסְקִין בְּאוֹרַיְתָא, דִּי בְאַתְרָא הָדֵין, וְדִי בְכָל אֲתַר
וַאֲתַר, יְהֵא לְהוֹן וּלְכוֹן שְׁלָמָא רַבָּא, חִנָּא וְחִסְדָּא, וְרַחֲמֵי, וְחַיֵּי אֲרִיכֵי,
וּמְזוֹנֵי רְוִיחֵי, וּפֻרְקָנָא מִן קֳדָם אֲבוּהוֹן דִּי בִשְׁמַיָּא, וְאִמְרוּ אָמֵן.
(קהל: אָמֵן)

יְהֵא שְׁלָמָא רַבָּא מִן שְׁמַיָּא וְחַיִּים, עָלֵינוּ וְעַל כָּל יִשְׂרָאֵל, וְאִמְרוּ
אָמֵן. (קהל: אָמֵן)

Bow, take three steps back, as if taking leave of the Divine Presence, then bow, first left, then right, then center, while saying:

עֹשֶׂה שָׁלוֹם /בשבת שובה: הַשָּׁלוֹם/ בִּמְרוֹמָיו, הוּא יַעֲשֶׂה שָׁלוֹם עָלֵינוּ,
וְעַל כָּל יִשְׂרָאֵל, וְאִמְרוּ אָמֵן. (קהל: אָמֵן)

לְאֹהֲבֵי תוֹרָתֶךָ – *Those who love Your Torah.* Not only those who study Torah, but even those who only *love* Torah can share in its blessing of

Jewish community (Yerushalmi, *Eiruvin* ch. 3), and Shabbat itself is the harbinger of a world fully at peace (R. Chaim Berlin).

Ps. 119 Those who love Your Torah enjoy great peace, and for them there is no stumbling. May your walls be enclosures of peace, Your mansions secure.
Ps. 122 For the sake of my brethren and friends I would say, Peace be with you. For
Ps. 29 the sake of the house of the Lord our God I will seek your good. ▸ The Lord will strengthen His people, the Lord will bless His people with peace.

THE RABBIS' KADDISH

The following prayer, said by mourners, requires the presence of a minyan. A transliteration can be found on page 1344.

Mourner: יִתְגַּדַּל EXALTED AND HALLOWED may God's great name be, in the world He created as He willed. May He reign in your lifetimes and in your days, and in the lifetime of the whole house of Israel, speedily and soon, and say, Amen.

All: May His great name be blessed forever and all time.

Mourner: Blessed and praised, honored, extolled, glorified, adored and exalted above all be the name of the Holy One, blessed is He, (*Between Rosh Hashana & Yom Kippur:* above and) beyond any blessing, hymn, praise, or expressions of consolation that may be uttered in this world, and say, Amen.

May the Jewish people, and our teachers, together with their students and all their students' students, as well as all who engage in Torah study here and in every other place, have abundant peace, grace, kindness, mercy, length of days, abundant food, and deliverance at the hands of their heavenly Father, and say, Amen.

May abundant peace descend from heaven, as well as life, for us and for all Israel, and say, Amen.

Bow, take three steps back, as if taking leave of the Divine Presence, then bow, first left, then right, then center, while saying:

May He Who makes peace in the highest heaven, make peace for us, and for all Israel, and say, Amen.

---

peace, even if they are not scholars. Thus the sages speak frequently of the reward awaiting those who support and respect Torah scholars (*Etz Yosef*).

מעריב לשבת וליום טוב

ברכות קריאת שמע

The following blessing and response are said only in the presence of a מנין.
The שליח ציבור *says the following (while bowing at* בָּרְכוּ *and straightening at Hashem).*
The קהל *followed by the* שליח ציבור *responds by bowing at* בָּרוּךְ *and standing straight at Hashem.*

ש״ץ: **בָּרְכוּ** אֶת יהוה הַמְבֹרָךְ.

קהל: בָּרוּךְ יהוה הַמְבֹרָךְ לְעוֹלָם וָעֶד.

ש״ץ: בָּרוּךְ יהוה הַמְבֹרָךְ לְעוֹלָם וָעֶד.

בָּרוּךְ אַתָּה יהוה אֱלֹהֵינוּ מֶלֶךְ הָעוֹלָם, אֲשֶׁר בִּדְבָרוֹ מַעֲרִיב עֲרָבִים, בְּחָכְמָה פּוֹתֵחַ שְׁעָרִים, וּבִתְבוּנָה מְשַׁנֶּה עִתִּים וּמַחֲלִיף אֶת הַזְּמַנִּים, וּמְסַדֵּר אֶת הַכּוֹכָבִים בְּמִשְׁמְרוֹתֵיהֶם בָּרָקִיעַ כִּרְצוֹנוֹ. בּוֹרֵא יוֹם וָלָיְלָה, גּוֹלֵל אוֹר מִפְּנֵי חֹשֶׁךְ וְחֹשֶׁךְ מִפְּנֵי אוֹר, ◂ וּמַעֲבִיר יוֹם וּמֵבִיא לָיְלָה, וּמַבְדִּיל בֵּין יוֹם וּבֵין לָיְלָה, יהוה צְבָאוֹת שְׁמוֹ. אֵל חַי וְקַיָּם, תָּמִיד יִמְלֹךְ עָלֵינוּ לְעוֹלָם וָעֶד. בָּרוּךְ אַתָּה יהוה, הַמַּעֲרִיב עֲרָבִים.

אַהֲבַת עוֹלָם בֵּית יִשְׂרָאֵל עַמְּךָ אָהָבְתָּ, תּוֹרָה וּמִצְוֹת, חֻקִּים וּמִשְׁפָּטִים, אוֹתָנוּ לִמַּדְתָּ, עַל כֵּן יהוה אֱלֹהֵינוּ

THE ABSENCE OF וְהוּא רַחוּם PRECEDING BAREKHU ON SHABBAT
On Shabbat we omit the usual *VeHu Raḥum* verses that precede *Barekhu*. This is because these verses ask God to forgive our transgressions and "answer us on the day that we cry out to Him." Such thoughts contradict the spirit of Shabbat, for it is neither a day of focusing on our failures, nor a day on which we feel in need or deprived. For the same reason the middle sections of the various *Amidot* throughout Shabbat do not feature the usual supplications and petitions (*Kol Bo*).

ה׳ צְבָאוֹת שְׁמוֹ – *Lord of hosts is His name.* The Gemara (*Berakhot* 31b) teaches that Hannah

ONE WHO COMES LATE TO MA'ARIV
If one comes late to *Ma'ariv*, the highest priority is to recite the *Amida* together with the congregation, even if one must skip *Keriat Shema* and its blessings and recite them after the prayers (*OḤ* 326:3).

MA'ARIV FOR SHABBAT AND YOM TOV

BLESSINGS OF THE SHEMA

The following blessing and response are said only in the presence of a minyan. The Leader says the following (while bowing at "Barekhu" and straightening at Hashem). The congregation followed by the Leader responds by bowing at "Barukh" and standing straight at Hashem.

Leader: בָּרְכוּ BLESS THE LORD, the blessed One.

Cong: Blessed is the Lord Who is blessed for all eternity.

Leader: Blessed is the Lord Who is blessed for all eternity.

בָּרוּךְ BLESSED ARE YOU, Lord, our God, King of the universe, at Whose command evening occurs, Who opens gates with wisdom, Who alters time periods and changes seasons with understanding, and Who places the stars in order according to their respective duties in heaven, in accordance with His will. He creates both day and night, making light give way to darkness, and darkness to light. ▸ He causes day to pass away and brings night, and separates day from night – Lord of hosts is His name. He is the living and enduring God, Who will always rule over us, forever and ever. Blessed are You, Lord, Who makes evening occur.

אַהֲבַת עוֹלָם WITH EVERLASTING LOVE have You loved the house of Israel Your people. You have taught us Torah and commandments,

---

was the first one to use the name "God of Hosts" when she asked God, "Given that You created all of the heavenly hosts, is it too difficult to grant me a child?" From this we learn that it took a brokenhearted woman to recognize that the same God Who creates and controls the cosmos can also respond to the heartfelt prayer of a single individual.

INTERRUPTIONS DURING THE BLESSINGS OF SHEMA

As a general rule during *Ma'ariv* one should not speak from *Barekhu* until after the *Amida*. As in *Shaharit* (see page 89), there are certain exceptions (*MB* 236:1). At *Ma'ariv* the *Gabbai* is permitted to announce the insertions of *Ya'aleh VeYavo, Tal uMatar* or *Al HaNissim* before the *Amida* (*OḤ* 236:2 and *MB* 236:7).

בְּשָׁכְבֵנוּ וּבְקוּמֵנוּ נָשִׂיחַ בְּחֻקֶּיךָ, וְנִשְׂמַח בְּדִבְרֵי תוֹרָתֶךָ וּבְמִצְוֹתֶיךָ
לְעוֹלָם וָעֶד, ◂ כִּי הֵם חַיֵּינוּ וְאֹרֶךְ יָמֵינוּ, וּבָהֶם נֶהְגֶּה יוֹמָם וָלָיְלָה.
וְאַהֲבָתְךָ אַל תָּסִיר מִמֶּנּוּ לְעוֹלָמִים. בָּרוּךְ אַתָּה יהוה, אוֹהֵב עַמּוֹ
יִשְׂרָאֵל.

שמע

The שמע must be said with intense concentration. In the first paragraph one should accept, with love, the sovereignty of God; in the second, accept the מצוות as the will of God. The end of the third paragraph constitutes fulfillment of the מצווה to remember, morning and evening, the Exodus from Egypt.

When not praying with a מנין, some say:

אֵל מֶלֶךְ נֶאֱמָן

The following verse should be said aloud, while covering the eyes with the right hand:

דברים ו

שְׁמַע יִשְׂרָאֵל, יהוה אֱלֹהֵינוּ, יהוה | אֶחָד:

Quietly בָּרוּךְ שֵׁם כְּבוֹד מַלְכוּתוֹ לְעוֹלָם וָעֶד.

דברים ו

וְאָהַבְתָּ אֵת יהוה אֱלֹהֶיךָ, בְּכָל־לְבָבְךָ וּבְכָל־נַפְשְׁךָ וּבְכָל־מְאֹדֶךָ:
וְהָיוּ הַדְּבָרִים הָאֵלֶּה, אֲשֶׁר אָנֹכִי מְצַוְּךָ הַיּוֹם, עַל־לְבָבֶךָ:
וְשִׁנַּנְתָּם לְבָנֶיךָ וְדִבַּרְתָּ בָּם, בְּשִׁבְתְּךָ בְּבֵיתֶךָ וּבְלֶכְתְּךָ בַדֶּרֶךְ, וּבְשָׁכְבְּךָ
וּבְקוּמֶךָ: וּקְשַׁרְתָּם לְאוֹת עַל־יָדֶךָ וְהָיוּ לְטֹטָפֹת בֵּין עֵינֶיךָ: וּכְתַבְתָּם
עַל־מְזֻזוֹת בֵּיתֶךָ וּבִשְׁעָרֶיךָ:

דברים יא

וְהָיָה אִם־שָׁמֹעַ תִּשְׁמְעוּ אֶל־מִצְוֺתַי אֲשֶׁר אָנֹכִי מְצַוֶּה אֶתְכֶם
הַיּוֹם, לְאַהֲבָה אֶת־יהוה אֱלֹהֵיכֶם וּלְעָבְדוֹ, בְּכָל־לְבַבְכֶם
וּבְכָל־נַפְשְׁכֶם: וְנָתַתִּי מְטַר־אַרְצְכֶם בְּעִתּוֹ, יוֹרֶה וּמַלְקוֹשׁ, וְאָסַפְתָּ
דְגָנֶךָ וְתִירֹשְׁךָ וְיִצְהָרֶךָ: וְנָתַתִּי עֵשֶׂב בְּשָׂדְךָ לִבְהֶמְתֶּךָ, וְאָכַלְתָּ
וְשָׂבָעְתָּ: הִשָּׁמְרוּ לָכֶם פֶּן־יִפְתֶּה לְבַבְכֶם, וְסַרְתֶּם וַעֲבַדְתֶּם אֱלֹהִים
אֲחֵרִים וְהִשְׁתַּחֲוִיתֶם לָהֶם: וְחָרָה אַף־יהוה בָּכֶם, וְעָצַר אֶת־
הַשָּׁמַיִם וְלֹא־יִהְיֶה מָטָר, וְהָאֲדָמָה לֹא תִתֵּן אֶת־יְבוּלָהּ, וַאֲבַדְתֶּם

וְאָהַבְתָּ – *You shall love.* Rambam (*Hil. Teshuva* 10:3) explains that the way we are to love God is with a passion so powerful that our souls are constantly consumed with Him, like a man who is so lovesick for a woman that he cannot stop thinking of her.

statutes and laws. Therefore, Lord our God, whenever we lie down to sleep, and whenever we arise, we will discuss Your statutes, and rejoice in the words of Your Torah and Your commandments forever and ever. ▸ For they are our life and our length of days, and we will meditate on them day and night. May You never deprive us of Your love. Blessed are You, Lord, Who loves His people Israel.

SHEMA

The Shema must be said with intense concentration. In the first paragraph one should accept, with love, the sovereignty of God; in the second, accept the mitzvot as the will of God. The end of the third paragraph constitutes fulfillment of the mitzva to remember, morning and evening, the Exodus from Egypt.

When not praying with a minyan, some say:

God, the King Who is faithful.

The following verse should be said aloud, while covering the eyes with the right hand:

Deut. 6 HEAR, O ISRAEL, the LORD is our God, the LORD is One.

Quietly: Blessed be His name and His glorious kingdom forever and ever.

Deut. 6 וְאָהַבְתָּ YOU SHALL LOVE the LORD your God with all your heart, and with all your soul, and with all your might. And these words which I command you this day shall be upon your heart. You shall teach them diligently to your children, speaking of them when you sit in your house and when you walk by the way, when you lie down and when you rise up. You shall bind them for a sign on your hand, and they shall be as *tefillin* between your eyes. And you shall write them upon the doorposts of your house and upon your gates.

Deut. 11 וְהָיָה IT SHALL COME to PASS pass that if you will listen diligently to My commandments with which I charge you this day, to love the Lord your God and to serve Him with all your heart and with all your soul, then will I send the rain for your land in its due season, the autumn rain and the spring rain, that you may gather in your corn, your wine, and your oil. And I will give grass in your field for your cattle, and you shall eat and be satisfied. Be careful lest your heart be deceived, and you turn aside and serve other gods and worship them. For then the Lord's wrath will be kindled against you, and He will shut the heavens so that there will be no rain, the land will not yield her produce, and

מְהֵרָה מֵעַל הָאָרֶץ הַטֹּבָה אֲשֶׁר יהוה נֹתֵן לָכֶם: וְשַׂמְתֶּם אֶת־דְּבָרַי אֵלֶּה עַל־לְבַבְכֶם וְעַל־נַפְשְׁכֶם, וּקְשַׁרְתֶּם אֹתָם לְאוֹת עַל־יֶדְכֶם, וְהָיוּ לְטוֹטָפֹת בֵּין עֵינֵיכֶם: וְלִמַּדְתֶּם אֹתָם אֶת־בְּנֵיכֶם לְדַבֵּר בָּם, בְּשִׁבְתְּךָ בְּבֵיתֶךָ וּבְלֶכְתְּךָ בַדֶּרֶךְ, וּבְשָׁכְבְּךָ וּבְקוּמֶךָ: וּכְתַבְתָּם עַל־מְזוּזוֹת בֵּיתֶךָ וּבִשְׁעָרֶיךָ: לְמַעַן יִרְבּוּ יְמֵיכֶם וִימֵי בְנֵיכֶם עַל הָאֲדָמָה אֲשֶׁר נִשְׁבַּע יהוה לַאֲבֹתֵיכֶם לָתֵת לָהֶם, כִּימֵי הַשָּׁמַיִם עַל־הָאָרֶץ:

במדבר טו **וַיֹּאמֶר** יהוה אֶל־מֹשֶׁה לֵּאמֹר: דַּבֵּר אֶל־בְּנֵי יִשְׂרָאֵל וְאָמַרְתָּ אֲלֵהֶם, וְעָשׂוּ לָהֶם צִיצִת עַל־כַּנְפֵי בִגְדֵיהֶם לְדֹרֹתָם, וְנָתְנוּ עַל־צִיצִת הַכָּנָף פְּתִיל תְּכֵלֶת: וְהָיָה לָכֶם לְצִיצִת, וּרְאִיתֶם אֹתוֹ וּזְכַרְתֶּם אֶת־כָּל־מִצְוֹת יהוה וַעֲשִׂיתֶם אֹתָם, וְלֹא תָתֻרוּ אַחֲרֵי לְבַבְכֶם וְאַחֲרֵי עֵינֵיכֶם, אֲשֶׁר־אַתֶּם זֹנִים אַחֲרֵיהֶם: לְמַעַן תִּזְכְּרוּ וַעֲשִׂיתֶם אֶת־כָּל־מִצְוֹתָי, וִהְיִיתֶם קְדֹשִׁים לֵאלֹהֵיכֶם: אֲנִי יהוה אֱלֹהֵיכֶם, אֲשֶׁר הוֹצֵאתִי אֶתְכֶם מֵאֶרֶץ מִצְרַיִם, לִהְיוֹת לָכֶם לֵאלֹהִים, אֲנִי יהוה אֱלֹהֵיכֶם: **אֱמֶת**

The שליח ציבור *repeats:*

◂ יהוה אֱלֹהֵיכֶם אֱמֶת

וֶאֱמוּנָה כָּל זֹאת וְקַיָּם עָלֵינוּ, כִּי הוּא יהוה אֱלֹהֵינוּ וְאֵין זוּלָתוֹ, וַאֲנַחְנוּ יִשְׂרָאֵל עַמּוֹ. הַפּוֹדֵנוּ מִיַּד מְלָכִים, מַלְכֵּנוּ הַגּוֹאֲלֵנוּ מִכַּף כָּל הֶעָרִיצִים. הָאֵל הַנִּפְרָע לָנוּ מִצָּרֵינוּ, וְהַמְשַׁלֵּם גְּמוּל לְכָל אוֹיְבֵי נַפְשֵׁנוּ. הָעוֹשֶׂה גְדוֹלוֹת עַד אֵין חֵקֶר, וְנִפְלָאוֹת
תהלים סו עַד אֵין מִסְפָּר, הַשָּׂם נַפְשֵׁנוּ בַּחַיִּים, וְלֹא־נָתַן לַמּוֹט רַגְלֵנוּ:
הַמַּדְרִיכֵנוּ עַל בָּמוֹת אוֹיְבֵינוּ, וַיָּרֶם קַרְנֵנוּ עַל כָּל שׂוֹנְאֵינוּ. הָעוֹשֶׂה לָּנוּ נִסִּים וּנְקָמָה בְּפַרְעֹה, אוֹתוֹת וּמוֹפְתִים בְּאַדְמַת בְּנֵי חָם. הַמַּכֶּה בְעֶבְרָתוֹ כָּל בְּכוֹרֵי מִצְרָיִם, וַיּוֹצֵא אֶת עַמּוֹ יִשְׂרָאֵל מִתּוֹכָם

you shall perish quickly from the good land which the Lord gives you. Therefore place these words of Mine upon your heart and upon your soul, and you shall bind them for a sign on your hand and they shall be as *tefillin* between your eyes. And you shall teach them to your children, speaking of them when you sit in your house and when you walk on the way, when you lie down and when you rise up. And you shall write them upon the doorposts of your house and upon your gates. That long as the days of the heavens above the earth may be your days and the days of your children in the land which the Lord promised your fathers to give to them.

Num. 15 וַיֹּאמֶר THE LORD SPOKE to Moses, saying: "Speak to the children of Israel and tell them to make for themselves *tzitzit* on the corners of their garments, throughout their generations, putting a thread of blue upon the *tzitzit* of each corner. It shall be to you a *tzitzit* which you may look upon and remember all the commandments of the LORD and do them, that you shall not stray after your heart and your eyes, after which you sinfully follow. So may you remember and do all My commandments and be holy for your God. I am the LORD your God who brought you out of the land of Egypt to be your God; I am the LORD your God." TRUE IT IS –

The Leader repeats:

▸ The LORD your God. True it is –

וֶאֱמוּנָה AND UNCHANGING in its entirety, and binding on us, that He is the Lord our God and there is none beside Him, and we Israel are His people. He redeems us from the might of kings, our King Who saves us from the hand of all oppressors. He is the God Who delivers us from our foes, Who brings retribution on all our mortal enemies. "Who does
Ps. 66 great things beyond our understanding, and innumerable wonders." He has bestowed life on our souls, and prevented our feet from stumbling He has led us to surmount our enemies, and has raised our strength above all who hate us. He performed miracles on our behalf, while bringing vengeance upon Pharaoh; with signs and wonders in the land of the children of Ham. In His wrath He struck down all the firstborn

לְחֵרוּת עוֹלָם. הַמַּעֲבִיר בָּנָיו בֵּין גִּזְרֵי יַם סוּף, אֶת רוֹדְפֵיהֶם וְאֶת שׂוֹנְאֵיהֶם בִּתְהוֹמוֹת טִבַּע, וְרָאוּ בָנָיו גְּבוּרָתוֹ, שִׁבְּחוּ וְהוֹדוּ לִשְׁמוֹ, ◂ וּמַלְכוּתוֹ בְּרָצוֹן קִבְּלוּ עֲלֵיהֶם. מֹשֶׁה וּבְנֵי יִשְׂרָאֵל, לְךָ עָנוּ שִׁירָה בְּשִׂמְחָה רַבָּה, וְאָמְרוּ כֻלָּם,

שמות טו מִי־כָמֹכָה בָּאֵלִם יהוה, מִי כָּמֹכָה נֶאְדָּר בַּקֹּדֶשׁ, נוֹרָא תְהִלֹּת עֹשֵׂה פֶלֶא:

◂ מַלְכוּתְךָ רָאוּ בָנֶיךָ, בּוֹקֵעַ יָם לִפְנֵי מֹשֶׁה, זֶה אֵלִי עָנוּ, וְאָמְרוּ,

שמות טו יהוה יִמְלֹךְ לְעֹלָם וָעֶד:

ירמיהו לא ◂ וְנֶאֱמַר, כִּי־פָדָה יהוה אֶת־יַעֲקֹב, וּגְאָלוֹ מִיַּד חָזָק מִמֶּנּוּ: בָּרוּךְ אַתָּה יהוה, גָּאַל יִשְׂרָאֵל.

הַשְׁכִּיבֵנוּ יהוה אֱלֹהֵינוּ לְשָׁלוֹם, וְהַעֲמִידֵנוּ מַלְכֵּנוּ לְחַיִּים, וּפְרֹשׂ עָלֵינוּ סֻכַּת שְׁלוֹמֶךָ, וְתַקְּנֵנוּ בְּעֵצָה טוֹבָה מִלְּפָנֶיךָ, וְהוֹשִׁיעֵנוּ לְמַעַן שְׁמֶךָ. וְהָגֵן בַּעֲדֵנוּ, וְהָסֵר מֵעָלֵינוּ אוֹיֵב, דֶּבֶר וְחֶרֶב וְרָעָב וְיָגוֹן, וְהָסֵר שָׂטָן מִלְּפָנֵינוּ וּמֵאַחֲרֵינוּ, וּבְצֵל כְּנָפֶיךָ תַּסְתִּירֵנוּ, כִּי אֵל שׁוֹמְרֵנוּ וּמַצִּילֵנוּ אָתָּה, כִּי אֵל מֶלֶךְ חַנּוּן וְרַחוּם אָתָּה. ◂ וּשְׁמֹר צֵאתֵנוּ וּבוֹאֵנוּ לְחַיִּים וּלְשָׁלוֹם מֵעַתָּה וְעַד עוֹלָם. וּפְרֹשׂ עָלֵינוּ סֻכַּת שְׁלוֹמֶךָ. בָּרוּךְ אַתָּה יהוה, הַפּוֹרֵשׂ סֻכַּת שָׁלוֹם עָלֵינוּ וְעַל כָּל עַמּוֹ יִשְׂרָאֵל וְעַל יְרוּשָׁלָיִם.

לְחֵרוּת עוֹלָם – *To everlasting freedom*. How can we declare that as a result of the Exodus we have "everlasting freedom" if subsequent to the Exodus there have been periods when the Jewish people has been subjugated by other nations, whether in the land of Israel or in the Diaspora? The answer is that "everlasting freedom" refers not to political servitude but to the spiritual emancipation that resulted from the Exodus and its ensuing Revelation at Sinai. This freedom of spirit has indeed been everlasting, irrespective of subjugation or exile, for ever since then the Jewish people has adhered to the Torah and its *mitzvot* (R. Shlomo Zalman Auerbach).

אֶת רוֹדְפֵיהֶם וְאֶת שׂוֹנְאֵיהֶם בִּתְהוֹמוֹת טִבַּע – *Drowned their pursuers and those who hated them, in its depths*. This phrase distinguishes

of Egypt, and brought out His people Israel from amongst them to everlasting freedom. He led His children through the divided Sea of Reeds, and drowned their pursuers and those who hated them, in its depths. When His children beheld His power, they gave praise and thanks to His name. ▸ It was then that they enthusiastically accepted His sovereignty over them. Then Moses and the children of Israel sang to You with great joy, all proclaiming:

Ex. 15 WHO IS LIKE YOU, Lord, among the mighty? Who is like You, glorious in holiness, awesome beyond praise, working wonders?

▸ Your children beheld Your sovereignty when You split the sea apart before Moses. "This is my God," they proclaimed, and then declared,

Ex. 15 "THE LORD shall reign forever and ever."

Jer. 31 ▸ And it is said: "For the Lord redeemed Jacob, and rescued him from the hand of one stronger than he." Blessed are You, Lord, Who redeemed Israel.

הַשְׁכִּיבֵנוּ LAY US DOWN in peace, Lord our God, and raise us up, our King, to life. Spread over us the canopy of Your peace, and direct us with Your wise guidance. Save us for the sake of Your name. Shield us and ward off from us enemies, epidemics, violence, hunger, and sorrow. Remove Satan from before us and from behind us. Shelter us in the shadow of Your wings, for You, God, are our Guardian and Deliverer, insofar as You are a gracious and merciful God and King. ▸ Guard our going out and our coming in, for the sake of life and peace now and forever. And spread over us the canopy of Your peace. Blessed are You, Lord, Who spreads a canopy of peace over us, and over all His people Israel, and over Jerusalem.

---

between "their pursuers" and "their haters," for the following reason. The Torah states that "Israel saw the great hand that God wielded against Egypt and they feared God" (Ex. 14:31). Why does it not say that they saw "God's great hand that saved Israel?" Furthermore why did this lead them to fear God any more than the earlier plagues or the fact of the Exodus itself? The answer to both questions is that it was precisely the way in which God destroyed the pursuers that caused great fear among the Israelites. Those Egyptians who hated them

On שבת*, the* קהל *stands and, together with the* שליח ציבור*, says:*

שמות לא
וְשָׁמְרוּ בְנֵי־יִשְׂרָאֵל אֶת־הַשַּׁבָּת, לַעֲשׂוֹת אֶת־הַשַּׁבָּת לְדֹרֹתָם בְּרִית עוֹלָם: בֵּינִי וּבֵין בְּנֵי יִשְׂרָאֵל, אוֹת הִוא לְעֹלָם, כִּי־שֵׁשֶׁת יָמִים עָשָׂה יהוה אֶת־הַשָּׁמַיִם וְאֶת־הָאָרֶץ, וּבַיּוֹם הַשְּׁבִיעִי שָׁבַת וַיִּנָּפַשׁ:

On יום טוב *of the* שלוש רגלים*, say:*

ויקרא כג
וַיְדַבֵּר מֹשֶׁה אֶת־מֹעֲדֵי יהוה אֶל־בְּנֵי יִשְׂרָאֵל:

חצי קדיש

ש״ץ: **יִתְגַּדַּל** וְיִתְקַדַּשׁ שְׁמֵהּ רַבָּא (קהל: אָמֵן) בְּעָלְמָא דִּי בְרָא כִרְעוּתֵהּ, וְיַמְלִיךְ מַלְכוּתֵהּ בְּחַיֵּיכוֹן וּבְיוֹמֵיכוֹן וּבְחַיֵּי דְכָל בֵּית יִשְׂרָאֵל, בַּעֲגָלָא וּבִזְמַן קָרִיב, וְאִמְרוּ אָמֵן. (קהל: אָמֵן)

קהל וש״ץ: יְהֵא שְׁמֵהּ רַבָּא מְבָרַךְ לְעָלַם וּלְעָלְמֵי עָלְמַיָּא.

ש״ץ: יִתְבָּרַךְ וְיִשְׁתַּבַּח וְיִתְפָּאַר וְיִתְרוֹמַם וְיִתְנַשֵּׂא, וְיִתְהַדָּר וְיִתְעַלֶּה וְיִתְהַלָּל שְׁמֵהּ דְּקֻדְשָׁא בְּרִיךְ הוּא (קהל: בְּרִיךְ הוּא), לְעֵלָּא מִן כָּל בִּרְכָתָא / בשבת שובה: לְעֵלָּא (וּ)לְעֵלָּא מִכָּל בִּרְכָתָא / וְשִׁירָתָא, תֻּשְׁבְּחָתָא וְנֶחֱמָתָא דַּאֲמִירָן בְּעָלְמָא, וְאִמְרוּ אָמֵן. (קהל: אָמֵן)

On יום טוב *(including one that falls on* שבת*)*
say the appropriate עמידה *on page 810.*

(שׂוֹנְאֵיהֶם) suffered a much more painful death than רוֹדְפֵיהֶם, i.e., those who only pursued them because they were under orders to do so. Seeing such all-knowing divine punishment at work, the Israelites became especially fearful of their own future fate when they themselves would be judged by God for their own actions (*Netziv*).

הַפּוֹרֵשׂ סֻכַּת שָׁלוֹם – *Who spreads a canopy of peace* (previous page). On week nights this prayer concludes with "He safeguards His people forever," but on Shabbat and Yom Tov we are not in need of extra divine protection, for it is the Shabbat itself that guards us (Abudarham).

לַעֲשׂוֹת אֶת־הַשַּׁבָּת – *Observing the Sabbath.* Shabbat observance is not only about abstaining from certain activities, but also

On Shabbat, the congregation stands and, together with the Leader, says:

Ex. 31 וְשָׁמְרוּ THE CHILDREN of Israel shall keep the Sabbath, observing the Sabbath throughout their generations as an everlasting covenant. It is a sign forever, between Me and the children of Israel, that the Lord made heaven and earth in six days, and He rested on the seventh day and was refreshed.

On Yom Tov of the Three Festivals, say:

Lev. 23 וַיְדַבֵּר MOSES DECLARED the appointed festival seasons of the Lord to the children of Israel.

HALF KADDISH

Leader: יִתְגַּדַּל EXALTED AND HALLOWED may God's great name be, in the world He created as He willed. May He reign in your lifetimes and in your days, and in the lifetime of the whole house of Israel, speedily and soon, and say, Amen.

All: May His great name be blessed forever and all time.

Leader: Blessed and praised, honored, extolled, glorified, adored and exalted above all be the name of the Holy One, blessed is He, (*Between Rosh Hashana & Yom Kippur:* above and) beyond any blessing, hymn, praise, or expressions of consolation that may be uttered in this world, and say, Amen.

On Yom Tov (including one that falls on Shabbat) say the appropriate Amida on page 811.

---

about performing positive acts. These include proactively extending Shabbat so that it begins before its designated time, and beginning the day by lighting candles and reciting *Kiddush*. Furthermore there are two rabbinically enacted Shabbat obligations derived from Isaiah 58:13, stating "you shall call Shabbat an עֹנֶג (a delight) and the holy day of the Lord מְכֻבָּד (honored)."

With the arrival of Shabbat, as the prefiguration of the Messianic era, we are to consider all of our labors completed (*Mekhilta*). In the Kabbalistic view of Shabbat as a day of mystical union of God and the Jewish people, the seven blessings of the Shabbat *Amida* parallel the שֶׁבַע בְּרָכוֹת, the seven blessings under the wedding canopy and the days that follow.

עמידה

One begins the עמידה *by taking three steps forward (OH 95:1). According to some traditions, one should first take three steps back before moving forward (MB 95:3). The* עמידה *is recited with one's feet together. One should try to concentrate on the simple meaning of the words of the* עמידה *with the awareness throughout that one is standing in the presence of the Almighty (OH 98:1 and MB 98:1). At the points indicated by ▾, bend the knees at the first word, bow at the second, and stand straight before saying God's name.*

אֲדֹנָי, שְׂפָתַי תִּפְתָּח, וּפִי יַגִּיד תְּהִלָּתֶךָ: תהלים נא

אבות

▾**בָּרוּךְ** אַתָּה יהוה, אֱלֹהֵינוּ וֵאלֹהֵי אֲבוֹתֵינוּ, אֱלֹהֵי אַבְרָהָם, אֱלֹהֵי יִצְחָק, וֵאלֹהֵי יַעֲקֹב, הָאֵל הַגָּדוֹל הַגִּבּוֹר וְהַנּוֹרָא, אֵל עֶלְיוֹן, גּוֹמֵל חֲסָדִים טוֹבִים, וְקוֹנֵה הַכֹּל, וְזוֹכֵר חַסְדֵי אָבוֹת, וּמֵבִיא גוֹאֵל לִבְנֵי בְנֵיהֶם לְמַעַן שְׁמוֹ בְּאַהֲבָה.

בשבת שובה: זָכְרֵנוּ לְחַיִּים, מֶלֶךְ חָפֵץ בַּחַיִּים, וְכָתְבֵנוּ בְּסֵפֶר הַחַיִּים, לְמַעַנְךָ אֱלֹהִים חַיִּים.

(If forgotten, no corrective action is necessary.)

מֶלֶךְ עוֹזֵר וּמוֹשִׁיעַ וּמָגֵן. ▾בָּרוּךְ אַתָּה יהוה, מָגֵן אַבְרָהָם.

גבורות

אַתָּה גִּבּוֹר לְעוֹלָם, אֲדֹנָי, מְחַיֵּה מֵתִים אַתָּה, רַב לְהוֹשִׁיעַ.

בחורף: מַשִּׁיב הָרוּחַ וּמוֹרִיד הַגֶּשֶׁם

עֲמִידָה שֶׁל שַׁבָּת / THE SHABBAT AMIDA

Unlike the weekday and even Yom Tov *Amidot* in which the middle section is the same throughout the day, on Shabbat the middle section changes with each *Amida*. This is because Shabbat prayer spans, and describes, the beginning, middle, and end of human history. The Friday night *Amida* focuses on the Shabbat of Creation, the *Shaharit Amida* corresponds to the Shabbat of Sinai, and the *Minha Amida* anticipates the Shabbat of the end of time (*Tur*).

The Arizal explains this prayer progression as reflecting, in marital terms, the intensifying stages of the love between God and His people. The Friday night *Amida* describes their betrothal (קִדּוּשִׁין\אַתָּה קִדַּשְׁתָּ) when the bride (Israel) is designated for the groom (God), precluding her from any similar relationship to others, but not yet permitted to join completely with her beloved. Historically this corresponds to the Exodus from Egypt when Israel was separated from the nations, but not yet "together with

For laws regarding "Omission/Insertion of *Mashiv Haru'ah*," see page 109.

AMIDA

One begins the Amida by taking three steps forward (OḤ 95:1). According to some traditions, one should first take three steps back before moving forward (MB 95:3). The Amida is recited with one's feet together. One should try to concentrate on the simple meaning of the words of the Amida with the awareness throughout that one is standing in the presence of the Almighty. (OḤ 98:1 and MB 98:1)
At the points indicated by ▾, bend the knees at the first word, bow at the second, and stand straight before saying God's name.

Ps. 51 "O MY MASTER, open my lips, and my mouth will relate Your praise."

PATRIARCHS

▾בָּרוּךְ BLESSED ARE YOU, LORD, our God and the God of our fathers, the God of Abraham, the God of Isaac, and the God of Jacob, the God Who is great, mighty, and awesome, God most exalted, Who bestows rewards of benevolent kindness, Who is the Creator of everything, Who remembers all the kind acts of the fathers, and Who brings a redeemer to their children's children, for the sake of His name, with love.

On Shabbat Shuva: Remember us for life, King Who desires life, and inscribe us in the book of life for Your sake, Living God.
(*If forgotten, no corrective action is necessary.*)

King Who helps, saves, and shields, ▾blessed are You, LORD, Shield of Abraham.

GOD'S MIGHT

אַתָּה YOU, my Master, are forever mighty, You are the Resurrector of the dead, with great power to save.

In winter: He makes the wind blow and the rain fall

God." The Shabbat morning *Amida* (יִשְׂמַח מֹשֶׁה) corresponds to the groom (God) bestowing gifts upon His bride (Israel). Historically this relates to the gifts of specific commandments, in particular Shabbat, that were given at Marah (Ex. 15:23–26.) The *Amida* of *Musaf* reflects the "additional" commitments (תּוֹסֶפֶת כְּתֻבָּה), and obligations, accompanied by a "great *Kiddush*" and its wedding meal. These correspond to the Revelation at Sinai. Finally, at *Minḥa* (אַתָּה אֶחָד) the *Amida* expresses יחוד, the coming together of groom and bride, God and Israel, to consummate their relationship. Historically this refers to the Messianic era in which God and Israel will finally be blissfully together as "one." This cathartic progression reflects עֹנֶג שַׁבָּת – the special enjoyment of Shabbat (*Benei Yisas'khar*).

מְכַלְכֵּל חַיִּים בְּחֶסֶד, מְחַיֵּה מֵתִים בְּרַחֲמִים רַבִּים, סוֹמֵךְ נוֹפְלִים, וְרוֹפֵא חוֹלִים, וּמַתִּיר אֲסוּרִים, וּמְקַיֵּם אֱמוּנָתוֹ לִישֵׁנֵי עָפָר. מִי כָמְוֹךָ, בַּעַל גְּבוּרוֹת, וּמִי דּוֹמֶה לָּךְ, מֶלֶךְ, מֵמִית וּמְחַיֶּה וּמַצְמִיחַ יְשׁוּעָה.

בשבת שובה: מִי כָמְוֹךָ אַב הָרַחֲמִים, זוֹכֵר יְצוּרָיו לְחַיִּים בְּרַחֲמִים.

(*If forgotten, no corrective action is necessary.*)

וְנֶאֱמָן אַתָּה לְהַחֲיוֹת מֵתִים. בָּרוּךְ אַתָּה יהוה, מְחַיֵּה הַמֵּתִים.

קדושת השם

אַתָּה קָדוֹשׁ וְשִׁמְךָ קָדוֹשׁ. וּקְדוֹשִׁים בְּכָל יוֹם יְהַלְלְוּךָ סֶּלָה. בָּרוּךְ אַתָּה יהוה, הָאֵל הַקָּדוֹשׁ. / בשבת שובה: הַמֶּלֶךְ הַקָּדוֹשׁ./

(*If forgotten, repeat the* עמידה.)

קדושת היום

אַתָּה קִדַּשְׁתָּ אֶת יוֹם הַשְּׁבִיעִי לִשְׁמֶךָ, תַּכְלִית מַעֲשֵׂה שָׁמַיִם וָאָרֶץ, וּבֵרַכְתּוֹ מִכָּל הַיָּמִים, וְקִדַּשְׁתּוֹ מִכָּל הַזְּמַנִּים, וְכֵן כָּתוּב בְּתוֹרָתֶךָ

בראשית ב **וַיְכֻלּוּ** הַשָּׁמַיִם וְהָאָרֶץ וְכָל־צְבָאָם: וַיְכַל אֱלֹהִים בַּיּוֹם הַשְּׁבִיעִי מְלַאכְתּוֹ אֲשֶׁר עָשָׂה, וַיִּשְׁבֹּת בַּיּוֹם הַשְּׁבִיעִי מִכָּל־מְלַאכְתּוֹ אֲשֶׁר עָשָׂה: וַיְבָרֶךְ אֱלֹהִים אֶת־יוֹם הַשְּׁבִיעִי, וַיְקַדֵּשׁ אֹתוֹ, כִּי בוֹ שָׁבַת מִכָּל־מְלַאכְתּוֹ, אֲשֶׁר־בָּרָא אֱלֹהִים לַעֲשׂוֹת:

This metaphor is reflected in the widespread practice, first mentioned in the *Magen Avraham*, and subsequently found in many *siddurim* including this one, to change the form of the pronoun referring to Shabbat in the paragraph that concludes the middle section. The Friday night version is the feminine בָהּ, in *Shaharit* and *Musaf* it is the masculine בוֹ, *while* at *Minha* it is the conjoint plural form בָם.

אֲשֶׁר־בָּרָא אֱלֹהִים לַעֲשׂוֹת – *He had created and performed*. God created an unfinished world for the use of humanity, but humanity is also charged to *complete what God had begun*. In this capacity, man becomes God's partner (*Hatam Sofer*).

For laws regarding "Omission of *HaMelekh HaKadosh*," see page 112.

He sustains the living with kindness, He resurrects the dead with great compassion, He supports those who are falling, He heals the sick, He sets the incarcerated free, and He fulfills what He has promised to those who sleep in the dust. Who is like You, O mighty One, and who can be compared to You, O King Who causes death and resurrects, and Who causes salvation to sprout?

On Shabbat Shuva: Who is like You, merciful Father, Who in compassion remembers for life those He has created.

(*If forgotten, no corrective action is necessary.*)

Trustworthy are You to resurrect the dead. Blessed are You, Lord, Resurrector of the dead.

HOLINESS

אַתָּה YOU ARE HOLY and Your name is holy, and holy ones will praise You every day, forever. Blessed are You, Lord, the holy God.

/*On Shabbat Shuva:* the holy King./

(*If forgotten, repeat the Amida.*)

HOLINESS OF THE DAY

אַתָּה קִדַּשְׁתָּ YOU SANCTIFIED the seventh day for the sake of Your name, the culmination of the creation of heaven and earth. You blessed it above all days, and sanctified it above all times, as it is written in Your Torah:

Gen. 2 **וַיְכֻלּוּ** THUS THE HEAVENS and the earth were finished, and all their multitudes. And by the seventh day God ended His work which He had done; and He rested on the seventh day from all His work which He had done. And God blessed the seventh day and sanctified it: because on it He rested from all the work He had created and performed.

INSTRUCTIONS FOR SOMEONE WHO MADE A MISTAKE AND RECITED THE WRONG AMIDA

If after the third *berakha* (*HaKel HaKadosh*) one accidentally began to recite the weekday *Amida*, even if one recited one word of that *berakha*, one should conclude the *berakha* that one has started and then continue with the middle *berakha* of Shabbat. (Regarding אַתָּה חוֹנֵן, one does not complete the *berakha* if one only recited the word אַתָּה, as long as one realized that it was Shabbat.) If one didn't realize the mistake until רְצֵה or one of the subsequent blessings, one should stop immediately and return to the middle *berakha* of Shabbat. If one didn't realize the mistake until after taking three steps back and didn't mention Shabbat at all in the *Amida*, one must repeat the *Amida*.

אֱלֹהֵֽינוּ וֵאלֹהֵי אֲבוֹתֵֽינוּ, רְצֵה בִמְנוּחָתֵֽנוּ. קַדְּשֵֽׁנוּ בְּמִצְוֹתֶֽיךָ, וְתֵן חֶלְקֵֽנוּ בְּתוֹרָתֶֽךָ, שַׂבְּעֵֽנוּ מִטּוּבֶֽךָ, וְשַׂמְּחֵֽנוּ בִּישׁוּעָתֶֽךָ, וְטַהֵר לִבֵּֽנוּ לְעָבְדְּךָ בֶּאֱמֶת. וְהַנְחִילֵֽנוּ, יהוה אֱלֹהֵֽינוּ, בְּאַהֲבָה וּבְרָצוֹן שַׁבַּת קָדְשֶֽׁךָ, וְיָנֽוּחוּ בָהּ יִשְׂרָאֵל מְקַדְּשֵׁי שְׁמֶֽךָ. בָּרוּךְ אַתָּה יהוה, מְקַדֵּשׁ הַשַּׁבָּת.

עבודה

רְצֵה יהוה אֱלֹהֵֽינוּ בְּעַמְּךָ יִשְׂרָאֵל, וּבִתְפִלָּתָם, וְהָשֵׁב אֶת הָעֲבוֹדָה לִדְבִיר בֵּיתֶֽךָ, וְאִשֵּׁי יִשְׂרָאֵל וּתְפִלָּתָם בְּאַהֲבָה תְקַבֵּל בְּרָצוֹן, וּתְהִי לְרָצוֹן תָּמִיד עֲבוֹדַת יִשְׂרָאֵל עַמֶּֽךָ.

On ראש חודש *and* חול המועד*, say:*

אֱלֹהֵֽינוּ וֵאלֹהֵי אֲבוֹתֵֽינוּ, יַעֲלֶה וְיָבוֹא וְיַגִּֽיעַ, וְיֵרָאֶה וְיֵרָצֶה וְיִשָּׁמַע, וְיִפָּקֵד וְיִזָּכֵר זִכְרוֹנֵֽנוּ וּפִקְדוֹנֵֽנוּ וְזִכְרוֹן אֲבוֹתֵֽינוּ, וְזִכְרוֹן מָשִֽׁיחַ בֶּן דָּוִד עַבְדֶּֽךָ, וְזִכְרוֹן יְרוּשָׁלַֽיִם עִיר קָדְשֶֽׁךָ, וְזִכְרוֹן כָּל עַמְּךָ בֵּית יִשְׂרָאֵל, לְפָנֶֽיךָ, לִפְלֵיטָה לְטוֹבָה, לְחֵן וּלְחֶֽסֶד וּלְרַחֲמִים, לְחַיִּים וּלְשָׁלוֹם בְּיוֹם

בראש חודש: רֹאשׁ הַחֹֽדֶשׁ / בפסח: חַג הַמַּצּוֹת / בסוכות: חַג הַסֻּכּוֹת

הַזֶּה. זָכְרֵֽנוּ יהוה אֱלֹהֵֽינוּ בּוֹ לְטוֹבָה, וּפָקְדֵֽנוּ בוֹ לִבְרָכָה, וְהוֹשִׁיעֵֽנוּ בוֹ לְחַיִּים. וּבִדְבַר יְשׁוּעָה וְרַחֲמִים, חוּס וְחָנֵּֽנוּ וְרַחֵם עָלֵֽינוּ וְהוֹשִׁיעֵֽנוּ, כִּי אֵלֶֽיךָ עֵינֵֽינוּ, כִּי אֵל מֶֽלֶךְ חַנּוּן וְרַחוּם אָֽתָּה.

אֱלֹהֵינוּ ... רְצֵה בִמְנוּחָתֵנוּ – *Our God... be pleased with our rest.* The term רְצֵה specifically connotes divine acceptance of sacrificial offerings. We ask God that He approve of our rest and physical indulgence on Shabbat in the same manner as an offering, for by abstaining from labor on Shabbat we sacrifice our earning potential in the service of God (R. Joseph B. Soloveitchik).

Shabbat prayers are particularly valuable insofar as they ask only for the needs of the soul, such as Torah, *mitzvot*, and purity of heart (R. Tzadok HaKohen of Lublin).

On Shabbat we eliminate all the requests and petitions from the middle section of the *Amida*, and instead focus on the uniqueness of Shabbat. During the week, our prayers have a dual nature: (a) they express our vulnerabilities, wants and desires, as we ask God to fulfill our needs; (b) they praise God in a way that leads to a sense of closeness and intimacy with our Father in heaven. But on Shabbat, when we enjoy a foretaste of the World to Come, our prayers express only the more elevated of these two modes of prayer, as we shift entirely to giving voice to our desire to draw closer to Him (*Netivot Shalom*).

אֱלֹהֵינוּ OUR GOD and God of our fathers, be pleased with our rest. Sanctify us through Your commandments and grant us our portion in Your Torah. Gratify us with Your goodness and gladden us with Your salvation. Purify our heart to serve You in truth. LORD our God, through Your loving favor may You grant that Your holy Sabbath will be our heritage, so that the people of Israel who sanctify Your name will rest on it. Blessed are You, LORD, Who sanctifies the Sabbath.

TEMPLE SERVICE

רְצֵה LOOK FAVORABLY, LORD our God, upon Your people Israel and their prayer, and restore the service to the Holy of Holies of Your House. Accept with love and favor the fire-offerings of Israel and their prayer. May the service of Israel Your people Israel always find favor with You.

On Rosh Ḥodesh and Ḥol HaMo'ed, say:

אֱלֹהֵינוּ וֵאלֹהֵי אֲבוֹתֵינוּ OUR GOD and God of our fathers, may there arise, arrive, reach, appear, be favored, heard, considered and remembered, our remembrance and recollection, Your remembrance of our fathers, of the Messiah son of David Your servant, of Jerusalem Your holy city and of all Your people the house of Israel. May they come before You for deliverance and benefit, for grace, kindness and mercy, for life and peace, on this day of:

On Rosh Ḥodesh: Rosh Ḥodesh.
On Pesaḥ: the Festival of Matzot.
On Sukkot: the Festival of Sukkot.

LORD our God, remember us this day for good. Be mindful of us this day for blessing, preserve us this day for life. Regarding redemption and mercy show us compassion and grace, and have pity on us and save us. For our eyes are lifted toward You, for You are a gracious and merciful God and King.

קַדְּשֵׁנוּ בְּמִצְוֹתֶיךָ – *Sanctify us through Your commandments.* While the *Shabbat Amida* indeed avoids explicit petition for material needs, the series of requests here correspond to, and briefly reference, the thirteen *berakhot* of the weekday *Amida* petition section: (1) the spiritual needs of the individual – קַדְּשֵׁנוּ בְּמִצְוֹתֶיךָ, וְתֵן חֶלְקֵנוּ בְּתוֹרָתֶךָ [blessings 4–6]; (2) the material needs of the individual – שַׂבְּעֵנוּ מִטּוּבֶךָ [blessings 7–9]; (3) the well-being and redemption of the Jewish people – וְשַׂמְּחֵנוּ בִּישׁוּעָתֶךָ [blessings 10–15]; and finally (4) the acceptance of our prayers – וְטַהֵר לִבֵּנוּ לְעָבְדְּךָ בֶּאֱמֶת [blessing 16, transition to 17] (R. Yaakov Rothschild).

For laws regarding "יַעֲלֶה וְיָבוֹא / *Ya'aleh VeYavo*," see page 125.

וְתֶחֱזֶינָה עֵינֵינוּ בְּשׁוּבְךָ לְצִיּוֹן בְּרַחֲמִים. בָּרוּךְ אַתָּה יהוה, הַמַּחֲזִיר שְׁכִינָתוֹ לְצִיּוֹן.

הודאה

Bow during the first five words.

מוֹדִים אֲנַחְנוּ לָךְ, שָׁאַתָּה הוּא יהוה אֱלֹהֵינוּ וֵאלֹהֵי אֲבוֹתֵינוּ לְעוֹלָם וָעֶד. צוּר חַיֵּינוּ, מָגֵן יִשְׁעֵנוּ, אַתָּה הוּא. לְדוֹר וָדוֹר נוֹדֶה לְּךָ וּנְסַפֵּר תְּהִלָּתֶךָ, עַל חַיֵּינוּ הַמְּסוּרִים בְּיָדֶךָ, וְעַל נִשְׁמוֹתֵינוּ הַפְּקוּדוֹת לָךְ, וְעַל נִסֶּיךָ שֶׁבְּכָל יוֹם עִמָּנוּ, וְעַל נִפְלְאוֹתֶיךָ וְטוֹבוֹתֶיךָ שֶׁבְּכָל עֵת, עֶרֶב וָבֹקֶר וְצָהֳרָיִם. הַטּוֹב, כִּי לֹא כָלוּ רַחֲמֶיךָ, וְהַמְרַחֵם, כִּי לֹא תַמּוּ חֲסָדֶיךָ, מֵעוֹלָם קִוִּינוּ לָךְ.

בחנוכה:

עַל הַנִּסִּים וְעַל הַפֻּרְקָן וְעַל הַגְּבוּרוֹת וְעַל הַתְּשׁוּעוֹת וְעַל הַמִּלְחָמוֹת שֶׁעָשִׂיתָ לַאֲבוֹתֵינוּ בַּיָּמִים הָהֵם בַּזְּמַן הַזֶּה.

בִּימֵי מַתִּתְיָהוּ בֶּן יוֹחָנָן כֹּהֵן גָּדוֹל חַשְׁמוֹנַאי וּבָנָיו, כְּשֶׁעָמְדָה מַלְכוּת יָוָן הָרְשָׁעָה עַל עַמְּךָ יִשְׂרָאֵל לְהַשְׁכִּיחָם תּוֹרָתֶךָ וּלְהַעֲבִירָם מֵחֻקֵּי רְצוֹנֶךָ, וְאַתָּה בְּרַחֲמֶיךָ הָרַבִּים עָמַדְתָּ לָהֶם בְּעֵת צָרָתָם, רַבְתָּ אֶת רִיבָם, דַּנְתָּ אֶת דִּינָם, נָקַמְתָּ אֶת נִקְמָתָם, מָסַרְתָּ גִבּוֹרִים בְּיַד חַלָּשִׁים, וְרַבִּים בְּיַד מְעַטִּים, וּטְמֵאִים בְּיַד טְהוֹרִים, וּרְשָׁעִים בְּיַד צַדִּיקִים, וְזֵדִים בְּיַד עוֹסְקֵי תוֹרָתֶךָ, וּלְךָ עָשִׂיתָ שֵׁם גָּדוֹל וְקָדוֹשׁ בְּעוֹלָמֶךָ, וּלְעַמְּךָ יִשְׂרָאֵל עָשִׂיתָ תְּשׁוּעָה גְדוֹלָה וּפֻרְקָן כְּהַיּוֹם הַזֶּה. וְאַחַר כֵּן בָּאוּ בָנֶיךָ לִדְבִיר בֵּיתֶךָ, וּפִנּוּ אֶת הֵיכָלֶךָ, וְטִהֲרוּ אֶת מִקְדָּשֶׁךָ, וְהִדְלִיקוּ נֵרוֹת בְּחַצְרוֹת קָדְשֶׁךָ, וְקָבְעוּ שְׁמוֹנַת יְמֵי חֲנֻכָּה אֵלּוּ, לְהוֹדוֹת וּלְהַלֵּל לְשִׁמְךָ הַגָּדוֹל.

Continue with וְעַל כֻּלָּם.

לְדוֹר וָדוֹר נוֹדֶה לְּךָ וּנְסַפֵּר תְּהִלָּתֶךָ – *From generation to generation we will thank You and recount Your praise*. In translating this phrase in the *Modim* paragraph of the *Amida*, this Siddur consistently follows the version of the text that is found in most early medieval siddur manuscripts, and which more recently has been favored by R. Chaim Kanievsky and R. Ovadia Yosef and adopted by many recent siddurim. The more common punctuation with a period after לְדוֹר וָדוֹר was favored by the Abudarham and R. Shabbetai Sofer (Dr. Jordan Pollack).

May our eyes witness Your return to Zion in compassion. Blessed are You, Lord, Who will restore His Divine Presence to Zion.

MODIM

Bow during the first seven words.

מוֹדִים WE THANK YOU, for You are the LORD our God and the God of our fathers for all eternity. You are the Rock of our life and Shield of our deliverance. From generation to generation we will thank You and recount Your praise for our lives that are in Your hands, for our souls that are given over to You, for Your miracles that are with us every day, and for Your constant wonders and favors, evening, morning and noon. You are good, for Your compassion does not cease, and You are compassionate, for Your kindness never ends. We have placed our hope in You forever and ever.

On Ḥanukka add:

עַל הַנִּסִּים [WE THANK YOU] for the miracles, the deliverance, and the triumphant victories and salvation, as well as wars which You wrought for our ancestors in those days at this season.

IT HAPPENED in the days of Mattathias son of Johanan, the Hasmonean high priest, and his sons. Then the cruel Hellenist power rose up to force Your people Israel to forget Your Torah and transgress the commands of Your will. In that hour of their distress, You in Your great mercy rose to take up their cause and defend their rights. Meting out retribution You delivered the strong into the hand of the weak, the many into the hand of the few, the impure into the hand of the pure, the evil ones into the hand of the righteous, and the wicked into the hand of devotees of Your Torah. You thereby made for Yourself a great and holy name throughout Your world, as well as bringing about great deliverance and salvation for Your people Israel (known) to this day. Then Your children came to the Holy of Holies in Your house, cleared Your Temple, purified Your holy place, kindled lights in Your holy courts, and instituted these eight days of Ḥanukka to give thanks and sing praise to Your great name.

Continue with "For all this."

For laws regarding "עַל הַנִּסִּים / *Al HaNissim*," see page 128.

וְעַל כֻּלָּם יִתְבָּרַךְ וְיִתְרוֹמַם שִׁמְךָ מַלְכֵּנוּ תָּמִיד לְעוֹלָם וָעֶד.

בשבת שובה: וּכְתֹב לְחַיִּים טוֹבִים כָּל בְּנֵי בְרִיתֶךָ.

(If forgotten, no corrective action is necessary.)

וְכֹל הַחַיִּים יוֹדוּךָ סֶּלָה, וִיהַלְלוּ אֶת שִׁמְךָ בֶּאֱמֶת, הָאֵל יְשׁוּעָתֵנוּ וְעֶזְרָתֵנוּ סֶלָה. ׳בָּרוּךְ אַתָּה יהוה, הַטּוֹב שִׁמְךָ וּלְךָ נָאֶה לְהוֹדוֹת.

ברכת שלום

שָׁלוֹם רָב עַל יִשְׂרָאֵל עַמְּךָ תָּשִׂים לְעוֹלָם, כִּי אַתָּה הוּא מֶלֶךְ אָדוֹן לְכָל הַשָּׁלוֹם. וְטוֹב בְּעֵינֶיךָ לְבָרֵךְ אֶת עַמְּךָ יִשְׂרָאֵל, בְּכָל עֵת וּבְכָל שָׁעָה בִּשְׁלוֹמֶךָ.

בשבת שובה: בְּסֵפֶר חַיִּים, בְּרָכָה וְשָׁלוֹם, וּפַרְנָסָה טוֹבָה, נִזָּכֵר וְנִכָּתֵב לְפָנֶיךָ, אֲנַחְנוּ וְכָל עַמְּךָ בֵּית יִשְׂרָאֵל, לְחַיִּים טוֹבִים וּלְשָׁלוֹם.*

בָּרוּךְ אַתָּה יהוה, הַמְבָרֵךְ אֶת עַמּוֹ יִשְׂרָאֵל בַּשָּׁלוֹם.

**On שבת שובה many end the blessing:*

בָּרוּךְ אַתָּה יהוה, עוֹשֵׂה הַשָּׁלוֹם.

Some say the following verse:

יִהְיוּ לְרָצוֹן אִמְרֵי־פִי וְהֶגְיוֹן לִבִּי לְפָנֶיךָ, יהוה צוּרִי וְגֹאֲלִי: תהלים יט

אֱלֹהַי, נְצֹר לְשׁוֹנִי מֵרָע וּשְׂפָתַי מִדַּבֵּר מִרְמָה, וְלִמְקַלְלַי נַפְשִׁי תִדֹּם, וְנַפְשִׁי כֶּעָפָר לַכֹּל תִּהְיֶה. פְּתַח לִבִּי בְּתוֹרָתֶךָ, וּבְמִצְוֹתֶיךָ תִּרְדֹּף נַפְשִׁי. וְכָל הַחוֹשְׁבִים עָלַי רָעָה, מְהֵרָה הָפֵר עֲצָתָם וְקַלְקֵל מַחֲשַׁבְתָּם. עֲשֵׂה לְמַעַן שְׁמֶךָ, עֲשֵׂה לְמַעַן יְמִינֶךָ, ברכות יז.

עֲשֵׂה לְמַעַן קְדֻשָּׁתֶךָ, עֲשֵׂה לְמַעַן תּוֹרָתֶךָ. לְמַעַן יֵחָלְצוּן יְדִידֶיךָ, תהלים ס

הוֹשִׁיעָה יְמִינְךָ וַעֲנֵנִי: יִהְיוּ לְרָצוֹן אִמְרֵי־פִי וְהֶגְיוֹן לִבִּי לְפָנֶיךָ, יהוה צוּרִי וְגֹאֲלִי: תהלים יט

For laws regarding "Interruptions during *Elokai Netzor*," see page 133.

For all this, our King, may Your name be blessed and exalted continually, forever and ever.

On Shabbat Shuva: Inscribe all the children of Your covenant for a life of goodness.

(If forgotten, no corrective action is necessary.)

All that lives will give thanks to You forever and praise Your name in truth, God, our salvation and our help forever. ▼Blessed are You, LORD, for Your name is "The Good One" and it is appropriate to give thanks to You.

PEACE

שָׁלוֹם רָב ESTABLISH ABUNDANT PEACE for Your people Israel forever, for You are the sovereign Master of all peace; and may it be good in Your eyes to bless Your people Israel at all times, at every hour, with Your peace.

On Shabbat Shuva: In the book of life and blessing, peace and prosperity, may we and all the house of Israel Your people be remembered before You and inscribed for a life of goodness and peace.*

Blessed are You, LORD, Who blesses His people Israel with peace.

**On Shabbat Shuva many end the blessing:*

Blessed are You, LORD, Who makes peace.

Some say the following verse:

Ps. 19 MAY THE WORDS of my mouth and the meditation of my heart find grace before You, LORD, my Rock and my Redeemer.

Berakhot 17a אֱלֹהַי MY GOD, guard my tongue from evil, and my lips from speaking deceit. Let my soul be silent to those who curse me; let my soul be humble toward everyone like the dust. Open my heart to Your Torah that my soul may follow Your commandments. As for all those who contemplate evil against me, speedily nullify their plans and spoil their schemes. Do so for the sake of Your name. Do so for Your right hand.
Ps. 60 Do so for Your holiness. Do so for Your Torah, that Your loved ones
Ps. 19 may be delivered. "Save with Your right hand, and answer me. May the words of my mouth and the meditation of my heart find grace before You, LORD, my Rock and my Redeemer."

Bow, take three steps back, then bow, first left, then right, then center, while saying:

עֹשֶׂה שָׁלוֹם / בשבת שובה: הַשָּׁלוֹם/ בִּמְרוֹמָיו, הוּא יַעֲשֶׂה שָׁלוֹם עָלֵינוּ, וְעַל כָּל יִשְׂרָאֵל, וְאִמְרוּ אָמֵן.

יְהִי רָצוֹן מִלְּפָנֶיךָ יהוה אֱלֹהֵינוּ וֵאלֹהֵי אֲבוֹתֵינוּ, שֶׁיִּבָּנֶה בֵּית הַמִּקְדָּשׁ בִּמְהֵרָה בְיָמֵינוּ, וְתֵן חֶלְקֵנוּ בְּתוֹרָתֶךָ, וְשָׁם נַעֲבָדְךָ בְּיִרְאָה כִּימֵי
עוֹלָם וּכְשָׁנִים קַדְמֹנִיּוֹת. וְעָרְבָה לַיהוה מִנְחַת יְהוּדָה וִירוּשָׁלָםִ כִּימֵי עוֹלָם וּכְשָׁנִים קַדְמֹנִיּוֹת: מלאכי ג

All stand and say:

וַיְכֻלּוּ הַשָּׁמַיִם וְהָאָרֶץ וְכָל־צְבָאָם: וַיְכַל אֱלֹהִים בַּיּוֹם הַשְּׁבִיעִי בראשית ב
מְלַאכְתּוֹ אֲשֶׁר עָשָׂה, וַיִּשְׁבֹּת בַּיּוֹם הַשְּׁבִיעִי מִכָּל־מְלַאכְתּוֹ אֲשֶׁר עָשָׂה: וַיְבָרֶךְ אֱלֹהִים אֶת־יוֹם הַשְּׁבִיעִי, וַיְקַדֵּשׁ אֹתוֹ, כִּי בוֹ שָׁבַת מִכָּל־מְלַאכְתּוֹ, אֲשֶׁר־בָּרָא אֱלֹהִים, לַעֲשׂוֹת:

On the first two nights of פסח*, some congregations recite* הלל *(page 766) at this point.*
The following until מְקַדֵּשׁ הַשַּׁבָּת *is omitted when praying alone or with a minyan that does not meet regularly (such as a minyan in a hotel that does not regularly have Shabbat services or a minyan in a home that does not meet on a weekly basis) (SA 268:8,10 and MB 24).*
It is also omitted when the first day of פסח *falls on* שבת*.*

מעין שבע

The שליח ציבור *continues:*

בָּרוּךְ אַתָּה יהוה, אֱלֹהֵינוּ וֵאלֹהֵי אֲבוֹתֵינוּ, אֱלֹהֵי אַבְרָהָם, אֱלֹהֵי יִצְחָק, וֵאלֹהֵי יַעֲקֹב, הָאֵל הַגָּדוֹל הַגִּבּוֹר וְהַנּוֹרָא, אֵל עֶלְיוֹן, קֹנֵה שָׁמַיִם וָאָרֶץ.

וַיְכֻלּוּ – *Were finished*. Three reasons have been provided for the repetition of וַיְכֻלּוּ: (1) Tosafot to *Pesaḥim* 106a explains that because it is important to affirm on both Shabbat

VAYEKHULU

Tur, Oraḥ Ḥayyim 268, quotes an opinion that the paragraph of *Vayekhulu* that is recited after the *Amida* should be recited out loud and in the standing position because it is considered testimony to the fact that God created the world. *Taz, Oraḥ Ḥayyim* 268:5, rules that since the purpose of the repetition of *Vayekhulu* is testimony, this can only be fulfilled if ten people recite it together. *Mishna Berura* 268:19, notes that if one cannot recite *Vayekhulu* together with a *minyan*, it should be recited in pairs to reflect the element of testimony. *Ḥazon Ish*, *Oraḥ Ḥayyim* 38:10, disagrees with *Mishna Berura,* as in his view there is nothing to be gained by reciting *Vayekhulu* in pairs insofar as it is intended to publicize the concept of the seven days of creation, and this can only be fulfilled if a *minyan* recites it together.

Bow, take three steps back, then bow, first left, then right, then center, while saying:

He Who makes peace in His heights, may He create peace for us and for all Israel. Amen.

יְהִי רָצוֹן MAY IT BE Your will, LORD our God and God of our fathers, that the Temple be rebuilt speedily in our days and may You grant our portion in Your Torah. We will serve You there in reverence as in the days of antiquity and in
Mal. 3 years gone by. "And may the offering of Judah and Jerusalem be pleasant to the LORD as in the days of antiquity and in years gone by."

All stand and say:

Gen. 2 וַיְכֻלּוּ THUS THE HEAVENS and the earth were finished, and all their multitudes. And by the seventh day God ended His work which He had done; and He rested on the seventh day from all His work which He had done. And God blessed the seventh day and sanctified it: because on it He rested from all the work He had created and performed.

On the first two nights of Pesaḥ, some congregations recite Hallel (page 767) at this point.
The following until "Who sanctifies the Sabbath" is omitted when praying alone or with a minyan that does not meet regularly (such as a minyan in a hotel that does not regularly have Shabbat services or a minyan in a home that does not meet on a weekly basis) (SA 268:8,10 and MB 24).
It is also omitted when the first day of Pesaḥ falls on Shabbat.

ME'EIN SHEVA

The Leader continues:

בָּרוּךְ BLESSED ARE YOU, Lord, our God and God of our fathers, God of Abraham, God of Isaac, and God of Jacob, the God Who is great, mighty, and awesome, God supreme, Creator of heaven and earth.

---

and Yom Tov that God was the Creator of the world, and the *Yom Tov Amida* does not contain that affirmation, the sages decreed that it be publically proclaimed following the *Amida*, whether on Shabbat or Yom Tov. (2) In case some of those in attendance were unable to make the affirmation by themselves, they could fulfill their obligation via the public recitation. (3) Ramban states that because the Torah designates Shabbat as a מִקְרָא קֹדֶשׁ (Lev. 23:3), literally a "holy proclamation," it is necessary to "sanctify" the day by means of a communal act of proclamation, which is accomplished by the group recital (R. Mosheh Lichtenstein).

מֵעֵין שֶׁבַע / ME'EIN SHEVA

The language of the *berakha*, and hence its name ("the *berakha* that derives from the seven *berakhot*"), consists of successive phrases alluding to the seven *berakhot* of the Friday evening *Amida*. In this respect it is similar to the repetition of the silent daytime *Amida* by the *Leader*. Its origin lies in the Talmudic discussion regarding whether

:שליח ציבור *then* ,קהל

מָגֵן אָבוֹת בִּדְבָרוֹ, מְחַיֵּה מֵתִים בְּמַאֲמָרוֹ, הָאֵל/ בשבת שובה: הַמֶּלֶךְ/ הַקָּדוֹשׁ שֶׁאֵין כָּמוֹהוּ, הַמֵּנִיחַ לְעַמּוֹ בְּיוֹם שַׁבַּת קָדְשׁוֹ, כִּי בָם רָצָה לְהָנִיחַ לָהֶם, לְפָנָיו נַעֲבֹד בְּיִרְאָה וָפַחַד, וְנוֹדֶה לִשְׁמוֹ בְּכָל יוֹם תָּמִיד, מֵעֵין הַבְּרָכוֹת, אֵל הַהוֹדָאוֹת, אֲדוֹן הַשָּׁלוֹם, מְקַדֵּשׁ הַשַּׁבָּת וּמְבָרֵךְ שְׁבִיעִי, וּמֵנִיחַ בִּקְדֻשָּׁה לְעַם מְדֻשְּׁנֵי עֹנֶג, זֵכֶר לְמַעֲשֵׂה בְרֵאשִׁית.

:שליח ציבור

אֱלֹהֵינוּ וֵאלֹהֵי אֲבוֹתֵינוּ, רְצֵה בִמְנוּחָתֵנוּ. קַדְּשֵׁנוּ בְּמִצְוֹתֶיךָ וְתֵן חֶלְקֵנוּ בְּתוֹרָתֶךָ, שַׂבְּעֵנוּ מִטּוּבֶךָ וְשַׂמְּחֵנוּ בִּישׁוּעָתֶךָ, וְטַהֵר לִבֵּנוּ לְעָבְדְּךָ בֶּאֱמֶת. וְהַנְחִילֵנוּ יהוה אֱלֹהֵינוּ בְּאַהֲבָה וּבְרָצוֹן שַׁבַּת קָדְשֶׁךָ, וְיָנוּחוּ בָהּ יִשְׂרָאֵל מְקַדְּשֵׁי שְׁמֶךָ. בָּרוּךְ אַתָּה יהוה, מְקַדֵּשׁ הַשַּׁבָּת.

קדיש שלם

ש״ץ: **יִתְגַּדַּל** וְיִתְקַדַּשׁ שְׁמֵהּ רַבָּא (קהל: אָמֵן) בְּעָלְמָא דִּי בְרָא כִרְעוּתֵהּ וְיַמְלִיךְ מַלְכוּתֵהּ בְּחַיֵּיכוֹן וּבְיוֹמֵיכוֹן וּבְחַיֵּי דְכָל בֵּית יִשְׂרָאֵל, בַּעֲגָלָא וּבִזְמַן קָרִיב, וְאִמְרוּ אָמֵן. (קהל: אָמֵן)

קהל וש״ץ: יְהֵא שְׁמֵהּ רַבָּא מְבָרַךְ לְעָלַם וּלְעָלְמֵי עָלְמַיָּא.

ש״ץ: יִתְבָּרַךְ וְיִשְׁתַּבַּח וְיִתְפָּאַר וְיִתְרוֹמַם וְיִתְנַשֵּׂא, וְיִתְהַדָּר וְיִתְעַלֶּה וְיִתְהַלָּל שְׁמֵהּ דְּקֻדְשָׁא בְּרִיךְ הוּא (קהל: בְּרִיךְ הוּא), לְעֵלָּא מִן כָּל

the *Ma'ariv* prayer is optional or obligatory (*Berakhot* 27b). The one-blessing abridgment represents a compromise position (Prof. Naftali Wieder).

The Talmud Yerushalmi (*Berakhot* 8:1) suggests that it was adopted in Babylonia to replace the synagogue recital of *Kiddush* when some communities could not afford wine. Another reason is that in earlier times synagogues were sometimes located in open areas outside the city limits. The Gemara (*Shabbat* 24b) explains that for this reason this prayer was included as a protective measure for those who might be late to the synagogue, and thus might have to return home alone. The custom has remained in place, even where such circum-

Congregation, then Leader:

מָגֵן HE WAS the shield of our forefathers with His word, Resurrector of the dead by his decree, the holy God / *On Shabbat Shuva:* the holy King / – there is none like Him. He gives rest to His people on His holy Sabbath day, for it was His desire for them to let them rest. Before Him we will serve with awe and fear, and give thanks to His name every day, continually, for He is the source of blessings. He is the God to Whom thanks are due, Master of peace, Who sanctifies the Sabbath and blesses the seventh day, and grants rest in holiness to the people abounding with delight, in remembrance of the act of Creation.

Leader:

אֱלֹהֵינוּ OUR GOD and God of our fathers, be pleased with our rest. Sanctify us through Your commandments and grant us our portion in Your Torah. Gratify us with Your goodness and gladden us with Your salvation. Purify our heart to serve You in truth. Lord our God, through Your loving favor may You grant that Your holy Sabbath will be our heritage, so that the people of Israel who sanctify Your name will rest on it. Blessed are You, Lord, Who sanctifies the Sabbath.

FULL KADDISH

Leader: **יִתְגַּדַּל** EXALTED AND HALLOWED may God's great name be, in the world He created as He willed. May He reign in your lifetimes and in your days, and in the lifetime of the whole house of Israel, speedily and soon, and say, Amen.

All: May His great name be blessed forever and all time.

Leader: Blessed and praised, honored, extolled, glorified, adored and exalted above all be the name of the Holy One, blessed

---

stances no longer exist, for the general rule is to maintain existing customs (Rashba; *Or Zarua*).

מֵעֵין הַבְּרָכוֹת – *He is the source of all blessings.* Various translations for this phrase have been attempted. Our translation is in accordance with the Gemara *Ḥagiga* 12b and Psalms 91:9 (as well as the Yemenite *nusaḥ*) that מָעוֹן (and thus here מֵעֵין too) refers to the aspect of heaven from where God's blessings emanate. Accordingly the term as used here refers to God as the source of all blessings (R. Barukh HaLevi Epstein).

בִּרְכָתָא / בשבת שובה: לְעֵלָּא (וּ)לְעֵלָּא מִכָּל בִּרְכָתָא/ וְשִׁירָתָא, תֻּשְׁבְּחָתָא וְנֶחֱמָתָא דַּאֲמִירָן בְּעָלְמָא, וְאִמְרוּ אָמֵן. (קהל: אָמֵן)

תִּתְקַבַּל צְלוֹתְהוֹן וּבָעוּתְהוֹן דְּכָל יִשְׂרָאֵל, קֳדָם אֲבוּהוֹן דִּי בִשְׁמַיָּא, וְאִמְרוּ אָמֵן. (קהל: אָמֵן)

יְהֵא שְׁלָמָא רַבָּא מִן שְׁמַיָּא וְחַיִּים, עָלֵינוּ וְעַל כָּל יִשְׂרָאֵל, וְאִמְרוּ אָמֵן. (קהל: אָמֵן)

Bow, take three steps back, as if taking leave of the Divine Presence, then bow, first left, then right, then center, while saying:

עֹשֶׂה שָׁלוֹם / בשבת שובה: הַשָּׁלוֹם/ בִּמְרוֹמָיו, הוּא יַעֲשֶׂה שָׁלוֹם עָלֵינוּ, וְעַל כָּל יִשְׂרָאֵל, וְאִמְרוּ אָמֵן. (קהל: אָמֵן)

קידוש בבית הכנסת

On יום טוב*, say the* קידוש *on page 794.*

The שליח ציבור *raises a cup of wine and says:*

בָּרוּךְ אַתָּה יהוה אֱלֹהֵינוּ מֶלֶךְ הָעוֹלָם, בּוֹרֵא פְּרִי הַגָּפֶן.

בָּרוּךְ אַתָּה יהוה אֱלֹהֵינוּ מֶלֶךְ הָעוֹלָם, אֲשֶׁר קִדְּשָׁנוּ בְּמִצְוֹתָיו, וְרָצָה בָנוּ, וְשַׁבַּת קָדְשׁוֹ בְּאַהֲבָה וּבְרָצוֹן הִנְחִילָנוּ, זִכָּרוֹן לְמַעֲשֵׂה בְרֵאשִׁית, כִּי הוּא יוֹם תְּחִלָּה לְמִקְרָאֵי קֹדֶשׁ, זֵכֶר לִיצִיאַת מִצְרָיִם, כִּי בָנוּ בָחַרְתָּ וְאוֹתָנוּ קִדַּשְׁתָּ מִכָּל הָעַמִּים, וְשַׁבַּת קָדְשְׁךָ בְּאַהֲבָה וּבְרָצוֹן הִנְחַלְתָּנוּ. בָּרוּךְ אַתָּה יהוה, מְקַדֵּשׁ הַשַּׁבָּת.

The wine should be drunk by children under the age of בר מצווה *or* בת מצווה *or, if there are none, by the* שליח ציבור*.*

קידוש / KIDDUSH

According to the Gemara (*Pesaḥim* 100b), *Kiddush* is recited in the synagogue "so that guests can fulfifill their *Kiddush* obligation." There are

KIDDUSH IN THE SYNAGOGUE

There are differing traditions regarding the recitation of *Kiddush* in the synagogue on Friday night. For those who do recite *Kiddush*, one should ensure that there is a child who understands the concept of *berakhot* (i.e., at least six or seven years old) but below the age of bar/bat *mitzva* and who is paying attention to the recitation of *Kiddush* and will subsequently drink the wine/grape juice (*MB* 269:1).

is He, (*Between Rosh Hashana & Yom Kippur:* above and) beyond any blessing, hymn, praise, or expressions of consolation that may be uttered in this world, and say, Amen.

May the prayers and pleas of all Israel be accepted before their Father Who is in heaven – and say, Amen.

May abundant peace descend from heaven, as well as life, for us and for all Israel, and say, Amen.

Bow, take three steps back, as if taking leave of the Divine Presence, then bow, first left, then right, then center, while saying:

May He Who makes peace in the highest heaven, make peace for us, and for all Israel, and say, Amen.

KIDDUSH IN THE SYNAGOGUE

On Yom Tov, say the Kiddush on *page 795*.

The Leader raises a cup of wine and says:

בָּרוּךְ BLESSED ARE YOU, Lord, our God, King of the universe, Who creates the fruit of the vine.

בָּרוּךְ BLESSED ARE YOU, Lord, our God, King of the universe, Who sanctified us with His commandments and favored us, Who with loving favor has given us the heritage of His holy Sabbath, in remembrance of the act of Creation. For this day is the first of the holy convocations, a remembrance of the Exodus from Egypt. For You have chosen us and sanctified us from among all peoples, and with love and favor You have given us the heritage of Your holy Sabbath. Blessed are You, Lord, Who sanctifies the Sabbath.

The wine should be drunk by children under the age of Bar/Bat Mitzva or, if there are none, by the Leader.

---

differing views if there are no guests present, or if it is clear that all those present will make *Kiddush* at home. Tosafot opposes *Kiddush* in the synagogue under such circumstances, on the grounds that the *Kiddush* would include a *berakha* made in vain. The Meiri, Ran, and others all favored it on the grounds that we should maintain existing customs whether or not the original reason for them still exists. This, similar to our continuing to recite the *Magen Avot berakha*, as explained above, reflects the principle formulated by Rambam

From the second night of פסח *until the night before* שבועות*,*
the עומר *is counted here* (*page 326*).

Stand while saying עָלֵינוּ*. Bow at* ˅.

עָלֵינוּ לְשַׁבֵּחַ לַאֲדוֹן הַכֹּל, לָתֵת גְּדֻלָּה לְיוֹצֵר בְּרֵאשִׁית, שֶׁלֹּא עָשָׂנוּ כְּגוֹיֵי הָאֲרָצוֹת, וְלֹא שָׂמָנוּ כְּמִשְׁפְּחוֹת הָאֲדָמָה, שֶׁלֹּא שָׂם חֶלְקֵנוּ כָּהֶם וְגוֹרָלֵנוּ כְּכָל הֲמוֹנָם. (שֶׁהֵם מִשְׁתַּחֲוִים לְהֶבֶל וָרִיק וּמִתְפַּלְלִים אֶל אֵל לֹא יוֹשִׁיעַ.) ˅וַאֲנַחְנוּ כּוֹרְעִים וּמִשְׁתַּחֲוִים וּמוֹדִים, לִפְנֵי מֶלֶךְ מַלְכֵי הַמְּלָכִים, הַקָּדוֹשׁ בָּרוּךְ הוּא, שֶׁהוּא נוֹטֶה שָׁמַיִם וְיוֹסֵד אָרֶץ, וּמוֹשַׁב יְקָרוֹ בַּשָּׁמַיִם מִמַּעַל, וּשְׁכִינַת עֻזּוֹ בְּגָבְהֵי מְרוֹמִים. הוּא אֱלֹהֵינוּ, אֵין עוֹד. אֱמֶת מַלְכֵּנוּ, אֶפֶס זוּלָתוֹ, כַּכָּתוּב בְּתוֹרָתוֹ, וְיָדַעְתָּ הַיּוֹם וַהֲשֵׁבֹתָ אֶל־לְבָבֶךָ, כִּי יהוה הוּא הָאֱלֹהִים דברים ד
בַּשָּׁמַיִם מִמַּעַל וְעַל־הָאָרֶץ מִתָּחַת, אֵין עוֹד:

עַל כֵּן נְקַוֶּה לְּךָ יהוה אֱלֹהֵינוּ, לִרְאוֹת מְהֵרָה בְּתִפְאֶרֶת עֻזֶּךָ, לְהַעֲבִיר גִּלּוּלִים מִן הָאָרֶץ, וְהָאֱלִילִים כָּרוֹת יִכָּרֵתוּן, לְתַקֵּן עוֹלָם בְּמַלְכוּת שַׁדַּי. וְכָל בְּנֵי בָשָׂר יִקְרְאוּ בִשְׁמֶךָ לְהַפְנוֹת אֵלֶיךָ כָּל רִשְׁעֵי אָרֶץ. יַכִּירוּ וְיֵדְעוּ כָּל יוֹשְׁבֵי תֵבֵל, כִּי לְךָ תִּכְרַע כָּל בֶּרֶךְ, תִּשָּׁבַע כָּל לָשׁוֹן. לְפָנֶיךָ יהוה אֱלֹהֵינוּ יִכְרְעוּ וְיִפֹּלוּ, וְלִכְבוֹד שִׁמְךָ יְקָר יִתֵּנוּ, וִיקַבְּלוּ כֻלָּם אֶת עֹל מַלְכוּתֶךָ, וְתִמְלֹךְ עֲלֵיהֶם מְהֵרָה לְעוֹלָם וָעֶד. כִּי הַמַּלְכוּת שֶׁלְּךָ הִיא וּלְעוֹלְמֵי עַד תִּמְלֹךְ בְּכָבוֹד, כַּכָּתוּב בְּתוֹרָתֶךָ, יהוה יִמְלֹךְ לְעֹלָם וָעֶד: ◂ וְנֶאֱמַר, וְהָיָה יהוה לְמֶלֶךְ עַל־כָּל־הָאָרֶץ, שמות טו / זכריה יד
בַּיּוֹם הַהוּא יִהְיֶה יהוה אֶחָד וּשְׁמוֹ אֶחָד:

Some add:

אַל־תִּירָא מִפַּחַד פִּתְאֹם וּמִשֹּׁאַת רְשָׁעִים כִּי תָבֹא: עֻצוּ עֵצָה וְתֻפָר, דַּבְּרוּ דָבָר וְלֹא יָקוּם, משלי ג / ישעיה ח
כִּי עִמָּנוּ אֵל: וְעַד־זִקְנָה אֲנִי הוּא, וְעַד־שֵׂיבָה אֲנִי אֶסְבֹּל, אֲנִי עָשִׂיתִי וַאֲנִי אֶשָּׂא ישעיה מו
וַאֲנִי אֶסְבֹּל וַאֲמַלֵּט:

that an enactment by a recognized Beit Din remains in effect unless and until it is voided by a subsequent, and greater, *Beit Din* (R. Israel Schepansky).

From the second night of Pesaḥ until the night before Shavuot, the Omer is counted here (page 327).

Stand while saying Aleinu. Bow at ▾.

עָלֵינוּ WE MUST, all of us, praise the Master of all, and ascribe greatness to He Who formed creation, for He did not make us like the nations of the world, nor render us like the families of the earth. He did not make our portion to be as theirs, nor our destiny like that of their masses. (For idolaters bow to vanity and emptiness and pray to a god who cannot save.) ▾We, however, bend our knees, bow, and give thanks before the King of the most exalted of kings, the Holy One, blessed is He. He is the One Who spreads out the heavens and establishes the earth. The seat of His glory is in the heavens above, and His Presence in all its strength is found in its highest abode. He is our God – there is no other. In truth
Deut. 4 He is our King; there is none but Him; as is written in His Torah: "On this day you should know, and take to heart, that the Lord is God in the heavens above and on the earth below – there is no other."

WE THEREFORE hope in You, Lord our God, that we may soon see the glory of Your might when You will remove abominations from the earth and the idols shall be utterly destroyed, when the world shall be perfected under the rule of the Almighty. Then all mankind shall invoke Your name, to turn all the wicked on earth toward You. All dwellers on earth will perceive and understand that to You every knee must bend, every tongue vow fealty. Before You, Lord our God, all will kneel and bow down, and give honor to Your glorious name. They will all accept the rule of Your dominion, and You will speedily rule over them forevermore. For the kingdom is Yours, and to all eternity You shall reign
Ex. 15 in glory, as it is written in Your Torah, "The Lord shall reign for ever and
Zech. 14 ever." ▸ And it is said, "And the Lord shall be King over all the earth; in that day shall the Lord be One, and His name One."

Some add:

Prov. 3 אַל־תִּירָא DO NOT FEAR sudden terror or the destruction when it comes to the
Is. 8 wicked. Devise a plan, and it will be thwarted; state a case and it will not stand,
Is. 46 for God is with us. And when you are old, I will remain; when you are aged, I will endure. I created you, I will carry you, I will endure, and I will rescue you.

קדיש יתום

The following prayer, said by mourners, requires the presence of a מנין*.*
A transliteration can be found on page 1345.

אבל: **יִתְגַּדַּל** וְיִתְקַדַּשׁ שְׁמֵהּ רַבָּא (קהל: אָמֵן) בְּעָלְמָא דִּי בְרָא
כִרְעוּתֵהּ, וְיַמְלִיךְ מַלְכוּתֵהּ, בְּחַיֵּיכוֹן וּבְיוֹמֵיכוֹן וּבְחַיֵּי
דְכָל בֵּית יִשְׂרָאֵל, בַּעֲגָלָא וּבִזְמַן קָרִיב, וְאִמְרוּ אָמֵן. (קהל: אָמֵן)

קהל ואבל: יְהֵא שְׁמֵהּ רַבָּא מְבָרַךְ לְעָלַם וּלְעָלְמֵי עָלְמַיָּא.

אבל: יִתְבָּרַךְ וְיִשְׁתַּבַּח וְיִתְפָּאַר, וְיִתְרוֹמַם וְיִתְנַשֵּׂא וְיִתְהַדָּר וְיִתְעַלֶּה
וְיִתְהַלָּל שְׁמֵהּ דְּקֻדְשָׁא בְּרִיךְ הוּא (קהל: בְּרִיךְ הוּא) לְעֵלָּא מִן כָּל
בִּרְכָתָא /בשבת שובה: לְעֵלָּא (וּ)לְעֵלָּא מִכָּל בִּרְכָתָא/ וְשִׁירָתָא, תֻּשְׁבְּחָתָא
וְנֶחֱמָתָא דַּאֲמִירָן בְּעָלְמָא, וְאִמְרוּ אָמֵן. (קהל: אָמֵן)

יְהֵא שְׁלָמָא רַבָּא מִן שְׁמַיָּא וְחַיִּים, עָלֵינוּ וְעַל כָּל יִשְׂרָאֵל,
וְאִמְרוּ אָמֵן. (קהל: אָמֵן)

Bow, take three steps back, as if taking leave of the Divine Presence,
then bow, first left, then right, then center, while saying:

עֹשֶׂה שָׁלוֹם / בשבת שובה: הַשָּׁלוֹם/ בִּמְרוֹמָיו, הוּא יַעֲשֶׂה שָׁלוֹם
עָלֵינוּ, וְעַל כָּל יִשְׂרָאֵל, וְאִמְרוּ אָמֵן. (קהל: אָמֵן)

From the second day of ראש חודש אלול *until and including* שמיני עצרת*,*
the following psalm is said:

תהלים כז **לְדָוִד**, יהוה אוֹרִי וְיִשְׁעִי, מִמִּי אִירָא, יהוה מָעוֹז־חַיַּי, מִמִּי
אֶפְחָד: בִּקְרֹב עָלַי מְרֵעִים לֶאֱכֹל אֶת־בְּשָׂרִי, צָרַי וְאֹיְבַי לִי,
הֵמָּה כָשְׁלוּ וְנָפָלוּ: אִם־תַּחֲנֶה עָלַי מַחֲנֶה, לֹא־יִירָא לִבִּי, אִם־תָּקוּם
עָלַי מִלְחָמָה, בְּזֹאת אֲנִי בוֹטֵחַ: אַחַת שָׁאַלְתִּי מֵאֵת־יהוה, אוֹתָהּ
אֲבַקֵּשׁ, שִׁבְתִּי בְּבֵית־יהוה כָּל־יְמֵי חַיַּי, לַחֲזוֹת בְּנֹעַם־יהוה, וּלְבַקֵּר
בְּהֵיכָלוֹ: כִּי יִצְפְּנֵנִי בְּסֻכֹּה בְּיוֹם רָעָה, יַסְתִּרֵנִי בְּסֵתֶר אָהֳלוֹ, בְּצוּר
יְרוֹמְמֵנִי: וְעַתָּה יָרוּם רֹאשִׁי עַל אֹיְבַי סְבִיבוֹתַי, וְאֶזְבְּחָה בְאָהֳלוֹ
זִבְחֵי תְרוּעָה, אָשִׁירָה וַאֲזַמְּרָה לַיהוה: שְׁמַע־יהוה קוֹלִי אֶקְרָא,

MOURNER'S KADDISH

The following prayer, said by mourners, requires the presence of a minyan. A transliteration can be found on page 1345.

Mourner: יִתְגַּדַּל EXALTED AND HALLOWED may God's great name be, in the world He created as He willed. May He reign in your lifetimes and in your days, and in the lifetime of the whole house of Israel, speedily and soon, and say, Amen.

All: May His great name be blessed forever and all time.

Mourner: Blessed and praised, honored, extolled, glorified, adored and exalted above all be the name of the Holy One, blessed is He, (*Between Rosh Hashana & Yom Kippur:* above and) beyond any blessing, hymn, praise, or expressions of consolation that may be uttered in this world, and say, Amen.

May abundant peace descend from heaven, as well as life, for us and for all Israel, and say, Amen.

Bow, take three steps back, as if taking leave of the Divine Presence, then bow, first left, then right, then center, while saying:

May He Who makes peace in the highest heaven, make peace for us, and for all Israel, and say, Amen.

From the second day of Rosh Ḥodesh Elul through Shemini Atzeret, the following psalm is said:

Ps. 27 לְדָוִד OF DAVID. The Lord is my light and my salvation. Whom shall I fear? The Lord is the refuge of my life. Whom shall I dread? When the evildoers came close to me to eat my flesh, those who were to me my adversaries and my enemies, it was they who stumbled and fell. If a host should encamp against me, my heart will not fear. If a war should rise against me, in this I trust. One thing have I asked of the Lord, that will I seek: That I may dwell in the house of the Lord all the days of my life, to behold the beauty of the Lord, and to contemplate His Temple, That He will hide me in His tabernacle on the day of evil, He will hide me in the shelter of His tent, He will lift me up upon a rock. And now my head will be lifted up above my enemies round about me, and I will offer in His tent sacrifices accompanied by the sound of trumpets. I will sing, and I will sing praises to the Lord. Hear, O Lord, my voice

וְחָנֵּנִי וַעֲנֵנִי: לְךָ אָמַר לִבִּי בַּקְּשׁוּ פָנָי, אֶת־פָּנֶיךָ יהוה אֲבַקֵּשׁ: אַל־תַּסְתֵּר פָּנֶיךָ מִמֶּנִּי, אַל תַּט־בְּאַף עַבְדֶּךָ, עֶזְרָתִי הָיִיתָ, אַל־תִּטְּשֵׁנִי וְאַל־תַּעַזְבֵנִי, אֱלֹהֵי יִשְׁעִי: כִּי־אָבִי וְאִמִּי עֲזָבוּנִי, וַיהוה יַאַסְפֵנִי: הוֹרֵנִי יהוה דַּרְכֶּךָ, וּנְחֵנִי בְּאֹרַח מִישׁוֹר, לְמַעַן שׁוֹרְרָי: אַל־תִּתְּנֵנִי בְּנֶפֶשׁ צָרָי, כִּי קָמוּ־בִי עֵדֵי־שֶׁקֶר, וִיפֵחַ חָמָס: ‹ לוּלֵא הֶאֱמַנְתִּי לִרְאוֹת בְּטוּב־יהוה בְּאֶרֶץ חַיִּים: קַוֵּה אֶל־יהוה, חֲזַק וְיַאֲמֵץ לִבֶּךָ, וְקַוֵּה אֶל־יהוה:

קדיש יתום *(previous page)*

Most congregations sing יגדל *at this point.*
Some congregations sing אדון עולם *(next page) instead.*

יִגְדַּל אֱלֹהִים חַי וְיִשְׁתַּבַּח, נִמְצָא וְאֵין עֵת אֶל מְצִיאוּתוֹ.

אֶחָד וְאֵין יָחִיד כְּיִחוּדוֹ, נֶעְלָם וְגַם אֵין סוֹף לְאַחְדוּתוֹ.

אֵין לוֹ דְּמוּת הַגּוּף וְאֵינוֹ גוּף, לֹא נַעֲרֹךְ אֵלָיו קְדֻשָּׁתוֹ.

קַדְמוֹן לְכָל דָּבָר אֲשֶׁר נִבְרָא, רִאשׁוֹן וְאֵין רֵאשִׁית לְרֵאשִׁיתוֹ.

הִנּוֹ אֲדוֹן עוֹלָם, וְכָל נוֹצָר יוֹרֶה גְדֻלָּתוֹ וּמַלְכוּתוֹ.

שֶׁפַע נְבוּאָתוֹ נְתָנוֹ אֶל־אַנְשֵׁי סְגֻלָּתוֹ וְתִפְאַרְתּוֹ.

לֹא קָם בְּיִשְׂרָאֵל כְּמֹשֶׁה עוֹד נָבִיא, וּמַבִּיט אֶת תְּמוּנָתוֹ.

יִגְדַּל אֱלֹהִים חַי – *Glorify... the living God.* This poem, composed in the fourteenth century, summarizes Rambam's Thirteen Principles of Faith. For a detailed analysis of these principles see the essay on page E93.

וְכָל נוֹצָר יוֹרֶה – *And every creature shall make ... known.* The common text of *Yigdal*, which has a ל preceding the כָּל, seems to be incorrect, for its meaning does not match Rambam's fifth principle on which it is based. The common text translates as "He is the Master of the universe to every creature; He demonstrates His greatness..." The problem with this text is that Rambam's principle actually affirms something else entirely: that we are "to serve Him and make His greatness known, while keeping His commandments – none of which we are to do for others less than He." For this reason we here use the text found in both a fifteenth-century Portuguese *siddur* and a sixteenth-century Italian *maḥzor*, and endorsed by R. Meir Mazuz, which reads וְכָל נוֹצָר יוֹרֶה גְדֻלָּתוֹ ("and every creature shall make His greatness and sovereignty known"). This is more faithful to Rambam's intent, that we are duty-bound to serve only God and to magnify His name and sovereignty as we do for none other (Prof. Marc B. Shapiro).

when I call, and show me favor and answer me. Of You my heart has said: Seek My face. Your face, O Lord, will I seek. Do not hide Your face from me. Do not turn Your servant away in anger. You have been my help, do not abandon me and do not forsake me, O God of my salvation. For my father and my mother have forsaken me, but the Lord will gather me in. Teach me Your way, O Lord, and lead me on an even path, because of my enemies. Do not deliver me to the desire of my enemies, for false witnesses have risen up against me, and a wicked witness. ▸ Were it not that I believed I would see the goodness of the Lord in the land of the living. Wait for the Lord, be strong and let your heart be encouraged, and wait for the Lord.

Mourner's Kaddish (*previous page*)

Most congregations sing "the Living God" at this point.
Some congregations sing "Eternal Master" (next page) instead.

יִגְדַּל THE LIVING GOD will be exalted and praised;
He exists, and His existence endures beyond time.

He is One and His oneness is like that of no other;
He is beyond our comprehension, for His unity is infinite.

He has no physical image, neither does He have a body;
nothing can be compared to Him in His Holiness.

He preceded everything that was created;
He was the first, and His primordial existence had no beginning.

Behold He is the eternal Master,
and every creature shall make His greatness and sovereignty known.

He bestowed His prophetic overflow
upon those individuals who were His treasured
and glorious ones.

Never did there arise in Israel another prophet like Moses,
who alone was able to view God's image.

כְּמֹשֶׁה – *Like Moses.* For Rambam, it is of paramount importance to affirm that Moses' prophecy was unique, qualitatively superior to that of every other prophet. The reason is that our foundational belief that the Torah can never be amended or replaced, whether by ill-informed Jews or by people professing other faiths, depends entirely on our

תּוֹרַת אֱמֶת נָתַן לְעַמּוֹ אֵל עַל יַד נְבִיאוֹ נֶאֱמַן בֵּיתוֹ.
לֹא יַחֲלִיף הָאֵל וְלֹא יָמִיר דָּתוֹ לְעוֹלָמִים לְזוּלָתוֹ.
צוֹפֶה וְיוֹדֵעַ סְתָרֵינוּ, מַבִּיט לְסוֹף דָּבָר בְּקַדְמָתוֹ.
גּוֹמֵל לְאִישׁ חֶסֶד כְּמִפְעָלוֹ, נוֹתֵן לְרָשָׁע רָע כְּרִשְׁעָתוֹ.
יִשְׁלַח לְקֵץ יָמִין מְשִׁיחֵנוּ לִפְדּוֹת מְחַכֵּי קֵץ יְשׁוּעָתוֹ.
מֵתִים יְחַיֶּה אֵל בְּרֹב חַסְדּוֹ, בָּרוּךְ עֲדֵי עַד שֵׁם תְּהִלָּתוֹ.

אֲדוֹן עוֹלָם אֲשֶׁר מָלַךְ בְּטֶרֶם כָּל־יְצִיר נִבְרָא.
לְעֵת נַעֲשָׂה בְחֶפְצוֹ כֹּל אֲזַי מֶלֶךְ שְׁמוֹ נִקְרָא.
וְאַחֲרֵי כִּכְלוֹת הַכֹּל לְבַדּוֹ יִמְלֹךְ נוֹרָא.
וְהוּא הָיָה וְהוּא הֹוֶה וְהוּא יִהְיֶה בְּתִפְאָרָה.
וְהוּא אֶחָד וְאֵין שֵׁנִי לְהַמְשִׁיל לוֹ לְהַחְבִּירָה.
בְּלִי רֵאשִׁית בְּלִי תַכְלִית וְלוֹ הָעֹז וְהַמִּשְׂרָה.
וְהוּא אֵלִי וְחַי גּוֹאֲלִי וְצוּר חֶבְלִי בְּעֵת צָרָה.
וְהוּא נִסִּי וּמָנוֹס לִי מְנָת כּוֹסִי בְּיוֹם אֶקְרָא.
בְּיָדוֹ אַפְקִיד רוּחִי בְּעֵת אִישַׁן וְאָעִירָה.
וְעִם רוּחִי גְּוִיָּתִי יהוה לִי וְלֹא אִירָא.

affirmation that Moses received it from God via his unique prophetic faculty, and thus no prophet or human being below his spiritual level is entitled to challenge, amend, supplement, or replace what he uniquely received from God. For this reason Rambam goes into great detail to show how Moses' prophecy, in which he alone beheld God's image as stated here, was one of a kind.

גּוֹמֵל לְאִישׁ חֶסֶד כְּמִפְעָלוֹ... כְּרִשְׁעָתוֹ – *He rewards the righteous in keeping with what they deserve; ... repays the evil.* We learn from this stanza that God's rewards are much greater than His punishments. For while it states that the rewards for our good deeds are in accordance with מִפְעָלוֹ (their impact on others), the punishments that God inflicts for our bad behavior reflect רִשְׁעָתוֹ (their inherent wickedness). Thus a good deed is rewarded for both the act and its consequences, whereas a hurtful action is punished only for its intrinsic immorality, not for its negative effect on others. This reflects God's infinite kindness, by which His rewards far outweigh His punishments (R. Levi Yitzḥak of Berditchev).

God gave His people the Torah of truth
by the hand of His prophet who was the most trusted in all His house.

God will not exchange or replace His law;
never will He alter it to become something else.

He sees and knows all that we conceal;
He discerns the end result of all that happens before it.

He rewards the compassionate person in accordance with his deeds;
He imposes punishment on the wicked person
in accordance with his evil.

He will send our Messiah at the end of days
to redeem with His salvation those who await the end of days.

God in His great kindness will resurrect the dead;
blessed is His illustrious name for ever and ever.

אֲדוֹן עוֹלָם ETERNAL MASTER,
Who reigned before anything was created –
when by His will all things were brought into being,
then as King was His name proclaimed.

After all things have ceased to be,
He will reign alone in awesome majesty.

He was. He is. He will always be;
His eternal glory can never fade.

He is One. There is no other;
beyond compare, or any metaphor.

He had no beginning, will have no end.
He above all others has strength and power.

He is my God, my living Redeemer,
a Rock when I am in pain in troubled times.

My banner and my refuge,
to Whom I will raise a cup on the day I proclaim my salvation.

I entrust my spirit to His hand,
when sleeping and when awake.

With my body my soul will stay;
the Lord is with me, I need not fear.

סעודת ליל שבת

It is the custom to bless one's children at the שבת *and* יום טוב *table prior to* קידוש.

To daughters, say:	To sons, say:	
יְשִׂימֵךְ אֱלֹהִים	**יְשִׂמְךָ** אֱלֹהִים	בראשית מח
כְּשָׂרָה רִבְקָה רָחֵל וְלֵאָה.	כְּאֶפְרַיִם וְכִמְנַשֶּׁה:	

במדבר ו

יְבָרֶכְךָ יהוה וְיִשְׁמְרֶךָ: יָאֵר יהוה פָּנָיו אֵלֶיךָ וִיחֻנֶּךָּ:
יִשָּׂא יהוה פָּנָיו אֵלֶיךָ וְיָשֵׂם לְךָ שָׁלוֹם:

שלום עליכם

Many people sing each of the four verses of the following song three times:

שָׁלוֹם עֲלֵיכֶם, מַלְאֲכֵי הַשָּׁרֵת, מַלְאֲכֵי עֶלְיוֹן, מִמֶּלֶךְ מַלְכֵי הַמְּלָכִים, הַקָּדוֹשׁ בָּרוּךְ הוּא.

בּוֹאֲכֶם לְשָׁלוֹם, מַלְאֲכֵי הַשָּׁלוֹם, מַלְאֲכֵי עֶלְיוֹן, מִמֶּלֶךְ מַלְכֵי הַמְּלָכִים, הַקָּדוֹשׁ בָּרוּךְ הוּא.

סְעוּדַת לֵיל שַׁבָּת / SABBATH EVE MEAL

בִּרְכַּת הַבָּנִים / BLESSING OF THE CHILDREN

The language of this *berakha* is taken directly from Genesis 48:20, where Jacob blesses his grandchildren with these very words, with a preface instructing that his words are to be the model for his future descendants. The blessing for daughters invoking Sarah, Rebecca, Rachel and Leah, does not have a clear source in the literature.

The *Magen Avraham* records the custom to kiss one's mother's hands at this point as a gesture of appreciation and love for all that she does for her household, especially in preparation for Shabbat (R. Yissachar Jacobson).

יְשִׂמְךָ אֱלֹהִים כְּאֶפְרַיִם וְכִמְנַשֶּׁה – *May God make you like Ephraim and Manasseh.* In blessing his two grandchildren, Jacob surprisingly gave priority to the younger brother Ephraim over his older sibling Menashe. The reason he did so is that parents (and grandparents) should certainly bless their offspring to enjoy material as well as spiritual blessings, but at the same time they should prioritize spiritual accomplishment, i.e., the study of Torah. After Jacob came down to Egypt he had taught Ephraim Torah, while Menashe had gone on to achieve material success. In this, the two siblings were similar to Yissachar (who excelled in Torah) and Zevulun, who supported his brother financially. In formulating their blessing, Jacob conveyed that while both realms are important, Torah study takes precedence even for a Menashe and Zevulun. Hence Jacob blessed Ephraim first, even though he was the younger brother.

SHABBAT EVE MEAL

It is the custom to bless one's children at the Shabbat and Yom Tov table prior to Kiddush.

To sons, say:

Gen. 48 יְשִׂמְךָ MAY God make you like Ephraim and Manasseh.

To daughters, say:

יְשִׂימֵךְ MAY God make you like Sarah, Rebecca, Rachel, and Leah.

Num. 6 May the Lord bless you and keep you. May the Lord make His countenance shine upon you and be gracious to you. May the Lord lift up His countenance to you and give you peace.

SHALOM ALEIKHEM

Many people sing each of the four verses of the following song three times:

שָׁלוֹם PEACE be with you, ministering angels, angels of the Most High, from the King Who is the King of the most exalted of kings, the Holy One, blessed is He.

MAY YOUR COMING be in peace, angels of peace, angels of the Most High, from the King Who is the King of the most exalted of kings, the Holy One, blessed is He.

So too every parent follows Jacob in blessing their children to enjoy the accomplishments of both Ephraim and Menashe, but always giving priority to Torah study. Similarly, Isaac blessed Jacob to receive "the dew of heaven" and only thereafter "the fat of the land" (Gen. 27:28) (*Ktav Sofer*).

Jacob's elevation of Joseph's two Egyptian sons, born of an Egyptian woman, to the same status as the tribes – was a conscious effort to extricate these sons from Egyptian culture, by planting them firmly in the national destiny of the Jewish people (R. Ezra Bick).

The Vilna Gaon insisted that the parent place only one hand on the child's head when reciting the priestly blessing, as only a *Kohen* is permitted to recite that benediction in its usual manner with two hands. Other authorities disagreed, insofar as this is not the conventional setting for the priestly blessing, and hence it is not subject to its laws.

שָׁלוֹם עֲלֵיכֶם / SHALOM ALEIKHEM
The Gemara (*Pesaḥim* 112b) says that on Friday evening harmful spirits abound, hence special angelic protection is needed. According to *Zohar Ḥadash* benevolent angels always accompany God's *Shekhina* and together they escort each Jew home on Friday evening from the synagogue. Upon glimpsing a serene home, the *Shekhina* and angels declare, "This is Mine – Israel, by whom I am glorified" (Isaiah 49:3). The *Shalom Aleikhem* poem greets the angels and

בָּרְכוּנִי לְשָׁלוֹם, מַלְאֲכֵי הַשָּׁלוֹם, מַלְאֲכֵי עֶלְיוֹן, מִמֶּלֶךְ מַלְכֵי הַמְּלָכִים, הַקָּדוֹשׁ בָּרוּךְ הוּא.

צֵאתְכֶם לְשָׁלוֹם ,מַלְאֲכֵי הַשָּׁלוֹם, מַלְאֲכֵי עֶלְיוֹן, מִמֶּלֶךְ מַלְכֵי הַמְּלָכִים, הַקָּדוֹשׁ בָּרוּךְ הוּא.

כִּי מַלְאָכָיו יְצַוֶּה־לָּךְ, לִשְׁמָרְךָ בְּכָל־דְּרָכֶיךָ: יהוה יִשְׁמָר־צֵאתְךָ תהלים צא
וּבוֹאֶךָ, מֵעַתָּה וְעַד־עוֹלָם: תהלים קכא

Some say:

רִבּוֹן כָּל הָעוֹלָמִים, אֲדוֹן כָּל הַנְּשָׁמוֹת, אֲדוֹן הַשָּׁלוֹם. מֶלֶךְ אַבִּיר, מֶלֶךְ בָּרוּךְ, מֶלֶךְ גָּדוֹל, מֶלֶךְ דּוֹבֵר שָׁלוֹם, מֶלֶךְ הָדוּר, מֶלֶךְ וָתִיק, מֶלֶךְ זַךְ, מֶלֶךְ חֵי הָעוֹלָמִים, מֶלֶךְ טוֹב וּמֵטִיב, מֶלֶךְ יָחִיד וּמְיֻחָד, מֶלֶךְ כַּבִּיר, מֶלֶךְ לוֹבֵשׁ רַחֲמִים, מֶלֶךְ מַלְכֵי הַמְּלָכִים, מֶלֶךְ נִשְׂגָּב, מֶלֶךְ סוֹמֵךְ נוֹפְלִים, מֶלֶךְ עֹשֶׂה מַעֲשֵׂה בְרֵאשִׁית, מֶלֶךְ פּוֹדֶה וּמַצִּיל, מֶלֶךְ צַח וְאָדֹם, מֶלֶךְ קָדוֹשׁ, מֶלֶךְ רָם וְנִשָּׂא, מֶלֶךְ שׁוֹמֵעַ תְּפִלָּה, מֶלֶךְ תָּמִים דַּרְכּוֹ. מוֹדֶה /*women* מוֹדָה/ אֲנִי לְפָנֶיךָ, יהוה אֱלֹהַי וֵאלֹהֵי אֲבוֹתַי, עַל כָּל הַחֶסֶד אֲשֶׁר עָשִׂיתָ עִמָּדִי וַאֲשֶׁר אַתָּה עָתִיד לַעֲשׂוֹת עִמִּי וְעִם כָּל בְּנֵי בֵיתִי וְעִם כָּל בְּרִיּוֹתֶיךָ, בְּנֵי בְרִיתִי. וּבְרוּכִים הֵם מַלְאָכֶיךָ הַקְּדוֹשִׁים וְהַטְּהוֹרִים שֶׁעוֹשִׂים רְצוֹנֶךָ. אֲדוֹן הַשָּׁלוֹם, מֶלֶךְ שֶׁהַשָּׁלוֹם שֶׁלּוֹ, בָּרְכֵנִי בַשָּׁלוֹם, וְתִפְקֹד אוֹתִי וְאֶת כָּל בְּנֵי בֵיתִי וְכָל עַמְּךָ בֵּית יִשְׂרָאֵל לְחַיִּים טוֹבִים וּלְשָׁלוֹם. מֶלֶךְ עֶלְיוֹן עַל כָּל צְבָא מָרוֹם,

---

asks for their blessing. The poem and the subsequent prayer (*Ribon Kol HaOlamim*) are one unit. It first appears in the work *Tikkunei Shabbat* (1613) and appears to have been compiled and formulated by its author, R. Yehuda ben David HaKohen of Budapest. The practice of greeting the angels – which is repeated at the end of the prayer (בּוֹאֲכֶם לְשָׁלוֹם, מַלְאֲכֵי הַשָּׁלוֹם... מֵעַתָּה וְעַד עוֹלָם אָמֵן סֶלָה) – first appears in a book of customs from thirteenth-century Italy, and is recorded as the practice of the Tosafist R. Aharon of Regensburg. Thereafter we sing the praises of the *Shekhina* as well, by reciting the *Eshet Ḥayyil*, which some take as a metaphor for the *Shekhina* (R. Moshe Isaac Blau).

בָּרְכוּנִי לְשָׁלוֹם – *Bless me in peace*. Some authorities, such as the Ḥatam Sofer and R. Jacob Emden, object to this phrase, and the recital of the poem altogether, on the grounds that it is forbidden to petition any spiritual being other than God Himself, even if the petition is no more than a desire that the angel bring one's request before God.

BLESS ME in peace, angels of peace, angels of the Most High from the King of the most exalted of kings, the Holy One, blessed is He.

MAY YOUR LEAVING be in peace, angels of peace, angels of the Most High, from the King of the most exalted of kings, the Holy One, blessed is He.

Ps. 91 INDEED, HE will give His angels charge over you, to keep you in all your
Ps. 121 ways. The Lord will guard your going out and your coming in from now
and forever.

Some say:

רִבּוֹן כָּל הָעוֹלָמִים RULER OF ALL WORLDS, Master of all souls, Master of peace – King Who is mighty, King Who is blessed, King Who is great, King Who speaks of peace, King Who is glorious, King Who is faithful, King Who is pure, King Who gives life to the universe, King Who is good and benevolent, King Who is unique and Whose uniqueness is proclaimed, King Who is powerful, King Who wears mercy, King Who reigns over kings, King Who is exalted, King Who supports the fallen, King Who maintains the works of creation, King Who redeems and rescues, King Who is pure yet ruddy, King Who is holy, King Who is exalted and upraised, King Who hears prayer, King Whose way is wholesome. I gratefully thank You, Lord, my God and the God of my fathers, for all the kindness You have done with me, and which You will do with me, with all my household, and with all Your creatures who are my fellows. Blessed are Your holy and pure angels who do Your will. Master of peace, King to Whom peace belongs, bless me with peace, and consider me and my entire household, and Your entire people, Israel, for a good life and for peace. King Who is exalted above all the heavenly legions,

---

One approach to this objection that may well deal with it persuasively is that בָּרְכוּנִי לְשָׁלוֹם is not a petition or prayer at all. It is a directive. We know that the angels are enjoined to bless the home when they see the lit candles and the table prepared for Shabbat. Thus, בָּרְכוּנִי לְשָׁלוֹם does not mean "Please bless me." It means, "Do what you are required to do" (Prof. David Berger).

כִּי מַלְאָכָיו יְצַוֶּה־לָּךְ – *For He will give His angels charge over you*. On Shabbat we remind ourselves that our achievements throughout the workweek are all thanks to God, Who constantly protects us with a "heavenly retinue" (*Zohar Ḥadash*). These verses serve as a bridge to רִבּוֹן כָּל הָעוֹלָמִים.

מֶלֶךְ אַבִּיר – *King Who is mighty*. The *Melekh* refrain is common in the prayers offered in the celestial "Temple," as found in *Heikhalot Rabbati*. It is recited following the *Shalom Aleikhem* to emphasize that our praise is truly directed only to God, Who rules over all the heavenly spheres.

יוֹצְרֵנוּ, יוֹצֵר בְּרֵאשִׁית, אֲחַלֶּה פָנֶיךָ הַמְּאִירִים, שֶׁתְּזַכֶּה אוֹתִי וְאֶת כָּל בְּנֵי בֵיתִי לִמְצֹא חֵן וְשֵׂכֶל טוֹב בְּעֵינֶיךָ וּבְעֵינֵי כָּל בְּנֵי אָדָם וּבְעֵינֵי כָל רוֹאֵינוּ לַעֲבוֹדָתֶךָ. וְזַכֵּנוּ לְקַבֵּל שַׁבָּתוֹת מִתּוֹךְ רֹב שִׂמְחָה וּמִתּוֹךְ עֹשֶׁר וְכָבוֹד וּמִתּוֹךְ מִעוּט עֲוֹנוֹת. וְהָסֵר מִמֶּנִּי וּמִכָּל בְּנֵי בֵיתִי וּמִכָּל עַמְּךָ בֵּית יִשְׂרָאֵל כָּל מִינֵי חֹלִי וְכָל מִינֵי מַדְוֶה וְכָל מִינֵי דַלּוּת וַעֲנִיּוּת וְאֶבְיוֹנוּת. וְתֵן בָּנוּ יֵצֶר טוֹב לְעָבְדְּךָ בֶּאֱמֶת וּבְיִרְאָה וּבְאַהֲבָה. וְנִהְיֶה מְכֻבָּדִים בְּעֵינֶיךָ וּבְעֵינֵי כָל רוֹאֵינוּ, כִּי אַתָּה הוּא מֶלֶךְ הַכָּבוֹד, כִּי לְךָ נָאֶה, כִּי לְךָ יָאֶה. אָנָּא, מֶלֶךְ מַלְכֵי הַמְּלָכִים, צַוֵּה לְמַלְאָכֶיךָ, מַלְאֲכֵי הַשָּׁרֵת, מְשָׁרְתֵי עֶלְיוֹן, שֶׁיִּפְקְדוּנִי בְּרַחֲמִים וִיבָרְכוּנִי בְּבוֹאָם לְבֵיתִי בְּיוֹם קָדְשֵׁנוּ, כִּי הִדְלַקְתִּי נֵרוֹתַי וְהִצַּעְתִּי מִטָּתִי וְהֶחֱלַפְתִּי שִׂמְלוֹתַי לִכְבוֹד יוֹם הַשַּׁבָּת וּבָאתִי לְבֵיתְךָ לְהַפִּיל תְּחִנָּתִי לְפָנֶיךָ, שֶׁתַּעֲבִיר אַנְחָתִי, וָאָעִיד אֲשֶׁר בָּרָאתָ בְשִׁשָּׁה יָמִים כָּל הַיְצוּר, וָאֶשְׁנֶה וַאֲשַׁלֵּשׁ עוֹד לְהָעִיד עַל כּוֹסִי בְּתוֹךְ שִׂמְחָתִי, כַּאֲשֶׁר צִוִּיתַנִי לְזָכְרוֹ וּלְהִתְעַנֵּג בְּיֶתֶר נִשְׁמָתִי אֲשֶׁר נָתַתָּ בִּי. בּוֹ אֶשְׁבֹּת כַּאֲשֶׁר צִוִּיתַנִי לְשָׁרְתֶךָ, וְכֵן אַגִּיד גְּדֻלָּתְךָ בְּרִנָּה, וְשִׁוִּיתִי יהוה לִקְרָאתִי שֶׁתְּרַחֲמֵנִי עוֹד בְּגָלוּתִי לִגְאָלֵנִי לְעוֹרֵר לִבִּי לְאַהֲבָתֶךָ. וְאָז אֶשְׁמֹר פִּקּוּדֶיךָ וְחֻקֶּיךָ בְּלִי עֶצֶב, וְאֶתְפַּלֵּל כַּדָּת כָּרָאוּי וְכַנָּכוֹן. מַלְאֲכֵי הַשָּׁלוֹם, בּוֹאֲכֶם לְשָׁלוֹם, בָּרְכוּנִי לְשָׁלוֹם, וְאִמְרוּ בָּרוּךְ לְשֻׁלְחָנִי הֶעָרוּךְ, וְצֵאתְכֶם לְשָׁלוֹם מֵעַתָּה וְעַד עוֹלָם, אָמֵן סֶלָה.

משלי לא
אֵשֶׁת־חַיִל מִי יִמְצָא, וְרָחֹק מִפְּנִינִים מִכְרָהּ:
בָּטַח בָּהּ לֵב בַּעְלָהּ, וְשָׁלָל לֹא יֶחְסָר:
גְּמָלַתְהוּ טוֹב וְלֹא־רָע, כֹּל יְמֵי חַיֶּיהָ:

אֵשֶׁת־חַיִל / A WOMAN OF VALOR

The *Eshet Ḥayyil* selection consists of the final twenty-two verses of the book of Proverbs, in which each verse starts with a succeeding letter of the alphabet. The *Midrash Yalkut Shimoni* quotes R. Isaac b. Nehemiah as saying that just as God's Torah uses the twenty-two letters of the alphabet, so God praises the virtuous woman with the same twenty-two letters. Some Midrashim identify the *Eshet Ḥayyil* with the Torah itself. Kabbalists consider these verses to be describing God's *Shekhina*, i.e., the "feminine" aspect of God that is encountered in this world. Meiri in the fourteenth century noted that the description of the ideal woman serves as a counterpoint to the allegorical "foreign woman" described in the opening chapters of Proverbs.

In any case the full range of virtues and accomplishments detailed in these twenty-two verses has been understood for centuries as describing the devotion of our wives and mothers, past and present, in caring for their families and households, both within the home setting and beyond its confines, displaying remarkable talent, energy, modesty, insight, and wisdom.

our Molder, Molder of the Creation, I beseech Your luminous countenance that You privilege me and all my household to find favor and good understanding – in Your eyes, and in the eyes of all descendants of Adam and Eve, and in the eyes of all who see us – that we may perform Your service. Privilege us to receive Sabbaths amid abundant gladness, amid wealth and honor, and amid fewness of sins. Remove from me, from all my household, and from Your entire people, Israel, every manner of illness, every manner of pain, and every manner of need, poverty, and destitution. Give us a virtuous desire to serve You with honesty, with awe, and with love. May we be honored in Your eyes and in the eyes of all who see us, for You are the King of glory – for to You it is seemly, for to You it is fitting. Please, King Who reigns over kings, instruct Your angels, the ministering angels, servants of the Most High, that they consider me with mercy and bless me when they enter my home on our holy day, for I have kindled my lights, spread my bed, and changed my clothes in honor of the Sabbath day. I have entered Your house to cast my plea before You that You banish my sighs; I bore witness that in six days You created the entire universe. I repeated it and will again repeat it over my cup amid my gladness as You commanded me to recall it, and to take pleasure in the additional soul which You have placed within me. On it shall I rest, as You have commanded me, to serve You, and so shall I tell Your greatness with joyous song. I have set the Lord before me that You should further show me mercy in my exile, to redeem me and to inspire my heart to Your love. Then I shall observe Your laws and Your decrees without suffering and I shall pray correctly as is fitting and right. Angels of peace, may your coming be in peace. Bless me in peace. Pronounce "Blessed" upon my set table. May your leaving be in peace, from now and forevermore. Amen. Selah.

Prov. 31 א אֵשֶׁת־חַיִל A WOMAN OF VALOR, who can find?
Her worth is beyond pearls.

ב Her husband's heart has faith in her,
and he will never lack good fortune.

ג She does him good and not harm all the days of her life.

A notable comment, found in the *Midrash Mishlei*, states that Beruria the wife of the Tanna R. Meir and also the daughter of R. Ḥanina b. Teradyon was the embodiment of an *Eshet Ḥayyil*. By way of illustration, it records the incident in which, following the untimely death of their two sons, she broke the news to her husband with surpassing wisdom and sensitivity, despite her own unspeakable grief. The *Midrash* concludes with the words of R. Ḥanina: "With her words she consoled him, as it says, 'A woman of valor who can find?'"

There is, however, an earlier embodiment of the woman of valor. As pointed out by R. Yehuda Kil, the only woman in Scripture who is described as an *Eshet Ḥayyil* is Ruth (Ruth 3:11), the great-great-grandmother of King Solomon, the author of Proverbs, whose

דָּרְשָׁה צֶמֶר וּפִשְׁתִּים, וַתַּעַשׂ בְּחֵפֶץ כַּפֶּיהָ:
הָיְתָה כָּאֳנִיּוֹת סוֹחֵר, מִמֶּרְחָק תָּבִיא לַחְמָהּ:
וַתָּקָם בְּעוֹד לַיְלָה, וַתִּתֵּן טֶרֶף לְבֵיתָהּ, וְחֹק לְנַעֲרֹתֶיהָ:
זָמְמָה שָׂדֶה וַתִּקָּחֵהוּ, מִפְּרִי כַפֶּיהָ נָטַע כָּרֶם:
חָגְרָה בְעוֹז מָתְנֶיהָ, וַתְּאַמֵּץ זְרוֹעֹתֶיהָ:
טָעֲמָה כִּי־טוֹב סַחְרָהּ, לֹא־יִכְבֶּה בַלַּיְל נֵרָהּ:
יָדֶיהָ שִׁלְּחָה בַכִּישׁוֹר, וְכַפֶּיהָ תָּמְכוּ פָלֶךְ:
כַּפָּהּ פָּרְשָׂה לֶעָנִי, וְיָדֶיהָ שִׁלְּחָה לָאֶבְיוֹן:
לֹא־תִירָא לְבֵיתָהּ מִשָּׁלֶג, כִּי כָל־בֵּיתָהּ לָבֻשׁ שָׁנִים:
מַרְבַדִּים עָשְׂתָה־לָּהּ, שֵׁשׁ וְאַרְגָּמָן לְבוּשָׁהּ:
נוֹדָע בַּשְּׁעָרִים בַּעְלָהּ, בְּשִׁבְתּוֹ עִם־זִקְנֵי־אָרֶץ:
סָדִין עָשְׂתָה וַתִּמְכֹּר, וַחֲגוֹר נָתְנָה לַכְּנַעֲנִי:
עוֹז־וְהָדָר לְבוּשָׁהּ, וַתִּשְׂחַק לְיוֹם אַחֲרוֹן:
פִּיהָ פָּתְחָה בְחָכְמָה, וְתוֹרַת־חֶסֶד עַל־לְשׁוֹנָהּ:
צוֹפִיָּה הֲלִיכוֹת בֵּיתָהּ, וְלֶחֶם עַצְלוּת לֹא תֹאכֵל:
קָמוּ בָנֶיהָ וַיְאַשְּׁרוּהָ, בַּעְלָהּ וַיְהַלְלָהּ:
רַבּוֹת בָּנוֹת עָשׂוּ חָיִל, וְאַתְּ עָלִית עַל־כֻּלָּנָה:
שֶׁקֶר הַחֵן וְהֶבֶל הַיֹּפִי, אִשָּׁה יִרְאַת־יהוה הִיא תִתְהַלָּל:
תְּנוּ־לָהּ מִפְּרִי יָדֶיהָ, וִיהַלְלוּהָ בַשְּׁעָרִים מַעֲשֶׂיהָ:

praises in these verses bear resemblance to the character and actions of Ruth (including her kindness, strength, resourcefulness, commitment to the Torah, and faithfulness). This parallel would explain the invocation of this chapter at the Friday evening Shabbat meal that commemorates Creation, as noted in its *Kiddush*, for these were the very qualities embedded in the universe by God at Creation, and epitomized by Ruth as a model for every Jew, male and female alike (Mrs. Shira Schechter).

ד She seeks out wool and flax and works willingly with her hands.
ה She is like a merchant ship, bringing food from afar.
ו She rises while it is still night,
and gives food to her household, as well as a portion for her maids.
ז She appraises a field and buys it;
she plants a vineyard with the fruit of her hand.
ח She girds herself with strength, and makes her arms powerful.
ט She knows when her output is of good quality, and then
(so as to produce more) she does not extinguish her light at night.
י She lays her hands on the distaff, her palms grasp the spindle.
כ She is generous to the poor, and extends a hand to the needy.
ל Her household has no fear of snow,
because they are all clothed in scarlet wool.
מ She makes luxurious covers for herself;
her clothing is fine linen and purple wool.
נ Her husband is well known at the gates of the city
where he sits among the elders of the land.
ס She makes linen cloth and sells it;
she delivers fine sashes to the merchant.
ע Strength and honor are her garb;
she faces the end of days with equanimity.
פ When she opens her mouth she speaks wisdom,
and the teaching of kindness is on her tongue.
צ She watches over the comings and goings of her household,
and she never partakes of the bread of idleness.
ק Her children stand up to declare her happiness,
as does her husband as he praises her, saying:
ר "There are many women of valorous deeds,
but you surpass them all."
ש Gracefulness can be deceptive and beauty can be without benefit,
whereas a God-fearing woman is indeed to be praised.
ת Therefore recognize her for the fruit of her hands,
and let her actions speak her praises at the gates of the city.

קידוש לליל שבת

For קידוש *on* יום טוב *see page 794, and on* ראש השנה*, see page 930.*

בראשית א *Quietly* וַיְהִי־עֶרֶב וַיְהִי־בֹקֶר

בראשית ב **יוֹם הַשִּׁשִּׁי:** וַיְכֻלּוּ הַשָּׁמַיִם וְהָאָרֶץ וְכָל־צְבָאָם: וַיְכַל אֱלֹהִים בַּיּוֹם הַשְּׁבִיעִי מְלַאכְתּוֹ אֲשֶׁר עָשָׂה, וַיִּשְׁבֹּת בַּיּוֹם הַשְּׁבִיעִי מִכָּל־מְלַאכְתּוֹ, אֲשֶׁר עָשָׂה: וַיְבָרֶךְ אֱלֹהִים אֶת־יוֹם הַשְּׁבִיעִי, וַיְקַדֵּשׁ אֹתוֹ, כִּי בוֹ שָׁבַת מִכָּל־מְלַאכְתּוֹ, אֲשֶׁר־בָּרָא אֱלֹהִים, לַעֲשׂוֹת:

When saying קידוש *for others, add:*

סַבְרִי מָרָנָן וְרַבָּנָן וְרַבּוֹתַי

בָּרוּךְ אַתָּה יהוה אֱלֹהֵינוּ מֶלֶךְ הָעוֹלָם, בּוֹרֵא פְּרִי הַגָּפֶן.

בָּרוּךְ אַתָּה יהוה אֱלֹהֵינוּ מֶלֶךְ הָעוֹלָם, אֲשֶׁר קִדְּשָׁנוּ בְּמִצְוֹתָיו, וְרָצָה בָנוּ, וְשַׁבַּת קָדְשׁוֹ בְּאַהֲבָה וּבְרָצוֹן הִנְחִילָנוּ, זִכָּרוֹן לְמַעֲשֵׂה בְרֵאשִׁית, כִּי הוּא יוֹם תְּחִלָּה לְמִקְרָאֵי קֹדֶשׁ, זֵכֶר לִיצִיאַת

קִדּוּשׁ / KIDDUSH

"It is a positive commandment of the Torah to sanctify Shabbat verbally, as it says, 'Remember the Shabbat day to sanctify it.' That is, remember it by way of praise and sanctification. And it must be sanctified both at its outset and its conclusion, via *Kiddush* and *Havdala*, by rabbinic edict (מִדִּבְרֵי סוֹפְרִים). *Kiddush* must be made on a cup of wine, hence we must recite a *berakha* over wine and then proceed to recite *Kiddush*." (Rambam)

וַיְבָרֶךְ... וַיְקַדֵּשׁ – *Blessed ... sanctified.* This declares that God "blessed" Shabbat and also "sanctified" it. This is to be understood as referring to two separate stages in the existence of Shabbat. The first occurred at Creation, when God *blessed* it to be a day of special significance. The second stage took place when the Israelites approached Sinai. At that point God sanctified it, by joining it via the equivalent of קִדּוּשִׁין, or betrothal, to the people of Israel, signifying its exclusive relationship with the

LAWS OF KIDDUSH

When reciting *Kiddush*, one holds a full cup of grape wine (or grape juice) in one's right hand, bearing in mind that one is fulfilling the *mitzva* of *Kiddush* for oneself and those who are listening. Listeners should bear in mind that they are fulfilling the *mitzva*, and should remain silent except for "Amen." Some stand during *Kiddush*, others sit, and still others stand until the blessing over the wine, then sit.

KIDDUSH FOR SHABBAT EVENING

For Kiddush on Yom Tov see page 795, and on Rosh HaShana, see page 931.

Gen. 1 *Quietly:* And it was evening, and it was morning.

Gen. 2 יוֹם הַשִּׁשִּׁי THE SIXTH DAY. Thus the heavens and the earth were finished, and all their multitudes. And by the seventh day God ended His work which He had done; and He rested on the seventh day from all His work which He had done. And God blessed the seventh day and sanctified it: because on it He rested from all the work He had created and performed.

When saying Kiddush for others, add:

With your permission, my masters, rabbis and esteemed companions:

בָּרוּךְ BLESSED ARE YOU, Lord, our God, King of the universe, Who creates the fruit of the vine.

בָּרוּךְ BLESSED ARE YOU, Lord, our God, King of the universe, Who sanctified us with His commandments and favored us, Who with loving favor gave us the heritage of His holy Sabbath, in remembrance of the act of Creation. For this day is the first of the holy convocations, a remembrance of the Exodus from Egypt.

Jewish people, who alone were to keep and observe Shabbat for all time (*Benei Yisas'khar*).

לַעֲשׂוֹת – *Performed.* This Hebrew verb refers to an act that brings its object to realize its intended purpose. Here the term indicates that every facet of God's creation was to realize its fullest purpose in due course, and with the help of man. Each of us is charged with the responsibility of finding our own unique role in realizing God's purpose through our own actions. The result will be the fulfillment of the ultimate purpose of all of Creation, i.e., the greater glory of God Himself (*Netziv*).

זִכָּרוֹן לְמַעֲשֵׂה בְרֵאשִׁית... זֵכֶר לִיצִיאַת מִצְרָיִם – *In remembrance of the act of Creation ... a remembrance of the Exodus from Egypt.* The text of the *Kiddush* first describes Shabbat as a זֵכֶר לְמַעֲשֵׂה בְרֵאשִׁית (a remembrance of the act of Creation) and then describes it as a זֵכֶר לִיצִיאַת מִצְרָיִם (a remembrance of the Exodus from Egypt). One can easily understand how Shabbat commemorates Creation, for the Torah describes how after the six days on which God created the heavens and the earth, He then rested on the seventh. Hence when we too rest on the seventh day of the week in imitation of

מִצְרָיִם, כִּי בָנוּ בָחַרְתָּ וְאוֹתָנוּ קִדַּשְׁתָּ מִכָּל הָעַמִּים, וְשַׁבַּת קָדְשְׁךָ בְּאַהֲבָה וּבְרָצוֹן הִנְחַלְתָּנוּ. בָּרוּךְ אַתָּה יהוה, מְקַדֵּשׁ הַשַּׁבָּת.

On שבת חול המועד סוכות*, if* קידוש *is made in the* סוכה*, add:*

בָּרוּךְ אַתָּה יהוה אֱלֹהֵינוּ מֶלֶךְ הָעוֹלָם, אֲשֶׁר קִדְּשָׁנוּ בְּמִצְוֹתָיו וְצִוָּנוּ לֵישֵׁב בַּסֻּכָּה.

It is customary for all present to drink of the wine.

לחם משנה

On washing hands before eating bread:

בָּרוּךְ אַתָּה יהוה אֱלֹהֵינוּ מֶלֶךְ הָעוֹלָם, אֲשֶׁר קִדְּשָׁנוּ בְּמִצְוֹתָיו וְצִוָּנוּ עַל נְטִילַת יָדָיִם.

Before eating bread:

בָּרוּךְ אַתָּה יהוה אֱלֹהֵינוּ מֶלֶךְ הָעוֹלָם, הַמּוֹצִיא לֶחֶם מִן הָאָרֶץ.

God, we attest to God's creation of the world. But how does our Shabbat observance act as a remembrance of the Exodus? To answer this question, we do well to recall that the Torah itself provides two separate reasons for Shabbat, one as found in the Ten Commandments in Exodus, and the other in the Ten Commandments in Deuteronomy. In Exodus it states, "Remember the Sabbath day… For in six days the Lord created the heavens and the earth… and He rested on the seventh day" (Ex. 20:8, 11). In Deuteronomy the reason given for keeping Shabbat is "For you shall remember that you were a slave in the land of Egypt, and the Lord your God took you out from there…" (Deut. 5:15). Hence Deuteronomy explicitly links Shabbat observance to the Egyptian Exodus. Even so, we need to clarify how exactly Shabbat observance attests to the Exodus. It is Rambam who provides an answer. As he explains in his *Guide for the Perplexed* (2:31), when we desist from labor on Shabbat we give concrete expression to the fact that we are no longer slaves beholden to Egyptian or any other earthly masters. Slaves have no day of rest. They must always be available to do the bidding of their owner or master. It is only thanks to the physical and spiritual redemption from Egypt that we can observe Shabbat. Hence our Shabbat rest is a testament to the Exodus. Moreover, this explains why when the Shabbat *Kiddush* mentions the Exodus it invokes the *Yamim Tovim* ("It is the first among the holy days of assembly, a remembrance of the Exodus from Egypt") which would seem to be out of place in the *Kiddush* of Shabbat. The answer is that the prohibitions of labor on the *Yamim Tovim* in Leviticus 23 follow immediately on the prohibition of Shabbat labor (i.e., it is literally "the first of the holy days" listed there),

For You have chosen us and sanctified us from among all peoples, and with love and favor You have given us the heritage of Your holy Sabbath. Blessed are You, Lord, Who sanctifies the Sabbath.

On Shabbat Ḥol HaMo'ed Sukkot, if Kiddush is made in the sukka, add:

בָּרוּךְ BLESSED ARE YOU, Lord our God, King of the universe, Who has sanctified us through his commandments and commanded us to dwell in the sukka.

It is customary for all present to drink of the wine.

LEḤEM MISHNEH

On washing hands before eating bread:

בָּרוּךְ BLESSED ARE YOU, Lord, our God, King of the universe, Who has sanctified us with His commandments, and has commanded us about washing hands.

Before eating bread:

בָּרוּךְ BLESSED ARE YOU, Lord, our God, King of the universe, Who brings forth bread from the earth.

---

and thus they reinforce the identical truth, i.e., our cessation from labor on all these days testifies to the freedom from slavery gained at the Exodus, hence these days are mentioned together in the Shabbat *Kiddush*. And this is true also of the *Kiddush* of Rosh HaShana and Yom Kippur, which also mention the Exodus even though ostensibly those days have nothing to do with the Exodus. But because they also are days of respite from labor (as commanded in Leviticus 23) they too testify to the Exodus (Prof. David Henshke).

LAWS OF LEḤEM MISHNEH

Before partaking of the *ḥalla*, one washes one's hands by pouring a cup of water two times over each hand and then recites the following blessing before drying one's hands: בָּרוּךְ אַתָּה ה׳ אֱלֹהֵינוּ מֶלֶךְ הָעוֹלָם, אֲשֶׁר קִדְּשָׁנוּ בְּמִצְוֹתָיו וְצִוָּנוּ עַל נְטִילַת יָדָיִם

It is customary to remain silent from the time one washes one's hands until one eats the bread. If one did speak, there is no need to repeat washing one's hands. The one reciting *Hamotzi* holds both loaves, bearing in mind that the *Hamotzi* will be recited on behalf all who are present. Listeners should bear in mind that they are fulfilling the *berakha*, and should remain silent except for "Amen." After reciting the *berakha*, the bottom *ḥalla* is cut first and distributed.

זמירות לליל שבת

כָּל מְקַדֵּשׁ שְׁבִיעִי כָּרָאוּי לוֹ

כָּל שׁוֹמֵר שַׁבָּת כַּדָּת, מֵחַלְּלוֹ

שְׂכָרוֹ הַרְבֵּה מְאֹד עַל פִּי פָעֳלוֹ

אִישׁ עַל־מַחֲנֵהוּ וְאִישׁ עַל־דִּגְלוֹ: במדבר א

אוֹהֲבֵי יהוה הַמְחַכִּים לְבִנְיַן אֲרִיאֵל

בְּיוֹם הַשַּׁבָּת שִׂישׂוּ וְשִׂמְחוּ כִּמְקַבְּלֵי מַתַּן נַחֲלִיאֵל

גַּם שְׂאוּ יְדֵיכֶם קֹדֶשׁ וְאִמְרוּ לָאֵל

בָּרוּךְ יהוה אֲשֶׁר נָתַן מְנוּחָה לְעַמּוֹ יִשְׂרָאֵל: מלכים א, ח

דּוֹרְשֵׁי יהוה זֶרַע אַבְרָהָם אוֹהֲבוֹ

הַמְאַחֲרִים לָצֵאת מִן הַשַּׁבָּת וּמְמַהֲרִים לָבוֹא

וּשְׂמֵחִים לְשָׁמְרוֹ וּלְעָרֵב עֵרוּבוֹ

זֶה־הַיּוֹם עָשָׂה יהוה, נָגִילָה וְנִשְׂמְחָה בוֹ: תהלים קיח

זִכְרוּ תּוֹרַת מֹשֶׁה בְּמִצְוַת שַׁבָּת גְּרוּסָה

חֲרוּתָה לַיּוֹם הַשְּׁבִיעִי, כְּכַלָּה בֵּין רֵעוֹתֶיהָ מְשֻׁבָּצָה

טְהוֹרִים יִירָשׁוּהָ, וִיקַדְּשׁוּהָ בְּמַאֲמַר כָּל אֲשֶׁר עָשָׂה

וַיְכַל אֱלֹהִים בַּיּוֹם הַשְּׁבִיעִי מְלַאכְתּוֹ אֲשֶׁר עָשָׂה: בראשית ב

יוֹם קָדוֹשׁ הוּא, מִבּוֹאוֹ וְעַד צֵאתוֹ

כָּל זֶרַע יַעֲקֹב יְכַבְּדוּהוּ, כִּדְבַר הַמֶּלֶךְ וְדָתוֹ

לָנוּחַ בּוֹ וְלִשְׂמֹחַ בְּתַעֲנוּג אָכוֹל וְשָׁתֹה

כָּל־עֲדַת יִשְׂרָאֵל יַעֲשׂוּ אֹתוֹ: שמות יב

זְמִירוֹת לְלֵיל שַׁבָּת / FRIDAY NIGHT ZEMIROT

The earliest halakhic source for the custom of singing Shabbat *zemirot* is found in the late eleventh-century *Maḥzor Vitri*. Many of the *zemirot* in our possession were actually composed before and during the period of the *Rishonim*, from the eleventh through the sixteenth century. Notable subsequent authorities who explicitly favored the singing of Shabbat meal *zemirot* include the Magen Avraham, R. Yaakov Emden, and the Ḥatam Sofer. In the sixteenth century the Kabbalistic school headed by the Arizal was particularly prolific in authoring *zemirot*. Subsequent Hasidic literature records numerous statements in favor of *zemirot*, a number of which were composed by Hasidic leaders. Among *Mitnagdim*, some (including R. Moshe Soloveichik and his son R. Joseph B. Soloveitchik) would recite the *zemirot* without singing them. In general one should make every effort to sing the *zemirot* on

FRIDAY NIGHT ZEMIROT

כָּל מְקַדֵּשׁ EVERYONE WHO SANCTIFIES the seventh day properly,
everyone who observes the Sabbath without desecrating it,
great will be his reward in accordance with his deeds,
Num. 1 "Each in accord with his place and station."

YOU WHO LOVE the Lord and yearn for the rebuilt Temple,
rejoice on the Sabbath and be happy for having received God's gift.
Lift your hands in holiness and declare unto God
1 Kings 8 "Blessed is the Lord Who gave His people Israel a day of rest."

THE DESCENDANTS of His beloved Abraham seek God;
they delay the departure of the Sabbath, and hasten to bring it early.
They rejoice in its observance and in staying within its boundaries,
Ps. 118 "This is the day on which the Lord has acted; let us be glad and rejoice in Him."

REMEMBER the Torah of Moses that taught the commandment of Shabbat,
which inscribed the commandment of the seventh day together with others similarly adorned.
Only pure ones will inherit it, by sanctifying it at the command of He Who created all.
Gen. 2 As it is said, "On the seventh day God completed all that He had created."

IT IS A SACRED day from beginning to end
and all the descendants of Jacob will respect it like a decree and proclamation of the king,
to rest upon it, rejoicing in its pleasures of eating and drinking;
Ex. 12 "All of the congregation of Israel will indeed make it so."

Shabbat in an appropriate manner, that is, with the intention of expressing the joy one feels on Shabbat to praise and thank God for giving us this special day (R. Michael Taubes).

כָּל מְקַדֵּשׁ שְׁבִיעִי / KOL MEKADESH SHEVI'I
This intricately rhyming *zemer* is first mentioned in the *Maḥzor Vitri*. The author is unknown. It sings the praises of Shabbat observance and the rich rewards accruing to one who is *Shomer Shabbat*. Each stanza concludes with a related scriptural verse. The stichs within the stanzas (except for the first stanza) follow an alphabetical order. The last four letters are, however, missing from our version of the *zemer*, and thus the rhythm terminates at that point, whereas the version found in *Maḥzor Vitri* (see the next page) has an alternative ending which completes the alphabetical and rhythmic scheme (*Zemirot Shabbat – Metivta*).

כְּכַלָּה בֵּין רֵעוֹתֶיהָ מְשֻׁבָּצָה – *Together with others similarly adorned.* This phrase refers to Shabbat as inscribed on the two tablets, in which it has particular length and prominence, like a bride surrounded by her attendants, the tablets

מְשֹׁךְ חַסְדְּךָ לְיוֹדְעֶיךָ, אֵל קַנּוֹא וְנוֹקֵם
נוֹטְרֵי יוֹם הַשְּׁבִיעִי זָכוֹר וְשָׁמוֹר לְהָקֵם
שַׂמְּחֵם בְּבִנְיַן שָׁלֵם, בְּאוֹר פָּנֶיךָ תַּבְהִיקֵם
יִרְוְיֻן מִדֶּשֶׁן בֵּיתֶךָ, וְנַחַל עֲדָנֶיךָ תַשְׁקֵם: תהלים לו

עֲזֹר לַשּׁוֹבְתִים בַּשְּׁבִיעִי, בֶּחָרִישׁ וּבַקָּצִיר עוֹלָמִים
פּוֹסְעִים בּוֹ פְּסִיעָה קְטַנָּה, סוֹעֲדִים בּוֹ, לְבָרֵךְ שָׁלֹשׁ פְּעָמִים
צִדְקָתָם תַּצְהִיר כְּאוֹר שִׁבְעַת הַיָּמִים
יהוה אֱלֹהֵי יִשְׂרָאֵל, הָבָה תָמִים: שמואל א, יד

(יהוה אֱלֹהֵי יִשְׂרָאֵל אַהֲבַת תָּמִים. / יהוה אֱלֹהֵי יִשְׂרָאֵל תְּשׁוּעַת עוֹלָמִים.)
(נ״א קַדְּשֵׁם בְּמִצְוֹתֶיךָ וְטַהֲרֵם כְּעֶצֶם הַשָּׁמַיִם לָטֹהַר / רוּחֲךָ תְּנִיחֵמוֹ כַּבְּהֵמָה תֵּרֵד בַּבִּקְעָה מִן הָהָר / שַׁבְּתֵיהֶם תַּשְׁכְּנֵם בְּנַחֲלַת הַסֹּהַר, כִּנְחָלִים נִטָּיוּ וּכְגַנֹּות עֲלֵי נָהָר.)

מְנוּחָה וְשִׂמְחָה אוֹר לַיְּהוּדִים, יוֹם שַׁבָּתוֹן, יוֹם מַחֲמַדִּים
שׁוֹמְרָיו וְזוֹכְרָיו הֵמָּה מְעִידִים,
כִּי לְשִׁשָּׁה כֹּל בְּרוּאִים וְעוֹמְדִים.

שְׁמֵי שָׁמַיִם, אֶרֶץ וְיַמִּים, כָּל צְבָא מָרוֹם גְּבוֹהִים וְרָמִים
תַּנִּין וְאָדָם וְחַיַּת רְאֵמִים, כִּי בְּיָהּ יהוה צוּר עוֹלָמִים.
הוּא אֲשֶׁר דִּבֶּר לְעַם סְגֻלָּתוֹ, שָׁמוֹר לְקַדְּשׁוֹ מִבּוֹאוֹ עַד צֵאתוֹ
שַׁבַּת קֹדֶשׁ יוֹם חֶמְדָּתוֹ, כִּי בוֹ שָׁבַת אֵל מִכָּל מְלַאכְתּוֹ.
בְּמִצְוַת שַׁבָּת אֵל יַחֲלִיצָךְ, קוּם קְרָא אֵלָיו, יָחִישׁ לְאַמְּצָךְ
נִשְׁמַת כָּל חַי וְגַם נַעֲרִיצָךְ, אֱכֹל בְּשִׂמְחָה כִּי כְבָר רָצָךְ.

---

themselves having been given on Shabbat day (*Iyyun Tefilla*).

מְנוּחָה וְשִׂמְחָה / MENUḤA VESIMḤA
This *zemer*, whose author is unknown, is first mentioned in the mid-sixteenth century. The focus is on Shabbat as testimony to God's creation of the cosmos in all its dimensions. Hence one who observes its minutiae, particularly in the context of *Kiddush* and the three Shabbat meals, is vouchsafed life in the World to Come.

שְׁמֵי שָׁמַיִם – *The heaven of heavens.* This paragraph references the six days of creation in succinct poetic form, following the order in which each is described in Genesis 1. The final line of the stanza refers to God by His name "י־ה." This is to be understood in light of the Gemara (*Menaḥot* 29b) which explains that God created the physical universe invoking

The commentary continues on page 434.

GOD OF JUSTICE, grant Your love to those who know Your ways,
who in holiness of Shabbat uphold "remember" and "observe it."
Make them joyous by rebuilding the Temple, and make them radiant with the light of Your presence,
Ps. 36 "To be satisfied by the fatness of Your house and to make them drink the river of Your pleasures."

ASSIST those who desist on the seventh day from planting and harvesting throughout,
as they walk modestly and sit down to eat and bless God on three occasions.
Make their goodness shine resplendent as creation's day,
1 Sam. 14 "O Lord, God of Israel, let it happen completely."

(O Lord, God of Israel, a perfect love. / O Lord, God of Israel, an eternal salvation.)

(*Alternate ending:* Sanctify them with Your commandments, / and purify them with heavenly splendor. / May Your spirit descend from on high to comfort them. / May
Nu. 24 they inherit the illumination of Your presence on their Sabbaths. / "To rest as planted aloes, and as cedars beside the waters.")

מְנוּחָה וְשִׂמְחָה* THE DAY of Shabbat, "Delight" is its name.
To Jews it brings rest, holiness, and all good.
Remember it, keep it; thus will you proclaim
that sealing God's work of creation it stood.

THE HEAVEN of heavens, the sea and the earth,
the heavenly hosts that encircle the sky,
alike man and beast and all that has birth,
through the Sabbath attest the one God enthroned on high.

TO ISRAEL, chosen by Him, God proclaimed
Shabbat to hallow and keep it as blessed.
Shabbat delight is with holiness framed;
for after God's work, on that day He found rest.

THROUGH Shabbat observance God gives to you strength.
With thanksgiving hymns of glad praise lift your voice,
in *nishmat kol ḥai* and the prayers at length.
Then go to your table at home and rejoice.

* The translation of this *zemer* is by R. David de Sola Pool, and uses a free-form poetic rhyming scheme rather than a literal translation.

בְּמִשְׁנֶה לֶחֶם וְקִדּוּשׁ רַבָּה, בְּרֹב מַטְעַמִּים וְרוּחַ נְדִיבָה
יִזְכּוּ לְרַב טוּב הַמִּתְעַנְּגִים בָּהּ, בְּבִיאַת גּוֹאֵל לְחַיֵּי הָעוֹלָם הַבָּא.

מַה־יְּדִידוּת מְנוּחָתֵךְ, אַתְּ שַׁבָּת הַמַּלְכָּה
בְּכֵן נָרוּץ לִקְרָאתֵךְ, בּוֹאִי כַלָּה נְסוּכָה
לְבוּשׁ בִּגְדֵי חֲמוּדוֹת, לְהַדְלִיק נֵר בִּבְרָכָה
וַתֵּכֶל כָּל הָעֲבוֹדוֹת, לֹא תַעֲשׂוּ מְלָאכָה.
לְהִתְעַנֵּג בְּתַעֲנוּגִים בַּרְבּוּרִים וּשְׂלָו וְדָגִים.

מֵעֶרֶב מַזְמִינִים כָּל מִינֵי מַטְעַמִּים
מִבְּעוֹד יוֹם מוּכָנִים תַּרְנְגוֹלִים מְפֻטָּמִים
וְלַעֲרֹךְ כַּמָּה מִינִים, שְׁתוֹת יֵינוֹת מְבֻשָּׂמִים
וְתַפְנוּקֵי מַעֲדַנִּים בְּכָל שָׁלֹשׁ פְּעָמִים.
לְהִתְעַנֵּג בְּתַעֲנוּגִים בַּרְבּוּרִים וּשְׂלָו וְדָגִים.

נַחֲלַת יַעֲקֹב יִירָשׁ, בְּלִי מְצָרִים נַחֲלָה
וִיכַבְּדוּהוּ עָשִׁיר וָרָשׁ, וְתִזְכּוּ לִגְאֻלָּה
יוֹם שַׁבָּת אִם תְּכַבְּדוּ וִהְיִיתֶם לִי סְגֻלָּה
שֵׁשֶׁת יָמִים תַּעֲבֹדוּ וּבַשְּׁבִיעִי נָגִילָה.
לְהִתְעַנֵּג בְּתַעֲנוּגִים בַּרְבּוּרִים וּשְׂלָו וְדָגִים.

חֲפָצֶיךָ אֲסוּרִים וְגַם לַחְשֹׁב חֶשְׁבּוֹנוֹת
הִרְהוּרִים מֻתָּרִים וּלְשַׁדֵּךְ הַבָּנוֹת
וְתִינוֹק לְלַמְּדוֹ סֵפֶר, לַמְנַצֵּחַ בִּנְגִינוֹת
וְלַהֲגוֹת בְּאִמְרֵי שֶׁפֶר בְּכָל פִּנּוֹת וּמַחֲנוֹת.
לְהִתְעַנֵּג בְּתַעֲנוּגִים בַּרְבּוּרִים וּשְׂלָו וְדָגִים.

מַה־יְּדִידוּת / MA YEDIDUT
This carefully rhyming *zemer*, known since the mid-sixteenth century, is by an unknown author. It describes numerous aspects of the Shabbat that relate to both a queen and a bride,

the letter *heh*, and the celestial world (or alternatively the World to Come) by invoking the letter *yud*. Thus it can be read as saying "God, Who is the Rock of both worlds, created them with יה – *yud-heh*" (*Etz Yosef*).

TAKE twin loaves of bread and good plenteous food,
and wine for Kiddush. Then wide open your door.
True joy will be yours through Shabbat's rich good.
Soon may our Redeemer bring life evermore!

מַה־יְּדִידוּת WE CHERISH the rest that comes with you, O Sabbath queen,
hastening to greet you as you draw near, O royal bride.
Wearing our best clothing, we kindle and bless the Sabbath lights,
when all our labors are completed, and mundane work forbidden.
It is indeed a day of joy, filled with the likes of succulent poultry, quail and fish.

ON THE SABBATH eve we prepare all kinds of delicacy,
while it is still day time fattened fowl are made ready
to be served with a variety of dishes, and slaked with properly-aged wines,
thus to indulge the palate over the course of the three festive meals.
It is indeed a day of joy, filled with the likes of succulent poultry, quail and fish.

SUCH is our unbounded legacy inherited from Jacob,
a day honored by rich and poor alike, bringing redemption as their reward,
for "If you will honor the Sabbath day you will be My treasure,"
then your six days of labor will be followed by rejoicing on the seventh.
It is indeed a day of joy, filled with the likes of succulent poultry, quail and fish.

BUSINESS MATTERS are beyond the pale, so too considerations of profit and loss,
whereas pleasurable thoughts are permitted, even discussing potential marital partners,
as well as teaching children sacred texts and the singing of songs,
while studying the words of the wise in every place and locale.
It is indeed a day of joy, filled with the likes of succulent poultry, quail and fish.

---

such as avoidance of manual work, adornment in festive garments, candle-lighting, extended rest and sleep, the three festive meals, and Shabbat-appropriate modes of thought, speech, and walking, all of which are rewarded with the enjoyment of eternal life.

בַּרְבּוּרִים – *Poultry.* In I Kings 5:3, *barburim* are listed as among the royal foods eaten by King Solomon. Alternatively, this refers to fattened poultry, so named insofar as Berbers fatten these birds in this fashion (*Metzudat David*). The second paragraph makes explicit reference to "fattened chickens."

יֵינוֹת מְבֻשָּׂמִים – *Properly-aged wines.* This phrase appears in *Bava Batra* 98a, where Rashba explains it to refer to choice aged wine.

וּלְשַׁדֵּךְ הַבָּנוֹת, וְתִינוֹק לְלַמְּדוֹ סֵפֶר – *Discussing potential marital partners, as well as teaching*

הַלּוֹכֵךְ יְהֵא בְנַחַת, עֹנֶג קְרָא לַשַּׁבָּת
וְהַשֵּׁנָה מְשֻׁבַּחַת כְּדָת נֶפֶשׁ מְשִׁיבַת
בְּכֵן נַפְשִׁי לְךָ עָרְגָה וְלָנוּחַ בְּחִבַּת
כַּשּׁוֹשַׁנִּים סוּגָה, בּוֹ יָנְוּחוּ בֵּן וּבַת.
לְהִתְעַנֵּג בְּתַעֲנוּגִים בַּרְבּוּרִים וּשְׂלָו וְדָגִים.

מֵעֵין עוֹלָם הַבָּא יוֹם שַׁבָּת מְנוּחָה
כָּל הַמִּתְעַנְּגִים בָּהּ יִזְכּוּ לְרֹב שִׂמְחָה
מֵחֶבְלֵי מָשִׁיחַ יֻצָּלוּ לִרְוָחָה
פְּדוּתֵנוּ תַצְמִיחַ, וְנָס יָגוֹן וַאֲנָחָה.
לְהִתְעַנֵּג בְּתַעֲנוּגִים בַּרְבּוּרִים וּשְׂלָו וְדָגִים.

יוֹם זֶה לְיִשְׂרָאֵל אוֹרָה וְשִׂמְחָה,
שַׁבַּת מְנוּחָה.

צִוִּיתָ פִּקּוּדִים בְּמַעֲמַד, סִינַי
שַׁבָּת וּמוֹעֲדִים לִשְׁמֹר בְּכָל שָׁנַי
לַעֲרֹךְ לְפָנַי מַשְׂאֵת וַאֲרוּחָה, שַׁבַּת מְנוּחָה.
יוֹם זֶה לְיִשְׂרָאֵל אוֹרָה וְשִׂמְחָה, שַׁבַּת מְנוּחָה.

חֶמְדַּת הַלְּבָבוֹת לְאֻמָּה שְׁבוּרָה
לִנְפָשׁוֹת נִכְאָבוֹת נְשָׁמָה יְתֵרָה
לְנֶפֶשׁ מְצֵרָה יָסִיר אֲנָחָה, שַׁבַּת מְנוּחָה.
יוֹם זֶה לְיִשְׂרָאֵל אוֹרָה וְשִׂמְחָה, שַׁבַּת מְנוּחָה.

---

children sacred texts. Even though the preceding phrases reflect the prohibition against thoughts or discussions of a financial nature on Shabbat, such discussions are permitted in the context of clarifying financial considerations involved in arranging a marriage or the Torah education of one's children (R. Yaakov Emden).

יוֹם זֶה לְיִשְׂרָאֵל / YOM ZEH LEYISRAEL
This *zemer* describes the many benefits bestowed upon those who observe Shabbat properly, including the blessings of closeness to God as well as ultimate redemption from exile. Based on the imbedded acrostic of the name Yitzḥak, some attribute the *zemer* to the Arizal. It is more accurately attributed to R. Yitzḥak Hendeli (or Chendeli) of Crimea, insofar as the first part of the *zemer* was already printed prior to 1534 when the Arizal was born.

WHEN you walk it shall be at a leisurely pace, as befits the joyous nature of the Sabbath,
when it is praiseworthy to sleep so as to restore the weary soul.
Therefore my soul longs for the Sabbath, when it will rest and be tranquil,
as if on a bed of roses, on which will rest male and female alike.

It is indeed a day of joy, filled with the likes of succulent poultry, quail and fish.

THE SABBATH DAY is a microcosm of the restful World to Come.
Doubtless all who delight on it will merit an overflow of happiness,
to be spared the sufferings that will precede the Messiah
when God will bring forth our redemption, and banish all sadness and sighing.

It is indeed a day of joy, filled with the likes of succulent poultry, quail and fish.

יוֹם זֶה לְיִשְׂרָאֵל THIS DAY is for the Jewish nation filled with light and joy,
a day of Shabbat rest.

YOU COMMANDED its laws when they stood at Sinai,
to observe Shabbat and the holidays throughout the years,
to set before You the choicest of tables. A day of Shabbat rest.

This day is for the Jewish nation filled with light and joy, a day of Shabbat rest.

THE SOULS of a broken nation long for this day;
it gives an additional soul to those who suffer pain,
and removes sighing from those who suffer. A day of Shabbat rest.

This day is for the Jewish nation filled with light and joy, a day of Shabbat rest.

Some have attributed it to the even earlier R. Yitzḥak Salameh, a Spanish exile living in the Ottoman Empire, probably Salonika.

לְאֻמָּה שְׁבוּרָה, לִנְפָשׁוֹת נִכְאָבוֹת – *A broken nation ... to those who suffer pain.* Via these and other similar phrases throughout the *zemer* the poet gently alludes to the harsh exilic conditions of the Jewish community in his time, as experienced under the Tartars in Crimea (or alternatively in the period following the expulsion from Spain), subject to the trepidations of intermittent warfare and oppression at the hands of various neighboring powers. In addition the Jewish community itself was divided between the traditionalists and powerful Karaite factions. The poet describes how Shabbat brings weekly respite and solace to his suffering fellow Jews, bringing them "light and joy" that will strengthen them to face the coming week (R. Basil Herring).

קִדַּשְׁתָּ בֵּרַכְתָּ אוֹתוֹ מִכָּל יָמִים
בְּשֵׁשֶׁת כִּלִּיתָ מְלֶאכֶת עוֹלָמִים
בּוֹ מָצְאוּ עֲגוּמִים הַשְׁקֵט וּבִטְחָה, שַׁבַּת מְנוּחָה.
יוֹם זֶה לְיִשְׂרָאֵל אוֹרָה וְשִׂמְחָה, שַׁבַּת מְנוּחָה.

לְאִסּוּר מְלָאכָה צִוִּיתָנוּ נוֹרָא
אֶזְכֶּה הוֹד מְלוּכָה אִם שַׁבָּת אֶשְׁמְרָה
אַקְרִיב שַׁי לַמּוֹרָא, מִנְחָה מֶרְקָחָה, שַׁבַּת מְנוּחָה.
יוֹם זֶה לְיִשְׂרָאֵל אוֹרָה וְשִׂמְחָה, שַׁבַּת מְנוּחָה.

חַדֵּשׁ מִקְדָּשֵׁנוּ, זָכְרָה נֶחֱרֶבֶת
טוּבְךָ, מוֹשִׁיעֵנוּ, תְּנָה לַנֶּעֱצֶבֶת
בְּשַׁבָּת יוֹשֶׁבֶת בְּזֶמֶר וּשְׁבָחָה, שַׁבַּת מְנוּחָה.
יוֹם זֶה לְיִשְׂרָאֵל אוֹרָה וְשִׂמְחָה, שַׁבַּת מְנוּחָה.

יָהּ רִבּוֹן עָלַם וְעָלְמַיָּא
אַנְתְּ הוּא מַלְכָּא מֶלֶךְ מַלְכַיָּא
עוֹבַד גְּבוּרְתָךְ וְתִמְהַיָּא
שְׁפַר קֳדָמָךְ לְהַחֲוָיָא.
יָהּ רִבּוֹן עָלַם וְעָלְמַיָּא, אַנְתְּ הוּא מַלְכָּא מֶלֶךְ מַלְכַיָּא.

שְׁבָחִין אֲסַדֵּר צַפְרָא וְרַמְשָׁא
לָךְ אֱלָהָא קַדִּישָׁא דִּי בְרָא כָּל נַפְשָׁא
עִירִין קַדִּישִׁין וּבְנֵי אֱנָשָׁא
חֵיוַת בָּרָא וְעוֹפֵי שְׁמַיָּא.
יָהּ רִבּוֹן עָלַם וְעָלְמַיָּא, אַנְתְּ הוּא מַלְכָּא מֶלֶךְ מַלְכַיָּא.

רַבְרְבִין עוֹבְדָיךְ וְתַקִּיפִין
מָכֵךְ רָמַיָּא וְזָקֵף כְּפִיפִין
לוּ יְחֵי גְבַר שְׁנִין אַלְפִין
לָא יֵעֹל גְּבוּרְתָךְ בְּחֻשְׁבְּנַיָּא.
יָהּ רִבּוֹן עָלַם וְעָלְמַיָּא, אַנְתְּ הוּא מַלְכָּא מֶלֶךְ מַלְכַיָּא.

YOU did bless it with sanctity more than all days,
when You completed Your cosmic creation after six days.
On it the weary find rest and repose. A day of Shabbat rest.
This day is for the Jewish nation filled with light and joy, a day of Shabbat rest.

GOD of awe, You bade us avoid every forbidden labor;
hence when I observe the Sabbath I acquire the dignity of royalty,
as I bring to God a scented gift. A day of Shabbat rest.
This day is for the Jewish nation filled with light and joy, a day of Shabbat rest.

RENEW our Temple, recall that it is destroyed.
May Your goodness, dear Savior, Your people delight,
as it experiences the Sabbath with song and praise. A day of Shabbat rest.
This day is for the Jewish nation filled with light and joy, a day of Shabbat rest.

יָהּ רִבּוֹן LORD of this world and all worlds to be,
You are supreme in Your majesty.
Your mighty work and marvelous ways
thrill and inspire my soul in Your praise.
Lord of this world and all worlds to be, You are supreme in Your majesty.
Your mighty work and marvelous ways thrill and inspire my soul in Your praise.

EVENING and morn Your praises I sing:
holy are You Who made everything,
all mortal men and angels on high,
beasts in their dens and birds of the sky.
Lord of this world and all worlds to be, You are supreme in Your majesty.
Your mighty work and marvelous ways thrill and inspire my soul in Your praise.

"HOW GREAT Your works!" all life cries aloud.
Humbling the proud, You raise the bowed.
Even if man lived a thousand years through,
never could he give Your glory its due.
Lord of this world and all worlds to be, You are supreme in Your majesty.
Your mighty work and marvelous ways thrill and inspire my soul in Your praise.

* The translation of this *zemer* is by R. David de Sola Pool, and uses a free-form poetic rhyming scheme rather than a literal translation..

יָהּ רִבּוֹן עָלַם / KA RIBON OLAM
This *zemer*, which makes no mention of Shabbat, was composed by the sixteenth-century Kabbalist R. Israel Najara, whose first name

אֱלָהָא דִּי לֵהּ יְקָר וּרְבוּתָא,
פְּרֹק יָת עָנָךְ מִפֻּם אַרְיָוָתָא
וְאַפֵּק יָת עַמָּךְ מִגּוֹ גָלוּתָא
עַמָּא דִּי בְחַרְתְּ מִכָּל אֻמַּיָּא.
יָהּ רִבּוֹן עָלַם וְעָלְמַיָּא, אַנְתְּ הוּא מַלְכָּא מֶלֶךְ מַלְכַיָּא.

לְמַקְדְּשָׁךְ תּוּב וּלְקֹדֶשׁ קֻדְשִׁין
אֲתַר דִּי בֵהּ יֶחֱדוּן רוּחִין וְנַפְשִׁין
וִיזַמְּרוּן לָךְ שִׁירִין וְרַחֲשִׁין
בִּירוּשְׁלֵם קַרְתָּא דְשֻׁפְרַיָּא.
יָהּ רִבּוֹן עָלַם וְעָלְמַיָּא, אַנְתְּ הוּא מַלְכָּא מֶלֶךְ מַלְכַיָּא.

צוּר מִשֶּׁלּוֹ אָכַלְנוּ, בָּרְכוּ אֱמוּנַי,
שָׂבַעְנוּ וְהוֹתַרְנוּ, כִּדְבַר יהוה.

הַזָּן אֶת עוֹלָמוֹ, רוֹעֵנוּ אָבִינוּ
אָכַלְנוּ אֶת לַחְמוֹ, וְיֵינוֹ שָׁתִינוּ
עַל כֵּן נוֹדֶה לִשְׁמוֹ, וּנְהַלְלוֹ בְּפִינוּ
אָמַרְנוּ וְעָנִינוּ, אֵין קָדוֹשׁ כַּיהוה.

צוּר מִשֶּׁלּוֹ אָכַלְנוּ, בָּרְכוּ אֱמוּנַי, שָׂבַעְנוּ וְהוֹתַרְנוּ כִּדְבַר יהוה.

---

appears in the *zemer* in acrostic form. He was born in Damascus, then lived in Safed, and later served as a rabbi in Gaza. In 1587 he published the *zemer* in his volume of poems titled *Zemirot Yisrael*. There the author explains that the language of this *zemer* was inspired by verses in Daniel (3:32–33) that record the effusive praise of God spoken by the Babylonian king Nebuchadnezzar at the miraculous salvation of Daniel's three colleagues from a fiery furnace. The Gemara (*Sanhedrin* 92b) is of the view that Nebuchadnezzar proclaimed his words of wonder when he witnessed Ezekiel bringing the dry bones to life, as recounted in Ezekiel 37 (*Zemirot Shabbat – Metivta*).

פְּרֹק יָת עָנָךְ מִפֻּם אַרְיָוָתָא – *Rescue Your flock from perilous plight*. The final two stanzas of the *zemer* do not reflect the words of Nebuchadnezzar, but rather express the heartfelt prayer of the Jewish people that it be saved "like a sheep from the mouths of marauding lions." Clearly this is a reference to Daniel chapter 6 that describes Daniel's own salvation in the lion's den, a metaphor for deliverance of the Jewish people from the sometimes devouring nations among whom they find themselves, so

GOD of all greatness, glory and light,
Rescue Your flock from perilous plight.
Bring from their exile wandering Jews;
They are the people whom You did choose.

Lord of this world and all worlds to be, You are supreme in Your majesty.
Your mighty work and marvelous ways thrill and inspire my soul in Your praise.

COME BACK to Zion, shrine of Your choice,
Spirit and soul in song to rejoice.
There we would bring our hymn's diadem
In Your fair city Jerusalem.

Lord of this world and all worlds to be, You are supreme in Your majesty.
Your mighty work and marvelous ways thrill and inspire my soul in Your praise.

צוּר מִשֶּׁלּוֹ* O ALL OF YOU of Jewish faith, as God has said in times of yore,
bless the Rock Who gives you food in plenty, yes, and more.

OUR SHEPHERD and our Father He, our food His gift divine.
His bread it is of which we eat, we drink with joy His wine.
For this we praise His holy name with thanks to Him outpoured.
Our theme shall ever be the same – none holy as the Lord.

O all of you of Jewish faith, as God has said in times of yore,
bless the Rock Who gives you food in plenty, yes, and more.

* The translation of this *zemer* is by R. David de Sola Pool, and uses a free-form poetic rhyming scheme rather than a literal translation..

that they might be redeemed and repatriated to "the beautiful city of Jerusalem" where the Temple will be rebuilt, there to sing their own songs of praise to God (R. Basil Herring).

צוּר מִשֶּׁלּוֹ אָכַלְנוּ / TZUR MISHELO AKHALNU
While the author of this *zemer* is unknown, it is likely of very early composition. It also makes no mention of Shabbat. It is customarily sung immediately prior to *Birkat HaMazon*, as it serves as a *reshut* (introduction or overture) in which the contents of each of the first three stanzas echo in turn the themes of the first three blessings of *Birkat HaMazon*, while the fourth corresponds to (and explicitly references) the blessing over wine that follows it. It is possible that a stanza corresponding to the fourth blessing was lost, or else was intentionally omitted by the author insofar as that blessing was (as the Gemara *Berakhot* 28b states) a later rabbinic addition. Given this parallel to the *Birkat HaMazon* there is a minority view (notably R. Ḥayyim of Volozhin) that omitted the *zemer* completely on the grounds that by reciting it one has technically fulfilled the obligation to recite Grace after Meals, and thus the *Birkat HaMazon*

בְּשִׁיר וְקוֹל תּוֹדָה, נְבָרֵךְ אֱלֹהֵינוּ
עַל אֶרֶץ חֶמְדָּה, שֶׁהִנְחִיל לַאֲבוֹתֵינוּ
מָזוֹן וְצֵידָה, הִשְׂבִּיעַ לְנַפְשֵׁנוּ
חַסְדּוֹ גָּבַר עָלֵינוּ, וֶאֱמֶת יהוה.
צוּר מִשֶּׁלּוֹ אָכַלְנוּ, בָּרְכוּ אֱמוּנַי, שָׂבַעְנוּ וְהוֹתַרְנוּ כִּדְבַר יהוה.

רַחֵם בְּחַסְדֶּךָ, עַל עַמְּךָ צוּרֵנוּ
עַל צִיּוֹן מִשְׁכַּן כְּבוֹדֶךָ, זְבוּל בֵּית תִּפְאַרְתֵּנוּ
בֶּן דָּוִד עַבְדֶּךָ, יָבוֹא וְיִגְאָלֵנוּ
רוּחַ אַפֵּינוּ, מְשִׁיחַ יהוה.
צוּר מִשֶּׁלּוֹ אָכַלְנוּ, בָּרְכוּ אֱמוּנַי, שָׂבַעְנוּ וְהוֹתַרְנוּ כִּדְבַר יהוה.

יִבָּנֶה הַמִּקְדָּשׁ, עִיר צִיּוֹן תְּמַלֵּא
וְשָׁם נָשִׁיר שִׁיר חָדָשׁ, וּבִרְנָנָה נַעֲלֶה
הָרַחֲמָן הַנִּקְדָּשׁ, יִתְבָּרַךְ וְיִתְעַלֶּה
עַל כּוֹס יַיִן מָלֵא, כְּבִרְכַּת יהוה.
צוּר מִשֶּׁלּוֹ אָכַלְנוּ, בָּרְכוּ אֱמוּנַי, שָׂבַעְנוּ וְהוֹתַרְנוּ כִּדְבַר יהוה.

itself becomes redundant (*Zemirot Shabbat – Metivta*).

שָׂבַעְנוּ וְהוֹתַרְנוּ – *Who gives you food in plenty, yes, and more*. This refers to the verse in the Torah (Deut. 8:10) commanding us to "eat, be satiated, and bless the Lord your God for the good land that He gave to you." As Ramban to that verse and its context explains, we are to remember the deprivations experienced prior to coming into the land of Israel, and thus to thank God not just for the food He provides, but for the land He gave us. This provides the framework for the subsequent blessings of *Birkat HaMazon*. The term הוֹתַרְנוּ ("we have leftover food") declares that we are indeed satiated to the point of leaving food on the table, and thus obligated to bless God in accordance with the verse. This accords with the *Shulḥan Arukh* that rules (*OḤ* 180:1) that some bread must be

WE BLESS Him now with song and happy praise and thanks
on behalf of Israel, our heritage of chosen happiness.
He richly rewards us with food and every other necessity.
His gracious love determines everything. How faithful is our Lord!

O all of you of Jewish faith, as God has said in times of yore,
bless the Rock Who gives you food in plenty, yes, and more.

O ROCK, have mercy on us, often so badly treated in Your world,
and have mercy, too, on the shrine where You once dwelled, the Temple of our pride.
Hasten the coming of David's son, Your servant, to restore us,
and breathe new life into us through the Messiah of the Lord.

O all of you of Jewish faith, as God has said in times of yore,
bless the Rock Who gives you food in plenty, yes, and more.

LET THE RENEWAL of Davidic leadership and the rebuilding of our Temple come about soon.
Enable the people of Zion to return with song and assemble there as in times long past.
You are compassionate and merciful, and we sing Your praises
over a brimming cup of happiness and blessing from You, Lord.

O all of you of Jewish faith, as God has said in times of yore,
bless the Rock Who gives you food in plenty, yes, and more.

---

left on the table until after *Birkat HaMazon* (R. Basil Herring).

כִּדְבַר ה' – *As God has said.* This *zemer* is unique in that it repeatedly invokes God's four-lettered name, at the conclusion of each stanza. This raises the question, much discussed in the halakhic literature, as to whether it is appropriate to pronounce this name when singing *zemirot*. While a number of authorities opposed it, the consensus (including the *Mishna Berura*, the *Arukh HaShulḥan*, and R. Shlomo Zalman Auerbach) permit full pronunciation of God's name where it occurs in a *zemer*, as long as it is done so as to praise, beseech, or thank God in a fully respectful fashion (R. Michael Taubes).

שחרית לשבת וליום טוב

Begin as on weekdays, from pages 2–54.

מזמור לפני פסוקי דזמרה

תהלים ל **מִזְמוֹר** שִׁיר־חֲנֻכַּת הַבַּיִת לְדָוִד: אֲרוֹמִמְךָ יהוה כִּי דִלִּיתָנִי, וְלֹא־שִׂמַּחְתָּ
אֹיְבַי לִי: יהוה אֱלֹהָי, שִׁוַּעְתִּי אֵלֶיךָ וַתִּרְפָּאֵנִי: יהוה, הֶעֱלִיתָ
מִן־שְׁאוֹל נַפְשִׁי, חִיִּיתַנִי מִיָּרְדִי־בוֹר: זַמְּרוּ לַיהוה חֲסִידָיו, וְהוֹדוּ לְזֵכֶר
קָדְשׁוֹ: כִּי רֶגַע בְּאַפּוֹ, חַיִּים בִּרְצוֹנוֹ, בָּעֶרֶב יָלִין בֶּכִי וְלַבֹּקֶר רִנָּה: וַאֲנִי
אָמַרְתִּי בְשַׁלְוִי, בַּל־אֶמּוֹט לְעוֹלָם: יהוה, בִּרְצוֹנְךָ הֶעֱמַדְתָּה לְהַרְרִי עֹז,
הִסְתַּרְתָּ פָנֶיךָ הָיִיתִי נִבְהָל: אֵלֶיךָ יהוה אֶקְרָא, וְאֶל־אֲדֹנָי אֶתְחַנָּן: מַה־
בֶּצַע בְּדָמִי, בְּרִדְתִּי אֶל שָׁחַת, הֲיוֹדְךָ עָפָר, הֲיַגִּיד אֲמִתֶּךָ: שְׁמַע־יהוה
וְחָנֵּנִי, יהוה הֱיֵה־עֹזֵר לִי: ◂ הָפַכְתָּ מִסְפְּדִי לְמָחוֹל לִי, פִּתַּחְתָּ שַׂקִּי,
וַתְּאַזְּרֵנִי שִׂמְחָה: לְמַעַן יְזַמֶּרְךָ כָבוֹד וְלֹא יִדֹּם, יהוה אֱלֹהַי, לְעוֹלָם אוֹדֶךָּ:

קדיש יתום

The following prayer, said by mourners, requires the presence of a מנין.
A transliteration can be found on page 1345.

אבל: **יִתְגַּדַּל** וְיִתְקַדַּשׁ שְׁמֵהּ רַבָּא (קהל: אָמֵן), בְּעָלְמָא דִּי בְרָא כִרְעוּתֵהּ.
וְיַמְלִיךְ מַלְכוּתֵהּ, בְּחַיֵּיכוֹן וּבְיוֹמֵיכוֹן וּבְחַיֵּי דְכָל בֵּית
יִשְׂרָאֵל, בַּעֲגָלָא וּבִזְמַן קָרִיב, וְאִמְרוּ אָמֵן. (קהל: אָמֵן)

קהל ואבל: יְהֵא שְׁמֵהּ רַבָּא מְבָרַךְ לְעָלַם וּלְעָלְמֵי עָלְמַיָּא.

אבל: יִתְבָּרַךְ וְיִשְׁתַּבַּח וְיִתְפָּאַר, וְיִתְרוֹמַם וְיִתְנַשֵּׂא וְיִתְהַדָּר וְיִתְעַלֶּה
וְיִתְהַלָּל שְׁמֵהּ דְּקֻדְשָׁא בְּרִיךְ הוּא (קהל: בְּרִיךְ הוּא), לְעֵלָּא מִן כָּל
בִּרְכָתָא /בשבת שובה: לְעֵלָּא (וּ)לְעֵלָּא מִכָּל בִּרְכָתָא/ וְשִׁירָתָא, תֻּשְׁבְּחָתָא
וְנֶחֱמָתָא דַּאֲמִירָן בְּעָלְמָא, וְאִמְרוּ אָמֵן. (קהל: אָמֵן)

יְהֵא שְׁלָמָא רַבָּא מִן שְׁמַיָּא וְחַיִּים, עָלֵינוּ וְעַל כָּל יִשְׂרָאֵל, וְאִמְרוּ
אָמֵן. (קהל: אָמֵן)

Bow, take three steps back, as if taking leave of the Divine Presence,
then bow, first left, then right, then center, while saying:

עֹשֶׂה שָׁלוֹם /בשבת שובה: הַשָּׁלוֹם/ בִּמְרוֹמָיו, הוּא יַעֲשֶׂה שָׁלוֹם עָלֵינוּ,
וְעַל כָּל יִשְׂרָאֵל, וְאִמְרוּ אָמֵן. (קהל: אָמֵן)

SHAḤARIT FOR SHABBAT AND YOM TOV

Begin as on weekdays, from pages 3–55.

A PSALM BEFORE VERSES OF PRAISE

Psalm 30 מִזְמוֹר A PSALM. A song at the dedication of the house. Of David. I will extol You, O Lord, for You have lifted me up, and You have not made my enemies rejoice over me. O Lord, my God, I cried out to You, and You healed me. O Lord, You brought me up from the underworld. You kept me alive, that I should not go down into the pit. Sing praise to the Lord, O you His pious ones, and give thanks to the remembrance of His holiness. For He remains a moment in His anger, a lifetime in His favor. In the evening one goes to sleep weeping, but in the morning there is joy. But I said in my prosperity: I will never stumble. O Lord, by Your favor You made my mountain stand strong. You hid Your face, and I was dismayed. I cried to You, O Lord, and to the Lord I made supplication. What profit is there in my blood, when I go down into the pit? Shall the dust give thanks to You? Shall it declare Your truth? Hear, O Lord, and be gracious to me. O Lord, be my helper. ▸ You turned for me my mourning into dancing. You loosened my sackcloth and girded me with gladness. Therefore glory will sing praise to You, and will not be silent. O Lord, my God, I will give thanks to You forever.

MOURNER'S KADDISH

The following prayer, said by mourners, requires the presence of a minyan. A transliteration can be found on page 1345.

Mourner: יִתְגַּדַּל EXALTED AND HALLOWED may God's great name be, in the world He created as He willed. May He reign in your lifetimes and in your days, and in the lifetime of the whole house of Israel, speedily and soon, and say, Amen.

All: May His great name be blessed forever and all time.

Mourner: Blessed and praised, honored, extolled, glorified, adored and exalted above all be the name of the Holy One, blessed is He, (*Between Rosh Hashana & Yom Kippur:* above and) beyond any blessing, hymn, praise, or expressions of consolation that may be uttered in this world, and say, Amen.

May abundant peace descend from heaven, as well as life, for us and for all Israel, and say, Amen.

Bow, take three steps back, as if taking leave of the Divine Presence, then bow, first left, then right, then center, while saying:

May He Who makes peace in the highest heaven, make peace for us, and for all Israel, and say, Amen.

פסוקי דזמרה

The introductory blessing to the פסוקי דזמרה *is said standing, while holding the two front* ציציות *of the* טלית*. They are kissed and released at the end of the blessing at* בַּתִּשְׁבָּחוֹת*. From the beginning of this prayer to the end of the* עמידה*, conversation is forbidden. See "Interruptions during Pesukei DeZimra" below.*

בָּרוּךְ שֶׁאָמַר וְהָיָה הָעוֹלָם, בָּרוּךְ הוּא. בָּרוּךְ עוֹשֶׂה בְרֵאשִׁית,
בָּרוּךְ אוֹמֵר וְעוֹשֶׂה, בָּרוּךְ גּוֹזֵר וּמְקַיֵּם, בָּרוּךְ
מְרַחֵם עַל הָאָרֶץ, בָּרוּךְ מְרַחֵם עַל הַבְּרִיּוֹת, בָּרוּךְ מְשַׁלֵּם שָׂכָר
טוֹב לִירֵאָיו, בָּרוּךְ חַי לָעַד וְקַיָּם לָנֶצַח, בָּרוּךְ פּוֹדֶה וּמַצִּיל, בָּרוּךְ
שְׁמוֹ. בָּרוּךְ אַתָּה יהוה אֱלֹהֵינוּ מֶלֶךְ הָעוֹלָם, הָאֵל הָאָב הָרַחֲמָן
הַמְהֻלָּל בְּפִי עַמּוֹ, מְשֻׁבָּח וּמְפֹאָר בִּלְשׁוֹן חֲסִידָיו וַעֲבָדָיו. וּבְשִׁירֵי
דָוִד עַבְדֶּךָ, נְהַלֶּלְךָ יהוה אֱלֹהֵינוּ. בִּשְׁבָחוֹת וּבִזְמִירוֹת, נְגַדֶּלְךָ
וּנְשַׁבֵּחֲךָ וּנְפָאֶרְךָ. וְנַזְכִּיר שִׁמְךָ וְנַמְלִיכְךָ, מַלְכֵּנוּ אֱלֹהֵינוּ, ◂ יָחִיד חֵי
הָעוֹלָמִים מֶלֶךְ, מְשֻׁבָּח וּמְפֹאָר עֲדֵי עַד שְׁמוֹ הַגָּדוֹל, בָּרוּךְ אַתָּה
יהוה, מֶלֶךְ מְהֻלָּל בַּתִּשְׁבָּחוֹת.

הוֹדוּ לַיהוה קִרְאוּ בִשְׁמוֹ, הוֹדִיעוּ בָעַמִּים עֲלִילֹתָיו: שִׁירוּ לוֹ, דברי הימים א, טז
זַמְּרוּ־לוֹ, שִׂיחוּ בְּכָל־נִפְלְאוֹתָיו: הִתְהַלְלוּ בְּשֵׁם קָדְשׁוֹ,

INTERRUPTIONS DURING PESUKEI DEZIMRA

As a general rule, from the time one recites *Barukh She'amar* until the conclusion of *Taḥanun* one should not speak (*OḤ* 51:4 and *MB* 51:6–11). However, there are certain interruptions that are permissible during *Pesukei DeZimra*:

- One may answer *amen* to a *berakha* that one heard (but not *barukh Hu uvarukh shemo*).
- One may recite *Asher Yatzar*.
- If one was called for an *aliya*, one may accept the *aliya* (ideally the *gabbai* should not call someone for an *aliya* who is in the middle of *Pesukei DeZimra*).
- If one is concerned about missing the final time to recite *Shema*, one may recite it during *Pesukei DeZimra*.
- If one forgot to recite *Birkhot HaTorah*, one may recite them with the accompanying verses during *Pesukei DeZimra*.
- If one did not yet put on the *tallit* (such as in a case where the congregation starts *Pesukei DeZimra* before the time for *tallit*), it is preferable to put it on after reciting *Yishtabaḥ* before *Kaddish* and recite the *berakhot* as usual. The *Leader*, however, should put on his *tallit* before reciting *Yishtabaḥ* (*OḤ* 53:3).

PESUKEI DEZIMRA

The introductory blessing to the Pesukei DeZimra (Verses of Praise) is said standing, while holding the two front tzitziot of the tallit. They are kissed and released at the end of the blessing at "songs of praise." From the beginning of this prayer to the end of the Amida, conversation is forbidden. See "Interruptions during Pesukei DeZimra" below.

בָּרוּךְ שֶׁאָמַר BLESSED IS HE Who spoke and the world came into being, blessed is He. Blessed is He Who creates the universe. Blessed is He Who speaks and it is done. Blessed is He Whose decrees are always fulfilled. Blessed is He Who has compassion for the world. Blessed is He Who has compassion for those He created. Blessed is He Who rewards those who revere Him. Blessed is He, ever living, existent forever. Blessed is He Who redeems and saves, blessed is His name. Blessed are You, Lord, our God, King of the universe, God the merciful Father, exalted on the lips on Your people, praised and glorified on the tongues of Your pious servants. We too, Lord our God, will sing Your praises with the psalms of Your servant David. With praises and hymns will we declare Your greatness, Your praise, and Your glory. We will acclaim Your name and Your sovereignty, our King and our God, ▸ Only One, Who gives life to the worlds. O King, lauded and praised be Your great name forever and ever. Blessed are You, Lord, the King Who is extolled with songs of praise.

I Chr. 16 הוֹדוּ GIVE THANKS to the Lord, call on His name. Proclaim His deeds among the peoples. Sing to Him, chant His praise, recite His wondrous

LAWS FOR ONE WHO HAS FALLEN BEHIND THE CONGREGATION:
If one cannot keep up with the congregation or one came late to synagogue, certain portions of *Pesukei DeZimra* can be skipped so that one can recite the *berakhot* of *Keriat Shema* with the congregation. The core of *Pesukei DeZimra*, which is *Barukh She'amar*, *Ashrei* and *Yishtabaḥ* cannot be skipped. (On Shabbat and Yom Tov, one should not skip *Nishmat*.) The other portions may be skipped, but if time allows, certain portions are given priority over others (*OḤ* 52:1 and *MB* 52:1–5). The order of priority is:

1. Psalms 148 and 150
2. Psalms 146, 147, and 148
3. *Vayevarech David* until *Leshem Tifartekha*
4. *Hodu* until *Vehu Raḥum*
5. On Shabbat and Yom Tov, the portions recited during the week precede those recited only on Shabbat and Yom Tov.

יִשְׂמַח לֵב מְבַקְשֵׁי יהוה: דִּרְשׁוּ יהוה וְעֻזּוֹ, בַּקְּשׁוּ פָנָיו תָּמִיד:
זִכְרוּ נִפְלְאֹתָיו אֲשֶׁר עָשָׂה, מֹפְתָיו וּמִשְׁפְּטֵי־פִיהוּ: זֶרַע יִשְׂרָאֵל
עַבְדּוֹ, בְּנֵי יַעֲקֹב בְּחִירָיו: הוּא יהוה אֱלֹהֵינוּ בְּכָל־הָאָרֶץ מִשְׁפָּטָיו:
זִכְרוּ לְעוֹלָם בְּרִיתוֹ, דָּבָר צִוָּה לְאֶלֶף דּוֹר: אֲשֶׁר כָּרַת אֶת־אַבְרָהָם,
וּשְׁבוּעָתוֹ לְיִצְחָק: וַיַּעֲמִידֶהָ לְיַעֲקֹב לְחֹק, לְיִשְׂרָאֵל בְּרִית עוֹלָם:
לֵאמֹר, לְךָ אֶתֵּן אֶרֶץ־כְּנָעַן, חֶבֶל נַחֲלַתְכֶם: בִּהְיוֹתְכֶם מְתֵי מִסְפָּר,
כִּמְעַט וְגָרִים בָּהּ: וַיִּתְהַלְּכוּ מִגּוֹי אֶל־גּוֹי, וּמִמַּמְלָכָה אֶל־עַם אַחֵר:
לֹא־הִנִּיחַ לְאִישׁ לְעָשְׁקָם, וַיּוֹכַח עֲלֵיהֶם מְלָכִים: אַל־תִּגְּעוּ בִּמְשִׁיחָי,
וּבִנְבִיאַי אַל־תָּרֵעוּ: שִׁירוּ לַיהוה כָּל־הָאָרֶץ, בַּשְּׂרוּ מִיּוֹם־אֶל־יוֹם
יְשׁוּעָתוֹ: סַפְּרוּ בַגּוֹיִם אֶת־כְּבוֹדוֹ, בְּכָל־הָעַמִּים נִפְלְאֹתָיו: כִּי גָדוֹל
יהוה וּמְהֻלָּל מְאֹד, וְנוֹרָא הוּא עַל־כָּל־אֱלֹהִים: ‹ כִּי כָּל־אֱלֹהֵי
הָעַמִּים אֱלִילִים (*pause*), וַיהוה שָׁמַיִם עָשָׂה:

הוֹד וְהָדָר לְפָנָיו, עֹז וְחֶדְוָה בִּמְקֹמוֹ: הָבוּ לַיהוה מִשְׁפְּחוֹת
עַמִּים, הָבוּ לַיהוה כָּבוֹד וָעֹז: הָבוּ לַיהוה כְּבוֹד שְׁמוֹ, שְׂאוּ מִנְחָה
וּבֹאוּ לְפָנָיו, הִשְׁתַּחֲווּ לַיהוה בְּהַדְרַת־קֹדֶשׁ: חִילוּ מִלְּפָנָיו כָּל־
הָאָרֶץ, אַף־תִּכּוֹן תֵּבֵל בַּל־תִּמּוֹט: יִשְׂמְחוּ הַשָּׁמַיִם וְתָגֵל הָאָרֶץ,
וְיֹאמְרוּ בַגּוֹיִם יהוה מָלָךְ: יִרְעַם הַיָּם וּמְלוֹאוֹ, יַעֲלֹץ הַשָּׂדֶה וְכָל־

הודו / GIVE THANKS (previous page)
This section of the *Pesukei DeZimra* is taken directly from I Chronicles 16, as well as Psalm 105, composed by King David, to be recited on the occasion of the transfer of the Ark containing the tablets of the Law from Givon to Jerusalem. See the commentary on page 61. It describes at length the special covenantal relationship between God and the patriarchs, the promise of the land of Israel to them and their descendants, as well as the protective shield that God extended over them in their multiple interactions with the surrounding nations and cultures. In light of these many kindnesses, both natural and supernatural, their descendants are called upon to sing God's praises, and appreciate His endless kindnesses and blessings. These verses thus appropriately set the tone and form the foundation of the *Pesukei DeZimra* that will follow, while also reaffirming the special relationship between God and His chosen nation, the Jewish people.

זֶרַע יִשְׂרָאֵל עַבְדּוֹ – *Seed of Israel His servant*. The term זֶרַע יִשְׂרָאֵל (the descendants of Israel) is not casually chosen. While in the original verse in Psalm 105 the phrase is זֶרַע אַבְרָהָם (the descendants of Abraham), the version in Chronicles is זֶרַע יִשְׂרָאֵל. The reason for this

works. Glorify His holiness. Let your hearts rejoice, you who seek the Lord. Seek out the Lord and His might. Seek His presence continually. Recall the wonders He has brought about, His many acts of providence and guidance. Seed of Israel His servant, children of Jacob His chosen one, never forget that He is the Lord our God; His judgments are in all the earth. Always remember His covenant, the words He ordained for a thousand generations, the covenant He made with Abraham, and His oath to Isaac, which He confirmed as a statute with Jacob, an everlasting covenant for Israel, saying: "To you will I give the land of Canaan as the portion of your inheritance." When you were but few in number, very few and sojourners in the land, and when you wandered from nation to nation, and from one realm to another, He permitted no one to oppress you. Truly, on your account He castigates kings: "Do not touch My anointed ones or harm My prophets." Therefore sing to the Lord, let the whole earth, from day to day, proclaim His saving power. Declare His glory among the nations, His wonders among all the peoples. For the Lord's greatness extends beyond any human praise; He stands above every other god, ▸ because the gods of the heathens are no more than idols (*pause*), whereas the Lord made the heavens.

His very presence is the essence of majesty and grandeur, of strength and gladness in His omnipresence. Ascribe to the Lord, you families of nations, ascribe to the Lord glory and might, ascribe to the Lord the glory due His name. Bring an offering and come before Him, worship the Lord in the beauty of holiness; the whole earth trembles before Him, though the world is fixed and cannot be moved. Let the heavens rejoice and the earth be glad, and let it be declared among the nations that the Lord reigns. Let

---

choice is that Abraham had other descendants (not by way of Isaac and Jacob) outside of the Jewish people, whereas the descendants of Israel (i.e., Jacob) were all included in the nation of Israel. Thus only the זֶרַע יִשְׂרָאֵל were "בְּחִירָיו" (His chosen ones) who inherited the blessings and the land of Israel as promised to the patriarchs (Radak).

דָּבָר צִוָּה לְאֶלֶף דּוֹר – *The words He ordained for a thousand generations.* This refers to the Torah that, according to a midrashic interpretation of this verse, God originally intended to reveal to the world in the thousandth generation after Creation. When, however, God in His infinite wisdom recognized that the world would not survive that long without the Torah, He created the Torah nine hundred and seventy-four generations prior to Creation, and then revealed it at Sinai, twenty-six generations after Creation, that is, a thousand generations after its creation (Rashi).

אֲשֶׁר־בּוֹ: אָז יְרַנְּנוּ עֲצֵי הַיָּעַר, מִלִּפְנֵי יהוה, כִּי־בָא לִשְׁפּוֹט אֶת־
הָאָרֶץ: הוֹדוּ לַיהוה כִּי טוֹב, כִּי לְעוֹלָם חַסְדּוֹ: וְאִמְרוּ, הוֹשִׁיעֵנוּ
אֱלֹהֵי יִשְׁעֵנוּ, וְקַבְּצֵנוּ וְהַצִּילֵנוּ מִן־הַגּוֹיִם, לְהֹדוֹת לְשֵׁם קָדְשֶׁךָ,
לְהִשְׁתַּבֵּחַ בִּתְהִלָּתֶךָ: בָּרוּךְ יהוה אֱלֹהֵי יִשְׂרָאֵל מִן־הָעוֹלָם וְעַד־
הָעֹלָם, וַיֹּאמְרוּ כָל־הָעָם אָמֵן, וְהַלֵּל לַיהוה:

◂ רוֹמְמוּ יהוה אֱלֹהֵינוּ וְהִשְׁתַּחֲווּ לַהֲדֹם רַגְלָיו, קָדוֹשׁ הוּא: רוֹמְמוּ תהלים צט
יהוה אֱלֹהֵינוּ וְהִשְׁתַּחֲווּ לְהַר קָדְשׁוֹ, כִּי־קָדוֹשׁ יהוה אֱלֹהֵינוּ:

וְהוּא רַחוּם, יְכַפֵּר עָוֹן וְלֹא־יַשְׁחִית, וְהִרְבָּה לְהָשִׁיב אַפּוֹ, וְלֹא־יָעִיר תהלים עח
כָּל־חֲמָתוֹ: אַתָּה יהוה לֹא־תִכְלָא רַחֲמֶיךָ מִמֶּנִּי, חַסְדְּךָ וַאֲמִתְּךָ תהלים מ
תָּמִיד יִצְּרוּנִי: זְכֹר־רַחֲמֶיךָ יהוה וַחֲסָדֶיךָ, כִּי מֵעוֹלָם הֵמָּה: תְּנוּ תהלים כה תהלים סח
עֹז לֵאלֹהִים, עַל־יִשְׂרָאֵל גַּאֲוָתוֹ, וְעֻזּוֹ בַּשְּׁחָקִים: נוֹרָא אֱלֹהִים
מִמִּקְדָּשֶׁיךָ, אֵל יִשְׂרָאֵל הוּא נֹתֵן עֹז וְתַעֲצֻמוֹת לָעָם, בָּרוּךְ אֱלֹהִים:
אֵל־נְקָמוֹת יהוה, אֵל נְקָמוֹת הוֹפִיעַ: הִנָּשֵׂא שֹׁפֵט הָאָרֶץ, הָשֵׁב תהלים צד
גְּמוּל עַל־גֵּאִים: לַיהוה הַיְשׁוּעָה, עַל־עַמְּךָ בִרְכָתֶךָ סֶּלָה: ◂ יהוה תהלים ג תהלים מו
צְבָאוֹת עִמָּנוּ, מִשְׂגָּב לָנוּ אֱלֹהֵי יַעֲקֹב סֶלָה: יהוה צְבָאוֹת, אַשְׁרֵי תהלים פד
אָדָם בֹּטֵחַ בָּךְ: יהוה הוֹשִׁיעָה, הַמֶּלֶךְ יַעֲנֵנוּ בְיוֹם־קָרְאֵנוּ: תהלים כ

הוֹשִׁיעָה אֶת־עַמֶּךָ, וּבָרֵךְ אֶת־נַחֲלָתֶךָ, וּרְעֵם וְנַשְּׂאֵם עַד־הָעוֹלָם: תהלים כח
נַפְשֵׁנוּ חִכְּתָה לַיהוה, עֶזְרֵנוּ וּמָגִנֵּנוּ הוּא: כִּי־בוֹ יִשְׂמַח לִבֵּנוּ, תהלים לג
כִּי בְשֵׁם קָדְשׁוֹ בָטָחְנוּ: יְהִי־חַסְדְּךָ יהוה עָלֵינוּ, כַּאֲשֶׁר יִחַלְנוּ
לָךְ: הַרְאֵנוּ יהוה חַסְדֶּךָ, וְיֶשְׁעֲךָ תִּתֶּן־לָנוּ: קוּמָה עֶזְרָתָה לָּנוּ, תהלים פה תהלים מד
וּפְדֵנוּ לְמַעַן חַסְדֶּךָ: אָנֹכִי יהוה אֱלֹהֶיךָ הַמַּעַלְךָ מֵאֶרֶץ מִצְרָיִם, תהלים פא
הַרְחֶב־פִּיךָ וַאֲמַלְאֵהוּ: אַשְׁרֵי הָעָם שֶׁכָּכָה לּוֹ, אַשְׁרֵי הָעָם שֶׁיהוה תהלים קמד
אֱלֹהָיו: ◂ וַאֲנִי בְּחַסְדְּךָ בָטַחְתִּי, יָגֵל לִבִּי בִּישׁוּעָתֶךָ, אָשִׁירָה לַיהוה, תהלים יג
כִּי גָמַל עָלָי:

the ocean and its fullness roar, the fields and all that is in them rejoice. The trees of the forest will sing for joy before the Lord when He comes to judge the earth. Give thanks to the Lord because He is good, because His mercy endures forever, and say, "Save us, God of our deliverance; gather us together and free us from the nations to laud Your holy name and triumph in Your praise." Blessed is the Lord God of Israel from everlasting to everlasting. And all the people said Amen and praised the Lord.

Ps. 99 ▸ Exalt the Lord our God, and worship at His footstool, because He
is holy. Exalt the Lord our God, and worship at His holy mountain,
because the Lord our God is holy.

Ps. 78 Yet He, being merciful, forgives iniquity and does not destroy; many
Ps. 40 times He has turned away His anger and not released His wrath. Lord,
do not withhold Your tender mercies from me. May Your love and truth
Ps. 25 always protect me. Lord, remember Your loving mercies and gentle acts
Ps. 68 of kindness enacted since the very beginning of time. Ascribe power
to God; His sublime presence rests over Israel, His power is in the
heavens. God of Israel, awesome God, from Your holy shrines You give
Ps. 94 strength and power to Your people, blessed is God. The Lord God of
retribution: God of retribution, shine forth. Arise, Judge of the earth,
Ps. 3 render to tyrants what they deserve. Salvation is in Your hand, O Lord,
Ps. 46 please bless Your people. Selah. ▸ Lord of hosts, be with us; God of Jacob,
Ps. 84 be our high refuge. Selah. Lord of hosts, happy is he who trusts in You.
Ps. 20 Lord, save us. Our King, answer us on the day we call.

Ps. 28 Save Your people and bless Your heritage; tend them and sustain them
Ps. 33 forever. Our souls await You, O Lord; You are our help and our shield.
Truly, our hearts rejoice in You, for we trust in Your holiness. May Your
Ps. 85 love, O Lord, embrace us, even as we hope in You. Lord, show us Your
Ps. 44 loving-kindness, and grant us freedom. Rise up to help us, and redeem
Ps. 81 us for Your mercy's sake. I am the Lord your God, Who brought you up
Ps. 144 from the land of Egypt. What you desire I will fulfill. Happy the people
Ps. 13 whose lot this is, happy the people whose God is the Lord. ▸ As for me,
I trust in Your mercy, my heart exults in Your saving strength; I will sing
to the Lord, because He has dealt generously with me.

On הושענא רבה *continue here:*

לַמְנַצֵּחַ מִזְמוֹר לְדָוִד: הַשָּׁמַיִם מְסַפְּרִים כְּבוֹד־אֵל, וּמַעֲשֵׂה יָדָיו תהלים יט
מַגִּיד הָרָקִיעַ: יוֹם לְיוֹם יַבִּיעַ אֹמֶר, וְלַיְלָה לְּלַיְלָה יְחַוֶּה־
דָּעַת: אֵין־אֹמֶר וְאֵין דְּבָרִים, בְּלִי נִשְׁמָע קוֹלָם: בְּכָל־הָאָרֶץ יָצָא
קַוָּם, וּבִקְצֵה תֵבֵל מִלֵּיהֶם, לַשֶּׁמֶשׁ שָׂם־אֹהֶל בָּהֶם: וְהוּא כְּחָתָן
יֹצֵא מֵחֻפָּתוֹ, יָשִׂישׂ כְּגִבּוֹר לָרוּץ אֹרַח: מִקְצֵה הַשָּׁמַיִם מוֹצָאוֹ,
וּתְקוּפָתוֹ עַל־קְצוֹתָם, וְאֵין נִסְתָּר מֵחַמָּתוֹ: תּוֹרַת יהוה תְּמִימָה,
מְשִׁיבַת נָפֶשׁ, עֵדוּת יהוה נֶאֱמָנָה, מַחְכִּימַת פֶּתִי: פִּקּוּדֵי יהוה
יְשָׁרִים, מְשַׂמְּחֵי־לֵב, מִצְוַת יהוה בָּרָה, מְאִירַת עֵינָיִם: יִרְאַת
יהוה טְהוֹרָה, עוֹמֶדֶת לָעַד, מִשְׁפְּטֵי־יהוה אֱמֶת, צָדְקוּ יַחְדָּו:
הַנֶּחֱמָדִים מִזָּהָב וּמִפַּז רָב, וּמְתוּקִים מִדְּבַשׁ וְנֹפֶת צוּפִים: גַּם־
עַבְדְּךָ נִזְהָר בָּהֶם, בְּשָׁמְרָם עֵקֶב רָב: שְׁגִיאוֹת מִי־יָבִין, מִנִּסְתָּרוֹת
נַקֵּנִי: גַּם מִזֵּדִים חֲשֹׂךְ עַבְדֶּךָ, אַל־יִמְשְׁלוּ־בִי אָז אֵיתָם, וְנִקֵּיתִי
מִפֶּשַׁע רָב: ‹ יִהְיוּ לְרָצוֹן אִמְרֵי־פִי וְהֶגְיוֹן לִבִּי לְפָנֶיךָ, יהוה,
צוּרִי וְגֹאֲלִי:

THE SHABBAT ADDITIONS TO THE DAILY PESUKEI DEZIMRA

To understand the choice of psalms for *Pesukei DeZimra* of Shabbat and Yom Tov, we can recall that according to R. Joseph B. Soloveitchik the sages chose the particular psalms of the daily *Pesukei DeZimra* because they highlight the everyday hidden miracles by which God's will sustains the world. It is these actions that are the basis of our faith, rather than the rare supernatural miracles that are the focus of the Yom Tov and Rosh Ḥodesh *Hallel*. The *Pesukei DeZimra* of Shabbat and Yom Tov include the same psalms, and thus they reaffirm this essential source of faith. But they also include other psalms pointing to additional aspects of Divine Providence to be encountered in our daily lives, each of which should serve to strengthen our faith.

לַמְנַצֵּחַ / PSALM 19

תּוֹרַת ה׳ תְּמִימָה – *The law of the Lord is perfect.* Psalm 19 consists of two equal sections. The first (verses 1–7) describes the forces of nature that testify to God's glory. The second (verses 8–15) speaks in praise of the Torah. The pivotal verse 8 declares that God's Torah embodies perfection, such that by embracing it we can achieve wholeness of spirit. In this, the Torah is unlike the sun which through overexposure can cause blindness, disease, death, and hallucinations, whereas the more we study Torah the more we achieve longevity, enlightenment, and fulfillment, even in

On Hoshana Raba continue here:

Ps. 19 **לַמְנַצֵּחַ** TO THE DIRECTOR of music. A psalm of David. The heavens declare the glory of God, and the firmament proclaims His handiwork. Day to day utters speech, and night to night expresses knowledge. There is no speech, nor are there words. Their voice is not heard. Their call goes out through all the earth, and their words to the end of the world. In them He has set a tent for the sun. And it is like a bridegroom coming out of his chamber. It rejoices like a mighty man running along a path. Its going forth is from the end of the heaven, and its circuit is to its ends, and nothing is hidden from its heat. The law of the Lord is perfect, restoring the soul. The testimony of the Lord is faithful, making the simple wise. The statutes of the Lord are upright, rejoicing the heart. The commandments of the Lord are pure, enlightening the eyes. The fear of the Lord is pure, standing forever. The judgments of the Lord are true: they are all righteous. How much more desirable they are than much gold and fine gold, and they are sweeter than honey and the honeycomb. Indeed, Your servant is careful about them. In the keeping of them there is great reward. Who can discern errors? Cleanse me from hidden transgressions. Also keep Your servant from willing sinners. Let them not rule over me. Then I shall be faultless, and let me be clean of many transgressions. ▸ May the words of my mouth and the meditation of my heart be acceptable before You, O Lord, my Rock and my Redeemer.

---

the darkest of nights. Thus while nature can be a source of life as well as death, the Torah by contrast brings only blessing and goodness (Radak).

עֵדוּת ה׳ נֶאֱמָנָה, מַחְכִּימַת פֶּתִי – *The testimony of the Lord is faithful, making the simple wise.* The Torah has two components: its laws and its narratives. The latter are known as עֵדוּת (testaments), for they affirm its truths in anecdotal form. Similarly, in the *Haggada* when the wise child asks regarding the *edot, ḥukim,* and *mishpatim*, he or she is referring to the narrative as well as the laws pertinent to the *Seder*. This verse teaches that even those who, being unable to delve into the Torah's laws, have been led astray by uncritically accepting false narratives, can still find the truth if they study the stories of the Torah (R. Yitzḥak Ze'ev Soloveitchik).

תהלים לד

לְדָוִד, בְּשַׁנּוֹתוֹ אֶת־טַעְמוֹ לִפְנֵי אֲבִימֶלֶךְ, וַיְגָרְשֵׁהוּ וַיֵּלַךְ:
אֲבָרְכָה אֶת־יהוה בְּכָל־עֵת, תָּמִיד תְּהִלָּתוֹ בְּפִי:
בַּיהוה תִּתְהַלֵּל נַפְשִׁי, יִשְׁמְעוּ עֲנָוִים וְיִשְׂמָחוּ:
גַּדְּלוּ לַיהוה אִתִּי, וּנְרוֹמְמָה שְׁמוֹ יַחְדָּו:
דָּרַשְׁתִּי אֶת־יהוה וְעָנָנִי, וּמִכָּל־מְגוּרוֹתַי הִצִּילָנִי:
הִבִּיטוּ אֵלָיו וְנָהָרוּ, וּפְנֵיהֶם אַל־יֶחְפָּרוּ:
זֶה עָנִי קָרָא, וַיהוה שָׁמֵעַ, וּמִכָּל־צָרוֹתָיו הוֹשִׁיעוֹ:
חֹנֶה מַלְאַךְ־יהוה סָבִיב לִירֵאָיו, וַיְחַלְּצֵם:
טַעֲמוּ וּרְאוּ כִּי־טוֹב יהוה, אַשְׁרֵי הַגֶּבֶר יֶחֱסֶה־בּוֹ:
יְראוּ אֶת־יהוה קְדֹשָׁיו, כִּי־אֵין מַחְסוֹר לִירֵאָיו:
כְּפִירִים רָשׁוּ וְרָעֵבוּ, וְדֹרְשֵׁי יהוה לֹא־יַחְסְרוּ כָל־טוֹב:
לְכוּ־בָנִים שִׁמְעוּ־לִי, יִרְאַת יהוה אֲלַמֶּדְכֶם:
מִי־הָאִישׁ הֶחָפֵץ חַיִּים, אֹהֵב יָמִים לִרְאוֹת טוֹב:
נְצֹר לְשׁוֹנְךָ מֵרָע, וּשְׂפָתֶיךָ מִדַּבֵּר מִרְמָה:
סוּר מֵרָע וַעֲשֵׂה־טוֹב, בַּקֵּשׁ שָׁלוֹם וְרָדְפֵהוּ:

לְדָוִד, בְּשַׁנּוֹתוֹ / PSALM 34
In I Samuel 21 the young David flees from Saul, finding temporary refuge in the Philistine city of Gat, where he resorts to feigning mental illness. From this experience David learned that every life experience, no matter how illogical or painful at the time, must be recognized as a potential blessing over time. This is the repeated theme of this psalm, which David composed upon his successful escape from Gat. From this we are to learn that even when we are in pain or despair we can find the inner strength to extract something positive from that experience. Rather than being driven to self-pity or loss of faith in difficult times, our faith in God's goodness can help us find a positive outcome (R. Levi Yitzḥak of Berditchev).

גַּדְּלוּ לַה' אִתִּי... יַחְדָּו – *Magnify the Lord with me ... together.* The two halves of this verse teach us how to approach God in prayer. At first the Psalmist calls on his fellows to proclaim the Lord's greatness "with him," implying that he remains at the center of the service, while they play only a supplementary role. The second half of the verse proclaims "let us extol His name together." That is, when we put aside our self-centeredness to come truly יַחְדָּו (together as one) into God's presence, only then are we able to truly "extol His name" (R. Akiva Eger).

אַשְׁרֵי הַגֶּבֶר יֶחֱסֶה־בּוֹ – *Happy is the man who seeks refuge in Him.* We ask neither about the cause of evil nor about its purpose, but rather about how it might be mended and elevated.

Ps. 34 לְדָוִד OF DAVID, when he feigned madness before Abimelech, who drove him away, and he departed.

א I will bless the Lord at all times. His praise is always in my mouth.

ב My soul glories in the Lord. But the humble hear and rejoice.

ג Magnify the Lord with me, and let us exalt His name together.

ד I sought the Lord and He answered me,
and He delivered me from all my fears.

ה They looked to Him, and were radiant.

ו Let their faces not be abashed.

ז Behold, a poor man cries and the Lord hears,
and He saves him from all his troubles.

ח The angel of the Lord encamps around those who fear Him,
and he rescues them.

ט Taste and see that the Lord is good.
Happy is the man who seeks refuge in Him.

י Fear the Lord, you His holy ones,
for those who fear Him have no lack.

כ The young lions are poor and hungry,
but those who seek the Lord will not lack any good thing.

ל Come, children, listen to me. I will teach you to fear the Lord.

מ The man who desires life, who loves days to see good,

נ Guard your tongue from evil,
and your lips from speaking deceit.

ס Turn away from evil, and do good. Seek peace, and pursue it.

How shall a person act in a time of trouble? What ought a man to do so that he not perish in his afflictions? The halakhic answer to this question is very simple. Afflictions come to elevate a person, to purify and sanctify his spirit… The Torah itself bears witness to man's powerful spiritual reaction to any trouble that may befall him when it states 'In your distress when all these things come upon you… you shall return unto the Lord your God' (Deut. 4:30). Suffering imposes upon man the obligation to return to God in complete and wholehearted repentance. Afflictions are designed to bestir us to repent, and what is repentance if not man's self-renewal and his supernal redemption? (R. Joseph B. Soloveitchik)

עֵינֵי יהוה אֶל־צַדִּיקִים, וְאָזְנָיו אֶל־שַׁוְעָתָם:
פְּנֵי יהוה בְּעֹשֵׂי רָע, לְהַכְרִית מֵאֶרֶץ זִכְרָם:
צָעֲקוּ וַיהוה שָׁמֵעַ, וּמִכׇּל־צָרוֹתָם הִצִּילָם:
קָרוֹב יהוה לְנִשְׁבְּרֵי־לֵב, וְאֶת־דַּכְּאֵי־רוּחַ יוֹשִׁיעַ:
רַבּוֹת רָעוֹת צַדִּיק, וּמִכֻּלָּם יַצִּילֶנּוּ יהוה:
שֹׁמֵר כׇּל־עַצְמוֹתָיו, אַחַת מֵהֵנָּה לֹא נִשְׁבָּרָה:
תְּמוֹתֵת רָשָׁע רָעָה, וְשֹׂנְאֵי צַדִּיק יֶאְשָׁמוּ:
◄ פּוֹדֶה יהוה נֶפֶשׁ עֲבָדָיו, וְלֹא יֶאְשְׁמוּ כׇּל־הַחֹסִים בּוֹ:

תְּפִלָּה לְמֹשֶׁה אִישׁ־הָאֱלֹהִים, אֲדֹנָי, מָעוֹן אַתָּה הָיִיתָ לָּנוּ בְּדֹר תהלים צ
וָדֹר: בְּטֶרֶם הָרִים יֻלָּדוּ, וַתְּחוֹלֵל אֶרֶץ וְתֵבֵל, וּמֵעוֹלָם
עַד־עוֹלָם אַתָּה אֵל: תָּשֵׁב אֱנוֹשׁ עַד־דַּכָּא, וַתֹּאמֶר שׁוּבוּ בְנֵי־אָדָם:
כִּי אֶלֶף שָׁנִים בְּעֵינֶיךָ, כְּיוֹם אֶתְמוֹל כִּי יַעֲבֹר, וְאַשְׁמוּרָה בַלָּיְלָה:
זְרַמְתָּם, שֵׁנָה יִהְיוּ, בַּבֹּקֶר כֶּחָצִיר יַחֲלֹף: בַּבֹּקֶר יָצִיץ וְחָלָף, לָעֶרֶב
יְמוֹלֵל וְיָבֵשׁ: כִּי־כָלִינוּ בְאַפֶּךָ, וּבַחֲמָתְךָ נִבְהָלְנוּ: שַׁתָּ עֲוֺנֹתֵינוּ
לְנֶגְדֶּךָ, עֲלֻמֵנוּ לִמְאוֹר פָּנֶיךָ: כִּי כׇל־יָמֵינוּ פָּנוּ בְעֶבְרָתֶךָ, כִּלִּינוּ
שָׁנֵינוּ כְמוֹ־הֶגֶה: יְמֵי־שְׁנוֹתֵינוּ בָהֶם שִׁבְעִים שָׁנָה, וְאִם בִּגְבוּרֹת

רַבּוֹת רָעוֹת צַדִּיק – *Many are the afflictions of the righteous*. Greatness is a product of challenges, brave attempts, and many mistakes. No one becomes truly *righteous* without his share of *mishaps* (*Sefat Emet*).

תְּפִלָּה לְמֹשֶׁה / PSALM 90
In this psalm the notion of time dominates. No less than sixteen words convey notions of time, such as morning, evening, days, and years (R. Ronald Benun).

The psalm is divided into two sections. The first nine verses express the feelings

קָרוֹב ה׳ לְנִשְׁבְּרֵי־לֵב, וְאֶת־דַּכְּאֵי־רוּחַ יוֹשִׁיעַ – *The Lord is near to those with a broken heart, and He saves those of contrite spirit*. The Psalmist here teaches us that the foundation of prayer is to come before God with a broken heart, with a feeling of complete worthlessness and dependence on Him. This is the reason that the preceding verses state that "The eyes of the Lord are toward the righteous, and His ears are open to their cry," i.e., when they are broken-hearted. So too in *Ashrei* it says that God is close to those who call out to Him בֶאֱמֶת, i.e., with all of their being (Meiri).

ע The eyes of the Lord are toward the righteous,
and His ears are open to their cry.
פ The face of the Lord is against those who do evil, to cut off
the remembrance of them from the earth.
צ They cry, and the Lord hears,
and He delivers them from all their troubles.
ק The Lord is near to those with a broken heart,
and He saves those of contrite spirit.
ר Many are the afflictions of the righteous,
but the Lord delivers him from them all.
ש He keeps all his bones. Not one of them is broken.
ת Evil will kill the wicked,
and those who hate the righteous will be held guilty.
▸ The Lord redeems the soul of His servant,
and none of those who seek refuge in Him will be held guilty.

Ps. 90 **תְּפִלָּה** A PRAYER of Moses, the man of God. O Lord, You have been our shelter in all generations. Before the mountains were born and You had formed the earth and the world, even from everlasting to everlasting, You are God. You turn man back to dust and You say, "Return, you children of man." Indeed, a thousand years in Your sight are like yesterday when it is past, and like a watch in the night. You engulf them, they are like sleepers. In the morning they are like the short-lived grass. In the morning it flowers and fades, in the evening it withers and dries. Indeed, we are consumed by Your anger, and through Your wrath we die. You set our iniquities before You, our secrets in the light of Your countenance. Indeed, all our days pass away in Your wrath, we consume our years like a sound. The days of our years are seventy, or even by reason of strength eighty

---

of a man in his twilight years, reflecting on the insignificance of the human life span in light of God's eternity. The second section, consisting of eight verses, asks for divine guidance to fill our lives with righteousness in the presence of God, and thereby to achieve lasting meaning and purpose (R. Yitzchak Etshalom).

שְׁמוֹנִים שָׁנָה, וְרָהְבָּם עָמָל וָאָוֶן, כִּי־גָז חִישׁ וַנָּעֻפָה: מִי־יוֹדֵעַ עֹז
אַפֶּךָ, וּכְיִרְאָתְךָ עֶבְרָתֶךָ, לִמְנוֹת יָמֵינוּ כֵּן הוֹדַע, וְנָבִא לְבַב חָכְמָה:
שׁוּבָה יהוה עַד־מָתָי, וְהִנָּחֵם עַל־עֲבָדֶיךָ: שַׂבְּעֵנוּ בַבֹּקֶר חַסְדֶּךָ,
וּנְרַנְּנָה וְנִשְׂמְחָה בְּכָל־יָמֵינוּ: שַׂמְּחֵנוּ כִּימוֹת עִנִּיתָנוּ, שְׁנוֹת רָאִינוּ
רָעָה: יֵרָאֶה אֶל־עֲבָדֶיךָ פָעֳלֶךָ, וַהֲדָרְךָ עַל־בְּנֵיהֶם: ◂ וִיהִי נֹעַם
אֲדֹנָי אֱלֹהֵינוּ עָלֵינוּ, וּמַעֲשֵׂה יָדֵינוּ כּוֹנְנָה עָלֵינוּ, וּמַעֲשֵׂה יָדֵינוּ
כּוֹנְנֵהוּ:

יֹשֵׁב בְּסֵתֶר עֶלְיוֹן, בְּצֵל שַׁדַּי יִתְלוֹנָן: אֹמַר לַיהוה מַחְסִי וּמְצוּדָתִי, תהלים צא
אֱלֹהַי אֶבְטַח־בּוֹ: כִּי הוּא יַצִּילְךָ מִפַּח יָקוּשׁ, מִדֶּבֶר הַוּוֹת:
בְּאֶבְרָתוֹ יָסֶךְ לָךְ, וְתַחַת־כְּנָפָיו תֶּחְסֶה, צִנָּה וְסֹחֵרָה אֲמִתּוֹ: לֹא־
תִירָא מִפַּחַד לָיְלָה, מֵחֵץ יָעוּף יוֹמָם: מִדֶּבֶר בָּאֹפֶל יַהֲלֹךְ, מִקֶּטֶב
יָשׁוּד צָהֳרָיִם: יִפֹּל מִצִּדְּךָ אֶלֶף, וּרְבָבָה מִימִינֶךָ, אֵלֶיךָ לֹא יִגָּשׁ:
רַק בְּעֵינֶיךָ תַבִּיט, וְשִׁלֻּמַת רְשָׁעִים תִּרְאֶה: כִּי־אַתָּה יהוה מַחְסִי,
עֶלְיוֹן שַׂמְתָּ מְעוֹנֶךָ: לֹא־תְאֻנֶּה אֵלֶיךָ רָעָה, וְנֶגַע לֹא־יִקְרַב בְּאָהֳלֶךָ:
כִּי מַלְאָכָיו יְצַוֶּה־לָּךְ, לִשְׁמָרְךָ בְּכָל־דְּרָכֶיךָ: עַל־כַּפַּיִם יִשָּׂאוּנְךָ,
פֶּן־תִּגֹּף בָּאֶבֶן רַגְלֶךָ: עַל־שַׁחַל וָפֶתֶן תִּדְרֹךְ, תִּרְמֹס כְּפִיר וְתַנִּין:
כִּי בִי חָשַׁק וַאֲפַלְּטֵהוּ, אֲשַׂגְּבֵהוּ כִּי־יָדַע שְׁמִי: יִקְרָאֵנִי וְאֶעֱנֵהוּ,

---

יֹשֵׁב בְּסֵתֶר / PSALM 91
The Gemara (*Shavuot* 15b) refers to this psalm as the "*Song of Plagues*" on account of its description of the many perils from which God shields His faithful servants. Many of the dangers mentioned here are those experienced by travelers, and thus it is possible that it was originally recited by or for those setting out on a long journey in the hope that they would enjoy God's protection for the duration of the trip. This would possibly account for the widespread custom to recite this psalm in its entirety, with its numerous references to God's protection of the faithful, as part of the funeral service, and in particular as the casket approaches its final resting place. The psalm would thus represent an apt reflection of our hope and prayer that (as it states) God's angels will accompany and protect the soul on its ultimate journey, i.e., from this world to the next. We can also identify a connection between this psalm and our Shabbat prayers. The verse "I will satisfy him with long life, and I will show him of My salvation" is echoed in our repeated Shabbat request to God to "Gratify us with Your goodness

years, but their pride is trouble and wretchedness, for it soars in haste, and we fly away. Who knows the power of Your anger, and that Your wrath is in accordance with Your fear? Teach us to number our days correctly. And may we get a heart of wisdom. Return, O Lord! How long? And relent concerning Your servants. Satisfy us in the morning with Your loving-kindness, and let us rejoice and be glad all our days. Make us glad according to the days in which You have afflicted us, the years in which we have seen evil. Let Your work be seen by Your servants, and Your glory through their children. ▸ And let the pleasantness of the Lord our God be upon us, and establish the work of our hands upon us, and establish it, the work of our hands.

Ps. 91 **יֹשֵׁב** HE WHO DWELLS in the secret place of the Most High abides in the shadow of the Almighty. I say to the Lord, my refuge and my fortress, my God, I trust in Him. Indeed, He will deliver you from the baited trap, from the deadly pestilence. He will cover you with His pinions, and under His wings you will find refuge. His truth will be your shield and buckler. You will not be afraid of the terror by night, of the arrow that flies by day, of the pestilence that walks in the darkness, of the destruction that wastes at noonday. A thousand will fall at your side and ten thousand at your right hand. It will not come near to you. Only with your eyes will you behold, and you will see the destruction of the wicked. Indeed, You, O Lord, are my refuge. You have made the Most High Your habitation. No evil will befall you, and plague will not come near to your tent. Indeed, He will give His angels charge over you, to keep you in all your ways. They will bear you up on their hands, lest you dash your foot against a stone. You will tread upon the lion and the adder. You will trample the young lion and the crocodile underfoot. Because he has clung to Me, I will deliver him. I will make him safe, because he has known My name. When he calls upon Me, I answer

---

and gladden us with Your salvation" (R. Amos Ḥakham).

כִּי־יָדַע שְׁמִי – *Because he has known My name.* God declares that He will rescue and protect us "because we know His name." This refers to our knowing the secret of His name of four

עִמּוֹ אָנֹכִי בְצָרָה, אֲחַלְּצֵהוּ וַאֲכַבְּדֵהוּ: ◂ אֹרֶךְ יָמִים אַשְׂבִּיעֵהוּ,
וְאַרְאֵהוּ בִּישׁוּעָתִי: אֹרֶךְ יָמִים אַשְׂבִּיעֵהוּ, וְאַרְאֵהוּ בִּישׁוּעָתִי:

תהלים קלה

הַלְלוּיָהּ, הַלְלוּ אֶת־שֵׁם יהוה, הַלְלוּ עַבְדֵי יהוה: שֶׁעֹמְדִים בְּבֵית
יהוה, בְּחַצְרוֹת בֵּית אֱלֹהֵינוּ: הַלְלוּיָהּ כִּי־טוֹב יהוה,
זַמְּרוּ לִשְׁמוֹ כִּי נָעִים: כִּי־יַעֲקֹב בָּחַר לוֹ יָהּ, יִשְׂרָאֵל לִסְגֻלָּתוֹ: כִּי
אֲנִי יָדַעְתִּי כִּי־גָדוֹל יהוה, וַאֲדֹנֵינוּ מִכָּל־אֱלֹהִים: כֹּל אֲשֶׁר־חָפֵץ
יהוה עָשָׂה, בַּשָּׁמַיִם וּבָאָרֶץ, בַּיַּמִּים וְכָל־תְּהֹמוֹת: מַעֲלֶה נְשִׂאִים
מִקְצֵה הָאָרֶץ, בְּרָקִים לַמָּטָר עָשָׂה, מוֹצֵא־רוּחַ מֵאוֹצְרוֹתָיו: שֶׁהִכָּה
בְּכוֹרֵי מִצְרָיִם, מֵאָדָם עַד־בְּהֵמָה: שָׁלַח אוֹתֹת וּמֹפְתִים בְּתוֹכֵכִי
מִצְרָיִם, בְּפַרְעֹה וּבְכָל־עֲבָדָיו: שֶׁהִכָּה גּוֹיִם רַבִּים, וְהָרַג מְלָכִים
עֲצוּמִים: לְסִיחוֹן מֶלֶךְ הָאֱמֹרִי, וּלְעוֹג מֶלֶךְ הַבָּשָׁן, וּלְכֹל מַמְלְכוֹת
כְּנָעַן: וְנָתַן אַרְצָם נַחֲלָה, נַחֲלָה לְיִשְׂרָאֵל עַמּוֹ: יהוה שִׁמְךָ לְעוֹלָם,
יהוה זִכְרְךָ לְדֹר־וָדֹר: כִּי־יָדִין יהוה עַמּוֹ, וְעַל־עֲבָדָיו יִתְנֶחָם: עֲצַבֵּי
הַגּוֹיִם כֶּסֶף וְזָהָב, מַעֲשֵׂה יְדֵי אָדָם: פֶּה־לָהֶם וְלֹא יְדַבֵּרוּ, עֵינַיִם
לָהֶם וְלֹא יִרְאוּ: אָזְנַיִם לָהֶם וְלֹא יַאֲזִינוּ, אַף אֵין־יֶשׁ־רוּחַ בְּפִיהֶם:

---

letters, knowledge of which leads to, and is essential for, the love of God (Radak). This is consistent with the approach of Rambam in the Guide, where he asserts that God's protective providence is extended to individuals only to the extent that they have acquired knowledge of God and the celestial world in relation to mankind. In this regard, see also the commentary on page 178.

עִמּוֹ אָנֹכִי בְצָרָה – *I am with him in trouble.* This phrase should not be understood to be saying that God Himself experiences distress. Rather, it is saying that God lowers Himself, so to speak, to be with or "visit" us, so as to comfort us and thus diminish our pain and suffering. But God's glory in and of itself remains absolutely intact, as we affirm in the *kedusha*, "Blessed is the glory of the Lord from His abode" (Maharal).

הַלְלוּיָהּ / PSALM 135

This psalm and the next are a liturgical pair, apparently first intended to be recited in the Temple, as indicated by the second verse. It urges the assembly to praise God, in recognition of His supreme power, as manifested by His mastery of nature and His victory over mighty kings and armies. Thereupon the assembly recited Psalm 136, probably responsively (R. Amos Ḥakham).

This psalm is a summons to recite *Hallel*, which is to be distinguished from other songs of praise in that it does not address God directly, but rather is about Him. It appears to have

him. I am with him in trouble. I deliver him and I will honor him. ▸ I will satisfy him with long life, and I will show him of My salvation. I will satisfy him with long life, and I will show him of My salvation.

Ps. 135 הַלְלוּיָהּ PRAISE THE LORD. Praise the name of the Lord, praise, you servants of the Lord, who stand in the house of the Lord, in the courtyards of the house of our God. Praise the Lord, for the Lord is good. Sing praises to His name, for it is pleasant. For the Lord has chosen Jacob for Himself, Israel for His special possession. Indeed, I know that the Lord is great, and that our Lord is greater than all gods. Whatever the Lord wishes He does, in the heavens and on the earth, in the seas and all the deep places. He causes clouds to rise from the end of the earth. He makes lightnings with the rain. He brings wind out of His treasure-houses. It was He Who smote the firstborn of Egypt, both of man and of beast, Who sent signs and wonders into the midst of Egypt, upon Pharaoh and upon all his servants, Who smote great nations, and slew mighty kings, Sihon King of the Amorites, and Og King of Bashan, and all the kingdoms of Canaan, and Who gave their land as a heritage, a heritage to Israel His people. O Lord, Your name is forever. O Lord, Your renown is for all generations. Indeed, the Lord will judge His people, and He will relent concerning His servants. The idols of the nations are silver and gold, the work of man's hands. They have a mouth but they do not speak, they have eyes but they do not see. They have ears but they do not hear, and there is even no breath in their mouths. Those who make them will become like them,

---

been recited in the presence of an assembly in order to proclaim God's wondrous deeds, and to evoke in those present a realization that they should fully rely on His salvation (R. Eric Levy).

פֶּה־לָהֶם וְלֹא יְדַבֵּרוּ – *They have a mouth but they do not speak.* There was no reason for the Psalmist to proclaim the obvious fact, recognized even by those who worship idols, that an object made of wood or stone cannot speak or see or hear. Rather, what this verse means is that just as a physical object cannot actually do these things, so too the heavenly powers that these objects supposedly represent are completely incapable of accomplishing anything on behalf of their believers. So, too, in our own time there are many who mistakenly believe that there are spiritual beings or forces other than the one true God that have the power to help them or control their fate for good or evil (R. Moshe Feinstein).

כְּמוֹהֶם יִהְיוּ עֹשֵׂיהֶם, כֹּל אֲשֶׁר־בֹּטֵחַ בָּהֶם: ◂ בֵּית יִשְׂרָאֵל בָּרְכוּ אֶת־
יהוה, בֵּית אַהֲרֹן בָּרְכוּ אֶת־יהוה: בֵּית הַלֵּוִי בָּרְכוּ אֶת־יהוה, יִרְאֵי
יהוה בָּרְכוּ אֶת־יהוה: בָּרוּךְ יהוה מִצִּיּוֹן, שֹׁכֵן יְרוּשָׁלָםִ, הַלְלוּיָהּ:

The custom is to stand for the following psalm.

תהלים קלו

הוֹדוּ לַיהוה כִּי־טוֹב — כִּי לְעוֹלָם חַסְדּוֹ:
הוֹדוּ לֵאלֹהֵי הָאֱלֹהִים — כִּי לְעוֹלָם חַסְדּוֹ:
הוֹדוּ לַאֲדֹנֵי הָאֲדֹנִים — כִּי לְעוֹלָם חַסְדּוֹ:
לְעֹשֵׂה נִפְלָאוֹת גְּדֹלוֹת לְבַדּוֹ — כִּי לְעוֹלָם חַסְדּוֹ:
לְעֹשֵׂה הַשָּׁמַיִם בִּתְבוּנָה — כִּי לְעוֹלָם חַסְדּוֹ:
לְרֹקַע הָאָרֶץ עַל־הַמָּיִם — כִּי לְעוֹלָם חַסְדּוֹ:
לְעֹשֵׂה אוֹרִים גְּדֹלִים — כִּי לְעוֹלָם חַסְדּוֹ:
אֶת־הַשֶּׁמֶשׁ לְמֶמְשֶׁלֶת בַּיּוֹם — כִּי לְעוֹלָם חַסְדּוֹ:
אֶת־הַיָּרֵחַ וְכוֹכָבִים לְמֶמְשְׁלוֹת בַּלָּיְלָה — כִּי לְעוֹלָם חַסְדּוֹ:
לְמַכֵּה מִצְרַיִם בִּבְכוֹרֵיהֶם — כִּי לְעוֹלָם חַסְדּוֹ:
וַיּוֹצֵא יִשְׂרָאֵל מִתּוֹכָם — כִּי לְעוֹלָם חַסְדּוֹ:
בְּיָד חֲזָקָה וּבִזְרוֹעַ נְטוּיָה — כִּי לְעוֹלָם חַסְדּוֹ:
לְגֹזֵר יַם־סוּף לִגְזָרִים — כִּי לְעוֹלָם חַסְדּוֹ:

יִרְאֵי ה׳ בָּרְכוּ – *You who fear the Lord, bless.* These are the Jewish sages, or even God-fearing individuals among the nations (Radak, Ibn Ezra).

הוֹדוּ לַה׳ / PSALM 136

The Gemara (*Pesaḥim* 118a) calls this psalm הַלֵּל הַגָּדוֹל (*Great Song of Praise*). A number of the sages of the Talmud contend that the song also includes the preceding psalm (135). Structurally, the psalm begins with three introductory verses, followed by twenty-two verses of praise. Each succeeding verse enumerates God's great deeds (including Creation, the Exodus, victory over the Canaanite kings, the gift of the land of Israel to the Jewish people, and His ongoing sustenance of all life). The psalm concludes with a verse that recalls the structure of the introductory verses (R. Amos Ḥakham).

The praises of this psalm are expressed over the course of twenty-six verses – the numerical value of the letters of God›s four-lettered name – each followed by the refrain "for His mercy endures forever." It thus conveys the meaning of that name, i.e., it represents God's attribute of mercy, reflecting His compassionate involvement in all of creation, from the heavenly luminaries to the lowest invertebrate (Maharal).

everyone who trusts in them. ▸ O house of Israel, bless the Lord. O house of Aaron, bless the Lord. O house of Levi, bless the Lord. You who fear the Lord, bless the Lord. Blessed is the Lord from Zion, He Who dwells in Jerusalem. Praise the Lord.

The custom is to stand for the following psalm.

Ps. 136 **הוֹדוּ** GIVE THANKS to the Lord,
for He is good, for His loving-kindness is forever.
Give thanks to the God of gods, for His loving-kindness is forever.
Give thanks to the Lord of Lords, for His loving-kindness is forever.
To Him Who alone performs great wonders, for His loving-kindness is forever.
To Him Who made the heavens with understanding, for His loving-kindness is forever.
To Him Who stretched out the earth over the water, for His loving-kindness is forever.
To Him Who made great lights, for His loving-kindness is forever.
The sun as ruler over the day, for His loving-kindness is forever.
The moon and the stars as rulers over the night, for His loving-kindness is forever.
To Him Who smote Egypt in their firstborn, for His loving-kindness is forever.
And brought Israel out from among them, for His loving-kindness is forever.
With a strong hand and with an outstretched arm, for His loving-kindness is forever.
To Him Who divided the Sea of Reeds into halves, for His loving-kindness is forever.

אוֹרִים ... הַשֶּׁמֶשׁ ... הַיָּרֵחַ – *Great lights ... the sun ... the moon.* The psalm devotes three separate verses to the subject of the "great lights," i.e., the sun, the moon, and the stars. The first of these verses describes their creation, while the subsequent two portray how God allocated their respective responsibilities. The very fact that the psalm gives equal weight to each of these divine activities teaches that just as it is important for us to engage in creative activity in perfecting God's world, so too it is important in our own lives to engage in bringing order,

וְהֶעֱבִיר יִשְׂרָאֵל בְּתוֹכוֹ כִּי לְעוֹלָם חַסְדּוֹ:
וְנִעֵר פַּרְעֹה וְחֵילוֹ בְיַם־סוּף כִּי לְעוֹלָם חַסְדּוֹ:
לְמוֹלִיךְ עַמּוֹ בַּמִּדְבָּר כִּי לְעוֹלָם חַסְדּוֹ:
לְמַכֵּה מְלָכִים גְּדֹלִים כִּי לְעוֹלָם חַסְדּוֹ:
וַיַּהֲרֹג מְלָכִים אַדִּירִים כִּי לְעוֹלָם חַסְדּוֹ:
לְסִיחוֹן מֶלֶךְ הָאֱמֹרִי כִּי לְעוֹלָם חַסְדּוֹ:
וּלְעוֹג מֶלֶךְ הַבָּשָׁן כִּי לְעוֹלָם חַסְדּוֹ:
וְנָתַן אַרְצָם לְנַחֲלָה כִּי לְעוֹלָם חַסְדּוֹ:
נַחֲלָה לְיִשְׂרָאֵל עַבְדּוֹ כִּי לְעוֹלָם חַסְדּוֹ:
שֶׁבְּשִׁפְלֵנוּ זָכַר לָנוּ כִּי לְעוֹלָם חַסְדּוֹ:
וַיִּפְרְקֵנוּ מִצָּרֵינוּ כִּי לְעוֹלָם חַסְדּוֹ:
◄ נֹתֵן לֶחֶם לְכָל־בָּשָׂר כִּי לְעוֹלָם חַסְדּוֹ:
הוֹדוּ לְאֵל הַשָּׁמָיִם כִּי לְעוֹלָם חַסְדּוֹ:

תהלים לג
רַנְּנוּ צַדִּיקִים בַּיהוה, לַיְשָׁרִים נָאוָה תְהִלָּה: הוֹדוּ לַיהוה בְּכִנּוֹר,
בְּנֵבֶל עָשׂוֹר זַמְּרוּ־לוֹ: שִׁירוּ־לוֹ שִׁיר חָדָשׁ, הֵיטִיבוּ נַגֵּן
בִּתְרוּעָה: כִּי־יָשָׁר דְּבַר־יהוה, וְכָל־מַעֲשֵׂהוּ בֶּאֱמוּנָה: אֹהֵב צְדָקָה
וּמִשְׁפָּט, חֶסֶד יהוה מָלְאָה הָאָרֶץ: בִּדְבַר יהוה שָׁמַיִם נַעֲשׂוּ, וּבְרוּחַ
פִּיו כָּל־צְבָאָם: כֹּנֵס כַּנֵּד מֵי הַיָּם, נֹתֵן בְּאוֹצָרוֹת תְּהוֹמוֹת: יִירְאוּ

---

balance, harmony, and rhythm into that which already exists (R. Yitzchok Hutner).

נֹתֵן לֶחֶם לְכָל־בָּשָׂר – *Who gives bread to all flesh.* From the proximity of this verse to the preceding account of the splitting of the sea, the Gemara (*Pesaḥim* 118a) derives that providing for our daily food is as "difficult" for God as the act by which He split the sea. This is to be understood as follows: When He split the sea God made it appear that this was the natural result of a strong wind, so that the Egyptians would throw caution to the wind and cause their own destruction. This is precisely what God does every day: He makes it appear as if our daily sustenance is a natural occurrence, when in fact it is a complex miracle dependent on the hidden hand of God. (R. Shlomo Zalman Auerbach).

רַנְּנוּ צַדִּיקִים / PSALM 33
Pesikta DeRav Kahana records the view that this psalm was not composed by David but by Moses, to be included later among the psalms.

And brought Israel through its midst, for His loving-kindness is forever.
And cast Pharaoh and his host into the Sea of Reeds, for His loving-kindness is forever.
To Him Who led His people through the wilderness, for His loving-kindness is forever.
To Him Who smote great kings, for His loving-kindness is forever.
And slew mighty kings, for His loving-kindness is forever.
Sihon King of the Amorites, for His loving-kindness is forever.
And Og King of Bashan, for His loving-kindness is forever.
And gave their land as an inheritance, for His loving-kindness is forever.
An inheritance to Israel His servant, for His loving-kindness is forever.
Who remembered us in our degradation, for His loving-kindness is forever.
And delivered us from our enemies, for His loving-kindness is forever.
▸ Who gives bread to all flesh, for His loving-kindness is forever.
Give thanks to the God of the heavens, for His loving-kindness is forever.

Ps. 33 **רַנְּנוּ** REJOICE in the Lord, O you righteous. Praise is seemly for the upright. Give thanks to the Lord with a lyre. Sing praises to Him with a harp of ten strings. Sing Him a new song. Play skillfully with a loud sound. For the word of the Lord is upright, and all His work is done in faithfulness. He loves righteousness and judgment. The earth is full of the loving-kindness of the Lord. By the word of the Lord were the heavens made, and by the breath of His mouth all their host. He gathers the

---

כִּי־יָשָׁר דְּבַר־ה' – *For the word of the Lord is upright*. This echoes Moses' statement (Deut. 32:4) that God is righteous and fair in all His ways (Radak).

This doctrine was epitomized in the life and teachings of the Tanna R. Naḥum of Gimzo. The Gemara (*Ta'anit* 21a) recounts the extreme difficulties in his life, suffering blindness, the loss of his arms and legs, being afflicted with boils and reduced to abject poverty. To all of this he would respond that these were inflicted by the righteous God upon him for

מֵיהוה כָּל־הָאָרֶץ, מִמֶּנּוּ יָגוּרוּ כָּל־יֹשְׁבֵי תֵבֵל: כִּי הוּא אָמַר וַיֶּהִי, הוּא־צִוָּה וַיַּעֲמֹד: יהוה הֵפִיר עֲצַת־גּוֹיִם, הֵנִיא מַחְשְׁבוֹת עַמִּים: עֲצַת יהוה לְעוֹלָם תַּעֲמֹד, מַחְשְׁבוֹת לִבּוֹ לְדֹר וָדֹר: אַשְׁרֵי הַגּוֹי אֲשֶׁר־יהוה אֱלֹהָיו, הָעָם בָּחַר לְנַחֲלָה לוֹ: מִשָּׁמַיִם הִבִּיט יהוה, רָאָה אֶת־כָּל־בְּנֵי הָאָדָם: מִמְּכוֹן־שִׁבְתּוֹ הִשְׁגִּיחַ, אֶל כָּל־יֹשְׁבֵי הָאָרֶץ: הַיֹּצֵר יַחַד לִבָּם, הַמֵּבִין אֶל־כָּל־מַעֲשֵׂיהֶם: אֵין־הַמֶּלֶךְ נוֹשָׁע בְּרָב־חָיִל, גִּבּוֹר לֹא־יִנָּצֵל בְּרָב־כֹּחַ: שֶׁקֶר הַסּוּס לִתְשׁוּעָה, וּבְרֹב חֵילוֹ לֹא יְמַלֵּט: הִנֵּה עֵין יהוה אֶל־יְרֵאָיו, לַמְיַחֲלִים לְחַסְדּוֹ: לְהַצִּיל מִמָּוֶת נַפְשָׁם, וּלְחַיּוֹתָם בָּרָעָב: נַפְשֵׁנוּ חִכְּתָה לַיהוה, עֶזְרֵנוּ וּמָגִנֵּנוּ הוּא: ◂ כִּי־בוֹ יִשְׂמַח לִבֵּנוּ, כִּי בְשֵׁם קָדְשׁוֹ בָטָחְנוּ: יְהִי־חַסְדְּךָ יהוה עָלֵינוּ, כַּאֲשֶׁר יִחַלְנוּ לָךְ:

תהלים צב **מִזְמוֹר שִׁיר** לְיוֹם הַשַּׁבָּת: טוֹב לְהֹדוֹת לַיהוה, וּלְזַמֵּר לְשִׁמְךָ עֶלְיוֹן: לְהַגִּיד בַּבֹּקֶר חַסְדֶּךָ, וֶאֱמוּנָתְךָ בַּלֵּילוֹת: עֲלֵי־עָשׂוֹר וַעֲלֵי־נָבֶל, עֲלֵי הִגָּיוֹן בְּכִנּוֹר: כִּי שִׂמַּחְתַּנִי יהוה בְּפָעֳלֶךָ, בְּמַעֲשֵׂי יָדֶיךָ אֲרַנֵּן: מַה־גָּדְלוּ מַעֲשֶׂיךָ יהוה, מְאֹד עָמְקוּ מַחְשְׁבֹתֶיךָ: אִישׁ־בַּעַר לֹא יֵדָע, וּכְסִיל לֹא־יָבִין אֶת־זֹאת: בִּפְרֹחַ רְשָׁעִים כְּמוֹ עֵשֶׂב, וַיָּצִיצוּ כָּל־פֹּעֲלֵי אָוֶן, לְהִשָּׁמְדָם עֲדֵי־עַד: וְאַתָּה מָרוֹם לְעֹלָם יהוה: כִּי הִנֵּה אֹיְבֶיךָ יהוה, כִּי־הִנֵּה אֹיְבֶיךָ יֹאבֵדוּ, יִתְפָּרְדוּ כָּל־פֹּעֲלֵי אָוֶן: וַתָּרֶם כִּרְאֵים קַרְנִי, בַּלֹּתִי בְּשֶׁמֶן רַעֲנָן: וַתַּבֵּט עֵינִי בְּשׁוּרָי, בַּקָּמִים עָלַי מְרֵעִים תִּשְׁמַעְנָה אָזְנָי: ◂ צַדִּיק כַּתָּמָר יִפְרָח,

see below in the commentary to the opening verses of the *Shema*.) Such affirmations of faith and trust in God's ways are eminently suited to our Shabbat and Yom Tov prayers, for they are days on which we experience a profound sense of being at peace with God, fortunate in being His faithful servants. Hence, we proclaim with the Psalmist the verse preceding this one,

good reason. As he would put it, גַּם זוּ לְטוֹבָה (this too is for the best). As a result he became known not as "Naḥum from Gimzo" but as "Naḥum of *Gamzu*." His student was R. Akiva, who similarly embodied this attitude in the face of misfortune and suffering, seeing God's benevolent ways in even the most horrific personal and national circumstances. (On this,

waters of the sea as a heap. He lays the great waters in storehouses. Let all the earth be in fear of the Lord. Let all the inhabitants of the world stand in awe of Him. For He spoke, and it was. He commanded, and it stood. The Lord confounds the plan of the nations. He makes the thoughts of the people of no effect. The plan of the Lord will stand forever, the thoughts of His heart for all generations. Happy is the nation whose God is the Lord, the people whom He has chosen for His own inheritance. The Lord looks down from heaven. He sees all the sons of man. From the place of His habitation He gazes upon all the inhabitants of the earth. It is He Who creates all their hearts, who discerns all their deeds. A king is not saved by a great host. A mighty man is not delivered by great strength. A horse is a vain thing for safety, and it will not save with its great strength. Behold, the eye of the Lord is on those who fear Him, on those who hope for His loving-kindness, To deliver their soul from death, and to keep them alive in famine. Our soul waits for the Lord. He is our help and our shield. Indeed, in Him does our heart rejoice. Indeed, in His holy name we trust. May Your loving-kindness, O Lord, be upon us, as we hope for You.

Ps. 92 **מִזְמוֹר שִׁיר** A PSALM. A song for thew Sabbath day. It is good to give thanks to the Lord, and to sing praise to Your name, O Most High, to relate Your loving-kindness in the morning and Your faithfulness in the nights. Upon an instrument of ten strings and upon the harp, to the melody of the lyre. For You, O Lord, make me glad through Your work. I rejoice in the works of Your hands. How great are Your works, O Lord! Your thoughts are very deep. A brutish man does not know, and a fool does not understand this. When the wicked spring forth, they are like grass, and when all the workers of iniquity flourish, it is only that they may be destroyed forever. But You, O Lord, are most high forever. Indeed, behold Your enemies, O Lord! Indeed, behold, Your enemies are perishing. All the workers of iniquity are being scattered. But You have exalted my horn like that of a wild ox. I have anointed myself with fresh oil. My eye has seen the downfall of my enemies, and my ears have heard the doom of the wicked who rise against me. ▸ The righteous man flourishes like the palm

---

שִׁירוּ־לוֹ שִׁיר חָדָשׁ (Sing Him a new song), i.e., whatever happens to us at any given moment, we will respond by singing His praises anew (R. Basil Herring).

כְּאֶרֶז בַּלְּבָנוֹן יִשְׂגֶּה: שְׁתוּלִים בְּבֵית יהוה, בְּחַצְרוֹת אֱלֹהֵינוּ יַפְרִיחוּ: עוֹד יְנוּבוּן בְּשֵׂיבָה, דְּשֵׁנִים וְרַעֲנַנִּים יִהְיוּ: לְהַגִּיד כִּי־יָשָׁר יהוה, צוּרִי, וְלֹא־עַוְלָתָה בּוֹ:

תהלים צג **יהוה מָלָךְ,** גֵּאוּת לָבֵשׁ, לָבֵשׁ יהוה עֹז הִתְאַזָּר, אַף־תִּכּוֹן תֵּבֵל בַּל־תִּמּוֹט: נָכוֹן כִּסְאֲךָ מֵאָז, מֵעוֹלָם אָתָּה: נָשְׂאוּ נְהָרוֹת יהוה, נָשְׂאוּ נְהָרוֹת קוֹלָם, יִשְׂאוּ נְהָרוֹת דָּכְיָם: ‹ מִקֹּלוֹת מַיִם רַבִּים, אַדִּירִים מִשְׁבְּרֵי־יָם, אַדִּיר בַּמָּרוֹם יהוה: עֵדֹתֶיךָ נֶאֶמְנוּ מְאֹד לְבֵיתְךָ נַאֲוָה־קֹדֶשׁ, יהוה לְאֹרֶךְ יָמִים:

On הושענא רבה *continue with* יְהִי כְבוֹד *on page 66.*

תהלים קד
תהלים קיג **יְהִי כְבוֹד** יהוה לְעוֹלָם, יִשְׂמַח יהוה בְּמַעֲשָׂיו: יְהִי שֵׁם יהוה מְבֹרָךְ, מֵעַתָּה וְעַד־עוֹלָם: מִמִּזְרַח־שֶׁמֶשׁ עַד־מְבוֹאוֹ,
תהלים קלה מְהֻלָּל שֵׁם יהוה: רָם עַל־כָּל־גּוֹיִם יהוה, עַל הַשָּׁמַיִם כְּבוֹדוֹ: יהוה
תהלים קג שִׁמְךָ לְעוֹלָם, יהוה זִכְרְךָ לְדֹר־וָדֹר: יהוה בַּשָּׁמַיִם הֵכִין כִּסְאוֹ,
דברי הימים א׳ טז וּמַלְכוּתוֹ בַּכֹּל מָשָׁלָה: יִשְׂמְחוּ הַשָּׁמַיִם וְתָגֵל הָאָרֶץ, וְיֹאמְרוּ בַגּוֹיִם
תהלים י יהוה מָלָךְ: יהוה מֶלֶךְ, יהוה מָלָךְ, יהוה יִמְלֹךְ לְעֹלָם וָעֶד. יהוה
תהלים לג מֶלֶךְ עוֹלָם וָעֶד, אָבְדוּ גוֹיִם מֵאַרְצוֹ: יהוה הֵפִיר עֲצַת־גּוֹיִם, הֵנִיא
משלי יט מַחְשְׁבוֹת עַמִּים: רַבּוֹת מַחֲשָׁבוֹת בְּלֶב־אִישׁ, וַעֲצַת יהוה הִיא
תהלים לג תָקוּם: עֲצַת יהוה לְעוֹלָם תַּעֲמֹד, מַחְשְׁבוֹת לִבּוֹ לְדֹר וָדֹר: כִּי הוּא
תהלים קלב אָמַר וַיֶּהִי, הוּא־צִוָּה וַיַּעֲמֹד: כִּי־בָחַר יהוה בְּצִיּוֹן, אִוָּהּ לְמוֹשָׁב לוֹ:
תהלים קלה
תהלים צד כִּי־יַעֲקֹב בָּחַר לוֹ יָהּ, יִשְׂרָאֵל לִסְגֻלָּתוֹ: כִּי לֹא־יִטֹּשׁ יהוה עַמּוֹ,
תהלים עח וְנַחֲלָתוֹ לֹא יַעֲזֹב: ‹ וְהוּא רַחוּם, יְכַפֵּר עָוֹן וְלֹא־יַשְׁחִית, וְהִרְבָּה
תהלים כ לְהָשִׁיב אַפּוֹ, וְלֹא־יָעִיר כָּל־חֲמָתוֹ: יהוה הוֹשִׁיעָה, הַמֶּלֶךְ יַעֲנֵנוּ בְיוֹם־קָרְאֵנוּ:

CONTINUATION OF *PESUKEI DEZIMRA:*

For commentary on this section see pages 66–86.

tree. He grows like a cedar in Lebanon. They are planted in the house of the Lord. They will flourish in the courts of our God. They will still bring forth fruit in old age. They will be fat and flourishing. To declare that the Lord is upright, that He is my Rock, and there is no unrighteousness in Him.

Ps. 93 יהוה מָלָךְ THE LORD REIGNS, He is clothed in majesty, the Lord is clothed, He has girded Himself with strength. The world, too, is established so that it cannot be moved. You throne is established from of old. You are from everlasting. The floodwaters have lifted up, O Lord, the floodwaters have lifted up their voice, the floodwaters have lifted up their pounding. ▸ Mightier than the voices of great, mighty waters, breakers of the sea, is the Lord on high. Your testimonies are very true, in Your house, Your holy habitation, O Lord, for length of days.

On Hoshana Raba continue with the weekday service from "May the glory" on page 67.

Ps. 104 יְהִי כְבוֹד MAY THE GLORY of the Lord be forever, may the Lord rejoice in
Ps. 113 His works. Blessed be the name of the Lord from now and forevermore.
From the rising of the sun to its going down – may the name of the Lord
be praised, now and forever. Supreme over all nations is the Lord; His
Ps. 135 glory is above the heavens. O Lord, Your name is forever. O Lord, Your
Ps. 103 renown is for all generations. The Lord has established His throne in the
I Chr. 16 heavens, and His kingdom rules over everything. Let the heavens rejoice
and the earth be glad, let the nations declare that the Lord reigns! The
Ps. 10 Lord reigns; the Lord reigned; the Lord shall reign forever and ever. The
Lord is King forever and ever. The nations have perished from His land.
Ps. 33 The Lord confounds the plan of the nations. He makes the thoughts of
Prov. 19 the people of no effect. Many are the thoughts in the heart of man, but
Ps. 33 the Lord's wise guidance shall stand. The plan of the Lord will stand
forever, the thoughts of His heart for all generations. For it was He Who
spoke and the world came into being, it was He Who commanded and
Ps. 132 it stood forth. Indeed, the Lord has chosen Zion, He had desired it for
Ps. 135 His habitation. For the Lord has chosen Jacob for Himself, Israel for His
Ps. 94 special possession. For the Lord will not abandon His people, and He
Ps. 78 will not forsake His inheritance. ▸ But He, the compassionate one, forgave
iniquity, and did not destroy them, and He often turned away His anger
Ps. 20 and did not stir up all His wrath. Lord, save us; answer us, divine King,
on the day that we call.

אשרי

The line beginning with פּוֹתֵחַ אֶת יָדֶךָ *should be said with special concentration, representing as it does the key idea of this psalm, and of* פסוקי דזמרה *as a whole, that God is the Creator and Sustainer of all.*

תהלים פד **אַשְׁרֵי** יוֹשְׁבֵי בֵיתֶךָ, עוֹד יְהַלְלְוּךָ סֶּלָה:

תהלים קמד אַשְׁרֵי הָעָם שֶׁכָּכָה לּוֹ, אַשְׁרֵי הָעָם שֶׁיהוה אֱלֹהָיו:

תהלים קמה תְּהִלָּה לְדָוִד

אֲרוֹמִמְךָ אֱלוֹהַי הַמֶּלֶךְ, וַאֲבָרְכָה שִׁמְךָ לְעוֹלָם וָעֶד:

בְּכָל־יוֹם אֲבָרְכֶךָּ, וַאֲהַלְלָה שִׁמְךָ לְעוֹלָם וָעֶד:

גָּדוֹל יהוה וּמְהֻלָּל מְאֹד, וְלִגְדֻלָּתוֹ אֵין חֵקֶר:

דּוֹר לְדוֹר יְשַׁבַּח מַעֲשֶׂיךָ, וּגְבוּרֹתֶיךָ יַגִּידוּ:

הֲדַר כְּבוֹד הוֹדֶךָ, וְדִבְרֵי נִפְלְאֹתֶיךָ אָשִׂיחָה:

וֶעֱזוּז נוֹרְאֹתֶיךָ יֹאמֵרוּ, וּגְדוּלָּתְךָ אֲסַפְּרֶנָּה:

זֵכֶר רַב־טוּבְךָ יַבִּיעוּ, וְצִדְקָתְךָ יְרַנֵּנוּ:

חַנּוּן וְרַחוּם יהוה, אֶרֶךְ אַפַּיִם וּגְדָל־חָסֶד:

טוֹב־יהוה לַכֹּל, וְרַחֲמָיו עַל־כָּל־מַעֲשָׂיו:

יוֹדְוּךָ יהוה כָּל־מַעֲשֶׂיךָ, וַחֲסִידֶיךָ יְבָרְכוּכָה:

כְּבוֹד מַלְכוּתְךָ יֹאמֵרוּ, וּגְבוּרָתְךָ יְדַבֵּרוּ:

לְהוֹדִיעַ לִבְנֵי הָאָדָם גְּבוּרֹתָיו, וּכְבוֹד הֲדַר מַלְכוּתוֹ:

מַלְכוּתְךָ מַלְכוּת כָּל־עֹלָמִים, וּמֶמְשַׁלְתְּךָ בְּכָל־דּוֹר וָדֹר:

סוֹמֵךְ יהוה לְכָל־הַנֹּפְלִים, וְזוֹקֵף לְכָל־הַכְּפוּפִים:

עֵינֵי־כֹל אֵלֶיךָ יְשַׂבֵּרוּ, וְאַתָּה נוֹתֵן־לָהֶם אֶת־אָכְלָם בְּעִתּוֹ:

פּוֹתֵחַ אֶת־יָדֶךָ, וּמַשְׂבִּיעַ לְכָל־חַי רָצוֹן:

צַדִּיק יהוה בְּכָל־דְּרָכָיו, וְחָסִיד בְּכָל־מַעֲשָׂיו:

קָרוֹב יהוה לְכָל־קֹרְאָיו, לְכֹל אֲשֶׁר יִקְרָאֻהוּ בֶאֱמֶת:

רְצוֹן־יְרֵאָיו יַעֲשֶׂה, וְאֶת־שַׁוְעָתָם יִשְׁמַע וְיוֹשִׁיעֵם:

שׁוֹמֵר יהוה אֶת־כָּל־אֹהֲבָיו, וְאֵת כָּל־הָרְשָׁעִים יַשְׁמִיד:

◂ **תְּ**הִלַּת יהוה יְדַבֶּר פִּי, וִיבָרֵךְ כָּל־בָּשָׂר שֵׁם קָדְשׁוֹ לְעוֹלָם וָעֶד:

תהלים קטו וַאֲנַחְנוּ נְבָרֵךְ יָהּ מֵעַתָּה וְעַד־עוֹלָם, הַלְלוּיָהּ:

ASHREI

The line beginning with "You open Your hand" should be said with special concentration, representing as it does the key idea of this psalm, and of Pesukei DeZimra as a whole, that God is the Creator and Sustainer of all.

Ps. 84 אַשְׁרֵי HAPPY are they who dwell in Your house,
They shall forever praise You. Selah.

Ps. 144 HAPPY are the people of whom this is so,
Happy are the people whose God is the Lord.

Ps. 145 A PRAISE OF DAVID.

א I exalt You, my God, the King, and I will bless Your name forever and ever. ב Every day I will bless You, and I will praise Your name forever and ever. ג Great is the Lord, and very praiseworthy, and His greatness is boundless. ד One generation lauds Your works to another, and they declare Your mighty deeds. ה I speak of the splendid glory of Your majesty and of Your wondrous works, ו And they speak of the might of Your awesome deeds, and I declare Your greatness. ז They express the renown of Your great goodness, and sing of Your righteousness. ח Gracious and merciful is the Lord, slow to anger and great in loving-kindness. ט The Lord is good to all, and His mercies are upon all His works. י All Your works thank You, O Lord, and Your pious ones bless You. כ They describe the glory of Your kingdom, and speak of Your might, ל To make known to the sons of man His mighty deeds, and the glorious splendor of His kingdom. מ Your kingdom is a kingdom for all times, and Your dominion is for every generation. ס The Lord supports all who fall and raises up all who are bowed down. ע The eyes of all await You, and You give them their food in its time. פ You open Your hand, and You satisfy the desire of every living thing. צ The Lord is righteous in all His ways and kind in all His works. ק The Lord is near to all who address Him, to all who address Him in truth. ר He does the will of those who fear Him, and He hears their cry and saves them. ש The Lord preserves all who love Him, but all the wicked He destroys. ת ▸ May my mouth speak the praise of the Lord, and may all flesh bless His holy name forever and ever.

Ps. 115 And we shall bless the Lord now and for evermore. Praise the Lord.

תהלים קמו **הַלְלוּיָהּ,** הַלְלִי נַפְשִׁי אֶת־יהוה: אֲהַלְלָה יהוה בְּחַיָּי, אֲזַמְּרָה לֵאלֹהַי בְּעוֹדִי: אַל־תִּבְטְחוּ בִנְדִיבִים, בְּבֶן־אָדָם שֶׁאֵין לוֹ תְשׁוּעָה: תֵּצֵא רוּחוֹ, יָשֻׁב לְאַדְמָתוֹ, בַּיּוֹם הַהוּא אָבְדוּ עֶשְׁתֹּנֹתָיו: אַשְׁרֵי שֶׁאֵל יַעֲקֹב בְּעֶזְרוֹ, שִׂבְרוֹ עַל־יהוה אֱלֹהָיו: עֹשֶׂה שָׁמַיִם וָאָרֶץ, אֶת־הַיָּם וְאֶת־כָּל־אֲשֶׁר־בָּם, הַשֹּׁמֵר אֱמֶת לְעוֹלָם: עֹשֶׂה מִשְׁפָּט לַעֲשׁוּקִים, נֹתֵן לֶחֶם לָרְעֵבִים, יהוה מַתִּיר אֲסוּרִים: יהוה פֹּקֵחַ עִוְרִים, יהוה זֹקֵף כְּפוּפִים, יהוה אֹהֵב צַדִּיקִים: יהוה שֹׁמֵר אֶת־גֵּרִים, יָתוֹם וְאַלְמָנָה יְעוֹדֵד, וְדֶרֶךְ רְשָׁעִים יְעַוֵּת: ◂ יִמְלֹךְ יהוה לְעוֹלָם, אֱלֹהַיִךְ צִיּוֹן לְדֹר וָדֹר, הַלְלוּיָהּ:

תהלים קמז **הַלְלוּיָהּ,** כִּי־טוֹב זַמְּרָה אֱלֹהֵינוּ, כִּי־נָעִים נָאוָה תְהִלָּה: בּוֹנֵה יְרוּשָׁלַםִ יהוה, נִדְחֵי יִשְׂרָאֵל יְכַנֵּס: הָרוֹפֵא לִשְׁבוּרֵי לֵב, וּמְחַבֵּשׁ לְעַצְּבוֹתָם: מוֹנֶה מִסְפָּר לַכּוֹכָבִים, לְכֻלָּם שֵׁמוֹת יִקְרָא: גָּדוֹל אֲדוֹנֵינוּ וְרַב־כֹּחַ, לִתְבוּנָתוֹ אֵין מִסְפָּר: מְעוֹדֵד עֲנָוִים יהוה, מַשְׁפִּיל רְשָׁעִים עֲדֵי־אָרֶץ: עֱנוּ לַיהוה בְּתוֹדָה, זַמְּרוּ לֵאלֹהֵינוּ בְכִנּוֹר: הַמְכַסֶּה שָׁמַיִם בְּעָבִים, הַמֵּכִין לָאָרֶץ מָטָר, הַמַּצְמִיחַ הָרִים חָצִיר: נוֹתֵן לִבְהֵמָה לַחְמָהּ, לִבְנֵי עֹרֵב אֲשֶׁר יִקְרָאוּ: לֹא בִגְבוּרַת הַסּוּס יֶחְפָּץ, לֹא־בְשׁוֹקֵי הָאִישׁ יִרְצֶה: רוֹצֶה יהוה אֶת־יְרֵאָיו, אֶת־הַמְיַחֲלִים לְחַסְדּוֹ: שַׁבְּחִי יְרוּשָׁלַםִ אֶת־יהוה, הַלְלִי אֱלֹהַיִךְ צִיּוֹן: כִּי־חִזַּק בְּרִיחֵי שְׁעָרָיִךְ, בֵּרַךְ בָּנַיִךְ בְּקִרְבֵּךְ: הַשָּׂם־גְּבוּלֵךְ שָׁלוֹם, חֵלֶב חִטִּים יַשְׂבִּיעֵךְ: הַשֹּׁלֵחַ אִמְרָתוֹ אָרֶץ, עַד־מְהֵרָה יָרוּץ דְּבָרוֹ: הַנֹּתֵן שֶׁלֶג כַּצָּמֶר, כְּפוֹר כָּאֵפֶר יְפַזֵּר: מַשְׁלִיךְ קַרְחוֹ כְפִתִּים, לִפְנֵי קָרָתוֹ מִי יַעֲמֹד: יִשְׁלַח דְּבָרוֹ וְיַמְסֵם, יַשֵּׁב רוּחוֹ יִזְּלוּ־מָיִם: ◂ מַגִּיד דְּבָרָו לְיַעֲקֹב, חֻקָּיו וּמִשְׁפָּטָיו לְיִשְׂרָאֵל: לֹא עָשָׂה כֵן לְכָל־גּוֹי, וּמִשְׁפָּטִים בַּל־יְדָעוּם, הַלְלוּיָהּ:

תהלים קמח **הַלְלוּיָהּ,** הַלְלוּ אֶת־יהוה מִן־הַשָּׁמַיִם, הַלְלוּהוּ בַּמְּרוֹמִים: הַלְלוּהוּ כָל־מַלְאָכָיו, הַלְלוּהוּ כָּל־צְבָאָו: הַלְלוּהוּ שֶׁמֶשׁ וְיָרֵחַ,

Ps. 146 הַלְלוּיָהּ PRAISE THE LORD. Praise the Lord, O my soul. I will praise the Lord while I live. I will sing praises to my God while I exist. Do not put your trust in princes, in a son of man in whom there is no help. His breath will leave, he will return to his earth. On that day his thoughts will perish. Happy is he who has the God of Jacob as his helper, whose hope is in the Lord his God, Who makes heaven and earth, the sea, and all that is in them, Who keeps truth forever, Who executes judgment for the oppressed, Who gives bread to the hungry, the Lord sets the prisoners free. The Lord opens the eyes of the blind, the Lord raises up those who are bowed down, the Lord loves the righteous. The Lord preserves the strangers, He strengthens the fatherless and the widow, and He makes crooked the way of the wicked. ▸ The Lord will reign forever, your God, O Zion, to all generations. Praise the Lord.

Ps. 147 הַלְלוּיָהּ PRAISE THE LORD. Indeed, it is good to sing to our God. Indeed, it is pleasant. Praise is seemly. The Lord is the builder of Jerusalem. He gathers the outcasts of Israel. He heals the broken-hearted, and binds their wounds. He counts the number of the stars. He calls them all by names. Great is our Master, and of great power. His understanding has no measure. The Lord lifts up the humble. He casts the wicked down to the ground. Sing to the Lord with thanksgiving, play the lyre to our God, Who covers heaven with clouds, Who prepares rain for the earth, Who makes grass grow upon the mountains. He gives to the beast its food, to the ravens that cry. He does not desire the strength of the horse. He does not want the thighs of man. The Lord wants those who fear Him, those who hope for His loving-kindness. Praise the Lord, O Jerusalem. Extol your God, O Zion. For He has strengthened the bars of your gates, He has blessed your sons in your midst. He places peace in your border. He satisfies you with the finest of wheat. He sends His command to the earth. His word runs very swiftly. He gives snow like wool. He scatters frost like ashes. He casts His ice like crumbs. Who can stand before His cold? He sends His word and melts them. He makes His wind blow, and the waters flow. ▸ He proclaimed His words to Jacob, His statutes and judgments to Israel. He has not done so for any other nation, and as for judgments, they do not know them. Praise the Lord.

Ps. 148 הַלְלוּיָהּ PRAISE THE LORD. Praise the Lord from the heavens, praise Him in the heights. Praise Him, all you His angels. Praise Him, all you His hosts. Praise Him, sun and moon. Praise Him, all you stars of light. Praise

הַלְלְוּהוּ כָּל־כּוֹכְבֵי אוֹר: הַלְלְוּהוּ שְׁמֵי הַשָּׁמָיִם, וְהַמַּיִם אֲשֶׁר מֵעַל
הַשָּׁמָיִם: יְהַלְלוּ אֶת־שֵׁם יהוה, כִּי הוּא צִוָּה וְנִבְרָאוּ: וַיַּעֲמִידֵם
לָעַד לְעוֹלָם, חָק־נָתַן וְלֹא יַעֲבוֹר: הַלְלוּ אֶת־יהוה מִן־הָאָרֶץ,
תַּנִּינִים וְכָל־תְּהֹמוֹת: אֵשׁ וּבָרָד שֶׁלֶג וְקִיטוֹר, רְוּחַ סְעָרָה עֹשָׂה
דְבָרוֹ: הֶהָרִים וְכָל־גְּבָעוֹת, עֵץ פְּרִי וְכָל־אֲרָזִים: הַחַיָּה וְכָל־בְּהֵמָה,
רֶמֶשׂ וְצִפּוֹר כָּנָף: מַלְכֵי־אֶרֶץ וְכָל־לְאֻמִּים, שָׂרִים וְכָל־שֹׁפְטֵי אָרֶץ:
בַּחוּרִים וְגַם־בְּתוּלוֹת, זְקֵנִים עִם־נְעָרִים: ◂ יְהַלְלוּ אֶת־שֵׁם יהוה,
כִּי־נִשְׂגָּב שְׁמוֹ לְבַדּוֹ, הוֹדוֹ עַל־אֶרֶץ וְשָׁמָיִם: וַיָּרֶם קֶרֶן לְעַמּוֹ,
תְּהִלָּה לְכָל־חֲסִידָיו, לִבְנֵי יִשְׂרָאֵל עַם קְרֹבוֹ, הַלְלוּיָהּ:

הַלְלוּיָהּ, שִׁירוּ לַיהוה שִׁיר חָדָשׁ, תְּהִלָּתוֹ בִּקְהַל חֲסִידִים: תהלים קמט
יִשְׂמַח יִשְׂרָאֵל בְּעֹשָׂיו, בְּנֵי־צִיּוֹן יָגִילוּ בְמַלְכָּם: יְהַלְלוּ
שְׁמוֹ בְמָחוֹל, בְּתֹף וְכִנּוֹר יְזַמְּרוּ־לוֹ: כִּי־רוֹצֶה יהוה בְּעַמּוֹ, יְפָאֵר
עֲנָוִים בִּישׁוּעָה: יַעְלְזוּ חֲסִידִים בְּכָבוֹד, יְרַנְּנוּ עַל־מִשְׁכְּבוֹתָם:
רוֹמְמוֹת אֵל בִּגְרוֹנָם, וְחֶרֶב פִּיפִיּוֹת בְּיָדָם: לַעֲשׂוֹת נְקָמָה בַּגּוֹיִם,
תּוֹכֵחוֹת בַּלְאֻמִּים: ◂ לֶאְסֹר מַלְכֵיהֶם בְּזִקִּים, וְנִכְבְּדֵיהֶם בְּכַבְלֵי
בַרְזֶל: לַעֲשׂוֹת בָּהֶם מִשְׁפָּט כָּתוּב, הָדָר הוּא לְכָל־חֲסִידָיו,
הַלְלוּיָהּ:

הַלְלוּיָהּ, הַלְלוּ־אֵל בְּקָדְשׁוֹ, הַלְלְוּהוּ בִּרְקִיעַ עֻזּוֹ: הַלְלְוּהוּ תהלים קנ
בִגְבוּרֹתָיו, הַלְלְוּהוּ כְּרֹב גֻּדְלוֹ: הַלְלְוּהוּ בְּתֵקַע שׁוֹפָר,
הַלְלְוּהוּ בְּנֵבֶל וְכִנּוֹר: הַלְלְוּהוּ בְּתֹף וּמָחוֹל, הַלְלְוּהוּ בְּמִנִּים וְעוּגָב:
הַלְלְוּהוּ בְצִלְצְלֵי־שָׁמַע, הַלְלְוּהוּ בְּצִלְצְלֵי תְרוּעָה: ◂ כֹּל הַנְּשָׁמָה
תְּהַלֵּל יָהּ, הַלְלוּיָהּ: כֹּל הַנְּשָׁמָה תְּהַלֵּל יָהּ, הַלְלוּיָהּ:

בָּרוּךְ יהוה לְעוֹלָם, אָמֵן וְאָמֵן: בָּרוּךְ יהוה מִצִּיּוֹן, שֹׁכֵן יְרוּשָׁלָיִם, תהלים פט תהלים קלה
הַלְלוּיָהּ: בָּרוּךְ יהוה אֱלֹהִים אֱלֹהֵי יִשְׂרָאֵל, עֹשֵׂה נִפְלָאוֹת תהלים עב
לְבַדּוֹ: ◂ וּבָרוּךְ שֵׁם כְּבוֹדוֹ לְעוֹלָם, וְיִמָּלֵא כְבוֹדוֹ אֶת־כָּל־הָאָרֶץ,
אָמֵן וְאָמֵן:

Him, heavens of the heavens, and the waters that are above the heavens. Let them praise the name of the Lord, that He commanded and they were created. And He established them forever and ever. He gave a command and it will not be annulled. Praise the Lord from the earth, O sea creatures and all depths. Fire and hail, snow and vapors, stormy wind fulfilling His word. The mountains and all hills, fruit trees and all cedars. Beasts and all cattle, creeping things, and winged birds. Kings of the earth and all peoples, princes, and all judges of the earth. Both young men and virgins, old men and boys. ‣ Let them praise the name of the Lord, that His name alone is exalted. His glory is over the earth and the heavens. And He has raised the horn of His people, praise for all His pious ones, for the children of Israel, the people near to Him. Praise the Lord.

Ps. 149 הַלְלוּיָהּ PRAISE THE LORD. Sing to the Lord a new song, His praise in the congregation of the pious. Let Israel rejoice in Him Who made him. Let the children of Zion be joyful in their King. Let them praise His name in dance. Let them play to Him on the timbrel and the lyre, That the Lord takes pleasure in His people, He honors the oppressed with salvation. Let the pious be joyful in glory, let them sing upon their beds. The praises of God are in their throat, and a two-edged sword in their hand, to execute vengeance upon the nations, chastisements upon the peoples, ‣ to bind their kings with chains, and their nobles with fetters of iron, to execute upon them the written judgment. He is an honor to all His pious ones. Praise the Lord.

Ps. 150 הַלְלוּיָהּ PRAISE THE LORD. Praise God for His sanctity, praise Him for His power in the firmament. Praise Him for His mighty acts, praise Him in accordance with His exceeding greatness. Praise Him with the sounding of the shofar, praise Him with the harp and lyre. Praise Him with the timbrel and the dance, praise Him with flutes and the pipe. Praise Him with sounding cymbals, praise Him with loud clashing cymbals. ‣ Let everything that has breath praise the Lord. Praise the Lord. Let everything that has breath praise the Lord. Praise the Lord.

Ps. 89
Ps. 135 בָּרוּךְ BLESSED is the Lord forever. Amen and amen. Blessed is the Lord
Ps. 72 from Zion, He Who dwells in Jerusalem. Praise the Lord. Blessed is the Lord God, the God of Israel, Who does wondrous things alone. ‣ And blessed be His glorious name forever, and may the whole earth be filled with His glory. Amen and amen.

Stand until נִשְׁמַת *on page 480.*

דברי הימים א, כט

וַיְבָרֶךְ דָּוִיד אֶת־יהוה לְעֵינֵי כָּל־הַקָּהָל, וַיֹּאמֶר דָּוִיד, בָּרוּךְ אַתָּה
יהוה, אֱלֹהֵי יִשְׂרָאֵל אָבִינוּ, מֵעוֹלָם וְעַד־עוֹלָם:
לְךָ יהוה הַגְּדֻלָּה וְהַגְּבוּרָה וְהַתִּפְאֶרֶת וְהַנֵּצַח וְהַהוֹד, כִּי־כֹל
בַּשָּׁמַיִם וּבָאָרֶץ, לְךָ יהוה הַמַּמְלָכָה וְהַמִּתְנַשֵּׂא לְכֹל לְרֹאשׁ:
וְהָעֹשֶׁר וְהַכָּבוֹד מִלְּפָנֶיךָ, וְאַתָּה מוֹשֵׁל בַּכֹּל, וּבְיָדְךָ כֹּחַ וּגְבוּרָה,
וּבְיָדְךָ לְגַדֵּל וּלְחַזֵּק לַכֹּל: וְעַתָּה אֱלֹהֵינוּ מוֹדִים אֲנַחְנוּ לָךְ, וּמְהַלְלִים
לְשֵׁם תִּפְאַרְתֶּךָ: אַתָּה־הוּא יהוה לְבַדֶּךָ, אַתָּ עָשִׂיתָ

נחמיה ט

אֶת־הַשָּׁמַיִם, שְׁמֵי הַשָּׁמַיִם וְכָל־צְבָאָם, הָאָרֶץ וְכָל־אֲשֶׁר עָלֶיהָ,
הַיַּמִּים וְכָל־אֲשֶׁר בָּהֶם, וְאַתָּה מְחַיֶּה אֶת־כֻּלָּם, וּצְבָא הַשָּׁמַיִם
לְךָ מִשְׁתַּחֲוִים: ◂ אַתָּה הוּא יהוה הָאֱלֹהִים אֲשֶׁר בָּחַרְתָּ בְּאַבְרָם,
וְהוֹצֵאתוֹ מֵאוּר כַּשְׂדִּים, וְשַׂמְתָּ שְׁמוֹ אַבְרָהָם: וּמָצָאתָ אֶת־
לְבָבוֹ נֶאֱמָן לְפָנֶיךָ,
וְכָרוֹת עִמּוֹ הַבְּרִית לָתֵת אֶת־אֶרֶץ הַכְּנַעֲנִי הַחִתִּי
הָאֱמֹרִי וְהַפְּרִזִּי וְהַיְבוּסִי וְהַגִּרְגָּשִׁי, לָתֵת לְזַרְעוֹ, וַתָּקֶם אֶת־דְּבָרֶיךָ,
כִּי צַדִּיק אָתָּה: וַתֵּרֶא אֶת־עֳנִי אֲבֹתֵינוּ בְּמִצְרָיִם, וְאֶת־זַעֲקָתָם
שָׁמַעְתָּ עַל־יַם־סוּף: וַתִּתֵּן אֹתֹת וּמֹפְתִים בְּפַרְעֹה וּבְכָל־עֲבָדָיו
וּבְכָל־עַם אַרְצוֹ, כִּי יָדַעְתָּ כִּי הֵזִידוּ עֲלֵיהֶם, וַתַּעַשׂ־לְךָ שֵׁם כְּהַיּוֹם
הַזֶּה: ◂ וְהַיָּם בָּקַעְתָּ לִפְנֵיהֶם, וַיַּעַבְרוּ בְתוֹךְ־הַיָּם בַּיַּבָּשָׁה, וְאֶת־
רֹדְפֵיהֶם הִשְׁלַכְתָּ בִמְצוֹלֹת כְּמוֹ־אֶבֶן, בְּמַיִם עַזִּים:

שירת הים

שמות יד

וַיּוֹשַׁע יהוה בַּיּוֹם הַהוּא אֶת־יִשְׂרָאֵל מִיַּד מִצְרָיִם וַיַּרְא יִשְׂרָאֵל
אֶת־מִצְרַיִם מֵת עַל־שְׂפַת הַיָּם: ◂ וַיַּרְא יִשְׂרָאֵל אֶת־הַיָּד
הַגְּדֹלָה אֲשֶׁר עָשָׂה יהוה בְּמִצְרַיִם וַיִּירְאוּ הָעָם אֶת־יהוה וַיַּאֲמִינוּ
בַּיהוה וּבְמֹשֶׁה עַבְדּוֹ:

Stand until "The soul" on page 481.

I Chr. 29 **וַיְבָרֶךְ דָּוִיד** THEN DAVID BLESSED the Lord in the sight of all the congregation. David said, "Blessed are You, Lord, God of our father Israel, forever and ever. Yours, O Lord, are greatness, and power, and glory, and victory, and majesty; yes, all that is in the heavens and on the earth. Yours, O Lord, is the dominion, and You are supreme over all. Riches and honor come from You, and You rule over all. In Your hand are power and might, it is in Your hand to make great and give strength to all. Now therefore we thank You, our God, and we praise Your glorious name."

Neh. 9 You are the Lord, You alone. You have made the heavens, the heaven of heavens and all their host, the earth and all that is on it, the seas and all that is therein. You give life to them all, and the hosts of heaven worship You. ▸ You are the Lord, the God Who chose Abram, and brought him forth from Ur of the Chaldees and gave him the name Abraham. Finding his heart faithful to You,

You made the covenant with him to give his seed the land of the Canaanite, the Hittite, the Amorite, the Perizzite, the Jebusite, and the Girgashite. You have fulfilled Your words, because You are true. You saw the affliction of our fathers in Egypt, and hearkened to their cry by the Sea of Reeds. There You performed signs and wonders on Pharaoh and all his servants and all the people of his land, because You knew that they had dealt tyrannously with our fathers. And in so doing You made a glorious name for Yourself known even to this day. ▸ The sea You divided before them, so that they went through the midst of the sea on dry ground, but their pursuers You cast into the depths like a stone in the mighty waters.

THE SONG AT THE SEA

Ex. 14 **וַיּוֹשַׁע** THUS THE LORD saved Israel that day from the power of the Egyptians, and Israel saw the Egyptians dead upon the seashore. ▸ Israel beheld the great power that the Lord had displayed against Egypt, and the people revered the Lord and believed in the Lord and in His servant Moses.

אָז יָשִׁיר־מֹשֶׁה וּבְנֵי יִשְׂרָאֵל אֶת־הַשִּׁירָה הַזֹּאת לַיהוה, וַיֹּאמְרוּ שמות טו
לֵאמֹר, אָשִׁירָה לַיהוה כִּי־גָאֹה גָּאָה, סוּס
וְרֹכְבוֹ רָמָה בַיָּם: עָזִּי וְזִמְרָת יָהּ וַיְהִי־לִי
לִישׁוּעָה, זֶה אֵלִי וְאַנְוֵהוּ, אֱלֹהֵי
אָבִי וַאֲרֹמְמֶנְהוּ: יהוה אִישׁ מִלְחָמָה, יהוה
שְׁמוֹ: מַרְכְּבֹת פַּרְעֹה וְחֵילוֹ יָרָה בַיָּם, וּמִבְחַר
שָׁלִשָׁיו טֻבְּעוּ בְיַם־סוּף: תְּהֹמֹת יְכַסְיֻמוּ, יָרְדוּ בִמְצוֹלֹת כְּמוֹ־
אָבֶן: יְמִינְךָ יהוה נֶאְדָּרִי בַּכֹּחַ, יְמִינְךָ
יהוה תִּרְעַץ אוֹיֵב: וּבְרֹב גְּאוֹנְךָ תַּהֲרֹס
קָמֶיךָ, תְּשַׁלַּח חֲרֹנְךָ יֹאכְלֵמוֹ כַּקַּשׁ: וּבְרוּחַ
אַפֶּיךָ נֶעֶרְמוּ מַיִם, נִצְּבוּ כְמוֹ־נֵד
נֹזְלִים, קָפְאוּ תְהֹמֹת בְּלֶב־יָם: אָמַר
אוֹיֵב אֶרְדֹּף, אַשִּׂיג, אֲחַלֵּק שָׁלָל, תִּמְלָאֵמוֹ
נַפְשִׁי, אָרִיק חַרְבִּי תּוֹרִישֵׁמוֹ יָדִי: נָשַׁפְתָּ
בְרוּחֲךָ כִּסָּמוֹ יָם, צָלְלוּ כַּעוֹפֶרֶת בְּמַיִם
אַדִּירִים: מִי־כָמֹכָה בָּאֵלִם יהוה, מִי
כָּמֹכָה נֶאְדָּר בַּקֹּדֶשׁ, נוֹרָא תְהִלֹּת עֹשֵׂה
פֶלֶא: נָטִיתָ יְמִינְךָ תִּבְלָעֵמוֹ אָרֶץ: נָחִיתָ
בְחַסְדְּךָ עַם־זוּ גָּאָלְתָּ, נֵהַלְתָּ בְעָזְּךָ אֶל־נְוֵה
קָדְשֶׁךָ: שָׁמְעוּ עַמִּים יִרְגָּזוּן, חִיל
אָחַז יֹשְׁבֵי פְּלָשֶׁת: אָז נִבְהֲלוּ אַלּוּפֵי
אֱדוֹם, אֵילֵי מוֹאָב יֹאחֲזֵמוֹ רָעַד, נָמֹגוּ
כֹּל יֹשְׁבֵי כְנָעַן: תִּפֹּל עֲלֵיהֶם אֵימָתָה
וָפַחַד, בִּגְדֹל זְרוֹעֲךָ יִדְּמוּ כָּאָבֶן, עַד־
יַעֲבֹר עַמְּךָ יהוה, עַד־יַעֲבֹר עַם־זוּ
קָנִיתָ: תְּבִאֵמוֹ וְתִטָּעֵמוֹ בְּהַר נַחֲלָתְךָ, מָכוֹן

Ex. 15 אָז THEN MOSES and the children of Israel sang this song to the Lord, and thus did they say: / I will sing to the Lord, for He has triumphed gloriously; / the horse and his rider He has thrown into the sea.

The Lord is my strength and song, and He has become my liberation. / This is my God and I will glorify Him, / my father's God and I will extol Him.

The Lord victorious, the Lord is His name.

Pharaoh's chariots and his host He has cast into the sea, / and in the Sea of Reeds are sunk his chosen captains.

The deeps cover them; they went down in the depths like a stone.

Your right hand, O Lord, glorious in power, / Your right hand, O Lord, crushes the enemy.

In the greatness of Your majesty You overthrow them who rise against You. / You send forth Your wrath; it consumes them like stubble.

At the blast of Your wind the waters piled up; / the tides stood upright as a heap, / the deeps congealed in the heart of the sea.

The enemy said, "I will pursue, overtake, / divide the spoil, my lust shall be glutted with them; / I will unsheathe my sword, my hand shall destroy them."

You did blow with Your wind, the sea covered them; / they sank like lead in the mighty waters.

Who is like You, Lord, among the mighty? / Who is like You, glorious in holiness, / inspiring in praises, working wonders?

You did stretch out Your right hand, the earth swallows them.

In Your love You guide the people You have redeemed; / You will lead them by Your strength to Your holy dwelling.

Peoples heard, they tremble; / pangs seized the inhabitants of Philistia.

Then were the chieftains of Edom frightened, / the mighty men of Moab, trembling takes hold of them, / all the inhabitants of Canaan melted away.

Terror and dread fall upon them; / by the greatness of Your arm they are still as stone – / until Your people pass over, O Lord, / until the people whom You have acquired pass over.

Bring them and settle them in the mountain of Your inheritance, / the

לְשִׁבְתְּךָ פָּעַלְתָּ יהוה, מִקְּדָשׁ אֲדֹנָי כּוֹנְנוּ
יָדֶיךָ: יהוה | יִמְלֹךְ לְעֹלָם וָעֶד:

יהוה יִמְלֹךְ לְעָלָם וָעֶד. יהוה מַלְכוּתֵהּ קָאֵם לְעָלַם וּלְעָלְמֵי עָלְמַיָּא.

כִּי
בָא סוּס פַּרְעֹה בְּרִכְבּוֹ וּבְפָרָשָׁיו בַּיָּם, וַיָּשֶׁב יהוה עֲלֵהֶם אֶת־מֵי
הַיָּם, וּבְנֵי יִשְׂרָאֵל הָלְכוּ בַיַּבָּשָׁה בְּתוֹךְ הַיָּם:

◂ כִּי לַיהוה הַמְּלוּכָה וּמֹשֵׁל בַּגּוֹיִם: וְעָלוּ מוֹשִׁעִים בְּהַר צִיּוֹן תהלים כב / עובדיה א
לִשְׁפֹּט אֶת־הַר עֵשָׂו, וְהָיְתָה לַיהוה הַמְּלוּכָה: וְהָיָה יהוה זכריה יד
לְמֶלֶךְ עַל־כָּל־הָאָרֶץ, בַּיּוֹם הַהוּא יִהְיֶה יהוה אֶחָד וּשְׁמוֹ אֶחָד:

(וּבְתוֹרָתְךָ כָּתוּב לֵאמֹר, שְׁמַע יִשְׂרָאֵל, יהוה אֱלֹהֵינוּ יהוה אֶחָד:) דברים ו

נִשְׁמַת כָּל חַי תְּבָרֵךְ אֶת שִׁמְךָ, יהוה אֱלֹהֵינוּ, וְרוּחַ כָּל בָּשָׂר
תְּפָאֵר וּתְרוֹמֵם זִכְרְךָ מַלְכֵּנוּ תָּמִיד. מִן הָעוֹלָם וְעַד
הָעוֹלָם אַתָּה אֵל, וּמִבַּלְעָדֶיךָ אֵין לָנוּ מֶלֶךְ גּוֹאֵל וּמוֹשִׁיעַ, פּוֹדֶה

נִשְׁמַת / THE SOUL

Sections of the *Nishmat* prayer are mentioned in the Mishna (*Pesaḥim* 10:7) as well as the Gemara (*Pesaḥim* 118a and *Berakhot* 59b). R. Yoḥanan refers to *Nishmat* as בִּרְכַּת הַשִּׁיר (the Blessing of Praise), insofar as it is recited on Shabbat and Yom Tov following the praises of *Pesukei DeZimra* (Tosafot).

The overall theme is clear from the opening words: נִשְׁמַת כָּל חַי – The soul of *every* living being shall bless Your name. It moves our focus beyond the particularistic redemption of the Jewish people described in the preceding Song at the Sea of Reeds to encompass the universal theme that all the nations, indeed every animate being, will in due course come to recognize God and sing His praises. *Nishmat* thus teaches that the Jew is not satisfied with his own salvation unless the whole world is redeemed with him. The same principled outlook explains the choice of the book of Jonah, with its universalistic themes, for the Yom Kippur *Minḥa haftara* – i.e., after spending much of that holiest of days praying for the Jewish people, the Jew turns his attention at *Minḥa* to the well-being of all of mankind (R. Joseph B. Soloveitchik).

It is significant that the structure of *Nishmat* progresses from the general to the specific. The entire first section describes the praises of God expressed by "every living being," the next section focuses more specifically on those of the Jewish people. The final section speaks of the various ways in which the comparatively few who are "upright, righteous, devout or holy, will (or do) praise, bless, elevate, and sanctify Him." These successive expressions of praise begin with the lowest and most inclusive

shrine, O Lord, that You make for Your dwelling, / the sanctuary, my Master, that Your own hands establish.

The Lord shall reign forever and ever.

The Lord shall reign forever and ever.
The sovereignty of the Lord is established forever.

When the horses of Pharaoh went into the sea with his chariots and his horsemen, / the Lord turned the waters of the sea back upon them, / while the children of Israel walked on dry ground in the midst / of the sea.

Ps. 22 ▸ כִּי FOR THE KINGDOM is the Lord's, and He is the ruler over the
Ob. 1 nations. Deliverers shall go up to Mount Zion to rule the hill
Zech. 14 country of Esau, and sovereignty shall be the Lord's. And the
Lord shall be King over all the earth; in that day shall the Lord be One, and His name One.

Deut. 6 (As it is written in Your Torah, saying: "Hear, O Israel, the Lord is our God, the Lord is One.")

נִשְׁמַת THE SOUL of every living being shall bless Your name, Lord our God. The spirit of all flesh shall ever praise and extol You, our King. From this world to the next You are God, and other than You we have

---

common denominator, and end with the exclusive and rarified spiritual realm inhabited by the singular few (R. Yissachar Jacobson).

We should also note that *Nishmat* begins with a paraphrase of the end of the preceding psalm (כֹּל הַנְּשָׁמָה תְּהַלֵּל יָהּ) and ends with the opening phrase of the *Amida* (הָאֵל הַגָּדוֹל, הַגִּבּוֹר וְהַנּוֹרָא, אֵל עֶלְיוֹן). So too its content serves as a bridge between the universalistic ending of the quoted psalm and the individual Jew's private audience with God in the *Amida* (R. Aton Holzer).

Nishmat at first proclaims the impossibility of adequately praising God for all that He has done for mankind and for the Jewish people in particular. Then it says that "the limbs... spirit and soul" will in fact be the ones to "thank and bless, praise and glorify" God for all that He has done. But if we cannot adequately sing God's praises, how can our organs and souls do so? One answer might be that while it is impossible to sufficiently articulate in words all that God has done and continues to do for us, the wondrous structure of our organs itself attests to and bespeaks God's infinite wisdom and kindness. If so, this would constitute an appropriate sequel to the preceding *Pesukei DeZimra*, by proclaiming that in addition to the wondrous nature of the world that surrounds us, our own

וּמַצִּיל וּמְפַרְנֵס וּמְרַחֵם, בְּכָל עֵת צָרָה וְצוּקָה אֵין לָנוּ מֶלֶךְ אֶלָּא אָתָּה. אֱלֹהֵי הָרִאשׁוֹנִים וְהָאַחֲרוֹנִים, אֱלוֹהַּ כָּל בְּרִיּוֹת, אֲדוֹן כָּל תּוֹלָדוֹת, הַמְהֻלָּל בְּרֹב הַתִּשְׁבָּחוֹת, הַמְנַהֵג עוֹלָמוֹ בְּחֶסֶד וּבְרִיּוֹתָיו בְּרַחֲמִים. וַיהוה לֹא יָנוּם וְלֹא יִישָׁן, הַמְעוֹרֵר יְשֵׁנִים וְהַמֵּקִיץ נִרְדָּמִים, וְהַמֵּשִׂיחַ אִלְּמִים וְהַמַּתִּיר אֲסוּרִים, וְהַסּוֹמֵךְ נוֹפְלִים וְהַזּוֹקֵף כְּפוּפִים.

לְךָ לְבַדְּךָ אֲנַחְנוּ מוֹדִים. אִלּוּ פִינוּ מָלֵא שִׁירָה כַּיָּם, וּלְשׁוֹנֵנוּ רִנָּה כַּהֲמוֹן גַּלָּיו, וְשִׂפְתוֹתֵינוּ שֶׁבַח כְּמֶרְחֲבֵי רָקִיעַ, וְעֵינֵינוּ מְאִירוֹת כַּשֶּׁמֶשׁ וְכַיָּרֵחַ, וְיָדֵינוּ פְרוּשׂוֹת כְּנִשְׁרֵי שָׁמָיִם, וְרַגְלֵינוּ קַלּוֹת כָּאַיָּלוֹת, אֵין אֲנַחְנוּ מַסְפִּיקִים לְהוֹדוֹת לְךָ, יהוה אֱלֹהֵינוּ וֵאלֹהֵי אֲבוֹתֵינוּ, וּלְבָרֵךְ אֶת שְׁמֶךָ, עַל אַחַת מֵאֶלֶף אֶלֶף אַלְפֵי אֲלָפִים, וְרִבֵּי רְבָבוֹת פְּעָמִים הַטּוֹבוֹת, שֶׁעָשִׂיתָ עִם אֲבוֹתֵינוּ וְעִמָּנוּ. מִמִּצְרַיִם גְּאַלְתָּנוּ, יהוה אֱלֹהֵינוּ, וּמִבֵּית עֲבָדִים פְּדִיתָנוּ, בְּרָעָב זַנְתָּנוּ וּבְשָׂבָע כִּלְכַּלְתָּנוּ, מֵחֶרֶב הִצַּלְתָּנוּ וּמִדֶּבֶר מִלַּטְתָּנוּ, וּמֵחֳלָיִים רָעִים וְנֶאֱמָנִים דִּלִּיתָנוּ. עַד הֵנָּה עֲזָרוּנוּ רַחֲמֶיךָ, וְלֹא עֲזָבוּנוּ חֲסָדֶיךָ, וְאַל תִּטְּשֵׁנוּ, יהוה אֱלֹהֵינוּ, לָנֶצַח.

עַל כֵּן אֵבָרִים שֶׁפִּלַּגְתָּ בָּנוּ, וְרוּחַ וּנְשָׁמָה שֶׁנָּפַחְתָּ בְּאַפֵּנוּ, וְלָשׁוֹן אֲשֶׁר שַׂמְתָּ בְּפִינוּ, הֵן הֵם יוֹדוּ וִיבָרְכוּ וִישַׁבְּחוּ וִיפָאֲרוּ, וִירוֹמְמוּ וְיַעֲרִיצוּ וְיַקְדִּישׁוּ וְיַמְלִיכוּ אֶת שִׁמְךָ מַלְכֵּנוּ, כִּי כָל פֶּה לְךָ יוֹדֶה וְכָל לָשׁוֹן לְךָ תִשָּׁבַע, וְכָל בֶּרֶךְ לְךָ תִכְרַע וְכָל קוֹמָה לְפָנֶיךָ תִשְׁתַּחֲוֶה,

---

bodies and spirits themselves silently attest to God's wisdom and compassion (R. Basil Herring).

נשמת ... וְרוּחַ – *The soul ... the spirit. Nishmat* contains the praises emanating from our *nefesh, ruaḥ, and neshama,* which are the means by which we cleave to God our King and Father. It is because of them that God constantly performs wonders and miracles for us. This is why it is recited on Shabbat, for on this day we possess a special נְשָׁמָה יְתֵרָה – "additional soul" (Shela HaKadosh).

no king, redeemer, or savior. It is You Who liberates, rescues, sustains, and shows mercy in every time of trouble and distress. We have no king other than You. God of those who came first and those who will come last, God of all creatures, Master of all that issues forth, He is celebrated with a multitude of praises, for it is He Who governs His world with kindness, and His creatures with mercy. The Lord neither slumbers nor sleeps. It is He Who awakens those who sleep and rouses the slumberers, Who causes the mute to speak and frees those who are bound, Who supports the falling and raises those who are bent over.

To You alone we give thanks, yet were our mouths as full of song as the sea, our tongues uplifted in song like its multitude of waves, our lips vibrant with praise like the expanses of the heavens, our eyes shining like the sun and moon, our hands outstretched like the wings of eagles of the sky, and our feet as swift as deer, we would still be unable to thank You enough, Lord our God and God of our fathers. Nor could we adequately bless Your name for even one of the millions upon millions and myriads upon myriads of favors You have done for our ancestors and for us. You redeemed us from Egypt, Lord, our God, and set us free from the house of bondage. In famine you nourished us; in plenty You sustained us. You have saved us from the sword, delivered us from pestilence, and spared us from terrible and chronic diseases. Therefore, just as Your mercies have helped us until now, and Your kindnesses have never departed from us, so may You never forsake us, Lord our God.

Therefore, the limbs with which You have endowed us, and the spirit and soul You have breathed into us, and the tongue You have placed in our mouth – it is that they will thank and bless, praise and glorify, exalt and revere, sanctify and declare the sovereignty of Your name, our King. For every mouth shall thank You, every tongue shall vow allegiance to You, every knee shall bend to You, and everything that stands upright shall bow down before You. Every heart shall revere

וְכָל לְבָבוֹת יִירָאוּךָ וְכָל קֶרֶב וּכְלָיוֹת יְזַמְּרוּ לִשְׁמֶךָ, כַּדָּבָר שֶׁכָּתוּב,
כָּל עַצְמֹתַי תֹּאמַרְנָה יהוה מִי כָמוֹךָ, מַצִּיל עָנִי מֵחָזָק מִמֶּנּוּ, וְעָנִי תהלים לה
וְאֶבְיוֹן מִגֹּזְלוֹ:

מִי יִדְמֶה לָּךְ וּמִי יִשְׁוֶה לָּךְ וּמִי יַעֲרָךְ לָךְ, הָאֵל הַגָּדוֹל, הַגִּבּוֹר וְהַנּוֹרָא,
אֵל עֶלְיוֹן, קֹנֵה שָׁמַיִם וָאָרֶץ. ‹ נְהַלֶּלְךָ וּנְשַׁבֵּחֲךָ וּנְפָאֶרְךָ וּנְבָרֵךְ
אֶת שֵׁם קָדְשֶׁךָ, כָּאָמוּר, לְדָוִד, בָּרְכִי נַפְשִׁי אֶת־יהוה, וְכָל־קְרָבַי תהלים קג
אֶת־שֵׁם קָדְשׁוֹ:

On יום טוב *the* שליח ציבור *begins here:*

הָאֵל בְּתַעֲצֻמוֹת עֻזֶּךָ, הַגָּדוֹל בִּכְבוֹד שְׁמֶךָ, הַגִּבּוֹר לָנֶצַח וְהַנּוֹרָא
בְּנוֹרְאוֹתֶיךָ, הַמֶּלֶךְ הַיּוֹשֵׁב עַל כִּסֵּא, רָם וְנִשָּׂא

On שבת *the* שליח ציבור *begins here:*

שׁוֹכֵן עַד, מָרוֹם וְקָדוֹשׁ שְׁמוֹ, וְכָתוּב, רַנְּנוּ צַדִּיקִים בַּיהוה, תהלים לג
לַיְשָׁרִים נָאוָה תְהִלָּה:

‹ בְּפִי יְשָׁרִים תִּתְהַלָּל
וּבְדִבְרֵי צַדִּיקִים תִּתְבָּרַךְ
וּבִלְשׁוֹן חֲסִידִים תִּתְרוֹמָם
וּבְקֶרֶב קְדוֹשִׁים תִּתְקַדָּשׁ

וּבְמַקְהֲלוֹת רִבְבוֹת עַמְּךָ בֵּית יִשְׂרָאֵל, בְּרִנָּה יִתְפָּאַר שִׁמְךָ
מַלְכֵּנוּ בְּכָל דּוֹר וָדוֹר, ‹ שֶׁכֵּן חוֹבַת כָּל הַיְצוּרִים,
לְפָנֶיךָ יהוה אֱלֹהֵינוּ וֵאלֹהֵי אֲבוֹתֵינוּ, לְהוֹדוֹת, לְהַלֵּל, לְשַׁבֵּחַ,

---

וּבִלְשׁוֹן חֲסִידִים תִּתְרוֹמָם – *And exalted in the language of the pious*. Hasidim, as classically defined, relate to God in ways that are above and beyond the proverbial letter of the law, or what could normally be demanded. This was true of Aaron when, at the sudden death of his two sons, he faithfully accepted God's will. For this reason Moses blessed the tribe of Levi after Aaron's death, referring to him as אִישׁ חֲסִידֶךָ (the man of *Hasidic* proportion) (Deut. 33:8). Thus this phrase affirms that the prayers of the righteous bring special glory to God's name (*Netziv*).

וּבְמַקְהֲלוֹת רִבְבוֹת – *In the assembled myriads*. The ultimate fulfillment of the universalistic vision of נִשְׁמַת כָּל חַי comes about gradually,

You, and every inner organ shall sing the praises of Your name, as it is
Ps. 35 written: "All my bones will say: O Lord, who is like You, who delivers the oppressed from him who is stronger than him, and the poor and the needy from him who robs him?"

Who is like You, who can equal You, who can be compared to You, God, great, mighty, awesome, God Most High, Creator of heaven and earth! ▸ We shall sing unto You, praise and glorify You,
Ps. 103 and bless Your holy name, as it is said: "Of David. Bless the Lord, O my soul, and all that is within me, bless His holy name."

On Yom Tov the Leader begins here:

הָאֵל YOU ARE GOD, in Your overwhelming strength, great in the glory of Your name, mighty in Your eternal existence and awesome in Your awe-inspiring actions, You are the King Who sits upon a high and exalted throne.

On Shabbat the Leader begins here:

Ps. 33 **שׁוֹכֵן עַד** HE DWELLS in eternity, exalted and holy is His name. And it is written: "Rejoice in the Lord, O you righteous. Praise is seemly for the upright.

▸ You shall be praised in the mouths of the upright;
and blessed in the words of the righteous;
and exalted in the language of the pious;
and sanctified in the midst of the holy ones.

וּבְמַקְהֲלוֹת IN THE ASSEMBLED myriads of Your people, the house of Israel, Your name, O our King, shall be glorified in song in every generation. ▸ For thus are all whom You have created duty bound before You, Lord, our God and God of our fathers, to thank, laud,

---

emerging in stages from the particularistic mission of the Jewish people. Thus the speech and deeds of the Jewish righteous יְשָׁרִים, צַדִּיקִים, חֲסִידִים, קְדוֹשִׁים radiate outward to become the chorus of the entire House of Israel. Then, this "kingdom of priests and holy nation" models proper praise of God to "all whom You have created," כָּל הַיְצוּרִים, until His name is praised eternally and universally, as it concludes יִשְׁתַּבַּח שִׁמְךָ לָעַד – May Your name be praised forever.

לְפָאֵר, לְרוֹמֵם, לְהַדֵּר, לְבָרֵךְ, לְעַלֵּה וּלְקַלֵּס, עַל כָּל דִּבְרֵי שִׁירוֹת וְתִשְׁבְּחוֹת, דָּוִד בֶּן יִשַׁי, עַבְדְּךָ מְשִׁיחֶךָ.

Stand until after בָּרְכוּ *on the next page.*

יִשְׁתַּבַּח שִׁמְךָ לָעַד, מַלְכֵּנוּ, הָאֵל הַמֶּלֶךְ הַגָּדוֹל וְהַקָּדוֹשׁ בַּשָּׁמַיִם וּבָאָרֶץ. כִּי לְךָ נָאֶה, יהוה אֱלֹהֵינוּ וֵאלֹהֵי אֲבוֹתֵינוּ, שִׁיר וּשְׁבָחָה, הַלֵּל וְזִמְרָה, עֹז וּמֶמְשָׁלָה, נֶצַח, גְּדֻלָּה וּגְבוּרָה, תְּהִלָּה וְתִפְאֶרֶת, קְדֻשָּׁה וּמַלְכוּת, ◂ בְּרָכוֹת וְהוֹדָאוֹת, מֵעַתָּה וְעַד עוֹלָם. בָּרוּךְ אַתָּה יהוה, אֵל מֶלֶךְ גָּדוֹל בַּתִּשְׁבָּחוֹת, אֵל הַהוֹדָאוֹת, אֲדוֹן הַנִּפְלָאוֹת, הַבּוֹחֵר בְּשִׁירֵי זִמְרָה, מֶלֶךְ, אֵל, חֵי הָעוֹלָמִים.

On שבת שובה*, many congregations open the* ארון קודש *and say this psalm responsively, verse by verse.*

שִׁיר הַמַּעֲלוֹת, מִמַּעֲמַקִּים קְרָאתִיךָ יהוה: אֲדֹנָי שִׁמְעָה בְקוֹלִי, תִּהְיֶינָה אָזְנֶיךָ קַשֻּׁבוֹת לְקוֹל תַּחֲנוּנָי: אִם־עֲוֹנוֹת תִּשְׁמָר־יָהּ, אֲדֹנָי מִי יַעֲמֹד: כִּי־עִמְּךָ הַסְּלִיחָה, לְמַעַן תִּוָּרֵא: קִוִּיתִי יהוה קִוְּתָה נַפְשִׁי, וְלִדְבָרוֹ הוֹחָלְתִּי: נַפְשִׁי לַאדֹנָי, מִשֹּׁמְרִים לַבֹּקֶר, שֹׁמְרִים לַבֹּקֶר: יַחֵל יִשְׂרָאֵל אֶל יהוה, כִּי־עִם־יהוה הַחֶסֶד, וְהַרְבֵּה עִמּוֹ פְדוּת: וְהוּא יִפְדֶּה אֶת־יִשְׂרָאֵל, מִכֹּל עֲוֹנוֹתָיו: תהלים קל

חצי קדיש

ש״ץ: **יִתְגַּדַּל** וְיִתְקַדַּשׁ שְׁמֵהּ רַבָּא (קהל: אָמֵן), בְּעָלְמָא דִּי בְרָא כִרְעוּתֵהּ. וְיַמְלִיךְ מַלְכוּתֵהּ, בְּחַיֵּיכוֹן וּבְיוֹמֵיכוֹן וּבְחַיֵּי דְכָל בֵּית יִשְׂרָאֵל, בַּעֲגָלָא וּבִזְמַן קָרִיב, וְאִמְרוּ אָמֵן. (קהל: אָמֵן)

קהל וש״ץ: יְהֵא שְׁמֵהּ רַבָּא מְבָרַךְ לְעָלַם וּלְעָלְמֵי עָלְמַיָּא.

ש״ץ: יִתְבָּרַךְ וְיִשְׁתַּבַּח וְיִתְפָּאַר, וְיִתְרוֹמַם וְיִתְנַשֵּׂא וְיִתְהַדָּר וְיִתְעַלֶּה וְיִתְהַלָּל שְׁמֵהּ דְּקֻדְשָׁא בְּרִיךְ הוּא (קהל: בְּרִיךְ הוּא), לְעֵלָּא מִן כָּל בִּרְכָתָא / בשבת שובה: לְעֵלָּא (וּ)לְעֵלָּא מִכָּל בִּרְכָתָא/ וְשִׁירָתָא, תֻּשְׁבְּחָתָא וְנֶחֱמָתָא דַּאֲמִירָן בְּעָלְמָא, וְאִמְרוּ אָמֵן. (קהל: אָמֵן)

praise, glorify, exalt, honor, bless, raise high and acclaim, beyond even all the words of song and praise of David son of Jesse, who was Your servant and anointed one.

Stand until after "Barekhu" on the next page.

יִשְׁתַּבַּח MAY YOUR NAME be praised forever, God our King, great and holy in heaven and on earth. For to You, Lord, our God and God of our fathers, are due song and praise, acclaim and hymn. Yours are strength and dominion, eternity, greatness and might, praise and glory, holiness and sovereignty, ▸ blessing and thanksgiving henceforth and evermore. Blessed are You, Lord, God and King, great in praises, God of thanksgivings, Master of wonders, Who chooses songs of praise, King, God, Who gives life to the worlds.

On Shabbat Shuva, many congregations open the Ark and say this psalm responsively, verse by verse.

Ps. 130 **שִׁיר הַמַּעֲלוֹת** A SONG OF ASCENTS. From the depths I call out to you, O Lord. My Master, hear my voice. Let Your ears be attentive to the sound of my supplications. If You, Lord, pay heed to iniquities, who, my Master, will stand? Indeed, forgiveness is with You, so that You may be feared. I wait for the Lord, my soul waits, and I hope for His word. My soul waits for my Master, among those who watch for the morning, who watch for the morning. Israel, hope for the Lord, for with the Lord is loving-kindness, and with Him is abundant redemption. And He will redeem Israel from all his iniquities.

HALF KADDISH

Leader: **יִתְגַּדַּל** EXALTED AND HALLOWED may God's great name be, in the world He created as He willed. May He reign in your lifetimes and in your days, and in the lifetime of the whole house of Israel, speedily and soon, and say, Amen.

All: May His great name be blessed forever and all time.

Leader: Blessed and praised, honored, extolled, glorified, adored and exalted above all be the name of the Holy One, blessed is He, (*Between Rosh Hashana & Yom Kippur:* above and) beyond any blessing, hymn, praise, or expressions of consolation that may be uttered in this world, and say, Amen.

ברכות קריאת שמע

The following blessing and response are said only in the presence of a מנין.
The שליח ציבור *says the following (while bowing at* בָּרְכוּ *and straightening at Hashem). The* קהל *followed by the* שליח ציבור *responds by bowing at* בָּרוּךְ *and standing straight at Hashem.*

ש״ץ: **בָּרְכוּ** אֶת יהוה הַמְבֹרָךְ.

קהל: בָּרוּךְ יהוה הַמְבֹרָךְ לְעוֹלָם וָעֶד.

ש״ץ: בָּרוּךְ יהוה הַמְבֹרָךְ לְעוֹלָם וָעֶד.

ישעיה מה **בָּרוּךְ** אַתָּה יהוה אֱלֹהֵינוּ מֶלֶךְ הָעוֹלָם, יוֹצֵר אוֹר וּבוֹרֵא חֹשֶׁךְ, עֹשֶׂה שָׁלוֹם וּבוֹרֵא אֶת הַכֹּל.

If יום טוב *falls on a weekday continue with* הַמֵּאִיר לָאָרֶץ *on the next page.*

הַכֹּל יוֹדְוּךָ וְהַכֹּל יְשַׁבְּחוּךָ, וְהַכֹּל יֹאמְרוּ אֵין קָדוֹשׁ כַּיהוה, הַכֹּל יְרוֹמְמוּךָ סֶּלָה, יוֹצֵר הַכֹּל. הָאֵל הַפּוֹתֵחַ בְּכָל יוֹם דַּלְתוֹת שַׁעֲרֵי מִזְרָח, וּבוֹקֵעַ חַלּוֹנֵי רָקִיעַ, מוֹצִיא חַמָּה מִמְּקוֹמָהּ וּלְבָנָה מִמְּכוֹן שִׁבְתָּהּ, וּמֵאִיר לָעוֹלָם כֻּלּוֹ וּלְיוֹשְׁבָיו, שֶׁבָּרָא בְּמִדַּת הָרַחֲמִים. הַמֵּאִיר לָאָרֶץ וְלַדָּרִים עָלֶיהָ בְּרַחֲמִים, וּבְטוּבוֹ

בִּרְכוֹת קְרִיאַת שְׁמַע / BLESSINGS OF THE SHEMA
For commentary on the overall structure of these blessings, see page 90.

הַכֹּל יוֹדְוּךָ – *All things shall thank You.* This section of the *berakha* echoes the words of Hannah upon the birth of Samuel, declaring that "None is holy like the Lord, for there is

INTERRUPTIONS DURING SHEMA AND ITS BLESSINGS
The following are generally permitted interruptions. As a general rule, one may not interrupt Shema and its blessings. There are certain "permitted responses" which should ideally be recited when one is "between paragraphs." Those four places are:

- Between the first blessing and the second blessing.
- Between the second blessing and *Shema*.
- Between the first and second paragraphs of *Shema*.
- Between the second and third paragraphs of *Shema*.

BLESSINGS OF THE SHEMA

The following blessing and response are said only in the presence of a minyan. The Leader says the following (while bowing at "Barekhu" and straightening at Hashem). The congregation followed by the Leader responds by bowing at "Barukh" and standing straight at Hashem.

Leader: בָּרְכוּ BLESS THE LORD, the blessed One.

Cong: Blessed is the Lord Who is blessed for all eternity.

Leader: Blessed is the Lord Who is blessed for all eternity.

Is. 45 בָּרוּךְ BLESSED ARE YOU, Lord our God, King of the universe, Who forms light and creates darkness, Who makes peace and creates all things.

If Yom Tov falls on a weekday continue with "He gives light" on the next page.

הַכֹּל יוֹדְוּךָ ALL THINGS shall thank You, all shall praise You, all shall declare, "None is so holy as the Lord!" All shall exalt You, Selah! – Creator of everything. The God Who each day opens the doors of the gates of the east, and cleaves the windows of the heavens, Who brings forth the sun from its place, and the moon from its dwelling, Who gives light to the whole world and its inhabitants, which He created with the attribute of compassion. He Who gives light to the earth and those who dwell on it, with compassion; and in

---

no one like You, and there is no rock like our God" (I Samuel 2:2). Her words similarly form the basis of the Rosh HaShana *Amida* (*Berakhot* 29a). Her words, like those of the prophetess

THE FOLLOWING ARE "PERMITTED RESPONSES":

- Answering *Barekhu* (by the Leader or by someone receiving an *aliya*); *Kedusha* (just the two verses "*Kadosh kadosh*" and "*Barukh kevod*"); the first three words of Modim; "*Amen yeheh shemeh raba* etc."; *Amen* to *da'amiran be'alema* and *HaKel HaKadosh* (*OḤ* 66:3 and *MB* 66:17).
- On Shabbat (but not Yom Tov) it is also permissible to make the above responses between *Ga'al Yisrael* and the *Amida* (*MB* 111:9).
- Between paragraphs, one may put on one's *tallit*. One should wait until the end of one's prayers to recite the *berakha* on the *tallit* (*OḤ* 66:2).

Some authorities permit answering *Amen* to all *berakhot* (*MB* 66:22).

מְחַדֵּשׁ בְּכָל יוֹם תָּמִיד מַעֲשֵׂה בְרֵאשִׁית. הַמֶּלֶךְ הַמְרוֹמָם לְבַדּוֹ מֵאָז, הַמְשֻׁבָּח וְהַמְפֹאָר וְהַמִּתְנַשֵּׂא מִימוֹת עוֹלָם. אֱלֹהֵי עוֹלָם, בְּרַחֲמֶיךָ הָרַבִּים רַחֵם עָלֵינוּ, אֲדוֹן עֻזֵּנוּ, צוּר מִשְׂגַּבֵּנוּ, מָגֵן יִשְׁעֵנוּ, מִשְׂגָּב בַּעֲדֵנוּ.

If יום טוב *falls on a weekday continue here:*

הַמֵּאִיר לָאָרֶץ וְלַדָּרִים עָלֶיהָ בְּרַחֲמִים, וּבְטוּבוֹ מְחַדֵּשׁ בְּכָל יוֹם תָּמִיד מַעֲשֵׂה בְרֵאשִׁית. מָה־רַבּוּ מַעֲשֶׂיךָ יהוה, כֻּלָּם בְּחָכְמָה עָשִׂיתָ, מָלְאָה הָאָרֶץ קִנְיָנֶךָ: הַמֶּלֶךְ הַמְרוֹמָם לְבַדּוֹ מֵאָז, הַמְשֻׁבָּח וְהַמְפֹאָר וְהַמִּתְנַשֵּׂא מִימוֹת עוֹלָם. אֱלֹהֵי עוֹלָם, בְּרַחֲמֶיךָ הָרַבִּים רַחֵם עָלֵינוּ, אֲדוֹן עֻזֵּנוּ, צוּר מִשְׂגַּבֵּנוּ, מָגֵן יִשְׁעֵנוּ, מִשְׂגָּב בַּעֲדֵנוּ. אֵל בָּרוּךְ גְּדוֹל דֵּעָה, הֵכִין וּפָעַל זָהֳרֵי חַמָּה, טוֹב יָצַר כָּבוֹד לִשְׁמוֹ, מְאוֹרוֹת נָתַן סְבִיבוֹת עֻזּוֹ, פִּנּוֹת צְבָאָיו קְדוֹשִׁים, רוֹמְמֵי שַׁדַּי, תָּמִיד מְסַפְּרִים כְּבוֹד אֵל וּקְדֻשָּׁתוֹ. ◂ תִּתְבָּרַךְ יהוה אֱלֹהֵינוּ, עַל שֶׁבַח מַעֲשֵׂה יָדֶיךָ. וְעַל מְאוֹרֵי אוֹר שֶׁעָשִׂיתָ, יְפָאֲרוּךָ סֶּלָה. תהלים קד

Continue with תִּתְבָּרַךְ, צוּרֵנוּ *on page 494.*

אֵין כְּעֶרְכֶּךָ, וְאֵין זוּלָתֶךָ, אֶפֶס בִּלְתֶּךָ, וּמִי דּוֹמֶה לָּךְ.

◂ אֵין כְּעֶרְכְּךָ, יהוה אֱלֹהֵינוּ, בָּעוֹלָם הַזֶּה, וְאֵין זוּלָתְךָ, מַלְכֵּנוּ, לְחַיֵּי הָעוֹלָם הַבָּא, אֶפֶס בִּלְתְּךָ, גּוֹאֲלֵנוּ, לִימוֹת הַמָּשִׁיחַ, וְאֵין דּוֹמֶה לְּךָ, מוֹשִׁיעֵנוּ, לִתְחִיַּת הַמֵּתִים.

Deborah, were unprecedented, and became the model that inspired the prayers of subsequent generations (*Zohar* 3:19).

הַמֵּאִיר לָאָרֶץ וְלַדָּרִים / HE GIVES LIGHT

מָה רַבּוּ מַעֲשֶׂיךָ – *How great are Your works.* The Gemara (*Ḥullin* 127a) understands the term רַבּוּ to mean "diverse," that is, God's creations are found on land, in the air, and under the sea. Another meaning of the word רַבּוּ is "maturity" (Ezek. 16:7). Thus we can understand this phrase as saying "how well developed and intricate are God's creatures" (R. Joseph B. Soloveitchik).

בָּעוֹלָם הַזֶּה... לִתְחִיַּת הַמֵּתִים – *In this world .... at the Resurrection of the Dead.* These four phrases, originating in the mystical work *Merkava Shelema,* elaborate on the phrase in *Nishmat,* "From this world to the next You are God, and other than You we have no king, redeemer, or savior." They describe four periods in human affairs

His goodness each day constantly renews the act of creation. King, exalted uniquely since the beginning, extolled, praised sublimely from days of old, God of all time, abounding in pity, have mercy on us, Master of our strength, our sheltering Rock, our saving Shield, our protecting Fortress.

If Yom Tov falls on a weekday continue here:

הַמֵּאִיר HE GIVES LIGHT to the earth and on all who dwell on it, with compassion; and in His goodness ever renews each day the work of
Ps. 104 creation. "How great are Your works, O Lord! You have made them all in wisdom. The earth is full of Your creatures." King, exalted uniquely since the beginning, extolled, praised sublimely from days of old, God of all time, abounding in pity, have mercy on us, Master of our strength, our sheltering Rock, our saving Shield, our protecting Fortress. God, blessed and all-knowing, planned and created the brilliance of the sun. The Beneficent One made glory for the sake of His name. He placed luminaries round about His majesty. The chiefs of His hosts are holy beings that extol the Almighty. They constantly describe the glory and holiness of God. ▸ Lord our God, may You be blessed in praise of the work of Your hands and for the light-emitting luminaries You created, may they praise You, Selah.

Continue with "May You be blessed, our Rock" on page 495.

אֵין כְּעֶרְכֶּךָ THERE IS NOTHING to compare to You, there is nothing besides You, there is nothing without You, who is like You?

▸ There is nothing to compare to You, Lord, our God, in this world; there will be nothing besides You, our King, in the life of the World to Come; there will be nothing without You, our Redeemer, in the days of the Messiah; and there will be nothing like You, our Savior, at the Resurrection of the Dead.

---

throughout which God alone is supreme. These span the present physical world, the World to Come where only deserving souls will reside while enjoying the radiance of God, the era of Messianic redemption, and the age in which there will be the Resurrection of the Dead.

אֵל אָדוֹן עַל כָּל הַמַּעֲשִׂים
בָּרוּךְ וּמְבֹרָךְ בְּפִי כָּל נְשָׁמָה
גָּדְלוֹ וְטוּבוֹ מָלֵא עוֹלָם
דַּעַת וּתְבוּנָה סוֹבְבִים אוֹתוֹ.

הַמִּתְגָּאֶה עַל חַיּוֹת הַקֹּדֶשׁ
וְנֶהְדָּר בְּכָבוֹד עַל הַמֶּרְכָּבָה
זְכוּת וּמִישׁוֹר לִפְנֵי כִסְאוֹ
חֶסֶד וְרַחֲמִים לִפְנֵי כְבוֹדוֹ.

טוֹבִים מְאוֹרוֹת שֶׁבָּרָא אֱלֹהֵינוּ
יְצָרָם בְּדַעַת בְּבִינָה וּבְהַשְׂכֵּל
כֹּחַ וּגְבוּרָה נָתַן בָּהֶם
לִהְיוֹת מוֹשְׁלִים בְּקֶרֶב תֵּבֵל.

מְלֵאִים זִיו וּמְפִיקִים נֹגַהּ
נָאֶה זִיוָם בְּכָל הָעוֹלָם
שְׂמֵחִים בְּצֵאתָם וְשָׂשִׂים בְּבוֹאָם
עוֹשִׂים בְּאֵימָה רְצוֹן קוֹנָם.

פְּאֵר וְכָבוֹד נוֹתְנִים לִשְׁמוֹ
צָהֳלָה וְרִנָּה לְזֵכֶר מַלְכוּתוֹ
קָרָא לַשֶּׁמֶשׁ וַיִּזְרַח אוֹר
רָאָה וְהִתְקִין צוּרַת הַלְּבָנָה.
שֶׁבַח נוֹתְנִים לוֹ כָּל צְבָא מָרוֹם
תִּפְאֶרֶת וּגְדֻלָּה, שְׂרָפִים וְאוֹפַנִּים וְחַיּוֹת הַקֹּדֶשׁ –

אֵל אָדוֹן – *God, Master*. When we stand before God in prayer we must be mindful that it is not just we and the creatures of the physical world who all sing God's praises. The celestial beings praise Him too. In fact their tributes are a model and inspiration for us to follow. This

אֵל אָדוֹן GOD, Master of all creation,
the Blessed, is blessed by the mouth of every soul.
His greatness and goodness fill the world;
knowledge and insight surround Him.

EXALTED above the holy Ḥayyot,
glorified with honor above the chariot;
merit and fairness are before His throne,
kindness and compassion before His glory.

GOOD are the luminaries our God created;
He formed them with knowledge,
understanding and discernment.
He gave them strength and power, to be rulers over the world.

THEY are filled with splendor and radiate light,
their fine splendor being found throughout the cosmos,
they are happy when they rise, and joyous when they set,
they do their Creator's will in awe.

THEY bestow distinction and glory upon His name,
with exultation and song at the mention of His sovereignty.
He called upon the sun and it radiated light;
He perceived the [changing] shape of the moon.

ALL the heavenly host give Him praise;
as the Seraphim, Ophanim and holy Ḥayyot attribute
distinction and greatness –

---

poem describes the heavenly hosts, particularly the sun and the moon, that express the splendor and glory of His name.

The first stich contains ten words corresponding to the Ten Commandments, while the final one has twelve words matching the twelve constellations of the Zodiac. Each of the nine middle stichs contains eight words, for a total of seventy-two, alluding to the Divine Name of seventy-two letters. Together they teach that God gave the Torah with its Ten Commandments to Israel that consists of twelve tribes, by means of His holy name of seventy-two letters. The verse "Behold I come to you via the *thickness* [עָב, this word's numerical value is seventy-two] of the cloud" (Ex. 19:9) alludes to this. Finally, the twenty-two letters of the *Alef-Beit* – each of which begins a

לָאֵל אֲשֶׁר שָׁבַת מִכָּל הַמַּעֲשִׂים, בַּיּוֹם הַשְּׁבִיעִי הִתְעַלָּה וְיָשַׁב עַל כִּסֵּא כְבוֹדוֹ. תִּפְאֶרֶת עָטָה לְיוֹם הַמְּנוּחָה, עֹנֶג קָרָא לְיוֹם הַשַּׁבָּת. זֶה שֶׁבַח שֶׁל יוֹם הַשְּׁבִיעִי, שֶׁבּוֹ שָׁבַת אֵל מִכָּל מְלַאכְתּוֹ.

וְיוֹם הַשְּׁבִיעִי מְשַׁבֵּחַ וְאוֹמֵר, מִזְמוֹר שִׁיר לְיוֹם הַשַּׁבָּת, טוֹב לְהֹדוֹת לַיהוה: תהלים צב
לְפִיכָךְ יְפָאֲרוּ וִיבָרְכוּ לָאֵל כָּל יְצוּרָיו, שֶׁבַח יְקָר וּגְדֻלָּה יִתְּנוּ לָאֵל מֶלֶךְ יוֹצֵר כֹּל, הַמַּנְחִיל מְנוּחָה לְעַמּוֹ יִשְׂרָאֵל בִּקְדֻשָּׁתוֹ בְּיוֹם שַׁבַּת קֹדֶשׁ. שִׁמְךָ יהוה אֱלֹהֵינוּ יִתְקַדַּשׁ, וְזִכְרְךָ מַלְכֵּנוּ יִתְפָּאַר, בַּשָּׁמַיִם מִמַּעַל וְעַל הָאָרֶץ מִתָּחַת. תִּתְבָּרַךְ מוֹשִׁיעֵנוּ עַל שֶׁבַח מַעֲשֵׂה יָדֶיךָ, וְעַל מְאוֹרֵי אוֹר שֶׁעָשִׂיתָ, יְפָאֲרוּךָ סֶּלָה.

All continue here:

תִּתְבָּרַךְ צוּרֵנוּ מַלְכֵּנוּ וְגוֹאֲלֵנוּ, בּוֹרֵא קְדוֹשִׁים, יִשְׁתַּבַּח שִׁמְךָ לָעַד, מַלְכֵּנוּ, יוֹצֵר מְשָׁרְתִים, וַאֲשֶׁר מְשָׁרְתָיו כֻּלָּם עוֹמְדִים בְּרוּם עוֹלָם, וּמַשְׁמִיעִים בְּיִרְאָה יַחַד בְּקוֹל, דִּבְרֵי אֱלֹהִים חַיִּים וּמֶלֶךְ עוֹלָם. כֻּלָּם אֲהוּבִים, כֻּלָּם בְּרוּרִים, כֻּלָּם גִּבּוֹרִים, וְכֻלָּם עוֹשִׂים בְּאֵימָה וּבְיִרְאָה רְצוֹן קוֹנָם, ◄ וְכֻלָּם פּוֹתְחִים אֶת פִּיהֶם בִּקְדֻשָּׁה וּבְטָהֳרָה, בְּשִׁירָה וּבְזִמְרָה, וּמְבָרְכִים וּמְשַׁבְּחִים וּמְפָאֲרִים, וּמַעֲרִיצִים וּמַקְדִּישִׁים וּמַמְלִיכִים

אֶת שֵׁם הָאֵל הַמֶּלֶךְ הַגָּדוֹל, הַגִּבּוֹר וְהַנּוֹרָא, קָדוֹשׁ הוּא. ◄ וְכֻלָּם מְקַבְּלִים עֲלֵיהֶם עֹל מַלְכוּת שָׁמַיִם זֶה מִזֶּה, וְנוֹתְנִים רְשׁוּת זֶה לָזֶה, לְהַקְדִּישׁ לְיוֹצְרָם בְּנַחַת רוּחַ, בְּשָׂפָה בְרוּרָה וּבִנְעִימָה, קְדֻשָּׁה כֻּלָּם כְּאֶחָד עוֹנִים, וְאוֹמְרִים בְּיִרְאָה

All say aloud:

קָדוֹשׁ, קָדוֹשׁ, קָדוֹשׁ יהוה צְבָאוֹת, מְלֹא כָל־הָאָרֶץ כְּבוֹדוֹ: ישעיה ו

זֶה שֶׁבַח שֶׁל יוֹם הַשְּׁבִיעִי – *This is the praise of the seventh day*. Whereas the weekday version of this *berakha* extols God from the perspective of the unfolding and not yet completed process of Creation, the Shabbat form of the *berakha*

successive phrase of the structure – point to the Torah that was written with twenty-two letters, to teach us that the heavens above and the earth below exist only by virtue of the Torah (Abudarham).

לָאֵל – TO GOD Who rested from all His works, Who on the seventh day ascended and sat upon the throne of His glory. He vested the day of rest with splendor; He called the Sabbath day a delight. This is the praise of the seventh day, for on it God rested from all His work.
Ps. 92 And the seventh day gives praise, saying: "A psalm. A song for the Sabbath day. It is good to give thanks to the Lord." Therefore let all His creations glorify and bless God. Let them bestow praise, honor and grandeur upon God, the King Who formed everything, and Who in His holiness bestows rest upon His people Israel on the holy Sabbath day. May Your name, Lord, our God, be sanctified; may Your renown, Our King, be glorified in the heavens above and on the earth below. May You be blessed, our Savior, for Your praiseworthy handiwork, and for the bright luminaries that You made, which bring glory upon You, Selah.

All continue here:

תִּתְבָּרַךְ MAY YOU BE BLESSED, our Rock, our King, our Redeemer, Creator of holy beings. May You be forever extolled, our King, Creator of the ministering angels who stand in the firmament on high, who reverently proclaim in unison, aloud, the words of the living God, the eternal King. All are beloved, all pure, all powerful, all performing in reverent awe the will of their Maker. ▸ Opening their mouths in holiness and purity, with song and hymn, they all bless and praise and glorify and revere and sanctify and declare the sovereignty of

God's name, the great, mighty and awe-inspiring King, holy is He. ▸ All accept upon themselves the yoke of the heavenly kingdom, from one to another, and grant permission, one to another, to sanctify their Maker in serenity, in clear and sweet utterance, all proclaiming His holiness in unison, and declaring in awe:

All say aloud:

Is. 6 "HOLY, HOLY, HOLY, is the Lord of hosts, the whole world is filled with His glory."

---

praises God from the joyous perspective of the completed creation, by quoting the psalm for the Sabbath day that proclaims "For You, O Lord, make me glad through Your work. I rejoice in the works of Your hands" (Psalms 92:3) (R. Joseph B. Soloveitchik).

◂ **וְהָאוֹפַנִּים** וְחַיּוֹת הַקֹּדֶשׁ, בְּרַעַשׁ גָּדוֹל מִתְנַשְּׂאִים לְעֻמַּת שְׂרָפִים, לְעֻמָּתָם מְשַׁבְּחִים, וְאוֹמְרִים

All say aloud:

בָּרוּךְ כְּבוֹד־יהוה מִמְּקוֹמוֹ: יחזקאל ג

לָאֵל בָּרוּךְ נְעִימוֹת יִתֵּנוּ, לַמֶּלֶךְ אֵל חַי וְקַיָּם, זְמִירוֹת יֹאמֵרוּ וְתִשְׁבָּחוֹת יַשְׁמִיעוּ, כִּי הוּא לְבַדּוֹ, פּוֹעֵל גְּבוּרוֹת, עוֹשֶׂה חֲדָשׁוֹת, בַּעַל מִלְחָמוֹת, זוֹרֵעַ צְדָקוֹת, מַצְמִיחַ יְשׁוּעוֹת, בּוֹרֵא רְפוּאוֹת, נוֹרָא תְהִלּוֹת, אֲדוֹן הַנִּפְלָאוֹת, הַמְחַדֵּשׁ בְּטוּבוֹ בְּכָל יוֹם תָּמִיד מַעֲשֵׂה בְרֵאשִׁית, כָּאָמוּר, לְעֹשֵׂה אוֹרִים גְּדֹלִים, כִּי לְעוֹלָם חַסְדּוֹ: תהלים קלו ◂ אוֹר חָדָשׁ עַל צִיּוֹן תָּאִיר וְנִזְכֶּה כֻלָּנוּ מְהֵרָה לְאוֹרוֹ. בָּרוּךְ אַתָּה יהוה, יוֹצֵר הַמְּאוֹרוֹת.

אַהֲבָה רַבָּה אֲהַבְתָּנוּ, יהוה אֱלֹהֵינוּ, חֶמְלָה גְדוֹלָה וִיתֵרָה חָמַלְתָּ עָלֵינוּ. אָבִינוּ מַלְכֵּנוּ, בַּעֲבוּר אֲבוֹתֵינוּ שֶׁבָּטְחוּ בְךָ, וַתְּלַמְּדֵם חֻקֵּי חַיִּים, כֵּן תְּחָנֵּנוּ וּתְלַמְּדֵנוּ. אָבִינוּ, הָאָב הָרַחֲמָן, הַמְרַחֵם, רַחֵם עָלֵינוּ, וְתֵן בְּלִבֵּנוּ לְהָבִין וּלְהַשְׂכִּיל, לִשְׁמֹעַ, לִלְמֹד וּלְלַמֵּד, לִשְׁמֹר וְלַעֲשׂוֹת, וּלְקַיֵּם, אֶת כָּל דִּבְרֵי תַלְמוּד תּוֹרָתֶךָ בְּאַהֲבָה. וְהָאֵר עֵינֵינוּ בְּתוֹרָתֶךָ, וְדַבֵּק לִבֵּנוּ בְּמִצְוֹתֶיךָ, וְיַחֵד

זוֹרֵעַ צְדָקוֹת, מַצְמִיחַ יְשׁוּעוֹת – *Sows the seeds of just outcomes, makes salvations sprout forth.* When we perform righteous deeds they are like seeds which God then expands to ultimately bear fruit in the form of a redeemed world (Vilna Gaon).

הַמְחַדֵּשׁ בְּטוּבוֹ בְּכָל יוֹם תָּמִיד מַעֲשֵׂה בְרֵאשִׁית – *In His goodness He every day constantly renews the work of Creation.* When God created the physical universe each entity was endowed with a hidden spiritual light. Our task is to bring this created world closer to perfection by bringing out these hidden sparks of light. Every day, constantly, God gives us the life, energy, and opportunity to accomplish this task by living in accordance with His will (R. Eliyahu Dessler).

אַהֲבָה רַבָּה אֲהַבְתָּנוּ – *With great love You have loved us.* Rambam, in the Epistle to Yemen, explains the origin and nature of God's love for the people of Israel. Quoting Deuteronomy 10:15, "Only on account of your forefathers to whom God was drawn out of love did He choose their descendants from out of all the nations," Rambam explains that God distinguished us from the rest of mankind, "not on the basis of our merits but rather as an act of grace on account of our ancestors who knew God and were obedient to Him." Moreover "He chose us by giving us His laws and statutes, obedience to which expresses our preeminence as a nation." Rambam's understanding

▸ וְהָאוֹפַנִּים THEN THE OPHANIM and holy Ḥayyot rise up toward the Seraphim with great noise and respond by praising and proclaiming:

All say aloud:

Ezek. 3 "BLESSED is the glory of the Lord from His place."

לְאֵל TO THE BLESSED GOD they offer sweet melodies; to the King, Who is God and Who lives forever, they pronounce hymns and proclaim praises. For He alone performs mighty deeds, initiates unprecedented events, determines the outcome of wars, sows the seeds of just outcomes, makes salvations sprout forth, creates healing, is the awesome object of praise, and controls miracles. In His goodness He
Ps. 136 every day constantly renews the work of Creation, as it says, "He makes great lights, for His loving-kindness is forever." ▸ May You shine a new light on Zion, and all of us soon merit its illumination. Blessed are You, Lord, Maker of the heavenly lights.

אַהֲבָה רַבָּה WITH GREAT LOVE You have loved us, Lord our God; with great and overflowing compassion You have pitied us. Our Father, our King, for the sake of our fathers who trusted in You, and whom You taught the statutes of life, please also be gracious to us and teach us. Our Father, merciful Father, always compassionate, have mercy on us. Give us understanding and discernment, so that we can grasp all the words of Your Torah's teaching – learning and transmitting them by lovingly observing, practicing, and fulfilling them. Open our eyes through Your Torah so that our hearts can cleave to Your

---

of our chosenness (i.e., it is not by virtue of any inherent superiority to others, but only in the merit of our forefathers and thereafter our ongoing adherence to His Torah) is fully reflected in this second of the *birkhot Shema*. First it describes God's love and special compassion for our people. Then it goes on to invoke the reason for this special relationship, i.e., "our forefathers who trusted in You and to whom You taught lessons of life." Finally, echoing the notion that our chosenness is reflected only to the extent that we adhere to the Torah, it asks God to facilitate our own study, teaching, and upholding of the Torah and its commandments (R. Basil Herring).

לִלְמֹד וּלְלַמֵּד, לִשְׁמֹר וְלַעֲשׂוֹת, וּלְקַיֵּם – *Learning and transmitting them by lovingly observing, practicing, and fulfilling them*. The term לַעֲשׂוֹת does not refer to performing the *mitzvot* of the Torah, for that is the meaning of the next word (לְקַיֵּם). Rather it refers to achieving new insights into the Torah via sustained study thereof. So too when a teacher explains Torah to a student, the teacher also gains new understanding and insight, derived from the give and take of the learning process (*Netziv*).

לְבָבֵנוּ לְאַהֲבָה וּלְיִרְאָה אֶת שְׁמֶךָ, וְלֹא נֵבוֹשׁ לְעוֹלָם וָעֶד. כִּי בְשֵׁם קָדְשְׁךָ הַגָּדוֹל וְהַנּוֹרָא בָּטָחְנוּ, נָגִילָה וְנִשְׂמְחָה בִּישׁוּעָתֶךָ. °וַהֲבִיאֵנוּ לְשָׁלוֹם (*At this point, one should gather the* ציציות *strands. See below.*) מֵאַרְבַּע כַּנְפוֹת הָאָרֶץ, וְתוֹלִיכֵנוּ קוֹמְמִיּוּת לְאַרְצֵנוּ. ‹ כִּי אֵל פּוֹעֵל יְשׁוּעוֹת אָתָּה, וּבָנוּ בָחַרְתָּ מִכָּל עַם וְלָשׁוֹן, וְקֵרַבְתָּנוּ לְשִׁמְךָ הַגָּדוֹל סֶלָה, בֶּאֱמֶת, לְהוֹדוֹת לְךָ וּלְיַחֶדְךָ בְּאַהֲבָה. בָּרוּךְ אַתָּה יהוה, הַבּוֹחֵר בְּעַמּוֹ יִשְׂרָאֵל בְּאַהֲבָה.

שמע

The שמע *must be said with intense concentration. In the first paragraph one should accept, with love, the sovereignty of God; in the second, accept the* מצוות *as the will of God. The end of the third paragraph constitutes fulfillment of the* מצווה *to remember, morning and evening, the Exodus from Egypt.*

When not praying with a מנין*, some say:*

אֵל מֶלֶךְ נֶאֱמָן

The following verse should be said aloud, while covering the eyes with the right hand:

דברים ו

שְׁמַע יִשְׂרָאֵל, יהוה אֱלֹהֵינוּ, יהוה | אֶחָד:

Quietly בָּרוּךְ שֵׁם כְּבוֹד מַלְכוּתוֹ לְעוֹלָם וָעֶד.

דברים ו

וְאָהַבְתָּ אֵת יהוה אֱלֹהֶיךָ, בְּכָל־לְבָבְךָ וּבְכָל־נַפְשְׁךָ וּבְכָל־מְאֹדֶךָ: וְהָיוּ הַדְּבָרִים הָאֵלֶּה, אֲשֶׁר אָנֹכִי מְצַוְּךָ הַיּוֹם, עַל־לְבָבֶךָ:

GATHERING OF TZITZIT

At this point, one should gather the four (some have the tradition of only gathering the front two) *tzitzit* strands (*Arukh HaShulḥan* 60:9). The *tzitzit* strands should be held in one's left hand between the pinky and ring-finger (*MB* 24:4).

הַבּוֹחֵר בְּעַמּוֹ יִשְׂרָאֵל בְּאַהֲבָה / HABOḤER BE'AMO YISRAEL

According to the *Mishna Berura*, it is preferable for the congregation to recite this blessing in an undertone simultaneously with the Leader so as to avoid having to answer *Amen* to the *berakha* (*MB* 59:25). However, those who follow the practice of reciting *Amen* to the *berakha* should complete the *berakha* before the Leader does, and then answer *Amen* to his *berakha*. The Leader should make sure to recite the *berakha* out loud.

שְׁמַע / THE SHEMA

בָּרוּךְ שֵׁם כְּבוֹד מַלְכוּתוֹ – *Blessed be His name and His glorious kingdom.* This is not a scriptural verse, but was rather, as recorded in the Gemara (*Pesaḥim* 56a), the response of Jacob on his deathbed, when upon hearing his children

commandments. Make our hearts a harmony of love and reverence for Your name, so that we will never feel shame. And insofar as we have trusted in Your holy, great, and awesome name, let us rejoice and be happy in Your saving power. (*At this point, one should gather the tzitziyot strands. See below.*) °Bring us in peace from the four corners of the earth and lead us, standing upright, to our land, ▸ for You are the God Who brings salvation. You have chosen us from among every other people and tongue, and have brought us near in truth to Your great name so that we can give thanks to You and lovingly proclaim Your unity. Blessed are You, Lord, Who so lovingly chooses His people Israel.

SHEMA

The Shema must be said with intense concentration. In the first paragraph one should accept, with love, the sovereignty of God; in the second, accept the mitzvot as the will of God. The end of the third paragraph constitutes fulfillment of the mitzva to remember, morning and evening, the Exodus from Egypt.

When not praying with a minyan, some say:
God, the King Who is faithful.

The following verse should be said aloud, while covering the eyes with the right hand:

Deut. 6 HEAR, O ISRAEL, the LORD is our God, the LORD is One.

Quietly: Blessed be His name and His glorious kingdom for ever and ever.

Deut. 6 וְאָהַבְתָּ YOU SHALL LOVE the LORD your God with all your heart, and with all your soul, and with all your might. And these words which I command you this day shall be upon your heart. You shall teach

---

declare (anticipating Deuteronomy 6:1) their faith in God's Oneness, he reaffirmed God's sovereignty (מַלְכוּת) in these words. Hence with these words we too proclaim our acceptance of God's sovereignty after reciting Deuteronomy 6:1, i.e., the opening verse of the *Shema*. We do so, however, merely in an undertone. The Gemara explains this by analogy to a princess who craves special delicacies not available to commoners. Were this to become publically known, she would be embarrassed – hence her attendants quietly supply her cravings. So it is with our soul. Descended from a divine Father, it is a "daughter of the King" who is consigned to dwell in this physical world, hidden within our bodies, while longing to submit unconditionally to God's will. Yet, in a world that is subject to the limitations of physical existence, it would be inappropriate for our soul to publicly proclaim that craving. Thus, like the servants of a hidden princess, we quietly recite Jacob's words that affirm God's sovereignty, and give expression to the hidden longing of our soul to unconditionally embrace God's will, through קַבָּלַת עֹל מַלְכוּת שָׁמַיִם (submission to the yoke of the kingdom of heaven) (Maharal).

וּבְכָל־נַפְשְׁךָ – *With all your soul.* The Talmud

וְשִׁנַּנְתָּם לְבָנֶיךָ וְדִבַּרְתָּ בָּם, בְּשִׁבְתְּךָ בְּבֵיתֶךָ וּבְלֶכְתְּךָ בַדֶּרֶךְ, וּבְשָׁכְבְּךָ
וּבְקוּמֶךָ: וּקְשַׁרְתָּם לְאוֹת עַל־יָדֶךָ וְהָיוּ לְטֹטָפֹת בֵּין עֵינֶיךָ: וּכְתַבְתָּם
עַל־מְזֻזוֹת בֵּיתֶךָ וּבִשְׁעָרֶיךָ:

דברים יא
וְהָיָה אִם־שָׁמֹעַ תִּשְׁמְעוּ אֶל־מִצְוֹתַי אֲשֶׁר אָנֹכִי מְצַוֶּה אֶתְכֶם
הַיּוֹם, לְאַהֲבָה אֶת־יהוה אֱלֹהֵיכֶם וּלְעָבְדוֹ, בְּכָל־לְבַבְכֶם
וּבְכָל־נַפְשְׁכֶם: וְנָתַתִּי מְטַר־אַרְצְכֶם בְּעִתּוֹ, יוֹרֶה וּמַלְקוֹשׁ, וְאָסַפְתָּ
דְגָנֶךָ וְתִירֹשְׁךָ וְיִצְהָרֶךָ: וְנָתַתִּי עֵשֶׂב בְּשָׂדְךָ לִבְהֶמְתֶּךָ, וְאָכַלְתָּ
וְשָׂבָעְתָּ: הִשָּׁמְרוּ לָכֶם פֶּן־יִפְתֶּה לְבַבְכֶם, וְסַרְתֶּם וַעֲבַדְתֶּם אֱלֹהִים
אֲחֵרִים וְהִשְׁתַּחֲוִיתֶם לָהֶם: וְחָרָה אַף־יהוה בָּכֶם, וְעָצַר אֶת־
הַשָּׁמַיִם וְלֹא־יִהְיֶה מָטָר, וְהָאֲדָמָה לֹא תִתֵּן אֶת־יְבוּלָהּ, וַאֲבַדְתֶּם
מְהֵרָה מֵעַל הָאָרֶץ הַטֹּבָה אֲשֶׁר יהוה נֹתֵן לָכֶם: וְשַׂמְתֶּם אֶת־
דְּבָרַי אֵלֶּה עַל־לְבַבְכֶם וְעַל־נַפְשְׁכֶם, וּקְשַׁרְתֶּם אֹתָם לְאוֹת עַל־
יֶדְכֶם, וְהָיוּ לְטוֹטָפֹת בֵּין עֵינֵיכֶם: וְלִמַּדְתֶּם אֹתָם אֶת־בְּנֵיכֶם
לְדַבֵּר בָּם, בְּשִׁבְתְּךָ בְּבֵיתֶךָ וּבְלֶכְתְּךָ בַדֶּרֶךְ, וּבְשָׁכְבְּךָ וּבְקוּמֶךָ:

Yerushalmi (*Berakhot* 9:5) records the death of R. Akiva during the second-century Hadrianic persecutions in the land of Israel. While tortured he joyously recited this verse, explaining to those present that "I have always loved God with 'all my heart' and served Him with 'all my means' but I was never sure if I was capable of serving Him with 'all my life,' as this verse commands. Now I am happily assured that I am able to do that too." With these words, R. Akiva articulated the doctrine of יִסּוּרֵי אַהֲבָה (sufferings of divine love), by which he affirmed that our suffering is not necessarily a punishment for having sinned. Sometimes, R. Akiva taught, it is imposed on us by God, without any preceding sin, but purely as an expression of divine love, so as to bring us some ultimate benefit, whether or not we can comprehend His ways. This doctrine was responsible for saving the Torah by immeasurably strengthening the resolve of Jews to remain lovingly faithful to God no matter the suffering or consequence, not just during those persecutions in the land of Israel in the second century, but for all time, and under all kinds of difficult circumstances (Prof. Ephraim Urbach).

בְּכָל־לְבַבְכֶם וּבְכָל־נַפְשְׁכֶם – *With all your heart and with all your soul.* In this second paragraph of the *Shema*, the verse does not say וּבְכָל מְאֹדְכֶם (and with all your might), as the first paragraph of the *Shema* does, for the following reason. The Gemara (*Berakhot* 54a) cites one view which explains that מְאֹדֶךָ in the first paragraph obligates us to bless God for both the benefits and the suffering that He brings upon us. As explained by Abaye (*Megilla* 31b), Reish Lakish argues that this applies only to the pain of an individual, but not when the Jewish people as a whole suffer, for then God

them diligently to your children, speaking of them when you sit in your house and when you walk by the way, when you lie down and when you rise up. You shall bind them for a sign on your hand, and they shall be as *tefillin* between your eyes. And you shall write them upon the doorposts of your house and upon your gates.

Deut. 11 **וְהָיָה** IT SHALL COME to PASS that if you will listen diligently to My commandments with which I charge you this day, to love the LORD your God and to serve Him with all your heart and with all your soul, then will I send the rain for your land in its due season, the autumn rain and the spring rain, that you may gather in your corn, your wine, and your oil. And I will give grass in your field for your cattle, and you shall eat and be satisfied. Be careful lest your heart be deceived, and you turn aside and serve other gods and worship them. For then the LORD's wrath will be kindled against you, and He will shut the heavens so that there will be no rain, the land will not yield her produce, and you shall perish quickly from the good land which the LORD gives you. Therefore place these words of Mine upon your heart and upon your soul, and you shall bind them for a sign on your hand and they shall be as *tefillin* between your eyes. And you shall teach them to your children, speaking of them when you sit in your house and when you walk on the way, when you lie down and when

---

Himself experiences their pain. As Isaiah (63:9) states, בְּכָל־צָרָתָם לוֹ צָר (whenever they suffer He too is in pain), which the *Mekhilta* to Exodus 14 understands as saying, "it is not appropriate that while My children are suffering I am being blessed." For this reason, too, we do not recite a *berakha* when reading the curses of Leviticus 26 (hence we include verses of blessings as well in that *aliya*) which being in the plural form refer to the future suffering of the Jewish people, unlike the curses of Deuteronomy 28 which refer to personal suffering in the singular form. Accordingly, because the second paragraph of the *Shema* (unlike the first) is framed entirely in the plural, it refers to the obligations that fall upon the Jewish people as a whole, and no *berakha* is recited with respect to collective suffering. Consequently וּבְכָל מְאֹדְכֶם would be inappropriate, and is therefore omitted (*Beit HaLevi*).

וְנָתַתִּי עֵשֶׂב בְּשָׂדְךָ לִבְהֶמְתֶּךָ, וְאָכַלְתָּ וְשָׂבָעְתָּ – *And I will give grass in your field for your cattle, and you shall eat and be satisfied.* The Gemara (*Berakhot* 40a) derives from this verse that we must first feed our animals before we sit down to eat. So too *Barkhi Nafshi* states, "He causes the grass to grow for the cattle and plants for the service of man" (Psalms 104:14), i.e., God Himself acts this way, as it says in *Ashrei*, "His mercies are upon all His works" (Psalms 145:9) (*Bekhor Shor*).

וּכְתַבְתָּם עַל־מְזֻזוֹת בֵּיתֶךָ וּבִשְׁעָרֶיךָ: לְמַעַן יִרְבּוּ יְמֵיכֶם וִימֵי
בְנֵיכֶם עַל הָאֲדָמָה אֲשֶׁר נִשְׁבַּע יהוה לַאֲבֹתֵיכֶם לָתֵת לָהֶם, כִּימֵי
הַשָּׁמַיִם עַל־הָאָרֶץ:

Hold the ציצית *in both hands, kissing them at* °.

במדבר טו
וַיֹּאמֶר יהוה אֶל־מֹשֶׁה לֵּאמֹר: דַּבֵּר אֶל־בְּנֵי יִשְׂרָאֵל וְאָמַרְתָּ
אֲלֵהֶם, וְעָשׂוּ לָהֶם °צִיצִת עַל־כַּנְפֵי בִגְדֵיהֶם לְדֹרֹתָם,
וְנָתְנוּ °עַל־צִיצִת הַכָּנָף פְּתִיל תְּכֵלֶת: וְהָיָה לָכֶם °לְצִיצִת, וּרְאִיתֶם
אֹתוֹ וּזְכַרְתֶּם אֶת־כׇּל־מִצְוֹת יהוה וַעֲשִׂיתֶם אֹתָם, וְלֹא תָתֻרוּ
אַחֲרֵי לְבַבְכֶם וְאַחֲרֵי עֵינֵיכֶם, אֲשֶׁר־אַתֶּם זֹנִים אַחֲרֵיהֶם: לְמַעַן
תִּזְכְּרוּ וַעֲשִׂיתֶם אֶת־כׇּל־מִצְוֹתָי, וִהְיִיתֶם קְדֹשִׁים לֵאלֹהֵיכֶם: אֲנִי
יהוה אֱלֹהֵיכֶם, אֲשֶׁר הוֹצֵאתִי אֶתְכֶם מֵאֶרֶץ מִצְרַיִם, לִהְיוֹת לָכֶם
לֵאלֹהִים, אֲנִי יהוה אֱלֹהֵיכֶם: °**אֱמֶת**

The שליח ציבור *repeats:*

◂ יהוה אֱלֹהֵיכֶם אֱמֶת

וְיַצִּיב, וְנָכוֹן וְקַיָּם, וְיָשָׁר וְנֶאֱמָן, וְאָהוּב וְחָבִיב, וְנֶחְמָד וְנָעִים,
וְנוֹרָא וְאַדִּיר, וּמְתֻקָּן וּמְקֻבָּל, וְטוֹב וְיָפֶה, הַדָּבָר
הַזֶּה עָלֵינוּ לְעוֹלָם וָעֶד. אֱמֶת אֱלֹהֵי עוֹלָם מַלְכֵּנוּ, צוּר יַעֲקֹב
מָגֵן יִשְׁעֵנוּ, ◂ לְדֹר וָדֹר הוּא קַיָּם וּשְׁמוֹ קַיָּם, וְכִסְאוֹ נָכוֹן,
וּמַלְכוּתוֹ וֶאֱמוּנָתוֹ לָעַד קַיָּמֶת. ◂ וּדְבָרָיו חָיִים וְקַיָּמִים, נֶאֱמָנִים
וְנֶחֱמָדִים לָעַד (*kiss the* ציצית *and release them*), וּלְעוֹלְמֵי עוֹלָמִים, עַל
אֲבוֹתֵינוּ וְעָלֵינוּ, עַל בָּנֵינוּ וְעַל דּוֹרוֹתֵינוּ, וְעַל כׇּל דּוֹרוֹת זֶרַע
יִשְׂרָאֵל עֲבָדֶיךָ.

עַל הָרִאשׁוֹנִים וְעַל הָאַחֲרוֹנִים, דָּבָר טוֹב וְקַיָּם לְעוֹלָם וָעֶד.
אֱמֶת וֶאֱמוּנָה, חֹק וְלֹא יַעֲבֹר. אֱמֶת שָׁאַתָּה הוּא יהוה אֱלֹהֵינוּ

וְלֹא תָתֻרוּ אַחֲרֵי לְבַבְכֶם וְאַחֲרֵי עֵינֵיכֶם – *That you shall not stray after your heart and your eyes.* Rambam (*Hilkhot Avoda Zara* 2:3) explains that these words forbid us to entertain any thoughts that might bring us to undermine the fundamental principles of the Torah. Persisting in contemplating these things can lead one to embrace heresy. He refers to this verse as

you rise up. And you shall write them upon the doorposts of your house and upon your gates. That long as the days of the heavens above the earth may be your days and the days of your children in the land which the LORD promised your fathers to give to them.

Hold the tzitziyot in both hands, kissing them at °.

Num. 15 וַיֹּאמֶר THE LORD SPOKE to Moses, saying: "Speak to the children of Israel and tell them to make for themselves °*tzitzit* on the corners of their garments, throughout their generations, putting a thread of blue upon the °*tzitzit* of each corner. It shall be to you a °*tzitzit* which you may look upon and remember all the commandments of the LORD and do them, that you shall not stray after your heart and your eyes, after which you sinfully follow. So may you remember and do all My commandments and be holy for your God. I am the LORD your God who brought you out of the land of Egypt to be your God; I am the LORD your God." °TRUE IT IS –

The Leader repeats:
▸ The LORD your God. True it is –

וְיַצִּיב AND FIRMLY GROUNDED, ordered and established, right and permanent, lovely and precious, pleasant and sweet, solemn and revered, accepted as well as good and beautiful, is this matter for us for all time. The eternal God is truly our King, the Rock of Jacob, our protecting shield. ▸ He endures, as does His name, to all generations. His throne is established, and His sovereignty and faithfulness endure forever. ◂ His words live and endure, faithful and precious forever (*kiss the tzitziot and release them*), and for all eternity. They were incumbent upon our forefathers, and so they are and will be for us, for our children and our descendants, and for every generation of the seed of Israel, Your servants.

For the early and the later generations, these words are a doctrine that is good and enduring forever; true and faithful, a law that shall not pass away. In truth, You are the Lord, our God and the God of our fathers;

---

support, saying, "As an individual do not be pulled by your weak intellect into thinking that you can arrive independently at the truth, as the sages said in the *Sifrei* 'after your hearts' refers to מִינוּת (heresy), while 'after your eyes' refers to זְנוּת (sexual impropriety)."

וֵאלֹהֵי אֲבוֹתֵינוּ, ‹ מַלְכֵּנוּ מֶלֶךְ אֲבוֹתֵינוּ, גּוֹאֲלֵנוּ גּוֹאֵל אֲבוֹתֵינוּ, יוֹצְרֵנוּ צוּר יְשׁוּעָתֵנוּ, פּוֹדֵנוּ וּמַצִּילֵנוּ מֵעוֹלָם שְׁמֶךָ, אֵין אֱלֹהִים זוּלָתֶךָ.

עֶזְרַת אֲבוֹתֵינוּ אַתָּה הוּא מֵעוֹלָם, מָגֵן וּמוֹשִׁיעַ לִבְנֵיהֶם אַחֲרֵיהֶם בְּכָל דּוֹר וָדוֹר. בְּרוּם עוֹלָם מוֹשָׁבֶךָ, וּמִשְׁפָּטֶיךָ וְצִדְקָתְךָ עַד אַפְסֵי אָרֶץ. אַשְׁרֵי אִישׁ שֶׁיִּשְׁמַע לְמִצְוֹתֶיךָ, וְתוֹרָתְךָ וּדְבָרְךָ יָשִׂים עַל לִבּוֹ. אֱמֶת אַתָּה הוּא אָדוֹן לְעַמֶּךָ, וּמֶלֶךְ גִּבּוֹר לָרִיב רִיבָם. אֱמֶת אַתָּה הוּא רִאשׁוֹן וְאַתָּה הוּא אַחֲרוֹן, וּמִבַּלְעָדֶיךָ אֵין לָנוּ מֶלֶךְ גּוֹאֵל וּמוֹשִׁיעַ. מִמִּצְרַיִם גְּאַלְתָּנוּ, יהוה אֱלֹהֵינוּ, וּמִבֵּית עֲבָדִים פְּדִיתָנוּ, כָּל בְּכוֹרֵיהֶם הָרַגְתָּ, וּבְכוֹרְךָ
גָּאַלְתָּ, וְיַם סוּף בָּקַעְתָּ, וְזֵדִים טִבַּעְתָּ, וִידִידִים הֶעֱבַרְתָּ, וַיְכַסּוּ־מַיִם תהלים קו
צָרֵיהֶם, אֶחָד מֵהֶם לֹא נוֹתָר: עַל זֹאת שִׁבְּחוּ אֲהוּבִים, וְרוֹמְמוּ אֵל, וְנָתְנוּ יְדִידִים זְמִירוֹת, שִׁירוֹת וְתִשְׁבָּחוֹת, בְּרָכוֹת וְהוֹדָאוֹת לְמֶלֶךְ אֵל חַי וְקַיָּם, רָם וְנִשָּׂא, גָּדוֹל וְנוֹרָא, מַשְׁפִּיל גֵּאִים וּמַגְבִּיהַּ שְׁפָלִים, מוֹצִיא אֲסִירִים, וּפוֹדֶה עֲנָוִים וְעוֹזֵר דַּלִּים, וְעוֹנֶה לְעַמּוֹ בְּעֵת שַׁוְּעָם אֵלָיו.

Stand in preparation for the עמידה*. Take three steps back before beginning the* עמידה*.*

‹ תְּהִלּוֹת לְאֵל עֶלְיוֹן, בָּרוּךְ הוּא וּמְבֹרָךְ, מֹשֶׁה וּבְנֵי יִשְׂרָאֵל, לְךָ עָנוּ שִׁירָה בְּשִׂמְחָה רַבָּה, וְאָמְרוּ כֻלָּם,

מִי־כָמֹכָה בָּאֵלִם, יהוה, מִי כָּמֹכָה נֶאְדָּר בַּקֹּדֶשׁ, נוֹרָא תְהִלֹּת, עֹשֵׂה פֶלֶא: שמות טו

‹ שִׁירָה חֲדָשָׁה שִׁבְּחוּ גְאוּלִים, לְשִׁמְךָ עַל שְׂפַת הַיָּם, יַחַד כֻּלָּם הוֹדוּ וְהִמְלִיכוּ, וְאָמְרוּ,

יהוה יִמְלֹךְ לְעֹלָם וָעֶד: שמות טו

▸ our King and the King of our fathers; our Redeemer and Redeemer of our fathers; our Maker, the Rock of our salvation; our Savior and Deliverer – this has ever been Your name; there is no other god besides You.

עֶזְרַת אֲבוֹתֵינוּ FROM OF OLD You have been the help of our fathers, a shield and a savior for their children after them in every generation. Although Your dwelling is in the heights above the cosmos, Your works of righteousness and justice extend to the ends of the earth. Happy is the man who hearkens to Your commandments, who sets Your Torah and Your word in his heart. True it is that You are the Master of Your people, their mighty King to champion their cause. True it is that You are the first and You are the last, and besides You we have no king who saves and redeems. From Egypt You redeemed us, Lord, our God, and from the house of bondage You delivered us; all their firstborn You slayed, but Your firstborn, You redeemed. You divided the Sea of Reeds and drowned those who had oppressed us. The people You loved
Ps. 106 You brought across the sea, but "the waters covered their enemies, not one of them remained." For this, the beloved ones praised and exalted God; the cherished ones sang hymns, songs and praises, blessings and thanksgivings to the King, the ever-living and enduring God. Supremely exalted, all-powerful and awe-inspiring, He brings low the arrogant and raises the meek, sets free those who are bound, rescues the lowly, helps the needy, and answers His people when they cry to Him.

Stand in preparation for the Amida. Take three steps back before beginning the Amida.

▸ Praises to the supreme God, ever blessed be He. To You Moses and all the children of Israel chanted songs with great joy, all proclaiming:

Ex. 15 WHO IS LIKE YOU, Lord, among the mighty? Who is like You, glorious in holiness, inspiring in praises, working wonders?

▸ By the shore of the sea the rescued people sang to Your name a new song of praise. Together they all acknowledged and proclaimed Your sovereignty, saying:

Ex. 15 THE LORD shall reign forever and ever.

◂ צוּר יִשְׂרָאֵל, קוּמָה בְּעֶזְרַת יִשְׂרָאֵל, וּפְדֵה כִנְאֻמֶךָ יְהוּדָה וְיִשְׂרָאֵל.
ישעיה מז גֹּאֲלֵנוּ יהוה צְבָאוֹת שְׁמוֹ, קְדוֹשׁ יִשְׂרָאֵל:

On פסח *some congregations say here a short piyut* *(pages 802–808)* *before the* עמידה.

בָּרוּךְ אַתָּה יהוה, גָּאַל יִשְׂרָאֵל.

On יום טוב *(including one that falls on* שבת*), but not on* חול המועד*, turn to page 810.*

עמידה

One begins the עמידה *by taking three steps forward (OḤ 95:1). According to some traditions, one should first take three steps back before moving forward (MB 95:3). The* עמידה *is recited with one's feet together. One should try to concentrate on the simple meaning of the words of the* עמידה *with the awareness throughout that one is standing in the presence of the Almighty (OḤ 98:1 and MB 98:1). At the points indicated by* ▾*, bend the knees at the first word, bow at the second, and stand straight before saying God's name.*

תהלים נא אֲדֹנָי, שְׂפָתַי תִּפְתָּח, וּפִי יַגִּיד תְּהִלָּתֶךָ:

אבות

▾בָּרוּךְ אַתָּה יהוה, אֱלֹהֵינוּ וֵאלֹהֵי אֲבוֹתֵינוּ, אֱלֹהֵי אַבְרָהָם, אֱלֹהֵי יִצְחָק, וֵאלֹהֵי יַעֲקֹב, הָאֵל הַגָּדוֹל הַגִּבּוֹר וְהַנּוֹרָא, אֵל עֶלְיוֹן, גּוֹמֵל חֲסָדִים טוֹבִים, וְקוֹנֵה הַכֹּל, וְזוֹכֵר חַסְדֵי אָבוֹת, וּמֵבִיא גוֹאֵל לִבְנֵי בְנֵיהֶם לְמַעַן שְׁמוֹ בְּאַהֲבָה.

בשבת שובה: זָכְרֵנוּ לְחַיִּים, מֶלֶךְ חָפֵץ בַּחַיִּים, וְכָתְבֵנוּ בְּסֵפֶר הַחַיִּים, לְמַעַנְךָ אֱלֹהִים חַיִּים.

(If forgotten, no corrective action is necessary.)

מֶלֶךְ עוֹזֵר וּמוֹשִׁיעַ וּמָגֵן. ▾בָּרוּךְ אַתָּה יהוה, מָגֵן אַבְרָהָם.

גָּאַל יִשְׂרָאֵל / GA'AL YISRAEL

It is preferable for the congregation to recite this blessing in an undertone simultaneously with the Leader (*MB* 66:35). The Leader should make sure to recite the *berakha* out loud (R. Yosef Eliyahu Henkin, *Edut LeYisrael*, p. 161).

For laws regarding "The repetition of the *Amida*," see page 107.

עֲמִידָה / THE AMIDA

וֵאלֹהֵי אֲבוֹתֵינוּ, אֱלֹהֵי אַבְרָהָם, אֱלֹהֵי יִצְחָק, וֵאלֹהֵי יַעֲקֹב – *Our God and God of our fathers, God of Abraham, God of Isaac and God of Jacob.* The *Amida* begins in this fashion because when God appeared to Moses for the first time at the Burning Bush, He identified Himself as "the God of your father, the God of Abraham, the God of Isaac and the God of Jacob" (Ex. 3:6). More pointedly, a few verses later (Ex. 3:15), using the same language, God instructs Moses to tell the people that "the Lord Who is the God

▸ Rock of Israel, rise up to the aid of Israel, and fulfill Your promised
Is. 47 word to deliver Judah and Israel. Our Redeemer, Whose name is the Lord of hosts, is the Holy One of Israel.

On Pesaḥ some congregations say here a short piyut (pages 803–809) before the Amida.

Blessed are You, Lord, Who redeemed Israel.

On Yom Tov (including one that falls on Shabbat), but not on Ḥol HaMo'ed, turn to page 811.

AMIDA

One begins the Amida by taking three steps forward (OḤ 95:1). According to some traditions, one should first take three steps back before moving forward (MB 95:3). The Amida is recited with one's feet together. One should try to concentrate on the simple meaning of the words of the Amida with the awareness throughout that one is standing in the presence of the Almighty. (OḤ 98:1 and MB 98:1) At the points indicated by ▾, bend the knees at the first word, bow at the second, and stand straight before saying God's name.

Ps. 51 "O MY MASTER, open my lips, and my mouth will relate Your praise."

PATRIARCHS

▾בָּרוּךְ▾ BLESSED ARE YOU, LORD, our God and the God of our fathers, the God of Abraham, the God of Isaac, and the God of Jacob, the God Who is great, mighty, and awesome, God most exalted, Who bestows rewards of benevolent kindness, Who is the Creator of everything, Who remembers all the kind acts of the fathers, and Who brings a redeemer to their children's children, for the sake of His name, with love.

On Shabbat Shuva: Remember us for life, King Who desires life, and inscribe us in the book of life for Your sake, Living God.
(If forgotten, no corrective action is necessary.)

King Who helps, saves, and shields, ▾blessed are You, LORD, Shield of Abraham.

---

of your fathers, the God of Abraham, the God of Isaac and the God of Jacob, has sent me to you; this is My name forever, and זֶה זִכְרִי לְדֹר דֹּר – this is how to invoke Me in each generation." From this we learn that throughout the generations when we want to approach God in prayer, we are to address Him using this exact formulation so that He will hear and answer us (Ramban).

The phrase "Our God and the God of our fathers" echoes the song of the Israelites at the Sea of Reeds, in declaring (in their case in the singular), "This is my God and I will glorify Him, my father's God and I will extol Him" (Ex. 15:2).

הַגָּדוֹל הַגִּבּוֹר וְהַנּוֹרָא – *Great, mighty and awesome.* The Gemara (*Yoma* 69b) explains that those primarily responsible for composing our prayers are known as the "Men of the *Great*

גבורות

אַתָּה גִּבּוֹר לְעוֹלָם, אֲדֹנָי, מְחַיֵּה מֵתִים אַתָּה, רַב לְהוֹשִׁיעַ.

בחורף: מַשִּׁיב הָרְוּחַ וּמוֹרִיד הַגֶּשֶׁם

מְכַלְכֵּל חַיִּים בְּחֶסֶד, מְחַיֵּה מֵתִים בְּרַחֲמִים רַבִּים, סוֹמֵךְ נוֹפְלִים, וְרוֹפֵא חוֹלִים, וּמַתִּיר אֲסוּרִים, וּמְקַיֵּם אֱמוּנָתוֹ לִישֵׁנֵי עָפָר. מִי כָמְוֹךָ, בַּעַל גְּבוּרוֹת, וּמִי דְּוֹמֶה לָּךְ, מֶלֶךְ, מֵמִית וּמְחַיֶּה וּמַצְמִיחַ יְשׁוּעָה.

בשבת שובה: מִי כָמְוֹךָ אַב הָרַחֲמִים, זוֹכֵר יְצוּרָיו לְחַיִּים בְּרַחֲמִים.

(*If forgotten, no corrective action is necessary.*)

וְנֶאֱמָן אַתָּה לְהַחֲיוֹת מֵתִים. בָּרוּךְ אַתָּה יהוה, מְחַיֵּה הַמֵּתִים.

During the חזרת הש"ץ*, the* קדושה *is said at this point on the next page.*

קדושת השם

אַתָּה קָדוֹשׁ וְשִׁמְךָ קָדוֹשׁ. וּקְדוֹשִׁים בְּכָל יוֹם יְהַלְלְוּךָ סֶּלָה. בָּרוּךְ אַתָּה יהוה, הָאֵל הַקָּדוֹשׁ./ בשבת שובה: הַמֶּלֶךְ הַקָּדוֹשׁ./

(*If forgotten, repeat the* עמידה*.*)

Assembly" because they restored the *greatness* of God's glory which had been diminished over time. For while Moses had addressed God as "the great, mighty, and awesome God" (Deut. 10:17), when Jeremiah saw the Babylonians strutting in the destroyed courtyard of the First Temple he asked, "Where is God's awesomeness now," and as a result omitted "awesome" from his prayer (Jer. 32:18). Thereafter, confronted with the servitude of his people in exile, Daniel said, "Where is God's might now," and thus He omitted "mighty" from his prayers (Dan. 9:4). But then the Men of the Great Assembly came and proclaimed, "On the contrary; this is precisely the proof of His *might*, in that He restrains Himself by showing patience to the wicked by not punishing them immediately, and proof of His *awesomeness*, in that were it not for the awe in which He is held, our solitary nation would not have survived among the nations of the world." They therefore restored Moses' original "great, mighty, and awesome" formulation. Based on this affirmation of the Men of the Great Assembly, the Shela HaKadosh taught that the most noteworthy spiritual accomplishment is not just to sing God's praises out of a sense of gratitude when all is going well. It is relatively easy to praise and believe in Him when He performs miracles to help or save us. The higher achievement is

For laws regarding "Omission/Insertion of *Mashiv Haru'aḥ*," see page 109.
For laws regarding "Omission of *HaMelekh HaKadosh*," see page 112.

GOD'S MIGHT

אַתָּה YOU, my Master, are forever mighty, You are the Resurrector of the dead, with great power to save.

In winter: He makes the wind blow and the rain fall

He sustains the living with kindness, He resurrects the dead with great compassion, He supports those who are falling, He heals the sick, He sets the incarcerated free, and He fulfills what He has promised to those who sleep in the dust. Who is like You, O mighty One, and who can be compared to You, O King Who causes death and resurrects, and Who causes salvation to sprout?

On Shabbat Shuva: Who is like You, merciful Father, Who in compassion remembers for life those He has created.

(*If forgotten, no corrective action is necessary.*)

Trustworthy are You to resurrect the dead. Blessed are YOU, LORD, Resurrector of the dead.

During the Leader's Repetition, the "Kedusha" is said at this point on the next page.

HOLINESS

אַתָּה YOU ARE HOLY and Your name is holy, and holy ones will praise You every day, forever. Blessed are You, LORD, the holy God.

/*On Shabbat Shuva:* the holy King./

(*If forgotten, repeat the Amida.*)

---

to believe so completely in God's salvation that even in the midst of pain and torment, one can pray to Him with undiminished affirmation of His awesome power and might, in the certain knowledge that in due course He will triumph over, and appropriately punish, His and our enemies (R. Moshe Weinberger).

אַתָּה גִּבּוֹר... הָרְוּחַ/הַגֶּשֶׁם/הַטָּל – *You are eternally mighty ... wind/rain/dew.* It is precisely in this *berakha* that speaks of God's power that we describe these elements of the cycle that produces rain or dew. For the more we understand what is involved in providing life-sustaining rain, the more we should be in awe of God's power. Water evaporates from the ocean to form vapor, which is then borne toward land by ocean breezes, where the land masses force the air higher into the cooler atmosphere, causing condensation in the form of clouds, which eventually deposit rain and dew onto land to form streams, rivers, and underground aquifers without all of which life on earth could not exist, before flowing back into the ocean. Thus does God's power maintain and support all of life in delicate ecological balance. This remarkable cycle, so indispensable to human life, is truly evidence of God's awesome strength (R. Eliyahu Dessler).

קדושה

During חזרת הש"ץ*, the following is said standing with feet together, rising on the toes at the words indicated by* ▲.

then קהל ש"ץ: **נְקַדֵּשׁ** אֶת שִׁמְךָ בָּעוֹלָם, כְּשֵׁם שֶׁמַּקְדִּישִׁים אוֹתוֹ בִּשְׁמֵי מָרוֹם,
כַּכָּתוּב עַל יַד נְבִיאֶךָ, וְקָרָא זֶה אֶל־זֶה וְאָמַר ישעיה ו

then קהל ש"ץ: ▲קָדוֹשׁ, ▲קָדוֹשׁ, ▲קָדוֹשׁ יהוה צְבָאוֹת, מְלֹא כָל־הָאָרֶץ כְּבוֹדוֹ:
אָז בְּקוֹל רַעַשׁ גָּדוֹל אַדִּיר וְחָזָק מַשְׁמִיעִים קוֹל, מִתְנַשְּׂאִים לְעֻמַּת שְׂרָפִים,

ש"ץ: לְעֻמָּתָם בָּרוּךְ יֹאמֵרוּ

then קהל ש"ץ: ▲בָּרוּךְ כְּבוֹד־יהוה מִמְּקוֹמוֹ: יחזקאל ג
מִמְּקוֹמְךָ מַלְכֵּנוּ תוֹפִיעַ וְתִמְלֹךְ עָלֵינוּ, כִּי מְחַכִּים אֲנַחְנוּ לָךְ מָתַי תִּמְלֹךְ בְּצִיּוֹן, בְּקָרוֹב בְּיָמֵינוּ לְעוֹלָם וָעֶד תִּשְׁכֹּן. תִּתְגַּדַּל וְתִתְקַדַּשׁ בְּתוֹךְ יְרוּשָׁלַיִם עִירְךָ, לְדוֹר וָדוֹר וּלְנֵצַח נְצָחִים. וְעֵינֵינוּ תִרְאֶינָה מַלְכוּתֶךָ, כַּדָּבָר הָאָמוּר בְּשִׁירֵי עֻזֶּךָ, עַל יְדֵי דָוִד מְשִׁיחַ צִדְקֶךָ

then קהל ש"ץ: ▲יִמְלֹךְ יהוה לְעוֹלָם, אֱלֹהַיִךְ צִיּוֹן לְדֹר וָדֹר, הַלְלוּיָהּ: תהלים קמו

ש"ץ: לְדוֹר וָדוֹר נַגִּיד גָּדְלֶךָ, וּלְנֵצַח נְצָחִים קְדֻשָּׁתְךָ נַקְדִּישׁ, וְשִׁבְחֲךָ אֱלֹהֵינוּ מִפִּינוּ לֹא יָמוּשׁ לְעוֹלָם וָעֶד, כִּי אֵל מֶלֶךְ גָּדוֹל וְקָדוֹשׁ אָתָּה. בָּרוּךְ אַתָּה יהוה, הָאֵל הַקָּדוֹשׁ. / בשבת שובה: הַמֶּלֶךְ הַקָּדוֹשׁ./

The שליח ציבור *continues with* יִשְׂמַח מֹשֶׁה *below.*

קדושת היום

יִשְׂמַח מֹשֶׁה בְּמַתְּנַת חֶלְקוֹ, כִּי עֶבֶד נֶאֱמָן קָרָאתָ לוֹ, כְּלִיל תִּפְאֶרֶת בְּרֹאשׁוֹ נָתַתָּ לוֹ, בְּעָמְדוֹ לְפָנֶיךָ עַל הַר

RESPONDING TO THE LEADER DURING KEDUSHA

The *Kedusha* must be recited responsively. It consists of a number of calls (or lead-in lines) by the Leader to the congregation to respond by reciting verses, which are then repeated by the Leader. There are differing views whether the congregation also recites the lead-in lines. If the lead-in lines are recited by the congregation, the congregation should hear the Leader reciting them (*MB* 125:1). Additionally, the congregation should hear the Leader reciting the verses (*Iggerot Moshe*, *OḤ* 3:4). On Shabbat and Yom Tov the *Kedusha* contains additional responses – but the congregation does not have to hear the Leader reciting them as they are not essential to the *Kedusha*.

For the *"Instructions for someone who made a mistake and recited the wrong Amida,"* see page 397.

KEDUSHA

During the Leader's Repetition, the following is said standing with feet together, rising on the toes at the words indicated by ▴.

Cong. then Leader: נְקַדֵּשׁ WE WILL SANCTIFY Your name in this world, as they sanctify
Is. 6 it in the heavenly heights, as is written by Your prophet: "They called to one another, saying":

Cong. then Leader: ▴"Holy, ▴holy, ▴holy is the LORD of hosts; the whole world is filled with His glory.'"

So too, with a great, mighty, and powerful sound they make their voices heard, raising themselves before the Seraphim,

Leader: and facing them proclaim:

Ezek. 3 *Cong. then Leader:* ▴"Blessed is the glory of the LORD from His place."

May You, our King, appear from Your place and rule over us, for we are waiting for You. When will You rule in Zion? May it be soon in our day that You will make Zion Your dwelling evermore. May You be exalted and sanctified in Jerusalem Your city for all generations and forever more. May our eyes behold Your sovereign rule, as it was described in the songs praising Your strength, as written by David, the one anointed by Your just decree.

Ps. 146 *Cong. then Leader:* ▴"The LORD will reign forever, Your God, O Zion, to all generations. Praise the LORD."

Leader: To all generations we will proclaim Your greatness, and forever declare Your holiness, and the praise of You, our God, will never leave our mouth, for You are God and King, great and holy; blessed are You, LORD, the holy God. / *On Shabbat Shuva:* the holy King. /

The Leader continues with "Moses rejoiced" below.

HOLINESS OF THE DAY

יִשְׂמַח מֹשֶׁה LET MOSES rejoice for the gift of his portion, on account of which You called him a faithful servant. You placed a crown of splendor upon his head when he stood before You on Mount Sinai.

יִשְׂמַח מֹשֶׁה – *Moses rejoiced.* Even though, as we noted at the Friday eve *Amida,* the three *Amida* middle sections for Shabbat are not alike, this was not always the universal practice. The most ancient *nusah* for the middle sections of the various Shabbat *Amidot* appears to have been constant for all three. By the time of the Geonim in the tenth century, separate texts for them were in use. Later authorities such as Rashi opposed the change, while his grandson Rabbeinu Tam favored it. In due course the Geonic practice became firmly established in all Ashkenazic Jewish communities (Prof. Naftali Wieder).

סִינַי, וּשְׁנֵי לוּחוֹת אֲבָנִים הוֹרִיד בְּיָדוֹ, וְכָתוּב בָּהֶם שְׁמִירַת שַׁבָּת, וְכֵן כָּתוּב בְּתוֹרָתֶךָ

וְשָׁמְרוּ בְנֵי־יִשְׂרָאֵל אֶת־הַשַּׁבָּת, לַעֲשׂוֹת אֶת־הַשַּׁבָּת לְדֹרֹתָם בְּרִית עוֹלָם: בֵּינִי וּבֵין בְּנֵי יִשְׂרָאֵל אוֹת הִוא לְעֹלָם, כִּי־שֵׁשֶׁת יָמִים עָשָׂה יהוה אֶת־הַשָּׁמַיִם וְאֶת־הָאָרֶץ, וּבַיּוֹם הַשְּׁבִיעִי שָׁבַת וַיִּנָּפַשׁ: שמות לא

וְלֹא נְתַתּוֹ, יהוה אֱלֹהֵינוּ, לְגוֹיֵי הָאֲרָצוֹת, וְלֹא הִנְחַלְתּוֹ, מַלְכֵּנוּ, לְעוֹבְדֵי פְסִילִים, וְגַם בִּמְנוּחָתוֹ לֹא יִשְׁכְּנוּ עֲרֵלִים, כִּי לְיִשְׂרָאֵל עַמְּךָ נְתַתּוֹ בְּאַהֲבָה, לְזֶרַע יַעֲקֹב אֲשֶׁר בָּם בָּחָרְתָּ. עַם מְקַדְּשֵׁי שְׁבִיעִי, כֻּלָּם יִשְׂבְּעוּ וְיִתְעַנְּגוּ מִטּוּבֶךָ, וּבַשְּׁבִיעִי רָצִיתָ בּוֹ וְקִדַּשְׁתּוֹ, חֶמְדַּת יָמִים אוֹתוֹ קָרָאתָ, זֵכֶר לְמַעֲשֵׂה בְרֵאשִׁית.

בְּמַתְּנַת חֶלְקוֹ – *For the gift of his portion* (previous page). The *Zohar* teaches that while the patriarchs came to the service of God through their sustained efforts to discover and then make God known in the world, Moses' path to God was more by way of a gift bestowed by God, facilitated by signs and miracles, without his having to spend a lifetime in search of God. This explains the phrase "the gift of his portion." Moreover, Moses' "gift" is mentioned in the Shabbat morning *Amida*, for it was granted to him in the spirit of Shabbat rest, while the Patriarchs' path to God was like the six days of the workweek, involving struggle and hard labor (*Sefat Emet*).

עֶבֶד נֶאֱמָן קָרָאתָ לּוֹ, כְּלִיל תִּפְאֶרֶת בְּרֹאשׁוֹ נָתַתָּ לּוֹ – *On account of which You called him a faithful servant. You placed a crown of splendor upon his head* (previous page). These two phrases point to the dual reasons for Moses to rejoice: he was both a servant who cared for the material needs of his people, as well as a leader imbued with spiritual authority over them. The Gemara (*Horayot* 10a) indicates that leadership in the socio-economic realm is really a form of indenture, whereas leadership in the spiritual realm constitutes authority (שְׂרָרָה) to implement the Torah and *mitzvot*. Moses was privileged in that he filled both aspects of communal leadership. On the one hand he was a "faithful servant" who saw to it that the material needs of the people were provided for in the wilderness; on the other hand he possessed real authority by virtue of wearing the crown of Torah on his head, as a result of which he directed their spiritual affairs (R. Avraham Yitzḥak HaKohen Kook).

An Aggadic passage found in several manuscript versions explains that when Moses first saw the suffering of his brethren, he argued with Pharaoh to give them one day a week to rest. Pharaoh offered him the choice of which day, and Moses chose the seventh day. When subsequently at Sinai God gave the Torah to the people on the very day of Shabbat, Moses saw this as divine endorsement of his choice, and he thus rejoiced (Maharal).

In his hand he brought down the two tablets of stone on which was inscribed the observance of the Sabbath as is written in Your Torah:

Ex. 31 וְשָׁמְרוּ THE CHILDREN of Israel shall keep the Sabbath, observing the Sabbath throughout their generations as an everlasting covenant. It is a sign between Me and the children of Israel forever that in six days the LORD made heaven and earth, and He rested on the seventh day and was refreshed.

וְלֹא נְתַתּוֹ LORD OUR GOD, You did not give it to the nations of the world, nor, our King, did You bequeath it to idol-worshipers, and neither may the uncircumcised take shelter in its tranquility. For You gave it lovingly to Israel Your people, the descendants of Jacob whom You chose. May the nation consisting of those who sanctify the seventh day all be sated and take pleasure in Your benevolence. For You have favored the seventh day and sanctified it, proclaiming it the most precious of all days, a remembrance of the work of creation.

וְכָתוּב בָּהֶם שְׁמִירַת שַׁבָּת – *Inscribed the observance of the Sabbath.* This is in accordance with Deuteronomy 5:19 which states that God "wrote these words on tablets of stone," in which "these" *refers* to the preceding account of the Ten Commandments that contain the words שָׁמוֹר אֶת־יוֹם הַשַּׁבָּת (keep the Shabbat day) as they appear in Deuteronomy 5:12. Accordingly, with these words, Moses emphasizes that God said, and Moses heard, both "keep Shabbat" and "remember Shabbat" the first time the tablets were given, even if at the time the people could not hear both phrases. Consequently we are to understand that both aspects of the *mitzva* of Shabbat as implied by these phrases are equal, essential, and complementary, even if the Torah, reflecting how they were recorded on the two sets of tablets, recorded them separately (*Netziv*).

לְזֶרַע יַעֲקֹב – *The descendants of Jacob.* This is a reference to Isaiah 58:13–14, which explicitly links the reward for Shabbat observance to the inheritance promised to the patriarch Jacob. To paraphrase those verses, "If you observe Shabbat by avoiding weekday activities, especially refraining from doing business, and instead you dedicate the day exclusively to spiritual priorities, then you will receive the inheritance that I promised to Jacob your Patriarch."

חֶמְדַּת יָמִים אוֹתוֹ קָרָאתָ – *Proclaiming it the most precious of all days.* While there is no explicit scriptural source indicating that God did this, the Ba'al HaTurim, R. Yosef Karo, and others, found an implicit source in the *Targum Yerushalmi* which (as found in a Paris manuscript version, according to R. Menaḥem Kasher) translated the first word of Genesis 2:2, וַיְכַל אֱלֹהִים בַּיּוֹם הַשְּׁבִיעִי (usually translated as "God completed on the seventh day") as וְחָמַד (God cherished the seventh day), reflecting Psalms 84:3. So too, the very fact that the other six days are merely called "the first day," "the second day," etc., while God's Torah refers to the Sabbath alone with a proper name –

אֱלֹהֵינוּ וֵאלֹהֵי אֲבוֹתֵינוּ, רְצֵה בִמְנוּחָתֵנוּ, קַדְּשֵׁנוּ בְּמִצְוֹתֶיךָ וְתֵן חֶלְקֵנוּ בְּתוֹרָתֶךָ, שַׂבְּעֵנוּ מִטּוּבֶךָ וְשַׂמְּחֵנוּ בִּישׁוּעָתֶךָ, וְטַהֵר לִבֵּנוּ לְעָבְדְּךָ בֶּאֱמֶת, וְהַנְחִילֵנוּ, יהוה אֱלֹהֵינוּ, בְּאַהֲבָה וּבְרָצוֹן שַׁבַּת קָדְשֶׁךָ, וְיָנוּחוּ בוֹ יִשְׂרָאֵל מְקַדְּשֵׁי שְׁמֶךָ. בָּרוּךְ אַתָּה יהוה, מְקַדֵּשׁ הַשַּׁבָּת.

עבודה

רְצֵה יהוה אֱלֹהֵינוּ בְּעַמְּךָ יִשְׂרָאֵל, וּבִתְפִלָּתָם, וְהָשֵׁב אֶת הָעֲבוֹדָה לִדְבִיר בֵּיתֶךָ, וְאִשֵּׁי יִשְׂרָאֵל וּתְפִלָּתָם בְּאַהֲבָה תְקַבֵּל בְּרָצוֹן, וּתְהִי לְרָצוֹן תָּמִיד עֲבוֹדַת יִשְׂרָאֵל עַמֶּךָ.

On ראש חודש *and* חול המועד*, say:*

אֱלֹהֵינוּ וֵאלֹהֵי אֲבוֹתֵינוּ, יַעֲלֶה וְיָבוֹא וְיַגִּיעַ, וְיֵרָאֶה וְיֵרָצֶה וְיִשָּׁמַע, וְיִפָּקֵד וְיִזָּכֵר זִכְרוֹנֵנוּ וּפִקְדוֹנֵנוּ וְזִכְרוֹן אֲבוֹתֵינוּ, וְזִכְרוֹן מָשִׁיחַ בֶּן דָּוִד עַבְדֶּךָ, וְזִכְרוֹן יְרוּשָׁלַיִם עִיר קָדְשֶׁךָ, וְזִכְרוֹן כָּל עַמְּךָ בֵּית יִשְׂרָאֵל, לְפָנֶיךָ, לִפְלֵיטָה לְטוֹבָה, לְחֵן וּלְחֶסֶד וּלְרַחֲמִים, לְחַיִּים וּלְשָׁלוֹם בְּיוֹם

בראש חודש: רֹאשׁ הַחֹדֶשׁ / בפסח: חַג הַמַּצּוֹת / בסוכות: חַג הַסֻּכּוֹת

הַזֶּה. זָכְרֵנוּ יהוה אֱלֹהֵינוּ בּוֹ לְטוֹבָה, וּפָקְדֵנוּ בוֹ לִבְרָכָה, וְהוֹשִׁיעֵנוּ בוֹ לְחַיִּים. וּבִדְבַר יְשׁוּעָה וְרַחֲמִים, חוּס וְחָנֵּנוּ וְרַחֵם עָלֵינוּ וְהוֹשִׁיעֵנוּ, כִּי אֵלֶיךָ עֵינֵינוּ, כִּי אֵל מֶלֶךְ חַנּוּן וְרַחוּם אָתָּה.

Shabbat – is itself a reflection of its precious nature (R. Yitzchak Mirsky).

Another approach to this phrase takes the word אותו to mean אוֹת שֶׁלּוֹ (its sign). Thus the translation would read, "You designated this choicest of days to be the special sign (or symbol) for the עַם מְקַדְּשֵׁי שְׁבִיעִי (the people who sanctify the seventh day") (Prof. Shmuel Sprecher).

רְצֵה בִמְנוּחָתֵנוּ – *Be pleased with our rest*. Even though the Talmud Yerushalmi (*Shabbat* 15:3) states that on Shabbat we are not permitted to petition God for our needs, every prayer – even that of Shabbat and Yom Tov – must contain an element of בַּקָּשָׁה (petition), as supplication constitutes the core experience of all prayer. Indeed, the vigor and power of prayer derive from its petitions (R. Joseph B. Soloveitchik).

בְּאַהֲבָה וּבְרָצוֹן – *Through Your loving favor*. We ask God to grant us His holy Shabbat בְּאַהֲבָה וּבְרָצוֹן (with love and enthusiasm) here in the *Amida*, as well as in the *Kiddush*, whether on a regular Shabbat or when Yom Tov and Shabbat coincide. The reason is that according

אֱלֹהֵינוּ OUR GOD and God of our fathers, be pleased with our rest. Sanctify us through Your commandments and grant us our portion in Your Torah. Gratify us with Your goodness and gladden us with Your salvation. Purify our heart to serve You in truth. LORD our God, through Your loving favor may You grant that Your holy Sabbath will be our heritage, so that the people of Israel who sanctify Your name will rest on it. Blessed are You, LORD, Who sanctifies the Sabbath.

TEMPLE SERVICE

רְצֵה LOOK FAVORABLY, LORD our God, upon Your people Israel and their prayer, and restore the service to the Holy of Holies of Your House. Accept with love and favor the fire-offerings of Israel and their prayer. May the service of Israel Your people Israel always find favor with You.

On Rosh Ḥodesh and Ḥol HaMo'ed, say:

אֱלֹהֵינוּ וֵאלֹהֵי אֲבוֹתֵינוּ OUR GOD and God of our fathers, may there arise, arrive, reach, appear, be favored, heard, considered and remembered, our remembrance and recollection, Your remembrance of our fathers, of the Messiah son of David Your servant, of Jerusalem Your holy city and of all Your people the house of Israel. May they come before You for deliverance and benefit, for grace, kindness and mercy, for life and peace, on this day of:

On Rosh Ḥodesh: Rosh Ḥodesh.
On Pesaḥ: the Festival of Matzot.
On Sukkot: the Festival of Sukkot.

LORD our God, remember us this day for good. Be mindful of us this day for blessing, preserve us this day for life. Regarding redemption and mercy show us compassion and grace, and have pity on us and save us. For our eyes are lifted toward You, for You are a gracious and merciful God and King.

---

to the Gemara (*Shabbat* 88a) Shabbat was commanded prior to Sinai, when the Israelites reached Marah (Ex. 15:25 and the *Mekhilta* there, as evidenced by the Torah's lengthy description at that point of the laws of the manna relating to Shabbat observance). Consequently, unlike most other *mitzvot* that according to the Gemara were given at Sinai under duress ("like a barrel hanging over their heads"), Shabbat was given, and the Israelites accepted it, with

For laws regarding "יַעֲלֶה וְיָבוֹא / *Ya'aleh VeYavo,*" see page 125.

וְתֶחֱזֶינָה עֵינֵינוּ בְּשׁוּבְךָ לְצִיּוֹן בְּרַחֲמִים. בָּרוּךְ אַתָּה יהוה, הַמַּחֲזִיר שְׁכִינָתוֹ לְצִיּוֹן.

הודאה

Bow during the first five words.

ׂ**מוֹדִים** אֲנַחְנוּ לָךְ, שָׁאַתָּה הוּא יהוה אֱלֹהֵינוּ וֵאלֹהֵי אֲבוֹתֵינוּ לְעוֹלָם וָעֶד. צוּר חַיֵּינוּ, מָגֵן יִשְׁעֵנוּ, אַתָּה הוּא. לְדוֹר וָדוֹר נוֹדֶה לְּךָ וּנְסַפֵּר תְּהִלָּתֶךָ, עַל חַיֵּינוּ הַמְּסוּרִים בְּיָדֶךָ, וְעַל נִשְׁמוֹתֵינוּ הַפְּקוּדוֹת לָךְ, וְעַל נִסֶּיךָ שֶׁבְּכָל יוֹם עִמָּנוּ, וְעַל נִפְלְאוֹתֶיךָ וְטוֹבוֹתֶיךָ, שֶׁבְּכָל עֵת, עֶרֶב וָבֹקֶר וְצָהֳרָיִם. הַטּוֹב, כִּי לֹא כָלוּ רַחֲמֶיךָ וְהַמְרַחֵם, כִּי לֹא תַמּוּ חֲסָדֶיךָ, מֵעוֹלָם קִוִּינוּ לָךְ.

During חזרת הש״ץ*, the* קהל *says quietly:*

ׂ**מוֹדִים** אֲנַחְנוּ לָךְ, שָׁאַתָּה הוּא יהוה אֱלֹהֵינוּ וֵאלֹהֵי אֲבוֹתֵינוּ, אֱלֹהֵי כָל בָּשָׂר, יוֹצְרֵנוּ, יוֹצֵר בְּרֵאשִׁית. בְּרָכוֹת וְהוֹדָאוֹת לְשִׁמְךָ הַגָּדוֹל וְהַקָּדוֹשׁ, עַל שֶׁהֶחֱיִיתָנוּ וְקִיַּמְתָּנוּ. כֵּן תְּחַיֵּנוּ וּתְקַיְּמֵנוּ, וְתֶאֱסֹף גָּלֻיּוֹתֵינוּ לְחַצְרוֹת קָדְשֶׁךָ, לִשְׁמֹר חֻקֶּיךָ וְלַעֲשׂוֹת רְצוֹנֶךָ וּלְעָבְדְּךָ בְּלֵבָב שָׁלֵם, עַל שֶׁאֲנַחְנוּ מוֹדִים לָךְ. בָּרוּךְ אֵל הַהוֹדָאוֹת.

בחנוכה:

עַל הַנִּסִּים וְעַל הַפֻּרְקָן וְעַל הַגְּבוּרוֹת וְעַל הַתְּשׁוּעוֹת וְעַל הַמִּלְחָמוֹת שֶׁעָשִׂיתָ לַאֲבוֹתֵינוּ בַּיָּמִים הָהֵם בַּזְּמַן הַזֶּה.

בִּימֵי מַתִּתְיָהוּ בֶּן יוֹחָנָן כֹּהֵן גָּדוֹל חַשְׁמוֹנַאי וּבָנָיו, כְּשֶׁעָמְדָה מַלְכוּת יָוָן הָרְשָׁעָה עַל עַמְּךָ יִשְׂרָאֵל לְהַשְׁכִּיחָם תּוֹרָתֶךָ וּלְהַעֲבִירָם מֵחֻקֵּי רְצוֹנֶךָ, וְאַתָּה בְּרַחֲמֶיךָ הָרַבִּים עָמַדְתָּ לָהֶם בְּעֵת צָרָתָם, רַבְתָּ אֶת רִיבָם, דַּנְתָּ אֶת דִּינָם, נָקַמְתָּ אֶת נִקְמָתָם, מָסַרְתָּ גִבּוֹרִים בְּיַד חַלָּשִׁים, וְרַבִּים בְּיַד מְעַטִּים, וּטְמֵאִים בְּיַד טְהוֹרִים, וּרְשָׁעִים בְּיַד צַדִּיקִים, וְזֵדִים בְּיַד עוֹסְקֵי תוֹרָתֶךָ, וּלְךָ עָשִׂיתָ שֵׁם גָּדוֹל וְקָדוֹשׁ בְּעוֹלָמֶךָ, וּלְעַמְּךָ יִשְׂרָאֵל עָשִׂיתָ תְּשׁוּעָה גְדוֹלָה וּפֻרְקָן כְּהַיּוֹם הַזֶּה. וְאַחַר

Continued on the top of the next page.

love and enthusiasm. Hence in these phrases we beseech God every Shabbat to once again bestow this precious gift on us in the same felicitous fashion (R. Barukh HaLevi Epstein).

For laws regarding "עַל הַנִּסִּים / *Al HaNissim,*" see page 128.

May our eyes witness Your return to Zion in compassion. Blessed are You, LORD, Who will restore His Divine Presence to Zion.

THANKSGIVING

Bow during the first seven words.

מוֹדִים WE THANK YOU, for You are the LORD our God and the God of our fathers for all eternity. You are the Rock of our life and Shield of our deliverance. From generation to generation we will thank You and recount Your praise for our lives that are in Your hands, for our souls that are given over to You, for Your miracles that are with us every day, and for Your constant wonders and favors, evening, morning and noon. You are good, for Your compassion does not cease, and You are compassionate, for Your kindness never ends. We have placed our hope in You forever and ever.

During the Leader's Repetition, the congregation says quietly:

מוֹדִים WE THANK YOU, for You are the LORD our God, the God of our fathers and God of all flesh. You are our Maker, the Maker of Creation. Blessings and thanks are due Your great and holy name for You have given us life and preserved us in life. May You continue to keep us in life and preserve us. Gather our exiles to the courtyards of Your Temple so that we may fulfill Your commandments and do Your will, serving You with a perfect heart, in the merit of our giving thanks to You now. Blessed be the God of all thanksgiving.

On Ḥanukka add:

עַל הַנִּסִּים [WE THANK YOU] for the miracles, the deliverance, and the triumphant victories and salvation, as well as wars which You wrought for our ancestors in those days at this season.

IT HAPPENED in the days of Mattathias son of Johanan, the Hasmonean high priest, and his sons. Then the cruel Hellenist power rose up to force Your people Israel to forget Your Torah and transgress the commands of Your will. In that hour of their distress, You in Your great mercy rose to take up their cause and defend their rights. Meting out retribution You delivered the strong into the hand of the weak, the many into the hand of the few, the impure into the hand of the pure, the evil ones into the hand of the righteous, and the wicked into the hand of devotees of Your Torah. You thereby made for Yourself a great and holy name throughout Your world, as well as bringing about great deliverance and salvation for Your people Israel

Continued on the top of the next page.

כֵּן בָּאוּ בָנֶיךָ לִדְבִיר בֵּיתֶךָ, וּפִנּוּ אֶת הֵיכָלֶךָ, וְטִהֲרוּ אֶת מִקְדָּשֶׁךָ, וְהִדְלִיקוּ נֵרוֹת בְּחַצְרוֹת קָדְשֶׁךָ, וְקָבְעוּ שְׁמוֹנַת יְמֵי חֲנֻכָּה אֵלּוּ, לְהוֹדוֹת וּלְהַלֵּל לְשִׁמְךָ הַגָּדוֹל.

Continue with וְעַל כֻּלָּם.

וְעַל כֻּלָּם יִתְבָּרַךְ וְיִתְרוֹמַם שִׁמְךָ מַלְכֵּנוּ תָּמִיד לְעוֹלָם וָעֶד.

בשבת שובה: וּכְתֹב לְחַיִּים טוֹבִים כָּל בְּנֵי בְרִיתֶךָ.

(If forgotten, no corrective action is necessary.)

וְכֹל הַחַיִּים יוֹדוּךָ סֶּלָה, וִיהַלְלוּ אֶת שִׁמְךָ בֶּאֱמֶת, הָאֵל יְשׁוּעָתֵנוּ וְעֶזְרָתֵנוּ סֶלָה. ׳בָּרוּךְ אַתָּה יהוה, הַטּוֹב שִׁמְךָ וּלְךָ נָאֶה לְהוֹדוֹת.

ברכת כהנים

The following is said by the שליח ציבור *during* חזרת הש״ץ:

אֱלֹהֵינוּ וֵאלֹהֵי אֲבוֹתֵינוּ, בָּרְכֵנוּ בַּבְּרָכָה הַמְשֻׁלֶּשֶׁת, בַּתּוֹרָה, הַכְּתוּבָה עַל יְדֵי מֹשֶׁה עַבְדֶּךָ, הָאֲמוּרָה מִפִּי אַהֲרֹן וּבָנָיו כֹּהֲנִים עַם קְדוֹשֶׁיךָ, כָּאָמוּר

במדבר ו

יְבָרֶכְךָ יהוה וְיִשְׁמְרֶךָ: קהל: כֵּן יְהִי רָצוֹן

יָאֵר יהוה פָּנָיו אֵלֶיךָ וִיחֻנֶּךָּ: קהל: כֵּן יְהִי רָצוֹן

יִשָּׂא יהוה פָּנָיו אֵלֶיךָ וְיָשֵׂם לְךָ שָׁלוֹם: קהל: כֵּן יְהִי רָצוֹן

בָּרְכֵנוּ בַּבְּרָכָה הַמְשֻׁלֶּשֶׁת – *Bless us with the three-fold blessing.* The בִּרְכַּת כֹּהֲנִים (Priestly Blessing) – and its substitute when the *Kohanim* do not ascend the *bima* – can be understood in light of the following passage in the Talmud Yerushalmi (*Ta'anit* 4:1): "What is the source for reciting the priestly blessing (in prayer)? It is the verse 'Thus shall you bless the children of Israel (Num. 6:23).' That verse suffices to explain why it is recited in *Shaḥarit* – what is the source for saying it in *Musaf*? It is the verse 'Aaron raised his hands over the people, blessed them, and then descended from offering the…sacrifices' (Lev. 9:22)." That is, he blessed the people before the conclusion of the sacrificial order, and only thereafter descended, for apparently the blessing was an integral part of the sacrifices. From this passage we learn that there are two separate obligations involved in the priestly blessing. The first, derived from Numbers 6, and unconnected to any particular sacrifice, is the priestly duty to bless the people of Israel by pronouncing the three verses petitioning God to bless the people. This priestly blessing stands on its own, and is unconnected to any other act or commandment. The second, derived from Leviticus 9 that describes Aaron's actions, is the priestly duty to bless the people as the concluding act of specific Temple sacrifices, i.e., at both the *Shaḥarit* and *Musaf* sacrifices, just as Aaron did. It is this latter aspect that accounts for the recital of the priestly blessing (whether by the *Kohanim* or the Leader) at the conclusion of the *Shaḥarit* and *Musaf* *Amidot*, which are after all the substitutes for those sacrifices.

(known) to this day. Then Your children came to the Holy of Holies in Your house, cleared Your Temple, purified Your holy place, kindled lights in Your holy courts, and instituted these eight days of Ḥanukka to give thanks and sing praise to Your great name. *Continue with "For all this."*

For all this, our King, may Your name be blessed and exalted continually, forever and ever.

On Shabbat Shuva: Inscribe all the children of Your covenant for a life of goodness.
(*If forgotten, no corrective action is necessary.*)

All that lives will give thanks to You forever and praise Your name in truth, God, our salvation and our help forever. ▾Blessed are You, LORD, for Your name is "The Good One" and it is appropriate to give thanks to You.

THE PRIESTLY BLESSING

The following is said by the Leader during the Repetition of the Amida:

אֱלֹהֵינוּ OUR GOD, God of our fathers, bless us with the threefold blessing, in the Torah, written by Your servant Moses and spoken by Aaron and his descendants, being priests, Your holy people, as it is said:

Num. 6 "May the LORD bless you and keep you." *Cong:* May this be His will.
"May the LORD make His countenance shine upon you and be gracious to you." *Cong:* May this be His will.
"May the LORD lift up His countenance toward you and grant you peace." *Cong:* May this be His will.

This in turn helps us understand the structure of the *Amida* itself. For these two aspects of the priestly blessing correspond to the two aspects of prayer. The first, derived from the prayers of the three patriarchs, takes the form of a שִׂיחָה (dialogue) between man and God, in which we pour out our thoughts, feelings, and aspirations before God. In the second, derived from the sacrificial service, prayer takes the form of a קָרְבָּן (sacrifice) in which we seek קֵרוּב (closeness) to Him by offering a sacrifice – not of an animal, bird, flour or libation, but of ourselves. The former is encountered in the middle section of the *Amida*, while the latter (sacrificial) aspect of prayer begins with רְצֵה ("Accept…the service") in the final section of the *Amida*, reaching its pinnacle with the priestly blessing (R. Joseph B. Soloveitchik).

Thus explained, the *Amida* facilitates both prayer experiences, and their outcome. In the middle section it engages us in conversation with God, as we pour out our hearts and describe our personal as well as national needs. In the last section we reverse course: it is no longer about us and our needs, but rather

שלום

שִׂים שָׁלוֹם טוֹבָה וּבְרָכָה, חֵן וָחֶסֶד וְרַחֲמִים עָלֵינוּ וְעַל כָּל יִשְׂרָאֵל עַמֶּךָ. בָּרְכֵנוּ אָבִינוּ כֻּלָּנוּ כְּאֶחָד בְּאוֹר פָּנֶיךָ, כִּי בְאוֹר פָּנֶיךָ נָתַתָּ לָּנוּ יהוה אֱלֹהֵינוּ, תּוֹרַת חַיִּים וְאַהֲבַת חֶסֶד, וּצְדָקָה וּבְרָכָה וְרַחֲמִים וְחַיִּים וְשָׁלוֹם. וְטוֹב בְּעֵינֶיךָ לְבָרֵךְ אֶת עַמְּךָ יִשְׂרָאֵל, בְּכָל עֵת וּבְכָל שָׁעָה בִּשְׁלוֹמֶךָ.

בשבת שובה: בְּסֵפֶר חַיִּים, בְּרָכָה וְשָׁלוֹם, וּפַרְנָסָה טוֹבָה, נִזָּכֵר וְנִכָּתֵב לְפָנֶיךָ, אֲנַחְנוּ וְכָל עַמְּךָ בֵּית יִשְׂרָאֵל, לְחַיִּים טוֹבִים וּלְשָׁלוֹם.*

בָּרוּךְ אַתָּה יהוה, הַמְבָרֵךְ אֶת עַמּוֹ יִשְׂרָאֵל בַּשָּׁלוֹם.

**On* שבת שובה *many end the blessing:*

בָּרוּךְ אַתָּה יהוה, עוֹשֵׂה הַשָּׁלוֹם.

At this point when the* שליח ציבור *repeats the* עמידה *he should complete the repetition by saying the verse beginning "*יִהְיוּ לְרָצוֹן*" out loud.

תהלים יט
יִהְיוּ לְרָצוֹן אִמְרֵי־פִי וְהֶגְיוֹן לִבִּי לְפָנֶיךָ, יהוה צוּרִי וְגֹאֲלִי:

ברכות יז.
אֱלֹהַי, נְצֹר לְשׁוֹנִי מֵרָע וּשְׂפָתַי מִדַּבֵּר מִרְמָה, וְלִמְקַלְלַי נַפְשִׁי תִדֹּם, וְנַפְשִׁי כֶּעָפָר לַכֹּל תִּהְיֶה. פְּתַח לִבִּי בְּתוֹרָתֶךָ, וּבְמִצְוֹתֶיךָ תִּרְדֹּף נַפְשִׁי. וְכָל הַחוֹשְׁבִים עָלַי רָעָה, מְהֵרָה הָפֵר עֲצָתָם וְקַלְקֵל מַחֲשַׁבְתָּם. עֲשֵׂה לְמַעַן שְׁמֶךָ, עֲשֵׂה לְמַעַן יְמִינֶךָ,

---

how we can overcome the self, sacrificing the personal and national ego, so to speak, in a sublime quest to come ever closer to Him. Together, they render us worthy of divine blessing and protection, favor and grace, in peace and tranquility, as described and accorded by the priestly blessing.

בָּרְכֵנוּ אָבִינוּ כֻּלָּנוּ כְּאֶחָד בְּאוֹר פָּנֶיךָ – *Bless us all together with the light of Your presence*. These words encapsulate both our personal individuality as well as our unity with the human race. The phrase "the light of Your face" reflects the sages' view that the face represents the uniqueness (יְחִידוּת) of every individual (as they said in the Talmud Yerushalmi *Berakhot* 9:1, "Just as human faces are not alike, neither are their dispositions"), while the preceding phrase "all of us together" teaches us that we must simultaneously recognize our unity (אַחְדוּת) with our fellow human beings. Our recognition of both our personal uniqueness as well as our unity with all others is tightly bound with the revelation of the light of God's countenance. Thus we ask God, our Father, to bless each one of us, His children, together with our fellows, with (or through) the light of His countenance (R. Yitzchok Hutner).

נְצֹר לְשׁוֹנִי מֵרָע – *Guard my tongue from evil*. For centuries, Jews lodged during a long Diaspora

PEACE

שִׂים שָׁלוֹם GRANT PEACE with welfare and blessing, and grace with loving-kindness and mercy on us and all Israel Your people. Bless us, our Father, all together, with the light of Your presence. For in that light, LORD our God, You have given us the Torah of life, and love of kindness with justice, blessing, tenderness, life and peace. May it be good in Your eyes to bless Your people Israel at all times, at every hour, with Your peace.

On Shabbat Shuva: In the book of life and blessing, peace and prosperity, may we and all the house of Israel Your people be remembered before You and inscribed for a life of goodness and peace.*

Blessed are You, LORD, Who blesses His people Israel with peace.

**On Shabbat Shuva many end the blessing:*
Blessed are You, LORD, Who makes peace.

At this point when the Leader repeats the Amida he should complete the repetition by saying the verse beginning "May the words" out loud.

Ps. 19 MAY THE WORDS of my mouth and the meditation of my heart find grace before You, LORD, my Rock and my Redeemer.

Berakhot 17a אֱלֹהַי MY GOD, guard my tongue from evil, and my lips from speaking deceit. Let my soul be silent to those who curse me; let my soul be humble toward everyone like the dust. Open my heart to Your Torah that my soul may follow Your commandments. As for all those who contemplate evil against me, speedily nullify their plans and spoil their schemes. Do so for the sake of Your name. Do so for Your right

---

night in all sorts of ghettos, unprotected, helpless, without rights, abandoned, despised, and alone. In the morning Jews would pray a remarkable prayer: "O God, I must soon go out to the street. I must earn something to support my family. I know perfectly well that my appearance will elicit the nasty expression, '*Jude*' or '*zhid*' or 'dirty Jew,' that a stone will strike my head, or a nasty dog will attack me. So I beg You, dear God, let me not get angry, and let my tongue and my lips not instinctively utter improper words. 'My God, guard my tongue from evil and my lips from speaking guile' [*Berakhot* 17a]. I beg You God for yet more – let me not feel insulted; let it not bother me at all. 'And let my soul be dumb to those who curse me, my soul insensitive unto all as the dust' [*ibid.*]. Let he who pursues me be ashamed, not me" (R. Joseph B. Soloveitchik).

For laws regarding "Interruptions during *Elokai Netzor*," see page 133.

תהלים ס עֲשֵׂה לְמַעַן קְדֻשָּׁתֶךָ, עֲשֵׂה לְמַעַן תּוֹרָתֶךָ. לְמַעַן יֵחָלְצוּן יְדִידֶיךָ,
תהלים יט הוֹשִׁיעָה יְמִינְךָ וַעֲנֵנִי: יִהְיוּ לְרָצוֹן אִמְרֵי־פִי וְהֶגְיוֹן לִבִּי לְפָנֶיךָ, יהוה צוּרִי וְגֹאֲלִי:

Bow, take three steps back, then bow, first left, then right, then center, while saying:

עֹשֶׂה שָׁלוֹם / בשבת שובה: הַשָּׁלוֹם/ בִּמְרוֹמָיו, הוּא יַעֲשֶׂה שָׁלוֹם עָלֵינוּ, וְעַל כָּל יִשְׂרָאֵל, וְאִמְרוּ אָמֵן.

יְהִי רָצוֹן מִלְּפָנֶיךָ יהוה אֱלֹהֵינוּ וֵאלֹהֵי אֲבוֹתֵינוּ, שֶׁיִּבָּנֶה בֵּית הַמִּקְדָּשׁ בִּמְהֵרָה בְיָמֵינוּ, וְתֵן חֶלְקֵנוּ בְּתוֹרָתֶךָ, וְשָׁם נַעֲבָדְךָ בְּיִרְאָה כִּימֵי
מלאכי ג עוֹלָם וּכְשָׁנִים קַדְמוֹנִיּוֹת. וְעָרְבָה לַיהוה מִנְחַת יְהוּדָה וִירוּשָׁלָםִ כִּימֵי עוֹלָם וּכְשָׁנִים קַדְמוֹנִיּוֹת:

On ראש חודש, חול המועד *and* חנוכה*, the service continues with* הלל *on page 766.*

קדיש שלם

ש״ץ: **יִתְגַּדַּל** וְיִתְקַדַּשׁ שְׁמֵהּ רַבָּא (קהל: אָמֵן) בְּעָלְמָא דִּי בְרָא כִרְעוּתֵהּ. וְיַמְלִיךְ מַלְכוּתֵהּ בְּחַיֵּיכוֹן וּבְיוֹמֵיכוֹן וּבְחַיֵּי דְכָל בֵּית יִשְׂרָאֵל, בַּעֲגָלָא וּבִזְמַן קָרִיב, וְאִמְרוּ אָמֵן. (קהל: אָמֵן)

קהל וש״ץ: יְהֵא שְׁמֵהּ רַבָּא מְבָרַךְ לְעָלַם וּלְעָלְמֵי עָלְמַיָּא.

ש״ץ: יִתְבָּרַךְ וְיִשְׁתַּבַּח וְיִתְפָּאַר וְיִתְרוֹמַם וְיִתְנַשֵּׂא, וְיִתְהַדָּר וְיִתְעַלֶּה וְיִתְהַלָּל שְׁמֵהּ דְּקֻדְשָׁא בְּרִיךְ הוּא (קהל: בְּרִיךְ הוּא), לְעֵלָּא מִן כָּל בִּרְכָתָא / בשבת שובה: לְעֵלָּא (וּ)לְעֵלָּא מִכָּל בִּרְכָתָא/ וְשִׁירָתָא, תֻּשְׁבְּחָתָא וְנֶחֱמָתָא דַּאֲמִירָן בְּעָלְמָא, וְאִמְרוּ אָמֵן. (קהל: אָמֵן)

תִּתְקַבַּל צְלוֹתְהוֹן וּבָעוּתְהוֹן דְּכָל יִשְׂרָאֵל, קֳדָם אֲבוּהוֹן דִּי בִשְׁמַיָּא, וְאִמְרוּ אָמֵן. (קהל: אָמֵן)

יְהֵא שְׁלָמָא רַבָּא מִן שְׁמַיָּא וְחַיִּים, עָלֵינוּ וְעַל כָּל יִשְׂרָאֵל, וְאִמְרוּ אָמֵן. (קהל: אָמֵן)

Bow, take three steps back, as if taking leave of the Divine Presence, then bow, first left, then right, then center, while saying:

עֹשֶׂה שָׁלוֹם / בשבת שובה: הַשָּׁלוֹם/ בִּמְרוֹמָיו, הוּא יַעֲשֶׂה שָׁלוֹם עָלֵינוּ, וְעַל כָּל יִשְׂרָאֵל, וְאִמְרוּ אָמֵן. (קהל: אָמֵן)

Some congregations recite the שיר הכבוד *(page 598) at this point, followed by* קדיש יתום*, rather than at the conclusion of* מוסף*.*

Ps. 60 hand. Do so for Your holiness. Do so for Your Torah, that Your loved ones may be delivered. "Save with Your right hand, and answer me.
Ps. 19 May the words of my mouth and the meditation of my heart find grace before You, LORD, my Rock and my Redeemer."

Bow, take three steps back, then bow, first left, then right, then center, while saying:

He Who makes peace in His heights, may He create peace for us and for all Israel. Amen.

יְהִי רָצוֹן MAY IT BE Your will, LORD our God and God of our fathers, that the Temple be rebuilt speedily in our days and may You grant our portion in Your Torah. We will serve You there in reverence as in the days of antiquity and in
Mal. 3 years gone by. "And may the offering of Judah and Jerusalem be pleasant to the LORD as in the days of antiquity and in years gone by."

On Rosh Ḥodesh, Ḥol HaMo'ed and Ḥanukka, the service continues with Hallel on page 767.

FULL KADDISH

Leader: יִתְגַּדַּל EXALTED AND HALLOWED may God's great name be, in the world He created as He willed. May He reign in your lifetimes and in your days, and in the lifetime of the whole house of Israel, speedily and soon, and say, Amen.

All: May His great name be blessed forever and all time.

Leader: Blessed and praised, honored, extolled, glorified, adored and exalted above all be the name of the Holy One, blessed is He, (*Between Rosh Hashana & Yom Kippur:* above and) beyond any blessing, hymn, praise, or expressions of consolation that may be uttered in this world, and say, Amen.

May the prayers and pleas of all Israel be accepted before their Father Who is in heaven – and say, Amen.

May abundant peace descend from heaven, as well as life, for us and for all Israel, and say, Amen.

Bow, take three steps back, as if taking leave of the Divine Presence, then bow, first left, then right, then center, while saying:

May He Who makes peace in the highest heaven, make peace for us, and for all Israel, and say, Amen.

Some congregations recite the Song of Glory (page 599) at this point, followed by the Mourner's Kaddish, rather than at the conclusion of Musaf.

הוצאת ספר תורה

A detailed description of many halakhot relating to the Reading of the Torah can be found on page E17.

תהלים פו
תהלים קמה
אֵין־כָּמְוֹךָ בָאֱלֹהִים, אֲדֹנָי, וְאֵין כְּמַעֲשֶׂיךָ: מַלְכוּתְךָ מַלְכוּת כָּל־עֹלָמִים, וּמֶמְשַׁלְתְּךָ בְּכָל־דּוֹר וָדֹר:

תהלים כט
יהוה מֶלֶךְ, יהוה מָלָךְ, יהוה יִמְלֹךְ לְעֹלָם וָעֶד. יהוה עֹז לְעַמּוֹ יִתֵּן, יהוה יְבָרֵךְ אֶת־עַמּוֹ בַשָּׁלוֹם:

תהלים נא
אַב הָרַחֲמִים, הֵיטִיבָה בִרְצוֹנְךָ אֶת־צִיּוֹן תִּבְנֶה חוֹמוֹת יְרוּשָׁלָםִ: כִּי בְךָ לְבַד בָּטָחְנוּ, מֶלֶךְ אֵל רָם וְנִשָּׂא, אֲדוֹן עוֹלָמִים.

במדבר י
ישעיה ב
וַיְהִי בִּנְסֹעַ הָאָרֹן וַיֹּאמֶר מֹשֶׁה, קוּמָה יהוה וְיָפֻצוּ אֹיְבֶיךָ וְיָנֻסוּ מְשַׂנְאֶיךָ מִפָּנֶיךָ: כִּי מִצִּיּוֹן תֵּצֵא תוֹרָה וּדְבַר־יהוה, מִירוּשָׁלָםִ: בָּרוּךְ שֶׁנָּתַן תּוֹרָה לְעַמּוֹ יִשְׂרָאֵל בִּקְדֻשָּׁתוֹ.

On שבת*, continue with* בְּרִיךְ שְׁמֵהּ *on the next page.*

On a יום טוב *that occurs on a weekday, and on* הושענא רבה*, recite the following up to and including* שְׁמַע*. On* שבת *(including* יום טוב *that occurs on* שבת*) continue with* בְּרִיךְ שְׁמֵהּ *on the next page.*

Say the following verses three times:

שמות לד
יהוה, יהוה, אֵל רַחוּם וְחַנּוּן, אֶרֶךְ אַפַּיִם וְרַב־חֶסֶד וֶאֱמֶת: נֹצֵר חֶסֶד לָאֲלָפִים, נֹשֵׂא עָוֹן וָפֶשַׁע וְחַטָּאָה, וְנַקֵּה:

הוֹצָאַת סֵפֶר תּוֹרָה / REMOVAL OF THE TORAH
When the Torah is removed from the Ark, the congregation should stand in awe, imagining that at that moment they are standing at Sinai to receive the Torah, listening carefully to every word. It is not permitted whatsoever to talk, even words of Torah, and certainly not of other things, as it says, "When it was opened the people stood" (Neh. 8:5), "Inclining their ears to the Torah" (Neh. 8:3). R. Shimon said, "When the doors of the Ark are opened the heavenly doors of mercy are opened too, to increase heavenly love." Then each person should recite *Berikh Shemeh* (*Zohar, Vayak-hel*).

The *Berikh Shemeh* that is recited before the Torah reading (next page) includes three references to the Torah, in which we proclaim that (a) we bow down in complete submission to the Torah, insofar as (b) it contains God's truth, and therefore we ask God to (c) open our hearts to understand and uphold it.

The public reading of the Torah is not simply proclaiming or studying the Torah; it is a re-enactment of the events at Sinai, as

REMOVING THE TORAH FROM THE ARK

A detailed description of many halakhot relating to the Reading of the Torah can be found on page E17.

Ps. 86 אֵין־כָּמְוֹךָ THERE IS NONE like You among the powers, O Lord, and
Ps. 145 there are none like Your deeds. Your kingdom is a kingdom for all times, and Your dominion is for every generation.

Ps. 29 יהוה מֶלֶךְ THE LORD REIGNS; the Lord has reigned; the Lord will reign forever and ever. The Lord will give strength to His people. The Lord will bless His people with peace.

Ps. 29 אַב הָרַחֲמִים FATHER OF MERCY, beautify Zion with Your favor. Build the walls of Jerusalem. We trust in You alone, King, God, sublime and exalted, Master of worlds.

Num. 10 וַיְהִי בִּנְסֹעַ WHEN THE ARK moved forward, Moses would say, "Arise, O Lord, and may Your enemies be dispersed, and they who hate You
Is. 2 flee from You." For from Zion shall go forth Torah, and the word of the Lord from Jerusalem. Blessed is He Who, in His holiness, has given the Torah to His people Israel.

On Shabbat, continue with "Blessed is Your name" on the next page.

On a Yom Tov that occurs on a weekday, and on Hoshana Raba, recite the following up to and including Shema. On Shabbat (including Yom Tov that occurs on Shabbat) continue with "Blessed is Your name" on the next page.

Say the following verses three times:

Ex. 34 יהוה THE LORD, the Lord, compassionate and gracious God, slow to anger and great in mercy and truth, keeping loving-kindness for thousands, forgiving iniquity, transgression, and sin, and offering absolution.

---

reflected in numerous laws pertaining to the reading of the Torah (R. Joseph B. Soloveitchik).

SPECIAL FESTIVAL PRAYERS

This part of the service found its way from Kabbalistic circles into the standard *nusaḥ* as early as the seventeenth century. The Thirteen Attributes of Mercy were revealed when God forgave the people for having worshiped the Golden Calf, and represent a new way in which God would relate to the Jewish people. They encapsulate God's merciful ways in forgiving the people of Israel throughout its subsequent history, and were a prerequisite for the renewed acceptance of the Torah that followed (R. Menachem Leibtag).

On יום טוב *(except on* שבת*) continue, inserting appropriate phrase/s in parentheses:*

רִבּוֹנוֹ שֶׁל עוֹלָם, מַלֵּא מִשְׁאֲלוֹת לִבִּי לְטוֹבָה, וְהָפֵק רְצוֹנִי וְתֵן שְׁאֵלָתִי, וְזַכֵּה לִי (פלוני/ת בֶּן/בַּת פלוני) (וְאִשְׁתִּי/בַּעֲלִי וּבָנַי וּבְנוֹתַי) וְכָל בְּנֵי בֵיתִי, לַעֲשׂוֹת רְצוֹנְךָ בְּלֵבָב שָׁלֵם, וּמַלְּטֵנוּ מִיֵּצֶר הָרָע, וְתֵן חֶלְקֵנוּ בְּתוֹרָתֶךָ, וְזַכֵּנוּ שֶׁתַּשְׁרֶה שְׁכִינָתְךָ עָלֵינוּ, וְהוֹפַע עָלֵינוּ רוּחַ חָכְמָה וּבִינָה. וְיִתְקַיֵּם בָּנוּ

ישעיה יא מִקְרָא שֶׁכָּתוּב: וְנָחָה עָלָיו רוּחַ יהוה, רוּחַ חָכְמָה וּבִינָה, רוּחַ עֵצָה וּגְבוּרָה, רוּחַ דַּעַת וְיִרְאַת יהוה:
וּבְכֵן יְהִי רָצוֹן מִלְּפָנֶיךָ יהוה אֱלֹהֵינוּ וֵאלֹהֵי אֲבוֹתֵינוּ, שֶׁתְּזַכֵּנוּ לַעֲשׂוֹת מַעֲשִׂים טוֹבִים בְּעֵינֶיךָ וְלָלֶכֶת בְּדַרְכֵי יְשָׁרִים לְפָנֶיךָ, וְקַדְּשֵׁנוּ בִּקְדֻשָּׁתֶךָ כְּדֵי שֶׁנִּזְכֶּה לְחַיִּים טוֹבִים וַאֲרוּכִים וּלְחַיֵּי הָעוֹלָם הַבָּא, וְתִשְׁמְרֵנוּ מִמַּעֲשִׂים רָעִים וּמִשָּׁעוֹת רָעוֹת הַמִּתְרַגְּשׁוֹת לָבוֹא לָעוֹלָם,

תהלים לב וְהַבּוֹטֵחַ בַּיהוה חֶסֶד יְסוֹבְבֶנּוּ: אָמֵן.

On הושענא רבה *continue:*

רִבּוֹנוֹ שֶׁל עוֹלָם, מַלֵּא מִשְׁאֲלוֹתַי לְטוֹבָה, וְהָפֵק רְצוֹנִי וְתֵן שְׁאֵלָתִי, וּמְחֹל לִי עַל כָּל עֲוֹנוֹתַי וְעַל כָּל עֲוֹנוֹת אַנְשֵׁי בֵיתִי, מְחִילָה בְּחֶסֶד מְחִילָה בְּרַחֲמִים, וְטַהֲרֵנוּ מֵחֲטָאֵינוּ וּמֵעֲוֹנוֹתֵינוּ וּמִפְּשָׁעֵינוּ, וְזָכְרֵנוּ בְּזִכָּרוֹן טוֹב לְפָנֶיךָ, וּפָקְדֵנוּ בִּפְקֻדַּת יְשׁוּעָה וְרַחֲמִים. וְזָכְרֵנוּ לְחַיִּים טוֹבִים וּלְשָׁלוֹם, וּפַרְנָסָה וְכַלְכָּלָה, וְלֶחֶם לֶאֱכֹל וּבֶגֶד לִלְבֹּשׁ, וְעֹשֶׁר וְכָבוֹד, וְאֹרֶךְ יָמִים לַהֲגוֹת בְּתוֹרָתֶךָ וּלְקַיֵּם מִצְוֹתֶיהָ, וְשֵׂכֶל וּבִינָה לְהָבִין וּלְהַשְׂכִּיל עִמְקֵי סוֹדוֹתֶיהָ. וְהָפֵק רְפוּאָה לְכָל מַכְאוֹבֵינוּ, וּבָרֵךְ כָּל מַעֲשֵׂה יָדֵינוּ, וּגְזֹר עָלֵינוּ גְּזֵרוֹת טוֹבוֹת יְשׁוּעוֹת וְנֶחָמוֹת, וּבַטֵּל מֵעָלֵינוּ כָּל גְּזֵרוֹת קָשׁוֹת וְרָעוֹת, וְתֵן בְּלֵב הַמַּלְכוּת וְיוֹעֲצֶיהָ וְשָׂרֶיהָ עָלֵינוּ לְטוֹבָה. אָמֵן וְכֵן יְהִי רָצוֹן.

תהלים יט **יִהְיוּ** לְרָצוֹן אִמְרֵי־פִי וְהֶגְיוֹן לִבִּי לְפָנֶיךָ, יהוה צוּרִי וְגֹאֲלִי:

Say the following verse three times:

תהלים סט **וַאֲנִי** תְפִלָּתִי־לְךָ יהוה, עֵת רָצוֹן, אֱלֹהִים בְּרָב־חַסְדֶּךָ, עֲנֵנִי בֶּאֱמֶת יִשְׁעֶךָ:

The ספר תורה *is removed from the* ארון קודש *before the recitation of* בְּרִיךְ שְׁמֵהּ *(Iggerot Moshe, OH 4:70:9).*

On שבת*,* יום טוב *and on* הושענא רבה*:*

זוהר ויקהל **בְּרִיךְ שְׁמֵהּ** דְּמָרֵא עָלְמָא, בְּרִיךְ כִּתְרָךְ וְאַתְרָךְ. יְהֵא רְעוּתָךְ עִם עַמָּךְ יִשְׂרָאֵל לְעָלַם, וּפֻרְקַן יְמִינָךְ אַחֲזֵי לְעַמָּךְ בְּבֵית מַקְדְּשָׁךְ, וּלְאַמְטוּיֵי לָנָא מִטּוּב נְהוֹרָךְ, וּלְקַבֵּל צְלוֹתָנָא בְּרַחֲמִין. יְהֵא רַעֲוָא קֳדָמָךְ דְּתוֹרִיךְ לָן חַיִּין בְּטִיבוּ,

---

עת רצון – *A time of favor.* According to the Gemara (*Berakhot* 8a), עֵת רָצוֹן (a time of favor) occurs whenever a congregation joins together in prayer. This reflects the general principle that praying with a minyan raises our prayers to a higher level, for then it is not merely a תְּפִלַּת הַיָּחִיד – prayer of an individual, but a תְּפִלַּת הַצִּבּוּר – prayer of the community (R. Joseph B. Soloveitchik).

On Yom Tov (except on Shabbat) continue, inserting appropriate phrase/s in parentheses:

רִבּוֹנוֹ RULER OF THE UNIVERSE, fulfill the prayers of my heart for good. Respond to my desires and answer my prayerful petition. Enable me, Your servant (*name*) son/daughter of (*mother's name*) Your maidservant, and grant me (and my wife/my husband, my sons, my daughters) and all my family to whole-heartedly carry out Your will. Deliver us from the evil impulse, and grant our lot in Your Torah, and make us worthy so that Your Presence will rest upon us. Bestow on us a spirit of wisdom and understanding, and may there
Is. 11 be fulfilled in us the verse: "A spirit of the Lord shall rest upon him, a spirit of wisdom and understanding, a spirit of counsel and might, a spirit of knowledge and reverence for the Lord. May it be Your will, Lord our God, and God of our fathers, that we be privileged to always do what is good in Your sight, and to walk before You in the ways of the upright. Make us holy through Your commandments, so that we may be worthy of a happy and long life in the World to Come. Guard us from evil deeds and from the evil times that may come upon this
Ps. 32 world. But he who trusts in the Lord – He will surround him with loving-kindness. Amen.

On Hoshana Raba continue:

רִבּוֹנוֹ RULER OF THE UNIVERSE, fulfill my prayers for good. Respond to my desires, and answer my prayerful petition. Forgive all my sins, and the sins of the members of my household. May it be a forgiveness based on kindness and mercy. Purify us of our transgressions, our sins, and our errors. Remember us for good before You. Be mindful of us for salvation and mercy. Remember us for life and peace, sustenance and security, food to eat, clothing to wear, riches and honor. Give us length of days so as to study Your Torah and fulfill its commandments, as well as to attain discernment and understanding of the depths of its secrets. Bring healing to all our ailments, bless the work of our hands, and bring upon us decrees of goodness, salvation, and consolation. Nullify all harsh and evil decrees, and put in the heart of the government, its advisers and leaders, to treat us with benevolence. Amen, may this be Your will.

Ps. 19 יִהְיוּ MAY the words of my mouth and the meditation of my heart find grace before You, Lord, my Rock and my Redeemer.

Say the following verse three times:

Ps. 69 וַאֲנִי BUT I pray to You, O Lord, for a time of favor. O God, in the greatness of Your loving-kindness, answer me, in the truth of Your salvation.

The Torah is removed from the Ark before the recitation of Berikh Shemeh (Iggerot Moshe, OH 4:70:9).

On Shabbat, Yom Tov and on Hoshana Raba:

Zohar, Vayak-hel בְּרִיךְ שְׁמֵהּ BLESSED IS YOUR NAME, Master of the universe; blessed is Your crown; blessed Your place. May You always favor Your people Israel. In Your Temple, reveal to Your people the redeeming power of Your right hand. Grant us of Your beneficent light and mercifully accept our prayer. May it be Your will

וְלֶהֱוֵי אֲנָא פְקִידָא בְּגוֹ צַדִּיקַיָּא, לְמִרְחַם עָלַי וּלְמִנְטַר יָתִי וְיָת כָּל דִּי לִי וְדִי לְעַמָּךְ יִשְׂרָאֵל. אַנְתְּ הוּא זָן לְכֹלָּא וּמְפַרְנֵס לְכֹלָּא, אַנְתְּ הוּא שַׁלִּיט עַל כֹּלָּא, אַנְתְּ הוּא דְּשַׁלִּיט עַל מַלְכַיָּא, וּמַלְכוּתָא דִּילָךְ הִיא. אֲנָא עַבְדָּא דְקֻדְשָׁא בְּרִיךְ הוּא, דְּסָגִדְנָא קַמֵּהּ וּמִקַּמֵּי דִּיקַר אוֹרַיְתֵהּ בְּכָל עִדָּן וְעִדָּן. לָא עַל אֱנָשׁ רָחִיצְנָא וְלָא עַל בַּר אֱלָהִין סָמִיכְנָא, אֶלָּא בֶּאֱלָהָא דִשְׁמַיָּא, דְּהוּא אֱלָהָא קְשׁוֹט, וְאוֹרַיְתֵהּ קְשׁוֹט, וּנְבִיאוֹהִי קְשׁוֹט, וּמַסְגֵּא לְמֶעְבַּד טַבְוָן וּקְשׁוֹט. ◂ בֵּהּ אֲנָא רָחִיץ, וְלִשְׁמֵהּ קַדִּישָׁא יַקִּירָא אֲנָא אֵמַר תֻּשְׁבְּחָן. יְהֵא רַעֲוָא קֳדָמָךְ דְּתִפְתַּח לִבַּאי בְּאוֹרַיְתָא, וְתַשְׁלִים מִשְׁאֲלִין דְּלִבַּאי וְלִבָּא דְכָל עַמָּךְ יִשְׂרָאֵל לְטָב וּלְחַיִּין וְלִשְׁלָם. (אָמֵן.)

The שליח ציבור *then* קהל*:*

דברים ו שְׁמַע יִשְׂרָאֵל, יהוה אֱלֹהֵינוּ, יהוה אֶחָד:

The שליח ציבור *then* קהל*:*

אֶחָד (הוּא) אֱלֹהֵינוּ, גָּדוֹל אֲדוֹנֵינוּ, קָדוֹשׁ (בהושענא רבה: וְנוֹרָא) שְׁמוֹ.

The שליח ציבור *turns to face the* ארון קודש*, bows and says:*

תהלים לד גַּדְּלוּ לַיהוה אִתִּי וּנְרוֹמְמָה שְׁמוֹ יַחְדָּו:

The ארון קודש *is closed. The* שליח ציבור *carries the* ספר תורה *to the* בימה *and the* קהל *says:*

דברי הימים א׳ כט לְךָ יהוה הַגְּדֻלָּה וְהַגְּבוּרָה וְהַתִּפְאֶרֶת וְהַנֵּצַח וְהַהוֹד, כִּי־כֹל בַּשָּׁמַיִם וּבָאָרֶץ, לְךָ יהוה הַמַּמְלָכָה וְהַמִּתְנַשֵּׂא לְכֹל לְרֹאשׁ:

תהלים צט רוֹמְמוּ יהוה אֱלֹהֵינוּ וְהִשְׁתַּחֲווּ לַהֲדֹם רַגְלָיו, קָדוֹשׁ הוּא: רוֹמְמוּ יהוה אֱלֹהֵינוּ וְהִשְׁתַּחֲווּ לְהַר קָדְשׁוֹ, כִּי־קָדוֹשׁ יהוה אֱלֹהֵינוּ:

עַל הַכֹּל יִתְגַּדַּל וְיִתְקַדַּשׁ וְיִשְׁתַּבַּח וְיִתְפָּאַר וְיִתְרוֹמַם וְיִתְנַשֵּׂא שְׁמוֹ שֶׁל מֶלֶךְ מַלְכֵי הַמְּלָכִים הַקָּדוֹשׁ בָּרוּךְ הוּא בָּעוֹלָמוֹת שֶׁבָּרָא, הָעוֹלָם הַזֶּה וְהָעוֹלָם הַבָּא, כִּרְצוֹנוֹ וְכִרְצוֹן יְרֵאָיו וְכִרְצוֹן כָּל בֵּית יִשְׂרָאֵל. צוּר הָעוֹלָמִים, אֲדוֹן כָּל הַבְּרִיּוֹת, אֱלוֹהַּ כָּל הַנְּפָשׁוֹת, הַיּוֹשֵׁב בְּמֶרְחֲבֵי מָרוֹם, הַשּׁוֹכֵן בִּשְׁמֵי שְׁמֵי קֶדֶם, קְדֻשָּׁתוֹ עַל הַחַיּוֹת, וּקְדֻשָּׁתוֹ עַל כִּסֵּא הַכָּבוֹד.

שְׁמַע יִשְׂרָאֵל — *Hear, O Israel.* The public recitation of these verses before reading from the Torah is first documented in the Mishna (*Soferim* 14:9).

to prolong our lives in goodness. Count me among the righteous to whom You show love, protecting me and all that is mine, as well as all that belongs to Your people Israel. You are He Who provides food for all and sustains all. You are He Who rules over all. You are He Who rules over monarchs, for the dominion is Yours. I am the servant of the Holy One, blessed is He, before Whom, and before Whose glorious Torah, I bow at all times. Not on man do I rely, nor do I trust in any angel, but only on the God of the heavens Who is the God of truth, Whose Torah is truth and Whose prophets are true, and Who acts with abundant love and truth. ▸ In Him alone is my trust, and it is to His holy and glorious name that I utter praises. May it be Your will to open my heart to Your Torah, and to fulfill the desires of my heart and the hearts of all Your people Israel for good, for life, and for peace. (Amen.)

Leader then congregation:

Deut. 6 שְׁמַע HEAR, O ISRAEL, the LORD is our God, the LORD is One.

Leader then congregation:

אֶחָד ONE IS OUR GOD, great is our Master,
holy (*On Hoshana Raba:* and awesome) is His name.

The Leader turns to face the Ark, bows and says:

Ps. 34 גַּדְּלוּ MAGNIFY the Lord with me,
and let us exalt His name together.

The Ark is closed. The Leader carries the Torah scroll to the bima and the congregation says:

I Chr. 29 לְךָ YOURS, O Lord, are greatness, power, glory, victory, and majesty;
indeed, everything that is in the heavens and on earth. Yours, O Lord,
Ps. 99 is the dominion, and You are supreme over all. Exalt the Lord our
God, and bow down before His footstool. He is holy. Exalt the Lord our God, and bow down before His holy mountain. Indeed, the Lord our God is holy.

עַל הַכֹּל ABOVE ALL may the name of the King of the most exalted of kings, the Holy One, blessed is He, be exalted and hallowed, praised and honored, extolled and glorified in the worlds He has created – this world and the World to Come – in accordance with His will, the will of those who revere Him, and the will of the whole house of Israel. Rock of the universe, Master of all created beings, God of all spirits, He Who dwells in the high expanses and rests in the ancient heavens – His holiness is upon the Ḥayyot; His holiness is upon His throne of glory. Now, therefore, Lord our God, may Your name be hallowed among us in the sight of all living beings. We sing before You a

וּבְכֵן יִתְקַדַּשׁ שִׁמְךָ בָּנוּ יהוה אֱלֹהֵינוּ לְעֵינֵי כָּל חָי, וְנֹאמַר לְפָנָיו שִׁיר
תהלים סח חָדָשׁ, כַּכָּתוּב: שִׁירוּ לֵאלֹהִים זַמְּרוּ שְׁמוֹ, סֹלּוּ לָרֹכֵב בָּעֲרָבוֹת, בְּיָהּ שְׁמוֹ,
ישעיה נב וְעִלְזוּ לְפָנָיו: וְנִרְאֵהוּ עַיִן בְּעַיִן בְּשׁוּבוֹ אֶל נָוֵהוּ, כַּכָּתוּב: כִּי עַיִן בְּעַיִן יִרְאוּ
ישעיה מ בְּשׁוּב יהוה צִיּוֹן: וְנֶאֱמַר: וְנִגְלָה כְּבוֹד יהוה, וְרָאוּ כָל־בָּשָׂר יַחְדָּו כִּי פִּי
יהוה דִּבֵּר:

אַב הָרַחֲמִים הוּא יְרַחֵם עַם עֲמוּסִים, וְיִזְכֹּר בְּרִית אֵיתָנִים, וְיַצִּיל נַפְשׁוֹתֵינוּ מִן הַשָּׁעוֹת הָרָעוֹת, וְיִגְעַר בְּיֵצֶר הָרָע מִן הַנְּשׂוּאִים, וְיָחֹן אוֹתָנוּ לִפְלֵיטַת עוֹלָמִים, וִימַלֵּא מִשְׁאֲלוֹתֵינוּ בְּמִדָּה טוֹבָה יְשׁוּעָה וְרַחֲמִים.

The ספר תורה *is placed on the* שולחן *and the* גבאי *calls a* כהן *to the* תורה.

וְיַעֲזֹר וְיָגֵן וְיוֹשִׁיעַ לְכָל הַחוֹסִים בּוֹ, וְנֹאמַר אָמֵן. הַכֹּל הָבוּ גֹדֶל לֵאלֹהֵינוּ וּתְנוּ כָבוֹד לַתּוֹרָה. *כֹּהֵן קְרַב, יַעֲמֹד (פלוני בֶּן פלוני) הַכֹּהֵן.

**If no* כהן *is present, a* לוי *or* ישראל *is called up as follows:*

/אֵין כָּאן כֹּהֵן, יַעֲמֹד (פלוני בֶּן פלוני) בִּמְקוֹם כֹּהֵן./

בָּרוּךְ שֶׁנָּתַן תּוֹרָה לְעַמּוֹ יִשְׂרָאֵל בִּקְדֻשָּׁתוֹ.

The קהל *followed by the* גבאי*:*

דברים ד וְאַתֶּם הַדְּבֵקִים בַּיהוה אֱלֹהֵיכֶם חַיִּים כֻּלְּכֶם הַיּוֹם:

הָבוּ גֹדֶל – *Ascribe greatness*. The Gemara (*Berakhot* 21a) explains that this verse is the source for reciting a *berakha* before the reading of the Torah.

כֹּהֵן קְרַב – *Let the Kohen come forward*. Just as at Sinai all the Israelites participated in the event, so in re-enacting that event, all Jews (*Kohanim*, Levites, and Israelites) are represented, by having at least one of them called to the Torah (R. Joseph B. Soloveitchik).

The Torah records that when God was about to give the Torah וַיַּעֲנוּ כָל־הָעָם (All the people answered) יַחְדָּו (together), and said כָּל (all) that the Lord has commanded we will do (Ex. 19:8). This apparently redundant emphasis on all of the people together committing to all of the commandments can be explained in light of the fact that no single individual or group can keep "all" of the *mitzvot*. Some can only be observed by *Kohanim*, some only by a king, others only by the Sanhedrin, and yet others exclusively by landowners in Israel, and so forth. It was only as a people in its entirety that they could say that they would uphold the entire Torah. The Jewish people in regard to the Torah is like a single body, with various types of Jews corresponding to organs of the body, each playing a unique role, like the heart, the head, the eyes, and so forth. This is the basis of the principle כָּל יִשְׂרָאֵל עֲרֵבִים זֶה לָזֶה (all Jews

Ps. 68 new song, as it is written: "Sing to God. Sing praise to His name. Raise your voice to Him Who rides upon the clouds by His name, YaH, and rejoice before Him." May we truly see eye to eye when He returns to His abode,
Is. 52 as is written: "For they shall see eye to eye when the Lord returns to Zion."
Is. 40 And it is said: "The glory of the Lord shall be revealed, and all flesh shall see it together, because the mouth of the Lord has spoken it."

אַב הָרַחֲמִים MAY THE FATHER OF MERCY have compassion on the people borne by Him. May He remember the covenant with the mighty (patriarchs), and deliver us from evil times. May He reproach the evil impulse in the people He carries, and graciously grant us eternal survival. May He fulfill in good measure our requests for salvation and mercy.

The Torah scroll is placed on the bima and the Gabbai calls a Kohen to the Torah.

וְיַעֲזֹר MAY HE HELP, protect, and save all who take refuge in Him, and let us say, Amen. Ascribe greatness to our God and give honor to the Torah. Let the *Kohen* come forward. *Arise (*name*) son of (*father's name*) the *Kohen*.

**If no Kohen is present, a Levi or Yisrael is called up as follows:*

Since there is no *Kohen*, arise (*name* son of *father's name*) in place of a *Kohen*.

Blessed is He Who, in His holiness, gave the Torah to His people Israel.

The congregation followed by the Gabbai:

Deut. 4 And you who cleave to the Lord your God, all of you are alive this day.

---

have a responsibility to each other), as found in the Gemara (*Shevuot* 39a). In short, we depend on each other to ensure that the entire Torah is upheld by us as a single people (R. Meir Simḥa of Dvinsk).

וְאַתֶּם הַדְּבֵקִים בַּיהוה אֱלֹהֵיכֶם חַיִּים כֻּלְּכֶם הַיּוֹם – *And you who cleave to the Lord your God, all of you are alive this day.* This verse teaches us that a life which is not Godly is not to be termed life at all. This conviction is inscribed on the soul of every Jew (R. Avraham Yitzḥak HaKohen Kook).

קְרִיאַת הַתּוֹרָה/ READING OF THE TORAH
The Talmud Yerushalmi (*Megilla* 4:1) traces the public reading of the Torah on Shabbat and Yom Tov to Moses, on the basis of וַיְדַבֵּר מֹשֶׁה אֶת־מֹעֲדֵי ה׳ אֶל־בְּנֵי יִשְׂרָאֵל: – Moses announced the Lord's appointed seasons to the children of Israel (Lev. 23:44). The Ritva takes the position that the Torah itself requires us to read it on Shabbat and Yom Tov, while Moses extended the obligation to Mondays and Thursdays as well. Others, such as Ramban (Lev. 23:2) are of the view that even Shabbat and Yom Tov readings originated with the rabbinic tradition to pray in the synagogue on those days.

Since the Torah reading is an expression of מִקְרָא קֹדֶשׁ (a holy convocation), it is appropriate that the number of *aliyot* fluctuates according to the sanctity of each day. Thus, on Mondays, Thursdays, Fast Days, Purim

ברכות התורה

The קורא *shows the* עולה *the section to be read.*

The עולה *touches the* ספר תורה, *but not the letters themselves, with his* ציצית *or the Torah belt or cover, which he then kisses. Holding the handles of the* ספר תורה, *he says:*

עולה: **בָּרְכוּ** אֶת יהוה הַמְבֹרָךְ.

קהל: בָּרוּךְ יהוה הַמְבֹרָךְ לְעוֹלָם וָעֶד.

עולה: בָּרוּךְ יהוה הַמְבֹרָךְ לְעוֹלָם וָעֶד.

בָּרוּךְ אַתָּה יהוה, אֱלֹהֵינוּ מֶלֶךְ הָעוֹלָם, אֲשֶׁר בָּחַר בָּנוּ מִכָּל הָעַמִּים וְנָתַן לָנוּ אֶת תּוֹרָתוֹ. בָּרוּךְ אַתָּה יהוה, נוֹתֵן הַתּוֹרָה.

The appropriate Torah portion is read.

At the conclusion of each portion, the עולה *recites this concluding* ברכה*:*

עולה: בָּרוּךְ אַתָּה יהוה אֱלֹהֵינוּ מֶלֶךְ הָעוֹלָם, אֲשֶׁר נָתַן לָנוּ תּוֹרַת אֱמֶת וְחַיֵּי עוֹלָם נָטַע בְּתוֹכֵנוּ. בָּרוּךְ אַתָּה יהוה, נוֹתֵן הַתּוֹרָה.

---

and Ḥanukka, there are three *aliyot*; on Rosh Ḥodesh and Ḥol HaMo'ed when there is *Musaf* there are four; on Yom Tov and Rosh HaShana when certain labors are prohibited (as a לֹא תַעֲשֶׂה) there are five; on Yom Kippur when those labors are more stringently prohibited (on pain of כָּרֵת – excision) there are six; and on Shabbat when those labors are punished by the death penalty, there are seven *aliyot*. Only three are called at Shabbat *Minḥa*, since the Torah has already been read in the morning (R. Yair Kahn).

בָּרְכוּ – *Bless*. Each *aliya* is preceded by *Barekhu* and the *berakha* that follows, even though at the outset of *Shaḥarit* a *berakha* over Torah study was recited. This is because the earlier *berakha* referred to Torah study in general, whereas the public reading of the Torah is a communal affirmation of the yoke of heaven, and constitutes a דָּבָר שֶׁבִּקְדֻשָּׁה (an act of special sanctity), that can only be said with a *minyan*. This follows the precedent of Nehemiah who required a *berakha* before reading from the Torah in public (R. Joseph B. Soloveitchik).

נָתַן לָנוּ... נָטַע בְּתוֹכֵנוּ... נוֹתֵן הַתּוֹרָה – *Who has given us... planting eternal life among us... Giver of the Torah*. The *berakha* starts with the past tense and ends in the present, because it first refers to the written Torah that was revealed in the past at Sinai, and then it concludes with the oral Torah whose development is ongoing. This accords with the Gemara (*Eiruvin* 21b) that explains חֲדָשִׁים גַּם־יְשָׁנִים דּוֹדִי צָפַנְתִּי לָךְ (both new and old have I hidden for you My beloved) (Song of Songs 7:14) as referring to the established words of the Torah as well as the rabbinic tradition that each generation reveals some-

BLESSINGS OF THE TORAH

The Reader shows the oleh the section to be read. The oleh touches the scroll, but not the letters themselves, with his tzitzit or the Torah belt or cover, which he then kisses. Holding the handles of the scroll, he says:

Oleh: בָּרְכוּ BLESS the Lord, the blessed One.

Cong: BLESSED is the Lord Who is blessed for all eternity.

Oleh: BLESSED is the Lord Who is blessed for all eternity.
BLESSED are You, Lord, our God, King of the universe, Who has chosen us from all peoples and has given us His Torah. Blessed are You, Lord, Giver of the Torah.

The appropriate Torah portion is read.

At the conclusion of each portion, the oleh recites this concluding blessing:

Oleh: BLESSED are You, Lord, our God, King of the universe, Who has given us the Torah of truth, planting eternal life among us. Blessed are You, Lord, Giver of the Torah.

---

thing hidden therein. This also accounts for the use of the term "planted" in this *berakha*. For while the written Torah never changes, the oral Torah is like a plant that continues to grow organically "in us," i.e., in the Jewish people, with shoots and blossoms appearing generation after generation, as insights are added – making explicit what until then was only implicit in the Torah. In this way, whatever Torah insights are gleaned by the sages of ensuing generations are to be considered as originating with God, in accordance with the verse, "My wisdom dwells within, to be uncovered through careful examination" (Song of Songs 8:12). Therefore this *berakha* states that God both "gave us [in the past] the Torah of truth" and "gives [in the present] the Torah" (Vilna Gaon).

תּוֹרַת אֱמֶת וְחַיֵּי עוֹלָם – *Torah of truth... eternal life.* According to the Gemara (*Nedarim* 81a) the land of Israel was destroyed, "Because they did not recite the *berakha* over the Torah properly." By this the sages meant that the people did not sufficiently appreciate the importance of the Torah as the supreme source of wisdom for the Jewish people, through which we inherit both this world and the next. Therefore we must recite this *berakha* with great concentration (R. Yeḥiel Mikhel HaLevi Epstein).

The *Siddur Vilna* points out that these two *berakhot* together contain forty words, twenty in the first and twenty in the second, corresponding to the forty days during which Moses received the Torah on Sinai. This serves to remind us that the public reading of the Torah for each *aliya* should be experienced as an occasion to once again receive the Torah, just as happened over the course of forty days at Sinai. In this sense, the very term *aliya* connotes, literally, a "going up" to receive the Torah, a personal re-enactment of Moses' original "*aliya*" on Mount Sinai (R. Basil Herring).

מי שברך

לעולה לתורה

מִי שֶׁבֵּרַךְ אֲבוֹתֵינוּ אַבְרָהָם יִצְחָק וְיַעֲקֹב, הוּא יְבָרֵךְ אֶת (פלוני בֶּן פלוני), בַּעֲבוּר שֶׁעָלָה לִכְבוֹד הַמָּקוֹם וְלִכְבוֹד הַתּוֹרָה

בשבת: וְלִכְבוֹד הַשַּׁבָּת / ביום טוב: וְלִכְבוֹד הָרֶגֶל

בִּשְׂכַר זֶה הַקָּדוֹשׁ בָּרוּךְ הוּא יִשְׁמְרֵהוּ וְיַצִּילֵהוּ מִכָּל צָרָה וְצוּקָה וּמִכָּל נֶגַע וּמַחֲלָה, וְיִשְׁלַח בְּרָכָה וְהַצְלָחָה בְּכָל מַעֲשֵׂה יָדָיו (ביום טוב: וְיִזְכֶּה לַעֲלוֹת לָרֶגֶל) עִם כָּל יִשְׂרָאֵל אֶחָיו, וְנֹאמַר אָמֵן.

לחולה

מִי שֶׁבֵּרַךְ אֲבוֹתֵינוּ אַבְרָהָם יִצְחָק וְיַעֲקֹב, מֹשֶׁה וְאַהֲרֹן דָּוִד וּשְׁלֹמֹה הוּא יְבָרֵךְ וִירַפֵּא אֶת הַחוֹלֶה (פלוני בֶּן פלונית) בַּעֲבוּר שֶׁ(פלוני בֶּן פלוני) יִתֵּן / שֶׁ(פלונית בַּת פלוני) תִּתֵּן / צְדָקָה בַּעֲבוּרוֹ. בִּשְׂכַר זֶה הַקָּדוֹשׁ בָּרוּךְ הוּא יִמָּלֵא רַחֲמִים עָלָיו לְהַחֲלִימוֹ וּלְרַפְּאתוֹ וּלְהַחֲזִיקוֹ וּלְהַחֲיוֹתוֹ וְיִשְׁלַח לוֹ מְהֵרָה רְפוּאָה שְׁלֵמָה מִן הַשָּׁמַיִם לִרְמַ״ח אֵבָרָיו וּשְׁסָ״ה גִּידָיו בְּתוֹךְ שְׁאָר חוֹלֵי יִשְׂרָאֵל, רְפוּאַת הַנֶּפֶשׁ וּרְפוּאַת הַגּוּף (בשבת: שַׁבָּת הִיא / ביום טוב: יוֹם טוֹב הוּא / מִלִּזְעֹק וּרְפוּאָה קְרוֹבָה לָבוֹא), הַשְׁתָּא בַּעֲגָלָא וּבִזְמַן קָרִיב, וְנֹאמַר אָמֵן.

לחולה

מִי שֶׁבֵּרַךְ אֲבוֹתֵינוּ אַבְרָהָם יִצְחָק וְיַעֲקֹב, מֹשֶׁה וְאַהֲרֹן דָּוִד וּשְׁלֹמֹה, אִמּוֹתֵינוּ שָׂרָה רִבְקָה רָחֵל וְלֵאָה, הוּא יְבָרֵךְ וִירַפֵּא אֶת הַחוֹלָה (פלונית בַּת פלונית) בַּעֲבוּר שֶׁ(פלוני בֶּן פלוני) יִתֵּן / שֶׁ(פלונית בַּת פלוני) תִּתֵּן / צְדָקָה בַּעֲבוּרָהּ. בִּשְׂכַר זֶה הַקָּדוֹשׁ בָּרוּךְ הוּא יִמָּלֵא רַחֲמִים עָלֶיהָ לְהַחֲלִימָהּ וּלְרַפְּאתָהּ וּלְהַחֲזִיקָהּ וּלְהַחֲיוֹתָהּ וְיִשְׁלַח לָהּ מְהֵרָה רְפוּאָה שְׁלֵמָה מִן

מִי שֶׁבֵּרַךְ / HE WHO BLESSED

בַּעֲבוּר שֶׁ... יִתֵּן צְדָקָה – *On whose behalf ... will make a charitable gift.* In offering a prayer for the sick, it is not appropriate to ask that God respond "because so-and-so prays on their behalf," for doing so implies that we expect God to heal someone by virtue of our having prayed to Him. This violates the Gemara (*Rosh HaShana* 16b) which opposes praying with excessive confidence that God will answer our prayers. In accordance with the Gemara (*Ta'anit* 9a) one should instead ask for healing on the grounds that charity will be given on behalf of the sick. This is based on Malachi 3:10 which says, "Bring tithes into the store-house that there be food in My house, and test Me to see if I will open the windows of heaven and bring forth a blessing" (R. Joseph B. Soloveitchik).

Additionally, it is preferable to use the

MI SHEBERAKH

FOR AN OLEH

מִי שֶׁבֵּרַךְ MAY HE Who blessed our fathers Abraham, Isaac, and Jacob bless (*name*) son of (*father's name*), who has come forward to the Torah, in honor of the Omnipresent, in honor of the Torah,

On Shabbat: and in honor of the Sabbath
On Yom Tov: and in honor of the festival.

As a reward for this, may the Holy One, blessed is He, protect him and spare him from all trouble and sorrow, and from every wound or illness. May He send blessing and bestow success on all that he does (*On Yom Tov:* and grant him the privilege to ascend to Jerusalem for the festivals), together with all Israel his brethren, and let us say, Amen.

FOR A SICK MAN

מִי שֶׁבֵּרַךְ MAY HE Who blessed our fathers Abraham, Isaac, and Jacob, Moses and Aaron, David and Solomon, bless and heal the sick person (*name*) son of (*mother's name*), on whose behalf (*name of supplicant*) will make a charitable gift. As a reward for this, may the Holy One, blessed is He, show him the fullness of compassion by restoring his health, healing him, strengthening him, and granting him life. May He speedily send him a complete healing from heaven, to all his two hundred and forty-eight organs and three hundred and sixty-five sinews, among the other sick people of Israel, a healing of the spirit and a healing of the body (*On Shabbat:* though on the Sabbath / *On Yom Tov:* though on Yom Tov / it is forbidden to cry out, may his healing be quick to come), now, swiftly and soon. And let us say, Amen.

FOR A SICK WOMAN

מִי שֶׁבֵּרַךְ MAY HE Who blessed our fathers Abraham, Isaac, and Jacob, Moses and Aaron, David and Solomon, our mothers Sarah, Rebecca, Rachel and Leah, bless and heal the sick person (*name*) daughter of (*mother's name*), on whose behalf (*name of supplicant*) will make a charitable gift. As a reward for this, may the Holy One, blessed is He, show her the fullness of compassion by restoring her health, healing her, strengthening her, and granting her life. May He speedily send her a complete healing from heaven, to all her organs and sinews, among the other sick people of Israel, a healing of the spirit and a

---

phrase יִתֵּן לִצְדָקָה (will give charity) rather than נָדַר לִצְדָקָה (has vowed to give to charity). For the Gemara (*Beitza* 36b) forbids making monetary vows on Shabbat or Yom Tov, whereas declaring that someone "will give charity" is not language indicating taking a vow.

הַשָּׁמַיִם לְכָל אֵבָרֶיהָ וּלְכָל גִּידֶיהָ בְּתוֹךְ שְׁאָר חוֹלֵי יִשְׂרָאֵל, רְפוּאַת הַנֶּפֶשׁ וּרְפוּאַת הַגּוּף (בשבת: שַׁבָּת הִיא / ביום טוב: יוֹם טוֹב הוּא / מִלִּזְעֹק וּרְפוּאָה קְרוֹבָה לָבוֹא), הַשְׁתָּא בַּעֲגָלָא וּבִזְמַן קָרִיב, וְנֹאמַר אָמֵן.

לחולים

מִי שֶׁבֵּרַךְ אֲבוֹתֵינוּ אַבְרָהָם יִצְחָק וְיַעֲקֹב, מֹשֶׁה וְאַהֲרֹן דָּוִד וּשְׁלֹמֹה הוּא יְבָרֵךְ וִירַפֵּא אֶת הַחוֹלִים (*for each sick person* – פלוני בֶּן פלונית) בַּעֲבוּר שֶׁ(פלוני בֶּן פלוני) יִתֵּן / שֶׁ(פלונית בַּת פלוני) תִּתֵּן / צְדָקָה בַּעֲבוּרָם. בִּשְׂכַר זֶה הַקָּדוֹשׁ בָּרוּךְ הוּא יִמָּלֵא רַחֲמִים עֲלֵיהֶם לְהַחֲלִימָם וּלְרַפְּאֹתָם וּלְהַחֲזִיקָם וּלְהַחֲיוֹתָם וְיִשְׁלַח לָהֶם מְהֵרָה רְפוּאָה שְׁלֵמָה מִן הַשָּׁמַיִם לִרְמַ״ח אֵבְרֵיהֶם וּשְׁסָ״ה גִּידֵיהֶם בְּתוֹךְ שְׁאָר חוֹלֵי יִשְׂרָאֵל, רְפוּאַת הַנֶּפֶשׁ וּרְפוּאַת הַגּוּף (בשבת: שַׁבָּת הִיא / ביום טוב: יוֹם טוֹב הוּא / מִלִּזְעֹק וּרְפוּאָה קְרוֹבָה לָבוֹא), הַשְׁתָּא בַּעֲגָלָא וּבִזְמַן קָרִיב, וְנֹאמַר אָמֵן.

לחולות

מִי שֶׁבֵּרַךְ אֲבוֹתֵינוּ אַבְרָהָם יִצְחָק וְיַעֲקֹב, מֹשֶׁה וְאַהֲרֹן דָּוִד וּשְׁלֹמֹה, אִמּוֹתֵינוּ שָׂרָה רִבְקָה רָחֵל וְלֵאָה, הוּא יְבָרֵךְ וִירַפֵּא אֶת הַחוֹלוֹת (*for each sick person* – פלונית בַּת פלונית) בַּעֲבוּר שֶׁ(פלוני בֶּן פלוני) יִתֵּן / שֶׁ(פלונית בַּת פלוני) תִּתֵּן / צְדָקָה בַּעֲבוּרָן. בִּשְׂכַר זֶה הַקָּדוֹשׁ בָּרוּךְ הוּא יִמָּלֵא רַחֲמִים עֲלֵיהֶן לְהַחֲלִימָן וּלְרַפְּאֹתָן וּלְהַחֲזִיקָן וּלְהַחֲיוֹתָן וְיִשְׁלַח לָהֶן מְהֵרָה רְפוּאָה שְׁלֵמָה מִן הַשָּׁמַיִם לְכָל אֵבְרֵיהֶן וּלְכָל גִּידֵיהֶן בְּתוֹךְ שְׁאָר חוֹלֵי יִשְׂרָאֵל, רְפוּאַת הַנֶּפֶשׁ וּרְפוּאַת הַגּוּף (בשבת: שַׁבָּת הִיא / ביום טוב: יוֹם טוֹב הוּא / מִלִּזְעֹק וּרְפוּאָה קְרוֹבָה לָבוֹא), הַשְׁתָּא בַּעֲגָלָא וּבִזְמַן קָרִיב, וְנֹאמַר אָמֵן.

לאנשים חולים ולנשים חולות

מִי שֶׁבֵּרַךְ אֲבוֹתֵינוּ אַבְרָהָם יִצְחָק וְיַעֲקֹב, מֹשֶׁה וְאַהֲרֹן דָּוִד וּשְׁלֹמֹה, אִמּוֹתֵינוּ שָׂרָה רִבְקָה רָחֵל וְלֵאָה, הוּא יְבָרֵךְ וִירַפֵּא אֶת הַחוֹלִים (*for each person* – פלוני/פלונית בֶּן/בַּת פלונית) בַּעֲבוּר שֶׁ(פלוני בֶּן פלוני) יִתֵּן / שֶׁ(פלונית בַּת פלוני) תִּתֵּן / צְדָקָה בַּעֲבוּרָם. בִּשְׂכַר זֶה הַקָּדוֹשׁ בָּרוּךְ הוּא יִמָּלֵא רַחֲמִים עֲלֵיהֶם לְהַחֲלִימָם וּלְרַפְּאֹתָם וּלְהַחֲזִיקָם וּלְהַחֲיוֹתָם וְיִשְׁלַח לָהֶם מְהֵרָה רְפוּאָה שְׁלֵמָה מִן הַשָּׁמַיִם לְכָל אֵבְרֵיהֶם וּלְכָל גִּידֵיהֶם בְּתוֹךְ שְׁאָר חוֹלֵי יִשְׂרָאֵל, רְפוּאַת הַנֶּפֶשׁ וּרְפוּאַת הַגּוּף (בשבת: שַׁבָּת הִיא / ביום טוב: יוֹם טוֹב הוּא / מִלִּזְעֹק וּרְפוּאָה קְרוֹבָה לָבוֹא), הַשְׁתָּא בַּעֲגָלָא וּבִזְמַן קָרִיב, וְנֹאמַר אָמֵן.

healing of the body (*On Shabbat:* though on the Sabbath / *On Yom Tov:* though on Yom Tov / it is forbidden to cry out, may her healing be quick to come), now, swiftly and soon. And let us say, Amen.

FOR SICK MEN

מִי שֶׁבֵּרַךְ MAY HE Who blessed our fathers Abraham, Isaac, and Jacob, Moses and Aaron, David and Solomon, bless and heal the sick people (*names*) son of (*mother's names*), on whose behalf (*name of supplicant*) will make a charitable gift. As a reward for this, may the Holy One, blessed is He, show them the fullness of compassion by restoring their health, healing them, strengthening them, and granting them life. May He speedily send them a complete healing from heaven, to all their two hundred and forty-eight organs and three hundred and sixty-five sinews, among the other sick people of Israel, a healing of the spirit and a healing of the body (*On Shabbat:* though on the Sabbath / *On Yom Tov:* though on Yom Tov / it is forbidden to cry out, may their healing be quick to come), now, swiftly and soon. And let us say, Amen.

FOR SICK WOMEN

מִי שֶׁבֵּרַךְ MAY HE Who blessed our fathers Abraham, Isaac, and Jacob, Moses and Aaron, David and Solomon, our mothers Sarah, Rebecca, Rachel and Leah, bless and heal the sick people (*names*) son of (*mother's names*), on whose behalf (*name of supplicant*) will make a charitable gift. As a reward for this, may the Holy One, blessed is He, show them the fullness of compassion by restoring their health, healing them, strengthening them, and granting them life. May He speedily send them a complete healing from heaven, to all their organs and sinews, among the other sick people of Israel, a healing of the spirit and a healing of the body (*On Shabbat:* though on the Sabbath / *On Yom Tov:* though on Yom Tov / it is forbidden to cry out, may their healing be quick to come), now, swiftly and soon. And let us say, Amen.

FOR SICK MEN AND WOMEN

מִי שֶׁבֵּרַךְ MAY HE Who blessed our fathers Abraham, Isaac, and Jacob, Moses and Aaron, David and Solomon, our mothers Sarah, Rebecca, Rachel and Leah, bless and heal the sick people (*names*) son of (*mother's names*), on whose behalf (*name of supplicant*) will make a charitable gift. As a reward for this, may the Holy One, blessed is He, show them the fullness of compassion by restoring their health, healing them, strengthening them, and granting them life. May He speedily send them a complete healing from heaven, to all their organs and sinews, among the other sick people of Israel, a healing of the spirit and a healing of the body (*On Shabbat:* though on the Sabbath / *On Yom Tov:* though on Yom Tov / it is forbidden to cry out, may their healing be quick to come), now, swiftly and soon. And let us say, Amen.

ליולדת בן

If the ברית *has not yet been performed, the bracketed words are added:*

מִי שֶׁבֵּרַךְ אֲבוֹתֵינוּ אַבְרָהָם יִצְחָק וְיַעֲקֹב, מֹשֶׁה וְאַהֲרֹן דָּוִד וּשְׁלֹמֹה, אִמּוֹתֵינוּ שָׂרָה רִבְקָה רָחֵל וְלֵאָה הוּא יְבָרֵךְ אֶת הָאִשָּׁה הַיּוֹלֶדֶת (פלונית בַּת פלוני) וְאֶת בְּנָהּ שֶׁנּוֹלַד לָהּ לְמַזָּל טוֹב בַּעֲבוּר שֶׁבַּעְלָהּ וְאָבִיו יִתֵּן צְדָקָה בַּעֲדָם. וְיִזְכּוּ אָבִיו וְאִמּוֹ [לְהַכְנִיסוֹ בִּבְרִיתוֹ שֶׁל אַבְרָהָם אָבִינוּ בְּעִתּוֹ וּבִזְמַנּוֹ, וּ]לְגַדְּלוֹ לְתוֹרָה וּלְחֻפָּה וּלְמַעֲשִׂים טוֹבִים, וְנֹאמַר אָמֵן.

ליולדת בת (עם קריאת שם)

If the baby is being named, the bracketed words are added:

מִי שֶׁבֵּרַךְ אֲבוֹתֵינוּ אַבְרָהָם יִצְחָק וְיַעֲקֹב, מֹשֶׁה וְאַהֲרֹן דָּוִד וּשְׁלֹמֹה, אִמּוֹתֵינוּ שָׂרָה רִבְקָה רָחֵל וְלֵאָה הוּא יְבָרֵךְ אֶת הָאִשָּׁה הַיּוֹלֶדֶת (פלונית בַּת פלוני) וְאֶת בִּתָּהּ שֶׁנּוֹלְדָה לָהּ לְמַזָּל טוֹב, בַּעֲבוּר שֶׁבַּעְלָהּ וְאָבִיהָ יִתֵּן צְדָקָה בַּעֲדָן. [וְיִקָּרֵא שְׁמָהּ בְּיִשְׂרָאֵל (פלונית בַּת פלוני)] וְיִזְכּוּ אָבִיהָ וְאִמָּהּ לְגַדְּלָהּ לְתוֹרָה וּלְחֻפָּה וּלְמַעֲשִׂים טוֹבִים, וְנֹאמַר אָמֵן.

ליולדת בנים

If the ברית *has not yet been performed, the bracketed words are added:*

מִי שֶׁבֵּרַךְ אֲבוֹתֵינוּ אַבְרָהָם יִצְחָק וְיַעֲקֹב, מֹשֶׁה וְאַהֲרֹן דָּוִד וּשְׁלֹמֹה, אִמּוֹתֵינוּ שָׂרָה רִבְקָה רָחֵל וְלֵאָה הוּא יְבָרֵךְ אֶת הָאִשָּׁה הַיּוֹלֶדֶת (פלונית בַּת פלוני) וְאֶת בָּנֶיהָ הַנּוֹלָדִים לָהּ לְמַזָּל טוֹב בַּעֲבוּר שֶׁבַּעְלָהּ וַאֲבִיהֶם יִתֵּן צְדָקָה בַּעֲדָם. וְיִזְכּוּ אֲבִיהֶם וְאִמָּם [לְהַכְנִיסָם בִּבְרִיתוֹ שֶׁל אַבְרָהָם אָבִינוּ בְּעִתָּם וּבִזְמַנָּם, וּ]לְגַדְּלָם לְתוֹרָה וּלְחֻפָּה וּלְמַעֲשִׂים טוֹבִים, וְנֹאמַר אָמֵן.

ליולדת בנות (עם קריאת שמות)

If the babies are being named, the bracketed words are added:

מִי שֶׁבֵּרַךְ אֲבוֹתֵינוּ אַבְרָהָם יִצְחָק וְיַעֲקֹב, מֹשֶׁה וְאַהֲרֹן דָּוִד וּשְׁלֹמֹה, אִמּוֹתֵינוּ שָׂרָה רִבְקָה רָחֵל וְלֵאָה הוּא יְבָרֵךְ אֶת הָאִשָּׁה הַיּוֹלֶדֶת (פלונית בַּת פלוני) וְאֶת בְּנוֹתֶיהָ הַנּוֹלָדוֹת לָהּ לְמַזָּל טוֹב, בַּעֲבוּר שֶׁבַּעְלָהּ וַאֲבִיהֶן יִתֵּן צְדָקָה בַּעֲדָן. [וְיִקָּרֵא שְׁמָן בְּיִשְׂרָאֵל (*for first baby* – פלונית בַּת פלוני),

FOR A MOTHER AND NEWBORN SON

If the brit has not yet been performed, the bracketed words are added:

מִי שֶׁבֵּרַךְ MAY HE Who blessed our fathers Abraham, Isaac, and Jacob, Moses and Aaron, David and Solomon, our mothers Sarah, Rebecca, Rachel and Leah, bless the woman who has given birth (*new mother's name*) daughter of (*her father's name*) and her son who was born at an auspicious time, insofar as her husband and the infant's father will make a charitable gift on their behalf. As a reward for this, may they merit to [bring him into the covenant of Abraham our forefather at the proper time and] raise him to Torah, the marriage canopy, and good deeds. And let us say, Amen.

FOR A MOTHER AND NEWBORN DAUGHTER (AND NAMING THE BABY)

If the baby is being named, the bracketed words are added:

מִי שֶׁבֵּרַךְ MAY HE Who blessed our fathers Abraham, Isaac, and Jacob, Moses and Aaron, David and Solomon, our mothers Sarah, Rebecca, Rachel and Leah, bless the woman who has given birth (*new mother's name*) daughter of (*her father's name*) and her daughter who was born at an auspicious time [and who will be known among the Jewish people by the name (*baby's name*) daughter of (*baby's father's name*)], insofar as her husband and the infant's father will make a charitable gift on their behalf. As a reward for this, may they merit to raise her to Torah, the marriage canopy, and good deeds. And let us say, Amen.

FOR A MOTHER AND NEWBORN SONS (TWINS/MULTIPLES)

If the brit has not yet been performed, the bracketed words are added:

מִי שֶׁבֵּרַךְ MAY HE Who blessed our fathers Abraham, Isaac, and Jacob, Moses and Aaron, David and Solomon, our mothers Sarah, Rebecca, Rachel and Leah, bless the woman who has given birth (*new mother's name*) daughter of (*her father's name*) and her sons who were born at an auspicious time, insofar as her husband and their father will make a charitable gift on their behalf. As a reward for this, may they merit to [bring them into the covenant of Abraham our forefather in the proper time and] raise them to Torah, the marriage canopy, and good deeds. And let us say, Amen.

FOR A MOTHER AND NEWBORN DAUGHTERS (AND NAMING THEM)

If the babies are being named, the bracketed words are added:

מִי שֶׁבֵּרַךְ MAY HE Who blessed our fathers Abraham, Isaac, and Jacob, Moses and Aaron, David and Solomon, our mothers Sarah, Rebecca, Rachel and Leah, bless the woman who has given birth (*new mother's name*) daughter of (*her father's name*) and her daughters who were born at an auspicious time [and who will be known among the Jewish people by the names (*first baby's name*) daughter of (*baby's father's name*) and (*subsequent baby's name*) daughter of (*baby's father's*

וּ(פלונית בַּת פלוני – *for second baby*)] וְיִזְכּוּ אֲבִיהֶן וְאִמָּן לְגַדְּלָן לְתוֹרָה וּלְחֻפָּה וּלְמַעֲשִׂים טוֹבִים, וְנֹאמַר אָמֵן.

ליולדת תאומים זכר ונקבה (וקריאת שם)

If the daughter is being named, the first bracketed words are added.
If the ברית *has not yet been performed, the later bracketed words are added:*

מִי שֶׁבֵּרַךְ אֲבוֹתֵינוּ אַבְרָהָם יִצְחָק וְיַעֲקֹב, מֹשֶׁה וְאַהֲרֹן דָּוִד וּשְׁלֹמֹה, אִמּוֹתֵינוּ שָׂרָה רִבְקָה רָחֵל וְלֵאָה הוּא יְבָרֵךְ אֶת הָאִשָּׁה הַיּוֹלֶדֶת (פלונית בַּת פלוני) וְאֶת בְּנָהּ וְאֶת בִּתָּהּ הַנּוֹלָדִים לָהּ לְמַזָּל טוֹב, בַּעֲבוּר שֶׁבַּעְלָהּ וַאֲבִיהֶם יִתֵּן צְדָקָה בַּעֲדָן. [וְיִקָּרֵא שֵׁם הַבַּת בְּיִשְׂרָאֵל (פלונית בַּת פלוני)] וְיִזְכּוּ אֲבִיהֶם וְאִמָּם [לְהַכְנִיסוֹ בִּבְרִיתוֹ שֶׁל אַבְרָהָם אָבִינוּ בְּעִתּוֹ וּבִזְמַנּוֹ, וּ]לְגַדְּלָם לְתוֹרָה וּלְחֻפָּה וּלְמַעֲשִׂים טוֹבִים, וְנֹאמַר אָמֵן.

לבר מצווה

מִי שֶׁבֵּרַךְ אֲבוֹתֵינוּ אַבְרָהָם יִצְחָק וְיַעֲקֹב הוּא יְבָרֵךְ אֶת (פלוני בֶּן פלוני) שֶׁמָּלְאוּ לוֹ שְׁלֹשׁ עֶשְׂרֵה שָׁנָה וְהִגִּיעַ לְמִצְוֹת, וְעָלָה לַתּוֹרָה, לָתֵת שֶׁבַח וְהוֹדָיָה לְהַשֵּׁם יִתְבָּרַךְ עַל כָּל הַטּוֹבָה שֶׁגָּמַל אִתּוֹ. יִשְׁמְרֵהוּ הַקָּדוֹשׁ בָּרוּךְ הוּא וִיחַיֵּהוּ, וִיכוֹנֵן אֶת לִבּוֹ לִהְיוֹת שָׁלֵם עִם יהוה וְלָלֶכֶת בִּדְרָכָיו וְלִשְׁמֹר מִצְוֹתָיו כָּל הַיָּמִים, וְנֹאמַר אָמֵן.

לבת מצווה

מִי שֶׁבֵּרַךְ אֲבוֹתֵינוּ אַבְרָהָם יִצְחָק וְיַעֲקֹב, אִמּוֹתֵינוּ שָׂרָה רִבְקָה רָחֵל וְלֵאָה, הוּא יְבָרֵךְ אֶת (פלונית בַּת פלוני) שֶׁמָּלְאוּ לָהּ שְׁתֵּים עֶשְׂרֵה שָׁנָה וְהִגִּיעָה לְמִצְוֹת, וְנוֹתֶנֶת שֶׁבַח וְהוֹדָיָה לְהַשֵּׁם יִתְבָּרַךְ עַל כָּל הַטּוֹבָה שֶׁגָּמַל אִתָּהּ. יִשְׁמְרֶהָ הַקָּדוֹשׁ בָּרוּךְ הוּא וִיחַיֶּהָ, וִיכוֹנֵן אֶת לִבָּהּ לִהְיוֹת שָׁלֵם עִם יהוה וְלָלֶכֶת בִּדְרָכָיו וְלִשְׁמֹר מִצְוֹתָיו כָּל הַיָּמִים, וְנֹאמַר אָמֵן.

לחיילי צה״ל

The שליח ציבור*, or the* רב*, says the following prayer:*

מִי שֶׁבֵּרַךְ אֲבוֹתֵינוּ אַבְרָהָם יִצְחָק וְיַעֲקֹב הוּא יְבָרֵךְ אֶת חַיָּלֵי צְבָא הַהֲגַנָּה לְיִשְׂרָאֵל וְאַנְשֵׁי כֹּחוֹת הַבִּטָּחוֹן, הָעוֹמְדִים עַל מִשְׁמַר אַרְצֵנוּ וְעָרֵי אֱלֹהֵינוּ, מִגְּבוּל הַלְּבָנוֹן וְעַד מִדְבַּר מִצְרַיִם וּמִן הַיָּם הַגָּדוֹל עַד לְבוֹא

name)], insofar as her husband and their father will make a charitable gift on their behalf. As a reward for this, may they merit to raise them to Torah, the marriage canopy, and good deeds. And let us say, Amen.

FOR A MOTHER AND NEWBORN MALE AND FEMALE TWINS (AND NAMING HER)

If the daughter is being named, the first bracketed words are added.
If the brit has not yet been performed, the later bracketed words are added:

מִי שֶׁבֵּרַךְ MAY HE Who blessed our fathers Abraham, Isaac, and Jacob, Moses and Aaron, David and Solomon, our mothers Sarah, Rebecca, Rachel and Leah, bless the woman who has given birth (*new mother's name*) daughter of (*her father's name*) and her son and daughter who were born at an auspicious time, [the daughter to be known among the Jewish people by the name (*baby's name*) daughter of (*baby's father's name*)], insofar as her husband and their father will make a charitable gift on their behalf. As a reward for this, may they merit to [bring him into the covenant of Abraham our forefather in the proper time and] raise them to Torah, the marriage canopy, and good deeds. And let us say, Amen.

FOR A BAR MITZVA

מִי שֶׁבֵּרַךְ MAY HE Who blessed our fathers Abraham, Isaac, and Jacob, bless (*name of bar mitzva boy*) son of (*father's name*) who has reached the age of thirteen years, and become subject to the commandments, and been called to the Torah to give praise and thanks to the Holy One, blessed is He, for all the goodness He has bestowed upon him. May the Holy One, blessed is He, watch over him and grant him life, preparing his heart to be whole with the Lord, to walk in His ways, and to keep His commandments all his days. And let us say, Amen.

FOR A BAT MITZVA

מִי שֶׁבֵּרַךְ MAY HE Who blessed our fathers Abraham, Isaac, and Jacob, and our mothers Sarah, Rebecca, Rachel, and Leah, bless (*name of bat mitzva girl*) daughter of (*father's name*) who has reached the age of twelve years, and become subject to the commandments, and who gives praise and thanks to the Holy One, blessed is He, for all the goodness He has bestowed upon her. May the Holy One, blessed is He, watch over her and grant her life, preparing her heart to be whole with the Lord, to walk in His ways, and to keep His commandments all her days. And let us say, Amen.

FOR THE ISRAEL DEFENSE FORCES

The Leader, or the rabbi, says the following prayer:

מִי שֶׁבֵּרַךְ MAY HE Who blessed our fathers, Abraham, Isaac and Jacob, bless those who serve in Israel's Defense Forces and its security services who stand guard over our land and the cities of our God from the Lebanese border to the Egyptian desert, from the Mediterranean Sea to the approach of the Aravah, and

הָעֲרָבָה וּבְכָל מָקוֹם שֶׁהֵם, בַּיַּבָּשָׁה, בָּאֲוִיר וּבַיָּם. יִתֵּן יהוה אֶת אוֹיְבֵינוּ הַקָּמִים
עָלֵינוּ נִגָּפִים לִפְנֵיהֶם. הַקָּדוֹשׁ בָּרוּךְ הוּא יִשְׁמֹר וְיַצִּיל אֶת חַיָּלֵינוּ מִכָּל צָרָה
וְצוּקָה וּמִכָּל נֶגַע וּמַחֲלָה, וְיִשְׁלַח בְּרָכָה וְהַצְלָחָה בְּכָל מַעֲשֵׂי יְדֵיהֶם. יַדְבֵּר
שׂוֹנְאֵינוּ תַּחְתֵּיהֶם וִיעַטְּרֵם בְּכֶתֶר יְשׁוּעָה וּבַעֲטֶרֶת נִצָּחוֹן. וִיקֻיַּם בָּהֶם הַכָּתוּב:
כִּי יהוה אֱלֹהֵיכֶם הַהֹלֵךְ עִמָּכֶם לְהִלָּחֵם לָכֶם עִם־אֹיְבֵיכֶם לְהוֹשִׁיעַ אֶתְכֶם: דברים כ
וְנֹאמַר אָמֵן.

לשבויים

If Israeli soldiers or civilians are being held in captivity, the שליח ציבור *says the following:*

מִי שֶׁבֵּרַךְ אֲבוֹתֵינוּ אַבְרָהָם יִצְחָק וְיַעֲקֹב, יוֹסֵף מֹשֶׁה וְאַהֲרֹן, דָּוִד וּשְׁלֹמֹה,
הוּא יְבָרֵךְ וְיִשְׁמֹר וְיִנְצֹר אֶת נֶעְדְּרֵי צְבָא הַהֲגָנָה לְיִשְׂרָאֵל וּשְׁבוּיָו,
וְאֶת כָּל אַחֵינוּ הַנְּתוּנִים בְּצָרָה וּבְשִׁבְיָה, בַּעֲבוּר שֶׁכָּל הַקָּהָל הַקָּדוֹשׁ הַזֶּה
יִתְּנוּ צְדָקָה בַּעֲבוּרָם. הַקָּדוֹשׁ בָּרוּךְ הוּא יִמָּלֵא רַחֲמִים עֲלֵיהֶם, וְיוֹצִיאֵם
מֵחֹשֶׁךְ וְצַלְמָוֶת, וּמוֹסְרוֹתֵיהֶם יְנַתֵּק, וּמִמְּצוּקוֹתֵיהֶם יוֹשִׁיעֵם, וִישִׁיבֵם מְהֵרָה
לְחֵיק מִשְׁפְּחוֹתֵיהֶם. וִיקֻיַּם בָּהֶם מִקְרָא שֶׁכָּתוּב: וּפְדוּיֵי יהוה יְשֻׁבוּן, וּבָאוּ ישעיה לה
צִיּוֹן בְּרִנָּה, וְשִׂמְחַת עוֹלָם עַל־רֹאשָׁם, שָׂשׂוֹן וְשִׂמְחָה יַשִּׂיגוּ, וְנָסוּ יָגוֹן וַאֲנָחָה:
וְנֹאמַר אָמֵן.

ברכת הגומל

One who has been delivered from danger recites this blessing.

בָּרוּךְ אַתָּה יהוה אֱלֹהֵינוּ מֶלֶךְ הָעוֹלָם הַגּוֹמֵל לְחַיָּבִים טוֹבוֹת, שֶׁגְּמָלַנִי
כָּל טוֹב.

If a man recites the ברכה*, the* קהל *responds:*

אָמֵן. מִי שֶׁגְּמָלְךָ כָּל טוֹב הוּא יִגְמָלְךָ כָּל טוֹב, סֶלָה.

If a woman recites the ברכה*, the* קהל *responds:*

אָמֵן. מִי שֶׁגְּמָלֵךְ כָּל טוֹב הוּא יִגְמְלֵךְ כָּל טוֹב, סֶלָה.

בִּרְכַּת הַגּוֹמֵל / THANKSGIVING BLESSING

For further commentary see pages 163–164. In Temple times one brought a thanksgiving offering after surviving a life-threatening peril. In the absence of the Temple this *berakha* is recited during the Torah reading, within three days of the event. Such dangers (based on Psalm 107) include hazardous land or sea journeys, serious illness, or incarceration. In practice we recite the *berakha* in the aftermath of any life-threatening experience (*Oraḥ Ḥayyim* 219:9).

The *berakha* must be recited in the presence of a *minyan*, even though it is not a דָּבָר שֶׁבִּקְדֻשָּׁה (possessing special sanctity like the *Barekhu*, *Kaddish*, or *Kedusha* prayers that

wherever else they are, on land, in the air and at sea. May the Lord cause our enemies who rise against us to be struck down before them. May the Holy One, blessed is He, protect and deliver our servicemen from all trouble and distress, injury and illness, and bring blessing and success upon all that they do. May those who hate us be vanquished before them, and may He crown them with deliverance and the laurels of victory. Through them may there be the fulfillment
Deut. 20 of the verse: "It is the Lord your God Who goes with you to fight for you against your enemies, to deliver you." And let us say, Amen.

FOR THOSE BEING HELD IN CAPTIVITY

If Israeli soldiers or civilians are being held in captivity, the Leader says the following:

מִי שֶׁבֵּרַךְ MAY HE Who blessed our fathers, Abraham, Isaac and Jacob, Joseph, Moses and Aaron, David and Solomon, bless, protect and guard the members of Israel's Defense Forces missing in action or held captive, and any others among our brethren, who are in distress or captivity, insofar as all the members of this holy congregation will make a charitable gift on their behalf. May the Holy One, blessed is He, have compassion on them and bring them out from darkness and the shadow of death; may He break their bonds, deliver them from their distress, and bring them swiftly back to their families' embrace. Through them
Is. 35 may there be the fulfillment of the verse: "Those redeemed by the Lord will return; they will enter Zion with singing, and everlasting joy will crown their heads. Gladness and joy will overtake them, and sorrow and sighing will flee away." And let us say, Amen.

BLESSING OF GRATITUDE

One who has been delivered from danger recites this blessing.

בָּרוּךְ BLESSED are You, Lord, our God, King of the universe, Who bestows favors on the undeserving, and Who has bestowed every good thing on me.

The congregation responds:

Amen. May He Who has bestowed every good thing on you continue to grant you every good thing, forever.

---

require a *minyan*). This can be understood in light of the *Netziv*'s explanation (see the commentary on *Hallel*, page 766) of the Torah's requirement that the thanksgiving sacrifice be accompanied by a public meal at which one's salvation by God is recounted at length, so that the others present can experience a heightened awareness of God's providence. The same would be true of the public recital of this *berakha*, and its unusual response, reflecting how that sacrifice and meal of thanksgiving were carried out (R. Basil Herring).

לְחַיָּבִים – *On the undeserving*. With this word the beneficiary declares that God bestows much goodness even on those, like himself, who are undeserving of it (*Mishna Berura*).

ברוך שפטרני

After a בר מצווה *has concluded the* תורה *blessings, his father says aloud:*

בָּרוּךְ (*Some say*: אַתָּה יהוה אֱלֹהֵינוּ מֶלֶךְ הָעוֹלָם) שֶׁפְּטָרַנִי מֵעָנְשׁוֹ שֶׁלָּזֶה.

חצי קדיש

קורא: **יִתְגַּדַּל** וְיִתְקַדַּשׁ שְׁמֵהּ רַבָּא (קהל: אָמֵן), בְּעָלְמָא דִּי בְרָא כִרְעוּתֵהּ.
וְיַמְלִיךְ מַלְכוּתֵהּ, בְּחַיֵּיכוֹן וּבְיוֹמֵיכוֹן וּבְחַיֵּי דְכָל בֵּית
יִשְׂרָאֵל, בַּעֲגָלָא וּבִזְמַן קָרִיב, וְאִמְרוּ אָמֵן. (קהל: אָמֵן)

קהל וקורא: יְהֵא שְׁמֵהּ רַבָּא מְבָרַךְ לְעָלַם וּלְעָלְמֵי עָלְמַיָּא.

קורא: יִתְבָּרַךְ וְיִשְׁתַּבַּח וְיִתְפָּאַר, וְיִתְרוֹמַם וְיִתְנַשֵּׂא וְיִתְהַדָּר וְיִתְעַלֶּה
וְיִתְהַלָּל שְׁמֵהּ דְּקֻדְשָׁא בְּרִיךְ הוּא (קהל: בְּרִיךְ הוּא), לְעֵלָּא מִן כָּל
בִּרְכָתָא / בשבת שובה: לְעֵלָּא (וּ)לְעֵלָּא מִכָּל בִּרְכָתָא/ וְשִׁירָתָא, תֻּשְׁבְּחָתָא
וְנֶחֱמָתָא דַּאֲמִירָן בְּעָלְמָא, וְאִמְרוּ אָמֵן. (קהל: אָמֵן)

הגבהה וגלילה

מִי שֶׁבֵּרַךְ אֲבוֹתֵינוּ אַבְרָהָם יִצְחָק וְיַעֲקֹב, הוּא יְבָרֵךְ אֶת (המגביה: פלוני
בֶּן פלוני), בַּעֲבוּר שֶׁעָלָה לְהַגְבָּהַת הַתּוֹרָה, וְאֶת (הגולל: פלוני
בֶּן פלוני), בַּעֲבוּר שֶׁעָלָה לִגְלִילַת הַתּוֹרָה. בִּשְׂכַר זֶה הַקָּדוֹשׁ בָּרוּךְ הוּא
יִשְׁמְרֵם וְיַצִּילֵם מִכָּל צָרָה וְצוּקָה וּמִכָּל נֶגַע וּמַחֲלָה, וְיִשְׁלַח בְּרָכָה
וְהַצְלָחָה בְּכָל מַעֲשֵׂה יְדֵיהֶם (ביום טוב: וְיִזְכּוּ לַעֲלוֹת לְרֶגֶל) עִם כָּל יִשְׂרָאֵל
אֲחֵיהֶם, וְנֹאמַר אָמֵן.

The ספר תורה *is lifted and the* קהל *says:*

דברים ד **וְזֹאת הַתּוֹרָה** אֲשֶׁר־שָׂם מֹשֶׁה לִפְנֵי בְּנֵי יִשְׂרָאֵל: עַל־פִּי יהוה
בְּיַד מֹשֶׁה:

בָּרוּךְ שֶׁפְּטָרַנִי / BAR MITZVA BLESSING
When a *bar mitzva* boy completes the *berakha* following his *aliya*, his father recites this *berakha*. Although in most congregations the *berakha* is said in abbreviated form by omitting God's name, others follow the view (attributed to the Vilna Gaon) that it should not be abbreviated. Some (such as R. Ovadia Yosef in Responsa *Yabia Omer* 6:29) are of the opinion that when God's name is omitted, the *berakha* (with an appropriate grammatical change – בָּרוּךְ שֶׁפְּטָרַנִי מֵעָנְשָׁהּ שֶׁל זוֹ) can also be recited for a girl upon her *bat mitzva* (R. Hershel Billet).

While it is certainly true that once young-

BAR MITZVA BLESSING

After a bar mitzva has concluded the Torah blessings, his father recites:

בָּרוּךְ BLESSED be (*Some say:* You, Lord, our God, King of the universe,) He Who has released me from further responsibility for this youth.

HALF KADDISH

Reader: יִתְגַּדַּל EXALTED AND HALLOWED may God's great name be, in the world He created as He willed. May He reign in your lifetimes and in your days, and in the lifetime of the whole house of Israel, speedily and soon, and say, Amen.

All: May His great name be blessed forever and all time.

Reader: Blessed and praised, honored, extolled, glorified, adored and exalted above all be the name of the Holy One, blessed is He, (*Between Rosh Hashana & Yom Kippur:* above and) beyond any blessing, hymn, praise, or expressions of consolation that may be uttered in this world, and say, Amen.

HAGBAHA AND GELILA

מִי שֶׁבֵּרַךְ MAY HE Who blessed our fathers Abraham, Isaac, and Jacob bless also (*honoree for Hagbaha's name*) son of (*father's name*), who will raise the Torah and (*honoree for Gelila's name*) son of (*father's name*), who will roll up the Torah. As a reward for this, may the Holy One, blessed is He, protect them and spare them from all trouble and sorrow, and from every wound or illness. May He send blessing and bestow success on all that they do (*On Yom Tov:* and grant them the privilege to ascend to Jerusalem for the festivals), together with all Israel their brethren, and let us say, Amen.

The Torah scroll is lifted and the congregations says:

Deut. 4 וְזֹאת הַתּוֹרָה THIS IS THE Torah that Moses set before the children of Israel. It was according to the Lord's command, at the hand of Moses.

---

sters become *bar* or *bat mitzva* parents have no formal obligation to further educate them, and thus they are no longer technically liable for their transgressions, there is still a parental obligation to discipline one's children for any improper behavior. As the Gemara (*Shabbat* 54b) states, "One who can prevent the members of his household from committing transgression but fails to do so will be punished for that transgression" (*Mishna Berura*).

וְזֹאת הַתּוֹרָה – *This is the Torah.* The custom of הַגְבָּהָה (raising the Torah for all to see)

Some add

משלי ג עֵץ־חַיִּים הִיא לַמַּחֲזִיקִים בָּהּ וְתֹמְכֶיהָ מְאֻשָּׁר: דְּרָכֶיהָ דַרְכֵי־נֹעַם וְכָל־
ישעיה מב נְתִיבֹתֶיהָ שָׁלוֹם: אֹרֶךְ יָמִים בִּימִינָהּ, בִּשְׂמֹאולָהּ עֹשֶׁר וְכָבוֹד: יהוה חָפֵץ
לְמַעַן צִדְקוֹ יַגְדִּיל תּוֹרָה וְיַאְדִּיר:

The ספר תורה *is bound and covered.*

ברכות ההפטרה

Before reading the הפטרה*, the person called up for* מפטיר *says:*

בָּרוּךְ אַתָּה יהוה אֱלֹהֵינוּ מֶלֶךְ הָעוֹלָם אֲשֶׁר בָּחַר בִּנְבִיאִים טוֹבִים, וְרָצָה בְדִבְרֵיהֶם הַנֶּאֱמָרִים בֶּאֱמֶת. בָּרוּךְ אַתָּה יהוה, הַבּוֹחֵר בַּתּוֹרָה וּבְמֹשֶׁה עַבְדּוֹ וּבְיִשְׂרָאֵל עַמּוֹ וּבִנְבִיאֵי הָאֱמֶת וָצֶדֶק.

The הפטרה *is read.*

After the הפטרה*, the person called up for* מפטיר *says the following blessings:*

בָּרוּךְ אַתָּה יהוה אֱלֹהֵינוּ מֶלֶךְ הָעוֹלָם, צוּר כָּל הָעוֹלָמִים, צַדִּיק בְּכָל הַדּוֹרוֹת, הָאֵל הַנֶּאֱמָן, הָאוֹמֵר וְעוֹשֶׂה, הַמְדַבֵּר וּמְקַיֵּם, שֶׁכָּל דְּבָרָיו אֱמֶת וָצֶדֶק. נֶאֱמָן אַתָּה הוּא יהוה אֱלֹהֵינוּ וְנֶאֱמָנִים

---

originated with Ezra, part of his efforts (see Neh. 8:5) to bring Torah to the people. Many recite וְזֹאת הַתּוֹרָה ("This is the Torah") with the understanding that it is all one verse, whereas it actually consists of two sections: one full verse, i.e., Deuteronomy 4:44, plus עַל־פִּי ה׳ בְּיַד מֹשֶׁה (By the word of the Lord, through the hand of Moses), which is a phrase from Numbers 9:23. One can ask why that last phrase, which deals with the travels of the Israelites in the wilderness at God's command, and not at all with the raised Torah per se, was added. One answer might be that there is a concern that if we only recite the first verse some present might erroneously think that the visible Torah scroll is what Moses gave to Israel, without being mindful of the Oral Law that Moses also received from God and taught to Israel. To avoid this, we add עַל־פִּי ה׳ בְּיַד מֹשֶׁה, a phrase that alludes to the Oral Law, which equally came from God, albeit not in writing but verbally, to be transmitted "through the hand of Moses" to Israel (R. Basil Herring).

The addition of עַל־פִּי ה׳ בְּיַד מֹשֶׁה may be intended to counter the Christian perception that Moses, though divinely inspired, should be seen as a lawgiver, and that his Torah could consequently be superseded by that of a later, superior lawgiver. We consequently proclaim that the true Giver of the Torah is God, and Moses was the instrument of His revelation. This suggestion could help explain why this addition is found only among Jews who lived in Christian countries (Prof. Elazar Touitou).

הַהַפְטָרָה / THE HAFTARA

Rabbeinu Tam is of the view that the *Haftara*

Some add:

Prov. 3 It is a tree of life for those who grasp it, and they who uphold it are made happy. Its ways are ways of pleasantness, and all its paths are peace. Length
Is. 42 of days is in its right hand, and wealth and honor in its left hand. The Lord was pleased, for the sake of [Israel's] righteousness, to magnify the Torah and glorify it.

The Torah scroll is bound and covered.

BLESSINGS OF THE HAFTARA

Before reading the Haftara, the person called up for Maftir says:

בָּרוּךְ BLESSED ARE YOU, Lord, our God, King of the universe, Who chose good prophets and was pleased with their words that spoke the truth. Blessed are You, Lord, Who has chosen the Torah, as well as His servant Moses, His people Israel, and the prophets of truth and righteousness.

The Haftara is read.
After the Haftara, the person called up for Maftir says the following blessings:

בָּרוּךְ BLESSED ARE YOU, Lord, our God, King of the universe, Rock of ages, righteous in every generation. God Who keeps faith, Who speaks and it is done, Who fulfills what He promises, for whatever He says is true and correct. You are faithful, Lord our God, and

---

was an enactment of Ezra. *Sefer HaPardes* traces its origin to an era in which Bible, Mishna and Talmud were studied every day in the synagogue, with the *Haftara* selections representing their scriptural study.

The recital of the *Haftara*, like the Torah reading itself, is intended as a re-enactment of prophetic revelation, not just that which occurred at Sinai, but in all its subsequent forms, i.e., in נְבִיאִים (the Prophets) and כְּתוּבִים (the so-called "Writings"). For this reason too, as stated in *Tosafot* (*Shabbat* 24a), in Talmudic times a *Haftara* from the Writings was read at Shabbat *Minḥa* services (R. Joseph B. Soloveitchik).

Another explanation of the *Haftara* is that it originated in the time of Antiochus when it was forbidden to read the Torah in public, and the sages substituted a thematically appropriate prophetic reading at a later point of the service. In this view, Haftarot for the most part consist of at least twenty-one verses that correspond to the missing seven *aliyot*, each containing at least three verses. These are preceded and followed by a total of seven *berakhot* corresponding to the omitted blessings of seven *aliyot*. After the decree was lifted, the established custom remained in place (Abudarham).

בְּרָכָה לִפְנֵי הַהַפְטָרָה / BLESSING BEFORE THE HAFTARA

וְרָצָה בְדִבְרֵיהֶם – *Was pleased with their words.* Unlike the Torah which consists of words dictated verbatim by God, the books of the

דְּבָרֶיךָ, וְדָבָר אֶחָד מִדְּבָרֶיךָ אָחוֹר, לֹא יָשׁוּב רֵיקָם, כִּי אֵל מֶלֶךְ נֶאֱמָן (וְרַחֲמָן) אָתָּה. בָּרוּךְ אַתָּה יהוה, הָאֵל הַנֶּאֱמָן בְּכָל דְּבָרָיו.

רַחֵם עַל צִיּוֹן כִּי הִיא בֵּית חַיֵּינוּ, וְלַעֲלוּבַת נֶפֶשׁ תּוֹשִׁיעַ בִּמְהֵרָה בְיָמֵינוּ. בָּרוּךְ אַתָּה יהוה, מְשַׂמֵּחַ צִיּוֹן בְּבָנֶיהָ.

שַׂמְּחֵנוּ יהוה אֱלֹהֵינוּ בְּאֵלִיָּהוּ הַנָּבִיא עַבְדֶּךָ, וּבְמַלְכוּת בֵּית דָּוִד מְשִׁיחֶךָ, בִּמְהֵרָה יָבוֹא וְיָגֵל לִבֵּנוּ. עַל כִּסְאוֹ לֹא יֵשֶׁב זָר, וְלֹא יִנְחֲלוּ עוֹד אֲחֵרִים אֶת כְּבוֹדוֹ, כִּי בְשֵׁם קָדְשְׁךָ נִשְׁבַּעְתָּ לּוֹ שֶׁלֹּא יִכְבֶּה נֵרוֹ לְעוֹלָם וָעֶד. בָּרוּךְ אַתָּה יהוה, מָגֵן דָּוִד.

On שבת*, including* שבת חול המועד פסח*, say:*

עַל הַתּוֹרָה וְעַל הָעֲבוֹדָה וְעַל הַנְּבִיאִים וְעַל יוֹם הַשַּׁבָּת הַזֶּה, שֶׁנָּתַתָּ לָּנוּ יהוה אֱלֹהֵינוּ לִקְדֻשָּׁה וְלִמְנוּחָה, לְכָבוֹד וּלְתִפְאָרֶת. עַל הַכֹּל יהוה אֱלֹהֵינוּ אֲנַחְנוּ מוֹדִים לָךְ וּמְבָרְכִים אוֹתָךְ, יִתְבָּרַךְ שִׁמְךָ בְּפִי כָּל חַי תָּמִיד לְעוֹלָם וָעֶד. בָּרוּךְ אַתָּה יהוה, מְקַדֵּשׁ הַשַּׁבָּת.

On יום טוב *and on* שבת חול המועד סוכות*, say (adding on* שבת *the words in parentheses):*

עַל הַתּוֹרָה וְעַל הָעֲבוֹדָה וְעַל הַנְּבִיאִים (וְעַל יוֹם הַשַּׁבָּת הַזֶּה), וְעַל יוֹם

בפסח: חַג הַמַּצּוֹת הַזֶּה / בשבועות: חַג הַשָּׁבוּעוֹת הַזֶּה

בסוכות: חַג הַסֻּכּוֹת הַזֶּה / בשמיני עצרת ובש"ת: הַשְּׁמִינִי חַג הָעֲצֶרֶת הַזֶּה

שֶׁנָּתַתָּ לָּנוּ, יהוה אֱלֹהֵינוּ (לִקְדֻשָּׁה וְלִמְנוּחָה) לְשָׂשׂוֹן וּלְשִׂמְחָה, לְכָבוֹד וּלְתִפְאָרֶת. עַל הַכֹּל יהוה אֱלֹהֵינוּ אֲנַחְנוּ מוֹדִים לָךְ וּמְבָרְכִים אוֹתָךְ. יִתְבָּרַךְ שִׁמְךָ בְּפִי כָּל חַי תָּמִיד לְעוֹלָם וָעֶד. בָּרוּךְ אַתָּה יהוה, מְקַדֵּשׁ (הַשַּׁבָּת וְ) יִשְׂרָאֵל וְהַזְּמַנִּים.

Prophets used words chosen by the prophets themselves. This phrase conveys that these words of the prophets were favorably received by God.

faithful are Your promises; not one of Your words of the past will remain unfulfilled, for You are the God Who is a faithful (and merciful) King. Blessed are You, Lord, Who is the God Who fulfills all that He promises.

רַחֵם HAVE COMPASSION on Zion, for it is the home of our [national] existence; and to the afflicted of spirit grant salvation speedily, in our days. Blessed are You, Lord, Who makes Zion rejoice in her children.

שַׂמְּחֵנוּ GRANT US JOY, Lord our God, through Elijah the prophet, Your servant, and through the sovereignty of the house of David Your anointed – may he come soon and gladden our hearts. May no stranger sit on his throne; let others no longer appropriate his glory, for by Your holy name You swore to David that his light would never be extinguished. Blessed are You, Lord, Shield of David.

On Shabbat, including Shabbat Ḥol HaMo'ed Pesaḥ, say:

עַל הַתּוֹרָה FOR THE TORAH, for divine worship, for the prophets, and for this Sabbath day that You have given us, Lord our God, for sanctity and rest, glory and beauty – for all these, Lord our God, we thank You and bless You. May Your name be blessed in the mouths of every living being, continually, forever and ever. Blessed are You, Lord, Who sanctifies the Sabbath.

On Yom Tov and on Shabbat Ḥol HaMo'ed Sukkot, say (adding on Shabbat the words in parentheses):

עַל הַתּוֹרָה FOR THE TORAH, for divine worship, for the prophets, (for this Sabbath day) and for this day of

On Pesaḥ: the Festival of Matzot

On Shavuot: the Festival of Shavuot

On Sukkot: the Festival of Sukkot

On Shemini Atzeret & Simḥat Torah: the eighth day, this Festival of Atzeret

that You have given us, Lord our God, for [sanctity and rest,] joy and happiness, glory and beauty– for all these, Lord our God, we thank You and bless You. May Your name be blessed in the mouths of every living being, continually, forever and ever. Blessed are You, Lord, Who sanctifies (the Sabbath,) Israel and the festive seasons.

The following three paragraphs are recited on שבת*, or on a* יום טוב *that falls on* שבת*, and only with a* מנין*.*

יְקוּם פֻּרְקָן מִן שְׁמַיָּא, חִנָּא וְחִסְדָּא וְרַחֲמֵי וְחַיֵּי אֲרִיכֵי וּמְזוֹנֵי רְוִיחֵי, וְסִיַּעְתָּא דִשְׁמַיָּא, וּבַרְיוּת גּוּפָא וּנְהוֹרָא מְעַלְּיָא, זַרְעָא חַיָּא וְקַיָּמָא, זַרְעָא דִּי לָא יִפְסֻק וְדִי לָא יִבְטֻל מִפִּתְגָּמֵי אוֹרַיְתָא, לְמָרָנָן וְרַבָּנָן חֲבוּרָתָא קַדִּישָׁתָא דִּי בְאַרְעָא דְיִשְׂרָאֵל וְדִי בְּבָבֶל, לְרֵישֵׁי כַלָּה, וּלְרֵישֵׁי גַלְוָתָא, וּלְרֵישֵׁי מְתִיבָתָא, וּלְדַיָּנֵי דְבָבָא, לְכָל תַּלְמִידֵיהוֹן, וּלְכָל תַּלְמִידֵי תַלְמִידֵיהוֹן, וּלְכָל מָאן דְּעָסְקִין בְּאוֹרַיְתָא. מַלְכָּא דְעָלְמָא יְבָרֵךְ יָתְהוֹן, יַפֵּשׁ חַיֵּיהוֹן וְיַסְגֵּא יוֹמֵיהוֹן, וְיִתֵּן אַרְכָא לִשְׁנֵיהוֹן, וְיִתְפָּרְקוּן וְיִשְׁתֵּיזְבוּן מִן כָּל עָקָא וּמִן כָּל מַרְעִין בִּישִׁין. מָרַן דִּי בִשְׁמַיָּא יְהֵא בְסַעְדְּהוֹן כָּל זְמַן וְעִדָּן, וְנֹאמַר אָמֵן.

יְקוּם פֻּרְקָן מִן שְׁמַיָּא, חִנָּא וְחִסְדָּא וְרַחֲמֵי וְחַיֵּי אֲרִיכֵי וּמְזוֹנֵי רְוִיחֵי, וְסִיַּעְתָּא דִשְׁמַיָּא, וּבַרְיוּת גּוּפָא וּנְהוֹרָא מְעַלְּיָא, זַרְעָא חַיָּא וְקַיָּמָא, זַרְעָא דִּי לָא יִפְסֻק וְדִי לָא יִבְטֻל מִפִּתְגָּמֵי אוֹרַיְתָא, לְכָל קְהָלָא קַדִּישָׁא הָדֵין, רַבְרְבַיָּא עִם זְעֵרַיָּא,

---

יְקוּם פֻּרְקָן – *May deliverance arise. Yekum Purkan* was instituted in the face of those, like the medieval Karaites, who in Babylonia and elsewhere denied the authority of the Oral Law. It is recited following the reading of the Written Torah in order to publically affirm the authenticity and authoritative nature of the Oral Law passed down through the generations, first by the sages of the Talmud, and then by the leading rabbinic authorities in each generation who were responsible for its further transmission and development. It asks God to bless them, their families, and their students, in light of all that they do for the Jewish people. For the same reason the sages inserted a parallel prayer for the well-being of the חַכְמֵי יִשְׂרָאֵל (sages of Israel) immediately following the Monday and Thursday Torah readings (R. Shlomo Zalman Auerbach).

The pair of *Yekum Purkan* prayers first appears in parallel in the twelfth-century *Maḥzor Vitri* (France) and *Ḥibbur Berakhot* (Italy). It developed from a pair of Babylonian blessings delivered after the *Pirka*, a *shiur* given after קְרִיאַת הַתּוֹרָה with its traditional translation (*Targum*), in which the congregation would bless the Yeshiva heads (known as Geonim in the two most prominent Babylonian Yeshivot) and the Exilarch, whereupon the Geonim would in turn bless the congregation and local leaders (Prof. Neil Danzig).

The following three paragraphs are recited on Shabbat, or on a Yom Tov that falls on Shabbat, and only with a minyan.

יְקוּם פֻּרְקָן MAY DELIVERANCE arise from heaven, to bring grace, loving-kindness, compassion, length of days, abundant sustenance, divine support, bodily health and superior vision, living and thriving children, children who will neither neglect nor desist from study of the Torah. As for our teachers and rabbis of the holy communities in the land of Israel and (as formerly) in Babylon; as well as the heads of the rabbinic academies, the leaders of the exile, the heads of the Talmudic academies, and the judges at the gates, all their disciples, and their disciples' disciples, and everyone who engages in learning Torah – may the King of the universe bless them all, prolonging their lives, increasing their days and lengthening their years. May they be spared all trouble and saved from every evil happening. May our Master in heaven be their help on every occasion at all times, and let us say, Amen.

יְקוּם פֻּרְקָן MAY DELIVERANCE arise from heaven, to bring grace, loving-kindness, compassion, length of days, abundant sustenance, divine support, bodily health and spiritual enlightenment, living and thriving children, children who will neither interrupt nor cease from the words of the Torah – to this entire holy congregation, great

---

From the first known appearance of our version of these prayers, some of these institutions were already defunct. However, invoking these leaders along with the heads of the community in the land of Israel was a way of showing respect to the traditional centers of Torah learning and political Jewish leadership, and the terms could be understood to represent the various new communal organizations and leaders (Prof. Shai Secunda).

וּלְרֵישֵׁי גַלְוָתָא – *The leaders of the exile.* These prayers, publically recited week after week, reflect the allegiance of local communities and their rabbis to the central rabbinic authorities of their time under whom they studied or to whom they turned for rulings in Jewish law, many of which are recorded in the Responsa literature. Despite enjoying wide autonomy, the practice of local community rabbis has been to coordinate with, and sometimes even subordinate their own authority to, leading halakhic authorities of their age, especially on sensitive or difficult issues confronting them. This approach has been a central feature of halakhic communal life over the generations.

טַפְלָא וּנְשַׁיָּא. מַלְכָּא דְעָלְמָא יְבָרֵךְ יָתְכוֹן, יַפֵּשׁ חַיֵּיכוֹן וְיַסְגֵּא יוֹמֵיכוֹן, וְיִתֵּן אַרְכָא לִשְׁנֵיכוֹן, וְתִתְפָּרְקוּן וְתִשְׁתֵּיזְבוּן מִן כָּל עָקָא וּמִן כָּל מַרְעִין בִּישִׁין. מָרַן דִּי בִשְׁמַיָּא יְהֵא בְסַעְדְּכוֹן כָּל זְמַן וְעִדָּן, וְנֹאמַר אָמֵן.

מִי שֶׁבֵּרַךְ אֲבוֹתֵינוּ אַבְרָהָם יִצְחָק וְיַעֲקֹב, הוּא יְבָרֵךְ אֶת כָּל הַקָּהָל הַקָּדוֹשׁ הַזֶּה עִם כָּל קְהִלּוֹת הַקֹּדֶשׁ, הֵם וּנְשֵׁיהֶם וּבְנֵיהֶם וּבְנוֹתֵיהֶם וְכָל אֲשֶׁר לָהֶם, וּמִי שֶׁמְּיַחֲדִים בָּתֵּי כְנֵסִיּוֹת לִתְפִלָּה, וּמִי שֶׁבָּאִים בְּתוֹכָם לְהִתְפַּלֵּל, וּמִי שֶׁנּוֹתְנִים נֵר לַמָּאוֹר וְיַיִן לְקִדּוּשׁ וּלְהַבְדָּלָה וּפַת לָאוֹרְחִים וּצְדָקָה לָעֲנִיִּים, וְכָל מִי שֶׁעוֹסְקִים בְּצָרְכֵי צִבּוּר בֶּאֱמוּנָה. הַקָּדוֹשׁ בָּרוּךְ הוּא יְשַׁלֵּם שְׂכָרָם, וְיָסִיר מֵהֶם כָּל מַחֲלָה, וְיִרְפָּא לְכָל גּוּפָם, וְיִסְלַח לְכָל עֲוֹנָם, וְיִשְׁלַח בְּרָכָה וְהַצְלָחָה בְּכָל מַעֲשֵׂי יְדֵיהֶם עִם כָּל יִשְׂרָאֵל אֲחֵיהֶם, וְנֹאמַר אָמֵן.

Some congregations recite the following prayer for those who refrain from talking throughout the prayer service.

מִי שֶׁבֵּרַךְ אֲבוֹתֵינוּ אַבְרָהָם יִצְחָק וְיַעֲקֹב, מֹשֶׁה וְאַהֲרֹן, דָּוִד וּשְׁלֹמֹה, הוּא יְבָרֵךְ אֶת הַשּׁוֹמֵר פִּיו וּלְשׁוֹנוֹ מִלְּהַפְסִיק בְּשׁוּם דִּבּוּר מִן 'בָּרוּךְ שֶׁאָמַר' עַד גְּמַר הַתְּפִלָּה וּבִשְׁעַת קְרִיאַת סֵפֶר הַתּוֹרָה שֶׁבְּצִבּוּר, אֲפִלּוּ בְּדִבְרֵי תוֹרָה כָּל שֶׁכֵּן בְּשִׂיחַת חֻלִּין וְסִפּוּרֵי שְׁמוּעוֹת. וְיָחוּלוּ עָלָיו כָּל הַבְּרָכוֹת הַכְּתוּבוֹת בְּתוֹרַת מֹשֶׁה רַבֵּנוּ עָלָיו הַשָּׁלוֹם וּבְכָל הַנְּבוּאוֹת, יִרְאֶה זֶרַע כָּשֵׁר חַיִּים וְקַיָּמִים, וְיִזְכֶּה לִשְׁנֵי שֻׁלְחָנוֹת שֶׁבִּשְׁנֵי עוֹלָמִים, שֶׁהֵם הָעוֹלָם הַזֶּה שֶׁעָלָיו נֶאֱמַר: 'וְהִנֵּה טוֹב', וְהָעוֹלָם הַבָּא שֶׁהוּא יוֹם שֶׁכֻּלּוֹ אָרוֹךְ וְגַם טוֹב, וְנֹאמַר אָמֵן.

PRAYER FOR THOSE WHO REFRAIN FROM TALKING
This prayer was composed in the seventeenth century by R. Yom Tov Lipmann Heller, (author of the *Tosfot* Yom Tov commentary on the *Mishna*, and whose name is alluded to in its closing phrases) in the immediate aftermath

and small, women and children. May the King of the universe bless you all, prolonging your lives, increasing your days and lengthening your years. May you be spared all trouble and saved from every evil happening. May our Master in heaven be your help on every occasion at all times, and let us say, Amen.

מִי שֶׁבֵּרַךְ MAY HE Who blessed our fathers Abraham, Isaac, and Jacob, bless this holy congregation together with all other holy congregations, them, their wives, their sons and daughters, and all that is theirs. May He bless those who consecrate synagogues for prayer and those who enter therein to pray, those who provide light for illumination, wine for Kiddush and Havdala, food for visitors, charity for the poor, and all who are faithfully involved in the needs of the community. May the Holy One, blessed is He, reward them and spare them from every illness, heal their entire body, forgive all their sins, and send blessing and success in all that they do, together with all Israel their brothers. And let us say, Amen.

Some congregations recite the following prayer for those who refrain from talking throughout the prayer service.

מִי שֶׁבֵּרַךְ MAY HE Who blessed our fathers Abraham, Isaac, and Jacob, Moses and Aaron, David and Solomon, bless one who guards his or her tongue from talking during prayer, starting with *Barukh She'amar*, till the end of services, including the Torah reading, even if the subject matter is one of Torah learning, and certainly if it is of a non-sacred or anecdotal nature. May that person enjoy all the blessings recorded in the Torah of Moses our teacher and the other prophecies, to bear righteous and long-living offspring, and be privileged to enjoy the rewards of two worlds, that is, this one of which it is said "it is good," and the next one which will be both long-lasting and good. And let us say, Amen.

---

of the Chmielnicki massacres that devastated many communities in Eastern Europe. In recent years it has been adopted by numerous congregations seeking to enhance the spiritual atmosphere and ambience of communal prayer.

תפילה לשלום המדינה

The שליח ציבור *or* רב *says the following:*

הַנּוֹתֵן תְּשׁוּעָה לַמְּלָכִים וּמֶמְשָׁלָה לַנְּסִיכִים, מַלְכוּתוֹ מַלְכוּת כָּל עוֹלָמִים, הַפּוֹצֶה אֶת דָּוִד עַבְדּוֹ מֵחֶרֶב רָעָה, הַנּוֹתֵן בַּיָּם דֶּרֶךְ וּבְמַיִם עַזִּים נְתִיבָה, הוּא יְבָרֵךְ אֶת (הַנָּשִׂיא/הַנְּשִׂיאָה וְאֶת מִשְׁנֵהוּ/מִשְׁנֶהָ) (אֶת רֹאשׁ הַמֶּמְשָׁלָה) (וְכוּ׳) וְאֶת כָּל שָׂרֵי הַמְּדִינוֹת הָאֵלּוּ. מֶלֶךְ מַלְכֵי הַמְּלָכִים, בְּרַחֲמָיו יְחַיֵּם וְיִשְׁמְרֵם, וּמִכָּל צָרָה וְיָגוֹן וָנֶזֶק יַצִּילֵם. וְיִתֵּן בְּלִבָּם וּבְלֵב כָּל יוֹעֲצֵיהֶם וְשָׂרֵיהֶם לַעֲשׂוֹת טוֹבוֹת עִמָּנוּ וְעִם כָּל יִשְׂרָאֵל אַחֵינוּ. בִּימֵיהֶם וּבְיָמֵינוּ תִּוָּשַׁע יְהוּדָה, וְיִשְׂרָאֵל יִשְׁכֹּן לָבֶטַח, וּבָא לְצִיּוֹן גּוֹאֵל. וְכֵן יְהִי רָצוֹן, וְנֹאמַר אָמֵן.

תפילה לשלום מדינת ישראל

The שליח ציבור *or* רב *says the following:*

אָבִינוּ שֶׁבַּשָּׁמַיִם, צוּר יִשְׂרָאֵל וְגוֹאֲלוֹ, בָּרֵךְ אֶת מְדִינַת יִשְׂרָאֵל, רֵאשִׁית צְמִיחַת גְּאֻלָּתֵנוּ. הָגֵן עָלֶיהָ בְּאֶבְרַת

תְּפִלָּה לִשְׁלוֹם הַמְּדִינָה / PRAYER FOR THE WELFARE OF THE GOVERNMENT

The earliest source advocating a prayer for the welfare of ruling authorities is Jeremiah 29:7 that instructs the Babylonian exiles to seek the peace of the city where they find themselves and "pray unto God for it; for in its peace will you have peace." Several decades later the custom was cited by the Babylonian King Darius as good reason to permit the Israelites to return to Israel to rebuild the Temple, saying "that they may offer sacrifices of sweet savor unto the God of heaven, and pray for the life of the king, and of his sons" (Ezra 6:10). The Mishna (*Avot* 3:2) similarly instructs us to pray for the well-being of the government, on the grounds that "Without a fear of governmental authority people might eat each other alive." The Gemara (*Yoma* 69a) relates that in the fourth century BCE Shimon HaTzaddik met with the conquering Alexander the Great near Jerusalem. The Samaritans had lobbied the powerful king to destroy Jerusalem as he made his way to Egypt. Shimon pleaded that Jerusalem be saved, arguing that it would be unjust to "do away with the very house in which the Jews regularly pray for the king and his empire." Alexander agreed, and as a result the Temple was spared. From this we learn that a prayer for the government (even a foreign one) was a regular feature of Second Temple procedure, instituted by the Men of the Great Assembly – a group to which, in its final years, Shimon HaTzaddik belonged.

The existence of a fixed text for this prayer is mentioned by Abudarham and *Kol Bo*. The widely accepted text used here was brought from Spain and Provence to Amsterdam in

PRAYER FOR THE WELFARE OF THE GOVERNMENT

The Leader or rabbi says the following:

הַנּוֹתֵן MAY GOD, Whose kingdom lasts forever, Who alone grants salvation to kings and sovereignty to rulers, Who delivered David His servant from an evil sword, and Who made a thoroughfare in the sea and a path through mighty waters – bless (the President, the Vice President) (the Prime Minister) (et al.), and all the (cabinet) ministers of this land. In His mercy, may the King Who rules over the most exalted of kings grant them life and well-being, and save them from every trouble, worry, and harm. May He inspire them and all their advisers and (cabinet) ministers to act in good faith toward us and all Israel our brothers. In their days and ours may Judah be saved and Israel dwell securely. May the Redeemer come to Zion. May this be Your will, and let us say, Amen.

PRAYER FOR THE STATE OF ISRAEL

The Leader or rabbi says the following:

אָבִינוּ שֶׁבַּשָּׁמַיִם HEAVENLY FATHER, Rock and Redeemer of Israel, bless the State of Israel, the first flowering of our redemption. Shield her beneath your protective wing, and spread over her the canopy of

---

the seventeenth century, and by the early eighteenth century had become the dominant version in Ashkenazi communities.

יִתֵּן בְּלִבָּם וּבְלֵב כָּל יוֹעֲצֵיהֶם וְשָׂרֵיהֶם – *May He inspire them and all their advisers and (cabinet) ministers.* The text of this traditional prayer has been amended in this Siddur to reflect modern institutions of government, and to recognize that in a democracy ultimate sovereignty resides with the people, rather than with an elected or even hereditary head of state. The particular phrases referring to such heads of state should be adapted to the system of government in whatever country it is said.

תְּפִלָּה לִשְׁלוֹם מְדִינַת יִשְׂרָאֵל / PRAYER FOR THE WELFARE OF THE STATE OF ISRAEL

With the founding of the State of Israel in 1948, it was recognized that a new prayer was necessary to address the phenomenon of an autonomous Jewish sovereign state. The Ashkenazi Chief Rabbi at the time, R. Isaac HaLevi Herzog, composed this text, with input from the renowned and observant author Shmuel Yosef Agnon.

The phrase describing the State of Israel as רֵאשִׁית צְמִיחַת גְּאֻלָּתֵנוּ (the beginning of the flowering of our redemption) is ambiguous. Some understand it as affirming that the State of Israel is a harbinger, or precursor, of the long-

חַסְדֶּךָ וּפְרֹשׂ עָלֶיהָ סֻכַּת שְׁלוֹמֶךָ, וּשְׁלַח אוֹרְךָ וַאֲמִתְּךָ לְרָאשֶׁיהָ, שָׂרֶיהָ וְיוֹעֲצֶיהָ, וְתַקְּנֵם בְּעֵצָה טוֹבָה מִלְּפָנֶיךָ.

חַזֵּק אֶת יְדֵי מְגִנֵּי אֶרֶץ קָדְשֵׁנוּ, וְהַנְחִילֵם אֱלֹהֵינוּ יְשׁוּעָה וַעֲטֶרֶת נִצָּחוֹן תְּעַטְּרֵם, וְנָתַתָּ שָׁלוֹם בָּאָרֶץ וְשִׂמְחַת עוֹלָם לְיוֹשְׁבֶיהָ.

וְאֶת אַחֵינוּ כָּל בֵּית יִשְׂרָאֵל, פְּקָד נָא בְּכָל אַרְצוֹת פְּזוּרֵיהֶם,
וְתוֹלִיכֵם מְהֵרָה קוֹמְמִיּוּת לְצִיּוֹן עִירֶךָ וְלִירוּשָׁלַיִם מִשְׁכַּן שְׁמֶךָ,
כַּכָּתוּב בְּתוֹרַת מֹשֶׁה עַבְדֶּךָ: אִם־יִהְיֶה נִדַּחֲךָ בִּקְצֵה הַשָּׁמָיִם, מִשָּׁם דברים ל
יְקַבֶּצְךָ יהוה אֱלֹהֶיךָ וּמִשָּׁם יִקָּחֶךָ: וֶהֱבִיאֲךָ יהוה אֱלֹהֶיךָ אֶל־הָאָרֶץ
אֲשֶׁר־יָרְשׁוּ אֲבֹתֶיךָ וִירִשְׁתָּהּ, וְהֵיטִבְךָ וְהִרְבְּךָ מֵאֲבֹתֶיךָ:

וְיַחֵד לְבָבֵנוּ לְאַהֲבָה וּלְיִרְאָה אֶת שְׁמֶךָ, וְלִשְׁמֹר אֶת כָּל דִּבְרֵי תוֹרָתֶךָ, וּשְׁלַח לָנוּ מְהֵרָה בֶּן דָּוִד מְשִׁיחַ צִדְקֶךָ, לִפְדּוֹת מְחַכֵּי קֵץ יְשׁוּעָתֶךָ.

וְהוֹפַע בַּהֲדַר גְּאוֹן עֻזֶּךָ עַל כָּל יוֹשְׁבֵי תֵּבֵל אַרְצֶךָ וְיֹאמַר כֹּל אֲשֶׁר נְשָׁמָה בְאַפּוֹ, יהוה אֱלֹהֵי יִשְׂרָאֵל מֶלֶךְ וּמַלְכוּתוֹ בַּכֹּל מָשָׁלָה, אָמֵן סֶלָה.

On the last day of פסח*, second day of* שבועות *and on* שמיני עצרת*,* יזכור *(on page 1098) is said. On other days of* יום טוב *continue with "*יָהּ אֵלִי*" on page 826; in some congregations, "*יָהּ אֵלִי*" is omitted on* שבת *and the service continues with "*אַשְׁרֵי*" on page 562.*

awaited Messianic redemption. To avoid making such a definitive declaration of Messianic certainty, some ardent Zionists, including R. Joseph B. Soloveitchik, choose to omit the phrase entirely. Others amend it by prefacing the phrase with the word שֶׁתְּהֵא ("may it be the beginning of our redemption"). Most, however, recite the prayer as found here, in the form originally composed by the Chief Rabbinate. In any case, it is clear that the author did not intend to imply that the State of Israel would replace the need for the Messiah, as seen from the fact that the final stanza asks God to "send us soon Your righteous Messiah, descended of David." For further discussion of this prayer see the essay on page E12.

וִירִשְׁתָּהּ – *And you shall inherit it*. The root יָרַשׁ means both "possess" and "inherit" (R. David Zvi Hoffman). Whereas some translate the word as "possess" or even as "occupy", we translate it as

Your peace. Bestow Your light and truth upon her leaders, (cabinet) ministers, and advisers, and guide them with Your good counsel.

STRENGTHEN the hands of those who defend our holy land. May You our God grant them salvation. May You crown them with the laurels of victory. May You bring peace in the land and everlasting joy for its inhabitants.

REMEMBER our brethren the whole house of Israel in all the lands of their dispersion, to lead them soon, unbowed and upright, to Zion Your city and to Jerusalem, the dwelling place of Your name. As it is
Deut. 30 written in the Torah of Moses Your servant, "Even if your outcasts will be at the end of the heavens the Lord Your God will gather and take you from there. The Lord Your God will bring you to the land which your fathers inherited, and you will inherit it. He will bring goodness upon you, increasing your numbers beyond those of your fathers."

UNITE our hearts in love and fear of Your name, and in observance of all the words of Your Torah. Send us soon Your righteous Messiah, descended of David, to redeem the people that longs for Your complete salvation.

MAY YOU be revealed to all the inhabitants of Your world in the brilliant glory of Your power, so that everything that possesses a soul will proclaim, "The Lord God of Israel is King, and His kingdom rules over all." Amen. Selah.

On the last day of Pesaḥ, second day of Shavuot, and on Shemini Atzeret, Yizkor (on page 1099) is said. On other days of Yom Tov continue with "Lord my God" on page 827; in some congregations, "Lord my God" is omitted on Shabbat and the service continues with "Happy are those" on page 563.

"inherit," insofar as Jewish sovereignty over the land of Israel is not merely the result of possession or occupation, and thus a mere technical matter of whether it is under Jewish control at a given point in history. It is rather an inheritance in the fullest sense, ours by right, having been granted by God to our forefathers, who in turn bequeathed it to their descendants for all time.

ברכת החודש

On the שבת *before* ראש חודש*, the following is said by the* קהל*, and repeated by the* שליח ציבור*:*

יְהִי רָצוֹן מִלְּפָנֶיךָ, יהוה אֱלֹהֵינוּ וֵאלֹהֵי אֲבוֹתֵינוּ, שֶׁתְּחַדֵּשׁ עָלֵינוּ אֶת הַחֹדֶשׁ הַזֶּה לְטוֹבָה וְלִבְרָכָה. וְתִתֶּן לָנוּ חַיִּים אֲרוּכִים, חַיִּים שֶׁל שָׁלוֹם, חַיִּים שֶׁל טוֹבָה, חַיִּים שֶׁל בְּרָכָה, חַיִּים שֶׁל פַּרְנָסָה, חַיִּים שֶׁל חִלּוּץ עֲצָמוֹת, חַיִּים שֶׁיֵּשׁ בָּהֶם יִרְאַת שָׁמַיִם וְיִרְאַת חֵטְא, חַיִּים שֶׁאֵין בָּהֶם בּוּשָׁה וּכְלִמָּה, חַיִּים שֶׁל עֹשֶׁר וְכָבוֹד, חַיִּים שֶׁתְּהֵא בָנוּ אַהֲבַת תּוֹרָה וְיִרְאַת שָׁמַיִם, חַיִּים שֶׁיִּמָּלְאוּ מִשְׁאֲלוֹת לִבֵּנוּ לְטוֹבָה, אָמֵן סֶלָה. ברכות טז:

The מולד *is announced, then the* שליח ציבור *takes the* ספר תורה *in his right arm and says:*

מִי שֶׁעָשָׂה נִסִּים לַאֲבוֹתֵינוּ וְגָאַל אוֹתָם מֵעַבְדוּת לְחֵרוּת, הוּא יִגְאַל אוֹתָנוּ בְּקָרוֹב וִיקַבֵּץ נִדָּחֵינוּ מֵאַרְבַּע כַּנְפוֹת הָאָרֶץ, חֲבֵרִים כָּל יִשְׂרָאֵל וְנֹאמַר אָמֵן.

The שליח ציבור*, then the* קהל*:*

רֹאשׁ חֹדֶשׁ *month* יִהְיֶה בְּיוֹם *day* (*וּבְיוֹם *day*) הַבָּא עָלֵינוּ וְעַל כָּל יִשְׂרָאֵל לְטוֹבָה.

*if the second day falls on Sunday, then substitute: וּלְמָחֳרָתוֹ בְּיוֹם

בִּרְכַּת הַחֹדֶשׁ / BLESSING OF THE NEW MONTH The text of this prayer is based on the Gemara (*Berakhot* 16b). During Temple times, the great Sanhedrin in Jerusalem established the Jewish calendar based on actual sighting of each new moon. In the absence of the Sanhedrin, at the dawn of Byzantine rule over the land of Israel in the fourth century CE, Hillel II established the Jewish calendar for future generations, based upon astronomical calculations.

While it is true that the calendar is fixed, and the dates of future occurrences of Rosh Ḥodesh are well established, it is still necessary to proclaim the occurrence of each Rosh Ḥodesh. The reason is that in fixing and proclaiming each new month, the Sanhedrin itself was not acting independently, but rather as the representative of the Jewish nation, which was commanded at the Exodus to sanctify each month. Accordingly, in the absence of the Sanhedrin, the responsibility to proclaim each month reverts back to the people. This is the reason that each congregation, in advance of the sanctification on Rosh Ḥodesh itself, publicly declares the precise day and time of the מולד (birth, or first possible moment for sighting) of the new moon, as the Sanhedrin used to do. Reflecting the nature of this declaration as representing the Jewish people as a whole, we

BLESSING OF THE NEW MONTH

On the Shabbat before Rosh Ḥodesh, the following is said by the congregation, and repeated by the Leader:

Berakhot 16b יְהִי רָצוֹן MAY IT BE Your will, Lord our God and God of our fathers, that You renew for us this coming month for good and for blessing. Grant us long life, a life of peace, a life of goodness, a life of blessing, a life of sustenance, a life of vigor and vitality, a life of fear of heaven and fear of sin, a life without shame or disgrace, a life of wealth and honor, a life marked by love of Torah and fear of heaven, a life in which our hearts' requests will be fulfilled for the good. Amen. Selah.

The molad (birth) of the new moon is announced, then the Leader takes the Torah scroll in his right arm and says:

מִי שֶׁעָשָׂה MAY HE WHO performed miracles for our fathers and redeemed them from slavery to freedom, speedily redeem us and gather our dispersed from the four corners of the earth, for all Israel are united in fellowship, and let us say, Amen.

The Leader, then the congregation:

The beginning of the month of (*Hebrew month*) will be on (*day/s of the week*), which will come to us and to all Israel for the good.

---

include the phrase חֲבֵרִים כָּל יִשְׂרָאֵל ("all Israel are united in fellowship"), and for the same reason the Leader takes hold of the Torah when proclaiming the occurrence of Rosh Ḥodesh, for ever since Sinai it is the Torah that has bound us together as a people (R. Joseph B. Soloveitchik).

יִרְאַת שָׁמַיִם וְיִרְאַת חֵטְא – *Fear of heaven and fear of sin.* "Fear of sin" refers to the fear we experience in contemplating the punishment that comes when we transgress God's will. "Fear of heaven," on the other hand, expresses the shame and pain that we experience in thinking about being separated and distanced from God as a result of sins we might commit (R. Avraham Yitzḥak HaKohen Kook).

אַהֲבַת תּוֹרָה וְיִרְאַת שָׁמַיִם – *Love of Torah and fear of heaven.* "Fear of heaven" is repeated a second time, following "love of Torah," for love of Torah, and the study thereof, is a powerful means to achieve the fear of heaven. When a person sets his heart to imitating the ways of God – the essence of keeping the Torah – the act of imitation breeds love. At the same time, comprehension of the greatness and perfection of divine ways breeds awe and fear of heaven (R. Avraham Yitzḥak HaKohen Kook).

ANNOUNCEMENT OF THE MOLAD

The מוֹלָד (the moment at which the new moon appears) occurs at a single moment, which is when it is sighted over Jerusalem. Thus, if it is announced that the *molad* will occur at 9:00 a.m., it refers to 9:00 a.m. in Jerusalem.

The שליח ציבור *and* קהל *continue:*

יְחַדְּשֵׁהוּ הַקָּדוֹשׁ בָּרוּךְ הוּא, עָלֵינוּ, וְעַל כָּל עַמּוֹ בֵּית יִשְׂרָאֵל, לְחַיִּים וּלְשָׁלוֹם, לְשָׂשׂוֹן וּלְשִׂמְחָה, לִישׁוּעָה וּלְנֶחָמָה, וְנֹאמַר אָמֵן.

In many congregations the following אֵל מָלֵא רַחֲמִים *is said at this point for those who passed away during the year and, in many congregations, for those whose yahrzeit falls during the coming week. It is not said on days that "*אב הָרַחֲמִים*" is omitted (see below). This prayer is recited while holding or touching the* ספר תורה*.*

אֵל מָלֵא רַחֲמִים, שׁוֹכֵן בַּמְּרוֹמִים, הַמְצֵא מְנוּחָה נְכוֹנָה תַּחַת (נ״א עַל) כַּנְפֵי הַשְּׁכִינָה, בְּמַעֲלוֹת קְדוֹשִׁים וּטְהוֹרִים, כְּזֹהַר הָרָקִיעַ מַזְהִירִים,

For a man:

לְנִשְׁמַת (פלוני בֶּן פלוני) שֶׁהָלַךְ לְעוֹלָמוֹ, בַּעֲבוּר שֶׁ(פלוני בֶּן פלוני) יִתֵּן / שֶׁ(פלונית בַּת פלוני) תִּתֵּן / צְדָקָה בְּעַד הַזְכָּרַת נִשְׁמָתוֹ, בְּגַן עֵדֶן תְּהֵא מְנוּחָתוֹ. לָכֵן, בַּעַל הָרַחֲמִים יַסְתִּירֵהוּ בְּסֵתֶר כְּנָפָיו לְעוֹלָמִים, וְיִצְרֹר בִּצְרוֹר הַחַיִּים אֶת נִשְׁמָתוֹ, יהוה הוּא נַחֲלָתוֹ, וְיָנְוּחַ בְּשָׁלוֹם עַל מִשְׁכָּבוֹ, וְנֹאמַר אָמֵן.

For a woman:

לְנִשְׁמַת (פלונית בַּת פלוני) שֶׁהָלְכָה לְעוֹלָמָהּ, בַּעֲבוּר שֶׁ(פלוני בֶּן פלוני) יִתֵּן / שֶׁ(פלונית בַּת פלוני) תִּתֵּן / צְדָקָה בְּעַד הַזְכָּרַת נִשְׁמָתָהּ, בְּגַן עֵדֶן תְּהֵא מְנוּחָתָהּ. לָכֵן, בַּעַל הָרַחֲמִים יַסְתִּירֶהָ בְּסֵתֶר כְּנָפָיו לְעוֹלָמִים, וְיִצְרֹר בִּצְרוֹר הַחַיִּים אֶת נִשְׁמָתָהּ, יהוה הוּא נַחֲלָתָהּ, וְתָנְוּחַ בְּשָׁלוֹם עַל מִשְׁכָּבָהּ, וְנֹאמַר אָמֵן.

The following is omitted on days when תחנון *would not be said on weekdays (see page 144). It is also omitted on* שבת מברכים *(except for the* שבת *before* ראש חודש אייר *and* ראש חודש סיון*) and on the "*ארבע פרשיות*,"* שקלים*,* זכור*,* פרה *and* החודש*.*

On the last day of פסח*, the second day of* שבועות *and* שמיני עצרת*,* יזכור *is said, page 1098.*

On other חגים *continue with* יָהּ אֵלִי*, page 826.*

אַב הָרַחֲמִים שׁוֹכֵן מְרוֹמִים, בְּרַחֲמָיו הָעֲצוּמִים הוּא יִפְקֹד בְּרַחֲמִים הַחֲסִידִים וְהַיְשָׁרִים וְהַתְּמִימִים, קְהִלּוֹת הַקֹּדֶשׁ שֶׁמָּסְרוּ נַפְשָׁם עַל קְדֻשַּׁת הַשֵּׁם, הַנֶּאֱהָבִים וְהַנְּעִימִים בְּחַיֵּיהֶם, וּבְמוֹתָם

אַב הָרַחֲמִים – *Father of mercy.* This memorial prayer honors those who have died עַל קִדּוּשׁ ה׳ (to sanctify God's name). According to R. Ephraim of Bonn (twelfth century) and the Maharil (fifteenth century), it was composed in the aftermath of the bloody massacres of the Jewish communities of Rhineland Germany in the First Crusade in 1096 (Prof. Shlomo Eidelberg).

The commentary continues on page 562.

The congregation and Leader continue:

יְחַדְּשֵׁהוּ MAY THE HOLY ONE, blessed is He, renew this new month for us and for all His people, the house of Israel, for life and peace, for gladness and joy, for salvation and consolation, and let us say, Amen.

In many congregations the following "God, full of mercy," is said at this point for those who passed away during the year and, in many congregations, for those whose yahrzeit falls during the coming week. It is not said on days that "Father of mercy" is omitted (see below). This prayer is recited while holding or touching the Sefer Torah.

אֵל O GOD, full of mercy, Who dwells on high, grant fitting rest beneath (*some say:* above) the protective wings of the Divine Presence, where the souls of the holy and pure ones – whose radiance is like that of the heavens – reside, to the soul of

For a man:

(*name of the deceased*) the son of (*father of the deceased*), who has gone to his eternal reward. May the Garden of Eden be his resting place, insofar as (*name of supplicant*) will make a charitable gift in memory of his soul. For this reason may the ever-merciful One shelter the deceased under His protective wings forever, and may He bind his soul in lasting life. For the Lord will surely be his benefactor, so that he can rest in peace in his allotted place. And let us say, Amen.

For a woman:

(*name of the deceased*) the daughter of (*father of the deceased*), who has gone to her eternal reward. May the Garden of Eden be her resting place, insofar as (*name of supplicant*) will make a charitable gift in memory of her soul. For this reason may the ever-merciful One shelter the deceased under His protective wings forever, and may He bind her soul in lasting life. For the Lord will surely be her benefactor, so that she can rest in peace in her allotted place. And let us say, Amen.

The following is omitted on days when Taḥanun would not be said on weekdays (see page 145). It is also omitted on a Shabbat before Rosh Ḥodesh (except for the Shabbat before Rosh Ḥodesh Iyar and Rosh Ḥodesh Sivan) and on Shabbat Shekalim, Zakhor, Para and HaḤodesh.

On the last day of Pesaḥ, the second day of Shavuot and Shemini Atzeret, Yizkor is said, page 1099.

On other Festivals continue with "Lord my God" (Ka Keli), page 827.

אַב הָרַחֲמִים FATHER OF MERCY Who dwells on high, in His sublime mercy may He recall compassionately the pious, the upright and unblemished ones, the holy congregations that gave their lives for the sanctification of His name. They were beloved and sweet in their lives, and in death they

לֹא נִפְרָדוּ, מִנְּשָׁרִים קַלּוּ וּמֵאֲרָיוֹת גָּבֵרוּ לַעֲשׂוֹת רְצוֹן קוֹנָם וְחֵפֶץ
צוּרָם. יִזְכְּרֵם אֱלֹהֵינוּ לְטוֹבָה עִם שְׁאָר צַדִּיקֵי עוֹלָם, וְיִנְקֹם לְעֵינֵינוּ
(דברים לב) נִקְמַת דַּם עֲבָדָיו הַשָּׁפוּךְ, כַּכָּתוּב בְּתוֹרַת מֹשֶׁה אִישׁ הָאֱלֹהִים: הַרְנִינוּ
גוֹיִם עַמּוֹ, כִּי דַם־עֲבָדָיו יִקּוֹם, וְנָקָם יָשִׁיב לְצָרָיו, וְכִפֶּר אַדְמָתוֹ עַמּוֹ:
(יואל ד) וְעַל יְדֵי עֲבָדֶיךָ הַנְּבִיאִים כָּתוּב לֵאמֹר: וְנִקֵּיתִי, דָּמָם לֹא־נִקֵּיתִי, וַיהוה
(תהלים עט) שֹׁכֵן בְּצִיּוֹן: וּבְכִתְבֵי הַקֹּדֶשׁ נֶאֱמַר: לָמָּה יֹאמְרוּ הַגּוֹיִם אַיֵּה אֱלֹהֵיהֶם,
(תהלים ט) יִוָּדַע בַּגּוֹיִם לְעֵינֵינוּ נִקְמַת דַּם־עֲבָדֶיךָ הַשָּׁפוּךְ: וְאוֹמֵר: כִּי־דֹרֵשׁ דָּמִים
(תהלים קי) אוֹתָם זָכָר, לֹא־שָׁכַח צַעֲקַת עֲנָוִים: וְאוֹמֵר: יָדִין בַּגּוֹיִם מָלֵא גְוִיּוֹת,
מָחַץ רֹאשׁ עַל־אֶרֶץ רַבָּה: מִנַּחַל בַּדֶּרֶךְ יִשְׁתֶּה, עַל־כֵּן יָרִים רֹאשׁ:

The line beginning with פּוֹתֵחַ אֶת יָדֶךָ *should be said with special concentration, representing as it does the key idea of this psalm, that God is the Creator and Sustainer of all.*

(תהלים פד) **אַשְׁרֵי** יוֹשְׁבֵי בֵיתֶךָ, עוֹד יְהַלְלוּךָ סֶּלָה:
(תהלים קמד) אַשְׁרֵי הָעָם שֶׁכָּכָה לּוֹ, אַשְׁרֵי הָעָם שֶׁיהוה אֱלֹהָיו:
(תהלים קמה) תְּהִלָּה לְדָוִד

אֲרוֹמִמְךָ אֱלוֹהַי הַמֶּלֶךְ, וַאֲבָרְכָה שִׁמְךָ לְעוֹלָם וָעֶד:
בְּכָל־יוֹם אֲבָרְכֶךָּ, וַאֲהַלְלָה שִׁמְךָ לְעוֹלָם וָעֶד:
גָּדוֹל יהוה וּמְהֻלָּל מְאֹד, וְלִגְדֻלָּתוֹ אֵין חֵקֶר:
דּוֹר לְדוֹר יְשַׁבַּח מַעֲשֶׂיךָ, וּגְבוּרֹתֶיךָ יַגִּידוּ:
הֲדַר כְּבוֹד הוֹדֶךָ, וְדִבְרֵי נִפְלְאֹתֶיךָ אָשִׂיחָה:
וֶעֱזוּז נוֹרְאֹתֶיךָ יֹאמֵרוּ, וּגְדוּלָּתְךָ אֲסַפְּרֶנָּה:
זֵכֶר רַב־טוּבְךָ יַבִּיעוּ, וְצִדְקָתְךָ יְרַנֵּנוּ:
חַנּוּן וְרַחוּם יהוה, אֶרֶךְ אַפַּיִם וּגְדָל־חָסֶד:
טוֹב־יהוה לַכֹּל, וְרַחֲמָיו עַל־כָּל־מַעֲשָׂיו:
יוֹדוּךָ יהוה כָּל־מַעֲשֶׂיךָ, וַחֲסִידֶיךָ יְבָרְכוּכָה:
כְּבוֹד מַלְכוּתְךָ יֹאמֵרוּ, וּגְבוּרָתְךָ יְדַבֵּרוּ:

Even though the memory of these bitter events contradicts the tranquil spirit of Shabbat, we nonetheless recall them publicly at this point because it is proper that on this day of peace and tranquility prayers be said for the peace of their souls. For this reason some congregations recite the אֵל מָלֵא (memorial prayer) for those whose *Yahrzeit* will occur in the coming week,

were not parted. They were swifter than eagles and stronger than lions in adhering to their Creator's will and their Rock's desire. May our God remember them for good, together with all other righteous people of the world. May we witness His vengeance visited upon those who spilled His servants' blood, as it is written in the Torah of Moses, the man of God:
Deut. 32 "Nations, cause His people to sing for joy, for He will avenge the blood of His servants and bring retribution on His enemies, and make atonement for the land of His people." So too, by Your servants the prophets, it is writ-
Joel 4 ten, saying: "And I shall avenge the shedding of their blood that I have not yet avenged, and the Lord shall dwell in Zion." And in the holy Writings it is
Ps. 79 said: "Why should the nations say, Where is their God? Let the avenging of the shed blood of Your servants be known to the nations before our eyes."
Ps. 9 And it is said: "For He Who avenges blood has remembered it. He has not
Ps. 110 forgotten the cry of the oppressed." And it is said: "He will judge among the nations, full of bodies. He will crush heads over a great region. He will drink from the brook on the way. Therefore he will lift up his head."

The line beginning with "You open Your hand" should be said with special concentration, representing as it does the key idea of this psalm, that God is the Creator and Sustainer of all.

Ps. 84 **אַשְׁרֵי** HAPPY are they who dwell in Your house,
They shall forever praise You. Selah.

Ps. 144 HAPPY are the people of whom this is so,
Happy are the people whose God is the Lord.

Ps. 145 A PRAISE OF DAVID.

א I exalt You, my God, the King, and I will bless Your name forever and ever. ב Every day I will bless You, and I will praise Your name forever and ever. ג Great is the Lord, and very praiseworthy, and His greatness is boundless. ד One generation lauds Your works to another, and they declare Your mighty deeds. ה I speak of the splendid glory of Your majesty and of Your wondrous works, ו And they speak of the might of Your awesome deeds, and I declare Your greatness. ז They express the renown of Your great goodness, and sing of Your righteousness. ח Gracious and merciful is the Lord, slow to anger and great in loving-kindness. ט The Lord is good to all, and His mercies are upon all His works. י All Your works thank You, O Lord, and Your pious ones bless You. כ They describe the glory of Your kingdom, and speak of Your

לְהוֹדִיעַ לִבְנֵי הָאָדָם גְּבוּרֹתָיו, וּכְבוֹד הֲדַר מַלְכוּתוֹ:
מַלְכוּתְךָ מַלְכוּת כָּל־עֹלָמִים, וּמֶמְשַׁלְתְּךָ בְּכָל־דּוֹר וָדֹר:
סוֹמֵךְ יהוה לְכָל־הַנֹּפְלִים, וְזוֹקֵף לְכָל־הַכְּפוּפִים:
עֵינֵי־כֹל אֵלֶיךָ יְשַׂבֵּרוּ, וְאַתָּה נוֹתֵן־לָהֶם אֶת־אָכְלָם בְּעִתּוֹ:
פּוֹתֵחַ אֶת־יָדֶךָ, וּמַשְׂבִּיעַ לְכָל־חַי רָצוֹן:
צַדִּיק יהוה בְּכָל־דְּרָכָיו, וְחָסִיד בְּכָל־מַעֲשָׂיו:
קָרוֹב יהוה לְכָל־קֹרְאָיו, לְכֹל אֲשֶׁר יִקְרָאֻהוּ בֶאֱמֶת:
רְצוֹן־יְרֵאָיו יַעֲשֶׂה, וְאֶת־שַׁוְעָתָם יִשְׁמַע וְיוֹשִׁיעֵם:
שׁוֹמֵר יהוה אֶת־כָּל־אֹהֲבָיו, וְאֵת כָּל־הָרְשָׁעִים יַשְׁמִיד:
◂ תְּהִלַּת יהוה יְדַבֶּר פִּי, וִיבָרֵךְ כָּל־בָּשָׂר שֵׁם קָדְשׁוֹ לְעוֹלָם וָעֶד:
תהלים קטו וַאֲנַחְנוּ נְבָרֵךְ יָהּ מֵעַתָּה וְעַד־עוֹלָם, הַלְלוּיָהּ:

הכנסת ספר תורה

The ארון קודש *is opened. All stand. The* שליח ציבור *takes the* ספר תורה *and says:*

תהלים קמח **יְהַלְלוּ** אֶת־שֵׁם יהוה, כִּי־נִשְׂגָּב שְׁמוֹ לְבַדּוֹ

The קהל *responds:*

הוֹדוֹ עַל־אֶרֶץ וְשָׁמָיִם: וַיָּרֶם קֶרֶן לְעַמּוֹ, תְּהִלָּה לְכָל־חֲסִידָיו, לִבְנֵי
יִשְׂרָאֵל עַם קְרֹבוֹ, הַלְלוּיָהּ:

While the ספר תורה *is being returned to the* ארון קודש*, on* שבת *say:*

תהלים כט **מִזְמוֹר לְדָוִד,** הָבוּ לַיהוה בְּנֵי אֵלִים, הָבוּ לַיהוה כָּבוֹד וָעֹז: הָבוּ
לַיהוה כְּבוֹד שְׁמוֹ, הִשְׁתַּחֲווּ לַיהוה בְּהַדְרַת־קֹדֶשׁ:

---

either at this point or at the conclusion of the Torah reading at Shabbat *Minḥa (Levush).*

פּוֹתֵחַ אֶת־יָדֶךָ – *You open Your hand.* This verse, which must be recited with special concentration, can be understood as follows: It is certainly true that emotional pleasure increases in proportion to our having been deprived of the source of that pleasure. The more we long for the object of our desire in its absence, the greater our joy when we finally receive it. Conversely, those who are granted much to start with, are likely to take correspondingly less pleasure in what they have been given. For this reason, this verse declares, in His infinite goodness, God facilitates our greatest eventual satisfaction by implanting in us numerous desires and hopes for what we do not have, and then satisfies them in due course, whether in this world or the next. It is as if the verse says, "God maximizes our benefit by granting our desires only after we have long desired them." This accounts for the importance of the verse,

might, ל To make known to the sons of man His mighty deeds, and the glorious splendor of His kingdom. מ Your kingdom is a kingdom for all times, and Your dominion is for every generation. ס The Lord supports all who fall and raises up all who are bowed down. ע The eyes of all await You, and You give them their food in its time. פ You open Your hand, and You satisfy the desire of every living thing. צ The Lord is righteous in all His ways and kind in all His works. ק The Lord is near to all who address Him, to all who address Him in truth. ר He does the will of those who fear Him, and He hears their cry and saves them. ש The Lord preserves all who love Him, but all the wicked He destroys. ת ▸ May my mouth speak the praise of the Lord, and may all flesh bless His holy name forever and ever.

Ps. 115 And we shall bless the Lord now and for evermore. Praise the Lord.

RETURNING THE TORAH TO THE ARK

The Ark is opened. All stand. The Leader takes the Torah scroll and says:

Ps. 148 **יְהַלְלוּ** LET THEM PRAISE the name of the Lord, that His name alone is exalted.

The congregation responds:

His glory is over the earth and the heavens. And He has raised the horn of His people, praise for all His pious ones, for the children of Israel, the people near to Him. Praise the Lord.

While the Torah scroll is being returned to the Ark, on Shabbat say:

Ps. 29 **מִזְמוֹר לְדָוִד** A PSALM of David. Ascribe to the Lord, O you divine beings, ascribe to the Lord glory and strength. Ascribe to the Lord the glory of His name. Bow down to the Lord in the splendor of holiness. The

---

as well as the unusual placement of the word רָצוֹן (desire) at its conclusion (*Ḥatam Sofer*).

Similarly R. Joseph D. Soloveitchik described the Torah principle of catharsis, encountered in many areas of *halakha*, by which we are required to temporarily deprive ourselves of otherwise permissible pleasures, and then enjoy correspondingly greater pleasure when we eventually are permitted to indulge our desires. This is a fundamental principle of Judaism.

מִזְמוֹר לְדָוִד – *A psalm of David*. The Gemara (*Berakhot* 29a) explains that while on weekdays (and Yom Tov that occurs on weekdays) Psalm 24 is recited when returning the Torah to the Ark, on Shabbat we recite Psalm 29 because it mentions God's קול (voice) seven times. This alludes to the seven *berakhot* of the *Musaf Amida* that will follow (*Tur*).

קוֹל יהוה עַל־הַמָּֽיִם, אֵל־הַכָּבוֹד הִרְעִים, יהוה עַל־מַֽיִם רַבִּים:
קוֹל־יהוה בַּכֹּֽחַ, קוֹל יהוה בֶּהָדָר: קוֹל יהוה שֹׁבֵר אֲרָזִים, וַיְשַׁבֵּר
יהוה אֶת־אַרְזֵי הַלְּבָנוֹן: וַיַּרְקִידֵם כְּמוֹ־עֵֽגֶל, לְבָנוֹן וְשִׂרְיוֹן כְּמוֹ בֶן־
רְאֵמִים: קוֹל־יהוה חֹצֵב לַהֲבוֹת אֵשׁ: קוֹל יהוה יָחִיל מִדְבָּר, יָחִיל
יהוה מִדְבַּר קָדֵשׁ: קוֹל יהוה יְחוֹלֵל אַיָּלוֹת וַיֶּחֱשֹׂף יְעָרוֹת, וּבְהֵיכָלוֹ,
כֻּלּוֹ אֹמֵר כָּבוֹד: יהוה לַמַּבּוּל יָשָׁב, וַיֵּשֶׁב יהוה מֶלֶךְ לְעוֹלָם: יהוה
עֹז לְעַמּוֹ יִתֵּן, יהוה יְבָרֵךְ אֶת־עַמּוֹ בַשָּׁלוֹם:

On a יום טוב occurring on a weekday say:

לְדָוִד מִזְמוֹר, לַיהוה הָאָֽרֶץ וּמְלוֹאָהּ, תֵּבֵל וְיֹֽשְׁבֵי בָהּ: כִּי־הוּא תהלים כד
עַל־יַמִּים יְסָדָהּ, וְעַל־נְהָרוֹת יְכוֹנְנֶֽהָ: מִי־יַעֲלֶה
בְהַר־יהוה, וּמִי־יָקוּם בִּמְקוֹם קָדְשׁוֹ: נְקִי כַפַּֽיִם וּבַר־לֵבָב, אֲשֶׁר
לֹא־נָשָׂא לַשָּׁוְא נַפְשִׁי וְלֹא נִשְׁבַּע לְמִרְמָה: יִשָּׂא בְרָכָה מֵאֵת יהוה,
וּצְדָקָה מֵאֱלֹהֵי יִשְׁעוֹ: זֶה דּוֹר דֹּרְשָׁיו, מְבַקְשֵׁי פָנֶֽיךָ, יַעֲקֹב, סֶֽלָה:
שְׂאוּ שְׁעָרִים רָאשֵׁיכֶם, וְהִנָּשְׂאוּ פִּתְחֵי עוֹלָם, וְיָבוֹא מֶֽלֶךְ הַכָּבוֹד:
מִי זֶה מֶֽלֶךְ הַכָּבוֹד, יהוה עִזּוּז וְגִבּוֹר, יהוה גִּבּוֹר מִלְחָמָה: שְׂאוּ
שְׁעָרִים רָאשֵׁיכֶם, וּשְׂאוּ פִּתְחֵי עוֹלָם, וְיָבֹא מֶֽלֶךְ הַכָּבוֹד: מִי הוּא
זֶה מֶֽלֶךְ הַכָּבוֹד, יהוה צְבָאוֹת הוּא מֶֽלֶךְ הַכָּבוֹד, סֶֽלָה:

As the ספר תורה is placed into the ארון קודש, all say:

וּבְנֻחֹה יֹאמַר, שׁוּבָה יהוה רִבְבוֹת אַלְפֵי יִשְׂרָאֵל: קוּמָה יהוה במדבר י תהלים קלב
לִמְנוּחָתֶךָ, אַתָּה וַאֲרוֹן עֻזֶּךָ: כֹּהֲנֶיךָ יִלְבְּשׁוּ־צֶדֶק, וַחֲסִידֶיךָ
יְרַנֵּֽנוּ: בַּעֲבוּר דָּוִד עַבְדֶּךָ אַל־תָּשֵׁב פְּנֵי מְשִׁיחֶךָ: כִּי לֶקַח טוֹב נָתַתִּי משלי ד
לָכֶם, תּוֹרָתִי אַל־תַּעֲזֹֽבוּ: עֵץ־חַיִּים הִיא לַמַּחֲזִיקִים בָּהּ, וְתֹמְכֶיהָ משלי ג
מְאֻשָּׁר: דְּרָכֶֽיהָ דַרְכֵי־נֹֽעַם וְכָל־נְתִיבֹתֶֽיהָ שָׁלוֹם: ◄ הֲשִׁיבֵנוּ יהוה איכה ה
אֵלֶֽיךָ וְנָשֽׁוּבָה, חַדֵּשׁ יָמֵֽינוּ כְּקֶֽדֶם:

The ארון קודש is closed.

וּבְנֻחֹה יֹאמַר – *And when the Ark rested, Moses would say.* This is the companion verse to וַיְהִי בִּנְסֹעַ הָאָרֹן ("When the Ark moved forward"), which Moses proclaimed when the Ark began to journey, and which we recite when removing the Torah from the Ark.

voice of the Lord is upon the waters. The God of glory thunders. The Lord is upon many waters. The voice of the Lord is powerful. The voice of the Lord is majestic. The voice of the Lord breaks cedars, and the Lord breaks the cedars of Lebanon. And He makes them skip like a calf, Lebanon and Sirion like a young wild ox. The voice of the Lord hews out flames of fire. The voice of the Lord shakes the wilderness. The Lord shakes the wilderness of Kadesh. The voice of the Lord causes the hinds to tremble, and strips the forests bare, and in His Temple all say: Glory. The Lord sat for a flood, but the Lord sits as King forever. The Lord will give strength to His people. The Lord will bless His people with peace.

On a Yom Tov occurring on a weekday say:

Ps. 24 **לְדָוִד מִזְמוֹר** OF DAVID. A psalm. The earth is the Lord's and the fullness thereof, the world and those who dwell in it. For He has founded it upon the seas, and has established it upon the floods. Who shall ascend the mountain of the Lord, and who shall stand in His holy place? He who has clean hands and a pure heart, who has not sworn in vain "by my soul," and has not sworn deceitfully, he shall receive the blessing from the Lord, and righteousness from the God of his salvation. This is the company of those who seek Him, who seek Your face, Jacob. Selah. Lift up your heads, O gates, and be lifted up, O everlasting doors, so that the King of glory may come in. Who is this King of glory? The Lord strong and mighty, the Lord mighty in battle. Lift up your heads, O gates, and lift them up, O everlasting doors, so that the King of glory may come in. Who is He, this King of glory? The Lord of hosts, He is the King of glory. Selah.

As the Torah scroll is placed into the Ark, say:

Num. 10 **וּבְנֻחֹה** AND WHEN the Ark rested, Moses would say: "Return, O Lord,
Ps. 132 to the myriad thousands of Israel." Arise, O Lord, to Your resting place,
You and the Ark of Your strength. May Your priests be clothed in
righteousness, and may Your pious ones shout for joy. For the sake of
Prov. 4 David Your servant, do not turn away the face of Your anointed. I have
Prov. 3 given you a good doctrine, My Torah, do not forsake it. It is a tree of
life for those who grasp it, and they who uphold it are made happy. Its
Lam. 5 ways are ways of pleasantness, and all its paths are peace. ▸ Lord, turn
us to You once again, for we wish to return; renew our days as of old.

The Ark is closed.

חצי קדיש

ש״ץ: **יִתְגַּדַּל** וְיִתְקַדַּשׁ שְׁמֵהּ רַבָּא (קהל: אָמֵן), בְּעָלְמָא דִּי בְרָא כִרְעוּתֵהּ.
וְיַמְלִיךְ מַלְכוּתֵהּ, בְּחַיֵּיכוֹן וּבְיוֹמֵיכוֹן וּבְחַיֵּי דְכָל בֵּית
יִשְׂרָאֵל, בַּעֲגָלָא וּבִזְמַן קָרִיב, וְאִמְרוּ אָמֵן. (קהל: אָמֵן)

קהל וש״ץ: יְהֵא שְׁמֵהּ רַבָּא מְבָרַךְ לְעָלַם וּלְעָלְמֵי עָלְמַיָּא.

ש״ץ: יִתְבָּרַךְ וְיִשְׁתַּבַּח וְיִתְפָּאַר, וְיִתְרוֹמַם וְיִתְנַשֵּׂא וְיִתְהַדָּר וְיִתְעַלֶּה
וְיִתְהַלָּל שְׁמֵהּ דְּקֻדְשָׁא בְּרִיךְ הוּא (קהל: בְּרִיךְ הוּא), לְעֵלָּא מִן כָּל
בִּרְכָתָא /בשבת שובה: לְעֵלָּא (וּ)לְעֵלָּא מִכָּל בִּרְכָתָא/ וְשִׁירָתָא, תֻּשְׁבְּחָתָא
וְנֶחֱמָתָא דַּאֲמִירָן בְּעָלְמָא, וְאִמְרוּ אָמֵן. (קהל: אָמֵן)

מוסף לשבת

On יום טוב (*including* שבת חול המועד) *say the* מוסף לשלוש רגלים *on page 828.*

עמידה

One begins the עמידה *by taking three steps forward (OḤ 95:1). According to some traditions, one should first take three steps back before moving forward (MB 95:3). The* עמידה *is recited with one's feet together. One should try to concentrate on the simple meaning of the words of the* עמידה *with the awareness throughout that one is standing in the presence of the Almighty (OḤ 98:1 and MB 98:1). At the points indicated by* ', *bend the knees at the first word, bow at the second, and stand straight before saying God's name.*

כִּי שֵׁם יהוה אֶקְרָא, הָבוּ גֹדֶל לֵאלֹהֵינוּ: דברים לב
אֲדֹנָי, שְׂפָתַי תִּפְתָּח, וּפִי יַגִּיד תְּהִלָּתֶךָ: תהלים נא

אבות

'**בָּרוּךְ** אַתָּה יהוה, אֱלֹהֵינוּ וֵאלֹהֵי אֲבוֹתֵינוּ, אֱלֹהֵי אַבְרָהָם, אֱלֹהֵי
יִצְחָק, וֵאלֹהֵי יַעֲקֹב, הָאֵל הַגָּדוֹל הַגִּבּוֹר וְהַנּוֹרָא, אֵל עֶלְיוֹן,
גּוֹמֵל חֲסָדִים טוֹבִים, וְקוֹנֵה הַכֹּל, וְזוֹכֵר חַסְדֵי אָבוֹת, וּמֵבִיא גוֹאֵל
לִבְנֵי בְנֵיהֶם לְמַעַן שְׁמוֹ בְּאַהֲבָה.

מוּסָף / MUSAF

אֱלֹהֵי אַבְרָהָם, אֱלֹהֵי יִצְחָק, וֵאלֹהֵי יַעֲקֹב – *God of Abraham, God of Isaac and God of Jacob.* Rather than saying "The God of Abraham, Isaac, and Jacob" which would be expected as we do not needlessly repeat God's names, the *Amida* starts by repeating His name three times, because each of the patriarchs served God differently, reflecting their own personalities. Taken together, this teaches us how to serve

HALF KADDISH

Leader: יִתְגַּדַּל EXALTED AND HALLOWED may God's great name be, in the world He created as He willed. May He reign in your lifetimes and in your days, and in the lifetime of the whole house of Israel, speedily and soon, and say, Amen.

All: May His great name be blessed forever and all time.

Leader: Blessed and praised, honored, extolled, glorified, adored and exalted above all be the name of the Holy One, blessed is He, (*Between Rosh Hashana & Yom Kippur:* above and) beyond any blessing, hymn, praise, or expressions of consolation that may be uttered in this world, and say, Amen.

MUSAF FOR SHABBAT

On Yom Tov (including Shabbat Ḥol HaMo'ed) say the Musaf for Festivals on page 829.

AMIDA

One begins the Amida by taking three steps forward (OḤ 95:1). According to some traditions, one should first take three steps back before moving forward (MB 95:3). The Amida is recited with one's feet together. One should try to concentrate on the simple meaning of the words of the Amida with the awareness throughout that one is standing in the presence of the Almighty (OḤ 98:1 and MB 98:1). At the points indicated by ▾, bend the knees at the first word, bow at the second, and stand straight before saying God's name.

Deut. 32 WHEN I proclaim the name of the LORD, ascribe greatness to our God.

Ps. 51 "O my Master, open my lips, and my mouth will relate Your praise."

PATRIARCHS

▾ בָּרוּךְ BLESSED ARE YOU, LORD, our God and the God of our fathers, the God of Abraham, the God of Isaac, and the God of Jacob, the God Who is great, mighty, and awesome, God most exalted, Who bestows rewards of benevolent kindness, Who is the Creator of everything, Who remembers all the kind acts of the fathers, and Who brings a redeemer to their children's children, for the sake of His name, with love.

God. Thus Abraham was a person of חֶסֶד (compassion), whose whole life was dedicated to helping others. Isaac was a man of גְּבוּרָה (self-discipline), while Jacob strove to achieve אֱמֶת (truth). At the outset of every *Amida*, when we seek to enter into the presence of God, we must follow in the footsteps of our patriarchs (R. Eliyahu Dessler).

בשבת שובה: זָכְרֵנוּ לְחַיִּים, מֶלֶךְ חָפֵץ בַּחַיִּים, וְכָתְבֵנוּ בְּסֵפֶר הַחַיִּים, לְמַעַנְךָ אֱלֹהִים חַיִּים.

(*If forgotten, no corrective action is necessary.*)

מֶלֶךְ עוֹזֵר וּמוֹשִׁיעַ וּמָגֵן. ׳בָּרוּךְ אַתָּה יהוה, מָגֵן אַבְרָהָם.

גבורות

אַתָּה גִּבּוֹר לְעוֹלָם, אֲדֹנָי, מְחַיֵּה מֵתִים אַתָּה, רַב לְהוֹשִׁיעַ.

בחורף: מַשִּׁיב הָרוּחַ וּמוֹרִיד הַגֶּשֶׁם

מְכַלְכֵּל חַיִּים בְּחֶסֶד, מְחַיֵּה מֵתִים בְּרַחֲמִים רַבִּים, סוֹמֵךְ נוֹפְלִים, וְרוֹפֵא חוֹלִים, וּמַתִּיר אֲסוּרִים, וּמְקַיֵּם אֱמוּנָתוֹ לִישֵׁנֵי עָפָר. מִי כָמְוֹךָ, בַּעַל גְּבוּרוֹת, וּמִי דּוֹמֶה לָּךְ, מֶלֶךְ, מֵמִית וּמְחַיֶּה וּמַצְמִיחַ יְשׁוּעָה.

בשבת שובה: מִי כָמְוֹךָ אַב הָרַחֲמִים, זוֹכֵר יְצוּרָיו לְחַיִּים בְּרַחֲמִים.

(*If forgotten, no corrective action is necessary.*)

וְנֶאֱמָן אַתָּה לְהַחֲיוֹת מֵתִים. בָּרוּךְ אַתָּה יהוה, מְחַיֵּה הַמֵּתִים.

When saying the עמידה *silently, continue with* אַתָּה קָדוֹשׁ *on the next page.*

קדושה

During the חזרת הש״ץ, *the following is said standing with feet together, rising on the toes at the words indicated by* ˄.

then קהל ש״ץ: **נַעֲרִיצְךָ** וְנַקְדִּישְׁךָ כְּסוֹד שִׂיחַ שַׂרְפֵי קֹדֶשׁ, הַמַּקְדִּישִׁים שִׁמְךָ בַּקֹּדֶשׁ, כַּכָּתוּב עַל יַד נְבִיאֶךָ: וְקָרָא זֶה אֶל־זֶה וְאָמַר ישעיה ו

then קהל ש״ץ: ˄קָדוֹשׁ, ˄קָדוֹשׁ, ˄קָדוֹשׁ יהוה צְבָאוֹת, מְלֹא כָל הָאָרֶץ כְּבוֹדוֹ:

כְּבוֹדוֹ מָלֵא עוֹלָם, מְשָׁרְתָיו שׁוֹאֲלִים זֶה לָזֶה, אַיֵּה מְקוֹם כְּבוֹדוֹ,

ש״ץ: לְעֻמָּתָם בָּרוּךְ יֹאמֵרוּ

קְדֻשָּׁה / KEDUSHA

אַיֵּה מְקוֹם כְּבוֹדוֹ – *Where is the place of His glory?* God is both immanent (i.e., His presence can be discovered in His created works), and transcendent (His existence is above and beyond any imaginable manifestation in His creation). His transcendent "place" is unknowable (and hence a סוד – secret) even to the angels who dwell in the heaven that He created, and thus they "ask" each other where His place might

For laws regarding "Omission/Insertion of *Mashiv Haru'aḥ,*" see page 109.
For laws regarding "*Responding to the Leader during Kedusha,*" see page 510.

On Shabbat Shuva: Remember us for life, King Who desires life, and inscribe us in the book of life for Your sake, Living God.

(If forgotten, no corrective action is necessary.)

King Who helps, saves, and shields, ▾blessed are You, LORD, Shield of Abraham.

GOD'S MIGHT

אַתָּה YOU, my Master, are forever mighty, You are the Resurrector of the dead, with great power to save.

In winter: He makes the wind blow and the rain fall

He sustains the living with kindness, He resurrects the dead with great compassion, He supports those who are falling, He heals the sick, He sets the incarcerated free, and He fulfills what He has promised to those who sleep in the dust. Who is like You, O mighty One, and who can be compared to You, O King Who causes death and resurrects, and Who causes salvation to sprout?

On Shabbat Shuva: Who is like You, merciful Father, Who in compassion remembers for life those He has created.

(If forgotten, no corrective action is necessary.)

Trustworthy are You to resurrect the dead. Blessed are You, LORD, Resurrector of the dead.

When saying the Amida silently, continue with "You are holy" on the next page.

KEDUSHA *During the Leader's Repetition, the following is said standing with feet together, rising on the toes at the words indicated by* ▴.

Cong. then Leader: נַעֲרִיצְךָ WE WILL REVERE You and sanctify You, in the manner of the gathered counsels of the holy Seraphim, who sanctify Your name in the celestial Sanctuary, as it is written by Your prophet:

Is. 6 "And they call to one another:

Cong. then Leader: ▴"Holy, ▴holy, ▴holy is the LORD of hosts; the whole world is filled with His glory.'"

His glory fills the world. His ministering angels ask each other, "Where is the place of His glory?"

Leader: Those facing them say: "Blessed –"

---

be. The souls of men and the angels all long to find God and to encounter Him in His celestial "place." This longing is the root of repentance (R. Naḥman of Breslov).

יחזקאל ג | קהל *then* ש״ץ: ▲בָּרוּךְ כְּבוֹד־יהוה מִמְּקוֹמוֹ:

מִמְּקוֹמוֹ הוּא יִפֶן בְּרַחֲמִים, וְיָחֹן עַם הַמְיַחֲדִים שְׁמוֹ, עֶרֶב וָבְקֶר בְּכָל יוֹם תָּמִיד, פַּעֲמַיִם בְּאַהֲבָה שְׁמַע אוֹמְרִים

דברים ו | קהל *then* ש״ץ: שְׁמַע יִשְׂרָאֵל, יהוה אֱלֹהֵינוּ, יהוה אֶחָד:

הוּא אֱלֹהֵינוּ, הוּא אָבִינוּ, הוּא מַלְכֵּנוּ, הוּא מוֹשִׁיעֵנוּ, וְהוּא יַשְׁמִיעֵנוּ

במדבר טו | בְּרַחֲמָיו שֵׁנִית לְעֵינֵי כָּל חָי, לִהְיוֹת לָכֶם לֵאלֹהִים, אֲנִי יהוה אֱלֹהֵיכֶם:

ש״ץ: וּבְדִבְרֵי קָדְשְׁךָ כָּתוּב לֵאמֹר

תהלים קמו | קהל *then* ש״ץ: ▲יִמְלֹךְ יהוה לְעוֹלָם, אֱלֹהַיִךְ צִיּוֹן לְדֹר וָדֹר, הַלְלוּיָהּ:

ש״ץ: לְדוֹר וָדוֹר נַגִּיד גָּדְלֶךָ, וּלְנֵצַח נְצָחִים קְדֻשָּׁתְךָ נַקְדִּישׁ, וְשִׁבְחֲךָ אֱלֹהֵינוּ מִפִּינוּ לֹא יָמוּשׁ לְעוֹלָם וָעֶד, כִּי אֵל מֶלֶךְ גָּדוֹל וְקָדוֹשׁ אָתָּה. בָּרוּךְ אַתָּה יהוה, הָאֵל הַקָּדוֹשׁ./ בשבת שובה: הַמֶּלֶךְ הַקָּדוֹשׁ./

The שליח ציבור ***continues on the next page with*** תִּכַּנְתָּ שַׁבָּת ***on*** שבת ***and*** אַתָּה יָצַרְתָּ ***on*** ראש חודש.

קדושת השם

אַתָּה קָדוֹשׁ וְשִׁמְךָ קָדוֹשׁ. וּקְדוֹשִׁים בְּכָל יוֹם יְהַלְלוּךָ סֶּלָה. בָּרוּךְ אַתָּה יהוה, הָאֵל הַקָּדוֹשׁ./ בשבת שובה: הַמֶּלֶךְ הַקָּדוֹשׁ./

(*If forgotten, repeat the* עמידה.)

The *Kedusha* reflects the disparate experiences of Isaiah and Ezekiel. The former, living during the glory days of the First Temple, felt God's presence in every place and at all times, thus reporting the angels' declaration, "מְלֹא כָל הָאָרֶץ כְּבוֹדוֹ – The whole world is filled with His glory." Ezekiel, on the other hand, was overcome by the bitter experience of destruction and exile to Babylon, and thus he speaks of God's place in more restrictive language introduced in the *Kedusha* by the plaintive angelic cry, "אַיֵּה מְקוֹם כְּבוֹדוֹ – Where is His place of glory?" So it is with the Jewish people at different stages of its history. And so too in our own lives there are times when we feel God's comforting presence, while at other times He withdraws "to His place" and is distant, leaving us feeling frightened and alone (R. Joseph B. Soloveitchik).

שְׁמַע יִשְׂרָאֵל – *Hear, O Israel*. R. Yehudai Gaon of eighth-century Babylonia writes that early seventh-century Christian authorities in the land of Israel forbade the public recital of the *Shema*. As a result those communities added the first and last phrases of the *Shema* to the *Kedusha* of *Musaf*, which could be recited at a later point in the day when the government enforcers had already left the synagogue. While the ban was lifted when the Muslims later conquered Israel, the communities maintained the established custom (R. Israel Schepansky).

By carefully examining numerous extant

Ezek. 3 *Cong. then Leader:* ▲"Blessed is the glory of the LORD from His place."
May He turn in mercy from His place, to be gracious to the people who proclaim the unity of His name, evening and morning, every day, continually, twice daily reciting the Shema with love.

Deut. 6 *Cong. then Leader:* Hear, O Israel, the LORD is our God, the LORD is One.
He is our God, He is our Father, He is our King, He is our Savior – and He, in His compassion, will let us hear a second time in the
Num. 15 presence of all that lives, [His promise] "to be your God. I am the LORD your God."

Leader: And in Your holy Writings it is written, saying:

Ps. 146 *Cong. then Leader:* ▲"The LORD will reign forever, Your God, O Zion, to all generations. Praise the LORD."

Leader: To all generations we will proclaim Your greatness, and forever declare Your holiness, and the praise of You, our God, will never leave our mouth, for You are God and King, great and holy; blessed are You, LORD, the holy God. / *On Shabbat Shuva:* the holy King. /

The Leader continues on the next page with "You established the Sabbath" on Shabbat and "You created" on Rosh Ḥodesh.

HOLINESS

אַתָּה YOU ARE HOLY and Your name is holy, and holy ones will praise You every day, forever. Blessed are You, LORD, the holy God.
/ *On Shabbat Shuva:* the holy King./
(*If forgotten, repeat the Amida.*)

---

versions of the *Kedusha* dating from the third until the seventh century, including those from Tannaitic, Amoraic, Midrashic, and *Geniza* texts, in particular a passage in *Pirkei deR. Eliezer*, we can provide an alternative explanation for the addition of these verses of the *Shema* as found in the *Musaf Kedusha*. Rather than seeing them as artificially and surreptitiously inserted in public prayer as a result of persecution, they actually are a logical extension of the regular *Kedusha*. Thus after recording how the angels in heaven praise God (as described by Isaiah and Ezekiel), the *Kedusha* carefully balances the events "above" with those "below" by describing how in our world the Jewish people praises God twice daily by reciting the *Shema* that proclaims His uniqueness to all the world. For this, we petition God to respond by revealing to all of humanity that the Lord is indeed our God. If He will do that, we in turn will proclaim before all that He Who is "the God of Zion," the God of the Jewish people, will rule over

For the *"Instructions for someone who made a mistake and recited the wrong Amida,"* see page 397.

On ראש חודש שבת *say* אַתָּה יָצַרְתָּ *below.*

קדושת היום

תִּכַּנְתָּ שַׁבָּת, רָצִיתָ קָרְבְּנוֹתֶיהָ, צִוִּיתָ פֵּרוּשֶׁיהָ עִם סִדּוּרֵי נְסָכֶיהָ, מְעַנְּגֶיהָ לְעוֹלָם כָּבוֹד יִנְחָלוּ, טוֹעֲמֶיהָ חַיִּים זָכוּ, וְגַם הָאוֹהֲבִים דְּבָרֶיהָ גְּדֻלָּה בָּחָרוּ. אָז מִסִּינַי נִצְטַוּוּ עָלֶיהָ, וַתְּצַוֵּנוּ יהוה אֱלֹהֵינוּ לְהַקְרִיב בָּהּ קָרְבַּן מוּסַף שַׁבָּת כָּרָאוּי.

acrostic, starting with ת and ending with א. R. Yosef Karo explained that the use of this literary device was intended to remind us of a similar usage by the prophet Zechariah in reference to the final redemption. For Zechariah 10:8 states אֶשְׁרְקָה לָהֶם וַאֲקַבְּצֵם כִּי פְדִיתִים ("I will whistle for them to gather together so I can redeem them"), in which the first word includes three of the last four letters of the alphabet in reverse order, immediately followed by a promise of redemption. So too, he explains, the reverse acrostic in *Musaf* here implies (as does Isaiah 56:4–7) that those who observe Shabbat will be rewarded to see the final redemption (*Beit Yosef*).

all forever and ever. Thus understood, the *Kedusha* embodies a finely balanced approach, fully reflecting the desire of the sages to acknowledge the heavenly sphere, while giving due consideration to the practical realm of human endeavor in the service of God and in the redemption of the Jewish people. This is consistent with the original intent of the third *berakha* of the *Amida*, as earlier described in a comment on the weekday *Shaharit Amida* (Prof. Ezra Fleischer).

תִּכַּנְתָּ שַׁבָּת – *You established the Sabbath.* The first twenty-two words of this prayer begin with the letters of the alphabet in a reverse

בשבת ראש חודש:

אַתָּה יָצַרְתָּ עוֹלָמְךָ מִקֶּדֶם, כִּלִּיתָ מְלַאכְתְּךָ בַּיּוֹם הַשְּׁבִיעִי, אָהַבְתָּ אוֹתָנוּ וְרָצִיתָ בָּנוּ, וְרוֹמַמְתָּנוּ מִכָּל הַלְּשׁוֹנוֹת, וְקִדַּשְׁתָּנוּ בְּמִצְוֹתֶיךָ, וְקֵרַבְתָּנוּ מַלְכֵּנוּ לַעֲבוֹדָתֶךָ, וְשִׁמְךָ הַגָּדוֹל וְהַקָּדוֹשׁ עָלֵינוּ קָרָאתָ. וַתִּתֶּן לָנוּ יהוה אֱלֹהֵינוּ בְּאַהֲבָה, שַׁבָּתוֹת לִמְנוּחָה וְרָאשֵׁי חֳדָשִׁים לְכַפָּרָה. וּלְפִי שֶׁחָטָאנוּ לְפָנֶיךָ אֲנַחְנוּ וַאֲבוֹתֵינוּ, חָרְבָה עִירֵנוּ, וְשָׁמֵם בֵּית מִקְדָּשֵׁנוּ, וְגָלָה יְקָרֵנוּ, וְנֻטַּל כָּבוֹד מִבֵּית חַיֵּינוּ, וְאֵין אֲנַחְנוּ יְכוֹלִים לַעֲשׂוֹת חוֹבוֹתֵינוּ בְּבֵית בְּחִירָתֶךָ, בַּבַּיִת הַגָּדוֹל וְהַקָּדוֹשׁ שֶׁנִּקְרָא שִׁמְךָ עָלָיו, מִפְּנֵי הַיָּד שֶׁנִּשְׁתַּלְּחָה בְּמִקְדָּשֶׁךָ.

Continue below the line on the next page.

אַתָּה יָצַרְתָּ / ATA YATZARTA

When Rosh Hodesh coincides with Shabbat, the fourth blessing of the *Amida* of *Musaf* incorporates both themes. If one accidentally recited the ordinary *Musaf Amida* for Shabbat, one must repeat the *Amida*. If one recited the proper text but in the conclusion of the blessing omitted וּבְרָאשֵׁי חָדְשֵׁיכֶם, one is not required to repeat the *Amida* (*MB* 425:15 and *Iggerot Moshe OH* 4:70 #14).

On Shabbat Rosh Ḥodesh say "You created" (Ata Yatzarta), below.

HOLINESS OF THE DAY

תִּכַּנְתָּ שַׁבָּת YOU ESTABLISHED the Sabbath, desired its sacrifices, and commanded its laws via detailed commentary that included the order of its sacrifices. Those who delight in it will always inherit honor, those who taste it have merited life, and those who cherish its teachings have chosen greatness. Then, at Sinai, they were commanded regarding it, when You, LORD our God, commanded us to offer on it the additional Sabbath sacrifice, properly.

A different explanation is provided by R. Yaakov Emden, who suggested that this reverse acrostic reminds us that one who observes Shabbat is able to "go back" to the very beginning of time, to recall and celebrate God's act of creation itself. Taking both explanations together, this literary structure teaches us, as does the Shabbat itself, that God directs all of history, infusing it with meaning and purpose, from the moment of creation until the ultimate redemption (R. Leonard Matanky).

צִוִּיתָ פֵּרוּשֶׁיהָ – *Commanded its laws.* The numerous and complex laws of Shabbat are not stated in detail in the Torah. They were revealed instead to Moses as part of the oral Torah. Without that tradition it would be impossible to know how to keep Shabbat. Thus in this phrase we quote God as saying, "I have elaborated on the written Torah's laws regarding Shabbat in its oral commentary."

אָז מִסִּינַי – *Then, at Sinai.* This phrase seems to contradict the Torah itself. As *Sanhedrin* 56b notes, in Exodus 16 (that describes the events at Marah preceding Sinai) we read at length that on Shabbat, which is there described as שַׁבַּת קֹדֶשׁ לַה' ("It is a Sabbath sacred unto the Lord" (v. 23,) the Israelites were forbidden to collect the manna. Thus Shabbat was commanded at Marah, and not, as stated here, at Sinai. We can answer this question as follows: there are two separate but overlapping ways in which the seventh day becomes sanctified as Shabbat. The first occurred on the seventh day of Creation, when God Himself sanctified

---

On Shabbat Rosh Ḥodesh:

אַתָּה יָצַרְתָּ YOU CREATED Your universe from the beginning of time, completing Your work on the seventh day. You have loved us and desired us, raising us above every other nation, sanctifying us with Your commandments, drawing us close to perform Your service, and calling us by Your great and holy name. In Your love, LORD our God, You have given us Sabbaths for rest and days of Rosh Ḥodesh for atonement. Yet because we and our fathers sinned, our city was destroyed and our Temple is desolate. Our splendor was exiled, and the glory was removed from the home of our [national] existence. We cannot carry out our duties in Your chosen Temple, that great and holy House that bore Your name, because of the hand that was unleashed against Your Sanctuary.

Continue below the line on the next page.

On an ordinary שבת*, except* שבת ראש חודש*, continue here:*

יְהִי רָצוֹן מִלְּפָנֶיךָ, יהוה אֱלֹהֵינוּ וֵאלֹהֵי אֲבוֹתֵינוּ, שֶׁתַּעֲלֵנוּ
בְשִׂמְחָה לְאַרְצֵנוּ וְתִטָּעֵנוּ בִּגְבוּלֵנוּ, וְשָׁם נַעֲשֶׂה לְפָנֶיךָ
אֶת קָרְבְּנוֹת חוֹבוֹתֵינוּ, תְּמִידִים כְּסִדְרָם וּמוּסָפִים כְּהִלְכָתָם.

וְאֶת מוּסַף יוֹם הַשַּׁבָּת הַזֶּה, נַעֲשֶׂה וְנַקְרִיב לְפָנֶיךָ בְּאַהֲבָה כְּמִצְוַת
רְצוֹנֶךָ, כְּמוֹ שֶׁכָּתַבְתָּ עָלֵינוּ בְּתוֹרָתֶךָ, עַל יְדֵי מֹשֶׁה עַבְדֶּךָ
מִפִּי כְבוֹדֶךָ, כָּאָמוּר

וּבְיוֹם הַשַּׁבָּת שְׁנֵי־כְבָשִׂים בְּנֵי־שָׁנָה תְּמִימִם, וּשְׁנֵי עֶשְׂרֹנִים במדבר כח
סֹלֶת מִנְחָה בְּלוּלָה בַשֶּׁמֶן וְנִסְכּוֹ: עֹלַת שַׁבַּת בְּשַׁבַּתּוֹ,
עַל־עֹלַת הַתָּמִיד וְנִסְכָּהּ:

---

it, as it says וַיְקַדֵּשׁ אוֹתוֹ (He sanctified it). We commemorate that divine sanctification every Shabbat passively, by resting just as God did, and desisting from forbidden labor, as did the Israelites at Marah. The second form of sanctification requires the active participation of the Jewish people. This action was commanded not at Marah but at Sinai, as described in Leviticus 23:1–3 when God instructs Israel saying (first regarding Shabbat and then regarding the festivals), "These are the festivals of the Lord which *you shall declare* to be מִקְרָאֵי קֹדֶשׁ (days which are declared holy)." The ensuing verses go on to describe the special sacrifices of those days. In other words, it is for the Jewish people to complete the sanctification of Shabbat which God began at Creation. This is accomplished every seventh day by (a) reciting *Kiddush* at its outset when we declare the holiness of the day, and (b) offering special Shabbat sacrifices (as found in that chapter, and later in Numbers 28.) We can thus well

---

On שבת ראש חודש*, continue here:*

יְהִי רָצוֹן מִלְּפָנֶיךָ, יהוה אֱלֹהֵינוּ וֵאלֹהֵי אֲבוֹתֵינוּ, שֶׁתַּעֲלֵנוּ בְשִׂמְחָה לְאַרְצֵנוּ
וְתִטָּעֵנוּ בִּגְבוּלֵנוּ, וְשָׁם נַעֲשֶׂה לְפָנֶיךָ אֶת קָרְבְּנוֹת חוֹבוֹתֵינוּ,
תְּמִידִים כְּסִדְרָם וּמוּסָפִים כְּהִלְכָתָם.

וְאֶת מוּסְפֵי יוֹם הַשַּׁבָּת הַזֶּה וְיוֹם רֹאשׁ הַחֹדֶשׁ הַזֶּה, נַעֲשֶׂה וְנַקְרִיב לְפָנֶיךָ
בְּאַהֲבָה כְּמִצְוַת רְצוֹנֶךָ, כְּמוֹ שֶׁכָּתַבְתָּ עָלֵינוּ בְּתוֹרָתֶךָ עַל יְדֵי מֹשֶׁה
עַבְדֶּךָ מִפִּי כְבוֹדֶךָ, כָּאָמוּר

וּבְיוֹם הַשַּׁבָּת שְׁנֵי־כְבָשִׂים בְּנֵי־שָׁנָה תְּמִימִם, וּשְׁנֵי עֶשְׂרֹנִים סֹלֶת מִנְחָה במדבר כח
בְּלוּלָה בַשֶּׁמֶן וְנִסְכּוֹ: עֹלַת שַׁבַּת בְּשַׁבַּתּוֹ, עַל־עֹלַת הַתָּמִיד וְנִסְכָּהּ:

Continue below the line on the next page.

On an ordinary Shabbat, except Shabbat Rosh Ḥodesh, continue here:

יְהִי רָצוֹן MAY IT BE Your will, LORD our God and God of our fathers, to bring us in joy to our land and implant us within its borders. There, in Your presence, we will bring the sacrifices required of us, including the daily ones in their order, and the additional sacrifices according to their laws.

וְאֶת AS TO the additional offering of this Sabbath day we will prepare and offer it before You with love, in accordance with the commandment that you willed, as You have written for us in Your Torah at the hand of Moses Your servant, at Your command, as it is said:

Num. 28 וּבְיוֹם "ON THE SABBATH day you shall bring two unblemished one-year-old male lambs, a grain-offering of two-tenths of an ephah of fine flour mixed with oil, and its libation. This is the burnt-offering for every Sabbath, in addition to the regular daily burnt-offering and its libation."

---

understand that the *Musaf* prayer, which focuses on the Shabbat sacrifices in detail, declares at the outset that these were commanded at Sinai, not at Marah, and in this regard Shabbat is like Yom Tov. This connection to the festivals, which are days of rejoicing, would also account for the subsequent statement that those who "keep the Sabbath...rejoice," even though there is no obligation per se of שִׂמְחָה on Shabbat (R. Joseph B. Soloveitchik).

On Shabbat Rosh Ḥodesh, continue here:

יְהִי רָצוֹן MAY IT BE Your will, LORD our God and God of our fathers, to bring us in joy to our land, and implant us within its borders. There, in Your presence, we will bring the sacrifices required of us, including the daily ones in their order and the additional sacrifices according to their laws.

וְאֶת AS TO the additional offerings of this Sabbath day and this day of Rosh Ḥodesh we will prepare and offer them before You with love, in accordance with the commandment that You willed, as You have written for us in Your Torah at the hand of Moses, Your servant, at Your command, as it is said:

Num. 28 וּבְיוֹם ON THE SABBATH day you shall bring two unblemished one-year-old male lambs, a grain-offering of two-tenths of an ephah of fine flour mixed with oil, and its libation. This is the burnt-offering for every Sabbath, in addition to the regular daily burnt-offering and its libation.

Continue below the line on the next page.

On an ordinary שבת*, except* שבת ראש חודש*, continue here:*

יִשְׂמְחוּ בְמַלְכוּתְךָ שׁוֹמְרֵי שַׁבָּת וְקוֹרְאֵי עֹנֶג, עַם מְקַדְּשֵׁי שְׁבִיעִי, כֻּלָּם יִשְׂבְּעוּ וְיִתְעַנְּגוּ מִטּוּבֶךָ, וּבַשְּׁבִיעִי רָצִיתָ בּוֹ וְקִדַּשְׁתּוֹ, חֶמְדַּת יָמִים אוֹתוֹ קָרָאתָ, זֵכֶר לְמַעֲשֵׂה בְרֵאשִׁית.

אֱלֹהֵינוּ וֵאלֹהֵי אֲבוֹתֵינוּ, רְצֵה בִמְנוּחָתֵנוּ, קַדְּשֵׁנוּ בְּמִצְוֹתֶיךָ וְתֵן חֶלְקֵנוּ בְּתוֹרָתֶךָ, שַׂבְּעֵנוּ מִטּוּבֶךָ, וְשַׂמְּחֵנוּ בִּישׁוּעָתֶךָ, וְטַהֵר לִבֵּנוּ לְעָבְדְּךָ בֶּאֱמֶת, וְהַנְחִילֵנוּ יהוה אֱלֹהֵינוּ בְּאַהֲבָה וּבְרָצוֹן שַׁבַּת קָדְשֶׁךָ, וְיָנוּחוּ בוֹ יִשְׂרָאֵל מְקַדְּשֵׁי שְׁמֶךָ. בָּרוּךְ אַתָּה יהוה, מְקַדֵּשׁ הַשַּׁבָּת.

Continue with רְצֵה *on the next page.*

On שבת ראש חודש*, continue here:*

וּבְרָאשֵׁי חָדְשֵׁיכֶם תַּקְרִיבוּ עֹלָה לַיהוה, פָּרִים בְּנֵי־בָקָר שְׁנַיִם, וְאַיִל אֶחָד, כְּבָשִׂים בְּנֵי־שָׁנָה שִׁבְעָה, תְּמִימִם: וּמִנְחָתָם וְנִסְכֵּיהֶם כִּמְדֻבָּר, שְׁלֹשָׁה עֶשְׂרֹנִים לַפָּר, וּשְׁנֵי עֶשְׂרֹנִים לָאַיִל, וְעִשָּׂרוֹן לַכֶּבֶשׂ, וְיַיִן כְּנִסְכּוֹ, וְשָׂעִיר לְכַפֵּר, וּשְׁנֵי תְמִידִים כְּהִלְכָתָם. במדבר כח

יִשְׂמְחוּ בְמַלְכוּתְךָ שׁוֹמְרֵי שַׁבָּת וְקוֹרְאֵי עֹנֶג, עַם מְקַדְּשֵׁי שְׁבִיעִי, כֻּלָּם יִשְׂבְּעוּ וְיִתְעַנְּגוּ מִטּוּבֶךָ, וּבַשְּׁבִיעִי רָצִיתָ בּוֹ וְקִדַּשְׁתּוֹ, חֶמְדַּת יָמִים אוֹתוֹ קָרָאתָ, זֵכֶר לְמַעֲשֵׂה בְרֵאשִׁית.

אֱלֹהֵינוּ וֵאלֹהֵי אֲבוֹתֵינוּ, רְצֵה בִמְנוּחָתֵנוּ, וְחַדֵּשׁ עָלֵינוּ בְּיוֹם הַשַּׁבָּת הַזֶּה אֶת הַחֹדֶשׁ הַזֶּה, לְטוֹבָה וְלִבְרָכָה, לְשָׂשׂוֹן וּלְשִׂמְחָה, לִישׁוּעָה וּלְנֶחָמָה, לְפַרְנָסָה וּלְכַלְכָּלָה, לְחַיִּים וּלְשָׁלוֹם, לִמְחִילַת חֵטְא וְלִסְלִיחַת עָוֹן (*in a Jewish leap year:* *From* מרחשון *to* אדר שני: וּלְכַפָּרַת פָּשַׁע), כִּי בְעַמְּךָ יִשְׂרָאֵל בָּחַרְתָּ מִכָּל הָאֻמּוֹת, וְשַׁבַּת קָדְשְׁךָ לָהֶם הוֹדַעְתָּ וְחֻקֵּי רָאשֵׁי חֳדָשִׁים לָהֶם קָבָעְתָּ. בָּרוּךְ אַתָּה יהוה, מְקַדֵּשׁ הַשַּׁבָּת וְיִשְׂרָאֵל וְרָאשֵׁי חֳדָשִׁים.

Continue with רְצֵה *on the next page.*

יִשְׂמְחוּ בְמַלְכוּתְךָ שׁוֹמְרֵי שַׁבָּת – *May they who keep the Sabbath.* The wording of this phrase should not be misunderstood to be saying that on Shabbat there is a *mitzva* of שִׂמְחָה (rejoicing) as there is on Yom Tov. On Shabbat there is only an obligation of עֹנֶג (pleasure). At the very most one can say that one who is joyous on Shabbat has thereby fulfilled the *mitzva* of pleasure, insofar as one who is joyous certainly experiences pleasure. That, however, does not mean that there is a requirement to rejoice on Shabbat. This distinction accords with the view of the Vilna

The commentary continues on page 580.

On an ordinary Shabbat, except Shabbat Rosh Ḥodesh, continue here:

יִשְׂמְחוּ MAY THEY who keep the Sabbath and call it a delight rejoice in Your sovereignty. May all Your people who sanctify the seventh day find satisfaction and delight in Your goodness. You desired and sanctified the seventh day, calling it the choicest of days, in remembrance of the act of Creation.

אֱלֹהֵינוּ OUR GOD and God of our fathers, be pleased with our rest. Sanctify us through Your commandments and grant us our portion in Your Torah. Gratify us with Your goodness and gladden us with Your salvation. Purify our heart to serve You in truth. LORD our God, through Your loving favor may You grant that Your holy Sabbath will be our heritage, so that the people of Israel who sanctify Your name will rest on it. Blessed are You, LORD, Who sanctifies the Sabbath.

Continue "May it be Your will" on the next page.

On Shabbat Rosh Ḥodesh, continue here:

Num. 28 וּבְרָאשֵׁי AND ON your days of Rosh Ḥodesh you shall bring as a burnt-offering to the LORD two young bullocks, one ram, and seven unblemished one-year-old male lambs. Together with these their grain-offerings and their libations, as stated in the Torah: three-tenths [of an ephah] for each bullock, two-tenths for the ram, one-tenth for each lamb, and wine for the libation, as well as a male goat for atonement, and the two regular daily burnt-offerings as specified.

יִשְׂמְחוּ MAY THEY who keep the Sabbath and call it a delight rejoice in Your sovereignty. May all Your people who sanctify the seventh day find satisfaction and delight in Your goodness. You desired and sanctified the seventh day, calling it the choicest of days, in remembrance of the act of Creation.

אֱלֹהֵינוּ OUR GOD and God of our fathers, be pleased with our rest, and on this Sabbath day renew for us this month for good and blessing, for joy and gladness, for salvation and consolation, for sustenance and support, for life and peace, for pardon of sin and forgiveness of wrongdoing, (*From Marḥeshvan to Adar Sheni in a Jewish leap year:* and for atonement of transgression). For You have chosen Your people Israel from among all the other nations, informing them of Your holy Sabbath and establishing the statutes of the days of Rosh Ḥodesh for them. Blessed are You, LORD, Who sanctifies the Sabbath, Israel, and the days of Rosh Ḥodesh.

Continue "May it be Your will" on the next page.

עבודה

רְצֵה יהוה אֱלֹהֵינוּ בְּעַמְּךָ יִשְׂרָאֵל, וּבִתְפִלָּתָם, וְהָשֵׁב אֶת הָעֲבוֹדָה לִדְבִיר בֵּיתֶךָ, וְאִשֵּׁי יִשְׂרָאֵל וּתְפִלָּתָם בְּאַהֲבָה תְקַבֵּל בְּרָצוֹן, וּתְהִי לְרָצוֹן תָּמִיד עֲבוֹדַת יִשְׂרָאֵל עַמֶּךָ. וְתֶחֱזֶינָה עֵינֵינוּ בְּשׁוּבְךָ לְצִיּוֹן בְּרַחֲמִים. בָּרוּךְ אַתָּה יהוה, הַמַּחֲזִיר שְׁכִינָתוֹ לְצִיּוֹן.

הודאה

Bow during the first five words.

׳מוֹדִים אֲנַחְנוּ לָךְ, שָׁאַתָּה הוּא יהוה אֱלֹהֵינוּ וֵאלֹהֵי אֲבוֹתֵינוּ לְעוֹלָם וָעֶד. צוּר חַיֵּינוּ, מָגֵן יִשְׁעֵנוּ, אַתָּה הוּא. לְדוֹר וָדוֹר נוֹדֶה לְּךָ וּנְסַפֵּר תְּהִלָּתֶךָ, עַל חַיֵּינוּ הַמְּסוּרִים בְּיָדֶךָ, וְעַל נִשְׁמוֹתֵינוּ הַפְּקוּדוֹת לָךְ, וְעַל נִסֶּיךָ שֶׁבְּכָל יוֹם עִמָּנוּ, וְעַל נִפְלְאוֹתֶיךָ וְטוֹבוֹתֶיךָ, שֶׁבְּכָל עֵת, עֶרֶב וָבֹקֶר וְצָהֳרָיִם. הַטּוֹב, כִּי לֹא כָלוּ רַחֲמֶיךָ, וְהַמְרַחֵם, כִּי לֹא תַמּוּ חֲסָדֶיךָ, מֵעוֹלָם קִוִּינוּ לָךְ.

During חזרת הש״ץ*, the* קהל *says quietly:*

׳מוֹדִים אֲנַחְנוּ לָךְ, שָׁאַתָּה הוּא יהוה אֱלֹהֵינוּ וֵאלֹהֵי אֲבוֹתֵינוּ, אֱלֹהֵי כָל בָּשָׂר, יוֹצְרֵנוּ, יוֹצֵר בְּרֵאשִׁית. בְּרָכוֹת וְהוֹדָאוֹת לְשִׁמְךָ הַגָּדוֹל וְהַקָּדוֹשׁ, עַל שֶׁהֶחֱיִיתָנוּ וְקִיַּמְתָּנוּ. כֵּן תְּחַיֵּנוּ וּתְקַיְּמֵנוּ, וְתֶאֱסֹף גָּלֻיּוֹתֵינוּ לְחַצְרוֹת קָדְשֶׁךָ, לִשְׁמֹר חֻקֶּיךָ וְלַעֲשׂוֹת רְצוֹנֶךָ וּלְעָבְדְּךָ בְּלֵבָב שָׁלֵם, עַל שֶׁאֲנַחְנוּ מוֹדִים לָךְ. בָּרוּךְ אֵל הַהוֹדָאוֹת.

בחנוכה:

עַל הַנִּסִּים וְעַל הַפֻּרְקָן וְעַל הַגְּבוּרוֹת וְעַל הַתְּשׁוּעוֹת וְעַל הַמִּלְחָמוֹת שֶׁעָשִׂיתָ לַאֲבוֹתֵינוּ בַּיָּמִים הָהֵם בַּזְּמַן הַזֶּה.

בִּימֵי מַתִּתְיָהוּ בֶּן יוֹחָנָן כֹּהֵן גָּדוֹל חַשְׁמוֹנַאי וּבָנָיו, כְּשֶׁעָמְדָה מַלְכוּת יָוָן הָרְשָׁעָה עַל עַמְּךָ יִשְׂרָאֵל לְהַשְׁכִּיחָם תּוֹרָתֶךָ וּלְהַעֲבִירָם מֵחֻקֵּי רְצוֹנֶךָ, וְאַתָּה בְּרַחֲמֶיךָ הָרַבִּים עָמַדְתָּ לָהֶם בְּעֵת צָרָתָם, רַבְתָּ

Continued on the top of the next page.

Gaon that only on Yom Tov are we obligated to rejoice. These words therefore say that, "Those who keep Shabbat will, as a result, rejoice in God's sovereignty" (R. Menaḥem Kasher).

For laws regarding "עַל הַנִּסִּים / *Al HaNissim*," see page 128.

TEMPLE SERVICE

רְצֵה LOOK FAVORABLY, LORD our God, upon Your people Israel and their prayer, and restore the service to the Holy of Holies of Your House. Accept with love and favor the fire-offerings of Israel and their prayer. May the service of Israel Your people Israel always find favor with You. May our eyes witness Your return to Zion in compassion. Blessed are You, LORD, Who will restore His Divine Presence to Zion.

THANKSGIVING

Bow during the first seven words.

מוֹדִים WE THANK YOU, for You are the LORD our God and the God of our fathers for all eternity. You are the Rock of our life and Shield of our deliverance. From generation to generation we will thank You and recount Your praise for our lives that are in Your hands, for our souls that are given over to You, for Your miracles that are with us every day, and for Your constant wonders and favors, evening, morning and noon. You are good, for Your compassion does not cease, and You are compassionate, for Your kindness never ends. We have placed our hope in You forever and ever.

During the Leader's Repetition, the congregation says quietly:

מוֹדִים WE THANK YOU, for You are the LORD our God, the God of our fathers and God of all flesh. You are our Maker, the Maker of Creation. Blessings and thanks are due Your great and holy name for You have given us life and preserved us in life. May You continue to keep us in life and preserve us. Gather our exiles to the courtyards of Your Temple so that we may fulfill Your commandments and do Your will, serving You with a perfect heart, in the merit of our giving thanks to You now. Blessed be the God of all thanksgiving.

On Ḥanukka add:

עַל הַנִּסִּים [WE THANK YOU] for the miracles, the deliverance, and the triumphant victories and salvation, as well as wars which You wrought for our ancestors in those days at this season.

IT HAPPENED in the days of Mattathias son of Johanan, the Hasmonean high priest, and his sons. Then the cruel Hellenist power rose up to force Your people Israel to forget Your Torah and transgress the commands of Your will. In that hour of their distress, You in Your great mercy rose to

Continued on the top of the next page.

אֶת רִיבָם, דַּנְתָּ אֶת דִּינָם, נָקַמְתָּ אֶת נִקְמָתָם, מָסַרְתָּ גִבּוֹרִים בְּיַד חַלָּשִׁים, וְרַבִּים בְּיַד מְעַטִּים, וּטְמֵאִים בְּיַד טְהוֹרִים, וּרְשָׁעִים בְּיַד צַדִּיקִים, וְזֵדִים בְּיַד עוֹסְקֵי תוֹרָתֶךָ, וּלְךָ עָשִׂיתָ שֵׁם גָּדוֹל וְקָדוֹשׁ בְּעוֹלָמֶךָ, וּלְעַמְּךָ יִשְׂרָאֵל עָשִׂיתָ תְּשׁוּעָה גְדוֹלָה וּפֻרְקָן כְּהַיּוֹם הַזֶּה. וְאַחַר כֵּן בָּאוּ בָנֶיךָ לִדְבִיר בֵּיתֶךָ, וּפִנּוּ אֶת הֵיכָלֶךָ, וְטִהֲרוּ אֶת מִקְדָּשֶׁךָ, וְהִדְלִיקוּ נֵרוֹת בְּחַצְרוֹת קָדְשֶׁךָ, וְקָבְעוּ שְׁמוֹנַת יְמֵי חֲנֻכָּה אֵלּוּ, לְהוֹדוֹת וּלְהַלֵּל לְשִׁמְךָ הַגָּדוֹל.

Continue with וְעַל כֻּלָּם.

וְעַל כֻּלָּם יִתְבָּרַךְ וְיִתְרוֹמַם שִׁמְךָ מַלְכֵּנוּ תָּמִיד לְעוֹלָם וָעֶד.

בשבת שובה: וּכְתֹב לְחַיִּים טוֹבִים כָּל בְּנֵי בְרִיתֶךָ.

(*If forgotten, no corrective action is necessary.*)

וְכֹל הַחַיִּים יוֹדוּךָ סֶּלָה, וִיהַלְלוּ אֶת שִׁמְךָ בֶּאֱמֶת, הָאֵל יְשׁוּעָתֵנוּ וְעֶזְרָתֵנוּ סֶלָה. ‏יבָּרוּךְ אַתָּה יהוה, הַטּוֹב שִׁמְךָ וּלְךָ נָאֶה לְהוֹדוֹת.

ברכת כהנים

The following is said by the שליח ציבור *during* חזרת הש״ץ*:*

אֱלֹהֵינוּ וֵאלֹהֵי אֲבוֹתֵינוּ, בָּרְכֵנוּ בַּבְּרָכָה הַמְשֻׁלֶּשֶׁת, בַּתּוֹרָה, הַכְּתוּבָה עַל יְדֵי מֹשֶׁה עַבְדֶּךָ, הָאֲמוּרָה מִפִּי אַהֲרֹן וּבָנָיו כֹּהֲנִים עַם קְדוֹשֶׁיךָ, כָּאָמוּר

יְבָרֶכְךָ יהוה וְיִשְׁמְרֶךָ: קהל: כֵּן יְהִי רָצוֹן במדבר ו

יָאֵר יהוה פָּנָיו אֵלֶיךָ וִיחֻנֶּךָּ: קהל: כֵּן יְהִי רָצוֹן

יִשָּׂא יהוה פָּנָיו אֵלֶיךָ וְיָשֵׂם לְךָ שָׁלוֹם: קהל: כֵּן יְהִי רָצוֹן

שלום

שִׂים שָׁלוֹם טוֹבָה וּבְרָכָה, חֵן וָחֶסֶד וְרַחֲמִים עָלֵינוּ וְעַל כָּל יִשְׂרָאֵל עַמֶּךָ. בָּרְכֵנוּ אָבִינוּ כֻּלָּנוּ כְּאֶחָד בְּאוֹר פָּנֶיךָ, כִּי בְאוֹר פָּנֶיךָ נָתַתָּ לָּנוּ יהוה אֱלֹהֵינוּ, תּוֹרַת חַיִּים וְאַהֲבַת חֶסֶד,

take up their cause and defend their rights. Meting out retribution You delivered the strong into the hand of the weak, the many into the hand of the few, the impure into the hand of the pure, the evil ones into the hand of the righteous, and the wicked into the hand of devotees of Your Torah. You thereby made for Yourself a great and holy name throughout Your world, as well as bringing about great deliverance and salvation for Your people Israel (known) to this day. Then Your children came to the Holy of Holies in Your house, cleared Your Temple, purified Your holy place, kindled lights in Your holy courts, and instituted these eight days of Ḥanukka to give thanks and sing praise to Your great name.

Continue with "For all this."

For all this, our King, may Your name be blessed and exalted continually, forever and ever.

On Shabbat Shuva: Between Rosh HaShana and Yom Kippur: Inscribe all the children of Your covenant for a life of goodness.

(*If forgotten, no corrective action is necessary.*)

All that lives will give thanks to You forever and praise Your name in truth, God, our salvation and our help forever. ▼Blessed are You, LORD, for Your name is "The Good One" and it is appropriate to give thanks to You.

THE PRIESTLY BLESSING

The following is said by the Leader during the Repetition of the Amida:

אֱלֹהֵינוּ OUR GOD, God of our fathers, bless us with the threefold blessing, in the Torah, written by Your servant Moses and spoken by Aaron and his descendants, being priests, Your holy people, as it is said:

Num. 6 "May the LORD bless you and keep you." *Cong:* May this be His will.
"May the LORD make His countenance shine upon you and be gracious to you." *Cong:* May this be His will.
"May the LORD lift up His countenance toward you and grant you peace." *Cong:* May this be His will.

PEACE

שִׂים שָׁלוֹם GRANT PEACE with welfare and blessing, and grace with loving-kindness and mercy on us and all Israel Your people. Bless us, our Father, all together, with the light of Your presence. For in that light, LORD our God, You have given us the Torah of life, and love

וּצְדָקָה וּבְרָכָה וְרַחֲמִים וְחַיִּים וְשָׁלוֹם. וְטוֹב בְּעֵינֶיךָ לְבָרֵךְ אֶת עַמְּךָ יִשְׂרָאֵל, בְּכָל עֵת וּבְכָל שָׁעָה בִּשְׁלוֹמֶךָ.

בשבת שובה: בְּסֵפֶר חַיִּים, בְּרָכָה וְשָׁלוֹם, וּפַרְנָסָה טוֹבָה, נִזָּכֵר וְנִכָּתֵב לְפָנֶיךָ, אֲנַחְנוּ וְכָל עַמְּךָ בֵּית יִשְׂרָאֵל, לְחַיִּים טוֹבִים וּלְשָׁלוֹם.*

בָּרוּךְ אַתָּה יהוה, הַמְבָרֵךְ אֶת עַמּוֹ יִשְׂרָאֵל בַּשָּׁלוֹם.

**On שבת שובה many end the blessing:*

בָּרוּךְ אַתָּה יהוה, עוֹשֶׂה הַשָּׁלוֹם.

At this point when the שליח ציבור repeats the עמידה he should complete the repetition by saying the verse beginning "יִהְיוּ לְרָצוֹן" out loud.

תהלים יט יִהְיוּ לְרָצוֹן אִמְרֵי־פִי וְהֶגְיוֹן לִבִּי לְפָנֶיךָ, יהוה צוּרִי וְגֹאֲלִי:

ברכות יז. **אֱלֹהַי**, נְצֹר לְשׁוֹנִי מֵרָע וּשְׂפָתַי מִדַּבֵּר מִרְמָה, וְלִמְקַלְלַי נַפְשִׁי תִדֹּם, וְנַפְשִׁי כֶּעָפָר לַכֹּל תִּהְיֶה. פְּתַח לִבִּי בְּתוֹרָתֶךָ, וּבְמִצְוֹתֶיךָ תִּרְדֹּף נַפְשִׁי. וְכָל הַחוֹשְׁבִים עָלַי רָעָה, מְהֵרָה הָפֵר עֲצָתָם וְקַלְקֵל מַחֲשַׁבְתָּם. עֲשֵׂה לְמַעַן שְׁמֶךָ, עֲשֵׂה לְמַעַן יְמִינֶךָ,

תהלים ס עֲשֵׂה לְמַעַן קְדֻשָּׁתֶךָ, עֲשֵׂה לְמַעַן תּוֹרָתֶךָ. לְמַעַן יֵחָלְצוּן יְדִידֶיךָ,

תהלים יט הוֹשִׁיעָה יְמִינְךָ וַעֲנֵנִי: יִהְיוּ לְרָצוֹן אִמְרֵי־פִי וְהֶגְיוֹן לִבִּי לְפָנֶיךָ, יהוה צוּרִי וְגֹאֲלִי:

Bow, take three steps back, then bow, first left, then right, then center, while saying:

עֹשֶׂה שָׁלוֹם/ בשבת שובה: הַשָּׁלוֹם/ בִּמְרוֹמָיו, הוּא יַעֲשֶׂה שָׁלוֹם עָלֵינוּ, וְעַל כָּל יִשְׂרָאֵל, וְאִמְרוּ אָמֵן.

יְהִי רָצוֹן מִלְּפָנֶיךָ יהוה אֱלֹהֵינוּ וֵאלֹהֵי אֲבוֹתֵינוּ, שֶׁיִּבָּנֶה בֵּית הַמִּקְדָּשׁ בִּמְהֵרָה בְיָמֵינוּ, וְתֵן חֶלְקֵנוּ בְּתוֹרָתֶךָ, וְשָׁם נַעֲבָדְךָ בְּיִרְאָה כִּימֵי

מלאכי ג עוֹלָם וּכְשָׁנִים קַדְמוֹנִיּוֹת. וְעָרְבָה לַיהוה מִנְחַת יְהוּדָה וִירוּשָׁלָםִ כִּימֵי עוֹלָם וּכְשָׁנִים קַדְמֹנִיּוֹת:

For laws regarding "Interruptions during *Elokai Netzor,*" see page 133.

of kindness with justice, blessing, tenderness, life and peace. May it be good in Your eyes to bless Your people Israel at all times, at every hour, with Your peace.

On Shabbat Shuva: In the book of life and blessing, peace and prosperity, may we and all the house of Israel Your people be remembered before You and inscribed for a life of goodness and peace.*

Blessed are You, LORD, Who blesses His people Israel with peace.

**On Shabbat Shuva many end the blessing:*
Blessed are You, LORD, Who makes peace.

At this point when the Leader repeats the Amida he should complete the repetition by saying the verse beginning "May the words" out loud.

Ps. 19 MAY THE WORDS of my mouth and the meditation of my heart find grace before You, LORD, my Rock and my Redeemer.

Berakhot 17a אֱלֹהַי MY GOD, guard my tongue from evil, and my lips from speaking deceit. Let my soul be silent to those who curse me; let my soul be humble toward everyone like the dust. Open my heart to Your Torah that my soul may follow Your commandments. As for all those who contemplate evil against me, speedily nullify their plans and spoil their schemes. Do so for the sake of Your name. Do so for Your right
Ps. 60 hand. Do so for Your holiness. Do so for Your Torah, that Your loved ones may be delivered. "Save with Your right hand, and answer me.
Ps. 19 May the words of my mouth and the meditation of my heart find grace before You, LORD, my Rock and my Redeemer."

Bow, take three steps back, then bow, first left, then right, then center, while saying:

He Who makes peace in His heights, may He create peace for us and for all Israel. Amen.

יְהִי רָצוֹן MAY IT BE Your will, LORD our God and God of our fathers, that the Temple be rebuilt speedily in our days and may You grant our portion in Your Torah. We will serve You there in reverence as in the days of antiquity and in
Mal. 3 years gone by. "And may the offering of Judah and Jerusalem be pleasant to the LORD as in the days of antiquity and in years gone by."

קדיש שלם

ש״ץ: **יִתְגַּדַּל** וְיִתְקַדַּשׁ שְׁמֵהּ רַבָּא (קהל: אָמֵן) בְּעָלְמָא דִּי בְרָא כִרְעוּתֵהּ. וְיַמְלִיךְ מַלְכוּתֵהּ בְּחַיֵּיכוֹן וּבְיוֹמֵיכוֹן וּבְחַיֵּי דְכָל בֵּית יִשְׂרָאֵל, בַּעֲגָלָא וּבִזְמַן קָרִיב, וְאִמְרוּ אָמֵן. (קהל: אָמֵן)

קהל וש״ץ: יְהֵא שְׁמֵהּ רַבָּא מְבָרַךְ לְעָלַם וּלְעָלְמֵי עָלְמַיָּא.

ש״ץ: יִתְבָּרַךְ וְיִשְׁתַּבַּח וְיִתְפָּאַר וְיִתְרוֹמַם וְיִתְנַשֵּׂא, וְיִתְהַדָּר וְיִתְעַלֶּה וְיִתְהַלָּל שְׁמֵהּ דְּקֻדְשָׁא בְּרִיךְ הוּא (קהל: בְּרִיךְ הוּא), לְעֵלָּא מִן כָּל בִּרְכָתָא / בשבת שובה: לְעֵלָּא (וּ)לְעֵלָּא מִכָּל בִּרְכָתָא/ וְשִׁירָתָא, תֻּשְׁבְּחָתָא וְנֶחֱמָתָא דַּאֲמִירָן בְּעָלְמָא, וְאִמְרוּ אָמֵן. (קהל: אָמֵן)

תִּתְקַבַּל צְלוֹתְהוֹן וּבָעוּתְהוֹן דְּכָל יִשְׂרָאֵל, קֳדָם אֲבוּהוֹן דִּי בִשְׁמַיָּא, וְאִמְרוּ אָמֵן. (קהל: אָמֵן)

יְהֵא שְׁלָמָא רַבָּא מִן שְׁמַיָּא וְחַיִּים, עָלֵינוּ וְעַל כָּל יִשְׂרָאֵל, וְאִמְרוּ אָמֵן. (קהל: אָמֵן)

Bow, take three steps back, as if taking leave of the Divine Presence, then bow, first left, then right, then center, while saying:

עֹשֶׂה שָׁלוֹם / בשבת שובה: הַשָּׁלוֹם/ בִּמְרוֹמָיו, הוּא יַעֲשֶׂה שָׁלוֹם עָלֵינוּ, וְעַל כָּל יִשְׂרָאֵל, וְאִמְרוּ אָמֵן. (קהל: אָמֵן)

קַוֵּה אֶל־יהוה, חֲזַק וְיַאֲמֵץ לִבֶּךָ, וְקַוֵּה אֶל־יהוה: אֵין־קָדוֹשׁ תהלים כז / שמואל א׳ ב
כַּיהוה, כִּי־אֵין בִּלְתֶּךָ, וְאֵין צוּר כֵּאלֹהֵינוּ: כִּי מִי אֱלוֹהַּ תהלים יח
מִבַּלְעֲדֵי יהוה, וּמִי צוּר זוּלָתִי אֱלֹהֵינוּ:

אֵין כֵּאלֹהֵינוּ, אֵין כַּאדוֹנֵינוּ, אֵין כְּמַלְכֵּנוּ, אֵין כְּמוֹשִׁיעֵנוּ. מִי כֵאלֹהֵינוּ, מִי כַאדוֹנֵינוּ, מִי כְמַלְכֵּנוּ, מִי כְמוֹשִׁיעֵנוּ.
נוֹדֶה לֵאלֹהֵינוּ, נוֹדֶה לַאדוֹנֵינוּ, נוֹדֶה לְמַלְכֵּנוּ, נוֹדֶה לְמוֹשִׁיעֵנוּ.
בָּרוּךְ אֱלֹהֵינוּ, בָּרוּךְ אֲדוֹנֵינוּ, בָּרוּךְ מַלְכֵּנוּ, בָּרוּךְ מוֹשִׁיעֵנוּ. אַתָּה הוּא אֱלֹהֵינוּ, אַתָּה הוּא אֲדוֹנֵינוּ, אַתָּה הוּא מַלְכֵּנוּ, אַתָּה הוּא מוֹשִׁיעֵנוּ.
אַתָּה הוּא שֶׁהִקְטִירוּ אֲבוֹתֵינוּ לְפָנֶיךָ אֶת קְטֹרֶת הַסַּמִּים.

FULL KADDISH

Leader: יִתְגַּדַּל EXALTED AND HALLOWED may God's great name be, in the world He created as He willed. May He reign in your lifetimes and in your days, and in the lifetime of the whole house of Israel, speedily and soon, and say, Amen.

All: May His great name be blessed forever and all time.

Leader: Blessed and praised, honored, extolled, glorified, adored and exalted above all be the name of the Holy One, blessed is He, (*Between Rosh Hashana & Yom Kippur:* above and) beyond any blessing, hymn, praise, or expressions of consolation that may be uttered in this world, and say, Amen.

May the prayers and pleas of all Israel be accepted before their Father Who is in heaven – and say, Amen.

May abundant peace descend from heaven, as well as life, for us and for all Israel, and say, Amen.

Bow, take three steps back, as if taking leave of the Divine Presence, then bow, first left, then right, then center, while saying:

May He Who makes peace in the highest heaven, make peace for us, and for all Israel, and say, Amen.

Ps. 27 קַוֵּה WAIT for the Lord, be strong and let your heart be encouraged,
I Sam. 2 and wait for the Lord. There is none so holy as the Lord, for there
Ps. 18 is none beside You, and there is no Rock like our God. For who is a
God beside the Lord, and who is a Rock except for our God?

אֵין כֵּאלֹהֵינוּ THERE IS NONE like our God; there is none like our Master; there is none like our King; there is none like our Savior. Who is like our God? Who is like our Master? Who is like our King? Who is like our Savior? Let us thank our God; let us thank our Master; let us thank our King; let us thank our Savior. Blessed is our God; blessed is our Master; blessed is our King; blessed is our Savior. You are our God, You are our Master, You are our King, You are our Savior. You are the One before Whom our ancestors offered the incense of spices.

כריתות ו.

פִּטּוּם הַקְּטֹרֶת. א הַצֳּרִי, ב וְהַצִּפֹּרֶן, ג וְהַחֶלְבְּנָה, ד וְהַלְּבוֹנָה מִשְׁקַל
שִׁבְעִים שִׁבְעִים מָנֶה, ה מֹר, ו וּקְצִיעָה, ז שִׁבֹּלֶת נֵרְדְּ,
ח וְכַרְכֹּם מִשְׁקַל שִׁשָּׁה עָשָׂר שִׁשָּׁה עָשָׂר מָנֶה, ט הַקֹּשְׁטְ שְׁנֵים עָשָׂר,
י קִלּוּפָה שְׁלֹשָׁה, יא וְקִנָּמוֹן תִּשְׁעָה, בֹּרִית כַּרְשִׁינָה תִּשְׁעָה קַבִּין, יֵין
קַפְרִיסִין סְאִין תְּלָתָא וְקַבִּין תְּלָתָא, וְאִם אֵין לוֹ יֵין קַפְרִיסִין, מֵבִיא חֲמַר
חִוַּרְיָן עַתִּיק. מֶלַח סְדוֹמִית רֹבַע, מַעֲלֶה עָשָׁן כָּל שֶׁהוּא. רַבִּי נָתָן הַבַּבְלִי
אוֹמֵר: אַף כִּפַּת הַיַּרְדֵּן כָּל שֶׁהוּא, וְאִם נָתַן בָּהּ דְּבַשׁ פְּסָלָהּ, וְאִם חִסַּר
אֶחָד מִכָּל סַמָּנֶיהָ, חַיָּב מִיתָה.

רַבָּן שִׁמְעוֹן בֶּן גַּמְלִיאֵל אוֹמֵר: הַצֳּרִי אֵינוֹ אֶלָּא שְׂרָף הַנּוֹטֵף מֵעֲצֵי
הַקְּטָף. בֹּרִית כַּרְשִׁינָה שֶׁשָּׁפִין בָּהּ אֶת הַצִּפֹּרֶן כְּדֵי שֶׁתְּהֵא
נָאָה, יֵין קַפְרִיסִין שֶׁשּׁוֹרִין בּוֹ אֶת הַצִּפֹּרֶן כְּדֵי שֶׁתְּהֵא עַזָּה, וַהֲלֹא מֵי
רַגְלַיִם יָפִין לָהּ, אֶלָּא שֶׁאֵין מַכְנִיסִין מֵי רַגְלַיִם בַּמִּקְדָּשׁ מִפְּנֵי הַכָּבוֹד.

משנה תמיד ז
תהלים כד
תהלים מח

הַשִּׁיר שֶׁהַלְוִיִּם הָיוּ אוֹמְרִים בְּבֵית הַמִּקְדָּשׁ: בַּיּוֹם הָרִאשׁוֹן הָיוּ אוֹמְרִים,
לַיהוה הָאָרֶץ וּמְלוֹאָהּ, תֵּבֵל וְיֹשְׁבֵי בָהּ: בַּשֵּׁנִי הָיוּ אוֹמְרִים, גָּדוֹל
יהוה וּמְהֻלָּל מְאֹד, בְּעִיר אֱלֹהֵינוּ הַר־קָדְשׁוֹ: בַּשְּׁלִישִׁי הָיוּ אוֹמְרִים,

---

אֵין כֵּאלֹהֵינוּ – *There is none like our God* (previous page). This poem appears in the Kabbalistic *Shiur Koma*, as well as *Sefer Raziel HaMalakh*. It stresses that despite our extended quotation and repetition of the praises that the angels give to God in the preceding *Musaf Kedusha*, ultimately in our prayers we turn to none but God, for He alone is our God, Master, King, and Savior.

The initial letters of the words אֵין, מִי, and נוֹדֶה spell אָמֵן (amen), thus hinting at the concept of blessing, followed by repeated instances of בָּרוּךְ and אַתָּה ("Blessed are You"), which is the standard form of blessing. Altogether, the poem consists of twenty blessing-like declarations. Some explain that this is needed on Shabbat and Yom Tov, as we are required to recite one hundred *berakhot* a day, but those days lack the thrice-repeated nineteen *berakhot* of the *Amida*, hence we must supplement them in other blessing-like ways (*Kol Bo*).

פִּטּוּם הַקְּטֹרֶת – *The incense was compounded.* The *Midrash Tanḥuma* refers to Psalms 141:2 ("May my prayer be set before You like incense") as teaching us that no sacrifice is as precious to God as the incense offering. For this reason David compared his prayers to incense in the hope that they too would be favored by God. R. Baḥya explains that the word קְטֹרֶת is derived from הִתְקַשְּׁרוּת (connection), for the incense offering connects to the celestial world and brings an overflow of blessing to the one who

Keritot 6a **פִּטּוּם הַקְּטֹרֶת** THE INCENSE mixture was compounded of: seventy manehs each of [1] balm, [2] onycha, [3] galbanum, [4] and frankincense; [5] sixteen manehs each of myrrh, [6] cassia, [7] spikenard, [8] and saffron; [9] twelve manehs of costus; [10] three manehs of aromatic bark; [11] nine manehs of cinnamon; nine kabs of lye of Karsina; three seahs and three kabs of Cyprus wine, but if Cyprus wine was not available, strong white wine could be substituted for it; a fourth of a kab of salt of Sodom, and a small quantity of an herb that caused the smoke to ascend straight upward. R. Nathan said that a small quantity of amber from the Jordan was also added. If honey was mixed in, the incense became unfit for sacred use. If the person who prepared the incense omitted any of the ingredients he was deemed guilty of a capital offense.

רַבָּן שִׁמְעוֹן RABBAN SIMEON son of Gamliel said that the balm required was the sap of the balsam tree. The lye of Karsina was rubbed on the onycha to refine its appearance. The onycha was steeped in the Cyprus wine to make it more pungent. Urine would have achieved the same purpose, but was not used because it would have been unseemly to bring it into the Temple.

Mishna, Tamid 7 **הַשִּׁיר** THE LEVITES chanted the following psalms of the day in the
Ps. 24 Temple: On the first day of the week they would say: "The earth is the Lord's and the fullness thereof, the world and those who dwell in it."
Ps. 48 On the second day since the Sabbath they would say: "The Lord is great and exceedingly praised in the city of our God, His holy mountain." On

---

offers it. From this we learn that the impact of our prayers is greater than any of us can understand, for they are just like the sacrifices connecting us to the realm of the divine (R. Ḥayyim of Volozhin).

וְהַחֶלְבְּנָה – *Galbanum.* The Gemara (*Keritot* 6b) quotes R. Shimon Ḥasida as saying that every fast day should include the participation of פּוֹשְׁעֵי יִשְׂרָאֵל (Jewish sinners), just as the incense in the Temple had to include foul-smelling galbanum. It also quotes Abaye who agrees to this inclusive attitude, but derives it from Amos 9:6, וַאֲגֻדָּתוֹ עַל־אֶרֶץ יְסָדָהּ ("He established the earth upon His *aguda*"), on which Rashi comments, "When they are מְאֻגָּדִים (together) God's world is established." From these sages we learn the importance of welcoming transgressors into our midst. While being careful to avoid endorsing values or behaviors that violate important Torah parameters, we should recognize that every Jew, like the galbanum in the incense, is important in his or her own right, in addition to having a significant role to play in the אֲגֻדָּה (totality) of Jewish communal

תהלים פב תהלים צד אֱלֹהִים נִצָּב בַּעֲדַת־אֵל, בְּקֶרֶב אֱלֹהִים יִשְׁפֹּט: בָּרְבִיעִי הָיוּ אוֹמְרִים, אֵל־
תהלים פא נְקָמוֹת יהוה, אֵל נְקָמוֹת הוֹפִיעַ: בַּחֲמִישִׁי הָיוּ אוֹמְרִים, הַרְנִינוּ לֵאלֹהִים
תהלים צג עוּזֵּנוּ, הָרִיעוּ לֵאלֹהֵי יַעֲקֹב: בַּשִּׁשִּׁי הָיוּ אוֹמְרִים, יהוה מָלָךְ גֵּאוּת לָבֵשׁ,
לָבֵשׁ יהוה עֹז הִתְאַזָּר, אַף־תִּכּוֹן תֵּבֵל בַּל־תִּמּוֹט: בַּשַּׁבָּת הָיוּ אוֹמְרִים,
תהלים צב מִזְמוֹר שִׁיר לְיוֹם הַשַּׁבָּת: מִזְמוֹר שִׁיר לֶעָתִיד לָבוֹא, לְיוֹם שֶׁכֻּלּוֹ שַׁבָּת
וּמְנוּחָה לְחַיֵּי הָעוֹלָמִים.

מגילה כח: **תָּנָא** דְבֵי אֵלִיָּהוּ: כָּל הַשּׁוֹנֶה הֲלָכוֹת בְּכָל יוֹם, מֻבְטָח לוֹ שֶׁהוּא בֶּן
חבקוק ג עוֹלָם הַבָּא, שֶׁנֶּאֱמַר, הֲלִיכוֹת עוֹלָם לוֹ: אַל תִּקְרֵי הֲלִיכוֹת אֶלָּא
הֲלָכוֹת.

ברכות סד. **אָמַר** רַבִּי אֶלְעָזָר, אָמַר רַבִּי חֲנִינָא: תַּלְמִידֵי חֲכָמִים מַרְבִּים שָׁלוֹם
ישעיה נד בָּעוֹלָם, שֶׁנֶּאֱמַר, וְכָל־בָּנַיִךְ לִמּוּדֵי יהוה, וְרַב שְׁלוֹם בָּנָיִךְ: אַל תִּקְרֵי
תהלים קיט תהלים קכב בָּנָיִךְ, אֶלָּא בּוֹנָיִךְ. שָׁלוֹם רָב לְאֹהֲבֵי תוֹרָתֶךָ, וְאֵין־לָמוֹ מִכְשׁוֹל: יְהִי־שָׁלוֹם
בְּחֵילֵךְ, שַׁלְוָה בְּאַרְמְנוֹתָיִךְ: לְמַעַן אַחַי וְרֵעָי אֲדַבְּרָה־נָּא שָׁלוֹם בָּךְ: לְמַעַן
תהלים כט בֵּית־יהוה אֱלֹהֵינוּ אֲבַקְשָׁה טוֹב לָךְ: ◂ יהוה עֹז לְעַמּוֹ יִתֵּן, יהוה יְבָרֵךְ
אֶת־עַמּוֹ בַשָּׁלוֹם:

---

life. Such a perspective is consistent with the Siddur's subsequent passage quoting *Berakhot* 64a, which cites R. Elazar's praise of Torah scholars who increase peace and harmony in the world by facilitating the inclusion of "all of our children" in the shared goal of strengthening the Jewish people (R. Basil Herring).

אָמַר רַבִּי אֶלְעָזָר – *R. Eleazar quoted.* Although in-depth study of the Torah sometimes involves disagreement and even argument, the very process of clarification of disparate views so as to resolve questions and difficulties can lead to agreement and reconciliation. Peace is achieved not through the single-minded pursuit of one's personal vision, but by a readiness by many to recognize that there can be a diversity of views and approaches, each expressing a different perspective on God's world (R. Avraham Yitzḥak HaKohen Kook).

וְכָל־בָּנַיִךְ לִמּוּדֵי ה׳, וְרַב שְׁלוֹם בָּנָיִךְ – *When all your children shall be taught of the Lord, great shall be the peace of your children.* This verse from Isaiah 54:13 requires clarification, given that it is not unusual for Torah scholars to disagree sharply in interpreting and applying the laws of the Torah. The Gemara (*Sanhedrin* 86b, *Shabbat* 130a) explains that the Torah itself (Deut. 17:8–13) not only anticipates and legitimizes such disagreements, it also provides the practical mechanism by which they are to be peacefully resolved. In Temple times this involved presenting such conflicting views to the Sanhedrin, for resolution by majority

Ps. 82 the third day since the Sabbath they would say: "God is standing in the congregation of God. He will judge in the midst of the congregation
Ps. 94 of God." On the fourth day since the Sabbath they would say: "God of vengeance, O Lord, God of vengeance, reveal Yourself." On the fifth day
Ps. 81 since the Sabbath they would say: "Sing for joy to God our strength. Make a joyful noise for the God of Jacob." On the sixth day since the
Ps. 93 Sabbath they would say: "The Lord reigns, He is clothed in majesty, the Lord is clothed, He has girded Himself with strength. The world, too, is
Ps. 92 established so that it cannot be moved." On Shabbat they would say: "A psalm. A song for the Sabbath day" – a psalm, a song for the time to come that shall be entirely Sabbath and the repose of life eternal.

Megilla 28b *Hab. 3* **תָּנָא** IT WAS TAUGHT in the Academy of Elijah: "Whoever studies the laws every day is assured of being in the World to Come, as it says 'The pathways of the world are His.' Do not read this as הֲלִיכוֹת (pathways) but as הֲלָכוֹת (the laws)."

Berakhot 64a **אָמַר** R. ELEAZAR quoted R. Ḥanina as saying that students of Torah
Is. 54 increase peace in the world. As it is said: "When all your children shall be taught of the Lord, great shall be the peace of your children." Do
Ps. 119 not read this as בָּנָיִךְ, "your children," but בּוֹנָיִךְ, "your builders." "Those who love Your law have great peace, and they have no stumbling-block."
Ps. 122 "May peace be within your walls, prosperity within your palaces. For my brothers' and companions' sakes may I now say: 'Peace be within you.' For the sake of the house of the Lord our God, I will seek your good."
Ps. 29 ▸ "The Lord will give strength to His people; the Lord will bless His people with peace."

---

vote, in accordance with Exodus 23:2. This was true even when, objectively speaking, the minority view was the more correct. Indeed we learn from the celebrated case of the תַּנּוּר שֶׁל עַכְנַאי ("the oven of the coiled snake"), discussed in *Bava Metzia* 59b, that even the greatest of sages is excommunicated if he persists in rejecting the majority view, and thus prolonging conflict. As that Gemara notes, God Himself happily accedes to whatever the majority decides. Thus the second phrase of this verse is teaching that the principle of רוב (majority rule) is so רַב (great or powerful) that it even supersedes objective truth, to become the law which every Jew must follow, and thus bring about שְׁלוֹם בָּנָיִךְ – harmony for the Jewish people (R. Moshe Feinstein).

קדיש דרבנן

The following prayer, said by mourners, requires the presence of a מנין.
A transliteration can be found on page 1344.

אבל: **יִתְגַּדַּל** וְיִתְקַדַּשׁ שְׁמֵהּ רַבָּא (קהל: אָמֵן) בְּעָלְמָא דִּי בְרָא כִרְעוּתֵהּ.
וְיַמְלִיךְ מַלְכוּתֵהּ בְּחַיֵּיכוֹן וּבְיוֹמֵיכוֹן וּבְחַיֵּי דְכָל בֵּית
יִשְׂרָאֵל, בַּעֲגָלָא וּבִזְמַן קָרִיב, וְאִמְרוּ אָמֵן. (קהל: אָמֵן)

קהל ואבל: יְהֵא שְׁמֵהּ רַבָּא מְבָרַךְ לְעָלַם וּלְעָלְמֵי עָלְמַיָּא.

אבל: יִתְבָּרַךְ וְיִשְׁתַּבַּח וְיִתְפָּאַר וְיִתְרוֹמַם וְיִתְנַשֵּׂא, וְיִתְהַדָּר וְיִתְעַלֶּה
וְיִתְהַלָּל שְׁמֵהּ דְּקֻדְשָׁא בְּרִיךְ הוּא (קהל: בְּרִיךְ הוּא), לְעֵלָּא מִן כָּל
בִּרְכָתָא / בשבת שובה: לְעֵלָּא (וּ)לְעֵלָּא מִכָּל בִּרְכָתָא/ וְשִׁירָתָא, תֻּשְׁבְּחָתָא
וְנֶחֱמָתָא דַּאֲמִירָן בְּעָלְמָא, וְאִמְרוּ אָמֵן. (קהל: אָמֵן)

עַל יִשְׂרָאֵל וְעַל רַבָּנָן, וְעַל תַּלְמִידֵיהוֹן וְעַל כָּל תַּלְמִידֵי תַלְמִידֵיהוֹן,
וְעַל כָּל מָאן דְּעָסְקִין בְּאוֹרַיְתָא, דִּי בְּאַתְרָא הָדֵין, וְדִי בְּכָל אֲתַר
וַאֲתַר, יְהֵא לְהוֹן וּלְכוֹן שְׁלָמָא רַבָּא, חִנָּא וְחִסְדָּא, וְרַחֲמֵי, וְחַיֵּי
אֲרִיכֵי, וּמְזוֹנֵי רְוִיחֵי, וּפֻרְקָנָא מִן קֳדָם אֲבוּהוֹן דִּי בִשְׁמַיָּא, וְאִמְרוּ
אָמֵן. (קהל: אָמֵן)

יְהֵא שְׁלָמָא רַבָּא מִן שְׁמַיָּא וְחַיִּים, עָלֵינוּ וְעַל כָּל יִשְׂרָאֵל, וְאִמְרוּ
אָמֵן. (קהל: אָמֵן)

Bow, take three steps back, as if taking leave of the Divine Presence, then bow, first left, then right, then center, while saying:

עֹשֶׂה שָׁלוֹם/בשבת שובה: הַשָּׁלוֹם/ בִּמְרוֹמָיו, הוּא יַעֲשֶׂה שָׁלוֹם עָלֵינוּ,
וְעַל כָּל יִשְׂרָאֵל, וְאִמְרוּ אָמֵן. (קהל: אָמֵן)

קַדִּישׁ דְּרַבָּנָן / THE RABBIS' KADDISH

בַּעֲגָלָא וּבִזְמַן קָרִיב – *Speedily and soon.* May the travail preceding the Messianic epoch be over swiftly and not be prolonged; and may it begin very soon (R. Yeḥiel Mikhel HaLevi Epstein).

יְהֵא שְׁמֵהּ רַבָּא – *May His great name. Berakhot* 3a explains that this response is so significant that upon hearing it God, so to speak, regrets having exiled His people. This response upon hearing *Kaddish* takes precedence over responding to other prayers, even *Kedusha* and *Barekhu* (*Mishna Berura*).

Shabbat 19b teaches that it should be recited with total concentration (Rashi, Tosafot).

THE RABBIS' KADDISH

The following prayer, said by mourners, requires the presence of a minyan. A transliteration can be found on page 1344.

Mourner: יִתְגַּדַּל EXALTED AND HALLOWED may God's great name be, in the world He created as He willed. May He reign in your lifetimes and in your days, and in the lifetime of the whole house of Israel, speedily and soon, and say, Amen.

All: May His great name be blessed forever and all time.

Mourner: Blessed and praised, honored, extolled, glorified, adored and exalted above all be the name of the Holy One, blessed is He, (*Between Rosh Hashana & Yom Kippur:* above and) beyond any blessing, hymn, praise, or expressions of consolation that may be uttered in this world, and say, Amen.

May the Jewish people, and our teachers, together with their students and all their students' students, as well as all who engage in Torah study here and in every other place, have abundant peace, grace, kindness, mercy, length of days, abundant food, and deliverance at the hands of their heavenly Father, and say, Amen.

May abundant peace descend from heaven, as well as life, for us and for all Israel, and say, Amen.

Bow, take three steps back, as if taking leave of the Divine Presence, then bow, first left, then right, then center, while saying:

May He Who makes peace in the highest heaven, make peace for us, and for all Israel, and say, Amen.

עַל יִשְׂרָאֵל וְעַל רַבָּנָן – *May the Jewish people, and our teachers.* Although this is a prayer for the benefit of Torah scholars, it begins with mention of Israel. Any prayer for Torah scholars is a prayer for the nation, because Israel's welfare depends on its attention to the covenant which is its *raison d'etre*, which in turn is entirely dependent on Torah study (R. Samson Raphael Hirsch).

חִנָּא וְחִסְדָּא, וְרַחֲמֵי – *Grace, kindness, mercy. Grace* is the quality that makes one loved by others. *Kindness* refers to considerate behavior toward others, even the undeserving. *Mercy* refers to compassion by which one withholds punishment even when a wrongdoer has earned it. These all refer to the ways in which God relates to us (R. Samson Raphael Hirsch).

Stand while saying עָלֵינוּ*. Bow at* ▾.

עָלֵינוּ לְשַׁבֵּחַ לַאֲדוֹן הַכֹּל, לָתֵת גְּדֻלָּה לְיוֹצֵר בְּרֵאשִׁית, שֶׁלֹּא עָשָׂנוּ
כְּגוֹיֵי הָאֲרָצוֹת, וְלֹא שָׂמָנוּ כְּמִשְׁפְּחוֹת הָאֲדָמָה, שֶׁלֹּא
שָׂם חֶלְקֵנוּ כָּהֶם וְגוֹרָלֵנוּ כְּכָל הֲמוֹנָם. (שֶׁהֵם מִשְׁתַּחֲוִים לְהֶבֶל
וָרִיק וּמִתְפַּלְלִים אֶל אֵל לֹא יוֹשִׁיעַ.) ▾וַאֲנַחְנוּ כּוֹרְעִים וּמִשְׁתַּחֲוִים
וּמוֹדִים, לִפְנֵי מֶלֶךְ מַלְכֵי הַמְּלָכִים, הַקָּדוֹשׁ בָּרוּךְ הוּא, שֶׁהוּא נוֹטֶה
שָׁמַיִם וְיוֹסֵד אָרֶץ, וּמוֹשַׁב יְקָרוֹ בַּשָּׁמַיִם מִמַּעַל, וּשְׁכִינַת עֻזּוֹ בְּגָבְהֵי
מְרוֹמִים. הוּא אֱלֹהֵינוּ, אֵין עוֹד. אֱמֶת מַלְכֵּנוּ, אֶפֶס זוּלָתוֹ, כַּכָּתוּב
בְּתוֹרָתוֹ, וְיָדַעְתָּ הַיּוֹם וַהֲשֵׁבֹתָ אֶל־לְבָבֶךָ, כִּי יהוה הוּא הָאֱלֹהִים דברים ד
בַּשָּׁמַיִם מִמַּעַל וְעַל־הָאָרֶץ מִתָּחַת, אֵין עוֹד:

עַל כֵּן נְקַוֶּה לְּךָ יהוה אֱלֹהֵינוּ, לִרְאוֹת מְהֵרָה בְּתִפְאֶרֶת עֻזֶּךָ, לְהַעֲבִיר
גִּלּוּלִים מִן הָאָרֶץ, וְהָאֱלִילִים כָּרוֹת יִכָּרֵתוּן, לְתַקֵּן עוֹלָם בְּמַלְכוּת
שַׁדַּי. וְכָל בְּנֵי בָשָׂר יִקְרְאוּ בִשְׁמֶךָ לְהַפְנוֹת אֵלֶיךָ כָּל רִשְׁעֵי אָרֶץ.
יַכִּירוּ וְיֵדְעוּ כָּל יוֹשְׁבֵי תֵבֵל, כִּי לְךָ תִּכְרַע כָּל בֶּרֶךְ, תִּשָּׁבַע כָּל
לָשׁוֹן. לְפָנֶיךָ יהוה אֱלֹהֵינוּ יִכְרְעוּ וְיִפֹּלוּ, וְלִכְבוֹד שִׁמְךָ יְקָר יִתֵּנוּ,
וִיקַבְּלוּ כֻלָּם אֶת עֹל מַלְכוּתֶךָ, וְתִמְלֹךְ עֲלֵיהֶם מְהֵרָה לְעוֹלָם וָעֶד.
כִּי הַמַּלְכוּת שֶׁלְּךָ הִיא וּלְעוֹלְמֵי עַד תִּמְלֹךְ בְּכָבוֹד, כַּכָּתוּב בְּתוֹרָתֶךָ,
יהוה יִמְלֹךְ לְעֹלָם וָעֶד: ◂ וְנֶאֱמַר, וְהָיָה יהוה לְמֶלֶךְ עַל־כָּל־הָאָרֶץ, שמות טו זכריה יד
בַּיּוֹם הַהוּא יִהְיֶה יהוה אֶחָד וּשְׁמוֹ אֶחָד:

עָלֵינוּ / ALEINU

שֶׁהֵם מִשְׁתַּחֲוִים – *For idolaters bow.* The passage in parentheses is drawn from the original version of *Aleinu* which referred to the idolaters of antiquity. In fact the phrase וּמִתְפַּלְלִים אֶל אֵל לֹא יוֹשִׁיעַ occurs in Isaiah 45:20 in reference to such pagans. During the Middle Ages, Christians became aware of this text and concluded that it must refer to them as well. They were offended by this, and retention of the passage came to be fraught with danger for the Jewish community. Consequently it was removed from most Ashkenazi *siddurim*, and the abridged version predominates to this day. However there are significant authorities who maintain that the original version should be restored. Hence it has been included but placed in parentheses. So too, our translation replaces the non-specific but easily misunderstood "they" with the more specific "idolaters" to accurately reflect the original intention of the prayer.

While *Aleinu* distinguishes between Jew and non-Jew, it also teaches that our distinctiveness is not racial, self-serving, or dismissive of the rest of humanity. Rather it conveys the universalistic message of the even-

Stand while saying Aleinu. Bow at ▼.

עָלֵינוּ WE MUST, all of us, praise the Master of all, and ascribe greatness to He Who formed creation, for He did not make us like the nations of the world, nor render us like the families of the earth. He did not make our portion to be as theirs, nor our destiny like that of their masses. (For idolaters bow to vanity and emptiness and pray to a god who cannot save.) ▼We, however, bend our knees, bow, and give thanks before the King of the most exalted of kings, the Holy One, blessed is He. He is the One Who spreads out the heavens and establishes the earth. The seat of His glory is in the heavens above, and His Presence in all its strength is found in its highest abode. He is our God – there is no other. In truth
Deut. 4 He is our King; there is none but Him; as is written in His Torah: "On this day you should know, and take to heart, that the Lord is God in the heavens above and on the earth below – there is no other."

WE THEREFORE hope in You, Lord our God, that we may soon see the glory of Your might when You will remove abominations from the earth and the idols shall be utterly destroyed, when the world shall be perfected under the rule of the Almighty. Then all mankind shall invoke Your name, to turn all the wicked on earth toward You. All dwellers on earth will perceive and understand that to You every knee must bend, every tongue vow fealty. Before You, Lord our God, all will kneel and bow down, and give honor to Your glorious name. They will all accept the rule of Your dominion, and You will speedily rule over them forevermore. For the kingdom is Yours, and to all eternity You shall reign
Ex. 15 in glory, as it is written in Your Torah, "The Lord shall reign for ever and
Zech. 14 ever." ▸ And it is said, "And the Lord shall be King over all the earth; in that day shall the Lord be One, and His name One."

---

tual redemption of all mankind (R. Yissachar Jacobson).

וְיָדַעְתָּ הַיּוֹם וַהֲשֵׁבֹתָ אֶל־לְבָבֶךָ – *On this day you should know, and take to heart.* This verse is perfectly balanced. The first phrase, "You should know," refers to abstract knowledge, while the second refers to the more powerful emotional awareness of "taking to heart" that leads to concrete action. In the second half of the verse the focus of each of these two types of knowledge is described. Abstract knowledge leads to the recognition that "the Lord is God in the heavens above," while our emotional awareness sensitizes us to God's power in the "earth below," i.e., where we translate abstract knowledge into concrete action. Together they bring us to a better understanding that, as the verse concludes, "There is no other" (R. Avraham Yitzḥak HaKohen Kook).

וְהָיָה ה׳ לְמֶלֶךְ עַל־כָּל־הָאָרֶץ – *The Lord shall reign over all the earth.* There is a difference between

Some add:

משלי ג אַל־תִּירָא מִפַּחַד פִּתְאֹם וּמִשֹּׁאַת רְשָׁעִים כִּי תָבֹא: עֻצוּ עֵצָה וְתֻפָר, דַּבְּרוּ דָבָר וְלֹא יָקוּם,
ישעיה ח כִּי עִמָּנוּ אֵל: וְעַד־זִקְנָה אֲנִי הוּא, וְעַד־שֵׂיבָה אֲנִי אֶסְבֹּל, אֲנִי עָשִׂיתִי וַאֲנִי אֶשָּׂא
ישעיה מו וַאֲנִי אֶסְבֹּל וַאֲמַלֵּט:

קדיש יתום

The following prayer, said by mourners, requires the presence of a מנין*.*
A transliteration can be found on page 1345.

אבל: **יִתְגַּדַּל** וְיִתְקַדַּשׁ שְׁמֵהּ רַבָּא (קהל: אָמֵן), בְּעָלְמָא דִּי בְרָא כִרְעוּתֵהּ.
וְיַמְלִיךְ מַלְכוּתֵהּ, בְּחַיֵּיכוֹן וּבְיוֹמֵיכוֹן וּבְחַיֵּי דְכָל בֵּית
יִשְׂרָאֵל, בַּעֲגָלָא וּבִזְמַן קָרִיב, וְאִמְרוּ אָמֵן. (קהל: אָמֵן)

קהל ואבל: יְהֵא שְׁמֵהּ רַבָּא מְבָרַךְ לְעָלַם וּלְעָלְמֵי עָלְמַיָּא.

אבל: יִתְבָּרַךְ וְיִשְׁתַּבַּח וְיִתְפָּאַר, וְיִתְרוֹמַם וְיִתְנַשֵּׂא וְיִתְהַדָּר וְיִתְעַלֶּה
וְיִתְהַלָּל שְׁמֵהּ דְּקֻדְשָׁא בְּרִיךְ הוּא (קהל: בְּרִיךְ הוּא), לְעֵלָּא מִן כָּל
בִּרְכָתָא /בשבת שובה: לְעֵלָּא (וּ)לְעֵלָּא מִכָּל בִּרְכָתָא/ וְשִׁירָתָא, תֻּשְׁבְּחָתָא
וְנֶחֱמָתָא דַּאֲמִירָן בְּעָלְמָא, וְאִמְרוּ אָמֵן. (קהל: אָמֵן)

יְהֵא שְׁלָמָא רַבָּא מִן שְׁמַיָּא וְחַיִּים, עָלֵינוּ וְעַל כָּל יִשְׂרָאֵל, וְאִמְרוּ
אָמֵן. (קהל: אָמֵן)

Bow, take three steps back, as if taking leave of the Divine Presence,
then bow, first left, then right, then center, while saying:

עֹשֶׂה שָׁלוֹם /בשבת שובה: הַשָּׁלוֹם/ בִּמְרוֹמָיו, הוּא יַעֲשֶׂה שָׁלוֹם עָלֵינוּ,
וְעַל כָּל יִשְׂרָאֵל, וְאִמְרוּ אָמֵן. (קהל: אָמֵן)

---

a מֶלֶךְ (king) and a מוֹשֵׁל (ruler). The former rules only by the will of the people, whereas the latter rules by imposing his will upon them. *Aleinu* proclaims our hope and expectation that one day all of mankind will come to freely accept God's kingship of their own volition, just as the Jewish people have always done (Vilna Gaon).

בַּיּוֹם הַהוּא יִהְיֶה ה׳ אֶחָד וּשְׁמוֹ אֶחָד – *On that day the Lord shall be One and His name One* (previous page). In the Gemara (*Pesaḥim* 50a) R. Naḥman b. Yitzḥak explains this verse as saying that whereas before the redemption we are not permitted to pronounce God's four-lettered proper name as it is written, but must instead pronounce it "*Adonai*," at the end of time we will all pronounce it exactly as it is written, and thus at that time "His name will be One." Rambam (Guide 1:69) explains this as follows: With the exception of the four-lettered name, all of God's other names describe His traits (or "attributes") as distinct from His essence, and thus people do not understand His absolute Oneness. At the final redemption, however, two things will happen: (1) All the misleading

Some add:

Prov. 3 אַל־תִּירָא DO NOT FEAR sudden terror or the destruction when it comes to the
Is. 8 wicked. Devise a plan, and it will be thwarted; state a case and it will not stand,
Is. 46 for God is with us. And when you are old, I will remain; when you are aged, I will
endure. I created you, I will carry you, I will endure, and I will rescue you.

MOURNER'S KADDISH

The following prayer, said by mourners, requires the presence of a minyan. A transliteration can be found on page 1345.

Mourner: יִתְגַּדַּל EXALTED AND HALLOWED may God's great name be, in the world He created as He willed. May He reign in your lifetimes and in your days, and in the lifetime of the whole house of Israel, speedily and soon, and say, Amen.

All: May His great name be blessed forever and all time.

Mourner: Blessed and praised, honored, extolled, glorified, adored and exalted above all be the name of the Holy One, blessed is He, (*Between Rosh Hashana & Yom Kippur:* above and) beyond any blessing, hymn, praise, or expressions of consolation that may be uttered in this world, and say, Amen.

May abundant peace descend from heaven, as well as life, for us and for all Israel, and say, Amen.

Bow, take three steps back, as if taking leave of the Divine Presence, then bow, first left, then right, then center, while saying:

May He Who makes peace in the highest heaven, make peace for us, and for all Israel, and say, Amen.

---

descriptive names of God will no longer be used; (2) even the four-lettered proper name will be pronounced exactly as it is written, to avoid the current pronunciation ("*Adonai*" meaning "My Master"), that is also descriptive and thus misleading. Thus, the verse teaches that He will finally be recognized as absolutely One ("God will be One") to be reflected in His proper name being written and pronounced in one and the same way ("and His name will be One"). This concluding verse thus fittingly echoes the preceding declaration that at the end of time all the nations of the world "will give honor to Your glorious name," by finally understanding and proclaiming the uniqueness of God and His name (R. Basil Herring).

קדיש יתום / THE MOURNER'S KADDISH

The custom for mourners to recite *Kaddish* is found for the first time in three twelfth-century sources – *Maḥzor Vitri*, *Sefer Roke'aḥ*, and *Or Zarua*. All three account for the custom by referring to an early *Midrash* according to which R. Akiva was able to ameliorate the suffering of a deceased sinner by prevailing upon his son to perform good deeds on his father's behalf.

שִׁיר הַכָּבוֹד

The ארון קודש *is opened and* שיר הכבוד *is said responsively.*

ש״ץ: **אַנְעִים זְמִירוֹת** וְשִׁירִים אֶאֱרֹג, כִּי אֵלֶיךָ נַפְשִׁי תַעֲרֹג.

קהל: נַפְשִׁי חִמְּדָה בְּצֵל יָדֶךָ, לָדַעַת כָּל רָז סוֹדֶךָ.

ש״ץ: מִדֵּי דַבְּרִי בִּכְבוֹדֶךָ, הוֹמֶה לִבִּי אֶל דּוֹדֶיךָ.

קהל: עַל כֵּן אֲדַבֵּר בְּךָ נִכְבָּדוֹת, וְשִׁמְךָ אֲכַבֵּד בְּשִׁירֵי יְדִידוֹת.

ש״ץ: אֲסַפְּרָה כְבוֹדְךָ וְלֹא רְאִיתִיךָ, אֲדַמְּךָ אֲכַנְּךָ וְלֹא יְדַעְתִּיךָ.

קהל: בְּיַד נְבִיאֶיךָ בְּסוֹד עֲבָדֶיךָ, דִּמִּיתָ הֲדַר כְּבוֹד הוֹדֶךָ.

ש״ץ: גְּדֻלָּתְךָ וּגְבוּרָתֶךָ, כִּנּוּ לְתֹקֶף פְּעֻלָּתֶךָ.

קהל: דִּמּוּ אוֹתְךָ וְלֹא כְּפִי יֶשְׁךָ, וַיְשַׁוּוּךָ (נ״א וַיְשַׁוּוּךָ) לְפִי מַעֲשֶׂיךָ.

ש״ץ: הִמְשִׁילוּךָ בְּרֹב חֶזְיוֹנוֹת, הִנְּךָ אֶחָד בְּכָל דִּמְיוֹנוֹת.

קהל: וַיֶּחֱזוּ בְךָ זִקְנָה וּבַחֲרוּת, וּשְׂעַר רֹאשְׁךָ בְּשֵׂיבָה וְשַׁחֲרוּת.

ש״ץ: זִקְנָה בְּיוֹם דִּין וּבַחֲרוּת בְּיוֹם קְרָב, כְּאִישׁ מִלְחָמוֹת יָדָיו לוֹ רָב.

קהל: חָבַשׁ כּוֹבַע־יְשׁוּעָה בְּרֹאשׁוֹ, הוֹשִׁיעָה לּוֹ יְמִינוֹ וּזְרוֹעַ קָדְשׁוֹ.

ש״ץ: טַלְלֵי אוֹרוֹת רֹאשׁוֹ נִמְלָא, קְוֻצּוֹתָיו רְסִיסֵי לָיְלָה.

קהל: יִתְפָּאֵר בִּי כִּי חָפֵץ בִּי, וְהוּא יִהְיֶה לִּי לַעֲטֶרֶת צְבִי.

ש״ץ: כֶּתֶם טָהוֹר פָּז דְּמוּת רֹאשׁוֹ, וְחַק עַל מֵצַח כְּבוֹד שֵׁם קָדְשׁוֹ.

קהל: לְחֵן וּלְכָבוֹד צְבִי תִפְאָרָה, אֻמָּתוֹ לוֹ עִטְּרָה עֲטָרָה.

All three sources give special weight to a son's recital of the *Kaddish* that sanctifies God's name. The *Maḥzor Vitri* states, "This is the reason that immediately following Shabbat one who has no father or mother recites *Barekhu* or *Kaddish*." According to this, the Mourner's *Kaddish* was originally recited only at *Ma'ariv* following Shabbat. Not surprisingly, this accords with the view of the same R. Akiva (*Sanhedrin* 65b), that sinners in the afterlife are granted a reprieve from their suffering for the duration of Shabbat, and thus it follows that a child who recites *Kaddish* on behalf of such a parent immediately following the conclusion of Shabbat can temporarily "extend" that dispensation.

שִׁיר הַכָּבוֹד / SONG OF GLORY
Levush writes that, due to the sanctity and

SONG OF GLORY

The Ark is opened and the Song of Glory is said responsively.

Leader: **אַנְעִים זְמִירוֹת** I SING sweet hymns and compose songs, because my heart yearns for You.

Cong: My soul longs to shelter in Your hand and understand Your mysteries.

Leader: As I search out words for Your glory, my heart desires to know Your love.

Cong: That is why I give voice to Your wonders and cajole You with songs of love.

Leader: I cannot see You, but seek to recount Your praise, I cannot know You, but dare to describe Your essence.

Cong: By the agency of Your prophets, and the secrets revealed to them, You tell us of Your awesome splendor.

Leader: Your greatness and Your strength show the measure of Your works.

Cong: They described You, not as You really are, but as Your actions let You be known.

Leader: The countless word-pictures spun by these visionaries are all and more encompassed in Your sacred Unity.

Cong: They saw You both as old and young, Your hair as gray yet also black.

Leader: As an aged judge on the day we are judged, a virile warrior when war beckons,

Cong: wearing the cap signifying redemption on His head, His right arm extended victoriously.

Leader: His hair shining with dewy light, His locks like the nighttime rain.

Cong: He delights in me, and shall ever be the crown of my joy.

Leader: His head is like the purest gold; His holy name is engraved on His brow.

Cong: And as further sign His hand bears a crown whereby His people have crowned Him.

---

loftiness of its themes, the Song of Glory is not to be recited daily, lest it become too familiar. Most Ashkenazi congregations recite it every Shabbat and Yom Tov. The Vilna Gaon favored saying it only on Yom Tov, and some congregations recite it only on Rosh HaShana and Yom Kippur. These concerns also led some to propose that it be recited only by a child

ש״ץ: מַחְלְפוֹת רֹאשׁוֹ כְּבִימֵי בְחוּרוֹת, קְוֻצּוֹתָיו תַּלְתַּלִּים שְׁחוֹרוֹת.

קהל: נְוֵה הַצֶּדֶק צְבִי תִפְאַרְתּוֹ, יַעֲלֶה נָּא עַל רֹאשׁ שִׂמְחָתוֹ.

ש״ץ: סְגֻלָּתוֹ תְּהִי בְיָדוֹ עֲטֶרֶת, וּצְנִיף מְלוּכָה צְבִי תִפְאֶרֶת.

קהל: עֲמוּסִים נְשָׂאָם, עֲטֶרֶת עִנְּדָם, מֵאֲשֶׁר יָקְרוּ בְעֵינָיו כִּבְּדָם.

ש״ץ: פְּאֵרוֹ עָלַי וּפְאֵרִי עָלָיו, וְקָרוֹב אֵלַי בְּקָרְאִי אֵלָיו.

קהל: צַח וְאָדֹם לִלְבוּשׁוֹ אָדֹם, פּוּרָה בְדָרְכוֹ בְּבוֹאוֹ מֵאֱדוֹם.

ש״ץ: קֶשֶׁר תְּפִלִּין הֶרְאָה לֶעָנָו, תְּמוּנַת יהוה לְנֶגֶד עֵינָיו.

קהל: רוֹצֶה בְעַמּוֹ עֲנָוִים יְפָאֵר, יוֹשֵׁב תְּהִלּוֹת בָּם לְהִתְפָּאֵר.

ש״ץ: רֹאשׁ דְּבָרְךָ אֱמֶת קוֹרֵא מֵרֹאשׁ דּוֹר וָדוֹר, עַם דּוֹרֶשְׁךָ דְּרֹשׁ.

קהל: שִׁית הֲמוֹן־שִׁירַי נָא עָלֶיךָ, וְרִנָּתִי תִּקְרַב אֵלֶיךָ.

ש״ץ: תְּהִלָּתִי תְּהִי לְרֹאשְׁךָ עֲטֶרֶת, וּתְפִלָּתִי תִּכּוֹן קְטֹרֶת.

קהל: תִּיקַר שִׁירַת רָשׁ בְּעֵינֶיךָ, כַּשִּׁיר יוּשַׁר עַל קָרְבָּנֶיךָ.

ש״ץ: בִּרְכָתִי תַעֲלֶה לְרֹאשׁ מַשְׁבִּיר, מְחוֹלֵל וּמוֹלִיד, צַדִּיק כַּבִּיר.

קהל: וּבְבִרְכָתִי תְנַעְנַע לִי רֹאשׁ, וְאוֹתָהּ קַח לְךָ כִּבְשָׂמִים רֹאשׁ.

ש״ץ: יֶעֱרַב נָא שִׂיחִי עָלֶיךָ, כִּי נַפְשִׁי תַעֲרֹג אֵלֶיךָ.

The ארון קודש *is closed.*

לְךָ יהוה הַגְּדֻלָּה וְהַגְּבוּרָה וְהַתִּפְאֶרֶת וְהַנֵּצַח וְהַהוֹד, כִּי־כֹל בַּשָּׁמַיִם וּבָאָרֶץ, לְךָ יהוה הַמַּמְלָכָה וְהַמִּתְנַשֵּׂא לְכֹל לְרֹאשׁ: ◂ מִי יְמַלֵּל גְּבוּרוֹת יהוה, יַשְׁמִיעַ כָּל־תְּהִלָּתוֹ: דברי הימים א׳ כט תהלים קו

קדיש יתום (*page 596*)

under *bar mitzva* age, who is "pure," that is, free of sin (R. Yissachar Jacobson).

This poem forms the last part of the שִׁיר הַיִּחוּד וְהַכָּבוֹד, attributed to R. Judah HeḤasid of Regensburg, or his father R. Samuel ben Kalonymus HeḤasid of Speyer, leaders of the German Pietists of the twelfth and thirteenth centuries.

As its name indicates, שִׁיר הַכָּבוֹד is an exploration of the concept of *Kavod* (God's glory). While the medieval Pietists recognized that God has no form whatsoever, they also spoke of *Kavod* as a divine creation reflecting God's presence in our midst. It assumes a form in the eye of the prophet. The poem begins, and ends, with an affirmation that we pursue knowledge of God because our souls thirst to

Leader: His hair is jet-black and curly, flowing like a youth's;

Cong: He values His righteous dwelling, Jerusalem, above any other source of joy.

Leader: The chosen nation He so values is like a crown in His hand, a royal crown of matchless beauty.

Cong: He raises them up and leads them on; He honors them as a rare treasure and source of delight.

Leader: His glory dotes on me, and mine on Him; when I call He is always near.

Cong: Glowing with ruddy vigor, He is garbed in red as He emerges from treading Edom's wine-press.

Leader: The *tefillin* knot was shown to humble Moses when the image of the Lord appeared before his eyes.

Cong: He loves His people and raises up the meek; enshrined in their prayers, He is glorified and praised.

Leader: Truth is the centerpiece of Your message in every generation, seeking those who seek You.

Cong: Be pleased with my many songs, hearken to them and draw them near.

Leader: May my praises crown Your head, and my prayers rise up to You like the sweet-smelling incense.

Cong: And please, deem my poor song as precious as the psalms that accompanied Your holy sacrifices.

Leader: May my blessing rise up to the head of the Sustainer – Creator, Life-Giver, mighty Righteous One.

Cong: And to my blessing incline Your head, and take it to Yourself as the most supreme incense.

Leader: May You find this meditation sweet, because my soul yearns for You.

The Ark is closed.

I Chr. 29 Yours, Lord, are greatness, power, glory, victory, and majesty. Indeed, everything that is in the heavens and on earth. Yours, Lord, is the dominion,
Ps. 106 and You are supreme over all. ▸ Who can recount all the Lord's mighty acts, or make all His praise heard?

Mourner's Kaddish (*page* 597)

---

know and cleave to Him. In between these lines are twenty-six stanzas, the numerical value of God's four-letter name. These stanzas elaborate on the often contradictory manifestations of God that occur in the visions of His prophets, and also describe the Jewish people who manifest His glory in the physical world (R. Aton Holzer).

הַיּוֹם יוֹם שַׁבַּת קֹדֶשׁ, שֶׁבּוֹ הָיוּ הַלְוִיִּם אוֹמְרִים בְּבֵית הַמִּקְדָּשׁ:

תהלים צב
מִזְמוֹר שִׁיר לְיוֹם הַשַּׁבָּת: טוֹב לְהֹדוֹת לַיהוה, וּלְזַמֵּר לְשִׁמְךָ עֶלְיוֹן: לְהַגִּיד בַּבֹּקֶר חַסְדֶּךָ, וֶאֱמוּנָתְךָ בַּלֵּילוֹת: עֲלֵי־עָשׂוֹר וַעֲלֵי־נָבֶל, עֲלֵי הִגָּיוֹן בְּכִנּוֹר: כִּי שִׂמַּחְתַּנִי יהוה בְּפָעֳלֶךָ, בְּמַעֲשֵׂי יָדֶיךָ אֲרַנֵּן: מַה־גָּדְלוּ מַעֲשֶׂיךָ יהוה, מְאֹד עָמְקוּ מַחְשְׁבֹתֶיךָ: אִישׁ־בַּעַר לֹא יֵדָע, וּכְסִיל לֹא־יָבִין אֶת־זֹאת: בִּפְרֹחַ רְשָׁעִים כְּמוֹ עֵשֶׂב, וַיָּצִיצוּ כָּל־פֹּעֲלֵי אָוֶן, לְהִשָּׁמְדָם עֲדֵי־עַד: וְאַתָּה מָרוֹם לְעֹלָם יהוה: כִּי הִנֵּה אֹיְבֶיךָ יהוה, כִּי־הִנֵּה אֹיְבֶיךָ יֹאבֵדוּ, יִתְפָּרְדוּ כָּל־פֹּעֲלֵי אָוֶן: וַתָּרֶם כִּרְאֵים קַרְנִי, בַּלֹּתִי בְּשֶׁמֶן רַעֲנָן: וַתַּבֵּט עֵינִי בְּשׁוּרָי, בַּקָּמִים עָלַי מְרֵעִים תִּשְׁמַעְנָה אָזְנָי: צַדִּיק כַּתָּמָר יִפְרָח, כְּאֶרֶז בַּלְּבָנוֹן יִשְׂגֶּה: שְׁתוּלִים בְּבֵית יהוה, בְּחַצְרוֹת אֱלֹהֵינוּ יַפְרִיחוּ: ‹ עוֹד יְנוּבוּן בְּשֵׂיבָה, דְּשֵׁנִים וְרַעֲנַנִּים יִהְיוּ: לְהַגִּיד כִּי־יָשָׁר יהוה, צוּרִי, וְלֹא־עַוְלָתָה בּוֹ:

קדיש יתום (*page 596*)

On יום טוב *that falls on a weekday, say the appropriate* שיר של יום (*page 184*).
On ראש חודש, *say* בָּרְכִי נַפְשִׁי *on page 194 followed by* קדיש יתום.
On חנוכה, *many congregations add* מִזְמוֹר שִׁיר־חֲנֻכַּת הַבַּיִת *on page 54 followed by* קדיש יתום.

From the second day of ראש חודש אלול *through* שמיני עצרת, *the following psalm is said:*

תהלים כז
לְדָוִד, יהוה אוֹרִי וְיִשְׁעִי, מִמִּי אִירָא, יהוה מָעוֹז־חַיַּי, מִמִּי אֶפְחָד: בִּקְרֹב עָלַי מְרֵעִים לֶאֱכֹל אֶת־בְּשָׂרִי, צָרַי וְאֹיְבַי לִי, הֵמָּה כָשְׁלוּ וְנָפָלוּ: אִם־תַּחֲנֶה עָלַי מַחֲנֶה, לֹא־יִירָא לִבִּי, אִם־תָּקוּם עָלַי מִלְחָמָה, בְּזֹאת אֲנִי בוֹטֵחַ: אַחַת שָׁאַלְתִּי מֵאֵת־יהוה, אוֹתָהּ אֲבַקֵּשׁ, שִׁבְתִּי בְּבֵית־יהוה כָּל־יְמֵי חַיַּי, לַחֲזוֹת בְּנֹעַם־יהוה, וּלְבַקֵּר בְּהֵיכָלוֹ: כִּי יִצְפְּנֵנִי בְּסֻכֹּה בְּיוֹם רָעָה, יַסְתִּרֵנִי בְּסֵתֶר אָהֳלוֹ, בְּצוּר יְרוֹמְמֵנִי: וְעַתָּה יָרוּם רֹאשִׁי עַל אֹיְבַי סְבִיבוֹתַי, וְאֶזְבְּחָה בְאָהֳלוֹ זִבְחֵי תְרוּעָה,

וַיָּצִיצוּ כָּל־פֹּעֲלֵי אָוֶן – *And when all the workers of iniquity flourish*. The Gemara (*Sota* 22b) critiques those who who falsely clothe themselves in a garment of piety. Accordingly this verse alludes to sinners who similarly wrap themselves in *tallitot* that have long *tzitziyot* (reflecting "*vayatzitzu*" in the verse), so as to appear pious, but who in reality are anything but devout. The verse declares that God will punish such deceptive behavior, if not sooner then later,

Today is the holy Sabbath, when the Levites in the Temple would say:

Ps. 92 מִזְמוֹר שִׁיר A PSALM. A song for the Sabbath day. It is good to give thanks to the Lord, and to sing praise to Your name, O Most High, to relate Your loving-kindness in the morning and Your faithfulness in the nights. Upon an instrument of ten strings and upon the harp, to the melody of the lyre. For You, O Lord, make me glad through Your work. I rejoice in the works of Your hands. How great are Your works, O Lord! Your thoughts are very deep. A brutish man does not know, and a fool does not understand this. When the wicked spring forth, they are like grass, and when all the workers of iniquity flourish, it is only that they may be destroyed forever. But You, O Lord, are most high forever. Indeed, behold Your enemies, O Lord! Indeed, behold, Your enemies are perishing. All the workers of iniquity are being scattered. But You have exalted my horn like that of a wild ox. I have anointed myself with fresh oil. My eye has seen the downfall of my enemies, and my ears have heard the doom of the wicked who rise against me. The righteous man flourishes like the palm tree. He grows like a cedar in Lebanon. They are planted in the house of the Lord. They will flourish in the courts of our God. ▸ They will still bring forth fruit in old age. They will be fat and flourishing. To declare that the Lord is upright, that He is my Rock, and there is no unrighteousness in Him.

Mourner's Kaddish (page 597)

On Yom Tov that falls on a weekday, say the appropriate Daily Psalm (page 185).
On Rosh Ḥodesh, say Barekhi Nafshi on page 195 followed by Mourner's Kaddish.
On Ḥanukka, many congregations add Psalm 30 on page 55
followed by Mourner's Kaddish.

From the second day of Rosh Ḥodesh Elul through Shemini Atzeret,
the following psalm is said:

Ps. 27 לְדָוִד OF DAVID. The Lord is my light and my salvation. Whom shall I fear? The Lord is the refuge of my life. Whom shall I dread? When the evildoers came close to me to eat my flesh, those who were to me my adversaries and my enemies, it was they who stumbled and fell. If a host should encamp against me, my heart will not fear. If a war should rise against me, in this I trust. One thing have I asked of the Lord, that will I seek: That I may dwell in the house of the Lord all the days of my life, to behold the beauty of the Lord, and to contemplate His Temple, That He will hide me in His tabernacle on the day of evil, He will hide me in the shelter of His tent, He will lift me up upon a rock. And now my head will be lifted up above my enemies round about me, and I will offer in His tent sacrifices accompanied

אָשִׁירָה וַאֲזַמְּרָה לַיהוה: שְׁמַע־יהוה קוֹלִי אֶקְרָא, וְחָנֵּנִי וַעֲנֵנִי: לְךָ אָמַר לִבִּי בַּקְּשׁוּ פָנָי, אֶת־פָּנֶיךָ יהוה אֲבַקֵּשׁ: אַל־תַּסְתֵּר פָּנֶיךָ מִמֶּנִּי, אַל תַּט־בְּאַף עַבְדֶּךָ, עֶזְרָתִי הָיִיתָ, אַל־תִּטְּשֵׁנִי וְאַל־תַּעַזְבֵנִי, אֱלֹהֵי יִשְׁעִי: כִּי־אָבִי וְאִמִּי עֲזָבוּנִי, וַיהוה יַאַסְפֵנִי: הוֹרֵנִי יהוה דַּרְכֶּךָ, וּנְחֵנִי בְּאֹרַח מִישׁוֹר, לְמַעַן שׁוֹרְרָי: אַל־תִּתְּנֵנִי בְּנֶפֶשׁ צָרָי, כִּי קָמוּ־בִי עֵדֵי־שֶׁקֶר, וִיפֵחַ חָמָס: ◂ לוּלֵא הֶאֱמַנְתִּי לִרְאוֹת בְּטוּב־יהוה בְּאֶרֶץ חַיִּים: קַוֵּה אֶל־יהוה, חֲזַק וְיַאֲמֵץ לִבֶּךָ, וְקַוֵּה אֶל־יהוה:

קדיש יתום (*page 596*)

קדיש יתום

The following prayer, said by mourners, requires the presence of a מנין.
A transliteration can be found on page 1345.

אבל: **יִתְגַּדַּל** וְיִתְקַדַּשׁ שְׁמֵהּ רַבָּא (קהל: אָמֵן), בְּעָלְמָא דִּי בְרָא כִרְעוּתֵהּ.
וְיַמְלִיךְ מַלְכוּתֵהּ, בְּחַיֵּיכוֹן וּבְיוֹמֵיכוֹן וּבְחַיֵּי דְכָל בֵּית
יִשְׂרָאֵל, בַּעֲגָלָא וּבִזְמַן קָרִיב, וְאִמְרוּ אָמֵן. (קהל: אָמֵן)

קהל ואבל: יְהֵא שְׁמֵהּ רַבָּא מְבָרַךְ לְעָלַם וּלְעָלְמֵי עָלְמַיָּא.

אבל: יִתְבָּרַךְ וְיִשְׁתַּבַּח וְיִתְפָּאַר, וְיִתְרוֹמַם וְיִתְנַשֵּׂא וְיִתְהַדָּר וְיִתְעַלֶּה
וְיִתְהַלָּל שְׁמֵהּ דְּקֻדְשָׁא בְּרִיךְ הוּא (קהל: בְּרִיךְ הוּא), לְעֵלָּא מִן כָּל
בִּרְכָתָא /בשבת שובה: לְעֵלָּא (וּ)לְעֵלָּא מִכָּל בִּרְכָתָא/ וְשִׁירָתָא, תֻּשְׁבְּחָתָא
וְנֶחֱמָתָא דַּאֲמִירָן בְּעָלְמָא, וְאִמְרוּ אָמֵן. (קהל: אָמֵן)

יְהֵא שְׁלָמָא רַבָּא מִן שְׁמַיָּא וְחַיִּים, עָלֵינוּ וְעַל כָּל יִשְׂרָאֵל, וְאִמְרוּ
אָמֵן. (קהל: אָמֵן)

Bow, take three steps back, as if taking leave of the Divine Presence, then bow, first left, then right, then center, while saying:

עֹשֶׂה שָׁלוֹם /בשבת שובה: הַשָּׁלוֹם/ בִּמְרוֹמָיו, הוּא יַעֲשֶׂה שָׁלוֹם עָלֵינוּ,
וְעַל כָּל יִשְׂרָאֵל, וְאִמְרוּ אָמֵן. (קהל: אָמֵן)

---

even if such people have to be "destroyed forever" (Me'iri)

כִּי־אָבִי וְאִמִּי עֲזָבוּנִי, וַה׳ יַאַסְפֵנִי. – *For my father and my mother have forsaken me, but the Lord will gather me in.* "I am lonely because at times I feel rejected and thrust away by everybody, not excluding my most intimate friends, and the words of the Psalmist ('my father and my mother have forsaken me') ring quite often in my ears like the plaintive cooing of the turtle-

by the sound of trumpets. I will sing, and I will sing praises to the Lord. Hear, O Lord, my voice when I call, and show me favor and answer me. Of You my heart has said: Seek My face. Your face, O Lord, will I seek. Do not hide Your face from me. Do not turn Your servant away in anger. You have been my help, do not abandon me and do not forsake me, O God of my salvation. For my father and my mother have forsaken me, but the Lord will gather me in. Teach me Your way, O Lord, and lead me on an even path, because of my enemies. Do not deliver me to the desire of my enemies, for false witnesses have risen up against me, and a wicked witness. ▸ Were it not that I believed I would see the goodness of the Lord in the land of the living. Wait for the Lord, be strong and let your heart be encouraged, and wait for the Lord.

Mourner's Kaddish (page 597)

MOURNER'S KADDISH

The following prayer, said by mourners, requires the presence of a minyan. A transliteration can be found on page 1345.

Mourner: **יִתְגַּדַּל** EXALTED AND HALLOWED may God's great name be, in the world He created as He willed. May He reign in your lifetimes and in your days, and in the lifetime of the whole house of Israel, speedily and soon, and say, Amen.

All: May His great name be blessed forever and all time.

Mourner: Blessed and praised, honored, extolled, glorified, adored and exalted above all be the name of the Holy One, blessed is He, (*Between Rosh Hashana & Yom Kippur:* above and) beyond any blessing, hymn, praise, or expressions of consolation that may be uttered in this world, and say, Amen.

May abundant peace descend from heaven, as well as life, for us and for all Israel, and say, Amen.

Bow, take three steps back, as if taking leave of the Divine Presence, then bow, first left, then right, then center, while saying:

May He Who makes peace in the highest heaven, make peace for us, and for all Israel, and say, Amen.

---

dove. It is a strange, alas, absurd experience engendering sharp, enervating pain as well as a stimulating, cathartic feeling. I despair because I am lonely, and, hence, feel frustrated. On the other hand, I also feel invigorated because this very experience of loneliness presses everything in me into the service of God… This service to which I, a lonely and solitary

אֲדוֹן עוֹלָם אֲשֶׁר מָלַךְ
בְּטֶרֶם כָּל־יְצִיר נִבְרָא.
לְעֵת נַעֲשָׂה בְחֶפְצוֹ כֹּל
אֲזַי מֶלֶךְ שְׁמוֹ נִקְרָא.
וְאַחֲרֵי כִּכְלוֹת הַכֹּל
לְבַדּוֹ יִמְלֹךְ נוֹרָא.
וְהוּא הָיָה וְהוּא הֹוֶה
וְהוּא יִהְיֶה בְּתִפְאָרָה.

וְהוּא אֶחָד וְאֵין שֵׁנִי
לְהַמְשִׁיל לוֹ לְהַחְבִּירָה.
בְּלִי רֵאשִׁית בְּלִי תַכְלִית
וְלוֹ הָעֹז וְהַמִּשְׂרָה.
וְהוּא אֵלִי וְחַי גּוֹאֲלִי
וְצוּר חֶבְלִי בְּעֵת צָרָה.

וְהוּא נִסִּי וּמָנוֹס לִי
מְנָת כּוֹסִי בְּיוֹם אֶקְרָא.
בְּיָדוֹ אַפְקִיד רוּחִי
בְּעֵת אִישַׁן וְאָעִירָה.

וְעִם רוּחִי גְּוִיָּתִי
יהוה לִי וְלֹא אִירָא.

individual, am committed is wanted and gracefully accepted by God in His transcendental loneliness and numinous solitude" (R. Joseph B. Soloveitchik).

אֲדוֹן עוֹלָם ETERNAL MASTER,
Who reigned before anything was created –

when by His will all things were brought into being,
then as King was His name proclaimed.

After all things have ceased to be,
He will reign alone in awesome majesty.

He was. He is. He will always be;
His eternal glory can never fade.

He is One. There is no other;
beyond compare, or any metaphor.

He had no beginning, will have no end.
He above all others has strength and power.

He is my God, my living Redeemer,
a Rock when I am in pain
in troubled times.

My banner and my refuge,
to Whom I will raise a cup
on the day I proclaim my salvation.

I entrust my spirit to His hand,
when sleeping and when awake.

With my body my soul will stay;
the Lord is with me,
I need not fear.

אֲדוֹן עוֹלָם – *Eternal Master.* This poem of praise is attributed to the great eleventh-century Spanish poet and philosopher R. Shlomo ibn Gabirol.

קידוש וזמירות ליום שבת

חַי יהוה וּבָרוּךְ צוּרִי, בַּיהוה תִּתְהַלֵּל נַפְשִׁי,
כִּי יהוה יָאִיר נֵרִי, בְּהִלּוֹ נֵרוֹ עֲלֵי רֹאשִׁי.
יהוה רוֹעִי לֹא אֶחְסָר, עַל מֵי מְנוּחוֹת יְנַהֲלֵנִי,
נוֹתֵן לֶחֶם לְכָל בָּשָׂר, לֶחֶם חֻקִּי הַטְרִיפֵנִי.
יְהִי רָצוֹן מִלְּפָנֶיךָ, אַתָּה אֱלֹהֵי קְדוֹשִׁי,
תַּעֲרֹךְ לְפָנַי שֻׁלְחָנְךָ, תְּדַשֵּׁן בַּשֶּׁמֶן רֹאשִׁי.
מִי יִתֵּן מְנוּחָתִי, לִפְנֵי אֲדוֹן הַשָּׁלוֹם,
וְהָיְתָה שְׁלֵמָה מִטָּתִי, הַחַיִּים וְהַשָּׁלוֹם.
יִשְׁלַח מַלְאָכוֹ לְפָנַי, לְלַוּוֹתִי לְוָיָה,
בְּכוֹס יְשׁוּעוֹת אֶשָּׂא פָנַי, מְנָת כּוֹסִי רְוָיָה.
צָמְאָה נַפְשִׁי אֶל יהוה, יְמַלֵּא שֹׂבַע אֲסָמַי,
אֶל הֶהָרִים אֶשָּׂא עֵינַי, כְּהִלֵּל וְלֹא כְשַׁמַּאי.
חֶדְוַת יָמִים וּשְׁנוֹת עוֹלָמִים, עוּרָה כְבוֹדִי עוּרָה,
וְעַל רֹאשִׁי יִהְיוּ תַמִּים, נֵר מִצְוָה וְאוֹר תּוֹרָה.
קוּמָה יהוה לִמְנוּחָתִי, אַתָּה וַאֲרוֹן עֻזֶּךָ,
קַח נָא אֵל אֶת בִּרְכָתִי, וְהַחֲזֵק מָגֵן חוֹזֶךָ.

תהלים כג **מִזְמוֹר לְדָוִד,** יהוה רֹעִי לֹא אֶחְסָר: בִּנְאוֹת דֶּשֶׁא יַרְבִּיצֵנִי, עַל־
מֵי מְנֻחוֹת יְנַהֲלֵנִי: נַפְשִׁי יְשׁוֹבֵב, יַנְחֵנִי בְמַעְגְּלֵי־
צֶדֶק לְמַעַן שְׁמוֹ: גַּם כִּי־אֵלֵךְ בְּגֵיא צַלְמָוֶת לֹא־אִירָא רָע, כִּי־אַתָּה
עִמָּדִי, שִׁבְטְךָ וּמִשְׁעַנְתֶּךָ הֵמָּה יְנַחֲמֻנִי: תַּעֲרֹךְ לְפָנַי שֻׁלְחָן נֶגֶד
צֹרְרָי, דִּשַּׁנְתָּ בַשֶּׁמֶן רֹאשִׁי, כּוֹסִי רְוָיָה: אַךְ טוֹב וָחֶסֶד יִרְדְּפוּנִי
כָּל־יְמֵי חַיָּי, וְשַׁבְתִּי בְּבֵית־יהוה לְאֹרֶךְ יָמִים:

סְעוּדַת יוֹם הַשַּׁבָּת / SABBATH-DAY MEAL

חַי ה׳ / THE LORD LIVES
The poem introduces Psalm 23 by interweaving its verses with other scriptural references. It also serves as a preamble to the verse אִם תָּשִׁיב, which is the source for כָּבוֹד and עֹנֶג (to honor and enjoy Shabbat).

KIDDUSH AND ZEMIROT FOR SHABBAT MORNING

ח **חַי יהוה** THE LORD LIVES and blessed is my Rock. My soul glories in the Lord, for the Lord gives light to my lamp when His lamp shines on my head.

י The Lord is my Shepherd. I lack for nothing; He leads me beside still waters. He Who gives bread for all flesh, feed me my allotted bread.

י May it be Your will – You, my holy God – prepare Your table before me, anoint my head with oil.

ם Who can place my contentment, before the Master of Peace, that my progeny be perfect, with life and peace?

י May He send His angel before me as my accompanying escort. With a cup of salvations I shall lift my face; the portion of my cup runs over.

צ My soul thirsts for the Lord; may He fill my storehouses with abundance. To the teachers I shall raise my eyes, like Hillel, not like Shammai.

ח So give me days of delight and eternal years – "Wake up, my soul, wake up!" Then above my head will unite as twins, the lamp of commandments and the light of Torah.

ק Rise up, Lord, be present in my contentment, You and the Ark of Your strength. Please accept, God, my blessing, and strengthen the shield of Your seer.

Ps. 23 **מִזְמוֹר לְדָוִד** A PSALM OF DAVID. The Lord is my shepherd. I lack for nothing. He makes me lie down in green pastures. He leads me beside still waters. He restores my soul. He leads me in the paths of righteousness for His name's sake. Even when I walk in a valley of darkness, I do not fear evil, for You are with me. Your rod and Your staff, they comfort me. You prepare a table before me in the presence of my enemies. You have anointed my head with oil. My cup runs over. Only goodness and loving-kindness will follow me all the days of my life, and I will dwell in tranquility in the house of the Lord forever.

קידושא רבא לשבת ולחגים

There are various starting points for Kiddush depending on one's custom, indicated below with.*

**Some say:*

אִם־תָּשִׁיב מִשַּׁבָּת רַגְלֶךָ עֲשׂוֹת חֲפָצֶךָ בְּיוֹם קָדְשִׁי, וְקָרָאתָ לַשַּׁבָּת עֹנֶג לִקְדוֹשׁ יהוה מְכֻבָּד, וְכִבַּדְתּוֹ מֵעֲשׂוֹת דְּרָכֶיךָ מִמְּצוֹא חֶפְצְךָ וְדַבֵּר דָּבָר: אָז תִּתְעַנַּג עַל־יהוה, וְהִרְכַּבְתִּיךָ עַל־בָּמֳתֵי אָרֶץ, וְהַאֲכַלְתִּיךָ נַחֲלַת יַעֲקֹב אָבִיךָ, כִּי פִּי יהוה דִּבֵּר: ישעיה נח

**Most begin קידוש here. On יום טוב that falls on a weekday, begin on the next page.*

וְשָׁמְרוּ בְנֵי־יִשְׂרָאֵל אֶת־הַשַּׁבָּת, לַעֲשׂוֹת אֶת־הַשַּׁבָּת לְדֹרֹתָם בְּרִית עוֹלָם: בֵּינִי וּבֵין בְּנֵי יִשְׂרָאֵל אוֹת הִוא לְעֹלָם, כִּי־שֵׁשֶׁת יָמִים עָשָׂה יהוה אֶת־הַשָּׁמַיִם וְאֶת־הָאָרֶץ וּבַיּוֹם הַשְּׁבִיעִי שָׁבַת וַיִּנָּפַשׁ: שמות לא

זָכוֹר אֶת־יוֹם הַשַּׁבָּת לְקַדְּשׁוֹ: שֵׁשֶׁת יָמִים תַּעֲבֹד, וְעָשִׂיתָ כָּל־מְלַאכְתֶּךָ: וְיוֹם הַשְּׁבִיעִי שַׁבָּת לַיהוה אֱלֹהֶיךָ, לֹא־תַעֲשֶׂה כָל־מְלָאכָה אַתָּה וּבִנְךָ וּבִתֶּךָ, עַבְדְּךָ וַאֲמָתְךָ וּבְהֶמְתֶּךָ, וְגֵרְךָ אֲשֶׁר בִּשְׁעָרֶיךָ: כִּי שֵׁשֶׁת־יָמִים עָשָׂה יהוה אֶת־הַשָּׁמַיִם וְאֶת־הָאָרֶץ אֶת־הַיָּם וְאֶת־כָּל־אֲשֶׁר־בָּם, וַיָּנַח בַּיּוֹם הַשְּׁבִיעִי, שמות כ

**On יום טוב that falls on שבת, some start קידוש here instead:*

עַל־כֵּן בֵּרַךְ יהוה אֶת־יוֹם הַשַּׁבָּת וַיְקַדְּשֵׁהוּ:

For weekday יום טוב continue on the next page.

When saying קידוש for others, add:

סַבְרִי מָרָנָן וְרַבָּנָן וְרַבּוֹתַי

בָּרוּךְ אַתָּה יהוה אֱלֹהֵינוּ מֶלֶךְ הָעוֹלָם, בּוֹרֵא פְּרִי הַגָּפֶן.

On סוכות when קידוש is made in the סוכה, add:

בָּרוּךְ אַתָּה יהוה אֱלֹהֵינוּ מֶלֶךְ הָעוֹלָם, אֲשֶׁר קִדְּשָׁנוּ בְּמִצְוֹתָיו וְצִוָּנוּ לֵישֵׁב בַּסֻּכָּה.

LAWS OF KIDDUSH

When reciting *Kiddush*, one holds a full cup of grape wine (or grape juice) in one's right hand, bearing in mind that one is fulfilling the *mitzva* of *Kiddush* for oneself and those who are listening. Listeners should bear in mind that they are fulfilling the *mitzva*, and should remain silent except for "Amen."

KIDDUSHA RABA FOR SHABBAT AND FESTIVALS

There are various starting points for Kiddush depending on one's custom, indicated below with.*

**Some say:*

Is. 58 אִם־תָּשִׁיב IF BECAUSE of the Sabbath you restrain your foot from pursuing your business on My holy day, and you call the Sabbath "a delight," the holy day of the Lord "honored," and you honor it by not following your customary ways, nor pursuing your business, nor speaking thereof, then shall you find delight in the Lord, and I will make you ride on the high places of the earth, and I will nourish you with the heritage of Jacob your forefather; for the mouth of the Lord has spoken.

**Most begin Kiddush here. On Yom Tov that falls on a weekday, begin on the next page.*

Ex. 31 וְשָׁמְרוּ THE CHILDREN OF ISRAEL shall keep the Sabbath, observing the Sabbath throughout their generations as an everlasting covenant. It is a sign between Me and the children of Israel forever that in six days the Lord made heaven and earth, and He rested on the seventh day and was refreshed.

Ex. 20 זָכוֹר REMEMBER THE SABBATH to keep it holy. Six days shall you labor and do all your work; but the seventh day is a Sabbath to the Lord your God, you shall not do any work, neither you, nor your son, nor your daughter, nor your manservant, nor your maidservant, nor your cattle, nor the stranger who is within your gates. For in six days the Lord made heaven and earth, the sea and all that is therein, and He rested on the seventh day –

**On Yom Tov that falls on Shabbat, some start Kiddush here instead:*

therefore the Lord blessed the Sabbath day and made it holy.

For weekday Yom Tov continue on the next page.

When saying kiddush for others, add:

By your leave, my masters, rabbis, and esteemed companions:

בָּרוּךְ BLESSED ARE YOU, Lord, our God, King of the universe, Who creates the fruit of the vine.

On Sukkot, when Kiddush is made in the sukka, add:

בָּרוּךְ BLESSED ARE YOU, Lord, our God, King of the universe, Who has sanctified us with His commandments and commanded us to dwell in the sukka.

קִדּוּשָׁא רַבָּא / THE GREAT KIDDUSH

אִם־תָּשִׁיב – *If... you restrain.* These verses conclude Isaiah 58, which is recited as the *Haftara* for Yom Kippur. It focuses on Shabbat as a day of faith as well as social responsibility.

On יום טוב*, say:*

ויקרא כג
אֵלֶּה מוֹעֲדֵי יהוה מִקְרָאֵי קֹדֶשׁ אֲשֶׁר־תִּקְרְאוּ אֹתָם בְּמוֹעֲדָם: וַיְדַבֵּר מֹשֶׁה אֶת־מֹעֲדֵי יהוה אֶל־בְּנֵי יִשְׂרָאֵל:

On ראש השנה *say:*

תהלים פא
תִּקְעוּ בַחֹדֶשׁ שׁוֹפָר, בַּכֶּסֶה לְיוֹם חַגֵּנוּ: כִּי חֹק לְיִשְׂרָאֵל הוּא, מִשְׁפָּט לֵאלֹהֵי יַעֲקֹב:

When saying קידוש *for others, add:*

סַבְרִי מָרָנָן וְרַבָּנָן וְרַבּוֹתַי

בָּרוּךְ אַתָּה יהוה אֱלֹהֵינוּ מֶלֶךְ הָעוֹלָם, בּוֹרֵא פְּרִי הַגָּפֶן.

On סוכות *when* קידוש *is made in the* סוכה*, add:*

בָּרוּךְ אַתָּה יהוה אֱלֹהֵינוּ מֶלֶךְ הָעוֹלָם, אֲשֶׁר קִדְּשָׁנוּ בְּמִצְוֹתָיו וְצִוָּנוּ לֵישֵׁב בַּסֻּכָּה.

לחם משנה

On washing hands before eating bread:

בָּרוּךְ אַתָּה יהוה אֱלֹהֵינוּ מֶלֶךְ הָעוֹלָם אֲשֶׁר קִדְּשָׁנוּ בְּמִצְוֹתָיו וְצִוָּנוּ עַל נְטִילַת יָדָיִם.

Before eating bread:

בָּרוּךְ אַתָּה יהוה אֱלֹהֵינוּ מֶלֶךְ הָעוֹלָם, הַמּוֹצִיא לֶחֶם מִן הָאָרֶץ.

KIDDUSHA RABA

As we read in the Torah (Gen. 2:3) on the seventh day of Creation God sanctified the seventh day. In addition, however, the Torah tells us that the seventh day was also sanctified during the Exodus from Egypt, as it says, "Remember that the Lord your God brought you forth from there… therefore the Lord your God commanded you to make the Sabbath day" (Deut. 5:15). This supplementary sanctification of the seventh day depends on the Jewish people "making" the day holy. This is the basis for reciting *Kiddush* by which we actually sanctify the day, over and above the sanctification by God at Creation, as Ramban states in commenting on Exodus 20:8. It is for this reason that we make Shabbat *Kiddush* on Friday night for it makes sense to sanctify it at its outset rather than during the subsequent daylight hours. It also accounts for "*Tosefet Shabbat*" by which a Jew can extend the sanctity of the seventh day beyond its usual twenty-four-hour cycle, for God has empowered us to add to His original sanctification.

This all applies to the *Kiddush* of Friday night. What about *Kiddush* on Shabbat morning? The answer, based on the Gemara *Pesaḥim* 105–106, is that while it is true that on Shabbat morning the *Kiddush* does not sanctify the day, as it has already been sanctified the night before, nonetheless by reciting it we bear witness to Creation and praise the greatness of the God Who is the Creator of all. For this reason the only required text of Shabbat morning *Kiddush* is the *berakha* of בּוֹרֵא פְּרִי הַגָּפֶן ("He

For laws of *Leḥem Mishneh*, see page 429.

On Yom Tov, say:

Lev. 23 אֵלֶּה THESE are the appointed festival seasons of the Lord, the holy assemblies that you shall proclaim in their appointed seasons. Moses declared the appointed festival seasons of the Lord, to the children of Israel.

On Rosh HaShana say:

Ps. 81 תִּקְעוּ SOUND A SHOFAR on the new moon, on the day of covering for our feast day. For this is a statute for Israel, an ordinance of the God of Jacob.

When saying kiddush for others, add:

By your leave, my masters, rabbis, and esteemed companions:

בָּרוּךְ BLESSED ARE YOU, Lord, our God, King of the universe, Who creates the fruit of the vine.

On Sukkot, when Kiddush is made in the sukka, add:

בָּרוּךְ BLESSED ARE YOU, Lord, our God, King of the universe, Who has sanctified us with His commandments and commanded us to dwell in the sukka.

LEḤEM MISHNEH

On washing hands before eating bread:

בָּרוּךְ BLESSED ARE YOU, Lord, our God, King of the universe, Who has sanctified us with His commandments, and has commanded us about washing hands.

Before eating bread:

בָּרוּךְ BLESSED ARE YOU, Lord, our God, King of the universe, Who brings forth bread from the earth.

---

is the Creator of the fruit of the vine"). For with these words we bear witness to the six days of Creation and we praise Him Who is the בּוֹרֵא עוֹלָם (Creator of the cosmos).

What is the nature of this particular blessing over wine? It is not simply a *berakha* like those we make over benefits we enjoy. Rather, as the Gemara *Pesaḥim* describes it, in reciting the *berakha* we also fulfill the obligation of שִׁירָה עַל הַיַּיִן, that is, it is an "ode of praise" that must be accompanied by wine. As the Rashbam on *Pesaḥim* 106a puts it: "We recite the *berakha* over a cup of wine and then drink it for the sake of honoring Shabbat and distinguishing it from the rest of the week, to fulfill our duty to sing His praises accompanied by wine, as explained in the *She'iltot*." This is also consistent with the view of Rambam regarding the nature of the Shabbat morning *Kiddush*.

In light of this, we can also account for the unusual name given to this *Kiddush* – "*Kiddusha Raba*" or "*Kiddush* of greatness." The name signifies that it is not a *Kiddush* of "sanctification," but rather one of "greatness," that is, by reciting it we testify to the "greatness" of (a) the Creator and (b) the Shabbat for all that it signifies (R. Joseph B. Soloveitchik).

Through Rav Soloveitchik's analysis of *Kiddusha Raba* we can perhaps better understand why the *halakha* strongly prefers that Shabbat morning *Kiddush* be recited over wine or grape juice, as opposed to other drinks that (a) do not fulfill the obligation of שִׁירָה עַל הַיַּיִן, (b) do not feature the *berakha* of בּוֹרֵא פְּרִי הַגָּפֶן, and (c) are difficult to consume in the volume that is required for *Kiddush* (R. Basil Herring).

זמירות ליום שבת

בָּרוּךְ אֲדֹנָי יוֹם יוֹם, יַעֲמָס לָנוּ יֶשַׁע וּפִדְיוֹם, וּבִשְׁמוֹ נָגִיל כָּל הַיּוֹם, וּבִישׁוּעָתוֹ
נָרִים רֹאשׁ עֶלְיוֹן. כִּי הוּא מָעוֹז לַדָּל וּמַחְסֶה לָאֶבְיוֹן.

שִׁבְטֵי יָהּ לְיִשְׂרָאֵל עֵדוּת, בְּצָרָתָם לוֹ צָר בְּסִבְלוּת וּבְעַבְדוּת, בְּלִבְנַת הַסַּפִּיר
הֶרְאָם עֹז יְדִידוּת, וְנִגְלָה לְהַעֲלוֹתָם מֵעֹמֶק בּוֹר וָדוּת. כִּי־עִם־יהוה הַחֶסֶד, וְהַרְבֵּה תהלים קל
עִמּוֹ פְדוּת:

מַה יָּקָר חַסְדּוֹ בְּצִלּוֹ לְגוֹנְנֵמוֹ, בְּגָלוּת בָּבֶלָה שֻׁלַּח לְמַעֲנֵמוֹ, לְהוֹרִיד בָּרִיחִים
נִמְנָה בֵינֵימוֹ, וַיִּתְּנֵם לְרַחֲמִים לִפְנֵי שׁוֹבֵימוֹ. כִּי לֹא יִטֹּשׁ יהוה אֶת עַמּוֹ, בַּעֲבוּר
הַגָּדוֹל שְׁמוֹ.

עֵילָם שָׁת כִּסְאוֹ לְהַצִּיל יְדִידָיו, לְהַאֲבִיד מִשָּׁם מָעֻזְנֵי מוֹרְדָיו, מֵעֲבֹר בַּשֶּׁלַח פָּדָה
אֶת עֲבָדָיו, קֶרֶן לְעַמּוֹ יָרִים, תְּהִלָּה לְכָל חֲסִידָיו. כִּי אִם־הוֹגָה, וְרִחַם כְּרֹב חֲסָדָו: איכה ג

וּצְפִיר הָעִזִּים הִגְדִּיל עֲצוּמָיו, וְגַם חָזוּת אַרְבַּע עָלוּ לִמְרוֹמָיו, וּבְלִבָּם דִּמּוּ
לְהַשְׁחִית אֶת רְחוּמָיו, עַל יְדֵי כֹהֲנָיו מִגֵּר מִתְקוֹמְמָיו. חַסְדֵי יהוה כִּי לֹא־תָמְנוּ,
כִּי לֹא כָלוּ רַחֲמָיו: איכה ג

נִסְגַּרְתִּי לֶאֱדוֹם בְּיַד רֵעַי מְדָנַי, שֶׁבְּכָל יוֹם מְמַלְּאִים כְּרֵסָם מֵעֲדָנַי, עֶזְרָתוֹ עִמִּי
לִסְמֹךְ אֶת אֲדָנַי, וְלֹא נְטַשְׁתַּנִי כָּל יְמֵי עִדָּנַי. כִּי לֹא יִזְנַח לְעוֹלָם אֲדֹנָי: איכה ג

בְּבוֹאוֹ מֵאֱדוֹם חֲמוּץ בְּגָדִים, זֶבַח לוֹ בְּבָצְרָה וְטֶבַח לוֹ בְּבוֹגְדִים, וְיֵז נִצְחָם מַלְבּוּשָׁיו
לְהַאְדִּים, בְּכֹחוֹ הַגָּדוֹל יִבְצֹר רוּחַ נְגִידִים. הָגָה בְּרוּחוֹ הַקָּשָׁה בְּיוֹם קָדִים: ישעיה כז

רְאוֹתוֹ כִּי כֵן אֲדוֹמִי הָעוֹצֵר, יַחְשָׁב לוֹ בָּצְרָה תִּקְלֹט כְּבֶצֶר, וּמַלְאָךְ כְּאָדָם בְּתוֹכָהּ
יִנָּצֵר, וּמֵזִיד כַּשּׁוֹגֵג בְּמִקְלָט יֵעָצֵר. אֶהֱבוּ אֶת־יהוה כָּל־חֲסִידָיו, אֱמוּנִים נֹצֵר: תהלים לא

יְצַוֶּה צוּר **חַ**סְדּוֹ **קְ**הִלּוֹתָיו לְקַבֵּץ, מֵאַרְבַּע רוּחוֹת עָדָיו לְהִקָּבֵץ, וּבְהַר מְרוֹם
הָרִים אוֹתָנוּ לְהַרְבֵּץ, וְאִתָּנוּ יָשׁוּב נִדָּחִים קוֹבֵץ. יָשִׁיב לֹא נֶאֱמַר, כִּי אִם וְשָׁב וְקִבֵּץ.

בָּרוּךְ הוּא אֱלֹהֵינוּ אֲשֶׁר טוֹב גְּמָלָנוּ, כְּרַחֲמָיו וּכְרֹב חֲסָדָיו הִגְדִּיל לָנוּ, אֵלֶּה וְכָאֵלֶּה
יוֹסֵף עִמָּנוּ, לְהַגְדִּיל שְׁמוֹ הַגָּדוֹל הַגִּבּוֹר וְהַנּוֹרָא, שֶׁנִּקְרָא עָלֵינוּ.

בָּרוּךְ הוּא אֱלֹהֵינוּ שֶׁבְּרָאָנוּ לִכְבוֹדוֹ, לְהַלְלוֹ וּלְשַׁבְּחוֹ וּלְסַפֵּר הוֹדוֹ, מִכָּל אֹם גָּבַר
עָלֵינוּ חַסְדּוֹ, לָכֵן בְּכָל לֵב וּבְכָל נֶפֶשׁ וּבְכָל מְאוֹדוֹ, נַמְלִיכוֹ וּנְיַחֲדוֹ.

שֶׁהַשָּׁלוֹם שֶׁלּוֹ יָשִׂים עָלֵינוּ בְּרָכָה וְשָׁלוֹם, מִשְּׂמֹאל וּמִיָּמִין עַל יִשְׂרָאֵל שָׁלוֹם,
הָרַחֲמָן הוּא יְבָרֵךְ אֶת עַמּוֹ בַשָּׁלוֹם, וְיִזְכּוּ לִרְאוֹת בָּנִים וּבְנֵי בָנִים, עוֹסְקִים, בַּתּוֹרָה
וּבְמִצְוֹת, עַל יִשְׂרָאֵל שָׁלוֹם. פֶּלֶא יוֹעֵץ אֵל גִּבּוֹר אֲבִי־עַד שַׂר־שָׁלוֹם: ישעיה ט

ZEMIROT FOR SHABBAT DAY

בָּרוּךְ אֲדֹנָי יוֹם יוֹם BLESSED be the Lord Who every day / sets on us salvation and His redemption. / In His name we delight at all times; / through His salvation we will hold our heads high. / A stronghold is He for the poor, for the needy a refuge.

THE TRIBES of the Lord have been witness for Israel. / In their burdens and bondage in Egypt He grieved. / In their brickwork He showed them love based as on sapphire. / He came forth to *Ps. 130* uplift them from the depths. / "For with the Lord is loving-kindness, and with Him is abundant redemption."

PROTECTING and shielding, how great was His kindness! / For them He went with them in Babylon's exile. / When their ships went down He was among them, / and from their harsh captors He won for them mercy. / "For His people the Lord will never forsake in keeping with His great name."

HIS THRONE was in Persia to rescue His loved ones / by foiling the ruthlessness planned by Haman. / His servants He saved from malevolent weapons. / He will raise the banner of His *Lam. 3* people, all His devoted ones will be praised. / "Though He sent them affliction, mercy He showed them in pity and kindness."

THEN GREECE, Daniel's he-goat, extended supremely; / the four horns which Daniel saw surged up on high. / While they thought in their heart to destroy God's loved people, / God *Lam. 3* vanquished His foes by His priests, Maccabees. / "Through the Lord's loving mercies we were not consumed, for His kindnesses did not fail."

THEN STRIFE with my fellows made me victim to Rome, / which gorged its fill daily on all my delights. / But God's help was still with me to aid and uphold me. / He did not forsake me through *Lam. 3* all those dark days, / "For it is not forever that the Lord will reject us."

HE WILL COME from Edom with garments encrimsoned. / In Botzra He will slaughter and destroy treasonous ones. / He will scatter their blood as it reddens His garments / Withpower He *Is. 27* will cut down their leader's life spirit / "When He sweeps them away as with blast of East wind."

WHEN EDOM will see all of this he will think / that Botzra will protect him as did Betzer, / and that his angel will be sheltered there like a man, / and willful misdoer be there safe as the *Ps. 31* erring. / "Love the Lord, all you pious, He cares for the faithful."

IN HIS LOVE our great Rock will regather His people, / from four corners of earth bring them back to Himself, / and root us on Zion, supreme among mountains. / Yes, He will return with His ingathered people: / for rather than saying, "He will return us," it states, "He (Himself) shall return."

BLESSED be our God Who has dealt with us graciously. / In His mercy and great kindness He has done great things for us. / So that His great, mighty, awesome name / that has been placed upon us, will be ever magnified.

BLESSED be our God Who for His glory created us / to sing praise and blessing and His majesty declare. / He has shown us above others His grace and His kindness. / So with all our heart, soul, and might / we proclaim Him the King and declare His unity.

MAY He, source of peace, give us blessing and peace. / From all sides may there come unto Israel peace. / May the Merciful One bless His people with peace, / that they may see their children and their children's children / busied with Torah, fulfilling its commands. / May Israel *Is. 9* know peace from Him Who is "wonderful in counsel, / God the mighty, the eternal Father, Prince of peace."

בָּרוּךְ אֵל עֶלְיוֹן אֲשֶׁר נָתַן מְנוּחָה, לְנַפְשֵׁנוּ פִדְיוֹן מִשֵּׁאת וַאֲנָחָה,
וְהוּא יִדְרֹשׁ לְצִיּוֹן, עִיר הַנִּדָּחָה, עַד אָנָה תּוּגְיוֹן נֶפֶשׁ נֶאֱנָחָה.
הַשּׁוֹמֵר שַׁבָּת הַבֵּן עִם הַבַּת, לָאֵל יֵרָצוּ כְּמִנְחָה עַל מַחֲבַת.

רוֹכֵב בָּעֲרָבוֹת, מֶלֶךְ עוֹלָמִים, אֶת עַמּוֹ לִשְׁבֹּת אִזֵּן בַּנְּעִימִים,
בְּמַאֲכָלוֹת עֲרֵבוֹת בְּמִינֵי מַטְעַמִּים, בְּמַלְבּוּשֵׁי כָבוֹד זֶבַח מִשְׁפָּחָה.
הַשּׁוֹמֵר שַׁבָּת הַבֵּן עִם הַבַּת, לָאֵל יֵרָצוּ כְּמִנְחָה עַל מַחֲבַת.

וְאַשְׁרֵי כָּל חוֹכֶה לְתַשְׁלוּמֵי כֵפֶל, מֵאֵת כֹּל סוֹכֶה, שׁוֹכֵן בָּעֲרָפֶל,
נַחֲלָה לוֹ יִזְכֶּה בָּהָר וּבַשָּׁפֶל, נַחֲלָה וּמְנוּחָה כַּשֶּׁמֶשׁ לוֹ זָרְחָה.
הַשּׁוֹמֵר שַׁבָּת הַבֵּן עִם הַבַּת, לָאֵל יֵרָצוּ כְּמִנְחָה עַל מַחֲבַת.

כָּל שׁוֹמֵר שַׁבָּת כַּדָּת מֵחַלְּלוֹ, הֵן הֶכְשַׁר חִבַּת קֹדֶשׁ גּוֹרָלוֹ,
וְאִם יֵצֵא חוֹבַת הַיּוֹם, אַשְׁרֵי לוֹ, אֶל אֵל אָדוֹן מְחוֹלְלוֹ מִנְחָה הִיא שְׁלוּחָה.
הַשּׁוֹמֵר שַׁבָּת הַבֵּן עִם הַבַּת, לָאֵל יֵרָצוּ כְּמִנְחָה עַל מַחֲבַת.

חֶמְדַּת הַיָּמִים קְרָאוֹ אֵלִי צוּר, וְאַשְׁרֵי לִתְמִימִים אִם יִהְיֶה נָצוּר,
כֶּתֶר הִלּוּמִים עַל רֹאשָׁם יָצוּר, צוּר הָעוֹלָמִים, רוּחוֹ בָּם נָחָה.
הַשּׁוֹמֵר שַׁבָּת הַבֵּן עִם הַבַּת, לָאֵל יֵרָצוּ כְּמִנְחָה עַל מַחֲבַת.

בָּרוּךְ אֵל עֶלְיוֹן / BLESSED IS THE SUPREME GOD
The author of this *zemer* was the early German Tosafist and community Dayan R. Barukh ben Shmuel of Mainz (1150–1221,) the author of the now lost *Sefer HaHokhma*. He composed numerous *piyutim* that reflect a deep knowledge of both scriptural and rabbinic law and literature. True to the Tosafist perspective, the seven stanzas of the *zemer* praise punctilious Shabbat observance. Between its lines are clear echoes of the persecution of the Jews of Mainz during the Crusades (in his own lifetime the Third Crusade occurred in 1189–1192), which the *zemer* places in contrast to God's Shabbat gift, that is portrayed as a weekly island of respite, refuge, and renewal.

בָּרוּךְ אֵל עֶלְיוֹן – *Blessed is the supreme God*. This first stanza declares that Shabbat is a powerful antidote to the travails of his time, providing much-needed spiritual sustenance and emotional fortitude, to be enjoyed until such time as God will rebuke the nations that oppress His people, and then bring them home to Zion, the city that itself is forlorn. This reflects the statement in the Gemara (*Shabbat* 118a) that one who partakes of the three Shabbat meals is saved from three evils (namely the birth-pangs of the Messiah, *Gehenna* , and the wars of Gog and Magog).

הַשּׁוֹמֵר שַׁבָּת הַבֵּן עִם הַבַּת – *Who observe the Sabbath, be they male or female*. This repeated refrain incorporates several halakhic themes. Firstly, it emphasizes that careful Shabbat observance (*HaShomer Shabbat*) is to be fully shared with one's children (reflecting Exodus 20:10, "You shall not perform forbidden labors, neither you nor your son and daughter"). Secondly, such observance is as pleasing to God as was a Minḥa (flour-offering) that was brought on a pan on the Temple altar. This virtual Minḥa offering is a poetic play on words that describes a grateful act of reciprocity in return for the

בָּרוּךְ אֵל עֶלְיוֹן BLESSED is the supreme God Who has granted rest / and redemption to our souls from our burdens and sighs. / So too may He seek the welfare of Zion, the desolate city, / for how long shall the soul that sighs suffer?

May God be pleased with those who observe the Sabbath, be they male or female, as if they have made a meal offering on its designated pan.

HE IS THE KING of the universe Who stands astride the heavens, / He brought rest to His people balancing sumptuous foods, various delicacies, / fine clothing, and family feasts.

May God be pleased with those who observe the Sabbath, be they male or female, as if they have made a meal offering on its designated pan.

HAPPY ARE THOSE who defer their rewards and thus receive twice as much, / from He Who sees all but Himself is hidden in darkness. / Such a person will inherit a fitting reward through life's ups and downs, / a tranquil heritage over which the sun will shine.

May God be pleased with those who observe the Sabbath, be they male or female, as if they have made a meal offering on its designated pan.

WHOEVER OBSERVES the Sabbath properly and does not desecrate it, / will be rewarded so as to embrace holiness. / Happy is the person who fulfills the obligations of the day, / for such observance is like a gift sent to one's Creator.

May God be pleased with those who observe the Sabbath, be they male or female, as if they have made a meal offering on its designated pan.

MY GOD Who is my rock called the Sabbath the choicest of days, / happy are those who faithfully keep it. / He will make a special crown to go on their heads, / reflecting the spirit of the Rock of the universe that rests upon them.

May God be pleased with those who observe the Sabbath, be they male or female, as if they have made a meal offering on its designated pan.

---

menuḥa (rest) that God has given to His people, as described in the first stanza and repeated at the end of the third stanza (R. Basil Herring).

אִזֵּן בְּנֶעְימִים – *Balancing sumptuous foods*. This phrase and those that follow refer to numerous pleasurable Shabbat activities that God's command entails, i.e., sweet and tasty foods, festive clothing, and uninterrupted family gatherings.

כַּשֶּׁמֶשׁ לוֹ זָרְחָה – *Which the sun will shine*. This alludes to Jacob upon whom (see Genesis 32:32) the sun arose after a night of grappling with the angel of Esau. The Gemara (*Shabbat* 118a) quotes Isaiah 58:14, that declares that one who faithfully observes Shabbat will be rewarded to "enjoy God's presence, to be raised up upon the high places of the land, and to possess the inheritance of the patriarch Jacob." Rashi there explains that God promised Jacob in particular that he would inherit the land of Israel without any limits or boundaries (Gen. 28:14:

זָכוֹר אֶת יוֹם הַשַּׁבָּת לְקַדְּשׁוֹ, קַרְנוֹ כִּי גָבְהָה נֵזֶר עַל רֹאשׁוֹ,
עַל כֵּן יִתֵּן הָאָדָם לְנַפְשׁוֹ, עֹנֶג וְגַם שִׂמְחָה בָּהֶם לְמָשְׁחָה.
הַשּׁוֹמֵר שַׁבָּת הַבֵּן עִם הַבַּת, לָאֵל יֵרָצוּ כְּמִנְחָה עַל מַחֲבַת.

קֹדֶשׁ הִיא לָכֶם שַׁבָּת הַמַּלְכָּה, אֶל תּוֹךְ בָּתֵּיכֶם לְהָנִיחַ בְּרָכָה,
בְּכָל מוֹשְׁבוֹתֵיכֶם לֹא תַעֲשׂוּ מְלָאכָה, בְּנֵיכֶם וּבְנוֹתֵיכֶם עֶבֶד וְגַם שִׁפְחָה.
הַשּׁוֹמֵר שַׁבָּת הַבֵּן עִם הַבַּת, לָאֵל יֵרָצוּ כְּמִנְחָה עַל מַחֲבַת.

יוֹם זֶה מְכֻבָּד מִכָּל יָמִים, כִּי בוֹ שָׁבַת צוּר עוֹלָמִים.

שֵׁשֶׁת יָמִים תַּעֲשֶׂה מְלַאכְתֶּךָ, וְיוֹם הַשְּׁבִיעִי לֵאלֹהֶיךָ,
שַׁבָּת לֹא תַעֲשֶׂה בוֹ מְלָאכָה, כִּי כֹל עָשָׂה שֵׁשֶׁת יָמִים.
יוֹם זֶה מְכֻבָּד מִכָּל יָמִים, כִּי בוֹ שָׁבַת צוּר עוֹלָמִים.

רִאשׁוֹן הוּא לְמִקְרָאֵי קֹדֶשׁ, יוֹם שַׁבָּתוֹן יוֹם שַׁבַּת קֹדֶשׁ,
עַל כֵּן כָּל אִישׁ בְּיֵינוֹ יְקַדֵּשׁ, עַל שְׁתֵּי לֶחֶם יִבְצְעוּ תְמִימִים.
יוֹם זֶה מְכֻבָּד מִכָּל יָמִים, כִּי בוֹ שָׁבַת צוּר עוֹלָמִים.

אֱכֹל מַשְׁמַנִּים, שְׁתֵה מַמְתַּקִּים, כִּי אֵל יִתֵּן לְכֹל בּוֹ דְבֵקִים,
בֶּגֶד לִלְבֹּשׁ, לֶחֶם חֻקִּים, בָּשָׂר וְדָגִים וְכָל מַטְעַמִּים.
יוֹם זֶה מְכֻבָּד מִכָּל יָמִים, כִּי בוֹ שָׁבַת צוּר עוֹלָמִים.

לֹא תֶחְסַר כֹּל בּוֹ וְאָכַלְתָּ, וְשָׂבָעְתָּ וּבֵרַכְתָּ,
אֶת יהוה אֱלֹהֶיךָ אֲשֶׁר אָהַבְתָּ, כִּי בֵרַכְךָ מִכָּל הָעַמִּים.
יוֹם זֶה מְכֻבָּד מִכָּל יָמִים, כִּי בוֹ שָׁבַת צוּר עוֹלָמִים.

"You shall burst forth to the West, East, North and South") (*Zemirot Shabbat – Mesivta*).

יוֹם זֶה מְכֻבָּד / MORE THAN ALL OTHER DAYS
The author and date of composition are unknown, although the name Israel appears as an acrostic at the beginning of the stanzas. Based on an implicit acrostic in the final stanza, some have attributed the *zemer* to a poet named Yisrael HaGer (the proselyte). A sixteenth-century collection of *zemirot* published in Cracow records an opinion that the author composed it prior to being martyred on Shabbat for having converted to Judaism, and he accordingly concluded the *zemer* with the classic statement of *Tzidduk HaDin* (acceptance of God's decree), found in Deuteronomy 32:4, כִּי הוּא הַצּוּר פָּעֳלוֹ תָמִים ("He is the Rock Whose work is perfect"). If true, the use of this phrase appropriately echoes the *zemer* refrain that describes God as צוּר עוֹלָמִים, i.e., He is the Rock and Foundation of both this world and the next (as in Isaiah 26:4) (*Zemirot Shabbat – Mesivta*).

REMEMBER the Sabbath day to sanctify it; / by raising its honor one earns a crown of distinction. / Therefore let us bring upon ourselves / pleasure and joy by which we will be anointed.

May God be pleased with those who observe the Sabbath, be they male or female, as if they have made a meal offering on its designated pan.

THE SABBATH Queen brings holiness upon you; / She comes into your homes to spread blessing. / Do not perform any labors wherever you dwell – / so too your sons and daughters, and your servants be they male or female.

May God be pleased with those who observe the Sabbath, be they male or female, as if they have made a meal offering on its designated pan.

*יוֹם זֶה מְכֻבָּד MORE THAN all other days is the Sabbath day blessed;
for the Rock of all time made it His day of rest.

FOR COMPLETING your work He has given six days; / But the seventh belongs to your God for His praise. / In creation's six days God His work did perfect; / So must you on that day all your labor reject.

More than all other days is the Sabbath day blessed;
for the Rock of all time made it His day of rest.

'TIS THE SABBATH which leads all the year's holy days / As a day for pure rest and for learning God's ways. / Sing glad song on this day; sanctify it with wine, / And bless God over two loaves for the Sabbath divine.

More than all other days is the Sabbath day blessed;
for the Rock of all time made it His day of rest.

THEN EAT good Sabbath food, and give wine its due place; / for to all who hold fast to Him, God gives His grace. / In choice Sabbath array eat your meal without haste, / with fine fish and fresh meats, and foods good to the taste.

More than all other days is the Sabbath day blessed;
for the Rock of all time made it His day of rest.

ON THIS DAY know no lack; let there be happiness, / for your blest Promised Land which your sires did possess. / To your God you must cleave and must bless His great name, / that 'twas you He did choose to be priest of His flame.

More than all other days is the Sabbath day blessed;
for the Rock of all time made it His day of rest.

*The translation of this *zemer* is by R. David de Sola Pool, and uses a free-form poetic rhyming scheme rather than a literal translation.

הַשָּׁמַיִם מְסַפְּרִים כְּבוֹדוֹ, וְגַם הָאָרֶץ מָלְאָה חַסְדּוֹ,
רְאוּ כָּל אֵלֶּה עָשְׂתָה יָדוֹ, כִּי הוּא הַצּוּר פָּעֳלוֹ תָמִים.
יוֹם זֶה מְכֻבָּד מִכָּל יָמִים, כִּי בוֹ שָׁבַת צוּר עוֹלָמִים.

יוֹם שַׁבָּתוֹן אֵין לִשְׁכֹּחַ, זִכְרוֹ כְּרֵיחַ הַנִּיחֹחַ,
יוֹנָה מָצְאָה בוֹ מָנוֹחַ וְשָׁם יָנוּחוּ יְגִיעֵי כֹחַ.

הַיּוֹם נִכְבָּד לִבְנֵי אֱמוּנִים, זְהִירִים לְשָׁמְרוֹ אָבוֹת וּבָנִים,
חָקוּק בִּשְׁנֵי לוּחוֹת אֲבָנִים, מֵרֹב אוֹנִים וְאַמִּיץ כֹּחַ.
יוֹנָה מָצְאָה בוֹ מָנוֹחַ וְשָׁם יָנוּחוּ יְגִיעֵי כֹחַ.

וּבָאוּ כֻלָּם בִּבְרִית יַחַד, נַעֲשֶׂה וְנִשְׁמַע אָמְרוּ כְּאֶחָד,
וּפָתְחוּ וְעָנוּ יהוה אֶחָד, בָּרוּךְ נֹתֵן לַיָּעֵף כֹּחַ.
יוֹנָה מָצְאָה בוֹ מָנוֹחַ וְשָׁם יָנוּחוּ יְגִיעֵי כֹחַ.

דִּבֶּר בְּקָדְשׁוֹ בְּהַר הַמֹּר, יוֹם הַשְּׁבִיעִי זָכוֹר וְשָׁמוֹר,
וְכָל פִּקּוּדָיו יַחַד לִגְמֹר, חַזֵּק מָתְנַיִם וְאַמֵּץ כֹּחַ.
יוֹנָה מָצְאָה בוֹ מָנוֹחַ וְשָׁם יָנוּחוּ יְגִיעֵי כֹחַ.

הָעָם אֲשֶׁר נָע, כַּצֹּאן תָּעָה, יִזְכֹּר לְפָקְדוֹ בְּרִית וּשְׁבוּעָה,
לְבַל יַעֲבָר בָּם מִקְרֵה רָעָה, כַּאֲשֶׁר נִשְׁבַּעְתָּ עַל מֵי נֹחַ.
יוֹנָה מָצְאָה בוֹ מָנוֹחַ וְשָׁם יָנוּחוּ יְגִיעֵי כֹחַ.

יוֹם שַׁבָּתוֹן / DAY OF REST

This *zemer* was composed by the illustrious poet and philosopher R. Yehuda HaLevi (1075–1141), whose name appears on it in acrostic form. Of its five stanzas it is generally accepted that the third and fourth were not in the original *zemer*, but were substituted at a later time out of fear that the original ones (that included phrases such as "stamp with a boot upon our enemies and oppressors"), which invoked God's ire against the enemies of the Jewish people, would incur the wrath of Gentile rulers (*Zemirot Shabbat – Mesivta*).

The *zemer*, or at least those stanzas composed by HaLevi, is constructed around the image of Noah's dove as a metaphor for the faithful Jewish people surrounded by stormy waters, while seeking safe harbor and renewed strength in the weekly observance of Shabbat. The metaphor has its roots in Isaiah 54:9, which links God's promise to Noah after the flood (to never again bring such destruction upon the world) to God's oath to the Jewish people that He will not vent His wrath upon the Jewish nation. So too Song of Songs 2:14 implicitly compares Israel to a faithful dove (Dr. Ilana Turetzky).

יוֹנָה מָצְאָה בוֹ מָנוֹחַ – *Even Noah's dove was able to rest on it.* The words of this repeated refrain can be understood in light of Genesis 8:12 that

THE LORD'S GLORY supreme let the heavens declare, / while the earth testifies to His love and His care. / For all nature alike bears witness each day – / He alone is the Rock, and perfected His way.

More than all other days is the Sabbath day blessed;
for the Rock of all time made it His day of rest.

יוֹם שַׁבָּתוֹן NEVER let us forget the Sabbath day of rest,
always let it be remembered like a welcomed aroma.
Even Noah's dove was able to rest on it;
so too do the weary find respite on it.

THE DAY is honored by the faithful,
who carefully observe its principles as well as its details,
as inscribed on the two stone tablets
that were given to us by the mighty and powerful God.

Even Noah's dove was able to rest on it; so too do the weary find respite on it.

THEY all gathered together to enter into the Covenant,
Declaring, "We will do and we will hear" as one nation.
Opening their mouths they replied, "God is One,"
blessed is He Who gives strength to the weary.

Even Noah's dove was able to rest on it; so too do the weary find respite on it.

IN HIS SANCTITY He declared upon the mountain of myrrh,
"Remember and Observe the seventh day,"
study all of its laws altogether,
and gird your loins while being of good strength.

Even Noah's dove was able to rest on it; so too do the weary find respite on it.

THE PEOPLE that wandered like an errant flock
will be remembered by God because of the covenant and promise,
so that no evil will befall them,
just as was promised after Noah's flood.

Even Noah's dove was able to rest on it; so too do the weary find respite on it.

---

states that Noah dispatched the dove "on the seventh day" whereupon it did not return, having found a place to rest. So too, the poet implies, Shabbat is the resting place (or safe harbor) of the Jewish people, where it can at least temporarily enjoy shelter from the threat of deluge and stormy waters at the hands of its enemies (*Mateh Yehuda*).

כִּי אֶשְׁמְרָה שַׁבָּת אֵל יִשְׁמְרֵנִי. אוֹת הִיא לְעוֹלְמֵי עַד בֵּינוֹ וּבֵינִי.
אוֹת הִיא לְעוֹלְמֵי עַד בֵּינוֹ וּבֵינִי.

אָסוּר מְצֹא חֵפֶץ, עֲשׂוֹת דְּרָכִים, גַּם מִלְּדַבֵּר בּוֹ דִּבְרֵי צְרָכִים
דִּבְרֵי סְחוֹרָה אַף דִּבְרֵי מְלָכִים, אֶהְגֶּה בְּתוֹרַת אֵל וּתְחַכְּמֵנִי.
אוֹת הִיא לְעוֹלְמֵי עַד בֵּינוֹ וּבֵינִי.

בּוֹ אֶמְצָא תָמִיד נֹפֶשׁ לְנַפְשִׁי, הִנֵּה לְדוֹר רִאשׁוֹן נָתַן קְדוֹשִׁי
מוֹפֵת, בְּתֵת לֶחֶם מִשְׁנֶה בַּשִּׁשִּׁי, כָּכָה בְּכָל שִׁשִּׁי יַכְפִּיל מְזוֹנִי.
אוֹת הִיא לְעוֹלְמֵי עַד בֵּינוֹ וּבֵינִי.

רָשַׁם בְּדַת הָאֵל חֹק אֶל סְגָנָיו, בּוֹ לַעֲרֹךְ לֶחֶם פָּנִים בְּפָנָיו
עַל כֵּן לְהִתְעַנּוֹת בּוֹ עַל פִּי נְבוֹנָיו, אָסוּר, לְבַד מִיּוֹם כִּפּוּר עֲוֹנִי.
אוֹת הִיא לְעוֹלְמֵי עַד בֵּינוֹ וּבֵינִי.

הוּא יוֹם מְכֻבָּד, הוּא יוֹם תַּעֲנוּגִים, לֶחֶם וְיַיִן טוֹב, בָּשָׂר וְדָגִים
הַמִּתְאַבְּלִים בּוֹ אָחוֹר נְסוֹגִים, כִּי יוֹם שְׂמָחוֹת הוּא וּתְשַׂמְּחֵנִי.
אוֹת הִיא לְעוֹלְמֵי עַד בֵּינוֹ וּבֵינִי.

מֵחֵל מְלָאכָה בּוֹ סוֹפוֹ לְהַכְרִית, עַל כֵּן אֲכַבֵּס בּוֹ לִבִּי כְּבוֹרִית
וְאֶתְפַּלְּלָה אֶל אֵל עַרְבִית וְשַׁחֲרִית, מוּסָף וְגַם מִנְחָה הוּא יַעֲנֵנִי.
אוֹת הִיא לְעוֹלְמֵי עַד בֵּינוֹ וּבֵינִי.

יִזָּכֵר לְפָקְדוֹ בְּרִית וּשְׁבוּעָה – *Will be remembered by God because of the covenant and promise* (previous page). In this stanza HaLevi makes explicit reference to the aforementioned Isaiah 54:9, which links God's covenantal commitment to never destroy the Jewish nation to His similar promise to Noah to never again destroy mankind. Here, however, the poet changes the metaphor of the Jewish people to that of an errant sheep straying from the proper path. Even then, the poet implies, we can be assured that God will ultimately remember His oath and covenant with our forefathers, and bring us salvation and redemption. The entire stanza brings to mind the words of Psalm 23 that invoke the image of God as the protective Shepherd of His people, Who uses His punishing שֵׁבֶט (rod) when they wander away, but also His supportive מִשְׁעֶנֶת (staff) when they are in need of succor and support (R. Basil Herring).

כִּי אֶשְׁמְרָה שַׁבָּת / IF I KEEP THE SABBATH
The author of this *zemer* is the famed Spanish Bible commentator, poet, and philosopher R. Abraham Ibn Ezra (1089–1164). As in many of his poems, this *zemer* reflects a tension between his enduring longing to achieve spiritual closeness to God and his appreciation of the physical pleasures of this world. The *zemer* highlights the ways in which the Shabbat experience embodies this duality. Thus, of the five stanzas, the first and fifth respectively emphasize Shabbat Torah study and prayer, while the second,

כִּי אֶשְׁמְרָה IF I WILL SAFEGUARD the Sabbath, God will safeguard me. For it is an everlasting symbol between Him and me.

For it is an everlasting symbol between Him and me.

ON THIS DAY we may not engage in trade, travel, or speak of our material needs. Neither may we think about business or politics, but instead we are to focus on the divine Torah that makes us wise.

For it is an everlasting symbol between Him and me.

ON THIS DAY my soul will be rejuvenated, just as happened when the Holy One notified the first generation that He would give them a double portion of bread on the sixth day. So may He double my sustenance on every sixth day.

For it is an everlasting symbol between Him and me.

INSCRIBED in God's law is the requirement that in the Temple the priests were to replace the showbreads every Sabbath in His presence. For this reason His sages forbade fasting on this day, except when it coincides with Yom Kippur on account of our sins.

For it is an everlasting symbol between Him and me.

IT IS A DAY of honor, many pleasures, breads, good wines, meats and various types of fish. Those who would mourn on it are to be rebuked, for it is a day of rejoicing that makes us happy.

For it is an everlasting symbol between Him and me.

THOSE who desecrate it by performing forbidden labors will be cut off in the end. For this reason I will make sure to wash my heart thoroughly as if cleansing it with soap. Then I will pray to God at Ma'ariv, Shaḥarit, Musaf and Minḥa, and He will surely answer me.

For it is an everlasting symbol between Him and me.

---

third, and fourth incorporate poetic descriptions of Shabbat food, wine, and joyous indulgence. Throughout there are allusions to Torah verses and Talmudic themes pertinent to these themes (e.g., Exodus 31:17, Isaiah 58:13, *Shabbat* 113a and 150b, and *Eiruvin* 38b) (R. Basil Herring).

אַף דִּבְרֵי מְלָכִים – *Neither may we think about business or politics.* The *Shulḥan Arukh* (*OḤ* 307:16) rules that on Shabbat it is forbidden to speak of non-spiritual matters, or to read "books regarding wars." The phrase "matters of trade and state" would appear to include talk related to politics or general society. Instead, the stanza concludes, in-depth Torah study leading to the attainment of wisdom is the order of the day.

הוּא יוֹם תַּעֲנוּגִים – *It is a day of... many pleasures.* As noted, this stanza, and the two preceding it, describe the sensory enjoyments of the day, as dictated by the Torah and the sages, including partaking of double loaves of bread,

דְּרוֹר יִקְרָא לְבֵן עִם בַּת, וְיִנְצָרְכֶם כְּמוֹ בָבַת,
נְעִים שִׁמְכֶם וְלֹא יֻשְׁבַּת, שְׁבוּ נוּחוּ בְּיוֹם שַׁבָּת

דְּרֹשׁ נָוִי וְאוּלַמִּי, וְאוֹת יֶשַׁע עֲשֵׂה עִמִּי,
נְטַע שׂוֹרֵק בְּתוֹךְ כַּרְמִי, שְׁעֵה שַׁוְעַת בְּנֵי עַמִּי.

דְּרֹךְ פּוּרָה בְּתוֹךְ בָּצְרָה, וְגַם בָּבֶל אֲשֶׁר גָּבְרָה,
נְתֹץ צָרַי בְּאַף עֶבְרָה, שְׁמַע קוֹלִי בְּיוֹם אֶקְרָא.

אֱלֹהִים תֵּן בְּמִדְבָּר הָר, הֲדַס שִׁטָּה בְּרוֹשׁ תִּדְהָר,
וְלַמַּזְהִיר וְלַנִּזְהָר, שְׁלוֹמִים תֵּן כְּמֵי נָהָר.

הֲדֹךְ קָמַי, אֵל קַנָּא, בְּמוֹג לֵבָב וּבִמְגִנָּה,
וְנַרְחִיב פֶּה וּנְמַלְאֶנָּה, לְשׁוֹנֵנוּ לְךָ רִנָּה.

דְּעֵה חָכְמָה לְנַפְשֶׁךָ, וְהִיא כֶתֶר לְרֹאשֶׁךָ,
נְצֹר מִצְוַת קְדוֹשֶׁךָ, שְׁמֹר שַׁבַּת קָדְשֶׁךָ.

---

superior wine, meat as well as fish, during the course of the three Shabbat meals. And yet in the next stanza the poet closes with a striking metaphor: violation of Shabbat prohibitions leads to spiritual demise, whereas observing them – in conjunction with the four prayer services of the day – is the spiritual equivalent of a cleansing agent that rids our souls of impurity (see Jeremiah 2:22, "If you will cleanse it… with much soap").

דְּרוֹר יִקְרָא / MAY GOD PROCLAIM
The composer of this *zemer* was the tenth-century grammarian and poet Dunash ben Labrat, a student of R. Sa'adia Gaon, who grew up in Baghdad, but later lived in Muslim Morocco and Spain. His name appears four times as the acrostic of the stiches in stanzas 1, 2, 3, and 6. His Hebrew name, *Adonim HaLevi*, is hinted at in stanzas 4 and 5, which begin with an *alef* and a *heh*, respectively (R. Yosef Serfati).

נְטַע שׂוֹרֵק בְּתוֹךְ כַּרְמִי – *When He will plant a Messianic offshoot in our vineyard.* In an oblique reference to the Messiah the poet pleads with God to plant a vine branch (i.e., the coming Messiah) in the vineyard of His people, and thus to respond to their prayers for redemption and the rebuilding of the Temple (*Siddur Beit Ya'akov*).

דְּרֹךְ פּוּרָה בְּתוֹךְ בָּצְרָה, וְגַם בָּבֶל אֲשֶׁר גָּבְרָה – *May He trample yet again upon the people of Botzra and the ascendant Babylonia.* This entire stanza is to be understood in light of Jeremiah 63:1–3, where the prophet has a vision in which God appears as coming from Edom and Botzra, His clothing soaked in what appears to be splatterings from a wine press. Asked for an explanation of His appearance, God responds in language, reflected in this stanza, that He has trampled upon those peoples as one would do when squeezing grapes in a wine press, and it is those peoples' blood which stains His clothing like wine drops. Here the poem as we have it addresses God with a plea to do the same again not just to Edom but to the "ascendant Babylonia" as well. While the lands in question were under the sovereignty of Islamic authorities during Dunash's lifetime, Edom in rabbinic literature generally refers to Christianity. The poet might thus be referring delicately to both faiths, each of which oppressed his people in their own ways and dominions, and thus

דְּרוֹר יִקְרָא MAY GOD proclaim freedom for men and women,
protecting them like the pupil of the eye,
ensuring the preservation of their good name without end,
as long as they themselves rest on the Sabbath day.

MAY HE RESTORE our Temple and its vestibules,
and grant us a sign of impending salvation
when He will plant a Messianic offshoot in our vineyard,
in response to the prayers of our people.

MAY HE TRAMPLE yet again upon the people
of Botzra and the ascendant Babylonia,
once more to crush our enemies with fierce anger,
as He hears the prayers of our people on the day that we call out to Him.

DEAR GOD GRANT us in the wilderness a place on high
where myrtle, pine, boxwood and fir trees will grow,
providing tranquility for those who have been properly conscientious,
like the waters of a gently flowing stream.

CRUSH OUR ENEMIES O zealous God, and instill terror in their hearts,
even as our own mouths will be filled to overflowing
and our tongues sing Your praises.

ON THE SABBATH day acquire wisdom for your soul,
that being a crown upon your head,
in conjunction with keeping the commandments of the Holy God
as you carefully observe the holy Sabbath day.

---

deserving of bloody punishment at the hands of a vengeful God. Such punishment would come as a precursor to the events to be described in the next stanza (R. Basil Herring).

אֱלֹהִים תֵּן בְּמִדְבָּר הָר – *Dear God grant us in the wilderness a place on high.* In contrast to the tumultuous preceding stanza, this one portrays an idyllic, even Edenic, scene. Evoking Isaiah 41:19, the poet asks God to create a verdant pasture in the desert with flowing rivers and filled with myrtle bushes as well as pine, boxwood and fir trees (*Rosh HaShana* 23a). As *Etz Yosef* explains, these are to provide shade and sustenance for the returning exiles traveling en-route to Israel (*Zemirot Shabbat – Mesivta*).

דְּעֶה חָכְמָה לְנַפְשֶׁךָ – *Acquire wisdom for your soul.* The final stanza returns to the first stanza's focus on Shabbat observance, but at this point raising the bar from the first stanza's mere abstinence from labor and physical rest, to the higher level of utilizing God's holy day for the pursuit of wisdom, which is the Jew's "crowning glory." In closing the *zemer* with this thought, Dunash gives expression to the rationalist tradition of his teacher Sa'adia Gaon, in which reason and revelation, logic and law (in this instance the laws of Shabbat), teach one and the same truth when properly understood and practiced (R. Basil Herring).

מנחה לשבת וליום טוב

אשרי

The line beginning with פּוֹתֵחַ אֶת־יָדֶךָ *should be said with special concentration.*

תהלים פד
אַשְׁרֵי יוֹשְׁבֵי בֵיתֶךָ, עוֹד יְהַלְלוּךָ סֶּלָה:

תהלים קמד
אַשְׁרֵי הָעָם שֶׁכָּכָה לּוֹ, אַשְׁרֵי הָעָם שֶׁיהוה אֱלֹהָיו:

תהלים קמה
תְּהִלָּה לְדָוִד

אֲרוֹמִמְךָ אֱלוֹהַי הַמֶּלֶךְ, וַאֲבָרְכָה שִׁמְךָ לְעוֹלָם וָעֶד:
בְּכָל־יוֹם אֲבָרְכֶךָּ, וַאֲהַלְלָה שִׁמְךָ לְעוֹלָם וָעֶד:
גָּדוֹל יהוה וּמְהֻלָּל מְאֹד, וְלִגְדֻלָּתוֹ אֵין חֵקֶר:
דּוֹר לְדוֹר יְשַׁבַּח מַעֲשֶׂיךָ, וּגְבוּרֹתֶיךָ יַגִּידוּ:
הֲדַר כְּבוֹד הוֹדֶךָ, וְדִבְרֵי נִפְלְאֹתֶיךָ אָשִׂיחָה:
וֶעֱזוּז נוֹרְאֹתֶיךָ יֹאמֵרוּ, וּגְדוּלָּתְךָ אֲסַפְּרֶנָּה:
זֵכֶר רַב־טוּבְךָ יַבִּיעוּ, וְצִדְקָתְךָ יְרַנֵּנוּ:
חַנּוּן וְרַחוּם יהוה, אֶרֶךְ אַפַּיִם וּגְדָל־חָסֶד:
טוֹב־יהוה לַכֹּל, וְרַחֲמָיו עַל־כָּל־מַעֲשָׂיו:
יוֹדוּךָ יהוה כָּל־מַעֲשֶׂיךָ, וַחֲסִידֶיךָ יְבָרְכוּכָה:
כְּבוֹד מַלְכוּתְךָ יֹאמֵרוּ, וּגְבוּרָתְךָ יְדַבֵּרוּ:
לְהוֹדִיעַ לִבְנֵי הָאָדָם גְּבוּרֹתָיו, וּכְבוֹד הֲדַר מַלְכוּתוֹ:
מַלְכוּתְךָ מַלְכוּת כָּל־עֹלָמִים, וּמֶמְשַׁלְתְּךָ בְּכָל־דּוֹר וָדֹר:
סוֹמֵךְ יהוה לְכָל־הַנֹּפְלִים, וְזוֹקֵף לְכָל־הַכְּפוּפִים:
עֵינֵי־כֹל אֵלֶיךָ יְשַׂבֵּרוּ, וְאַתָּה נוֹתֵן־לָהֶם אֶת־אָכְלָם בְּעִתּוֹ:
פּוֹתֵחַ אֶת־יָדֶךָ, וּמַשְׂבִּיעַ לְכָל־חַי רָצוֹן:
צַדִּיק יהוה בְּכָל־דְּרָכָיו, וְחָסִיד בְּכָל־מַעֲשָׂיו:
קָרוֹב יהוה לְכָל־קֹרְאָיו, לְכֹל אֲשֶׁר יִקְרָאֻהוּ בֶאֱמֶת:
רְצוֹן־יְרֵאָיו יַעֲשֶׂה, וְאֶת־שַׁוְעָתָם יִשְׁמַע וְיוֹשִׁיעֵם:

מִנְחָה לְשַׁבָּת וְלְיוֹם טוֹב / MINHA FOR SHABBAT AND YOM TOV
The afternoon is a particularly auspicious time for prayer, for it was in the afternoon that God answered Elijah in his confrontation with the prophets of Ba'al (*Berakhot* 6b).

MINḤA FOR SHABBAT AND YOM TOV

ASHREI

The line beginning with "You open Your hand" should be said with special concentration.

Ps. 84 אַשְׁרֵי HAPPY are they who dwell in Your house,
They shall forever praise You. Selah.

Ps. 144 HAPPY are the people of whom this is so,
Happy are the people whose God is the Lord.

Ps. 145 A PRAISE OF DAVID.
א I exalt You, my God, the King, and I will bless Your name forever and ever. ב Every day I will bless You, and I will praise Your name forever and ever. ג Great is the Lord, and very praiseworthy, and His greatness is boundless. ד One generation lauds Your works to another, and they declare Your mighty deeds. ה I speak of the splendid glory of Your majesty and of Your wondrous works, ו And they speak of the might of Your awesome deeds, and I declare Your greatness. ז They express the renown of Your great goodness, and sing of Your righteousness. ח Gracious and merciful is the Lord, slow to anger and great in loving-kindness. ט The Lord is good to all, and His mercies are upon all His works. י All Your works thank You, O Lord, and Your pious ones bless You. כ They describe the glory of Your kingdom, and speak of Your might, ל To make known to the sons of man His mighty deeds, and the glorious splendor of His kingdom. מ Your kingdom is a kingdom for all times, and Your dominion is for every generation. ס The Lord supports all who fall and raises up all who are bowed down. ע The eyes of all await You, and You give them their food in its time. פ You open Your hand, and You satisfy the desire of every living thing. צ The Lord is righteous in all His ways and kind in all His works. ק The Lord is near to all who address Him, to all who address Him in truth. ר He does the will of those who fear Him, and He hears their cry and saves them.

שׁוֹמֵר יהוה אֶת־כָּל־אֹהֲבָיו, וְאֵת כָּל־הָרְשָׁעִים יַשְׁמִיד:
◂ תְּהִלַּת יהוה יְדַבֶּר פִּי, וִיבָרֵךְ כָּל־בָּשָׂר שֵׁם קָדְשׁוֹ לְעוֹלָם וָעֶד:
תהלים קטו וַאֲנַחְנוּ נְבָרֵךְ יָהּ מֵעַתָּה וְעַד־עוֹלָם, הַלְלוּיָהּ:

ישעיה נט **וּבָא לְצִיּוֹן** גּוֹאֵל, וּלְשָׁבֵי פֶשַׁע בְּיַעֲקֹב, נְאֻם יהוה: וַאֲנִי זֹאת בְּרִיתִי אוֹתָם, אָמַר יהוה, רוּחִי אֲשֶׁר עָלֶיךָ וּדְבָרַי אֲשֶׁר־שַׂמְתִּי בְּפִיךָ, לֹא־יָמוּשׁוּ מִפִּיךָ וּמִפִּי זַרְעֲךָ וּמִפִּי זֶרַע זַרְעֲךָ, אָמַר יהוה, מֵעַתָּה וְעַד־עוֹלָם:

תהלים כב ישעיה ו ◂ **וְאַתָּה קָדוֹשׁ** יוֹשֵׁב תְּהִלּוֹת יִשְׂרָאֵל: וְקָרָא זֶה אֶל־זֶה וְאָמַר, קָדוֹשׁ, קָדוֹשׁ, קָדוֹשׁ יהוה צְבָאוֹת, מְלֹא כָל־הָאָרֶץ כְּבוֹדוֹ:

תרגום יונתן ישעיה ו וּמְקַבְּלִין דֵּין מִן דֵּין וְאָמְרִין, קַדִּישׁ בִּשְׁמֵי מְרוֹמָא עִלָּאָה בֵּית שְׁכִינְתֵּהּ, קַדִּישׁ עַל אַרְעָא עוֹבַד גְּבוּרְתֵּהּ, קַדִּישׁ לְעָלַם וּלְעָלְמֵי עָלְמַיָּא, יהוה צְבָאוֹת, מַלְיָא כָל אַרְעָא זִיו יְקָרֵהּ.

יחזקאל ג ◂ וַתִּשָּׂאֵנִי רוּחַ, וָאֶשְׁמַע אַחֲרַי קוֹל רַעַשׁ גָּדוֹל, בָּרוּךְ כְּבוֹד־יהוה מִמְּקוֹמוֹ:

תרגום יונתן יחזקאל ג וּנְטָלַתְנִי רוּחָא, וּשְׁמָעִית בַּתְרַי קָל זִיעַ סַגִּיא, דִּמְשַׁבְּחִין וְאָמְרִין, בְּרִיךְ יְקָרָא דַיהוה מֵאֲתַר בֵּית שְׁכִינְתֵּהּ.

שמות טו יהוה יִמְלֹךְ לְעֹלָם וָעֶד:

תרגום אונקלוס שמות טו יהוה מַלְכוּתֵהּ קָאֵם לְעָלַם וּלְעָלְמֵי עָלְמַיָּא.

דברי הימים א׳ כט **יהוה** אֱלֹהֵי אַבְרָהָם יִצְחָק וְיִשְׂרָאֵל אֲבֹתֵינוּ, שָׁמְרָה־זֹּאת לְעוֹלָם לְיֵצֶר מַחְשְׁבוֹת לְבַב עַמֶּךָ, וְהָכֵן לְבָבָם אֵלֶיךָ: וְהוּא רַחוּם
תהלים עח יְכַפֵּר עָוֹן וְלֹא־יַשְׁחִית, וְהִרְבָּה לְהָשִׁיב אַפּוֹ, וְלֹא־יָעִיר כָּל־חֲמָתוֹ:

וּבָא לְצִיּוֹן גּוֹאֵל – *A redeemer shall come to Zion.* Shabbat afternoon prior to *Minḥa* was a time of communal Torah study, and these verses were recited to conclude the synagogue study session in Geonic times. The central section of this prayer highlights the importance and benefits of Talmud Torah (R. Shlomo Bar Shimshon of Worms).

ש The Lord preserves all who love Him, but all the wicked He destroys. ת ▸ May my mouth speak the praise of the Lord, and may all flesh bless His holy name forever and ever.

Ps. 115 And we shall bless the Lord now and for evermore. Praise the Lord.

Is. 59 **וּבָא לְצִיּוֹן** A REDEEMER shall come to Zion and to those in Jacob who turn away from sin – the Lord has said so. As for me, the Lord has said, "This is My covenant with them. My spirit which is upon you, and My words which I have put in your mouth, shall not depart out of your mouth, nor out of the mouths of your children, nor out of the mouths of your children's children, not now and not ever," so the Lord has said

Ps. 22 ▸ **וְאַתָּה קָדוֹשׁ** BUT YOU are holy. You sit among the praises of Israel. The
Is. 6 angels called to one another and said, Holy, holy, holy is the Lord of hosts, the whole world is filled with His glory.

Targum Yonatan Is. 6 And they receive word from each other and say, Holy in the highest heaven, the abode of His Divine Presence, holy upon earth, the work of His mighty power, holy forever and to all eternity is the Lord of hosts. The whole earth is full of His glorious splendor

Ezek. 3 ▸ Then a spirit uplifted me, and I heard behind me a powerful moving sound, Blessed is the glory of the Lord from His place.

Targum Yonatan Ezek. 3 Then a spirit lifted me up and I heard behind me the powerful moving sound of those who uttered His praise, proclaiming, "Blessed be the glory of the Lord from the abode of His Divine Presence"

Ex. 15 The Lord shall reign forever and ever

Targum Onkelos Ex. 15 The sovereignty of the Lord is established forever and ever

I Chr. 29 **יהוה** LORD GOD of our fathers Abraham, Isaac, and Israel, forever forming the thoughts in Your people's heart, and directing their
Ps. 78 hearts toward You. But He, the compassionate one, forgave iniquity, and did not destroy them, and He often turned away His anger

---

We recite וּבָא לְצִיּוֹן גּוֹאֵל following *Ashrei* at Shabbat *Minḥa*, and not at the conclusion of Shabbat morning prayers as we do on weekdays, for on Shabbat morning we do not want to burden the congregation (especially the elderly, and pregnant or nursing women) at that point. Thus it is deferred to *Minḥa* (*Orḥot Ḥayyim*).

כִּי־אַתָּה אֲדֹנָי טוֹב וְסַלָּח, וְרַב־חֶסֶד לְכָל־קֹרְאֶיךָ: צִדְקָתְךָ צֶדֶק תהלים פו / תהלים קיט
לְעוֹלָם וְתוֹרָתְךָ אֱמֶת: תִּתֵּן אֱמֶת לְיַעֲקֹב, חֶסֶד לְאַבְרָהָם, אֲשֶׁר־ מיכה ז
נִשְׁבַּעְתָּ לַאֲבֹתֵינוּ מִימֵי קֶדֶם: בָּרוּךְ אֲדֹנָי יוֹם יוֹם יַעֲמָס־לָנוּ, הָאֵל תהלים סח
יְשׁוּעָתֵנוּ סֶלָה: יהוה צְבָאוֹת עִמָּנוּ, מִשְׂגָּב לָנוּ אֱלֹהֵי יַעֲקֹב סֶלָה: תהלים מו
יהוה צְבָאוֹת, אַשְׁרֵי אָדָם בֹּטֵחַ בָּךְ: יהוה הוֹשִׁיעָה, הַמֶּלֶךְ יַעֲנֵנוּ תהלים פד / תהלים כ
בְיוֹם־קָרְאֵנוּ:

בָּרוּךְ הוּא אֱלֹהֵינוּ שֶׁבְּרָאָנוּ לִכְבוֹדוֹ, וְהִבְדִּילָנוּ מִן הַתּוֹעִים, וְנָתַן לָנוּ תּוֹרַת אֱמֶת, וְחַיֵּי עוֹלָם נָטַע בְּתוֹכֵנוּ. הוּא יִפְתַּח לִבֵּנוּ בְּתוֹרָתוֹ, וְיָשֵׂם בְּלִבֵּנוּ אַהֲבָתוֹ וְיִרְאָתוֹ וְלַעֲשׂוֹת רְצוֹנוֹ וּלְעָבְדוֹ בְּלֵבָב שָׁלֵם, לְמַעַן לֹא נִיגַע לָרִיק וְלֹא נֵלֵד לַבֶּהָלָה.

יְהִי רָצוֹן מִלְּפָנֶיךָ יהוה אֱלֹהֵינוּ וֵאלֹהֵי אֲבוֹתֵינוּ, שֶׁנִּשְׁמֹר חֻקֶּיךָ בָּעוֹלָם הַזֶּה, וְנִזְכֶּה וְנִחְיֶה וְנִרְאֶה וְנִירַשׁ טוֹבָה וּבְרָכָה,
לִשְׁנֵי יְמוֹת הַמָּשִׁיחַ וּלְחַיֵּי הָעוֹלָם הַבָּא. לְמַעַן יְזַמֶּרְךָ כָבוֹד וְלֹא תהלים ל
יִדֹּם, יהוה אֱלֹהַי, לְעוֹלָם אוֹדֶךָּ: בָּרוּךְ הַגֶּבֶר אֲשֶׁר יִבְטַח בַּיהוה, ירמיה יז
וְהָיָה יהוה מִבְטַחוֹ: בִּטְחוּ בַיהוה עֲדֵי־עַד, כִּי בְּיָהּ יהוה צוּר ישעיה כו
עוֹלָמִים: ▸ וְיִבְטְחוּ בְךָ יוֹדְעֵי שְׁמֶךָ, כִּי לֹא־עָזַבְתָּ דֹרְשֶׁיךָ, יהוה: תהלים ט
יהוה חָפֵץ לְמַעַן צִדְקוֹ, יַגְדִּיל תּוֹרָה וְיַאְדִּיר: ישעיה מב

חצי קדיש

ש״ץ: **יִתְגַּדַּל** וְיִתְקַדַּשׁ שְׁמֵהּ רַבָּא (קהל: אָמֵן), בְּעָלְמָא דִּי בְרָא כִרְעוּתֵהּ, וְיַמְלִיךְ מַלְכוּתֵהּ, בְּחַיֵּיכוֹן וּבְיוֹמֵיכוֹן וּבְחַיֵּי דְכָל בֵּית יִשְׂרָאֵל, בַּעֲגָלָא וּבִזְמַן קָרִיב, וְאִמְרוּ אָמֵן. (קהל: אָמֵן)

קהל וש״ץ: יְהֵא שְׁמֵהּ רַבָּא מְבָרַךְ לְעָלַם וּלְעָלְמֵי עָלְמַיָּא.

ש״ץ: יִתְבָּרַךְ וְיִשְׁתַּבַּח וְיִתְפָּאַר, וְיִתְרוֹמַם וְיִתְנַשֵּׂא וְיִתְהַדָּר וְיִתְעַלֶּה וְיִתְהַלָּל שְׁמֵהּ דְּקֻדְשָׁא בְּרִיךְ הוּא (קהל: בְּרִיךְ הוּא), לְעֵלָּא מִן כָּל בִּרְכָתָא /בשבת שובה: לְעֵלָּא (וּ)לְעֵלָּא מִכָּל בִּרְכָתָא/ וְשִׁירָתָא, תֻּשְׁבְּחָתָא וְנֶחֱמָתָא דַּאֲמִירָן בְּעָלְמָא, וְאִמְרוּ אָמֵן. (קהל: אָמֵן)

Ps. 86 and did not stir up all His wrath. Indeed, You, O Lord, are good and
forgiving, and of bountiful loving-kindness to all who call upon You.
Ps. 119 Your righteousness is an everlasting righteousness, and Your law is truth.
Mic. 7 Grant truth to Jacob, loving-kindness to Abraham, as You have sworn to
Ps. 68 our fathers from days of old. Blessed is the Lord day by day. The God of
Ps. 46 our salvation will load us generously. The Lord of hosts is with us. The
Ps. 84 God of Jacob is our refuge. Selah. O Lord of hosts, happy is the man who
Ps. 20 trusts in You. Lord, save! The King will answer us on the day that we call.

בָּרוּךְ BLESSED BE our God, Who created us for His glory, separated us from those who stray, gave us the Torah of truth, and implanted in us eternal life. May He open our hearts through His Torah and arouse in us such love and reverence for Him that we shall perform His will and serve Him with perfect hearts, rather than labor in vain or bring forth disaster.

יְהִי רָצוֹן MAY IT BE Your will, Lord our God and God of our fathers,
that we keep Your statutes in this world, and thus be worthy to inherit
a life of goodness and blessing in the days of the Messiah and in the
Ps. 30 life of the World to Come. Grant that I sing Your praises and not be
Jer. 17 silent; O Lord, my God, I will give thanks to You forever. Blessed is the
person who trusts in the Lord, for then the Lord will be his security.
Is. 26 Trust always in the Lord, for the Lord is God, an everlasting Rock.
Ps. 9 ▸ And those who know Your name will trust in You, for You, Lord,
Is. 42 have not abandoned those who seek You. The Lord desired, for the
sake of its [Israel's] righteousness, to magnify the Torah and glorify it.

HALF KADDISH

Leader: יִתְגַּדַּל EXALTED AND HALLOWED may God's great name be, in the world He created as He willed. May He reign in your lifetimes and in your days, and in the lifetime of the whole house of Israel, speedily and soon, and say, Amen.

All: May His great name be blessed forever and all time.

Leader: Blessed and praised, honored, extolled, glorified, adored and exalted above all be the name of the Holy One, blessed is He, (*Between Rosh Hashana & Yom Kippur:* above and) beyond any blessing, hymn, praise, or expressions of consolation that may be uttered in this world, and say, Amen.

On שבת *continue below. On* יום טוב *falling on a weekday, say the* עמידה *on page 810.*

וַאֲנִי תְפִלָּתִי־לְךָ יהוה, עֵת רָצוֹן, אֱלֹהִים בְּרָב־חַסְדֶּךָ, עֲנֵנִי בֶּאֱמֶת יִשְׁעֶךָ: תהלים סט

The ארון קודש *is opened and the* קהל *stands. All say:*

וַיְהִי בִּנְסֹעַ הָאָרֹן וַיֹּאמֶר מֹשֶׁה, קוּמָה יהוה וְיָפֻצוּ אֹיְבֶיךָ וְיָנֻסוּ מְשַׂנְאֶיךָ מִפָּנֶיךָ: כִּי מִצִּיּוֹן תֵּצֵא תוֹרָה וּדְבַר־יהוה, מִירוּשָׁלָםִ: בָּרוּךְ שֶׁנָּתַן תּוֹרָה לְעַמּוֹ יִשְׂרָאֵל בִּקְדֻשָּׁתוֹ. במדבר י ישעיה ב

בְּרִיךְ שְׁמֵהּ דְּמָרֵא עָלְמָא, בְּרִיךְ כִּתְרָךְ וְאַתְרָךְ. יְהֵא רְעוּתָךְ עִם עַמָּךְ יִשְׂרָאֵל לְעָלַם, וּפֻרְקַן יְמִינָךְ אַחֲזֵי לְעַמָּךְ בְּבֵית מַקְדְּשָׁךְ, וּלְאַמְטוּיֵי לַנָא מִטּוּב נְהוֹרָךְ, וּלְקַבֵּל צְלוֹתַנָא בְּרַחֲמִין. יְהֵא רַעֲוָא קֳדָמָךְ דְּתוֹרִיךְ לַן חַיִּין בְּטִיבוּ, וְלֶהֱוֵי אֲנָא פְּקִידָא בְּגוֹ צַדִּיקַיָּא, לְמִרְחַם עָלַי וּלְמִנְטַר יָתִי וְיַת כָּל דִּי לִי וְדִי לְעַמָּךְ יִשְׂרָאֵל. אַנְתְּ הוּא זָן לְכֹלָּא וּמְפַרְנֵס לְכֹלָּא, אַנְתְּ הוּא שַׁלִּיט עַל כֹּלָּא, אַנְתְּ הוּא דְּשַׁלִּיט עַל מַלְכַיָּא, וּמַלְכוּתָא דִּילָךְ הִיא. אֲנָא עַבְדָּא דְקֻדְשָׁא בְּרִיךְ הוּא, דְּסָגֵדְנָא קַמֵּהּ וּמִקַּמֵּי דִּיקַר אוֹרַיְתֵהּ בְּכָל עִדָּן וְעִדָּן. לָא עַל אֱנָשׁ רָחִיצְנָא וְלָא עַל בַּר אֱלָהִין סָמִיכְנָא, אֶלָּא בֵּאלָהָא דִשְׁמַיָּא, דְּהוּא אֱלָהָא קְשׁוֹט, וְאוֹרַיְתֵהּ קְשׁוֹט, וּנְבִיאוֹהִי קְשׁוֹט, וּמַסְגֵּא לְמֶעְבַּד טַבְוָן וּקְשׁוֹט. ◂ בֵּהּ אֲנָא רָחִיץ, וְלִשְׁמֵהּ קַדִּישָׁא יַקִּירָא אֲנָא אֵמַר תֻּשְׁבְּחָן. יְהֵא רַעֲוָא קֳדָמָךְ דְּתִפְתַּח לִבַּאי בְּאוֹרַיְתָא, וְתַשְׁלִים מִשְׁאֲלִין דְּלִבַּאי וְלִבָּא דְכָל עַמָּךְ יִשְׂרָאֵל לְטָב וּלְחַיִּין וְלִשְׁלָם. (אָמֵן.) זוהר ויקהל

The שליח ציבור *bows toward the* ארון קודש *and says:*

גַּדְּלוּ לַיהוה אִתִּי וּנְרוֹמְמָה שְׁמוֹ יַחְדָּו: תהלים לד

The ארון קודש *is closed. The* שליח ציבור *carries the* ספר תורה *to the* בימה *and the* קהל *says:*

לְךָ יהוה הַגְּדֻלָּה וְהַגְּבוּרָה וְהַתִּפְאֶרֶת וְהַנֵּצַח וְהַהוֹד, כִּי־כֹל בַּשָּׁמַיִם וּבָאָרֶץ, לְךָ יהוה הַמַּמְלָכָה וְהַמִּתְנַשֵּׂא לְכֹל לְרֹאשׁ: דברי הימים א׳ כט

וַאֲנִי תְפִלָּתִי – *But I pray*. This verse is found in Psalms 69:14. The preceding verse states, "Those who sit at the gates talk of me, and I am the song of those who drink wine." The two verses are linked by the letter *vav*, which the sages in the *Midrash* took as a disjunctive, i.e., David proclaims "my detractors spend their time in public places drinking wine and gossiping about me, whereas I seek only to find an עֵת רָצוֹן (time of favor) to pray so that my supplications can be answered compassionately." This sentiment is particularly appropriate at Shabbat afternoon *Minḥa*, when many spend their time eating and drinking, as opposed to those who set aside such enjoyable activities when the time for heartfelt prayer arrives (R. Amos Ḥakham).

The *Arukh HaShulḥan* explains that the afternoon *Minḥa* service is particularly appropriate for the acceptance of our prayers, for it replaces the Temple's afternoon sacrifice, which, accompanied by a wine offering and

On Shabbat continue below. On Yom Tov falling on a weekday, say the Amida on page 811.

Ps. 69 וַאֲנִי BUT I PRAY to You, O Lord, for a time of favor. O God, in the greatness of Your loving-kindness, answer me, in the truth of Your salvation.

The Ark is opened and the congregation stands. All say:

Num. 10 וַיְהִי בִּנְסֹעַ WHEN THE ARK moved forward, Moses would say, "Arise, O Lord, and may Your enemies be dispersed, and they who hate You
Is. 2 flee from You." For from Zion shall go forth Torah, and the word of the Lord from Jerusalem. Blessed is He Who, in His holiness, has given the Torah to His people Israel.

Zohar, Vayak-hel בְּרִיךְ שְׁמֵהּ BLESSED IS YOUR NAME, Master of the universe; blessed is Your crown; blessed Your place. May You always favor Your people Israel. In Your Temple, reveal to Your people the redeeming power of Your right hand. Grant us of Your beneficent light and mercifully accept our prayer. May it be Your will to prolong our lives in goodness. Count me among the righteous to whom You show love, protecting me and all that is mine, as well as all that belongs to Your people Israel. You are He Who provides food for all and sustains all. You are He Who rules over all. You are He Who rules over monarchs, for the dominion is Yours. I am the servant of the Holy One, blessed is He, before Whom, and before Whose glorious Torah, I bow at all times. Not on man do I rely, nor do I trust in any angel, but only on the God of the heavens Who is the God of truth, Whose Torah is truth and Whose prophets are true, and Who acts with abundant love and truth. ▸ In Him alone is my trust, and it is to His holy and glorious name that I utter praises. May it be Your will to open my heart to Your Torah, and to fulfill the desires of my heart and the hearts of all Your people Israel for good, for life, and for peace. (Amen.)

The Leader bows toward the Ark and says:

Ps. 34 גַּדְּלוּ MAGNIFY the Lord with me, and let us exalt His name together.

The Ark is closed. The Leader carries the Torah scroll to the bima and the congregation says:

I Chr. 29 לְךָ YOURS, O Lord, are greatness, power, glory, victory, and majesty; indeed, everything that is in the heavens and on earth. Yours, Lord, is the dominion, and You are supreme over all.

Levitical song, was the culmination and high point of each day's sacrificial order. This made it "especially beloved of God, just like *Ne'ila*, that similarly concludes Yom Kippur." Thus one might say, we recite this verse at the outset of our *Minḥa* prayers on this choicest of days, to emphasize that this is a most propitious time to approach God (R. Shalom Axelrod).

תהלים צט
רוֹמְמוּ יהוה אֱלֹהֵינוּ וְהִשְׁתַּחֲווּ לַהֲדֹם רַגְלָיו, קָדוֹשׁ הוּא: רוֹמְמוּ יהוה אֱלֹהֵינוּ וְהִשְׁתַּחֲווּ לְהַר קָדְשׁוֹ, כִּי־קָדוֹשׁ יהוה אֱלֹהֵינוּ:

אַב הָרַחֲמִים הוּא יְרַחֵם עַם עֲמוּסִים, וְיִזְכֹּר בְּרִית אֵיתָנִים, וְיַצִּיל נַפְשׁוֹתֵינוּ מִן הַשָּׁעוֹת הָרָעוֹת, וְיִגְעַר בְּיֵצֶר הָרָע מִן הַנְּשׂוּאִים, וְיָחֹן אוֹתָנוּ לִפְלֵיטַת עוֹלָמִים, וִימַלֵּא מִשְׁאֲלוֹתֵינוּ בְּמִדָּה טוֹבָה יְשׁוּעָה וְרַחֲמִים.

The ספר תורה *is placed on the* שולחן *and the* גבאי *calls a* כהן *to the* תורה.

וְתִגָּלֶה וְתֵרָאֶה מַלְכוּתוֹ עָלֵינוּ בִּזְמַן קָרוֹב, וְיָחֹן פְּלֵיטָתֵנוּ וּפְלֵיטַת עַמּוֹ בֵּית יִשְׂרָאֵל לְחֵן וּלְחֶסֶד וּלְרַחֲמִים וּלְרָצוֹן וְנֹאמַר אָמֵן. הַכֹּל הָבוּ גֹדֶל לֵאלֹהֵינוּ וּתְנוּ כָבוֹד לַתּוֹרָה. *כֹּהֵן קְרַב, יַעֲמֹד (פלוני בֶּן פלוני) הַכֹּהֵן.

**If no* כהן *is present, a* לוי *or* ישראל *is called up as follows:*

/אֵין כָּאן כֹּהֵן, יַעֲמֹד (פלוני בֶּן פלוני) בִּמְקוֹם כֹּהֵן./

בָּרוּךְ שֶׁנָּתַן תּוֹרָה לְעַמּוֹ יִשְׂרָאֵל בִּקְדֻשָּׁתוֹ.

קהל *followed by the* גבאי*:*

דברים ד
וְאַתֶּם הַדְּבֵקִים בַּיהוה אֱלֹהֵיכֶם חַיִּים כֻּלְּכֶם הַיּוֹם:

ברכות התורה

The קורא *shows the* עולה *the section to be read. The* עולה *touches the scroll, but not the letters themselves, with his* ציצית *or the Torah belt or cover, which he then kisses. Holding the handles of the scroll, he says:*

עולה: **בָּרְכוּ** אֶת יהוה הַמְבֹרָךְ.

קהל: בָּרוּךְ יהוה הַמְבֹרָךְ לְעוֹלָם וָעֶד.

עולה: בָּרוּךְ יהוה הַמְבֹרָךְ לְעוֹלָם וָעֶד.

בָּרוּךְ אַתָּה יהוה, אֱלֹהֵינוּ מֶלֶךְ הָעוֹלָם, אֲשֶׁר בָּחַר בָּנוּ מִכָּל הָעַמִּים וְנָתַן לָנוּ אֶת תּוֹרָתוֹ. בָּרוּךְ אַתָּה יהוה, נוֹתֵן הַתּוֹרָה.

The appropriate Torah portion is read (see page 1108–1132).

At the conclusion of each portion, the עולה *recites this concluding* ברכה*:*

עולה: בָּרוּךְ אַתָּה יהוה אֱלֹהֵינוּ מֶלֶךְ הָעוֹלָם, אֲשֶׁר נָתַן לָנוּ תּוֹרַת אֱמֶת וְחַיֵּי עוֹלָם נָטַע בְּתוֹכֵנוּ. בָּרוּךְ אַתָּה יהוה, נוֹתֵן הַתּוֹרָה.

Special מי שבירך *prayers may be said at this point. See pages 534–540.*

SHABBAT AFTERNOON TORAH READING
According to the Gemara (*Bava Kama* 82a), Ezra instituted Shabbat *Minḥa* Torah reading for the benefit of those whose weekday business activities made it difficult to attend Monday and Thursday Torah readings. This provided an additional opportunity for them to hear the words of the Torah.

Ps. 99 Exalt the Lord our God, and bow down before His footstool. He is holy. Exalt the Lord our God, and bow down before His holy mountain. Indeed, the Lord our God is holy.

אַב הָרַחֲמִים MAY THE FATHER OF MERCY have compassion on the people borne by Him. May He remember the covenant with the mighty (patriarchs), and deliver us from evil times. May He reproach the evil impulse in the people He carries, and graciously grant us eternal survival. May He fulfill in good measure our requests for salvation and mercy.

The Torah scroll is placed on the bima and the Gabbai calls a Kohen to the Torah.

וְתִגָּלֶה AND MAY HIS SOVEREIGNTY over us soon be revealed and made apparent. May He be gracious to our surviving remnant and the surviving remnant of His people, the house of Israel, in grace, loving-kindness, compassion, and favor, and let us say: Amen. Let us all declare greatness to our God and give honor to the Torah. Let the *Kohen* come forward. Arise (*name* son of *father's name*), the *Kohen*.

**If no Kohen is present, a Levi or Yisrael is called up as follows:*
Since there is no *Kohen*, arise (*name* son of *father's name*) in place of a *Kohen*.

Blessed is He Who, in His holiness, gave the Torah to His people Israel.

Congregation followed by the Gabbai:

Deut. 4 And you who cleave to the Lord your God, all of you are alive this day.

BLESSINGS OF THE TORAH

The Reader shows the oleh the section to be read. The oleh touches the scroll, but not the letters themselves, with his tzitzit or the Torah belt or cover, which he then kisses. Holding the handles of the scroll, he says:

Oleh: בָּרְכוּ BLESS the Lord, the blessed One.

Cong: BLESSED is the Lord Who is blessed for all eternity.

Oleh: BLESSED is the Lord Who is blessed for all eternity.
BLESSED are You, Lord, our God, King of the universe, Who has chosen us from all peoples and has given us His Torah. Blessed are You, Lord, Giver of the Torah.

The appropriate Torah portion is read *(see page 1108–1132).*

At the conclusion of each portion, the oleh recites this concluding blessing:

Oleh: BLESSED are You, Lord, our God, King of the universe, Who has given us the Torah of truth, planting eternal life among us. Blessed are You, Lord, Giver of the Torah.

Special Mi Sheberakh prayers may be said at this point. *See pages 535–541.*

ברכת הגומל

One who has been delivered from danger recites this blessing.

בָּרוּךְ אַתָּה יהוה אֱלֹהֵינוּ מֶלֶךְ הָעוֹלָם הַגּוֹמֵל לְחַיָּבִים טוֹבוֹת, שֶׁגְּמָלַנִי כָּל טוֹב.

If a man recites the ברכה*, the* קהל *responds:*

אָמֵן. מִי שֶׁגְּמָלְךָ כָּל טוֹב הוּא יִגְמָלְךָ כָּל טוֹב, סֶלָה.

If a woman recites the ברכה*, the* קהל *responds:*

אָמֵן. מִי שֶׁגְּמָלֵךְ כָּל טוֹב הוּא יִגְמָלֵךְ כָּל טוֹב, סֶלָה.

The ספר תורה *is lifted and the* קהל *says:*

דברים ד **וְזֹאת הַתּוֹרָה** אֲשֶׁר־שָׂם מֹשֶׁה לִפְנֵי בְּנֵי יִשְׂרָאֵל: עַל־פִּי יהוה בְּיַד־מֹשֶׁה:

Some add:

משלי ג עֵץ־חַיִּים הִיא לַמַּחֲזִיקִים בָּהּ וְתֹמְכֶיהָ מְאֻשָּׁר: דְּרָכֶיהָ דַרְכֵי־נֹעַם וְכָל־נְתִיבֹתֶיהָ שָׁלוֹם: אֹרֶךְ יָמִים בִּימִינָהּ, בִּשְׂמֹאולָהּ עֹשֶׁר וְכָבוֹד: יהוה חָפֵץ לְמַעַן צִדְקוֹ
ישעיה מב יַגְדִּיל תּוֹרָה וְיַאְדִּיר:

The ספר תורה *is bound and covered.*

In some congregations, on the שבת *preceding a yahrzeit,* אֵל מָלֵא רַחֲמִים *is said.*

אֵל מָלֵא רַחֲמִים, שׁוֹכֵן בַּמְּרוֹמִים, הַמְצֵא מְנוּחָה נְכוֹנָה תַּחַת (נ״א עַל) כַּנְפֵי הַשְּׁכִינָה, בְּמַעֲלוֹת קְדוֹשִׁים וּטְהוֹרִים, כְּזֹהַר הָרָקִיעַ מַזְהִירִים, לְנִשְׁמַת

For a male close relative:

(פלוני בֶּן פלוני) שֶׁהָלַךְ לְעוֹלָמוֹ, בַּעֲבוּר שֶׁ(פלוני בֶּן פלוני) יִתֵּן / שֶׁ(פלונית בַּת פלוני) תִּתֵּן / צְדָקָה בְּעַד הַזְכָּרַת נִשְׁמָתוֹ, בְּגַן עֵדֶן תְּהֵא מְנוּחָתוֹ. לָכֵן, בַּעַל הָרַחֲמִים יַסְתִּירֵהוּ בְּסֵתֶר כְּנָפָיו לְעוֹלָמִים, וְיִצְרֹר בִּצְרוֹר הַחַיִּים אֶת נִשְׁמָתוֹ, יהוה הוּא נַחֲלָתוֹ, וְיָנוּחַ בְּשָׁלוֹם עַל מִשְׁכָּבוֹ, וְנֹאמַר אָמֵן.

For a female close relative:

(פלונית בַּת פלוני) שֶׁהָלְכָה לְעוֹלָמָהּ, בַּעֲבוּר שֶׁ(פלוני בֶּן פלוני) יִתֵּן / שֶׁ(פלונית בַּת פלוני) תִּתֵּן / צְדָקָה בְּעַד הַזְכָּרַת נִשְׁמָתָהּ, בְּגַן עֵדֶן תְּהֵא מְנוּחָתָהּ. לָכֵן, בַּעַל הָרַחֲמִים יַסְתִּירֶהָ בְּסֵתֶר כְּנָפָיו לְעוֹלָמִים, וְיִצְרֹר בִּצְרוֹר הַחַיִּים אֶת נִשְׁמָתָהּ, יהוה הוּא נַחֲלָתָהּ, וְתָנוּחַ בְּשָׁלוֹם עַל מִשְׁכָּבָהּ, וְנֹאמַר אָמֵן.

The ארון קודש *is opened. The* שליח ציבור *takes the* ספר תורה *and says:*

תהלים קמח **יְהַלְלוּ** אֶת־שֵׁם יהוה, כִּי נִשְׂגָּב־שְׁמוֹ לְבַדּוֹ

The קהל *responds:*

הוֹדוֹ עַל־אֶרֶץ וְשָׁמָיִם: וַיָּרֶם קֶרֶן לְעַמּוֹ, תְּהִלָּה לְכָל־חֲסִידָיו, לִבְנֵי יִשְׂרָאֵל עַם קְרֹבוֹ, הַלְלוּיָהּ:

BLESSING OF GRATITUDE

One who has been delivered from danger recites this blessing.

בָּרוּךְ BLESSED are You, Lord, our God, King of the universe, Who bestows favors on the undeserving, and Who has bestowed every good thing on me.

Congregation responds:

Amen. May He Who has bestowed every good thing on you continue to grant you every good thing, forever.

The Torah scroll is lifted and the congregation says:

Deut. 4 וְזֹאת הַתּוֹרָה THIS IS THE Torah that Moses set before the children of Israel. It was according to the Lord's command, at the hand of Moses.

Some add:

Prov. 3 It is a tree of life for those who grasp it, and they who uphold it are made happy. Its ways are ways of pleasantness, and all its paths are peace. Length of days is in its right
Is. 42 hand, and wealth and honor in its left hand. The Lord was pleased, for the sake of its [Israel's] righteousness, to magnify the Torah and glorify it.

The Torah scroll is bound and covered.

In some congregations, on the Shabbat preceding a yahrzeit, "God, full of mercy" is said.

אֵל O GOD, FULL OF MERCY, Who dwells on high, grant fitting rest beneath (*Some say:* above) the protective wings of the Divine Presence, where the souls of the holy and pure ones – whose radiance is like that of the heavens – reside, to the soul of

For a man:

(*name of the deceased*) the son of (*father of the deceased*), who has gone to his eternal reward, insofar as (*name of supplicant*) will make a charitable gift in memory of his soul, may the Garden of Eden be his resting place. For this reason may the ever-merciful One shelter the deceased under His protective wings forever, and may He bind his soul in lasting life. For the Lord will surely be his benefactor, so that he can rest in peace in his allotted place. And let us say, Amen.

For a woman:

(*name of the deceased*) the daughter of (*father of the deceased*), who has gone to her eternal reward, insofar as (*name of supplicant*) will make a charitable gift in memory of her soul, may the Garden of Eden be her resting place. For this reason may the ever-merciful One shelter the deceased under His protective wings forever, and may He bind her soul in lasting life. For the Lord will surely be her benefactor, so that she can rest in peace in her allotted place. And let us say, Amen.

The Ark is opened. The Leader takes the Torah scroll and says:

Ps. 148 יְהַלְלוּ LET THEM PRAISE the name of the Lord, that His name alone is exalted.

The congregation responds:

His glory is over the earth and the heavens. And He has raised the horn of His people, praise for all His pious ones, for the children of Israel, the people near to Him. Praise the Lord.

As the ספר תורה *is returned to the* ארון קודש*, say:*

תהלים כד **לְדָוִד מִזְמוֹר**, לַיהוה הָאָרֶץ וּמְלוֹאָהּ, תֵּבֵל וְיֽשְׁבֵי בָהּ: כִּי־הוּא
עַל־יַמִּים יְסָדָהּ, וְעַל־נְהָרוֹת יְכוֹנְנֶהָ: מִי־יַעֲלֶה
בְהַר־יהוה, וּמִי־יָקוּם בִּמְקוֹם קָדְשׁוֹ: נְקִי כַפַּיִם וּבַר־לֵבָב, אֲשֶׁר
לֹא־נָשָׂא לַשָּׁוְא נַפְשִׁי וְלֹא נִשְׁבַּע לְמִרְמָה: יִשָּׂא בְרָכָה מֵאֵת יהוה,
וּצְדָקָה מֵאֱלֹהֵי יִשְׁעוֹ: זֶה דּוֹר דֹּרְשָׁו, מְבַקְשֵׁי פָנֶיךָ, יַעֲקֹב, סֶלָה:
שְׂאוּ שְׁעָרִים רָאשֵׁיכֶם, וְהִנָּשְׂאוּ פִּתְחֵי עוֹלָם, וְיָבוֹא מֶלֶךְ הַכָּבוֹד:
מִי זֶה מֶלֶךְ הַכָּבוֹד, יהוה עִזּוּז וְגִבּוֹר, יהוה גִּבּוֹר מִלְחָמָה: שְׂאוּ
שְׁעָרִים רָאשֵׁיכֶם, וּשְׂאוּ פִּתְחֵי עוֹלָם, וְיָבֹא מֶלֶךְ הַכָּבוֹד: מִי הוּא
זֶה מֶלֶךְ הַכָּבוֹד, יהוה צְבָאוֹת הוּא מֶלֶךְ הַכָּבוֹד, סֶלָה:

As the ספר תורה *is placed into the* ארון קודש*, say:*

במדבר י תהלים קלב **וּבְנֻחֹה** יֹאמַר, שׁוּבָה יהוה רִבְבוֹת אַלְפֵי יִשְׂרָאֵל: קוּמָה יהוה
לִמְנוּחָתֶךָ, אַתָּה וַאֲרוֹן עֻזֶּךָ: כֹּהֲנֶיךָ יִלְבְּשׁוּ־צֶדֶק, וַחֲסִידֶיךָ
משלי ד יְרַנֵּנוּ: בַּעֲבוּר דָּוִד עַבְדֶּךָ אַל־תָּשֵׁב פְּנֵי מְשִׁיחֶךָ: כִּי לֶקַח טוֹב
משלי ג נָתַתִּי לָכֶם, תּוֹרָתִי אַל־תַּעֲזֹבוּ: עֵץ־חַיִּים הִיא לַמַּחֲזִיקִים בָּהּ,
איכה ה וְתֹמְכֶיהָ מְאֻשָּׁר: דְּרָכֶיהָ דַרְכֵי־נֹעַם וְכָל־נְתִיבוֹתֶיהָ שָׁלוֹם: ‹ הֲשִׁיבֵנוּ
יהוה אֵלֶיךָ וְנָשׁוּבָה, חַדֵּשׁ יָמֵינוּ כְּקֶדֶם:

The ארון קודש *is closed.*

חצי קדיש

ש״ץ: **יִתְגַּדַּל** וְיִתְקַדַּשׁ שְׁמֵהּ רַבָּא (קהל: אָמֵן) בְּעָלְמָא דִּי בְרָא כִרְעוּתֵהּ.
וְיַמְלִיךְ מַלְכוּתֵהּ, בְּחַיֵּיכוֹן וּבְיוֹמֵיכוֹן וּבְחַיֵּי דְכָל בֵּית
יִשְׂרָאֵל, בַּעֲגָלָא וּבִזְמַן קָרִיב, וְאִמְרוּ אָמֵן. (קהל: אָמֵן)

קהל וש״ץ: יְהֵא שְׁמֵהּ רַבָּא מְבָרַךְ לְעָלַם וּלְעָלְמֵי עָלְמַיָּא.

ש״ץ: יִתְבָּרַךְ וְיִשְׁתַּבַּח וְיִתְפָּאַר, וְיִתְרוֹמַם וְיִתְנַשֵּׂא וְיִתְהַדָּר וְיִתְעַלֶּה
וְיִתְהַלָּל שְׁמֵהּ דְּקֻדְשָׁא בְּרִיךְ הוּא (קהל: בְּרִיךְ הוּא) לְעֵלָּא מִן כָּל
בִּרְכָתָא / בשבת שובה: לְעֵלָּא (וּ)לְעֵלָּא מִכָּל בִּרְכָתָא/ וְשִׁירָתָא, תֻּשְׁבְּחָתָא
וְנֶחֱמָתָא דַּאֲמִירָן בְּעָלְמָא, וְאִמְרוּ אָמֵן. (קהל: אָמֵן)

As the Torah scroll is returned to the Ark, say:

Ps. 24 **לְדָוִד מִזְמוֹר** OF DAVID. A psalm. The earth is the Lord's and the fullness thereof, the world and those who dwell in it. For He has founded it upon the seas, and has established it upon the floods. Who shall ascend the mountain of the Lord, and who shall stand in His holy place? He who has clean hands and a pure heart, who has not sworn in vain "by my soul," and has not sworn deceitfully, he shall receive the blessing from the Lord, and righteousness from the God of his salvation. This is the company of those who seek Him, who seek Your face, Jacob. Selah. Lift up your heads, O gates, and be lifted up, O everlasting doors, so that the King of glory may come in. Who is this King of glory? The Lord strong and mighty, the Lord mighty in battle. Lift up your heads, O gates, and lift them up, O everlasting doors, so that the King of glory may come in. Who is He, this King of glory? The Lord of hosts, He is the King of glory. Selah.

As the Torah scroll is placed into the Ark, say:

Num. 10 **וּבְנֻחֹה** AND WHEN the Ark rested, Moses would say: "Return, O Lord,
Ps. 132 to the myriad thousands of Israel." Arise, O Lord, to Your resting place,
You and the Ark of Your strength. May Your priests be clothed in
righteousness, and may Your pious ones shout for joy. For the sake of
Prov. 4 David Your servant, do not turn away the face of Your anointed. I have
Prov. 3 given you a good doctrine, My Torah, do not forsake it. It is a tree of life
for those who grasp it, and they who uphold it are made happy. Its ways
Lam. 5 are ways of pleasantness, and all its paths are peace. ▸ Lord, turn us to You
once again, for we wish to return; renew our days as of old.

The Ark is closed.

HALF KADDISH

Leader: **יִתְגַּדַּל** EXALTED AND HALLOWED may God's great name be, in the world He created as He willed. May He reign in your lifetimes and in your days, and in the lifetime of the whole house of Israel, speedily and soon, and say, Amen.

All: May His great name be blessed forever and all time.

Leader: Blessed and praised, honored, extolled, glorified, adored and exalted above all be the name of the Holy One, blessed is He, (*Between Rosh Hashana & Yom Kippur:* above and) beyond any blessing, hymn, praise, or expressions of consolation that may be uttered in this world, and say, Amen.

On יום טוב *(including one that falls on* שבת*), but not on* חול המועד*,*
say the appropriate עמידה *on page 810.*

עמידה

One begins the עמידה *by taking three steps forward (OḤ 95:1). According to some traditions, one should first take three steps back before moving forward (MB 95:3). The* עמידה *is recited with one's feet together. One should try to concentrate on the simple meaning of the words of the* עמידה *with the awareness throughout that one is standing in the presence of the Almighty (OḤ 98:1 and MB 98:1).*
At the points indicated by ˺*, bend the knees at the first word, bow at the second, and stand straight before saying God's name.*

כִּי שֵׁם יהוה אֶקְרָא, הָבוּ גֹדֶל לֵאלֹהֵינוּ: דברים לב
אֲדֹנָי, שְׂפָתַי תִּפְתָּח, וּפִי יַגִּיד תְּהִלָּתֶךָ: תהלים נא

אבות

˺**בָּרוּךְ** אַתָּה יהוה, אֱלֹהֵינוּ וֵאלֹהֵי אֲבוֹתֵינוּ, אֱלֹהֵי אַבְרָהָם, אֱלֹהֵי יִצְחָק, וֵאלֹהֵי יַעֲקֹב, הָאֵל הַגָּדוֹל הַגִּבּוֹר וְהַנּוֹרָא, אֵל עֶלְיוֹן, גּוֹמֵל חֲסָדִים טוֹבִים, וְקוֹנֵה הַכֹּל, וְזוֹכֵר חַסְדֵי אָבוֹת, וּמֵבִיא גוֹאֵל לִבְנֵי בְנֵיהֶם לְמַעַן שְׁמוֹ בְּאַהֲבָה.

בשבת שובה: זָכְרֵנוּ לְחַיִּים, מֶלֶךְ חָפֵץ בַּחַיִּים, וְכָתְבֵנוּ בְּסֵפֶר הַחַיִּים, לְמַעַנְךָ אֱלֹהִים חַיִּים.

(If forgotten, no corrective action is necessary.)

מֶלֶךְ עוֹזֵר וּמוֹשִׁיעַ וּמָגֵן. ˺בָּרוּךְ אַתָּה יהוה, מָגֵן אַבְרָהָם.

גבורות

אַתָּה גִּבּוֹר לְעוֹלָם, אֲדֹנָי, מְחַיֵּה מֵתִים אַתָּה, רַב לְהוֹשִׁיעַ.

בחורף: מַשִּׁיב הָרְוּחַ וּמוֹרִיד הַגֶּשֶׁם

וְזוֹכֵר חַסְדֵי אָבוֹת – *Who remembers all the kind acts of the fathers.* The Gemara (*Shabbat* 55a) states that in the days of the prophet Ezekiel (at the end of the First Temple period), *zekhut avot* (the merits of the patriarchs) ceased to exist. The Tosafist Rabbeinu Tam asks the following question: If this is the case, how can we invoke the merits of Abraham, Isaac, and Jacob, at the beginning of every *Amida*, as protection for us? He answers that while it is true that the *zekhut avot* has ended, the *brit avot* (the covenant with our patriarchs) continues uninterrupted. This *brit avot* is not based on God's love for us, for we have sinned and defiled ourselves, and no longer deserve the love that God had for the patriarchs. Rather the covenant is based on the agreement God made with our patriarchs, which is a legally binding contractual

For laws regarding "The repetition of the *Amida*," see page 107.

On Yom Tov (including one that falls on Shabbat), but not on Ḥol HaMo'ed, say the appropriate Amida on page 811.

AMIDA

One begins the Amida by taking three steps forward (OḤ 95:1). According to some traditions, one should first take three steps back before moving forward (MB 95:3). The Amida is recited with one's feet together. One should try to concentrate on the simple meaning of the words of the Amida with the awareness throughout that one is standing in the presence of the Almighty (OḤ 98:1 and MB 98:1). At the points indicated by ▾, bend the knees at the first word, bow at the second, and stand straight before saying God's name.

Deut. 32 WHEN I proclaim the name of the LORD, ascribe greatness to our God.

Ps. 51 "O my Master, open my lips, and my mouth will relate Your praise."

PATRIARCHS

▾בָּרוּךְ BLESSED ARE YOU, LORD, our God and the God of our fathers, the God of Abraham, the God of Isaac, and the God of Jacob, the God Who is great, mighty, and awesome, God most exalted, Who bestows rewards of benevolent kindness, Who is the Creator of everything, Who remembers all the kind acts of the fathers, and Who brings a redeemer to their children's children, for the sake of His name, with love.

On Shabbat Shuva: Remember us for life, King Who desires life, and inscribe us in the book of life for Your sake, Living God.
(If forgotten, no corrective action is necessary.)

King Who helps, saves, and shields, ▾blessed are You, LORD, Shield of Abraham.

GOD'S MIGHT

אַתָּה YOU, my Master, are forever mighty, You are the Resurrector of the dead, with great power to save.

In winter: He makes the wind blow and the rain fall

---

obligation that remains in force to this day. This is reflected in the verse (that in fact refers to the period following the destruction of the Temple), "Then will I remember My covenant with Jacob, and also My covenant with Isaac, and also My covenant with Abraham will I remember" (Lev. 26:42). At the outset of the *Amida* we invoke that obligation in asking God to answer the prayers that will follow (R. Joseph B. Soloveitchik).

For laws regarding "Omission/Insertion of *Mashiv Haru'ah*," see page 109.

מְכַלְכֵּל חַיִּים בְּחֶסֶד, מְחַיֵּה מֵתִים בְּרַחֲמִים רַבִּים, סוֹמֵךְ נוֹפְלִים, וְרוֹפֵא חוֹלִים, וּמַתִּיר אֲסוּרִים, וּמְקַיֵּם אֱמוּנָתוֹ לִישֵׁנֵי עָפָר. מִי כָמְוֹךָ, בַּעַל גְּבוּרוֹת, וּמִי דְּוֹמֶה לָּךְ, מֶלֶךְ, מֵמִית וּמְחַיֶּה וּמַצְמִיחַ יְשׁוּעָה.

בשבת שובה: מִי כָמְוֹךָ אַב הָרַחֲמִים, זוֹכֵר יְצוּרָיו לְחַיִּים בְּרַחֲמִים.

(If forgotten, no corrective action is necessary.)

וְנֶאֱמָן אַתָּה לְהַחֲיוֹת מֵתִים. בָּרוּךְ אַתָּה יהוה, מְחַיֵּה הַמֵּתִים.

When saying the עמידה *silently, continue with* אַתָּה קָדוֹשׁ *below.*

קדושה

During חזרת הש"ץ*, the following is said standing with feet together, rising on the toes at the words indicated by* ▲.

קהל *then* ש"ץ: **נְקַדֵּשׁ** אֶת שִׁמְךָ בָּעוֹלָם, כְּשֵׁם שֶׁמַּקְדִּישִׁים אוֹתוֹ בִּשְׁמֵי מָרוֹם, כַּכָּתוּב עַל יַד נְבִיאֶךָ, וְקָרָא זֶה אֶל־זֶה וְאָמַר ישעיה ו

קהל *then* ש"ץ: ▲קָדוֹשׁ, ▲קָדוֹשׁ, ▲קָדוֹשׁ יהוה צְבָאוֹת, מְלֹא כָל־הָאָרֶץ כְּבוֹדוֹ:

ש"ץ: לְעֻמָּתָם בָּרוּךְ יֹאמֵרוּ

קהל *then* ש"ץ: ▲בָּרוּךְ כְּבוֹד־יהוה מִמְּקוֹמוֹ: יחזקאל ג

ש"ץ: וּבְדִבְרֵי קָדְשְׁךָ כָּתוּב לֵאמֹר

קהל *then* ש"ץ: ▲יִמְלֹךְ יהוה לְעוֹלָם, אֱלֹהַיִךְ צִיּוֹן לְדֹר וָדֹר, הַלְלוּיָהּ: תהלים קמו

ש"ץ: לְדוֹר וָדוֹר נַגִּיד גָּדְלֶךָ, וּלְנֵצַח נְצָחִים קְדֻשָּׁתְךָ נַקְדִּישׁ, וְשִׁבְחֲךָ אֱלֹהֵינוּ מִפִּינוּ לֹא יָמוּשׁ לְעוֹלָם וָעֶד, כִּי אֵל מֶלֶךְ גָּדוֹל וְקָדוֹשׁ אָתָּה. בָּרוּךְ אַתָּה יהוה, הָאֵל הַקָּדוֹשׁ./בשבת שובה: הַמֶּלֶךְ הַקָּדוֹשׁ./

The שליח ציבור *continues with* אַתָּה אֶחָד *on the next page.*

קדושת השם

אַתָּה קָדוֹשׁ וְשִׁמְךָ קָדוֹשׁ, וּקְדוֹשִׁים בְּכָל יוֹם יְהַלְלוּךָ סֶּלָה. בָּרוּךְ אַתָּה יהוה, הָאֵל הַקָּדוֹשׁ./בשבת שובה: הַמֶּלֶךְ הַקָּדוֹשׁ./

(If forgotten, repeat the עמידה*.)*

For laws regarding "*Responding to the Leader during Kedusha,*" see page 510.
For laws regarding "Omission of *HaMelekh HaKadosh,*" see page 112.

He sustains the living with kindness, He resurrects the dead with great compassion, He supports those who are falling, He heals the sick, He sets the incarcerated free, and He fulfills what He has promised to those who sleep in the dust. Who is like You, O mighty One, and who can be compared to You, O King Who causes death and resurrects, and Who causes salvation to sprout?

On Shabbat Shuva: Who is like You, merciful Father, Who in compassion remembers for life those He has created.

(If forgotten, no corrective action is necessary.)

Trustworthy are You to resurrect the dead. Blessed are You, LORD, Resurrector of the dead.

When saying the Amida silently, continue with "You are holy" below.

KEDUSHA *During the Leader's Repetition, the following is said standing with feet together, rising on the toes at the words indicated by ▲.*

Cong. then Leader: נְקַדֵּשׁ WE WILL SANCTIFY Your name in this world, as they sanctify it in the heavenly heights, as is written by Your prophet: "They called to one another, saying": *Is. 6*

Cong. then Leader: "▲Holy, ▲holy, ▲holy is the LORD of hosts; the whole world is filled with His glory."

Leader: Those who face them declare, "Blessed –"

Ezek. 3 *Cong. then Leader:* ▲"Blessed is the glory of the LORD from His place."

Leader: And in Your holy Writings it is written as follows:

Ps. 146 *Cong. then Leader:* ▲"The LORD will reign forever, Your God, O Zion, to all generations. Praise the LORD."

Leader: To all generations we will proclaim Your greatness, and forever declare Your holiness, and the praise of You, our God, will never leave our mouth, for You are God and King, great and holy; blessed are You, LORD, the holy God. / *On Shabbat Shuva:* the holy King. /

The Leader continues with "You are One" on the next page.

HOLINESS

אַתָּה YOU ARE HOLY and Your name is holy, and holy ones will praise You every day, forever. Blessed are You, LORD, the holy God. / *On Shabbat Shuva:* the holy King./

(If forgotten, repeat the Amida.)

קדושת היום

אַתָּה אֶחָד וְשִׁמְךָ אֶחָד, וּמִי כְּעַמְּךָ יִשְׂרָאֵל גּוֹי אֶחָד בָּאָרֶץ.
תִּפְאֶרֶת גְּדֻלָּה וַעֲטֶרֶת יְשׁוּעָה, יוֹם מְנוּחָה וּקְדֻשָּׁה לְעַמְּךָ נָתָתָּ. אַבְרָהָם יָגֵל, יִצְחָק יְרַנֵּן, יַעֲקֹב וּבָנָיו יָנְוּחוּ בוֹ. מְנוּחַת אַהֲבָה וּנְדָבָה, מְנוּחַת אֱמֶת וֶאֱמוּנָה, מְנוּחַת שָׁלוֹם וְשַׁלְוָה וְהַשְׁקֵט וָבֶטַח, מְנוּחָה שְׁלֵמָה שֶׁאַתָּה רוֹצֶה בָּהּ. יַכִּירוּ בָנֶיךָ וְיֵדְעוּ, כִּי מֵאִתְּךָ הִיא מְנוּחָתָם, וְעַל מְנוּחָתָם יַקְדִּישׁוּ אֶת שְׁמֶךָ.

אַתָּה אֶחָד – *You are One*. This paragraph contains fifty-five words, corresponding to the fifty-five words in the Ten Commandments that command the Shabbat (Ex. 20:8–11) (*Tur*, *Perisha*).

The affirmation that "God is One and His name is One" is of course taken from Zechariah 14:9, as quoted at the conclusion of *Aleinu*. In that context, however, it is not a description of current reality but of בַּיּוֹם הַהוּא ("on that future day") of hoped-for Messianic redemption when God and His name will finally be one. Yet it is invoked here as if that unity of God and His name are already a present reality, which is clearly not yet the case. Rather we are to understand that, as explained in the commentary to the Friday night *Amida*, Shabbat *Minḥa* represents the realization of the final redemption, as if it has already materialized. Thus our prayers describe a virtual reality in which God and His name are already one (R. Basil Herring).

וּמִי כְּעַמְּךָ יִשְׂרָאֵל גּוֹי אֶחָד בָּאָרֶץ – *And who is like Your people Israel, a nation unique in the world*. These words are taken from II Samuel 7:23, as spoken by King David. In the context of the preceding phrase this too is an affirmation of faith that at the future redemption the people of Israel too will, like God, be one, unified, able to finally overcome its divisions, and recognized by all as unique in the world. That state of complete fellowship with our fellow Jews, and the awareness of our uniqueness

INSTRUCTIONS FOR SOMEONE WHO MADE A MISTAKE AND RECITED THE WRONG AMIDA

If after the third *berakha* (*HaKel HaKadosh)* one accidentally began to recite the weekday *Amida*, even if one recited one word of that *berakha*, one should conclude the *berakha* that one has started and then continue with the middle *berakha* of Shabbat. (Regarding אַתָּה חוֹנֵן, one does not complete the *berakha* if one only recited the word אַתָּה, as long as one realized that it was Shabbat.) If one didn't realize the mistake until רְצֵה or one of the subsequent blessings, one should stop immediately and return to the middle *berakha* of Shabbat. If one didn't realize the mistake until after taking three steps back and didn't mention Shabbat at all in the *Amida*, one must repeat the *Amida*.

HOLINESS OF THE DAY

אַתָּה YOU ARE ONE and Your name is One; and who is like Your people Israel, a nation unique in the world? The day of rest and holiness that You gave to Your people bestows upon them the splendor of greatness and the crown of the future salvation. Then Abraham will rejoice and Isaac will sing in exultation, when Jacob and his descendants will rest on it. It will indeed be a rest filled with love and generosity, a respite of truth and faith, a repose of peace and tranquility, as well as serenity and trust, a complete rest in accordance with Your will. Then will Your children recognize and know that their rest comes from You, and that by their resting they will be sanctifying Your name.

---

as a people, is likewise to be experienced mentally and emotionally as we recite *Minḥa* (R. Basil Herring).

תִּפְאֶרֶת גְּדֻלָּה וַעֲטֶרֶת יְשׁוּעָה – *The splendor of greatness and the crown of the future salvation.* Shabbat is the crown of the Jewish people, allowing even the most downtrodden Jew to feel like royalty for its duration (R. Shlomo ben Shimshon of Worms).

As explained earlier, the central section of the Shabbat *Minḥa Amida* focuses on the end of history when the people and the land of Israel will finally be redeemed. With this phrase ("the crown of the future salvation") we declare that it is in the merit of Shabbat observance that redemption will come, hence our fidelity to Shabbat will be worn as our crowning glory, so to speak. This focus on the future redemption in its various dimensions ties together the disparate phrases found in this paragraph. Thus, as Abudarham explains, as part of that eschatology Abraham and Isaac, who will of course be resurrected, will rejoice when they will see that Jacob and those of his descendants (who are indeed known as the children of *Israel*) who will live at that time (including those to be resurrected) will observe Shabbat as a day of rest and rejuvenation in every conceivable sense. For this reason we have translated the paragraph as an affirmation of faith that at the end of days Shabbat will be a time of complete individual and national respite and renewal (R. Basil Herring).

By invoking the patriarchs in the context of the final redemption, this prayer ties together our end history with its beginning foundations. It emphasizes that what began as the sanctification of God by a few heroic individuals will culminate in the glorious sanctification of His name by an entire nation when it will keep His Shabbat and proclaim His Oneness (Dr. Yaakov Rothschild).

יוֹם מְנוּחָה וּקְדֻשָּׁה – *Day of holy rest.* The word מְנוּחָה (rest) appears here seven times, alluding to the seventh day, i.e., Shabbat.

אֱלֹהֵינוּ וֵאלֹהֵי אֲבוֹתֵינוּ, רְצֵה בִמְנוּחָתֵנוּ, קַדְּשֵׁנוּ בְּמִצְוֹתֶיךָ וְתֵן חֶלְקֵנוּ בְּתוֹרָתֶךָ, שַׂבְּעֵנוּ מִטּוּבֶךָ וְשַׂמְּחֵנוּ בִּישׁוּעָתֶךָ, וְטַהֵר לִבֵּנוּ לְעָבְדְּךָ בֶּאֱמֶת. וְהַנְחִילֵנוּ יהוה אֱלֹהֵינוּ בְּאַהֲבָה וּבְרָצוֹן שַׁבְּתוֹת קָדְשֶׁךָ, וְיָנוּחוּ בָם יִשְׂרָאֵל מְקַדְּשֵׁי שְׁמֶךָ. בָּרוּךְ אַתָּה יהוה, מְקַדֵּשׁ הַשַּׁבָּת.

עבודה

רְצֵה יהוה אֱלֹהֵינוּ בְּעַמְּךָ יִשְׂרָאֵל, וּבִתְפִלָּתָם, וְהָשֵׁב אֶת הָעֲבוֹדָה לִדְבִיר בֵּיתֶךָ, וְאִשֵּׁי יִשְׂרָאֵל וּתְפִלָּתָם בְּאַהֲבָה תְקַבֵּל בְּרָצוֹן, וּתְהִי לְרָצוֹן תָּמִיד עֲבוֹדַת יִשְׂרָאֵל עַמֶּךָ.

On ראש חודש *and* חול המועד*, say:*

אֱלֹהֵינוּ וֵאלֹהֵי אֲבוֹתֵינוּ, יַעֲלֶה וְיָבוֹא וְיַגִּיעַ, וְיֵרָאֶה וְיֵרָצֶה וְיִשָּׁמַע, וְיִפָּקֵד וְיִזָּכֵר זִכְרוֹנֵנוּ וּפִקְדוֹנֵנוּ וְזִכְרוֹן אֲבוֹתֵינוּ, וְזִכְרוֹן מָשִׁיחַ בֶּן דָּוִד עַבְדֶּךָ, וְזִכְרוֹן יְרוּשָׁלַיִם עִיר קָדְשֶׁךָ, וְזִכְרוֹן כָּל עַמְּךָ בֵּית יִשְׂרָאֵל, לְפָנֶיךָ, לִפְלֵיטָה לְטוֹבָה, לְחֵן וּלְחֶסֶד וּלְרַחֲמִים, לְחַיִּים וּלְשָׁלוֹם בְּיוֹם

בראש חודש: רֹאשׁ הַחֹדֶשׁ

בפסח: חַג הַמַּצּוֹת

בסוכות: חַג הַסֻּכּוֹת

הַזֶּה. זָכְרֵנוּ יהוה אֱלֹהֵינוּ בּוֹ לְטוֹבָה, וּפָקְדֵנוּ בוֹ לִבְרָכָה, וְהוֹשִׁיעֵנוּ בוֹ לְחַיִּים. וּבִדְבַר יְשׁוּעָה וְרַחֲמִים, חוּס וְחָנֵּנוּ וְרַחֵם עָלֵינוּ וְהוֹשִׁיעֵנוּ, כִּי אֵלֶיךָ עֵינֵינוּ, כִּי אֵל מֶלֶךְ חַנּוּן וְרַחוּם אָתָּה.

וְתֶחֱזֶינָה עֵינֵינוּ בְּשׁוּבְךָ לְצִיּוֹן בְּרַחֲמִים. בָּרוּךְ אַתָּה יהוה, הַמַּחֲזִיר שְׁכִינָתוֹ לְצִיּוֹן.

For laws regarding "יַעֲלֶה וְיָבוֹא / *Ya'aleh VeYavo,*" see page 125.

אֱלֹהֵינוּ OUR GOD and God of our fathers, be pleased with our rest. Sanctify us through Your commandments and grant us our portion in Your Torah. Gratify us with Your goodness and gladden us with Your salvation. Purify our heart to serve You in truth. LORD our God, through Your loving favor may You grant that Your holy Sabbaths will be our heritage, so that the people of Israel who sanctify Your name will rest on them. Blessed are You, LORD, Who sanctifies the Sabbath.

TEMPLE SERVICE

רְצֵה LOOK FAVORABLY, LORD our God, upon Your people Israel and their prayer, and restore the service to the Holy of Holies of Your House. Accept with love and favor the fire-offerings of Israel and their prayer. May the service of Israel Your people Israel always find favor with You.

On Rosh Ḥodesh and Ḥol HaMo'ed, say:

אֱלֹהֵינוּ וֵאלֹהֵי אֲבוֹתֵינוּ OUR GOD and God of our fathers, may there arise, arrive, reach, appear, be favored, heard, considered and remembered, our remembrance and recollection, Your remembrance of our fathers, of the Messiah son of David Your servant, of Jerusalem Your holy city and of all Your people the house of Israel. May they come before You for deliverance and benefit, for grace, kindness and mercy, for life and peace, on this day of:

On Rosh Ḥodesh: Rosh Ḥodesh.
On Pesaḥ: the Festival of Matzot.
On Sukkot: the Festival of Sukkot.

LORD our God, remember us this day for good. Be mindful of us this day for blessing, preserve us this day for life. Regarding redemption and mercy show us compassion and grace, and have pity on us and save us. For our eyes are lifted toward You, for You are a gracious and merciful God and King.

May our eyes witness Your return to Zion in compassion. Blessed are You, LORD, Who will restore His Divine Presence to Zion.

הודאה

Bow during the first five words.

ימודים אֲנַחְנוּ לָךְ, שָׁאַתָּה הוּא יהוה אֱלֹהֵינוּ וֵאלֹהֵי אֲבוֹתֵינוּ לְעוֹלָם וָעֶד. צוּר חַיֵּינוּ, מָגֵן יִשְׁעֵנוּ, אַתָּה הוּא. לְדוֹר וָדוֹר נוֹדֶה לְּךָ וּנְסַפֵּר תְּהִלָּתֶךָ, עַל חַיֵּינוּ הַמְּסוּרִים בְּיָדֶךָ, וְעַל נִשְׁמוֹתֵינוּ הַפְּקוּדוֹת לָךְ, וְעַל נִסֶּיךָ שֶׁבְּכָל יוֹם עִמָּנוּ, וְעַל נִפְלְאוֹתֶיךָ וְטוֹבוֹתֶיךָ, שֶׁבְּכָל עֵת, עֶרֶב וָבֹקֶר וְצָהֳרָיִם. הַטּוֹב, כִּי לֹא כָלוּ רַחֲמֶיךָ וְהַמְרַחֵם, כִּי לֹא תַמּוּ חֲסָדֶיךָ, מֵעוֹלָם קִוִּינוּ לָךְ.

During חזרת הש״ץ*, the* קהל *says quietly:*

ימודים אֲנַחְנוּ לָךְ, שָׁאַתָּה הוּא יהוה אֱלֹהֵינוּ וֵאלֹהֵי אֲבוֹתֵינוּ, אֱלֹהֵי כָל בָּשָׂר, יוֹצְרֵנוּ, יוֹצֵר בְּרֵאשִׁית. בְּרָכוֹת וְהוֹדָאוֹת לְשִׁמְךָ הַגָּדוֹל וְהַקָּדוֹשׁ, עַל שֶׁהֶחֱיִיתָנוּ וְקִיַּמְתָּנוּ. כֵּן תְּחַיֵּנוּ וּתְקַיְּמֵנוּ, וְתֶאֱסֹף גָּלֻיּוֹתֵינוּ לְחַצְרוֹת קָדְשֶׁךָ, לִשְׁמֹר חֻקֶּיךָ וְלַעֲשׂוֹת רְצוֹנֶךָ וּלְעָבְדְּךָ בְּלֵבָב שָׁלֵם, עַל שֶׁאֲנַחְנוּ מוֹדִים לָךְ. בָּרוּךְ אֵל הַהוֹדָאוֹת.

בחנוכה:

עַל הַנִּסִּים וְעַל הַפֻּרְקָן וְעַל הַגְּבוּרוֹת וְעַל הַתְּשׁוּעוֹת וְעַל הַמִּלְחָמוֹת שֶׁעָשִׂיתָ לַאֲבוֹתֵינוּ בַּיָּמִים הָהֵם בַּזְּמַן הַזֶּה.

בִּימֵי מַתִּתְיָהוּ בֶּן יוֹחָנָן כֹּהֵן גָּדוֹל חַשְׁמוֹנַאי וּבָנָיו, כְּשֶׁעָמְדָה מַלְכוּת יָוָן הָרְשָׁעָה עַל עַמְּךָ יִשְׂרָאֵל לְהַשְׁכִּיחָם תּוֹרָתֶךָ וּלְהַעֲבִירָם מֵחֻקֵּי רְצוֹנֶךָ, וְאַתָּה בְּרַחֲמֶיךָ הָרַבִּים עָמַדְתָּ לָהֶם בְּעֵת צָרָתָם, רַבְתָּ אֶת רִיבָם, דַּנְתָּ אֶת דִּינָם, נָקַמְתָּ אֶת נִקְמָתָם, מָסַרְתָּ גִבּוֹרִים בְּיַד חַלָּשִׁים, וְרַבִּים בְּיַד מְעַטִּים, וּטְמֵאִים בְּיַד טְהוֹרִים, וּרְשָׁעִים בְּיַד צַדִּיקִים, וְזֵדִים בְּיַד עוֹסְקֵי תוֹרָתֶךָ, וּלְךָ עָשִׂיתָ שֵׁם גָּדוֹל וְקָדוֹשׁ בְּעוֹלָמֶךָ, וּלְעַמְּךָ יִשְׂרָאֵל עָשִׂיתָ תְּשׁוּעָה גְדוֹלָה וּפֻרְקָן כְּהַיּוֹם הַזֶּה. וְאַחַר כֵּן בָּאוּ בָנֶיךָ לִדְבִיר בֵּיתֶךָ, וּפִנּוּ אֶת הֵיכָלֶךָ, וְטִהֲרוּ אֶת מִקְדָּשֶׁךָ, וְהִדְלִיקוּ נֵרוֹת בְּחַצְרוֹת קָדְשֶׁךָ, וְקָבְעוּ שְׁמוֹנַת יְמֵי חֲנֻכָּה אֵלּוּ, לְהוֹדוֹת וּלְהַלֵּל לְשִׁמְךָ הַגָּדוֹל.

Continue with וְעַל כֻּלָּם.

For laws regarding "עַל הַנִּסִּים / *Al HaNissim,*" see page 128.

THANKSGIVING

Bow during the first seven words.

מוֹדִים WE THANK YOU, for You are the LORD our God and the God of our fathers for all eternity. You are the Rock of our life and Shield of our deliverance. From generation to generation we will thank You and recount Your praise for our lives that are in Your hands, for our souls that are given over to You, for Your miracles that are with us every day, and for Your constant wonders and favors, evening, morning and noon. You are good, for Your compassion does not cease, and You are compassionate, for Your kindness never ends. We have placed our hope in You forever and ever.

During the Leader's Repetition, the congregation says quietly:

מוֹדִים WE THANK YOU, for You are the LORD our God, the God of our fathers and God of all flesh. You are our Maker, the Maker of Creation. Blessings and thanks are due Your great and holy name for You have given us life and preserved us in life. May You continue to keep us in life and preserve us. Gather our exiles to the courtyards of Your Temple so that we may fulfill Your commandments and do Your will, serving You with a perfect heart, in the merit of our giving thanks to You now. Blessed be the God of all thanksgiving.

On Ḥanukka add:

עַל הַנִּסִּים [WE THANK YOU] for the miracles, the deliverance, and the triumphant victories and salvation, as well as wars which You wrought for our ancestors in those days at this season.

IT HAPPENED in the days of Mattathias son of Johanan, the Hasmonean high priest, and his sons. Then the cruel Hellenist power rose up to force Your people Israel to forget Your Torah and transgress the commands of Your will. In that hour of their distress, You in Your great mercy rose to take up their cause and defend their rights. Meting out retribution You delivered the strong into the hand of the weak, the many into the hand of the few, the impure into the hand of the pure, the evil ones into the hand of the righteous, and the wicked into the hand of devotees of Your Torah. You thereby made for Yourself a great and holy name throughout Your world, as well as bringing about great deliverance and salvation for Your people Israel (known) to this day. Then Your children came to the Holy of Holies in Your house, cleared Your Temple, purified Your holy place, kindled lights in Your holy courts, and instituted these eight days of Ḥanukka to give thanks and sing praise to Your great name.

Continue with "For all this."

וְעַל כֻּלָּם יִתְבָּרַךְ וְיִתְרוֹמַם שִׁמְךָ מַלְכֵּנוּ תָּמִיד לְעוֹלָם וָעֶד.

בשבת שובה: וּכְתֹב לְחַיִּים טוֹבִים כָּל בְּנֵי בְרִיתֶךָ.

(*If forgotten, no corrective action is necessary.*)

וְכֹל הַחַיִּים יוֹדוּךָ סֶּלָה, וִיהַלְלוּ אֶת שִׁמְךָ בֶּאֱמֶת, הָאֵל יְשׁוּעָתֵנוּ וְעֶזְרָתֵנוּ סֶלָה. בָּרוּךְ אַתָּה יהוה, הַטּוֹב שִׁמְךָ וּלְךָ נָאֶה לְהוֹדוֹת.

ברכת שלום

שָׁלוֹם רָב עַל יִשְׂרָאֵל עַמְּךָ תָּשִׂים לְעוֹלָם, כִּי אַתָּה הוּא מֶלֶךְ אָדוֹן לְכָל הַשָּׁלוֹם. וְטוֹב בְּעֵינֶיךָ לְבָרֵךְ אֶת עַמְּךָ יִשְׂרָאֵל, בְּכָל עֵת וּבְכָל שָׁעָה בִּשְׁלוֹמֶךָ.

בשבת שובה: בְּסֵפֶר חַיִּים, בְּרָכָה וְשָׁלוֹם, וּפַרְנָסָה טוֹבָה, נִזָּכֵר וְנִכָּתֵב לְפָנֶיךָ, אֲנַחְנוּ וְכָל עַמְּךָ בֵּית יִשְׂרָאֵל, לְחַיִּים טוֹבִים וּלְשָׁלוֹם.*

בָּרוּךְ אַתָּה יהוה, הַמְבָרֵךְ אֶת עַמּוֹ יִשְׂרָאֵל בַּשָּׁלוֹם.

**On* שבת שובה *many end the blessing:*

בָּרוּךְ אַתָּה יהוה, עוֹשֵׂה הַשָּׁלוֹם.

At this point when the שליח ציבור *repeats the* עמידה *he should complete the repetition by saying the verse beginning "*יִהְיוּ לְרָצוֹן*" out loud.*

תהלים יט יִהְיוּ לְרָצוֹן אִמְרֵי־פִי וְהֶגְיוֹן לִבִּי לְפָנֶיךָ, יהוה צוּרִי וְגֹאֲלִי:

ברכות יז. **אֱלֹהַי,** נְצֹר לְשׁוֹנִי מֵרָע וּשְׂפָתַי מִדַּבֵּר מִרְמָה, וְלִמְקַלְלַי נַפְשִׁי תִדֹּם, וְנַפְשִׁי כֶּעָפָר לַכֹּל תִּהְיֶה. פְּתַח לִבִּי בְּתוֹרָתֶךָ, וּבְמִצְוֹתֶיךָ תִּרְדֹּף נַפְשִׁי. וְכָל הַחוֹשְׁבִים עָלַי רָעָה, מְהֵרָה הָפֵר עֲצָתָם וְקַלְקֵל מַחֲשַׁבְתָּם. עֲשֵׂה לְמַעַן שְׁמֶךָ, עֲשֵׂה לְמַעַן יְמִינֶךָ,

תהלים ס עֲשֵׂה לְמַעַן קְדֻשָּׁתֶךָ, עֲשֵׂה לְמַעַן תּוֹרָתֶךָ. לְמַעַן יֵחָלְצוּן יְדִידֶיךָ,

תהלים יט הוֹשִׁיעָה יְמִינְךָ וַעֲנֵנִי: יִהְיוּ לְרָצוֹן אִמְרֵי־פִי וְהֶגְיוֹן לִבִּי לְפָנֶיךָ, יהוה צוּרִי וְגֹאֲלִי:

For laws regarding "Interruptions during *Elokai Netzor,*" see page 133.

For all this, our King, may Your name be blessed and exalted continually, forever and ever.

On Shabbat Shuva: Inscribe all the children of Your covenant for a life of goodness. (*If forgotten, no corrective action is necessary.*)

All that lives will give thanks to You forever and praise Your name in truth, God, our salvation and our help forever. Blessed are You, LORD, for Your name is "The Good One" and it is appropriate to give thanks to You.

PEACE

שָׁלוֹם רָב ESTABLISH ABUNDANT PEACE for Your people Israel forever, for You are the sovereign Master of all peace; and may it be good in Your eyes to bless Your people Israel at all times, at every hour, with Your peace.

On Shabbat Shuva: In the book of life and blessing, peace and prosperity, may we and all the house of Israel Your people be remembered before You and inscribed for a life of goodness and peace.*

Blessed are You, LORD, Who blesses His people Israel with peace.

**On Shabbat Shuva many end the blessing:*
Blessed are You, LORD, Who makes peace.

At this point when the Leader repeats the Amida he should complete the repetition by saying the verse beginning "May the words" out loud.

Ps. 19 MAY THE WORDS of my mouth and the meditation of my heart find grace before You, LORD, my Rock and my Redeemer.

Berakhot 17a אֱלֹהַי MY GOD, guard my tongue from evil, and my lips from speaking deceit. Let my soul be silent to those who curse me; let my soul be humble toward everyone like the dust. Open my heart to Your Torah that my soul may follow Your commandments. As for all those who contemplate evil against me, speedily nullify their plans and spoil their schemes. Do so for the sake of Your name. Do so for Your right hand. Do
Ps. 60 so for Your holiness. Do so for Your Torah, that Your loved ones may be
Ps. 19 delivered. "Save with Your right hand, and answer me. May the words of my mouth and the meditation of my heart find grace before You, LORD, my Rock and my Redeemer."

Bow, take three steps back, then bow, first left, then right, then center, while saying:

עֹשֶׂה שָׁלוֹם/ בשבת שובה: הַשָּׁלוֹם/ בִּמְרוֹמָיו, הוּא יַעֲשֶׂה שָׁלוֹם עָלֵינוּ, וְעַל כָּל יִשְׂרָאֵל, וְאִמְרוּ אָמֵן.

יְהִי רָצוֹן מִלְּפָנֶיךָ יהוה אֱלֹהֵינוּ וֵאלֹהֵי אֲבוֹתֵינוּ, שֶׁיִּבָּנֶה בֵּית הַמִּקְדָּשׁ בִּמְהֵרָה בְיָמֵינוּ, וְתֵן חֶלְקֵנוּ בְּתוֹרָתֶךָ, וְשָׁם נַעֲבָדְךָ בְּיִרְאָה כִּימֵי
עוֹלָם וּכְשָׁנִים קַדְמֹנִיּוֹת. וְעָרְבָה לַיהוה מִנְחַת יְהוּדָה וִירוּשָׁלָםִ כִּימֵי עוֹלָם מלאכי ג
וּכְשָׁנִים קַדְמֹנִיּוֹת:

The following is omitted on days when תחנון *would not be said on weekdays* (*see page 144*).

צִדְקָתְךָ צֶדֶק לְעוֹלָם וְתוֹרָתְךָ אֱמֶת: וְצִדְקָתְךָ אֱלֹהִים עַד־ תהלים קיט תהלים עא
מָרוֹם, אֲשֶׁר־עָשִׂיתָ גְדֹלוֹת, אֱלֹהִים, מִי כָמוֹךָ: צִדְקָתְךָ תהלים לו
כְּהַרְרֵי־אֵל, מִשְׁפָּטֶךָ תְּהוֹם רַבָּה, אָדָם וּבְהֵמָה תוֹשִׁיעַ יהוה:

קדיש שלם

ש״ץ: **יִתְגַּדַּל** וְיִתְקַדַּשׁ שְׁמֵהּ רַבָּא (קהל: אָמֵן) בְּעָלְמָא דִּי בְרָא כִרְעוּתֵהּ, וְיַמְלִיךְ מַלְכוּתֵהּ בְּחַיֵּיכוֹן וּבְיוֹמֵיכוֹן וּבְחַיֵּי דְכָל בֵּית יִשְׂרָאֵל, בַּעֲגָלָא וּבִזְמַן קָרִיב, וְאִמְרוּ אָמֵן. (קהל: אָמֵן)

צִדְקָתְךָ – *Your righteousness.* These three verses have long been understood as a derivative form of צִדּוּק הַדִּין (faithful acceptance of God's justice in the face of the death of a loved one). It is recited at Shabbat *Minḥa* in memory of Moses, who by tradition died on Shabbat afternoon (*Maḥzor Vitri*). Others accept the view that this was also the time when Joseph and David died (Baḥ), as well as Aaron and Miriam (Rashash).

According to the Gemara (*Sanhedrin* 65b), R. Akiva told his Roman interlocutor Turnus Rufus that on Shabbat the souls of sinners in Gehenna enjoy a temporary reprieve from their suffering, and thus as the resumption of their suffering draws closer we reaffirm on their behalf our acceptance of the justice of God's decree.

אֲשֶׁר־עָשִׂיתָ גְדֹלוֹת – *Who have done great things.* In this psalm David recalls God's many interventions on his behalf. This verse declares that God's accomplishments are so great that they defy specific description (*Alshikh*), as is conveyed by the verse (Job 5:9), עֹשֶׂה גְדֹלוֹת וְאֵין חֵקֶר נִפְלָאוֹת עַד אֵין מִסְפָּר (He does great and incomprehensible things, marvelous things without number). In that instance Eliphaz points to God's omnipotence to demonstrate that man's limited perspective renders inappropriate any complaints in the face of what appears to be divine injustice. Recited at this time of the day, the psalm teaches us that in the coming week we are to remain mindful of God's ability to overturn our troubles; and in these waning moments of Shabbat, we recall that the twilight period at

Bow, take three steps back, then bow, first left, then right, then center, while saying:

He Who makes peace in His heights, may He create peace for us and for all Israel. Amen.

יְהִי רָצוֹן MAY IT BE Your will, LORD our God and God of our fathers, that the Temple be rebuilt speedily in our days and may You grant our portion in Your Torah. We will serve You there in reverence as in the days of antiquity and in
Mal. 3 years gone by. "And may the offering of Judah and Jerusalem be pleasant to the LORD as in the days of antiquity and in years gone by."

The following is omitted on days when Taḥanun would not be said on weekdays (see page 144).

Ps. 119 צִדְקָתְךָ YOUR RIGHTEOUSNESS is an everlasting righteousness, and
Ps. 71 Your law is truth. And Your righteousness, O God, reaches the high heavens. O God, You Who have done great things, who is like You?
Ps. 36 Your righteousness is like the mighty mountains, Your judgments reach the great deep. O Lord, You deliver both man and beast.

FULL KADDISH

Leader: יִתְגַּדַּל EXALTED AND HALLOWED may God's great name be, in the world He created as He willed. May He reign in your lifetimes and in your days, and in the lifetime of the whole house of Israel, speedily and soon, and say, Amen.

---

the end of life can be as hopeful as the rising sun.

אָדָם וּבְהֵמָה תוֹשִׁיעַ ה׳ – *O Lord, You deliver both man and beast.* The Gemara (*Ḥullin* 5b), faced with the surprising implication in this verse that humans and animals are somehow equally saved by God, explains it to mean that God saves those people who render themselves like animals that are bereft of intelligence. To understand this Gemara we must recall that at Sinai, when Israel declared נַעֲשֶׂה וְנִשְׁמָע (we will do and listen), they committed themselves in the first place to performing God's will and commandments, whether or not they could understand them intellectually. The understanding (or "listening") would come later. More generally, those words represented a commitment to serve God only in ways that He had commanded. They recognized at that moment that creating novel modalities of divine worship could eventually lead to disaster. Sadly, however, that was precisely what happened at the Golden Calf, when in Moses' absence some of the people chose out of desperation to serve God in a creative fashion of their own making. Accordingly, this verse declares that while it is certainly true that מִשְׁפָּטֶיךָ תְּהוֹם רַבָּה (God's commandments contain profound and deep truths), we must, initially at least, serve God by keeping His laws, as if we were like animals bereft of intellect. Only thus will we merit His salvation (Beit HaLevi).

קהל וש״ץ: יְהֵא שְׁמֵהּ רַבָּא מְבָרַךְ לְעָלַם וּלְעָלְמֵי עָלְמַיָּא.

ש״ץ: יִתְבָּרַךְ וְיִשְׁתַּבַּח וְיִתְפָּאַר וְיִתְרוֹמַם וְיִתְנַשֵּׂא, וְיִתְהַדָּר וְיִתְעַלֶּה
וְיִתְהַלָּל שְׁמֵהּ דְּקֻדְשָׁא בְּרִיךְ הוּא (קהל: בְּרִיךְ הוּא), לְעֵלָּא מִן כָּל
בִּרְכָתָא / בשבת שובה: לְעֵלָּא (וּ)לְעֵלָּא מִכָּל בִּרְכָתָא/ וְשִׁירָתָא, תֻּשְׁבְּחָתָא
וְנֶחֱמָתָא דַּאֲמִירָן בְּעָלְמָא, וְאִמְרוּ אָמֵן. (קהל: אָמֵן)

תִּתְקַבַּל צְלוֹתְהוֹן וּבָעוּתְהוֹן דְּכָל יִשְׂרָאֵל, קֳדָם אֲבוּהוֹן דִּי בִשְׁמַיָּא,
וְאִמְרוּ אָמֵן. (קהל: אָמֵן)

יְהֵא שְׁלָמָא רַבָּא מִן שְׁמַיָּא וְחַיִּים, עָלֵינוּ וְעַל כָּל יִשְׂרָאֵל, וְאִמְרוּ
אָמֵן. (קהל: אָמֵן)

Bow, take three steps back, as if taking leave of the Divine Presence, then bow, first left, then right, then center, while saying:

עֹשֶׂה שָׁלוֹם / בשבת שובה: הַשָּׁלוֹם/ בִּמְרוֹמָיו, הוּא יַעֲשֶׂה שָׁלוֹם עָלֵינוּ,
וְעַל כָּל יִשְׂרָאֵל, וְאִמְרוּ אָמֵן. (קהל: אָמֵן)

Between סוכות *and* פסח*, some recite* תהלים למנחה של שבת*, page 658, at this point.*
Between פסח *and* ראש השנה *some recite* פרקי אבות*, page 674, at this point.*

Stand while saying עָלֵינוּ*. Bow at* ▾*.*

עָלֵינוּ לְשַׁבֵּחַ לַאֲדוֹן הַכֹּל, לָתֵת גְּדֻלָּה לְיוֹצֵר בְּרֵאשִׁית, שֶׁלֹּא
עָשָׂנוּ כְּגוֹיֵי הָאֲרָצוֹת, וְלֹא שָׂמָנוּ כְּמִשְׁפְּחוֹת הָאֲדָמָה,
שֶׁלֹּא שָׂם חֶלְקֵנוּ כָּהֶם וְגוֹרָלֵנוּ כְּכָל הֲמוֹנָם. (שֶׁהֵם מִשְׁתַּחֲוִים
לְהֶבֶל וָרִיק וּמִתְפַּלְלִים אֶל אֵל לֹא יוֹשִׁיעַ.) ▾וַאֲנַחְנוּ כּוֹרְעִים
וּמִשְׁתַּחֲוִים וּמוֹדִים, לִפְנֵי מֶלֶךְ מַלְכֵי הַמְּלָכִים, הַקָּדוֹשׁ בָּרוּךְ
הוּא, שֶׁהוּא נוֹטֶה שָׁמַיִם וְיוֹסֵד אָרֶץ, וּמוֹשַׁב יְקָרוֹ בַּשָּׁמַיִם
מִמַּעַל, וּשְׁכִינַת עֻזּוֹ בְּגָבְהֵי מְרוֹמִים. הוּא אֱלֹהֵינוּ, אֵין עוֹד. אֱמֶת
מַלְכֵּנוּ, אֶפֶס זוּלָתוֹ, כַּכָּתוּב בְּתוֹרָתוֹ, וְיָדַעְתָּ הַיּוֹם וַהֲשֵׁבֹתָ אֶל־ דברים ד
לְבָבֶךָ, כִּי יהוה הוּא הָאֱלֹהִים בַּשָּׁמַיִם מִמַּעַל וְעַל־הָאָרֶץ מִתָּחַת,
אֵין עוֹד:

עַל כֵּן נְקַוֶּה לְּךָ יהוה אֱלֹהֵינוּ, לִרְאוֹת מְהֵרָה בְּתִפְאֶרֶת עֻזֶּךָ,
לְהַעֲבִיר גִּלּוּלִים מִן הָאָרֶץ, וְהָאֱלִילִים כָּרוֹת יִכָּרֵתוּן, לְתַקֵּן עוֹלָם

All: May His great name be blessed forever and all time.

Leader: Blessed and praised, honored, extolled, glorified, adored and exalted above all be the name of the Holy One, blessed is He, (*Between Rosh Hashana & Yom Kippur:* above and) beyond any blessing, hymn, praise, or expressions of consolation that may be uttered in this world, and say, Amen.

May the prayers and pleas of all Israel be accepted before their Father Who is in heaven – and say, Amen.

May abundant peace descend from heaven, as well as life, for us and for all Israel, and say, Amen.

Bow, take three steps back, as if taking leave of the Divine Presence, then bow, first left, then right, then center, while saying:

May He Who makes peace in the highest heaven, make peace for us, and for all Israel, and say, Amen.

Between Sukkot and Pesaḥ, some recite Tehillim for Shabbat Minḥa, *page 659,* *at this point. Between Pesaḥ and Rosh HaShana some recite Ethics of the Fathers,* *page 675,* *at this point.*

Stand while saying Aleinu. Bow at ▾.

עָלֵינוּ WE MUST, all of us, praise the Master of all, and ascribe greatness to He Who formed creation, for He did not make us like the nations of the world, nor render us like the families of the earth. He did not make our portion to be as theirs, nor our destiny like that of their masses. (For idolaters bow to vanity and emptiness and pray to a god who cannot save.) ▾We, however, bend our knees, bow, and give thanks before the King of the most exalted of kings, the Holy One, blessed is He. He is the One Who spreads out the heavens and establishes the earth. The seat of His glory is in the heavens above, and His Presence in all its strength is found in its highest abode. He is our God – there is no other. In truth
Deut. 4 He is our King; there is none but Him; as is written in His Torah: "On this day you should know, and take to heart, that the Lord is God in the heavens above and on the earth below – there is no other."

WE THEREFORE hope in You, Lord our God, that we may soon see the glory of Your might when You will remove abominations from the earth and the idols shall be utterly destroyed, when the world shall

בְּמַלְכוּת שַׁדַּי. וְכָל בְּנֵי בָשָׂר יִקְרְאוּ בִשְׁמֶךָ לְהַפְנוֹת אֵלֶיךָ כָּל רִשְׁעֵי אָרֶץ. יַכִּירוּ וְיֵדְעוּ כָּל יוֹשְׁבֵי תֵבֵל, כִּי לְךָ תִּכְרַע כָּל בֶּרֶךְ, תִּשָּׁבַע כָּל לָשׁוֹן. לְפָנֶיךָ יהוה אֱלֹהֵינוּ יִכְרְעוּ וְיִפֹּלוּ, וְלִכְבוֹד שִׁמְךָ יְקָר יִתֵּנוּ, וִיקַבְּלוּ כֻלָּם אֶת עֹל מַלְכוּתֶךָ, וְתִמְלֹךְ עֲלֵיהֶם מְהֵרָה לְעוֹלָם וָעֶד. כִּי הַמַּלְכוּת שֶׁלְּךָ הִיא וּלְעוֹלְמֵי עַד תִּמְלֹךְ בְּכָבוֹד,
כַּכָּתוּב בְּתוֹרָתֶךָ, יהוה יִמְלֹךְ לְעֹלָם וָעֶד: ◄ וְנֶאֱמַר, וְהָיָה יהוה לְמֶלֶךְ עַל־כָּל־הָאָרֶץ, בַּיּוֹם הַהוּא יִהְיֶה יהוה אֶחָד וּשְׁמוֹ אֶחָד: שמות טו / זכריה יד

Some add:

אַל־תִּירָא מִפַּחַד פִּתְאֹם וּמִשֹּׁאַת רְשָׁעִים כִּי תָבֹא: עֻצוּ עֵצָה וְתֻפָר, דַּבְּרוּ דָבָר וְלֹא יָקוּם, כִּי עִמָּנוּ אֵל: וְעַד־זִקְנָה אֲנִי הוּא, וְעַד־שֵׂיבָה אֲנִי אֶסְבֹּל, אֲנִי עָשִׂיתִי וַאֲנִי אֶשָּׂא וַאֲנִי אֶסְבֹּל וַאֲמַלֵּט: משלי ג / ישעיה ח / ישעיה מו

קדיש יתום

The following prayer, said by mourners, requires the presence of a מנין*.*
A transliteration can be found on page 1345.

אבל: **יִתְגַּדַּל** וְיִתְקַדַּשׁ שְׁמֵהּ רַבָּא (קהל: אָמֵן), בְּעָלְמָא דִּי בְרָא כִרְעוּתֵהּ. וְיַמְלִיךְ מַלְכוּתֵהּ, בְּחַיֵּיכוֹן וּבְיוֹמֵיכוֹן וּבְחַיֵּי דְכָל בֵּית יִשְׂרָאֵל, בַּעֲגָלָא וּבִזְמַן קָרִיב, וְאִמְרוּ אָמֵן. (קהל: אָמֵן)

קהל ואבל: יְהֵא שְׁמֵהּ רַבָּא מְבָרַךְ לְעָלַם וּלְעָלְמֵי עָלְמַיָּא.

אבל: יִתְבָּרַךְ וְיִשְׁתַּבַּח וְיִתְפָּאַר, וְיִתְרוֹמַם וְיִתְנַשֵּׂא וְיִתְהַדָּר וְיִתְעַלֶּה וְיִתְהַלָּל שְׁמֵהּ דְּקֻדְשָׁא בְּרִיךְ הוּא (קהל: בְּרִיךְ הוּא), לְעֵלָּא מִן כָּל בִּרְכָתָא / בשבת שובה: לְעֵלָּא (וּ)לְעֵלָּא מִכָּל בִּרְכָתָא/ וְשִׁירָתָא, תֻּשְׁבְּחָתָא וְנֶחֱמָתָא דַּאֲמִירָן בְּעָלְמָא, וְאִמְרוּ אָמֵן. (קהל: אָמֵן)

יְהֵא שְׁלָמָא רַבָּא מִן שְׁמַיָּא וְחַיִּים, עָלֵינוּ וְעַל כָּל יִשְׂרָאֵל, וְאִמְרוּ אָמֵן. (קהל: אָמֵן)

Bow, take three steps back, as if taking leave of the Divine Presence, then bow, first left, then right, then center, while saying:

עֹשֶׂה שָׁלוֹם / בשבת שובה: הַשָּׁלוֹם/ בִּמְרוֹמָיו, הוּא יַעֲשֶׂה שָׁלוֹם עָלֵינוּ, וְעַל כָּל יִשְׂרָאֵל, וְאִמְרוּ אָמֵן. (קהל: אָמֵן)

be perfected under the rule of the Almighty. Then all mankind shall invoke Your name, to turn all the wicked on earth toward You. All dwellers on earth will perceive and understand that to You every knee must bend, every tongue vow fealty. Before You, Lord our God, all will kneel and bow down, and give honor to Your glorious name. They will all accept the rule of Your dominion, and You will speedily rule over them forevermore. For the kingdom is Yours, and to all eternity You
Ex. 15 shall reign in glory, as it is written in Your Torah, "The Lord shall reign
Zech. 14 for ever and ever." ▸ And it is said, "And the Lord shall be King over all the earth; in that day shall the Lord be One, and His name One."

Some add:

Prov. 3 אַל־תִּירָא DO NOT FEAR sudden terror or the destruction when it comes to the
Is. 8 wicked. Devise a plan, and it will be thwarted; state a case and it will not stand,
Is. 46 for God is with us. And when you are old, I will remain; when you are aged, I will endure. I created you, I will carry you, I will endure, and I will rescue you.

MOURNER'S KADDISH

The following prayer, said by mourners, requires the presence of a minyan. A transliteration can be found on page 1345.

Mourner: יִתְגַּדַּל EXALTED AND HALLOWED may God's great name be, in the world He created as He willed. May He reign in your lifetimes and in your days, and in the lifetime of the whole house of Israel, speedily and soon, and say, Amen.

All: May His great name be blessed forever and all time.

Mourner: Blessed and praised, honored, extolled, glorified, adored and exalted above all be the name of the Holy One, blessed is He, (*Between Rosh Hashana & Yom Kippur:* above and) beyond any blessing, hymn, praise, or expressions of consolation that may be uttered in this world, and say, Amen.

May abundant peace descend from heaven, as well as life, for us and for all Israel, and say, Amen.

Bow, take three steps back, as if taking leave of the Divine Presence, then bow, first left, then right, then center, while saying:

May He Who makes peace in the highest heaven, make peace for us, and for all Israel, and say, Amen.

תהלים למנחה של שבת

The following psalms are said from שבת בראשית *until* (*but not including*) שבת הגדול.

תהלים קד **בָּרְכִי נַפְשִׁי** אֶת־יהוה, יהוה אֱלֹהַי גָּדַלְתָּ מְּאֹד, הוֹד וְהָדָר לָבָשְׁתָּ: עֹטֶה־אוֹר
כַּשַּׂלְמָה, נוֹטֶה שָׁמַיִם כַּיְרִיעָה: הַמְקָרֶה בַמַּיִם עֲלִיּוֹתָיו, הַשָּׂם־
עָבִים רְכוּבוֹ, הַמְהַלֵּךְ עַל־כַּנְפֵי־רוּחַ: עֹשֶׂה מַלְאָכָיו רוּחוֹת, מְשָׁרְתָיו אֵשׁ
לֹהֵט: יָסַד־אֶרֶץ עַל־מְכוֹנֶיהָ, בַּל־תִּמּוֹט עוֹלָם וָעֶד: תְּהוֹם כַּלְּבוּשׁ כִּסִּיתוֹ,
עַל־הָרִים יַעַמְדוּ־מָיִם: מִן־גַּעֲרָתְךָ יְנוּסוּן, מִן־קוֹל רַעַמְךָ יֵחָפֵזוּן: יַעֲלוּ הָרִים,
יֵרְדוּ בְקָעוֹת, אֶל־מְקוֹם זֶה יָסַדְתָּ לָהֶם: גְּבוּל־שַׂמְתָּ בַּל־יַעֲבֹרוּן, בַּל־יְשׁוּבוּן
לְכַסּוֹת הָאָרֶץ: הַמְשַׁלֵּחַ מַעְיָנִים בַּנְּחָלִים, בֵּין הָרִים יְהַלֵּכוּן: יַשְׁקוּ כָּל־חַיְתוֹ
שָׂדָי, יִשְׁבְּרוּ פְרָאִים צְמָאָם: עֲלֵיהֶם עוֹף־הַשָּׁמַיִם יִשְׁכּוֹן, מִבֵּין עֳפָאיִם יִתְּנוּ־
קוֹל: מַשְׁקֶה הָרִים מֵעֲלִיּוֹתָיו, מִפְּרִי מַעֲשֶׂיךָ תִּשְׂבַּע הָאָרֶץ: מַצְמִיחַ חָצִיר
לַבְּהֵמָה, וְעֵשֶׂב לַעֲבֹדַת הָאָדָם, לְהוֹצִיא לֶחֶם מִן־הָאָרֶץ: וְיַיִן יְשַׂמַּח לְבַב־
אֱנוֹשׁ, לְהַצְהִיל פָּנִים מִשָּׁמֶן, וְלֶחֶם לְבַב־אֱנוֹשׁ יִסְעָד: יִשְׂבְּעוּ עֲצֵי יהוה, אַרְזֵי
לְבָנוֹן אֲשֶׁר נָטָע: אֲשֶׁר־שָׁם צִפֳּרִים יְקַנֵּנוּ, חֲסִידָה בְּרוֹשִׁים בֵּיתָהּ: הָרִים
הַגְּבֹהִים לַיְּעֵלִים, סְלָעִים מַחְסֶה לַשְׁפַנִּים: עָשָׂה יָרֵחַ לְמוֹעֲדִים, שֶׁמֶשׁ יָדַע
מְבוֹאוֹ: תָּשֶׁת־חֹשֶׁךְ וִיהִי לָיְלָה, בּוֹ־תִרְמֹשׂ כָּל־חַיְתוֹ־יָעַר: הַכְּפִירִים שֹׁאֲגִים
לַטָּרֶף, וּלְבַקֵּשׁ מֵאֵל אָכְלָם: תִּזְרַח הַשֶּׁמֶשׁ יֵאָסֵפוּן, וְאֶל־מְעוֹנֹתָם יִרְבָּצוּן:

PSALM 104

In the early Middle Ages there were varying customs regarding the final hours of Shabbat. Mishna *Avot* was studied on certain Shabbatot (R. Amram Gaon), while others occupied themselves with recitation of the fifteen Songs of Ascent that constitute Psalms 120–134 (Abudarham). A third custom was to recite various psalms for every Shabbat of the year (Avodat Yisrael).

בָּרְכִי נַפְשִׁי אֶת־ה' – *Bless O Lord, O my soul.* This psalm is recited at Shabbat *Minḥa*, beginning on the Shabbat on which we read *Parashat Bereshit*, for Shabbat itself commemorates the six days of creation, and it is therefore appropriate to contemplate the natural world of God's creation in detail (*Levush*).

This psalm expresses the exultation of our souls in contemplating nature. It praises God for His wondrous acts of creation, listed here in the same order as the account in Genesis 1: the creation of light, heavenly and earthly waters, the vegetative world, the heavenly luminaries, the fish of the sea, and then the wild animals on land (Ibn Ezra).

R. Meir Weiss noted that while it is true that in this psalm the creations are mentioned following the order in Genesis, it is significant that interspersed among them are references to mankind and various animal species, even though the latter were only created on the sixth day. The effect is to highlight the harmony and sharing of resources and outputs that properly govern the interactions between

TEHILLIM FOR SHABBAT MINḤA

The following psalms are said from the Shabbat after Simḥat Torah until (but not including) the Shabbat before Pesaḥ.

Ps. 104 **בָּרְכִי נַפְשִׁי** BLESS O LORD, O my soul. O Lord, my God, You are very great. You are clothed with splendor and majesty. He covers Himself with light as a garment. He spreads the heavens like a curtain. Who roofs His chambers with water, Who makes the clouds His chariot, Who walks upon the wings of the wind. He makes His angels winds, His ministers flaming fire. He established the earth on its foundations, so that it should never collapse. You covered it with great waters as with a garment. The water stood above the mountains. At Your rebuke they fled. At the sound of Your thunder they hastened away. They went up the mountains, they went down the valleys, to the place that You prepared for them. You set a boundary that they could not pass over, that they would not return to cover the earth. He sends the springs into the streams. They go between the mountains. They water every beast of the field. The wild asses quench their thirst. Beside them dwell the birds of the sky. From among the branches they give voice. He waters the mountains from His upper chambers. The earth is satisfied with the fruit of Your works. He causes the grass to grow for the cattle, and plants for the service of man, and He brings forth food from the earth. And wine gladdens the heart of man, to brighten his face with oil, and bread sustains the heart of man. The trees of the Lord are satisfied, the cedars of Lebanon that He planted, Where the birds make their nests. As for the stork, the cypress trees are her house. The high hills are for the wild goats, the rocks are a refuge for the badgers. He made the moon for the seasons. The sun knows its setting place. You put down darkness, and it is night, when all the forest beasts creep out. The young lions roar for their prey, and seek their food from God. The sun rises, they gather together, and lie within their dens. Man goes forth to his work,

---

man, the animal world, and inanimate nature, by day and by night. Explicitly the Psalmist proclaims that through עֲבֹדַת הָאָדָם (human labor), nature is to be cultivated and developed in partnership with God, thus bringing benefit to man, but also preserving nature rather than despoiling it (Dr. Deena Rabinovich).

ה׳ אֱלֹהַי גָּדַלְתָּ מְּאֹד – *O Lord, my God, You are very great.* We cannot describe the full extent of God's greatness; we say only that He is "very great." Man can merely begin to enumerate His blessings, which are truly beyond number (Ibn Ezra). The Psalmist conveys the paradoxical truth that God is so much greater than man, but also so close to us that He feeds each and every creature and takes care of each one's individual needs (R. Amos Ḥakham).

יֵצֵא אָדָם לְפָעֳלוֹ, וְלַעֲבֹדָתוֹ עֲדֵי־עָרֶב: מָה־רַבּוּ מַעֲשֶׂיךָ יהוה, כֻּלָּם בְּחָכְמָה
עָשִׂיתָ, מָלְאָה הָאָרֶץ קִנְיָנֶךָ: זֶה הַיָּם גָּדוֹל וּרְחַב יָדָיִם, שָׁם־רֶמֶשׂ וְאֵין מִסְפָּר,
חַיּוֹת קְטַנּוֹת עִם־גְּדֹלוֹת: שָׁם אֳנִיּוֹת יְהַלֵּכוּן, לִוְיָתָן זֶה־יָצַרְתָּ לְשַׂחֶק־בּוֹ: כֻּלָּם
אֵלֶיךָ יְשַׂבֵּרוּן, לָתֵת אָכְלָם בְּעִתּוֹ: תִּתֵּן לָהֶם יִלְקֹטוּן, תִּפְתַּח יָדְךָ יִשְׂבְּעוּן טוֹב:
תַּסְתִּיר פָּנֶיךָ יִבָּהֵלוּן, תֹּסֵף רוּחָם יִגְוָעוּן, וְאֶל־עֲפָרָם יְשׁוּבוּן: תְּשַׁלַּח רוּחֲךָ
יִבָּרֵאוּן, וּתְחַדֵּשׁ פְּנֵי אֲדָמָה: יְהִי כְבוֹד יהוה לְעוֹלָם, יִשְׂמַח יהוה בְּמַעֲשָׂיו:
הַמַּבִּיט לָאָרֶץ וַתִּרְעָד, יִגַּע בֶּהָרִים וְיֶעֱשָׁנוּ: אָשִׁירָה לַיהוה בְּחַיָּי, אֲזַמְּרָה
לֵאלֹהַי בְּעוֹדִי: יֶעֱרַב עָלָיו שִׂיחִי, אָנֹכִי אֶשְׂמַח בַּיהוה: יִתַּמּוּ חַטָּאִים מִן־
הָאָרֶץ, וּרְשָׁעִים עוֹד אֵינָם, בָּרְכִי נַפְשִׁי אֶת־יהוה, הַלְלוּיָהּ:

תהלים קכ **שִׁיר הַמַּעֲלוֹת,** אֶל־יהוה בַּצָּרָתָה לִּי, קָרָאתִי וַיַּעֲנֵנִי: יהוה הַצִּילָה נַפְשִׁי
מִשְּׂפַת־שֶׁקֶר, מִלָּשׁוֹן רְמִיָּה: מַה־יִּתֵּן לְךָ וּמַה־יֹּסִיף לָךְ,

---

יִתַּמּוּ חַטָּאִים מִן־הָאָרֶץ, וּרְשָׁעִים עוֹד אֵינָם – *May the sinners be removed from the earth, and may the wicked be no more.* The Gemara (*Berakhot* 10a) recounts an incident in the lives of R. Meir and his wife Beruria (second century). R. Meir was suffering greatly at the hands of neighborhood bullies. Apparently in fear of their lives, R. Meir prayed to God to end the lives of their tormentors. In response Beruria urged him to instead pray for their repentance and rehabilitation, explaining that we are to learn from this verse that in similar circumstances David did not ask God to remove the חוֹטְאִים (sinners) from the earth, but rather to eliminate חַטָּאִים (sins), so that, in the absence of sin, וּרְשָׁעִים עוֹד אֵינָם (there would no longer be evildoers).

This Gemara, in particular as regarding Beruria's understanding of the verse, raises a number of questions. On a grammatical level the word חַטָּאִים as vocalized in this verse is in fact used scripturally to mean "sinners," or more precisely "repeat offenders," for whom sin has become ingrained in their nature (see for instance Genesis 13:13 regarding the people of Sodom). On a philosophical level there is the problem of free will, for as we learn from the Gemara (*Berakhot* 33b), whether or not we commit wrongful acts is for us to choose. If so, how could Beruria suggest that R. Meir ask God to make them repent of their evil ways? Among those attempting to answer these questions, R. Dovber Kahana Shapiro answered that Beruria understood the verse to teach that David indeed asked God to end the lives of sinners, but only those whose evil ways had become so ingrained that (like Pharaoh after the sixth plague) they were no longer able to repent. Beruria wanted R. Meir to see that his tormentors had not reached that stage, and were thus still capable of repentance (R. Gil Student).

What brought Beruria to such forbearance? A possible answer is to be found in the martyrdom of her father R. Ḥanina b. Tradyon. The Gemara (*Avoda Zara* 17b) relates that the Roman executioner overseeing his torture hastened his death to spare him further suffering, while at the same time jumping into the same fire to die with R. Ḥanina. At that moment a heavenly voice proclaimed that the Roman had earned his eternal reward "in a single moment." One can suggest that the death of this Roman taught Beruria that if a heretofore murderous mass executioner could

and to his labor until evening. How great are Your works, O Lord! You have made them all in wisdom. The earth is full of Your creatures. Behold, the great and wide sea, where creeping things are innumerable, small beasts and big ones. There go the ships, the leviathan that You made to play with. All of them wait upon You, to give them their food in its season. You give them, they gather it. You open Your hand, they are filled with good. You hide Your face, they are terrified. You take away their breath, they die and return to their dust. You send forth Your breath, they are created, and You renew the face of the earth. May the glory of the Lord be forever, may the Lord rejoice in His works. He looks upon the earth, and it trembles. He touches the hills, and they smoke. I will sing to the Lord while I live. I will sing praises to my God while I exist. My meditation will be sweet to Him. I will rejoice in the Lord. May the sinners be removed from the earth, and may the wicked be no more. Bless the Lord, O my soul. Praise the Lord.

Ps. 120 **שִׁיר הַמַּעֲלוֹת** A SONG OF ASCENTS. In my distress I call upon the Lord that He may answer me. O Lord, deliver my soul from lying lips, from a deceitful tongue. What will He give to you and what will He add to you, O deceitful

---

thus transform himself to find favor in God's eyes, surely anyone (including their violent neighbors) could undergo life-changing repentance. Thus she urged her husband to pray for that outcome (R. Basil Herring).

PSALM 120

Shabbat *Minḥa* concludes during the winter months with Psalms 120–134. They form a distinct literary unit with each psalm beginning with the phrase שִׁיר הַמַּעֲלוֹת (A Song of Ascents), which is unique among the Psalms. R. Sa'adia Gaon understands the phrase to refer to the fact that these psalms were to be sung in a high musical octave. Meiri understands it to derive from it being sung in several octaves, from low to high. R. Amos Ḥakham explains that the phrase refers to the unusual poetic structure of each of these psalms, known as anadiplosis or "staircase parallelism," i.e., consecutive verses often starting with words that appear earlier in the same psalm. Thus Psalm 121 declares, "From where will my help come? My help is from...."

The Mishna (*Sukka* 5:4) teaches that the fifteen psalms correspond to the fifteen steps leading from the women's section to the main Temple courtyard, to be sung by the Levites as they went up these successive steps (or "ascents"). R. Amos Ḥakham suggests that the pilgrims recited them as they ascended the Temple Mount at the onset of the three pilgrimage festivals.

Overall, these psalms are arranged in four groups of three to five psalms each, with the fifteenth acting as a general conclusion to the entire liturgy (R. Yoel Bin Nun). The first in every group asks God to protect the people from danger or to provide for essential needs; the second conveys a core theological teaching; and the third is usually a blessing relating to Jerusalem and the Temple (R. Eliav Levy). The fourth group includes not three, but five psalms, with Psalms 131 and 133 introducing and following Psalm 132. Psalm 132 breaks the pattern, as it portrays David's request to build the Temple.

הַצִּילָה נַפְשִׁי מִשְּׂפַת־שֶׁקֶר – *Deliver my soul from lying lips.* Sometimes it is permitted, and even

לָשׁוֹן רְמִיָּה: חִצֵּי גִבּוֹר שְׁנוּנִים, עִם גַּחֲלֵי רְתָמִים: אוֹיָה־לִי כִּי־גַרְתִּי מֶשֶׁךְ,
שָׁכַנְתִּי עִם־אָהֳלֵי קֵדָר: רַבַּת שָׁכְנָה־לָּהּ נַפְשִׁי, עִם שׂוֹנֵא שָׁלוֹם: אֲנִי־שָׁלוֹם
וְכִי אֲדַבֵּר, הֵמָּה לַמִּלְחָמָה:

תהלים קכא **שִׁיר לַמַּעֲלוֹת,** אֶשָּׂא עֵינַי אֶל־הֶהָרִים, מֵאַיִן יָבֹא עֶזְרִי: עֶזְרִי מֵעִם יהוה,
עֹשֵׂה שָׁמַיִם וָאָרֶץ: אַל־יִתֵּן לַמּוֹט רַגְלֶךָ, אַל־יָנוּם שֹׁמְרֶךָ:
הִנֵּה לֹא־יָנוּם וְלֹא יִישָׁן, שׁוֹמֵר יִשְׂרָאֵל: יהוה שֹׁמְרֶךָ, יהוה צִלְּךָ עַל־יַד יְמִינֶךָ:
יוֹמָם הַשֶּׁמֶשׁ לֹא־יַכֶּכָּה, וְיָרֵחַ בַּלָּיְלָה: יהוה יִשְׁמָרְךָ מִכָּל־רָע, יִשְׁמֹר אֶת־
נַפְשֶׁךָ: יהוה יִשְׁמָר־צֵאתְךָ וּבוֹאֶךָ, מֵעַתָּה וְעַד־עוֹלָם:

תהלים קכב **שִׁיר הַמַּעֲלוֹת** לְדָוִד, שָׂמַחְתִּי בְּאֹמְרִים לִי בֵּית יהוה נֵלֵךְ: עֹמְדוֹת הָיוּ
רַגְלֵינוּ, בִּשְׁעָרַיִךְ יְרוּשָׁלָםִ: יְרוּשָׁלַםִ הַבְּנוּיָה, כְּעִיר שֶׁחֻבְּרָה־
לָּהּ יַחְדָּו: שֶׁשָּׁם עָלוּ שְׁבָטִים שִׁבְטֵי־יָהּ, עֵדוּת לְיִשְׂרָאֵל, לְהֹדוֹת לְשֵׁם יהוה:
כִּי שָׁמָּה יָשְׁבוּ כִסְאוֹת לְמִשְׁפָּט, כִּסְאוֹת לְבֵית דָּוִד: שַׁאֲלוּ שְׁלוֹם יְרוּשָׁלָםִ,
יִשְׁלָיוּ אֹהֲבָיִךְ: יְהִי־שָׁלוֹם בְּחֵילֵךְ, שַׁלְוָה בְּאַרְמְנוֹתָיִךְ: לְמַעַן אַחַי וְרֵעָי,
אֲדַבְּרָה־נָּא שָׁלוֹם בָּךְ: לְמַעַן בֵּית־יהוה אֱלֹהֵינוּ, אֲבַקְשָׁה טוֹב לָךְ:

---

correct, to utter a so-called "white lie" if one's intent is to benefit the one so addressed, as long as doing so does not devolve into a habit. Accordingly, this verse asks God, "Please help me make sure that such misleading words on my part are extremely rare and alien to my usual behavior." The Sefat Emet explains that this verse refers to Jacob's prayer, having misled his father in order to receive Esau's blessing. Similarly, when Abraham had to resort to battle in order to free his nephew Lot, God assured him that actions such as those would remain alien to his core. We learn from this that while under highly exceptional circumstances we might need to engage in deceitful behavior, we must at the same time strive to not become habituated to it. This lesson is consistent with the principle that we should avoid being overly compassionate, insofar as there are rare times when seemingly cruel action is necessary and justified. As the sages said, those who are compassionate when they should be harsh will end up being unduly punitive when they should be merciful (R. Yechiel Yaakov Weinberg).

אֲנִי־שָׁלוֹם וְכִי אֲדַבֵּר, הֵמָּה לַמִּלְחָמָה – *I am for peace; but when I speak, they are for war*. The Psalmist bemoans the fact that whereas Israel has always sought peace and harmony with its neighbors, it has often been surrounded by deceitful nations and dubious allies, who even as they have pretended to be our friends, were preparing to wage war against us.

PSALM 121

מֵאַיִן יָבֹא עֶזְרִי – *From where will my help come?* While we should certainly value and seek material and financial security, it is important that we give due priority to the spiritual security resulting from our Torah studies. For this reason Isaac's blessing to Jacob prioritized the dew of heaven over the fat of the land (Gen. 27:28), and Jacob's blessing placed Ephraim before Menasheh (Gen. 48:20). In this Psalm עֶזְרִי

tongue? Sharp arrows of the mighty, with coals of broom. Woe is me, that I sojourn with Meshech, that I dwell among the tents of Kedar! My soul has long dwelt with him who hates peace. I am for peace; but when I speak, they are for war.

Ps. 121 **שִׁיר לַמַּעֲלוֹת** A SONG FOR ASCENTS. I lift up my eyes to the hills. From where will my help come? My help is from the Lord, the Maker of heaven and earth. May He not suffer your foot to slip. May He Who guards you not slumber. Behold, He Who guards Israel neither slumbers nor sleeps. The Lord is your guardian. The Lord is your shade upon your right hand. The sun will not smite you by day, nor the moon by night. The Lord will guard you from all evil. He will guard your soul. The Lord will guard your going out and your coming in from now and forever.

Ps. 122 **שִׁיר הַמַּעֲלוֹת** A SONG OF ASCENTS of David. I was glad when they said to me: We are going to the house of the Lord. Our feet were standing within your gates, O Jerusalem. Jerusalem that is built. It is like a city that is united together. For the tribes went up there, the tribes of the Lord, a testimony to Israel, to give thanks to the name of the Lord. For there they sat on thrones for judgment, the thrones of the house of David. Pray for the peace of Jerusalem. May they prosper who love you. May peace be within your walls, prosperity within your palaces. For my brothers' and companions' sakes may I now say: "Peace be within you." For the sake of the house of the Lord our God, I will seek your good.

(my help) also refers to a עֵזֶר כְּנֶגְדּוֹ (helpmate), as found in Genesis 2:18. Thus in seeking our future spouse we should place special emphasis on finding someone who will share our spiritual priorities. For this reason the verse concludes that God Who is the Maker of "heaven and earth," i.e., Who prioritizes heavenly ahead of earthly matters, will help us find such a person, for that is what we sincerely seek (R. Yitzchok Yaakov Weiss).

PSALM 122

שָׂמַחְתִּי בְּאֹמְרִים לִי בֵּית ה׳ נֵלֵךְ – *I was glad when they said to me: We are going to the house of the Lord.* These words reflect David's desire to see the Temple built so that he could spend less time fighting Israel's wars, and more time devoted to Torah study within its walls. The Gemara (*Makkot* 10a) records that David on one occasion overheard some people expressing their hope that he pass on so that his successor Solomon could at long last build the Temple. At this, David responded joyously with the words of this verse, for which he was rewarded by God so that on the day that Solomon eventually dedicated the Temple, all the people came to recognize (*Shabbat* 10a) that it was only in David's merit that the gates of the Temple finally opened to welcome the Ark (R. Shmuel HaLevi Wosner).

This psalm forms the high point of the first set of three psalms. After praying for deliverance from bitter enemies (Psalm 120),

תהלים קכג **שִׁיר הַמַּעֲלוֹת,** אֵלֶיךָ נָשָׂאתִי אֶת־עֵינַי, הַיֹּשְׁבִי בַּשָּׁמָיִם: הִנֵּה כְעֵינֵי עֲבָדִים אֶל־יַד אֲדוֹנֵיהֶם, כְּעֵינֵי שִׁפְחָה אֶל־יַד גְּבִרְתָּהּ, כֵּן עֵינֵינוּ אֶל־יהוה אֱלֹהֵינוּ, עַד שֶׁיְּחָנֵּנוּ: חָנֵּנוּ יהוה חָנֵּנוּ, כִּי־רַב שָׂבַעְנוּ בוּז: רַבַּת שָׂבְעָה־לָּהּ נַפְשֵׁנוּ, הַלַּעַג הַשַּׁאֲנַנִּים, הַבּוּז לִגְאֵי יוֹנִים:

תהלים קכד **שִׁיר הַמַּעֲלוֹת** לְדָוִד, לוּלֵי יהוה שֶׁהָיָה לָנוּ, יֹאמַר־נָא יִשְׂרָאֵל: לוּלֵי יהוה שֶׁהָיָה לָנוּ, בְּקוּם עָלֵינוּ אָדָם: אֲזַי חַיִּים בְּלָעוּנוּ, בַּחֲרוֹת אַפָּם בָּנוּ: אֲזַי הַמַּיִם שְׁטָפוּנוּ, נַחְלָה עָבַר עַל־נַפְשֵׁנוּ: אֲזַי עָבַר עַל־נַפְשֵׁנוּ, הַמַּיִם הַזֵּידוֹנִים: בָּרוּךְ יהוה, שֶׁלֹּא נְתָנָנוּ טֶרֶף לְשִׁנֵּיהֶם: נַפְשֵׁנוּ כְּצִפּוֹר נִמְלְטָה מִפַּח יוֹקְשִׁים, הַפַּח נִשְׁבָּר וַאֲנַחְנוּ נִמְלָטְנוּ: עֶזְרֵנוּ בְּשֵׁם יהוה, עֹשֵׂה שָׁמַיִם וָאָרֶץ:

תהלים קכה **שִׁיר הַמַּעֲלוֹת,** הַבֹּטְחִים בַּיהוה, כְּהַר־צִיּוֹן לֹא־יִמּוֹט, לְעוֹלָם יֵשֵׁב: יְרוּשָׁלַםִ, הָרִים סָבִיב לָהּ, וַיהוה סָבִיב לְעַמּוֹ, מֵעַתָּה וְעַד־עוֹלָם: כִּי לֹא יָנוּחַ שֵׁבֶט הָרֶשַׁע עַל גּוֹרַל הַצַּדִּיקִים, לְמַעַן לֹא־יִשְׁלְחוּ הַצַּדִּיקִים בְּעַוְלָתָה יְדֵיהֶם: הֵיטִיבָה יהוה לַטּוֹבִים, וְלִישָׁרִים בְּלִבּוֹתָם: וְהַמַּטִּים עֲקַלְקַלּוֹתָם יוֹלִיכֵם יהוה אֶת־פֹּעֲלֵי הָאָוֶן, שָׁלוֹם עַל־יִשְׂרָאֵל:

תהלים קכו **שִׁיר הַמַּעֲלוֹת,** בְּשׁוּב יהוה אֶת־שִׁיבַת צִיּוֹן, הָיִינוּ כְּחֹלְמִים: אָז יִמָּלֵא שְׂחוֹק פִּינוּ וּלְשׁוֹנֵנוּ רִנָּה, אָז יֹאמְרוּ בַגּוֹיִם הִגְדִּיל יהוה לַעֲשׂוֹת עִם־אֵלֶּה: הִגְדִּיל יהוה לַעֲשׂוֹת עִמָּנוּ, הָיִינוּ שְׂמֵחִים: שׁוּבָה יהוה אֶת־שְׁבִיתֵנוּ, כַּאֲפִיקִים בַּנֶּגֶב: הַזֹּרְעִים בְּדִמְעָה בְּרִנָּה יִקְצֹרוּ: הָלוֹךְ יֵלֵךְ וּבָכֹה נֹשֵׂא מֶשֶׁךְ־הַזָּרַע, בֹּא־יָבֹא בְרִנָּה נֹשֵׂא אֲלֻמֹּתָיו:

---

and after leaving home to travel to Jerusalem (Psalm 121), the pilgrim reaches the holy city in awe of its beauty. There the tribes assemble to praise God, and from there justice spreads throughout the land.

PSALM 126

בְּשׁוּב ה׳ אֶת־שִׁיבַת צִיּוֹן – *When the Lord brought back the return of Zion*. There are several opinions among the sages regarding who, in addition to David, authored various Psalms. Some see this one, which describes a future redemption, as authored by David in prophetic mode, while others considered it the work of a later psalmist, perhaps Ezra the Scribe, who personally experienced the return to Zion that it describes (R. Amos Ḥakham).

אָז יִמָּלֵא שְׂחוֹק פִּינוּ וּלְשׁוֹנֵנוּ רִנָּה – *Then our mouth was filled with laughter and our tongue with joy*. When God bestows a reward upon us there are two reasons to rejoice. The first is that we have received something of value from which we will benefit. The second – and by far the greater – is that His kindness to us brings about a *Kiddush Hashem* by which others

Ps. 123 **שִׁיר הַמַּעֲלוֹת** A SONG OF ASCENTS. To You I lift up my eyes, O You Who dwell in the heavens. Behold, as the eyes of servants to the hand of their masters, as the eyes of a maidservant to the hand of her mistress, so are our eyes to the Lord our God until He is gracious unto us. Be gracious unto us, O Lord, be gracious unto us, for we have suffered our fill of contempt. Our soul has suffered its fill of the scorn of those who are at ease, of the contempt of the proud.

Ps. 124 **שִׁיר הַמַּעֲלוֹת** A SONG OF ASCENTS of David. Were it not for the Lord Who was with us, let Israel say, Were it not for the Lord Who was with us, when people rose against us. Then they would have swallowed us alive, in their burning fury against us. Then the waters would have flooded us. The torrent would have passed over our soul. Then over our soul the treacherous waters would have passed. Blessed is the Lord, Who did not make us prey to their teeth. Our soul is like a bird escaped from the snare of the hunters. The snare broke, and we escaped. Our help is in the name of the Lord, the Maker of heaven and earth.

Ps. 125 **שִׁיר הַמַּעֲלוֹת** A SONG OF ASCENTS. Those who trust in the Lord are like Mount Zion, which will not be moved and will abide forever. Jerusalem, mountains surround it, and the Lord surrounds His people from now and forever. Indeed, the rod of wickedness will not rest upon the lot of the righteous, so that the righteous will not put forth their hands unto iniquity. Do good, O Lord, to the good, and to the upright in their hearts. But as for those who turn aside their crooked ways, may the Lord carry away the workers of iniquity. Peace be upon Israel.

Ps. 126 **שִׁיר הַמַּעֲלוֹת** A SONG OF ASCENTS. When the Lord brought back the return of Zion, we were like those who dream. Then our mouth was filled with laughter and our tongue with joy. Then they said among the nations: "the Lord did great things for these." The Lord did great things for us. We were glad. Bring back our return, O Lord, like the streams in the south. Those that sow in tears will reap in joy. May he who goes out weeping, bearing the sack of seed, come home in joy, bearing his sheaves.

---

will come to recognize His greatness. This distinction accounts for the repetition in this verse. First it describes our joy when God will return us to Zion even if the nations will not recognize His great name. Such rejoicing will however be incomplete, "as if in a dream." But if our return to Zion will be accompanied by the realization among the nations that "the Lord has performed great things" for us, then, and only then, will "our mouths be filled with genuine joy and laughter" (R. Akiva Eger).

כַּאֲפִיקִים בַּנֶּגֶב – *Like the streams in the south*. Just

תהלים קכז **שִׁיר הַמַּעֲלוֹת** לִשְׁלֹמֹה, אִם־יהוה לֹא־יִבְנֶה בַיִת, שָׁוְא עָמְלוּ בוֹנָיו בּוֹ,
אִם־יהוה לֹא־יִשְׁמָר־עִיר, שָׁוְא שָׁקַד שׁוֹמֵר: שָׁוְא לָכֶם
מַשְׁכִּימֵי קוּם מְאַחֲרֵי־שֶׁבֶת, אֹכְלֵי לֶחֶם הָעֲצָבִים, כֵּן יִתֵּן לִידִידוֹ שֵׁנָא:
הִנֵּה נַחֲלַת יהוה בָּנִים, שָׂכָר פְּרִי הַבָּטֶן: כְּחִצִּים בְּיַד־גִּבּוֹר כֵּן בְּנֵי הַנְּעוּרִים:
אַשְׁרֵי הַגֶּבֶר אֲשֶׁר מִלֵּא אֶת־אַשְׁפָּתוֹ מֵהֶם, לֹא־יֵבֹשׁוּ כִּי־יְדַבְּרוּ אֶת־אוֹיְבִים
בַּשָּׁעַר:

תהלים קכח **שִׁיר הַמַּעֲלוֹת,** אַשְׁרֵי כָּל־יְרֵא יהוה, הַהֹלֵךְ בִּדְרָכָיו: יְגִיעַ כַּפֶּיךָ כִּי תֹאכֵל,
אַשְׁרֶיךָ וְטוֹב לָךְ: אֶשְׁתְּךָ כְּגֶפֶן פֹּרִיָּה בְּיַרְכְּתֵי בֵיתֶךָ, בָּנֶיךָ
כִּשְׁתִלֵי זֵיתִים, סָבִיב לְשֻׁלְחָנֶךָ: הִנֵּה כִי־כֵן יְבֹרַךְ גָּבֶר יְרֵא יהוה: יְבָרֶכְךָ יהוה
מִצִּיּוֹן, וּרְאֵה בְּטוּב יְרוּשָׁלָיִם, כֹּל יְמֵי חַיֶּיךָ: וּרְאֵה־בָנִים לְבָנֶיךָ, שָׁלוֹם עַל־
יִשְׂרָאֵל:

תהלים קכט **שִׁיר הַמַּעֲלוֹת,** רַבַּת צְרָרוּנִי מִנְּעוּרָי, יֹאמַר־נָא יִשְׂרָאֵל: רַבַּת צְרָרוּנִי
מִנְּעוּרָי, גַּם לֹא־יָכְלוּ לִי: עַל־גַּבִּי חָרְשׁוּ חֹרְשִׁים, הֶאֱרִיכוּ
לְמַעֲנִיתָם: יהוה צַדִּיק, קִצֵּץ עֲבוֹת רְשָׁעִים: יֵבֹשׁוּ וְיִסֹּגוּ אָחוֹר כֹּל שֹׂנְאֵי

as the streams in the south are dry for most of the year and suddenly become filled with powerful currents and sweeping torrents, so may all the good that we need come suddenly upon us. Another possibility is that this is a prayer that the desolate land may become filled with people who have returned from exile, like dry streams that become filled with water (R. Amos Ḥakham).

PSALM 127

שָׁוְא לָכֶם מַשְׁכִּימֵי קוּם מְאַחֲרֵי־שֶׁבֶת – *It is vain for you who rise early, who sit late*. The *Taz* understands this to refer to two types of study habits. The first approach values spending long hours, both early in the morning and late at night in study, even if it means being short of adequate sleep. The other approach is to get sufficient sleep so that we can be mentally sharp and focused. This verse teaches us that there is no inherent benefit in longer hours of study if the result is sleep deprivation that causes us to be less alert. A similar lesson is found in the words in *Ma'ariv* בְּשָׁכְבֵנוּ וּבְקוּמֵנוּ נָשִׂיחַ בְּחֻקֶּיךָ (when we lie down and when we get up we will speak of Your Torah), i.e., not just our waking hours, but even our sleeping hours are conducive to Torah, for when we have enough sleep we can arise refreshed and eager to learn (R. Eliezer Yehuda Waldenberg).

This focus on healthy study habits reflects Rambam's view. In the fifth chapter of his Introduction to *Pirkei Avot*, he writes that our goal in life should be to know God to the best of our ability, and therefore we must cultivate proper behaviors, among which Rambam includes healthy eating, drinking, and sleeping habits. This, says Rambam, will facilitate strength of character and intellect necessary to reaching the goal (Proverbs 3:6) of בְּכָל דְּרָכֶיךָ דָעֵהוּ (know Him in all your ways). Needless to say, this Maimonidean approach to healthy habits fully reflects his medical expertise (R. Basil Herring).

Ps. 127 **שִׁיר הַמַּעֲלוֹת** A SONG OF ASCENTS of Solomon. If the Lord does not build a house, those that built it have labored on it in vain. If the Lord does not guard the city, the watchman has persevered in vain. It is vain for you who rise early, who sit late, who eat the bread of toil, truly He gives His loved one sleep. Behold, children are an inheritance of the Lord, the fruit of the womb is a reward. Like arrows in the hand of a mighty man, so are the sons of one's youth. Happy is the man who has filled his quiver with them. They will not be put to shame, when they speak with the enemies in the gate.

Ps. 128 **שִׁיר הַמַּעֲלוֹת** A SONG OF ASCENTS. Happy is everyone who fears the Lord, who walks in His ways. If you eat the labor of your hands, you will be happy and it will be well with you. Your wife will be like a fruitful vine in the innermost parts of your house, your children like olive plants around your table. Behold, truly the man who fears the Lord will be blessed. May the Lord bless you from Zion, and may you see the good of Jerusalem all the days of your life. And may you see your children's children. Peace be upon Israel.

Ps. 129 **שִׁיר הַמַּעֲלוֹת** A SONG OF ASCENTS. They have greatly afflicted me from my youth, let Israel now say. They have greatly afflicted me from my youth, yet they have not prevailed over me. The plowers have plowed upon my back, they have made their furrow long. The Lord is righteous, He has cut apart the cord of the wicked. Let all who hate Zion be confounded and turned back.

PSALM 128

אֶשְׁתְּךָ כְּגֶפֶן פֹּרִיָּה בְּיַרְכְּתֵי בֵיתֶךָ, בָּנֶיךָ כִּשְׁתִלֵי זֵיתִים – *Your wife will be like a fruitful vine in the innermost parts of your house, your children like olive plants.* Olive trees can live for many years, developing strong, gnarled roots. If these are not pruned they will be surrounded by young shoots growing from the original root system, while also developing their own independent roots. The comparison in this verse of children to such olive shoots portends a dual blessing. Such children will remain connected to each other by virtue of being rooted in one tree-trunk, but they will also flourish as a result of their own strengths. The olive tree imagery is all the more striking as it follows a depiction of the family matriarch as a grapevine, which is a symbol of fertility, insofar as a vine branches out far beyond its deceptively frail trunk to produce abundant fruit (R. Elchanan Samet).

וּרְאֵה־בָנִים לְבָנֶיךָ, שָׁלוֹם עַל־יִשְׂרָאֵל – *And may you see your children's children. Peace be upon Israel.* The two halves of this verse can be connected to express a single idea. It sometimes happens that parents and children become estranged. The child might feel that the parent is not sufficiently supportive or does not truly understand the needs of the child. The parent, in turn, might feel that the child does not sufficiently appreciate what the parent has sacrificed for him or her. When in due course the child becomes a parent, this dynamic often changes for the better, for then the child can better recognize the challenges of parenthood. So it is that "when we see our children having children of their own" there is greater "peace and harmony in Israel" (R. Aryeh Levine).

צִיּוֹן: יִהְיוּ כַּחֲצִיר גַּגּוֹת שֶׁקַּדְמַת שָׁלַף יָבֵשׁ: שֶׁלֹּא מִלֵּא כַפּוֹ קוֹצֵר, וְחִצְנוֹ
מְעַמֵּר: וְלֹא אָמְרוּ הָעֹבְרִים, בִּרְכַּת־יהוה אֲלֵיכֶם, בֵּרַכְנוּ אֶתְכֶם בְּשֵׁם
יהוה:

תהלים קל **שִׁיר הַמַּעֲלוֹת,** מִמַּעֲמַקִּים קְרָאתִיךָ יהוה: אֲדֹנָי שִׁמְעָה בְקוֹלִי, תִּהְיֶינָה
אָזְנֶיךָ קַשֻּׁבוֹת לְקוֹל תַּחֲנוּנָי: אִם־עֲוֹנוֹת תִּשְׁמָר־יָהּ,
אֲדֹנָי מִי יַעֲמֹד: כִּי־עִמְּךָ הַסְּלִיחָה, לְמַעַן תִּוָּרֵא: קִוִּיתִי יהוה קִוְּתָה נַפְשִׁי,
וְלִדְבָרוֹ הוֹחָלְתִּי: נַפְשִׁי לַאדֹנָי, מִשֹּׁמְרִים לַבֹּקֶר, שֹׁמְרִים לַבֹּקֶר: יַחֵל יִשְׂרָאֵל
אֶל־יהוה, כִּי־עִם־יהוה הַחֶסֶד, וְהַרְבֵּה עִמּוֹ פְדוּת: וְהוּא יִפְדֶּה אֶת־יִשְׂרָאֵל,
מִכֹּל עֲוֹנוֹתָיו:

תהלים קלא **שִׁיר הַמַּעֲלוֹת** לְדָוִד, יהוה לֹא־גָבַהּ לִבִּי, וְלֹא־רָמוּ עֵינַי, וְלֹא־הִלַּכְתִּי
בִּגְדֹלוֹת וּבְנִפְלָאוֹת מִמֶּנִּי: אִם־לֹא שִׁוִּיתִי וְדוֹמַמְתִּי
נַפְשִׁי, כְּגָמֻל עֲלֵי אִמּוֹ, כַּגָּמֻל עָלַי נַפְשִׁי: יַחֵל יִשְׂרָאֵל אֶל־יהוה, מֵעַתָּה
וְעַד־עוֹלָם:

PSALM 130

שִׁיר הַמַּעֲלוֹת מִמַּעֲמַקִּים קְרָאתִיךָ ה׳ – *A Song of Ascents. From the depths I call out to you, O Lord.* Rambam rules that, "If a person who may be legally compelled to divorce his wife refuses to do so, a *Beit Din* may impose lashes until he says, "I consent…." This, Rambam goes on to explain, is not considered a forced, and therefore invalid, divorce, because duress only applies when one is compelled to do that which the Torah does not require. Therefore, if our evil inclination leads us to transgress the Torah, and the experience of being lashed helps us overcome its influence, that is not considered duress at all. To the contrary, it is the evil inclination that forced us to act against our true selves. Such is the case with a man who refuses to divorce his wife, inasmuch as he really desires to be part of the Jewish people, abiding by the Torah's commandments, and keeping away from transgressions, except that he has succumbed to his evil inclination (*Hilkhot Gerushin* 2:20). This psalm reflects the same principle by saying that when we pray for our own needs, that request expresses our physical self and its superficial desires. But deep down, what we really want is for God's sake, not ours. Thus the Psalmist proclaims, "מִמַּעֲמַקִּים – deep down inside of me, in my soul – קְרָאתִיךָ – I pray only for what is for Your sake. Therefore, please hear my inner, not my outer, voice" (R. Shlomo Kluger).

In biblical usage מִמַּעֲמַקִּים (out of the depths), refers to deep water. The Psalmist feels as if he is drowning. As we discover later in the psalm, however, his fear of drowning is only metaphorical, for what he is drowning in are his past sins and his resultant great distress. Thus he longs for a sign from God that He has forgiven his sins, as if to hear God say סָלַחְתִּי (I have forgiven you) (R. Yitzchak Etshalom).

יַחֵל יִשְׂרָאֵל אֶל־ה׳ – *Israel, hope for the Lord.* Generally a request might be turned down for one of three reasons: the person approached might

Let them be as the grass of the rooftops, which has withered before it is cut down, with which the reaper has not filled his hand, nor the binder of sheaves the fold of his garment. And the passers-by have not said: The blessing of the Lord be upon you. We bless you in the name of the Lord.

Ps. 130 **שִׁיר הַמַּעֲלוֹת** A SONG OF ASCENTS. From the depths I call out to you, O Lord. My Master, hear my voice. Let Your ears be attentive to the sound of my supplications. If You, Lord, pay heed to iniquities, who, my Master, will stand? Indeed, forgiveness is with You, so that You may be feared. I wait for the Lord, my soul waits, and I hope for His word. My soul waits for my Master, among those who watch for the morning, who watch for the morning. Israel, hope for the Lord, for with the Lord is loving-kindness, and with Him is abundant redemption. And He will redeem Israel from all his iniquities.

Ps. 131 **שִׁיר הַמַּעֲלוֹת** A SONG OF ASCENTS of David. O Lord, my heart is not haughty, nor are my eyes lofty. And I do not occupy myself with great things, or with things beyond my power. Surely I compose and still my soul, like a weaned child beside its mother: my soul is to me like a weaned child. Israel, hope for the Lord, from now and forever.

---

for unrelated reasons be in an angry state, he might not be in a position to help, or he might feel that the supplicant is undeserving. These verses teach that because none of these apply to God, we can always hope that He will fulfill our request without delay. Thus it states עִם ה' הַחֶסֶד (the Lord is always compassionate and not angry), and thus His state of mind is not an impediment; וְהַרְבֵּה עִמּוֹ פְדוּת (He has infinite ways to grant our request), and thus He is certainly in a position to help, and finally וְהוּא יִפְדֶּה אֶת־יִשְׂרָאֵל, מִכֹּל עֲוֹנוֹתָיו (He will redeem Israel from all its sins, meaning that He can void our sins completely), and thus we will no longer be undeserving of His redemption. For these reasons, we should always pray for the full and immediate redemption of our people, and not consider such a request to be inappropriate or impractical (Ḥafetz Ḥayyim).

PSALM 131

לֹא־גָבַהּ לִבִּי – *My heart is not haughty.* This psalm instructs us to love one another, in a spirit of humility, brotherhood and fellowship. From it we learn the value of humility, to avoid arrogance or any feeling of superior status relative to our fellows (Meiri).

אִם־לֹא שִׁוִּיתִי וְדוֹמַמְתִּי נַפְשִׁי – *Surely I compose and still my soul.* This phrase refers to two levels of humility, illustrated by how we respond to being insulted. The first is when we are so humble that if someone affronts us we absorb the hurt without responding to the perpetrator in any way. The second is when we not only do not respond to such abuse, we don't even feel aggrieved in the first place, because we are so self-effacing that honor and insult at the hands of others are all the same to us, neither are of special significance. Thus the Psalmist proclaims, "If I have not reached the level where honor and insult are equal in my eyes, at least I am able to overcome the urge to respond to those who abuse me" (R. Ḥayyim Pelaggi).

תהלים קלב **שִׁיר הַמַּעֲלוֹת,** זְכוֹר־יהוה לְדָוִד אֵת כָּל־עֻנּוֹתוֹ: אֲשֶׁר נִשְׁבַּע לַיהוה, נָדַר
לַאֲבִיר יַעֲקֹב: אִם־אָבֹא בְּאֹהֶל בֵּיתִי, אִם־אֶעֱלֶה עַל־עֶרֶשׂ
יְצוּעָי: אִם־אֶתֵּן שְׁנָת לְעֵינָי, לְעַפְעַפַּי תְּנוּמָה: עַד־אֶמְצָא מָקוֹם לַיהוה,
מִשְׁכָּנוֹת לַאֲבִיר יַעֲקֹב: הִנֵּה־שְׁמַעֲנוּהָ בְאֶפְרָתָה, מְצָאנוּהָ בִּשְׂדֵי־יָעַר: נָבוֹאָה
לְמִשְׁכְּנוֹתָיו, נִשְׁתַּחֲוֶה לַהֲדֹם רַגְלָיו: קוּמָה יהוה לִמְנוּחָתֶךָ, אַתָּה וַאֲרוֹן
עֻזֶּךָ: כֹּהֲנֶיךָ יִלְבְּשׁוּ־צֶדֶק, וַחֲסִידֶיךָ יְרַנֵּנוּ: בַּעֲבוּר דָּוִד עַבְדֶּךָ, אַל־תָּשֵׁב פְּנֵי
מְשִׁיחֶךָ: נִשְׁבַּע־יהוה לְדָוִד, אֱמֶת לֹא־יָשׁוּב מִמֶּנָּה, מִפְּרִי בִטְנְךָ אָשִׁית לְכִסֵּא־
לָךְ: אִם־יִשְׁמְרוּ בָנֶיךָ בְּרִיתִי, וְעֵדֹתִי זוֹ אֲלַמְּדֵם, גַּם־בְּנֵיהֶם עֲדֵי־עַד, יֵשְׁבוּ
לְכִסֵּא־לָךְ: כִּי־בָחַר יהוה בְּצִיּוֹן, אִוָּהּ לְמוֹשָׁב לוֹ: זֹאת־מְנוּחָתִי עֲדֵי־עַד, פֹּה
אֵשֵׁב כִּי אִוִּתִיהָ: צֵידָהּ בָּרֵךְ אֲבָרֵךְ, אֶבְיוֹנֶיהָ אַשְׂבִּיעַ לָחֶם: וְכֹהֲנֶיהָ אַלְבִּישׁ
יֶשַׁע, וַחֲסִידֶיהָ רַנֵּן יְרַנֵּנוּ: שָׁם אַצְמִיחַ קֶרֶן לְדָוִד, עָרַכְתִּי נֵר לִמְשִׁיחִי: אוֹיְבָיו
אַלְבִּישׁ בֹּשֶׁת, וְעָלָיו יָצִיץ נִזְרוֹ:

תהלים קלג **שִׁיר הַמַּעֲלוֹת** לְדָוִד, הִנֵּה מַה־טּוֹב וּמַה־נָּעִים, שֶׁבֶת אַחִים גַּם־יָחַד: כַּשֶּׁמֶן
הַטּוֹב עַל־הָרֹאשׁ, יֹרֵד עַל־הַזָּקָן, זְקַן־אַהֲרֹן שֶׁיֹּרֵד עַל־פִּי

PSALM 132

אִם־אָבֹא בְּאֹהֶל בֵּיתִי... עַד־אֶמְצָא מָקוֹם לַה׳ – *I will not come under the roof of my house... Until I find a place for the Lord.* With these words David proclaims that he will not settle into the royal palace as long as he has not found the right place to build God's house, i.e., the Temple. The problem with this statement is that, as the Gemara (*Zevaḥim* 54b) teaches, we learn from Deuteronomy 12:11 that God Himself, and not David, chose the location for the future Temple. The answer is found in the *Midrash Sifrei* quoting Deuteronomy 12:5, לְשִׁכְנוֹ תִדְרְשׁוּ וּבָאתָ שָׁמָּה (You shall seek His habitation and there will you go). That is, the people are to look for an appropriate location, and once found, they should request God's confirmation of their choice, via a prophetic vision. This teaches us the importance of engaging in human effort and initiative, as opposed to always waiting passively for God's will to materialize (R. Yitzḥak Ze'ev Soloveitchik).

הִנֵּה־שְׁמַעֲנוּהָ בְאֶפְרָתָה – *Behold, we heard it in Ephratah.* Prophets had told us that the previous stations of the Tabernacle, in Shilo and Nov, were temporary locations, and that eventually, the Temple would be built near Efrata, but the precise location had not yet been revealed to us (Radak).

PSALMS 133

מַה־טּוֹב וּמַה־נָּעִים... כַּשֶּׁמֶן הַטּוֹב עַל־הָרֹאשׁ... – *Behold, how good and how pleasant... Like the good oil upon the head.* This verse refers to the important benefits that accrue when Jews study Torah together. The Psalmist illustrates the point by referring to the oil with which Moses anointed Aaron. The Torah states that Moses "took oil," "poured it" on Aaron's head, and "sanctified him" by "anointing him" (Lev. 8:10–12). The duplicative final phrase can be accounted for if we understand that the anointing oil itself was sanctified as it was

Ps. 132 **שִׁיר הַמַּעֲלוֹת** A SONG OF ASCENTS. O Lord, remember for David all his affliction, What he swore to the Lord, what he vowed to the mighty One of Jacob: I will not come under the roof of my house, nor will I mount my bed, I will not give sleep to my eyes, or slumber to my eyelids, Until I find a place for the Lord, a habitation for the mighty One of Jacob. Behold, we heard it in Ephratah, we found it in Sedei-Ya'ar. Let us come into His dwelling places, let us bow down to His footstool. Arise, O Lord, to Your resting place, You and the Ark of Your strength. May Your priests be clothed in righteousness, and may Your pious ones shout for joy. For the sake of David your servant, do not turn away the face of Your anointed. The Lord has sworn to David, in truth, He will not turn back from it: From the fruit of your body I will place upon your throne. If your children will keep My covenant and My testimony that I will teach them, then their children will sit on your throne forevermore. Indeed, the Lord has chosen Zion, He had desired it for His habitation: This is My resting place forever. Here I will dwell, for I desire it. I will abundantly bless her food. I will satisfy her poor with bread. And I will clothe her priests with salvation, and her pious ones will surely shout for joy. There will I make the horn of David flourish, I prepare a lamp for My anointed. I will clothe his enemies with shame, but on him will his crown shine.

Ps. 133 **שִׁיר הַמַּעֲלוֹת** A SONG OF ASCENTS of David. Behold, how good and how pleasant it is for brothers to sit together. Like the good oil upon the head that descends upon the beard, the beard of Aaron, that descends over the border

---

poured on Aaron's head. Moses then took that newly sanctified oil and anointed Aaron with it, a reciprocal process consistent with Aaron's own peace-seeking character. So it is too, as the Psalmist puts it, when "colleagues sit together" and study Torah, arguing for their respective positions, and thereby stimulating greater understanding. The Gemara (*Ta'anit* 7a) similarly compares Torah study to iron, in which two blunt rods can be sharpened by rubbing them against each other. This is the case when students question their teachers, thereby helping both student and teacher to gain better understanding of the subject at hand. This, says this verse, is like the oil that was sanctified by contact with Aaron's head, which in due course anointed Aaron himself, in accordance with his own special character (R. Shlomo Kluger).

Aaron loved and pursued peace at all times, seeking always to bring people together in harmony. Even for himself, he did not resent the fact that his younger brother, and not he himself, was chosen, for he genuinely rejoiced at Moses' election. Thus he epitomized "brothers who dwell together" without rancor or argument, but in peace and harmony. This is why he was chosen as the High Priest, and as a result he enjoyed the blessings described in the ensuing verse (*Netziv*).

מְדּוֹתָיו: כְּטַל־חֶרְמוֹן שֶׁיֹּרֵד עַל־הַרְרֵי צִיּוֹן, כִּי שָׁם צִוָּה יהוה אֶת־הַבְּרָכָה, חַיִּים עַד־הָעוֹלָם:

תהלים קלד **שִׁיר הַמַּעֲלוֹת,** הִנֵּה בָּרְכוּ אֶת־יהוה כָּל־עַבְדֵי יהוה, הָעֹמְדִים בְּבֵית־יהוה בַּלֵּילוֹת: שְׂאוּ־יְדֵכֶם קֹדֶשׁ, וּבָרְכוּ אֶת־יהוה: יְבָרֶכְךָ יהוה מִצִּיּוֹן, עֹשֵׂה שָׁמַיִם וָאָרֶץ:

קדיש יתום

The following prayer, said by mourners, requires the presence of a מנין*.*
A transliteration can be found on page 1345.

אבל: **יִתְגַּדַּל** וְיִתְקַדַּשׁ שְׁמֵהּ רַבָּא (קהל: אָמֵן), בְּעָלְמָא דִּי בְרָא כִרְעוּתֵהּ. וְיַמְלִיךְ מַלְכוּתֵהּ, בְּחַיֵּיכוֹן וּבְיוֹמֵיכוֹן וּבְחַיֵּי דְכָל בֵּית יִשְׂרָאֵל, בַּעֲגָלָא וּבִזְמַן קָרִיב, וְאִמְרוּ אָמֵן. (קהל: אָמֵן)

קהל ואבל: יְהֵא שְׁמֵהּ רַבָּא מְבָרַךְ לְעָלַם וּלְעָלְמֵי עָלְמַיָּא.

אבל: יִתְבָּרַךְ וְיִשְׁתַּבַּח וְיִתְפָּאַר, וְיִתְרוֹמַם וְיִתְנַשֵּׂא וְיִתְהַדָּר וְיִתְעַלֶּה וְיִתְהַלָּל שְׁמֵהּ דְּקֻדְשָׁא בְּרִיךְ הוּא (קהל: בְּרִיךְ הוּא), לְעֵלָּא מִן כָּל בִּרְכָתָא / בשבת שובה: לְעֵלָּא (וּ)לְעֵלָּא מִכָּל בִּרְכָתָא/ וְשִׁירָתָא, תֻּשְׁבְּחָתָא וְנֶחֱמָתָא דַּאֲמִירָן בְּעָלְמָא, וְאִמְרוּ אָמֵן. (קהל: אָמֵן)

יְהֵא שְׁלָמָא רַבָּא מִן שְׁמַיָּא וְחַיִּים, עָלֵינוּ וְעַל כָּל יִשְׂרָאֵל, וְאִמְרוּ אָמֵן. (קהל: אָמֵן)

Bow, take three steps back, as if taking leave of the Divine Presence, then bow, first left, then right, then center, while saying:

עֹשֶׂה שָׁלוֹם / בשבת שובה: הַשָּׁלוֹם/ בִּמְרוֹמָיו, הוּא יַעֲשֶׂה שָׁלוֹם עָלֵינוּ, וְעַל כָּל יִשְׂרָאֵל, וְאִמְרוּ אָמֵן. (קהל: אָמֵן)

כְּשֶׁמֶן הַטּוֹב עַל־הָרֹאשׁ... כְּטַל־חֶרְמוֹן – *Like the good oil upon the head... So the dew of Hermon* (previous page). These two verses are a blessing for the assembly of pilgrims, and thus for all of Israel: May the dew of the Ḥermon – a tall mountain, which here stands in for all hills and mountains of the entire land – be as plentiful as the oil that one applies to the head. It was customary to anoint oneself with oil, especially on festive occasions, and the oil would drip down onto one's beard and collar. Since the Songs of Ascent were spoken at or after visiting the Temple, the psalm refers to the oil on the heads of the priests, particularly the High Priest. These two verses are thus a blessing for plentiful dew and rain (R. Amos Ḥakham).

of his garments. So the dew of Hermon that descends upon the mountains of Zion. For there the Lord has commanded the blessing, life forevermore.

Ps. 134 **שִׁיר הַמַּעֲלוֹת** A SONG OF ASCENTS. Behold, bless the Lord, all you servants of the Lord, who stand in the house of the Lord in the nights. Raise your hands to the sanctuary, and bless the Lord. May the Lord, the Maker of heaven and earth, bless you from Zion.

MOURNER'S KADDISH

The following prayer, said by mourners, requires the presence of a minyan. A transliteration can be found on page 1345.

Mourner: **יִתְגַּדַּל** EXALTED AND HALLOWED may God's great name be, in the world He created as He willed. May He reign in your lifetimes and in your days, and in the lifetime of the whole house of Israel, speedily and soon, and say, Amen.

All: May His great name be blessed forever and all time.

Mourner: Blessed and praised, honored, extolled, glorified, adored and exalted above all be the name of the Holy One, blessed is He, (*Between Rosh Hashana & Yom Kippur:* above and) beyond any blessing, hymn, praise, or expressions of consolation that may be uttered in this world, and say, Amen.

May abundant peace descend from heaven, as well as life, for us and for all Israel, and say, Amen.

Bow, take three steps back, as if taking leave of the Divine Presence, then bow, first left, then right, then center, while saying:

May He Who makes peace in the highest heaven, make peace for us, and for all Israel, and say, Amen.

PSALM 134

הָעֹמְדִים בְּבֵית־ה' בַּלֵּילוֹת – *Who stand in the house of the Lord in the nights.* This refers to the pilgrims who were in the Temple at night, either to attend the preparations before the beginning of the morning service (Mishna *Yoma* 1:8), or for holiday festivities in the Women's Courtyard. According to the view that these Songs of Ascent were intended to be recited on Sukkot, this may refer to the special festivities of the drawing of the water.

יְבָרֶכְךָ ה' מִצִּיּוֹן – *May the Lord... bless you from Zion.* As this psalm concludes the entire Songs of Ascent liturgy, it might have been the priests' parting blessing to the pilgrims as they took their leave to return to their homes (R. Amos Ḥakham).

פרקי אבות*

One of the following chapters is read each שבת *after* פסח *until the* שבת *before* ראש השנה*.*
On the last three שבתות *before* ראש השנה*, two chapters are read.*

פרק ראשון

סנהדרין צ.
ישעיה ס

כָּל יִשְׂרָאֵל יֵשׁ לָהֶם חֵלֶק לָעוֹלָם הַבָּא. שֶׁנֶּאֱמַר: וְעַמֵּךְ כֻּלָּם צַדִּיקִים, לְעוֹלָם יִירְשׁוּ אָרֶץ, נֵצֶר מַטָּעַי, מַעֲשֵׂה יָדַי לְהִתְפָּאֵר:

א **מֹשֶׁה** קִבֵּל תּוֹרָה מִסִּינַי וּמְסָרָהּ לִיהוֹשֻׁעַ, וִיהוֹשֻׁעַ לִזְקֵנִים, וּזְקֵנִים לִנְבִיאִים, וּנְבִיאִים מְסָרוּהָ לְאַנְשֵׁי כְנֶסֶת הַגְּדוֹלָה. הֵם אָמְרוּ שְׁלֹשָׁה דְבָרִים: הֱווּ מְתוּנִים בַּדִּין, וְהַעֲמִידוּ תַלְמִידִים הַרְבֵּה, וַעֲשׂוּ סְיָג לַתּוֹרָה:

* The text of *Pirkei Avot* found here follows that of the authoritative *Mehadurat Albeck*.

פִּרְקֵי אָבוֹת / PIRKEI AVOT
Pirkei Avot translates literally as "Chapters of the Fathers." A title that would more accurately reflect the nature and content of these Mishnaic chapters would be "Moral Aphorisms of the Sages." It constitutes a self-contained Mishnaic Tractate of the Talmud, albeit one that has no explanatory Gemara.

The practice of studying *Pirkei Avot* between *Minḥa* and *Ma'ariv* on Shabbat afternoon first appears in the *Seder R. Amram Gaon* in the name of R. Sar Shalom Gaon, where it is described as intended to honor the memory of Moses who passed away on Shabbat afternoon.

Avot is written in the style of biblical wisdom literature, such as Proverbs, Ecclesiastes, and Job. Like those books it employs riddles, numerical sayings, metaphor, and parallelism. It is replete with subtle literary devices that help to imprint its ideas in the reader's mind. It likewise employs themes familiar from those wisdom works, focusing on rabbinic advice on how to live a good life, with an emphasis on ethics. It is also unique in praising Torah study as the pillar of the world and the crown of the Jewish people, indeed the highest form of wisdom. The overall structure centers around the Torah's chain of transmission, from Sinai through the Tannaitic period (Prof. Amram Tropper).

There are additional explanations for studying *Avot* on Shabbat afternoon. *Maḥzor Vitry* writes that *Avot* was introduced because one learns from it fear of heaven and proper behavior (cf. *Bava Kama* 30a), and since the masses assemble in the synagogue for the Torah reading on Shabbat afternoon, it is a propitious time for communal study. *Sefer HaMaḥkim* adds that this is particularly true in the summer months, when there is time to expound at length. Moreover, in the summer, one can accommodate a study session without concern for missing the third meal (Maharal).

The first five chapters are Mishnaic in origin, while a sixth chapter, known as קִנְיַן תּוֹרָה (acquisition of Torah), found in the minor tractate *Kalla Rabbati* and *Seder Eliyahu Zuta*, is appended to the five of *Avot* to complete the six Shabbatot in the *Sefira* period. Its themes are congruent with those of *Avot*, and it is an apt prelude to the Yom Tov of Shavuot.

כָּל יִשְׂרָאֵל יֵשׁ לָהֶם חֵלֶק לָעוֹלָם הַבָּא – *All Israel have a share in the World to Come.* The Jewish people as a whole possesses a soul that encompasses every individual Jew throughout history. The soul of every individual Jew has its share in the next world, by virtue of its deep desire to be connected to that world. The encompassing soul of the Jewish people illuminates each individual soul, and the result is that its well-being is in proportion to the strength

ETHICS OF THE FATHERS

One of the following chapters is read each Shabbat after Pesaḥ until the Shabbat before Rosh HaShana. On the last three Shabbatot before Rosh HaShana, two chapters are read.

CHAPTER ONE

Sanhedrin 90a
Is. 60

ALL ISRAEL have a share in the World to Come. As it is said, "Your people shall all be righteous and shall inherit the land forever. They are the shoot of My planting, the work of My hands in which I glory."

1. מֹשֶׁה MOSES received the Torah from Sinai. He transmitted it to Joshua, Joshua to the elders, and they to the prophets, who transmitted it to the Men of the Great Assembly. The Men of the Great Assembly established three principles: Be deliberate in judgment; raise up many disciples; and make a fence around the Torah.

---

of its connection to the soul of the nation. The illumination of the next world shines on every individual in proportion to his embrace of that larger soul (R. Avraham Yitzḥak HaKohen Kook).

CHAPTER 1

מֹשֶׁה קִבֵּל תּוֹרָה מִסִּינַי – *Moses received the Torah from Sinai.* This phrase precedes all the teachings that follow in this tractate to teach us a fundamental principle of Jewish ethics. While all the other ethical codes, developed and taught by the wise men of the nations of the world, have their origin in reason and logic, that is not true of Jewish ethics. Therefore the first *mishna* states clearly that these ethical teachings did not originate with mere rational deduction, but were indeed given by God to Moses (R. Ovadia of Bartenura).

וּמְסָרָהּ לִיהוֹשֻׁעַ – *He transmitted it to Joshua.* In his introduction to his *Mishne Torah*, Rambam states that Moses taught the תּוֹרָה שֶׁבְּעַל פֶּה (Oral Law) to the seventy elders as well as to Eleazar, Pinḥas, and Joshua. Then he adds, "And to Joshua who was the disciple of Moses he gave (מָסַר) the Oral Law and commanded him regarding it." Apparently Rambam understood this *mishna* to say that the obligation to ensure the transmission (in Hebrew "*mesira*") of the Oral Law to the next generation was entrusted to Joshua. This *Mesora* had two aspects. The first was the commentary received from God explaining the written Torah. The second consisted of various decrees, enactments and safeguards enacted by Moses. This dual aspect of the *Mesora* continued generation after generation. That is, the commentary was transmitted by way of teaching textual Torah analysis with resulting practice to follow majority rule, while the decrees and enactments of that and subsequent generations of prophets and sages were transmitted by way of personal testimony regarding past decrees or practices. This latter form of transmission even took precedence over textual analysis and majority rule (R. Joseph B. Soloveitchik).

וַעֲשׂוּ סְיָג לַתּוֹרָה – *Make a fence around the Torah.* There are numerous halakhot intended to minimize danger to life. Some are explicit in the Torah (such as the obligation in Deuteronomy 22:8 to build a parapet on the roof of a house), while others are rabbinic in origin (such as the requirement to cover an open pit or other obstacle). But we are also vulnerable in the spiritual realm, where we are continually exposed to disaster in areas of religious observance. This *mishna* accordingly prescribes that regulatory

ב שִׁמְעוֹן הַצַּדִּיק הָיָה מִשְּׁיָרֵי כְנֶסֶת הַגְּדוֹלָה. הוּא הָיָה אוֹמֵר: עַל שְׁלֹשָׁה
דְבָרִים הָעוֹלָם עוֹמֵד, עַל הַתּוֹרָה, וְעַל הָעֲבוֹדָה, וְעַל גְּמִילוּת חֲסָדִים.

ג אַנְטִיגְנוֹס אִישׁ סוֹכוֹ קִבֵּל מִשִּׁמְעוֹן הַצַּדִּיק. הוּא הָיָה אוֹמֵר: אַל תִּהְיוּ
כַּעֲבָדִים הַמְשַׁמְּשִׁים אֶת הָרַב עַל מְנָת לְקַבֵּל פְּרָס, אֶלָּא הֱווּ כַּעֲבָדִים
הַמְשַׁמְּשִׁים אֶת הָרַב שֶׁלֹּא עַל מְנָת לְקַבֵּל פְּרָס, וִיהִי מוֹרָא שָׁמַיִם עֲלֵיכֶם.

ד יוֹסֵי בֶּן יוֹעֶזֶר אִישׁ צְרֵדָה וְיוֹסֵי בֶּן יוֹחָנָן אִישׁ יְרוּשָׁלַיִם קִבְּלוּ מֵהֶם. יוֹסֵי בֶּן
יוֹעֶזֶר אִישׁ צְרֵדָה אוֹמֵר: יְהִי בֵיתְךָ בֵּית וַעַד לַחֲכָמִים, וֶהֱוֵי מִתְאַבֵּק בַּעֲפַר
רַגְלֵיהֶם, וֶהֱוֵי שׁוֹתֶה בַצָּמָא אֶת דִּבְרֵיהֶם.

ה יוֹסֵי בֶּן יוֹחָנָן אִישׁ יְרוּשָׁלַיִם אוֹמֵר: יְהִי בֵיתְךָ פָּתוּחַ לִרְוָחָה, וְיִהְיוּ עֲנִיִּים
בְּנֵי בֵיתֶךָ, וְאַל תַּרְבֶּה שִׂיחָה עִם הָאִשָּׁה. בְּאִשְׁתּוֹ אָמְרוּ, קַל וָחֹמֶר בְּאֵשֶׁת
חֲבֵרוֹ. מִכָּאן אָמְרוּ חֲכָמִים: כָּל הַמַּרְבֶּה שִׂיחָה עִם הָאִשָּׁה, גּוֹרֵם רָעָה לְעַצְמוֹ,
וּבוֹטֵל מִדִּבְרֵי תוֹרָה, וְסוֹפוֹ יוֹרֵשׁ גֵּיהִנֹּם.

ו יְהוֹשֻׁעַ בֶּן פְּרַחְיָה וְנִתַּאי הָאַרְבֵּלִי קִבְּלוּ מֵהֶם. יְהוֹשֻׁעַ בֶּן פְּרַחְיָה אוֹמֵר:
עֲשֵׂה לְךָ רַב, וּקְנֵה לְךָ חָבֵר, וֶהֱוֵי דָן אֶת כָּל הָאָדָם לְכַף זְכוּת.

ז נִתַּאי הָאַרְבֵּלִי אוֹמֵר: הַרְחֵק מִשָּׁכֵן רָע, וְאַל תִּתְחַבֵּר לָרָשָׁע, וְאַל תִּתְיָאֵשׁ
מִן הַפֻּרְעָנוּת.

ח יְהוּדָה בֶּן טַבַּאי וְשִׁמְעוֹן בֶּן שָׁטָח קִבְּלוּ מֵהֶם. יְהוּדָה בֶּן טַבַּאי אוֹמֵר: אַל
תַּעַשׂ עַצְמְךָ כְּעוֹרְכֵי הַדַּיָּנִין, וּכְשֶׁיִּהְיוּ בַּעֲלֵי הַדִּין עוֹמְדִים לְפָנֶיךָ יִהְיוּ
בְעֵינֶיךָ כִּרְשָׁעִים, וּכְשֶׁנִּפְטָרִים מִלְּפָנֶיךָ יִהְיוּ בְעֵינֶיךָ כְּזַכָּאִין, כְּשֶׁקִּבְּלוּ
עֲלֵיהֶם אֶת הַדִּין.

ט שִׁמְעוֹן בֶּן שָׁטָח אוֹמֵר: הֱוֵי מַרְבֶּה לַחֲקֹר אֶת הָעֵדִים, וֶהֱוֵי זָהִיר בִּדְבָרֶיךָ,
שֶׁמָּא מִתּוֹכָם יִלְמְדוּ לְשַׁקֵּר.

The words of Rambam carry particular resonance in an age when so many acquire their knowledge primarily through long distance and on-line learning, while having very limited face-to-face access to teachers and fellow students.

וּקְנֵה לְךָ חָבֵר – *Get yourself ... a study partner*. Rambam explains this *mishna* by saying that there are three types of friendship.

1. Pragmatic friendships in which two people have a practical relationship with agreed upon benefits, as happens with a business

"fences" or restrictions be enacted around basic religious laws, because we are often distracted by temptation (R. Joseph B. Soloveitchik).

עֲשֵׂה לְךָ רַב – *Get yourself a teacher*. Self-tutoring is not as good as when we learn from a teacher, for what is learned from someone else is generally better understood and remembered. This is true even if the only available person is not objectively qualified to be your teacher. The very act of discussion, give and take, and mutually respectful dialogue, brings great benefit (Rambam).

2. Simon the Just, one of the last members of the Great Assembly, used to say that the world endures on account of three things: Torah study, serving God, and acts of kindness.
3. Antigonos of Sokho, who received the tradition from Simon the Just, used to say, "Do not be like servants who serve their master in order to receive a reward; instead, be like servants who serve their master without thought of reward, and let the fear of heaven be upon you."
4. Yose ben Yoezer of Tzereida and Yose ben Yoḥanan of Jerusalem were next in the line of tradition. Yose ben Yoezer of Tzereida said, "Make your house a meeting place for the sages; sit in the dust at their feet and thirstily drink in their words."
5. Yose ben Yoḥanan of Jerusalem used to say, "Let your house be open wide so that the poor may join your household. Do not engage in too much conversation with a woman." If he said this of one's own wife, how much the more does it apply to the wife of another. Based on this the sages said, "One who converses too much with a woman causes himself harm, is distracted from Torah study, and eventually will inherit Gehenna."
6. Joshua of Peraḥya and Nittai of Arbel received the tradition from them. Joshua ben Peraḥya used to say, "Get yourself a teacher and arrange for a study partner. When judging people, give everyone the benefit of the doubt."
7. Nittai of Arbel said, "Stay far from a bad neighbor. Do not associate with an evil man. Never doubt the certainty of retribution."
8. Judah ben Tabbai and Simeon ben Shataḥ received the tradition from them. Judah ben Tabbai used to say, "When presiding as a judge, do not act as an advocate. Treat both of the litigants standing before you as if they were guilty; but after the verdict is given, treat them both as innocent, after they will have accepted the ruling of the court."
9. Simeon ben Shataḥ would say, "Examine the witnesses thoroughly; be careful what you say, so as not to give the witnesses an opening to testify falsely."

---

partnership. This kind of friendship lasts only so long as each one is useful to the other, for there is no deeper bond between them. See 5:19 below, describing a similar love relationship.

2. Empathetic friendships that share feelings, both sad and joyful. This relationship lightens life's burdens and heightens its celebrations. Such friendships endure longer than pragmatic ones.
3. Value friendships that are based on a shared commitment and dedication to a noble ideal or value, a unity of purpose and goal, transcending personal concerns.

י שְׁמַעְיָה וְאַבְטַלְיוֹן קִבְּלוּ מֵהֶם. שְׁמַעְיָה אוֹמֵר: אֱהֹב אֶת הַמְּלָאכָה, וּשְׂנָא אֶת הָרַבָּנוּת, וְאַל תִּתְוַדַּע לָרָשׁוּת.

יא אַבְטַלְיוֹן אוֹמֵר: חֲכָמִים הִזָּהֲרוּ בְּדִבְרֵיכֶם, שֶׁמָּא תָחוֹבוּ חוֹבַת גָּלוּת, וְתִגְלוּ לִמְקוֹם מַיִם הָרָעִים, וְיִשְׁתּוּ הַתַּלְמִידִים הַבָּאִים אַחֲרֵיכֶם וְיָמוּתוּ, וְנִמְצָא שֵׁם שָׁמַיִם מִתְחַלֵּל.

יב הִלֵּל וְשַׁמַּאי קִבְּלוּ מֵהֶם. הִלֵּל אוֹמֵר: הֱוֵי מִתַּלְמִידָיו שֶׁל אַהֲרֹן, אוֹהֵב שָׁלוֹם וְרוֹדֵף שָׁלוֹם, אוֹהֵב אֶת הַבְּרִיּוֹת וּמְקָרְבָן לַתּוֹרָה.

יג הוּא הָיָה אוֹמֵר: נְגַד שְׁמָא אֲבַד שְׁמֵהּ, וּדְלָא מוֹסִיף יָסוּף, וּדְלָא יָלֵף קְטָלָא חַיָּב, וּדְאִשְׁתַּמַּשׁ בְּתָגָא חֲלָף.

יד הוּא הָיָה אוֹמֵר: אִם אֵין אֲנִי לִי מִי לִי, וּכְשֶׁאֲנִי לְעַצְמִי מָה אֲנִי, וְאִם לֹא עַכְשָׁו אֵימָתָי.

טו שַׁמַּאי אוֹמֵר: עֲשֵׂה תוֹרָתְךָ קֶבַע, אֱמֹר מְעַט וַעֲשֵׂה הַרְבֵּה, וֶהֱוֵי מְקַבֵּל אֶת כָּל הָאָדָם בְּסֵבֶר פָּנִים יָפוֹת.

טז רַבָּן גַּמְלִיאֵל אוֹמֵר: עֲשֵׂה לְךָ רַב, וְהִסְתַּלֵּק מִן הַסָּפֵק, וְאַל תַּרְבֶּה לְעַשֵּׂר אֻמָּדוֹת.

יז שִׁמְעוֹן בְּנוֹ אוֹמֵר: כָּל יָמַי גָּדַלְתִּי בֵּין הַחֲכָמִים, וְלֹא מָצָאתִי לַגּוּף טוֹב מִשְּׁתִיקָה, וְלֹא הַמִּדְרָשׁ עִקָּר אֶלָּא הַמַּעֲשֶׂה, וְכָל הַמַּרְבֶּה דְבָרִים מֵבִיא חֵטְא.

This third level of friendship is what the partners in a marriage should strive to accomplish, for when there is a higher ideal to which their union is devoted their marriage will thrive. It is also the ideal relationship between a *rebbe* and his student (R. Joseph B. Soloveitchik).

הֱוֵי מִתַּלְמִידָיו שֶׁל אַהֲרֹן, אוֹהֵב שָׁלוֹם וְרוֹדֵף שָׁלוֹם – *Be of the disciples of Aaron, loving peace and pursuing peace.* This is a world of separation, division and opposition. God Himself created the cosmos by separating its parts, and human history begins with separation and conflict, as seen in the lives of Cain and Abel. Our highest task is to overcome those separations and divisions to the best of our ability. Aaron was uniquely suited to this task, for by nature he was an אוֹהֵב אֶת הַבְּרִיּוֹת (he loved people). His appointment as the High Priest was intended to unify the people at its central point (i.e., the Tabernacle) via communal sacrifices offered on their behalf, and by means of teaching the Torah, which is the great unifying force in Jewish life. In this, Aaron was the opposite of Koraḥ. In this *mishna* Hillel urges us to imitate Aaron, who not only loved peace in principle, he practiced it in detail, by pursuing every opportunity to increase it. Furthermore he not only ran after people who were distancing themselves from each other in dispute, he also ran after them when they were running away from God. This he accomplished in the main by teaching them God's Torah, which is not only filled with wisdom but also peace and harmony, like God Himself, one of Whose names is Shalom. Finally, it is significant that this *mishna* was formulated by none other than Hillel, for he was himself the unifying leader of his generation, distinguished by

10. Shemaya and Avtalyon received the tradition from them. Shemaya said, "Love work, despise being in a position of authority, and do not make yourself known to the political authorities."

11. Avtalyon used to say, "Sages, be careful what you say, lest you condemn yourselves to exile someplace where the waters of learning are impure, because then the disciples who follow you will drink of them and die, and God's name will be desecrated."

12. Hillel and Shammai received the tradition from them. Hillel used to say, "Be of the disciples of Aaron, loving peace and pursuing peace, loving your fellow human beings, and drawing them near to Torah."

13. He also would say, "One who seeks fame destroys his name. One who does not increase one's knowledge decreases it. One who does not study is deserving of death. One who uses the crown of Torah for self-gratification will have a premature death."

14. He also used to say, "If I am not for myself, who will be for me? But if I am for myself alone, what am I? And if not now, when?"

15. Shammai would say, "Set a fixed time for Torah study. Say little but do much. Receive all people in a friendly manner."

16. Rabban Gamliel used to say, "Get yourself a teacher to keep you free of doubt. Do not make a practice of estimating your tithe rather than calculating it."

17. Simeon ben Rabban Gamliel used to say, "All my days I have lived among the sages, and I have found there is nothing better than silence. Theoretical learning is not the goal, but rather its practical application. Talking too much leads to sin."

---

virtue of the Torah he taught and the humility he practiced (*Shabbat* 31a) (Maharal).

אִם אֵין אֲנִי לִי מִי לִי... וְאִם לֹא עַכְשָׁו אֵימָתַי – *If I am not for myself, who will be for me? ... And if not now, when?* We must take responsibility for developing our character traits. We cannot escape that duty by claiming "I have a bad nature" or "I have no choice but to act in negative ways," for we are completely free to make the ethical decisions before us. Hillel here urges us to take deliberate steps toward self-improvement and moral responsibility, for if we do not work on our ethical behavior no one else can do it on our behalf. Even if we feel that we will never be fully ethical, no matter our efforts, we should never stop trying to change for the better, for we are creatures of habit, and with each passing day change and self-improvement become more and more difficult. This is certainly true as we grow older and more set it in our ways. As Proverbs 22:6 states, "Teach the young in their ways, for when they grow older they will not depart therefrom" (Rambam).

וְלֹא מָצָאתִי לַגּוּף טוֹב מִשְּׁתִיקָה – *And I have found there is nothing better than silence*. The Gemara (*Ḥullin* 89a) says that we should make it our

יח רַבָּן שִׁמְעוֹן בֶּן גַּמְלִיאֵל אוֹמֵר: עַל שְׁלֹשָׁה דְבָרִים הָעוֹלָם קַיָּם, עַל הַדִּין,
זכריה ח וְעַל הָאֱמֶת, וְעַל הַשָּׁלוֹם. שֶׁנֶּאֱמַר: אֱמֶת וּמִשְׁפַּט שָׁלוֹם שִׁפְטוּ בְּשַׁעֲרֵיכֶם:

מכות כג: רַבִּי חֲנַנְיָא בֶּן עֲקַשְׁיָא אוֹמֵר: רָצָה הַקָּדוֹשׁ בָּרוּךְ הוּא לְזַכּוֹת אֶת יִשְׂרָאֵל, לְפִיכָךְ הִרְבָּה
ישעיה מב לָהֶם תּוֹרָה וּמִצְוֹת. שֶׁנֶּאֱמַר: יהוה חָפֵץ לְמַעַן צִדְקוֹ, יַגְדִּיל תּוֹרָה וְיַאְדִּיר:

If there is a מנין*, mourners say* קדיש דרבנן *(page 724).*

פרק שני

סנהדרין צ. ישעיה ס כָּל יִשְׂרָאֵל יֵשׁ לָהֶם חֵלֶק לָעוֹלָם הַבָּא. שֶׁנֶּאֱמַר: וְעַמֵּךְ כֻּלָּם צַדִּיקִים, לְעוֹלָם יִירְשׁוּ אָרֶץ, נֵצֶר מַטָּעַי, מַעֲשֵׂה יָדַי לְהִתְפָּאֵר:

א **רַבִּי** אוֹמֵר: אֵיזוֹ הִיא דֶּרֶךְ יְשָׁרָה שֶׁיָּבֹר לוֹ הָאָדָם, כָּל שֶׁהִיא תִּפְאֶרֶת לְעֹשֶׂיהָ וְתִפְאֶרֶת לוֹ מִן הָאָדָם. וֶהֱוֵי זָהִיר בְּמִצְוָה קַלָּה כְּבַחֲמוּרָה, שֶׁאֵין אַתָּה יוֹדֵעַ מַתַּן שְׂכָרָן שֶׁל מִצְוֹת. וֶהֱוֵי מְחַשֵּׁב הֶפְסֵד מִצְוָה כְּנֶגֶד שְׂכָרָהּ, וּשְׂכַר עֲבֵרָה כְּנֶגֶד הֶפְסֵדָהּ. הִסְתַּכֵּל בִּשְׁלֹשָׁה דְבָרִים, וְאֵין אַתָּה בָא לִידֵי עֲבֵרָה. דַּע מַה לְּמַעְלָה מִמְּךָ, עַיִן רוֹאָה, וְאֹזֶן שׁוֹמַעַת, וְכָל מַעֲשֶׂיךָ בְּסֵפֶר נִכְתָּבִים.

ב רַבָּן גַּמְלִיאֵל בְּנוֹ שֶׁל רַבִּי יְהוּדָה הַנָּשִׂיא אוֹמֵר: יָפֶה תַּלְמוּד תּוֹרָה עִם דֶּרֶךְ אֶרֶץ, שֶׁיְּגִיעַת שְׁנֵיהֶם מְשַׁכַּחַת עָוֹן. וְכָל תּוֹרָה שֶׁאֵין עִמָּהּ מְלָאכָה, סוֹפָהּ

אֻמָּנוּת (vocation) to cultivate silence. The use of this term is significant. It signifies that a person has, through sustained practice, become a professional in that field. While an amateur might also produce a result, it will never be as good as when done by a professional. Thus we must strive to be professional at the practice of silence, because only a sustained and disciplined avoidance of unnecessary (even if permitted) speech can prevent improper speech patterns. For this reason, a wise person prefers to be silent rather than to respond to unjust criticism, knowing that any verbal response will only lead to more of the same. It is better if people say, "Why are you so quiet?" than "Why don't you keep silent!" Thus this *mishna* says that the most precious human attribute is speech, for it is what separates us from the lower beings, and since it is so valuable it should be safeguarded and hidden by recourse to silence (Ḥafetz Ḥayyim).

This entire *mishna* is a call to balance intellect, speech, and action, in the right proportion. Thus, the *Zohar* emphasizes the importance of verbal confession when repenting, for it is not enough to have mental remorse if we do not also verbally express our thoughts. Moreover, even when we say what is on our minds, such words must also be translated into concrete deeds. Similarly, actions that do not truly reflect our mental state are not sufficient either, for it is only to the extent that our deeds reflect our spiritual state of mind, that we can achieve wholeness and eternal life (R. Avraham Yitzḥak HaKohen Kook).

CHAPTER 2

אֵיזוֹ הִיא דֶּרֶךְ יְשָׁרָה שֶׁיָּבֹר לוֹ הָאָדָם – *What is the right way for a person to conduct oneself?* R. Yehuda (Judah) HaNasi distinguishes between permitted behavior and required behavior. The first part of the *mishna* refers to the former, i.e., activities that are halakhically neutral, and

18. Rabban Simeon ben Gamliel used to say, "The continued existence of the world is dependent on three pillars: justice, truth, and peace, as declared by the prophet Zechariah, 'In your gates judge with truth and the justice of peace.'" *Zech. 8*

Makkot 23b R. ḤANANYA ben Akashya used to say, "The Holy One, blessed is He, wishing to render Israel more worthy, enlarged the Torah and its commandments for them, as it is said, 'The Lord desired, for the sake of its [Israel's] righteousness, to magnify the Torah and glorify it.'" *Is. 42*

If a minyan is present, mourners say the Rabbis' Kaddish (page 725).

CHAPTER TWO

Sanhedrin 90a *Is. 60* ALL ISRAEL have a share in the World to Come. As it is said, "Your people shall all be righteous and shall inherit the land forever. They are the shoot of My planting, the work of My hands in which I glory."

1. רַבִּי R. (Judah HaNasi) used to say, "What is the right way for a person to conduct oneself? Whatever way is honorable for oneself and brings one honor from one's fellow. Be as careful with an easy commandment as with a difficult one, for you do not know the rewards for the commandments. Reckon any loss incurred in fulfilling a commandment against the reward for observing it, and balance any benefit that comes through a transgression against the loss. Ponder three things and you will not fall into sin: Know what is above you – a seeing eye, a hearing ear, and a detailed record of everything you do."
2. Rabban Gamliel ben R. Judah HaNasi used to say, "Combining Torah study with a worldly occupation is desirable, because the work the two require will leave no opportunity to think about sin. Torah study that

---

therefore voluntary. We should engage in such activities if we judge them to be good in themselves, as well as socially approved. This will result for the most part in our doing what is right, as well as allowing us to avoid unjustified criticism. The second half of the *mishna* refers to the obligatory commandments of the Torah, which we are to fulfill irrespective of whether they appear to be more or less important, more or less a good thing, or more or less socially correct (R. Avraham Yitzḥak HaKohen Kook).

יָפֶה תַּלְמוּד תּוֹרָה עִם דֶּרֶךְ אֶרֶץ – *Combining Torah study with a worldly occupation is desirable. Derekh Eretz* refers to any situation dependent on circumstances in which we live, fulfill our destiny, and co-exist with others. Thus it includes how we earn a living, the social order in any given place and time, as well as things pertinent to good breeding and general education. Rabban Gamliel teaches that to flourish as individuals and as a people, it is essential to cultivate Torah, *derekh eretz*

בְּטֵלָה וְגוֹרֶרֶת עָוֹן. וְכָל הָעוֹסְקִים עִם הַצִּבּוּר, יִהְיוּ עוֹסְקִים עִמָּהֶם לְשֵׁם שָׁמַיִם, שֶׁזְּכוּת אֲבוֹתָם מְסַיַּעְתָּם, וְצִדְקָתָם עוֹמֶדֶת לָעַד. וְאַתֶּם, מַעֲלֶה אֲנִי עֲלֵיכֶם שָׂכָר הַרְבֵּה כְּאִלּוּ עֲשִׂיתֶם.

ג הֱווּ זְהִירִין בָּרָשׁוּת, שֶׁאֵין מְקָרְבִין לוֹ לָאָדָם אֶלָּא לְצֹרֶךְ עַצְמָן. נִרְאִין כְּאוֹהֲבִין בִּשְׁעַת הֲנָאָתָן, וְאֵין עוֹמְדִין לוֹ לָאָדָם בִּשְׁעַת דָּחְקוֹ.

ד הוּא הָיָה אוֹמֵר: עֲשֵׂה רְצוֹנוֹ כִּרְצוֹנְךָ, כְּדֵי שֶׁיַּעֲשֶׂה רְצוֹנְךָ כִּרְצוֹנוֹ. בַּטֵּל רְצוֹנְךָ מִפְּנֵי רְצוֹנוֹ, כְּדֵי שֶׁיְּבַטֵּל רְצוֹן אֲחֵרִים מִפְּנֵי רְצוֹנֶךָ.

ה הִלֵּל אוֹמֵר: אַל תִּפְרֹשׁ מִן הַצִּבּוּר, וְאַל תַּאֲמִין בְּעַצְמְךָ עַד יוֹם מוֹתְךָ, וְאַל תָּדִין אֶת חֲבֵרְךָ עַד שֶׁתַּגִּיעַ לִמְקוֹמוֹ. וְאַל תֹּאמַר דָּבָר שֶׁאִי אֶפְשָׁר לִשְׁמֹעַ, שֶׁסּוֹפוֹ לְהִשָּׁמַע. וְאַל תֹּאמַר לִכְשֶׁאֶפָּנֶה אֶשְׁנֶה, שֶׁמָּא לֹא תִפָּנֶה.

ו הוּא הָיָה אוֹמֵר: אֵין בּוּר יְרֵא חֵטְא, וְלֹא עַם הָאָרֶץ חָסִיד, וְלֹא הַבַּיְשָׁן לָמֵד, וְלֹא הַקַּפְּדָן מְלַמֵּד, וְלֹא כָל הַמַּרְבֶּה בִסְחוֹרָה מַחְכִּים. וּבְמָקוֹם שֶׁאֵין אֲנָשִׁים, הִשְׁתַּדֵּל לִהְיוֹת אִישׁ.

ז אַף הוּא רָאָה גֻּלְגֹּלֶת אַחַת שֶׁצָּפָה עַל פְּנֵי הַמָּיִם. אָמַר לָהּ: עַל דַּאֲטֵפְתְּ אֲטִיפוּךְ, וְסוֹף מְטִיפַיִךְ יְטוּפוּן.

ח הוּא הָיָה אוֹמֵר: מַרְבֶּה בָשָׂר, מַרְבֶּה רִמָּה. מַרְבֶּה נְכָסִים, מַרְבֶּה דְאָגָה. מַרְבֶּה נָשִׁים, מַרְבֶּה כְשָׁפִים. מַרְבֶּה שְׁפָחוֹת, מַרְבֶּה זִמָּה. מַרְבֶּה עֲבָדִים, מַרְבֶּה

אַל תִּפְרֹשׁ מִן הַצִּבּוּר – *Do not separate yourself from the community*. Rambam rules that if we separate from the Jewish community we forfeit our share in the World to Come, and are in the same halakhic category as a heretic, even if we commit no other transgressions. A Jew who fully observes the Torah – but does so in isolation from the Jewish community, as if he or she is a Gentile – is excluded from any eternal reward. The exception to this rule is where the community itself has become corrupted. If we find ourselves in such a community, we must leave it to find one that is more conducive to our moral and spiritual growth, for we are greatly influenced by our peers.

In his introduction to *Pirkei Avot*, when praising moderation and the Golden Mean, Rambam warns us not to be misled when we

and *melakha* (healthy work habits). In a similar vein, those responsible for communal affairs should always act for the sake of heaven, i.e., motivated by a sense of duty without ulterior motive (R. Samson Raphael Hirsch).

R. Hirsch similarly explains the *mishna* 2:21 (If there is no Torah there is no *derekh eretz*, if there is no *derekh eretz* there is no Torah) as teaching that without the spiritual guidance and moral ennoblement in the Torah, any attempt to establish and maintain a civilized society will be in vain. Conversely, if an orderly way of life is not fostered, then the teachings of the Torah will lack a foundation in reality, as the understanding needed for a great many situations covered by the Torah's teachings in their application to daily living will be lost.

is not combined with work is ineffectual and induces sin. Let everyone who labors on behalf of the community do so for the sake of heaven; because the merit of their forefathers facilitates their success and their virtue endures. To those who do communal work, God says, 'I count you as worthy of a rich reward as if the work were solely yours.'"

3. "Be cautious with those in political authority, because they will draw you near to them only for their own purposes. They pretend to be friends when it profits them, but they do not stand by a man in his time of trouble."
4. He also used to say, "Do His will as if it were your will, so that He may do your will as if it were His will. Set aside your will before His will, so that He may set aside the will of others before your will."
5. Hillel used to say, "Do not separate yourself from the community. Do not trust yourself until the day of your death. Do not judge your fellows unless you are in their place. Do not confide secrets to others in the belief that they will not be repeated, for they will indeed be heard by others. Do not say, 'When I have leisure I will study'; you may never have leisure."
6. He would say, "A crude man will not fear sin, an ignorant person cannot be pious, a timid person will not be able to learn properly, an irritable person cannot teach, nor can someone overly engrossed in business ever be a scholar. In a place where there are no people to learn from, you should strive to acquire knowledge on your own."
7. Seeing a skull floating on the water, Hillel said to it, "Because you drowned others, they have drowned you, and in turn, they who drowned you shall themselves be drowned."
8. He used to say, "The more flesh, the more worms; the more wealth, the more worry; the more women, the more witchcraft; the more maid-servants, the more debauchery; the more menservants, the more theft.

---

see righteous people who sometimes engage in extreme behaviors. He illustrates this by referring to the righteous who sometimes choose to live in isolation in order to avoid the influence of degenerate people. Such extraordinary behavior must be seen for what it is, i.e., it is not a rejection of the general requirement to be part and parcel of communal life, for as a rule we must always strive "to build up society in justice and righteousness, and not dwell in caves or mountains."

Finally, says Rambam, while being part of the community and subject to its influences, we should not rely only on what the community expects, but should seek self-improvement wherever possible. This means engaging

גָזֵל. מַרְבֶּה תוֹרָה, מַרְבֶּה חַיִּים. מַרְבֶּה יְשִׁיבָה, מַרְבֶּה חָכְמָה. מַרְבֶּה עֵצָה, מַרְבֶּה תְבוּנָה. מַרְבֶּה צְדָקָה, מַרְבֶּה שָׁלוֹם. קָנָה שֵׁם טוֹב, קָנָה לְעַצְמוֹ. קָנָה לוֹ דִבְרֵי תוֹרָה, קָנָה לוֹ חַיֵּי הָעוֹלָם הַבָּא.

ט רַבָּן יוֹחָנָן בֶּן זַכַּאי קִבֵּל מֵהִלֵּל וּמִשַּׁמַּאי. הוּא הָיָה אוֹמֵר: אִם לָמַדְתָּ תּוֹרָה הַרְבֵּה, אַל תַּחֲזִיק טוֹבָה לְעַצְמְךָ, כִּי לְכָךְ נוֹצָרְתָּ.

י חֲמִשָּׁה תַלְמִידִים הָיוּ לְרַבָּן יוֹחָנָן בֶּן זַכַּאי. וְאֵלוּ הֵן: רַבִּי אֱלִיעֶזֶר בֶּן הוֹרְקְנוֹס, רַבִּי יְהוֹשֻׁעַ בֶּן חֲנַנְיָה, רַבִּי יוֹסֵי הַכֹּהֵן, רַבִּי שִׁמְעוֹן בֶּן נְתַנְאֵל, רַבִּי אֶלְעָזָר בֶּן עֲרָךְ.

יא הוּא הָיָה מוֹנֶה שְׁבָחָם: אֱלִיעֶזֶר בֶּן הוֹרְקְנוֹס, בּוֹר סוּד שֶׁאֵינוֹ מְאַבֵּד טִפָּה. יְהוֹשֻׁעַ בֶּן חֲנַנְיָה, אַשְׁרֵי יוֹלַדְתּוֹ. יוֹסֵי הַכֹּהֵן, חָסִיד. שִׁמְעוֹן בֶּן נְתַנְאֵל, יְרֵא חֵטְא. אֶלְעָזָר בֶּן עֲרָךְ, כְּמַעְיָן הַמִּתְגַּבֵּר.

יב הוּא הָיָה אוֹמֵר: אִם יִהְיוּ כָּל חַכְמֵי יִשְׂרָאֵל בְּכַף מֹאזְנַיִם, וֶאֱלִיעֶזֶר בֶּן הוֹרְקְנוֹס בְּכַף שְׁנִיָּה, מַכְרִיעַ אֶת כֻּלָּם. אַבָּא שָׁאוּל אוֹמֵר מִשְּׁמוֹ: אִם יִהְיוּ כָּל חַכְמֵי יִשְׂרָאֵל בְּכַף מֹאזְנַיִם, וֶאֱלִיעֶזֶר בֶּן הוֹרְקְנוֹס אַף עִמָּהֶם, וְאֶלְעָזָר בֶּן עֲרָךְ בְּכַף שְׁנִיָּה, מַכְרִיעַ אֶת כֻּלָּם.

יג אָמַר לָהֶם: צְאוּ וּרְאוּ אֵיזוֹ הִיא דֶּרֶךְ טוֹבָה, שֶׁיִּדְבַּק בָּהּ הָאָדָם. רַבִּי אֱלִיעֶזֶר אוֹמֵר: עַיִן טוֹבָה. רַבִּי יְהוֹשֻׁעַ אוֹמֵר: חָבֵר טוֹב. רַבִּי יוֹסֵי אוֹמֵר: שָׁכֵן טוֹב. רַבִּי שִׁמְעוֹן אוֹמֵר: הָרוֹאֶה אֶת הַנּוֹלָד. רַבִּי אֶלְעָזָר אוֹמֵר: לֵב טוֹב. אָמַר לָהֶם, רוֹאֶה אֲנִי אֶת דִּבְרֵי אֶלְעָזָר בֶּן עֲרָךְ מִדִּבְרֵיכֶם, שֶׁבִּכְלַל דְּבָרָיו דִּבְרֵיכֶם.

יד אָמַר לָהֶם: צְאוּ וּרְאוּ, אֵיזוֹ הִיא דֶּרֶךְ רָעָה, שֶׁיִּתְרַחֵק מִמֶּנָּה הָאָדָם. רַבִּי אֱלִיעֶזֶר אוֹמֵר: עַיִן רָעָה. רַבִּי יְהוֹשֻׁעַ אוֹמֵר: חָבֵר רָע. רַבִּי יוֹסֵי אוֹמֵר: שָׁכֵן רָע. רַבִּי שִׁמְעוֹן אוֹמֵר: הַלֹּוֶה וְאֵינוֹ מְשַׁלֵּם, אֶחָד הַלֹּוֶה מִן הָאָדָם כְּלֹוֶה מִן הַמָּקוֹם, שֶׁנֶּאֱמַר: לֹוֶה רָשָׁע וְלֹא יְשַׁלֵּם, וְצַדִּיק חוֹנֵן וְנוֹתֵן: (תהלים לז) רַבִּי אֶלְעָזָר אוֹמֵר: לֵב רָע. אָמַר לָהֶם: רוֹאֶה אֲנִי אֶת דִּבְרֵי אֶלְעָזָר בֶּן עֲרָךְ מִדִּבְרֵיכֶם, שֶׁבִּכְלַל דְּבָרָיו דִּבְרֵיכֶם.

טו הֵם אָמְרוּ שְׁלֹשָׁה דְבָרִים. רַבִּי אֱלִיעֶזֶר אוֹמֵר: יְהִי כְבוֹד חֲבֵרְךָ חָבִיב עָלֶיךָ כְּשֶׁלְּךָ, וְאַל תְּהִי נוֹחַ לִכְעוֹס. וְשׁוּב יוֹם אֶחָד לִפְנֵי מִיתָתְךָ. וֶהֱוֵי מִתְחַמֵּם כְּנֶגֶד

in concrete positive actions to achieve self-improvement, for our character is molded by our actions. And, being creatures of habit, many small acts of charity or good deeds are better than one large one. Finally, as long as we are alive we should seek self-improvement, for we never know how we might fail, no matter our age.

But the more Torah, the more life; the more study, the more wisdom; the more counsel, the more understanding; the more charity, the more peace. Gain a good name and you have gained it for yourself; but gain knowledge of Torah and you have gained life in the World to Come."

9. Rabban Yoḥanan ben Zakkai received the tradition from Hillel and Shammai. He used to say, "If you have learned much Torah, do not think that what you have done is beyond what was required of you, for you were created only for that purpose."

10. Rabban Yoḥanan ben Zakkai had five disciples, R. Eliezer ben Hyrcanus, R. Joshua ben Ḥananya, R. Yose the priest, R. Simeon ben Nethanel, and R. Eleazar ben Arakh.

11. This is how he evaluated them: Eliezer ben Hyrcanus is a plastered cistern that does not lose a drop. Joshua ben Ḥananya, happy is she who bore him. Yose the priest, he is pious. Simeon ben Nethanel fears sin. Eleazar ben Arakh is like a perennial spring.

12. He said further, "If all the sages of Israel were in one scale of the balance, and Eliezer ben Hyrcanus in the other, he would outweigh all of them." But Abba Shaul said in his name that if all the sages of Israel were together with Eliezer ben Hyrcanus in one scale of the balance, and Eleazar ben Arakh in the other, it is he who would outweigh all the others.

13. Rabban Yoḥanan ben Zakkai also said to them, "Go find out what is the best personal quality to cultivate." R. Eliezer said, "Having a good eye." R. Joshua said, "Being a good friend." R. Yose said, "Being a good neighbor." R. Simeon said, "The ability to anticipate the outcome of one's actions." R. Eleazar said, "Having a good heart." Said Rabban Yoḥanan ben Zakkai, "I approve the words of Eleazar ben Arakh the most, because they include what the rest of you said."

14. Again he said to them, "Go find out what evil is most to be shunned." R. Eliezer said, "Having an evil eye." R. Joshua said, "Being a bad friend." R. Yose said, "Being a bad neighbor." R. Simeon said, "To borrow and not
Ps. 37 repay, whether from man or from God, as it says in the psalm, 'The wicked borrows but does not pay back, but the righteous gives with grace.'" R. Eleazar said, "Having an evil heart." Said Rabban Yoḥanan ben Zakkai, "I approve the words of Eleazar ben Arakh the most, because they include what the rest of you said."

15. Each of them said three things. R. Eliezer (ben Hyrcanus) used to say, "Let the honor of your fellow be as dear to you as your own, and do not be easily angered. Repent one day before your death. Warm yourself at

אוּרָן שֶׁל חֲכָמִים, וֶהֱוֵי זָהִיר בְּגַחַלְתָּן שֶׁלֹּא תִכָּוֶה, שֶׁנְּשִׁיכָתָן נְשִׁיכַת שׁוּעָל, וַעֲקִיצָתָן עֲקִיצַת עַקְרָב, וּלְחִישָׁתָן לְחִישַׁת שָׂרָף, וְכָל דִּבְרֵיהֶם כְּגַחֲלֵי אֵשׁ.

טז רַבִּי יְהוֹשֻׁעַ אוֹמֵר: עַיִן הָרָע וְיֵצֶר הָרָע וְשִׂנְאַת הַבְּרִיּוֹת, מוֹצִיאִין אֶת הָאָדָם מִן הָעוֹלָם.

יז רַבִּי יוֹסֵי אוֹמֵר: יְהִי מָמוֹן חֲבֵרְךָ חָבִיב עָלֶיךָ כְּשֶׁלָּךְ. וְהַתְקֵן עַצְמְךָ לִלְמֹד תּוֹרָה, שֶׁאֵינָהּ יְרֻשָּׁה לָךְ. וְכָל מַעֲשֶׂיךָ יִהְיוּ לְשֵׁם שָׁמָיִם.

יח רַבִּי שִׁמְעוֹן אוֹמֵר: הֱוֵי זָהִיר בִּקְרִיאַת שְׁמַע וּבִתְפִלָּה. וּכְשֶׁאַתָּה מִתְפַּלֵּל
אַל תַּעַשׂ תְּפִלָּתְךָ קֶבַע, אֶלָּא רַחֲמִים וְתַחֲנוּנִים לִפְנֵי הַמָּקוֹם, שֶׁנֶּאֱמַר: כִּי יואל ב
חַנּוּן וְרַחוּם הוּא, אֶרֶךְ אַפַּיִם וְרַב־חֶסֶד וְנִחָם עַל־הָרָעָה: וְאַל תְּהִי רָשָׁע
בִּפְנֵי עַצְמֶךָ.

וְכָל דִּבְרֵיהֶם כְּגַחֲלֵי אֵשׁ – *All their words like coals of fire*. This provides an important lesson for how to educate our children. Some parents believe it is enough to raise their children in a warm Jewish home, in contact with Jewish traditions and behaviors in the family setting. Other parents feel strongly that it is necessary to give their children a thorough Torah education, so that learning Torah becomes their lifelong passion. The difference between them is the difference between heat emanating from a pot that has been on a cooktop, and heat coming directly from the flame that heated that pot in the first place. A hot pot removed from its flame slowly loses its heat, and can only heat another to a lesser degree (known as a כְּלִי שֵׁנִי – a derivative container), whereas a flame can continue to heat multiple objects and even set them on fire, as long as it is supplied with combustible material. So it is with the education of our children. Giving them direct contact with the endless "fiery coals" of Torah will ensure that they themselves remain "hot" throughout their lifetime, retaining a love of Torah study, and equipped with the tools to study it on their own. But when a child absorbs only the "heat of the pot" by proximity to the traditions experienced in the home, without serious study of the Torah that generated those traditions in the first place, his or her Jewish commitment will likely cool over time (Ḥafetz Ḥayyim).

וְהַתְקֵן עַצְמְךָ לִלְמֹד תּוֹרָה, שֶׁאֵינָהּ יְרֻשָּׁה לָךְ – *Work hard to learn Torah, because it does not come to you as an inheritance*. Rambam, in commenting on this *mishna* in the eighth chapter of his introduction, as well as in the Guide, explains that even if we are naturally talented or intelligent, we must engage in sustained effort to translate our potential into reality. So too with Torah, no matter how bright we are, we must engage in serious and disciplined study on successively more difficult levels, to convert our great potential into reality. Elsewhere Rambam compares Torah to precious pearls on the ocean floor. To retrieve them a diver must first undergo proper training and preparation. If one jumps into the depths without the necessary preparation one is likely to drown. So too, the ability to retrieve the deep pearls of Torah wisdom is not something we are born with. It requires training and ongoing effort.

וְכָל מַעֲשֶׂיךָ יִהְיוּ לְשֵׁם שָׁמָיִם – *Let all your actions be for the sake of heaven*. Unlike in some other faiths, for Jews serving God is not to be restricted to worship or ceremonial ritual. It involves every aspect of life. Nothing – from

the fire of the sages, but beware lest you burn yourself with their glowing coals, because their bite can be like that of a fox, their sting like the scorpion, their hiss like the serpent, and all their words like coals of fire."

16. R. Joshua (ben Ḥananya) would talk about three things, namely one who has an evil eye, or an evil inclination, or who despises people – all cause one to die before one's time.

17. R. Yose used to say, "Let your neighbor's money be as precious to you as your own. Work hard to learn Torah, because it does not come to you as an inheritance. Let all your actions be for the sake of heaven."

18. R. Simeon (ben Nethanel) used to say, "Be scrupulous in reciting the Shema and the Amida. When you pray, do not treat your prayer as a fixed obligation but make it a heart-felt plea for divine mercy. As the prophet
Joel 2 Joel said, 'Gracious and compassionate is He, slow to anger and abundant in mercy, and repenting of evil.' Do not think that you are a bad person."

---

the most intimate to the most public – is devoid of this service. We have one goal: to do God's will. This includes our physiological functions such as digestion and reproduction, our innermost feelings such as love for parents, and how we relate to friends, fellows, business activities, political activity, and everything else. The *halakha* imprints itself on every aspect of our lives. Thus R. Yose teaches that everything we do should be for the sake of heaven (R. Joseph B. Soloveitchik).

וּכְשֶׁאַתָּה מִתְפַּלֵּל אַל תַּעַשׂ תְּפִלָּתְךָ קֶבַע – *When you pray, do not treat your prayer as a fixed obligation.* R. Shimon distinguishes between *Shema* and the *Amida*. The former must be recited with a sense of obligation to accept the yoke of God's kingdom with conviction and love, in accordance with the Torah's commandment. The *Amida*, on the other hand, requires even more. It is to be recited as an outpouring of supplication soliciting God's compassion. The primary motive in reciting the *Amida* should not be a sense of duty, but rather to express one's heartfelt longing to merit God's compassion. This is why this *mishna* quotes the verse from Joel describing God's compassion at length. So too, even though women are technically exempt from the *Amida*, nonetheless they are expected to recite it as an expression of their inner longing to solicit God's compassion. In this respect the *mitzva* of prayer via the *Amida* differs from all the other *mitzvot*, as it alone does not emanate primarily from a sense of obligation (R. Joseph B. Soloveitchik).

Alternatively the term קֶבַע can be understood in the sense of "a fixed time." Thus we should try to extend the time we spend in prayer in the synagogue past the end of services. Optimally we should take our time when leaving, in the spirit of the opening verse of the *Ashrei*, as explained earlier in the Siddur (see page 68) (R. Joseph B. Soloveitchik).

וְאַל תְּהִי רָשָׁע בִּפְנֵי עַצְמְךָ – *Do not think that you are a bad person.* Rambam explains that if we think that we are spiritual failures we might succumb to even greater sin because we think we are unable to withstand temptation. Rabbeinu Yona similarly explains that a negative self-image will stand in the way of repentance, for in our loss of self-esteem we might despair of all hope of self-improvement. As a result when confronted with the possibility of

יט רַבִּי אֶלְעָזָר אוֹמֵר: הֱוֵי שָׁקוּד לִלְמֹד תּוֹרָה. וְדַע מַה שֶּׁתָּשִׁיב לְאֶפִּיקוֹרוֹס. וְדַע לִפְנֵי מִי אַתָּה עָמֵל, וּמִי הוּא בַּעַל מְלַאכְתְּךָ, שֶׁיְּשַׁלֶּם לְךָ שְׂכַר פְּעֻלָּתֶךָ.

כ רַבִּי טַרְפוֹן אוֹמֵר: הַיּוֹם קָצֵר, וְהַמְּלָאכָה מְרֻבָּה, וְהַפּוֹעֲלִים עֲצֵלִים, וְהַשָּׂכָר הַרְבֵּה, וּבַעַל הַבַּיִת דּוֹחֵק.

כא הוּא הָיָה אוֹמֵר: לֹא עָלֶיךָ הַמְּלָאכָה לִגְמֹר, וְלֹא אַתָּה בֶן חוֹרִין לִבָּטֵל מִמֶּנָּה. אִם לָמַדְתָּ תּוֹרָה הַרְבֵּה, נוֹתְנִין לְךָ שָׂכָר הַרְבֵּה. וְנֶאֱמָן הוּא בַּעַל מְלַאכְתְּךָ, שֶׁיְּשַׁלֶּם לְךָ שְׂכַר פְּעֻלָּתֶךָ. וְדַע, שֶׁמַּתַּן שְׂכָרָן שֶׁל צַדִּיקִים לֶעָתִיד לָבוֹא.

מכות כג: רַבִּי חֲנַנְיָא בֶּן עֲקַשְׁיָא אוֹמֵר: רָצָה הַקָּדוֹשׁ בָּרוּךְ הוּא לְזַכּוֹת אֶת יִשְׂרָאֵל, לְפִיכָךְ הִרְבָּה
ישעיה מב לָהֶם תּוֹרָה וּמִצְוֹת. שֶׁנֶּאֱמַר: יהוה חָפֵץ לְמַעַן צִדְקוֹ, יַגְדִּיל תּוֹרָה וְיַאְדִּיר:

If there is a מנין*, mourners say* קדיש דרבנן *(page 724).*

פרק שלישי

סנהדרין צ. כָּל יִשְׂרָאֵל יֵשׁ לָהֶם חֵלֶק לָעוֹלָם הַבָּא. שֶׁנֶּאֱמַר: וְעַמֵּךְ כֻּלָּם צַדִּיקִים, לְעוֹלָם יִירְשׁוּ אָרֶץ,
ישעיה ס נֵצֶר מַטָּעַי, מַעֲשֵׂה יָדַי לְהִתְפָּאֵר:

א **עֲקַבְיָא** בֶּן מַהֲלַלְאֵל אוֹמֵר: הִסְתַּכֵּל בִּשְׁלֹשָׁה דְבָרִים, וְאֵין אַתָּה בָא לִידֵי עֲבֵרָה. דַּע מֵאַיִן בָּאתָ, וּלְאָן אַתָּה הוֹלֵךְ, וְלִפְנֵי מִי אַתָּה עָתִיד לִתֵּן דִּין וְחֶשְׁבּוֹן. מֵאַיִן בָּאתָ, מִטִּפָּה סְרוּחָה. וּלְאָן אַתָּה הוֹלֵךְ, לִמְקוֹם עָפָר, רִמָּה וְתוֹלֵעָה. וְלִפְנֵי מִי אַתָּה עָתִיד לִתֵּן דִּין וְחֶשְׁבּוֹן, לִפְנֵי מֶלֶךְ מַלְכֵי הַמְּלָכִים, הַקָּדוֹשׁ בָּרוּךְ הוּא.

ב רַבִּי חֲנִינָא סְגַן הַכֹּהֲנִים אוֹמֵר: הֱוֵי מִתְפַּלֵּל בִּשְׁלוֹמָהּ שֶׁל מַלְכוּת, שֶׁאִלְמָלֵא מוֹרָאָהּ, אִישׁ אֶת רֵעֵהוּ חַיִּים בְּלָעוֹ.

---

sin, it will be all the more difficult to withstand temptation. We should never feel so ashamed that we despair of ever being able to achieve a rapprochement with God, for the gates of repentance are always open.

CHAPTER 3

דַּע מֵאַיִן בָּאתָ, וּלְאָן אַתָּה הוֹלֵךְ, וְלִפְנֵי מִי אַתָּה עָתִיד לִתֵּן דִּין וְחֶשְׁבּוֹן – *Know what you came from, where you are going, and before Whom you are destined to give an accounting.* The repeated use of the second person "you" in this *mishna* is unusual. Akavia understood our natural tendency to avoid thinking about our own death. The use of the second person is constructively intended to make us the more aware of our own mortality. Often we attend a funeral or a *shiva* house, and mourn the deceased while commiserating with the family. But on all such occasions we should make every effort to confront our own mortality, so we can draw the proper lessons while we still live (Ḥafetz Ḥayyim).

הֱוֵי מִתְפַּלֵּל בִּשְׁלוֹמָהּ שֶׁל מַלְכוּת – *Pray for the welfare of the government.* It is noteworthy that in this *mishna* R. Ḥanina urges us to pray for the well-being of the ruling authorities even though he lived in Israel under the oppressive rule of Rome. As human beings, Jews have more than one identity. We are part of the

19. R. Eleazar (ben Arakh) said, "Be prepared to study Torah with great effort. Know how to answer a heretic. Know before Whom you are laboring and Who is the Master Who will pay the reward due for your labor."

20. R. Tarfon used to say, "The day is short, the work great, the workers are lazy, the reward is abundant, and the Master of the house is impatient."

21. He used to say, "You are not obligated to complete the work, but neither are you free to abstain from it. If you have learned much Torah, you will receive an abundant reward, because your Master can be relied upon to pay the reward for your labor. But know this: the righteous will receive their reward in the World to Come."

Makkot 23b R. ḤANANYA ben Akashya used to say, "The Holy One, blessed is He, wishing to render Israel more worthy, enlarged the Torah and its commandments for them, as
Is. 42 it is said, 'The Lord desired, for the sake of its [Israel's] righteousness, to magnify the Torah and glorify it.'"

If a minyan is present, mourners say the Rabbis' Kaddish (page 725).

CHAPTER THREE

Sanhedrin 90a ALL ISRAEL have a share in the World to Come. As it is said, "Your people shall all
Is. 60 be righteous and shall inherit the land forever. They are the shoot of My planting, the work of My hands in which I glory."

1. עֲקַבְיָא AKAVYA ben Mahalalel used to say, "Ponder three things and you will not come into the power of sin: know what you came from, where you are going, and before Whom you are destined to give an accounting. Where did you come from? A filthy drop. Where you are going? To a place of dust, maggots, and worms. Before Whom are you destined to give an accounting? Before the King of the most exalted of kings, the Holy One, blessed is He."

2. R. Ḥanina, the deputy high priest, would say, "Pray for the welfare of the government, because without the fear thereof people would swallow one another alive."

---

larger family of mankind, but we also have a specific Jewish character that separates us from others. Each of these imposes on us particular responsibilities. Therefore in addition to our unique responsibilities toward our fellow Jews, we must as citizens assume our social and political obligations to enhance the general welfare, by combating common dangers such as famine, corruption, disease and foreign enemies. Where the freedom, dignity and security of human life are at stake, all people, irrespective of ethnic diversity, are expected to join as brothers in shouldering their responsibilities. This echoes Jeremiah's

ג רַבִּי חֲנִינָא בֶּן תְּרַדְיוֹן אוֹמֵר: שְׁנַיִם שֶׁיּוֹשְׁבִין, וְאֵין בֵּינֵיהֶם דִּבְרֵי תוֹרָה, הֲרֵי
תהלים א זֶה מוֹשַׁב לֵצִים, שֶׁנֶּאֱמַר: וּבְמוֹשַׁב לֵצִים לֹא יָשָׁב: אֲבָל שְׁנַיִם שֶׁיּוֹשְׁבִין, וְיֵשׁ
מלאכי ג בֵּינֵיהֶם דִּבְרֵי תוֹרָה, שְׁכִינָה שְׁרוּיָה בֵינֵיהֶם, שֶׁנֶּאֱמַר: אָז נִדְבְּרוּ יִרְאֵי יהוה
אִישׁ אֶל־רֵעֵהוּ, וַיַּקְשֵׁב יהוה וַיִּשְׁמָע, וַיִּכָּתֵב סֵפֶר זִכָּרוֹן לְפָנָיו לְיִרְאֵי יהוה
וּלְחֹשְׁבֵי שְׁמוֹ: אֵין לִי אֶלָּא שְׁנַיִם, מִנַּיִן אֲפִלּוּ אֶחָד שֶׁיּוֹשֵׁב וְעוֹסֵק בַּתּוֹרָה
איכה ג שֶׁהַקָּדוֹשׁ בָּרוּךְ הוּא קוֹבֵעַ לוֹ שָׂכָר, שֶׁנֶּאֱמַר: יֵשֵׁב בָּדָד וְיִדֹּם כִּי נָטַל עָלָיו:

ד רַבִּי שִׁמְעוֹן אוֹמֵר: שְׁלֹשָׁה שֶׁאָכְלוּ עַל שֻׁלְחָן אֶחָד וְלֹא אָמְרוּ עָלָיו דִּבְרֵי
ישעיה כח תוֹרָה, כְּאִלּוּ אָכְלוּ מִזִּבְחֵי מֵתִים, שֶׁנֶּאֱמַר: כִּי כָּל־שֻׁלְחָנוֹת מָלְאוּ קִיא
צֹאָה בְּלִי מָקוֹם: אֲבָל שְׁלֹשָׁה שֶׁאָכְלוּ עַל שֻׁלְחָן אֶחָד, וְאָמְרוּ עָלָיו דִּבְרֵי
יחזקאל מא תוֹרָה, כְּאִלּוּ אָכְלוּ מִשֻּׁלְחָנוֹ שֶׁל מָקוֹם, שֶׁנֶּאֱמַר: וַיְדַבֵּר אֵלַי, זֶה הַשֻּׁלְחָן
אֲשֶׁר לִפְנֵי יהוה:

ה רַבִּי חֲנִינָא בֶּן חֲכִינַאי אוֹמֵר: הַנֵּעוֹר בַּלַּיְלָה, וְהַמְהַלֵּךְ בַּדֶּרֶךְ יְחִידִי, וְהַמְפַנֶּה
לִבּוֹ לְבַטָּלָה, הֲרֵי זֶה מִתְחַיֵּב בְּנַפְשׁוֹ.

ו רַבִּי נְחוּנְיָא בֶּן הַקָּנָה אוֹמֵר: כָּל הַמְקַבֵּל עָלָיו עֹל תּוֹרָה, מַעֲבִירִין מִמֶּנּוּ
עֹל מַלְכוּת וְעֹל דֶּרֶךְ אֶרֶץ. וְכָל הַפּוֹרֵק מִמֶּנּוּ עֹל תּוֹרָה, נוֹתְנִין עָלָיו עֹל
מַלְכוּת וְעֹל דֶּרֶךְ אֶרֶץ.

ז רַבִּי חֲלַפְתָּא בֶּן דּוֹסָא אִישׁ כְּפַר חֲנַנְיָה אוֹמֵר: עֲשָׂרָה שֶׁיּוֹשְׁבִין וְעוֹסְקִין
תהלים פב בַּתּוֹרָה שְׁכִינָה שְׁרוּיָה בֵינֵיהֶם, שֶׁנֶּאֱמַר: אֱלֹהִים נִצָּב בַּעֲדַת־אֵל: וּמִנַּיִן אֲפִלּוּ
עמוס ט חֲמִשָּׁה, שֶׁנֶּאֱמַר: וַאֲגֻדָּתוֹ עַל־אֶרֶץ יְסָדָהּ: וּמִנַּיִן אֲפִלּוּ שְׁלֹשָׁה, שֶׁנֶּאֱמַר:

---

counsel to the Jewish inhabitants of Babylonia to "seek the welfare of the city" (Jer. 29:7), and the principle of Shmuel of Nehardea that in civil matters the law of the land is as binding upon the Jews as the religious commandments of their own faith (*Gittin* 10b). The precise details of how *halakha* relates to local rules and regulations in any given society, and when one takes precedence over the other, require careful study. But the general principle is that a Jew must respect and obey the law of the land (R. Joseph B. Soloveitchik).

שְׁלֹשָׁה שֶׁאָכְלוּ עַל שֻׁלְחָן אֶחָד – *Three who have eaten together at a table.* A meal is basically a biological act, although modern man has made of it a social experience with table manners and esthetic enhancements. Judaism, even as it acknowledges the social aspect of eating, also tries to elevate it into a holy experience. That is what R. Shimon intends in this *mishna* (R. Joseph B. Soloveitchik).

כָּל הַמְקַבֵּל עָלָיו עֹל תּוֹרָה – *Whoever accepts the yoke of Torah.* The Maharal explains that this *mishna* refers to the study of Torah as a "yoke" or imposition, rather than as a purely joyous activity, because while Torah study does indeed give us joy and satisfaction, it is also true that Torah study is not optional – it is obligatory, for without it we and the world cannot survive. It is for this reason that the Gemara (*Shabbat* 88a) tells us that when giving the Torah God threatened the people with

3. R. Ḥananya ben Teradyon used to say, "When two persons sit together and no words of Torah pass between them, it is a 'seat of the scornful,' as
Ps. 1 it says, '[Do] not sit in the seat of the scornful.' But when two sit together and words of Torah pass between them, the Divine Presence rests on
Mal. 3 them. For as the prophet Malachi said, 'Then those who revere the Lord spoke with one another, and the Lord hearkened and heard, and it was written before Him in the book of remembrance for those who revere the Lord and think on His name.' This applies to two persons. What verse shows that the Holy One, blessed is He, has a reward even for one person who sits and occupies himself with Torah? The verse from Lamentations,
Lam. 3 'Let him sit alone and meditate, for [God[has laid it [a reward] on him.'"

4. R. Simeon said, "Three who have eaten together at a table and have not spoken words of Torah are as though they had eaten of sacrifices to the
Is. 28 dead. For we read the verse of Isaiah as saying, 'For all tables without God are covered by filthy vomit.' But three who have eaten together at a table and have said words of Torah are as though they had eaten of the table of
Ezek. 41 God, as suggested by the words of Ezekiel, 'And he said unto me, This is the table which is before the Lord.'"

5. R. Ḥanina ben Ḥakhinai used to say, "Those who stay up all night, and those who travel alone in dangerous places, and those who waste their mind to no good purpose, cause themselves and their souls great harm."

6. R. Neḥunya ben HaKana used to say, "Whoever accepts the yoke of Torah is exempted from governmental obligations as well as from having to perform excessive labor to earn a livelihood. But one who casts off the yoke of Torah will have to bear the burdens of both the government and earning a livelihood."

7. R. Ḥalafta ben Dosa of Kfar Ḥananya used to say, "When ten sit down and occupy themselves with Torah, the Divine Presence rests among
Ps. 82 them, as is suggested by the words of the psalm, 'God is standing in the congregation of God.' What biblical verse shows that this is also true of
Amos 9 five? The words of Amos, 'And He has established His group over the earth.' What verse suggests it also of three? The words of the psalm,

---

death if they refused to accept it. Even though they were anxious to accept it, God wanted them to know that without it they would be doomed. This is the dual nature of Torah study: it provides the greatest of pleasures, but it is also a necessity of life, and an unconditional duty. Thus even while experiencing the sheer joy of Torah one should never forget that it is a yoke to be carried consciously throughout life (R. Yitzchok Hutner).

תהלים פב בְּקֶרֶב אֱלֹהִים יִשְׁפֹּט: וּמִנַּיִן אֲפִלּוּ שְׁנַיִם, שֶׁנֶּאֱמַר: אָז נִדְבְּרוּ יִרְאֵי יהוה אִישׁ
מלאכי ג
שמות כ אֶל־רֵעֵהוּ, וַיַּקְשֵׁב יהוה וַיִּשְׁמָע: וּמִנַּיִן אֲפִלּוּ אֶחָד, שֶׁנֶּאֱמַר: בְּכָל־הַמָּקוֹם
אֲשֶׁר אַזְכִּיר אֶת־שְׁמִי, אָבוֹא אֵלֶיךָ וּבֵרַכְתִּיךָ:

עמוס ט ח רַבִּי אֶלְעָזָר אִישׁ בַּרְתּוֹתָא אוֹמֵר: תֶּן לוֹ מִשֶּׁלּוֹ, שֶׁאַתָּה וְשֶׁלְּךָ שֶׁלּוֹ. וְכֵן בְּדָוִד
דברי הימים א׳ כט הוּא אוֹמֵר: כִּי־מִמְּךָ הַכֹּל, וּמִיָּדְךָ נָתַנּוּ לָךְ:

ט רַבִּי יַעֲקֹב אוֹמֵר: הַמְהַלֵּךְ בַּדֶּרֶךְ וְשׁוֹנֶה, וּמַפְסִיק מִמִּשְׁנָתוֹ וְאוֹמֵר, מַה
נָּאֶה אִילָן זֶה, מַה נָּאֶה נִיר זֶה, מַעֲלֶה עָלָיו הַכָּתוּב כְּאִלּוּ מִתְחַיֵּב בְּנַפְשׁוֹ.

י רַבִּי דוֹסְתַּאי בְּרַבִּי יַנַּאי מִשּׁוּם רַבִּי מֵאִיר אוֹמֵר: כָּל הַשּׁוֹכֵחַ דָּבָר אֶחָד
דברים ד מִמִּשְׁנָתוֹ, מַעֲלֶה עָלָיו הַכָּתוּב כְּאִלּוּ מִתְחַיֵּב בְּנַפְשׁוֹ, שֶׁנֶּאֱמַר: רַק הִשָּׁמֶר
לְךָ וּשְׁמֹר נַפְשְׁךָ מְאֹד, פֶּן־תִּשְׁכַּח אֶת־הַדְּבָרִים אֲשֶׁר־רָאוּ עֵינֶיךָ: יָכוֹל אֲפִלּוּ
דברים ד תָּקְפָה עָלָיו מִשְׁנָתוֹ, תַּלְמוּד לוֹמַר: וּפֶן יָסוּרוּ מִלְּבָבְךָ כֹּל יְמֵי חַיֶּיךָ: הָא אֵינוֹ
מִתְחַיֵּב בְּנַפְשׁוֹ, עַד שֶׁיֵּשֵׁב וִיסִירֵם מִלִּבּוֹ.

יא רַבִּי חֲנִינָא בֶּן דּוֹסָא אוֹמֵר: כָּל שֶׁיִּרְאַת חֶטְאוֹ קוֹדֶמֶת לְחָכְמָתוֹ, חָכְמָתוֹ
מִתְקַיֶּמֶת. וְכָל שֶׁחָכְמָתוֹ קוֹדֶמֶת לְיִרְאַת חֶטְאוֹ, אֵין חָכְמָתוֹ מִתְקַיֶּמֶת.

יב הוּא הָיָה אוֹמֵר: כָּל שֶׁמַּעֲשָׂיו מְרֻבִּין מֵחָכְמָתוֹ, חָכְמָתוֹ מִתְקַיֶּמֶת. וְכָל
שֶׁחָכְמָתוֹ מְרֻבָּה מִמַּעֲשָׂיו, אֵין חָכְמָתוֹ מִתְקַיֶּמֶת.

יג הוּא הָיָה אוֹמֵר: כָּל שֶׁרוּחַ הַבְּרִיּוֹת נוֹחָה הֵימֶנּוּ, רוּחַ הַמָּקוֹם נוֹחָה הֵימֶנּוּ.
וְכָל שֶׁאֵין רוּחַ הַבְּרִיּוֹת נוֹחָה הֵימֶנּוּ, אֵין רוּחַ הַמָּקוֹם נוֹחָה הֵימֶנּוּ.

יד רַבִּי דוֹסָא בֶּן הַרְכִּינַס אוֹמֵר: שֵׁנָה שֶׁל שַׁחֲרִית, וְיַיִן שֶׁל צָהֳרַיִם, וְשִׂיחַת
הַיְלָדִים, וִישִׁיבַת בָּתֵּי כְנֵסִיּוֹת שֶׁל עַמֵּי הָאָרֶץ, מוֹצִיאִין אֶת הָאָדָם מִן הָעוֹלָם.

שֵׁנָה שֶׁל שַׁחֲרִית, וְיַיִן שֶׁל צָהֳרַיִם, וְשִׂיחַת הַיְלָדִים, וִישִׁיבַת בָּתֵּי כְנֵסִיּוֹת שֶׁל עַמֵּי הָאָרֶץ, מוֹצִיאִין אֶת הָאָדָם מִן הָעוֹלָם – *Morning sleep, noonday wine, children's talk, and frequenting the synagogues of the ignorant deprive a person of eternal life.*. Why do these actions or habits, and not others, have such a terrible effect? Surely there are others that are even worse? The answer is that R. Dosa ben Harkinas is speaking metaphorically of the successive stages of one's life. At each stage we can easily fail to earn a share in the afterlife. Thus, in the "morning" of our youth, when we are spiritually underdeveloped, we are like late-sleeping teenagers who should be using that time for spiritual growth. In subsequent

מִתְחַיֵּב בְּנַפְשׁוֹ – *Incurred a life-threatening punishment.* We are forbidden at all times to be unmindful of Torah learning, for the failure to engage in regular Torah study leads to spiritual atrophy. The source of this prohibition is precisely in the verses that R. Dostai quotes in this *mishna*. They forbid us to forget that it is Torah that raises the Jewish nation to greatness, wisdom and understanding. The Torah requires us to be a prodigious and wise nation, and forbids us to be a foolish and inconsequential one. Thus the spiritual lethargy that results when we separate ourselves from Torah study is prohibited, and the Jew who fails in this responsibility commits a grave sin (R. Joseph B. Soloveitchik).

Ps. 82 'He will judge in the midst of judges.' What verse suggests it even of two?
Mal. 3 The words of Malachi, 'Then those who revere the Lord spoke with one another, and the Lord hearkened and heard.' And what verse suggests it
Ex. 20 even of one? The words of Exodus, 'In every place where I cause My name to be mentioned, I will come to you and I will bless you.'"

Amos 9 8. R. Eleazar of Bertota would say, "Give Him what is His, for you and what
I Chr. 29 is yours are His. The same thought is expressed in David's words, 'For all is from You, and from Your own hand we give to You.'"

9. R. Jacob used to say, "Those who study the Torah while traveling, and interrupt their learning to proclaim, 'How beautiful is that tree, how beautiful is that field,' are considered to have incurred a life-threatening punishment."

10. R. Dostai ben Yannai would say in R. Meir's name, "Anyone who deliberately forgets any of his Torah learning is considered to have incurred
Deut. 4 a life-threatening punishment. As it says, 'Only take heed to yourself and guard your soul diligently, so that you do not forget the things which your eyes have seen.' In case you think that this applies even when your
Deut. 4 memory unintentionally fails you, the verse continues, 'and that they be not removed from your heart all the days of your life.' In other words, you risk your life only when you deliberately remove God's words from your heart."

11. R. Ḥanina ben Dosa used to say, "Everyone in whom fear of sin takes precedence over learning, his learning will endure; but everyone whose learning takes precedence over fear of sin, his learning will not endure."

12. He also used to say, "Everyone whose works exceed his learning, his learning will endure; but everyone whose learning exceeds his works, his learning will not endure."

13. He also used to say, "Everyone in whom the spirit of his fellow men takes pleasure, the spirit of God also takes pleasure; but everyone in whom the spirit of his fellow men does not take pleasure, the spirit of God takes no pleasure in him."

14. R. Dosa ben Harkinas said, "Morning sleep, noonday wine, children's talk, and frequenting the synagogues of the ignorant deprive a person of eternal life."

---

years we often indulge in sensory pleasures, symbolized by alcohol in the middle of the day. Thereafter we are preoccupied with establishing our families, exposed to "children's chatter" that leaves little time for spiritual priorities. Finally, after a lifetime of pursuing these other priorities, we often find ourselves in a twilight stage of spiritual deprivation, spending our

טו רַבִּי אֶלְעָזָר הַמּוֹדָעִי אוֹמֵר: הַמְחַלֵּל אֶת הַקֳּדָשִׁים, וְהַמְבַזֶּה אֶת הַמּוֹעֲדוֹת,
וְהַמַּלְבִּין פְּנֵי חֲבֵרוֹ בָּרַבִּים, וְהַמֵּפֵר בְּרִיתוֹ שֶׁל אַבְרָהָם אָבִינוּ, וְהַמְגַלֶּה פָנִים
בַּתּוֹרָה שֶׁלֹּא כַהֲלָכָה, אַף עַל פִּי שֶׁיֵּשׁ בְּיָדוֹ תּוֹרָה וּמַעֲשִׂים טוֹבִים, אֵין לוֹ
חֵלֶק לָעוֹלָם הַבָּא.

טז רַבִּי יִשְׁמָעֵאל אוֹמֵר: הֱוֵי קַל לְרֹאשׁ וְנוֹחַ לְתִשְׁחֹרֶת, וֶהֱוֵי מְקַבֵּל אֶת כָּל
הָאָדָם בְּשִׂמְחָה.

יז רַבִּי עֲקִיבָא אוֹמֵר: שְׂחוֹק וְקַלּוּת רֹאשׁ מַרְגִּילִין אֶת הָאָדָם לְעֶרְוָה. מָסֹרֶת
סְיָג לַתּוֹרָה, מַעְשְׂרוֹת סְיָג לָעֹשֶׁר, נְדָרִים סְיָג לַפְּרִישׁוּת, סְיָג לַחָכְמָה
שְׁתִיקָה.

יח הוּא הָיָה אוֹמֵר, חָבִיב אָדָם שֶׁנִּבְרָא בְצֶלֶם, חִבָּה יְתֵרָה נוֹדַעַת לוֹ שֶׁנִּבְרָא
בראשית ט בְּצֶלֶם, שֶׁנֶּאֱמַר: כִּי בְּצֶלֶם אֱלֹהִים עָשָׂה אֶת־הָאָדָם: חֲבִיבִין יִשְׂרָאֵל שֶׁנִּקְרְאוּ
דברים יד בָנִים לַמָּקוֹם, חִבָּה יְתֵרָה נוֹדַעַת לָהֶם שֶׁנִּקְרְאוּ בָנִים לַמָּקוֹם, שֶׁנֶּאֱמַר: בָּנִים
אַתֶּם לַיהוה אֱלֹהֵיכֶם: חֲבִיבִין יִשְׂרָאֵל שֶׁנִּתַּן לָהֶם כְּלִי חֶמְדָּה, חִבָּה יְתֵרָה
משלי ד נוֹדַעַת לָהֶם שֶׁנִּתַּן לָהֶם כְּלִי חֶמְדָּה שֶׁבּוֹ נִבְרָא הָעוֹלָם, שֶׁנֶּאֱמַר: כִּי לֶקַח
טוֹב נָתַתִּי לָכֶם, תּוֹרָתִי אַל־תַּעֲזֹבוּ:

יט הַכֹּל צָפוּי, וְהָרְשׁוּת נְתוּנָה, וּבְטוּב הָעוֹלָם נִדּוֹן, וְהַכֹּל לְפִי רֹב הַמַּעֲשֶׂה.

---

later years in the company of similarly ignorant people. R. Dosa urges us to avoid this sad fate, by striving at every stage of our lives to seek transformative spiritual accomplishments that will allow us to earn and enjoy eternal life (R. Barukh HaLevi Epstein).

חָבִיב אָדָם שֶׁנִּבְרָא בְצֶלֶם, חִבָּה יְתֵרָה נוֹדַעַת לוֹ שֶׁנִּבְרָא בְּצֶלֶם – *Beloved is man in that he was created in the image of God; but greater yet is the divine love that made this known to him.* The *mishna* repeats itself in almost identical phrasing to express the two levels of divine love manifested in our creation in the image of God. As animal-like physical beings we are capable of acting like brutes, or worse. At the same time we are endowed with a moral spark reflecting God Himself. This aspect allows us to live ethically and spiritually in imitation of God. We experience constant struggle between these two sides of our nature. Which side wins out at any given moment depends on our upbringing, education, social influences, and prior choices. In the end, however, the outcome is entirely up to us. This, says the *mishna*, is the first act of God's love – that by creating us in His image He granted us the privilege of forming our own moral character. The second, and even greater, manifestation of divine love is that we can become joyously aware over time that we have succeeded in empowering the divine image within us, and that as a result we have acted in accordance with God's will (R. Moshe Feinstein).

הַכֹּל צָפוּי, וְהָרְשׁוּת נְתוּנָה, וּבְטוּב הָעוֹלָם נִדּוֹן, וְהַכֹּל לְפִי רֹב הַמַּעֲשֶׂה – *All is foreseen, but free-will is given to man. The world is judged compassionately for the good, in accordance with the preponderance of one's actions.* Rambam explains this *mishna* briefly in his commentary to the *mishna* itself, and at length in the eighth chapter of his introduction. We cannot escape responsibility for our actions or our moral

15. R. Eleazar of Modiim would say, "These have no share in the World to Come even if they possess Torah and good deeds: One who desecrates holy things, one who disrespects [the intermediate days of] Yom Tov, one who embarrasses one's fellow in public, one who deliberately avoids performing or undoes a circumcision which is the covenant of our father Abraham, and one who makes allegorical interpretations of the Torah's laws in a way that would prevent them being observed."

16. R. Yishmael used to say, "Be respectful in serving those who are in a position of authority, but also treat those younger than you with due civility. receive everyone cheerfully."

17. R. Akiva used to say, "Merrymaking and frivolity are conducive to immorality. Tradition is a fence that safeguards the Torah; tithing is conducive to wealth; vows are conducive to abstinence; silence is conducive to wisdom."

18. He used to say, "Beloved is man in that he was created in the image of God; but greater yet is the divine love that made this known to him, as it says,
Gen. 9 'In the image of God He made man.' Beloved are Israel in that they are called children of God; but greater yet is the love that made this known to
Deut. 14 them, as it says, 'You are children to the Lord your God.' Beloved are Israel in that they have been given the Torah that is the precious instrument by which the world was created; but greater yet is the love that made this
Prov. 4 known to them, as it says, 'For I have given you a good doctrine; do not abandon My Torah.'"

19. "All is foreseen, but free-will is given to man. The world is judged compassionately for the good, in accordance with the preponderance of one's actions."

---

character by claiming that causal chains allow us no choice. Neither can we disclaim responsibility for our actions on the grounds that we are the products of our upbringing, our parents, our teachers, or our environment. We cannot even claim on theological grounds that we are not free to choose because God always knows in advance of our "choices" as to what we will do. To such arguments R. Akiva replies that unlike the rest of the cosmos, man is uniquely endowed with the ability to choose what he will or will not do at any given moment. Our actions mold our moral character, so we cannot claim innocence on the grounds that we are born with a certain moral character. Even God's foreknowledge, which transcends our understanding because He and His knowledge are incomprehensibly one, does not allow us to escape responsibility for our choices. Thus we can freely choose and He can also know. In sum God knows all, man is granted the ability to choose, we are judged compassionately for those choices, and the more we make the right choices, the better it will be for us.

כ הוּא הָיָה אוֹמֵר: הַכֹּל נָתוּן בְּעֵרָבוֹן, וּמְצוּדָה פְרוּסָה עַל כָּל הַחַיִּים. הֶחָנוּת פְּתוּחָה, וְהַחֶנְוָנִי מַקִּיף, וְהַפִּנְקָס פָּתְוּחַ, וְהַיָּד כּוֹתֶבֶת, וְכָל הָרוֹצֶה לִלְווֹת יָבֹא וְיִלְוֶה. וְהַגַּבָּאִין מַחֲזִירִין תָּדִיר בְּכָל יוֹם, וְנִפְרָעִין מִן הָאָדָם מִדַּעְתּוֹ וְשֶׁלֹּא מִדַּעְתּוֹ, וְיֵשׁ לָהֶם עַל מַה שֶּׁיִּסְמֹכוּ. וְהַדִּין, דִּין אֱמֶת. וְהַכֹּל מְתֻקָּן לִסְעוּדָה.

כא רַבִּי אֶלְעָזָר בֶּן עֲזַרְיָה אוֹמֵר: אִם אֵין תּוֹרָה אֵין דֶּרֶךְ אֶרֶץ, אִם אֵין דֶּרֶךְ אֶרֶץ אֵין תּוֹרָה. אִם אֵין חָכְמָה אֵין יִרְאָה, אִם אֵין יִרְאָה אֵין חָכְמָה. אִם אֵין דַּעַת אֵין בִּינָה, אִם אֵין בִּינָה אֵין דַּעַת. אִם אֵין קֶמַח אֵין תּוֹרָה, אִם אֵין תּוֹרָה אֵין קֶמַח.

כב הוּא הָיָה אוֹמֵר: כָּל שֶׁחָכְמָתוֹ מְרֻבָּה מִמַּעֲשָׂיו, לְמָה הוּא דוֹמֶה, לְאִילָן שֶׁעֲנָפָיו מְרֻבִּין וְשָׁרָשָׁיו מֻעָטִין, וְהָרְוּחַ בָּאָה וְעוֹקַרְתּוֹ וְהוֹפַכְתּוֹ עַל פָּנָיו.
ירמיה יז שֶׁנֶּאֱמַר, וְהָיָה כְּעַרְעָר בָּעֲרָבָה, וְלֹא יִרְאֶה כִּי־יָבוֹא טוֹב, וְשָׁכַן חֲרֵרִים בַּמִּדְבָּר, אֶרֶץ מְלֵחָה וְלֹא תֵשֵׁב: אֲבָל כָּל שֶׁמַּעֲשָׂיו מְרֻבִּין מֵחָכְמָתוֹ, לְמָה הוּא דוֹמֶה, לְאִילָן שֶׁעֲנָפָיו מֻעָטִין וְשָׁרָשָׁיו מְרֻבִּין, שֶׁאֲפִלּוּ כָּל הָרוּחוֹת שֶׁבָּעוֹלָם בָּאוֹת
ירמיה יז וְנוֹשְׁבוֹת בּוֹ, אֵין מְזִיזִין אוֹתוֹ מִמְּקוֹמוֹ. שֶׁנֶּאֱמַר: וְהָיָה כְּעֵץ שָׁתוּל עַל־מַיִם, וְעַל־יוּבַל יְשַׁלַּח שָׁרָשָׁיו, וְלֹא יִרְאֶה כִּי־יָבֹא חֹם, וְהָיָה עָלֵהוּ רַעֲנָן, וּבִשְׁנַת בַּצֹּרֶת לֹא יִדְאָג, וְלֹא יָמִישׁ מֵעֲשׂוֹת פֶּרִי:

כג רַבִּי אֱלִיעֶזֶר בֶּן חִסְמָא אוֹמֵר: קִנִּין וּפִתְחֵי נִדָּה הֵן הֵן גּוּפֵי הֲלָכוֹת, תְּקוּפוֹת וְגִימַטְרִיָּאוֹת פַּרְפְּרָאוֹת לַחָכְמָה.

מכות כג: רַבִּי חֲנַנְיָא בֶּן עֲקַשְׁיָא אוֹמֵר: רָצָה הַקָּדוֹשׁ בָּרוּךְ הוּא לְזַכּוֹת אֶת יִשְׂרָאֵל, לְפִיכָךְ הִרְבָּה
ישעיה מב לָהֶם תּוֹרָה וּמִצְוֹת. שֶׁנֶּאֱמַר: יהוה חָפֵץ לְמַעַן צִדְקוֹ, יַגְדִּיל תּוֹרָה וְיַאְדִּיר:

If there is a מנין, *mourners say* קדיש דרבנן *(page 724).*

אִם אֵין תּוֹרָה אֵין דֶּרֶךְ אֶרֶץ, אִם אֵין דֶּרֶךְ אֶרֶץ אֵין תּוֹרָה – *If one has not studied Torah one cannot act with virtue, and if one does not act with virtue then one's Torah study is useless.* R. Israel Lipschutz, the *Tiferet Yisrael*, affirms that this *mishna* is not saying that one cannot be moral unless one has Torah, for after all we know that there are Torah-ignorant Jews who are בַּעֲלֵי מוּסָר וְדֶרֶךְ אֶרֶץ (ethical and decent people), as well as righteous Gentiles who certainly do not possess Torah. Rather, every nation – he was presumably speaking of Christians and Muslims – has a דַּת אֱלֹקִי (religious framework) that includes three principles: that there is a God-given text, that there is divine reward and punishment, and that the soul survives after death. They only differ in the understanding of these beliefs. The *mishna* teaches that if a person does not accept these three beliefs (i.e., without this "Torah") then that person cannot be trusted to treat the souls of others with due respect. Likewise, someone who has no respect for the souls of others cannot truly be a person of Torah (as thus defined), for those three beliefs are predicated on the acknowledgment that all humans have a soul, and are higher than animals, and hence are to be treated with respect and dignity. Without the one there cannot be the other.

20. R. Akiva would also say, "We will be held accountable for all that we do with that which God has given to us, and there can be no escaping this. The store is open, the owner extends credit, the ledger is open, the hand records, and anyone who wishes to borrow can come and borrow. But the collectors unfailingly make their daily rounds and exact payment whether or not one remembers the debts, for they have reliable proof of indebtedness, and the divine judgment is always accurate. The result will be that after everyone will have paid their debt they will qualify to partake of the World to Come."

21. R. Eleazar ben Azarya used to say, "If one has not studied Torah one cannot act with virtue, and if one does not act with virtue then one's Torah study is useless. Where there is no wisdom, there is no reverence, and where there is no reverence, there is no wisdom. Where there is no knowledge, there is no understanding, and where there is no understanding, there is no knowledge. Where there is no food, there is no Torah, and where there is no Torah, there is no food."

22. He would also say, "He whose wisdom is greater than his works, to what is he likened? To a tree with many branches but few roots. The wind
Jer. 17 blows, uproots it, and it falls to the ground, as it says, 'For he shall be like a tamarisk in the steppes, not seeing when good comes, but abiding in the parched places of the wilderness, in a land that is salt and uninhabited.' But he whose works are greater than his wisdom, to what is he likened? To a tree with few branches but many roots. All the winds in the world may come and blow against it, but they cannot move it from its place, as
Jer. 17 it says, 'For he shall be as a tree planted by water, striking down its roots to the river, and not feeling when heat comes, but its foliage remains green, and in the year of drought it has no cares and does not cease to bear fruit.'"

23. R. Eleazar Ḥisma used to say, "The study of the laws pertaining to the sacrifices of various kinds of birds as well as how to keep track of fluctuations in menstrual cycles are essential to upholding the Oral Law, whereas the study of astronomy and geometry are to be undertaken only in due course."

Makkot 23b R. ḤANANYA ben Akashya used to say, "The Holy One, blessed is He, wishing to render Israel more worthy, enlarged the Torah and its commandments for them, as
Is. 42 it is said, 'The Lord desired, for the sake of its [Israel's] righteousness, to magnify the Torah and glorify it.'"

If a minyan is present, mourners say the Rabbis' Kaddish (page 725).

פרק רביעי

סנהדרין צ. ישעיה ס כָּל יִשְׂרָאֵל יֵשׁ לָהֶם חֵלֶק לָעוֹלָם הַבָּא. שֶׁנֶּאֱמַר: וְעַמֵּךְ כֻּלָּם צַדִּיקִים, לְעוֹלָם יִירְשׁוּ אָרֶץ, נֵצֶר מַטָּעַי, מַעֲשֵׂה יָדַי לְהִתְפָּאֵר:

תהלים קיט א **בֶּן זוֹמָא** אוֹמֵר: אֵיזֶהוּ חָכָם, הַלּוֹמֵד מִכָּל אָדָם, שֶׁנֶּאֱמַר: מִכָּל־מְלַמְּדַי הִשְׂכַּלְתִּי, כִּי עֵדְוֹתֶיךָ שִׂיחָה לִי: אֵיזֶהוּ גִבּוֹר, הַכּוֹבֵשׁ אֶת יִצְרוֹ,
משלי טז שֶׁנֶּאֱמַר: טוֹב אֶרֶךְ אַפַּיִם מִגִּבּוֹר וּמֹשֵׁל בְּרוּחוֹ מִלֹּכֵד עִיר: אֵיזֶהוּ עָשִׁיר,
תהלים קכח הַשָּׂמֵחַ בְּחֶלְקוֹ, שֶׁנֶּאֱמַר: יְגִיעַ כַּפֶּיךָ כִּי תֹאכֵל אַשְׁרֶיךָ וְטוֹב לָךְ: אַשְׁרֶיךָ בָּעוֹלָם הַזֶּה וְטוֹב לָךְ לָעוֹלָם הַבָּא. אֵיזֶהוּ מְכֻבָּד, הַמְכַבֵּד אֶת הַבְּרִיּוֹת,
שמואל א׳ ב שֶׁנֶּאֱמַר: כִּי־מְכַבְּדַי אֲכַבֵּד, וּבֹזַי יֵקָלּוּ:

ב בֶּן עַזַּאי אוֹמֵר: הֱוֵי רָץ לְמִצְוָה קַלָּה וּבוֹרֵחַ מִן הָעֲבֵרָה. שֶׁמִּצְוָה גוֹרֶרֶת מִצְוָה, וַעֲבֵרָה גוֹרֶרֶת עֲבֵרָה. שֶׁשְּׂכַר מִצְוָה מִצְוָה, וּשְׂכַר עֲבֵרָה עֲבֵרָה.

ג הוּא הָיָה אוֹמֵר: אַל תְּהִי בָז לְכָל אָדָם, וְאַל תְּהִי מַפְלִיג לְכָל דָּבָר. שֶׁאֵין לְךָ אָדָם שֶׁאֵין לוֹ שָׁעָה, וְאֵין לְךָ דָבָר שֶׁאֵין לוֹ מָקוֹם.

ד רַבִּי לְוִיטַס אִישׁ יַבְנֶה אוֹמֵר: מְאֹד מְאֹד הֱוֵי שְׁפַל רוּחַ, שֶׁתִּקְוַת אֱנוֹשׁ רִמָּה.

CHAPTER 4

אֵיזֶהוּ חָכָם, הַלּוֹמֵד מִכָּל אָדָם – *Who is wise? He who learns from every person.* Wisdom is not a function of how much one knows, but rather how much one thirsts for knowledge. One who loves knowledge, and has a passion for it, can be considered wise even while still acquiring it, as the very desire makes it likely that one will ultimately attain it. Thus true wisdom is the appreciation of wisdom, and the readiness to seek it anywhere, without embarrassment, at every stage of one's life, even by examining the ways of those who may be on a lower level than oneself (Rabbeinu Yona).

הֱוֵי רָץ לְמִצְוָה קַלָּה – *Be eager to do even an easy commandment.* The Gemara (*Makkot* 10a) invokes Moses as the embodiment of this principle. By the end of his life he had reached the pinnacle of spiritual accomplishment, yet he did everything in his power to perform the *mitzva* of setting aside three cities of refuge in the trans-Jordan. Even though he was technically exempt from the obligation on the grounds that the three corresponding cities in Israel proper were not yet designated, and thus all six could not be designated at once, as a strict reading of *halakha* would indicate, Moses nonetheless argued, "If I can perform this *mitzva*, how can I not do so, even if I am technically excused?" How much more should we, who are so much less than Moses, run to perform every *mitzva* that comes our way (Rambam).

אַל תְּהִי בָז לְכָל אָדָם – *Do not treat any person with disrespect.* Ben Azzai teaches us that no person is self-sufficient. God made His world such that is impossible for one person to survive in isolation, given everything involved in providing for even our most basic needs. In *Berakhot* 58a, Ben Zoma declares his good

CHAPTER FOUR

Sanhedrin 90a Is. 60 ALL ISRAEL have a share in the World to Come. As it is said, "Your people shall all be righteous and shall inherit the land forever. They are the shoot of My planting, the work of My hands in which I glory."

1. בֶּן זוֹמָא BEN ZOMA used to say, "Who is wise? He who learns from every person, as it says, 'I gain wisdom from all who teach me.' Who is strong? He who controls his passions, as it says, 'Better is he who is slow to anger than the mighty, and the one who controls himself than he who captures a city.' Who is rich? He who is happy in his lot, as it says, 'If you eat the labor of your hands, you will be happy and it will be well with you': 'Happy are you' in this world, 'and it will be well with you' in the World to Come. Who is honored? He who honors his fellow men, as it says, 'For I honor those who honor Me, and those who despise Me shall be lightly esteemed.'"

Ps. 119 / Prov. 16 / Ps. 128 / I Sam. 2

2. Ben Azzai used to say, "Be eager to do even an easy commandment, and flee from transgression; for one commandment leads to another, and one transgression leads to another. The reward for performing a commandment is the opportunity to perform another one, whereas the punishment for committing one transgression is the opportunity to sin again."

3. He also used to say, "Do not treat any person with disrespect, and do not consider anything to be without a purpose. For there is no person whose time will not come, neither is there anything that is not needed somewhere in the world."

4. R. Levitas of Yavneh used to say, "Be very, very humble, because the aspirations of every person end with maggots."

---

fortune in having everything at his disposal, whereas Adam had to do all kinds of things before he could eat or be dressed. What is true of the individual is equally true on the global level, because no country can survive by itself, given that the resources to sustain the world are scattered all over the globe. Accordingly, we must always seek harmony with our fellows, for God created His world in such a way that ultimately we all need each other, if not in the present then in the future. We can never know when we may need others, no matter how insignificant they may appear. (R. Moshe Feinstein).

הֱוֵי שְׁפַל רוּחַ– *Be very, very humble*. The fact that we are susceptible to accidental turns of fortune is not necessarily a tragic condition. It can also be the source of virtue and nobility of character. Being aware of our vulnerability

ה רַבִּי יוֹחָנָן בֶּן בְּרוֹקָא אוֹמֵר: כָּל הַמְחַלֵּל שֵׁם שָׁמַיִם בַּסֵּתֶר, נִפְרָעִין מִמֶּנּוּ בַּגָּלוּי. אֶחָד שׁוֹגֵג וְאֶחָד מֵזִיד בְּחִלּוּל הַשֵּׁם.

ו רַבִּי יִשְׁמָעֵאל בְּנוֹ אוֹמֵר: הַלּוֹמֵד עַל מְנָת לְלַמֵּד, מַסְפִּיקִין בְּיָדוֹ לִלְמֹד וּלְלַמֵּד. וְהַלּוֹמֵד עַל מְנָת לַעֲשׂוֹת, מַסְפִּיקִין בְּיָדוֹ לִלְמֹד וּלְלַמֵּד, לִשְׁמֹר וְלַעֲשׂוֹת.

ז רַבִּי צָדוֹק אוֹמֵר: אַל תִּפְרֹשׁ מִן הַצִּבּוּר, וְאַל תַּעַשׂ עַצְמְךָ כְּעוֹרְכֵי הַדַּיָּנִין, וְאַל תַּעֲשֵׂם עֲטָרָה לְהִתְגַּדֵּל בָּהּ, וְלֹא קַרְדֹּם לַחְפֹּר בָּהּ. וְכָךְ הָיָה הִלֵּל אוֹמֵר: וּדְאִשְׁתַּמֵּשׁ בְּתָגָא חֲלָף. הָא לָמַדְתָּ, כָּל הַנֶּהֱנֶה מִדִּבְרֵי תוֹרָה, נוֹטֵל חַיָּיו מִן הָעוֹלָם.

ח רַבִּי יוֹסֵי אוֹמֵר: כָּל הַמְכַבֵּד אֶת הַתּוֹרָה, גּוּפוֹ מְכֻבָּד עַל הַבְּרִיּוֹת. וְכָל הַמְחַלֵּל אֶת הַתּוֹרָה, גּוּפוֹ מְחֻלָּל עַל הַבְּרִיּוֹת.

ט רַבִּי יִשְׁמָעֵאל בְּנוֹ אוֹמֵר: הַחוֹשֵׂךְ עַצְמוֹ מִן הַדִּין, פּוֹרֵק מִמֶּנּוּ אֵיבָה וְגָזֵל וּשְׁבוּעַת שָׁוְא. וְהַגַּס לִבּוֹ בְּהוֹרָאָה, שׁוֹטֶה, רָשָׁע וְגַס רוּחַ.

י הוּא הָיָה אוֹמֵר: אַל תְּהִי דָן יְחִידִי, שֶׁאֵין דָּן יְחִידִי אֶלָּא אֶחָד. וְאַל תֹּאמַר קַבְּלוּ דַעְתִּי, שֶׁהֵן רַשָּׁאִין וְלֹא אָתָּה.

יא רַבִּי יוֹנָתָן אוֹמֵר: כָּל הַמְקַיֵּם אֶת הַתּוֹרָה מֵעֹנִי, סוֹפוֹ לְקַיְּמָהּ מֵעֹשֶׁר. וְכָל הַמְבַטֵּל אֶת הַתּוֹרָה מֵעֹשֶׁר, סוֹפוֹ לְבַטְּלָהּ מֵעֹנִי.

יב רַבִּי מֵאִיר אוֹמֵר: הֱוֵי מְמַעֵט בְּעֵסֶק וַעֲסֹק בַּתּוֹרָה, וֶהֱוֵי שְׁפַל רוּחַ בִּפְנֵי כָל אָדָם. וְאִם בָּטַלְתָּ מִן הַתּוֹרָה, יֵשׁ לְךָ בְּטֵלִים הַרְבֵּה כְּנֶגְדְּךָ. וְאִם עָמַלְתָּ בַּתּוֹרָה, יֶשׁ לוֹ שָׂכָר הַרְבֵּה לִתֶּן לָךְ.

יג רַבִּי אֱלִיעֶזֶר בֶּן יַעֲקֹב אוֹמֵר: הָעוֹשֶׂה מִצְוָה אַחַת, קוֹנֶה לוֹ פְּרַקְלִיט אֶחָד. וְהָעוֹבֵר עֲבֵרָה אַחַת, קוֹנֶה לוֹ קַטֵּגוֹר אֶחָד. תְּשׁוּבָה וּמַעֲשִׂים טוֹבִים, כִּתְרִיס בִּפְנֵי הַפֻּרְעָנוּת.

יד רַבִּי יוֹחָנָן הַסַּנְדְּלָר אוֹמֵר: כָּל כְּנֵסִיָּה שֶׁהִיא לְשֵׁם שָׁמַיִם, סוֹפָהּ לְהִתְקַיֵּם. וְשֶׁאֵינָהּ לְשֵׁם שָׁמַיִם, אֵין סוֹפָהּ לְהִתְקַיֵּם.

---

makes us humble, and dispels arrogance and pride. Rambam regarded humility as the highest ethical quality of man. Though he consistently counseled the golden mean with respect to other human characteristics, he suspended moderation when speaking of humility, saying that we should be humble in the extreme, and he cited the language of this *mishna* in support of this exception (R. Joseph B. Soloveitchik).

5. R. Yoḥanan ben Beroka used to say, "Whoever profanes God's name in secret will pay the penalty in public. When it comes to profaning the name of God there is no difference between acting deliberately or unintentionally."
6. R. Yishmael, his son, used to say, "He who learns in order to teach will be able both to learn and to teach; but he who learns in order to act will be able to learn, to teach, to take heed and to act."
7. R. Tzadok repeated the statements of Hillel: "Do not separate from the community," and of Judah ben Tabbai: "When presiding as a judge, do not act as an advocate." He would also say, "Do not use the words of the Torah like a crown for self-promotion, nor like a spade to make a living." Similarly Hillel used to say, "He who uses the Torah for personal gain will die." From this we learn that anyone who uses the Torah for personal honor or gain forfeits his life.
8. R. Yose used to say, "Everyone who honors the Torah will in turn be honored by others, and everyone who profanes the Torah will himself be disrespected by others."
9. R. Yishmael, his son, used to say, "He who shuns the office of judge avoids being despised, causing unjust loss to another, and causing another to take an unnecessary oath. And one who judges arrogantly without proper consideration is a fool, wicked, and arrogant."
10. He used to say, "Judge not alone, for there is but One Who may judge alone. Do not say 'Accept my opinion' because the majority are entitled to decide, not you alone."
11. R. Yonatan would say, "Everyone who fulfills the Torah in poverty will in the end fulfill it in wealth, and everyone who disregards the Torah in wealth will in the end disregard it in poverty."
12. R. Meir used to say, "Spend less time at your worldly occupation and devote yourself to studying Torah. Be humble of spirit before all men. If you neglect to study Torah sufficiently there will be many distractions to limit your study even further; but if you work diligently in the Torah, God has a rich reward for you."
13. R. Eliezer ben Jacob used to say, "For every commandment one performs one acquires one defense attorney. And for every transgression one acquires one prosecutor. Repentance and good deeds are an obstacle preventing punishment."
14. R. Yoḥanan the sandal-maker would say, "Every gathering that comes together strictly for the sake of heaven will achieve its purpose, whereas one that is not for the sake of heaven will not achieve its purpose."

טו רַבִּי אֶלְעָזָר בֶּן שַׁמּוּעַ אוֹמֵר: יְהִי כְבוֹד תַּלְמִידְךָ חָבִיב עָלֶיךָ כְּשֶׁלָּךְ, וּכְבוֹד
חֲבֵרְךָ כְּמוֹרָא רַבָּךְ, וּמוֹרָא רַבָּךְ כְּמוֹרָא שָׁמָיִם.

טז רַבִּי יְהוּדָה אוֹמֵר: הֱוֵי זָהִיר בְּתַלְמוּד, שֶׁשִּׁגְגַת תַּלְמוּד עוֹלָה זָדוֹן.

יז רַבִּי שִׁמְעוֹן אוֹמֵר: שְׁלֹשָׁה כְתָרִים הֵן, כֶּתֶר תּוֹרָה וְכֶתֶר כְּהֻנָּה וְכֶתֶר מַלְכוּת,
וְכֶתֶר שֵׁם טוֹב עוֹלֶה עַל גַּבֵּיהֶן.

יח רַבִּי נְהוֹרַאי אוֹמֵר: הֱוֵי גוֹלֶה לִמְקוֹם תּוֹרָה. וְאַל תֹּאמַר שֶׁהִיא תָבוֹא אַחֲרֶיךָ,
שֶׁחֲבֵרֶיךָ יְקַיְּמוּהָ בְּיָדֶךָ. וְאֶל־בִּינָתְךָ אַל־תִּשָּׁעֵן: משלי ג

יט רַבִּי יַנַּאי אוֹמֵר: אֵין בְּיָדֵינוּ לֹא מִשַּׁלְוַת הָרְשָׁעִים וְאַף לֹא מִיִּסּוּרֵי הַצַּדִּיקִים.

כ רַבִּי מַתְיָא בֶּן חָרָשׁ אוֹמֵר: הֱוֵי מַקְדִּים בִּשְׁלוֹם כָּל אָדָם, וֶהֱוֵי זָנָב לָאֲרָיוֹת,
וְאַל תְּהִי רֹאשׁ לַשּׁוּעָלִים.

כא רַבִּי יַעֲקֹב אוֹמֵר: הָעוֹלָם הַזֶּה דּוֹמֶה לִפְרוֹזְדוֹר בִּפְנֵי הָעוֹלָם הַבָּא. הַתְקֵן
עַצְמְךָ בִּפְרוֹזְדוֹר, כְּדֵי שֶׁתִּכָּנֵס לַטְּרַקְלִין.

כב הוּא הָיָה אוֹמֵר: יָפָה שָׁעָה אַחַת בִּתְשׁוּבָה וּמַעֲשִׂים טוֹבִים בָּעוֹלָם הַזֶּה,
מִכֹּל חַיֵּי הָעוֹלָם הַבָּא. וְיָפָה שָׁעָה אַחַת שֶׁל קוֹרַת רוּחַ בָּעוֹלָם הַבָּא, מִכֹּל
חַיֵּי הָעוֹלָם הַזֶּה.

כג רַבִּי שִׁמְעוֹן בֶּן אֶלְעָזָר אוֹמֵר: אַל תְּרַצֶּה אֶת חֲבֵרְךָ בִּשְׁעַת כַּעְסוֹ, וְאַל
תְּנַחֲמֶהוּ בְּשָׁעָה שֶׁמֵּתוֹ מֻטָּל לְפָנָיו, וְאַל תִּשְׁאַל לוֹ בִּשְׁעַת נִדְרוֹ, וְאַל
תִּשְׁתַּדֵּל לִרְאוֹתוֹ בִּשְׁעַת קַלְקָלָתוֹ.

וּמוֹרָא רַבָּךְ כְּמוֹרָא שָׁמָיִם – *And respect for your teacher as precious to you as your fear of heaven.* In general *halakha* seeks to limit the power of anyone who wields a position of authority. The only exception is the respect due a *rebbe*, which is unlimited. Thus the Gemara (*Pesahim* 22b) understands "You must revere the Lord your God" (Deut. 10:20) to include reverence for Torah scholars. The reason is that while in the political realm God is reluctant to share His kingship with men, in the scholarly realm there is no hesitation to do so (R. Joseph B. Soloveitchik).

הָעוֹלָם הַזֶּה דּוֹמֶה לִפְרוֹזְדוֹר בִּפְנֵי הָעוֹלָם הַבָּא – *This world is like an entrance way leading to the World to Come.* This *mishna* teaches that this world and the next are not complete opposites. Even in our lifetimes we can experience something like the spiritual rewards of the World to Come. Judaism is not an otherworldly faith that considers our existence here to be opposed to the hereafter. While it is true that the revelation of God there will be vastly superior, it is also true that we can live our years in this world so as to be better prepared for what we will experience in the next. Those who do not set this as their goal will never come to recognize the fullness of God's glory, neither here nor there. Hence a wise person cultivates intellectual, spiritual, as well as ethical sensitivities and greatness, the better to enjoy both worlds (R. Avraham Yitzḥak HaKohen Kook).

15. R. Eleazar ben Shammua used to say, "Let the dignity of your student be as precious to you as your own dignity, the dignity of your colleague as precious to you as the respect due your teacher, and respect for your teacher as precious to you as your fear of heaven."

16. R. Judah used to say, "Be extremely careful when studying Torah, for any transgressions that result from careless study are considered to be deliberate."

17. R. Simeon (ben Yoḥai) would say, "There are three crowns: the crown of Torah, the crown of the priesthood, and the crown of kingship; but the crown of a good name supersedes all of them."

18. R. Nehorai used to say, "Exile yourself to a place of Torah, and do not think that the Torah will follow you. Neither should you think that your colleagues rather than your teachers will maintain your Torah study
Prov. 3 sufficiently. And you should never rely on your own understanding of Torah."

19. R. Yannai said, "We cannot answer the question why the wicked prosper nor why the righteous suffer."

20. R. Matya ben Ḥarash used to say, "Greet every person first even before they greet you. Be a tail to lions, not a head to foxes."

21. R. Jacob would say, "This world is like an entrance way leading to the World to Come; prepare yourself in the entrance way so that you will be permitted to enter and celebrate in the inner sanctum."

22. He also said, "Better is one hour of repentance and good deeds in this world than all the life of the World to Come; but better is one hour of spiritual joy in the World to Come than all the life of this world."

23. R. Simeon ben Eleazar used to say, "Do not try to placate your fellow man when he is angry, or to comfort him in the hour that his dead lies still unburied before him, or to question him when he is making a vow, or to visit him at the moment he is caught up in transgression."

יָפָה שָׁעָה אַחַת בִּתְשׁוּבָה וּמַעֲשִׂים טוֹבִים – *Better is one hour of repentance and good deeds. Halakha* insists that God must be experienced by living a disciplined life, for it is only through the purifying influence of *mitzvot* that we are sanctified and cleansed. The Torah aspires to bring the Divine Presence into the worldly arena of space and time, in the midst of earthly life. Our goal is not simply to achieve a flight to a higher world, but rather to superimpose, however imperfectly, the eternal world upon "those who dwell in bodies of clay" (Job 4:19). This *mishna* teaches accordingly that a redeemed life, even if it is brief, is better than all of eternity (R. Joseph B. Soloveitchik).

משלי כד כד שְׁמוּאֵל הַקָּטָן אוֹמֵר: בִּנְפֹל אוֹיִבְךָ אַל־תִּשְׂמָח, וּבִכָּשְׁלוֹ אַל־יָגֵל לִבֶּךָ: פֶּן־
יִרְאֶה יהוה וְרַע בְּעֵינָיו, וְהֵשִׁיב מֵעָלָיו אַפּוֹ:

כה אֱלִישָׁע בֶּן אֲבוּיָה אוֹמֵר: הַלּוֹמֵד יֶלֶד, לְמָה הוּא דוֹמֶה, לִדְיוֹ כְתוּבָה עַל נְיָר
חָדָשׁ. וְהַלּוֹמֵד זָקֵן, לְמָה הוּא דוֹמֶה, לִדְיוֹ כְתוּבָה עַל נְיָר מָחוּק.

כו רַבִּי יוֹסֵי בַּר יְהוּדָה אִישׁ כְּפַר הַבַּבְלִי אוֹמֵר: הַלּוֹמֵד מִן הַקְּטַנִּים, לְמָה הוּא
דוֹמֶה, לְאוֹכֵל עֲנָבִים קֵהוֹת וְשׁוֹתֶה יַיִן מִגִּתּוֹ. וְהַלּוֹמֵד מִן הַזְּקֵנִים, לְמָה הוּא
דוֹמֶה, לְאוֹכֵל עֲנָבִים בְּשׁוּלוֹת וְשׁוֹתֶה יַיִן יָשָׁן.

כז רַבִּי אוֹמֵר: אַל תִּסְתַּכֵּל בַּקַּנְקָן, אֶלָּא בְּמַה שֶּׁיֵּשׁ בּוֹ. יֵשׁ קַנְקָן חָדָשׁ מָלֵא
יָשָׁן, וְיָשָׁן שֶׁאֲפִלּוּ חָדָשׁ אֵין בּוֹ.

כח רַבִּי אֶלְעָזָר הַקַּפָּר אוֹמֵר: הַקִּנְאָה וְהַתַּאֲוָה וְהַכָּבוֹד, מוֹצִיאִין אֶת הָאָדָם
מִן הָעוֹלָם.

בִּנְפֹל אוֹיִבְךָ אַל־תִּשְׂמָח – *When your enemy falls, do not rejoice*. This statement refers only to the downfall of one's personal enemies, not to the enemies of the Jewish people. It is not relevant in the public realm, i.e., in reacting to the fate of the enemies of the Jews (*Midrash Shmuel*).

It was precisely because Shmuel HaKatan favored these verses out of his abundant determination not to rejoice at the fall of his personal enemies, that he was elected by Rabban Gamliel to compose the supplementary *berakha* in the daily *Amida* that asks God to neutralize the enemies of God and the Jewish people. For his motivation in composing so sensitive a prayer would not in any way include any personal desire to see his own opponents brought low by God. It would be motivated purely by the good of the Jewish people, and the name of God (R. Avraham Yitzḥak HaKohen Kook).

It is significant that this is the only *mishna* in all of *Pirkei Avot* in which the quoted Tanna simply quotes a verse from Scripture without articulating a saying or commentary of his own. Here Shmuel HaKatan quotes (as he apparently often did) two verses from Proverbs. His reticence was likely the result of extreme humility (as similarly reflected in *Sanhedrin* 11a describing his selflessness) for which, perhaps, he was known as "HaKatan" (the small, or modest, one). Indeed the key lesson of these two verses is to teach us the virtues of humility, even when we are vindicated by the course of events. Instead of seeing the fall of an opponent as a sign that we are favored by God and by fate, we should humbly recognize that the downfall of a detractor could simply be a temporary turn subject to eventual reversal, as explained by the *Metzudat David* to that verse. As the seventeenth-century English poet John Donne said, "Each man's death diminishes me, for I am involved in mankind. Therefore, send not to know for whom the bell tolls, it tolls for thee" (R. Basil Herring).

הַקִּנְאָה וְהַתַּאֲוָה וְהַכָּבוֹד, מוֹצִיאִין אֶת הָאָדָם מִן הָעוֹלָם – *Jealousy, the pursuit of physical pleasure, and the longing for honor cause a person to be removed prematurely from the world.* Of all the destructive behaviors that could be listed, R. Elazar HaKapar chose these three, because these are the most conducive to self-defeating behaviors. First, if we did not constantly look at what others have we would feel no envy, but instead be satisfied to have our basic needs fulfilled. Instead we spend much of our time and energy, in ways both permitted and forbidden, pursuing things that enable us to acquire

Prov. 24 24. Samuel HaKatan would say, "When your enemy falls, do not rejoice, and when he stumbles, do not let your heart be glad, lest the Lord see and it be evil in His eyes, and He turn away His anger from him [to you]."

25. Elisha ben Avuya used to say, "One who learns when a youth, what is he like? He is like ink written on fresh paper. But one who learns when old, what is he like? He is like ink written on paper that has been written on and erased for reuse."

26. R. Yose ben Judah of Kfar HaBavli used to say, "He who learns from the young, what is he like? He is like someone who eats unripe grapes and drinks wine fresh from his winepress. But he who learns from his elders, what is he like? He is like one who eats ripe grapes and drinks old wine."

27. R. (Judah HaNasi) would say [in disagreement], "Do not pass judgment by looking at the flask but at what it contains, for a new flask may be filled with old wine, while an old flask may be empty, not even containing new wine."

28. R. Eleazar HaKappar used to say, "Jealousy, the pursuit of physical pleasure, and the longing for honor cause a person to be removed prematurely from the world."

---

what we really do not need, and in the process put ourselves at risk of losing our peace of mind in this world as well as our optimal place in the next. Second, when we spend our lives in pursuit of the pleasures of the flesh, we are likely to engage in spiritually destructive behaviors, and thus come to forfeit a redeemed life. Third, the urge to achieve honor exposes us to risky behavior and a heightened possibility of eventual ruin, whether physical or spiritual. So too on the broader level of how nations behave when they believe that their "national honor" must be protected or enhanced at all costs, they will engage in policies that likely lead to their eventual defeat and ruin. Fortunate are we who have the Torah and its laws. For only in following them faithfully can we be assured that we do not ourselves fall victim to these self-destructive behaviors, but instead can always do what is right and proper, and at the same time acquire true life and happiness in this world and the next (R. Moshe Feinstein, writing in 1921 in Soviet Russia in the aftermath of the First World War and the rise of Communism).

This *mishna* condemns the pursuit of honor in such stark terms, even though the Torah tells us that the garments of the High Priest were intended precisely to bring him honor and dignity. For the Torah teaches us that these two virtues do have an important place in life. If the pursuit of honor stems from selfishness, and results in diminishing the honor of others, then it is nothing more than vanity. But when it is motivated by a desire to honor all people, recognizing that every human is created in God's image, then the pursuit of honor is essential to a dignified life. This is true for parents and children, as well as husbands and wives. The same is true of the pursuit of beauty, for as pointed out by the Vilna Gaon, it is with good reason that the Torah pointed out the beauty of Sarah, Rebecca, and Rachel, as the Torah knew that eye appeal has a great deal to do with heart appeal. Thus

כט הוּא הָיָה אוֹמֵר: הַיִּלּוֹדִים לָמוּת, וְהַמֵּתִים לִחְיוֹת, וְהַחַיִּים לִדּוֹן, לֵידַע וּלְהוֹדִיעַ וּלְהִוָּדַע, שֶׁהוּא אֵל, הוּא הַיּוֹצֵר, הוּא הַבּוֹרֵא, הוּא הַמֵּבִין, הוּא הַדַּיָּן, הוּא הָעֵד, הוּא בַּעַל דִּין, הוּא עָתִיד לָדוּן. בָּרוּךְ הוּא, שֶׁאֵין לְפָנָיו לֹא עַוְלָה וְלֹא שִׁכְחָה, וְלֹא מַשּׂוֹא פָנִים וְלֹא מִקַּח שֹׁחַד, שֶׁהַכֹּל שֶׁלּוֹ. וְדַע, שֶׁהַכֹּל לְפִי הַחֶשְׁבּוֹן. וְאַל יַבְטִיחֲךָ יִצְרְךָ שֶׁהַשְּׁאוֹל בֵּית מָנוֹס לָךְ, שֶׁעַל כָּרְחֲךָ אַתָּה נוֹצָר, וְעַל כָּרְחֲךָ אַתָּה נוֹלָד, וְעַל כָּרְחֲךָ אַתָּה חַי, וְעַל כָּרְחֲךָ אַתָּה מֵת, וְעַל כָּרְחֲךָ אַתָּה עָתִיד לִתֵּן דִּין וְחֶשְׁבּוֹן לִפְנֵי מֶלֶךְ מַלְכֵי הַמְּלָכִים הַקָּדוֹשׁ בָּרוּךְ הוּא.

מכות כג: רַבִּי חֲנַנְיָא בֶּן עֲקַשְׁיָא אוֹמֵר: רָצָה הַקָּדוֹשׁ בָּרוּךְ הוּא לְזַכּוֹת אֶת יִשְׂרָאֵל, לְפִיכָךְ הִרְבָּה
ישעיה מב לָהֶם תּוֹרָה וּמִצְווֹת. שֶׁנֶּאֱמַר: יהוה חָפֵץ לְמַעַן צִדְקוֹ, יַגְדִּיל תּוֹרָה וְיַאְדִּיר:

If there is a מנין*, mourners say* קדיש דרבנן *(page 724).*

פרק חמישי

סנהדרין צ. כָּל יִשְׂרָאֵל יֵשׁ לָהֶם חֵלֶק לָעוֹלָם הַבָּא. שֶׁנֶּאֱמַר: וְעַמֵּךְ כֻּלָּם צַדִּיקִים, לְעוֹלָם יִירְשׁוּ אָרֶץ,
ישעיה ס נֵצֶר מַטָּעַי, מַעֲשֵׂה יָדַי לְהִתְפָּאֵר:

א **בַּעֲשָׂרָה** מַאֲמָרוֹת נִבְרָא הָעוֹלָם. וּמַה תַּלְמוּד לוֹמַר, וַהֲלֹא בְּמַאֲמָר אֶחָד יָכוֹל לְהִבָּרְאוֹת, אֶלָּא לְהִפָּרַע מִן הָרְשָׁעִים, שֶׁמְּאַבְּדִין אֶת הָעוֹלָם שֶׁנִּבְרָא בַּעֲשָׂרָה מַאֲמָרוֹת, וְלִתֵּן שָׂכָר טוֹב לַצַּדִּיקִים, שֶׁמְּקַיְּמִין אֶת הָעוֹלָם שֶׁנִּבְרָא בַּעֲשָׂרָה מַאֲמָרוֹת.

ב עֲשָׂרָה דוֹרוֹת מֵאָדָם וְעַד נֹחַ, לְהוֹדִיעַ כַּמָּה אֶרֶךְ אַפַּיִם לְפָנָיו, שֶׁכָּל הַדּוֹרוֹת הָיוּ מַכְעִיסִין וּבָאִין, עַד שֶׁהֵבִיא עֲלֵיהֶם אֶת מֵי הַמַּבּוּל.

ג עֲשָׂרָה דוֹרוֹת מִנֹּחַ וְעַד אַבְרָהָם, לְהוֹדִיעַ כַּמָּה אֶרֶךְ אַפַּיִם לְפָנָיו, שֶׁכָּל הַדּוֹרוֹת הָיוּ מַכְעִיסִין וּבָאִין, עַד שֶׁבָּא אַבְרָהָם אָבִינוּ וְקִבֵּל שְׂכַר כֻּלָּם.

"beauty is vain" in Proverbs 31:30 refers only to beauty which is uncoupled from morality (R. Ahron Soloveichik).

CHAPTER 5

בַּעֲשָׂרָה מַאֲמָרוֹת נִבְרָא הָעוֹלָם... לְהִפָּרַע מִן הָרְשָׁעִים, שֶׁמְּאַבְּדִין אֶת הָעוֹלָם – *By ten statements was the world created...that the wicked are punished for bringing about the destruction of the world.* With each succeeding utterance of "And God said," the world was brought to a higher level of completion. While each successive creation completed the preceding ones, it was also more dependent on them. Man, the last to be created, is thus the highest of God's creations, but also the most dependent on the well-being of the rest of nature. Thus we must care for even the tiniest creature, for thereby we not only preserve the natural world, we also strengthen our own well-being. If we needlessly destroy even the least significant part of God's world, we

29. He also used to say, "They who are born will die, but the dead shall be resurrected, and all living beings will be judged, to become aware, to know, and to make known that He is God, He is the Maker, He is the Creator, He is the One Who understands, He is the Judge, He is the Witness, He is the Prosecutor. He will sit in judgment, and before Him there is neither iniquity nor forgetting, neither favoring one person over another, nor the taking of bribes, for all is His. Know that everything will be taken into consideration. Do not let your evil inclination fool you into thinking that in the afterlife you will escape judgment. For just as you were formed, born, live, and die, whether you like it or not, so too, whether you like it or not, you will one day have to give an accounting of your deeds before the King of the most exalted of kings, the Holy One, blessed is He."

Makkot 23b R. ḤANANYA ben Akashya used to say, "The Holy One, blessed is He, wishing to render Israel more worthy, enlarged the Torah and its commandments for them, as
Is. 42 it is said, 'The Lord desired, for the sake of its [Israel's] righteousness, to magnify the Torah and glorify it.'"

If a minyan is present, mourners say the Rabbis' Kaddish (page 725).

CHAPTER FIVE

Sanhedrin 90a
Is. 60 ALL ISRAEL have a share in the World to Come. As it is said, "Your people shall all be righteous and shall inherit the land forever. They are the shoot of My planting, the work of My hands in which I glory."

1. בַּעֲשָׂרָה BY TEN statements was the world created. What does this teach us? It teaches that the wicked are punished for bringing about the destruction of the world that was created by means of ten statements – even though it could have been created with one statement – and that the righteous are rewarded for maintaining the world that was created by ten statements.
2. There were ten generations from Adam to Noah to demonstrate God's patience, because every one of those generations persisted in angering Him, until in the end He brought upon them the waters of the flood.
3. There were ten generations from Noah to Abraham, to demonstrate God's patience, because every one of those generations persisted in angering Him, until in the end our father Abraham came and received the reward that should have gone to all of them.

---

have committed a grievous error. A Jew must therefore always preserve and protect nature, and never engage in wanton destruction (R. Samson Raphael Hirsch).

ד עֲשָׂרָה נִסְיוֹנוֹת נִתְנַסָּה אַבְרָהָם אָבִינוּ וְעָמַד בְּכֻלָּם, לְהוֹדִיעַ כַּמָּה חִבָּתוֹ שֶׁל אַבְרָהָם אָבִינוּ.

ה עֲשָׂרָה נִסִּים נַעֲשׂוּ לַאֲבוֹתֵינוּ בְּמִצְרַיִם, וַעֲשָׂרָה עַל הַיָּם. עֶשֶׂר מַכּוֹת הֵבִיא הַקָּדוֹשׁ בָּרוּךְ הוּא עַל הַמִּצְרִיִּים בְּמִצְרַיִם, וְעֶשֶׂר עַל הַיָּם.

ו עֲשָׂרָה נִסְיוֹנוֹת נִסּוּ אֲבוֹתֵינוּ אֶת הַקָּדוֹשׁ בָּרוּךְ הוּא בַּמִּדְבָּר, שֶׁנֶּאֱמַר: וַיְנַסּוּ אֹתִי זֶה עֶשֶׂר פְּעָמִים, וְלֹא שָׁמְעוּ בְּקוֹלִי: במדבר יד

ז עֲשָׂרָה נִסִּים נַעֲשׂוּ לַאֲבוֹתֵינוּ בְּבֵית הַמִּקְדָּשׁ. לֹא הִפִּילָה אִשָּׁה מֵרֵיחַ בְּשַׂר הַקֹּדֶשׁ, וְלֹא הִסְרִיחַ בְּשַׂר הַקֹּדֶשׁ מֵעוֹלָם, וְלֹא נִרְאָה זְבוּב בְּבֵית הַמִּטְבְּחַיִם, וְלֹא אֵרַע קֶרִי לְכֹהֵן גָּדוֹל בְּיוֹם הַכִּפּוּרִים, וְלֹא כִבּוּ הַגְּשָׁמִים אֵשׁ שֶׁל עֲצֵי הַמַּעֲרָכָה, וְלֹא נִצְּחָה הָרוּחַ אֶת עַמּוּד הֶעָשָׁן, וְלֹא נִמְצָא פְסוּל בָּעֹמֶר וּבִשְׁתֵּי הַלֶּחֶם וּבְלֶחֶם הַפָּנִים, עוֹמְדִים צְפוּפִים וּמִשְׁתַּחֲוִים רְוָחִים, וְלֹא הִזִּיק נָחָשׁ וְעַקְרָב בִּירוּשָׁלַיִם מֵעוֹלָם, וְלֹא אָמַר אָדָם לַחֲבֵרוֹ: צַר לִי הַמָּקוֹם שֶׁאָלִין בִּירוּשָׁלַיִם.

ח עֲשָׂרָה דְבָרִים נִבְרְאוּ בְּעֶרֶב שַׁבָּת בֵּין הַשְּׁמָשׁוֹת. וְאֵלוּ הֵן, פִּי הָאָרֶץ, פִּי הַבְּאֵר, פִּי הָאָתוֹן, הַקֶּשֶׁת, וְהַמָּן, וְהַמַּטֶּה, וְהַשָּׁמִיר, הַכְּתָב, וְהַמִּכְתָּב, וְהַלּוּחוֹת. וְיֵשׁ אוֹמְרִים, אַף הַמַּזִּיקִין, וּקְבוּרָתוֹ שֶׁל מֹשֶׁה, וְאֵילוֹ שֶׁל אַבְרָהָם אָבִינוּ. וְיֵשׁ אוֹמְרִים, אַף צְבָת בִּצְבָת עֲשׂוּיָה.

ט שִׁבְעָה דְבָרִים בַּגֹּלֶם, וְשִׁבְעָה בֶּחָכָם. חָכָם אֵינוֹ מְדַבֵּר לִפְנֵי מִי שֶׁגָּדוֹל מִמֶּנּוּ בְּחָכְמָה, וְאֵינוֹ נִכְנָס לְתוֹךְ דִּבְרֵי חֲבֵרוֹ, וְאֵינוֹ נִבְהָל לְהָשִׁיב, שׁוֹאֵל כָּעִנְיָן וּמֵשִׁיב כַּהֲלָכָה, וְאוֹמֵר עַל רִאשׁוֹן רִאשׁוֹן וְעַל אַחֲרוֹן אַחֲרוֹן, וְעַל מַה שֶּׁלֹּא שָׁמַע אוֹמֵר לֹא שָׁמַעְתִּי, וּמוֹדֶה עַל הָאֱמֶת. וְחִלּוּפֵיהֶן בַּגֹּלֶם.

וּמוֹדֶה עַל הָאֱמֶת – *He concedes the truth.* The language of this *mishna* is precise. It enumerates seven qualities of the wise because wisdom reflects balance and equilibrium, symbolized by the number seven. Numbers one through six refer to the three spatial dimensions (left/right, up/down, front/back,) while the number seven refers to the center point, which corresponds to the virtue of acknowledging the truth. Thus the wise can honestly consider the views of those "all around" them and if necessary admit that the truth is in accordance with their views. The Hebrew term **אֱמֶת** (truth) illustrates this point. For its three letters occur precisely in the beginning, middle, and end of the alphabet, creating a finely centered equilibrium. As opposed to this, the Hebrew word for falsehood is שֶׁקֶר. These three letters occur almost at the end of the alphabet, right before the final letter, i.e. at one extremity rather than being balanced around the center point. Furthermore, the letters are out of alphabetical order, for that is the nature of falsehood – it reflects disorder and confusion. Thus the wise adhere to truth, balance, and order, seeing the larger picture on all sides, and thus are able to sustain the world (Maharal).

4. Our father Abraham was tested ten times, and he passed them all, thereby demonstrating how great was his love.
5. Ten miracles were performed for our ancestors in Egypt, and ten at the Sea of Reeds. The Holy One, blessed is He, brought ten plagues on the Egyptians in Egypt, and ten more at the Sea of Reeds.
6. With ten tests our ancestors in the wilderness tested the Holy One, blessed is He, as it says, "They have tested Me these ten times and have not hearkened to My voice." *Num. 14*
7. Ten miracles were performed for our ancestors in connection with the Temple: no woman miscarried from the odor of the flesh of the offerings; the sanctified meat never became putrid; no fly was ever seen in the place of slaughter; the high priest never experienced a bodily emission on Yom Kippur; rain never extinguished the fire of the wood arranged on the altar; wind never scattered the column of smoke; no defilement was ever found in the offering of the omer of barley, nor in the two loaves of the first fruits of the wheat harvest, nor in the showbread; there was always room for the worshipers to prostrate themselves even though they were jammed closely together; snakes and scorpions never harmed anyone in Jerusalem; and no pilgrim ever said to his fellow, "It is too congested in Jerusalem for me to find a place of lodging."
8. Ten things were created at twilight on the eve of the first Sabbath: the mouth of the earth that would open for Koraḥ and his followers; the mouth of the well that would open for Miriam; the mouth of the ass that would open for Balaam; the rainbow of Noah; the manna; the staff of Moses; the stone-cutting worm that split the stones for the Temple; the shape of the letters used on the two tablets; the inscription on the tablets; and the tablets themselves. Some also include the evil spirits, the grave of Moses, and the ram of the patriarch Abraham, and others add the original tongs of Creation used to shape metal in fire, because tongs must be made with tongs.
9. Seven are the characteristics of an ignorant person, and seven those of a scholar. The scholar does not speak in the presence of someone who is more learned; he does not interrupt his fellow; he does not reply in haste; he raises questions that are in context, and gives answers that are in accordance with the halakha; he answers questions in the precise order that they are posed; if he answers a question by his own reasoning he avoids saying that he heard it from his teacher; when arguing a point he concedes the truth when the opposing view is correct. The opposite characteristics typify the ignorant person.

י שִׁבְעָה מִינֵי פֻרְעָנִיּוֹת בָּאִין לָעוֹלָם עַל שִׁבְעָה גוּפֵי עֲבֵרָה. מִקְצָתָן מְעַשְּׂרִין וּמִקְצָתָן אֵינָן מְעַשְּׂרִין, רָעָב שֶׁל בַּצֹּרֶת בָּא, מִקְצָתָן רְעֵבִים וּמִקְצָתָן שְׂבֵעִים. גָּמְרוּ שֶׁלֹּא לְעַשֵּׂר, רָעָב שֶׁל מְהוּמָה וְשֶׁל בַּצֹּרֶת בָּא. וְשֶׁלֹּא לִטּוֹל אֶת הַחַלָּה, רָעָב שֶׁל כְּלָיָה בָּא.

יא דֶּבֶר בָּא לָעוֹלָם עַל מִיתוֹת הָאֲמוּרוֹת בַּתּוֹרָה שֶׁלֹּא נִמְסְרוּ לְבֵית דִּין, וְעַל פֵּרוֹת שְׁבִיעִית. חֶרֶב בָּאָה לָעוֹלָם עַל עִנּוּי הַדִּין, וְעַל עִוּוּת הַדִּין, וְעַל הַמּוֹרִים בַּתּוֹרָה שֶׁלֹּא כַהֲלָכָה. חַיָּה רָעָה בָּאָה לָעוֹלָם עַל שְׁבוּעַת שָׁוְא וְעַל חִלּוּל הַשֵּׁם. גָּלוּת בָּאָה לָעוֹלָם עַל עֲבוֹדָה זָרָה, וְעַל גִּלּוּי עֲרָיוֹת, וְעַל שְׁפִיכוּת דָּמִים, וְעַל שְׁמִטַּת הָאָרֶץ.

יב בְּאַרְבָּעָה פְרָקִים הַדֶּבֶר מִתְרַבֶּה, בָּרְבִיעִית, וּבַשְּׁבִיעִית, וּבְמוֹצָאֵי שְׁבִיעִית, וּבְמוֹצָאֵי הֶחָג שֶׁבְּכָל שָׁנָה וְשָׁנָה. בָּרְבִיעִית, מִפְּנֵי מַעְשַׂר עָנִי שֶׁבַּשְּׁלִישִׁית. בַּשְּׁבִיעִית, מִפְּנֵי מַעְשַׂר עָנִי שֶׁבַּשִּׁשִּׁית. בְּמוֹצָאֵי שְׁבִיעִית, מִפְּנֵי פֵּרוֹת שְׁבִיעִית. בְּמוֹצָאֵי הֶחָג שֶׁבְּכָל שָׁנָה וְשָׁנָה, מִפְּנֵי גֶזֶל מַתְּנוֹת עֲנִיִּים.

יג אַרְבַּע מִדּוֹת בָּאָדָם. הָאוֹמֵר שֶׁלִּי שֶׁלִּי וְשֶׁלְּךָ שֶׁלָּךְ, זוֹ מִדָּה בֵינוֹנִית, וְיֵשׁ אוֹמְרִים, זוֹ מִדַּת סְדוֹם. שֶׁלִּי שֶׁלָּךְ וְשֶׁלְּךָ שֶׁלִּי, עַם הָאָרֶץ. שֶׁלִּי שֶׁלָּךְ וְשֶׁלְּךָ שֶׁלָּךְ, חָסִיד. שֶׁלְּךָ שֶׁלִּי וְשֶׁלִּי שֶׁלִּי, רָשָׁע.

יד אַרְבַּע מִדּוֹת בַּדֵּעוֹת. נוֹחַ לִכְעוֹס וְנוֹחַ לִרְצוֹת, יָצָא הֶפְסֵדוֹ בִּשְׂכָרוֹ. קָשֶׁה לִכְעוֹס וְקָשֶׁה לִרְצוֹת, יָצָא שְׂכָרוֹ בְּהֶפְסֵדוֹ. קָשֶׁה לִכְעוֹס וְנוֹחַ לִרְצוֹת, חָסִיד. נוֹחַ לִכְעוֹס וְקָשֶׁה לִרְצוֹת, רָשָׁע.

טו אַרְבַּע מִדּוֹת בַּתַּלְמִידִים. מָהִיר לִשְׁמֹעַ וּמָהִיר לְאַבֵּד, יָצָא שְׂכָרוֹ בְּהֶפְסֵדוֹ. קָשֶׁה לִשְׁמֹעַ וְקָשֶׁה לְאַבֵּד, יָצָא הֶפְסֵדוֹ בִּשְׂכָרוֹ. מָהִיר לִשְׁמֹעַ וְקָשֶׁה לְאַבֵּד, זֶה חֵלֶק טוֹב. קָשֶׁה לִשְׁמֹעַ וּמָהִיר לְאַבֵּד, זֶה חֵלֶק רָע.

חֶרֶב בָּאָה לָעוֹלָם עַל עִנּוּי הַדִּין – *The sword of war comes upon the land because of justice withheld.* Both here and in the Gemara (*Shabbat* 33a, 139a) the curse of war is said to be the result of delayed justice in the law courts of the land, rather than – as one might expect – being the result of the sinful behavior of the people themselves. The reason is that it is the judges of any given society who are responsible for its moral fiber. They are to be models of ethical behavior and the virtues of civil society, and when they see unjust behavior by others they are duty-bound to reprove, and thereby improve, them. As the Gemara (*Arakhin* 16b) says, when a judge is himself guilty of improper actions or behavior, he becomes ineffectual, for then criminals will justifiably tell him to examine his own reprehensible behavior. This

The commentary continues on page 712.

10. Seven punishments come to the world for seven major transgressions. Famine of normal drought proportions comes when only some people pay their tithes and others do not; as a result, some go hungry, whereas others have enough. Famine of catastrophic proportions comes when the whole population does not pay its tithes. Famine leading to mass death comes when people refuse to give the offering of the first of the dough.

11. Epidemics occur when capital offenses detailed in the Torah are not properly adjudicated by the courts and when the laws of the Sabbatical year are not adhered to. The sword of war comes upon the land because of justice withheld and perverted, and because of judges who do not rule in accordance with the halakha. Marauding wild animals wreak havoc in the land because of oaths taken in vain, and because of the desecration of God's name. Exile comes about as a result of idolatry, sexual immorality, bloodshed, and failure to observe the Sabbatical year.

12. During the years of the Sabbatical cycle there are four times in which epidemics increase: in the fourth year, the seventh year, at the end of the seventh year, and at the end of Sukkot every year. In the fourth and seventh years because of failure to give the tithe of the poor that is due in the third and sixth years; at the end of the seventh year because of failure to leave the fruits of the seventh year for all; at the end of Sukkot every year for robbing the poor of the harvest gifts that are their due at the festival.

13. There are four types of people when it comes to their possessions. One who says, "What is mine is mine, and what is yours is yours," is the average person, although some say that is the type of Sodom. One who says, "What is mine is yours, and what is yours is mine," is a fool. One who says, "What is mine is yours, and what is yours is yours," is saintly. But one who says, "What is yours is mine, and what is mine is mine," is wicked.

14. There are four human temperaments. Those who are easily angered and easily appeased; their loss is canceled by their gain. Those who are slow to anger and slow to appeasement; their gain is canceled by their loss. Those who are slow to anger and quick to appeasement; they are saintly. Those who are easily angered and appeased with difficulty; they are wicked.

15. There are four kinds of students: Quick to learn and quick to forget; their gain is cancelled by their loss. Slow to learn and slow to forget; their loss is cancelled by their gain. Quick to learn and slow to forget; their lot is a happy one. Slow to learn and quick to forget; their lot is an unhappy one.

טז אַרְבַּע מִדּוֹת בְּנוֹתְנֵי צְדָקָה. הָרוֹצֶה שֶׁיִּתֵּן וְלֹא יִתְּנוּ אֲחֵרִים, עֵינוֹ רָעָה בְּשֶׁל אֲחֵרִים. יִתְּנוּ אֲחֵרִים וְהוּא לֹא יִתֵּן, עֵינוֹ רָעָה בְּשֶׁלּוֹ. יִתֵּן וְיִתְּנוּ אֲחֵרִים, חָסִיד. לֹא יִתֵּן וְלֹא יִתְּנוּ אֲחֵרִים, רָשָׁע.

יז אַרְבַּע מִדּוֹת בְּהוֹלְכֵי בֵית הַמִּדְרָשׁ. הוֹלֵךְ וְאֵינוֹ עוֹשֶׂה, שְׂכַר הֲלִיכָה בְּיָדוֹ. עוֹשֶׂה וְאֵינוֹ הוֹלֵךְ, שְׂכַר מַעֲשֶׂה בְּיָדוֹ. הוֹלֵךְ וְעוֹשֶׂה, חָסִיד. לֹא הוֹלֵךְ וְלֹא עוֹשֶׂה, רָשָׁע.

יח אַרְבַּע מִדּוֹת בְּיוֹשְׁבִים לִפְנֵי חֲכָמִים, סְפוֹג, וּמַשְׁפֵּךְ, מְשַׁמֶּרֶת, וְנָפָה. סְפוֹג, שֶׁהוּא סוֹפֵג אֶת הַכֹּל. וּמַשְׁפֵּךְ, שֶׁמַּכְנִיס בְּזוֹ וּמוֹצִיא בְזוֹ. מְשַׁמֶּרֶת, שֶׁמּוֹצִיאָה אֶת הַיַּיִן וְקוֹלֶטֶת אֶת הַשְּׁמָרִים. וְנָפָה, שֶׁמּוֹצִיאָה אֶת הַקֶּמַח וְקוֹלֶטֶת אֶת הַסֹּלֶת.

יט כָּל אַהֲבָה שֶׁהִיא תְלוּיָה בְדָבָר, בָּטֵל דָּבָר, בְּטֵלָה אַהֲבָה. וְשֶׁאֵינָהּ תְּלוּיָה בְדָבָר, אֵינָהּ בְּטֵלָה לְעוֹלָם. אֵיזוֹ הִיא אַהֲבָה שֶׁהִיא תְלוּיָה בְדָבָר, זוֹ אַהֲבַת אַמְנוֹן וְתָמָר. וְשֶׁאֵינָהּ תְּלוּיָה בְדָבָר, זוֹ אַהֲבַת דָּוִד וִיהוֹנָתָן.

כ כָּל מַחֲלֹקֶת שֶׁהִיא לְשֵׁם שָׁמַיִם, סוֹפָהּ לְהִתְקַיֵּם. וְשֶׁאֵינָהּ לְשֵׁם שָׁמַיִם, אֵין סוֹפָהּ לְהִתְקַיֵּם. אֵיזוֹ הִיא מַחֲלֹקֶת שֶׁהִיא לְשֵׁם שָׁמַיִם, זוֹ מַחֲלֹקֶת הִלֵּל וְשַׁמַּאי. וְשֶׁאֵינָהּ לְשֵׁם שָׁמַיִם, זוֹ מַחֲלֹקֶת קֹרַח וְכָל עֲדָתוֹ.

כא כָּל הַמְזַכֶּה אֶת הָרַבִּים, אֵין חֵטְא בָּא עַל יָדוֹ. וְכָל הַמַּחֲטִיא אֶת הָרַבִּים, אֵין מַסְפִּיקִין בְּיָדוֹ לַעֲשׂוֹת תְּשׁוּבָה. מֹשֶׁה זָכָה וְזִכָּה אֶת הָרַבִּים, זְכוּת הָרַבִּים
דברים לג תָּלוּי בּוֹ, שֶׁנֶּאֱמַר: צִדְקַת יהוה עָשָׂה וּמִשְׁפָּטָיו עִם־יִשְׂרָאֵל: יָרָבְעָם בֶּן נְבָט,
מלכים א׳ טו חָטָא וְהֶחֱטִיא אֶת הָרַבִּים, חֵטְא הָרַבִּים תָּלוּי בּוֹ, שֶׁנֶּאֱמַר: עַל־חַטֹּאות יָרָבְעָם אֲשֶׁר חָטָא וַאֲשֶׁר הֶחֱטִיא אֶת־יִשְׂרָאֵל:

כב כָּל מִי שֶׁיֶּשׁ בּוֹ שְׁלֹשָׁה דְבָרִים הַלָּלוּ, הוּא מִתַּלְמִידָיו שֶׁל אַבְרָהָם אָבִינוּ, וּשְׁלֹשָׁה דְבָרִים אֲחֵרִים, הוּא מִתַּלְמִידָיו שֶׁל בִּלְעָם הָרָשָׁע. עַיִן טוֹבָה, וְרוּחַ נְמוּכָה, וְנֶפֶשׁ שְׁפָלָה, תַּלְמִידָיו שֶׁל אַבְרָהָם אָבִינוּ. עַיִן רָעָה, וְרוּחַ גְּבוֹהָה וְנֶפֶשׁ רְחָבָה, תַּלְמִידָיו שֶׁל בִּלְעָם הָרָשָׁע. מַה בֵּין תַּלְמִידָיו שֶׁל אַבְרָהָם אָבִינוּ לְתַלְמִידָיו שֶׁל בִּלְעָם הָרָשָׁע. תַּלְמִידָיו שֶׁל אַבְרָהָם אָבִינוּ אוֹכְלִין
משלי ח בָּעוֹלָם הַזֶּה וְנוֹחֲלִין הָעוֹלָם הַבָּא, שֶׁנֶּאֱמַר: לְהַנְחִיל אֹהֲבַי יֵשׁ וְאֹצְרֹתֵיהֶם אֲמַלֵּא: אֲבָל תַּלְמִידָיו שֶׁל בִּלְעָם הָרָשָׁע יוֹרְשִׁין גֵּיהִנֹּם וְיוֹרְדִין לִבְאֵר שַׁחַת,

---

is why in the weekday *Amida* we ask God to give us judges who will "relieve our sorrows and our troubles," i.e., guide and rebuke the people, and thus prevent the unraveling of social justice and all that might follow (R. Barukh HaLevi Epstein).

16. There are four types in giving charity: Those who give but do not wish others to give, begrudge others. Those who wish others to give but do not themselves give, begrudge themselves. Those who give and wish others to give are saintly. Those who neither give nor wish others to give are wicked.

17. Four types of individuals attend the house of study: Those who attend but do not apply what they learn have the reward for attending. Those who apply the teachings but do not attend have the reward for applying the teachings. Those who both attend and apply the teachings are saintly. But those who neither attend nor apply the teachings are wicked.

18. Four types of individuals seek out the company of sages: the sponge, the funnel, the strainer, and the sieve. The sponge absorbs everything, the funnel receives in one ear and lets it out at the other, the strainer lets the good wine through and retains the dregs, and the sieve eliminates the coarse meal and collects the fine flour.

19. Love that is dependent on an external factor will disappear if that factor disappears, but if it is not dependent on an external factor it will never end. What is an example of the former? That of Amnon for Tamar. And an example of the latter? That of David and Jonathan.

20. Every argument for the sake of heaven will in the end be of lasting benefit. But if it is not for the sake of heaven in the end it will not be of lasting benefit. An example of the former is the arguments of Hillel and Shamai. An example of the latter is the argument involving Koraḥ and his followers.

21. Whoever leads the people in the right path will not bring about sin; but one who leads the people astray will never have an opportunity to repent. Moses was virtuous and led the people in the right path, and thus their
Deut. 33 merit is ascribed to him, as it is said: "He performed the righteousness of the Lord and His judgments are with Israel." But Jeroboam sinned and led the people astray, and thus the sin of the people is ascribed to him, as
1 Kings 15 it is said: "For the sins of Jeroboam which he sinned and which he caused Israel to sin."

22. Whoever possesses these three qualities is a disciple of our father Abraham: modest expectation, humility, and acceptance of one's lot. One who possesses the three opposite qualities is a disciple of the wicked Balaam. What is the difference between the disciples of these two men? The disciples of our father Abraham enjoy this world and inherit the World
Prov. 8 to Come, as it is said: "That I may cause those who love Me to inherit substance, and fill their treasuries." But the disciples of the wicked Balaam

תהלים נה שֶׁנֶּאֱמַר: וְאַתָּה אֱלֹהִים תּוֹרִדֵם לִבְאֵר שַׁחַת, אַנְשֵׁי דָמִים וּמִרְמָה לֹא־יֶחֱצוּ
יְמֵיהֶם, וַאֲנִי אֶבְטַח־בָּךְ:

כג יְהוּדָה בֶּן תֵּימָא אוֹמֵר: הֱוֵי עַז כַּנָּמֵר וְקַל כַּנֶּשֶׁר, רָץ כַּצְּבִי וְגִבּוֹר כָּאֲרִי,
לַעֲשׂוֹת רְצוֹן אָבִיךָ שֶׁבַּשָּׁמַיִם. הוּא הָיָה אוֹמֵר: עַז פָּנִים לְגֵיהִנָּם, וּבֹשֶׁת
פָּנִים לְגַן עֵדֶן. יְהִי רָצוֹן מִלְּפָנֶיךָ, יהוה אֱלֹהֵינוּ וֵאלֹהֵי אֲבוֹתֵינוּ, שֶׁיִּבָּנֶה בֵּית
הַמִּקְדָּשׁ בִּמְהֵרָה בְיָמֵינוּ, וְתֵן חֶלְקֵנוּ בְּתוֹרָתֶךָ.

כד הוּא הָיָה אוֹמֵר: בֶּן חָמֵשׁ שָׁנִים לַמִּקְרָא, בֶּן עֶשֶׂר שָׁנִים לַמִּשְׁנָה, בֶּן שְׁלֹשׁ
עֶשְׂרֵה לַמִּצְוֹת, בֶּן חֲמֵשׁ עֶשְׂרֵה לַגְּמָרָא, בֶּן שְׁמוֹנֶה עֶשְׂרֵה לַחֻפָּה, בֶּן עֶשְׂרִים
לִרְדֹּף, בֶּן שְׁלֹשִׁים לַכֹּחַ, בֶּן אַרְבָּעִים לַבִּינָה, בֶּן חֲמִשִּׁים לָעֵצָה, בֶּן שִׁשִּׁים
לַזִּקְנָה, בֶּן שִׁבְעִים לַשֵּׂיבָה, בֶּן שְׁמוֹנִים לַגְּבוּרָה, בֶּן תִּשְׁעִים לָשׁוּחַ, בֶּן מֵאָה
כְּאִלּוּ מֵת וְעָבַר וּבָטֵל מִן הָעוֹלָם.

כה בֶּן בַּג בַּג אוֹמֵר: הֲפָךְ בָּהּ וַהֲפָךְ בָּהּ דְּכֹלָּא בַהּ, וּבַהּ תֶּחֱזֵי, וְסִיב וּבְלֵה בַהּ, וּמִנַּהּ
לָא תְזוּעַ, שֶׁאֵין לְךָ מִדָּה טוֹבָה הֵימֶנָּה. בֶּן הֵא הֵא אוֹמֵר: לְפוּם צַעֲרָא אַגְרָא.

מכות כג: רַבִּי חֲנַנְיָא בֶּן עֲקַשְׁיָא אוֹמֵר: רָצָה הַקָּדוֹשׁ בָּרוּךְ הוּא לְזַכּוֹת אֶת יִשְׂרָאֵל, לְפִיכָךְ הִרְבָּה
ישעיה מב לָהֶם תּוֹרָה וּמִצְוֹת. שֶׁנֶּאֱמַר: יהוה חָפֵץ לְמַעַן צִדְקוֹ, יַגְדִּיל תּוֹרָה וְיַאְדִּיר:

If there is a מנין*, mourners say* קדיש דרבנן *(page 724).*

הֱוֵי עַז כַּנָּמֵר... עַז פָּנִים לְגֵיהִנָּם... יְהִי רָצוֹן מִלְּפָנֶיךָ, יהוה אֱלֹהֵינוּ וֵאלֹהֵי אֲבוֹתֵינוּ, שֶׁיִּבָּנֶה בֵּית הַמִּקְדָּשׁ בִּמְהֵרָה בְיָמֵינוּ, וְתֵן חֶלְקֵנוּ בְּתוֹרָתֶךָ – *Be strong as the leopard... The arrogant are doomed to Gehenna... May it be Your will, Lord our God and God of our fathers, that the Temple be rebuilt speedily in our days and may You grant our portion in Your Torah*. Being עַז (bold) is generally not a virtue but a vice. After all, extreme humility and meekness are considered great virtues. The reason this *mishna* praises boldness, however, is found in the second part of the *mishna* which states that although boldness generally leads to eternal punishment, when it is utilized only to do God's will, or to act for His glory, then even boldness is a virtue. So too the Mishna (*Sota* 9:2) states that immediately preceding the advent of the Messiah, חֻצְפָּה (brazenness) will prevail. The *mishna* here concludes with a request that we be granted our share in God's Torah in accordance with the teaching in *Beitza* 25b that God gave His Torah to the Jews because עַזִּין הֵם (they are a bold people) in need of the antidote of the Torah. It is the Torah that ensures that our boldness as a nation will be used only in humble fulfillment of God's will. As it says (Psalms 20:11), "The Lord will give His people עֹז (the Torah), and as a result the Lord will bless His people with peace" (R. Barukh HaLevi Epstein).

בֶּן עֶשְׂרִים לִרְדֹּף – *At twenty one must engage in pursuit*. There are various views as to which goal is to be pursued. The Me'iri links the term to the preceding – if one has not found a wife by twenty one should pursue the matter with great diligence. Bartenura views this as the obligation to find ways to support one's family. *Maḥzor Vitri* links it to Numbers 4:47, where military conscription begins at twenty, thus the reference here is to military service.

בֶּן חֲמִשִּׁים לָעֵצָה, בֶּן שִׁשִּׁים לַזִּקְנָה – *Fifty is the*

Ps. 55 inherit Gehenna and go down to destruction in the grave, as it is said: "But You, O God, will bring them down into the deep pit. Bloody and deceitful men, may they not live out half their days. But I will trust in You."

23. Judah ben Tema used to say, "Be strong as the leopard, swift as the eagle, graceful as the gazelle, and powerful as the lion, to do the will of your Father in heaven." He also used to say, "The arrogant are doomed to Gehenna, but the modest are destined for the Garden of Eden. May it be Your will, Lord our God and God of our fathers, that the Temple be rebuilt speedily in our days and may You grant our portion in Your Torah."

24. He also used to say, "At five years of age one should begin studying the Scriptures; at ten one should begin studying the Mishna; at thirteen one must observe the commandments; at fifteen one must start to study the Talmud; at eighteen one should marry; at twenty one must engage in pursuit; thirty is the age of full strength; forty is the age of understanding; fifty is the age of wisdom; at sixty one has reached old age; at seventy one has reached advanced old age; eighty is the age of heroic strength; ninety is the age of being bent over; when one turns a hundred it is as if one were already dead and had left the world."

25. Ben Bag Bag used to say of the Torah, "Turn its pages and return to it again and again, for everything is in it. Pore over it, grow old and weary in it, and never depart from it, for nothing surpasses it."

26. Ben Hei Hei used to say, "The reward is proportionate to the difficulty."

Makkot 23b R. ḤANANYA ben Akashya used to say, "The Holy One, blessed is He, wishing to render Israel more worthy, enlarged the Torah and its commandments for them, as
Is. 42 it is said, 'The Lord desired, for the sake of its [Israel's] righteousness, to magnify the Torah and glorify it.'"

If a minyan is present, mourners say the Rabbis' Kaddish (page 725).

---

age of wisdom; at sixty one has reached old age. The seven days of the week can be compared to the seventy years of an average lifespan, one day for every ten years. On day five, i.e., in our forties, it is appropriate to offer – and take – counsel, by reviewing the purpose of our lives in light of all that came before. On day six, in our fifties, we should arise early to begin to prepare for that we will need for the seventh day, i.e., the last decade of the typical seventy-year lifespan. Therefore, that is a time when we should go beyond preoccupation with the needs of this world, and instead devote more time and energy to Torah and good deeds, in preparation for the time that is "continually Shabbat." As the Torah says (Num. 8:25) regarding the Levites, when they turn fifty they are to return from their regular labor, and work no more (Ḥafetz Ḥayyim).

וְסִיב וּבְלֵה בַהּ... שֶׁאֵין לְךָ מִדָּה טוֹבָה הֵימֶנָּה – *Pore over it, grow old and weary in it... for nothing is better.* The study of Torah is both restricted

פרק ששי

פרק קנין תורה

כָּל יִשְׂרָאֵל יֵשׁ לָהֶם חֵלֶק לָעוֹלָם הַבָּא. שֶׁנֶּאֱמַר: וְעַמֵּךְ כֻּלָּם צַדִּיקִים, לְעוֹלָם יִירְשׁוּ אָרֶץ, נֵצֶר מַטָּעַי, מַעֲשֵׂה יָדַי לְהִתְפָּאֵר: סנהדרין צ. ישעיה ס

שָׁנוּ חֲכָמִים בִּלְשׁוֹן הַמִּשְׁנָה, בָּרוּךְ שֶׁבָּחַר בָּהֶם וּבְמִשְׁנָתָם.

א רַבִּי מֵאִיר אוֹמֵר: כָּל הָעוֹסֵק בַּתּוֹרָה לִשְׁמָהּ, זוֹכֶה לִדְבָרִים הַרְבֵּה. וְלֹא עוֹד, אֶלָּא שֶׁכָּל הָעוֹלָם כֻּלּוֹ כְּדַאי הוּא לוֹ. נִקְרָא רֵעַ, אָהוּב, אוֹהֵב אֶת הַמָּקוֹם, אוֹהֵב אֶת הַבְּרִיּוֹת, מְשַׂמֵּחַ אֶת הַמָּקוֹם, מְשַׂמֵּחַ אֶת הַבְּרִיּוֹת, וּמַלְבַּשְׁתּוֹ עֲנָוָה וְיִרְאָה, וּמַכְשַׁרְתּוֹ לִהְיוֹת צַדִּיק, חָסִיד, יָשָׁר, וְנֶאֱמָן, וּמְרַחַקְתּוֹ מִן הַחֵטְא, וּמְקָרַבְתּוֹ לִידֵי זְכוּת, וְנֶהֱנִין מִמֶּנּוּ עֵצָה וְתוּשִׁיָּה, בִּינָה וּגְבוּרָה, שֶׁנֶּאֱמַר: לִי־עֵצָה וְתוּשִׁיָּה, אֲנִי בִינָה, לִי גְבוּרָה: (משלי ח) וְנוֹתֶנֶת לוֹ מַלְכוּת וּמֶמְשָׁלָה, וְחִקּוּר דִּין, וּמְגַלִּין לוֹ רָזֵי תוֹרָה, וְנַעֲשֶׂה כְּמַעְיָן הַמִּתְגַּבֵּר וּכְנָהָר שֶׁאֵינוֹ פוֹסֵק, וְהֹוֶה צָנְוּעַ, וְאֶרֶךְ רוּחַ, וּמוֹחֵל עַל עֶלְבּוֹנוֹ, וּמְגַדַּלְתּוֹ וּמְרוֹמַמְתּוֹ עַל כָּל הַמַּעֲשִׂים.

ב אָמַר רַבִּי יְהוֹשֻׁעַ בֶּן לֵוִי: בְּכָל יוֹם וָיוֹם, בַּת קוֹל יוֹצֵאת מֵהַר חוֹרֵב וּמַכְרֶזֶת וְאוֹמֶרֶת, אוֹי לָהֶם לַבְּרִיּוֹת מֵעֶלְבּוֹנָהּ שֶׁל תּוֹרָה, שֶׁכָּל מִי שֶׁאֵינוֹ עוֹסֵק בַּתּוֹרָה נִקְרָא נָזוּף, שֶׁנֶּאֱמַר: (משלי יא) נֶזֶם זָהָב בְּאַף חֲזִיר, אִשָּׁה יָפָה וְסָרַת טָעַם: וְאוֹמֵר: (שמות לב) וְהַלֻּחֹת מַעֲשֵׂה אֱלֹהִים הֵמָּה, וְהַמִּכְתָּב מִכְתַּב אֱלֹהִים הוּא, חָרוּת עַל־הַלֻּחֹת: אַל תִּקְרָא חָרוּת אֶלָּא חֵרוּת, שֶׁאֵין לְךָ בֶּן חוֹרִין אֶלָּא מִי שֶׁעוֹסֵק בְּתַלְמוּד תּוֹרָה. וְכָל מִי שֶׁעוֹסֵק בְּתַלְמוּד תּוֹרָה, הֲרֵי זֶה מִתְעַלֶּה, שֶׁנֶּאֱמַר: (במדבר כא) וּמִמַּתָּנָה נַחֲלִיאֵל, וּמִנַּחֲלִיאֵל בָּמוֹת:

God-questing individual. It is not determined by the brilliance of the performance. The *gaon* and the dull person, the great mind and the simpleton, share in the redemptive hallowing experience each according to his effort. Hence, the *mishna* states, the reward is in proportion to the exertion (R. Joseph B. Soloveitchik).

CHAPTER 6

כָּל הָעוֹסֵק בַּתּוֹרָה לִשְׁמָהּ, זוֹכֶה לִדְבָרִים הַרְבֵּה – *Whoever occupies himself with Torah for its own sake merits many things.* The study of Torah must be undertaken in two frameworks. The first is to fulfill the obligation to study Torah

to a small group and open to the public. It is restricted in the sense that a brilliant mind can certainly accomplish more, while a dull person accomplishes less. There is indeed an aristocracy of intellectual capacity, which nothing can change. However when we view the study of Torah as a rendezvous with God's *Shekhina*, then it becomes completely democratized. Then it is the effort that counts, not the results. The value of the meeting of the Jew who studies Torah and the *Shekhina* is determined by the sincerity of the commitment, the intensity of the dedication, the warmth of the encounter, and the love and passion of the

CHAPTER SIX

In Praise of the Virtues of Torah Study

Sanhedrin 90a *Is. 60* ALL ISRAEL have a share in the World to Come. As it is said, "Your people shall all be righteous and shall inherit the land forever. They are the shoot of My planting, the work of My hands in which I glory."

שָׁנוּ THE SAGES (blessed be He Who chose them and their teaching) also taught the following in the style of the Mishna.

1. R. MEIR used to say, "Whoever occupies himself with Torah for its own sake merits many things; moreover, the whole world is regarded as worthy because of his presence. He is called friend, beloved, lover of God, and lover of mankind. God and mankind rejoice because of him. He is robed in modesty and reverence; it prepares him to be virtuous, pious, upright, and faithful. It keeps him far from sin, and draws him near to virtue. He provides his fellow men with counsel and sound wisdom, *Prov. 8* understanding and might, as is said: 'Mine are counsel and sound wisdom; I am understanding, mine is might.' It gives him rule and authority and insight into justice. To him are revealed the secrets of the Torah. He is like a never-failing spring and a river that flows without cease. He is modest and patient, and ignores insults, because the Torah magnifies him and raises him above worldly concerns."

2. R. Joshua ben Levi would say, "Every day a heavenly voice goes forth from Mount Horeb, proclaiming, 'Woe to mankind for not respecting the Torah.' Those who do not occupy themselves with Torah are called *Prov. 11* 'rebuked,' as it is said: 'Like a gold ring in a pig's snout is an attractive *Ex. 32* woman who lacks good sense.' And it says: 'The tablets were the work of God, and the writing was the writing of God (*ḥarut*) engraved upon the tablets.' Do not read (*ḥarut*) 'engraved' but (*ḥerut*) 'freedom' for no one is truly free unless he occupies himself with learning Torah. But those who do occupy themselves with the study of Torah are raised up on high, as it *Num. 21* is said: 'From Mattanah (the gift of Torah) to Naḥaliel (the inheritance of God) and from Naḥaliel to Bamot (the heights).'"

---

and master its wisdom to the best of one's ability. The second is to study Torah so that we can be elevated and enriched by that experience. For this reason we recite a two-part blessing every morning prior to studying Torah: (1) לַעֲסֹק בְּדִבְרֵי תוֹרָה – to be occupied in the words of the Torah, and (2) וְהַעֲרֶב נָא – may the words of Torah sweeten our mouths. The first refers to the study of Torah per se. The second refers to the impact of that study on us: that through that study we should be uplifted, spiritually purified, and worthy of bearing

ג הַלּוֹמֵד מֵחֲבֵרוֹ פֶּרֶק אֶחָד, אוֹ הֲלָכָה אַחַת, אוֹ פָּסוּק אֶחָד, אוֹ דִבּוּר אֶחָד, אוֹ אֲפִלּוּ אוֹת אַחַת, צָרִיךְ לִנְהָג בּוֹ כָּבוֹד. שֶׁכֵּן מָצִינוּ בְּדָוִד מֶלֶךְ יִשְׂרָאֵל, שֶׁלֹּא לָמַד מֵאֲחִיתֹפֶל אֶלָּא שְׁנֵי דְבָרִים בִּלְבָד, קְרָאוֹ רַבּוֹ אַלּוּפוֹ וּמְיֻדָּעוֹ, שֶׁנֶּאֱמַר: וְאַתָּה אֱנוֹשׁ כְּעֶרְכִּי, אַלּוּפִי וּמְיֻדָּעִי: וַהֲלֹא דְבָרִים קַל וָחֹמֶר. וּמַה דָּוִד מֶלֶךְ יִשְׂרָאֵל, שֶׁלֹּא לָמַד מֵאֲחִיתֹפֶל אֶלָּא שְׁנֵי דְבָרִים בִּלְבָד, קְרָאוֹ רַבּוֹ אַלּוּפוֹ וּמְיֻדָּעוֹ, הַלּוֹמֵד מֵחֲבֵרוֹ פֶּרֶק אֶחָד, אוֹ הֲלָכָה אַחַת, אוֹ פָּסוּק אֶחָד, אוֹ דִבּוּר אֶחָד, אוֹ אֲפִלּוּ אוֹת אַחַת, עַל אַחַת כַּמָּה וְכַמָּה שֶׁצָּרִיךְ לִנְהָג בּוֹ כָּבוֹד. וְאֵין כָּבוֹד אֶלָּא תוֹרָה, שֶׁנֶּאֱמַר: כָּבוֹד חֲכָמִים יִנְחָלוּ: וּתְמִימִים יִנְחֲלוּ־טוֹב: וְאֵין טוֹב אֶלָּא תוֹרָה, שֶׁנֶּאֱמַר: כִּי לֶקַח טוֹב נָתַתִּי לָכֶם, תּוֹרָתִי אַל־תַּעֲזֹבוּ:

תהלים נה | משלי ג | משלי כח | משלי ד

ד כָּךְ הִיא דַּרְכָּהּ שֶׁל תּוֹרָה. פַּת בַּמֶּלַח תֹּאכֵל, וּמַיִם בַּמְּשׂוּרָה תִּשְׁתֶּה, וְעַל הָאָרֶץ תִּישָׁן, וְחַיֵּי צַעַר תִּחְיֶה, וּבַתּוֹרָה אַתָּה עָמֵל. אִם אַתָּה עוֹשֶׂה כֵּן, אַשְׁרֶיךָ וְטוֹב לָךְ, אַשְׁרֶיךָ בָּעוֹלָם הַזֶּה, וְטוֹב לָךְ לָעוֹלָם הַבָּא.

ה אַל תְּבַקֵּשׁ גְּדֻלָּה לְעַצְמְךָ, וְאַל תַּחְמֹד כָּבוֹד. יוֹתֵר מִלִּמּוּדְךָ עֲשֵׂה. וְאַל תִּתְאַוֶּה לְשֻׁלְחָנָם שֶׁל מְלָכִים, שֶׁשֻּׁלְחָנְךָ גָּדוֹל מִשֻּׁלְחָנָם, וְכִתְרְךָ גָּדוֹל מִכִּתְרָם. וְנֶאֱמָן הוּא בַּעַל מְלַאכְתְּךָ, שֶׁיְּשַׁלֶּם לְךָ שְׂכַר פְּעֻלָּתֶךָ.

ו גְּדוֹלָה תוֹרָה יוֹתֵר מִן הַכְּהֻנָּה וּמִן הַמַּלְכוּת. שֶׁהַמַּלְכוּת נִקְנֵית בִּשְׁלֹשִׁים מַעֲלוֹת, וְהַכְּהֻנָּה בְּעֶשְׂרִים וְאַרְבַּע, וְהַתּוֹרָה נִקְנֵית בְּאַרְבָּעִים וּשְׁמוֹנָה דְבָרִים. וְאֵלּוּ הֵן, בְּתַלְמוּד, בִּשְׁמִיעַת הָאֹזֶן, בַּעֲרִיכַת שְׂפָתַיִם, בְּבִינַת הַלֵּב, בְּאֵימָה, בְּיִרְאָה, בַּעֲנָוָה, בְּשִׂמְחָה, בְּטָהֳרָה, בְּשִׁמּוּשׁ חֲכָמִים, בְּדִקְדּוּק חֲבֵרִים, בְּפִלְפּוּל הַתַּלְמִידִים, בְּיִשּׁוּב, בְּמִקְרָא, בְּמִשְׁנָה, בְּמִעוּט סְחוֹרָה, בְּמִעוּט דֶּרֶךְ אֶרֶץ, בְּמִעוּט תַּעֲנוּג, בְּמִעוּט שֵׁנָה, בְּמִעוּט שִׂיחָה, בְּמִעוּט שְׂחוֹק, בְּאֶרֶךְ אַפַּיִם, בְּלֵב טוֹב, בֶּאֱמוּנַת חֲכָמִים, בְּקַבָּלַת הַיִּסּוּרִין, הַמַּכִּיר אֶת מְקוֹמוֹ, וְהַשָּׂמֵחַ בְּחֶלְקוֹ, וְהָעוֹשֶׂה סְיָג לִדְבָרָיו, וְאֵינוֹ מַחֲזִיק טוֹבָה לְעַצְמוֹ, אָהוּב, אוֹהֵב אֶת הַמָּקוֹם, אוֹהֵב אֶת הַבְּרִיּוֹת, אוֹהֵב אֶת הַצְּדָקוֹת, אוֹהֵב אֶת הַמֵּישָׁרִים, אוֹהֵב אֶת הַתּוֹכָחוֹת, וּמִתְרַחֵק מִן הַכָּבוֹד, וְלֹא מֵגִיס לִבּוֹ בְּתַלְמוּדוֹ, וְאֵינוֹ שָׂמֵחַ בְּהוֹרָאָה, נוֹשֵׂא בְעֹל עִם חֲבֵרוֹ, וּמַכְרִיעוֹ לְכַף זְכוּת, וּמַעֲמִידוֹ עַל הָאֱמֶת, וּמַעֲמִידוֹ עַל הַשָּׁלוֹם, וּמִתְיַשֵּׁב לִבּוֹ בְּתַלְמוּדוֹ, שׁוֹאֵל וּמֵשִׁיב, שׁוֹמֵעַ וּמוֹסִיף, הַלּוֹמֵד עַל מְנָת לְלַמֵּד, וְהַלּוֹמֵד

---

the name of God in the world. This *mishna* describes the many ways in which proper Torah study purifies our souls, strengthens our spirits, disciplines our lives and our bodies, and raises our existence to ever greater heights (R. Joseph B. Soloveitchik).

3. One who learns from one's fellow only one chapter, or halakha, or verse, or saying, or even just a single letter, must treat him with respect. This is exemplified by David King of Israel. He learned only two things from Achitophel but nonetheless called him his teacher, familiar friend, and
Ps. 55 companion, as it is said: "But it is you, a man like me, my familiar friend and my companion." It necessarily follows that if David King of Israel learned only two things from Achitophel but nonetheless called him his teacher and close friend, then how much more honor must be shown by someone who learns from his associate just a single chapter, halakha, verse, or saying, or even a single letter of Torah. For honor only comes
Prov. 3 from knowledge of Torah, as it is said: "The wise inherit honor" and "the
Prov. 28 *Prov. 4* virtuous inherit good." And only Torah is good, as it is said: "For I have given you a good doctrine; do not abandon My Torah."

4. This is the way that Torah is acquired: a diet of bread and salt, minimal amounts of water, sleeping on the ground, and living a life of hardship while laboring to acquire Torah. If you do so, "Happy are you, and it shall be well with you." "Happy are you" in this world, "and it shall be well with you" in the World to Come.

5. Do not seek greatness and and do not envy those who are honored. You should study, but even more you should act. Do not yearn to dine at the table of kings, because your table is greater than theirs, and your crown nobler. Moreover, the Master for Whom you have worked can be trusted to pay the reward you deserve.

6. Torah is greater than the priesthood or royalty, because royalty is attained through thirty qualifications and the priesthood through twenty-four, but Torah is acquired through forty-eight qualifications, namely: diligent study, careful listening, oral review, understanding and insight, respect, reverence, humility, joyousness, association with sages, cooperation with fellow students, discussion with fellow students, knowledge of Scripture and Mishna, all while limiting one's trading activities as well as one's worldly interests, indulgence in pleasure, sleep, conversation and frivolity, while increasing one's patience and cultivating a good heart, confidence in the sages, acceptance of criticism, knowing one's place, rejoicing in one's lot, setting a limit to one's words, not claiming merit for oneself, being beloved, loving God, loving one's fellow, loving righteousness, loving rectitude, loving reproof, fleeing honor, not being arrogant about one's learning, not delighting in laying down the law, sharing the burden of one's fellow, judging him favorably, pointing him in the direction of truth and peace, having time to calmly review one's studies, questioning and answering, hearing and

עַל מְנָת לַעֲשׂוֹת, הַמַּחְכִּים אֶת רַבּוֹ, וְהַמְכַוֵּן אֶת שְׁמוּעָתוֹ, וְהָאוֹמֵר דָּבָר
בְּשֵׁם אוֹמְרוֹ. הָא לָמַדְתָּ, כָּל הָאוֹמֵר דָּבָר בְּשֵׁם אוֹמְרוֹ, מֵבִיא גְאֻלָּה
לָעוֹלָם, שֶׁנֶּאֱמַר: וַתֹּאמֶר אֶסְתֵּר לַמֶּלֶךְ בְּשֵׁם מָרְדֳּכָי: אסתר ב

ז גְּדוֹלָה תוֹרָה, שֶׁהִיא נוֹתֶנֶת חַיִּים לְעוֹשֶׂיהָ בָּעוֹלָם הַזֶּה וּבָעוֹלָם הַבָּא,
שֶׁנֶּאֱמַר: כִּי־חַיִּים הֵם לְמֹצְאֵיהֶם, וּלְכָל־בְּשָׂרוֹ מַרְפֵּא: וְאוֹמֵר: רִפְאוּת תְּהִי משלי ד משלי ג
לְשָׁרֶּךָ, וְשִׁקּוּי לְעַצְמוֹתֶיךָ: וְאוֹמֵר: עֵץ־חַיִּים הִיא לַמַּחֲזִיקִים בָּהּ, וְתֹמְכֶיהָ
מְאֻשָּׁר: וְאוֹמֵר: כִּי לִוְיַת חֵן הֵם לְרֹאשֶׁךָ, וַעֲנָקִים לְגַרְגְּרֹתֶיךָ: וְאוֹמֵר: תִּתֵּן משלי א משלי ד
לְרֹאשְׁךָ לִוְיַת־חֵן, עֲטֶרֶת תִּפְאֶרֶת תְּמַגְּנֶךָּ: וְאוֹמֵר: כִּי־בִי יִרְבּוּ יָמֶיךָ, וְיוֹסִיפוּ משלי ט
לְךָ שְׁנוֹת חַיִּים: וְאוֹמֵר: אֹרֶךְ יָמִים בִּימִינָהּ, בִּשְׂמֹאולָהּ עֹשֶׁר וְכָבוֹד: וְאוֹמֵר: משלי ג
כִּי אֹרֶךְ יָמִים וּשְׁנוֹת חַיִּים וְשָׁלוֹם יוֹסִיפוּ לָךְ: משלי ג

ח רַבִּי שִׁמְעוֹן בֶּן מְנַסְיָא מִשּׁוּם רַבִּי שִׁמְעוֹן בֶּן יוֹחַאי אוֹמֵר: הַנּוֹי, וְהַכֹּחַ,
וְהָעֹשֶׁר, וְהַכָּבוֹד, וְהַחָכְמָה, וְהַזִּקְנָה, וְהַשֵּׂיבָה, וְהַבָּנִים, נָאֶה לַצַּדִּיקִים
וְנָאֶה לָעוֹלָם, שֶׁנֶּאֱמַר: עֲטֶרֶת תִּפְאֶרֶת שֵׂיבָה, בְּדֶרֶךְ צְדָקָה תִּמָּצֵא: משלי טז
וְאוֹמֵר: עֲטֶרֶת חֲכָמִים עָשְׁרָם: וְאוֹמֵר: עֲטֶרֶת זְקֵנִים בְּנֵי בָנִים, וְתִפְאֶרֶת משלי יד משלי יז
בָּנִים אֲבוֹתָם: וְאוֹמֵר: תִּפְאֶרֶת בַּחוּרִים כֹּחָם, וַהֲדַר זְקֵנִים שֵׂיבָה: משלי כ
וְאוֹמֵר: וְחָפְרָה הַלְּבָנָה וּבוֹשָׁה הַחַמָּה, כִּי־מָלַךְ יהוה צְבָאוֹת בְּהַר צִיּוֹן ישעיה כד
וּבִירוּשָׁלִַם, וְנֶגֶד זְקֵנָיו כָּבוֹד: רַבִּי שִׁמְעוֹן בֶּן מְנַסְיָא אוֹמֵר: אֵלּוּ שֶׁבַע מִדּוֹת
שֶׁמָּנוּ חֲכָמִים לַצַּדִּיקִים, כֻּלָּם נִתְקַיְּמוּ בְּרַבִּי וּבְבָנָיו.

ט אָמַר רַבִּי יוֹסֵי בֶּן קִסְמָא: פַּעַם אַחַת הָיִיתִי מְהַלֵּךְ בַּדֶּרֶךְ, וּפָגַע בִּי אָדָם
אֶחָד, וְנָתַן לִי שָׁלוֹם וְהֶחֱזַרְתִּי לוֹ שָׁלוֹם. אָמַר לִי, רַבִּי, מֵאֵיזֶה מָקוֹם אָתָּה.
אָמַרְתִּי לוֹ, מֵעִיר גְּדוֹלָה שֶׁל חֲכָמִים וְשֶׁל סוֹפְרִים אָנִי. אָמַר לִי, רַבִּי, רְצוֹנְךָ
שֶׁתָּדוּר עִמָּנוּ בִּמְקוֹמֵנוּ, וַאֲנִי אֶתֵּן לְךָ אֶלֶף אֲלָפִים דִּינְרֵי זָהָב וַאֲבָנִים טוֹבוֹת
וּמַרְגָּלִיּוֹת. אָמַרְתִּי לוֹ, אִם אַתָּה נוֹתֵן לִי כָּל כֶּסֶף וְזָהָב וַאֲבָנִים טוֹבוֹת
וּמַרְגָּלִיּוֹת שֶׁבָּעוֹלָם, אֵינִי דָר אֶלָּא בִּמְקוֹם תּוֹרָה, וְכֵן כָּתוּב בְּסֵפֶר תְּהִלִּים

רַבִּי יוֹסֵי בֶּן קִסְמָא – *R.* Yose ben Kisma. This is the same R. Yose b. Kisma who, as recorded in the Gemara (*Avoda Zara* 18a), counseled R. Ḥananya b. Teradyon against risking the wrath of the Roman authorities by teaching Torah in public. Without doubt R. Yose himself taught Torah, but only in private, and thus was able to maintain positive relations with the ruling authorities, so that, as the Gemara continues, when he died "all the great men of Rome attended his funeral." Taken together, that Gemara and this Beraita illustrate R. Yose's complex outlook. While he would not openly violate a Roman edict, so as to minimize further religious repression, he nonetheless insisted on living only in "a place of Torah," i.e., where

The commentary continues on page 722.

adding to what one hears, learning in order to teach, learning in order to practice, enlightening one's teacher, thoroughly organizing what one hears, and citing scholarly dicta in the name of whoever first said them. For we have learned that whoever repeats a saying in the name of its author brings
Esther 2 salvation to the world, as it is said: "And Esther told the king in the name of Mordecai."

7. Great is Torah; those who fulfill it earn life both in this world and in the
Prov. 4 World to Come, as it is said: "For they [the teachings of the Torah] are life
Prov. 3 to those who find them and healing for all their flesh." And it says: "For it is health to your body and marrow to your bones." And it says, "It is a tree of life for those who grasp it, and they who uphold it are made happy." And
Prov. 1 it says, "For it is a wreath of grace on your head and a necklace for your
Prov. 4 throat." And it says, "It gives your head a wreath of grace, a crown of glory
Prov. 9 it will bestow on you." And it says, "For by Me shall your days be multiplied
Prov. 3 and the years of your life increased." And it says, "Length of days are in its
Prov. 3 right hand, wealth and honor in its left." And it says, "For it shall give you length of days and years of life and peace."

8. R. Simeon ben Judah said in the name of R. Simeon ben Yoḥai, "Beauty, strength, wealth, honor, wisdom, age, the hoary head, and children are
Prov. 16 beautiful for the righteous and beautiful for the world, as it is said, 'The hoary head is a crown of glory; it will be found in the way of righteousness.
Prov. 14 *Prov. 17* The crown of the wise is their wealth. Children's children are the crown of
Prov. 20 old men, and parents are the glory of children. The glory of young men is their strength, and the beauty of old men is the hoary head.' And it says,
Is. 24 'The moon shall be confounded and the sun ashamed; for the Lord of hosts will reign in Mount Zion and in Jerusalem, and before His elders shall be glory.'" R. Simeon ben Menasya said, "These seven qualities, which were enumerated by the sages as characteristics of the righteous, were all realized in R. (Judah HaNasi) and his sons."

9. R. Yose ben Kisma related: Once, when I was on a journey, I met a man. He greeted me and I returned his greeting. Said he, "Rabbi, where do you come from?" I replied, "From a city great in sages and scribes." He said, "Rabbi, if you will dwell with us in our place, I will give you a thousand thousands of gold pieces, and pearls, and precious stones." Whereupon I said to him, "Even if you were to give me all the silver, gold, pearls, and precious stones in the world, I would not dwell anywhere except in a place where there is Torah." As David King of Israel says in the book of Psalms,

עַל יְדֵי דָוִד מֶלֶךְ יִשְׂרָאֵל: טוֹב־לִי תוֹרַת־פִּיךָ מֵאַלְפֵי זָהָב וָכָסֶף: וְלֹא עוֹד, (תהלים קיט)
אֶלָּא שֶׁבִּשְׁעַת פְּטִירָתוֹ שֶׁל אָדָם, אֵין מְלַוִּין לוֹ לְאָדָם לֹא כֶסֶף וְלֹא זָהָב
וְלֹא אֲבָנִים טוֹבוֹת וּמַרְגָּלִיּוֹת, אֶלָּא תּוֹרָה וּמַעֲשִׂים טוֹבִים בִּלְבָד, שֶׁנֶּאֱמַר:
בְּהִתְהַלֶּכְךָ תַּנְחֶה אֹתָךְ, בְּשָׁכְבְּךָ תִּשְׁמֹר עָלֶיךָ, וַהֲקִיצוֹתָ הִיא תְשִׂיחֶךָ: (משלי ו)
בְּהִתְהַלֶּכְךָ תַּנְחֶה אֹתָךְ, בָּעוֹלָם הַזֶּה. בְּשָׁכְבְּךָ תִּשְׁמֹר עָלֶיךָ, בַּקֶּבֶר. וַהֲקִיצוֹתָ
הִיא תְשִׂיחֶךָ, לָעוֹלָם הַבָּא. וְאוֹמֵר: לִי הַכֶּסֶף וְלִי הַזָּהָב, נְאֻם יהוה צְבָאוֹת: (חגי ב)

י חֲמִשָּׁה קִנְיָנִים קָנָה הַקָּדוֹשׁ בָּרוּךְ הוּא בְּעוֹלָמוֹ. וְאֵלּוּ הֵן, תּוֹרָה קִנְיָן אֶחָד,
שָׁמַיִם וָאָרֶץ קִנְיָן אֶחָד, אַבְרָהָם קִנְיָן אֶחָד, יִשְׂרָאֵל קִנְיָן אֶחָד, בֵּית הַמִּקְדָּשׁ
קִנְיָן אֶחָד. תּוֹרָה מִנַּיִן, דִּכְתִיב: יהוה קָנָנִי רֵאשִׁית דַּרְכּוֹ, קֶדֶם מִפְעָלָיו מֵאָז: (משלי ח)
שָׁמַיִם וָאָרֶץ מִנַּיִן, דִּכְתִיב: כֹּה אָמַר יהוה הַשָּׁמַיִם כִּסְאִי וְהָאָרֶץ הֲדֹם רַגְלָי, (ישעיה סו)
אֵי־זֶה בַיִת אֲשֶׁר תִּבְנוּ־לִי, וְאֵי־זֶה מָקוֹם מְנוּחָתִי: וְאוֹמֵר: מָה־רַבּוּ מַעֲשֶׂיךָ (תהלים קד)
יהוה, כֻּלָּם בְּחָכְמָה עָשִׂיתָ, מָלְאָה הָאָרֶץ קִנְיָנֶךָ: אַבְרָהָם מִנַּיִן, דִּכְתִיב:
וַיְבָרְכֵהוּ וַיֹּאמַר, בָּרוּךְ אַבְרָם לְאֵל עֶלְיוֹן, קֹנֵה שָׁמַיִם וָאָרֶץ: יִשְׂרָאֵל מִנַּיִן, (בראשית יד)
דִּכְתִיב: עַד־יַעֲבֹר עַמְּךָ יהוה, עַד־יַעֲבֹר עַם־זוּ קָנִיתָ: וְאוֹמֵר: לִקְדוֹשִׁים (שמות טו) (תהלים טז)
אֲשֶׁר־בָּאָרֶץ הֵמָּה, וְאַדִּירֵי כָּל־חֶפְצִי־בָם: בֵּית הַמִּקְדָּשׁ מִנַּיִן, דִּכְתִיב: מָכוֹן (שמות טו)
לְשִׁבְתְּךָ פָּעַלְתָּ יהוה, מִקְּדָשׁ אֲדֹנָי כּוֹנְנוּ יָדֶיךָ: וְאוֹמֵר: וַיְבִיאֵם אֶל־גְּבוּל (תהלים עח)
קָדְשׁוֹ, הַר־זֶה קָנְתָה יְמִינוֹ:

יא כָּל מַה שֶּׁבָּרָא הַקָּדוֹשׁ בָּרוּךְ הוּא בְּעוֹלָמוֹ, לֹא בְרָאוֹ אֶלָּא לִכְבוֹדוֹ, שֶׁנֶּאֱמַר:
כֹּל הַנִּקְרָא בִשְׁמִי וְלִכְבוֹדִי בְּרָאתִיו, יְצַרְתִּיו אַף־עֲשִׂיתִיו: וְאוֹמֵר: יהוה (ישעיה מג) (שמות טו)
יִמְלֹךְ לְעֹלָם וָעֶד:

רַבִּי חֲנַנְיָא בֶּן עֲקַשְׁיָא אוֹמֵר: רָצָה הַקָּדוֹשׁ בָּרוּךְ הוּא לְזַכּוֹת אֶת יִשְׂרָאֵל, לְפִיכָךְ הִרְבָּה (מכות כג:)
לָהֶם תּוֹרָה וּמִצְוֹת. שֶׁנֶּאֱמַר: יהוה חָפֵץ לְמַעַן צִדְקוֹ, יַגְדִּיל תּוֹרָה וְיַאְדִּיר: (ישעיה מב)

If a מנין *is present, mourners say* קדיש דרבנן *(on the next page).*

Torah was intensively – and apparently legally – studied, taught, and lived in non-public fashion, with Roman blessing, even if it meant choosing a life of hardship, poverty and material deprivation, as was clearly the case in second-century Israel (R. Basil Herring).

כָּל מַה שֶּׁבָּרָא הַקָּדוֹשׁ בָּרוּךְ הוּא בְּעוֹלָמוֹ, לֹא בְרָאוֹ אֶלָּא לִכְבוֹדוֹ – *Everything that the Holy One, blessed is He, created in His world, He created only for His glory*. We learn from this *mishna* that we must do everything in our power to avoid the desecration of God's name, whether in the eyes of our fellow Jews, or in the eyes of Gentiles. The Gemara (*Yoma* 86a) explains that this matter depends on our religious standing, for a greater person is held to a higher standard than a lesser person. In general, the greater we are, the more the

The commentary continues on page 724.

Ps. 119 "The law of Your mouth is better for me than thousands of pieces of gold and
silver." Moreover, when the time comes to depart from this world, neither
silver nor gold nor pearls nor precious stones will accompany you, but only
Prov. 6 Torah and good deeds, as it is said: "When you walk, it shall guide you;
when you lie down it shall watch over you, and when you awaken it shall
converse with you." "When you walk it shall guide you" in this world; "when
you lie down it shall watch over you" in the grave; "and when you wake it
Hag. 2 shall talk with you" in the World to Come. And it says, "Mine is the silver,
Mine the gold, says the Lord of hosts."

10. Five possessions did the Holy One, blessed is He, acquire in His world,
namely: the Torah, heaven and earth, Abraham, Israel, and the Temple.
Prov. 8 The Torah, as it is written, "The Lord formed me as the first of His way, the
beginning of His works of old." Of heaven and earth, from where do we
Is. 66 learn this? It is written: "Thus says the Lord, The heavens are My throne
and the earth is My footstool. What house, then, can you build for Me,
Ps. 104 and what is the place where I may rest?" And it says, "How great are Your
works, O Lord! You have made them all in wisdom. The earth is full of
Your creatures." Of Abraham, from where do we learn this? It is written:
Gen. 14 "Blessed be Abram of God Most High, Who acquired heaven and earth."
Ex. 15 Of Israel, from where do we learn this? It is written: "Until Your people
pass over, O Lord, until the people whom You have acquired pass over."
Ps. 16 And it says: "To the holy that are in the land, and the mighty in whom
is all my desire." Of the holy Temple, from where do we learn this? It is
Ex. 15 written: "The shrine, O Lord, that You have made for Your dwelling; the
sanctuary, my Master, that Your own hands have established." And it says:
Ps. 78 "And He brought them to His holy border, to the mountain that His right
hand had established."

11. Everything that the Holy One, blessed is He, created in His world, He
Is. 43 created only for His glory, as it is said: "All that is called by My name, it is
for My glory that I have created it, formed it, and made it." And it is said:
Ex. 15 "The Lord shall reign forever and ever."

Makkot 23b R. ḤANANYA ben Akashya used to say, "The Holy One, blessed is He, wishing to
render Israel more worthy, enlarged the Torah and its commandments for them, as
Is. 42 it is said, 'The Lord desired, for the sake of its [Israel's] righteousness, to magnify the
Torah and glorify it.'"

If a minyan is present, mourners say the Rabbis' Kaddish (on the next page).

קדיש דרבנן

The following prayer, said by mourners, requires the presence of a מנין.
A transliteration can be found on page 1344.

אבל: **יִתְגַּדַּל** וְיִתְקַדַּשׁ שְׁמֵהּ רַבָּא (קהל: אָמֵן) בְּעָלְמָא דִּי בְרָא כִרְעוּתֵהּ.
וְיַמְלִיךְ מַלְכוּתֵהּ בְּחַיֵּיכוֹן וּבְיוֹמֵיכוֹן וּבְחַיֵּי דְכָל בֵּית
יִשְׂרָאֵל, בַּעֲגָלָא וּבִזְמַן קָרִיב, וְאִמְרוּ אָמֵן. (קהל: אָמֵן)

קהל ואבל: יְהֵא שְׁמֵהּ רַבָּא מְבָרַךְ לְעָלַם וּלְעָלְמֵי עָלְמַיָּא.

אבל: יִתְבָּרַךְ וְיִשְׁתַּבַּח וְיִתְפָּאַר וְיִתְרוֹמַם וְיִתְנַשֵּׂא, וְיִתְהַדָּר וְיִתְעַלֶּה
וְיִתְהַלָּל שְׁמֵהּ דְּקֻדְשָׁא בְּרִיךְ הוּא (קהל: בְּרִיךְ הוּא), לְעֵלָּא מִן כָּל
בִּרְכָתָא / בשבת שובה: לְעֵלָּא (וּ)לְעֵלָּא מִכָּל בִּרְכָתָא/ וְשִׁירָתָא, תֻּשְׁבְּחָתָא
וְנֶחֱמָתָא דַּאֲמִירָן בְּעָלְמָא, וְאִמְרוּ אָמֵן. (קהל: אָמֵן)

עַל יִשְׂרָאֵל וְעַל רַבָּנָן, וְעַל תַּלְמִידֵיהוֹן וְעַל כָּל תַּלְמִידֵי תַלְמִידֵיהוֹן,
וְעַל כָּל מָאן דְּעָסְקִין בְּאוֹרַיְתָא, דִּי בְאַתְרָא הָדֵין, וְדִי בְכָל אֲתַר
וַאֲתַר, יְהֵא לְהוֹן וּלְכוֹן שְׁלָמָא רַבָּא, חִנָּא וְחִסְדָּא, וְרַחֲמֵי, וְחַיֵּי
אֲרִיכֵי, וּמְזוֹנֵי רְוִיחֵי, וּפֻרְקָנָא מִן קֳדָם אֲבוּהוֹן דִּי בִשְׁמַיָּא, וְאִמְרוּ
אָמֵן. (קהל: אָמֵן)

יְהֵא שְׁלָמָא רַבָּא מִן שְׁמַיָּא וְחַיִּים, עָלֵינוּ וְעַל כָּל יִשְׂרָאֵל, וְאִמְרוּ
אָמֵן. (קהל: אָמֵן)

Bow, take three steps back, as if taking leave of the Divine Presence,
then bow, first left, then right, then center, while saying:

עֹשֶׂה שָׁלוֹם/ בשבת שובה: הַשָּׁלוֹם/ בִּמְרוֹמָיו, הוּא יַעֲשֶׂה שָׁלוֹם עָלֵינוּ,
וְעַל כָּל יִשְׂרָאֵל, וְאִמְרוּ אָמֵן. (קהל: אָמֵן)

---

halakha demands of us. And if from our improper actions others are encouraged to act in similar ways, then our behavior constitutes a desecration of God's name. In this context it is not what we do, but how others perceive our actions. Hence we must always bring glory to God's name, in accordance with the verse (Isaiah 49:3), "Israel in whom I am glorified" (Ḥafetz Ḥayyim).

This teaches us how to relate to the natural

THE RABBIS' KADDISH

The following prayer, said by mourners, requires the presence of a minyan. A transliteration can be found on page 1344.

Mourner: יִתְגַּדַּל EXALTED AND HALLOWED may God's great name be, in the world He created as He willed. May He reign in your lifetimes and in your days, and in the lifetime of the whole house of Israel, speedily and soon, and say, Amen.

All: May His great name be blessed forever and all time.

Mourner: Blessed and praised, honored, extolled, glorified, adored and exalted above all be the name of the Holy One, blessed is He, (*Between Rosh Hashana & Yom Kippur:* above and) beyond any blessing, hymn, praise, or expressions of consolation that may be uttered in this world, and say, Amen.

May the Jewish people, and our teachers, together with their students and all their students' students, as well as all who engage in Torah study here and in every other place, have abundant peace, grace, kindness, mercy, length of days, abundant food, and deliverance at the hands of their heavenly Father, and say, Amen.

May abundant peace descend from heaven, as well as life, for us and for all Israel, and say, Amen.

Bow, take three steps back, as if taking leave of the Divine Presence, then bow, first left, then right, then center, while saying:

May He Who makes peace in the highest heaven, make peace for us, and for all Israel, and say, Amen.

---

world. Man alone has a נְשָׁמָה (soul) which elevates us to the extent that we realize our spiritual potential. To achieve this we depend on all that God made to serve our needs. Thus when we utilize the world around us to this spiritual end we realize not only our own greatest potential, but that of nature too (R. Moshe Feinstein).

סעודה שלישית

אַתְקִינוּ סְעוּדָתָא דִּמְהֵימְנוּתָא שְׁלִימְתָא, חֶדְוְתָא דְּמַלְכָּא קַדִּישָׁא. אַתְקִינוּ סְעוּדָתָא דְמַלְכָּא. דָּא הִיא סְעוּדָתָא דִזְעֵיר אַנְפִּין, וְעַתִּיקָא קַדִּישָׁא וַחֲקַל תַּפּוּחִין קַדִּישִׁין אָתַיִן לְסַעֲדָה בַּהֲדֵהּ.

בְּנֵי הֵיכְלָא, דְּכַסִּיפִין לְמֶחֱזֵי זִיו זְעֵיר אַנְפִּין

יְהוֹן הָכָא, בְּהַאי תַּכָּא, דְּבֵהּ מַלְכָּא בְּגִלּוּפִין.

צְבוּ לְחַדָא, בְּהַאי וַעְדָא, בְּגוֹ עִירִין וְכָל גַּדְפִין.

חֲדוּ הַשְׁתָּא, בְּהַאי שַׁעְתָּא, דְּבֵהּ רַעֲוָא וְלֵית זַעְפִין.

קְרִיבוּ לִי, חֲזוּ חֵילִי, דְּלֵית דִּינִין דְּתַקִּיפִין.

לְבַר נָטְלִין, וְלָא עָלִין, הָנֵי כַלְבִּין דַּחֲצִיפִין.

וְהָא אַזְמִין עַתִּיק יוֹמִין, לְמִצְחֵהּ עֲד יְהוֹן חָלְפִין.

רְעוּ דִי לֵהּ, דְּגַלֵּי לֵהּ, לְבַטָּלָה בְּכָל קְלִיפִין.

יְשַׁוֵּי לוֹן, בְּנִקְבְהוֹן, וִיטַמְּרוּן בְּגוֹ כֵפִין.

אֲרֵי הַשְׁתָּא, בְּמִנְחָתָא, בְּחֶדְוְתָא דִּזְעֵיר אַנְפִּין.

מִזְמוֹר לְדָוִד יהוה רֹעִי לֹא אֶחְסָר: בִּנְאוֹת דֶּשֶׁא יַרְבִּיצֵנִי, עַל־מֵי תהלים כג
מְנֻחוֹת יְנַהֲלֵנִי: נַפְשִׁי יְשׁוֹבֵב, יַנְחֵנִי בְמַעְגְּלֵי־צֶדֶק
לְמַעַן שְׁמוֹ: גַּם כִּי־אֵלֵךְ בְּגֵיא צַלְמָוֶת לֹא־אִירָא רָע, כִּי־אַתָּה עִמָּדִי,

---

סְעוּדָה שְׁלִישִׁית / SEUDA SHELISHIT (SHALESHUDES) Yiddish speaking Jews and their descendants tend to call *seuda shelishit*, which means the third meal, *shaleshudes*, a contraction for *shalosh seudot*, i.e., three meals. A homiletical explanation for this practice is that one eats the first two Shabbat meals while one is hungry. Consequently, it is not evident that it is being eaten for the sake of the *mitzva*. The third meal, however, especially in the winter, is often eaten when one is not hungry. This demonstrates that the meal is indeed being eaten to fulfill the *mitzva*, and it also indicates that this was true of the first two meals as well. Thus, the third meal provides reward for all three Shabbat meals and is properly called *shaleshudes* (R. Menaḥem Naḥum Rabinowitz).

The Gemara (*Shabbat* 118a) states that the three Shabbat meals correspond to the periods of suffering from which we will be redeemed at the end of time: (1) The birth-pangs of the Messiah, (2) *Gehenna*, and (3) the war of Gog and Magog.

In Kabbalistic literature, the *Seuda Shelishit* is referred to as רַעֲוָא דְרַעֲוִין (the time of highest favor), i.e., it is when God is most kindly disposed toward Israel and most receptive of our efforts to achieve spiritual growth.

The concluding moments of Shabbat are much like the World to Come, when, as described in *Berakhot* 17a, the earthly mission of the Jewish people will have been completed, leaving them to bask in the glow of God's celestial radiance (R. Joseph B. Soloveitchik).

SE'UDA SHELISHIT

אַתְקִינוּ סְעוּדְתָא PREPARE THE MEAL of complete faithfulness which is the joy of the holy King. Prepare the King's meal, which is the Sabbath meal that reflects the sefira of Tiferet known as Ze'ir Anpin, as well as the sefira of Keter which is known as Hazaken Hakadosh, as well as the sefira of Malkhut which is known as Sedeh Tapuḥin Kadishin. May they all come to partake with Him.

בְּנֵי הֵיכְלָא MAY THE WISE SCHOLARS who long to see the countenance of the Ze'eir Anpin / be present at this table which is designated for the presence of the King. / For it is their sincere desire to sit at this gathering amidst the angels and winged ones. / Rejoice therefore at this hour of divine favor, when there is no anger or wrath. / Draw near unto me and witness my strength, in the absence of all harsh judgments. / When the brazen dogs are expelled and excluded from this gathering / to which I have invited the Atik Yomin at the hour of Minḥa to stay until every accuser has left. / For His will as it has been revealed will nullify every impure shell / and banish them to their hidden lairs, consigned to remain among the rocks. / For now is the time, at Minḥa, to rejoice with the Ze'eir Anpin.

Ps. 23 מִזְמוֹר לְדָוִד A PSALM OF DAVID. The Lord is my shepherd. I lack for nothing. He makes me lie down in green pastures. He leads me beside still waters. He restores my soul. He leads me in the paths of righteousness for His name's sake. Even when I walk in a valley of darkness, I do not fear evil, for You are with me. Your rod and Your

---

בְּנֵי הֵיכְלָא / BNEI HEICHALA
This zemer was composed by the Arizal (d. 1572). His name Yitzḥak Luria is found in acrostic form at the beginning of each of the nine stanzas that follow the first stanza. It is filled with mystical allusions as studied by devotees of the Kabbalah. The first three stanzas refer to the righteous who are privileged to enjoy the intimate radiance of the Divine Presence, and who, together with the celestial angels, are invited to be present in spirit to attend this third Shabbat meal (*Zemirot Shabbat – Mesivta*).

דְּבֵהּ רַעֲוָא וְלֵית זַעְפִּין – *When there is no anger or wrath.* The period following Shabbat *Minḥa* is considered particularly conducive to divine favor and thus spiritual peacefulness, as we declare during *Minḥa, Lekha Hashem eit ratzon* (it is a time of special divine favor). For this reason too the *Minḥa Amida* emphasizes the unity of God, together with His name, in harmony with His people Israel. Hence the next stanzas speak of drawing closer to God at this hour, to witness His overwhelming protective power, and (as the light of the sun weakens toward evening) to see the spiritual light of His *Shekhina* (*Minḥat Yaakov*).

מִזְמוֹר לְדָוִד / PSALM 23
This psalm invokes the metaphor of a caring shepherd tending to his flock to portray a

שִׁבְטְךָ וּמִשְׁעַנְתֶּךָ הֵמָּה יְנַחֲמֻנִי: תַּעֲרֹךְ לְפָנַי שֻׁלְחָן נֶגֶד צֹרְרָי, דִּשַּׁנְתָּ בַשֶּׁמֶן רֹאשִׁי, כּוֹסִי רְוָיָה: אַךְ טוֹב וָחֶסֶד יִרְדְּפוּנִי כָּל־יְמֵי חַיָּי, וְשַׁבְתִּי בְּבֵית־יהוה לְאֹרֶךְ יָמִים:

The following is the commonly used version.
An alternative version can be found on page 1342.

יְדִיד נֶפֶשׁ, אָב הָרַחֲמָן, מְשֹׁךְ עַבְדְּךָ אֶל רְצוֹנֶךָ
יָרוּץ עַבְדְּךָ כְּמוֹ אַיָּל, יִשְׁתַּחֲוֶה אֶל מוּל הֲדָרֶךָ
יֶעֱרַב לוֹ יְדִידוֹתֶיךָ, מִנֹּפֶת צוּף וְכָל טָעַם.

הָדוּר, נָאֶה, זִיו הָעוֹלָם, נַפְשִׁי חוֹלַת אַהֲבָתֶךָ
אָנָּא, אֵל נָא, רְפָא נָא לָהּ, בְּהַרְאוֹת לָהּ נֹעַם זִיוֶךָ
אָז תִּתְחַזֵּק וְתִתְרַפֵּא, וְהָיְתָה לָהּ שִׂמְחַת עוֹלָם.

וָתִיק, יֶהֱמוּ נָא רַחֲמֶיךָ, וְחוּסָה נָא עַל בֵּן אֲהוּבֶךָ
כִּי זֶה כַּמָּה נִכְסֹף נִכְסַפְתִּי לִרְאוֹת מְהֵרָה בְּתִפְאֶרֶת עֻזֶּךָ,
אֵלֶּה חָמְדָה לִבִּי, וְחוּסָה נָּא, וְאַל תִּתְעַלָּם.

הִגָּלֵה נָא וּפְרֹשׂ, חֲבִיבִי, עָלַי אֶת סֻכַּת שְׁלוֹמֶךָ
תָּאִיר אֶרֶץ מִכְּבוֹדֶךָ, נָגִילָה וְנִשְׂמְחָה בָּךְ.
מַהֵר, אֱהֹב, כִּי בָא מוֹעֵד, וְחָנֵּנוּ כִּימֵי עוֹלָם.

---

trusting relationship to God. A good shepherd makes sure that his flock lacks for nothing. Sometimes, however, due to its limited perspective, a sheep may try to run to what it mistakenly thinks are greener pastures. Then, the ever-protective shepherd stands in its way to keep it on the "straight and narrow." At other times a sheep might mistakenly balk at what the shepherd provides for its own good. When that happens, the shepherd finds a way to gently induce the sheep to submit to his protective hand. So it is with us and our divine Shepherd. Our perspective, like that of the sheep, is limited, our understanding inadequate. Sometimes we want what we really do not need, or we resist those things that He sends to us that are truly for our benefit. With this metaphor in mind, David tells us to be mindful at all times that even though life can be difficult and filled with suffering or even death, we should have no fear, for God is undoubtedly caring for us, like a good shepherd, appearances notwithstanding. More specifically, it is sometimes necessary for God's punishing rod to discipline us for our own good, while at other times His supporting staff is there to help us overcome life's challenges. Throughout we must trust that everything that happens is for the good. If such will be our

staff, they comfort me. You prepare a table before me in the presence of my enemies. You have anointed my head with oil. My cup runs over. Only goodness and loving-kindness will follow me all the days of my life, and I will dwell in tranquility in the house of the Lord forever.

The following is the commonly used version.
An alternative version can be found on page 1343.

יְדִיד נֶפֶשׁ BELOVED of the soul, compassionate Father, help me, Your servant, to do Your will. / May I, Your servant, run like a deer, and bow down before Your glory. / For the sweetness of your love will be better than a honeycomb or any other taste.

MY SOUL is love-sick for You Who are the glorious, pleasant, splendor of the universe. / Please dear God, heal her by revealing the pleasantness of Your splendor, / thus strengthening and healing her, to enjoy everlasting happiness.

ANCIENT ONE – may Your mercy be aroused. Take pity, please, on Your beloved son. / For I have long and passionately yearned to behold the splendor of Your might without delay. / This alone my heart desires, so please, take pity and do not hide from me.

PLEASE REVEAL Yourself, my Beloved, by spreading over me the canopy of Your peace. / Light up the world with Your glory so that we may be gladdened by rejoicing in You. / Hasten to show Your love, for the time has come to grace us just as in the days of yore.

---

attitude, our cup will indeed be filled to overflowing with joy and tranquility, "throughout our lives," i.e., not only in this life, but the next one as well, when we can be sure "we will dwell in the house of the Lord forever" (R. Ḥayyim of Volozhin).

The message of complete trust is further conveyed by the Psalmist by progressing from a third person perspective (conveying distance) in the first three verses, to a direct second person address (conveying closeness) in the last three. This reflects the Psalmist's increasing sense of closeness and intimacy with God, culminating in the desire to feel at home in God's Temple and to cleave ever closer to Him (R. Amos Ḥakham).

נֶגֶד צֹרְרָי – *In the presence of my enemies.* Trust in God does not also imply a life free of pain or danger, for even the person of faith sometimes endures loss and must deal with cruel adversaries (R. Asher Oser).

יְדִיד נֶפֶשׁ / BELOVED OF THE SOUL
See the commentary on page 358.

מעריב למוצאי שבת

In many congregations, the following two psalms are sung before מעריב *on* מוצאי שבת.

תהלים קמד

לְדָוִד, בָּרוּךְ יהוה צוּרִי, הַמְלַמֵּד יָדַי לַקְרָב, אֶצְבְּעוֹתַי לַמִּלְחָמָה:
חַסְדִּי וּמְצוּדָתִי מִשְׂגַּבִּי וּמְפַלְטִי לִי, מָגִנִּי וּבוֹ חָסִיתִי,
הָרוֹדֵד עַמִּי תַחְתָּי: יהוה מָה־אָדָם וַתֵּדָעֵהוּ, בֶּן־אֱנוֹשׁ וַתְּחַשְּׁבֵהוּ:
אָדָם לַהֶבֶל דָּמָה, יָמָיו כְּצֵל עוֹבֵר: יהוה הַט־שָׁמֶיךָ וְתֵרֵד, גַּע בֶּהָרִים
וְיֶעֱשָׁנוּ: בְּרוֹק בָּרָק וּתְפִיצֵם, שְׁלַח חִצֶּיךָ וּתְהֻמֵּם: שְׁלַח יָדֶיךָ
מִמָּרוֹם, פְּצֵנִי וְהַצִּילֵנִי מִמַּיִם רַבִּים, מִיַּד בְּנֵי נֵכָר: אֲשֶׁר פִּיהֶם דִּבֶּר־
שָׁוְא, וִימִינָם יְמִין שָׁקֶר: אֱלֹהִים שִׁיר חָדָשׁ אָשִׁירָה לָּךְ, בְּנֵבֶל עָשׂוֹר
אֲזַמְּרָה־לָּךְ: הַנּוֹתֵן תְּשׁוּעָה לַמְּלָכִים, הַפּוֹצֶה אֶת־דָּוִד עַבְדּוֹ מֵחֶרֶב
רָעָה: פְּצֵנִי וְהַצִּילֵנִי מִיַּד בְּנֵי נֵכָר, אֲשֶׁר פִּיהֶם דִּבֶּר־שָׁוְא, וִימִינָם
יְמִין שָׁקֶר: אֲשֶׁר בָּנֵינוּ כִּנְטִעִים, מְגֻדָּלִים בִּנְעוּרֵיהֶם, בְּנוֹתֵינוּ
כְזָוִיֹּת, מְחֻטָּבוֹת תַּבְנִית הֵיכָל: מְזָוֵינוּ מְלֵאִים, מְפִיקִים מִזַּן אֶל־
זַן, צֹאונֵנוּ מַאֲלִיפוֹת מְרֻבָּבוֹת בְּחוּצוֹתֵינוּ: אַלּוּפֵינוּ מְסֻבָּלִים, אֵין
פֶּרֶץ וְאֵין יוֹצֵאת, וְאֵין צְוָחָה בִּרְחֹבֹתֵינוּ: אַשְׁרֵי הָעָם שֶׁכָּכָה לּוֹ,
אַשְׁרֵי הָעָם שֶׁיהוה אֱלֹהָיו:

תהלים סז

לַמְנַצֵּחַ בִּנְגִינֹת, מִזְמוֹר שִׁיר: אֱלֹהִים יְחָנֵּנוּ וִיבָרְכֵנוּ, יָאֵר פָּנָיו
אִתָּנוּ סֶלָה: לָדַעַת בָּאָרֶץ דַּרְכֶּךָ, בְּכָל־גּוֹיִם

PSALM 144 / לְדָוִד, בָּרוּךְ

אַשְׁרֵי הָעָם שֶׁכָּכָה לּוֹ – *Happy is the people that has this.* As the Gemara (*Berakhot* 17a) records, the students of R. Ḥisda and R. Shmuel bar Naḥmani would recite this verse when leaving the house of study, because it encapsulated their regret at leaving, just as David regretted interrupting his study in order to lead his armies against their enemies. As we prepare to leave Shabbat, we experience a similar feeling, for we want the Shabbat aura to stay with us for as long as possible, and so we too recite it (R. Joseph B. Soloveitchik).

אֲשֶׁר פִּיהֶם דִּבֶּר־שָׁוְא, וִימִינָם יְמִין שָׁקֶר – *Whose mouth speaks deceit, and whose right hand is a right hand of falsehood.* This verse portrays David's enemies as false allies who had deviously betrayed their word and his trust. Throughout Jewish history we have had to deal with those who profess friendship and support, but who turn out to be anything but friends and supporters. This too stands as a warning to us at the conclusion of Shabbat, as we prepare to deal with the outside world.

MA'ARIV FOR THE CONCLUSION OF SHABBAT

In many congregations, the following two psalms are sung before Ma'ariv at the end of Shabbat.

Ps. 144 לְדָוִד, בָּרוּךְ OF DAVID. Blessed be the Lord, my rock, Who teaches my hands for battle, my fingers for war. My gracious One, and my fortress, my high tower, and my deliverer, my shield, and the One in Whom I find shelter, Who subdues people under me. O Lord, what is man, that You know him, the son of man, that You consider him! Man is like a breath. His days are like a passing shadow. O Lord, bow Your heavens and come down. Touch the mountains so that they smoke. Fire lightning and scatter them. Send Your arrows and destroy them. Send Your hands from on high. Rescue me and deliver me from many waters, from the hand of strangers, whose mouth speaks deceit, and whose right hand is a right hand of falsehood. O God, I will sing a new song to You, upon a ten-string harp I will sing praises to You. He Who gives salvation to kings, Who rescues David, His servant, from the evil sword, Rescue me and deliver me from the hand of strangers, whose mouth speaks deceit, and whose right hand is a right hand of falsehood. So that our sons will be like saplings raised in their youth, our daughters like cornerstones, carved in the fashion of a palace. Our storehouses are full, supplying all kinds of produce, our sheep bring forth thousands, tens of thousands in our markets. Our rams are stout. There is no breach and there is no leaving, and there is no outcry in our streets. Happy is the people that has this. Happy is the people whose God is the Lord.

Ps. 67 לַמְנַצֵּחַ TO THE DIRECTOR of music for instruments. A psalm. A song. May God be gracious to us and bless us. May He cause His face to shine upon us. Selah. That Your way may become known upon the earth, Your salvation among all nations. The peoples will praise You,

---

מְחֻטָּבוֹת תַּבְנִית הֵיכָל – *Carved in the fashion of a palace.* Jewish mothers, wives, and daughters are the pillars and cornerstones of the edifice of the Jewish nation (R. Amos Ḥakham).

לַמְנַצֵּחַ־בִּנְגִינֹת / PSALM 67 Following the superscription, the psalm forms a perfect seven verse chiasmus. In the middle is verse 5, which is longer than the other verses,

יְשׁוּעָתֶךָ: יוֹדְוּךָ עַמִּים אֱלֹהִים, יוֹדְוּךָ עַמִּים כֻּלָּם: יִשְׂמְחוּ וִירַנְּנוּ לְאֻמִּים, כִּי־תִשְׁפֹּט עַמִּים מִישֹׁר, וּלְאֻמִּים בָּאָרֶץ תַּנְחֵם סֶלָה: יוֹדְוּךָ עַמִּים אֱלֹהִים, יוֹדְוּךָ עַמִּים כֻּלָּם: אֶרֶץ נָתְנָה יְבוּלָהּ, יְבָרְכֵנוּ אֱלֹהִים אֱלֹהֵינוּ: יְבָרְכֵנוּ אֱלֹהִים, וְיִירְאוּ אוֹתוֹ כָּל־אַפְסֵי־אָרֶץ:

The service continues with מעריב לחול *on page 290. After the* עמידה, *the* שליח ציבור *says* חצי קדיש *and the* קהל *continues below.*

If a יום טוב *(or according to some authorities even* ערב פסח*) falls during the coming week the* שליח ציבור *says* קדיש שלם *(page 736), and the service continues there.*

On פורים, מגילת אסתר *is read at this point. On* תשעה באב, מגילת איכה *and* קינות *are read at this point. On weeknights, both are followed by* וְאַתָּה קָדוֹשׁ *(next page) and* עָלֵינוּ *(page 746).*

If פורים *occurs on* מוצאי שבת, מגילת אסתר *is followed by* וִיהִי נְעַם *below:*

תהלים צ **וִיהִי נְעַם** אֲדֹנָי אֱלֹהֵינוּ עָלֵינוּ וּמַעֲשֵׂה יָדֵינוּ כּוֹנְנָה עָלֵינוּ וּמַעֲשֵׂה יָדֵינוּ כּוֹנְנֵהוּ:

תהלים צא **יֹשֵׁב** בְּסֵתֶר עֶלְיוֹן, בְּצֵל שַׁדַּי יִתְלוֹנָן: אֹמַר לַיהוה מַחְסִי וּמְצוּדָתִי, אֱלֹהַי אֶבְטַח־בּוֹ: כִּי הוּא יַצִּילְךָ מִפַּח יָקוּשׁ, מִדֶּבֶר הַוּוֹת: בְּאֶבְרָתוֹ יָסֶךְ לָךְ, וְתַחַת־כְּנָפָיו תֶּחְסֶה, צִנָּה וְסֹחֵרָה אֲמִתּוֹ: לֹא־תִירָא מִפַּחַד לָיְלָה, מֵחֵץ יָעוּף יוֹמָם: מִדֶּבֶר בָּאֹפֶל יַהֲלֹךְ, מִקֶּטֶב יָשׁוּד צָהֳרָיִם: יִפֹּל מִצִּדְּךָ אֶלֶף, וּרְבָבָה מִימִינֶךָ, אֵלֶיךָ לֹא יִגָּשׁ: רַק בְּעֵינֶיךָ תַבִּיט, וְשִׁלֻּמַת רְשָׁעִים תִּרְאֶה: כִּי־אַתָּה יהוה מַחְסִי, עֶלְיוֹן שַׂמְתָּ מְעוֹנֶךָ: לֹא־תְאֻנֶּה אֵלֶיךָ רָעָה, וְנֶגַע לֹא־יִקְרַב בְּאָהֳלֶךָ: כִּי מַלְאָכָיו יְצַוֶּה־לָּךְ, לִשְׁמָרְךָ בְּכָל־דְּרָכֶיךָ: עַל־כַּפַּיִם יִשָּׂאוּנְךָ, פֶּן־תִּגֹּף בָּאֶבֶן רַגְלֶךָ: עַל־שַׁחַל וָפֶתֶן תִּדְרֹךְ, תִּרְמֹס כְּפִיר וְתַנִּין: כִּי בִי חָשַׁק

---

and includes all the nations of the world in the joy engendered by divine blessing, for God judges fairly as He guides humanity. On either side of the verse is the identical refrain, "The peoples will acknowledge You, o God, the peoples will acknowledge You, all of them." On the next rung, verses 3 and 7 speak of the earth: "The earth has yielded its produce" (v. 7), and it is particularly through this blessing of Israel that the nations learn of God's salvations and His ways "on the earth" (v. 3). Finally, the outer verses, 2 and 8, envelop these five verses, and each is a petition for divine blessing. The chiasmus is so perfect, the verses so balanced, that the psalm is said to display with its seven verses (after the superscription) a seven branched *menora* structure (R. Amos Ḥakham).

O God. All the peoples will praise You. The nations will rejoice and sing. For You judge the peoples equitably and govern the nations upon the earth. Selah. The peoples will praise You, O God. All the peoples will praise You. The earth has yielded its produce. God, our God, will bless us. God will bless us, and all the ends of the earth will fear Him.

The service continues with Ma'ariv for Weekdays on page 291. After the Amida, the Leader says Half Kaddish and the congregation continues below.

If a Yom Tov (or according to some authorities even Erev Pesaḥ) falls during the coming week the Leader says Full Kaddish (page 737), and the service continues there.

On Purim, Megillat Esther is read at this point. On Tisha B'Av, Megillat Eikha and Kinnot are read at this point. On weeknights, both are followed by "But, You are holy" (next page) and Aleinu (page 747).

If Purim occurs at the conclusion of Shabbat, Megillat Esther is followed by "And let the pleasantness" below:

Ps. 90 **וִיהִי נֹעַם** AND LET the pleasantness of the Lord our God be upon us, and establish the work of our hands upon us, and establish it, the work of our hands.

Ps. 91 **יֹשֵׁב** HE WHO DWELLS in the secret place of the Most High abides in the shadow of the Almighty. I say to the Lord, my refuge and my fortress, my God, I trust in Him. Indeed, He will deliver you from the baited trap, from the deadly pestilence. He will cover you with His pinions, and under His wings you will find refuge. His truth will be your shield and buckler. You will not be afraid of the terror by night, of the arrow that flies by day, of the pestilence that walks in the darkness, of the destruction that wastes at noonday. A thousand will fall at your side and ten thousand at your right hand. It will not come near to you. Only with your eyes will you behold, and you will see the destruction of the wicked. Indeed, You, O Lord, are my refuge. You have made the Most High Your habitation. No evil will befall you, and plague will not come near to your tent. Indeed, He will give His angels charge over you, to keep you in all your ways. They will bear you up on their hands, lest you dash your foot against a stone. You will tread upon the lion and the adder. You will trample the young lion and the crocodile underfoot. Because he has clung to Me, I will deliver him. I will make him safe,

---

וִיהִי נֹעַם / PSALM 90
The final verse of Psalm 90, anticipating the labors of the coming week, asks that God establish "the work of our hands," to ensure their

וַאֲפַלְּטֵהוּ, אֲשַׂגְּבֵהוּ כִּי־יָדַע שְׁמִי: יִקְרָאֵנִי וְאֶעֱנֵהוּ, עִמּוֹ אָנֹכִי בְצָרָה,
אֲחַלְּצֵהוּ וַאֲכַבְּדֵהוּ: ◂ אֹרֶךְ יָמִים אַשְׂבִּיעֵהוּ, וְאַרְאֵהוּ בִּישׁוּעָתִי:
אֹרֶךְ יָמִים אַשְׂבִּיעֵהוּ, וְאַרְאֵהוּ בִּישׁוּעָתִי:

תהלים כב ישעיה ו ◂ **וְאַתָּה קָדוֹשׁ** יוֹשֵׁב תְּהִלּוֹת יִשְׂרָאֵל: וְקָרָא זֶה אֶל־זֶה וְאָמַר,
קָדוֹשׁ, קָדוֹשׁ, קָדוֹשׁ יהוה צְבָאוֹת, מְלֹא כָל־
הָאָרֶץ כְּבוֹדוֹ:

תרגום יונתן ישעיה ו וּמְקַבְּלִין דֵּין מִן דֵּין וְאָמְרִין, קַדִּישׁ בִּשְׁמֵי מְרוֹמָא עִלָּאָה בֵּית שְׁכִינְתֵהּ, קַדִּישׁ
עַל אַרְעָא עוֹבַד גְּבוּרְתֵהּ, קַדִּישׁ לְעָלַם וּלְעָלְמֵי עָלְמַיָּא, יהוה צְבָאוֹת, מַלְיָא
כָל אַרְעָא זִיו יְקָרֵהּ.

יחזקאל ג ◂ וַתִּשָּׂאֵנִי רוּחַ, וָאֶשְׁמַע אַחֲרַי קוֹל רַעַשׁ גָּדוֹל, בָּרוּךְ כְּבוֹד־יהוה
מִמְּקוֹמוֹ:

תרגום יונתן יחזקאל ג וּנְטָלַתְנִי רוּחָא, וּשְׁמָעִית בַּתְרַי קָל זִיעַ סַגִּיא, דִּמְשַׁבְּחִין וְאָמְרִין, בְּרִיךְ יְקָרָא
דַיהוה מֵאֲתַר בֵּית שְׁכִינְתֵהּ.

שמות טו יהוה יִמְלֹךְ לְעֹלָם וָעֶד:

תרגום אונקלוס שמות טו יהוה מַלְכוּתֵהּ קָאֵם לְעָלַם וּלְעָלְמֵי עָלְמַיָּא.

דברי הימים א׳ כט **יהוה** אֱלֹהֵי אַבְרָהָם יִצְחָק וְיִשְׂרָאֵל אֲבֹתֵינוּ, שָׁמְרָה־זֹּאת לְעוֹלָם
תהלים עח לְיֵצֶר מַחְשְׁבוֹת לְבַב עַמֶּךָ, וְהָכֵן לְבָבָם אֵלֶיךָ: וְהוּא רַחוּם
תהלים פו יְכַפֵּר עָוֹן וְלֹא־יַשְׁחִית, וְהִרְבָּה לְהָשִׁיב אַפּוֹ, וְלֹא־יָעִיר כָּל־חֲמָתוֹ: כִּי־
תהלים קיט אַתָּה אֲדֹנָי טוֹב וְסַלָּח, וְרַב־חֶסֶד לְכָל־קֹרְאֶיךָ: צִדְקָתְךָ צֶדֶק לְעוֹלָם
מיכה ז וְתוֹרָתְךָ אֱמֶת: תִּתֵּן אֱמֶת לְיַעֲקֹב, חֶסֶד לְאַבְרָהָם, אֲשֶׁר־נִשְׁבַּעְתָּ
תהלים סח לַאֲבֹתֵינוּ מִימֵי קֶדֶם: בָּרוּךְ אֲדֹנָי יוֹם יוֹם יַעֲמָס־לָנוּ, הָאֵל יְשׁוּעָתֵנוּ
תהלים מו תהלים פד סֶלָה: יהוה צְבָאוֹת עִמָּנוּ, מִשְׂגָּב לָנוּ אֱלֹהֵי יַעֲקֹב סֶלָה: יהוה צְבָאוֹת,
תהלים כ אַשְׁרֵי אָדָם בֹּטֵחַ בָּךְ: יהוה הוֹשִׁיעָה, הַמֶּלֶךְ יַעֲנֵנוּ בְיוֹם־קָרְאֵנוּ:

---

success. This is immediately followed by Psalm 91 that once again addresses the challenges which we will experience in an oft-hostile world. Most of the dangers enumerated here are those usually faced by a traveler – including obstacles, rough roads, wild animals, snakes, alligators, and the like. It was possibly intended to refer to those traveling to Jerusalem on the three pilgrimage festivals (R. Amos Ḥakham).

This psalm is recited as an expansion of

because he has known My name. When he calls upon Me, I answer him. I am with him in trouble. I deliver him and I will honor him. ▸ I will satisfy him with long life, and I will show him of My salvation. I will satisfy him with long life, and I will show him of My salvation.

Ps. 22 ▸ **וְאַתָּה קָדוֹשׁ** BUT YOU ARE HOLY. You sit among the praises of Israel.
Is. 6 The angels called to one another and said, Holy, holy, holy is the Lord of hosts, the whole world is filled with His glory.

Targum Yonatan Is. 6 And they receive word from each other and say, Holy in the highest heaven, the abode of His Divine Presence, holy upon earth, the work of His mighty power, holy forever and to all eternity is the Lord of hosts. The whole earth is full of His glorious splendor.

Ezek. 3 ▸ Then a spirit uplifted me, and I heard behind me a powerful moving sound, Blessed is the glory of the Lord from His place.

Targum Yonatan Ezek. 3 Then a spirit lifted me up and I heard behind me the powerful moving sound of those who uttered His praise, proclaiming, "Blessed be the glory of the Lord from the abode of His Divine Presence."

Ex. 15 The Lord shall reign forever and ever.

Targum Onkelos Ex. 15 The sovereignty of the Lord is established forever and ever.

I Chr. 29 **יהוה** LORD GOD of our fathers Abraham, Isaac, and Israel, forever
forming the thoughts in Your people's heart, and directing their hearts
Ps. 78 toward You. But He, the compassionate one, forgave iniquity, and did
not destroy them, and He often turned away His anger and did not stir
Ps. 86 up all His wrath. Indeed, You, O Lord, are good and forgiving, and of
Ps. 119 bountiful loving-kindness to all who call upon You. Your righteousness
Mic. 7 is an everlasting righteousness, and Your law is truth. Grant truth to
Jacob, loving-kindness to Abraham, as You have sworn to our fathers
Ps. 68 from days of old. Blessed is the Lord day by day. The God of our
Ps. 46 salvation will load us generously. The Lord of hosts is with us. The God
Ps. 84 of Jacob is our refuge. Selah. O Lord of hosts, happy is the man who
Ps. 20 trusts in You. Lord, save! The King will answer us on the day that we call.

Havdala intended to protect us from danger once Shabbat has departed, when the forces of evil in the world (referred to at *seuda shelishit* as הֲנֵי כַּלְבִין דַּחֲצִיפִין – the "brazen dogs") once again manifest themselves (*Havdala deR. Akiva*).

וְאַתָּה קָדוֹשׁ / IN TRUTH, YOU ARE HOLY
Having recited a Scriptural passage, we now recite the *Kedusha* to infuse the coming workweek with the holiness of the just completed Shabbat.

בָּרוּךְ הוּא אֱלֹהֵינוּ שֶׁבְּרָאָנוּ לִכְבוֹדוֹ, וְהִבְדִּילָנוּ מִן הַתּוֹעִים, וְנָתַן לָנוּ תּוֹרַת אֱמֶת, וְחַיֵּי עוֹלָם נָטַע בְּתוֹכֵנוּ. הוּא יִפְתַּח לִבֵּנוּ בְּתוֹרָתוֹ, וְיָשֵׂם בְּלִבֵּנוּ אַהֲבָתוֹ וְיִרְאָתוֹ וְלַעֲשׂוֹת רְצוֹנוֹ וּלְעָבְדוֹ בְּלֵבָב שָׁלֵם, לְמַעַן לֹא נִיגַע לָרִיק וְלֹא נֵלֵד לַבֶּהָלָה.

יְהִי רָצוֹן מִלְּפָנֶיךָ יהוה אֱלֹהֵינוּ וֵאלֹהֵי אֲבוֹתֵינוּ, שֶׁנִּשְׁמֹר חֻקֶּיךָ בָּעוֹלָם הַזֶּה, וְנִזְכֶּה וְנִחְיֶה וְנִרְאֶה וְנִירַשׁ טוֹבָה וּבְרָכָה,

תהלים ל לִשְׁנֵי יְמוֹת הַמָּשִׁיחַ וּלְחַיֵּי הָעוֹלָם הַבָּא. לְמַעַן יְזַמֶּרְךָ כָבוֹד וְלֹא

ירמיה יז יִדֹּם, יהוה אֱלֹהַי, לְעוֹלָם אוֹדֶךָּ: בָּרוּךְ הַגֶּבֶר אֲשֶׁר יִבְטַח בַּיהוה,

ישעיה כו וְהָיָה יהוה מִבְטַחוֹ: בִּטְחוּ בַיהוה עֲדֵי־עַד, כִּי בְּיָהּ יהוה צוּר

תהלים ט עוֹלָמִים: ‹ וְיִבְטְחוּ בְךָ יוֹדְעֵי שְׁמֶךָ, כִּי לֹא־עָזַבְתָּ דֹרְשֶׁיךָ, יהוה:

ישעיה מב יהוה חָפֵץ לְמַעַן צִדְקוֹ, יַגְדִּיל תּוֹרָה וְיַאְדִּיר:

קדיש שלם

ש״ץ: **יִתְגַּדַּל** וְיִתְקַדַּשׁ שְׁמֵהּ רַבָּא (קהל: אָמֵן) בְּעָלְמָא דִּי בְרָא כִרְעוּתֵהּ. וְיַמְלִיךְ מַלְכוּתֵהּ, בְּחַיֵּיכוֹן וּבְיוֹמֵיכוֹן וּבְחַיֵּי דְכָל בֵּית יִשְׂרָאֵל, בַּעֲגָלָא וּבִזְמַן קָרִיב, וְאִמְרוּ אָמֵן. (קהל: אָמֵן)

קהל וש״ץ: יְהֵא שְׁמֵהּ רַבָּא מְבָרַךְ לְעָלַם וּלְעָלְמֵי עָלְמַיָּא.

ש״ץ: יִתְבָּרַךְ וְיִשְׁתַּבַּח וְיִתְפָּאַר, וְיִתְרוֹמַם וְיִתְנַשֵּׂא וְיִתְהַדָּר וְיִתְעַלֶּה וְיִתְהַלָּל שְׁמֵהּ דְּקֻדְשָׁא בְּרִיךְ הוּא (קהל: בְּרִיךְ הוּא) לְעֵלָּא מִן כָּל בִּרְכָתָא / בעשרת ימי תשובה: לְעֵלָּא (וּ)לְעֵלָּא מִכָּל בִּרְכָתָא/ וְשִׁירָתָא, תֻּשְׁבְּחָתָא וְנֶחֱמָתָא דַּאֲמִירָן בְּעָלְמָא, וְאִמְרוּ אָמֵן. (קהל: אָמֵן)

תִּתְקַבַּל צְלוֹתְהוֹן וּבָעוּתְהוֹן דְּכָל יִשְׂרָאֵל, קֳדָם אֲבוּהוֹן דִּי בִשְׁמַיָּא, וְאִמְרוּ אָמֵן. (קהל: אָמֵן)

יְהֵא שְׁלָמָא רַבָּא מִן שְׁמַיָּא וְחַיִּים, עָלֵינוּ וְעַל כָּל יִשְׂרָאֵל, וְאִמְרוּ אָמֵן. (קהל: אָמֵן)

Bow, take three steps back, as if taking leave of the Divine Presence, then bow, first left, then right, then center, while saying:

עֹשֶׂה שָׁלוֹם / בעשרת ימי תשובה: הַשָּׁלוֹם/ בִּמְרוֹמָיו, הוּא יַעֲשֶׂה שָׁלוֹם עָלֵינוּ, וְעַל כָּל יִשְׂרָאֵל, וְאִמְרוּ אָמֵן. (קהל: אָמֵן)

בָּרוּךְ BLESSED BE OUR God, Who created us for His glory, separated us from those who stray, gave us the Torah of truth, and implanted in us eternal life. May He open our hearts through His Torah and arouse in us such love and reverence for Him that we shall perform His will and serve Him with perfect hearts, rather than labor in vain or bring forth disaster.

יְהִי רָצוֹן MAY IT BE Your will, Lord our God and God of our fathers, that we keep Your statutes in this world, and thus be worthy to inherit a life of goodness and blessing in the days of the Messiah and in the life
Ps. 30 of the World to Come. Grant that I sing Your praises and not be silent;
Jer. 17 O Lord, my God, I will give thanks to You forever. Blessed is the person
Is. 26 who trusts in the Lord, for then the Lord will be his security. Trust always
Ps. 9 in the Lord, for the Lord is God, an everlasting Rock. ▸ And those who
know Your name will trust in You, for You, Lord, have not abandoned
Is. 42 those who seek You. The Lord desired, for the sake of its [Israel's]
righteousness, to magnify the Torah and glorify it.

FULL KADDISH

Leader: יִתְגַּדַּל EXALTED AND HALLOWED may God's great name be, in the world He created as He willed. May He reign in your lifetimes and in your days, and in the lifetime of the whole house of Israel, speedily and soon, and say, Amen.

All: May His great name be blessed forever and all time.

Leader: Blessed and praised, honored, extolled, glorified, adored and exalted above all be the name of the Holy One, blessed is He, (*Between Rosh Hashana & Yom Kippur:* above and) beyond any blessing, hymn, praise, or expressions of consolation that may be uttered in this world, and say, Amen.

May the prayers and pleas of all Israel be accepted before their Father Who is in heaven – and say, Amen.

May abundant peace descend from heaven, as well as life, for us and for all Israel, and say, Amen.

Bow, take three steps back, as if taking leave of the Divine Presence, then bow, first left, then right, then center, while saying:

May He Who makes peace in the highest heaven, make peace for us, and for all Israel, and say, Amen.

Between פסח *and* שבועות *the* עומר *is counted at this point.* *See page 326.*

On חנוכה*, the candles are lit at this point.* *See page 950.*

On תשעה באב*, the following prayers are omitted and the service continues with* עָלֵינוּ *on page 746.*

פסוקי ברכה

וְיִתֶּן־לְךָ הָאֱלֹהִים מִטַּל הַשָּׁמַיִם וּמִשְׁמַנֵּי הָאָרֶץ, וְרֹב דָּגָן וְתִירֹשׁ: בראשית כז
יַעַבְדוּךָ עַמִּים וְיִשְׁתַּחֲוֻ לְךָ לְאֻמִּים, הֱוֵה גְבִיר לְאַחֶיךָ
וְיִשְׁתַּחֲווּ לְךָ בְּנֵי אִמֶּךָ, אֹרְרֶיךָ אָרוּר וּמְבָרְכֶיךָ בָּרוּךְ:

וְאֵל שַׁדַּי יְבָרֵךְ אֹתְךָ וְיַפְרְךָ וְיַרְבֶּךָ, וְהָיִיתָ לִקְהַל עַמִּים: וְיִתֶּן־לְךָ אֶת־ בראשית כח
בִּרְכַּת אַבְרָהָם, לְךָ וּלְזַרְעֲךָ אִתָּךְ, לְרִשְׁתְּךָ אֶת־אֶרֶץ מְגֻרֶיךָ
אֲשֶׁר־נָתַן אֱלֹהִים לְאַבְרָהָם: מֵאֵל אָבִיךָ וְיַעְזְרֶךָּ וְאֵת שַׁדַּי וִיבָרְכֶךָּ, בראשית מט
בִּרְכֹת שָׁמַיִם מֵעָל בִּרְכֹת תְּהוֹם רֹבֶצֶת תָּחַת, בִּרְכֹת שָׁדַיִם וָרָחַם:
בִּרְכֹת אָבִיךָ גָּבְרוּ עַל־בִּרְכֹת הוֹרַי עַד־תַּאֲוַת גִּבְעֹת עוֹלָם, תִּהְיֶיןָ לְרֹאשׁ
יוֹסֵף וּלְקָדְקֹד נְזִיר אֶחָיו: וַאֲהֵבְךָ וּבֵרַכְךָ וְהִרְבֶּךָ, וּבֵרַךְ פְּרִי־בִטְנְךָ דברים ז
וּפְרִי־אַדְמָתֶךָ, דְּגָנְךָ וְתִירֹשְׁךָ וְיִצְהָרֶךָ, שְׁגַר־אֲלָפֶיךָ וְעַשְׁתְּרֹת צֹאנֶךָ,
עַל הָאֲדָמָה אֲשֶׁר־נִשְׁבַּע לַאֲבֹתֶיךָ לָתֶת לָךְ: בָּרוּךְ תִּהְיֶה מִכָּל־הָעַמִּים,
לֹא־יִהְיֶה בְךָ עָקָר וַעֲקָרָה וּבִבְהֶמְתֶּךָ: וְהֵסִיר יהוה מִמְּךָ כָּל־חֹלִי, וְכָל־
מַדְוֵי מִצְרַיִם הָרָעִים אֲשֶׁר יָדַעְתָּ, לֹא יְשִׂימָם בָּךְ, וּנְתָנָם בְּכָל־שֹׂנְאֶיךָ:

הַמַּלְאָךְ הַגֹּאֵל אֹתִי מִכָּל־רָע יְבָרֵךְ אֶת־הַנְּעָרִים, וְיִקָּרֵא בָהֶם שְׁמִי בראשית מח
וְשֵׁם אֲבֹתַי אַבְרָהָם וְיִצְחָק, וְיִדְגּוּ לָרֹב בְּקֶרֶב הָאָרֶץ: יהוה דברים א
אֱלֹהֵיכֶם הִרְבָּה אֶתְכֶם, וְהִנְּכֶם הַיּוֹם כְּכוֹכְבֵי הַשָּׁמַיִם לָרֹב: יהוה אֱלֹהֵי
אֲבוֹתֵיכֶם יֹסֵף עֲלֵיכֶם כָּכֶם אֶלֶף פְּעָמִים, וִיבָרֵךְ אֶתְכֶם כַּאֲשֶׁר דִּבֶּר לָכֶם:

בָּרוּךְ אַתָּה בָּעִיר, וּבָרוּךְ אַתָּה בַּשָּׂדֶה: בָּרוּךְ אַתָּה בְּבֹאֶךָ, וּבָרוּךְ אַתָּה דברים כח
בְּצֵאתֶךָ: בָּרוּךְ טַנְאֲךָ וּמִשְׁאַרְתֶּךָ: בָּרוּךְ פְּרִי־בִטְנְךָ וּפְרִי אַדְמָתְךָ
וּפְרִי בְהֶמְתֶּךָ, שְׁגַר אֲלָפֶיךָ וְעַשְׁתְּרוֹת צֹאנֶךָ: יְצַו יהוה אִתְּךָ אֶת־

וְיִתֶּן־לְךָ / VEYITEN LEKHA

The following prayer is a collection of biblical verses containing blessings for financial well-being and continues with the verses recommended by R. Yoḥanan bar Nafḥa as blessings for the transformation of bad to good, redemption and peace (*Berakhot* 54b).

Between Pesaḥ and Shavuot the Omer is counted at this point. *See page 327.*
On Ḥanukka, the candles are lit at this point. *See page 951.*
On Tisha B'Av, the following prayers are omitted and the service continues with Aleinu on page 747.

VEYITEN LEKHA

Gen. 27 וְיִתֶּן־לְךָ MAY GOD give you of the dew of the heavens and the richness of the earth, an abundance of grain and wine. May peoples serve you and nations bow down to you. Be the leader of your brethren, and may your mother's sons bow down to you. Cursed be everyone who curses you, and blessed be everyone who blesses you.

Gen. 28 וְאֵל שַׁדַּי AND MAY ALMIGHTY GOD bless you and make you fruitful and multiply you, so that you become an association of peoples. And may He give you the blessing of Abraham, to you and to your seed with you, so that
Gen. 49 you inherit the land of your sojourning that God gave to Abraham. Be blessed by the God of your fathers – may He help you – and by the Almighty, with the blessings of heaven above, the blessings of the deep couching beneath, the blessings of the breasts and the womb. The blessings of your fathers are mighty beyond the blessings of my progenitors unto the utmost bounds of the everlasting hills. May they be on the head of Joseph, and on the crown
Deut. 7 of the head of the prince among his brethren. He will love you and bless you and multiply you, and He will bless the fruit of your body and the fruit of your land, your grain and your wine and your oil, the increase of your cattle and the young of your flock, in the land which He swore to your fathers to give you. Blessed shall you be above all peoples. No male or female among you or among your cattle will be barren. The Lord will take away all sickness from you, and none of the evil diseases that you knew in Egypt will afflict you, but He will lay them on everyone who hates you.

Gen. 48 הַמַּלְאָךְ MAY THE ANGEL who redeems me from all evil bless the lads; and let them be called by my name and the name of my fathers Abraham and Isaac,
Deut. 1 and may they grow into a multitude in the midst of the earth. The Lord your God has multiplied you, and behold, you are this day like the stars of the heaven for multitude. The Lord God of your fathers will make you a thousand times as many as you are, and bless you as He promised you.

Deut. 28 בָּרוּךְ BLESSED shall you be in the city, and blessed shall you be in the country. Blessed shall you be when you come in, and blessed shall you be when you go out. Blessed shall be your basket and your kneading-trough. Blessed shall be the fruit of your body and the fruit of your land and the fruit of your cattle, the increase of your cattle and the young of your flock. The Lord will command

הַבְּרָכָה בַּאֲסָמֶיךָ וּבְכֹל מִשְׁלַח יָדֶךָ, וּבֵרַכְךָ בָּאָרֶץ אֲשֶׁר־יהוה אֱלֹהֶיךָ
נֹתֵן לָךְ: יִפְתַּח יהוה לְךָ אֶת־אוֹצָרוֹ הַטּוֹב אֶת־הַשָּׁמַיִם, לָתֵת מְטַר־
אַרְצְךָ בְּעִתּוֹ, וּלְבָרֵךְ אֵת כָּל־מַעֲשֵׂה יָדֶךָ, וְהִלְוִיתָ גּוֹיִם רַבִּים וְאַתָּה
דברים טו לֹא תִלְוֶה: כִּי־יהוה אֱלֹהֶיךָ בֵּרַכְךָ כַּאֲשֶׁר דִּבֶּר־לָךְ, וְהַעֲבַטְתָּ גּוֹיִם
דברים לג רַבִּים וְאַתָּה לֹא תַעֲבֹט, וּמָשַׁלְתָּ בְּגוֹיִם רַבִּים וּבְךָ לֹא יִמְשֹׁלוּ: אַשְׁרֶיךָ
יִשְׂרָאֵל, מִי כָמוֹךָ, עַם נוֹשַׁע בַּיהוה, מָגֵן עֶזְרֶךָ וַאֲשֶׁר־חֶרֶב גַּאֲוָתֶךָ,
וְיִכָּחֲשׁוּ אֹיְבֶיךָ לָךְ, וְאַתָּה עַל־בָּמוֹתֵימוֹ תִדְרֹךְ:

ישעיה מד **מָחִיתִי** כָעָב פְּשָׁעֶיךָ וְכֶעָנָן חַטֹּאותֶיךָ, שׁוּבָה אֵלַי כִּי גְאַלְתִּיךָ: רָנּוּ
שָׁמַיִם כִּי־עָשָׂה יהוה, הָרִיעוּ תַּחְתִּיּוֹת אָרֶץ, פִּצְחוּ הָרִים
ישעיה מז רִנָּה, יַעַר וְכָל־עֵץ בּוֹ, כִּי־גָאַל יהוה יַעֲקֹב וּבְיִשְׂרָאֵל יִתְפָּאָר: גֹּאֲלֵנוּ,
יהוה צְבָאוֹת שְׁמוֹ, קְדוֹשׁ יִשְׂרָאֵל:

ישעיה מה **יִשְׂרָאֵל** נוֹשַׁע בַּיהוה תְּשׁוּעַת עוֹלָמִים, לֹא־תֵבֹשׁוּ וְלֹא־תִכָּלְמוּ עַד־
יואל ב עוֹלְמֵי עַד: וַאֲכַלְתֶּם אָכוֹל וְשָׂבוֹעַ, וְהִלַּלְתֶּם אֶת־שֵׁם יהוה
אֱלֹהֵיכֶם אֲשֶׁר־עָשָׂה עִמָּכֶם לְהַפְלִיא, וְלֹא־יֵבֹשׁוּ עַמִּי לְעוֹלָם: וִידַעְתֶּם
כִּי בְקֶרֶב יִשְׂרָאֵל אָנִי, וַאֲנִי יהוה אֱלֹהֵיכֶם וְאֵין עוֹד, וְלֹא־יֵבֹשׁוּ עַמִּי
ישעיה נה לְעוֹלָם: כִּי־בְשִׂמְחָה תֵצֵאוּ וּבְשָׁלוֹם תּוּבָלוּן, הֶהָרִים וְהַגְּבָעוֹת יִפְצְחוּ
ישעיה יב לִפְנֵיכֶם רִנָּה, וְכָל־עֲצֵי הַשָּׂדֶה יִמְחֲאוּ־כָף: הִנֵּה אֵל יְשׁוּעָתִי אֶבְטַח,
וְלֹא אֶפְחָד, כִּי־עָזִּי וְזִמְרָת יָהּ יהוה, וַיְהִי־לִי לִישׁוּעָה: וּשְׁאַבְתֶּם־מַיִם
בְּשָׂשׂוֹן, מִמַּעַיְנֵי הַיְשׁוּעָה: וַאֲמַרְתֶּם בַּיּוֹם הַהוּא, הוֹדוּ לַיהוה קִרְאוּ
בִשְׁמוֹ, הוֹדִיעוּ בָעַמִּים עֲלִילֹתָיו, הַזְכִּירוּ כִּי נִשְׂגָּב שְׁמוֹ: זַמְּרוּ יהוה
כִּי גֵאוּת עָשָׂה, מוּדַעַת זֹאת בְּכָל־הָאָרֶץ: צַהֲלִי וָרֹנִּי יוֹשֶׁבֶת צִיּוֹן,
ישעיה כה כִּי־גָדוֹל בְּקִרְבֵּךְ קְדוֹשׁ יִשְׂרָאֵל: וְאָמַר בַּיּוֹם הַהוּא, הִנֵּה אֱלֹהֵינוּ זֶה
קִוִּינוּ לוֹ וְיוֹשִׁיעֵנוּ, זֶה יהוה קִוִּינוּ לוֹ, נָגִילָה וְנִשְׂמְחָה בִּישׁוּעָתוֹ:

ישעיה ב
ישעיה לב **בֵּית** יַעֲקֹב לְכוּ וְנֵלְכָה בְּאוֹר יהוה: וְהָיָה אֱמוּנַת עִתֶּיךָ, חֹסֶן יְשׁוּעֹת
שמואל א׳ יח חָכְמַת וָדָעַת, יִרְאַת יהוה הִיא אוֹצָרוֹ: וַיְהִי דָוִד לְכָל־דְּרָכָו
מַשְׂכִּיל, וַיהוה עִמּוֹ:

As R. Avraham ben Natan wrote in his work, *Sefer HaManhig*, the purpose of this prayer is so that we may be blessed in the coming week and forever after.

blessings upon you in your storehouses and in everything to which you put
your hand, and He will bless you in the land which the Lord your God gives
you. The Lord will open His goodly treasure for you, the heavens, to give the
rain for your land in its season, and to bless all the work of your hands so that
Deut. 15 you will lend to many nations and have no need to borrow. For the Lord your
God will surely bless you as He has promised you; and you shall lend to many
nations and not borrow; and you shall be set over many nations and they shall
Deut. 33 not be set over you. Happy are you, Israel. Who is like you, a people saved by
the Lord, your helping shield and the sword of your triumph! Your enemies
shall give in to you, and you shall tread upon their high places.

Is. 44 מָחִיתִי I HAVE BLOTTED out your transgressions as a thick cloud, and your sins
as mist; return to Me, for I have redeemed you. Sing for joy, O ye heavens,
for the Lord has done it; shout for joy, ye depths of earth, break forth into
singing, ye mountains, forests, and every tree therein; for the Lord has
Is. 47 redeemed Jacob, and through Israel He will be glorified. Our Redeemer,
Whose name is the Lord of hosts, is the Holy One of Israel.

Is. 45 יִשְׂרָאֵל ISRAEL shall be saved by the Lord with everlasting redemption. You
Joel 2 will never again be shamed or confused. You shall have enough to eat and
be satisfied, and shall praise the name of the Lord your God Who has dealt
wondrously with you, and My people shall never more be shamed. And you
shall know that I am in the midst of Israel, and that I am the Lord your God;
Is. 55 that there is none else, and My people shall never more be shamed. Yes,
you shall go forth joyously and be led forward in peace; the mountains and
the hills shall break into song before you, and all the trees of the field shall
Is. 12 applaud. Behold, God is my salvation, I trust and am not afraid; for the Lord
Eternal is my strength and song, and He has become my liberation. Therefore
shall you joyously draw water from the wells of salvation. And you shall say
on that day, "Give thanks to the Lord, call on His name, make known His
mighty deeds among the peoples, proclaim that His name is exalted." Sing
to the Lord, for He has worked wonders; make this known in all the earth.
Cry aloud and sing for joy, O Zion restored, for great in the midst of you is
Is. 25 the Holy One of Israel. On that day it shall be said, "Behold, this is our God,
of Whom we hoped that He might save us; this is the Lord for Whom we
hoped; let us rejoice and be glad in His redemption."

Is. 2
Is. 32 בֵּית HOUSE OF JACOB, come and let us walk in the light of the Lord. He will
be the secure focus of your lives, the abundance of liberation, wisdom, and
I Sam. 18 knowledge; reverence for the Lord, that is His treasure. David was successful
in everything, and the Lord was with him.

תהלים נה
שמואל א׳ יד
פָּדָה בְשָׁלוֹם נַפְשִׁי מִקְּרָב־לִי, כִּי־בְרַבִּים הָיוּ עִמָּדִי: וַיֹּאמֶר הָעָם אֶל־שָׁאוּל, הֲיוֹנָתָן יָמוּת אֲשֶׁר עָשָׂה הַיְשׁוּעָה הַגְּדוֹלָה הַזֹּאת בְּיִשְׂרָאֵל, חָלִילָה, חַי־יהוה אִם־יִפֹּל מִשַּׂעֲרַת רֹאשׁוֹ אַרְצָה, כִּי־עִם־
ישעיה לה
אֱלֹהִים עָשָׂה הַיּוֹם הַזֶּה, וַיִּפְדּוּ הָעָם אֶת־יוֹנָתָן וְלֹא־מֵת: וּפְדוּיֵי יהוה יְשֻׁבוּן וּבָאוּ צִיּוֹן בְּרִנָּה, וְשִׂמְחַת עוֹלָם עַל־רֹאשָׁם, שָׂשׂוֹן וְשִׂמְחָה יַשִּׂיגוּ, וְנָסוּ יָגוֹן וַאֲנָחָה:

תהלים ל
דברים כג
הָפַכְתָּ מִסְפְּדִי לְמָחוֹל לִי, פִּתַּחְתָּ שַׂקִּי, וַתְּאַזְּרֵנִי שִׂמְחָה: וְלֹא־אָבָה יהוה אֱלֹהֶיךָ לִשְׁמֹעַ אֶל־בִּלְעָם, וַיַּהֲפֹךְ יהוה אֱלֹהֶיךָ לְּךָ אֶת־
ירמיה לא
הַקְּלָלָה לִבְרָכָה, כִּי אֲהֵבְךָ יהוה אֱלֹהֶיךָ: אָז תִּשְׂמַח בְּתוּלָה בְּמָחוֹל, וּבַחֻרִים וּזְקֵנִים יַחְדָּו, וְהָפַכְתִּי אֶבְלָם לְשָׂשׂוֹן, וְנִחַמְתִּים, וְשִׂמַּחְתִּים מִיגוֹנָם:

ישעיה נז
בּוֹרֵא נִיב שְׂפָתָיִם, שָׁלוֹם שָׁלוֹם לָרָחוֹק וְלַקָּרוֹב אָמַר יהוה, וּרְפָאתִיו:
דברי
הימים א׳ יב
וְרוּחַ לָבְשָׁה אֶת־עֲמָשַׂי רֹאשׁ הַשָּׁלִישִׁים, לְךָ דָוִיד וְעִמְּךָ בֶן־יִשַׁי, שָׁלוֹם שָׁלוֹם לְךָ וְשָׁלוֹם לְעֹזְרֶךָ, כִּי עֲזָרְךָ אֱלֹהֶיךָ, וַיְקַבְּלֵם דָּוִיד
שמואל א׳ כה
וַיִּתְּנֵם בְּרָאשֵׁי הַגְּדוּד: וַאֲמַרְתֶּם כֹּה לֶחָי, וְאַתָּה שָׁלוֹם וּבֵיתְךָ שָׁלוֹם
תהלים כט
וְכֹל אֲשֶׁר־לְךָ שָׁלוֹם: יהוה עֹז לְעַמּוֹ יִתֵּן, יהוה יְבָרֵךְ אֶת־עַמּוֹ בַשָּׁלוֹם:

מגילה לא.
אָמַר רַבִּי יוֹחָנָן: בְּכָל מָקוֹם שֶׁאַתָּה מוֹצֵא גְּדֻלָּתוֹ שֶׁל הַקָּדוֹשׁ בָּרוּךְ הוּא, שָׁם אַתָּה מוֹצֵא עַנְוְתָנוּתוֹ. דָּבָר זֶה כָּתוּב בַּתּוֹרָה,
דברים י
וְשָׁנוּי בַּנְּבִיאִים, וּמְשֻׁלָּשׁ בַּכְּתוּבִים. כָּתוּב בַּתּוֹרָה: כִּי יהוה אֱלֹהֵיכֶם הוּא אֱלֹהֵי הָאֱלֹהִים וַאֲדֹנֵי הָאֲדֹנִים, הָאֵל הַגָּדֹל הַגִּבֹּר וְהַנּוֹרָא, אֲשֶׁר לֹא־יִשָּׂא פָנִים וְלֹא יִקַּח שֹׁחַד: וּכְתִיב בַּתְרֵהּ: עֹשֶׂה מִשְׁפַּט יָתוֹם וְאַלְמָנָה, וְאֹהֵב גֵּר לָתֶת לוֹ לֶחֶם וְשִׂמְלָה: שָׁנוּי בַּנְּבִיאִים, דִּכְתִיב:
ישעיה נז
כִּי כֹה אָמַר רָם וְנִשָּׂא שֹׁכֵן עַד וְקָדוֹשׁ שְׁמוֹ, מָרוֹם וְקָדוֹשׁ אֶשְׁכּוֹן, וְאֶת־דַּכָּא וּשְׁפַל־רוּחַ, לְהַחֲיוֹת רוּחַ שְׁפָלִים וּלְהַחֲיוֹת לֵב נִדְכָּאִים:
תהלים סח
מְשֻׁלָּשׁ בַּכְּתוּבִים, דִּכְתִיב: שִׁירוּ לֵאלֹהִים, זַמְּרוּ שְׁמוֹ, סֹלּוּ לָרֹכֵב בָּעֲרָבוֹת בְּיָהּ שְׁמוֹ, וְעִלְזוּ לְפָנָיו: וּכְתִיב בַּתְרֵהּ: אֲבִי יְתוֹמִים וְדַיַּן אַלְמָנוֹת, אֱלֹהִים בִּמְעוֹן קָדְשׁוֹ:

Ps. 55 פָּדָה GOD HAS REDEEMED my soul in peace, so that no one can approach me,
I Sam. 14 even if I am outnumbered by those who fight against me. The people said to Saul, "Shall Jonathan die, who has brought about this great deliverance for Israel? Far from it. As the Lord lives, not a hair of his head shall fall to the ground, for he acted with God this day." So the people saved Jonathan and
Is. 35 he did not die. Those rescued by the Lord shall return and come singing to Zion, with enduring joy upon their heads. Joy and gladness shall come to them, whereas sorrow and sighing shall flee.

Ps. 30 הָפַכְתָּ YOU HAVE TURNED my mourning into dancing, loosed my sackcloth,
Deut. 23 and garbed me with joy. The Lord your God would not hearken to Balaam, but the Lord your God turned Balaam's curse into a blessing for you, for the
Jer. 31 Lord your God loved you. Then shall the maiden rejoice in dancing, and young men and old together, for I, the Lord, will turn their mourning into joy, and will comfort them and make them glad after their sorrow.

Is. 57 בּוֹרֵא I WHO CREATE the words your lips utter will create peace – peace to him
I Chr. 12 who is far away and to him who is near, the Lord has said, and I will heal him. A spirit embraced Amasai, the chief captain, [and he said,] "We are yours, David, and on your side, son of Jesse. Peace, peace be to you, and peace be to whoever who helps you. For God is your helper." Then David welcomed them and set
I Sam. 25 them at the head of the troops. And thus shall you say, "All hail! For life! Peace
Ps. 29 to you and peace be your house, and may everything you have be peace." The Lord will give strength to His people, the Lord will bless His people with peace.

Megilla 31a אָמַר R. YOḤANAN said, Wherever Scripture mentions the greatness of the Holy One, blessed is He, there it also mentions His gentleness. This is found in the Torah, it is repeated in the Prophets, and reiterated in the Holy
Deut. 10 Writings. Thus in the Torah it is written, "For the Lord your God, He is the God of gods and the Lord of lords, the God great, powerful, and awe-inspiring, Who favors no one and cannot be bribed." And immediately after this, it is written, "He does justice for orphan and widow, and shows love for the stranger by giving him food and clothing." This is repeated in the
Is. 57 Prophets, where it is written by Isaiah, "For thus has said the exalted and sublime One Who dwells in eternity and Whose name is holy, 'In sublime holiness I dwell, and also with the contrite and humble of spirit, to revive the spirits of the lowly and revive the hearts of the contrite.'" It is found also in
Ps. 68 the Holy Writings, where it is said in the Psalms, "Sing to God. Sing praise to His name. Raise your voice to Him Who rides upon the clouds by His name, *YaH*, and rejoice before Him." Then this verse is followed by, "The father of orphans and the judge of widows is God in His holy habitation."

מלכים א׳ ח יְהִי יהוה אֱלֹהֵינוּ עִמָּנוּ כַּאֲשֶׁר הָיָה עִם־אֲבֹתֵינוּ, אַל־יַעַזְבֵנוּ וְאַל־
דברים ד יִטְּשֵׁנוּ: וְאַתֶּם הַדְּבֵקִים בַּיהוה אֱלֹהֵיכֶם, חַיִּים כֻּלְּכֶם הַיּוֹם:
ישעיה נא כִּי־נִחַם יהוה צִיּוֹן, נִחַם כָּל־חָרְבֹתֶיהָ, וַיָּשֶׂם מִדְבָּרָהּ כְּעֵדֶן וְעַרְבָתָהּ
ישעיה מב כְּגַן־יהוה, שָׂשׂוֹן וְשִׂמְחָה יִמָּצֵא בָהּ, תּוֹדָה וְקוֹל זִמְרָה: יהוה חָפֵץ
לְמַעַן צִדְקוֹ, יַגְדִּיל תּוֹרָה וְיַאְדִּיר:

תהלים קכח **שִׁיר הַמַּעֲלוֹת,** אַשְׁרֵי כָּל־יְרֵא יהוה, הַהֹלֵךְ בִּדְרָכָיו: יְגִיעַ כַּפֶּיךָ
כִּי תֹאכֵל, אַשְׁרֶיךָ וְטוֹב לָךְ: אֶשְׁתְּךָ כְּגֶפֶן פֹּרִיָּה
בְּיַרְכְּתֵי בֵיתֶךָ, בָּנֶיךָ כִּשְׁתִלֵי זֵיתִים, סָבִיב לְשֻׁלְחָנֶךָ: הִנֵּה כִי־כֵן יְבֹרַךְ
גָּבֶר יְרֵא יהוה: יְבָרֶכְךָ יהוה מִצִּיּוֹן, וּרְאֵה בְּטוּב יְרוּשָׁלָםִ, כֹּל יְמֵי חַיֶּיךָ:
וּרְאֵה־בָנִים לְבָנֶיךָ, שָׁלוֹם עַל־יִשְׂרָאֵל:

In some congregations, mourners recite קדיש יתום *(on the next page).*

הבדלה בבית הכנסת

Some say the full הבדלה *on page 756.*
On מוצאי יום טוב *that is not a* מוצאי שבת*, the blessings for the spices and flame are omitted.*
At the end of יום כפור*, only the blessing for the spices is omitted.*

The שליח ציבור *takes the cup of wine in his right hand, and says:*

סַבְרִי מָרָנָן וְרַבָּנָן וְרַבּוֹתַי

בָּרוּךְ אַתָּה יהוה אֱלֹהֵינוּ מֶלֶךְ הָעוֹלָם, בּוֹרֵא פְּרִי הַגָּפֶן.

Holding the spice box, the שליח ציבור *says:*

בָּרוּךְ אַתָּה יהוה אֱלֹהֵינוּ מֶלֶךְ הָעוֹלָם, בּוֹרֵא מִינֵי בְשָׂמִים.

The שליח ציבור *smells the spices and puts the spice box down.*
He lifts his hands toward the flame of the הבדלה *candle, and says:*

בָּרוּךְ אַתָּה יהוה אֱלֹהֵינוּ מֶלֶךְ הָעוֹלָם, בּוֹרֵא מְאוֹרֵי הָאֵשׁ.

He lifts the cup of wine in his right hand, and says:

בָּרוּךְ אַתָּה יהוה אֱלֹהֵינוּ מֶלֶךְ הָעוֹלָם, הַמַּבְדִּיל בֵּין קֹדֶשׁ לְחוֹל, בֵּין אוֹר לְחֹשֶׁךְ, בֵּין יִשְׂרָאֵל לָעַמִּים, בֵּין יוֹם הַשְּׁבִיעִי לְשֵׁשֶׁת יְמֵי הַמַּעֲשֶׂה. בָּרוּךְ אַתָּה יהוה, הַמַּבְדִּיל בֵּין קֹדֶשׁ לְחוֹל.

I Kings 8 יְהִי MAY THE LORD our God be with us as He was with our fathers; may He
Deut. 4 not forsake us or abandon us. And you who cleave to the Lord your God,
Is. 51 every one of you is alive today. The Lord will surely comfort Zion, He will comfort all her waste places; He will make her wilderness like Eden, and her desert like the garden of the Lord; joy and gladness will be found in her,
Is. 42 thanksgiving and the sound of song. The Lord was pleased for the sake of His righteousness to magnify His teaching and glorify it.

Ps. 128 שִׁיר הַמַּעֲלוֹת A SONG OF ASCENTS. Happy is everyone who fears the Lord, who walks in His ways. If you eat the labor of your hands, you will be happy and it will be well with you. Your wife will be like a fruitful vine in the innermost parts of your house, your children like olive plants around your table. Behold, truly the man who fears the Lord will be blessed. May the Lord bless you from Zion, and may you see the good of Jerusalem all the days of your life. And may you see your children's children. Peace be upon Israel.

In some congregations, mourners recite the Mourner's Kaddish (on the next page).

HAVDALA IN THE SYNAGOGUE

Some say the full Havdala on page 757.
On Motza'ei Yom Tov that is not a Motza'ei Shabbat, the blessings for the spices and flame are omitted. At the end of Yom Kippur, only the blessing for the spices is omitted.

The Leader takes the cup of wine in his right hand, and says:

With your permission, my masters, rabbis and esteemed companions:

BLESSED ARE YOU, Lord, our God, King of the universe, Who creates the fruit of the vine.

Holding the spice box, the Leader says:

BLESSED ARE YOU, Lord, our God, King of the universe, Who creates the many different spices.

The Leader smells the spices and puts the spice box down.
He lifts his hands toward the flame of the Havdala candle, and says:

BLESSED ARE YOU, Lord, our God, King of the universe, Who creates the lights of fire.

He lifts the cup of wine in his right hand, and says:

BLESSED ARE YOU, Lord, our God, King of the universe, Who separates sacred from secular, light from darkness, Israel from the nations, and the seventh day from the six days of labor. Blessed are You, Lord, Who separates sacred from secular.

Stand while saying עָלֵינוּ. *Bow at* ׳.

עָלֵינוּ לְשַׁבֵּחַ לַאֲדוֹן הַכֹּל, לָתֵת גְּדֻלָּה לְיוֹצֵר בְּרֵאשִׁית, שֶׁלֹּא עָשָׂנוּ כְּגוֹיֵי הָאֲרָצוֹת, וְלֹא שָׂמָנוּ כְּמִשְׁפְּחוֹת הָאֲדָמָה, שֶׁלֹּא שָׂם חֶלְקֵנוּ כָּהֶם וְגוֹרָלֵנוּ כְּכָל הֲמוֹנָם. (שֶׁהֵם מִשְׁתַּחֲוִים לְהֶבֶל וָרִיק וּמִתְפַּלְלִים אֶל אֵל לֹא יוֹשִׁיעַ.) ׳וַאֲנַחְנוּ כּוֹרְעִים וּמִשְׁתַּחֲוִים וּמוֹדִים, לִפְנֵי מֶלֶךְ מַלְכֵי הַמְּלָכִים, הַקָּדוֹשׁ בָּרוּךְ הוּא, שֶׁהוּא נוֹטֶה שָׁמַיִם וְיוֹסֵד אָרֶץ, וּמוֹשַׁב יְקָרוֹ בַּשָּׁמַיִם מִמַּעַל, וּשְׁכִינַת עֻזּוֹ בְּגָבְהֵי מְרוֹמִים. הוּא אֱלֹהֵינוּ, אֵין עוֹד. אֱמֶת מַלְכֵּנוּ, אֶפֶס זוּלָתוֹ, כַּכָּתוּב בְּתוֹרָתוֹ, וְיָדַעְתָּ הַיּוֹם וַהֲשֵׁבֹתָ אֶל־לְבָבֶךָ, כִּי יהוה הוּא הָאֱלֹהִים בַּשָּׁמַיִם מִמַּעַל וְעַל־הָאָרֶץ מִתָּחַת, אֵין עוֹד: דברים ד

עַל כֵּן נְקַוֶּה לְּךָ יהוה אֱלֹהֵינוּ, לִרְאוֹת מְהֵרָה בְּתִפְאֶרֶת עֻזֶּךָ, לְהַעֲבִיר גִּלּוּלִים מִן הָאָרֶץ, וְהָאֱלִילִים כָּרוֹת יִכָּרֵתוּן, לְתַקֵּן עוֹלָם בְּמַלְכוּת שַׁדַּי. וְכָל בְּנֵי בָשָׂר יִקְרְאוּ בִשְׁמֶךָ לְהַפְנוֹת אֵלֶיךָ כָּל רִשְׁעֵי אָרֶץ. יַכִּירוּ וְיֵדְעוּ כָּל יוֹשְׁבֵי תֵבֵל, כִּי לְךָ תִּכְרַע כָּל בֶּרֶךְ, תִּשָּׁבַע כָּל לָשׁוֹן. לְפָנֶיךָ יהוה אֱלֹהֵינוּ יִכְרְעוּ וְיִפֹּלוּ, וְלִכְבוֹד שִׁמְךָ יְקָר יִתֵּנוּ, וִיקַבְּלוּ כֻלָּם אֶת עֹל מַלְכוּתֶךָ, וְתִמְלֹךְ עֲלֵיהֶם מְהֵרָה לְעוֹלָם וָעֶד. כִּי הַמַּלְכוּת שֶׁלְּךָ הִיא וּלְעוֹלְמֵי עַד תִּמְלֹךְ בְּכָבוֹד, כַּכָּתוּב בְּתוֹרָתֶךָ, יהוה יִמְלֹךְ לְעֹלָם וָעֶד: ◄ וְנֶאֱמַר, וְהָיָה יהוה לְמֶלֶךְ עַל־כָּל־הָאָרֶץ, בַּיּוֹם הַהוּא יִהְיֶה יהוה אֶחָד וּשְׁמוֹ אֶחָד: שמות טו / זכריה יד

Some add:

אַל־תִּירָא מִפַּחַד פִּתְאֹם וּמִשֹּׁאַת רְשָׁעִים כִּי תָבֹא: עֻצוּ עֵצָה וְתֻפָר, דַּבְּרוּ דָבָר וְלֹא יָקוּם, כִּי עִמָּנוּ אֵל: וְעַד־זִקְנָה אֲנִי הוּא, וְעַד־שֵׂיבָה אֲנִי אֶסְבֹּל, אֲנִי עָשִׂיתִי וַאֲנִי אֶשָּׂא וַאֲנִי אֶסְבֹּל וַאֲמַלֵּט: משלי ג / ישעיה ח / ישעיה מו

קדיש יתום

The following prayer, said by mourners, requires the presence of a מנין*.*
A transliteration can be found on page 1345.

אבל: **יִתְגַּדַּל** וְיִתְקַדַּשׁ שְׁמֵהּ רַבָּא (קהל: אָמֵן) בְּעָלְמָא דִּי בְרָא כִרְעוּתֵהּ וְיַמְלִיךְ מַלְכוּתֵהּ, בְּחַיֵּיכוֹן וּבְיוֹמֵיכוֹן וּבְחַיֵּי דְכָל בֵּית יִשְׂרָאֵל, בַּעֲגָלָא וּבִזְמַן קָרִיב, וְאִמְרוּ אָמֵן. (קהל: אָמֵן)

Stand while saying Aleinu. Bow at ▾.

עָלֵינוּ WE MUST, all of us, praise the Master of all, and ascribe greatness to He Who formed creation, for He did not make us like the nations of the world, nor render us like the families of the earth. He did not make our portion to be as theirs, nor our destiny like that of their masses. (For idolaters bow to vanity and emptiness and pray to a god who cannot save.) ▾We, however, bend our knees, bow, and give thanks before the King of the most exalted of kings, the Holy One, blessed is He. He is the One Who spreads out the heavens and establishes the earth. The seat of His glory is in the heavens above, and His Presence in all its strength is found in its highest abode. He is our God – there is no other. In truth He is our King;
Deut. 4 there is none but Him; as is written in His Torah: "On this day you should know, and take to heart, that the Lord is God in the heavens above and on the earth below – there is no other."

WE THEREFORE hope in You, Lord our God, that we may soon see the glory of Your might when You will remove abominations from the earth and the idols shall be utterly destroyed, when the world shall be perfected under the rule of the Almighty. Then all mankind shall invoke Your name, to turn all the wicked on earth toward You. All dwellers on earth will perceive and understand that to You every knee must bend, every tongue vow fealty. Before You, Lord our God, all will kneel and bow down, and give honor to Your glorious name. They will all accept the rule of Your dominion, and You will speedily rule over them forevermore. For the kingdom is Yours, and to
Ex. 15 all eternity You shall reign in glory, as it is written in Your Torah, "The Lord
Zech. 14 shall reign for ever and ever." ▸ And it is said, "And the Lord shall be King over all the earth; in that day shall the Lord be One, and His name One."

Some add:

Prov. 3 **אַל־תִּירָא** DO NOT FEAR sudden terror or the destruction when it comes to the
Is. 8 wicked. Devise a plan, and it will be thwarted; state a case and it will not stand,
Is. 46 for God is with us. And when you are old, I will remain; when you are aged, I will endure. I created you, I will carry you, I will endure, and I will rescue you.

MOURNER'S KADDISH

The following prayer, said by mourners, requires the presence of a minyan. *A transliteration can be found on page 1345.*

Mourner: **יִתְגַּדַּל** EXALTED AND HALLOWED may God's great name be, in the world He created as He willed. May He reign in your lifetimes and in your days, and in the lifetime of the whole house of Israel, speedily and soon, and say, Amen.

קהל ואבל: יְהֵא שְׁמֵהּ רַבָּא מְבָרַךְ לְעָלַם וּלְעָלְמֵי עָלְמַיָּא.

אבל: יִתְבָּרַךְ וְיִשְׁתַּבַּח וְיִתְפָּאַר, וְיִתְרוֹמַם וְיִתְנַשֵּׂא וְיִתְהַדָּר וְיִתְעַלֶּה וְיִתְהַלָּל שְׁמֵהּ דְּקֻדְשָׁא בְּרִיךְ הוּא (קהל: בְּרִיךְ הוּא), לְעֵלָּא מִן כָּל בִּרְכָתָא / בעשרת ימי תשובה: לְעֵלָּא (וּ)לְעֵלָּא מִכָּל בִּרְכָתָא / וְשִׁירָתָא, תֻּשְׁבְּחָתָא וְנֶחֱמָתָא דַּאֲמִירָן בְּעָלְמָא, וְאִמְרוּ אָמֵן. (קהל: אָמֵן)

יְהֵא שְׁלָמָא רַבָּא מִן שְׁמַיָּא וְחַיִּים, עָלֵינוּ וְעַל כָּל יִשְׂרָאֵל, וְאִמְרוּ אָמֵן. (קהל: אָמֵן)

Bow, take three steps back, as if taking leave of the Divine Presence, then bow, first left, then right, then center, while saying:

עֹשֶׂה שָׁלוֹם / בעשרת ימי תשובה: הַשָּׁלוֹם/ בִּמְרוֹמָיו, הוּא יַעֲשֶׂה שָׁלוֹם עָלֵינוּ, וְעַל כָּל יִשְׂרָאֵל, וְאִמְרוּ אָמֵן. (קהל: אָמֵן)

From the second day of ראש חודש אלול *through* שמיני עצרת *the following psalm is said:*

תהלים כז **לְדָוִד,** יהוה אוֹרִי וְיִשְׁעִי, מִמִּי אִירָא, יהוה מָעוֹז־חַיַּי, מִמִּי אֶפְחָד: בִּקְרֹב עָלַי מְרֵעִים לֶאֱכֹל אֶת־בְּשָׂרִי, צָרַי וְאֹיְבַי לִי, הֵמָּה כָשְׁלוּ וְנָפָלוּ: אִם־תַּחֲנֶה עָלַי מַחֲנֶה, לֹא־יִירָא לִבִּי, אִם־תָּקוּם עָלַי מִלְחָמָה, בְּזֹאת אֲנִי בוֹטֵחַ: אַחַת שָׁאַלְתִּי מֵאֵת־יהוה, אוֹתָהּ אֲבַקֵּשׁ, שִׁבְתִּי בְּבֵית־יהוה כָּל־יְמֵי חַיַּי, לַחֲזוֹת בְּנֹעַם־יהוה, וּלְבַקֵּר בְּהֵיכָלוֹ: כִּי יִצְפְּנֵנִי בְּסֻכֹּה בְּיוֹם רָעָה, יַסְתִּרֵנִי בְּסֵתֶר אָהֳלוֹ, בְּצוּר יְרוֹמְמֵנִי: וְעַתָּה יָרוּם רֹאשִׁי עַל אֹיְבַי סְבִיבוֹתַי, וְאֶזְבְּחָה בְאָהֳלוֹ זִבְחֵי תְרוּעָה, אָשִׁירָה וַאֲזַמְּרָה לַיהוה: שְׁמַע־יהוה קוֹלִי אֶקְרָא, וְחָנֵּנִי וַעֲנֵנִי: לְךָ אָמַר לִבִּי בַּקְּשׁוּ פָנָי, אֶת־פָּנֶיךָ יהוה אֲבַקֵּשׁ: אַל־תַּסְתֵּר פָּנֶיךָ מִמֶּנִּי, אַל תַּט־בְּאַף עַבְדֶּךָ, עֶזְרָתִי הָיִיתָ, אַל־תִּטְּשֵׁנִי וְאַל־תַּעַזְבֵנִי, אֱלֹהֵי יִשְׁעִי: כִּי־אָבִי וְאִמִּי עֲזָבוּנִי, וַיהוה יַאַסְפֵנִי: הוֹרֵנִי יהוה דַּרְכֶּךָ, וּנְחֵנִי בְּאֹרַח מִישׁוֹר, לְמַעַן שׁוֹרְרָי: אַל־תִּתְּנֵנִי בְּנֶפֶשׁ צָרָי, כִּי קָמוּ־בִי עֵדֵי־שֶׁקֶר, וִיפֵחַ חָמָס: ◂ לוּלֵא הֶאֱמַנְתִּי לִרְאוֹת בְּטוּב־יהוה בְּאֶרֶץ חַיִּים: קַוֵּה אֶל־יהוה, חֲזַק וְיַאֲמֵץ לִבֶּךָ, וְקַוֵּה אֶל־יהוה:

קדיש יתום (previous page)

In a שבעה *house the service continues on page 198.*

All: May His great name be blessed forever and all time.

Mourner: Blessed and praised, honored, extolled, glorified, adored and exalted above all be the name of the Holy One, blessed is He, (*Between Rosh Hashana & Yom Kippur:* above and) beyond any blessing, hymn, praise, or expressions of consolation that may be uttered in this world, and say, Amen.

May abundant peace descend from heaven, as well as life, for us and for all Israel, and say, Amen.

Bow, take three steps back, as if taking leave of the Divine Presence, then bow, first left, then right, then center, while saying:

May He Who makes peace in the highest heaven, make peace for us, and for all Israel, and say, Amen.

From the second day of Rosh Ḥodesh Elul through Shemini Atzeret the following psalm is said:

Ps. 27 לְדָוִד OF DAVID. The Lord is my light and my salvation. Whom shall I fear? The Lord is the refuge of my life. Whom shall I dread? When the evildoers came close to me to eat my flesh, those who were to me my adversaries and my enemies, it was they who stumbled and fell. If a host should encamp against me, my heart will not fear. If a war should rise against me, in this I trust. One thing have I asked of the Lord, that will I seek: That I may dwell in the house of the Lord all the days of my life, to behold the beauty of the Lord, and to contemplate His Temple, that He will hide me in His tabernacle on the day of evil, He will hide me in the shelter of His tent, He will lift me up upon a rock. And now my head will be lifted up above my enemies round about me, and I will offer in His tent sacrifices accompanied by the sound of trumpets. I will sing, and I will sing praises to the Lord. Hear, O Lord, my voice when I call, and show me favor and answer me. Of You my heart has said: Seek My face. Your face, O Lord, will I seek. Do not hide Your face from me. Do not turn Your servant away in anger. You have been my help, do not abandon me and do not forsake me, O God of my salvation. For my father and my mother have forsaken me, but the Lord will gather me in. Teach me Your way, O Lord, and lead me on an even path, because of my enemies. Do not deliver me to the desire of my enemies, for false witnesses have risen up against me, and a wicked witness. ▸ Were it not that I believed I would see the goodness of the Lord in the land of the living. Wait for the Lord, be strong and let your heart be encouraged, and wait for the Lord.

Mourner's Kaddish (previous page)

In a shiva house the service continues on page 199.

קידוש לבנה

קידוש לבנה is said between seventy-two hours after the Molad and the middle day of the month. If possible, it should be said at the end of שבת, under the open sky, and in the presence of a מנין.

הַלְלוּיָהּ, הַלְלוּ אֶת־יהוה מִן־הַשָּׁמַיִם, הַלְלוּהוּ בַּמְּרוֹמִים: הַלְלוּהוּ כָל־מַלְאָכָיו, הַלְלוּהוּ כָּל־צְבָאָו: הַלְלוּהוּ שֶׁמֶשׁ וְיָרֵחַ, הַלְלוּהוּ כָּל־כּוֹכְבֵי אוֹר: הַלְלוּהוּ שְׁמֵי הַשָּׁמָיִם, וְהַמַּיִם אֲשֶׁר מֵעַל הַשָּׁמָיִם: יְהַלְלוּ אֶת־שֵׁם יהוה, כִּי הוּא צִוָּה וְנִבְרָאוּ: וַיַּעֲמִידֵם לָעַד לְעוֹלָם, חָק־נָתַן וְלֹא יַעֲבוֹר: תהלים קמח

Look at the moon, then say:

בָּרוּךְ אַתָּה יהוה אֱלֹהֵינוּ מֶלֶךְ הָעוֹלָם, אֲשֶׁר בְּמַאֲמָרוֹ בָּרָא שְׁחָקִים, וּבְרוּחַ פִּיו כָּל צְבָאָם, חֹק וּזְמַן נָתַן לָהֶם שֶׁלֹּא יְשַׁנּוּ אֶת תַּפְקִידָם. שָׂשִׂים וּשְׂמֵחִים לַעֲשׂוֹת רְצוֹן קוֹנָם, פּוֹעֵל

קִדּוּשׁ לְבָנָה / BLESSING THE NEW MOON
Kiddush Levana compares the Jewish people to the moon. Indeed, the history of the Jewish people is entirely parallel to the lunar cycle, in which the historical pendulum swings between grandeur and lowliness. The process continuously repeats itself: the people grows slowly until it reaches its pinnacle... and that very power brings about a sense that כֹּחִי וְעֹצֶם יָדִי עָשָׂה לִי אֶת־הַחַיִל הַזֶּה, "my power and the might of my hand has gotten me this wealth" (Deut. 8:17). When that occurs, the Jewish people forgets its life source and loses its sense of being a receptacle [as the moon is to the light of the sun, merely a reflection of the divine light]... thus that very grandeur brings to lowliness... until the Jewish people recognize the limitations of their own powers, and the cycle repeats itself. A day will come when the light of the moon will not diminish, and the Jewish people will add light, strength and life force beyond measure. On that day the "flaw" of the moon will be rectified, and we will understand ourselves as mere receptacles, at every moment and in every situation, as did King David [and the Davidic line]... On that day, God's light will shine upon us in all its completeness (R. Moshe Shapira).

This cyclical pattern of Jewish history, especially the recurring suffering at the hands of other nations, explains the perpetual survival of the Jewish people. Every nation engages in actions that deserve God's punishment. In the case of the Jewish people, after we have sinned God does not allow our "account" to accumulate, but instead brings punishment upon us, so that thereafter we have a clean slate to start over again. With other nations, however, God allows them to flourish and prosper over many generations, all the while allowing their sins to accumulate. When they are finally called to account, their punishment is so great that they go into decline, often to disappear from history (R. Yehuda HaLevi).

In the Gemara (*Ḥullin* 60b) R. Shimon ben Pazi related the *midrash* that when God created "the two great luminaries" (Gen. 1:16), i.e., the sun and the moon, the latter immodestly complained that "when two rulers sit on one

SANCTIFYING THE NEW MOON

The Sanctification of the New Moon is recited between seventy-two hours after the Molad and the middle day of the month. If possible, it should be said at the end of Shabbat, under the open sky, and in the presence of a minyan.

Ps. 148 הַלְלוּיָהּ PRAISE THE LORD. Praise the Lord from the heavens, praise Him in the heights. Praise Him, all you His angels. Praise Him, all you His hosts. Praise Him, sun and moon. Praise Him, all you stars of light. Praise Him, heavens of the heavens, and the waters that are above the heavens. Let them praise the name of the Lord, that He commanded and they were created. And He established them forever and ever. He gave a command and it will not be annulled.

Look at the moon, then say:

בָּרוּךְ BLESSED ARE YOU, Lord, our God, King of the universe, Who with His word created the heavens, and with the breath of His mouth all their host. He set for them a decree and a schedule so that they would not alter their appointed task. They are joyous and glad to perform the

---

throne the result is conflict." For subtly implying its desire to dominate the sun, the moon was punished, relegated to being junior to the sun, incapable of generating its own light. When the moon objected that it had simply stated the obvious, God placated it by promising that in due course the Jewish people would bring a special monthly offering in honor of the lunar renewal. That sacrifice would, as the Torah puts it (Num. 28:15), be a חַטָּאת לַה' (sin-offering "on behalf of" God). This unusual phrase implies that God regretted what might be construed as an excessive punishment. As the Maharal explains, that sacrifice honors the moon by making it the monthly catalyst by which the Jewish people furthers the ultimate purpose of all of creation, which is to serve God.

The thrust of this Talmudic passage is to emphasize in various ways the virtues of humility: The moon was punished for its presumptuousness, God Himself humbly recognizes that He too needs atonement, so to speak, and (as the same Gemara notes) we are to imitate the unpretentiousness of the patriarch Jacob, King David, and the *tanna* Shmuel Hakatan. Of course the epitome of humility was Moses – the singular law-giver, greatest of all prophets, and leader of the Jewish people par excellence, who was ready to sink into oblivion so that his people could be saved after the Golden Calf episode (Ex. 32:32). R. Zalman Sorotzkin makes the trenchant observation that with all of Moses' centrality to the Jewish faith, Judaism is utterly unlike other faiths whose central religious holidays revolve around the birth and death of their founders, and whose prescriptions for achieving eternal life demand unconditional identification with the founders of their faith. Moses' humility was such that he neither sought, nor was he given, such a role (R. Basil Herring).

הַלְלוּיָהּ, הַלְלוּ אֶת־ה' מִן־הַשָּׁמַיִם – *Praise the Lord. Praise the Lord from the heavens.* The first six verses of Psalm 148 describe how the heavens praise God, and they are therefore used as the preface to *Kiddush Levana.* They remind us that

אֱמֶת שֶׁפְּעֻלָּתוֹ אֱמֶת. וְלַלְּבָנָה אָמַר שֶׁתִּתְחַדֵּשׁ, עֲטֶרֶת תִּפְאֶרֶת לַעֲמוּסֵי בָטֶן, שֶׁהֵם עֲתִידִים לְהִתְחַדֵּשׁ כְּמוֹתָהּ וּלְפָאֵר לְיוֹצְרָם עַל שֵׁם כְּבוֹד מַלְכוּתוֹ. בָּרוּךְ אַתָּה יהוה, מְחַדֵּשׁ חֳדָשִׁים.

The following five verses are each said three times:

בָּרוּךְ יוֹצְרֵךְ, בָּרוּךְ עוֹשֵׂךְ, בָּרוּךְ קוֹנֵךְ, בָּרוּךְ בּוֹרְאֵךְ.

The following verse is said rising on the toes.

כְּשֵׁם שֶׁאֲנִי רוֹקֵד כְּנֶגְדֵּךְ וְאֵינִי יָכוֹל לִנְגֹּעַ בָּךְ, כָּךְ לֹא יוּכְלוּ כָּל אוֹיְבַי לִנְגֹּעַ בִּי לְרָעָה.

תִּפֹּל עֲלֵיהֶם אֵימָתָה וָפַחַד, בִּגְדֹל זְרוֹעֲךָ יִדְּמוּ כָּאָבֶן: שמות טו

כָּאָבֶן יִדְּמוּ זְרוֹעֲךָ בִּגְדֹל, וָפַחַד אֵימָתָה עֲלֵיהֶם תִּפֹּל.

דָּוִד מֶלֶךְ יִשְׂרָאֵל חַי וְקַיָּם.

Turn to three people and say to each: שָׁלוֹם עֲלֵיכֶם.

They respond: עֲלֵיכֶם שָׁלוֹם.

Say three times:

סִימָן טוֹב וּמַזָּל טוֹב יְהֵא לָנוּ וּלְכָל יִשְׂרָאֵל, אָמֵן.

קוֹל דּוֹדִי הִנֵּה־זֶה בָּא, מְדַלֵּג עַל־הֶהָרִים, מְקַפֵּץ עַל־הַגְּבָעוֹת: שיר השירים ב
דּוֹמֶה דוֹדִי לִצְבִי אוֹ לְעֹפֶר הָאַיָּלִים, הִנֵּה־זֶה עוֹמֵד אַחַר כָּתְלֵנוּ, מַשְׁגִּיחַ מִן־הַחַלֹּנוֹת, מֵצִיץ מִן־הַחֲרַכִּים:

---

what follows is directed not at the moon itself, but at its divine Creator.

בָּרוּךְ יוֹצְרֵךְ – *Blessed is He Who formed you.* This and most of the following verses find their origin in the eighth-century Tractate *Soferim* (19:10). Three-fold repetitions were commonly used in *segulot* (commonly used when invoking divine protection) (Rashi, *Shabbat* 66b), as is seen in verses said after the bedtime *Shema*.

דָּוִד מֶלֶךְ יִשְׂרָאֵל חַי וְקַיָּם – *David, King of Israel, lives and endures.* As recorded in the Gemara (*Rosh HaShana* 25a), this phrase served on occasion as a secret code to validate the truthfulness of witnesses to a new moon. This became necessary in the face of Sadducean attempts to undermine the accuracy of the lunar calendar which depended on reliable witnesses. Coincidentally, the combined numerical value of the five words is 819, identical to the numerical value of רֹאשׁ חוֹדֶשׁ.

שָׁלוֹם עֲלֵיכֶם – *Peace upon you.* According to the Arizal this thrice-repeated act symbolically declares our desire to put aside our differences, to peaceably seek harmony as equals before

will of their Owner, the Worker of truth Whose work is truth. To the moon He said that it should renew itself as a crown of splendor for those borne by Him from the womb, those destined to renew themselves like it, and to glorify their Creator for the name of His glorious kingdom. Blessed are You, Lord, Who renews the months.

The following five verses are each said three times:

BLESSED IS HE Who formed you; blessed is He Who made you; blessed is He Who owns you; blessed is He Who created you.

The following verse is said rising on the toes.

JUST AS I dance toward you but cannot touch you, so may none of my enemies be able to touch me to do me harm.

Ex. 15 LET FEAR AND dread fall upon them; by the power of Your arm may they be still as stone.

LET THEM BE still as stone through the power of Your arm, when dread and fear fall upon them.

DAVID, KING OF Israel, lives and endures.

Turn to three people and say to each: PEACE UPON YOU.

They respond: UPON YOU, PEACE.

Say three times:

MAY IT BE a good sign and an auspicious omen for us and all Israel. Amen.

Song. 2 קול HARK! My beloved! Here he comes, leaping over the mountains, bounding over the hills. My beloved is like a gazelle, like a young deer. There he stands outside our wall, peering in through the windows, gazing through the lattice.

God, and to avoid all forms of jealousy that might, as happened with the moon, lead to conflict and punishment. This sets the stage for a higher celestial harmony (*Benei Yissasḥar*).

On a halakhic level, this greeting reenacts the Sanhedrin's procedure for establishing the month. When witnesses would come before the panel of three judges to attest that they had seen the appearance of the new moon, they would first give the password and then greet each judge in turn. Hence we too greet three fellow Jews when sanctifying the new moon (R. Joseph B. Soloveitchik).

Despite the moon's complaint in the narrative quoted above, the sun continues to illuminate the moon. This teaches us that we too should not harbor a grudge against others who have sought to harm us. We express this by giving each other a blessing of peace and wholeness (*Anaf Yosef*).

תהלים קכא **שִׁיר לַמַּעֲלוֹת,** אֶשָּׂא עֵינַי אֶל־הֶהָרִים, מֵאַיִן יָבֹא עֶזְרִי: עֶזְרִי מֵעִם יהוה, עֹשֵׂה שָׁמַיִם וָאָרֶץ: אַל־יִתֵּן לַמּוֹט רַגְלֶךָ, אַל־יָנוּם שֹׁמְרֶךָ: הִנֵּה לֹא־יָנוּם וְלֹא יִישָׁן, שׁוֹמֵר יִשְׂרָאֵל: יהוה שֹׁמְרֶךָ, יהוה צִלְּךָ עַל־יַד יְמִינֶךָ: יוֹמָם הַשֶּׁמֶשׁ לֹא־יַכֶּכָּה, וְיָרֵחַ בַּלָּיְלָה: יהוה יִשְׁמָרְךָ מִכָּל־רָע, יִשְׁמֹר אֶת־נַפְשֶׁךָ: יהוה יִשְׁמָר־צֵאתְךָ וּבוֹאֶךָ, מֵעַתָּה וְעַד־עוֹלָם:

תהלים קנ **הַלְלוּיָהּ,** הַלְלוּ־אֵל בְּקָדְשׁוֹ, הַלְלוּהוּ בִּרְקִיעַ עֻזּוֹ: הַלְלוּהוּ בִגְבוּרֹתָיו, הַלְלוּהוּ כְּרֹב גֻּדְלוֹ: הַלְלוּהוּ בְּתֵקַע שׁוֹפָר, הַלְלוּהוּ בְּנֵבֶל וְכִנּוֹר: הַלְלוּהוּ בְתֹף וּמָחוֹל, הַלְלוּהוּ בְּמִנִּים וְעוּגָב: הַלְלוּהוּ בְצִלְצְלֵי־שָׁמַע, הַלְלוּהוּ בְּצִלְצְלֵי תְרוּעָה: כֹּל הַנְּשָׁמָה תְּהַלֵּל יָהּ, הַלְלוּיָהּ:

סנהדרין מב. **תָּנָא** דְבֵי רַבִּי יִשְׁמָעֵאל: אִלְמָלֵי לֹא זָכוּ יִשְׂרָאֵל אֶלָּא לְהַקְבִּיל פְּנֵי אֲבִיהֶם שֶׁבַּשָּׁמַיִם פַּעַם אַחַת בַּחֹדֶשׁ, דַּיָּם. אָמַר אַבַּיֵי: הִלְכָּךְ צָרִיךְ לְמֵימְרָא מְעֻמָּד. מִי זֹאת עֹלָה מִן־הַמִּדְבָּר, מִתְרַפֶּקֶת עַל־דּוֹדָהּ: שיר השירים ח

וִיהִי רָצוֹן מִלְּפָנֶיךָ יהוה אֱלֹהַי וֵאלֹהֵי אֲבוֹתַי, לְמַלֹּאת פְּגִימַת הַלְּבָנָה וְלֹא יִהְיֶה בָּהּ שׁוּם מִעוּט. וִיהִי אוֹר הַלְּבָנָה כְּאוֹר הַחַמָּה וּכְאוֹר שִׁבְעַת יְמֵי בְרֵאשִׁית, כְּמוֹ שֶׁהָיְתָה קֹדֶם מִעוּטָהּ, שֶׁנֶּאֱמַר: אֶת־שְׁנֵי הַמְּאֹרֹת הַגְּדֹלִים: וְיִתְקַיֵּם בָּנוּ מִקְרָא שֶׁכָּתוּב: וּבִקְשׁוּ אֶת־יהוה אֱלֹהֵיהֶם וְאֵת דָּוִיד מַלְכָּם: אָמֵן. בראשית א הושע ג

תהלים סז **לַמְנַצֵּחַ** בִּנְגִינֹת, מִזְמוֹר שִׁיר: אֱלֹהִים יְחָנֵּנוּ וִיבָרְכֵנוּ, יָאֵר פָּנָיו אִתָּנוּ סֶלָה: לָדַעַת בָּאָרֶץ דַּרְכֶּךָ, בְּכָל־גּוֹיִם יְשׁוּעָתֶךָ: יוֹדוּךָ עַמִּים אֱלֹהִים, יוֹדוּךָ עַמִּים כֻּלָּם: יִשְׂמְחוּ וִירַנְּנוּ לְאֻמִּים, כִּי־תִשְׁפֹּט עַמִּים מִישֹׁר, וּלְאֻמִּים בָּאָרֶץ תַּנְחֵם סֶלָה: יוֹדוּךָ עַמִּים אֱלֹהִים, יוֹדוּךָ עַמִּים כֻּלָּם: אֶרֶץ נָתְנָה יְבוּלָהּ, יְבָרְכֵנוּ אֱלֹהִים אֱלֹהֵינוּ: יְבָרְכֵנוּ אֱלֹהִים, וְיִירְאוּ אוֹתוֹ כָּל־אַפְסֵי־אָרֶץ:

מעריב *continues with* עָלֵינוּ *and* קדיש יתום (*page 746*).

מִי זֹאת עֹלָה – *Who is this rising.* The Jewish people were elevated as a result of their humbling forty-year sojourn in the wilderness of Sinai. There they received the Torah, there they built the Tabernacle, and there the first Sanhedrin was formed. Likewise, as we pray for God

Ps. 121 **שִׁיר לַמַּעֲלוֹת** A SONG FOR ASCENTS. I lift up my eyes to the hills. From where will my help come? My help is from the Lord, the Maker of heaven and earth. May He not suffer your foot to slip. May He Who guards you not slumber. Behold, He Who guards Israel neither slumbers nor sleeps. The Lord is your guardian. The Lord is your shade upon your right hand. The sun will not smite you by day, nor the moon by night. The Lord will guard you from all evil. He will guard your soul. The Lord will guard your going out and your coming in from now and forever.

Ps. 150 **הַלְלוּיָהּ** PRAISE THE LORD. Praise God for His sanctity, praise Him for His power in the firmament. Praise Him for His mighty acts, praise Him in accordance with His exceeding greatness. Praise Him with the sounding of the shofar, praise Him with the harp and lyre. Praise Him with the timbrel and the dance, praise Him with flutes and the pipe. Praise Him with sounding cymbals, praise Him with loud clashing cymbals. Let everything that has breath praise the Lord. Praise the Lord.

Sanhedrin 42a **תָּנָא** THE ACADEMY of R. Yishmael taught: Had Israel not been privileged to greet the countenance of their Father in heaven except for once a month – it would have sufficed them. Abaye said: Therefore it should be said while
Song. 8 standing. Who is this rising from the desert, leaning on her beloved?

וִיהִי MAY IT BE Your will, Lord, my God and the God of my fathers, to make whole the deficiency of the moon, so that it is no longer diminished. May the light of the moon be like the light of the sun and like the light of the seven
Gen. 1 days of Creation, as it was before it was diminished, as it is said: "The two great luminaries." And may there be fulfilled for us the verse that is written:
Hos. 3 "They shall seek the Lord their God, and David, their king." Amen.

Ps. 67 **לַמְנַצֵּחַ** TO THE DIRECTOR of music for instruments. A psalm. A song. May God be gracious to us and bless us. May He cause His face to shine upon us. Selah. That Your way may become known upon the earth, Your salvation among all nations. The peoples will praise You, O God. All the peoples will praise You. The nations will rejoice and sing. For You judge the peoples equitably and govern the nations upon the earth. Selah. The peoples will praise You, O God. All the peoples will praise You. The earth has yielded its produce. God, our God, will bless us. God will bless us, and all the ends of the earth will fear Him.

Ma'ariv continues with Aleinu and Mourner's Kaddish *(page 747)*.

to "make whole the deficiency of the moon," we yearn that our exile and suffering will be revealed as the precursor of the fulfillment of our historic destiny (*Shir HaShirim Raba*).

סדר הבדלה בבית

Many follow the custom to precede הבדלה
by reciting the following phrases and verses.

אֵלִיָּהוּ הַנָּבִיא אֵלִיָּהוּ הַתִּשְׁבִּי, אֵלִיָּהוּ הַגִּלְעָדִי, בִּמְהֵרָה יָבוֹא אֵלֵינוּ עִם
מָשִׁיחַ בֶּן דָּוִד. תִּתֵּן אֱמֶת לְיַעֲקֹב, אַל תִּירָא עַבְדִּי יַעֲקֹב. מיכה ז

On מוצאי יום טוב *that is not a* מוצאי שבת*, the first paragraph and the blessings for the spices and flame are omitted. At the end of* יום כפור*, only the blessing for the spices is omitted.*
Taking a cup of wine in the right hand, say:

הִנֵּה אֵל יְשׁוּעָתִי אֶבְטַח, וְלֹא אֶפְחָד, כִּי־עָזִּי וְזִמְרָת יָהּ יהוה, ישעיה יב
וַיְהִי־לִי לִישׁוּעָה: וּשְׁאַבְתֶּם־מַיִם בְּשָׂשׂוֹן, מִמַּעַיְנֵי הַיְשׁוּעָה:
לַיהוה הַיְשׁוּעָה, עַל־עַמְּךָ בִרְכָתֶךָ סֶּלָה: יהוה צְבָאוֹת עִמָּנוּ, תהלים ג תהלים מו
מִשְׂגָּב לָנוּ אֱלֹהֵי יַעֲקֹב סֶלָה: יהוה צְבָאוֹת, אַשְׁרֵי אָדָם בֹּטֵחַ בָּךְ: תהלים פד
יהוה הוֹשִׁיעָה, הַמֶּלֶךְ יַעֲנֵנוּ בְיוֹם־קָרְאֵנוּ: לַיְּהוּדִים הָיְתָה אוֹרָה תהלים כ אסתר ח
וְשִׂמְחָה וְשָׂשֹׂן וִיקָר: כֵּן תִּהְיֶה לָּנוּ. כּוֹס־יְשׁוּעוֹת אֶשָּׂא, וּבְשֵׁם תהלים קטז
יהוה אֶקְרָא:

הַבְדָּלָה / HAVDALA
According to Rambam the obligation to recite *Havdala* is required by the Torah. He states "it is a positive *mitzva* of the Torah to sanctify Shabbat by a verbal declaration, in accordance with 'remember the Shabbat day to sanctify it.' We must remember it at its beginning with *Kiddush* and at its end with *Havdala*." Others consider *Havdala* to be of rabbinic origin.

אֵלִיָּהוּ הַנָּבִיא / ELIJAH THE PROPHET
As these words of the prophet Malakhi indicate, Elijah the Prophet will reappear shortly before the Messiah will be revealed in the world. He will not only be the harbinger of universal repentance in the Messianic age, he will also, as the Mishna (*Eduyot* 8:7) explains, "bring peace to the world." Over the course of Shabbat we have traversed the full arc of history, from the Shabbat of Creation that is celebrated on Friday evening, through the Revelation at Sinai that is the central focus of Shabbat morning, and then the culmination of eschatological redemption that is the theme of Shabbat afternoon. As the Shabbat Queen takes her leave, we celebrate the coming redemption, whose symbol is the prophet Elijah who according to the sages never died, but arose alive to heaven in a whirlwind borne on a fiery chariot, as recounted in II Kings 2:11.

It is significant that the same Elijah who was so identified with confrontation and conflict in his uncompromising relations with his contemporaries, whether they were the tyrannical rulers of Israel or the common folk themselves, is also the symbol of future peace and harmony throughout the world. The sages recognized that in this Elijah's alter-ego was Pinchas b. Elazar (as described in Numbers 25),

HAVDALA AT HOME

Many follow the custom to precede Havdala by reciting the following phrases and verses.

אֵלִיָּהוּ הַנָּבִיא ELIJAH THE PROPHET, Elijah the Tishbite, Elijah of Gilead, may
Micha 7 he come to us soon, together with the Messiah son of David. You will show truth to Jacob, fear not, My servant Jacob."

On Motza'ei Yom Tov that is not a Motza'ei Shabbat, the first paragraph and the blessings for the spices and flame are omitted. At the end of Yom Kippur, only the blessing for the spices is omitted.

Taking a cup of wine in the right hand, say:

Is. 12 הִנֵּה BEHOLD, God is my salvation, I trust and am not afraid; for
the Lord is my strength and my song, and He is the source of my
liberation. Therefore shall we joyously draw water from the wells of
Ps. 3 salvation. O Lord, salvation comes from You; please bless Your people.
Ps. 46 Selah. Lord of hosts, be with us; God of Jacob, be our high refuge.
Ps. 84 *Ps. 20* Selah. Lord of hosts, those who trust in You are happy. Lord, save!
Esther 8 The King will answer us on the day that we call. The Jews had light
Ps. 116 and gladness, joy and honor. So may it be with us. I lift up the cup of
salvation, and I call upon the name of the Lord.

---

with whom he is identified. In their tumultuous lives and actions both displayed undiluted zealotry for God, but paradoxically also came in due course to embody the realization of peace and harmony in the world. Accordingly, this ode to the life and work of Elijah, both past and future, is a fitting capstone to the Shabbat experience that similarly provides respite and peaceful resolution after six days of struggle and strife (R. Basil Herring).

The various Scriptural verses preceding the *berakhot* of *Havdala* are first mentioned in the medieval *Maḥzor Vitri*.

וּשְׁאַבְתֶּם־מַיִם בְּשָׂשׂוֹן – *Therefore shall we joyously draw water.* When King Hezekiah sealed the Giḥon spring outside of Jerusalem in advance of the Assyrian siege (II Chron. 32:2–4), Isaiah prophesied that the "spring of salvation" would one day spring forth, its waters to be drawn not in fear but in joy.

לַיְּהוּדִים הָיְתָה אוֹרָה – *The Jews had light.* This corresponds to the *berakha* on the light which will follow (*Levush*).

כּוֹס־יְשׁוּעוֹת אֶשָּׂא – *I will raise up the cup of salvation.* This is a reference to the cup of wine (or its substitute) over which a *berakha* is about to be recited, providing fulfillment of the rest of the verse (Psalms 116:13), וּבְשֵׁם ה׳ אֶקְרָא – "I call upon the name of the Lord" (*Levush*).

The Rema explains that the "cup of deliverance" of *Havdala* is synonymous with plenitude and fullness. We fill the cup to overflowing in accordance with the Gemara (*Eiruvin* 65a) that says "a house in which wine does not flow like water is without blessing."

When making הבדלה *for others, add:*

סַבְרִי מָרָנָן וְרַבָּנָן וְרַבּוֹתַי

בָּרוּךְ אַתָּה יהוה אֱלֹהֵינוּ מֶלֶךְ הָעוֹלָם, בּוֹרֵא פְּרִי הַגָּפֶן.

Hold the spice box and say:

בָּרוּךְ אַתָּה יהוה אֱלֹהֵינוּ מֶלֶךְ הָעוֹלָם, בּוֹרֵא מִינֵי בְשָׂמִים.

Smell the spices and put the spice box down.
Lift the hands toward the flame of the הבדלה *candle and say:*

בָּרוּךְ אַתָּה יהוה אֱלֹהֵינוּ מֶלֶךְ הָעוֹלָם, בּוֹרֵא מְאוֹרֵי הָאֵשׁ.

Holding the cup of wine again in the right hand, say:

בָּרוּךְ אַתָּה יהוה אֱלֹהֵינוּ מֶלֶךְ הָעוֹלָם, הַמַּבְדִּיל בֵּין קֹדֶשׁ לְחֹל, בֵּין אוֹר לְחֹשֶׁךְ, בֵּין יִשְׂרָאֵל לָעַמִּים, בֵּין יוֹם הַשְּׁבִיעִי לְשֵׁשֶׁת יְמֵי הַמַּעֲשֶׂה. בָּרוּךְ אַתָּה יהוה, הַמַּבְדִּיל בֵּין קֹדֶשׁ לְחֹל.

The order of the four *berakhot* of *Havdala* has been explained in a variety of ways. The *Shulḥan Arukh* explains that their first letters together form the acrostic "Yavneh" (יַיִן, בְּשָׂמִים, נֵר, הַבְדָּלָה). The *Rashbatz* points out the ascending location of the senses involved: the tongue which tastes the wine, the nose which inhales the spices, the eyes which see the light, and finally the brain that understands the difference between the holy and the profane. So too, we are to seek always to elevate our own spiritual and moral selves.

בּוֹרֵא מִינֵי בְשָׂמִים – *Who creates the many different spices.* The Gemara (*Beitza* 16a) explains that the *berakha* over spice is to recover from the loss of the נְשָׁמָה יְתֵרָה (additional soul) of the just-departed Shabbat, by inhaling the invigorating aroma of spice. This might also allude to the creation of man when God breathed נִשְׁמַת חַיִּים (the soul of life) into his nostrils (Gen. 2:7). Just as man's soul was instilled through his nostrils, so too, following the departure of Shabbat, are we rejuvenated and restored through our nose by what we might call "the spices of life."

בּוֹרֵא מְאוֹרֵי הָאֵשׁ – *Who creates the light of fire.* The Torah considers kindling fire to be the archetype of forbidden activity on Shabbat (Ex. 35:3). Therefore, having restrained ourselves over Shabbat from engaging in any activities that might convey our mastery over nature, especially as they relate to fire in its various forms, we immediately light a fire at the conclusion of Shabbat. (*Rashba*)

The Gemara (*Pesaḥim* 54a) explains that God created fire immediately following the seventh day of creation, showing Adam and Eve how to rub two stones together to create their own fire to harness and develop the forces embedded in nature, as a partner to God. Using this skill, man attains dignity, as he exercises his "capability of dominating our environment and exercising control over it" (R. Joseph B. Soloveitchik).

When making Havdala for others, add:

With your permission, my masters, rabbis and esteemed companions:

בָּרוּךְ BLESSED ARE YOU, Lord, our God, King of the universe, Who creates the fruit of the vine.

Hold the spice box and say:

בָּרוּךְ BLESSED ARE YOU, Lord, our God, King of the universe, Who creates the many different spices.

Smell the spices and put the spice box down.
Lift the hands toward the flame of the Havdala candle and say:

בָּרוּךְ BLESSED ARE YOU, Lord, our God, King of the universe, Who creates the lights of fire.

Holding the cup of wine again in the right hand, say:

בָּרוּךְ BLESSED ARE YOU, Lord, our God, King of the universe, Who separates sacred from secular, light from darkness, Israel from the nations, and the seventh day from the six days of labor. Blessed are You, Lord, Who separates sacred from secular.

The ancient Greeks took a very different approach to the origin of fire, and man's creative role, in the world. They taught that Prometheus stole the original fire from Zeus, an act for which he was severely punished. This illuminates a key difference between Athens and Jerusalem: For the Greeks, the gods opposed man having the use of fire, while for the sages of Israel, God Himself initiated the gift of fire, through which He granted man the responsibility and privilege of becoming His partner in building a better world.

לְחֹל – *Secular*. The term חל does not mean "profane," or imply an object devoid of holiness. It is instead similar to חֻלִּין שֶׁנַּעֲשׂוּ עַל טַהֲרַת הַקֹּדֶשׁ – mundane foods that can be raised to a higher level of sanctity – when they are prepared in a pure and sacred state of mind. So too the mundane activities of the work-week can provide opportunities for us to serve God, and thus to infuse sanctity into ordinary events and objects (R. Shneur Zalman of Liadi).

בֵּין קֹדֶשׁ לְחֹל, בֵּין אוֹר לְחֹשֶׁךְ – *Who separates sacred from secular, light from darkness*. This *berakha* speaks of three distinctions, each with its own level of visibility. The first is the difference between sacred and secular, which is not visible at all. The second is between light and darkness, which is certainly evident to anyone with eyes to see. An intermediate category is the third distinction – the difference between the Jewish people and other nations. This requires that our actions lead others who see us to recognize that our unique way of life radiates from our relationship to God. As the Torah declares (Deut. 28:10), "All the people of the earth will see that the name of God is proclaimed upon you, and they will revere you" (R. Joseph B. Soloveitchik).

גָאט פוּן אַבְרָהָם אוּן פוּן יִצְחָק אוּן פוּן יַעֲקֹב, בַּאהִיט דַיין פָאלְק יִשְׂרָאֵל פוּן אַלֶעם בֵּייזִין אִין דַיינֶעם לוֹיב, אַז דֶער לִיבֶּער שַׁבַּת קֹדֶשׁ גֵייט אַוֶועק, אַז דִיא וָואךְ זָאל אוּנְז קוּמֶען צוּ אֱמוּנָה שְׁלֵמָה, צוּ אֱמוּנַת חֲכָמִים, צוּ אַהֲבַת וְדִבּוּק חֲבֵרִים טוֹבִים, צוּ דְּבֵקוּת הַבּוֹרֵא בָּרוּךְ הוּא, מַאֲמִין צוּ זַיין בִּשְׁלֹשָׁה עָשָׂר עִקָּרִים שֶׁלְּךָ, וּבִגְאֻלָּה שְׁלֵמָה וּקְרוֹבָה בִמְהֵרָה בְּיָמֵינוּ, וּבִתְחִיַּת הַמֵּתִים, וּבִנְבוּאַת מֹשֶׁה רַבֵּנוּ עָלָיו הַשָּׁלוֹם.

רִבּוֹנוֹ שֶׁל עוֹלָם, דוּא בִּיסְט דָאךְ הַנּוֹתֵן לַיָּעֵף כֹּחַ, גִיב דַיינֶע לִיבֶּע אִידִישֶׁע קִינְדֶערְלֶעךְ אוֹיךְ כֹּחַ דִיךְ צוּ לוֹיבִּין, אוּן דִיךְ צוּ דִינֶען אוּן ווייטֶער קֵיינֶעם נִישְׁט. אוּן דִיא וָואךְ זָאל אוּנְז קוּמֶען צוּ חֶסֶד, אוּן צוּ מַזָּל, אוּן צוּ בְּרָכָה, אוּן צוּ הַצְלָחָה, אוּן צוּ גֶעזוּנְט, אוּן צוּ עֹשֶׁר וְכָבוֹד, אוּן צוּ בָּנֵי חַיֵּי וּמְזוֹנֵי, לָנוּ וּלְכָל יִשְׂרָאֵל. אָמֵן.

זמירות של מוצאי שבת

הַמַּבְדִּיל בֵּין קֹדֶשׁ לְחֹל, חַטֹּאתֵינוּ הוּא יִמְחֹל
זַרְעֵנוּ וְכַסְפֵּנוּ יַרְבֶּה כַּחוֹל וְכַכּוֹכָבִים בַּלָּיְלָה.

יוֹם פָּנָה כְּצֵל תֹּמֶר, אֶקְרָא לָאֵל עָלַי גּוֹמֵר
אָמַר שֹׁמֵר, אָתָא בֹקֶר וְגַם־לָיְלָה: ישעיה כא

צִדְקָתְךָ כְּהַר תָּבוֹר, עַל חֲטָאַי עָבוֹר תַּעֲבֹר
כְּיוֹם אֶתְמוֹל כִּי יַעֲבֹר, וְאַשְׁמוּרָה בַלָּיְלָה: תהלים צ

חָלְפָה עוֹנַת מִנְחָתִי, מִי יִתֵּן מְנוּחָתִי
יָגַעְתִּי בְאַנְחָתִי, אַשְׂחֶה בְכָל־לַיְלָה: תהלים ו

קוֹלִי בַּל יֻנְטַל, פְּתַח לִי שַׁעַר הַמְּנֻטָּל
שֶׁרֹּאשִׁי נִמְלָא טָל, קְוֻצּוֹתַי רְסִיסֵי לָיְלָה: שיר השירים ה

הֵעָתֵר נוֹרָא וְאָיֹם, אֲשַׁוֵּעַ, תְּנָה פִדְיוֹם
בְּנֶשֶׁף־בְּעֶרֶב יוֹם, בְּאִישׁוֹן לָיְלָה: משלי ז

גָאט פוּן אַבְרָהָם – *Dear God of Abraham.* This *teḥina* was originally recited by pious women before or after *Havdala.* It has achieved widespread usage by men and women of all ages, and is a fitting parallel to the *teḥinot* that precede *Kabbalat Shabbat.*

גאָט DEAR GOD of Abraham, Isaac, and Jacob, safeguard and shelter Your beloved people Israel from all evil as the beloved holy Sabbath departs. May the coming week, month, and year bring upon us undiminished belief, faithfulness to the teachings of the sages, the love of friends, and attachment to the Creator, blessed be He. To affirm the thirteen articles of faith, including the final redemption, may it come soon in our days, as well as the resurrection of the dead, and the truth of the prophecy of Moses our teacher, may he rest in peace.

RULER OF THE UNIVERSE, You are the one Who gives strength to the weary. Therefore grant Your beloved Jewish people the strength to praise You and to serve only You and no other, God forbid. So that this week, month and year will come upon us in good health, with good fortune, blessing and success, as well as compassion, offspring, long life, food aplenty, and divine assistance, for us and all Israel – and let us say Amen.

SONGS FOR THE CONCLUSION OF SHABBAT

הַמַּבְדִּיל MAY THE ONE Who differentiates between sacred and secular forgive our sins, / and multiply our seed and our silver like the sand of the shore and the stars of the night.

THE DAY has passed like the shadow of a palm tree, and I call unto God to
Is. 21 complete His promise to me, / when the Guardian of Israel foretold the
shining morning of the righteous, and the dark of the wicked.

YOUR RIGHTEOUSNESS, O God, is as great as Mount Tavor, thus please
Ps. 80 forgive my sins, / rendering them non-existent like a day that has passed,
and a night-watch gone by.

MY MINḤA prayer of Messianic redemption is passed, let my prayer to
Ps. 6 find rest be accepted, / for I sigh in my weariness, and every night my bed
is filled with tears.

LET MY SUPPLICATION not be rejected, rather may the gates of heaven be
Song. 5 opened to me, / for in my suffering my head is soaked in dew-like night-
sweat, my hair wet as if caught in the rain.

I IMPLORE YOU to answer my prayers O Awesome One, to redeem and save
Mishle 7 me /from the darkness of exile that has fallen at the end of the day, and
from the depths of the night.

קְרָאתִֽיךָ יָהּ, הוֹשִׁיעֵֽנִי, אֹֽרַח חַיִּים תּוֹדִיעֵֽנִי
מִדַּלָּה תְבַצְּעֵֽנִי, מִיּוֹם עַד לָֽיְלָה.
טַהֵר טִנּוּף מַעֲשַׂי, פֶּן יֹאמְרוּ מַכְעִיסַי
איוב לה אַיֵּה אֱלֽוֹהַּ עֹשָׂי, נֹתֵן זְמִרוֹת בַּלָּֽיְלָה:
נַֽחְנוּ בְיָדְךָ כַּחֹֽמֶר, סְלַח נָא עַל קַל וָחֹֽמֶר
תהלים יט יוֹם לְיוֹם יַבִּֽיעַ אֹֽמֶר, וְלַֽיְלָה לְּלָֽיְלָה:

אָמַר יהוה לְיַעֲקֹב, אַל תִּירָא עַבְדִּי יַעֲקֹב.
בָּחַר יהוה בְּיַעֲקֹב, אַל תִּירָא עַבְדִּי יַעֲקֹב.
גָּאַל יהוה אֶת יַעֲקֹב, אַל תִּירָא עַבְדִּי יַעֲקֹב.
במדבר כד דָּרַךְ כּוֹכָב מִיַּעֲקֹב, אַל תִּירָא עַבְדִּי יַעֲקֹב.
ישעיה כז הַבָּאִים יַשְׁרֵשׁ יַעֲקֹב, אַל תִּירָא עַבְדִּי יַעֲקֹב.
במדבר כד וְיֵרְדְּ מִיַּעֲקֹב, אַל תִּירָא עַבְדִּי יַעֲקֹב.
זְכֹר זֹאת לְיַעֲקֹב, אַל תִּירָא עַבְדִּי יַעֲקֹב.
חֶדְוַת יְשׁוּעוֹת יַעֲקֹב, אַל תִּירָא עַבְדִּי יַעֲקֹב.
טֹבוּ אֹהָלֶיךָ יַעֲקֹב, אַל תִּירָא עַבְדִּי יַעֲקֹב.
דברים לג יוֹרוּ מִשְׁפָּטֶיךָ לְיַעֲקֹב, אַל תִּירָא עַבְדִּי יַעֲקֹב.
במדבר כג כִּי לֹא נַחַשׁ בְּיַעֲקֹב, אַל תִּירָא עַבְדִּי יַעֲקֹב.
לֹא הִבִּיט אָוֶן בְּיַעֲקֹב, אַל תִּירָא עַבְדִּי יַעֲקֹב.
מִי מָנָה עֲפַר יַעֲקֹב, אַל תִּירָא עַבְדִּי יַעֲקֹב.
נִשְׁבַּע יהוה לְיַעֲקֹב, אַל תִּירָא עַבְדִּי יַעֲקֹב.
סְלַח נָא לַעֲוֹן יַעֲקֹב, אַל תִּירָא עַבְדִּי יַעֲקֹב.
עַתָּה הָשֵׁב שְׁבוּת יַעֲקֹב, אַל תִּירָא עַבְדִּי יַעֲקֹב.
פָּדָה יהוה אֶת יַעֲקֹב, אַל תִּירָא עַבְדִּי יַעֲקֹב.
צַוֵּה יְשׁוּעוֹת יַעֲקֹב, אַל תִּירָא עַבְדִּי יַעֲקֹב.
קוֹל קוֹל יַעֲקֹב, אַל תִּירָא עַבְדִּי יַעֲקֹב.
רָנּוּ שִׂמְחָה לְיַעֲקֹב, אַל תִּירָא עַבְדִּי יַעֲקֹב.
שָׁב יהוה אֶת גְּאוֹן יַעֲקֹב, אַל תִּירָא עַבְדִּי יַעֲקֹב.
מיכה ז תִּתֵּן אֱמֶת לְיַעֲקֹב, אַל תִּירָא עַבְדִּי יַעֲקֹב.

I BESEECH YOU O God, please save me, as You show me the path to eternal life / and heal me from my sickness, as quickly as day turns into night.

PURIFY ME from the pollution of my actions lest my enemies declare, /
Lam. 35 "Where is their God Who created them, Who is supposed to punish the wicked of the night?"

WE ARE in Your hands but works of pottery, thus please forgive our sins
Ps. 19 both minor and major, / allowing us to sing Your praises day after day and night after night.

אָמַר THE LORD has said to
the house of Jacob, fear not, My servant Jacob.
The Lord has chosen Jacob, fear not, My servant Jacob.
The Lord has redeemed Jacob, fear not, My servant Jacob.
Num. 24 There has stepped forth a star from Jacob, fear not, My servant Jacob.
Is. 27 In days to come rooted will be Jacob, fear not, My servant Jacob.
Num. 24 Dominion shall be exercised by Jacob, fear not, My servant Jacob.
Remember these things, O Jacob, fear not, My servant Jacob.
There will be joy in
the redemption of Jacob, fear not, My servant Jacob.
Goodly are your tents, O Jacob, fear not, My servant Jacob.
Deut. 33 They shall teach Your judgments to Jacob, fear not, My servant Jacob.
Num. 23 For there is no enchantment against Jacob, fear not, My servant Jacob.
None has beheld iniquity in Jacob, fear not, My servant Jacob.
Who can count the dust of Jacob? Fear not, My servant Jacob.
The Lord has sworn by the pride of Jacob, fear not, My servant Jacob.
Forgive, we pray, the sin of Jacob, fear not, My servant Jacob.
Now God will turn back
the captivity of Jacob, Fear not, My servant Jacob.
The Lord will indeed redeem Jacob, fear not, My servant Jacob.
Ordain salvation for Jacob, fear not, My servant Jacob.
The voice is the voice of Jacob, fear not, My servant Jacob.
Sing with gladness for Jacob, fear not, My servant Jacob.
The Lord will surely restore
the majesty of Jacob, Fear not, My servant Jacob.
Micha 7 You will show truth to Jacob, fear not, My servant Jacob.

סדר נטילת לולב

Each morning of סוכות*, before the recitation of* הלל *(on the next page), the* לולב *with the* הדסים *and the* ערבות *are taken in the right hand and the* אתרוג *in the left hand, with its pointed end toward the floor. While one stands, they are held together and waved after the following prayer and blessings. The taking of the* לולב *is omitted on* שבת.

At this point some follow the Hasidic custom of reciting additional prayers, which can be found on page 1338.

בָּרוּךְ אַתָּה יהוה אֱלֹהֵינוּ מֶלֶךְ הָעוֹלָם, אֲשֶׁר קִדְּשָׁנוּ בְּמִצְוֹתָיו וְצִוָּנוּ עַל נְטִילַת לוּלָב.

On the first day the לולב *is taken, add:*

בָּרוּךְ אַתָּה יהוה אֱלֹהֵינוּ מֶלֶךְ הָעוֹלָם, שֶׁהֶחֱיָנוּ וְקִיְּמָנוּ וְהִגִּיעָנוּ לַזְּמַן הַזֶּה.

Invert the* אתרוג*, so that its pointed end is facing up. Face the front of the* בית כנסת *and wave the* לולב *and* אתרוג *in the following sequence, three times in each direction: ahead, right, back, left, up, down.

Continue to hold the לולב *and* אתרוג *during* הלל.

אַרְבַּעַת הַמִּינִים / THE FOUR SPECIES

Leviticus 23:40 commands us to "take" (וּלְקַחְתֶּם) the Four Species, and rejoice with them before God for the seven days of Sukkot. Halakhic authorities (including the *Netziv*, the *Binyan Shlomo*, and the Ḥazon Ish) differ as to the nature of this "taking." That is, does the term לְקִיחָה refer to the act of "taking the species into one's hands," or is the obligation to "hold the species in one's hands." A practical consequence of this distinction occurs when someone takes the species before dawn and continues to hold them until after sunrise. Whether or not that person has fulfilled the *mitzva* will depend on this question, as the "taking into" was done prior to the time of *mitzva* obligation (which is during the day,) while the "holding in" occurred during daylight. As a practical matter, one satisfies both opinions by (as is commonly done) taking the Four Species with the *etrog* inverted, then reciting the blessing, and thereafter reversing (and thus "taking") the *etrog* into the correct posture so as to fulfill the *mitzva* at that point. A related question (discussed by the Rashash and R. Akiva Eiger) is whether in "taking" the Four Species it suffices to take a hold of them even without raising them up, or must one actually lift them into the air. The consensus view among later authorities is that one must have physically lifted them up (R. Shlomo Yosef Zevin).

SHAKING THE LULAV

There are three approaches to the shaking of the *lulav*. One approach is to shake the leaves. A second approach is to wave the *lulav* back and forth. A third approach is to combine these two approaches and stretch out the arms and then to draw it close to the chest while shaking strongly enough to rustle the *lulav*'s leaves. This is repeated three times in each direction. The third approach is the generally accepted practice for Ashkenazim (Rema, *OḤ* 651:9), but there are some who follow one of the first two approaches.

BLESSINGS OVER THE LULAV

Each morning of Sukkot, before the recitation of Hallel (on the next page), the lulav, myrtle and willow are taken in the right hand and the etrog in the left hand. While one stands, they are held together and waved after the following prayer and blessings. The taking of the lulav is omitted on Shabbat.

At this point some follow the Hasidic custom of reciting additional prayers, which can be found on page 1339.

בָּרוּךְ BLESSED are You, Lord, our God, King of the universe, Who has sanctified us with His commandments and has commanded us about the taking of the lulav.

On the first day the lulav is taken, add:

בָּרוּךְ BLESSED are You, Lord, our God, King of the universe, Who has given us life and sustenance, and brought us to this happy season.

Invert the etrog, so that its pointed end is facing up. Face the front of the synagogue and wave the lulav and etrog in the following sequence, three times in each direction: ahead, right, back, left, up, down.

Continue to hold the lulav and etrog during Hallel.

הָאֶתְרוֹג / THE ETROG

The Torah (Lev. 23:40) refers to the *etrog* as פְּרִי עֵץ הָדָר. This is to be understood as the name of the fruit, not a description of its properties, i.e., it is "the Hadar-tree fruit." This is why we refer to it as an "*etrog*" which is the Aramaic for the Hebrew term הָדָר, as well as חֲמֻדָּה, and how Onkelos translates these terms as they appear in Genesis 3:6 and Exodus 20:14. In this light, we should understand that the various descriptive terms that the Gemara (*Sukka* 35a) uses to explain the name of this fruit are merely by way of *asmakhta* (terms that can be associated with the Hebrew name) (Ramban).

The various explanations of the phrase פְּרִי עֵץ הָדָר suggested by the Gemara should not be taken as indicating any doubt by the sages as to which fruit the Torah was referring to, for from the days of Joshua until our own time every succeeding generation has been witness to the use of the *etrog* as one of the Four Species. The explanations offered by the Gemara were merely intended to explain why the Torah used that particular phrase in referring to the *etrog* (Rambam).

These comments of the Ramban and Rambam together illustrate how the mimetic tradition (i.e. the oral record of how earlier

PRAYERS PREPARATORY TO MITZVOT

Traditionally, Ashkenazi Jews did not recite prayers prior to performance of *mitzvot*. One simply recited the *berakha* and then performed the *mitzva*. In the eighteenth century, under Hasidic influence, some siddurim started to include various statements, including *LeShem Yiḥud,* to be recited before performing selected – but not all – *mitzvot* that are fulfilled during prayer. R. Yechezkel Landau (*Noda BeYehuda* Vol. I, *YD* no. 93) and other authorities, including at least one Hasidic one, opposed the recital of *LeShem Yiḥud* by the masses, for they would not understand its highly esoteric nature. Others, however, favored its recital. The matter has remained in dispute. In this Siddur we provide the text for those whose custom is to recite it. See page 1336.

סדר הלל

On the first two days of פסח, *on* שבועות; *the entire festival of* סוכות, שמיני עצרת *and* שמחת תורה, *and* חנוכה, הלל שלם *is said.*
On ראש חודש *and the last six days of* פסח, הלל בדילוג *is said.*
Regarding יום העצמאות *and* יום ירושלים, *see the commentary below.*

בָּרוּךְ אַתָּה יהוה אֱלֹהֵינוּ מֶלֶךְ הָעוֹלָם, אֲשֶׁר קִדְּשָׁנוּ בְּמִצְוֹתָיו וְצִוָּנוּ לִקְרֹא אֶת הַהַלֵּל.

הַלְלוּיָהּ, הַלְלוּ עַבְדֵי יהוה, הַלְלוּ אֶת־שֵׁם יהוה: יְהִי שֵׁם יהוה מְבֹרָךְ, מֵעַתָּה וְעַד־עוֹלָם: מִמִּזְרַח־שֶׁמֶשׁ עַד־מְבוֹאוֹ, מְהֻלָּל שֵׁם יהוה: רָם עַל־כָּל־גּוֹיִם יהוה, עַל הַשָּׁמַיִם כְּבוֹדוֹ: מִי כַּיהוה אֱלֹהֵינוּ, הַמַּגְבִּיהִי לָשָׁבֶת: הַמַּשְׁפִּילִי לִרְאוֹת, בַּשָּׁמַיִם וּבָאָרֶץ: ◂ מְקִימִי מֵעָפָר דָּל, מֵאַשְׁפֹּת יָרִים אֶבְיוֹן: לְהוֹשִׁיבִי עִם־נְדִיבִים, עִם נְדִיבֵי עַמּוֹ: מוֹשִׁיבִי עֲקֶרֶת הַבַּיִת, אֵם־הַבָּנִים שְׂמֵחָה, הַלְלוּיָהּ: תהלים קיג

generations observed the Torah, as communicated from one generation to the next,) exists side by side with the text-based interpretive tradition that follows accepted hermeneutic rules to understand the words of the Torah. In complementary fashion they clarify for each succeeding generation the halakhic practices of the *Mesora* which we are to follow. Similarly on a personal level: we learn the *Mesora* by observing how our parents, grandparents, and teachers act, and we also learn it by studying Torah texts. This distinction is further clarified in our commentary to the first *mishna* of *Pirkei Avot*, as explained by R. Joseph B. Soloveitchik (R. Basil Herring).

הַלֵּל / HALLEL

The sages referred to this prayer (that we refer to as *Hallel*) as "the Egyptian *Hallel*" because the six psalms (113–118) that are at its core refer repeatedly to the events surrounding the Exodus from Egypt. The Gemara (*Pesaḥim* 117a) understands *Hallel* to also be commemorating the events at Sinai, the Messianic era, and the Resurrection of the Dead.

According to the Gemara (*Arakhin* 11a) *Hallel* is recited on Yom Tov to commemorate the *Hallel* recited by the Levites during the Yom Tov *Musaf* sacrifice. It explains further that on the last six days of Pesaḥ, when the *Musaf* sacrifices offered each day were identical in number, only "half-*Hallel*" (so-called in reference to omitted verses from some of those psalms) was recited. On Rosh Ḥodesh Ashkenazic custom is also to recite half-*Hallel*, as Rosh Ḥodesh is neither a Yom Tov nor a commemoration of a historical event.

We recite *Hallel* on Ḥanukka for the sake of פִּרְסוּמֵי נִסָּא (publicizing the miracle) of the Maccabean restoration of national sovereignty. From this derives the view of the Vilna Gaon that *Hallel* is said following *Ma'ariv* on the night of the *Seder* to publicize the miracles of the Exodus. On the other hand *Hallel* is not recited on Purim for (a) it did not lead to sovereignty,

HALLEL

On the first two days of Pesaḥ, on Shavuot; the entire festival of Sukkot, Shemini Atzeret and Simḥat Torah, and Ḥanukka, Full Hallel is said. On Rosh Ḥodesh and the last six days of Pesaḥ, Half Hallel is said. Regarding Yom HaAtzma'ut and Yom Yerushalayim, see the commentary below.

בָּרוּךְ BLESSED are You, Lord, our God, King of the universe, Who has sanctified us with His commandments and has commanded us about the reading of the Hallel.

Ps. 113 הַלְלוּיָהּ PRAISE THE LORD. Praise, you servants of the Lord. Praise the name of the Lord. Blessed be the name of the Lord from now and forevermore. From the rising of the sun to its going down the Lord's name is praised. The Lord is high above all nations. His glory is above the heavens. Who is like the Lord our God, Who dwells on high, Who looks down low upon the heavens and upon the earth? ▸ He raises the poor from the dust, from the dunghill He lifts the needy, to seat him with princes, with the princes of his people. He seats the barren woman in her house as the joyful mother of children. Praise the Lord.

---

and (b) the reading of the *Megilla* is in lieu of *Hallel* (R. Joseph B. Soloveitchik).

According to R. Ḥai Gaon *Hallel* is also recited in commemoration of a particular miracle, hence it is recited at the *Seder* in commemoration of the events described in the *Haggada*. For this reason, R. Yitzḥak Ze'ev Soloveitchik considers the *Hallel* recited at the *Seder* to be the basis for the *Hallel* recited on the other festivals that similarly commemorate the Exodus.

This in turn leads to the contemporary issue whether *Hallel* is to be recited as a result of what many consider to be miraculous events surrounding the establishment and subsequent military victories of the State of Israel against all odds. R. Ovadia Yosef rules that on these days *Hallel* is optional and hence to be recited without a *berakha*. R. Meshulam Roth and R. Shlomo Goren require *Hallel* with a *berakha*. Advocates of such recital note that the Gemara (*Sanhedrin* 94a) criticizes Hezekiah for failing to sing God's praises when the nation was saved from Sennacherib. R. Joseph B. Soloveitchik advised those who recite *Hallel* on these days to do so after the *Kaddish Titkabel*, and without the *berakhot* with which it opens and closes.

הַלְלוּיָהּ, הַלְלוּ עַבְדֵי ה' – *Praise the Lord. Praise, you servants of the Lord.* The Exodus involved two redemptions, one physical and the other spiritual. These verses first praise God for terminating our enslavement to Pharaoh so that we could instead become עַבְדֵי ה' (God's servants.) Then they praise שֵׁם ה' (His name) to reflect the resulting mission of the Jewish people to promote God's name in the world. Even though the first redemption can be temporarily interrupted if we are exiled and become subject to others, the second redemption is never suspended, for we are always duty-bound to sanctify God's name in the world. Hence the next verse declares "may

תהלים קיד **בְּצֵאת יִשְׂרָאֵל** מִמִּצְרָיִם, בֵּית יַעֲקֹב מֵעַם לֹעֵז: הָיְתָה יְהוּדָה
לְקָדְשׁוֹ, יִשְׂרָאֵל מַמְשְׁלוֹתָיו: הַיָּם רָאָה וַיָּנֹס,
הַיַּרְדֵּן יִסֹּב לְאָחוֹר: הֶהָרִים רָקְדוּ כְאֵילִים, גְּבָעוֹת כִּבְנֵי־צֹאן:
› מַה־לְּךָ הַיָּם כִּי תָנוּס, הַיַּרְדֵּן תִּסֹּב לְאָחוֹר: הֶהָרִים תִּרְקְדוּ
כְאֵילִים, גְּבָעוֹת כִּבְנֵי־צֹאן: מִלִּפְנֵי אָדוֹן חוּלִי אָרֶץ, מִלִּפְנֵי אֱלוֹהַּ
יַעֲקֹב: הַהֹפְכִי הַצּוּר אֲגַם־מָיִם, חַלָּמִישׁ לְמַעְיְנוֹ־מָיִם:

Omit on ראש חודש (*except on* חנוכה) *and the last six days of* פסח*:*

תהלים קטו **לֹא לָנוּ** יהוה לֹא לָנוּ, כִּי־לְשִׁמְךָ תֵּן כָּבוֹד, עַל־חַסְדְּךָ עַל־אֲמִתֶּךָ: לָמָּה
יֹאמְרוּ הַגּוֹיִם אַיֵּה־נָא אֱלֹהֵיהֶם: וֵאלֹהֵינוּ בַשָּׁמָיִם, כֹּל אֲשֶׁר־
חָפֵץ עָשָׂה: עֲצַבֵּיהֶם כֶּסֶף וְזָהָב, מַעֲשֵׂה יְדֵי אָדָם: פֶּה־לָהֶם וְלֹא יְדַבֵּרוּ,
עֵינַיִם לָהֶם וְלֹא יִרְאוּ: אָזְנַיִם לָהֶם וְלֹא יִשְׁמָעוּ, אַף לָהֶם וְלֹא יְרִיחוּן:
יְדֵיהֶם וְלֹא יְמִישׁוּן, רַגְלֵיהֶם וְלֹא יְהַלֵּכוּ, לֹא־יֶהְגּוּ בִּגְרוֹנָם: כְּמוֹהֶם יִהְיוּ
עֹשֵׂיהֶם, כֹּל אֲשֶׁר־בֹּטֵחַ בָּהֶם: › יִשְׂרָאֵל בְּטַח בַּיהוה, עֶזְרָם וּמָגִנָּם הוּא:
בֵּית אַהֲרֹן בִּטְחוּ בַיהוה, עֶזְרָם וּמָגִנָּם הוּא: יִרְאֵי יהוה בִּטְחוּ בַיהוה,
עֶזְרָם וּמָגִנָּם הוּא:

---

the name of the Lord be blessed from now and forevermore" (*Ḥatam Sofer*).

לְהוֹשִׁיבִי עִם־נְדִיבִים, עִם נְדִיבֵי עַמּוֹ – *To seat him with princes, with the princes of his people* (previous page). The duplication of "princes" and "princes of His people" refers to two levels of honor bestowed on the faithful. The lower occurs when traveling to a distant place and there meeting well-known "princes" who do not know the traveler. A more significant validation is when we are recognized by "princes of our people," i.e., those princes among whom we live, and who consequently know us well. God rewards the faithful in both contexts – bringing us to where we can feel honored, but also by helping us to be truly deserving of respect (*Hayyei Adam*).

PSALMS 114/115

These two psalms should be seen as forming a single unit within *Hallel*, as the first does not end nor the second begin with the usual opening and closing phrases. In fact in the Aleppo Codex, the Septuagint, and the Arabic translation of the Psalms by Sa'adia Gaon, they are joined together. It is likely that they were originally recited at festive Temple gatherings following sacrifices, alternating between Israelites, Levites, *Kohanim*, and "those who fear the Lord" (R. Amos Ḥakham).

PSALM 114

הָיְתָה יְהוּדָה לְקָדְשׁוֹ – *Judah became His sanctuary*. The tribe of Judah is singled out for special praise because of the selflessness of its leaders. These included Naḥshon ben Aminadav (who waded into the Sea of Reeds even before it split), and Ḥur (who sacrificed his life in a desperate effort to prevent the worship of the Golden Calf) (R. Meir Simḥa of Dvinsk).

Ps. 114 **בְּצֵאת יִשְׂרָאֵל** WHEN ISRAEL WENT out of Egypt, the house of Jacob from a people of a foreign language, Judah became His sanctuary, Israel His dominion. The sea saw and fled, the Jordan turned backward. The mountains skipped like rams, the hills like lambs. ▸ What has happened to you, O sea, that you flee? O Jordan, that you turn backward? You mountains, that you skip like rams? You hills, like lambs? Tremble, O earth, at the presence of the Lord, at the presence of the God of Jacob, Who turned the rock into a pool of water, the flint into a fountain of water.

Omit on Rosh Ḥodesh (except on Ḥanukka) and the last six days of Pesaḥ:

Ps. 115 **לֹא לָנוּ** NOT TO US, O Lord, not to us, but to Your name give glory, for Your loving-kindness and for Your truth. Why should the nations say: "Where, pray, is their God?" But our God is in the heavens. All that He wishes He does. Their idols are silver and gold, the work of man's hands. They have a mouth but they do not speak; they have eyes but they do not see. They have ears but they do not hear; they have a nose but they do not smell. They have hands but they do not touch; they have legs but they do not walk; they do not emit sound with their throat. They that make them shall be like them, everyone who trusts in them. ▸ Israel, trust in the Lord. He is their help and their shield. House of Aaron, trust in the Lord. He is their help and their shield. You who fear the Lord, trust in the Lord. He is their help and their shield.

אֱלוֹהַּ יַעֲקֹב – *God of Jacob.* The correct pronunciation of God's name in this phrase is *"Elo-ah"*, insofar as the *pataḥ* under the *heh* is a *pataḥ genuva*, similar to the usage found in the word *No'aḥ*.

PSALM 115

עֲצַבֵּיהֶם – *Their idols.* The root of the word for idols used here is עָצָב which has a connotation of both "sadness" as well as "shaped." That is, idols that are shaped by humans bring nothing but sadness to their devotees (Ibn Ezra).

יִשְׂרָאֵל בְּטַח בַּה׳, עֶזְרָם וּמָגִנָּם הוּא – *Israel, trust in the Lord. He is their help and their shield.* These three verses teach that we do not trust in God *because* He protects us. It is the other way around, i.e., His providence protects us only to the extent that we fully trust in Him. Thus the verses declare that when we trust in Him, He will be our help and shield. For the same reason God led the Israelites out of Egypt along a lengthy route (Ex. 13:17) to avoid war, because they had no faith in Him, and as a result He would not protect them from their enemies. Taking the direct route would have resulted in military defeat or a return to Egyptian slavery. To emphasize this lesson the verses in this Psalm repeat three times that we must trust in God, for then, and only then, will He be our help and our shield (R. Moshe Feinstein).

יהוה זְכָרָנוּ יְבָרֵךְ, יְבָרֵךְ אֶת־בֵּית יִשְׂרָאֵל, יְבָרֵךְ אֶת־בֵּית אַהֲרֹן: יְבָרֵךְ יִרְאֵי יהוה, הַקְּטַנִּים עִם־הַגְּדֹלִים: יֹסֵף יהוה עֲלֵיכֶם, עֲלֵיכֶם וְעַל־בְּנֵיכֶם: בְּרוּכִים אַתֶּם לַיהוה, עֹשֵׂה שָׁמַיִם וָאָרֶץ: › הַשָּׁמַיִם שָׁמַיִם לַיהוה, וְהָאָרֶץ נָתַן לִבְנֵי־אָדָם: לֹא הַמֵּתִים יְהַלְלוּ־יָהּ, וְלֹא כָּל־יֹרְדֵי דוּמָה: וַאֲנַחְנוּ נְבָרֵךְ יָהּ, מֵעַתָּה וְעַד־עוֹלָם, הַלְלוּיָהּ:

Omit on ראש חודש (*except on* חנוכה) *and the last six days of* פסח*:*

תהלים קטז

אָהַבְתִּי, כִּי־יִשְׁמַע יהוה, אֶת־קוֹלִי תַּחֲנוּנָי: כִּי־הִטָּה אָזְנוֹ לִי, וּבְיָמַי אֶקְרָא: אֲפָפוּנִי חֶבְלֵי־מָוֶת, וּמְצָרֵי שְׁאוֹל מְצָאוּנִי, צָרָה וְיָגוֹן אֶמְצָא: וּבְשֵׁם־יהוה אֶקְרָא, אָנָּה יהוה מַלְּטָה נַפְשִׁי: חַנּוּן יהוה וְצַדִּיק, וֵאלֹהֵינוּ מְרַחֵם: שֹׁמֵר פְּתָאִים יהוה, דַּלּוֹתִי וְלִי יְהוֹשִׁיעַ: שׁוּבִי נַפְשִׁי לִמְנוּחָיְכִי, כִּי־יהוה גָּמַל עָלָיְכִי: כִּי חִלַּצְתָּ נַפְשִׁי מִמָּוֶת, אֶת־עֵינִי מִן־דִּמְעָה, אֶת־רַגְלִי מִדֶּחִי: › אֶתְהַלֵּךְ לִפְנֵי יהוה, בְּאַרְצוֹת הַחַיִּים: הֶאֱמַנְתִּי כִּי אֲדַבֵּר, אֲנִי עָנִיתִי מְאֹד: אֲנִי אָמַרְתִּי בְחָפְזִי, כָּל־הָאָדָם כֹּזֵב:

מָה־אָשִׁיב לַיהוה, כָּל־תַּגְמוּלוֹהִי עָלָי: כּוֹס־יְשׁוּעוֹת אֶשָּׂא, וּבְשֵׁם יהוה אֶקְרָא: נְדָרַי לַיהוה אֲשַׁלֵּם, נֶגְדָה־נָּא לְכָל־עַמּוֹ: יָקָר בְּעֵינֵי יהוה, הַמָּוְתָה לַחֲסִידָיו: אָנָּה יהוה כִּי־אֲנִי עַבְדֶּךָ, אֲנִי־עַבְדְּךָ בֶּן־אֲמָתֶךָ, פִּתַּחְתָּ לְמוֹסֵרָי: › לְךָ־אֶזְבַּח זֶבַח

יְבָרֵךְ יִרְאֵי ה׳, הַקְּטַנִּים עִם־הַגְּדֹלִים – *He will bless those who fear the Lord, the small together with the great*. It is only when the "small ones" walk with the "great ones," consulting with them and following their advice, that God blesses them. But if the "small ones" act only according to their independent views without turning to the "great ones" to help them become truly God-fearing, then God does not provide His *berakha*. Rashi comments that in this verse "God-fearing" refers to converts. Righteous converts are especially God-fearing as shown by their courageous choice to embrace God and the Jewish people. Thus we also learn from this verse that when קְטַנִּים (minors) are converted it must be עִם־הַגְּדֹלִים (with their adults), that is, at the initiative of parents whose God-fearing ways are a model for the minor to follow (R. Chaim Kanievsky).

יֹסֵף ה׳ עֲלֵיכֶם, עֲלֵיכֶם וְעַל־בְּנֵיכֶם – *The Lord will make you increase, you and your children*. God shall extend His blessing of fertility and abundance into the third generation. By using the particular verb יוֹסֵף (He will increase), the Psalmist evokes the great blessings and increase bestowed by יוֹסֵף (Joseph) on four generations of his descendants (Gen. 50:23) (R. Yitzchak Etshalom).

יהוה THE LORD has remembered us, He will bless us. He will bless the house of Israel; He will bless the house of Aaron. He will bless those who fear the Lord, the small together with the great. The Lord will make you increase, you and your children. May you be blessed of the Lord, the Maker of heaven and earth. ▸ The heavens are the heavens of the Lord, but He has given the earth to the children of man. The dead do not praise the Lord, nor all who go down into silence. But we will bless the Lord from now and forevermore. Praise the Lord.

Omit on Rosh Ḥodesh (except on Ḥanukka) and the last six days of Pesaḥ:

Ps. 116 אָהַבְתִּי I LOVE that the Lord has heard my voice, my supplications, that He has inclined His ear to me, and all my days I will call. The pangs of death encompassed me, and the straits of the underworld beset me. I found trouble and sorrow. But I called upon the name of the Lord: "I beseech You, O Lord, deliver my soul." Gracious is the Lord and righteous, and our God is merciful. The Lord preserves the simple. I was brought low and He saved me. Return to your rest, O my soul, for the Lord has dealt bountifully with you. Indeed, You have delivered my soul from death, my eyes from tears, my feet from stumbling. ▸ I will walk before the Lord in the lands of the living. I believed even when I said: "I have been greatly afflicted." I said in my haste: "The whole of man is delusive."

מָה־אָשִׁיב WHAT CAN I RENDER to the Lord for all His benefits toward me? I lift up the cup of salvation, and I call upon the name of the Lord. I pay my vows to the Lord in the presence of all His people. Precious in the eyes of the Lord is the death of His pious ones. I beseech You, O Lord, for I am Your servant. I am Your servant, the son of Your handmaid. You have loosened my bonds. ▸ I offer to You a sacrifice

---

PSALM 116

אָהַבְתִּי – *I love*. This psalm is intended to accompany an offering pledged in great distress. Although it is written in the first person singular, it is also the voice of the People of Israel as a whole, thanking God for His salvation (R. Amos Ḥakham).

לְךָ־אֶזְבַּח זֶבַח תּוֹדָה, וּבְשֵׁם ה׳ אֶקְרָא – *I offer to You a sacrifice of thanksgiving, and I call upon the name of the Lord*. This entire paragraph relates to the קָרְבַּן תּוֹדָה (thanksgiving offering) whose purpose was to acknowledge God's indispensable role in saving us from peril. The thanksgiving sacrifice and *berakha* acknowledge the role of natural cause as well as human effort in overcoming our perils, but they also make it clear that we recognize that these natural processes are ultimately governed by God's will and His laws. Thus when we are saved from

תּוֹדָה, וּבְשֵׁם יהוה אֶקְרָא: נְדָרַי לַיהוה אֲשַׁלֵּם, נֶגְדָה־נָּא לְכָל־עַמּוֹ:
בְּחַצְרוֹת בֵּית יהוה, בְּתוֹכֵכִי יְרוּשָׁלָםִ, הַלְלוּיָהּ:

תהלים קיז **הַלְלוּ** אֶת־יהוה כָּל־גּוֹיִם, שַׁבְּחוּהוּ כָּל־הָאֻמִּים: כִּי גָבַר עָלֵינוּ
חַסְדּוֹ, וֶאֱמֶת־יהוה לְעוֹלָם, הַלְלוּיָהּ:

The following verses are chanted by the שליח ציבור. *At the end of each verse, the* קהל *responds:* הודו ליהוה כי־טוב, כי לעולם חסדו *and then recites the next verse.*

On סוכות, *the* לולב *and* אתרוג *are waved, three waves for each word of the verse (except God's name). On the first word, wave forward, then, on subsequent words, wave right, back, left, up and down respectively. The* שליח ציבור *waves only for the first two verses. The* קהל *waves each time the first verse is said in response.*

תהלים קיח **הוֹדוּ** לַיהוה כִּי־טוֹב כִּי לְעוֹלָם חַסְדּוֹ:
יֹאמַר־נָא יִשְׂרָאֵל כִּי לְעוֹלָם חַסְדּוֹ:
יֹאמְרוּ־נָא בֵית־אַהֲרֹן כִּי לְעוֹלָם חַסְדּוֹ:
יֹאמְרוּ־נָא יִרְאֵי יהוה כִּי לְעוֹלָם חַסְדּוֹ:

misfortune and peril, or recover from sickness, we must make sure to thank and praise Him. That is why in the *Amida* prayer for healing we declare כִּי תְהִלָּתֵנוּ אָתָּה (For You are the One we praise) (R. Shlomo Zalman Auerbach).

נְדָרַי לַה׳ אֲשַׁלֵּם... בְּתוֹכֵכִי יְרוּשָׁלָםִ – *I pay my vows to the Lord... in your midst, O Jerusalem.* These verses refer to the process by which the thanksgiving-offering was brought, as described in Leviticus 7:12–13. In addition to making the sacrifice in the Temple itself, the individual would also host a public festive meal, during which he or she would recount in detail the events that were the reason for thanksgiving. Hence the psalm makes a point of stating that the ceremony take place in the presence of "all His people" and "in the midst of Jerusalem," not just within the Temple limits. In sum, a manifestation of God's providence requires a סְעוּדַת הוֹדָאָה (thanksgiving meal) so that others can share in the recognition of divine compassion (*Netziv*).

This insight is consistent with the Mishna (*Zevaḥim* 5:6), which we recite each morning in *Eizehu Mekoman* before the *Pesukei DeZimra* that the meat of the thanksgiving offering could be prepared in any way desired, and eaten by all Jews anywhere in the city of Jerusalem until the hour of midnight that follows the sacrifice.

It is not uncommon that, when imperiled and anxious for God's salvation, we vow that if only God will save us, we will reciprocate by acting in specific ways that God would approve. It may well be that this is why the Psalmist here pointedly declares "I will fulfill my vows to the Lord," i.e., "I have not forgotten what I undertook to do at the time were God to save me, and so in the presence of all present I declare that I will indeed honor that commitment" (R. Basil Herring).

כִּי גָבַר עָלֵינוּ חַסְדּוֹ, וֶאֱמֶת־ה׳ לְעוֹלָם – *For His loving-kindness is mighty toward us, and the truth of the Lord is forever.* The question is well known: why should the nations praise God for the kindnesses shown to "us," i.e., the Jewish people? Furthermore, why does this verse connect God's kindnesses to His eternal truth?

of thanksgiving, and I call upon the name of the Lord. I pay my vows to the Lord in the presence of all His people, in the courtyards of the house of the Lord, in your midst, O Jerusalem. Praise the Lord.

Ps. 117 הַלְלוּ PRAISE the Lord, all nations. Laud Him, all the peoples. For His loving-kindness is mighty toward us, and the truth of the Lord is forever. Praise the Lord.

The following verses are chanted by the Leader. At the end of each verse, the congregation responds, "Thank the Lord for He is good; His loving-kindness is for ever" and then recites the next verse.

On Sukkot, the lulav and etrog are waved, three waves for each word of the verse (except God's name). On the first word, wave forward, then, on subsequent words, wave right, back, left, up and down respectively. The Leader waves only for the first two verses. The congregation waves each time the first verse is said in response.

Ps. 118 הודו GIVE THANKS to the Lord, for He is good,
for His loving-kindness is forever.

LET ISRAEL NOW say,
for His loving-kindness is forever.

LET THE HOUSE of Aaron now say,
for His loving-kindness is forever.

LET THOSE who fear the Lord now say,
for His loving-kindness is forever.

The answer can be derived from the Gemara (*Avoda Zara* 3a) which teaches that God made the continued existence of His creation dependent on the Jewish people accepting the Torah. Accordingly this verse is saying that there will come a time when the nations will all recognize that their own existence and well-being has always depended on God's kindness to Israel in giving us the Torah that embodies universal and eternal truth (R. Yaakov Ettlinger).

Compassion and truth are generally mutually exclusive. When someone is compassionate that means they bestow something that has not been earned. This, however, is not the case with God's compassion, for in Him all contradictions are reconciled. We too should always seek to imitate this attribute of God, by always pursuing truth in compassionate ways, which is what the Torah, which embodies both truth and compassion, teaches us. Beit Shammai and Beit Hillel embodied this principle, for even though they often strongly disagreed in their pursuit of the truth, nonetheless, as the Gemara (*Yevamot* 14b) tells us, "they demonstrated love and fellowship toward each other in accordance with the prophet's exhortation to 'love truth *and* peace'" (Zechariah 8:19) (R. Yerucham Levovitz).

PSALM 118

Hallel from this point until (but not including)

מִן־הַמֵּצַר קָרָֽאתִי יָּהּ, עָנָֽנִי בַמֶּרְחָב יָהּ: יהוה לִי לֹא אִירָא, מַה־
יַּעֲשֶׂה לִי אָדָם: יהוה לִי בְּעֹזְרָי, וַאֲנִי אֶרְאֶה בְשֹׂנְאָי:
טוֹב לַחֲסוֹת בַּיהוה, מִבְּטֹחַ בָּאָדָם: טוֹב לַחֲסוֹת בַּיהוה, מִבְּטֹחַ
בִּנְדִיבִים: כָּל־גּוֹיִם סְבָבֽוּנִי, בְּשֵׁם יהוה כִּי אֲמִילַם: סַבּֽוּנִי גַם־
סְבָבֽוּנִי, בְּשֵׁם יהוה כִּי אֲמִילַם: סַבּֽוּנִי כִדְבֹרִים, דֹּעֲכוּ כְּאֵשׁ קוֹצִים,
בְּשֵׁם יהוה כִּי אֲמִילַם: דָּחֹה דְחִיתַֽנִי לִנְפֹּל, וַיהוה עֲזָרָֽנִי: עָזִּי
וְזִמְרָת יָהּ, וַיְהִי־לִי לִישׁוּעָה: קוֹל רִנָּה וִישׁוּעָה בְּאָהֳלֵי צַדִּיקִים,
יְמִין יהוה עֹשָׂה חָֽיִל: יְמִין יהוה רוֹמֵמָה, יְמִין יהוה עֹשָׂה חָֽיִל:
לֹא־אָמוּת כִּי־אֶחְיֶה, וַאֲסַפֵּר מַעֲשֵׂי יָהּ: יַסֹּר יִסְּרַֽנִּי יָּהּ, וְלַמָּֽוֶת לֹא
נְתָנָֽנִי: ‹ פִּתְחוּ־לִי שַׁעֲרֵי־צֶֽדֶק, אָבֹא־בָם אוֹדֶה יָהּ: זֶה־הַשַּֽׁעַר
לַיהוה, צַדִּיקִים יָבֹֽאוּ בוֹ:

---

the final paragraph consists of only one psalm. The Gemara (*Pesaḥim* 118a) teaches that in the Temple period this psalm was recited following a military victory, when the leadership would lead the people in public acknowledgment of God's salvation. This also accounts for its being recited on the three pilgrim festivals that mark the various divine protections experienced during the Exodus and forty years sojourn in Sinai. When recited on those occasions the language of the psalm was understood in the context of the particular festival (R. Amos Ḥakham).

ה׳ לִי בְּעֹזְרָי, וַאֲנִי אֶרְאֶה בְשֹׂנְאָי – *The Lord is for me among my helpers, and I will see the downfall of those who hate me.* There are two kinds of enemies. The first does not disguise its harmful intentions, whereas the second pretends to be a friend or ally but in reality seeks our harm. Of these two, the second is far more dangerous. Here David, whose life and rule were repeatedly exposed to danger, asks God to help him recognize such "friends" who are not to be trusted, recognizing as he did that only God can know a person's real thoughts and intentions (Vilna Gaon).

However, such betrayals did not lead David to cynicism or blanket distrust of everyone professing to be his friend or supporter. After all, he had every reason to suspect that Jonathan the son of King Saul was not, and could not be, a genuine friend, given Jonathan's clear interest in succeeding his royal father. Yet David trusted Jonathan with his life and their friendship became the very model of mutual devotion. This sensitive balance is subsequently reflected, as recounted in the Gemara (*Berakhot* 16b), in the prayer of R. Yehuda HaNasi, who would always conclude his *Amida* by petitioning God to protect him from a חָבֵר רָע (false friend), a prayer that we repeat every morning following בִּרְכוֹת הַשַּׁחַר (morning blessings) (R. Basil Herring).

כָּל־גּוֹיִם סְבָבֽוּנִי – *All nations encompassed me.* These verses repeat סְבָבֽוּנִי (surround me) with

מִן־הַמֵּצַר FROM DISTRESS I called upon the Lord. The Lord answered me with enlargement. The Lord is for me, I will not fear. What can man do to me? The Lord is for me among my helpers, and I will see the downfall of those who hate me. It is better to seek refuge in the Lord than to trust in man. It is better to seek refuge in the Lord than to trust in princes. All nations encompassed me. In the name of the Lord I surely destroyed them. They encompassed me, yes, they encompassed me. In the name of the Lord I surely destroyed them. They encompassed me like bees. They crackled like the fire of thorns. In the name of the Lord I surely destroyed them. You harshly pushed me to fall, but the Lord helped me. The Lord is my strength and my song, and He has become my salvation. The voice of rejoicing and salvation is in the tents of the righteous. The right hand of the Lord does valiantly. The right hand of the Lord is exalted. The right hand of the Lord does valiantly. I did not die but I lived, and I declare the deeds of the Lord. The Lord made me suffer severely, but He did not give me over to death. ▸ Open to me the gates of righteousness. Let me enter them and I will thank the Lord. This is the gate of the Lord. Let the righteous enter it.

---

slight variations four times. This is because some of our enemies, like Pharaoh, have sought to destroy us by frontal attack, while others, like Balaam, did so by pretending to be our friends. In these verses David references both groups. סְבָבוּנִי can be understood as "they surrounded (or have surrounded) me," to openly threaten harm, whereas סַבּוּנִי can be understood as "they (have) turned me around," i.e., to disorient and confuse me so that I will follow in their ways. David proclaims that "either way I will resist and defeat them in the name of God." The Psalmist then invokes a second metaphor to underscore the point. The enemy who pretends to be a friend is like the beekeeper who uses smoke from a burning bush to neutralize the bees' defense mechanism, allowing the keeper to draw close without being bitten. The Psalmist declares that such "smokescreens" will be resisted by the faithful, who will see them for what they are (R. Chaim Berlin).

Throughout its history the Jewish people has been subject to both predations, the one resulting in physical harm and destruction, the other leading to assimilation and abandonment of Jewish identity. Echoing the Psalmist, it is only by virtue of an undiluted commitment over the generations to sanctify "the name of God" that we have survived and flourished as a nation apart.

אוֹדְךָ כִּי עֲנִיתָנִי, וַתְּהִי־לִי לִישׁוּעָה:
אוֹדְךָ כִּי עֲנִיתָנִי, וַתְּהִי־לִי לִישׁוּעָה:
אֶבֶן מָאֲסוּ הַבּוֹנִים, הָיְתָה לְרֹאשׁ פִּנָּה:
אֶבֶן מָאֲסוּ הַבּוֹנִים, הָיְתָה לְרֹאשׁ פִּנָּה:
מֵאֵת יהוה הָיְתָה זֹּאת, הִיא נִפְלָאת בְּעֵינֵינוּ:
מֵאֵת יהוה הָיְתָה זֹּאת, הִיא נִפְלָאת בְּעֵינֵינוּ:
זֶה־הַיּוֹם עָשָׂה יהוה, נָגִילָה וְנִשְׂמְחָה בוֹ:
זֶה־הַיּוֹם עָשָׂה יהוה, נָגִילָה וְנִשְׂמְחָה בוֹ:

On סוכות*, the* לולב *and* אתרוג *are waved while saying* אָנָּא יהוה הוֹשִׁיעָה נָּא*,*
three waves for each word of the verse (except God's name). On the first word, wave forward and right; third word: back and left; fourth word: up and down.

followed by קהל*:* שליח ציבור

אָנָּא יהוה הוֹשִׁיעָה נָּא:
אָנָּא יהוה הוֹשִׁיעָה נָּא:
אָנָּא יהוה הַצְלִיחָה נָא:
אָנָּא יהוה הַצְלִיחָה נָא:

בָּרוּךְ הַבָּא בְּשֵׁם יהוה, בֵּרַכְנוּכֶם מִבֵּית יהוה:
בָּרוּךְ הַבָּא בְּשֵׁם יהוה, בֵּרַכְנוּכֶם מִבֵּית יהוה:

REPETITION OF VERSES
The Gemara (*Sukka* 32a) accounts for various customs regarding repetition of some verses of this psalm. Starting in the early medieval period it became the widespread Ashkenazic custom to repeat the verses starting with אוֹדְךָ, to reflect the pattern of repetition in the earlier verses of the psalm.

אֶבֶן מָאֲסוּ הַבּוֹנִים, הָיְתָה לְרֹאשׁ פִּנָּה – *The stone that the builders rejected has become the chief cornerstone.* The Gemara (*Pesaḥim* 117a) records two opinions regarding this entire chapter of Psalms: one is that it refers to the events of David's life; the other sees it as referring to the exile of the Jewish people. According to the second opinion, this verse describes the Jewish people as a cornerstone upholding the edifice of humanity by virtue of its upholding the laws of the Torah, whether those of a purely religious nature, or those intended to further social justice. Throughout our exiles we have been rejected by those claiming to uphold civilization. One day, however, we will be recognized for what we have always been, i.e., the foundation of mankind (Radak).

אוֹדְךָ I GIVE THANKS to You, for You have answered me,
and You have become my salvation.

I give thanks to You, for You have answered me, and You have become my salvation.

THE STONE that the builders rejected has become
the chief cornerstone.

The stone that the builders rejected has become the chief cornerstone.

THIS WAS from the Lord; it is marvelous in our eyes.

This was from the Lord; it is marvelous in our eyes.

THIS IS the day on which the Lord has acted.
Let us be glad and rejoice in Him.

This is the day on which the Lord has acted. Let us be glad and rejoice in Him.

On Sukkot, the lulav and etrog are waved while saying "Lord, please, save us," three waves for each word of the verse (except God's name). On the first word, wave forward and right; third word: back and left; fourth word: up and down.

Leader followed by congregation:

אָנָּא WE BESEECH YOU, O Lord, please save us.
WE BESEECH YOU, O Lord, please save us.
WE BESEECH YOU, O Lord, please give us success.
WE BESEECH YOU, O Lord, please give us success.

בָּרוּךְ BLESSED in the name of the Lord is he who comes.
We bless you from the house of the Lord.

Blessed in the name of the Lord is he who comes.
We bless you from the house of the Lord.

זֶה־הַיּוֹם עָשָׂה ה׳, נָגִילָה וְנִשְׂמְחָה בוֹ – *This is the day on which the Lord has acted. Let us be glad and rejoice in Him.* The *Midrash* teaches us that when something good transpires it is better to rejoice not at the event itself but rather at the larger lesson implied by that event. After all, an event might be fleeting and subject to reversal, but if we see in it the hand of God, our joy is complete because we recognize that God's will must prevail. Thus the verse is to be understood as saying "we will rejoice and be happy on account of You God" (R. Yaakov Ariel).

בָּרוּךְ הַבָּא – *Blessed... is he who comes.* These final four verses were likely spoken at the climax of the sacrificial ceremony, as the animals were handed over to be slaughtered. The first verse was uttered by the *Kohen* blessing the pilgrim, the ensuing verses were spoken by the pilgrim – first recognizing that God had inspired him to make this sacrifice, then instructing

אֵל יהוה וַיָּאֶר לָנוּ, אִסְרוּ־חַג בַּעֲבֹתִים עַד־קַרְנוֹת הַמִּזְבֵּחַ:
אֵל יהוה וַיָּאֶר לָנוּ, אִסְרוּ־חַג בַּעֲבֹתִים עַד־קַרְנוֹת הַמִּזְבֵּחַ:

אֵלִי אַתָּה וְאוֹדֶךָּ, אֱלֹהַי אֲרוֹמְמֶךָּ:
אֵלִי אַתָּה וְאוֹדֶךָּ, אֱלֹהַי אֲרוֹמְמֶךָּ:

On סוכות*, the* לולב *and* אתרוג *are waved while saying* הוֹדוּ לַיהוה כִּי־טוֹב, כִּי לְעוֹלָם חַסְדּוֹ*, three waves for each word of the verse (except God's name). On the first word, wave forward, then, on subsequent words, wave right, back, left, up and down respectively.*

הוֹדוּ לַיהוה כִּי־טוֹב, כִּי לְעוֹלָם חַסְדּוֹ:
הוֹדוּ לַיהוה כִּי־טוֹב, כִּי לְעוֹלָם חַסְדּוֹ:

יְהַלְלוּךָ יהוה אֱלֹהֵינוּ כָּל מַעֲשֶׂיךָ, וַחֲסִידֶיךָ צַדִּיקִים עוֹשֵׂי רְצוֹנֶךָ, וְכָל עַמְּךָ בֵּית יִשְׂרָאֵל בְּרִנָּה יוֹדוּ וִיבָרְכוּ וִישַׁבְּחוּ וִיפָאֲרוּ וִירוֹמְמוּ וְיַעֲרִיצוּ וְיַקְדִּישׁוּ וְיַמְלִיכוּ אֶת שִׁמְךָ מַלְכֵּנוּ, ‹ כִּי לְךָ טוֹב לְהוֹדוֹת וּלְשִׁמְךָ נָאֶה לְזַמֵּר, כִּי מֵעוֹלָם וְעַד עוֹלָם אַתָּה אֵל. בָּרוּךְ אַתָּה יהוה, מֶלֶךְ מְהֻלָּל בַּתִּשְׁבָּחוֹת.

On ראש חודש *and* חול המועד*, say* קדיש שלם *on page 180 and continue the service with* קריאת התורה *on page 158 (on* הושענא רבה *on page 524).*

On סוכות *some say* הושענות *at this point on page 880, then* קדיש שלם *on page 180.*

On שבת *and* יום טוב*, the service continues with* קדיש שלם *on page 522.*

On weekday חנוכה *(except* ראש חודש טבת*),* יום העצמאות *and* יום ירושלים*, the service continues with* חצי קדיש *on page 156.*

---

the *Kohen* to bind the animal and ready it for slaughter near the altar, and finally proclaiming his loyalty and gratitude to God as the sacrifice was made (R. Amos Ḥakham).

אֵלִי אַתָּה וְאוֹדֶךָּ, אֱלֹהַי אֲרוֹמְמֶךָּ – *You are my God and I give You thanks. You are my God, and I exalt You.* This verse reflects a similar one in the Song of the Israelites at the Sea of Reeds. There they sang זֶה אֵלִי וְאַנְוֵהוּ, אֱלֹהֵי אָבִי וַאֲרֹמְמֶנְהוּ, where God's name אֵל signifies His attribute of mercy (as in אֵל רַחוּם in the Thirteen Attributes of Mercy), while אֱלֹהִים reflects His attribute of judgment. At the Sea of Reeds Israel affirmed זֶה אֵלִי וְאַנְוֵהוּ – i.e., when God is merciful to us (as at the Red Sea) we naturally praise Him, but even אֱלֹהֵי אָבִי וַאֲרֹמְמֶנְהוּ – when He allows us to suffer and thus appears distant or far above us (as during the slavery of our fathers in Egypt) then too we must praise Him. So too this verse in *Hallel* states that we must praise God either way – whether for the kindnesses that He bestows on us, or for the hardships that we cannot understand, because only in the course of time will we, like the generation that left Egypt, be able to comprehend His earlier

GOD is the Lord and He has given us light.
Tie the sacrifice with cords to the horns of the altar.
God is the Lord and He has given us light.
Tie the sacrifice with cords to the horns of the altar.

YOU ARE my God and I give You thanks.
You are my God, and I exalt You.
You are my God and I give You thanks. You are my God, and I exalt You.

On Sukkot, the lulav and etrog are waved while saying "Thank the Lord…," three waves for each word of the verse (except God's name). On the first word, wave forward, then, on subsequent words, wave right, back, left, up and down respectively.

GIVE THANKS TO the Lord, for He is good,
for His loving-kindness is forever.
Give thanks to the Lord, for He is good, for His loving-kindness is forever.

יְהַלְלוּךָ ALL YOUR WORKS will praise You, Lord our God. And Your pious and righteous ones who perform Your will, and all Your people of the house of Israel, will joyously thank, bless, praise, glorify, exalt, extol, sanctify, and proclaim the sovereignty of Your name, O our King. ▸ For it is good to give thanks to You and becoming to sing praises to Your name; from everlasting to everlasting You are God. Blessed are You, Lord, the King Who is extolled with praises.

On Rosh Ḥodesh and Ḥol HaMo'ed, say Full Kaddish on page 181 and continue the service with the Reading of the Torah on page 159 (on Hoshana Raba on page 525).

On Sukkot some say Hoshanot at this point on page 881, then Full Kaddish on page 181.

On Shabbat and Yom Tov, the service continues with Full Kaddish on page 523.

On weekday Ḥanukka (except Rosh Ḥodesh Tevet), Yom HaAtzma'ut and Yom Yerushalayim, the service continues with Half Kaddish on page 157.

---

ways, as God told Moses (Ex. 33:23), "you shall see in hindsight" (*Netziv*).

יְהַלְלוּךָ – *Will praise You.* The entire final paragraph of the *Hallel* refers to the future Messianic redemption. Having expressed our gratitude and praise to God for all that He has done for us and our people since time immemorial, we conclude by proclaiming our utter conviction that in due course "His people the House of Israel" will lead not only all of the nations of the world, but even the inanimate beings in praising, sanctifying, and accepting the sovereignty of "You Who are God from eternity to eternity" (R. Joseph B. Soloveitchik).

מוסף לראש חודש

עמידה

One begins the עמידה *by taking three steps forward (OḤ 95:1). According to some traditions, one should first take three steps back before moving forward (MB 95:3). The* עמידה *is recited with one's feet together. One should try to concentrate on the simple meaning of the words of the* עמידה *with the awareness throughout that one is standing in the presence of the Almighty (OḤ 98:1 and MB 98:1). At the points indicated by* ˚, *bend the knees at the first word, bow at the second, and stand straight before saying God's name.*

דברים לב כִּי שֵׁם יהוה אֶקְרָא, הָבוּ גֹדֶל לֵאלֹהֵינוּ:
תהלים נא אֲדֹנָי, שְׂפָתַי תִּפְתָּח, וּפִי יַגִּיד תְּהִלָּתֶךָ:

אבות

˚בָּרוּךְ אַתָּה יהוה, אֱלֹהֵינוּ וֵאלֹהֵי אֲבוֹתֵינוּ, אֱלֹהֵי אַבְרָהָם, אֱלֹהֵי יִצְחָק, וֵאלֹהֵי יַעֲקֹב, הָאֵל הַגָּדוֹל הַגִּבּוֹר וְהַנּוֹרָא, אֵל עֶלְיוֹן, גּוֹמֵל חֲסָדִים טוֹבִים, וְקוֹנֵה הַכֹּל, וְזוֹכֵר חַסְדֵי אָבוֹת, וּמֵבִיא גוֹאֵל לִבְנֵי בְנֵיהֶם לְמַעַן שְׁמוֹ בְּאַהֲבָה. מֶלֶךְ עוֹזֵר וּמוֹשִׁיעַ וּמָגֵן. ˚בָּרוּךְ אַתָּה יהוה, מָגֵן אַבְרָהָם.

גבורות

אַתָּה גִּבּוֹר לְעוֹלָם, אֲדֹנָי, מְחַיֵּה מֵתִים אַתָּה, רַב לְהוֹשִׁיעַ.

בחורף: מַשִּׁיב הָרוּחַ וּמוֹרִיד הַגֶּשֶׁם

מְכַלְכֵּל חַיִּים בְּחֶסֶד, מְחַיֵּה מֵתִים בְּרַחֲמִים רַבִּים, סוֹמֵךְ נוֹפְלִים, וְרוֹפֵא חוֹלִים, וּמַתִּיר אֲסוּרִים, וּמְקַיֵּם אֱמוּנָתוֹ לִישֵׁנֵי עָפָר. מִי כָמוֹךָ, בַּעַל גְּבוּרוֹת, וּמִי דּוֹמֶה לָּךְ, מֶלֶךְ, מֵמִית וּמְחַיֶּה וּמַצְמִיחַ

מוּסָף לְרֹאשׁ חֹדֶשׁ / ROSH ḤODESH *MUSAF*

Rosh Ḥodesh holds a special place in the heart of the Jewish people. Like the moon, our fate waxes and wanes over time. As the moon reflects the light of the sun, so do we as a nation reflect God's radiance. The moon symbolizes the power granted by God to Israel at the Exodus to determine the lunar calendar. Thus the central section of the Rosh Ḥodesh *Musaf* declares, "You gave Rosh Ḥodesh to Your people," i.e., You handed Your own prerogative over to the Jewish people by empowering the *Sanhedrin*, acting on behalf of all Israel, to regulate the calendar and the precise occurrence of the *Yamim Tovim* (R. Basil Herring).

MUSAF FOR ROSH ḤODESH

AMIDA

One begins the Amida by taking three steps forward (OḤ 95:1). According to some traditions, one should first take three steps back before moving forward (MB 95:3). The Amida is recited with one's feet together. One should try to concentrate on the simple meaning of the words of the Amida with the awareness throughout that one is standing in the presence of the Almighty (OḤ 98:1 and MB 98:1). At the points indicated by ▾, bend the knees at the first word, bow at the second, and stand straight before saying God's name.

Deut. 32 WHEN I proclaim the name of the LORD, ascribe greatness to our God.
Ps. 51 "O my Master, open my lips, and my mouth will relate Your praise."

PATRIARCHS

▾בָּרוּךְ BLESSED ARE YOU, LORD, our God and the God of our fathers, the God of Abraham, the God of Isaac, and the God of Jacob, the God Who is great, mighty, and awesome, God most exalted, Who bestows rewards of benevolent kindness, Who is the Creator of everything, Who remembers all the kind acts of the fathers, and Who brings a redeemer to their children's children, for the sake of His name, with love. King Who helps, saves, and shields, ▾blessed are You, LORD, Shield of Abraham.

GOD'S MIGHT

אַתָּה YOU, my Master, are forever mighty, You are the Resurrector of the dead, with great power to save.

In winter: He makes the wind blow and the rain fall

He sustains the living with kindness, He resurrects the dead with great compassion, He supports those who are falling, He heals the sick, He sets the incarcerated free, and He fulfills what He has promised to those who sleep in the dust. Who is like You, O mighty One, and who can be compared to You, O King Who causes death and resurrects, and Who causes salvation to sprout? Trustworthy

For laws regarding "The repetition of the *Amida,*" see page 107.
For laws regarding "Omission/Insertion of *Mashiv Haru'aḥ,*" see page 109.

יְשׁוּעָה. וְנֶאֱמָן אַתָּה לְהַחֲיוֹת מֵתִים. בָּרוּךְ אַתָּה יהוה, מְחַיֵּה הַמֵּתִים.

When saying the עמידה *silently, continue with* אַתָּה קָדוֹשׁ *below.*

קדושה

During חזרת הש״ץ*, the following is said standing with feet together, rising on the toes at the words indicated by* ^.

קהל *then* ש״ץ: **נְקַדֵּשׁ** אֶת שִׁמְךָ בָּעוֹלָם, כְּשֵׁם שֶׁמַּקְדִּישִׁים אוֹתוֹ בִּשְׁמֵי מָרוֹם, כַּכָּתוּב עַל יַד נְבִיאֶךָ, וְקָרָא זֶה אֶל־זֶה וְאָמַר

ישעיה ו

קהל *then* ש״ץ: ^קָדוֹשׁ, ^קָדוֹשׁ, ^קָדוֹשׁ יהוה צְבָאוֹת, מְלֹא כָל־הָאָרֶץ כְּבוֹדוֹ:

ש״ץ: לְעֻמָּתָם בָּרוּךְ יֹאמֵרוּ

יחזקאל ג

קהל *then* ש״ץ: ^בָּרוּךְ כְּבוֹד־יהוה מִמְּקוֹמוֹ:

ש״ץ: וּבְדִבְרֵי קָדְשְׁךָ כָּתוּב לֵאמֹר

תהלים קמו

קהל *then* ש״ץ: ^יִמְלֹךְ יהוה לְעוֹלָם, אֱלֹהַיִךְ צִיּוֹן לְדֹר וָדֹר, הַלְלוּיָהּ:

ש״ץ: לְדוֹר וָדוֹר נַגִּיד גָּדְלֶךָ, וּלְנֵצַח נְצָחִים קְדֻשָּׁתְךָ נַקְדִּישׁ, וְשִׁבְחֲךָ אֱלֹהֵינוּ מִפִּינוּ לֹא יָמוּשׁ לְעוֹלָם וָעֶד, כִּי אֵל מֶלֶךְ גָּדוֹל וְקָדוֹשׁ אָתָּה. בָּרוּךְ אַתָּה יהוה, הָאֵל הַקָּדוֹשׁ.

The שליח ציבור *continues with* רָאשֵׁי חֳדָשִׁים *below.*

קדושת השם

אַתָּה קָדוֹשׁ וְשִׁמְךָ קָדוֹשׁ. וּקְדוֹשִׁים בְּכָל יוֹם יְהַלְלוּךָ סֶּלָה. בָּרוּךְ אַתָּה יהוה, הָאֵל הַקָּדוֹשׁ.

קדושת היום

רָאשֵׁי חֳדָשִׁים לְעַמְּךָ נָתַתָּ, זְמַן כַּפָּרָה לְכָל תּוֹלְדוֹתָם, בִּהְיוֹתָם מַקְרִיבִים לְפָנֶיךָ זִבְחֵי רָצוֹן, וּשְׂעִירֵי חַטָּאת לְכַפֵּר בַּעֲדָם. זִכָּרוֹן לְכֻלָּם יִהְיוּ, וּתְשׁוּעַת נַפְשָׁם מִיַּד שׂוֹנֵא. מִזְבֵּחַ

זְמַן כַּפָּרָה – *A time of atonement*. The Gemara (*Shevuot* 2b) teaches that the Rosh Ḥodesh sacrifices atone for actions that might have brought impurity into the Temple or its

For laws regarding "*Responding to the Leader during Kedusha,*" see page 510.
For the "*Instructions for someone who made a mistake and recited the wrong Amida,*" see page 397.

are You to resurrect the dead. Blessed are You, LORD, Resurrector of the dead.

When saying the Amida silently, continue with "You are holy" below.

KEDUSHA

During the Leader's Repetition, the following is said standing with feet together, rising on the toes at the words indicated by ▲.

Cong. then Leader: נְקַדֵּשׁ WE WILL SANCTIFY Your name in this world, as they sanctify it in the heavenly heights, as is written by Your prophet:

Is. 6 "They called to one another, saying":

Cong. then Leader: "▲Holy, ▲holy, ▲holy is the LORD of hosts; the whole world is filled with His glory."

Leader: Those who face them declare, "Blessed –"

Ezek. 3 *Cong. then Leader:* ▲"Blessed is the glory of the LORD from His place."

Leader: And in Your holy Writings it is written as follows:

Ps. 146 *Cong. then Leader:* ▲"The LORD will reign forever, Your God, O Zion, to all generations. Praise the LORD."

Leader: To all generations we will proclaim Your greatness, and forever declare Your holiness, and the praise of You, our God, will never leave our mouth, for You are God and King, great and holy; blessed are You, LORD, the holy God.

The Leader continues with "You gave days of Rosh Ḥodesh" below.

HOLINESS

אַתָּה YOU ARE HOLY and Your name is holy, and holy ones will praise You every day, forever. Blessed are You, LORD, the holy God.

KEDUSHAT HAYOM

רָאשֵׁי חֳדָשִׁים YOU GAVE days of Rosh Ḥodesh to Your people, a time of atonement for all their offspring, when they would bring before You offerings for favor and goats of sin-offering to atone on their behalf. They would serve as a remembrance for them all and as a deliverance of their soul from the hand of the hater. May You establish

---

sacrifices (טֻמְאַת מִקְדָּשׁ וְקָדָשָׁיו). For further discussion of this aspect of Rosh Ḥodesh see the Siddur commentary at *Kiddush Levana*, page 751.

זִכָּרוֹן לְכֻלָּם יִהְיוּ – *A remembrance for them all.* Numbers 10:10 states that on the days of our rejoicing, festivals, and Rosh Ḥodesh, we are

חֹדֶשׁ בְּצִיּוֹן תָּכִין, וְעוֹלַת רֹאשׁ חֹדֶשׁ נַעֲלֶה עָלָיו, וּשְׂעִירֵי עִזִּים נַעֲשֶׂה בְרָצוֹן, וּבַעֲבוֹדַת בֵּית הַמִּקְדָּשׁ נִשְׂמַח כֻּלָּנוּ, וּבְשִׁירֵי דָוִד עַבְדְּךָ הַנִּשְׁמָעִים בְּעִירֶךָ, הָאֲמוּרִים לִפְנֵי מִזְבְּחֶךָ. אַהֲבַת עוֹלָם תָּבִיא לָהֶם, וּבְרִית אָבוֹת לַבָּנִים תִּזְכֹּר.

וַהֲבִיאֵנוּ לְצִיּוֹן עִירְךָ בְּרִנָּה, וְלִירוּשָׁלַיִם בֵּית מִקְדָּשְׁךָ בְּשִׂמְחַת עוֹלָם, וְשָׁם נַעֲשֶׂה לְפָנֶיךָ אֶת קָרְבְּנוֹת חוֹבוֹתֵינוּ, תְּמִידִים כְּסִדְרָם וּמוּסָפִים כְּהִלְכָתָם.

וְאֶת מוּסַף יוֹם רֹאשׁ הַחֹדֶשׁ הַזֶּה, נַעֲשֶׂה וְנַקְרִיב לְפָנֶיךָ בְּאַהֲבָה כְּמִצְוַת רְצוֹנֶךָ, כְּמוֹ שֶׁכָּתַבְתָּ עָלֵינוּ בְּתוֹרָתֶךָ, עַל יְדֵי מֹשֶׁה עַבְדֶּךָ מִפִּי כְבוֹדֶךָ, כָּאָמוּר

וּבְרָאשֵׁי חָדְשֵׁיכֶם תַּקְרִיבוּ עֹלָה לַיהוה, פָּרִים בְּנֵי־בָקָר שְׁנַיִם וְאַיִל אֶחָד, כְּבָשִׂים בְּנֵי־שָׁנָה שִׁבְעָה, תְּמִימִם: במדבר כח

וּמִנְחָתָם וְנִסְכֵּיהֶם כִּמְדֻבָּר, שְׁלֹשָׁה עֶשְׂרֹנִים לַפָּר, וּשְׁנֵי עֶשְׂרֹנִים לָאָיִל, וְעִשָּׂרוֹן לַכֶּבֶשׂ, וְיַיִן כְּנִסְכּוֹ, וְשָׂעִיר לְכַפֵּר, וּשְׁנֵי תְמִידִים כְּהִלְכָתָם.

אֱלֹהֵינוּ וֵאלֹהֵי אֲבוֹתֵינוּ, חַדֵּשׁ עָלֵינוּ אֶת הַחֹדֶשׁ הַזֶּה לְטוֹבָה וְלִבְרָכָה (אָמֵן), לְשָׂשׂוֹן וּלְשִׂמְחָה (אָמֵן), לִישׁוּעָה וּלְנֶחָמָה (אָמֵן), לְפַרְנָסָה וּלְכַלְכָּלָה (אָמֵן), לְחַיִּים וּלְשָׁלוֹם (אָמֵן), לִמְחִילַת חֵטְא וְלִסְלִיחַת עָוֹן (אָמֵן), (*From* מרחשון *to* אדר שני *in a Jewish leap year*: וּלְכַפָּרַת פֶּשַׁע (אָמֵן)), כִּי בְעַמְּךָ יִשְׂרָאֵל בָּחַרְתָּ מִכָּל הָאֻמּוֹת, וְחֻקֵּי רָאשֵׁי חֳדָשִׁים לָהֶם קָבָעְתָּ. בָּרוּךְ אַתָּה יהוה, מְקַדֵּשׁ יִשְׂרָאֵל וְרָאשֵׁי חֳדָשִׁים.

---

to sound the trumpets over the sacrifices, and "they shall be a remembrance for you before your God."

וּתְשׁוּעַת נַפְשָׁם מִיַּד שׂוֹנֵא – *A deliverance of their soul from the hand of the hater* (previous page). This "hater" is the Evil Inclination that lies in wait like an enemy to tempt Israel to sin. By remembering to be on guard against his evil schemes, our souls will be saved from him (Abudarham).

a new altar in Zion, and may we offer upon it the elevation-offering of Rosh Ḥodesh, and prepare he-goats with favor. May we all rejoice in the service of the Holy Temple by means of the songs of Your servant David that were heard in Your city, and proclaimed before Your altar. May You bring upon them everlasting love, and remember the covenant of the forefathers for the benefit of their descendants.

וַהֲבִיאֵנוּ MAY YOU BRING US to Zion, Your city, in song, and to Jerusalem, Your Holy Temple, in eternal rejoicing. There in Your presence will we bring our obligatory offerings, the continual offerings according to their order and the additional offerings according to their law.

וְאֶת AND we will prepare and bring before You the additional offering of this Rosh Ḥodesh with love, in accordance with the commandment that you willed. For so did You write for us in Your Torah, by the hand of Moses Your servant, as spoken in Your glory. As it is said:

Num. 28 וּבְרָאשֵׁי חָדְשֵׁיכֶם AND ON YOUR DAYS OF ROSH ḤODESH you shall bring as a burnt-offering to the LORD two young bullocks, one ram, and seven unblemished one-year-old male lambs. Together with these their grain-offerings and their libations, as stated in the Torah: three-tenths [of an ephah] for each bullock, two-tenths for the ram, one-tenth for each lamb, and wine for the libation, as well as a male goat for atonement, and the two regular daily burnt-offerings as specified.

אֱלֹהֵינוּ OUR GOD and God of our fathers, renew for us this month for good and blessing (Amen), for joy and gladness (Amen), for salvation and consolation (Amen), for sustenance and support (Amen), for life and peace (Amen), for pardon of sin and forgiveness of wrongdoing (Amen), (*From Marḥeshvan to Adar Sheni in a Jewish leap year:* and for atonement of transgression (Amen)). For You have chosen Your people Israel from among all the other nations, establishing the statutes of the days of Rosh Ḥodesh for them. Blessed are You, LORD, Who sanctifies Israel and the days of Rosh Ḥodesh.

עבודה

רְצֵה יהוה אֱלֹהֵינוּ בְּעַמְּךָ יִשְׂרָאֵל, וּבִתְפִלָּתָם, וְהָשֵׁב אֶת הָעֲבוֹדָה לִדְבִיר בֵּיתֶךָ, וְאִשֵּׁי יִשְׂרָאֵל וּתְפִלָּתָם בְּאַהֲבָה תְקַבֵּל בְּרָצוֹן, וּתְהִי לְרָצוֹן תָּמִיד עֲבוֹדַת יִשְׂרָאֵל עַמֶּךָ. וְתֶחֱזֶינָה עֵינֵינוּ בְּשׁוּבְךָ לְצִיּוֹן בְּרַחֲמִים. בָּרוּךְ אַתָּה יהוה, הַמַּחֲזִיר שְׁכִינָתוֹ לְצִיּוֹן.

הודאה

Bow during the first five words.

ᐟמוֹדִים אֲנַחְנוּ לָךְ, שָׁאַתָּה הוּא יהוה אֱלֹהֵינוּ וֵאלֹהֵי אֲבוֹתֵינוּ לְעוֹלָם וָעֶד. צוּר חַיֵּינוּ, מָגֵן יִשְׁעֵנוּ, אַתָּה הוּא. לְדוֹר וָדוֹר נוֹדֶה לְּךָ וּנְסַפֵּר תְּהִלָּתֶךָ, עַל חַיֵּינוּ הַמְּסוּרִים בְּיָדֶךָ, וְעַל נִשְׁמוֹתֵינוּ הַפְּקוּדוֹת לָךְ, וְעַל נִסֶּיךָ שֶׁבְּכָל יוֹם עִמָּנוּ, וְעַל נִפְלְאוֹתֶיךָ וְטוֹבוֹתֶיךָ, שֶׁבְּכָל עֵת, עֶרֶב וָבֹקֶר וְצָהֳרָיִם. הַטּוֹב, כִּי לֹא כָלוּ רַחֲמֶיךָ, וְהַמְרַחֵם, כִּי לֹא תַמּוּ חֲסָדֶיךָ, מֵעוֹלָם קִוִּינוּ לָךְ.

During חזרת הש"ץ, *the* קהל *says quietly:*

ᐟמוֹדִים אֲנַחְנוּ לָךְ, שָׁאַתָּה הוּא יהוה אֱלֹהֵינוּ וֵאלֹהֵי אֲבוֹתֵינוּ, אֱלֹהֵי כָל בָּשָׂר, יוֹצְרֵנוּ, יוֹצֵר בְּרֵאשִׁית. בְּרָכוֹת וְהוֹדָאוֹת לְשִׁמְךָ הַגָּדוֹל וְהַקָּדוֹשׁ, עַל שֶׁהֶחֱיִיתָנוּ וְקִיַּמְתָּנוּ. כֵּן תְּחַיֵּנוּ וּתְקַיְּמֵנוּ, וְתֶאֱסֹף גָּלֻיּוֹתֵינוּ לְחַצְרוֹת קָדְשֶׁךָ, לִשְׁמֹר חֻקֶּיךָ וְלַעֲשׂוֹת רְצוֹנֶךָ וּלְעָבְדְּךָ בְּלֵבָב שָׁלֵם, עַל שֶׁאֲנַחְנוּ מוֹדִים לָךְ. בָּרוּךְ אֵל הַהוֹדָאוֹת.

בחנוכה:

עַל הַנִּסִּים וְעַל הַפֻּרְקָן וְעַל הַגְּבוּרוֹת וְעַל הַתְּשׁוּעוֹת וְעַל הַמִּלְחָמוֹת שֶׁעָשִׂיתָ לַאֲבוֹתֵינוּ בַּיָּמִים הָהֵם בַּזְּמַן הַזֶּה.

בִּימֵי מַתִּתְיָהוּ בֶּן יוֹחָנָן כֹּהֵן גָּדוֹל חַשְׁמוֹנַאי וּבָנָיו, כְּשֶׁעָמְדָה מַלְכוּת יָוָן הָרְשָׁעָה עַל עַמְּךָ יִשְׂרָאֵל לְהַשְׁכִּיחָם תּוֹרָתֶךָ וּלְהַעֲבִירָם מֵחֻקֵּי רְצוֹנֶךָ, וְאַתָּה בְּרַחֲמֶיךָ הָרַבִּים עָמַדְתָּ לָהֶם בְּעֵת צָרָתָם, רַבְתָּ אֶת רִיבָם,

Continued on the top of the next page.

For laws regarding "עַל הַנִּסִּים / *Al HaNissim,*" see page 128.

TEMPLE SERVICE

רְצֵה LOOK FAVORABLY, LORD our God, upon Your people Israel and their prayer, and restore the service to the Holy of Holies of Your House. Accept with love and favor the fire-offerings of Israel and their prayer. May the service of Israel Your people Israel always find favor with You. May our eyes witness Your return to Zion in compassion. Blessed are You, LORD, Who will restore His Divine Presence to Zion.

THANKSGIVING

Bow during the first seven words.

מוֹדִים WE THANK YOU, for You are the LORD our God and the God of our fathers for all eternity. You are the Rock of our life and Shield of our deliverance. From generation to generation we will thank You and recount Your praise for our lives that are in Your hands, for our souls that are given over to You, for Your miracles that are with us every day, and for Your constant wonders and favors, evening, morning and noon. You are good, for Your compassion does not cease, and You are compassionate, for Your kindness never ends. We have placed our hope in You forever and ever.

During the Leader's Repetition, the congregation says quietly:

מוֹדִים WE THANK YOU, for You are the LORD our God, the God of our fathers and God of all flesh. You are our Maker, the Maker of Creation. Blessings and thanks are due Your great and holy name for You have given us life and preserved us in life. May You continue to keep us in life and preserve us. Gather our exiles to the courtyards of Your Temple so that we may fulfill Your commandments and do Your will, serving You with a perfect heart, in the merit of our giving thanks to You now. Blessed is the God of all thanksgiving.

On Ḥanukka add:

עַל הַנִּסִּים [WE THANK YOU] for the miracles, the deliverance, and the triumphant victories and salvation, as well as wars which You wrought for our ancestors in those days at this season.

IT HAPPENED in the days of Mattathias son of Johanan, the Hasmonean high priest, and his sons. Then the cruel Hellenist power rose up to force Your people Israel to forget Your Torah and transgress the commands of Your will. In that hour of their distress, You in Your great mercy rose to take up their cause and defend their rights. Meting out retribution You

Continued on the top of the next page.

דַּנְתָּ אֶת דִּינָם, נָקַמְתָּ אֶת נִקְמָתָם, מָסַרְתָּ גִּבּוֹרִים בְּיַד חַלָּשִׁים,
וְרַבִּים בְּיַד מְעַטִּים, וּטְמֵאִים בְּיַד טְהוֹרִים, וּרְשָׁעִים בְּיַד צַדִּיקִים,
וְזֵדִים בְּיַד עוֹסְקֵי תוֹרָתֶךָ, וּלְךָ עָשִׂיתָ שֵׁם גָּדוֹל וְקָדוֹשׁ בְּעוֹלָמֶךָ,
וּלְעַמְּךָ יִשְׂרָאֵל עָשִׂיתָ תְּשׁוּעָה גְדוֹלָה וּפֻרְקָן כְּהַיּוֹם הַזֶּה. וְאַחַר
כֵּן בָּאוּ בָנֶיךָ לִדְבִיר בֵּיתֶךָ, וּפִנּוּ אֶת הֵיכָלֶךָ, וְטִהֲרוּ אֶת מִקְדָּשֶׁךָ,
וְהִדְלִיקוּ נֵרוֹת בְּחַצְרוֹת קָדְשֶׁךָ, וְקָבְעוּ שְׁמוֹנַת יְמֵי חֲנֻכָּה אֵלּוּ, לְהוֹדוֹת
וּלְהַלֵּל לְשִׁמְךָ הַגָּדוֹל.

Continue with וְעַל כֻּלָּם.

וְעַל כֻּלָּם יִתְבָּרַךְ וְיִתְרוֹמַם שִׁמְךָ מַלְכֵּנוּ תָּמִיד לְעוֹלָם וָעֶד. וְכֹל
הַחַיִּים יוֹדְוּךָ סֶּלָה, וִיהַלְלוּ אֶת שִׁמְךָ בֶּאֱמֶת, הָאֵל יְשׁוּעָתֵנוּ וְעֶזְרָתֵנוּ
סֶלָה. ·בָּרוּךְ אַתָּה יהוה, הַטּוֹב שִׁמְךָ וּלְךָ נָאֶה לְהוֹדוֹת.

ברכת כהנים

The following is said by the שליח ציבור *during* חזרת הש"ץ *except in a* שבעה *house.*

אֱלֹהֵינוּ וֵאלֹהֵי אֲבוֹתֵינוּ, בָּרְכֵנוּ בַבְּרָכָה הַמְשֻׁלֶּשֶׁת, בַּתּוֹרָה, הַכְּתוּבָה עַל
יְדֵי מֹשֶׁה עַבְדֶּךָ, הָאֲמוּרָה מִפִּי אַהֲרֹן וּבָנָיו כֹּהֲנִים עַם קְדוֹשֶׁיךָ,
כָּאָמוּר

יְבָרֶכְךָ יהוה וְיִשְׁמְרֶךָ: קהל: כֵּן יְהִי רָצוֹן במדבר ו
יָאֵר יהוה פָּנָיו אֵלֶיךָ וִיחֻנֶּךָּ: קהל: כֵּן יְהִי רָצוֹן
יִשָּׂא יהוה פָּנָיו אֵלֶיךָ וְיָשֵׂם לְךָ שָׁלוֹם: קהל: כֵּן יְהִי רָצוֹן

שלום

שִׂים שָׁלוֹם טוֹבָה וּבְרָכָה, חֵן וָחֶסֶד וְרַחֲמִים עָלֵינוּ וְעַל כָּל
יִשְׂרָאֵל עַמֶּךָ. בָּרְכֵנוּ אָבִינוּ כֻּלָּנוּ כְּאֶחָד בְּאוֹר פָּנֶיךָ,
כִּי בְאוֹר פָּנֶיךָ נָתַתָּ לָּנוּ יהוה אֱלֹהֵינוּ, תּוֹרַת חַיִּים וְאַהֲבַת חֶסֶד,
וּצְדָקָה וּבְרָכָה וְרַחֲמִים וְחַיִּים וְשָׁלוֹם. וְטוֹב בְּעֵינֶיךָ לְבָרֵךְ אֶת עַמְּךָ
יִשְׂרָאֵל, בְּכָל עֵת וּבְכָל שָׁעָה בִּשְׁלוֹמֶךָ. בָּרוּךְ אַתָּה יהוה, הַמְבָרֵךְ
אֶת עַמּוֹ יִשְׂרָאֵל בַּשָּׁלוֹם.

delivered the strong into the hand of the weak, the many into the hand of the few, the impure into the hand of the pure, the evil ones into the hand of the righteous, and the wicked into the hand of devotees of Your Torah. You thereby made for Yourself a great and holy name throughout Your world, as well as bringing about great deliverance and salvation for Your people Israel (known) to this day. Then Your children came to the Holy of Holies in Your house, cleared Your Temple, purified Your holy place, kindled lights in Your holy courts, and instituted these eight days of Ḥanukka to give thanks and sing praise to Your great name.

Continue with "For all this."

For all this, our King, may Your name be blessed and exalted continually, forever and ever. All that lives will give thanks to You forever and praise Your name in truth, God, our salvation and our help forever. ▼Blessed are You, LORD, for Your name is "The Good One" and it is appropriate to give thanks to You.

THE PRIESTLY BLESSING

The following is said by the Leader during the Repetition of the Amida, except in a shiva house.

אֱלֹהֵינוּ OUR GOD, God of our fathers, bless us with the threefold blessing, in the Torah, written by Your servant Moses and spoken by Aaron and his descendants, being priests, Your holy people, as it is said:

Num. 6 "May the LORD bless you and keep you." *Cong:* May this be His will.
"May the LORD make His countenance shine upon you and be gracious to you." *Cong:* May this be His will.
"May the LORD lift up His countenance toward you and grant you peace." *Cong:* May this be His will.

PEACE

שִׂים שָׁלוֹם GRANT PEACE with welfare and blessing, and grace with loving-kindness and mercy on us and all Israel Your people. Bless us, our Father, all together, with the light of Your presence. For in that light, LORD our God, You have given us the Torah of life, and love of kindness with justice, blessing, tenderness, life and peace. May it be good in Your eyes to bless Your people Israel at all times, at every hour, with Your peace. Blessed are You, LORD, Who blesses His people Israel with peace.

At this point when the שליח ציבור *repeats the* עמידה *he should complete the repetition by saying the verse beginning "*יִהְיוּ לְרָצוֹן*" out loud.*

תהלים יט יִהְיוּ לְרָצוֹן אִמְרֵי־פִי וְהֶגְיוֹן לִבִּי לְפָנֶיךָ, יהוה צוּרִי וְגֹאֲלִי:

ברכות יז. **אֱלֹהַי,** נְצֹר לְשׁוֹנִי מֵרָע וּשְׂפָתַי מִדַּבֵּר מִרְמָה, וְלִמְקַלְלַי נַפְשִׁי תִדֹּם, וְנַפְשִׁי כֶּעָפָר לַכֹּל תִּהְיֶה. פְּתַח לִבִּי בְּתוֹרָתֶךָ, וּבְמִצְוֹתֶיךָ תִּרְדֹּף נַפְשִׁי. וְכָל הַחוֹשְׁבִים עָלַי רָעָה, מְהֵרָה הָפֵר עֲצָתָם וְקַלְקֵל מַחֲשַׁבְתָּם. עֲשֵׂה לְמַעַן שְׁמֶךָ, עֲשֵׂה לְמַעַן יְמִינֶךָ,
תהלים ס עֲשֵׂה לְמַעַן קְדֻשָּׁתֶךָ, עֲשֵׂה לְמַעַן תּוֹרָתֶךָ. לְמַעַן יֵחָלְצוּן יְדִידֶיךָ,
תהלים יט הוֹשִׁיעָה יְמִינְךָ וַעֲנֵנִי: יִהְיוּ לְרָצוֹן אִמְרֵי־פִי וְהֶגְיוֹן לִבִּי לְפָנֶיךָ, יהוה צוּרִי וְגֹאֲלִי:

Bow, take three steps back, then bow, first left, then right, then center, while saying:

עֹשֶׂה שָׁלוֹם בִּמְרוֹמָיו, הוּא יַעֲשֶׂה שָׁלוֹם עָלֵינוּ, וְעַל כָּל יִשְׂרָאֵל, וְאִמְרוּ אָמֵן.

יְהִי רָצוֹן מִלְּפָנֶיךָ יהוה אֱלֹהֵינוּ וֵאלֹהֵי אֲבוֹתֵינוּ, שֶׁיִּבָּנֶה בֵּית הַמִּקְדָּשׁ בִּמְהֵרָה בְיָמֵינוּ, וְתֵן חֶלְקֵנוּ בְּתוֹרָתֶךָ, וְשָׁם נַעֲבָדְךָ בְּיִרְאָה כִּימֵי
מלאכי ג עוֹלָם וּכְשָׁנִים קַדְמֹנִיּוֹת. וְעָרְבָה לַיהוה מִנְחַת יְהוּדָה וִירוּשָׁלָיִם כִּימֵי עוֹלָם וּכְשָׁנִים קַדְמֹנִיּוֹת:

After the חזרת הש״ץ, *the service continues with* קדיש שלם,
followed by עָלֵינוּ *(page 180),* שיר של יום *(page 184) and* בָּרְכִי נַפְשִׁי *(page 194)*
together with the various קדיש יתום *recitals indicated on those pages.*

For laws regarding "Interruptions during *Elokai Netzor,*" see page 133.

At this point when the Leader repeats the Amida he should complete the repetition by saying the verse beginning "May the words" out loud.

Ps. 19 MAY THE WORDS of my mouth and the meditation of my heart be acceptable before You, LORD, my Rock and my Redeemer.

Berakhot 17a אֱלֹהַי MY GOD, guard my tongue from evil, and my lips from speaking deceit. Let my soul be silent to those who curse me; let my soul be humble toward everyone like the dust. Open my heart to Your Torah that my soul may follow Your commandments. As for all those who contemplate evil against me, speedily nullify their plans and spoil their schemes. Do so for the sake of Your name. Do so for Your right hand.
Ps. 60 Do so for Your holiness. Do so for Your Torah, that Your loved ones may
Ps. 19 be delivered. Save with Your right hand, and answer me. May the words of my mouth and the meditation of my heart be acceptable before You, LORD, my Rock and my Redeemer.

Bow, take three steps back, then bow, first left, then right, then center, while saying:

He Who makes peace in His heights, may He create peace for us and for all Israel. Amen.

יְהִי רָצוֹן MAY IT BE Your will, LORD our God and God of our fathers, that the Temple be rebuilt speedily in our days and may You grant our portion in Your Torah. We will serve You there in reverence as in the days of antiquity and in
Mal. 3 years gone by. "And may the offering of Judah and Jerusalem be pleasant to the LORD as in the days of antiquity and in years gone by."

After the Leader's Repetition, the service continues with Full Kaddish, followed by Aleinu (page 181), the Daily Psalm (page 185) and Barekhi Nafshi (page 195) together with the various Mourner's Kaddish recitals indicated on those pages.

בדיקת/ביעור חמץ

Instructions for בדיקת/ביעור חמץ *are found below.*

Before the search, make the following blessing:

בָּרוּךְ אַתָּה יהוה אֱלֹהֵינוּ מֶלֶךְ הָעוֹלָם, אֲשֶׁר קִדְּשָׁנוּ בְּמִצְוֹתָיו וְצִוָּנוּ עַל בִּעוּר חָמֵץ.

After the search, say:

כָּל חֲמִירָא וַחֲמִיעָא דְּאִכָּא בִרְשׁוּתִי, דְּלָא חֲמִתֵּהּ וּדְלָא בִעַרְתֵּהּ, לִבְטִיל וְלֶהֱוֵי הֶפְקֵר כְּעַפְרָא דְאַרְעָא.

On the following morning after burning the חמץ*, say:*

כָּל חֲמִירָא וַחֲמִיעָא דְּאִכָּא בִרְשׁוּתִי, דַּחֲמִתֵּהּ וּדְלָא חֲמִתֵּהּ, דְּבִעַרְתֵּהּ וּדְלָא בִעַרְתֵּהּ, לִבְטִיל וְלֶהֱוֵי הֶפְקֵר כְּעַפְרָא דְאַרְעָא.

עירוב תבשילין

Instructions for עירוב תבשילין *are found below.*

בָּרוּךְ אַתָּה יהוה אֱלֹהֵינוּ מֶלֶךְ הָעוֹלָם, אֲשֶׁר קִדְּשָׁנוּ בְּמִצְוֹתָיו וְצִוָּנוּ עַל מִצְוַת עֵרוּב.

בְּדֵין עֵרוּבָא יְהֵא שְׁרֵא לָנָא לְמֵיפֵא וּלְבַשָּׁלָא וּלְאַטְמָנָא וּלְאַדְלָקָא שְׁרָגָא, וּלְמֶעְבַּד כָּל צָרְכָּנָא מִיּוֹמָא טָבָא לְשַׁבְּתָא, (לָנוּ וּלְכָל יִשְׂרָאֵל הַדָּרִים בָּעִיר הַזֹּאת).

For עירוב תחומין *see page 348. For* הדלקת נרות *see page 350.*

EIRUV TAVSHILIN

When Yom Tov occurs on a Friday, whether it is the first day of Yom Tov or the second day, there is an obligation to establish an *eiruv tavshilin* prior to Yom Tov. This allows one to prepare food on Yom Tov that is going to be served on Shabbat. The *eiruv tavshilin* consists of one cooked item and one baked item. If one wants to include others – beyond immediate family – in the *eiruv*, one should give the food items to an adult and the other person should lift the food items more than a *tefaḥ* (approximately four inches) for the purpose of acquiring the *eiruv* on behalf of the others. The individual establishing the *eiruv* then retrieves the items and while holding both items, recites the above *berakha* and then the declaration. If one included the entire community in the *eiruv*, one should recite the portion in brackets: לָנוּ וּלְכָל יִשְׂרָאֵל הַדָּרִים בָּעִיר הַזֹּאת.

BEDIKAT/BIUR ḤAMETZ

Instructions for Bedikat/Biur Ḥametz are found below.

Before the search, make the following blessing:

בָּרוּךְ BLESSED ARE YOU, Lord, our God, King of the universe, Who has sanctified us with His commandments and has commanded us about the removal of leaven.

After the search, say:

May any ḥametz or leaven that is in my possession, which I have not seen, have not removed, and do not know about, be annulled and become ownerless, like dust of the earth.

On the following morning after burning the ḥametz, say:

May any ḥametz or leaven that is in my possession, whether I have recognized it or not, (whether I have seen it or not,) whether I have removed it or not, be annulled and become ownerless, like dust of the earth.

EIRUV TAVSHILIN

Instructions for Eiruv Tavshilin are found below.

בָּרוּךְ BLESSED ARE YOU, Lord, our God, King of the universe, Who has sanctified us with His commandments, and has commanded us about the mitzva of Eiruv.

THROUGH THIS EIRUV may we be permitted to bake, cook, insulate food, light a flame and do everything necessary on the festival for the sake of Shabbat (for us and for all Jews living in this city).

For Eiruv Teḥumin see page 349. For Candle Lighting see page 351.

BEDIKAT / BIUR ḤAMETZ

On the night before Pesaḥ, a search for *ḥametz*, such as breadcrumbs, products containing leaven and grain alcohol, is made in the house. The custom is to do so at night by the light of a candle. However, nowadays once the search has begun, many transition to using a flashlight. If Pesaḥ falls on Motza'ei Shabbat, the search is made on Thursday night. Those who plan to be away on Pesaḥ should conduct the search the night before their departure, but without making a blessing.

קידוש לליל שלוש רגלים

On שבת *add:*

בראשית א *Quietly* וַיְהִי־עֶרֶב וַיְהִי־בֹקֶר

בראשית ב **יוֹם הַשִּׁשִּׁי:** וַיְכֻלּוּ הַשָּׁמַיִם וְהָאָרֶץ וְכָל־צְבָאָם: וַיְכַל אֱלֹהִים בַּיּוֹם הַשְּׁבִיעִי מְלַאכְתּוֹ אֲשֶׁר עָשָׂה, וַיִּשְׁבֹּת בַּיּוֹם הַשְּׁבִיעִי מִכָּל־מְלַאכְתּוֹ, אֲשֶׁר עָשָׂה: וַיְבָרֶךְ אֱלֹהִים אֶת־יוֹם הַשְּׁבִיעִי, וַיְקַדֵּשׁ אֹתוֹ, כִּי בוֹ שָׁבַת מִכָּל־מְלַאכְתּוֹ, אֲשֶׁר־בָּרָא אֱלֹהִים, לַעֲשׂוֹת:

On other evenings the קידוש *starts here:*

When making קידוש *for others, add:*

סַבְרִי מָרָנָן וְרַבָּנָן וְרַבּוֹתַי

בָּרוּךְ אַתָּה יהוה אֱלֹהֵינוּ מֶלֶךְ הָעוֹלָם, בּוֹרֵא פְּרִי הַגָּפֶן.

On שבת*, add the words in parentheses.*

בָּרוּךְ אַתָּה יהוה אֱלֹהֵינוּ מֶלֶךְ הָעוֹלָם, אֲשֶׁר בָּחַר בָּנוּ מִכָּל עָם, וְרוֹמְמָנוּ מִכָּל לָשׁוֹן, וְקִדְּשָׁנוּ בְּמִצְוֹתָיו, וַתִּתֶּן לָנוּ יהוה אֱלֹהֵינוּ בְּאַהֲבָה, (שַׁבָּתוֹת לִמְנוּחָה וּ) מוֹעֲדִים לְשִׂמְחָה, חַגִּים וּזְמַנִּים לְשָׂשׂוֹן, אֶת יוֹם (הַשַּׁבָּת הַזֶּה וְאֶת יוֹם)

בפסח: חַג הַמַּצּוֹת הַזֶּה, זְמַן חֵרוּתֵנוּ

בשבועות: חַג הַשָּׁבוּעוֹת הַזֶּה, זְמַן מַתַּן תּוֹרָתֵנוּ

בסוכות: חַג הַסֻּכּוֹת הַזֶּה, זְמַן שִׂמְחָתֵנוּ

בשמע״צ ובש״ת: הַשְּׁמִינִי חַג הָעֲצֶרֶת הַזֶּה, זְמַן שִׂמְחָתֵנוּ

קִדּוּשׁ לְלֵיל שָׁלֹשׁ רְגָלִים / KIDDUSH FOR FESTIVAL EVENING

זְמַן מַתַּן תּוֹרָתֵנוּ – *The time of the giving of our Torah.* The *Halakha* accepts the view of R. Yossi in the Gemara (*Shabbat* 87a) that the Revelation on Sinai occurred on the seventh day of *Sivan*, insofar as Moses unilaterally added an additional day of preparation beyond what God had commanded (see Rashi to Exodus 19:15). How then can we declare on Shavuot, which always occurs on the sixth day of Sivan, that the day is זְמַן מַתַּן תּוֹרָתֵנוּ (when the Torah was given), when it was only given on the seventh? The answer is that legal ownership of the Torah was transferred to us on the sixth for it was on that day that God, by delaying His Revelation to accord with Moses' view, ratified Moses' (and by extension the Jewish people's) authority to interpret God's word as they saw fit. Thus on the sixth of Sivan we took ownership of the Torah,

For "*Laws of Kiddush*" see page 426.

KIDDUSH FOR FESTIVAL EVENING

On Shabbat add:

Gen. 1 *Quietly:* And it was evening, and it was morning.

Gen. 2 **יוֹם הַשִּׁשִּׁי** THE SIXTH DAY. Thus the heavens and the earth were finished, and all their multitudes. And by the seventh day God ended His work which He had done; and He rested on the seventh day from all His work which He had done. And God blessed the seventh day and sanctified it: because on it He rested from all the work He had created and performed.

On other evenings the Kiddush starts here:

When saying Kiddush for others, add:

With your permission, my masters, rabbis and esteemed companions:

בָּרוּךְ BLESSED ARE YOU, LORD, our God, King of the universe, Who creates the fruit of the vine.

On Shabbat, add the words in parentheses.

בָּרוּךְ BLESSED ARE YOU, Lord, our God, King of the universe, Who has chosen us from all peoples, raised us above all languages, and sanctified us with His commandments. In Your love, Lord our God, You have given us (Sabbaths for rest), festivals for rejoicing, holidays and seasons for joy, (this Sabbath day and)

On Pesaḥ: this day of the Festival of Matzot, the time of our freedom

On Shavuot: this day of the Festival of Shavuot, the time of the giving of our Torah

On Sukkot: this day of the Festival of Sukkot, the time of our rejoicing

On Shemini Atzeret & Simḥat Torah: the eighth day, this Festival of Atzeret, the time of our rejoicing

---

as expressed in תּוֹרָה שֶׁבְּעַל פֶּה (the Oral Law) – even though the formal handing over of תּוֹרָה שֶׁבִּכְתָב (the Written Law) only occurred the next day. That is why we declare on the sixth of Sivan that today is זְמַן מַתַּן תּוֹרָתֵנוּ, i.e., on this day it became ours to interpret and apply. For this reason too the sages instituted two *berakhot* over the reading of the Torah. The first refers to the written Torah. The second describes the oral Torah in saying נָתַן לָנוּ תּוֹרַת אֱמֶת וְחַיֵּי עוֹלָם

(בְּאַהֲבָה) מִקְרָא קֹדֶשׁ, זֵכֶר לִיצִיאַת מִצְרָיִם, כִּי בָנוּ בָחַרְתָּ וְאוֹתָנוּ קִדַּשְׁתָּ מִכָּל הָעַמִּים (וְשַׁבָּת), וּמוֹעֲדֵי קָדְשֶׁךָ (בְּאַהֲבָה וּבְרָצוֹן), בְּשִׂמְחָה וּבְשָׂשׂוֹן הִנְחַלְתָּנוּ. בָּרוּךְ אַתָּה יהוה, מְקַדֵּשׁ (הַשַּׁבָּת וְ) יִשְׂרָאֵל וְהַזְּמַנִּים.

On מוצאי שבת*, the following* הבדלה *is added:*

בָּרוּךְ אַתָּה יהוה אֱלֹהֵינוּ מֶלֶךְ הָעוֹלָם, בּוֹרֵא מְאוֹרֵי הָאֵשׁ.

בָּרוּךְ אַתָּה יהוה אֱלֹהֵינוּ מֶלֶךְ הָעוֹלָם, הַמַּבְדִּיל בֵּין קֹדֶשׁ לְחֹל, בֵּין אוֹר לְחֹשֶׁךְ, בֵּין יִשְׂרָאֵל לָעַמִּים, בֵּין יוֹם הַשְּׁבִיעִי לְשֵׁשֶׁת יְמֵי הַמַּעֲשֶׂה. בֵּין קְדֻשַּׁת שַׁבָּת לִקְדֻשַּׁת יוֹם טוֹב הִבְדַּלְתָּ, וְאֶת יוֹם הַשְּׁבִיעִי מִשֵּׁשֶׁת יְמֵי הַמַּעֲשֶׂה קִדַּשְׁתָּ, הִבְדַּלְתָּ וְקִדַּשְׁתָּ אֶת עַמְּךָ יִשְׂרָאֵל בִּקְדֻשָּׁתֶךָ. בָּרוּךְ אַתָּה יהוה, הַמַּבְדִּיל בֵּין קֹדֶשׁ לְקֹדֶשׁ.

On סוכות*, say the following blessing. On the first night it is said before the blessing* שֶׁהֶחֱיָנוּ*; on the second night, after it (some say it before on both nights).*

בָּרוּךְ אַתָּה יהוה אֱלֹהֵינוּ מֶלֶךְ הָעוֹלָם, אֲשֶׁר קִדְּשָׁנוּ בְּמִצְוֹתָיו וְצִוָּנוּ לֵישֵׁב בַּסֻּכָּה.

The following blessing is omitted on the last two nights of פסח*.*

בָּרוּךְ אַתָּה יהוה אֱלֹהֵינוּ מֶלֶךְ הָעוֹלָם, שֶׁהֶחֱיָנוּ וְקִיְּמָנוּ וְהִגִּיעָנוּ לַזְּמַן הַזֶּה.

It is customary for all present to drink of the wine.

לחם משנה

On washing hands before eating bread:

בָּרוּךְ אַתָּה יהוה אֱלֹהֵינוּ מֶלֶךְ הָעוֹלָם, אֲשֶׁר קִדְּשָׁנוּ בְּמִצְוֹתָיו וְצִוָּנוּ עַל נְטִילַת יָדָיִם.

Before eating bread:

בָּרוּךְ אַתָּה יהוה אֱלֹהֵינוּ מֶלֶךְ הָעוֹלָם, הַמּוֹצִיא לֶחֶם מִן הָאָרֶץ.

נָטַע בְּתוֹכֵנוּ (He gave us the Torah of truth, and thereby implanted in us eternal life), i.e., the Jewish nation is constantly renewed by the ever-revitalized Torah, as each succeeding generation of sages adds to the interpretations of its predecessors (R. Ḥayyim HaLevi Soloveitchik).

(with love,) a holy convocation, a remembrance of the Exodus from Egypt. For You have chosen us and You have sanctified us above all peoples, and You have given us (the Sabbath and) Your holy festivals (in love and favor,) in joy, and in gladness, as a heritage. Blessed are You, Lord, Who sanctifies (the Sabbath and) Israel and the festive seasons.

On Motza'ei Shabbat, the following Havdala is added:

בָּרוּךְ BLESSED ARE YOU, Lord, our god, King of the universe, Who creates the lights of fire.

בָּרוּךְ BLESSED ARE YOU, Lord, our God, King of the universe, Who separates sacred from secular, light from darkness, Israel from the nations, and the seventh day from the six days of labor. Between the holiness of the Sabbath and the holiness of the festivals You have made a separation, and You have sanctified the seventh day above the six days of labor. You have separated and sanctified Your people Israel with Your holiness. Blessed are You, Lord, Who separates sacred from sacred.

On Sukkot, say the following blessing. On the first night it is said before the blessing "Who has given us life"; on the second night, after it (some say it before on both nights).

בָּרוּךְ BLESSED ARE YOU, Lord, our God, King of the universe, Who has sanctified us with His commandments and commanded us to dwell in the sukka.

The following blessing is omitted on the last two nights of פסח.

בָּרוּךְ BLESSED ARE YOU, Lord, our God, King of the universe, Who has given us life, sustained us, and brought us to this time.

It is customary for all present to drink of the wine.

LEḤEM MISHNEH

On washing hands before eating bread:

בָּרוּךְ BLESSED ARE YOU, Lord, our God, King of the universe, Who has sanctified us with His commandments, and has commanded us about washing hands.

Before eating bread:

בָּרוּךְ BLESSED ARE YOU, Lord, our God, King of the universe, Who brings forth bread from the earth.

For laws of *Leḥem Mishneh*, see page 429.

אושפיזין

On entering the סוכה *and before saying* קידוש*, many have the custom to welcome "guests" from the biblical past, who are said to join us as we sit in the* סוכה.
At this point some follow the Hasidic custom of reciting additional prayers, which can be found on page 1340.

אֲזַמִּין לִסְעוּדָתִי אֻשְׁפִּיזִין עִלָּאִין, אַבְרָהָם יִצְחָק יַעֲקֹב יוֹסֵף מֹשֶׁה אַהֲרֹן וְדָוִד.

On the first day בְּמָטוּ מִנָּךְ אַבְרָהָם אֻשְׁפִּיזִי עִלָּאִי דְּתֵיתֵב עִמִּי, וְעִמָּךְ כָּל אֻשְׁפִּיזֵי עִלָּאֵי: יִצְחָק יַעֲקֹב יוֹסֵף מֹשֶׁה אַהֲרֹן וְדָוִד.

On the second day בְּמָטוּ מִנָּךְ יִצְחָק אֻשְׁפִּיזִי עִלָּאִי דְּתֵיתֵב עִמִּי, וְעִמָּךְ כָּל אֻשְׁפִּיזֵי עִלָּאֵי: אַבְרָהָם יַעֲקֹב יוֹסֵף מֹשֶׁה אַהֲרֹן וְדָוִד.

On the third day בְּמָטוּ מִנָּךְ יַעֲקֹב אֻשְׁפִּיזִי עִלָּאִי דְּתֵיתֵב עִמִּי, וְעִמָּךְ כָּל אֻשְׁפִּיזֵי עִלָּאֵי: אַבְרָהָם יִצְחָק יוֹסֵף מֹשֶׁה אַהֲרֹן וְדָוִד.

On the fourth day בְּמָטוּ מִנָּךְ יוֹסֵף אֻשְׁפִּיזִי עִלָּאִי דְּתֵיתֵב עִמִּי, וְעִמָּךְ כָּל אֻשְׁפִּיזֵי עִלָּאֵי: אַבְרָהָם יִצְחָק יַעֲקֹב מֹשֶׁה אַהֲרֹן וְדָוִד.

On the fifth day בְּמָטוּ מִנָּךְ מֹשֶׁה אֻשְׁפִּיזִי עִלָּאִי דְּתֵיתֵב עִמִּי, וְעִמָּךְ כָּל אֻשְׁפִּיזֵי עִלָּאֵי: אַבְרָהָם יִצְחָק יַעֲקֹב יוֹסֵף אַהֲרֹן וְדָוִד.

On the sixth day בְּמָטוּ מִנָּךְ אַהֲרֹן אֻשְׁפִּיזִי עִלָּאִי דְּתֵיתֵב עִמִּי, וְעִמָּךְ כָּל אֻשְׁפִּיזֵי עִלָּאֵי: אַבְרָהָם יִצְחָק יַעֲקֹב יוֹסֵף מֹשֶׁה וְדָוִד.

On הושענא רבה בְּמָטוּ מִנָּךְ דָּוִד אֻשְׁפִּיזִי עִלָּאִי דְּתֵיתֵב עִמִּי, וְעִמָּךְ כָּל אֻשְׁפִּיזֵי עִלָּאֵי: אַבְרָהָם יִצְחָק יַעֲקֹב יוֹסֵף מֹשֶׁה וְאַהֲרֹן.

On the last day of סוכות *on leaving the* סוכה*:*

יְהִי רָצוֹן מִלְּפָנֶיךָ יהוה אֱלֹהֵינוּ וֵאלֹהֵי אֲבוֹתֵינוּ, כְּשֵׁם שֶׁקִּיַּמְתִּי וְיָשַׁבְתִּי בְּסֻכָּה זוֹ, כֵּן אֶזְכֶּה לַשָּׁנָה הַבָּאָה לֵישֵׁב בְּסֻכַּת עוֹרוֹ שֶׁל לִוְיָתָן.

אֻשְׁפִּיזִין / USHPIZIN

The *Zohar* derives from Leviticus 23:42 that when a Jew dwells in the *sukka*, seven "righteous ones" (in Aramaic, *ushpizin)* visit the *sukka* too, and thus Rav Hamnuna Saba would invite the "guests" to sit with him. The *Zohar* insists that one allot a meal to these heavenly guests, which being uneaten, is then to be given to the poor. *Arizal* recommends that one be sure to invite the needy to one's meals on Sukkot to fulfill this prescription. He adds that generally speaking, the righteous seek to share their own portion with the poor (*Pri Etz Ḥayyim*).

The seven righteous guests are: Abraham, Isaac, Jacob, Moses, Aaron, Joseph, and David. Kabbalists view these seven Biblical figures as personifications of the seven lower *Sefirot*,

USHPIZIN

On entering the sukka and before saying Kiddush, many have the custom to welcome "guests" from the biblical past, who are said to join us as we sit in the sukka.
At this point some follow the Hasidic custom of reciting additional prayers, which can be found on page 1341.

אֲזַמִּין I INVITE to my meal exalted guests, Abraham, Isaac, Jacob, Joseph, Moses, Aaron and David.

On the first day I PRAY you, Abraham, exalted guest, may there abide here wit me and with you all the other exalted guests, Isaac, Jacob, Joseph, Moses, Aaron and David.

On the second day I PRAY you, Isaac, exalted guest, may there abide here with me and with you all the other exalted guests, Abraham, Jacob, Joseph, Moses, Aaron and David.

On the third day I PRAY you, Jacob, exalted guest, may there abide here with me and with you all the other exalted guests, Abraham, Isaac, Joseph, Moses, Aaron and David.

On the fourth day I PRAY you, Joseph, exalted guest, may there abide here with me and with you all the other exalted guests, Abraham, Isaac, Jacob, Moses, Aaron and David.

On the fifth day I PRAY you, Moses, exalted guest, may there abide here with me and with you all the other exalted guests, Abraham, Isaac, Jacob, Joseph, Aaron and David.

On the sixth day I PRAY you, Aaron, exalted guest, may there abide here with me and with you all the other exalted guests, Abraham, Isaac, Jacob, Joseph, Moses and David.

On Hoshana Raba I PRAY you, David, exalted guest, may there abide here with me and with you all the other exalted guests, Abraham, Isaac, Jacob, Joseph, Moses and Aaron.

On the last day of Sukkot, on leaving the sukka:

יְהִי רָצוֹן MAY IT BE Your will, Lord our God and God of our fathers, that as I have fulfilled Your commandment and have dwelt in this sukka, so may I merit to dwell next year in the sukka made from the skin of the Leviathan.

---

which manifest seven qualities of the Divine: חֶסֶד (lovingkindness), גְּבוּרָה (might), תִּפְאֶרֶת (splendor), נֶצַח (eternity), הוֹד (glory), יְסוֹד (foundation), and מַלְכוּת (majesty), respectively. The *Zohar* portrays all seven as guests in every *sukka* throughout the seven days of the festival, but the *Arizal* describes how each one of the seven personified traits is conveyed over the seven days of the festival; hence the focus of the first day is Abraham, the personification of חֶסֶד; of the second, Isaac, the personification of גְּבוּרָה, etc.

קידושא רבא לשלוש רגלים

On שבת חול המועד *turn to page 610.*

On יום טוב *that falls on* שבת*, start* קידוש *here:*

שמות לא

וְשָׁמְרוּ בְנֵי־יִשְׂרָאֵל אֶת־הַשַּׁבָּת, לַעֲשׂוֹת אֶת־הַשַּׁבָּת לְדֹרֹתָם בְּרִית עוֹלָם: בֵּינִי וּבֵין בְּנֵי יִשְׂרָאֵל אוֹת הִוא לְעֹלָם, כִּי־שֵׁשֶׁת יָמִים עָשָׂה יהוה אֶת־הַשָּׁמַיִם וְאֶת־הָאָרֶץ וּבַיּוֹם הַשְּׁבִיעִי שָׁבַת וַיִּנָּפַשׁ:

שמות כ

זָכוֹר אֶת־יוֹם הַשַּׁבָּת לְקַדְּשׁוֹ: שֵׁשֶׁת יָמִים תַּעֲבֹד, וְעָשִׂיתָ כָּל־מְלַאכְתֶּךָ: וְיוֹם הַשְּׁבִיעִי שַׁבָּת לַיהוה אֱלֹהֶיךָ, לֹא־תַעֲשֶׂה כָל־מְלָאכָה אַתָּה וּבִנְךָ וּבִתֶּךָ, עַבְדְּךָ וַאֲמָתְךָ וּבְהֶמְתֶּךָ, וְגֵרְךָ אֲשֶׁר בִּשְׁעָרֶיךָ: כִּי שֵׁשֶׁת־יָמִים עָשָׂה יהוה אֶת־הַשָּׁמַיִם וְאֶת־הָאָרֶץ אֶת־הַיָּם וְאֶת־כָּל־אֲשֶׁר־בָּם, וַיָּנַח בַּיּוֹם הַשְּׁבִיעִי

On יום טוב *that falls on* שבת*, some start* קידוש *here instead:*

עַל־כֵּן בֵּרַךְ יהוה אֶת־יוֹם הַשַּׁבָּת וַיְקַדְּשֵׁהוּ:

On יום טוב *that falls on a weekday, start here:*

ויקרא כג

אֵלֶּה מוֹעֲדֵי יהוה מִקְרָאֵי קֹדֶשׁ אֲשֶׁר־תִּקְרְאוּ אֹתָם בְּמוֹעֲדָם:
וַיְדַבֵּר מֹשֶׁה אֶת־מֹעֲדֵי יהוה אֶל־בְּנֵי יִשְׂרָאֵל:

When saying קידוש *for others, add:*

סַבְרִי מָרָנָן וְרַבָּנָן וְרַבּוֹתַי

בָּרוּךְ אַתָּה יהוה אֱלֹהֵינוּ מֶלֶךְ הָעוֹלָם, בּוֹרֵא פְּרִי הַגָּפֶן.

On סוכות *when* קידוש *is made in the* סוכה*, add:*

בָּרוּךְ אַתָּה יהוה אֱלֹהֵינוּ מֶלֶךְ הָעוֹלָם, אֲשֶׁר קִדְּשָׁנוּ בְּמִצְוֹתָיו וְצִוָּנוּ לֵישֵׁב בַּסֻּכָּה.

For "*Laws of Kiddush*" see page 426.

KIDDUSH FOR YOM TOV MORNING

On Shabbat Ḥol HaMo'ed, turn to page 611.

On a Yom Tov that falls on Shabbat, start Kiddush here:

Ex. 31 וְשָׁמְרוּ THE CHILDREN of ISRAEL shall keep the Sabbath, observing the Sabbath throughout their generations as an everlasting covenant. It is a sign between Me and the children of Israel forever that in six days the Lord made heaven and earth, and He rested on the seventh day and was refreshed.

Ex. 20 זָכוֹר REMEMBER THE SABBATH to keep it holy. Six days shall you labor and do all your work; but the seventh day is a Sabbath to the Lord your God, you shall not do any work, neither you, nor your son, nor your daughter, nor your manservant, nor your maidservant, nor your cattle, nor the stranger who is within your gates. For in six days the Lord made heaven and earth, the sea and all that is therein, and He rested on the seventh day –

**On Yom Tov that falls on Shabbat, some start Kiddush here instead:*

therefore the Lord blessed the Sabbath day and made it holy.

On Yom Tov that falls on a weekday, start here:

Lev. 23 אֵלֶּה THESE are the appointed festival seasons of the Lord, the holy assemblies that you shall proclaim in their appointed seasons. Moses declared the appointed festival seasons of the Lord, to the children of Israel.

When saying Kiddush for others, add:

By your leave, my masters, rabbis, and esteemed companions:

בָּרוּךְ BLESSED ARE YOU, Lord, our God, King of the universe, Who creates the fruit of the vine.

On Sukkot, when Kiddush is made in the sukka, add:

בָּרוּךְ BLESSED ARE YOU, Lord, our God, King of the universe, Who has sanctified us with His commandments and commanded us to dwell in the sukka.

In many congregations, on פסח*, a short piyut is said before the* עמידה *of* שחרית*.* *See page 506.*
No such piyut is said on the eighth day of פסח*, unless it falls on a* שבת *in which case* בְּרַח דּוֹדִי אֶל שֶׁאָנָן נָוֶה *(page 806) is said.*

ברח דודי

ליום טוב ראשון של פסח

בְּרַח דּוֹדִי עַד שֶׁתְּחַפֵּץ אַהֲבַת כְּלוּלֵינוּ
שׁוּב לְרַחֵם, כִּי כָלִינוּ
מַלְכֵי רִשְׁעָה, שׁוֹבֵינוּ, תּוֹלָלֵינוּ
הֲרֹס וְקַעְקֵעַ בִּצָּתָם מִתְּלֵנוּ
הָקֵם טוּרְךָ, נְגֹן שְׁתִילֵינוּ
הִנֵּה־זֶה עוֹמֵד אַחַר כָּתְלֵנוּ: שיר השירים ב

בְּרַח דּוֹדִי עַד שֶׁיָּפוּחַ קֵץ מַחֲזֶה
חִישׁ וְנָסוּ הַצְּלָלִים מִזֶּה
יָרוּם וְנִשָּׂא, וְגָבֹהַּ נִבְזֶה
יַשְׂכִּיל וְיוֹכִיחַ, וְגוֹיִם רַבִּים יַזֶּה
חֲשֹׂף זְרוֹעֲךָ, קְרָא כָזֶה
קוֹל דּוֹדִי הִנֵּה־זֶה: שיר השירים ב

בְּרַח דּוֹדִי וּדְמֵה־לְךָ לִצְבִי: שיר השירים ח
יָגַל, יָגֵשׁ, קֵץ קִצְבִּי / דַּלְתוֹתַי מִשְּׁבִי
לַעֲטֶרֶת צְבִי / תְּעוּבִים, תְּאֵבִים הַר צְבִי
וְאֵין מֵבִיא וְנָבִיא / וְלֹא תַשְׁבִּי
מְשׁוּי, מְשִׁיבִי / רִיבָה רִיבִי
הָסֵר חוֹבִי וּכְאֵבִי/ וְיֵרָא וְיֵבוֹשׁ אוֹיְבִי
וְאָשִׁיבָה חוֹרְפִי בְּנִיבִי/ זֶה דוֹדִי, גּוֹאֲלִי, קְרוֹבִי
רֵעִי וַאֲהוּבִי / אֵל אֱלֹהֵי אָבִי.

בִּגְלַל אָבוֹת תּוֹשִׁיעַ בָּנִים, וְתָבִיא גְאֻלָּה לִבְנֵי בְנֵיהֶם.
בָּרוּךְ אַתָּה יהוה, גָּאַל יִשְׂרָאֵל.

Continue with the עמידה *on page 810.*

In many congregations, on Pesaḥ, a short piyut is said before the Amida of Shaḥarit. See page 507. No such piyut is said on the eighth day of Pesaḥ, unless it falls on a Shabbat, in which case "Beloved, hasten to Your hallowed dwelling" (page 807) is said.

BERAḤ DODI

FIRST DAY OF PESAḤ

בְּרַח דּוֹדִי FLEE, MY BELOVED, till our love shall please You,
Then turn in pity. Base kings would sweep
Us hence; shall their despoiling not appease You?
O tear their roots up from our ruined heap!
Then raise our rampart; let our songful children call,
Song. 2 "Behold, He stands now behind our wall."

FLEE, MY BELOVED, till the day be breaking
Beyond the end of vision – then arise
And chase these shadows – him You were forsaking,
Despised, shall be exalted, high and wise,
Sprinkling the nations. Bare Your arm, Lord, when we cry,
Song. 2 "The voice of my Beloved sounded nigh."

Song. 8 FLEE, MY BELOVED, like a roe be flying,
Till You reveal the end of my account.
Despoiled, and for my crown of beauty sighing,
Contemned, but longing for the glorious mount,
So with no leader and no prophet leave me,
With yet no Tishbite to renew my fame;
But plead my cause at last; the bonds that grieve me
Break; and my foe shall turn away in shame
When these that do reproach me and deceive me
I answer with sweet words that speak Your name:
"This is my Beloved, my Redeemer, Lover, Friend,
My father's God, my God until the end."

ON ACCOUNT of the fathers please save the children and bring redemption to their children's children.
Blessed are You, Lord, Who redeemed Israel.

Continue with the Amida on page 811.

*This translation is based on that of Nina Salaman, and uses a free-form poetic rhyming scheme rather than a literal translation.

ליום טוב שני של פסח

בְּרַח דּוֹדִי אֶל מָכוֹן לְשִׁבְתָּךְ
וְאִם עָבַֽרְנוּ אֶת בְּרִיתָךְ
אָנָּא זְכֹר אִוּוּי חֻפָּתָךְ
הָקֵם קֹשְׁטְ מִלָּתָךְ
כּוֹנֵן מְשׂוֹשׂ קִרְיָתָךְ
הַעֲלוֹתָהּ עַל רֹאשׁ שִׂמְחָתָךְ

בְּרַח דּוֹדִי אֶל שָׁלֵם סֻכָּךְ
וְאִם תָּעִֽינוּ מִדַּרְכָּךְ
אָנָּא הָצֵץ מֵחֲרַכָּךְ
וְתוֹשִֽׁיעַ עַם עָנִי וּמִתְּכָךְ
חֲמָתְךָ מֵהֶם לְשַׁכֵּךְ
וּבְאֶבְרָתְךָ סֶֽלָה לְהִסְתּוֹכֵךְ

בְּרַח דּוֹדִי אֶל לִבְּךָ וְעֵינֶֽיךָ שָׁם
וְאִם זָנַֽחְנוּ טוֹב מְרֻשָּׁם
אָנָּא שְׁמַע שַׁאֲגַת קוֹל צוֹרְרֶֽיךָ וְרִגְשָׁם
רַוֵּה מִדָּם גּוּשָׁם
וַעֲפָרָם מֵחֵלֶב יְדֻשָּׁם
וּפִגְרֵיהֶם, יַעֲלֶה בְאָשָׁם

בְּרַח דּוֹדִי אֶל מָרוֹם מֵרִאשׁוֹן
וְאִם בָּגַדְנוּ בְּכַחְשׁוֹן
אָנָּא סְכוֹת צָקוּן לַחֲשׁוֹן
דְּלוֹתִי מִטְּבֽוּעַ רִפְשׁוֹן
גְּאֹל נְצוּרֵי כְּאִישׁוֹן
כְּאָז בַּחֹֽדֶשׁ הָרִאשׁוֹן.

בִּגְלַל אָבוֹת תּוֹשִֽׁיעַ בָּנִים, וְתָבִיא גְאֻלָּה לִבְנֵי בְנֵיהֶם.
בָּרוּךְ אַתָּה יהוה, גָּאַל יִשְׂרָאֵל.

Continue with the עמידה *on page 810.*

SECOND DAY OF PESAH

בְּרַח דּוֹדִי* BELOVED, hasten to Your chosen habitation.
Though we have transgressed Your covenant,
Remember, we beseech You, the tabernacle of Your desire.
Confirm Your promise to us,
And reestablish in its joy Your city
Which I set above my chiefest joys.

BELOVED, hasten to Your tabernacle in Jerusalem.
Though we have strayed from Your way,
Yet look upon us and have compassion
On Your helpless and oppressed people.
Avert Your wrath from us,
And shelter us beneath Your wings for ever.

BELOVED, hasten to Your shrine
For which Your heart and eyes long.
Though we have shrunk from that which is good,
Please listen to the roaring and the raging,
And see the foulness poured out on earth
By those who oppress Your people.

BELOVED, hasten to Your temple exalted from of old.
Though we may have acted falsely and wrongly,
Yet, we beseech You, hearken to our inward prayer.
Draw us out of the depths of the mire,
And redeem and preserve us as the apple of the eye,
As You did aforetime in this opening month of the year.

ON ACCOUNT of the fathers please save the children and bring redemption to their children's children.
Blessed are You, Lord, Who redeemed Israel.

Continue with the Amida on page 811.

*This translation is based on that of R. David Aaron de Sola, and uses a free-form poetic scheme rather than a literal translation.

לשבת חול המועד פסח

On שבת חול המועד, or on the eighth day of פסח that occurs on שבת,
some congregations say the following:

בְּרַח דּוֹדִי אֶל שַׁאֲנָן נָוֶה
אִם הֶלְאֵינוּ דֶּרֶךְ הָעִוָּה
הִנֵּה לָקִינוּ בְּכָל מַדְוֶה
וְאַתָּה יהוה מָעוֹז וּמִקְוֶה
עָלֶיךָ כָּל הַיּוֹם נְקַוֶּה   לְגָאֳלֵנוּ וּלְשִׁיתֵנוּ כְּגַן רָוֶה.

בְּרַח דּוֹדִי אֶל מְקוֹם מִקְדָּשֵׁנוּ
אִם עֲוֹנוֹת עָבְרוּ רֹאשֵׁנוּ
הִנֵּה בַּרְזֶל בָּאָה נַפְשֵׁנוּ
וְאַתָּה יהוה אוֹרֵנוּ, קְדוֹשֵׁנוּ
עָלֶיךָ נִשְׁפֹּךְ שִׂיחַ רַחֲשֵׁנוּ   לְגָאֳלֵנוּ מִמְּעוֹן קָדְשְׁךָ לְהַחְפִּישֵׁנוּ.

בְּרַח דּוֹדִי אֶל עִיר צִדְקֵנוּ
אִם לֹא שָׁמַעְנוּ לְקוֹל מַצְדִּיקֵנוּ
הִנֵּה אֲכָלוּנוּ בְּכָל פֶּה מְדִקֵּינוּ
וְאַתָּה יהוה שׁוֹפְטֵנוּ, מְחוֹקְקֵנוּ
עָלֶיךָ נַשְׁלִיךְ יְהַב חֶלְקֵנוּ   לְגָאֳלֵנוּ בְּהַשְׁקֵט וּבְבִטְחָה לְהַחֲזִיקֵנוּ.

בְּרַח דּוֹדִי אֶל וַעַד הַזְּבוּל
עִם עֻלְּךָ סָבַלְנוּ בְּלִי סִבּוּל
הִנֵּה שִׁחֲתוּנוּ בְּכָל מִינֵי חִבּוּל
וְאַתָּה יהוה מְשַׂמֵּחַ אָבוּל
עָלֶיךָ נְסַבִּיר לְהַתִּיר כָּבוּל   לְגָאֳלֵנוּ לְהִתְגַּדֵּל מֵעַל גְּבוּל.

בְּרַח דּוֹדִי אֶל נִשָּׂא מִגְּבָעוֹת
אִם זַדְנוּ בִּפְרֹעַ פְּרָעוֹת
הִנֵּה הִשִּׂיגוּנוּ צָרוֹת רַבּוֹת וְרָעוֹת
וְאַתָּה יהוה אֵל לְמוֹשָׁעוֹת
עָלֶיךָ נִתְחַנֵּן שִׂיחַ שְׁוָעוֹת   לְגָאֳלֵנוּ וּלְעַטְּרֵנוּ נֹעַם יְשׁוּעוֹת.

בִּגְלַל אָבוֹת תּוֹשִׁיעַ בָּנִים, וְתָבִיא גְאֻלָּה לִבְנֵי בְנֵיהֶם.
בָּרוּךְ אַתָּה יהוה, גָּאַל יִשְׂרָאֵל.

On יום טוב, say the עמידה on page 810. On שבת חול המועד, say the עמידה on page 506.

SHABBAT ḤOL HAMO'ED PESAḤ

On Shabbat Ḥol HaMo'ed, or on the eighth day of Pesaḥ that occurs on Shabbat, some congregations say the following:

בְּרַח דוֹדִי* BELOVED, hasten to Your hallowed dwelling,
And though our wanton ways have vexed Your face,
Behold our woe, all other woe excelling,
You are our only strength and resting-place;
With hope in You our hearts are daily swelling,
O make us watered gardens of Your grace.

BELOVED, hasten to our shrine all-holy,
And though sin claims us almost for its own,
Behold how bound in chains we cower lowly,
You are the sacred Savior, You alone;
To You we give ourselves in prayer wholly,
O grant redemption from Your lofty throne.

BELOVED, hasten to our righteous city,
And though we lent no ear to lore divine,
Behold us now consumed, a thing of pity,
You are our Judge, we make our burden Thine.
Our Legislator, hear our mournful ditty,
O send the strength and peace for which we pine.

BELOVED, hasten to Your habitation,
And though impatiently we spurned Your rein,
Behold the measure of our tribulation,
You are the comforter of every pain;
We look to You to free our captive nation,
And in our boundaries be hymned again.

BELOVED, hasten to Your seat uplifted,
And though presumption did our duty whelm,
Behold to what distresses we have drifted,
You are the liberator of our realm;
Our pleading trust in You has never shifted,
O place upon our head salvation's helm.

ON ACCOUNT of the fathers please save the children and bring redemption to their children's children. Blessed are You, Lord, Who redeemed Israel.

On Yom Tov, say the Amida on page 811. On Shabbat Ḥol HaMo'ed, say the Amida on page 507.

* This translation is based on that of Israel Zangwill, and uses a free-form poetic rhyming scheme rather than a literal translation.

גאולה לשביעי של פסח

יוֹם לְיַבָּשָׁה נֶהֶפְכוּ מְצוּלִים
שִׁירָה חֲדָשָׁה שִׁבְּחוּ גְאוּלִים.

הִטְבַּעְתָּ בְּתַרְמִית / רַגְלֵי בַּת עֲנָמִית
וּפַעֲמֵי שׁוּלַמִּית / יָפוּ בַּנְּעָלִים. שִׁירָה חֲדָשָׁה שִׁבְּחוּ גְאוּלִים.

וְכָל רוֹאַי יְשׁוּרוּן / בְּעֵת הוֹדְךָ יְשָׁרוֹן
אֵין כָּאֵל יְשֻׁרוּן / וְאוֹיְבֵינוּ פְּלִילִים. שִׁירָה חֲדָשָׁה שִׁבְּחוּ גְאוּלִים.

דְּגָלַי כֵּן תָּרִים / עַל הַנִּשְׁאָרִים
וּתְלַקֵּט נִפְזָרִים / כִּמְלַקֵּט שִׁבֳּלִים. שִׁירָה חֲדָשָׁה שִׁבְּחוּ גְאוּלִים.

הַבָּאִים עִמְּךָ / בִּבְרִית חוֹתָמְךָ
וּמִבֶּטֶן לְשִׁמְךָ / הֵמָּה נִמּוֹלִים. שִׁירָה חֲדָשָׁה שִׁבְּחוּ גְאוּלִים.

הֶרְאוּ אוֹתוֹתָם / לְכָל רוֹאֶה אוֹתָם
וְעַל כַּנְפֵי כְּסוּתָם / עָשׂוּ גְּדִילִים. שִׁירָה חֲדָשָׁה שִׁבְּחוּ גְאוּלִים.

לְמִי זֹאת נִרְשֶׁמֶת / הַכֶּר נָא דְּבַר אֱמֶת
לְמִי הַחוֹתֶמֶת / וּלְמִי הַפְּתִילִים. שִׁירָה חֲדָשָׁה שִׁבְּחוּ גְאוּלִים.

וְשׁוּב שֵׁנִית לְקַדְּשָׁהּ / וְאַל תּוֹסֵף לְגָרְשָׁהּ
וְהַעֲלֵה אוֹר שִׁמְשָׁהּ / וְנָסוּ הַצְּלָלִים. שִׁירָה חֲדָשָׁה שִׁבְּחוּ גְאוּלִים.

יְדִידִים רוֹמְמוּךָ / בְּשִׁירָה קִדְּמוּךָ
מִי כָמְכָה / יהוה בָּאֵלִים. שִׁירָה חֲדָשָׁה שִׁבְּחוּ גְאוּלִים.

בִּגְלַל אָבוֹת תּוֹשִׁיעַ בָּנִים, וְתָבִיא גְאֻלָּה לִבְנֵי בְנֵיהֶם.
בָּרוּךְ אַתָּה יהוה גָּאַל יִשְׂרָאֵל.

Continue with the עמידה *on the next page.*

יוֹם לְיַבָּשָׁה – *On the day...became dry land.* This *piyut* was crafted by the famed eleventh-century poet and philosopher R. Yehuda HaLevi, author of the *Kuzari*. His name appears in the acrostic formed by the initial letters of each stanza. True to his oft-expressed love for the Jewish people and the land of Israel, it describes the epochal salvation of Israel at the Sea of Reeds, as celebrated on the seventh day of Pesaḥ. It expresses the poet's own longing for God to once again redeem His people, by renewing the covenantal bond, gathering in the exiles, and returning the Jewish people to Israel, its ancient homeland. Then once again, as the repeating refrain states, the redeemed Jewish people will sing a new song of praise to God, just as they did at the first redemption.

SEVENTH DAY OF PESAḤ

יוֹם לְיַבָּשָׁה ON THE day that the deep waters became dry land,
Those who were redeemed gave praise with a new song.

DROWNED in her deceit were the Anamite daughter's feet,
while the footsteps of the Shulamit were secured in their shoes.
Those who were redeemed gave praise with a new song.

THEREFORE will all who see Yeshurun give praise in My House of Glory,
declaring "There is none like Yeshurun's God" when our enemies will be judged.
Those who were redeemed gave praise with a new song.

SURELY You will raise our banners over those who will remain,
when You will gather our dispersed as one who brings sheaves together.
Those who were redeemed gave praise with a new song.

THOSE who go with You bear Your seal of the covenant,
being circumcised they are dedicated to Your name from the womb.
Those who were redeemed gave praise with a new song.

MAKE KNOWN their sign of the covenant to all who will see them,
just as they in turn make fringes on the corners of their garments.
Those who were redeemed gave praise with a new song.

TO WHOM is this one assigned, please recognize the truth,
Whose is this seal, and Whose these threads?
Those who were redeemed gave praise with a new song.

RETURN once more to betroth her, do not again send her away;
make the light of her sun arise once more, that the shadows flee away.
Those who were redeemed gave praise with a new song.

YOUR BELOVED ones raised You on high, greeted You with song, saying,
Who is like You, O Lord, among the mighty ones?
Those who were redeemed gave praise with a new song.

ON ACCOUNT of the fathers please save the children and bring redemption to their children's children.
Blessed are You, Lord, Who redeemed Israel.

Continue with the Amida on the next page.

שלוש רגלים

The following עמידה *is said at* שחרית, מנחה *and* מעריב *of* פסח, שבועות, סוכות, שמיני עצרת *and* שמחת תורה*, but not on* חול המועד.

עמידה לשחרית, מנחה ומעריב

One begins the עמידה *by taking three steps forward (OH 95:1). According to some traditions, one should first take three steps back before moving forward (MB 95:3). The* עמידה *is recited with one's feet together. One should try to concentrate on the simple meaning of the words of the* עמידה *with the awareness throughout that one is standing in the presence of the Almighty (OH 98:1 and MB 98:1). At the points indicated by* ˺*, bend the knees at the first word, bow at the second, and stand straight before saying God's name.*

כִּי שֵׁם יהוה אֶקְרָא, הָבוּ גֹדֶל לֵאלֹהֵינוּ: דברים לב

אֲדֹנָי, שְׂפָתַי תִּפְתָּח, וּפִי יַגִּיד תְּהִלָּתֶךָ: תהלים נא

אבות

˺**בָּרוּךְ** אַתָּה יהוה, אֱלֹהֵינוּ וֵאלֹהֵי אֲבוֹתֵינוּ, אֱלֹהֵי אַבְרָהָם, אֱלֹהֵי יִצְחָק, וֵאלֹהֵי יַעֲקֹב, הָאֵל הַגָּדוֹל הַגִּבּוֹר וְהַנּוֹרָא, אֵל עֶלְיוֹן, גּוֹמֵל חֲסָדִים טוֹבִים, וְקוֹנֵה הַכֹּל, וְזוֹכֵר חַסְדֵי אָבוֹת, וּמֵבִיא גוֹאֵל לִבְנֵי בְנֵיהֶם לְמַעַן שְׁמוֹ בְּאַהֲבָה. מֶלֶךְ עוֹזֵר וּמוֹשִׁיעַ וּמָגֵן. ˺בָּרוּךְ אַתָּה יהוה, מָגֵן אַבְרָהָם.

גבורות

אַתָּה גִּבּוֹר לְעוֹלָם, אֲדֹנָי, מְחַיֵּה מֵתִים אַתָּה, רַב לְהוֹשִׁיעַ.

From מנחה *of* שמיני עצרת *through* שחרית *on the first day of* פסח*:*

מַשִּׁיב הָרְוּחַ וּמוֹרִיד הַגֶּשֶׁם

מְכַלְכֵּל חַיִּים בְּחֶסֶד, מְחַיֵּה מֵתִים בְּרַחֲמִים רַבִּים, סוֹמֵךְ נוֹפְלִים, וְרוֹפֵא חוֹלִים, וּמַתִּיר אֲסוּרִים, וּמְקַיֵּם אֱמוּנָתוֹ לִישֵׁנֵי עָפָר. מִי

For laws regarding "The repetition of the *Amida*," see page 107.
For laws regarding "Omission/Insertion of *Mashiv Haru'aḥ*," see page 109.

SERVICE FOR FESTIVALS

The following Amida is said at Shaḥarit, Minḥa and Ma'ariv on Yom Tov Pesaḥ, Shavuot, Sukkot, Shemini Atzeret and Simḥat Torah, but not on Ḥol HaMo'ed.

AMIDA FOR SHAḤARIT, MINḤA AND MA'ARIV

One begins the Amida by taking three steps forward (OḤ 95:1). According to some traditions, one should first take three steps back before moving forward (MB 95:3). The Amida is recited with one's feet together. One should try to concentrate on the simple meaning of the words of the Amida with the awareness throughout that one is standing in the presence of the Almighty (OḤ 98:1 and MB 98:1). At the points indicated by ▾, bend the knees at the first word, bow at the second, and stand straight before saying God's name.

Deut. 32 WHEN I proclaim the name of the LORD, ascribe greatness to our God.
Ps. 51 "O my Master, open my lips, and my mouth will relate Your praise."

PATRIARCHS

▾ בָּרוּךְ BLESSED ARE YOU, LORD, our God and the God of our fathers, the God of Abraham, the God of Isaac, and the God of Jacob, the God Who is great, mighty, and awesome, God most exalted, Who bestows rewards of benevolent kindness, Who is the Creator of everything, Who remembers all the kind acts of the fathers, and Who brings a redeemer to their children's children, for the sake of His name, with love. King Who helps, saves, and shields, ▾blessed are You, LORD, Shield of Abraham.

GOD'S MIGHT

אַתָּה YOU, my Master, are forever mighty, You are the Resurrector of the dead, with great power to save.

From Minḥa of Shemini Atzeret, through Shaḥarit on the first day of Pesaḥ:
He makes the wind blow and the rain fall

He sustains the living with kindness, He resurrects the dead with great compassion, He supports those who are falling, He heals the sick, He sets the incarcerated free, and He fulfills what He has promised to those who sleep in the dust. Who is like You, O mighty

כָּמְוֹךָ, בַּעַל גְּבוּרוֹת, וּמִי דּוֹמֶה לָּךְ, מֶלֶךְ, מֵמִית וּמְחַיֶּה וּמַצְמִיחַ יְשׁוּעָה. וְנֶאֱמָן אַתָּה לְהַחֲיוֹת מֵתִים. בָּרוּךְ אַתָּה יהוה, מְחַיֵּה הַמֵּתִים.

When saying the עמידה *silently, continue with* אַתָּה קָדוֹשׁ *on the next page.*
During the חזרת הש״ץ *of* מנחה*, turn to the* קדושה *on the next page.*

קדושה לשחרית

During חזרת הש״ץ *of* שחרית*, the following is said standing with feet together, rising on the toes at the words indicated by* ▲.

then קהל / ש״ץ: **נְקַדֵּשׁ** אֶת שִׁמְךָ בָּעוֹלָם, כְּשֵׁם שֶׁמַּקְדִּישִׁים אוֹתוֹ בִּשְׁמֵי מָרוֹם, כַּכָּתוּב עַל יַד נְבִיאֶךָ, וְקָרָא זֶה אֶל־זֶה וְאָמַר

ישעיה ו

then קהל / ש״ץ: ▲קָדוֹשׁ, ▲קָדוֹשׁ, ▲קָדוֹשׁ יהוה צְבָאוֹת, מְלֹא כָל־הָאָרֶץ כְּבוֹדוֹ:

אָז בְּקוֹל רַעַשׁ גָּדוֹל אַדִּיר וְחָזָק מַשְׁמִיעִים קוֹל, מִתְנַשְּׂאִים לְעֻמַּת שְׂרָפִים,

ש״ץ: לְעֻמָּתָם בָּרוּךְ יֹאמֵרוּ

יחזקאל ג

then קהל / ש״ץ: ▲בָּרוּךְ כְּבוֹד־יהוה מִמְּקוֹמוֹ:

מִמְּקוֹמְךָ מַלְכֵּנוּ תוֹפִיעַ וְתִמְלֹךְ עָלֵינוּ, כִּי מְחַכִּים אֲנַחְנוּ לָךְ. מָתַי תִּמְלֹךְ בְּצִיּוֹן, בְּקָרוֹב בְּיָמֵינוּ לְעוֹלָם וָעֶד תִּשְׁכֹּן. תִּתְגַּדַּל וְתִתְקַדַּשׁ בְּתוֹךְ יְרוּשָׁלַיִם עִירְךָ, לְדוֹר וָדוֹר וּלְנֵצַח נְצָחִים. וְעֵינֵינוּ תִרְאֶינָה מַלְכוּתֶךָ, כַּדָּבָר הָאָמוּר בְּשִׁירֵי עֻזֶּךָ, עַל יְדֵי דָוִד מְשִׁיחַ צִדְקֶךָ

תהלים קמו

then קהל / ש״ץ: ▲יִמְלֹךְ יהוה לְעוֹלָם, אֱלֹהַיִךְ צִיּוֹן לְדֹר וָדֹר, הַלְלוּיָהּ:

ש״ץ: לְדוֹר וָדוֹר נַגִּיד גָּדְלֶךָ, וּלְנֵצַח נְצָחִים קְדֻשָּׁתְךָ נַקְדִּישׁ, וְשִׁבְחֲךָ אֱלֹהֵינוּ מִפִּינוּ לֹא יָמוּשׁ לְעוֹלָם וָעֶד, כִּי אֵל מֶלֶךְ גָּדוֹל וְקָדוֹשׁ אָתָּה. בָּרוּךְ אַתָּה יהוה, הָאֵל הַקָּדוֹשׁ.

The שליח ציבור *continues with* אַתָּה בְחַרְתָּנוּ *on the next page.*

For laws regarding "*Responding to the Leader during Kedusha,*" see page 510.

One, and who can be compared to You, O King Who causes death and resurrects, and Who causes salvation to sprout? Trustworthy are You to resurrect the dead. Blessed are You, Lord, Resurrector of the dead.

When saying the Amida silently, continue with "You are holy" on the next page.
During the Leader's Repetition of Minḥa, turn to the Kedusha on the next page.

KEDUSHA FOR SHAḤARIT

During the Leader's Repetition of Shaḥarit, the following is said standing with feet together, rising on the toes at the words indicated by ▴.

Cong. then Leader: נְקַדֵּשׁ WE WILL SANCTIFY Your name in this world, as they sanctify it in the heavenly heights, as is written by Your prophet:
Is. 6 "They called to one another, saying":

Cong. then Leader: ▴"Holy, ▴holy, ▴holy is the Lord of hosts; the whole world is filled with His glory.'"

So too, with a great, mighty, and powerful sound they make their voices heard, raising themselves before the Seraphim,

Leader: and facing them proclaim:

Ezek. 3 *Cong. then Leader:* ▴"Blessed is the glory of the Lord from His place."

May You, our King, appear from Your place and rule over us, for we are waiting for You. When will You rule in Zion? May it be soon in our day that You will make Zion Your dwelling evermore. May You be exalted and sanctified in Jerusalem Your city for all generations and forever more. May our eyes behold Your sovereign rule, as it was described in the songs praising Your strength, as written by David, the one anointed by Your just decree.

Ps. 146 *Cong. then Leader:* ▴"The Lord will reign forever, Your God, O Zion, to all generations. Praise the Lord."

Leader: To all generations we will proclaim Your greatness, and forever declare Your holiness, and the praise of You, our God, will never leave our mouth, for You are God and King, great and holy; blessed are You, Lord, the holy God.

The Leader continues with "You have chosen us" on the next page.

קדושה למנחה

During חזרת הש״ץ *of* מנחה*, the following is said standing with feet together, rising on the toes at the words indicated by* ▲.

קהל *then* ש״ץ: **נְקַדֵּשׁ** אֶת שִׁמְךָ בָּעוֹלָם, כְּשֵׁם שֶׁמַּקְדִּישִׁים אוֹתוֹ בִּשְׁמֵי מָרוֹם,
ישעיה ו כַּכָּתוּב עַל יַד נְבִיאֶךָ, וְקָרָא זֶה אֶל־זֶה וְאָמַר

קהל *then* ש״ץ: ▲קָדוֹשׁ, ▲קָדוֹשׁ, ▲קָדוֹשׁ יהוה צְבָאוֹת, מְלֹא כָל־הָאָרֶץ כְּבוֹדוֹ:

ש״ץ: לְעֻמָּתָם בָּרוּךְ יֹאמֵרוּ

יחזקאל ג קהל *then* ש״ץ: ▲בָּרוּךְ כְּבוֹד־יהוה מִמְּקוֹמוֹ:

ש״ץ: וּבְדִבְרֵי קָדְשְׁךָ כָּתוּב לֵאמֹר

תהלים קמו קהל *then* ש״ץ: ▲יִמְלֹךְ יהוה לְעוֹלָם, אֱלֹהַיִךְ צִיּוֹן לְדֹר וָדֹר, הַלְלוּיָהּ:

ש״ץ: לְדוֹר וָדוֹר נַגִּיד גָּדְלֶךָ, וּלְנֵצַח נְצָחִים קְדֻשָּׁתְךָ נַקְדִּישׁ, וְשִׁבְחֲךָ אֱלֹהֵינוּ מִפִּינוּ לֹא יָמוּשׁ לְעוֹלָם וָעֶד, כִּי אֵל מֶלֶךְ גָּדוֹל וְקָדוֹשׁ אָתָּה. בָּרוּךְ אַתָּה יהוה, הָאֵל הַקָּדוֹשׁ.

The שליח ציבור *continues with* אַתָּה בְחַרְתָּנוּ *below.*

When saying the עמידה *silently, continue here:*

קדושת השם

אַתָּה קָדוֹשׁ וְשִׁמְךָ קָדוֹשׁ. וּקְדוֹשִׁים בְּכָל יוֹם יְהַלְלוּךָ סֶּלָה. בָּרוּךְ אַתָּה יהוה, הָאֵל הַקָּדוֹשׁ.

קדושת היום

אַתָּה בְחַרְתָּנוּ מִכָּל הָעַמִּים, אָהַבְתָּ אוֹתָנוּ וְרָצִיתָ בָּנוּ, וְרוֹמַמְתָּנוּ מִכָּל הַלְּשׁוֹנוֹת, וְקִדַּשְׁתָּנוּ בְּמִצְוֹתֶיךָ, וְקֵרַבְתָּנוּ מַלְכֵּנוּ לַעֲבוֹדָתֶךָ, וְשִׁמְךָ הַגָּדוֹל וְהַקָּדוֹשׁ עָלֵינוּ קָרָאתָ.

וְקֵרַבְתָּנוּ מַלְכֵּנוּ לַעֲבוֹדָתֶךָ – *You have drawn us close to You, Our King, to Your service.* We thank God for yet another aspect of election – the privilege of being allowed to approach Him in

INSTRUCTIONS FOR SOMEONE WHO MADE A MISTAKE AND RECITED THE WRONG AMIDA ON YOM TOV

If one accidentally recited the weekday or Shabbat *Amida* on Yom Tov, even if *Ya'aleh VeYavo* was recited, one must recite the proper Yom Tov *Amida*. If one realized the mistake before concluding the *Amida*, one can return to *Ata Veḥartanu*.

When Yom Tov coincides with Shabbat, the Yom Tov *Amida* is recited with specific insertions for Shabbat. If these insertions were omitted, no corrective action is necessary as long as the conclusion of the blessing was recited properly. If one recited the blessing properly but omitted *"Yisrael vehazmanim"* from the conclusion, no corrective action is necessary. If *"HaShabbat"* was omitted, see *MB* 487:7 and *Biur Halakha* there.

KEDUSHA FOR MINHA

During the Leader's Repetition of Minha, the following is said standing with feet together, rising on the toes at the words indicated by ▴.

Cong. then Leader: נְקַדֵּשׁ WE WILL SANCTIFY Your name in this world, as they sanctify it in the heavenly heights, as is written by Your prophet: "They called to one another, saying": *Is. 6*

Cong. then Leader: "▴Holy, ▴holy, ▴holy is the LORD of hosts; the whole world is filled with His glory."

Leader: Those who face them declare, "Blessed –"

Ezek. 3 *Cong. then Leader:* ▴"Blessed is the glory of the LORD from His place."

Leader: And in Your holy Writings it is written as follows:

Ps. 146 *Cong. then Leader:* ▴"The LORD will reign forever, Your God, O Zion, to all generations. Praise the LORD."

Leader: To all generations we will proclaim Your greatness, and forever declare Your holiness, and the praise of You, our God, will never leave our mouth, for You are God and King, great and holy; blessed are You, LORD, the holy God.

The Leader continues with "You have chosen us" below.

When saying the Amida silently, continue here:

HOLINESS

אַתָּה YOU ARE HOLY and Your name is holy, and holy ones will praise You every day, forever. Blessed are You, LORD, the holy God.

אַתָּה בְחַרְתָּנוּ YOU HAVE CHOSEN US from among all the peoples; You have loved us and favored us. You have raised us above all languages and You have sanctified us with Your commandments. You have drawn us close to You, Our King, to Your service, and have proclaimed upon us Your great and holy name.

---

prayer and service in His sanctuary (cf. Psalms 65:4), all of which was inaugurated when קֵרְבָנוּ לִפְנֵי הַר סִינַי (we were 'drawn close' at Sinai), the prototype of the future Temple. Our thanksgiving for chosenness encompasses the gifts of both Torah and prayer.

וְשִׁמְךָ... עָלֵינוּ קָרָאתָ – *And have proclaimed upon us Your... holy name.* God is known as "the God of Israel;" He has chosen the Jewish people as the vehicle of His name and His reputation in the universe (R. Yehuda ben Yakar). For the same reason, throughout our prayers when we ask God to save or redeem us, we often declare that doing so will be not just for our sake but also "for the sake of Your name." If we are punished, that will constitute a desecration of God's name, given that the nations identify the Jewish people with God Himself.

On מוצאי שבת*:*

וַתּוֹדִיעֵנוּ יהוה אֱלֹהֵינוּ אֶת מִשְׁפְּטֵי צִדְקֶךָ, וַתְּלַמְּדֵנוּ לַעֲשׂוֹת חֻקֵּי רְצוֹנֶךָ, וַתִּתֶּן לָנוּ יהוה אֱלֹהֵינוּ מִשְׁפָּטִים יְשָׁרִים וְתוֹרוֹת אֱמֶת, חֻקִּים וּמִצְוֹת טוֹבִים, וַתַּנְחִילֵנוּ זְמַנֵּי שָׂשׂוֹן וּמוֹעֲדֵי קֹדֶשׁ וְחַגֵּי נְדָבָה, וַתּוֹרִישֵׁנוּ קְדֻשַּׁת שַׁבָּת וּכְבוֹד מוֹעֵד וַחֲגִיגַת הָרֶגֶל. וַתַּבְדֵּל יהוה אֱלֹהֵינוּ בֵּין קֹדֶשׁ לְחֹל, בֵּין אוֹר לְחֹשֶׁךְ, בֵּין יִשְׂרָאֵל לָעַמִּים, בֵּין יוֹם הַשְּׁבִיעִי לְשֵׁשֶׁת יְמֵי הַמַּעֲשֶׂה. בֵּין קְדֻשַּׁת שַׁבָּת לִקְדֻשַּׁת יוֹם טוֹב הִבְדַּלְתָּ, וְאֶת יוֹם הַשְּׁבִיעִי מִשֵּׁשֶׁת יְמֵי הַמַּעֲשֶׂה קִדַּשְׁתָּ, הִבְדַּלְתָּ וְקִדַּשְׁתָּ אֶת עַמְּךָ יִשְׂרָאֵל בִּקְדֻשָּׁתֶךָ.

(*If forgotten, no corrective action is necessary.*)

On שבת*, add the words in parentheses:*

וַתִּתֶּן לָנוּ יהוה אֱלֹהֵינוּ בְּאַהֲבָה, (שַׁבָּתוֹת לִמְנוּחָה וּ)מוֹעֲדִים לְשִׂמְחָה, חַגִּים וּזְמַנִּים לְשָׂשׂוֹן, אֶת יוֹם (הַשַּׁבָּת הַזֶּה וְאֶת יוֹם)

בפסח: חַג הַמַּצּוֹת הַזֶּה, זְמַן חֵרוּתֵנוּ

בשבועות: חַג הַשָּׁבוּעוֹת הַזֶּה, זְמַן מַתַּן תּוֹרָתֵנוּ

בסוכות: חַג הַסֻּכּוֹת הַזֶּה, זְמַן שִׂמְחָתֵנוּ

בשמע״צ ובש״ת: הַשְּׁמִינִי חַג הָעֲצֶרֶת הַזֶּה, זְמַן שִׂמְחָתֵנוּ

(בְּאַהֲבָה) מִקְרָא קֹדֶשׁ, זֵכֶר לִיצִיאַת מִצְרָיִם.

וַתַּבְדֵּל – *You made a separation.* The following list parallels the one found in the weekday Amida recited at the conclusion of Shabbat, except that this one adds the distinction between the respective sanctities of Shabbat and Yom Tov.

שַׁבָּתוֹת לִמְנוּחָה וּמוֹעֲדִים לְשִׂמְחָה – *Sabbaths for rest, festivals for rejoicing.* When Shabbat occurs in the course of a Yom Tov we recite the regular Yom Tov *Amida*, while inserting brief references to Shabbat. Given the central importance of Shabbat in the life of the Jew one might have thought that the Shabbat *Amida* should take precedence, with only brief Yom Tov insertions. The explanation, according to the Arizal, is that because the occurrence of Yom Tov is determined by the actions and declarations of the Jewish people, whereas Shabbat occurs automatically every seven days, it is essential that the *Amida* of Yom Tov remain intact even on Shabbat, so that we not diminish the sanctity of Yom Tov. This distinction between Shabbat and Yom Tov is reflected in the way the Torah refers to them: Shabbat is referred to as קֹדֶשׁ (holy), i.e., its holiness occurs independently of us, while Yom Tov is called מִקְרָא קֹדֶשׁ (a day to be designated as holy), through our making it so (*Bnei Yissaschar*).

The same insight would explain why when Shabbat and Yom Tov coincide we recite the Yom Tov *Kiddush* with a Shabbat insertion, rather than the other way around. Our Yom Tov

On Motza'ei Shabbat:

וַתּוֹדִיעֵנוּ YOU MADE KNOWN to us, LORD, our God, Your righteous laws, and You taught us to do the decrees of Your will. You gave us, LORD, our God, just laws and true teachings, good decrees and commandments. You gave us as our heritage seasons of gladness, holy festivals, and holidays of voluntary offerings. You made us heir to the holiness of the Sabbath, the glory of the festival, and the festive offering of the pilgrimage. You made a separation, LORD, our God, between sacred and secular, between light and darkness, between Israel and the nations, between the seventh day and the six days of labor. You made a separation between the holiness of the Sabbath and the holiness of the festivals, and You sanctified the seventh day above the six days of labor. You separated and sanctified Your people Israel with Your holiness. *(If forgotten, no corrective action is necessary.)*

On Shabbat, add the words in parentheses:

וַתִּתֶּן לָנוּ IN YOUR LOVE, LORD our God, You have given us (Sabbaths for rest), festivals for rejoicing, holidays and seasons for joy, (this Sabbath day and)

On Pesaḥ: this day of the Festival of Matzot,
the time of our freedom

On Shavuot: this day of the Festival of Shavuot,
the time of the giving of our Torah

On Sukkot: this day of the Festival of Sukkot,
the time of our rejoicing

On Shemini Atzeret & Simḥat Torah: the eighth day, this Festival of Atzeret,
the time of our rejoicing

(with love,) a holy convocation, a remembrance of the Exodus from Egypt.

Kiddush enhances the sanctity of Yom Tov itself, whereas when we recite *Kiddush* on Shabbat, we are not "sanctifying the day" for it is sacred even without our declaring it so; we are rather bringing its sanctity upon ourselves.

זְמַן חֵרוּתֵנוּ – *The time of our freedom.* There is a difference between the term חֵרוּת (liberation) that characterizes the purpose and outcome of the festival of Pesaḥ, and the term חוֹפֶשׁ (freedom). As can be derived from the Mishna (*Avot* 6:2), חֵרוּת connotes the removal of impediments that prevent us from acting in uplifting and redemptive ways (in a Torah context these would include the study of Torah and

אֱלֹהֵינוּ וֵאלֹהֵי אֲבוֹתֵינוּ, יַעֲלֶה וְיָבוֹא וְיַגִּיעַ, וְיֵרָאֶה וְיֵרָצֶה וְיִשָּׁמַע, וְיִפָּקֵד וְיִזָּכֵר זִכְרוֹנֵנוּ וּפִקְדוֹנֵנוּ, וְזִכְרוֹן אֲבוֹתֵינוּ, וְזִכְרוֹן מָשִׁיחַ בֶּן דָּוִד עַבְדֶּךָ, וְזִכְרוֹן יְרוּשָׁלַיִם עִיר קָדְשֶׁךָ, וְזִכְרוֹן כָּל עַמְּךָ בֵּית יִשְׂרָאֵל, לְפָנֶיךָ, לִפְלֵיטָה, לְטוֹבָה, לְחֵן וּלְחֶסֶד וּלְרַחֲמִים, לְחַיִּים וּלְשָׁלוֹם בְּיוֹם

בפסח: חַג הַמַּצּוֹת הַזֶּה.

בשבועות: חַג הַשָּׁבוּעוֹת הַזֶּה.

בסוכות: חַג הַסֻּכּוֹת הַזֶּה.

בשמע״צ ובש״ת: הַשְּׁמִינִי חַג הָעֲצֶרֶת הַזֶּה.

זָכְרֵנוּ יהוה אֱלֹהֵינוּ בּוֹ לְטוֹבָה, וּפָקְדֵנוּ בוֹ לִבְרָכָה, וְהוֹשִׁיעֵנוּ בוֹ לְחַיִּים. וּבִדְבַר יְשׁוּעָה וְרַחֲמִים, חוּס וְחָנֵּנוּ, וְרַחֵם עָלֵינוּ וְהוֹשִׁיעֵנוּ, כִּי אֵלֶיךָ עֵינֵינוּ, כִּי אֵל מֶלֶךְ חַנּוּן וְרַחוּם אָתָּה.

On שבת*, add the words in parentheses:*

וְהַשִּׂיאֵנוּ יהוה אֱלֹהֵינוּ אֶת בִּרְכַּת מוֹעֲדֶיךָ, לְחַיִּים וּלְשָׁלוֹם, לְשִׂמְחָה וּלְשָׂשׂוֹן, כַּאֲשֶׁר רָצִיתָ וְאָמַרְתָּ לְבָרְכֵנוּ. (אֱלֹהֵינוּ וֵאלֹהֵי אֲבוֹתֵינוּ, רְצֵה בִמְנוּחָתֵנוּ) קַדְּשֵׁנוּ בְּמִצְוֹתֶיךָ, וְתֵן חֶלְקֵנוּ בְּתוֹרָתֶךָ, שַׂבְּעֵנוּ מִטּוּבֶךָ, וְשַׂמְּחֵנוּ בִּישׁוּעָתֶךָ, וְטַהֵר לִבֵּנוּ לְעָבְדְּךָ בֶּאֱמֶת. וְהַנְחִילֵנוּ יהוה אֱלֹהֵינוּ (בְּאַהֲבָה וּבְרָצוֹן), בְּשִׂמְחָה וּבְשָׂשׂוֹן

---

the performance of *mitzvot*), whereas the latter represents the freedom from all constraint and thus to do whatever one wants. If I am truly free to do *whatever I want* then I am completely unpredictable. If everyone acts in this manner, it results in chaos, and often leads to the loss of freedom by necessitating the imposition of authority. How then do we establish order in a free society? We do so by educating ourselves as to the necessity of the laws – חָרוּת עַל הַלֻּחֹת – inscribing the Law on our hearts, as it were – and voluntarily making a covenant. We create order, which is indispensable for a free society to flourish, by limiting freedom to a certain extent – by committing ourselves to that which we know to be just, and keeping our word. For this reason the liberation we celebrate on Pesaḥ commemorates the Israelite preparation to assume the covenantal obligations of Sinai, rather than a mere casting off of the shackles of slavery (R. Jonathan Sacks).

זְמַן מַתַּן תּוֹרָתֵנוּ – *The time of the giving of our Torah* (previous page). Nowhere in the Torah itself is the festival of Shavuot explicitly identified as the day on which God gave us the Torah. Rather, the association is implicit in the description of the festival in Deuteronomy 16:12, where we are commanded וְעָשִׂיתָ אֶת־

אֱלֹהֵינוּ OUR GOD and God of our fathers, may there arise, arrive, reach, appear, be favored, heard, considered and remembered, our remembrance and recollection, Your remembrance of our fathers, of the Messiah son of David Your servant, of Jerusalem Your holy city and of all Your people the house of Israel. May they come before You for deliverance and benefit, for grace, kindness and mercy, for life and peace, on

On Pesaḥ:	this day of the Festival of Matzot.
On Shavuot:	this day of the Festival of Shavuot.
On Sukkot:	this day of the Festival of Sukkot.
On Shemini Atzeret & Simḥat Torah:	the eighth day, this Festival of Atzeret,

LORD our God, remember us this day for good. Be mindful of us this day for blessing, preserve us this day for life. Regarding redemption and mercy show us compassion and grace, and have pity on us and save us. For our eyes are lifted toward You, for You are a gracious and merciful God and King.

On Shabbat, add the words in parentheses:

וְהַשִּׂיאֵנוּ BESTOW UPON US, LORD, our God, the blessing of Your festivals for life and peace, joy and gladness, as You desired and promised to bless us. (Our God and the God of our fathers, may You find favor with our rest.) Sanctify us with Your commandments and grant us our share in Your Torah. Satisfy us from Your goodness, gladden us with Your salvation, and purify our heart to serve you in truth. And grant us as a heritage, LORD, our God, (with love and favor,) with joy and gladness, (the Sabbath and) the festivals of Your

---

הַחֻקִּים הָאֵלֶּה (you shall examine these laws). This refers to remembering and studying the general principles by which the conclusions and teachings of the Gemara are arrived at. Such activity is particularly appropriate when commemorating the day on which the Torah was given, and in doing that we reaffirm our commitment to remember and study those principles. This is consistent with the words of the Rashba who explained that each of the six days of creation is particularly suited to the renewal of the creations of that day. So too Shavuot is a propitious day to renew our acceptance of the teachings of the Torah (*Netziv*).

כַּאֲשֶׁר רָצִיתָ – *As You desired.* The term רָצוֹן (desire) implies acceptance of our service, typically in the context of the sacrificial order. We pray

(שַׁבָּת וּ) מוֹעֲדֵי קָדְשֶׁךָ, וְיִשְׂמְחוּ בְךָ יִשְׂרָאֵל מְקַדְּשֵׁי שְׁמֶךָ. בָּרוּךְ אַתָּה יהוה, מְקַדֵּשׁ (הַשַּׁבָּת וְ) יִשְׂרָאֵל וְהַזְּמַנִּים.

עבודה

רְצֵה יהוה אֱלֹהֵינוּ בְּעַמְּךָ יִשְׂרָאֵל, וּבִתְפִלָּתָם, וְהָשֵׁב אֶת הָעֲבוֹדָה לִדְבִיר בֵּיתֶךָ, וְאִשֵּׁי יִשְׂרָאֵל וּתְפִלָּתָם בְּאַהֲבָה תְקַבֵּל בְּרָצוֹן, וּתְהִי לְרָצוֹן תָּמִיד עֲבוֹדַת יִשְׂרָאֵל עַמֶּךָ. וְתֶחֱזֶינָה עֵינֵינוּ בְּשׁוּבְךָ לְצִיּוֹן בְּרַחֲמִים. בָּרוּךְ אַתָּה יהוה, הַמַּחֲזִיר שְׁכִינָתוֹ לְצִיּוֹן.

הודאה

Bow during the first five words.

׳מוֹדִים אֲנַחְנוּ לָךְ, שָׁאַתָּה הוּא יהוה אֱלֹהֵינוּ וֵאלֹהֵי אֲבוֹתֵינוּ לְעוֹלָם וָעֶד. צוּר חַיֵּינוּ, מָגֵן יִשְׁעֵנוּ, אַתָּה הוּא. לְדוֹר וָדוֹר נוֹדֶה לְּךָ וּנְסַפֵּר תְּהִלָּתֶךָ, עַל חַיֵּינוּ הַמְּסוּרִים בְּיָדֶךָ, וְעַל נִשְׁמוֹתֵינוּ הַפְּקוּדוֹת לָךְ, וְעַל נִסֶּיךָ שֶׁבְּכָל יוֹם עִמָּנוּ, וְעַל נִפְלְאוֹתֶיךָ וְטוֹבוֹתֶיךָ, שֶׁבְּכָל עֵת, עֶרֶב וָבֹקֶר וְצָהֳרָיִם. הַטּוֹב, כִּי לֹא כָלוּ רַחֲמֶיךָ, וְהַמְרַחֵם, כִּי לֹא תַמּוּ חֲסָדֶיךָ, מֵעוֹלָם קִוִּינוּ לָךְ.

During חזרת הש״ץ, *the* קהל *says quietly:*

׳מוֹדִים אֲנַחְנוּ לָךְ, שָׁאַתָּה הוּא יהוה אֱלֹהֵינוּ וֵאלֹהֵי אֲבוֹתֵינוּ, אֱלֹהֵי כָל בָּשָׂר, יוֹצְרֵנוּ, יוֹצֵר בְּרֵאשִׁית. בְּרָכוֹת וְהוֹדָאוֹת לְשִׁמְךָ הַגָּדוֹל וְהַקָּדוֹשׁ, עַל שֶׁהֶחֱיִיתָנוּ וְקִיַּמְתָּנוּ. כֵּן תְּחַיֵּנוּ וּתְקַיְּמֵנוּ, וְתֶאֱסֹף גָּלֻיּוֹתֵינוּ לְחַצְרוֹת קָדְשֶׁךָ, לִשְׁמֹר חֻקֶּיךָ וְלַעֲשׂוֹת רְצוֹנֶךָ וּלְעָבְדְּךָ בְּלֵבָב שָׁלֵם, עַל שֶׁאֲנַחְנוּ מוֹדִים לָךְ. בָּרוּךְ אֵל הַהוֹדָאוֹת.

וְעַל כֻּלָּם יִתְבָּרַךְ וְיִתְרוֹמַם שִׁמְךָ מַלְכֵּנוּ תָּמִיד לְעוֹלָם וָעֶד. וְכֹל

---

that when God accepts our 'service' – in the form of the ideal observance of this festival – with favor, He also grant us His blessing.

מְקַדֵּשׁ יִשְׂרָאֵל וְהַזְּמַנִּים – *Who sanctifies Israel and the festive seasons*. The Gemara (*Berakhot* 49a) establishes the principle that a single *berakha* cannot conclude by blessing God on two separate accounts. It then asks why the conclusion of this *berakha* blesses Him for two separate things: sanctifying Israel and sanctifying the seasons. It answers that the *berakha* in fact refers only to one divine act, i.e., He sanctifies Israel who are thereby empowered to sanctify the seasons. The Gemara similarly explains the Rosh Ḥodesh *Amida* formulation, which blesses God for sanctifying Israel who are thereby empowered to determine the date of Rosh Ḥodesh.

holiness. And may Israel, who sanctify Your name, rejoice in You. Blessed are You, LORD, Who sanctifies (the Sabbath and) Israel and the festive seasons.

TEMPLE SERVICE

רְצֵה LOOK FAVORABLY, LORD our God, upon Your people Israel and their prayer, and restore the service to the Holy of Holies of Your House. Accept with love and favor the fire-offerings of Israel and their prayer. May the service of Israel Your people Israel always find favor with You. May our eyes witness Your return to Zion in compassion. Blessed are You, LORD, Who will restore His Divine Presence to Zion.

THANKSGIVING

Bow during the first seven words.

מוֹדִים WE THANK YOU, for You are the LORD our God and the God of our fathers for all eternity. You are the Rock of our life and Shield of our deliverance. From generation to generation we will thank You and recount Your praise for our lives that are in Your hands, for our souls that are given over to You, for Your miracles that are with us every day, and for Your constant wonders and favors, evening, morning and noon. You are good, for Your compassion does not cease, and You are compassionate, for Your kindness never ends. We have placed our hope in You forever and ever.

During the Leader's Repetition, the congregation says quietly:

מוֹדִים WE THANK YOU, for You are the LORD our God, the God of our fathers and God of all flesh. You are our Maker, the Maker of Creation. Blessings and thanks are due Your great and holy name for You have given us life and preserved us in life. May You continue to keep us in life and preserve us. Gather our exiles to the courtyards of Your Temple so that we may fulfill Your commandments and do Your will, serving You with a perfect heart, in the merit of our giving thanks to You now. Blessed is the God of all thanksgiving.

For all this, our King, may Your name be blessed and exalted continually, forever and ever. All that lives will give thanks to You

הַחַיִּים יוֹדְוּךָ סֶּלָה, וִיהַלְלוּ אֶת שִׁמְךָ בֶּאֱמֶת, הָאֵל יְשׁוּעָתֵנוּ וְעֶזְרָתֵנוּ סֶלָה. ׳בָּרוּךְ אַתָּה יהוה, הַטּוֹב שִׁמְךָ וּלְךָ נָאֶה לְהוֹדוֹת.

When saying the עמידה *silently, continue with* שִׂים שָׁלוֹם *below.*

ברכת כהנים

The following is said by the שליח ציבור *during* חזרת הש״ץ.
In many congregations, in שחרית *of* שמחת תורה,
the כהנים *ascend for the* ברכת כהנים.

אֱלֹהֵינוּ וֵאלֹהֵי אֲבוֹתֵינוּ, בָּרְכֵנוּ בַּבְּרָכָה הַמְשֻׁלֶּשֶׁת, בַּתּוֹרָה, הַכְּתוּבָה עַל יְדֵי מֹשֶׁה עַבְדֶּךָ, הָאֲמוּרָה מִפִּי אַהֲרֹן וּבָנָיו כֹּהֲנִים עַם קְדוֹשֶׁיךָ, כָּאָמוּר

יְבָרֶכְךָ יהוה וְיִשְׁמְרֶךָ: קהל: כֵּן יְהִי רָצוֹן במדבר ו

יָאֵר יהוה פָּנָיו אֵלֶיךָ וִיחֻנֶּךָּ: קהל: כֵּן יְהִי רָצוֹן

יִשָּׂא יהוה פָּנָיו אֵלֶיךָ וְיָשֵׂם לְךָ שָׁלוֹם: קהל: כֵּן יְהִי רָצוֹן

ברכת שלום

בשחרית:

שִׂים שָׁלוֹם טוֹבָה וּבְרָכָה, חֵן וָחֶסֶד וְרַחֲמִים עָלֵינוּ וְעַל כָּל יִשְׂרָאֵל עַמֶּךָ. בָּרְכֵנוּ אָבִינוּ כֻּלָּנוּ כְּאֶחָד בְּאוֹר פָּנֶיךָ, כִּי בְאוֹר פָּנֶיךָ נָתַתָּ לָּנוּ יהוה אֱלֹהֵינוּ, תּוֹרַת חַיִּים וְאַהֲבַת חֶסֶד, וּצְדָקָה וּבְרָכָה וְרַחֲמִים וְחַיִּים וְשָׁלוֹם. וְטוֹב בְּעֵינֶיךָ לְבָרֵךְ אֶת עַמְּךָ יִשְׂרָאֵל, בְּכָל עֵת וּבְכָל שָׁעָה בִּשְׁלוֹמֶךָ.

במנחה ובמעריב:

שָׁלוֹם רָב עַל יִשְׂרָאֵל עַמְּךָ תָּשִׂים לְעוֹלָם, כִּי אַתָּה הוּא מֶלֶךְ אָדוֹן לְכָל הַשָּׁלוֹם. וְטוֹב בְּעֵינֶיךָ לְבָרֵךְ אֶת עַמְּךָ יִשְׂרָאֵל, בְּכָל עֵת וּבְכָל שָׁעָה בִּשְׁלוֹמֶךָ.

בָּרוּךְ אַתָּה יהוה, הַמְבָרֵךְ אֶת עַמּוֹ יִשְׂרָאֵל בַּשָּׁלוֹם.

At this point when the שליח ציבור *repeats the* עמידה *he should complete the repetition by saying the verse beginning "*יִהְיוּ לְרָצוֹן*" out loud.*

יִהְיוּ לְרָצוֹן אִמְרֵי־פִי וְהֶגְיוֹן לִבִּי לְפָנֶיךָ, יהוה צוּרִי וְגֹאֲלִי: תהלים יט

forever and praise Your name in truth, God, our salvation and our help forever. Blessed are You, LORD, for Your name is "The Good One" and it is appropriate to give thanks to You.

When saying the Amida silently, continue with "Grant peace" below.

THE PRIESTLY BLESSING

The following is said by the Leader during the Repetition of the Amida. In many congregations, in Shaharit of Simhat Torah, the Kohanim ascend for the Priestly Blessing.

אֱלֹהֵינוּ OUR GOD, God of our fathers, bless us with the threefold blessing, in the Torah, written by Your servant Moses and spoken by Aaron and his descendants, being priests, Your holy people, as it is said:

Num. 6 "May the LORD bless you and keep you." *Cong:* May this be His will.
"May the LORD make His countenance shine upon you and be gracious to you." *Cong:* May this be His will.
"May the LORD lift up His countenance toward you and grant you peace." *Cong:* May this be His will.

PEACE

At Shaharit

שִׂים שָׁלוֹם GRANT PEACE with welfare and blessing, and grace with loving-kindness and mercy on us and all Israel Your people. Bless us, our Father, all together, with the light of Your presence. For in that light, LORD our God, You have given us the Torah of life, and love of kindness with justice, blessing, tenderness, life and peace. May it be good in Your eyes to bless Your people Israel at all times, at every hour, with Your peace.

At Minha and Ma'ariv:

שָׁלוֹם רָב ESTABLISH ABUNDANT PEACE for Your people Israel forever, for You are the sovereign Master of all peace; and may it be good in Your eyes to bless Your people Israel at all times, at every hour, with Your peace.

Blessed are You, LORD, Who blesses His people Israel with peace.

At this point when the Leader repeats the Amida he should complete the repetition by saying the verse beginning "May the words" out loud.

Ps. 19 MAY THE WORDS of my mouth and the meditation of my heart be acceptable before You, LORD, my Rock and my Redeemer.

אֱלֹהַי, נְצֹר לְשׁוֹנִי מֵרָע וּשְׂפָתַי מִדַּבֵּר מִרְמָה, וְלִמְקַלְלַי נַפְשִׁי ברכות יז.
תִדֹּם, וְנַפְשִׁי כֶּעָפָר לַכֹּל תִּהְיֶה. פְּתַח לִבִּי בְּתוֹרָתֶךָ, וּבְמִצְוֹתֶיךָ
תִּרְדֹּף נַפְשִׁי. וְכָל הַחוֹשְׁבִים עָלַי רָעָה, מְהֵרָה הָפֵר עֲצָתָם וְקַלְקֵל
מַחֲשַׁבְתָּם. עֲשֵׂה לְמַעַן שְׁמֶךָ, עֲשֵׂה לְמַעַן יְמִינֶךָ, עֲשֵׂה לְמַעַן קְדֻשָּׁתֶךָ,
עֲשֵׂה לְמַעַן תּוֹרָתֶךָ. לְמַעַן יֵחָלְצוּן יְדִידֶיךָ, הוֹשִׁיעָה יְמִינְךָ וַעֲנֵנִי: יִהְיוּ תהלים ס תהלים יט
לְרָצוֹן אִמְרֵי־פִי וְהֶגְיוֹן לִבִּי לְפָנֶיךָ, יהוה צוּרִי וְגֹאֲלִי:

Bow, take three steps back, then bow, first left, then right, then center, while saying:

עֹשֶׂה שָׁלוֹם בִּמְרוֹמָיו, הוּא יַעֲשֶׂה שָׁלוֹם עָלֵינוּ, וְעַל כָּל יִשְׂרָאֵל,
וְאִמְרוּ אָמֵן.

יְהִי רָצוֹן מִלְּפָנֶיךָ יהוה אֱלֹהֵינוּ וֵאלֹהֵי אֲבוֹתֵינוּ, שֶׁיִּבָּנֶה בֵּית הַמִּקְדָּשׁ
בִּמְהֵרָה בְיָמֵינוּ, וְתֵן חֶלְקֵנוּ בְּתוֹרָתֶךָ, וְשָׁם נַעֲבָדְךָ בְּיִרְאָה כִּימֵי
עוֹלָם וּכְשָׁנִים קַדְמֹנִיּוֹת. וְעָרְבָה לַיהוה מִנְחַת יְהוּדָה וִירוּשָׁלָםִ כִּימֵי עוֹלָם מלאכי ג
וּכְשָׁנִים קַדְמֹנִיּוֹת:

After מנחה*:*

Continue with קדיש שלם *(page 406) and* עָלֵינוּ *(page 410).*

After מעריב*:*

1. *On* יום טוב*,* קדיש שלם *is said (page 406), except for* ליל הסדר *when many first say* הלל שלם *(page 766) followed by* קדיש שלם *(page 406) and* עָלֵינוּ *(page 410).*
2. *If* יום טוב *coincides with Friday night, the service continues with* וַיְכֻלּוּ *and* מעין שבע *(page 404) and then* קדיש שלם *(page 406) and* עָלֵינוּ *(page 410).*
3. *On the second and last nights of* פסח*, after* קדיש שלם *(page 406), the* עומר *is counted (page 326) followed by* עָלֵינוּ *(page 322).*
4. *On* שמחת תורה*, after* קדיש שלם *(page 406) continue with* אַתָּה הָרְאֵתָ *and* הקפות *(page 920).*

After שחרית*:*

1. *Continue with* הלל שלם *(page 766) (except on the last days of* פסח *when* חצי הלל *is said),* קדיש שלם *(page 522),* קריאת התורה *(page 524) and* מוסף *(page 828).*
2. *On* פסח*,* שיר השירים *(page 1168) is read on* שבת חול המועד *before* קריאת התורה*. But if there is no* שבת חול המועד *it is read on either the seventh or the eighth day, whichever falls on* שבת*.*
3. *On the second day of* שבועות*,* מגילת רות *(page 1170) is read before* קריאת התורה*.*
4. *On* סוכות*,* קהלת *(page 1176) is read on* שבת חול המועד *before* קריאת התורה*. But if there is no* שבת חול המועד*, it is read on* שמיני עצרת*.*

For laws regarding "Interruptions during *Elokai Netzor,*" see page 133.

Berakhot 17a אֱלֹהַי MY GOD, guard my tongue from evil, and my lips from speaking deceit. Let my soul be silent to those who curse me; let my soul be humble toward everyone like the dust. Open my heart to Your Torah that my soul may follow Your commandments. As for all those who contemplate evil against me, speedily nullify their plans and spoil their schemes. Do so for the sake of Your name. Do so for Your right hand.
Ps. 60 Do so for Your holiness. Do so for Your Torah, that Your loved ones
Ps. 19 may be delivered. Save with Your right hand, and answer me. May the words of my mouth and the meditation of my heart be acceptable before You, LORD, my Rock and my Redeemer.

Bow, take three steps back, then bow, first left, then right, then center, while saying:

He Who makes peace in His heights, may He create peace for us and for all Israel. Amen.

יְהִי רָצוֹן MAY IT BE Your will, LORD our God and God of our fathers, that the Temple be rebuilt speedily in our days and may You grant our portion in Your Torah. We will serve You there in reverence as in the days of antiquity and in
Mal. 3 years gone by. "And may the offering of Judah and Jerusalem be pleasant to the LORD as in the days of antiquity and in years gone by."

After Minḥa:
Continue with Full Kaddish (page 407) and Aleinu (page 411).

After Ma'ariv:

1. *On Yom Tov, Full Kaddish is said (page 407), except for Seder nights when many first say Full Hallel (page 767) followed by Full Kaddish (page 407) and Aleinu (page 411).*
2. *If Yom Tov coincides with Friday night, the service continues with "Then the heavens and the earth" (page 405) and then Full Kaddish (page 407) and Aleinu (page 411).*
3. *On the second and last nights of Pesaḥ, after Full Kaddish (page 407), the Omer is counted (page 327) followed by Aleinu (page 323).*
4. *On Simḥat Torah, after Full Kaddish (page 407) continue with "You have been shown" and Hakafot (page 921).*

After Shaḥarit:

1. *Continue with Full Hallel (page 767) (except on the last days of Pesaḥ when Half Hallel is said), Full Kaddish (page 523), Torah Reading (page 525), and Musaf (page 829).*
2. *On Pesaḥ, Shir HaShirim (page 1168) is read on Shabbat Ḥol Hamo'ed before the Torah Reading. But if there is no Shabbat Ḥol Hamo'ed it is read on either the seventh or the eighth day, whichever falls on Shabbat.*
3. *On the second day of Shavuot, Megillat Rut (page 1170) is read before the Torah Reading.*
4. *On Sukkot, Kohelet (page 1176) is read on Shabbat Ḥol HaMo'ed before the Torah Reading. But if there is no Shabbat Ḥol HaMo'ed, it is read on Shemini Atzeret.*

Most congregations omit the following on days that יזכור *is said. Some also omit on* שבת.

יָהּ אֵלִי וְגוֹאֲלִי, אֶתְיַצְּבָה לִקְרָאתֶךָ / הָיָה וְיִהְיֶה, הָיָה וְהֹוֶה, כָּל גּוֹי אַדְמָתֶךָ.

וְתוֹרָה לָעוֹלָה (נ״א וְתוֹדָה וְלָעוֹלָה) וְלַמִּנְחָה וְלַחַטָּאת וְלָאָשָׁם, וְלַשְּׁלָמִים וְלַמִּלּוּאִים כָּל קָרְבָּנֶךָ. זְכֹר נִלְאָה אֲשֶׁר נָשְׂאָה וְהָשִׁיבָה לְאַדְמָתֶךָ, סֶלָה אֲהַלֶּלְךָ בְּאַשְׁרֵי יוֹשְׁבֵי בֵיתֶךָ.

דַּק עַל דַּק, עַד אֵין נִבְדָּק, וְלִתְבוּנָתוֹ אֵין חֵקֶר / הָאֵל נוֹרָא, בְּאַחַת סְקִירָה, בֵּין טוֹב לְרַע יְבַקֵּר.

וְתוֹרָה לָעוֹלָה (נ״א וְתוֹדָה וְלָעוֹלָה) וְלַמִּנְחָה וְלַחַטָּאת וְלָאָשָׁם, וְלַשְּׁלָמִים וְלַמִּלּוּאִים כָּל קָרְבָּנֶךָ. זְכֹר נִלְאָה אֲשֶׁר נָשְׂאָה וְהָשִׁיבָה לְאַדְמָתֶךָ, סֶלָה אֲהַלֶּלְךָ בְּאַשְׁרֵי יוֹשְׁבֵי בֵיתֶךָ.

אֲדוֹן צְבָאוֹת, בְּרֹב פְּלָאוֹת, חִבֵּר כָּל אָהֳלוֹ / בִּנְתִיבוֹת לֵב לִבְלֵב, הַצּוּר תָּמִים פָּעֳלוֹ.

וְתוֹרָה לָעוֹלָה (נ״א וְתוֹדָה וְלָעוֹלָה) וְלַמִּנְחָה וְלַחַטָּאת וְלָאָשָׁם, וְלַשְּׁלָמִים וְלַמִּלּוּאִים כָּל קָרְבָּנֶךָ. זְכֹר נִלְאָה אֲשֶׁר נָשְׂאָה וְהָשִׁיבָה לְאַדְמָתֶךָ, סֶלָה אֲהַלֶּלְךָ בְּאַשְׁרֵי יוֹשְׁבֵי בֵיתֶךָ.

יָהּ אֵלִי – *Lord my God*. This *piyut* first appeared in the *Siddur Sha'ar HaShamayim* with the commentary of the Shela, published in 1717, from whence it spread to communities throughout Eastern Europe. The author is unknown, but its content indicates he was a late seventeenth-century Kabbalist (Prof. Daniel Goldschmidt).

וְתוֹרָה לָעוֹלָה (נ״א וְתוֹדָה וְלָעוֹלָה) – *May our recital of the Torah passages regarding the burnt-offering, the meal-offering*. The *piyut's* refrain, as it has reached us, is probably corrupt. A list of sacrifices unconnected to the body of the *piyut* would be odd. The list largely follows Leviticus 7:37: "This is the law for the burnt-offering, the meal-offering, the sin-offering, the guilt-offering, the consecration-offering, and the peace-offering" (**זֹאת הַתּוֹרָה לָעֹלָה** etc.), but it begins with the redundant thanksgiving-offering (*toda*), which in the verse is subsumed under the peace-offering. We may, therefore, surmise that the refrain originally began *ve-Torah la'ola*, more closely echoing the verse. (*Torah* was mistaken for *toda* because of the similarity of *dalet* and *resh*, and a *vav* was added to *la'ola*,, to graft the *toda* to the list.) The reconstructed refrain reflects the homiletical reading of Leviticus 7:37 found in *Menaḥot* 110a: study of "this Torah" can substitute for the sacrifices. For the *paytan* (following R. Baḥya ben Asher), the reference is probably to the Torah on the sacrifices. Accordingly, the *piyut* petitions God to accept our reading of the day's prescribed sacrifices, in the *Maftir* and *Musaf* (similarly see Tosafot, *Rosh HaShana* 35a), as sacrifice-equivalents (Prof. Bernard Septimus).

Most congregations omit the following on days that Yizkor is said. Some also omit on Shabbat.

יָהּ אֵלִי LORD MY GOD and my Redeemer, I stand upright to greet You. Who is, was, and will always be, the ruler over all the nations of Your world.

May our recital of the Torah passages regarding the burnt-offering, the meal-offering, the sin-offering, the guilt-offering, the peace-offering, and the consecration-offering, be accepted in lieu of all of Your sacrifices. Remember the nation that was lifted up by You in the past, and bring it back to Your land. I will forever sing Your praises, with the words "Happy are those that dwell in Your house."

GOD IS EVER MORE inscrutable, beyond any human knowledge or attempt to understand Him. / He is the awesome God Who in one glance distinguishes between good and evil.

May our recital of the Torah passages regarding the burnt-offering, the meal-offering, the sin-offering, the guilt-offering, the peace-offering, and the consecration-offering, be accepted in lieu of all of Your sacrifices. Remember the nation that was lifted up by You in the past, and bring it back to Your land. I will forever sing Your praises, with the words "Happy are those that dwell in Your house."

HE IS THE MASTER of the hosts Who with many wonders stitched the fabric of His world into existence. / Creating it by His spoken word in thirty-two ways, for He is the Rock Whose work is perfect.

May our recital of the Torah passages regarding the burnt-offering, the meal-offering, the sin-offering, the guilt-offering, the peace-offering, and the consecration-offering, be accepted in lieu of all of Your sacrifices. Remember the nation that was lifted up by You in the past, and bring it back to Your land. I will forever sing Your praises, with the words "Happy are those that dwell in Your house."

בִּנְתִיבוֹת לֵב לְבַלֵּב – *Creating it by His spoken word in thirty-two ways*. This phrase praises God for having created the universe through the thirty-two paths of wisdom (לב equals 32): namely the ten *Sefirot* plus the twenty-two letters of the alphabet, by which, as taught in the mystical text *Sefer Yetzira*, God established creation, even including evil. The stanza then cites the key verse of *tzidduk hadin*, (the acceptance of God's decree) proclaiming the righteousness of God, despite finding ourselves in exile, distant from the Temple, and far from eschatological fulfillment.

מוסף לשלוש רגלים

The following עמידה *is said on* יום טוב *and* חול המועד (*including* שבת חול המועד).
On the first day of פסח, *the* שליח ציבור *begins the* חזרת הש"ץ *with* תפילת טל *on page 862;*
on שמיני עצרת, *with* תפילת גשם *on page 866.*

One begins the עמידה *by taking three steps forward (OḤ 95:1). According to some traditions, one should first take three steps back before moving forward (MB 95:3). The* עמידה *is recited with one's feet together. One should try to concentrate on the simple meaning of the words of the* עמידה *with the awareness throughout that one is standing in the presence of the Almighty (OḤ 98:1 and MB 98:1). At the points indicated by* ', *bend the knees at the first word, bow at the second, and stand straight before saying God's name.*

דברים לב כִּי שֵׁם יהוה אֶקְרָא, הָבוּ גֹדֶל לֵאלֹהֵינוּ:

תהלים נא אֲדֹנָי, שְׂפָתַי תִּפְתָּח, וּפִי יַגִּיד תְּהִלָּתֶךָ:

אבות

'**בָּרוּךְ** אַתָּה יהוה, אֱלֹהֵינוּ וֵאלֹהֵי אֲבוֹתֵינוּ, אֱלֹהֵי אַבְרָהָם, אֱלֹהֵי יִצְחָק, וֵאלֹהֵי יַעֲקֹב, הָאֵל הַגָּדוֹל הַגִּבּוֹר וְהַנּוֹרָא, אֵל עֶלְיוֹן, גּוֹמֵל חֲסָדִים טוֹבִים, וְקוֹנֵה הַכֹּל, וְזוֹכֵר חַסְדֵי אָבוֹת, וּמֵבִיא גוֹאֵל לִבְנֵי בְנֵיהֶם לְמַעַן שְׁמוֹ בְּאַהֲבָה. מֶלֶךְ עוֹזֵר וּמוֹשִׁיעַ וּמָגֵן. 'בָּרוּךְ אַתָּה יהוה, מָגֵן אַבְרָהָם.

גבורות

אַתָּה גִּבּוֹר לְעוֹלָם, אֲדֹנָי, מְחַיֵּה מֵתִים אַתָּה, רַב לְהוֹשִׁיעַ.

בחורף: מַשִּׁיב הָרוּחַ וּמוֹרִיד הַגֶּשֶׁם

מְכַלְכֵּל חַיִּים בְּחֶסֶד, מְחַיֵּה מֵתִים בְּרַחֲמִים רַבִּים, סוֹמֵךְ נוֹפְלִים, וְרוֹפֵא חוֹלִים, וּמַתִּיר אֲסוּרִים, וּמְקַיֵּם אֱמוּנָתוֹ לִישֵׁנֵי עָפָר. מִי

מוּסָף / MUSAF

לְמַעַן שְׁמוֹ – *For the sake of His name.* Rambam in the Guide (1:61) explains that God's four-lettered name is unique in that it alone is His proper name describing His essence, unlike the other names by which He is known that describe His actions. Rambam explains that that proper name is the one that Zechariah (14:9, so familiar to us from the closing words of the *Aleinu*) declares will be the one and only name by which God will be known to all of mankind when the Messiah will come. One can thus suggest that this final phrase of the first paragraph of the Amida affirms our belief that God will indeed bring the Messiah, not for our sake but "for the sake of His name," i.e., because in doing so His full four-lettered name, and all that it signifies about God and His relationship to the world, will finally be revealed and understood by mankind. Consistent with this approach, the passage found toward the end of every *Amida* stating, "All that lives will give thanks to You forever, and praise Your name *in truth*," can be understood as affirming

MUSAF FOR FESTIVALS

The following Amida is said on Yom Tov and Ḥol HaMo'ed (including Shabbat Ḥol HaMo'ed). On the first day of Pesaḥ, the Leader begins the Repetition with "Prayer for Dew" on page 863; on Shemini Atzeret, with "Prayer for Rain" on page 867.

One begins the Amida by taking three steps forward (OḤ 95:1). According to some traditions, one should first take three steps back before moving forward (MB 95:3). The Amida is recited with one's feet together. One should try to concentrate on the simple meaning of the words of the Amida with the awareness throughout that one is standing in the presence of the Almighty (OḤ 98:1 and MB 98:1). At the points indicated by ▾, bend the knees at the first word, bow at the second, and stand straight before saying God's name.

Deut. 32 WHEN I proclaim the name of the LORD, ascribe greatness to our God.
Ps. 51 "O my Master, open my lips, and my mouth will relate Your praise."

PATRIARCHS

▾ בָּרוּךְ BLESSED ARE YOU, LORD, our God and the God of our fathers, the God of Abraham, the God of Isaac, and the God of Jacob, the God Who is great, mighty, and awesome, God most exalted, Who bestows rewards of benevolent kindness, Who is the Creator of everything, Who remembers all the kind acts of the fathers, and Who brings a redeemer to their children's children, for the sake of His name, with love. King Who helps, saves, and shields, ▾blessed are You, LORD, Shield of Abraham.

GOD'S MIGHT

אַתָּה YOU, my Master, are forever mighty, You are the Resurrector of the dead, with great power to save.

In winter: He makes the wind blow and the rain fall

He sustains the living with kindness, He resurrects the dead with great compassion, He supports those who are falling, He heals the sick, He sets the incarcerated free, and He fulfills what He has promised to those who sleep in the dust. Who is like You, O mighty One, and who can be compared to You, O King Who causes death

---

not merely that they will indeed praise God, but that at that future time because all of humanity will accurately understand God's four-lettered name as it will be revealed, they

For laws regarding "The repetition of the *Amida*," see page 107.
For laws regarding "Omission/Insertion of *Mashiv Haru'aḥ*," see page 109.

כָמְוֹךָ, בַּעַל גְּבוּרוֹת, וּמִי דּוֹמֶה לָּךְ, מֶלֶךְ, מֵמִית וּמְחַיֶּה וּמַצְמִיחַ יְשׁוּעָה. וְנֶאֱמָן אַתָּה לְהַחֲיוֹת מֵתִים. בָּרוּךְ אַתָּה יהוה, מְחַיֵּה הַמֵּתִים.

When saying the עמידה *silently, continue with* אַתָּה קָדוֹשׁ *on the next page.*

קדושה

On חול המועד*, turn to the* קדושה *on the next page.*

On יום טוב*,* שבת חול המועד *and* הושענא רבה*, during the* חזרת הש״ץ*, the following is said standing with feet together, rising on the toes at the words indicated by* ⁺.

then קהל ש״ץ: **נַעֲרִיצְךָ** וְנַקְדִּישְׁךָ כְּסוֹד שִׂיחַ שַׂרְפֵי קֹדֶשׁ, הַמַּקְדִּישִׁים שִׁמְךָ בַּקֹּדֶשׁ,

ישעיה ו כַּכָּתוּב עַל יַד נְבִיאֶךָ: וְקָרָא זֶה אֶל־זֶה וְאָמַר

then קהל ש״ץ: ⁺קָדוֹשׁ, ⁺קָדוֹשׁ, ⁺קָדוֹשׁ יהוה צְבָאוֹת, מְלֹא כָל הָאָרֶץ כְּבוֹדוֹ:

כְּבוֹדוֹ מָלֵא עוֹלָם, מְשָׁרְתָיו שׁוֹאֲלִים זֶה לָזֶה, אַיֵּה מְקוֹם כְּבוֹדוֹ,

ש״ץ: לְעֻמָּתָם בָּרוּךְ יֹאמֵרוּ

יחזקאל ג *then* קהל ש״ץ: ⁺בָּרוּךְ כְּבוֹד־יהוה מִמְּקוֹמוֹ:

מִמְּקוֹמוֹ הוּא יִפֶן בְּרַחֲמִים, וְיָחֹן עַם הַמְיַחֲדִים שְׁמוֹ, עֶרֶב וָבֹקֶר בְּכָל יוֹם תָּמִיד, פַּעֲמַיִם בְּאַהֲבָה שְׁמַע אוֹמְרִים

דברים ו *then* קהל ש״ץ: שְׁמַע יִשְׂרָאֵל, יהוה אֱלֹהֵינוּ, יהוה אֶחָד:

הוּא אֱלֹהֵינוּ, הוּא אָבִינוּ, הוּא מַלְכֵּנוּ, הוּא מוֹשִׁיעֵנוּ, וְהוּא יַשְׁמִיעֵנוּ

במדבר טו בְּרַחֲמָיו שֵׁנִית לְעֵינֵי כָּל חָי, לִהְיוֹת לָכֶם לֵאלֹהִים, אֲנִי יהוה אֱלֹהֵיכֶם:

On שבת חול המועד*, the following paragraph is omitted:*

תהלים ח / זכריה יד *then* קהל ש״ץ: אַדִּיר אַדִּירֵנוּ, יהוה אֲדֹנֵינוּ, מָה־אַדִּיר שִׁמְךָ בְּכָל־הָאָרֶץ: וְהָיָה יהוה לְמֶלֶךְ עַל־כָּל־הָאָרֶץ, בַּיּוֹם הַהוּא יִהְיֶה יהוה אֶחָד וּשְׁמוֹ אֶחָד:

ש״ץ: וּבְדִבְרֵי קָדְשְׁךָ כָּתוּב לֵאמֹר

תהלים קמו *then* קהל ש״ץ: ⁺יִמְלֹךְ יהוה לְעוֹלָם, אֱלֹהַיִךְ צִיּוֹן לְדֹר וָדֹר, הַלְלוּיָהּ:

ש״ץ: לְדוֹר וָדוֹר נַגִּיד גָּדְלֶךָ, וּלְנֵצַח נְצָחִים קְדֻשָּׁתְךָ נַקְדִּישׁ, וְשִׁבְחֲךָ אֱלֹהֵינוּ מִפִּינוּ לֹא יָמוּשׁ לְעוֹלָם וָעֶד, כִּי אֵל מֶלֶךְ גָּדוֹל וְקָדוֹשׁ אָתָּה. בָּרוּךְ אַתָּה יהוה, הָאֵל הַקָּדוֹשׁ.

The שליח ציבור *continues with* אַתָּה בְחַרְתָּנוּ *on the next page.*

שְׁמַע יִשְׂרָאֵל – *Hear, O Israel.* See the commentary to the Shabbat *Musaf Kedusha*. Additionally, will praise it, i.e., in accordance with its true meaning. (R. Basil Herring).

For laws regarding "*Responding to the Leader during Kedusha,*" see page 510.

and resurrects, and Who causes salvation to sprout? Trustworthy are You to resurrect the dead. Blessed are You, LORD, Resurrector of the dead.

When saying the Amida silently, continue with "You are holy" on the next page.

KEDUSHA

On Ḥol HaMo'ed, turn to the Kedusha on the next page.
On Yom Tov, Shabbat Ḥol HaMo'ed and Hoshana Raba, during the Repetition, the following is said standing with feet together, rising on the toes at the words indicated by ▴.

Cong. then Leader: נַעֲרִיצְךָ WE WILL REVERE You and sanctify You, in the manner of the gathered counsels of the holy Seraphim, who sanctify Your name
Is. 6 in the celestial Sanctuary, as it is written by Your prophet: "And they call to one another:

Cong. then Leader: ▴"Holy, ▴holy, ▴holy is the LORD of hosts; the whole world is filled with His glory.'"

His glory fills the world. His ministering angels ask each other, "Where is the place of His glory?"

Leader: Those facing them say: "Blessed –"

Ezek. 3 *Cong. then Leader:* ▴"Blessed is the glory of the LORD from His place."

May He turn in mercy from His place, to be gracious to the people who proclaim the unity of His name, evening and morning, every day, continually, twice daily reciting the Shema with love.

Deut. 6 *Cong. then Leader:* Hear, O Israel, the LORD is our God, the LORD is One.

He is our God, He is our Father, He is our King, He is our Savior – and He, in His compassion, will let us hear a second time in the
Num. 15 presence of all that lives, [His promise] "to be your God. I am the LORD your God."

On Shabbat Ḥol HaMo'ed, the following paragraph is omitted:

Ps. 8 *Cong. then Leader:* Majestic is our Majestic One. LORD, our Master, how majestic is Your
Zech. 14 name in all the earth. And the LORD shall be King over all the earth; in that day shall the LORD be One, and His name One.

Leader: And in Your holy Writings it is written, saying:

Ps. 146 *Cong. then Leader:* ▴"'The LORD will reign forever, Your God, O Zion, to all generations. Praise the LORD.'"

Leader: To all generations we will proclaim Your greatness, and forever declare Your holiness, and the praise of You, our God, will never leave our mouth, for You are God and King, great and holy; blessed are You, LORD, the holy God.

The Leader continues with "You have chosen us" on the next page.

קדושה לחול המועד

During חזרת הש״ץ*, the following is said standing with feet together, rising on the toes at the words indicated by* ˄.

then קהל ש״ץ: **נְקַדֵּשׁ** אֶת שִׁמְךָ בָּעוֹלָם, כְּשֵׁם שֶׁמַּקְדִּישִׁים אוֹתוֹ בִּשְׁמֵי מָרוֹם, כַּכָּתוּב עַל יַד נְבִיאֶךָ, וְקָרָא זֶה אֶל־זֶה וְאָמַר

ישעיה ו

then קהל ש״ץ: ˄קָדוֹשׁ, ˄קָדוֹשׁ, ˄קָדוֹשׁ יהוה צְבָאוֹת, מְלֹא כָל־הָאָרֶץ כְּבוֹדוֹ:

ש״ץ: לְעֻמָּתָם בָּרוּךְ יֹאמֵרוּ

יחזקאל ג

then קהל ש״ץ: ˄בָּרוּךְ כְּבוֹד־יהוה מִמְּקוֹמוֹ:

ש״ץ: וּבְדִבְרֵי קָדְשְׁךָ כָּתוּב לֵאמֹר

תהלים קמו

then קהל ש״ץ: ˄יִמְלֹךְ יהוה לְעוֹלָם, אֱלֹהַיִךְ צִיּוֹן לְדֹר וָדֹר, הַלְלוּיָהּ:

ש״ץ: לְדוֹר וָדוֹר נַגִּיד גָּדְלֶךָ, וּלְנֵצַח נְצָחִים קְדֻשָּׁתְךָ נַקְדִּישׁ, וְשִׁבְחֲךָ אֱלֹהֵינוּ מִפִּינוּ לֹא יָמוּשׁ לְעוֹלָם וָעֶד, כִּי אֵל מֶלֶךְ גָּדוֹל וְקָדוֹשׁ אָתָּה. בָּרוּךְ אַתָּה יהוה, הָאֵל הַקָּדוֹשׁ.

The שליח ציבור *continues with* אַתָּה בְחַרְתָּנוּ *below.*

When saying the עמידה *silently, continue here with* אַתָּה קָדוֹשׁ:

קדושת השם

אַתָּה קָדוֹשׁ וְשִׁמְךָ קָדוֹשׁ. וּקְדוֹשִׁים בְּכָל יוֹם יְהַלְלוּךָ סֶּלָה. בָּרוּךְ אַתָּה יהוה, הָאֵל הַקָּדוֹשׁ.

קדושת היום

אַתָּה בְחַרְתָּנוּ מִכָּל הָעַמִּים, אָהַבְתָּ אוֹתָנוּ וְרָצִיתָ בָּנוּ, וְרוֹמַמְתָּנוּ מִכָּל הַלְּשׁוֹנוֹת, וְקִדַּשְׁתָּנוּ בְּמִצְוֹתֶיךָ, וְקֵרַבְתָּנוּ מַלְכֵּנוּ לַעֲבוֹדָתֶךָ, וְשִׁמְךָ הַגָּדוֹל וְהַקָּדוֹשׁ עָלֵינוּ קָרָאתָ.

---

the Gemara (*Ḥullin* 91b, quoting Job 38:7) states that the celestial angels are permitted to recite "Holy, holy, holy" as it appears in the *Kedusha* only after Israel has recited its own praise of God, i.e., the *Shema Yisrael*, as it appears here, for Israel and its praises are even more beloved by God than are the angels and their praises. So too the *Pirkei deR. Eliezer* juxtaposes the praises of Israel and the angels, praising the former above the latter, and thus God declares to Israel (as the *Kedusha* proceeds to say), "I am the Lord your God." By including the *Shema* in

For the *"Instructions for someone who made a mistake and recited the wrong Amida on Yom Tov,"* see page 814.

KEDUSHA FOR ḤOL HAMO'ED

During the Leader's Repetition, the following is said standing with feet together, rising on the toes at the words indicated by ▲.

Cong. then Leader: נְקַדֵּשׁ WE WILL SANCTIFY Your name in this world, as they sanctify it in the heavenly heights, as is written by Your prophet: "They called to one another, saying": *Is. 6*

Cong. then Leader: "▲Holy, ▲holy, ▲holy is the LORD of hosts; the whole world is filled with His glory.'"

Leader: Those who face them declare, "Blessed –"

Cong. then Leader: ▲"Blessed is the glory of the LORD from His place." *Ezek. 3*

Leader: And in Your holy Writings it is written as follows:

Cong. then Leader: ▲"The LORD will reign forever, Your God, O Zion, to all generations. Praise the LORD." *Ps. 146*

Leader: To all generations we will proclaim Your greatness, and forever declare Your holiness, and the praise of You, our God, will never leave our mouth, for You are God and King, great and holy; blessed are You, LORD, the holy God.

The Leader continues with "You have chosen us" below.

When saying the Amida silently, continue here with "You are holy":

HOLINESS

אַתָּה YOU ARE HOLY and Your name is holy, and holy ones will praise You every day, forever. Blessed are You, LORD, the holy God.

אַתָּה בְחַרְתָּנוּ YOU HAVE CHOSEN US from among all the peoples; You have loved us and favored us. You have raised us above all languages and You have sanctified us with Your commandments. You have drawn us close to You, Our King, to Your service, and have proclaimed upon us Your great and holy name.

---

the *Kedusha* we emphasize that without Israel, the angels could not declare "Holy, holy, holy." This is echoed too in the pairing of these selfsame angelic declarations with the *Shema* that occurs earlier in *Shaḥarit*. This approach to the *Kedusha* was adopted in Geonic times in the Jewish community of Palestine, which (as *Tosafot* to *Sanhedrin* 37b records) restricted recital of the *Kedusha* to Shabbat and Yom Tov, and it thus subsequently became part of the *Kedusha* of *Nusaḥ Ashkenaz* only on those days (R. Daniel Korobkin).

וְקִדַּשְׁתָּנוּ בְּמִצְוֹתֶיךָ – *You have sanctified us with Your commandments.* The *mitzvot* should not

On שבת*, add the words in parentheses:*

וַתִּתֶּן לָנוּ יהוה אֱלֹהֵינוּ בְּאַהֲבָה, (שַׁבָּתוֹת לִמְנוּחָה וּ)מוֹעֲדִים לְשִׂמְחָה, חַגִּים וּזְמַנִּים לְשָׂשׂוֹן, אֶת יוֹם (הַשַּׁבָּת הַזֶּה וְאֶת יוֹם)

בפסח: חַג הַמַּצּוֹת הַזֶּה, זְמַן חֵרוּתֵנוּ

בשבועות: חַג הַשָּׁבוּעוֹת הַזֶּה, זְמַן מַתַּן תּוֹרָתֵנוּ

בסוכות: חַג הַסֻּכּוֹת הַזֶּה, זְמַן שִׂמְחָתֵנוּ

בשמע"צ ובש"ת: הַשְּׁמִינִי חַג הָעֲצֶרֶת הַזֶּה, זְמַן שִׂמְחָתֵנוּ

(בְּאַהֲבָה) מִקְרָא קֹדֶשׁ, זֵכֶר לִיצִיאַת מִצְרָיִם.

וּמִפְּנֵי חֲטָאֵינוּ גָּלִינוּ מֵאַרְצֵנוּ, וְנִתְרַחַקְנוּ מֵעַל אַדְמָתֵנוּ, וְאֵין אֲנַחְנוּ יְכוֹלִים לַעֲלוֹת וְלֵרָאוֹת וּלְהִשְׁתַּחֲווֹת לְפָנֶיךָ, וְלַעֲשׂוֹת חוֹבוֹתֵינוּ בְּבֵית בְּחִירָתֶךָ, בַּבַּיִת הַגָּדוֹל וְהַקָּדוֹשׁ שֶׁנִּקְרָא שִׁמְךָ עָלָיו, מִפְּנֵי הַיָּד שֶׁנִּשְׁתַּלְּחָה בְּמִקְדָּשֶׁךָ. יְהִי רָצוֹן מִלְּפָנֶיךָ יהוה אֱלֹהֵינוּ וֵאלֹהֵי אֲבוֹתֵינוּ, מֶלֶךְ רַחֲמָן, שֶׁתָּשׁוּב וּתְרַחֵם עָלֵינוּ וְעַל מִקְדָּשְׁךָ בְּרַחֲמֶיךָ הָרַבִּים, וְתִבְנֵהוּ מְהֵרָה וּתְגַדֵּל כְּבוֹדוֹ. אָבִינוּ מַלְכֵּנוּ, גַּלֵּה כְּבוֹד מַלְכוּתְךָ עָלֵינוּ מְהֵרָה, וְהוֹפַע וְהִנָּשֵׂא עָלֵינוּ לְעֵינֵי כָּל חַי, וְקָרֵב פְּזוּרֵינוּ מִבֵּין הַגּוֹיִם, וּנְפוּצוֹתֵינוּ כַּנֵּס

---

only be written on the parchment of the Torah, we must strive to inscribe them in our hearts and on our limbs, at all times and in all places. For this reason it is wrong to teach that the commandments must be observed only in the privacy of our homes or in the synagogue, but not when we venture out into the public domain. The way of the Torah, as taught in this phrase, is for the *mitzvot* to sanctify every aspect of our lives. Thus too we precede the performance of *mitzvot* by declaring אֲשֶׁר קִדְּשָׁנוּ בְּמִצְוֹתָיו (He has sanctified us with His commandments), that is, the commandments sanctify our lives in their totality (R. Moshe Feinstein).

The Gemara (*Avoda Zara* 18a) relates that when the Romans wrapped R. Ḥanina b. Teradyon in a Torah scroll and proceeded to burn him to death, he informed his disciples that he could see "the parchment burning but the letters taking flight." From this we learn that when non-Jews burn a Torah it is only the parchment that is burned, for the letters rise up intact to heaven. This, however, is not the case when it is a Jew who deliberately burns a Torah, for those letters which should be in the heart of every Jew are violated, and hence the letters of that *Sefer Torah* are also annihilated in that fire (R. Joseph B. Soloveitchik).

On Shabbat, add the words in parentheses:

וַתִּתֶּן לָנוּ IN YOUR LOVE, LORD our God, You have given us (Sabbaths for rest), festivals for rejoicing, holidays and seasons for joy, (this Sabbath day and) this day of

On Pesaḥ: the Festival of Matzot,
the time of our freedom

On Shavuot: the Festival of Shavuot,
the time of the giving of our Torah

On Sukkot: the Festival of Sukkot,
the time of our rejoicing

On Shemini Atzeret & Simḥat Torah: the eighth day, this Festival of Atzeret,
the time of our rejoicing

(with love,) a holy convocation, a remembrance of the Exodus from Egypt.

וּמִפְּנֵי חֲטָאֵינוּ BUT BECAUSE OF OUR SINS we were exiled from our land and driven far from our soil. We cannot go up to appear and bow down before You and perform our obligations in Your chosen House – the great and holy House upon which Your name was proclaimed – because of the hand that was sent out against Your Sanctuary. May it be Your will, LORD, our God and God of our fathers, merciful King, that you once more, in Your abundant mercy, have compassion on us and on Your Sanctuary, and rebuild it soon and magnify its glory. Our Father, our King, swiftly reveal the glory of Your sovereignty over us, and appear and be exalted over us in the sight of all living things. Draw near our scattered ones from among the nations, and gather our dispersed ones from the

---

וּמִפְּנֵי חֲטָאֵינוּ – *But because of our sins.* This admission of sin in the *Musaf Amida* of Yom Tov and Rosh Ḥodesh corresponds to the sin-offering offered on those days (*Kol Bo, Roke'aḥ*).

וְתִבְנֵהוּ מְהֵרָה וּתְגַדֵּל כְּבוֹדוֹ – *And rebuild it soon and magnify its glory.* The Land of Israel and the Temple are more than geographical or structural entities. Their continued existence and well-being are dependent on the spiritual condition of the inhabitants of the land. When our ancestors became morally and spiritually unworthy of the land, punishment and exile resulted. Conversely, the return to the land and its restoration are accomplished when those

מֵיַּרְכְּתֵי אָרֶץ. וַהֲבִיאֵנוּ לְצִיּוֹן עִירְךָ בְּרִנָּה, וְלִירוּשָׁלַיִם בֵּית מִקְדָּשְׁךָ בְּשִׂמְחַת עוֹלָם, וְשָׁם נַעֲשֶׂה לְפָנֶיךָ אֶת קָרְבְּנוֹת חוֹבוֹתֵינוּ, תְּמִידִים כְּסִדְרָם וּמוּסָפִים כְּהִלְכָתָם, וְאֶת מוּסַף יוֹם /וְאֶת מוּסְפֵי יוֹם הַשַּׁבָּת הַזֶּה וְיוֹם/

בפסח: חַג הַמַּצּוֹת הַזֶּה,

בשבועות: חַג הַשָּׁבוּעוֹת הַזֶּה,

בסוכות: חַג הַסֻּכּוֹת הַזֶּה,

בשמע"צ ובש"ת: הַשְּׁמִינִי חַג הָעֲצֶרֶת הַזֶּה,

נַעֲשֶׂה וְנַקְרִיב לְפָנֶיךָ בְּאַהֲבָה כְּמִצְוַת רְצוֹנֶךָ, כְּמוֹ שֶׁכָּתַבְתָּ עָלֵינוּ בְּתוֹרָתֶךָ, עַל יְדֵי מֹשֶׁה עַבְדֶּךָ מִפִּי כְבוֹדֶךָ, כָּאָמוּר

On שבת *add:*

במדבר כח **וּבְיוֹם הַשַּׁבָּת,** שְׁנֵי־כְבָשִׂים בְּנֵי־שָׁנָה תְּמִימִם, וּשְׁנֵי עֶשְׂרֹנִים סֹלֶת מִנְחָה בְּלוּלָה בַשֶּׁמֶן וְנִסְכּוֹ: עֹלַת שַׁבַּת בְּשַׁבַּתּוֹ, עַל־עֹלַת הַתָּמִיד וְנִסְכָּהּ:

---

who aspire to live on the land live spiritually redeemed lives, as individuals and as a people The longing for this transformation expresses itself in the particular wording of this passage: it asks that גָּלִינוּ (we were exiled) become its opposite, an occasion for גִּלָּה (God to reveal His glory), so that with the rebuilding of the Temple, we will be able to once more fulfill the commandment of יֵרָאֶה (appearing before God) on the three Festivals.

קָרְבְּנוֹת חוֹבוֹתֵינוּ – *The sacrifices required of us.* In general, it is only during the *Musaf Amida* of Shabbat and the Yamim Tovim, and not during the other *Amidas* of those days, that we incorporate a detailed account of the sacrifices offered in the Temple. The reason for this can be derived from a principle found in *Tosafot* (*Berakhot* 26a), which states that generally our prayer services were instituted by the sages to correspond to specific Temple sacrifices. However, that correspondence relates only to the time of the day recited, not to the essence of the prayers themselves which were instituted as what the Gemara refers to as expressions of רַחֲמֵי (petition and pleading with God), rather than as sacrifice substitutes. This, says *Tosafot*, is not the case with *Musaf*, which was indeed intended as a substitute fulfillment of the obligatory sacrifices offered on the days when *Musaf* is recited (i.e., Shabbat and Yom Tov), in the spirit of the verse וּנְשַׁלְּמָה פָרִים שְׂפָתֵינוּ (we will render the offering of our lips in place of sacrificial bulls) (Hosea 14:3). In accordance with this principle of *Tosafot* we well understand why it is precisely during *Musaf* that we incorporate the Torah texts that delineate the sacrificial requirements of the day at hand, so as to at least verbally and intellectually fulfill our sacrificial obligation, in

ends of the earth. Bring us to Zion, Your city, in joyful song, and to Jerusalem, home of Your Sanctuary, in everlasting joy. There, in Your presence, we will bring the sacrifices required of us, including the daily ones in their order, and the additional sacrifices according to their laws. As to the additional offering(s of this Sabbath day and) of

On Pesaḥ: this day of the Festival of Matzot,
On Shavuot: this day of the Festival of Shavuot,
On Sukkot: this day of the Festival of Sukkot,
On Shemini Atzeret & Simḥat Torah: the eighth day, this Festival of Atzeret,

we will prepare and offer it (them) before You with love, in accordance with the commandment that you willed, as You have written for us in Your Torah at the hand of Moses Your servant, at Your command, as it is said:

On Shabbat add:

Num. 28 **וּבְיוֹם הַשַּׁבָּת** "ON THE SABBATH DAY you shall bring two unblemished one-year-old male lambs, a grain-offering of two-tenths of an ephah of fine flour mixed with oil, and its libation. This is the burnt-offering for every Sabbath, in addition to the regular daily burnt-offering and its libation."

---

the absence of the actual sacrifice. This also explains the assertion by Rambam and Alfasi that it is not permitted to recite a voluntary additional *Musaf Amida*, unlike other *Amidas*. For the same restriction was true of the *Musaf* sacrifice alone, i.e., one is not permitted to offer a voluntary *Musaf* sacrifice (R. Joseph B. Soloveitchik).

A key component of the sin-offering is confession of sin; a sin-offering proffered without confession is invalid. (*Shevuot* 12b) A sin-offering is not rote ritual, and a sinner cannot be forgiven without his or her genuine acknowledgment of having sinned. Although this obligation is ordinarily waived for communal offerings – the entire community is presumed righteous – individual repentance is still necessary for individuals to achieve atonement by means of the communal offering. Regarding Rosh Ḥodesh and Festival offerings, the Talmud teaches that the sin-offering atones for defilement of the sanctuary and its sacred items. Thus on these festive days, by acknowledging these sins, whether in causing exile in the first place, or in failing to bring it to an end in subsequent generations, we offer our sincere confession for our part in the defilement of the Temple and our sacred land and pray in earnest for redemption and the sacrificial atonements that will ensue.

On the first two days of פסח *say:*

במדבר כח

וּבַחֹדֶשׁ הָרִאשׁוֹן בְּאַרְבָּעָה עָשָׂר יוֹם לַחֹדֶשׁ, פֶּסַח לַיהוה: וּבַחֲמִשָּׁה עָשָׂר יוֹם לַחֹדֶשׁ הַזֶּה חָג, שִׁבְעַת יָמִים מַצּוֹת יֵאָכֵל: בַּיּוֹם הָרִאשׁוֹן מִקְרָא־קֹדֶשׁ, כָּל־מְלֶאכֶת עֲבֹדָה לֹא תַעֲשׂוּ: וְהִקְרַבְתֶּם אִשֶּׁה עֹלָה לַיהוה, פָּרִים בְּנֵי־בָקָר שְׁנַיִם וְאַיִל אֶחָד, וְשִׁבְעָה כְבָשִׂים בְּנֵי שָׁנָה תְּמִימִם יִהְיוּ לָכֶם: וּמִנְחָתָם וְנִסְכֵּיהֶם כִּמְדֻבָּר, שְׁלֹשָׁה עֶשְׂרֹנִים לַפָּר וּשְׁנֵי עֶשְׂרֹנִים לָאָיִל, וְעִשָּׂרוֹן לַכֶּבֶשׂ, וְיַיִן כְּנִסְכּוֹ, וְשָׂעִיר לְכַפֵּר, וּשְׁנֵי תְמִידִים כְּהִלְכָתָם.

On weekdays, continue with אֱלֹהֵינוּ וֵאלֹהֵי אֲבוֹתֵינוּ *on page 844.*
On שבת*, continue with* יִשְׂמְחוּ בְמַלְכוּתְךָ *on page 844.*

On the last six days of פסח *say:*

במדבר כח

וְהִקְרַבְתֶּם אִשֶּׁה עֹלָה לַיהוה, פָּרִים בְּנֵי־בָקָר שְׁנַיִם וְאַיִל אֶחָד, וְשִׁבְעָה כְבָשִׂים בְּנֵי שָׁנָה, תְּמִימִם יִהְיוּ לָכֶם: וּמִנְחָתָם וְנִסְכֵּיהֶם כִּמְדֻבָּר, שְׁלֹשָׁה עֶשְׂרֹנִים לַפָּר וּשְׁנֵי עֶשְׂרֹנִים לָאָיִל, וְעִשָּׂרוֹן לַכֶּבֶשׂ, וְיַיִן כְּנִסְכּוֹ, וְשָׂעִיר לְכַפֵּר, וּשְׁנֵי תְמִידִים כְּהִלְכָתָם.

On weekdays, continue with אֱלֹהֵינוּ וֵאלֹהֵי אֲבוֹתֵינוּ *on page 844.*
On שבת*, continue with* יִשְׂמְחוּ בְמַלְכוּתְךָ *on page 844.*

On שבועות *say:*

במדבר כח

וּבְיוֹם הַבִּכּוּרִים, בְּהַקְרִיבְכֶם מִנְחָה חֲדָשָׁה לַיהוה בְּשָׁבֻעֹתֵיכֶם, מִקְרָא־קֹדֶשׁ יִהְיֶה לָכֶם, כָּל־מְלֶאכֶת עֲבֹדָה לֹא תַעֲשׂוּ: וְהִקְרַבְתֶּם עוֹלָה לְרֵיחַ נִיחֹחַ לַיהוה, פָּרִים בְּנֵי־בָקָר שְׁנַיִם, אַיִל אֶחָד, שִׁבְעָה כְבָשִׂים בְּנֵי שָׁנָה: וּמִנְחָתָם וְנִסְכֵּיהֶם כִּמְדֻבָּר, שְׁלֹשָׁה עֶשְׂרֹנִים לַפָּר וּשְׁנֵי עֶשְׂרֹנִים לָאָיִל, וְעִשָּׂרוֹן לַכֶּבֶשׂ, וְיַיִן כְּנִסְכּוֹ, וְשָׂעִיר לְכַפֵּר, וּשְׁנֵי תְמִידִים כְּהִלְכָתָם.

On weekdays, continue with אֱלֹהֵינוּ וֵאלֹהֵי אֲבוֹתֵינוּ *on page 844.*
On שבת*, continue with* יִשְׂמְחוּ בְמַלְכוּתְךָ *on page 844.*

On the first two days of סוכות *say:*

במדבר כט

וּבַחֲמִשָּׁה עָשָׂר יוֹם לַחֹדֶשׁ הַשְּׁבִיעִי, מִקְרָא־קֹדֶשׁ יִהְיֶה לָכֶם, כָּל־מְלֶאכֶת עֲבֹדָה לֹא תַעֲשׂוּ, וְחַגֹּתֶם חַג לַיהוה שִׁבְעַת יָמִים: וְהִקְרַבְתֶּם עֹלָה אִשֵּׁה רֵיחַ נִיחֹחַ לַיהוה, פָּרִים בְּנֵי־בָקָר שְׁלֹשָׁה

On the first two days of Pesaḥ say:

Num. 28 וּבַחֹדֶשׁ הָרִאשׁוֹן AND IN THE FIRST MONTH, on the fourteenth day of the month, is the LORD's Passover. And on the fifteenth day of this month shall be a feast; seven days shall unleavened bread be eaten. On the first day shall be a holy convocation; you shall do no manner of servile work; but you shall present an offering made by fire, a burnt-offering to the LORD: two young bulls, and one ram, and seven one-year-old male lambs; they shall be for you without blemish. And their meal-offerings and their wine-libations as ordained: three-tenths of an ephah for each bull, two-tenths of an ephah for the ram; one-tenth of an ephah for each lamb, and wine for its libation. A male goat for atonement, and two daily offerings according to their law.

On weekdays, continue with "Our God and God of our fathers" on page 845.
On Shabbat, continue with "Those who keep the Sabbath" on page 845.

On the last six days of Pesaḥ say:

Num. 28 וְהִקְרַבְתֶּם AND YOU SHALL present an offering made by fire, a burnt-offering to the LORD: two young bulls, and one ram, and seven one-year-old male lambs; they shall be for you without blemish. And their meal-offerings and their wine-libations as ordained: three-tenths of an ephah for each bull, two-tenths of an ephah for the ram; one-tenth of an ephah for each lamb, and wine for its libation. A male goat for atonement, and two daily offerings according to their law.

On weekdays, continue with "Our God and God of our fathers" on page 845.
On Shabbat, continue with "Those who keep the Sabbath" on page 845.

On Shavuot say:

Num. 28 וּבְיוֹם הַבִּכּוּרִים AND ON THE DAY of the first fruits, when you bring a new meal-offering to the LORD on your Festival of Shavuot, you shall have a holy convocation: you shall do no manner of servile work; but you shall present a burnt-offering for a sweet savor to the LORD: two young bulls, one ram, seven one-year-old male lambs. And their meal-offerings and their wine-libations as ordained: three-tenths of an ephah for each bull, two-tenths of an ephah for the ram; one-tenth of an ephah for each lamb, and wine for its libation. A male goat for atonement, and two daily offerings according to their law.

On weekdays, continue with "Our God and God of our fathers" on page 845.
On Shabbat, continue with "Those who keep the Sabbath" on page 845.

On the first two days of Sukkot say:

Num. 29 וּבַחֲמִשָּׁה עָשָׂר AND ON THE FIFTEENTH DAY of the seventh month you shall have a holy convocation: you shall do no manner of servile work, and you shall keep a feast for the LORD seven days; and you shall present

עָשָׂר, אֵילִם שְׁנָיִם, כְּבָשִׂים בְּנֵי־שָׁנָה אַרְבָּעָה עָשָׂר, תְּמִימִם יִהְיוּ: וּמִנְחָתָם וְנִסְכֵּיהֶם כִּמְדֻבָּר, שְׁלֹשָׁה עֶשְׂרֹנִים לַפָּר וּשְׁנֵי עֶשְׂרֹנִים לָאָיִל, וְעִשָּׂרוֹן לַכֶּבֶשׂ, וְיַיִן כְּנִסְכּוֹ, וְשָׂעִיר לְכַפֵּר, וּשְׁנֵי תְמִידִים כְּהִלְכָתָם.

On weekdays, continue with אֱלֹהֵינוּ וֵאלֹהֵי אֲבוֹתֵינוּ *on page 844.*
On שבת*, continue with* יִשְׂמְחוּ בְמַלְכוּתְךָ *on page 844.*

On the first day of חול המועד סוכות *say:*

במדבר כט **וּבַיּוֹם הַשֵּׁנִי,** פָּרִים בְּנֵי־בָקָר שְׁנֵים עָשָׂר, אֵילִם שְׁנָיִם, כְּבָשִׂים בְּנֵי־שָׁנָה אַרְבָּעָה עָשָׂר, תְּמִימִם: וּמִנְחָתָם וְנִסְכֵּיהֶם כִּמְדֻבָּר, שְׁלֹשָׁה עֶשְׂרֹנִים לַפָּר, וּשְׁנֵי עֶשְׂרֹנִים לָאָיִל, וְעִשָּׂרוֹן לַכֶּבֶשׂ, וְיַיִן כְּנִסְכּוֹ, וְשָׂעִיר לְכַפֵּר, וּשְׁנֵי תְמִידִים כְּהִלְכָתָם.

במדבר כט **וּבַיּוֹם הַשְּׁלִישִׁי,** פָּרִים עַשְׁתֵּי־עָשָׂר, אֵילִם שְׁנָיִם, כְּבָשִׂים בְּנֵי־שָׁנָה אַרְבָּעָה עָשָׂר, תְּמִימִם: וּמִנְחָתָם וְנִסְכֵּיהֶם כִּמְדֻבָּר, שְׁלֹשָׁה עֶשְׂרֹנִים לַפָּר, וּשְׁנֵי עֶשְׂרֹנִים לָאָיִל, וְעִשָּׂרוֹן לַכֶּבֶשׂ, וְיַיִן כְּנִסְכּוֹ, וְשָׂעִיר לְכַפֵּר, וּשְׁנֵי תְמִידִים כְּהִלְכָתָם.

On weekdays, continue with אֱלֹהֵינוּ וֵאלֹהֵי אֲבוֹתֵינוּ *on page 844.*
On שבת*, continue with* יִשְׂמְחוּ בְמַלְכוּתְךָ *on page 844.*

On the second day of חול המועד סוכות*, say:*

במדבר כט **וּבַיּוֹם הַשְּׁלִישִׁי,** פָּרִים עַשְׁתֵּי־עָשָׂר, אֵילִם שְׁנָיִם, כְּבָשִׂים בְּנֵי־שָׁנָה אַרְבָּעָה עָשָׂר, תְּמִימִם: וּמִנְחָתָם וְנִסְכֵּיהֶם כִּמְדֻבָּר, שְׁלֹשָׁה עֶשְׂרֹנִים לַפָּר, וּשְׁנֵי עֶשְׂרֹנִים לָאָיִל, וְעִשָּׂרוֹן לַכֶּבֶשׂ, וְיַיִן כְּנִסְכּוֹ, וְשָׂעִיר לְכַפֵּר, וּשְׁנֵי תְמִידִים כְּהִלְכָתָם.

במדבר כט **וּבַיּוֹם הָרְבִיעִי,** פָּרִים עֲשָׂרָה, אֵילִם שְׁנָיִם, כְּבָשִׂים בְּנֵי־שָׁנָה אַרְבָּעָה עָשָׂר, תְּמִימִם: וּמִנְחָתָם וְנִסְכֵּיהֶם כִּמְדֻבָּר, שְׁלֹשָׁה עֶשְׂרֹנִים לַפָּר, וּשְׁנֵי עֶשְׂרֹנִים לָאָיִל, וְעִשָּׂרוֹן לַכֶּבֶשׂ, וְיַיִן כְּנִסְכּוֹ, וְשָׂעִיר לְכַפֵּר, וּשְׁנֵי תְמִידִים כְּהִלְכָתָם.

On weekdays, continue with אֱלֹהֵינוּ וֵאלֹהֵי אֲבוֹתֵינוּ *on page 844.*
On שבת*, continue with* יִשְׂמְחוּ בְמַלְכוּתְךָ *on page 844.*

---

a burnt-offering, an offering made by fire, of a sweet savor to the LORD: thirteen young bulls, two rams, fourteen one-year-old male lambs; they shall be without blemish. And their meal-offerings and their wine-libations as ordained: three-tenths of an ephah for each bull, two-tenths of an ephah for each ram; one-tenth of an ephah for each lamb, and wine for its libation. A male goat for atonement, and two daily offerings according to their law.

On weekdays, continue with "Our God and God of our fathers" on page 845.
On Shabbat, continue with "Those who keep the Sabbath" on page 845.

On the first day of Ḥol HaMo'ed Sukkot say:

Num. 29 וּבַיּוֹם הַשֵּׁנִי AND ON THE SECOND DAY you shall present twelve young bulls, two rams, fourteen one-year-old male lambs without blemish. And their meal-offerings and their wine-libations as ordained: three-tenths of an ephah for each bull, two-tenths of an ephah for each ram; one-tenth of an ephah for each lamb, and wine for its libation.

Num. 29 וּבַיּוֹם הַשְּׁלִישִׁי AND ON THE THIRD DAY eleven bulls, two rams, fourteen one-year-old male lambs without blemish. And their meal-offerings and their wine-libations as ordained: three-tenths of an ephah for each bull, two-tenths of an ephah for each ram; one-tenth of an ephah for each lamb, and wine for its libation. A male goat for atonement, and two daily offerings according to their law.

On weekdays, continue with "Our God and God of our fathers" on page 845.
On Shabbat, continue with "Those who keep the Sabbath" on page 845.

On the second day of Ḥol HaMo'ed Sukkot say:

Num. 29 וּבַיּוֹם הַשְּׁלִישִׁי AND ON THE THIRD DAY eleven bulls, two rams, fourteen one-year-old male lambs without blemish. And their meal-offerings and their wine-libations as ordained: three-tenths of an ephah for each bull, two-tenths of an ephah for each ram; one-tenth of an ephah for each lamb, and wine for its libation. A male goat for atonement, and two daily offerings according to their law.

Num. 29 וּבַיּוֹם הָרְבִיעִי AND ON THE FOURTH DAY ten bulls, two rams, fourteen one-year-old male lambs without blemish. And their meal-offerings and their wine-libations as ordained: three-tenths of an ephah for each bull, two-tenths of an ephah for each ram; one-tenth of an ephah for each lamb, and wine for its libation. A male goat for atonement, and two daily offerings according to their law.

On weekdays, continue with "Our God and God of our fathers" on page 845.
On Shabbat, continue with "Those who keep the Sabbath" on page 845.

On the third day of חול המועד סוכות*, say:*

במדבר כט **וּבַיּוֹם הָרְבִיעִי,** פָּרִים עֲשָׂרָה, אֵילִם שְׁנָיִם, כְּבָשִׂים בְּנֵי־שָׁנָה אַרְבָּעָה עָשָׂר, תְּמִימִם: וּמִנְחָתָם וְנִסְכֵּיהֶם כִּמְדֻבָּר, שְׁלֹשָׁה עֶשְׂרֹנִים לַפָּר, וּשְׁנֵי עֶשְׂרֹנִים לָאָיִל, וְעִשָּׂרוֹן לַכֶּבֶשׂ, וְיַיִן כְּנִסְכּוֹ, וְשָׂעִיר לְכַפֵּר, וּשְׁנֵי תְמִידִים כְּהִלְכָתָם.

במדבר כט **וּבַיּוֹם הַחֲמִישִׁי,** פָּרִים תִּשְׁעָה, אֵילִם שְׁנָיִם, כְּבָשִׂים בְּנֵי־שָׁנָה אַרְבָּעָה עָשָׂר, תְּמִימִם: וּמִנְחָתָם וְנִסְכֵּיהֶם כִּמְדֻבָּר, שְׁלֹשָׁה עֶשְׂרֹנִים לַפָּר, וּשְׁנֵי עֶשְׂרֹנִים לָאָיִל, וְעִשָּׂרוֹן לַכֶּבֶשׂ, וְיַיִן כְּנִסְכּוֹ, וְשָׂעִיר לְכַפֵּר, וּשְׁנֵי תְמִידִים כְּהִלְכָתָם.

On weekdays, continue with אֱלֹהֵינוּ וֵאלֹהֵי אֲבוֹתֵינוּ *on the next page.*
On שבת*, continue with* יִשְׂמְחוּ בְמַלְכוּתְךָ *on the next page.*

On the fourth day of חול המועד סוכות*, say:*

במדבר כט **וּבַיּוֹם הַחֲמִישִׁי,** פָּרִים תִּשְׁעָה, אֵילִם שְׁנָיִם, כְּבָשִׂים בְּנֵי־שָׁנָה אַרְבָּעָה עָשָׂר, תְּמִימִם: וּמִנְחָתָם וְנִסְכֵּיהֶם כִּמְדֻבָּר, שְׁלֹשָׁה עֶשְׂרֹנִים לַפָּר, וּשְׁנֵי עֶשְׂרֹנִים לָאָיִל, וְעִשָּׂרוֹן לַכֶּבֶשׂ, וְיַיִן כְּנִסְכּוֹ, וְשָׂעִיר לְכַפֵּר, וּשְׁנֵי תְמִידִים כְּהִלְכָתָם.

במדבר כט **וּבַיּוֹם הַשִּׁשִּׁי,** פָּרִים שְׁמֹנָה, אֵילִם שְׁנָיִם, כְּבָשִׂים בְּנֵי־שָׁנָה אַרְבָּעָה עָשָׂר, תְּמִימִם: וּמִנְחָתָם וְנִסְכֵּיהֶם כִּמְדֻבָּר, שְׁלֹשָׁה עֶשְׂרֹנִים לַפָּר, וּשְׁנֵי עֶשְׂרֹנִים לָאָיִל, וְעִשָּׂרוֹן לַכֶּבֶשׂ, וְיַיִן כְּנִסְכּוֹ, וְשָׂעִיר לְכַפֵּר, וּשְׁנֵי תְמִידִים כְּהִלְכָתָם.

On weekdays, continue with אֱלֹהֵינוּ וֵאלֹהֵי אֲבוֹתֵינוּ *on the next page.*
On שבת*, continue with* יִשְׂמְחוּ בְמַלְכוּתְךָ *on the next page.*

On הושענא רבה*, say:*

במדבר כט **וּבַיּוֹם הַשִּׁשִּׁי,** פָּרִים שְׁמֹנָה, אֵילִם שְׁנָיִם, כְּבָשִׂים בְּנֵי־שָׁנָה אַרְבָּעָה עָשָׂר, תְּמִימִם: וּמִנְחָתָם וְנִסְכֵּיהֶם כִּמְדֻבָּר, שְׁלֹשָׁה

On the third day of Ḥol HaMo'ed Sukkot say:

Num. 29 **וּבַיּוֹם הָרְבִיעִי** AND ON THE FOURTH DAY ten bulls, two rams, fourteen one-year-old male lambs without blemish. And their meal-offerings and their wine-libations as ordained: three-tenths of an ephah for each bull, two-tenths of an ephah for each ram; one-tenth of an ephah for each lamb, and wine for its libation. A male goat for atonement, and two daily offerings according to their law.

Num. 29 **וּבַיּוֹם הַחֲמִישִׁי** AND ON THE FIFTH DAY nine bulls, two rams, fourteen one-year-old male lambs without blemish. And their meal-offerings and their wine-libations as ordained: three-tenths of an ephah for each bull, two-tenths of an ephah for each ram; one-tenth of an ephah for each lamb, and wine for its libation. A male goat for atonement, and two daily offerings according to their law.

On weekdays, continue with "Our God and God of our fathers" on the next page.
On Shabbat, continue with "Those who keep the Sabbath" on the next page.

On the fourth day of Ḥol HaMo'ed Sukkot say:

Num. 29 **וּבַיּוֹם הַחֲמִישִׁי** AND ON THE FIFTH DAY nine bulls, two rams, fourteen one-year-old male lambs without blemish. And their meal-offerings and their wine-libations as ordained: three-tenths of an ephah for each bull, two-tenths of an ephah for each ram; one-tenth of an ephah for each lamb, and wine for its libation. A male goat for atonement, and two daily offerings according to their law.

Num. 29 **וּבַיּוֹם הַשִּׁשִּׁי** AND ON THE SIXTH DAY eight bulls, two rams, fourteen one-year-old male lambs without blemish. And their meal-offerings and their wine-libations as ordained: three-tenths of an ephah for each bull, two-tenths of an ephah for each ram; one-tenth of an ephah for each lamb, and wine for its libation. A male goat for atonement, and two daily offerings according to their law.

On weekdays, continue with "Our God and God of our fathers" on the next page.
On Shabbat, continue with "Those who keep the Sabbath" on the next page.

On Hoshana Raba, say:

Num. 29 **וּבַיּוֹם הַשִּׁשִּׁי** AND ON THE SIXTH DAY eight bulls, two rams, fourteen one-year-old male lambs without blemish. And their meal-offerings and their wine-libations as ordained: three-tenths of an ephah for each bull, two-tenths

עֶשְׂרֹנִים לַפָּר, וּשְׁנֵי עֶשְׂרֹנִים לָאָיִל, וְעִשָּׂרוֹן לַכֶּבֶשׂ, וְיַיִן כְּנִסְכּוֹ, וְשָׂעִיר לְכַפֵּר, וּשְׁנֵי תְמִידִים כְּהִלְכָתָם.

וּבַיּוֹם הַשְּׁבִיעִי, פָּרִים שִׁבְעָה, אֵילִם שְׁנָיִם, כְּבָשִׂים בְּנֵי־שָׁנָה אַרְבָּעָה עָשָׂר, תְּמִימִם: וּמִנְחָתָם וְנִסְכֵּיהֶם כִּמְדֻבָּר, שְׁלֹשָׁה עֶשְׂרֹנִים לַפָּר, וּשְׁנֵי עֶשְׂרֹנִים לָאָיִל, וְעִשָּׂרוֹן לַכֶּבֶשׂ, וְיַיִן כְּנִסְכּוֹ, וְשָׂעִיר לְכַפֵּר, וּשְׁנֵי תְמִידִים כְּהִלְכָתָם. במדבר כט

Continue with אֱלֹהֵינוּ וֵאלֹהֵי אֲבוֹתֵינוּ *below.*

On שמחת תורה *and* שמיני עצרת*, say:*

בַּיּוֹם הַשְּׁמִינִי, עֲצֶרֶת תִּהְיֶה לָכֶם, כָּל־מְלֶאכֶת עֲבֹדָה לֹא תַעֲשׂוּ: וְהִקְרַבְתֶּם עֹלָה אִשֵּׁה רֵיחַ נִיחֹחַ לַיהוה, פַּר אֶחָד, אַיִל אֶחָד, כְּבָשִׂים בְּנֵי־שָׁנָה שִׁבְעָה, תְּמִימִם: וּמִנְחָתָם וְנִסְכֵּיהֶם כִּמְדֻבָּר, שְׁלֹשָׁה עֶשְׂרֹנִים לַפָּר וּשְׁנֵי עֶשְׂרֹנִים לָאָיִל, וְעִשָּׂרוֹן לַכֶּבֶשׂ, וְיַיִן כְּנִסְכּוֹ, וְשָׂעִיר לְכַפֵּר, וּשְׁנֵי תְמִידִים כְּהִלְכָתָם. במדבר כט

On weekdays, continue with אֱלֹהֵינוּ וֵאלֹהֵי אֲבוֹתֵינוּ *below.*
On שבת*, continue with* יִשְׂמְחוּ בְמַלְכוּתְךָ *below the line.*

On שבת *say:*

יִשְׂמְחוּ בְמַלְכוּתְךָ שׁוֹמְרֵי שַׁבָּת וְקוֹרְאֵי עֹנֶג. עַם מְקַדְּשֵׁי שְׁבִיעִי כֻּלָּם יִשְׂבְּעוּ וְיִתְעַנְּגוּ מִטּוּבֶךָ, וּבַשְּׁבִיעִי רָצִיתָ בּוֹ וְקִדַּשְׁתּוֹ, חֶמְדַּת יָמִים אוֹתוֹ קָרָאתָ, זֵכֶר לְמַעֲשֵׂה בְרֵאשִׁית.

On all days continue:

אֱלֹהֵינוּ וֵאלֹהֵי אֲבוֹתֵינוּ, מֶלֶךְ רַחֲמָן רַחֵם עָלֵינוּ, טוֹב וּמֵטִיב הִדָּרֶשׁ לָנוּ, שׁוּבָה אֵלֵינוּ בַּהֲמוֹן רַחֲמֶיךָ, בִּגְלַל אָבוֹת שֶׁעָשׂוּ רְצוֹנֶךָ. בְּנֵה בֵיתְךָ כְּבַתְּחִלָּה, וְכוֹנֵן מִקְדָּשְׁךָ עַל מְכוֹנוֹ, וְהַרְאֵנוּ בְּבִנְיָנוֹ, וְשַׂמְּחֵנוּ בְּתִקּוּנוֹ, וְהָשֵׁב כֹּהֲנִים לַעֲבוֹדָתָם, וּלְוִיִּם לְשִׁירָם וּלְזִמְרָם, וְהָשֵׁב יִשְׂרָאֵל לִנְוֵיהֶם. וְשָׁם נַעֲלֶה וְנֵרָאֶה
וְנִשְׁתַּחֲוֶה לְפָנֶיךָ בְּשָׁלֹשׁ פַּעֲמֵי רְגָלֵינוּ, כַּכָּתוּב בְּתוֹרָתֶךָ, שָׁלוֹשׁ דברים טז

of an ephah for each ram; one-tenth of an ephah for each lamb, and wine for its libation. A male goat for atonement, and two daily offerings according to their law.

Num. 29 וּבַיּוֹם הַשְּׁבִיעִי AND ON THE SEVENTH DAY seven bulls, two rams, fourteen one-year-old male lambs without blemish. And their meal-offerings and their wine-libations as ordained: three-tenths of an ephah for each bull, two-tenths of an ephah for each ram; one-tenth of an ephah for each lamb, and wine for its libation. A male goat for atonement, and two daily offerings according to their law.

Continue with "Our God and God of our fathers" below.

On Shemini Atzeret and Simḥat Torah, say:

Num. 29 בַּיּוֹם הַשְּׁמִינִי AND ON THE EIGHTH DAY you shall have a solemn assembly: you shall do no manner of servile work; but you shall present a burnt-offering, an offering made by fire, of a sweet savor to the LORD: one bull, one ram, seven one-year-old male lambs without blemish. And their meal-offerings and their wine-libations as ordained: three-tenths of an ephah for each bull, two-tenths of an ephah for each ram; one-tenth of an ephah for each lamb, and wine for its libation. A male goat for atonement, and two daily offerings according to their law.

On weekdays, continue with "Our God and God of our fathers" below.
On Shabbat, continue with "Those who keep the Sabbath" below the line.

On Shabbat say:

יִשְׂמְחוּ MAY THEY who keep the Sabbath and call it a delight rejoice in Your sovereignty. May all Your people who sanctify the seventh day find satisfaction and delight in Your goodness. You desired and sanctified the seventh day, calling it the choicest of days, in remembrance of the act of Creation.

On all days continue:

אֱלֹהֵינוּ OUR GOD and God of our fathers, merciful King, have mercy on us. Good and beneficent One respond to us. Return to us in Your abundant mercy, for the sake of the forefathers who did Your will. Rebuild Your House as at the beginning, and establish Your Sanctuary on its site. Show us its rebuilding and gladden us with its restoration. Return the priests to their service, and the Levites to their song and music, and return Israel to their homes. There we will go up and appear and bow down before You on our three pilgrimage festivals, as is written in Your Torah: "Three times in a year shall all your males appear before the LORD

פְּעָמִים בַּשָּׁנָה יֵרָאֶה כָל־זְכוּרְךָ אֶת־פְּנֵי יהוה אֱלֹהֶיךָ, בַּמָּקוֹם אֲשֶׁר יִבְחָר, בְּחַג הַמַּצּוֹת, וּבְחַג הַשָּׁבֻעוֹת, וּבְחַג הַסֻּכּוֹת, וְלֹא יֵרָאֶה אֶת־פְּנֵי יהוה רֵיקָם: אִישׁ כְּמַתְּנַת יָדוֹ, כְּבִרְכַּת יהוה אֱלֹהֶיךָ אֲשֶׁר נָתַן־לָךְ:

On שבת *add the words in parentheses:*

וְהַשִּׂיאֵנוּ יהוה אֱלֹהֵינוּ אֶת בִּרְכַּת מוֹעֲדֶיךָ, לְחַיִּים וּלְשָׁלוֹם, לְשִׂמְחָה וּלְשָׂשׂוֹן, כַּאֲשֶׁר רָצִיתָ וְאָמַרְתָּ לְבָרְכֵנוּ. (אֱלֹהֵינוּ וֵאלֹהֵי אֲבוֹתֵינוּ, רְצֵה בִמְנוּחָתֵנוּ) קַדְּשֵׁנוּ בְּמִצְוֹתֶיךָ, וְתֵן חֶלְקֵנוּ בְּתוֹרָתֶךָ, שַׂבְּעֵנוּ מִטּוּבֶךָ, וְשַׂמְּחֵנוּ בִּישׁוּעָתֶךָ, וְטַהֵר לִבֵּנוּ לְעָבְדְּךָ בֶּאֱמֶת, וְהַנְחִילֵנוּ יהוה אֱלֹהֵינוּ (בְּאַהֲבָה וּבְרָצוֹן), בְּשִׂמְחָה וּבְשָׂשׂוֹן (שַׁבָּת וּ) מוֹעֲדֵי קָדְשֶׁךָ, וְיִשְׂמְחוּ בְךָ יִשְׂרָאֵל מְקַדְּשֵׁי שְׁמֶךָ. בָּרוּךְ אַתָּה יהוה, מְקַדֵּשׁ (הַשַּׁבָּת וְ) יִשְׂרָאֵל וְהַזְּמַנִּים.

עבודה

רְצֵה יהוה אֱלֹהֵינוּ בְּעַמְּךָ יִשְׂרָאֵל, וּבִתְפִלָּתָם, וְהָשֵׁב אֶת הָעֲבוֹדָה לִדְבִיר בֵּיתֶךָ, וְאִשֵּׁי יִשְׂרָאֵל וּתְפִלָּתָם בְּאַהֲבָה תְקַבֵּל בְּרָצוֹן, וּתְהִי לְרָצוֹן תָּמִיד עֲבוֹדַת יִשְׂרָאֵל עַמֶּךָ.

On Yom Tov (but not on שבת חול המועד *or* חול המועד*), when Kohanim bless the congregation* *continue on page 852.*

וְתֶחֱזֶינָה עֵינֵינוּ בְּשׁוּבְךָ לְצִיּוֹן בְּרַחֲמִים. בָּרוּךְ אַתָּה יהוה, הַמַּחֲזִיר שְׁכִינָתוֹ לְצִיּוֹן.

כַּאֲשֶׁר רָצִיתָ וְאָמַרְתָּ לְבָרְכֵנוּ – *As You desired and promised to bless us.* This phrase implies that God has promised a special reward for those who keep Yom Tov. We do not, however, find such an explicit promise in the Torah. The answer is that in the preceding paragraph we quote the verse "they shall not appear before the Lord empty-handed" (Deut. 16:16). The Gemara (*Ḥagiga* 2b) explains that this verse is ambiguous, as the verb can be understood to mean either "appear" or "be seen." The former conveys the obligation to come with an offering, whereas the latter declares that one who comes to celebrate Yom Tov is promised that he will not be seen to be empty-handed. Our phrase teaches that the latter interpretation is correct, i.e., in celebrating Yom Tov we will be blessed to come before God laden with the many fruits of our preceding labors (*Netziv*).

בְּשִׂמְחָה וּבְשָׂשׂוֹן מוֹעֲדֵי קָדְשֶׁךָ – *With joy and*

your God in the place which He shall choose; on the Festival of Matzot, and on the Festival of Shavuot, and on the Festival of Sukkot; and they shall not appear before the LORD empty-handed; every man shall give as he is able, according to the blessing of the LORD your God which He has given you.

On Shabbat add the words in parentheses:

וְהַשִּׂיאֵנוּ BESTOW UPON US, LORD, our God, the blessing of Your festivals for life and peace, joy and gladness, as You desired and promised to bless us. (Our God and the God of our fathers, may You find favor with our rest.) Sanctify us with Your commandments and grant us our share in Your Torah. Satisfy us from Your goodness, gladden us with Your salvation, and purify our heart to serve you in truth. And grant us as a heritage, LORD, our God, (with love and favor,) with joy and gladness, (the Sabbath and) the festivals of Your holiness. And may Israel, who sanctify Your name, rejoice in You. Blessed are You, LORD, Who sanctifies (the Sabbath and) Israel and the festive seasons.

TEMPLE SERVICE

רְצֵה LOOK FAVORABLY, LORD our God, upon Your people Israel and their prayer, and restore the service to the Holy of Holies of Your House. Accept with love and favor the fire-offerings of Israel and their prayer. May the service of Israel Your people Israel always find favor with You.

On Yom Tov (but not on Ḥol HaMo'ed or Shabbat Ḥol HaMo'ed), when Kohanim bless the congregation continue on page 853.

May our eyes witness Your return to Zion in compassion. Blessed are You, LORD, Who will restore His Divine Presence to Zion.

---

gladness, the festivals of Your holiness. Rambam (*Sefer HaMitzvot* #54) explains that while the primary fulfillment of the obligation to rejoice on Yom Tov is via the *Shelamim* sacrifice (otherwise known as שַׁלְמֵי שִׂמְחָה), the sages also included other forms of rejoicing, including the consumption of meat and wine, wearing new clothing, distribution of delicacies, and singing and dancing to musical accompaniment. He adds that "the Torah also obligates us to include the weak, the poor, and the convert when we fulfill this *mitzva*, as it says 'you shall rejoice… as well as the convert, the orphan, and the widow' (Deut. 16:11)."

הודאה

Bow during the first five words.

מוֹדִים אֲנַחְנוּ לָךְ, שָׁאַתָּה הוּא יהוה אֱלֹהֵינוּ וֵאלֹהֵי אֲבוֹתֵינוּ לְעוֹלָם וָעֶד. צוּר חַיֵּינוּ, מָגֵן יִשְׁעֵנוּ, אַתָּה הוּא. לְדוֹר וָדוֹר נוֹדֶה לְּךָ וּנְסַפֵּר תְּהִלָּתֶךָ, עַל חַיֵּינוּ הַמְּסוּרִים בְּיָדֶךָ, וְעַל נִשְׁמוֹתֵינוּ הַפְּקוּדוֹת לָךְ, וְעַל נִסֶּיךָ שֶׁבְּכָל יוֹם עִמָּנוּ, וְעַל נִפְלְאוֹתֶיךָ וְטוֹבוֹתֶיךָ, שֶׁבְּכָל עֵת, עֶרֶב וָבֹקֶר וְצָהֳרָיִם. הַטּוֹב, כִּי לֹא כָלוּ רַחֲמֶיךָ וְהַמְרַחֵם, כִּי לֹא תַמּוּ חֲסָדֶיךָ, מֵעוֹלָם קִוִּינוּ לָךְ.

During חזרת הש״ץ, the קהל says quietly:

מוֹדִים אֲנַחְנוּ לָךְ, שָׁאַתָּה הוּא יהוה אֱלֹהֵינוּ וֵאלֹהֵי אֲבוֹתֵינוּ, אֱלֹהֵי כָל בָּשָׂר, יוֹצְרֵנוּ, יוֹצֵר בְּרֵאשִׁית. בְּרָכוֹת וְהוֹדָאוֹת לְשִׁמְךָ הַגָּדוֹל וְהַקָּדוֹשׁ, עַל שֶׁהֶחֱיִיתָנוּ וְקִיַּמְתָּנוּ. כֵּן תְּחַיֵּנוּ וּתְקַיְּמֵנוּ, וְתֶאֱסֹף גָּלֻיּוֹתֵינוּ לְחַצְרוֹת קָדְשֶׁךָ, לִשְׁמֹר חֻקֶּיךָ וְלַעֲשׂוֹת רְצוֹנֶךָ וּלְעָבְדְּךָ בְּלֵבָב שָׁלֵם, עַל שֶׁאֲנַחְנוּ מוֹדִים לָךְ. בָּרוּךְ אֵל הַהוֹדָאוֹת.

וְעַל כֻּלָּם יִתְבָּרַךְ וְיִתְרוֹמַם שִׁמְךָ מַלְכֵּנוּ תָּמִיד לְעוֹלָם וָעֶד. וְכֹל הַחַיִּים יוֹדוּךָ סֶּלָה, וִיהַלְלוּ אֶת שִׁמְךָ בֶּאֱמֶת, הָאֵל יְשׁוּעָתֵנוּ וְעֶזְרָתֵנוּ סֶלָה. בָּרוּךְ אַתָּה יהוה, הַטּוֹב שִׁמְךָ וּלְךָ נָאֶה לְהוֹדוֹת.

When saying the עמידה silently, continue with שִׂים שָׁלוֹם on the next page.

ברכת כהנים

If Kohanim do not ascend, the following is said.

אֱלֹהֵינוּ וֵאלֹהֵי אֲבוֹתֵינוּ, בָּרְכֵנוּ בַּבְּרָכָה הַמְשֻׁלֶּשֶׁת, בַּתּוֹרָה, הַכְּתוּבָה עַל יְדֵי מֹשֶׁה עַבְדֶּךָ, הָאֲמוּרָה מִפִּי אַהֲרֹן וּבָנָיו כֹּהֲנִים עַם קְדוֹשֶׁךָ, כָּאָמוּר

יְבָרֶכְךָ יהוה וְיִשְׁמְרֶךָ: קהל: כֵּן יְהִי רָצוֹן במדבר ו

יָאֵר יהוה פָּנָיו אֵלֶיךָ וִיחֻנֶּךָּ: קהל: כֵּן יְהִי רָצוֹן

יִשָּׂא יהוה פָּנָיו אֵלֶיךָ וְיָשֵׂם לְךָ שָׁלוֹם: קהל: כֵּן יְהִי רָצוֹן

THANKSGIVING

Bow during the first seven words.

מוֹדִים ᵛ WE THANK YOU, for You are the LORD our God and the God of our fathers for all eternity. You are the Rock of our life and Shield of our deliverance. From generation to generation we will thank You and recount Your praise for our lives that are in Your hands, for our souls that are given over to You, for Your miracles that are with us every day, and for Your constant wonders and favors, evening, morning and noon. You are good, for Your compassion does not cease, and You are compassionate, for Your kindness never ends. We have placed our hope in You forever and ever.

During the Leader's Repetition, the congregation says quietly:

מוֹדִים ᵛ WE THANK YOU, for You are the LORD our God, the God of our fathers and God of all flesh. You are our Maker, the Maker of Creation. Blessings and thanks are due Your great and holy name for You have given us life and preserved us in life. May You continue to keep us in life and preserve us. Gather our exiles to the courtyards of Your Temple so that we may fulfill Your commandments and do Your will, serving You with a perfect heart, in the merit of our giving thanks to You now. Blessed is the God of all thanksgiving.

For all this, our King, may Your name be blessed and exalted continually, forever and ever. All that lives will give thanks to You forever and praise Your name in truth, God, our salvation and our help forever. ᵛBlessed are You, LORD, for Your name is "The Good One" and it is appropriate to give thanks to You.

When saying the Amida silently, continue with "Grant peace" on the next page.

BIRKAT KOHANIM

If Kohanim do not ascend, the following is said.

אֱלֹהֵינוּ OUR GOD, God of our fathers, bless us with the threefold blessing, in the Torah, written by Your servant Moses and spoken by Aaron and his descendants, being priests, Your holy people, as it is said:

Num. 6 "May the LORD bless you and keep you." *Cong:* May this be His will.
"May the LORD make His countenance shine upon you and be gracious to you." *Cong:* May this be His will.
"May the LORD lift up His countenance toward you and grant you peace." *Cong:* May this be His will.

שלום

שִׂים שָׁלוֹם טוֹבָה וּבְרָכָה, חֵן וָחֶסֶד וְרַחֲמִים עָלֵינוּ וְעַל כָּל יִשְׂרָאֵל עַמֶּךָ. בָּרְכֵנוּ אָבִינוּ כֻּלָּנוּ כְּאֶחָד בְּאוֹר פָּנֶיךָ, כִּי בְאוֹר פָּנֶיךָ נָתַתָּ לָּנוּ יהוה אֱלֹהֵינוּ, תּוֹרַת חַיִּים וְאַהֲבַת חֶסֶד, וּצְדָקָה וּבְרָכָה וְרַחֲמִים וְחַיִּים וְשָׁלוֹם. וְטוֹב בְּעֵינֶיךָ לְבָרֵךְ אֶת עַמְּךָ יִשְׂרָאֵל, בְּכָל עֵת וּבְכָל שָׁעָה בִּשְׁלוֹמֶךָ. בָּרוּךְ אַתָּה יהוה, הַמְבָרֵךְ אֶת עַמּוֹ יִשְׂרָאֵל בַּשָּׁלוֹם.

At this point when the שליח ציבור *repeats the* עמידה *he should complete the repetition by saying the verse beginning "*יִהְיוּ לְרָצוֹן*" out loud.*

יִהְיוּ לְרָצוֹן אִמְרֵי־פִי וְהֶגְיוֹן לִבִּי לְפָנֶיךָ, יהוה צוּרִי וְגֹאֲלִי: תהלים יט

אֱלֹהַי, נְצֹר לְשׁוֹנִי מֵרָע וּשְׂפָתַי מִדַּבֵּר מִרְמָה, וְלִמְקַלְלַי נַפְשִׁי תִדֹּם, וְנַפְשִׁי כֶּעָפָר לַכֹּל תִּהְיֶה. פְּתַח לִבִּי בְּתוֹרָתֶךָ, וּבְמִצְוֹתֶיךָ תִּרְדֹּף נַפְשִׁי. וְכָל הַחוֹשְׁבִים עָלַי רָעָה, מְהֵרָה הָפֵר עֲצָתָם וְקַלְקֵל מַחֲשַׁבְתָּם. עֲשֵׂה לְמַעַן שְׁמֶךָ, עֲשֵׂה לְמַעַן יְמִינֶךָ, ברכות יז.
עֲשֵׂה לְמַעַן קְדֻשָּׁתֶךָ, עֲשֵׂה לְמַעַן תּוֹרָתֶךָ. לְמַעַן יֵחָלְצוּן יְדִידֶיךָ, תהלים ס
הוֹשִׁיעָה יְמִינְךָ וַעֲנֵנִי: יִהְיוּ לְרָצוֹן אִמְרֵי־פִי וְהֶגְיוֹן לִבִּי לְפָנֶיךָ, יהוה צוּרִי וְגֹאֲלִי: תהלים יט

Bow, take three steps back, then bow, first left, then right, then center, while saying:

עֹשֶׂה שָׁלוֹם בִּמְרוֹמָיו, הוּא יַעֲשֶׂה שָׁלוֹם עָלֵינוּ, וְעַל כָּל יִשְׂרָאֵל, וְאִמְרוּ אָמֵן.

יְהִי רָצוֹן מִלְּפָנֶיךָ יהוה אֱלֹהֵינוּ וֵאלֹהֵי אֲבוֹתֵינוּ, שֶׁיִּבָּנֶה בֵּית הַמִּקְדָּשׁ בִּמְהֵרָה בְיָמֵינוּ, וְתֵן חֶלְקֵנוּ בְּתוֹרָתֶךָ, וְשָׁם נַעֲבָדְךָ בְּיִרְאָה כִּימֵי
עוֹלָם וּכְשָׁנִים קַדְמֹנִיּוֹת. וְעָרְבָה לַיהוה מִנְחַת יְהוּדָה וִירוּשָׁלָםִ כִּימֵי עוֹלָם וּכְשָׁנִים קַדְמֹנִיּוֹת: מלאכי ג

On סוכות, הושענות *(page 880) are said at this point. On other days of* יום טוב *and* שבת חול המועד *the service continues with* קדיש שלם *and* אֵין כֵּאלֹהֵינוּ *(page 586). On* חול המועד פסח *the service continues with* קדיש שלם *and* עָלֵינוּ *(page 180).*

For laws regarding "Interruptions during *Elokai Netzor,*" see page 133.

PEACE

שִׂים שָׁלוֹם GRANT PEACE with welfare and blessing, and grace with loving-kindness and mercy on us and all Israel Your people. Bless us, our Father, all together, with the light of Your presence. For in that light, LORD our God, You have given us the Torah of life, and love of kindness with justice, blessing, tenderness, life and peace. May it be good in Your eyes to bless Your people Israel at all times, at every hour, with Your peace. Blessed are You, LORD, Who blesses His people Israel with peace.

At this point when the Leader repeats the Amida he should complete the repetition by saying the verse beginning "May the words" out loud.

Ps. 19 MAY THE WORDS of my mouth and the meditation of my heart be acceptable before You, LORD, my Rock and my Redeemer.

Berakhot 17a אֱלֹהַי MY GOD, guard my tongue from evil, and my lips from speaking deceit. Let my soul be silent to those who curse me; let my soul be humble toward everyone like the dust. Open my heart to Your Torah that my soul may follow Your commandments. As for all those who contemplate evil against me, speedily nullify their plans and spoil their schemes. Do so for the sake of Your name. Do so for Your right hand.
Ps. 60 Do so for Your holiness. Do so for Your Torah, that Your loved ones
Ps. 19 may be delivered. Save with Your right hand, and answer me. May the words of my mouth and the meditation of my heart be acceptable before You, LORD, my Rock and my Redeemer.

Bow, take three steps back, then bow, first left, then right, then center, while saying:

He Who makes peace in His heights, may He create peace for us and for all Israel. Amen.

יְהִי רָצוֹן MAY IT BE Your will, LORD our God and God of our fathers, that the Temple be rebuilt speedily in our days and may You grant our portion in Your Torah. We will serve You there in reverence as in the days of antiquity and in years
Mal. 3 gone by. "And may the offering of Judah and Jerusalem be pleasant to the LORD as in the days of antiquity and in years gone by."

On Sukkot, Hoshanot (page 881) are said at this point. On other days of Yom Tov and Shabbat Ḥol HaMo'ed the service continues with Full Kaddish and "There is none like our God" (page 587). On Ḥol HaMo'ed Pesaḥ the service continues with Full Kaddish and Aleinu (page 181).

ברכת כהנים

If כהנים *say* ברכת כהנים *during* חזרת הש״ץ, *the following is said.*

קהל וש״ץ: **וְתֶעֱרַב** (נ״א וְתֵעָרֵב) עָלֶיךָ עֲתִירָתֵנוּ כְּעוֹלָה וּכְקָרְבָּן. אָנָּא רַחוּם, בְּרַחֲמֶיךָ הָרַבִּים הָשֵׁב שְׁכִינָתְךָ לְצִיּוֹן עִירְךָ, וְסֵדֶר הָעֲבוֹדָה לִירוּשָׁלָיִם. וְתֶחֱזֶינָה עֵינֵינוּ בְּשׁוּבְךָ לְצִיּוֹן בְּרַחֲמִים. וְשָׁם נַעֲבָדְךָ בְּיִרְאָה כִּימֵי עוֹלָם וּכְשָׁנִים קַדְמוֹנִיּוֹת.

ש״ץ: בָּרוּךְ אַתָּה יהוה, שֶׁאוֹתְךָ לְבַדְּךָ בְּיִרְאָה נַעֲבֹד.

הודאה

Bow during the first five words.

מוֹדִים אֲנַחְנוּ לָךְ, שָׁאַתָּה הוּא יהוה אֱלֹהֵינוּ וֵאלֹהֵי אֲבוֹתֵינוּ לְעוֹלָם וָעֶד. צוּר חַיֵּינוּ, מָגֵן יִשְׁעֵנוּ, אַתָּה הוּא. לְדוֹר וָדוֹר נוֹדֶה לְּךָ וּנְסַפֵּר תְּהִלָּתֶךָ, עַל חַיֵּינוּ הַמְּסוּרִים בְּיָדֶךָ, וְעַל נִשְׁמוֹתֵינוּ הַפְּקוּדוֹת לָךְ, וְעַל נִסֶּיךָ שֶׁבְּכָל יוֹם עִמָּנוּ, וְעַל נִפְלְאוֹתֶיךָ וְטוֹבוֹתֶיךָ, שֶׁבְּכָל עֵת, עֶרֶב וָבֹקֶר וְצָהֳרָיִם. הַטּוֹב, כִּי לֹא כָלוּ רַחֲמֶיךָ, וְהַמְרַחֵם, כִּי לֹא תַמּוּ חֲסָדֶיךָ, מֵעוֹלָם קִוִּינוּ לָךְ.

During חזרת הש״ץ, *the* קהל *says quietly:*

מוֹדִים אֲנַחְנוּ לָךְ, שָׁאַתָּה הוּא יהוה אֱלֹהֵינוּ וֵאלֹהֵי אֲבוֹתֵינוּ, אֱלֹהֵי כָל בָּשָׂר, יוֹצְרֵנוּ, יוֹצֵר בְּרֵאשִׁית. בְּרָכוֹת וְהוֹדָאוֹת לְשִׁמְךָ הַגָּדוֹל וְהַקָּדוֹשׁ, עַל שֶׁהֶחֱיִיתָנוּ וְקִיַּמְתָּנוּ. כֵּן תְּחַיֵּנוּ וּתְקַיְּמֵנוּ, וְתֶאֱסֹף גָּלֻיּוֹתֵינוּ לְחַצְרוֹת קָדְשֶׁךָ, לִשְׁמֹר חֻקֶּיךָ וְלַעֲשׂוֹת רְצוֹנֶךָ וּלְעָבְדְּךָ בְּלֵבָב שָׁלֵם, עַל שֶׁאֲנַחְנוּ מוֹדִים לָךְ. בָּרוּךְ אֵל הַהוֹדָאוֹת.

וְעַל כֻּלָּם יִתְבָּרַךְ וְיִתְרוֹמַם שִׁמְךָ מַלְכֵּנוּ תָּמִיד לְעוֹלָם וָעֶד.

בִּרְכַּת כֹּהֲנִים / THE PRIESTLY BLESSING
With the advent of the patriarchs, God made them the conduit of blessing to all mankind (Bemidbar Raba 11:2). Subsequently at the inauguration of the Tabernacle, God declared that the *Kohanim* would be the conduit of blessing for the Jewish people. Thus, the upraised hands of the *Kohanim*, with their hands and fingers extended to signify total generosity, are the vehicle through which God's blessing flows upon His chosen people (R. Joseph B. Soloveitchik).

וְתֶעֱרַב – *May our entreaty.* The Gemara (*Sota* 38b) stipulates that the *Kohanim* are to approach the platform prior to the conclusion

BIRKAT KOHANIM

If Kohanim bless the congregation during the Leader's Repetition, the following is said.

All: **וְתֶעֱרַב** MAY OUR ENTREATY be pleasing to You as a burnt-offering and sacrifice. Please, Merciful One, in Your abundant compassion restore Your Divine Presence to Zion, Your city, and the order of the Temple service to Jerusalem. May our eyes witness Your return to Zion in compassion. And may we worship You there with due reverence, as in days of old and times long past.

Leader: BLESSED are You, LORD, for You alone in awe we serve.

THANKSGIVING

Bow during the first seven words.

מוֹדִים WE THANK YOU, for You are the LORD our God and the God of our fathers for all eternity. You are the Rock of our life and Shield of our deliverance. From generation to generation we will thank You and recount Your praise for our lives that are in Your hands, for our souls that are given over to You, for Your miracles that are with us every day, and for Your constant wonders and favors, evening, morning and noon. You are good, for Your compassion does not cease, and You are compassionate, for Your kindness never ends. We have placed our hope in You forever and ever.

During the Leader's Repetition, the congregation says quietly:

מוֹדִים WE THANK YOU, for You are the LORD our God, the God of our fathers and God of all flesh. You are our Maker, the Maker of Creation. Blessings and thanks are due Your great and holy name for You have given us life and preserved us in life. May You continue to keep us in life and preserve us. Gather our exiles to the courtyards of Your Temple so that we may fulfill Your commandments and do Your will, serving You with a perfect heart, in the merit of our giving thanks to You now. Blessed is the God of all thanksgiving.

For all this, our King, may Your name be blessed and exalted continually, forever and ever.

---

of רְצֵה. The reason is that רְצֵה transforms our prayers into the equivalent of the temple sacrifices, which were always completed with the *Birkat Kohanim*, as it says at the conclusion

וְכֹל הַחַיִּים יוֹדְוּךָ סֶּלָה, וִיהַלְלוּ אֶת שִׁמְךָ בֶּאֱמֶת, הָאֵל יְשׁוּעָתֵנוּ וְעֶזְרָתֵנוּ סֶלָה. ׳בָּרוּךְ אַתָּה יהוה, הַטּוֹב שִׁמְךָ וּלְךָ נָאֶה לְהוֹדוֹת.

The following supplication is recited quietly while the שליח ציבור *says* וְכֹל הַחַיִּים *(above):*

In some communities, the קהל *says:*

יְהִי רָצוֹן מִלְּפָנֶיךָ, יהוה אֱלֹהֵינוּ וֵאלֹהֵי אֲבוֹתֵינוּ, שֶׁתְּהֵא הַבְּרָכָה הַזֹּאת שֶׁצִּוִּיתָ לְבָרֵךְ אֶת עַמְּךָ יִשְׂרָאֵל בְּרָכָה שְׁלֵמָה, וְלֹא יִהְיֶה בָּהּ שׁוּם מִכְשׁוֹל וְעָוֹן מֵעַתָּה וְעַד עוֹלָם.

The כהנים *say:*

יְהִי רָצוֹן מִלְּפָנֶיךָ, יהוה אֱלֹהֵינוּ וֵאלֹהֵי אֲבוֹתֵינוּ, שֶׁתְּהֵא הַבְּרָכָה הַזֹּאת שֶׁצִּוִּיתָנוּ לְבָרֵךְ אֶת עַמְּךָ יִשְׂרָאֵל בְּרָכָה שְׁלֵמָה, וְלֹא יִהְיֶה בָּהּ שׁוּם מִכְשׁוֹל וְעָוֹן מֵעַתָּה וְעַד עוֹלָם.

The following is recited quietly by the שליח ציבור*:*

אֱלֹהֵינוּ וֵאלֹהֵי אֲבוֹתֵינוּ, בָּרְכֵנוּ בַּבְּרָכָה הַמְשֻׁלֶּשֶׁת, בַּתּוֹרָה, הַכְּתוּבָה עַל יְדֵי מֹשֶׁה עַבְדֶּךָ, הָאֲמוּרָה מִפִּי אַהֲרֹן וּבָנָיו

The שליח ציבור *says aloud:*

כֹּהֲנִים

In most places, the קהל *responds:*

עַם קְדוֹשֶׁךָ, כָּאָמוּר:

The כהנים *say the following blessing in unison:*

בָּרוּךְ אַתָּה יהוה אֱלֹהֵינוּ מֶלֶךְ הָעוֹלָם, אֲשֶׁר קִדְּשָׁנוּ בִּקְדֻשָּׁתוֹ שֶׁל אַהֲרֹן, וְצִוָּנוּ לְבָרֵךְ אֶת עַמּוֹ יִשְׂרָאֵל בְּאַהֲבָה.

---

of the induction of the *Kohanim*, "Aaron lifted up his hands towards the people, blessed them, and then descended from sacrificing the sin offering, burnt-offering, and peace offering" (Lev. 9:22). Thus the approach of the *Kohanim* to the platform during רְצֵה sets the stage for them to bless the people, just as Aaron did at the conclusion of that sacrificial service (R. Joseph B. Soloveitchik).

The Rema (*OḤ* 128) writes that the priestly blessing is not recited in exile because the blessing requires one to be happy, and amid the difficulties of exile, *Kohanim* do not experience enough joy to convey it to the community. At this moment of *Musaf* on Yom Tov, we can imagine our Temple built, our people gathered in, our festival offerings rendered, and thus we are able to summon the joy that allows the recitation of the priestly blessing (R. Aton Holzer).

עַם קְדוֹשֶׁךָ – *Your holy people, as it is said.* An alternate version reads כֹּהֲנֵי עַם קְדוֹשֶׁךָ (priests of Your holy nation – i.e., Israel). The usual version (Your holy *Kohanim*) reflects the status of *Kohanim* as agents of God, while

All that lives will give thanks to You forever and praise Your name in truth, God, our salvation and our help forever. ▾Blessed are You, Lord, for Your name is "The Good One" and it is appropriate to give thanks to You.

The following supplication is recited quietly while the Leader says "All that lives" (above):

יְהִי רָצוֹן MAY IT BE Your will, LORD or God and God of our fathers, that this blessing with which You have commanded (*Kohanim say:* us) to bless Your people Israel be a complete blessing, and that there be in it neither stumbling block nor sin from now and forevermore.

The following is recited quietly by the Leader:

אֱלֹהֵינוּ OUR GOD, God of our fathers, bless us with the threefold blessing, in the Torah, written by Your servant Moses and spoken by Aaron and his descendants, the

The Leader says aloud:

KOHANIM!

In most places, the congregation responds:

Your holy people, as it is said:

The Kohanim say the following blessing in unison:

בָּרוּךְ BLESSED ARE YOU, LORD, our God, King of the universe, Who has sanctified us with the holiness of Aaron, and has commanded us to bless His people Israel with love.

---

the variant highlights the role of the *Kohanim* as agents of the Jewish people (*Meimei Shelomo*).

בְּאַהֲבָה – *With love.* It is essential, and obligatory, for the *Kohen* to feel genuine love for his fellow Jews when blessing them. It is this feeling that elevates the priestly blessing above being a mere recital of words (R. Joseph B. Soloveitchik).

R. Akiva considered "love your fellow as yourself" to be the great principle of the Torah, for the mutual love of Jews for each other binds us together. It is only when we are bound together that God relates to us as a father. Only when we practice this love are we called His children. Only within unity do we merit the blessings of His compassion and lovingkindness. Divisiveness among Jews, on the other hand, tears asunder the bond that makes us special. We do not become Jewish sinners through it. We become something less than Jews, at least in the sense of no longer being members of a single vibrant entity (*Netivot Shalom*).

The first word in each sentence is said by the שליח ציבור*, followed by the* כהנים*. Some follow a custom to read (but not pronounce) the adjacent verses. One should remain silent and not look at the* כהנים *while the blessings are being said.*

יְבָרֶכְךָ יְבָרֶכְךָ יהוה מִצִּיּוֹן, עֹשֵׂה שָׁמַיִם וָאָרֶץ: תהלים קלד

יהוה יהוה אֲדֹנֵינוּ, מָה־אַדִּיר שִׁמְךָ בְּכָל־הָאָרֶץ: תהלים ח

וְיִשְׁמְרֶךָ: שָׁמְרֵנִי אֵל, כִּי־חָסִיתִי בָךְ: תהלים טז

Read the following silently while the כהנים *chant. Omit on* שבת*.*

רִבּוֹנוֹ שֶׁל עוֹלָם, אֲנִי שֶׁלָּךְ וַחֲלוֹמוֹתַי שֶׁלָּךְ. חֲלוֹם חָלַמְתִּי וְאֵינִי יוֹדֵעַ מַה הוּא. יְהִי רָצוֹן מִלְּפָנֶיךָ, יהוה אֱלֹהַי וֵאלֹהֵי אֲבוֹתַי, שֶׁיִּהְיוּ כָּל חֲלוֹמוֹתַי עָלַי וְעַל כָּל יִשְׂרָאֵל לְטוֹבָה, בֵּין שֶׁחָלַמְתִּי עַל עַצְמִי, וּבֵין שֶׁחָלַמְתִּי עַל אֲחֵרִים, וּבֵין שֶׁחָלְמוּ אֲחֵרִים עָלָי. אִם טוֹבִים הֵם, חַזְּקֵם וְאַמְּצֵם, וְיִתְקַיְּמוּ בִי וּבָהֶם, כַּחֲלוֹמוֹתָיו שֶׁל יוֹסֵף הַצַּדִּיק. וְאִם צְרִיכִים רְפוּאָה, רְפָאֵם כְּחִזְקִיָּהוּ מֶלֶךְ יְהוּדָה מֵחָלְיוֹ, וּכְמִרְיָם הַנְּבִיאָה מִצָּרַעְתָּהּ, וּכְנַעֲמָן מִצָּרַעְתּוֹ, וּכְמֵי מָרָה עַל יְדֵי מֹשֶׁה רַבֵּנוּ, וּכְמֵי יְרִיחוֹ עַל יְדֵי אֱלִישָׁע. וּכְשֵׁם שֶׁהָפַכְתָּ אֶת קִלְלַת בִּלְעָם הָרָשָׁע מִקְּלָלָה לִבְרָכָה, כֵּן תַּהֲפֹךְ כָּל חֲלוֹמוֹתַי עָלַי וְעַל כָּל יִשְׂרָאֵל לְטוֹבָה, **וְתִשְׁמְרֵנִי**. אָמֵן.

יָאֵר אֱלֹהִים יְחָנֵּנוּ וִיבָרְכֵנוּ, יָאֵר פָּנָיו אִתָּנוּ סֶלָה: תהלים סז

יהוה יהוה, יהוה, אֵל רַחוּם וְחַנּוּן, אֶרֶךְ אַפַּיִם וְרַב־חֶסֶד וֶאֱמֶת: שמות לד

פָּנָיו פְּנֵה־אֵלַי וְחָנֵּנִי, כִּי־יָחִיד וְעָנִי אָנִי: תהלים כה

אֵלֶיךָ אֵלֶיךָ יהוה נַפְשִׁי אֶשָּׂא: תהלים כה

וִיחֻנֶּךָּ: הִנֵּה כְעֵינֵי עֲבָדִים אֶל־יַד אֲדוֹנֵיהֶם, כְּעֵינֵי שִׁפְחָה אֶל־יַד גְּבִרְתָּהּ, כֵּן עֵינֵינוּ אֶל־יהוה אֱלֹהֵינוּ, עַד שֶׁיְּחָנֵּנוּ: תהלים קכג

יְבָרֶכְךָ – *May the Lord bless you*. The Leader proclaims each word of the בִּרְכַּת כֹּהֲנִים not simply to assist the *Kohanim* to recite the words properly. Rather, by pronouncing these words he brings blessing upon the *Kohanim* so that they in turn can direct the overflow from their own blessing onto the people before them. Without this they would not have the wherewithal to be a source of blessing. This is why God tells Abraham "I will bless those who bless

---

In Ashkenazi tradition, while the *Kohanim* chant, the prayer "*Ribono Shel Olam*" is recited three times. The first *berakha* ends with וְתִשְׁמְרֵנִי – "protect me," the second וּתְחָנֵּנִי – "Be gracious to me," and the third, וְתִרְצֵנִי – "And accept me." These three conclusions correspond with the themes of each blessing of the *Kohanim*. Over time, the three variations were erroneously merged and repeated (R. Baruch HaLevi Epstein). Those who prefer to recite the "*Yehi Ratzon*" prayer that is of Hasidic origin for the third blessing can find it on page 1342.

The first word in each sentence is said by the Leader, followed by the Kohanim. Some follow a custom to read (but not pronounce) the adjacent verses. One should remain silent and not look at the Kohanim while the blessings are being said.

Ps. 134 MAY [HE] BLESS YOU — May the Lord, the Maker of heaven and earth, bless you from Zion.

Ps. 8 THE LORD — Lord, our Lord, how majestic is Your name in all the earth!

Ps. 16 AND KEEP YOU. — Preserve me, O God, for I seek refuge in You.

Read the following silently while the Kohanim chant. Omit on Shabbat.

רִבּוֹנוֹ שֶׁל עוֹלָם RULER OF THE UNIVERSE, I am Yours and my dreams are Yours. I have dreamed a dream but I do not know its meaning. May it be Your will, Lord, my God and God of my fathers, that all my dreams regarding myself and regarding all of Israel be for good – whether I dreamed about myself, or about others, or whether others dreamed them about me. If they are for good, strengthen them, fortify them, make them endure in me and in them like the dreams of the righteous Joseph. But if they require healing, heal them like Hezekiah, King of Judah, from his sickness; like Miriam the prophetess from her *tzara'at*; like Na'aman from his *tzara'at*; and like the waters of Marah through the hand of Moses our teacher; and like the waters of Jericho through the hand of Elisha. And just as You turned the curse of the wicked Balaam from a curse to a blessing, so may You turn all of my dreams about myself and about all Israel for the good. PROTECT ME. Amen.

Ps. 67 MAY [HE] SHINE — May God be gracious to us and bless us. May He cause His face to shine upon us. Selah.

Ex. 34 THE LORD — The Lord, the Lord, God of mercy and grace, full of forbearance and much kindness and truth.

Ps. 25 HIS COUNTENANCE — Turn to me and favor me, for I am alone and oppressed.

Ps. 25 UPON YOU — To You, O Lord, I lift up my soul.

Ps. 123 AND BE GRACIOUS TO YOU. — Behold, as the eyes of servants to the hand of their masters, as the eyes of a maidservant to the hand of her mistress, so are our eyes to the Lord our God until He is gracious unto us.

---

you" (Gen. 12:3), i.e., "I will first bless them, so they can bless you." Furthermore, as the Gemara (*Ḥullin* 49a) explains, this is the reason that the Torah concludes the priestly blessing by saying "when they come to place My name upon the Children of Israel, I will bless them" (Num. 6:27), i.e., the *Kohanim* will be blessed by the Leader acting on God's behalf when he first proclaims, "May the Lord bless you" (R. Efraim Lunshitz).

צָרַעַת – *Tzara'at.* While some translate the word צָרַעַת that appears in Leviticus chapters 13–14 as "leprosy," we prefer to avoid translating it altogether, here and on the next page, insofar as it is not certain that the Torah is referring to that physical disease.

וִיחֻנֶּךָּ – *And be gracious to you.* May you find favor in God's eyes (Ramban); or, may you find favor in the eyes of others. (Or HaḤayyim)

Read the following silently while the כהנים *chant. Omit on* שבת.

רִבּוֹנוֹ שֶׁל עוֹלָם, אֲנִי שֶׁלָּךְ וַחֲלוֹמוֹתַי שֶׁלָּךְ. חֲלוֹם חָלַמְתִּי וְאֵינִי יוֹדֵעַ מַה הוּא. יְהִי רָצוֹן מִלְּפָנֶיךָ, יהוה אֱלֹהַי וֵאלֹהֵי אֲבוֹתַי, שֶׁיִּהְיוּ כָּל חֲלוֹמוֹתַי עָלַי וְעַל כָּל יִשְׂרָאֵל לְטוֹבָה, בֵּין שֶׁחָלַמְתִּי עַל עַצְמִי, וּבֵין שֶׁחָלַמְתִּי עַל אֲחֵרִים, וּבֵין שֶׁחָלְמוּ אֲחֵרִים עָלַי. אִם טוֹבִים הֵם, חַזְּקֵם וְאַמְּצֵם, וְיִתְקַיְּמוּ בִי וּבָהֶם, כַּחֲלוֹמוֹתָיו שֶׁל יוֹסֵף הַצַּדִּיק. וְאִם צְרִיכִים רְפוּאָה, רְפָאֵם כְּחִזְקִיָּהוּ מֶלֶךְ יְהוּדָה מֵחָלְיוֹ, וּכְמִרְיָם הַנְּבִיאָה מִצָּרַעְתָּהּ, וּכְנַעֲמָן מִצָּרַעְתּוֹ, וּכְמֵי מָרָה עַל יְדֵי מֹשֶׁה רַבֵּנוּ, וּכְמֵי יְרִיחוֹ עַל יְדֵי אֱלִישָׁע. וּכְשֵׁם שֶׁהָפַכְתָּ אֶת קִלְלַת בִּלְעָם הָרָשָׁע מִקְּלָלָה לִבְרָכָה, כֵּן תַּהֲפֹךְ כָּל חֲלוֹמוֹתַי עָלַי וְעַל כָּל יִשְׂרָאֵל לְטוֹבָה, **וְתִשְׁמְרֵנִי וּתְחָנֵּנִי** וְתִרְצֵנִי. אָמֵן.

יִשָּׂא יִשָּׂא בְרָכָה מֵאֵת יהוה, וּצְדָקָה מֵאֱלֹהֵי יִשְׁעוֹ: וּמְצָא־חֵן וְשֵׂכֶל־טוֹב בְּעֵינֵי אֱלֹהִים וְאָדָם: תהלים כד / משלי ג

יהוה יהוה חָנֵּנוּ, לְךָ קִוִּינוּ, הֱיֵה זְרֹעָם לַבְּקָרִים, אַף־יְשׁוּעָתֵנוּ בְּעֵת צָרָה: ישעיה לג

פָּנָיו אַל־תַּסְתֵּר פָּנֶיךָ מִמֶּנִּי בְּיוֹם צַר לִי, הַטֵּה־אֵלַי אָזְנֶךָ, בְּיוֹם אֶקְרָא מַהֵר עֲנֵנִי: תהלים קב

אֵלֶיךָ אֵלֶיךָ נָשָׂאתִי אֶת־עֵינַי, הַיֹּשְׁבִי בַּשָּׁמָיִם: תהלים קכג

וְיָשֵׂם וְשָׂמוּ אֶת־שְׁמִי עַל־בְּנֵי יִשְׂרָאֵל, וַאֲנִי אֲבָרְכֵם: במדבר ו

לְךָ לְךָ יהוה הַגְּדֻלָּה וְהַגְּבוּרָה וְהַתִּפְאֶרֶת וְהַנֵּצַח וְהַהוֹד, כִּי־כֹל בַּשָּׁמַיִם וּבָאָרֶץ, לְךָ יהוה הַמַּמְלָכָה, וְהַמִּתְנַשֵּׂא לְכֹל לְרֹאשׁ: דברי הימים א׳ כט

שָׁלוֹם: שָׁלוֹם שָׁלוֹם לָרָחוֹק וְלַקָּרוֹב, אָמַר יהוה, וּרְפָאתִיו: ישעיה נז

יִשָּׂא ה׳ פָּנָיו אֵלֶיךָ – *May the Lord lift up His countenance toward you.* The Gemara (*Berakhot* 20a) records that the angels questioned this phrase in light of Deuteronomy 10:17 that states, לֹא־יִשָּׂא פָנִים וְלֹא יִקַּח שֹׁחַד (God does not lift his face or take a bribe), and thus asked God how this verse instructs *Kohanim* to proclaim יִשָּׂא ה׳ פָּנָיו אֵלֶיךָ (May God lift His face unto you), i.e., treat you with favoritism? The Gemara quotes God's response, saying that Jews deserve special treatment by virtue of blessing Him even when not obligated, as when they recite Grace after Meals having eaten only an olive or egg-sized portion, beyond the satiety requirement of Deuteronomy 8:10. This celestial exchange has been explained by various halakhic authorities. Among them were (1) R. Ḥayyim of Volozhin who understood God's words to be referring to the extraordinary hospitality of poor Jews who, able to afford only olive-size meals for themselves, generously serve their guests who then bless God on a full stomach, while the

Read the following silently while the Kohanim chant. Omit on Shabbat.

רִבּוֹנוֹ שֶׁל עוֹלָם RULER OF THE UNIVERSE, I am Yours and my dreams are Yours. I have dreamed a dream but I do not know its meaning. May it be Your will, Lord, my God and God of my fathers, that all my dreams regarding myself and regarding all of Israel be for good – whether I dreamed about myself, or about others, or whether others dreamed them about me. If they are for good, strengthen them, fortify them, make them endure in me and in them like the dreams of the righteous Joseph. But if they require healing, heal them like Hezekiah, King of Judah, from his sickness; like Miriam the prophetess from her *tzara'at*; like Na'aman from his *tzara'at*; and like the waters of Marah through the hand of Moses our teacher; and like the waters of Jericho through the hand of Elisha. And just as You turned the curse of the wicked Balaam from a curse to a blessing, so may You turn all of my dreams about myself and about all Israel for the good. BE GRACIOUS TO ME. Amen.

Ps. 24 *Prov. 3* MAY [HE] LIFT UP He shall receive the blessing from the Lord, and righteousness from the God of his salvation. So shall you find grace and good favor in the sight of God and man.

Is. 33 THE LORD O Lord, be gracious to us; we have waited for You; be their arm every morning, our salvation also in the time of trouble.

Ps. 102 HIS COUNTENANCE Do not hide Your face from me on the day that I am in trouble. Incline Your ear to me. On the day that I call answer me speedily.

Ps. 123 TOWARD YOU To You I lift up my eyes, O You Who dwell in the heavens.

Num. 6 AND GRANT So shall they put My name upon the children of Israel, and I will bless them.

I Chr. 29 YOU Yours, O Lord, are greatness, power, glory, victory, and majesty; indeed, everything that is in the heavens and on earth. Yours, O Lord, is the dominion, and You are supreme over all.

Is. 57 PEACE. Peace, peace, to him that is far off and to him that is near, says the Lord, and I will heal him.

---

still-hungry hosts bless God, out of personal stringency. R. Yechiel Yaakov Weinberg attested to such generosity, having witnessed it in even the most poverty-stricken ghettoes of Eastern Europe. (2) R. Yehoshua of Kutno explained the double phrase "up to an olive or egg-sized portion" as referring to the disagreement between the *Tannaim* R. Meir (who required Grace after eating an olive-size portion) and R. Yehuda (who required it after an egg-size meal). He explained that when their respective students would share a meal, rather than

Read the following silently while the כהנים *chant. Omit on* שבת.

רִבּוֹנוֹ שֶׁל עוֹלָם, אֲנִי שֶׁלָּךְ וַחֲלוֹמוֹתַי שֶׁלָּךְ. חֲלוֹם חָלַמְתִּי וְאֵינִי יוֹדֵעַ מַה הוּא. יְהִי רָצוֹן מִלְּפָנֶיךָ, יהוה אֱלֹהַי וֵאלֹהֵי אֲבוֹתַי, שֶׁיִּהְיוּ כָּל חֲלוֹמוֹתַי עָלַי וְעַל כָּל יִשְׂרָאֵל לְטוֹבָה, בֵּין שֶׁחָלַמְתִּי עַל עַצְמִי, וּבֵין שֶׁחָלַמְתִּי עַל אֲחֵרִים, וּבֵין שֶׁחָלְמוּ אֲחֵרִים עָלָי. אִם טוֹבִים הֵם, חַזְּקֵם וְאַמְּצֵם, וְיִתְקַיְּמוּ בִי וּבָהֶם, כַּחֲלוֹמוֹתָיו שֶׁל יוֹסֵף הַצַּדִּיק. וְאִם צְרִיכִים רְפוּאָה, רְפָאֵם כְּחִזְקִיָּהוּ מֶלֶךְ יְהוּדָה מֵחָלְיוֹ, וּכְמִרְיָם הַנְּבִיאָה מִצָּרַעְתָּהּ, וּכְנַעֲמָן מִצָּרַעְתּוֹ, וּכְמֵי מָרָה עַל יְדֵי מֹשֶׁה רַבֵּנוּ, וּכְמֵי יְרִיחוֹ עַל יְדֵי אֱלִישָׁע. וּכְשֵׁם שֶׁהָפַכְתָּ אֶת קִלְלַת בִּלְעָם הָרָשָׁע מִקְּלָלָה לִבְרָכָה, כֵּן תַּהֲפֹךְ כָּל חֲלוֹמוֹתַי עָלַי וְעַל כָּל יִשְׂרָאֵל לְטוֹבָה, **וְתִרְצֵנִי**. אָמֵן.

The כהנים *say:*

רִבּוֹנוֹ שֶׁל עוֹלָם, עָשִׂינוּ מַה שֶּׁגָּזַרְתָּ עָלֵינוּ, אַף אַתָּה עֲשֵׂה עִמָּנוּ כְּמוֹ שֶׁהִבְטַחְתָּנוּ.
הַשְׁקִיפָה מִמְּעוֹן קָדְשְׁךָ מִן־הַשָּׁמַיִם, וּבָרֵךְ אֶת־עַמְּךָ אֶת־יִשְׂרָאֵל, וְאֵת הָאֲדָמָה אֲשֶׁר נָתַתָּה לָנוּ, כַּאֲשֶׁר נִשְׁבַּעְתָּ לַאֲבֹתֵינוּ, אֶרֶץ זָבַת חָלָב וּדְבָשׁ: דברים כו

The קהל *says:*

אַדִּיר בַּמָּרוֹם שׁוֹכֵן בִּגְבוּרָה, אַתָּה שָׁלוֹם וְשִׁמְךָ שָׁלוֹם. יְהִי רָצוֹן שֶׁתָּשִׂים עָלֵינוּ וְעַל כָּל עַמְּךָ בֵּית יִשְׂרָאֵל חַיִּים וּבְרָכָה לְמִשְׁמֶרֶת שָׁלוֹם.

The שליח ציבור *continues with* שִׂים שָׁלוֹם *on page 850.*

---

critique each other for either failing to say Grace, or for reciting a *berakha* in vain, they would avoid all conflict by making sure to eat either less than an olive-size portion or more than an egg-size one. (3) R. Moshe Feinstein explained God's words by pointing to the behavior of even well-to-do Jews who, not satisfied with having already thanked God in their prayers for their many blessings, still make sure to recite the Grace over even a small olive-size portion, in recognition of His having granted them the ability to bless God for even the smallest things (R. Avraham Yisrael Rosenthal).

In his commentary to *Avot* 4:28, Rambam explains that it is self-evident that God cannot be bribed – after all with what shall we bribe Him? Rather the verse refers to how God rewards or punishes us. For instance, if a

Read the following silently while the Kohanim chant. Omit on Shabbat.

רִבּוֹנוֹ שֶׁל עוֹלָם RULER OF THE UNIVERSE, I am Yours and my dreams are Yours. I have dreamed a dream but I do not know its meaning. May it be Your will, Lord, my God and God of my fathers, that all my dreams regarding myself and regarding all of Israel be for good – whether I dreamed about myself, or about others, or whether others dreamed them about me. If they are for good, strengthen them, fortify them, make them endure in me and in them like the dreams of the righteous Joseph. But if they require healing, heal them like Hezekiah, King of Judah, from his sickness; like Miriam the prophetess from her *tzara'at*; like Na'aman from his *tzara'at*; and like the waters of Marah through the hand of Moses our teacher; and like the waters of Jericho through the hand of Elisha. And just as You turned the curse of the wicked Balaam from a curse to a blessing, so may You turn all of my dreams about myself and about all Israel for the good. AND ACCEPT ME. Amen.

The Kohanim say:

רִבּוֹנוֹ שֶׁל עוֹלָם RULER OF THE universe, we have done what You have decreed for us, so now may You deal with us as You have promised us. Look down from Your holy dwelling place, from heaven, and bless Your people Israel and the land You have given us as You swore to our fathers, a land flowing with milk and honey. *Deut. 26*

The congregation says:

אַדִּיר MIGHTY ONE on high, dwelling in power, You are peace and Your name is peace. May it be Your will to bestow upon us and upon all Your people the house of Israel, life and blessing for a safeguard of peace.

The Leader continues with "Grant peace" on page 851.

person has one thousand merits and one demerit, God will not simply deduct the one from the thousand, rather He will fully reward him for one thousand merits on the one hand, while punishing him for the one demerit on the other.

וְיָשֵׂם לְךָ שָׁלוֹם – *And grant you peace* (previous page). שָׁלוֹם (peace) is a derivative of שְׁלֵמוּת (perfection), and hence peace is the ultimate, perfect, blessing. So too cleaving unto God Whose name is שָׁלוֹם renders interpersonal strife null, even absurd (*Sefat Emet*).

תפילת טל

On the first day of פסח, *the* ארון קודש *is opened at the* חזרת הש"ץ *of the* מוסף עמידה.

All stand.

דברים לב כִּי שֵׁם יהוה אֶקְרָא, הָבוּ גֹדֶל לֵאלֹהֵינוּ:
תהלים נא אֲדֹנָי, שְׂפָתַי תִּפְתָּח, וּפִי יַגִּיד תְּהִלָּתֶךָ:

אבות

בָּרוּךְ אַתָּה יהוה, אֱלֹהֵינוּ וֵאלֹהֵי אֲבוֹתֵינוּ, אֱלֹהֵי אַבְרָהָם, אֱלֹהֵי יִצְחָק, וֵאלֹהֵי יַעֲקֹב, הָאֵל הַגָּדוֹל הַגִּבּוֹר וְהַנּוֹרָא, אֵל עֶלְיוֹן, גּוֹמֵל חֲסָדִים טוֹבִים, וְקוֹנֵה הַכֹּל, וְזוֹכֵר חַסְדֵי אָבוֹת, וּמֵבִיא גוֹאֵל לִבְנֵי בְנֵיהֶם לְמַעַן שְׁמוֹ בְּאַהֲבָה. מֶלֶךְ עוֹזֵר וּמוֹשִׁיעַ וּמָגֵן.

בְּדַעְתּוֹ אַבִּיעָה חִידוֹת
בְּעַם זוּ בְּזוּ בְּטַל לְהַחֲדוֹת.
טַל גַּיְא וּדְשָׁאֶיהָ לַחֲדוֹת
דָּצִים בְּצִלּוֹ לְהַחֲדוֹת.
אוֹת יַלְדוּת טַל, לְהָגֵן לְתוֹלָדוֹת

בָּרוּךְ אַתָּה יהוה, מָגֵן אַבְרָהָם.

גבורות

אַתָּה גִּבּוֹר לְעוֹלָם, אֲדֹנָי, מְחַיֵּה מֵתִים אַתָּה, רַב לְהוֹשִׁיעַ.

תְּפִלַּת טַל / THE PRAYER FOR DEW

There are several reasons to associate the blessings of dew with Pesaḥ. The *Midrash* (*Pirkei deR. Eliezer* Ch. 32) finds multiple allusions to Pesaḥ in the blessing bestowed by Isaac on his son Jacob, which opened with a blessing for dew (Genesis 27:28). It also correlates the 'opening of the heavenly chambers of dew' with the first day of Pesaḥ. So too, Pesaḥ is an auspicious time to pray for dew (*Mateh Moshe*). This association fits well with the agricultural component of Pesaḥ by which it is paired with חֹדֶשׁ הָאָבִיב, the season of ripening of the grain, when produce is particularly dependent upon the moisture of dew.

PRAYER FOR DEW

On the first day of Pesaḥ, the Ark is opened at the Repetition of the Musaf Amida.

All stand.

Deut. 32 WHEN I proclaim the name of the LORD, ascribe greatness to our God.

Ps. 51 "O my Master, open my lips, and my mouth will relate Your praise."

PATRIARCHS

▼בָּרוּךְ BLESSED ARE YOU, LORD, our God and the God of our fathers, the God of Abraham, the God of Isaac, and the God of Jacob, the God Who is great, mighty, and awesome, God most exalted, Who bestows rewards of benevolent kindness, Who is the Creator of everything, Who remembers all the kind acts of the fathers, and Who brings a redeemer to their children's children, for the sake of His name, with love. King Who helps, saves, and shields.

בְּדַעְתּוֹ WITH DEEP AWE in Your presence I utter my thought,
for Your people who here Your protection have sought.
They rejoice in Your gift of the blessing of dew
that makes herbs of the valley exultant anew.
That sweet dew which is symbol of coming rebirth,
that blessed dew which gives promise of new life on earth.

▼Blessed are You, LORD, Shield of Abraham.

GOD'S MIGHT

אַתָּה YOU, my Master, are forever mighty, You are the Resurrector of the dead, with great power to save.

אוֹת יַלְדוּת – *New life on earth.* The *Midrash* (*Bereshit Raba*) compares dew to Abraham: just as night-time dew evaporates quickly in the light of day, even as it continues to enrich the vegetation, so too Abraham's youthful worship of his father's idols quickly faded away when he saw the light, and went on to bring great blessing to mankind. His deeds continue to serve as a blessing for the generations of his offspring.

תְּהוֹמוֹת הֲדוֹם לִרְסִיסוֹ כְּסוּפִים
וְכָל נְאוֹת דֶּשֶׁא לוֹ נִכְסָפִים.
טַל זִכְרוֹ גְּבוּרוֹת מוֹסִיפִים
חָקוּק בְּגִישַׁת מוּסָפִים
טַל, לְהַחֲיוֹת בּוֹ נְקוּקֵי סְעִיפִים.

אֱלֹהֵינוּ וֵאלֹהֵי אֲבוֹתֵינוּ

טַל תֵּן לִרְצוֹת אַרְצָךְ — **שִׁ**יתֵנוּ בְרָכָה בְּדִיצָךְ
רֹב דָּגָן וְתִירוֹשׁ בְּהַפְרִיצָךְ — **קוֹ**מֵם עִיר בָּהּ חֶפְצָךְ — בְּטָל.

טַל צַוֵּה שָׁנָה טוֹבָה וּמְעֻטֶּרֶת — **פְּ**רִי הָאָרֶץ לְגָאוֹן וּלְתִפְאֶרֶת
עִיר כַּסֻּכָּה נוֹתֶרֶת — **שִׂ**ימָהּ בְּיָדְךָ עֲטֶרֶת — בְּטָל.

טַל נוֹפֵף עֲלֵי אֶרֶץ בְּרוּכָה — **מִ**מֶּגֶד שָׁמַיִם שַׂבְּעֵנוּ בְרָכָה
לְהָאִיר מִתּוֹךְ חֲשֵׁכָה — **כַּ**נָּה אַחֲרֶיךָ מְשׁוּכָה — בְּטָל.

טַל יַעֲסִיס צוּף הָרִים — **טְ**עֵם בִּמְאוֹדֶיךָ מֻבְחָרִים
חֲנוּנֶיךָ חַלֵּץ מִמַּסְגְּרִים — **זִ**מְרָה נַנְעִים וְקוֹל נָרִים — בְּטָל.

טַל וְשֹׂבַע מַלֵּא אֲסָמֵינוּ — **הֲ**כָעֵת תְּחַדֵּשׁ יָמֵינוּ
דּוֹד, כְּעֶרְכְּךָ הַעֲמֵד שְׁמֵנוּ — **גַּ**ן רָוֶה שִׂימֵנוּ — בְּטָל.

טַל בּוֹ תְּבָרֵךְ מָזוֹן — **בְּ**מַשְׁמַנֵּינוּ אַל יְהִי רָזוֹן
אֲיֻמָּה אֲשֶׁר הִסַּעְתָּ כַּצֹּאן — **אָ**נָּא תָּפֵק לָהּ רָצוֹן — בְּטָל.

תְּהוֹמוֹת הֲדוֹם – *Every cleft on Your footstool.* The earth is referred to as God's footstool (Isaiah 66:1). The *paytan* uplifts us subtly, deftly building heavenward in each of three stanzas – which describe successively how dew resuscitates vegetation by watering belowground roots, above-ground flowering, and finally the sprouting of vegetation in the clefts of mountains (R. Yosef Kara).

עִיר כַּסֻּכָּה נוֹתֶרֶת – *That the city now so desolate.* This simile is used to describe the isolation of Jerusalem in a desolate land, which was the situation of Judea in the time of Sennacherib's onslaught (Isaiah 1:8).

גַּן רָוֶה שִׂימֵנוּ בטל – *Make us as a richly-watered garden with dew.* As a striking historical footnote, in May 1790, shortly after becoming president, George Washington wrote the following sentiments mirroring these very words, to the Savannah, Georgia, Hebrew

תְּהוֹמוֹת EVERY CLEFT on Your footstool is yearning for dew,
every meadow, each field thirsts for Your dew.
It revives arid soil as hardened as stone.
So we pray that the dew may be sent from Your throne,
and we sing of Your might as these prayers we intone.

OUR GOD and God of our fathers:

*טַל DEW, precious dew, to Your land forlorn!
Pour out our blessing in Your exultation,
to strengthen us with ample wine and corn
and give your chosen city safe foundation in dew.

DEW, precious dew, the good year's crown, we wait
that earth in pride and glory may be fruited,
and that the city now so desolate
into a gleaming crown may be transmuted by dew.

DEW, precious dew, let fall upon the land,
from heaven's treasury be this accorded,
so shall the darkness by a beam be spanned,
the faithful of Your vineyard be rewarded with dew.

DEW, precious dew, to make the mountains sweet,
the savor of Your excellence recalling!
Deliver us from exile, we entreat,
so we may sing Your praises, softly falling as dew.

DEW, precious dew, our granaries to fill,
and us with youthful freshness to enharden!
Beloved God, uplift us at Your will
and make us as a richly-watered garden with dew.

DEW, precious dew, that we our harvest reap,
and guard our fatted flocks and herds from leanness!
Behold our people follows You like sheep,
and looks to You to give
the earth her greenness with dew.

* This translation is based on that of Israel Zangwill, and uses a free-form poetic rhyming scheme rather than a literal translation.

שליח ציבור:

שָׁאַתָּה הוּא יהוה אֱלֹהֵינוּ,

מַשִּׁיב הָרְוּחַ וּמוֹרִיד הַטָּל

The קהל *then* שליח ציבור*, responsively:*

לִבְרָכָה וְלֹא לִקְלָלָה קהל: אָמֵן

לְחַיִּים וְלֹא לְמָוֶת קהל: אָמֵן

לְשֹׂבַע וְלֹא לְרָזוֹן קהל: אָמֵן

The ארון קודש *is closed.*

The שליח ציבור *continues the* חזרת הש"ץ *with* מְכַלְכֵּל חַיִּים *on page 828.*

תפילת גשם

On שמיני עצרת*, the* ארון קודש *is opened at the* חזרת הש"ץ *of the* מוסף עמידה.

All stand.

כִּי שֵׁם יהוה אֶקְרָא, הָבוּ גֹדֶל לֵאלֹהֵינוּ: דברים לב

אֲדֹנָי, שְׂפָתַי תִּפְתָּח, וּפִי יַגִּיד תְּהִלָּתֶךָ: תהלים נא

אבות

בָּרוּךְ אַתָּה יהוה, אֱלֹהֵינוּ וֵאלֹהֵי אֲבוֹתֵינוּ, אֱלֹהֵי אַבְרָהָם, אֱלֹהֵי יִצְחָק, וֵאלֹהֵי יַעֲקֹב, הָאֵל הַגָּדוֹל הַגִּבּוֹר וְהַנּוֹרָא, אֵל עֶלְיוֹן, גּוֹמֵל חֲסָדִים טוֹבִים, וְקוֹנֵה הַכֹּל, וְזוֹכֵר חַסְדֵי אָבוֹת, וּמֵבִיא גוֹאֵל לִבְנֵי בְנֵיהֶם לְמַעַן שְׁמוֹ בְּאַהֲבָה. מֶלֶךְ עוֹזֵר וּמוֹשִׁיעַ וּמָגֵן.

תְּפִלַּת גֶּשֶׁם / THE PRAYER FOR RAIN

We recite a prayer for rain on Shemini Atzeret for several reasons. First is the fact that in the land of Israel the rainy season begins in the early autumn, and thus we ask for the blessing of rain only when there is reasonable likelihood that our prayers will be answered. Second, all of the *mitzvot* of the preceding days of Sukkot teach us that while we are certainly

Congregation: "May the same wonder-working deity, Who long since delivered the Hebrews from their Egyptian oppressors (and) planted them in the Promised Land – whose providential agency has lately been conspicuous in establishing these United States as an independent nation – still continue to water them with the dews of heaven."

Leader:

שָׁאַתָּה FOR YOU are the Lord our God
Who makes the wind blow and the dew fall

Congregation then Leader, responsively:

FOR blessing and not for curse, *Cong:* Amen.
FOR life and not for death, *Cong:* Amen.
FOR plenty and not for scarcity, *Cong:* Amen.

The Ark is closed.

The Leader continues the Repetition with "He sustains the living" on page 829.

PRAYER FOR RAIN

On Shemini Atzeret, the Ark is opened at the Repetition of the Musaf Amida.

All stand.

Deut. 32 WHEN I proclaim the name of the LORD, ascribe greatness to our God.
Ps. 51 "O my Master, open my lips, and my mouth will relate Your praise."

PATRIARCHS

▾ בָּרוּךְ BLESSED ARE YOU, LORD, our God and the God of our fathers, the God of Abraham, the God of Isaac, and the God of Jacob, the God Who is great, mighty, and awesome, God most exalted, Who bestows rewards of benevolent kindness, Who is the Creator of everything, Who remembers all the kind acts of the fathers, and Who brings a redeemer to their children's children, for the sake of His name, with love. King Who helps, saves, and shields.

---

subject to the forces of nature, they themselves are dependent on God's will. A person might dig a hole, plant a seed, and put a protective fence round about, but unless there is water to sustain it the seed will not survive to produce food – and whether or not there will be such water in the right time and measure is fully dependent on God. Even a man-made dam will eventually dry up unless there is sufficient rainfall. Hence by reciting a prayer for rain on

אַף־בְּרִי אֻתַּת שֵׁם שַׂר מָטָר
לְהַעֲבִיב וּלְהַעֲנִין לְהָרִיק וּלְהַמְטַר
מַיִם אִבִּים בָּם גַּיְא לַעֲטַר
לְבַל יֵעָצְרוּ בְּנִשְׁיוֹן שְׁטָר
אֱמוּנִים גְּנוֹן בָּם, שׁוֹאֲלֵי מָטָר.

°בָּרוּךְ אַתָּה יהוה, מָגֵן אַבְרָהָם.

גבורות

אַתָּה גִּבּוֹר לְעוֹלָם, אֲדֹנָי, מְחַיֵּה מֵתִים אַתָּה, רַב לְהוֹשִׁיעַ.

יַטְרִיחַ לְפַלַּג מִפֶּלֶג גֶּשֶׁם
לְמוֹגֵג פְּנֵי נֶשִׁי בְּצַחוּת לֶשֶׁם
מַיִם לְאַדְרָךְ כִּנִּית בְּרֶשֶׁם
לְהַרְגִּיעַ בְּרַעְפָּם לְנִפּוּחֵי נֶשֶׁם
לְהַחֲיוֹת מַזְכִּירִים גְּבוּרוֹת הַגֶּשֶׁם.

אֱלֹהֵינוּ וֵאלֹהֵי אֲבוֹתֵינוּ

זְכוֹר אָב נִמְשַׁךְ אַחֲרֶיךָ כַּמַּיִם
בֵּרַכְתּוֹ כְּעֵץ שָׁתוּל עַל פַּלְגֵי מַיִם
גְּנַנְתּוֹ, הִצַּלְתּוֹ מֵאֵשׁ וּמִמַּיִם
דְּרַשְׁתּוֹ בְּזָרְעוֹ עַל כָּל מָיִם.
קהל: בַּעֲבוּרוֹ אַל תִּמְנַע מָיִם.

זְכוֹר הַנּוֹלָד בִּבְשׂוֹרַת יֻקַּח־נָא מְעַט־מַיִם — בראשית יח:ד
וְשַׂחְתָּ לְהוֹרוֹ לְשָׁחֲטוֹ לִשְׁפּךְ דָּמוֹ כַּמַּיִם
זְהֵר גַּם הוּא לִשְׁפּךְ לֵב כַּמַּיִם
חָפַר וּמָצָא בְּאֵרוֹת מָיִם.
קהל: בְּצִדְקוֹ חֹן חַשְׁרַת מָיִם.

אַף־בְּרִי MAY YOUR MESSENGER seen as saturation through rain,
bring on vaporous clouds to be emptied in rain,
making valleys to flourish with burgeoning green.
May rain not be withheld as a debt overdue.
So look to our fathers who prayed for rain.

ᵛBlessed are You, LORD, Shield of Abraham.

GOD'S MIGHT

אַתָּה YOU, my Master, are forever mighty, You are the Resurrector of the dead, with great power to save.

יַטְרִיחַ WE NEED the rain water above and below,
that the soil else hardened as stone become soft,
through the rain which reechoes with Your revered name,
bringing ease to mankind else sore burdened with care,
giving life as we pray for the blessing of rain.

OUR GOD and God of our fathers:

*זְכוֹר REMEMBER one [Abraham] who followed You as to the sea flows water,
Your blessed son, like a tree well set where rivers met of water.
Wherever he moved, You were his shield; in fire or field or water,
and heaven-proved, his seed he sowed, wherever flowed water.

Cong: For his sake, do not withhold water!

Gen. 18 REMEMBER one [Issaac] whose heralds three beneath the tree had water,
whose sire was won to do Your will, his blood to spill like water.
Himself as high in faith could soar, his heart to pour like water.
Where earth lay dry, he dug and found deep underground the water.

Cong: For the sake of his righteousness, send abundant water!

* This translation is based on that of Israel Zangwill, and uses a free-form poetic rhyming scheme rather than a literal translation.

Shemini Atzeret we give concrete expression to our dependence on God for water, the most basic commodity necessary for life.

בְּנִשְׁיוֹן שְׁטָר – *As a debt overdue.* The Torah is our "contract" with God; if we fail to observe it, God withholds rain (Deuteronomy 11:17).

זְכוֹר טָעַן מַקְלוֹ וְעָבַר יַרְדֵּן מַיִם
יִחַד לֵב וְגָל אֶבֶן מִפִּי בְּאֵר מַיִם
כְּנֶאֱבַק לוֹ שַׂר בָּלוּל מֵאֵשׁ וּמִמַּיִם
לָכֵן הִבְטַחְתּוֹ הֱיוֹת עִמּוֹ בָּאֵשׁ וּבַמָּיִם.
קהל: בַּעֲבוּרוֹ אַל תִּמְנַע מָיִם.

זְכוֹר מָשׁוּי בְּתֵבַת גֹּמֶא מִן הַמַּיִם
נָמוּ דָּלֹה דָלָה וְהִשְׁקָה צֹאן מַיִם
סְגוּלֶיךָ עֵת צָמְאוּ לַמַּיִם
עַל הַסֶּלַע הָךְ, וַיֵּצְאוּ מָיִם.
קהל: בְּצִדְקוֹ חֹן חַשְׁרַת מָיִם.

זְכוֹר פְּקִיד שָׁתוֹת, טוֹבֵל חָמֵשׁ טְבִילוֹת בַּמַּיִם
צוֹעֶה וּמַרְחִיץ כַּפָּיו בְּקִדּוּשׁ מַיִם
קוֹרֵא וּמַזֶּה טָהֳרַת מַיִם
רֻחַק מֵעַם פַּחַז כַּמָּיִם.
קהל: בַּעֲבוּרוֹ אַל תִּמְנַע מָיִם.

זְכוֹר שְׁנֵים עָשָׂר שְׁבָטִים, שֶׁהֶעֱבַרְתָּ בְּגִזְרַת מַיִם
שֶׁהִמְתַּקְתָּ לָמוֹ מְרִירוּת מַיִם
תּוֹלְדוֹתָם נִשְׁפַּךְ דָּמָם עָלֶיךָ כַּמַּיִם
תֵּפֶן, כִּי נַפְשֵׁנוּ אָפְפוּ מָיִם.
קהל: בְּצִדְקָם חֹן חַשְׁרַת מָיִם.

שליח ציבור:

שָׁאַתָּה הוּא יהוה אֱלֹהֵינוּ,
מַשִּׁיב הָרְוּחַ וּמוֹרִיד הַגֶּשֶׁם

שליח ציבור then קהל, responsively:

לִבְרָכָה וְלֹא לִקְלָלָה — קהל: אָמֵן
לְחַיִּים וְלֹא לְמָוֶת — קהל: אָמֵן
לְשֹׂבַע וְלֹא לְרָזוֹן — קהל: אָמֵן

The ארון קודש is closed.

The שליח ציבור continues the חזרת הש״ץ with מְכַלְכֵּל חַיִּים on page 828.

REMEMBER one [Jacob], who bore his staff from Jordan's shore over water,
and rolled the stone – his love to tell – from off the well of water,
and, wrestling hard, achieved to tire a prince of fire and water.
Therefore You promised to be with him through fire and water.
Cong: For his sake, do not withhold water!

REMEMBER one [Moses] who in an ark of bulrushes
was drawn from the water,
Your shepherd son who could not sleep before his sheep had water.
And when Your flock did likewise burn with thirst
and yearn for water,
he struck the rock, there gushed a rill, to give their fill of water.
Cong: For the sake of his righteousness, send abundant water!

REMEMBER one [Aaron], Your Temple-priest,
who immersed five times in water.
He went and washed his hands with the sanctification of water.
He called out and sprinkled blood,
purifying [the people] as if with water.
He kept apart from the people unruly as water.
Cong: For his sake, do not withhold water!

REMEMBER the twelve tribes You brought across the divided water,
for whom turned sweet the bitter sheet of water.
For Your sake their descendants' blood was spilled like water.
Turn to us – troubles engulf our souls like water.
Cong: For the sake of his righteousness, send abundant water!

Leader:

שָׁאַתָּה FOR YOU are the Lord our God
Who makes the wind blow and the rain fall

Congregation then Leader, responsively:

FOR blessing and not for curse, *Cong:* Amen.
FOR life and not for death, *Cong:* Amen.
FOR plenty and not for scarcity, *Cong:* Amen.

The Ark is closed.

The Leader continues the Repetition with "He sustains the living" on page 829.

פָּקִיד – *Temple-priest.* The stanza goes on to depict service in the Temple, built centuries after Aaron's death, and so it may be speaking of all high priests, more generally.

אקדמות

On שבועות*, after the* כהן *is called up to the* תורה *and before he makes the* ברכה*, the following is said responsively by the* שליח ציבור *and the* קהל.

ש״ץ: **אַקְדָּמוּת** מִלִּין, וְשָׁרָיוּת שׁוּתָא
אַוְלָא שָׁקֵלְנָא, הַרְמָן וּרְשׁוּתָא.

קהל: **בְּ**בָבֵי תְרֵי וּתְלָת, דְּאֶפְתַּח בְּנַקְשׁוּתָא
בְּבָרֵי דְבָרֵי וְטָרֵי, עֲדֵי לְקַשִּׁישׁוּתָא.

ש״ץ: **גְּ**בוּרָן עָלְמִין לֵהּ, וְלָא סָפֵק פְּרִישׁוּתָא
גְּוִיל אִלּוּ רְקִיעֵי, קְנֵי כָּל חֻרְשָׁתָא.

קהל: **דְּ**יוֹ אִלּוּ יַמֵּי, וְכָל מֵי כְנִישׁוּתָא
דָּיְרֵי אַרְעָא סָפְרֵי, וְרָשְׁמֵי רַשְׁוָתָא.

ש״ץ: **הֲ**דַר מָרֵי שְׁמַיָּא, וְשַׁלִּיט בְּיַבֶּשְׁתָּא
הֲקֵים עָלְמָא יְחִידָאי, וְכַבְשֵׁהּ בְּכַבְשׁוּתָא.

קהל: **וּ**בְלָא לֵאוּ שַׁכְלְלֵהּ, וּבְלָא תְשָׁשׁוּתָא
וּבְאָתָא קַלִּילָא, דְּלֵית בַּהּ מְשָׁשׁוּתָא.

ש״ץ: **זַ**מֵּן כָּל עֲבִידְתֵּהּ, בְּהַךְ יוֹמֵי שִׁתָּא
זְהוֹר יְקָרֵהּ עֲלִי, עֲלֵי כָּרְסְיֵהּ דְּאֶשָּׁתָא.

אַקְדָּמוּת / AKDAMUT

As explained by Rambam and the *Shulḥan Arukh* it became customary during the Second Temple period to read an Aramaic translation (or *Targum*) of the Torah and Haftara readings of the day, as many people no longer understood the Hebrew original. This practice continued throughout the Talmudic period. In the early Middle Ages it became customary to preface those translations with an Aramaic *piyut* (technically referred to as a *reshut*, or "congregational consent"). Of those *piyutim*, the two that continued to be widely used in Ashkenazic congregations, long after the custom to publicly read the *Targum* had ceased, are those read on Shavuot, i.e., *Akdamut* (on the first day) and *Yetziv Pitgam* (on the second) (R. Michael Taubes).

Akdamut (the very name implies that it is intended as an introduction to the Torah reading) was composed in Worms in the late eleventh century by R. Meir ben Yitzḥak *Shaliaḥ Tzibbur* (or *Sha"tz*), who died shortly before the First Crusade struck Worms in 1096, but whose son and daughter-in-law were martyred in that event. He was a prolific and highly respected author of many Hebrew and Aramaic *piyutim*, being well regarded by Rashi and Tosafot

AKDAMUT

On Shavuot, after the Kohen is called up to the Torah and before he makes the blessing, the following is said responsively by the Leader and the congregation.

Leader: א **אַקְדָמוּת*** BEFORE the words of God Supreme, to us are read, for this my theme Approbation will I seek

Cong.: ב These my sentences to speak, Just two or three,
ב while tremblingly On Him I meditate,

Leader: ג The Pure Who doth bear, the world for e'er; His power who can relate?
ג Were the sky of parchment made, a quill each reed, each twig and blade,

Cong.: ד Could we with ink fill sea and brook,
ד were every man to write a book,

Leader: ה The marvelous story, of God's great glory, would still remain untold.
ה For He, Most High, the earth and sky, created alone of old,

Cong.: ו Without fatigue or weary hand, He spoke the word, He breathed command.
ו The world and that that therein dwell, field and meadow, fen and fell, mount and sea,

Leader: ז In six days He with life did then inspire.
ז The work when ended, His glory ascended upon His throne of fire.

* This translation is by R. Joseph Marcus, and uses a free-form poetic rhyming scheme rather than a literal translation.

---

as a reliable authority for numerous prayer practices. The striking power and beauty of *Akdamut* in the context of the major themes of Shavuot, particularly the Revelation of the Torah, its refined dramatic form, and stirring contents, certainly account for its persistence and popularity (Prof. Ezra Fleischer).

The *piyut* is carefully structured. The first letters of the initial forty-four lines constitute a double alphabetic acrostic, while the first letters of the remaining lines spell out the author's name, followed by a three word prayer to grow in Torah and good deeds. All of the lines end with תָא, i.e., the last and the first letters of the alphabet. The overall thrust of this form conveys the notion that the alphabet and human language are entirely incapable of properly praising or comprehending the grandeur of God and the Torah that He has given His chosen people.

קהל: חֲיַל אֶלֶף אַלְפִין, וְרִבּוֹא לְשַׁמָּשׁוּתָא
חַדְתִּין נְבוֹט לְצַפְרִין, סַגִּיאָה טְרָשׁוּתָא.

ש״ץ: טְפֵי יְקִידִין שְׂרָפִין, כְּלוּל גַּפֵּי שִׁתָּא
טְעֵם עַד יִתְיְהֵב לְהוֹן, שְׁתִיקִין בְּאַדִּישְׁתָּא.

קהל: יְקַבְּלוּן דֵּין מִן דֵּין, שָׁוֵי דְּלָא בְשַׁשְׁתָּא
יְקָר מְלֵי כָל אַרְעָא, לְתַלּוֹתֵי קְדֻשְׁתָּא.

ש״ץ: כְּקָל מִן קֳדָם שַׁדַּי, כְּקָל מֵי נְפִישׁוּתָא
כְּרוּבִין קֳבֵל גַּלְגִּלִּין, מְרוֹמְמִין בְּאַוְשָׁתָא.

קהל: לְמֶחֱזֵי בְּאַנְפָּא עֵין, כְּוָת גִּירֵי קַשְׁתָּא
לְכָל אֲתַר דְּמִשְׁתַּלְּחִין, זְרִיזִין בְּאַשְׁוָתָא.

ש״ץ: מְבָרְכִין בְּרִיךְ יְקָרֵהּ, בְּכָל לִשָּׁן לְחִישׁוּתָא
מֵאֲתַר בֵּית שְׁכִינְתֵּהּ, דְּלָא צְרִיךְ בְּחִישׁוּתָא.

קהל: נְהֵם כָּל חֵיל מְרוֹמָא, מְקַלְּסִין בַּחֲשַׁשְׁתָּא
נְהִירָא מַלְכוּתֵהּ, לְדָר וְדָר לְאַפְרַשְׁתָּא.

ש״ץ: סְדִירָא בְהוֹן קְדֻשְׁתָּא, וְכַד חָלְפָא שַׁעְתָּא
סִיּוּמָא דִלְעָלַם, וְאוֹף לָא לִשְׁבוּעֲתָא.

קהל: עֲדַב יְקַר אַחְסַנְתֵּהּ, חֲבִיבִין, דִּבְקַבַּעְתָּא
עֲבִידִין לֵהּ חֲטִיבָא, בִּדְנַח וּשְׁקַעְתָּא.

ש״ץ: פְּרִישָׁן לְמָנָתֵהּ, לְמֶעְבַּד לֵהּ רְעוּתָא
פְּרִישָׁתֵי שְׁבָחֵהּ, יְחַוּוּן בְּשָׁעוּתָא.

קהל: צָבֵי וְחָמֵד וְרָגֵג, דְּיִלְאוּן בְּלָעוּתָא
צְלוֹתְהוֹן בְּכֵן מְקַבֵּל, וְהָנְיָא בָעוּתָא.

ש״ץ: קְטִירָא לְחַי עָלְמָא, בְּתָגָא בִּשְׁבוּעֲתָא
קֳבֵל יְקַר טוֹטֶפְתָּא, יְתִיבָא בִקְבִיעֲתָא.

קהל: רְשִׁימָא הִיא גוּפָא, בְּחָכְמְתָא וּבְדַעְתָּא
רְבוּתְהוֹן דְּיִשְׂרָאֵל, קָרָאֵי בִשְׁמַעְתָּא.

ש״ץ: שְׁבַח רִבּוֹן עָלְמָא, אֲמִירָא דַכְוָתָא
שְׁפַר עֲלַי לְחַוּוֹיֵהּ, בְּאַפֵּי מַלְכְּוָתָא.

Cong.: ח Before Him myriad angels flash, to do His will they run and dash;
ח Each day new hosts gleam forth to praise, the Mighty One, Ancient of Days.

Leader: ט Six-winged hosts, stand at their posts – the brilliant Seraphim
ט In hushed awe, together draw, to chant their morning hymn.

Cong.: י The angels, together, without delay, call to one another in rapturous lay:
י Thrice holy He, Whose majesty "Fills earth from end to end."

Leader: כ The Cherubim soar, like the ocean's roar,
כ On celestial spheres they ascend, to gaze upon the light on high,

Cong.: ל Which, like the bow in cloudy sky,
ל Is iris-colored, silver-lined; while hasting on their task assigned,

Leader: מ In every tongue, they utter song, and bless and praise the Lord,
מ Whose secret and source, Whose light and force, can ne'er be fully explored.

Cong.: נ The heavenly hosts in awe reply:
נ "His Kingdom be blessed for e'er and aye."

Leader: ס Their song being hushed, they vanished away;
ס They may ne'er again offer rapturous lay.

Cong.: ע But Israel, His dear gazelle, in faith and troth well tried,
ע His glory share, Him One declare, at morn and eventide.

Leader: פ His portion they, His will obey, His power declare by night and day;
פ A precious Law, dearer than gold,

Cong.: צ He bade them study, their life to enfold,
צ That He may be near, their prayer to hear,

Leader: ק For always wear will He As diadem fair,
ק His people's prayer in His phylactery,

Cong.: ר Wherein is told of Israel's fame,
ר Who oft God's unity proclaim.

Leader: ש 'Tis also meet God's praise to sing,
ש in presence of both prince and king.

קהל: תָּאִין וּמִתְכַּנְּשִׁין, כְּחֵזוּ אַדְוָתָא
תְּמֵהִין וְשָׁיְלִין לֵהּ, בְּעֵסֶק אָתְוָתָא.

ש״ץ: מְנָן וּמַאן הוּא רְחִימָךְ, שַׁפִּירָא בְּרֵוְתָא
אֲרוּם בְּגִינֵהּ סָפִית, מְדוֹר אַרְיָוָתָא.

קהל: יְקָרָא וְיָאָה אַתְּ, אִין תְּעָרְבִי לְמָרְוָתָא
רְעוּתֵךְ נַעֲבֵד לִיךְ, בְּכָל אַתְרְוָתָא.

ש״ץ: בְּחָכְמְתָא מְתִיבְתָא לְהוֹן, קְצָת לְהוֹדָעוּתָא
יְדַעְתּוּן חַכְּמִין לֵהּ, בְּאִשְׁתְּמוֹדָעוּתָא.

קהל: רְבוּתְכוֹן מָה חֲשִׁיבָא, קֳבֵל הַהִיא שְׁבַחְתָּא
רְבוּתָא דְיַעֲבֵד לִי, כַּד מָטְיָא יְשׁוּעָתָא.

ש״ץ: בְּמֵיתֵי לִי נְהוֹרָא, וְתַחֲפֵי לְכוֹן בַּהֲתָא
יְקָרֵהּ כַּד אִתְגְּלֵי, בְּתָקְפָּא וּבְגֵיוְתָא.

קהל: יְשַׁלֵּם גְּמֻלַיָּא, לְשַׂנְאֵי וְנַגְוָתָא
צִדְקָתָא לְעַם חָבִיב, וְסַגֵּי זַכְוָתָא.

ש״ץ: חֲדוּ שְׁלֵמָא בְּמֵיתֵי, וּמָנָא דַכְוָתָא
קִרְיְתָא דִירוּשְׁלֵם, כַּד יְכַנֵּשׁ גָּלְוָתָא.

קהל: יְקָרֵהּ מַטֵּל עֲלַהּ, בְּיוֹמֵי וְלֵילְוָתָא
גְּנוּנֵהּ לְמֶעְבַּד בַּהּ, בְּתֻשְׁבְּחָן כְּלִילָתָא.

ש״ץ: דְּזֵהוֹר עֲנָנַיָּא, לְמִשְׁפַּר כִּילָתָא
לְפֻמֵּהּ דַעֲבִידְתָּא, עֲבִידָן מְטַלַּלְתָּא.

תָּאִין וּמִתְכַּנְּשִׁין – *With tempestuous glee.* This and the following lines portray the dramatic confrontation between the Jewish people, faithful to God under every circumstance to the point of martyrdom, and their non-Jewish neighbors who seek to seduce them into apostasy by accepting Gentile beliefs and thereby to be accorded honor, prosperity, security, and peace. Yet time and again, echoing the words of the Shunamite in the second and fifth chapters of the Song of Songs, the Jewish people refuse every such offer. As the *Mekhilta deR. Yishmael* on those verses states, "Said R. Akiva: 'I shall speak of the prophecies and the praises of Him by Whose word the world came into being, before all the nations of the world who ask Israel "why is your beloved more than another that you so refuse us (Song 5:9), that you are ready to die for Him and let yourselves be killed for Him… you

Cong.: ת With tempestuous glee, like a storming sea
ת They surge and ask: "Who, then,

Leader: מ Is the friend of thy heart
א For whom thou art cast in the lion's den?

Cong.: י How fairer wilt thou be to sight, if thou with us in faith unite;
ר Thy favor we shall always seek."

Leader: ב But Israel's sons with wisdom speak:
י "Oh ye, who are wise, in your own eyes,

Cong.: ר How can your trumpery at all compare,
י with our great share, when God proclaims us free,

Leader: ב And shined on us in glorious light,
י While you are wrapped in gloom of night?

Cong.: י His glory then will shine and gleam – Almighty God o'er all supreme!"
His enemies, on isles and seas, will suffering endure,
צ But He'll increase, abundant peace

Leader: ח To upright men and pure. Then perfect joy will bring our Lord, the sacred things will be restored;
ק The exiles, He will gather them, into rebuilt Jerusalem; ק

Cong.: י Day and night, shall be His light, a canopy of splendor;
ג A crown of praise, His people shall raise

Leader: ד To crown their Lord and defender. With brilliant clouds He'll ornament
ל Each deserving festive tent.

---

are handsome and mighty, come intermingle with us." To which the Israelites respond saying "Do you know Him? Let us tell you some of his praises… you shall have no share in Him, for my Beloved is mine and I am His (Song 2:16)." R. Akiva's subsequent death at the hands of his Roman persecutors is eloquent testimony to the accuracy of his understanding of these verses, and his own unwavering belief in the faithfulness of the Jew, come what may.

"In subsequent generations of persecution, whenever and wherever a sharp sword hung over the neck of Jews, and Jew-haters prepared bonfires to burn them alive on account of their persistence in remaining loyal to their faith in the living God, Jews throughout the lands of Central Europe drew strength and courage from the words of *Akdamut* ringing in their ears, to not submit to their enemies" (R. Eliyahu Kitov).

קהל: בְּתַכְתְּקֵי דְּהַב פִּזָא, וּשְׁבַע מַעֲלָתָא
תְּחִימִין צַדִּיקֵי, קֳדָם רַב פָּעֳלָתָא.

ש״ץ: וְרֵוִיהוֹן דָּמֵי, לְשָׂבְעָא חֶדְוָתָא
רְקִיעָא בְּזֵהוֹרֵהּ, וְכוֹכְבֵי זִיוָתָא.

קהל: הֲדָרָא דְּלָא אֶפְשָׁר, לְמִפְרַט שִׂפְוָתָא
וְלָא אִשְׁתְּמַע וַחֲמֵי, נְבִיאָן חֶזְוָתָא.

ש״ץ: בְּלָא שָׁלְטָא בֵהּ עֵין, בְּגוֹ עֵדֶן גִּנְּתָא
מְטַיְּלֵי בֵהּ חִנְגָּא, לְבַהֲדֵי דִשְׁכִינְתָּא.

קהל: עֲלֵהּ רָמְזֵי דֵּין הוּא, בְּרַם בְּאֵימְתָנוּתָא
שְׂבַרְנָא לֵהּ בְּשִׁבְיַן, תְּקוֹף הֵמָנוּתָא.

ש״ץ: יַדְבֵּר לַן עָלְמִין, עָלְמִין מְדַמּוּתָא
מְנָת דִּילַן דְּמִלְּקַדְמִין, פָּרֵשׁ בַּאֲרָמוּתָא.

קהל: טְלוּלָא דְלִוְיָתָן, וְתוֹר טוּר רָמוּתָא
וְחַד בְּחַד כִּי סָבֵךְ, וְעָבֵד קְרָבוּתָא.

ש״ץ: בְּקַרְנוֹהִי מְנַגַּח בְּהֵמוֹת, בִּרְבוּתָא
יְקַרְטַע נוּן לְקִבְלֵהּ, בְּצִיצוֹי בִּגְבוּרְתָא.

קהל: מְקָרֵב לֵהּ בָּרְיֵהּ, בְּחַרְבֵּהּ בְּרַבְרְבוּתָא
אֲרִסְטוֹן לְצַדִּיקֵי יְתַקֵּן, וְשֵׁרוּתָא.

ש״ץ: מְסַחֲרִין עֲלֵי תַכֵּי, דְּכַדְכֹּד וְגוּמַרְתָּא
נְגִידִין קָמֵיהוֹן, אֲפַרְסְמוֹן נַהֲרָתָא.

קהל: וּמִתְפַּנְּקִין וְרָווֹ, בְּכָסֵי רְוָיָתָא
חֲמַר מְרַת דְּמִבְּרֵאשִׁית, נְטִיר בֵּי נַעֲוָתָא.

ש״ץ: זַכָּאִין, כַּד שְׁמַעְתּוּן, שְׁבַח דָּא שִׁירָתָא
קְבִיעִין כֵּן תֶּהֱווּן, בְּהַנְהוּ חֲבוּרָתָא.

קהל: וְתִזְכּוּן דִּי תֵיתְבוּן, בְּעֵלָּא דָרָתָא
אֲרֵי תְצִיתוּן לְמִלּוֹי, דְּנָפְקִין בְּהַדְרָתָא.

ש״ץ: מְרוֹמַם הוּא אֱלָהִין, בְּקַדְמָתָא וּבַתְרַיְתָא
צְבִי וְאִתְרְעִי בַן, וּמְסַר לַן אוֹרַיְתָא.

The service continues with קריאת התורה *on page 1155.*

Cong.: ב The pure, on stools with gold inlaid;
ת Before the Lord shall be arrayed;

Leader: ו Their countenance bright, with sevenfold light,
ר Will dim the heavenly sheen.

Cong.: ה Such beauty rare, none can declare,
ו No prophet's eye has seen.

Leader: ב The glories of the Paradise, have not been seen by human eyes,
מ Where the pure rejoice and dance in the light of His countenance,

Cong.: ע And point: "'Tis He
ש We patiently hoped and waited for

Leader: י To set us free, from captivity
מ And guide us as of yore."

Cong.: ט Behold the fish in ocean deep, and the ox in its mountain keep
ו One day to meet face-to-face, to wage war and fight apace

Leader: ב The ox will gore, more and more
י And the fish will leap without fail propelled on high, as if to fly

Cong.: מ Till the sword of God prevail
א Then God will prepare, for the righteous sweet fare

Leader: מ To enjoy at His will, precious gems lacking nil
נ Before them will flow, rivers of balsam below

Cong.: ו As they drink from goblets galore overflowing with wine, so delightful and fine
ח Being aged since Creation of yore.

Leader: ז You upright who heard the voice of my song,
ק May you merit to join this glorious throng;

Cong.: ו In heavenly halls you shall meet them in time,
א If you hearken His words, melodious, sublime.

Leader: מ Exalted on high, for e'er and aye, Our Lord in glory and awe!
צ We are His choice, then let us rejoice that He blessed us and gave us the Law.

The service continues with the Torah Reading on page 1155.

הושענות

הושענות are said after the חזרת הש״ץ *of the* מוסף עמידה
(and in some congregations after הלל*) on every day of* סוכות*.*
On weekdays, the ארון קודש *is opened, and a* ספר תורה *is taken to the* בימה*.*
Male members of the congregation make a circuit around the בימה *while holding the* לולב *and* אתרוג *and reciting the* הושענות*. Mourners do not participate in the circuit.*
On שבת *the* ספר תורה *is not removed from the* ארון קודש*.*

On sixth day	*On fifth day*	*On fourth day*	*On third day*	*On second day*	*On first day*	*If first day of* סוכות *falls on*
אֹם נְצוּרָה	אֵל לְמוֹשָׁעוֹת	אֹם אֲנִי חוֹמָה	אֶעֱרֹךְ שׁוּעִי	אֶבֶן שְׁתִיָּה	לְמַעַן אֲמִתָּךְ	*Monday*
אָדוֹן הַמּוֹשִׁיעַ	אֹם נְצוּרָה	אֵל לְמוֹשָׁעוֹת	אֶעֱרֹךְ שׁוּעִי	אֶבֶן שְׁתִיָּה	לְמַעַן אֲמִתָּךְ	*Tuesday*
אָדוֹן הַמּוֹשִׁיעַ	אֵל לְמוֹשָׁעוֹת	אֶעֱרֹךְ שׁוּעִי	אֹם נְצוּרָה	אֶבֶן שְׁתִיָּה	לְמַעַן אֲמִתָּךְ	*Thursday*
אָדוֹן הַמּוֹשִׁיעַ	אֵל לְמוֹשָׁעוֹת	אֶבֶן שְׁתִיָּה	אֶעֱרֹךְ שׁוּעִי	לְמַעַן אֲמִתָּךְ	אֹם נְצוּרָה	שבת

The הושענות *service begins on each day with the following introductory stanza, chanted responsively,* שליח ציבור *then* קהל*:*

הוֹשַׁע נָא לְמַעַנְךָ אֱלֹהֵינוּ הוֹשַׁע נָא.
הוֹשַׁע נָא לְמַעַנְךָ בּוֹרְאֵנוּ הוֹשַׁע נָא.
הוֹשַׁע נָא לְמַעַנְךָ גּוֹאֲלֵנוּ הוֹשַׁע נָא.
הוֹשַׁע נָא לְמַעַנְךָ דּוֹרְשֵׁנוּ הוֹשַׁע נָא.

הוֹשַׁעְנוֹת / HOSHANOT

The Mishna (*Sukka* 4:5) states that in the Temple "on each day of Sukkot they would circle the altar once while saying 'please Lord save us, please Lord grant us success,' while in the view of R. Yehuda they would say '*ani veho*, please save us'; then on the seventh day they would circle the altar seven times." Thus the practice of circling the *bima* during Sukkot commemorates this Temple practice. Insofar as the synagogue lacks an altar, the *bima* which replaces the altar is circled instead. This reflects the principle (see *Megilla* 31b) that God promised Abraham that in the future absence of the Temple He would accept our public Torah readings regarding the offerings as an interim substitute for the sacrificial service. For this reason too, a *Sefer Torah* is kept at the *bima* during the *hakafot*. The Gemara there offers various views whether the four species were held during these circuits with or without a separate *arava*. We follow the view (codified by the Rema and *Mishna Berura*) that we take only the four species (R. Elchanan Adler).

HOSHANOT

Hoshanot are said after the Repetition of the Musaf Amida (and in some congregations after Hallel) on every day of Sukkot.

On weekdays, the Ark is opened, and a Torah Scroll is taken to the bima. Male members of the congregation make a circuit around the bima while holding the lulav and etrog and reciting the Hoshanot. Mourners do not participate in the circuit.On Shabbat the Torah Scroll is not removed from the Ark.

If first day of Sukkot falls on	*On first day*	*On second day*	*On third day*	*On fourth day*	*On fifth day*	*On sixth day*
Monday	*For the sake of Your Approach-ability*	*Save Your Temple, Abode of Your majesty*	*This the prayer I would chant*	*Save now this nation once firm as a rampart*	*God of salvation*	*Israel, cherished*
Tuesday	*For the sake of Your Approach-ability*	*Save Your Temple, Abode of Your majesty*	*This the prayer I would chant*	*God of salvation*	*Israel, cherished*	*Lord Who does save*
Thursday	*For the sake of Your Approach-ability*	*Save Your Temple, Abode of Your majesty*	*Israel, cherished*	*This the prayer I would chant*	*God of salvation*	*Lord Who does save*
Shabbat	*Israel, cherished*	*For the sake of Your Approach-ability*	*This the prayer I would chant*	*Save Your Temple, Abode of Your majesty*	*God of salvation*	*Lord Who does save*

The Hoshanot service begins on each day with the following introductory stanza, chanted responsively, Leader then congregation:

הוֹשַׁע נָא* PLEASE SAVE – for Your sake, our God, please save!
PLEASE SAVE – for Your sake, our Creator, please save!
PLEASE SAVE – for Your sake, our Redeemer, please save!
PLEASE SAVE – for Your sake, You Who seeks us, please save!

*The translation of *Hoshanot* is based on that of R. David de Sola Pool (unless stated otherwise), and uses a free-form poetic scheme rather than a literal translation.

The encircling of the altar (and in its absence, of the *bima*) can also be understood as symbolizing God's protection of His people, as it says "the angel of the Lord encamps around those who fear Him, and he rescues them" (Ps. 34:8). The Tur, based on the Talmud Yerushalmi, notes a parallel to Joshua's capture of Jericho (Joshua 6) in which the Israelites circled the city once each day for six days, and then seven times on the seventh day, when the city walls collapsed. So too, beating the *arava* "down to the ground" on Hoshana Raba after the

לְמַעַן אֲמִתָּךְ. לְמַעַן **בְּ**רִיתָךְ. לְמַעַן **גָּ**דְלְךָ וְתִפְאַרְתָּךְ. לְמַעַן **דָּ**תָךְ. לְמַעַן **הוֹ**דָךְ. לְמַעַן **וִ**עוּדָךְ. לְמַעַן **זִ**כְרָךְ. לְמַעַן **חַ**סְדָּךְ. לְמַעַן **טוּ**בָךְ. לְמַעַן **יִ**חוּדָךְ. לְמַעַן **כְּ**בוֹדָךְ. לְמַעַן **לִ**מּוּדָךְ. לְמַעַן **מַ**לְכוּתָךְ. לְמַעַן **נִ**צְחָךְ. לְמַעַן **סוֹ**דָךְ. לְמַעַן **עֻ**זָּךְ. לְמַעַן **פְּ**אֵרָךְ. לְמַעַן **צִ**דְקָתָךְ. לְמַעַן **קְ**דֻשָּׁתָךְ. לְמַעַן **רַ**חֲמֶיךָ הָרַבִּים. לְמַעַן **שְׁ**כִינָתָךְ. לְמַעַן **תְּ**הִלָּתָךְ. הוֹשַׁע נָא.

During the first six days continue with אֲנִי וָהוֹ הוֹשִׁיעָה נָּא *(page 892). On* הושענא רבה *continue:*

כִּי־אָמַרְתִּי עוֹלָם חֶסֶד יִבָּנֶה: תהלים פט

אֶבֶן שְׁתִיָּה. **בֵּ**ית הַבְּחִירָה. **גֹּ**רֶן אָרְנָן. **דְּ**בִיר הַמֻּצְנָע. **הַ**ר הַמּוֹרִיָּה. **וְ**הַר יֵרָאֶה. **זְ**בוּל תִּפְאַרְתֶּךָ. **חָ**נָה דָוִד. **טוֹ**ב הַלְּבָנוֹן. **יְ**פֵה נוֹף מְשׂוֹשׂ כָּל הָאָרֶץ. **כְּ**לִילַת יֹפִי. **לִ**ינַת הַצֶּדֶק. **מָ**כוֹן לְשִׁבְתֶּךָ. **נָ**וֶה שַׁאֲנָן. **סֻ**כַּת שָׁלֵם. **עֲ**לִיַּת שְׁבָטִים. **פִּ**נַּת יִקְרַת. **צִ**יּוֹן הַמְצֻיֶּנֶת. **קֹ**דֶשׁ הַקֳּדָשִׁים. **רָ**צוּף אַהֲבָה. **שְׁ**כִינַת כְּבוֹדֶךָ. **תֵּ**ל תַּלְפִּיּוֹת. הוֹשַׁע נָא.

During the first six days continue with אֲנִי וָהוֹ הוֹשִׁיעָה נָּא *(page 892). On* הושענא רבה *continue:*

לְךָ זְרוֹעַ עִם־גְּבוּרָה, תָּעֹז יָדְךָ תָּרוּם יְמִינֶךָ: תהלים פט

אֹם אֲנִי חוֹמָה. **בָּ**רָה כַּחַמָּה. **גּוֹ**לָה וְסוּרָה. **דָּ**מְתָה לְתָמָר. **הַ**הֲרוּגָה עָלֶיךָ. **וְ**נֶחְשֶׁבֶת כְּצֹאן טִבְחָה. **זְ**רוּיָה בֵּין מַכְעִיסֶיהָ. **חֲ**בוּקָה וּדְבוּקָה בָךְ. **טוֹ**עֶנֶת עֻלָּךְ. **יְ**חִידָה לְיַחֲדָךְ. **כְּ**בוּשָׁה בַגּוֹלָה. **לוֹ**מֶדֶת יִרְאָתָךְ. **מְ**רוּטַת לֶחִי. **נְ**תוּנָה לְמַכִּים. **סוֹ**בֶלֶת סִבְלָךְ. **עֲ**נִיָּה סוֹעֲרָה. **פְּ**דוּיַת טוֹבִיָּה. **צֹ**אן קָדָשִׁים. **קְ**הִלּוֹת יַעֲקֹב. **רְ**שׁוּמִים בִּשְׁמֶךָ. **שׁוֹ**אֲגִים הוֹשַׁע נָא. **תְּ**מוּכִים עָלֶיךָ. הוֹשַׁע נָא.

During the first six days continue with אֲנִי וָהוֹ הוֹשִׁיעָה נָּא *(page 892). On* הושענא רבה *continue:*

תִּתֵּן אֱמֶת לְיַעֲקֹב, חֶסֶד לְאַבְרָהָם: מיכה ז

---

seventh day's seven circuits can be seen as emblematic of the fall of Jericho (Maharsha).

אֶבֶן שְׁתִיָּה / SAVE YOUR TEMPLE – ABODE OF YOUR MAJESTY

The twenty-two verses of this *piyut* trace the stages of historical development of the Temple site, from the foundation stone of all creation, to the site of the binding of Isaac, to the threshing-floor of Ornan the Jebusite that was purchased by David for Solomon's Temple. The phrases are replete with Scriptural expressions and Talmudic paraphrases.

The thrust of this prayer, in the context of *Hoshanot*, is a supplication that the Temple Mount no longer remain desolate (Beit Avraham), but be rebuilt speedily (Sha'ar HaShamayim). The nostalgic *Hoshana* prayer, commemorating a Temple service intended to beautify the altar, is an apt place for such a supplication.

לְמַעַן אֲמִתָּךְ FOR THE SAKE OF YOUR APPROACHABILITY and Your **B**eauty, Your **C**ovenant and Your **D**ominion, Your **E**ternity and Your **F**aithfulness, Your **G**oodness and Your **H**oliness, Your **I**nspiration and Your **J**ustice, Your **K**indness and Your **L**aw, Your **M**ajesty and Your **N**ame, Your **O**mnipotence and Your **P**ity, Your **Q**uality of glory and Your **R**emembering, Your **S**acred Presence and Your **T**orah, Your **U**nity and Your **V**eneration, Your **W**isdom and Your **Y**oke of heaven, Yea, for the sake of Your **Z**eal. PLEASE, SAVE.

During the first six days continue with "Ani Vaho, please save us" (page 893).
On Hoshana Raba continue:

Ps. 89 Indeed, I have said that loving-kindness will be built forever.

אֶבֶן שְׁתִיָּה SAVE YOUR TEMPLE – ABODE OF YOUR MAJESTY, **B**uilt on Ornan's threshing floor, **C**hosen cornerstone, **D**welling place of righteousness, **E**stablished as Your shrine, **F**ane of Your worship, **G**oodliest of Lebanon's cedars, **H**oly of holies, **I**ndwelling of Your glory, **J**oy of the whole earth, **K**ing's residence, **L**ovely height, **M**ount Moriah, **N**oble in beauty, **O**verlaid with love, **P**erfect in loveliness, **Q**uest of the pilgrim people, **R**evelation's mountain, **S**erene habitation, **T**abernacle of Salem, **U**prising in beauty, **V**eiled shrine, **W**here David dwelt, Yea, **Z**ion in her distinction. PLEASE, SAVE.

During the first six days continue with "Ani Vaho, please save us" (page 893).
On Hoshana Raba continue:

Ps. 89 You have an arm and might. Your hand is strong, Your right hand is high.

*אֹם אֲנִי חוֹמָה SAVE NOW THIS NATION ONCE FIRM AS A RAMPART and clear as the sun; She is exiled, a wandering one. Likened of yore to a palm tree, today she is borne to the stake, Today she is slain for Your sake. Scattered amid her oppressors she flies to You from their stroke, She bends to the love of Your yoke. One to proclaim You are One, crushed by the far and the near, She waits, she is learning Your fear. Giving the cheek to the smiters, Your burden of sorrow she bears, Tossed in the storm of the years. Moses delivered her once; the sanctified sheep of his fold Were Jacob's assembly of old Marked by Your Name. O save! They are falling, they grasp You, they crave, They are calling, beseeching You, "Save!" Lord, save, we beseech You. PLEASE, SAVE.

During the first six days continue with "Ani Vaho, please save us" (page 893).
On Hoshana Raba continue:

Mic 7 You will show faithfulness to Jacob, mercy to Abraham.

* This translation is based on that of Nina Salaman, and uses a free-form poetic rhyming scheme rather than a literal translation.

אָדוֹן הַמּוֹשִֽׁיעַ. **בּ**ִלְתְּךָ אֵין לְהוֹשִֽׁיעַ. **גּ**ִבּוֹר וְרַב לְהוֹשִֽׁיעַ. **דַּ**לּוֹתִי וְלִי
יְהוֹשִֽׁיעַ. **הָ**אֵל הַמּוֹשִֽׁיעַ. **וּ**מַצִּיל וּמוֹשִֽׁיעַ. **ז**וֹעֲקֶֽיךָ תּוֹשִֽׁיעַ.
חוֹכֶֽיךָ הוֹשִֽׁיעַ. **טְ**לָאֶֽיךָ תַּשְׂבִּֽיעַ. **יְ**בוּל לְהַשְׁפִּֽיעַ. **כָּ**ל שִֽׂיחַ תַּדְשֵׁא וְתוֹשִֽׁיעַ.
לְגֵיא בַּל תַּרְשִֽׁיעַ. **מְ**גָדִים תַּמְתִּיק וְתוֹשִֽׁיעַ. **נְ**שִׂיאִים לְהַסִּֽיעַ. **שְׂ**עִירִים
לְהָנִֽיעַ. **עֲ**נָנִים מִלְּהַמְנִֽיעַ. **פּ**וֹתֵֽחַ יָד וּמַשְׂבִּֽיעַ. **צְ**מֵאֶֽיךָ תַּשְׂבִּֽיעַ. **ק**וֹרְאֶֽיךָ
תּוֹשִֽׁיעַ. **רְ**חוּמֶֽיךָ תּוֹשִֽׁיעַ. **ש**וֹחֲרֶֽיךָ הוֹשִֽׁיעַ. **תְּ**מִימֶֽיךָ תּוֹשִֽׁיעַ. הוֹשַֽׁע נָא.

During the first six days continue with אֲנִי וָהוֹ הוֹשִֽׁיעָה נָּא *(page 892). On* הושענא רבה *continue:*

נְעִמוֹת בִּימִינְךָ נֶֽצַח: תהלים טז

אָדָם וּבְהֵמָה. **בָּ**שָׂר וְרֽוּחַ וּנְשָׁמָה. **גִּ**יד וְעֶֽצֶם וְקָרְמָה. **דְּ**מוּת וְצֶֽלֶם וְרִקְמָה.
הוֹד לַהֶֽבֶל דָּמָה. **וְ**נִמְשַׁל כַּבְּהֵמוֹת נִדְמָה. **זִ**יו וְתֹֽאַר וְקוֹמָה.
חִדּוּשׁ פְּנֵי אֲדָמָה. **טִ**יעַת עֲצֵי נְשַׁמָּה. **יְ**קָבִים וְקָמָה. **כְּ**רָמִים וְשִׁקְמָה. **לְ**תֵבֵל
הַמְסֻיָּמָה. **מִ**טְרוֹת עֹז לְסַמְּמָה. **נְ**שִׁיָּה לְקַיְּמָה. **שִׂ**יחִים לְקוֹמְמָה. **עֲ**דָנִים
לְעָצְמָה. **פְּ**רָחִים לְהַעֲצִימָה. **צְ**מָחִים לְגָשְׁמָה. **קָ**רִים לְזָרְמָה. **רְ**בִיבִים
לְשַׁלְּמָה. **שְׁ**תִיָּה לְרוֹמְמָה. **תְּ**לוּיָה עַל בְּלִימָה. הוֹשַֽׁע נָא.

יהוה אֲדֹנֵֽינוּ מָה־אַדִּיר שִׁמְךָ בְּכָל־הָאָֽרֶץ תהלים ח
אֲשֶׁר־תְּנָה הוֹדְךָ עַל־הַשָּׁמָֽיִם:

אֲדָמָה מֵאֶֽרֶר. **בְּ**הֵמָה מִמְּשַׁכֶּֽלֶת. **גֹּ**רֶן מִגָּזָם. **דָּ**גָן מִדַּלֶּֽקֶת. **ה**וֹן מִמְּאֵרָה.
וְאֹֽכֶל מִמְּהוּמָה. **זַ**יִת מִנֶּֽשֶׁל. **חִ**טָּה מֵחָגָב. **טֶ**רֶף מִגּוֹבַי. **יֶ**קֶב
מִיֶּֽלֶק. **כֶּ**רֶם מִתּוֹלַֽעַת. **לֶ**קֶשׁ מֵאַרְבֶּה. **מֶ**גֶד מִצְּלָצַל. **נֶ**פֶשׁ מִבֶּהָלָה. **שֹׂ**בַע
מִסָּלְעָם. **עֲ**דָרִים מִדַּלּוּת. **פֵּ**רוֹת מִשִּׁדָּפוֹן. **צֹ**אן מִצְּמִיתוּת. **קָ**צִיר מִקְּלָלָה.
רֹב מֵרָזוֹן. **שִׁ**בֹּֽלֶת מִצִּנָּמוֹן. **תְּ**בוּאָה מֵחָסִיל. הוֹשַֽׁע נָא.

צַדִּיק יהוה בְּכָל־דְּרָכָיו, וְחָסִיד בְּכָל־מַעֲשָׂיו: תהלים קמה

אָדוֹן הַמּוֹשִֽׁיעַ / LORD WHO DOES SAVE

This *piyut* is a supplication for the all-important rains, and the agricultural bounty and natural beauty that is dependent on rainfall. Because rain poses many hardships for outdoor dwelling during Sukkot (*Ta'anit* 2a), this poem is typically reserved for the latter part of the intermediate days. The *piyut* begins as is prescribed for Jewish prayer, with praise of God as the Unique Savior (א-ו); a request that God save, and then bless His people (ז-ט); a description of the agricultural manifestations of divine bounty for which we yearn (י-ע); and finally, a return to the first two themes: God as the One Who provides for man (פ) and a request for salvation for His people (צ-ת).

אָדָם וּבְהֵמָה / SAVE, WE BESEECH YOU, BOTH MAN AND BEAST

The premise of this *Hoshana* is derived from the verse in Psalms (36:7), אָדָם וּבְהֵמָה תוֹשִׁיעַ יְהוָה,

אָדוֹן הַמּוֹשִׁיעַ LORD WHO DOES SAVE, besides You who will save? You are mighty to save. Those brought low You save. Those who hope that You will save, those who pray You will save. Give food to Your flock through a harvest abundant. Make herbage spring forth from the valleys abloom, Sweet fruits all to ripen through Your rain not withheld. So gather the clouds that the showers may fall, With Your open hand slake our thirsting for You. Save those who invoke You, Your beloved ones save. Save all those who seek You; save, we beseech You. Those seeking perfection, save, we beseech You. PLEASE, SAVE.

During the first six days continue with "Ani Vaho, please save us" (*page* 893).
On Hoshana Raba continue:

Ps. 16 At Your right hand are pleasures forevermore.

אָדָם וּבְהֵמָה SAVE, WE BESEECH YOU, BOTH MAN AND BEAST, in flesh, spirit and soul, sinew, bone and skin, likeness, shape and finished form, though for all his beauty, form and stature, his glory may be likened to a breath or to the beasts that perish. Save him by renewal of the face of the earth, through the trees planted even in arid soil, the wine press, the standing grain, the vineyards, the sycamores of the world within its set bounds, through steady reviving rains to invigorate forgotten soil, through vegetation yielding sweet produce in abundance, blossoming flowers, the rain which brings budding life, cool flowing waters for irrigation and showers for ripening harvests. PLEASE SAVE.

Ps. 8 Lord, our Lord, how majestic is Your name in all the earth,
Whose splendor is set upon the heavens!

אֲדָמָה מֵאָרֶר OUR ABUNDANCE FROM LOCUSTS, **B**read wheat from grasshoppers, **C**attle from barrenness, **D**aily food from insect pests, **E**arth from evil hap, **F**ruits from blight, **G**rain from parching heat, **H**erbage from devouring swarms, **I**ngathering from being blasted, **J**uicy olives from dropping off, **L**ambs from extermination, our **M**eans from scarcity, **N**ourishing food from spoilage, **O**il from cicada, **P**rovender from destructive insects, **R**ipe fruits from winged pests, **S**heep from languishing, **T**hreshing floor from whirring swarms, **U**pright corn from drying up, **V**ineyards from worms, Our **W**ealth from ruin, our **Y**earning soul from terror, PLEASE SAVE.

Ps. 145 The Lord is righteous in all His ways and kind in all His works.

(man and beast You preserve, O Lord). A major theme in the book of Ecclesiastes is the ultimate futility of human endeavors; that man is like the beasts, susceptible to the same needs and urges, and subject to the same ultimate end. This *Hoshana* prays for our sustenance as part of the natural order, with a keen awareness of human frailty and dependency on God.

לְמַעַן אֵיתָן הַנִּזְרָק בְּלַהַב אֵשׁ.
לְמַעַן **בֵּ**ן הַנֶּעֱקַד עַל עֵצִים וָאֵשׁ.
לְמַעַן **גִּ**בּוֹר הַנֶּאֱבַק עִם שַׂר אֵשׁ.
לְמַעַן **דְּ**גָלִים נָחִיתָ בְּאוֹר וַעֲנַן אֵשׁ.
לְמַעַן **הָ**עֲלָה לַמָּרוֹם, וְנִתְעַלָּה כְּמַלְאֲכֵי אֵשׁ.
לְמַעַן **וְ**הוּא לָךְ כְּסֶגֶן בְּאֶרְאֱלֵּי אֵשׁ.
לְמַעַן **זֶ**בֶד דִּבְּרוֹת הַנִּתּוּנוֹת מֵאֵשׁ.
לְמַעַן **חִ**פּוּי יְרִיעוֹת וַעֲנַן אֵשׁ.
לְמַעַן **טֶ**כֶס הַר יָרַדְתָּ עָלָיו בָּאֵשׁ.
לְמַעַן **יְ**דִידוּת בַּיִת אֲשֶׁר אָהַבְתָּ מִשְּׁמֵי אֵשׁ.
לְמַעַן **כָּ**מַהּ עַד שָׁקְעָה הָאֵשׁ.
לְמַעַן **לָ**קַח מַחְתַּת אֵשׁ וְהֵסִיר חֲרוֹן אֵשׁ.
לְמַעַן **מְ**קַנֵּא קִנְאָה גְדוֹלָה בָּאֵשׁ.
לְמַעַן **נָ**ף יָדוֹ וְיָרְדוּ אַבְנֵי אֵשׁ.
לְמַעַן **שָׂ**ם טְלֵה חָלָב כְּלִיל אֵשׁ.
לְמַעַן **עָ**מַד בַּגֹּרֶן וְנִתְרַצָּה בָאֵשׁ.
לְמַעַן **פִּ**לֵּל בָּעֲזָרָה וְיָרְדָה הָאֵשׁ.
לְמַעַן **צִ**יר עָלָה וְנִתְעַלָּה בְּרֶכֶב וְסוּסֵי אֵשׁ.
לְמַעַן **קְ**דוֹשִׁים מֻשְׁלָכִים בָּאֵשׁ.
לְמַעַן **רִ**בּוֹ רִבְבָן חָז וְנַהֲרֵי אֵשׁ.
לְמַעַן **שְׁ**מְמוֹת עִירְךָ הַשְּׂרוּפָה בָאֵשׁ.
לְמַעַן **תּ**וֹלְדוֹת אַלּוּפֵי יְהוּדָה, תָּשִׂים כְּכִיּוֹר אֵשׁ. הוֹשַׁע נָא.

דברי הימים א׳ כט **לְךָ** יהוה הַגְּדֻלָּה וְהַגְּבוּרָה וְהַתִּפְאֶרֶת וְהַנֵּצַח וְהַהוֹד, כִּי־כֹל בַּשָּׁמַיִם וּבָאָרֶץ,
זכריה יד לְךָ יהוה הַמַּמְלָכָה וְהַמִּתְנַשֵּׂא לְכֹל לְרֹאשׁ: וְהָיָה יהוה לְמֶלֶךְ עַל־כָּל־
דברים ו הָאָרֶץ, בַּיּוֹם הַהוּא יִהְיֶה יהוה אֶחָד וּשְׁמוֹ אֶחָד: וּבְתוֹרָתְךָ כָּתוּב לֵאמֹר: שְׁמַע
יִשְׂרָאֵל, יהוה אֱלֹהֵינוּ, יהוה אֶחָד: בָּרוּךְ שֵׁם כְּבוֹד מַלְכוּתוֹ לְעוֹלָם וָעֶד.

On הושענא רבה *continue with* אֲנִי וָהוֹ הוֹשִׁיעָה נָּא *on page 892.*

לְמַעַן אֵיתָן / FOR THE SAKE OF THE PATRIARCH Each stanza of this final *Hoshana* ends with the word אֵשׁ (fire). It takes us on a tour of Scripture, from Abraham's experience in Babylonia until Daniel's return to the same land (א-ר), and concludes with our contemporary situation (ש).

לְמַעַן אֵיתָן FOR THE SAKE OF THE PATRIARCH Abraham cast into flames of fire;
for the sake of Isaac his son bound on the wood for the fire;
for the sake of Jacob the mighty who wrestled with a prince of fire;
for the sake of Israel's hosts whom You led by cloud and light of fire;
for the sake of Moses taken up on high and exalted as the angels of fire;
for the sake of Aaron Your minister among the host of fire;
for the sake of the Ten Commandments, a gift from out of fire;
for the sake of the tabernacle covered by curtains and cloud of fire;
for the sake of Mount Sinai upon which You came down in fire;
for the sake of the beloved shrine which You loved more than the heavens of fire;
for the sake of Moses who remained in prayer until sank down the fire;
for the sake of Aaron who took the censer and allayed Your wrath of fire;
for the sake of Phineas who flamed with a zeal as of fire;
for the sake of Joshua at the wave of whose hand there descended stones of fire;
for the sake of Samuel who placed on the altar a suckling lamb as an offering burned by fire;
for the sake of David who stood at the threshing-floor and won grace by fire;
for the sake of Solomon who prayed in the Temple court until there descended fire;
for the sake of Elijah Your messenger taken by chariot and horses of fire;
for the sake of the three holy men cast into a furnace of fire;
for the sake of Daniel who beheld myriads of angels and streams of fire;
for the sake of the desolations of Your city burned by fire;
for the sake of the generations of princes of Judah whom You will make as a refining furnace of fire, PLEASE SAVE.

I Chr. 29 לְךָ YOURS, O Lord, are greatness, power, glory, victory, and majesty; indeed,
everything that is in the heavens and on earth. Yours, O Lord, is the
Zech. 14 dominion, and You are supreme over all. And the Lord shall be King over all
the earth; in that day shall the Lord be One, and His name One. And in Your
Deut. 6 Torah it is written, saying, "Hear, O Israel, the Lord is our God, the Lord
is One." Blessed be His name and His glorious kingdom for ever and ever.

On Hoshana Raba continue with "Ani Vaho, please save us" on page 893.

Initially, the fire imagery is one of hardship and trial for Abraham and Isaac. However, in the bulk of the *piyut*, it becomes a manifestation of the Divine Presence, and shifts, near the end,

אֶעֱרֹךְ שׁוּעִי. בְּבֵית שַׁוְעִי. גִּלִּיתִי בַצּוֹם פִּשְׁעִי. דְּרַשְׁתִּיךָ בּוֹ לְהוֹשִׁיעִי. הַקְשִׁיבָה לְקוֹל שַׁוְעִי. וְקוּמָה וְהוֹשִׁיעִי. זְכֹר וְרַחֵם מוֹשִׁיעִי. חַי כֵּן תְּשַׁעְשְׁעִי. טוֹב בְּאֶנֶק שַׁעְיִ. יוֹחַשׁ מוֹשִׁיעִי. כַּלֵּה מַרְשִׁיעִי. לְבַל עוֹד יַרְשִׁיעִי. מַהֵר אֱלֹהֵי יִשְׁעִי. נֶצַח לְהוֹשִׁיעִי. שָׂא נָא עֲוֹן רִשְׁעִי. עֲבֹר עַל פִּשְׁעִי. פְּנֵה נָא לְהוֹשִׁיעִי. צוּר צַדִּיק מוֹשִׁיעִי. קַבֵּל נָא שַׁוְעִי. רוֹמֵם קֶרֶן יִשְׁעִי. שַׁדַּי מוֹשִׁיעִי. תּוֹפִיעַ וְתוֹשִׁיעִי. הוֹשַׁע נָא.

Continue with אֲנִי וָהוֹ הוֹשִׁיעָה נָּא *below.*

אֵל לְמוֹשָׁעוֹת. בְּאַרְבַּע שְׁבוּעוֹת. גָּשִׁים בְּשַׁוְעוֹת. דּוֹפְקֵי עֶרֶךְ שׁוּעוֹת. הוֹגֵי שַׁעֲשׁוּעוֹת. וְחִידוֹת מִשְׁתַּעְשְׁעוֹת. זוֹעֲקִים לְהִשָּׁעוֹת. חוֹכֵי יְשׁוּעוֹת. טְפוּלִים בְּךָ שְׁעוֹת. יוֹדְעֵי בִין שָׁעוֹת. כּוֹרְעֶיךָ בְּשַׁוְעוֹת. לְהָבִין שְׁמוּעוֹת. מֵפִיק נִשְׁמָעוֹת. נוֹתֵן תְּשׁוּעוֹת. סְפוּרוֹת מַשְׁמָעוֹת. עֵדוּת מַשְׁמִיעוֹת. פּוֹעֵל יְשׁוּעוֹת. צַדִּיק נוֹשָׁעוֹת. קִרְיַת תְּשׁוּעוֹת. רֶגֶשׁ תְּשׁוּאוֹת. שָׁלֹשׁ שָׁעוֹת. תָּחִישׁ לִתְשׁוּעוֹת. הוֹשַׁע נָא.

After each day's הקפות *(except on* שבת*) the following* הושענא *is said:*

אֲנִי וָהוֹ הוֹשִׁיעָה נָּא.

כְּהוֹשַׁעְתָּ אֵלִים בְּלוּד עִמָּךְ.
בְּצֵאתְךָ לְיֵשַׁע עַמָּךְ.   כֵּן הוֹשַׁע נָא.

כְּהוֹשַׁעְתָּ גּוֹי וֵאלֹהִים.
דְּרוּשִׁים לְיֵשַׁע אֱלֹהִים.   כֵּן הוֹשַׁע נָא.

כְּהוֹשַׁעְתָּ הֲמוֹן צְבָאוֹת.
וְעִמָּם מַלְאֲכֵי צְבָאוֹת.   כֵּן הוֹשַׁע נָא.

---

again to trial, hardship and the sufferings of destruction and exile. It invokes two kinds of merit: that of trial by fire, and of the righteousness that brought about Divine revelation in fire throughout our history. The conclusion of this piece (ת), which also concludes the seven *Hoshana* circuits, paraphrases the ultimate rebuilding and salvation of Jerusalem as described in Zechariah 12:6–7.

אֶעֱרֹךְ שׁוּעִי / THIS THE PRAYER I WOULD CHANT This intensely personal *piyut* reflects the emotional journey of the individual over the course of Yom Kippur and the ensuing period leading up to Hoshana Raba. It describes, in the first person singular, how we lay our sins bare (ג) seek out God for salvation (ד); ask God to listen to our cry (ה-ו); ask for divine mercy to come to our rescue and restore His delight in us (ז-י). The prayer then alternates between asking God to punish our persecutors (כ-ל), and to overlook our sins (ע-ש). It ends with a request for divine revelation.

אֶעֶרֹךְ שׁוּעִי THIS THE PRAYER I WOULD CHANT in this house of my worship: On the fast day I sought from my sin Your salvation; Give ear now to my prayer and rise up to save me. Look on me in Your pity, my joy, my salvation. O God Who is good, turn to me, haste, redeem me, And destroy the accuser, that mine be salvation. Haste to save evermore; You are God Who will save me, Forgive sin and my guilt, and reveal my salvation. Savior and Rock, turn to me now, save me, Accept my prayer and make firm my salvation. Almighty, my Savior, O save, I beseech You, Shine forth and redeem; I beseech Your salvation. PLEASE, SAVE.

Continue with "Ani Vaho, please save us" below.

אֵל לְמוֹשָׁעוֹת GOD OF SALVATION, strengthened by Your fourfold covenant we approach Your gate in suppliant prayer. We who ponder on the joys of Your Torah and who delight in its deep wisdom, pray to You to win Your grace, hoping for Your salvation. We who count the sacred hours depend on Your grace. In our prayers we bend the knee before You, for we would understand the teachings You have proclaimed. You Who will give salvation through the destined tidings, the testimony to be proclaimed, You Who works salvation and are righteous to save, save Zion, city of salvation, from violence and tumult. At the destined hour, save, we beseech You; hasten to our salvation and save, we beseech You. PLEASE, SAVE.

After each day's Hakafot (except on Shabbat) the following Hoshana is said:

אֲנִי וָהוֹ ANI VAHO, please save us.

כְּהוֹשַׁעְתָּ* SAVIOR OF MIGHTY ones that dwelt with Thee
In Lud, the land where You set them free; So, please, save us.

As You did save together God and nation,
The people singled out for God's salvation; So, please, save us.

The hosts of Your redeemed, with manifold
Angelic hosts were saved by You of old. So, please, save us.

*This translation is based on that of Elsie Davis, and uses a free-form poetic rhyming scheme rather than a literal translation.

כְּהוֹשַׁעְתָּ אֵלִים / SAVIOR OF MIGHTY
This *Hoshana,* which is recited after each day's circuit (except on Shabbat) includes an emphasis on God's own redemption, or perhaps the redemption of His *Shekhina,* as it were, along with the salvation of the Jewish people. The crux of the passage derives from the most straightforward understanding of the Mishnaic phrase אֲנִי וָהוֹ הוֹשִׁיעָה נָּא – *ani vaho, bring salvation now.* As *Tosafot* (*Sukka*

כְּהוֹשַׁעְתָּ זַכִּים מְבֵית עֲבָדִים.
חַנּוּן בְּיָדָם מַעֲבִידִים. כֵּן הוֹשַׁע נָא.

כְּהוֹשַׁעְתָּ טְבוּעִים בְּצוּל גְּזָרִים.
יְקָרְךָ עִמָּם מַעֲבִירִים. כֵּן הוֹשַׁע נָא.

כְּהוֹשַׁעְתָּ כַּנָּה מְשׁוֹרֶרֶת וַיּוֹשַׁע.
לְגוֹחָהּ מְצֻיֶּנֶת וַיִּוָּשַׁע. כֵּן הוֹשַׁע נָא.

כְּהוֹשַׁעְתָּ מַאֲמַר וְהוֹצֵאתִי אֶתְכֶם.
נָקוּב וְהוּצֵאתִי אִתְּכֶם. כֵּן הוֹשַׁע נָא.

כְּהוֹשַׁעְתָּ סוֹבְבֵי מִזְבֵּחַ.
עוֹמְסֵי עֲרָבָה לְהַקִּיף מִזְבֵּחַ. כֵּן הוֹשַׁע נָא.

כְּהוֹשַׁעְתָּ פִּלְאֵי אָרוֹן כְּהֻפְשַׁע.
צִעֵר פְּלֶשֶׁת בַּחֲרוֹן אַף, וְנוֹשַׁע. כֵּן הוֹשַׁע נָא.

כְּהוֹשַׁעְתָּ קְהִלּוֹת בָּבֶלָה שִׁלַּחְתָּ.
רַחוּם לְמַעֲנָם שֻׁלַּחְתָּ. כֵּן הוֹשַׁע נָא.

כְּהוֹשַׁעְתָּ שְׁבוּת שִׁבְטֵי יַעֲקֹב.
תָּשׁוּב וְתָשִׁיב שְׁבוּת אָהֳלֵי יַעֲקֹב. וְהוֹשִׁיעָה נָּא.

כְּהוֹשַׁעְתָּ שׁוֹמְרֵי מִצְוֹת וְחוֹכֵי יְשׁוּעוֹת.
אֵל לְמוֹשָׁעוֹת. וְהוֹשִׁיעָה נָּא.

אֲנִי וָהוֹ הוֹשִׁיעָה נָּא.

On Hoshana Raba continue with תִּתְּנֵנוּ *(page 896). On the first six days continue here.*

הוֹשִׁיעָה אֶת־עַמֶּךָ, וּבָרֵךְ אֶת־נַחֲלָתֶךָ, וּרְעֵם וְנַשְּׂאֵם עַד־הָעוֹלָם: וְיִהְיוּ דְבָרַי אֵלֶּה, אֲשֶׁר הִתְחַנַּנְתִּי לִפְנֵי יהוה, קְרֹבִים אֶל־יהוה אֱלֹהֵינוּ יוֹמָם וָלָיְלָה, לַעֲשׂוֹת מִשְׁפַּט עַבְדּוֹ וּמִשְׁפַּט עַמּוֹ יִשְׂרָאֵל, דְּבַר־יוֹם בְּיוֹמוֹ: לְמַעַן דַּעַת כָּל־עַמֵּי הָאָרֶץ כִּי יהוה הוּא הָאֱלֹהִים, אֵין עוֹד: תהלים כח / מלכים א׳ ח

The ספר תורה *is returned to the* ארון קודש, *and the* ארון קודש *is closed.*
On יום טוב *the* שליח ציבור *continues the service with* קדיש שלם *on page 586;*
on חול המועד, *with* קדיש שלם *on page 180.*

45a) notes, these words literally mean "I and He bring salvation now." Similarly the Yerushalmi has the spelling אֲנִי וְהוּא which conveys this notion directly. The words encapsulate the

From bondage grim Your power brought forth the pure;
You, Gracious One, did all their grief endure. So, please, save us.

They passed between the deep divided sea;
And with them for their guide, the light from Thee. So, please, save us.

"He saved": Your stock with joyful singing told;
Then saved was He, Who gave them birth of old. So, please, save us.

"And I will bring you out," the mandate said;
"And I went out with you," the mystics read. So, please, save us.

Your sons with circling step, (their guardian Thou!),
Around Your altar bore the willow bough. So, please, save us.

Your Ark was won by marvels from the foe,
Philistia, sinful, by Your wrath laid low. So, please, save us.

And with Your banished throngs to Babylon
Journeyed in love Your Presence, Gracious One! So, please, save us.

Helper of Jacob's captive tribes of yore,
Return, and Jacob's exiled tents restore. And please save us.

For those who kept Your law and hoped for Your salvation,
God, You have ever been the savior of our nation. And please save us.

ANI VAHO, please save us.

On Hoshana Raba continue with "Zestful" (page 897).
On the first six days continue here.

Ps. 28 הוֹשִׁיעָה SAVE YOUR PEOPLE and bless Your inheritance, and tend them and
I Kings 8 carry them forever. And may these my words with which I have entreated before the Lord, be near to the Lord our God day and night, so that He shall maintain the cause of His servant and of His people Israel day by day, that all the peoples of the earth may know that the Lord He is God, there is none else.

The Torah scroll is returned to the Ark, and the Ark is closed.
On Festival days the Leader continues the service with Full Kaddish on page 587;
on Ḥol HaMo'ed, with Full Kaddish on page 181.

---

essence of the statement of R. Aḥa in the *Midrash* (*Eikha Raba Petiḥta* 34), that when the Jews were led into exile God ("וְהוּא" in Jeremiah 40:1) was bound in chains, as it were, and Himself ("וַאֲנִי" in Ezekiel 1:1) sent into exile (R. Aton Holzer).

On שבת *whether* יום טוב *or* חול המועד *the following Hoshanot are said:*

אֹם נְצוּרָה כְּבָבַת. **בּ**וֹנֶנֶת בְּדַת נֶפֶשׁ מְשִׁיבַת. **ג**וֹמֶרֶת הִלְכוֹת שַׁבָּת. **ד**וֹרֶשֶׁת מַשְׂאַת שַׁבָּת. **ה**ַקּוֹבַעַת אַלְפַּיִם תְּחוּם שַׁבָּת. **וּ**מְשִׁיבַת רֶגֶל מִשַּׁבָּת. **ז**ָכוֹר וְשָׁמוֹר מְקַיֶּמֶת בַּשַּׁבָּת. **ח**ָשָׁה לְמַהֵר בִּיאַת שַׁבָּת. **ט**וֹרַחַת כֹּל מִשִּׁשָּׁה לַשַּׁבָּת. **י**וֹשֶׁבֶת וּמְמַתֶּנֶת עַד כְּלוֹת שַׁבָּת. **כּ**ָבוֹד וָעֹנֶג קוֹרְאָה לַשַּׁבָּת. **ל**ְבוּשׁ וּכְסוּת מְחַלֶּפֶת בַּשַּׁבָּת. **מ**ַאֲכָל וּמִשְׁתֶּה מְכִינָה לַשַּׁבָּת. **נ**ְעַם מְגָדִים מַנְעֶמֶת לַשַּׁבָּת. **ס**ְעוּדוֹת שָׁלֹשׁ מְקַיֶּמֶת בַּשַּׁבָּת. **ע**ַל שְׁתֵּי כִכָּרוֹת בּוֹצַעַת בַּשַּׁבָּת. **פּ**וֹרֶטֶת אַרְבַּע רְשֻׁיּוֹת שַׁבָּת. **צ**ִוּוּי הַדְלָקַת נֵר מַדְלֶקֶת בַּשַּׁבָּת. **ק**ִדּוּשׁ הַיּוֹם מְקַדֶּשֶׁת בַּשַּׁבָּת. **ר**ֶנֶן שֶׁבַע מְפַלֶּלֶת בַּשַּׁבָּת. **שִׁ**בְעָה בְּדַת קוֹרְאָה בַּשַּׁבָּת. **תּ**ַנְחִילֶנָּה לְיוֹם שֶׁכֻּלּוֹ שַׁבָּת. הוֹשַׁע נָא.

אֲנִי וָהוֹ הוֹשִׁיעָה נָּא.

כְּהוֹשַׁעְתָּ אָדָם יְצִיר כַּפֶּיךָ לְגוֹנְנָה.
בְּשַׁבַּת קֹדֶשׁ הִמְצֵאתוֹ כֹּפֶר וַחֲנִינָה. כֵּן הוֹשַׁע נָא.

כְּהוֹשַׁעְתָּ גּוֹי מְצֻיָּן מְקַוִּים חֹפֶשׁ.
דֵּעָה כִּוְּנוּ לָבוּר שְׁבִיעִי לְנֹפֶשׁ. כֵּן הוֹשַׁע נָא.

כְּהוֹשַׁעְתָּ הָעָם נִהַגְתָּ כַּצֹּאן לְהַנְחוֹת.
וְחֹק שַׂמְתָּ בְּמָרָה עַל מֵי מְנוּחוֹת. כֵּן הוֹשַׁע נָא.

כְּהוֹשַׁעְתָּ זְבוּדֶיךָ בְּמִדְבַּר סִין בַּמַּחֲנֶה.
חָכְמוּ וְלָקְטוּ בַּשִּׁשִּׁי לֶחֶם מִשְׁנֶה. כֵּן הוֹשַׁע נָא.

כְּהוֹשַׁעְתָּ טְפוּלֶיךָ הוֹרוּ הֲכָנָה בְּמַדָּעָם.
יָשַׁר כֹּחָם, וְהוֹדָה לָמוֹ רוֹעָם. כֵּן הוֹשַׁע נָא.

כְּהוֹשַׁעְתָּ כָּלְכְּלוּ בְּעֹנֶג מָן הַמִּשְׁמָר.
לֹא הָפַךְ עֵינוֹ וְרֵיחוֹ לֹא נָמָר. כֵּן הוֹשַׁע נָא.

אֹם נְצוּרָה / ISRAEL, CHERISHED
The Four Species are not taken on Shabbat. While the *lulav*-bundle is left aside, the aspect of "praise" that the *lulav* conveys is replaced by meticulous observance of Shabbat itself, which is the focus of this *Hoshana*.

כְּהוֹשַׁעְתָּ אָדָם / AS YOU SAVED AND SHIELDED THE FIRST MAN
Like the preceding *Hoshana* this one was written specifically for Shabbat. It contains allusions to Shabbat as observed throughout Jewish and human history. Like its weekday

On Shabbat whether Yom Tov or Ḥol HaMo'ed the following Hoshanot are said:

אֹם נְצוּרָה ISRAEL, CHERISHED as the apple of the eye, "remember" and "keep" the Sabbath day. They hasten to welcome the coming of the Sabbath, toiling for six days to honor the Sabbath. Their garments of beauty they don for the Sabbath, fine food and good drink they prepare for the Sabbath, setting the table with dainties and sweets for every Sabbath day. They kindle with blessing the lights of the Sabbath. With kiddush wine blessing they hallow the Sabbath, and break the twin bread loaves of blessing on the Sabbath, of three meals with worship and joy they partake every Sabbath day. They study Torah that gives solace on the Sabbath, and con all the happy directions for the Sabbath, such as not bearing burdens or loads on the Sabbath, or moving beyond the set limits on the Sabbath, or passing beyond the domains of the Sabbath, thus keeping their feet from profaning the rest of every Sabbath day. Sevenfold blessing they utter on the Sabbath, and seven they call to the Torah on the Sabbath. Acclaiming the glory and joy of the Sabbath, they cling to the very last moment of the Sabbath. May Israel inherit a rest to be ever one glorious Sabbath day. Please, save.

אֲנִי וָהוֹ ANI VAHO, please save us.

כְּהוֹשַׁעְתָּ AS YOU SAVED and shielded the first man, the work of Your hands,
and on the holy Sabbath let him find atonement and grace –
so, please, save us.

As You saved Your distinguished people who longing for freedom sought
out the Torah's teaching by choosing the seventh day for rest –
so, please, save us.

As You saved the people whom You led as a flock to their rest, and ordained
for them a statute at Marah by still waters – so, please, save us.

As You saved Your chosen portion encamped in the Sin wilderness, where
in their Wisdom they gathered a double measure of manna for
food on the sixth day – so, please, save us.

As You saved Your children clinging to You, who in their knowledge made
preparation for the Sabbath so that Moses their shepherd
approved and praised their work – so, please, save us.

As You saved those joyously sustained on the Sabbath by the manna stored in
readiness while neither its appearance nor its savor changed –
so, please, save us.

כְּהוֹשַׁעְתָּ מִשְׁפְּטֵי מַשְׂאוֹת שַׁבָּת גְּמָרוּ.
נָחוּ וְשָׁבְתוּ, רְשֻׁיּוֹת וּתְחוּמִים שָׁמָרוּ. כֵּן הוֹשַׁע נָא.

כְּהוֹשַׁעְתָּ סִינַי הָשְׁמְעוּ בְּדִבּוּר רְבִיעִי.
עִנְיַן זָכוֹר וְשָׁמוֹר לְקַדֵּשׁ שְׁבִיעִי. כֵּן הוֹשַׁע נָא.

כְּהוֹשַׁעְתָּ פְּקְדוּ יְרִיחוֹ שֶׁבַע לְהַקִּיף.
צָרוּ עַד רִדְתָּהּ בַּשַּׁבָּת לְתַקֵּף. כֵּן הוֹשַׁע נָא.

כְּהוֹשַׁעְתָּ קֹהֶלֶת וְעַמּוֹ בְּבֵית עוֹלָמִים.
רְצוּף בְּחָגְגָם שִׁבְעָה וְשִׁבְעָה יָמִים. כֵּן הוֹשַׁע נָא.

כְּהוֹשַׁעְתָּ שָׁבִים עוֹלֵי גוֹלָה לפדיום.
תּוֹרָתְךָ בְּקָרְאָם בְּחַג יוֹם יוֹם. כֵּן הוֹשַׁע נָא.

כְּהוֹשַׁעְתָּ מְשַׂמְּחֶיךָ בְּבִנְיַן שֵׁנִי הַמְחֻדָּשׁ.
נוֹטְלִין לוּלָב כָּל שִׁבְעָה בַּמִּקְדָּשׁ. כֵּן הוֹשַׁע נָא.

כְּהוֹשַׁעְתָּ חִבּוּט עֲרָבָה שַׁבָּת מַדְחִים.
מְרַבִּיּוֹת מוֹצָא לִיסוֹד מִזְבֵּחַ מַנִּיחִים. כֵּן הוֹשַׁע נָא.

כְּהוֹשַׁעְתָּ בְּרָכּוֹת וַאֲרֻכּוֹת וּגְבוֹהוֹת מְעַלְּסִים.
בְּפְטִירָתָן יֹפִי לְךָ מִזְבֵּחַ מְקַלְּסִים. כֵּן הוֹשַׁע נָא.

כְּהוֹשַׁעְתָּ מוֹדִים וּמְיַחֲלִים וְלֹא מְשַׁנִּים.
כֻּלָּנוּ אָנוּ לְיָהּ וְעֵינֵינוּ לְיָהּ שׁוֹנִים. כֵּן הוֹשַׁע נָא.

כְּהוֹשַׁעְתָּ יֶקֶב מַחְצְבֶיךָ סוֹבְבִים בִּרְנָנָה.
רוֹנְנִים אֲנִי וָהוֹ הוֹשִׁיעָה נָּא. כֵּן הוֹשַׁע נָא.

כְּהוֹשַׁעְתָּ חֵיל זְרִיזִים מְשָׁרְתִים בִּמְנוּחָה.
קָרְבַּן שַׁבָּת כָּפוּל, עוֹלָה וּמִנְחָה. כֵּן הוֹשַׁע נָא.

כְּהוֹשַׁעְתָּ לְוִיֶּיךָ עַל דּוּכָנָם לְהַרְבַּת.
אוֹמְרִים מִזְמוֹר שִׁיר לְיוֹם הַשַּׁבָּת. כֵּן הוֹשַׁע נָא.

---

counterpart כְּהוֹשַׁעְתָּ אֵלִים, it explores the theme of אֲנִי וָהוֹ הוֹשִׁיעָה נָּא by approaching Shabbat as a mechanism by which the Jewish people cleaves to God – starting with Adam, through the generations of Egypt, Sinai, Joshua, as well as the first and second Temple periods.

As You saved those who established the prohibitions of Sabbath burdens, who rested in repose on the Sabbath day, observing its domains and bounds – so, please, save us.

As You saved those who at Sinai in Your fourth utterance were made to hear the command "Remember" and "Keep" the Sabbath in sanctity– so, please, save us.

As You saved those who were bidden encircle Jericho seven times, who beleaguered it until it fell into their power on the Sabbath – so, please, save us.

As You saved in Your eternal shrine Solomon and his people who sought Your favor with their festival of twice seven days – so, please, save us.

As You saved those who returned redeemed from exile in Babylon when they read from Your Torah each day of this festival – so, please, save us.

As You saved those who brought You joy in rebuilding the Temple renewed, in the holiness of which they carried the palm-branch all seven days of this festival – so, please, save us.

As You saved those who even on the Sabbath beat the willow-branch and laid boughs from Motza at the altar's base – so, please, save us.

As You saved those who praised You with slender, long, lofty willow-branches, and on leaving acclaimed the altar saying, "Beauty is yours, O altar," – so, please, save us.

As You saved those who thanked You and steadfastly hoped in You, antiphonally chanting, "We are all His and our eyes are toward Him," – so, please, save us.

As You saved those who with green shoots encircled Your hewn-out altar, singing, "We beseech You, O Lord, to save us," – so, please, save us.

As You saved the host of Your zealous priests ministering on the day of rest with double oblation of burnt-offering and grain sacrifice – so, please, save us.

As You saved Your Levites who on their platform sang "A psalm, a song, for the Sabbath day," – so, please, save us.

כְּהוֹשַׁעְתָּ **נ**ְחוּמֶיךָ בְּמִצְוֹתֶיךָ תָּמִיד יִשְׁתַּעְשְׁעוּן.
וּרְצֵם וְהַחֲלִיצֵם בְּשׁוּבָה וָנַחַת יִוָּשֵׁעוּן. כֵּן הוֹשַׁע נָא.

כְּהוֹשַׁעְתָּ שְׁבוּת שִׁבְטֵי יַעֲקֹב.
תָּשׁוּב וְתָשִׁיב שְׁבוּת אָהֳלֵי יַעֲקֹב. וְהוֹשִׁיעָה נָּא.

כְּהוֹשַׁעְתָּ שׁוֹמְרֵי מִצְוֹת וְחוֹכֵי יְשׁוּעוֹת.
אֵל לְמוֹשָׁעוֹת. וְהוֹשִׁיעָה נָּא.
אֲנִי וָהוֹ הוֹשִׁיעָה נָּא.

הוֹשִׁיעָה אֶת־עַמֶּךָ, וּבָרֵךְ אֶת־נַחֲלָתֶךָ, וּרְעֵם וְנַשְּׂאֵם עַד־הָעוֹלָם: וְיִהְיוּ תהלים כח / מלכים א׳ ח
דְבָרַי אֵלֶּה, אֲשֶׁר הִתְחַנַּנְתִּי לִפְנֵי יהוה, קְרֹבִים אֶל־יהוה אֱלֹהֵינוּ
יוֹמָם וָלָיְלָה, לַעֲשׂוֹת מִשְׁפַּט עַבְדּוֹ וּמִשְׁפַּט עַמּוֹ יִשְׂרָאֵל, דְּבַר־יוֹם בְּיוֹמוֹ:
לְמַעַן דַּעַת כָּל־עַמֵּי הָאָרֶץ כִּי יהוה הוּא הָאֱלֹהִים, אֵין עוֹד:

The ארון קודש *is closed and the* שליח ציבור *continues the service with* קדיש שלם *on page 586.*

הושענות נוספות להושענא רבה

On הושענא רבה *continue here:*

תְּתְנֵנוּ לְשֵׁם וְלִתְהִלָּה. תְּ**שִׁ**יבֵנוּ אֶל הַחֶבֶל וְאֶל הַנַּחֲלָה. תְּ**ר**וֹמְמֵנוּ לְמַעְלָה לְמַעְלָה. תְּ**ק**ַבְּצֵנוּ לְבֵית הַתְּפִלָּה. תַּ**צִּ**יבֵנוּ כְּעֵץ עַל פַּלְגֵי מַיִם שְׁתוּלָה. תִּ**פְ**דֵּנוּ מִכָּל נֶגַע וּמַחֲלָה. תְּ**עַ**טְּרֵנוּ בְּאַהֲבָה כְּלוּלָה. תְּ**שַׂ**מְּחֵנוּ בְּבֵית הַתְּפִלָּה. תְּ**נַ**הֲלֵנוּ עַל מֵי מְנוּחוֹת סֶלָה. תְּ**מַ**לְּאֵנוּ חָכְמָה וְשִׂכְלָה. תַּ**לְ**בִּישֵׁנוּ עֹז וּגְדֻלָּה. תַּ**כְ**תִּירֵנוּ בְּכֶתֶר כְּלוּלָה. תְּ**יַ**שְּׁרֵנוּ בְּאֹרַח סְלוּלָה. תִּ**טָּ**עֵנוּ בְּיֹשֶׁר מְסִלָּה. תְּ**חָ**נֵּנוּ בְּרַחֲמִים וּבְחֶמְלָה. תַּ**זְ**כִּירֵנוּ בְּמִי זֹאת עוֹלָה. תּ**וֹ**שִׁיעֵנוּ לְקֵץ הַגְּאֻלָּה. תְּ**הַ**דְּרֵנוּ בְּזִיו הַמְּלָה. תַּ**דְ**בִּיקֵנוּ כְּאֵזוֹר חֲתוּלָה. תְּ**גַ**דְּלֵנוּ בְּיָד הַגְּדוֹלָה. תְּ**בִ**יאֵנוּ לְבֵיתְךָ

הוֹשַׁעְנָא רַבָּה / HOSHANA RABA

On Sukkot the rainfall for the coming year is decreed in heaven. Hoshana Raba is the last day of Sukkot, and thus is the day when the "final note" (in Yiddish "*kvittel*") carrying the verdict that was pronounced on Yom Kippur reaches those angels who will implement it. Hence it is the last day on which to plead for a good year ahead.

תְּתְנֵנוּ / ZESTFUL

This is the first in a series of seven additional *Hoshanot* for Hoshana Raba. The first three of this series focus on the theme of future redemption; the second three focus on the request for rain. The final *Hoshana* focuses on the Messianic arrival and beyond, leading to the Resurrection of the Dead.

As You saved those who found comfort through their constant delight in Your commandments, so take pleasure in them and give them vigor, that by return to You and by their rest they may be saved – so, please, save us.

As You saved the captive tribes of Jacob, so turn again and restore the captive tents of Jacob, – and please save us.

As You saved those who keep Your commandments and hope for salvation from You, God of salvation – and please save us.

ANI VAHO, please save us.

Ps. 28 הוֹשִׁיעָה SAVE YOUR PEOPLE and bless Your inheritance, and tend them and
I Kings 8 carry them forever. And may these my words with which I have entreated before the Lord, be near to the Lord our God day and night, so that He shall maintain the cause of His servant and of His people Israel day by day, that all the peoples of the earth may know that the Lord He is God, there is none else.

The Ark is closed and the Leader continues the service with Full Kaddish on *page 587.*

ADDITIONAL HOSHANOT FOR HOSHANA RABA

On Hoshana Raba continue here:

תִּתְּנֵנוּ ZESTFUL let us be through Your rescue and deliverance, Yea, be our song resounding with our gladness and rejoicing. Ward off from us all evil plague and every fell disease. Vest us with radiant garments of Your power and Your strength. Uplift us and raise us up yet nearer to You. To Zion, our great heritage, return us as of yore. Save us through Your power that we rest in pasture rich. Restore us to Your Temple as we sing Your praise with joy. Quicken us that we may walk on Your clear road of truth. Plant us as a fruitful tree by welling springs of water, and set us up securely as the vineyard of Your choice. Once more let it be said of us, "Who is this that goes up!" Near to You O let us be as an encircling girdle. Make our name be known on earth for glory and men's praise. Lead us to pastures green beside the peaceful waters. Keep us marching forward on the path of love and justice. Jerusalem, O be it built through Israel's return. Increase our joy through worship in the Temple of our prayers. Hearten us as we behold it built up as of old. Glorify us with the day of Your triumphant saving. Fill us with discernment and with wisdom of the heart. Exalt our strength for evermore, beloved God of Jacob.

בְּרִנָּה וְצָהֳלָה. תְּאַדְּרֵנוּ בְּיֶשַׁע וְגִילָה. תְּאַמְּצֵנוּ בְּרֶוַח וְהַצָּלָה. תְּלַבְּבֵנוּ בְּבִנְיַן עִירְךָ כְּבַתְּחִלָּה. תְּעוֹרְרֵנוּ לְצִיּוֹן בְּשִׁכְלוּלָה. תְּזַכֵּנוּ בְּנִבְנְתָה הָעִיר עַל תִּלָּהּ. תְּרַבִּיצֵנוּ בְּשָׂשׂוֹן וְגִילָה. תְּחַזְּקֵנוּ אֱלֹהֵי יַעֲקֹב סֶלָה.

followed by the קהל *:* שליח ציבור

אָנָּא, הוֹשִׁיעָה נָּא.

אָנָּא **אֵ**זֶן חִין תְּאַבֵּי יִשְׁעָךְ.
בְּ**עַ**רְבֵי נַחַל לְשַׁעְשְׁעָךְ. וְהוֹשִׁיעָה נָּא.

אָנָּא **גְּ**אַל כַּנַּת נִטְעָךְ.
דוּמָה בְּטַאטְאָךְ. וְהוֹשִׁיעָה נָּא.

אָנָּא **הַ**בֵּט לַבְּרִית טִבְעָךְ.
וּמַחֲשַׁכֵּי אֶרֶץ בְּהַטְבִּיעָךְ. וְהוֹשִׁיעָה נָּא.

אָנָּא **זְ**כָר לָנוּ אָב יְדָעָךְ.
חַסְדְּךָ לָמוֹ בְּהוֹדִיעָךְ. וְהוֹשִׁיעָה נָּא.

אָנָּא **טְ**הוֹרֵי לֵב בְּהַפְלִיאָךְ.
יָדַע כִּי הוּא פִּלְאָךְ. וְהוֹשִׁיעָה נָּא.

אָנָּא **כַּ**בִּיר כֹּחַ תֵּן לָנוּ יִשְׁעָךְ.
לַאֲבוֹתֵינוּ כְּהִשָּׁבְעָךְ. וְהוֹשִׁיעָה נָּא.

אָנָּא **מְ**לֵא מִשְׁאֲלוֹת עַם מְשַׁוְּעָךְ.
נֶעֱקַד בְּהַר מוֹר כְּמוֹ שַׁוְעָךְ. וְהוֹשִׁיעָה נָּא.

אָנָּא **סַ**גֵּב אֶשְׁלֵי נִטְעָךְ.
עֲרִיצִים בְּהָנִיעָךְ. וְהוֹשִׁיעָה נָּא.

אָנָּא **פְּ**תַח לָנוּ אוֹצְרוֹת רִבְעָךְ.
צִיָּה מֵהֶם בְּהַרְבִּיעָךְ. וְהוֹשִׁיעָה נָּא.

אָנָּא אֵזֶן / I BESEECH YOU, GIVE EAR
The *Hoshanot* service of Hoshana Raba centers on the *aravot*, or brook-willows, a species which grows near rivers, and is particularly sensitive to a shortage of water; it is the first of the four species to dry out and usually must be replaced over the course of the holiday. The *Hoshana* begins with words that evoke an association with words of different meanings but similar sounds that appear in a very different context: the *Ketuba* marriage contract in which the words "וְאָנָא...אֵזֹן," (I will provide…

Deck us with the radiance of a host in victory. Crown us with Your coronet of all-embracing love. Be gracious to us in Your compassion and Your mercy. Adorn us with the diadem of perfect love of You. PLEASE SAVE.

Leader followed by the congregation:
אָנָּא LORD, please save us.

אָנָּא אֵזוֹן* I BESEECH YOU, give ear to their cry that implores You to save,
That seek to bring You joy with the willows that wave –
and please save us.

I beseech You, deliver the stock You have planted, and say
On the day when You sweep the remnant of nations away –
and please save us.

I beseech You to look to the covenant sealed at our birth,
When You cast men down to the darkness under the earth –
and please save us.

I beseech You, remember the father who knew You alone,
When we say, "To his children today make Your kindness known" –
and please save us.

I beseech You, O worker of wonders for hearts without stain
Be it known that herein is the wonder of You that saves again –
and please save us.

I beseech You, O honored in strength, give salvation to us,
For in ages of yore You swore to our forefathers thus –
and please save us.

I beseech You, fulfill the desires of Your entreating nation,
As the bound one on the mountain pleaded for salvation –
and please save us.

I beseech You, the trees of Your planting! – give shelter to these,
When uprooting the mighty – Almighty, remember Your trees –
and please save us.

I beseech You, throw open Your treasures of rain; let us see
The good of the land that is thirsting for showers from Thee –
and please save us.

* This translation is based on that of Nina Salaman, and uses a free-form poetic rhyming scheme rather than a literal translation.

subsistence…,) are a key part of a husband's commitment to provide for his wife. Thus, this *piyut* evokes the marital bond of the Jewish people with God – sealed with the covenant

אָנָּא קוֹרְאֶיךָ אֶרֶץ בְּרוֹעֲעָךְ.
רְעֵם בְּטוּב מֵרְעָךְ. וְהוֹשִׁיעָה נָּא.

אָנָּא שְׁעָרֶיךָ תָּעַל מִמְּשׁוֹאָךְ.
תֵּל תַּלְפִּיּוֹת בְּהַשִּׂיאָךְ. וְהוֹשִׁיעָה נָּא.

קהל *followed by the* שליח ציבור:

אָנָּא, אֵל נָא, הוֹשַׁע נָא וְהוֹשִׁיעָה נָּא.

אֵל נָא תָּעִינוּ כְּשֶׂה אוֹבֵד
שְׁמֵנוּ מִסִּפְרְךָ אַל תְּאַבֵּד הוֹשַׁע נָא וְהוֹשִׁיעָה נָּא.

אֵל נָא רְעֵה אֶת צֹאן הַהֲרֵגָה
קְצוּפָה, וְעָלֶיךָ הֲרוּגָה הוֹשַׁע נָא וְהוֹשִׁיעָה נָּא.

אֵל נָא צֹאנְךָ וְצֹאן מַרְעִיתֶךָ
פְּעֻלָּתְךָ וְרַעְיָתֶךָ הוֹשַׁע נָא וְהוֹשִׁיעָה נָּא.

אֵל נָא עֲנִיֵּי הַצֹּאן
שִׂיחָם עֲנֵה בְּעֵת רָצוֹן הוֹשַׁע נָא וְהוֹשִׁיעָה נָּא.

אֵל נָא נוֹשְׂאֵי לְךָ עַיִן
מִתְקוֹמְמֶיךָ יִהְיוּ כְאַיִן הוֹשַׁע נָא וְהוֹשִׁיעָה נָּא.

אֵל נָא לִמְנַסְּכֵי לְךָ מַיִם
כְּמִמַּעַיְנֵי הַיְשׁוּעָה יִשְׁאֲבוּן מַיִם הוֹשַׁע נָא וְהוֹשִׁיעָה נָּא.

אֵל נָא יַעֲלוּ לְצִיּוֹן מוֹשִׁיעִים
טְפוּלִים בְּךָ וּבְשִׁמְךָ נוֹשָׁעִים הוֹשַׁע נָא וְהוֹשִׁיעָה נָּא.

אֵל נָא חֲמוּץ בְּגָדִים
זְעֹם לְנַעֵר כָּל בּוֹגְדִים הוֹשַׁע נָא וְהוֹשִׁיעָה נָּא.

אֵל נָא וְזָכוֹר תִּזְכֹּר
הַנְּכוּרִים בִּלְתְּךָ וָכֹר הוֹשַׁע נָא וְהוֹשִׁיעָה נָּא.

---

at Sinai — in order to request that He provide for our sustenance, which in this case are the life-giving rains for the year ahead (R. Aton Holzer).

I beseech You, give friendship to those who have called You and feed
With the goodness and fat of Your pasture their hunger and need – and please save us.

I beseech You, O lift up Your gates from their desolate fall,
O lift up that ruinous heap for Your people that call – and please save us.

Leader followed by the congregation:

אָנָּא PLEASE, GOD, please! Save us, O please save us.

אֵל נָא תָּעִינוּ* PLEASE GOD! Like sheep we all have gone astray;
From out Your book wipe not our name away.
Save us, O please save us.

Please God! Sustain the sheep for slaughter; see
These dealt with wrathfully and slain for Thee.
Save us, O please save us.

Please God! Your sheep, the sheep You did tend
In pasture; Your creation and Your friend.
Save us, O please save us.

Please God! The poor among the sheep! Give heed;
Answer in time of favor to their need.
Save us, O please save us.

Please God! They lift their eyes to You, long sought;
Let those who rise against You count as naught.
Save us, O please save us.

Please God; They pour out water, worshiping;
Let them be drawing from salvation's spring.
Save us, O please save us.

Please God! To Zion saviors send at length,
Endowed of You, and saved by Your Name's strength.
Save us, O please save us.

Please God! In garb of vengeance clad about,
In mighty wrath cast all deceivers out.
Save us, O please save us.

Please God! And You will surely not forget
Her, by love-tokens bought, that still hopes yet.
Save us, O please save us.

---

*This translation is based on that of Nina Salaman, and uses a free-form poetic rhyming scheme rather than a literal translation.

אֵל נָא דּוֹרְשֶׁיךָ בְּעַנְפֵי עֲרָבוֹת
גֹּעִים שְׁעֵה מֵעֲרָבוֹת הוֹשַׁע נָא וְהוֹשִׁיעָה נָּא.

אֵל נָא בָּרֵךְ בְּעִטּוּר שָׁנָה
אֲמָרַי רְצֵה בְּפִלּוּלִי בְּיוֹם הוֹשַׁעְנָא הוֹשַׁע נָא וְהוֹשִׁיעָה נָּא.

קהל *followed by the* שליח ציבור:

אָנָּא, אֵל נָא,
הוֹשַׁע נָא וְהוֹשִׁיעָה נָּא,
אָבִינוּ אָתָּה.

לְמַעַן **תָּ**מִים בְּדוֹרוֹתָיו,
הַנִּמְלָט בְּרֹב צִדְקוֹתָיו
מֻצָּל מִשֶּׁטֶף בְּבוֹא מַבּוּל מַיִם.
לְאֹם אֲנִי חוֹמָה הוֹשַׁע נָא וְהוֹשִׁיעָה נָּא, אָבִינוּ אָתָּה.

לְמַעַן **שָׁ**לֵם בְּכָל מַעֲשִׂים,
הַמְנֻסֶּה בַּעֲשָׂרָה נִסִּים
כְּשָׂר מַלְאָכִים, נָם יֻקַּח נָא מְעַט מַיִם.
לְבָרָה כַּחַמָּה הוֹשַׁע נָא וְהוֹשִׁיעָה נָּא, אָבִינוּ אָתָּה.

לְמַעַן **רַ**ךְ וְיָחִיד נֶחֱנַט פְּרִי לְמֵאָה,
זָעַק אַיֵּה הַשֶּׂה לְעֹלָה
בִּשְּׂרוּהוּ עֲבָדָיו מָצָאנוּ מַיִם.
לְגוֹלָה וְסוּרָה הוֹשַׁע נָא וְהוֹשִׁיעָה נָּא, אָבִינוּ אָתָּה.

לְמַעַן **קָ**דַם שְׂאֵת בְּרָכָה,
הַנִּשְׂטָם וּלְשִׁמְךָ חִכָּה
מְיַחֵם בְּמַקְלוֹת בְּשִׁקְתוֹת הַמָּיִם.
לְדָמְתָה לְתָמָר הוֹשַׁע נָא וְהוֹשִׁיעָה נָּא, אָבִינוּ אָתָּה.

לְמַעַן **צָ**דַק הֱיוֹת לְךָ לְכֹהֵן,
כְּחָתָן פְּאֵר יְכַהֵן
מְנֻסֶּה בְּמַסָּה בְּמֵי מְרִיבַת מַיִם.
לְהָהָר הַטּוֹב הוֹשַׁע נָא וְהוֹשִׁיעָה נָּא, אָבִינוּ אָתָּה.

Please God! They seeking You with willow bough,
Regard their crying from Your Heaven now.
Save us, O please save us.
Please God! As with a crown bless the year;
Yea, Lord, my singing, I beseech You, hear.
Save us, O please save us.

Leader followed by the congregation:

אָנָּא PLEASE, God, please! Save us, O please save us,
for You are our Father.

לְמַעַן תָּמִים* FOR HIM who was a perfect man 'mid all,
Who once was saved through goodness at Your call,
Redeemed from overflowing floods of water –
Save her who standeth steadfast as a wall,
Please, God, please! Save us, O please save us, for You are our Father.

For one unblemished in his works and ways
Though tried tenfold; who, lifting up his gaze,
Saw angel forms, and ran to give them water –
Save her that shineth as the sunlight's rays,
Please, God, please! Save us, O please save us, for You are our Father.

For that loved son who asked his aged sire,
"Where is the lamb for offering made by fire?"
For him who heard the tidings, "Here is water" –
Save her that wandereth in exile dire,
Please, God, please! Save us, O please save us, for You are our Father.

For his sake who before his brother came
To take his blessing – hoping in Your Name;
For him whose flocks increased by troughs of water –
Save her that was a palm-tree in her fame,
Please, God, please! Save us, O please save us, for You are our Father.

For him who meet to serve You, You did deem,
Appareled as a bridegroom doth beseem;
At Massah tried, at Meribah's sad water –
O save that goodly mountain of our dream,
Please, God, please! Save us, O please save us, for You are our Father.

* This translation is based on that of Nina Salaman, and uses a free-form poetic rhyming scheme rather than a literal translation.

לְמַעַן פְּאַר הֱיוֹת גְּבִיר לְאֶחָיו,
יְהוּדָה אֲשֶׁר גָּבַר בְּאֶחָיו
מִסְפַּר רֹבַע מִדָּלְיָו יִזַּל מַיִם.
לֹא לָנוּ כִּי אִם לְמַעַנְךָ הוֹשַׁע נָא וְהוֹשִׁיעָה נָּא, אָבִינוּ אָתָּה.

לְמַעַן עָנָו מִכֹּל וְנֶאֱמָן,
אֲשֶׁר בְּצִדְקוֹ כִּלְכֵּל הַמָּן
מָשׁוּךְ לְגוֹאֵל וּמָשׁוּי מִמַּיִם.
לְזֹאת הַנִּשְׁקָפָה הוֹשַׁע נָא וְהוֹשִׁיעָה נָּא, אָבִינוּ אָתָּה.

לְמַעַן שַׁמָּתוֹ כְּמַלְאֲכֵי מְרוֹמִים,
הַלּוֹבֵשׁ אוּרִים וְתֻמִּים
מְצֻוֶּה לָבוֹא בַמִּקְדָּשׁ בְּקִדּוּשׁ יָדַיִם וְרַגְלַיִם וּרְחִיצַת מַיִם.
לְחוֹלַת אַהֲבָה הוֹשַׁע נָא וְהוֹשִׁיעָה נָּא, אָבִינוּ אָתָּה.

לְמַעַן נְבִיאָה מְחוֹלַת מַחֲנַיִם,
לְכַמְהֵי לֵב הוּשְׂמָה עֵינַיִם
לְרַגְלָהּ רָצָה עָלוֹת וָרֶדֶת בְּאֵר מָיִם.
לְטוֹבוּ אֹהָלָיו הוֹשַׁע נָא וְהוֹשִׁיעָה נָּא, אָבִינוּ אָתָּה.

לְמַעַן מְשָׁרֵת לֹא מָשׁ מֵאֹהֶל,
וְרוּחַ הַקֹּדֶשׁ עָלָיו אָהֵל
בְּעָבְרוֹ בַיַּרְדֵּן נִכְרְתוּ הַמַּיִם.
לְיָפָה וּבָרָה הוֹשַׁע נָא וְהוֹשִׁיעָה נָּא, אָבִינוּ אָתָּה.

לְמַעַן לָמַד רְאוֹת לְטוֹבָה אוֹת,
זָעַק אַיֵּה נִפְלָאוֹת
מִצָּה טַל מִגִּזָּה מְלֹא הַסֵּפֶל מָיִם.
לְכַלַּת לְבָנוֹן הוֹשַׁע נָא וְהוֹשִׁיעָה נָּא, אָבִינוּ אָתָּה.

לְמַעַן כְּלוּלֵי עֲשׂוֹת מִלְחַמְתֶּךָ,
אֲשֶׁר בְּיָדָם תַּתָּה יְשׁוּעָתֶךָ
צְרוּפֵי מִגּוֹי בְּלָקְקָם בְּיָדָם מָיִם.
לְלֹא בָגְדוּ בָךְ הוֹשַׁע נָא וְהוֹשִׁיעָה נָּא, אָבִינוּ אָתָּה.

For him above his brethren set to shine –
Yet we be but a fourth of Judah's line –
Whereof 'tis said "His buckets flowed with water" –
So save not, Lord, for our sake, but for Thine,
Please, God, please! Save us, O please save us, for You are our Father.

For one more meek than all men and more true
Whose merit brought down manna on the dew,
Chosen redeemer, drawn from out the water –
Save her that ever looketh forth anew,
Please, God, please! Save us, O please save us, for You are our Father.

For one who was as angels are above,
Who, meetly clad, did in Your precincts move
In holiness, all purified with water –
Save her, O Lord, her that is sick with love,
Please, God, please! Save us, O please save us, for You are our Father.

For that glad prophetess who danced before
The camp, to them whose heart was sad and sore,
For whom there rose and sank a well of water –
Save them that dwelt in goodly tents of yore,
Please, God, please! Save us, O please save us, for You are our Father.

For him who in the tent was fain to stay,
On whom the spirit shone, who went his way
o'er Jordan, and You did divide the water –
Save her, the beautiful and pure as day,
Please, God, please! Save us, O please save us, for You are our Father.

For his sake who besought a sign, who cried
"Where be Your wonders?" and at morning-tide
Wringed dew from out the fleece, a bowl of water –
Save her who was in Lebanon a bride,
Please, God, please! Save us, O please save us, for You are our Father.

For those of old who went Your wars to fight
Whole-hearted, in their hands Your saving might;
Chosen when gathering in their palms the water –
Save them forever faithful in Your sight,
Please, God, please! Save us, O please save us, for You are our Father.

לְמַעַן יָחִיד צוֹרְרִים דָּשׁ,
אֲשֶׁר מֵרֶחֶם לְנָזִיר הֻקְדָּשׁ
מִמַּכְתֵּשׁ לֶחִי הִבְקַעְתָּ לוֹ מַיִם.
לְמַעַן שֵׁם קָדְשֶׁךָ הוֹשַׁע נָא וְהוֹשִׁיעָה נָּא, אָבִינוּ אָתָּה.

לְמַעַן טוֹב הוֹלֵךְ וְגָדֵל,
אֲשֶׁר מֵעֹשֶׁק עֵדָה חִדֵּל
בְּשׁוּב עַם מֵחֵטְא צִוָּה שְׁאֹב מַיִם.
לְנָאוָה כִּירוּשָׁלָיִם הוֹשַׁע נָא וְהוֹשִׁיעָה נָּא, אָבִינוּ אָתָּה.

לְמַעַן חִכָּךְ מְכַרְכֵּר בְּשִׁיר,
הַמְלַמֵּד תּוֹרָה בְּכָל כְּלֵי שִׁיר
מְנַסֵּךְ לְפָנֶיךָ כְּתָאֵב שְׁתוֹת מַיִם.
לִשְׁמוּ בְּךָ סִבְרָם הוֹשַׁע נָא וְהוֹשִׁיעָה נָּא, אָבִינוּ אָתָּה.

לְמַעַן זָךְ עָלָה בִּסְעָרָה,
הַמְקַנֵּא וּמֵשִׁיב עֶבְרָה
לְפִלּוּלוֹ יָרְדָה אֵשׁ וְלִחֲכָה עָפָר וּמַיִם.
לְעֵינֶיהָ בְּרֵכוֹת הוֹשַׁע נָא וְהוֹשִׁיעָה נָּא, אָבִינוּ אָתָּה.

לְמַעַן וְשֵׁרֵת בֶּאֱמֶת לְרַבּוֹ,
פִּי שְׁנַיִם בְּרוּחוֹ נֶאֱצַל בּוֹ
בְּקַחְתּוֹ מְנַגֵּן נִתְמַלְּאוּ גֵּבִים מַיִם.
לְפָצוּ מִי כָמֹכָה הוֹשַׁע נָא וְהוֹשִׁיעָה נָּא, אָבִינוּ אָתָּה.

לְמַעַן הִרְהֵר עֲשׂוֹת רְצוֹנֶךָ,
הַמַּכְרִיז תְּשׁוּבָה לְצֹאנֶךָ
אָז בְּבוֹא מְחָרֵף סָתַם עֵינוֹת מַיִם.
לְצִיּוֹן מִכְלַל יֹפִי הוֹשַׁע נָא וְהוֹשִׁיעָה נָּא, אָבִינוּ אָתָּה.

לְמַעַן דָּרְשׁוּךָ בְּתוֹךְ הַגּוֹלָה,
וְסוֹדְךָ לָמוֹ נִגְלָה
בְּלִי לְהִתְגָּאֵל דָּרְשׁוּ זֵרְעוֹנִים וּמַיִם.
לְקוֹרְאֶיךָ בַּצָּר הוֹשַׁע נָא וְהוֹשִׁיעָה נָּא, אָבִינוּ אָתָּה.

For him, that only son, who crushed the foe,
Sacred from birth, a Nazirite to grow,
For whom from out a jaw-bone gushed forth water–
Save! even for Your holy Name save now!
Please, God, please! Save us, O please save us, for You are our Father.

For his sake who in favor yet grew on
When through their sinfulness the throngs had gone;
Who, turning men from sin, spake, "Now draw water" –
Save her more fair than Zion when she shone,
Please, God, please! Save us, O please save us, for You are our Father.

For his sake who did play and dance and sing,
Who taught the Law with sound of pipe and string,
Who, thirsting sore, poured out to You the water –
Save those who trust salvation You will bring,
Please, God, please! Save us, O please save us, for You are our Father.

For his sake whom a whirlwind once did bear
To Heav'n, whose zeal turned back Your wrath, whose prayer
Drew fire from Heav'n, which licked up dust and water –
Save her, O God, whose eyes are fountains fair,
Please, God, please! Save us, O please save us, for You are our Father.

For him who served his lord in deed and thought
On whom twofold the spirit fell; who sought
A minstrel ere the ditches filled with water –
Save them that sang "Lord, Who such deeds have wrought?"
Please, God, please! Save us, O please save us, for You are our Father.

For his sake, swift to do the word from Thee,
Who bid Your sheep repent, and set them free
From the blasphemer, staying founts of water–
Save Zion, beautiful and fair to see,
Please, God, please! Save us, O please save us, for You are our Father.

For those who sought in exile for Your face,
Who knew Your secret; who to gather grace
And shun defilement, ate but pulse and water –
Save them that call You, grieving from their place,
Please, God, please! Save us, O please save us, for You are our Father.

לְמַעַן גֹּמֵר חָכְמָה וּבִינָה, סוֹפֵר מָהִיר מְפַלֵּשׁ אֲמָנָה
מַחְכִּימֵנוּ אֲמָרִים הַמְּשׁוּלִים בְּרַהֲבֵי מָיִם.
לְרַבֹּתַי עַם הוֹשַׁע נָא וְהוֹשִׁיעָה נָּא, אָבִינוּ אָתָּה.

לְמַעַן בָּאֵי לְךָ הַיּוֹם בְּכָל לֵב, שׁוֹפְכִים לְךָ שִׂיחַ בְּלֹא לֵב וָלֵב
שׁוֹאֲלִים מִמְּךָ עֹז מִטְרוֹת מָיִם.
לְשׁוֹרְרוּ בַּיָּם הוֹשַׁע נָא וְהוֹשִׁיעָה נָּא, אָבִינוּ אָתָּה.

לְמַעַן אוֹמְרֵי יִגְדַּל שְׁמֶךָ, וְהֵם נַחֲלָתְךָ וְעַמֶּךָ
צְמֵאִים לְיִשְׁעֲךָ כְּאֶרֶץ עֲיֵפָה לַמָּיִם.
לְתַרְתָּ לָמוֹ מְנוּחָה הוֹשַׁע נָא וְהוֹשִׁיעָה נָּא, אָבִינוּ אָתָּה.

קהל *then* שליח ציבור:

הוֹשַׁע נָא, אֵל נָא, אָנָּא הוֹשִׁיעָה נָּא.
הוֹשַׁע נָא, סְלַח נָא, וְהַצְלִיחָה נָא, וְהוֹשִׁיעֵנוּ אֵל מָעֻזֵּנוּ.

Put down the לולב *and* אתרוג *and pick up the* הושענות.

תַּעֲנֶה אֱמוּנִים שׁוֹפְכִים לְךָ לֵב כַּמַּיִם וְהוֹשִׁיעָה נָּא.
לְמַעַן בָּא בָאֵשׁ וּבַמַּיִם וְהַצְלִיחָה נָא.
גָּזַר וְנָם יֻקַּח נָא מְעַט מַיִם וְהוֹשִׁיעֵנוּ אֵל מָעֻזֵּנוּ.

תַּעֲנֶה דְגָלִים גָּזוּ גִּזְרֵי מַיִם וְהוֹשִׁיעָה נָּא.
לְמַעַן הַנֶּעֱקַד בְּשַׁעַר הַשָּׁמַיִם וְהַצְלִיחָה נָא.
וְשָׁב וְחָפַר בְּאֵרוֹת מָיִם וְהוֹשִׁיעֵנוּ אֵל מָעֻזֵּנוּ.

תַּעֲנֶה זַכִּים חוֹנִים עֲלֵי מַיִם וְהוֹשִׁיעָה נָּא.
לְמַעַן חָלָק מְפַצֵּל מַקְלוֹת בְּשִׁקְתוֹת הַמַּיִם וְהַצְלִיחָה נָא.
טָעַן וְגָל אֶבֶן מִבְּאֵר מַיִם וְהוֹשִׁיעֵנוּ אֵל מָעֻזֵּנוּ.

תַּעֲנֶה יְדִידִים נוֹחֲלֵי דָת מְשׁוּלֶּת מַיִם וְהוֹשִׁיעָה נָּא.
לְמַעַן כָּרוּ בְּמִשְׁעֲנוֹתָם מַיִם וְהַצְלִיחָה נָא.
לְהָכִין לָמוֹ וּלְצֶאֱצָאֵימוֹ מַיִם וְהוֹשִׁיעֵנוּ אֵל מָעֻזֵּנוּ.

תַּעֲנֶה אֱמוּנִים / ANSWER THE FAITHFUL
This *Hoshana* follows the theme of the preceding one, but each stanza opens by praising the Jewish people, and continues by invoking the merit of our righteous forebears in requesting life-giving rain. This time, both components are woven into one alphabetical acrostic.

For one who witnessed wisdom's light arise,
The ready scribe of yore, who made us wise
With outspread truth like spaces wide of water –
O save that once full city, when she cries,
Please, God, please! Save us, O please save us, for You are our Father.

For their sake who with all their soul this day
Have come to pour their heart out and to pray,
Begging from You Your rains of mighty water –
Save them who sang to You upon their way,
Please, God, please! Save us, O please save us, for You are our Father.

For their sake who have said "Your Name be blest,"
Your heritage, the sons of Your behest,
Longing for You like land that faints for water –
Save them for whom so long You seekest rest,
Please, God, please! Save us, O please save us, for You are our Father.

Leader followed by the congregation:

הוֹשַׁע נָא PLEASE, God, please! Save us, O please save us.
Please save us, please forgive us, and please prosper us.
And save us, God, our Stronghold.

Put down the lulav and etrog and pick up the Hoshanot.

תַּעֲנֶה* GIVE RAIN! Your lieges pour their hearts as water, and please save us.
For Abram's sake who went through fire and water, and please prosper us.
In courtesy he gave the angels water, and save us, God, our Stronghold.

Give rain! For us to pass was cleft the water, and please save us.
For Isaac's sake on mountain bound for slaughter, and please prosper us.
He turned and digged his people wells of water,
and save us, God, our Stronghold.

Give rain! We are the pure who camped by water, and please save us.
For Jacob's sake who set the rods in water, and please prosper us.
He strained and rolled the stone from off the water,
and save us, God, our Stronghold.

Give rain! Blest heirs to Torah's quickening water, and please save us.
Because of those who digged with staves for water, and please prosper us.
To win for them and for their offspring water,
and save us, God, our Stronghold.

*This translation is based on that of Israel Zangwill, and uses a free-form poetic rhyming scheme rather than a literal translation.

תַּעֲנֶה מִתְחַנְּנִים כְּבִישִׁימוֹן עֲלֵי מַיִם — וְהוֹשִׁיעָה נָּא.
לְמַעַן נֶאֱמַן בַּיִת מַסְפִּיק לָעָם מַיִם — וְהַצְלִיחָה נָא.
סֶלַע הָךְ וַיָּזוּבוּ מַיִם — וְהוֹשִׁיעֵנוּ אֵל מָעֻזֵּנוּ.

תַּעֲנֶה עוֹנִים עֲלֵי בְאֵר מַיִם — וְהוֹשִׁיעָה נָּא.
לְמַעַן פְּקַד בְּמֵי מְרִיבַת מַיִם — וְהַצְלִיחָה נָא.
צְמֵאִים לְהַשְׁקוֹת מַיִם — וְהוֹשִׁיעֵנוּ אֵל מָעֻזֵּנוּ.

תַּעֲנֶה קְדוֹשִׁים מְנַסְּכִים לְךָ מַיִם — וְהוֹשִׁיעָה נָּא.
לְמַעַן רֹאשׁ מְשׁוֹרְרִים כְּתָאֵב שְׁתוֹת מַיִם — וְהַצְלִיחָה נָא.
שָׁב וְנָסַךְ לְךָ מַיִם — וְהוֹשִׁיעֵנוּ אֵל מָעֻזֵּנוּ.

תַּעֲנֶה שׁוֹאֲלִים בְּרִבּוּעַ אֶשְׁלֵי מַיִם — וְהוֹשִׁיעָה נָּא.
לְמַעַן תֵּל תַּלְפִּיּוֹת מוֹצָא מַיִם — וְהַצְלִיחָה נָא.
תִּפְתַּח אֶרֶץ וְתַרְעִיף שָׁמַיִם — וְהוֹשִׁיעֵנוּ אֵל מָעֻזֵּנוּ.

קהל *followed by the* שליח ציבור*:*

רַחֶם נָא קְהַל עֲדַת יְשׁוּרוּן, סְלַח וּמְחַל עֲוֹנָם
וְהוֹשִׁיעֵנוּ אֱלֹהֵי יִשְׁעֵנוּ.

אָז כְּעֵינֵי עֲבָדִים
אֶל יַד אֲדוֹנִים
בָּאנוּ לְפָנֶיךָ נְדוֹנִים. — וְהוֹשִׁיעֵנוּ אֱלֹהֵי יִשְׁעֵנוּ.

גֵּאֶה אֲדוֹנֵי הָאֲדוֹנִים,
נִתְגָּרוּ בָנוּ מְדָנִים
דְּשׁוּנוּ וּבְעָלוּנוּ זוּלָתְךָ אֲדוֹנִים. — וְהוֹשִׁיעֵנוּ אֱלֹהֵי יִשְׁעֵנוּ.

הֵן גַּשְׁנוּ הַיּוֹם בְּתַחֲנוּן,
עָדֶיךָ רַחוּם וְחַנּוּן
וְסִפַּרְנוּ נִפְלְאוֹתֶיךָ בְּשִׁנּוּן. — וְהוֹשִׁיעֵנוּ אֱלֹהֵי יִשְׁעֵנוּ.

זָבַת חָלָב וּדְבָשׁ,
נָא אַל תִּיבָשׁ
חֲשְׁרַת מַיִם כְּאֵבָה תְּחֻבָּשׁ. — וְהוֹשִׁיעֵנוּ אֱלֹהֵי יִשְׁעֵנוּ.

Give rain! Today as then we cry for water, and please save us.
For Moses' sake who found his people water, and please prosper us.
He smote the rock and lo! out gushed the water,
and save us, God, our Stronghold.

Give rain! Our sires sang round the well of water, and please save us.
Because of Moses at Meribah's water, and please prosper us.
At Your command he gave the thirsting water,
and save us, God, our Stronghold.

Give rain! Your holy servants poured You water, and please save us.
For Your chief minstrel's sake who longed for water, and please prosper us.
Yet turned and made libation with the water,
and save us, God, our Stronghold.

Give rain! Four plants we wave that love the water, and please save us.
For Zion's sake, the home of living water, and please prosper us.
The parched earth open to the heavens' water,
and save us, God, our Stronghold.

Leader followed by the congregation:

רַחֵם נָא HAVE MERCY, please, on this congregation, an assembly of Jeshurun; forgive and pardon their wrongdoing; and save us, God of our salvation.

אָז כְּעֵינֵי* AS SLAVES, with eyes beseeching, seek their lord,
We came before You stricken, and implored:
And save us, God of our salvation.

Triumphant Lord of lords, to You we pray;
Strife like a whirlwind scattered us, and we
Your sons lay crushed beneath the tyrant's sway.
And save us, God of our salvation.

Behold! with supplication how we throng
O Lord of grace and mercy, unto Thee;
Your wondrous deeds, our never-ceasing song.
And save us, God of our salvation.

"Flowing with milk and honey": this Your land
Spare You from drought. O stay her tears of woe;
Bind up her torrents with Your healing hand.
And save us, God of our salvation.

---

*This translation is based on that of Elsie Davis, and uses a free-form poetic rhyming scheme rather than a literal translation.

טְעֵנוּ בַּשְּׁמֵנָה,
בְּיַד שִׁבְעָה וּשְׁמוֹנָה
יָשָׁר צַדִּיק אֵל אֱמוּנָה. וְהוֹשִׁיעֵנוּ אֱלֹהֵי יִשְׁעֵנוּ.

כָּרַתָּ בְּרִית לָאָרֶץ,
עוֹד כָּל יְמֵי הָאָרֶץ
לְבִלְתִּי פְּרָץ בָּהּ פֶּרֶץ. וְהוֹשִׁיעֵנוּ אֱלֹהֵי יִשְׁעֵנוּ.

מִתְחַנְּנִים עֲלֵי מָיִם,
כַּעֲרָבִים עַל יִבְלֵי מָיִם
נָא זְכָר לָמוֹ נִסּוּךְ הַמָּיִם. וְהוֹשִׁיעֵנוּ אֱלֹהֵי יִשְׁעֵנוּ.

שִׂיחִים בְּדֶרֶךְ מַטָּעָתָם,
עוֹמְסִים בְּשַׁוְעָתָם
עֲנֵם בְּקוֹל פְּגִיעָתָם. וְהוֹשִׁיעֵנוּ אֱלֹהֵי יִשְׁעֵנוּ.

פּוֹעֵל יְשׁוּעוֹת,
פְּנֵה לִפְלוּלָם שְׁעוֹת
צַדִּיקִם אֵל לְמוֹשָׁעוֹת. וְהוֹשִׁיעֵנוּ אֱלֹהֵי יִשְׁעֵנוּ.

קוֹל רִגְשָׁם תִּשַׁע,
תִּפְתַּח אֶרֶץ וְיִפְרוּ יֶשַׁע
רַב לְהוֹשִׁיעַ וְלֹא חָפֵץ רֶשַׁע. וְהוֹשִׁיעֵנוּ אֱלֹהֵי יִשְׁעֵנוּ.

followed by the שליח ציבור קהל:

שַׁעֲרֵי שָׁמַיִם פְּתַח,
וְאוֹצָרְךָ הַטּוֹב לָנוּ תִפְתַּח.
תּוֹשִׁיעֵנוּ וְרִיב אַל תִּמְתַּח.
וְהוֹשִׁיעֵנוּ אֱלֹהֵי יִשְׁעֵנוּ.

followed by the שליח ציבור קהל:

קוֹל מְבַשֵּׂר מְבַשֵּׂר וְאוֹמֵר.

אָמְנָן יִשְׁעֲךָ בָּא,
קוֹל דּוֹדִי הִנֵּה זֶה בָּא. מְבַשֵּׂר וְאוֹמֵר.

Plant us, we pray, upon a fruitful sod;
Send as of old defenders from the foe,
You just and righteous One, You faithful God!
And save us, God of our salvation.

Recall Your covenant with the earth of yore,
Your sign, that while the earth still yet abide,
Your anger break and rend it nevermore. And save us, God of our salvation.

The while for water we entreat You now,
Athirst as willows by the waterside,
The pouring forth of old, remember Thou!
And save us, God of our salvation.

These bearing boughs held upward in the way
They sprout from earth; these burdened by their plea,
O answer, when in sudden need they pray.
And save us, God of our salvation.

You worker of deliverance alone!
Turn to them, hear the words that mount to Thee;
God of salvation, justify Your own. And save us, God of our salvation.

List to the surging voices of Your throng,
Open the earth, let help spring forth, O Thou
Delighting not in evil; Savior strong! And save us, God of our salvation.

Leader followed by the congregation:

שַׁעֲרֵי שָׁמַיִם OPEN FOR US THE GATES of heaven, we crave;
Open for us Your goodly treasure now;
Ah! Strife prolong not endlessly, but save!
And save us, God of our salvation.

Leader followed by the congregation:

קוֹל מְבַשֵּׂר THE VOICE OF THE HERALD, he heralds and proclaims:

אֹמֶן יֶשְׁעֲךָ* O HARK to the herald of sure salvation.
I hear my Beloved, his voice is nigh, He heralds and proclaims.

*This translation is based on that of Israel Zangwill and uses a free-form poetic rhyming scheme rather than a literal translation.

קוֹל מְבַשֵּׂר / THE VOICE OF THE HERALD
This *piyut* opens and closes with a phrase abridging Isaiah's description of the herald of the future redemption: How beautiful upon

בָּא בְּרִבְבוֹת כִּתִּים,
לַעֲמֹד עַל הַר הַזֵּיתִים. מְבַשֵּׂר וְאוֹמֵר.
גִּשְׁתּוֹ בַּשּׁוֹפָר לִתְקֹעַ,
תַּחְתָּיו הַר יִבָּקֵעַ. מְבַשֵּׂר וְאוֹמֵר.
דָּפַק וְהֵצִיץ וְזָרַח,
וּמָשׁ חֲצִי הָהָר מִמִּזְרָח. מְבַשֵּׂר וְאוֹמֵר.
הֵקִים מִלּוּל נְאֻמוֹ,
וּבָא הוּא וְכָל קְדוֹשָׁיו עִמּוֹ. מְבַשֵּׂר וְאוֹמֵר.
וּלְכָל בָּאֵי הָעוֹלָם,
בַּת קוֹל יִשָּׁמַע בָּעוֹלָם. מְבַשֵּׂר וְאוֹמֵר.
זֶרַע עֲמוּסֵי רַחְמוֹ,
נוֹלְדוּ כְּיֶלֶד מִמְּעֵי אִמּוֹ. מְבַשֵּׂר וְאוֹמֵר.
ישעיה סו חָלָה וְיָלְדָה מִי זֹאת,
מִי־שָׁמַע כָּזֹאת. מְבַשֵּׂר וְאוֹמֵר.
ישעיה סו טָהוֹר פָּעַל כָּל אֵלֶּה,
מִי רָאָה כָּאֵלֶּה. מְבַשֵּׂר וְאוֹמֵר.
ישעיה סו יֶשַׁע וּזְמַן הוּחַד,
הֲיוּחַל אֶרֶץ בְּיוֹם אֶחָד. מְבַשֵּׂר וְאוֹמֵר.
ישעיה סו כַּבִּיר רוּם וָתַחַת,
אִם־יִוָּלֵד גּוֹי פַּעַם אֶחָת. מְבַשֵּׂר וְאוֹמֵר.
זכריה יד לְעֵת יִגְאַל עַמּוֹ נָאוֹר,
וְהָיָה לְעֵת־עֶרֶב יִהְיֶה־אוֹר. מְבַשֵּׂר וְאוֹמֵר.
ישעיה סו מוֹשִׁיעִים יַעֲלוּ לְהַר צִיּוֹן,
כִּי־חָלָה גַּם־יָלְדָה צִיּוֹן. מְבַשֵּׂר וְאוֹמֵר.
ישעיה נד נִשְׁמַע בְּכָל גְּבוּלֵךְ,
הַרְחִיבִי מְקוֹם אָהֳלֵךְ. מְבַשֵּׂר וְאוֹמֵר.

the mountains are the feet of the messenger (מְבַשֵּׂר) announcing peace, heralding (מְבַשֵּׂר) good tidings, announcing salvation (Isaiah 52:7). The *piyut* concludes the prayers for rain with a detailed description of the nature of the messianic redemption and the Resurrection

He comes with his myriads of hovering angels,
On the Mount of Olives to stand and cry. He heralds and proclaims.

The herald comes – be the trumpet sounded,
Beneath his tread be the mountain cleft. He heralds and proclaims.

He knocks – at his radiant glance
The hill-side shall half from the eastward be rent and reft.
He heralds and proclaims.

Fulfilled is his ancient prophetic saying,
The herald is come with his saints around; He heralds and proclaims.

By all upon earth shall a still small voice
To the uttermost islands be heard resound. He heralds and proclaims.

The seed he begot and the seed he reared
Has been born as a child from its mother's womb. He heralds and proclaims.

Is. 66 But who then has travailed and who brought forth,
And a similar thing has been told to whom? He heralds and proclaims.

Is. 66 The perfectly pure has achieved this marvel,
What mortal has seen such a wondrous way? He heralds and proclaims.

Is. 66 Salvation, redemption in one united,
The earth bringing forth in a single day! He heralds and proclaims.

Is. 66 Though He in the heights and the depths be potent,
Yet how can a nation at once be born? He heralds and proclaims.

Zech. 14 The radiant One shall redeem His people,
And then at the evening it shall be morn! He heralds and proclaims.

Is. 66 And up to Mount Zion shall march her saviors,
For Zion has travailed and now brings forth, He heralds and proclaims.

Is. 54 A voice is proclaiming in all her borders,
Your tent-place enlarge both to south and north, He heralds and proclaims.

---

of the Dead. This juxtaposition paraphrases the *Amida*, in which the reminder (אַזְכָּרָה) to God for rain is interpolated in the blessing of the Resurrection of the Dead. This theme is often echoed in the Gemara and the *Midrash* (*Ta'anit 7a, Bereshit Raba 13:6*). R. Yehuda Ben Yakar explains that the annual revitalization of the land resulting from life-giving rains is an apt metaphor for the ultimate Resurrection of the Dead.

שִׂימִי עַד דַּמֶּשֶׂק מִשְׁכְּנוֹתַיִךְ,
קַבְּלִי בָנַיִךְ וּבְנוֹתַיִךְ. מְבַשֵּׂר וְאוֹמֵר.

עִלְזִי חֲבַצֶּלֶת הַשָּׁרוֹן,
כִּי קָמוּ יְשֵׁנֵי חֶבְרוֹן. מְבַשֵּׂר וְאוֹמֵר.

פְּנוּ אֵלַי וְהִוָּשְׁעוּ,
הַיּוֹם אִם בְּקוֹלִי תִשְׁמָעוּ. מְבַשֵּׂר וְאוֹמֵר.

צֶמַח אִישׁ צֶמַח שְׁמוֹ,
הוּא דָוִד בְּעַצְמוֹ. מְבַשֵּׂר וְאוֹמֵר.

קוּמוּ כְּפוּשֵׁי עָפָר, ישעיה כו
הָקִיצוּ וְרַנְּנוּ שֹׁכְנֵי עָפָר. מְבַשֵּׂר וְאוֹמֵר.

רַבָּתִי עָם בְּהַמְלִיכוֹ, שמואל ב׳ כב
מגדּוֹל ישׁוּעוֹת מלכּוֹ. מְבַשֵּׂר וְאוֹמֵר.

שֵׁם רְשָׁעִים לְהַאֲבִיד, שמואל ב׳ כב
עֹשֶׂה־חֶסֶד לִמְשִׁיחוֹ לְדָוִד. מְבַשֵּׂר וְאוֹמֵר.

תְּנָה יְשׁוּעוֹת לְעַם עוֹלָם, שמואל ב׳ כב
לְדָוִד וּלְזַרְעוֹ עַד־עוֹלָם. מְבַשֵּׂר וְאוֹמֵר.

שליח ציבור *says three times then* קהל *repeats three times:*

קוֹל מְבַשֵּׂר מְבַשֵּׂר וְאוֹמֵר.

Beat the הושענות *against a chair or the floor five times, then say the following:*

תהלים כח / מלכים א׳ ח
הוֹשִׁיעָה אֶת־עַמֶּךָ, וּבָרֵךְ אֶת־נַחֲלָתֶךָ, וּרְעֵם וְנַשְּׂאֵם עַד־הָעוֹלָם: וְיִהְיוּ
דְבָרַי אֵלֶּה, אֲשֶׁר הִתְחַנַּנְתִּי לִפְנֵי יהוה, קְרֹבִים אֶל־יהוה אֱלֹהֵינוּ
יוֹמָם וָלָיְלָה, לַעֲשׂוֹת מִשְׁפַּט עַבְדּוֹ וּמִשְׁפַּט עַמּוֹ יִשְׂרָאֵל, דְּבַר־יוֹם בְּיוֹמוֹ:
לְמַעַן דַּעַת כָּל־עַמֵּי הָאָרֶץ כִּי יהוה הוּא הָאֱלֹהִים, אֵין עוֹד:

The ספרי תורה *are returned to the* ארון קודש, *which is then closed.*

יְהִי רָצוֹן מִלְּפָנֶיךָ יהוה אֱלֹהֵינוּ וֵאלֹהֵי אֲבוֹתֵינוּ, הַבּוֹחֵר בִּנְבִיאִים טוֹבִים
וּבְמִנְהֲגֵיהֶם הַטּוֹבִים, שֶׁתְּקַבֵּל בְּרַחֲמִים וּבְרָצוֹן אֶת תְּפִלָּתֵנוּ
וְהַקָּפוֹתֵינוּ. וּזְכָר לָנוּ זְכוּת שִׁבְעַת תְּמִימֶיךָ, וְתָסִיר מְחִצַּת הַבַּרְזֶל הַמַּפְסֶקֶת

BEATING THE *ARAVOT*
The imagery in this prayer references the Kabbalistic understanding of the procedure. Kabbalists see in the beating of the *arava*

Your dwelling extend unto far Damascus,
Your sons and your daughters again to take, He heralds and proclaims.

Exult and be joyful, O rose of Sharon,
Beholding the sleepers of Hebron wake. He heralds and proclaims.

Return unto Me and be saved, O Israel,
If only today you would hear My voice! He heralds and proclaims.

A man has sprung forth, and the Branch his name is –
Yea David himself, 'tis King David, rejoice! He heralds and proclaims.

Is. 26 Up, up! in the dust lie no longer buried!
Ye dwellers in ashes awake and sing! He heralds and proclaims.

I Shmuel 22 The desolate city shall rise imperial
To hail as aforetime her ransomed king. He heralds and proclaims.

I Shmuel 22 The name of the wicked shall God extinguish –
He grants His anointed celestial grace. He heralds and proclaims.

I Shmuel 22 Then make of our seed an eternal people,
Preserving for ever King David's race. He heralds and proclaims.

The Leader says three times then the congregation repeats three times:

THE VOICE of the herald, he heralds and proclaims.

Beat the Hoshanot against a chair or the floor five times, then say the following:

Ps. 28 הוֹשִׁיעָה SAVE YOUR PEOPLE and bless Your inheritance, and tend them and
I Kings 8 carry them forever. And may these my words with which I have entreated before the Lord, be near to the Lord our God day and night, so that He shall maintain the cause of His servant and of His people Israel day by day, that all the peoples of the earth may know that the Lord He is God, there is none else.

The Torah Scrolls are returned to the Ark, which is then closed.

יְהִי רָצוֹן MAY IT BE YOUR WILL, Lord our God and God of our fathers, Who has chosen our true prophets and their good teachings, in Your compassionate favor may it be Your will to accept our prayer and our *hakafot*. Recall for us the merit of Your seven devotees and free us from the iron curtain which divides

---

the dramatic end of a three-week process of detaching, constructing and softening the nascent new year, conceived as an empty, bounded vessel, for infusion with divine blessing symbolized by rains on the morrow; this symbolism is extended to the Jewish people vis a vis God and the individual supplicant toward his Maker (R. Aton Holzer).

יְהִי רָצוֹן / MAY IT BE YOUR WILL

מְחִצַּת הַבַּרְזֶל – *The iron curtain which divides us*

בֵּינֵינוּ וּבֵינֶךָ, וְתַאֲזִין שַׁוְעָתֵנוּ, וְתֵיטִיב לָנוּ הַחֲתִימָה, תּוֹלֶה אֶרֶץ עַל בְּלִימָה, וְחָתְמֵנוּ בְּסֵפֶר חַיִּים טוֹבִים. וְהַיּוֹם הַזֶּה תִּתֵּן בִּשְׁכִינַת עֻזֶּךָ חָמֵשׁ גְּבוּרוֹת מְמֻתָּקוֹת, עַל יְדֵי חֲבִיטַת עֲרָבָה מִנְהַג נְבִיאֶיךָ הַקְּדוֹשִׁים, וְתִתְעוֹרֵר הָאַהֲבָה בֵּינֵיהֶם. וּתְנַשְּׁקֵנוּ מִנְּשִׁיקוֹת פִּיךָ, מַמְתֶּקֶת כָּל הַגְּבוּרוֹת וְכָל הַדִּינִין. וְתָאִיר לִשְׁכִינַת עֻזֶּךָ בְּשֵׁם יו״ד הֵ״א וָא״ו שֶׁהוּא טַל אוֹרוֹת טַלֶּךָ, וּמִשָּׁם תַּשְׁפִּיעַ שֶׁפַע לְעַבְדְּךָ הַמִּתְפַּלֵּל לְפָנֶיךָ, שֶׁתַּאֲרִיךְ יָמָיו וְתִמְחַל לוֹ חֲטָאָיו וַעֲוֹנוֹתָיו וּפְשָׁעָיו. וְתִפְשֹׁט יְמִינְךָ וְיָדְךָ לְקַבְּלוֹ בִתְשׁוּבָה שְׁלֵמָה לְפָנֶיךָ. וְאוֹצָרְךָ הַטּוֹב
תִּפְתַּח לְהַשְׂבִּיעַ מַיִם נֶפֶשׁ שׁוֹקֵקָה, כְּמוֹ שֶׁכָּתוּב: יִפְתַּח יהוה לְךָ אֶת־אוֹצָרוֹ דברים כח
הַטּוֹב אֶת־הַשָּׁמַיִם לָתֵת מְטַר־אַרְצְךָ בְּעִתּוֹ, וּלְבָרֵךְ אֵת כָּל־מַעֲשֵׂה יָדֶךָ: אָמֵן.

קדיש שלם

ש״ץ: **יִתְגַּדַּל** וְיִתְקַדַּשׁ שְׁמֵהּ רַבָּא (קהל: אָמֵן), בְּעָלְמָא דִּי בְרָא כִרְעוּתֵהּ. וְיַמְלִיךְ מַלְכוּתֵהּ, בְּחַיֵּיכוֹן וּבְיוֹמֵיכוֹן וּבְחַיֵּי דְכָל בֵּית יִשְׂרָאֵל, בַּעֲגָלָא וּבִזְמַן קָרִיב, וְאִמְרוּ אָמֵן. (קהל: אָמֵן)

קהל וש״ץ: יְהֵא שְׁמֵהּ רַבָּא מְבָרַךְ לְעָלַם וּלְעָלְמֵי עָלְמַיָּא.

ש״ץ: יִתְבָּרַךְ וְיִשְׁתַּבַּח וְיִתְפָּאַר, וְיִתְרוֹמַם וְיִתְנַשֵּׂא וְיִתְהַדָּר וְיִתְעַלֶּה וְיִתְהַלָּל שְׁמֵהּ דְּקֻדְשָׁא בְּרִיךְ הוּא (קהל: בְּרִיךְ הוּא), לְעֵלָּא מִן כָּל בִּרְכָתָא וְשִׁירָתָא, תֻּשְׁבְּחָתָא וְנֶחֱמָתָא דַּאֲמִירָן בְּעָלְמָא, וְאִמְרוּ אָמֵן. (קהל: אָמֵן)

תִּתְקַבַּל צְלוֹתְהוֹן וּבָעוּתְהוֹן דְּכָל יִשְׂרָאֵל, קֳדָם אֲבוּהוֹן דִּי בִשְׁמַיָּא, וְאִמְרוּ אָמֵן. (קהל: אָמֵן)

יְהֵא שְׁלָמָא רַבָּא מִן שְׁמַיָּא וְחַיִּים, עָלֵינוּ וְעַל כָּל יִשְׂרָאֵל, וְאִמְרוּ אָמֵן. (קהל: אָמֵן)

Bow, take three steps back, as if taking leave of the Divine Presence, then bow, first left, then right, then center, while saying:

עֹשֶׂה שָׁלוֹם בִּמְרוֹמָיו, הוּא יַעֲשֶׂה שָׁלוֹם עָלֵינוּ, וְעַל כָּל יִשְׂרָאֵל, וְאִמְרוּ אָמֵן. (קהל: אָמֵן)

The שליח ציבור *continues with* קַוֵּה אֶל־ה׳ *on page 586.*

---

from You. This metaphor (famously invoked by Sir Winston Churchill in 1946 to describe the post-war division of Europe) is derived from the Gemara *Berachot* 32b: "Said R. Elazar (based

us from You. Hear our cry that we may be inscribed and sealed for good. May He Who suspends the world in space, inscribe and seal us for good in the book of good life. And on this day may You grant, with the Divine Presence of Your strength, five strictures sweetened by the beating of willows, the custom of Your holy prophets. Awaken love between them and kiss us with the kisses of Your mouth, which sweeten all the strictures and all the judgments. And illuminate the Divine Presence of Your strength with the [Tetragrammaton] Name *Y-K-V-K*, which corresponds to the dew – Your dew is like lights. And from there pour absolving grace upon Your servant prostrated before You, that my days may be lengthened, and my sins, iniquities, and transgressions forgiven. Stretch out Your right arm and Your hand to accept me in complete repentance before You. Open Your goodly treasury to satisfy with water a soul
Deut. 28 that thirsts. May there be fulfilled in me the verse as it is written: "The Lord will open for you His good treasure the heaven to give the rain of your land in its season, and to bless all the work of your hand." Amen.

FULL KADDISH

Leader: **יִתְגַּדַּל** EXALTED AND HALLOWED may God's great name be, in the world He created as He willed. May He reign in your lifetimes and in your days, and in the lifetime of the whole house of Israel, speedily and soon, and say, Amen.

All: May His great name be blessed forever and all time.

Leader: Blessed and praised, honored, extolled, glorified, adored and exalted above all be the name of the Holy One, blessed is He, (*Between Rosh Hashana & Yom Kippur:* above and) beyond any blessing, hymn, praise, or expressions of consolation that may be uttered in this world, and say, Amen.

May the prayers and pleas of all Israel be accepted before their Father Who is in heaven – and say, Amen.

May abundant peace descend from heaven, as well as life, for us and for all Israel, and say, Amen.

Bow, take three steps back, as if taking leave of the Divine Presence, then bow, first left, then right, then center, while saying:

May He Who makes peace in the highest heaven, make peace for us, and for all Israel, and say, Amen.

The Leader continues with "Wait for the Lord" on page 587.

---

on Ezekiel 4:3): 'since the day the Temple was destroyed an iron curtain has separated the Jewish people from their Father in heaven.'" (R. Basil Herring)

סדר הקפות

At מעריב *and* שחרית *of* שמחת תורה*, the following is said after* קדיש שלם *(page 522).*

אַתָּה הָרְאֵתָ לָדַעַת, כִּי יהוה הוּא הָאֱלֹהִים, אֵין עוֹד מִלְּבַדּוֹ: דברים ד

לְעֹשֵׂה נִפְלָאוֹת גְּדֹלוֹת לְבַדּוֹ, כִּי לְעוֹלָם חַסְדּוֹ: תהלים קלו

אֵין־כָּמוֹךָ בָאֱלֹהִים, אֲדֹנָי, וְאֵין כְּמַעֲשֶׂיךָ: תהלים פו

יְהִי כְבוֹד יהוה לְעוֹלָם, יִשְׂמַח יהוה בְּמַעֲשָׂיו: תהלים קד

יְהִי שֵׁם יהוה מְבֹרָךְ, מֵעַתָּה וְעַד־עוֹלָם: תהלים קיג

יְהִי יהוה אֱלֹהֵינוּ עִמָּנוּ, כַּאֲשֶׁר הָיָה עִם־אֲבֹתֵינוּ, אַל־יַעַזְבֵנוּ וְאַל־יִטְּשֵׁנוּ: מלכים א׳ ח

וְאִמְרוּ, הוֹשִׁיעֵנוּ אֱלֹהֵי יִשְׁעֵנוּ, וְקַבְּצֵנוּ וְהַצִּילֵנוּ מִן־הַגּוֹיִם, לְהֹדוֹת לְשֵׁם קָדְשֶׁךָ, לְהִשְׁתַּבֵּחַ בִּתְהִלָּתֶךָ: דברי הימים א׳ טז

יהוה מֶלֶךְ, יהוה מָלָךְ, יהוה יִמְלֹךְ לְעֹלָם וָעֶד.

יהוה עֹז לְעַמּוֹ יִתֵּן, יהוה יְבָרֵךְ אֶת־עַמּוֹ בַשָּׁלוֹם: תהלים כט

וְיִהְיוּ נָא אֲמָרֵינוּ לְרָצוֹן, לִפְנֵי אֲדוֹן כֹּל.

The ארון קודש *is opened.*

וַיְהִי בִּנְסֹעַ הָאָרֹן וַיֹּאמֶר מֹשֶׁה, קוּמָה יהוה וְיָפֻצוּ אֹיְבֶיךָ וְיָנֻסוּ מְשַׂנְאֶיךָ מִפָּנֶיךָ: במדבר י

קוּמָה יהוה לִמְנוּחָתֶךָ, אַתָּה וַאֲרוֹן עֻזֶּךָ: תהלים קלב

כֹּהֲנֶיךָ יִלְבְּשׁוּ־צֶדֶק, וַחֲסִידֶיךָ יְרַנֵּנוּ:

בַּעֲבוּר דָּוִד עַבְדֶּךָ, אַל־תָּשֵׁב פְּנֵי מְשִׁיחֶךָ:

וְאָמַר בַּיּוֹם הַהוּא, הִנֵּה אֱלֹהֵינוּ זֶה קִוִּינוּ לוֹ, וְיוֹשִׁיעֵנוּ, זֶה יהוה קִוִּינוּ לוֹ, נָגִילָה וְנִשְׂמְחָה בִּישׁוּעָתוֹ: ישעיה כה

מַלְכוּתְךָ מַלְכוּת כָּל־עֹלָמִים, וּמֶמְשַׁלְתְּךָ בְּכָל־דּוֹר וָדֹר: תהלים קמה

כִּי מִצִּיּוֹן תֵּצֵא תוֹרָה, וּדְבַר־יהוה מִירוּשָׁלָםִ: ישעיה ב

אַב הָרַחֲמִים, הֵיטִיבָה בִרְצוֹנְךָ אֶת־צִיּוֹן, תִּבְנֶה חוֹמוֹת יְרוּשָׁלָםִ: תהלים נא

כִּי בְךָ לְבַד בָּטָחְנוּ, מֶלֶךְ אֵל רָם וְנִשָּׂא, אֲדוֹן עוֹלָמִים.

שמחת תורה / SIMHAT TORAH

Both the Vilna Gaon and the Ba'al HaTanya understood the rejoicing of Simḥat Torah as reflecting the words of the verse "the King

HAKAFOT

At Ma'ariv and Shaḥarit of Simḥat Torah the following is said after Full Kaddish (page 523).

Deut. 4 אַתָּה TO YOU it was shown, that you might know that the Lord, He is
Ps. 136 God; there is none else beside Him. To Him Who alone performs great
Ps. 86 wonders, for His loving-kindness is forever. There is none like You
Ps. 104 among the powers, O Lord, and there are none like Your deeds. May
the glory of the Lord be forever, may the Lord rejoice in His works.
Ps. 113 Blessed be the name of the Lord from now and forevermore. The Lord
I Kings 8 our God be with us, as He was with our fathers; let Him not leave us,
I Chr. 16 nor forsake us. And say, "Save us, God of our salvation, and gather us
together and deliver us from the nations, that we may give thanks to
Your holy name, that we may triumph in Your praise." The Lord reigns;
Ps. 29 the Lord reigned; the Lord shall reign for ever and ever. The Lord will
give strength to His people. The Lord will bless His people with peace.
And may our words find favor before the Master of all.

The Ark is opened.

Num. 10 וַיְהִי WHEN THE ARK moved forward, Moses would say, "Arise, O
Lord, and may Your enemies be dispersed, and they who hate You
Ps. 132 flee from You." Arise, O Lord, to Your resting place, You and the Ark
of Your strength. May Your priests be clothed in righteousness, and
may Your pious ones shout for joy. For the sake of David Your servant,
Is. 25 do not turn away the face of Your anointed. And it shall be said in
that day: "This is our God, for Whom we waited, that He might save
us; this is the Lord, for Whom we waited, we will be glad and rejoice
Ps. 145 in His salvation." Your kingdom is a kingdom for all times, and Your
Is. 2 dominion is for every generation. For from Zion shall go forth Torah,
and the word of the Lord from Jerusalem.

Ps. 51 אַב FATHER OF MERCY, beautify Zion with Your favor. Build the walls of Jerusalem. We trust in You alone, King, God, sublime and exalted, Master of worlds.

---

has brought me to His chambers; I will be gladdened and rejoice in Him (Song of Songs 1:4). Yom Kippur is the day on which we "come into God's chambers" to achieve extraordinary closeness and intimacy with Him, to be followed some days later by Simḥat Torah on which we celebrate that reconciliation with God (R. Joseph B. Soloveitchik).

All the ספרי תורה *are taken from the* ארון קודש.

First הקפה

תהלים קיח

אָנָּא יהוה הוֹשִׁיעָה נָּא,
אָנָּא יהוה הַצְלִיחָה נָא
אָנָּא יהוה עֲנֵנוּ בְּיוֹם קָרְאֵנוּ.

אֱלֹהֵי הָרוּחוֹת הוֹשִׁיעָה נָּא,
בּוֹחֵן לְבָבוֹת הַצְלִיחָה נָא
גּוֹאֵל חָזָק עֲנֵנוּ בְּיוֹם קָרְאֵנוּ.

Second הקפה

דּוֹבֵר צְדָקוֹת הוֹשִׁיעָה נָּא,
הָדוּר בִּלְבוּשׁוֹ הַצְלִיחָה נָא
וָתִיק וְחָסִיד עֲנֵנוּ בְּיוֹם קָרְאֵנוּ.

Third הקפה

זַךְ וְיָשָׁר הוֹשִׁיעָה נָּא,
חַנּוּן וְרַחוּם הַצְלִיחָה נָא
טוֹב וּמֵטִיב עֲנֵנוּ בְּיוֹם קָרְאֵנוּ.

Fourth הקפה

יוֹדֵעַ מַחֲשָׁבוֹת הוֹשִׁיעָה נָּא,
כַּבִּיר כֹּחַ הַצְלִיחָה נָא
לוֹבֵשׁ צְדָקוֹת עֲנֵנוּ בְּיוֹם קָרְאֵנוּ.

Fifth הקפה

מֶלֶךְ עוֹלָמִים הוֹשִׁיעָה נָּא,
נָאוֹר וְאַדִּיר הַצְלִיחָה נָא
סוֹמֵךְ וְסוֹעֵד עֲנֵנוּ בְּיוֹם קָרְאֵנוּ.

Sixth הקפה

עוֹזֵר דַּלִּים הוֹשִׁיעָה נָּא,
פּוֹדֶה וּמַצִּיל הַצְלִיחָה נָא
צוּר עוֹלָמִים עֲנֵנוּ בְּיוֹם קָרְאֵנוּ.

All the Torah scrolls are taken from the Ark.

First Hakafa

Ps. 118 אָנָּא WE BESEECH YOU, Lord, please save us.
We beseech You, Lord, please prosper us.
We beseech You, Lord, answer us on the day we call.

God of all spirits, please save us.
Questing our hearts, please prosper us.
Invincible Redeemer, answer us on the day we call.

Second Hakafa

Justice declaring, please save us.
Clad in glory, please prosper us.
Omnipotent yet loving, answer us on the day we call.

Third Hakafa

Pure and upright, please save us.
Gracious to the poor, please prosper us.
Good and benevolent, answer us on the day we call.

Fourth Hakafa

Diviner of thoughts, please save us.
Mighty and resplendent, please prosper us.
Vested in righteousness, answer us on the day we call.

Fifth Hakafa

Regal eternally, please save us.
Resplendent in glory, please prosper us.
Upholder of the falling, answer us on the day we call.

Sixth Hakafa

Helper of the needy, please save us.
Redeemer and Deliverer, please prosper us.
Rock of eternity, answer us on the day we call.

Seventh הקפה

קָדוֹשׁ וְנוֹרָא הוֹשִׁיעָה נָּא,
רַחוּם וְחַנּוּן הַצְלִיחָה נָא
שׁוֹכֵן שְׁחָקִים עֲנֵנוּ בְּיוֹם קָרְאֵנוּ.

תּוֹמֵךְ תְּמִימִים הוֹשִׁיעָה נָּא,
תַּקִּיף לָעַד הַצְלִיחָה נָא
תָּמִים בְּמַעֲשָׂיו עֲנֵנוּ בְּיוֹם קָרְאֵנוּ.

The ספרי תורה *are returned to the* ארון קודש *except for the one used in the* קריאת התורה*.*
At מעריב*, three (in some congregations, five) are called up and the* קריאה
of וְזֹאת הַבְּרָכָה *(**page 1165**) is read. During* שחרית*, the prevalent custom is to call up every adult male in the congregation.*

In most congregations, this piyut is said during the הקפות *or after* קריאת התורה*.*

שִׂישׂוּ וְשִׂמְחוּ בְּשִׂמְחַת תּוֹרָה
וּתְנוּ כָבוֹד לַתּוֹרָה
כִּי טוֹב סַחְרָהּ מִכָּל סְחוֹרָה
מִפָּז וּמִפְּנִינִים יְקָרָה.
נָגִיל וְנָשִׂישׂ בְּזֹאת הַתּוֹרָה / כִּי הִיא לָנוּ עֹז וְאוֹרָה.

אֲהַלֵּל אֱלֹהַי וְאֶשְׂמְחָה בוֹ
וְאָשִׂימָה תִקְוָתִי בּוֹ
אֲהוֹדֶנּוּ בְּסוֹד עַם קְרוֹבוֹ
אֱלֹהֵי צוּרִי, אֶחֱסֶה בּוֹ.
נָגִיל וְנָשִׂישׂ בְּזֹאת הַתּוֹרָה / כִּי הִיא לָנוּ עֹז וְאוֹרָה.

בְּכָל לֵב אֲרַנֵּן צִדְקוֹתֶיךָ
וַאֲסַפְּרָה תְּהִלָּתֶךָ
בְּעוֹדִי אַגִּיד נִפְלְאוֹתֶיךָ
עַל חַסְדְּךָ וְעַל אֲמִתֶּךָ.
נָגִיל וְנָשִׂישׂ בְּזֹאת הַתּוֹרָה / כִּי הִיא לָנוּ עֹז וְאוֹרָה.

Seventh Hakafa

Holy and revered One, please save us.
Forbearing and gracious, please prosper us.
Keeper of the covenant, answer us on the day we call.

Stay of the innocent, please save us.
Eternal in strength, please prosper us.
Perfect in His ways, answer us on the day we call.

The Torah scrolls are returned to the Ark except for the one used in the Torah Reading. At Ma'ariv, three (in some congregations, five) are called up and the "VeZot HaBerakha" Torah portion (page 1165) is read. During Shaḥarit, the prevalent custom is to call up every adult male in the congregation.

In most congregations, this piyut is said during the Hakafot or after the Torah Reading.

שִׂישׂוּ BE HAPPY, rejoice on Simḥat Torah,
and thereby give honor to Israel's Torah.
For rich its reward beyond treasures untold,
far richer than jewels and finest of gold.

In this our Torah we rejoice and delight,
for it is the source of our strength and our light.

FOREVER IN God is my hope which upraises
as with gladness and joy I sing of His praises.
Chanted by Israel, nigh unto Him
Who is Rock divine. My trust is in Him.

In this our Torah we rejoice and delight,
for it is the source of our strength and our light.

I SING of Your goodness with heart rising to You,
for I would discourse on the praises of You.
While life breathes in me of Your wonders I'll sing
and Your kindness unfailing and truth, divine King.

In this our Torah we rejoice and delight,
for it is the source of our strength and our light.

התרת נדרים

On the morning before ראש השנה*, one should annul vows before three men, who sit as judges. Women should substitute with the word immediately following the slash.*

שִׁמְעוּ נָא רַבּוֹתַי (דַּיָּנִים מֻמְחִים), כָּל נֶדֶר אוֹ שְׁבוּעָה אוֹ אִסָּר אוֹ קוֹנָם אוֹ חֵרֶם שֶׁנָּדַרְתִּי אוֹ נִשְׁבַּעְתִּי בְּהָקִיץ אוֹ בַחֲלוֹם, אוֹ נִשְׁבַּעְתִּי בְּשֵׁמוֹת הַקְּדוֹשִׁים שֶׁאֵינָם נִמְחָקִים וּבְשֵׁם הוי״ה בָּרוּךְ הוּא, וְכָל מִינֵי נְזִירוּת שֶׁקִּבַּלְתִּי עָלַי וַאֲפִלּוּ נְזִירוּת שִׁמְשׁוֹן, וְכָל שׁוּם אִסּוּר וַאֲפִלּוּ אִסּוּר הֲנָאָה שֶׁאָסַרְתִּי עָלַי אוֹ עַל אֲחֵרִים בְּכָל לָשׁוֹן שֶׁל אִסּוּר בֵּין בִּלְשׁוֹן אִסּוּר אוֹ חֵרֶם אוֹ קוֹנָם, וְכָל שׁוּם קַבָּלָה אֲפִלּוּ שֶׁל מִצְוָה שֶׁקִּבַּלְתִּי עָלַי בֵּין בִּלְשׁוֹן נֶדֶר בֵּין בִּלְשׁוֹן נְדָבָה בֵּין בִּלְשׁוֹן שְׁבוּעָה בֵּין בִּלְשׁוֹן נְזִירוּת בֵּין בְּכָל לָשׁוֹן, וְגַם הַנַּעֲשֶׂה בִּתְקִיעַת כַּף. בֵּין כָּל נֶדֶר וּבֵין כָּל נְדָבָה וּבֵין שׁוּם מִנְהָג שֶׁל מִצְוָה שֶׁנָּהַגְתִּי אֶת עַצְמִי, וְכָל מוֹצָא שְׂפָתַי שֶׁיָּצָא מִפִּי אוֹ שֶׁנָּדַרְתִּי וְגָמַרְתִּי בְלִבִּי לַעֲשׂוֹת שׁוּם מִצְוָה מֵהַמִּצְוֹת אוֹ אֵיזוֹ הַנְהָגָה טוֹבָה אוֹ אֵיזֶה דָבָר טוֹב שֶׁנָּהַגְתִּי שָׁלֹשׁ פְּעָמִים, וְלֹא הִתְנֵיתִי שֶׁיְּהֵא בְּלִי נֶדֶר. הֵן דָּבָר שֶׁעָשִׂיתִי, הֵן עַל עַצְמִי הֵן עַל אֲחֵרִים, הֵן אוֹתָן הַיְדוּעִים לִי הֵן אוֹתָן שֶׁכְּבָר שָׁכַחְתִּי. בְּכֻלְּהוֹן אִתְחֲרַטְנָא בְהוֹן מֵעִקָּרָא, וְשׁוֹאֵל/וְשׁוֹאֶלֶת וּמְבַקֵּשׁ/וּמְבַקֶּשֶׁת אֲנִי מִמַּעֲלַתְכֶם הַתָּרָה עֲלֵיהֶם, כִּי יָרֵאתִי פֶּן אֶכָּשֵׁל וְנִלְכַּדְתִּי, חַס וְשָׁלוֹם, בַּעֲוֹן נְדָרִים וּשְׁבוּעוֹת וּנְזִירוֹת וַחֲרָמוֹת וְאִסּוּרִין וְקוֹנָמוֹת וְהַסְכָּמוֹת. וְאֵין אֲנִי תוֹהֵא/תוֹהָא, חַס וְשָׁלוֹם, עַל קִיּוּם הַמַּעֲשִׂים הַטּוֹבִים הָהֵם שֶׁעָשִׂיתִי, רַק אֲנִי מִתְחָרֵט/מִתְחָרֶטֶת עַל קַבָּלַת הָעִנְיָנִים בִּלְשׁוֹן נֶדֶר אוֹ שְׁבוּעָה אוֹ נְזִירוּת אוֹ אִסּוּר אוֹ חֵרֶם אוֹ קוֹנָם אוֹ הַסְכָּמָה אוֹ קַבָּלָה בְלֵב, וּמִתְחָרֵט/וּמִתְחָרֶטֶת אֲנִי עַל

הַתָּרַת נְדָרִים / **RELEASE FROM VOWS**
Release from vows reflects the essence of repentance. When a person regrets having taken a vow, the proper halakhic mechanism

RELEASE FROM VOWS

On the morning before Rosh HaShana, one should annul vows before three men, who sit as judges.

שִׁמְעוּ נָא LISTEN, PLEASE, my esteemed masters (expert judges): every vow or oath or prohibition or restriction or ban that I have vowed or sworn, whether awake or in a dream, or that I swore with one of the holy names that may not be erased, or by the holy four-letter name of God, blessed be He, or any naziriteship that I accepted on myself, even a naziriteship like that of Samson, or any prohibition, even against enjoyment, whether I forbade it to myself or others, by any expression of prohibition, whether using the language of prohibition or restriction or ban, or any positive commitment, even to perform a [non-obligatory] commandment, that I undertook by way of a vow or voluntary undertaking or oath or naziriteship or any other such expression, whether it was done by handshake or vow or voluntary undertaking or commandment-mandated custom I have customarily practiced, or any utterance that I have verbalized, or any non-obligatory commandment or good practice or conduct I have vowed and resolved in my heart to do, and have done three times without specifying that it does not have the force of a vow, whether it relates to myself or others, both those known to me and those I have already forgotten – regarding all of them, I hereby express my retroactive regret, and ask and seek their annulment from you, my eminences. For I fear that I may stumble and be trapped, heaven forbid, in the sin of vows, oaths, naziriteships, bans, prohibitions, restrictions and agreements. I do not regret, heaven forbid, the performance of the good deeds I have done. I regret, rather, having accepted them on myself in the

---

to remove the vow involves finding a פֶּתַח or "opening," so that it can be declared that the vow was originally undertaken in error. This is analogous to repentance, in which we regret our past words or actions, and seek to undo or cancel them by declaring that they were done בִּשְׁגָגָה (unintentionally) – not reflecting our true selves (R. Joseph B. Soloveitchik).

זֶה שֶׁלֹּא אָמַרְתִּי הִנְנִי עוֹשֶׂה/עוֹשָׂה דָּבָר זֶה בְּלִי נֶדֶר וּשְׁבוּעָה וּנְזִירוּת וְחֵרֶם וְאִסּוּר וְקוֹנָם וְקַבָּלָה בְלֵב.

לָכֵן אֲנִי שׁוֹאֵל/שׁוֹאֶלֶת הַתָּרָה בְּכֻלְּהוֹן.

אֲנִי מִתְחָרֵט /מִתְחָרֶטֶת עַל כָּל הַנִּזְכָּר, בֵּין אִם הָיוּ הַמַּעֲשִׂים מִדְּבָרִים הַנּוֹגְעִים בְּמָמוֹן, בֵּין מֵהַדְּבָרִים הַנּוֹגְעִים בְּגוּף, בֵּין מֵהַדְּבָרִים הַנּוֹגְעִים אֶל הַנְּשָׁמָה. בְּכֻלְּהוֹן אֲנִי מִתְחָרֵט/מִתְחָרֶטֶת עַל לְשׁוֹן נֶדֶר וּשְׁבוּעָה וּנְזִירוּת וְאִסּוּר וְחֵרֶם וְקוֹנָם וְקַבָּלָה בְלֵב. וְהִנֵּה מִצַּד הַדִּין הַמִּתְחָרֵט וְהַמְבַקֵּשׁ הַתָּרָה צָרִיךְ לִפְרֹט הַנֶּדֶר, אַךְ דְּעוּ נָא רַבּוֹתַי, כִּי אִי אֶפְשָׁר לְפָרְטָם, כִּי רַבִּים הֵם. וְאֵין אֲנִי מְבַקֵּשׁ/מְבַקֶּשֶׁת הַתָּרָה עַל אוֹתָם הַנְּדָרִים שֶׁאֵין לְהַתִּיר אוֹתָם, עַל כֵּן יִהְיוּ נָא בְעֵינֵיכֶם כְּאִלּוּ הָיִיתִי פוֹרְטָם.

The judges repeat three times:

הַכֹּל יִהְיוּ מֻתָּרִים לָךְ, הַכֹּל מְחוּלִים לָךְ, הַכֹּל שְׁרוּיִים לָךְ. אֵין כָּאן לֹא נֶדֶר וְלֹא שְׁבוּעָה וְלֹא נְזִירוּת וְלֹא חֵרֶם וְלֹא אִסּוּר וְלֹא קוֹנָם וְלֹא נִדּוּי וְלֹא שַׁמְתָּא וְלֹא אָרוּר. אֲבָל יֵשׁ כָּאן מְחִילָה וּסְלִיחָה וְכַפָּרָה. וּכְשֵׁם שֶׁמַּתִּירִים בְּבֵית דִּין שֶׁל מַטָּה, כָּךְ יִהְיוּ מֻתָּרִים מִבֵּית דִּין שֶׁל מַעְלָה.

The petitioner declares:

הֲרֵי אֲנִי מוֹסֵר/מוֹסֶרֶת מוֹדָעָה לִפְנֵיכֶם, וַאֲנִי מְבַטֵּל/מְבַטֶּלֶת מִכָּאן וּלְהַבָּא כָּל הַנְּדָרִים וְכָל שְׁבוּעוֹת וּנְזִירוּת וְאִסּוּרִין וְקוֹנָמוֹת וַחֲרָמוֹת וְהַסְכָּמוֹת וְקַבָּלָה בְלֵב שֶׁאֲקַבֵּל עָלַי בְּעַצְמִי, הֵן בְּהָקִיץ הֵן בַּחֲלוֹם, חוּץ מִנִּדְרֵי תַעֲנִית בִּשְׁעַת מִנְחָה. וּבְאִם אֶשְׁכַּח לְתְנַאי מוֹדָעָה הַזֹּאת וְאֶדֹּר מֵהַיּוֹם עוֹד, מֵעַתָּה אֲנִי מִתְחָרֵט/מִתְחָרֶטֶת עֲלֵיהֶם וּמַתְנֶה/וּמַתְנָה עֲלֵיהֶם שֶׁיִּהְיוּ כֻלָּן בְּטֵלִין וּמְבֻטָּלִין, לָא שְׁרִירִין וְלָא קַיָּמִין, וְלָא יְהוֹן חָלִין כְּלָל וּכְלָל. בְּכֻלָּן אִתְחֲרַטְנָא בְּהוֹן מֵעַתָּה וְעַד עוֹלָם.

language of vow, oath, naziriteship, prohibition, ban, restriction, agreement or acceptance of the heart.

Therefore I request annulment for them all.

אֲנִי מִתְחָרֵט I REGRET all these things I have mentioned, whether they related to monetary matters, or to the body or to the soul. In relation to them all, I regret the language of vow, oath, naziriteship, prohibition, ban, penalty, and acceptance of the heart. To be sure, according to the law, one who regrets and seeks annulment must specify the vow [from which he seeks release]. But please know, my esteemed masters, that it is impossible to specify them, for they are many. I do not seek release from vows that cannot be annulled. Therefore, may it be in your eyes as if I had specified them.

The judges repeat three times:

הַכֹּל MAY ALL be permitted to you. May all be forgiven you. May all be allowed to you. There is now no vow, oath, naziriteship, ban, prohibition, penalty, ostracism, excommunication, or curse. There is now pardon, forgiveness and atonement. And just as the earthly court has granted permission, so may the heavenly court grant permission.

The petitioner declares:

הֲרֵי BEHOLD I make a formal declaration before you that I cancel from now onward all vows and all oaths, naziriteships, prohibitions, penalties, bans, agreements and acceptances of the heart that I may accept upon myself, whether awake or in a dream, except a vow to fast that I undertake at the time of the afternoon prayer. If I forget the conditions of this declaration and make a vow from this day onward, as of now I retroactively regret them and declare them to be null and void, without effect or validity, and they shall have no force whatsoever. Regarding them all, I regret them from now and forever.

קידוש לליל ראש השנה

On שבת *add:*

בראשית א *Quietly* וַיְהִי־עֶרֶב וַיְהִי־בֹקֶר

בראשית ב **יוֹם הַשִּׁשִּׁי:** וַיְכֻלּוּ הַשָּׁמַיִם וְהָאָרֶץ וְכָל־צְבָאָם: וַיְכַל אֱלֹהִים בַּיּוֹם הַשְּׁבִיעִי מְלַאכְתּוֹ אֲשֶׁר עָשָׂה, וַיִּשְׁבֹּת בַּיּוֹם הַשְּׁבִיעִי מִכָּל־מְלַאכְתּוֹ, אֲשֶׁר עָשָׂה: וַיְבָרֶךְ אֱלֹהִים אֶת־יוֹם הַשְּׁבִיעִי, וַיְקַדֵּשׁ אֹתוֹ, כִּי בוֹ שָׁבַת מִכָּל־מְלַאכְתּוֹ, אֲשֶׁר־בָּרָא אֱלֹהִים, לַעֲשׂוֹת:

On other evenings the קידוש *starts here:*

When making קידוש *for others, add:*

סַבְרִי מָרָנָן וְרַבָּנָן וְרַבּוֹתַי

בָּרוּךְ אַתָּה יהוה אֱלֹהֵינוּ מֶלֶךְ הָעוֹלָם, בּוֹרֵא פְּרִי הַגָּפֶן.

On שבת*, add the words in parentheses.*

בָּרוּךְ אַתָּה יהוה אֱלֹהֵינוּ מֶלֶךְ הָעוֹלָם, אֲשֶׁר בָּחַר בָּנוּ מִכָּל עָם, וְרוֹמְמָנוּ מִכָּל לָשׁוֹן, וְקִדְּשָׁנוּ בְּמִצְוֹתָיו, וַתִּתֶּן לָנוּ יהוה אֱלֹהֵינוּ בְּאַהֲבָה, אֶת יוֹם (הַשַּׁבָּת הַזֶּה וְאֶת יוֹם) הַזִּכָּרוֹן הַזֶּה, יוֹם (זִכְרוֹן) תְּרוּעָה, (בְּאַהֲבָה) מִקְרָא קֹדֶשׁ, זֵכֶר לִיצִיאַת מִצְרָיִם, כִּי בָנוּ בָחַרְתָּ וְאוֹתָנוּ קִדַּשְׁתָּ מִכָּל הָעַמִּים, וּדְבָרְךָ אֱמֶת וְקַיָּם לָעַד. בָּרוּךְ אַתָּה יהוה, מֶלֶךְ עַל כָּל הָאָרֶץ, מְקַדֵּשׁ (הַשַּׁבָּת וְ) יִשְׂרָאֵל וְיוֹם הַזִּכָּרוֹן.

On מוצאי שבת*, the following* הבדלה *is added:*

בָּרוּךְ אַתָּה יהוה אֱלֹהֵינוּ מֶלֶךְ הָעוֹלָם, בּוֹרֵא מְאוֹרֵי הָאֵשׁ.

בָּרוּךְ אַתָּה יהוה אֱלֹהֵינוּ מֶלֶךְ הָעוֹלָם, הַמַּבְדִּיל בֵּין קֹדֶשׁ לְחֹל, בֵּין אוֹר לְחֹשֶׁךְ, בֵּין יִשְׂרָאֵל לָעַמִּים, בֵּין יוֹם הַשְּׁבִיעִי לְשֵׁשֶׁת יְמֵי הַמַּעֲשֶׂה. בֵּין קְדֻשַּׁת שַׁבָּת לִקְדֻשַּׁת יוֹם טוֹב הִבְדַּלְתָּ, וְאֶת יוֹם הַשְּׁבִיעִי מִשֵּׁשֶׁת יְמֵי הַמַּעֲשֶׂה קִדַּשְׁתָּ, הִבְדַּלְתָּ וְקִדַּשְׁתָּ אֶת עַמְּךָ יִשְׂרָאֵל בִּקְדֻשָּׁתֶךָ. בָּרוּךְ אַתָּה יהוה, הַמַּבְדִּיל בֵּין קֹדֶשׁ לְקֹדֶשׁ.

The following blessing is said on both nights of ראש השנה*. On the second night, new fruit is placed on the table, and one should have in mind that the blessing is also on the new fruit.*

בָּרוּךְ אַתָּה יהוה אֱלֹהֵינוּ מֶלֶךְ הָעוֹלָם, שֶׁהֶחֱיָנוּ וְקִיְּמָנוּ וְהִגִּיעָנוּ לַזְּמַן הַזֶּה.

It is customary for all present to drink of the wine.

For "*Laws of Kiddush*" see page 426.
For laws of *Leḥem Mishneh*, see page 429.

KIDDUSH FOR ROSH HASHANA EVENING

On Shabbat add:

Gen. 1 *Quietly:* And it was evening, and it was morning.

Gen. 2 יוֹם הַשִּׁשִּׁי THE SIXTH DAY. Thus the heavens and the earth were finished, and all their multitudes. And by the seventh day God ended His work which He had done; and He rested on the seventh day from all His work which He had done. And God blessed the seventh day and sanctified it: because on it He rested from all the work He had created and performed.

On other evenings the Kiddush starts here:

When saying Kiddush for others, add:

With your permission, my masters, rabbis and esteemed companions:

בָּרוּךְ BLESSED ARE YOU, Lord, our God, King of the universe, Who creates the fruit of the vine.

On Shabbat, add the words in parentheses.

בָּרוּךְ BLESSED ARE YOU, Lord, our God, King of the universe, Who has chosen us from all peoples and raised us above every language, and sanctified us with His commandments. You have given us, Lord our God, with love, this (Sabbath day and) Day of Remembrance, a day of (remembrance of) blowing the shofar (with love), a holy convocation, a remembrance of the Exodus from Egypt. For You have chosen us and sanctified us from among all peoples, and Your word is true and endures forever. Blessed are You, Lord, King over all the earth, Who sanctifies (the Sabbath and) Israel and the Day of Remembrance.

On Motza'ei Shabbat, the following Havdala is added:

בָּרוּךְ BLESSED ARE YOU, Lord, our god, King of the universe, Who creates the lights of fire.

בָּרוּךְ BLESSED ARE YOU, Lord, our God, King of the universe, Who separates sacred from secular, light from darkness, Israel from the nations, and the seventh day from the six days of labor. Between the holiness of the Sabbath and the holiness of the festivals You have made a separation, and You have sanctified the seventh day above the six days of labor. You have separated and sanctified Your people Israel with Your holiness. Blessed are You, Lord, Who separates sacred from sacred.

The following blessing is said on both nights of Rosh HaShana. On the second night, new fruit is placed on the table, and one should have in mind that the blessing is also on the new fruit.

בָּרוּךְ BLESSED ARE YOU, Lord, our God, King of the universe, Who has given us life, sustained us, and brought us to this time.

It is customary for all present to drink of the wine.

On the night of ראש השנה *it is customary to dip the first piece of* חלה *into honey. After the* חלה *has been eaten, a piece of apple dipped in honey is given to each participant and the following blessing is recited:*

בָּרוּךְ אַתָּה יהוה אֱלֹהֵינוּ מֶלֶךְ הָעוֹלָם, בּוֹרֵא פְּרִי הָעֵץ.

After eating some of the apple and honey, say:

יְהִי רָצוֹן מִלְּפָנֶיךָ יהוה אֱלֹהֵינוּ וֵאלֹהֵי אֲבוֹתֵינוּ, שֶׁתְּחַדֵּשׁ עָלֵינוּ שָׁנָה טוֹבָה וּמְתוּקָה.

סימנים

Some have the custom to eat the following symbolic foods:

תמרים

יְהִי רָצוֹן מִלְּפָנֶיךָ יהוה אֱלֹהֵינוּ וֵאלֹהֵי אֲבוֹתֵינוּ שֶׁיִּתַּמּוּ שׂוֹנְאֵינוּ.

רימון

יְהִי רָצוֹן מִלְּפָנֶיךָ יהוה אֱלֹהֵינוּ וֵאלֹהֵי אֲבוֹתֵינוּ שֶׁנִּרְבֶּה זְכֻיּוֹת כְּרִמּוֹן.

רוביא (חילבה)

בָּרוּךְ אַתָּה יהוה אֱלֹהֵינוּ מֶלֶךְ הָעוֹלָם, בּוֹרֵא פְּרִי הָאֲדָמָה.

יְהִי רָצוֹן מִלְּפָנֶיךָ יהוה אֱלֹהֵינוּ וֵאלֹהֵי אֲבוֹתֵינוּ שֶׁיִּרְבּוּ זְכֻיּוֹתֵינוּ.

כרתי (כרישה)

יְהִי רָצוֹן מִלְּפָנֶיךָ יהוה אֱלֹהֵינוּ וֵאלֹהֵי אֲבוֹתֵינוּ שֶׁיִּכָּרְתוּ שׂוֹנְאֵינוּ.

סלק

יְהִי רָצוֹן מִלְּפָנֶיךָ יהוה אֱלֹהֵינוּ וֵאלֹהֵי אֲבוֹתֵינוּ שֶׁיִּסְתַּלְּקוּ שׂוֹנְאֵינוּ.

קרא (דלעת קטנה)

יְהִי רָצוֹן מִלְּפָנֶיךָ יהוה אֱלֹהֵינוּ וֵאלֹהֵי אֲבוֹתֵינוּ שֶׁתִּקְרַע רֹעַ גְּזַר דִּינֵנוּ, וְיִקָּרְאוּ לְפָנֶיךָ זְכֻיּוֹתֵינוּ.

ראש כבש, או דג

יְהִי רָצוֹן מִלְּפָנֶיךָ יהוה אֱלֹהֵינוּ וֵאלֹהֵי אֲבוֹתֵינוּ שֶׁנִּהְיֶה לְרֹאשׁ וְלֹא לְזָנָב.

דגים

יְהִי רָצוֹן מִלְּפָנֶיךָ יהוה אֱלֹהֵינוּ וֵאלֹהֵי אֲבוֹתֵינוּ שֶׁנִּפְרֶה וְנִרְבֶּה כְּדָגִים.

סִימָנָא מִילְתָא / SYMBOLIC FOODS
Various symbolic foods are eaten at the festive meal on the first night of Rosh HaShana. The choice of these foods sometimes reflects their Hebrew (or even Yiddish) name, or alternatively reflects one or another characteristic of that food item, suggestive of a desired outcome in the coming year. It should be noted that Leviticus 19:26 and Deuteronomy 18:10 forbid any form of superstition or omens to influence future events. Nonetheless use of these symbolic foods is permitted by various commentators for

On the night of Rosh HaShana it is customary to dip the first piece of ḥalla into honey. After the ḥalla has been eaten, a piece of apple dipped in honey is given to each participant and the following blessing is recited:

בָּרוּךְ BLESSED ARE YOU, Lord, our God, King of the universe, Who creates the fruit of the tree.

After eating some of the apple and honey, say:

יְהִי רָצוֹן MAY IT BE Your will, Lord our God and God of our fathers, that You renew for us a good and sweet year.

SYMBOLIC FOODS

Some have the custom to eat the following symbolic foods:

ON DATES

יְהִי רָצוֹן MAY it be Your will, Lord our God and God of our fathers, that our enemies meet their end.

ON POMEGRANATE

יְהִי רָצוֹן MAY it be Your will, Lord our God and God of our fathers, that we produce as much merit as the pomegranate produces seeds.

ON BLACK-EYED BEANS OR CARROTS

בָּרוּךְ BLESSED are You, Lord our God, King of the Universe, Who creates fruit of the ground.

יְהִי רָצוֹן MAY it be Your will, Lord our God and God of our fathers, that our merits grow abundant.

ON LEEK

יְהִי רָצוֹן MAY it be Your will, Lord our God and God of our fathers, that our enemies be cut off.

ON BEET

יְהִי רָצוֹן MAY it be Your will, Lord our God and God of our fathers, that our enemies vanish.

ON SQUASH

יְהִי רָצוֹן MAY it be Your will, Lord our God and God of our fathers, that the evil decree against us be torn apart, and our merit be read out before You.

ON THE HEAD OF A SHEEP, OR A FISH

יְהִי רָצוֹן MAY it be Your will, Lord our God and God of our fathers, that we be the head, not the tail.

ON FISH

יְהִי רָצוֹן MAY it be Your will, Lord our God and God of our fathers, that we multiply like fish.

---

several reasons: (1) They induce a positive state of mind conducive to these desired outcomes, (2) they facilitate the steps necessary to repent and ensure good outcomes, and (3) they symbolically begin the implementation of a positive divine decree (R. Mordechai Torczyner).

קידושא רבא לראש השנה

On שבת *first say* וְשָׁמְרוּ *and* זָכוֹר.
**Most begin Kiddush here.*

וְשָׁמְרוּ בְנֵי־יִשְׂרָאֵל אֶת־הַשַּׁבָּת, לַעֲשׂוֹת אֶת־הַשַּׁבָּת לְדֹרֹתָם בְּרִית עוֹלָם: בֵּינִי וּבֵין בְּנֵי יִשְׂרָאֵל אוֹת הִוא לְעֹלָם, כִּי־שֵׁשֶׁת יָמִים עָשָׂה יהוה אֶת־הַשָּׁמַיִם וְאֶת־הָאָרֶץ וּבַיּוֹם הַשְּׁבִיעִי שָׁבַת וַיִּנָּפַשׁ: שמות לא

זָכוֹר אֶת־יוֹם הַשַּׁבָּת לְקַדְּשׁוֹ: שֵׁשֶׁת יָמִים תַּעֲבֹד, וְעָשִׂיתָ כָּל־מְלַאכְתֶּךָ: וְיוֹם הַשְּׁבִיעִי שַׁבָּת לַיהוה אֱלֹהֶיךָ, לֹא־תַעֲשֶׂה כָל־מְלָאכָה אַתָּה וּבִנְךָ וּבִתֶּךָ, עַבְדְּךָ וַאֲמָתְךָ וּבְהֶמְתֶּךָ, וְגֵרְךָ אֲשֶׁר בִּשְׁעָרֶיךָ: כִּי שֵׁשֶׁת־יָמִים עָשָׂה יהוה אֶת־הַשָּׁמַיִם וְאֶת־הָאָרֶץ אֶת־הַיָּם וְאֶת־כָּל־אֲשֶׁר־בָּם, וַיָּנַח בַּיּוֹם הַשְּׁבִיעִי, שמות כ

**On* שבת*, some start* קידוש *here instead:*

עַל־כֵּן בֵּרַךְ יהוה אֶת־יוֹם הַשַּׁבָּת וַיְקַדְּשֵׁהוּ:

On יום טוב *that falls on a weekday, some start here:*

אֵלֶּה מוֹעֲדֵי יהוה מִקְרָאֵי קֹדֶשׁ אֲשֶׁר־תִּקְרְאוּ אֹתָם בְּמוֹעֲדָם: וַיְדַבֵּר מֹשֶׁה אֶת־מֹעֲדֵי יהוה אֶל־בְּנֵי יִשְׂרָאֵל: ויקרא כג

On יום טוב *that falls on a weekday, start here:*

תִּקְעוּ בַחֹדֶשׁ שׁוֹפָר, בַּכֵּסֶה לְיוֹם חַגֵּנוּ: כִּי חֹק לְיִשְׂרָאֵל הוּא, מִשְׁפָּט לֵאלֹהֵי יַעֲקֹב: תהלים פא

When making קידוש *for others, add:*

סַבְרִי מָרָנָן וְרַבָּנָן וְרַבּוֹתַי

בָּרוּךְ אַתָּה יהוה אֱלֹהֵינוּ מֶלֶךְ הָעוֹלָם, בּוֹרֵא פְּרִי הַגָּפֶן.

It is customary for all present to drink of the wine.

For "*Laws of Kiddush*" see page 426.

KIDDUSH FOR ROSH HASHANA MORNING

On Shabbat first say "The children of Israel" and "Remember the Sabbath."
**Most begin Kiddush here.*

Ex. 31 וְשָׁמְרוּ THE CHILDREN OF ISRAEL shall keep the Sabbath, observing the Sabbath throughout their generations as an everlasting covenant. It is a sign between Me and the children of Israel forever that in six days the Lord made heaven and earth, and He rested on the seventh day and was refreshed.

Ex. 20 זָכוֹר REMEMBER THE SABBATH to keep it holy. Six days shall you labor and do all your work; but the seventh day is a Sabbath to the Lord your God, you shall not do any work, neither you, nor your son, nor your daughter, nor your manservant, nor your maidservant, nor your cattle, nor the stranger who is within your gates. For in six days the Lord made heaven and earth, the sea and all that is therein, and He rested on the seventh day –

**On Shabbat, some start Kiddush here instead:*

therefore the Lord blessed the Sabbath day and made it holy.

On Yom Tov that falls on a weekday, some start here:

Lev. 23 אֵלֶּה THESE are the appointed festival seasons of the Lord, the holy assemblies that you shall proclaim in their appointed seasons. Moses declared the appointed festival seasons of the Lord, to the children of Israel.

On a Yom Tov that falls on a weekday, start here:

Ps. 81 תִּקְעוּ SOUND THE SHOFAR on the new moon, on our feast day when the moon is hidden. For it is a statute for Israel, an ordinance of the God of Jacob.

When saying Kiddush for others, add:

By your leave, my masters, rabbis, and esteemed companions:

בָּרוּךְ BLESSED ARE YOU, Lord, our God, King of the universe, Who creates the fruit of the vine.

It is customary for all present to drink of the wine.

סדר תשליך

On the first day of ראש השנה *(or, if that day is* שבת*, on the second day), it is customary, in the afternoon after* מנחה*, to go to the banks of a river, or of any stretch of flowing water, and say the following:*

מיכה ז **מִי־אֵל כָּמְוֹךָ** נֹשֵׂא עָוֹן וְעֹבֵר עַל־פֶּשַׁע לִשְׁאֵרִית נַחֲלָתוֹ, לֹא־הֶחֱזִיק
לָעַד אַפּוֹ, כִּי־חָפֵץ חֶסֶד הוּא: יָשׁוּב יְרַחֲמֵנוּ, יִכְבֹּשׁ
עֲוֺנֹתֵינוּ, וְתַשְׁלִיךְ בִּמְצֻלוֹת יָם כָּל־חַטֹּאתָם: תִּתֵּן אֱמֶת לְיַעֲקֹב,
חֶסֶד לְאַבְרָהָם, אֲשֶׁר־נִשְׁבַּעְתָּ לַאֲבֹתֵינוּ מִימֵי קֶדֶם:

תהלים קיח **מִן־הַמֵּצַר** קָרָאתִי יָּהּ, עָנָנִי בַמֶּרְחָב יָהּ: יהוה לִי לֹא אִירָא, מַה־
יַּעֲשֶׂה לִי אָדָם: יהוה לִי בְּעֹזְרָי, וַאֲנִי אֶרְאֶה בְשֹׂנְאָי:
טוֹב לַחֲסוֹת בַּיהוה, מִבְּטֹחַ בָּאָדָם: טוֹב לַחֲסוֹת בַּיהוה, מִבְּטֹחַ
בִּנְדִיבִים:

תהלים לג **רַנְּנוּ** צַדִּיקִים בַּיהוה, לַיְשָׁרִים נָאוָה תְהִלָּה: הוֹדוּ לַיהוה בְּכִנּוֹר,
בְּנֵבֶל עָשׂוֹר זַמְּרוּ־לוֹ: שִׁירוּ־לוֹ שִׁיר חָדָשׁ, הֵיטִיבוּ נַגֵּן
בִּתְרוּעָה: כִּי־יָשָׁר דְּבַר־יהוה, וְכָל־מַעֲשֵׂהוּ בֶּאֱמוּנָה: אֹהֵב צְדָקָה
וּמִשְׁפָּט, חֶסֶד יהוה מָלְאָה הָאָרֶץ: בִּדְבַר יהוה שָׁמַיִם נַעֲשׂוּ, וּבְרוּחַ
פִּיו כָּל־צְבָאָם: כֹּנֵס כַּנֵּד מֵי הַיָּם, נֹתֵן בְּאוֹצָרוֹת תְּהוֹמוֹת: יִירְאוּ
מֵיהוה כָּל־הָאָרֶץ, מִמֶּנּוּ יָגוּרוּ כָּל־יֹשְׁבֵי תֵבֵל: כִּי הוּא אָמַר וַיֶּהִי,
הוּא־צִוָּה וַיַּעֲמֹד: יהוה הֵפִיר עֲצַת־גּוֹיִם, הֵנִיא מַחְשְׁבוֹת עַמִּים:
עֲצַת יהוה לְעוֹלָם תַּעֲמֹד, מַחְשְׁבוֹת לִבּוֹ לְדֹר וָדֹר: אַשְׁרֵי הַגּוֹי
אֲשֶׁר־יהוה אֱלֹהָיו, הָעָם בָּחַר לְנַחֲלָה לוֹ: מִשָּׁמַיִם הִבִּיט יהוה, רָאָה
אֶת־כָּל־בְּנֵי הָאָדָם: מִמְּכוֹן־שִׁבְתּוֹ הִשְׁגִּיחַ, אֶל כָּל־יֹשְׁבֵי הָאָרֶץ:

תַּשְׁלִיךְ / TASHLIKH
The custom of Tashlikh first appears in the works of the fourteenth-century Ashkenazic authority Maharil, but allusions to a Jewish custom practiced in proximity to flowing water can be found throughout earlier mystical and classical rabbinic literature.

TASHLIKH

On the first day of Rosh HaShana (or, if that day is Shabbat, on the second day), it is customary, in the afternoon after Minḥa, to go to the banks of a river, or of any stretch of flowing water, and say the following:

Mic. 7 מִי־אֵל כָּמוֹךָ WHO IS A GOD like You, that pardons the iniquity, and passes by the transgression of the remnant of His heritage? He retains not His anger forever, because He delights in mercy. He will again have compassion upon us; He will subdue our iniquities; and You will cast all their sins into the depths of the sea. You will show faithfulness to Jacob, mercy to Abraham, as You have sworn to our fathers from the days of old.

Ps. 118 מִן־הַמֵּצַר FROM DISTRESS I called upon the Lord. The Lord answered me with enlargement. The Lord is for me, I will not fear. What can man do to me? The Lord is for me among my helpers, and I will see the downfall of those who hate me. It is better to seek refuge in the Lord than to trust in man. It is better to seek refuge in the Lord than to trust in princes.

Ps. 33 רַנְּנוּ REJOICE IN THE LORD, O you righteous. Praise is seemly for the upright. Give thanks to the Lord with a lyre. Sing praises to Him with a harp of ten strings. Sing Him a new song. Play skillfully with a loud sound. For the word of the Lord is upright, and all His work is done in faithfulness. He loves righteousness and judgment. The earth is full of the loving-kindness of the Lord. By the word of the Lord were the heavens made, and by the breath of His mouth all their host. He gathers the waters of the sea as a heap. He lays the great waters in storehouses. Let all the earth be in fear of the Lord. Let all the inhabitants of the world stand in awe of Him. For He spoke, and it was. He commanded, and it stood. The Lord confounds the plan of the nations. He makes the thoughts of the people of no effect. The plan of the Lord will stand forever, the thoughts of His heart for all generations. Happy is the nation whose God is the Lord, the people whom He has chosen for His own inheritance. The Lord looks down from heaven. He sees all the sons of man. From the place of His habitation He gazes upon all the inhabitants of the earth. It is He Who creates all their hearts, Who

הַיֹּצֵר יַחַד לִבָּם, הַמֵּבִין אֶל־כׇּל־מַעֲשֵׂיהֶם: אֵין־הַמֶּלֶךְ נוֹשָׁע בְּרׇב־חָיִל, גִּבּוֹר לֹא־יִנָּצֵל בְּרׇב־כֹּחַ: שֶׁקֶר הַסּוּס לִתְשׁוּעָה, וּבְרֹב חֵילוֹ לֹא יְמַלֵּט: הִנֵּה עֵין יהוה אֶל־יְרֵאָיו, לַמְיַחֲלִים לְחַסְדּוֹ: לְהַצִּיל מִמָּוֶת נַפְשָׁם, וּלְחַיּוֹתָם בָּרָעָב: נַפְשֵׁנוּ חִכְּתָה לַיהוה, עֶזְרֵנוּ וּמָגִנֵּנוּ הוּא: ‹ כִּי־בוֹ יִשְׂמַח לִבֵּנוּ, כִּי בְשֵׁם קׇדְשׁוֹ בָטָחְנוּ: יְהִי־חַסְדְּךָ יהוה עָלֵינוּ, כַּאֲשֶׁר יִחַלְנוּ לָךְ:

תהלים קל

שִׁיר הַמַּעֲלוֹת, מִמַּעֲמַקִּים קְרָאתִיךָ יהוה: אֲדֹנָי שִׁמְעָה בְקוֹלִי, תִּהְיֶינָה אׇזְנֶיךָ קַשֻּׁבוֹת לְקוֹל תַּחֲנוּנָי: אִם־עֲוֹנוֹת תִּשְׁמׇר־יָהּ, אֲדֹנָי מִי יַעֲמֹד: כִּי־עִמְּךָ הַסְּלִיחָה, לְמַעַן תִּוָּרֵא: קִוִּיתִי יהוה קִוְּתָה נַפְשִׁי, וְלִדְבָרוֹ הוֹחָלְתִּי: נַפְשִׁי לַאדֹנָי, מִשֹּׁמְרִים לַבֹּקֶר, שֹׁמְרִים לַבֹּקֶר: יַחֵל יִשְׂרָאֵל אֶל יהוה, כִּי־עִם־יהוה הַחֶסֶד, וְהַרְבֵּה עִמּוֹ פְדוּת: וְהוּא יִפְדֶּה אֶת־יִשְׂרָאֵל, מִכֹּל עֲוֹנוֹתָיו:

סדר כפרות

Taking a rooster (men), or a hen (women) in the right hand (alternatively one may use money), say the following paragraph three times:

תהלים קז

בְּנֵי אָדָם יֹשְׁבֵי חֹשֶׁךְ וְצַלְמָוֶת, אֲסִירֵי עֳנִי וּבַרְזֶל: יוֹצִיאֵם מֵחֹשֶׁךְ וְצַלְמָוֶת, וּמוֹסְרוֹתֵיהֶם יְנַתֵּק: אֱוִלִים מִדֶּרֶךְ פִּשְׁעָם,

KAPPAROT

The custom of *Kapparot* can be fulfilled by using either live fowl or money as a substitute. Those who use live fowl should be very careful to ensure that (a) the fowl is treated before, during and after the ceremony with full consideration of the prohibition against inflicting pain or discomfort on animal life, as well as (b) sensitivity to all local health and safety ordinances relating to livestock. For these and other reasons, many people prefer to observe *Kapparot* by using coins or bills to be given afterward to a worthy charity.

discerns all their deeds. A king is not saved by a great host. A mighty man is not delivered by great strength. A horse is a vain thing for safety, and it will not save with its great strength. Behold, the eye of the Lord is on those who fear Him, on those who hope for His loving-kindness, To deliver their soul from death, and to keep them alive in famine. Our soul waits for the Lord. He is our help and our shield. Indeed, in Him does our heart rejoice. Indeed, in His holy name we trust. May Your loving-kindness, O Lord, be upon us, as we hope for You.

Ps. 130 **שִׁיר הַמַּעֲלוֹת** A SONG OF ASCENTS. From the depths I call out to You, O Lord. My Master, hear my voice. Let Your ears be attentive to the sound of my supplications. If You, Lord, pay heed to iniquities, who, my Master, will stand? Indeed, forgiveness is with You, so that You may be feared. I wait for the Lord, my soul waits, and I hope for His word. My soul waits for my Master, among those who watch for the morning, who watch for the morning. Israel, hope for the Lord, for with the Lord is loving-kindness, and with Him is abundant redemption. And He will redeem Israel from all his iniquities.

KAPPAROT

Taking a rooster (men), or a hen (women) in the right hand (alternatively one may use money), say the following paragraph three times:

Ps. 107 **בְּנֵי אָדָם** CHILDREN OF MAN, who sat in darkness and the shadow of death, bound in affliction and iron – He brought them out from darkness and the shadow of death, and He broke their bonds

---

כפרות / KAPPAROT

Kapparot is an ancient practice of the land of Israel, first attested in Geonic literature. In its origin, it was likely practiced on behalf of small children, who are unable to express remorse and achieve atonement through conventional means. The practice is of the same nature as the symbolic foods on Rosh HaShana night, i.e., to serve as a symbolic act for the forthcoming year, in this case that the one performing *Kapparot* should feel that he or she enters the new year relieved of the crushing burden of sin. Meiri argues to the contrary, that *Kapparot* are intended to inculcate the

וּמֵעֲוֹנֹתֵיהֶם יִתְעַנּוּ: כָּל־אֹכֶל תְּתַעֵב נַפְשָׁם, וַיַּגִּיעוּ עַד־שַׁעֲרֵי
מָוֶת: וַיִּזְעֲקוּ אֶל־יהוה בַּצַּר לָהֶם, מִמְּצֻקוֹתֵיהֶם יוֹשִׁיעֵם: יִשְׁלַח
דְּבָרוֹ וְיִרְפָּאֵם, וִימַלֵּט מִשְּׁחִיתוֹתָם: יוֹדוּ לַיהוה חַסְדּוֹ, וְנִפְלְאוֹתָיו
לִבְנֵי אָדָם: אִם־יֵשׁ עָלָיו מַלְאָךְ מֵלִיץ אֶחָד מִנִּי־אָלֶף, לְהַגִּיד לְאָדָם איוב לג
יָשְׁרוֹ: וַיְחֻנֶּנּוּ, וַיֹּאמֶר פְּדָעֵהוּ מֵרֶדֶת שַׁחַת, מָצָאתִי כֹפֶר:

A man revolves the rooster around his head and says:

זֶה חֲלִיפָתִי, זֶה תְּמוּרָתִי, זֶה כַּפָּרָתִי. זֶה הַתַּרְנְגוֹל יֵלֵךְ לְמִיתָה, וַאֲנִי אֵלֵךְ וְאֶכָּנֵס לְחַיִּים טוֹבִים אֲרֻכִּים וּלְשָׁלוֹם.

A woman revolves the hen around her head and says:

זֹאת חֲלִיפָתִי, זֹאת תְּמוּרָתִי, זֹאת כַּפָּרָתִי. זֹאת הַתַּרְנְגֹלֶת תֵּלֵךְ לְמִיתָה, וַאֲנִי אֵלֵךְ וְאֶכָּנֵס לְחַיִּים טוֹבִים אֲרֻכִּים וּלְשָׁלוֹם.

If money is used, then revolve the money around the head and say:

אֵלּוּ חֲלִיפָתִי, אֵלּוּ תְּמוּרָתִי, אֵלּוּ כַּפָּרָתִי. אֵלּוּ הַמָּעוֹת יֵלְכוּ לִצְדָקָה, וַאֲנִי אֵלֵךְ וְאֶכָּנֵס לְחַיִּים טוֹבִים אֲרֻכִּים וּלְשָׁלוֹם.

---

gravity of sin and spur genuine repentance. Meiri and Radbaz note, based on the earliest Geonic source, that actual reprieve comes not from the ritual but from the donation of the bird, along with other goods and funds, to charity, in line with the Talmudic dictum "he who says 'this coin to charity so that my son should live... is completely righteous'" (*Rosh HaShana* 4a). In early medieval Marseille, *Kapparot* took on a second meaning: the bird was conceived as a sin-offering, *semikha* (laying hands on the head of the offering) was done, and liturgy was added to reflect a sacrificial element. This remains in our contemporary practice (cf. *Mishna Temura* 5:5). The practice met opposition from Sephardic authorities such as Rashba, Ramban and R. Yosef Karo due to its perceived similarities to pagan magical practices, as well as the sin of offering sacrifices outside the Temple precincts. Early Ashkenazic

asunder. The foolish who can be recognized by their way of sin, and who are afflicted on account of their iniquities, whose soul abhors all food, and who have come near the gates of death – then they cried to the Lord in their distress, and He saved them from their troubles. He sent His word and healed them, and He rescued them from their destructions. Let them praise the Lord for His loving-kindness, and
Job 33 for His wondrous works to the children of man. If there be for him an angel, an intercessor, one among a thousand, to vouch for a man's uprightness; then He is gracious to him, and says: "Deliver him from going down to the pit, I have found a ransom."

A man revolves the rooster around his head and says:

זֶה חֲלִיפָתִי THIS IS MY EXCHANGE, this is my substitute, this is my atonement, this is the rooster that will go to its death, while I go and enter a good, long life and peace.

A woman revolves the hen around her head and says:

זֹאת חֲלִיפָתִי THIS IS MY EXCHANGE, this is my substitute, this is my atonement, this is the hen that will go to its death, while I go and enter a good, long life and peace.

If money is used, then revolve the money around the head and say:

אֵלּוּ חֲלִיפָתִי THIS IS MY EXCHANGE, this is my substitute, this is my atonement, This is the money that will go to charity, while I go and enter a good, long life and peace.

---

authorities generally accepted it (Prof. Yaakov Gartner).

Later authorities urged that *Kapparot* be done earlier in the week so as to not overburden the one who would slaughter the bird and lead to invalid slaughter (Pri Megadim, Ḥatam Sofer). In modern times, most Jews do not live in proximity to livestock, and mass *Kapparot* in urban areas have led to mistreatment of chickens in storage and transport; as a result, contemporary authorities have stressed that those who do *Kapparot* do so either with careful attention to humane treatment of animals, or not at all (R. Hayyim David HaLevi, R. David Lau).

וידוי למנחה ערב יום הכיפורים

The following is said on ערב יום הכיפורים *(and by a* חתן *and* כלה *on the eve of their wedding), in the* עמידה *before* אֱלֹהַי, נְצֹר:

אֱלֹהֵינוּ וֵאלֹהֵי אֲבוֹתֵינוּ, תָּבוֹא לְפָנֶיךָ תְּפִלָּתֵנוּ, וְאַל תִּתְעַלַּם מִתְּחִנָּתֵנוּ. שֶׁאֵין אֲנַחְנוּ עַזֵּי פָנִים וּקְשֵׁי עֹרֶף לוֹמַר לְפָנֶיךָ, יהוה אֱלֹהֵינוּ וֵאלֹהֵי אֲבוֹתֵינוּ, צַדִּיקִים אֲנַחְנוּ וְלֹא חָטָאנוּ. אֲבָל אֲנַחְנוּ וַאֲבוֹתֵינוּ חָטָאנוּ.

Strike the left side of the chest with the right fist while saying each of the sins:

אָשַׁמְנוּ, בָּגַדְנוּ, גָּזַלְנוּ, דִּבַּרְנוּ דֹפִי, הֶעֱוִינוּ, וְהִרְשַׁעְנוּ, זַדְנוּ, חָמַסְנוּ, טָפַלְנוּ שֶׁקֶר, יָעַצְנוּ רָע, כִּזַּבְנוּ, לַצְנוּ, מָרַדְנוּ, נִאַצְנוּ, סָרַרְנוּ, עָוִינוּ, פָּשַׁעְנוּ, צָרַרְנוּ, קִשִּׁינוּ עֹרֶף, רָשַׁעְנוּ, שִׁחַתְנוּ, תִּעַבְנוּ, תָּעִינוּ, תִּעְתָּעְנוּ.

סַרְנוּ מִמִּצְוֹתֶיךָ וּמִמִּשְׁפָּטֶיךָ הַטּוֹבִים, וְלֹא שָׁוָה לָנוּ. וְאַתָּה צַדִּיק עַל כָּל הַבָּא עָלֵינוּ, כִּי אֱמֶת עָשִׂיתָ, וַאֲנַחְנוּ הִרְשָׁעְנוּ.

מַה נֹּאמַר לְפָנֶיךָ יוֹשֵׁב מָרוֹם, וּמַה נְּסַפֵּר לְפָנֶיךָ שׁוֹכֵן שְׁחָקִים, הֲלֹא כָּל הַנִּסְתָּרוֹת וְהַנִּגְלוֹת אַתָּה יוֹדֵעַ.

אַתָּה יוֹדֵעַ רָזֵי עוֹלָם וְתַעֲלוּמוֹת סִתְרֵי כָּל חָי. אַתָּה חוֹפֵשׂ כָּל חַדְרֵי בָטֶן וּבוֹחֵן כְּלָיוֹת וָלֵב. אֵין דָּבָר נֶעְלָם מִמֶּךָּ וְאֵין נִסְתָּר מִנֶּגֶד עֵינֶיךָ. וּבְכֵן, יְהִי רָצוֹן מִלְּפָנֶיךָ, יהוה אֱלֹהֵינוּ וֵאלֹהֵי אֲבוֹתֵינוּ, שֶׁתִּסְלַח לָנוּ עַל כָּל חַטֹּאתֵינוּ, וְתִמְחַל לָנוּ עַל כָּל עֲוֹנוֹתֵינוּ, וּתְכַפֵּר לָנוּ עַל כָּל פְּשָׁעֵינוּ.

Strike the left side of the chest with the right fist while saying each of the sins.

עַל חֵטְא שֶׁחָטָאנוּ לְפָנֶיךָ בְּאֹנֶס וּבְרָצוֹן
וְעַל חֵטְא שֶׁחָטָאנוּ לְפָנֶיךָ בְּאִמּוּץ הַלֵּב
עַל חֵטְא שֶׁחָטָאנוּ לְפָנֶיךָ בִּבְלִי דָעַת
וְעַל חֵטְא שֶׁחָטָאנוּ לְפָנֶיךָ בְּבִטּוּי שְׂפָתָיִם
עַל חֵטְא שֶׁחָטָאנוּ לְפָנֶיךָ בְּגִלּוּי עֲרָיוֹת
וְעַל חֵטְא שֶׁחָטָאנוּ לְפָנֶיךָ בְּגָלוּי וּבַסָּתֶר

VIDUY FOR MINḤA OF EREV YOM KIPPUR

The following is said on Erev Yom Kippur (and by a bride and groom on the eve of their wedding), in the Amida before "My God, guard":

אֱלֹהֵינוּ OUR GOD and God of our fathers, let our prayer come before You, and do not hide Yourself from our plea, for we are not so arrogant or obstinate as to say before You, LORD, our God and God of our fathers, we are righteous and have not sinned, for in truth, we and our fathers have sinned.

Strike the left side of the chest with the right fist while saying each of the sins:

אָשַׁמְנוּ WE HAVE SINNED, we have acted treacherously, we have robbed, we have spoken slander. We have acted perversely, we have acted wickedly, we have acted presumptuously, we have been violent, we have framed lies. We have given bad advice, we have deceived, we have scorned, we have rebelled, we have provoked, we have turned away, we have committed iniquity, we have transgressed, we have persecuted, we have been obstinate. We have acted wickedly, we have corrupted, we have acted abominably, we have strayed, we have led others astray.

סַרְנוּ WE HAVE TURNED AWAY from Your commandments and good laws, to no avail, for You are just in all that has befallen us, for You have acted faithfully while we have done wickedly.

מַה נֹּאמַר WHAT CAN WE SAY before You, You Who dwell on high? What can we declare before You, You Who abide in heaven? Do You not know all, the hidden and revealed alike?

אַתָּה יוֹדֵעַ YOU KNOW EVERY SECRET since the world began, and what is hidden deep inside every living thing. You search each person's inner chambers examining conscience and mind. Nothing is shrouded from You, and nothing is hidden, before Your eyes. And so, may it be Your will, LORD our God and God of our fathers, that You forgive us all our sins, pardon all our iniquities and grant us atonement for all of our transgressions.

Strike the left side of the chest with the right fist while saying each of the sins.

א עַל חֵטְא FOR THE SIN we have sinned before You under duress or freewill,
and for the sin we have sinned before You in hardness of heart.

ב For the sin we have sinned before You unwittingly,
and for the sin we have sinned before You by an utterance of our lips.

ג For the sin we have sinned before You by unchastity,
and for the sin we have sinned before You openly or secretly.

עַל חֵטְא שֶׁחָטָאנוּ לְפָנֶיךָ בְּדַעַת וּבְמִרְמָה
וְעַל חֵטְא שֶׁחָטָאנוּ לְפָנֶיךָ בְּדִבּוּר פֶּה

עַל חֵטְא שֶׁחָטָאנוּ לְפָנֶיךָ בְּהוֹנָאַת רֵעַ
וְעַל חֵטְא שֶׁחָטָאנוּ לְפָנֶיךָ בְּהַרְהוֹר הַלֵּב

עַל חֵטְא שֶׁחָטָאנוּ לְפָנֶיךָ בִּוְעִידַת זְנוּת
וְעַל חֵטְא שֶׁחָטָאנוּ לְפָנֶיךָ בְּוִדּוּי פֶּה

עַל חֵטְא שֶׁחָטָאנוּ לְפָנֶיךָ בְּזִלְזוּל הוֹרִים וּמוֹרִים
וְעַל חֵטְא שֶׁחָטָאנוּ לְפָנֶיךָ בְּזָדוֹן וּבִשְׁגָגָה

עַל חֵטְא שֶׁחָטָאנוּ לְפָנֶיךָ בְּחֹזֶק יָד
וְעַל חֵטְא שֶׁחָטָאנוּ לְפָנֶיךָ בְּחִלּוּל הַשֵּׁם

עַל חֵטְא שֶׁחָטָאנוּ לְפָנֶיךָ בְּטֻמְאַת שְׂפָתָיִם
וְעַל חֵטְא שֶׁחָטָאנוּ לְפָנֶיךָ בְּטִפְשׁוּת פֶּה

עַל חֵטְא שֶׁחָטָאנוּ לְפָנֶיךָ בְּיֵצֶר הָרָע
וְעַל חֵטְא שֶׁחָטָאנוּ לְפָנֶיךָ בְּיוֹדְעִים וּבְלֹא יוֹדְעִים

וְעַל כֻּלָּם אֱלוֹהַּ סְלִיחוֹת סְלַח לָנוּ, מְחַל לָנוּ, כַּפֶּר לָנוּ.

עַל חֵטְא שֶׁחָטָאנוּ לְפָנֶיךָ בְּכַחַשׁ וּבְכָזָב
וְעַל חֵטְא שֶׁחָטָאנוּ לְפָנֶיךָ בְּכַפַּת שֹׁחַד

עַל חֵטְא שֶׁחָטָאנוּ לְפָנֶיךָ בְּלָצוֹן
וְעַל חֵטְא שֶׁחָטָאנוּ לְפָנֶיךָ בְּלָשׁוֹן הָרָע

עַל חֵטְא שֶׁחָטָאנוּ לְפָנֶיךָ בְּמַשָּׂא וּבְמַתָּן
וְעַל חֵטְא שֶׁחָטָאנוּ לְפָנֶיךָ בְּמַאֲכָל וּבְמִשְׁתֶּה

עַל חֵטְא שֶׁחָטָאנוּ לְפָנֶיךָ בְּנֶשֶׁךְ וּבְמַרְבִּית
וְעַל חֵטְא שֶׁחָטָאנוּ לְפָנֶיךָ בִּנְטִיַּת גָּרוֹן

עַל חֵטְא שֶׁחָטָאנוּ לְפָנֶיךָ בְּשִׂיחַ שִׂפְתוֹתֵינוּ
וְעַל חֵטְא שֶׁחָטָאנוּ לְפָנֶיךָ בְּשִׂקּוּר עָיִן

ד For the sin we have sinned before You knowingly and deceitfully,
and for the sin we have sinned before You in speech.

ה For the sin we have sinned before You by wronging a neighbor,
and for the sin we have sinned before You by thoughts of the heart.

ו For the sin we have sinned before You in a gathering for immorality,
and for the sin we have sinned before You by insincere confession.

ז For the sin we have sinned before You by contempt for parents and teachers,
and for the sin we have sinned before You willfully or in error.

ח For the sin we have sinned before You by force,
and for the sin we have sinned before You by desecrating Your name.

ט For the sin we have sinned before You by impure lips,
and for the sin we have sinned before You by foolish speech.

י For the sin we have sinned before You by the evil inclination,
and for the sin we have sinned before You knowingly or unwittingly.

FOR ALL THESE, God of forgiveness,
forgive us, pardon us, grant us atonement.

כ For the sin we have sinned before You by deceit and lies,
and for the sin we have sinned before You by bribery.

ל For the sin we have sinned before You by scorn,
and for the sin we have sinned before You by evil speech.

מ For the sin we have sinned before You in business,
and for the sin we have sinned before You with food and drink.

נ For the sin we have sinned before You by interest and extortion,
and for the sin we have sinned before You by being haughty.

ס For the sin we have sinned before You by the idle chatter of our lips,
and for the sin we have sinned before You by prying eyes.

עַל חֵטְא שֶׁחָטָאנוּ לְפָנֶיךָ **בְּעֵ**ינַיִם רָמוֹת
וְעַל חֵטְא שֶׁחָטָאנוּ לְפָנֶיךָ בְּעַזּוּת מֵצַח

וְעַל כֻּלָּם אֱלוֹהַּ סְלִיחוֹת סְלַח לָנוּ, מְחַל לָנוּ, כַּפֶּר לָנוּ.

עַל חֵטְא שֶׁחָטָאנוּ לְפָנֶיךָ **בִּפְ**רִיקַת עֹל
וְעַל חֵטְא שֶׁחָטָאנוּ לְפָנֶיךָ בִּפְלִילוּת

עַל חֵטְא שֶׁחָטָאנוּ לְפָנֶיךָ **בִּצְ**דִיַּת רֵעַ
וְעַל חֵטְא שֶׁחָטָאנוּ לְפָנֶיךָ בְּצָרוּת עָיִן

עַל חֵטְא שֶׁחָטָאנוּ לְפָנֶיךָ **בְּקַ**לּוּת רֹאשׁ
וְעַל חֵטְא שֶׁחָטָאנוּ לְפָנֶיךָ בְּקַשְׁיוּת עֹרֶף

עַל חֵטְא שֶׁחָטָאנוּ לְפָנֶיךָ **בְּ**רִיצַת רַגְלַיִם לְהָרַע
וְעַל חֵטְא שֶׁחָטָאנוּ לְפָנֶיךָ בִּרְכִילוּת

עַל חֵטְא שֶׁחָטָאנוּ לְפָנֶיךָ **בִּשְׁ**בוּעַת שָׁוְא
וְעַל חֵטְא שֶׁחָטָאנוּ לְפָנֶיךָ בְּשִׂנְאַת חִנָּם

עַל חֵטְא שֶׁחָטָאנוּ לְפָנֶיךָ **בִּתְ**שׂוּמֶת יָד
וְעַל חֵטְא שֶׁחָטָאנוּ לְפָנֶיךָ בְּתִמְהוֹן לֵבָב

וְעַל כֻּלָּם אֱלוֹהַּ סְלִיחוֹת סְלַח לָנוּ, מְחַל לָנוּ, כַּפֶּר לָנוּ.

וְעַל חֲטָאִים שֶׁאָנוּ חַיָּבִים עֲלֵיהֶם עוֹלָה
וְעַל חֲטָאִים שֶׁאָנוּ חַיָּבִים עֲלֵיהֶם חַטָּאת
וְעַל חֲטָאִים שֶׁאָנוּ חַיָּבִים עֲלֵיהֶם קָרְבָּן עוֹלֶה וְיוֹרֵד
וְעַל חֲטָאִים שֶׁאָנוּ חַיָּבִים עֲלֵיהֶם אָשָׁם וַדַּאי וְתָלוּי
וְעַל חֲטָאִים שֶׁאָנוּ חַיָּבִים עֲלֵיהֶם מַכַּת מַרְדּוּת
וְעַל חֲטָאִים שֶׁאָנוּ חַיָּבִים עֲלֵיהֶם מַלְקוּת אַרְבָּעִים
וְעַל חֲטָאִים שֶׁאָנוּ חַיָּבִים עֲלֵיהֶם מִיתָה בִּידֵי שָׁמַיִם
וְעַל חֲטָאִים שֶׁאָנוּ חַיָּבִים עֲלֵיהֶם כָּרֵת וַעֲרִירִי
וְעַל חֲטָאִים שֶׁאָנוּ חַיָּבִים עֲלֵיהֶם אַרְבַּע מִיתוֹת בֵּית דִּין,
סְקִילָה, שְׂרֵפָה, הֶרֶג, וְחֶנֶק.

ע For the sin we have sinned before You by arrogance,
and for the sin we have sinned before You by insolence.

FOR ALL THESE, God of forgiveness,
forgive us, pardon us, grant us atonement.

פ For the sin we have sinned before You by casting off the yoke,
and for the sin we have sinned before You by perverting judgment.

צ For the sin we have sinned before You by entrapping a neighbor,
and for the sin we have sinned before You by envy.

ק For the sin we have sinned before You by lack of seriousness,
and for the sin we have sinned before You by obstinacy.

ר For the sin we have sinned before You by running to do evil,
and for the sin we have sinned before You by gossip.

ש For the sin we have sinned before You by vain oath,
and for the sin we have sinned before You by baseless hatred.

ת For the sin we have sinned before You by breach of trust,
and for the sin we have sinned before You by confusion of heart.

FOR ALL THESE, God of forgiveness,
forgive us, pardon us, grant us atonement.

וְעַל חֲטָאִים AND FOR THE SINS for which we are liable to bring a burnt-offering,
and for the sins for which we are liable to bring a sin-offering,
and for the sins for which we are liable to bring an offering according to our means,
and for the sins for which we are liable to bring a guilt-offering for certain or possible sin,
and for the sins for which we are liable to lashes for rebellion,
and for the sins for which we are liable to forty lashes,
and for the sins for which we are liable to death by the hands of heaven,
and for the sins for which we are liable to be cut off and childless,
and for the sins for which we are liable to the four death penalties inflicted by the court: stoning, burning, beheading and strangling.

עַל מִצְוַת עֲשֵׂה וְעַל מִצְוַת לֹא תַעֲשֶׂה. בֵּין שֶׁיֵּשׁ בָּהּ קוּם עֲשֵׂה וּבֵין
שֶׁאֵין בָּהּ קוּם עֲשֵׂה. אֶת הַגְּלוּיִים לָנוּ וְאֶת שֶׁאֵינָם גְּלוּיִים לָנוּ, אֶת
הַגְּלוּיִים לָנוּ, כְּבָר אֲמַרְנוּם לְפָנֶיךָ, וְהוֹדִינוּ לְךָ עֲלֵיהֶם, וְאֶת שֶׁאֵינָם
דברים כט גְּלוּיִים לָנוּ, לְפָנֶיךָ הֵם גְּלוּיִים וִידוּעִים, כַּדָּבָר שֶׁנֶּאֱמַר, הַנִּסְתָּרֹת
לַיהוה אֱלֹהֵינוּ, וְהַנִּגְלֹת לָנוּ וּלְבָנֵינוּ עַד־עוֹלָם, לַעֲשׂוֹת אֶת־כָּל־דִּבְרֵי
הַתּוֹרָה הַזֹּאת: כִּי אַתָּה סָלְחָן לְיִשְׂרָאֵל וּמָחֳלָן לְשִׁבְטֵי יְשֻׁרוּן בְּכָל
דּוֹר וָדוֹר, וּמִבַּלְעָדֶיךָ אֵין לָנוּ מֶלֶךְ מוֹחֵל וְסוֹלֵחַ אֶלָּא אָתָּה.

אֱלֹהַי עַד שֶׁלֹּא נוֹצַרְתִּי אֵינִי כְדַאי, וְעַכְשָׁיו שֶׁנּוֹצַרְתִּי, כְּאִלּוּ לֹא
נוֹצַרְתִּי, עָפָר אֲנִי בְּחַיַּי, קַל וָחֹמֶר בְּמִיתָתִי. הֲרֵי אֲנִי לְפָנֶיךָ
כִּכְלִי מָלֵא בּוּשָׁה וּכְלִמָּה. יְהִי רָצוֹן מִלְּפָנֶיךָ, יהוה אֱלֹהַי וֵאלֹהֵי אֲבוֹתַי,
שֶׁלֹּא אֶחֱטָא עוֹד. וּמַה שֶּׁחָטָאתִי לְפָנֶיךָ, מְחֹק בְּרַחֲמֶיךָ הָרַבִּים, אֲבָל
לֹא עַל יְדֵי יִסּוּרִים וָחֳלָיִים רָעִים.

ברכות יז. **אֱלֹהַי,** נְצֹר לְשׁוֹנִי מֵרָע וּשְׂפָתַי מִדַּבֵּר מִרְמָה, וְלִמְקַלְלַי נַפְשִׁי
תִדֹּם, וְנַפְשִׁי כֶּעָפָר לַכֹּל תִּהְיֶה. פְּתַח לִבִּי בְּתוֹרָתֶךָ, וּבְמִצְוֹתֶיךָ
תִּרְדֹּף נַפְשִׁי. וְכָל הַחוֹשְׁבִים עָלַי רָעָה, מְהֵרָה הָפֵר עֲצָתָם וְקַלְקֵל
מַחֲשַׁבְתָּם. עֲשֵׂה לְמַעַן שְׁמֶךָ, עֲשֵׂה לְמַעַן יְמִינֶךָ, עֲשֵׂה לְמַעַן קְדֻשָּׁתֶךָ,
תהלים ס עֲשֵׂה לְמַעַן תּוֹרָתֶךָ. לְמַעַן יֵחָלְצוּן יְדִידֶיךָ, הוֹשִׁיעָה יְמִינְךָ וַעֲנֵנִי:
תהלים יט יִהְיוּ לְרָצוֹן אִמְרֵי־פִי וְהֶגְיוֹן לִבִּי לְפָנֶיךָ, יהוה צוּרִי וְגֹאֲלִי:

Bow, take three steps back, then bow, first left, then right, then center, while saying:

עֹשֶׂה שָׁלוֹם/ בעשרת ימי תשובה: הַשָּׁלוֹם/ בִּמְרוֹמָיו, הוּא יַעֲשֶׂה שָׁלוֹם
עָלֵינוּ, וְעַל כָּל יִשְׂרָאֵל, וְאִמְרוּ אָמֵן.

יְהִי רָצוֹן מִלְּפָנֶיךָ יהוה אֱלֹהֵינוּ וֵאלֹהֵי אֲבוֹתֵינוּ, שֶׁיִּבָּנֶה בֵּית הַמִּקְדָּשׁ
בִּמְהֵרָה בְיָמֵינוּ, וְתֵן חֶלְקֵנוּ בְּתוֹרָתֶךָ, וְשָׁם נַעֲבָדְךָ בְּיִרְאָה כִּימֵי
מלאכי ג עוֹלָם וּכְשָׁנִים קַדְמֹנִיּוֹת. וְעָרְבָה לַיהוה מִנְחַת יְהוּדָה וִירוּשָׁלָםִ כִּימֵי עוֹלָם
וּכְשָׁנִים קַדְמֹנִיּוֹת:

For positive and negative commandments, whether they can be remedied by an act or not, for sins known to us and for those that are unknown – for those that are known, we have already declared them before You and confessed them to You; and for those that are unknown, before You they are revealed
Deut. 29 and known, as it is said, "The secret things belong to the LORD our God, but the things that are revealed are for us and our children for ever, that we may fulfill all the words of this Torah." For You are He Who forgives Israel and pardons the tribes of Yeshurun in every generation, and besides You we have no king who pardons and forgives, only You.

אֱלֹהַי MY GOD, before I was formed I was unworthy, and now that I have been formed it is as if I had not been formed. I am dust while alive, how much more so when I am dead. See, I am before You like a vessel filled with shame and disgrace. May it be Your will, LORD my God and God of my fathers, that I may sin no more, and as for the sins I have committed before You, erase them in Your great compassion, but not by suffering or severe illness.

Berakhot 17a אֱלֹהַי MY GOD, guard my tongue from evil, and my lips from speaking deceit. Let my soul be silent to those who curse me; let my soul be humble toward everyone like the dust. Open my heart to Your Torah that my soul may follow Your commandments. As for all those who contemplate evil against me, speedily nullify their plans and spoil their schemes. Do so for the sake of Your name. Do so for Your right hand. Do so for Your holiness.
Ps. 60 Do so for Your Torah, that Your loved ones may be delivered. Save with Your
Ps. 19 right hand, and answer me. May the words of my mouth and the meditation of my heart be acceptable before You, LORD, my Rock and my Redeemer.

Bow, take three steps back, then bow, first left, then right, then center, while saying:

He Who makes peace in His heights, may He create peace for us and for all Israel. Amen.

יְהִי רָצוֹן MAY IT BE Your will, LORD our God and God of our fathers, that the Temple be rebuilt speedily in our days and may You grant our portion in Your Torah. We will
Mal. 3 serve You there in reverence as in the days of antiquity and in years gone by. "And may the offering of Judah and Jerusalem be pleasant to the LORD as in the days of antiquity and in years gone by."

סדר הדלקת נרות חנוכה

On each of the eight nights of חנוכה*, the lights of the* חנוכיה *are lit: one on the first night, two on the second, and so on. On the first night, the rightmost branch of the* חנוכיה *is used; on each subsequent night, an additional light is added to the left. Each night, the new light is lit first, then the others, moving rightwards. The lighting should be carried out as soon as possible after nightfall. On Friday night, it must be done before the beginning of* שבת*.*

Before lighting the חנוכה *lights, say:*

בָּרוּךְ אַתָּה יהוה אֱלֹהֵינוּ מֶלֶךְ הָעוֹלָם, אֲשֶׁר קִדְּשָׁנוּ בְּמִצְוֹתָיו וְצִוָּנוּ לְהַדְלִיק נֵר שֶׁל חֲנֻכָּה.

בָּרוּךְ אַתָּה יהוה אֱלֹהֵינוּ מֶלֶךְ הָעוֹלָם, שֶׁעָשָׂה נִסִּים לַאֲבוֹתֵינוּ בַּיָּמִים הָהֵם בַּזְּמַן הַזֶּה.

On the first night, add:

בָּרוּךְ אַתָּה יהוה אֱלֹהֵינוּ מֶלֶךְ הָעוֹלָם, שֶׁהֶחֱיָנוּ וְקִיְּמָנוּ וְהִגִּיעָנוּ לַזְּמַן הַזֶּה.

After lighting the first light, say:

הַנֵּרוֹת הַלָּלוּ אָנוּ מַדְלִיקִים, עַל הַנִּסִּים וְעַל הַנִּפְלָאוֹת וְעַל הַתְּשׁוּעוֹת וְעַל הַמִּלְחָמוֹת, שֶׁעָשִׂיתָ לַאֲבוֹתֵינוּ בַּיָּמִים הָהֵם בַּזְּמַן הַזֶּה, עַל יְדֵי כֹּהֲנֶיךָ הַקְּדוֹשִׁים. וְכָל שְׁמוֹנַת יְמֵי חֲנֻכָּה, הַנֵּרוֹת הַלָּלוּ קֹדֶשׁ הֵם, וְאֵין לָנוּ רְשׁוּת לְהִשְׁתַּמֵּשׁ בָּהֶם, אֶלָּא לִרְאוֹתָם בִּלְבָד, כְּדֵי לְהוֹדוֹת וּלְהַלֵּל לְשִׁמְךָ הַגָּדוֹל, עַל נִסֶּיךָ וְעַל נִפְלְאוֹתֶיךָ וְעַל יְשׁוּעָתֶךָ. מסכת סופרים פרק כ

חנוכה / ḤANUKKA

In *Hilkhot Ḥanukka*, Rambam explained that we are to perform two *mitzvot* on this festival: recitation of *Hallel* and lighting the candles. The former is performed in the morning, the latter at night. In essence, these are not two separate *mitzvot*, but one *mitzva*, that of פִּרְסוּמֵי נִסָּא (publicizing the miracle). The sages decreed that the *mitzva* is fulfilled in two ways, one via speech (*Hallel*) and the other via action

ADDITIONAL HALAKHOT REGARDING THE MENORA

One should not leave the home while the lights are burning. If one needs to leave during the time for candle-lighting, it is better to delay the lighting until returning home, as there should always be someone watching or near the open flame. Those who must use an electric *menorah* instead of oil (e.g., in a hospital room) should not recite the *berakhot*.

LIGHTING THE ḤANUKKA MENORA

On each of the eight nights of Ḥanukka, the lights of the menora are lit: one on the first night, two on the second, and so on. On the first night, the rightmost branch of the menora is used; on each subsequent night, an additional light is added to the left. Each night, the new light is lit first, then the others, moving rightwards. The lighting should be carried out as soon as possible after nightfall. On Friday night, it must be done before the beginning of Shabbat.

Before lighting the Ḥanukka lights, say:

בָּרוּךְ BLESSED ARE YOU, Lord, our God, King of the universe, Who has made us holy through His commandments, and has commanded us to light the Ḥanukka lights.

בָּרוּךְ BLESSED ARE YOU, Lord, our God, King of the universe, Who performed miracles for our ancestors in those days, at this time.

On the first night, add:

בָּרוּךְ BLESSED ARE YOU, Lord, our God, King of the universe, Who has given us life, sustained us, and brought us to this time.

After lighting the first light, say:

Sofrim ch. 20 הַנֵּרוֹת הַלָּלוּ WE LIGHT these lights because of the miracles and wonders, deliverances and victories You performed for our ancestors in those days, at this time, through Your holy priests. Throughout the eight days of Ḥanukka these lights are holy and we are not permitted to make any other use of them, except to look at them, that we may give thanks and praise to Your great name for Your miracles, Your wonders and Your deliverances.

(lighting candles). It is quite possible that if one lights the candles and omits *Hallel*, or vice versa, one's fulfillment of the *mitzva* is incomplete.

Moreover, the nature of the obligation to publicize the story of Ḥanukka is different from the obligation of publicizing the miracles of Purim and Pesaḥ. On those other days we publicize it only to our fellow Jews, through actions that amount to teaching Torah (on Purim by reading the *Megilla*, on *Pesaḥ* by studying appropriate Torah passages at the Seder), which by its very nature is to be restricted to Jews alone. But on Ḥanukka, when we are required to publicize it even to the non-Jewish population, publicizing the miracle and the story is accomplished simply by lighting candles, an act which in itself involves no Torah study whatsoever, and is hence the means by which the story of Ḥanukka is to be universally propagated (R. Joseph B. Soloveitchik).

הַנֵּרוֹת הַלָּלוּ – *We light these lights*. This prayer first appears in Tractate *Soferim*, which dates

After all the lights are lit:

מָעוֹז צוּר יְשׁוּעָתִי   לְךָ נָאֶה לְשַׁבֵּחַ
תִּכּוֹן בֵּית תְּפִלָּתִי   וְשָׁם תּוֹדָה נְזַבֵּחַ
לְעֵת תָּכִין מַטְבֵּחַ   מִצָּר הַמְנַבֵּחַ
אָז אֶגְמֹר, בְּשִׁיר מִזְמוֹר   חֲנֻכַּת הַמִּזְבֵּחַ.

רָעוֹת שָׂבְעָה נַפְשִׁי   בְּיָגוֹן כֹּחִי כָּלָה (נ״א כִּלָּה)
חַיַּי מֵרְרוּ בְּקֹשִׁי   בְּשִׁעְבּוּד מַלְכוּת עֶגְלָה
וּבְיָדוֹ הַגְּדוֹלָה   הוֹצִיא אֶת הַסְּגֻלָּה
חֵיל פַּרְעֹה, וְכָל זַרְעוֹ   יָרְדוּ כְּאֶבֶן בִּמְצוּלָה (נ״א מְצוּלָה).

דְּבִיר קָדְשׁוֹ הֱבִיאַנִי   וְגַם שָׁם לֹא שָׁקַטְתִּי
וּבָא נוֹגֵשׂ וְהִגְלַנִי   כִּי זָרִים עָבַדְתִּי
וְיֵין רַעַל מָסַכְתִּי   כִּמְעַט שֶׁעָבַרְתִּי
קֵץ בָּבֶל, זְרֻבָּבֶל   לְקֵץ שִׁבְעִים נוֹשַׁעְתִּי.

כְּרֹת קוֹמַת בְּרוֹשׁ בִּקֵּשׁ   אֲגָגִי בֶּן הַמְּדָתָא
וְנִהְיָתָה לּוֹ לְפַח וּלְמוֹקֵשׁ   וְגַאֲוָתוֹ נִשְׁבָּתָה
רֹאשׁ יְמִינִי נִשֵּׂאתָ   וְאוֹיֵב שְׁמוֹ מָחִיתָ
רֹב בָּנָיו, וְקִנְיָנָיו   עַל הָעֵץ תָּלִיתָ.

---

from the land of Israel in Geonic times. It immediately follows the first *berakha*. One version reads מַתְנֶה וְאוֹמֵר the one who lights "stipulates" this declaration; that is, the recital of the paragraph is a "stipulation" prior to kindling, a declaration which establishes the proper context for the kindling and thereby serves to render it a *mitzva* performance. For this reason some authorities (*Tashbetz, Hagahot Maimoniyot*) consider its recital obligatory. Others do not, likely following the alternate version of *Soferim* that omits וּמַתְנֶה. Some suggest that it is intended as a warning to the assembled household not to make use of the lights due to their sanctity (Prof. Daniel Goldschmidt).

מָעוֹז צוּר – *Refuge, Rock of my salvation. Maoz Tzur* is comprised of six stanzas structured around the five nations under whom the Jewish people were subjugated – Egypt, Babylon, Persia, Greece and Edom (Rome/Christendom). The sixth stanza was absent from manuscripts for five-hundred years due to external or self-censorship. The poet who wrote it in thirteenth-century Germany, celebrates the divine redemptions from past exiles and subjugation, and prays fervently for delivery from

After all the lights are lit:

מָעוֹז צוּר REFUGE, Rock of my salvation: to You it is a delight to give praise.
Restore my House of prayer, so that there I may offer You thanksgiving.
When You silence the loud-mouthed foe,
Then will I complete, with song and psalm, the altar's dedication.

רָעוֹת TROUBLES sated my soul; my strength was spent with sorrow.
They embittered my life with hardship, when I was enslaved under Egyptian rule.
But God with His great power brought out His treasured people,
While Pharaoh's host and followers sank like a stone into the deep.

דְּבִיר HE BROUGHT ME to His holy abode, but even there I found no rest.
The oppressor came and exiled me, because I had served strange gods.
I had drunk poisoned wine. I almost perished.
Then Babylon fell, Zerubbabel came: within seventy years I was saved.

כְּרֹת THE AGAGITE, son of Hammedatha, sought to cut down the tall fir tree,
But it became a trap to him, and his arrogance was brought to an end.
You raised the head of the Benjaminite, and the enemy's name You blotted out.
His many sons and his household You hanged on the gallows.

---

his own. The term אדמון may well refer to Esau, described in the Bible as אַדְמוֹנִי (red) (Genesis 25:25), who represents Edom. צַלְמוֹן can be a poetic form for צֶלֶם (icon, specifically the cross) or it can be derived from צֵל or צַלְמָוֶת (darkness) referring to the relegation of Edom to perdition.

Some scholars have suggested a more specific meaning for this line, to wit, that it refers to Frederick Barbarossa (Redbeard), the Emperor of the Holy Roman Empire, who died during the Third Crusade near the city of Iconium (thus צַלְמוֹן in the sense of icon) (Prof. Yom Tov Levinsky).

This is not meant as the primary understanding of our passage since Frederick's defeat was a past event and this stanza is a prayer for future redemption. We evoke the memory of the major persecutions at the hands of our historic enemies, recall the salvation that God granted us, and look forward to the destruction of the final evil empire with the advent of the messianic age. Nonetheless, we may gain a richer understanding of the passage by considering the possibility that the poet saw the recent defeat of the ruler of Edom as a foreshadowing of the imminent redemption.

יְוָנִים נִקְבְּצוּ עָלַי אֲזַי בִּימֵי חַשְׁמַנִּים
וּפָרְצוּ חוֹמוֹת מִגְדָּלַי וְטִמְּאוּ כָּל הַשְּׁמָנִים
וּמִנּוֹתַר קַנְקַנִּים נַעֲשָׂה נֵס לַשּׁוֹשַׁנִּים
בְּנֵי בִינָה, יְמֵי שְׁמוֹנָה קָבְעוּ שִׁיר וּרְנָנִים.

חֲשׂף זְרוֹעַ קָדְשֶׁךָ וְקָרֵב קֵץ הַיְשׁוּעָה
נְקֹם נִקְמַת עֲבָדֶיךָ מֵאֻמָּה הָרְשָׁעָה
כִּי אָרְכָה לָנוּ הַיְשׁוּעָה (נ״א הַשָּׁעָה) וְאֵין קֵץ לִימֵי הָרָעָה
דְּחֵה אַדְמוֹן, בְּצֵל צַלְמוֹן הָקֵם לָנוּ רוֹעִים שִׁבְעָה.

סדר קריאת המגילה בפורים

Before the reading of the מגילה, the קהל stands and the קורא says the following three blessings:

בָּרוּךְ אַתָּה יהוה אֱלֹהֵינוּ מֶלֶךְ הָעוֹלָם, אֲשֶׁר קִדְּשָׁנוּ בְּמִצְוֹתָיו וְצִוָּנוּ עַל מִקְרָא מְגִלָּה.

בָּרוּךְ אַתָּה יהוה אֱלֹהֵינוּ מֶלֶךְ הָעוֹלָם, שֶׁעָשָׂה נִסִּים לַאֲבוֹתֵינוּ בַּיָּמִים הָהֵם בַּזְּמַן הַזֶּה.

בָּרוּךְ אַתָּה יהוה אֱלֹהֵינוּ מֶלֶךְ הָעוֹלָם, שֶׁהֶחֱיָנוּ וְקִיְּמָנוּ וְהִגִּיעָנוּ לַזְּמַן הַזֶּה.

The מגילה is read. When the reading is completed, the scroll is rolled up and, if a מנין is present, the קורא continues:

בָּרוּךְ אַתָּה יהוה אֱלֹהֵינוּ מֶלֶךְ הָעוֹלָם, הָרָב אֶת רִיבֵנוּ, וְהַדָּן אֶת דִּינֵנוּ, וְהַנּוֹקֵם אֶת נִקְמָתֵנוּ, וְהַמְשַׁלֵּם גְּמוּל לְכָל אוֹיְבֵי

The primary reference is to Esau's punishment at the end of days, but the formulation was inspired by the fate of the ruler of "Edom" in the late twelfth century (Prof. David Berger).

While the sixth stanza was absent, and even after it was restored, the poem was supplemented by scholars and poets with compositions reflecting each generation's

יְוָנִים THEN THE GREEKS gathered against me, in the days of the Hasmoneans.
They broke down the walls of my towers, and defiled all the oils.
But from the last remaining flask a miracle was wrought for Your beloved.
Therefore the sages ordained these eight days for song and praise.

חֲשׂף BARE YOUR HOLY arm, and hasten the time of salvation.
Take retribution against the evil nation on behalf of Your servants,
For deliverance has been too long delayed; there seems no end to the evil days.
Thrust the enemy into the darkness of death,
and establish for us the seven Shepherds.

MEGILLA READING FOR PURIM

Before the reading of the Megilla, the congregation stands and the Reader says the following three blessings:

בָּרוּךְ BLESSED ARE YOU, Lord, our God, King of the universe, Who has made us holy through His commandments, and has commanded us about reading the Megilla.

בָּרוּךְ BLESSED ARE YOU, Lord, our God, King of the universe, Who performed miracles for our ancestors in those days at this time.

בָּרוּךְ BLESSED ARE YOU, Lord, our God, King of the universe, Who has given us life, sustained us, and brought us to this time.

The Megilla is read. When the reading is completed, the scroll is rolled up and, if a minyan is present, the Reader continues:

בָּרוּךְ BLESSED ARE YOU, Lord, our God, King of the universe, Who pleads our cause, judges our claim, avenges our wrong, brings

---

own troubles and hopes for redemption, consistent with the Ḥanukka theme of שֶׁעָשָׂה נִסִּים לַאֲבוֹתֵינוּ בַּיָּמִים הָהֵם בַּזְּמַן הַזֶּה (Who performed miracles for our fathers in those days, and in our own time) (R. Aton Holzer).

נַפְשֵׁנוּ, וְהַנִּפְרָע לָנוּ מִצָּרֵינוּ. בָּרוּךְ אַתָּה יהוה, הַנִּפְרָע לְעַמּוֹ יִשְׂרָאֵל מִכָּל צָרֵיהֶם, הָאֵל הַמּוֹשִׁיעַ.

The following is said after the night reading of the מגילה:

אֲשֶׁר הֵנִיא עֲצַת גּוֹיִם, וַיָּפֶר מַחְשְׁבוֹת עֲרוּמִים.
בְּקוּם עָלֵינוּ אָדָם רָשָׁע, נֵצֶר זָדוֹן מִזֶּרַע עֲמָלֵק.
גָּאָה בְעָשְׁרוֹ וְכָרָה לוֹ בּוֹר, וּגְדֻלָּתוֹ יָקְשָׁה לוֹ לָכֶד.
דִּמָּה בְנַפְשׁוֹ לִלְכֹּד וְנִלְכַּד, בִּקֵּשׁ לְהַשְׁמִיד וְנִשְׁמַד מְהֵרָה.
הָמָן הוֹדִיעַ אֵיבַת אֲבוֹתָיו, וְעוֹרֵר שִׂנְאַת אַחִים לַבָּנִים.
וְלֹא זָכַר רַחֲמֵי שָׁאוּל, כִּי בְחֶמְלָתוֹ עַל אֲגָג נוֹלַד אוֹיֵב.
זָמַם רָשָׁע לְהַכְרִית צַדִּיק, וְנִלְכַּד טָמֵא בִּידֵי טָהוֹר.
חֶסֶד גָּבַר עַל שִׁגְגַת אָב, וְרָשָׁע הוֹסִיף חֵטְא עַל חֲטָאָיו.
טָמַן בְּלִבּוֹ מַחְשְׁבוֹת עֲרוּמָיו, וַיִּתְמַכֵּר לַעֲשׂוֹת רָעָה.
יָדוֹ שָׁלַח בִּקְדוֹשֵׁי אֵל, כַּסְפּוֹ נָתַן לְהַכְרִית זִכְרָם.
כִּרְאוֹת מָרְדְּכַי כִּי יָצָא קֶצֶף, וְדָתֵי הָמָן נִתְּנוּ בְשׁוּשָׁן.
לָבַשׁ שַׂק וְקָשַׁר מִסְפֵּד וְגָזַר צוֹם וַיֵּשֶׁב עַל הָאֵפֶר.
מִי זֶה יַעֲמֹד לְכַפֵּר שְׁגָגָה, וְלִמְחֹל חַטַּאת עֲוֹן אֲבוֹתֵינוּ.
נֵץ פָּרַח מִלּוּלָב, הֵן הֲדַסָּה עָמְדָה לְעוֹרֵר יְשֵׁנִים.
סָרִיסֶיהָ הִבְהִילוּ לְהָמָן, לְהַשְׁקוֹתוֹ יֵין חֲמַת תַּנִּינִים.

פורים / PURIM

אֲשֶׁר הֵנִיא – *[God] frustrated the plan.* The Gemara (*Megilla* 21b) records two opinions as to the proper blessing to be recited after the *Megilla* reading, either הָרָב אֶת רִיבֵנוּ or הָאֵל הַמּוֹשִׁיעַ. Our current single blessing reflects the Gemara's conclusion, to synthesize the two blessings into one. However, in the land of Israel in Talmudic times, the blessing of הָאֵל הַמּוֹשִׁיעַ was said; it began with the standard blessing formula בָּרוּךְ אַתָּה ה׳ אֱלֹהֵינוּ מֶלֶךְ הָעוֹלָם, continued with the extended poem *"Asher Heini"* and concluded with the words תְּשׁוּעָתָם הָיִיתָ לָנֶצַח, וְתִקְוָתָם בְּכָל דּוֹר וָדוֹר, followed with a blessing, בָּרוּךְ אַתָּה ה׳ הָאֵל הַמּוֹשִׁיעַ. In the early pre-Ashkenazic communities the ruling of the Babylonian Talmud was accepted so that one synthesized blessing was recited, but in deference to the custom of the land of Israel, the ancient central portion of the הָאֵל הַמּוֹשִׁיעַ blessing was retained and recited afterward. The verses that follow (אָרוּר הָמָן...לְהוֹדִיעַ) relate back to the first blessing (Avraham Frankel). After the daytime reading, the poem is abbreviated to its last stanza, which is composed of the last two verses (שׁוֹשַׁנַּת יַעֲקֹב and תְּשׁוּעָתָם הָיִיתָ, concluding with בְּכָל דּוֹר וָדוֹר), which constitutes an apt abbreviation (R. Aton Holzer).

retribution to our enemies, and punishes our foes. Blessed are You, Lord, Who on behalf of His people Israel, exacts punishment from all their foes, the God Who brings salvation.

The following is said after the night reading of the Megilla:

א אֲשֶׁר הֵנִיא [GOD] FRUSTRATED THE PLAN of the nations,
Thwarted the intentions of the crafty.

ב An evil man rose up against us,
an arrogant branch of Amalek's tree,

ג Haughty, rich, he dug his own pit.
His hubris became his own snare.

ד He was trapped in the trap he set for others.
Seeking to destroy, he was destroyed.

ה Haman shared his ancestors' hate,
and stirred against children the hostility of brothers.

ו He did not remember Saul's act of mercy,
his pity for Agag, through which a new enemy was born.

ז The wicked planned to cut off the righteous,
but the impure was defeated by the pure.

ח [Mordekhai's] goodness overcame the father's [Saul's] error,
but the evil [Haman] piled sin upon sin.

ט He hid in his heart his cunning schemes,
intent on his evildoing.

י He stretched out his hand against God's holy ones;
he spent his wealth to destroy every memory of them.

כ When Mordekhai saw the wrath go forth,
and Haman's decrees issued in Shushan,

ל he put on sackcloth, wrapped himself in mourning,
decreed a fast and sat on ashes.

מ "Who will arise to atone for error,
and find forgiveness for our ancestors' sins?"

נ A flower blossomed from the palm tree;
Hadassa arose to wake those who slept.

ס Her servants hastened Haman to come,
to serve him wine with the venom of serpents.

עָמַד בְּעָשְׁרוֹ וְנָפַל בְּרִשְׁעוֹ, עָשָׂה לּוֹ עֵץ וְנִתְלָה עָלָיו.
פִּיהֶם פָּתְחוּ כָּל יוֹשְׁבֵי תֵבֵל, כִּי פוּר הָמָן נֶהְפַּךְ לְפוּרֵנוּ.
צַדִּיק נֶחֱלַץ מִיַּד רָשָׁע, אוֹיֵב נִתַּן תַּחַת נַפְשׁוֹ.
קִיְּמוּ עֲלֵיהֶם לַעֲשׂוֹת פּוּרִים וְלִשְׂמֹחַ בְּכָל שָׁנָה וְשָׁנָה.
רָאִיתָ אֶת תְּפִלַּת מָרְדְּכַי וְאֶסְתֵּר, הָמָן וּבָנָיו עַל הָעֵץ תָּלִיתָ.

The following is said after both night and morning readings of the מגילה:

שׁוֹשַׁנַּת יַעֲקֹב צָהֲלָה וְשָׂמֵחָה בִּרְאוֹתָם יַחַד תְּכֵלֶת מָרְדְּכָי.
תְּשׁוּעָתָם הָיִיתָ לָנֶצַח, וְתִקְוָתָם בְּכָל דּוֹר וָדוֹר.
לְהוֹדִיעַ שֶׁכָּל קוֶֹיךָ לֹא יֵבֹשׁוּ, וְלֹא יִכָּלְמוּ לָנֶצַח כָּל הַחוֹסִים בָּךְ.
אָרוּר הָמָן אֲשֶׁר בִּקֵּשׁ לְאַבְּדִי,
בָּרוּךְ מָרְדְּכַי הַיְּהוּדִי.
אֲרוּרָה זֶרֶשׁ אֵשֶׁת מַפְחִידִי,
בְּרוּכָה אֶסְתֵּר בַּעֲדִי.
אֲרוּרִים כָּל הָרְשָׁעִים,
בְּרוּכִים כָּל יִשְׂרָאֵל,
וְגַם חַרְבוֹנָה זָכוּר לַטּוֹב.

After the night reading, מעריב *continues with* וְאַתָּה קָדוֹשׁ *to* וַיְאַדִּיר *on pages 734–736 (on* מוצאי שבת*, begin with* וִיהִי נֹעַם *on page 732). The* שליח ציבור *then continues with* קדיש שלם *on page 736 (omitting the line* תִּתְקַבַּל*). (On* מוצאי שבת*, continue with* וְיִתֶּן לְךָ *on page 738.) The service continues with* עָלֵינוּ *and* קדיש יתום *on page 746.*
In the morning, continue with אַשְׁרֵי *on page 172 and* וּבָא לְצִיּוֹן *on page 176.*

בָּרוּךְ מָרְדְּכַי... בְּרוּכָה אֶסְתֵּר – *Blessed be Mordekhai... Blessed be Esther.* "God willed that both male and female appear as actors on the historical stage. Judaism has never discriminated against women. From the days of Sarah, the woman was on a par with man as a history maker. Both Mordekhai and Esther were endowed with dignity and majesty; both possessed great talent; both were charismatic personae, both were called to service, to make history. Their assignments differed not only physiologically but psychologically and spiritually as well. A historical masculine role cannot be assigned to a woman. A feminine task must not be imposed on a man... The inspired charismatic woman is superior to inspired charismatic man in two areas: practical thinking and prayer. Our sages said, "Many important rules can be derived from the verses relating to Hannah's prayer" (*Berakhot* 31a). It is true that Hannah would not have been counted in a *minyan*. Nevertheless she is our teacher regarding prayer. If not for her we would not know how to pray. While

ע He had risen by his wealth, but fell by his evil.
He made the very gallows by which he was hanged.

פ All the inhabitants of the world were amazed
when Haman's ploy (*pur*) became our joy (*Purim*).

צ The righteous one was saved from evil hands,
the perpetrator suffered the fate of his intended victim.

ק They undertook to celebrate Purim,
and to rejoice on it year after year.

ר You heeded the prayer of Mordekhai and Esther;
and Haman and his sons were hanged on the gallows.

The following is said after both night and morning readings of the Megilla:

ש **שׁוֹשַׁנַּת יַעֲקֹב** THE LILY OF Jacob rejoiced and was glad,
when, together, they saw Mordekhai robed in royal blue.

ת You have been their eternal salvation, their hope in every generation;
to make known that all who hope in You will not be put to shame,
all who trust in You will never be humiliated.

Cursed be Haman who sought to destroy me.
Blessed be Mordekhai the Yehudi.
Cursed be Zeresh, wife of the one who terrified me.
Blessed be Esther [whose actions saved] me.
Cursed be all the wicked;
blessed be all Israel.
And may Ḥarvona, too, be remembered for good.

After the night reading, Ma'ariv continues with "You are Holy" to "and glorify it" on pages 735–737 (on Motza'ei Shabbat, begin with "May the pleasantness" on page 733). The Leader then continues with Full Kaddish on page 737 (omitting the line "May the prayers and pleas"). (On Motza'ei Shabbat, continue with "May God give you" on page 739.) The service continues with Aleinu and Mourner's Kaddish on page 747. In the morning, continue with Ashrei on page 173 and "A redeemer shall come" on page 177.

Hannah taught the individual, the lonely man or woman, how to pour out his or her soul in times of distress, Esther taught Mordekhai, the Jews, and all future generations how to pray in assembly, in community, when disaster strikes the nation... When called upon to act as God's agent, a Jew must be mature, but when it is time to pray he must shed his maturity to achieve the enthusiasm or grief of a child. The woman is more of an expert in playing this double role. Esther performed it magnificently. She knew how to be cunning and how to pray. Therefore the *Megilla* is named for Esther" (R. Joseph B. Soloveitchik).

סליחות

סליחות are said on Fast Days, immediately following the repetition of the עמידה לשחרית. On תשעה באב, קינות are said instead. On צום גדליה, the סליחות for the עשרת ימי תשובה are said.

סליחות לעשרה בטבת

סְלַח לָֽנוּ, אָבִֽינוּ, כִּי בְּרֹב אִוַּלְתֵּֽנוּ שָׁגִֽינוּ. מְחַל לָֽנוּ, מַלְכֵּֽנוּ, כִּי רַבּוּ עֲוֹנֵֽינוּ.

אֵל אֶֽרֶךְ אַפַּֽיִם אַתָּה, וּבַֽעַל הָרַחֲמִים נִקְרֵֽאתָ, וְדֶֽרֶךְ תְּשׁוּבָה הוֹרֵֽיתָ.
גְּדֻלַּת רַחֲמֶֽיךָ וַחֲסָדֶֽיךָ, תִּזְכֹּר הַיּוֹם וּבְכָל יוֹם לְזֶֽרַע יְדִידֶֽיךָ.
תֵּֽפֶן אֵלֵֽינוּ בְּרַחֲמִים, כִּי אַתָּה הוּא בַּֽעַל הָרַחֲמִים. בְּתַחֲנוּן וּבִתְפִלָּה

סְלִיחוֹת / SELIḤOT

The prototypical fast day is Yom Kippur. Scripture records numerous additional fast days adopted when Jews were endangered by natural calamities or military threats. The practice of responding to communal threats with prayer-gatherings and fasting is codified in the Mishna *Ta'anit*.

Zechariah the prophet (Zech. 8:16–18) mentions four communal fasts established on a fixed basis in the Second Temple era to commemorate four key events leading to the destruction of the First Temple and the exile from the land. These are observed as the fasts of *Asara B'Tevet, Shiva Asar B'Tammuz, Tisha B'Av* and *Tzom Gedalya*. Another fast day, *Ta'anit Esther*, on the eve of Purim, is first attested in the works of the Geonim, while the fast of the firstborn, *Ta'anit Bekhorim*, on the eve of Pesaḥ, appears in tractate *Soferim*.

The purpose of fasting is explained by Isaiah, as read in the *Haftara* for Yom Kippur morning, which emphasizes that fasting is intended to open our eyes, hearts and hands to our fellows in need. This is true not only for individuals but for entire communities. *Ta'anit* 12b describes how, during fasts declared for communal calamities, the leaders would examine the deeds of the entire community, with special attention paid to unacceptable acts of social injustice.

Hence, on the fast days, we should engage in communal repentance and self-scrutiny in relation to others.

In their origin, the special prayers for fast days were part of the *Amida*. In Babylonia, *Seliḥot* were said on all fast days as an expansion of the sixth blessing of the *Amida*, סְלַח לָֽנוּ אָבִֽינוּ. In the land of Israel, *Kinot* were recited on all four fasts for the loss of the Temple and sovereignty, and were read as an expansion of the fourteenth blessing, which covered the restoration of Davidic rule and rebuilding of Jerusalem (Prof. Avi Shmidman).

The Thirteen Attributes are listed in Exodus 34:6–7 where, following the disastrous episode of the Golden Calf, and Moses' pleas for forgiveness, God passes in front of Moses while proclaiming His attributes of mercy and forgiveness. There are five views among medieval halakhic authorities as to precisely how the attributes listed in these verses are to be understood and enumerated (Rabbeinu Tam, Nissim Gaon, Hagaha"h in Tosafot, the Arizal, and R. Yehuda Haḥasid, the first three being found in comments to the Gemara *Rosh*

SELIḤOT

Seliḥot are said on Fast Days, immediately following the repetition of the Shaḥarit Amida. On Tisha B'Av, Kinot are said instead. On the Fast of Gedalya, the Seliḥot for the Ten Days of Repentance are said.

SELIḤOT FOR THE TENTH OF TEVET

סְלַח לָנוּ FORGIVE US, our Father, for in our great foolishness we have blundered. Pardon us, our King, for our iniquities are many.

אֵל אֶרֶךְ YOU ARE A GOD slow to anger, You are called the Master of Compassion, and You have taught the way of repentance. May You remember today and every day the greatness of Your compassion and kindness, for the sake of the descendants of Your beloved ones. Turn toward us in compassion, for You are the Master of Compassion. We come before You in plea and prayer, as You in

---

HaShana 17b). The implication of that divine proclamation was that the people would be forgiven then and in the future, by prayerfully invoking this very list verbatim, just as God had done (R. Ahron Soloveichik).

In fact, that Gemara records the view of R. Yoḥanan that God Himself demonstrated to Moses how forgiveness was to be sought and achieved, i.e., God assumed the human form of a prayer-leader wrapped in a *tallit*, and then pronounced the list of attributes. Hence, following God's model, we too proclaim the list of these attributes when seeking divine forgiveness. Yet it should be noted that several late medieval commentators develop a most repercussive understanding of this Gemara. The late fifteenth-century R. Avraham Sava (in the *Zeror Hamor*), who was among those expelled from Spain in 1492, notes that R. Yoḥanan quotes God as saying "when Israel will sin, יַעֲשׂוּ לְפָנַי (they should act – i.e. not merely verbally proclaim) before Me in ways that are consistent with the following list of qualities, and then I will forgive them." He goes on to explain "after all we ourselves have witnessed many times that we wrapped ourselves in a *tallit* and proclaimed these words, yet God did not answer us. The reason is that it is only when we act in accordance with the ethical attributes of God, having mercy on the weak, being long-suffering toward those who wrong us, and in general acting compassionately with each other, that we can be assured that our prayers will be answered. But if we are cruel toward each other, or commit evil deeds, then our invocation of God's mercies will only serve to highlight our failures, and condemn us. That is why the Torah introduces this section by saying that if we will act in these ways 'I will have mercy on those whom I will choose to be merciful toward (v. 19).'" We find a similar interpretation of these verses by R. Ḥayyim of Friedberg (the brother of the Maharal of Prague), who in 1578 wrote "what is crucial is not our words but our actions, and because in our time people proclaim these words but do not act according to them, therefore our prayers for mercy are not answered" (Dr. Eliezer Brodt).

In short, it is not enough to passionately proclaim the Thirteen Attributes of Mercy, as many do during Seliḥot, on Yom Kippur, or on other occasions. The words are not some kind of magical incantation, which if proclaimed

פָּנֶיךָ נְקַדֵּם, כְּהוֹדַעְתָּ לֶעָנָו מִקֶּדֶם. מֵחֲרוֹן אַפְּךָ שׁוּב, כְּמוֹ בְּתוֹרָתְךָ כָּתוּב. וּבְצֵל כְּנָפֶיךָ נֶחֱסֶה וְנִתְלוֹנָן, כְּיוֹם וַיֵּרֶד יהוה בֶּעָנָן. ‹ תַּעֲבֹר עַל פֶּשַׁע וְתִמְחֶה אָשָׁם, כְּיוֹם וַיִּתְיַצֵּב עִמּוֹ שָׁם. תַּאֲזִין שַׁוְעָתֵנוּ וְתַקְשִׁיב מֶנּוּ מַאֲמָר, כְּיוֹם וַיִּקְרָא בְשֵׁם יהוה, וְשָׁם נֶאֱמַר

:שליח ציבור then קהל

שמות לד וַיַּעֲבֹר יהוה עַל־פָּנָיו וַיִּקְרָא

All say aloud:

שמות לד **יהוה,** יהוה, אֵל רַחוּם וְחַנּוּן, אֶרֶךְ אַפַּיִם, וְרַב־חֶסֶד וֶאֱמֶת: נֹצֵר חֶסֶד לָאֲלָפִים, נֹשֵׂא עָוֹן וָפֶשַׁע וְחַטָּאָה, וְנַקֵּה: וְסָלַחְתָּ לַעֲוֺנֵנוּ וּלְחַטָּאתֵנוּ, וּנְחַלְתָּנוּ:

Continue:

תהלים פו **סְלַח לָנוּ** אָבִינוּ כִּי חָטָאנוּ, מְחַל לָנוּ מַלְכֵּנוּ כִּי פָשָׁעְנוּ. כִּי־אַתָּה אֲדֹנָי טוֹב וְסַלָּח, וְרַב־חֶסֶד לְכָל־קֹרְאֶיךָ:

תהלים קל
תהלים כה **כִּי־עִם־יהוה** הַחֶסֶד, וְהַרְבֵּה עִמּוֹ פְדוּת: פְּדֵה אֱלֹהִים אֶת־יִשְׂרָאֵל
תהלים קל מִכֹּל צָרוֹתָיו: וְהוּא יִפְדֶּה אֶת־יִשְׂרָאֵל מִכֹּל עֲוֺנֹתָיו: פּוֹדֶה
תהלים לד יהוה נֶפֶשׁ עֲבָדָיו, וְלֹא יֶאְשְׁמוּ כָּל־הַחֹסִים בּוֹ:

תהלים ג **כְּרַחֵם** אָב עַל בָּנִים, כֵּן תְּרַחֵם יהוה עָלֵינוּ. לַיהוה הַיְשׁוּעָה, עַל־עַמְּךָ
תהלים מו בִרְכָתֶךָ סֶּלָה: יהוה צְבָאוֹת עִמָּנוּ, מִשְׂגָּב לָנוּ אֱלֹהֵי יַעֲקֹב סֶלָה:

---

with sufficient enthusiasm or heartfelt pleading will bring forgiveness or salvation. To the contrary, unless they are understood for what they are, i.e., as an aid to facilitate our fullest remorse and repentance, and our very real commitment to pursue proper behavior, they can, God forbid, only serve to highlight our own shortcomings in living up to God's example.

עֲשָׂרָה בְּטֵבֵת / THE TENTH OF TEVET
Three tragedies occurred in Tevet:
8 Tevet – The Gemara (*Megilla* 9a) relates that in the reign of the third-century BCE Egyptian king Ptolemy II seventy-two Jewish sages were forced to translate all of Scripture into Greek, producing the Septuagint. *Soferim* 1:7 refers to that translation as cause for mourning insofar as the translation necessarily failed to convey the full meaning of the original.

9 Tevet – It is widely believed that Ezra the Scribe died on this date. Some identify Ezra with Malachi, with whose death prophecy came to an end.

10 Tevet – On this day Nebuchadnezzar laid siege to Jerusalem, leading to the destruction

ancient times showed the humble one [Moses]. Turn from Your fierce anger, as is written in Your Torah. In the shadow of Your wings may we shelter and abide, as on the day when the Lord descended in the cloud. ▸ Overlook sin and wipe away guilt, as on the day when "He stood beside him there." Give ear to our pleading and listen to our speech, as on the day when "he called upon the name of the Lord," and in that place is said –

Congregation then Leader:

Ex. 34 AND THE LORD passed by before him and proclaimed:

All say aloud:

Ex. 34 יהוה THE LORD, the Lord, compassionate and gracious God, slow to anger and great in mercy and truth, keeping loving-kindness for thousands, forgiving iniquity, transgression, and sin, and offering absolution. Forgive us our iniquity and our sin, and take us as Your inheritance.

Continue:

סְלַח לָנוּ FORGIVE US, our Father, for we have sinned. Pardon us, our King, for
Ps. 86 we have transgressed. For You, Lord, are good and forgiving, abounding in loving-kindness to all who call on You.

Ps. 130 כִּי־עִם־יהוה FOR WITH THE LORD there is loving-kindness, and great is His power
Ps. 25 Ps. 130 to redeem. Lord, save Israel from all its troubles. It is He Who will redeem Israel
Ps. 34 from all its sins. The Lord redeems His servants; those who take refuge in Him shall not be condemned.

כְּרַחֵם AS A FATHER has compassion for his children, so, Lord, have com-
Ps. 3 passion for us. Salvation is the Lord's; on Your people is Your blessing, Selah!
Ps. 46 The Lord of hosts is with us, the God of Jacob is our stronghold, Selah!

---

of the First Temple some eighteen months later. Ezekiel, sent to Babylonia with the early wave of exiles, was informed by God to take note of "the very day" that the siege had begun. Word of the ultimate destruction, on the ninth of Av, reached the Babylonian exiles on the fifth of Tevet of the following year.

In the early days of the State of Israel, Chief Rabbis Yitzḥak HaLevi Herzog and Ben-Zion Uziel established the Tenth of Tevet as the "general day of *Kaddish*" for all those eligible to recite *Kaddish* on behalf of Holocaust victims whose *Yahrzeits* remain unknown. This decision was made on the basis of the Gemara (*Berakhot* 32b) that the siege of the Tenth of Tevet marked the beginning of divine concealment, when a "wall of iron" came between God and the Jewish people. The Holocaust, seen as the ultimate concealment of God from His people Israel, was fittingly to be mourned on the Tenth of Tevet by the recital of *Kaddish* for its victims.

תהלים פד / תהלים כ — יהוה צְבָאוֹת, אַשְׁרֵי אָדָם בֹּטֵחַ בָּךְ: יהוה הוֹשִׁיעָה, הַמֶּלֶךְ יַעֲנֵנוּ בְיוֹם־קָרְאֵנוּ:

במדבר יד ◂ **סְלַח־נָא** לַעֲוֹן הָעָם הַזֶּה כְּגֹדֶל חַסְדֶּךָ, וְכַאֲשֶׁר נָשָׂאתָה לָעָם הַזֶּה מִמִּצְרַיִם וְעַד־הֵנָּה: וְשָׁם נֶאֱמַר

:שליח ציבור then קהל

וַיֹּאמֶר יהוה, סָלַחְתִּי כִּדְבָרֶךָ:

Continue:

דניאל ט — **הַטֵּה** אֱלֹהַי אָזְנְךָ וּשְׁמָע, פְּקַח עֵינֶיךָ וּרְאֵה שֹׁמְמֹתֵינוּ וְהָעִיר אֲשֶׁר־נִקְרָא שִׁמְךָ עָלֶיהָ, כִּי לֹא עַל־צִדְקֹתֵינוּ אֲנַחְנוּ מַפִּילִים תַּחֲנוּנֵינוּ לְפָנֶיךָ, כִּי עַל־רַחֲמֶיךָ הָרַבִּים: אֲדֹנָי שְׁמָעָה, אֲדֹנָי סְלָחָה, אֲדֹנָי הַקְשִׁיבָה וַעֲשֵׂה אַל־תְּאַחַר, לְמַעַנְךָ אֱלֹהַי, כִּי־שִׁמְךָ נִקְרָא עַל־עִירְךָ וְעַל־עַמֶּךָ:

אֱלֹהֵינוּ וֵאלֹהֵי אֲבוֹתֵינוּ

אֶזְכְּרָה מָצוֹק אֲשֶׁר קְרָאַנִי. / **בְּ**שָׁלֹשׁ מַכּוֹת בַּחֹדֶשׁ הַזֶּה הִכַּנִי.
איוב טז — **גְּ**דָעַנִי הֱנִיאַנִי הִכְאַנִי. אַף־עַתָּה הֶלְאָנִי:
דְּעָכַנִי בִּשְׁמוֹנָה בוֹ שְׂמָאלִית וִימָנִית. / **הֲ**לֹא שְׁלָשְׁתָּן קָבַעְתִּי תַעֲנִית.
וּמֶלֶךְ יָוָן אֲנָסַנִי לִכְתֹּב דָּת, יְוָנִית. עַל גַּבִּי חָרְשׁוּ חוֹרְשִׁים, הֶאֱרִיכוּ מַעֲנִית.
זְעַמְתִּי בְּתִשְׁעָה בוֹ בִּכְלִמָּה וְחֵפֶר. / **חָ**שַׁךְ מֵעָלַי מְעִיל הוֹד וָצֶפֶר.
טָרֹף טֹרַף בּוֹ הַנּוֹתֵן אִמְרֵי שֶׁפֶר. הוּא עֶזְרָא הַסּוֹפֵר.
יוֹם עֲשִׂירִי, צֻוָּה בֶן בּוּזִי הַחוֹזֶה. / **כְּ**תָב לְךָ בַּסֵּפֶר הַמַּחֲזֶה.
יחזקאל כד — **לְ**זִכָּרוֹן לְעַם נָמֵס וְנִבְזֶה. אֶת־עֶצֶם הַיּוֹם הַזֶּה:
מִנְיַן סֵדֶר חֳדָשִׁים בַּעֲשָׂרָה בוֹ הָעִיר. / **נְ**הִי וִילֵל בָּמוֹ פִּי אַפְעִיר.
סֵדֶר פֻּרְעָנִיּוֹת בְּתוֹךְ לְבָבִי יַבְעִיר. בְּבֹא אֵלַי הַפָּלִיט לֵאמֹר הֻכְּתָה הָעִיר.
עַל אֵלֶּה, עַל פְּנֵי אָבָק זֵרִיתִי. / **פַּ**צְתִּי עַל אַרְבַּעְתָּן, לוּ חֵץ בְּלִבִּי יָרִיתִי.
איכה א — **צָ**רוֹת עַל אֵלֶּה, קֶבֶר לִי כָּרִיתִי. צַדִּיק הוּא יהוה, כִּי פִיהוּ מָרִיתִי:
קָרָאתִי שִׁמְךָ, מִתְנַחֵם עַל רָעָתִי. / **רְ**אֵה עָנְיִי וּשְׁמַע קוֹל פְּגִיעָתִי.
איכה ג — **שְׁ**מַע תְּחִנָּתִי, חִישׁ נָא יְשׁוּעָתִי. אַל־תַּעְלֵם אָזְנְךָ לְרַוְחָתִי לְשַׁוְעָתִי:
◂ **יֶ**רַח טֵבֵת, מְאֹד לָקִיתִי בוֹ. / **וְ**נִשְׁתְּנוּ עָלַי סְדָרַי נְתִיבוֹ.
סְרַרְתִּי, **פְּ**שַׁעְתִּי, יְגַלֶּה לִי טוּבוֹ. הָאוֹמֵר לַיָּם עַד פֹּה תָבוֹא.

Ps. 84 Ps. 20 Lord of hosts, happy is the one who trusts in You. Lord, save! May the King answer us on the day we call.

Num. 14 ▸ סְלַח־נָא FORGIVE, PLEASE, this people's iniquity, in the abundance of Your kindness,and as You have forgiven this people from the time of Egypt until now, and there it is written:

Congregation then Leader:

AND THE LORD said, I have forgiven as you asked.

Continue:

Dan. 9 הַטֵּה GIVE EAR, my God and hear; open Your eyes and see our desolation, and the city that bears Your name, for it is not on the strength of our righteousness that we throw down our pleadings before You, but on the strength of Your great compassion. Lord, hear me; Lord, forgive; Lord, listen and act and do not delay – for Your sake, my God; for Your city and Your people bear Your name.

OUR GOD and God of our fathers:

אֶזְכְּרָה I SHALL RECALL the anguish that came to me; He inflicted three blows
Job 16 upon me in this month. He cut me off, He veered me aside, He beat me – but now He has finally drained me out. On the eighth of the month He darkened my right and my left; I marked out all three days for fasting. The king of Greece forced me to write the Torah in his tongue. The ploughmen have ploughed across my back; they made the furrows long. I raged, on the ninth, in shame and disgrace, my mantle of glory and my wreath were taken from me. The man who gave us the words of heaven was torn from us on that day – that was Ezra the Scribe. On the tenth, Ezekiel the Seer, son of Buzi was commanded, "Write this happening in the scroll, for the remembrance of a people melted away
Ezek. 24 and disgraced; write this very day." The tenth was listed last among the fasts to show the order of the months. My own mouth gapes open with weeping and wailing, and this chronicle of troubles burns within my heart – as the fugitive came to me and said, "The city is crushed." For these things I have scattered dust upon my face. I have spoken now of all four – would that I could shoot an arrow through my heart. For these great torments, I have dug my own grave.
Lam. 1 "The Lord is righteous; I have rebelled against His word." I have called out Your name as I grieve my troubles. Witness my oppression and hear my voice in its
Lam. 3 entreaty. Hear my pleading, please, hasten my salvation. Do not block Your ears to my sighing, to my cry. ▸ In the month of Tevet I was stricken sorely. The world changed its course, from where I stand. I was stubborn, I sinned – yet may He reveal His goodness to me; the One Who told the ocean, "Only thus far, come."

אֵל מֶלֶךְ יוֹשֵׁב עַל כִּסֵּא רַחֲמִים, מִתְנַהֵג בַּחֲסִידוּת. מוֹחֵל עֲוֹנוֹת עַמּוֹ, מַעֲבִיר רִאשׁוֹן רִאשׁוֹן. מַרְבֶּה מְחִילָה לְחַטָּאִים, וּסְלִיחָה לְפוֹשְׁעִים. עֹשֶׂה צְדָקוֹת עִם כָּל בָּשָׂר וָרְוּחַ, לֹא כְרָעָתָם תִּגְמֹל. ◂ אֵל, הוֹרֵיתָ לָּנוּ לוֹמַר שְׁלֹשׁ עֶשְׂרֵה, וּזְכָר לָנוּ הַיּוֹם בְּרִית שְׁלֹשׁ עֶשְׂרֵה, כְּמוֹ

שמות לד שֶׁהוֹדַעְתָּ לֶעָנָו מִקֶּדֶם, כְּמוֹ שֶׁכָּתוּב: וַיֵּרֶד יהוה בֶּעָנָן, וַיִּתְיַצֵּב עִמּוֹ שָׁם, וַיִּקְרָא בְשֵׁם, יהוה:

then שליח ציבור *:*קהל

שמות לד וַיַּעֲבֹר יהוה עַל־פָּנָיו וַיִּקְרָא

All say aloud:

שמות לד **יהוה,** יהוה, אֵל רַחוּם וְחַנּוּן, אֶרֶךְ אַפַּיִם, וְרַב־חֶסֶד וֶאֱמֶת: נֹצֵר חֶסֶד לָאֲלָפִים, נֹשֵׂא עָוֹן וָפֶשַׁע וְחַטָּאָה, וְנַקֵּה: וְסָלַחְתָּ לַעֲוֹנֵנוּ וּלְחַטָּאתֵנוּ, וּנְחַלְתָּנוּ:

Continue:

תהלים פו **סְלַח לָנוּ** אָבִינוּ כִּי חָטָאנוּ, מְחַל לָנוּ מַלְכֵּנוּ כִּי פָשָׁעְנוּ. כִּי־אַתָּה אֲדֹנָי טוֹב וְסַלָּח, וְרַב־חֶסֶד לְכָל־קֹרְאֶיךָ:

תהלים עט **אֱלֹהִים** בָּאוּ גוֹיִם בְּנַחֲלָתֶךָ, טִמְּאוּ אֶת־הֵיכַל קָדְשֶׁךָ, שָׂמוּ אֶת־יְרוּשָׁלִַם לְעִיִּים: אֱלֹהִים, זֵדִים קָמוּ עָלֵינוּ, וַעֲדַת עָרִיצִים בִּקְשׁוּ נַפְשֵׁנוּ, וְלֹא שָׂמוּךָ לְנֶגְדָּם.

תהלים ג **כְּרַחֵם** אָב עַל בָּנִים, כֵּן תְּרַחֵם יהוה עָלֵינוּ. לַיהוה הַיְשׁוּעָה, עַל־עַמְּךָ

תהלים מו בִרְכָתֶךָ סֶּלָה: יהוה צְבָאוֹת עִמָּנוּ, מִשְׂגָּב לָנוּ אֱלֹהֵי יַעֲקֹב סֶלָה:

תהלים פד תהלים כ יהוה צְבָאוֹת, אַשְׁרֵי אָדָם בֹּטֵחַ בָּךְ: יהוה הוֹשִׁיעָה, הַמֶּלֶךְ יַעֲנֵנוּ בְיוֹם־קָרְאֵנוּ:

אֱלֹהֵינוּ וֵאלֹהֵי אֲבוֹתֵינוּ

אֶבֶן הָרֹאשָׁה, לְעִיִּים וְלַחֲרִישָׁה, וְנוֹחֲלֵי מוֹרָשָׁה, מְנוֹד רֹאשׁ בִּלְאֻמִּים.
בְּקִרְבִּי לֵב נִכְאָב, נִדְוֶה וְנִדְאָב, נִשְׁאַרְנוּ כְּאֵין אָב, וְהָיִינוּ כִּיתוֹמִים.
רַכָּה וַעֲנֻגָּה, בַּשּׁוֹשַׁנִּים סוּגָה, וְעַתָּה הִיא נוּגָה, מְסוּרָה בְּיַד קָמִים.
הָיְתָה כְּאַלְמָנָה, קִרְיָה נֶאֱמָנָה, וְזֶרַע מִי מָנָה, נִמְכְּרוּ בְּלֹא דָמִים.
מְעֻנָּגָה וְרַכָּה, צָלְחָה לִמְלוּכָה, וּמַעֲנִיתָהּ אָרְכָה, זֶה כַּמָּה שָׁנִים וְיָמִים.

אֵל מֶלֶךְ GOD, KING Who sits upon a throne of compassion, Who acts with loving-kindness, Who pardons the iniquities of His people, passing them before Him in order; Who forgives sinners and pardons transgressors; Who performs righteousness with all flesh and spirit, do not repay their bad actions in kind. ▸ God, You taught us to speak thirteen attributes: recall for us today the covenant of the thirteen attributes, as You in ancient times showed the humble
Ex. 34 one [Moses], as is written: The Lord descended in the cloud and stood with him there, and proclaimed in the name of the Lord:

Congregation then Leader:

Ex. 34 AND THE LORD passed by before him and proclaimed:

All say aloud:

Ex. 34 יהוה THE LORD, the Lord, compassionate and gracious God, slow to anger and great in mercy and truth, keeping loving-kindness for thousands, forgiving iniquity, transgression, and sin, and offering absolution. Forgive us our iniquity and our sin, and take us as Your inheritance.

Continue:

סְלַח לָנוּ FORGIVE US, our Father, for we have sinned. Pardon us, our King, for we
Ps. 86 have transgressed. For You, Lord, are good and forgiving, abounding in loving-kindness to all who call on You.

Ps. 79 אֱלֹהִים GOD, nations came into Your inheritance, they made Your holy Sanctuary impure, they reduced Jerusalem to ruins. God, wanton people came up against us and a gang of oppressors sought out our lives, and did not place You before them.

כְּרַחֵם AS A FATHER has compassion for his children, so, Lord, have compassion
Ps. 3 Ps. 46 for us. Salvation is the Lord's; on Your people is Your blessing, Selah! The Lord
Ps. 84 of hosts is with us, the God of Jacob is our stronghold, Selah! Lord of hosts,
Ps. 20 happy is the one who trusts in You. Lord, save! May the King answer us on the day we call.

OUR GOD and God of our fathers:

אֶבֶן THE TEMPLE, TOP Stone, is laid to ruin and ploughed over, and the Torah's heirs, Israel, a derision among nations. Within me an aching heart, sickened and pained – we are left as if fatherless, become like orphans. Israel, delicate and refined, fenced by lilies of the Law, has now become mournful, given over to assailants. The faithful city has become like a widow, the countless descendants of Jacob have been sold for no price. Refined and delicate, worthy of royalty, they have been ploughed across in long furrows over many years and days. The house of Jacob is given over to plunder, to

בֵּית יַעֲקֹב לְבִזָּה, לְלַעַג וּלְעִזָּה, וְהָעִיר הָעַלִּיזָה, לְמַטְּעֵי כְרָמִים.
רְווּיָה תַרְעֵלָה, בְּיַד בְּנֵי עַוְלָה, הָרְצוּיָה כְּעוֹלָה, וְכִקְטֹרֶת הַסַּמִּים.
מְאָסָה לִזְנֹחַ, תּוֹרַת אֲבִי זָנוֹחַ, וְלֹא מָצְאָה מָנוֹחַ, לֵילוֹת וְגַם יָמִים.
נוֹרָא אֵל עֶלְיוֹן, מִמְּךָ יְהִי צִבְיוֹן, לְהָשִׁיב לְרִיב צִיּוֹן, שְׁנַת שִׁלּוּמִים.
חַדֵּשׁ יָמֵינוּ כְּקֶדֶם, מְעוֹנָה אֱלֹהֵי קֶדֶם, וְלַבֵּן כְּצֶמֶר אָדֹם, וְכַשֶּׁלֶג כְּתָמִים.
◂ חַזְּקֵנוּ בְּיִרְאָתֶךָ, וּבְקִיּוּם תּוֹרָתֶךָ, וּפָקְדֵנוּ בִּישׁוּעָתֶךָ, אֵל מָלֵא רַחֲמִים.

אֵל מֶלֶךְ יוֹשֵׁב עַל כִּסֵּא רַחֲמִים, מִתְנַהֵג בַּחֲסִידוּת. מוֹחֵל עֲוֹנוֹת עַמּוֹ, מַעֲבִיר רִאשׁוֹן רִאשׁוֹן. מַרְבֶּה מְחִילָה לְחַטָּאִים, וּסְלִיחָה לְפוֹשְׁעִים. עֹשֶׂה צְדָקוֹת עִם כָּל בָּשָׂר וָרוּחַ, לֹא כְרָעָתָם תִּגְמֹל. ◂ אֵל, הוֹרֵיתָ לָּנוּ לוֹמַר שְׁלֹשׁ עֶשְׂרֵה, וּזְכֹר לָנוּ הַיּוֹם בְּרִית שְׁלֹשׁ עֶשְׂרֵה, כְּמוֹ
שֶׁהוֹדַעְתָּ לֶעָנָו מִקֶּדֶם, כְּמוֹ שֶׁכָּתוּב: וַיֵּרֶד יהוה בֶּעָנָן, וַיִּתְיַצֵּב עִמּוֹ שָׁם, שמות לד
וַיִּקְרָא בְשֵׁם, יהוה:

שליח ציבור *then* קהל:

וַיַּעֲבֹר יהוה עַל־פָּנָיו וַיִּקְרָא שמות לד

All say aloud:

יהוה, יהוה, אֵל רַחוּם וְחַנּוּן, אֶרֶךְ אַפַּיִם, וְרַב־חֶסֶד וֶאֱמֶת: נֹצֵר חֶסֶד לָאֲלָפִים, נֹשֵׂא עָוֹן וָפֶשַׁע וְחַטָּאָה, וְנַקֵּה: וְסָלַחְתָּ לַעֲוֹנֵנוּ וּלְחַטָּאתֵנוּ, וּנְחַלְתָּנוּ: שמות לד

Continue:

סְלַח לָנוּ אָבִינוּ כִּי חָטָאנוּ, מְחַל לָנוּ מַלְכֵּנוּ כִּי פָשָׁעְנוּ. כִּי־אַתָּה אֲדֹנָי טוֹב וְסַלָּח, וְרַב־חֶסֶד לְכָל־קֹרְאֶיךָ: תהלים פו

The following is said responsively:

אֲבוֹתַי כִּי בָטְחוּ בְּשֵׁם אֱלֹהֵי צוּרִי
גָּדְלוּ וְהִצְלִיחוּ וְגַם עָשׂוּ פְרִי
וּמֵעֵת הֻדְּחוּ וְהָלְכוּ עִמּוֹ קֶרִי
הָיוּ הָלוֹךְ וְחָסוֹר עַד הַחֹדֶשׁ הָעֲשִׂירִי. בראשית ח

jeering and slander, and the joyous city to plantations of vines. Doused in poison by lawless ones, is the people once desired like offerings, like fragrant incense. They have despised and neglected the Torah of Moses Avi-Zanoaḥ, they can find no rest by night or by day. Awesome, highest God, may the desire arise in You to bring a year of recompense for Israel's strife. Renew our days as of old, Dwelling Place Who is our God of old. And wash our red guilt white as wool; our stains as snow. ▸ Strengthen us in awe of You, and in the keeping of Your Law. And come to us, in Your salvation, God Who is full of compassion.

אֵל מֶלֶךְ GOD, KING Who sits upon a throne of compassion, Who acts with loving-kindness, Who pardons the iniquities of His people, passing them before Him in order; Who forgives sinners and pardons transgressors; Who performs righteousness with all flesh and spirit, do not repay their bad actions in kind. ▸ God, You taught us to speak thirteen attributes: recall for us today the covenant of the thirteen attributes, as You in ancient times showed the
Ex. 34 humble one [Moses], as is written: The Lord descended in the cloud and stood with him there, and proclaimed in the name of the Lord:

Congregation then Leader:

Ex. 34 AND THE LORD passed by before him and proclaimed:

All say aloud:

Ex. 34 **יהוה** THE LORD, the Lord, compassionate and gracious God, slow to anger and great in mercy and truth, keeping loving-kindness for thousands, forgiving iniquity, transgression, and sin, and offering absolution. Forgive us our iniquity and our sin, and take us as Your inheritance.

Continue:

סְלַח לָנוּ FORGIVE US, our Father, for we have sinned. Pardon us, our King, for
Ps. 86 we have transgressed. For You, Lord, are good and forgiving, abounding in loving-kindness to all who call on You.

The following is said responsively:

אֲבוֹתַי WHEN MY FOREBEARS trusted in the name of God, my Rock,
they grew and were successful and also gave forth fruit.
And from the time when they were drawn away
to walk with Him in enmity,
Gen. 8 they diminished and diminished until the tenth month.

בָּעֲשִׂירִי לַחֹדֶשׁ סָמַךְ מֶלֶךְ בָּבֶל
וְצָר עַל עִיר הַקֹּדֶשׁ, וְנִקְרַב רַב הַחוֹבֵל
נְתַתִּי הָדֵשׁ וְעֻנֵּיתִי בַכֶּבֶל
וְהָיָה מִדֵּי חֹדֶשׁ לְאֵבֶל כִּנּוֹרִי.

רֵאשִׁית בִּכּוּרָה לְרֵאשִׁית הַחֵרֶם
שֵׁם אֲחֵרִים הִזְכִּירָה, וְהֶעָוֹן גּוֹרֵם
פְּנֵי אֵל לֹא הִכִּירָה, וְשָׁטְפָה בְזֶרֶם
צָרָה כְּמַבְכִּירָה כָּעֵת בַּמָּרוֹם תַּמְרִיא.

הָאֱלֹהִים הֵבִיא יוֹם רָעָה וּמָצוֹר
צִוָּה צָרֵי סְבִיבַי עוֹלְלַי לִבְצֹר
יוֹם הֵרַךְ לְבָבִי וְאֵין כֹּחַ לַעְצֹר
וְדִבֵּר אֶל נָבִיא, מְשֹׁל אֶל בֵּית הַמֶּרִי.

מִיּוֹשְׁבֵי שַׁעַר הֶעֱבִיר אַדֶּרֶת
חֲמָתוֹ כָּאֵשׁ בָּעַר, וְהֵרִים עֲטֶרֶת
וּמִלְּבָנוֹן יַעַר הִשְׁלִיךְ תִּפְאֶרֶת
וְרוּחַ סוֹעָה וָסַעַר תְּסַמֵּר שַׂעֲרַת בְּשָׂרִי.

יְפֵיפִיָּת נִמְשַׁלְתְּ, וְעַתָּה קְדוֹרַנִּית
בְּעָוֹן כִּי כָשַׁלְתְּ, וְלִבֵּךְ אֲחוֹרַנִּית
זָנַבוּךְ וְנֶחְשַׁלְתְּ רִאשׁוֹנָה וְשֵׁנִית
וְהָחֵל לֹא חָתַלְתְּ מְעַט צֳרִי.

צַדִּיק הַצּוּר תָּם, נָשָׂא עָוֹן נִלְאָה
מִכְּרוּב לְמִפְתָּן, לְפִנַּת גַּג דָּאָה
מֵעֲוֹן הִכְּתָם, וְצַעֲקָתָם בָּאָה
רַבָּה רָעָתָם כְּעֵץ עֹשֶׂה פֶּרִי.

חִזֵּק כָּל קָמַי, תּוֹכֵן הָעֲלִילוֹת
כִּי מָלְאוּ יָמַי בֶּרַע מִפְעָלוֹת
וּמִבֹּשֶׁת עֲלוּמַי שָׁכַחְתִּי גְמוּלוֹת
נוֹתֵן לַחְמִי וּמֵימַי, פִּשְׁתִּי וְצַמְרִי.

ON THE TENTH, the king of Babylon laid siege on the city,
and beleaguered it. The chief of the army arrived,
and I was yielded to be trampled, was tormented in fetters,
and from month to month my harp turned to grief.

ONCE like the first figs of a new tree,
they were the very first to be destroyed.
They spoke the names of others, and sin closed their destiny.
They did not recognize God's face and were swept off by the flood –
agony like that of a first childbirth, soars up as high as heaven.

GOD brought us a day of evil and siege,
ordered enemies about me to harvest my last fruits.
The day my heart was quelled, no strength to resist,
and He said to the prophet,
"Preach this to the rebellious house."

HE TOOK the cloak of authority from the judges at the gate.
His rage burned like fire and He raised the crown away,
and He cast down the splendor of the Temple, Forest of Lebanon,
and rushing wind and storm make my flesh bristle and shiver.

ONCE you were called most beautiful; now you are darkened,
for you have stumbled over iniquity and your heart has turned back.
You have been attacked from behind,
have been weakened, once, then twice,
and even the slightest dressing or balm not offered you.

THE RIGHTEOUS One, perfect Rock,
Who forgives iniquity almost too great to bear,
flew from the cherubs to the threshold,
and from there to a corner of the roof,
because of the iniquity marked out; the scream of it rose up,
their evil as abundant as a fruit-tree's crop.

THE ONE Who weighs the actions of people,
strengthened all my attackers,
for my days had been filled with malignant deeds,
and in the shamefulness of my youth I forgot the good granted me,
and the One Who gives me my bread and water,
my flax and my wool.

קָמַי פִּיהֶם פָּעֲרוּ וְנַחֲלָתִי בִּלְּעוּ
מְאֹד עָלַי גָּבְרוּ וְדָמִי שָׁתוּ וְלָעוּ
נָכְרִים עָלַי צָרוּ וְאֶת אַחַי הֵרֵעוּ
הָאוֹמְרִים עָרוּ עָרוּ, בְּנֵי שֵׂעִיר הַחֹרִי.

אָמְרוּ לְכוּ נְכַלֵּם, וְנַשְׁבִּיתָה זִכְרָם
אֵל קַנּוֹא וְנוֹקֵם, גְּמֹלֵם, יִשְׂאוּ אֶת שִׁבְרָם
כְּמַעֲשֵׂיהֶם שַׁלֵּם וְיֵבוֹשׁוּ מִשִּׁבְרָם
כְּאִישׁ חֲלוֹם חוֹלֵם שְׁלֹשָׁה סַלֵּי חֹרִי.

פְּצָעַי לֹא רֻכְּכָה וְחַבּוּרוֹתַי רֶצַח
וְעֵינַי הִכְהֲתָה, צוֹפָה לְדוֹדִי צַח
הַעוֹד לֹא שָׁכְכָה חֲמָתוֹ לָנֶצַח
עַל מֶה עָשָׂה כָּכָה וּמֶה חֳרִי.

רַחוּם זֶה אֵלִי, אַל לָעַד תִּזְנַח
אָרְכוּ יְמֵי אֶבְלִי וְעוֹד לִבִּי נֶאֱנָח
שׁוּבָה אֵל לְאָהֳלִי, מְקוֹמְךָ אַל תַּנַּח
שַׁלֵּם יְמֵי אֶבְלִי כִּי תָבוֹא עַל שְׂכָרִי.

יהוה מְנָת חֶלְקִי, חוּשָׁה לִּי לְעֶזְרָה
וּפִתַּחְתָּ שַׂקִּי, שִׂמְחָה לִי לְאַזְּרָה
וְתַגִּיהַּ אֶת חָשְׁכִּי בְּאוֹרְךָ לְהָאִירָה
אֶת נֶשֶׁף חִשְׁקִי, כִּי אַתָּה נֵרִי.

מִיָּגוֹן וַאֲנָחָה, פְּדֵה אֵל אֶת נַפְשִׁי
עֲשֵׂה לְעַמְּךָ הֲנָחָה, מַלְכִּי וּקְדוֹשִׁי
תַּהֲפוֹךְ לִרְוָחָה אֶת צוֹם הַחֲמִישִׁי
לְשָׂשׂוֹן וּלְשִׂמְחָה, צוֹם הָרְבִיעִי וְצוֹם הָעֲשִׂירִי.

Continue with אֵל מֶלֶךְ יוֹשֵׁב *on page 998.*

MY ATTACKERS opened wide their mouths
and swallowed up my legacy.
They overcame me utterly, drank my blood and gulped it down.
Strangers became my enemies, they injured my brothers –
strangers who called out, "Destroy, destroy!"
Descendants of Seir the Horite.

THEY SAID, "Come, let us finish them off,
and put an end to their memory."
Jealous, vengeful God, grant retribution;
let them load the burden of their own ruin.
Pay them back for their actions and have their hopes disgrace them,
like the baker who dreamt his dream
of three baskets of white bread.

MY WOUND was not softened, my bruise enough to kill me,
and my eyes have grown dim
with watching for my bright-faced Love.
Is His anger even now not forever forgotten?
Why has He done this; why this burning rage?

THIS GOD of mine is compassionate; He shall not forever reject.
The days of my grief have grown long and still my heart sighs.
Return, God, to my tent; do not abandon Your place.
Close the days of my grief. Bring my recompense.

LORD Who is the portion allotted me, come to me quickly, help me,
and loosen my sackcloth, wrap me around in joy,
and dazzle my darkness with Your light – light up
the twilight I once longed for, for it is You Who are my lamp.

REDEEM my soul from anguish and sighing,
grant Your people remission, my King and my Holy One.
And turn into relief the fast of Av;
into gladness and joy, the fast of Tammuz and the fast of Tevet.

Continue with "God, King Who sits" on page 999.

סליחות לתענית אסתר

סְלַח לָנוּ, אָבִינוּ, כִּי בְּרֹב אִוַּלְתֵּנוּ שָׁגִינוּ. מְחַל לָנוּ, מַלְכֵּנוּ, כִּי רַבּוּ עֲוֹנֵינוּ.

אֵל אֶרֶךְ אַפַּיִם אַתָּה, וּבַעַל הָרַחֲמִים נִקְרֵאתָ, וְדֶרֶךְ תְּשׁוּבָה הוֹרֵיתָ. גְּדֻלַּת רַחֲמֶיךָ וַחֲסָדֶיךָ, תִּזְכֹּר הַיּוֹם וּבְכָל יוֹם לְזֶרַע יְדִידֶיךָ. תֵּפֶן אֵלֵינוּ בְּרַחֲמִים, כִּי אַתָּה הוּא בַּעַל הָרַחֲמִים. בְּתַחֲנוּן וּבִתְפִלָּה פָּנֶיךָ נְקַדֵּם, כְּהוֹדַעְתָּ לֶעָנָו מִקֶּדֶם. מֵחֲרוֹן אַפְּךָ שׁוּב, כְּמוֹ בְּתוֹרָתְךָ כָּתוּב. וּבְצֵל כְּנָפֶיךָ נֶחֱסֶה וְנִתְלוֹנָן, כְּיוֹם וַיֵּרֶד יהוה בֶּעָנָן. ◂ תַּעֲבֹר עַל פֶּשַׁע וְתִמְחֶה אָשָׁם, כְּיוֹם וַיִּתְיַצֵּב עִמּוֹ שָׁם. תַּאֲזִין שַׁוְעָתֵנוּ וְתַקְשִׁיב מֶנּוּ מַאֲמָר, כְּיוֹם וַיִּקְרָא בְשֵׁם יהוה, וְשָׁם נֶאֱמַר

שליח ציבור then קהל:

שמות לד וַיַּעֲבֹר יהוה עַל־פָּנָיו וַיִּקְרָא

All say aloud:

שמות לד **יהוה,** יהוה, אֵל רַחוּם וְחַנּוּן, אֶרֶךְ אַפַּיִם, וְרַב־חֶסֶד וֶאֱמֶת: נֹצֵר חֶסֶד לָאֲלָפִים, נֹשֵׂא עָוֹן וָפֶשַׁע וְחַטָּאָה, וְנַקֵּה: וְסָלַחְתָּ לַעֲוֹנֵנוּ וּלְחַטָּאתֵנוּ וּנְחַלְתָּנוּ:

Continue:

תהלים פו **סְלַח לָנוּ** אָבִינוּ כִּי חָטָאנוּ, מְחַל לָנוּ מַלְכֵּנוּ כִּי פָשָׁעְנוּ. כִּי־אַתָּה אֲדֹנָי טוֹב וְסַלָּח, וְרַב־חֶסֶד לְכָל־קֹרְאֶיךָ:

ישעיה כו **קַוֵּה** קִוִּינוּ יהוה, וַיֵּט אֵלֵינוּ וַיִּשְׁמַע שַׁוְעָתֵנוּ. אַף אֹרַח מִשְׁפָּטֶיךָ יהוה קִוִּינוּךָ, לְשִׁמְךָ וּלְזִכְרְךָ תַּאֲוַת־נָפֶשׁ:

תהלים ג **כְּרַחֵם** אָב עַל בָּנִים, כֵּן תְּרַחֵם יהוה עָלֵינוּ. לַיהוה הַיְשׁוּעָה, עַל־עַמְּךָ
תהלים מו בִרְכָתֶךָ סֶּלָה: יהוה צְבָאוֹת עִמָּנוּ, מִשְׂגָּב לָנוּ אֱלֹהֵי יַעֲקֹב סֶלָה: יהוה
תהלים פד
תהלים כ צְבָאוֹת, אַשְׁרֵי אָדָם בֹּטֵחַ בָּךְ: יהוה הוֹשִׁיעָה, הַמֶּלֶךְ יַעֲנֵנוּ בְיוֹם־קָרְאֵנוּ:

תענית אסתר / THE FAST OF ESTHER

The origins of the fast are a matter of debate among the early authorities. Some, such as Rashi, traced its origins to Geonic times, while some of the Geonim themselves (see *Sheiltot R. Aḥai Gaon*) trace it back to the *Megilla* itself (9:31) and the Gemara (*Megilla* 2a).

The Purim experience, which was the prototypical experience of the Jews in exile, lends itself to two conflicting emotions – celebration of the fact that God will never allow the Jewish people's total destruction, but also fear and trepidation regarding the vulnerability of exilic existence. The latter aspect is commemorated by the Fast of Esther, on the very day that the פור (lot) chose for our destruction. This aspect was eclipsed during the Second Temple period by the victories of the Hasmoneans, which

SELIḤOT FOR THE FAST OF ESTHER

סְלַח לָנוּ FORGIVE US, our Father, for in our great foolishness we have blundered. Pardon us, our King, for our iniquities are many.

אֵל אֶרֶךְ YOU ARE A GOD slow to anger, You are called the Master of Compassion, and You have taught the way of repentance. May You remember today and every day the greatness of Your compassion and kindness, for the sake of the descendants of Your beloved ones. Turn toward us in compassion, for You are the Master of Compassion. We come before You in plea and prayer, as You in ancient times showed the humble one [Moses]. Turn from Your fierce anger, as is written in Your Torah. In the shadow of Your wings may we shelter and abide, as on the day when the Lord descended in the cloud. ▸ Overlook sin and wipe away guilt, as on the day when "He stood beside him there." Give ear to our pleading and listen to our speech, as on the day when "he called upon the name of the Lord," and in that place is said –

Congregation then Leader:

Ex. 34 AND THE LORD passed by before him and proclaimed:

All say aloud:

Ex. 34 יהוה THE LORD, the Lord, compassionate and gracious God, slow to anger and great in mercy and truth, keeping loving-kindness for thousands, forgiving iniquity, transgression, and sin, and offering absolution. Forgive us our iniquity and our sin, and take us as Your inheritance.

Continue:

סְלַח לָנוּ FORGIVE US, our Father, for we have sinned. Pardon us, our King, for
Ps. 86 we have transgressed. For You, Lord, are good and forgiving, abounding in loving-kindness to all who call on You.

Is. 26 קַוֵּה WE HAVE WAITED patiently for the Lord, and He has turned toward us and heard our cry. And on the path of Your laws, Lord, we have waited for You, for it is Your name and Your memory that are our souls' desire.

כְּרַחֵם AS A FATHER has compassion for his children, so, Lord, have compassion
Ps. 3 Ps. 46 for us. Salvation is the Lord's; on Your people is Your blessing, Selah! The Lord
Ps. 84 of hosts is with us, the God of Jacob is our stronghold, Selah! Lord of hosts,
Ps. 20 happy is the one who trusts in You. Lord, save! May the King answer us on the day we call.

---

restored national sovereignty and ended exilic subjugation – and was replaced by a celebration of an early Maccabean triumph, *Yom Nicanor*. After the destruction of 70 CE, exilic conditions again prevailed, and the Fast of Esther was reinstated (R. Elchanan Samet).

במדבר יד ◂ **סְלַח־נָא** לַעֲוֹן הָעָם הַזֶּה כְּגֹדֶל חַסְדֶּךָ, וְכַאֲשֶׁר נָשָׂאתָה לָעָם הַזֶּה
מִמִּצְרַיִם וְעַד־הֵנָּה: וְשָׁם נֶאֱמַר

:קהל then שליח ציבור

וַיֹּאמֶר יהוה, סָלַחְתִּי כִּדְבָרֶךָ:

Continue:

דניאל ט **הַטֵּה** אֱלֹהַי אָזְנְךָ וּשְׁמָע, פְּקַח עֵינֶיךָ וּרְאֵה שֹׁמְמֹתֵינוּ וְהָעִיר אֲשֶׁר־נִקְרָא
שִׁמְךָ עָלֶיהָ, כִּי לֹא עַל־צִדְקֹתֵינוּ אֲנַחְנוּ מַפִּילִים תַּחֲנוּנֵינוּ לְפָנֶיךָ,
כִּי עַל־רַחֲמֶיךָ הָרַבִּים: אֲדֹנָי שְׁמָעָה, אֲדֹנָי סְלָחָה, אֲדֹנָי הַקְשִׁיבָה וַעֲשֵׂה
אַל־תְּאַחַר, לְמַעַנְךָ אֱלֹהַי, כִּי־שִׁמְךָ נִקְרָא עַל־עִירְךָ וְעַל־עַמֶּךָ:

אֱלֹהֵינוּ וֵאלֹהֵי אֲבוֹתֵינוּ

אָדָם בְּקוּם עָלֵינוּ, חִיל אֲחָזַתְנוּ לִרְעֹד.
בְּהִסְתַּפְּחוֹ לְמַלְכוּת חָנֵף, כִּמְעַט כָּשַׁלְנוּ לִמְעֹד.
גָּמְרוּ לְמִכְרֵנוּ כְּתֵל וְחָרִיץ בְּלִי מִסְעוֹד.
תהלים פג אָמְרוּ לְכוּ וְנַכְחִידֵם מִגּוֹי, וְלֹא־יִזָּכֵר שֵׁם־יִשְׂרָאֵל עוֹד:

דַּלּוּ עֵינַי לַמָּרוֹם, קְרָאתִיךָ אוֹיְבַי לָקֹב.
הַכְרֵת שֵׁם וּשְׁאָר, וּמְחֵה שֵׁם לִרְקֹב.
וְצַר צוֹרְרֵי בְּנִכְלֵיהֶם אֲשֶׁר נִכְּלוּ לַעֲקֹב.
תהלים צד וַיֹּאמְרוּ, לֹא יִרְאֶה־יָּהּ, וְלֹא־יָבִין אֱלֹהֵי יַעֲקֹב:

זְרוּיִים עָנָה וְיָגָה, וְלֹא מִלֵּב לְכַלּוֹתָם.
חָבוּ לְפָנִים, וְרָדָם בַּהֲסָרַת טַבַּעַת לְהַחֲלוֹתָם.
טוֹב דְּבָרוֹ הֵקִים לְעֵינֵי הַגּוֹיִם לְהַעֲלוֹתָם.
ויקרא כו בְּאֶרֶץ אֹיְבֵיהֶם לֹא־מְאַסְתִּים וְלֹא־גְעַלְתִּים לְכַלֹּתָם:

יָדַע רֶמֶז הַקּוֹרוֹת לָעַם מְאֹפֶר וּמְהֻדָּס.
כָּתַב הַסְתֵּר אַסְתִּיר וּמַר דְּרוֹר מְפֻרְדָּס.
לְשַׁבַּת הַמָּן מִמָּחֳרָת, הֲמִן הָעֵץ קָנְדָּס.
ישעיה נה תַּחַת הַנַּעֲצוּץ יַעֲלֶה בְרוֹשׁ וְתַחַת הַסִּרְפַּד יַעֲלֶה הֲדַס:

מַקְשִׁיב דְּבַר שֶׁקֶר כָּתַב שִׂטְנָה וָעֶצֶב.
נִתְעַטֵּף בְּבִגְדֵי שְׂרָד כְּטָעָה בְּמִנְיַן קֶצֶב.
סֵדֶר לְהִשְׁתַּמֵּשׁ בְּשׁוֹנִים כְּלֵי הַמַּחְצֵב.
איוב ב וַיָּבוֹא גַם־הַשָּׂטָן בְּתֹכָם לְהִתְיַצֵּב:

Num. 14 ▸ סְלַח־נָא FORGIVE, PLEASE, this people's iniquity, in the abundance of Your kindness,and as You have forgiven this people from the time of Egypt until now, and there it is written:

Congregation then Leader:

AND THE LORD said, I have forgiven as you asked.

Continue:

Dan. 9 הַטֵּה GIVE EAR, my God and hear; open Your eyes and see our desolation, and the city that bears Your name, for it is not on the strength of our righteousness that we throw down our pleadings before You, but on the strength of Your great compassion. Lord, hear me; Lord, forgive; Lord, listen and act and do not delay – for Your sake, my God; for Your city and Your people bear Your name.

OUR GOD and God of our fathers:

אָדָם WHEN A MAN rose up against us, convulsions of trembling seized us. When he attached himself to a government of flattery, we almost stumbled and fell. They cheerfully closed an agreement to sell us, as a person with an unwanted mound gives it away quite freely to one with an unwanted pit. There was no
Ps. 83 defense. They said, "Come, let us annihilate them from among nations: the name of Israel shall be recalled no more."

MY EYES turned heavenward and I called on You to curse my enemies: "Cut off name and remnant; expunge their name, let it rot. And be Enemy to my enemies; bring them down in the very deceptions with which they deceived
Ps. 94 the people of Jacob." And they said, "The Lord will not see; the God of Jacob will not comprehend."

Yet God tormented the scattered ones and made them mournful – but did not mean to destroy them utterly. They were guilty on the face of things, and so He terrorized them. By the taking off of a ring, He made them tremble. But God fulfilled the good of His word, raising them up in the view of nations.
Lev. 26 "In their enemies' land He did not reject them, and did not detest them to the point of destruction."

HE REVEALED the premonition of events for a nation begrimed and scratched over. He wrote "I shall surely hide (*astir*) Myself" to hint at Esther, and fragrant "pure myrrh," translated "mar-dokh," to hint at Mordekhai; all to put an end to Haman on the morrow, "From (*hamin*) the tree" foreshadowing his
Is. 55 gallows. "In place of the thorn bush, shall rise up a cypress, and in place of the nettle, shall rise up myrtle."

THE KING who listened to lies, dictated accusation and sorrow. He wrapped himself in priestly clothes, Ahasuerus, having mistaken his reckoning of the End. He ordered "other vessels" to be used, from the Quarry from which the
Job 2 world was hewn; and the devil too, came and placed himself among them.

עַם הַנִּמְצְאִים בְּשׁוּשָׁן, בְּאָכְלָם מִזֶּבַח עוֹכְרָם.
פָּעַר פִּיו לְהַשְׂטִינָם, וּלְהַסְגִּירָם בְּיַד נוֹתֵן מִכְרָם.
צוּר הִסְכִּים לִכְתֹּב אִגֶּרֶת לְאַבֵּד שִׁבְרָם.
אָמַרְתִּי אַפְאֵיהֶם, אַשְׁבִּיתָה מֵאֱנוֹשׁ זִכְרָם: דברים לב

קְדוֹשִׁים מַלְאֲכֵי שָׁלוֹם מַר יִבְכָּיוּן בִּצְעָקָה.
רַחוּם הַבֵּט לַבְּרִית וְאַל תָּפֵר לְהַרְחִיקָה.
שָׁמְעָה מוֹרָשָׁה, וַתִּלְבַּשׁ בִּגְדֵי אַלְמְנוּת וּמוּעָקָה.
וַתָּשֶׂם יָדָהּ עַל־רֹאשָׁהּ, וַתֵּלֶךְ הָלוֹךְ וְזָעָקָה: שמואל ב׳ יג

תִּשְׁבִּי שָׂם אֵזוֹר שַׂק בְּמָתְנָיו תַּחְבֹּשֶׁת.
מִהֵר וְהוֹדִיעַ יְשֵׁנֵי מַכְפֵּל, אָבוֹת שְׁלֹשֶׁת.
נָחַץ לְרוֹעֶה, מַה לְּךָ נִרְדָּם לְהִתְעַשֵּׁת.
קוּם קְרָא אֶל־אֱלֹהֶיךָ, אוּלַי יִתְעַשֵּׁת: יונה א

חוֹתַם טִיט אֲשֶׁר נַעֲשָׂה, לְבִלְשָׁן סֵפֶר.
מִנִּינְוֵה לָמְדוּ לְאַחַר גְּזֵרָה כַּעַס לְהָפֵר.
בֶּן קִישׁ הִקִּישׁ דַּלְתוֹת בֵּית הַסֵּפֶר.
וַיְכַס שַׂק, וַיֵּשֶׁב עַל־הָאֵפֶר: יונה ג

רִבֵּץ תִּינוֹקוֹת לְפָנָיו יָמִים שְׁלֹשָׁה, צְמֵאִים וּמְכֻפָּנִים.
בְּקוֹל יַעֲקֹב לַחֲלֹשׁ יְדֵי עַז פָּנִים.
יָדָיו אֱמוּנָה לָאֵל, הַצִּילֵנִי נָא מֵעֶלְבּוֹנִים.
פֶּן־יָבוֹא וְהִכַּנִי אֵם עַל־בָּנִים: בראשית לב

מִזֶּה אֵלֶּה וּמִזֶּה אֵלֶּה, בְּנֵי אֵיתָנַי וְרַבָּנָי.
כֻּלָּם צָעֲקוּ, וַתַּעַל שַׁוְעָתָם אֶל יהוה.
יָהּ, לְקוֹל רִנּוּן כְּבוֹא, שָׁאַל לִפְנָי.
וּמֶה קוֹל־הַצֹּאן הַזֶּה בְּאָזְנָי: שמואל א׳ טו

רוֹעֶה הֱשִׁיבוֹ, הֵם קְטַנֵּי קֹדֶשׁ זֶרַע.
יָהּ, הַצֵּל לְקוּחִים לַמָּוֶת מֵאוֹיֵב הָרָע.
חַנּוּן נִכְמְרוּ רַחֲמָיו וַיְבַקֵּשׁ לִבְכּוֹת הַמְאֹרָע.
וַיְהִי כִּקְרֹא מֶלֶךְ־יִשְׂרָאֵל אֶת־הַסֵּפֶר, וַיִּקְרַע: מלכים ב׳ ה

WHEN THE PEOPLE in Shushan ate of their destroyer's meat, the king opened his mouth wide to accuse them, to give them over into the hands of the one who was ready to pay their price. The Rock, meanwhile, agreed to write a
Deut. 32 letter to destroy their hope; "I said that I would yield them up, would put an end to their memory among mankind."

THE ANGELS, messengers of peace, wept bitterly, crying out, "Compassionate One, look to the covenant and do not break it, pushing it away!" The Torah, too, heard of it and put on clothes of widowhood and sorrow;
II Sam. 13 and she laid her hands upon her head and walked along, crying as she went.

[ELIJAH] THE TISHBITE wrapped a covering of sackcloth around his waist. He hurried and told the three fathers who sleep in the Cave of Makhpela, and
Jonah 1 then hastened to the Shepherd, [Moses] – "What do you mean by sleeping?

ROUSE YOURSELF! Get up and call out to your God – perhaps He may change His mind!" He told [Mordekhai] Bilshan of the pronouncement that had been sealed in clay – but not in blood. They learnt from the example of Nineveh how to overturn anger after a decree; the son of Kish knocked at
Jonah 3 the door of the school, and covered himself in sackcloth and sat down on the earth.

FOR THREE DAYS he gathered the children before him – thirsty, hidden from by God – so that, in the voice of Jacob, they might weaken the hand of the bold-faced king. His hands raised steadily to God, Mordekhai prayed,
Gen. 32 "Save us now from insult; that he should not come and slaughter us, mothers and children together."

THOSE and those, from all sides, the children of my mighty ones and teachers, all cried out, and their plea rose up to the Lord. And God, when those
I Sam. 15 plaintive calls reached Him, asked, "And what is this bleating of sheep that meets My ears?"

THE SHEPHERD Moses answered Him, "These are the little ones of the holy offspring. Lord, save ones condemned to die, from the evil enemy." The compassion of the Gracious One was stirred, and He was moved to weep
II Kings 5 for what had happened. And so it was that when the King of Israel read the letter, He tore it to pieces.

יְהוּדִי הוֹקִיעַ, יְלָדָיו לְמַטָּה וַאֲבִיהֶם לְמַעְלָה.
אִישׁ אִישׁ בְּשָׁלֹשׁ אַמּוֹת, וְהָרְבִיעִית אֲוִיר מְגֻלָּה.
מִשְׁנֶה נָקַם חֲזֵה, וְשָׂמַח וְשָׁח תְּהִלָּה.
בראשית מא אֹתִי הֵשִׁיב עַל־כַּנִּי וְאֹתוֹ תָלָה:

▸ וַתִּכְתֹּב אֶסְתֵּר תֹּקֶף, לִקְרֹא כְּבַהֵלֵל מְהוֹדִים.
מִלְמַעְלָה קִיְּמוּ מַה שֶּׁקִּבְּלוּ לְמַטָּה דוֹדִים.
נֵס יָנוֹסֵס לְפַרְסֵם כְּאָז פְּלָאוֹ מַסְהִידִים.
אסתר ד בָּעֵת הַזֹּאת רֶוַח וְהַצָּלָה יַעֲמוֹד לַיְּהוּדִים:

אֵל מֶלֶךְ יוֹשֵׁב עַל כִּסֵּא רַחֲמִים, מִתְנַהֵג בַּחֲסִידוּת. מוֹחֵל עֲוֹנוֹת עַמּוֹ, מַעֲבִיר רִאשׁוֹן רִאשׁוֹן. מַרְבֶּה מְחִילָה לְחַטָּאִים, וּסְלִיחָה לְפוֹשְׁעִים. עֹשֶׂה צְדָקוֹת עִם כָּל בָּשָׂר וָרְוּחַ, לֹא כְרָעָתָם תִּגְמֹל. ▸ אֵל, הוֹרֵיתָ לָּנוּ לוֹמַר שְׁלֹשׁ עֶשְׂרֵה, וּזְכֹר לָנוּ הַיּוֹם בְּרִית שְׁלֹשׁ עֶשְׂרֵה, כְּמוֹ שֶׁהוֹדַעְתָּ לֶעָנָו מִקֶּדֶם,
שמות לד כְּמוֹ שֶׁכָּתוּב: וַיֵּרֶד יהוה בֶּעָנָן, וַיִּתְיַצֵּב עִמּוֹ שָׁם, וַיִּקְרָא בְשֵׁם, יהוה:

then קהל *:*שליח ציבור

שמות לד וַיַּעֲבֹר יהוה עַל־פָּנָיו וַיִּקְרָא

All say aloud:

שמות לד **יהוה,** יהוה, אֵל רַחוּם וְחַנּוּן, אֶרֶךְ אַפַּיִם, וְרַב־חֶסֶד וֶאֱמֶת: נֹצֵר חֶסֶד לָאֲלָפִים, נֹשֵׂא עָוֹן וָפֶשַׁע וְחַטָּאָה, וְנַקֵּה: וְסָלַחְתָּ לַעֲוֹנֵנוּ וּלְחַטָּאתֵנוּ, וּנְחַלְתָּנוּ:

Continue:

תהלים פו **סְלַח לָנוּ** אָבִינוּ כִּי חָטָאנוּ, מְחַל לָנוּ מַלְכֵּנוּ כִּי פָשָׁעְנוּ. כִּי־אַתָּה אֲדֹנָי טוֹב וְסַלָּח, וְרַב־חֶסֶד לְכָל־קֹרְאֶיךָ:

תהלים לו **כִּי־עִמְּךָ** מְקוֹר חַיִּים, בְּאוֹרְךָ נִרְאֶה־אוֹר: בְּקָרְאֵנוּ עֲנֵנוּ אֱלֹהֵי צִדְקֵנוּ, בַּצָּר
במדבר יד הִרְחַבְתָּ לָּנוּ, חָנֵּנוּ וּשְׁמַע תְּפִלָּתֵנוּ. וְעַתָּה יִגְדַּל־נָא כֹּחַ אֲדֹנָי, כַּאֲשֶׁר דִּבַּרְתָּ לֵאמֹר:

תהלים ג **כְּרַחֵם** אָב עַל בָּנִים, כֵּן תְּרַחֵם יהוה עָלֵינוּ. לַיהוה הַיְשׁוּעָה, עַל־עַמְּךָ
תהלים מו בִרְכָתֶךָ סֶּלָה: יהוה צְבָאוֹת עִמָּנוּ, מִשְׂגָּב לָנוּ אֱלֹהֵי יַעֲקֹב סֶלָה:
תהלים פד / תהלים כ יהוה צְבָאוֹת, אַשְׁרֵי אָדָם בֹּטֵחַ בָּךְ: יהוה הוֹשִׁיעָה, הַמֶּלֶךְ יַעֲנֵנוּ בְיוֹם־קָרְאֵנוּ:

THE JEW suspended sons below and father above. Each man covered three *amot*; the fourth *amah* above was space exposed. Mordekhai saw a double
Gen. 41 revenge, was delighted, and spoke praises: "I was returned to my post and he was hanged!"

ESTHER wrote with emphasis, that a Hallel of thanks should be read on that day; and what the beloved ones accepted down below was established above. A banner shall be raised by those who bear witness, to make the
Esther 4 wonder known now, as it was then. And at this time – may relief and salvation rise up for the Jews.

אֵל מֶלֶךְ GOD, KING Who sits upon a throne of compassion, Who acts with loving-kindness, Who pardons the iniquities of His people, passing them before Him in order; Who forgives sinners and pardons transgressors; Who performs righteousness with all flesh and spirit, do not repay their bad actions in kind. ▸ God, You taught us to speak thirteen attributes: recall for us today the covenant of the thirteen attributes, as You in ancient times showed the humble
Ex. 34 one [Moses], as is written: The Lord descended in the cloud and stood with him there, and proclaimed in the name of the Lord:

Congregation then Leader:

Ex. 34 AND THE LORD passed by before him and proclaimed:

All say aloud:

Ex. 34 יהוה THE LORD, the Lord, compassionate and gracious God, slow to anger and great in mercy and truth, keeping loving-kindness for thousands, forgiving iniquity, transgression, and sin, and offering absolution. Forgive us our iniquity and our sin, and take us as Your inheritance.

Continue:

סְלַח לָנוּ FORGIVE US, our Father, for we have sinned. Pardon us, our King, for
Ps. 86 we have transgressed. For You, Lord, are good and forgiving, abounding in loving-kindness to all who call on You.

Ps. 36 כִּי־עִמְּךָ FOR IN YOU there is a wellspring of life; in Your light shall we see light. As we call You, God of our righteousness, answer us. In a narrow place You have
Num. 14 opened out our horizon; be gracious to us and hear our prayer. And now let the strength of the Lord be great, as You have said.

כְּרַחֵם AS A FATHER has compassion for his children, so, Lord, have compassion
Ps. 3 *Ps. 46* for us. Salvation is the Lord's; on Your people is Your blessing, Selah! The Lord
Ps. 84 of hosts is with us, the God of Jacob is our stronghold, Selah! Lord of hosts,
Ps. 20 happy is the one who trusts in You. Lord, save! May the King answer us on the day we call.

אֱלֹהֵינוּ וֵאלֹהֵי אֲבוֹתֵינוּ

אַתָּה הָאֵל עוֹשֵׂה פְלָאוֹת, / **בְּ**עַמִּים הוֹדַעְתָּ עֹז נוֹרָאוֹת,
גָּאַלְתָּ בִּזְרוֹעַ עַמְּךָ מִתְּלָאוֹת, / **דִּ**כִּיתָ צָרֵיהֶם בְּמוֹתֵי תַחֲלוּאוֹת.
הָאוֹיֵב בְּקוּמוֹ לְעוֹרֵר מְדָנִים, / **וְ**דִמָּה לְהַכְרִית פִּרְחֵי עֲדָנִים,
זָמַם לִשְׁקֹל לְגִנְזֵי אֲדוֹנִים, / **חֲ**לִיפֵי מְאַת כִּכְּרֵי אֲדָנִים.
טְלָאֶיךָ הִזְהַרְתָּ שִׁקְלֵיהֶם לְהַקְדִּים, / **יָ**דַעְתָּ הָעֲתִידוֹת וְדָרַשְׁתָּ נִשְׁקָדִים,
כִּבּוּי לְהַמְצִיא לְלַהַב יוֹקְדִים, / **לְ**קוּחִים לַמָּוֶת לְתֶחִי נִפְקָדִים.
מַסֵּכָה צָרָה בְּעָבְדָם לְפָנִים, / **נִ**מְסְרוּ לְהַתֵּז קְנוֹקְנוֹת וּגְפָנִים,
סְבָבוּם מוֹקְשִׁים בְּכָל דְּפָנִים, / **עֵ**ינֵיהֶם לְךָ תּוֹלִים וּבְסִתְרְךָ נִצְפָּנִים.
פּוּר נֶהְפַּךְ בְּאוֹיְבִים לִשְׁלֹט, / **צְ**לִיבָה הוּכַן אֲגָגִי לִקְלֹט,
קַלַּע וּבַלַּע פְּנֵי הַלּוֹט הַלּוֹט, / **רִ**יבֵי עָם בְּאַשְׁמַנִּים לַעֲלֹט.
שָׁלוֹם וֶאֱמֶת נִכְתַּב מִכָּל צַד, / **תֹּ**קֶף יֶשַׁע סֶלַע וּמְצָד,
שׁוֹדֵד הַשְׁדַּד וּבְרִשְׁתּוֹ נוּצַד, / **מְ**לָשְׁנִי נִסְחַף נִצְמַת וְנִרְצָד.
עָשׂוּ שְׂמָחוֹת וְלַדּוֹרוֹת קְבָעוּם, / **וּ**מִקְרָאוֹת שִׁלְּשׁוּם וְלֹא רִבְּעוּם,
נִסְכְּמוּ מִמַּעַל וּלְמַטָּה טְבָעוּם, / **בְּ**סֵפֶר נֶחֱקַק עַל מָה קְבָעוּם.
רָמָה יָדְךָ לִסְלֹחַ לַפּוֹשְׁעִים, / **יְ**הוּדִי וַהֲדַסָּה הֵקַמְתָּ מוֹשִׁיעִים,
צִדְקָתָם עוֹמֶדֶת לָעַד לְשַׁעֲשׁוּעִים, / **חֵ**קֶר כְּבוֹדָם לְהִזָּכֵר לְנוֹשָׁעִים.
קַנֵּא לְשִׁמְךָ נוֹרָא וְנִקְדָּשׁ, / **חֲ**זֵה כַּרְמְךָ נֶהֱרַס וְנִדָּשׁ,
זְרוּיֵינוּ קַבֵּץ וְשִׁיר לְךָ יְחֻדָּשׁ, / **קַ**יְּמֵם וְהַחַיִּם בְּבִנְיַן בֵּית הַמִּקְדָּשׁ.
◂ **וְ**כַעֲשׂוֹתְךָ נוֹרָאוֹת בְּאוֹתָן הַיָּמִים, / **אִ**תָּנוּ הַפְלֵא תְּשׁוּעַת עוֹלָמִים,
מְצוֹא לְפָנֶיךָ כֹּפֶר וְתַנְחוּמִים, אֵל מֶלֶךְ יוֹשֵׁב עַל כִּסֵּא רַחֲמִים.

אֵל מֶלֶךְ יוֹשֵׁב עַל כִּסֵּא רַחֲמִים, מִתְנַהֵג בַּחֲסִידוּת. מוֹחֵל עֲוֹנוֹת עַמּוֹ, מַעֲבִיר רִאשׁוֹן רִאשׁוֹן. מַרְבֶּה מְחִילָה לְחַטָּאִים, וּסְלִיחָה לְפוֹשְׁעִים. עֹשֶׂה צְדָקוֹת עִם כָּל בָּשָׂר וָרוּחַ, לֹא כְרָעָתָם תִּגְמֹל. ◂ אֵל, הוֹרֵיתָ לָּנוּ לוֹמַר שְׁלֹשׁ עֶשְׂרֵה, וּזְכָר לָנוּ הַיּוֹם בְּרִית שְׁלֹשׁ עֶשְׂרֵה,
שמות לד כְּמוֹ שֶׁהוֹדַעְתָּ לֶעָנָו מִקֶּדֶם, כְּמוֹ שֶׁכָּתוּב: וַיֵּרֶד יהוה בֶּעָנָן, וַיִּתְיַצֵּב עִמּוֹ שָׁם, וַיִּקְרָא בְשֵׁם, יהוה:

שליח ציבור then קהל:

שמות לד וַיַּעֲבֹר יהוה עַל־פָּנָיו וַיִּקְרָא

OUR GOD and God of our fathers:

אַתָּה הָאֵל IT IS YOU Who are the God of wonders. You have made known among nations Your terrifying strength. You redeemed Your people by might from torments, suppressed their foes with ignominious death, when the enemy rose to awaken strife, and seemed about to cut down the exquisite flowers, Israel. He plotted to measure out into the masters' treasuries, a hundred times the silver talents of the sockets in the Tabernacle. You warned Your lambs to announce the shekel offering early; You knew what would be. You warned us to be punctual, and to find a way to douse the fire of ones who sought to burn us. And so, those once condemned to death – are marked out for resurrection. When (for appearances,) they worshiped a narrow image, they were yielded up to be clipped off: all those offshoots and grapes. Traps surrounded them on all sides; they turned their eyes to You, they were concealed in Your hiddenness. The lots were overturned, they ruled over their enemies, and the gallows was prepared to receive Haman the Agagite. God struck and swallowed the façade of covering that covered, and He entombed His people's enemies in darkness. Peace and truth were written on all sides; power of salvation, steady rock and fortress. The plunderer was plundered, he was caught in his own trap. The one who spoke against me was swept away; destroyed; eyed disdainfully. The people made celebrations, and these were fixed for all generations. Amalek had entered the Scriptures three times – how could there be a fourth? Yet on High it was agreed and here below it was sealed, and the reason for all that had been fixed, was inscribed in the scroll. Your hand is lifted high to forgive sinners. You set Mordekhai the Jew and Hadassah Esther in their place as saviors, and now their righteousness remains forever to delight us, and the study of their honor to recall to You those who were saved. Be zealous for Your name, Awesome and Sanctified One. Witness Your vineyard, destroyed, trampled; gather our scattered ones and their song to You will be renewed. Sustain them and revive them with the building of the Temple. ▸ And as You did awe-inspiring things in those days, so perform with us the wonder of salvation for all time. Find in Your presence our ransom, our appeasement – God, King Who sits upon a throne of compassion.

אֵל מֶלֶךְ GOD, KING Who sits upon a throne of compassion, Who acts with loving-kindness, Who pardons the iniquities of His people, passing them before Him in order; Who forgives sinners and pardons transgressors; Who performs righteousness with all flesh and spirit, do not repay their bad actions in kind. ▸ God, You taught us to speak thirteen attributes: recall for us today the covenant of the thirteen attributes, as You in ancient times showed the humble one [Moses], as is
Ex. 34 written: The Lord descended in the cloud and stood with him there, and proclaimed in the name of the Lord:

Congregation then Leader:

Ex. 34 AND THE LORD passed by before him and proclaimed:

All say aloud:

יהוה, יהוה, אֵל רַחוּם וְחַנּוּן, אֶרֶךְ אַפַּיִם, וְרַב־חֶסֶד וֶאֱמֶת: נֹצֵר חֶסֶד לָאֲלָפִים, נֹשֵׂא עָוֹן וָפֶשַׁע וְחַטָּאָה, וְנַקֵּה: וְסָלַחְתָּ לַעֲוֹנֵנוּ וּלְחַטָּאתֵנוּ, וּנְחַלְתָּנוּ: שמות לד

Continue:

סְלַח לָנוּ אָבִינוּ כִּי חָטָאנוּ, מְחַל לָנוּ מַלְכֵּנוּ כִּי פָשָׁעְנוּ. כִּי־אַתָּה אֲדֹנָי טוֹב וְסַלָּח, וְרַב־חֶסֶד לְכָל־קֹרְאֶיךָ: תהלים פו

The following is said responsively:

בְּמֹתֵי מִסְפָּר חִלִּינוּ פָּנֶיךָ. / לְשַׁוְעַת נִכְאִים אַל תַּעְלֵם אָזְנֶךָ.
הַקְשֵׁב תְּחִנָּתָם מִשְּׁמֵי מְעוֹנֶךָ.
כְּבִימֵי מֹר וַהֲדַס הוֹשַׁעְתָּ בָנֶיךָ.

תְּהִלּוֹת יִשְׂרָאֵל אַתָּה יוֹשֵׁב. / **שַׁ**וְעָתָם מַאֲזִין וְרִנָּתָם קוֹשֵׁב.
רְפָאוּת לְמַחַץ מַקְדִּים וּמְחַשֵּׁב. / **קְ**נוּיֶיךָ לְהֵיטִיב וְנָוֵיהֶם לְיַשֵּׁב.

צַר וְאוֹיֵב הִלְטִישׁ עֵינָיו. / **פִּ**יהוּ פָּעַר לִשְׁאֹף עָנָו.
עָשַׂת בְּשַׁלְוֹ לְהַשְׁמִיד קְהַל הֲמוֹנָיו. / **סָ**גַל לְאַבֵּד חָרַת בְּנִשְׁתְּוָנָיו.

נוֹקֵם לְצָרִים וְנוֹטֵר לְאוֹיְבִים. / **מָ**דַדְתָּ מִדָּתָם כְּזָדוּ לַאֲהוּבִים.
לוֹחֵם וּבָנָיו הָתְלוּ מְצֻלָּבִים. / **כְּ**בַחֲרֶזֶת דָּגִים חֹרְזוּ תְּחוּבִים.

יוֹם אֲשֶׁר שִׂבְּרוּ צוֹרְרִים. / **טִ**בְחָה לָשִׁית בְּעַם נְצוּרִים.
חָלְפָה הַדָּת וְנָפְלוּ פְגָרִים. / **זָ**לְעֲפוּ זָעֲמוּ מוּבָסִים מְגֻרִים.

וּבְכֵן יִתְעַלֶּה שִׁמְךָ וְיִתְנַשָּׂא. / **ה**וֹדְךָ שְׁמֵי שָׁמַיִם כִּסָּה.
דַּכִּים בִּרוֹמִמְךָ נְתוּנִים לִמְשִׁסָּה. / **גַּ**יְא וְאַפְסֶיהָ תְּהִלָּתְךָ מְכַסָּה.

בִּינָה הֲגִיגֵנוּ עַתָּה, וּרְאֵה בַצָּר. / **בְּ**אַפְּךָ קוּמָה עַל צוֹרֵר הַצָּר.
אָדוֹן, קְרָאנוּךָ מִן הַמֵּצַר. / **אָ**נָּא הוֹצִיאֵנוּ לַמֶּרְחָב וְחַלְּצֵנוּ מִצָּר.

מְאֹד תַּרְבֶּה לָנוּ מְחִילָה. / **שְׁ**מַע תְּפִלָּה, וְהַעֲבֵר תִּפְלָה.
לוֹחֲצֵינוּ הַמְעֵד וּמַלֵּא חַלְחָלָה. / **מִ**מֶּנּוּ רַחֲמֶיךָ לָעַד לֹא תִכְלָא.

Continue with אֵל מֶלֶךְ יוֹשֵׁב *on page 998.*

All say aloud:

Ex. 34 יהוה THE LORD, the Lord, compassionate and gracious God, slow to anger and great in mercy and truth, keeping loving-kindness for thousands, forgiving iniquity, transgression, and sin, and offering absolution. Forgive us our iniquity and our sin, and take us as Your inheritance.

Continue:

סְלַח לָנוּ FORGIVE US, our Father, for we have sinned. Pardon us, our King, for we
Ps. 86 have transgressed. For You, Lord, are good and forgiving, abounding in loving-kindness to all who call on You.

The following is said responsively:

בִּמְתֵי SMALL of number we stand pleading before You: do not block Your ears to the cry of people crushed. Listen to their entreaty from the heaven where You dwell, as You saved Your children in the days of Myrrh and Myrtle [Mordekhai and Esther].

ON ISRAEL'S PRAISES You sit enthroned, hearing their cry, listening to their prayer. Bringing healing even before the blow, counting it out to help the ones You have acquired; to settle their homes again.

A FOE and enemy fixed his eyes like knives on Israel; he opened wide his mouth to swallow up the humble man. He deliberated within him to destroy Mordekhai's great community; in the letter, he etched his intent to destroy the treasured people.

YOU WHO TAKE revenge upon foes and persist in Your claim against enemies; You measured them out with the very measure they used against Your loved ones. The fighter and his descendants were hanged, suspended; they were strung up together, like fish on a thread.

ON THE DAY on which the enemies hoped to lay carnage among the people You harbor, the rule was overturned and bodies fell; they bore the brunt and fury of Your rage – they were trodden underfoot and washed away.

AND SO may Your name be raised up, exalted. Your glory covers all the highest heavens. As You lift the downtrodden, those yielded up as plunder, Your praise fills up the valleys to their very ends.

CONSIDER our thoughts, now, and witness our suffering. Rise up, in Your rage, against the bitter enemy. Master, we have called You from a narrow place. Please, take us out into the open, and release us from anguish.

BRING US much, abundant pardon. Hear our prayer, and what is crude in us – pass over. Bring down those who press us and fill them with horror. And as for us – do not forever withhold Your compassion.

Continue with "God, King Who sits" on page 999.

סליחות לשבעה עשר בתמוז

סְלַח לָנוּ, אָבִינוּ, כִּי בְּרֹב אִוַּלְתֵּנוּ שָׁגִינוּ. מְחַל לָנוּ, מַלְכֵּנוּ, כִּי רַבּוּ עֲוֹנֵינוּ.

אֵל אֶרֶךְ אַפַּיִם אַתָּה, וּבַעַל הָרַחֲמִים נִקְרֵאתָ, וְדֶרֶךְ תְּשׁוּבָה הוֹרֵיתָ.
גְּדֻלַּת רַחֲמֶיךָ וַחֲסָדֶיךָ, תִּזְכֹּר הַיּוֹם וּבְכָל יוֹם לְזֶרַע יְדִידֶיךָ.
תֵּפֶן אֵלֵינוּ בְּרַחֲמִים, כִּי אַתָּה הוּא בַּעַל הָרַחֲמִים. בְּתַחֲנוּן וּבִתְפִלָּה פָּנֶיךָ נְקַדֵּם, כְּהוֹדַעְתָּ לֶעָנָו מִקֶּדֶם. מֵחֲרוֹן אַפְּךָ שׁוּב, כְּמוֹ בְּתוֹרָתְךָ כָּתוּב. וּבְצֵל כְּנָפֶיךָ נֶחֱסֶה וְנִתְלוֹנָן, כְּיוֹם וַיֵּרֶד יהוה בֶּעָנָן. ‹ תַּעֲבֹר עַל פֶּשַׁע וְתִמְחֶה אָשָׁם, כְּיוֹם וַיִּתְיַצֵּב עִמּוֹ שָׁם. תַּאֲזִין שַׁוְעָתֵנוּ וְתַקְשִׁיב מֶנּוּ מַאֲמָר, כְּיוֹם וַיִּקְרָא בְשֵׁם יהוה, וְשָׁם נֶאֱמַר

:שליח ציבור then קהל

שמות לד וַיַּעֲבֹר יהוה עַל־פָּנָיו וַיִּקְרָא

All say aloud:

שמות לד **יהוה,** יהוה, אֵל רַחוּם וְחַנּוּן, אֶרֶךְ אַפַּיִם, וְרַב־חֶסֶד וֶאֱמֶת: נֹצֵר חֶסֶד לָאֲלָפִים, נֹשֵׂא עָוֹן וָפֶשַׁע וְחַטָּאָה, וְנַקֵּה: וְסָלַחְתָּ לַעֲוֹנֵנוּ וּלְחַטָּאתֵנוּ, וּנְחַלְתָּנוּ:

Continue:

תהלים פו **סְלַח לָנוּ** אָבִינוּ כִּי חָטָאנוּ, מְחַל לָנוּ מַלְכֵּנוּ כִּי פָשָׁעְנוּ. כִּי־אַתָּה אֲדֹנָי טוֹב וְסַלָּח, וְרַב־חֶסֶד לְכָל־קֹרְאֶיךָ:

שבעה עשר בתמוז / SEVENTEENTH OF TAMMUZ

The five tragedies of this day are enumerated in the Mishna (*Ta'anit* 4:6):

1. Moses broke the first Tablets of the Covenant.
2. The Babylonians breached the wall of Jerusalem, in preparation for the destruction of the First Temple.
3. The Romans broke through the defenses of Second Temple in Jerusalem.
4. Apostomos publicly burned a *Sefer Torah*. Some suggest that this event took place during the reign of Antiochus IV Epiphanes, and Apostomos refers to Antiochus himself or to his emissary. Nonetheless, both the identity of Apostomos and the time of the event, which have been the subject of considerable speculation, remain obscure.
5. An idol was placed in the Second Temple.

SELIḤOT FOR THE SEVENTEENTH OF TAMMUZ

סְלַח לָנוּ FORGIVE US, our Father, for in our great foolishness we have blundered. Pardon us, our King, for our iniquities are many.

אֵל אֶרֶךְ YOU ARE A GOD slow to anger, You are called the Master of Compassion, and You have taught the way of repentance. May You remember today and every day the greatness of Your compassion and kindness, for the sake of the descendants of Your beloved ones. Turn toward us in compassion, for You are the Master of Compassion. We come before You in plea and prayer, as You in ancient times showed the humble one [Moses]. Turn from Your fierce anger, as is written in Your Torah. In the shadow of Your wings may we shelter and abide, as on the day when the Lord descended in the cloud. ▸ Overlook sin and wipe away guilt, as on the day when "He stood beside him there." Give ear to our pleading and listen to our speech, as on the day when "he called upon the name of the Lord," and in that place is said –

Congregation then Leader:

Ex. 34 AND THE LORD passed by before him and proclaimed:

All say aloud:

Ex. 34 יהוה THE LORD, the Lord, compassionate and gracious God, slow to anger and great in mercy and truth, keeping loving-kindness for thousands, forgiving iniquity, transgression, and sin, and offering absolution. Forgive us our iniquity and our sin, and take us as Your inheritance.

Continue:

סְלַח לָנוּ FORGIVE US, our Father, for we have sinned. Pardon us, our King,
Ps. 86 for we have transgressed. For You, Lord, are good and forgiving, abounding in loving-kindness to all who call on You.

This may refer to Antiochus' transformation of the Temple into an idolatrous shrine or to the golden imperial eagle erected in the Temple by Herod. Here too the precise reference cannot be established with certainty.

In later times, the Seventeenth of Tammuz marked the massacre of the Jews of Jerusalem by the Crusaders on July 15, 1099. Jews were barred from Jerusalem for the ensuing eighty-eight years of Christian rule.

ישעיה סב **וְאַל־תִּתְּנוּ** דֳמִי לוֹ, עַד־יְכוֹנֵן וְעַד־יָשִׂים אֶת־יְרוּשָׁלַ͏ִם תְּהִלָּה בָּאָרֶץ:
תהלים לו כִּי־עִמְּךָ מְקוֹר חַיִּים, בְּאוֹרְךָ נִרְאֶה־אוֹר: אֱלֹהֵינוּ, בֹּשְׁנוּ
בְּמַעֲשֵׂינוּ וְנִכְלַמְנוּ בַּעֲוֹנֵינוּ.

תהלים ג **כְּרַחֵם** אָב עַל בָּנִים, כֵּן תְּרַחֵם יהוה עָלֵינוּ. לַיהוה הַיְשׁוּעָה, עַל־עַמְּךָ
תהלים מו בִרְכָתֶךָ סֶּלָה: יהוה צְבָאוֹת עִמָּנוּ, מִשְׂגָּב לָנוּ אֱלֹהֵי יַעֲקֹב סֶלָה:
תהלים פד יהוה צְבָאוֹת, אַשְׁרֵי אָדָם בֹּטֵחַ בָּךְ: יהוה הוֹשִׁיעָה, הַמֶּלֶךְ יַעֲנֵנוּ בְיוֹם־
תהלים כ קָרְאֵנוּ:

במדבר יד ◂ **סְלַח־נָא** לַעֲוֹן הָעָם הַזֶּה כְּגֹדֶל חַסְדֶּךָ, וְכַאֲשֶׁר נָשָׂאתָה לָעָם הַזֶּה
מִמִּצְרַיִם וְעַד־הֵנָּה: וְשָׁם נֶאֱמַר

:קהל then שליח ציבור

וַיֹּאמֶר יהוה, סָלַחְתִּי כִּדְבָרֶךָ:

Continue:

דניאל ט **הַטֵּה** אֱלֹהַי אָזְנְךָ וּשְׁמָע, פְּקַח עֵינֶיךָ וּרְאֵה שֹׁמְמֹתֵינוּ וְהָעִיר אֲשֶׁר־נִקְרָא
שִׁמְךָ עָלֶיהָ, כִּי לֹא עַל־צִדְקֹתֵינוּ אֲנַחְנוּ מַפִּילִים תַּחֲנוּנֵינוּ לְפָנֶיךָ,
כִּי עַל־רַחֲמֶיךָ הָרַבִּים: אֲדֹנָי שְׁמָעָה, אֲדֹנָי סְלָחָה, אֲדֹנָי הַקְשִׁיבָה וַעֲשֵׂה
אַל־תְּאַחַר, לְמַעַנְךָ אֱלֹהַי, כִּי־שִׁמְךָ נִקְרָא עַל־עִירְךָ וְעַל־עַמֶּךָ:

אֱלֹהֵינוּ וֵאלֹהֵי אֲבוֹתֵינוּ

אָתָנוּ לְךָ יוֹצֵר רוּחוֹת, **בְּ**רוֹב עֲוֹנֵינוּ כָּבְדוּ אֲנָחוֹת, **גְּ**זֵרוֹת עָצְמוּ וְרַבּוּ צְרִיחוֹת,
כִּי בְּשִׁבְעָה עָשָׂר בְּתַמּוּז נִשְׁתַּבְּרוּ הַלֻּחוֹת.

גָּלִינוּ מִבֵּית הַבְּחִירָה, **דִּ**ינֵנוּ נֶחְתַּם וְנִגְזְרָה גְּזֵרָה, וְחָשַׁךְ בַּעֲדֵנוּ אוֹרָה,
כִּי בְּשִׁבְעָה עָשָׂר בְּתַמּוּז נִשְׂרְפָה הַתּוֹרָה.

הָרְסוּ אוֹיְבֵינוּ הַהֵיכָל, **וּ**בָרְחָה שְׁכִינָה מִזָּוִית הֵיכָל, וְנִמְסַרְנוּ בִּידֵי זֵדִים לְהִתְאַכָּל,
כִּי בְּשִׁבְעָה עָשָׂר בְּתַמּוּז הָעֳמַד צֶלֶם בַּהֵיכָל.

זֵרוּנוּ מֵעִיר אֶל עִיר, וְנִלְכַּד מִמֶּנּוּ רַב וְצָעִיר, **חָ**רְבָה מְשׂוֹשֵׂנוּ וְאֵשׁ בָּהּ הִבְעִיר,
כִּי בְּשִׁבְעָה עָשָׂר בְּתַמּוּז הָבְקְעָה הָעִיר.

טָפַשׂ מִקְדָּשֵׁנוּ צַר הַמַּשְׁמִיד, וְנָטַל מֵחָתָן וְכַלָּה אֶצְעָדָה וְצָמִיד, **יַ**עַן כַּעַסְנוּךְ
נִתַּנּוּ לְהַשְׁמִיד,
כִּי בְּשִׁבְעָה עָשָׂר בְּתַמּוּז בֻּטַּל הַתָּמִיד.

Is. 62 וְאַל־תִּתְּנוּ AND DO NOT LET Him rest, until He establishes, until He makes
Ps. 36 Jerusalem the praise of all the earth. For in You there is a wellspring of life; in Your light shall we see light. Our God, we are ashamed of our actions, distraught at our sins.

כְּרַחֵם AS A FATHER has compassion for his children, so, Lord, have compassion
Ps. 3 for us. Salvation is the Lord's; on Your people is Your blessing, Selah!
Ps. 46 The Lord of hosts is with us, the God of Jacob is our stronghold, Selah!
Ps. 84 Lord of hosts, happy is the one who trusts in You.
Ps. 20 Lord, save! May the King answer us on the day we call.

Num. 14 ▸ סְלַח־נָא FORGIVE, PLEASE, this people's iniquity, in the abundance of Your kindness,and as You have forgiven this people from the time of Egypt until now, and there it is written:

Congregation then Leader:

AND THE LORD said, I have forgiven as you asked.

Continue:

Dan. 9 הַטֵּה GIVE EAR, my God and hear; open Your eyes and see our desolation, and the city that bears Your name, for it is not on the strength of our righteousness that we throw down our pleadings before You, but on the strength of Your great compassion. Lord, hear me; Lord, forgive; Lord, listen and act and do not delay – for Your sake, my God; for Your city and Your people bear Your name.

OUR GOD and God of our fathers:

אָתָֽנוּ WE COME before You, Former of the winds. In our many iniquities our sighs have grown heavy; the decrees against us powerful and our screams so many –

for on the Seventeenth of Tammuz, the Tablets were smashed.

WE HAVE been exiled from the House of Your choosing; our judgment was sealed, the decree laid down. And the light has darkened over us –

for on the Seventeenth of Tammuz, the Torah scroll was burnt.

OUR ENEMIES destroyed the Sanctuary, the Divine Presence fled from Its corner, and we were yielded up to the hands of the wanton, to be consumed –

for on the Seventeenth of Tammuz, an idol was set up in the Temple.

WE WERE scattered from city to city, and old and young of us were seized. The place of our delight was destroyed, and fire raged through her –

for on the Seventeenth of Tammuz the city was broken through.

THE LETHAL foe took hold of our Temple, and the cherubs, bride and bridegroom were deprived of all their ornament. Because we angered You we were given up to destruction –

for on the Seventeenth of Tammuz, the daily offering ceased.

כָּלָה מֶנּוּ כָּל הוֹד וָשֶׁבַח, חַרְבּוֹ שָׁלַף אוֹיֵב עָלֵינוּ לָאֶבַח, לִהְיוֹת עוֹלְלִים וְיוֹנְקִים מוּכָנִים לַטֶּבַח,
כִּי בְּשִׁבְעָה עָשָׂר בְּתַמּוּז בָּטְלוּ עוֹלָה וָזֶבַח.

מָרַדְנוּ לְשׁוֹכֵן מְעוֹנוֹת, לָכֵן נִתְפַּזַּרְנוּ בְּכָל פִּנּוֹת, נֶהְפַּךְ מְחוֹלֵנוּ לְקִינוֹת,
כִּי בְּשִׁבְעָה עָשָׂר בְּתַמּוּז בָּטְלוּ קָרְבָּנוֹת.

סָרַרְנוּ לְפָנֶיךָ מֵרִיב לְשׁוֹנוֹת, לָכֵן לָמְדָה לְשׁוֹנֵנוּ לוֹמַר קִינוֹת, עֲזָבְנוּ בְּלִי לְהַמְּנוֹת,
כִּי בְּשִׁבְעָה עָשָׂר בְּתַמּוּז גָּרְמוּ לָנוּ עֲוֹנוֹת.

פֹּזַּרְנוּ בְּלִי מְצוֹא רְוָחָה, לָכֵן רַבְּתָה בָּנוּ אֲנָחָה, צוּר רְאֵה נַפְשֵׁנוּ כִּי שָׁחָה,
וְשִׁבְעָה עָשָׂר בְּתַמּוּז הֲפָךְ לָנוּ לְשָׂשׂוֹן וּלְשִׂמְחָה.

קָשִׁינוּ עֹרֶף וְרַבְּתָה בָּנוּ אָסוֹן, לָכֵן נִתְּנוּ לִמְשִׁסָּה וְרִפְשׁוֹן, רְאֵה יהוה וְחַלְּצֵנוּ מֵאָסוֹן,
וְשִׁבְעָה עָשָׂר בְּתַמּוּז הֲפָךְ לָנוּ לְשִׂמְחָה וּלְשָׂשׂוֹן.

◂ שְׁעֵנוּ שׁוֹכֵן רוּמָה, וְקַבֵּץ נְפוּצוֹתֵינוּ מִקְּצוֹוֹת אֲדָמָה, תֹּאמַר לְצִיּוֹן קוּמָה,
וְשִׁבְעָה עָשָׂר בְּתַמּוּז הֲפָךְ לָנוּ לְיוֹם יְשׁוּעָה וְנֶחָמָה.

אֵל מֶלֶךְ יוֹשֵׁב עַל כִּסֵּא רַחֲמִים, מִתְנַהֵג בַּחֲסִידוּת. מוֹחֵל עֲוֹנוֹת עַמּוֹ, מַעֲבִיר רִאשׁוֹן רִאשׁוֹן. מַרְבֶּה מְחִילָה לְחַטָּאִים, וּסְלִיחָה לְפוֹשְׁעִים. עֹשֶׂה צְדָקוֹת עִם כָּל בָּשָׂר וָרוּחַ, לֹא כְרָעָתָם תִּגְמֹל. ◂ אֵל, הוֹרֵיתָ לָּנוּ לוֹמַר שְׁלֹשׁ עֶשְׂרֵה, וּזְכֹר לָנוּ הַיּוֹם בְּרִית שְׁלֹשׁ עֶשְׂרֵה, כְּמוֹ
שמות לד שֶׁהוֹדַעְתָּ לֶעָנָו מִקֶּדֶם, כְּמוֹ שֶׁכָּתוּב: וַיֵּרֶד יהוה בֶּעָנָן, וַיִּתְיַצֵּב עִמּוֹ שָׁם, וַיִּקְרָא בְשֵׁם, יהוה:

שליח ציבור then קהל:

שמות לד וַיַּעֲבֹר יהוה עַל־פָּנָיו וַיִּקְרָא

All say aloud:

שמות לד **יהוה,** יהוה, אֵל רַחוּם וְחַנּוּן, אֶרֶךְ אַפַּיִם, וְרַב־חֶסֶד וֶאֱמֶת: נֹצֵר חֶסֶד לָאֲלָפִים, נֹשֵׂא עָוֹן וָפֶשַׁע וְחַטָּאָה, וְנַקֵּה: וְסָלַחְתָּ לַעֲוֹנֵנוּ וּלְחַטָּאתֵנוּ, וּנְחַלְתָּנוּ:

ALL GLORY and praise there ended. The enemy drew his sword and brandished its point against us; small children and babies were prepared for the slaughter –
for on the Seventeenth of Tammuz, the offerings and sacrifices ceased.

WE REBELLED against the One Who inhabits the heavens, and so we were dispersed to all the corners of the world. All our dancing was turned to lament –
for on the Seventeenth of Tammuz, the Temple service ended.

WE ACTED obstinately with You in the discord of tongues, and so our own tongue has learnt lamentation; we have been abandoned in countless numbers –
for on the Seventeenth of Tammuz, sin decided our destiny.

We have been dispersed and found no relief, and so our sighs have multiplied within us; Rock, see how our souls have been bowed low –
and turn our Seventeenth of Tammuz into gladness and joy.

We have been obstinate and many calamities have met us; and so we have been yielded up to the plunder, have been pushed into the mud. See, Lord, and release us from disaster –
and turn our Seventeenth of Tammuz into joy and gladness.

▸ Turn to us, You Who reside on High, and gather in our scattered ones from the very ends of the earth. Say to Zion, "Come, get up," –
and turn our Seventeenth of Tammuz to a day of salvation and comfort.

אֵל מֶלֶךְ GOD, KING Who sits upon a throne of compassion, Who acts with loving-kindness, Who pardons the iniquities of His people, passing them before Him in order; Who forgives sinners and pardons transgressors; Who performs righteousness with all flesh and spirit, do not repay their bad actions in kind. ▸ God, You taught us to speak thirteen attributes: recall for us today the covenant of the thirteen attributes, as You in ancient times showed the
Ex. 34 humble one [Moses], as is written: The Lord descended in the cloud and stood with him there, and proclaimed in the name of the Lord:

Congregation then Leader:

Ex. 34 AND THE LORD passed by before him and proclaimed:

All say aloud:

Ex. 34 יהוה THE LORD, the Lord, compassionate and gracious God, slow to anger and great in mercy and truth, keeping loving-kindness for thousands, forgiving iniquity, transgression, and sin, and offering absolution. Forgive us our iniquity and our sin, and take us as Your inheritance.

Continue:

תהלים פו **סְלַח לָֽנוּ** אָבִֽינוּ כִּי חָטָֽאנוּ, מְחַל לָֽנוּ מַלְכֵּֽנוּ כִּי פָשָֽׁעְנוּ. כִּי־אַתָּה אֲדֹנָי
טוֹב וְסַלָּח, וְרַב־חֶסֶד לְכָל־קֹרְאֶיךָ:

תהלים פג **אֱלֹהִים** אַל־דֳּמִי־לָךְ, אַל־תֶּחֱרַשׁ וְאַל־תִּשְׁקֹט אֵל: כִּי־הִנֵּה אוֹיְבֶיךָ יֶהֱמָיוּן,
תהלים צד וּמְשַׂנְאֶיךָ נָֽשְׂאוּ רֹאשׁ: אֵל־נְקָמוֹת יהוה, אֵל נְקָמוֹת הוֹפִֽיעַ:

תהלים ג **כְּרַחֵם** אָב עַל בָּנִים, כֵּן תְּרַחֵם יהוה עָלֵֽינוּ. לַיהוה הַיְשׁוּעָה, עַל־עַמְּךָ
תהלים מו בִרְכָתֶֽךָ סֶּֽלָה: יהוה צְבָאוֹת עִמָּֽנוּ, מִשְׂגָּב לָֽנוּ אֱלֹהֵי יַעֲקֹב סֶֽלָה:
תהלים פד יהוה צְבָאוֹת, אַשְׁרֵי אָדָם בֹּטֵֽחַ בָּךְ: יהוה הוֹשִֽׁיעָה, הַמֶּֽלֶךְ יַעֲנֵֽנוּ בְיוֹם־
תהלים כ קָרְאֵֽנוּ:

אֱלֹהֵֽינוּ וֵאלֹהֵי אֲבוֹתֵֽינוּ

אֱמָרַר בִּבְכִי מִפְּנֵי יָד שְׁלוּחָה בְּעִי.
בְּנַאֲצִי בְּתוֹךְ בֵּיתוֹ בִּבְגָדַי וְקָבְעִי.
גָּח וּבָרַח וְנָסַע עָשׂר וְעָלָה לַשְּׁבִיעִי.
דִּמַּנִי הֱצִיקַנִי הִשִּׂיקַנִי בְּחֹדֶשׁ הָרְבִיעִי.
הֵבִיא מוֹעֵד בִּמְלַאכְתּוֹ לִשְׁבֹּר בַּחוּרַי גָּמוּז.
וְרִבָּה בוֹ פְּעָמִים בְּמִסְמוּס וּמִזְמוּז.
זְבוּלוֹ כְּשֶׁר שֶׁאִנְּנוּת מְבַכּוֹת אֶת הַתַּמּוּז.
חִיְּבַנִי וְאִיְּבַנִי אֲזַי בְּיֶֽרַח תַּמּוּז.
טָמְנוּ פַחִים חֲמִשָּׁה בְּמִקְרָא תְּלָאוֹת מְשֻׁלָּחוֹת.
יָכְלוּ לִי בְּשִׁבְעָה עָשָׂר בּוֹ בַּאֲלִיחוֹת.
כִּי נוֹקַשְׁתִּי כְּכַלָּה עֲלוּבָה בְּחֻפַּת שַׁלְוָה וְהַצְלָחוֹת.
לְרוֹעִי לֹא הִמְתַּנְתִּי שֵׁשׁ, וְנִשְׁתַּבְּרוּ הַלֻּחוֹת.
מִיָּדוֹ עָדִֽיתִי חֲלִי כֶֽתֶם, אֶצְעָדָה וְצָמִיד.
נִגְּרוֹת בְּיוֹם אַפּוֹ, כְּשִׁחַתִּי דְּרָכַי לְהַשְׁמִיד.
סֵֽדֶר עֲבוֹדָתוֹ וְקֵץ מִזְבְּחוֹ קִצַּֽתִּי לְהַעֲמִיד.
עַל כֵּן מִלִּשְׁכַּת הַטְּלָאִים בָּטַל הַתָּמִיד.
פּוֹר הִתְפּוֹרְרָה וְנִתְפַּזְּרָה סֹעֲרָה עֲנִיָּה.
צִי נִמְשְׁלָה מִבְּלִי חוֹבֵל, וְנִטְרְפָה כָּאֳנִיָּה.
קַחְתָּהּ בְּחַטָּאתָהּ בְּרֹאשָׁהּ, וּבְכֶֽפֶל תַּאֲנִיָּה וַאֲנִיָּה.

Continue:

סְלַח לָנוּ FORGIVE US, our Father, for we have sinned. Pardon us, our King, for
Ps. 86 we have transgressed. For You, Lord, are good and forgiving, abounding in
loving-kindness to all who call on You.

Ps. 83 אֱלֹהִים GOD, DO NOT rest, do not be silent and do not be still, for Your enemies
Ps. 94 clamor and those who hate You hold their heads high. God of retribution,
Lord; God of retribution, appear

כְּרַחֵם AS A FATHER has compassion for his children, so, Lord, have compassion
Ps. 3 *Ps. 46* for us. Salvation is the Lord's; on Your people is Your blessing, Selah! The Lord
Ps. 84 of hosts is with us, the God of Jacob is our stronghold, Selah! Lord of hosts,
Ps. 20 happy is the one who trusts in You. Lord, save! May the King answer us on the
day we call.

OUR GOD and God of our fathers:

אֲמָרֵר IT IS BITTERLY that I weep, over the Hand raised against our ruins.
I blasphemed Him in His House, in my unfaithfulness and thieving.
The Holy Presence broke out and fled, flew ten stretches and rose up to the seventh heaven.
God cut me off, tormented me, burnt me, in the fourth month.
He closed the time set for Him to break those young boys, who were like boughs just sprouting.
He shot us with His arrows twice, melted and weakened us, as heedless women wept for Tammuz in the Temple.
He condemned me and became Enemy to me, then, in the month of Tammuz.
Five traps were laid for me, deep in the Scripture of sufferings sent.
Those people overcame me for my impurity on the seventeenth of the month.
For I was ensnared like a wretched bride, unfaithful beneath a wedding canopy of peace and success.
I did not wait for Moses, my shepherd, until the sixth hour, and the Tablets were smashed.
From His hand was I ornamented with jewelry of fine gold, brooch and bracelet.
They flowed away on the day of His rage, when I corrupted my way, and denounced my faith.
I broke off the order of His service and the constant supplies of the altar –
from the Chamber of the Lambs, the daily offering is ended.
Israel is crumbled to pieces, scattered, storm battered, oppressed.
Likened to a ship without a captain, tossed about like a boat.
You have taken her by the head for her sins, exposed her twice over to mourning and moaning.

רִבְּוֹהָ צָרֶיהָ כְּהַיּוֹם, וְהָבְקְעָה הָעִיר בַּשְּׁנִיָּה.
שִׁלְּחָה כִּצְבִי מֻדָּח מֵאֵין דּוֹרֵשׁ לְהַסְתִּירָה.
שָׁנְנוּ לְשׁוֹנָם וּנְתָנוּהָ כְּשֶׂה, צַמְרָהּ וַחֲלָבָהּ לְהַתִּירָה.
תִּצְעַק עַל כְּלִי חֶמְדָּה שֶׁבּוֹ נִכְתְּרָה.
תַּחֲמוֹד עֵינֶיהָ נְצַל כְּשָׂרַף אַפּוֹסְטְמוֹס הַתּוֹרָה.
חֵרֵף עֲשׁוּקִים וּרְצוּצִים בַּעֲבוּר הַרְעִימָם סָכָל.
יְרוּדִים בְּוֹהָיָה לֶאֱכֹל וּבְהַסְתֵּר פָּנִים מִלְּהִסְתַּכֵּל.
יַד הַשְּׁלִים מִכְּנַף שִׁקּוּצִים נֶאֱכָל.
עֵת צָרָה כְּהִתְכַּנֵּס וְהָעֳמַד צֶלֶם בְּהֵיכָל.
דְּוּוּיִם סְגוּפִים בָּנִים הָיוּ מִקֶּדֶם רִאשׁוֹנִים.
סְמוּכוֹת צָרוֹתֵיהֶם זוֹ לְזוֹ כַּמָּה שָׁנִים.
לוֹקִים כַּאֲשֶׁר תַּעֲשֶׂינָה הַדְּבוֹרִים, וְהָעַקְרַבִּים שׁוֹנִים.
הוֹגִים אָבַד שִׂבְרָם וּבָטֵל סִכּוּיָם בָּאִישׁוֹנִים.
‣ אֵל קַנָּא, בְּהִתְאַפֵּק בְּמְקַנְאֶיךָ דְּשֵׁנִים רְטוּבִים.
מְחַכִּים תְּקִים עוֹמְדִים לְעוֹלָמִים,
כִּנְטִיעִים מְחֻטָּבִים בָּאֲהָבִים.
הָאֱמֶת וְהַשָּׁלוֹם בְּצוֹמוֹת חֲטוּבִים.
נֶצַח הֱיוֹתָם לְשִׂמְחָה וּלְשָׂשׂוֹן וּלְמוֹעֲדִים טוֹבִים.

אֵל מֶלֶךְ יוֹשֵׁב עַל כִּסֵּא רַחֲמִים, מִתְנַהֵג בַּחֲסִידוּת. מוֹחֵל עֲוֹנוֹת עַמּוֹ, מַעֲבִיר רִאשׁוֹן רִאשׁוֹן. מַרְבֶּה מְחִילָה לְחַטָּאִים, וּסְלִיחָה לְפוֹשְׁעִים. עֹשֶׂה צְדָקוֹת עִם כָּל בָּשָׂר וָרוּחַ, לֹא כְרָעָתָם תִּגְמֹל. ‣ אֵל, הוֹרֵיתָ לָּנוּ לוֹמַר שְׁלֹשׁ עֶשְׂרֵה, וּזְכָר לָנוּ הַיּוֹם בְּרִית שְׁלֹשׁ עֶשְׂרֵה, כְּמוֹ שֶׁהוֹדַעְתָּ לֶעָנָו מִקֶּדֶם, כְּמוֹ שֶׁכָּתוּב: וַיֵּרֶד יהוה בֶּעָנָן, וַיִּתְיַצֵּב עִמּוֹ שָׁם, וַיִּקְרָא בְשֵׁם, יהוה: שמות לד

קהל *then* שליח ציבור:

וַיַּעֲבֹר יהוה עַל־פָּנָיו וַיִּקְרָא שמות לד

All say aloud:

יהוה, יהוה, אֵל רַחוּם וְחַנּוּן, אֶרֶךְ אַפַּיִם, וְרַב־חֶסֶד וֶאֱמֶת: נֹצֵר חֶסֶד לָאֲלָפִים, נֹשֵׂא עָוֹן וָפֶשַׁע וְחַטָּאָה, וְנַקֵּה: וְסָלַחְתָּ לַעֲוֹנֵנוּ וּלְחַטָּאתֵנוּ, וּנְחַלְתָּנוּ: שמות לד

Her enemies waged war on her on this day, and the city was broken through again.
She fled out like a chased gazelle to hide, when none sought her.
They sharpened their tongues, they made her like a lamb, and left her wool and milk for all takers.
She cries out for the cherished thing with which she was crowned:
the beloved of her eyes eluded her as Apostomus burnt the Torah.
A fool cursed those oppressed and broken to vex them; he taunted abject people:
"They shall be consumed;" "God shall hide His face from seeing."
When idols were placed in the Temple,
God avenged one's hand at the hand of the other, a disgusting item consumed.
This, at the time when He gathered anguish over us; for an image was set up in the Sanctuary of God.
Miserable and plagued are these children, who were once the very first.
Their troubles have come close on one another's heels these many years;
stricken as if by the stings of bees and scorpions.
They think their hope is gone, that as they sit in this darkness they have no more chance.
▸ Zealous God, in Your restraint towards those who incite You they have flourished fat and succulent.
Raise up those who still await You;
let them stand firm always, like something planted, or carved out with love.
It is on fast days that truth and peace are hewn out.
May they become forever times of joy and celebration – festive days.

אֵל מֶלֶךְ GOD, KING Who sits upon a throne of compassion, Who acts with loving-kindness, Who pardons the iniquities of His people, passing them before Him in order; Who forgives sinners and pardons transgressors; Who performs righteousness with all flesh and spirit, do not repay their bad actions in kind. ▸ God, You taught us to speak thirteen attributes: recall for us today the covenant of the thirteen attributes, as You in ancient times showed the humble
Ex. 34 one [Moses], as is written: The Lord descended in the cloud and stood with him there, and proclaimed in the name of the Lord:

Congregation then Leader:

Ex. 34 AND THE LORD passed by before him and proclaimed:

All say aloud:

Ex. 34 יהוה THE LORD, the Lord, compassionate and gracious God, slow to anger and great in mercy and truth, keeping loving-kindness for thousands, forgiving iniquity, transgression, and sin, and offering absolution. Forgive us our iniquity and our sin, and take us as Your inheritance.

Continue:

סְלַח לָנוּ אָבִינוּ כִּי חָטָאנוּ, מְחַל לָנוּ מַלְכֵּנוּ כִּי פָשָׁעְנוּ. כִּי־אַתָּה אֲדֹנָי טוֹב וְסַלָּח, וְרַב־חֶסֶד לְכָל־קֹרְאֶיךָ: תהלים פו

The following is said responsively:

שְׁעֵה נֶאֱסַר, אֲשֶׁר נִמְסַר, בְּיַד בָּבֶל וְגַם שֵׂעִיר.
לְךָ יֶהֱמֶה, זֶה כַּמֶּה, וְיִתְחַנֵּן כְּבֶן צָעִיר.
יוֹם גָּבַר הָאוֹיֵב וַתִּבָּקַע הָעִיר.

לְזֹאת אַכֶּה, וְאֶסְפֹּק כַּף, בְּיוֹם חֲמֵשׁ פִּזְרוֹנִי.
וְעַל רֶגֶל הָעֵגֶל, הַלֻּחוֹת יְצָאוּנִי.
וְגַם הֻשְׁמַד הַתָּמִיד, וּבַסּוּגַר הֱבִיאָנִי.
וְהוּשַׂם אֱלִיל בְּהֵיכַל כְּלִיל, וּמֵעֲצָתוֹ כְּלָאָנִי.
וְהַמִּנְחָה הוּנָחָה, וְדָתְךָ, צָר בָּאֵשׁ הִבְעִיר.
יוֹם גָּבַר הָאוֹיֵב וַתִּבָּקַע הָעִיר.

מְאֹד אֶתְחַל, וְאֶתְחַלְחַל, בְּיוֹם שַׁדַּי דְּחָפַנִי.
וְהַשְּׁפִיפוֹן מִצָּפוֹן, כְּשִׁבֹּלֶת שְׁטָפָנִי.
מְאוֹר חָשַׁךְ, וְגַם שֵׁשַׁךְ, כְּמוֹ כַדּוּר צְנָפַנִי.
וְהַצַּיָּד שָׁלַח יָד, וְהַצָּפִיר וְהַשָּׂעִיר.
יוֹם גָּבַר הָאוֹיֵב וַתִּבָּקַע הָעִיר.

הוֹד לִבִּי וּמִשְׂגַּבִּי, הֲלָעַד אַפְּךָ יֶעְשַׁן.
הֲלֹא תִרְאֶה עַם נִלְאֶה, אֲשֶׁר הֻשְׁחַר כְּמוֹ כִבְשָׁן.
גְּדֹר פִּרְצִי בְּבֶן פַּרְצִי, וּמְחַדֵּק לְקַט שׁוֹשָׁן.
בְּנֵה בֵּית זְבוּל, וְהָשֵׁב גְּבוּל הַכַּרְמֶל וְהַבָּשָׁן.
וְעַיִן פְּקַח, וְנָקָם קַח מֵאֱצֶר וּמִדִּישָׁן.
שְׁפֹט אִלֵּם, וְאָז יְשַׁלֵּם הַמַּבְעֶה וְהַמַּבְעִיר.
יוֹם גָּבַר הָאוֹיֵב וַתִּבָּקַע הָעִיר.

Continue with אֵל מֶלֶךְ יוֹשֵׁב *on the next page.*

Continue:

סְלַח לָנוּ FORGIVE US, our Father, for we have sinned. Pardon us, our King,
Ps. 86 for we have transgressed. For You, Lord, are good and forgiving, abounding in loving-kindness to all who call on You.

The following is said responsively:

שְׁעֵה TURN to this prisoner who has been yielded up, to the hand of Babylon and then of Seir; to You he has been calling all these years, and he pleads like a small child,

on the day the enemy prevailed and the city was broken through.

AND SO I bow myself and strike my hands together, on this day of five disasters that scattered me about, for at the time of the golden calf, the Tablets left me. And the daily offering was annulled, and they brought me away in a cage. And an idol was placed in the Sanctuary that was my crowning glory, and I was deprived of His counsel. The meal-offering was ended, and Your Law – the foe sent it up in flames,

on the day the enemy prevailed and the city was broken through.

I TREMBLE terribly, I stand horrified, on the day the Lord pushed me aside, And Sennacherib, the Viper of the north, swept me away like a deluge. My light grew dark, and Sheshakh [Babylon] too, tossed me about like a ball. And the hunter stretched out his hand, and the goat of Greece, the hairy one of Rome,

on the day the enemy prevailed and the city was broken through.

THE GLORY of my heart, my Stronghold, will Your rage fume forever? Will You not see this weary nation, blackened as if by the furnace? Close, with the descendant of Peretz, the breach in my fence, and, from among the thorns, pick out the lily. Build the Temple, and return the borders of the Carmel and of Bashan. And open Your eyes, exact vengeance from Etzer and Dishan. Judge a people struck dumb, so that the damages be paid, by the one who destroys, the one who burns –

on the day the enemy prevailed and the city was broken through.

Continue with "God, King Who sits" on the next page.

כל הימים

אֵל מֶֽלֶךְ יוֹשֵׁב עַל כִּסֵּא רַחֲמִים, מִתְנַהֵג בַּחֲסִידוּת. מוֹחֵל עֲוֹנוֹת עַמּוֹ, מַעֲבִיר רִאשׁוֹן רִאשׁוֹן. מַרְבֶּה מְחִילָה לְחַטָּאִים, וּסְלִיחָה לְפוֹשְׁעִים. עֹשֶׂה צְדָקוֹת עִם כָּל בָּשָׂר וָרְוּחַ, לֹא כְרָעָתָם תִּגְמֹל. ◂ אֵל, הוֹרֵיתָ לָּנוּ לוֹמַר שְׁלֹשׁ עֶשְׂרֵה, וּזְכָר לָנוּ הַיּוֹם בְּרִית שְׁלֹשׁ עֶשְׂרֵה, כְּמוֹ
שמות לד שֶׁהוֹדַעְתָּ לֶעָנָו מִקֶּדֶם, כְּמוֹ שֶׁכָּתוּב: וַיֵּרֶד יהוה בֶּעָנָן, וַיִּתְיַצֵּב עִמּוֹ שָׁם, וַיִּקְרָא בְשֵׁם, יהוה:

:קהל *then* שליח ציבור

שמות לד וַיַּעֲבֹר יהוה עַל־פָּנָיו וַיִּקְרָא

All say aloud:

שמות לד **יהוה,** יהוה, אֵל רַחוּם וְחַנּוּן, אֶרֶךְ אַפַּיִם, וְרַב־חֶסֶד וֶאֱמֶת: נֹצֵר חֶסֶד לָאֲלָפִים, נֹשֵׂא עָוֹן וָפֶשַׁע וְחַטָּאָה, וְנַקֵּה: וְסָלַחְתָּ לַעֲוֹנֵנוּ וּלְחַטָּאתֵנוּ, וּנְחַלְתָּנוּ:

Continue:

תהלים פו **סְלַח לָנוּ** אָבִינוּ כִּי חָטָאנוּ, מְחַל לָנוּ מַלְכֵּנוּ כִּי פָשָׁעְנוּ. כִּי־אַתָּה אֲדֹנָי טוֹב וְסַלָּח, וְרַב־חֶסֶד לְכָל־קֹרְאֶיךָ:

תהלים כה **זְכֹר־רַחֲמֶיךָ** יהוה וַחֲסָדֶיךָ, כִּי מֵעוֹלָם הֵמָּה: זָכְרֵנוּ יהוה בִּרְצוֹן עַמֶּךָ, פָּקְדֵנוּ בִּישׁוּעָתֶךָ.

תהלים עד זְכֹר עֲדָתְךָ קָנִיתָ קֶּדֶם, גָּאַלְתָּ שֵׁבֶט נַחֲלָתֶךָ, הַר־צִיּוֹן זֶה שָׁכַנְתָּ בּוֹ:

תהלים קב זְכֹר יהוה חִבַּת יְרוּשָׁלַיִם, אַהֲבַת צִיּוֹן אַל תִּשְׁכַּח לָנֶצַח. אַתָּה תָקוּם תְּרַחֵם צִיּוֹן, כִּי־עֵת לְחֶנְנָהּ, כִּי־בָא מוֹעֵד:

תהלים קלז זְכֹר יהוה לִבְנֵי אֱדוֹם אֵת יוֹם יְרוּשָׁלָֽםִ, הָאֹמְרִים עָרוּ עָרוּ, עַד הַיְסוֹד בָּהּ:

שמות לב זְכֹר לְאַבְרָהָם לְיִצְחָק וּלְיִשְׂרָאֵל עֲבָדֶיךָ, אֲשֶׁר נִשְׁבַּעְתָּ לָהֶם בָּךְ וַתְּדַבֵּר אֲלֵהֶם, אַרְבֶּה אֶת־זַרְעֲכֶם כְּכוֹכְבֵי הַשָּׁמָיִם, וְכָל־הָאָרֶץ הַזֹּאת אֲשֶׁר אָמַרְתִּי אֶתֵּן לְזַרְעֲכֶם, וְנָחֲלוּ לְעֹלָם:

דברים ט זְכֹר לַעֲבָדֶיךָ לְאַבְרָהָם לְיִצְחָק וּלְיַעֲקֹב, אַל־תֵּפֶן אֶל־קְשִׁי הָעָם הַזֶּה וְאֶל־רִשְׁעוֹ וְאֶל־חַטָּאתוֹ:

במדבר יב **אַל־נָא** תָשֵׁת עָלֵינוּ חַטָּאת אֲשֶׁר נוֹאַלְנוּ וַאֲשֶׁר חָטָאנוּ:
חָטָאנוּ צוּרֵנוּ, סְלַח לָנוּ יוֹצְרֵנוּ.

ALL DAYS

אֵל מֶֽלֶךְ GOD, KING Who sits upon a throne of compassion, Who acts with loving-kindness, Who pardons the iniquities of His people, passing them before Him in order; Who forgives sinners and pardons transgressors; Who performs righteousness with all flesh and spirit, do not repay their bad actions in kind. ▸ God, You taught us to speak thirteen attributes: recall for us today the covenant of the thirteen attributes, as You in ancient times showed the humble
Ex. 34 one [Moses], as is written: The Lord descended in the cloud and stood with him there, and proclaimed in the name of the Lord:

Congregation then Leader:

Ex. 34 AND THE LORD passed by before him and proclaimed:

All say aloud:

Ex. 34 יהוה THE LORD, the Lord, compassionate and gracious God, slow to anger and great in mercy and truth, keeping loving-kindness for thousands, forgiving iniquity, transgression, and sin, and offering absolution. Forgive us our iniquity and our sin, and take us as Your inheritance.

Continue:

סְלַח לָֽנוּ FORGIVE US, our Father, for we have sinned. Pardon us, our King, for we
Ps. 86 have transgressed. For You, Lord, are good and forgiving, abounding in loving-kindness to all who call on You.

Ps. 25 זְכֹר REMEMBER, Lord, Your compassion and loving-kindness, for they are everlasting. Remember us, Lord, in favoring Your people; redeem us with Your salvation.

Ps. 74 REMEMBER Your congregation, the one that You acquired long ago, the tribe of Your inheritance that You redeemed, this Mount Zion that You have dwelt in.

REMEMBER, Lord, the fondness of Jerusalem; do not forever forget the love of
Ps. 102 Zion. You shall rise up and have compassion for Zion, for now it is right to be gracious, for the time has come.

Ps. 137 REMEMBER, Lord, what the Edomites did on the day Jerusalem fell. They said, "Tear it down, tear it down to its very foundations!"

Ex. 32 REMEMBER Abraham, Isaac and Jacob, to whom You swore by Your own self, when You said to them, "I shall make Your descendants as numerous as the stars in the sky, and I shall give all this Land that I spoke of to your descendants, and they shall inherit it forever."

Deut. 9 REMEMBER Your servants, Abraham, Isaac and Jacob; do not attend to the stubbornness of this people, to their wickedness or sinfulness.

Num. 12 אַל־נָא PLEASE, DO NOT hold against us the sin that we committed so foolishly, that we have sinned. We have sinned, our Rock; forgive us, our Creator.

זְכֹר לָנוּ בְּרִית אָבוֹת כַּאֲשֶׁר אָמַרְתָּ: וְזָכַרְתִּי אֶת־בְּרִיתִי יַעֲקוֹב, וְאַף ויקרא כו
אֶת־בְּרִיתִי יִצְחָק וְאַף אֶת־בְּרִיתִי אַבְרָהָם אֶזְכֹּר, וְהָאָרֶץ
אֶזְכֹּר: זְכֹר לָנוּ בְּרִית רִאשׁוֹנִים כַּאֲשֶׁר אָמַרְתָּ: וְזָכַרְתִּי לָהֶם בְּרִית ויקרא כו
רִאשֹׁנִים אֲשֶׁר הוֹצֵאתִי־אֹתָם מֵאֶרֶץ מִצְרַיִם לְעֵינֵי הַגּוֹיִם, לִהְיוֹת
לָהֶם לֵאלֹהִים, אֲנִי יהוה:

עֲשֵׂה עִמָּנוּ כְּמָה שֶׁהִבְטַחְתָּנוּ: וְאַף גַּם־זֹאת בִּהְיוֹתָם בְּאֶרֶץ אֹיְבֵיהֶם, ויקרא כו
לֹא־מְאַסְתִּים וְלֹא־גְעַלְתִּים לְכַלֹּתָם, לְהָפֵר בְּרִיתִי אִתָּם, כִּי
אֲנִי יהוה אֱלֹהֵיהֶם: הָשֵׁב שְׁבוּתֵנוּ וְרַחֲמֵנוּ כְּמָה שֶׁכָּתוּב: וְשָׁב יהוה דברים ל
אֱלֹהֶיךָ אֶת־שְׁבוּתְךָ וְרִחֲמֶךָ, וְשָׁב וְקִבֶּצְךָ מִכָּל־הָעַמִּים אֲשֶׁר הֱפִיצְךָ
יהוה אֱלֹהֶיךָ שָׁמָּה: קַבֵּץ נִדָּחֵינוּ כְּמָה שֶׁכָּתוּב: אִם־יִהְיֶה נִדַּחֲךָ בִּקְצֵה דברים ל
הַשָּׁמָיִם, מִשָּׁם יְקַבֶּצְךָ יהוה אֱלֹהֶיךָ וּמִשָּׁם יִקָּחֶךָ: מְחֵה פְשָׁעֵינוּ כָּעָב
וְכֶעָנָן כְּמָה שֶׁכָּתוּב: מָחִיתִי כָעָב פְּשָׁעֶיךָ וְכֶעָנָן חַטֹּאותֶיךָ, שׁוּבָה ישעיה מד
אֵלַי כִּי גְאַלְתִּיךָ: מְחֵה פְשָׁעֵינוּ לְמַעַנְךָ כַּאֲשֶׁר אָמַרְתָּ: אָנֹכִי אָנֹכִי ישעיה מג
הוּא מֹחֶה פְשָׁעֶיךָ לְמַעֲנִי, וְחַטֹּאתֶיךָ לֹא אֶזְכֹּר: הַלְבֵּן חֲטָאֵינוּ כַּשֶּׁלֶג
וְכַצֶּמֶר כְּמָה שֶׁכָּתוּב: לְכוּ־נָא וְנִוָּכְחָה יֹאמַר יהוה, אִם־יִהְיוּ חֲטָאֵיכֶם ישעיה א
כַּשָּׁנִים כַּשֶּׁלֶג יַלְבִּינוּ, אִם־יַאְדִּימוּ כַתּוֹלָע כַּצֶּמֶר יִהְיוּ: זְרֹק עָלֵינוּ
מַיִם טְהוֹרִים וְטַהֲרֵנוּ כְּמָה שֶׁכָּתוּב: וְזָרַקְתִּי עֲלֵיכֶם מַיִם טְהוֹרִים יחזקאל לו
וּטְהַרְתֶּם, מִכֹּל טֻמְאוֹתֵיכֶם וּמִכָּל־גִּלּוּלֵיכֶם אֲטַהֵר אֶתְכֶם: רַחֵם עָלֵינוּ
וְאַל תַּשְׁחִיתֵנוּ כְּמָה שֶׁכָּתוּב: כִּי אֵל רַחוּם יהוה אֱלֹהֶיךָ, לֹא יַרְפְּךָ וְלֹא דברים ד
יַשְׁחִיתֶךָ, וְלֹא יִשְׁכַּח אֶת־בְּרִית אֲבֹתֶיךָ אֲשֶׁר נִשְׁבַּע לָהֶם: מוֹל אֶת
לְבָבֵנוּ לְאַהֲבָה אֶת שְׁמֶךָ כְּמָה שֶׁכָּתוּב: וּמָל יהוה אֱלֹהֶיךָ אֶת־לְבָבְךָ דברים ל
וְאֶת־לְבַב זַרְעֶךָ, לְאַהֲבָה אֶת־יהוה אֱלֹהֶיךָ בְּכָל־לְבָבְךָ וּבְכָל־נַפְשְׁךָ,
לְמַעַן חַיֶּיךָ: הִמָּצֵא לָנוּ בְּבַקָּשָׁתֵנוּ כְּמָה שֶׁכָּתוּב: וּבִקַּשְׁתֶּם מִשָּׁם אֶת־ דברים ד
יהוה אֱלֹהֶיךָ וּמָצָאתָ, כִּי תִדְרְשֶׁנּוּ בְּכָל־לְבָבְךָ וּבְכָל־נַפְשֶׁךָ: תְּבִיאֵנוּ
אֶל הַר קָדְשֶׁךָ וְשַׂמְּחֵנוּ בְּבֵית תְּפִלָּתֶךָ כְּמָה שֶׁכָּתוּב: וַהֲבִיאוֹתִים ישעיה נו
אֶל־הַר קָדְשִׁי וְשִׂמַּחְתִּים בְּבֵית תְּפִלָּתִי, עוֹלֹתֵיהֶם וְזִבְחֵיהֶם לְרָצוֹן
עַל־מִזְבְּחִי, כִּי בֵיתִי בֵּית־תְּפִלָּה יִקָּרֵא לְכָל־הָעַמִּים:

Lev. 26 זְכֹר REMEMBER the covenant of our fathers, as You have said, "I shall remember My covenant with Jacob, and My covenant with Isaac, and I shall remember My covenant with Abraham, and I shall remember the Land." Remember the
Lev. 26 covenant of the early ones, as You have said, "I shall remember for them the covenant of the early ones, those I took out of the Land of Egypt before the eyes of the nations, in order to be their God: I am the Lord."

Lev. 26 עֲשֵׂה DEAL KINDLY WITH us as You have promised, "Even so, when they are in the land of their enemies I shall not reject them and shall not detest them to the point of destruction, to the point of breaking My covenant with them, for I am the Lord their God." Restore our fortunes, and have compassion for
Deut. 30 us as is written, "And God shall restore your fortunes and have compassion for you, and shall return and gather you in from all the nations among whom the Lord has scattered you." Gather those of us who have been distanced, as is
Deut. 30 written, "If your distanced ones are at the very ends of the heavens, from there shall the Lord your God gather you; from there shall He bring You." Wipe
Is. 44 out our crimes as if they were a cloud, as if they were a haze, as is written, "I have wiped out your crimes like a cloud, and as a haze your sins; come back to Me for I have redeemed you." Wipe out our crimes for Your sake, as You
Is. 43 have said, "I, I am the one Who shall wipe out your crimes for My sake, and I shall not recall your sins." Whiten our sins as snow and as wool, as is written,
Is. 1 "Come now, let us reason together, says the Lord; If your sins are like scarlet, they shall be whitened like snow; should they be as red as crimson, they shall
Ezek. 36 become like wool." Throw over us pure waters and purify us, as is written, "I shall throw pure waters over you and you shall be pure. I shall purify you of all your impurities and of all your idolatry." Have compassion for us and do not
Deut. 4 destroy us, as is written, "For the Lord your God is a compassionate God; He will not cease to hold you and He will not destroy you, and will not forget the covenant of your fathers that He pledged to them." Circumcise our hearts to
Deut. 30 love Your name, as is written, "And the Lord will circumcise your heart and the heart of your descendants to love the Lord your God with all your heart and with all your soul, so that you shall live." Let us find You when we seek You, as
Deut. 4 is written, "And if from there you seek the Lord your God, you shall find Him, when you seek Him out with all your heart and with all your soul." Bring us to Your holy mountain, and let us rejoice in Your house of prayer, as is written,
Is. 56 "I shall bring them to My holy mountain, and I shall make them rejoice in My house of prayer; their offerings and their sacrifices will be accepted, desired on My altar, for My House will be called a house of prayer for all peoples."

The ארון קודש *is opened. The following until* ◂ *is said responsively, verse by verse:*

שְׁמַע קוֹלֵנוּ, יהוה אֱלֹהֵינוּ, חוּס וְרַחֵם עָלֵינוּ וְקַבֵּל בְּרַחֲמִים וּבְרָצוֹן אֶת תְּפִלָּתֵנוּ.

איכה ה
הֲשִׁיבֵנוּ יהוה אֵלֶיךָ וְנָשׁוּבָה, חַדֵּשׁ יָמֵינוּ כְּקֶדֶם:

אַל תַּשְׁלִיכֵנוּ מִלְּפָנֶיךָ, וְרוּחַ קָדְשְׁךָ אַל תִּקַּח מִמֶּנּוּ.

אַל תַּשְׁלִיכֵנוּ לְעֵת זִקְנָה, כִּכְלוֹת כֹּחֵנוּ אַל תַּעַזְבֵנוּ. ◂

אַל תַּעַזְבֵנוּ יהוה, אֱלֹהֵינוּ אַל תִּרְחַק מִמֶּנּוּ.

עֲשֵׂה עִמָּנוּ אוֹת לְטוֹבָה, וְיִרְאוּ שׂוֹנְאֵינוּ וְיֵבֹשׁוּ, כִּי אַתָּה יהוה עֲזַרְתָּנוּ וְנִחַמְתָּנוּ.

אֲמָרֵינוּ הַאֲזִינָה יהוה, בִּינָה הֲגִיגֵנוּ.

יִהְיוּ לְרָצוֹן אִמְרֵי פִינוּ וְהֶגְיוֹן לִבֵּנוּ לְפָנֶיךָ, יהוה צוּרֵנוּ וְגוֹאֲלֵנוּ.

כִּי לְךָ יהוה הוֹחָלְנוּ, אַתָּה תַעֲנֶה אֲדֹנָי אֱלֹהֵינוּ.

The ארון קודש *is closed.*

וידוי

אֱלֹהֵינוּ וֵאלֹהֵי אֲבוֹתֵינוּ, תָּבֹא לְפָנֶיךָ תְּפִלָּתֵנוּ, וְאַל תִּתְעַלַּם מִתְּחִנָּתֵנוּ. שֶׁאֵין אָנוּ עַזֵּי פָנִים וּקְשֵׁי עֹרֶף לוֹמַר לְפָנֶיךָ, יהוה אֱלֹהֵינוּ וֵאלֹהֵי אֲבוֹתֵינוּ, צַדִּיקִים אֲנַחְנוּ וְלֹא חָטָאנוּ. אֲבָל אֲנַחְנוּ וַאֲבוֹתֵינוּ חָטָאנוּ.

Strike the left side of the chest with the right fist while saying each of the sins.

אָשַׁמְנוּ, בָּגַדְנוּ, גָּזַלְנוּ, דִּבַּרְנוּ דֹפִי. הֶעֱוִינוּ, וְהִרְשַׁעְנוּ, זַדְנוּ, חָמַסְנוּ, טָפַלְנוּ שֶׁקֶר. יָעַצְנוּ רָע, כִּזַּבְנוּ, לַצְנוּ, מָרַדְנוּ, נִאַצְנוּ, סָרַרְנוּ, עָוִינוּ, פָּשַׁעְנוּ, צָרַרְנוּ, קִשִּׁינוּ עֹרֶף. רָשַׁעְנוּ, שִׁחַתְנוּ, תִּעַבְנוּ, תָּעִינוּ, תִּעְתָּעְנוּ.

נחמיה ט
סַרְנוּ מִמִּצְוֹתֶיךָ וּמִמִּשְׁפָּטֶיךָ הַטּוֹבִים, וְלֹא שָׁוָה לָנוּ. וְאַתָּה צַדִּיק עַל כָּל־הַבָּא עָלֵינוּ, כִּי־אֱמֶת עָשִׂיתָ וַאֲנַחְנוּ הִרְשָׁעְנוּ.

הִרְשַׁעְנוּ וּפָשַׁעְנוּ לָכֵן לֹא נוֹשָׁעְנוּ. וְתֵן בְּלִבֵּנוּ לַעֲזֹב דֶּרֶךְ רֶשַׁע, וְחִישׁ
ישעיה נה
לָנוּ יֶשַׁע, כַּכָּתוּב עַל יַד נְבִיאֶךָ: יַעֲזֹב רָשָׁע דַּרְכּוֹ וְאִישׁ אָוֶן מַחְשְׁבֹתָיו, וְיָשֹׁב אֶל־יהוה וִירַחֲמֵהוּ וְאֶל־אֱלֹהֵינוּ כִּי־יַרְבֶּה לִסְלוֹחַ:

The Ark is opened. The following until ◂ is said responsively, verse by verse:

שְׁמַע קוֹלֵנוּ LISTEN TO OUR VOICE, Lord our God. Spare us and have compassion on us, and in compassion and favor accept our prayer.

Lam. 5 Turn us back, O Lord, to You, and we will return. Renew our days as of old.

Do not cast us away from You, and do not take Your holy spirit from us.

Do not cast us away in our old age; when our strength is gone do not desert us.◂

Do not desert us, Lord; our God, do not be distant from us.

Give us a sign of good things, and those who hate us shall see it and be ashamed, for You, Lord, will help us and console us.

Hear our speech, Lord, consider our thoughts.

May the words of our mouths and the thoughts within our hearts be pleasing to You, Lord, our Rock and our Redeemer.

For it is You, Lord, that we have longed for; You shall answer us, Lord our God.

The Ark is closed.

CONFESSION

אֱלֹהֵינוּ OUR GOD AND God of our fathers, let our prayer come before You, and do not hide Yourself from our plea, for we are not so arrogant or obstinate as to say before You, Lord, our God and God of our fathers, we are righteous and have not sinned, for in truth, we and our fathers have sinned.

Strike the left side of the chest with the right fist while saying each of the sins.

אָשַׁמְנוּ WE HAVE BEEN guilty, we have acted treacherously, we have robbed, we have spoken slander. We have acted perversely, we have acted wickedly, we have acted presumptuously, we have been violent, we have framed lies. We have given bad advice, we have deceived, we have scorned, we have rebelled, we have provoked, we have turned away, we have committed iniquity, we have transgressed, we have persecuted, we have been obstinate. We have acted wickedly, we have corrupted, we have acted abominably, we have strayed, we have led others astray.

סַרְנוּ WE HAVE TURNED away from Your commandments, and good laws, to no
Neh. 9 avail, for You are just in all that has befallen us, for You have acted faithfully while we have done wickedly.

הִרְשַׁעְנוּ WE HAVE BEEN wicked and we have done wrong, and so we have not been saved. Place it in our hearts to abandon the way of wickedness, and hasten
Is. 55 our salvation, as is written by Your prophet, "Let each wicked person abandon his ways, each man of iniquity his thoughts, and let him come back to the Lord and He will have compassion for him; back to our God for He will forgive abundantly."

תהלים יט **מְשִׁיחַ** צִדְקֶךָ אָמַר לְפָנֶיךָ: שְׁגִיאוֹת מִי־יָבִין, מִנִּסְתָּרוֹת נַקֵּנִי: נַקֵּנוּ יהוה אֱלֹהֵינוּ מִכָּל פְּשָׁעֵינוּ וְטַהֲרֵנוּ מִכָּל טֻמְאוֹתֵינוּ וּזְרֹק עָלֵינוּ מַיִם
יחזקאל לו טְהוֹרִים וְטַהֲרֵנוּ, כַּכָּתוּב עַל יַד נְבִיאֶךָ: וְזָרַקְתִּי עֲלֵיכֶם מַיִם טְהוֹרִים וּטְהַרְתֶּם, מִכֹּל טֻמְאוֹתֵיכֶם וּמִכָּל־גִּלּוּלֵיכֶם אֲטַהֵר אֶתְכֶם: עַמְּךָ וְנַחֲלָתְךָ רְעֵבֵי טוּבְךָ, צְמֵאֵי חַסְדְּךָ, תְּאֵבֵי יִשְׁעֶךָ. יַכִּירוּ וְיֵדְעוּ, כִּי לַיהוה אֱלֹהֵינוּ הָרַחֲמִים וְהַסְּלִיחוֹת.

אֵל רַחוּם שְׁמֶךָ. אֵל חַנּוּן שְׁמֶךָ. בָּנוּ נִקְרָא שְׁמֶךָ. יהוה עֲשֵׂה לְמַעַן שְׁמֶךָ. עֲשֵׂה לְמַעַן **א**ֲמִתָּךְ. עֲשֵׂה לְמַעַן **ב**ְּרִיתָךְ. עֲשֵׂה לְמַעַן **ג**ָּדְלְךָ וְתִפְאַרְתָּךְ. עֲשֵׂה לְמַעַן **ד**ָּתָךְ. עֲשֵׂה לְמַעַן **ה**וֹדָךְ. עֲשֵׂה לְמַעַן **ו**ִעוּדָךְ. עֲשֵׂה לְמַעַן **ז**ִכְרָךְ. עֲשֵׂה לְמַעַן **ח**ַסְדָּךְ. עֲשֵׂה לְמַעַן **ט**וּבָךְ. עֲשֵׂה לְמַעַן **י**ִחוּדָךְ. עֲשֵׂה לְמַעַן **כ**ְּבוֹדָךְ. עֲשֵׂה לְמַעַן **ל**ִמּוּדָךְ. עֲשֵׂה לְמַעַן **מ**ַלְכוּתָךְ. עֲשֵׂה לְמַעַן **נ**ִצְחָךְ. עֲשֵׂה לְמַעַן **ס**וֹדָךְ. עֲשֵׂה לְמַעַן **ע**ֻזָּךְ. עֲשֵׂה לְמַעַן **פ**ְּאֵרָךְ. עֲשֵׂה לְמַעַן **צ**ִדְקָתָךְ. עֲשֵׂה לְמַעַן **ק**ְדֻשָּׁתָךְ. עֲשֵׂה לְמַעַן **ר**ַחֲמֶיךָ הָרַבִּים. עֲשֵׂה לְמַעַן **ש**ְׁכִינָתָךְ. עֲשֵׂה לְמַעַן **ת**ְּהִלָּתָךְ. עֲשֵׂה לְמַעַן אוֹהֲבֶיךָ שׁוֹכְנֵי עָפָר. עֲשֵׂה לְמַעַן אַבְרָהָם יִצְחָק וְיַעֲקֹב. עֲשֵׂה לְמַעַן מֹשֶׁה וְאַהֲרֹן. עֲשֵׂה לְמַעַן דָּוִד וּשְׁלֹמֹה. עֲשֵׂה לְמַעַן יְרוּשָׁלַיִם עִיר קָדְשֶׁךָ. עֲשֵׂה לְמַעַן צִיּוֹן מִשְׁכַּן כְּבוֹדֶךָ. עֲשֵׂה לְמַעַן שִׁמְמוֹת הֵיכָלֶךָ. עֲשֵׂה לְמַעַן הֲרִיסוּת מִזְבְּחֶךָ. עֲשֵׂה לְמַעַן הֲרוּגִים עַל שֵׁם קָדְשֶׁךָ. עֲשֵׂה לְמַעַן טְבוּחִים עַל יִחוּדֶךָ. עֲשֵׂה לְמַעַן בָּאֵי בָאֵשׁ וּבַמַּיִם עַל קִדּוּשׁ שְׁמֶךָ. עֲשֵׂה לְמַעַן יוֹנְקֵי שָׁדַיִם שֶׁלֹּא חָטְאוּ. עֲשֵׂה לְמַעַן גְּמוּלֵי חָלָב שֶׁלֹּא פָשְׁעוּ. עֲשֵׂה לְמַעַן תִּינוֹקוֹת שֶׁל בֵּית רַבָּן. עֲשֵׂה לְמַעַנְךָ אִם לֹא לְמַעֲנֵנוּ. עֲשֵׂה לְמַעַנְךָ וְהוֹשִׁיעֵנוּ.

עֲנֵנוּ יהוה עֲנֵנוּ. עֲנֵנוּ **א**ֱלֹהֵינוּ עֲנֵנוּ. עֲנֵנוּ **א**ָבִינוּ עֲנֵנוּ. עֲנֵנוּ **ב**ּוֹרְאֵנוּ עֲנֵנוּ. עֲנֵנוּ **ג**ּוֹאֲלֵנוּ עֲנֵנוּ. עֲנֵנוּ **ד**ּוֹרְשֵׁנוּ עֲנֵנוּ. עֲנֵנוּ **ה**ָאֵל הַנֶּאֱמָן עֲנֵנוּ. עֲנֵנוּ **ו**ָתִיק וְחָסִיד עֲנֵנוּ. עֲנֵנוּ **ז**ַךְ וְיָשָׁר עֲנֵנוּ. עֲנֵנוּ **ח**ַי וְקַיָּם עֲנֵנוּ. עֲנֵנוּ **ט**וֹב וּמֵטִיב עֲנֵנוּ. עֲנֵנוּ **י**וֹדֵעַ יֵצֶר עֲנֵנוּ. עֲנֵנוּ **כ**ּוֹבֵשׁ כְּעָסִים עֲנֵנוּ. עֲנֵנוּ **ל**וֹבֵשׁ צְדָקוֹת עֲנֵנוּ. עֲנֵנוּ **מ**ֶלֶךְ מַלְכֵי הַמְּלָכִים עֲנֵנוּ. עֲנֵנוּ **נ**וֹרָא וְנִשְׂגָּב עֲנֵנוּ. עֲנֵנוּ **ס**וֹלֵחַ וּמוֹחֵל עֲנֵנוּ. עֲנֵנוּ **ע**וֹנֶה בְּעֵת צָרָה עֲנֵנוּ. עֲנֵנוּ **פ**ּוֹדֶה וּמַצִּיל עֲנֵנוּ. עֲנֵנוּ **צ**ַדִּיק וְיָשָׁר עֲנֵנוּ. עֲנֵנוּ **ק**ָרוֹב לְקוֹרְאָיו עֲנֵנוּ. עֲנֵנוּ **ר**ַחוּם וְחַנּוּן עֲנֵנוּ. עֲנֵנוּ **ש**ׁוֹמֵעַ אֶל אֶבְיוֹנִים עֲנֵנוּ. עֲנֵנוּ **ת**ּוֹמֵךְ תְּמִימִים עֲנֵנוּ. עֲנֵנוּ אֱלֹהֵי אֲבוֹתֵינוּ

Ps. 19 מְשִׁיחַ YOUR RIGHTEOUS anointed one said to You, "Who can discern his own mistakes? Cleanse me of my hidden faults." Cleanse us, Lord our God, of all our sins, and purify us of all our impurities and throw clear waters over us to purify us,
Ezek. 36 as was written by Your prophet, "I shall throw clear waters over you and you shall be pure. I shall purify you of all your impurities and of all your idolatry." Your people, Your inheritance, famished of Your good, thirsting for Your loving-kindness, craving Your salvation – they shall recognize and know that compassion and forgiveness belong to the Lord our God.

אֵל רַחוּם COMPASSIONATE GOD is Your name; Gracious God is Your name. We are called by Your name; Lord, act for the sake of Your name. Act for the sake of Your truth. Act for the sake of Your covenant. Act for the sake of Your greatness and glory. Act for the sake of Your Law. Act for the sake of Your majesty. Act for the sake of Your promise. Act for the sake of Your remembrance. Act for the sake of Your loving-kindness. Act for the sake of Your goodness. Act for the sake of Your oneness. Act for the sake of Your honor. Act for the sake of Your wisdom. Act for the sake of Your kingship. Act for the sake of Your eternity. Act for the sake of Your mystery. Act for the sake of Your might. Act for the sake of Your splendor. Act for the sake of Your righteousness. Act for the sake of Your holiness. Act for the sake of Your great compassion. Act for the sake of Your Presence. Act for the sake of Your praise. Act for the sake of those who loved You, who now dwell in the dust. Act for the sake of Abraham, Isaac and Jacob. Act for the sake of Moses and Aaron. Act for the sake of David and Solomon. Act for the sake of Jerusalem, Your holy city. Act for the sake of Zion, the dwelling place of Your glory. Act for the sake of the desolate site of Your Temple. Act for the sake of the ruins of Your altar. Act for the sake of those killed in sanctification of Your name. Act for the sake of those slaughtered over Your unity. Act for the sake of those who have gone through fire and water in sanctification of Your name. Act for the sake of suckling infants who have not sinned. Act for the sake of little ones just weaned who have done no wrong. Act for the sake of schoolchildren. Act for Your own sake if not for ours. Act for Your own sake, and save us.

עֲנֵנוּ ANSWER US, LORD, answer us. Answer us, our God, answer us. Answer us, our Father, answer us. Answer us, our Creator, answer us. Answer us, our Redeemer, answer us. Answer us, You Who seek us, answer us. Answer us, God Who is faithful, answer us. Answer us, You Who are ancient and kind, answer us. Answer us, You Who are pure and upright, answer us. Answer us, You Who are alive and remain, answer us. Answer us, You Who are good and do good, answer us. Answer us, You Who know our impulses, answer us. Answer us, You Who conquer rage, answer us. Answer us, You Who clothe Yourself in righteousness, answer us. Answer us, Supreme King of kings, answer us. Answer us, You Who are awesome and elevated, answer us. Answer us, You Who forgive and pardon, answer us. Answer us, You Who answer in times of trouble, answer us. Answer us, You Who redeem and save, answer us. Answer

עֲנֵנוּ. עֲנֵנוּ אֱלֹהֵי אַבְרָהָם עֲנֵנוּ. עֲנֵנוּ פַּחַד יִצְחָק עֲנֵנוּ. עֲנֵנוּ אֲבִיר יַעֲקֹב עֲנֵנוּ. עֲנֵנוּ עֶזְרַת הַשְּׁבָטִים עֲנֵנוּ. עֲנֵנוּ מִשְׂגַּב אִמָּהוֹת עֲנֵנוּ. עֲנֵנוּ קָשֶׁה לִכְעוֹס עֲנֵנוּ. עֲנֵנוּ רַךְ לִרְצוֹת עֲנֵנוּ. עֲנֵנוּ עוֹנֶה בְּעֵת רָצוֹן עֲנֵנוּ. עֲנֵנוּ אֲבִי יְתוֹמִים עֲנֵנוּ. עֲנֵנוּ דַּיַּן אַלְמָנוֹת עֲנֵנוּ.

מִי שֶׁעָנָה לְאַבְרָהָם אָבִינוּ בְּהַר הַמּוֹרִיָּה, הוּא יַעֲנֵנוּ.

מִי שֶׁעָנָה לְיִצְחָק בְּנוֹ כְּשֶׁנֶּעֱקַד עַל גַּבֵּי הַמִּזְבֵּחַ, הוּא יַעֲנֵנוּ.

מִי שֶׁעָנָה לְיַעֲקֹב בְּבֵית אֵל, הוּא יַעֲנֵנוּ.

מִי שֶׁעָנָה לְיוֹסֵף בְּבֵית הָאֲסוּרִים, הוּא יַעֲנֵנוּ.

מִי שֶׁעָנָה לַאֲבוֹתֵינוּ עַל יַם סוּף, הוּא יַעֲנֵנוּ.

מִי שֶׁעָנָה לְמֹשֶׁה בְּחוֹרֵב, הוּא יַעֲנֵנוּ.

מִי שֶׁעָנָה לְאַהֲרֹן בַּמַּחְתָּה, הוּא יַעֲנֵנוּ.

מִי שֶׁעָנָה לְפִינְחָס בְּקוּמוֹ מִתּוֹךְ הָעֵדָה, הוּא יַעֲנֵנוּ.

מִי שֶׁעָנָה לִיהוֹשֻׁעַ בַּגִּלְגָּל, הוּא יַעֲנֵנוּ.

מִי שֶׁעָנָה לִשְׁמוּאֵל בַּמִּצְפָּה, הוּא יַעֲנֵנוּ.

מִי שֶׁעָנָה לְדָוִד וּשְׁלֹמֹה בְנוֹ בִּירוּשָׁלָיִם, הוּא יַעֲנֵנוּ.

מִי שֶׁעָנָה לְאֵלִיָּהוּ בְּהַר הַכַּרְמֶל, הוּא יַעֲנֵנוּ.

מִי שֶׁעָנָה לֶאֱלִישָׁע בִּירִיחוֹ, הוּא יַעֲנֵנוּ.

מִי שֶׁעָנָה לְיוֹנָה בִּמְעֵי הַדָּגָה, הוּא יַעֲנֵנוּ.

מִי שֶׁעָנָה לְחִזְקִיָּהוּ מֶלֶךְ יְהוּדָה בְּחָלְיוֹ, הוּא יַעֲנֵנוּ.

מִי שֶׁעָנָה לַחֲנַנְיָה מִישָׁאֵל וַעֲזַרְיָה בְּתוֹךְ כִּבְשַׁן הָאֵשׁ, הוּא יַעֲנֵנוּ.

מִי שֶׁעָנָה לְדָנִיֵּאל בְּגוֹב הָאֲרָיוֹת, הוּא יַעֲנֵנוּ.

מִי שֶׁעָנָה לְמָרְדְּכַי וְאֶסְתֵּר בְּשׁוּשַׁן הַבִּירָה, הוּא יַעֲנֵנוּ.

מִי שֶׁעָנָה לְעֶזְרָא בַּגּוֹלָה, הוּא יַעֲנֵנוּ.

מִי שֶׁעָנָה לְכָל הַצַּדִּיקִים וְהַחֲסִידִים וְהַתְּמִימִים וְהַיְשָׁרִים, הוּא יַעֲנֵנוּ.

רַחֲמָנָא דְּעָנֵי לַעֲנִיֵּי עֲנִינָן. רַחֲמָנָא דְּעָנֵי לִתְבִירֵי לִבָּא עֲנִינָן. רַחֲמָנָא דְּעָנֵי לְמַכִּיכֵי רוּחָא עֲנִינָן. רַחֲמָנָא עֲנִינָן. רַחֲמָנָא חוּס, רַחֲמָנָא פְּרוֹק, רַחֲמָנָא שֵׁיזִב. רַחֲמָנָא רְחֵם עֲלָן, הַשְׁתָּא בַּעֲגָלָא וּבִזְמַן קָרִיב.

Continue with אבינו מלכנו *on page 138.*

us, You Who are righteous and straightforward, answer us. Answer us, You Who are close to those who call, answer us. Answer us, You Who are compassionate and gracious, answer us. Answer us, You Who listen to the destitute, answer us. Answer us, You Who support the innocent, answer us. Answer us, God of our fathers, answer us. Answer us, God of Abraham, answer us. Answer us, Terror of Isaac, answer us. Answer us, Champion of Jacob, answer us. Answer us, Help of the tribes, answer us. Answer us, Stronghold of the mothers, answer us. Answer us, You Who are slow to anger, answer us. Answer us, You Who are lightly appeased, answer us. Answer us, You Who answer at times of favor, answer us. Answer us, Father of orphans, answer us. Answer us, Justice of widows, answer us.

מִי שֶׁעָנָה THE ONE Who answered Abraham our father on Mount Moriah – answer us.
THE ONE Who answered Isaac his son, when he was bound upon the altar – answer us.
THE ONE Who answered Jacob in Beth-El – answer us.
THE ONE Who answered Joseph in prison – answzer us.
THE ONE Who answered our fathers at the Reed Sea – answer us.
THE ONE Who answered Moses at Horeb – answer us.
THE ONE Who answered Aaron over his firepan – answer us.
THE ONE Who answered Pinehas when he stood up from among the congregation – answer us.
THE ONE Who answered Joshua at Gilgal – answer us.
THE ONE Who answered Samuel at Mitzpah – answer us.
THE ONE Who answered David and Solomon his son in Jerusalem – answer us.
THE ONE Who answered Elijah on Mount Carmel – answer us.
THE ONE Who answered Elisha at Jericho – answer us.
THE ONE Who answered Jonah in the belly of the fish – answer us.
THE ONE Who answered Hezekiah the king of Judah in his illness – answer us.
THE ONE Who answered Hananiah, Mishael and Azariah in the furnace of fire – answer us.
THE ONE Who answered Daniel in the lions' den – answer us.
THE ONE Who answered Mordekhai and Esther in Shushan the capital city – answer us.
THE ONE Who answered Ezra in his exile – answer us.
THE ONE Who answered so many righteous, devoted, innocent and upright people – answer us.

רַחֲמָנָא LOVING GOD, Who answers the oppressed: answer us. Loving God, Who answers the broken hearted: answer us. Loving God, Who answers those of humbled spirit: answer us. Loving God, answer us. Loving God, spare; Loving God, release; Loving God, save us. Loving God, have compassion for us now, swiftly, at a time soon coming.

Continue with "Avinu Malkenu" on page 139.

Some say סליחות *on the first Monday, the Thursday, and the second Monday following* פסח *and* סוכות*. This custom is known by the acronym* בה״ב *(second, fifth, and second days of the week).*

סליחות לשני קמא

SELIHOT FOR THE FIRST MONDAY

סְלַח לָנוּ, אָבִינוּ, כִּי בְּרֹב אִוַּלְתֵּנוּ שָׁגִינוּ. מְחַל לָנוּ, מַלְכֵּנוּ, כִּי רַבּוּ עֲוֹנֵינוּ.

אֵל אֶרֶךְ אַפַּיִם אַתָּה, וּבַעַל הָרַחֲמִים נִקְרֵאתָ, וְדֶרֶךְ תְּשׁוּבָה הוֹרֵיתָ.
גְּדֻלַּת רַחֲמֶיךָ וַחֲסָדֶיךָ, תִּזְכֹּר הַיּוֹם וּבְכָל יוֹם לְזֶרַע יְדִידֶיךָ.
תֵּפֶן אֵלֵינוּ בְּרַחֲמִים, כִּי אַתָּה הוּא בַּעַל הָרַחֲמִים. בְּתַחֲנוּן וּבִתְפִלָּה
פָּנֶיךָ נְקַדֵּם, כְּהוֹדַעְתָּ לֶעָנָו מִקֶּדֶם. מֵחֲרוֹן אַפְּךָ שׁוּב, כְּמוֹ בְּתוֹרָתְךָ כָּתוּב.
וּבְצֵל כְּנָפֶיךָ נֶחֱסֶה וְנִתְלוֹנָן, כְּיוֹם וַיֵּרֶד יהוה בֶּעָנָן. ‹ תַּעֲבֹר עַל פֶּשַׁע
וְתִמְחֶה אָשָׁם, כְּיוֹם וַיִּתְיַצֵּב עִמּוֹ שָׁם. תַּאֲזִין שַׁוְעָתֵנוּ וְתַקְשִׁיב מֶנּוּ מַאֲמָר,
כְּיוֹם וַיִּקְרָא בְשֵׁם יהוה, וְשָׁם נֶאֱמַר

then שליח ציבור *then* קהל:

שמות לד וַיַּעֲבֹר יהוה עַל־פָּנָיו וַיִּקְרָא

All say aloud:

שמות לד **יהוה, יהוה,** אֵל רַחוּם וְחַנּוּן, אֶרֶךְ אַפַּיִם, וְרַב־חֶסֶד וֶאֱמֶת: נֹצֵר
חֶסֶד לָאֲלָפִים, נֹשֵׂא עָוֹן וָפֶשַׁע וְחַטָּאָה, וְנַקֵּה: וְסָלַחְתָּ
לַעֲוֹנֵנוּ וּלְחַטָּאתֵנוּ, וּנְחַלְתָּנוּ:

Continue:

תהלים פו **סְלַח לָנוּ** אָבִינוּ כִּי חָטָאנוּ, מְחַל לָנוּ מַלְכֵּנוּ כִּי פָשָׁעְנוּ. כִּי־אַתָּה אֲדֹנָי
טוֹב וְסַלָּח, וְרַב־חֶסֶד לְכָל־קֹרְאֶיךָ:

תהלים יב **הוֹשִׁיעָה** יהוה, כִּי־גָמַר חָסִיד, כִּי־פַסּוּ אֱמוּנִים מִבְּנֵי אָדָם: לוּלֵי יהוה
תהלים קכד שֶׁהָיָה לָנוּ, בְּקוּם עָלֵינוּ אָדָם: אֲזַי חַיִּים בְּלָעוּנוּ, בַּחֲרוֹת אַפָּם בָּנוּ:

תהלים ג **כְּרַחֵם** אָב עַל בָּנִים, כֵּן תְּרַחֵם יהוה עָלֵינוּ. לַיהוה הַיְשׁוּעָה, עַל־עַמְּךָ
תהלים מו בִרְכָתֶךָ סֶּלָה: יהוה צְבָאוֹת עִמָּנוּ, מִשְׂגָּב לָנוּ אֱלֹהֵי יַעֲקֹב סֶלָה:
תהלים פד יהוה צְבָאוֹת, אַשְׁרֵי אָדָם בֹּטֵחַ בָּךְ: יהוה הוֹשִׁיעָה, הַמֶּלֶךְ יַעֲנֵנוּ בְיוֹם־
תהלים כ קָרְאֵנוּ:

סְלַח־נָא לַעֲוֹן הָעָם הַזֶּה כְּגֹדֶל חַסְדֶּךָ, וְכַאֲשֶׁר נָשָׂאתָה לָעָם הַזֶּה במדבר יד
מִמִּצְרַיִם וְעַד־הֵנָּה: וְשָׁם נֶאֱמַר

then קהל :שליח ציבור

וַיֹּאמֶר יהוה, סָלַחְתִּי כִּדְבָרֶךָ:

Continue:

הַטֵּה אֱלֹהַי אָזְנְךָ וּשְׁמָע, פְּקַח עֵינֶיךָ וּרְאֵה שֹׁמְמֹתֵינוּ וְהָעִיר אֲשֶׁר־ דניאל ט
נִקְרָא שִׁמְךָ עָלֶיהָ, כִּי לֹא עַל־צִדְקֹתֵינוּ אֲנַחְנוּ מַפִּילִים תַּחֲנוּנֵינוּ
לְפָנֶיךָ, כִּי עַל־רַחֲמֶיךָ הָרַבִּים: אֲדֹנָי שְׁמָעָה, אֲדֹנָי סְלָחָה, אֲדֹנָי הַקְשִׁיבָה
וַעֲשֵׂה אַל־תְּאַחַר, לְמַעַנְךָ אֱלֹהַי, כִּי־שִׁמְךָ נִקְרָא עַל־עִירְךָ וְעַל־עַמֶּךָ:

אֱלֹהֵינוּ וֵאלֹהֵי אֲבוֹתֵינוּ

יִשְׂרָאֵל עַמְּךָ תְּחִנָּה עוֹרְכִים,
שֶׁהֵם מְצֵרִים וּלְהִוָּשַׁע צְרִיכִים,
צָרֵיהֶם עֲלֵיהֶם עֹל מַאֲרִיכִים,
כָּל זֹאת הִגַּעְתָּם וְשִׁמְךָ מְבָרְכִים.

חֳלִי וּמַכְאוֹב לְהִכָּתֵב לֹא נִמְסַר,
עֲלוּבִים מִנֹּעַר וּמֵהֶם לֹא הוּסַר,
קָדוֹשׁ בְּיָדְךָ לְפַתֵּחַ מוּסָר,
כֶּאֱמוּנָתְךָ הַנְּקִיָּה וְלֹא כֶּאֱמוּנַת בָּשָׂר.

הַלּוֹבֵשׁ צְדָקָה וְלוֹ כַּמְּעִיל עֲטוּיָה,
וּמִמַּכָּה עַצְמָהּ מְתַקֵּן רְטִיָּה,
קוֹמֵם עֲדָתְךָ מִנְּפִילָתָהּ הַמְּטוּיָה,
בְּכֹחֲךָ הַגָּדוֹל וּבִזְרוֹעֲךָ הַנְּטוּיָה.

טְמֵאִים אוֹמְרִים נַחֲלָתְךָ לְחַבֵּל,
כְּבוֹדְךָ לְהָמִיר וּבְהֶבְלָם לְהִתְהַבֵּל,
נֵצֶר נִתְעָב לֶאֱלוֹהַּ לְקַבֵּל,
וְיִרְאָתְךָ הַקְּדוֹשָׁה לִנְטֹשׁ וּלְנַבֵּל.

בְּאַהֲבָתְךָ וּבְחֶמְלָתְךָ מְנַשֵּׂא וּמְנַטֵּל,
עֲצָתָם תְּסַכֵּל וּמַחְשְׁבֹתָם תְּבַטֵּל,
רַבָּה הַמְּהוּמָה בֵּינֵיהֶם הַטֵּל,
וּמַלְאָךְ אַכְזָרִי דּוֹחֶה וּמְטַלְטֵל.

בַּעֲבוּר כְּבוֹד שִׁמְךָ שֵׁם קָדְשְׁךָ הַמְּהֻלָּל,
נוֹרָאוֹת הַפְלֵא לְבַל בַּגּוֹיִם יִתְחַלָּל,
יוֹעֲצֵיהֶם וְאֵיתָנֵיהֶם תּוֹלִיךְ שׁוֹלָל,
וּבָהֶם תִּעוֹלֵל כַּאֲשֶׁר בִּי הִתְעוֹלָל.

מֵקִים מֵעָפָר דָּל וְאֶבְיוֹן מֵאַשְׁפָּה,
כְּנֵסָתְךָ בַּל תִּתֵּן לְכָלָה וּלְחֶרְפָּה,
אִם בְּפִקּוּדֶיךָ מִתְעַצֶּלֶת וּמְרַפָּה,
עַל כָּל פְּשָׁעֶיהָ אַהֲבָתְךָ תְּהֵא מְחַפָּה.

יְתֵרָה חִבָּתָם לְפָנֶיךָ אֲדוֹנֵי הָאֲדוֹנִים,
בֵּין כָּךְ וּבֵין כָּךְ קְרוּאִים לְךָ בָּנִים,
רַחֲמֶיךָ יְקַדְּמוּנוּ אֱלֹהֵי עֶלְיוֹנִים וְתַחְתּוֹנִים,
טֶרֶם יִשְׁטְפוּנוּ הַמַּיִם הַזֵּידוֹנִים.

◂ חֲפֵצֵי קִרְבָתְךָ עַל כָּל הַבָּאוֹת,
הָחִישָׁה לָמוֹ יְשׁוּעוֹת הַנִּבָּאוֹת,
קָדוֹשׁ עֲשֵׂה עִמָּהֶם לְטוֹבָה אוֹת,
חָזָק וְאַמִּיץ גּוֹאֲלָם, יהוה צְבָאוֹת.

אֵל מֶלֶךְ יוֹשֵׁב עַל כִּסֵּא רַחֲמִים, מִתְנַהֵג בַּחֲסִידוּת. מוֹחֵל עֲוֹנוֹת עַמּוֹ, מַעֲבִיר רִאשׁוֹן רִאשׁוֹן. מַרְבֶּה מְחִילָה לְחַטָּאִים, וּסְלִיחָה לְפוֹשְׁעִים. עֹשֶׂה צְדָקוֹת עִם כָּל בָּשָׂר וָרוּחַ, לֹא כְרָעָתָם תִּגְמֹל. ◂ אֵל, הוֹרֵיתָ לָּנוּ לוֹמַר שְׁלֹשׁ עֶשְׂרֵה, וּזְכָר לָנוּ הַיּוֹם בְּרִית שְׁלֹשׁ עֶשְׂרֵה, כְּמוֹ
שמות לד שֶׁהוֹדַעְתָּ לֶעָנָו מִקֶּדֶם, כְּמוֹ שֶׁכָּתוּב: וַיֵּרֶד יהוה בֶּעָנָן, וַיִּתְיַצֵּב עִמּוֹ שָׁם, וַיִּקְרָא בְשֵׁם, יהוה:

:קהל *then* שליח ציבור

שמות לד וַיַּעֲבֹר יהוה עַל־פָּנָיו וַיִּקְרָא

All say aloud:

יהוה, יהוה, אֵל רַחוּם וְחַנּוּן, אֶרֶךְ אַפַּיִם, וְרַב־חֶסֶד וֶאֱמֶת: נֹצֵר שמות לד
חֶסֶד לָאֲלָפִים, נֹשֵׂא עָוֹן וָפֶשַׁע וְחַטָּאָה, וְנַקֵּה: וְסָלַחְתָּ
לַעֲוֹנֵנוּ וּלְחַטָּאתֵנוּ, וּנְחַלְתָּנוּ:

Continue:

סְלַח לָנוּ אָבִינוּ כִּי חָטָאנוּ, מְחַל לָנוּ מַלְכֵּנוּ כִּי פָשָׁעְנוּ. כִּי־אַתָּה אֲדֹנָי תהלים פו
טוֹב וְסַלָּח, וְרַב־חֶסֶד לְכָל־קֹרְאֶיךָ:

נִשָּׂא לְבָבֵנוּ אֶל־כַּפָּיִם אֶל־אֵל בַּשָּׁמָיִם: תָּבוֹא לְפָנֶיךָ אֶנְקַת אָסִיר, כְּגֹדֶל איכה ג תהלים עט
זְרוֹעֲךָ הוֹתֵר בְּנֵי תְמוּתָה: לַאדֹנָי אֱלֹהֵינוּ הָרַחֲמִים וְהַסְּלִיחוֹת כִּי דניאל ט
מָרַדְנוּ בּוֹ:

כְּרַחֵם אָב עַל בָּנִים, כֵּן תְּרַחֵם יהוה עָלֵינוּ. לַיהוה הַיְשׁוּעָה, עַל־עַמְּךָ תהלים ג
בִרְכָתֶךָ סֶּלָה: יהוה צְבָאוֹת עִמָּנוּ, מִשְׂגָּב לָנוּ אֱלֹהֵי יַעֲקֹב סֶלָה: תהלים מו
יהוה צְבָאוֹת, אַשְׁרֵי אָדָם בֹּטֵחַ בָּךְ: יהוה הוֹשִׁיעָה, הַמֶּלֶךְ יַעֲנֵנוּ בְיוֹם־ תהלים פד תהלים כ
קָרְאֵנוּ:

אֱלֹהִים בְּיִשְׂרָאֵל גָּדוֹל נוֹדַעְתָּ. / אַתָּה יהוה אָבִינוּ אָתָּה.
בְּכָל קָרְאֵנוּ אֵלֶיךָ קָרְבֵנוּ. / רָם וְנִשָּׂא אַתָּה בְּקִרְבֵּנוּ.
גְּמַלְתָּנוּ הַטּוֹבוֹת גַּם בְּחוֹבֵנוּ. / לֹא בְצִדְקוֹתֵינוּ וּבְיֹשֶׁר לְבָבֵנוּ.
דוֹדֵנוּ, גַּם כִּי זָנַחְנוּ. / גְּאָלֵנוּ כִּי עֲבָדִים אֲנָחְנוּ.
הִנְנוּ בַּעֲוֹנֵינוּ עַד דַּכָּא. / וַתִּקְצַר נֶפֶשׁ לְךָ מְחַכָּה.
וְאַיֵּה חֲסָדֶיךָ הָרִאשׁוֹנִים עִמָּנוּ. / מֵעוֹלָם וְעַד עוֹלָם נֶאֱמָנוּ.
זַעַף נִשָּׂא וְתַשׁ כֹּחֵנוּ. / יהוה, אַל בְּאַפְּךָ תוֹכִיחֵנוּ.
חַלְחָלוֹת רַבּוֹת בְּלוּ בְשָׂרֵנוּ. / נָא אַל בַּחֲמָתְךָ תְּיַסְּרֵנוּ.
טֹרַח הַצָּרוֹת אֵין לְהִסָּפֵר. / אַיֵּה שׁוֹקֵל וְאַיֵּה סוֹפֵר.
יָדַעְנוּ רִשְׁעֵנוּ כִּי פָשַׁעְנוּ. / כִּי אֱמֶת עָשִׂיתָ וַאֲנַחְנוּ הִרְשָׁעְנוּ.
כַּעַס וְחָרוֹן מֶנּוּ יֶחְדָּל. / כִּי קָטֹן יַעֲקֹב וָדָל.
לַחַץ יוֹסֵר וְעֹל מֶנּוּ יְחֻבַּל. / כִּי כָשַׁל כֹּחַ הַסַּבָּל.
מְנָת מִדָּתֵנוּ לֹא תִגְבֶּה. / כִּי נִשְׁאַרְנוּ מְעַט מֵהַרְבֵּה.
נִחָם עַל הָרָעָה לְאָמָּתֶךָ. / מַטֵּה כְּלַפֵּי חֶסֶד אֱמוּנָתֶךָ.

סְלָחָה אִם עֲוֹנֵינוּ עָנוּ בָנוּ. / עָזְרֵנוּ כִּי עָלֶיךָ נִשְׁעָנוּ.
עָרְפֵּנוּ כֹּף לְךָ לְהִשְׁתַּעְבֵּד. / לְאַהֲבָה וּלְיִרְאָה אוֹתְךָ, וּלְכַבֵּד.
פּוֹקְדֶיךָ קִדְּשׁוּ צוֹמוֹת לִקְבֹּעַ. / דַּעְתָּם קְצָרָה צָרְכָּם לִתְבֹּעַ.
צָקוּן לַחֲשָׁם אֵלֶיךָ יָבוֹא. / חַתֵּל לְאִישׁ אִישׁ נִגְעוֹ וּמַכְאוֹבוֹ.
קוֹל יַעֲקֹב נוֹהֵם מִתְּהוֹמוֹתֶיךָ. / תִּשְׁמַע הַשָּׁמַיִם מְכוֹן שִׁבְתֶּךָ.
רוֹדֶה רוֹדֵף בְּאַף תְּכַלֶּה. / שְׁנַת שִׁלּוּמִים לְרִיב צִיּוֹן תְּגַלֶּה.
שֵׁרַתָּ וְרָדְתָּ מִנֹּעַר קְנוֹתֵנוּ. / וְאַל תַּשְׁלִיכֵנוּ לְעֵת זִקְנָתֵנוּ.
תָּעִינוּ לִשְׂמֹאל וִימִינְךָ תְּקָרְבֵנוּ. / כִּכְלוֹת כֹּחֵנוּ אַל תַּעַזְבֵנוּ.
תַּבִּיט וְתָצִיץ וְתַשְׁגִּיחַ לְרַחוּמֶיךָ.
◂ תִּתְאַזֵּר בַּחֲנִינוּתֶךָ, תִּתְלַבֵּשׁ בִּצְדָקוֹתֶיךָ.
תִּתְכַּסֶּה בְרַחֲמֶיךָ וְתִתְעַטֵּף בַּחֲסִידוּתֶךָ.
וְתָבוֹא לְפָנֶיךָ מִדַּת טוּבְךָ וְעַנְוְתָנוּתֶךָ.

אֵל מֶלֶךְ יוֹשֵׁב עַל כִּסֵּא רַחֲמִים, מִתְנַהֵג בַּחֲסִידוּת. מוֹחֵל עֲוֹנוֹת עַמּוֹ, מַעֲבִיר רִאשׁוֹן רִאשׁוֹן. מַרְבֶּה מְחִילָה לְחַטָּאִים, וּסְלִיחָה לְפוֹשְׁעִים. עֹשֶׂה צְדָקוֹת עִם כָּל בָּשָׂר וָרוּחַ, לֹא כְרָעָתָם תִּגְמֹל. ◂ אֵל, הוֹרֵיתָ לָּנוּ לוֹמַר שְׁלֹשׁ עֶשְׂרֵה, וּזְכֹר לָנוּ הַיּוֹם בְּרִית שְׁלֹשׁ עֶשְׂרֵה, כְּמוֹ
שמות לד שֶׁהוֹדַעְתָּ לֶעָנָו מִקֶּדֶם, כְּמוֹ שֶׁכָּתוּב: וַיֵּרֶד יהוה בֶּעָנָן, וַיִּתְיַצֵּב עִמּוֹ שָׁם, וַיִּקְרָא בְשֵׁם, יהוה:

then שליח ציבור *:*קהל

שמות לד וַיַּעֲבֹר יהוה עַל־פָּנָיו וַיִּקְרָא

All say aloud:

שמות לד **יהוה**, יהוה, אֵל רַחוּם וְחַנּוּן, אֶרֶךְ אַפַּיִם, וְרַב־חֶסֶד וֶאֱמֶת: נֹצֵר חֶסֶד לָאֲלָפִים, נֹשֵׂא עָוֹן וָפֶשַׁע וְחַטָּאָה, וְנַקֵּה: וְסָלַחְתָּ לַעֲוֹנֵנוּ וּלְחַטָּאתֵנוּ, וּנְחַלְתָּנוּ:

Continue:

תהלים פו **סְלַח לָנוּ** אָבִינוּ כִּי חָטָאנוּ, מְחַל לָנוּ מַלְכֵּנוּ כִּי פָשָׁעְנוּ. כִּי־אַתָּה אֲדֹנָי טוֹב וְסַלָּח, וְרַב־חֶסֶד לְכָל־קֹרְאֶיךָ:

The following is said responsively:

יִשְׂרָאֵל נוֹשַׁע בַּיהוה תְּשׁוּעַת עוֹלָמִים ישעיה מה
גַּם הַיּוֹם יִוָּשְׁעוּ מִפִּיךָ, שׁוֹכֵן מְרוֹמִים
כִּי אַתָּה רַב סְלִיחוֹת וּבַעַל הָרַחֲמִים.

שְׁעָרֶיךָ הֵם דּוֹפְקִים כַּעֲנִיִּים וְדַלִּים
צָקוּן לַחֲשָׁם קְשֹׁב יָהּ שׁוֹכֵן מְעָלִים
כִּי אַתָּה רַב סְלִיחוֹת וּבַעַל הָרַחֲמִים.

פְּחוּדִים הֵם מִכָּל צָרוֹת
מִמְּחָרְפֵיהֶם וּמִלּוֹחֲצֵיהֶם
נָא אַל תַּעַזְבֵם יהוה אֱלֹהֵי אֲבוֹתֵיהֶם
כִּי אַתָּה רַב סְלִיחוֹת וּבַעַל הָרַחֲמִים.

טוֹבוֹתֶיךָ יְקַדְּמוּ לָהֶם בְּיוֹם תּוֹכֵחָה
וּמִתּוֹךְ צָרָה הַמְצִיאֵם פְּדוּת וּרְוָחָה
כִּי אַתָּה רַב סְלִיחוֹת וּבַעַל הָרַחֲמִים.

יִוָּשְׁעוּ לְעֵין כֹּל, וְאַל יִמְשְׁלוּ בָם רְשָׁעִים
כַּלֵּה שֵׂעִיר וְחוֹתְנוֹ, וְיַעֲלוּ לְצִיּוֹן מוֹשִׁיעִים
כִּי אַתָּה רַב סְלִיחוֹת וּבַעַל הָרַחֲמִים.

הַקְשִׁיבָה אָדוֹן לְקוֹל שַׁוְעָתָם
וְלִמְכוֹן שִׁבְתְּךָ הַשָּׁמַיִם תַּעֲלֶה תְּפִלָּתָם
כִּי אַתָּה רַב סְלִיחוֹת וּבַעַל הָרַחֲמִים.

Continue with אֵל מֶלֶךְ יוֹשֵׁב *on page 998.*

סליחות לחמישי

SELIḤOT FOR THURSDAY

סְלַח לָנוּ, אָבִינוּ, כִּי בְּרֹב אִוַּלְתֵּנוּ שָׁגִינוּ. מְחַל לָנוּ, מַלְכֵּנוּ, כִּי רַבּוּ עֲוֹנֵינוּ.

אֵל אֶרֶךְ אַפַּיִם אַתָּה, וּבַעַל הָרַחֲמִים נִקְרֵאתָ, וְדֶרֶךְ תְּשׁוּבָה הוֹרֵיתָ.
גְּדֻלַּת רַחֲמֶיךָ וַחֲסָדֶיךָ, תִּזְכֹּר הַיּוֹם וּבְכָל יוֹם לְזֶרַע יְדִידֶיךָ.
תֵּפֶן אֵלֵינוּ בְּרַחֲמִים, כִּי אַתָּה הוּא בַּעַל הָרַחֲמִים. בְּתַחֲנוּן וּבִתְפִלָּה

פָּנֶיךָ נְקַדֵּם, כְּהוֹדַעְתָּ לֶעָנָו מִקֶּדֶם. מֵחֲרוֹן אַפְּךָ שׁוּב, כְּמוֹ בְּתוֹרָתְךָ כָּתוּב. וּבְצֵל כְּנָפֶיךָ נֶחְסֶה וְנִתְלוֹנָן, כְּיוֹם וַיֵּרֶד יהוה בֶּעָנָן. ◂ תַּעֲבֹר עַל פֶּשַׁע וְתִמְחֶה אָשָׁם, כְּיוֹם וַיִּתְיַצֵּב עִמּוֹ שָׁם. תַּאֲזִין שַׁוְעָתֵנוּ וְתַקְשִׁיב מֶנּוּ מַאֲמָר, כְּיוֹם וַיִּקְרָא בְשֵׁם יהוה, וְשָׁם נֶאֱמַר

then שליח ציבור קהל:

שמות לד וַיַּעֲבֹר יהוה עַל־פָּנָיו וַיִּקְרָא

All say aloud:

שמות לד **יהוה,** יהוה, אֵל רַחוּם וְחַנּוּן, אֶרֶךְ אַפַּיִם, וְרַב־חֶסֶד וֶאֱמֶת: נֹצֵר חֶסֶד לָאֲלָפִים, נֹשֵׂא עָוֹן וָפֶשַׁע וְחַטָּאָה, וְנַקֵּה: וְסָלַחְתָּ לַעֲוֹנֵנוּ וּלְחַטָּאתֵנוּ, וּנְחַלְתָּנוּ:

Continue:

תהלים פו **סְלַח לָנוּ** אָבִינוּ כִּי חָטָאנוּ, מְחַל לָנוּ מַלְכֵּנוּ כִּי פָשָׁעְנוּ. כִּי־אַתָּה אֲדֹנָי טוֹב וְסַלָּח, וְרַב־חֶסֶד לְכָל־קֹרְאֶיךָ:

הַאֲזִינָה יהוה תְּפִלָּתֵנוּ, הַקְשִׁיבָה לְקוֹל תַּחֲנוּנוֹתֵינוּ. הַקְשִׁיבָה לְקוֹל שַׁוְעֵנוּ מַלְכֵּנוּ וֵאלֹהֵינוּ כִּי אֵלֶיךָ נִתְפַּלָּל. שְׁמַע יהוה וְחָנֵּנוּ, יהוה הֱיֵה עוֹזֵר לָנוּ.

תהלים ג **כְּרַחֵם** אָב עַל בָּנִים, כֵּן תְּרַחֵם יהוה עָלֵינוּ. לַיהוה הַיְשׁוּעָה, עַל־עַמְּךָ
תהלים מו בִרְכָתֶךָ סֶּלָה: יהוה צְבָאוֹת עִמָּנוּ, מִשְׂגָּב לָנוּ אֱלֹהֵי יַעֲקֹב סֶלָה:
תהלים פד תהלים כ יהוה צְבָאוֹת, אַשְׁרֵי אָדָם בֹּטֵחַ בָּךְ: יהוה הוֹשִׁיעָה, הַמֶּלֶךְ יַעֲנֵנוּ בְיוֹם־קָרְאֵנוּ:

במדבר יד ◂ **סְלַח־נָא** לַעֲוֹן הָעָם הַזֶּה כְּגֹדֶל חַסְדֶּךָ, וְכַאֲשֶׁר נָשָׂאתָה לָעָם הַזֶּה מִמִּצְרַיִם וְעַד־הֵנָּה: וְשָׁם נֶאֱמַר

then שליח ציבור קהל:

וַיֹּאמֶר יהוה, סָלַחְתִּי כִּדְבָרֶךָ:

Continue:

דניאל ט **הַטֵּה** אֱלֹהַי אָזְנְךָ וּשְׁמָע, פְּקַח עֵינֶיךָ וּרְאֵה שֹׁמְמֹתֵינוּ וְהָעִיר אֲשֶׁר־נִקְרָא שִׁמְךָ עָלֶיהָ, כִּי לֹא עַל־צִדְקֹתֵינוּ אֲנַחְנוּ מַפִּילִים תַּחֲנוּנֵינוּ לְפָנֶיךָ, כִּי עַל־רַחֲמֶיךָ הָרַבִּים: אֲדֹנָי שְׁמָעָה, אֲדֹנָי סְלָחָה, אֲדֹנָי הַקְשִׁיבָה וַעֲשֵׂה אַל־תְּאַחַר, לְמַעַנְךָ אֱלֹהַי, כִּי־שִׁמְךָ נִקְרָא עַל־עִירְךָ וְעַל־עַמֶּךָ:

אֱלֹהֵינוּ וֵאלֹהֵי אֲבוֹתֵינוּ

תַּעֲנִית צִבּוּר (תְּפִלָּה) קָבְעוּ תְּבֹעַ צְרָכִים,
שׁוּב עָדֶיךָ חַפֵּשׂ וְלַחֲקֹר דְּרָכִים,
רַךְ לִרְצוֹת בִּשְׁלֹשׁ עֶשְׂרֵה עֲרָכִים,
קָשֶׁה לִכְעֹס תֵּת לְאַפַּיִם אֲרֻכִּים.

צְדָדֶיךָ מְקֻשָּׁטִים עֲדָיִם בְּלִי תַפְשִׁיט,
פְּאֵר הָרַחֲמִים וְהַסְּלִיחוֹת הוֹד תַּכְשִׁיט,
עֶרְךָ שַׁוְעָתֵנוּ לְךָ לְבַד נוֹשִׁיט,
סֵדֶר חַיִּים וּפַרְנָסָה לִיצוּרִים תּוֹשִׁיט.

נִסְתְּמָה הַכִּירָה וְנִתְרוֹקַן טֹהַר הַשֻּׁלְחָן,
מֵזִין וּמֵזִיחַ סְתַר מֵעֲבוֹדַת פָּלְחָן,
לְשִׁפִיכַת הַנֶּפֶשׁ חֲשֹׁב כְּבַשִׁית זָלְחָן,
כִּמְעַטֵּר וּמַשְׂבִּיעַ גּוֹאֵל וְרוֹפֵא וְסָלְחָן.

יֵאוֹת לְךָ, יַעַן מִמְּנָתְךָ נִשְׁנֶסֶת,
טוֹב רוּחֲךָ הֱיוֹת נִזּוֹנֶת וּמִתְפַּרְנֶסֶת,
חֵלֶף שׁוֹאֶלֶת קוֹבֶלֶת וּמִתְנוֹסֶסֶת,
זֵכֶר דַּאֲגוֹתֶיהָ לְפָנֶיךָ מְשִׂיחָה וּמַכְנֶסֶת.

וְאֵלֶיךָ הִיא נְשׂוּיָה וּבְךָ חָסָיָה,
הַוּוֹתֶיהָ הַעֲבֵר מִי כָמוֹךָ חֲסִין יָהּ,
דֶּרֶךְ אֻמָּנוּתְךָ בְּחַלֶּקְךָ לִלְגְיוֹנְךָ אַפְסַנְיָא,
גְּמֹל חֶסֶד לַעֲלוּבָה הַלֵּזוּ אַכְסַנְיָא.

בְּקִיאִים וּמְיֻשָּׁבִים לְרַצּוֹתְךָ בִּדְבָרִים עֲרֵבִים,
אָפְסוּ פַּסּוּ בְּכֹחָם קַטֵּגוֹר מְעַרְבְּבִים,
מְאַהֲבֵי לַאֲבִיהֶם שֶׁבַּשָּׁמַיִם זְרִיזִים וּמְעָרְבָּבִים,
יְרֵאָיו נִדְבָּרִים דָּתוֹ שְׁחָרִים וַעֲרָבִים.

הִקְדַּשְׁנוּ צוֹם (תְּפִלַּת) עוֹלְלִים וְזִקְנֵי אֲסָפוֹת,
יִשַּׁרְנוּ רִנָּה וּתְפִלָּה וְשָׁקַדְנוּ סִפּוֹת,

חֲשֹׂךְ לְמַטֵּה מֵעָוֹן וּשְׁלוּמֵנוּ תִּשְׁפֹּת,
זְקֹף דַּל מֵעָפָר וְאֶבְיוֹן מֵאַשְׁפּוֹת.

◂ בְּתוֹר הַמַּעֲלָה וּבְמִדּוֹת הֲגוּנוֹת תְּרוּמוֹת,
עֲרָבָתֵנוּ שִׂים לְטוֹב יוֹשֵׁב מְרוֹמוֹת,
וּבְמִקְוֵה טֹהַר תָּדִיחַ קַלּוֹת וְרָמוֹת,
מְצוֹא תְפִלָּתֵנוּ חֶסֶד לְאַדֶּרֶךְ רוֹמֵמוֹת.

אֵל מֶלֶךְ יוֹשֵׁב עַל כִּסֵּא רַחֲמִים, מִתְנַהֵג בַּחֲסִידוּת. מוֹחֵל עֲוֹנוֹת עַמּוֹ, מַעֲבִיר רִאשׁוֹן רִאשׁוֹן. מַרְבֶּה מְחִילָה לְחַטָּאִים, וּסְלִיחָה לְפוֹשְׁעִים. עֹשֶׂה צְדָקוֹת עִם כָּל בָּשָׂר וָרוּחַ, לֹא כְרָעָתָם תִּגְמֹל. ◂ אֵל, הוֹרֵיתָ לָּנוּ לוֹמַר שְׁלֹשׁ עֶשְׂרֵה, וּזְכָר לָנוּ הַיּוֹם בְּרִית שְׁלֹשׁ עֶשְׂרֵה, כְּמוֹ
שמות לד שֶׁהוֹדַעְתָּ לֶעָנָו מִקֶּדֶם, כְּמוֹ שֶׁכָּתוּב: וַיֵּרֶד יהוה בֶּעָנָן, וַיִּתְיַצֵּב עִמּוֹ שָׁם, וַיִּקְרָא בְשֵׁם, יהוה:

קהל then שליח ציבור:

שמות לד וַיַּעֲבֹר יהוה עַל־פָּנָיו וַיִּקְרָא

All say aloud:

שמות לד **יהוה,** יהוה, אֵל רַחוּם וְחַנּוּן, אֶרֶךְ אַפַּיִם, וְרַב־חֶסֶד וֶאֱמֶת: נֹצֵר חֶסֶד לָאֲלָפִים, נֹשֵׂא עָוֹן וָפֶשַׁע וְחַטָּאָה, וְנַקֵּה: וְסָלַחְתָּ לַעֲוֹנֵנוּ וּלְחַטָּאתֵנוּ, וּנְחַלְתָּנוּ:

Continue:

תהלים פו **סְלַח לָנוּ** אָבִינוּ כִּי חָטָאנוּ, מְחַל לָנוּ מַלְכֵּנוּ כִּי פָשָׁעְנוּ. כִּי־אַתָּה אֲדֹנָי טוֹב וְסַלָּח, וְרַב־חֶסֶד לְכָל־קֹרְאֶיךָ:

תהלים יב קהלת ז **הוֹשִׁיעָה,** יהוה, כִּי־גָמַר חָסִיד, כִּי־פַסּוּ אֱמוּנִים מִבְּנֵי אָדָם: כִּי אָדָם אֵין
ירמיה לא צַדִּיק בָּאָרֶץ, אֲשֶׁר יַעֲשֶׂה־טּוֹב וְלֹא יֶחֱטָא: הוֹשַׁע, יהוה,
ישעיה מה אֶת־עַמְּךָ, אֵת שְׁאֵרִית יִשְׂרָאֵל: יִשְׂרָאֵל נוֹשַׁע בַּיהוה תְּשׁוּעַת עוֹלָמִים.

תהלים ג **כְּרַחֵם** אָב עַל בָּנִים, כֵּן תְּרַחֵם יהוה עָלֵינוּ. לַיהוה הַיְשׁוּעָה, עַל־עַמְּךָ
תהלים מו בִרְכָתֶךָ סֶּלָה: יהוה צְבָאוֹת עִמָּנוּ, מִשְׂגָּב לָנוּ אֱלֹהֵי יַעֲקֹב סֶלָה:
תהלים פד תהלים כ יהוה צְבָאוֹת, אַשְׁרֵי אָדָם בֹּטֵחַ בָּךְ: יהוה הוֹשִׁיעָה, הַמֶּלֶךְ יַעֲנֵנוּ בְיוֹם־קָרְאֵנוּ:

אֱלֹהֵינוּ וֵאלֹהֵי אֲבוֹתֵינוּ

אַנְשֵׁי אֱמָנָה אָבָדוּ, / **בָּ**אִים בְּכֹחַ מַעֲשֵׂיהֶם.
גִּבּוֹרִים לַעֲמֹד בַּפֶּרֶץ, / **דּ**וֹחִים אֶת הַגְּזֵרוֹת.
הָיוּ לָנוּ לְחוֹמָה, / **וּ**לְמַחְסֶה בְּיוֹם זָעַם.
זוֹעֲכִים אַף בְּלַחֲשָׁם, / **חֵ**מָה עוֹצְרִים בְּשַׁוְעָם.
טֶרֶם קְרָאוּךָ עֲנִיתָם, / **י**וֹדְעִים לַעְתֹּר וּלְרַצֵּךְ.
כְּאָב רִחַמְתָּ לְמַעֲנָם, / **לֹ**א הֱשִׁיבוֹתָ פְּנֵיהֶם רֵיקָם.
מֵרֹב עֲוֹנֵינוּ אֲבַדְנוּם, / **נֶ**אֶסְפוּ מֶנּוּ בַּחֲטָאֵינוּ.
סָעוּ הֵמָּה לִמְנוּחוֹת, / **עָ**זְבוּ אוֹתָנוּ לַאֲנָחוֹת.
פַּסּוּ גּוֹדְרֵי פֶרֶץ, / **צֻ**מְּתוּ מְשִׁיבֵי חֵמָה.
קָמִים בַּפֶּרֶץ אַיִן, / **רְ**אוּיִם לְרַצּוֹתְךָ בְּעֶתֶר.
◂ **שֹׁ**טַטְנוּ בְּאַרְבַּע פִּנּוֹת, / **תְּ**רוּפָה לֹא מָצָאנוּ.
שַׁבְנוּ אֵלֶיךָ בְּבֹשֶׁת פָּנִים, / לְשַׁחֶרְךָ אֵל, בְּעֵת צָרוֹתֵינוּ.

אֵל מֶלֶךְ יוֹשֵׁב עַל כִּסֵּא רַחֲמִים, מִתְנַהֵג בַּחֲסִידוּת. מוֹחֵל עֲוֹנוֹת עַמּוֹ, מַעֲבִיר רִאשׁוֹן רִאשׁוֹן. מַרְבֶּה מְחִילָה לְחַטָּאִים, וּסְלִיחָה לְפוֹשְׁעִים. עֹשֶׂה צְדָקוֹת עִם כָּל בָּשָׂר וָרוּחַ, לֹא כְרָעָתָם תִּגְמֹל. ◂ אֵל, הוֹרֵיתָ לָּנוּ לוֹמַר שְׁלֹשׁ עֶשְׂרֵה, וּזְכֹר לָנוּ הַיּוֹם בְּרִית שְׁלֹשׁ עֶשְׂרֵה, כְּמוֹ
שמות לד שֶׁהוֹדַעְתָּ לֶעָנָו מִקֶּדֶם, כְּמוֹ שֶׁכָּתוּב: וַיֵּרֶד יהוה בֶּעָנָן, וַיִּתְיַצֵּב עִמּוֹ שָׁם, וַיִּקְרָא בְשֵׁם, יהוה:

then קהל *:*שליח ציבור

שמות לד וַיַּעֲבֹר יהוה עַל־פָּנָיו וַיִּקְרָא

All say aloud:

שמות לד **יהוה,** יהוה, אֵל רַחוּם וְחַנּוּן, אֶרֶךְ אַפַּיִם, וְרַב־חֶסֶד וֶאֱמֶת: נֹצֵר חֶסֶד לָאֲלָפִים, נֹשֵׂא עָוֹן וָפֶשַׁע וְחַטָּאָה, וְנַקֵּה: וְסָלַחְתָּ לַעֲוֹנֵנוּ וּלְחַטָּאתֵנוּ, וּנְחַלְתָּנוּ:

Continue:

תהלים פו **סְלַח לָנוּ** אָבִינוּ כִּי חָטָאנוּ, מְחַל לָנוּ מַלְכֵּנוּ כִּי פָשָׁעְנוּ. כִּי־אַתָּה אֲדֹנָי טוֹב וְסַלָּח, וְרַב־חֶסֶד לְכָל־קֹרְאֶיךָ:

The following is said responsively:

מַלְאֲכֵי רַחֲמִים, מְשָׁרְתֵי עֶלְיוֹן
חַלּוּ נָא פְּנֵי אֵל בְּמֵיטַב הִגָּיוֹן
אוּלַי יָחוּס עַם עָנִי וְאֶבְיוֹן, אוּלַי יְרַחֵם.

אוּלַי יְרַחֵם שְׁאֵרִית יוֹסֵף
שְׁפָלִים וְנִבְזִים, פְּשׁוּחֵי שֶׁסֶף
שְׁבוּיֵי חִנָּם, מְכוּרֵי בְּלֹא כֶסֶף
שׁוֹאֲגִים בִּתְפִלָּה וּמְבַקְשִׁים רִשָּׁיוֹן.
אוּלַי יָחוּס עַם עָנִי וְאֶבְיוֹן, אוּלַי יְרַחֵם.

אוּלַי יְרַחֵם מְעֻנֵּי כֶבֶל
מְלֻמְּדֵי מַכּוֹת בְּעִנּוּי סֵבֶל
מְנוֹד רֹאשׁ נְתוּנִים לְיוֹשְׁבֵי תֵבֵל
מָשָׁל בָּעַמִּים קֶצֶף וּבִזָּיוֹן.
אוּלַי יָחוּס עַם עָנִי וְאֶבְיוֹן, אוּלַי יְרַחֵם.

אוּלַי יְרַחֵם וְיִרְאֶה בָּעֳנִי עַמּוֹ
וְיַקְשִׁיב וְיִשְׁמַע הַצָּגִים לְעֻמּוֹ
וְעוֹדִים בְּלַחַשׁ מוּסָר לָמוֹ
וְעֵינֵיהֶם תּוֹלִים לִמְצוֹא רִצָּיוֹן.
אוּלַי יָחוּס עַם עָנִי וְאֶבְיוֹן, אוּלַי יְרַחֵם.

אוּלַי יְרַחֵם אוֹמְרֵי סְלַח נָא
אוֹמְצֵי שְׁבָחוֹ בְּכָל עֵת וְעוֹנָה
אֲגוּדִים בְּצָרָה לִשְׁפֹּךְ תְּחִנָּה
אֶת פְּנֵי אֱלֹהֵיהֶם שׁוֹפְכִים לֵב דִּוָּיוֹן.
אוּלַי יָחוּס עַם עָנִי וְאֶבְיוֹן, אוּלַי יְרַחֵם.

אוּלַי יְרַחֵם לָקְחָה בְּכִפְלַיִם
לְעוּטָה אֲרָיוֹת כְּמוֹ בְּפִי שַׁחֲלַיִם
לוֹקָה וּמִשְׁתַּלֶּמֶת בַּעֲוֹן שׁוּלַיִם
לֹא שָׁכְחָה בְּכָל זֹאת מִכְתַּב עֹז חֶבְיוֹן.
אוּלַי יָחוּס עַם עָנִי וְאֶבְיוֹן, אוּלַי יְרַחֵם.

אוּלַי יְרַחֵם כְּבוּשֵׁי פָנִים
הַשּׁוֹמְעִים חֶרְפָּתָם וְלֹא מְשִׁיבִים וְעוֹנִים
נִצְחָם מְקַוִּים וּלְיִשְׁעוֹ נִשְׁעָנִים
כִּי לֹא כָלוּ רַחֲמָיו בְּכִלָּיוֹן.
אוּלַי יָחוּס עַם עָנִי וְאֶבְיוֹן, אוּלַי יְרַחֵם.

אוּלַי יְרַחֵם יְחַלֵּץ עָנִי בְּעָנְיוֹ
חֲבוּשׁוֹ יַתִּיר מֵאֶרֶץ שִׁבְיוֹ
יַגְהֶה מְזוֹרוֹ וְיַחְבֹּשׁ חֳלָיוֹ
צַעֲקָתוֹ יִשְׁמַע וְיָחִישׁ עֵת פִּדְיוֹן.
אוּלַי יָחוּס עַם עָנִי וְאֶבְיוֹן, אוּלַי יְרַחֵם.

Continue with אֵל מֶלֶךְ יוֹשֵׁב *on page 998.*

סליחות לשני תנינא
SELIḤOT FOR THE SECOND MONDAY

סְלַח לָנוּ, אָבִינוּ, כִּי בְּרֹב אִוַּלְתֵּנוּ שָׁגִינוּ. מְחַל לָנוּ, מַלְכֵּנוּ, כִּי רַבּוּ עֲוֹנֵינוּ.

אֵל אֶרֶךְ אַפַּיִם אַתָּה, וּבַעַל הָרַחֲמִים נִקְרֵאתָ, וְדֶרֶךְ תְּשׁוּבָה הוֹרֵיתָ. גְּדֻלַּת רַחֲמֶיךָ וַחֲסָדֶיךָ, תִּזְכֹּר הַיּוֹם וּבְכָל יוֹם לְזֶרַע יְדִידֶיךָ. תֵּפֶן אֵלֵינוּ בְּרַחֲמִים, כִּי אַתָּה הוּא בַּעַל הָרַחֲמִים. בְּתַחֲנוּן וּבִתְפִלָּה פָּנֶיךָ נְקַדֵּם, כְּהוֹדַעְתָּ לֶעָנָו מִקֶּדֶם. מֵחֲרוֹן אַפְּךָ שׁוּב, כְּמוֹ בְּתוֹרָתְךָ כָּתוּב. וּבְצֵל כְּנָפֶיךָ נֶחֱסֶה וְנִתְלוֹנָן, כְּיוֹם וַיֵּרֶד יהוה בֶּעָנָן. ◂ תַּעֲבֹר עַל פֶּשַׁע וְתִמְחֶה אָשָׁם, כְּיוֹם וַיִּתְיַצֵּב עִמּוֹ שָׁם. תַּאֲזִין שַׁוְעָתֵנוּ וְתַקְשִׁיב מֶנּוּ מַאֲמָר, כְּיוֹם וַיִּקְרָא בְשֵׁם יהוה, וְשָׁם נֶאֱמַר

then שליח ציבור קהל:

וַיַּעֲבֹר יהוה עַל־פָּנָיו וַיִּקְרָא — שמות לד

All say aloud:

יהוה, יהוה, אֵל רַחוּם וְחַנּוּן, אֶרֶךְ אַפַּיִם, וְרַב־חֶסֶד וֶאֱמֶת: נֹצֵר חֶסֶד לָאֲלָפִים, נֹשֵׂא עָוֺן וָפֶשַׁע וְחַטָּאָה, וְנַקֵּה: וְסָלַחְתָּ לַעֲוֹנֵנוּ וּלְחַטָּאתֵנוּ, וּנְחַלְתָּנוּ: — שמות לד

Continue:

תהלים פו **סְלַח לָנוּ** אָבִינוּ כִּי חָטָאנוּ, מְחַל לָנוּ מַלְכֵּנוּ כִּי פָשָׁעְנוּ. כִּי־אַתָּה אֲדֹנָי טוֹב וְסַלָּח, וְרַב־חֶסֶד לְכָל־קֹרְאֶיךָ:

ישעיה סד **אַל־תִּקְצֹף** יהוה עַד־מְאֹד, וְאַל־לָעַד תִּזְכֹּר עָוֹן, הֵן הַבֶּט־נָא עַמְּךָ כֻלָּנוּ: הַעַל־אֵלֶּה תִתְאַפַּק יהוה, תֶּחֱשֶׁה וּתְעַנֵּנוּ עַד־
תהלים צ מְאֹד: שׁוּבָה יהוה עַד־מָתָי, וְהִנָּחֵם עַל־עֲבָדֶיךָ:

תהלים ג **כְּרַחֵם** אָב עַל בָּנִים, כֵּן תְּרַחֵם יהוה עָלֵינוּ. לַיהוה הַיְשׁוּעָה, עַל־עַמְּךָ
תהלים מו בִרְכָתֶךָ סֶּלָה: יהוה צְבָאוֹת עִמָּנוּ, מִשְׂגָּב לָנוּ אֱלֹהֵי יַעֲקֹב סֶלָה:
תהלים פד
תהלים כ יהוה צְבָאוֹת, אַשְׁרֵי אָדָם בֹּטֵחַ בָּךְ: יהוה הוֹשִׁיעָה, הַמֶּלֶךְ יַעֲנֵנוּ בְיוֹם־קָרְאֵנוּ:

במדבר יד ◂ **סְלַח־נָא** לַעֲוֹן הָעָם הַזֶּה כְּגֹדֶל חַסְדֶּךָ, וְכַאֲשֶׁר נָשָׂאתָה לָעָם הַזֶּה מִמִּצְרַיִם וְעַד־הֵנָּה: וְשָׁם נֶאֱמַר

קהל then שליח ציבור:

וַיֹּאמֶר יהוה, סָלַחְתִּי כִּדְבָרֶךָ:

Continue:

דניאל ט **הַטֵּה** אֱלֹהַי אָזְנְךָ וּשְׁמָע, פְּקַח עֵינֶיךָ וּרְאֵה שֹׁמְמֹתֵינוּ וְהָעִיר אֲשֶׁר־נִקְרָא שִׁמְךָ עָלֶיהָ, כִּי לֹא עַל־צִדְקֹתֵינוּ אֲנַחְנוּ מַפִּילִים תַּחֲנוּנֵינוּ לְפָנֶיךָ, כִּי עַל־רַחֲמֶיךָ הָרַבִּים: אֲדֹנָי שְׁמָעָה, אֲדֹנָי סְלָחָה, אֲדֹנָי הַקְשִׁיבָה וַעֲשֵׂה אַל־תְּאַחַר, לְמַעַנְךָ אֱלֹהַי, כִּי־שִׁמְךָ נִקְרָא עַל־עִירְךָ וְעַל־עַמֶּךָ:

אֱלֹהֵינוּ וֵאלֹהֵי אֲבוֹתֵינוּ

אֲפָפוּנוּ מַיִם עַד נֶפֶשׁ. / **בָּ**אנוּ בְּעִמְקֵי מְצוּלָה.
גַּלֵּי יָם עָבְרוּ עָלֵינוּ. / **דָּ**כְיוֹת תְּהוֹם כִּסָּתְנוּ.
הוֹדֵנוּ נֶהְפַּךְ לְמַשְׁחִית. / **וְ**עוֹד לֹא עָצַרְנוּ כֹחַ.
זָלְעָפְנוּ עַל חַטֹּאתֵינוּ. / **חָ**לְחַלְנוּ עַל רֹב פְּשָׁעֵינוּ.
טִכַּסְנוּ עֵצָה מַה לַּעֲשׂוֹת. / **יוֹ**עֵץ בְּקִרְבֵּנוּ אָיִן.
כּוֹנַנּוּ בְּלֵב מַחֲשָׁבוֹת. / **לְ**מֵרָחוֹק שְׂאֵת דֵּעָה.
מָסֹרֶת בְּיָדֵינוּ מֵאֲבוֹתֵינוּ. / **נְ**אָקָה תְּשׁוּבָה וּצְדָקָה.
סוֹתְרוֹת רֹעַ גְּזֵרוֹת. / **עוֹ**ד מֵעֲנוֹת עָם.

פַּצְנוּ בְּהַסְכָּמָה אַחַת. / (**צ**וֹם) שֵׁנִי וַחֲמִישִׁי וְשֵׁנִי.
קָדוֹשׁ אוּלַי יַשְׁקִיף. / **ר**ַחֲמָיו לְקַדֵּם לְרֹגֶז.
שַׁדַּי עָשִׂינוּ אֶת שֶׁלָּנוּ. / **תּ**ַקִּיף עֲשֵׂה אֶת שֶׁלָּךְ.
אַל תְּשֵׁב עִמָּנוּ בַּדִּין. / מִדֶּבֶר וּמֵחֶרֶב וּמֵרָעָב מַלְּטֵנוּ.
תִּיקַר נַפְשֵׁנוּ בְּעֵינֶיךָ.
יָהּ, סְלַח לָנוּ, מְחַל לָנוּ, כַּפֵּר לָנוּ, כְּיוֹם רִדְתְּךָ בֶּעָנָן.

אֵל מֶלֶךְ יוֹשֵׁב עַל כִּסֵּא רַחֲמִים, מִתְנַהֵג בַּחֲסִידוּת. מוֹחֵל עֲוֹנוֹת עַמּוֹ, מַעֲבִיר רִאשׁוֹן רִאשׁוֹן. מַרְבֶּה מְחִילָה לְחַטָּאִים, וּסְלִיחָה לְפוֹשְׁעִים. עֹשֶׂה צְדָקוֹת עִם כָּל בָּשָׂר וָרוּחַ, לֹא כְרָעָתָם תִּגְמֹל. ◂ אֵל, הוֹרֵיתָ לָנוּ לוֹמַר שְׁלֹשׁ עֶשְׂרֵה, וּזְכָר לָנוּ הַיּוֹם בְּרִית שְׁלֹשׁ עֶשְׂרֵה, כְּמוֹ
שמות לד שֶׁהוֹדַעְתָּ לֶעָנָו מִקֶּדֶם, כְּמוֹ שֶׁכָּתוּב: וַיֵּרֶד יהוה בֶּעָנָן, וַיִּתְיַצֵּב עִמּוֹ שָׁם, וַיִּקְרָא בְשֵׁם, יהוה:

:שליח ציבור then קהל

שמות לד וַיַּעֲבֹר יהוה עַל־פָּנָיו וַיִּקְרָא

All say aloud:

שמות לד **יהוה,** יהוה, אֵל רַחוּם וְחַנּוּן, אֶרֶךְ אַפַּיִם, וְרַב־חֶסֶד וֶאֱמֶת: נֹצֵר חֶסֶד לָאֲלָפִים, נֹשֵׂא עָוֹן וָפֶשַׁע וְחַטָּאָה, וְנַקֵּה: וְסָלַחְתָּ לַעֲוֹנֵנוּ וּלְחַטָּאתֵנוּ, וּנְחַלְתָּנוּ:

Continue:

תהלים פו **סְלַח לָנוּ** אָבִינוּ כִּי חָטָאנוּ, מְחַל לָנוּ מַלְכֵּנוּ כִּי פָשָׁעְנוּ. כִּי־אַתָּה אֲדֹנָי טוֹב וְסַלָּח, וְרַב־חֶסֶד לְכָל־קֹרְאֶיךָ:

הַאֲזִינָה, יהוה, תְּפִלָּתֵנוּ וְהַקְשִׁיבָה בְּקוֹל תַּחֲנוּנוֹתֵינוּ. שְׁמַע, יהוה, קוֹלֵנוּ נִקְרָא וְחָנֵּנוּ וַעֲנֵנוּ. שִׁמְעָה, יהוה, צֶדֶק הַקְשִׁיבָה רִנָּתֵנוּ, הַאֲזִינָה תְּפִלָּתֵנוּ. שְׁמַע, יהוה, וְחָנֵּנוּ. יהוה, הֱיֵה עוֹזֵר לָנוּ.

תהלים ג **כְּרַחֵם** אָב עַל בָּנִים, כֵּן תְּרַחֵם יהוה עָלֵינוּ. לַיהוה הַיְשׁוּעָה, עַל־עַמְּךָ
תהלים מו בִרְכָתֶךָ סֶּלָה: יהוה צְבָאוֹת עִמָּנוּ, מִשְׂגָּב לָנוּ אֱלֹהֵי יַעֲקֹב סֶלָה:
תהלים פד
תהלים כ יהוה צְבָאוֹת, אַשְׁרֵי אָדָם בֹּטֵחַ בָּךְ: יהוה הוֹשִׁיעָה, הַמֶּלֶךְ יַעֲנֵנוּ בְיוֹם־קָרְאֵנוּ:

אֱלֹהֵינוּ וֵאלֹהֵי אֲבוֹתֵינוּ

אֹזֶן תַּחַן וְהַסְכֵּת עֲתִירָה, / אַף הָפֵר וְשַׁכֵּךְ עֶבְרָה.
בָּאֵי לְחַלּוֹתְךָ בְּנֶפֶשׁ מָרָה, / בְּשִׁמְךָ הַגָּדוֹל יִמְצְאוּ עֶזְרָה.
גַּעְיַת נֶאֱנָחִים וַעֲנוּתָם חֱזֵה, / גְּחִינַת קוֹמָתָם נָא לֹא תִבְזֶה.
דְּרֹשׁ עֶלְבּוֹנָם מִצַּר בּוֹזֶה, / דְּרֹךְ פּוּרָה וְנִצְחָם יִזֶּה.
הֲלֹא אַתָּה הָיִיתָ וְהִנְּךָ, / הָיֹה תִהְיֶה בַּהֲדַר גְּאוֹנֶךָ.
וְנָמַתָּ יִכּוֹן זֶרַע אֱמוּנֶיךָ, / וְהִנָּם כָּלִים מִתִּגְרַת חֲרוֹנֶךָ.
זָעֲמוּ בְּעִוּוּיָם וּמִמַּאֲוָיָם נִסָּחוּ, / זֹרוּ בָּאֲפָסִים וְלֹא נָחוּ.
חֻבְּלָה רוּחָם וְלֶעָפָר שָׁחוּ, / חָרְשׁוּ חוֹרְשִׁים וּמַעֲנִית הִמְתִּיחוּ.
טָבְעוּ בַבֹּץ וְאֵין פּוֹצֶה, / טוֹרְפֵיהֶם שָׁלוּ מִקָּצֶה אֶל קָצֶה.
יוֹם יוֹם לוֹחֲמָם מְנַצֵּחַ, / יַד פּוֹרְשִׂים מִלַּחַץ לֵיצֵא.
כָּלוּ חַיֵּיהֶם בְּיָגוֹן וַאֲנָחָה, / כּוֹשֵׁל רָבָה וְעָרְבָה שִׂמְחָה.
לְיֶשַׁע חוֹכִים וְהִנֵּה צְוָחָה, / לִבְטוֹם קָמִים וְכָרוּ שׁוּחָה.
מַעֲרִימִים סוֹד מִמְּךָ לְהַדִּיחָם, / מַכְבִּידִים עֹל לְהַכְשִׁיל כֹּחָם.
נוֹאֲקִים אֵלֶיךָ בְּהִתְעַטֵּף רוּחָם, / נַחַת מְצוֹא מִכֹּבֶד טָרְחָם.
שִׂיחַ צָקִים בְּמַעֲמָד צָפוּף, / סְלִיחָה מְבַקְשִׁים בְּקָדְקֹד כָּפוּף.
עוֹשְׁקֵיהֶם יְקַנִּיאוּם בְּנֵצֶר נַאֲפוּף, / עוֹיְעִים יְמַסְּכוּ וְיִהְיוּ לְסִפּוּף.
פְּדֵה דְבֵקֶיךָ מֵחֶרֶץ וְכִלּוּי, / פַּלְּטֵם מִצּוֹרֵר וּתְנֵם לְעִלּוּי.
צַוֵּה יְשׁוּעוֹת מְשַׁחֲרֶיךָ בְּחִלּוּי, / צוּר עוֹלָמִים הוֹשִׁיעֵנוּ בְּגָלוּי.
קַנּוֹא וְנוֹקֵם קַנֵּא לִשְׁמֶךָ, / קַצֵּץ סִמְלוֹנִים מִצַּוַּאר עַמֶּךָ.
רְאֵה עֲמָלֵנוּ וְשׁוּב מִזַּעְמֶךָ, / רִיבָה רִיבֵנוּ מֵעִם חֶרְמֶךָ.
◂ שִׁבְעָתַיִם הָשֵׁב לְחֵיק מְאַנְנֵי, / שַׁכֵּר חִצֶּיךָ מִדַּם מְעַנַּי.
תַּטֶּה אָזְנְךָ לְקוֹל תַּחֲנוּנַי, / תִּרְצֵנִי בְּקָרְאִי יהוה יהוה.

אֵל מֶלֶךְ יוֹשֵׁב עַל כִּסֵּא רַחֲמִים, מִתְנַהֵג בַּחֲסִידוּת. מוֹחֵל עֲוֹנוֹת עַמּוֹ, מַעֲבִיר רִאשׁוֹן רִאשׁוֹן. מַרְבֶּה מְחִילָה לְחַטָּאִים, וּסְלִיחָה לְפוֹשְׁעִים. עֹשֶׂה צְדָקוֹת עִם כָּל בָּשָׂר וָרוּחַ, לֹא כְרָעָתָם תִּגְמֹל. ◂ אֵל, הוֹרֵיתָ לָּנוּ לוֹמַר שְׁלֹשׁ עֶשְׂרֵה, וּזְכָר לָנוּ הַיּוֹם בְּרִית שְׁלֹשׁ עֶשְׂרֵה, כְּמוֹ
שמות לד שֶׁהוֹדַעְתָּ לֶעָנָו מִקֶּדֶם, כְּמוֹ שֶׁכָּתוּב: וַיֵּרֶד יהוה בֶּעָנָן, וַיִּתְיַצֵּב עִמּוֹ שָׁם, וַיִּקְרָא בְשֵׁם, יהוה:

קהל then שליח ציבור:

שמות לד וַיַּעֲבֹר יהוה עַל־פָּנָיו וַיִּקְרָא

All say aloud:

יהוה, יהוה, אֵל רַחוּם וְחַנּוּן, אֶרֶךְ אַפַּיִם, וְרַב־חֶסֶד וֶאֱמֶת: נֹצֵר חֶסֶד לָאֲלָפִים, נֹשֵׂא עָוֹן וָפֶשַׁע וְחַטָּאָה, וְנַקֵּה: וְסָלַחְתָּ לַעֲוֺנֵנוּ וּלְחַטָּאתֵנוּ, וּנְחַלְתָּנוּ: שמות לד

Continue:

סְלַח לָנוּ אָבִינוּ כִּי חָטָאנוּ, מְחַל לָנוּ מַלְכֵּנוּ כִּי פָשָׁעְנוּ. כִּי־אַתָּה אֲדֹנָי טוֹב וְסַלָּח, וְרַב־חֶסֶד לְכָל־קֹרְאֶיךָ: תהלים פו

The following is said responsively:

יהוה, יהוה, אֵל רַחוּם וְחַנּוּן, אֶרֶךְ אַפַּיִם, וְרַב־חֶסֶד וֶאֱמֶת: שמות לד
נֹצֵר חֶסֶד לָאֲלָפִים, נֹשֵׂא עָוֹן וָפֶשַׁע וְחַטָּאָה, וְנַקֵּה
וְסָלַחְתָּ לַעֲוֺנֵנוּ וּלְחַטָּאתֵנוּ וּנְחַלְתָּנוּ:

אֶזְכְּרָה אֱלֹהִים וְאֶהֱמָיָה
בִּרְאוֹתִי כָּל עִיר עַל תִּלָּהּ בְּנוּיָה
וְעִיר הָאֱלֹהִים מֻשְׁפֶּלֶת עַד שְׁאוֹל תַּחְתִּיָּה
וּבְכָל זֹאת אָנוּ לְיָהּ וְעֵינֵינוּ לְיָהּ.

מִדַּת הָרַחֲמִים עָלֵינוּ הִתְגַּלְגְּלִי
וְלִפְנֵי קוֹנֵךְ תְּחִנָּתֵנוּ הַפִּילִי
וּבְעַד עַמֵּךְ רַחֲמִים שַׁאֲלִי
כִּי כָל לֵבָב דַּוָּי וְכָל רֹאשׁ לָחֳלִי.

תָּמַכְתִּי יְתֵדוֹתַי בִּשְׁלֹשׁ עֶשְׂרֵה תֵבוֹת
וּבְשַׁעֲרֵי דְמָעוֹת כִּי לֹא נִשְׁלָבוֹת
לָכֵן שָׁפַכְתִּי שִׂיחַ פְּנֵי בוֹחֵן לִבּוֹת
בָּטוּחַ אֲנִי בְּאֵלֶּה וּבִזְכוּת שְׁלֹשֶׁת אָבוֹת.

יְהִי רָצוֹן מִלְּפָנֶיךָ, שׁוֹמֵעַ קוֹל בְּכִיּוֹת
שֶׁתָּשִׂים דִּמְעוֹתֵינוּ בְּנֹאדְךָ לִהְיוֹת
וְתַצִּילֵנוּ מִכָּל גְּזֵרוֹת אַכְזָרִיּוֹת
כִּי לְךָ לְבַד עֵינֵינוּ תְלוּיוֹת.

Continue with אֵל מֶלֶךְ יוֹשֵׁב *on page 998.*

יום הזיכרון לחללי חורבן אירופה

The historical background and halakhic perspective for the following service, can be found in the Essay section on page E7.

תהלים מד **לַמְנַצֵּחַ** לִבְנֵי־קֹרַח מַשְׂכִּיל:
אֱלֹהִים בְּאָזְנֵינוּ שָׁמַעְנוּ אֲבוֹתֵינוּ סִפְּרוּ־לָנוּ פֹּעַל־פָּעַלְתָּ בִימֵיהֶם
בִּימֵי קֶדֶם:
אַתָּה יָדְךָ גּוֹיִם הוֹרַשְׁתָּ וַתִּטָּעֵם תָּרַע לְאֻמִּים וַתְּשַׁלְּחֵם:
כִּי לֹא בְחַרְבָּם יָרְשׁוּ אָרֶץ וּזְרוֹעָם לֹא־הוֹשִׁיעָה לָּמוֹ כִּי־יְמִינְךָ וּזְרוֹעֲךָ
וְאוֹר פָּנֶיךָ כִּי רְצִיתָם:
אַתָּה־הוּא מַלְכִּי אֱלֹהִים צַוֵּה יְשׁוּעוֹת יַעֲקֹב:
בְּךָ צָרֵינוּ נְנַגֵּחַ בְּשִׁמְךָ נָבוּס קָמֵינוּ:
כִּי לֹא בְקַשְׁתִּי אֶבְטָח וְחַרְבִּי לֹא תוֹשִׁיעֵנִי:
כִּי הוֹשַׁעְתָּנוּ מִצָּרֵינוּ וּמְשַׂנְאֵינוּ הֱבִישׁוֹתָ:
בֵּאלֹהִים הִלַּלְנוּ כָל־הַיּוֹם וְשִׁמְךָ לְעוֹלָם נוֹדֶה סֶלָה:
אַף־זָנַחְתָּ וַתַּכְלִימֵנוּ וְלֹא־תֵצֵא בְּצִבְאוֹתֵינוּ:
תְּשִׁיבֵנוּ אָחוֹר מִנִּי־צָר וּמְשַׂנְאֵינוּ שָׁסוּ לָמוֹ:
תִּתְּנֵנוּ כְּצֹאן מַאֲכָל וּבַגּוֹיִם זֵרִיתָנוּ:
תִּמְכֹּר־עַמְּךָ בְלֹא־הוֹן וְלֹא־רִבִּיתָ בִּמְחִירֵיהֶם:
תְּשִׂימֵנוּ חֶרְפָּה לִשְׁכֵנֵינוּ לַעַג וָקֶלֶס לִסְבִיבוֹתֵינוּ:
תְּשִׂימֵנוּ מָשָׁל בַּגּוֹיִם מְנוֹד־רֹאשׁ בַּלְאֻמִּים:
כָּל־הַיּוֹם כְּלִמָּתִי נֶגְדִּי וּבֹשֶׁת פָּנַי כִּסָּתְנִי:
מִקּוֹל מְחָרֵף וּמְגַדֵּף מִפְּנֵי אוֹיֵב וּמִתְנַקֵּם:
כָּל־זֹאת בָּאַתְנוּ וְלֹא שְׁכַחֲנוּךָ וְלֹא־שִׁקַּרְנוּ בִּבְרִיתֶךָ:

* The following is a suggested ceremony by R. Arie Folger and R. David Mescheloff.

יום הזכרון לחללי חורבן אירופה / REMEMBRANCE SERVICE
During the Holocaust (Shoah), the Nazis and their accomplices murdered a third of the Jewish people, some six million men, women and children. This extended crescendo of brutality was unparalleled in human history.

It has become the custom in many communities to commemorate those murdered in the Holocaust. Various dates have been

SERVICE FOR HOLOCAUST MEMORIAL DAYS

The historical background and halakhic perspective for the following service, can be found in the Essay section on page E7.

Ps. 44 לַמְנַצֵּחַ TO THE DIRECTOR of music, a *maskil* for the sons of Koraḥ. O God, we have heard with our ears, our fathers have told us, of the deed You did in their days, in days of old. You with Your hand drove out the nations, and planted them. You broke the peoples and cast them out. For they did not take possession of the land by their own sword, and their own arm did not save them, but Your right hand and Your arm, and the light of Your countenance, for You blessed them. You alone are my King, O God. Command salvations for Jacob. Through You we have smitten our enemies. Through Your name we have trampled on those who rose up against us. Indeed, I did not trust in my bow, and my sword did not save me. But You have saved us from our enemies, and You have put to shame those who hate us. We praise God all the day, and we thank Your name forever. Selah. But You have abandoned us and put us to shame, and You do not go out with our armies. You have made us turn back from the enemy, and those who hate us have plundered us for themselves. You have given us like sheep to be eaten, and You have scattered us among the nations. You have sold Your people for no sum, and You have not set their prices high. You have made us a reproach to our neighbors, a scorn and a derision to those round about us. You have made us a byword among the nations, a shaking of the head among the peoples. All the day my humiliation is before me, and shame covers my face. From the voice of him who taunts and blasphemes, from the enemy and the avenger. All this has come upon us, yet we have

---

suggested for Holocaust Remembrance. The Chief Rabbinate of Israel designated the fast day of *Asara beTevet* for reciting *Kaddish* for the merit of those whose date of death is unknown; in 1951 the Israeli Knesset designated the 27th of Nisan as Yom HaShoah, Holocaust Remembrance Day. R. Joseph B. Soloveitchik advocated that the Holocaust be mourned on Tisha B'Av; some communities commemorate the martyrs on the first Sunday of *Seliḥot*.

The remembrance service we offer here can be used in whole or in part on any of the days on which a community chooses to memorialize the Shoah, except for Tisha B'Av, when Torah study is prohibited.

לֹא־נָסוֹג אָחוֹר לִבֵּנוּ וַתֵּט אֲשֻׁרֵינוּ מִנִּי אָרְחֶךָ:
כִּי דִכִּיתָנוּ בִּמְקוֹם תַּנִּים וַתְּכַס עָלֵינוּ בְצַלְמָוֶת:
אִם־שָׁכַחְנוּ שֵׁם אֱלֹהֵינוּ וַנִּפְרֹשׂ כַּפֵּינוּ לְאֵל זָר:
הֲלֹא אֱלֹהִים יַחֲקָר־זֹאת כִּי־הוּא יֹדֵעַ תַּעֲלֻמוֹת לֵב:
כִּי־עָלֶיךָ הֹרַגְנוּ כָל־הַיּוֹם נֶחְשַׁבְנוּ כְּצֹאן טִבְחָה:
עוּרָה לָמָּה תִישַׁן אֲדֹנָי הָקִיצָה אַל־תִּזְנַח לָנֶצַח:
לָמָּה־פָנֶיךָ תַסְתִּיר תִּשְׁכַּח עָנְיֵנוּ וְלַחֲצֵנוּ:
כִּי שָׁחָה לֶעָפָר נַפְשֵׁנוּ דָּבְקָה לָאָרֶץ בִּטְנֵנוּ:
קוּמָה עֶזְרָתָה לָּנוּ וּפְדֵנוּ לְמַעַן חַסְדֶּךָ:

לימוד משניות

Six משנה *selections are to be studied by all present, for the merit of the six million souls, one from each of the* שישה סדרי משנה.

סדר זרעים

One must bless God for the evil as one must bless God for the good.

ברכות ט, ה **חַיָּב** אָדָם לְבָרֵךְ עַל הָרָעָה, כְּשֵׁם שֶׁהוּא מְבָרֵךְ עַל הַטּוֹבָה, שֶׁנֶּאֱמַר:
דברים ו וְאָהַבְתָּ אֵת ה׳ אֱלֹהֶיךָ, בְּכָל־לְבָבְךָ וּבְכָל־נַפְשְׁךָ וּבְכָל־מְאֹדֶךָ:
בְּכָל־לְבָבְךָ – בִּשְׁנֵי יְצָרֶיךָ, בְּיֵצֶר טוֹב וּבְיֵצֶר רָע; וּבְכָל־נַפְשְׁךָ – אֲפִלּוּ הוּא נוֹטֵל אֶת נַפְשְׁךָ; וּבְכָל־מְאֹדֶךָ – בְּכָל מָמוֹנְךָ. דָּבָר אַחֵר: בְּכָל־מְאֹדֶךָ – בְּכָל מִדָּה וּמִדָּה שֶׁהוּא מוֹדֵד לְךָ, הֱוֵי מוֹדֶה לוֹ בִּמְאֹד מְאֹד.

סדר מועד

God purifies Israel; death is one form of atonement.

יומא ח, ח **חַטָּאת** וְאָשָׁם וַדַּאי מְכַפְּרִין. מִיתָה וְיוֹם הַכִּפּוּרִים מְכַפְּרִין עִם הַתְּשׁוּבָה. הַתְּשׁוּבָה מְכַפֶּרֶת עַל עֲבֵרוֹת הַקַּלּוֹת, עַל עֲשֵׂה וְעַל לֹא תַעֲשֶׂה, וְעַל הַחֲמוּרוֹת הִיא תוֹלָה עַד שֶׁיָּבֹא יוֹם הַכִּפּוּרִים וִיכַפֵּר.

יומא ח, ט אָמַר רַבִּי עֲקִיבָא: אַשְׁרֵיכֶם יִשְׂרָאֵל! לִפְנֵי מִי אַתֶּם מִטַּהֲרִין? מִי מְטַהֵר
יחזקאל לו אֶתְכֶם? אֲבִיכֶם שֶׁבַּשָּׁמַיִם, שֶׁנֶּאֱמַר: וְזָרַקְתִּי עֲלֵיכֶם מַיִם טְהוֹרִים, וּטְהַרְתֶּם:

לימוד משניות / THE LEARNING OF MISHNAYOT
It is a long-standing Jewish custom to study *mishnayot* to honor the souls of the departed. The Oral Torah, recorded in the Mishna, is the hidden, internal, eternal soul of Judaism, that gives life to the revealed word of God recorded in the Torah. Thus Mishna study memorializes the hidden, internal, eternal soul of the departed. This association is hinted at by the Hebrew words *mishna* (מִשְׁנָה) and *neshama*

not forgotten You, nor have we been false to Your covenant. Our heart has not turned back, nor have our steps turned from Your way, Though You have broken us in the place of jackals, and You have covered us with darkness. I swear that we have not forgotten the name of our God, nor have we stretched out our hands to a strange god. Surely God has searched this out, for He knows the secrets of the heart. Indeed, for Your sake we are being killed all the day, we are regarded as sheep for the slaughter. Awake, why do you sleep, O Lord? Arise, do not abandon us forever. Why do You hide Your face? Why do You forget our affliction and oppression? For our soul is bowed down to the dust, our belly cleaves to the ground. Arise and help us, and redeem us for the sake of Your loving-kindness.

THE LEARNING OF MISHNAYOT

Six Mishna selections are to be studied by all present, for the merit of the six million souls, one from each of the Six Orders of the Mishna.

SEDER ZERAIM

One must bless God for the evil as one must bless God for the good.

Berakhot 9:5 **חייב** A PERSON is obligted to recite a blessing for the bad just as he recites a
Deut. 6 blessing for the good, as it says: "You shall love the Lord your God with all your heart, and with all your soul, and with all your might."
With all your heart: with both your inclinations, with the good inclination and with the evil inclination. *With all your soul*: even if He takes your life. *And with all your might:* with all your wealth. An alternative interpretation: *With all your might:* whatever measure He metes out to you, praise Him very much.

SEDER MO'ED

God purifies Israel; death is one form of atonement.

Yoma 8:8 **חַטָּאת** A SIN OFFERING and a guilt offering for a definite sin provide atonement. Death or Yom Kippur provide atonement together with repentance. [However] repentance [alone] atones for lesser transgressions: for positive commandments and negative commandments. But for the graver [sins], it suspends [punishment] until Yom Kippur comes and provides atonement.
Yoma 8:9 R. Akiva said: Praiseworthy are you, O Israel! Before Whom do you cleanse
Ezek. 36 yourselves? Who cleanses you? Your Father in heaven! As it is said: "And I will

---

(soul, נְשָׁמָה), which consist of the same four Hebrew letters.

The following *mishnayot* have been selected from each of the six orders of the Mishna, to symbolize the six million Jews who perished in the Holocaust. These *mishnayot*

ירמיה יז וְאוֹמֵר: מִקְוֵה יִשְׂרָאֵל ה׳: מָה הַמִּקְוֶה מְטַהֵר אֶת הַטְּמֵאִים, אַף הַקָּדוֹשׁ בָּרוּךְ הוּא מְטַהֵר אֶת יִשְׂרָאֵל.

סדר נשים

The footsteps of Messiah.

סוטה ט, טו **בְּעִקְּבוֹת מְשִׁיחָא** – חוּצְפָּא יִסְגֵּא, וְיוֹקֶר יַאֲמִיר, הַגֶּפֶן תִּתֵּן פִּרְיָהּ וְהַיַּיִן בְּיוֹקֶר, וּמַלְכוּת תֵּהָפֵךְ לְמִינוּת, וְאֵין תּוֹכַחַת, בֵּית וַועַד יִהְיֶה לִזְנוּת. וְהַגָּלִיל יֶחֱרַב, וְהַגַּבְלָן יִשּׁוֹם, וְאַנְשֵׁי הַגְּבוּל יְסוֹבְבוּ מֵעִיר לְעִיר וְלֹא יְחוֹנָּנוּ, וְחָכְמוֹת סוֹפְרִים תִּסְרַח, וְיִרְאֵי חֵטְא יִמָּאֲסוּ, וְהָאֱמֶת תְּהֵא נֶעְדֶּרֶת.
מיכה ז נְעָרִים פְּנֵי זְקֵנִים יַלְבִּינוּ, זְקֵנִים יַעַמְדוּ מִפְּנֵי קְטַנִּים, בֵּן מְנַוֵּל אָב, בַּת קָמָה בְאִמָּהּ, כַּלָּה בַּחֲמוֹתָהּ, אֹיְבֵי אִישׁ אַנְשֵׁי בֵיתוֹ: פְּנֵי הַדּוֹר כִּפְנֵי הַכֶּלֶב, הַבֵּן אֵינוֹ מִתְבַּיֵּשׁ מֵאָבִיו. וְעַל מָה יֵשׁ לָנוּ לְהִשָּׁעֵן? עַל אָבִינוּ שֶׁבַּשָּׁמַיִם.

סדר נזיקין

Every one of Israel has a share in the World to Come.

סנהדרין י, א ישעיה ס **כָּל יִשְׂרָאֵל** יֵשׁ לָהֶם חֵלֶק לָעוֹלָם הַבָּא. שֶׁנֶּאֱמַר: וְעַמֵּךְ כֻּלָּם צַדִּיקִים, לְעוֹלָם יִירְשׁוּ אָרֶץ, נֵצֶר מַטָּעַי, מַעֲשֵׂה יָדַי לְהִתְפָּאֵר:

סדר קדשים

One's closeness to God depends on one's intentions while doing the most one can.

מנחות יג, יא ויקרא א **נֶאֱמַר** בְּעוֹלַת בְּהֵמָה, אִשֵּׁה רֵיחַ נִיחוֹחַ, וּבְעוֹלַת עוֹף, אִשֵּׁה רֵיחַ נִיחוֹחַ, וּבַמִּנְחָה, אִשֵּׁה רֵיחַ נִיחוֹחַ – לוֹמַר לְךָ: אֶחָד הַמַּרְבֶּה וְאֶחָד הַמַּמְעִיט, וּבִלְבַד שֶׁיְּכַוֵּן לִבּוֹ לַשָּׁמַיִם.

סדר טהרות

God will give every righteous person great reward, and peace to His people.

עוקצין ג, יב **אָמַר** רַבִּי יְהוֹשֻׁעַ בֶּן לֵוִי: עָתִיד הַקָּדוֹשׁ בָּרוּךְ הוּא לְהַנְחִיל לְכָל צַדִּיק
משלי ח וְצַדִּיק שְׁלֹשׁ מֵאוֹת וַעֲשָׂרָה עוֹלָמוֹת, שֶׁנֶּאֱמַר: לְהַנְחִיל אֹהֲבַי יֵשׁ, וְאֹצְרֹתֵיהֶם אֲמַלֵּא: אָמַר רַבִּי שִׁמְעוֹן בֶּן חֲלַפְתָּא: לֹא מָצָא הַקָּדוֹשׁ בָּרוּךְ
תהלים כט הוּא כְּלִי מַחֲזִיק בְּרָכָה לְיִשְׂרָאֵל אֶלָּא הַשָּׁלוֹם, שֶׁנֶּאֱמַר: יהוה עֹז לְעַמּוֹ יִתֵּן, יהוה יְבָרֵךְ אֶת עַמּוֹ בַשָּׁלוֹם:

---

have been chosen as particularly appropriate as we attempt to comprehend the enormity of the national tragedy of the Shoah, our traditional Jewish response to suffering, and our search for meaning in the unparalleled sacrifice of our people.

Jer. 17 sprinkle pure water upon you and you shall be cleansed," and He also says: "The mikveh of Israel is God." Just as a mikveh purifies the contaminated, so does the Holy One, blessed is He, purify Israel.

SEDER NASHIM

The footsteps of Messiah.

Sota 9:15 **בְּעִקְּבוֹת מְשִׁיחָא** WITH THE FOOTSTEPS of the Messiah insolence will increase, and inflation will soar, the vine will give its fruit but wine will be dear, and the government will turn to heresy, and there will be rebuke, the meeting place [of sages] will be used for immorality, and the Galilee will be destroyed and the Gavlian desolated, and the border dwellers will wander about from city to city but will not be pited, the knowledge of scholars will be lost, those who fear sin will be despised, and the truth will be hidden; youths will shame old men and
Mic. 7 old men will stand up for youngsters; [it will be a time when] a son shames his father, a daughter rebels against her mother, a daughter-in-law against her mother-in-law [and] a man's enemies are the members of his household; the face of the generation will be like the face of the dog; [and] the son is not ashamed before his father. On whom can we rely? [Only] on our Father in heaven.

SEDER NEZIKIN

Every one of Israel has a share in the World to Come.

Sanhedrin 10:1 *Is. 60* **כָּל יִשְׂרָאֵל** ALL ISRAEL have a share in the World to Come. As it is said, "Your people also shall be all righteous, they shall inherit the land for ever; the branch of My planting, the work of My hands, wherein I glory."

SEDER KODASHIM

One's closeness to God depends on one's intentions while doing the most one can.

Menaḥot 13:11 *Lev. 1* **נֶאֱמַר** IT IS SAID regarding the animal *olah: a fire-offering, a pleasing aroma,* and regarding the bird *olah: a fire-offering, a pleasing aroma.* and regarding the *Minḥa*-offering: *a fire-offering, a pleasing aroma.* this teaches that [there is no difference] between the one who offers much and the one who offers little, as long as he directs his mind to heaven.

SEDER TEHAROT

God will give every righteous person great reward, and peace to His people.

Uktzin 3:12 **אָמַר** R. YEHOSHUA ben Levi said: The time will come when the Holy One, blessed is He, will endow each and every righteous person with three hundred
Prov. 8 and ten worlds, as it is stated: "That I may cause those that love Me to inherit substance, and that I may fill their treasuries." R. Shimon ben Ḥalafta said: the Holy One, Blessed is He, found no vessel to hold blessing for Israel other than
Ps. 29 peace, as it is stated: "The Lord will give strength to His people. The Lord will bless His people with peace."

תפילות אל מלא

The אֵל מָלֵא *prayer for the victims of the Holocaust ("For Martyrs") is recited, as found on page 1106.*

קדיש דרבנן

The following prayer, said by mourners, requires the presence of a מנין.
A transliteration can be found on page 1344.

אבל: **יִתְגַּדַּל** וְיִתְקַדַּשׁ שְׁמֵהּ רַבָּא (קהל: אָמֵן). בְּעָלְמָא דִּי בְרָא כִרְעוּתֵהּ.
וְיַמְלִיךְ מַלְכוּתֵהּ בְּחַיֵּיכוֹן וּבְיוֹמֵיכוֹן וּבְחַיֵּי דְכָל בֵּית
יִשְׂרָאֵל, בַּעֲגָלָא וּבִזְמַן קָרִיב, וְאִמְרוּ אָמֵן. (קהל: אָמֵן)

קהל ואבל: יְהֵא שְׁמֵהּ רַבָּא מְבָרַךְ לְעָלַם וּלְעָלְמֵי עָלְמַיָּא.

אבל: יִתְבָּרַךְ וְיִשְׁתַּבַּח וְיִתְפָּאַר וְיִתְרוֹמַם וְיִתְנַשֵּׂא, וְיִתְהַדָּר וְיִתְעַלֶּה
וְיִתְהַלָּל שְׁמֵהּ דְּקֻדְשָׁא בְּרִיךְ הוּא (קהל: בְּרִיךְ הוּא), לְעֵלָּא מִן כָּל
בִּרְכָתָא / בעשרת ימי תשובה: לְעֵלָּא (וּ)לְעֵלָּא מִכָּל בִּרְכָתָא / וְשִׁירָתָא,
תֻּשְׁבְּחָתָא וְנֶחֱמָתָא דַּאֲמִירָן בְּעָלְמָא, וְאִמְרוּ אָמֵן. (קהל: אָמֵן)

עַל יִשְׂרָאֵל וְעַל רַבָּנָן, וְעַל תַּלְמִידֵיהוֹן וְעַל כָּל תַּלְמִידֵי תַלְמִידֵיהוֹן,
וְעַל כָּל מָאן דְּעָסְקִין בְּאוֹרַיְתָא, דִּי בְאַתְרָא הָדֵין, וְדִי בְכָל אֲתַר
וַאֲתַר, יְהֵא לְהוֹן וּלְכוֹן שְׁלָמָא רַבָּא, חִנָּא וְחִסְדָּא, וְרַחֲמֵי, וְחַיֵּי
אֲרִיכֵי, וּמְזוֹנֵי רְוִיחֵי, וּפֻרְקָנָא מִן קֳדָם אֲבוּהוֹן דִּי בִשְׁמַיָּא, וְאִמְרוּ
אָמֵן. (קהל: אָמֵן)

יְהֵא שְׁלָמָא רַבָּא מִן שְׁמַיָּא וְחַיִּים, עָלֵינוּ וְעַל כָּל יִשְׂרָאֵל, וְאִמְרוּ
אָמֵן. (קהל: אָמֵן)

Bow, take three steps back, as if taking leave of the Divine Presence, then bow, first left, then right, then center, while saying:

עֹשֶׂה שָׁלוֹם/ בעשרת ימי תשובה: הַשָּׁלוֹם/ בִּמְרוֹמָיו, הוּא יַעֲשֶׂה שָׁלוֹם
עָלֵינוּ, וְעַל כָּל יִשְׂרָאֵל, וְאִמְרוּ אָמֵן. (קהל: אָמֵן)

MEMORIAL PRAYERS

The "El Male" prayer for the victims of the Holocaust ("For Martyrs") is recited, as found on page 1107.

THE RABBIS' KADDISH

The following prayer, said by mourners, requires the presence of a minyan. A transliteration can be found on page 1344.

Mourner: **יִתְגַּדַּל** EXALTED AND HALLOWED may God's great name be, in the world He created as He willed. May He reign in your lifetimes and in your days, and in the lifetime of the whole house of Israel, speedily and soon, and say, Amen.

All: May His great name be blessed forever and all time.

Mourner: Blessed and praised, honored, extolled, glorified, adored and exalted above all be the name of the Holy One, blessed is He, (*Between Rosh Hashana & Yom Kippur:* above and) beyond any blessing, hymn, praise, or expressions of consolation that may be uttered in this world, and say, Amen.

May the Jewish people, and our teachers, together with their students and all their students' students, as well as all who engage in Torah study here and in every other place, have abundant peace, grace, kindness, mercy, length of days, abundant food, and deliverance at the hands of their heavenly Father, and say, Amen.

May abundant peace descend from heaven, as well as life, for us and for all Israel, and say, Amen.

Bow, take three steps back, as if taking leave of the Divine Presence, then bow, first left, then right, then center, while saying:

May He Who makes peace in the highest heaven, make peace for us, and for all Israel, and say, Amen.

יום הזיכרון לחללי צה״ל

The historical background and halakhic perspective for the following service can be found in the Essay section on page E12.

Some congregations utilize the following special service for this day as recommended by the Chief Rabbinate of Israel.

At the end of שחרית, after קדיש שלם, the ארון קודש is opened and the following is said by some congregations:

לַמְנַצֵּחַ עַל־מוּת לַבֵּן מִזְמוֹר לְדָוִד: אוֹדֶה יהוה בְּכָל־לִבִּי, אֲסַפְּרָה כָּל־נִפְלְאוֹתֶיךָ: תהלים ט
אֶשְׂמְחָה וְאֶעֶלְצָה בָךְ, אֲזַמְּרָה שִׁמְךָ עֶלְיוֹן:
בְּשׁוּב־אוֹיְבַי אָחוֹר, יִכָּשְׁלוּ וְיֹאבְדוּ מִפָּנֶיךָ:
כִּי־עָשִׂיתָ מִשְׁפָּטִי וְדִינִי, יָשַׁבְתָּ לְכִסֵּא שׁוֹפֵט צֶדֶק:
גָּעַרְתָּ גוֹיִם אִבַּדְתָּ רָשָׁע, שְׁמָם מָחִיתָ לְעוֹלָם וָעֶד:
הָאוֹיֵב תַּמּוּ חֳרָבוֹת לָנֶצַח, וְעָרִים נָתַשְׁתָּ, אָבַד זִכְרָם הֵמָּה:
וַיהוה לְעוֹלָם יֵשֵׁב, כּוֹנֵן לַמִּשְׁפָּט כִּסְאוֹ:
וְהוּא יִשְׁפֹּט־תֵּבֵל בְּצֶדֶק, יָדִין לְאֻמִּים בְּמֵישָׁרִים:
וִיהִי יהוה מִשְׂגָּב לַדָּךְ, מִשְׂגָּב לְעִתּוֹת בַּצָּרָה:
וְיִבְטְחוּ בְךָ יוֹדְעֵי שְׁמֶךָ, כִּי לֹא־עָזַבְתָּ דֹרְשֶׁיךָ, יהוה:
זַמְּרוּ לַיהוה יֹשֵׁב צִיּוֹן, הַגִּידוּ בָעַמִּים עֲלִילוֹתָיו:
כִּי־דֹרֵשׁ דָּמִים אוֹתָם זָכָר, לֹא־שָׁכַח צַעֲקַת עֲנָוִים:
חָנְנֵנִי יהוה רְאֵה עָנְיִי מִשֹּׂנְאָי, מְרוֹמְמִי מִשַּׁעֲרֵי־מָוֶת:
לְמַעַן אֲסַפְּרָה כָּל־תְּהִלָּתֶיךָ,
בְּשַׁעֲרֵי בַת־צִיּוֹן אָגִילָה בִּישׁוּעָתֶךָ:
טָבְעוּ גוֹיִם בְּשַׁחַת עָשׂוּ, בְּרֶשֶׁת־זוּ טָמָנוּ נִלְכְּדָה רַגְלָם:
נוֹדַע יהוה מִשְׁפָּט עָשָׂה, בְּפֹעַל כַּפָּיו נוֹקֵשׁ רָשָׁע, הִגָּיוֹן סֶלָה:
יָשׁוּבוּ רְשָׁעִים לִשְׁאוֹלָה, כָּל־גּוֹיִם שְׁכֵחֵי אֱלֹהִים:
כִּי לֹא לָנֶצַח יִשָּׁכַח אֶבְיוֹן, תִּקְוַת עֲנִיִּים תֹּאבַד לָעַד:
קוּמָה יהוה אַל־יָעֹז אֱנוֹשׁ, יִשָּׁפְטוּ גוֹיִם עַל־פָּנֶיךָ:
שִׁיתָה יהוה מוֹרָה לָהֶם, יֵדְעוּ גוֹיִם, אֱנוֹשׁ הֵמָּה סֶּלָה:

The ארון קודש is closed.

MEMORIAL DAY FOR THE FALLEN OF THE ISRAEL DEFENSE FORCES

The historical background and halakhic perspective for the following service can be found in the Essay section on page E12.

Some congregations utilize the following special service for this day as recommended by the Chief Rabbinate of Israel.

At the end of Shaḥarit, after Full Kaddish, the Ark is opened and the following is said by some congregations:

Ps. 9 לַמְנַצֵּחַ TO THE DIRECTOR of music *al-mut laben*. A psalm of David. I thank the Lord with all my heart. I will relate all Your wondrous works. I will rejoice in exulting You. I will sing praise to Your name, O Most High, When my enemies turn back, when they stumble and perish from before You, For You have executed my judgment and my cause. You have sat upon the throne, O judge of righteousness. You have rebuked nations. You have destroyed the wicked. You have erased their name forever and ever. As for the enemy, its cities have come to an end and become perpetual ruins, and You have destroyed the cities, their memorial is gone. But the Lord will sit for ever. He has established His throne for judgment. And He will judge the world in righteousness. He will judge the peoples in uprightness. And the Lord will be a refuge for the oppressed, a refuge in times of trouble. And those who know Your name will trust in You, for You, Lord, have not abandoned those who seek You. Sing praises to the Lord Who dwells in Zion, declare His works among the peoples. For He Who avenges blood has remembered it. He has not forgotten the cry of the oppressed. Be gracious unto me, Lord. Look upon my affliction from those who hate me, You Who lift me up from the gates of death, So that I may relate all Your praise in the gates of the daughter of Zion. I will rejoice in Your salvation. The nations have drowned in the pit that they made. In the net that they concealed their own foot has been caught. The Lord has become known through the judgment that He executed. The wicked is snared in the work of his own hands. *Higgayon*. Selah. May the wicked turn toward the underworld, all the nations that forget God. For may the needy not always be forgotten, and may the hope of the oppressed not perish forever. Arise, Lord, let man not prevail. Let the nations be judged before You. Set fear over them, Lord. The nations will know that they are but men. Selah.

The Ark is closed.

Memorial Prayer for Fallen Israeli Soldiers:

אָבִינוּ שֶׁבַּשָּׁמַיִם, אֵל אֱלֹהֵי הָרוּחוֹת לְכָל בָּשָׂר, זְכֹר נָא אֶת הַנְּשָׁמוֹת הַזַּכּוֹת וְהַטְּהוֹרוֹת שֶׁל בָּנֵינוּ וּבְנוֹתֵינוּ, אֲשֶׁר הֶעֱרוּ אֶת נַפְשָׁם לָמוּת מוֹת גִּבּוֹרִים, בְּהֵחָלְצָם לְעֶזְרַת הָעָם וְהָאָרֶץ. מִנְּשָׁרִים קַלּוּ מֵאֲרָיוֹת גָּבֵרוּ, בְּמִלְחַמְתָּם לְמַעַן שִׁחְרוּר עַמָּם וּמוֹלַדְתָּם. בַּעֲלוֹתָם עַל מִזְבַּח תְּקוּמַת יִשְׂרָאֵל בְּאֶרֶץ קָדְשׁוֹ, הֵפִיחוּ רוּחַ עֹז וּגְבוּרָה בְּכָל בֵּית יִשְׂרָאֵל בָּאָרֶץ וּבַתְּפוּצוֹת, וַיִּתְעוֹרֵר לִקְרַאת גְּאֻלָּתוֹ וּפְדוּת נַפְשׁוֹ. יִזְכְּרֵם אֱלֹהֵינוּ לְטוֹבָה עִם רִבְבוֹת אַלְפֵי קְדוֹשֵׁי יִשְׂרָאֵל וְגִבּוֹרָיו מִימֵי עוֹלָם, בִּצְרוֹר הַחַיִּים יִצְרֹר אֶת נִשְׁמוֹתֵיהֶם, בְּגַן עֵדֶן תְּהֵא מְנוּחָתָם, וְיָנוּחוּ בְשָׁלוֹם עַל מִשְׁכָּבָם, וְיַעַמְדוּ לְגוֹרָלָם לְקֵץ הַיָּמִין, אָמֵן.

לְדָוִד בָּרוּךְ יהוה צוּרִי הַמְלַמֵּד יָדַי לַקְרָב, אֶצְבְּעוֹתַי לַמִּלְחָמָה: חַסְדִּי וּמְצוּדָתִי מִשְׂגַּבִּי וּמְפַלְטִי לִי מָגִנִּי וּבוֹ חָסִיתִי הָרוֹדֵד עַמִּי תַחְתָּי: יהוה מָה־אָדָם וַתֵּדָעֵהוּ, בֶּן־אֱנוֹשׁ וַתְּחַשְּׁבֵהוּ: אָדָם לַהֶבֶל דָּמָה יָמָיו כְּצֵל עוֹבֵר: יהוה הַט־שָׁמֶיךָ וְתֵרֵד גַּע בֶּהָרִים וְיֶעֱשָׁנוּ: בְּרוֹק בָּרָק וּתְפִיצֵם, שְׁלַח חִצֶּיךָ וּתְהֻמֵּם: שְׁלַח יָדֶיךָ מִמָּרוֹם פְּצֵנִי וְהַצִּילֵנִי מִמַּיִם רַבִּים מִיַּד בְּנֵי נֵכָר: אֲשֶׁר פִּיהֶם דִּבֶּר־שָׁוְא, וִימִינָם יְמִין שָׁקֶר: אֱלֹהִים שִׁיר חָדָשׁ אָשִׁירָה לָּךְ, בְּנֵבֶל עָשׂוֹר אֲזַמְּרָה־לָּךְ: הַנּוֹתֵן תְּשׁוּעָה לַמְּלָכִים הַפּוֹצֶה אֶת־דָּוִד עַבְדּוֹ מֵחֶרֶב רָעָה: פְּצֵנִי וְהַצִּילֵנִי מִיַּד בְּנֵי־נֵכָר אֲשֶׁר־פִּיהֶם דִּבֶּר־שָׁוְא וִימִינָם יְמִין שָׁקֶר: אֲשֶׁר בָּנֵינוּ כִּנְטִעִים מְגֻדָּלִים בִּנְעוּרֵיהֶם בְּנוֹתֵינוּ כְזָוִיֹּת מְחֻטָּבוֹת תַּבְנִית הֵיכָל: מְזָוֵינוּ מְלֵאִים מְפִיקִים מִזַּן אֶל־זַן צֹאונֵנוּ מַאֲלִיפוֹת מְרֻבָּבוֹת בְּחוּצוֹתֵינוּ: אַלּוּפֵינוּ מְסֻבָּלִים אֵין פֶּרֶץ וְאֵין יוֹצֵאת וְאֵין צְוָחָה בִּרְחֹבֹתֵינוּ: אַשְׁרֵי הָעָם שֶׁכָּכָה לּוֹ אַשְׁרֵי הָעָם שֶׁיהוה אֱלֹהָיו: תהלים קמד

Memorial Prayer for Fallen Israeli Soldiers:

אָבִינוּ שֶׁבַּשָּׁמַיִם HEAVENLY FATHER, God, Source of the spirits of all flesh, remember, we pray You, the pure souls of our sons and daughters who heroically gave their lives in defense of the people and the Land. Swifter than eagles, stronger than lions, they fought for the liberation of their people and homeland, sacrificing their lives for Israel's rebirth in its holy land. They breathed a spirit of strength and courage into the whole house of Israel, in the Land and the Diaspora, inspiring it to go forward toward its redemption and liberation. Remember them, our God, for good, together with the myriad holy ones and heroes of Israel from ancient times. May their souls be bound in lasting life, may the Garden of Eden be their resting place, may they rest in peace and receive their reward at the End of Days. Amen.

Ps. 144 **לְדָוִד** OF DAVID. Blessed be the Lord, my rock, Who teaches my hands for battle, my fingers for war. My gracious One, and my fortress, my high tower, and my deliverer, my shield, and the One in Whom I find shelter, Who subdues people under me. O Lord, what is man, that You know him, the son of man, that You consider him! Man is like a breath. His days are like a passing shadow. O Lord, bow Your heavens and come down. Touch the mountains so that they smoke. Fire lightning and scatter them. Send Your arrows and destroy them. Send Your hands from on high. Rescue me and deliver me from many waters, from the hand of strangers, whose mouth speaks deceit, and whose right hand is a right hand of falsehood. O God, I will sing a new song to You, upon a ten-string harp I will sing praises to You. He Who gives salvation to kings, Who rescues David, His servant, from the evil sword, Rescue me and deliver me from the hand of strangers, whose mouth speaks deceit, and whose right hand is a right hand of falsehood. So that our sons will be like saplings raised in their youth, our daughters like cornerstones, carved in the fashion of a palace. Our storehouses are full, supplying all kinds of produce, our sheep bring forth thousands, tens of thousands in our markets. Our rams are stout. There is no breach and there is no leaving, and there is no outcry in our streets. Happy is the people that has this. Happy is the people whose God is the Lord.

מעריב ליום העצמאות

The historical background and halakhic perspective for the following service, can be found in the Essay section on page E12.
Some congregations utilize the following special service for this day as recommended by the Chief Rabbinate of Israel.

The following is said before מעריב*:*

תהלים קז **הֹדוּ** לַיהוה כִּי־טוֹב, כִּי לְעוֹלָם חַסְדּוֹ: יֹאמְרוּ גְּאוּלֵי יהוה, אֲשֶׁר
גְּאָלָם מִיַּד־צָר: וּמֵאֲרָצוֹת קִבְּצָם, מִמִּזְרָח וּמִמַּעֲרָב, מִצָּפוֹן
וּמִיָּם: תָּעוּ בַמִּדְבָּר, בִּישִׁימוֹן דָּרֶךְ, עִיר מוֹשָׁב לֹא מָצָאוּ: רְעֵבִים
גַּם־צְמֵאִים, נַפְשָׁם בָּהֶם תִּתְעַטָּף: וַיִּצְעֲקוּ אֶל־יהוה בַּצַּר לָהֶם,
מִמְּצוּקוֹתֵיהֶם יַצִּילֵם: וַיַּדְרִיכֵם בְּדֶרֶךְ יְשָׁרָה, לָלֶכֶת אֶל־עִיר מוֹשָׁב:
יוֹדוּ לַיהוה חַסְדּוֹ, וְנִפְלְאוֹתָיו לִבְנֵי אָדָם: כִּי־הִשְׂבִּיעַ נֶפֶשׁ שֹׁקֵקָה,
וְנֶפֶשׁ רְעֵבָה מִלֵּא־טוֹב: יֹשְׁבֵי חֹשֶׁךְ וְצַלְמָוֶת, אֲסִירֵי עֳנִי וּבַרְזֶל: כִּי־
הִמְרוּ אִמְרֵי־אֵל, וַעֲצַת עֶלְיוֹן נָאָצוּ: וַיַּכְנַע בֶּעָמָל לִבָּם, כָּשְׁלוּ וְאֵין
עֹזֵר: וַיִּזְעֲקוּ אֶל־יהוה בַּצַּר לָהֶם, מִמְּצֻקוֹתֵיהֶם יוֹשִׁיעֵם: יוֹצִיאֵם
מֵחֹשֶׁךְ וְצַלְמָוֶת, וּמוֹסְרוֹתֵיהֶם יְנַתֵּק: יוֹדוּ לַיהוה חַסְדּוֹ, וְנִפְלְאוֹתָיו
לִבְנֵי אָדָם: כִּי־שִׁבַּר דַּלְתוֹת נְחֹשֶׁת, וּבְרִיחֵי בַרְזֶל גִּדֵּעַ: אֱוִלִים
מִדֶּרֶךְ פִּשְׁעָם, וּמֵעֲוֺנֹתֵיהֶם יִתְעַנּוּ: כָּל־אֹכֶל תְּתַעֵב נַפְשָׁם, וַיַּגִּיעוּ
עַד־שַׁעֲרֵי מָוֶת: וַיִּזְעֲקוּ אֶל־יהוה בַּצַּר לָהֶם, מִמְּצֻקוֹתֵיהֶם יוֹשִׁיעֵם:
יִשְׁלַח דְּבָרוֹ וְיִרְפָּאֵם, וִימַלֵּט מִשְּׁחִיתוֹתָם: יוֹדוּ לַיהוה חַסְדּוֹ,
וְנִפְלְאוֹתָיו לִבְנֵי אָדָם: וְיִזְבְּחוּ זִבְחֵי תוֹדָה וִיסַפְּרוּ מַעֲשָׂיו בְּרִנָּה:
יוֹרְדֵי הַיָּם בָּאֳנִיּוֹת, עֹשֵׂי מְלָאכָה בְּמַיִם רַבִּים: הֵמָּה רָאוּ מַעֲשֵׂי
יהוה, וְנִפְלְאוֹתָיו בִּמְצוּלָה: וַיֹּאמֶר, וַיַּעֲמֵד רוּחַ סְעָרָה, וַתְּרוֹמֵם
גַּלָּיו: יַעֲלוּ שָׁמַיִם, יֵרְדוּ תְהוֹמוֹת, נַפְשָׁם בְּרָעָה תִתְמוֹגָג: יָחוֹגּוּ
וְיָנוּעוּ כַּשִּׁכּוֹר, וְכָל־חָכְמָתָם תִּתְבַּלָּע: וַיִּצְעֲקוּ אֶל־יהוה בַּצַּר לָהֶם,
וּמִמְּצוּקֹתֵיהֶם יוֹצִיאֵם: יָקֵם סְעָרָה לִדְמָמָה, וַיֶּחֱשׁוּ גַּלֵּיהֶם: וַיִּשְׂמְחוּ
כִי־יִשְׁתֹּקוּ, וַיַּנְחֵם אֶל־מְחוֹז חֶפְצָם: יוֹדוּ לַיהוה חַסְדּוֹ, וְנִפְלְאוֹתָיו
לִבְנֵי אָדָם: וִירוֹמְמוּהוּ בִּקְהַל־עָם, וּבְמוֹשַׁב זְקֵנִים יְהַלְלוּהוּ: יָשֵׂם
נְהָרוֹת לְמִדְבָּר, וּמֹצָאֵי מַיִם לְצִמָּאוֹן: אֶרֶץ פְּרִי לִמְלֵחָה, מֵרָעַת

MA'ARIV FOR YOM HAATZMA'UT

The historical background and halakhic perspective for the following service, can be found in the Essay section on page E12.

Some congregations utilize the following special service for this day as recommended by the Chief Rabbinate of Israel.

The following is said before Ma'ariv:

Ps. 107 הודו GIVE THANKS to the Lord, for He is good, for His loving-kindness is forever. Let the redeemed of the Lord say this, whom He has redeemed from the hand of distress, And whom He has gathered from the lands, from the east, and from the west, from the north, and from the south. They lost themselves in the wilderness, their way in the desert. They did not find a city of habitation. Hungry and thirsty, their spirit fainted within them. Then they cried to the Lord in their distress, and He delivered them from their troubles. And He led them on the straight path, to go to a city of habitation. Let them praise the Lord for His loving-kindness, and for His wondrous works to the children of man, That He has satisfied the thirsty soul, and He has filled the hungry soul with good. Those who sat in darkness and the shadow of death, bound in affliction and iron, Because they had rebelled against the words of God, and derided the counsel of the Most High. So He brought down their heart with affliction, they fell down and there was none to help. Then they cried to the Lord in their distress, and He saved them from their troubles. He brought them out from darkness and the shadow of death, and He broke their bonds asunder. Let them praise the Lord for His loving-kindness, and for His wondrous works to the children of man, That He has broken the gates of brass, and He has cut the bars of iron asunder. The foolish who can be recognized by their way of sin, and who are afflicted on account of their iniquities, Whose soul abhors all food, and who have come near the gates of death, Then they cried to the Lord in their distress, and He saved them from their troubles. He sent His word and healed them, and He rescued them from their destructions. Let them praise the Lord for His loving-kindness, and for His wondrous works to the children of man, And let them sacrifice sacrifices of thanksgiving, and let them declare His works with rejoicing. Those who go down to the sea in ships, who do work in great waters, They have seen the works of the Lord, and His wonders in the deep. For He commanded and raised a stormy wind, and it lifted up its waves. They rose up to the sky, they went down to the depths, their soul trembled because of the trouble. They reeled and staggered like a drunkard, and all their skill disappeared. Then they cried to the Lord in their distress, and He brought them out from their troubles. He made the storm a calm, and their waves became still. And they were glad because they became quiet, and He guided them to their desired harbor. Let them praise the Lord for His loving-kindness, and for His wondrous works to the

יֽוֹשְׁבֵי בָהּ: יָשֵׂם מִדְבָּר לַאֲגַם־מַיִם, וְאֶרֶץ צִיָּה לְמֹצָאֵי מָיִם: וַיּוֹשֶׁב
שָׁם רְעֵבִים, וַיְכוֹנְנוּ עִיר מוֹשָׁב: וַיִּזְרְעוּ שָׂדוֹת, וַיִּטְּעוּ כְרָמִים, וַיַּעֲשׂוּ
פְּרִי תְבוּאָה: וַיְבָרְכֵם וַיִּרְבּוּ מְאֹד, וּבְהֶמְתָּם לֹא יַמְעִיט: וַיִּמְעֲטוּ
וַיָּשֹׁחוּ, מֵעֹצֶר רָעָה וְיָגוֹן: שֹׁפֵךְ בּוּז עַל־נְדִיבִים, וַיַּתְעֵם בְּתֹהוּ לֹא־
דָרֶךְ: ◂ וַיְשַׂגֵּב אֶבְיוֹן מֵעוֹנִי, וַיָּשֶׂם כַּצֹּאן מִשְׁפָּחוֹת: יִרְאוּ יְשָׁרִים
וְיִשְׂמָחוּ, וְכָל־עַוְלָה קָפְצָה פִּיהָ: מִי־חָכָם וְיִשְׁמָר־אֵלֶּה, וְיִתְבּוֹנְנוּ
חַסְדֵי יהוה:

יהוה מָלָךְ תָּגֵל הָאָרֶץ, יִשְׂמְחוּ אִיִּים רַבִּים: עָנָן וַעֲרָפֶל סְבִיבָיו, תהלים צז
צֶדֶק וּמִשְׁפָּט מְכוֹן כִּסְאוֹ: אֵשׁ לְפָנָיו תֵּלֵךְ, וּתְלַהֵט
סָבִיב צָרָיו: הֵאִירוּ בְרָקָיו תֵּבֵל, רָאֲתָה וַתָּחֵל הָאָרֶץ: הָרִים
כַּדּוֹנַג נָמַסּוּ מִלִּפְנֵי יהוה, מִלִּפְנֵי אֲדוֹן כָּל־הָאָרֶץ: הִגִּידוּ
הַשָּׁמַיִם צִדְקוֹ, וְרָאוּ כָל־הָעַמִּים כְּבוֹדוֹ: יֵבֹשׁוּ כָּל־עֹבְדֵי פֶסֶל
הַמִּתְהַלְלִים בָּאֱלִילִים, הִשְׁתַּחֲווּ־לוֹ כָּל־אֱלֹהִים: שָׁמְעָה וַתִּשְׂמַח
צִיּוֹן, וַתָּגֵלְנָה בְּנוֹת יְהוּדָה, לְמַעַן מִשְׁפָּטֶיךָ יהוה: כִּי־אַתָּה יהוה
עֶלְיוֹן עַל־כָּל־הָאָרֶץ, מְאֹד נַעֲלֵיתָ עַל־כָּל־אֱלֹהִים: אֹהֲבֵי יהוה
שִׂנְאוּ רָע, שֹׁמֵר נַפְשׁוֹת חֲסִידָיו, מִיַּד רְשָׁעִים יַצִּילֵם: ◂ אוֹר
זָרֻעַ לַצַּדִּיק, וּלְיִשְׁרֵי־לֵב שִׂמְחָה: שִׂמְחוּ צַדִּיקִים בַּיהוה, וְהוֹדוּ
לְזֵכֶר קָדְשׁוֹ:

מִזְמוֹר, שִׁירוּ לַיהוה שִׁיר חָדָשׁ כִּי־נִפְלָאוֹת עָשָׂה, הוֹשִׁיעָה־לּוֹ תהלים צח
יְמִינוֹ וּזְרוֹעַ קָדְשׁוֹ: הוֹדִיעַ יהוה יְשׁוּעָתוֹ, לְעֵינֵי הַגּוֹיִם
גִּלָּה צִדְקָתוֹ: זָכַר חַסְדּוֹ וֶאֱמוּנָתוֹ לְבֵית יִשְׂרָאֵל, רָאוּ כָל־אַפְסֵי־
אָרֶץ אֵת יְשׁוּעַת אֱלֹהֵינוּ: הָרִיעוּ לַיהוה כָּל־הָאָרֶץ, פִּצְחוּ וְרַנְּנוּ
וְזַמֵּרוּ: זַמְּרוּ לַיהוה בְּכִנּוֹר, בְּכִנּוֹר וְקוֹל זִמְרָה: בַּחֲצֹצְרוֹת וְקוֹל
שׁוֹפָר, הָרִיעוּ לִפְנֵי הַמֶּלֶךְ יהוה: ◂ יִרְעַם הַיָּם וּמְלֹאוֹ, תֵּבֵל וְיֹשְׁבֵי
בָהּ: נְהָרוֹת יִמְחֲאוּ־כָף, יַחַד הָרִים יְרַנֵּנוּ: לִפְנֵי־יהוה כִּי בָא לִשְׁפֹּט
הָאָרֶץ, יִשְׁפֹּט־תֵּבֵל בְּצֶדֶק, וְעַמִּים בְּמֵישָׁרִים:

children of men, And let them exalt Him in the congregation of the people, and let them praise Him in the assembly of the elders. He turned rivers into wilderness, and springs of water into dry ground, A fruitful land into desolation, because of the wickedness of those who dwelled therein. He turned wilderness into a pool of water, and dry ground into springs of water. And He settled the hungry there, and they established a city of habitation. And they sowed the fields and planted vineyards, and they yielded fruits of increase. And He blessed them, and they multiplied greatly, and He did not diminish their cattle. But they were diminished and brought low by the dominion of evil and sorrow. He pours contempt upon nobles, and He makes them wander in the wilderness where there is no way. ▸ But He has set the needy on high from poverty, and He has made their families like a flock. The upright see this and rejoice, and all iniquity shuts its mouth. Whoever is wise must keep these things, and let them contemplate the acts of loving-kindness of the Lord.

Ps. 97 יהוה מָלָךְ THE LORD is King, may the earth rejoice. May the many islands be happy. Cloud and mist are about Him. Justice and law are the foundation of His throne. Fire walks before Him, and it burns His enemies on every side. His lightnings illuminate the world. The earth sees and shudders. The mountains melt like wax before the Lord, before the Lord of all the earth. The heavens proclaim His righteousness, and all the peoples see His glory. Let all those who worship statues be ashamed, those who exult in false gods. All gods bow down to Him. Zion has heard and is glad, and the daughters of Judah rejoice, on account of Your judgments, O Lord. Indeed, You, O Lord, are high above all the earth. You are exalted far above all gods. Those who love the Lord, hate evil. He preserves the souls of His pious ones. He saves them from the hand of the wicked. ▸ Light is sown for the righteous, and gladness for the upright in heart. Rejoice, O righteous, in the Lord, and give thanks to the memory of His holiness.

Ps. 98 מִזְמוֹר A PSALM. Sing to the Lord a new song, for He has done marvels. His right hand and His holy arm have gained Him the victory. The Lord has made known His salvation. He has revealed His righteousness in the sight of the nations. He has remembered His loving-kindness in His faithfulness to the house of Israel. All the ends of the earth have seen the salvation of our God. Make a joyful noise to the Lord, all the earth. Make a loud noise, and sing, and sing praise. Sing praise to the Lord with the lyre, with the lyre and the sound of song. With trumpets and the sound of a shofar, make a joyful noise before the Lord, the King. ▸ May the sea roar and the fullness of it, the world and those who dwell in it. May the rivers clap hands. May the mountains sing for joy together, Before the Lord Who is coming to judge the earth. He will judge the world in righteousness, and the peoples with equity.

It is customary to sing:

התְעוֹרְרִי הִתְעוֹרְרִי
כִּי בָא אוֹרֵךְ קוּמִי אוֹרִי
עוּרִי עוּרִי, שִׁיר דַּבֵּרִי
כְּבוֹד יהוה עָלַיִךְ נִגְלָה.
זֶה־הַיּוֹם עָשָׂה יהוה, נָגִילָה וְנִשְׂמְחָה בוֹ: תהלים קיח

לֹא תֵבֹשִׁי וְלֹא תִכָּלְמִי
מַה תִּשְׁתּוֹחֲחִי וּמַה תֶּהֱמִי
בָּךְ יֶחֱסוּ עֲנִיֵּי עַמִּי
וְנִבְנְתָה עִיר עַל תִּלָּהּ.
זֶה־הַיּוֹם עָשָׂה יהוה, נָגִילָה וְנִשְׂמְחָה בוֹ:

יָמִין וּשְׂמֹאל תִּפְרֹצִי
וְאֶת יהוה תַּעֲרִיצִי
עַל יַד אִישׁ בֶּן פַּרְצִי
וְנִשְׂמְחָה וְנָגִילָה.
זֶה־הַיּוֹם עָשָׂה יהוה, נָגִילָה וְנִשְׂמְחָה בוֹ:

מעריב לחול (page 290) is said at this point, in the יום טוב melody. After קדיש שלם, the ארון קודש is opened and the following is said responsively by the שליח ציבור and the קהל.

שְׁמַע יִשְׂרָאֵל, יהוה אֱלֹהֵינוּ, יהוה אֶחָד: דברים ו

The following is said three times responsively:

יהוה הוּא הָאֱלֹהִים.

The שליח ציבור says the following which is repeated by the קהל.

מִי שֶׁעָשָׂה נִסִּים לַאֲבוֹתֵינוּ וְלָנוּ, וּגְאָלָנוּ מֵעַבְדוּת לְחֵרוּת, הוּא יִגְאָלֵנוּ גְּאֻלָּה שְׁלֵמָה בְּקָרוֹב, וִיקַבֵּץ נִדָּחֵינוּ מֵאַרְבַּע כַּנְפוֹת הָאָרֶץ, חֲבֵרִים כָּל יִשְׂרָאֵל, וְנֹאמַר אָמֵן.

The ארון קודש is closed.

It is customary to sing:

GET UP, get up, for your light has come, so rise and shine.
Arise, arise, call out in song,
for the glory of the Lord
has been revealed upon you.

Ps. 118 This is the day on which the Lord has acted.
Let us be glad and rejoice in Him.

NO LONGER will you be embarrassed or humiliated;
why are you depressed and why are you distraught?
For in you will the impoverished of My people take shelter,
and soon will the city be rebuilt over its ruins.

This is the day on which the Lord has acted.
Let us be glad and rejoice in Him.

YOU will break out to the right and to the left
and you will praise the Lord,
together with the descendant of Peretz
we will rejoice and sing out in exultation.

This is the day on which the Lord has acted.
Let us be glad and rejoice in Him.

Ma'ariv for Weekdays (page 291) is said at this point, in the Yom Tov melody. After Full Kaddish, the Ark is opened and the following is said responsively by the Leader and the congregation.

Deut. 6 שְׁמַע HEAR, O ISRAEL, the LORD is our God, the LORD is One.

The following is said three times responsively:

THE LORD, He is God

The Leader says the following which is repeated by the congregation.

מִי שֶׁעָשָׂה MAY HE Who performed miracles for our ancestors and for us, redeeming us from slavery to freedom, grant us a complete redemption soon, and gather in our dispersed people from the four quarters of the earth, so that all Israel may be united in friendship, and let us say: Amen.

The Ark is closed.

The שליח ציבור *continues:*

וְכִי־תָבֹאוּ מִלְחָמָה בְּאַרְצְכֶם עַל־הַצַּר הַצֹּרֵר אֶתְכֶם, וַהֲרֵעֹתֶם בַּחֲצֹצְרֹת, וְנִזְכַּרְתֶּם לִפְנֵי יהוה אֱלֹהֵיכֶם, וְנוֹשַׁעְתֶּם מֵאֹיְבֵיכֶם: וּבְיוֹם שִׂמְחַתְכֶם וּבְמוֹעֲדֵיכֶם וּבְרָאשֵׁי חָדְשֵׁכֶם, וּתְקַעְתֶּם בַּחֲצֹצְרֹת עַל עֹלֹתֵיכֶם וְעַל זִבְחֵי שַׁלְמֵיכֶם, וְהָיוּ לָכֶם לְזִכָּרוֹן לִפְנֵי אֱלֹהֵיכֶם, אֲנִי יהוה אֱלֹהֵיכֶם: במדבר י

The שופר *is sounded with a* תקיעה גדולה *and the following is said aloud:*

לַשָּׁנָה הַבָּאָה בִּירוּשָׁלַיִם הַבְּנוּיָה.

All:

יְהִי רָצוֹן מִלְּפָנֶיךָ יהוה אֱלֹהֵינוּ וֵאלֹהֵי אֲבוֹתֵינוּ, שֶׁכְּשֵׁם שֶׁזָּכִינוּ לְאַתְחַלְתָּא דִגְאֻלָּה, כֵּן נִזְכֶּה לִשְׁמֹעַ קוֹל שׁוֹפָרוֹ שֶׁל מְשִׁיחַ צִדְקֵנוּ בִּמְהֵרָה בְיָמֵינוּ.

All sing:

שִׁיר הַמַּעֲלוֹת, בְּשׁוּב יהוה אֶת־שִׁיבַת צִיּוֹן, הָיִינוּ כְּחֹלְמִים: תהלים קכו
אָז יִמָּלֵא שְׂחוֹק פִּינוּ וּלְשׁוֹנֵנוּ רִנָּה, אָז יֹאמְרוּ בַגּוֹיִם הִגְדִּיל יהוה לַעֲשׂוֹת עִם־אֵלֶּה: הִגְדִּיל יהוה לַעֲשׂוֹת עִמָּנוּ, הָיִינוּ שְׂמֵחִים: שׁוּבָה יהוה אֶת־שְׁבִיתֵנוּ, כַּאֲפִיקִים בַּנֶּגֶב: הַזֹּרְעִים בְּדִמְעָה בְּרִנָּה יִקְצֹרוּ: הָלוֹךְ יֵלֵךְ וּבָכֹה נֹשֵׂא מֶשֶׁךְ־הַזָּרַע, בֹּא־יָבֹא בְרִנָּה נֹשֵׂא אֲלֻמֹּתָיו:

The עומר *is counted* *(page 326)**, followed by* עָלֵינוּ *(page 322)*.

All sing:

אֲנִי מַאֲמִין בֶּאֱמוּנָה שְׁלֵמָה בְּבִיאַת הַמָּשִׁיחַ, וְאַף עַל פִּי שֶׁיִּתְמַהְמֵהַּ, עִם כָּל זֶה אֲחַכֶּה לּוֹ בְּכָל יוֹם שֶׁיָּבוֹא.

It is customary to greet each other with the following phrase:

מוֹעֲדִים לְשִׂמְחָה לִגְאֻלָּה שְׁלֵמָה

The Leader continues:

Num. 10 **וְכִי־תָבֹאוּ** WHEN YOU GO into battle in your land against an enemy who is attacking you, sound a staccato blast on the trumpets. Then you will be remembered by the Lord your God and you will be delivered from your enemies. On your days of rejoicing – your festivals and new moon celebrations – you shall sound a note on the trumpets over your burnt- and peace-offerings, and they will be a remembrance for you before your God. I am the Lord your God.

The shofar is sounded with a Tekia Gedola and the following is said aloud:

לְשָׁנָה הַבָּאָה NEXT YEAR in Jerusalem rebuilt.

All:

יְהִי רָצוֹן MAY IT BE Your will, Lord our God and God of our fathers, That as we have merited to witness the beginning of redemption, So may we merit to hear the sound of the shofar of our righteous anointed one, swiftly in our days.

All sing:

Ps. 126 **שִׁיר הַמַּעֲלוֹת** A SONG OF ASCENTS. When the Lord brought back the return of Zion, we were like those who dream. Then our mouth was filled with laughter and our tongue with joy. Then they said among the nations: "the Lord did great things for these." The Lord did great things for us. We were glad. Bring back our return, O Lord, like the streams in the south. Those that sow in tears will reap in joy. May he who goes out weeping, bearing the sack of seed, come home in joy, bearing his sheaves.

The Omer is counted (page 327), followed by Aleinu (page 323).

All sing:

אֲנִי מַאֲמִין I BELIEVE with complete faith in the coming of the Messiah, and though he may delay, I wait daily for his coming.

It is customary to greet each other with the following phrase:

Happy festival; to a complete redemption!

שחרית ליום העצמאות

The historical background and halakhic perspective for the following service, can be found in the Essay section on page E12.

Some congregations utilize the following special service for this day as recommended by the Chief Rabbinate of Israel.

Many congregations say פסוקי דזמרה *of* יום טוב *(pages 452–468), then continue with* יְהִי כְבוֹד *on page 66.* שירת הים *(page 82) is said verse by verse. After* חזרת הש״ץ, הלל שלם *(page 766) is said followed by* חצי קדיש *(page 156). On Thursdays the* תורה *is read (page 158). Some also have the custom to recite the following* הפטרה *(without the blessings before and after).*

ישעיה י:לב-יב:ו **עוֹד הַיּוֹם** בְּנֹב לַעֲמֹד יְנֹפֵף יָדוֹ הַר בַּת־צִיּוֹן גִּבְעַת
יְרוּשָׁלִָם: הִנֵּה הָאָדוֹן יהוה צְבָאוֹת
מְסָעֵף פֻּארָה בְּמַעֲרָצָה וְרָמֵי הַקּוֹמָה גְּדֻעִים וְהַגְּבֹהִים יִשְׁפָּלוּ:
וְנִקַּף סִבְכֵי הַיַּעַר בַּבַּרְזֶל וְהַלְּבָנוֹן בְּאַדִּיר יִפּוֹל: וְיָצָא
חֹטֶר מִגֵּזַע יִשָׁי וְנֵצֶר מִשָּׁרָשָׁיו יִפְרֶה: וְנָחָה עָלָיו רוּחַ יהוה רוּחַ
חָכְמָה וּבִינָה רוּחַ עֵצָה וּגְבוּרָה רוּחַ דַּעַת וְיִרְאַת יהוה: וַהֲרִיחוֹ
בְּיִרְאַת יהוה וְלֹא־לְמַרְאֵה עֵינָיו יִשְׁפּוֹט וְלֹא־לְמִשְׁמַע אָזְנָיו
יוֹכִיחַ: וְשָׁפַט בְּצֶדֶק דַּלִּים וְהוֹכִיחַ בְּמִישׁוֹר לְעַנְוֵי־אָרֶץ וְהִכָּה־
אֶרֶץ בְּשֵׁבֶט פִּיו וּבְרוּחַ שְׂפָתָיו יָמִית רָשָׁע: וְהָיָה צֶדֶק אֵזוֹר
מָתְנָיו וְהָאֱמוּנָה אֵזוֹר חֲלָצָיו: וְגָר זְאֵב עִם־כֶּבֶשׂ וְנָמֵר עִם־גְּדִי
יִרְבָּץ וְעֵגֶל וּכְפִיר וּמְרִיא יַחְדָּו וְנַעַר קָטֹן נֹהֵג בָּם: וּפָרָה וָדֹב
תִּרְעֶינָה יַחְדָּו יִרְבְּצוּ יַלְדֵיהֶן וְאַרְיֵה כַּבָּקָר יֹאכַל־תֶּבֶן: וְשִׁעֲשַׁע
יוֹנֵק עַל־חֻר פָּתֶן וְעַל מְאוּרַת צִפְעוֹנִי גָּמוּל יָדוֹ הָדָה: לֹא־יָרֵעוּ
וְלֹא־יַשְׁחִיתוּ בְּכָל־הַר קָדְשִׁי כִּי־מָלְאָה הָאָרֶץ דֵּעָה אֶת־יהוה
כַּמַּיִם לַיָּם מְכַסִּים: וְהָיָה בַּיּוֹם הַהוּא שֹׁרֶשׁ יִשַׁי
אֲשֶׁר עֹמֵד לְנֵס עַמִּים אֵלָיו גּוֹיִם יִדְרֹשׁוּ וְהָיְתָה מְנֻחָתוֹ
כָּבוֹד: וְהָיָה | בַּיּוֹם הַהוּא יוֹסִיף אֲדֹנָי | שֵׁנִית יָדוֹ לִקְנוֹת
אֶת־שְׁאָר עַמּוֹ אֲשֶׁר יִשָּׁאֵר מֵאַשּׁוּר וּמִמִּצְרַיִם וּמִפַּתְרוֹס וּמִכּוּשׁ
וּמֵעֵילָם וּמִשִּׁנְעָר וּמֵחֲמָת וּמֵאִיֵּי הַיָּם: וְנָשָׂא נֵס לַגּוֹיִם וְאָסַף
נִדְחֵי יִשְׂרָאֵל וּנְפֻצוֹת יְהוּדָה יְקַבֵּץ מֵאַרְבַּע כַּנְפוֹת הָאָרֶץ: וְסָרָה

SHAḤARIT FOR YOM HAATZMA'UT

The historical background and halakhic perspective for the following service, can be found in the Essay section on page E12.

Some congregations utilize the following special service for this day as recommended by the Chief Rabbinate of Israel.

Many congregations say Pesukei DeZimra of Yom Tov (pages 453–469), then continue with "May the glory" on page 67. Shirat HaYam (page 83) is said verse by verse. After the Leader's Repetition, Full Hallel (page 767) is said followed by Half Kaddish (page 157). On Thursdays the Torah is read (page 159). Some also have the custom to recite the following haftara (without the blessings before and after).

Is. 10:32–12:6 **עוֹד הַיּוֹם** This day he will halt at Nob; he will wave his hand, mountain of the daughter of Zion, hill of Jerusalem. See, the sovereign Lord of hosts will lop off the boughs with an axe. The tall trees will be felled, the lofty ones laid low. He will cut down the forest thickets with an axe. Lebanon will fall before the Mighty One. A shoot will grow from the stump of Jesse; from his roots a branch will bear fruit. The spirit of the Lord will rest on him – a spirit of wisdom and understanding, a spirit of counsel and power, a spirit of knowledge and the fear of the Lord, and he will delight in the fear of the Lord. He will not judge by what his eyes see, or decide by what his ears hear; with justice he will judge the poor, and with equity defend the humble in the land. He will strike the earth with the rod of his mouth; with the breath of his lips he will slay the wicked. Justice will be his belt and faithfulness the sash around his waist. The wolf will live with the lamb, the leopard will lie down with the kid, the calf and the lion and the yearling together; and a little child will lead them. The cow will graze with the bear, their young will lie down together, and the lion will eat straw like the ox. An infant will play near the cobra's hole, and a young child put his hand into the viper's nest. They will neither harm nor destroy on all My holy mountain, for the earth will be full of the knowledge of the Lord as the waters cover the sea. On that day the stock of Jesse will stand as a banner for the peoples; nations will rally to him, and his place of rest will be glorious. On that day the Lord will reach out His hand a second time to reclaim the remnant that is left of His people from Assyria, Lower Egypt, Pathros, Cush, Elam, Shinar, Hamath and the islands of the sea. He will raise a banner for the nations and gather the exiles of Israel; He will assemble the scattered people of Judah from the four quarters of the earth.

קִנְאַת אֶפְרַיִם וְצֹרְרֵי יְהוּדָה יִכָּרֵתוּ אֶפְרַיִם לֹא־יְקַנֵּא אֶת־יְהוּדָה
וִיהוּדָה לֹא־יָצֹר אֶת־אֶפְרָיִם: וְעָפוּ בְכָתֵף פְּלִשְׁתִּים יָמָּה יַחְדָּו יָבֹזּוּ
אֶת־בְּנֵי־קֶדֶם אֱדוֹם וּמוֹאָב מִשְׁלוֹחַ יָדָם וּבְנֵי עַמּוֹן מִשְׁמַעְתָּם:
וְהֶחֱרִים יהוה אֵת לְשׁוֹן יַם־מִצְרַיִם וְהֵנִיף יָדוֹ עַל־הַנָּהָר בַּעְיָם
רוּחוֹ וְהִכָּהוּ לְשִׁבְעָה נְחָלִים וְהִדְרִיךְ בַּנְּעָלִים: וְהָיְתָה מְסִלָּה
לִשְׁאָר עַמּוֹ אֲשֶׁר יִשָּׁאֵר מֵאַשּׁוּר כַּאֲשֶׁר הָיְתָה לְיִשְׂרָאֵל בְּיוֹם
עֲלֹתוֹ מֵאֶרֶץ מִצְרָיִם: וְאָמַרְתָּ בַּיּוֹם הַהוּא אוֹדְךָ יהוה כִּי אָנַפְתָּ
בִּי יָשֹׁב אַפְּךָ וּתְנַחֲמֵנִי: הִנֵּה אֵל יְשׁוּעָתִי אֶבְטַח וְלֹא אֶפְחָד כִּי־עָזִּי
וְזִמְרָת יָהּ יהוה וַיְהִי־לִי לִישׁוּעָה: וּשְׁאַבְתֶּם־מַיִם בְּשָׂשׂוֹן מִמַּעַיְנֵי
הַיְשׁוּעָה: וַאֲמַרְתֶּם בַּיּוֹם הַהוּא הוֹדוּ לַיהוה קִרְאוּ בִשְׁמוֹ הוֹדִיעוּ
בָעַמִּים עֲלִילֹתָיו הַזְכִּירוּ כִּי נִשְׂגָּב שְׁמוֹ: זַמְּרוּ יהוה כִּי גֵאוּת
עָשָׂה מוּדַעַת זֹאת בְּכָל־הָאָרֶץ: צַהֲלִי וָרֹנִּי יוֹשֶׁבֶת צִיּוֹן כִּי־גָדוֹל
בְּקִרְבֵּךְ קְדוֹשׁ יִשְׂרָאֵל:

After the הפטרה*, the Prayer for the State of Israel (page 554) followed by the* אזכרה *for Fallen Israeli Soldiers (page 1034) is said. The service then continues with* אַשְׁרֵי *and* וּבָא לְצִיּוֹן *until the end of* שחרית *(page 172).*

At the end of the service, sing:

אֲנִי מַאֲמִין בֶּאֱמוּנָה שְׁלֵמָה, בְּבִיאַת הַמָּשִׁיחַ, וְאַף עַל פִּי
שֶׁיִּתְמַהְמֵהַּ, עִם כָּל זֶה אֲחַכֶּה לּוֹ בְּכָל יוֹם שֶׁיָּבוֹא.

יום ירושלים

At מנחה *before* יום ירושלים, תחנון *is omitted. (If* שבת, צִדְקָתְךָ *on page 652 is omitted.) In the evening,* מעריב לחול *is said in the* יום טוב *melody. The* עומר *is counted. Many have the custom to add prayers of thanksgiving at the end of* מעריב.

In many communities in ארץ ישראל *and in* חוץ לארץ *say the* פסוקי דזמרה *of* יום טוב שחרית *(pages 452–468), then continue with* יְהִי כְבוֹד *on page 66. After* חזרת הש״ץ, הלל שלם *(page 766) is said and the regular service continues.*

Ephraim's jealousy will vanish, and Judah's harassment will end. Ephraim will not be jealous of Judah, nor will Judah be hostile toward Ephraim. They will swoop down on the slopes of Philistia to the west; together they will plunder the people to the east. Edom and Moab will be subject to them, and the Ammonites shall obey them. The Lord will dry up the gulf of the Egyptian sea; with a scorching wind He will sweep His hand over the Euphrates River. He will break it up into seven streams so that people can cross over in sandals. There will be a highway for the remnant of His people that is left from Assyria, as there was for Israel when they came up from Egypt. In that day you will say: "I will praise You, O Lord. Although You were angry with me, Your anger has turned away and You have comforted me. Surely God is my salvation; I will trust and not be afraid. The Lord, the Lord, is my strength and my song; He has become my salvation." With joy you will draw water from the wells of salvation. In that day you will say: "Give thanks to the Lord, call on His name; make known among the nations what He has done, and proclaim that His name is exalted. Sing to the Lord, for He has done glorious things; let this be known to all the world. Shout aloud and sing for joy, people of Zion, for great is the Holy One of Israel among you."

After the Haftara, the Prayer for the State of Israel (page 555) followed by the Memorial Prayer for Fallen Israeli Soldiers (page 1035) is said. The service then continues with Ashrei until the end of Shaḥarit (page 173).

At the end of the service, sing:

I BELIEVE with complete faith in the coming of the Messiah, and though he may delay, I wait daily for his coming.

YOM YERUSHALAYIM

At Minḥa before Yom Yerushalayim, Taḥanun is omitted. (If Shabbat, Tzidkatekha on page 653 is omitted.) In the evening, Ma'ariv for weekdays is said in the Yom Tov melody. The Omer is counted. Many have the custom to add prayers of thanksgiving at the end of Ma'ariv.

In Shaḥarit, many communities outside Israel and in Israel say the Pesukei DeZimra of Yom Tov (pages 453–469), then continue with "May the glory" on page 67. After the Leader's Repetition, Full Hallel (page 767) is said and the regular service continues.

סדר קידושין ונישואין

When the חתן *reaches the* חופה, *the following is said:*

בָּרוּךְ הַבָּא. מִי אַדִּיר עַל הַכֹּל, מִי בָּרוּךְ עַל הַכֹּל, מִי גָּדוֹל עַל הַכֹּל, מִי דָּגוּל עַל הַכֹּל, הוּא יְבָרֵךְ אֶת הֶחָתָן וְאֶת הַכַּלָּה.

When the כלה *reaches the* חופה, *the following is said:*

בְּרוּכָה הַבָּאָה. מִי בָּן שִׂיחַ שׁוֹשַׁן חוֹחִים, אַהֲבַת כַּלָּה מְשׂוֹשׂ דּוֹדִים, הוּא יְבָרֵךְ אֶת הֶחָתָן וְאֶת הַכַּלָּה.

ברכות האירוסין

The מסדר קידושין *takes a cup of wine and says:*

בָּרוּךְ אַתָּה יהוה אֱלֹהֵינוּ מֶלֶךְ הָעוֹלָם, בּוֹרֵא פְּרִי הַגָּפֶן.

בָּרוּךְ אַתָּה יהוה אֱלֹהֵינוּ מֶלֶךְ הָעוֹלָם, אֲשֶׁר קִדְּשָׁנוּ בְּמִצְוֹתָיו וְצִוָּנוּ עַל הָעֲרָיוֹת, וְאָסַר לָנוּ אֶת הָאֲרוּסוֹת, וְהִתִּיר לָנוּ אֶת הַנְּשׂוּאוֹת לָנוּ עַל יְדֵי חֻפָּה וְקִדּוּשִׁין. בָּרוּךְ אַתָּה יהוה, מְקַדֵּשׁ עַמּוֹ יִשְׂרָאֵל עַל יְדֵי חֻפָּה וְקִדּוּשִׁין.

The חתן *and* כלה *both drink from the wine.*

אֵרוּסִין וְנִשּׂוּאִין / THE MARRIAGE SERVICE
As explained by the Kabbalistic *Iggeret HaKodesh* and later authors such as R. Yaakov Emden, marriage is not merely a functional institution to facilitate physical and spiritual procreation, but a "blessed and pure" reflection of the mystical union of the celestial *Tiferet* and *Shekhina*. As such, it provides a means for an energized religious life by integrating sexuality, and its cycles of physical denial and realization, within a totally sanctified existence, and by establishing a carnal yet powerfully existential

HALAKHIC PRENUPTIAL AGREEMENTS
It has become the widespread custom that prior to the marriage day every couple completes a halakhic prenuptial agreement. The RCA and its halakhic authorities strongly urge that this be done, and that no marriage take place without it. For more information, and to access and download the prenuptial forms and instructions in their various formats, see www.theprenup.org.

MARRIAGE SERVICE

When the bridegroom reaches the ḥuppa, the following is said:

בָּרוּךְ הַבָּא BLESSED is he who has come! May He Who is supreme in power, as well as blessed above all, greater than all, and exalted above all – bless the groom and the bride.

When the bride reaches the ḥuppa, the following is said:

בְּרוּכָה הַבָּאָה BLESSED is she who has come! May the one who is about to officiate, who understands the deeper meaning of the phrase "the rose among the thorns," as well as the love of a bride who is celebrated by those who cherish her – bless the groom and the bride.

BLESSINGS OF BETROTHAL

The officiating rabbi takes a cup of wine and says:

בָּרוּךְ BLESSED ARE YOU, Lord, our God, King of the universe, Who creates the fruit of the vine.

בָּרוּךְ BLESSED ARE YOU, Lord, our God, King of the universe, Who has sanctified us with His commandments, and has commanded us regarding forbidden unions; Who has forbidden us from betrothed women while permitting us to those whom we have married by means of *Ḥuppa* and *Kiddushin*/consecration. Blessed are You, Lord, Who sanctifies His people Israel by means of *Ḥuppa* and *Kiddushin*/consecration.

The bride and bridegroom both drink from the wine.

---

relationship suffused with spiritual content (R. Aharon Lichtenstein).

It is customary for the bride to circle the groom under the *Ḥuppa*. Some see the source for this custom in the verse "God has created a new thing in the land: a woman shall encircle (תְּסוֹבֵב) a man" (Jer. 31:21). The Malbim explains this to mean that when a population that comes from afar to settle a land it usually does so with force, whereas when Israel will return to the land of Israel, which, in relation to its people, is portrayed as a wife, the land will desire her nation's return. As applied to the wedding ceremony, when a bride circles

The חתן *takes the ring and, holding it ready to be placed on the forefinger of the* כלה*'s right hand, says:*

הֲרֵי אַתְּ מְקֻדֶּשֶׁת לִי בְּטַבַּעַת זוֹ כְּדַת מֹשֶׁה וְיִשְׂרָאֵל.

He then places the ring on the forefinger of the כלה*'s right hand. The* כתובה *is read and the* חתן *hands it to the* כלה.

A second cup of wine is taken, and over it, the שבע ברכות *are said; the same person should preferably say the first two blessings.*

שבע ברכות מתחת לחופה

בָּרוּךְ אַתָּה יהוה אֱלֹהֵינוּ מֶלֶךְ הָעוֹלָם, בּוֹרֵא פְּרִי הַגָּפֶן.

בָּרוּךְ אַתָּה יהוה אֱלֹהֵינוּ מֶלֶךְ הָעוֹלָם, שֶׁהַכֹּל בָּרָא לִכְבוֹדוֹ.

בָּרוּךְ אַתָּה יהוה אֱלֹהֵינוּ מֶלֶךְ הָעוֹלָם, יוֹצֵר הָאָדָם.

בָּרוּךְ אַתָּה יהוה אֱלֹהֵינוּ מֶלֶךְ הָעוֹלָם, אֲשֶׁר יָצַר אֶת הָאָדָם בְּצַלְמוֹ, בְּצֶלֶם דְּמוּת תַּבְנִיתוֹ, וְהִתְקִין לוֹ מִמֶּנּוּ בִּנְיַן עֲדֵי עַד. בָּרוּךְ אַתָּה יהוה, יוֹצֵר הָאָדָם.

The union of bride and groom evokes the events at Sinai when God (the Groom) and Israel (His bride) were joined together. Some take the analogy one step further, and see the *ketuba* as symbolic of the Torah, both of which delineate the terms of their union.

These seven consist of one *berakha* over wine followed by six *berakhot* over the marriage. The six are arranged in a double three-fold structure. The first three have a universalistic character, praising God (1) for all of creation, (2) for the creation of man, and (3) for having created male and female. The next three pray (4) for the Jewish nation, (5) for the happiness of the couple, and (6) for the full redemption of the Jewish people, as symbolized by the rapturous marriage celebrations that will take place in the cities of Judea, especially in a rebuilt Jerusalem.

her groom she actively signals her desire to enter into this union. The Gemara (*Yevamot* 62b) further derives from Jeremiah's prophecy that the wife is the protector of her husband. In some communities, the bride circles seven times, reminiscent of the seven heavens, thus dedicating their marriage to the service of God. In other communities, she circles three times, for the phrase "when a man marries a woman" occurs three times in the Torah, in Deuteronomy 22:13, 24:1 and 24:5 (*Tashbetz Katan*).

שֶׁבַע בְּרָכוֹת / SHEVA BERAKHOT

The number seven also evokes the revelation at Sinai, insofar as the Torah mentions "sounds" seven times at Sinai, and God's name occurs fourteen times in the Ten Commandments (*Tashbetz*).

The bridegroom takes the ring and, holding it ready to be placed on the forefinger of the bride's right hand, says:

הֲרֵי אַתְּ YOU ARE CONSECRATED to me by means of this ring, in accordance with the laws of Moses and Israel.

He then places the ring on the forefinger of the bride's right hand. The Ketuba is read and the bridegroom hands it to the bride.

A second cup of wine is taken, and over it, the Sheva Berakhot are said; the same person should preferably say the first two blessings.

SHEVA BERAKHOT UNDER THE ḤUPPA

בָּרוּךְ BLESSED ARE YOU, Lord, our God, King of the universe, Who creates the fruit of the vine.

בָּרוּךְ BLESSED ARE YOU, Lord, our God, King of the universe, in that He created all that exists for His glory.

בָּרוּךְ BLESSED ARE YOU, Lord, our God, King of the universe, Who forms all of humanity.

בָּרוּךְ BLESSED ARE YOU, Lord, our God, King of the universe, Who formed man in His image, in the image of his likeness, and Who for his sake and from him made an everlasting being. Blessed are You, Lord, Who forms all of humanity.

שֶׁהַכֹּל בָּרָא לִכְבוֹדוֹ – *In that He created all that exists for His glory.* We praise God for creating the entire world, which leads to procreation and settlement (Rema).

יוֹצֵר הָאָדָם – *Who forms all of humanity.* Marriage is more than a social institution for the purpose of satisfying particular personal and social needs. It establishes a spiritual relationship. Therefore this *berakha*, in which no reference is made to woman, refers to man's physical creation, but makes no mention of man's spiritual nature. Only in the next *berakha*, which speaks of woman, is reference made to man being made in God's image. When woman enters man's life in marriage, as described in Genesis 2, man transcends his animal nature and his egocentricity, and only then does he reflect a divine image (R. Joseph B. Soloveitchik).

בְּצֶלֶם דְּמוּת תַּבְנִיתוֹ – *In the image of his likeness.* R. Sa'adia Gaon's version וּבְצֶלֶם דְּמוּת תַּבְנִיתוֹ הִתְקִין connects this phrase to the latter part of the blessing – that God created for Adam a helpmate in Adam's own image. R. Yehuda Ben Yakar understands the reference as being to God, i.e., although God has no body, humankind is created in His image. The Kabbalists understand that the construction of the human anatomy reflects the heavenly blueprint by which God created physical reality,

שׂוֹשׂ תָּשִׂישׂ וְתָגֵל הָעֲקָרָה בְּקִבּוּץ בָּנֶיהָ לְתוֹכָהּ בְּשִׂמְחָה. בָּרוּךְ אַתָּה יהוה, מְשַׂמֵּחַ צִיּוֹן בְּבָנֶיהָ.

שַׂמֵּחַ תְּשַׂמַּח רֵעִים הָאֲהוּבִים כְּשַׂמֵּחֲךָ יְצִירְךָ בְּגַן עֵדֶן מִקֶּדֶם. בָּרוּךְ אַתָּה יהוה, מְשַׂמֵּחַ חָתָן וְכַלָּה.

בָּרוּךְ אַתָּה יהוה אֱלֹהֵינוּ מֶלֶךְ הָעוֹלָם, אֲשֶׁר בָּרָא שָׂשׂוֹן וְשִׂמְחָה, חָתָן וְכַלָּה, גִּילָה, רִנָּה, דִּיצָה וְחֶדְוָה, אַהֲבָה וְאַחֲוָה וְשָׁלוֹם וְרֵעוּת. מְהֵרָה יהוה אֱלֹהֵינוּ, יִשָּׁמַע בְּעָרֵי יְהוּדָה וּבְחוּצוֹת יְרוּשָׁלָיִם, קוֹל שָׂשׂוֹן וְקוֹל שִׂמְחָה, קוֹל חָתָן וְקוֹל כַּלָּה, קוֹל מִצְהֲלוֹת חֲתָנִים מֵחֻפָּתָם וּנְעָרִים מִמִּשְׁתֵּה נְגִינָתָם. בָּרוּךְ אַתָּה יהוה, מְשַׂמֵּחַ הֶחָתָן עִם הַכַּלָּה.

The חתן *and* כלה *both drink from the wine.*

The חתן *breaks a glass in memory of the destruction of the* בית המקדש.
Some say the following beforehand:

אִם־אֶשְׁכָּחֵךְ יְרוּשָׁלָםִ, תִּשְׁכַּח יְמִינִי: תהלים קלז
תִּדְבַּק לְשׁוֹנִי לְחִכִּי אִם־לֹא אֶזְכְּרֵכִי,
אִם־לֹא אַעֲלֶה אֶת־יְרוּשָׁלַםִ
עַל רֹאשׁ שִׂמְחָתִי:

---

as the verse declares, "From our very flesh, we perceive God's ways" (Job 19:26).

מְהֵרָה... יִשָּׁמַע – *May there soon be heard.* This *berakha* relates the personal happiness of the groom and bride to the Messianic fulfillment. We find a similar correlation in "as the bridegroom rejoices over bride, so shall God rejoice over thee (Zion)" (Is. 62:5). The couple is challenged to reach out to the Jewish people to identify with the strivings of the broader community, its travails and its triumphs, and thereby to hasten the coming of the Messiah. It is noteworthy that whereas the preceding *berakha* concludes with חָתָן וְכַלָּה (the groom

שׂוֹשׂ BRING GREAT REJOICING and exultation to the desolate land by gathering in its children in celebration. Blessed are You, Lord, Who gladdens Zion through her children.

שַׂמֵּחַ BRING GREAT HAPPINESS to this couple who are so beloved of each other, just as You brought happiness to those whom You formed in the Garden of Eden of old. Blessed are You, Lord, Who causes both groom and bride to rejoice.

בָּרוּךְ BLESSED ARE YOU, Lord, our God, King of the universe, Who created joy and happiness, groom and bride, rejoicing and song, joy and delight, love and brotherhood, peace and fellowship. Lord our God, may there soon be heard in the cities of Judea and the streets of Jerusalem the sounds of jubilation and rejoicing, celebratory noises of grooms and brides, echoes of grooms exalting under their marriage canopy, and youths feasting in song. Blessed are You, Lord, Who causes groom and bride to rejoice together.

The bridegroom and bride both drink from the wine.

The bridegroom breaks a glass in memory of the destruction of the Temple. Some say the following beforehand:

Ps. 137 אִם־אֶשְׁכָּחֵךְ IF I FORGET YOU, O Jerusalem,
may my right hand forget.
May my tongue cleave to the roof of my mouth,
if I do not make mention of you,
if I do not raise Jerusalem to the head of my joy.

---

and the bride) this *berakha* ends חָתָן עִם כַּלָּה (the groom *together with* the bride). The connecting עִם implies a stronger bond or connection than the simple conjunctive "and." The implication is that the marital relationship is the stronger and more joyous when the couple, as described at length in this *berakha*, form their union based on an unconditional commitment to the destiny of the Jewish people (R. Joseph B. Soloveitchik).

זימון לסעודת שבע ברכות

The Leader takes a cup of wine in his hand and says:

Leader רַבּוֹתַי, נְבָרֵךְ.

תהלים קיג Others יְהִי שֵׁם יהוה מְבֹרָךְ מֵעַתָּה וְעַד־עוֹלָם:

Leader יְהִי שֵׁם יהוה מְבֹרָךְ מֵעַתָּה וְעַד־עוֹלָם:

דְּוַי הָסֵר וְגַם חָרוֹן,
וְאָז אִלֵּם בְּשִׁיר יָרֹן.
נְחֵנוּ בְּמַעְגְּלֵי צֶדֶק,
שְׁעֵה בִּרְכַּת בְּנֵי אַהֲרֹן.

Add the appropriate words in parentheses:

Traditionally, the terms אבי מורי *("my father and teacher") and* בעל הבית *("the head of the household") were understood to include "mother and teacher" as well as the female head of the household, respectively. However, for those who prefer to be more explicit, the feminine versions are included in parentheses below.*

בִּרְשׁוּת (אָבִי מוֹרִי / אִמִּי מוֹרָתִי / כֹּהֲנִים / מוֹרֵנוּ הָרַב / בַּעַל הַבַּיִת הַזֶּה / בַּעֲלַת הַבַּיִת הַזֶּה) מָרָנָן וְרַבָּנָן וְרַבּוֹתַי, נְבָרֵךְ אֱלֹהֵינוּ שֶׁהַשִּׂמְחָה בִּמְעוֹנוֹ וְשֶׁאָכַלְנוּ מִשֶּׁלּוֹ.

Others בָּרוּךְ אֱלֹהֵינוּ שֶׁהַשִּׂמְחָה בִּמְעוֹנוֹ, שֶׁאָכַלְנוּ מִשֶּׁלּוֹ וּבְטוּבוֹ חָיִינוּ.

Leader בָּרוּךְ אֱלֹהֵינוּ שֶׁהַשִּׂמְחָה בִּמְעוֹנוֹ, שֶׁאָכַלְנוּ מִשֶּׁלּוֹ וּבְטוּבוֹ חָיִינוּ.

בָּרוּךְ הוּא וּבָרוּךְ שְׁמוֹ.

Continue with ברכת המזון *on page 222, at the end of which say the* שבע ברכות *(on the next page) over a second cup of wine.*

ZIMMUN FOR SHEVA BERAKHOT

דְּוַי הָסֵר – *Remove all sorrow.* This poetic couplet was composed by the highly regarded tenth-century poet and grammarian Dunash ibn Labrat (who also composed the *Deror Yikra* Shabbat *zemer*), who imbedded his name in the opening letters of each succeeding phrase of the poem. It asks God to remove all trouble and sorrow from the conjoined lives of the new couple, and to ensure that their new home be continually filled with joyous song. It furthermore invokes Psalm 23 in

GRACE AFTER MEALS FOLLOWED BY SHEVA BERAKHOT

The Leader takes a cup of wine in his hand and says:

Leader: רַבּוֹתַי ESTEEMED COMPANIONS, let us say grace.

Ps. 113 *Others:* BLESSED be the name of the Lord from now and forevermore.

Leader: BLESSED be the name of the Lord from now and forevermore.

דְּוַי הָסֵר REMOVE ALL SORROW and anger,
so that all – even the mute – will rejoice in song;
Lead us in the ways of righteousness,
so as to merit the blessing of the descendants of Aaron.

Add the appropriate words in parentheses:
Traditionally, the terms "my father and teacher" and "the head of the household" were understood to include "mother and teacher" as well as the female head of the household, respectively. However, for those who prefer to be more explicit, the feminine versions are included in parentheses below.

With your permission, (my father and teacher / my mother and teacher / the *Kohanim* / our teacher the rabbi / the head of this household) my masters and teachers, let us bless our God, in Whose abode there is rejoicing, (and) of Whose bounty we have partaken.

Others: BLESSED be our God, in Whose abode there is rejoicing, (and) of Whose bounty we have partaken and through Whose goodness we live.

Leader: BLESSED be our God, in Whose abode there is rejoicing, (and) of Whose bounty we have partaken and through Whose goodness we live.
Blessed be He, and blessed be His name.

Continue with the Grace after Meals on page 223, at the end of which say the Sheva Berakhot (on the next page) over a second cup of wine.

---

asking God's assistance to ensure that the couple always walk "in righteous paths," and thus be rewarded to enjoy the priestly blessings conveyed by "the sons of Aharon," as found in the Torah.

שֶׁהַשִּׂמְחָה בִּמְעוֹנוֹ, שֶׁאָכַלְנוּ מִשֶּׁלּוֹ – *In Whose abode there is rejoicing, (and) of Whose bounty we have partaken.* In accordance with Maḥzor Vitri, Rambam, Abudarham, the *Shulḥan Arukh* and others, the correct text is שֶׁאָכַלְנוּ without a

שבע ברכות בסעודה

בָּרוּךְ אַתָּה יהוה אֱלֹהֵינוּ מֶלֶךְ הָעוֹלָם, שֶׁהַכֹּל בָּרָא לִכְבוֹדוֹ.

בָּרוּךְ אַתָּה יהוה אֱלֹהֵינוּ מֶלֶךְ הָעוֹלָם, יוֹצֵר הָאָדָם.

בָּרוּךְ אַתָּה יהוה אֱלֹהֵינוּ מֶלֶךְ הָעוֹלָם, אֲשֶׁר יָצַר אֶת הָאָדָם בְּצַלְמוֹ, בְּצֶלֶם דְּמוּת תַּבְנִיתוֹ, וְהִתְקִין לוֹ מִמֶּנּוּ בִּנְיַן עֲדֵי עַד. בָּרוּךְ אַתָּה יהוה, יוֹצֵר הָאָדָם.

שׂוֹשׂ תָּשִׂישׂ וְתָגֵל הָעֲקָרָה בְּקִבּוּץ בָּנֶיהָ לְתוֹכָהּ בְּשִׂמְחָה. בָּרוּךְ אַתָּה יהוה, מְשַׂמֵּחַ צִיּוֹן בְּבָנֶיהָ.

שַׂמֵּחַ תְּשַׂמַּח רֵעִים הָאֲהוּבִים כְּשַׂמֵּחֲךָ יְצִירְךָ בְּגַן עֵדֶן מִקֶּדֶם. בָּרוּךְ אַתָּה יהוה, מְשַׂמֵּחַ חָתָן וְכַלָּה.

בָּרוּךְ אַתָּה יהוה אֱלֹהֵינוּ מֶלֶךְ הָעוֹלָם, אֲשֶׁר בָּרָא שָׂשׂוֹן וְשִׂמְחָה, חָתָן וְכַלָּה, גִּילָה, רִנָּה, דִּיצָה וְחֶדְוָה, אַהֲבָה וְאַחֲוָה וְשָׁלוֹם וְרֵעוּת. מְהֵרָה יהוה אֱלֹהֵינוּ, יִשָּׁמַע בְּעָרֵי יְהוּדָה וּבְחוּצוֹת יְרוּשָׁלָיִם, קוֹל שָׂשׂוֹן וְקוֹל שִׂמְחָה, קוֹל חָתָן וְקוֹל כַּלָּה, קוֹל מִצְהֲלוֹת חֲתָנִים מֵחֻפָּתָם וּנְעָרִים מִמִּשְׁתֵּה נְגִינָתָם. בָּרוּךְ אַתָּה יהוה, מְשַׂמֵּחַ הֶחָתָן עִם הַכַּלָּה.

The Leader makes the following blessing over his cup of wine:

בָּרוּךְ אַתָּה יהוה אֱלֹהֵינוּ מֶלֶךְ הָעוֹלָם, בּוֹרֵא פְּרִי הַגָּפֶן.

The two cups of wine are mixed, then poured into separate cups, one for the כלה *and one for the* חתן.

The specific mention of God's מְעוֹן (abode) is on account of Deuteronomy 26:15, which asks God to look from מְעוֹן קָדְשְׁךָ (Your holy abode) in heaven to "bless Your people Israel," which the Gemara (*Ḥagiga* 12b) considers to be the location in heaven from whence the angels joyously sing God's praises. Accord-

preceding vav (*Tzelota DeAvraham*). This makes sense insofar as שֶׁהַשִּׂמְחָה בִּמְעוֹנוֹ is a parenthetical phrase, i.e., it is not intended to separately bless God for "the rejoicing that occurs in His abode," but only to describe God's abode, while the *berakha* itself blesses Him for the food that He has given us (R. Yehiel Michel Epstein).

SHEVA BERAKHOT AFTER THE MEAL

בָּרוּךְ BLESSED ARE YOU, Lord, our God, King of the universe, in that He created all that exists for His glory.

בָּרוּךְ BLESSED ARE YOU, Lord, our God, King of the universe, Who forms all of humanity.

בָּרוּךְ BLESSED ARE YOU, Lord, our God, King of the universe, Who formed man in His image, in the image of his likeness, and Who for his sake and from him made an everlasting being. Blessed are You, Lord, Who forms all of humanity.

שׂוֹשׂ BRING GREAT REJOICING and exultation to the desolate land by gathering in its children in celebration. Blessed are You, Lord, Who gladdens Zion through her children.

שַׂמֵּחַ BRING GREAT HAPPINESS to this couple who are so beloved of each other, just as You brought happiness to those whom You formed in the Garden of Eden of old. Blessed are You, Lord, Who causes both groom and bride to rejoice.

בָּרוּךְ BLESSED ARE YOU, Lord, our God, King of the universe, Who created joy and happiness, groom and bride, rejoicing and song, joy and delight, love and brotherhood, peace and fellowship. Lord our God, may there soon be heard in the cities of Judea and the streets of Jerusalem the sounds of jubilation and rejoicing, celebratory noises of grooms and brides, echoes of grooms exalting under their marriage canopy, and youths feasting in song. Blessed are You, Lord, Who causes groom and bride to rejoice together.

The Leader makes the following blessing over his cup of wine:

בָּרוּךְ BLESSED ARE YOU, Lord, our God, King of the universe, Who creates the fruit of the vine.

The two cups of wine are mixed, then poured into separate cups, one for the bride and one for the bridegroom.

---

ingly, on this happy occasion on which we too praise God, we ask Him to shower His blessings upon the new couple from His heavenly abode (R. Yeḥiel Michel Epstein).

תפילת הודיה לאחר הלידה

Upon the birth of a boy the parents recite the following blessing:

בָּרוּךְ אַתָּה יהוה אֱלֹהֵינוּ מֶלֶךְ הָעוֹלָם, הַטּוֹב וְהַמֵּטִיב.

Upon the birth of a girl:

בָּרוּךְ אַתָּה יהוה אֱלֹהֵינוּ מֶלֶךְ הָעוֹלָם, שֶׁהֶחֱיָנוּ וְקִיְּמָנוּ
וְהִגִּיעָנוּ לַזְּמַן הַזֶּה.

The following is a suggested ceremony.
On entering the בית כנסת *after the childbirth the mother says:*

תהלים ה **וַאֲנִי** בְּרֹב חַסְדְּךָ אָבוֹא בֵיתֶךָ, אֶשְׁתַּחֲוֶה אֶל־הֵיכַל־קָדְשְׁךָ בְּיִרְאָתֶךָ:

תהלים קטז **אָהַבְתִּי**, כִּי־יִשְׁמַע יהוה, אֶת־קוֹלִי תַּחֲנוּנָי: כִּי־הִטָּה אָזְנוֹ לִי, וּבְיָמַי אֶקְרָא: אֲפָפוּנִי חֶבְלֵי־מָוֶת, וּמְצָרֵי שְׁאוֹל מְצָאוּנִי, צָרָה וְיָגוֹן אֶמְצָא: וּבְשֵׁם־יהוה אֶקְרָא, אָנָּה יהוה מַלְּטָה נַפְשִׁי: חַנּוּן יהוה וְצַדִּיק, וֵאלֹהֵינוּ מְרַחֵם: שֹׁמֵר פְּתָאִים יהוה, דַּלּוֹתִי וְלִי יְהוֹשִׁיעַ: שׁוּבִי נַפְשִׁי לִמְנוּחָיְכִי, כִּי־יהוה גָּמַל עָלָיְכִי: כִּי חִלַּצְתָּ נַפְשִׁי מִמָּוֶת, אֶת־עֵינִי מִן־דִּמְעָה, אֶת־רַגְלִי מִדֶּחִי: אֶתְהַלֵּךְ לִפְנֵי יהוה, בְּאַרְצוֹת הַחַיִּים: הֶאֱמַנְתִּי כִּי אֲדַבֵּר, אֲנִי עָנִיתִי מְאֹד: אֲנִי אָמַרְתִּי בְחָפְזִי, כָּל־הָאָדָם כֹּזֵב:
מָה־אָשִׁיב לַיהוה, כָּל־תַּגְמוּלוֹהִי עָלָי: לְךָ־אֶזְבַּח זֶבַח תּוֹדָה, וּבְשֵׁם יהוה אֶקְרָא: נְדָרַי לַיהוה אֲשַׁלֵּם, נֶגְדָה־נָּא לְכָל־עַמּוֹ: בְּחַצְרוֹת בֵּית יהוה, בְּתוֹכֵכִי יְרוּשָׁלָםִ, הַלְלוּיָהּ:

ON THE BIRTH OF A CHILD

The Gemara (*Berakhot* 59b) teaches that a new father may recite the blessing of *HaTov VeHaMeitiv* (which is found on page 246/7) upon hearing of the birth of a son. Recent Halakhic authorities are divided as to the proper blessing to be recited upon the birth of a daughter. The *Arukh HaShulḥan* (*OḤ* 223:1) records no blessing, while the *Mishna Berura* (*OḤ* 223.2) and *Iggerot Moshe* (*OḤ* 5:43:5) advise that the father may recite the *Sheheḥeyanu* blessing (which is found on page 246/7) upon seeing his new daughter. R. Shlomo Zalman Auerbach notes that the mother may also recite this blessing (*Minḥat Shlomo* 2:32). Some contemporary authorities suggest that the *HaTov VeHaMeitiv* blessing may be recited upon the joy of hearing of the birth of a daughter, just as that of a son (R. Naḥum Rabinovitch in *Yad Peshuta*, *Berakhot* 10:7). R. Hershel Schachter agrees that this is a halakhically valid practice.

THANKSGIVING PRAYER AFTER CHILDBIRTH

Upon the birth of a boy the parents recite the following blessing:

בָּרוּךְ BLESSED ARE YOU, Lord, our God, King of the universe, Who is good and does good.

Upon the birth of a girl:

בָּרוּךְ BLESSED ARE YOU, Lord, our God, King of the universe, Who has given us life, sustained us, and brought us to this time.

The following is a suggested ceremony.
On entering the synagogue after the childbirth, the mother says:

Ps. 5 וַאֲנִי BUT as for me, I will come into Your house in the abundance of Your loving-kindness. I will bow down toward Your holy Temple in the fear of You.

Ps. 116 אָהַבְתִּי I LOVE that the Lord has heard my voice, my supplications, that He has inclined His ear to me, and all my days I will call. The pangs of death encompassed me, and the straits of the underworld beset me. I found trouble and sorrow. But I called upon the name of the Lord: "I beseech You, O Lord, deliver my soul." Gracious is the Lord and righteous, and our God is merciful. The Lord preserves the simple. I was brought low and He saved me. Return to your rest, O my soul, for the Lord has dealt bountifully with you. Indeed, You have delivered my soul from death, my eyes from tears, my feet from stumbling. I will walk before the Lord in the lands of the living. I believed even when I said: "I have been greatly afflicted." I said in my haste: "The whole of man is delusive."

WHAT CAN I RENDER to the Lord for all His benefits toward me? I offer to You a sacrifice of thanksgiving, and I call upon the name of the Lord. I pay my vows to the Lord in the presence of all His people, in the courtyards of the house of the Lord, in your midst, O Jerusalem. Praise the Lord.

The mother says:

בָּרוּךְ אַתָּה יהוה אֱלֹהֵינוּ מֶלֶךְ הָעוֹלָם, הַגּוֹמֵל לְחַיָּבִים טוֹבוֹת, שֶׁגְּמָלַנִי כָּל טוֹב.

Those present respond:

אָמֵן. מִי שֶׁגְּמָלֵךְ כָּל טוֹב הוּא יִגְמְלֵךְ כָּל טוֹב, סֶלָה.

אָנָּא הָאֵל הַגָּדוֹל הַגִּבּוֹר וְהַנּוֹרָא, בְּרֹב חַסְדְּךָ אָבוֹא בֵיתֶךָ, לִזְבֹּחַ לְךָ זֶבַח תּוֹדָה עַל כָּל הַטּוֹבוֹת אֲשֶׁר גְּמַלְתָּ עָלַי. אֲפָפוּנִי חֲבָלִים וְצִירִים אֲחָזוּנִי, בַּצַּר לִי קָרָאתִי אֵלֶיךָ, וְשָׁמַעְתָּ מֵהֵיכָלְךָ קוֹלִי וְהָיִיתָ בְּעוֹזְרָי, רִפֵּאתָ לְכָל תַּחֲלוּאַי, עִטַּרְתַּנִי חֶסֶד וְרַחֲמִים, עַד הֵנָּה עֲזָרוּנִי רַחֲמֶיךָ, אָנָּא אַל תִּטְּשֵׁנִי לָנֶצַח. הוֹאֵל אֱלוֹהַּ, וּבָרֵךְ אֶת אֲמָתֶךָ, חַזְּקֵנִי וְאַמְּצֵנִי, אוֹתִי וְאֶת בַּעְלִי, וּנְגַדֵּל אֶת

For a boy:

הַיֶּלֶד אֲשֶׁר יֻלַּד לָנוּ, לְיִרְאָתְךָ וּלְעָבְדְּךָ בֶּאֱמֶת, וְלָלֶכֶת אֹרַח מֵישָׁרִים. שְׁמֹר אֶת הַיֶּלֶד הָרַךְ בְּכָל דְּרָכָיו, חָנֵּהוּ דֵּעָה בִּינָה וְהַשְׂכֵּל, וְתֵן חֶלְקוֹ בְּתוֹרָתֶךָ, וִיקַדֵּשׁ אֶת שִׁמְךָ הַגָּדוֹל, וְהָיָה לָנוּ לְמֵשִׁיב נֶפֶשׁ בִּימֵי שֵׂיבָתֵנוּ. וַאֲנִי תְפִלָּתִי־לְךָ יהוה עֵת רָצוֹן, אֱלֹהִים בְּרָב־חַסְדֶּךָ, עֲנֵנִי בֶּאֱמֶת יִשְׁעֶךָ: תהלים סט

For a girl:

הַיַּלְדָּה אֲשֶׁר יֻלְּדָה לָנוּ, לְיִרְאָתְךָ וּלְעָבְדְּךָ בֶּאֱמֶת, וְלָלֶכֶת אֹרַח מֵישָׁרִים. שְׁמֹר אֶת הַיַּלְדָּה הָרַכָּה בְּכָל דְּרָכֶיהָ, חָנֶּהָ דֵּעָה בִּינָה וְהַשְׂכֵּל, וְתֵן חֶלְקָהּ בְּתוֹרָתֶךָ, וּתְקַדֵּשׁ אֶת שִׁמְךָ הַגָּדוֹל, וְהָיְתָה לָנוּ לְמְשִׁיבַת נֶפֶשׁ בִּימֵי שֵׂיבָתֵנוּ. וַאֲנִי תְפִלָּתִי־לְךָ יהוה עֵת רָצוֹן, אֱלֹהִים בְּרָב־חַסְדֶּךָ, עֲנֵנִי בֶּאֱמֶת יִשְׁעֶךָ: תהלים סט

If the baby is brought to the בית כנסת*,*
the rabbi says the following blessings over him/her:

יְבָרֶכְךָ יהוה וְיִשְׁמְרֶךָ: יָאֵר יהוה פָּנָיו אֵלֶיךָ וִיחֻנֶּךָּ: יִשָּׂא יהוה פָּנָיו אֵלֶיךָ, וְיָשֵׂם לְךָ שָׁלוֹם: במדבר ו

The mother says:

בָּרוּךְ BLESSED are You, Lord, our God, King of the universe, Who bestows favors on the undeserving, and Who has bestowed every good thing on me.

Those present respond:

Amen. May He Who has bestowed every good thing on you continue to grant you every good thing, forever.

אָנָּא O GREAT, mighty and revered God. By Your great love I now come into Your House, to offer You a thanksgiving-offering for all the good You have bestowed on me. Travail beset me, pains seized me. In my distress I cried to You, and from Your habitation You heard my voice and helped me. You healed all my sickness, and crowned me with kindness and compassion. Until now Your mercy has helped me. I pray to You, God, never forsake me. Bestow Your blessing upon Your handmaid. Strengthen and support me together with my husband, that we may raise

For a boy:

הַיֶּלֶד THE BOY that has been born to us, to revere You and serve You in truth, and to walk in the path of righteousness. Protect our tender child in all his ways. Favor him with knowledge, understanding and discernment, and let his portion be in Your Torah, so that he may sanctify Your great name, and
Ps. 69 become a comfort to us as we grow old. But I pray to You, O Lord, for a time of favor. O God, in the greatness of Your loving-kindness, answer me, in the truth of Your salvation.

For a girl:

הַיַּלְדָּה THE GIRL that has been born to us, to revere You and serve You in truth, and to walk in the path of righteousness. Protect our tender child in all her ways. Favor her with knowledge, understanding and discernment, and let her portion be in Your Torah, so that she may sanctify Your great name,
Ps. 69 and become a comfort to us as we grow old. But I pray to You, O Lord, for a time of favor. O God, in the greatness of Your loving-kindness, answer me, in the truth of Your salvation.

If the baby is brought to the synagogue, the rabbi says the following blessings over him/her:

Num. 6 יְבָרֶכְךָ MAY THE LORD bless you and keep you. May the Lord make His countenance shine upon you and be gracious to you. May the Lord lift up His countenance to you and give you peace.

סדר ברית מילה

When the baby is brought in, all stand and say:

בָּרוּךְ הַבָּא.

The מוהל *says:*

במדבר כה

וַיְדַבֵּר יהוה אֶל־מֹשֶׁה לֵּאמֹר: פִּינְחָס בֶּן־אֶלְעָזָר בֶּן־אַהֲרֹן הַכֹּהֵן הֵשִׁיב אֶת־חֲמָתִי מֵעַל בְּנֵי־יִשְׂרָאֵל, בְּקַנְאוֹ אֶת־קִנְאָתִי בְּתוֹכָם, וְלֹא־כִלִּיתִי אֶת־בְּנֵי־יִשְׂרָאֵל בְּקִנְאָתִי: לָכֵן אֱמֹר, הִנְנִי נֹתֵן לוֹ אֶת־בְּרִיתִי שָׁלוֹם:

The baby is placed on the כסא של אליהו*, and the* מוהל *says:*

זֶה הַכִּסֵּא שֶׁל אֵלִיָּהוּ הַנָּבִיא זָכוּר לַטּוֹב.

The מוהל *declares:*

בראשית מט
תהלים קיט

לִישׁוּעָתְךָ קִוִּיתִי יהוה: שִׂבַּרְתִּי לִישׁוּעָתְךָ יהוה, וּמִצְוֹתֶיךָ עָשִׂיתִי: אֵלִיָּהוּ מַלְאַךְ הַבְּרִית, הִנֵּה שֶׁלְּךָ לְפָנֶיךָ, עֲמֹד

תהלים קיט

עַל יְמִינִי וְסָמְכֵנִי. שִׂבַּרְתִּי לִישׁוּעָתְךָ יהוה: שָׂשׂ אָנֹכִי עַל־אִמְרָתֶךָ, כְּמוֹצֵא שָׁלָל רָב: שָׁלוֹם רָב לְאֹהֲבֵי תוֹרָתֶךָ, וְאֵין־לָמוֹ מִכְשׁוֹל:

תהלים סה

אַשְׁרֵי תִּבְחַר וּתְקָרֵב, יִשְׁכֹּן חֲצֵרֶיךָ

All present respond:

נִשְׂבְּעָה בְּטוּב בֵּיתֶךָ, קְדֹשׁ הֵיכָלֶךָ:

בְּרִית מִילָה / CIRCUMCISION

בָּרוּךְ הַבָּא – *Blessed is the one who has arrived.* The numerical value of the word הַבָּא is eight. This alludes to the *Brit Mila* that is performed on the eighth day after birth (Abudarham).

The number eight represents the metaphysical world, following the seven days of Creation. Circumcision on the eighth day represents a new dimension of physical existence in which one is challenged to elevate one's own life, and more generally the physical world, to accord with the realm of the spirit, by embracing the covenant of Abraham. Unlike the ancient Greeks who regarded the physical body as perfectly formed from birth, we are commanded to elevate the imperfect body via *Brit Mila*. So too the Hanukka oil lasted for eight days, that number representing the Hasmonean triumph over the Greeks who idealized the natural body in its form at birth.

BRIT MILA

When the baby is brought in, all stand and say:

בָּרוּךְ הַבָּא BLESSED is the one who has arrived!

The mohel says:

Num. 25 וַיְדַבֵּר THE LORD SPOKE to Moses, saying: Pinehas the son of Elazar, the son of Aaron the priest, has turned My wrath away from the children of Israel, in that he was very jealous for My sake among them, so that I consumed not the children of Israel in My jealousy. Therefore say: Behold, I give to him My covenant of peace.

The baby is placed on Eliyahu's seat, and the Mohel says:

זֶה הַכִּסֵּא THIS IS THE THRONE of Elijah the prophet, who is remembered for good.

The mohel declares:

Gen. 49 *Ps. 119* לִישׁוּעָתְךָ I WAIT for Your salvation, O Lord. I hope for Your salvation,
O Lord, and I perform Your commandments. Elijah, angel of the
covenant, the one who belongs to you is in your presence. Stand
Ps. 119 to my right and be close to me. I hope for Your salvation, O Lord.
I rejoice at Your word, like one who finds great spoil. Those who
love Your law have great peace, and they have no stumbling-block.
Ps. 65 Happy is he whom You choose and bring near, that he may dwell in
Your courts.

All present respond:

May we be sated with the goodness of Your House, Your holy Temple.

This is why the Greeks forbade *Brit Mila*, and the Hellenizing Jews physically sought to reverse their own *Brit Mila* (Maharal).

פִּינְחָס – *Pinehas.* Pinḥas acts as protector of the Covenant at the first moment of confrontation with Canaanite idol worship and pagan culture. A rabbinic tradition (cf. Rashi, *Bava Metzia* 114b) identifies Pinḥas with Elijah, the ultimate zealot for God's covenant in its confrontation with *Ba'al* worship. A chair is set aside for Elijah at each *Brit*, and he is said to attend each (*Pirkei DeR. Eliezer* 29), either as a reward for his zeal for the Covenant, or as a rebuke for expressing despair with the nation's erstwhile neglect of the Covenant (cf. I Kings 19:10).

Father of the baby:

הִנְנִי מוּכָן וּמְזֻמָּן לְקַיֵּם מִצְוַת עֲשֵׂה שֶׁצִּוַּנִי הַבּוֹרֵא יִתְבָּרַךְ, לָמוֹל אֶת בְּנִי.

The מוהל:

אָמַר הַקָּדוֹשׁ בָּרוּךְ הוּא לְאַבְרָהָם אָבִינוּ, הִתְהַלֵּךְ לְפָנַי וֶהְיֵה תָמִים. הִנְנִי מוּכָן וּמְזֻמָּן לְקַיֵּם מִצְוַת עֲשֵׂה שֶׁצִּוָּנוּ הַבּוֹרֵא יִתְבָּרַךְ, לָמוֹל. בראשית יז

The baby is placed on the knees of the סנדק*, and the* מוהל *says:*

בָּרוּךְ אַתָּה יהוה אֱלֹהֵינוּ מֶלֶךְ הָעוֹלָם, אֲשֶׁר קִדְּשָׁנוּ בְּמִצְוֹתָיו וְצִוָּנוּ עַל הַמִּילָה.

Immediately after the circumcision, the father says:

בָּרוּךְ אַתָּה יהוה אֱלֹהֵינוּ מֶלֶךְ הָעוֹלָם, אֲשֶׁר קִדְּשָׁנוּ בְּמִצְוֹתָיו, וְצִוָּנוּ לְהַכְנִיסוֹ בִּבְרִיתוֹ שֶׁל אַבְרָהָם אָבִינוּ.

All present respond:

אָמֵן. כְּשֵׁם שֶׁנִּכְנַס לַבְּרִית, כֵּן יִכָּנֵס לְתוֹרָה וּלְחֻפָּה וּלְמַעֲשִׂים טוֹבִים.

After the circumcision has been completed, the מוהל *(or another honoree) takes a cup of wine and says:*

בָּרוּךְ אַתָּה יהוה אֱלֹהֵינוּ מֶלֶךְ הָעוֹלָם, בּוֹרֵא פְּרִי הַגָּפֶן.

בָּרוּךְ אַתָּה יהוה אֱלֹהֵינוּ מֶלֶךְ הָעוֹלָם, אֲשֶׁר קִדַּשׁ יְדִיד מִבֶּטֶן, וְחֹק בִּשְׁאֵרוֹ שָׂם, וְצֶאֱצָאָיו חָתַם בְּאוֹת בְּרִית קֹדֶשׁ. עַל

THE BERAKHOT OF BRIT MILA

The two *berakhot* of the circumcision refer to two separate aspects of the *mitzva*. At the circumcision of Abraham, the God says (Gen. 17:9–10), "You shall keep My covenant…. Every male among you shall be circumcised." The first phrase refers to the drawing of the blood immediately following the circumcision, while the second refers to the cutting of the foreskin. So too, the first *berakha* (עַל הַמִּילָה), recited by the *Mohel*, refers to the cutting of the foreskin, while the second (לְהַכְנִיסוֹ בִּבְרִיתוֹ), recited by the father, refers to the drawing of the blood, by which the child is inducted into the covenant of Abraham (R. Ḥayyim HaLevi Soloveitchik).

Cutting the foreskin represents that aspect of the covenant intended to counteract the destructive forces that arise within us. This is accomplished when we overcome our instincts

Father of the baby:

הִנְנִי I AM READY and prepared to fulfill the positive commandment which the Creator, blessed be He, has commanded me to perform, to circumcise my son.

The mohel:

Gen. 17 אָמַר THE HOLY ONE, blessed is He, said to Abraham our father, walk before Me and be whole-hearted. I am ready and prepared to fulfill the positive commandment of circumcision which the Creator, blessed be He, has commanded us to perform.

The baby is placed on the knees of the sandak, and the mohel says:

בָּרוּךְ BLESSED ARE YOU, Lord, our God, King of the universe, Who has sanctified us with His commandments, and has commanded us regarding circumcision.

Immediately after the circumcision, the father says:

בָּרוּךְ BLESSED ARE YOU, Lord, our God, King of the universe, Who has sanctified us with His commandments, and has commanded us to bring him into the covenant of Abraham our father.

All present respond:

אָמֵן JUST as he has entered into the covenant, so may he enter into Torah, the marriage canopy, and good deeds.

After the circumcision has been completed, the mohel (or another honoree) takes a cup of wine and says:

בָּרוּךְ BLESSED ARE YOU, Lord, our God, King of the universe, Who creates the fruit of the vine.

בָּרוּךְ BLESSED ARE YOU, Lord, our God, King of the universe, Who consecrated His beloved (Isaac) while still in the womb, and marked his flesh by means of the decree (of circumcision), and sealed his progeny with the sign of the holy covenant. Therefore as a reward for this act, dear living

---

by dedicating ourselves to a life of *mitzvot*. Separately, drawing the blood represents the covenant between God and the Jewish people, by which the suffering of every Jew is coupled with a commitment to serve God and perfect His world in accordance with His will (R. Ahron Soloveichik).

אֲשֶׁר קִדֵּשׁ יְדִיד מִבֶּטֶן – *Who consecrated His beloved (Isaac) while still in the womb*. The difference between this *berakha* following the act of circumcision and the preceding two *berakhot* is that the earlier ones are בִּרְכוֹת מִצְוָה (*berakhot* that precede the performance of a *mitzva*), whereas this one is a בִּרְכַּת שֶׁבַח (a *berakha* that praises God for a new reality that has come into existence). In this case, this refers to the fact that the circumcised child has become a בֶּן בְּרִית (member of the Covenant of Israel

כֵּן בִּשְׂכַר זֹאת, אֵל חַי חֶלְקֵנוּ צוּרֵנוּ צַוֵּה (נ״א צִוָּה) לְהַצִּיל יְדִידוּת שְׁאֵרֵנוּ מִשַּׁחַת, לְמַעַן בְּרִיתוֹ אֲשֶׁר שָׂם בִּבְשָׂרֵנוּ. בָּרוּךְ אַתָּה יהוה, כּוֹרֵת הַבְּרִית.

Giving the name:

אֱלֹהֵינוּ וֵאלֹהֵי אֲבוֹתֵינוּ, קַיֵּם אֶת הַיֶּלֶד הַזֶּה לְאָבִיו וּלְאִמּוֹ, וְיִקָּרֵא שְׁמוֹ בְּיִשְׂרָאֵל (פלוני בֶּן פלוני). יִשְׂמַח הָאָב בְּיוֹצֵא חֲלָצָיו
משלי כג וְתָגֵל אִמּוֹ בִּפְרִי בִטְנָהּ, כַּכָּתוּב: יִשְׂמַח־אָבִיךָ וְאִמֶּךָ, וְתָגֵל יוֹלַדְתֶּךָ:
וְנֶאֱמַר:

All respond (the phrases marked by arrows are recited aloud by those present, then repeated by the honoree):

יחזקאל טז וָאֶעֱבֹר עָלַיִךְ וָאֶרְאֵךְ מִתְבּוֹסֶסֶת בְּדָמָיִךְ, ◂ וָאֹמַר לָךְ בְּדָמַיִךְ חֲיִי,
תהלים קה וָאֹמַר לָךְ בְּדָמַיִךְ חֲיִי: ◂ וְנֶאֱמַר: זָכַר לְעוֹלָם בְּרִיתוֹ, דָּבָר צִוָּה לְאֶלֶף
דּוֹר: אֲשֶׁר כָּרַת אֶת־אַבְרָהָם, וּשְׁבוּעָתוֹ לְיִשְׂחָק: וַיַּעֲמִידֶהָ לְיַעֲקֹב
בראשית כא לְחֹק, לְיִשְׂרָאֵל בְּרִית עוֹלָם: וְנֶאֱמַר: וַיָּמָל אַבְרָהָם אֶת־יִצְחָק בְּנוֹ
תהלים קיח בֶּן־שְׁמֹנַת יָמִים, כַּאֲשֶׁר צִוָּה אֹתוֹ אֱלֹהִים: ◂ הוֹדוּ לַיהוה כִּי־טוֹב,
כִּי לְעוֹלָם חַסְדּוֹ: ◂

All respond:

הוֹדוּ לַיהוה כִּי־טוֹב, כִּי לְעוֹלָם חַסְדּוֹ:

The מוהל *(or honoree) continues:*

(פלוני בֶּן פלוני) זֶה הַקָּטָן גָּדוֹל יִהְיֶה,

All present respond:

כְּשֵׁם שֶׁנִּכְנַס לַבְּרִית, כֵּן יִכָּנֵס לְתוֹרָה וּלְחֻפָּה וּלְמַעֲשִׂים טוֹבִים.

The one who recited the blessings drinks some of the wine; some drops are given to the baby. The cup is then sent to the mother, who also drinks from it.

The מוהל *blesses the child:*

מִי שֶׁבֵּרַךְ אֲבוֹתֵינוּ אַבְרָהָם יִצְחָק וְיַעֲקֹב, הוּא יְבָרֵךְ אֶת הַיֶּלֶד הָרַךְ הַנִּמּוֹל (פלוני בֶּן פלונית) וְיִשְׁלַח לוֹ רְפוּאָה שְׁלֵמָה בַּעֲבוּר שֶׁנִּכְנַס לַבְּרִית, כֵּן יִכָּנֵס לְתוֹרָה וּלְחֻפָּה וּלְמַעֲשִׂים טוֹבִים. וְנֹאמַר אָמֵן.

---

that started with the circumcision of Isaac), and his קְדֻשַּׁת יִשְׂרָאֵל (sanctity as a Jew) has been raised to a higher level. Prior to this moment the uncircumcised child had been a Jew by birth, but as long as he would have remained uncircumcised his sanctity as a Jew would have been incomplete, and thus, for instance, he would have been disqualified from serving

The commentary continues on page 1068.

God Who is our Portion and our Rock, command (*some say:* Who has commanded) the salvation from destruction of our soul that is connected to our bodies, on account of His covenant that He has inscribed in our flesh. Blessed are You, Lord, Who establishes the covenant.

Giving the name:

אֱלֹהֵינוּ OUR GOD and the God of our fathers, safeguard this boy for his father and mother. He will be known among the Jewish people as (*baby's name*) the son of (*father's name*). May the father rejoice in the one who has come forth from his loins, and may his mother be gladdened by the fruit
Prov. 23 of her womb. As it is written: "Let your father and your mother be glad, and let her that bore you rejoice." And as it says:

All respond (the phrases marked by arrows are recited aloud by those present, then repeated by the honoree):

Ezek. 16 "AND WHEN I passed by you, and saw you wallowing in your blood, ▸ I said to you: 'In your blood, live; and I said to you: In your blood, live.'" ◂
Ps. 105 And as it further says: "He has remembered His covenant forever, the word that He has commanded to a thousand generations, which He made with Abraham, and His oath to Isaac, and He confirmed it to
Gen. 21 Jacob as a law, to Israel as an everlasting covenant." So too it says: "And Abraham circumcised his son Isaac when he was eight days old, as God
Ps. 118 had commanded him." ▸ Give thanks to the Lord, for He is good, for His loving-kindness is forever. ◂

All respond:

GIVE THANKS to the Lord, for He is good, for His loving-kindness is forever.

The mohel (or honoree) continues:

MAY this little one (*baby's name*) the son of (*father's name*) become great.

All present respond:

JUST as he has entered into the covenant, so may he enter into Torah, the marriage canopy, and good deeds.

The one who recited the blessings drinks some of the wine; some drops are given to the baby. The cup is then sent to the mother, who also drinks from it.

The mohel blesses the child:

מִי שֶׁבֵּרַךְ MAY HE Who blessed our fathers, Abraham, Isaac and Jacob, bless this tender circumcised boy (*baby's name*) the son of (*mother's name*), sending him a complete recovery in the merit of his having entered into the covenant. And just as he has entered into the covenant, so may he enter into Torah, the marriage canopy, and good deeds, and let us say, Amen.

ברכת המזון לברית מילה

יוֹם לְיַבָּשָׁה נֶהֶפְכוּ מְצוּלִים
שִׁירָה חֲדָשָׁה שִׁבְּחוּ גְאוּלִים.

הִטְבַּעְתָּ בְּתַרְמִית / רַגְלֵי בַּת עֲנָמִית
וּפַעֲמֵי שׁוּלַמִּית / יָפוּ בַּנְּעָלִים. שִׁירָה חֲדָשָׁה שִׁבְּחוּ גְאוּלִים.

וְכָל רוֹאֵי יְשׁוּרוּן / בְּעֵת הוֹדְךָ יְשָׁרוּן
אֵין כָּאֵל יְשֻׁרוּן / וְאוֹיְבֵינוּ פְּלִילִים. שִׁירָה חֲדָשָׁה שִׁבְּחוּ גְאוּלִים.

דְּגָלֵי כֵּן תָּרִים / עַל הַנִּשְׁאָרִים
וּתְלַקֵּט נִפְזָרִים / כִּמְלַקֵּט שִׁבֳּלִים. שִׁירָה חֲדָשָׁה שִׁבְּחוּ גְאוּלִים.

הַבָּאִים עִמְּךָ / בִּבְרִית חוֹתָמְךָ
וּמִבֶּטֶן לְשִׁמְךָ / הֵמָּה נִמּוֹלִים. שִׁירָה חֲדָשָׁה שִׁבְּחוּ גְאוּלִים.

הַרְאוּ אוֹתוֹתָם / לְכָל רוֹאֶה אוֹתָם
וְעַל כַּנְפֵי כְסוּתָם / עֲשׂוּ גְדִילִים. שִׁירָה חֲדָשָׁה שִׁבְּחוּ גְאוּלִים.

לְמִי זֹאת נִרְשֶׁמֶת / הַכֶּר נָא דְּבַר אֱמֶת
לְמִי הַחוֹתֶמֶת / וּלְמִי הַפְּתִילִים. שִׁירָה חֲדָשָׁה שִׁבְּחוּ גְאוּלִים.

וְשׁוּב שֵׁנִית לְקַדְּשָׁהּ / וְאַל תּוֹסֵף לְגָרְשָׁהּ
וְהַעֲלֵה אוֹר שִׁמְשָׁהּ / וְנָסוּ הַצְּלָלִים. שִׁירָה חֲדָשָׁה שִׁבְּחוּ גְאוּלִים.

יְדִידִים רוֹמְמוּךָ / בְּשִׁירָה קִדְּמוּךָ
מִי כָּמֹכָה / יהוה בָּאֵלִים. שִׁירָה חֲדָשָׁה שִׁבְּחוּ גְאוּלִים.

בִּגְלַל אָבוֹת תּוֹשִׁיעַ בָּנִים, וְתָבִיא גְאֻלָּה לִבְנֵי בְנֵיהֶם.

---

in the Temple. But once circumcised, his Jewish sanctity has been completed, a reality and status which this *berakha* celebrates and praises. It thus does not precede the circumcision, but follows it, once the new status is in place (R. Joseph B. Soloveitchik).

יוֹם לְיַבָּשָׁה נֶהֶפְכוּ מְצוּלִים – *The day the depths turned to dry land.* This poem was crafted by R. Yehuda HaLevi (eleventh to twelfth century), whose name appears in the acrostic formed by the initial letters. It is customarily recited at the *Brit Mila* meal, because (a) it speaks of *Brit Mila*, and (b) the opening words refer to the splitting of the sea which, according to the Midrash, was in the merit of the Covenant of circumcision.

CIRCUMCISION FEAST

יוֹם לְיַבָּשָׁה ON THE day that the deep waters became dry land,
Those who were redeemed gave praise with a new song.

DROWNED in her deceit were the Anamite daughter's feet,
while the footsteps of the Shulamit were secured in their shoes.
Those who were redeemed gave praise with a new song.

THEREFORE will all who see Yeshurun give praise in My House of Glory,
declaring "There is none like Yeshurun's God" when our enemies will be judged.
Those who were redeemed gave praise with a new song.

SURELY You will raise our banners over those who will remain,
when You will gather our dispersed as one who brings sheaves together.
Those who were redeemed gave praise with a new song.

THOSE who go with You bear Your seal of the covenant,
being circumcised they are dedicated to Your name from the womb.
Those who were redeemed gave praise with a new song.

MAKE KNOWN their sign of the covenant to all who will see them,
just as they in turn make fringes on the corners of their garments.
Those who were redeemed gave praise with a new song.

TO WHOM is this one assigned, please recognize the truth,
Whose is this seal, and Whose these threads?
Those who were redeemed gave praise with a new song.

RETURN once more to betroth her, do not again send her away;
make the light of her sun arise once more, that the shadows flee away.
Those who were redeemed gave praise with a new song.

YOUR BELOVED ones raised You on high, greeted You with song, saying,
Who is like You, O Lord, among the mighty ones?
Those who were redeemed gave praise with a new song.

ON ACCOUNT of the fathers please save the children
and bring redemption to their children's children.

עָשׂוּ גְּדִילִים – *They will make fringes.* The eight-stringed fringes and *Brit Mila* on the eighth day share a common eight-themed symbolism with the splitting of the sea which occurred on the eighth day following the *Pesaḥ* sacrifice (R. Mordechai Willig).

זימון לסעודת ברית מילה

The zimmun when three or more men are present:

Leader רַבּוֹתַי, נְבָרֵךְ.

Others יְהִי שֵׁם יהוה מְבֹרָךְ מֵעַתָּה וְעַד־עוֹלָם: תהלים קיג

Leader יְהִי שֵׁם יהוה מְבֹרָךְ מֵעַתָּה וְעַד־עוֹלָם:

Leader then others נוֹדֶה לְשִׁמְךָ בְּתוֹךְ אֱמוּנַי, בְּרוּכִים אַתֶּם לַיהוה.

Leader **בִּרְשׁוּת** אֵל אָיֹם וְנוֹרָא / מִשְׂגָּב לְעִתּוֹת בַּצָּרָה
אֵל נֶאְזָר בִּגְבוּרָה / אַדִּיר בַּמָּרוֹם יהוה.

Others נוֹדֶה לְשִׁמְךָ בְּתוֹךְ אֱמוּנַי, בְּרוּכִים אַתֶּם לַיהוה.

Leader **בִּרְשׁוּת** הַתּוֹרָה הַקְּדוֹשָׁה / טְהוֹרָה הִיא וְגַם פְּרוּשָׁה
צִוָּה לָנוּ מוֹרָשָׁה / מֹשֶׁה עֶבֶד יהוה.

Others נוֹדֶה לְשִׁמְךָ בְּתוֹךְ אֱמוּנַי, בְּרוּכִים אַתֶּם לַיהוה.

Leader **בִּרְשׁוּת** הַכֹּהֲנִים וְהַלְוִיִּם / אֶקְרָא לֵאלֹהֵי הָעִבְרִיִּים
אֲהוֹדֶנּוּ בְּכָל אִיִּים / אֲבָרְכָה אֶת יהוה.

Others נוֹדֶה לְשִׁמְךָ בְּתוֹךְ אֱמוּנַי, בְּרוּכִים אַתֶּם לַיהוה.

Leader **בִּרְשׁוּת** מָרָנָן וְרַבָּנָן וְרַבּוֹתַי / אֶפְתְּחָה בְּשִׁיר פִּי וּשְׂפָתַי
וְתֹאמַרְנָה עַצְמוֹתַי / בָּרוּךְ הַבָּא בְּשֵׁם יהוה.

Others נוֹדֶה לְשִׁמְךָ בְּתוֹךְ אֱמוּנַי, בְּרוּכִים אַתֶּם לַיהוה.

Leader בִּרְשׁוּת מָרָנָן וְרַבָּנָן וְרַבּוֹתַי נְבָרֵךְ (במנין: אֱלֹהֵינוּ) שֶׁאָכַלְנוּ מִשֶּׁלּוֹ.

Others בָּרוּךְ (במנין: אֱלֹהֵינוּ) שֶׁאָכַלְנוּ מִשֶּׁלּוֹ וּבְטוּבוֹ חָיִינוּ.

Leader בָּרוּךְ (במנין: אֱלֹהֵינוּ) שֶׁאָכַלְנוּ מִשֶּׁלּוֹ וּבְטוּבוֹ חָיִינוּ.
בָּרוּךְ הוּא וּבָרוּךְ שְׁמוֹ.

Continue with ברכת המזון *on page 222 until* בְּעֵינֵי אֱלֹהִים וְאָדָם *on page 232. Then continue on the next page.*

BIRKAT HAMAZON FOR BRIT MILA

נוֹדֶה לְשִׁמְךָ – *We give thanks to Your name.* There are indications that this poem, originating in twelfth- or thirteenth-century France, was recited by Polish Jews following all festive meals. Over time, the custom was discontinued except at circumcisions, insofar as the circumcision meal is accorded particular significance and joy (*Shabbat* 130a). It also reflects the custom in the ancient world to partake of a shared meal following covenantal ceremonies (R. Joshua Berman).

GRACE FOR THE CIRCUMCISION MEAL

The zimmun when three or more men are present:

Leader: רַבּוֹתַי ESTEEMED COMPANIONS, let us say grace.

Ps. 113 *Others:* BLESSED be the name of the Lord from now and forevermore.

Leader: BLESSED be the name of the Lord from now and forevermore.

Leader then others: WE GIVE THANKS to Your name among my faithful ones, blessed are you to the Lord

Leader: WITH THE PERMISSION of the God Who is awesome and revered, / a fortress whenever there is trouble, / God Who is girded in might, / mighty is the Lord on high.

Others: WE GIVE THANKS to Your name among my faithful ones, blessed are you to the Lord

Leader: WITH THE PERMISSION of the sacred Torah, / which is both pure and clear, / and which Moses, the servant of the Lord, / commanded us as our inheritance.

Others: WE GIVE THANKS to Your name among my faithful ones, blessed are you to the Lord

Leader: WITH THE PERMISSION of the *Kohanim* and Levites, / I call upon the God of the Hebrews / to Whom I give thanks in every island, / and bless the Lord.

Others: WE GIVE THANKS to Your name among my faithful ones, blessed are you to the Lord

Leader: WITH YOUR PERMISSION my masters, teachers, and esteemed companions / I will open my mouth and my lips in song, / and my bones will declare / "Blessed is the one who comes in the name of the Lord."

Others: WE GIVE THANKS to Your name among my faithful ones, blessed are you to the Lord

Leader: With your permission masters, teachers, and esteemed companions let us bless (*with a minyan:* our God) the One of Whose bounty we have partaken.

Others: BLESSED be (*in a minyan:* our God,) the One of Whose bounty we have partaken and through Whose goodness we live.

Leader: BLESSED be (*in a minyan:* our God,) the One of Whose bounty we have partaken and through Whose goodness we live.
Blessed be He, and blessed be His name.

Continue with Birkat HaMazon on page 223 until "in the eyes of God and man" on page 232. Then continue on the next page.

Someone other than the father says:

הָרַחֲמָן הוּא יְבָרֵךְ אֲבִי הַיֶּלֶד וְאִמּוֹ
וְיִזְכּוּ לְגַדְּלוֹ וּלְחַנְּכוֹ וּלְחַכְּמוֹ
מִיּוֹם הַשְּׁמִינִי וָהָלְאָה יֵרָצֶה דָמוֹ / וִיהִי יהוה אֱלֹהָיו עִמּוֹ.

Someone other than the סנדק *says:*

הָרַחֲמָן הוּא יְבָרֵךְ בַּעַל בְּרִית הַמִּילָה
אֲשֶׁר שָׂשׂ לַעֲשׂוֹת צֶדֶק בְּגִילָה
וִישַׁלֵּם פָּעֳלוֹ וּמַשְׂכֻּרְתּוֹ כְּפוּלָה / וְיִתְּנֵהוּ לְמַעְלָה לְמָעְלָה.

הָרַחֲמָן הוּא יְבָרֵךְ רַךְ הַנִּמּוֹל לִשְׁמוֹנָה
וְיִהְיוּ יָדָיו וְלִבּוֹ לָאֵל אֱמוּנָה
וְיִזְכֶּה לִרְאוֹת פְּנֵי הַשְּׁכִינָה / שָׁלֹשׁ פְּעָמִים בַּשָּׁנָה.

Someone other than the מוהל *says:*

הָרַחֲמָן הוּא יְבָרֵךְ הַמָּל בְּשַׂר הָעָרְלָה
וּפָרַע וּמָצַץ דְּמֵי הַמִּילָה
אִישׁ הַיָּרֵא וְרַךְ הַלֵּבָב עֲבוֹדָתוֹ פְּסוּלָה
אִם שְׁלָשׁ אֵלֶּה לֹא יַעֲשֶׂה לָהּ.

הָרַחֲמָן הוּא יִשְׁלַח לָנוּ מְשִׁיחוֹ הוֹלֵךְ תָּמִים
בִּזְכוּת חֲתַן לַמּוּלוֹת דָּמִים
לְבַשֵּׂר בְּשׂוֹרוֹת טוֹבוֹת וְנִחוּמִים
לְעַם אֶחָד מְפֻזָּר וּמְפֹרָד בֵּין הָעַמִּים.

הָרַחֲמָן הוּא יִשְׁלַח לָנוּ כֹּהֵן צֶדֶק אֲשֶׁר לֻקַּח לְעֵילֹם
עַד הוּכַן כִּסְאוֹ כַּשֶּׁמֶשׁ וְיַהֲלֹם
וַיָּלֶט פָּנָיו בְּאַדַּרְתּוֹ וַיִּגְלֹם / בְּרִיתִי הָיְתָה אִתּוֹ הַחַיִּים וְהַשָּׁלוֹם.

Continue with הָרַחֲמָן הוּא יְזַכֵּנוּ לִימוֹת הַמָּשִׁיחַ *on page 232.*
On שבת, ראש חודש *or* יום טוב, *continue with the appropriate* הָרַחֲמָן *on page 232.*
The Leader then recites the blessing over wine before drinking,
and then recites ברכה מעין שלוש, *page 234.*

הָרַחֲמָן / THE COMPASSIONATE ONE
At the end of every *Birkat HaMazon*, it is customary to insert prayers calling upon הָרַחֲמָן, the Compassionate One, to bless the nation, participants in a meal, or the particular festive day. The following brief and poetic prayers are

Someone other than the father says:

הָרַחֲמָן MAY THE COMPASSIONATE ONE bless the father and mother / of the boy, to merit raising and educating him to attain wisdom. / From this eighth day onward may his (circumcision) blood be accepted, / so that the Lord his God be with him.

Someone other than the sandak says:

MAY THE COMPASSIONATE ONE bless the *Sandak* who officiated during the *Brit Mila,* / while rejoicing in the performance of a righteous deed with joy. / May He reward his deed in double measure, / raising him ever higher.

MAY THE COMPASSIONATE ONE bless the tender boy circumcised on the eighth day. / May his hands and heart be faithful to God, / and merit seeing the Divine Presence / three times a year.

Someone other than the mohel says:

MAY THE COMPASSIONATE ONE bless the one who circumcised the flesh, / and also uncovered the membrane and drew the blood of circumcision. / Had he been fearful and faint-hearted and thus failed to perform / all three acts, his labors would have been disqualified.

MAY THE COMPASSIONATE ONE send us the anointed Messiah of perfect faith, / in the merit of the one whose circumcision blood has initiated him. / May the Messiah be the herald of good news and consolation / for the singular nation scattered and dispersed among the nations.

MAY THE COMPASSIONATE ONE send us Elijah the righteous *Kohen* who went into hiding / to reappear as bright as the sun and a diamond whenever a chair would be prepared for him. / It was he who covered his face with his cloak when he heard God say / "My covenant of life and peace will accompany him."

Continue with "May the Compassionate One make us worthy of the Messianic Age" on page 233.

On Shabbat, Rosh Ḥodesh or Yom Tov, continue with the appropriate "May the Compassionate One" on page 233.

The Leader then recites the blessing over wine before drinking, and then recites Al HaGefen, page 235.

---

recited in honor of the *Brit Mila* celebration. The author, Abraham ben Isaac HaKohen, or Kohen-Tzedek, is recalled in an acrostic formed by each stanza. The first and fourth stanzas respectively bless the father and the *mohel* who fulfill the divine command. The second one blesses the *sandak*, whose lap serves as the "altar" and basis for the *Mila*. The fifth stanza blesses the Messiah, who will facilitate optimal divine service. Finally, the third and sixth stanzas respectively bless the circumcised child and Elijah, the righteous priest, the ultimate teacher. These figures are tasked with conveying and fulfilling the divine revelation.

סדר פדיון הבן

A firstborn male child, must be redeemed on the 31st day of his birth – unless the father is a כהן or לוי, or the mother is a daughter of a כהן or a לוי. If the 31st day falls on שבת or יום טוב, the ceremony is postponed to the following weekday.

The father, presenting his child to the כהן, declares:

זֶה בְּנִי בְכוֹרִי הוּא פֶּטֶר רֶחֶם לְאִמּוֹ, וְהַקָּדוֹשׁ בָּרוּךְ הוּא צִוָּה
לִפְדּוֹתוֹ, שֶׁנֶּאֱמַר, וּפְדוּיָו מִבֶּן־חֹדֶשׁ תִּפְדֶּה, בְּעֶרְכְּךָ כֶּסֶף חֲמֵשֶׁת במדבר יח
שְׁקָלִים בְּשֶׁקֶל הַקֹּדֶשׁ, עֶשְׂרִים גֵּרָה הוּא: וְנֶאֱמַר, קַדֶּשׁ־לִי כָל־בְּכוֹר שמות יג
פֶּטֶר כָּל־רֶחֶם בִּבְנֵי יִשְׂרָאֵל בָּאָדָם וּבַבְּהֵמָה, לִי הוּא:

The כהן then asks the father:

מַאי בָּעֵית טְפֵי, לִתֵּן לִי בִּנְךָ בְּכוֹרְךָ שֶׁהוּא פֶּטֶר רֶחֶם לְאִמּוֹ, אוֹ בָּעֵית לִפְדּוֹתוֹ בְּעַד חָמֵשׁ סְלָעִים, כִּדְמְחֻיַּבְתְּ מִדְּאוֹרָיְתָא.

The father replies:

חָפֵץ אֲנִי לִפְדּוֹת אֶת בְּנִי, וְהֵילָךְ דְּמֵי פִדְיוֹנוֹ כִּדְמְחֻיַּבְנָא מִדְּאוֹרָיְתָא.

Holding the redemption money, the father says:

בָּרוּךְ אַתָּה יהוה אֱלֹהֵינוּ מֶלֶךְ הָעוֹלָם, אֲשֶׁר קִדְּשָׁנוּ בְּמִצְוֹתָיו וְצִוָּנוּ עַל פִּדְיוֹן הַבֵּן.

בָּרוּךְ אַתָּה יהוה אֱלֹהֵינוּ מֶלֶךְ הָעוֹלָם, שֶׁהֶחֱיָנוּ וְקִיְּמָנוּ וְהִגִּיעָנוּ לַזְּמַן הַזֶּה.

The redemption money is given to the כהן, who then returns the child to his father.

זֶה תַּחַת זֶה. זֶה חִלּוּף זֶה. זֶה מָחוּל עַל זֶה. וְיִכָּנֵס זֶה הַבֵּן לַחַיִּים, לְתוֹרָה וּלְיִרְאַת שָׁמַיִם. יְהִי רָצוֹן שֶׁכְּשֵׁם שֶׁנִּכְנַס לְפִדְיוֹן, כֵּן יִכָּנֵס לְתוֹרָה וּלְחֻפָּה וּלְמַעֲשִׂים טוֹבִים.

פִּדְיוֹן הַבֵּן / REDEMPTION OF THE FIRSTBORN
Pidyon HaBen reenacts the drama of the Binding of Isaac. The presentation of the child to the *Kohen* is symbolic of Abraham's

חֲמֵשֶׁת שְׁקָלִים / FIVE SHEKELS OF SILVER
There is some dispute as to how much silver is needed for a valid *Pidyon HaBen*, with opinions ranging from 100 grams to 117 grams, and the use of five pre-1936 United States silver dollars certainly satisfies all of the halakhic views, as do many other coins.

PIDYON HABEN

A firstborn male child, must be redeemed on the 31st day of his birth – unless the father is a Kohen or Levi, or the mother is a daughter of a Kohen or a Levi. If the 31st day falls on Shabbat or Yom Tov, the ceremony is postponed to the following weekday.
The father, presenting his child to the Kohen, declares:

זֶה THIS is my firstborn son, the first to issue from his mother's womb. The Holy One, blessed is He, has commanded to redeem him, as it says,
Num. 18 "And their redemption-money – from a month old shall you redeem them – shall be, according to your valuation, five shekels of silver, after the shekel of the Sanctuary, which is twenty gerahs." And as it further
Ex. 13 says, "Sanctify to Me all the firstborn, the first issue of every womb among the children of Israel, both of man and of beast, it is Mine."

The Kohen then asks the father:

מַאי WHICH do you prefer: to give your firstborn son, who is the first issue of his mother's womb, to me, or do you prefer to redeem him for five Selas, as you are obligated by Torah law?

The father replies:

חָפֵץ I WISH to redeem my son, and accordingly I give you the money to effect his redemption in accordance with my obligation by Torah law.

Holding the redemption money, the father says:

בָּרוּךְ BLESSED ARE YOU, Lord, our God, King of the universe, Who has sanctified us with His commandments, and has commanded us regarding the redemption of a son.

בָּרוּךְ BLESSED ARE YOU, Lord, our God, King of the universe, Who has given us life, sustained us, and brought us to this time.

The redemption money is given to the Kohen, who then returns the child to his father.

זֶה THIS (silver) is in place of this (child). This (silver) is in exchange for this (child). This (child) is desanctified because of this (silver). As a result of this exchange may this boy be initiated fully into life, Torah, and the fear of Heaven. May it be God's will that just as he has been initiated into being redeemed, so may he be initiated into Torah, Ḥuppa, and good deeds.

---

performance. The father of today, as Abraham of old, acknowledges God's absolute ownership of the child. God wills the consecration of the firstborn son because the emotional

Placing his right hand on the head of the child, the כהן *blesses him as follows:*

בראשית מח / במדבר ו — **יְשִׂמְךָ** אֱלֹהִים כְּאֶפְרַיִם וְכִמְנַשֶּׁה: יְבָרֶכְךָ יהוה וְיִשְׁמְרֶךָ: יָאֵר יהוה
משלי ג — פָּנָיו אֵלֶיךָ וִיחֻנֶּךָּ: יִשָּׂא יהוה פָּנָיו אֵלֶיךָ וְיָשֵׂם לְךָ שָׁלוֹם: כִּי
תהלים קכא — אֹרֶךְ יָמִים וּשְׁנוֹת חַיִּים וְשָׁלוֹם יוֹסִיפוּ לָךְ: יהוה יִשְׁמָרְךָ מִכָּל־רָע,
יִשְׁמֹר אֶת־נַפְשֶׁךָ:

The כהן *takes a cup of wine and says:*

בָּרוּךְ אַתָּה יהוה אֱלֹהֵינוּ מֶלֶךְ הָעוֹלָם, בּוֹרֵא פְּרִי הַגָּפֶן.

סדר זבד הבת

The ספר טעמי המנהגים *records the view of the* מאור הגדול *that it is appropriate to celebrate the birth and/or naming of a baby girl with a* סעודה*, "with song and praise of God." Among certain* ספרדים *(see the commentary) this took the following form, known as* זבד הבת*. The* מִי שֶׁבֵּרַךְ *for naming the baby (page 538) may be recited here, even if it has been recited already in the* בית כנסת*, when the father – whether or not in the presence of the mother – received an* עליה*.*

Leader:

שיר השירים ב — **יוֹנָתִי** בְּחַגְוֵי הַסֶּלַע, בְּסֵתֶר הַמַּדְרֵגָה, הַרְאִינִי אֶת־מַרְאַיִךְ,
הַשְׁמִיעִנִי אֶת־קוֹלֵךְ, כִּי־קוֹלֵךְ עָרֵב וּמַרְאֵיךְ נָאוֶה:

If this is their first daughter, the mother or father adds:

שיר השירים ו — **אַחַת** הִיא יוֹנָתִי תַמָּתִי, אַחַת הִיא לְאִמָּהּ, בָּרָה הִיא לְיוֹלַדְתָּהּ,
רָאוּהָ בָנוֹת וַיְאַשְּׁרוּהָ, מְלָכוֹת וּפִילַגְשִׁים וַיְהַלְלוּהָ:

בראשית כד — **וַיְבָרְכוּ** אֶת־רִבְקָה וַיֹּאמְרוּ לָהּ אֲחֹתֵנוּ אַתְּ, הֲיִי לְאַלְפֵי רְבָבָה,
וְיִירַשׁ זַרְעֵךְ אֵת שַׁעַר שֹׂנְאָיו:

---

involvement of the parent with his firstborn is of the most intricate and intimate nature, and the closer the relation and the more deep-rooted the commitment of the father to the child, the more sublime and hallowed is the sacrifice. When the *Kohen* returns the child to the father and accepts the five shekels, he presents him on behalf of God with a new child; something precious is re-entrusted to him. The dialectical drama of Mount Moriah consisting in losing and finding a son is re-staged in all its magnificence (R. Joseph B. Soloveitchik).

זבד הבת / CELEBRATION OF THE BIRTH OF A GIRL

R. Yaakov Emden of Altona (1697–1776) records a ceremony that he had witnessed among Sephardim marking the birth of a girl. Relatives would visit the mother and her newborn daughter on Shabbat, when treats would be distributed to children, and verses of blessing were recited together with a special *Mi Sheberakh* blessing. In some communities this ceremony was held on the day of the naming or on the baby's thirtieth day of life. The

Placing his right hand on the head of the child, the Kohen blesses him as follows:

Gen. 48 Num. 6 יְשִׂמְךָ MAY God make you like Ephraim and Menashe. May the Lord bless you and keep you. May the Lord make His countenance shine upon you and be gracious to you. May the Lord lift up His countenance to you and
Prov. 3 give you peace. For length of days, years of life, and peace He will increase
Ps. 121 for you. The Lord will guard you from all evil. He will guard your soul.

The Kohen takes a cup of wine and says:

בָּרוּךְ BLESSED ARE YOU, Lord, our God, King of the universe, Who creates the fruit of the vine.

ZEVED HABAT

The Sefer Ta'amei HaMinhagim records the view of the Maor HaGadol that it is appropriate to celebrate the birth and/or naming of a baby girl with a festive meal, "with song and praise of God." Among certain Sephardim (see the commentary) this took the following form, known as Zeved HaBat. The Mi Sheberakh prayer for naming the baby (page 539) may be recited here, even if it has been recited already in the synagogue, when the father – whether or not in the presence of the mother – was called to the Torah.

Leader:

Song. 2 יוֹנָתִי O MY DOVE, who is in the clefts of the rock, in the covert of the cliff, let me see your countenance, let me hear your voice; for sweet is your voice, and your countenance is comely.

If this is their first daughter, the mother or father adds:

Song. 6 אַחַת MY DOVE, my undefiled, is but one; she is the only one of her mother; she is the choice one of her that bore her. The daughters saw her, and called her happy; the queens and the concubines, and they praised her.

Gen. 24 וַיְבָרְכוּ AND THEY BLESSED Rebecca, and said to her: "Our sister, may you be the mother of thousands of ten thousands, and may your seed possess the gate of those that hate them."

---

baby would be placed in a basket and passed around among the participants, each of whom would bless the baby with health and longevity, placing a coin in the basket as a gift for the mother. Hence the ceremony was referred to as a *Zeved HaBat*, a Hebraization of the original Spanish *El Pagamiento*, "the payment." See too Genesis 30:20 ("*zeved tov*") and the commentaries thereon (Sarah Hammer).

יוֹנָתִי – *O my dove.* The love poetry of the Song of Songs is taken by most classic commentators as a metaphor for the vicissitudes of the relationship between God and the Jewish people. The verse citations, and the hymn of *Yefat Ayin*, appear to cast the new arrival of a baby girl as a metaphor for the beloved in the Song of Songs, representing the Jewish nation.

Leader:

מִי שֶׁבֵּרַךְ אִמּוֹתֵינוּ שָׂרָה רִבְקָה, רָחֵל וְלֵאָה וּמִרְיָם הַנְּבִיאָה וַאֲבִיגַיִל וְאֶסְתֵּר הַמַּלְכָּה בַּת אֲבִיחַיִל, הוּא יְבָרֵךְ אֶת הַיַּלְדָּה הַנְּעִימָה הַזֹּאת, וְיִקָּרֵא שְׁמָהּ בְּיִשְׂרָאֵל (פלונית בַּת פלוני) בְּמַזָּל טוֹב וּבִשְׁעַת בְּרָכָה, וִיגַדְּלוּהָ לְתוֹרָה וּלְמִצְוֹת בִּבְרִיאוּת, שָׁלוֹם וּמְנוּחָה, וִיזַכֶּה אֶת אָבִיהָ וְאֶת אִמָּהּ לִרְאוֹת בְּשִׂמְחָתָהּ וּבְחֻפָּתָהּ, בְּבָנִים וּבְבָנוֹת, עֹשֶׁר וְכָבוֹד. עוֹד יְנוּבוּן בְּשֵׂיבָה, דְּשֵׁנִים וְרַעֲנַנִּים יִהְיוּ, וְכֵן יְהִי רָצוֹן וְנֹאמַר, אָמֵן. תהלים צב

If the mother did not recite ברכת הגומל *yet, she recites it in the presence of a* מנין *of men (Minḥat Shlomo 2–3:60:10).*

בָּרוּךְ אַתָּה יהוה אֱלֹהֵינוּ מֶלֶךְ הָעוֹלָם הַגּוֹמֵל לְחַיָּבִים טוֹבוֹת, שֶׁגְּמָלַנִי כָּל טוֹב.

Those present respond:

אָמֵן. מִי שֶׁגְּמָלֵךְ כָּל טוֹב הוּא יִגְמְלֵךְ כָּל טוֹב, סֶלָה.

The parents each put their hands on their newborn child's head and bless her:

במדבר ו **יְשִׂמֵךְ** אֱלֹהִים כְּשָׂרָה רִבְקָה רָחֵל וְלֵאָה. יְבָרֶכְךָ יהוה וְיִשְׁמְרֶךָ: יָאֵר יהוה פָּנָיו אֵלֶיךָ וִיחֻנֶּךָּ: יִשָּׂא יהוה פָּנָיו אֵלֶיךָ, וְיָשֵׂם לְךָ שָׁלוֹם:

יְפַת עַיִן לִבַּבְתִּינִי / זֹהַר פָּנַיִךְ הַרְאִינִי
בְּעִיר צִיּוֹן שִׁיר הַרְנִינִי / וְאָז אָשִׁיב שְׁבוּתֵךְ שָׁם

שִׁבַּרְתִּי לִגְאֻלָּתֵךְ / קְרוֹבָה יְשׁוּעָתֵךְ
אֵלַי שׁוּבָה לִמְנוּחָתֵךְ / בִּגְדֵי יֶשַׁע הַלְבִּישֵׁנִי

עוּרִי כַלָּה בַּת אֲהוּבָה / חִזְקִי וְשׁוּבִי בִתְשׁוּבָה
וְלָךְ יִקָּרֵא חֶפְצִי בָהּ / לְמוּל קוֹלֵךְ הַשְׁמִיעִינִי

יָהּ בְּנֵה לִי בֵּית תִּפְאַרְתִּי / וְהָשֵׁב אֶת עֲבוֹדָתִי
וְשָׁם אָשִׁיר אֶת שִׁירָתִי / אֶמְצָא חֵן כִּי נִחַמְתָּנִי

יְפַת עַיִן – *You, of beautiful eye.* This *pizmon* originated in the Syrian Jewish community, and was composed by R. Ezra ben Yeshaya Attiya of Aleppo (d. 1874), a scion of the distinguished Attiya rabbinical family and a prolific *paytan.* It refers to aspects of the feminine metaphor in Jewish mystical thought, including the Jewish people as the betrothed of God (stanzas 1 and 3) and the *Shekhina*, the "feminine" aspect of the Divine that dwells within physical reality (stanzas 2 and 4). In imagery and language borrowed from the

Leader:

מִי שֶׁבֵּרַךְ MAY He Who blessed our mothers Sarah, Rebecca, Rachel, Leah, Miriam the Prophetess, and Queen Esther daughter of Aviḥayil, bless this pleasant child, and she will be known among the Jewish people by the name (*baby's name*) daughter of (*baby's father's name*), at an auspicious time and in a time of blessing, and may she be raised to Torah and commandments in good health, peace and tranquility, and may her father and mother merit to witness her in joy and under the marriage canopy, with sons and daughters,
Ps. 92 wealth and honor. "They will still bring forth fruit in old age. They will be fat and flourishing." And may it be His will, and let us say, Amen.

If the mother did not recite the HaGomel blessing yet, she recites it in the presence of a minyan of men (Minḥat Shlomo 2–3:60:10).

בָּרוּךְ BLESSED are You, Lord, our God, King of the universe, Who bestows favors on the undeserving, and Who has bestowed every good thing on me.

Those present respond:

Amen. May He Who has bestowed every good thing on you continue to grant you every good thing, forever.

The parents each put their hands on their newborn child's head and bless her:

Num. 6 יְשִׂימֵךְ MAY God make you like Sarah, Rebecca, Rachel, and Leah. May the Lord bless you and keep you. May the Lord make His countenance shine upon you and be gracious to you. May the Lord lift up His countenance to you and give you peace.

יְפַת עַיִן YOU, OF BEAUTIFUL EYE, have captured my heart,
Show me your glowing coutenance!
Sing your joyful song in the city of Zion,
Then will I return your captivity to there.
I have hoped for your redemption, / Your salvation is near,
My God, return to Your resting place,
Clothe me in garments of salvation.
Awaken, bride, beloved daughter, / Be strong and return through repentance,
You will be called Hefzibah, / Let me hear your voice facing me!
Build me my glorious house, God, / And restore my worship,
And I will sing my song there,
I will find favor, for You will have comforted me.

Song of Songs the poem alternatively reflects God's call to the Jewish nation to return to Him; and the Jews' call to God to return His presence to Zion.

סעודת הודיה

When a person has experienced Divine Providence (see A MEAL OF PERSONAL THANKSGIVING *below), it is appropriate to invite guests to a festive meal, and in their presence to tell of that deliverance while expressing gratitude to God. One should, where appropriate, recite* ברכת הגומל *(see page 162). In addition, Psalms 30, 100, and 107 (pages 1216, 1282, 1292, respectively) are particularly appropriate for this occasion. Torah study should also be part of such an event.*

סדר חנוכת הבית

What follows here is a suggested liturgy based on one found in the סידור מנחת ירושלים*.*
Before affixing the first מזוזה*, the following verse is recited responsively, led by the homeowner:*

תהלים צ **וִיהִי נֹעַם** אֲדֹנָי אֱלֹהֵינוּ עָלֵינוּ וּמַעֲשֵׂה יָדֵינוּ כּוֹנְנָה עָלֵינוּ וּמַעֲשֵׂה
יָדֵינוּ כּוֹנְנֵהוּ:

תהלים צא **יֹשֵׁב** בְּסֵתֶר עֶלְיוֹן, בְּצֵל שַׁדַּי יִתְלוֹנָן: אֹמַר לַיהוה מַחְסִי וּמְצוּדָתִי,
אֱלֹהַי אֶבְטַח־בּוֹ: כִּי הוּא יַצִּילְךָ מִפַּח יָקוּשׁ, מִדֶּבֶר הַוּוֹת:
בְּאֶבְרָתוֹ יָסֶךְ לָךְ, וְתַחַת־כְּנָפָיו תֶּחְסֶה, צִנָּה וְסֹחֵרָה אֲמִתּוֹ: לֹא־
תִירָא מִפַּחַד לָיְלָה, מֵחֵץ יָעוּף יוֹמָם: מִדֶּבֶר בָּאֹפֶל יַהֲלֹךְ, מִקֶּטֶב
יָשׁוּד צָהֳרָיִם: יִפֹּל מִצִּדְּךָ אֶלֶף, וּרְבָבָה מִימִינֶךָ, אֵלֶיךָ לֹא יִגָּשׁ: רַק

A MEAL OF PERSONAL THANKSGIVING

The Gemara (*Berakhot* 54b) states that one who has been delivered from any of four kinds of life-threatening experiences should recite *Birkat HaGomel*. While the Temple stood, as stipulated in Leviticus 6:11–15 (and echoed in Psalm 116:11–19) an animal and grain offering was offered on the altar, with its remainder to be feasted upon by invited guests by midnight of that day within the confines of Jerusalem. In the absence of a Temple service the custom arose to invite guests to a similar "meal of gratitude."

Interestingly, there is a historical echo of this practice, from the earliest days of the American experience, in a Jewish context. As Prof. Moshe Sokolow has pointed out, when the Pilgrims arrived in America in 1620 they celebrated their safe deliverance with a meal of thanksgiving to God, at which they recited the entirely apposite Psalm 107. In doing so they specifically referenced Rambam's *Hilkhot Berakhot* 10:8 as noted on a copy of the Psalms that they had, and that included the notes of the Puritan scholar Henry Ainsworth referencing Rambam, whose writings he greatly admired.

A MEAL OF PERSONAL THANKSGIVING

When a person has experienced Divine Providence (see A MEAL OF PERSONAL THANKSGIVING *below), it is appropriate to invite guests to a festive meal, and in their presence to tell of that deliverance while expressing gratitude to God. One should, where appropriate, recite Birkat HaGomel (see page 163). In addition, Psalms 30, 100, and 107 (pages 1217, 1283, 1293, respectively) are particularly appropriate for this occasion. Torah study should also be part of such an event.*

THE DEDICATION OF A NEW HOME

What follows here is a suggested liturgy based on one found in the Siddur Minḥat Yerushalayim. Before affixing the first mezuza, the following verse is recited responsively, led by the homeowner:

Ps. 90 **וִיהִי נֹעַם** AND LET the pleasantness of the Lord our God be upon us, and establish the work of our hands upon us, and establish it, the work of our hands.

Ps. 91 **יֹשֵׁב** HE WHO DWELLS in the secret place of the Most High abides in the shadow of the Almighty. I say to the Lord, my refuge and my fortress, my God, I trust in Him. Indeed, He will deliver you from the baited trap, from the deadly pestilence. He will cover you with His pinions, and under His wings you will find refuge. His truth will be your shield and buckler. You will not be afraid of the terror by night, of the arrow that flies by day, of the pestilence that walks in the darkness,

---

THE DEDICATION OF A NEW HOME – חנוכת הבית
Magen Avraham 568:5 quotes a dispute as to whether a meal convened for the purpose of dedicating one's home in the Diaspora constitutes a *se'udat mitzva*. According to some, there is no *mitzva*. According to others, if one is planning on dedicating one's home to upholding Torah values, then it constitutes a *se'udat mitzva*. Accordingly, while building a home is technically a *mitzva* only in the Land of Israel (Yerushalmi, *Sota* 8:4), it is nonetheless cause for spiritual celebration and thanksgiving wherever the home may be, for it is in the home that we live our daily Jewish lives to the fullest, observing *kashrut* in the kitchen, engaging in Torah study in the dining and living room, and engaging in many other

בְּעֵינֶיךָ תַבִּיט, וְשִׁלֻּמַת רְשָׁעִים תִּרְאֶה: כִּי־אַתָּה יהוה מַחְסִי, עֶלְיוֹן שַׂמְתָּ מְעוֹנֶךָ: לֹא־תְאֻנֶּה אֵלֶיךָ רָעָה, וְנֶגַע לֹא־יִקְרַב בְּאָהֳלֶךָ: כִּי מַלְאָכָיו יְצַוֶּה־לָּךְ, לִשְׁמָרְךָ בְּכָל־דְּרָכֶיךָ: עַל־כַּפַּיִם יִשָּׂאוּנְךָ, פֶּן־תִּגֹּף בָּאֶבֶן רַגְלֶךָ: עַל־שַׁחַל וָפֶתֶן תִּדְרֹךְ, תִּרְמֹס כְּפִיר וְתַנִּין: כִּי בִי חָשַׁק וַאֲפַלְּטֵהוּ, אֲשַׂגְּבֵהוּ כִּי־יָדַע שְׁמִי: יִקְרָאֵנִי וְאֶעֱנֵהוּ, עִמּוֹ אָנֹכִי בְצָרָה, אֲחַלְּצֵהוּ וַאֲכַבְּדֵהוּ: אֹרֶךְ יָמִים אַשְׂבִּיעֵהוּ, וְאַרְאֵהוּ בִּישׁוּעָתִי:

מִזְמוֹר לְתוֹדָה, הָרִיעוּ לַיהוה כָּל־הָאָרֶץ: עִבְדוּ אֶת־יהוה בְּשִׂמְחָה, בֹּאוּ לְפָנָיו בִּרְנָנָה: דְּעוּ כִּי־יהוה הוּא אֱלֹהִים, הוּא עָשָׂנוּ וְלוֹ אֲנַחְנוּ, עַמּוֹ וְצֹאן מַרְעִיתוֹ: בֹּאוּ שְׁעָרָיו בְּתוֹדָה, חֲצֵרֹתָיו בִּתְהִלָּה, הוֹדוּ לוֹ, בָּרְכוּ שְׁמוֹ: כִּי־טוֹב יהוה, לְעוֹלָם חַסְדּוֹ, וְעַד־דֹּר וָדֹר אֱמוּנָתוֹ: תהלים ק

The homeowners then recite the following prayer:
If ownership of the home is shared by a number of people, each recites (MB 223:11):

בָּרוּךְ אַתָּה יהוה אֱלֹהֵינוּ מֶלֶךְ הָעוֹלָם, הַטּוֹב וְהַמֵּטִיב.

If the home is owned by only person, he or she recites:

בָּרוּךְ אַתָּה יהוה אֱלֹהֵינוּ מֶלֶךְ הָעוֹלָם, שֶׁהֶחֱיָנוּ וְקִיְּמָנוּ וְהִגִּיעָנוּ לַזְּמַן הַזֶּה.

During the meal, תורה *is studied, beginning with the recitation of three* משניות *whose first letters together form the word* בית *"home," for example,* אבות ה, א; א, ד *(pages 706, 676). This is followed by studying* ברכות ד, א*. The following* תהלים *appropriate to the occasion can be recited:* תהילים קיא, ל, סז, טז, קכז, קנ.

activities of religious significance. Indeed, the Torah considers the dedication of a new home to be sufficient reason to free a person from a wartime draft (Deut. 20:5). In Jewish daily life, our home – even more than our synagogue – is our "sacred space."

The dedication of a home centers around affixing the *mezuzot* (*Targum Yonatan*, Deut. 20:5). It is customary (although not an obligation) to celebrate this event with a festive meal during which there is Torah study, prayer, and song. Through this meal we dedicate our homes to the service of God, beyond mere idle talk or frivolity (*Magen*

of the destruction that wastes at noonday. A thousand will fall at your side and ten thousand at your right hand. It will not come near to you. Only with your eyes will you behold, and you will see the destruction of the wicked. Indeed, You, O Lord, are my refuge. You have made the Most High Your habitation. No evil will befall you, and plague will not come near to your tent. Indeed, He will give His angels charge over you, to keep you in all your ways. They will bear you up on their hands, lest you dash your foot against a stone. You will tread upon the lion and the adder. You will trample the young lion and the crocodile underfoot. Because he has clung to Me, I will deliver him. I will make him safe, because he has known My name. When he calls upon Me, I answer him. I am with him in trouble. I deliver him and I will honor him. I will satisfy him with long life, and I will show him of My salvation.

Ps. 100 **מִזְמוֹר לְתוֹדָה** A PSALM OF THANKSGIVING. Make a joyful noise to the Lord, all the earth. Serve the Lord with gladness, come before Him with singing. Know that the Lord is God. He made us, and we belong to Him. We are His people, and the sheep of His pasture. Enter His gates with thanksgiving, His courtyards with praise. Give thanks to Him, and bless His name. For the Lord is good, His loving-kindness is forever, and His faithfulness is for all generations.

The homeowners then recite the following prayer:
If ownership of the home is shared by a number of people, each recites (MB 223:11):

בָּרוּךְ BLESSED ARE YOU, Lord, our God, King of the universe, Who is good and does good.

If the home is owned by only person, he or she recites:

בָּרוּךְ BLESSED ARE YOU, Lord, our God, King of the universe, by Whose word all things came to be.

During the meal, Torah is studied, beginning with the recitation of three mishnayot whose first letters together form the word בית *"home," for example, Avot 5:1 and 1:4 (pages 707, 677). This is followed by studying Berakhot 4:1. The following psalms appropriate to the occasion can be recited: Ps. 111, 30, 67, 16, 127, 150.*

Avraham, OḤ 568:2). If *mezuzot* have already been affixed, a festive meal accompanied by Torah and prayer can still be held to inaugurate the home.

The program concludes with the following prayer:

יְהִי רָצוֹן מִלְּפָנֶיךָ אֲדֹנָי אֱלֹהֵינוּ וֵאלֹהֵי אֲבוֹתֵינוּ, אֱלֹהֵי אַבְרָהָם, אֱלֹהֵי יִצְחָק, וֵאלֹהֵי יַעֲקֹב, אֵל רַחוּם וְחַנּוּן, אַב הָרַחֲמִים, שֶׁיְּהֵא חָשׁוּב וּמְרֻצֶּה לְפָנֶיךָ הַלִּמּוּד שֶׁלָּמַדְנוּ בְּתוֹרָתְךָ הַקְּדוֹשָׁה כְּרֵיחַ נִיחוֹחַ. וּבְרֹב רַחֲמֶיךָ תְּרַחֵם עַל (פלוני/ת בֶּן/בַּת פלוני), בַּעֲלֵי הַבַּיִת הַזֶּה, אֲשֶׁר בְּבוֹאָם לִשְׁכֹּן בַּבַּיִת הַזֶּה, נַפְשָׁם אִוּוּ וְעָשׂוּ חֲנֻכַּת הַבַּיִת בְּדִבְרֵי תוֹרָתְךָ הַקְּדוֹשָׁה, לְיַסֵּד אֶת הַבַּיִת וּלְחָנְכוֹ בְּדִבְרֵי תוֹרָה. וּבְכֵן בִּזְכוּת תּוֹרָתְךָ הַקְּדוֹשָׁה תְּבָרֵךְ אֶת (פלוני/ת בֶּן/בַּת פלוני), בַּעֲלֵי הַבַּיִת הַזֶּה, בְּרָכוֹת לָעַד, וּתְמַלֵּא כָּל מִשְׁאֲלוֹת לִבָּם לְטוֹבָה, וְיִהְיֶה לָהֶם הַבַּיִת הַזֶּה מֻצְלָח וּמְבֹרָךְ בַּכֹּל מִכֹּל כֹּל, וְיִשָּׁמַע בַּבַּיִת הַזֶּה וּבְבָתֵּי כָל יִשְׂרָאֵל קוֹל שָׂשׂוֹן וְקוֹל שִׂמְחָה.

אָנָּא בְּרַחֲמֶיךָ הָרַבִּים, הֱיֵה עֲלֵיהֶם סִתְרָה, צִנָּה וְסֹחֵרָה, וּתְבַטֵּל מֵהֶם כָּל גְּזֵרוֹת וָנֶגַע וּמַחֲלָה וְכָל רָעוֹת, וּבְהַרְמָנָא מַלְכָּא עִלָּאָה, תִּשְׁמֹר מִכָּל עַיִן רָע, וְתִשְׁלַח בְּרָכָה וְהַצְלָחָה בְּכָל מַעֲשֵׂי יְדֵיהֶם, וְיַאֲרִיכוּ יָמִים וְשָׁנִים דְּשֵׁנִים וְרַעֲנַנִּים, כִּי אַתָּה שׁוֹמֵעַ תְּפִלּוֹת כָּל פֶּה עַמְּךָ יִשְׂרָאֵל בְּרַחֲמִים.

יִהְיוּ לְרָצוֹן אִמְרֵי־פִי וְהֶגְיוֹן לִבִּי לְפָנֶיךָ, יהוה צוּרִי וְגֹאֲלִי: תהלים יט

The program concludes with the following prayer:

יְהִי May it be Your will, Lord, our God and the God of our fathers, the God of Abraham, the God of Isaac, and the God of Jacob; God, compassionate and gracious, merciful Father, that the study that we have done of Your holy Torah be as satisfactory to You as a sweet fragrance. And in Your great compassion have mercy upon (*name*) the son/daughter of (*father's name*), the owners of this house, who, upon coming to live in this house, followed the promptings of their souls and dedicated their home with words of Your holy Torah, in order to establish and inaugurate it with words of Torah. Therefore, in the merit of Your holy Torah, bless (*name*) the son/daughter of (*father's name*), the owners of this house, with eternal blessings, and fulfill all their hearts' desires for good. May this house be blessed with everything, and may there be heard in this home – and in the homes of all of Israel – the sound of joy and the sound of gladness.

Please, in Your abundant compassion, be a protection for them, nullify all decrees, sickness, and all evil things from upon them. By decree of the heavenly King, may they be protected against every evil eye. Send blessing and success to all of their handiwork, and let them have long days and years of vigor and abundance, for You are the One Who hears the prayers of Your nation, Israel, with compassion.

Ps. 19 May the words of our mouths and the meditations of our hearts be acceptable before You, Lord, our Rock and our Redeemer.

תפילה לחולה

When praying for recovery from illness, Psalms 23, 102, 103, and 139 are often recited. After reciting such psalms, the following prayer is said.

אָנָּא יהוה רוֹפֵא כָל בָּשָׂר, רַחֵם עָלַי, וּסְעָדֵנִי בְּחַסְדְּךָ הַגָּדוֹל עַל עֶרֶשׂ דְּוַי, כִּי אֻמְלַל אָנִי. שְׁלַח לִי תְּרוּפָה וּתְעָלָה, בְּתוֹךְ שְׁאָר חוֹלֵי יִשְׂרָאֵל. רְפָא אֶת מַכְאוֹבִי, וְחַדֵּשׁ כַּנֶּשֶׁר נְעוּרָי. תֵּן בִּינָה לָרוֹפֵא, וְיִגְהֶה מִמֶּנִּי מְזוֹרִי, וַאֲרוּכָתִי מְהֵרָה תִצְמַח. שְׁמַע תְּפִלָּתִי, וְהוֹסֵף יָמִים עַל יָמַי, וַאֲכַלֶּה שְׁנוֹתַי בַּנְּעִימִים, לְמַעַן אוּכַל לַעֲבֹד אוֹתְךָ, וְלִשְׁמֹר פִּקּוּדֶיךָ בְּלֵב שָׁלֵם. הֲבִינֵנִי וְאֵדְעָה, כִּי לְשָׁלוֹמִי מַר לִי מָר. וְאַל אֶמְאַס אֶת מוּסָרְךָ, וּבְתוֹכַחְתְּךָ אַל אָקוּץ.

אֱלוֹהַּ סְלִיחוֹת, חַנּוּן וְרַחוּם אֶרֶךְ אַפַּיִם וְרַב חֶסֶד, מוֹדֶה אֲנִי לְפָנֶיךָ בְּלֵב נִשְׁבָּר וְנִדְכֶּה כִּי חָטָאתִי, וְהָרַע בְּעֵינֶיךָ עָשִׂיתִי. הִנֵּה נִחַמְתִּי עַל רָעָתִי, וְאָשׁוּב בִּתְשׁוּבָה שְׁלֵמָה לְפָנֶיךָ. עָזְרֵנִי אֱלֹהֵי יִשְׁעִי, וְלֹא
תהלים פו אָשׁוּב לְכִסְלָה, וְאֶתְהַלֵּךְ לְפָנֶיךָ בֶּאֱמֶת וּבְתָמִים. שַׂמֵּחַ נֶפֶשׁ עַבְדֶּךָ,
ירמיה יז כִּי־אֵלֶיךָ אֲדֹנָי, נַפְשִׁי אֶשָּׂא: רְפָאֵנִי יהוה וְאֵרָפֵא, הוֹשִׁיעֵנִי וְאִוָּשֵׁעָה, כִּי תְהִלָּתִי אָתָּה: אָמֵן וְאָמֵן.

ON PRAYER IN THE FACE OF SERIOUS ILLNESS OR DEATH

According to our tradition, God's very presence (the *Shekhina*) resides at the patient's bedside. Since the Almighty understands every language, reads our thoughts, and knows what is in our hearts, we may speak to Him openly, as one might talk to an intimate friend, and sincerely appeal for His help. The prophet Jeremiah cried out, "Heal me, God, and I will be healed; save me, and I will be saved, for You are my praise" (Jeremiah 17:14). To this very day, Jeremiah's plea is enshrined in the daily *Amida*. King David, feeling abandoned and rejected by God, implores, "My God, my God why have You forsaken me; why so far from saving me, from the words of my roar? O, my God! I called out by day, but You answer not; and by night, but there is no respite for me" (Psalms 22:2–3). Such hopes and fears have been echoed in the personal prayers of the sick and suffering throughout history.

We believe that God is the true "Physician Who heals our people." He is the One Who "creates cures..." and is the "Master of wonders." He promises us that if we remain faithful to our Torah, "I will put none of the diseases on you that I have put on the Egyptians; for I am God, your healer." We pray, then, that God guide our physicians and grant them the wisdom and skills to provide us with the best possible medical care.

PRAYER FOR RECOVERY FROM ILLNESS

When praying for recovery from illness, Psalms 23, 102, 103, and 139 are often recited. After reciting such psalms, the following prayer is said.

אָנָּא PLEASE, Lord, Healer of all flesh, have pity on me, and support me on my sick bed, in Your great love, for I am weak. Send relief and healing to me and to the others of Your children who are sick. Heal my pain and renew my youth as the eagle's. Grant wisdom to the physician that he may cure my illness, so that my healing may spring up swiftly. Hear my prayer, prolong my life, and let me complete my years in happiness, so that I may be able to serve You and keep Your precepts with a perfect heart. Grant me the understanding to know that this bitter trial has come upon me for my welfare. Let me not reject Your discipline or spurn Your rebuke.

אֱלוֹהַּ GOD of forgiveness, gracious and compassionate, slow to anger, abounding in love, I acknowledge before You with a broken and contrite heart that I have sinned and done evil in Your sight. I hereby repent of my evil and turn to You in complete repentance. Help me, God of my salvation, that I may not turn to folly again, but instead walk before You in truth and
Ps. 86 integrity. Make the soul of Your servant rejoice, for to You, O Lord, I lift up
Jer. 17 my soul. Heal me, O Lord, and I shall be healed; save me, and I shall be saved; for You are my praise. Amen and Amen.

Patients who recognize that the end is near often seek assurance that though God may not heal them, He will accompany them on their final journey. At that point Psalm 23 – *Even though I walk through the valley of the shadow of death, I fear no evil for You are with me* – captures the essence of God's providence and compassion – no matter how dire the prognosis.

Finally, when death is imminent, prayers for healing, such as the *Mi Sheberakh* prayers, are no longer warranted (cf. *Ran* to *Nedarim* 40a). At that point the patient should recite the *Viduy*, final confessional prayers, assisted by a rabbi, if necessary.

GUIDELINES FOR VISITING THE SICK
According to the rabbinic tradition, *bikkur ḥolim* is not simply an admirable act of *ḥesed*, or compassion, it is also an important source of recovery for the one visited – and even (as we say every day during the Morning Blessings) assures a special reward for the visitor him or herself in the next world.

The visit itself should be carefully planned and carried out, with due consideration for both the *halakhic*, medical and ethical considerations involved.

One should not presume that because one is a family member or close friend, a visit is at all times welcome or even expected. Patients are often uncomfortable as a result of their illness, medications or treatments, and thus might not wish to receive visitors

The commentary continues on page 1089.

שינוי השם

If a person is desperately ill, rabbinical authorities may advise that the name of the sick person be changed. When the name is changed, the following formula is recited:

If the sick person is a male:

וְאַף אִם נִגְזַר עָלָיו בְּבֵית דִּינְךָ הַצֶּדֶק שֶׁיָּמוּת מֵחׇלְיוֹ זֶה, הִנֵּה רַבּוֹתֵינוּ הַקְּדוֹשִׁים אָמְרוּ: שְׁלֹשָׁה דְבָרִים קוֹרְעִים גְּזַר דִּינוֹ שֶׁל אָדָם. וְאֶחָד מֵהֶם שִׁנּוּי הַשֵּׁם, שֶׁיִּשַּׁנּוּ הַשֵּׁם שֶׁל הַחוֹלֶה. וְקִיַּמְנוּ דִּבְרֵיהֶם וְנִשְׁתַּנָּה שְׁמוֹ וְלָכֵן אַחֶרֶת הִיא וְאִם עַל (*sick person's name*) נִגְזַר גְּזַר הַדִּין, עַל (*sick person's new name*) לֹא נִגְזַר כִּי אַחֵר הוּא וְאֵינוֹ הוּא הַנִּקְרָא בַּשֵּׁם הָרִאשׁוֹן. וּכְשֵׁם שֶׁנִּשְׁתַּנָּה שְׁמוֹ כֵּן יִשְׁתַּנֶּה גְּזַר הַדִּין מֵעָלָיו מִדִּין לְרַחֲמִים וּמִמִּיתָה לְחַיִּים וּמִמַּחֲלָה לִרְפוּאָה שְׁלֵמָה לְ(*new name*) בֶּן (*mother's name*) בְּשֵׁם כָּל הַשֵּׁמוֹת הַכְּתוּבִים בְּסֵפֶר תּוֹרָה זֶה וּבְשֵׁם כָּל הַמַּלְאָכִים הַמְמֻנִּים עַל כָּל הָרְפוּאוֹת וְהַהַצָּלוֹת, וְתִשְׁלַח מְהֵרָה רְפוּאָה שְׁלֵמָה לְ(*new name*) בֶּן (*mother's name*) וְתַאֲרִיךְ יָמָיו וּשְׁנוֹתָיו בַּנְּעִימִים, וִיבַלֶּה בְּטוֹב יָמָיו בְּרֹב עֹז וְשָׁלוֹם מֵעַתָּה וְעַד עוֹלָם, אָמֵן סֶלָה.

If the sick person is a female:

וְאַף אִם נִגְזַר עָלֶיהָ בְּבֵית דִּינְךָ הַצֶּדֶק שֶׁתָּמוּת מֵחׇלְיֹה זֶה, הִנֵּה רַבּוֹתֵינוּ הַקְּדוֹשִׁים אָמְרוּ: שְׁלֹשָׁה דְבָרִים קוֹרְעִים גְּזַר דִּינוֹ שֶׁל אָדָם. וְאֶחָד מֵהֶם שִׁנּוּי הַשֵּׁם, שֶׁיִּשַּׁנּוּ הַשֵּׁם שֶׁל הַחוֹלֶה. וְקִיַּמְנוּ דִּבְרֵיהֶם וְנִשְׁתַּנָּה שְׁמָהּ וְלָכֵן אַחֶרֶת הִיא וְאִם עַל (*sick person's name*) נִגְזַר גְּזַר הַדִּין, עַל (*sick person's new name*) לֹא נִגְזַר כִּי אַחֶרֶת הִיא וְאֵינָהּ הִיא הַנִּקְרֵאת בַּשֵּׁם הָרִאשׁוֹן. וּכְשֵׁם שֶׁנִּשְׁתַּנָּה שְׁמָהּ כֵּן יִשְׁתַּנֶּה גְּזַר הַדִּין מֵעָלֶיהָ מִדִּין לְרַחֲמִים וּמִמִּיתָה לְחַיִּים וּמִמַּחֲלָה לִרְפוּאָה שְׁלֵמָה לְ(*new name*) בַּת (*mother's name*) בְּשֵׁם כָּל הַשֵּׁמוֹת הַכְּתוּבִים בְּסֵפֶר תּוֹרָה זֶה וּבְשֵׁם כָּל הַמַּלְאָכִים הַמְמֻנִּים עַל כָּל הָרְפוּאוֹת וְהַהַצָּלוֹת, וְתִשְׁלַח מְהֵרָה רְפוּאָה שְׁלֵמָה לְ(*new name*) בַּת (*mother's name*) וְתַאֲרִיךְ יָמֶיהָ וּשְׁנוֹתֶיהָ בַּנְּעִימִים, וּתְבַלֶּה בְּטוֹב יָמֶיהָ בְּרֹב עֹז וְשָׁלוֹם מֵעַתָּה וְעַד עוֹלָם, אָמֵן סֶלָה.

CHANGING THE NAME

This is based on *Rosh HaShana* 16b, which teaches that certain things can annul the decree against a person: charity, prayer, change of name, and change of deeds (i.e., repentance). In ancient times, the name was changed completely. In more recent times, a name is generally added to the sick person's name. the additional name is often one that alludes to life and recovery, such as חַיִּים, Ḥayyim (lit., "life"), or רְפָאֵל, Raphael (lit., "God has cured").

CHANGING THE NAME

If a person is desperately ill, rabbinical authorities may advise that the name of the sick person be changed. When the name is changed, the following formula is recited:

If the sick person is a male:

וְאִף IF IT has been decreed upon him in Your Court of Justice that he must die of this illness, our holy rabbis have said: Three things annul a decree against a person. One of those is changing the name; that is, that they should change the name of the person who is sick. We have fulfilled their words and have changed his name, and it is therefore different. And if on (*sick person's name*) there is a decree, on (*sick person's new name*) there is no decree, for he is different and is no longer the one called by that previous name. And just as his name has been changed so may the decree be changed from strict justice to mercy, from death to life, from sickness to complete recovery, for (*new name*) son of (*mother's name*). In the name of all the names written in this Torah Scroll, and in the name of all the angels appointed over all healing and salvation, swiftly send a complete recovery to (*new name*) son of (*mother's name*). Lengthen his days and years in pleasantness, let him spend his days well, with abundant strength and peace, from now and through eternity. Amen, Selah.

If the sick person is a male:

וְאִף IF IT has been decreed upon her in Your Court of Justice that she must die of this illness, our holy rabbis have said: Three things annul a decree against a person. One of those is changing the name; that is, that they should change the name of the person who is sick. We have fulfilled their words and have changed her name, and it is therefore different. And if on (*sick person's name*) there is a decree, on (*sick person's new name*) there is no decree, for she is different and is no longer the one called by that previous name. And just as her name has been changed so may the decree be changed from strict justice to mercy, from death to life, from sickness to complete recovery, for (*new name*) daughter of (*mother's name*). In the name of all the names written in this Torah Scroll, and in the name of all the angels appointed over all healing and salvation, swiftly send a complete recovery to (*new name*) daughter of (*mother's name*). Lengthen her days and years in pleasantness, let her spend her days well, with abundant strength and peace, from now and through eternity. Amen, Selah.

---

altogether — or at the time that it is convenient for the visitor but not for the patient. It is a good idea to call the patient (or appropriate family members) ahead of time to determine

תפילה לעומד מחליו

Say תהלים כג *and* קג *(pages 1210 and 1284 respectively). Then continue with:*

אָנָּא הָאֵל הַגָּדוֹל הַגִּבּוֹר וְהַנּוֹרָא, בְּרֹב חַסְדְּךָ אָבוֹא לְפָנֶיךָ לְהוֹדוֹת
לְךָ עַל כָּל הַטּוֹבוֹת אֲשֶׁר גָּמַלְתָּ עָלַי. מִן הַמֵּצַר קְרָאתִיךָ וַתַּעֲנֵנִי,
מֵעֶרֶשׂ דְּוָי שִׁוַּעְתִּי אֵלֶיךָ, וַתִּשְׁמַע אֶת קוֹלִי תַּחֲנוּנָי. יַסֹּר יִסְּרַנִּי יָהּ,
וְלַמָּוֶת לֹא נְתָנָנִי. בְּאַהֲבָתְךָ וּבְחֶמְלָתְךָ הֶעֱלִיתָ מִן שְׁאוֹל נַפְשִׁי. כִּי רֶגַע
בְּאַפּוֹ, חַיִּים בִּרְצוֹנוֹ, בָּעֶרֶב יָלִין בֶּכִי וְלַבֹּקֶר רִנָּה. חַי חַי הוּא יוֹדֶךָ, כָּמוֹנִי ישעיה לח
הַיּוֹם: וְנַפְשִׁי אֲשֶׁר פָּדִיתָ, תְּסַפֵּר נִפְלְאוֹתֶיךָ לִבְנֵי אָדָם. בָּרוּךְ אַתָּה, רוֹפֵא
נֶאֱמָן לְכָל בָּשָׂר.

אֵל רַחוּם וְחַנּוּן, הַגּוֹמֵל לְחַיָּבִים טוֹבוֹת, קָטֹנְתִּי מִכֹּל הַחֲסָדִים אֲשֶׁר
עָשִׂיתָ עִמָּדִי עַד הֵנָּה. אָנָּא טַהֵר לְבָבִי, וְזַכֵּנִי לָלֶכֶת בְּדֶרֶךְ יְשָׁרִים
לְפָנֶיךָ, וּמְשֹׁךְ עֶזְרְךָ לְעַבְדֶּךָ. חַזְּקֵנִי וְאַמְּצֵנִי מֵרִפְיוֹן, וּבְחִלּוּץ עֲצָמוֹת
תְּבָרְכֵנִי. הַרְחֵק מֵעָלַי כָּל צָרָה וְתוּגָה, שָׁמְרֵנִי מִכָּל רָע, וּבַעֲצָתְךָ תַּנְחֵנִי.
וְזָרְחָה לִי שֶׁמֶשׁ צְדָקָה, וּמַרְפֵּא בִּכְנָפֶיהָ. יִהְיוּ לְרָצוֹן אִמְרֵי־פִי וְהֶגְיוֹן לִבִּי תהלים יט
לְפָנֶיךָ, יהוה צוּרִי וְגוֹאֲלִי: אָמֵן.

whether a visit would be appropriate, and if so, the most convenient time.

Visiting in person is halakhically preferable where possible, as our sages tell us that seeing a patient can be a spur to heightened prayer. Furthermore, prayers recited at the bedside are considered more effective. Being at the bedside one can see first-hand what is needed, and thus be in a better position to really help the patient.

Nonetheless there are times when it is not necessary or even preferable to make a face-to-face visit. Thus for instance a visitor who is himself not well should not enter the room of a patient who might be vulnerable to infection. In such cases it is preferable to perform *bikkur ḥolim* visit via telephone, email, texting, get-well card, or the like. Such actions can partially fulfil the *mitzva* of *bikkur ḥolim*. Other such scenarios would occur if one lives at a great distance, or there is a request for no visitors. This would also be appropriate halakhically if a person has already seen the patient and wants to follow up.

Whether the visit takes place in a home, a hospital, or a nursing home setting, it is essential to knock before entering the room. Where feasible, one should ask if it is convenient to enter right away or at a later time. If the door is closed, one should check with a nurse or family member. If a physician enters the room one should offer to step outside. One should pay strict attention to any infection control signs that require wearing a disposable gown, gloves and/or a mask before entering. The visitor should be prepared for the

PRAYER AFTER RECOVERY FROM ILLNESS

Say Psalms 23 and 103 (page 1211 and 1285 respectively). Then continue with:

אָנָּא O GREAT, mighty and awesome God: By Your great love I come before You to offer thanks for all the good You have bestowed on me. In my distress I called to You and You answered me; from my sick bed I cried to You, and You heard my voice and my pleas. You chastened me severely, Lord, but You did not hand me over to death. In Your love and compassion You lifted my soul from the grave. For Your anger is for a moment, Your favor for a lifetime. At
Is. 38 night there may be weeping, but in the morning there is joy. The living, the living, he shall praise You, as I do this day. My soul which You have redeemed shall tell of Your wonders to the children of men. Blessed are You, the faithful Healer of all flesh.

אֵל O GOD, compassionate and gracious, Who grants favors to the undeserving: I am not worthy of all the kindness You have shown to me until now. Purify, please, my heart that I may be worthy to walk before You in the way of the upright. Extend Your help to Your servant. Grant me the strength and resolution to overcome my weakness, and bless me with physical health. Keep sorrow and grief far from me; protect me from all harm, and guide me with Your counsel. May the sun of righteousness shine for me, bringing healing
Ps. 19 in its wings. May the words of my mouth and the meditation of my heart be acceptable before You, O Lord, my Rock and my Redeemer. Amen.

---

possibility that the patient may look "worse" than usual, and thus not react in an unhelpful fashion.

One should let the patient take the lead in the conversation, and make every effort to be an empathetic listener. Visitors should follow the conversational lead of the patient, and thus if the patient does not want to talk about "it," neither should the visitor. Indeed when God visited Abraham after his circumcision there is no record of God saying anything to him. God's mere presence made all the difference. So, too, we emulate God by just being there, showing we care and by being as supportive as possible – even if we just listen. However, many patients are tired, so one should be prepared to initiate whatever conversation seems most appropriate.

A critical component of *bikkur ḥolim* is to offer a bedside prayer. The Torah's first recorded prayer for the sick was Moses' prayer for his sister's complete recovery, in five brief Hebrew words: "God, please, heal her, please!" (Numbers 12:13). It is appropriate to recite the *Mi Sheberakh* for healing and recovery at the bedside, and also where appropriate during communal prayer. Before reciting it, the visitor should ask for the Hebrew names of the patient and his/her mother, although it is not essential to specify the person's name.

For the full Hebrew and English text of the *Mi Sheberakh* for the sick, see pages 534–537.

וידוי שכיב מרע

If one is unable to recite the entire וידוי*, then this abbreviated phrase should be said. If even that is not possible, this phrase should be contemplated in one's thoughts*

אִם חַס וְשָׁלוֹם אָמוּת, תְּהֵא מִיתָתִי כַּפָּרָה עַל כָּל עֲוֹנוֹתָי.

The lengthier verson is as follows:

מוֹדֶה / *women* מוֹדָה/ אֲנִי לְפָנֶיךָ, יהוה אֱלֹהַי וֵאלֹהֵי אֲבוֹתַי שֶׁרְפוּאָתִי וּמִיתָתִי בְּיָדֶךָ עַל כָּל הַחַיִּים וְצָרְכֵי הַחַיִּים שֶׁנָּתַתָּ לִּי. יְהִי רָצוֹן מִלְּפָנֶיךָ, שֶׁתִּרְפָּאֵנִי רְפוּאָה שְׁלֵמָה, וְאִם חַס וְשָׁלוֹם אָמוּת, תְּהֵא מִיתָתִי כַּפָּרָה עַל כָּל הַחֲטָאִים וַעֲוֹנוֹת וְהַפְּשָׁעִים שֶׁחָטָאתִי וְשֶׁעָוִיתִי וְשֶׁפָּשַׁעְתִּי לְפָנֶיךָ. וְתֵן חֶלְקִי בְּגַן עֵדֶן, וְזַכֵּנִי לָעוֹלָם הַבָּא הַצָּפוּן לַצַּדִּיקִים. אֵל נָא רְפָא נָא לִי.

Women should substitute with the word immediately following the slash.

אֲנִי מַאֲמִין /מַאֲמִינָה בֶּאֱמוּנָה שְׁלֵמָה, שֶׁאֱלֹהִים אֱמֶת וּשְׁמוֹ אֱמֶת, וּבִשְׁלֹשָׁה עָשָׂר הָעִקָּרִים. וְהִנְנִי מוֹחֵל/מוֹחֶלֶת לְכָל אָדָם וּמְבַקֵּשׁ/וּמְבַקֶּשֶׁת שֶׁכֻּלָּם יִמְחֲלוּ לִי.

WHEN DEATH IS NEAR

We realize that cure and complete recovery are not always possible. Sometimes, a loved one may suffer from an end-stage, terminal illness, or experience a sudden, severe traumatic episode such as a stroke, where medical treatment or rehabilitation will not reverse the inevitable outcome. The patient may experience significant physical pain and emotional trauma, be unable to communicate, and have little, if any, quality of life. Critical decisions must be made about whether to provide aggressive medical interventions or offer comfort care or hospice. Hopefully, patients who are unable to make their own decisions at such a time will have previously appointed a health care proxy and a knowledgable Orthodox rabbi to represent their wishes in accordance with halacha, Jewish law. In order to facilitate the appointment of a health care proxy and provide end-of-life halakhic guidelines, the Rabbinical Council of America offers the appropriate documents and information online for free download at its website: http://www.rabbis.org/pdfs/hcp.pdf. Wherever possible completed health-care proxy forms, along with other essential legal documents, such as a durable power of attorney, last will and testament, ethical will, burial plot and deed information should be prepared well in advance of a crisis and be readily accessible to those who will need them.

One should make every effort to address

CONFESSION BEFORE DEATH

If one is unable to recite the entire Viduy, then this abbreviated phrase should be said. If even that is not possible, this phrase should be contemplated in one's thoughts

אִם IF heaven forfend I will die, may my death be an atonement for all my sins.

The lengthier verson is as follows:

מוֹדֶה I GIVE thanks to You, Lord my God and the God of my fathers, in Whose hands is my recovery and my death, for all the life and the necessities of life that You have provided for me. May it be Your will that You grant me a full recovery, and if heaven forfend I will die, may my death be an atonement for all my sins, iniquities, and transgressions that I have perpetrated before You. Grant that my portion will be in the Garden of Eden and allow me to merit the World to Come that is reserved for the righteous. Please God, please heal me.

אֲנִי מַאֲמִין I BELIEVE with complete faith that God is true, that His name is true, and that the thirteen principles of faith are true. I hereby forgive every person, and request that they all will forgive me.

---

one's financial and moral obligations before leaving this world. This includes repayment of debts and asking forgiveness of those one may have offended. If at all possible this should be done in person or, if need be, by phone. Wills should be updated where necessary. Burial plots should be purchased, providing survivors with vital contact and other information. Finally, they might want to follow in the footsteps of our Patriarchs and meet with each of their loved ones, share their ethical will and values with them, and bless them.

FINAL PRAYERS AND CONFESSION – VIDUY
Our rabbis prescribe that those close to death should confess their sins. This brief prayer is known as *Viduy* (or "confessional prayer"). Through it, one achieves atonement for one's sins, and leaves this world with a pure soul, just as one entered it. Where necessary, someone else who is present can assist in the recital. If no one is available to assist, and one is unable to speak, one should confess in one's heart.

Recitation of *Viduy* does not mean that hope is abandoned. *Viduy* combines the request for forgiveness with hope for the future – either in this world or in *Olam Haba*, the next world. In the words of the formula we use in explaining the importance of reciting *Viduy* by a patient facing death, "many have confessed and lived; while many who never confessed, have died." In other words, better to recite it and live, than to die without reciting it.

It is absolutely vital that the dying person not be left alone.

In the last hours, if it is at all possible, the sick person should endeavor to recite or think the following:

מיכה ז **מִי־אֵל כָּמְוֹךָ** נֹשֵׂא עָוֹן וְעֹבֵר עַל־פֶּשַׁע לִשְׁאֵרִית נַחֲלָתוֹ, לֹא־הֶחֱזִיק לָעַד אַפּוֹ, כִּי־חָפֵץ חֶסֶד הוּא: יָשׁוּב יְרַחֲמֵנוּ, יִכְבֹּשׁ עֲוֹנֹתֵינוּ, וְתַשְׁלִיךְ בִּמְצֻלוֹת יָם כָּל־חַטֹּאתָם:

תהלים לא **בְּיָדְךָ** אַפְקִיד רוּחִי, פָּדִיתָה אוֹתִי יהוה אֵל אֱמֶת:

במדבר ו **יְבָרֶכְךָ** יהוה וְיִשְׁמְרֶךָ: יָאֵר יהוה פָּנָיו אֵלֶיךָ וִיחֻנֶּךָּ: יִשָּׂא יהוה פָּנָיו אֵלֶיךָ וְיָשֵׂם לְךָ שָׁלוֹם:

בראשית מט **לִישׁוּעָתְךָ** קִוִּיתִי יהוה: קִוִּיתִי יהוה לִישׁוּעָתְךָ, יהוה לִישׁוּעָתְךָ קִוִּיתִי

יהוה אֵל אֱמֶת, מֹשֶׁה אֱמֶת וְתוֹרָתוֹ אֱמֶת.

As the soul departs the following is recited:

דברים ו **שְׁמַע יִשְׂרָאֵל,** יהוה אֱלֹהֵינוּ, יהוה אֶחָד:

Recite three times:

בָּרוּךְ שֵׁם כְּבוֹד מַלְכוּתוֹ לְעוֹלָם וָעֶד.

Recite seven times:

יהוה הוּא הָאֱלֹהִים.

Once:

יהוה מֶלֶךְ, יהוה מָלָךְ, יהוה יִמְלֹךְ לְעוֹלָם וָעֶד.

If possible, the last words recited in the presence of the dying person should be the שְׁמַע.
At the moment of death, those present should say the following:

איוב א **יהוה** נָתַן וַיהוה לָקָח, יְהִי שֵׁם יהוה מְבֹרָךְ:

דברים לב **הַצּוּר** תָּמִים פָּעֳלוֹ כִּי כָל־דְּרָכָיו מִשְׁפָּט, אֵל אֱמוּנָה וְאֵין עָוֶל צַדִּיק וְיָשָׁר הוּא:

It is absolutely vital that the dying person not be left alone.

In the last hours, if it is at all possible, the sick person should endeavor to recite or think the following:

Mic. 7 **מִי־אֵל כָּמוֹךָ** WHO IS LIKE YOU, God, pardoning iniquity and overlooking transgression for the remnanat of God's people, Who has not retained wrath forever for God desires mercifulness. God will return us in compassion, God will suppress our iniquities, and will cast all their sins into the sea-depths.

Ps. 31 **בְּיָדְךָ** INTO YOUR HAND I entrust my spirit. Redeem me, O Lord, God of truth.

Num. 6 **יְבָרֶכְךָ** MAY THE LORD bless you and keep you. May the Lord make His countenance shine upon you and be gracious to you. May the Lord lift up His countenance toward you and grant you peace.

Gen. 49 **לִישׁוּעָתְךָ** FOR YOUR SALVATION I hope, Lord. I hope, Lord, for Your salvation. Lord, for Your salvation, I hope.

יהוה THE LORD is the true God, Moses is true, as is His Torah.

As the soul departs the following is recited:

Deut. 6 **שְׁמַע יִשְׂרָאֵל** HEAR, O ISRAEL, the Lord is our God, the Lord is One.

Recite three times:

בָּרוּךְ BLESSED is the name of His glorious kingdom forever and ever.

Recite seven times:

יהוה THE LORD, He is God.

Once:

יהוה מֶלֶךְ THE LORD is King, the Lord was King,
and the Lord will be King for ever and ever.

If possible, the last words recited in the presence of the dying person should be the Shema.
At the moment of death, those present should say the following:

Job 1 **יהוה** THE LORD has given and the Lord has taken away: blessed be the name of the Lord.

Deut. 32 **הַצּוּר** THE ROCK, His work is perfect, for all His ways are just; a faithful God Who does no wrong, righteous and fair is He.

FUNERAL SERVICE

Given the nature of the funeral and burial services, this Siddur does not contain a full order of prayers for such occasions. For the full customary order of these prayers consult the *RCA Lifecycle Madrikh* pp. 139–163. This can be ordered directly from the Rabbinical Council of America at 212 807-9000.

ברכת המזון בבית האבל

Leader רַבּוֹתַי, נְבָרֵךְ.

Others יְהִי שֵׁם יהוה מְבֹרָךְ מֵעַתָּה וְעַד־עוֹלָם: תהלים קיג

Leader יְהִי שֵׁם יהוה מְבֹרָךְ מֵעַתָּה וְעַד־עוֹלָם: בִּרְשׁוּת רַבּוֹתַי, נְבָרֵךְ מְנַחֵם אֲבֵלִים שֶׁאָכַלְנוּ מִשֶּׁלּוֹ.

Others בָּרוּךְ מְנַחֵם אֲבֵלִים, שֶׁאָכַלְנוּ מִשֶּׁלּוֹ וּבְטוּבוֹ חָיִינוּ.

**People present who have not taken part in the meal say:*

*בָּרוּךְ מְנַחֵם אֲבֵלִים, וּמְבֹרָךְ שְׁמוֹ תָּמִיד לְעוֹלָם וָעֶד.

Leader בָּרוּךְ מְנַחֵם אֲבֵלִים, שֶׁאָכַלְנוּ מִשֶּׁלּוֹ וּבְטוּבוֹ חָיִינוּ.

בָּרוּךְ הוּא וּבָרוּךְ שְׁמוֹ.

Continue with בִּרְכַּת הַמָּזוֹן *on page 222 until* וּבְנֵה יְרוּשָׁלַיִם *on page 228.*

Then say:

נַחֵם יהוה אֱלֹהֵינוּ אֶת אֲבֵלֵי יְרוּשָׁלַיִם, וְאֶת הָאֲבֵלִים הַמִּתְאַבְּלִים בָּאֵבֶל הַזֶּה. נַחֲמֵם מֵאֶבְלָם וְשַׂמְּחֵם מִיגוֹנָם, כָּאָמוּר: כְּאִישׁ אֲשֶׁר אִמּוֹ תְּנַחֲמֶנּוּ, כֵּן אָנֹכִי אֲנַחֶמְכֶם וּבִירוּשָׁלַםִ תְּנֻחָמוּ: בָּרוּךְ אַתָּה יהוה, מְנַחֵם צִיּוֹן בְּבִנְיַן יְרוּשָׁלָיִם. אָמֵן. ישעיה סו

בָּרוּךְ אַתָּה יהוה אֱלֹהֵינוּ מֶלֶךְ הָעוֹלָם, הָאֵל אָבִינוּ מַלְכֵּנוּ אַדִּירֵנוּ בּוֹרְאֵנוּ גּוֹאֲלֵנוּ יוֹצְרֵנוּ קְדוֹשֵׁנוּ קְדוֹשׁ יַעֲקֹב, רוֹעֵנוּ רוֹעֵה יִשְׂרָאֵל, הַמֶּלֶךְ הַחַי, הַטּוֹב וְהַמֵּטִיב. אֵל אֱמֶת, דַּיַּן אֱמֶת, שׁוֹפֵט צֶדֶק, לוֹקֵחַ נְפָשׁוֹת בְּמִשְׁפָּט, וְשַׁלִּיט בְּעוֹלָמוֹ לַעֲשׂוֹת בּוֹ כִּרְצוֹנוֹ, כִּי כָל דְּרָכָיו מִשְׁפָּט, וַאֲנַחְנוּ עַמּוֹ וַעֲבָדָיו, וְעַל הַכֹּל אֲנַחְנוּ חַיָּבִים לְהוֹדוֹת לוֹ וּלְבָרְכוֹ. גּוֹדֵר פִּרְצוֹת יִשְׂרָאֵל, הוּא יִגְדֹּר אֶת הַפִּרְצָה הַזֹּאת מֵעָלֵינוּ לְחַיִּים וּלְשָׁלוֹם. הוּא יִגְמְלֵנוּ לָעַד חֵן וָחֶסֶד וְרַחֲמִים וְכָל טוֹב, וּמִכָּל טוּב לְעוֹלָם אַל יְחַסְּרֵנוּ.

Continue with הָרַחֲמָן הוּא יִמְלֹךְ *on page 228.*

GRACE AFTER MEALS IN A SHIVA HOUSE

Leader: רַבּוֹתַי ESTEEMED COMPANIONS, let us say grace.

Ps. 113 *Others:* BLESSED be the name of the Lord from now and forevermore.

Leader: BLESSED be the name of the Lord from now and forevermore. With your permission, my esteemed companions, let us bless the One Who comforts mourners, of Whose bounty we have partaken.

Others: BLESSED be the One Who comforts mourners, of Whose bounty we have partaken and through Whose goodness we live.

**People present who have not taken part in the meal say:*

*BLESSED be the One Who comforts mourners, and Whose name is blessed continually, forever and ever.

Leader: BLESSED be the One Who comforts mourners, of Whose bounty we have partaken and through Whose goodness we live.

BLESSED be He, and blessed be His name.

Continue with Grace after Meals on page 223 until "Please rebuild Jerusalem" on page 229. Then say:

נַחֵם COMFORT, O Lord our God, the mourners of Jerusalem and those who mourn here. Grant them consolation in their mourning and gladness in their
Is. 66 grief, as it is said, "As one whom his mother comforts, so will I comfort you; and you shall be comforted in Jerusalem." Blessed are You, Lord, Who brings comfort to Zion through the rebuilding of Jerusalem. Amen.

בָּרוּךְ BLESSED ARE YOU, Lord our God, King of the universe, God our Father, our King, our Sovereign, our Creator, our Redeemer, our Maker, our Holy One, Holy One of Jacob. You are our Shepherd, Shepherd of Israel, You are the Living King Who is good and Who does good. The true God, the true Judge, Who judges righteously and takes back souls in judgment. He rules the world according to His will, for all His ways are just, and we are His people and His servants. For everything, we are duty bound to acknowledge and bless Him. May He Who repairs the breaches in Israel, repair this breach in us and grant us life and peace. May He forever bestow upon us grace, kindness, mercy, and all manner of good things. And may He never deprive us of any good thing.

Continue with "May the Compassionate One reign" on page 229.

סדר הזכרת נשמות

The יזכור *service is said on the last day of* פסח*, the second day of* שבועות*,* יום כיפור *and* שמיני עצרת*. In some communities, those who have not been bereaved of a parent or immediate relative do not participate in the service, but leave the* בית כנסת *and return at the end of* סדר הזכרת נשמות*.*

תהלים קמד **יהוה** מָה־אָדָם וַתֵּדָעֵהוּ, בֶּן־אֱנוֹשׁ וַתְּחַשְּׁבֵהוּ:
אָדָם לַהֶבֶל דָּמָה, יָמָיו כְּצֵל עוֹבֵר:

תהלים צ בַּבֹּקֶר יָצִיץ וְחָלָף, לָעֶרֶב יְמוֹלֵל וְיָבֵשׁ:
לִמְנוֹת יָמֵינוּ כֵּן הוֹדַע, וְנָבִא לְבַב חָכְמָה:

תהלים לז שְׁמָר־תָּם וּרְאֵה יָשָׁר, כִּי־אַחֲרִית לְאִישׁ שָׁלוֹם:

תהלים מט אַךְ־אֱלֹהִים יִפְדֶּה נַפְשִׁי מִיַּד שְׁאוֹל, כִּי יִקָּחֵנִי סֶלָה:

תהלים עג כָּלָה שְׁאֵרִי וּלְבָבִי, צוּר־לְבָבִי וְחֶלְקִי אֱלֹהִים לְעוֹלָם:

קהלת יב וְיָשֹׁב הֶעָפָר עַל־הָאָרֶץ כְּשֶׁהָיָה, וְהָרוּחַ תָּשׁוּב אֶל־הָאֱלֹהִים אֲשֶׁר נְתָנָהּ:

תהלים צא **יֹשֵׁב** בְּסֵתֶר עֶלְיוֹן, בְּצֵל שַׁדַּי יִתְלוֹנָן: אֹמַר לַיהוה מַחְסִי וּמְצוּדָתִי, אֱלֹהַי אֶבְטַח־בּוֹ: כִּי הוּא יַצִּילְךָ מִפַּח יָקוּשׁ, מִדֶּבֶר הַוּוֹת: בְּאֶבְרָתוֹ יָסֶךְ לָךְ, וְתַחַת־כְּנָפָיו תֶּחְסֶה, צִנָּה וְסֹחֵרָה אֲמִתּוֹ: לֹא־תִירָא מִפַּחַד לָיְלָה, מֵחֵץ יָעוּף יוֹמָם: מִדֶּבֶר בָּאֹפֶל יַהֲלֹךְ, מִקֶּטֶב יָשׁוּד צָהֳרָיִם: יִפֹּל מִצִּדְּךָ אֶלֶף, וּרְבָבָה מִימִינֶךָ, אֵלֶיךָ לֹא יִגָּשׁ: רַק בְּעֵינֶיךָ תַבִּיט, וְשִׁלֻּמַת רְשָׁעִים תִּרְאֶה: כִּי־אַתָּה יהוה מַחְסִי, עֶלְיוֹן שַׂמְתָּ מְעוֹנֶךָ: לֹא־תְאֻנֶּה אֵלֶיךָ רָעָה, וְנֶגַע לֹא־יִקְרַב בְּאָהֳלֶךָ: כִּי מַלְאָכָיו יְצַוֶּה־לָּךְ, לִשְׁמָרְךָ בְּכָל־דְּרָכֶיךָ: עַל־כַּפַּיִם יִשָּׂאוּנְךָ, פֶּן־תִּגֹּף בָּאֶבֶן רַגְלֶךָ: עַל־שַׁחַל וָפֶתֶן תִּדְרֹךְ, תִּרְמֹס כְּפִיר וְתַנִּין: כִּי בִי חָשַׁק וַאֲפַלְּטֵהוּ, אֲשַׂגְּבֵהוּ כִּי־יָדַע שְׁמִי: יִקְרָאֵנִי וְאֶעֱנֵהוּ, עִמּוֹ־אָנֹכִי בְצָרָה, אֲחַלְּצֵהוּ וַאֲכַבְּדֵהוּ: אֹרֶךְ יָמִים אַשְׂבִּיעֵהוּ, וְאַרְאֵהוּ בִּישׁוּעָתִי: אֹרֶךְ יָמִים אַשְׂבִּיעֵהוּ, וְאַרְאֵהוּ בִּישׁוּעָתִי:

יִזְכֹּר / YIZKOR

The earliest mention of praying for atonement for the departed souls appears in the Tannaitic *Midrash Sifrei*, Deuteronomy 21:8. The practice of reciting *Yizkor* on Yom Kippur is attested to in the later *Midrash Tanḥuma, Ha'azinu*. The remembrance of past lives serves another purpose on Yom Kippur – to link us to the ongoing Jewish mission, the process begun by our forefathers and continued by our grandparents and parents, so that the merits of our ancestors can be reckoned for us as well on the Day of Judgment (*Orḥot Ḥayyim*).

The custom of reciting *Yizkor* at the end of the three pilgrimage festivals stems from an ancient practice cited by *Maḥzor Vitri*

YIZKOR

The Yizkor service is said on the last day of Pesaḥ, the second day of Shavuot, Shemini Atzeret and Yom Kippur. In some communities, those who have not been bereaved of a parent or immediate relative do not participate in the service, but leave the synagogue and return at the end of Yizkor.

Ps. 144 יהוה O LORD, what is man, that You know him, the son of man, that You
Ps. 90 consider him! Man is like a breath. His days are like a passing shadow. In the
morning it flowers and fades, in the evening it withers and dries. Teach us
Ps. 37 to number our days correctly. And may we get a heart of wisdom. Preserve
innocence and behold uprightness, for there is a future for the man of peace.
Ps. 49 But God will redeem my soul from the hand of the underworld, for He will
Ps. 73 take me. Selah. My flesh and my heart fail. God is the rock of my heart and my
Eccl. 12 portion forever. And the dust returns to the earth as it was, and the spirit returns
to God Who gave it.

Ps. 91 יֹשֵׁב HE WHO DWELLS in the secret place of the Most High abides in the shadow of the Almighty. I say to the Lord, my refuge and my fortress, my God, I trust in Him. Indeed, He will deliver you from the baited trap, from the deadly pestilence. He will cover you with His pinions, and under His wings you will find refuge. His truth will be your shield and buckler. You will not be afraid of the terror by night, of the arrow that flies by day, of the pestilence that walks in the darkness, of the destruction that wastes at noonday. A thousand will fall at your side and ten thousand at your right hand. It will not come near to you. Only with your eyes will you behold, and you will see the destruction of the wicked. Indeed, You, O Lord, are my refuge. You have made the Most High Your habitation. No evil will befall you, and plague will not come near to your tent. Indeed, He will give His angels charge over you, to keep you in all your ways. They will bear you up on their hands, lest you dash your foot against a stone. You will tread upon the lion and the adder. You will trample the young lion and the crocodile underfoot. Because he has clung to Me, I will deliver him. I will make him safe, because he has known My name. When he calls upon Me, I answer him. I am with him in trouble. I deliver him and I will honor him. I will satisfy him with long life, and I will show him of My salvation. I will satisfy him with long life, and I will show him of My salvation.

---

known as *matnat yad* (gift of one's hand). This custom involved making pledges to charity on days when the Torah reading dealt with charity. This included charitable activity on the festivals, as it says "each person shall give, according to *the gift of his hand*, per the blessing that God has bestowed upon him" (Deut. 14:22–16:17). Thus on these days pledges would be made in memory of departed loved ones (*Levush*).

Regarding the mourning practices of *Shiva* and *Sheloshim*, the *Halakha* requires

For one's father:

יִזְכֹּר אֱלֹהִים נִשְׁמַת אָבִי מוֹרִי (פלוני בֶּן פלוני) שֶׁהָלַךְ לְעוֹלָמוֹ, בַּעֲבוּר שֶׁאֶתֵּן צְדָקָה בְּעַד הַזְכָּרַת נִשְׁמָתוֹ. בִּשְׂכַר זֶה תְּהֵא נַפְשׁוֹ צְרוּרָה בִּצְרוֹר הַחַיִּים עִם נִשְׁמוֹת אַבְרָהָם יִצְחָק וְיַעֲקֹב, שָׂרָה רִבְקָה רָחֵל וְלֵאָה, וְעִם שְׁאָר צַדִּיקִים וְצִדְקָנִיּוֹת שֶׁבְּגַן עֵדֶן, וְנֹאמַר אָמֵן.

For one's mother:

יִזְכֹּר אֱלֹהִים נִשְׁמַת אִמִּי מוֹרָתִי (פלונית בַּת פלוני) שֶׁהָלְכָה לְעוֹלָמָהּ, בַּעֲבוּר שֶׁאֶתֵּן צְדָקָה בְּעַד הַזְכָּרַת נִשְׁמָתָהּ. בִּשְׂכַר זֶה תְּהֵא נַפְשָׁהּ צְרוּרָה בִּצְרוֹר הַחַיִּים עִם נִשְׁמוֹת אַבְרָהָם יִצְחָק וְיַעֲקֹב, שָׂרָה רִבְקָה רָחֵל וְלֵאָה, וְעִם שְׁאָר צַדִּיקִים וְצִדְקָנִיּוֹת שֶׁבְּגַן עֵדֶן, וְנֹאמַר אָמֵן.

For a male relative:

יִזְכֹּר אֱלֹהִים נִשְׁמַת (*my grandfather* זְקֵנִי / *my uncle* דּוֹדִי / *my brother* אָחִי / *my son* בְּנִי / *my husband* בַּעֲלִי) (פלוני בֶּן פלוני) שֶׁהָלַךְ לְעוֹלָמוֹ, בַּעֲבוּר שֶׁאֶתֵּן צְדָקָה בְּעַד הַזְכָּרַת נִשְׁמָתוֹ. בִּשְׂכַר זֶה תְּהֵא נַפְשׁוֹ צְרוּרָה בִּצְרוֹר הַחַיִּים עִם נִשְׁמוֹת אַבְרָהָם יִצְחָק וְיַעֲקֹב, שָׂרָה רִבְקָה רָחֵל וְלֵאָה, וְעִם שְׁאָר צַדִּיקִים וְצִדְקָנִיּוֹת שֶׁבְּגַן עֵדֶן, וְנֹאמַר אָמֵן.

For a female relative:

יִזְכֹּר אֱלֹהִים נִשְׁמַת (*my grandmother* זְקֵנָתִי / *my aunt* דּוֹדָתִי / *my sister* אֲחוֹתִי / *my daughter* בִּתִּי / *my wife* אִשְׁתִּי) (פלונית בַּת פלוני) שֶׁהָלְכָה לְעוֹלָמָהּ, בַּעֲבוּר שֶׁאֶתֵּן צְדָקָה בְּעַד הַזְכָּרַת נִשְׁמָתָהּ. בִּשְׂכַר זֶה תְּהֵא נַפְשָׁהּ צְרוּרָה בִּצְרוֹר הַחַיִּים עִם נִשְׁמוֹת אַבְרָהָם יִצְחָק וְיַעֲקֹב, שָׂרָה רִבְקָה רָחֵל וְלֵאָה, וְעִם שְׁאָר צַדִּיקִים וְצִדְקָנִיּוֹת שֶׁבְּגַן עֵדֶן, וְנֹאמַר אָמֵן.

---

that all public manifestations of mourning be suspended on Yom Tov, and yet we say *Yizkor* on every Yom Tov, which for many is accompanied by tears and sadness in recalling the passing of loved ones and martyrs. The justification for this is that *Yizkor* is less an act of mourning and more a redemptive gesture, perhaps even a joyous one. When the deceased are recalled for their goodness and devotion to Jewish life and Torah values, their

For one's father:

יִזְכֹּר MAY GOD REMEMBER the soul of my father, my teacher, (*name* son of *father's name*) who has gone on to his eternal reward, insofar as I will make a charitable gift in memory of his soul. As reward for this, may his soul be bound in lasting life, together with the souls of Abraham, Isaac, and Jacob; Sarah, Rebecca, Rachel, and Leah; and together with the other righteous men and women who are in the Garden of Eden. And let us say, Amen.

For one's mother:

יִזְכֹּר MAY GOD REMEMBER the soul of my mother, my teacher, (*name* daughter of *father's name*) who has gone on to her eternal reward, insofar as I will make a charitable gift in memory of her soul. As reward for this, may her soul be bound in lasting life, together with the souls of Abraham, Isaac, and Jacob; Sarah, Rebecca, Rachel, and Leah; and together with the other righteous men and women who are in the Garden of Eden. And let us say, Amen.

For a male relative:

יִזְכֹּר MAY GOD REMEMBER the soul of my grandfather / uncle / brother / son / husband, (*name* son of *father's name*) who has gone on to his eternal reward, insofar as I will make a charitable gift in memory of his soul. As reward for this, may his soul be bound in lasting life, together with the souls of Abraham, Isaac, and Jacob; Sarah, Rebecca, Rachel, and Leah; and together with the other righteous men and women who are in the Garden of Eden. And let us say, Amen.

For a female relative:

יִזְכֹּר MAY GOD REMEMBER the soul of my grandmother / aunt / sister / daughter / wife, (*name* daughter of *father's name*) who has gone on to her eternal reward, insofar as I will make a charitable gift in memory of her soul. As reward for this, may her soul be bound in lasting life, together with the souls of Abraham, Isaac, and Jacob; Sarah, Rebecca, Rachel, and Leah; and together with the other righteous men and women who are in the Garden of Eden. And let us say, Amen.

---

memory becomes an inspiration and a source of strength to the living. In this light the words of *Yizkor* should be understood in balanced fashion: imbued with a sense of loss but also with thankfulness for the lives our loved ones lived; with sadness, but also with hope for the living, and a determination to learn from the departed how to use our own time and energies in the service of God.

יִזְכּוֹר אֱלֹהִים – *May God remember.* Since God knows all and does not forget anything, the

For one's extended family:

יִזְכֹּר אֱלֹהִים נִשְׁמוֹת זְקֵנַי וּזְקֵנוֹתַי, דּוֹדַי וְדוֹדוֹתַי, אַחַי וְאַחְיוֹתַי, מִצַּד אָבִי וּמִצַּד אִמִּי, שֶׁהָלְכוּ לְעוֹלָמָם, בַּעֲבוּר שֶׁאֶתֵּן צְדָקָה בְּעַד הַזְכָּרַת נִשְׁמוֹתֵיהֶם. בִּשְׂכַר זֶה תִּהְיֶינָה נַפְשׁוֹתֵיהֶם צְרוּרוֹת בִּצְרוֹר הַחַיִּים עִם נִשְׁמוֹת אַבְרָהָם יִצְחָק וְיַעֲקֹב, שָׂרָה רִבְקָה רָחֵל וְלֵאָה, וְעִם שְׁאָר צַדִּיקִים וְצִדְקָנִיּוֹת שֶׁבְּגַן עֵדֶן, וְנֹאמַר אָמֵן.

For martyrs:

יִזְכֹּר אֱלֹהִים נִשְׁמַת (*male* פלוני בֶּן פלוני / *female* פלונית בַּת פלוני) וְנִשְׁמוֹת כָּל קְרוֹבַי וּקְרוֹבוֹתַי, הֵן מִצַּד אָבִי הֵן מִצַּד אִמִּי, שֶׁהוּמְתוּ וְשֶׁנֶּהֶרְגוּ וְשֶׁנִּשְׁחֲטוּ וְשֶׁנִּשְׂרְפוּ וְשֶׁנִּטְבְּעוּ וְשֶׁנֶּחְנְקוּ עַל קִדּוּשׁ הַשֵּׁם, בַּעֲבוּר שֶׁאֶתֵּן צְדָקָה בְּעַד הַזְכָּרַת נִשְׁמוֹתֵיהֶם. בִּשְׂכַר זֶה תִּהְיֶינָה נַפְשׁוֹתֵיהֶם צְרוּרוֹת בִּצְרוֹר הַחַיִּים עִם נִשְׁמוֹת אַבְרָהָם יִצְחָק וְיַעֲקֹב, שָׂרָה רִבְקָה רָחֵל וְלֵאָה, וְעִם שְׁאָר צַדִּיקִים וְצִדְקָנִיּוֹת שֶׁבְּגַן עֵדֶן, וְנֹאמַר אָמֵן.

After reciting the above יזכור *texts, it is customary to also recite the following* אֵל מָלֵא *paragraphs, as applicable.*

For an individual:

אֵל מָלֵא רַחֲמִים, שׁוֹכֵן בַּמְּרוֹמִים, הַמְצֵא מְנוּחָה נְכוֹנָה תַּחַת (נ״א עַל) כַּנְפֵי הַשְּׁכִינָה, בְּמַעֲלוֹת קְדוֹשִׁים וּטְהוֹרִים, כְּזֹהַר הָרָקִיעַ מַזְהִירִים, לְנִשְׁמַת

For a man:

(פלוני בֶּן פלוני) שֶׁהָלַךְ לְעוֹלָמוֹ, בַּעֲבוּר שֶׁאֶתֵּן צְדָקָה בְּעַד הַזְכָּרַת נִשְׁמָתוֹ, בְּגַן עֵדֶן תְּהֵא מְנוּחָתוֹ. לָכֵן, בַּעַל הָרַחֲמִים יַסְתִּירֵהוּ

---

term here is primarily a prayer for atonement of the souls of the departed (R. Joseph B. Soloveitchik).

בצרור החיים – *Bond of life.* The Gemara (*Shabbat* 152b) identifies this as the "concealment of righteous souls under the divine throne." The *Zohar* explains that those who act to further the divine mission in this world are invested with eternal life, and retain a bond to the divine source after physical life has ended.

אֵל מָלֵא רַחֲמִים – *God, full of mercy.* The earliest mention of this prayer, whose author is unknown, is found in the *Ma'avar Yabok* (published in 1626). The text, apparently written in Germany, reflects the understanding of the thirteenth-century Ramban, as found in his *Shaar HaGemul* (and as further refined by the *Rosh*). As they explain, immediately after death the soul goes to the world of the souls. The righteous are immediately rewarded, while the

For one's extended family:

יִזְכֹּר MAY GOD REMEMBER the souls of my grandfathers and grandmothers, uncles and aunts, brothers and sisters, both on my father's side and on my mother's side, who have gone on to their eternal reward, insofar as I will make a charitable gift in memory of their souls. As reward for this, may their souls be bound in lasting life, together with the souls of Abraham, Isaac, and Jacob; Sarah, Rebecca, Rachel, and Leah; and together with the other righteous men and women who are in the Garden of Eden. And let us say, Amen.

For martyrs:

יִזְכֹּר MAY GOD REMEMBER the souls of (all my relatives, both on my father's side and on my mother's side,) the holy and pure ones who were killed, murdered, slaughtered, burned, drowned, and strangled for the sanctification of the Name, insofar as I will make a charitable gift in memory of their souls. As reward for this, may their souls be bound in lasting life, together with the souls of Abraham, Isaac, and Jacob; Sarah, Rebecca, Rachel, and Leah; and together with the other righteous men and women who are in the Garden of Eden. And let us say, Amen.

After reciting the above Yizkor texts, it is customary to also recite the following Kel Maleh paragraphs, as applicable.

For an individual:

אֵל GOD, full of mercy, Who dwells on high, grant fitting rest beneath (*some say:* above) the protective wings of the Divine Presence, where the souls of the holy and pure ones – whose radiance is like that of the heavens – reside, to the soul of

For a man:

(*name of the deceased*) the son of (*father of the deceased*), who has gone to his eternal reward, insofar as I will make a charitable gift in memory of his soul, may the Garden of Eden be his resting place. For

---

unrepentant most serious sinners suffer eternal punishment in *Gehennom*. Less serious sinners are sent to *Gehennom* for twelve months, and depending on their sins, can ascend from there at some point to receive their earned reward in *Gan Eden*. Thus the prayer beseeches God to raise the soul of the beloved departed one from *Gehennom* to reach *Gan Eden*, to be in the company of the souls of the righteous and holy ones that reside there.

תַּחַת כַּנְפֵי הַשְּׁכִינָה – *Beneath the protective wings of the Divine Presence.* There are two versions of this phrase. One reads תַּחַת (beneath), while the other reads עַל (on). The former reading is likely the correct one, for a number of reasons. Numerous Scriptural passages (particularly in Psalms 17:8, 61:4–5, 36:8) invoke the language "under the wings" or "in the shadow of the wings" to express God's protective covering or His concealing someone in the face of

בְּסֵתֶר כְּנָפָיו לְעוֹלָמִים, וְיִצְרֹר בִּצְרוֹר הַחַיִּים אֶת נִשְׁמָתוֹ, יהוה הוּא נַחֲלָתוֹ, וְיָנְוּחַ בְּשָׁלוֹם עַל מִשְׁכָּבוֹ, וְנֹאמַר אָמֵן.

For a woman:

(פלונית בַּת פלוני) שֶׁהָלְכָה לְעוֹלָמָהּ, בַּעֲבוּר שֶׁאֶתֵּן צְדָקָה בְּעַד הַזְכָּרַת נִשְׁמָתָהּ, בְּגַן עֵדֶן תְּהֵא מְנוּחָתָהּ. לָכֵן, בַּעַל הָרַחֲמִים יַסְתִּירֶהָ בְּסֵתֶר כְּנָפָיו לְעוֹלָמִים, וְיִצְרֹר בִּצְרוֹר הַחַיִּים אֶת נִשְׁמָתָהּ, יהוה הוּא נַחֲלָתָהּ, וְתָנְוּחַ בְּשָׁלוֹם עַל מִשְׁכָּבָהּ, וְנֹאמַר אָמֵן.

For a group:

אֵל מָלֵא רַחֲמִים, שׁוֹכֵן בַּמְּרוֹמִים, הַמְצֵא מְנוּחָה נְכוֹנָה תַּחַת (נ״א עַל) כַּנְפֵי הַשְּׁכִינָה, בְּמַעֲלוֹת קְדוֹשִׁים וּטְהוֹרִים, כְּזְהַר הָרָקִיעַ מַזְהִירִים, לְנִשְׁמוֹת

For a group of men:

(פלוני בֶּן פלוני) שֶׁהָלְכוּ לְעוֹלָמָם, בַּעֲבוּר שֶׁאֶתֵּן צְדָקָה בְּעַד הַזְכָּרַת נִשְׁמוֹתֵיהֶם, בְּגַן עֵדֶן תְּהֵא מְנוּחָתָם. לָכֵן, בַּעַל הָרַחֲמִים יַסְתִּירֵם בְּסֵתֶר כְּנָפָיו לְעוֹלָמִים, וְיִצְרֹר בִּצְרוֹר הַחַיִּים אֶת נִשְׁמוֹתֵיהֶם, יהוה הוּא נַחֲלָתָם, וְיָנְוּחוּ בְּשָׁלוֹם עַל מִשְׁכְּבָם, וְנֹאמַר אָמֵן.

For a group of women:

(פלונית בַּת פלוני) שֶׁהָלְכוּ לְעוֹלָמָן, בַּעֲבוּר שֶׁאֶתֵּן צְדָקָה בְּעַד הַזְכָּרַת נִשְׁמוֹתֵיהֶן, בְּגַן עֵדֶן תְּהֵא מְנוּחָתָן. לָכֵן, בַּעַל הָרַחֲמִים יַסְתִּירֵן בְּסֵתֶר כְּנָפָיו לְעוֹלָמִים, וְיִצְרֹר בִּצְרוֹר הַחַיִּים אֶת נִשְׁמוֹתֵיהֶן, יהוה הוּא נַחֲלָתָן, וְיָנְוּחוּ בְּשָׁלוֹם עַל מִשְׁכְּבָן, וְנֹאמַר אָמֵן.

---

danger. So too in the above-quoted Gemara (*Shabbat* 152b), the souls of the righteous are concealed under the divine throne. This sense is also reflected in the subsequent language of the *Kel Malei* itself, which describes God as concealing the deceased under His wings. While there are certainly other sources that prefer the "on the wings" formulation, based primarily on R. Isaiah Horowitz (the *Shela*), the preponderance of medieval (especially

this reason may the ever-merciful One shelter the deceased under His protective wings forever, and may He bind his soul in lasting life. For the Lord will surely be his benefactor, so that he can rest in peace in his allotted place. And let us say, Amen.

For a woman:

(*name of the deceased*) the daughter of (*father of the deceased*), who has gone to her eternal reward, insofar as I will make a charitable gift in memory of her soul, may the Garden of Eden be her resting place. For this reason may the ever-merciful One shelter the deceased under His protective wings forever, and may He bind her soul in lasting life. For the Lord will surely be her benefactor, so that she can rest in peace in her allotted place. And let us say, Amen.

For a group:

אֵל GOD, full of mercy, Who dwells on high, grant fitting rest beneath (some say: above) the protective wings of the Divine Presence, where the souls of the holy and pure ones – whose radiance is like that of the heavens – reside, to the souls of

For a group of men:

(*names of the deceased*), who have gone to their eternal reward, insofar as I will make a charitable gift in memory of their souls, may the Garden of Eden be their resting place. For this reason may the ever-merciful One shelter the deceased under His protective wings forever, and may He bind their souls in lasting life. For the Lord will surely be their benefactor, so that they can rest in peace in their allotted place. And let us say, Amen.

For a group of women:

(*names of the deceased*), who have gone to their eternal reward, insofar as I will make a charitable gift in memory of their souls, may the Garden of Eden be their resting place. For this reason may the ever-merciful One shelter the deceased under His protective wings forever, and may He bind their souls in lasting life. For the Lord will surely be their benefactor, so that they can rest in peace in their allotted place. And let us say, Amen.

Rambam) and early modern texts give priority to "beneath." This indeed was the preference and practice of R. Joseph B. Soloveitchik (R. Yaakov Jaffe).

תפילות מיוחדות לזכר אירועים היסטוריים ולאומיים

Some congregations recite the following for the Six Million martyrs of the Holocaust.

אֵל מָלֵא רַחֲמִים, דַּיַּן אַלְמָנוֹת וַאֲבִי יְתוֹמִים, אַל נָא תֶחֱשֶׁה וְתִתְאַפַּק לְדַם יִשְׂרָאֵל שֶׁנִּשְׁפַּךְ כַּמָּיִם. הַמְצֵא מְנוּחָה נְכוֹנָה תַּחַת (נ״א עַל) כַּנְפֵי הַשְּׁכִינָה, בְּמַעֲלוֹת קְדוֹשִׁים וּטְהוֹרִים, כְּזֹהַר הָרָקִיעַ מַזְהִירִים, אֶת נִשְׁמוֹת שֵׁשׁ מֵאוֹת רִבְבוֹת אַלְפֵי יִשְׂרָאֵל, אֲנָשִׁים וְנָשִׁים, יְלָדִים וִילָדוֹת, חַלְלֵי הַשּׁוֹאָה בְּאֵירוֹפָּה, שֶׁנֶּהֶרְגוּ וְשֶׁנִּשְׁחֲטוּ וְשֶׁנִּשְׂרְפוּ וְשֶׁנִּטְבְּעוּ וְשֶׁנֶּחְנְקוּ וְשֶׁנִּקְבְּרוּ חַיִּים, עַל קִדּוּשׁ הַשֵּׁם, בִּידֵי הַמְרַצְּחִים הַנָּאצִים הָאֲרוּרִים וְעוֹזְרֵיהֶם מִשְּׁאָר הָעַמִּים יִמַּח שְׁמָם וְזִכְרָם. כֻּלָּם קְדוֹשִׁים וּטְהוֹרִים, וּבָהֶם גְּאוֹנִים וְצַדִּיקִים, אַרְזֵי הַלְּבָנוֹן וְאַדִּירֵי הַתּוֹרָה. בְּגַן עֵדֶן תְּהֵא מְנוּחָתָם, בַּעֲבוּר שֶׁכָּל הַקָּהָל הַקָּדוֹשׁ הַזֶּה יִתְּנוּ צְדָקָה בְּעַד הַזְכָּרַת נִשְׁמוֹתֵיהֶם. לָכֵן, בַּעַל הָרַחֲמִים יַסְתִּירֵם בְּסֵתֶר כְּנָפָיו לְעוֹלָמִים, וְיִצְרֹר בִּצְרוֹר הַחַיִּים אֶת נִשְׁמוֹתֵיהֶם, יהוה הוּא נַחֲלָתָם, וְיִזְכֹּר לָנוּ עֲקֵדָתָם, וְתַעֲמֹד לָנוּ וּלְכָל יִשְׂרָאֵל זְכוּתָם. אֶרֶץ אַל תְּכַסִּי דָמָם, וְאַל יְהִי מָקוֹם לְזַעֲקָתָם. בְּגַן עֵדֶן תְּהֵא מְנוּחָתָם, וְיַעַמְדוּ לְגוֹרָלָם לְקֵץ הַיָּמִין, וְנֹאמַר אָמֵן.

Some congregations recite the following for those who have given their lives in defense of the State of Israel.

אֵל מָלֵא רַחֲמִים, שׁוֹכֵן בַּמְּרוֹמִים, הַמְצֵא מְנוּחָה נְכוֹנָה תַּחַת (נ״א עַל) כַּנְפֵי הַשְּׁכִינָה, בְּמַעֲלוֹת קְדוֹשִׁים טְהוֹרִים וְגִבּוֹרִים, כְּזֹהַר הָרָקִיעַ מַזְהִירִים, לְנִשְׁמוֹת הַקְּדוֹשִׁים שֶׁנִּלְחֲמוּ בְּכָל מַעַרְכוֹת יִשְׂרָאֵל, בַּמַּחְתֶּרֶת וּבִצְבָא הַהֲגָנָה לְיִשְׂרָאֵל, וְשֶׁנָּפְלוּ בְּמִלְחַמְתָּם וּמָסְרוּ נַפְשָׁם עַל קְדֻשַּׁת הַשֵּׁם, הָעָם וְהָאָרֶץ, בַּעֲבוּר שֶׁכָּל הַקָּהָל הַקָּדוֹשׁ הַזֶּה יִתְּנוּ צְדָקָה בְּעַד הַזְכָּרַת נִשְׁמוֹתֵיהֶם. לָכֵן, בַּעַל הָרַחֲמִים יַסְתִּירֵם בְּסֵתֶר כְּנָפָיו לְעוֹלָמִים, וְיִצְרֹר בִּצְרוֹר הַחַיִּים אֶת נִשְׁמוֹתֵיהֶם, יהוה הוּא נַחֲלָתָם, בְּגַן עֵדֶן תְּהֵא מְנוּחָתָם, וְיָנוּחוּ בְשָׁלוֹם עַל מִשְׁכְּבוֹתֵיהֶם וְתַעֲמֹד לְכָל יִשְׂרָאֵל זְכוּתָם, וְיַעַמְדוּ לְגוֹרָלָם לְקֵץ הַיָּמִין, וְנֹאמַר אָמֵן.

The service continues on page 560.

קְדוֹשִׁים וּטְהוֹרִים – *The holy and pure ones.* There is particular significance to perpetuating the memory of the martyrs of the Holocaust, just as our sages instituted the *Av haRaḥamim* for each Shabbat, and just as we recite *Yizkor* on behalf of those slaughtered for the sanctification of God's name. The purpose is to connect with them, and to be included together with them in the category of sacred Israel, thereby associating our commitment

SPECIAL PRAYERS FOR OCCASIONS BEARING HISTORICAL OR NATIONAL SIGNIFICANCE

Some congregations recite the following for the Six Million martyrs of the Holocaust.

אֵל GOD, full of mercy, Who dwells on high, Judge of the widows and Father of the orphans, do not be silent or restrained before the blood of Israel, spilled like water. Grant proper rest beneath (*some say:* above) the protective wings of the Divine Presence, in the heights of the holy and pure ones whose radiance is like that of the heavens, for the souls of the six million, – men and women, boys and girls – the victims of the European Holocaust, who were killed, murdered, slaughtered, burned, drowned, strangled and buried alive, for the sanctification of the Name, in the hands of the murderous, cursed Nazis and their collaborators from other nations, may their names and memories be blotted out. The martyrs were all holy and pure, and among them were geniuses and righteous men, cedars of Lebanon and mighty Torah giants. May the Garden of Eden be their resting place, insofar as this entire holy congregation will make a charitable gift in remembrance of their souls. For this, may the ever-merciful One shelter the deceased under His protective wings forever, and may He bind their souls in lasting life. For the Lord will surely be their benefactor, and He shall remember for us their Binding. Their merit shall stand for us and all of Israel. May the land not conceal their blood, may there not be a hiding place for their screams. May the Garden of Eden be their resting place, and may they meet their destiny during the End of Days. And let us say, Amen.

Some congregations recite the following for those who have given their lives in defense of the State of Israel.

אֵל GOD, full of mercy, who dwells on high, grant fitting rest beneath (*some say:* above) the wings of the Divine Presence, in the heights of the holy, the pure and the brave, who shine like the radiance of heaven, to the souls of the holy ones who fought in any of Israel's battles, in clandestine operations and in Israel's Defense Forces, who fell in battle and sacrificed their lives for the consecration of God's name, for the people and the land, insofar as this entire holy congregation will make a charitable gift in remembrance of their souls. Therefore, Master of compassion, shelter them in the shadow of Your wings forever, and bind their souls in lasting life. The Lord is their heritage; may the Garden of Eden be their resting place, may they rest in peace, may their merit stand for all Israel, and may they receive their reward at the End of Days, and let us say: Amen.

The service continues on page 561.

---

to *Kiddush Hashem* with the actual *Kiddush Hashem* of those martyrs. The bond with all of the martyrs is a connection that precipitates blessing, for through this connection their sanctity and purity will guard us (*Netivot Shalom*).

קריאת התורה
THE READING OF THE TORAH

לימי שני וחמישי ולמנחה של שבת
FOR MONDAYS, THURSDAYS, AND SHABBAT MINḤA

BERESHIT / בראשית

בראשית א: א-כג

בְּרֵאשִׁ֖ית בָּרָ֣א אֱלֹהִ֑ים אֵ֥ת הַשָּׁמַ֖יִם וְאֵ֥ת
הָאָֽרֶץ׃ וְהָאָ֗רֶץ הָיְתָ֥ה תֹ֙הוּ֙ וָבֹ֔הוּ וְחֹ֖שֶׁךְ עַל־
פְּנֵ֣י תְה֑וֹם וְר֣וּחַ אֱלֹהִ֔ים מְרַחֶ֖פֶת עַל־פְּנֵ֥י
הַמָּֽיִם׃ וַיֹּ֥אמֶר אֱלֹהִ֖ים יְהִ֣י א֑וֹר וַֽיְהִי־אֽוֹר׃
וַיַּ֧רְא אֱלֹהִ֛ים אֶת־הָא֖וֹר כִּי־ט֑וֹב וַיַּבְדֵּ֣ל
אֱלֹהִ֔ים בֵּ֥ין הָא֖וֹר וּבֵ֥ין הַחֹֽשֶׁךְ׃ וַיִּקְרָ֨א
אֱלֹהִ֤ים ׀ לָאוֹר֙ י֔וֹם וְלַחֹ֖שֶׁךְ קָ֣רָא לָ֑יְלָה וַֽיְהִי־
עֶ֥רֶב וַֽיְהִי־בֹ֖קֶר י֥וֹם אֶחָֽד׃
לוי: וַיֹּ֣אמֶר אֱלֹהִ֔ים יְהִ֥י רָקִ֖יעַ בְּת֣וֹךְ הַמָּ֑יִם
וִיהִ֣י מַבְדִּ֔יל בֵּ֥ין מַ֖יִם לָמָֽיִם׃ וַיַּ֣עַשׂ אֱלֹהִים֮
אֶת־הָרָקִיעַ֒ וַיַּבְדֵּ֗ל בֵּ֤ין הַמַּ֙יִם֙ אֲשֶׁר֙ מִתַּ֣חַת
לָרָקִ֔יעַ וּבֵ֣ין הַמַּ֔יִם אֲשֶׁ֖ר מֵעַ֣ל לָרָקִ֑יעַ וַֽיְהִי־
כֵֽן׃ וַיִּקְרָ֧א אֱלֹהִ֛ים לָֽרָקִ֖יעַ שָׁמָ֑יִם וַֽיְהִי־עֶ֥רֶב
וַֽיְהִי־בֹ֖קֶר י֥וֹם שֵׁנִֽי׃
ישראל: וַיֹּ֣אמֶר אֱלֹהִ֗ים יִקָּו֨וּ הַמַּ֜יִם מִתַּ֤חַת
הַשָּׁמַ֙יִם֙ אֶל־מָק֣וֹם אֶחָ֔ד וְתֵרָאֶ֖ה הַיַּבָּשָׁ֑ה
וַֽיְהִי־כֵֽן׃ וַיִּקְרָ֨א אֱלֹהִ֤ים ׀ לַיַּבָּשָׁה֙ אֶ֔רֶץ
וּלְמִקְוֵ֥ה הַמַּ֖יִם קָרָ֣א יַמִּ֑ים וַיַּ֥רְא אֱלֹהִ֖ים כִּי־
טֽוֹב׃ וַיֹּ֣אמֶר אֱלֹהִ֗ים תַּֽדְשֵׁ֤א הָאָ֙רֶץ֙ דֶּ֔שֶׁא
עֵ֚שֶׂב מַזְרִ֣יעַ זֶ֔רַע עֵ֣ץ פְּרִ֞י עֹ֤שֶׂה פְּרִי֙ לְמִינ֔וֹ
אֲשֶׁ֥ר זַרְעוֹ־ב֖וֹ עַל־הָאָ֑רֶץ וַֽיְהִי־כֵֽן׃ וַתּוֹצֵ֨א
הָאָ֜רֶץ דֶּ֠שֶׁא עֵ֣שֶׂב מַזְרִ֤יעַ זֶ֙רַע֙ לְמִינֵ֔הוּ וְעֵ֧ץ
עֹֽשֶׂה־פְּרִ֛י אֲשֶׁ֥ר זַרְעוֹ־ב֖וֹ לְמִינֵ֑הוּ וַיַּ֥רְא
אֱלֹהִ֖ים כִּי־טֽוֹב׃ וַֽיְהִי־עֶ֥רֶב וַֽיְהִי־בֹ֖קֶר י֥וֹם
שְׁלִישִֽׁי׃

NOAḤ / נח

בראשית ו: ט-כב

אֵ֚לֶּה תּוֹלְדֹ֣ת נֹ֔חַ נֹ֗חַ אִ֥ישׁ צַדִּ֛יק תָּמִ֥ים הָיָ֖ה
בְּדֹֽרֹתָ֑יו אֶת־הָֽאֱלֹהִ֖ים הִֽתְהַלֶּךְ־נֹֽחַ׃ וַיּ֥וֹלֶד
נֹ֖חַ שְׁלֹשָׁ֣ה בָנִ֑ים אֶת־שֵׁ֖ם אֶת־חָ֥ם וְאֶת־
יָֽפֶת׃ וַתִּשָּׁחֵ֥ת הָאָ֖רֶץ לִפְנֵ֣י הָֽאֱלֹהִ֑ים וַתִּמָּלֵ֥א
הָאָ֖רֶץ חָמָֽס׃ וַיַּ֧רְא אֱלֹהִ֛ים אֶת־הָאָ֖רֶץ וְהִנֵּ֣ה
נִשְׁחָ֑תָה כִּֽי־הִשְׁחִ֧ית כָּל־בָּשָׂ֛ר אֶת־דַּרְכּ֖וֹ
עַל־הָאָֽרֶץ׃ וַיֹּ֨אמֶר אֱלֹהִ֜ים לְנֹ֗חַ קֵ֤ץ כָּל־בָּשָׂר֙
בָּ֣א לְפָנַ֔י כִּֽי־מָלְאָ֥ה הָאָ֛רֶץ חָמָ֖ס מִפְּנֵיהֶ֑ם
וְהִנְנִ֥י מַשְׁחִיתָ֖ם אֶת־הָאָֽרֶץ׃ עֲשֵׂ֤ה לְךָ֙ תֵּבַ֣ת
עֲצֵי־גֹ֔פֶר קִנִּ֖ים תַּעֲשֶׂ֣ה אֶת־הַתֵּבָ֑ה וְכָֽפַרְתָּ֥
אֹתָ֛הּ מִבַּ֥יִת וּמִח֖וּץ בַּכֹּֽפֶר׃ וְזֶ֕ה אֲשֶׁ֥ר תַּעֲשֶׂ֖ה
אֹתָ֑הּ שְׁלֹ֨שׁ מֵא֤וֹת אַמָּה֙ אֹ֣רֶךְ הַתֵּבָ֔ה חֲמִשִּׁ֤ים
אַמָּה֙ רָחְבָּ֔הּ וּשְׁלֹשִׁ֥ים אַמָּ֖ה קוֹמָתָֽהּ׃ צֹ֣הַר ׀
תַּעֲשֶׂ֣ה לַתֵּבָ֗ה וְאֶל־אַמָּה֙ תְּכַלֶּ֣נָּה מִלְמַ֔עְלָה
וּפֶ֥תַח הַתֵּבָ֖ה בְּצִדָּ֣הּ תָּשִׂ֑ים תַּחְתִּיִּ֛ם שְׁנִיִּ֥ם
וּשְׁלִשִׁ֖ים תַּעֲשֶֽׂהָ׃ לוי: וַאֲנִ֗י הִנְנִי֩ מֵבִ֨יא אֶת־
הַמַּבּ֥וּל מַ֙יִם֙ עַל־הָאָ֔רֶץ לְשַׁחֵ֣ת כָּל־בָּשָׂ֗ר
אֲשֶׁר־בּוֹ֙ ר֣וּחַ חַיִּ֔ים מִתַּ֖חַת הַשָּׁמָ֑יִם כֹּ֥ל
אֲשֶׁר־בָּאָ֖רֶץ יִגְוָֽע׃ וַהֲקִמֹתִ֥י אֶת־בְּרִיתִ֖י אִתָּ֑ךְ
וּבָאתָ֙ אֶל־הַתֵּבָ֔ה אַתָּ֕ה וּבָנֶ֛יךָ וְאִשְׁתְּךָ֥ וּנְשֵֽׁי־
בָנֶ֖יךָ אִתָּֽךְ׃ וּמִכָּל־הָ֠חַי מִֽכָּל־בָּשָׂ֞ר שְׁנַ֧יִם
מִכֹּ֛ל תָּבִ֥יא אֶל־הַתֵּבָ֖ה לְהַחֲיֹ֣ת אִתָּ֑ךְ זָכָ֥ר
וּנְקֵבָ֖ה יִהְיֽוּ׃ ישראל: מֵהָע֣וֹף לְמִינֵ֗הוּ וּמִן־
הַבְּהֵמָה֙ לְמִינָ֔הּ מִכֹּ֛ל רֶ֥מֶשׂ הָאֲדָמָ֖ה לְמִינֵ֑הוּ
שְׁנַ֧יִם מִכֹּ֛ל יָבֹ֥אוּ אֵלֶ֖יךָ לְהַחֲיֽוֹת׃ וְאַתָּ֣ה קַח־
לְךָ֗ מִכָּל־מַֽאֲכָל֙ אֲשֶׁ֣ר יֵֽאָכֵ֔ל וְאָסַפְתָּ֖ אֵלֶ֑יךָ
וְהָיָ֥ה לְךָ֛ וְלָהֶ֖ם לְאָכְלָֽה׃ וַיַּ֖עַשׂ נֹ֑חַ כְּ֠כֹל אֲשֶׁ֨ר
צִוָּ֥ה אֹת֛וֹ אֱלֹהִ֖ים כֵּ֥ן עָשָֽׂה׃

LEKH LEKHA / לך לך

בראשית יב: א-יג

וַיֹּ֤אמֶר יהוה֙ אֶל־אַבְרָ֔ם לֶךְ־לְךָ֛ מֵאַרְצְךָ֥

וּמִמּוֹלַדְתְּךָ וּמִבֵּית אָבִיךָ אֶל־הָאָרֶץ אֲשֶׁר אַרְאֶךָּ: וְאֶעֶשְׂךָ לְגוֹי גָּדוֹל וַאֲבָרֶכְךָ וַאֲגַדְּלָה שְׁמֶךָ וֶהְיֵה בְּרָכָה: וַאֲבָרְכָה מְבָרְכֶיךָ וּמְקַלֶּלְךָ אָאֹר וְנִבְרְכוּ בְךָ כֹּל מִשְׁפְּחֹת הָאֲדָמָה:

לוי: וַיֵּלֶךְ אַבְרָם כַּאֲשֶׁר דִּבֶּר אֵלָיו יהוה וַיֵּלֶךְ אִתּוֹ לוֹט וְאַבְרָם בֶּן־חָמֵשׁ שָׁנִים וְשִׁבְעִים שָׁנָה בְּצֵאתוֹ מֵחָרָן: וַיִּקַּח אַבְרָם אֶת־שָׂרַי אִשְׁתּוֹ וְאֶת־לוֹט בֶּן־אָחִיו וְאֶת־כָּל־רְכוּשָׁם אֲשֶׁר רָכָשׁוּ וְאֶת־הַנֶּפֶשׁ אֲשֶׁר־עָשׂוּ בְחָרָן וַיֵּצְאוּ לָלֶכֶת אַרְצָה כְּנַעַן וַיָּבֹאוּ אַרְצָה כְּנָעַן: וַיַּעֲבֹר אַבְרָם בָּאָרֶץ עַד מְקוֹם שְׁכֶם עַד אֵלוֹן מוֹרֶה וְהַכְּנַעֲנִי אָז בָּאָרֶץ: וַיֵּרָא יהוה אֶל־אַבְרָם וַיֹּאמֶר לְזַרְעֲךָ אֶתֵּן אֶת־הָאָרֶץ הַזֹּאת וַיִּבֶן שָׁם מִזְבֵּחַ לַיהוה הַנִּרְאֶה אֵלָיו: וַיַּעְתֵּק מִשָּׁם הָהָרָה מִקֶּדֶם לְבֵית־אֵל וַיֵּט אָהֳלֹה בֵּית־אֵל מִיָּם וְהָעַי מִקֶּדֶם וַיִּבֶן־שָׁם מִזְבֵּחַ לַיהוה וַיִּקְרָא בְּשֵׁם יהוה: וַיִּסַּע אַבְרָם הָלוֹךְ וְנָסוֹעַ הַנֶּגְבָּה:

ישראל: וַיְהִי רָעָב בָּאָרֶץ וַיֵּרֶד אַבְרָם מִצְרַיְמָה לָגוּר שָׁם כִּי־כָבֵד הָרָעָב בָּאָרֶץ: וַיְהִי כַּאֲשֶׁר הִקְרִיב לָבוֹא מִצְרָיְמָה וַיֹּאמֶר אֶל־שָׂרַי אִשְׁתּוֹ הִנֵּה־נָא יָדַעְתִּי כִּי אִשָּׁה יְפַת־מַרְאֶה אָתְּ: וְהָיָה כִּי־יִרְאוּ אֹתָךְ הַמִּצְרִים וְאָמְרוּ אִשְׁתּוֹ זֹאת וְהָרְגוּ אֹתִי וְאֹתָךְ יְחַיּוּ: אִמְרִי־נָא אֲחֹתִי אָתְּ לְמַעַן יִיטַב־לִי בַעֲבוּרֵךְ וְחָיְתָה נַפְשִׁי בִּגְלָלֵךְ:

VAYERA / וירא

בראשית יח: א–יד

וַיֵּרָא אֵלָיו יהוה בְּאֵלֹנֵי מַמְרֵא וְהוּא יֹשֵׁב פֶּתַח־הָאֹהֶל כְּחֹם הַיּוֹם: וַיִּשָּׂא עֵינָיו וַיַּרְא וְהִנֵּה שְׁלֹשָׁה אֲנָשִׁים נִצָּבִים עָלָיו וַיַּרְא וַיָּרָץ לִקְרָאתָם מִפֶּתַח הָאֹהֶל וַיִּשְׁתַּחוּ אָרְצָה: וַיֹּאמַר אֲדֹנָי אִם־נָא מָצָאתִי חֵן בְּעֵינֶיךָ אַל־נָא תַעֲבֹר מֵעַל עַבְדֶּךָ: יֻקַּח־נָא מְעַט־מַיִם וְרַחֲצוּ רַגְלֵיכֶם וְהִשָּׁעֲנוּ תַּחַת הָעֵץ: וְאֶקְחָה פַת־לֶחֶם וְסַעֲדוּ לִבְּכֶם אַחַר תַּעֲבֹרוּ כִּי־עַל־כֵּן עֲבַרְתֶּם עַל־עַבְדְּכֶם וַיֹּאמְרוּ כֵּן תַּעֲשֶׂה כַּאֲשֶׁר דִּבַּרְתָּ:

לוי: וַיְמַהֵר אַבְרָהָם הָאֹהֱלָה אֶל־שָׂרָה וַיֹּאמֶר מַהֲרִי שְׁלֹשׁ סְאִים קֶמַח סֹלֶת לוּשִׁי וַעֲשִׂי עֻגוֹת: וְאֶל־הַבָּקָר רָץ אַבְרָהָם וַיִּקַּח בֶּן־בָּקָר רַךְ וָטוֹב וַיִּתֵּן אֶל־הַנַּעַר וַיְמַהֵר לַעֲשׂוֹת אֹתוֹ: וַיִּקַּח חֶמְאָה וְחָלָב וּבֶן־הַבָּקָר אֲשֶׁר עָשָׂה וַיִּתֵּן לִפְנֵיהֶם וְהוּא עֹמֵד עֲלֵיהֶם תַּחַת הָעֵץ וַיֹּאכֵלוּ:

ישראל: וַיֹּאמְרוּ אֵלָיו אַיֵּה שָׂרָה אִשְׁתֶּךָ וַיֹּאמֶר הִנֵּה בָאֹהֶל: וַיֹּאמֶר שׁוֹב אָשׁוּב אֵלֶיךָ כָּעֵת חַיָּה וְהִנֵּה־בֵן לְשָׂרָה אִשְׁתֶּךָ וְשָׂרָה שֹׁמַעַת פֶּתַח הָאֹהֶל וְהוּא אַחֲרָיו: וְאַבְרָהָם וְשָׂרָה זְקֵנִים בָּאִים בַּיָּמִים חָדַל לִהְיוֹת לְשָׂרָה אֹרַח כַּנָּשִׁים: וַתִּצְחַק שָׂרָה בְּקִרְבָּהּ לֵאמֹר אַחֲרֵי בְלֹתִי הָיְתָה־לִּי עֶדְנָה וַאדֹנִי זָקֵן: וַיֹּאמֶר יהוה אֶל־אַבְרָהָם לָמָּה זֶּה צָחֲקָה שָׂרָה לֵאמֹר הַאַף אֻמְנָם אֵלֵד וַאֲנִי זָקַנְתִּי: הֲיִפָּלֵא מֵיהוה דָּבָר לַמּוֹעֵד אָשׁוּב אֵלֶיךָ כָּעֵת חַיָּה וּלְשָׂרָה בֵן:

HAYYEI SARA / חיי שרה

בראשית כג: א–טז

וַיִּהְיוּ חַיֵּי שָׂרָה מֵאָה שָׁנָה וְעֶשְׂרִים שָׁנָה וְשֶׁבַע שָׁנִים שְׁנֵי חַיֵּי שָׂרָה: וַתָּמָת שָׂרָה בְּקִרְיַת אַרְבַּע הִוא חֶבְרוֹן בְּאֶרֶץ כְּנָעַן וַיָּבֹא אַבְרָהָם לִסְפֹּד לְשָׂרָה וְלִבְכֹּתָהּ: וַיָּקָם אַבְרָהָם מֵעַל פְּנֵי מֵתוֹ וַיְדַבֵּר אֶל־בְּנֵי־חֵת לֵאמֹר: גֵּר־וְתוֹשָׁב אָנֹכִי עִמָּכֶם תְּנוּ לִי אֲחֻזַּת־קֶבֶר עִמָּכֶם וְאֶקְבְּרָה מֵתִי מִלְּפָנָי: וַיַּעֲנוּ בְנֵי־חֵת אֶת־אַבְרָהָם לֵאמֹר לוֹ: שְׁמָעֵנוּ ׀ אֲדֹנִי נְשִׂיא אֱלֹהִים אַתָּה בְּתוֹכֵנוּ בְּמִבְחַר קְבָרֵינוּ קְבֹר אֶת־מֵתֶךָ אִישׁ מִמֶּנּוּ אֶת־קִבְרוֹ לֹא־יִכְלֶה מִמְּךָ מִקְּבֹר מֵתֶךָ: וַיָּקָם אַבְרָהָם וַיִּשְׁתַּחוּ לְעַם־הָאָרֶץ לִבְנֵי־חֵת:

לוי: וַיְדַבֵּר אִתָּם לֵאמֹר אִם־יֵשׁ אֶת־נַפְשְׁכֶם לִקְבֹּר אֶת־מֵתִי מִלְּפָנַי שְׁמָעוּנִי וּפִגְעוּ־לִי בְּעֶפְרוֹן בֶּן־צֹחַר: וְיִתֶּן־לִי אֶת־

מְעָרַת הַמַּכְפֵּלָה אֲשֶׁר־לוֹ אֲשֶׁר בִּקְצֵה שָׂדֵהוּ בְּכֶסֶף מָלֵא יִתְּנֶנָּה לִּי בְּתוֹכְכֶם לַאֲחֻזַּת־קָבֶר׃ וְעֶפְרוֹן יֹשֵׁב בְּתוֹךְ בְּנֵי־חֵת וַיַּעַן עֶפְרוֹן הַחִתִּי אֶת־אַבְרָהָם בְּאָזְנֵי בְנֵי־חֵת לְכֹל בָּאֵי שַׁעַר־עִירוֹ לֵאמֹר׃ לֹא־אֲדֹנִי שְׁמָעֵנִי הַשָּׂדֶה נָתַתִּי לָךְ וְהַמְּעָרָה אֲשֶׁר־בּוֹ לְךָ נְתַתִּיהָ לְעֵינֵי בְנֵי־עַמִּי נְתַתִּיהָ לָּךְ קְבֹר מֵתֶךָ׃ וַיִּשְׁתַּחוּ אַבְרָהָם לִפְנֵי עַם־הָאָרֶץ׃ ישראל: וַיְדַבֵּר אֶל־עֶפְרוֹן בְּאָזְנֵי עַם־הָאָרֶץ לֵאמֹר אַךְ אִם־אַתָּה לוּ שְׁמָעֵנִי נָתַתִּי כֶּסֶף הַשָּׂדֶה קַח מִמֶּנִּי וְאֶקְבְּרָה אֶת־מֵתִי שָׁמָּה׃ וַיַּעַן עֶפְרוֹן אֶת־אַבְרָהָם לֵאמֹר לוֹ׃ אֲדֹנִי שְׁמָעֵנִי אֶרֶץ אַרְבַּע מֵאֹת שֶׁקֶל־כֶּסֶף בֵּינִי וּבֵינְךָ מַה־הִוא וְאֶת־מֵתְךָ קְבֹר׃ וַיִּשְׁמַע אַבְרָהָם אֶל־עֶפְרוֹן וַיִּשְׁקֹל אַבְרָהָם לְעֶפְרֹן אֶת־הַכֶּסֶף אֲשֶׁר דִּבֶּר בְּאָזְנֵי בְנֵי־חֵת אַרְבַּע מֵאוֹת שֶׁקֶל כֶּסֶף עֹבֵר לַסֹּחֵר׃

תולדות / TOLEDOT

בראשית כה:יט-כו:ה

וְאֵלֶּה תּוֹלְדֹת יִצְחָק בֶּן־אַבְרָהָם אַבְרָהָם הוֹלִיד אֶת־יִצְחָק׃ וַיְהִי יִצְחָק בֶּן־אַרְבָּעִים שָׁנָה בְּקַחְתּוֹ אֶת־רִבְקָה בַּת־בְּתוּאֵל הָאֲרַמִּי מִפַּדַּן אֲרָם אֲחוֹת לָבָן הָאֲרַמִּי לוֹ לְאִשָּׁה׃ וַיֶּעְתַּר יִצְחָק לַיהוָה לְנֹכַח אִשְׁתּוֹ כִּי עֲקָרָה הִוא וַיֵּעָתֶר לוֹ יְהוָה וַתַּהַר רִבְקָה אִשְׁתּוֹ׃ וַיִּתְרֹצְצוּ הַבָּנִים בְּקִרְבָּהּ וַתֹּאמֶר אִם־כֵּן לָמָּה זֶּה אָנֹכִי וַתֵּלֶךְ לִדְרֹשׁ אֶת־יְהוָה׃ לוי: וַיֹּאמֶר יְהוָה לָהּ שְׁנֵי גיים [גוֹיִם] בְּבִטְנֵךְ וּשְׁנֵי לְאֻמִּים מִמֵּעַיִךְ יִפָּרֵדוּ וּלְאֹם מִלְאֹם יֶאֱמָץ וְרַב יַעֲבֹד צָעִיר׃ וַיִּמְלְאוּ יָמֶיהָ לָלֶדֶת וְהִנֵּה תוֹמִם בְּבִטְנָהּ׃ וַיֵּצֵא הָרִאשׁוֹן אַדְמוֹנִי כֻּלּוֹ כְּאַדֶּרֶת שֵׂעָר וַיִּקְרְאוּ שְׁמוֹ עֵשָׂו׃ וְאַחֲרֵי־כֵן יָצָא אָחִיו וְיָדוֹ אֹחֶזֶת בַּעֲקֵב עֵשָׂו וַיִּקְרָא שְׁמוֹ יַעֲקֹב וְיִצְחָק בֶּן־שִׁשִּׁים שָׁנָה בְּלֶדֶת אֹתָם׃ ישראל: וַיִּגְדְּלוּ הַנְּעָרִים וַיְהִי עֵשָׂו אִישׁ יֹדֵעַ צַיִד אִישׁ שָׂדֶה וְיַעֲקֹב אִישׁ תָּם יֹשֵׁב אֹהָלִים׃ וַיֶּאֱהַב יִצְחָק אֶת־עֵשָׂו כִּי־צַיִד בְּפִיו וְרִבְקָה אֹהֶבֶת אֶת־יַעֲקֹב׃ וַיָּזֶד יַעֲקֹב נָזִיד וַיָּבֹא עֵשָׂו מִן־הַשָּׂדֶה וְהוּא עָיֵף׃ וַיֹּאמֶר עֵשָׂו אֶל־יַעֲקֹב הַלְעִיטֵנִי נָא מִן־הָאָדֹם הָאָדֹם הַזֶּה כִּי עָיֵף אָנֹכִי עַל־כֵּן קָרָא־שְׁמוֹ אֱדוֹם׃ וַיֹּאמֶר יַעֲקֹב מִכְרָה כַיּוֹם אֶת־בְּכֹרָתְךָ לִי׃ וַיֹּאמֶר עֵשָׂו הִנֵּה אָנֹכִי הוֹלֵךְ לָמוּת וְלָמָּה־זֶּה לִי בְּכֹרָה׃ וַיֹּאמֶר יַעֲקֹב הִשָּׁבְעָה לִּי כַּיּוֹם וַיִּשָּׁבַע לוֹ וַיִּמְכֹּר אֶת־בְּכֹרָתוֹ לְיַעֲקֹב׃ וְיַעֲקֹב נָתַן לְעֵשָׂו לֶחֶם וּנְזִיד עֲדָשִׁים וַיֹּאכַל וַיֵּשְׁתְּ וַיָּקָם וַיֵּלַךְ וַיִּבֶז עֵשָׂו אֶת־הַבְּכֹרָה׃

וַיְהִי רָעָב בָּאָרֶץ מִלְּבַד הָרָעָב הָרִאשׁוֹן אֲשֶׁר הָיָה בִּימֵי אַבְרָהָם וַיֵּלֶךְ יִצְחָק אֶל־אֲבִימֶלֶךְ מֶלֶךְ־פְּלִשְׁתִּים גְּרָרָה׃ וַיֵּרָא אֵלָיו יְהוָה וַיֹּאמֶר אַל־תֵּרֵד מִצְרָיְמָה שְׁכֹן בָּאָרֶץ אֲשֶׁר אֹמַר אֵלֶיךָ׃ גּוּר בָּאָרֶץ הַזֹּאת וְאֶהְיֶה עִמְּךָ וַאֲבָרְכֶךָּ כִּי־לְךָ וּלְזַרְעֲךָ אֶתֵּן אֶת־כָּל־הָאֲרָצֹת הָאֵל וַהֲקִמֹתִי אֶת־הַשְּׁבֻעָה אֲשֶׁר נִשְׁבַּעְתִּי לְאַבְרָהָם אָבִיךָ׃ וְהִרְבֵּיתִי אֶת־זַרְעֲךָ כְּכוֹכְבֵי הַשָּׁמַיִם וְנָתַתִּי לְזַרְעֲךָ אֵת כָּל־הָאֲרָצֹת הָאֵל וְהִתְבָּרְכוּ בְזַרְעֲךָ כֹּל גּוֹיֵי הָאָרֶץ׃ עֵקֶב אֲשֶׁר־שָׁמַע אַבְרָהָם בְּקֹלִי וַיִּשְׁמֹר מִשְׁמַרְתִּי מִצְוֹתַי חֻקּוֹתַי וְתוֹרֹתָי׃

ויצא / VAYETZEH

בראשית כח:י-כב

וַיֵּצֵא יַעֲקֹב מִבְּאֵר שָׁבַע וַיֵּלֶךְ חָרָנָה׃ וַיִּפְגַּע בַּמָּקוֹם וַיָּלֶן שָׁם כִּי־בָא הַשֶּׁמֶשׁ וַיִּקַּח מֵאַבְנֵי הַמָּקוֹם וַיָּשֶׂם מְרַאֲשֹׁתָיו וַיִּשְׁכַּב בַּמָּקוֹם הַהוּא׃ וַיַּחֲלֹם וְהִנֵּה סֻלָּם מֻצָּב אַרְצָה וְרֹאשׁוֹ מַגִּיעַ הַשָּׁמָיְמָה וְהִנֵּה מַלְאֲכֵי אֱלֹהִים עֹלִים וְיֹרְדִים בּוֹ׃ לוי: וְהִנֵּה יְהוָה נִצָּב עָלָיו וַיֹּאמַר אֲנִי יְהוָה אֱלֹהֵי אַבְרָהָם אָבִיךָ וֵאלֹהֵי יִצְחָק הָאָרֶץ אֲשֶׁר אַתָּה שֹׁכֵב עָלֶיהָ לְךָ אֶתְּנֶנָּה וּלְזַרְעֶךָ׃ וְהָיָה זַרְעֲךָ כַּעֲפַר הָאָרֶץ וּפָרַצְתָּ יָמָּה וָקֵדְמָה וְצָפֹנָה וָנֶגְבָּה וְנִבְרְכוּ בְךָ כָּל־

מִשְׁפְּחֹת הָאֲדָמָה וּבְזַרְעֶךָ׃ וְהִנֵּה אָנֹכִי עִמָּךְ וּשְׁמַרְתִּיךָ בְּכֹל אֲשֶׁר־תֵּלֵךְ וַהֲשִׁבֹתִיךָ אֶל־הָאֲדָמָה הַזֹּאת כִּי לֹא אֶעֱזָבְךָ עַד אֲשֶׁר אִם־עָשִׂיתִי אֵת אֲשֶׁר־דִּבַּרְתִּי לָךְ׃ וַיִּיקַץ יַעֲקֹב מִשְּׁנָתוֹ וַיֹּאמֶר אָכֵן יֵשׁ יהוה בַּמָּקוֹם הַזֶּה וְאָנֹכִי לֹא יָדָעְתִּי׃ וַיִּירָא וַיֹּאמַר מַה־נּוֹרָא הַמָּקוֹם הַזֶּה אֵין זֶה כִּי אִם־בֵּית אֱלֹהִים וְזֶה שַׁעַר הַשָּׁמָיִם׃ ישראל: וַיַּשְׁכֵּם יַעֲקֹב בַּבֹּקֶר וַיִּקַּח אֶת־הָאֶבֶן אֲשֶׁר־שָׂם מְרַאֲשֹׁתָיו וַיָּשֶׂם אֹתָהּ מַצֵּבָה וַיִּצֹק שֶׁמֶן עַל־רֹאשָׁהּ׃ וַיִּקְרָא אֶת־שֵׁם־הַמָּקוֹם הַהוּא בֵּית־אֵל וְאוּלָם לוּז שֵׁם־הָעִיר לָרִאשֹׁנָה׃ וַיִּדַּר יַעֲקֹב נֶדֶר לֵאמֹר אִם־יִהְיֶה אֱלֹהִים עִמָּדִי וּשְׁמָרַנִי בַּדֶּרֶךְ הַזֶּה אֲשֶׁר אָנֹכִי הוֹלֵךְ וְנָתַן־לִי לֶחֶם לֶאֱכֹל וּבֶגֶד לִלְבֹּשׁ׃ וְשַׁבְתִּי בְשָׁלוֹם אֶל־בֵּית אָבִי וְהָיָה יהוה לִי לֵאלֹהִים׃ וְהָאֶבֶן הַזֹּאת אֲשֶׁר־שַׂמְתִּי מַצֵּבָה יִהְיֶה בֵּית אֱלֹהִים וְכֹל אֲשֶׁר תִּתֶּן־לִי עַשֵּׂר אֲעַשְּׂרֶנּוּ לָךְ׃

VAYISHLAḤ / וישלח

בראשית לב:ג-יב

וַיִּשְׁלַח יַעֲקֹב מַלְאָכִים לְפָנָיו אֶל־עֵשָׂו אָחִיו אַרְצָה שֵׂעִיר שְׂדֵה אֱדוֹם׃ וַיְצַו אֹתָם לֵאמֹר כֹּה תֹאמְרוּן לַאדֹנִי לְעֵשָׂו כֹּה אָמַר עַבְדְּךָ יַעֲקֹב עִם־לָבָן גַּרְתִּי וָאֵחַר עַד־עָתָּה׃ וַיְהִי־לִי שׁוֹר וַחֲמוֹר צֹאן וְעֶבֶד וְשִׁפְחָה וָאֶשְׁלְחָה לְהַגִּיד לַאדֹנִי לִמְצֹא־חֵן בְּעֵינֶיךָ׃ לוי: וַיָּשֻׁבוּ הַמַּלְאָכִים אֶל־יַעֲקֹב לֵאמֹר בָּאנוּ אֶל־אָחִיךָ אֶל־עֵשָׂו וְגַם הֹלֵךְ לִקְרָאתְךָ וְאַרְבַּע־מֵאוֹת אִישׁ עִמּוֹ׃ וַיִּירָא יַעֲקֹב מְאֹד וַיֵּצֶר לוֹ וַיַּחַץ אֶת־הָעָם אֲשֶׁר־אִתּוֹ וְאֶת־הַצֹּאן וְאֶת־הַבָּקָר וְהַגְּמַלִּים לִשְׁנֵי מַחֲנוֹת׃ וַיֹּאמֶר אִם־יָבוֹא עֵשָׂו אֶל־הַמַּחֲנֶה הָאַחַת וְהִכָּהוּ וְהָיָה הַמַּחֲנֶה הַנִּשְׁאָר לִפְלֵיטָה׃ ישראל: וַיֹּאמֶר יַעֲקֹב אֱלֹהֵי אָבִי אַבְרָהָם וֵאלֹהֵי אָבִי יִצְחָק יהוה הָאֹמֵר אֵלַי שׁוּב לְאַרְצְךָ וּלְמוֹלַדְתְּךָ וְאֵיטִיבָה עִמָּךְ׃ קָטֹנְתִּי מִכֹּל הַחֲסָדִים וּמִכָּל־הָאֱמֶת אֲשֶׁר עָשִׂיתָ אֶת־עַבְדֶּךָ כִּי בְמַקְלִי עָבַרְתִּי אֶת־הַיַּרְדֵּן הַזֶּה וְעַתָּה הָיִיתִי לִשְׁנֵי מַחֲנוֹת׃ הַצִּילֵנִי נָא מִיַּד אָחִי מִיַּד עֵשָׂו כִּי־יָרֵא אָנֹכִי אֹתוֹ פֶּן־יָבוֹא וְהִכַּנִי אֵם עַל־בָּנִים׃ וְאַתָּה אָמַרְתָּ הֵיטֵב אֵיטִיב עִמָּךְ וְשַׂמְתִּי אֶת־זַרְעֲךָ כְּחוֹל הַיָּם אֲשֶׁר לֹא־יִסָּפֵר מֵרֹב׃

VAYESHEV / וישב

בראשית לז:א-יא

וַיֵּשֶׁב יַעֲקֹב בְּאֶרֶץ מְגוּרֵי אָבִיו בְּאֶרֶץ כְּנָעַן׃ אֵלֶּה ׀ תֹּלְדוֹת יַעֲקֹב יוֹסֵף בֶּן־שְׁבַע־עֶשְׂרֵה שָׁנָה הָיָה רֹעֶה אֶת־אֶחָיו בַּצֹּאן וְהוּא נַעַר אֶת־בְּנֵי בִלְהָה וְאֶת־בְּנֵי זִלְפָּה נְשֵׁי אָבִיו וַיָּבֵא יוֹסֵף אֶת־דִּבָּתָם רָעָה אֶל־אֲבִיהֶם׃ וְיִשְׂרָאֵל אָהַב אֶת־יוֹסֵף מִכָּל־בָּנָיו כִּי־בֶן־זְקֻנִים הוּא לוֹ וְעָשָׂה לוֹ כְּתֹנֶת פַּסִּים׃ לוי: וַיִּרְאוּ אֶחָיו כִּי־אֹתוֹ אָהַב אֲבִיהֶם מִכָּל־אֶחָיו וַיִּשְׂנְאוּ אֹתוֹ וְלֹא יָכְלוּ דַּבְּרוֹ לְשָׁלֹם׃ וַיַּחֲלֹם יוֹסֵף חֲלוֹם וַיַּגֵּד לְאֶחָיו וַיּוֹסִפוּ עוֹד שְׂנֹא אֹתוֹ׃ וַיֹּאמֶר אֲלֵיהֶם שִׁמְעוּ־נָא הַחֲלוֹם הַזֶּה אֲשֶׁר חָלָמְתִּי׃ וְהִנֵּה אֲנַחְנוּ מְאַלְּמִים אֲלֻמִּים בְּתוֹךְ הַשָּׂדֶה וְהִנֵּה קָמָה אֲלֻמָּתִי וְגַם־נִצָּבָה וְהִנֵּה תְסֻבֶּינָה אֲלֻמֹּתֵיכֶם וַתִּשְׁתַּחֲוֶיןָ לַאֲלֻמָּתִי׃ ישראל: וַיֹּאמְרוּ לוֹ אֶחָיו הֲמָלֹךְ תִּמְלֹךְ עָלֵינוּ אִם־מָשׁוֹל תִּמְשֹׁל בָּנוּ וַיּוֹסִפוּ עוֹד שְׂנֹא אֹתוֹ עַל־חֲלֹמֹתָיו וְעַל־דְּבָרָיו׃ וַיַּחֲלֹם עוֹד חֲלוֹם אַחֵר וַיְסַפֵּר אֹתוֹ לְאֶחָיו וַיֹּאמֶר הִנֵּה חָלַמְתִּי חֲלוֹם עוֹד וְהִנֵּה הַשֶּׁמֶשׁ וְהַיָּרֵחַ וְאַחַד עָשָׂר כּוֹכָבִים מִשְׁתַּחֲוִים לִי׃ וַיְסַפֵּר אֶל־אָבִיו וְאֶל־אֶחָיו וַיִּגְעַר־בּוֹ אָבִיו וַיֹּאמֶר לוֹ מָה הַחֲלוֹם הַזֶּה אֲשֶׁר חָלָמְתָּ הֲבוֹא נָבוֹא אֲנִי וְאִמְּךָ וְאַחֶיךָ לְהִשְׁתַּחֲוֹת לְךָ אָרְצָה׃ וַיְקַנְאוּ־בוֹ אֶחָיו וְאָבִיו שָׁמַר אֶת־הַדָּבָר׃

MIKETZ / מקץ

בראשית מא:א-יד

וַיְהִ֕י מִקֵּ֖ץ שְׁנָתַ֣יִם יָמִ֑ים וּפַרְעֹ֣ה חֹלֵ֔ם וְהִנֵּ֖ה עֹמֵ֥ד עַל־הַיְאֹֽר׃ וְהִנֵּ֣ה מִן־הַיְאֹ֗ר עֹלֹת֙ שֶׁ֣בַע פָּר֔וֹת יְפ֥וֹת מַרְאֶ֖ה וּבְרִיאֹ֣ת בָּשָׂ֑ר וַתִּרְעֶ֖ינָה בָּאָֽחוּ׃ וְהִנֵּ֞ה שֶׁ֧בַע פָּר֣וֹת אֲחֵר֗וֹת עֹל֤וֹת אַחֲרֵיהֶן֙ מִן־הַיְאֹ֔ר רָע֥וֹת מַרְאֶ֖ה וְדַקּ֣וֹת בָּשָׂ֑ר וַֽתַּעֲמֹ֛דְנָה אֵ֥צֶל הַפָּר֖וֹת עַל־שְׂפַ֥ת הַיְאֹֽר׃ וַתֹּאכַ֣לְנָה הַפָּר֗וֹת רָע֤וֹת הַמַּרְאֶה֙ וְדַקֹּ֣ת הַבָּשָׂ֔ר אֵ֚ת שֶׁ֣בַע הַפָּר֔וֹת יְפֹ֥ת הַמַּרְאֶ֖ה וְהַבְּרִיאֹ֑ת וַיִּיקַ֖ץ פַּרְעֹֽה׃ לוי: וַיִּישָׁ֕ן וַיַּחֲלֹ֖ם שֵׁנִ֑ית וְהִנֵּ֣ה ׀ שֶׁ֣בַע שִׁבֳּלִ֗ים עֹל֛וֹת בְּקָנֶ֥ה אֶחָ֖ד בְּרִיא֥וֹת וְטֹבֽוֹת׃ וְהִנֵּה֙ שֶׁ֣בַע שִׁבֳּלִ֔ים דַּקּ֖וֹת וּשְׁדוּפֹ֣ת קָדִ֑ים צֹֽמְח֖וֹת אַחֲרֵיהֶֽן׃ וַתִּבְלַ֙עְנָה֙ הַשִּׁבֳּלִ֣ים הַדַּקּ֔וֹת אֵ֚ת שֶׁ֣בַע הַשִּׁבֳּלִ֔ים הַבְּרִיא֖וֹת וְהַמְּלֵא֑וֹת וַיִּיקַ֥ץ פַּרְעֹ֖ה וְהִנֵּ֥ה חֲלֽוֹם׃ ישראל: וַיְהִ֤י בַבֹּ֙קֶר֙ וַתִּפָּ֣עֶם רוּח֔וֹ וַיִּשְׁלַ֛ח וַיִּקְרָ֥א אֶת־כָּל־חַרְטֻמֵּ֥י מִצְרַ֖יִם וְאֶת־כָּל־חֲכָמֶ֑יהָ וַיְסַפֵּ֨ר פַּרְעֹ֤ה לָהֶם֙ אֶת־חֲלֹמ֔וֹ וְאֵין־פּוֹתֵ֥ר אוֹתָ֖ם לְפַרְעֹֽה׃ וַיְדַבֵּר֙ שַׂ֣ר הַמַּשְׁקִ֔ים אֶת־פַּרְעֹ֖ה לֵאמֹ֑ר אֶת־חֲטָאַ֕י אֲנִ֖י מַזְכִּ֥יר הַיּֽוֹם׃ פַּרְעֹ֖ה קָצַ֣ף עַל־עֲבָדָ֑יו וַיִּתֵּ֨ן אֹתִ֜י בְּמִשְׁמַ֗ר בֵּ֚ית שַׂ֣ר הַטַּבָּחִ֔ים אֹתִ֕י וְאֵ֖ת שַׂ֥ר הָאֹפִֽים׃ וַנַּחַלְמָ֥ה חֲל֛וֹם בְּלַ֥יְלָה אֶחָ֖ד אֲנִ֣י וָה֑וּא אִ֛ישׁ כְּפִתְר֥וֹן חֲלֹמ֖וֹ חָלָֽמְנוּ׃ וְשָׁ֨ם אִתָּ֜נוּ נַ֣עַר עִבְרִ֗י עֶ֚בֶד לְשַׂ֣ר הַטַּבָּחִ֔ים וַנְּסַפֶּר־ל֕וֹ וַיִּפְתָּר־לָ֖נוּ אֶת־חֲלֹמֹתֵ֑ינוּ אִ֥ישׁ כַּחֲלֹמ֖וֹ פָּתָֽר׃ וַיְהִ֛י כַּאֲשֶׁ֥ר פָּֽתַר־לָ֖נוּ כֵּ֣ן הָיָ֑ה אֹתִ֛י הֵשִׁ֥יב עַל־כַּנִּ֖י וְאֹת֥וֹ תָלָֽה׃ וַיִּשְׁלַ֤ח פַּרְעֹה֙ וַיִּקְרָ֣א אֶת־יוֹסֵ֔ף וַיְרִיצֻ֖הוּ מִן־הַבּ֑וֹר וַיְגַלַּח֙ וַיְחַלֵּ֣ף שִׂמְלֹתָ֔יו וַיָּבֹ֖א אֶל־פַּרְעֹֽה׃

VAYIGASH / ויגש

בראשית מד:יח-ל

וַיִּגַּ֨שׁ אֵלָ֜יו יְהוּדָ֗ה וַיֹּאמֶר֮ בִּ֣י אֲדֹנִי֒ יְדַבֶּר־נָ֨א עַבְדְּךָ֤ דָבָר֙ בְּאָזְנֵ֣י אֲדֹנִ֔י וְאַל־יִ֥חַר אַפְּךָ֖ בְּעַבְדֶּ֑ךָ כִּ֥י כָמ֖וֹךָ כְּפַרְעֹֽה׃ אֲדֹנִ֣י שָׁאַ֔ל אֶת־עֲבָדָ֖יו לֵאמֹ֑ר הֲיֵשׁ־לָכֶ֥ם אָ֖ב אוֹ־אָֽח׃ וַנֹּ֙אמֶר֙ אֶל־אֲדֹנִ֔י יֶשׁ־לָ֙נוּ֙ אָ֣ב זָקֵ֔ן וְיֶ֥לֶד זְקֻנִ֖ים קָטָ֑ן וְאָחִ֣יו מֵ֗ת וַיִּוָּתֵ֨ר ה֧וּא לְבַדּ֛וֹ לְאִמּ֖וֹ וְאָבִ֥יו אֲהֵבֽוֹ׃ לוי: וַתֹּ֙אמֶר֙ אֶל־עֲבָדֶ֔יךָ הוֹרִדֻ֖הוּ אֵלָ֑י וְאָשִׂ֥ימָה עֵינִ֖י עָלָֽיו׃ וַנֹּ֙אמֶר֙ אֶל־אֲדֹנִ֔י לֹא־יוּכַ֥ל הַנַּ֖עַר לַעֲזֹ֣ב אֶת־אָבִ֑יו וְעָזַ֥ב אֶת־אָבִ֖יו וָמֵֽת׃ וַתֹּ֙אמֶר֙ אֶל־עֲבָדֶ֔יךָ אִם־לֹ֥א יֵרֵ֛ד אֲחִיכֶ֥ם הַקָּטֹ֖ן אִתְּכֶ֑ם לֹ֥א תֹסִפ֖וּן לִרְא֥וֹת פָּנָֽי׃ וַיְהִי֙ כִּ֣י עָלִ֔ינוּ אֶֽל־עַבְדְּךָ֖ אָבִ֑י וַנַּ֨גֶּד־ל֔וֹ אֵ֖ת דִּבְרֵ֥י אֲדֹנִֽי׃ ישראל: וַיֹּ֖אמֶר אָבִ֑ינוּ שֻׁ֖בוּ שִׁבְרוּ־לָ֥נוּ מְעַט־אֹֽכֶל׃ וַנֹּ֕אמֶר לֹ֥א נוּכַ֖ל לָרֶ֑דֶת אִם־יֵשׁ֩ אָחִ֨ינוּ הַקָּטֹ֤ן אִתָּ֙נוּ֙ וְיָרַ֔דְנוּ כִּי־לֹ֣א נוּכַ֗ל לִרְאוֹת֙ פְּנֵ֣י הָאִ֔ישׁ וְאָחִ֥ינוּ הַקָּטֹ֖ן אֵינֶ֥נּוּ אִתָּֽנוּ׃ וַיֹּ֛אמֶר עַבְדְּךָ֥ אָבִ֖י אֵלֵ֑ינוּ אַתֶּ֣ם יְדַעְתֶּ֔ם כִּ֥י שְׁנַ֖יִם יָֽלְדָה־לִּ֥י אִשְׁתִּֽי׃ וַיֵּצֵ֤א הָאֶחָד֙ מֵֽאִתִּ֔י וָאֹמַ֕ר אַ֖ךְ טָרֹ֣ף טֹרָ֑ף וְלֹ֥א רְאִיתִ֖יו עַד־הֵֽנָּה׃ וּלְקַחְתֶּ֧ם גַּם־אֶת־זֶ֛ה מֵעִ֥ם פָּנַ֖י וְקָרָ֣הוּ אָס֑וֹן וְהוֹרַדְתֶּ֧ם אֶת־שֵׂיבָתִ֛י בְּרָעָ֖ה שְׁאֹֽלָה׃ וְעַתָּ֗ה כְּבֹאִי֙ אֶל־עַבְדְּךָ֣ אָבִ֔י וְהַנַּ֖עַר אֵינֶ֣נּוּ אִתָּ֑נוּ וְנַפְשׁ֖וֹ קְשׁוּרָ֥ה בְנַפְשֽׁוֹ׃

VAYHI / ויחי

בראשית מז:כח-מח:ט

וַיְחִ֤י יַעֲקֹב֙ בְּאֶ֣רֶץ מִצְרַ֔יִם שְׁבַ֥ע עֶשְׂרֵ֖ה שָׁנָ֑ה וַיְהִ֤י יְמֵֽי־יַעֲקֹב֙ שְׁנֵ֣י חַיָּ֔יו שֶׁ֣בַע שָׁנִ֔ים וְאַרְבָּעִ֖ים וּמְאַ֥ת שָׁנָֽה׃ וַיִּקְרְב֣וּ יְמֵֽי־יִשְׂרָאֵל֮ לָמוּת֒ וַיִּקְרָ֣א ׀ לִבְנ֣וֹ לְיוֹסֵ֗ף וַיֹּ֤אמֶר לוֹ֙ אִם־נָ֨א מָצָ֤אתִי חֵן֙ בְּעֵינֶ֔יךָ שִֽׂים־נָ֥א יָדְךָ֖ תַּ֣חַת יְרֵכִ֑י וְעָשִׂ֤יתָ עִמָּדִי֙ חֶ֣סֶד וֶֽאֱמֶ֔ת אַל־נָ֥א תִקְבְּרֵ֖נִי בְּמִצְרָֽיִם׃ וְשָֽׁכַבְתִּי֙ עִם־אֲבֹתַ֔י וּנְשָׂאתַ֙נִי֙ מִמִּצְרַ֔יִם וּקְבַרְתַּ֖נִי בִּקְבֻרָתָ֑ם וַיֹּאמַ֕ר אָנֹכִ֖י אֶֽעֱשֶׂ֥ה כִדְבָרֶֽךָ׃ וַיֹּ֗אמֶר הִשָּֽׁבְעָה֙ לִ֔י וַיִּשָּׁבַ֖ע ל֑וֹ וַיִּשְׁתַּ֥חוּ יִשְׂרָאֵ֖ל עַל־רֹ֥אשׁ הַמִּטָּֽה׃

לוי: וַיְהִ֗י אַחֲרֵי֙ הַדְּבָרִ֣ים הָאֵ֔לֶּה וַיֹּ֣אמֶר לְיוֹסֵ֔ף הִנֵּ֥ה אָבִ֖יךָ חֹלֶ֑ה וַיִּקַּ֞ח אֶת־שְׁנֵ֤י בָנָיו֙ עִמּ֔וֹ אֶת־מְנַשֶּׁ֖ה וְאֶת־אֶפְרָֽיִם׃ וַיַּגֵּ֣ד לְיַעֲקֹ֔ב וַיֹּ֕אמֶר

הִנֵּה בִּנְךָ יוֹסֵף בָּא אֵלֶיךָ וַיִּתְחַזֵּק יִשְׂרָאֵל
וַיֵּשֶׁב עַל־הַמִּטָּה׃ וַיֹּאמֶר יַעֲקֹב אֶל־יוֹסֵף אֵל
שַׁדַּי נִרְאָה־אֵלַי בְּלוּז בְּאֶרֶץ כְּנָעַן וַיְבָרֶךְ אֹתִי׃
ישראל: וַיֹּאמֶר אֵלַי הִנְנִי מַפְרְךָ וְהִרְבִּיתִךָ
וּנְתַתִּיךָ לִקְהַל עַמִּים וְנָתַתִּי אֶת־הָאָרֶץ
הַזֹּאת לְזַרְעֲךָ אַחֲרֶיךָ אֲחֻזַּת עוֹלָם׃ וְעַתָּה
שְׁנֵי־בָנֶיךָ הַנּוֹלָדִים לְךָ בְּאֶרֶץ מִצְרַיִם עַד־
בֹּאִי אֵלֶיךָ מִצְרַיְמָה לִי־הֵם אֶפְרַיִם וּמְנַשֶּׁה
כִּרְאוּבֵן וְשִׁמְעוֹן יִהְיוּ־לִי׃ וּמוֹלַדְתְּךָ אֲשֶׁר־
הוֹלַדְתָּ אַחֲרֵיהֶם לְךָ יִהְיוּ עַל שֵׁם אֲחֵיהֶם
יִקָּרְאוּ בְּנַחֲלָתָם׃ וַאֲנִי ׀ בְּבֹאִי מִפַּדָּן מֵתָה
עָלַי רָחֵל בְּאֶרֶץ כְּנַעַן בַּדֶּרֶךְ בְּעוֹד כִּבְרַת־
אֶרֶץ לָבֹא אֶפְרָתָה וָאֶקְבְּרֶהָ שָּׁם בְּדֶרֶךְ
אֶפְרָת הִוא בֵּית לָחֶם׃ וַיַּרְא יִשְׂרָאֵל אֶת־
בְּנֵי יוֹסֵף וַיֹּאמֶר מִי־אֵלֶּה׃ וַיֹּאמֶר יוֹסֵף אֶל־
אָבִיו בָּנַי הֵם אֲשֶׁר־נָתַן־לִי אֱלֹהִים בָּזֶה
וַיֹּאמַר קָחֶם־נָא אֵלַי וַאֲבָרֲכֵם׃

SHEMOT / שמות

שמות א:א-יז

וְאֵלֶּה שְׁמוֹת בְּנֵי יִשְׂרָאֵל הַבָּאִים מִצְרָיְמָה
אֵת יַעֲקֹב אִישׁ וּבֵיתוֹ בָּאוּ׃ רְאוּבֵן שִׁמְעוֹן
לֵוִי וִיהוּדָה׃ יִשָּׂשכָר זְבוּלֻן וּבִנְיָמִן׃ דָּן
וְנַפְתָּלִי גָּד וְאָשֵׁר׃ וַיְהִי כָּל־נֶפֶשׁ יֹצְאֵי יֶרֶךְ־
יַעֲקֹב שִׁבְעִים נָפֶשׁ וְיוֹסֵף הָיָה בְמִצְרָיִם׃
וַיָּמָת יוֹסֵף וְכָל־אֶחָיו וְכֹל הַדּוֹר הַהוּא׃ וּבְנֵי
יִשְׂרָאֵל פָּרוּ וַיִּשְׁרְצוּ וַיִּרְבּוּ וַיַּעַצְמוּ בִּמְאֹד
מְאֹד וַתִּמָּלֵא הָאָרֶץ אֹתָם׃

לוי: וַיָּקָם מֶלֶךְ־חָדָשׁ עַל־מִצְרָיִם אֲשֶׁר לֹא־
יָדַע אֶת־יוֹסֵף׃ וַיֹּאמֶר אֶל־עַמּוֹ הִנֵּה עַם
בְּנֵי יִשְׂרָאֵל רַב וְעָצוּם מִמֶּנּוּ׃ הָבָה נִתְחַכְּמָה
לוֹ פֶּן־יִרְבֶּה וְהָיָה כִּי־תִקְרֶאנָה מִלְחָמָה
וְנוֹסַף גַּם־הוּא עַל־שֹׂנְאֵינוּ וְנִלְחַם־בָּנוּ וְעָלָה
מִן־הָאָרֶץ׃ וַיָּשִׂימוּ עָלָיו שָׂרֵי מִסִּים לְמַעַן
עַנֹּתוֹ בְּסִבְלֹתָם וַיִּבֶן עָרֵי מִסְכְּנוֹת לְפַרְעֹה
אֶת־פִּתֹם וְאֶת־רַעַמְסֵס׃ וְכַאֲשֶׁר יְעַנּוּ אֹתוֹ
כֵּן יִרְבֶּה וְכֵן יִפְרֹץ וַיָּקֻצוּ מִפְּנֵי בְּנֵי יִשְׂרָאֵל׃
ישראל: וַיַּעֲבִדוּ מִצְרַיִם אֶת־בְּנֵי יִשְׂרָאֵל בְּפָרֶךְ׃
וַיְמָרְרוּ אֶת־חַיֵּיהֶם בַּעֲבֹדָה קָשָׁה בְּחֹמֶר
וּבִלְבֵנִים וּבְכָל־עֲבֹדָה בַּשָּׂדֶה אֵת כָּל־
עֲבֹדָתָם אֲשֶׁר־עָבְדוּ בָהֶם בְּפָרֶךְ׃ וַיֹּאמֶר
מֶלֶךְ מִצְרַיִם לַמְיַלְּדֹת הָעִבְרִיֹּת אֲשֶׁר שֵׁם
הָאַחַת שִׁפְרָה וְשֵׁם הַשֵּׁנִית פּוּעָה׃ וַיֹּאמֶר
בְּיַלֶּדְכֶן אֶת־הָעִבְרִיּוֹת וּרְאִיתֶן עַל־הָאָבְנָיִם
אִם־בֵּן הוּא וַהֲמִתֶּן אֹתוֹ וְאִם־בַּת הִוא
וָחָיָה׃ וַתִּירֶאןָ הַמְיַלְּדֹת אֶת־הָאֱלֹהִים וְלֹא
עָשׂוּ כַּאֲשֶׁר דִּבֶּר אֲלֵיהֶן מֶלֶךְ מִצְרָיִם וַתְּחַיֶּיןָ
אֶת־הַיְלָדִים׃

VA'ERA / וארא

שמות ו:ב-יג

וַיְדַבֵּר אֱלֹהִים אֶל־מֹשֶׁה וַיֹּאמֶר אֵלָיו אֲנִי
יהוה׃ וָאֵרָא אֶל־אַבְרָהָם אֶל־יִצְחָק וְאֶל־
יַעֲקֹב בְּאֵל שַׁדָּי וּשְׁמִי יהוה לֹא נוֹדַעְתִּי
לָהֶם׃ וְגַם הֲקִמֹתִי אֶת־בְּרִיתִי אִתָּם לָתֵת
לָהֶם אֶת־אֶרֶץ כְּנָעַן אֵת אֶרֶץ מְגֻרֵיהֶם
אֲשֶׁר־גָּרוּ בָהּ׃ וְגַם ׀ אֲנִי שָׁמַעְתִּי אֶת־נַאֲקַת
בְּנֵי יִשְׂרָאֵל אֲשֶׁר מִצְרַיִם מַעֲבִדִים אֹתָם
וָאֶזְכֹּר אֶת־בְּרִיתִי׃ לוי: לָכֵן אֱמֹר לִבְנֵי־
יִשְׂרָאֵל אֲנִי יהוה וְהוֹצֵאתִי אֶתְכֶם מִתַּחַת
סִבְלֹת מִצְרַיִם וְהִצַּלְתִּי אֶתְכֶם מֵעֲבֹדָתָם
וְגָאַלְתִּי אֶתְכֶם בִּזְרוֹעַ נְטוּיָה וּבִשְׁפָטִים
גְּדֹלִים׃ וְלָקַחְתִּי אֶתְכֶם לִי לְעָם וְהָיִיתִי לָכֶם
לֵאלֹהִים וִידַעְתֶּם כִּי אֲנִי יהוה אֱלֹהֵיכֶם
הַמּוֹצִיא אֶתְכֶם מִתַּחַת סִבְלוֹת מִצְרָיִם׃
וְהֵבֵאתִי אֶתְכֶם אֶל־הָאָרֶץ אֲשֶׁר נָשָׂאתִי
אֶת־יָדִי לָתֵת אֹתָהּ לְאַבְרָהָם לְיִצְחָק
וּלְיַעֲקֹב וְנָתַתִּי אֹתָהּ לָכֶם מוֹרָשָׁה אֲנִי
יהוה׃ וַיְדַבֵּר מֹשֶׁה כֵּן אֶל־בְּנֵי יִשְׂרָאֵל וְלֹא
שָׁמְעוּ אֶל־מֹשֶׁה מִקֹּצֶר רוּחַ וּמֵעֲבֹדָה
קָשָׁה׃

ישראל: וַיְדַבֵּר יהוה אֶל־מֹשֶׁה לֵּאמֹר׃ בֹּא
דַבֵּר אֶל־פַּרְעֹה מֶלֶךְ מִצְרָיִם וִישַׁלַּח אֶת־
בְּנֵי־יִשְׂרָאֵל מֵאַרְצוֹ׃ וַיְדַבֵּר מֹשֶׁה לִפְנֵי יהוה

לֵאמֹר הֵן בְּנֵי־יִשְׂרָאֵל לֹא־שָׁמְעוּ אֵלַי וְאֵיךְ יִשְׁמָעֵנִי פַרְעֹה וַאֲנִי עֲרַל שְׂפָתָיִם: וַיְדַבֵּר יהוה אֶל־מֹשֶׁה וְאֶל־אַהֲרֹן וַיְצַוֵּם אֶל־בְּנֵי יִשְׂרָאֵל וְאֶל־פַּרְעֹה מֶלֶךְ מִצְרָיִם לְהוֹצִיא אֶת־בְּנֵי־יִשְׂרָאֵל מֵאֶרֶץ מִצְרָיִם:

BO / בא

שמות י:א-יא

וַיֹּאמֶר יהוה אֶל־מֹשֶׁה בֹּא אֶל־פַּרְעֹה כִּי־אֲנִי הִכְבַּדְתִּי אֶת־לִבּוֹ וְאֶת־לֵב עֲבָדָיו לְמַעַן שִׁתִי אֹתֹתַי אֵלֶּה בְּקִרְבּוֹ: וּלְמַעַן תְּסַפֵּר בְּאָזְנֵי בִנְךָ וּבֶן־בִּנְךָ אֵת אֲשֶׁר הִתְעַלַּלְתִּי בְּמִצְרַיִם וְאֶת־אֹתֹתַי אֲשֶׁר־שַׂמְתִּי בָם וִידַעְתֶּם כִּי־אֲנִי יהוה: וַיָּבֹא מֹשֶׁה וְאַהֲרֹן אֶל־פַּרְעֹה וַיֹּאמְרוּ אֵלָיו כֹּה־אָמַר יהוה אֱלֹהֵי הָעִבְרִים עַד־מָתַי מֵאַנְתָּ לֵעָנֹת מִפָּנָי שַׁלַּח עַמִּי וְיַעַבְדֻנִי: לוי: כִּי אִם־מָאֵן אַתָּה לְשַׁלֵּחַ אֶת־עַמִּי הִנְנִי מֵבִיא מָחָר אַרְבֶּה בִּגְבֻלֶךָ: וְכִסָּה אֶת־עֵין הָאָרֶץ וְלֹא יוּכַל לִרְאֹת אֶת־הָאָרֶץ וְאָכַל ׀ אֶת־יֶתֶר הַפְּלֵטָה הַנִּשְׁאֶרֶת לָכֶם מִן־הַבָּרָד וְאָכַל אֶת־כָּל־הָעֵץ הַצֹּמֵחַ לָכֶם מִן־הַשָּׂדֶה: וּמָלְאוּ בָתֶּיךָ וּבָתֵּי כָל־עֲבָדֶיךָ וּבָתֵּי כָל־מִצְרַיִם אֲשֶׁר לֹא־רָאוּ אֲבֹתֶיךָ וַאֲבוֹת אֲבֹתֶיךָ מִיּוֹם הֱיוֹתָם עַל־הָאֲדָמָה עַד הַיּוֹם הַזֶּה וַיִּפֶן וַיֵּצֵא מֵעִם פַּרְעֹה: ישראל: וַיֹּאמְרוּ עַבְדֵי פַרְעֹה אֵלָיו עַד־מָתַי יִהְיֶה זֶה לָנוּ לְמוֹקֵשׁ שַׁלַּח אֶת־הָאֲנָשִׁים וְיַעַבְדוּ אֶת־יהוה אֱלֹהֵיהֶם הֲטֶרֶם תֵּדַע כִּי אָבְדָה מִצְרָיִם: וַיּוּשַׁב אֶת־מֹשֶׁה וְאֶת־אַהֲרֹן אֶל־פַּרְעֹה וַיֹּאמֶר אֲלֵהֶם לְכוּ עִבְדוּ אֶת־יהוה אֱלֹהֵיכֶם מִי וָמִי הַהֹלְכִים: וַיֹּאמֶר מֹשֶׁה בִּנְעָרֵינוּ וּבִזְקֵנֵינוּ נֵלֵךְ בְּבָנֵינוּ וּבִבְנוֹתֵנוּ בְּצֹאנֵנוּ וּבִבְקָרֵנוּ נֵלֵךְ כִּי חַג־יהוה לָנוּ: וַיֹּאמֶר אֲלֵהֶם יְהִי כֵן יהוה עִמָּכֶם כַּאֲשֶׁר אֲשַׁלַּח אֶתְכֶם וְאֶת־טַפְּכֶם רְאוּ כִּי רָעָה נֶגֶד פְּנֵיכֶם: לֹא כֵן לְכוּ־נָא הַגְּבָרִים וְעִבְדוּ אֶת־יהוה כִּי אֹתָהּ אַתֶּם מְבַקְשִׁים וַיְגָרֶשׁ אֹתָם מֵאֵת פְּנֵי פַרְעֹה:

BESHALLAH / בשלח

שמות יג:יז-יד:ח

וַיְהִי בְּשַׁלַּח פַּרְעֹה אֶת־הָעָם וְלֹא־נָחָם אֱלֹהִים דֶּרֶךְ אֶרֶץ פְּלִשְׁתִּים כִּי קָרוֹב הוּא כִּי ׀ אָמַר אֱלֹהִים פֶּן־יִנָּחֵם הָעָם בִּרְאֹתָם מִלְחָמָה וְשָׁבוּ מִצְרָיְמָה: וַיַּסֵּב אֱלֹהִים ׀ אֶת־הָעָם דֶּרֶךְ הַמִּדְבָּר יַם־סוּף וַחֲמֻשִׁים עָלוּ בְנֵי־יִשְׂרָאֵל מֵאֶרֶץ מִצְרָיִם: וַיִּקַּח מֹשֶׁה אֶת־עַצְמוֹת יוֹסֵף עִמּוֹ כִּי הַשְׁבֵּעַ הִשְׁבִּיעַ אֶת־בְּנֵי יִשְׂרָאֵל לֵאמֹר פָּקֹד יִפְקֹד אֱלֹהִים אֶתְכֶם וְהַעֲלִיתֶם אֶת־עַצְמֹתַי מִזֶּה אִתְּכֶם: וַיִּסְעוּ מִסֻּכֹּת וַיַּחֲנוּ בְאֵתָם בִּקְצֵה הַמִּדְבָּר: וַיהוה הֹלֵךְ לִפְנֵיהֶם יוֹמָם בְּעַמּוּד עָנָן לַנְחֹתָם הַדֶּרֶךְ וְלַיְלָה בְּעַמּוּד אֵשׁ לְהָאִיר לָהֶם לָלֶכֶת יוֹמָם וָלָיְלָה: לֹא־יָמִישׁ עַמּוּד הֶעָנָן יוֹמָם וְעַמּוּד הָאֵשׁ לָיְלָה לִפְנֵי הָעָם:

לוי: וַיְדַבֵּר יהוה אֶל־מֹשֶׁה לֵּאמֹר: דַּבֵּר אֶל־בְּנֵי יִשְׂרָאֵל וְיָשֻׁבוּ וְיַחֲנוּ לִפְנֵי פִּי הַחִירֹת בֵּין מִגְדֹּל וּבֵין הַיָּם לִפְנֵי בַּעַל צְפֹן נִכְחוֹ תַחֲנוּ עַל־הַיָּם: וְאָמַר פַּרְעֹה לִבְנֵי יִשְׂרָאֵל נְבֻכִים הֵם בָּאָרֶץ סָגַר עֲלֵיהֶם הַמִּדְבָּר: וְחִזַּקְתִּי אֶת־לֵב־פַּרְעֹה וְרָדַף אַחֲרֵיהֶם וְאִכָּבְדָה בְּפַרְעֹה וּבְכָל־חֵילוֹ וְיָדְעוּ מִצְרַיִם כִּי־אֲנִי יהוה וַיַּעֲשׂוּ־כֵן: ישראל: וַיֻּגַּד לְמֶלֶךְ מִצְרַיִם כִּי בָרַח הָעָם וַיֵּהָפֵךְ לְבַב פַּרְעֹה וַעֲבָדָיו אֶל־הָעָם וַיֹּאמְרוּ מַה־זֹּאת עָשִׂינוּ כִּי־שִׁלַּחְנוּ אֶת־יִשְׂרָאֵל מֵעָבְדֵנוּ: וַיֶּאְסֹר אֶת־רִכְבּוֹ וְאֶת־עַמּוֹ לָקַח עִמּוֹ: וַיִּקַּח שֵׁשׁ־מֵאוֹת רֶכֶב בָּחוּר וְכֹל רֶכֶב מִצְרָיִם וְשָׁלִשִׁם עַל־כֻּלּוֹ: וַיְחַזֵּק יהוה אֶת־לֵב פַּרְעֹה מֶלֶךְ מִצְרַיִם וַיִּרְדֹּף אַחֲרֵי בְּנֵי יִשְׂרָאֵל וּבְנֵי יִשְׂרָאֵל יֹצְאִים בְּיָד רָמָה:

YITRO / יתרו

שמות יח:א-יב

וַיִּשְׁמַע יִתְרוֹ כֹהֵן מִדְיָן חֹתֵן מֹשֶׁה אֵת כָּל־אֲשֶׁר עָשָׂה אֱלֹהִים לְמֹשֶׁה וּלְיִשְׂרָאֵל עַמּוֹ כִּי־הוֹצִיא יהוה אֶת־יִשְׂרָאֵל מִמִּצְרָיִם: וַיִּקַּח

יִתְרוֹ חֹתֵן מֹשֶׁה אֶת־צִפֹּרָה אֵשֶׁת מֹשֶׁה אַחַר שִׁלּוּחֶיהָ: וְאֵת שְׁנֵי בָנֶיהָ אֲשֶׁר שֵׁם הָאֶחָד גֵּרְשֹׁם כִּי אָמַר גֵּר הָיִיתִי בְּאֶרֶץ נָכְרִיָּה: וְשֵׁם הָאֶחָד אֱלִיעֶזֶר כִּי־אֱלֹהֵי אָבִי בְּעֶזְרִי וַיַּצִּלֵנִי מֵחֶרֶב פַּרְעֹה: לוי: וַיָּבֹא יִתְרוֹ חֹתֵן מֹשֶׁה וּבָנָיו וְאִשְׁתּוֹ אֶל־מֹשֶׁה אֶל־הַמִּדְבָּר אֲשֶׁר־הוּא חֹנֶה שָׁם הַר הָאֱלֹהִים: וַיֹּאמֶר אֶל־מֹשֶׁה אֲנִי חֹתֶנְךָ יִתְרוֹ בָּא אֵלֶיךָ וְאִשְׁתְּךָ וּשְׁנֵי בָנֶיהָ עִמָּהּ: וַיֵּצֵא מֹשֶׁה לִקְרַאת חֹתְנוֹ וַיִּשְׁתַּחוּ וַיִּשַּׁק־לוֹ וַיִּשְׁאֲלוּ אִישׁ־לְרֵעֵהוּ לְשָׁלוֹם וַיָּבֹאוּ הָאֹהֱלָה: וַיְסַפֵּר מֹשֶׁה לְחֹתְנוֹ אֵת כָּל־אֲשֶׁר עָשָׂה יהוה לְפַרְעֹה וּלְמִצְרַיִם עַל אוֹדֹת יִשְׂרָאֵל אֵת כָּל־הַתְּלָאָה אֲשֶׁר מְצָאָתַם בַּדֶּרֶךְ וַיַּצִּלֵם יהוה: ישראל: וַיִּחַדְּ יִתְרוֹ עַל כָּל־הַטּוֹבָה אֲשֶׁר־עָשָׂה יהוה לְיִשְׂרָאֵל אֲשֶׁר הִצִּילוֹ מִיַּד מִצְרָיִם: וַיֹּאמֶר יִתְרוֹ בָּרוּךְ יהוה אֲשֶׁר הִצִּיל אֶתְכֶם מִיַּד מִצְרַיִם וּמִיַּד פַּרְעֹה אֲשֶׁר הִצִּיל אֶת־הָעָם מִתַּחַת יַד־מִצְרָיִם: עַתָּה יָדַעְתִּי כִּי־גָדוֹל יהוה מִכָּל־הָאֱלֹהִים כִּי בַדָּבָר אֲשֶׁר זָדוּ עֲלֵיהֶם: וַיִּקַּח יִתְרוֹ חֹתֵן מֹשֶׁה עֹלָה וּזְבָחִים לֵאלֹהִים וַיָּבֹא אַהֲרֹן וְכֹל ׀ זִקְנֵי יִשְׂרָאֵל לֶאֱכָל־לֶחֶם עִם־חֹתֵן מֹשֶׁה לִפְנֵי הָאֱלֹהִים:

MISHPATIM / משפטים

שמות כא:א–יט

וְאֵלֶּה הַמִּשְׁפָּטִים אֲשֶׁר תָּשִׂים לִפְנֵיהֶם: כִּי תִקְנֶה עֶבֶד עִבְרִי שֵׁשׁ שָׁנִים יַעֲבֹד וּבַשְּׁבִעִת יֵצֵא לַחָפְשִׁי חִנָּם: אִם־בְּגַפּוֹ יָבֹא בְּגַפּוֹ יֵצֵא אִם־בַּעַל אִשָּׁה הוּא וְיָצְאָה אִשְׁתּוֹ עִמּוֹ: אִם־אֲדֹנָיו יִתֶּן־לוֹ אִשָּׁה וְיָלְדָה־לוֹ בָנִים אוֹ בָנוֹת הָאִשָּׁה וִילָדֶיהָ תִּהְיֶה לַאדֹנֶיהָ וְהוּא יֵצֵא בְגַפּוֹ: וְאִם־אָמֹר יֹאמַר הָעֶבֶד אָהַבְתִּי אֶת־אֲדֹנִי אֶת־אִשְׁתִּי וְאֶת־בָּנָי לֹא אֵצֵא חָפְשִׁי: וְהִגִּישׁוֹ אֲדֹנָיו אֶל־הָאֱלֹהִים וְהִגִּישׁוֹ אֶל־הַדֶּלֶת אוֹ אֶל־הַמְּזוּזָה וְרָצַע אֲדֹנָיו אֶת־אָזְנוֹ בַּמַּרְצֵעַ וַעֲבָדוֹ לְעֹלָם: לוי: וְכִי־יִמְכֹּר אִישׁ אֶת־בִּתּוֹ לְאָמָה לֹא תֵצֵא כְּצֵאת הָעֲבָדִים: אִם־רָעָה בְּעֵינֵי אֲדֹנֶיהָ אֲשֶׁר־לֹא [לוֹ] יְעָדָהּ וְהֶפְדָּהּ לְעַם נָכְרִי לֹא־יִמְשֹׁל לְמָכְרָהּ בְּבִגְדוֹ־בָהּ: וְאִם־לִבְנוֹ יִיעָדֶנָּה כְּמִשְׁפַּט הַבָּנוֹת יַעֲשֶׂה־לָּהּ: אִם־אַחֶרֶת יִקַּח־לוֹ שְׁאֵרָהּ כְּסוּתָהּ וְעֹנָתָהּ לֹא יִגְרָע: וְאִם־שְׁלָשׁ־אֵלֶּה לֹא יַעֲשֶׂה לָהּ וְיָצְאָה חִנָּם אֵין כָּסֶף: ישראל: מַכֵּה אִישׁ וָמֵת מוֹת יוּמָת: וַאֲשֶׁר לֹא צָדָה וְהָאֱלֹהִים אִנָּה לְיָדוֹ וְשַׂמְתִּי לְךָ מָקוֹם אֲשֶׁר יָנוּס שָׁמָּה: וְכִי־יָזִד אִישׁ עַל־רֵעֵהוּ לְהָרְגוֹ בְעָרְמָה מֵעִם מִזְבְּחִי תִּקָּחֶנּוּ לָמוּת: וּמַכֵּה אָבִיו וְאִמּוֹ מוֹת יוּמָת: וְגֹנֵב אִישׁ וּמְכָרוֹ וְנִמְצָא בְיָדוֹ מוֹת יוּמָת: וּמְקַלֵּל אָבִיו וְאִמּוֹ מוֹת יוּמָת: וְכִי־יְרִיבֻן אֲנָשִׁים וְהִכָּה־אִישׁ אֶת־רֵעֵהוּ בְּאֶבֶן אוֹ בְאֶגְרֹף וְלֹא יָמוּת וְנָפַל לְמִשְׁכָּב: אִם־יָקוּם וְהִתְהַלֵּךְ בַּחוּץ עַל־מִשְׁעַנְתּוֹ וְנִקָּה הַמַּכֶּה רַק שִׁבְתּוֹ יִתֵּן וְרַפֹּא יְרַפֵּא:

TERUMA / תרומה

שמות כה:א–טז

וַיְדַבֵּר יהוה אֶל־מֹשֶׁה לֵּאמֹר: דַּבֵּר אֶל־בְּנֵי יִשְׂרָאֵל וְיִקְחוּ־לִי תְּרוּמָה מֵאֵת כָּל־אִישׁ אֲשֶׁר יִדְּבֶנּוּ לִבּוֹ תִּקְחוּ אֶת־תְּרוּמָתִי: וְזֹאת הַתְּרוּמָה אֲשֶׁר תִּקְחוּ מֵאִתָּם זָהָב וָכֶסֶף וּנְחֹשֶׁת: וּתְכֵלֶת וְאַרְגָּמָן וְתוֹלַעַת שָׁנִי וְשֵׁשׁ וְעִזִּים: וְעֹרֹת אֵילִם מְאָדָּמִים וְעֹרֹת תְּחָשִׁים וַעֲצֵי שִׁטִּים: לוי: שֶׁמֶן לַמָּאֹר בְּשָׂמִים לְשֶׁמֶן הַמִּשְׁחָה וְלִקְטֹרֶת הַסַּמִּים: אַבְנֵי־שֹׁהַם וְאַבְנֵי מִלֻּאִים לָאֵפֹד וְלַחֹשֶׁן: וְעָשׂוּ לִי מִקְדָּשׁ וְשָׁכַנְתִּי בְּתוֹכָם: כְּכֹל אֲשֶׁר אֲנִי מַרְאֶה אוֹתְךָ אֵת תַּבְנִית הַמִּשְׁכָּן וְאֵת תַּבְנִית כָּל־כֵּלָיו וְכֵן תַּעֲשׂוּ: ישראל: וְעָשׂוּ אֲרוֹן עֲצֵי שִׁטִּים אַמָּתַיִם וָחֵצִי אָרְכּוֹ וְאַמָּה וָחֵצִי רָחְבּוֹ וְאַמָּה וָחֵצִי קֹמָתוֹ: וְצִפִּיתָ אֹתוֹ זָהָב טָהוֹר מִבַּיִת וּמִחוּץ תְּצַפֶּנּוּ וְעָשִׂיתָ עָלָיו זֵר זָהָב סָבִיב:

וְיָצַקְתָּ לּוֹ אַרְבַּע טַבְּעֹת זָהָב וְנָתַתָּה עַל
אַרְבַּע פַּעֲמֹתָיו וּשְׁתֵּי טַבָּעֹת עַל־צַלְעוֹ
הָאֶחָת וּשְׁתֵּי טַבָּעֹת עַל־צַלְעוֹ הַשֵּׁנִית:
וְעָשִׂיתָ בַדֵּי עֲצֵי שִׁטִּים וְצִפִּיתָ אֹתָם זָהָב:
וְהֵבֵאתָ אֶת־הַבַּדִּים בַּטַּבָּעֹת עַל צַלְעֹת
הָאָרֹן לָשֵׂאת אֶת־הָאָרֹן בָּהֶם: בְּטַבְּעֹת
הָאָרֹן יִהְיוּ הַבַּדִּים לֹא יָסֻרוּ מִמֶּנּוּ: וְנָתַתָּ
אֶל־הָאָרֹן אֵת הָעֵדֻת אֲשֶׁר אֶתֵּן אֵלֶיךָ:

TETZAVEH / תצוה

שמות כז:כ-כח:יב

וְאַתָּה תְּצַוֶּה | אֶת־בְּנֵי יִשְׂרָאֵל וְיִקְחוּ אֵלֶיךָ
שֶׁמֶן זַיִת זָךְ כָּתִית לַמָּאוֹר לְהַעֲלֹת נֵר תָּמִיד:
בְּאֹהֶל מוֹעֵד מִחוּץ לַפָּרֹכֶת אֲשֶׁר עַל־הָעֵדֻת
יַעֲרֹךְ אֹתוֹ אַהֲרֹן וּבָנָיו מֵעֶרֶב עַד־בֹּקֶר לִפְנֵי
יהוה חֻקַּת עוֹלָם לְדֹרֹתָם מֵאֵת בְּנֵי יִשְׂרָאֵל:
וְאַתָּה הַקְרֵב אֵלֶיךָ אֶת־אַהֲרֹן אָחִיךָ וְאֶת־
בָּנָיו אִתּוֹ מִתּוֹךְ בְּנֵי יִשְׂרָאֵל לְכַהֲנוֹ־לִי
אַהֲרֹן נָדָב וַאֲבִיהוּא אֶלְעָזָר וְאִיתָמָר בְּנֵי
אַהֲרֹן: וְעָשִׂיתָ בִגְדֵי־קֹדֶשׁ לְאַהֲרֹן אָחִיךָ
לְכָבוֹד וּלְתִפְאָרֶת: וְאַתָּה תְּדַבֵּר אֶל־כָּל־
חַכְמֵי־לֵב אֲשֶׁר מִלֵּאתִיו רוּחַ חָכְמָה וְעָשׂוּ
אֶת־בִּגְדֵי אַהֲרֹן לְקַדְּשׁוֹ לְכַהֲנוֹ־לִי: וְאֵלֶּה
הַבְּגָדִים אֲשֶׁר יַעֲשׂוּ חֹשֶׁן וְאֵפוֹד וּמְעִיל
וּכְתֹנֶת תַּשְׁבֵּץ מִצְנֶפֶת וְאַבְנֵט וְעָשׂוּ בִגְדֵי־
קֹדֶשׁ לְאַהֲרֹן אָחִיךָ וּלְבָנָיו לְכַהֲנוֹ־לִי: וְהֵם
יִקְחוּ אֶת־הַזָּהָב וְאֶת־הַתְּכֵלֶת וְאֶת־הָאַרְגָּמָן
וְאֶת־תּוֹלַעַת הַשָּׁנִי וְאֶת־הַשֵּׁשׁ:
לוי: וְעָשׂוּ אֶת־הָאֵפֹד זָהָב תְּכֵלֶת וְאַרְגָּמָן
תּוֹלַעַת שָׁנִי וְשֵׁשׁ מָשְׁזָר מַעֲשֵׂה חֹשֵׁב:
שְׁתֵּי כְתֵפֹת חֹבְרֹת יִהְיֶה־לּוֹ אֶל־שְׁנֵי
קְצוֹתָיו וְחֻבָּר: וְחֵשֶׁב אֲפֻדָּתוֹ אֲשֶׁר עָלָיו
כְּמַעֲשֵׂהוּ מִמֶּנּוּ יִהְיֶה זָהָב תְּכֵלֶת וְאַרְגָּמָן
וְתוֹלַעַת שָׁנִי וְשֵׁשׁ מָשְׁזָר: וְלָקַחְתָּ אֶת־
שְׁתֵּי אַבְנֵי־שֹׁהַם וּפִתַּחְתָּ עֲלֵיהֶם שְׁמוֹת
בְּנֵי יִשְׂרָאֵל: ישראל: שִׁשָּׁה מִשְּׁמֹתָם עַל הָאֶבֶן
הָאֶחָת וְאֶת־שְׁמוֹת הַשִּׁשָּׁה הַנּוֹתָרִים עַל־
הָאֶבֶן הַשֵּׁנִית כְּתוֹלְדֹתָם: מַעֲשֵׂה חָרַשׁ אֶבֶן
פִּתּוּחֵי חֹתָם תְּפַתַּח אֶת־שְׁתֵּי הָאֲבָנִים
עַל־שְׁמֹת בְּנֵי יִשְׂרָאֵל מֻסַבֹּת מִשְׁבְּצוֹת זָהָב
תַּעֲשֶׂה אֹתָם: וְשַׂמְתָּ אֶת־שְׁתֵּי הָאֲבָנִים עַל
כִּתְפֹת הָאֵפֹד אַבְנֵי זִכָּרֹן לִבְנֵי יִשְׂרָאֵל וְנָשָׂא
אַהֲרֹן אֶת־שְׁמוֹתָם לִפְנֵי יהוה עַל־שְׁתֵּי
כְתֵפָיו לְזִכָּרֹן:

KI TISSA / כי תשא

שמות ל:יא-כא

וַיְדַבֵּר יהוה אֶל־מֹשֶׁה לֵּאמֹר: כִּי תִשָּׂא אֶת־
רֹאשׁ בְּנֵי־יִשְׂרָאֵל לִפְקֻדֵיהֶם וְנָתְנוּ אִישׁ כֹּפֶר
נַפְשׁוֹ לַיהוה בִּפְקֹד אֹתָם וְלֹא־יִהְיֶה בָהֶם
נֶגֶף בִּפְקֹד אֹתָם: זֶה | יִתְּנוּ כָּל־הָעֹבֵר עַל־
הַפְּקֻדִים מַחֲצִית הַשֶּׁקֶל בְּשֶׁקֶל הַקֹּדֶשׁ
עֶשְׂרִים גֵּרָה הַשֶּׁקֶל מַחֲצִית הַשֶּׁקֶל תְּרוּמָה
לַיהוה: לוי: כֹּל הָעֹבֵר עַל־הַפְּקֻדִים מִבֶּן
עֶשְׂרִים שָׁנָה וָמָעְלָה יִתֵּן תְּרוּמַת יהוה:
הֶעָשִׁיר לֹא־יַרְבֶּה וְהַדַּל לֹא יַמְעִיט מִמַּחֲצִית
הַשָּׁקֶל לָתֵת אֶת־תְּרוּמַת יהוה לְכַפֵּר עַל־
נַפְשֹׁתֵיכֶם: וְלָקַחְתָּ אֶת־כֶּסֶף הַכִּפֻּרִים מֵאֵת
בְּנֵי יִשְׂרָאֵל וְנָתַתָּ אֹתוֹ עַל־עֲבֹדַת אֹהֶל
מוֹעֵד וְהָיָה לִבְנֵי יִשְׂרָאֵל לְזִכָּרוֹן לִפְנֵי יהוה
לְכַפֵּר עַל־נַפְשֹׁתֵיכֶם:
ישראל: וַיְדַבֵּר יהוה אֶל־מֹשֶׁה לֵּאמֹר: וְעָשִׂיתָ
כִּיּוֹר נְחֹשֶׁת וְכַנּוֹ נְחֹשֶׁת לְרָחְצָה וְנָתַתָּ אֹתוֹ
בֵּין־אֹהֶל מוֹעֵד וּבֵין הַמִּזְבֵּחַ וְנָתַתָּ שָׁמָּה
מָיִם: וְרָחֲצוּ אַהֲרֹן וּבָנָיו מִמֶּנּוּ אֶת־יְדֵיהֶם
וְאֶת־רַגְלֵיהֶם: בְּבֹאָם אֶל־אֹהֶל מוֹעֵד
יִרְחֲצוּ־מַיִם וְלֹא יָמֻתוּ אוֹ בְגִשְׁתָּם אֶל־
הַמִּזְבֵּחַ לְשָׁרֵת לְהַקְטִיר אִשֶּׁה לַיהוה:
וְרָחֲצוּ יְדֵיהֶם וְרַגְלֵיהֶם וְלֹא יָמֻתוּ וְהָיְתָה
לָהֶם חָק־עוֹלָם לוֹ וּלְזַרְעוֹ לְדֹרֹתָם:

VAYAK-HEL / ויקהל

שמות לה:א-כ

וַיַּקְהֵל מֹשֶׁה אֶת־כָּל־עֲדַת בְּנֵי יִשְׂרָאֵל
וַיֹּאמֶר אֲלֵהֶם אֵלֶּה הַדְּבָרִים אֲשֶׁר־צִוָּה

יְהוָה לַעֲשֹׂת אֹתָם: שֵׁשֶׁת יָמִים תֵּעָשֶׂה
מְלָאכָה וּבַיּוֹם הַשְּׁבִיעִי יִהְיֶה לָכֶם קֹדֶשׁ
שַׁבַּת שַׁבָּתוֹן לַיהוָה כָּל־הָעֹשֶׂה בוֹ מְלָאכָה
יוּמָת: לֹא־תְבַעֲרוּ אֵשׁ בְּכֹל מֹשְׁבֹתֵיכֶם
בְּיוֹם הַשַּׁבָּת:

לוי: וַיֹּאמֶר מֹשֶׁה אֶל־כָּל־עֲדַת בְּנֵי־יִשְׂרָאֵל
לֵאמֹר זֶה הַדָּבָר אֲשֶׁר־צִוָּה יְהוָה לֵאמֹר:
קְחוּ מֵאִתְּכֶם תְּרוּמָה לַיהוָה כֹּל נְדִיב לִבּוֹ
יְבִיאֶהָ אֵת תְּרוּמַת יְהוָה זָהָב וָכֶסֶף וּנְחֹשֶׁת:
וּתְכֵלֶת וְאַרְגָּמָן וְתוֹלַעַת שָׁנִי וְשֵׁשׁ וְעִזִּים:
וְעֹרֹת אֵילִם מְאָדָּמִים וְעֹרֹת תְּחָשִׁים וַעֲצֵי
שִׁטִּים: וְשֶׁמֶן לַמָּאוֹר וּבְשָׂמִים לְשֶׁמֶן
הַמִּשְׁחָה וְלִקְטֹרֶת הַסַּמִּים: וְאַבְנֵי־שֹׁהַם
וְאַבְנֵי מִלֻּאִים לָאֵפוֹד וְלַחֹשֶׁן: וְכָל־חֲכַם־לֵב
בָּכֶם יָבֹאוּ וְיַעֲשׂוּ אֵת כָּל־אֲשֶׁר צִוָּה יְהוָה:
ישראל: אֶת־הַמִּשְׁכָּן אֶת־אָהֳלוֹ וְאֶת־מִכְסֵהוּ
אֶת־קְרָסָיו וְאֶת־קְרָשָׁיו אֶת־בְּרִיחָו אֶת־
עַמֻּדָיו וְאֶת־אֲדָנָיו: אֶת־הָאָרֹן וְאֶת־בַּדָּיו
אֶת־הַכַּפֹּרֶת וְאֵת פָּרֹכֶת הַמָּסָךְ: אֶת־
הַשֻּׁלְחָן וְאֶת־בַּדָּיו וְאֶת־כָּל־כֵּלָיו וְאֵת לֶחֶם
הַפָּנִים: וְאֶת־מְנֹרַת הַמָּאוֹר וְאֶת־כֵּלֶיהָ
וְאֶת־נֵרֹתֶיהָ וְאֵת שֶׁמֶן הַמָּאוֹר: וְאֶת־מִזְבַּח
הַקְּטֹרֶת וְאֶת־בַּדָּיו וְאֵת שֶׁמֶן הַמִּשְׁחָה
וְאֵת קְטֹרֶת הַסַּמִּים וְאֶת־מָסַךְ הַפֶּתַח
לְפֶתַח הַמִּשְׁכָּן: אֵת ׀ מִזְבַּח הָעֹלָה וְאֶת־
מִכְבַּר הַנְּחֹשֶׁת אֲשֶׁר־לוֹ אֶת־בַּדָּיו וְאֶת־
כָּל־כֵּלָיו אֶת־הַכִּיֹּר וְאֶת־כַּנּוֹ: אֵת קַלְעֵי
הֶחָצֵר אֶת־עַמֻּדָיו וְאֶת־אֲדָנֶיהָ וְאֵת מָסַךְ
שַׁעַר הֶחָצֵר: אֶת־יִתְדֹת הַמִּשְׁכָּן וְאֶת־
יִתְדֹת הֶחָצֵר וְאֶת־מֵיתְרֵיהֶם: אֶת־בִּגְדֵי
הַשְּׂרָד לְשָׁרֵת בַּקֹּדֶשׁ אֶת־בִּגְדֵי הַקֹּדֶשׁ
לְאַהֲרֹן הַכֹּהֵן וְאֶת־בִּגְדֵי בָנָיו לְכַהֵן: וַיֵּצְאוּ
כָּל־עֲדַת בְּנֵי־יִשְׂרָאֵל מִלִּפְנֵי מֹשֶׁה:

PEKUDEI / פקודי

שמות לח:כא-לט:א

אֵלֶּה פְקוּדֵי הַמִּשְׁכָּן מִשְׁכַּן הָעֵדֻת אֲשֶׁר פֻּקַּד
עַל־פִּי מֹשֶׁה עֲבֹדַת הַלְוִיִּם בְּיַד אִיתָמָר
בֶּן־אַהֲרֹן הַכֹּהֵן: וּבְצַלְאֵל בֶּן־אוּרִי בֶן־חוּר
לְמַטֵּה יְהוּדָה עָשָׂה אֵת כָּל־אֲשֶׁר־צִוָּה יְהוָה
אֶת־מֹשֶׁה: וְאִתּוֹ אָהֳלִיאָב בֶּן־אֲחִיסָמָךְ
לְמַטֵּה־דָן חָרָשׁ וְחֹשֵׁב וְרֹקֵם בַּתְּכֵלֶת
וּבָאַרְגָּמָן וּבְתוֹלַעַת הַשָּׁנִי וּבַשֵּׁשׁ: לוי: כָּל־
הַזָּהָב הֶעָשׂוּי לַמְּלָאכָה בְּכֹל מְלֶאכֶת הַקֹּדֶשׁ
וַיְהִי ׀ זְהַב הַתְּנוּפָה תֵּשַׁע וְעֶשְׂרִים כִּכָּר
וּשְׁבַע מֵאוֹת וּשְׁלֹשִׁים שֶׁקֶל בְּשֶׁקֶל הַקֹּדֶשׁ:
וְכֶסֶף פְּקוּדֵי הָעֵדָה מְאַת כִּכָּר וְאֶלֶף וּשְׁבַע
מֵאוֹת וַחֲמִשָּׁה וְשִׁבְעִים שֶׁקֶל בְּשֶׁקֶל הַקֹּדֶשׁ:
בֶּקַע לַגֻּלְגֹּלֶת מַחֲצִית הַשֶּׁקֶל בְּשֶׁקֶל הַקֹּדֶשׁ
לְכֹל הָעֹבֵר עַל־הַפְּקֻדִים מִבֶּן עֶשְׂרִים שָׁנָה
וָמַעְלָה לְשֵׁשׁ־מֵאוֹת אֶלֶף וּשְׁלֹשֶׁת אֲלָפִים
וַחֲמֵשׁ מֵאוֹת וַחֲמִשִּׁים: וַיְהִי מְאַת כִּכַּר
הַכֶּסֶף לָצֶקֶת אֵת אַדְנֵי הַקֹּדֶשׁ וְאֵת אַדְנֵי
הַפָּרֹכֶת מְאַת אֲדָנִים לִמְאַת הַכִּכָּר כִּכָּר
לָאָדֶן: ישראל: וְאֶת־הָאֶלֶף וּשְׁבַע הַמֵּאוֹת
וַחֲמִשָּׁה וְשִׁבְעִים עָשָׂה וָוִים לָעַמּוּדִים וְצִפָּה
רָאשֵׁיהֶם וְחִשַּׁק אֹתָם: וּנְחֹשֶׁת הַתְּנוּפָה
שִׁבְעִים כִּכָּר וְאַלְפַּיִם וְאַרְבַּע־מֵאוֹת שָׁקֶל:
וַיַּעַשׂ בָּהּ אֶת־אַדְנֵי פֶּתַח אֹהֶל מוֹעֵד וְאֵת
מִזְבַּח הַנְּחֹשֶׁת וְאֶת־מִכְבַּר הַנְּחֹשֶׁת אֲשֶׁר־
לוֹ וְאֵת כָּל־כְּלֵי הַמִּזְבֵּחַ: וְאֶת־אַדְנֵי הֶחָצֵר
סָבִיב וְאֶת־אַדְנֵי שַׁעַר הֶחָצֵר וְאֵת כָּל־
יִתְדֹת הַמִּשְׁכָּן וְאֶת־כָּל־יִתְדֹת הֶחָצֵר סָבִיב:
וּמִן־הַתְּכֵלֶת וְהָאַרְגָּמָן וְתוֹלַעַת הַשָּׁנִי עָשׂוּ
בִגְדֵי־שְׂרָד לְשָׁרֵת בַּקֹּדֶשׁ וַיַּעֲשׂוּ אֶת־בִּגְדֵי
הַקֹּדֶשׁ אֲשֶׁר לְאַהֲרֹן כַּאֲשֶׁר צִוָּה יְהוָה אֶת־
מֹשֶׁה:

VAYIKRA / ויקרא

ויקרא א:א-יג

וַיִּקְרָא אֶל־מֹשֶׁה וַיְדַבֵּר יְהוָה אֵלָיו מֵאֹהֶל
מוֹעֵד לֵאמֹר: דַּבֵּר אֶל־בְּנֵי יִשְׂרָאֵל וְאָמַרְתָּ
אֲלֵהֶם אָדָם כִּי־יַקְרִיב מִכֶּם קָרְבָּן לַיהוָה
מִן־הַבְּהֵמָה מִן־הַבָּקָר וּמִן־הַצֹּאן תַּקְרִיבוּ

אֶת־קָרְבַּנְכֶֽם׃ אִם־עֹלָ֤ה קָרְבָּנוֹ֙ מִן־הַבָּקָ֔ר זָכָ֥ר תָּמִ֖ים יַקְרִיבֶ֑נּוּ אֶל־פֶּ֜תַח אֹ֤הֶל מוֹעֵד֙ יַקְרִ֣יב אֹת֔וֹ לִרְצֹנ֖וֹ לִפְנֵ֥י יהוה׃ וְסָמַ֣ךְ יָד֔וֹ עַ֖ל רֹ֣אשׁ הָעֹלָ֑ה וְנִרְצָ֥ה ל֖וֹ לְכַפֵּ֥ר עָלָֽיו׃ לוי: וְשָׁחַ֛ט אֶת־בֶּ֥ן הַבָּקָ֖ר לִפְנֵ֣י יהוה וְהִקְרִ֡יבוּ בְּנֵי֩ אַהֲרֹ֨ן הַכֹּהֲנִ֜ים אֶת־הַדָּ֗ם וְזָרְק֨וּ אֶת־הַדָּ֤ם עַל־הַמִּזְבֵּ֙חַ֙ סָבִ֔יב אֲשֶׁר־פֶּ֖תַח אֹ֥הֶל מוֹעֵֽד׃ וְהִפְשִׁ֖יט אֶת־הָעֹלָ֑ה וְנִתַּ֥ח אֹתָ֖הּ לִנְתָחֶֽיהָ׃ וְ֠נָתְנוּ בְּנֵ֨י אַהֲרֹ֧ן הַכֹּהֵ֛ן אֵ֖שׁ עַל־הַמִּזְבֵּ֑חַ וְעָרְכ֥וּ עֵצִ֖ים עַל־הָאֵֽשׁ׃ וְעָרְכ֗וּ בְּנֵ֤י אַהֲרֹן֙ הַכֹּ֣הֲנִ֔ים אֵ֚ת הַנְּתָחִ֔ים אֶת־הָרֹ֖אשׁ וְאֶת־הַפָּ֑דֶר עַל־הָעֵצִים֙ אֲשֶׁ֣ר עַל־הָאֵ֔שׁ אֲשֶׁ֖ר עַל־הַמִּזְבֵּֽחַ׃ וְקִרְבּ֥וֹ וּכְרָעָ֖יו יִרְחַ֣ץ בַּמָּ֑יִם וְהִקְטִ֨יר הַכֹּהֵ֤ן אֶת־הַכֹּל֙ הַמִּזְבֵּ֔חָה עֹלָ֛ה אִשֵּׁ֥ה רֵֽיחַ־נִיח֖וֹחַ לַיהוה׃ ישראל: וְאִם־מִן־הַצֹּ֨אן קָרְבָּנ֧וֹ מִן־הַכְּשָׂבִ֛ים א֥וֹ מִן־הָעִזִּ֖ים לְעֹלָ֑ה זָכָ֥ר תָּמִ֖ים יַקְרִיבֶֽנּוּ׃ וְשָׁחַ֨ט אֹת֜וֹ עַ֣ל יֶ֧רֶךְ הַמִּזְבֵּ֛חַ צָפֹ֖נָה לִפְנֵ֣י יהוה וְזָרְק֡וּ בְּנֵי֩ אַהֲרֹ֨ן הַכֹּהֲנִ֧ים אֶת־דָּמ֛וֹ עַל־הַמִּזְבֵּ֖חַ סָבִֽיב׃ וְנִתַּ֤ח אֹתוֹ֙ לִנְתָחָ֔יו וְאֶת־רֹאשׁ֖וֹ וְאֶת־פִּדְר֑וֹ וְעָרַ֤ךְ הַכֹּהֵן֙ אֹתָ֔ם עַל־הָעֵצִים֙ אֲשֶׁ֣ר עַל־הָאֵ֔שׁ אֲשֶׁ֖ר עַל־הַמִּזְבֵּֽחַ׃ וְהַקֶּ֥רֶב וְהַכְּרָעַ֖יִם יִרְחַ֣ץ בַּמָּ֑יִם וְהִקְרִ֨יב הַכֹּהֵ֤ן אֶת־הַכֹּל֙ וְהִקְטִ֣יר הַמִּזְבֵּ֔חָה עֹלָ֣ה ה֗וּא אִשֵּׁ֛ה רֵ֥יחַ נִיחֹ֖חַ לַיהוה׃

TZAV / צו

ויקרא ו:א-יא

וַיְדַבֵּ֥ר יהוה אֶל־מֹשֶׁ֥ה לֵּאמֹֽר׃ צַ֤ו אֶֽת־אַהֲרֹן֙ וְאֶת־בָּנָ֣יו לֵאמֹ֔ר זֹ֥את תּוֹרַ֖ת הָעֹלָ֑ה הִ֣וא הָעֹלָ֡ה עַל֩ מוֹקְדָ֨ה עַל־הַמִּזְבֵּ֤חַ כָּל־הַלַּ֙יְלָה֙ עַד־הַבֹּ֔קֶר וְאֵ֥שׁ הַמִּזְבֵּ֖חַ תּ֥וּקַד בּֽוֹ׃ וְלָבַ֨שׁ הַכֹּהֵ֜ן מִדּ֣וֹ בַ֗ד וּמִֽכְנְסֵי־בַד֮ יִלְבַּ֣שׁ עַל־בְּשָׂרוֹ֒ וְהֵרִ֣ים אֶת־הַדֶּ֗שֶׁן אֲשֶׁ֨ר תֹּאכַ֥ל הָאֵ֛שׁ אֶת־הָעֹלָ֖ה עַל־הַמִּזְבֵּ֑חַ וְשָׂמ֕וֹ אֵ֖צֶל הַמִּזְבֵּֽחַ׃ לוי: וּפָשַׁט֙ אֶת־בְּגָדָ֔יו וְלָבַ֖שׁ בְּגָדִ֣ים אֲחֵרִ֑ים וְהוֹצִ֤יא אֶת־הַדֶּ֙שֶׁן֙ אֶל־מִח֣וּץ לַֽמַּחֲנֶ֔ה אֶל־מָק֖וֹם טָהֽוֹר׃ וְהָאֵ֨שׁ עַל־הַמִּזְבֵּ֤חַ תּֽוּקַד־בּוֹ֙ לֹ֣א תִכְבֶּ֔ה וּבִעֵ֨ר עָלֶ֧יהָ הַכֹּהֵ֛ן עֵצִ֖ים בַּבֹּ֣קֶר בַּבֹּ֑קֶר וְעָרַ֤ךְ עָלֶ֙יהָ֙ הָעֹלָ֔ה וְהִקְטִ֥יר עָלֶ֖יהָ חֶלְבֵ֥י הַשְּׁלָמִֽים׃ אֵ֗שׁ תָּמִ֛יד תּוּקַ֥ד עַל־הַמִּזְבֵּ֖חַ לֹ֥א תִכְבֶּֽה׃ ישראל: וְזֹ֥את תּוֹרַ֖ת הַמִּנְחָ֑ה הַקְרֵ֨ב אֹתָ֤הּ בְּנֵֽי־אַהֲרֹן֙ לִפְנֵ֣י יהוה אֶל־פְּנֵ֖י הַמִּזְבֵּֽחַ׃ וְהֵרִ֨ים מִמֶּ֜נּוּ בְּקֻמְצ֗וֹ מִסֹּ֤לֶת הַמִּנְחָה֙ וּמִשַּׁמְנָ֔הּ וְאֵת֙ כָּל־הַלְּבֹנָ֔ה אֲשֶׁ֖ר עַל־הַמִּנְחָ֑ה וְהִקְטִ֣יר הַמִּזְבֵּ֗חַ רֵ֣יחַ נִיחֹ֛חַ אַזְכָּרָתָ֖הּ לַיהוה׃ וְהַנּוֹתֶ֣רֶת מִמֶּ֔נָּה יֹאכְל֖וּ אַהֲרֹ֣ן וּבָנָ֑יו מַצּ֤וֹת תֵּֽאָכֵל֙ בְּמָק֣וֹם קָדֹ֔שׁ בַּחֲצַ֥ר אֹֽהֶל־מוֹעֵ֖ד יֹאכְלֽוּהָ׃ לֹ֤א תֵאָפֶה֙ חָמֵ֔ץ חֶלְקָ֛ם נָתַ֥תִּי אֹתָ֖הּ מֵאִשָּׁ֑י קֹ֤דֶשׁ קָֽדָשִׁים֙ הִ֔וא כַּֽחַטָּ֖את וְכָאָשָֽׁם׃ כָּל־זָכָ֞ר בִּבְנֵ֤י אַהֲרֹן֙ יֹֽאכֲלֶ֔נָּה חָק־עוֹלָם֙ לְדֹרֹ֣תֵיכֶ֔ם מֵאִשֵּׁ֖י יהוה כֹּ֛ל אֲשֶׁר־יִגַּ֥ע בָּהֶ֖ם יִקְדָּֽשׁ׃

SHEMINI / שמיני

ויקרא ט:א-טז

וַיְהִי֙ בַּיּ֣וֹם הַשְּׁמִינִ֔י קָרָ֣א מֹשֶׁ֔ה לְאַהֲרֹ֖ן וּלְבָנָ֑יו וּלְזִקְנֵ֖י יִשְׂרָאֵֽל׃ וַיֹּ֣אמֶר אֶֽל־אַהֲרֹ֗ן קַח־לְךָ֞ עֵ֨גֶל בֶּן־בָּקָ֧ר לְחַטָּ֛את וְאַ֥יִל לְעֹלָ֖ה תְּמִימִ֑ם וְהַקְרֵ֖ב לִפְנֵ֥י יהוה׃ וְאֶל־בְּנֵ֥י יִשְׂרָאֵ֖ל תְּדַבֵּ֣ר לֵאמֹ֑ר קְח֤וּ שְׂעִֽיר־עִזִּים֙ לְחַטָּ֔את וְעֵ֨גֶל וָכֶ֧בֶשׂ בְּנֵֽי־שָׁנָ֛ה תְּמִימִ֖ם לְעֹלָֽה׃ וְשׁ֨וֹר וָאַ֜יִל לִשְׁלָמִ֗ים לִזְבֹּ֙חַ֙ לִפְנֵ֣י יהוה וּמִנְחָ֖ה בְּלוּלָ֣ה בַשָּׁ֑מֶן כִּ֣י הַיּ֔וֹם יהוה נִרְאָ֥ה אֲלֵיכֶֽם׃ וַיִּקְח֗וּ אֵ֚ת אֲשֶׁ֣ר צִוָּ֣ה מֹשֶׁ֔ה אֶל־פְּנֵ֖י אֹ֣הֶל מוֹעֵ֑ד וַיִּקְרְבוּ֙ כָּל־הָ֣עֵדָ֔ה וַיַּֽעַמְד֖וּ לִפְנֵ֥י יהוה׃ וַיֹּ֣אמֶר מֹשֶׁ֔ה זֶ֧ה הַדָּבָ֛ר אֲשֶׁר־צִוָּ֥ה יהוה תַּעֲשׂ֑וּ וְיֵרָ֥א אֲלֵיכֶ֖ם כְּב֥וֹד יהוה׃ לוי: וַיֹּ֨אמֶר מֹשֶׁ֜ה אֶֽל־אַהֲרֹ֗ן קְרַ֤ב אֶל־הַמִּזְבֵּ֙חַ֙ וַעֲשֵׂ֞ה אֶת־חַטָּֽאתְךָ֙ וְאֶת־עֹ֣לָתֶ֔ךָ וְכַפֵּ֥ר בַּֽעַדְךָ֖ וּבְעַ֣ד הָעָ֑ם וַעֲשֵׂ֞ה אֶת־קָרְבַּ֤ן הָעָם֙ וְכַפֵּ֣ר בַּֽעֲדָ֔ם כַּאֲשֶׁ֖ר צִוָּ֥ה יהוה׃ וַיִּקְרַ֥ב אַהֲרֹ֖ן אֶל־הַמִּזְבֵּ֑חַ וַיִּשְׁחַ֛ט אֶת־עֵ֥גֶל הַחַטָּ֖את אֲשֶׁר־לֽוֹ׃ וַ֠יַּקְרִבוּ בְּנֵ֨י אַהֲרֹ֣ן אֶת־הַדָּם֮ אֵלָיו֒ וַיִּטְבֹּ֤ל אֶצְבָּעוֹ֙

בדם ויתן על־קרנות המזבח ואת־הדם יצק אל־יסוד המזבח: ואת־החלב ואת־הכלית ואת־היתרת מן־הכבד מן־החטאת הקטיר המזבחה כאשר צוה יהוה את־משה: ישראל: ואת־הבשר ואת־העור שרף באש מחוץ למחנה: וישחט את־העלה וימצאו בני אהרן אליו את־הדם ויזרקהו על־המזבח סביב: ואת־העלה המציאו אליו לנתחיה ואת־הראש ויקטר על־המזבח: וירחץ את־הקרב ואת־הכרעים ויקטר על־העלה המזבחה: ויקרב את קרבן העם ויקח את־שעיר החטאת אשר לעם וישחטהו ויחטאהו כראשון: ויקרב את־העלה ויעשה כמשפט:

TAZRIA / תזריע

ויקרא יב:א־יג:ה

וידבר יהוה אל־משה לאמר: דבר אל־בני ישראל לאמר אשה כי תזריע וילדה זכר וטמאה שבעת ימים כימי נדת דותה תטמא: וביום השמיני ימול בשר ערלתו: ושלשים יום ושלשת ימים תשב בדמי טהרה בכל־קדש לא־תגע ואל־המקדש לא תבא עד־מלאת ימי טהרה: לוי: ואם־נקבה תלד וטמאה שבעים כנדתה וששים יום וששת ימים תשב על־דמי טהרה: ובמלאת | ימי טהרה לבן או לבת תביא כבש בן־שנתו לעלה ובן־יונה או־תר לחטאת אל־פתח אהל־מועד אל־הכהן: והקריבו לפני יהוה וכפר עליה וטהרה ממקר דמיה זאת תורת הילדת לזכר או לנקבה: ואם־לא תמצא ידה די שה ולקחה שתי־תרים או שני בני יונה אחד לעלה ואחד לחטאת וכפר עליה הכהן וטהרה:

ישראל: וידבר יהוה אל־משה ואל־אהרן לאמר: אדם כי־יהיה בעור־בשרו שאת או־ספחת או בהרת והיה בעור־בשרו לנגע צרעת והובא אל־אהרן הכהן או אל־אחד מבניו הכהנים: וראה הכהן את־הנגע בעור־הבשר ושער בנגע הפך | לבן ומראה הנגע עמק מעור בשרו נגע צרעת הוא וראהו הכהן וטמא אתו: ואם־בהרת לבנה הוא בעור בשרו ועמק אין־מראה מן־העור ושערה לא־הפך לבן והסגיר הכהן את־הנגע שבעת ימים: וראהו הכהן ביום השביעי והנה הנגע עמד בעיניו לא־פשה הנגע בעור והסגירו הכהן שבעת ימים שנית:

METZORA / מצורע

ויקרא יד:א־יב

וידבר יהוה אל־משה לאמר: זאת תהיה תורת המצרע ביום טהרתו והובא אל־הכהן: ויצא הכהן אל־מחוץ למחנה וראה הכהן והנה נרפא נגע־הצרעת מן־הצרוע: וצוה הכהן ולקח למטהר שתי־צפרים חיות טהרות ועץ ארז ושני תולעת ואזב: וצוה הכהן ושחט את־הצפור האחת אל־כלי־חרש על־מים חיים: לוי: את־הצפר החיה יקח אתה ואת־עץ הארז ואת־שני התולעת ואת־האזב וטבל אותם ואת | הצפר החיה בדם הצפר השחטה על המים החיים: והזה על המטהר מן־הצרעת שבע פעמים וטהרו ושלח את־הצפר החיה על־פני השדה: וכבס המטהר את־בגדיו וגלח את־כל־שערו ורחץ במים וטהר ואחר יבוא אל־המחנה וישב מחוץ לאהלו שבעת ימים: והיה ביום השביעי יגלח את־כל־שערו את־ראשו ואת־זקנו ואת גבת עיניו ואת־כל־שערו יגלח וכבס את־בגדיו ורחץ את־בשרו במים וטהר: ישראל: וביום השמיני יקח שני־כבשים תמימם וכבשה אחת בת־שנתה תמימה ושלשה עשרנים

סֹלֶת מִנְחָה בְּלוּלָה בַשֶּׁמֶן וְלֹג אֶחָד שָׁמֶן: וְהֶעֱמִיד הַכֹּהֵן הַמְטַהֵר אֵת הָאִישׁ הַמִּטַּהֵר וְאֹתָם לִפְנֵי יהוה פֶּתַח אֹהֶל מוֹעֵד: וְלָקַח הַכֹּהֵן אֶת־הַכֶּבֶשׂ הָאֶחָד וְהִקְרִיב אֹתוֹ לְאָשָׁם וְאֶת־לֹג הַשָּׁמֶן וְהֵנִיף אֹתָם תְּנוּפָה לִפְנֵי יהוה:

AHAREI MOT / אחרי מות

ויקרא טז:א-יז

וַיְדַבֵּר יהוה אֶל־מֹשֶׁה אַחֲרֵי מוֹת שְׁנֵי בְּנֵי אַהֲרֹן בְּקָרְבָתָם לִפְנֵי־יהוה וַיָּמֻתוּ: וַיֹּאמֶר יהוה אֶל־מֹשֶׁה דַּבֵּר אֶל־אַהֲרֹן אָחִיךָ וְאַל־יָבֹא בְכָל־עֵת אֶל־הַקֹּדֶשׁ מִבֵּית לַפָּרֹכֶת אֶל־פְּנֵי הַכַּפֹּרֶת אֲשֶׁר עַל־הָאָרֹן וְלֹא יָמוּת כִּי בֶּעָנָן אֵרָאֶה עַל־הַכַּפֹּרֶת: בְּזֹאת יָבֹא אַהֲרֹן אֶל־הַקֹּדֶשׁ בְּפַר בֶּן־בָּקָר לְחַטָּאת וְאַיִל לְעֹלָה: כְּתֹנֶת־בַּד קֹדֶשׁ יִלְבָּשׁ וּמִכְנְסֵי־בַד יִהְיוּ עַל־בְּשָׂרוֹ וּבְאַבְנֵט בַּד יַחְגֹּר וּבְמִצְנֶפֶת בַּד יִצְנֹף בִּגְדֵי־קֹדֶשׁ הֵם וְרָחַץ בַּמַּיִם אֶת־בְּשָׂרוֹ וּלְבֵשָׁם: וּמֵאֵת עֲדַת בְּנֵי יִשְׂרָאֵל יִקַּח שְׁנֵי־שְׂעִירֵי עִזִּים לְחַטָּאת וְאַיִל אֶחָד לְעֹלָה: וְהִקְרִיב אַהֲרֹן אֶת־פַּר הַחַטָּאת אֲשֶׁר־לוֹ וְכִפֶּר בַּעֲדוֹ וּבְעַד בֵּיתוֹ: לוי: וְלָקַח אֶת־שְׁנֵי הַשְּׂעִירִם וְהֶעֱמִיד אֹתָם לִפְנֵי יהוה פֶּתַח אֹהֶל מוֹעֵד: וְנָתַן אַהֲרֹן עַל־שְׁנֵי הַשְּׂעִירִם גֹּרָלוֹת גּוֹרָל אֶחָד לַיהוה וְגוֹרָל אֶחָד לַעֲזָאזֵל: וְהִקְרִיב אַהֲרֹן אֶת־הַשָּׂעִיר אֲשֶׁר עָלָה עָלָיו הַגּוֹרָל לַיהוה וְעָשָׂהוּ חַטָּאת: וְהַשָּׂעִיר אֲשֶׁר עָלָה עָלָיו הַגּוֹרָל לַעֲזָאזֵל יָעֳמַד־חַי לִפְנֵי יהוה לְכַפֵּר עָלָיו לְשַׁלַּח אֹתוֹ לַעֲזָאזֵל הַמִּדְבָּרָה: וְהִקְרִיב אַהֲרֹן אֶת־פַּר הַחַטָּאת אֲשֶׁר־לוֹ וְכִפֶּר בַּעֲדוֹ וּבְעַד בֵּיתוֹ וְשָׁחַט אֶת־פַּר הַחַטָּאת אֲשֶׁר־לוֹ: ישראל: וְלָקַח מְלֹא־הַמַּחְתָּה גַּחֲלֵי־אֵשׁ מֵעַל הַמִּזְבֵּחַ מִלִּפְנֵי יהוה וּמְלֹא חָפְנָיו קְטֹרֶת סַמִּים דַּקָּה וְהֵבִיא מִבֵּית לַפָּרֹכֶת: וְנָתַן אֶת־הַקְּטֹרֶת עַל־הָאֵשׁ לִפְנֵי יהוה וְכִסָּה ׀ עֲנַן הַקְּטֹרֶת אֶת־הַכַּפֹּרֶת אֲשֶׁר עַל־הָעֵדוּת וְלֹא יָמוּת: וְלָקַח מִדַּם הַפָּר וְהִזָּה בְאֶצְבָּעוֹ עַל־פְּנֵי הַכַּפֹּרֶת קֵדְמָה וְלִפְנֵי הַכַּפֹּרֶת יַזֶּה שֶׁבַע־פְּעָמִים מִן־הַדָּם בְּאֶצְבָּעוֹ: וְשָׁחַט אֶת־שְׂעִיר הַחַטָּאת אֲשֶׁר לָעָם וְהֵבִיא אֶת־דָּמוֹ אֶל־מִבֵּית לַפָּרֹכֶת וְעָשָׂה אֶת־דָּמוֹ כַּאֲשֶׁר עָשָׂה לְדַם הַפָּר וְהִזָּה אֹתוֹ עַל־הַכַּפֹּרֶת וְלִפְנֵי הַכַּפֹּרֶת: וְכִפֶּר עַל־הַקֹּדֶשׁ מִטֻּמְאֹת בְּנֵי יִשְׂרָאֵל וּמִפִּשְׁעֵיהֶם לְכָל־חַטֹּאתָם וְכֵן יַעֲשֶׂה לְאֹהֶל מוֹעֵד הַשֹּׁכֵן אִתָּם בְּתוֹךְ טֻמְאֹתָם: וְכָל־אָדָם לֹא־יִהְיֶה ׀ בְּאֹהֶל מוֹעֵד בְּבֹאוֹ לְכַפֵּר בַּקֹּדֶשׁ עַד־צֵאתוֹ וְכִפֶּר בַּעֲדוֹ וּבְעַד בֵּיתוֹ וּבְעַד כָּל־קְהַל יִשְׂרָאֵל:

KEDOSHIM / קדושים

ויקרא יט:א-יד

וַיְדַבֵּר יהוה אֶל־מֹשֶׁה לֵּאמֹר: דַּבֵּר אֶל־כָּל־עֲדַת בְּנֵי־יִשְׂרָאֵל וְאָמַרְתָּ אֲלֵהֶם קְדֹשִׁים תִּהְיוּ כִּי קָדוֹשׁ אֲנִי יהוה אֱלֹהֵיכֶם: אִישׁ אִמּוֹ וְאָבִיו תִּירָאוּ וְאֶת־שַׁבְּתֹתַי תִּשְׁמֹרוּ אֲנִי יהוה אֱלֹהֵיכֶם: אַל־תִּפְנוּ אֶל־הָאֱלִילִם וֵאלֹהֵי מַסֵּכָה לֹא תַעֲשׂוּ לָכֶם אֲנִי יהוה אֱלֹהֵיכֶם: לוי: וְכִי תִזְבְּחוּ זֶבַח שְׁלָמִים לַיהוה לִרְצֹנְכֶם תִּזְבָּחֻהוּ: בְּיוֹם זִבְחֲכֶם יֵאָכֵל וּמִמָּחֳרָת וְהַנּוֹתָר עַד־יוֹם הַשְּׁלִישִׁי בָּאֵשׁ יִשָּׂרֵף: וְאִם הֵאָכֹל יֵאָכֵל בַּיּוֹם הַשְּׁלִישִׁי פִּגּוּל הוּא לֹא יֵרָצֶה: וְאֹכְלָיו עֲוֺנוֹ יִשָּׂא כִּי־אֶת־קֹדֶשׁ יהוה חִלֵּל וְנִכְרְתָה הַנֶּפֶשׁ הַהִוא מֵעַמֶּיהָ: וּבְקֻצְרְכֶם אֶת־קְצִיר אַרְצְכֶם לֹא תְכַלֶּה פְּאַת שָׂדְךָ לִקְצֹר וְלֶקֶט קְצִירְךָ לֹא תְלַקֵּט: וְכַרְמְךָ לֹא תְעוֹלֵל וּפֶרֶט כַּרְמְךָ לֹא תְלַקֵּט לֶעָנִי וְלַגֵּר תַּעֲזֹב אֹתָם אֲנִי יהוה אֱלֹהֵיכֶם: ישראל: לֹא תִּגְנֹבוּ וְלֹא־תְכַחֲשׁוּ וְלֹא־תְשַׁקְּרוּ אִישׁ בַּעֲמִיתוֹ: וְלֹא־תִשָּׁבְעוּ בִשְׁמִי לַשָּׁקֶר וְחִלַּלְתָּ אֶת־שֵׁם אֱלֹהֶיךָ אֲנִי יהוה: לֹא־תַעֲשֹׁק אֶת־רֵעֲךָ וְלֹא תִגְזֹל לֹא־תָלִין פְּעֻלַּת שָׂכִיר אִתְּךָ עַד־בֹּקֶר: לֹא־

תְקַלֵּל חֵרֵשׁ וְלִפְנֵי עִוֵּר לֹא תִתֵּן מִכְשֹׁל
וְיָרֵאתָ מֵּאֱלֹהֶיךָ אֲנִי יהוה׃

EMOR / אמור

ויקרא כא:א-טו

וַיֹּאמֶר יהוה אֶל־מֹשֶׁה אֱמֹר אֶל־הַכֹּהֲנִים
בְּנֵי אַהֲרֹן וְאָמַרְתָּ אֲלֵהֶם לְנֶפֶשׁ לֹא־יִטַּמָּא
בְּעַמָּיו׃ כִּי אִם־לִשְׁאֵרוֹ הַקָּרֹב אֵלָיו לְאִמּוֹ
וּלְאָבִיו וְלִבְנוֹ וּלְבִתּוֹ וּלְאָחִיו׃ וְלַאֲחֹתוֹ
הַבְּתוּלָה הַקְּרוֹבָה אֵלָיו אֲשֶׁר לֹא־הָיְתָה
לְאִישׁ לָהּ יִטַּמָּא׃ לֹא יִטַּמָּא בַּעַל בְּעַמָּיו
לְהֵחַלּוֹ׃ לֹא־יקרחה [יִקְרְחוּ] קָרְחָה בְּרֹאשָׁם
וּפְאַת זְקָנָם לֹא יְגַלֵּחוּ וּבִבְשָׂרָם לֹא יִשְׂרְטוּ
שָׂרָטֶת׃ קְדֹשִׁים יִהְיוּ לֵאלֹהֵיהֶם וְלֹא יְחַלְּלוּ
שֵׁם אֱלֹהֵיהֶם כִּי אֶת־אִשֵּׁי יהוה לֶחֶם
אֱלֹהֵיהֶם הֵם מַקְרִיבִם וְהָיוּ קֹדֶשׁ׃ לוי: אִשָּׁה
זֹנָה וַחֲלָלָה לֹא יִקָּחוּ וְאִשָּׁה גְּרוּשָׁה מֵאִישָׁהּ
לֹא יִקָּחוּ כִּי־קָדֹשׁ הוּא לֵאלֹהָיו׃ וְקִדַּשְׁתּוֹ
כִּי־אֶת־לֶחֶם אֱלֹהֶיךָ הוּא מַקְרִיב קָדֹשׁ
יִהְיֶה־לָּךְ כִּי קָדוֹשׁ אֲנִי יהוה מְקַדִּשְׁכֶם׃ וּבַת
אִישׁ כֹּהֵן כִּי תֵחֵל לִזְנוֹת אֶת־אָבִיהָ הִיא
מְחַלֶּלֶת בָּאֵשׁ תִּשָּׂרֵף׃ וְהַכֹּהֵן הַגָּדוֹל מֵאֶחָיו
אֲשֶׁר־יוּצַק עַל־רֹאשׁוֹ ׀ שֶׁמֶן הַמִּשְׁחָה וּמִלֵּא
אֶת־יָדוֹ לִלְבֹּשׁ אֶת־הַבְּגָדִים אֶת־רֹאשׁוֹ לֹא
יִפְרָע וּבְגָדָיו לֹא יִפְרֹם׃ וְעַל כָּל־נַפְשֹׁת מֵת
לֹא יָבֹא לְאָבִיו וּלְאִמּוֹ לֹא יִטַּמָּא׃ וּמִן־
הַמִּקְדָּשׁ לֹא יֵצֵא וְלֹא יְחַלֵּל אֵת מִקְדַּשׁ
אֱלֹהָיו כִּי נֵזֶר שֶׁמֶן מִשְׁחַת אֱלֹהָיו עָלָיו אֲנִי
יהוה׃ ישראל: וְהוּא אִשָּׁה בִבְתוּלֶיהָ יִקָּח׃
אַלְמָנָה וּגְרוּשָׁה וַחֲלָלָה זֹנָה אֶת־אֵלֶּה לֹא
יִקָּח כִּי אִם־בְּתוּלָה מֵעַמָּיו יִקַּח אִשָּׁה׃
וְלֹא־יְחַלֵּל זַרְעוֹ בְּעַמָּיו כִּי אֲנִי יהוה מְקַדְּשׁוֹ׃

BEHAR / בהר

ויקרא כה:א-יג

וַיְדַבֵּר יהוה אֶל־מֹשֶׁה בְּהַר סִינַי לֵאמֹר׃ דַּבֵּר
אֶל־בְּנֵי יִשְׂרָאֵל וְאָמַרְתָּ אֲלֵהֶם כִּי תָבֹאוּ
אֶל־הָאָרֶץ אֲשֶׁר אֲנִי נֹתֵן לָכֶם וְשָׁבְתָה
הָאָרֶץ שַׁבָּת לַיהוה׃ שֵׁשׁ שָׁנִים תִּזְרַע שָׂדֶךָ
וְשֵׁשׁ שָׁנִים תִּזְמֹר כַּרְמֶךָ וְאָסַפְתָּ אֶת־
תְּבוּאָתָהּ׃ לוי: וּבַשָּׁנָה הַשְּׁבִיעִת שַׁבַּת שַׁבָּתוֹן
יִהְיֶה לָאָרֶץ שַׁבָּת לַיהוה שָׂדְךָ לֹא תִזְרָע
וְכַרְמְךָ לֹא תִזְמֹר׃ אֵת סְפִיחַ קְצִירְךָ לֹא
תִקְצוֹר וְאֶת־עִנְּבֵי נְזִירֶךָ לֹא תִבְצֹר שְׁנַת
שַׁבָּתוֹן יִהְיֶה לָאָרֶץ׃ וְהָיְתָה שַׁבַּת הָאָרֶץ
לָכֶם לְאָכְלָה לְךָ וּלְעַבְדְּךָ וְלַאֲמָתֶךָ וְלִשְׂכִירְךָ
וּלְתוֹשָׁבְךָ הַגָּרִים עִמָּךְ׃ וְלִבְהֶמְתְּךָ וְלַחַיָּה
אֲשֶׁר בְּאַרְצֶךָ תִּהְיֶה כָל־תְּבוּאָתָהּ לֶאֱכֹל׃
ישראל: וְסָפַרְתָּ לְךָ שֶׁבַע שַׁבְּתֹת שָׁנִים שֶׁבַע
שָׁנִים שֶׁבַע פְּעָמִים וְהָיוּ לְךָ יְמֵי שֶׁבַע שַׁבְּתֹת
הַשָּׁנִים תֵּשַׁע וְאַרְבָּעִים שָׁנָה׃ וְהַעֲבַרְתָּ
שׁוֹפַר תְּרוּעָה בַּחֹדֶשׁ הַשְּׁבִעִי בֶּעָשׂוֹר לַחֹדֶשׁ
בְּיוֹם הַכִּפֻּרִים תַּעֲבִירוּ שׁוֹפָר בְּכָל־אַרְצְכֶם׃
וְקִדַּשְׁתֶּם אֵת שְׁנַת הַחֲמִשִּׁים שָׁנָה וּקְרָאתֶם
דְּרוֹר בָּאָרֶץ לְכָל־יֹשְׁבֶיהָ יוֹבֵל הִוא תִּהְיֶה
לָכֶם וְשַׁבְתֶּם אִישׁ אֶל־אֲחֻזָּתוֹ וְאִישׁ אֶל־
מִשְׁפַּחְתּוֹ תָּשֻׁבוּ׃ יוֹבֵל הִוא שְׁנַת הַחֲמִשִּׁים
שָׁנָה תִּהְיֶה לָכֶם לֹא תִזְרָעוּ וְלֹא תִקְצְרוּ
אֶת־סְפִיחֶיהָ וְלֹא תִבְצְרוּ אֶת־נְזִרֶיהָ׃ כִּי
יוֹבֵל הִוא קֹדֶשׁ תִּהְיֶה לָכֶם מִן־הַשָּׂדֶה
תֹּאכְלוּ אֶת־תְּבוּאָתָהּ׃ בִּשְׁנַת הַיּוֹבֵל הַזֹּאת
תָּשֻׁבוּ אִישׁ אֶל־אֲחֻזָּתוֹ׃

BEḤUKKOTAI / בחוקותי

ויקרא כו:ג-יג

אִם־בְּחֻקֹּתַי תֵּלֵכוּ וְאֶת־מִצְוֺתַי תִּשְׁמְרוּ
וַעֲשִׂיתֶם אֹתָם׃ וְנָתַתִּי גִשְׁמֵיכֶם בְּעִתָּם
וְנָתְנָה הָאָרֶץ יְבוּלָהּ וְעֵץ הַשָּׂדֶה יִתֵּן פִּרְיוֹ׃
וְהִשִּׂיג לָכֶם דַּיִשׁ אֶת־בָּצִיר וּבָצִיר יַשִּׂיג אֶת־
זָרַע וַאֲכַלְתֶּם לַחְמְכֶם לָשֹׂבַע וִישַׁבְתֶּם
לָבֶטַח בְּאַרְצְכֶם׃ לוי: וְנָתַתִּי שָׁלוֹם בָּאָרֶץ
וּשְׁכַבְתֶּם וְאֵין מַחֲרִיד וְהִשְׁבַּתִּי חַיָּה רָעָה
מִן־הָאָרֶץ וְחֶרֶב לֹא־תַעֲבֹר בְּאַרְצְכֶם׃
וּרְדַפְתֶּם אֶת־אֹיְבֵיכֶם וְנָפְלוּ לִפְנֵיכֶם

לֶחָרֶב: וְרָדְפוּ מִכֶּם חֲמִשָּׁה מֵאָה וּמֵאָה מִכֶּם רְבָבָה יִרְדֹּפוּ וְנָפְלוּ אֹיְבֵיכֶם לִפְנֵיכֶם לֶחָרֶב: וּפָנִיתִי אֲלֵיכֶם וְהִפְרֵיתִי אֶתְכֶם וְהִרְבֵּיתִי אֶתְכֶם וַהֲקִימֹתִי אֶת־בְּרִיתִי אִתְּכֶם: ישראל: וַאֲכַלְתֶּם יָשָׁן נוֹשָׁן וְיָשָׁן מִפְּנֵי חָדָשׁ תּוֹצִיאוּ: וְנָתַתִּי מִשְׁכָּנִי בְּתוֹכְכֶם וְלֹא־תִגְעַל נַפְשִׁי אֶתְכֶם: וְהִתְהַלַּכְתִּי בְּתוֹכְכֶם וְהָיִיתִי לָכֶם לֵאלֹהִים וְאַתֶּם תִּהְיוּ־לִי לְעָם: אֲנִי יהוה אֱלֹהֵיכֶם אֲשֶׁר הוֹצֵאתִי אֶתְכֶם מֵאֶרֶץ מִצְרַיִם מִהְיֹת לָהֶם עֲבָדִים וָאֶשְׁבֹּר מֹטֹת עֻלְּכֶם וָאוֹלֵךְ אֶתְכֶם קוֹמְמִיּוּת:

במדבר / BEMIDBAR

במדבר א:א-יט

וַיְדַבֵּר יהוה אֶל־מֹשֶׁה בְּמִדְבַּר סִינַי בְּאֹהֶל מוֹעֵד בְּאֶחָד לַחֹדֶשׁ הַשֵּׁנִי בַּשָּׁנָה הַשֵּׁנִית לְצֵאתָם מֵאֶרֶץ מִצְרַיִם לֵאמֹר: שְׂאוּ אֶת־רֹאשׁ כָּל־עֲדַת בְּנֵי־יִשְׂרָאֵל לְמִשְׁפְּחֹתָם לְבֵית אֲבֹתָם בְּמִסְפַּר שֵׁמוֹת כָּל־זָכָר לְגֻלְגְּלֹתָם: מִבֶּן עֶשְׂרִים שָׁנָה וָמַעְלָה כָּל־יֹצֵא צָבָא בְּיִשְׂרָאֵל תִּפְקְדוּ אֹתָם לְצִבְאֹתָם אַתָּה וְאַהֲרֹן: וְאִתְּכֶם יִהְיוּ אִישׁ אִישׁ לַמַּטֶּה אִישׁ רֹאשׁ לְבֵית־אֲבֹתָיו הוּא: לוי: וְאֵלֶּה שְׁמוֹת הָאֲנָשִׁים אֲשֶׁר יַעַמְדוּ אִתְּכֶם לִרְאוּבֵן אֱלִיצוּר בֶּן־שְׁדֵיאוּר: לְשִׁמְעוֹן שְׁלֻמִיאֵל בֶּן־צוּרִישַׁדָּי: לִיהוּדָה נַחְשׁוֹן בֶּן־עַמִּינָדָב: לְיִשָּׂשכָר נְתַנְאֵל בֶּן־צוּעָר: לִזְבוּלֻן אֱלִיאָב בֶּן־חֵלֹן: לִבְנֵי יוֹסֵף לְאֶפְרַיִם אֱלִישָׁמָע בֶּן־עַמִּיהוּד לִמְנַשֶּׁה גַּמְלִיאֵל בֶּן־פְּדָהצוּר: לְבִנְיָמִן אֲבִידָן בֶּן־גִּדְעֹנִי: לְדָן אֲחִיעֶזֶר בֶּן־עַמִּישַׁדָּי: לְאָשֵׁר פַּגְעִיאֵל בֶּן־עָכְרָן: לְגָד אֶלְיָסָף בֶּן־דְּעוּאֵל: לְנַפְתָּלִי אֲחִירַע בֶּן־עֵינָן: אֵלֶּה קריאי [קְרוּאֵי] הָעֵדָה נְשִׂיאֵי מַטּוֹת אֲבוֹתָם רָאשֵׁי אַלְפֵי יִשְׂרָאֵל הֵם: ישראל: וַיִּקַּח מֹשֶׁה וְאַהֲרֹן אֵת הָאֲנָשִׁים הָאֵלֶּה אֲשֶׁר נִקְּבוּ בְּשֵׁמוֹת: וְאֵת כָּל־הָעֵדָה הִקְהִילוּ בְּאֶחָד לַחֹדֶשׁ הַשֵּׁנִי וַיִּתְיַלְדוּ עַל־מִשְׁפְּחֹתָם לְבֵית אֲבֹתָם בְּמִסְפַּר שֵׁמוֹת מִבֶּן עֶשְׂרִים שָׁנָה וָמַעְלָה לְגֻלְגְּלֹתָם: כַּאֲשֶׁר צִוָּה יהוה אֶת־מֹשֶׁה וַיִּפְקְדֵם בְּמִדְבַּר סִינָי:

נשא / NASO

במדבר ד:כא-לז

וַיְדַבֵּר יהוה אֶל־מֹשֶׁה לֵּאמֹר: נָשֹׂא אֶת־רֹאשׁ בְּנֵי גֵרְשׁוֹן גַּם־הֵם לְבֵית אֲבֹתָם לְמִשְׁפְּחֹתָם: מִבֶּן שְׁלֹשִׁים שָׁנָה וָמַעְלָה עַד בֶּן־חֲמִשִּׁים שָׁנָה תִּפְקֹד אוֹתָם כָּל־הַבָּא לִצְבֹא צָבָא לַעֲבֹד עֲבֹדָה בְּאֹהֶל מוֹעֵד: זֹאת עֲבֹדַת מִשְׁפְּחֹת הַגֵּרְשֻׁנִּי לַעֲבֹד וּלְמַשָּׂא: לוי: וְנָשְׂאוּ אֶת־יְרִיעֹת הַמִּשְׁכָּן וְאֶת־אֹהֶל מוֹעֵד מִכְסֵהוּ וּמִכְסֵה הַתַּחַשׁ אֲשֶׁר־עָלָיו מִלְמָעְלָה וְאֶת־מָסַךְ פֶּתַח אֹהֶל מוֹעֵד: וְאֵת קַלְעֵי הֶחָצֵר וְאֶת־מָסַךְ ׀ פֶּתַח ׀ שַׁעַר הֶחָצֵר אֲשֶׁר עַל־הַמִּשְׁכָּן וְעַל־הַמִּזְבֵּחַ סָבִיב וְאֵת מֵיתְרֵיהֶם וְאֶת־כָּל־כְּלֵי עֲבֹדָתָם וְאֵת כָּל־אֲשֶׁר יֵעָשֶׂה לָהֶם וְעָבָדוּ: עַל־פִּי אַהֲרֹן וּבָנָיו תִּהְיֶה כָּל־עֲבֹדַת בְּנֵי הַגֵּרְשֻׁנִּי לְכָל־מַשָּׂאָם וּלְכֹל עֲבֹדָתָם וּפְקַדְתֶּם עֲלֵהֶם בְּמִשְׁמֶרֶת אֵת כָּל־מַשָּׂאָם: זֹאת עֲבֹדַת מִשְׁפְּחֹת בְּנֵי הַגֵּרְשֻׁנִּי בְּאֹהֶל מוֹעֵד וּמִשְׁמַרְתָּם בְּיַד אִיתָמָר בֶּן־אַהֲרֹן הַכֹּהֵן: ישראל: בְּנֵי מְרָרִי לְמִשְׁפְּחֹתָם לְבֵית־אֲבֹתָם תִּפְקֹד אֹתָם: מִבֶּן שְׁלֹשִׁים שָׁנָה וָמַעְלָה וְעַד בֶּן־חֲמִשִּׁים שָׁנָה תִּפְקְדֵם כָּל־הַבָּא לַצָּבָא לַעֲבֹד אֶת־עֲבֹדַת אֹהֶל מוֹעֵד: וְזֹאת מִשְׁמֶרֶת מַשָּׂאָם לְכָל־עֲבֹדָתָם בְּאֹהֶל מוֹעֵד קַרְשֵׁי הַמִּשְׁכָּן וּבְרִיחָיו וְעַמּוּדָיו וַאֲדָנָיו: וְעַמּוּדֵי הֶחָצֵר סָבִיב וְאַדְנֵיהֶם וִיתֵדֹתָם וּמֵיתְרֵיהֶם לְכָל־כְּלֵיהֶם וּלְכֹל עֲבֹדָתָם וּבְשֵׁמֹת תִּפְקְדוּ אֶת־כְּלֵי מִשְׁמֶרֶת מַשָּׂאָם: זֹאת עֲבֹדַת מִשְׁפְּחֹת בְּנֵי מְרָרִי לְכָל־עֲבֹדָתָם בְּאֹהֶל מוֹעֵד בְּיַד אִיתָמָר בֶּן־אַהֲרֹן הַכֹּהֵן:

Some extend the ישראל *portion:*

וַיִּפְקֹד מֹשֶׁה וְאַהֲרֹן וּנְשִׂיאֵי הָעֵדָה אֶת־

בְּנֵי הַקְּהָתִי לְמִשְׁפְּחֹתָם וּלְבֵית אֲבֹתָם: מִבֶּן
שְׁלֹשִׁים שָׁנָה וָמַעְלָה וְעַד בֶּן־חֲמִשִּׁים שָׁנָה
כָּל־הַבָּא לַצָּבָא לַעֲבֹדָה בְּאֹהֶל מוֹעֵד: וַיִּהְיוּ
פְקֻדֵיהֶם לְמִשְׁפְּחֹתָם אַלְפַּיִם שְׁבַע מֵאוֹת
וַחֲמִשִּׁים: אֵלֶּה פְקוּדֵי מִשְׁפְּחֹת הַקְּהָתִי
כָּל־הָעֹבֵד בְּאֹהֶל מוֹעֵד אֲשֶׁר פָּקַד מֹשֶׁה
וְאַהֲרֹן עַל־פִּי יהוה בְּיַד־מֹשֶׁה:

BEHA'ALOTEKHA / בהעלותך

במדבר ח:א-יד

וַיְדַבֵּר יהוה אֶל־מֹשֶׁה לֵּאמֹר: דַּבֵּר אֶל־אַהֲרֹן
וְאָמַרְתָּ אֵלָיו בְּהַעֲלֹתְךָ אֶת־הַנֵּרֹת אֶל־מוּל
פְּנֵי הַמְּנוֹרָה יָאִירוּ שִׁבְעַת הַנֵּרוֹת: וַיַּעַשׂ כֵּן
אַהֲרֹן אֶל־מוּל פְּנֵי הַמְּנוֹרָה הֶעֱלָה נֵרֹתֶיהָ
כַּאֲשֶׁר צִוָּה יהוה אֶת־מֹשֶׁה: וְזֶה מַעֲשֵׂה
הַמְּנֹרָה מִקְשָׁה זָהָב עַד־יְרֵכָהּ עַד־פִּרְחָהּ
מִקְשָׁה הִוא כַּמַּרְאֶה אֲשֶׁר הֶרְאָה יהוה
אֶת־מֹשֶׁה כֵּן עָשָׂה אֶת־הַמְּנֹרָה:
לוי: וַיְדַבֵּר יהוה אֶל־מֹשֶׁה לֵּאמֹר: קַח אֶת־
הַלְוִיִּם מִתּוֹךְ בְּנֵי יִשְׂרָאֵל וְטִהַרְתָּ אֹתָם:
וְכֹה־תַעֲשֶׂה לָהֶם לְטַהֲרָם הַזֵּה עֲלֵיהֶם מֵי
חַטָּאת וְהֶעֱבִירוּ תַעַר עַל־כָּל־בְּשָׂרָם
וְכִבְּסוּ בִגְדֵיהֶם וְהִטֶּהָרוּ: וְלָקְחוּ פַּר בֶּן־בָּקָר
וּמִנְחָתוֹ סֹלֶת בְּלוּלָה בַשָּׁמֶן וּפַר־שֵׁנִי בֶן־
בָּקָר תִּקַּח לְחַטָּאת: וְהִקְרַבְתָּ אֶת־הַלְוִיִּם
לִפְנֵי אֹהֶל מוֹעֵד וְהִקְהַלְתָּ אֶת־כָּל־עֲדַת
בְּנֵי יִשְׂרָאֵל: ישראל: וְהִקְרַבְתָּ אֶת־הַלְוִיִּם
לִפְנֵי יהוה וְסָמְכוּ בְנֵי־יִשְׂרָאֵל אֶת־יְדֵיהֶם
עַל־הַלְוִיִּם: וְהֵנִיף אַהֲרֹן אֶת־הַלְוִיִּם תְּנוּפָה
לִפְנֵי יהוה מֵאֵת בְּנֵי יִשְׂרָאֵל וְהָיוּ לַעֲבֹד
אֶת־עֲבֹדַת יהוה: וְהַלְוִיִּם יִסְמְכוּ אֶת־
יְדֵיהֶם עַל רֹאשׁ הַפָּרִים וַעֲשֵׂה אֶת־הָאֶחָד
חַטָּאת וְאֶת־הָאֶחָד עֹלָה לַיהוה לְכַפֵּר עַל־
הַלְוִיִּם: וְהַעֲמַדְתָּ אֶת־הַלְוִיִּם לִפְנֵי אַהֲרֹן
וְלִפְנֵי בָנָיו וְהֵנַפְתָּ אֹתָם תְּנוּפָה לַיהוה:
וְהִבְדַּלְתָּ אֶת־הַלְוִיִּם מִתּוֹךְ בְּנֵי יִשְׂרָאֵל וְהָיוּ
לִי הַלְוִיִּם:

SHELAḤ / שלח

במדבר יג:א-כ

וַיְדַבֵּר יהוה אֶל־מֹשֶׁה לֵּאמֹר: שְׁלַח־לְךָ
אֲנָשִׁים וְיָתֻרוּ אֶת־אֶרֶץ כְּנַעַן אֲשֶׁר־אֲנִי נֹתֵן
לִבְנֵי יִשְׂרָאֵל אִישׁ אֶחָד אִישׁ אֶחָד לְמַטֵּה
אֲבֹתָיו תִּשְׁלָחוּ כֹּל נָשִׂיא בָהֶם: וַיִּשְׁלַח אֹתָם
מֹשֶׁה מִמִּדְבַּר פָּארָן עַל־פִּי יהוה כֻּלָּם
אֲנָשִׁים רָאשֵׁי בְנֵי־יִשְׂרָאֵל הֵמָּה: לוי: וְאֵלֶּה
שְׁמוֹתָם לְמַטֵּה רְאוּבֵן שַׁמּוּעַ בֶּן־זַכּוּר:
לְמַטֵּה שִׁמְעוֹן שָׁפָט בֶּן־חוֹרִי: לְמַטֵּה יְהוּדָה
כָּלֵב בֶּן־יְפֻנֶּה: לְמַטֵּה יִשָּׂשכָר יִגְאָל בֶּן־
יוֹסֵף: לְמַטֵּה אֶפְרָיִם הוֹשֵׁעַ בִּן־נוּן: לְמַטֵּה
בִנְיָמִן פַּלְטִי בֶּן־רָפוּא: לְמַטֵּה זְבוּלֻן גַּדִּיאֵל
בֶּן־סוֹדִי: לְמַטֵּה יוֹסֵף לְמַטֵּה מְנַשֶּׁה גַּדִּי
בֶּן־סוּסִי: לְמַטֵּה דָן עַמִּיאֵל בֶּן־גְּמַלִּי: לְמַטֵּה
אָשֵׁר סְתוּר בֶּן־מִיכָאֵל: לְמַטֵּה נַפְתָּלִי נַחְבִּי
בֶּן־וָפְסִי: לְמַטֵּה גָד גְּאוּאֵל בֶּן־מָכִי: אֵלֶּה
שְׁמוֹת הָאֲנָשִׁים אֲשֶׁר־שָׁלַח מֹשֶׁה לָתוּר
אֶת־הָאָרֶץ וַיִּקְרָא מֹשֶׁה לְהוֹשֵׁעַ בִּן־נוּן
יְהוֹשֻׁעַ: ישראל: וַיִּשְׁלַח אֹתָם מֹשֶׁה לָתוּר
אֶת־אֶרֶץ כְּנָעַן וַיֹּאמֶר אֲלֵהֶם עֲלוּ זֶה בַּנֶּגֶב
וַעֲלִיתֶם אֶת־הָהָר: וּרְאִיתֶם אֶת־הָאָרֶץ
מַה־הִוא וְאֶת־הָעָם הַיֹּשֵׁב עָלֶיהָ הֶחָזָק
הוּא הֲרָפֶה הַמְעַט הוּא אִם־רָב: וּמָה הָאָרֶץ
אֲשֶׁר־הוּא יֹשֵׁב בָּהּ הֲטוֹבָה הִוא אִם־
רָעָה וּמָה הֶעָרִים אֲשֶׁר־הוּא יוֹשֵׁב בָּהֵנָּה
הַבְּמַחֲנִים אִם בְּמִבְצָרִים: וּמָה הָאָרֶץ
הַשְּׁמֵנָה הִוא אִם־רָזָה הֲיֵשׁ־בָּהּ עֵץ אִם־
אַיִן וְהִתְחַזַּקְתֶּם וּלְקַחְתֶּם מִפְּרִי הָאָרֶץ
וְהַיָּמִים יְמֵי בִּכּוּרֵי עֲנָבִים:

KORAḤ / קרח

במדבר טז:א-יג

וַיִּקַּח קֹרַח בֶּן־יִצְהָר בֶּן־קְהָת בֶּן־לֵוִי וְדָתָן
וַאֲבִירָם בְּנֵי אֱלִיאָב וְאוֹן בֶּן־פֶּלֶת בְּנֵי
רְאוּבֵן: וַיָּקֻמוּ לִפְנֵי מֹשֶׁה וַאֲנָשִׁים מִבְּנֵי־
יִשְׂרָאֵל חֲמִשִּׁים וּמָאתָיִם נְשִׂיאֵי עֵדָה קְרִאֵי

מוֹעֵד אַנְשֵׁי־שֵׁם: וַיִּקָּהֲלוּ עַל־מֹשֶׁה וְעַל־אַהֲרֹן וַיֹּאמְרוּ אֲלֵהֶם רַב־לָכֶם כִּי כָל־הָעֵדָה כֻּלָּם קְדֹשִׁים וּבְתוֹכָם יהוה וּמַדּוּעַ תִּתְנַשְּׂאוּ עַל־קְהַל יהוה: לוי: וַיִּשְׁמַע מֹשֶׁה וַיִּפֹּל עַל־פָּנָיו: וַיְדַבֵּר אֶל־קֹרַח וְאֶל־כָּל־עֲדָתוֹ לֵאמֹר בֹּקֶר וְיֹדַע יהוה אֶת־אֲשֶׁר־לוֹ וְאֶת־הַקָּדוֹשׁ וְהִקְרִיב אֵלָיו וְאֵת אֲשֶׁר יִבְחַר־בּוֹ יַקְרִיב אֵלָיו: זֹאת עֲשׂוּ קְחוּ־לָכֶם מַחְתּוֹת קֹרַח וְכָל־עֲדָתוֹ: וּתְנוּ־בָהֵן ׀ אֵשׁ וְשִׂימוּ עֲלֵיהֶן ׀ קְטֹרֶת לִפְנֵי יהוה מָחָר וְהָיָה הָאִישׁ אֲשֶׁר־יִבְחַר יהוה הוּא הַקָּדוֹשׁ רַב־לָכֶם בְּנֵי לֵוִי: ישראל: וַיֹּאמֶר מֹשֶׁה אֶל־קֹרַח שִׁמְעוּ־נָא בְּנֵי לֵוִי: הַמְעַט מִכֶּם כִּי־הִבְדִּיל אֱלֹהֵי יִשְׂרָאֵל אֶתְכֶם מֵעֲדַת יִשְׂרָאֵל לְהַקְרִיב אֶתְכֶם אֵלָיו לַעֲבֹד אֶת־עֲבֹדַת מִשְׁכַּן יהוה וְלַעֲמֹד לִפְנֵי הָעֵדָה לְשָׁרְתָם: וַיַּקְרֵב אֹתְךָ וְאֶת־כָּל־אַחֶיךָ בְנֵי־לֵוִי אִתָּךְ וּבִקַּשְׁתֶּם גַּם־כְּהֻנָּה: לָכֵן אַתָּה וְכָל־עֲדָתְךָ הַנֹּעָדִים עַל־יהוה וְאַהֲרֹן מַה־הוּא כִּי תלונו [תַלִּינוּ] עָלָיו: וַיִּשְׁלַח מֹשֶׁה לִקְרֹא לְדָתָן וְלַאֲבִירָם בְּנֵי אֱלִיאָב וַיֹּאמְרוּ לֹא נַעֲלֶה: הַמְעַט כִּי הֶעֱלִיתָנוּ מֵאֶרֶץ זָבַת חָלָב וּדְבַשׁ לַהֲמִיתֵנוּ בַּמִּדְבָּר כִּי־תִשְׂתָּרֵר עָלֵינוּ גַּם־הִשְׂתָּרֵר:

ḤUKAT / חוקת

במדבר יט:א-יז

וַיְדַבֵּר יהוה אֶל־מֹשֶׁה וְאֶל־אַהֲרֹן לֵאמֹר: זֹאת חֻקַּת הַתּוֹרָה אֲשֶׁר־צִוָּה יהוה לֵאמֹר דַּבֵּר ׀ אֶל־בְּנֵי יִשְׂרָאֵל וְיִקְחוּ אֵלֶיךָ פָרָה אֲדֻמָּה תְּמִימָה אֲשֶׁר אֵין־בָּהּ מוּם אֲשֶׁר לֹא־עָלָה עָלֶיהָ עֹל: וּנְתַתֶּם אֹתָהּ אֶל־אֶלְעָזָר הַכֹּהֵן וְהוֹצִיא אֹתָהּ אֶל־מִחוּץ לַמַּחֲנֶה וְשָׁחַט אֹתָהּ לְפָנָיו: וְלָקַח אֶלְעָזָר הַכֹּהֵן מִדָּמָהּ בְּאֶצְבָּעוֹ וְהִזָּה אֶל־נֹכַח פְּנֵי אֹהֶל־מוֹעֵד מִדָּמָהּ שֶׁבַע פְּעָמִים: וְשָׂרַף אֶת־הַפָּרָה לְעֵינָיו אֶת־עֹרָהּ וְאֶת־בְּשָׂרָהּ וְאֶת־דָּמָהּ עַל־פִּרְשָׁהּ יִשְׂרֹף: וְלָקַח הַכֹּהֵן עֵץ אֶרֶז וְאֵזוֹב וּשְׁנִי תוֹלָעַת וְהִשְׁלִיךְ אֶל־תּוֹךְ שְׂרֵפַת הַפָּרָה: לוי: וְכִבֶּס בְּגָדָיו הַכֹּהֵן וְרָחַץ בְּשָׂרוֹ בַּמַּיִם וְאַחַר יָבֹא אֶל־הַמַּחֲנֶה וְטָמֵא הַכֹּהֵן עַד־הָעָרֶב: וְהַשֹּׂרֵף אֹתָהּ יְכַבֵּס בְּגָדָיו בַּמַּיִם וְרָחַץ בְּשָׂרוֹ בַּמָּיִם וְטָמֵא עַד־הָעָרֶב: וְאָסַף ׀ אִישׁ טָהוֹר אֵת אֵפֶר הַפָּרָה וְהִנִּיחַ מִחוּץ לַמַּחֲנֶה בְּמָקוֹם טָהוֹר וְהָיְתָה לַעֲדַת בְּנֵי־יִשְׂרָאֵל לְמִשְׁמֶרֶת לְמֵי נִדָּה חַטָּאת הִוא: ישראל: וְכִבֶּס הָאֹסֵף אֶת־אֵפֶר הַפָּרָה אֶת־בְּגָדָיו וְטָמֵא עַד־הָעָרֶב וְהָיְתָה לִבְנֵי יִשְׂרָאֵל וְלַגֵּר הַגָּר בְּתוֹכָם לְחֻקַּת עוֹלָם: הַנֹּגֵעַ בְּמֵת לְכָל־נֶפֶשׁ אָדָם וְטָמֵא שִׁבְעַת יָמִים: הוּא יִתְחַטָּא־בוֹ בַּיּוֹם הַשְּׁלִישִׁי וּבַיּוֹם הַשְּׁבִיעִי יִטְהָר וְאִם־לֹא יִתְחַטָּא בַּיּוֹם הַשְּׁלִישִׁי וּבַיּוֹם הַשְּׁבִיעִי לֹא יִטְהָר: כָּל־הַנֹּגֵעַ בְּמֵת בְּנֶפֶשׁ הָאָדָם אֲשֶׁר־יָמוּת וְלֹא יִתְחַטָּא אֶת־מִשְׁכַּן יהוה טִמֵּא וְנִכְרְתָה הַנֶּפֶשׁ הַהִוא מִיִּשְׂרָאֵל כִּי מֵי נִדָּה לֹא־זֹרַק עָלָיו טָמֵא יִהְיֶה עוֹד טֻמְאָתוֹ בוֹ: זֹאת הַתּוֹרָה אָדָם כִּי־יָמוּת בְּאֹהֶל כָּל־הַבָּא אֶל־הָאֹהֶל וְכָל־אֲשֶׁר בָּאֹהֶל יִטְמָא שִׁבְעַת יָמִים: וְכֹל כְּלִי פָתוּחַ אֲשֶׁר אֵין־צָמִיד פָּתִיל עָלָיו טָמֵא הוּא: וְכֹל אֲשֶׁר־יִגַּע עַל־פְּנֵי הַשָּׂדֶה בַּחֲלַל־חֶרֶב אוֹ בְמֵת אוֹ־בְעֶצֶם אָדָם אוֹ בְקָבֶר יִטְמָא שִׁבְעַת יָמִים: וְלָקְחוּ לַטָּמֵא מֵעֲפַר שְׂרֵפַת הַחַטָּאת וְנָתַן עָלָיו מַיִם חַיִּים אֶל־כֶּלִי:

BALAK / בלק

במדבר כב:ב-יב

וַיַּרְא בָּלָק בֶּן־צִפּוֹר אֵת כָּל־אֲשֶׁר־עָשָׂה יִשְׂרָאֵל לָאֱמֹרִי: וַיָּגָר מוֹאָב מִפְּנֵי הָעָם מְאֹד כִּי רַב־הוּא וַיָּקָץ מוֹאָב מִפְּנֵי בְּנֵי יִשְׂרָאֵל: וַיֹּאמֶר מוֹאָב אֶל־זִקְנֵי מִדְיָן עַתָּה יְלַחֲכוּ הַקָּהָל אֶת־כָּל־סְבִיבֹתֵינוּ כִּלְחֹךְ הַשּׁוֹר אֵת יֶרֶק הַשָּׂדֶה וּבָלָק בֶּן־צִפּוֹר מֶלֶךְ לְמוֹאָב בָּעֵת הַהִוא: לוי: וַיִּשְׁלַח מַלְאָכִים אֶל־בִּלְעָם בֶּן־בְּעוֹר פְּתוֹרָה אֲשֶׁר עַל־הַנָּהָר אֶרֶץ בְּנֵי־עַמּוֹ לִקְרֹא־לוֹ לֵאמֹר הִנֵּה עַם יָצָא מִמִּצְרַיִם הִנֵּה כִסָּה אֶת־עֵין הָאָרֶץ

וְהוּא יֹשֵׁב מִמֻּלִי׃ וְעַתָּה לְכָה־נָּא אָרָה־לִּי
אֶת־הָעָם הַזֶּה כִּי־עָצוּם הוּא מִמֶּנִּי אוּלַי
אוּכַל נַכֶּה־בּוֹ וַאֲגָרְשֶׁנּוּ מִן־הָאָרֶץ כִּי יָדַעְתִּי
אֵת אֲשֶׁר־תְּבָרֵךְ מְבֹרָךְ וַאֲשֶׁר תָּאֹר יוּאָר׃
וַיֵּלְכוּ זִקְנֵי מוֹאָב וְזִקְנֵי מִדְיָן וּקְסָמִים בְּיָדָם
וַיָּבֹאוּ אֶל־בִּלְעָם וַיְדַבְּרוּ אֵלָיו דִּבְרֵי בָלָק׃
ישראל: וַיֹּאמֶר אֲלֵיהֶם לִינוּ פֹה הַלַּיְלָה
וַהֲשִׁבֹתִי אֶתְכֶם דָּבָר כַּאֲשֶׁר יְדַבֵּר יהוה אֵלָי
וַיֵּשְׁבוּ שָׂרֵי־מוֹאָב עִם־בִּלְעָם׃ וַיָּבֹא אֱלֹהִים
אֶל־בִּלְעָם וַיֹּאמֶר מִי הָאֲנָשִׁים הָאֵלֶּה עִמָּךְ׃
וַיֹּאמֶר בִּלְעָם אֶל־הָאֱלֹהִים בָּלָק בֶּן־צִפֹּר
מֶלֶךְ מוֹאָב שָׁלַח אֵלָי׃ הִנֵּה הָעָם הַיֹּצֵא
מִמִּצְרַיִם וַיְכַס אֶת־עֵין הָאָרֶץ עַתָּה לְכָה
קָבָה־לִּי אֹתוֹ אוּלַי אוּכַל לְהִלָּחֶם בּוֹ
וְגֵרַשְׁתִּיו׃ וַיֹּאמֶר אֱלֹהִים אֶל־בִּלְעָם לֹא תֵלֵךְ
עִמָּהֶם לֹא תָאֹר אֶת־הָעָם כִּי בָרוּךְ הוּא׃

PINEHAS / פינחס

במדבר כה:י–כו:ד

וַיְדַבֵּר יהוה אֶל־מֹשֶׁה לֵּאמֹר׃ פִּינְחָס בֶּן־
אֶלְעָזָר בֶּן־אַהֲרֹן הַכֹּהֵן הֵשִׁיב אֶת־חֲמָתִי
מֵעַל בְּנֵי־יִשְׂרָאֵל בְּקַנְאוֹ אֶת־קִנְאָתִי בְּתוֹכָם
וְלֹא־כִלִּיתִי אֶת־בְּנֵי־יִשְׂרָאֵל בְּקִנְאָתִי׃
לָכֵן אֱמֹר הִנְנִי נֹתֵן לוֹ אֶת־בְּרִיתִי שָׁלוֹם׃
לוי: וְהָיְתָה לּוֹ וּלְזַרְעוֹ אַחֲרָיו בְּרִית כְּהֻנַּת
עוֹלָם תַּחַת אֲשֶׁר קִנֵּא לֵאלֹהָיו וַיְכַפֵּר עַל־
בְּנֵי יִשְׂרָאֵל׃ וְשֵׁם אִישׁ יִשְׂרָאֵל הַמֻּכֶּה אֲשֶׁר
הֻכָּה אֶת־הַמִּדְיָנִית זִמְרִי בֶּן־סָלוּא נְשִׂיא
בֵית־אָב לַשִּׁמְעֹנִי׃ וְשֵׁם הָאִשָּׁה הַמֻּכָּה
הַמִּדְיָנִית כָּזְבִּי בַת־צוּר רֹאשׁ אֻמּוֹת בֵּית־
אָב בְּמִדְיָן הוּא׃
ישראל: וַיְדַבֵּר יהוה אֶל־מֹשֶׁה לֵּאמֹר׃ צָרוֹר
אֶת־הַמִּדְיָנִים וְהִכִּיתֶם אוֹתָם׃ כִּי־צֹרְרִים
הֵם לָכֶם בְּנִכְלֵיהֶם אֲשֶׁר־נִכְּלוּ לָכֶם עַל־
דְּבַר פְּעוֹר וְעַל־דְּבַר כָּזְבִּי בַת־נְשִׂיא מִדְיָן
אֲחֹתָם הַמֻּכָּה בְיוֹם־הַמַּגֵּפָה עַל־דְּבַר
פְּעוֹר׃ וַיְהִי אַחֲרֵי הַמַּגֵּפָה
וַיֹּאמֶר יהוה אֶל־מֹשֶׁה וְאֶל אֶלְעָזָר בֶּן־
אַהֲרֹן הַכֹּהֵן לֵאמֹר׃ שְׂאוּ אֶת־רֹאשׁ ׀ כָּל־
עֲדַת בְּנֵי־יִשְׂרָאֵל מִבֶּן עֶשְׂרִים שָׁנָה וָמַעְלָה
לְבֵית אֲבֹתָם כָּל־יֹצֵא צָבָא בְּיִשְׂרָאֵל׃ וַיְדַבֵּר
מֹשֶׁה וְאֶלְעָזָר הַכֹּהֵן אֹתָם בְּעַרְבֹת מוֹאָב
עַל־יַרְדֵּן יְרֵחוֹ לֵאמֹר׃ מִבֶּן עֶשְׂרִים שָׁנָה
וָמָעְלָה כַּאֲשֶׁר צִוָּה יהוה אֶת־מֹשֶׁה וּבְנֵי
יִשְׂרָאֵל הַיֹּצְאִים מֵאֶרֶץ מִצְרָיִם׃

MATOT / מטות

במדבר ל:ב–יז

וַיְדַבֵּר מֹשֶׁה אֶל־רָאשֵׁי הַמַּטּוֹת לִבְנֵי יִשְׂרָאֵל
לֵאמֹר זֶה הַדָּבָר אֲשֶׁר צִוָּה יהוה׃ אִישׁ כִּי־
יִדֹּר נֶדֶר לַיהוה אוֹ־הִשָּׁבַע שְׁבֻעָה לֶאְסֹר
אִסָּר עַל־נַפְשׁוֹ לֹא יַחֵל דְּבָרוֹ כְּכָל־הַיֹּצֵא
מִפִּיו יַעֲשֶׂה׃ וְאִשָּׁה כִּי־תִדֹּר נֶדֶר לַיהוה
וְאָסְרָה אִסָּר בְּבֵית אָבִיהָ בִּנְעֻרֶיהָ׃ וְשָׁמַע
אָבִיהָ אֶת־נִדְרָהּ וֶאֱסָרָהּ אֲשֶׁר אָסְרָה עַל־
נַפְשָׁהּ וְהֶחֱרִישׁ לָהּ אָבִיהָ וְקָמוּ כָּל־נְדָרֶיהָ
וְכָל־אִסָּר אֲשֶׁר־אָסְרָה עַל־נַפְשָׁהּ יָקוּם׃
וְאִם־הֵנִיא אָבִיהָ אֹתָהּ בְּיוֹם שָׁמְעוֹ כָּל־
נְדָרֶיהָ וֶאֱסָרֶיהָ אֲשֶׁר־אָסְרָה עַל־נַפְשָׁהּ לֹא
יָקוּם וַיהוה יִסְלַח־לָהּ כִּי־הֵנִיא אָבִיהָ אֹתָהּ׃
וְאִם־הָיוֹ תִהְיֶה לְאִישׁ וּנְדָרֶיהָ עָלֶיהָ אוֹ
מִבְטָא שְׂפָתֶיהָ אֲשֶׁר אָסְרָה עַל־נַפְשָׁהּ׃
וְשָׁמַע אִישָׁהּ בְּיוֹם שָׁמְעוֹ וְהֶחֱרִישׁ לָהּ וְקָמוּ
נְדָרֶיהָ וֶאֱסָרֶהָ אֲשֶׁר־אָסְרָה עַל־נַפְשָׁהּ
יָקֻמוּ׃ וְאִם בְּיוֹם שְׁמֹעַ אִישָׁהּ יָנִיא אוֹתָהּ
וְהֵפֵר אֶת־נִדְרָהּ אֲשֶׁר עָלֶיהָ וְאֵת מִבְטָא
שְׂפָתֶיהָ אֲשֶׁר אָסְרָה עַל־נַפְשָׁהּ וַיהוה
יִסְלַח־לָהּ׃ לוי: וְנֵדֶר אַלְמָנָה וּגְרוּשָׁה כֹּל
אֲשֶׁר־אָסְרָה עַל־נַפְשָׁהּ יָקוּם עָלֶיהָ׃ וְאִם־
בֵּית אִישָׁהּ נָדָרָה אוֹ־אָסְרָה אִסָּר עַל־נַפְשָׁהּ
בִּשְׁבֻעָה׃ וְשָׁמַע אִישָׁהּ וְהֶחֱרִשׁ לָהּ לֹא הֵנִיא
אֹתָהּ וְקָמוּ כָּל־נְדָרֶיהָ וְכָל־אִסָּר אֲשֶׁר־
אָסְרָה עַל־נַפְשָׁהּ יָקוּם׃ וְאִם־הָפֵר יָפֵר
אֹתָם ׀ אִישָׁהּ בְּיוֹם שָׁמְעוֹ כָּל־מוֹצָא שְׂפָתֶיהָ
לִנְדָרֶיהָ וּלְאִסַּר נַפְשָׁהּ לֹא יָקוּם אִישָׁהּ הֲפֵרָם
וַיהוה יִסְלַח־לָהּ׃ ישראל: כָּל־נֵדֶר וְכָל־שְׁבֻעַת

אִסָּר לְעַנֹּת נָפֶשׁ אִישָׁהּ יְקִימֶנּוּ וְאִישָׁהּ יְפֵרֶנּוּ: וְאִם־הַחֲרֵשׁ יַחֲרִישׁ לָהּ אִישָׁהּ מִיּוֹם אֶל־יוֹם וְהֵקִים אֶת־כָּל־נְדָרֶיהָ אוֹ אֶת־כָּל־אֱסָרֶיהָ אֲשֶׁר עָלֶיהָ הֵקִים אֹתָם כִּי־הֶחֱרִשׁ לָהּ בְּיוֹם שָׁמְעוֹ: וְאִם־הָפֵר יָפֵר אֹתָם אַחֲרֵי שָׁמְעוֹ וְנָשָׂא אֶת־עֲוֺנָהּ: אֵלֶּה הַחֻקִּים אֲשֶׁר צִוָּה יהוה אֶת־מֹשֶׁה בֵּין אִישׁ לְאִשְׁתּוֹ בֵּין־אָב לְבִתּוֹ בִּנְעֻרֶיהָ בֵּית אָבִיהָ:

MASEI / מסעי

במדבר לג:א–נג

אֵלֶּה מַסְעֵי בְנֵי־יִשְׂרָאֵל אֲשֶׁר יָצְאוּ מֵאֶרֶץ מִצְרַיִם לְצִבְאֹתָם בְּיַד־מֹשֶׁה וְאַהֲרֹן: וַיִּכְתֹּב מֹשֶׁה אֶת־מוֹצָאֵיהֶם לְמַסְעֵיהֶם עַל־פִּי יהוה וְאֵלֶּה מַסְעֵיהֶם לְמוֹצָאֵיהֶם: וַיִּסְעוּ מֵרַעְמְסֵס בַּחֹדֶשׁ הָרִאשׁוֹן בַּחֲמִשָּׁה עָשָׂר יוֹם לַחֹדֶשׁ הָרִאשׁוֹן מִמָּחֳרַת הַפֶּסַח יָצְאוּ בְנֵי־יִשְׂרָאֵל בְּיָד רָמָה לְעֵינֵי כָּל־מִצְרָיִם:

לוי: וּמִצְרַיִם מְקַבְּרִים אֵת אֲשֶׁר הִכָּה יהוה בָּהֶם כָּל־בְּכוֹר וּבֵאלֹהֵיהֶם עָשָׂה יהוה שְׁפָטִים: וַיִּסְעוּ בְנֵי־יִשְׂרָאֵל מֵרַעְמְסֵס וַיַּחֲנוּ בְּסֻכֹּת: וַיִּסְעוּ מִסֻּכֹּת וַיַּחֲנוּ בְאֵתָם אֲשֶׁר בִּקְצֵה הַמִּדְבָּר:

ישראל: וַיִּסְעוּ מֵאֵתָם וַיָּשָׁב עַל־פִּי הַחִירֹת אֲשֶׁר עַל־פְּנֵי בַּעַל צְפוֹן וַיַּחֲנוּ לִפְנֵי מִגְדֹּל: וַיִּסְעוּ מִפְּנֵי הַחִירֹת וַיַּעַבְרוּ בְתוֹךְ־הַיָּם הַמִּדְבָּרָה וַיֵּלְכוּ דֶּרֶךְ שְׁלֹשֶׁת יָמִים בְּמִדְבַּר אֵתָם וַיַּחֲנוּ בְּמָרָה: וַיִּסְעוּ מִמָּרָה וַיָּבֹאוּ אֵילִמָה וּבְאֵילִם שְׁתֵּים עֶשְׂרֵה עֵינֹת מַיִם וְשִׁבְעִים תְּמָרִים וַיַּחֲנוּ־שָׁם: וַיִּסְעוּ מֵאֵילִם וַיַּחֲנוּ עַל־יַם־סוּף:

Some extend the לוי portion:

וַיִּסְעוּ מִיַּם־סוּף וַיַּחֲנוּ בְּמִדְבַּר־סִין: וַיִּסְעוּ מִמִּדְבַּר־סִין וַיַּחֲנוּ בְּדָפְקָה: וַיִּסְעוּ מִדָּפְקָה וַיַּחֲנוּ בְּאָלוּשׁ: וַיִּסְעוּ מֵאָלוּשׁ וַיַּחֲנוּ בִּרְפִידִם וְלֹא־הָיָה שָׁם מַיִם לָעָם לִשְׁתּוֹת: וַיִּסְעוּ מֵרְפִידִם וַיַּחֲנוּ בְּמִדְבַּר סִינָי: וַיִּסְעוּ מִמִּדְבַּר סִינָי וַיַּחֲנוּ בְּקִבְרֹת הַתַּאֲוָה: וַיִּסְעוּ מִקִּבְרֹת הַתַּאֲוָה וַיַּחֲנוּ בַּחֲצֵרֹת: וַיִּסְעוּ מֵחֲצֵרֹת וַיַּחֲנוּ בְּרִתְמָה: וַיִּסְעוּ מֵרִתְמָה וַיַּחֲנוּ בְּרִמֹּן פָּרֶץ: וַיִּסְעוּ מֵרִמֹּן פָּרֶץ וַיַּחֲנוּ בְּלִבְנָה: וַיִּסְעוּ מִלִּבְנָה וַיַּחֲנוּ בְּרִסָּה: וַיִּסְעוּ מֵרִסָּה וַיַּחֲנוּ בִּקְהֵלָתָה: וַיִּסְעוּ מִקְּהֵלָתָה וַיַּחֲנוּ בְּהַר־שָׁפֶר: וַיִּסְעוּ מֵהַר־שָׁפֶר וַיַּחֲנוּ בַּחֲרָדָה: וַיִּסְעוּ מֵחֲרָדָה וַיַּחֲנוּ בְּמַקְהֵלֹת: וַיִּסְעוּ מִמַּקְהֵלֹת וַיַּחֲנוּ בְּתָחַת: וַיִּסְעוּ מִתָּחַת וַיַּחֲנוּ בְּתָרַח: וַיִּסְעוּ מִתָּרַח וַיַּחֲנוּ בְּמִתְקָה: וַיִּסְעוּ מִמִּתְקָה וַיַּחֲנוּ בְּחַשְׁמֹנָה: וַיִּסְעוּ מֵחַשְׁמֹנָה וַיַּחֲנוּ בְּמֹסֵרוֹת: וַיִּסְעוּ מִמֹּסֵרוֹת וַיַּחֲנוּ בִּבְנֵי יַעֲקָן: וַיִּסְעוּ מִבְּנֵי יַעֲקָן וַיַּחֲנוּ בְּחֹר הַגִּדְגָּד: וַיִּסְעוּ מֵחֹר הַגִּדְגָּד וַיַּחֲנוּ בְּיָטְבָתָה: וַיִּסְעוּ מִיָּטְבָתָה וַיַּחֲנוּ בְּעַבְרֹנָה: וַיִּסְעוּ מֵעַבְרֹנָה וַיַּחֲנוּ בְּעֶצְיֹן גָּבֶר: וַיִּסְעוּ מֵעֶצְיֹן גָּבֶר וַיַּחֲנוּ בְמִדְבַּר־צִן הִוא קָדֵשׁ: וַיִּסְעוּ מִקָּדֵשׁ וַיַּחֲנוּ בְּהֹר הָהָר בִּקְצֵה אֶרֶץ אֱדוֹם: וַיַּעַל אַהֲרֹן הַכֹּהֵן אֶל־הֹר הָהָר עַל־פִּי יהוה וַיָּמָת שָׁם בִּשְׁנַת הָאַרְבָּעִים לְצֵאת בְּנֵי־יִשְׂרָאֵל מֵאֶרֶץ מִצְרַיִם בַּחֹדֶשׁ הַחֲמִישִׁי בְּאֶחָד לַחֹדֶשׁ: וְאַהֲרֹן בֶּן־שָׁלֹשׁ וְעֶשְׂרִים וּמְאַת שָׁנָה בְּמֹתוֹ בְּהֹר הָהָר: וַיִּשְׁמַע הַכְּנַעֲנִי מֶלֶךְ עֲרָד וְהוּא־יֹשֵׁב בַּנֶּגֶב בְּאֶרֶץ כְּנָעַן בְּבֹא בְּנֵי יִשְׂרָאֵל: וַיִּסְעוּ מֵהֹר הָהָר וַיַּחֲנוּ בְּצַלְמֹנָה: וַיִּסְעוּ מִצַּלְמֹנָה וַיַּחֲנוּ בְּפוּנֹן: וַיִּסְעוּ מִפּוּנֹן וַיַּחֲנוּ בְּאֹבֹת: וַיִּסְעוּ מֵאֹבֹת וַיַּחֲנוּ בְּעִיֵּי הָעֲבָרִים בִּגְבוּל מוֹאָב: וַיִּסְעוּ מֵעִיִּים וַיַּחֲנוּ בְּדִיבֹן גָּד: וַיִּסְעוּ מִדִּיבֹן גָּד וַיַּחֲנוּ בְּעַלְמֹן דִּבְלָתָיְמָה: וַיִּסְעוּ מֵעַלְמֹן דִּבְלָתָיְמָה וַיַּחֲנוּ בְּהָרֵי הָעֲבָרִים לִפְנֵי נְבוֹ: וַיִּסְעוּ מֵהָרֵי הָעֲבָרִים וַיַּחֲנוּ בְּעַרְבֹת מוֹאָב עַל יַרְדֵּן יְרֵחוֹ: וַיַּחֲנוּ עַל־הַיַּרְדֵּן מִבֵּית הַיְשִׁמֹת עַד אָבֵל הַשִּׁטִּים בְּעַרְבֹת מוֹאָב:

ישראל: וַיְדַבֵּר יהוה אֶל־מֹשֶׁה בְּעַרְבֹת מוֹאָב עַל־יַרְדֵּן יְרֵחוֹ לֵאמֹר: דַּבֵּר אֶל־בְּנֵי יִשְׂרָאֵל וְאָמַרְתָּ אֲלֵהֶם כִּי אַתֶּם עֹבְרִים אֶת־הַיַּרְדֵּן אֶל־אֶרֶץ כְּנָעַן: וְהוֹרַשְׁתֶּם אֶת־כָּל־יֹשְׁבֵי

הָאָרֶץ מִפְּנֵיכֶם וְאִבַּדְתֶּם אֵת כָּל־מַשְׂכִּיֹּתָם וְאֵת כָּל־צַלְמֵי מַסֵּכֹתָם תְּאַבֵּדוּ וְאֵת כָּל־בָּמוֹתָם תַּשְׁמִידוּ: וְהוֹרַשְׁתֶּם אֶת־הָאָרֶץ וִישַׁבְתֶּם־בָּהּ כִּי לָכֶם נָתַתִּי אֶת־הָאָרֶץ לָרֶשֶׁת אֹתָהּ:

DEVARIM / דברים

דברים א:א–יא

אֵלֶּה הַדְּבָרִים אֲשֶׁר דִּבֶּר מֹשֶׁה אֶל־כָּל־יִשְׂרָאֵל בְּעֵבֶר הַיַּרְדֵּן בַּמִּדְבָּר בָּעֲרָבָה מוֹל סוּף בֵּין־פָּארָן וּבֵין־תֹּפֶל וְלָבָן וַחֲצֵרֹת וְדִי זָהָב: אַחַד עָשָׂר יוֹם מֵחֹרֵב דֶּרֶךְ הַר־שֵׂעִיר עַד קָדֵשׁ בַּרְנֵעַ: וַיְהִי בְּאַרְבָּעִים שָׁנָה בְּעַשְׁתֵּי־עָשָׂר חֹדֶשׁ בְּאֶחָד לַחֹדֶשׁ דִּבֶּר מֹשֶׁה אֶל־בְּנֵי יִשְׂרָאֵל כְּכֹל אֲשֶׁר צִוָּה יְהוָה אֹתוֹ אֲלֵהֶם: לוי: אַחֲרֵי הַכֹּתוֹ אֵת סִיחֹן מֶלֶךְ הָאֱמֹרִי אֲשֶׁר יוֹשֵׁב בְּחֶשְׁבּוֹן וְאֵת עוֹג מֶלֶךְ הַבָּשָׁן אֲשֶׁר־יוֹשֵׁב בְּעַשְׁתָּרֹת בְּאֶדְרֶעִי: בְּעֵבֶר הַיַּרְדֵּן בְּאֶרֶץ מוֹאָב הוֹאִיל מֹשֶׁה בֵּאֵר אֶת־הַתּוֹרָה הַזֹּאת לֵאמֹר: יְהוָה אֱלֹהֵינוּ דִּבֶּר אֵלֵינוּ בְּחֹרֵב לֵאמֹר רַב־לָכֶם שֶׁבֶת בָּהָר הַזֶּה: פְּנוּ | וּסְעוּ לָכֶם וּבֹאוּ הַר הָאֱמֹרִי וְאֶל־כָּל־שְׁכֵנָיו בָּעֲרָבָה בָהָר וּבַשְּׁפֵלָה וּבַנֶּגֶב וּבְחוֹף הַיָּם אֶרֶץ הַכְּנַעֲנִי וְהַלְּבָנוֹן עַד־הַנָּהָר הַגָּדֹל נְהַר־פְּרָת: ישראל: רְאֵה נָתַתִּי לִפְנֵיכֶם אֶת־הָאָרֶץ בֹּאוּ וּרְשׁוּ אֶת־הָאָרֶץ אֲשֶׁר נִשְׁבַּע יְהוָה לַאֲבֹתֵיכֶם לְאַבְרָהָם לְיִצְחָק וּלְיַעֲקֹב לָתֵת לָהֶם וּלְזַרְעָם אַחֲרֵיהֶם: וָאֹמַר אֲלֵכֶם בָּעֵת הַהִוא לֵאמֹר לֹא־אוּכַל לְבַדִּי שְׂאֵת אֶתְכֶם: יְהוָה אֱלֹהֵיכֶם הִרְבָּה אֶתְכֶם וְהִנְּכֶם הַיּוֹם כְּכוֹכְבֵי הַשָּׁמַיִם לָרֹב: יְהוָה אֱלֹהֵי אֲבוֹתֵכֶם יֹסֵף עֲלֵיכֶם כָּכֶם אֶלֶף פְּעָמִים וִיבָרֵךְ אֶתְכֶם כַּאֲשֶׁר דִּבֶּר לָכֶם:

VA'ET-ḤANAN / ואתחנן

דברים ג:כג–ד:ח

וָאֶתְחַנַּן אֶל־יְהוָה בָּעֵת הַהִוא לֵאמֹר: אֲדֹנָי יְהוִה אַתָּה הַחִלּוֹתָ לְהַרְאוֹת אֶת־עַבְדְּךָ אֶת־גָּדְלְךָ וְאֶת־יָדְךָ הַחֲזָקָה אֲשֶׁר מִי־אֵל בַּשָּׁמַיִם וּבָאָרֶץ אֲשֶׁר־יַעֲשֶׂה כְמַעֲשֶׂיךָ וְכִגְבוּרֹתֶךָ: אֶעְבְּרָה־נָּא וְאֶרְאֶה אֶת־הָאָרֶץ הַטּוֹבָה אֲשֶׁר בְּעֵבֶר הַיַּרְדֵּן הָהָר הַטּוֹב הַזֶּה וְהַלְּבָנֹן: לוי: וַיִּתְעַבֵּר יְהוָה בִּי לְמַעַנְכֶם וְלֹא שָׁמַע אֵלָי וַיֹּאמֶר יְהוָה אֵלַי רַב־לָךְ אַל־תּוֹסֶף דַּבֵּר אֵלַי עוֹד בַּדָּבָר הַזֶּה: עֲלֵה | רֹאשׁ הַפִּסְגָּה וְשָׂא עֵינֶיךָ יָמָּה וְצָפֹנָה וְתֵימָנָה וּמִזְרָחָה וּרְאֵה בְעֵינֶיךָ כִּי־לֹא תַעֲבֹר אֶת־הַיַּרְדֵּן הַזֶּה: וְצַו אֶת־יְהוֹשֻׁעַ וְחַזְּקֵהוּ וְאַמְּצֵהוּ כִּי־הוּא יַעֲבֹר לִפְנֵי הָעָם הַזֶּה וְהוּא יַנְחִיל אוֹתָם אֶת־הָאָרֶץ אֲשֶׁר תִּרְאֶה: וַנֵּשֶׁב בַּגָּיְא מוּל בֵּית פְּעוֹר:

וְעַתָּה יִשְׂרָאֵל שְׁמַע אֶל־הַחֻקִּים וְאֶל־הַמִּשְׁפָּטִים אֲשֶׁר אָנֹכִי מְלַמֵּד אֶתְכֶם לַעֲשׂוֹת לְמַעַן תִּחְיוּ וּבָאתֶם וִירִשְׁתֶּם אֶת־הָאָרֶץ אֲשֶׁר יְהוָה אֱלֹהֵי אֲבֹתֵיכֶם נֹתֵן לָכֶם: לֹא תֹסִפוּ עַל־הַדָּבָר אֲשֶׁר אָנֹכִי מְצַוֶּה אֶתְכֶם וְלֹא תִגְרְעוּ מִמֶּנּוּ לִשְׁמֹר אֶת־מִצְוֹת יְהוָה אֱלֹהֵיכֶם אֲשֶׁר אָנֹכִי מְצַוֶּה אֶתְכֶם: עֵינֵיכֶם הָרֹאוֹת אֵת אֲשֶׁר־עָשָׂה יְהוָה בְּבַעַל פְּעוֹר כִּי כָל־הָאִישׁ אֲשֶׁר הָלַךְ אַחֲרֵי בַעַל־פְּעוֹר הִשְׁמִידוֹ יְהוָה אֱלֹהֶיךָ מִקִּרְבֶּךָ: וְאַתֶּם הַדְּבֵקִים בַּיהוָה אֱלֹהֵיכֶם חַיִּים כֻּלְּכֶם הַיּוֹם: ישראל: רְאֵה | לִמַּדְתִּי אֶתְכֶם חֻקִּים וּמִשְׁפָּטִים כַּאֲשֶׁר צִוַּנִי יְהוָה אֱלֹהָי לַעֲשׂוֹת כֵּן בְּקֶרֶב הָאָרֶץ אֲשֶׁר אַתֶּם בָּאִים שָׁמָּה לְרִשְׁתָּהּ: וּשְׁמַרְתֶּם וַעֲשִׂיתֶם כִּי הִוא חָכְמַתְכֶם וּבִינַתְכֶם לְעֵינֵי הָעַמִּים אֲשֶׁר יִשְׁמְעוּן אֵת כָּל־הַחֻקִּים הָאֵלֶּה וְאָמְרוּ רַק עַם־חָכָם וְנָבוֹן הַגּוֹי הַגָּדוֹל הַזֶּה: כִּי מִי־גוֹי גָדוֹל אֲשֶׁר־לוֹ אֱלֹהִים קְרֹבִים אֵלָיו כַּיהוָה אֱלֹהֵינוּ בְּכָל־קָרְאֵנוּ אֵלָיו: וּמִי גּוֹי גָּדוֹל אֲשֶׁר־לוֹ חֻקִּים וּמִשְׁפָּטִים צַדִּיקִם כְּכֹל הַתּוֹרָה הַזֹּאת אֲשֶׁר אָנֹכִי נֹתֵן לִפְנֵיכֶם הַיּוֹם:

עקב / EKEV

דברים ז:יב-ח:י

וְהָיָה | עֵקֶב תִּשְׁמְעוּן אֵת הַמִּשְׁפָּטִים הָאֵלֶּה וּשְׁמַרְתֶּם וַעֲשִׂיתֶם אֹתָם וְשָׁמַר יהוה אֱלֹהֶיךָ לְךָ אֶת־הַבְּרִית וְאֶת־הַחֶסֶד אֲשֶׁר נִשְׁבַּע לַאֲבֹתֶיךָ: וַאֲהֵבְךָ וּבֵרַכְךָ וְהִרְבֶּךָ וּבֵרַךְ פְּרִי־בִטְנְךָ וּפְרִי־אַדְמָתֶךָ דְּגָנְךָ וְתִירֹשְׁךָ וְיִצְהָרֶךָ שְׁגַר־אֲלָפֶיךָ וְעַשְׁתְּרֹת צֹאנֶךָ עַל הָאֲדָמָה אֲשֶׁר־נִשְׁבַּע לַאֲבֹתֶיךָ לָתֶת לָךְ: בָּרוּךְ תִּהְיֶה מִכָּל־הָעַמִּים לֹא־יִהְיֶה בְךָ עָקָר וַעֲקָרָה וּבִבְהֶמְתֶּךָ: וְהֵסִיר יהוה מִמְּךָ כָּל־חֹלִי וְכָל־מַדְוֵי מִצְרַיִם הָרָעִים אֲשֶׁר יָדַעְתָּ לֹא יְשִׂימָם בָּךְ וּנְתָנָם בְּכָל־שֹׂנְאֶיךָ: וְאָכַלְתָּ אֶת־כָּל־הָעַמִּים אֲשֶׁר יהוה אֱלֹהֶיךָ נֹתֵן לָךְ לֹא־תָחוֹס עֵינְךָ עֲלֵיהֶם וְלֹא תַעֲבֹד אֶת־אֱלֹהֵיהֶם כִּי־מוֹקֵשׁ הוּא לָךְ: כִּי תֹאמַר בִּלְבָבְךָ רַבִּים הַגּוֹיִם הָאֵלֶּה מִמֶּנִּי אֵיכָה אוּכַל לְהוֹרִישָׁם: לֹא תִירָא מֵהֶם זָכֹר תִּזְכֹּר אֵת אֲשֶׁר־עָשָׂה יהוה אֱלֹהֶיךָ לְפַרְעֹה וּלְכָל־מִצְרָיִם: הַמַּסֹּת הַגְּדֹלֹת אֲשֶׁר־רָאוּ עֵינֶיךָ וְהָאֹתֹת וְהַמֹּפְתִים וְהַיָּד הַחֲזָקָה וְהַזְּרֹעַ הַנְּטוּיָה אֲשֶׁר הוֹצִאֲךָ יהוה אֱלֹהֶיךָ כֵּן־יַעֲשֶׂה יהוה אֱלֹהֶיךָ לְכָל־הָעַמִּים אֲשֶׁר־אַתָּה יָרֵא מִפְּנֵיהֶם: וְגַם אֶת־הַצִּרְעָה יְשַׁלַּח יהוה אֱלֹהֶיךָ בָּם עַד־אֲבֹד הַנִּשְׁאָרִים וְהַנִּסְתָּרִים מִפָּנֶיךָ: לֹא תַעֲרֹץ מִפְּנֵיהֶם כִּי־יהוה אֱלֹהֶיךָ בְּקִרְבֶּךָ אֵל גָּדוֹל וְנוֹרָא: לוי: וְנָשַׁל יהוה אֱלֹהֶיךָ אֶת־הַגּוֹיִם הָאֵל מִפָּנֶיךָ מְעַט מְעָט לֹא תוּכַל כַּלֹּתָם מַהֵר פֶּן־תִּרְבֶּה עָלֶיךָ חַיַּת הַשָּׂדֶה: וּנְתָנָם יהוה אֱלֹהֶיךָ לְפָנֶיךָ וְהָמָם מְהוּמָה גְדֹלָה עַד הִשָּׁמְדָם: וְנָתַן מַלְכֵיהֶם בְּיָדֶךָ וְהַאֲבַדְתָּ אֶת־שְׁמָם מִתַּחַת הַשָּׁמָיִם לֹא־יִתְיַצֵּב אִישׁ בְּפָנֶיךָ עַד הִשְׁמִדְךָ אֹתָם: פְּסִילֵי אֱלֹהֵיהֶם תִּשְׂרְפוּן בָּאֵשׁ לֹא־תַחְמֹד כֶּסֶף וְזָהָב עֲלֵיהֶם וְלָקַחְתָּ לָךְ פֶּן תִּוָּקֵשׁ בּוֹ כִּי תוֹעֲבַת יהוה אֱלֹהֶיךָ הוּא: וְלֹא־תָבִיא תוֹעֵבָה אֶל־בֵּיתֶךָ וְהָיִיתָ חֵרֶם כָּמֹהוּ שַׁקֵּץ | תְּשַׁקְּצֶנּוּ וְתַעֵב | תְּתַעֲבֶנּוּ כִּי־חֵרֶם הוּא: כָּל־הַמִּצְוָה אֲשֶׁר אָנֹכִי מְצַוְּךָ הַיּוֹם תִּשְׁמְרוּן לַעֲשׂוֹת לְמַעַן תִּחְיוּן וּרְבִיתֶם וּבָאתֶם וִירִשְׁתֶּם אֶת־הָאָרֶץ אֲשֶׁר־נִשְׁבַּע יהוה לַאֲבֹתֵיכֶם: וְזָכַרְתָּ אֶת־כָּל־הַדֶּרֶךְ אֲשֶׁר הוֹלִיכְךָ יהוה אֱלֹהֶיךָ זֶה אַרְבָּעִים שָׁנָה בַּמִּדְבָּר לְמַעַן עַנֹּתְךָ לְנַסֹּתְךָ לָדַעַת אֶת־אֲשֶׁר בִּלְבָבְךָ הֲתִשְׁמֹר מִצְוֺתָו אִם־לֹא: וַיְעַנְּךָ וַיַּרְעִבֶךָ וַיַּאֲכִלְךָ אֶת־הַמָּן אֲשֶׁר לֹא־יָדַעְתָּ וְלֹא יָדְעוּן אֲבֹתֶיךָ לְמַעַן הוֹדִיעֲךָ כִּי לֹא עַל־הַלֶּחֶם לְבַדּוֹ יִחְיֶה הָאָדָם כִּי עַל־כָּל־מוֹצָא פִי־יהוה יִחְיֶה הָאָדָם: ישראל: שִׂמְלָתְךָ לֹא בָלְתָה מֵעָלֶיךָ וְרַגְלְךָ לֹא בָצֵקָה זֶה אַרְבָּעִים שָׁנָה: וְיָדַעְתָּ עִם־לְבָבֶךָ כִּי כַּאֲשֶׁר יְיַסֵּר אִישׁ אֶת־בְּנוֹ יהוה אֱלֹהֶיךָ מְיַסְּרֶךָּ: וְשָׁמַרְתָּ אֶת־מִצְוֺת יהוה אֱלֹהֶיךָ לָלֶכֶת בִּדְרָכָיו וּלְיִרְאָה אֹתוֹ: כִּי יהוה אֱלֹהֶיךָ מְבִיאֲךָ אֶל־אֶרֶץ טוֹבָה אֶרֶץ נַחֲלֵי מָיִם עֲיָנֹת וּתְהֹמֹת יֹצְאִים בַּבִּקְעָה וּבָהָר: אֶרֶץ חִטָּה וּשְׂעֹרָה וְגֶפֶן וּתְאֵנָה וְרִמּוֹן אֶרֶץ־זֵית שֶׁמֶן וּדְבָשׁ: אֶרֶץ אֲשֶׁר לֹא בְמִסְכֵּנֻת תֹּאכַל־בָּהּ לֶחֶם לֹא־תֶחְסַר כֹּל בָּהּ אֶרֶץ אֲשֶׁר אֲבָנֶיהָ בַרְזֶל וּמֵהֲרָרֶיהָ תַּחְצֹב נְחֹשֶׁת: וְאָכַלְתָּ וְשָׂבָעְתָּ וּבֵרַכְתָּ אֶת־יהוה אֱלֹהֶיךָ עַל־הָאָרֶץ הַטֹּבָה אֲשֶׁר נָתַן־לָךְ:

ראה / RE'EH

דברים יא:כו-יב:י

רְאֵה אָנֹכִי נֹתֵן לִפְנֵיכֶם הַיּוֹם בְּרָכָה וּקְלָלָה: אֶת־הַבְּרָכָה אֲשֶׁר תִּשְׁמְעוּ אֶל־מִצְוֺת יהוה אֱלֹהֵיכֶם אֲשֶׁר אָנֹכִי מְצַוֶּה אֶתְכֶם הַיּוֹם: וְהַקְּלָלָה אִם־לֹא תִשְׁמְעוּ אֶל־מִצְוֺת יהוה אֱלֹהֵיכֶם וְסַרְתֶּם מִן־הַדֶּרֶךְ אֲשֶׁר אָנֹכִי מְצַוֶּה אֶתְכֶם הַיּוֹם לָלֶכֶת אַחֲרֵי אֱלֹהִים אֲחֵרִים אֲשֶׁר לֹא־יְדַעְתֶּם: וְהָיָה כִּי יְבִיאֲךָ יהוה אֱלֹהֶיךָ אֶל־הָאָרֶץ אֲשֶׁר־אַתָּה בָא־שָׁמָּה לְרִשְׁתָּהּ וְנָתַתָּה אֶת־הַבְּרָכָה עַל־הַר גְּרִזִּים וְאֶת־הַקְּלָלָה עַל־הַר עֵיבָל: הֲלֹא־

הֵמָּה בְּעֵבֶר הַיַּרְדֵּן אַחֲרֵי דֶּרֶךְ מְבוֹא הַשֶּׁמֶשׁ בְּאֶרֶץ הַכְּנַעֲנִי הַיֹּשֵׁב בָּעֲרָבָה מוּל הַגִּלְגָּל אֵצֶל אֵלוֹנֵי מֹרֶה׃ כִּי אַתֶּם עֹבְרִים אֶת־הַיַּרְדֵּן לָבֹא לָרֶשֶׁת אֶת־הָאָרֶץ אֲשֶׁר־יְהוָה אֱלֹהֵיכֶם נֹתֵן לָכֶם וִירִשְׁתֶּם אֹתָהּ וִישַׁבְתֶּם־בָּהּ׃ לוי: וּשְׁמַרְתֶּם לַעֲשׂוֹת אֵת כָּל־הַחֻקִּים וְאֶת־הַמִּשְׁפָּטִים אֲשֶׁר אָנֹכִי נֹתֵן לִפְנֵיכֶם הַיּוֹם׃ אֵלֶּה הַחֻקִּים וְהַמִּשְׁפָּטִים אֲשֶׁר תִּשְׁמְרוּן לַעֲשׂוֹת בָּאָרֶץ אֲשֶׁר נָתַן יְהוָה אֱלֹהֵי אֲבֹתֶיךָ לְךָ לְרִשְׁתָּהּ כָּל־הַיָּמִים אֲשֶׁר־אַתֶּם חַיִּים עַל־הָאֲדָמָה׃ אַבֵּד תְּאַבְּדוּן אֶת־כָּל־הַמְּקֹמוֹת אֲשֶׁר עָבְדוּ־שָׁם הַגּוֹיִם אֲשֶׁר אַתֶּם יֹרְשִׁים אֹתָם אֶת־אֱלֹהֵיהֶם עַל־הֶהָרִים הָרָמִים וְעַל־הַגְּבָעוֹת וְתַחַת כָּל־עֵץ רַעֲנָן׃ וְנִתַּצְתֶּם אֶת־מִזְבְּחֹתָם וְשִׁבַּרְתֶּם אֶת־מַצֵּבֹתָם וַאֲשֵׁרֵיהֶם תִּשְׂרְפוּן בָּאֵשׁ וּפְסִילֵי אֱלֹהֵיהֶם תְּגַדֵּעוּן וְאִבַּדְתֶּם אֶת־שְׁמָם מִן־הַמָּקוֹם הַהוּא׃ לֹא־תַעֲשׂוּן כֵּן לַיהוָה אֱלֹהֵיכֶם׃ כִּי אִם־אֶל־הַמָּקוֹם אֲשֶׁר־יִבְחַר יְהוָה אֱלֹהֵיכֶם מִכָּל־שִׁבְטֵיכֶם לָשׂוּם אֶת־שְׁמוֹ שָׁם לְשִׁכְנוֹ תִדְרְשׁוּ וּבָאתָ שָׁמָּה׃ ישראל: וַהֲבֵאתֶם שָׁמָּה עֹלֹתֵיכֶם וְזִבְחֵיכֶם וְאֵת מַעְשְׂרֹתֵיכֶם וְאֵת תְּרוּמַת יֶדְכֶם וְנִדְרֵיכֶם וְנִדְבֹתֵיכֶם וּבְכֹרֹת בְּקַרְכֶם וְצֹאנְכֶם׃ וַאֲכַלְתֶּם־שָׁם לִפְנֵי יְהוָה אֱלֹהֵיכֶם וּשְׂמַחְתֶּם בְּכֹל מִשְׁלַח יֶדְכֶם אַתֶּם וּבָתֵּיכֶם אֲשֶׁר בֵּרַכְךָ יְהוָה אֱלֹהֶיךָ׃ לֹא תַעֲשׂוּן כְּכֹל אֲשֶׁר אֲנַחְנוּ עֹשִׂים פֹּה הַיּוֹם אִישׁ כָּל־הַיָּשָׁר בְּעֵינָיו׃ כִּי לֹא־בָאתֶם עַד־עָתָּה אֶל־הַמְּנוּחָה וְאֶל־הַנַּחֲלָה אֲשֶׁר־יְהוָה אֱלֹהֶיךָ נֹתֵן לָךְ׃ וַעֲבַרְתֶּם אֶת־הַיַּרְדֵּן וִישַׁבְתֶּם בָּאָרֶץ אֲשֶׁר־יְהוָה אֱלֹהֵיכֶם מַנְחִיל אֶתְכֶם וְהֵנִיחַ לָכֶם מִכָּל־אֹיְבֵיכֶם מִסָּבִיב וִישַׁבְתֶּם־בֶּטַח׃

SHOFETIM / שופטים

דברים טז:יח-יז:יג

שֹׁפְטִים וְשֹׁטְרִים תִּתֶּן־לְךָ בְּכָל־שְׁעָרֶיךָ אֲשֶׁר יְהוָה אֱלֹהֶיךָ נֹתֵן לְךָ לִשְׁבָטֶיךָ וְשָׁפְטוּ אֶת־הָעָם מִשְׁפַּט־צֶדֶק׃ לֹא־תַטֶּה מִשְׁפָּט לֹא תַכִּיר פָּנִים וְלֹא־תִקַּח שֹׁחַד כִּי הַשֹּׁחַד יְעַוֵּר עֵינֵי חֲכָמִים וִיסַלֵּף דִּבְרֵי צַדִּיקִם׃ צֶדֶק צֶדֶק תִּרְדֹּף לְמַעַן תִּחְיֶה וְיָרַשְׁתָּ אֶת־הָאָרֶץ אֲשֶׁר־יְהוָה אֱלֹהֶיךָ נֹתֵן לָךְ׃ לוי: לֹא־תִטַּע לְךָ אֲשֵׁרָה כָּל־עֵץ אֵצֶל מִזְבַּח יְהוָה אֱלֹהֶיךָ אֲשֶׁר תַּעֲשֶׂה־לָּךְ׃ וְלֹא־תָקִים לְךָ מַצֵּבָה אֲשֶׁר שָׂנֵא יְהוָה אֱלֹהֶיךָ׃ לֹא־תִזְבַּח לַיהוָה אֱלֹהֶיךָ שׁוֹר וָשֶׂה אֲשֶׁר יִהְיֶה בוֹ מוּם כֹּל דָּבָר רָע כִּי תוֹעֲבַת יְהוָה אֱלֹהֶיךָ הוּא׃ כִּי־יִמָּצֵא בְקִרְבְּךָ בְּאַחַד שְׁעָרֶיךָ אֲשֶׁר־יְהוָה אֱלֹהֶיךָ נֹתֵן לָךְ אִישׁ אוֹ־אִשָּׁה אֲשֶׁר יַעֲשֶׂה אֶת־הָרַע בְּעֵינֵי יְהוָה־אֱלֹהֶיךָ לַעֲבֹר בְּרִיתוֹ׃ וַיֵּלֶךְ וַיַּעֲבֹד אֱלֹהִים אֲחֵרִים וַיִּשְׁתַּחוּ לָהֶם וְלַשֶּׁמֶשׁ ׀ אוֹ לַיָּרֵחַ אוֹ לְכָל־צְבָא הַשָּׁמַיִם אֲשֶׁר לֹא־צִוִּיתִי׃ וְהֻגַּד־לְךָ וְשָׁמָעְתָּ וְדָרַשְׁתָּ הֵיטֵב וְהִנֵּה אֱמֶת נָכוֹן הַדָּבָר נֶעֶשְׂתָה הַתּוֹעֵבָה הַזֹּאת בְּיִשְׂרָאֵל׃ וְהוֹצֵאתָ אֶת־הָאִישׁ הַהוּא אוֹ אֶת־הָאִשָּׁה הַהִוא אֲשֶׁר עָשׂוּ אֶת־הַדָּבָר הָרָע הַזֶּה אֶל־שְׁעָרֶיךָ אֶת־הָאִישׁ אוֹ אֶת־הָאִשָּׁה וּסְקַלְתָּם בָּאֲבָנִים וָמֵתוּ׃ עַל־פִּי ׀ שְׁנַיִם עֵדִים אוֹ שְׁלֹשָׁה עֵדִים יוּמַת הַמֵּת לֹא יוּמַת עַל־פִּי עֵד אֶחָד׃ יַד הָעֵדִים תִּהְיֶה־בּוֹ בָרִאשֹׁנָה לַהֲמִיתוֹ וְיַד כָּל־הָעָם בָּאַחֲרֹנָה וּבִעַרְתָּ הָרָע מִקִּרְבֶּךָ׃

כִּי יִפָּלֵא מִמְּךָ דָבָר לַמִּשְׁפָּט בֵּין־דָּם ׀ לְדָם בֵּין־דִּין לְדִין וּבֵין נֶגַע לָנֶגַע דִּבְרֵי רִיבֹת בִּשְׁעָרֶיךָ וְקַמְתָּ וְעָלִיתָ אֶל־הַמָּקוֹם אֲשֶׁר יִבְחַר יְהוָה אֱלֹהֶיךָ בּוֹ׃ וּבָאתָ אֶל־הַכֹּהֲנִים הַלְוִיִּם וְאֶל־הַשֹּׁפֵט אֲשֶׁר יִהְיֶה בַּיָּמִים הָהֵם וְדָרַשְׁתָּ וְהִגִּידוּ לְךָ אֵת דְּבַר הַמִּשְׁפָּט׃ וְעָשִׂיתָ עַל־פִּי הַדָּבָר אֲשֶׁר יַגִּידוּ לְךָ מִן־הַמָּקוֹם הַהוּא אֲשֶׁר יִבְחַר יְהוָה וְשָׁמַרְתָּ לַעֲשׂוֹת כְּכֹל אֲשֶׁר יוֹרוּךָ׃ ישראל: עַל־פִּי הַתּוֹרָה אֲשֶׁר יוֹרוּךָ וְעַל־הַמִּשְׁפָּט אֲשֶׁר־יֹאמְרוּ לְךָ תַּעֲשֶׂה לֹא תָסוּר מִן־הַדָּבָר אֲשֶׁר־יַגִּידוּ לְךָ יָמִין וּשְׂמֹאל׃ וְהָאִישׁ אֲשֶׁר־יַעֲשֶׂה בְזָדוֹן לְבִלְתִּי

שְׁמֹעַ אֶל־הַכֹּהֵן הָעֹמֵד לְשָׁרֶת שָׁם אֶת־יהוה אֱלֹהֶיךָ אוֹ אֶל־הַשֹּׁפֵט וּמֵת הָאִישׁ הַהוּא וּבִעַרְתָּ הָרָע מִיִּשְׂרָאֵל: וְכָל־הָעָם יִשְׁמְעוּ וְיִרָאוּ וְלֹא יְזִידוּן עוֹד:

KI TETZEH / כי תצא

דברים כא:י-כא

כִּי־תֵצֵא לַמִּלְחָמָה עַל־אֹיְבֶיךָ וּנְתָנוֹ יהוה אֱלֹהֶיךָ בְּיָדֶךָ וְשָׁבִיתָ שִׁבְיוֹ: וְרָאִיתָ בַּשִּׁבְיָה אֵשֶׁת יְפַת־תֹּאַר וְחָשַׁקְתָּ בָהּ וְלָקַחְתָּ לְךָ לְאִשָּׁה: וַהֲבֵאתָהּ אֶל־תּוֹךְ בֵּיתֶךָ וְגִלְּחָה אֶת־רֹאשָׁהּ וְעָשְׂתָה אֶת־צִפָּרְנֶיהָ: וְהֵסִירָה אֶת־שִׂמְלַת שִׁבְיָהּ מֵעָלֶיהָ וְיָשְׁבָה בְּבֵיתֶךָ וּבָכְתָה אֶת־אָבִיהָ וְאֶת־אִמָּהּ יֶרַח יָמִים וְאַחַר כֵּן תָּבוֹא אֵלֶיהָ וּבְעַלְתָּהּ וְהָיְתָה לְךָ לְאִשָּׁה: וְהָיָה אִם־לֹא חָפַצְתָּ בָּהּ וְשִׁלַּחְתָּהּ לְנַפְשָׁהּ וּמָכֹר לֹא־תִמְכְּרֶנָּה בַּכָּסֶף לֹא־תִתְעַמֵּר בָּהּ תַּחַת אֲשֶׁר עִנִּיתָהּ: לוי: כִּי־תִהְיֶיןָ לְאִישׁ שְׁתֵּי נָשִׁים הָאַחַת אֲהוּבָה וְהָאַחַת שְׂנוּאָה וְיָלְדוּ־לוֹ בָנִים הָאֲהוּבָה וְהַשְּׂנוּאָה וְהָיָה הַבֵּן הַבְּכֹר לַשְּׂנִיאָה: וְהָיָה בְּיוֹם הַנְחִילוֹ אֶת־בָּנָיו אֵת אֲשֶׁר־יִהְיֶה לוֹ לֹא יוּכַל לְבַכֵּר אֶת־בֶּן־הָאֲהוּבָה עַל־פְּנֵי בֶן־הַשְּׂנוּאָה הַבְּכֹר: כִּי אֶת־הַבְּכֹר בֶּן־הַשְּׂנוּאָה יַכִּיר לָתֶת לוֹ פִּי שְׁנַיִם בְּכֹל אֲשֶׁר־יִמָּצֵא לוֹ כִּי־הוּא רֵאשִׁית אֹנוֹ לוֹ מִשְׁפַּט הַבְּכֹרָה: ישראל: כִּי־יִהְיֶה לְאִישׁ בֵּן סוֹרֵר וּמוֹרֶה אֵינֶנּוּ שֹׁמֵעַ בְּקוֹל אָבִיו וּבְקוֹל אִמּוֹ וְיִסְּרוּ אֹתוֹ וְלֹא יִשְׁמַע אֲלֵיהֶם: וְתָפְשׂוּ בוֹ אָבִיו וְאִמּוֹ וְהוֹצִיאוּ אֹתוֹ אֶל־זִקְנֵי עִירוֹ וְאֶל־שַׁעַר מְקֹמוֹ: וְאָמְרוּ אֶל־זִקְנֵי עִירוֹ בְּנֵנוּ זֶה סוֹרֵר וּמֹרֶה אֵינֶנּוּ שֹׁמֵעַ בְּקֹלֵנוּ זוֹלֵל וְסֹבֵא: וּרְגָמֻהוּ כָּל־אַנְשֵׁי עִירוֹ בָאֲבָנִים וָמֵת וּבִעַרְתָּ הָרָע מִקִּרְבֶּךָ וְכָל־יִשְׂרָאֵל יִשְׁמְעוּ וְיִרָאוּ:

KI TAVO / כי תבוא

דברים כו:א-טו

וְהָיָה כִּי־תָבוֹא אֶל־הָאָרֶץ אֲשֶׁר יהוה אֱלֹהֶיךָ נֹתֵן לְךָ נַחֲלָה וִירִשְׁתָּהּ וְיָשַׁבְתָּ בָּהּ: וְלָקַחְתָּ מֵרֵאשִׁית | כָּל־פְּרִי הָאֲדָמָה אֲשֶׁר תָּבִיא מֵאַרְצְךָ אֲשֶׁר יהוה אֱלֹהֶיךָ נֹתֵן לָךְ וְשַׂמְתָּ בַטֶּנֶא וְהָלַכְתָּ אֶל־הַמָּקוֹם אֲשֶׁר יִבְחַר יהוה אֱלֹהֶיךָ לְשַׁכֵּן שְׁמוֹ שָׁם: וּבָאתָ אֶל־הַכֹּהֵן אֲשֶׁר יִהְיֶה בַּיָּמִים הָהֵם וְאָמַרְתָּ אֵלָיו הִגַּדְתִּי הַיּוֹם לַיהוה אֱלֹהֶיךָ כִּי־בָאתִי אֶל־הָאָרֶץ אֲשֶׁר נִשְׁבַּע יהוה לַאֲבֹתֵינוּ לָתֶת לָנוּ: לוי: וְלָקַח הַכֹּהֵן הַטֶּנֶא מִיָּדֶךָ וְהִנִּיחוֹ לִפְנֵי מִזְבַּח יהוה אֱלֹהֶיךָ: וְעָנִיתָ וְאָמַרְתָּ לִפְנֵי | יהוה אֱלֹהֶיךָ אֲרַמִּי אֹבֵד אָבִי וַיֵּרֶד מִצְרַיְמָה וַיָּגָר שָׁם בִּמְתֵי מְעָט וַיְהִי־שָׁם לְגוֹי גָּדוֹל עָצוּם וָרָב: וַיָּרֵעוּ אֹתָנוּ הַמִּצְרִים וַיְעַנּוּנוּ וַיִּתְּנוּ עָלֵינוּ עֲבֹדָה קָשָׁה: וַנִּצְעַק אֶל־יהוה אֱלֹהֵי אֲבֹתֵינוּ וַיִּשְׁמַע יהוה אֶת־קֹלֵנוּ וַיַּרְא אֶת־עָנְיֵנוּ וְאֶת־עֲמָלֵנוּ וְאֶת־לַחֲצֵנוּ: וַיּוֹצִאֵנוּ יהוה מִמִּצְרַיִם בְּיָד חֲזָקָה וּבִזְרֹעַ נְטוּיָה וּבְמֹרָא גָּדֹל וּבְאֹתוֹת וּבְמֹפְתִים: וַיְבִאֵנוּ אֶל־הַמָּקוֹם הַזֶּה וַיִּתֶּן־לָנוּ אֶת־הָאָרֶץ הַזֹּאת אֶרֶץ זָבַת חָלָב וּדְבָשׁ: וְעַתָּה הִנֵּה הֵבֵאתִי אֶת־רֵאשִׁית פְּרִי הָאֲדָמָה אֲשֶׁר־נָתַתָּה לִּי יהוה וְהִנַּחְתּוֹ לִפְנֵי יהוה אֱלֹהֶיךָ וְהִשְׁתַּחֲוִיתָ לִפְנֵי יהוה אֱלֹהֶיךָ: וְשָׂמַחְתָּ בְכָל־הַטּוֹב אֲשֶׁר נָתַן־לְךָ יהוה אֱלֹהֶיךָ וּלְבֵיתֶךָ אַתָּה וְהַלֵּוִי וְהַגֵּר אֲשֶׁר בְּקִרְבֶּךָ: ישראל: כִּי תְכַלֶּה לַעְשֵׂר אֶת־כָּל־מַעְשַׂר תְּבוּאָתְךָ בַּשָּׁנָה הַשְּׁלִישִׁת שְׁנַת הַמַּעֲשֵׂר וְנָתַתָּה לַלֵּוִי לַגֵּר לַיָּתוֹם וְלָאַלְמָנָה וְאָכְלוּ בִשְׁעָרֶיךָ וְשָׂבֵעוּ: וְאָמַרְתָּ לִפְנֵי יהוה אֱלֹהֶיךָ בִּעַרְתִּי הַקֹּדֶשׁ מִן־הַבַּיִת וְגַם נְתַתִּיו לַלֵּוִי וְלַגֵּר לַיָּתוֹם וְלָאַלְמָנָה כְּכָל־מִצְוָתְךָ אֲשֶׁר צִוִּיתָנִי לֹא־עָבַרְתִּי מִמִּצְוֹתֶיךָ וְלֹא שָׁכָחְתִּי: לֹא־אָכַלְתִּי בְאֹנִי מִמֶּנּוּ וְלֹא־בִעַרְתִּי מִמֶּנּוּ בְּטָמֵא וְלֹא־נָתַתִּי מִמֶּנּוּ לְמֵת שָׁמַעְתִּי בְּקוֹל יהוה אֱלֹהָי עָשִׂיתִי כְּכֹל אֲשֶׁר צִוִּיתָנִי: הַשְׁקִיפָה מִמְּעוֹן קָדְשְׁךָ מִן־הַשָּׁמַיִם וּבָרֵךְ אֶת־עַמְּךָ אֶת־יִשְׂרָאֵל

וְאֶת הָאֲדָמָה אֲשֶׁר נָתַתָּה לָנוּ כַּאֲשֶׁר נִשְׁבַּעְתָּ לַאֲבֹתֵינוּ אֶרֶץ זָבַת חָלָב וּדְבָשׁ׃

נצבים / NITZAVIM

דברים כט:ט-כח

אַתֶּם נִצָּבִים הַיּוֹם כֻּלְּכֶם לִפְנֵי יְהוָה אֱלֹהֵיכֶם רָאשֵׁיכֶם שִׁבְטֵיכֶם זִקְנֵיכֶם וְשֹׁטְרֵיכֶם כֹּל אִישׁ יִשְׂרָאֵל׃ טַפְּכֶם נְשֵׁיכֶם וְגֵרְךָ אֲשֶׁר בְּקֶרֶב מַחֲנֶיךָ מֵחֹטֵב עֵצֶיךָ עַד שֹׁאֵב מֵימֶיךָ׃ לְעָבְרְךָ בִּבְרִית יְהוָה אֱלֹהֶיךָ וּבְאָלָתוֹ אֲשֶׁר יְהוָה אֱלֹהֶיךָ כֹּרֵת עִמְּךָ הַיּוֹם׃ לוי: לְמַעַן הָקִים־אֹתְךָ הַיּוֹם ׀ לוֹ לְעָם וְהוּא יִהְיֶה־לְּךָ לֵאלֹהִים כַּאֲשֶׁר דִּבֶּר־לָךְ וְכַאֲשֶׁר נִשְׁבַּע לַאֲבֹתֶיךָ לְאַבְרָהָם לְיִצְחָק וּלְיַעֲקֹב׃ וְלֹא אִתְּכֶם לְבַדְּכֶם אָנֹכִי כֹּרֵת אֶת־הַבְּרִית הַזֹּאת וְאֶת־הָאָלָה הַזֹּאת׃ כִּי אֶת־אֲשֶׁר יֶשְׁנוֹ פֹּה עִמָּנוּ עֹמֵד הַיּוֹם לִפְנֵי יְהוָה אֱלֹהֵינוּ וְאֵת אֲשֶׁר אֵינֶנּוּ פֹּה עִמָּנוּ הַיּוֹם׃ ישראל: כִּי־אַתֶּם יְדַעְתֶּם אֵת אֲשֶׁר־יָשַׁבְנוּ בְּאֶרֶץ מִצְרָיִם וְאֵת אֲשֶׁר־עָבַרְנוּ בְּקֶרֶב הַגּוֹיִם אֲשֶׁר עֲבַרְתֶּם׃ וַתִּרְאוּ אֶת־שִׁקּוּצֵיהֶם וְאֵת גִּלֻּלֵיהֶם עֵץ וָאֶבֶן כֶּסֶף וְזָהָב אֲשֶׁר עִמָּהֶם׃ פֶּן־יֵשׁ בָּכֶם אִישׁ אוֹ־אִשָּׁה אוֹ מִשְׁפָּחָה אוֹ־שֵׁבֶט אֲשֶׁר לְבָבוֹ פֹנֶה הַיּוֹם מֵעִם יְהוָה אֱלֹהֵינוּ לָלֶכֶת לַעֲבֹד אֶת־אֱלֹהֵי הַגּוֹיִם הָהֵם פֶּן־יֵשׁ בָּכֶם שֹׁרֶשׁ פֹּרֶה רֹאשׁ וְלַעֲנָה׃ וְהָיָה בְּשָׁמְעוֹ אֶת־דִּבְרֵי הָאָלָה הַזֹּאת וְהִתְבָּרֵךְ בִּלְבָבוֹ לֵאמֹר שָׁלוֹם יִהְיֶה־לִּי כִּי בִּשְׁרִרוּת לִבִּי אֵלֵךְ לְמַעַן סְפוֹת הָרָוָה אֶת־הַצְּמֵאָה׃ לֹא־יֹאבֶה יְהוָה סְלֹחַ לוֹ כִּי אָז יֶעְשַׁן אַף־יְהוָה וְקִנְאָתוֹ בָּאִישׁ הַהוּא וְרָבְצָה בּוֹ כָּל־הָאָלָה הַכְּתוּבָה בַּסֵּפֶר הַזֶּה וּמָחָה יְהוָה אֶת־שְׁמוֹ מִתַּחַת הַשָּׁמָיִם׃ וְהִבְדִּילוֹ יְהוָה לְרָעָה מִכֹּל שִׁבְטֵי יִשְׂרָאֵל כְּכֹל אָלוֹת הַבְּרִית הַכְּתוּבָה בְּסֵפֶר הַתּוֹרָה הַזֶּה׃ וְאָמַר הַדּוֹר הָאַחֲרוֹן בְּנֵיכֶם אֲשֶׁר יָקוּמוּ מֵאַחֲרֵיכֶם וְהַנָּכְרִי אֲשֶׁר יָבֹא מֵאֶרֶץ רְחוֹקָה וְרָאוּ אֶת־מַכּוֹת הָאָרֶץ הַהִוא וְאֶת־תַּחֲלֻאֶיהָ אֲשֶׁר־חִלָּה יְהוָה בָּהּ׃ גָּפְרִית וָמֶלַח שְׂרֵפָה כָל־אַרְצָהּ לֹא תִזָּרַע וְלֹא תַצְמִחַ וְלֹא־יַעֲלֶה בָהּ כָּל־עֵשֶׂב כְּמַהְפֵּכַת סְדֹם וַעֲמֹרָה אַדְמָה וצביים [וּצְבוֹיִם] אֲשֶׁר הָפַךְ יְהוָה בְּאַפּוֹ וּבַחֲמָתוֹ׃ וְאָמְרוּ כָּל־הַגּוֹיִם עַל־מֶה עָשָׂה יְהוָה כָּכָה לָאָרֶץ הַזֹּאת מֶה חֳרִי הָאַף הַגָּדוֹל הַזֶּה׃ וְאָמְרוּ עַל אֲשֶׁר עָזְבוּ אֶת־בְּרִית יְהוָה אֱלֹהֵי אֲבֹתָם אֲשֶׁר כָּרַת עִמָּם בְּהוֹצִיאוֹ אֹתָם מֵאֶרֶץ מִצְרָיִם׃ וַיֵּלְכוּ וַיַּעַבְדוּ אֱלֹהִים אֲחֵרִים וַיִּשְׁתַּחֲווּ לָהֶם אֱלֹהִים אֲשֶׁר לֹא־יְדָעוּם וְלֹא חָלַק לָהֶם׃ וַיִּחַר־אַף יְהוָה בָּאָרֶץ הַהִוא לְהָבִיא עָלֶיהָ אֶת־כָּל־הַקְּלָלָה הַכְּתוּבָה בַּסֵּפֶר הַזֶּה׃ וַיִּתְּשֵׁם יְהוָה מֵעַל אַדְמָתָם בְּאַף וּבְחֵמָה וּבְקֶצֶף גָּדוֹל וַיַּשְׁלִכֵם אֶל־אֶרֶץ אַחֶרֶת כַּיּוֹם הַזֶּה׃ הַנִּסְתָּרֹת לַיהוָה אֱלֹהֵינוּ וְהַנִּגְלֹת לָנוּ וּלְבָנֵינוּ עַד־עוֹלָם לַעֲשׂוֹת אֶת־כָּל־דִּבְרֵי הַתּוֹרָה הַזֹּאת׃

וילך / VAYELEKH

דברים לא:א-יג

וַיֵּלֶךְ מֹשֶׁה וַיְדַבֵּר אֶת־הַדְּבָרִים הָאֵלֶּה אֶל־כָּל־יִשְׂרָאֵל׃ וַיֹּאמֶר אֲלֵהֶם בֶּן־מֵאָה וְעֶשְׂרִים שָׁנָה אָנֹכִי הַיּוֹם לֹא־אוּכַל עוֹד לָצֵאת וְלָבוֹא וַיהוָה אָמַר אֵלַי לֹא תַעֲבֹר אֶת־הַיַּרְדֵּן הַזֶּה׃ יְהוָה אֱלֹהֶיךָ הוּא ׀ עֹבֵר לְפָנֶיךָ הוּא־יַשְׁמִיד אֶת־הַגּוֹיִם הָאֵלֶּה מִלְּפָנֶיךָ וִירִשְׁתָּם יְהוֹשֻׁעַ הוּא עֹבֵר לְפָנֶיךָ כַּאֲשֶׁר דִּבֶּר יְהוָה׃ לוי: וְעָשָׂה יְהוָה לָהֶם כַּאֲשֶׁר עָשָׂה לְסִיחוֹן וּלְעוֹג מַלְכֵי הָאֱמֹרִי וּלְאַרְצָם אֲשֶׁר הִשְׁמִיד אֹתָם׃ וּנְתָנָם יְהוָה לִפְנֵיכֶם וַעֲשִׂיתֶם לָהֶם כְּכָל־הַמִּצְוָה אֲשֶׁר צִוִּיתִי אֶתְכֶם׃ חִזְקוּ וְאִמְצוּ אַל־תִּירְאוּ וְאַל־תַּעַרְצוּ מִפְּנֵיהֶם כִּי ׀ יְהוָה אֱלֹהֶיךָ הוּא הַהֹלֵךְ עִמָּךְ לֹא יַרְפְּךָ וְלֹא יַעַזְבֶךָּ׃ ישראל: וַיִּקְרָא מֹשֶׁה לִיהוֹשֻׁעַ וַיֹּאמֶר אֵלָיו לְעֵינֵי כָל־יִשְׂרָאֵל חֲזַק וֶאֱמָץ כִּי אַתָּה תָּבוֹא אֶת־הָעָם הַזֶּה אֶל־הָאָרֶץ אֲשֶׁר

נִשְׁבַּע יהוה לַאֲבֹתָם לָתֵת לָהֶם וְאַתָּה
תַּנְחִילֶנָּה אוֹתָם: וַיהוה הוּא | הַהֹלֵךְ לְפָנֶיךָ
הוּא יִהְיֶה עִמָּךְ לֹא יַרְפְּךָ וְלֹא יַעַזְבֶךָּ לֹא
תִירָא וְלֹא תֵחָת: וַיִּכְתֹּב מֹשֶׁה אֶת־הַתּוֹרָה
הַזֹּאת וַיִּתְּנָהּ אֶל־הַכֹּהֲנִים בְּנֵי לֵוִי הַנֹּשְׂאִים
אֶת־אֲרוֹן בְּרִית יהוה וְאֶל־כָּל־זִקְנֵי יִשְׂרָאֵל:
וַיְצַו מֹשֶׁה אוֹתָם לֵאמֹר מִקֵּץ | שֶׁבַע שָׁנִים
בְּמֹעֵד שְׁנַת הַשְּׁמִטָּה בְּחַג הַסֻּכּוֹת: בְּבוֹא
כָל־יִשְׂרָאֵל לֵרָאוֹת אֶת־פְּנֵי יהוה אֱלֹהֶיךָ
בַּמָּקוֹם אֲשֶׁר יִבְחָר תִּקְרָא אֶת־הַתּוֹרָה
הַזֹּאת נֶגֶד כָּל־יִשְׂרָאֵל בְּאָזְנֵיהֶם: הַקְהֵל
אֶת־הָעָם הָאֲנָשִׁים וְהַנָּשִׁים וְהַטַּף וְגֵרְךָ
אֲשֶׁר בִּשְׁעָרֶיךָ לְמַעַן יִשְׁמְעוּ וּלְמַעַן
יִלְמְדוּ וְיָרְאוּ אֶת־יהוה אֱלֹהֵיכֶם וְשָׁמְרוּ
לַעֲשׂוֹת אֶת־כָּל־דִּבְרֵי הַתּוֹרָה הַזֹּאת:
וּבְנֵיהֶם אֲשֶׁר לֹא־יָדְעוּ יִשְׁמְעוּ וְלָמְדוּ
לְיִרְאָה אֶת־יהוה אֱלֹהֵיכֶם כָּל־הַיָּמִים
אֲשֶׁר אַתֶּם חַיִּים עַל־הָאֲדָמָה אֲשֶׁר אַתֶּם
עֹבְרִים אֶת־הַיַּרְדֵּן שָׁמָּה לְרִשְׁתָּהּ:

HAʼAZINU / האזינו

דברים לב:א-יח

הַאֲזִינוּ הַשָּׁמַיִם וַאֲדַבֵּרָה וְתִשְׁמַע הָאָרֶץ
אִמְרֵי־פִי: יַעֲרֹף כַּמָּטָר לִקְחִי תִּזַּל כַּטַּל
אִמְרָתִי כִּשְׂעִירִם עֲלֵי־דֶשֶׁא וְכִרְבִיבִים עֲלֵי־
עֵשֶׂב: כִּי שֵׁם יהוה אֶקְרָא הָבוּ גֹדֶל לֵאלֹהֵינוּ:
לוי: הַצּוּר תָּמִים פָּעֳלוֹ כִּי כָל־דְּרָכָיו מִשְׁפָּט
אֵל אֱמוּנָה וְאֵין עָוֶל צַדִּיק וְיָשָׁר הוּא: שִׁחֵת
לוֹ לֹא בָּנָיו מוּמָם דּוֹר עִקֵּשׁ וּפְתַלְתֹּל: הַ
לְיהוה תִּגְמְלוּ־זֹאת עַם נָבָל וְלֹא חָכָם
הֲלוֹא־הוּא אָבִיךָ קָּנֶךָ הוּא עָשְׂךָ וַיְכֹנְנֶךָ:
ישראל: זְכֹר יְמוֹת עוֹלָם בִּינוּ שְׁנוֹת דֹּר־וָדֹר
שְׁאַל אָבִיךָ וְיַגֵּדְךָ זְקֵנֶיךָ וְיֹאמְרוּ לָךְ: בְּהַנְחֵל
עֶלְיוֹן גּוֹיִם בְּהַפְרִידוֹ בְּנֵי אָדָם יַצֵּב גְּבֻלֹת
עַמִּים לְמִסְפַּר בְּנֵי יִשְׂרָאֵל: כִּי חֵלֶק יהוה עַמּוֹ
יַעֲקֹב חֶבֶל נַחֲלָתוֹ: יִמְצָאֵהוּ בְּאֶרֶץ מִדְבָּר
וּבְתֹהוּ יְלֵל יְשִׁמֹן יְסֹבְבֶנְהוּ יְבוֹנְנֵהוּ יִצְּרֶנְהוּ
כְּאִישׁוֹן עֵינוֹ: כְּנֶשֶׁר יָעִיר קִנּוֹ עַל־גּוֹזָלָיו
יְרַחֵף יִפְרֹשׂ כְּנָפָיו יִקָּחֵהוּ יִשָּׂאֵהוּ עַל־
אֶבְרָתוֹ: יהוה בָּדָד יַנְחֶנּוּ וְאֵין עִמּוֹ אֵל נֵכָר:

VEZOT HABERAKHA / וזאת הברכה

דברים לג:א-יז

וְזֹאת הַבְּרָכָה אֲשֶׁר בֵּרַךְ מֹשֶׁה אִישׁ הָאֱלֹהִים
אֶת־בְּנֵי יִשְׂרָאֵל לִפְנֵי מוֹתוֹ: וַיֹּאמַר יהוה
מִסִּינַי בָּא וְזָרַח מִשֵּׂעִיר לָמוֹ הוֹפִיעַ מֵהַר
פָּארָן וְאָתָה מֵרִבְבֹת קֹדֶשׁ מִימִינוֹ אשדת
[אֵשׁ דָּת] לָמוֹ: אַף חֹבֵב עַמִּים כָּל־קְדֹשָׁיו
בְּיָדֶךָ וְהֵם תֻּכּוּ לְרַגְלֶךָ יִשָּׂא מִדַּבְּרֹתֶיךָ: תּוֹרָה
צִוָּה־לָנוּ מֹשֶׁה מוֹרָשָׁה קְהִלַּת יַעֲקֹב: וַיְהִי
בִישֻׁרוּן מֶלֶךְ בְּהִתְאַסֵּף רָאשֵׁי עָם יַחַד
שִׁבְטֵי יִשְׂרָאֵל: יְחִי רְאוּבֵן וְאַל־יָמֹת וִיהִי
מְתָיו מִסְפָּר: וְזֹאת לִיהוּדָה וַיֹּאמַר שְׁמַע
יהוה קוֹל יְהוּדָה וְאֶל־עַמּוֹ תְּבִיאֶנּוּ יָדָיו רָב
לוֹ וְעֵזֶר מִצָּרָיו תִּהְיֶה:
לוי: וּלְלֵוִי אָמַר תֻּמֶּיךָ וְאוּרֶיךָ לְאִישׁ חֲסִידֶךָ
אֲשֶׁר נִסִּיתוֹ בְּמַסָּה תְּרִיבֵהוּ עַל־מֵי מְרִיבָה:
הָאֹמֵר לְאָבִיו וּלְאִמּוֹ לֹא רְאִיתִיו וְאֶת־אֶחָיו
לֹא הִכִּיר וְאֶת־בָּנָו לֹא יָדָע כִּי שָׁמְרוּ אִמְרָתֶךָ
וּבְרִיתְךָ יִנְצֹרוּ: יוֹרוּ מִשְׁפָּטֶיךָ לְיַעֲקֹב וְתוֹרָתְךָ
לְיִשְׂרָאֵל יָשִׂימוּ קְטוֹרָה בְּאַפֶּךָ וְכָלִיל עַל־
מִזְבְּחֶךָ: בָּרֵךְ יהוה חֵילוֹ וּפֹעַל יָדָיו תִּרְצֶה
מְחַץ מָתְנַיִם קָמָיו וּמְשַׂנְאָיו מִן־יְקוּמוּן:
לְבִנְיָמִן אָמַר יְדִיד יהוה יִשְׁכֹּן לָבֶטַח עָלָיו
חֹפֵף עָלָיו כָּל־הַיּוֹם וּבֵין כְּתֵפָיו שָׁכֵן:
ישראל: וּלְיוֹסֵף אָמַר מְבֹרֶכֶת יהוה אַרְצוֹ
מִמֶּגֶד שָׁמַיִם מִטָּל וּמִתְּהוֹם רֹבֶצֶת תָּחַת:
וּמִמֶּגֶד תְּבוּאֹת שָׁמֶשׁ וּמִמֶּגֶד גֶּרֶשׁ יְרָחִים:
וּמֵרֹאשׁ הַרְרֵי־קֶדֶם וּמִמֶּגֶד גִּבְעוֹת עוֹלָם:
וּמִמֶּגֶד אֶרֶץ וּמְלֹאָהּ וּרְצוֹן שֹׁכְנִי סְנֶה
תָּבוֹאתָה לְרֹאשׁ יוֹסֵף וּלְקָדְקֹד נְזִיר אֶחָיו:
בְּכוֹר שׁוֹרוֹ הָדָר לוֹ וְקַרְנֵי רְאֵם קַרְנָיו בָּהֶם
עַמִּים יְנַגַּח יַחְדָּו אַפְסֵי־אָרֶץ וְהֵם רִבְבוֹת
אֶפְרַיִם וְהֵם אַלְפֵי מְנַשֶּׁה:

לראש חודש, לתעניות ציבור לחנוכה ולפורים
ROSH HODESH, FAST DAYS, HANUKKA AND PURIM

קריאה לראש חודש
READING FOR ROSH HODESH

במדבר כח:א–טו

For the כהן, the first three verses are read up to עֹלָה תָּמִיד. For the לוי, the third verse is repeated and starts with וְאָמַרְתָּ לָהֶם. For שלישי, continue from עֹלַת תָּמִיד up to וְנִסְכֹּה. For רביעי, read from וּבְרָאשֵׁי חָדְשֵׁיכֶם until the end. On ראש חודש טבת, the כהן reads until רְבִיעִת הַהִין, the לוי reads the portion for שלישי and the שלישי the portion of רביעי; the fourth עולה reads the appropriate day of חנוכה on page 1138.

וַיְדַבֵּר יהוה אֶל־מֹשֶׁה לֵּאמֹר: צַו אֶת־בְּנֵי יִשְׂרָאֵל וְאָמַרְתָּ אֲלֵהֶם אֶת־קָרְבָּנִי לַחְמִי לְאִשַּׁי רֵיחַ נִיחֹחִי תִּשְׁמְרוּ לְהַקְרִיב לִי בְּמוֹעֲדוֹ: לוי: וְאָמַרְתָּ לָהֶם זֶה הָאִשֶּׁה אֲשֶׁר תַּקְרִיבוּ לַיהוה כְּבָשִׂים בְּנֵי־שָׁנָה תְמִימִם שְׁנַיִם לַיּוֹם עֹלָה תָמִיד: עד כאן לכהן אֶת־הַכֶּבֶשׂ אֶחָד תַּעֲשֶׂה בַבֹּקֶר וְאֵת הַכֶּבֶשׂ הַשֵּׁנִי תַּעֲשֶׂה בֵּין הָעַרְבָּיִם: וַעֲשִׂירִית הָאֵיפָה סֹלֶת לְמִנְחָה בְּלוּלָה בְּשֶׁמֶן כָּתִית רְבִיעִת הַהִין: שלישי: עֹלַת תָּמִיד הָעֲשֻׂיָה בְּהַר סִינַי לְרֵיחַ נִיחֹחַ אִשֶּׁה לַיהוה: וְנִסְכּוֹ רְבִיעִת הַהִין לַכֶּבֶשׂ הָאֶחָד בַּקֹּדֶשׁ הַסֵּךְ נֶסֶךְ שֵׁכָר לַיהוה: וְאֵת הַכֶּבֶשׂ הַשֵּׁנִי תַּעֲשֶׂה בֵּין הָעַרְבָּיִם כְּמִנְחַת הַבֹּקֶר וּכְנִסְכּוֹ תַּעֲשֶׂה אִשֵּׁה רֵיחַ נִיחֹחַ לַיהוה:

וּבְיוֹם הַשַּׁבָּת שְׁנֵי־כְבָשִׂים בְּנֵי־שָׁנָה תְּמִימִם וּשְׁנֵי עֶשְׂרֹנִים סֹלֶת מִנְחָה בְּלוּלָה בַשֶּׁמֶן וְנִסְכּוֹ: עֹלַת שַׁבַּת בְּשַׁבַּתּוֹ עַל־עֹלַת הַתָּמִיד וְנִסְכָּהּ:

רביעי: וּבְרָאשֵׁי חָדְשֵׁיכֶם תַּקְרִיבוּ עֹלָה לַיהוה פָּרִים בְּנֵי־בָקָר שְׁנַיִם וְאַיִל אֶחָד כְּבָשִׂים בְּנֵי־שָׁנָה שִׁבְעָה תְּמִימִם: וּשְׁלֹשָׁה עֶשְׂרֹנִים סֹלֶת מִנְחָה בְּלוּלָה בַשֶּׁמֶן לַפָּר הָאֶחָד וּשְׁנֵי עֶשְׂרֹנִים סֹלֶת מִנְחָה בְּלוּלָה בַשֶּׁמֶן לָאַיִל הָאֶחָד: וְעִשָּׂרֹן עִשָּׂרוֹן סֹלֶת מִנְחָה בְּלוּלָה בַשֶּׁמֶן לַכֶּבֶשׂ הָאֶחָד עֹלָה רֵיחַ נִיחֹחַ אִשֶּׁה לַיהוה: וְנִסְכֵּיהֶם חֲצִי הַהִין יִהְיֶה לַפָּר וּשְׁלִישִׁת הַהִין לָאַיִל וּרְבִיעִת הַהִין לַכֶּבֶשׂ יָיִן זֹאת עֹלַת חֹדֶשׁ בְּחָדְשׁוֹ לְחָדְשֵׁי הַשָּׁנָה: וּשְׂעִיר עִזִּים אֶחָד לְחַטָּאת לַיהוה עַל־עֹלַת הַתָּמִיד יֵעָשֶׂה וְנִסְכּוֹ:

קריאה לתענית ציבור
READING FOR FAST DAYS

שמות לב:יא–יד

The following is read on a תענית ציבור (except תשעה באב) in both שחרית and מנחה. At מנחה, the person called up for שלישי also reads the הפטרה.

It is customary for the קהל to say aloud the passages marked by arrows, followed by the קורא.

וַיְחַל מֹשֶׁה אֶת־פְּנֵי יהוה אֱלֹהָיו וַיֹּאמֶר לָמָה יהוה יֶחֱרֶה אַפְּךָ בְּעַמֶּךָ אֲשֶׁר הוֹצֵאתָ מֵאֶרֶץ מִצְרַיִם בְּכֹחַ גָּדוֹל וּבְיָד חֲזָקָה: לָמָּה יֹאמְרוּ מִצְרַיִם לֵאמֹר בְּרָעָה הוֹצִיאָם לַהֲרֹג אֹתָם בֶּהָרִים וּלְכַלֹּתָם מֵעַל פְּנֵי הָאֲדָמָה ◂ שׁוּב מֵחֲרוֹן אַפֶּךָ וְהִנָּחֵם עַל־הָרָעָה לְעַמֶּךָ: ◂ זְכֹר לְאַבְרָהָם לְיִצְחָק וּלְיִשְׂרָאֵל עֲבָדֶיךָ אֲשֶׁר נִשְׁבַּעְתָּ לָהֶם בָּךְ וַתְּדַבֵּר אֲלֵהֶם אַרְבֶּה אֶת־זַרְעֲכֶם כְּכוֹכְבֵי הַשָּׁמָיִם וְכָל־הָאָרֶץ הַזֹּאת אֲשֶׁר אָמַרְתִּי אֶתֵּן לְזַרְעֲכֶם וְנָחֲלוּ לְעֹלָם: וַיִּנָּחֶם יהוה עַל־הָרָעָה אֲשֶׁר דִּבֶּר לַעֲשׂוֹת לְעַמּוֹ:

שמות לד:א–י

לוי: וַיֹּאמֶר יהוה אֶל־מֹשֶׁה פְּסָל־לְךָ שְׁנֵי־לֻחֹת אֲבָנִים כָּרִאשֹׁנִים וְכָתַבְתִּי עַל־הַלֻּחֹת אֶת־הַדְּבָרִים אֲשֶׁר הָיוּ עַל־הַלֻּחֹת הָרִאשֹׁנִים אֲשֶׁר שִׁבַּרְתָּ: וֶהְיֵה נָכוֹן לַבֹּקֶר וְעָלִיתָ בַבֹּקֶר אֶל־הַר סִינַי וְנִצַּבְתָּ לִי שָׁם

עַל־רֹאשׁ הָהָר׃ וְאִישׁ לֹא־יַעֲלֶה עִמָּךְ וְגַם־אִישׁ אַל־יֵרָא בְּכָל־הָהָר גַּם־הַצֹּאן וְהַבָּקָר אַל־יִרְעוּ אֶל־מוּל הָהָר הַהוּא׃ ישראל: וַיִּפְסֹל שְׁנֵי־לֻחֹת אֲבָנִים כָּרִאשֹׁנִים וַיַּשְׁכֵּם מֹשֶׁה בַבֹּקֶר וַיַּעַל אֶל־הַר סִינַי כַּאֲשֶׁר צִוָּה יהוה אֹתוֹ וַיִּקַּח בְּיָדוֹ שְׁנֵי לֻחֹת אֲבָנִים׃ וַיֵּרֶד יהוה בֶּעָנָן וַיִּתְיַצֵּב עִמּוֹ שָׁם וַיִּקְרָא בְשֵׁם יהוה׃ וַיַּעֲבֹר יהוה ׀ עַל־פָּנָיו וַיִּקְרָא • יהוה ׀ יהוה אֵל רַחוּם וְחַנּוּן אֶרֶךְ אַפַּיִם וְרַב־חֶסֶד וֶאֱמֶת׃ נֹצֵר חֶסֶד לָאֲלָפִים נֹשֵׂא עָוֺן וָפֶשַׁע וְחַטָּאָה וְנַקֵּה • לֹא יְנַקֶּה פֹּקֵד ׀ עֲוֺן אָבוֹת עַל־בָּנִים וְעַל־בְּנֵי בָנִים עַל־שִׁלֵּשִׁים וְעַל־רִבֵּעִים׃ וַיְמַהֵר מֹשֶׁה וַיִּקֹּד אַרְצָה וַיִּשְׁתָּחוּ׃ וַיֹּאמֶר אִם־נָא מָצָאתִי חֵן בְּעֵינֶיךָ אֲדֹנָי יֵלֶךְ־נָא אֲדֹנָי בְּקִרְבֵּנוּ כִּי עַם־קְשֵׁה־עֹרֶף הוּא • וְסָלַחְתָּ לַעֲוֺנֵנוּ וּלְחַטָּאתֵנוּ וּנְחַלְתָּנוּ׃ • וַיֹּאמֶר הִנֵּה אָנֹכִי כֹּרֵת בְּרִית נֶגֶד כָּל־עַמְּךָ אֶעֱשֶׂה נִפְלָאֹת אֲשֶׁר לֹא־נִבְרְאוּ בְכָל־הָאָרֶץ וּבְכָל־הַגּוֹיִם וְרָאָה כָל־הָעָם אֲשֶׁר־אַתָּה בְקִרְבּוֹ אֶת־מַעֲשֵׂה יהוה כִּי־נוֹרָא הוּא אֲשֶׁר אֲנִי עֹשֶׂה עִמָּךְ׃

הפטרה לתענית ציבור

HAFTARA FOR FAST DAYS

ישעיה נה:ו–נו:ח

The blessings for the הפטרה *can be found on page 546.*

דִּרְשׁוּ יהוה בְּהִמָּצְאוֹ קְרָאֻהוּ בִּהְיוֹתוֹ קָרוֹב׃ יַעֲזֹב רָשָׁע דַּרְכּוֹ וְאִישׁ אָוֶן מַחְשְׁבֹתָיו וְיָשֹׁב אֶל־יהוה וִירַחֲמֵהוּ וְאֶל־אֱלֹהֵינוּ כִּי־יַרְבֶּה לִסְלוֹחַ׃ כִּי לֹא מַחְשְׁבוֹתַי מַחְשְׁבוֹתֵיכֶם וְלֹא דַרְכֵיכֶם דְּרָכָי נְאֻם יהוה׃ כִּי־גָבְהוּ שָׁמַיִם מֵאָרֶץ כֵּן גָּבְהוּ דְרָכַי מִדַּרְכֵיכֶם וּמַחְשְׁבֹתַי מִמַּחְשְׁבֹתֵיכֶם׃ כִּי כַּאֲשֶׁר יֵרֵד הַגֶּשֶׁם וְהַשֶּׁלֶג מִן־הַשָּׁמַיִם וְשָׁמָּה לֹא יָשׁוּב כִּי אִם־הִרְוָה אֶת־הָאָרֶץ וְהוֹלִידָהּ וְהִצְמִיחָהּ וְנָתַן זֶרַע לַזֹּרֵעַ וְלֶחֶם לָאֹכֵל׃ כֵּן יִהְיֶה דְבָרִי אֲשֶׁר יֵצֵא מִפִּי לֹא־יָשׁוּב אֵלַי רֵיקָם כִּי אִם־עָשָׂה אֶת־אֲשֶׁר חָפַצְתִּי וְהִצְלִיחַ אֲשֶׁר שְׁלַחְתִּיו׃ כִּי־בְשִׂמְחָה תֵצֵאוּ וּבְשָׁלוֹם תּוּבָלוּן הֶהָרִים וְהַגְּבָעוֹת יִפְצְחוּ לִפְנֵיכֶם רִנָּה וְכָל־עֲצֵי הַשָּׂדֶה יִמְחֲאוּ־כָף׃ תַּחַת הַנַּעֲצוּץ יַעֲלֶה בְרוֹשׁ תחת [וְתַחַת] הַסִּרְפַּד יַעֲלֶה הֲדַס וְהָיָה לַיהוה לְשֵׁם לְאוֹת עוֹלָם לֹא יִכָּרֵת׃ כֹּה אָמַר יהוה שִׁמְרוּ מִשְׁפָּט וַעֲשׂוּ צְדָקָה כִּי־קְרוֹבָה יְשׁוּעָתִי לָבוֹא וְצִדְקָתִי לְהִגָּלוֹת׃ אַשְׁרֵי אֱנוֹשׁ יַעֲשֶׂה־זֹּאת וּבֶן־אָדָם יַחֲזִיק בָּהּ שֹׁמֵר שַׁבָּת מֵחַלְּלוֹ וְשֹׁמֵר יָדוֹ מֵעֲשׂוֹת כָּל־רָע׃ וְאַל־יֹאמַר בֶּן־הַנֵּכָר הַנִּלְוָה אֶל־יהוה לֵאמֹר הַבְדֵּל יַבְדִּילַנִי יהוה מֵעַל עַמּוֹ וְאַל־יֹאמַר הַסָּרִיס הֵן אֲנִי עֵץ יָבֵשׁ׃ כִּי־כֹה ׀ אָמַר יהוה לַסָּרִיסִים אֲשֶׁר יִשְׁמְרוּ אֶת־שַׁבְּתוֹתַי וּבָחֲרוּ בַּאֲשֶׁר חָפָצְתִּי וּמַחֲזִיקִים בִּבְרִיתִי׃ וְנָתַתִּי לָהֶם בְּבֵיתִי וּבְחוֹמֹתַי יָד וָשֵׁם טוֹב מִבָּנִים וּמִבָּנוֹת שֵׁם עוֹלָם אֶתֶּן־לוֹ אֲשֶׁר לֹא יִכָּרֵת׃ וּבְנֵי הַנֵּכָר הַנִּלְוִים עַל־יהוה לְשָׁרְתוֹ וּלְאַהֲבָה אֶת־שֵׁם יהוה לִהְיוֹת לוֹ לַעֲבָדִים כָּל־שֹׁמֵר שַׁבָּת מֵחַלְּלוֹ וּמַחֲזִיקִים בִּבְרִיתִי׃ וַהֲבִיאוֹתִים אֶל־הַר קָדְשִׁי וְשִׂמַּחְתִּים בְּבֵית תְּפִלָּתִי עוֹלֹתֵיהֶם וְזִבְחֵיהֶם לְרָצוֹן עַל־מִזְבְּחִי כִּי בֵיתִי בֵּית־תְּפִלָּה יִקָּרֵא לְכָל־הָעַמִּים׃ נְאֻם אֲדֹנָי יֱהֹוִה מְקַבֵּץ נִדְחֵי יִשְׂרָאֵל עוֹד אֲקַבֵּץ עָלָיו לְנִקְבָּצָיו׃

קריאה לתשעה באב

READING FOR TISHA B'AV

דברים ד:כה–מ

The following is read during שחרית *of* תשעה באב. *The person called up for* שלישי *also reads the* הפטרה. *At* מנחה, *the* קריאת התורה *and* הפטרה *are those for regular Fast Days.*

כִּי־תוֹלִיד בָּנִים וּבְנֵי בָנִים וְנוֹשַׁנְתֶּם בָּאָרֶץ וְהִשְׁחַתֶּם וַעֲשִׂיתֶם פֶּסֶל תְּמוּנַת כֹּל וַעֲשִׂיתֶם הָרַע בְּעֵינֵי־יהוה אֱלֹהֶיךָ לְהַכְעִיסוֹ׃ הַעִידֹתִי

בָּכֶם הַיּוֹם אֶת־הַשָּׁמַיִם וְאֶת־הָאָרֶץ כִּי־אָבֹד תֹּאבֵדוּן מַהֵר מֵעַל הָאָרֶץ אֲשֶׁר אַתֶּם עֹבְרִים אֶת־הַיַּרְדֵּן שָׁמָּה לְרִשְׁתָּהּ לֹא־תַאֲרִיכֻן יָמִים עָלֶיהָ כִּי הִשָּׁמֵד תִּשָּׁמֵדוּן׃ וְהֵפִיץ יְהוָה אֶתְכֶם בָּעַמִּים וְנִשְׁאַרְתֶּם מְתֵי מִסְפָּר בַּגּוֹיִם אֲשֶׁר יְנַהֵג יְהוָה אֶתְכֶם שָׁמָּה׃ וַעֲבַדְתֶּם־שָׁם אֱלֹהִים מַעֲשֵׂה יְדֵי אָדָם עֵץ וָאֶבֶן אֲשֶׁר לֹא־יִרְאוּן וְלֹא יִשְׁמְעוּן וְלֹא יֹאכְלוּן וְלֹא יְרִיחֻן׃ וּבִקַּשְׁתֶּם מִשָּׁם אֶת־יְהוָה אֱלֹהֶיךָ וּמָצָאתָ כִּי תִדְרְשֶׁנּוּ בְּכָל־לְבָבְךָ וּבְכָל־נַפְשֶׁךָ׃ לוי בַּצַּר לְךָ וּמְצָאוּךָ כֹּל הַדְּבָרִים הָאֵלֶּה בְּאַחֲרִית הַיָּמִים וְשַׁבְתָּ עַד־יְהוָה אֱלֹהֶיךָ וְשָׁמַעְתָּ בְּקֹלוֹ׃ כִּי אֵל רַחוּם יְהוָה אֱלֹהֶיךָ לֹא יַרְפְּךָ וְלֹא יַשְׁחִיתֶךָ וְלֹא יִשְׁכַּח אֶת־בְּרִית אֲבֹתֶיךָ אֲשֶׁר נִשְׁבַּע לָהֶם׃ כִּי שְׁאַל־נָא לְיָמִים רִאשֹׁנִים אֲשֶׁר־הָיוּ לְפָנֶיךָ לְמִן־הַיּוֹם אֲשֶׁר בָּרָא אֱלֹהִים ׀ אָדָם עַל־הָאָרֶץ וּלְמִקְצֵה הַשָּׁמַיִם וְעַד־קְצֵה הַשָּׁמָיִם הֲנִהְיָה כַּדָּבָר הַגָּדוֹל הַזֶּה אוֹ הֲנִשְׁמַע כָּמֹהוּ׃ הֲשָׁמַע עָם קוֹל אֱלֹהִים מְדַבֵּר מִתּוֹךְ־הָאֵשׁ כַּאֲשֶׁר־שָׁמַעְתָּ אַתָּה וַיֶּחִי׃ אוֹ ׀ הֲנִסָּה אֱלֹהִים לָבוֹא לָקַחַת לוֹ גוֹי מִקֶּרֶב גּוֹי בְּמַסֹּת בְּאֹתֹת וּבְמוֹפְתִים וּבְמִלְחָמָה וּבְיָד חֲזָקָה וּבִזְרוֹעַ נְטוּיָה וּבְמוֹרָאִים גְּדֹלִים כְּכֹל אֲשֶׁר־עָשָׂה לָכֶם יְהוָה אֱלֹהֵיכֶם בְּמִצְרַיִם לְעֵינֶיךָ׃ אַתָּה הָרְאֵתָ לָדַעַת כִּי יְהוָה הוּא הָאֱלֹהִים אֵין עוֹד מִלְּבַדּוֹ׃ ישראל מִן־הַשָּׁמַיִם הִשְׁמִיעֲךָ אֶת־קֹלוֹ לְיַסְּרֶךָּ וְעַל־הָאָרֶץ הֶרְאֲךָ אֶת־אִשּׁוֹ הַגְּדוֹלָה וּדְבָרָיו שָׁמַעְתָּ מִתּוֹךְ הָאֵשׁ׃ וְתַחַת כִּי אָהַב אֶת־אֲבֹתֶיךָ וַיִּבְחַר בְּזַרְעוֹ אַחֲרָיו וַיּוֹצִאֲךָ בְּפָנָיו בְּכֹחוֹ הַגָּדֹל מִמִּצְרָיִם׃ לְהוֹרִישׁ גּוֹיִם גְּדֹלִים וַעֲצֻמִים מִמְּךָ מִפָּנֶיךָ לַהֲבִיאֲךָ לָתֶת־לְךָ אֶת־אַרְצָם נַחֲלָה כַּיּוֹם הַזֶּה׃ וְיָדַעְתָּ הַיּוֹם וַהֲשֵׁבֹתָ אֶל־לְבָבֶךָ כִּי יְהוָה הוּא הָאֱלֹהִים בַּשָּׁמַיִם מִמַּעַל וְעַל־הָאָרֶץ מִתָּחַת אֵין עוֹד׃ וְשָׁמַרְתָּ אֶת־חֻקָּיו וְאֶת־מִצְוֹתָיו אֲשֶׁר אָנֹכִי מְצַוְּךָ הַיּוֹם אֲשֶׁר יִיטַב לְךָ וּלְבָנֶיךָ אַחֲרֶיךָ וּלְמַעַן תַּאֲרִיךְ יָמִים עַל־הָאֲדָמָה אֲשֶׁר יְהוָה אֱלֹהֶיךָ נֹתֵן לְךָ כָּל־הַיָּמִים׃

הפטרה לתשעה באב

HAFTARA FOR TISHA B'AV

ירמיהו ח:יג–ט:כג

אָסֹף אֲסִיפֵם נְאֻם־יְהוָה אֵין עֲנָבִים בַּגֶּפֶן וְאֵין תְּאֵנִים בַּתְּאֵנָה וְהֶעָלֶה נָבֵל וָאֶתֵּן לָהֶם יַעַבְרוּם׃ עַל־מָה אֲנַחְנוּ יֹשְׁבִים הֵאָסְפוּ וְנָבוֹא אֶל־עָרֵי הַמִּבְצָר וְנִדְּמָה־שָּׁם כִּי יְהוָה אֱלֹהֵינוּ הֲדִמָּנוּ וַיַּשְׁקֵנוּ מֵי־רֹאשׁ כִּי חָטָאנוּ לַיהוָה׃ קַוֵּה לְשָׁלוֹם וְאֵין טוֹב לְעֵת מַרְפֵּה וְהִנֵּה בְעָתָה׃ מִדָּן נִשְׁמַע נַחְרַת סוּסָיו מִקּוֹל מִצְהֲלוֹת אַבִּירָיו רָעֲשָׁה כָּל־הָאָרֶץ וַיָּבוֹאוּ וַיֹּאכְלוּ אֶרֶץ וּמְלוֹאָהּ עִיר וְיֹשְׁבֵי בָהּ׃ כִּי הִנְנִי מְשַׁלֵּחַ בָּכֶם נְחָשִׁים צִפְעֹנִים אֲשֶׁר אֵין־לָהֶם לָחַשׁ וְנִשְּׁכוּ אֶתְכֶם נְאֻם־יְהוָה׃ מַבְלִיגִיתִי עֲלֵי יָגוֹן עָלַי לִבִּי דַוָּי׃ הִנֵּה־קוֹל שַׁוְעַת בַּת־עַמִּי מֵאֶרֶץ מַרְחַקִּים הַיהוָה אֵין בְּצִיּוֹן אִם־מַלְכָּהּ אֵין בָּהּ מַדּוּעַ הִכְעִסוּנִי בִּפְסִלֵיהֶם בְּהַבְלֵי נֵכָר׃ עָבַר קָצִיר כָּלָה קָיִץ וַאֲנַחְנוּ לוֹא נוֹשָׁעְנוּ׃ עַל־שֶׁבֶר בַּת־עַמִּי הָשְׁבָּרְתִּי קָדַרְתִּי שַׁמָּה הֶחֱזִקָתְנִי׃ הַצֳרִי אֵין בְּגִלְעָד אִם־רֹפֵא אֵין שָׁם כִּי מַדּוּעַ לֹא עָלְתָה אֲרֻכַת בַּת־עַמִּי׃ מִי־יִתֵּן רֹאשִׁי מַיִם וְעֵינִי מְקוֹר דִּמְעָה וְאֶבְכֶּה יוֹמָם וָלַיְלָה אֵת חַלְלֵי בַת־עַמִּי׃ מִי־יִתְּנֵנִי בַמִּדְבָּר מְלוֹן אֹרְחִים וְאֶעֶזְבָה אֶת־עַמִּי וְאֵלְכָה מֵאִתָּם כִּי כֻלָּם מְנָאֲפִים עֲצֶרֶת בֹּגְדִים׃ וַיַּדְרְכוּ אֶת־לְשׁוֹנָם קַשְׁתָּם שֶׁקֶר וְלֹא לֶאֱמוּנָה גָּבְרוּ בָאָרֶץ כִּי מֵרָעָה אֶל־רָעָה ׀ יָצָאוּ וְאֹתִי לֹא־יָדָעוּ נְאֻם־יְהוָה׃ אִישׁ מֵרֵעֵהוּ הִשָּׁמֵרוּ וְעַל־כָּל־אָח אַל־תִּבְטָחוּ כִּי כָל־אָח עָקוֹב יַעְקֹב וְכָל־רֵעַ רָכִיל יַהֲלֹךְ׃ וְאִישׁ בְּרֵעֵהוּ יְהָתֵלּוּ וֶאֱמֶת לֹא יְדַבֵּרוּ לִמְּדוּ לְשׁוֹנָם דַּבֶּר־שֶׁקֶר הַעֲוֵה נִלְאוּ׃ שִׁבְתְּךָ בְּתוֹךְ מִרְמָה בְּמִרְמָה מֵאֲנוּ דַעַת־אוֹתִי נְאֻם־יְהוָה׃ לָכֵן

כֹּה אָמַר יְהוָה צְבָאוֹת הִנְנִי צוֹרְפָם
וּבְחַנְתִּים כִּי־אֵיךְ אֶעֱשֶׂה מִפְּנֵי בַּת־עַמִּי:
חֵץ שׁוֹחֵט [שָׁחוּט] לְשׁוֹנָם מִרְמָה דִבֵּר בְּפִיו
שָׁלוֹם אֶת־רֵעֵהוּ יְדַבֵּר וּבְקִרְבּוֹ יָשִׂים אָרְבּוֹ:
הַעַל־אֵלֶּה לֹא־אֶפְקָד־בָּם נְאֻם־יְהוָה אִם
בְּגוֹי אֲשֶׁר־כָּזֶה לֹא תִתְנַקֵּם נַפְשִׁי: עַל־
הֶהָרִים אֶשָּׂא בְכִי וָנֶהִי וְעַל־נְאוֹת מִדְבָּר
קִינָה כִּי נִצְּתוּ מִבְּלִי־אִישׁ עֹבֵר וְלֹא שָׁמְעוּ
קוֹל מִקְנֶה מֵעוֹף הַשָּׁמַיִם וְעַד־בְּהֵמָה נָדְדוּ
הָלָכוּ: וְנָתַתִּי אֶת־יְרוּשָׁלִַם לְגַלִּים מְעוֹן
תַּנִּים וְאֶת־עָרֵי יְהוּדָה אֶתֵּן שְׁמָמָה מִבְּלִי
יוֹשֵׁב: מִי־הָאִישׁ הֶחָכָם וְיָבֵן אֶת־זֹאת
וַאֲשֶׁר דִּבֶּר פִּי־יְהוָה אֵלָיו וְיַגִּדָהּ עַל־מָה
אָבְדָה הָאָרֶץ נִצְּתָה כַמִּדְבָּר מִבְּלִי עֹבֵר:
וַיֹּאמֶר יְהוָה עַל־עָזְבָם אֶת־תּוֹרָתִי אֲשֶׁר
נָתַתִּי לִפְנֵיהֶם וְלֹא־שָׁמְעוּ בְקוֹלִי וְלֹא־
הָלְכוּ בָהּ: וַיֵּלְכוּ אַחֲרֵי שְׁרִרוּת לִבָּם וְאַחֲרֵי
הַבְּעָלִים אֲשֶׁר לִמְּדוּם אֲבוֹתָם: לָכֵן כֹּה־
אָמַר יְהוָה צְבָאוֹת אֱלֹהֵי יִשְׂרָאֵל הִנְנִי
מַאֲכִילָם אֶת־הָעָם הַזֶּה לַעֲנָה וְהִשְׁקִיתִים
מֵי־רֹאשׁ: וַהֲפִצוֹתִים בַּגּוֹיִם אֲשֶׁר לֹא יָדְעוּ
הֵמָּה וַאֲבוֹתָם וְשִׁלַּחְתִּי אַחֲרֵיהֶם אֶת־הַחֶרֶב
עַד כַּלּוֹתִי אוֹתָם: כֹּה אָמַר יְהוָה צְבָאוֹת
הִתְבּוֹנְנוּ וְקִרְאוּ לַמְקוֹנְנוֹת וּתְבוֹאֶינָה וְאֶל־
הַחֲכָמוֹת שִׁלְחוּ וְתָבוֹאנָה: וּתְמַהֵרְנָה וְתִשֶּׂנָה
עָלֵינוּ נֶהִי וְתֵרַדְנָה עֵינֵינוּ דִּמְעָה וְעַפְעַפֵּינוּ
יִזְּלוּ־מָיִם: כִּי קוֹל נְהִי נִשְׁמַע מִצִּיּוֹן אֵיךְ
שֻׁדָּדְנוּ בֹּשְׁנוּ מְאֹד כִּי־עָזַבְנוּ אָרֶץ כִּי הִשְׁלִיכוּ
מִשְׁכְּנוֹתֵינוּ: כִּי־שְׁמַעְנָה נָשִׁים דְּבַר־יְהוָה
וְתִקַּח אָזְנְכֶם דְּבַר־פִּיו וְלַמֵּדְנָה בְנוֹתֵיכֶם
נֶהִי וְאִשָּׁה רְעוּתָהּ קִינָה: כִּי־עָלָה מָוֶת
בְּחַלּוֹנֵינוּ בָּא בְּאַרְמְנוֹתֵינוּ לְהַכְרִית עוֹלָל
מִחוּץ בַּחוּרִים מֵרְחֹבוֹת: דַּבֵּר כֹּה נְאֻם־יְהוָה
וְנָפְלָה נִבְלַת הָאָדָם כְּדֹמֶן עַל־פְּנֵי הַשָּׂדֶה
וּכְעָמִיר מֵאַחֲרֵי הַקֹּצֵר וְאֵין מְאַסֵּף: כֹּה ׀
אָמַר יְהוָה אַל־יִתְהַלֵּל חָכָם בְּחָכְמָתוֹ וְאַל־
יִתְהַלֵּל הַגִּבּוֹר בִּגְבוּרָתוֹ אַל־יִתְהַלֵּל עָשִׁיר
בְּעָשְׁרוֹ: כִּי אִם־בְּזֹאת יִתְהַלֵּל הַמִּתְהַלֵּל
הַשְׂכֵּל וְיָדֹעַ אוֹתִי כִּי אֲנִי יְהוָה עֹשֶׂה חֶסֶד
מִשְׁפָּט וּצְדָקָה בָּאָרֶץ כִּי־בְאֵלֶּה חָפַצְתִּי
נְאֻם־יְהוָה:

קריאה ליום הראשון של חנוכה
FIRST DAY OF ḤANUKKA

במדבר ז: א–יז

וַיְהִי בְּיוֹם כַּלּוֹת מֹשֶׁה לְהָקִים אֶת־הַמִּשְׁכָּן
וַיִּמְשַׁח אֹתוֹ וַיְקַדֵּשׁ אֹתוֹ וְאֶת־כָּל־כֵּלָיו
וְאֶת־הַמִּזְבֵּחַ וְאֶת־כָּל־כֵּלָיו וַיִּמְשָׁחֵם וַיְקַדֵּשׁ
אֹתָם: וַיַּקְרִיבוּ נְשִׂיאֵי יִשְׂרָאֵל רָאשֵׁי בֵּית
אֲבֹתָם הֵם נְשִׂיאֵי הַמַּטֹּת הֵם הָעֹמְדִים עַל־
הַפְּקֻדִים: וַיָּבִיאוּ אֶת־קָרְבָּנָם לִפְנֵי יְהוָה
שֵׁשׁ־עֶגְלֹת צָב וּשְׁנֵי־עָשָׂר בָּקָר עֲגָלָה עַל־
שְׁנֵי הַנְּשִׂאִים וְשׁוֹר לְאֶחָד וַיַּקְרִיבוּ אוֹתָם
לִפְנֵי הַמִּשְׁכָּן: וַיֹּאמֶר יְהוָה אֶל־מֹשֶׁה לֵּאמֹר:
קַח מֵאִתָּם וְהָיוּ לַעֲבֹד אֶת־עֲבֹדַת אֹהֶל
מוֹעֵד וְנָתַתָּה אוֹתָם אֶל־הַלְוִיִּם אִישׁ כְּפִי
עֲבֹדָתוֹ: וַיִּקַּח מֹשֶׁה אֶת־הָעֲגָלֹת וְאֶת־הַבָּקָר
וַיִּתֵּן אוֹתָם אֶל־הַלְוִיִּם: אֵת ׀ שְׁתֵּי הָעֲגָלוֹת
וְאֵת אַרְבַּעַת הַבָּקָר נָתַן לִבְנֵי גֵרְשׁוֹן כְּפִי
עֲבֹדָתָם: וְאֵת ׀ אַרְבַּע הָעֲגָלֹת וְאֵת שְׁמֹנַת
הַבָּקָר נָתַן לִבְנֵי מְרָרִי כְּפִי עֲבֹדָתָם בְּיַד
אִיתָמָר בֶּן־אַהֲרֹן הַכֹּהֵן: וְלִבְנֵי קְהָת לֹא
נָתָן כִּי־עֲבֹדַת הַקֹּדֶשׁ עֲלֵהֶם בַּכָּתֵף יִשָּׂאוּ:
וַיַּקְרִיבוּ הַנְּשִׂאִים אֵת חֲנֻכַּת הַמִּזְבֵּחַ בְּיוֹם
הִמָּשַׁח אֹתוֹ וַיַּקְרִיבוּ הַנְּשִׂיאִם אֶת־קָרְבָּנָם
לִפְנֵי הַמִּזְבֵּחַ: וַיֹּאמֶר יְהוָה אֶל־מֹשֶׁה נָשִׂיא
אֶחָד לַיּוֹם נָשִׂיא אֶחָד לַיּוֹם יַקְרִיבוּ אֶת־
קָרְבָּנָם לַחֲנֻכַּת הַמִּזְבֵּחַ: לוי: וַיְהִי הַמַּקְרִיב
בַּיּוֹם הָרִאשׁוֹן אֶת־קָרְבָּנוֹ נַחְשׁוֹן בֶּן־עַמִּינָדָב
לְמַטֵּה יְהוּדָה: וְקָרְבָּנוֹ קַעֲרַת־כֶּסֶף אַחַת
שְׁלֹשִׁים וּמֵאָה מִשְׁקָלָהּ מִזְרָק אֶחָד כֶּסֶף
שִׁבְעִים שֶׁקֶל בְּשֶׁקֶל הַקֹּדֶשׁ שְׁנֵיהֶם ׀ מְלֵאִים
סֹלֶת בְּלוּלָה בַשֶּׁמֶן לְמִנְחָה: כַּף אַחַת עֲשָׂרָה

זָהָב מְלֵאָה קְטֹרֶת: ישראל: פַּר אֶחָד בֶּן־בָּקָר אַיִל אֶחָד כֶּבֶשׂ־אֶחָד בֶּן־שְׁנָתוֹ לְעֹלָה: שְׂעִיר־עִזִּים אֶחָד לְחַטָּאת: וּלְזֶבַח הַשְּׁלָמִים בָּקָר שְׁנַיִם אֵילִם חֲמִשָּׁה עַתּוּדִים חֲמִשָּׁה כְּבָשִׂים בְּנֵי־שָׁנָה חֲמִשָּׁה זֶה קָרְבַּן נַחְשׁוֹן בֶּן־עַמִּינָדָב:

קריאה ליום השני של חנוכה

SECOND DAY OF ḤANUKKA

במדבר ז: יח-כט

בַּיּוֹם הַשֵּׁנִי הִקְרִיב נְתַנְאֵל בֶּן־צוּעָר נְשִׂיא יִשָּׂשכָר: הִקְרִב אֶת־קָרְבָּנוֹ קַעֲרַת־כֶּסֶף אַחַת שְׁלֹשִׁים וּמֵאָה מִשְׁקָלָהּ מִזְרָק אֶחָד כֶּסֶף שִׁבְעִים שֶׁקֶל בְּשֶׁקֶל הַקֹּדֶשׁ שְׁנֵיהֶם ׀ מְלֵאִים סֹלֶת בְּלוּלָה בַשֶּׁמֶן לְמִנְחָה: כַּף אַחַת עֲשָׂרָה זָהָב מְלֵאָה קְטֹרֶת: לוי: פַּר אֶחָד בֶּן־בָּקָר אַיִל אֶחָד כֶּבֶשׂ־אֶחָד בֶּן־שְׁנָתוֹ לְעֹלָה: שְׂעִיר־עִזִּים אֶחָד לְחַטָּאת: וּלְזֶבַח הַשְּׁלָמִים בָּקָר שְׁנַיִם אֵילִם חֲמִשָּׁה עַתֻּדִים חֲמִשָּׁה כְּבָשִׂים בְּנֵי־שָׁנָה חֲמִשָּׁה זֶה קָרְבַּן נְתַנְאֵל בֶּן־צוּעָר:

ישראל: בַּיּוֹם הַשְּׁלִישִׁי נָשִׂיא לִבְנֵי זְבוּלֻן אֱלִיאָב בֶּן־חֵלֹן: קָרְבָּנוֹ קַעֲרַת־כֶּסֶף אַחַת שְׁלֹשִׁים וּמֵאָה מִשְׁקָלָהּ מִזְרָק אֶחָד כֶּסֶף שִׁבְעִים שֶׁקֶל בְּשֶׁקֶל הַקֹּדֶשׁ שְׁנֵיהֶם ׀ מְלֵאִים סֹלֶת בְּלוּלָה בַשֶּׁמֶן לְמִנְחָה: כַּף אַחַת עֲשָׂרָה זָהָב מְלֵאָה קְטֹרֶת: פַּר אֶחָד בֶּן־בָּקָר אַיִל אֶחָד כֶּבֶשׂ־אֶחָד בֶּן־שְׁנָתוֹ לְעֹלָה: שְׂעִיר־עִזִּים אֶחָד לְחַטָּאת: וּלְזֶבַח הַשְּׁלָמִים בָּקָר שְׁנַיִם אֵילִם חֲמִשָּׁה עַתֻּדִים חֲמִשָּׁה כְּבָשִׂים בְּנֵי־שָׁנָה חֲמִשָּׁה זֶה קָרְבַּן אֱלִיאָב בֶּן־חֵלֹן:

קריאה ליום השלישי של חנוכה

THIRD DAY OF ḤANUKKA

במדבר ז: כד-לה

בַּיּוֹם הַשְּׁלִישִׁי נָשִׂיא לִבְנֵי זְבוּלֻן אֱלִיאָב בֶּן־חֵלֹן: קָרְבָּנוֹ קַעֲרַת־כֶּסֶף אַחַת שְׁלֹשִׁים וּמֵאָה מִשְׁקָלָהּ מִזְרָק אֶחָד כֶּסֶף שִׁבְעִים שֶׁקֶל בְּשֶׁקֶל הַקֹּדֶשׁ שְׁנֵיהֶם ׀ מְלֵאִים סֹלֶת בְּלוּלָה בַשֶּׁמֶן לְמִנְחָה: כַּף אַחַת עֲשָׂרָה זָהָב מְלֵאָה קְטֹרֶת: לוי: פַּר אֶחָד בֶּן־בָּקָר אַיִל אֶחָד כֶּבֶשׂ־אֶחָד בֶּן־שְׁנָתוֹ לְעֹלָה: שְׂעִיר־עִזִּים אֶחָד לְחַטָּאת: וּלְזֶבַח הַשְּׁלָמִים בָּקָר שְׁנַיִם אֵילִם חֲמִשָּׁה עַתֻּדִים חֲמִשָּׁה כְּבָשִׂים בְּנֵי־שָׁנָה חֲמִשָּׁה זֶה קָרְבַּן אֱלִיאָב בֶּן־חֵלֹן:

ישראל: בַּיּוֹם הָרְבִיעִי נָשִׂיא לִבְנֵי רְאוּבֵן אֱלִיצוּר בֶּן־שְׁדֵיאוּר: קָרְבָּנוֹ קַעֲרַת־כֶּסֶף אַחַת שְׁלֹשִׁים וּמֵאָה מִשְׁקָלָהּ מִזְרָק אֶחָד כֶּסֶף שִׁבְעִים שֶׁקֶל בְּשֶׁקֶל הַקֹּדֶשׁ שְׁנֵיהֶם ׀ מְלֵאִים סֹלֶת בְּלוּלָה בַשֶּׁמֶן לְמִנְחָה: כַּף אַחַת עֲשָׂרָה זָהָב מְלֵאָה קְטֹרֶת: פַּר אֶחָד בֶּן־בָּקָר אַיִל אֶחָד כֶּבֶשׂ־אֶחָד בֶּן־שְׁנָתוֹ לְעֹלָה: שְׂעִיר־עִזִּים אֶחָד לְחַטָּאת: וּלְזֶבַח הַשְּׁלָמִים בָּקָר שְׁנַיִם אֵילִם חֲמִשָּׁה עַתֻּדִים חֲמִשָּׁה כְּבָשִׂים בְּנֵי־שָׁנָה חֲמִשָּׁה זֶה קָרְבַּן אֱלִיצוּר בֶּן־שְׁדֵיאוּר:

קריאה ליום הרביעי של חנוכה

FOURTH DAY OF ḤANUKKA

במדבר ז: ל-מא

בַּיּוֹם הָרְבִיעִי נָשִׂיא לִבְנֵי רְאוּבֵן אֱלִיצוּר בֶּן־שְׁדֵיאוּר: קָרְבָּנוֹ קַעֲרַת־כֶּסֶף אַחַת שְׁלֹשִׁים וּמֵאָה מִשְׁקָלָהּ מִזְרָק אֶחָד כֶּסֶף שִׁבְעִים שֶׁקֶל בְּשֶׁקֶל הַקֹּדֶשׁ שְׁנֵיהֶם ׀ מְלֵאִים סֹלֶת בְּלוּלָה בַשֶּׁמֶן לְמִנְחָה: כַּף אַחַת עֲשָׂרָה זָהָב מְלֵאָה קְטֹרֶת: לוי: פַּר אֶחָד בֶּן־בָּקָר אַיִל אֶחָד כֶּבֶשׂ־אֶחָד בֶּן־שְׁנָתוֹ לְעֹלָה: שְׂעִיר־עִזִּים אֶחָד לְחַטָּאת: וּלְזֶבַח הַשְּׁלָמִים בָּקָר שְׁנַיִם אֵילִם חֲמִשָּׁה עַתֻּדִים חֲמִשָּׁה כְּבָשִׂים בְּנֵי־שָׁנָה חֲמִשָּׁה זֶה קָרְבַּן אֱלִיצוּר בֶּן־שְׁדֵיאוּר:

ישראל: בַּיּוֹם הַחֲמִישִׁי נָשִׂיא לִבְנֵי שִׁמְעוֹן

שְׁלֻמִיאֵל בֶּן־צוּרִישַׁדָּי: קָרְבָּנוֹ קַעֲרַת־כֶּסֶף
אַחַת שְׁלֹשִׁים וּמֵאָה מִשְׁקָלָהּ מִזְרָק אֶחָד
כֶּסֶף שִׁבְעִים שֶׁקֶל בְּשֶׁקֶל הַקֹּדֶשׁ שְׁנֵיהֶם ׀
מְלֵאִים סֹלֶת בְּלוּלָה בַשֶּׁמֶן לְמִנְחָה: כַּף
אַחַת עֲשָׂרָה זָהָב מְלֵאָה קְטֹרֶת: פַּר אֶחָד
בֶּן־בָּקָר אַיִל אֶחָד כֶּבֶשׂ־אֶחָד בֶּן־שְׁנָתוֹ
לְעֹלָה: שְׂעִיר־עִזִּים אֶחָד לְחַטָּאת: וּלְזֶבַח
הַשְּׁלָמִים בָּקָר שְׁנַיִם אֵילִם חֲמִשָּׁה עַתֻּדִים
חֲמִשָּׁה כְּבָשִׂים בְּנֵי־שָׁנָה חֲמִשָּׁה זֶה קָרְבַּן
שְׁלֻמִיאֵל בֶּן־צוּרִישַׁדָּי:

קריאה ליום החמישי של חנוכה
FIFTH DAY OF ḤANUKKA

במדבר ז:לו–מז

בַּיּוֹם הַחֲמִישִׁי נָשִׂיא לִבְנֵי שִׁמְעוֹן שְׁלֻמִיאֵל
בֶּן־צוּרִישַׁדָּי: קָרְבָּנוֹ קַעֲרַת־כֶּסֶף אַחַת
שְׁלֹשִׁים וּמֵאָה מִשְׁקָלָהּ מִזְרָק אֶחָד כֶּסֶף
שִׁבְעִים שֶׁקֶל בְּשֶׁקֶל הַקֹּדֶשׁ שְׁנֵיהֶם ׀ מְלֵאִים
סֹלֶת בְּלוּלָה בַשֶּׁמֶן לְמִנְחָה: כַּף אַחַת עֲשָׂרָה
זָהָב מְלֵאָה קְטֹרֶת: לוי: פַּר אֶחָד בֶּן־בָּקָר
אַיִל אֶחָד כֶּבֶשׂ־אֶחָד בֶּן־שְׁנָתוֹ לְעֹלָה:
שְׂעִיר־עִזִּים אֶחָד לְחַטָּאת: וּלְזֶבַח הַשְּׁלָמִים
בָּקָר שְׁנַיִם אֵילִם חֲמִשָּׁה עַתֻּדִים חֲמִשָּׁה
כְּבָשִׂים בְּנֵי־שָׁנָה חֲמִשָּׁה זֶה קָרְבַּן שְׁלֻמִיאֵל
בֶּן־צוּרִישַׁדָּי:

ישראל: בַּיּוֹם הַשִּׁשִּׁי נָשִׂיא לִבְנֵי גָד אֶלְיָסָף
בֶּן־דְּעוּאֵל: קָרְבָּנוֹ קַעֲרַת־כֶּסֶף אַחַת
שְׁלֹשִׁים וּמֵאָה מִשְׁקָלָהּ מִזְרָק אֶחָד כֶּסֶף
שִׁבְעִים שֶׁקֶל בְּשֶׁקֶל הַקֹּדֶשׁ שְׁנֵיהֶם ׀ מְלֵאִים
סֹלֶת בְּלוּלָה בַשֶּׁמֶן לְמִנְחָה: כַּף אַחַת עֲשָׂרָה
זָהָב מְלֵאָה קְטֹרֶת: פַּר אֶחָד בֶּן־בָּקָר אַיִל
אֶחָד כֶּבֶשׂ־אֶחָד בֶּן־שְׁנָתוֹ לְעֹלָה: שְׂעִיר־
עִזִּים אֶחָד לְחַטָּאת: וּלְזֶבַח הַשְּׁלָמִים בָּקָר
שְׁנַיִם אֵילִם חֲמִשָּׁה עַתֻּדִים חֲמִשָּׁה כְּבָשִׂים
בְּנֵי־שָׁנָה חֲמִשָּׁה זֶה קָרְבַּן אֶלְיָסָף בֶּן־
דְּעוּאֵל:

קריאה ליום השישי של חנוכה וראש חודש
SIXTH DAY OF ḤANUKKA AND ROSH ḤODESH

במדבר ז:מב–מז

The sixth day is ראש חודש טבת*. Two* ספרי תורה *are taken out of the* ארון קודש*. From the first, read the* קריאת התורה *for* ראש חודש *(page 1133); from the second, read* בַּיּוֹם הַשִּׁשִּׁי*:*

(page 1133)

בַּיּוֹם הַשִּׁשִּׁי נָשִׂיא לִבְנֵי גָד אֶלְיָסָף בֶּן־
דְּעוּאֵל: קָרְבָּנוֹ קַעֲרַת־כֶּסֶף אַחַת שְׁלֹשִׁים
וּמֵאָה מִשְׁקָלָהּ מִזְרָק אֶחָד כֶּסֶף שִׁבְעִים
שֶׁקֶל בְּשֶׁקֶל הַקֹּדֶשׁ שְׁנֵיהֶם ׀ מְלֵאִים סֹלֶת
בְּלוּלָה בַשֶּׁמֶן לְמִנְחָה: כַּף אַחַת עֲשָׂרָה זָהָב
מְלֵאָה קְטֹרֶת: פַּר אֶחָד בֶּן־בָּקָר אַיִל אֶחָד
כֶּבֶשׂ־אֶחָד בֶּן־שְׁנָתוֹ לְעֹלָה: שְׂעִיר־עִזִּים
אֶחָד לְחַטָּאת: וּלְזֶבַח הַשְּׁלָמִים בָּקָר שְׁנַיִם
אֵילִם חֲמִשָּׁה עַתֻּדִים חֲמִשָּׁה כְּבָשִׂים בְּנֵי־
שָׁנָה חֲמִשָּׁה זֶה קָרְבַּן אֶלְיָסָף בֶּן־דְּעוּאֵל:

קריאה ליום השביעי של חנוכה וראש חודש
SEVENTH DAY OF ḤANUKKA AND ROSH ḤODESH

במדבר ז:מח–נג

If the seventh day is also ראש חודש*, then two* ספרי תורה *are taken out of the* ארון קודש*. From the first, read the* קריאת התורה *for* ראש חודש *(page 1133); from the second, read* בַּיּוֹם הַשְּׁבִיעִי*:*

בַּיּוֹם הַשְּׁבִיעִי נָשִׂיא לִבְנֵי אֶפְרָיִם אֱלִישָׁמָע
בֶּן־עַמִּיהוּד: קָרְבָּנוֹ קַעֲרַת־כֶּסֶף אַחַת
שְׁלֹשִׁים וּמֵאָה מִשְׁקָלָהּ מִזְרָק אֶחָד כֶּסֶף
שִׁבְעִים שֶׁקֶל בְּשֶׁקֶל הַקֹּדֶשׁ שְׁנֵיהֶם ׀
מְלֵאִים סֹלֶת בְּלוּלָה בַשֶּׁמֶן לְמִנְחָה: כַּף
אַחַת עֲשָׂרָה זָהָב מְלֵאָה קְטֹרֶת: פַּר אֶחָד
בֶּן־בָּקָר אַיִל אֶחָד כֶּבֶשׂ־אֶחָד בֶּן־שְׁנָתוֹ
לְעֹלָה: שְׂעִיר־עִזִּים אֶחָד לְחַטָּאת: וּלְזֶבַח
הַשְּׁלָמִים בָּקָר שְׁנַיִם אֵילִם חֲמִשָּׁה עַתֻּדִים
חֲמִשָּׁה כְּבָשִׂים בְּנֵי־שָׁנָה חֲמִשָּׁה זֶה קָרְבַּן
אֱלִישָׁמָע בֶּן־עַמִּיהוּד:

קריאה ליום השביעי של חנוכה
SEVENTH DAY OF ḤANUKKA

במדבר ז: מח–נט

If the seventh day is not ראש חודש*, then read as below.*

בַּיּוֹם הַשְּׁבִיעִי נָשִׂיא לִבְנֵי אֶפְרָיִם אֱלִישָׁמָע בֶּן־עַמִּיהוּד: קָרְבָּנוֹ קַעֲרַת־כֶּסֶף אַחַת שְׁלֹשִׁים וּמֵאָה מִשְׁקָלָהּ מִזְרָק אֶחָד כֶּסֶף שִׁבְעִים שֶׁקֶל בְּשֶׁקֶל הַקֹּדֶשׁ שְׁנֵיהֶם ׀ מְלֵאִים סֹלֶת בְּלוּלָה בַשֶּׁמֶן לְמִנְחָה: כַּף אַחַת עֲשָׂרָה זָהָב מְלֵאָה קְטֹרֶת: לוי: פַּר אֶחָד בֶּן־בָּקָר אַיִל אֶחָד כֶּבֶשׂ־אֶחָד בֶּן־שְׁנָתוֹ לְעֹלָה: שְׂעִיר־עִזִּים אֶחָד לְחַטָּאת: וּלְזֶבַח הַשְּׁלָמִים בָּקָר שְׁנַיִם אֵילִם חֲמִשָּׁה עַתֻּדִים חֲמִשָּׁה כְּבָשִׂים בְּנֵי־שָׁנָה חֲמִשָּׁה זֶה קָרְבַּן אֱלִישָׁמָע בֶּן־עַמִּיהוּד:

ישראל: בַּיּוֹם הַשְּׁמִינִי נָשִׂיא לִבְנֵי מְנַשֶּׁה גַּמְלִיאֵל בֶּן־פְּדָהצוּר: קָרְבָּנוֹ קַעֲרַת־כֶּסֶף אַחַת שְׁלֹשִׁים וּמֵאָה מִשְׁקָלָהּ מִזְרָק אֶחָד כֶּסֶף שִׁבְעִים שֶׁקֶל בְּשֶׁקֶל הַקֹּדֶשׁ שְׁנֵיהֶם ׀ מְלֵאִים סֹלֶת בְּלוּלָה בַשֶּׁמֶן לְמִנְחָה: כַּף אַחַת עֲשָׂרָה זָהָב מְלֵאָה קְטֹרֶת: פַּר אֶחָד בֶּן־בָּקָר אַיִל אֶחָד כֶּבֶשׂ־אֶחָד בֶּן־שְׁנָתוֹ לְעֹלָה: שְׂעִיר־עִזִּים אֶחָד לְחַטָּאת: וּלְזֶבַח הַשְּׁלָמִים בָּקָר שְׁנַיִם אֵילִם חֲמִשָּׁה עַתֻּדִים חֲמִשָּׁה כְּבָשִׂים בְּנֵי־שָׁנָה חֲמִשָּׁה זֶה קָרְבַּן גַּמְלִיאֵל בֶּן־פְּדָהצוּר:

קריאה ליום השמיני של חנוכה
EIGHTH DAY OF ḤANUKKA

במדבר ז: נד–ח: ד

בַּיּוֹם הַשְּׁמִינִי נָשִׂיא לִבְנֵי מְנַשֶּׁה גַּמְלִיאֵל בֶּן־פְּדָהצוּר: קָרְבָּנוֹ קַעֲרַת־כֶּסֶף אַחַת שְׁלֹשִׁים וּמֵאָה מִשְׁקָלָהּ מִזְרָק אֶחָד כֶּסֶף שִׁבְעִים שֶׁקֶל בְּשֶׁקֶל הַקֹּדֶשׁ שְׁנֵיהֶם ׀ מְלֵאִים סֹלֶת בְּלוּלָה בַשֶּׁמֶן לְמִנְחָה: כַּף אַחַת עֲשָׂרָה זָהָב מְלֵאָה קְטֹרֶת: לוי: פַּר אֶחָד בֶּן־בָּקָר אַיִל אֶחָד כֶּבֶשׂ־אֶחָד בֶּן־שְׁנָתוֹ לְעֹלָה: שְׂעִיר־עִזִּים אֶחָד לְחַטָּאת: וּלְזֶבַח הַשְּׁלָמִים בָּקָר שְׁנַיִם אֵילִם חֲמִשָּׁה עַתֻּדִים חֲמִשָּׁה כְּבָשִׂים בְּנֵי־שָׁנָה חֲמִשָּׁה זֶה קָרְבַּן גַּמְלִיאֵל בֶּן־פְּדָהצוּר:

ישראל: בַּיּוֹם הַתְּשִׁיעִי נָשִׂיא לִבְנֵי בִנְיָמִן אֲבִידָן בֶּן־גִּדְעֹנִי: קָרְבָּנוֹ קַעֲרַת־כֶּסֶף אַחַת שְׁלֹשִׁים וּמֵאָה מִשְׁקָלָהּ מִזְרָק אֶחָד כֶּסֶף שִׁבְעִים שֶׁקֶל בְּשֶׁקֶל הַקֹּדֶשׁ שְׁנֵיהֶם ׀ מְלֵאִים סֹלֶת בְּלוּלָה בַשֶּׁמֶן לְמִנְחָה: כַּף אַחַת עֲשָׂרָה זָהָב מְלֵאָה קְטֹרֶת: פַּר אֶחָד בֶּן־בָּקָר אַיִל אֶחָד כֶּבֶשׂ־אֶחָד בֶּן־שְׁנָתוֹ לְעֹלָה: שְׂעִיר־עִזִּים אֶחָד לְחַטָּאת: וּלְזֶבַח הַשְּׁלָמִים בָּקָר שְׁנַיִם אֵילִם חֲמִשָּׁה עַתֻּדִים חֲמִשָּׁה כְּבָשִׂים בְּנֵי־שָׁנָה חֲמִשָּׁה זֶה קָרְבַּן אֲבִידָן בֶּן־גִּדְעֹנִי:

בַּיּוֹם הָעֲשִׂירִי נָשִׂיא לִבְנֵי דָן אֲחִיעֶזֶר בֶּן־עַמִּישַׁדָּי: קָרְבָּנוֹ קַעֲרַת־כֶּסֶף אַחַת שְׁלֹשִׁים וּמֵאָה מִשְׁקָלָהּ מִזְרָק אֶחָד כֶּסֶף שִׁבְעִים שֶׁקֶל בְּשֶׁקֶל הַקֹּדֶשׁ שְׁנֵיהֶם ׀ מְלֵאִים סֹלֶת בְּלוּלָה בַשֶּׁמֶן לְמִנְחָה: כַּף אַחַת עֲשָׂרָה זָהָב מְלֵאָה קְטֹרֶת: פַּר אֶחָד בֶּן־בָּקָר אַיִל אֶחָד כֶּבֶשׂ־אֶחָד בֶּן־שְׁנָתוֹ לְעֹלָה: שְׂעִיר־עִזִּים אֶחָד לְחַטָּאת: וּלְזֶבַח הַשְּׁלָמִים בָּקָר שְׁנַיִם אֵילִם חֲמִשָּׁה עַתֻּדִים חֲמִשָּׁה כְּבָשִׂים בְּנֵי־שָׁנָה חֲמִשָּׁה זֶה קָרְבַּן אֲחִיעֶזֶר בֶּן־עַמִּישַׁדָּי:

בְּיוֹם עַשְׁתֵּי עָשָׂר יוֹם נָשִׂיא לִבְנֵי אָשֵׁר פַּגְעִיאֵל בֶּן־עָכְרָן: קָרְבָּנוֹ קַעֲרַת־כֶּסֶף אַחַת שְׁלֹשִׁים וּמֵאָה מִשְׁקָלָהּ מִזְרָק אֶחָד כֶּסֶף שִׁבְעִים שֶׁקֶל בְּשֶׁקֶל הַקֹּדֶשׁ שְׁנֵיהֶם ׀ מְלֵאִים סֹלֶת בְּלוּלָה בַשֶּׁמֶן לְמִנְחָה: כַּף אַחַת עֲשָׂרָה זָהָב מְלֵאָה קְטֹרֶת: פַּר אֶחָד בֶּן־בָּקָר אַיִל אֶחָד כֶּבֶשׂ־אֶחָד בֶּן־שְׁנָתוֹ לְעֹלָה: שְׂעִיר־עִזִּים אֶחָד לְחַטָּאת: וּלְזֶבַח הַשְּׁלָמִים בָּקָר שְׁנַיִם אֵילִם חֲמִשָּׁה עַתֻּדִים

חֲמִשָּׁה כְּבָשִׂים בְּנֵי־שָׁנָה חֲמִשָּׁה זֶה קָרְבַּן פַּגְעִיאֵל בֶּן־עָכְרָן:

בְּיוֹם שְׁנֵים עָשָׂר יוֹם נָשִׂיא לִבְנֵי נַפְתָּלִי אֲחִירַע בֶּן־עֵינָן: קָרְבָּנוֹ קַעֲרַת־כֶּסֶף אַחַת שְׁלֹשִׁים וּמֵאָה מִשְׁקָלָהּ מִזְרָק אֶחָד כֶּסֶף שִׁבְעִים שֶׁקֶל בְּשֶׁקֶל הַקֹּדֶשׁ שְׁנֵיהֶם ׀ מְלֵאִים סֹלֶת בְּלוּלָה בַשֶּׁמֶן לְמִנְחָה: כַּף אַחַת עֲשָׂרָה זָהָב מְלֵאָה קְטֹרֶת: פַּר אֶחָד בֶּן־בָּקָר אַיִל אֶחָד כֶּבֶשׂ־אֶחָד בֶּן־שְׁנָתוֹ לְעֹלָה: שְׂעִיר־עִזִּים אֶחָד לְחַטָּאת: וּלְזֶבַח הַשְּׁלָמִים בָּקָר שְׁנַיִם אֵילִם חֲמִשָּׁה עַתֻּדִים חֲמִשָּׁה כְּבָשִׂים בְּנֵי־שָׁנָה חֲמִשָּׁה זֶה קָרְבַּן אֲחִירַע בֶּן־עֵינָן:

זֹאת ׀ חֲנֻכַּת הַמִּזְבֵּחַ בְּיוֹם הִמָּשַׁח אֹתוֹ מֵאֵת נְשִׂיאֵי יִשְׂרָאֵל קַעֲרֹת כֶּסֶף שְׁתֵּים עֶשְׂרֵה מִזְרְקֵי־כֶסֶף שְׁנֵים עָשָׂר כַּפּוֹת זָהָב שְׁתֵּים עֶשְׂרֵה: שְׁלֹשִׁים וּמֵאָה הַקְּעָרָה הָאַחַת כֶּסֶף וְשִׁבְעִים הַמִּזְרָק הָאֶחָד כֹּל כֶּסֶף הַכֵּלִים אַלְפַּיִם וְאַרְבַּע־מֵאוֹת בְּשֶׁקֶל הַקֹּדֶשׁ: כַּפּוֹת זָהָב שְׁתֵּים־עֶשְׂרֵה מְלֵאֹת קְטֹרֶת עֲשָׂרָה עֲשָׂרָה הַכַּף בְּשֶׁקֶל הַקֹּדֶשׁ כָּל־זְהַב הַכַּפּוֹת עֶשְׂרִים וּמֵאָה: כָּל־הַבָּקָר לָעֹלָה שְׁנֵים עָשָׂר פָּרִים אֵילִם שְׁנֵים־עָשָׂר כְּבָשִׂים בְּנֵי־שָׁנָה שְׁנֵים עָשָׂר וּמִנְחָתָם וּשְׂעִירֵי עִזִּים שְׁנֵים עָשָׂר לְחַטָּאת: וְכֹל בְּקַר ׀ זֶבַח הַשְּׁלָמִים עֶשְׂרִים וְאַרְבָּעָה פָּרִים אֵילִם שִׁשִּׁים עַתֻּדִים שִׁשִּׁים כְּבָשִׂים בְּנֵי־שָׁנָה שִׁשִּׁים זֹאת חֲנֻכַּת הַמִּזְבֵּחַ אַחֲרֵי הִמָּשַׁח אֹתוֹ: וּבְבֹא מֹשֶׁה אֶל־אֹהֶל מוֹעֵד לְדַבֵּר אִתּוֹ וַיִּשְׁמַע אֶת־הַקּוֹל מִדַּבֵּר אֵלָיו מֵעַל הַכַּפֹּרֶת אֲשֶׁר עַל־אֲרֹן הָעֵדֻת מִבֵּין שְׁנֵי הַכְּרֻבִים וַיְדַבֵּר אֵלָיו:

וַיְדַבֵּר יהוה אֶל־מֹשֶׁה לֵּאמֹר: דַּבֵּר אֶל־אַהֲרֹן וְאָמַרְתָּ אֵלָיו בְּהַעֲלֹתְךָ אֶת־הַנֵּרֹת אֶל־מוּל פְּנֵי הַמְּנוֹרָה יָאִירוּ שִׁבְעַת הַנֵּרוֹת: וַיַּעַשׂ כֵּן אַהֲרֹן אֶל־מוּל פְּנֵי הַמְּנוֹרָה הֶעֱלָה נֵרֹתֶיהָ כַּאֲשֶׁר צִוָּה יהוה אֶת־מֹשֶׁה: וְזֶה מַעֲשֵׂה הַמְּנֹרָה מִקְשָׁה זָהָב עַד־יְרֵכָהּ עַד־פִּרְחָהּ מִקְשָׁה הִוא כַּמַּרְאֶה אֲשֶׁר הֶרְאָה יהוה אֶת־מֹשֶׁה כֵּן עָשָׂה אֶת־הַמְּנֹרָה:

קריאה לפורים / PURIM

שמות יז:ח־טז

וַיָּבֹא עֲמָלֵק וַיִּלָּחֶם עִם־יִשְׂרָאֵל בִּרְפִידִם: וַיֹּאמֶר מֹשֶׁה אֶל־יְהוֹשֻׁעַ בְּחַר־לָנוּ אֲנָשִׁים וְצֵא הִלָּחֵם בַּעֲמָלֵק מָחָר אָנֹכִי נִצָּב עַל־רֹאשׁ הַגִּבְעָה וּמַטֵּה הָאֱלֹהִים בְּיָדִי: וַיַּעַשׂ יְהוֹשֻׁעַ כַּאֲשֶׁר אָמַר־לוֹ מֹשֶׁה לְהִלָּחֵם בַּעֲמָלֵק וּמֹשֶׁה אַהֲרֹן וְחוּר עָלוּ רֹאשׁ הַגִּבְעָה:

לוי: וְהָיָה כַּאֲשֶׁר יָרִים מֹשֶׁה יָדוֹ וְגָבַר יִשְׂרָאֵל וְכַאֲשֶׁר יָנִיחַ יָדוֹ וְגָבַר עֲמָלֵק: וִידֵי מֹשֶׁה כְּבֵדִים וַיִּקְחוּ־אֶבֶן וַיָּשִׂימוּ תַחְתָּיו וַיֵּשֶׁב עָלֶיהָ וְאַהֲרֹן וְחוּר תָּמְכוּ בְיָדָיו מִזֶּה אֶחָד וּמִזֶּה אֶחָד וַיְהִי יָדָיו אֱמוּנָה עַד־בֹּא הַשָּׁמֶשׁ: וַיַּחֲלֹשׁ יְהוֹשֻׁעַ אֶת־עֲמָלֵק וְאֶת־עַמּוֹ לְפִי־חָרֶב:

ישראל: וַיֹּאמֶר יהוה אֶל־מֹשֶׁה כְּתֹב זֹאת זִכָּרוֹן בַּסֵּפֶר וְשִׂים בְּאָזְנֵי יְהוֹשֻׁעַ כִּי־מָחֹה אֶמְחֶה אֶת־זֵכֶר עֲמָלֵק מִתַּחַת הַשָּׁמָיִם: וַיִּבֶן מֹשֶׁה מִזְבֵּחַ וַיִּקְרָא שְׁמוֹ יהוה ׀ נִסִּי: וַיֹּאמֶר כִּי־יָד עַל־כֵּס יָהּ מִלְחָמָה לַיהוה בַּעֲמָלֵק מִדֹּר דֹּר:

לפסח, שבועות וסוכות

FOR PESAḤ, SHAVUOT AND SUKKOT

קריאה ליום הראשון של פסח

FIRST DAY OF PESAḤ

שמות יב: כא–נא

וַיִּקְרָא מֹשֶׁה לְכׇל־זִקְנֵי יִשְׂרָאֵל וַיֹּאמֶר אֲלֵהֶם מִשְׁכוּ וּקְחוּ לָכֶם צֹאן לְמִשְׁפְּחֹתֵיכֶם וְשַׁחֲטוּ הַפָּסַח: וּלְקַחְתֶּם אֲגֻדַּת אֵזוֹב וּטְבַלְתֶּם בַּדָּם אֲשֶׁר־בַּסַּף וְהִגַּעְתֶּם אֶל־הַמַּשְׁקוֹף וְאֶל־שְׁתֵּי הַמְּזוּזֹת מִן־הַדָּם אֲשֶׁר בַּסָּף וְאַתֶּם לֹא תֵצְאוּ אִישׁ מִפֶּתַח־בֵּיתוֹ עַד־בֹּקֶר: וְעָבַר יהוה לִנְגֹּף אֶת־מִצְרַיִם וְרָאָה אֶת־הַדָּם עַל־הַמַּשְׁקוֹף וְעַל שְׁתֵּי הַמְּזוּזֹת וּפָסַח יהוה עַל־הַפֶּתַח וְלֹא יִתֵּן הַמַּשְׁחִית לָבֹא אֶל־בָּתֵּיכֶם לִנְגֹּף: וּשְׁמַרְתֶּם אֶת־הַדָּבָר הַזֶּה לְחׇק־לְךָ וּלְבָנֶיךָ עַד־עוֹלָם: לוי: וְהָיָה כִּי־תָבֹאוּ אֶל־הָאָרֶץ אֲשֶׁר יִתֵּן יהוה לָכֶם כַּאֲשֶׁר דִּבֵּר וּשְׁמַרְתֶּם אֶת־הָעֲבֹדָה הַזֹּאת: וְהָיָה כִּי־יֹאמְרוּ אֲלֵיכֶם בְּנֵיכֶם מָה הָעֲבֹדָה הַזֹּאת לָכֶם: וַאֲמַרְתֶּם זֶבַח־פֶּסַח הוּא לַיהוה אֲשֶׁר פָּסַח עַל־בָּתֵּי בְנֵי־יִשְׂרָאֵל בְּמִצְרַיִם בְּנׇגְפּוֹ אֶת־מִצְרַיִם וְאֶת־בָּתֵּינוּ הִצִּיל וַיִּקֹּד הָעָם וַיִּשְׁתַּחֲווּ: וַיֵּלְכוּ וַיַּעֲשׂוּ בְּנֵי יִשְׂרָאֵל כַּאֲשֶׁר צִוָּה יהוה אֶת־מֹשֶׁה וְאַהֲרֹן כֵּן עָשׂוּ:

שלישי: וַיְהִי | בַּחֲצִי הַלַּיְלָה וַיהוה הִכָּה כׇל־בְּכוֹר בְּאֶרֶץ מִצְרַיִם מִבְּכֹר פַּרְעֹה הַיֹּשֵׁב עַל־כִּסְאוֹ עַד בְּכוֹר הַשְּׁבִי אֲשֶׁר בְּבֵית הַבּוֹר וְכֹל בְּכוֹר בְּהֵמָה: וַיָּקׇם פַּרְעֹה לַיְלָה הוּא וְכׇל־עֲבָדָיו וְכׇל־מִצְרַיִם וַתְּהִי צְעָקָה גְדֹלָה בְּמִצְרָיִם כִּי־אֵין בַּיִת אֲשֶׁר אֵין־שָׁם מֵת: וַיִּקְרָא לְמֹשֶׁה וּלְאַהֲרֹן לַיְלָה וַיֹּאמֶר קוּמוּ צְּאוּ מִתּוֹךְ עַמִּי גַּם־אַתֶּם גַּם־בְּנֵי יִשְׂרָאֵל וּלְכוּ עִבְדוּ אֶת־יהוה כְּדַבֶּרְכֶם: גַּם־צֹאנְכֶם גַּם־בְּקַרְכֶם קְחוּ כַּאֲשֶׁר דִּבַּרְתֶּם וָלֵכוּ וּבֵרַכְתֶּם גַּם־אֹתִי: (בשבת רביעי) וַתֶּחֱזַק מִצְרַיִם עַל־הָעָם לְמַהֵר לְשַׁלְּחָם מִן־הָאָרֶץ כִּי אָמְרוּ כֻּלָּנוּ מֵתִים: וַיִּשָּׂא הָעָם אֶת־בְּצֵקוֹ טֶרֶם יֶחְמָץ מִשְׁאֲרֹתָם צְרֻרֹת בְּשִׂמְלֹתָם עַל־שִׁכְמָם: וּבְנֵי־יִשְׂרָאֵל עָשׂוּ כִּדְבַר מֹשֶׁה וַיִּשְׁאֲלוּ מִמִּצְרַיִם כְּלֵי־כֶסֶף וּכְלֵי זָהָב וּשְׂמָלֹת: וַיהוה נָתַן אֶת־חֵן הָעָם בְּעֵינֵי מִצְרַיִם וַיַּשְׁאִלוּם וַיְנַצְּלוּ אֶת־מִצְרָיִם:

רביעי (בשבת חמישי) וַיִּסְעוּ בְנֵי־יִשְׂרָאֵל מֵרַעְמְסֵס סֻכֹּתָה כְּשֵׁשׁ־מֵאוֹת אֶלֶף רַגְלִי הַגְּבָרִים לְבַד מִטָּף: וְגַם־עֵרֶב רַב עָלָה אִתָּם וְצֹאן וּבָקָר מִקְנֶה כָּבֵד מְאֹד: וַיֹּאפוּ אֶת־הַבָּצֵק אֲשֶׁר הוֹצִיאוּ מִמִּצְרַיִם עֻגֹת מַצּוֹת כִּי לֹא חָמֵץ כִּי־גֹרְשׁוּ מִמִּצְרַיִם וְלֹא יָכְלוּ לְהִתְמַהְמֵהַּ וְגַם־צֵדָה לֹא־עָשׂוּ לָהֶם: וּמוֹשַׁב בְּנֵי יִשְׂרָאֵל אֲשֶׁר יָשְׁבוּ בְּמִצְרָיִם שְׁלֹשִׁים שָׁנָה וְאַרְבַּע מֵאוֹת שָׁנָה: וַיְהִי מִקֵּץ שְׁלֹשִׁים שָׁנָה וְאַרְבַּע מֵאוֹת שָׁנָה וַיְהִי בְּעֶצֶם הַיּוֹם הַזֶּה יָצְאוּ כׇּל־צִבְאוֹת יהוה מֵאֶרֶץ מִצְרָיִם: לֵיל שִׁמֻּרִים הוּא לַיהוה לְהוֹצִיאָם מֵאֶרֶץ מִצְרָיִם הוּא־הַלַּיְלָה הַזֶּה לַיהוה שִׁמֻּרִים לְכׇל־בְּנֵי יִשְׂרָאֵל לְדֹרֹתָם:

חמישי (בשבת ששי) וַיֹּאמֶר יהוה אֶל־מֹשֶׁה וְאַהֲרֹן זֹאת חֻקַּת הַפָּסַח כׇּל־בֶּן־נֵכָר לֹא־יֹאכַל בּוֹ: וְכׇל־עֶבֶד אִישׁ מִקְנַת־כָּסֶף וּמַלְתָּה אֹתוֹ אָז יֹאכַל בּוֹ: תּוֹשָׁב וְשָׂכִיר לֹא־יֹאכַל בּוֹ: בְּבַיִת אֶחָד יֵאָכֵל לֹא־תוֹצִיא מִן־הַבַּיִת מִן־הַבָּשָׂר חוּצָה וְעֶצֶם לֹא תִשְׁבְּרוּ־בוֹ: כׇּל־עֲדַת יִשְׂרָאֵל יַעֲשׂוּ אֹתוֹ: (בשבת שביעי) וְכִי־יָגוּר אִתְּךָ גֵּר וְעָשָׂה פֶסַח לַיהוה הִמּוֹל לוֹ כׇל־זָכָר וְאָז יִקְרַב לַעֲשֹׂתוֹ וְהָיָה כְּאֶזְרַח הָאָרֶץ וְכׇל־עָרֵל לֹא־יֹאכַל בּוֹ: תּוֹרָה אַחַת יִהְיֶה לָאֶזְרָח וְלַגֵּר הַגָּר בְּתוֹכְכֶם: וַיַּעֲשׂוּ כׇּל־בְּנֵי יִשְׂרָאֵל כַּאֲשֶׁר צִוָּה יהוה אֶת־מֹשֶׁה וְאֶת־אַהֲרֹן כֵּן עָשׂוּ:

וַיְהִ֗י בְּעֶ֨צֶם֙ הַיּ֣וֹם הַזֶּ֔ה הוֹצִ֨יא יהו֜ה אֶת־בְּנֵ֧י יִשְׂרָאֵ֛ל מֵאֶ֥רֶץ מִצְרַ֖יִם עַל־צִבְאֹתָֽם׃

מפטיר / MAFTIR

במדבר כח: טז–כה

חצי קדיש (page 544) is said, and then the following מפטיר is read from the second ספר תורה on both the first and second days of פסח.

וּבַחֹ֣דֶשׁ הָֽרִאשׁ֗וֹן בְּאַרְבָּעָ֨ה עָשָׂ֥ר י֛וֹם לַחֹ֖דֶשׁ פֶּ֥סַח לַֽיהוֽה׃ וּבַחֲמִשָּׁ֨ה עָשָׂ֥ר י֛וֹם לַחֹ֥דֶשׁ הַזֶּ֖ה חָ֑ג שִׁבְעַ֣ת יָמִ֔ים מַצּ֖וֹת יֵאָכֵֽל׃ בַּיּ֥וֹם הָרִאשׁ֖וֹן מִקְרָא־קֹ֑דֶשׁ כָּל־מְלֶ֥אכֶת עֲבֹדָ֖ה לֹ֥א תַעֲשֽׂוּ׃ וְהִקְרַבְתֶּ֨ם אִשֶּׁ֤ה עֹלָה֙ לַֽיהוה פָּרִ֧ים בְּנֵי־בָקָ֛ר שְׁנַ֖יִם וְאַ֣יִל אֶחָ֑ד וְשִׁבְעָ֤ה כְבָשִׂים֙ בְּנֵ֣י שָׁנָ֔ה תְּמִימִ֖ם יִהְי֥וּ לָכֶֽם׃ וּמִ֨נְחָתָ֔ם סֹ֖לֶת בְּלוּלָ֣ה בַשָּׁ֑מֶן שְׁלֹשָׁ֨ה עֶשְׂרֹנִ֜ים לַפָּ֗ר וּשְׁנֵ֧י עֶשְׂרֹנִ֛ים לָאַ֖יִל תַּעֲשֽׂוּ׃ עִשָּׂר֤וֹן עִשָּׂרוֹן֙ תַּעֲשֶׂ֔ה לַכֶּ֖בֶשׂ הָאֶחָ֑ד לְשִׁבְעַ֖ת הַכְּבָשִֽׂים׃ וּשְׂעִ֥יר חַטָּ֖את אֶחָ֑ד לְכַפֵּ֖ר עֲלֵיכֶֽם׃ מִלְּבַד֙ עֹלַ֣ת הַבֹּ֔קֶר אֲשֶׁ֖ר לְעֹלַ֣ת הַתָּמִ֑יד תַּעֲשׂ֖וּ אֶת־אֵֽלֶּה׃ כָּאֵ֜לֶּה תַּעֲשׂ֤וּ לַיּוֹם֙ שִׁבְעַ֣ת יָמִ֔ים לֶ֛חֶם אִשֵּׁ֥ה רֵֽיחַ־נִיחֹ֖חַ לַֽיהוה עַל־עוֹלַ֧ת הַתָּמִ֛יד יֵעָשֶׂ֖ה וְנִסְכּֽוֹ׃ וּבַיּוֹם֙ הַשְּׁבִיעִ֔י מִקְרָא־קֹ֖דֶשׁ יִהְיֶ֣ה לָכֶ֑ם כָּל־מְלֶ֥אכֶת עֲבֹדָ֖ה לֹ֥א תַעֲשֽׂוּ׃

הפטרה ליום הראשון של פסח / HAFTARA FOR THE FIRST DAY OF PESAḤ

יהושע ג: ה–ז

Some start from the first verse and some start from the fourth verse.

וַיֹּ֧אמֶר יְהוֹשֻׁ֛עַ אֶל־הָעָ֖ם הִתְקַדָּ֑שׁוּ כִּ֣י מָחָ֔ר יַעֲשֶׂ֧ה יהוה בְּקִרְבְּכֶ֖ם נִפְלָאֽוֹת׃ וַיֹּ֤אמֶר יְהוֹשֻׁ֙עַ֙ אֶל־הַכֹּהֲנִ֣ים לֵאמֹ֔ר שְׂאוּ֙ אֶת־אֲר֣וֹן הַבְּרִ֔ית וְעִבְר֖וּ לִפְנֵ֣י הָעָ֑ם וַיִּשְׂאוּ֙ אֶת־אֲר֣וֹן הַבְּרִ֔ית וַיֵּלְכ֖וּ לִפְנֵ֥י הָעָֽם׃ וַיֹּ֤אמֶר יהוה֙ אֶל־יְהוֹשֻׁ֔עַ הַיּ֣וֹם הַזֶּ֗ה אָחֵל֙ גַּדֶּלְךָ֔ בְּעֵינֵ֖י כָּל־יִשְׂרָאֵ֑ל אֲשֶׁר֙ יֵֽדְע֔וּן כִּ֗י כַּאֲשֶׁ֛ר הָיִ֥יתִי עִם־מֹשֶׁ֖ה אֶהְיֶ֥ה עִמָּֽךְ׃

יהושע ה: ב–ו: א

בָּעֵ֣ת הַהִ֗יא אָמַ֤ר יהוה֙ אֶל־יְהוֹשֻׁ֔עַ עֲשֵׂ֥ה לְךָ֖ חַֽרְב֣וֹת צֻרִ֑ים וְשׁ֛וּב מֹ֥ל אֶת־בְּנֵֽי־יִשְׂרָאֵ֖ל שֵׁנִֽית׃ וַיַּעַשׂ־ל֥וֹ יְהוֹשֻׁ֖עַ חַֽרְב֣וֹת צֻרִ֑ים וַיָּ֙מָל֙ אֶת־בְּנֵ֣י יִשְׂרָאֵ֔ל אֶל־גִּבְעַ֖ת הָעֲרָלֽוֹת׃ וְזֶ֥ה הַדָּבָ֖ר אֲשֶׁר־מָ֣ל יְהוֹשֻׁ֑עַ כָּל־הָעָ֣ם הַיֹּצֵא֩ מִמִּצְרַ֨יִם הַזְּכָרִ֜ים כֹּ֣ל ׀ אַנְשֵׁ֣י הַמִּלְחָמָ֗ה מֵ֤תוּ בַמִּדְבָּר֙ בַּדֶּ֔רֶךְ בְּצֵאתָ֖ם מִמִּצְרָֽיִם׃ כִּֽי־מֻלִ֣ים הָי֔וּ כָּל־הָעָ֖ם הַיֹּצְאִ֑ים וְכָל־הָ֠עָם הַיִּלֹּדִ֨ים בַּמִּדְבָּ֤ר בַּדֶּ֙רֶךְ֙ בְּצֵאתָ֣ם מִמִּצְרַ֔יִם לֹא־מָֽלוּ׃ כִּ֣י ׀ אַרְבָּעִ֣ים שָׁנָ֗ה הָלְכ֣וּ בְנֵֽי־יִשְׂרָאֵל֮ בַּמִּדְבָּר֒ עַד־תֹּ֨ם כָּל־הַגּ֜וֹי אַנְשֵׁ֤י הַמִּלְחָמָה֙ הַיֹּצְאִ֣ים מִמִּצְרַ֔יִם אֲשֶׁ֥ר לֹא־שָׁמְע֖וּ בְּק֣וֹל יהוה אֲשֶׁר֩ נִשְׁבַּ֨ע יהוה לָהֶ֗ם לְבִלְתִּ֞י הַרְאוֹתָ֣ם אֶת־הָאָ֗רֶץ אֲשֶׁר֩ נִשְׁבַּ֨ע יהוה לַאֲבוֹתָם֙ לָ֣תֶת לָ֔נוּ אֶ֛רֶץ זָבַ֥ת חָלָ֖ב וּדְבָֽשׁ׃ וְאֶת־בְּנֵיהֶם֙ הֵקִ֣ים תַּחְתָּ֔ם אֹתָ֖ם מָ֣ל יְהוֹשֻׁ֑עַ כִּֽי־עֲרֵלִ֣ים הָי֔וּ כִּ֛י לֹא־מָ֥לוּ אוֹתָ֖ם בַּדָּֽרֶךְ׃ וַיְהִ֛י כַּאֲשֶׁר־תַּ֥מּוּ כָל־הַגּ֖וֹי לְהִמּ֑וֹל וַיֵּשְׁב֥וּ תַחְתָּ֛ם בַּֽמַּחֲנֶ֖ה עַ֥ד חֲיוֹתָֽם׃ וַיֹּ֤אמֶר יהוה֙ אֶל־יְהוֹשֻׁ֔עַ הַיּ֗וֹם גַּלּ֛וֹתִי אֶת־חֶרְפַּ֥ת מִצְרַ֖יִם מֵעֲלֵיכֶ֑ם וַיִּקְרָ֞א שֵׁ֣ם הַמָּק֤וֹם הַהוּא֙ גִּלְגָּ֔ל עַ֖ד הַיּ֥וֹם הַזֶּֽה׃ וַיַּחֲנ֥וּ בְנֵֽי־יִשְׂרָאֵ֖ל בַּגִּלְגָּ֑ל וַיַּעֲשׂ֣וּ אֶת־הַפֶּ֡סַח בְּאַרְבָּעָה֩ עָשָׂ֨ר י֥וֹם לַחֹ֛דֶשׁ בָּעֶ֖רֶב בְּעַֽרְב֥וֹת יְרִיחֽוֹ׃ וַיֹּ֨אכְל֜וּ מֵעֲב֥וּר הָאָ֛רֶץ מִמָּֽחֳרַ֥ת הַפֶּ֖סַח מַצּ֣וֹת וְקָל֑וּי בְּעֶ֖צֶם הַיּ֥וֹם הַזֶּֽה׃ וַיִּשְׁבֹּ֨ת הַמָּ֜ן מִֽמָּחֳרָ֗ת בְּאָכְלָם֙ מֵעֲב֣וּר הָאָ֔רֶץ וְלֹא־הָ֥יָה ע֛וֹד לִבְנֵ֥י יִשְׂרָאֵ֖ל מָ֑ן וַיֹּאכְל֗וּ מִתְּבוּאַת֙ אֶ֣רֶץ כְּנַ֔עַן בַּשָּׁנָ֖ה הַהִֽיא׃ וַיְהִ֗י בִּֽהְי֣וֹת יְהוֹשֻׁעַ֮ בִּירִיחוֹ֒ וַיִּשָּׂ֤א עֵינָיו֙ וַיַּ֔רְא וְהִנֵּה־אִישׁ֙ עֹמֵ֣ד לְנֶגְדּ֔וֹ וְחַרְבּ֥וֹ שְׁלוּפָ֖ה בְּיָד֑וֹ וַיֵּ֨לֶךְ יְהוֹשֻׁ֤עַ אֵלָיו֙ וַיֹּ֣אמֶר ל֔וֹ הֲלָ֥נוּ אַתָּ֖ה אִם־לְצָרֵֽינוּ׃ וַיֹּ֣אמֶר ׀ לֹ֗א כִּ֛י אֲנִ֥י שַׂר־צְבָֽא־יהוה עַתָּ֣ה בָ֑אתִי וַיִּפֹּל֩ יְהוֹשֻׁ֨עַ אֶל־פָּנָ֥יו אַ֙רְצָה֙ וַיִּשְׁתָּ֔חוּ וַיֹּ֣אמֶר ל֔וֹ מָ֥ה אֲדֹנִ֖י מְדַבֵּ֥ר אֶל־עַבְדּֽוֹ׃ וַיֹּאמֶר֩ שַׂר־צְבָ֨א יהוה אֶל־יְהוֹשֻׁ֗עַ שַׁל־נַֽעַלְךָ֙ מֵעַ֣ל רַגְלֶ֔ךָ כִּ֣י הַמָּק֗וֹם אֲשֶׁ֛ר אַתָּ֛ה עֹמֵ֥ד עָלָ֖יו קֹ֣דֶשׁ ה֑וּא

וַיַּעַשׂ יְהוֹשֻׁעַ כֵּן׃ וִירִיחוֹ סֹגֶרֶת וּמְסֻגֶּרֶת מִפְּנֵי בְּנֵי יִשְׂרָאֵל אֵין יוֹצֵא וְאֵין בָּא׃

Some add:

יהושע ו: כז

וַיְהִי יהוה אֶת־יְהוֹשֻׁעַ וַיְהִי שָׁמְעוֹ בְּכָל־הָאָרֶץ׃

קריאה ליום השני של פסח, וכן ליום טוב ראשון ושני של סוכות / READING FOR THE SECOND DAY OF PESAḤ; THE FIRST DAY AND THE SECOND DAY OF SUKKOT

ויקרא כב: כו–כג: מד

וַיְדַבֵּר יהוה אֶל־מֹשֶׁה לֵּאמֹר׃ שׁוֹר אוֹ־כֶשֶׂב אוֹ־עֵז כִּי יִוָּלֵד וְהָיָה שִׁבְעַת יָמִים תַּחַת אִמּוֹ וּמִיּוֹם הַשְּׁמִינִי וָהָלְאָה יֵרָצֶה לְקָרְבַּן אִשֶּׁה לַיהוה׃ וְשׁוֹר אוֹ־שֶׂה אֹתוֹ וְאֶת־בְּנוֹ לֹא תִשְׁחֲטוּ בְּיוֹם אֶחָד׃ וְכִי־תִזְבְּחוּ זֶבַח־תּוֹדָה לַיהוה לִרְצֹנְכֶם תִּזְבָּחוּ׃ בַּיּוֹם הַהוּא יֵאָכֵל לֹא־תוֹתִירוּ מִמֶּנּוּ עַד־בֹּקֶר אֲנִי יהוה׃ וּשְׁמַרְתֶּם מִצְוֹתַי וַעֲשִׂיתֶם אֹתָם אֲנִי יהוה׃ וְלֹא תְחַלְּלוּ אֶת־שֵׁם קָדְשִׁי וְנִקְדַּשְׁתִּי בְּתוֹךְ בְּנֵי יִשְׂרָאֵל אֲנִי יהוה מְקַדִּשְׁכֶם׃ הַמּוֹצִיא אֶתְכֶם מֵאֶרֶץ מִצְרַיִם לִהְיוֹת לָכֶם לֵאלֹהִים אֲנִי יהוה׃

(בשבת לוי) וַיְדַבֵּר יהוה אֶל־מֹשֶׁה לֵּאמֹר׃ דַּבֵּר אֶל־בְּנֵי יִשְׂרָאֵל וְאָמַרְתָּ אֲלֵהֶם מוֹעֲדֵי יהוה אֲשֶׁר־תִּקְרְאוּ אֹתָם מִקְרָאֵי קֹדֶשׁ אֵלֶּה הֵם מוֹעֲדָי׃ שֵׁשֶׁת יָמִים תֵּעָשֶׂה מְלָאכָה וּבַיּוֹם הַשְּׁבִיעִי שַׁבַּת שַׁבָּתוֹן מִקְרָא־קֹדֶשׁ כָּל־מְלָאכָה לֹא תַעֲשׂוּ שַׁבָּת הִוא לַיהוה בְּכֹל מוֹשְׁבֹתֵיכֶם׃

לוי (בשבת שלישי) אֵלֶּה מוֹעֲדֵי יהוה מִקְרָאֵי קֹדֶשׁ אֲשֶׁר־תִּקְרְאוּ אֹתָם בְּמוֹעֲדָם׃ בַּחֹדֶשׁ הָרִאשׁוֹן בְּאַרְבָּעָה עָשָׂר לַחֹדֶשׁ בֵּין הָעַרְבָּיִם פֶּסַח לַיהוה׃ וּבַחֲמִשָּׁה עָשָׂר יוֹם לַחֹדֶשׁ הַזֶּה חַג הַמַּצּוֹת לַיהוה שִׁבְעַת יָמִים מַצּוֹת תֹּאכֵלוּ׃ בַּיּוֹם הָרִאשׁוֹן מִקְרָא־קֹדֶשׁ יִהְיֶה לָכֶם כָּל־מְלֶאכֶת עֲבֹדָה לֹא תַעֲשׂוּ׃ וְהִקְרַבְתֶּם אִשֶּׁה לַיהוה שִׁבְעַת יָמִים בַּיּוֹם הַשְּׁבִיעִי מִקְרָא־קֹדֶשׁ כָּל־מְלֶאכֶת עֲבֹדָה לֹא תַעֲשׂוּ׃

לוי בחוה״מ פסח (בשבת רביעי): וַיְדַבֵּר יהוה אֶל־מֹשֶׁה לֵּאמֹר׃ דַּבֵּר אֶל־בְּנֵי יִשְׂרָאֵל וְאָמַרְתָּ אֲלֵהֶם כִּי־תָבֹאוּ אֶל־הָאָרֶץ אֲשֶׁר אֲנִי נֹתֵן לָכֶם וּקְצַרְתֶּם אֶת־קְצִירָהּ וַהֲבֵאתֶם אֶת־עֹמֶר רֵאשִׁית קְצִירְכֶם אֶל־הַכֹּהֵן׃ וְהֵנִיף אֶת־הָעֹמֶר לִפְנֵי יהוה לִרְצֹנְכֶם מִמָּחֳרַת הַשַּׁבָּת יְנִיפֶנּוּ הַכֹּהֵן׃ וַעֲשִׂיתֶם בְּיוֹם הֲנִיפְכֶם אֶת־הָעֹמֶר כֶּבֶשׂ תָּמִים בֶּן־שְׁנָתוֹ לְעֹלָה לַיהוה׃ וּמִנְחָתוֹ שְׁנֵי עֶשְׂרֹנִים סֹלֶת בְּלוּלָה בַשֶּׁמֶן אִשֶּׁה לַיהוה רֵיחַ נִיחֹחַ וְנִסְכֹּה יַיִן רְבִיעִת הַהִין׃ וְלֶחֶם וְקָלִי וְכַרְמֶל לֹא תֹאכְלוּ עַד־עֶצֶם הַיּוֹם הַזֶּה עַד הֲבִיאֲכֶם אֶת־קָרְבַּן אֱלֹהֵיכֶם חֻקַּת עוֹלָם לְדֹרֹתֵיכֶם בְּכֹל מֹשְׁבֹתֵיכֶם׃

שלישי ביו״ט ובחוה״מ פסח (בשבת חמישי): וּסְפַרְתֶּם לָכֶם מִמָּחֳרַת הַשַּׁבָּת מִיּוֹם הֲבִיאֲכֶם אֶת־עֹמֶר הַתְּנוּפָה שֶׁבַע שַׁבָּתוֹת תְּמִימֹת תִּהְיֶינָה׃ עַד מִמָּחֳרַת הַשַּׁבָּת הַשְּׁבִיעִת תִּסְפְּרוּ חֲמִשִּׁים יוֹם וְהִקְרַבְתֶּם מִנְחָה חֲדָשָׁה לַיהוה׃ מִמּוֹשְׁבֹתֵיכֶם תָּבִיאוּ ׀ לֶחֶם תְּנוּפָה שְׁתַּיִם שְׁנֵי עֶשְׂרֹנִים סֹלֶת תִּהְיֶינָה חָמֵץ תֵּאָפֶינָה בִּכּוּרִים לַיהוה׃ וְהִקְרַבְתֶּם עַל־הַלֶּחֶם שִׁבְעַת כְּבָשִׂים תְּמִימִם בְּנֵי שָׁנָה וּפַר בֶּן־בָּקָר אֶחָד וְאֵילִם שְׁנָיִם יִהְיוּ עֹלָה לַיהוה וּמִנְחָתָם וְנִסְכֵּיהֶם אִשֵּׁה רֵיחַ־נִיחֹחַ לַיהוה׃ וַעֲשִׂיתֶם שְׂעִיר־עִזִּים אֶחָד לְחַטָּאת וּשְׁנֵי כְבָשִׂים בְּנֵי שָׁנָה לְזֶבַח שְׁלָמִים׃ וְהֵנִיף הַכֹּהֵן ׀ אֹתָם עַל לֶחֶם הַבִּכֻּרִים תְּנוּפָה לִפְנֵי יהוה עַל־שְׁנֵי כְּבָשִׂים קֹדֶשׁ יִהְיוּ לַיהוה לַכֹּהֵן׃ וּקְרָאתֶם בְּעֶצֶם ׀ הַיּוֹם הַזֶּה מִקְרָא־קֹדֶשׁ יִהְיֶה לָכֶם כָּל־מְלֶאכֶת עֲבֹדָה לֹא תַעֲשׂוּ חֻקַּת עוֹלָם בְּכָל־מוֹשְׁבֹתֵיכֶם לְדֹרֹתֵיכֶם׃ וּבְקֻצְרְכֶם אֶת־קְצִיר אַרְצְכֶם לֹא־תְכַלֶּה פְּאַת שָׂדְךָ בְּקֻצְרֶךָ וְלֶקֶט קְצִירְךָ לֹא תְלַקֵּט לֶעָנִי וְלַגֵּר תַּעֲזֹב אֹתָם אֲנִי יהוה אֱלֹהֵיכֶם׃

רביעי (בשבת ששי) וַיְדַבֵּר יהוה אֶל־מֹשֶׁה לֵּאמֹר: דַּבֵּר אֶל־בְּנֵי יִשְׂרָאֵל לֵאמֹר בַּחֹדֶשׁ הַשְּׁבִיעִי בְּאֶחָד לַחֹדֶשׁ יִהְיֶה לָכֶם שַׁבָּתוֹן זִכְרוֹן תְּרוּעָה מִקְרָא־קֹדֶשׁ: כָּל־מְלֶאכֶת עֲבֹדָה לֹא תַעֲשׂוּ וְהִקְרַבְתֶּם אִשֶּׁה לַיהוה: וַיְדַבֵּר יהוה אֶל־מֹשֶׁה לֵּאמֹר: אַךְ בֶּעָשׂוֹר לַחֹדֶשׁ הַשְּׁבִיעִי הַזֶּה יוֹם הַכִּפֻּרִים הוּא מִקְרָא־קֹדֶשׁ יִהְיֶה לָכֶם וְעִנִּיתֶם אֶת־נַפְשֹׁתֵיכֶם וְהִקְרַבְתֶּם אִשֶּׁה לַיהוה: וְכָל־מְלָאכָה לֹא תַעֲשׂוּ בְּעֶצֶם הַיּוֹם הַזֶּה כִּי יוֹם כִּפֻּרִים הוּא לְכַפֵּר עֲלֵיכֶם לִפְנֵי יהוה אֱלֹהֵיכֶם: כִּי כָל־הַנֶּפֶשׁ אֲשֶׁר לֹא־תְעֻנֶּה בְּעֶצֶם הַיּוֹם הַזֶּה וְנִכְרְתָה מֵעַמֶּיהָ: וְכָל־הַנֶּפֶשׁ אֲשֶׁר תַּעֲשֶׂה כָּל־מְלָאכָה בְּעֶצֶם הַיּוֹם הַזֶּה וְהַאֲבַדְתִּי אֶת־הַנֶּפֶשׁ הַהִוא מִקֶּרֶב עַמָּהּ: כָּל־מְלָאכָה לֹא תַעֲשׂוּ חֻקַּת עוֹלָם לְדֹרֹתֵיכֶם בְּכֹל מֹשְׁבֹתֵיכֶם: שַׁבַּת שַׁבָּתוֹן הוּא לָכֶם וְעִנִּיתֶם אֶת־נַפְשֹׁתֵיכֶם בְּתִשְׁעָה לַחֹדֶשׁ בָּעֶרֶב מֵעֶרֶב עַד־עֶרֶב תִּשְׁבְּתוּ שַׁבַּתְּכֶם:

חמישי (בשבת שביעי) וַיְדַבֵּר יהוה אֶל־מֹשֶׁה לֵּאמֹר: דַּבֵּר אֶל־בְּנֵי יִשְׂרָאֵל לֵאמֹר בַּחֲמִשָּׁה עָשָׂר יוֹם לַחֹדֶשׁ הַשְּׁבִיעִי הַזֶּה חַג הַסֻּכּוֹת שִׁבְעַת יָמִים לַיהוה: בַּיּוֹם הָרִאשׁוֹן מִקְרָא־קֹדֶשׁ כָּל־מְלֶאכֶת עֲבֹדָה לֹא תַעֲשׂוּ: שִׁבְעַת יָמִים תַּקְרִיבוּ אִשֶּׁה לַיהוה בַּיּוֹם הַשְּׁמִינִי מִקְרָא־קֹדֶשׁ יִהְיֶה לָכֶם וְהִקְרַבְתֶּם אִשֶּׁה לַיהוה עֲצֶרֶת הִוא כָּל־מְלֶאכֶת עֲבֹדָה לֹא תַעֲשׂוּ: אֵלֶּה מוֹעֲדֵי יהוה אֲשֶׁר־תִּקְרְאוּ אֹתָם מִקְרָאֵי קֹדֶשׁ לְהַקְרִיב אִשֶּׁה לַיהוה עֹלָה וּמִנְחָה זֶבַח וּנְסָכִים דְּבַר־יוֹם בְּיוֹמוֹ: מִלְּבַד שַׁבְּתֹת יהוה וּמִלְּבַד מַתְּנוֹתֵיכֶם וּמִלְּבַד כָּל־נִדְרֵיכֶם וּמִלְּבַד כָּל־נִדְבֹתֵיכֶם אֲשֶׁר תִּתְּנוּ לַיהוה: אַךְ בַּחֲמִשָּׁה עָשָׂר יוֹם לַחֹדֶשׁ הַשְּׁבִיעִי בְּאָסְפְּכֶם אֶת־תְּבוּאַת הָאָרֶץ תָּחֹגּוּ אֶת־חַג־יהוה שִׁבְעַת יָמִים בַּיּוֹם הָרִאשׁוֹן שַׁבָּתוֹן וּבַיּוֹם הַשְּׁמִינִי שַׁבָּתוֹן: וּלְקַחְתֶּם לָכֶם בַּיּוֹם הָרִאשׁוֹן פְּרִי עֵץ הָדָר כַּפֹּת תְּמָרִים וַעֲנַף עֵץ־עָבֹת וְעַרְבֵי־נָחַל וּשְׂמַחְתֶּם לִפְנֵי יהוה אֱלֹהֵיכֶם שִׁבְעַת יָמִים: וְחַגֹּתֶם אֹתוֹ חַג לַיהוה שִׁבְעַת יָמִים בַּשָּׁנָה חֻקַּת עוֹלָם לְדֹרֹתֵיכֶם בַּחֹדֶשׁ הַשְּׁבִיעִי תָּחֹגּוּ אֹתוֹ: בַּסֻּכֹּת תֵּשְׁבוּ שִׁבְעַת יָמִים כָּל־הָאֶזְרָח בְּיִשְׂרָאֵל יֵשְׁבוּ בַּסֻּכֹּת: לְמַעַן יֵדְעוּ דֹרֹתֵיכֶם כִּי בַסֻּכּוֹת הוֹשַׁבְתִּי אֶת־בְּנֵי יִשְׂרָאֵל בְּהוֹצִיאִי אוֹתָם מֵאֶרֶץ מִצְרָיִם אֲנִי יהוה אֱלֹהֵיכֶם: וַיְדַבֵּר מֹשֶׁה אֶת־מֹעֲדֵי יהוה אֶל־בְּנֵי יִשְׂרָאֵל:

חצי קדיש (page 544) is said. The מפטיר *for the second day of* פסח *is the same as for the first day (page 1142). The* מפטיר *and* הפטרה *for* סוכות *appear on pages 1159–1161.*

הפטרה ליום טוב שני של פסח / HAFTARA FOR SECOND DAY OF PESAḤ

מלכים ב׳ כג:א–ט

Some start with וַיִּשְׁלַח הַמֶּלֶךְ *and some start with* וַיְצַו הַמֶּלֶךְ *on the facing page.*

וַיִּשְׁלַח הַמֶּלֶךְ וַיַּאַסְפוּ אֵלָיו כָּל־זִקְנֵי יְהוּדָה וִירוּשָׁלָםִ: וַיַּעַל הַמֶּלֶךְ בֵּית־יהוה וְכָל־אִישׁ יְהוּדָה וְכָל־יֹשְׁבֵי יְרוּשָׁלַםִ אִתּוֹ וְהַכֹּהֲנִים וְהַנְּבִיאִים וְכָל־הָעָם לְמִקָּטֹן וְעַד־גָּדוֹל וַיִּקְרָא בְאָזְנֵיהֶם אֶת־כָּל־דִּבְרֵי סֵפֶר הַבְּרִית הַנִּמְצָא בְּבֵית יהוה: וַיַּעֲמֹד הַמֶּלֶךְ עַל־הָעַמּוּד וַיִּכְרֹת אֶת־הַבְּרִית ׀ לִפְנֵי יהוה לָלֶכֶת אַחַר יהוה וְלִשְׁמֹר מִצְוֺתָיו וְאֶת־עֵדְוֺתָיו וְאֶת־חֻקֹּתָיו בְּכָל־לֵב וּבְכָל־נֶפֶשׁ לְהָקִים אֶת־דִּבְרֵי הַבְּרִית הַזֹּאת הַכְּתֻבִים עַל־הַסֵּפֶר הַזֶּה וַיַּעֲמֹד כָּל־הָעָם בַּבְּרִית: *וַיְצַו הַמֶּלֶךְ אֶת־חִלְקִיָּהוּ הַכֹּהֵן הַגָּדוֹל וְאֶת־כֹּהֲנֵי הַמִּשְׁנֶה וְאֶת־שֹׁמְרֵי הַסַּף לְהוֹצִיא מֵהֵיכַל יהוה אֵת כָּל־הַכֵּלִים הָעֲשׂוּיִם לַבַּעַל וְלָאֲשֵׁרָה וּלְכֹל צְבָא הַשָּׁמָיִם וַיִּשְׂרְפֵם מִחוּץ לִירוּשָׁלַםִ בְּשַׁדְמוֹת קִדְרוֹן וְנָשָׂא אֶת־עֲפָרָם בֵּית־אֵל: וְהִשְׁבִּית אֶת־הַכְּמָרִים אֲשֶׁר נָתְנוּ מַלְכֵי יְהוּדָה וַיְקַטֵּר בַּבָּמוֹת בְּעָרֵי יְהוּדָה וּמְסִבֵּי יְרוּשָׁלָםִ וְאֶת־

הַֽמְקַטְּרִים לַבַּעַל לַשֶּׁמֶשׁ וְלַיָּרֵחַ וְלַמַּזָּלוֹת וּלְכֹל צְבָא הַשָּׁמָיִם: וַיֹּצֵא אֶת־הָאֲשֵׁרָה מִבֵּית יהוה מִחוּץ לִירוּשָׁלַםִ אֶל־נַחַל קִדְרוֹן וַיִּשְׂרֹף אֹתָהּ בְּנַחַל קִדְרוֹן וַיָּדֶק לְעָפָר וַיַּשְׁלֵךְ אֶת־עֲפָרָהּ עַל־קֶבֶר בְּנֵי הָעָם: וַיִּתֹּץ אֶת־בָּתֵּי הַקְּדֵשִׁים אֲשֶׁר בְּבֵית יהוה אֲשֶׁר הַנָּשִׁים אֹרְגוֹת שָׁם בָּתִּים לָאֲשֵׁרָה: וַיָּבֵא אֶת־כָּל־הַכֹּהֲנִים מֵעָרֵי יְהוּדָה וַיְטַמֵּא אֶת־הַבָּמוֹת אֲשֶׁר קִטְּרוּ־שָׁמָּה הַכֹּהֲנִים מִגֶּבַע עַד־בְּאֵר שָׁבַע וְנָתַץ אֶת־בָּמוֹת הַשְּׁעָרִים אֲשֶׁר־פֶּתַח שַׁעַר יְהוֹשֻׁעַ שַׂר־הָעִיר אֲשֶׁר־עַל־שְׂמֹאול אִישׁ בְּשַׁעַר הָעִיר: אַךְ לֹא יַעֲלוּ כֹּהֲנֵי הַבָּמוֹת אֶל־מִזְבַּח יהוה בִּירוּשָׁלָםִ כִּי אִם־אָכְלוּ מַצּוֹת בְּתוֹךְ אֲחֵיהֶם:

מלכים ב׳ כג:כא-כה

וַיְצַו הַמֶּלֶךְ אֶת־כָּל־הָעָם לֵאמֹר עֲשׂוּ פֶסַח לַיהוה אֱלֹהֵיכֶם כַּכָּתוּב עַל סֵפֶר הַבְּרִית הַזֶּה: כִּי לֹא נַעֲשָׂה כַּפֶּסַח הַזֶּה מִימֵי הַשֹּׁפְטִים אֲשֶׁר שָׁפְטוּ אֶת־יִשְׂרָאֵל וְכֹל יְמֵי מַלְכֵי יִשְׂרָאֵל וּמַלְכֵי יְהוּדָה: כִּי אִם־בִּשְׁמֹנֶה עֶשְׂרֵה שָׁנָה לַמֶּלֶךְ יֹאשִׁיָּהוּ נַעֲשָׂה הַפֶּסַח הַזֶּה לַיהוה בִּירוּשָׁלָםִ: וְגַם אֶת־הָאֹבוֹת וְאֶת־הַיִּדְּעֹנִים וְאֶת־הַתְּרָפִים וְאֶת־הַגִּלֻּלִים וְאֵת כָּל־הַשִּׁקֻּצִים אֲשֶׁר נִרְאוּ בְּאֶרֶץ יְהוּדָה וּבִירוּשָׁלַםִ בִּעֵר יֹאשִׁיָּהוּ לְמַעַן הָקִים אֶת־דִּבְרֵי הַתּוֹרָה הַכְּתֻבִים עַל־הַסֵּפֶר אֲשֶׁר מָצָא חִלְקִיָּהוּ הַכֹּהֵן בֵּית יהוה: וְכָמֹהוּ לֹא־הָיָה לְפָנָיו מֶלֶךְ אֲשֶׁר־שָׁב אֶל־יהוה בְּכָל־לְבָבוֹ וּבְכָל־נַפְשׁוֹ וּבְכָל־מְאֹדוֹ כְּכֹל תּוֹרַת מֹשֶׁה וְאַחֲרָיו לֹא־קָם כָּמֹהוּ:

קריאה ליום השלישי של פסח

THIRD DAY OF PESAḤ

שמות יג:א-טז

If the third day of פסח *falls on* שבת, *the* קריאת התורה *for* שבת חול המועד *is read* (*page 1148*).

וַיְדַבֵּר יהוה אֶל־מֹשֶׁה לֵּאמֹר: קַדֶּשׁ־לִי כָל־בְּכוֹר פֶּטֶר כָּל־רֶחֶם בִּבְנֵי יִשְׂרָאֵל בָּאָדָם וּבַבְּהֵמָה לִי הוּא: וַיֹּאמֶר מֹשֶׁה אֶל־הָעָם זָכוֹר אֶת־הַיּוֹם הַזֶּה אֲשֶׁר יְצָאתֶם מִמִּצְרַיִם מִבֵּית עֲבָדִים כִּי בְּחֹזֶק יָד הוֹצִיא יהוה אֶתְכֶם מִזֶּה וְלֹא יֵאָכֵל חָמֵץ: הַיּוֹם אַתֶּם יֹצְאִים בְּחֹדֶשׁ הָאָבִיב: לוי: וְהָיָה כִי־יְבִיאֲךָ יהוה אֶל־אֶרֶץ הַכְּנַעֲנִי וְהַחִתִּי וְהָאֱמֹרִי וְהַחִוִּי וְהַיְבוּסִי אֲשֶׁר נִשְׁבַּע לַאֲבֹתֶיךָ לָתֶת לָךְ אֶרֶץ זָבַת חָלָב וּדְבָשׁ וְעָבַדְתָּ אֶת־הָעֲבֹדָה הַזֹּאת בַּחֹדֶשׁ הַזֶּה: שִׁבְעַת יָמִים תֹּאכַל מַצֹּת וּבַיּוֹם הַשְּׁבִיעִי חַג לַיהוה: מַצּוֹת יֵאָכֵל אֵת שִׁבְעַת הַיָּמִים וְלֹא־יֵרָאֶה לְךָ חָמֵץ וְלֹא־יֵרָאֶה לְךָ שְׂאֹר בְּכָל־גְּבֻלֶךָ: וְהִגַּדְתָּ לְבִנְךָ בַּיּוֹם הַהוּא לֵאמֹר בַּעֲבוּר זֶה עָשָׂה יהוה לִי בְּצֵאתִי מִמִּצְרָיִם: וְהָיָה לְךָ לְאוֹת עַל־יָדְךָ וּלְזִכָּרוֹן בֵּין עֵינֶיךָ לְמַעַן תִּהְיֶה תּוֹרַת יהוה בְּפִיךָ כִּי בְּיָד חֲזָקָה הוֹצִאֲךָ יהוה מִמִּצְרָיִם: וְשָׁמַרְתָּ אֶת־הַחֻקָּה הַזֹּאת לְמוֹעֲדָהּ מִיָּמִים יָמִימָה:

שלישי: וְהָיָה כִּי־יְבִאֲךָ יהוה אֶל־אֶרֶץ הַכְּנַעֲנִי כַּאֲשֶׁר נִשְׁבַּע לְךָ וְלַאֲבֹתֶיךָ וּנְתָנָהּ לָךְ: וְהַעֲבַרְתָּ כָל־פֶּטֶר־רֶחֶם לַיהוה וְכָל־פֶּטֶר ׀ שֶׁגֶר בְּהֵמָה אֲשֶׁר יִהְיֶה לְךָ הַזְּכָרִים לַיהוה: וְכָל־פֶּטֶר חֲמֹר תִּפְדֶּה בְשֶׂה וְאִם־לֹא תִפְדֶּה וַעֲרַפְתּוֹ וְכֹל בְּכוֹר אָדָם בְּבָנֶיךָ תִּפְדֶּה: וְהָיָה כִּי־יִשְׁאָלְךָ בִנְךָ מָחָר לֵאמֹר מַה־זֹּאת וְאָמַרְתָּ אֵלָיו בְּחֹזֶק יָד הוֹצִיאָנוּ יהוה מִמִּצְרַיִם מִבֵּית עֲבָדִים: וַיְהִי כִּי־הִקְשָׁה פַרְעֹה לְשַׁלְּחֵנוּ וַיַּהֲרֹג יהוה כָּל־בְּכוֹר בְּאֶרֶץ מִצְרַיִם מִבְּכֹר אָדָם וְעַד־בְּכוֹר בְּהֵמָה עַל־כֵּן אֲנִי זֹבֵחַ לַיהוה כָּל־פֶּטֶר רֶחֶם הַזְּכָרִים וְכָל־בְּכוֹר בָּנַי אֶפְדֶּה: וְהָיָה לְאוֹת עַל־יָדְכָה וּלְטוֹטָפֹת בֵּין עֵינֶיךָ כִּי בְּחֹזֶק יָד הוֹצִיאָנוּ יהוה מִמִּצְרָיִם:

רביעי *is read from the second* ספר תורה*:*

במדבר כח:יט-כה

וְהִקְרַבְתֶּם אִשֶּׁה עֹלָה לַיהוה פָּרִים בְּנֵי־בָקָר שְׁנַיִם וְאַיִל אֶחָד וְשִׁבְעָה כְבָשִׂים בְּנֵי שָׁנָה תְּמִימִם יִהְיוּ לָכֶם: וּמִנְחָתָם סֹלֶת בְּלוּלָה בַשָּׁמֶן שְׁלֹשָׁה עֶשְׂרֹנִים לַפָּר וּשְׁנֵי

עֶשְׂרֹנִים לָאַיִל תַּעֲשׂוּ: עִשָּׂרוֹן עִשָּׂרוֹן תַּעֲשֶׂה לַכֶּבֶשׂ הָאֶחָד לְשִׁבְעַת הַכְּבָשִׂים: וּשְׂעִיר חַטָּאת אֶחָד לְכַפֵּר עֲלֵיכֶם: מִלְּבַד עֹלַת הַבֹּקֶר אֲשֶׁר לְעֹלַת הַתָּמִיד תַּעֲשׂוּ אֶת־אֵלֶּה: כָּאֵלֶּה תַּעֲשׂוּ לַיּוֹם שִׁבְעַת יָמִים לֶחֶם אִשֵּׁה רֵיחַ־נִיחֹחַ לַיהוָה עַל־עוֹלַת הַתָּמִיד יֵעָשֶׂה וְנִסְכּוֹ: וּבַיּוֹם הַשְּׁבִיעִי מִקְרָא־קֹדֶשׁ יִהְיֶה לָכֶם כָּל־מְלֶאכֶת עֲבֹדָה לֹא תַעֲשׂוּ:

קריאה ליום הרביעי של פסח
FOURTH DAY OF PESAḤ

שמות כב:כד-כג:יט

If the fourth day of פסח *falls on Sunday, the* קריאת התורה *for the third day is read (page 1145).*

אִם־כֶּסֶף ׀ תַּלְוֶה אֶת־עַמִּי אֶת־הֶעָנִי עִמָּךְ לֹא־תִהְיֶה לוֹ כְּנֹשֶׁה לֹא־תְשִׂימוּן עָלָיו נֶשֶׁךְ: אִם־חָבֹל תַּחְבֹּל שַׂלְמַת רֵעֶךָ עַד־בֹּא הַשֶּׁמֶשׁ תְּשִׁיבֶנּוּ לוֹ: כִּי הִוא כְסוּתֹה לְבַדָּהּ הִוא שִׂמְלָתוֹ לְעֹרוֹ בַּמֶּה יִשְׁכָּב וְהָיָה כִּי־יִצְעַק אֵלַי וְשָׁמַעְתִּי כִּי־חַנּוּן אָנִי: לוי: אֱלֹהִים לֹא תְקַלֵּל וְנָשִׂיא בְעַמְּךָ לֹא תָאֹר: מְלֵאָתְךָ וְדִמְעֲךָ לֹא תְאַחֵר בְּכוֹר בָּנֶיךָ תִּתֶּן־לִּי: כֵּן־תַּעֲשֶׂה לְשֹׁרְךָ לְצֹאנֶךָ שִׁבְעַת יָמִים יִהְיֶה עִם־אִמּוֹ בַּיּוֹם הַשְּׁמִינִי תִּתְּנוֹ־לִי: וְאַנְשֵׁי־קֹדֶשׁ תִּהְיוּן לִי וּבָשָׂר בַּשָּׂדֶה טְרֵפָה לֹא תֹאכֵלוּ לַכֶּלֶב תַּשְׁלִכוּן אֹתוֹ: לֹא תִשָּׂא שֵׁמַע שָׁוְא אַל־תָּשֶׁת יָדְךָ עִם־רָשָׁע לִהְיֹת עֵד חָמָס: לֹא־תִהְיֶה אַחֲרֵי־רַבִּים לְרָעֹת וְלֹא־תַעֲנֶה עַל־רִב לִנְטֹת אַחֲרֵי רַבִּים לְהַטֹּת: וְדָל לֹא תֶהְדַּר בְּרִיבוֹ: כִּי תִפְגַּע שׁוֹר אֹיִבְךָ אוֹ חֲמֹרוֹ תֹּעֶה הָשֵׁב תְּשִׁיבֶנּוּ לוֹ: כִּי־תִרְאֶה חֲמוֹר שֹׂנַאֲךָ רֹבֵץ תַּחַת מַשָּׂאוֹ וְחָדַלְתָּ מֵעֲזֹב לוֹ עָזֹב תַּעֲזֹב עִמּוֹ: שלישי: לֹא תַטֶּה מִשְׁפַּט אֶבְיֹנְךָ בְּרִיבוֹ: מִדְּבַר־שֶׁקֶר תִּרְחָק וְנָקִי וְצַדִּיק אַל־תַּהֲרֹג כִּי לֹא־אַצְדִּיק רָשָׁע: וְשֹׁחַד לֹא תִקָּח כִּי הַשֹּׁחַד יְעַוֵּר פִּקְחִים וִיסַלֵּף דִּבְרֵי צַדִּיקִים: וְגֵר לֹא תִלְחָץ וְאַתֶּם יְדַעְתֶּם אֶת־נֶפֶשׁ הַגֵּר כִּי־גֵרִים הֱיִיתֶם בְּאֶרֶץ מִצְרָיִם: וְשֵׁשׁ שָׁנִים תִּזְרַע אֶת־אַרְצֶךָ וְאָסַפְתָּ אֶת־תְּבוּאָתָהּ: וְהַשְּׁבִיעִת תִּשְׁמְטֶנָּה וּנְטַשְׁתָּהּ וְאָכְלוּ אֶבְיֹנֵי עַמֶּךָ וְיִתְרָם תֹּאכַל חַיַּת הַשָּׂדֶה כֵּן־תַּעֲשֶׂה לְכַרְמְךָ לְזֵיתֶךָ: שֵׁשֶׁת יָמִים תַּעֲשֶׂה מַעֲשֶׂיךָ וּבַיּוֹם הַשְּׁבִיעִי תִּשְׁבֹּת לְמַעַן יָנוּחַ שׁוֹרְךָ וַחֲמֹרֶךָ וְיִנָּפֵשׁ בֶּן־אֲמָתְךָ וְהַגֵּר: וּבְכֹל אֲשֶׁר־אָמַרְתִּי אֲלֵיכֶם תִּשָּׁמֵרוּ וְשֵׁם אֱלֹהִים אֲחֵרִים לֹא תַזְכִּירוּ לֹא יִשָּׁמַע עַל־פִּיךָ: שָׁלֹשׁ רְגָלִים תָּחֹג לִי בַּשָּׁנָה: אֶת־חַג הַמַּצּוֹת תִּשְׁמֹר שִׁבְעַת יָמִים תֹּאכַל מַצּוֹת כַּאֲשֶׁר צִוִּיתִךָ לְמוֹעֵד חֹדֶשׁ הָאָבִיב כִּי־בוֹ יָצָאתָ מִמִּצְרָיִם וְלֹא־יֵרָאוּ פָנַי רֵיקָם: וְחַג הַקָּצִיר בִּכּוּרֵי מַעֲשֶׂיךָ אֲשֶׁר תִּזְרַע בַּשָּׂדֶה וְחַג הָאָסִף בְּצֵאת הַשָּׁנָה בְּאָסְפְּךָ אֶת־מַעֲשֶׂיךָ מִן־הַשָּׂדֶה: שָׁלֹשׁ פְּעָמִים בַּשָּׁנָה יֵרָאֶה כָּל־זְכוּרְךָ אֶל־פְּנֵי הָאָדֹן ׀ יהוה: לֹא־תִזְבַּח עַל־חָמֵץ דַּם־זִבְחִי וְלֹא־יָלִין חֵלֶב־חַגִּי עַד־בֹּקֶר: רֵאשִׁית בִּכּוּרֵי אַדְמָתְךָ תָּבִיא בֵּית יהוה אֱלֹהֶיךָ לֹא־תְבַשֵּׁל גְּדִי בַּחֲלֵב אִמּוֹ:

רביעי (וְהִקְרַבְתֶּם) *is read from the second* ספר תורה *(above).*

קריאה ליום החמישי של פסח
FIFTH DAY OF PESAḤ

שמות לד:א-כו

If the fifth day of פסח *falls on* שבת*, the* קריאת התורה *for* שבת חול המועד *is read (page 1148), if it falls on Monday, the* קריאת התורה *for the fourth day is read (this page).*

וַיֹּאמֶר יהוה אֶל־מֹשֶׁה פְּסָל־לְךָ שְׁנֵי־לֻחֹת אֲבָנִים כָּרִאשֹׁנִים וְכָתַבְתִּי עַל־הַלֻּחֹת אֶת־הַדְּבָרִים אֲשֶׁר הָיוּ עַל־הַלֻּחֹת הָרִאשֹׁנִים אֲשֶׁר שִׁבַּרְתָּ: וֶהְיֵה נָכוֹן לַבֹּקֶר וְעָלִיתָ בַבֹּקֶר אֶל־הַר סִינַי וְנִצַּבְתָּ לִי שָׁם עַל־רֹאשׁ הָהָר: וְאִישׁ לֹא־יַעֲלֶה עִמָּךְ וְגַם־אִישׁ אַל־יֵרָא בְּכָל־הָהָר גַּם־הַצֹּאן וְהַבָּקָר אַל־יִרְעוּ אֶל־מוּל הָהָר הַהוּא: לוי: וַיִּפְסֹל שְׁנֵי־לֻחֹת אֲבָנִים כָּרִאשֹׁנִים וַיַּשְׁכֵּם מֹשֶׁה בַבֹּקֶר וַיַּעַל

אֶל־הַר סִינַי כַּאֲשֶׁר צִוָּה יהוה אֹתוֹ וַיִּקַּח בְּיָדוֹ שְׁנֵי לֻחֹת אֲבָנִים׃ וַיֵּרֶד יהוה בֶּעָנָן וַיִּתְיַצֵּב עִמּוֹ שָׁם וַיִּקְרָא בְשֵׁם יהוה׃ וַיַּעֲבֹר יהוה ׀ עַל־פָּנָיו וַיִּקְרָא יהוה ׀ יהוה אֵל רַחוּם וְחַנּוּן אֶרֶךְ אַפַּיִם וְרַב־חֶסֶד וֶאֱמֶת׃ נֹצֵר חֶסֶד לָאֲלָפִים נֹשֵׂא עָוֺן וָפֶשַׁע וְחַטָּאָה וְנַקֵּה לֹא יְנַקֶּה פֹּקֵד ׀ עֲוֺן אָבוֹת עַל־בָּנִים וְעַל־בְּנֵי בָנִים עַל־שִׁלֵּשִׁים וְעַל־רִבֵּעִים׃ וַיְמַהֵר מֹשֶׁה וַיִּקֹּד אַרְצָה וַיִּשְׁתָּחוּ׃ וַיֹּאמֶר אִם־נָא מָצָאתִי חֵן בְּעֵינֶיךָ אֲדֹנָי יֵלֶךְ־נָא אֲדֹנָי בְּקִרְבֵּנוּ כִּי עַם־קְשֵׁה־עֹרֶף הוּא וְסָלַחְתָּ לַעֲוֺנֵנוּ וּלְחַטָּאתֵנוּ וּנְחַלְתָּנוּ׃ וַיֹּאמֶר הִנֵּה אָנֹכִי כֹּרֵת בְּרִית נֶגֶד כָּל־עַמְּךָ אֶעֱשֶׂה נִפְלָאֹת אֲשֶׁר לֹא־נִבְרְאוּ בְכָל־הָאָרֶץ וּבְכָל־הַגּוֹיִם וְרָאָה כָל־הָעָם אֲשֶׁר־אַתָּה בְקִרְבּוֹ אֶת־מַעֲשֵׂה יהוה כִּי־נוֹרָא הוּא אֲשֶׁר אֲנִי עֹשֶׂה עִמָּךְ׃ שלישי: שְׁמָר־לְךָ אֵת אֲשֶׁר אָנֹכִי מְצַוְּךָ הַיּוֹם הִנְנִי גֹרֵשׁ מִפָּנֶיךָ אֶת־הָאֱמֹרִי וְהַכְּנַעֲנִי וְהַחִתִּי וְהַפְּרִזִּי וְהַחִוִּי וְהַיְבוּסִי׃ הִשָּׁמֶר לְךָ פֶּן־תִּכְרֹת בְּרִית לְיוֹשֵׁב הָאָרֶץ אֲשֶׁר אַתָּה בָּא עָלֶיהָ פֶּן־יִהְיֶה לְמוֹקֵשׁ בְּקִרְבֶּךָ׃ כִּי אֶת־מִזְבְּחֹתָם תִּתֹּצוּן וְאֶת־מַצֵּבֹתָם תְּשַׁבֵּרוּן וְאֶת־אֲשֵׁרָיו תִּכְרֹתוּן׃ כִּי לֹא תִשְׁתַּחֲוֶה לְאֵל אַחֵר כִּי יהוה קַנָּא שְׁמוֹ אֵל קַנָּא הוּא׃ פֶּן־תִּכְרֹת בְּרִית לְיוֹשֵׁב הָאָרֶץ וְזָנוּ ׀ אַחֲרֵי אֱלֹהֵיהֶם וְזָבְחוּ לֵאלֹהֵיהֶם וְקָרָא לְךָ וְאָכַלְתָּ מִזִּבְחוֹ׃ וְלָקַחְתָּ מִבְּנֹתָיו לְבָנֶיךָ וְזָנוּ בְנֹתָיו אַחֲרֵי אֱלֹהֵיהֶן וְהִזְנוּ אֶת־בָּנֶיךָ אַחֲרֵי אֱלֹהֵיהֶן׃ אֱלֹהֵי מַסֵּכָה לֹא תַעֲשֶׂה־לָּךְ׃ אֶת־חַג הַמַּצּוֹת תִּשְׁמֹר שִׁבְעַת יָמִים תֹּאכַל מַצּוֹת אֲשֶׁר צִוִּיתִךָ לְמוֹעֵד חֹדֶשׁ הָאָבִיב כִּי בְּחֹדֶשׁ הָאָבִיב יָצָאתָ מִמִּצְרָיִם׃ כָּל־פֶּטֶר רֶחֶם לִי וְכָל־מִקְנְךָ תִּזָּכָר פֶּטֶר שׁוֹר וָשֶׂה׃ וּפֶטֶר חֲמוֹר תִּפְדֶּה בְשֶׂה וְאִם־לֹא תִפְדֶּה וַעֲרַפְתּוֹ כֹּל בְּכוֹר בָּנֶיךָ תִּפְדֶּה וְלֹא־יֵרָאוּ פָנַי רֵיקָם׃ שֵׁשֶׁת יָמִים תַּעֲבֹד וּבַיּוֹם הַשְּׁבִיעִי תִּשְׁבֹּת בֶּחָרִישׁ וּבַקָּצִיר תִּשְׁבֹּת׃ וְחַג שָׁבֻעֹת תַּעֲשֶׂה לְךָ בִּכּוּרֵי קְצִיר חִטִּים וְחַג הָאָסִיף תְּקוּפַת הַשָּׁנָה׃ שָׁלֹשׁ פְּעָמִים בַּשָּׁנָה יֵרָאֶה כָּל־זְכוּרְךָ אֶת־פְּנֵי הָאָדֹן ׀ יהוה אֱלֹהֵי יִשְׂרָאֵל׃ כִּי־אוֹרִישׁ גּוֹיִם מִפָּנֶיךָ וְהִרְחַבְתִּי אֶת־גְּבֻלֶךָ וְלֹא־יַחְמֹד אִישׁ אֶת־אַרְצְךָ בַּעֲלֹתְךָ לֵרָאוֹת אֶת־פְּנֵי יהוה אֱלֹהֶיךָ שָׁלֹשׁ פְּעָמִים בַּשָּׁנָה׃ לֹא־תִשְׁחַט עַל־חָמֵץ דַּם־זִבְחִי וְלֹא־יָלִין לַבֹּקֶר זֶבַח חַג הַפָּסַח׃ רֵאשִׁית בִּכּוּרֵי אַדְמָתְךָ תָּבִיא בֵּית יהוה אֱלֹהֶיךָ לֹא־תְבַשֵּׁל גְּדִי בַּחֲלֵב אִמּוֹ׃

רביעי (וְהִקְרַבְתֶּם) *is read from the second* ספר תורה *(page 1145).*

קריאה ליום הששי של פסח

SIXTH DAY OF PESAḤ

במדבר ט:א-יד

וַיְדַבֵּר יהוה אֶל־מֹשֶׁה בְמִדְבַּר־סִינַי בַּשָּׁנָה הַשֵּׁנִית לְצֵאתָם מֵאֶרֶץ מִצְרַיִם בַּחֹדֶשׁ הָרִאשׁוֹן לֵאמֹר׃ וְיַעֲשׂוּ בְנֵי־יִשְׂרָאֵל אֶת־הַפָּסַח בְּמוֹעֲדוֹ׃ בְּאַרְבָּעָה עָשָׂר־יוֹם בַּחֹדֶשׁ הַזֶּה בֵּין הָעַרְבַּיִם תַּעֲשׂוּ אֹתוֹ בְּמֹעֲדוֹ כְּכָל־חֻקֹּתָיו וּכְכָל־מִשְׁפָּטָיו תַּעֲשׂוּ אֹתוֹ׃ וַיְדַבֵּר מֹשֶׁה אֶל־בְּנֵי יִשְׂרָאֵל לַעֲשֹׂת הַפָּסַח׃ וַיַּעֲשׂוּ אֶת־הַפֶּסַח בָּרִאשׁוֹן בְּאַרְבָּעָה עָשָׂר יוֹם לַחֹדֶשׁ בֵּין הָעַרְבַּיִם בְּמִדְבַּר סִינָי כְּכֹל אֲשֶׁר צִוָּה יהוה אֶת־מֹשֶׁה כֵּן עָשׂוּ בְּנֵי יִשְׂרָאֵל׃ לוי: וַיְהִי אֲנָשִׁים אֲשֶׁר הָיוּ טְמֵאִים לְנֶפֶשׁ אָדָם וְלֹא־יָכְלוּ לַעֲשֹׂת־הַפֶּסַח בַּיּוֹם הַהוּא וַיִּקְרְבוּ לִפְנֵי מֹשֶׁה וְלִפְנֵי אַהֲרֹן בַּיּוֹם הַהוּא׃ וַיֹּאמְרוּ הָאֲנָשִׁים הָהֵמָּה אֵלָיו אֲנַחְנוּ טְמֵאִים לְנֶפֶשׁ אָדָם לָמָּה נִגָּרַע לְבִלְתִּי הַקְרִיב אֶת־קָרְבַּן יהוה בְּמֹעֲדוֹ בְּתוֹךְ בְּנֵי יִשְׂרָאֵל׃ וַיֹּאמֶר אֲלֵהֶם מֹשֶׁה עִמְדוּ וְאֶשְׁמְעָה מַה־יְצַוֶּה יהוה לָכֶם׃

שלישי: וַיְדַבֵּר יהוה אֶל־מֹשֶׁה לֵּאמֹר׃ דַּבֵּר אֶל־בְּנֵי יִשְׂרָאֵל לֵאמֹר אִישׁ אִישׁ כִּי־יִהְיֶה טָמֵא ׀ לָנֶפֶשׁ אוֹ בְדֶרֶךְ רְחֹקָה לָכֶם אוֹ לְדֹרֹתֵיכֶם וְעָשָׂה פֶסַח לַיהוה׃ בַּחֹדֶשׁ הַשֵּׁנִי בְּאַרְבָּעָה עָשָׂר יוֹם בֵּין הָעַרְבַּיִם יַעֲשׂוּ אֹתוֹ

עַל־מַצּוֹת וּמְרֹרִים יֹאכְלֻהוּ׃ לֹא־יַשְׁאִירוּ מִמֶּנּוּ עַד־בֹּקֶר וְעֶצֶם לֹא יִשְׁבְּרוּ־בוֹ כְּכָל־חֻקַּת הַפֶּסַח יַעֲשׂוּ אֹתוֹ׃ וְהָאִישׁ אֲשֶׁר־הוּא טָהוֹר וּבְדֶרֶךְ לֹא־הָיָה וְחָדַל לַעֲשׂוֹת הַפֶּסַח וְנִכְרְתָה הַנֶּפֶשׁ הַהִוא מֵעַמֶּיהָ כִּי ׀ קָרְבַּן יהוה לֹא הִקְרִיב בְּמֹעֲדוֹ חֶטְאוֹ יִשָּׂא הָאִישׁ הַהוּא׃ וְכִי־יָגוּר אִתְּכֶם גֵּר וְעָשָׂה פֶסַח לַיהוה כְּחֻקַּת הַפֶּסַח וּכְמִשְׁפָּטוֹ כֵּן יַעֲשֶׂה חֻקָּה אַחַת יִהְיֶה לָכֶם וְלַגֵּר וּלְאֶזְרַח הָאָרֶץ׃

רביעי (וְהִקְרַבְתֶּם) *is read from the second* ספר תורה *(page 1145).*

קריאה לשבת חול המועד פסח וסוכות
SHABBAT ḤOL HAMO'ED PESAḤ AND SUKKOT

שמות לג: יב-לד:כו

וַיֹּאמֶר מֹשֶׁה אֶל־יהוה רְאֵה אַתָּה אֹמֵר אֵלַי הַעַל אֶת־הָעָם הַזֶּה וְאַתָּה לֹא הוֹדַעְתַּנִי אֵת אֲשֶׁר־תִּשְׁלַח עִמִּי וְאַתָּה אָמַרְתָּ יְדַעְתִּיךָ בְשֵׁם וְגַם־מָצָאתָ חֵן בְּעֵינָי׃ וְעַתָּה אִם־נָא מָצָאתִי חֵן בְּעֵינֶיךָ הוֹדִעֵנִי נָא אֶת־דְּרָכֶךָ וְאֵדָעֲךָ לְמַעַן אֶמְצָא־חֵן בְּעֵינֶיךָ וּרְאֵה כִּי עַמְּךָ הַגּוֹי הַזֶּה׃ וַיֹּאמַר פָּנַי יֵלֵכוּ וַהֲנִחֹתִי לָךְ׃ וַיֹּאמֶר אֵלָיו אִם־אֵין פָּנֶיךָ הֹלְכִים אַל־תַּעֲלֵנוּ מִזֶּה׃ וּבַמֶּה ׀ יִוָּדַע אֵפוֹא כִּי־מָצָאתִי חֵן בְּעֵינֶיךָ אֲנִי וְעַמֶּךָ הֲלוֹא בְּלֶכְתְּךָ עִמָּנוּ וְנִפְלֵינוּ אֲנִי וְעַמְּךָ מִכָּל־הָעָם אֲשֶׁר עַל־פְּנֵי הָאֲדָמָה׃

לוי: וַיֹּאמֶר יהוה אֶל־מֹשֶׁה גַּם אֶת־הַדָּבָר הַזֶּה אֲשֶׁר דִּבַּרְתָּ אֶעֱשֶׂה כִּי־מָצָאתָ חֵן בְּעֵינַי וָאֵדָעֲךָ בְּשֵׁם׃ וַיֹּאמַר הַרְאֵנִי נָא אֶת־כְּבֹדֶךָ׃ וַיֹּאמֶר אֲנִי אַעֲבִיר כָּל־טוּבִי עַל־פָּנֶיךָ וְקָרָאתִי בְשֵׁם יהוה לְפָנֶיךָ וְחַנֹּתִי אֶת־אֲשֶׁר אָחֹן וְרִחַמְתִּי אֶת־אֲשֶׁר אֲרַחֵם׃

שלישי: וַיֹּאמֶר לֹא תוּכַל לִרְאֹת אֶת־פָּנָי כִּי לֹא־יִרְאַנִי הָאָדָם וָחָי׃ וַיֹּאמֶר יהוה הִנֵּה מָקוֹם אִתִּי וְנִצַּבְתָּ עַל־הַצּוּר׃ וְהָיָה בַּעֲבֹר כְּבֹדִי וְשַׂמְתִּיךָ בְּנִקְרַת הַצּוּר וְשַׂכֹּתִי כַפִּי עָלֶיךָ עַד־עָבְרִי׃ וַהֲסִרֹתִי אֶת־כַּפִּי וְרָאִיתָ אֶת־אֲחֹרָי וּפָנַי לֹא יֵרָאוּ׃

רביעי: וַיֹּאמֶר יהוה אֶל־מֹשֶׁה פְּסָל־לְךָ שְׁנֵי־לֻחֹת אֲבָנִים כָּרִאשֹׁנִים וְכָתַבְתִּי עַל־הַלֻּחֹת אֶת־הַדְּבָרִים אֲשֶׁר הָיוּ עַל־הַלֻּחֹת הָרִאשֹׁנִים אֲשֶׁר שִׁבַּרְתָּ׃ וֶהְיֵה נָכוֹן לַבֹּקֶר וְעָלִיתָ בַבֹּקֶר אֶל־הַר סִינַי וְנִצַּבְתָּ לִי שָׁם עַל־רֹאשׁ הָהָר׃ וְאִישׁ לֹא־יַעֲלֶה עִמָּךְ וְגַם־אִישׁ אַל־יֵרָא בְּכָל־הָהָר גַּם־הַצֹּאן וְהַבָּקָר אַל־יִרְעוּ אֶל־מוּל הָהָר הַהוּא׃ חמישי: וַיִּפְסֹל שְׁנֵי־לֻחֹת אֲבָנִים כָּרִאשֹׁנִים וַיַּשְׁכֵּם מֹשֶׁה בַבֹּקֶר וַיַּעַל אֶל־הַר סִינַי כַּאֲשֶׁר צִוָּה יהוה אֹתוֹ וַיִּקַּח בְּיָדוֹ שְׁנֵי לֻחֹת אֲבָנִים׃ וַיֵּרֶד יהוה בֶּעָנָן וַיִּתְיַצֵּב עִמּוֹ שָׁם וַיִּקְרָא בְשֵׁם יהוה׃ וַיַּעֲבֹר יהוה ׀ עַל־פָּנָיו וַיִּקְרָא יהוה ׀ יהוה אֵל רַחוּם וְחַנּוּן אֶרֶךְ אַפַּיִם וְרַב־חֶסֶד וֶאֱמֶת׃ נֹצֵר חֶסֶד לָאֲלָפִים נֹשֵׂא עָוֺן וָפֶשַׁע וְחַטָּאָה וְנַקֵּה לֹא יְנַקֶּה פֹּקֵד ׀ עֲוֺן אָבוֹת עַל־בָּנִים וְעַל־בְּנֵי בָנִים עַל־שִׁלֵּשִׁים וְעַל־רִבֵּעִים׃ וַיְמַהֵר מֹשֶׁה וַיִּקֹּד אַרְצָה וַיִּשְׁתָּחוּ׃ וַיֹּאמֶר אִם־נָא מָצָאתִי חֵן בְּעֵינֶיךָ אֲדֹנָי יֵלֶךְ־נָא אֲדֹנָי בְּקִרְבֵּנוּ כִּי עַם־קְשֵׁה־עֹרֶף הוּא וְסָלַחְתָּ לַעֲוֺנֵנוּ וּלְחַטָּאתֵנוּ וּנְחַלְתָּנוּ׃ וַיֹּאמֶר הִנֵּה אָנֹכִי כֹּרֵת בְּרִית נֶגֶד כָּל־עַמְּךָ אֶעֱשֶׂה נִפְלָאֹת אֲשֶׁר לֹא־נִבְרְאוּ בְכָל־הָאָרֶץ וּבְכָל־הַגּוֹיִם וְרָאָה כָל־הָעָם אֲשֶׁר־אַתָּה בְקִרְבּוֹ אֶת־מַעֲשֵׂה יהוה כִּי־נוֹרָא הוּא אֲשֶׁר אֲנִי עֹשֶׂה עִמָּךְ׃ ששי: שְׁמָר־לְךָ אֵת אֲשֶׁר אָנֹכִי מְצַוְּךָ הַיּוֹם הִנְנִי גֹרֵשׁ מִפָּנֶיךָ אֶת־הָאֱמֹרִי וְהַכְּנַעֲנִי וְהַחִתִּי וְהַפְּרִזִּי וְהַחִוִּי וְהַיְבוּסִי׃ הִשָּׁמֶר לְךָ פֶּן־תִּכְרֹת בְּרִית לְיוֹשֵׁב הָאָרֶץ אֲשֶׁר אַתָּה בָּא עָלֶיהָ פֶּן־יִהְיֶה לְמוֹקֵשׁ בְּקִרְבֶּךָ׃ כִּי אֶת־מִזְבְּחֹתָם תִּתֹּצוּן וְאֶת־מַצֵּבֹתָם תְּשַׁבֵּרוּן וְאֶת־אֲשֵׁרָיו תִּכְרֹתוּן׃ כִּי

לֹא תִשְׁתַּחֲוֶה לְאֵל אַחֵר כִּי יהוה קַנָּא שְׁמוֹ אֵל קַנָּא הוּא: פֶּן־תִּכְרֹת בְּרִית לְיוֹשֵׁב הָאָרֶץ וְזָנוּ ׀ אַחֲרֵי אֱלֹהֵיהֶם וְזָבְחוּ לֵאלֹהֵיהֶם וְקָרָא לְךָ וְאָכַלְתָּ מִזִּבְחוֹ: וְלָקַחְתָּ מִבְּנֹתָיו לְבָנֶיךָ וְזָנוּ בְנֹתָיו אַחֲרֵי אֱלֹהֵיהֶן וְהִזְנוּ אֶת־בָּנֶיךָ אַחֲרֵי אֱלֹהֵיהֶן: אֱלֹהֵי מַסֵּכָה לֹא תַעֲשֶׂה־לָּךְ: שביעי אֶת־חַג הַמַּצּוֹת תִּשְׁמֹר שִׁבְעַת יָמִים תֹּאכַל מַצּוֹת אֲשֶׁר צִוִּיתִךָ לְמוֹעֵד חֹדֶשׁ הָאָבִיב כִּי בְּחֹדֶשׁ הָאָבִיב יָצָאתָ מִמִּצְרָיִם: כָּל־פֶּטֶר רֶחֶם לִי וְכָל־מִקְנְךָ תִּזָּכָר פֶּטֶר שׁוֹר וָשֶׂה: וּפֶטֶר חֲמוֹר תִּפְדֶּה בְשֶׂה וְאִם־לֹא תִפְדֶּה וַעֲרַפְתּוֹ כֹּל בְּכוֹר בָּנֶיךָ תִּפְדֶּה וְלֹא־יֵרָאוּ פָנַי רֵיקָם: שֵׁשֶׁת יָמִים תַּעֲבֹד וּבַיּוֹם הַשְּׁבִיעִי תִּשְׁבֹּת בֶּחָרִישׁ וּבַקָּצִיר תִּשְׁבֹּת: וְחַג שָׁבֻעֹת תַּעֲשֶׂה לְךָ בִּכּוּרֵי קְצִיר חִטִּים וְחַג הָאָסִיף תְּקוּפַת הַשָּׁנָה: שָׁלֹשׁ פְּעָמִים בַּשָּׁנָה יֵרָאֶה כָּל־זְכוּרְךָ אֶת־פְּנֵי הָאָדֹן ׀ יהוה אֱלֹהֵי יִשְׂרָאֵל: כִּי־אוֹרִישׁ גּוֹיִם מִפָּנֶיךָ וְהִרְחַבְתִּי אֶת־גְּבֻלֶךָ וְלֹא־יַחְמֹד אִישׁ אֶת־אַרְצְךָ בַּעֲלֹתְךָ לֵרָאוֹת אֶת־פְּנֵי יהוה אֱלֹהֶיךָ שָׁלֹשׁ פְּעָמִים בַּשָּׁנָה: לֹא־תִשְׁחַט עַל־חָמֵץ דַּם־זִבְחִי וְלֹא־יָלִין לַבֹּקֶר זֶבַח חַג הַפָּסַח: רֵאשִׁית בִּכּוּרֵי אַדְמָתְךָ תָּבִיא בֵּית יהוה אֱלֹהֶיךָ לֹא־תְבַשֵּׁל גְּדִי בַּחֲלֵב אִמּוֹ:

The מפטיר *for* שבת חול המועד פסח *is the same as that for the other days of* חול המועד פסח, *page 1145. The* מפטיר *for* שבת חול המועד סוכות *is the* קריאת התורה *of the day of* חול המועד סוכות *on which* שבת *falls (pages 1161–1163).*

הפטרה לשבת חול המועד פסח
HAFTARA FOR SHABBAT ḤOL HAMO'ED PESAḤ

יחזקאל לז:א–יד

הָיְתָה עָלַי יַד־יהוה וַיּוֹצִאֵנִי בְרוּחַ יהוה וַיְנִיחֵנִי בְּתוֹךְ הַבִּקְעָה וְהִיא מְלֵאָה עֲצָמוֹת: וְהֶעֱבִירַנִי עֲלֵיהֶם סָבִיב ׀ סָבִיב וְהִנֵּה רַבּוֹת מְאֹד עַל־פְּנֵי הַבִּקְעָה וְהִנֵּה יְבֵשׁוֹת מְאֹד: וַיֹּאמֶר אֵלַי בֶּן־אָדָם הֲתִחְיֶינָה הָעֲצָמוֹת הָאֵלֶּה וָאֹמַר אֲדֹנָי יֱהֹוִה אַתָּה יָדָעְתָּ: וַיֹּאמֶר אֵלַי הִנָּבֵא עַל־הָעֲצָמוֹת הָאֵלֶּה וְאָמַרְתָּ אֲלֵיהֶם הָעֲצָמוֹת הַיְבֵשׁוֹת שִׁמְעוּ דְּבַר־יהוה: כֹּה אָמַר אֲדֹנָי יֱהֹוִה לָעֲצָמוֹת הָאֵלֶּה הִנֵּה אֲנִי מֵבִיא בָכֶם רוּחַ וִחְיִיתֶם: וְנָתַתִּי עֲלֵיכֶם גִּידִים וְהַעֲלֵתִי עֲלֵיכֶם בָּשָׂר וְקָרַמְתִּי עֲלֵיכֶם עוֹר וְנָתַתִּי בָכֶם רוּחַ וִחְיִיתֶם וִידַעְתֶּם כִּי־אֲנִי יהוה: וְנִבֵּאתִי כַּאֲשֶׁר צֻוֵּיתִי וַיְהִי־קוֹל כְּהִנָּבְאִי וְהִנֵּה־רַעַשׁ וַתִּקְרְבוּ עֲצָמוֹת עֶצֶם אֶל־עַצְמוֹ: וְרָאִיתִי וְהִנֵּה־עֲלֵיהֶם גִּדִים וּבָשָׂר עָלָה וַיִּקְרַם עֲלֵיהֶם עוֹר מִלְמָעְלָה וְרוּחַ אֵין בָּהֶם: וַיֹּאמֶר אֵלַי הִנָּבֵא אֶל־הָרוּחַ הִנָּבֵא בֶן־אָדָם וְאָמַרְתָּ אֶל־הָרוּחַ כֹּה־אָמַר ׀ אֲדֹנָי יֱהֹוִה מֵאַרְבַּע רוּחוֹת בֹּאִי הָרוּחַ וּפְחִי בַּהֲרוּגִים הָאֵלֶּה וְיִחְיוּ: וְהִנַּבֵּאתִי כַּאֲשֶׁר צִוָּנִי וַתָּבוֹא בָהֶם הָרוּחַ וַיִּחְיוּ וַיַּעַמְדוּ עַל־רַגְלֵיהֶם חַיִל גָּדוֹל מְאֹד מְאֹד: וַיֹּאמֶר אֵלַי בֶּן־אָדָם הָעֲצָמוֹת הָאֵלֶּה כָּל־בֵּית יִשְׂרָאֵל הֵמָּה הִנֵּה אֹמְרִים יָבְשׁוּ עַצְמוֹתֵינוּ וְאָבְדָה תִקְוָתֵנוּ נִגְזַרְנוּ לָנוּ: לָכֵן הִנָּבֵא וְאָמַרְתָּ אֲלֵיהֶם כֹּה־אָמַר אֲדֹנָי יֱהֹוִה הִנֵּה אֲנִי פֹתֵחַ אֶת־קִבְרוֹתֵיכֶם וְהַעֲלֵיתִי אֶתְכֶם מִקִּבְרוֹתֵיכֶם עַמִּי וְהֵבֵאתִי אֶתְכֶם אֶל־אַדְמַת יִשְׂרָאֵל: וִידַעְתֶּם כִּי־אֲנִי יהוה בְּפִתְחִי אֶת־קִבְרוֹתֵיכֶם וּבְהַעֲלוֹתִי אֶתְכֶם מִקִּבְרוֹתֵיכֶם עַמִּי: וְנָתַתִּי רוּחִי בָכֶם וִחְיִיתֶם וְהִנַּחְתִּי אֶתְכֶם עַל־אַדְמַתְכֶם וִידַעְתֶּם כִּי אֲנִי יהוה דִּבַּרְתִּי וְעָשִׂיתִי נְאֻם־יהוה:

קריאה לשביעי של פסח
SEVENTH DAY OF PESAḤ

שמות יג:יז–טו:כו

וַיְהִי בְּשַׁלַּח פַּרְעֹה אֶת־הָעָם וְלֹא־נָחָם אֱלֹהִים דֶּרֶךְ אֶרֶץ פְּלִשְׁתִּים כִּי קָרוֹב הוּא

כִּי ׀ אָמַר אֱלֹהִים פֶּן־יִנָּחֵם הָעָם בִּרְאֹתָם מִלְחָמָה וְשָׁבוּ מִצְרָיְמָה: וַיַּסֵּב אֱלֹהִים ׀ אֶת־הָעָם דֶּרֶךְ הַמִּדְבָּר יַם־סוּף וַחֲמֻשִׁים עָלוּ בְנֵי־יִשְׂרָאֵל מֵאֶרֶץ מִצְרָיִם: וַיִּקַּח מֹשֶׁה אֶת־עַצְמוֹת יוֹסֵף עִמּוֹ כִּי הַשְׁבֵּעַ הִשְׁבִּיעַ אֶת־בְּנֵי יִשְׂרָאֵל לֵאמֹר פָּקֹד יִפְקֹד אֱלֹהִים אֶתְכֶם וְהַעֲלִיתֶם אֶת־עַצְמֹתַי מִזֶּה אִתְּכֶם: (בשבת לוי): וַיִּסְעוּ מִסֻּכֹּת וַיַּחֲנוּ בְאֵתָם בִּקְצֵה הַמִּדְבָּר: וַיהוָה הֹלֵךְ לִפְנֵיהֶם יוֹמָם בְּעַמּוּד עָנָן לַנְחֹתָם הַדֶּרֶךְ וְלַיְלָה בְּעַמּוּד אֵשׁ לְהָאִיר לָהֶם לָלֶכֶת יוֹמָם וָלָיְלָה: לֹא־יָמִישׁ עַמּוּד הֶעָנָן יוֹמָם וְעַמּוּד הָאֵשׁ לָיְלָה לִפְנֵי הָעָם:

לוי (בשבת שלישי): וַיְדַבֵּר יהוה אֶל־מֹשֶׁה לֵּאמֹר: דַּבֵּר אֶל־בְּנֵי יִשְׂרָאֵל וְיָשֻׁבוּ וְיַחֲנוּ לִפְנֵי פִּי הַחִירֹת בֵּין מִגְדֹּל וּבֵין הַיָּם לִפְנֵי בַּעַל צְפֹן נִכְחוֹ תַחֲנוּ עַל־הַיָּם: וְאָמַר פַּרְעֹה לִבְנֵי יִשְׂרָאֵל נְבֻכִים הֵם בָּאָרֶץ סָגַר עֲלֵיהֶם הַמִּדְבָּר: וְחִזַּקְתִּי אֶת־לֵב־פַּרְעֹה וְרָדַף אַחֲרֵיהֶם וְאִכָּבְדָה בְּפַרְעֹה וּבְכָל־חֵילוֹ וְיָדְעוּ מִצְרַיִם כִּי־אֲנִי יהוה וַיַּעֲשׂוּ־כֵן: (בשבת רביעי): וַיֻּגַּד לְמֶלֶךְ מִצְרַיִם כִּי בָרַח הָעָם וַיֵּהָפֵךְ לְבַב פַּרְעֹה וַעֲבָדָיו אֶל־הָעָם וַיֹּאמְרוּ מַה־זֹּאת עָשִׂינוּ כִּי־שִׁלַּחְנוּ אֶת־יִשְׂרָאֵל מֵעָבְדֵנוּ: וַיֶּאְסֹר אֶת־רִכְבּוֹ וְאֶת־עַמּוֹ לָקַח עִמּוֹ: וַיִּקַּח שֵׁשׁ־מֵאוֹת רֶכֶב בָּחוּר וְכֹל רֶכֶב מִצְרָיִם וְשָׁלִשִׁם עַל־כֻּלּוֹ: וַיְחַזֵּק יהוה אֶת־לֵב פַּרְעֹה מֶלֶךְ מִצְרַיִם וַיִּרְדֹּף אַחֲרֵי בְּנֵי יִשְׂרָאֵל וּבְנֵי יִשְׂרָאֵל יֹצְאִים בְּיָד רָמָה: שלישי (בשבת חמישי): וַיִּרְדְּפוּ מִצְרַיִם אַחֲרֵיהֶם וַיַּשִּׂיגוּ אוֹתָם חֹנִים עַל־הַיָּם כָּל־סוּס רֶכֶב פַּרְעֹה וּפָרָשָׁיו וְחֵילוֹ עַל־פִּי הַחִירֹת לִפְנֵי בַּעַל צְפֹן: וּפַרְעֹה הִקְרִיב וַיִּשְׂאוּ בְנֵי־יִשְׂרָאֵל אֶת־עֵינֵיהֶם וְהִנֵּה מִצְרַיִם ׀ נֹסֵעַ אַחֲרֵיהֶם וַיִּירְאוּ מְאֹד וַיִּצְעֲקוּ בְנֵי־יִשְׂרָאֵל אֶל־יהוה: וַיֹּאמְרוּ אֶל־מֹשֶׁה הֲמִבְּלִי אֵין־קְבָרִים בְּמִצְרַיִם לְקַחְתָּנוּ לָמוּת בַּמִּדְבָּר מַה־זֹּאת עָשִׂיתָ לָּנוּ לְהוֹצִיאָנוּ מִמִּצְרָיִם: הֲלֹא־זֶה הַדָּבָר אֲשֶׁר דִּבַּרְנוּ אֵלֶיךָ בְמִצְרַיִם לֵאמֹר חֲדַל מִמֶּנּוּ וְנַעַבְדָה אֶת־מִצְרָיִם כִּי טוֹב לָנוּ עֲבֹד אֶת־מִצְרַיִם מִמֻּתֵנוּ בַּמִּדְבָּר: וַיֹּאמֶר מֹשֶׁה אֶל־הָעָם אַל־תִּירָאוּ הִתְיַצְּבוּ וּרְאוּ אֶת־יְשׁוּעַת יהוה אֲשֶׁר־יַעֲשֶׂה לָכֶם הַיּוֹם כִּי אֲשֶׁר רְאִיתֶם אֶת־מִצְרַיִם הַיּוֹם לֹא תֹסִפוּ לִרְאֹתָם עוֹד עַד־עוֹלָם: יהוה יִלָּחֵם לָכֶם וְאַתֶּם תַּחֲרִשׁוּן:

רביעי (בשבת ששי): וַיֹּאמֶר יהוה אֶל־מֹשֶׁה מַה־תִּצְעַק אֵלָי דַּבֵּר אֶל־בְּנֵי־יִשְׂרָאֵל וְיִסָּעוּ: וְאַתָּה הָרֵם אֶת־מַטְּךָ וּנְטֵה אֶת־יָדְךָ עַל־הַיָּם וּבְקָעֵהוּ וְיָבֹאוּ בְנֵי־יִשְׂרָאֵל בְּתוֹךְ הַיָּם בַּיַּבָּשָׁה: וַאֲנִי הִנְנִי מְחַזֵּק אֶת־לֵב מִצְרַיִם וְיָבֹאוּ אַחֲרֵיהֶם וְאִכָּבְדָה בְּפַרְעֹה וּבְכָל־חֵילוֹ בְּרִכְבּוֹ וּבְפָרָשָׁיו: וְיָדְעוּ מִצְרַיִם כִּי־אֲנִי יהוה בְּהִכָּבְדִי בְּפַרְעֹה בְּרִכְבּוֹ וּבְפָרָשָׁיו: וַיִּסַּע מַלְאַךְ הָאֱלֹהִים הַהֹלֵךְ לִפְנֵי מַחֲנֵה יִשְׂרָאֵל וַיֵּלֶךְ מֵאַחֲרֵיהֶם וַיִּסַּע עַמּוּד הֶעָנָן מִפְּנֵיהֶם וַיַּעֲמֹד מֵאַחֲרֵיהֶם: וַיָּבֹא בֵּין ׀ מַחֲנֵה מִצְרַיִם וּבֵין מַחֲנֵה יִשְׂרָאֵל וַיְהִי הֶעָנָן וְהַחֹשֶׁךְ וַיָּאֶר אֶת־הַלָּיְלָה וְלֹא־קָרַב זֶה אֶל־זֶה כָּל־הַלָּיְלָה: וַיֵּט מֹשֶׁה אֶת־יָדוֹ עַל־הַיָּם וַיּוֹלֶךְ יהוה ׀ אֶת־הַיָּם בְּרוּחַ קָדִים עַזָּה כָּל־הַלַּיְלָה וַיָּשֶׂם אֶת־הַיָּם לֶחָרָבָה וַיִּבָּקְעוּ הַמָּיִם: וַיָּבֹאוּ בְנֵי־יִשְׂרָאֵל בְּתוֹךְ הַיָּם בַּיַּבָּשָׁה וְהַמַּיִם לָהֶם חוֹמָה מִימִינָם וּמִשְּׂמֹאלָם: וַיִּרְדְּפוּ מִצְרַיִם וַיָּבֹאוּ אַחֲרֵיהֶם כֹּל סוּס פַּרְעֹה רִכְבּוֹ וּפָרָשָׁיו אֶל־תּוֹךְ הַיָּם: וַיְהִי בְּאַשְׁמֹרֶת הַבֹּקֶר וַיַּשְׁקֵף יהוה אֶל־מַחֲנֵה מִצְרַיִם בְּעַמּוּד אֵשׁ וְעָנָן וַיָּהָם אֵת מַחֲנֵה מִצְרָיִם: וַיָּסַר אֵת אֹפַן מַרְכְּבֹתָיו וַיְנַהֲגֵהוּ בִּכְבֵדֻת וַיֹּאמֶר מִצְרַיִם אָנוּסָה מִפְּנֵי יִשְׂרָאֵל כִּי יהוה נִלְחָם לָהֶם בְּמִצְרָיִם:

חמישי (בשבת שביעי): וַיֹּאמֶר יהוה אֶל־מֹשֶׁה נְטֵה אֶת־יָדְךָ עַל־הַיָּם וְיָשֻׁבוּ הַמַּיִם עַל־מִצְרַיִם עַל־רִכְבּוֹ וְעַל־פָּרָשָׁיו: וַיֵּט מֹשֶׁה אֶת־יָדוֹ

עַל־הַיָּם וַיָּשָׁב הַיָּם לִפְנוֹת בֹּקֶר לְאֵיתָנוֹ וּמִצְרַיִם נָסִים לִקְרָאתוֹ וַיְנַעֵר יהוה אֶת־מִצְרַיִם בְּתוֹךְ הַיָּם: וַיָּשֻׁבוּ הַמַּיִם וַיְכַסּוּ אֶת־הָרֶכֶב וְאֶת־הַפָּרָשִׁים לְכֹל חֵיל פַּרְעֹה הַבָּאִים אַחֲרֵיהֶם בַּיָּם לֹא־נִשְׁאַר בָּהֶם עַד־אֶחָד: וּבְנֵי יִשְׂרָאֵל הָלְכוּ בַיַּבָּשָׁה בְּתוֹךְ הַיָּם וְהַמַּיִם לָהֶם חֹמָה מִימִינָם וּמִשְּׂמֹאלָם: וַיּוֹשַׁע יהוה בַּיּוֹם הַהוּא אֶת־יִשְׂרָאֵל מִיַּד מִצְרָיִם וַיַּרְא יִשְׂרָאֵל אֶת־מִצְרַיִם מֵת עַל־שְׂפַת הַיָּם: וַיַּרְא יִשְׂרָאֵל אֶת־הַיָּד הַגְּדֹלָה אֲשֶׁר עָשָׂה יהוה בְּמִצְרַיִם וַיִּירְאוּ הָעָם אֶת־יהוה וַיַּאֲמִינוּ בַּיהוה וּבְמֹשֶׁה עַבְדּוֹ:

אָז יָשִׁיר־מֹשֶׁה וּבְנֵי יִשְׂרָאֵל אֶת־הַשִּׁירָה הַזֹּאת לַיהוה וַיֹּאמְרוּ לֵאמֹר אָשִׁירָה לַיהוה כִּי־גָאֹה גָּאָה סוּס וְרֹכְבוֹ רָמָה בַיָּם: עָזִּי וְזִמְרָת יָהּ וַיְהִי־לִי לִישׁוּעָה זֶה אֵלִי וְאַנְוֵהוּ אֱלֹהֵי אָבִי וַאֲרֹמְמֶנְהוּ: יהוה אִישׁ מִלְחָמָה יהוה שְׁמוֹ: מַרְכְּבֹת פַּרְעֹה וְחֵילוֹ יָרָה בַיָּם וּמִבְחַר שָׁלִשָׁיו טֻבְּעוּ בְיַם־סוּף: תְּהֹמֹת יְכַסְיֻמוּ יָרְדוּ בִמְצוֹלֹת כְּמוֹ־אָבֶן: יְמִינְךָ יהוה נֶאְדָּרִי בַּכֹּחַ יְמִינְךָ יהוה תִּרְעַץ אוֹיֵב: וּבְרֹב גְּאוֹנְךָ תַּהֲרֹס קָמֶיךָ תְּשַׁלַּח חֲרֹנְךָ יֹאכְלֵמוֹ כַּקַּשׁ: וּבְרוּחַ אַפֶּיךָ נֶעֶרְמוּ מַיִם נִצְּבוּ כְמוֹ־נֵד נֹזְלִים קָפְאוּ תְהֹמֹת בְּלֶב־יָם: אָמַר אוֹיֵב אֶרְדֹּף אַשִּׂיג אֲחַלֵּק שָׁלָל תִּמְלָאֵמוֹ נַפְשִׁי אָרִיק חַרְבִּי תּוֹרִישֵׁמוֹ יָדִי: נָשַׁפְתָּ בְרוּחֲךָ כִּסָּמוֹ יָם צָלְלוּ כַּעוֹפֶרֶת בְּמַיִם אַדִּירִים: מִי־כָמֹכָה בָּאֵלִם יהוה מִי כָּמֹכָה נֶאְדָּר בַּקֹּדֶשׁ נוֹרָא תְהִלֹּת עֹשֵׂה פֶלֶא: נָטִיתָ יְמִינְךָ תִּבְלָעֵמוֹ אָרֶץ: נָחִיתָ בְחַסְדְּךָ עַם־זוּ גָּאָלְתָּ נֵהַלְתָּ בְעָזְּךָ אֶל־נְוֵה קָדְשֶׁךָ: שָׁמְעוּ עַמִּים יִרְגָּזוּן חִיל אָחַז יֹשְׁבֵי פְּלָשֶׁת: אָז נִבְהֲלוּ אַלּוּפֵי אֱדוֹם אֵילֵי מוֹאָב יֹאחֲזֵמוֹ רָעַד נָמֹגוּ כֹּל יֹשְׁבֵי כְנָעַן: תִּפֹּל עֲלֵיהֶם אֵימָתָה וָפַחַד בִּגְדֹל זְרוֹעֲךָ יִדְּמוּ כָּאָבֶן עַד־יַעֲבֹר עַמְּךָ יהוה עַד־יַעֲבֹר עַם־זוּ קָנִיתָ: תְּבִאֵמוֹ וְתִטָּעֵמוֹ בְּהַר נַחֲלָתְךָ מָכוֹן לְשִׁבְתְּךָ פָּעַלְתָּ יהוה מִקְּדָשׁ אֲדֹנָי כּוֹנְנוּ יָדֶיךָ: יהוה ׀ יִמְלֹךְ לְעֹלָם וָעֶד: כִּי בָא סוּס פַּרְעֹה בְּרִכְבּוֹ וּבְפָרָשָׁיו בַּיָּם וַיָּשֶׁב יהוה עֲלֵהֶם אֶת־מֵי הַיָּם וּבְנֵי יִשְׂרָאֵל הָלְכוּ בַיַּבָּשָׁה בְּתוֹךְ הַיָּם:

וַתִּקַּח מִרְיָם הַנְּבִיאָה אֲחוֹת אַהֲרֹן אֶת־הַתֹּף בְּיָדָהּ וַתֵּצֶאןָ כָל־הַנָּשִׁים אַחֲרֶיהָ בְּתֻפִּים וּבִמְחֹלֹת: וַתַּעַן לָהֶם מִרְיָם שִׁירוּ לַיהוה כִּי־גָאֹה גָּאָה סוּס וְרֹכְבוֹ רָמָה בַיָּם: וַיַּסַּע מֹשֶׁה אֶת־יִשְׂרָאֵל מִיַּם־סוּף וַיֵּצְאוּ אֶל־מִדְבַּר־שׁוּר וַיֵּלְכוּ שְׁלֹשֶׁת־יָמִים בַּמִּדְבָּר וְלֹא־מָצְאוּ מָיִם: וַיָּבֹאוּ מָרָתָה וְלֹא יָכְלוּ לִשְׁתֹּת מַיִם מִמָּרָה כִּי מָרִים הֵם עַל־כֵּן קָרָא־שְׁמָהּ מָרָה: וַיִּלֹּנוּ הָעָם עַל־מֹשֶׁה לֵּאמֹר מַה־נִּשְׁתֶּה: וַיִּצְעַק אֶל־יהוה וַיּוֹרֵהוּ יהוה עֵץ וַיַּשְׁלֵךְ אֶל־הַמַּיִם וַיִּמְתְּקוּ הַמָּיִם שָׁם שָׂם לוֹ חֹק וּמִשְׁפָּט וְשָׁם נִסָּהוּ: וַיֹּאמֶר אִם־שָׁמוֹעַ תִּשְׁמַע לְקוֹל ׀ יהוה אֱלֹהֶיךָ וְהַיָּשָׁר בְּעֵינָיו תַּעֲשֶׂה וְהַאֲזַנְתָּ לְמִצְוֹתָיו וְשָׁמַרְתָּ כָּל־חֻקָּיו כָּל־הַמַּחֲלָה אֲשֶׁר־שַׂמְתִּי בְמִצְרַיִם לֹא־אָשִׂים עָלֶיךָ כִּי אֲנִי יהוה רֹפְאֶךָ:

The מפטיר (וְהִקְרַבְתֶּם) *is read from the second* ספר תורה *page 1145.*

הפטרה לשביעי של פסח

HAFTARA FOR SEVENTH DAY OF PESAḤ

שמואל ב׳ כב:א–נא

וַיְדַבֵּר דָּוִד לַיהוה אֶת־דִּבְרֵי הַשִּׁירָה הַזֹּאת בְּיוֹם הִצִּיל יהוה אֹתוֹ מִכַּף כָּל־אֹיְבָיו וּמִכַּף שָׁאוּל: וַיֹּאמַר יהוה סַלְעִי וּמְצֻדָתִי וּמְפַלְטִי־לִי: אֱלֹהֵי צוּרִי אֶחֱסֶה־בּוֹ מָגִנִּי וְקֶרֶן יִשְׁעִי מִשְׂגַּבִּי וּמְנוּסִי מֹשִׁעִי מֵחָמָס תֹּשִׁעֵנִי: מְהֻלָּל אֶקְרָא יהוה וּמֵאֹיְבַי אִוָּשֵׁעַ: כִּי אֲפָפֻנִי מִשְׁבְּרֵי־מָוֶת נַחֲלֵי בְלִיַּעַל יְבַעֲתֻנִי: חֶבְלֵי שְׁאוֹל סַבֻּנִי קִדְּמֻנִי מֹקְשֵׁי־מָוֶת: בַּצַּר־לִי אֶקְרָא יהוה וְאֶל־אֱלֹהַי

אֶקְרָא וַיִּשְׁמַע מֵהֵיכָלוֹ קוֹלִי וְשַׁוְעָתִי בְּאׇזְנָיו: ותגעש [וַיִּתְגָּעַשׁ] וַתִּרְעַשׁ הָאָרֶץ מוֹסְדוֹת הַשָּׁמַיִם יִרְגָּזוּ וַיִּתְגָּעֲשׁוּ כִּי־חָרָה לוֹ: עָלָה עָשָׁן בְּאַפּוֹ וְאֵשׁ מִפִּיו תֹּאכֵל גֶּחָלִים בָּעֲרוּ מִמֶּנּוּ: וַיֵּט שָׁמַיִם וַיֵּרַד וַעֲרָפֶל תַּחַת רַגְלָיו: וַיִּרְכַּב עַל־כְּרוּב וַיָּעֹף וַיֵּרָא עַל־כַּנְפֵי־רוּחַ: וַיָּשֶׁת חֹשֶׁךְ סְבִיבֹתָיו סֻכּוֹת חַשְׁרַת־מַיִם עָבֵי שְׁחָקִים: מִנֹּגַהּ נֶגְדּוֹ בָּעֲרוּ גַּחֲלֵי־אֵשׁ: יַרְעֵם מִן־שָׁמַיִם יְהֹוָה וְעֶלְיוֹן יִתֵּן קוֹלוֹ: וַיִּשְׁלַח חִצִּים וַיְפִיצֵם בָּרָק ויהמם [וַיָּהֹם]: וַיֵּרָאוּ אֲפִקֵי יָם יִגָּלוּ מֹסְדוֹת תֵּבֵל בְּגַעֲרַת יְהֹוָה מִנִּשְׁמַת רוּחַ אַפּוֹ: יִשְׁלַח מִמָּרוֹם יִקָּחֵנִי יַמְשֵׁנִי מִמַּיִם רַבִּים: יַצִּילֵנִי מֵאֹיְבִי עָז מִשֹּׂנְאַי כִּי אָמְצוּ מִמֶּנִּי: יְקַדְּמֻנִי בְּיוֹם אֵידִי וַיְהִי יְהֹוָה מִשְׁעָן לִי: וַיֹּצֵא לַמֶּרְחָב אֹתִי יְחַלְּצֵנִי כִּי־חָפֵץ בִּי: יִגְמְלֵנִי יְהֹוָה כְּצִדְקָתִי כְּבֹר יָדַי יָשִׁיב לִי: כִּי שָׁמַרְתִּי דַּרְכֵי יְהֹוָה וְלֹא רָשַׁעְתִּי מֵאֱלֹהָי: כִּי כׇל־מִשְׁפָּטָו לְנֶגְדִּי וְחֻקֹּתָיו לֹא־אָסוּר מִמֶּנָּה: וָאֶהְיֶה תָמִים לוֹ וָאֶשְׁתַּמְּרָה מֵעֲוֺנִי: וַיָּשֶׁב יְהֹוָה לִי כְּצִדְקָתִי כְּבֹרִי לְנֶגֶד עֵינָיו: עִם־חָסִיד תִּתְחַסָּד עִם־גִּבּוֹר תָּמִים תִּתַּמָּם: עִם־נָבָר תִּתָּבָר וְעִם־עִקֵּשׁ תִּתַּפָּל: וְאֶת־עַם עָנִי תּוֹשִׁיעַ וְעֵינֶיךָ עַל־רָמִים תַּשְׁפִּיל: כִּי־אַתָּה נֵירִי יְהֹוָה וַיהֹוָה יַגִּיהַּ חׇשְׁכִּי: כִּי בְכָה אָרוּץ גְּדוּד בֵּאלֹהַי אֲדַלֶּג־שׁוּר: הָאֵל תָּמִים דַּרְכּוֹ אִמְרַת יְהֹוָה צְרוּפָה מָגֵן הוּא לְכֹל הַחֹסִים בּוֹ: כִּי מִי־אֵל מִבַּלְעֲדֵי יְהֹוָה וּמִי צוּר מִבַּלְעֲדֵי אֱלֹהֵינוּ: הָאֵל מָעוּזִּי חָיִל וַיַּתֵּר תָּמִים דרכו [דַּרְכִּי]: מְשַׁוֶּה רגליו [רַגְלַי] כָּאַיָּלוֹת וְעַל־בָּמֹתַי יַעֲמִידֵנִי: מְלַמֵּד יָדַי לַמִּלְחָמָה וְנִחַת קֶשֶׁת־נְחוּשָׁה זְרֹעֹתָי: וַתִּתֶּן־לִי מָגֵן יִשְׁעֶךָ וַעֲנֹתְךָ תַּרְבֵּנִי: תַּרְחִיב צַעֲדִי תַּחְתֵּנִי וְלֹא מָעֲדוּ קַרְסֻלָּי: אֶרְדְּפָה אֹיְבַי וָאַשְׁמִידֵם וְלֹא אָשׁוּב עַד־כַּלּוֹתָם: וָאֲכַלֵּם וָאֶמְחָצֵם וְלֹא יְקוּמוּן וַיִּפְּלוּ תַּחַת רַגְלָי: וַתַּזְרֵנִי חַיִל לַמִּלְחָמָה תַּכְרִיעַ קָמַי תַּחְתֵּנִי: וְאֹיְבַי תַּתָּה לִּי עֹרֶף מְשַׂנְאַי וָאַצְמִיתֵם: יִשְׁעוּ וְאֵין מֹשִׁיעַ אֶל־יְהֹוָה וְלֹא עָנָם: וְאֶשְׁחָקֵם כַּעֲפַר־אָרֶץ כְּטִיט־חוּצוֹת אֲדִקֵּם אֶרְקָעֵם: וַתְּפַלְּטֵנִי מֵרִיבֵי עַמִּי תִּשְׁמְרֵנִי לְרֹאשׁ גּוֹיִם עַם לֹא־יָדַעְתִּי יַעַבְדֻנִי: בְּנֵי נֵכָר יִתְכַּחֲשׁוּ־לִי לִשְׁמוֹעַ אֹזֶן יִשָּׁמְעוּ לִי: בְּנֵי נֵכָר יִבֹּלוּ וְיַחְגְּרוּ מִמִּסְגְּרוֹתָם: חַי־יְהֹוָה וּבָרוּךְ צוּרִי וְיָרֻם אֱלֹהֵי צוּר יִשְׁעִי: הָאֵל הַנֹּתֵן נְקָמֹת לִי וּמוֹרִיד עַמִּים תַּחְתֵּנִי: וּמוֹצִיאִי מֵאֹיְבָי וּמִקָּמַי תְּרוֹמְמֵנִי מֵאִישׁ חֲמָסִים תַּצִּילֵנִי: עַל־כֵּן אוֹדְךָ יְהֹוָה בַּגּוֹיִם וּלְשִׁמְךָ אֲזַמֵּר: מגדיל [מִגְדּוֹל] יְשׁוּעוֹת מַלְכּוֹ וְעֹשֶׂה־חֶסֶד לִמְשִׁיחוֹ לְדָוִד וּלְזַרְעוֹ עַד־עוֹלָם:

קריאה ליום אחרון של פסח או שבועות, ולשמיני עצרת / LAST DAY OF PESAḤ AND SHAVUOT, AND SHEMINI ATZERET

דברים יד:כב–טז:יז

If the eighth day of פסח *or the second day of* שבועות *falls on* שבת*, start here.*
If it falls on a weekday, start with כׇּל־הַבְּכוֹר *on the facing page. On* שמיני עצרת *start here.*

עַשֵּׂר תְּעַשֵּׂר אֵת כׇּל־תְּבוּאַת זַרְעֶךָ הַיֹּצֵא הַשָּׂדֶה שָׁנָה שָׁנָה: וְאָכַלְתָּ לִפְנֵי ׀ יְהֹוָה אֱלֹהֶיךָ בַּמָּקוֹם אֲשֶׁר־יִבְחַר לְשַׁכֵּן שְׁמוֹ שָׁם מַעְשַׂר דְּגָנְךָ תִּירֹשְׁךָ וְיִצְהָרֶךָ וּבְכֹרֹת בְּקָרְךָ וְצֹאנֶךָ לְמַעַן תִּלְמַד לְיִרְאָה אֶת־יְהֹוָה אֱלֹהֶיךָ כׇּל־הַיָּמִים: וְכִי־יִרְבֶּה מִמְּךָ הַדֶּרֶךְ כִּי לֹא תוּכַל שְׂאֵתוֹ כִּי־יִרְחַק מִמְּךָ הַמָּקוֹם אֲשֶׁר יִבְחַר יְהֹוָה אֱלֹהֶיךָ לָשׂוּם שְׁמוֹ שָׁם כִּי יְבָרֶכְךָ יְהֹוָה אֱלֹהֶיךָ: וְנָתַתָּה בַּכָּסֶף וְצַרְתָּ הַכֶּסֶף בְּיָדְךָ וְהָלַכְתָּ אֶל־הַמָּקוֹם אֲשֶׁר יִבְחַר יְהֹוָה אֱלֹהֶיךָ בּוֹ: וְנָתַתָּה הַכֶּסֶף בְּכֹל אֲשֶׁר־

תַאֲוֶה נַפְשְׁךָ בַּבָּקָר וּבַצֹּאן וּבַיַּיִן וּבַשֵּׁכָר וּבְכֹל אֲשֶׁר תִּשְׁאָלְךָ נַפְשֶׁךָ וְאָכַלְתָּ שָּׁם לִפְנֵי יהוה אֱלֹהֶיךָ וְשָׂמַחְתָּ אַתָּה וּבֵיתֶךָ׃ וְהַלֵּוִי אֲשֶׁר־בִּשְׁעָרֶיךָ לֹא תַעַזְבֶנּוּ כִּי אֵין לוֹ חֵלֶק וְנַחֲלָה עִמָּךְ׃ מִקְצֵה ׀ שָׁלֹשׁ שָׁנִים תּוֹצִיא אֶת־כָּל־מַעְשַׂר תְּבוּאָתְךָ בַּשָּׁנָה הַהִוא וְהִנַּחְתָּ בִּשְׁעָרֶיךָ׃ וּבָא הַלֵּוִי כִּי אֵין־לוֹ חֵלֶק וְנַחֲלָה עִמָּךְ וְהַגֵּר וְהַיָּתוֹם וְהָאַלְמָנָה אֲשֶׁר בִּשְׁעָרֶיךָ וְאָכְלוּ וְשָׂבֵעוּ לְמַעַן יְבָרֶכְךָ יהוה אֱלֹהֶיךָ בְּכָל־מַעֲשֵׂה יָדְךָ אֲשֶׁר תַּעֲשֶׂה׃

(בשבת לוי) מִקֵּץ שֶׁבַע־שָׁנִים תַּעֲשֶׂה שְׁמִטָּה׃ וְזֶה דְּבַר הַשְּׁמִטָּה שָׁמוֹט כָּל־בַּעַל מַשֵּׁה יָדוֹ אֲשֶׁר יַשֶּׁה בְּרֵעֵהוּ לֹא־יִגֹּשׂ אֶת־רֵעֵהוּ וְאֶת־אָחִיו כִּי־קָרָא שְׁמִטָּה לַיהוה׃ אֶת־הַנָּכְרִי תִּגֹּשׂ וַאֲשֶׁר יִהְיֶה לְךָ אֶת־אָחִיךָ תַּשְׁמֵט יָדֶךָ׃ אֶפֶס כִּי לֹא יִהְיֶה־בְּךָ אֶבְיוֹן כִּי־בָרֵךְ יְבָרֶכְךָ יהוה בָּאָרֶץ אֲשֶׁר יהוה אֱלֹהֶיךָ נֹתֵן־לְךָ נַחֲלָה לְרִשְׁתָּהּ׃ רַק אִם־שָׁמוֹעַ תִּשְׁמַע בְּקוֹל יהוה אֱלֹהֶיךָ לִשְׁמֹר לַעֲשׂוֹת אֶת־כָּל־הַמִּצְוָה הַזֹּאת אֲשֶׁר אָנֹכִי מְצַוְּךָ הַיּוֹם׃ כִּי־יהוה אֱלֹהֶיךָ בֵּרַכְךָ כַּאֲשֶׁר דִּבֶּר־לָךְ וְהַעֲבַטְתָּ גּוֹיִם רַבִּים וְאַתָּה לֹא תַעֲבֹט וּמָשַׁלְתָּ בְּגוֹיִם רַבִּים וּבְךָ לֹא יִמְשֹׁלוּ׃ כִּי־יִהְיֶה בְךָ אֶבְיוֹן מֵאַחַד אַחֶיךָ בְּאַחַד שְׁעָרֶיךָ בְּאַרְצְךָ אֲשֶׁר־יהוה אֱלֹהֶיךָ נֹתֵן לָךְ לֹא תְאַמֵּץ אֶת־לְבָבְךָ וְלֹא תִקְפֹּץ אֶת־יָדְךָ מֵאָחִיךָ הָאֶבְיוֹן׃ כִּי־פָתֹחַ תִּפְתַּח אֶת־יָדְךָ לוֹ וְהַעֲבֵט תַּעֲבִיטֶנּוּ דֵּי מַחְסֹרוֹ אֲשֶׁר יֶחְסַר לוֹ׃ הִשָּׁמֶר לְךָ פֶּן־יִהְיֶה דָבָר עִם־לְבָבְךָ בְלִיַּעַל לֵאמֹר קָרְבָה שְׁנַת־הַשֶּׁבַע שְׁנַת הַשְּׁמִטָּה וְרָעָה עֵינְךָ בְּאָחִיךָ הָאֶבְיוֹן וְלֹא תִתֵּן לוֹ וְקָרָא עָלֶיךָ אֶל־יהוה וְהָיָה בְךָ חֵטְא׃ נָתוֹן תִּתֵּן לוֹ וְלֹא־יֵרַע לְבָבְךָ בְּתִתְּךָ לוֹ כִּי בִּגְלַל ׀ הַדָּבָר הַזֶּה יְבָרֶכְךָ יהוה אֱלֹהֶיךָ בְּכָל־מַעֲשֶׂךָ וּבְכֹל מִשְׁלַח יָדֶךָ׃ כִּי לֹא־יֶחְדַּל אֶבְיוֹן מִקֶּרֶב הָאָרֶץ עַל־כֵּן אָנֹכִי מְצַוְּךָ לֵאמֹר פָּתֹחַ תִּפְתַּח אֶת־יָדְךָ לְאָחִיךָ לַעֲנִיֶּךָ וּלְאֶבְיֹנְךָ בְּאַרְצֶךָ׃ כִּי־יִמָּכֵר לְךָ אָחִיךָ הָעִבְרִי אוֹ הָעִבְרִיָּה וַעֲבָדְךָ שֵׁשׁ שָׁנִים וּבַשָּׁנָה הַשְּׁבִיעִת תְּשַׁלְּחֶנּוּ חָפְשִׁי מֵעִמָּךְ׃ וְכִי־תְשַׁלְּחֶנּוּ חָפְשִׁי מֵעִמָּךְ לֹא תְשַׁלְּחֶנּוּ רֵיקָם׃ הַעֲנֵיק תַּעֲנִיק לוֹ מִצֹּאנְךָ וּמִגָּרְנְךָ וּמִיִּקְבֶךָ אֲשֶׁר בֵּרַכְךָ יהוה אֱלֹהֶיךָ תִּתֶּן־לוֹ׃ וְזָכַרְתָּ כִּי עֶבֶד הָיִיתָ בְּאֶרֶץ מִצְרַיִם וַיִּפְדְּךָ יהוה אֱלֹהֶיךָ עַל־כֵּן אָנֹכִי מְצַוְּךָ אֶת־הַדָּבָר הַזֶּה הַיּוֹם׃ וְהָיָה כִּי־יֹאמַר אֵלֶיךָ לֹא אֵצֵא מֵעִמָּךְ כִּי אֲהֵבְךָ וְאֶת־בֵּיתֶךָ כִּי־טוֹב לוֹ עִמָּךְ׃ וְלָקַחְתָּ אֶת־הַמַּרְצֵעַ וְנָתַתָּה בְאָזְנוֹ וּבַדֶּלֶת וְהָיָה לְךָ עֶבֶד עוֹלָם וְאַף לַאֲמָתְךָ תַּעֲשֶׂה־כֵּן׃ לֹא־יִקְשֶׁה בְעֵינֶךָ בְּשַׁלֵּחֲךָ אֹתוֹ חָפְשִׁי מֵעִמָּךְ כִּי מִשְׁנֶה שְׂכַר שָׂכִיר עֲבָדְךָ שֵׁשׁ שָׁנִים וּבֵרַכְךָ יהוה אֱלֹהֶיךָ בְּכֹל אֲשֶׁר תַּעֲשֶׂה׃

If the eighth day of פסח *or the second day of* שבועות *falls on a weekday, start here:*

(בשבת שלישי) כָּל־הַבְּכוֹר אֲשֶׁר יִוָּלֵד בִּבְקָרְךָ וּבְצֹאנְךָ הַזָּכָר תַּקְדִּישׁ לַיהוה אֱלֹהֶיךָ לֹא תַעֲבֹד בִּבְכֹר שׁוֹרֶךָ וְלֹא תָגֹז בְּכוֹר צֹאנֶךָ׃ לִפְנֵי יהוה אֱלֹהֶיךָ תֹאכְלֶנּוּ שָׁנָה בְשָׁנָה בַּמָּקוֹם אֲשֶׁר־יִבְחַר יהוה אַתָּה וּבֵיתֶךָ׃ וְכִי־יִהְיֶה בוֹ מוּם פִּסֵּחַ אוֹ עִוֵּר כֹּל מוּם רָע לֹא תִזְבָּחֶנּוּ לַיהוה אֱלֹהֶיךָ׃ בִּשְׁעָרֶיךָ תֹּאכְלֶנּוּ הַטָּמֵא וְהַטָּהוֹר יַחְדָּו כַּצְּבִי וְכָאַיָּל׃ רַק אֶת־דָּמוֹ לֹא תֹאכֵל עַל־הָאָרֶץ תִּשְׁפְּכֶנּוּ כַּמָּיִם׃

לוי (בשבת רביעי) שָׁמוֹר אֶת־חֹדֶשׁ הָאָבִיב וְעָשִׂיתָ פֶּסַח לַיהוה אֱלֹהֶיךָ כִּי בְּחֹדֶשׁ הָאָבִיב הוֹצִיאֲךָ יהוה אֱלֹהֶיךָ מִמִּצְרַיִם לָיְלָה׃ וְזָבַחְתָּ פֶּסַח לַיהוה אֱלֹהֶיךָ צֹאן וּבָקָר בַּמָּקוֹם אֲשֶׁר יִבְחַר יהוה לְשַׁכֵּן שְׁמוֹ שָׁם׃ לֹא־תֹאכַל עָלָיו חָמֵץ שִׁבְעַת יָמִים

תֹאכַל־עָלָיו מַצּוֹת לֶחֶם עֹנִי כִּי בְחִפָּזוֹן יָצָאתָ מֵאֶרֶץ מִצְרַיִם לְמַעַן תִּזְכֹּר אֶת־יוֹם צֵאתְךָ מֵאֶרֶץ מִצְרַיִם כֹּל יְמֵי חַיֶּיךָ: שלישי (בשבת חמישי): וְלֹא־יֵרָאֶה לְךָ שְׂאֹר בְּכָל־גְּבֻלְךָ שִׁבְעַת יָמִים וְלֹא־יָלִין מִן־הַבָּשָׂר אֲשֶׁר תִּזְבַּח בָּעֶרֶב בַּיּוֹם הָרִאשׁוֹן לַבֹּקֶר: לֹא תוּכַל לִזְבֹּחַ אֶת־הַפָּסַח בְּאַחַד שְׁעָרֶיךָ אֲשֶׁר־יהוה אֱלֹהֶיךָ נֹתֵן לָךְ: כִּי אִם־אֶל־הַמָּקוֹם אֲשֶׁר־יִבְחַר יהוה אֱלֹהֶיךָ לְשַׁכֵּן שְׁמוֹ שָׁם תִּזְבַּח אֶת־הַפֶּסַח בָּעָרֶב כְּבוֹא הַשֶּׁמֶשׁ מוֹעֵד צֵאתְךָ מִמִּצְרָיִם: וּבִשַּׁלְתָּ וְאָכַלְתָּ בַּמָּקוֹם אֲשֶׁר יִבְחַר יהוה אֱלֹהֶיךָ בּוֹ וּפָנִיתָ בַבֹּקֶר וְהָלַכְתָּ לְאֹהָלֶיךָ: שֵׁשֶׁת יָמִים תֹּאכַל מַצּוֹת וּבַיּוֹם הַשְּׁבִיעִי עֲצֶרֶת לַיהוה אֱלֹהֶיךָ לֹא תַעֲשֶׂה מְלָאכָה: רביעי (בשבת ששי): שִׁבְעָה שָׁבֻעֹת תִּסְפָּר־לָךְ מֵהָחֵל חֶרְמֵשׁ בַּקָּמָה תָּחֵל לִסְפֹּר שִׁבְעָה שָׁבֻעוֹת: וְעָשִׂיתָ חַג שָׁבֻעוֹת לַיהוה אֱלֹהֶיךָ מִסַּת נִדְבַת יָדְךָ אֲשֶׁר תִּתֵּן כַּאֲשֶׁר יְבָרֶכְךָ יהוה אֱלֹהֶיךָ: וְשָׂמַחְתָּ לִפְנֵי ׀ יהוה אֱלֹהֶיךָ אַתָּה וּבִנְךָ וּבִתֶּךָ וְעַבְדְּךָ וַאֲמָתֶךָ וְהַלֵּוִי אֲשֶׁר בִּשְׁעָרֶיךָ וְהַגֵּר וְהַיָּתוֹם וְהָאַלְמָנָה אֲשֶׁר בְּקִרְבֶּךָ בַּמָּקוֹם אֲשֶׁר יִבְחַר יהוה אֱלֹהֶיךָ לְשַׁכֵּן שְׁמוֹ שָׁם: וְזָכַרְתָּ כִּי־עֶבֶד הָיִיתָ בְּמִצְרָיִם וְשָׁמַרְתָּ וְעָשִׂיתָ אֶת־הַחֻקִּים הָאֵלֶּה:

חמישי (בשבת שביעי): חַג הַסֻּכֹּת תַּעֲשֶׂה לְךָ שִׁבְעַת יָמִים בְּאָסְפְּךָ מִגָּרְנְךָ וּמִיִּקְבֶךָ: וְשָׂמַחְתָּ בְּחַגֶּךָ אַתָּה וּבִנְךָ וּבִתֶּךָ וְעַבְדְּךָ וַאֲמָתֶךָ וְהַלֵּוִי וְהַגֵּר וְהַיָּתוֹם וְהָאַלְמָנָה אֲשֶׁר בִּשְׁעָרֶיךָ: שִׁבְעַת יָמִים תָּחֹג לַיהוה אֱלֹהֶיךָ בַּמָּקוֹם אֲשֶׁר־יִבְחַר יהוה כִּי יְבָרֶכְךָ יהוה אֱלֹהֶיךָ בְּכֹל־תְּבוּאָתְךָ וּבְכֹל מַעֲשֵׂה יָדֶיךָ וְהָיִיתָ אַךְ שָׂמֵחַ: שָׁלוֹשׁ פְּעָמִים ׀ בַּשָּׁנָה יֵרָאֶה כָל־זְכוּרְךָ אֶת־פְּנֵי ׀ יהוה אֱלֹהֶיךָ בַּמָּקוֹם אֲשֶׁר יִבְחָר בְּחַג הַמַּצּוֹת וּבְחַג הַשָּׁבֻעוֹת וּבְחַג הַסֻּכּוֹת וְלֹא יֵרָאֶה אֶת־פְּנֵי יהוה רֵיקָם: אִישׁ כְּמַתְּנַת יָדוֹ כְּבִרְכַּת יהוה אֱלֹהֶיךָ אֲשֶׁר נָתַן־לָךְ:

The מפטיר *for* יום שמיני של פסח *is the same as that for the other days of* חול המועד פסח*, page 1145. The* מפטיר *for* שבועות *appears on page 1156. The* הפטרה *for* יום טוב שני של שבועות *appears on page 1158 and that of* שמיני עצרת *on page 1164.*

הפטרה ליום אחרון של פסח

HAFTARA FOR LAST DAY OF PESAḤ

ישעיהו י:לב–יב:ו

עוֹד הַיּוֹם בְּנֹב לַעֲמֹד יְנֹפֵף יָדוֹ הַר בית־[בַּת־]צִיּוֹן גִּבְעַת יְרוּשָׁלָםִ: הִנֵּה הָאָדוֹן יהוה צְבָאוֹת מְסָעֵף פֻּארָה בְּמַעֲרָצָה וְרָמֵי הַקּוֹמָה גְּדֻעִים וְהַגְּבֹהִים יִשְׁפָּלוּ: וְנִקַּף סִבְכֵי הַיַּעַר בַּבַּרְזֶל וְהַלְּבָנוֹן בְּאַדִּיר יִפּוֹל: וְיָצָא חֹטֶר מִגֵּזַע יִשָׁי וְנֵצֶר מִשָּׁרָשָׁיו יִפְרֶה: וְנָחָה עָלָיו רוּחַ יהוה רוּחַ חָכְמָה וּבִינָה רוּחַ עֵצָה וּגְבוּרָה רוּחַ דַּעַת וְיִרְאַת יהוה: וַהֲרִיחוֹ בְּיִרְאַת יהוה וְלֹא־לְמַרְאֵה עֵינָיו יִשְׁפּוֹט וְלֹא־לְמִשְׁמַע אָזְנָיו יוֹכִיחַ: וְשָׁפַט בְּצֶדֶק דַּלִּים וְהוֹכִיחַ בְּמִישׁוֹר לְעַנְוֵי־אָרֶץ וְהִכָּה־אֶרֶץ בְּשֵׁבֶט פִּיו וּבְרוּחַ שְׂפָתָיו יָמִית רָשָׁע: וְהָיָה צֶדֶק אֵזוֹר מָתְנָיו וְהָאֱמוּנָה אֵזוֹר חֲלָצָיו: וְגָר זְאֵב עִם־כֶּבֶשׂ וְנָמֵר עִם־גְּדִי יִרְבָּץ וְעֵגֶל וּכְפִיר וּמְרִיא יַחְדָּו וְנַעַר קָטֹן נֹהֵג בָּם: וּפָרָה וָדֹב תִּרְעֶינָה יַחְדָּו יִרְבְּצוּ יַלְדֵיהֶן וְאַרְיֵה כַּבָּקָר יֹאכַל־תֶּבֶן: וְשִׁעֲשַׁע יוֹנֵק עַל־חֻר פָּתֶן וְעַל מְאוּרַת צִפְעוֹנִי גָּמוּל יָדוֹ הָדָה: לֹא־יָרֵעוּ וְלֹא־יַשְׁחִיתוּ בְּכָל־הַר קָדְשִׁי כִּי־מָלְאָה הָאָרֶץ דֵּעָה אֶת־יהוה כַּמַּיִם לַיָּם מְכַסִּים: וְהָיָה בַּיּוֹם הַהוּא שֹׁרֶשׁ יִשַׁי אֲשֶׁר עֹמֵד לְנֵס עַמִּים אֵלָיו גּוֹיִם יִדְרֹשׁוּ וְהָיְתָה מְנֻחָתוֹ כָּבוֹד: וְהָיָה ׀ בַּיּוֹם הַהוּא יוֹסִיף אֲדֹנָי ׀ שֵׁנִית יָדוֹ לִקְנוֹת אֶת־שְׁאָר עַמּוֹ אֲשֶׁר יִשָּׁאֵר מֵאַשּׁוּר וּמִמִּצְרַיִם וּמִפַּתְרוֹס

וּמִכּוּשׁ וּמֵעֵילָם וּמִשִּׁנְעָר וּמֵחֲמָת וּמֵאִיֵּי הַיָּם: וְנָשָׂא נֵס לַגּוֹיִם וְאָסַף נִדְחֵי יִשְׂרָאֵל וּנְפֻצוֹת יְהוּדָה יְקַבֵּץ מֵאַרְבַּע כַּנְפוֹת הָאָרֶץ: וְסָרָה קִנְאַת אֶפְרַיִם וְצֹרְרֵי יְהוּדָה יִכָּרֵתוּ אֶפְרַיִם לֹא־יְקַנֵּא אֶת־יְהוּדָה וִיהוּדָה לֹא־יָצֹר אֶת־אֶפְרָיִם: וְעָפוּ בְכָתֵף פְּלִשְׁתִּים יָמָּה יַחְדָּו יָבֹזּוּ אֶת־בְּנֵי־קֶדֶם אֱדוֹם וּמוֹאָב מִשְׁלוֹח יָדָם וּבְנֵי עַמּוֹן מִשְׁמַעְתָּם: וְהֶחֱרִים יהוה אֵת לְשׁוֹן יָם־מִצְרַיִם וְהֵנִיף יָדוֹ עַל־הַנָּהָר בַּעְיָם רוּחוֹ וְהִכָּהוּ לְשִׁבְעָה נְחָלִים וְהִדְרִיךְ בַּנְּעָלִים: וְהָיְתָה מְסִלָּה לִשְׁאָר עַמּוֹ אֲשֶׁר יִשָּׁאֵר מֵאַשּׁוּר כַּאֲשֶׁר הָיְתָה לְיִשְׂרָאֵל בְּיוֹם עֲלֹתוֹ מֵאֶרֶץ מִצְרָיִם: וְאָמַרְתָּ בַּיּוֹם הַהוּא אוֹדְךָ יהוה כִּי אָנַפְתָּ בִּי יָשֹׁב אַפְּךָ וּתְנַחֲמֵנִי: הִנֵּה אֵל יְשׁוּעָתִי אֶבְטַח וְלֹא אֶפְחָד כִּי־עָזִּי וְזִמְרָת יָהּ יהוה וַיְהִי־לִי לִישׁוּעָה: וּשְׁאַבְתֶּם־מַיִם בְּשָׂשׂוֹן מִמַּעַיְנֵי הַיְשׁוּעָה: וַאֲמַרְתֶּם בַּיּוֹם הַהוּא הוֹדוּ לַיהוה קִרְאוּ בִשְׁמוֹ הוֹדִיעוּ בָעַמִּים עֲלִילֹתָיו הַזְכִּירוּ כִּי נִשְׂגָּב שְׁמוֹ: זַמְּרוּ יהוה כִּי גֵאוּת עָשָׂה מידעת [מוּדַעַת] זֹאת בְּכָל־הָאָרֶץ: צַהֲלִי וָרֹנִּי יוֹשֶׁבֶת צִיּוֹן כִּי־גָדוֹל בְּקִרְבֵּךְ קְדוֹשׁ יִשְׂרָאֵל:

קריאה ליום טוב ראשון של שבועות
FIRST DAY OF SHAVUOT

אקדמות *appears on page 872.*

שמות יט:א–כ:כג

בַּחֹדֶשׁ הַשְּׁלִישִׁי לְצֵאת בְּנֵי־יִשְׂרָאֵל מֵאֶרֶץ מִצְרָיִם בַּיּוֹם הַזֶּה בָּאוּ מִדְבַּר סִינָי: וַיִּסְעוּ מֵרְפִידִים וַיָּבֹאוּ מִדְבַּר סִינַי וַיַּחֲנוּ בַּמִּדְבָּר וַיִּחַן־שָׁם יִשְׂרָאֵל נֶגֶד הָהָר: וּמֹשֶׁה עָלָה אֶל־הָאֱלֹהִים וַיִּקְרָא אֵלָיו יהוה מִן־הָהָר לֵאמֹר כֹּה תֹאמַר לְבֵית יַעֲקֹב וְתַגֵּיד לִבְנֵי יִשְׂרָאֵל: אַתֶּם רְאִיתֶם אֲשֶׁר עָשִׂיתִי לְמִצְרָיִם וָאֶשָּׂא אֶתְכֶם עַל־כַּנְפֵי נְשָׁרִים וָאָבִא אֶתְכֶם אֵלָי: וְעַתָּה אִם־שָׁמוֹעַ תִּשְׁמְעוּ בְּקֹלִי וּשְׁמַרְתֶּם אֶת־בְּרִיתִי וִהְיִיתֶם לִי סְגֻלָּה מִכָּל־הָעַמִּים כִּי־לִי כָּל־הָאָרֶץ: וְאַתֶּם תִּהְיוּ־לִי מַמְלֶכֶת כֹּהֲנִים וְגוֹי קָדוֹשׁ אֵלֶּה הַדְּבָרִים אֲשֶׁר תְּדַבֵּר אֶל־בְּנֵי יִשְׂרָאֵל: לוי: וַיָּבֹא מֹשֶׁה וַיִּקְרָא לְזִקְנֵי הָעָם וַיָּשֶׂם לִפְנֵיהֶם אֵת כָּל־הַדְּבָרִים הָאֵלֶּה אֲשֶׁר צִוָּהוּ יהוה: וַיַּעֲנוּ כָל־הָעָם יַחְדָּו וַיֹּאמְרוּ כֹּל אֲשֶׁר־דִּבֶּר יהוה נַעֲשֶׂה וַיָּשֶׁב מֹשֶׁה אֶת־דִּבְרֵי הָעָם אֶל־יהוה: וַיֹּאמֶר יהוה אֶל־מֹשֶׁה הִנֵּה אָנֹכִי בָּא אֵלֶיךָ בְּעַב הֶעָנָן בַּעֲבוּר יִשְׁמַע הָעָם בְּדַבְּרִי עִמָּךְ וְגַם־בְּךָ יַאֲמִינוּ לְעוֹלָם וַיַּגֵּד מֹשֶׁה אֶת־דִּבְרֵי הָעָם אֶל־יהוה: וַיֹּאמֶר יהוה אֶל־מֹשֶׁה לֵךְ אֶל־הָעָם וְקִדַּשְׁתָּם הַיּוֹם וּמָחָר וְכִבְּסוּ שִׂמְלֹתָם: וְהָיוּ נְכֹנִים לַיּוֹם הַשְּׁלִישִׁי כִּי ׀ בַּיּוֹם הַשְּׁלִשִׁי יֵרֵד יהוה לְעֵינֵי כָל־הָעָם עַל־הַר סִינָי: וְהִגְבַּלְתָּ אֶת־הָעָם סָבִיב לֵאמֹר הִשָּׁמְרוּ לָכֶם עֲלוֹת בָּהָר וּנְגֹעַ בְּקָצֵהוּ כָּל־הַנֹּגֵעַ בָּהָר מוֹת יוּמָת: לֹא־תִגַּע בּוֹ יָד כִּי־סָקוֹל יִסָּקֵל אוֹ־יָרֹה יִיָּרֶה אִם־בְּהֵמָה אִם־אִישׁ לֹא יִחְיֶה בִּמְשֹׁךְ הַיֹּבֵל הֵמָּה יַעֲלוּ בָהָר: שלישי: וַיֵּרֶד מֹשֶׁה מִן־הָהָר אֶל־הָעָם וַיְקַדֵּשׁ אֶת־הָעָם וַיְכַבְּסוּ שִׂמְלֹתָם: וַיֹּאמֶר אֶל־הָעָם הֱיוּ נְכֹנִים לִשְׁלֹשֶׁת יָמִים אַל־תִּגְּשׁוּ אֶל־אִשָּׁה: וַיְהִי בַיּוֹם הַשְּׁלִישִׁי בִּהְיֹת הַבֹּקֶר וַיְהִי קֹלֹת וּבְרָקִים וְעָנָן כָּבֵד עַל־הָהָר וְקֹל שֹׁפָר חָזָק מְאֹד וַיֶּחֱרַד כָּל־הָעָם אֲשֶׁר בַּמַּחֲנֶה: וַיּוֹצֵא מֹשֶׁה אֶת־הָעָם לִקְרַאת הָאֱלֹהִים מִן־הַמַּחֲנֶה וַיִּתְיַצְּבוּ בְּתַחְתִּית הָהָר: וְהַר סִינַי עָשַׁן כֻּלּוֹ מִפְּנֵי אֲשֶׁר יָרַד עָלָיו יהוה בָּאֵשׁ וַיַּעַל עֲשָׁנוֹ כְּעֶשֶׁן הַכִּבְשָׁן וַיֶּחֱרַד כָּל־הָהָר מְאֹד: וַיְהִי קוֹל הַשֹּׁפָר הוֹלֵךְ וְחָזֵק מְאֹד מֹשֶׁה יְדַבֵּר וְהָאֱלֹהִים יַעֲנֶנּוּ בְקוֹל: רביעי: וַיֵּרֶד יהוה עַל־הַר סִינַי אֶל־רֹאשׁ הָהָר וַיִּקְרָא יהוה לְמֹשֶׁה אֶל־רֹאשׁ

הָהָר וַיַּעַל מֹשֶׁה: וַיֹּאמֶר יהוה אֶל־מֹשֶׁה רֵד הָעֵד בָּעָם פֶּן־יֶהֶרְסוּ אֶל־יהוה לִרְאוֹת וְנָפַל מִמֶּנּוּ רָב: וְגַם הַכֹּהֲנִים הַנִּגָּשִׁים אֶל־יהוה יִתְקַדָּשׁוּ פֶּן־יִפְרֹץ בָּהֶם יהוה: וַיֹּאמֶר מֹשֶׁה אֶל־יהוה לֹא־יוּכַל הָעָם לַעֲלֹת אֶל־הַר סִינָי כִּי־אַתָּה הַעֵדֹתָה בָּנוּ לֵאמֹר הַגְבֵּל אֶת־הָהָר וְקִדַּשְׁתּוֹ: וַיֹּאמֶר אֵלָיו יהוה לֶךְ־רֵד וְעָלִיתָ אַתָּה וְאַהֲרֹן עִמָּךְ וְהַכֹּהֲנִים וְהָעָם אַל־יֶהֶרְסוּ לַעֲלֹת אֶל־יהוה פֶּן־יִפְרָץ־בָּם: וַיֵּרֶד מֹשֶׁה אֶל־הָעָם וַיֹּאמֶר אֲלֵהֶם:

וַיְדַבֵּר אֱלֹהִים אֵת כָּל־הַדְּבָרִים הָאֵלֶּה לֵאמֹר: אָנֹכִי יהוה אֱלֹהֶיךָ אֲשֶׁר הוֹצֵאתִיךָ מֵאֶרֶץ מִצְרַיִם מִבֵּית עֲבָדִים: לֹא־יִהְיֶה לְךָ אֱלֹהִים אֲחֵרִים עַל־פָּנָי לֹא תַעֲשֶׂה־לְךָ פֶסֶל ׀ וְכָל־תְּמוּנָה אֲשֶׁר בַּשָּׁמַיִם ׀ מִמַּעַל וַאֲשֶׁר בָּאָרֶץ מִתָּחַת וַאֲשֶׁר בַּמַּיִם ׀ מִתַּחַת לָאָרֶץ לֹא־תִשְׁתַּחֲוֶה לָהֶם וְלֹא תָעָבְדֵם כִּי אָנֹכִי יהוה אֱלֹהֶיךָ אֵל קַנָּא פֹּקֵד עֲוֹן אָבֹת עַל־בָּנִים עַל־שִׁלֵּשִׁים וְעַל־רִבֵּעִים לְשֹׂנְאָי וְעֹשֶׂה חֶסֶד לַאֲלָפִים לְאֹהֲבַי וּלְשֹׁמְרֵי מִצְוֺתָי: לֹא תִשָּׂא אֶת־שֵׁם־יהוה אֱלֹהֶיךָ לַשָּׁוְא כִּי לֹא יְנַקֶּה יהוה אֵת אֲשֶׁר־יִשָּׂא אֶת־שְׁמוֹ לַשָּׁוְא:

זָכוֹר אֶת־יוֹם הַשַּׁבָּת לְקַדְּשׁוֹ שֵׁשֶׁת יָמִים תַּעֲבֹד וְעָשִׂיתָ כָּל־מְלַאכְתֶּךָ וְיוֹם הַשְּׁבִיעִי שַׁבָּת ׀ לַיהוה אֱלֹהֶיךָ לֹא תַעֲשֶׂה כָל־מְלָאכָה אַתָּה וּבִנְךָ וּבִתֶּךָ עַבְדְּךָ וַאֲמָתְךָ וּבְהֶמְתֶּךָ וְגֵרְךָ אֲשֶׁר בִּשְׁעָרֶיךָ כִּי שֵׁשֶׁת־יָמִים עָשָׂה יהוה אֶת־הַשָּׁמַיִם וְאֶת־הָאָרֶץ אֶת־הַיָּם וְאֶת־כָּל־אֲשֶׁר־בָּם וַיָּנַח בַּיּוֹם הַשְּׁבִיעִי עַל־כֵּן בֵּרַךְ יהוה אֶת־יוֹם הַשַּׁבָּת וַיְקַדְּשֵׁהוּ: כַּבֵּד אֶת־אָבִיךָ וְאֶת־אִמֶּךָ לְמַעַן יַאֲרִכוּן יָמֶיךָ עַל הָאֲדָמָה אֲשֶׁר־יהוה אֱלֹהֶיךָ נֹתֵן לָךְ: לֹא תִרְצָח: לֹא תִנְאָף: לֹא תִגְנֹב: לֹא־תַעֲנֶה בְרֵעֲךָ עֵד שָׁקֶר: לֹא תַחְמֹד בֵּית רֵעֶךָ לֹא־תַחְמֹד אֵשֶׁת רֵעֶךָ וְעַבְדּוֹ וַאֲמָתוֹ וְשׁוֹרוֹ וַחֲמֹרוֹ וְכֹל אֲשֶׁר לְרֵעֶךָ:

חמישי: וְכָל־הָעָם רֹאִים אֶת־הַקּוֹלֹת וְאֶת־הַלַּפִּידִם וְאֵת קוֹל הַשֹּׁפָר וְאֶת־הָהָר עָשֵׁן וַיַּרְא הָעָם וַיָּנֻעוּ וַיַּעַמְדוּ מֵרָחֹק: וַיֹּאמְרוּ אֶל־מֹשֶׁה דַּבֵּר־אַתָּה עִמָּנוּ וְנִשְׁמָעָה וְאַל־יְדַבֵּר עִמָּנוּ אֱלֹהִים פֶּן־נָמוּת: וַיֹּאמֶר מֹשֶׁה אֶל־הָעָם אַל־תִּירָאוּ כִּי לְבַעֲבוּר נַסּוֹת אֶתְכֶם בָּא הָאֱלֹהִים וּבַעֲבוּר תִּהְיֶה יִרְאָתוֹ עַל־פְּנֵיכֶם לְבִלְתִּי תֶחֱטָאוּ: וַיַּעֲמֹד הָעָם מֵרָחֹק וּמֹשֶׁה נִגַּשׁ אֶל־הָעֲרָפֶל אֲשֶׁר־שָׁם הָאֱלֹהִים: וַיֹּאמֶר יהוה אֶל־מֹשֶׁה כֹּה תֹאמַר אֶל־בְּנֵי יִשְׂרָאֵל אַתֶּם רְאִיתֶם כִּי מִן־הַשָּׁמַיִם דִּבַּרְתִּי עִמָּכֶם: לֹא תַעֲשׂוּן אִתִּי אֱלֹהֵי כֶסֶף וֵאלֹהֵי זָהָב לֹא תַעֲשׂוּ לָכֶם: מִזְבַּח אֲדָמָה תַּעֲשֶׂה־לִּי וְזָבַחְתָּ עָלָיו אֶת־עֹלֹתֶיךָ וְאֶת־שְׁלָמֶיךָ אֶת־צֹאנְךָ וְאֶת־בְּקָרֶךָ בְּכָל־הַמָּקוֹם אֲשֶׁר אַזְכִּיר אֶת־שְׁמִי אָבוֹא אֵלֶיךָ וּבֵרַכְתִּיךָ: וְאִם־מִזְבַּח אֲבָנִים תַּעֲשֶׂה־לִּי לֹא־תִבְנֶה אֶתְהֶן גָּזִית כִּי חַרְבְּךָ הֵנַפְתָּ עָלֶיהָ וַתְּחַלְלֶהָ: וְלֹא־תַעֲלֶה בְמַעֲלֹת עַל־מִזְבְּחִי אֲשֶׁר לֹא־תִגָּלֶה עֶרְוָתְךָ עָלָיו:

The following מפטיר *is read from the second* ספר תורה *on both days of* שבועות*:*

במדבר כח:כו-לא

וּבְיוֹם הַבִּכּוּרִים בְּהַקְרִיבְכֶם מִנְחָה חֲדָשָׁה לַיהוה בְּשָׁבֻעֹתֵיכֶם מִקְרָא־קֹדֶשׁ יִהְיֶה לָכֶם כָּל־מְלֶאכֶת עֲבֹדָה לֹא תַעֲשׂוּ: וְהִקְרַבְתֶּם עוֹלָה לְרֵיחַ נִיחֹחַ לַיהוה פָּרִים בְּנֵי־בָקָר שְׁנַיִם אַיִל אֶחָד שִׁבְעָה כְבָשִׂים בְּנֵי שָׁנָה: וּמִנְחָתָם סֹלֶת בְּלוּלָה בַשָּׁמֶן שְׁלֹשָׁה עֶשְׂרֹנִים לַפָּר הָאֶחָד שְׁנֵי עֶשְׂרֹנִים לָאַיִל הָאֶחָד: עִשָּׂרוֹן עִשָּׂרוֹן לַכֶּבֶשׂ הָאֶחָד לְשִׁבְעַת הַכְּבָשִׂים: שְׂעִיר עִזִּים אֶחָד לְכַפֵּר עֲלֵיכֶם: מִלְּבַד עֹלַת הַתָּמִיד וּמִנְחָתוֹ תַּעֲשׂוּ תְּמִימִם יִהְיוּ־לָכֶם וְנִסְכֵּיהֶם:

הפטרה ליום טוב ראשון של שבועות / HAFTARA FOR FIRST DAY OF SHAVUOT

יחזקאל א:א-כח

וַיְהִי ׀ בִּשְׁלֹשִׁים שָׁנָה בָּרְבִיעִי בַּחֲמִשָּׁה לַחֹדֶשׁ וַאֲנִי בְתוֹךְ־הַגּוֹלָה עַל־נְהַר־כְּבָר נִפְתְּחוּ הַשָּׁמַיִם וָאֶרְאֶה מַרְאוֹת אֱלֹהִים: בַּחֲמִשָּׁה לַחֹדֶשׁ הִיא הַשָּׁנָה הַחֲמִישִׁית לְגָלוּת הַמֶּלֶךְ יוֹיָכִין: הָיֹה הָיָה דְבַר־יהוה אֶל־יְחֶזְקֵאל בֶּן־בּוּזִי הַכֹּהֵן בְּאֶרֶץ כַּשְׂדִּים עַל־נְהַר־כְּבָר וַתְּהִי עָלָיו שָׁם יַד־יהוה: וָאֵרֶא וְהִנֵּה רוּחַ סְעָרָה בָּאָה מִן־הַצָּפוֹן עָנָן גָּדוֹל וְאֵשׁ מִתְלַקַּחַת וְנֹגַהּ לוֹ סָבִיב וּמִתּוֹכָהּ כְּעֵין הַחַשְׁמַל מִתּוֹךְ הָאֵשׁ: וּמִתּוֹכָהּ דְּמוּת אַרְבַּע חַיּוֹת וְזֶה מַרְאֵיהֶן דְּמוּת אָדָם לָהֵנָּה: וְאַרְבָּעָה פָנִים לְאֶחָת וְאַרְבַּע כְּנָפַיִם לְאַחַת לָהֶם: וְרַגְלֵיהֶם רֶגֶל יְשָׁרָה וְכַף רַגְלֵיהֶם כְּכַף רֶגֶל עֵגֶל וְנֹצְצִים כְּעֵין נְחֹשֶׁת קָלָל: וידו [וִידֵי] אָדָם מִתַּחַת כַּנְפֵיהֶם עַל אַרְבַּעַת רִבְעֵיהֶם וּפְנֵיהֶם וְכַנְפֵיהֶם לְאַרְבַּעְתָּם: חֹבְרֹת אִשָּׁה אֶל־אֲחוֹתָהּ כַּנְפֵיהֶם לֹא־יִסַּבּוּ בְלֶכְתָּן אִישׁ אֶל־עֵבֶר פָּנָיו יֵלֵכוּ: וּדְמוּת פְּנֵיהֶם פְּנֵי אָדָם וּפְנֵי אַרְיֵה אֶל־הַיָּמִין לְאַרְבַּעְתָּם וּפְנֵי־שׁוֹר מֵהַשְּׂמֹאול לְאַרְבַּעְתָּן וּפְנֵי־נֶשֶׁר לְאַרְבַּעְתָּן: וּפְנֵיהֶם וְכַנְפֵיהֶם פְּרֻדוֹת מִלְמָעְלָה לְאִישׁ שְׁתַּיִם חֹבְרוֹת אִישׁ וּשְׁתַּיִם מְכַסּוֹת אֵת גְּוִיֹּתֵיהֶנָה: וְאִישׁ אֶל־עֵבֶר פָּנָיו יֵלֵכוּ אֶל אֲשֶׁר יִהְיֶה־שָׁמָּה הָרוּחַ לָלֶכֶת יֵלֵכוּ לֹא יִסַּבּוּ בְּלֶכְתָּן: וּדְמוּת הַחַיּוֹת מַרְאֵיהֶם כְּגַחֲלֵי־אֵשׁ בֹּעֲרוֹת כְּמַרְאֵה הַלַּפִּדִים הִיא מִתְהַלֶּכֶת בֵּין הַחַיּוֹת וְנֹגַהּ לָאֵשׁ וּמִן־הָאֵשׁ יוֹצֵא בָרָק: וְהַחַיּוֹת רָצוֹא וָשׁוֹב כְּמַרְאֵה הַבָּזָק: וָאֵרֶא הַחַיּוֹת וְהִנֵּה אוֹפַן אֶחָד בָּאָרֶץ אֵצֶל הַחַיּוֹת לְאַרְבַּעַת פָּנָיו: מַרְאֵה הָאוֹפַנִּים וּמַעֲשֵׂיהֶם כְּעֵין תַּרְשִׁישׁ וּדְמוּת אֶחָד לְאַרְבַּעְתָּן וּמַרְאֵיהֶם וּמַעֲשֵׂיהֶם כַּאֲשֶׁר יִהְיֶה הָאוֹפַן בְּתוֹךְ הָאוֹפָן: עַל־אַרְבַּעַת רִבְעֵיהֶן בְּלֶכְתָּם יֵלֵכוּ לֹא יִסַּבּוּ בְּלֶכְתָּן: וְגַבֵּיהֶן וְגֹבַהּ לָהֶם וְיִרְאָה לָהֶם וְגַבֹּתָם מְלֵאֹת עֵינַיִם סָבִיב לְאַרְבַּעְתָּן: וּבְלֶכֶת הַחַיּוֹת יֵלְכוּ הָאוֹפַנִּים אֶצְלָם וּבְהִנָּשֵׂא הַחַיּוֹת מֵעַל הָאָרֶץ יִנָּשְׂאוּ הָאוֹפַנִּים: עַל אֲשֶׁר יִהְיֶה־שָּׁם הָרוּחַ לָלֶכֶת יֵלֵכוּ שָׁמָּה הָרוּחַ לָלֶכֶת וְהָאוֹפַנִּים יִנָּשְׂאוּ לְעֻמָּתָם כִּי רוּחַ הַחַיָּה בָּאוֹפַנִּים: בְּלֶכְתָּם יֵלֵכוּ וּבְעָמְדָם יַעֲמֹדוּ וּבְהִנָּשְׂאָם מֵעַל הָאָרֶץ יִנָּשְׂאוּ הָאוֹפַנִּים לְעֻמָּתָם כִּי רוּחַ הַחַיָּה בָּאוֹפַנִּים: וּדְמוּת עַל־רָאשֵׁי הַחַיָּה רָקִיעַ כְּעֵין הַקֶּרַח הַנּוֹרָא נָטוּי עַל־רָאשֵׁיהֶם מִלְמָעְלָה: וְתַחַת הָרָקִיעַ כַּנְפֵיהֶם יְשָׁרוֹת אִשָּׁה אֶל־אֲחוֹתָהּ לְאִישׁ שְׁתַּיִם מְכַסּוֹת לָהֵנָּה וּלְאִישׁ שְׁתַּיִם מְכַסּוֹת לָהֵנָּה אֵת גְּוִיֹּתֵיהֶם: וָאֶשְׁמַע אֶת־קוֹל כַּנְפֵיהֶם כְּקוֹל מַיִם רַבִּים כְּקוֹל־שַׁדַּי בְּלֶכְתָּם קוֹל הֲמֻלָּה כְּקוֹל מַחֲנֶה בְּעָמְדָם תְּרַפֶּינָה כַנְפֵיהֶן: וַיְהִי־קוֹל מֵעַל לָרָקִיעַ אֲשֶׁר עַל־רֹאשָׁם בְּעָמְדָם תְּרַפֶּינָה כַנְפֵיהֶן: וּמִמַּעַל לָרָקִיעַ אֲשֶׁר עַל־רֹאשָׁם כְּמַרְאֵה אֶבֶן־סַפִּיר דְּמוּת כִּסֵּא וְעַל דְּמוּת הַכִּסֵּא דְּמוּת כְּמַרְאֵה אָדָם עָלָיו מִלְמָעְלָה: וָאֵרֶא ׀ כְּעֵין חַשְׁמַל כְּמַרְאֵה־אֵשׁ בֵּית־לָהּ סָבִיב מִמַּרְאֵה מָתְנָיו וּלְמָעְלָה וּמִמַּרְאֵה מָתְנָיו וּלְמַטָּה רָאִיתִי כְּמַרְאֵה־אֵשׁ וְנֹגַהּ לוֹ סָבִיב: כְּמַרְאֵה הַקֶּשֶׁת אֲשֶׁר יִהְיֶה בֶעָנָן בְּיוֹם הַגֶּשֶׁם כֵּן מַרְאֵה הַנֹּגַהּ סָבִיב הוּא מַרְאֵה דְּמוּת כְּבוֹד־יהוה וָאֶרְאֶה וָאֶפֹּל עַל־פָּנַי וָאֶשְׁמַע קוֹל מְדַבֵּר:

יחזקאל ג:יב

וַתִּשָּׂאֵנִי רוּחַ וָאֶשְׁמַע אַחֲרַי קוֹל רַעַשׁ גָּדוֹל בָּרוּךְ כְּבוֹד־יהוה מִמְּקוֹמוֹ:

The קריאת התורה *for the second day of* שבועות *is the same as that of the eighth day of* פסח *on page 1152. The* מפטיר *is the same as that of the first day of* שבועות *(page 1156).*

הפטרה ליום טוב שני של שבועות / HAFTARA FOR SECOND DAY OF SHAVUOT

חבקוק ב:כ-ג:יט

וַיהֹוָה בְּהֵיכַל קׇדְשׁוֹ הַס מִפָּנָיו כׇּל־הָאָרֶץ׃ תְּפִלָּה לַחֲבַקּוּק הַנָּבִיא עַל שִׁגְיֹנוֹת׃

Many say the following יַצִּיב פִּתְגָם *in the* הפטרה.

יַצִּיב פִּתְגָם, לְאָת וּדְגַם,
בְּרִבּוֹ רִבְבָן עִירִין.
עָנֵה אֲנָא, בְּמִנְיָנָא,
דְּפַסְלִין אַרְבְּעָה טוּרִין.
קֳדָמוֹהִי, לְגוֹ מוֹהִי,
נְגִיד וּנְפִיק נְהַר דִּי נוּרִין.
בְּטוּר תַּלְגָּא, נְהוֹר שְׁרָגָא,
וְזִיקִין דִּי נוּר וּבְעוּרִין.
בְּרָא וּסְכָא, מַה בַּחֲשׁוֹכָא,
וְעִמֵּהּ שָׁרְיָין נְהוֹרִין.
רְחִיקִין צָפָא, בְּלָא שִׁטְפָּא,
וּגְלְיָן לֵהּ דְּמִטַּמְרִין.
בְּעֵית מִנֵּהּ, יַת הַרְמָנֵהּ,
וּבָתְרוֹהִי עֲדֵי גַּבְרִין.
יָדְעֵי הִלְכְתָא, וּמַתְנִיתָא,
וְתוֹסֶפְתָּא סִפְרָא וְסִפְרִין.
מֶלֶךְ חַיָּא, לְעָלְמַיָּא,
יְמַגַּר עַם לְהוֹן מְשַׁחֲרִין.
אֲמִיר עֲלֵיהוֹן, כְּחָלָא יְהוֹן,
וְלָא יִתְמְנוּן הֵיךְ עַפְרִין.
יְחַוְּרוּן כְּעַן, לְהוֹן בִּקְעָן,
יְטוּפוּן נַעֲוֵי חַמְרִין.
רְעוּתְהוֹן הַב, וְאַפֵּיהוֹן צְהַב,
יְנַהֲרוּן כִּנְהוֹר צַפְרִין.
לִי הַב תְּקֹף, וְעֵינָךְ זְקֹף,
חֲזִי עָרָךְ דְּבָךְ כָּפְרִין.

* THE MYRIAD angels' songs of praise
On high have loudly pealed;
On earth I too am glorying
God's law this day revealed.
A stream of flame goes forth from Him
Toward the watery flood.
A light shines on a mount of snow
With flames as red as blood.
Creator He, He sees through dark,
He is the source of light;
He sees afar with naught to bar;
To Him the dark shines bright.
Approval for my song I ask
Of Him, and of those versed
In books derived from Scripture's text
And codes from last to first.
Guard Thou, O ever-living King,
Thy people seeking Thee;
Make them to be as dust of earth,
And as the sand of sea.
Yea, may their valleys shine with flocks,
Their presses flow with wine,
And grant their prayer, and make their face
As radiant sun to shine. Let me be strong
Weak must they be
Whose life by Thee is blamed,
May they be dumb as inmost stone
May they be ever shamed.

*This translation is by R. David de Sola Pool, and uses a free-form poetic rhyming scheme rather than a literal translation.

יַצִּיב פִּתְגָם / YETZIV PITGAM
This is one of many *piyutim* composed by Rabbeinu Tam (the grandson of Rashi, d. 1171), and whose full name it spells out in acrostic form, i.e., R. Yaakov b. Meir (Prof. Ezra Fleischer).

Rabbeinu Tam valued the recital of *piyutim*

יְהוֹן כְּתַבְנָא, בְּגוֹ לִבְנָא,
כְּאַבְנָא יִשְׁתְּקוּן חָפְרִין.
כְּקָאֵמְנָא, וְתַרְגְּמְנָא,
בְּמִלּוֹי דִּבְחִיר סָפְרִין.
יְהוֹנָתָן, גְּבַר עִנְוְתָן,
בְּכֵן נַמְטִין אַפְרִין.

While we enjoy words of truth without fail,
From the pen of Yonatan ben Uziel,
Peerless translator, seeker of truth,
and a man of modesty,
Thus will we elevate and carry him forth,
To thank him till eternity.

יְהוָה שָׁמַעְתִּי שִׁמְעֲךָ יָרֵאתִי יְהוָה פָּעָלְךָ
בְּקֶרֶב שָׁנִים חַיֵּיהוּ בְּקֶרֶב שָׁנִים תּוֹדִיעַ בְּרֹגֶז
רַחֵם תִּזְכּוֹר: אֱלוֹהַּ מִתֵּימָן יָבוֹא וְקָדוֹשׁ
מֵהַר־פָּארָן סֶלָה כִּסָּה שָׁמַיִם הוֹדוֹ וּתְהִלָּתוֹ
מָלְאָה הָאָרֶץ: וְנֹגַהּ כָּאוֹר תִּהְיֶה קַרְנַיִם מִיָּדוֹ
לוֹ וְשָׁם חֶבְיוֹן עֻזֹּה: לְפָנָיו יֵלֶךְ דָּבֶר וְיֵצֵא
רֶשֶׁף לְרַגְלָיו: עָמַד | וַיְמֹדֶד אֶרֶץ רָאָה וַיַּתֵּר
גּוֹיִם וַיִּתְפֹּצְצוּ הַרְרֵי־עַד שַׁחוּ גִּבְעוֹת עוֹלָם
הֲלִיכוֹת עוֹלָם לוֹ: תַּחַת אָוֶן רָאִיתִי אָהֳלֵי
כוּשָׁן יִרְגְּזוּן יְרִיעוֹת אֶרֶץ מִדְיָן: הֲבִנְהָרִים
חָרָה יְהוָה אִם בַּנְּהָרִים אַפֶּךָ אִם־בַּיָּם
עֶבְרָתֶךָ כִּי תִרְכַּב עַל־סוּסֶיךָ מַרְכְּבֹתֶיךָ
יְשׁוּעָה: עֶרְיָה תֵעוֹר קַשְׁתֶּךָ שְׁבֻעוֹת מַטּוֹת
אֹמֶר סֶלָה נְהָרוֹת תְּבַקַּע־אָרֶץ: רָאוּךָ יָחִילוּ
הָרִים זֶרֶם מַיִם עָבָר נָתַן תְּהוֹם קוֹלוֹ רוֹם
יָדֵיהוּ נָשָׂא: שֶׁמֶשׁ יָרֵחַ עָמַד זְבֻלָה לְאוֹר
חִצֶּיךָ יְהַלֵּכוּ לְנֹגַהּ בְּרַק חֲנִיתֶךָ: בְּזַעַם
תִּצְעַד־אָרֶץ בְּאַף תָּדוּשׁ גּוֹיִם: יָצָאתָ לְיֵשַׁע
עַמֶּךָ לְיֵשַׁע אֶת־מְשִׁיחֶךָ מָחַצְתָּ רֹּאשׁ
מִבֵּית רָשָׁע עָרוֹת יְסוֹד עַד־צַוָּאר סֶלָה:
נָקַבְתָּ בְמַטָּיו רֹאשׁ פְּרָזָו יִסְעֲרוּ לַהֲפִיצֵנִי
עֲלִיצֻתָם כְּמוֹ־לֶאֱכֹל עָנִי בַּמִּסְתָּר: דָּרַכְתָּ
בַיָּם סוּסֶיךָ חֹמֶר מַיִם רַבִּים: שָׁמַעְתִּי |
וַתִּרְגַּז בִּטְנִי לְקוֹל צָלֲלוּ שְׂפָתַי יָבוֹא רָקָב
בַּעֲצָמַי וְתַחְתַּי אֶרְגָּז אֲשֶׁר אָנוּחַ לְיוֹם
צָרָה לַעֲלוֹת לְעַם יְגוּדֶנּוּ: כִּי־תְאֵנָה לֹא־
תִפְרָח וְאֵין יְבוּל בַּגְּפָנִים כִּחֵשׁ מַעֲשֵׂה־זַיִת
וּשְׁדֵמוֹת לֹא־עָשָׂה אֹכֶל גָּזַר מִמִּכְלָה צֹאן
וְאֵין בָּקָר בָּרְפָתִים: וַאֲנִי בַּיהוָה אֶעְלוֹזָה
אָגִילָה בֵּאלֹהֵי יִשְׁעִי: יֱהוִה אֲדֹנָי חֵילִי וַיָּשֶׂם
רַגְלַי כָּאַיָּלוֹת וְעַל־בָּמוֹתַי יַדְרִכֵנִי לַמְנַצֵּחַ
בִּנְגִינוֹתָי:

מפטיר ליום הראשון ושני של סוכות / MAFTIR FOR FIRST DAY AND SECOND DAY OF SUKKOT

במדבר כט: יב–טז

The קריאת התורה *for the first two days of* סוכות *is the same as that of the second day of* פסח *(page 1143). The following* מפטיר *is then read from the second* ספר תורה:

וּבַחֲמִשָּׁה עָשָׂר יוֹם לַחֹדֶשׁ הַשְּׁבִיעִי מִקְרָא־
קֹדֶשׁ יִהְיֶה לָכֶם כָּל־מְלֶאכֶת עֲבֹדָה לֹא
תַעֲשׂוּ וְחַגֹּתֶם חַג לַיהוָה שִׁבְעַת יָמִים:
וְהִקְרַבְתֶּם עֹלָה אִשֵּׁה רֵיחַ נִיחֹחַ לַיהוָה
פָּרִים בְּנֵי־בָקָר שְׁלֹשָׁה עָשָׂר אֵילִם שְׁנָיִם
כְּבָשִׂים בְּנֵי־שָׁנָה אַרְבָּעָה עָשָׂר תְּמִימִם
יִהְיוּ: וּמִנְחָתָם סֹלֶת בְּלוּלָה בַשָּׁמֶן שְׁלֹשָׁה
עֶשְׂרֹנִים לַפָּר הָאֶחָד לִשְׁלֹשָׁה עָשָׂר פָּרִים
שְׁנֵי עֶשְׂרֹנִים לָאַיִל הָאֶחָד לִשְׁנֵי הָאֵילִם:
וְעִשָּׂרוֹן עִשָּׂרוֹן לַכֶּבֶשׂ הָאֶחָד לְאַרְבָּעָה עָשָׂר
כְּבָשִׂים: וּשְׂעִיר־עִזִּים אֶחָד חַטָּאת מִלְּבַד
עֹלַת הַתָּמִיד מִנְחָתָהּ וְנִסְכָּהּ:

---

highly, and ruled that not only is it permissible to interrupt the flow of prayer to recite them, but "it is highly desirable insofar as they facilitate proper concentration." He even utilized them as sources when issuing halakhic rulings (Prof. Efraim Urbach).

הפטרה ליום הראשון של סוכות / HAFTARA FOR FIRST DAY OF SUKKOT

זכריה יד:א-כא

הִנֵּה יוֹם־בָּא לַיהוָה וְחֻלַּק שְׁלָלֵךְ בְּקִרְבֵּךְ: וְאָסַפְתִּי אֶת־כָּל־הַגּוֹיִם ׀ אֶל־יְרוּשָׁלִַם לַמִּלְחָמָה וְנִלְכְּדָה הָעִיר וְנָשַׁסּוּ הַבָּתִּים וְהַנָּשִׁים תשגלנה [תִּשָּׁכַבְנָה] וְיָצָא חֲצִי הָעִיר בַּגּוֹלָה וְיֶתֶר הָעָם לֹא יִכָּרֵת מִן־הָעִיר: וְיָצָא יהוה וְנִלְחַם בַּגּוֹיִם הָהֵם כְּיוֹם הִלָּחֲמוֹ בְּיוֹם קְרָב: וְעָמְדוּ רַגְלָיו בַּיּוֹם־הַהוּא עַל־הַר הַזֵּיתִים אֲשֶׁר עַל־פְּנֵי יְרוּשָׁלִַם מִקֶּדֶם וְנִבְקַע הַר הַזֵּיתִים מֵחֶצְיוֹ מִזְרָחָה וָיָמָּה גֵּיא גְּדוֹלָה מְאֹד וּמָשׁ חֲצִי הָהָר צָפוֹנָה וְחֶצְיוֹ נֶגְבָּה: וְנַסְתֶּם גֵּיא־הָרַי כִּי־יַגִּיעַ גֵּי־הָרִים אֶל־אָצַל וְנַסְתֶּם כַּאֲשֶׁר נַסְתֶּם מִפְּנֵי הָרַעַשׁ בִּימֵי עֻזִּיָּה מֶלֶךְ־יְהוּדָה וּבָא יהוה אֱלֹהַי כָּל־קְדֹשִׁים עִמָּךְ: וְהָיָה בַּיּוֹם הַהוּא לֹא־יִהְיֶה אוֹר יְקָרוֹת יקפאון [וְקִפָּאוֹן]: וְהָיָה יוֹם־אֶחָד הוּא יִוָּדַע לַיהוָה לֹא־יוֹם וְלֹא־לָיְלָה וְהָיָה לְעֵת־עֶרֶב יִהְיֶה־אוֹר: וְהָיָה ׀ בַּיּוֹם הַהוּא יֵצְאוּ מַיִם־חַיִּים מִירוּשָׁלִַם חֶצְיָם אֶל־הַיָּם הַקַּדְמוֹנִי וְחֶצְיָם אֶל־הַיָּם הָאַחֲרוֹן בַּקַּיִץ וּבַחֹרֶף יִהְיֶה: וְהָיָה יהוה לְמֶלֶךְ עַל־כָּל־הָאָרֶץ בַּיּוֹם הַהוּא יִהְיֶה יהוה אֶחָד וּשְׁמוֹ אֶחָד: יִסּוֹב כָּל־הָאָרֶץ כָּעֲרָבָה מִגֶּבַע לְרִמּוֹן נֶגֶב יְרוּשָׁלִָם וְרָאֲמָה וְיָשְׁבָה תַחְתֶּיהָ לְמִשַּׁעַר בִּנְיָמִן עַד־מְקוֹם שַׁעַר הָרִאשׁוֹן עַד־שַׁעַר הַפִּנִּים וּמִגְדַּל חֲנַנְאֵל עַד יִקְבֵי הַמֶּלֶךְ: וְיָשְׁבוּ בָהּ וְחֵרֶם לֹא יִהְיֶה־עוֹד וְיָשְׁבָה יְרוּשָׁלִַם לָבֶטַח: וְזֹאת ׀ תִּהְיֶה הַמַּגֵּפָה אֲשֶׁר יִגֹּף יהוה אֶת־כָּל־הָעַמִּים אֲשֶׁר צָבְאוּ עַל־יְרוּשָׁלִָם הָמֵק ׀ בְּשָׂרוֹ וְהוּא עֹמֵד עַל־רַגְלָיו וְעֵינָיו תִּמַּקְנָה בְחֹרֵיהֶן וּלְשׁוֹנוֹ תִּמַּק בְּפִיהֶם: וְהָיָה בַּיּוֹם הַהוּא תִּהְיֶה מְהוּמַת־יהוה רַבָּה בָּהֶם וְהֶחֱזִיקוּ אִישׁ יַד רֵעֵהוּ וְעָלְתָה יָדוֹ עַל־יַד רֵעֵהוּ: וְגַם־יְהוּדָה תִּלָּחֵם בִּירוּשָׁלִָם וְאֻסַּף חֵיל כָּל־הַגּוֹיִם סָבִיב זָהָב וָכֶסֶף וּבְגָדִים לָרֹב מְאֹד: וְכֵן תִּהְיֶה מַגֵּפַת הַסּוּס הַפֶּרֶד הַגָּמָל וְהַחֲמוֹר וְכָל־הַבְּהֵמָה אֲשֶׁר יִהְיֶה בַּמַּחֲנוֹת הָהֵמָּה כַּמַּגֵּפָה הַזֹּאת: וְהָיָה כָּל־הַנּוֹתָר מִכָּל־הַגּוֹיִם הַבָּאִים עַל־יְרוּשָׁלִָם וְעָלוּ מִדֵּי שָׁנָה בְשָׁנָה לְהִשְׁתַּחֲוֹת לְמֶלֶךְ יהוה צְבָאוֹת וְלָחֹג אֶת־חַג הַסֻּכּוֹת: וְהָיָה אֲשֶׁר לֹא־יַעֲלֶה מֵאֵת מִשְׁפְּחוֹת הָאָרֶץ אֶל־יְרוּשָׁלִַם לְהִשְׁתַּחֲוֹת לְמֶלֶךְ יהוה צְבָאוֹת וְלֹא עֲלֵיהֶם יִהְיֶה הַגָּשֶׁם: וְאִם־מִשְׁפַּחַת מִצְרַיִם לֹא־תַעֲלֶה וְלֹא בָאָה וְלֹא עֲלֵיהֶם תִּהְיֶה הַמַּגֵּפָה אֲשֶׁר יִגֹּף יהוה אֶת־הַגּוֹיִם אֲשֶׁר לֹא יַעֲלוּ לָחֹג אֶת־חַג הַסֻּכּוֹת: זֹאת תִּהְיֶה חַטַּאת מִצְרָיִם וְחַטַּאת כָּל־הַגּוֹיִם אֲשֶׁר לֹא יַעֲלוּ לָחֹג אֶת־חַג הַסֻּכּוֹת: בַּיּוֹם הַהוּא יִהְיֶה עַל־מְצִלּוֹת הַסּוּס קֹדֶשׁ לַיהוָה וְהָיָה הַסִּירוֹת בְּבֵית יהוה כַּמִּזְרָקִים לִפְנֵי הַמִּזְבֵּחַ: וְהָיָה כָּל־סִיר בִּירוּשָׁלִַם וּבִיהוּדָה קֹדֶשׁ לַיהוָה צְבָאוֹת וּבָאוּ כָּל־הַזֹּבְחִים וְלָקְחוּ מֵהֶם וּבִשְּׁלוּ בָהֶם וְלֹא־יִהְיֶה כְנַעֲנִי עוֹד בְּבֵית־יהוה צְבָאוֹת בַּיּוֹם הַהוּא:

הפטרה ליום טוב שני של סוכות / HAFTARA FOR SECOND DAY OF SUKKOT

מלכים א׳ ח:ב-כא

וַיִּקָּהֲלוּ אֶל־הַמֶּלֶךְ שְׁלֹמֹה כָּל־אִישׁ יִשְׂרָאֵל בְּיֶרַח הָאֵתָנִים בֶּחָג הוּא הַחֹדֶשׁ הַשְּׁבִיעִי: וַיָּבֹאוּ כֹּל זִקְנֵי יִשְׂרָאֵל וַיִּשְׂאוּ הַכֹּהֲנִים אֶת־הָאָרוֹן: וַיַּעֲלוּ אֶת־אֲרוֹן יהוה וְאֶת־אֹהֶל מוֹעֵד וְאֶת־כָּל־כְּלֵי הַקֹּדֶשׁ אֲשֶׁר בָּאֹהֶל וַיַּעֲלוּ אֹתָם הַכֹּהֲנִים וְהַלְוִיִּם: וְהַמֶּלֶךְ שְׁלֹמֹה וְכָל־עֲדַת יִשְׂרָאֵל הַנּוֹעָדִים עָלָיו אִתּוֹ לִפְנֵי הָאָרוֹן מְזַבְּחִים צֹאן וּבָקָר אֲשֶׁר לֹא־יִסָּפְרוּ וְלֹא יִמָּנוּ מֵרֹב: וַיָּבִאוּ הַכֹּהֲנִים אֶת־אֲרוֹן בְּרִית־יהוה אֶל־מְקוֹמוֹ אֶל־דְּבִיר הַבַּיִת אֶל־קֹדֶשׁ הַקֳּדָשִׁים אֶל־תַּחַת כַּנְפֵי הַכְּרוּבִים: כִּי הַכְּרוּבִים פֹּרְשִׂים כְּנָפַיִם אֶל־

מְקוֹם הָאָרוֹן וַיָּסֹכּוּ הַכְּרֻבִים עַל־הָאָרוֹן וְעַל־בַּדָּיו מִלְמָעְלָה: וַיַּאֲרִכוּ הַבַּדִּים וַיֵּרָאוּ רָאשֵׁי הַבַּדִּים מִן־הַקֹּדֶשׁ עַל־פְּנֵי הַדְּבִיר וְלֹא יֵרָאוּ הַחוּצָה וַיִּהְיוּ שָׁם עַד הַיּוֹם הַזֶּה: אֵין בָּאָרוֹן רַק שְׁנֵי לֻחוֹת הָאֲבָנִים אֲשֶׁר הִנִּחַ שָׁם מֹשֶׁה בְּחֹרֵב אֲשֶׁר כָּרַת יהוה עִם־בְּנֵי יִשְׂרָאֵל בְּצֵאתָם מֵאֶרֶץ מִצְרָיִם: וַיְהִי בְּצֵאת הַכֹּהֲנִים מִן־הַקֹּדֶשׁ וְהֶעָנָן מָלֵא אֶת־בֵּית יהוה: וְלֹא־יָכְלוּ הַכֹּהֲנִים לַעֲמֹד לְשָׁרֵת מִפְּנֵי הֶעָנָן כִּי־מָלֵא כְבוֹד־יהוה אֶת־בֵּית יהוה: אָז אָמַר שְׁלֹמֹה יהוה אָמַר לִשְׁכֹּן בָּעֲרָפֶל: בָּנֹה בָנִיתִי בֵּית זְבֻל לָךְ מָכוֹן לְשִׁבְתְּךָ עוֹלָמִים: וַיַּסֵּב הַמֶּלֶךְ אֶת־פָּנָיו וַיְבָרֶךְ אֵת כָּל־קְהַל יִשְׂרָאֵל וְכָל־קְהַל יִשְׂרָאֵל עֹמֵד: וַיֹּאמֶר בָּרוּךְ יהוה אֱלֹהֵי יִשְׂרָאֵל אֲשֶׁר דִּבֶּר בְּפִיו אֵת דָּוִד אָבִי וּבְיָדוֹ מִלֵּא לֵאמֹר: מִן־הַיּוֹם אֲשֶׁר הוֹצֵאתִי אֶת־עַמִּי אֶת־יִשְׂרָאֵל מִמִּצְרַיִם לֹא־בָחַרְתִּי בְעִיר מִכֹּל שִׁבְטֵי יִשְׂרָאֵל לִבְנוֹת בַּיִת לִהְיוֹת שְׁמִי שָׁם וָאֶבְחַר בְּדָוִד לִהְיוֹת עַל־עַמִּי יִשְׂרָאֵל: וַיְהִי עִם־לְבַב דָּוִד אָבִי לִבְנוֹת בַּיִת לְשֵׁם יהוה אֱלֹהֵי יִשְׂרָאֵל: וַיֹּאמֶר יהוה אֶל־דָּוִד אָבִי יַעַן אֲשֶׁר הָיָה עִם־לְבָבְךָ לִבְנוֹת בַּיִת לִשְׁמִי הֱטִיבֹתָ כִּי הָיָה עִם־לְבָבֶךָ: רַק אַתָּה לֹא תִבְנֶה הַבָּיִת כִּי אִם־בִּנְךָ הַיֹּצֵא מֵחֲלָצֶיךָ הוּא־יִבְנֶה הַבַּיִת לִשְׁמִי: וַיָּקֶם יהוה אֶת־דְּבָרוֹ אֲשֶׁר דִּבֵּר וָאָקֻם תַּחַת דָּוִד אָבִי וָאֵשֵׁב ׀ עַל־כִּסֵּא יִשְׂרָאֵל כַּאֲשֶׁר דִּבֶּר יהוה וָאֶבְנֶה הַבַּיִת לְשֵׁם יהוה אֱלֹהֵי יִשְׂרָאֵל: וָאָשִׂם שָׁם מָקוֹם לָאָרוֹן אֲשֶׁר־שָׁם בְּרִית יהוה אֲשֶׁר כָּרַת עִם־אֲבֹתֵינוּ בְּהוֹצִיאוֹ אֹתָם מֵאֶרֶץ מִצְרָיִם:

קריאה ליום הראשון דחול המועד סוכות / FIRST DAY OF ḤOL HAMO'ED SUKKOT

במדבר כט:יז-כה

וּבַיּוֹם הַשֵּׁנִי פָּרִים בְּנֵי־בָקָר שְׁנֵים עָשָׂר אֵילִם שְׁנָיִם כְּבָשִׂים בְּנֵי־שָׁנָה אַרְבָּעָה עָשָׂר תְּמִימִם: וּמִנְחָתָם וְנִסְכֵּיהֶם לַפָּרִים לָאֵילִם וְלַכְּבָשִׂים בְּמִסְפָּרָם כַּמִּשְׁפָּט: וּשְׂעִיר־עִזִּים אֶחָד חַטָּאת מִלְּבַד עֹלַת הַתָּמִיד וּמִנְחָתָהּ וְנִסְכֵּיהֶם: לוי: וּבַיּוֹם הַשְּׁלִישִׁי פָּרִים עַשְׁתֵּי־עָשָׂר אֵילִם שְׁנָיִם כְּבָשִׂים בְּנֵי־שָׁנָה אַרְבָּעָה עָשָׂר תְּמִימִם: וּמִנְחָתָם וְנִסְכֵּיהֶם לַפָּרִים לָאֵילִם וְלַכְּבָשִׂים בְּמִסְפָּרָם כַּמִּשְׁפָּט: וּשְׂעִיר חַטָּאת אֶחָד מִלְּבַד עֹלַת הַתָּמִיד וּמִנְחָתָהּ וְנִסְכָּהּ: שלישי: וּבַיּוֹם הָרְבִיעִי פָּרִים עֲשָׂרָה אֵילִם שְׁנָיִם כְּבָשִׂים בְּנֵי־שָׁנָה אַרְבָּעָה עָשָׂר תְּמִימִם: מִנְחָתָם וְנִסְכֵּיהֶם לַפָּרִים לָאֵילִם וְלַכְּבָשִׂים בְּמִסְפָּרָם כַּמִּשְׁפָּט: וּשְׂעִיר־עִזִּים אֶחָד חַטָּאת מִלְּבַד עֹלַת הַתָּמִיד מִנְחָתָהּ וְנִסְכָּהּ:

רביעי: וּבַיּוֹם הַשֵּׁנִי פָּרִים בְּנֵי־בָקָר שְׁנֵים עָשָׂר אֵילִם שְׁנָיִם כְּבָשִׂים בְּנֵי־שָׁנָה אַרְבָּעָה עָשָׂר תְּמִימִם: וּמִנְחָתָם וְנִסְכֵּיהֶם לַפָּרִים לָאֵילִם וְלַכְּבָשִׂים בְּמִסְפָּרָם כַּמִּשְׁפָּט: וּשְׂעִיר־עִזִּים אֶחָד חַטָּאת מִלְּבַד עֹלַת הַתָּמִיד וּמִנְחָתָהּ וְנִסְכֵּיהֶם: וּבַיּוֹם הַשְּׁלִישִׁי פָּרִים עַשְׁתֵּי־עָשָׂר אֵילִם שְׁנָיִם כְּבָשִׂים בְּנֵי־שָׁנָה אַרְבָּעָה עָשָׂר תְּמִימִם: וּמִנְחָתָם וְנִסְכֵּיהֶם לַפָּרִים לָאֵילִם וְלַכְּבָשִׂים בְּמִסְפָּרָם כַּמִּשְׁפָּט: וּשְׂעִיר חַטָּאת אֶחָד מִלְּבַד עֹלַת הַתָּמִיד וּמִנְחָתָהּ וְנִסְכָּהּ:

קריאה ליום השני דחול המועד סוכות / SECOND DAY OF ḤOL HAMO'ED SUKKOT

במדבר כט:כ-כח

וּבַיּוֹם הַשְּׁלִישִׁי פָּרִים עַשְׁתֵּי־עָשָׂר אֵילִם שְׁנָיִם כְּבָשִׂים בְּנֵי־שָׁנָה אַרְבָּעָה עָשָׂר תְּמִימִם: וּמִנְחָתָם וְנִסְכֵּיהֶם לַפָּרִים לָאֵילִם וְלַכְּבָשִׂים בְּמִסְפָּרָם כַּמִּשְׁפָּט: וּשְׂעִיר חַטָּאת אֶחָד מִלְּבַד עֹלַת הַתָּמִיד וּמִנְחָתָהּ וְנִסְכָּהּ: לוי: וּבַיּוֹם הָרְבִיעִי פָּרִים עֲשָׂרָה אֵילִם שְׁנָיִם כְּבָשִׂים בְּנֵי־שָׁנָה אַרְבָּעָה עָשָׂר תְּמִימִם:

מִנְחָתָם וְנִסְכֵּיהֶם לַפָּרִים לָאֵילִם וְלַכְּבָשִׂים בְּמִסְפָּרָם כַּמִּשְׁפָּט: וּשְׂעִיר־עִזִּים אֶחָד חַטָּאת מִלְּבַד עֹלַת הַתָּמִיד מִנְחָתָהּ וְנִסְכָּהּ:

שלישי: וּבַיּוֹם הַחֲמִישִׁי פָּרִים תִּשְׁעָה אֵילִם שְׁנָיִם כְּבָשִׂים בְּנֵי־שָׁנָה אַרְבָּעָה עָשָׂר תְּמִימִם: וּמִנְחָתָם וְנִסְכֵּיהֶם לַפָּרִים לָאֵילִם וְלַכְּבָשִׂים בְּמִסְפָּרָם כַּמִּשְׁפָּט: וּשְׂעִיר חַטָּאת אֶחָד מִלְּבַד עֹלַת הַתָּמִיד וּמִנְחָתָהּ וְנִסְכָּהּ:

רביעי: וּבַיּוֹם הַשְּׁלִישִׁי פָּרִים עַשְׁתֵּי־עָשָׂר אֵילִם שְׁנָיִם כְּבָשִׂים בְּנֵי־שָׁנָה אַרְבָּעָה עָשָׂר תְּמִימִם: וּמִנְחָתָם וְנִסְכֵּיהֶם לַפָּרִים לָאֵילִם וְלַכְּבָשִׂים בְּמִסְפָּרָם כַּמִּשְׁפָּט: וּשְׂעִיר חַטָּאת אֶחָד מִלְּבַד עֹלַת הַתָּמִיד וּמִנְחָתָהּ וְנִסְכָּהּ: וּבַיּוֹם הָרְבִיעִי פָּרִים עֲשָׂרָה אֵילִם שְׁנָיִם כְּבָשִׂים בְּנֵי־שָׁנָה אַרְבָּעָה עָשָׂר תְּמִימִם: מִנְחָתָם וְנִסְכֵּיהֶם לַפָּרִים לָאֵילִם וְלַכְּבָשִׂים בְּמִסְפָּרָם כַּמִּשְׁפָּט: וּשְׂעִיר־עִזִּים אֶחָד חַטָּאת מִלְּבַד עֹלַת הַתָּמִיד מִנְחָתָהּ וְנִסְכָּהּ:

קריאה ליום השלישי דחול המועד סוכות
THIRD DAY OF ḤOL HAMO’ED SUKKOT

במדבר כט:כג-לא

וּבַיּוֹם הָרְבִיעִי פָּרִים עֲשָׂרָה אֵילִם שְׁנָיִם כְּבָשִׂים בְּנֵי־שָׁנָה אַרְבָּעָה עָשָׂר תְּמִימִם: מִנְחָתָם וְנִסְכֵּיהֶם לַפָּרִים לָאֵילִם וְלַכְּבָשִׂים בְּמִסְפָּרָם כַּמִּשְׁפָּט: וּשְׂעִיר־עִזִּים אֶחָד חַטָּאת מִלְּבַד עֹלַת הַתָּמִיד מִנְחָתָהּ וְנִסְכָּהּ:

לוי: וּבַיּוֹם הַחֲמִישִׁי פָּרִים תִּשְׁעָה אֵילִם שְׁנָיִם כְּבָשִׂים בְּנֵי־שָׁנָה אַרְבָּעָה עָשָׂר תְּמִימִם: וּמִנְחָתָם וְנִסְכֵּיהֶם לַפָּרִים לָאֵילִם וְלַכְּבָשִׂים בְּמִסְפָּרָם כַּמִּשְׁפָּט: וּשְׂעִיר חַטָּאת אֶחָד מִלְּבַד עֹלַת הַתָּמִיד וּמִנְחָתָהּ וְנִסְכָּהּ:

שלישי: וּבַיּוֹם הַשִּׁשִּׁי פָּרִים שְׁמֹנָה אֵילִם שְׁנָיִם כְּבָשִׂים בְּנֵי־שָׁנָה אַרְבָּעָה עָשָׂר תְּמִימִם: וּמִנְחָתָם וְנִסְכֵּיהֶם לַפָּרִים לָאֵילִם וְלַכְּבָשִׂים בְּמִסְפָּרָם כַּמִּשְׁפָּט: וּשְׂעִיר חַטָּאת אֶחָד מִלְּבַד עֹלַת הַתָּמִיד מִנְחָתָהּ וּנְסָכֶיהָ:

רביעי: וּבַיּוֹם הָרְבִיעִי פָּרִים עֲשָׂרָה אֵילִם שְׁנָיִם כְּבָשִׂים בְּנֵי־שָׁנָה אַרְבָּעָה עָשָׂר תְּמִימִם: מִנְחָתָם וְנִסְכֵּיהֶם לַפָּרִים לָאֵילִם וְלַכְּבָשִׂים בְּמִסְפָּרָם כַּמִּשְׁפָּט: וּשְׂעִיר־עִזִּים אֶחָד חַטָּאת מִלְּבַד עֹלַת הַתָּמִיד מִנְחָתָהּ וְנִסְכָּהּ: וּבַיּוֹם הַחֲמִישִׁי פָּרִים תִּשְׁעָה אֵילִם שְׁנָיִם כְּבָשִׂים בְּנֵי־שָׁנָה אַרְבָּעָה עָשָׂר תְּמִימִם: וּמִנְחָתָם וְנִסְכֵּיהֶם לַפָּרִים לָאֵילִם וְלַכְּבָשִׂים בְּמִסְפָּרָם כַּמִּשְׁפָּט: וּשְׂעִיר חַטָּאת אֶחָד מִלְּבַד עֹלַת הַתָּמִיד וּמִנְחָתָהּ וְנִסְכָּהּ:

קריאה ליום הרביעי דחול המועד סוכות
FOURTH DAY OF ḤOL HAMO’ED SUKKOT

במדבר כט:כו-לד

וּבַיּוֹם הַחֲמִישִׁי פָּרִים תִּשְׁעָה אֵילִם שְׁנָיִם כְּבָשִׂים בְּנֵי־שָׁנָה אַרְבָּעָה עָשָׂר תְּמִימִם: וּמִנְחָתָם וְנִסְכֵּיהֶם לַפָּרִים לָאֵילִם וְלַכְּבָשִׂים בְּמִסְפָּרָם כַּמִּשְׁפָּט: וּשְׂעִיר חַטָּאת אֶחָד מִלְּבַד עֹלַת הַתָּמִיד וּמִנְחָתָהּ וְנִסְכָּהּ:

לוי: וּבַיּוֹם הַשִּׁשִּׁי פָּרִים שְׁמֹנָה אֵילִם שְׁנָיִם כְּבָשִׂים בְּנֵי־שָׁנָה אַרְבָּעָה עָשָׂר תְּמִימִם: וּמִנְחָתָם וְנִסְכֵּיהֶם לַפָּרִים לָאֵילִם וְלַכְּבָשִׂים בְּמִסְפָּרָם כַּמִּשְׁפָּט: וּשְׂעִיר חַטָּאת אֶחָד מִלְּבַד עֹלַת הַתָּמִיד מִנְחָתָהּ וּנְסָכֶיהָ:

שלישי: וּבַיּוֹם הַשְּׁבִיעִי פָּרִים שִׁבְעָה אֵילִם שְׁנָיִם כְּבָשִׂים בְּנֵי־שָׁנָה אַרְבָּעָה עָשָׂר תְּמִימִם: וּמִנְחָתָם וְנִסְכֵּהֶם לַפָּרִים לָאֵילִם וְלַכְּבָשִׂים בְּמִסְפָּרָם כְּמִשְׁפָּטָם: וּשְׂעִיר חַטָּאת אֶחָד מִלְּבַד עֹלַת הַתָּמִיד מִנְחָתָהּ וְנִסְכָּהּ:

רביעי: וּבַיּוֹם הַחֲמִישִׁי פָּרִים תִּשְׁעָה אֵילִם שְׁנָיִם כְּבָשִׂים בְּנֵי־שָׁנָה אַרְבָּעָה עָשָׂר תְּמִימִם: וּמִנְחָתָם וְנִסְכֵּיהֶם לַפָּרִים לָאֵילִם וְלַכְּבָשִׂים בְּמִסְפָּרָם כַּמִּשְׁפָּט: וּשְׂעִיר חַטָּאת אֶחָד מִלְּבַד עֹלַת הַתָּמִיד וּמִנְחָתָהּ וְנִסְכָּהּ: וּבַיּוֹם הַשִּׁשִּׁי פָּרִים שְׁמֹנָה אֵילִם שְׁנָיִם כְּבָשִׂים בְּנֵי־שָׁנָה אַרְבָּעָה עָשָׂר תְּמִימִם: וּמִנְחָתָם וְנִסְכֵּיהֶם לַפָּרִים לָאֵילִם וְלַכְּבָשִׂים

בְּמִסְפָּרָם כַּמִּשְׁפָּט: וּשְׂעִיר חַטָּאת אֶחָד מִלְּבַד עֹלַת הַתָּמִיד מִנְחָתָהּ וּנְסָכֶיהָ:

קריאה להושענא רבא
HOSHANA RABA

במדבר כט:כו–לד

וּבַיּוֹם הַחֲמִישִׁי פָּרִים תִּשְׁעָה אֵילִם שְׁנָיִם כְּבָשִׂים בְּנֵי־שָׁנָה אַרְבָּעָה עָשָׂר תְּמִימִם: וּמִנְחָתָם וְנִסְכֵּיהֶם לַפָּרִים לָאֵילִם וְלַכְּבָשִׂים בְּמִסְפָּרָם כַּמִּשְׁפָּט: וּשְׂעִיר חַטָּאת אֶחָד מִלְּבַד עֹלַת הַתָּמִיד וּמִנְחָתָהּ וְנִסְכָּהּ:

לוי: וּבַיּוֹם הַשִּׁשִּׁי פָּרִים שְׁמֹנָה אֵילִם שְׁנָיִם כְּבָשִׂים בְּנֵי־שָׁנָה אַרְבָּעָה עָשָׂר תְּמִימִם: וּמִנְחָתָם וְנִסְכֵּיהֶם לַפָּרִים לָאֵילִם וְלַכְּבָשִׂים בְּמִסְפָּרָם כַּמִּשְׁפָּט: וּשְׂעִיר חַטָּאת אֶחָד מִלְּבַד עֹלַת הַתָּמִיד מִנְחָתָהּ וּנְסָכֶיהָ:

שלישי: וּבַיּוֹם הַשְּׁבִיעִי פָּרִים שִׁבְעָה אֵילִם שְׁנָיִם כְּבָשִׂים בְּנֵי־שָׁנָה אַרְבָּעָה עָשָׂר תְּמִימִם: וּמִנְחָתָם וְנִסְכֵּהֶם לַפָּרִים לָאֵילִם וְלַכְּבָשִׂים בְּמִסְפָּרָם כְּמִשְׁפָּטָם: וּשְׂעִיר חַטָּאת אֶחָד מִלְּבַד עֹלַת הַתָּמִיד מִנְחָתָהּ וְנִסְכָּהּ:

רביעי: וּבַיּוֹם הַשִּׁשִּׁי פָּרִים שְׁמֹנָה אֵילִם שְׁנָיִם כְּבָשִׂים בְּנֵי־שָׁנָה אַרְבָּעָה עָשָׂר תְּמִימִם: וּמִנְחָתָם וְנִסְכֵּיהֶם לַפָּרִים לָאֵילִם וְלַכְּבָשִׂים בְּמִסְפָּרָם כַּמִּשְׁפָּט: וּשְׂעִיר חַטָּאת אֶחָד מִלְּבַד עֹלַת הַתָּמִיד מִנְחָתָהּ וּנְסָכֶיהָ: וּבַיּוֹם הַשְּׁבִיעִי פָּרִים שִׁבְעָה אֵילִם שְׁנָיִם כְּבָשִׂים בְּנֵי־שָׁנָה אַרְבָּעָה עָשָׂר תְּמִימִם: וּמִנְחָתָם וְנִסְכֵּהֶם לַפָּרִים לָאֵילִם וְלַכְּבָשִׂים בְּמִסְפָּרָם כְּמִשְׁפָּטָם: וּשְׂעִיר חַטָּאת אֶחָד מִלְּבַד עֹלַת הַתָּמִיד מִנְחָתָהּ וְנִסְכָּהּ:

קריאה לשבת חול המועד סוכות
SHABBAT ḤOL HAMO'ED SUKKOT

The קריאת התורה *for* שבת חול המועד סוכות *is the same as that of* שבת חול המועד פסח *(page 1148). The* מפטיר *is the* קריאת התורה *of the day of* חול המועד סוכות *on which* שבת *falls.*

הפטרה לשבת חול המועד סוכות / HAFTARA FOR SHABBAT ḤOL HAMO'ED SUKKOT

יחזקאל לח:יח–לט:טז

וְהָיָה | בַּיּוֹם הַהוּא בְּיוֹם בּוֹא גוֹג עַל־אַדְמַת יִשְׂרָאֵל נְאֻם אֲדֹנָי יֱהוִה תַּעֲלֶה חֲמָתִי בְּאַפִּי: וּבְקִנְאָתִי בְאֵשׁ־עֶבְרָתִי דִּבַּרְתִּי אִם־לֹא | בַּיּוֹם הַהוּא יִהְיֶה רַעַשׁ גָּדוֹל עַל אַדְמַת יִשְׂרָאֵל: וְרָעֲשׁוּ מִפָּנַי דְּגֵי הַיָּם וְעוֹף הַשָּׁמַיִם וְחַיַּת הַשָּׂדֶה וְכָל־הָרֶמֶשׂ הָרֹמֵשׂ עַל־הָאֲדָמָה וְכֹל הָאָדָם אֲשֶׁר עַל־פְּנֵי הָאֲדָמָה וְנֶהֶרְסוּ הֶהָרִים וְנָפְלוּ הַמַּדְרֵגוֹת וְכָל־חוֹמָה לָאָרֶץ תִּפּוֹל: וְקָרָאתִי עָלָיו לְכָל־הָרַי חֶרֶב נְאֻם אֲדֹנָי יֱהוִה חֶרֶב אִישׁ בְּאָחִיו תִּהְיֶה: וְנִשְׁפַּטְתִּי אִתּוֹ בְּדֶבֶר וּבְדָם וְגֶשֶׁם שׁוֹטֵף וְאַבְנֵי אֶלְגָּבִישׁ אֵשׁ וְגָפְרִית אַמְטִיר עָלָיו וְעַל־אֲגַפָּיו וְעַל־עַמִּים רַבִּים אֲשֶׁר אִתּוֹ: וְהִתְגַּדִּלְתִּי וְהִתְקַדִּשְׁתִּי וְנוֹדַעְתִּי לְעֵינֵי גּוֹיִם רַבִּים וְיָדְעוּ כִּי־אֲנִי יהוה: וְאַתָּה בֶן־אָדָם הִנָּבֵא עַל־גּוֹג וְאָמַרְתָּ כֹּה אָמַר אֲדֹנָי יֱהוִה הִנְנִי אֵלֶיךָ גּוֹג נְשִׂיא רֹאשׁ מֶשֶׁךְ וְתֻבָל: וְשֹׁבַבְתִּיךָ וְשִׁשֵּׁאתִיךָ וְהַעֲלִיתִיךָ מִיַּרְכְּתֵי צָפוֹן וַהֲבִאוֹתִךָ עַל־הָרֵי יִשְׂרָאֵל: וְהִכֵּיתִי קַשְׁתְּךָ מִיַּד שְׂמֹאולֶךָ וְחִצֶּיךָ מִיַּד יְמִינְךָ אַפִּיל: עַל־הָרֵי יִשְׂרָאֵל תִּפּוֹל אַתָּה וְכָל־אֲגַפֶּיךָ וְעַמִּים אֲשֶׁר אִתָּךְ לְעֵיט צִפּוֹר כָּל־כָּנָף וְחַיַּת הַשָּׂדֶה נְתַתִּיךָ לְאָכְלָה: עַל־פְּנֵי הַשָּׂדֶה תִּפּוֹל כִּי אֲנִי דִּבַּרְתִּי נְאֻם אֲדֹנָי יֱהוִה: וְשִׁלַּחְתִּי־אֵשׁ בְּמָגוֹג וּבְיֹשְׁבֵי הָאִיִּים לָבֶטַח וְיָדְעוּ כִּי־אֲנִי יהוה: וְאֶת־שֵׁם קָדְשִׁי אוֹדִיעַ בְּתוֹךְ עַמִּי יִשְׂרָאֵל וְלֹא־אַחֵל אֶת־שֵׁם־קָדְשִׁי עוֹד וְיָדְעוּ הַגּוֹיִם כִּי־אֲנִי יהוה קָדוֹשׁ בְּיִשְׂרָאֵל: הִנֵּה בָאָה וְנִהְיָתָה נְאֻם אֲדֹנָי יֱהוִה הוּא הַיּוֹם אֲשֶׁר דִּבַּרְתִּי: וְיָצְאוּ יֹשְׁבֵי | עָרֵי יִשְׂרָאֵל וּבִעֲרוּ וְהִשִּׂיקוּ בְּנֶשֶׁק וּמָגֵן וְצִנָּה בְּקֶשֶׁת וּבְחִצִּים וּבְמַקֵּל יָד וּבְרֹמַח וּבִעֲרוּ בָהֶם אֵשׁ שֶׁבַע שָׁנִים: וְלֹא־יִשְׂאוּ עֵצִים מִן־הַשָּׂדֶה וְלֹא יַחְטְבוּ מִן־הַיְּעָרִים כִּי בַנֶּשֶׁק

יְבַעֲרוּ־אֵשׁ וְשָׁלְלוּ אֶת־שֹׁלְלֵיהֶם וּבָזְזוּ אֶת־בֹּזְזֵיהֶם נְאֻם אֲדֹנָי יֱהֹוִה׃ וְהָיָה בַיּוֹם הַהוּא אֶתֵּן לְגוֹג ׀ מְקוֹם־שָׁם קֶבֶר בְּיִשְׂרָאֵל גֵּי הָעֹבְרִים קִדְמַת הַיָּם וְחֹסֶמֶת הִיא אֶת־הָעֹבְרִים וְקָבְרוּ שָׁם אֶת־גּוֹג וְאֶת־כָּל־הֲמוֹנֹה וְקָרְאוּ גֵּיא הֲמוֹן גּוֹג׃ וּקְבָרוּם בֵּית יִשְׂרָאֵל לְמַעַן טַהֵר אֶת־הָאָרֶץ שִׁבְעָה חֳדָשִׁים׃ וְקָבְרוּ כָּל־עַם הָאָרֶץ וְהָיָה לָהֶם לְשֵׁם יוֹם הִכָּבְדִי נְאֻם אֲדֹנָי יֱהֹוִה׃ וְאַנְשֵׁי תָמִיד יַבְדִּילוּ עֹבְרִים בָּאָרֶץ מְקַבְּרִים אֶת־הָעֹבְרִים אֶת־הַנּוֹתָרִים עַל־פְּנֵי הָאָרֶץ לְטַהֲרָהּ מִקְצֵה שִׁבְעָה־חֳדָשִׁים יַחְקֹרוּ׃ וְעָבְרוּ הָעֹבְרִים בָּאָרֶץ וְרָאָה עֶצֶם אָדָם וּבָנָה אֶצְלוֹ צִיּוּן עַד קָבְרוּ אֹתוֹ הַמְקַבְּרִים אֶל־גֵּיא הֲמוֹן גּוֹג׃ וְגַם שֶׁם־עִיר הֲמוֹנָה וְטִהֲרוּ הָאָרֶץ׃

מפטיר לשמיני עצרת
MAFTIR FOR SHEMINI ATZERET

במדבר כט:לה-ל:א

The קריאת התורה *for* שמיני עצרת *is the same as that of the eighth day of* פסח*, page 1152. The following* מפטיר *is then read:*

בַּיּוֹם הַשְּׁמִינִי עֲצֶרֶת תִּהְיֶה לָכֶם כָּל־מְלֶאכֶת עֲבֹדָה לֹא תַעֲשׂוּ׃ וְהִקְרַבְתֶּם עֹלָה אִשֵּׁה רֵיחַ נִיחֹחַ לַיהוה פַּר אֶחָד אַיִל אֶחָד כְּבָשִׂים בְּנֵי־שָׁנָה שִׁבְעָה תְּמִימִם׃ מִנְחָתָם וְנִסְכֵּיהֶם לַפָּר לָאַיִל וְלַכְּבָשִׂים בְּמִסְפָּרָם כַּמִּשְׁפָּט׃ וּשְׂעִיר חַטָּאת אֶחָד מִלְּבַד עֹלַת הַתָּמִיד וּמִנְחָתָהּ וְנִסְכָּהּ׃ אֵלֶּה תַּעֲשׂוּ לַיהוה בְּמוֹעֲדֵיכֶם לְבַד מִנִּדְרֵיכֶם וְנִדְבֹתֵיכֶם לְעֹלֹתֵיכֶם וּלְמִנְחֹתֵיכֶם וּלְנִסְכֵּיכֶם וּלְשַׁלְמֵיכֶם׃ וַיֹּאמֶר מֹשֶׁה אֶל־בְּנֵי יִשְׂרָאֵל כְּכֹל אֲשֶׁר־צִוָּה יהוה אֶת־מֹשֶׁה׃

הפטרה לשמיני עצרת
HAFTARA FOR SHEMINI ATZERET

מלכים א׳ ח:נד-ט:א

וַיְהִי ׀ כְּכַלּוֹת שְׁלֹמֹה לְהִתְפַּלֵּל אֶל־יהוה אֵת כָּל־הַתְּפִלָּה וְהַתְּחִנָּה הַזֹּאת קָם מִלִּפְנֵי מִזְבַּח יהוה מִכְּרֹעַ עַל־בִּרְכָּיו וְכַפָּיו פְּרֻשׂוֹת הַשָּׁמָיִם׃ וַיַּעֲמֹד וַיְבָרֶךְ אֵת כָּל־קְהַל יִשְׂרָאֵל קוֹל גָּדוֹל לֵאמֹר׃ בָּרוּךְ יהוה אֲשֶׁר נָתַן מְנוּחָה לְעַמּוֹ יִשְׂרָאֵל כְּכֹל אֲשֶׁר דִּבֵּר לֹא־נָפַל דָּבָר אֶחָד מִכֹּל דְּבָרוֹ הַטּוֹב אֲשֶׁר דִּבֶּר בְּיַד מֹשֶׁה עַבְדּוֹ׃ יְהִי יהוה אֱלֹהֵינוּ עִמָּנוּ כַּאֲשֶׁר הָיָה עִם־אֲבֹתֵינוּ אַל־יַעַזְבֵנוּ וְאַל־יִטְּשֵׁנוּ׃ לְהַטּוֹת לְבָבֵנוּ אֵלָיו לָלֶכֶת בְּכָל־דְּרָכָיו וְלִשְׁמֹר מִצְוֺתָיו וְחֻקָּיו וּמִשְׁפָּטָיו אֲשֶׁר צִוָּה אֶת־אֲבֹתֵינוּ׃ וְיִהְיוּ דְבָרַי אֵלֶּה אֲשֶׁר הִתְחַנַּנְתִּי לִפְנֵי יהוה קְרֹבִים אֶל־יהוה אֱלֹהֵינוּ יוֹמָם וָלָיְלָה לַעֲשׂוֹת ׀ מִשְׁפַּט עַבְדּוֹ וּמִשְׁפַּט עַמּוֹ יִשְׂרָאֵל דְּבַר־יוֹם בְּיוֹמוֹ׃ לְמַעַן דַּעַת כָּל־עַמֵּי הָאָרֶץ כִּי יהוה הוּא הָאֱלֹהִים אֵין עוֹד׃ וְהָיָה לְבַבְכֶם שָׁלֵם עִם יהוה אֱלֹהֵינוּ לָלֶכֶת בְּחֻקָּיו וְלִשְׁמֹר מִצְוֺתָיו כַּיּוֹם הַזֶּה׃ וְהַמֶּלֶךְ וְכָל־יִשְׂרָאֵל עִמּוֹ זֹבְחִים זֶבַח לִפְנֵי יהוה׃ וַיִּזְבַּח שְׁלֹמֹה אֵת זֶבַח הַשְּׁלָמִים אֲשֶׁר זָבַח לַיהוה בָּקָר עֶשְׂרִים וּשְׁנַיִם אֶלֶף וְצֹאן מֵאָה וְעֶשְׂרִים אָלֶף וַיַּחְנְכוּ אֶת־בֵּית יהוה הַמֶּלֶךְ וְכָל־בְּנֵי יִשְׂרָאֵל׃ בַּיּוֹם הַהוּא קִדַּשׁ הַמֶּלֶךְ אֶת־תּוֹךְ הֶחָצֵר אֲשֶׁר לִפְנֵי בֵית־יהוה כִּי־עָשָׂה שָׁם אֶת־הָעֹלָה וְאֶת־הַמִּנְחָה וְאֵת חֶלְבֵי הַשְּׁלָמִים כִּי־מִזְבַּח הַנְּחֹשֶׁת אֲשֶׁר לִפְנֵי יהוה קָטֹן מֵהָכִיל אֶת־הָעֹלָה וְאֶת־הַמִּנְחָה וְאֵת חֶלְבֵי הַשְּׁלָמִים׃ וַיַּעַשׂ שְׁלֹמֹה בָעֵת־הַהִיא ׀ אֶת־הֶחָג וְכָל־יִשְׂרָאֵל עִמּוֹ קָהָל גָּדוֹל מִלְּבוֹא חֲמָת ׀ עַד־נַחַל מִצְרַיִם לִפְנֵי יהוה אֱלֹהֵינוּ שִׁבְעַת יָמִים וְשִׁבְעַת יָמִים אַרְבָּעָה עָשָׂר יוֹם׃ בַּיּוֹם הַשְּׁמִינִי שִׁלַּח אֶת־הָעָם וַיְבָרְכוּ אֶת־הַמֶּלֶךְ וַיֵּלְכוּ לְאָהֳלֵיהֶם שְׂמֵחִים וְטוֹבֵי לֵב עַל כָּל־הַטּוֹבָה אֲשֶׁר עָשָׂה יהוה לְדָוִד עַבְדּוֹ וּלְיִשְׂרָאֵל עַמּוֹ׃ וַיְהִי כְּכַלּוֹת שְׁלֹמֹה לִבְנוֹת אֶת־בֵּית־יהוה וְאֶת־בֵּית הַמֶּלֶךְ וְאֵת כָּל־חֵשֶׁק שְׁלֹמֹה אֲשֶׁר חָפֵץ לַעֲשׂוֹת׃

קריאה לשמחת תורה
SIMHAT TORAH

דברים לג:א–כו

וְזֹאת הַבְּרָכָה אֲשֶׁר בֵּרַךְ מֹשֶׁה אִישׁ הָאֱלֹהִים אֶת־בְּנֵי יִשְׂרָאֵל לִפְנֵי מוֹתוֹ: וַיֹּאמַר יהוה מִסִּינַי בָּא וְזָרַח מִשֵּׂעִיר לָמוֹ הוֹפִיעַ מֵהַר פָּארָן וְאָתָה מֵרִבְבֹת קֹדֶשׁ מִימִינוֹ אשדת [אֵשׁ דָּת] לָמוֹ: אַף חֹבֵב עַמִּים כָּל־קְדֹשָׁיו בְּיָדֶךָ וְהֵם תֻּכּוּ לְרַגְלֶךָ יִשָּׂא מִדַּבְּרֹתֶיךָ: תּוֹרָה צִוָּה־לָנוּ מֹשֶׁה מוֹרָשָׁה קְהִלַּת יַעֲקֹב: וַיְהִי בִישֻׁרוּן מֶלֶךְ בְּהִתְאַסֵּף רָאשֵׁי עָם יַחַד שִׁבְטֵי יִשְׂרָאֵל: יְחִי רְאוּבֵן וְאַל־יָמֹת וִיהִי מְתָיו מִסְפָּר: וְזֹאת לִיהוּדָה וַיֹּאמַר שְׁמַע יהוה קוֹל יְהוּדָה וְאֶל־עַמּוֹ תְּבִיאֶנּוּ יָדָיו רָב לוֹ וְעֵזֶר מִצָּרָיו תִּהְיֶה:

לוי: וּלְלֵוִי אָמַר תֻּמֶּיךָ וְאוּרֶיךָ לְאִישׁ חֲסִידֶךָ אֲשֶׁר נִסִּיתוֹ בְּמַסָּה תְּרִיבֵהוּ עַל־מֵי מְרִיבָה: הָאֹמֵר לְאָבִיו וּלְאִמּוֹ לֹא רְאִיתִיו וְאֶת־אֶחָיו לֹא הִכִּיר וְאֶת־בָּנָו לֹא יָדָע כִּי שָׁמְרוּ אִמְרָתֶךָ וּבְרִיתְךָ יִנְצֹרוּ: יוֹרוּ מִשְׁפָּטֶיךָ לְיַעֲקֹב וְתוֹרָתְךָ לְיִשְׂרָאֵל יָשִׂימוּ קְטוֹרָה בְּאַפֶּךָ וְכָלִיל עַל־מִזְבְּחֶךָ: בָּרֵךְ יהוה חֵילוֹ וּפֹעַל יָדָיו תִּרְצֶה מְחַץ מָתְנַיִם קָמָיו וּמְשַׂנְאָיו מִן־יְקוּמוּן: לְבִנְיָמִן אָמַר יְדִיד יהוה יִשְׁכֹּן לָבֶטַח עָלָיו חֹפֵף עָלָיו כָּל־הַיּוֹם וּבֵין כְּתֵפָיו שָׁכֵן:

שלישי: וּלְיוֹסֵף אָמַר מְבֹרֶכֶת יהוה אַרְצוֹ מִמֶּגֶד שָׁמַיִם מִטָּל וּמִתְּהוֹם רֹבֶצֶת תָּחַת: וּמִמֶּגֶד תְּבוּאֹת שָׁמֶשׁ וּמִמֶּגֶד גֶּרֶשׁ יְרָחִים: וּמֵרֹאשׁ הַרְרֵי־קֶדֶם וּמִמֶּגֶד גִּבְעוֹת עוֹלָם: וּמִמֶּגֶד אֶרֶץ וּמְלֹאָהּ וּרְצוֹן שֹׁכְנִי סְנֶה תָּבוֹאתָה לְרֹאשׁ יוֹסֵף וּלְקָדְקֹד נְזִיר אֶחָיו: בְּכוֹר שׁוֹרוֹ הָדָר לוֹ וְקַרְנֵי רְאֵם קַרְנָיו בָּהֶם עַמִּים יְנַגַּח יַחְדָּו אַפְסֵי־אָרֶץ וְהֵם רִבְבוֹת אֶפְרַיִם וְהֵם אַלְפֵי מְנַשֶּׁה:

רביעי: וְלִזְבוּלֻן אָמַר שְׂמַח זְבוּלֻן בְּצֵאתֶךָ וְיִשָּׂשכָר בְּאֹהָלֶיךָ: עַמִּים הַר־יִקְרָאוּ שָׁם יִזְבְּחוּ זִבְחֵי־צֶדֶק כִּי שֶׁפַע יַמִּים יִינָקוּ וּשְׂפֻנֵי טְמוּנֵי חוֹל: וּלְגָד אָמַר בָּרוּךְ מַרְחִיב גָּד כְּלָבִיא שָׁכֵן וְטָרַף זְרוֹעַ אַף־קָדְקֹד: וַיַּרְא רֵאשִׁית לוֹ כִּי־שָׁם חֶלְקַת מְחֹקֵק סָפוּן וַיֵּתֵא רָאשֵׁי עָם צִדְקַת יהוה עָשָׂה וּמִשְׁפָּטָיו עִם־יִשְׂרָאֵל:

חמישי: וּלְדָן אָמַר דָּן גּוּר אַרְיֵה יְזַנֵּק מִן־הַבָּשָׁן: וּלְנַפְתָּלִי אָמַר נַפְתָּלִי שְׂבַע רָצוֹן וּמָלֵא בִּרְכַּת יהוה יָם וְדָרוֹם יְרָשָׁה: וּלְאָשֵׁר אָמַר בָּרוּךְ מִבָּנִים אָשֵׁר יְהִי רְצוּי אֶחָיו וְטֹבֵל בַּשֶּׁמֶן רַגְלוֹ: בַּרְזֶל וּנְחֹשֶׁת מִנְעָלֶךָ וּכְיָמֶיךָ דָּבְאֶךָ: אֵין כָּאֵל יְשֻׁרוּן רֹכֵב שָׁמַיִם בְּעֶזְרֶךָ וּבְגַאֲוָתוֹ שְׁחָקִים:

קריאה לחתן תורה
READING FOR THE HATAN TORAH

דברים לג:כז–לד:יב

מְעֹנָה אֱלֹהֵי קֶדֶם וּמִתַּחַת זְרֹעֹת עוֹלָם וַיְגָרֶשׁ מִפָּנֶיךָ אוֹיֵב וַיֹּאמֶר הַשְׁמֵד: וַיִּשְׁכֹּן יִשְׂרָאֵל בֶּטַח בָּדָד עֵין יַעֲקֹב אֶל־אֶרֶץ דָּגָן וְתִירוֹשׁ אַף־שָׁמָיו יַעַרְפוּ־טָל: אַשְׁרֶיךָ יִשְׂרָאֵל מִי כָמוֹךָ עַם נוֹשַׁע בַּיהוה מָגֵן עֶזְרֶךָ וַאֲשֶׁר־חֶרֶב גַּאֲוָתֶךָ וְיִכָּחֲשׁוּ אֹיְבֶיךָ לָךְ וְאַתָּה עַל־בָּמוֹתֵימוֹ תִדְרֹךְ: וַיַּעַל מֹשֶׁה מֵעַרְבֹת מוֹאָב אֶל־הַר נְבוֹ רֹאשׁ הַפִּסְגָּה אֲשֶׁר עַל־פְּנֵי יְרֵחוֹ וַיַּרְאֵהוּ יהוה אֶת־כָּל־הָאָרֶץ אֶת־הַגִּלְעָד עַד־דָּן: וְאֵת כָּל־נַפְתָּלִי וְאֶת־אֶרֶץ אֶפְרַיִם וּמְנַשֶּׁה וְאֵת כָּל־אֶרֶץ יְהוּדָה עַד הַיָּם הָאַחֲרוֹן: וְאֶת־הַנֶּגֶב וְאֶת־הַכִּכָּר בִּקְעַת יְרֵחוֹ עִיר הַתְּמָרִים עַד־צֹעַר: וַיֹּאמֶר יהוה אֵלָיו זֹאת הָאָרֶץ אֲשֶׁר נִשְׁבַּעְתִּי לְאַבְרָהָם לְיִצְחָק וּלְיַעֲקֹב לֵאמֹר לְזַרְעֲךָ אֶתְּנֶנָּה הֶרְאִיתִיךָ בְעֵינֶיךָ וְשָׁמָּה לֹא תַעֲבֹר: וַיָּמָת שָׁם מֹשֶׁה עֶבֶד־יהוה בְּאֶרֶץ מוֹאָב עַל־פִּי יהוה: וַיִּקְבֹּר אֹתוֹ בַגַּי בְּאֶרֶץ מוֹאָב מוּל בֵּית פְּעוֹר וְלֹא־יָדַע אִישׁ אֶת־קְבֻרָתוֹ עַד הַיּוֹם הַזֶּה: וּמֹשֶׁה בֶּן־מֵאָה וְעֶשְׂרִים שָׁנָה בְּמֹתוֹ לֹא־כָהֲתָה עֵינוֹ וְלֹא־נָס לֵחֹה: וַיִּבְכּוּ בְנֵי יִשְׂרָאֵל אֶת־מֹשֶׁה בְּעַרְבֹת מוֹאָב שְׁלֹשִׁים

יוֹם וַיִּתְּמוּ יְמֵי בְכִי אֵבֶל מֹשֶׁה: וִיהוֹשֻׁעַ בִּן־נוּן מָלֵא רוּחַ חָכְמָה כִּי־סָמַךְ מֹשֶׁה אֶת־יָדָיו עָלָיו וַיִּשְׁמְעוּ אֵלָיו בְּנֵי־יִשְׂרָאֵל וַיַּעֲשׂוּ כַּאֲשֶׁר צִוָּה יהוה אֶת־מֹשֶׁה: וְלֹא־קָם נָבִיא עוֹד בְּיִשְׂרָאֵל כְּמֹשֶׁה אֲשֶׁר יְדָעוֹ יהוה פָּנִים אֶל־פָּנִים: לְכָל־הָאֹתֹת וְהַמּוֹפְתִים אֲשֶׁר שְׁלָחוֹ יהוה לַעֲשׂוֹת בְּאֶרֶץ מִצְרָיִם לְפַרְעֹה וּלְכָל־עֲבָדָיו וּלְכָל־אַרְצוֹ: וּלְכֹל הַיָּד הַחֲזָקָה וּלְכֹל הַמּוֹרָא הַגָּדוֹל אֲשֶׁר עָשָׂה מֹשֶׁה לְעֵינֵי כָּל־יִשְׂרָאֵל:

The קהל *followed by*
the קורא *proclaims:*

חֲזַק חֲזַק וְנִתְחַזֵּק

קריאה לחתן בראשית

READING FOR THE ḤATAN BERESHIT

בראשית א:א–ב:ג

Various passages in this chapter are read by the קהל*, then repeated by the* קורא*. These passages are marked by arrows.*

בְּרֵאשִׁית בָּרָא אֱלֹהִים אֵת הַשָּׁמַיִם וְאֵת הָאָרֶץ: וְהָאָרֶץ הָיְתָה תֹהוּ וָבֹהוּ וְחֹשֶׁךְ עַל־פְּנֵי תְהוֹם וְרוּחַ אֱלֹהִים מְרַחֶפֶת עַל־פְּנֵי הַמָּיִם: וַיֹּאמֶר אֱלֹהִים יְהִי־אוֹר וַיְהִי־אוֹר: וַיַּרְא אֱלֹהִים אֶת־הָאוֹר כִּי־טוֹב וַיַּבְדֵּל אֱלֹהִים בֵּין הָאוֹר וּבֵין הַחֹשֶׁךְ: וַיִּקְרָא אֱלֹהִים | לָאוֹר יוֹם וְלַחֹשֶׁךְ קָרָא לָיְלָה ◂ וַיְהִי־עֶרֶב וַיְהִי־בֹקֶר יוֹם אֶחָד: ◂

וַיֹּאמֶר אֱלֹהִים יְהִי רָקִיעַ בְּתוֹךְ הַמָּיִם וִיהִי מַבְדִּיל בֵּין מַיִם לָמָיִם: וַיַּעַשׂ אֱלֹהִים אֶת־הָרָקִיעַ וַיַּבְדֵּל בֵּין הַמַּיִם אֲשֶׁר מִתַּחַת לָרָקִיעַ וּבֵין הַמַּיִם אֲשֶׁר מֵעַל לָרָקִיעַ וַיְהִי־כֵן: וַיִּקְרָא אֱלֹהִים לָרָקִיעַ שָׁמָיִם ◂ וַיְהִי־עֶרֶב וַיְהִי־בֹקֶר יוֹם שֵׁנִי: ◂

וַיֹּאמֶר אֱלֹהִים יִקָּווּ הַמַּיִם מִתַּחַת הַשָּׁמַיִם אֶל־מָקוֹם אֶחָד וְתֵרָאֶה הַיַּבָּשָׁה וַיְהִי־כֵן: וַיִּקְרָא אֱלֹהִים | לַיַּבָּשָׁה אֶרֶץ וּלְמִקְוֵה הַמַּיִם קָרָא יַמִּים וַיַּרְא אֱלֹהִים כִּי־טוֹב: וַיֹּאמֶר אֱלֹהִים תַּדְשֵׁא הָאָרֶץ דֶּשֶׁא עֵשֶׂב מַזְרִיעַ זֶרַע עֵץ פְּרִי עֹשֶׂה פְּרִי לְמִינוֹ אֲשֶׁר זַרְעוֹ־בוֹ עַל־הָאָרֶץ וַיְהִי־כֵן: וַתּוֹצֵא הָאָרֶץ דֶּשֶׁא עֵשֶׂב מַזְרִיעַ זֶרַע לְמִינֵהוּ וְעֵץ עֹשֶׂה־פְּרִי אֲשֶׁר זַרְעוֹ־בוֹ לְמִינֵהוּ וַיַּרְא אֱלֹהִים כִּי־טוֹב: ◂ וַיְהִי־עֶרֶב וַיְהִי־בֹקֶר יוֹם שְׁלִישִׁי: ◂

וַיֹּאמֶר אֱלֹהִים יְהִי מְאֹרֹת בִּרְקִיעַ הַשָּׁמַיִם לְהַבְדִּיל בֵּין הַיּוֹם וּבֵין הַלָּיְלָה וְהָיוּ לְאֹתֹת וּלְמוֹעֲדִים וּלְיָמִים וְשָׁנִים: וְהָיוּ לִמְאוֹרֹת בִּרְקִיעַ הַשָּׁמַיִם לְהָאִיר עַל־הָאָרֶץ וַיְהִי־כֵן: וַיַּעַשׂ אֱלֹהִים אֶת־שְׁנֵי הַמְּאֹרֹת הַגְּדֹלִים אֶת־הַמָּאוֹר הַגָּדֹל לְמֶמְשֶׁלֶת הַיּוֹם וְאֶת־הַמָּאוֹר הַקָּטֹן לְמֶמְשֶׁלֶת הַלַּיְלָה וְאֵת הַכּוֹכָבִים: וַיִּתֵּן אֹתָם אֱלֹהִים בִּרְקִיעַ הַשָּׁמָיִם לְהָאִיר עַל־הָאָרֶץ: וְלִמְשֹׁל בַּיּוֹם וּבַלַּיְלָה וּלְהַבְדִּיל בֵּין הָאוֹר וּבֵין הַחֹשֶׁךְ וַיַּרְא אֱלֹהִים כִּי־טוֹב: ◂ וַיְהִי־עֶרֶב וַיְהִי־בֹקֶר יוֹם רְבִיעִי: ◂

וַיֹּאמֶר אֱלֹהִים יִשְׁרְצוּ הַמַּיִם שֶׁרֶץ נֶפֶשׁ חַיָּה וְעוֹף יְעוֹפֵף עַל־הָאָרֶץ עַל־פְּנֵי רְקִיעַ הַשָּׁמָיִם: וַיִּבְרָא אֱלֹהִים אֶת־הַתַּנִּינִם הַגְּדֹלִים וְאֵת כָּל־נֶפֶשׁ הַחַיָּה | הָרֹמֶשֶׂת אֲשֶׁר שָׁרְצוּ הַמַּיִם לְמִינֵהֶם וְאֵת כָּל־עוֹף כָּנָף לְמִינֵהוּ וַיַּרְא אֱלֹהִים כִּי־טוֹב: וַיְבָרֶךְ אֹתָם אֱלֹהִים לֵאמֹר פְּרוּ וּרְבוּ וּמִלְאוּ אֶת־הַמַּיִם בַּיַּמִּים וְהָעוֹף יִרֶב בָּאָרֶץ: ◂ וַיְהִי־עֶרֶב וַיְהִי־בֹקֶר יוֹם חֲמִישִׁי: ◂

וַיֹּאמֶר אֱלֹהִים תּוֹצֵא הָאָרֶץ נֶפֶשׁ חַיָּה לְמִינָהּ בְּהֵמָה וָרֶמֶשׂ וְחַיְתוֹ־אֶרֶץ לְמִינָהּ וַיְהִי־כֵן: וַיַּעַשׂ אֱלֹהִים אֶת־חַיַּת הָאָרֶץ לְמִינָהּ וְאֶת־הַבְּהֵמָה לְמִינָהּ וְאֵת כָּל־רֶמֶשׂ הָאֲדָמָה לְמִינֵהוּ וַיַּרְא אֱלֹהִים כִּי־טוֹב: וַיֹּאמֶר אֱלֹהִים נַעֲשֶׂה אָדָם בְּצַלְמֵנוּ כִּדְמוּתֵנוּ וְיִרְדּוּ בִדְגַת הַיָּם וּבְעוֹף הַשָּׁמַיִם וּבַבְּהֵמָה וּבְכָל־הָאָרֶץ וּבְכָל־הָרֶמֶשׂ הָרֹמֵשׂ

עַל־הָאָרֶץ׃ וַיִּבְרָא אֱלֹהִים ׀ אֶת־הָאָדָם בְּצַלְמוֹ בְּצֶלֶם אֱלֹהִים בָּרָא אֹתוֹ זָכָר וּנְקֵבָה בָּרָא אֹתָם׃ וַיְבָרֶךְ אֹתָם אֱלֹהִים וַיֹּאמֶר לָהֶם אֱלֹהִים פְּרוּ וּרְבוּ וּמִלְאוּ אֶת־הָאָרֶץ וְכִבְשֻׁהָ וּרְדוּ בִּדְגַת הַיָּם וּבְעוֹף הַשָּׁמַיִם וּבְכָל־חַיָּה הָרֹמֶשֶׂת עַל־הָאָרֶץ׃ וַיֹּאמֶר אֱלֹהִים הִנֵּה נָתַתִּי לָכֶם אֶת־כָּל־עֵשֶׂב ׀ זֹרֵעַ זֶרַע אֲשֶׁר עַל־פְּנֵי כָל־הָאָרֶץ וְאֶת־כָּל־הָעֵץ אֲשֶׁר־בּוֹ פְרִי־עֵץ זֹרֵעַ זָרַע לָכֶם יִהְיֶה לְאָכְלָה׃ וּלְכָל־חַיַּת הָאָרֶץ וּלְכָל־עוֹף הַשָּׁמַיִם וּלְכֹל ׀ רוֹמֵשׂ עַל־הָאָרֶץ אֲשֶׁר־בּוֹ נֶפֶשׁ חַיָּה אֶת־כָּל־יֶרֶק עֵשֶׂב לְאָכְלָה וַיְהִי־כֵן׃ וַיַּרְא אֱלֹהִים אֶת־כָּל־אֲשֶׁר עָשָׂה וְהִנֵּה־טוֹב מְאֹד • וַיְהִי־עֶרֶב וַיְהִי־בֹקֶר יוֹם הַשִּׁשִּׁי׃ •

• וַיְכֻלּוּ הַשָּׁמַיִם וְהָאָרֶץ וְכָל־צְבָאָם׃ וַיְכַל אֱלֹהִים בַּיּוֹם הַשְּׁבִיעִי מְלַאכְתּוֹ אֲשֶׁר עָשָׂה וַיִּשְׁבֹּת בַּיּוֹם הַשְּׁבִיעִי מִכָּל־מְלַאכְתּוֹ אֲשֶׁר עָשָׂה׃ וַיְבָרֶךְ אֱלֹהִים אֶת־יוֹם הַשְּׁבִיעִי וַיְקַדֵּשׁ אֹתוֹ כִּי בוֹ שָׁבַת מִכָּל־מְלַאכְתּוֹ אֲשֶׁר־בָּרָא אֱלֹהִים לַעֲשׂוֹת׃ •

The מפטיר *for* שמחת תורה *is the same as that of* שמיני עצרת *on page 1164.*

הפטרה לשמחת תורה

HAFTARA FOR SIMḤAT TORAH

יהושע א:א-יח

וַיְהִי אַחֲרֵי מוֹת מֹשֶׁה עֶבֶד יהוה וַיֹּאמֶר יהוה אֶל־יְהוֹשֻׁעַ בִּן־נוּן מְשָׁרֵת מֹשֶׁה לֵאמֹר׃ מֹשֶׁה עַבְדִּי מֵת וְעַתָּה קוּם עֲבֹר אֶת־הַיַּרְדֵּן הַזֶּה אַתָּה וְכָל־הָעָם הַזֶּה אֶל־הָאָרֶץ אֲשֶׁר אָנֹכִי נֹתֵן לָהֶם לִבְנֵי יִשְׂרָאֵל׃ כָּל־מָקוֹם אֲשֶׁר תִּדְרֹךְ כַּף־רַגְלְכֶם בּוֹ לָכֶם נְתַתִּיו כַּאֲשֶׁר דִּבַּרְתִּי אֶל־מֹשֶׁה׃ מֵהַמִּדְבָּר וְהַלְּבָנוֹן הַזֶּה וְעַד־הַנָּהָר הַגָּדוֹל נְהַר־פְּרָת כֹּל אֶרֶץ הַחִתִּים וְעַד־הַיָּם הַגָּדוֹל מְבוֹא הַשָּׁמֶשׁ יִהְיֶה גְּבוּלְכֶם׃ לֹא־יִתְיַצֵּב אִישׁ לְפָנֶיךָ כֹּל יְמֵי חַיֶּיךָ כַּאֲשֶׁר הָיִיתִי עִם־מֹשֶׁה אֶהְיֶה עִמָּךְ לֹא אַרְפְּךָ וְלֹא אֶעֶזְבֶךָּ׃ חֲזַק וֶאֱמָץ כִּי אַתָּה תַּנְחִיל אֶת־הָעָם הַזֶּה אֶת־הָאָרֶץ אֲשֶׁר־נִשְׁבַּעְתִּי לַאֲבוֹתָם לָתֵת לָהֶם׃ רַק חֲזַק וֶאֱמַץ מְאֹד לִשְׁמֹר לַעֲשׂוֹת כְּכָל־הַתּוֹרָה אֲשֶׁר צִוְּךָ מֹשֶׁה עַבְדִּי אַל־תָּסוּר מִמֶּנּוּ יָמִין וּשְׂמֹאול לְמַעַן תַּשְׂכִּיל בְּכֹל אֲשֶׁר תֵּלֵךְ׃ לֹא־יָמוּשׁ סֵפֶר הַתּוֹרָה הַזֶּה מִפִּיךָ וְהָגִיתָ בּוֹ יוֹמָם וָלַיְלָה לְמַעַן תִּשְׁמֹר לַעֲשׂוֹת כְּכָל־הַכָּתוּב בּוֹ כִּי־אָז תַּצְלִיחַ אֶת־דְּרָכֶךָ וְאָז תַּשְׂכִּיל׃ הֲלוֹא צִוִּיתִיךָ חֲזַק וֶאֱמָץ אַל־תַּעֲרֹץ וְאַל־תֵּחָת כִּי עִמְּךָ יהוה אֱלֹהֶיךָ בְּכֹל אֲשֶׁר תֵּלֵךְ׃ וַיְצַו יְהוֹשֻׁעַ אֶת־שֹׁטְרֵי הָעָם לֵאמֹר׃ עִבְרוּ ׀ בְּקֶרֶב הַמַּחֲנֶה וְצַוּוּ אֶת־הָעָם לֵאמֹר הָכִינוּ לָכֶם צֵידָה כִּי בְּעוֹד ׀ שְׁלֹשֶׁת יָמִים אַתֶּם עֹבְרִים אֶת־הַיַּרְדֵּן הַזֶּה לָבוֹא לָרֶשֶׁת אֶת־הָאָרֶץ אֲשֶׁר יהוה אֱלֹהֵיכֶם נֹתֵן לָכֶם לְרִשְׁתָּהּ׃ וְלָרְאוּבֵנִי וְלַגָּדִי וְלַחֲצִי שֵׁבֶט הַמְנַשֶּׁה אָמַר יְהוֹשֻׁעַ לֵאמֹר׃ זָכוֹר אֶת־הַדָּבָר אֲשֶׁר צִוָּה אֶתְכֶם מֹשֶׁה עֶבֶד־יהוה לֵאמֹר יהוה אֱלֹהֵיכֶם מֵנִיחַ לָכֶם וְנָתַן לָכֶם אֶת־הָאָרֶץ הַזֹּאת׃ נְשֵׁיכֶם טַפְּכֶם וּמִקְנֵיכֶם יֵשְׁבוּ בָּאָרֶץ אֲשֶׁר נָתַן לָכֶם מֹשֶׁה בְּעֵבֶר הַיַּרְדֵּן וְאַתֶּם תַּעַבְרוּ חֲמֻשִׁים לִפְנֵי אֲחֵיכֶם כֹּל גִּבּוֹרֵי הַחַיִל וַעֲזַרְתֶּם אוֹתָם׃ עַד אֲשֶׁר־יָנִיחַ יהוה ׀ לַאֲחֵיכֶם כָּכֶם וְיָרְשׁוּ גַם־הֵמָּה אֶת־הָאָרֶץ אֲשֶׁר־יהוה אֱלֹהֵיכֶם נֹתֵן לָהֶם וְשַׁבְתֶּם לְאֶרֶץ יְרֻשַּׁתְכֶם וִירִשְׁתֶּם אוֹתָהּ אֲשֶׁר ׀ נָתַן לָכֶם מֹשֶׁה עֶבֶד יהוה בְּעֵבֶר הַיַּרְדֵּן מִזְרַח הַשָּׁמֶשׁ׃ וַיַּעֲנוּ אֶת־יְהוֹשֻׁעַ לֵאמֹר כֹּל אֲשֶׁר־צִוִּיתָנוּ נַעֲשֶׂה וְאֶל־כָּל־אֲשֶׁר תִּשְׁלָחֵנוּ נֵלֵךְ׃ כְּכֹל אֲשֶׁר־שָׁמַעְנוּ אֶל־מֹשֶׁה כֵּן נִשְׁמַע אֵלֶיךָ רַק יִהְיֶה יהוה אֱלֹהֶיךָ עִמָּךְ כַּאֲשֶׁר הָיָה עִם־מֹשֶׁה׃ כָּל־אִישׁ אֲשֶׁר־יַמְרֶה אֶת־פִּיךָ וְלֹא־יִשְׁמַע אֶת־דְּבָרֶיךָ לְכֹל אֲשֶׁר־תְּצַוֶּנּוּ יוּמָת רַק חֲזַק וֶאֱמָץ׃

חמש מגילות

THE FIVE MEGILLOT

שיר השירים / THE SONG OF SONGS

שיר השירים is read before קריאת התורה *on the* שבת *of* חול המועד פסח*. In the event there is no* שבת *during* חול המועד*, it is read on either the seventh or eighth day of* פסח*, whichever fall on* שבת*.*

In some congregations individuals recite שיר השירים *on Friday afternoon before* מנחה*.*

א שיר השירים אשר לשלמה: ישקני
מנשיקות פיהו כי־טובים דדיך מיין: לריח
שמניך טובים שמן תורק שמך על־כן
עלמות אהבוך: משכני אחריך נרוצה
הביאני המלך חדריו נגילה ונשמחה בך
נזכירה דדיך מיין מישרים אהבוך: שחורה
אני ונאוה בנות ירושלם כאהלי קדר
כיריעות שלמה: אל־תראוני שאני שחרחרת
ששזפתני השמש בני אמי נחרו־בי שמני
נטרה את־הכרמים כרמי שלי לא נטרתי:
הגידה לי שאהבה נפשי איכה תרעה איכה
תרביץ בצהרים שלמה אהיה כעטיה על
עדרי חבריך: אם־לא תדעי לך היפה
בנשים צאי־לך בעקבי הצאן ורעי את־
גדיתיך על משכנות הרעים: לססתי ברכבי
פרעה דמיתיך רעיתי: נאוו לחייך בתרים
צוארך בחרוזים: תורי זהב נעשה־לך עם
נקדות הכסף: עד־שהמלך במסבו נרדי
נתן ריחו: צרור המר | דודי לי בין שדי ילין:
אשכל הכפר | דודי לי בכרמי עין גדי: הנך
יפה רעיתי הנך יפה עיניך יונים: הנך יפה
דודי אף נעים אף־ערשנו רעננה: קרות
בתינו ארזים רחיטנו [רהיטנו] ברותים:
ב אני חבצלת השרון שושנת העמקים:
כשושנה בין החוחים כן רעיתי בין הבנות:
כתפוח בעצי היער כן דודי בין הבנים
בצלו חמדתי וישבתי ופריו מתוק לחכי:
הביאני אל־בית היין ודגלו עלי אהבה:
סמכוני באשישות רפדוני בתפוחים כי־
חולת אהבה אני: שמאלו תחת לראשי
וימינו תחבקני: השבעתי אתכם בנות
ירושלם בצבאות או באילות השדה אם־
תעירו | ואם־תעוררו את־האהבה עד
שתחפץ: קול דודי הנה־זה בא מדלג על־
ההרים מקפץ על־הגבעות: דומה דודי
לצבי או לעפר האילים הנה־זה עומד אחר
כתלנו משגיח מן־החלנות מציץ מן־
החרכים: ענה דודי ואמר לי קומי לך רעיתי
יפתי ולכי־לך: כי־הנה הסתו עבר הגשם
חלף הלך לו: הנצנים נראו בארץ עת הזמיר
הגיע וקול התור נשמע בארצנו: התאנה
חנטה פגיה והגפנים | סמדר נתנו ריח קומי
לכי [לך] רעיתי יפתי ולכי־לך: יונתי בחגוי
הסלע בסתר המדרגה הראיני את־מראיך
השמיעני את־קולך כי־קולך ערב ומראיך
נאוה: אחזו־לנו שועלים שעלים קטנים
מחבלים כרמים וכרמינו סמדר: דודי לי
ואני לו הרעה בשושנים: עד שיפוח היום
ונסו הצללים סב דמה־לך דודי לצבי או
ג לעפר האילים על־הרי בתר: על־משכבי
בלילות בקשתי את שאהבה נפשי בקשתיו
ולא מצאתיו: אקומה נא ואסובבה בעיר
בשוקים וברחבות אבקשה את שאהבה
נפשי בקשתיו ולא מצאתיו: מצאוני
השמרים הסבבים בעיר את שאהבה נפשי
ראיתם: כמעט שעברתי מהם עד שמצאתי
את שאהבה נפשי אחזתיו ולא ארפנו עד־
שהביאתיו אל־בית אמי ואל־חדר הורתי:
השבעתי אתכם בנות ירושלם בצבאות
או באילות השדה אם־תעירו | ואם־

תְּעוֹרְרוּ אֶת־הָאַהֲבָה עַד שֶׁתֶּחְפָּץ: מִי זֹאת
עֹלָה מִן־הַמִּדְבָּר כְּתִימְרוֹת עָשָׁן מְקֻטֶּרֶת
מֹר וּלְבוֹנָה מִכֹּל אַבְקַת רוֹכֵל: הִנֵּה מִטָּתוֹ
שֶׁלִּשְׁלֹמֹה שִׁשִּׁים גִּבֹּרִים סָבִיב לָהּ מִגִּבֹּרֵי
יִשְׂרָאֵל: כֻּלָּם אֲחֻזֵי חֶרֶב מְלֻמְּדֵי מִלְחָמָה
אִישׁ חַרְבּוֹ עַל־יְרֵכוֹ מִפַּחַד בַּלֵּילוֹת: אַפִּרְיוֹן
עָשָׂה לוֹ הַמֶּלֶךְ שְׁלֹמֹה מֵעֲצֵי הַלְּבָנוֹן: עַמּוּדָיו
עָשָׂה כֶסֶף רְפִידָתוֹ זָהָב מֶרְכָּבוֹ אַרְגָּמָן תּוֹכוֹ
רָצוּף אַהֲבָה מִבְּנוֹת יְרוּשָׁלִָם: צְאֶינָה | וּרְאֶינָה
בְּנוֹת צִיּוֹן בַּמֶּלֶךְ שְׁלֹמֹה בָּעֲטָרָה שֶׁעִטְּרָה־
לּוֹ אִמּוֹ בְּיוֹם חֲתֻנָּתוֹ וּבְיוֹם שִׂמְחַת לִבּוֹ:
ד הִנָּךְ יָפָה רַעְיָתִי הִנָּךְ יָפָה עֵינַיִךְ יוֹנִים מִבַּעַד
לְצַמָּתֵךְ שַׂעְרֵךְ כְּעֵדֶר הָעִזִּים שֶׁגָּלְשׁוּ מֵהַר
גִּלְעָד: שִׁנַּיִךְ כְּעֵדֶר הַקְּצוּבוֹת שֶׁעָלוּ מִן־
הָרַחְצָה שֶׁכֻּלָּם מַתְאִימוֹת וְשַׁכֻּלָה אֵין
בָּהֶם: כְּחוּט הַשָּׁנִי שִׂפְתֹתַיִךְ וּמִדְבָּרֵיךְ
נָאוֶה כְּפֶלַח הָרִמּוֹן רַקָּתֵךְ מִבַּעַד לְצַמָּתֵךְ:
כְּמִגְדַּל דָּוִיד צַוָּארֵךְ בָּנוּי לְתַלְפִּיּוֹת אֶלֶף
הַמָּגֵן תָּלוּי עָלָיו כֹּל שִׁלְטֵי הַגִּבֹּרִים: שְׁנֵי
שָׁדַיִךְ כִּשְׁנֵי עֳפָרִים תְּאוֹמֵי צְבִיָּה הָרוֹעִים
בַּשּׁוֹשַׁנִּים: עַד שֶׁיָּפוּחַ הַיּוֹם וְנָסוּ הַצְּלָלִים
אֵלֶךְ לִי אֶל־הַר הַמּוֹר וְאֶל־גִּבְעַת הַלְּבוֹנָה:
כֻּלָּךְ יָפָה רַעְיָתִי וּמוּם אֵין בָּךְ: אִתִּי מִלְּבָנוֹן
כַּלָּה אִתִּי מִלְּבָנוֹן תָּבוֹאִי תָּשׁוּרִי | מֵרֹאשׁ
אֲמָנָה מֵרֹאשׁ שְׂנִיר וְחֶרְמוֹן מִמְּעֹנוֹת אֲרָיוֹת
מֵהַרְרֵי נְמֵרִים: לִבַּבְתִּנִי אֲחֹתִי כַלָּה לִבַּבְתִּנִי
באחד [בְּאַחַת] מֵעֵינַיִךְ בְּאַחַד עֲנָק מִצַּוְּרֹנָיִךְ:
מַה־יָּפוּ דֹדַיִךְ אֲחֹתִי כַלָּה מַה־טֹּבוּ דֹדַיִךְ
מִיַּיִן וְרֵיחַ שְׁמָנַיִךְ מִכָּל־בְּשָׂמִים: נֹפֶת
תִּטֹּפְנָה שִׂפְתוֹתַיִךְ כַּלָּה דְּבַשׁ וְחָלָב תַּחַת
לְשׁוֹנֵךְ וְרֵיחַ שַׂלְמֹתַיִךְ כְּרֵיחַ לְבָנוֹן: גַּן | נָעוּל
אֲחֹתִי כַלָּה גַּל נָעוּל מַעְיָן חָתוּם: שְׁלָחַיִךְ
פַּרְדֵּס רִמּוֹנִים עִם פְּרִי מְגָדִים כְּפָרִים עִם־
נְרָדִים: נֵרְדְּ | וְכַרְכֹּם קָנֶה וְקִנָּמוֹן עִם כָּל־
עֲצֵי לְבוֹנָה מֹר וַאֲהָלוֹת עִם כָּל־רָאשֵׁי
בְשָׂמִים: מַעְיַן גַּנִּים בְּאֵר מַיִם חַיִּים וְנֹזְלִים
מִן־לְבָנוֹן: עוּרִי צָפוֹן וּבוֹאִי תֵימָן הָפִיחִי גַנִּי
יִזְּלוּ בְשָׂמָיו יָבֹא דוֹדִי לְגַנּוֹ וְיֹאכַל פְּרִי מְגָדָיו:
ה בָּאתִי לְגַנִּי אֲחֹתִי כַלָּה אָרִיתִי מוֹרִי עִם־
בְּשָׂמִי אָכַלְתִּי יַעְרִי עִם־דִּבְשִׁי שָׁתִיתִי יֵינִי
עִם־חֲלָבִי אִכְלוּ רֵעִים שְׁתוּ וְשִׁכְרוּ דּוֹדִים:
אֲנִי יְשֵׁנָה וְלִבִּי עֵר קוֹל | דּוֹדִי דוֹפֵק פִּתְחִי־
לִי אֲחֹתִי רַעְיָתִי יוֹנָתִי תַמָּתִי שֶׁרֹּאשִׁי
נִמְלָא־טָל קְוֻצּוֹתַי רְסִיסֵי לָיְלָה: פָּשַׁטְתִּי
אֶת־כֻּתָּנְתִּי אֵיכָכָה אֶלְבָּשֶׁנָּה רָחַצְתִּי אֶת־
רַגְלַי אֵיכָכָה אֲטַנְּפֵם: דּוֹדִי שָׁלַח יָדוֹ מִן־
הַחוֹר וּמֵעַי הָמוּ עָלָיו: קַמְתִּי אֲנִי לִפְתֹּחַ
לְדוֹדִי וְיָדַי נָטְפוּ־מוֹר וְאֶצְבְּעֹתַי מוֹר עֹבֵר
עַל כַּפּוֹת הַמַּנְעוּל: פָּתַחְתִּי אֲנִי לְדוֹדִי וְדוֹדִי
חָמַק עָבָר נַפְשִׁי יָצְאָה בְדַבְּרוֹ בִּקַּשְׁתִּיהוּ
וְלֹא מְצָאתִיהוּ קְרָאתִיו וְלֹא עָנָנִי: מְצָאֻנִי
הַשֹּׁמְרִים הַסֹּבְבִים בָּעִיר הִכּוּנִי פְצָעוּנִי
נָשְׂאוּ אֶת־רְדִידִי מֵעָלַי שֹׁמְרֵי הַחֹמוֹת:
הִשְׁבַּעְתִּי אֶתְכֶם בְּנוֹת יְרוּשָׁלִָם אִם־תִּמְצְאוּ
אֶת־דּוֹדִי מַה־תַּגִּידוּ לוֹ שֶׁחוֹלַת אַהֲבָה אָנִי:
מַה־דּוֹדֵךְ מִדּוֹד הַיָּפָה בַּנָּשִׁים מַה־דּוֹדֵךְ
מִדּוֹד שֶׁכָּכָה הִשְׁבַּעְתָּנוּ: דּוֹדִי צַח וְאָדוֹם
דָּגוּל מֵרְבָבָה: רֹאשׁוֹ כֶּתֶם פָּז קְוֻצּוֹתָיו
תַּלְתַּלִּים שְׁחֹרוֹת כָּעוֹרֵב: עֵינָיו כְּיוֹנִים עַל־
אֲפִיקֵי מָיִם רֹחֲצוֹת בֶּחָלָב יֹשְׁבוֹת עַל־
מִלֵּאת: לְחָיָו כַּעֲרוּגַת הַבֹּשֶׂם מִגְדְּלוֹת
מֶרְקָחִים שִׂפְתוֹתָיו שׁוֹשַׁנִּים נֹטְפוֹת מוֹר
עֹבֵר: יָדָיו גְּלִילֵי זָהָב מְמֻלָּאִים בַּתַּרְשִׁישׁ
מֵעָיו עֶשֶׁת שֵׁן מְעֻלֶּפֶת סַפִּירִים: שׁוֹקָיו
עַמּוּדֵי שֵׁשׁ מְיֻסָּדִים עַל־אַדְנֵי־פָז מַרְאֵהוּ
כַּלְּבָנוֹן בָּחוּר כָּאֲרָזִים: חִכּוֹ מַמְתַקִּים וְכֻלּוֹ
מַחֲמַדִּים זֶה דוֹדִי וְזֶה רֵעִי בְּנוֹת יְרוּשָׁלִָם:
ו אָנָה הָלַךְ דּוֹדֵךְ הַיָּפָה בַּנָּשִׁים אָנָה פָּנָה דוֹדֵךְ
וּנְבַקְשֶׁנּוּ עִמָּךְ: דּוֹדִי יָרַד לְגַנּוֹ לַעֲרֻגוֹת
הַבֹּשֶׂם לִרְעוֹת בַּגַּנִּים וְלִלְקֹט שׁוֹשַׁנִּים: אֲנִי
לְדוֹדִי וְדוֹדִי לִי הָרֹעֶה בַּשּׁוֹשַׁנִּים:
יָפָה אַתְּ רַעְיָתִי כְּתִרְצָה נָאוָה כִּירוּשָׁלִָם

אימה כנדגלות: הסבי עיניך מנגדי שהם
הרהיבני שערך כעדר העזים שגלשו מן־
הגלעד: שניך כעדר הרחלים שעלו מן־
הרחצה שכלם מתאימות ושכלה אין בהם:
כפלח הרמון רקתך מבעד לצמתך: ששים
המה מלכות ושמנים פילגשים ועלמות
אין מספר: אחת היא יונתי תמתי אחת
היא לאמה ברה היא ליולדתה ראוה בנות
ויאשרוה מלכות ופילגשים ויהללוה: מי־
זאת הנשקפה כמו־שחר יפה כלבנה ברה
כחמה אימה כנדגלות: אל־גנת אגוז ירדתי
לראות באבי הנחל לראות הפרחה הגפן
הנצו הרמנים: לא ידעתי נפשי שמתני
ז מרכבות עמי נדיב: שובי שובי השולמית
שובי שובי ונחזה־בך מה־תחזו בשולמית
כמחלת המחנים: מה־יפו פעמיך בנעלים
בת־נדיב חמוקי ירכיך כמו חלאים מעשה
ידי אמן: שררך אגן הסהר אל־יחסר המזג
בטנך ערמת חטים סוגה בשושנים: שני
שדיך כשני עפרים תאמי צביה: צוארך
כמגדל השן עיניך ברכות בחשבון על־
שער בת־רבים אפך כמגדל הלבנון צופה
פני דמשק: ראשך עליך ככרמל ודלת
ראשך כארגמן מלך אסור ברהטים: מה־
יפית ומה־נעמת אהבה בתענוגים: זאת
קומתך דמתה לתמר ושדיך לאשכלות:
אמרתי אעלה בתמר אחזה בסנסניו
ויהיו־נא שדיך כאשכלות הגפן וריח אפך
כתפוחים: וחכך כיין הטוב הולך לדודי
למישרים דובב שפתי ישנים: אני לדודי
ועלי תשוקתו: לכה דודי נצא השדה נלינה
בכפרים: נשכימה לכרמים נראה אם־פרחה
הגפן פתח הסמדר הנצו הרמונים שם אתן
את־דדי לך: הדודאים נתנו־ריח ועל־
פתחינו כל־מגדים חדשים גם־ישנים דודי
ח צפנתי לך: מי יתנך כאח לי יונק שדי אמי
אמצאך בחוץ אשקך גם לא־יבזו לי: אנהגך
אביאך אל־בית אמי תלמדני אשקך מיין
הרקח מעסיס רמני: שמאלו תחת ראשי
וימינו תחבקני: השבעתי אתכם בנות
ירושלם מה־תעירו | ומה־תעררו את־
האהבה עד שתחפץ: מי זאת עלה מן־
המדבר מתרפקת על־דודה תחת התפוח
עוררתיך שמה חבלתך אמך שמה חבלה
ילדתך: שימני כחותם על־לבך כחותם על־
זרועך כי־עזה כמות אהבה קשה כשאול
קנאה רשפיה רשפי אש שלהבתיה: מים
רבים לא יוכלו לכבות את־האהבה ונהרות
לא ישטפוה אם־יתן איש את־כל־הון
ביתו באהבה בוז יבוזו לו: אחות לנו קטנה
ושדים אין לה מה־נעשה לאחתנו ביום
שידבר־בה: אם־חומה היא נבנה עליה
טירת כסף ואם־דלת היא נצור עליה לוח
ארז: אני חומה ושדי כמגדלות אז הייתי
בעיניו כמוצאת שלום: כרם היה לשלמה
בבעל המון נתן את־הכרם לנטרים איש
יבא בפריו אלף כסף: כרמי שלי לפני האלף
לך שלמה ומאתים לנטרים את־פריו:
היושבת בגנים חברים מקשיבים לקולך
השמיעני: ברח | דודי ודמה־לך לצבי או
לעפר האילים על הרי בשמים:

רות / RUTH

רות *is read before* קריאת התורה *on the second day of* שבועות.

א ויהי בימי שפט השפטים ויהי רעב בארץ
וילך איש מבית לחם יהודה לגור בשדי
מואב הוא ואשתו ושני בניו: ושם האיש
אלימלך ושם אשתו נעמי ושם שני־בניו |
מחלון וכליון אפרתים מבית לחם יהודה
ויבאו שדי־מואב ויהיו־שם: וימת אלימלך
איש נעמי ותשאר היא ושני בניה: וישאו

לָהֶם נָשִׁים מֹאֲבִיּוֹת שֵׁם הָאַחַת עָרְפָּה וְשֵׁם
הַשֵּׁנִית רוּת וַיֵּשְׁבוּ שָׁם כְּעֶשֶׂר שָׁנִים: וַיָּמֻתוּ
גַם־שְׁנֵיהֶם מַחְלוֹן וְכִלְיוֹן וַתִּשָּׁאֵר הָאִשָּׁה
מִשְּׁנֵי יְלָדֶיהָ וּמֵאִישָׁהּ: וַתָּקָם הִיא וְכַלֹּתֶיהָ
וַתָּשָׁב מִשְּׂדֵי מוֹאָב כִּי שָׁמְעָה בִּשְׂדֵה מוֹאָב
כִּי־פָקַד יהוה אֶת־עַמּוֹ לָתֵת לָהֶם לָחֶם:
וַתֵּצֵא מִן־הַמָּקוֹם אֲשֶׁר הָיְתָה־שָׁמָּה וּשְׁתֵּי
כַלֹּתֶיהָ עִמָּהּ וַתֵּלַכְנָה בַדֶּרֶךְ לָשׁוּב אֶל־אֶרֶץ
יְהוּדָה: וַתֹּאמֶר נָעֳמִי לִשְׁתֵּי כַלֹּתֶיהָ לֵכְנָה
שֹּׁבְנָה אִשָּׁה לְבֵית אִמָּהּ יעשה [יַעַשׂ] יהוה
עִמָּכֶם חֶסֶד כַּאֲשֶׁר עֲשִׂיתֶם עִם־הַמֵּתִים
וְעִמָּדִי: יִתֵּן יהוה לָכֶם וּמְצֶאןָ מְנוּחָה אִשָּׁה
בֵּית אִישָׁהּ וַתִּשַּׁק לָהֶן וַתִּשֶּׂאנָה קוֹלָן
וַתִּבְכֶּינָה: וַתֹּאמַרְנָה־לָּהּ כִּי־אִתָּךְ נָשׁוּב
לְעַמֵּךְ: וַתֹּאמֶר נָעֳמִי שֹׁבְנָה בְנֹתַי לָמָּה
תֵלַכְנָה עִמִּי הַעוֹד־לִי בָנִים בְּמֵעַי וְהָיוּ לָכֶם
לַאֲנָשִׁים: שֹׁבְנָה בְנֹתַי לֵכְןָ כִּי זָקַנְתִּי מִהְיוֹת
לְאִישׁ כִּי אָמַרְתִּי יֶשׁ־לִי תִקְוָה גַּם הָיִיתִי
הַלַּיְלָה לְאִישׁ וְגַם יָלַדְתִּי בָנִים: הֲלָהֵן ׀
תְּשַׂבֵּרְנָה עַד אֲשֶׁר יִגְדָּלוּ הֲלָהֵן תֵּעָגֵנָה
לְבִלְתִּי הֱיוֹת לְאִישׁ אַל בְּנֹתַי כִּי־מַר־לִי
מְאֹד מִכֶּם כִּי־יָצְאָה בִי יַד־יהוה: וַתִּשֶּׂנָה
קוֹלָן וַתִּבְכֶּינָה עוֹד וַתִּשַּׁק עָרְפָּה לַחֲמוֹתָהּ
וְרוּת דָּבְקָה בָּהּ: וַתֹּאמֶר הִנֵּה שָׁבָה יְבִמְתֵּךְ
אֶל־עַמָּהּ וְאֶל־אֱלֹהֶיהָ שׁוּבִי אַחֲרֵי יְבִמְתֵּךְ:
וַתֹּאמֶר רוּת אַל־תִּפְגְּעִי־בִי לְעָזְבֵךְ לָשׁוּב
מֵאַחֲרָיִךְ כִּי אֶל־אֲשֶׁר תֵּלְכִי אֵלֵךְ וּבַאֲשֶׁר
תָּלִינִי אָלִין עַמֵּךְ עַמִּי וֵאלֹהַיִךְ אֱלֹהָי: בַּאֲשֶׁר
תָּמוּתִי אָמוּת וְשָׁם אֶקָּבֵר כֹּה יַעֲשֶׂה יהוה
לִי וְכֹה יֹסִיף כִּי הַמָּוֶת יַפְרִיד בֵּינִי וּבֵינֵךְ:
וַתֵּרֶא כִּי־מִתְאַמֶּצֶת הִיא לָלֶכֶת אִתָּהּ
וַתֶּחְדַּל לְדַבֵּר אֵלֶיהָ: וַתֵּלַכְנָה שְׁתֵּיהֶם עַד־
בּוֹאָנָה בֵּית לָחֶם וַיְהִי כְּבוֹאָנָה בֵּית לֶחֶם
וַתֵּהֹם כָּל־הָעִיר עֲלֵיהֶן וַתֹּאמַרְנָה הֲזֹאת
נָעֳמִי: וַתֹּאמֶר אֲלֵיהֶן אַל־תִּקְרֶאנָה לִי
נָעֳמִי קְרֶאןָ לִי מָרָא כִּי־הֵמַר שַׁדַּי לִי
מְאֹד: אֲנִי מְלֵאָה הָלַכְתִּי וְרֵיקָם הֱשִׁיבַנִי
יהוה לָמָּה תִקְרֶאנָה לִי נָעֳמִי וַיהוה עָנָה בִי
וְשַׁדַּי הֵרַע־לִי: וַתָּשָׁב נָעֳמִי וְרוּת הַמּוֹאֲבִיָּה
כַלָּתָהּ עִמָּהּ הַשָּׁבָה מִשְּׂדֵי מוֹאָב וְהֵמָּה
בָּאוּ בֵּית לֶחֶם בִּתְחִלַּת קְצִיר שְׂעֹרִים:
ב וּלְנָעֳמִי מידע [מוֹדַע] לְאִישָׁהּ אִישׁ גִּבּוֹר
חַיִל מִמִּשְׁפַּחַת אֱלִימֶלֶךְ וּשְׁמוֹ בֹּעַז: וַתֹּאמֶר
רוּת הַמּוֹאֲבִיָּה אֶל־נָעֳמִי אֵלְכָה־נָּא הַשָּׂדֶה
וַאֲלַקֳטָה בַשִּׁבֳּלִים אַחַר אֲשֶׁר אֶמְצָא־חֵן
בְּעֵינָיו וַתֹּאמֶר לָהּ לְכִי בִתִּי: וַתֵּלֶךְ וַתָּבוֹא
וַתְּלַקֵּט בַּשָּׂדֶה אַחֲרֵי הַקֹּצְרִים וַיִּקֶר מִקְרֶהָ
חֶלְקַת הַשָּׂדֶה לְבֹעַז אֲשֶׁר מִמִּשְׁפַּחַת
אֱלִימֶלֶךְ: וְהִנֵּה־בֹעַז בָּא מִבֵּית לֶחֶם וַיֹּאמֶר
לַקּוֹצְרִים יהוה עִמָּכֶם וַיֹּאמְרוּ לוֹ יְבָרֶכְךָ
יהוה: וַיֹּאמֶר בֹּעַז לְנַעֲרוֹ הַנִּצָּב עַל־
הַקּוֹצְרִים לְמִי הַנַּעֲרָה הַזֹּאת: וַיַּעַן הַנַּעַר
הַנִּצָּב עַל־הַקּוֹצְרִים וַיֹּאמַר נַעֲרָה מוֹאֲבִיָּה
הִיא הַשָּׁבָה עִם־נָעֳמִי מִשְּׂדֵי מוֹאָב: וַתֹּאמֶר
אֲלַקֳטָה־נָּא וְאָסַפְתִּי בָעֳמָרִים אַחֲרֵי
הַקּוֹצְרִים וַתָּבוֹא וַתַּעֲמוֹד מֵאָז הַבֹּקֶר וְעַד־
עַתָּה זֶה שִׁבְתָּהּ הַבַּיִת מְעָט: וַיֹּאמֶר בֹּעַז
אֶל־רוּת הֲלוֹא שָׁמַעַתְּ בִּתִּי אַל־תֵּלְכִי לִלְקֹט
בְּשָׂדֶה אַחֵר וְגַם לֹא תַעֲבוּרִי מִזֶּה וְכֹה
תִדְבָּקִין עִם־נַעֲרֹתָי: עֵינַיִךְ בַּשָּׂדֶה אֲשֶׁר־
יִקְצֹרוּן וְהָלַכְתְּ אַחֲרֵיהֶן הֲלוֹא צִוִּיתִי אֶת־
הַנְּעָרִים לְבִלְתִּי נָגְעֵךְ וְצָמִת וְהָלַכְתְּ אֶל־
הַכֵּלִים וְשָׁתִית מֵאֲשֶׁר יִשְׁאֲבוּן הַנְּעָרִים:
וַתִּפֹּל עַל־פָּנֶיהָ וַתִּשְׁתַּחוּ אָרְצָה וַתֹּאמֶר
אֵלָיו מַדּוּעַ מָצָאתִי חֵן בְּעֵינֶיךָ לְהַכִּירֵנִי
וְאָנֹכִי נָכְרִיָּה: וַיַּעַן בֹּעַז וַיֹּאמֶר לָהּ הֻגֵּד הֻגַּד
לִי כֹּל אֲשֶׁר־עָשִׂית אֶת־חֲמוֹתֵךְ אַחֲרֵי מוֹת
אִישֵׁךְ וַתַּעַזְבִי אָבִיךְ וְאִמֵּךְ וְאֶרֶץ מוֹלַדְתֵּךְ
וַתֵּלְכִי אֶל־עַם אֲשֶׁר לֹא־יָדַעַתְּ תְּמוֹל
שִׁלְשׁוֹם: יְשַׁלֵּם יהוה פָּעֳלֵךְ וּתְהִי מַשְׂכֻּרְתֵּךְ
שְׁלֵמָה מֵעִם יהוה אֱלֹהֵי יִשְׂרָאֵל אֲשֶׁר־בָּאת
לַחֲסוֹת תַּחַת־כְּנָפָיו: וַתֹּאמֶר אֶמְצָא־חֵן

בְּעֵינֶיךָ אֲדֹנִי כִּי נִחַמְתָּנִי וְכִי דִבַּרְתָּ עַל־לֵב
שִׁפְחָתֶךָ וְאָנֹכִי לֹא אֶהְיֶה כְּאַחַת שִׁפְחֹתֶיךָ׃
וַיֹּאמֶר לָה בֹעַז לְעֵת הָאֹכֶל גֹּשִׁי הֲלֹם וְאָכַלְתְּ
מִן־הַלֶּחֶם וְטָבַלְתְּ פִּתֵּךְ בַּחֹמֶץ וַתֵּשֶׁב מִצַּד
הַקֹּצְרִים וַיִּצְבָּט־לָהּ קָלִי וַתֹּאכַל וַתִּשְׂבַּע
וַתֹּתַר׃ וַתָּקָם לְלַקֵּט וַיְצַו בֹּעַז אֶת־נְעָרָיו
לֵאמֹר גַּם בֵּין הָעֳמָרִים תְּלַקֵּט וְלֹא
תַכְלִימוּהָ׃ וְגַם שֹׁל־תָּשֹׁלּוּ לָהּ מִן־הַצְּבָתִים
וַעֲזַבְתֶּם וְלִקְּטָה וְלֹא תִגְעֲרוּ־בָהּ׃ וַתְּלַקֵּט
בַּשָּׂדֶה עַד־הָעָרֶב וַתַּחְבֹּט אֵת אֲשֶׁר־לִקֵּטָה
וַיְהִי כְּאֵיפָה שְׂעֹרִים׃ וַתִּשָּׂא וַתָּבוֹא הָעִיר
וַתֵּרֶא חֲמוֹתָהּ אֵת אֲשֶׁר־לִקֵּטָה וַתּוֹצֵא
וַתִּתֶּן־לָהּ אֵת אֲשֶׁר־הוֹתִרָה מִשָּׂבְעָהּ׃
וַתֹּאמֶר לָהּ חֲמוֹתָהּ אֵיפֹה לִקַּטְתְּ הַיּוֹם
וְאָנָה עָשִׂית יְהִי מַכִּירֵךְ בָּרוּךְ וַתַּגֵּד לַחֲמוֹתָהּ
אֵת אֲשֶׁר־עָשְׂתָה עִמּוֹ וַתֹּאמֶר שֵׁם הָאִישׁ
אֲשֶׁר עָשִׂיתִי עִמּוֹ הַיּוֹם בֹּעַז׃ וַתֹּאמֶר נָעֳמִי
לְכַלָּתָהּ בָּרוּךְ הוּא לַיהוה אֲשֶׁר לֹא־עָזַב
חַסְדּוֹ אֶת־הַחַיִּים וְאֶת־הַמֵּתִים וַתֹּאמֶר
לָהּ נָעֳמִי קָרוֹב לָנוּ הָאִישׁ מִגֹּאֲלֵנוּ הוּא׃
וַתֹּאמֶר רוּת הַמּוֹאֲבִיָּה גַּם ׀ כִּי־אָמַר אֵלַי
עִם־הַנְּעָרִים אֲשֶׁר־לִי תִּדְבָּקִין עַד אִם־כִּלּוּ
אֵת כָּל־הַקָּצִיר אֲשֶׁר־לִי׃ וַתֹּאמֶר נָעֳמִי אֶל־
רוּת כַּלָּתָהּ טוֹב בִּתִּי כִּי תֵצְאִי עִם־נַעֲרוֹתָיו
וְלֹא יִפְגְּעוּ־בָךְ בְּשָׂדֶה אַחֵר׃ וַתִּדְבַּק בְּנַעֲרוֹת
בֹּעַז לְלַקֵּט עַד־כְּלוֹת קְצִיר־הַשְּׂעֹרִים
ג וּקְצִיר הַחִטִּים וַתֵּשֶׁב אֶת־חֲמוֹתָהּ׃ וַתֹּאמֶר
לָהּ נָעֳמִי חֲמוֹתָהּ בִּתִּי הֲלֹא אֲבַקֶּשׁ־לָךְ
מָנוֹחַ אֲשֶׁר יִיטַב־לָךְ׃ וְעַתָּה הֲלֹא בֹעַז
מֹדַעְתָּנוּ אֲשֶׁר הָיִית אֶת־נַעֲרוֹתָיו הִנֵּה־הוּא
זֹרֶה אֶת־גֹּרֶן הַשְּׂעֹרִים הַלָּיְלָה׃ וְרָחַצְתְּ ׀
וָסַכְתְּ וְשַׂמְתְּ שמלתך [שִׂמְלֹתַיִךְ] עָלַיִךְ
וירדתי [וְיָרַדְתְּ] הַגֹּרֶן אַל־תִּוָּדְעִי לָאִישׁ עַד
כַּלֹּתוֹ לֶאֱכֹל וְלִשְׁתּוֹת׃ וִיהִי בְשָׁכְבוֹ וְיָדַעַתְּ
אֶת־הַמָּקוֹם אֲשֶׁר יִשְׁכַּב־שָׁם וּבָאת וְגִלִּית
מַרְגְּלֹתָיו ושכבתי [וְשָׁכָבְתְּ] וְהוּא יַגִּיד לָךְ
אֵת אֲשֶׁר תַּעֲשִׂין׃ וַתֹּאמֶר אֵלֶיהָ כֹּל אֲשֶׁר־
תֹּאמְרִי [אֵלַי] אֶעֱשֶׂה׃ וַתֵּרֶד הַגֹּרֶן
וַתַּעַשׂ כְּכֹל אֲשֶׁר־צִוַּתָּה חֲמוֹתָהּ׃ וַיֹּאכַל
בֹּעַז וַיֵּשְׁתְּ וַיִּיטַב לִבּוֹ וַיָּבֹא לִשְׁכַּב בִּקְצֵה
הָעֲרֵמָה וַתָּבֹא בַלָּט וַתְּגַל מַרְגְּלֹתָיו וַתִּשְׁכָּב׃
וַיְהִי בַּחֲצִי הַלַּיְלָה וַיֶּחֱרַד הָאִישׁ וַיִּלָּפֵת וְהִנֵּה
אִשָּׁה שֹׁכֶבֶת מַרְגְּלֹתָיו׃ וַיֹּאמֶר מִי־אָתְּ
וַתֹּאמֶר אָנֹכִי רוּת אֲמָתֶךָ וּפָרַשְׂתָּ כְנָפֶךָ עַל־
אֲמָתְךָ כִּי גֹאֵל אָתָּה׃ וַיֹּאמֶר בְּרוּכָה אַתְּ
לַיהוה בִּתִּי הֵיטַבְתְּ חַסְדֵּךְ הָאַחֲרוֹן מִן־
הָרִאשׁוֹן לְבִלְתִּי־לֶכֶת אַחֲרֵי הַבַּחוּרִים אִם־
דַּל וְאִם־עָשִׁיר׃ וְעַתָּה בִּתִּי אַל־תִּירְאִי כֹּל
אֲשֶׁר־תֹּאמְרִי אֶעֱשֶׂה־לָּךְ כִּי יוֹדֵעַ כָּל־שַׁעַר
עַמִּי כִּי אֵשֶׁת חַיִל אָתְּ׃ וְעַתָּה כִּי אָמְנָם כִּי
אם גֹאֵל אָנֹכִי וְגַם יֵשׁ גֹּאֵל קָרוֹב מִמֶּנִּי׃ לִינִי ׀
הַלַּיְלָה וְהָיָה בַבֹּקֶר אִם־יִגְאָלֵךְ טוֹב יִגְאָל
וְאִם־לֹא יַחְפֹּץ לְגָאֳלֵךְ וּגְאַלְתִּיךְ אָנֹכִי חַי־
יהוה שִׁכְבִי עַד־הַבֹּקֶר׃ וַתִּשְׁכַּב מַרְגְּלוֹתָו
עַד־הַבֹּקֶר וַתָּקָם בטרום [בְּטֶרֶם] יַכִּיר אִישׁ
אֶת־רֵעֵהוּ וַיֹּאמֶר אַל־יִוָּדַע כִּי־בָאָה הָאִשָּׁה
הַגֹּרֶן׃ וַיֹּאמֶר הָבִי הַמִּטְפַּחַת אֲשֶׁר־עָלַיִךְ
וְאֶחֳזִי־בָהּ וַתֹּאחֶז בָּהּ וַיָּמָד שֵׁשׁ־שְׂעֹרִים
וַיָּשֶׁת עָלֶיהָ וַיָּבֹא הָעִיר׃ וַתָּבוֹא אֶל־חֲמוֹתָהּ
וַתֹּאמֶר מִי־אַתְּ בִּתִּי וַתַּגֶּד־לָהּ אֵת כָּל־אֲשֶׁר
עָשָׂה־לָהּ הָאִישׁ׃ וַתֹּאמֶר שֵׁשׁ־הַשְּׂעֹרִים
הָאֵלֶּה נָתַן לִי כִּי אָמַר [אֵלַי] אַל־תָּבוֹאִי
רֵיקָם אֶל־חֲמוֹתֵךְ׃ וַתֹּאמֶר שְׁבִי בִתִּי עַד
אֲשֶׁר תֵּדְעִין אֵיךְ יִפֹּל דָּבָר כִּי לֹא יִשְׁקֹט
ד הָאִישׁ כִּי־אִם־כִּלָּה הַדָּבָר הַיּוֹם׃ וּבֹעַז עָלָה
הַשַּׁעַר וַיֵּשֶׁב שָׁם וְהִנֵּה הַגֹּאֵל עֹבֵר אֲשֶׁר
דִּבֶּר־בֹּעַז וַיֹּאמֶר סוּרָה שְׁבָה־פֹּה פְּלֹנִי
אַלְמֹנִי וַיָּסַר וַיֵּשֵׁב׃ וַיִּקַּח עֲשָׂרָה אֲנָשִׁים
מִזִּקְנֵי הָעִיר וַיֹּאמֶר שְׁבוּ־פֹה וַיֵּשֵׁבוּ׃ וַיֹּאמֶר
לַגֹּאֵל חֶלְקַת הַשָּׂדֶה אֲשֶׁר לְאָחִינוּ לֶאֱלִימֶלֶךְ
מָכְרָה נָעֳמִי הַשָּׁבָה מִשְּׂדֵה מוֹאָב׃ וַאֲנִי
אָמַרְתִּי אֶגְלֶה אָזְנְךָ לֵאמֹר קְנֵה נֶגֶד הַיֹּשְׁבִים

וְנֶגֶד זִקְנֵי עַמִּי אִם־תִּגְאַל גְּאָל וְאִם־לֹא
יִגְאַל הַגִּידָה לִּי וְאֵדַע כִּי אֵין זוּלָתְךָ לִגְאוֹל
וְאָנֹכִי אַחֲרֶיךָ וַיֹּאמֶר אָנֹכִי אֶגְאָל: וַיֹּאמֶר
בֹּעַז בְּיוֹם־קְנוֹתְךָ הַשָּׂדֶה מִיַּד נָעֳמִי וּמֵאֵת
רוּת הַמּוֹאֲבִיָּה אֵשֶׁת־הַמֵּת קניתי [קָנִיתָה]
לְהָקִים שֵׁם־הַמֵּת עַל־נַחֲלָתוֹ: וַיֹּאמֶר הַגֹּאֵל
לֹא אוּכַל לגאול־[לִגְאָל־]לִי פֶּן־אַשְׁחִית
אֶת־נַחֲלָתִי גְּאַל־לְךָ אַתָּה אֶת־גְּאֻלָּתִי כִּי
לֹא־אוּכַל לִגְאֹל: וְזֹאת לְפָנִים בְּיִשְׂרָאֵל עַל־
הַגְּאוּלָּה וְעַל־הַתְּמוּרָה לְקַיֵּם כָּל־דָּבָר שָׁלַף
אִישׁ נַעֲלוֹ וְנָתַן לְרֵעֵהוּ וְזֹאת הַתְּעוּדָה
בְּיִשְׂרָאֵל: וַיֹּאמֶר הַגֹּאֵל לְבֹעַז קְנֵה־לָךְ
וַיִּשְׁלֹף נַעֲלוֹ: וַיֹּאמֶר בֹּעַז לַזְּקֵנִים וְכָל־הָעָם
עֵדִים אַתֶּם הַיּוֹם כִּי קָנִיתִי אֶת־כָּל־אֲשֶׁר
לֶאֱלִימֶלֶךְ וְאֵת כָּל־אֲשֶׁר לְכִלְיוֹן וּמַחְלוֹן
מִיַּד נָעֳמִי: וְגַם אֶת־רוּת הַמֹּאֲבִיָּה אֵשֶׁת
מַחְלוֹן קָנִיתִי לִי לְאִשָּׁה לְהָקִים שֵׁם־הַמֵּת
עַל־נַחֲלָתוֹ וְלֹא־יִכָּרֵת שֵׁם־הַמֵּת מֵעִם אֶחָיו
וּמִשַּׁעַר מְקוֹמוֹ עֵדִים אַתֶּם הַיּוֹם: וַיֹּאמְרוּ
כָּל־הָעָם אֲשֶׁר־בַּשַּׁעַר וְהַזְּקֵנִים עֵדִים יִתֵּן
יהוה אֶת־הָאִשָּׁה הַבָּאָה אֶל־בֵּיתֶךָ כְּרָחֵל ׀
וּכְלֵאָה אֲשֶׁר בָּנוּ שְׁתֵּיהֶם אֶת־בֵּית יִשְׂרָאֵל
וַעֲשֵׂה־חַיִל בְּאֶפְרָתָה וּקְרָא־שֵׁם בְּבֵית לָחֶם:
וִיהִי בֵיתְךָ כְּבֵית פֶּרֶץ אֲשֶׁר־יָלְדָה תָמָר
לִיהוּדָה מִן־הַזֶּרַע אֲשֶׁר יִתֵּן יהוה לְךָ מִן־
הַנַּעֲרָה הַזֹּאת: וַיִּקַּח בֹּעַז אֶת־רוּת וַתְּהִי־לוֹ
לְאִשָּׁה וַיָּבֹא אֵלֶיהָ וַיִּתֵּן יהוה לָהּ הֵרָיוֹן
וַתֵּלֶד בֵּן: וַתֹּאמַרְנָה הַנָּשִׁים אֶל־נָעֳמִי בָּרוּךְ
יהוה אֲשֶׁר לֹא הִשְׁבִּית לָךְ גֹּאֵל הַיּוֹם וְיִקָּרֵא
שְׁמוֹ בְּיִשְׂרָאֵל: וְהָיָה לָךְ לְמֵשִׁיב נֶפֶשׁ וּלְכַלְכֵּל
אֶת־שֵׂיבָתֵךְ כִּי כַלָּתֵךְ אֲשֶׁר־אֲהֵבַתֶךְ יְלָדַתּוּ
אֲשֶׁר־הִיא טוֹבָה לָךְ מִשִּׁבְעָה בָּנִים: וַתִּקַּח
נָעֳמִי אֶת־הַיֶּלֶד וַתְּשִׁתֵהוּ בְחֵיקָהּ וַתְּהִי־לוֹ
לְאֹמֶנֶת: וַתִּקְרֶאנָה לוֹ הַשְּׁכֵנוֹת שֵׁם לֵאמֹר
יֻלַּד־בֵּן לְנָעֳמִי וַתִּקְרֶאנָה שְׁמוֹ עוֹבֵד הוּא
אֲבִי־יִשַׁי אֲבִי דָוִד:
וְאֵלֶּה תּוֹלְדוֹת פָּרֶץ פֶּרֶץ הוֹלִיד אֶת־חֶצְרוֹן:
וְחֶצְרוֹן הוֹלִיד אֶת־רָם וְרָם הוֹלִיד אֶת־
עַמִּינָדָב: וְעַמִּינָדָב הוֹלִיד אֶת־נַחְשׁוֹן וְנַחְשׁוֹן
הוֹלִיד אֶת־שַׂלְמָה: וְשַׂלְמוֹן הוֹלִיד אֶת־בֹּעַז
וּבֹעַז הוֹלִיד אֶת־עוֹבֵד: וְעֹבֵד הוֹלִיד אֶת־
יִשָׁי וְיִשַׁי הוֹלִיד אֶת־דָּוִד:

LAMENTATIONS / איכה

איכה *is read on* תשעה באב.

א אֵיכָה ׀ יָשְׁבָה בָדָד הָעִיר רַבָּתִי עָם הָיְתָה
כְּאַלְמָנָה רַבָּתִי בַגּוֹיִם שָׂרָתִי בַּמְּדִינוֹת
הָיְתָה לָמַס: בָּכוֹ תִבְכֶּה בַּלַּיְלָה וְדִמְעָתָהּ
עַל לֶחֱיָהּ אֵין־לָהּ מְנַחֵם מִכָּל־אֹהֲבֶיהָ כָּל־
רֵעֶיהָ בָּגְדוּ בָהּ הָיוּ לָהּ לְאֹיְבִים: גָּלְתָה
יְהוּדָה מֵעֹנִי וּמֵרֹב עֲבֹדָה הִיא יָשְׁבָה בַגּוֹיִם
לֹא מָצְאָה מָנוֹחַ כָּל־רֹדְפֶיהָ הִשִּׂיגוּהָ בֵּין
הַמְּצָרִים: דַּרְכֵי צִיּוֹן אֲבֵלוֹת מִבְּלִי בָּאֵי
מוֹעֵד כָּל־שְׁעָרֶיהָ שׁוֹמֵמִין כֹּהֲנֶיהָ נֶאֱנָחִים
בְּתוּלֹתֶיהָ נּוּגוֹת וְהִיא מַר־לָהּ: הָיוּ צָרֶיהָ
לְרֹאשׁ אֹיְבֶיהָ שָׁלוּ כִּי־יהוה הוֹגָהּ עַל־רֹב
פְּשָׁעֶיהָ עוֹלָלֶיהָ הָלְכוּ שְׁבִי לִפְנֵי־צָר: וַיֵּצֵא
מן בת־[מִבַּת־]צִיּוֹן כָּל־הֲדָרָהּ הָיוּ שָׂרֶיהָ
כְּאַיָּלִים לֹא־מָצְאוּ מִרְעֶה וַיֵּלְכוּ בְלֹא־
כֹחַ לִפְנֵי רוֹדֵף: זָכְרָה יְרוּשָׁלִַם יְמֵי עָנְיָהּ
וּמְרוּדֶיהָ כֹּל מַחֲמֻדֶיהָ אֲשֶׁר הָיוּ מִימֵי קֶדֶם
בִּנְפֹל עַמָּהּ בְּיַד־צָר וְאֵין עוֹזֵר לָהּ רָאוּהָ
צָרִים שָׂחֲקוּ עַל־מִשְׁבַּתֶּהָ: חֵטְא חָטְאָה
יְרוּשָׁלִַם עַל־כֵּן לְנִידָה הָיָתָה כָּל־מְכַבְּדֶיהָ
הִזִּילוּהָ כִּי־רָאוּ עֶרְוָתָהּ גַּם־הִיא נֶאֶנְחָה
וַתָּשָׁב אָחוֹר: טֻמְאָתָהּ בְּשׁוּלֶיהָ לֹא זָכְרָה
אַחֲרִיתָהּ וַתֵּרֶד פְּלָאִים אֵין מְנַחֵם לָהּ רְאֵה
יהוה אֶת־עָנְיִי כִּי הִגְדִּיל אוֹיֵב: יָדוֹ פָּרַשׂ צָר
עַל כָּל־מַחֲמַדֶּיהָ כִּי־רָאֲתָה גוֹיִם בָּאוּ
מִקְדָּשָׁהּ אֲשֶׁר צִוִּיתָה לֹא־יָבֹאוּ בַקָּהָל לָךְ:
כָּל־עַמָּהּ נֶאֱנָחִים מְבַקְּשִׁים לֶחֶם נָתְנוּ
מחמודיהם [מַחֲמַדֵּיהֶם] בְּאֹכֶל לְהָשִׁיב נָפֶשׁ

רְאֵה יהוה וְהַבִּיטָה כִּי הָיִיתִי זוֹלֵלָה: לוֹא
אֲלֵיכֶם כָּל־עֹבְרֵי דֶרֶךְ הַבִּיטוּ וּרְאוּ אִם־יֵשׁ
מַכְאוֹב כְּמַכְאֹבִי אֲשֶׁר עוֹלַל לִי אֲשֶׁר הוֹגָה
יהוה בְּיוֹם חֲרוֹן אַפּוֹ: מִמָּרוֹם שָׁלַח־אֵשׁ
בְּעַצְמֹתַי וַיִּרְדֶּנָּה פָּרַשׂ רֶשֶׁת לְרַגְלַי הֱשִׁיבַנִי
אָחוֹר נְתָנַנִי שֹׁמֵמָה כָּל־הַיּוֹם דָּוָה: נִשְׂקַד
עֹל פְּשָׁעַי בְּיָדוֹ יִשְׂתָּרְגוּ עָלוּ עַל־צַוָּארִי
הִכְשִׁיל כֹּחִי נְתָנַנִי אֲדֹנָי בִּידֵי לֹא־אוּכַל
קוּם: סִלָּה כָל־אַבִּירַי ׀ אֲדֹנָי בְּקִרְבִּי קָרָא
עָלַי מוֹעֵד לִשְׁבֹּר בַּחוּרָי גַּת דָּרַךְ אֲדֹנָי
לִבְתוּלַת בַּת־יְהוּדָה: עַל־אֵלֶּה ׀ אֲנִי בוֹכִיָּה
עֵינִי ׀ עֵינִי יֹרְדָה מַּיִם כִּי־רָחַק מִמֶּנִּי מְנַחֵם
מֵשִׁיב נַפְשִׁי הָיוּ בָנַי שׁוֹמֵמִים כִּי גָבַר אוֹיֵב:
פֵּרְשָׂה צִיּוֹן בְּיָדֶיהָ אֵין מְנַחֵם לָהּ צִוָּה יהוה
לְיַעֲקֹב סְבִיבָיו צָרָיו הָיְתָה יְרוּשָׁלִַם לְנִדָּה
בֵּינֵיהֶם: צַדִּיק הוּא יהוה כִּי פִיהוּ מָרִיתִי
שִׁמְעוּ־נָא כָל־עמים [הָעַמִּים] וּרְאוּ מַכְאֹבִי
בְּתוּלֹתַי וּבַחוּרַי הָלְכוּ בַשֶּׁבִי: קָרָאתִי
לַמְאַהֲבַי הֵמָּה רִמּוּנִי כֹּהֲנַי וּזְקֵנַי בָּעִיר גָּוָעוּ
כִּי־בִקְשׁוּ אֹכֶל לָמוֹ וְיָשִׁיבוּ אֶת־נַפְשָׁם: רְאֵה
יהוה כִּי־צַר־לִי מֵעַי חֳמַרְמָרוּ נֶהְפַּךְ לִבִּי
בְּקִרְבִּי כִּי מָרוֹ מָרִיתִי מִחוּץ שִׁכְּלָה־חֶרֶב
בַּבַּיִת כַּמָּוֶת: שָׁמְעוּ כִּי נֶאֱנָחָה אָנִי אֵין
מְנַחֵם לִי כָּל־אֹיְבַי שָׁמְעוּ רָעָתִי שָׂשׂוּ כִּי
אַתָּה עָשִׂיתָ הֵבֵאתָ יוֹם־קָרָאתָ וְיִהְיוּ כָמוֹנִי:
תָּבֹא כָל־רָעָתָם לְפָנֶיךָ וְעוֹלֵל לָמוֹ כַּאֲשֶׁר
עוֹלַלְתָּ לִי עַל כָּל־פְּשָׁעָי כִּי־רַבּוֹת אַנְחֹתַי
וְלִבִּי דַוָּי:

ב אֵיכָה יָעִיב בְּאַפּוֹ ׀ אֲדֹנָי אֶת־בַּת־צִיּוֹן
הִשְׁלִיךְ מִשָּׁמַיִם אֶרֶץ תִּפְאֶרֶת יִשְׂרָאֵל
וְלֹא־זָכַר הֲדֹם־רַגְלָיו בְּיוֹם אַפּוֹ: בִּלַּע אֲדֹנָי
לא [וְלֹא] חָמַל אֵת כָּל־נְאוֹת יַעֲקֹב הָרַס
בְּעֶבְרָתוֹ מִבְצְרֵי בַת־יְהוּדָה הִגִּיעַ לָאָרֶץ
חִלֵּל מַמְלָכָה וְשָׂרֶיהָ: גָּדַע בָּחֳרִי־אַף כֹּל קֶרֶן
יִשְׂרָאֵל הֵשִׁיב אָחוֹר יְמִינוֹ מִפְּנֵי אוֹיֵב וַיִּבְעַר
בְּיַעֲקֹב כְּאֵשׁ לֶהָבָה אָכְלָה סָבִיב: דָּרַךְ קַשְׁתּוֹ
כְּאוֹיֵב נִצָּב יְמִינוֹ כְּצָר וַיַּהֲרֹג כֹּל מַחֲמַדֵּי־
עָיִן בְּאֹהֶל בַּת־צִיּוֹן שָׁפַךְ כָּאֵשׁ חֲמָתוֹ:
הָיָה אֲדֹנָי ׀ כְּאוֹיֵב בִּלַּע יִשְׂרָאֵל בִּלַּע כָּל־
אַרְמְנוֹתֶיהָ שִׁחֵת מִבְצָרָיו וַיֶּרֶב בְּבַת־יְהוּדָה
תַּאֲנִיָּה וַאֲנִיָּה: וַיַּחְמֹס כַּגַּן שֻׂכּוֹ שִׁחֵת מֹעֲדוֹ
שִׁכַּח יהוה ׀ בְּצִיּוֹן מוֹעֵד וְשַׁבָּת וַיִּנְאַץ בְּזַעַם־
אַפּוֹ מֶלֶךְ וְכֹהֵן: זָנַח אֲדֹנָי ׀ מִזְבְּחוֹ נִאֵר
מִקְדָּשׁוֹ הִסְגִּיר בְּיַד־אוֹיֵב חוֹמֹת אַרְמְנוֹתֶיהָ
קוֹל נָתְנוּ בְּבֵית־יהוה כְּיוֹם מוֹעֵד: חָשַׁב
יהוה ׀ לְהַשְׁחִית חוֹמַת בַּת־צִיּוֹן נָטָה קָו
לֹא־הֵשִׁיב יָדוֹ מִבַּלֵּעַ וַיַּאֲבֶל־חֵל וְחוֹמָה
יַחְדָּו אֻמְלָלוּ: טָבְעוּ בָאָרֶץ שְׁעָרֶיהָ אִבַּד
וְשִׁבַּר בְּרִיחֶיהָ מַלְכָּהּ וְשָׂרֶיהָ בַגּוֹיִם אֵין
תּוֹרָה גַּם־נְבִיאֶיהָ לֹא־מָצְאוּ חָזוֹן מֵיהוה:
יֵשְׁבוּ לָאָרֶץ יִדְּמוּ זִקְנֵי בַת־צִיּוֹן הֶעֱלוּ
עָפָר עַל־רֹאשָׁם חָגְרוּ שַׂקִּים הוֹרִידוּ לָאָרֶץ
רֹאשָׁן בְּתוּלֹת יְרוּשָׁלִָם: כָּלוּ בַדְּמָעוֹת עֵינַי
חֳמַרְמְרוּ מֵעַי נִשְׁפַּךְ לָאָרֶץ כְּבֵדִי עַל־שֶׁבֶר
בַּת־עַמִּי בֵּעָטֵף עוֹלֵל וְיוֹנֵק בִּרְחֹבוֹת קִרְיָה:
לְאִמֹּתָם יֹאמְרוּ אַיֵּה דָּגָן וָיָיִן בְּהִתְעַטְּפָם
כֶּחָלָל בִּרְחֹבוֹת עִיר בְּהִשְׁתַּפֵּךְ נַפְשָׁם אֶל־
חֵיק אִמֹּתָם: מָה־אעודך [אֲעִידֵךְ] מָה
אֲדַמֶּה־לָּךְ הַבַּת יְרוּשָׁלִַם מָה אַשְׁוֶה־לָּךְ
וַאֲנַחֲמֵךְ בְּתוּלַת בַּת־צִיּוֹן כִּי־גָדוֹל כַּיָּם שִׁבְרֵךְ
מִי יִרְפָּא־לָךְ: נְבִיאַיִךְ חָזוּ לָךְ שָׁוְא וְתָפֵל
וְלֹא־גִלּוּ עַל־עֲוֺנֵךְ לְהָשִׁיב שביתך [שְׁבוּתֵךְ]
וַיֶּחֱזוּ לָךְ מַשְׂאוֹת שָׁוְא וּמַדּוּחִים: סָפְקוּ עָלַיִךְ
כַּפַּיִם כָּל־עֹבְרֵי דֶרֶךְ שָׁרְקוּ וַיָּנִעוּ רֹאשָׁם עַל־
בַּת יְרוּשָׁלִָם הֲזֹאת הָעִיר שֶׁיֹּאמְרוּ כְּלִילַת
יֹפִי מָשׂוֹשׂ לְכָל־הָאָרֶץ: פָּצוּ עָלַיִךְ פִּיהֶם כָּל־
אֹיְבַיִךְ שָׁרְקוּ וַיַּחַרְקוּ־שֵׁן אָמְרוּ בִּלָּעְנוּ אַךְ
זֶה הַיּוֹם שֶׁקִּוִּינֻהוּ מָצָאנוּ רָאִינוּ: עָשָׂה יהוה
אֲשֶׁר זָמָם בִּצַּע אֶמְרָתוֹ אֲשֶׁר צִוָּה מִימֵי־
קֶדֶם הָרַס וְלֹא חָמָל וַיְשַׂמַּח עָלַיִךְ אוֹיֵב הֵרִים
קֶרֶן צָרָיִךְ: צָעַק לִבָּם אֶל־אֲדֹנָי חוֹמַת בַּת־
צִיּוֹן הוֹרִידִי כַנַּחַל דִּמְעָה יוֹמָם וָלַיְלָה אַל־

תִּתְּנִי פוּגַת לָךְ אַל־תִּדֹּם בַּת־עֵינֵךְ: קוּמִי
רֹנִּי בַלַּיְלָ לְרֹאשׁ אַשְׁמֻרוֹת שִׁפְכִי כַמַּיִם לִבֵּךְ
נֹכַח פְּנֵי אֲדֹנָי שְׂאִי אֵלָיו כַּפַּיִךְ עַל־נֶפֶשׁ
עוֹלָלַיִךְ הָעֲטוּפִים בְּרָעָב בְּרֹאשׁ כָּל־חוּצוֹת:
רְאֵה יהוה וְהַבִּיטָה לְמִי עוֹלַלְתָּ כֹּה אִם־
תֹּאכַלְנָה נָשִׁים פִּרְיָם עֹלְלֵי טִפֻּחִים אִם־יֵהָרֵג
בְּמִקְדַּשׁ אֲדֹנָי כֹּהֵן וְנָבִיא: שָׁכְבוּ לָאָרֶץ
חוּצוֹת נַעַר וְזָקֵן בְּתוּלֹתַי וּבַחוּרַי נָפְלוּ בֶחָרֶב
הָרַגְתָּ בְּיוֹם אַפֶּךָ טָבַחְתָּ לֹא חָמָלְתָּ: תִּקְרָא
כְיוֹם מוֹעֵד מְגוּרַי מִסָּבִיב וְלֹא הָיָה בְּיוֹם
אַף־יהוה פָּלִיט וְשָׂרִיד אֲשֶׁר־טִפַּחְתִּי וְרִבִּיתִי
אֹיְבִי כִלָּם:
ג אֲנִי הַגֶּבֶר רָאָה עֳנִי בְּשֵׁבֶט עֶבְרָתוֹ: אוֹתִי
נָהַג וַיֹּלַךְ חֹשֶׁךְ וְלֹא־אוֹר: אַךְ בִּי יָשֻׁב יַהֲפֹךְ
יָדוֹ כָּל־הַיּוֹם: בִּלָּה בְשָׂרִי וְעוֹרִי שִׁבַּר
עַצְמוֹתָי: בָּנָה עָלַי וַיַּקַּף רֹאשׁ וּתְלָאָה:
בְּמַחֲשַׁכִּים הוֹשִׁיבַנִי כְּמֵתֵי עוֹלָם: גָּדַר בַּעֲדִי
וְלֹא אֵצֵא הִכְבִּיד נְחָשְׁתִּי: גַּם כִּי אֶזְעַק
וַאֲשַׁוֵּעַ שָׂתַם תְּפִלָּתִי: גָּדַר דְּרָכַי בְּגָזִית
נְתִיבֹתַי עִוָּה: דֹּב אֹרֵב הוּא לִי אריה [אֲרִי]
בְּמִסְתָּרִים: דְּרָכַי סוֹרֵר וַיְפַשְּׁחֵנִי שָׂמַנִי
שׁוֹמֵם: דָּרַךְ קַשְׁתּוֹ וַיַּצִּיבֵנִי כַּמַּטָּרָא לַחֵץ:
הֵבִיא בְּכִלְיוֹתָי בְּנֵי אַשְׁפָּתוֹ: הָיִיתִי שְּׂחֹק
לְכָל־עַמִּי נְגִינָתָם כָּל־הַיּוֹם: הִשְׂבִּיעַנִי
בַמְּרוֹרִים הִרְוַנִי לַעֲנָה: וַיַּגְרֵס בֶּחָצָץ שִׁנָּי
הִכְפִּישַׁנִי בָּאֵפֶר: וַתִּזְנַח מִשָּׁלוֹם נַפְשִׁי
נָשִׁיתִי טוֹבָה: וָאֹמַר אָבַד נִצְחִי וְתוֹחַלְתִּי
מֵיהוה: זְכָר־עָנְיִי וּמְרוּדִי לַעֲנָה וָרֹאשׁ: זָכוֹר
תִּזְכּוֹר ותשיח [וְתָשׁוֹחַ] עָלַי נַפְשִׁי: זֹאת
אָשִׁיב אֶל־לִבִּי עַל־כֵּן אוֹחִיל: חַסְדֵי יהוה
כִּי לֹא־תָמְנוּ כִּי לֹא־כָלוּ רַחֲמָיו: חֲדָשִׁים
לַבְּקָרִים רַבָּה אֱמוּנָתֶךָ: חֶלְקִי יהוה אָמְרָה
נַפְשִׁי עַל־כֵּן אוֹחִיל לוֹ: טוֹב יהוה לְקֹוָו
לְנֶפֶשׁ תִּדְרְשֶׁנּוּ: טוֹב וְיָחִיל וְדוּמָם לִתְשׁוּעַת
יהוה: טוֹב לַגֶּבֶר כִּי־יִשָּׂא עֹל בִּנְעוּרָיו: יֵשֵׁב
בָּדָד וְיִדֹּם כִּי נָטַל עָלָיו: יִתֵּן בֶּעָפָר פִּיהוּ
אוּלַי יֵשׁ תִּקְוָה: יִתֵּן לְמַכֵּהוּ לֶחִי יִשְׂבַּע
בְּחֶרְפָּה: כִּי לֹא יִזְנַח לְעוֹלָם אֲדֹנָי: כִּי אִם־
הוֹגָה וְרִחַם כְּרֹב חֲסָדָו: כִּי לֹא עִנָּה מִלִּבּוֹ
וַיַּגֶּה בְּנֵי־אִישׁ: לְדַכֵּא תַּחַת רַגְלָיו כֹּל אֲסִירֵי
אָרֶץ: לְהַטּוֹת מִשְׁפַּט־גָּבֶר נֶגֶד פְּנֵי עֶלְיוֹן:
לְעַוֵּת אָדָם בְּרִיבוֹ אֲדֹנָי לֹא רָאָה: מִי זֶה
אָמַר וַתֶּהִי אֲדֹנָי לֹא צִוָּה: מִפִּי עֶלְיוֹן לֹא
תֵצֵא הָרָעוֹת וְהַטּוֹב: מַה־יִּתְאוֹנֵן אָדָם חָי
גֶּבֶר עַל־חֲטָאָו: נַחְפְּשָׂה דְרָכֵינוּ וְנַחְקֹרָה
וְנָשׁוּבָה עַד־יהוה: נִשָּׂא לְבָבֵנוּ אֶל־כַּפָּיִם
אֶל־אֵל בַּשָּׁמָיִם: נַחְנוּ פָשַׁעְנוּ וּמָרִינוּ אַתָּה
לֹא סָלָחְתָּ: סַכֹּתָה בָאַף וַתִּרְדְּפֵנוּ הָרַגְתָּ
לֹא חָמָלְתָּ: סַכֹּתָה בֶעָנָן לָךְ מֵעֲבוֹר תְּפִלָּה:
סְחִי וּמָאוֹס תְּשִׂימֵנוּ בְּקֶרֶב הָעַמִּים: פָּצוּ
עָלֵינוּ פִּיהֶם כָּל־אֹיְבֵינוּ: פַּחַד וָפַחַת הָיָה
לָנוּ הַשֵּׁאת וְהַשָּׁבֶר: פַּלְגֵי־מַיִם תֵּרַד עֵינִי
עַל־שֶׁבֶר בַּת־עַמִּי: עֵינִי נִגְּרָה וְלֹא תִדְמֶה
מֵאֵין הֲפֻגוֹת: עַד־יַשְׁקִיף וְיֵרֶא יהוה מִשָּׁמָיִם:
עֵינִי עוֹלְלָה לְנַפְשִׁי מִכֹּל בְּנוֹת עִירִי: צוֹד
צָדוּנִי כַּצִּפּוֹר אֹיְבַי חִנָּם: צָמְתוּ בַבּוֹר חַיָּי
וַיַּדּוּ־אֶבֶן בִּי: צָפוּ־מַיִם עַל־רֹאשִׁי אָמַרְתִּי
נִגְזָרְתִּי: קָרָאתִי שִׁמְךָ יהוה מִבּוֹר תַּחְתִּיּוֹת:
קוֹלִי שָׁמָעְתָּ אַל־תַּעְלֵם אָזְנְךָ לְרַוְחָתִי
לְשַׁוְעָתִי: קָרַבְתָּ בְּיוֹם אֶקְרָאֶךָּ אָמַרְתָּ אַל־
תִּירָא: רַבְתָּ אֲדֹנָי רִיבֵי נַפְשִׁי גָּאַלְתָּ חַיָּי:
רָאִיתָה יהוה עַוָּתָתִי שָׁפְטָה מִשְׁפָּטִי:
רָאִיתָה כָּל־נִקְמָתָם כָּל־מַחְשְׁבֹתָם לִי:
שָׁמַעְתָּ חֶרְפָּתָם יהוה כָּל־מַחְשְׁבֹתָם עָלָי:
שִׂפְתֵי קָמַי וְהֶגְיוֹנָם עָלַי כָּל־הַיּוֹם: שִׁבְתָּם
וְקִימָתָם הַבִּיטָה אֲנִי מַנְגִּינָתָם: תָּשִׁיב לָהֶם
גְּמוּל יהוה כְּמַעֲשֵׂה יְדֵיהֶם: תִּתֵּן לָהֶם מְגִנַּת־
לֵב תַּאֲלָתְךָ לָהֶם: תִּרְדֹּף בְּאַף וְתַשְׁמִידֵם
מִתַּחַת שְׁמֵי יהוה:
ד אֵיכָה יוּעַם זָהָב יִשְׁנֶא הַכֶּתֶם הַטּוֹב
תִּשְׁתַּפֵּכְנָה אַבְנֵי־קֹדֶשׁ בְּרֹאשׁ כָּל־חוּצוֹת:
בְּנֵי צִיּוֹן הַיְקָרִים הַמְסֻלָּאִים בַּפָּז אֵיכָה

נֶחְשְׁבוּ לְנִבְלֵי־חֶרֶשׂ מַעֲשֵׂה יְדֵי יוֹצֵר: גַּם־
תנין [תַּנִּים] חָלְצוּ שַׁד הֵינִיקוּ גּוּרֵיהֶן בַּת־
עַמִּי לְאַכְזָר כי ענים [כַּיְעֵנִים] בַּמִּדְבָּר: דָּבַק
לְשׁוֹן יוֹנֵק אֶל־חִכּוֹ בַּצָּמָא עוֹלָלִים שָׁאֲלוּ
לֶחֶם פֹּרֵשׂ אֵין לָהֶם: הָאֹכְלִים לְמַעֲדַנִּים
נָשַׁמּוּ בַּחוּצוֹת הָאֱמֻנִים עֲלֵי תוֹלָע חִבְּקוּ
אַשְׁפַּתּוֹת: וַיִּגְדַּל עֲוֺן בַּת־עַמִּי מֵחַטַּאת
סְדֹם הַהֲפוּכָה כְמוֹ־רָגַע וְלֹא־חָלוּ בָהּ יָדָיִם:
זַכּוּ נְזִירֶיהָ מִשֶּׁלֶג צַחוּ מֵחָלָב אָדְמוּ עֶצֶם
מִפְּנִינִים סַפִּיר גִּזְרָתָם: חָשַׁךְ מִשְּׁחוֹר תָּאֳרָם
לֹא נִכְּרוּ בַּחוּצוֹת צָפַד עוֹרָם עַל־עַצְמָם
יָבֵשׁ הָיָה כָעֵץ: טוֹבִים הָיוּ חַלְלֵי־חֶרֶב
מֵחַלְלֵי רָעָב שֶׁהֵם יָזוּבוּ מְדֻקָּרִים מִתְּנוּבֹת
שָׂדָי: יְדֵי נָשִׁים רַחֲמָנִיּוֹת בִּשְּׁלוּ יַלְדֵיהֶן הָיוּ
לְבָרוֹת לָמוֹ בְּשֶׁבֶר בַּת־עַמִּי: כִּלָּה יהוה
אֶת־חֲמָתוֹ שָׁפַךְ חֲרוֹן אַפּוֹ וַיַּצֶּת־אֵשׁ בְּצִיּוֹן
וַתֹּאכַל יְסוֹדֹתֶיהָ: לֹא הֶאֱמִינוּ מַלְכֵי־אֶרֶץ
וכל [כֹּל] יֹשְׁבֵי תֵבֵל כִּי יָבֹא צַר וְאוֹיֵב
בְּשַׁעֲרֵי יְרוּשָׁלָ͏ִם: מֵחַטֹּאת נְבִיאֶיהָ עֲוֺנֹת
כֹּהֲנֶיהָ הַשֹּׁפְכִים בְּקִרְבָּהּ דַּם צַדִּיקִים: נָעוּ
עִוְרִים בַּחוּצוֹת נְגֹאֲלוּ בַּדָּם בְּלֹא יוּכְלוּ
יִגְּעוּ בִּלְבֻשֵׁיהֶם: סוּרוּ טָמֵא קָרְאוּ לָמוֹ
סוּרוּ סוּרוּ אַל־תִּגָּעוּ כִּי נָצוּ גַּם־נָעוּ אָמְרוּ
בַּגּוֹיִם לֹא יוֹסִפוּ לָגוּר: פְּנֵי יהוה חִלְּקָם לֹא
יוֹסִיף לְהַבִּיטָם פְּנֵי כֹהֲנִים לֹא נָשָׂאוּ
זקנים [וּזְקֵנִים] לֹא חָנָנוּ: עודינה [עוֹדֵינוּ]
תִּכְלֶינָה עֵינֵינוּ אֶל־עֶזְרָתֵנוּ הָבֶל בְּצִפִּיָּתֵנוּ
צִפִּינוּ אֶל־גּוֹי לֹא יוֹשִׁעַ: צָדוּ צְעָדֵינוּ מִלֶּכֶת
בִּרְחֹבֹתֵינוּ קָרַב קִצֵּנוּ מָלְאוּ יָמֵינוּ כִּי־בָא
קִצֵּנוּ: קַלִּים הָיוּ רֹדְפֵינוּ מִנִּשְׁרֵי שָׁמָיִם עַל־
הֶהָרִים דְּלָקֻנוּ בַּמִּדְבָּר אָרְבוּ לָנוּ: רוּחַ אַפֵּינוּ
מְשִׁיחַ יהוה נִלְכַּד בִּשְׁחִיתוֹתָם אֲשֶׁר אָמַרְנוּ
בְּצִלּוֹ נִחְיֶה בַגּוֹיִם: שִׂישִׂי וְשִׂמְחִי בַּת־אֱדוֹם
יושבתי [יוֹשֶׁבֶת] בְּאֶרֶץ עוּץ גַּם־עָלַיִךְ
תַּעֲבָר־כּוֹס תִּשְׁכְּרִי וְתִתְעָרִי: תַּם־עֲוֺנֵךְ
בַּת־צִיּוֹן לֹא יוֹסִיף לְהַגְלוֹתֵךְ פָּקַד עֲוֺנֵךְ
בַּת־אֱדוֹם גִּלָּה עַל־חַטֹּאתָיִךְ:

ה זְכֹר יהוה מֶה־הָיָה לָנוּ הַבִּיטָ וּרְאֵה אֶת־
חֶרְפָּתֵנוּ: נַחֲלָתֵנוּ נֶהֶפְכָה לְזָרִים בָּתֵּינוּ
לְנָכְרִים: יְתוֹמִים הָיִינוּ אין [וְאֵין] אָב
אִמֹּתֵינוּ כְּאַלְמָנוֹת: מֵימֵינוּ בְּכֶסֶף שָׁתִינוּ
עֵצֵינוּ בִּמְחִיר יָבֹאוּ: עַל צַוָּארֵנוּ נִרְדָּפְנוּ
יָגַעְנוּ לא [וְלֹא] הוּנַח־לָנוּ: מִצְרַיִם נָתַנּוּ
יָד אַשּׁוּר לִשְׂבֹּעַ לָחֶם: אֲבֹתֵינוּ חָטְאוּ
אינם [וְאֵינָם] אנחנו [וַאֲנַחְנוּ] עֲוֺנֹתֵיהֶם
סָבָלְנוּ: עֲבָדִים מָשְׁלוּ בָנוּ פֹּרֵק אֵין מִיָּדָם:
בְּנַפְשֵׁנוּ נָבִיא לַחְמֵנוּ מִפְּנֵי חֶרֶב הַמִּדְבָּר:
עוֹרֵנוּ כְּתַנּוּר נִכְמָרוּ מִפְּנֵי זַלְעֲפוֹת רָעָב:
נָשִׁים בְּצִיּוֹן עִנּוּ בְּתֻלֹת בְּעָרֵי יְהוּדָה: שָׂרִים
בְּיָדָם נִתְלוּ פְּנֵי זְקֵנִים לֹא נֶהְדָּרוּ: בַּחוּרִים
טְחוֹן נָשָׂאוּ וּנְעָרִים בָּעֵץ כָּשָׁלוּ: זְקֵנִים
מִשַּׁעַר שָׁבָתוּ בַּחוּרִים מִנְּגִינָתָם: שָׁבַת
מְשׂוֹשׂ לִבֵּנוּ נֶהְפַּךְ לְאֵבֶל מְחֹלֵנוּ: נָפְלָה
עֲטֶרֶת רֹאשֵׁנוּ אוֹי־נָא לָנוּ כִּי חָטָאנוּ: עַל־
זֶה הָיָה דָוֶה לִבֵּנוּ עַל־אֵלֶּה חָשְׁכוּ עֵינֵינוּ:
עַל הַר־צִיּוֹן שֶׁשָּׁמֵם שׁוּעָלִים הִלְּכוּ־בוֹ:
אַתָּה יהוה לְעוֹלָם תֵּשֵׁב כִּסְאֲךָ לְדֹר וָדוֹר:
לָמָּה לָנֶצַח תִּשְׁכָּחֵנוּ תַּעַזְבֵנוּ לְאֹרֶךְ יָמִים:
הֲשִׁיבֵנוּ יהוה ׀ אֵלֶיךָ וְנָשׁוּבָה חַדֵּשׁ יָמֵינוּ
כְּקֶדֶם: כִּי אִם־מָאֹס מְאַסְתָּנוּ קָצַפְתָּ עָלֵינוּ
עַד־מְאֹד:

השיבנו יהוה אליך ונשובה חדש ימינו כקדם

ECCLESIASTES / קהלת

קהלת is read before קריאת התורה on the שבת of חול המועד סוכות. In the event there is no שבת during חול המועד, it is read on שמיני עצרת.

א דִּבְרֵי קֹהֶלֶת בֶּן־דָּוִד מֶלֶךְ בִּירוּשָׁלָ͏ִם: הֲבֵל
הֲבָלִים אָמַר קֹהֶלֶת הֲבֵל הֲבָלִים הַכֹּל הָבֶל:
מַה־יִּתְרוֹן לָאָדָם בְּכָל־עֲמָלוֹ שֶׁיַּעֲמֹל תַּחַת
הַשָּׁמֶשׁ: דּוֹר הֹלֵךְ וְדוֹר בָּא וְהָאָרֶץ לְעוֹלָם
עֹמָדֶת: וְזָרַח הַשֶּׁמֶשׁ וּבָא הַשָּׁמֶשׁ וְאֶל־
מְקוֹמוֹ שׁוֹאֵף זוֹרֵחַ הוּא שָׁם: הוֹלֵךְ אֶל־
דָּרוֹם וְסוֹבֵב אֶל־צָפוֹן סוֹבֵב ׀ סֹבֵב הוֹלֵךְ

הָרֽוּחַ וְעַל־סְבִיבֹתָיו שָׁב הָרֽוּחַ: כָּל־הַנְּחָלִים
הֹלְכִים אֶל־הַיָּם וְהַיָּם אֵינֶנּוּ מָלֵא אֶל־מְקוֹם
שֶׁהַנְּחָלִים הֹלְכִים שָׁם הֵם שָׁבִים לָלָֽכֶת:
כָּל־הַדְּבָרִים יְגֵעִים לֹא־יוּכַל אִישׁ לְדַבֵּר לֹא־
תִשְׂבַּע עַיִן לִרְאוֹת וְלֹא־תִמָּלֵא אֹזֶן מִשְּׁמֹֽעַ:
מַה־שֶּׁהָיָה הוּא שֶׁיִּהְיֶה וּמַה־שֶּׁנַּעֲשָׂה הוּא
שֶׁיֵּעָשֶׂה וְאֵין כָּל־חָדָשׁ תַּחַת הַשָּֽׁמֶשׁ: יֵשׁ
דָּבָר שֶׁיֹּאמַר רְאֵה־זֶה חָדָשׁ הוּא כְּבָר הָיָה
לְעֹלָמִים אֲשֶׁר הָיָה מִלְּפָנֵֽנוּ: אֵין זִכְרוֹן
לָרִאשֹׁנִים וְגַם לָאַחֲרֹנִים שֶׁיִּהְיוּ לֹא־יִהְיֶה
לָהֶם זִכָּרוֹן עִם שֶׁיִּהְיוּ לָאַחֲרֹנָֽה:
אֲנִי קֹהֶלֶת הָיִיתִי מֶלֶךְ עַל־יִשְׂרָאֵל
בִּירוּשָׁלָֽם: וְנָתַתִּי אֶת־לִבִּי לִדְרוֹשׁ וְלָתוּר
בַּחָכְמָה עַל כָּל־אֲשֶׁר נַעֲשָׂה תַּחַת הַשָּׁמָיִם
הוּא ׀ עִנְיַן רָע נָתַן אֱלֹהִים לִבְנֵי הָאָדָם
לַעֲנוֹת בּֽוֹ: רָאִיתִי אֶת־כָּל־הַמַּעֲשִׂים
שֶׁנַּעֲשׂוּ תַּחַת הַשָּׁמֶשׁ וְהִנֵּה הַכֹּל הֶבֶל
וּרְעוּת רֽוּחַ: מְעֻוָּת לֹא־יוּכַל לִתְקֹן וְחֶסְרוֹן
לֹא־יוּכַל לְהִמָּנֽוֹת: דִּבַּרְתִּי אֲנִי עִם־לִבִּי
לֵאמֹר אֲנִי הִנֵּה הִגְדַּלְתִּי וְהוֹסַפְתִּי חָכְמָה
עַל כָּל־אֲשֶׁר־הָיָה לְפָנַי עַל־יְרוּשָׁלָם וְלִבִּי
רָאָה הַרְבֵּה חָכְמָה וָדָֽעַת: וָאֶתְּנָה לִבִּי לָדַעַת
חָכְמָה וְדַעַת הֹלֵלוֹת וְשִׂכְלוּת יָדַעְתִּי שֶׁגַּם־
זֶה הוּא רַעְיוֹן רֽוּחַ: כִּי בְּרֹב חָכְמָה רָב־
ב כָּעַס וְיוֹסִיף דַּעַת יוֹסִיף מַכְאֽוֹב: אָמַרְתִּי
אֲנִי בְּלִבִּי לְכָה־נָּא אֲנַסְּכָה בְשִׂמְחָה וּרְאֵה
בְטוֹב וְהִנֵּה גַם־הוּא הָֽבֶל: לִשְׂחוֹק אָמַרְתִּי
מְהוֹלָל וּלְשִׂמְחָה מַה־זֹּה עֹשָֽׂה: תַּרְתִּי בְלִבִּי
לִמְשׁוֹךְ בַּיַּיִן אֶת־בְּשָׂרִי וְלִבִּי נֹהֵג בַּחָכְמָה
וְלֶאֱחֹז בְּסִכְלוּת עַד אֲשֶׁר־אֶרְאֶה אֵי־זֶה
טוֹב לִבְנֵי הָאָדָם אֲשֶׁר יַעֲשׂוּ תַּחַת הַשָּׁמַיִם
מִסְפַּר יְמֵי חַיֵּיהֶֽם: הִגְדַּלְתִּי מַעֲשָׂי בָּנִיתִי לִי
בָּתִּים נָטַעְתִּי לִי כְּרָמִֽים: עָשִׂיתִי לִי גַּנּוֹת
וּפַרְדֵּסִים וְנָטַעְתִּי בָהֶם עֵץ כָּל־פֶּֽרִי: עָשִׂיתִי
לִי בְּרֵכוֹת מָיִם לְהַשְׁקוֹת מֵהֶם יַעַר צוֹמֵחַ
עֵצִֽים: קָנִיתִי עֲבָדִים וּשְׁפָחוֹת וּבְנֵי־בַיִת
הָיָה לִי גַּם מִקְנֶה בָקָר וָצֹאן הַרְבֵּה הָיָה לִי
מִכֹּל שֶׁהָיוּ לְפָנַי בִּירוּשָׁלָֽם: כָּנַסְתִּי לִי גַּם־
כֶּסֶף וְזָהָב וּסְגֻלַּת מְלָכִים וְהַמְּדִינוֹת עָשִׂיתִי
לִי שָׁרִים וְשָׁרוֹת וְתַעֲנֻגוֹת בְּנֵי הָאָדָם שִׁדָּה
וְשִׁדּֽוֹת: וְגָדַלְתִּי וְהוֹסַפְתִּי מִכֹּל שֶׁהָיָה לְפָנַי
בִּירוּשָׁלָם אַף חָכְמָתִי עָמְדָה לִּֽי: וְכֹל אֲשֶׁר
שָׁאֲלוּ עֵינַי לֹא אָצַלְתִּי מֵהֶם לֹא־מָנַעְתִּי
אֶת־לִבִּי מִכָּל־שִׂמְחָה כִּֽי־לִבִּי שָׂמֵחַ מִכָּל־
עֲמָלִי וְזֶה־הָיָה חֶלְקִי מִכָּל־עֲמָלִֽי: וּפָנִיתִי
אֲנִי בְּכָל־מַעֲשַׂי שֶׁעָשׂוּ יָדַי וּבֶעָמָל שֶׁעָמַלְתִּי
לַעֲשׂוֹת וְהִנֵּה הַכֹּל הֶבֶל וּרְעוּת רוּחַ וְאֵין
יִתְרוֹן תַּחַת הַשָּֽׁמֶשׁ: וּפָנִיתִי אֲנִי לִרְאוֹת
חָכְמָה וְהוֹלֵלוֹת וְסִכְלוּת כִּי ׀ מֶה הָאָדָם
שֶׁיָּבוֹא אַחֲרֵי הַמֶּלֶךְ אֵת אֲשֶׁר־כְּבָר עָשֽׂוּהוּ:
וְרָאִיתִי אָנִי שֶׁיֵּשׁ יִתְרוֹן לַחָכְמָה מִן־
הַסִּכְלוּת כִּיתְרוֹן הָאוֹר מִן־הַחֹֽשֶׁךְ: הֶחָכָם
עֵינָיו בְּרֹאשׁוֹ וְהַכְּסִיל בַּחֹשֶׁךְ הוֹלֵךְ וְיָדַעְתִּי
גַם־אָנִי שֶׁמִּקְרֶה אֶחָד יִקְרֶה אֶת־כֻּלָּֽם:
וְאָמַרְתִּי אֲנִי בְּלִבִּי כְּמִקְרֵה הַכְּסִיל גַּם־אֲנִי
יִקְרֵנִי וְלָמָּה חָכַמְתִּי אֲנִי אָז יוֹתֵר וְדִבַּרְתִּי
בְלִבִּי שֶׁגַּם־זֶה הָֽבֶל: כִּי אֵין זִכְרוֹן לֶחָכָם
עִם־הַכְּסִיל לְעוֹלָם בְּשֶׁכְּבָר הַיָּמִים הַבָּאִים
הַכֹּל נִשְׁכָּח וְאֵיךְ יָמוּת הֶחָכָם עִם־הַכְּסִֽיל:
וְשָׂנֵאתִי אֶת־הַחַיִּים כִּי רַע עָלַי הַמַּעֲשֶׂה
שֶׁנַּעֲשָׂה תַּחַת הַשָּׁמֶשׁ כִּי־הַכֹּל הֶבֶל וּרְעוּת
רֽוּחַ: וְשָׂנֵאתִי אֲנִי אֶת־כָּל־עֲמָלִי שֶׁאֲנִי
עָמֵל תַּחַת הַשָּׁמֶשׁ שֶׁאַנִּיחֶנּוּ לָאָדָם שֶׁיִּהְיֶה
אַחֲרָֽי: וּמִי יוֹדֵעַ הֶחָכָם יִהְיֶה אוֹ סָכָל וְיִשְׁלַט
בְּכָל־עֲמָלִי שֶׁעָמַלְתִּי וְשֶׁחָכַמְתִּי תַּחַת
הַשָּׁמֶשׁ גַּם־זֶה הָֽבֶל: וְסַבּוֹתִי אֲנִי לְיַאֵשׁ
אֶת־לִבִּי עַל כָּל־הֶעָמָל שֶׁעָמַלְתִּי תַּחַת
הַשָּֽׁמֶשׁ: כִּי־יֵשׁ אָדָם שֶׁעֲמָלוֹ בְּחָכְמָה
וּבְדַעַת וּבְכִשְׁרוֹן וּלְאָדָם שֶׁלֹּא עָמַל־בּוֹ
יִתְּנֶנּוּ חֶלְקוֹ גַּם־זֶה הֶבֶל וְרָעָה רַבָּֽה: כִּי מֶה־
הֹוֶה לָאָדָם בְּכָל־עֲמָלוֹ וּבְרַעְיוֹן לִבּוֹ שֶׁהוּא
עָמֵל תַּחַת הַשָּֽׁמֶשׁ: כִּי כָל־יָמָיו מַכְאֹבִים
וָכַעַס עִנְיָנוֹ גַּם־בַּלַּיְלָה לֹא־שָׁכַב לִבּוֹ גַּם־
זֶה הֶבֶל הֽוּא: אֵין־טוֹב בָּאָדָם שֶׁיֹּאכַל

וְשָׁתָה וְהֶרְאָה אֶת־נַפְשׁוֹ טוֹב בַּעֲמָלוֹ גַּם־
זֹה רָאִיתִי אָנִי כִּי מִיַּד הָאֱלֹהִים הִיא׃ כִּי
מִי יֹאכַל וּמִי יָחוּשׁ חוּץ מִמֶּנִּי׃ כִּי לְאָדָם
שֶׁטּוֹב לְפָנָיו נָתַן חָכְמָה וְדַעַת וְשִׂמְחָה
וְלַחוֹטֶא נָתַן עִנְיָן לֶאֱסֹף וְלִכְנוֹס לָתֵת לְטוֹב
לִפְנֵי הָאֱלֹהִים גַּם־זֶה הֶבֶל וּרְעוּת רוּחַ׃
ג לַכֹּל זְמָן וְעֵת לְכָל־חֵפֶץ תַּחַת הַשָּׁמָיִם׃

עֵת לָלֶדֶת וְעֵת לָמוּת
עֵת לָטַעַת וְעֵת לַעֲקוֹר נָטוּעַ׃
עֵת לַהֲרוֹג וְעֵת לִרְפּוֹא
עֵת לִפְרוֹץ וְעֵת לִבְנוֹת׃
עֵת לִבְכּוֹת וְעֵת לִשְׂחוֹק
עֵת סְפוֹד וְעֵת רְקוֹד׃
עֵת לְהַשְׁלִיךְ אֲבָנִים וְעֵת כְּנוֹס אֲבָנִים
עֵת לַחֲבוֹק וְעֵת לִרְחֹק מֵחַבֵּק׃
עֵת לְבַקֵּשׁ וְעֵת לְאַבֵּד
עֵת לִשְׁמוֹר וְעֵת לְהַשְׁלִיךְ׃
עֵת לִקְרוֹעַ וְעֵת לִתְפּוֹר
עֵת לַחֲשׁוֹת וְעֵת לְדַבֵּר׃
עֵת לֶאֱהֹב וְעֵת לִשְׂנֹא
עֵת מִלְחָמָה וְעֵת שָׁלוֹם׃

מַה־יִּתְרוֹן הָעוֹשֶׂה בַּאֲשֶׁר הוּא עָמֵל׃ רָאִיתִי
אֶת־הָעִנְיָן אֲשֶׁר נָתַן אֱלֹהִים לִבְנֵי הָאָדָם
לַעֲנוֹת בּוֹ׃ אֶת־הַכֹּל עָשָׂה יָפֶה בְעִתּוֹ גַּם
אֶת־הָעֹלָם נָתַן בְּלִבָּם מִבְּלִי אֲשֶׁר לֹא־
יִמְצָא הָאָדָם אֶת־הַמַּעֲשֶׂה אֲשֶׁר־עָשָׂה
הָאֱלֹהִים מֵרֹאשׁ וְעַד־סוֹף׃ יָדַעְתִּי כִּי אֵין
טוֹב בָּם כִּי אִם־לִשְׂמוֹחַ וְלַעֲשׂוֹת טוֹב
בְּחַיָּיו׃ וְגַם כָּל־הָאָדָם שֶׁיֹּאכַל וְשָׁתָה וְרָאָה
טוֹב בְּכָל־עֲמָלוֹ מַתַּת אֱלֹהִים הִיא׃ יָדַעְתִּי
כִּי כָּל־אֲשֶׁר יַעֲשֶׂה הָאֱלֹהִים הוּא יִהְיֶה
לְעוֹלָם עָלָיו אֵין לְהוֹסִיף וּמִמֶּנּוּ אֵין לִגְרֹעַ
וְהָאֱלֹהִים עָשָׂה שֶׁיִּרְאוּ מִלְּפָנָיו׃ מַה־שֶּׁהָיָה
כְּבָר הוּא וַאֲשֶׁר לִהְיוֹת כְּבָר הָיָה וְהָאֱלֹהִים
יְבַקֵּשׁ אֶת־נִרְדָּף׃ וְעוֹד רָאִיתִי תַּחַת הַשָּׁמֶשׁ
מְקוֹם הַמִּשְׁפָּט שָׁמָּה הָרֶשַׁע וּמְקוֹם הַצֶּדֶק
שָׁמָּה הָרָשַׁע׃ אָמַרְתִּי אֲנִי בְּלִבִּי אֶת־הַצַּדִּיק
וְאֶת־הָרָשָׁע יִשְׁפֹּט הָאֱלֹהִים כִּי־עֵת לְכָל־
חֵפֶץ וְעַל כָּל־הַמַּעֲשֶׂה שָׁם׃ אָמַרְתִּי אֲנִי
בְּלִבִּי עַל־דִּבְרַת בְּנֵי הָאָדָם לְבָרָם הָאֱלֹהִים
וְלִרְאוֹת שְׁהֶם־בְּהֵמָה הֵמָּה לָהֶם׃ כִּי מִקְרֶה
בְנֵי־הָאָדָם וּמִקְרֶה הַבְּהֵמָה וּמִקְרֶה אֶחָד
לָהֶם כְּמוֹת זֶה כֵּן מוֹת זֶה וְרוּחַ אֶחָד לַכֹּל
וּמוֹתַר הָאָדָם מִן־הַבְּהֵמָה אָיִן כִּי הַכֹּל הָבֶל׃
הַכֹּל הוֹלֵךְ אֶל־מָקוֹם אֶחָד הַכֹּל הָיָה מִן־
הֶעָפָר וְהַכֹּל שָׁב אֶל־הֶעָפָר׃ מִי יוֹדֵעַ רוּחַ
בְּנֵי הָאָדָם הָעֹלָה הִיא לְמָעְלָה וְרוּחַ
הַבְּהֵמָה הַיֹּרֶדֶת הִיא לְמַטָּה לָאָרֶץ׃ וְרָאִיתִי
כִּי אֵין טוֹב מֵאֲשֶׁר יִשְׂמַח הָאָדָם בְּמַעֲשָׂיו
כִּי־הוּא חֶלְקוֹ כִּי מִי יְבִיאֶנּוּ לִרְאוֹת בְּמֶה
ד שֶׁיִּהְיֶה אַחֲרָיו׃ וְשַׁבְתִּי אֲנִי וָאֶרְאֶה אֶת־כָּל־
הָעֲשֻׁקִים אֲשֶׁר נַעֲשִׂים תַּחַת הַשָּׁמֶשׁ
וְהִנֵּה ׀ דִּמְעַת הָעֲשֻׁקִים וְאֵין לָהֶם מְנַחֵם
וּמִיַּד עֹשְׁקֵיהֶם כֹּחַ וְאֵין לָהֶם מְנַחֵם׃ וְשַׁבֵּחַ
אֲנִי אֶת־הַמֵּתִים שֶׁכְּבָר מֵתוּ מִן־הַחַיִּים
אֲשֶׁר הֵמָּה חַיִּים עֲדֶנָה׃ וְטוֹב מִשְּׁנֵיהֶם אֵת
אֲשֶׁר־עֲדֶן לֹא הָיָה אֲשֶׁר לֹא־רָאָה אֶת־
הַמַּעֲשֶׂה הָרָע אֲשֶׁר נַעֲשָׂה תַּחַת הַשָּׁמֶשׁ׃
וְרָאִיתִי אֲנִי אֶת־כָּל־עָמָל וְאֵת כָּל־כִּשְׁרוֹן
הַמַּעֲשֶׂה כִּי הִיא קִנְאַת־אִישׁ מֵרֵעֵהוּ גַּם־זֶה
הֶבֶל וּרְעוּת רוּחַ׃ הַכְּסִיל חֹבֵק אֶת־יָדָיו
וְאֹכֵל אֶת־בְּשָׂרוֹ׃ טוֹב מְלֹא כַף נָחַת מִמְּלֹא
חָפְנַיִם עָמָל וּרְעוּת רוּחַ׃ וְשַׁבְתִּי אֲנִי וָאֶרְאֶה
הֶבֶל תַּחַת הַשָּׁמֶשׁ׃ יֵשׁ אֶחָד וְאֵין שֵׁנִי גַּם
בֵּן וָאָח אֵין־לוֹ וְאֵין קֵץ לְכָל־עֲמָלוֹ גַּם־
עֵינָיו [עינו] לֹא־תִשְׂבַּע עֹשֶׁר וּלְמִי ׀ אֲנִי
עָמֵל וּמְחַסֵּר אֶת־נַפְשִׁי מִטּוֹבָה גַּם־זֶה הֶבֶל
וְעִנְיַן רָע הוּא׃ טוֹבִים הַשְּׁנַיִם מִן־הָאֶחָד
אֲשֶׁר יֵשׁ־לָהֶם שָׂכָר טוֹב בַּעֲמָלָם׃ כִּי אִם־
יִפֹּלוּ הָאֶחָד יָקִים אֶת־חֲבֵרוֹ וְאִילוֹ הָאֶחָד
שֶׁיִּפּוֹל וְאֵין שֵׁנִי לַהֲקִימוֹ׃ גַּם אִם־יִשְׁכְּבוּ
שְׁנַיִם וְחַם לָהֶם וּלְאֶחָד אֵיךְ יֵחָם׃ וְאִם־

יִתְקְפוֹ הָאֶחָד הַשְּׁנַיִם יַעַמְדוּ נֶגְדּוֹ וְהַחוּט
הַמְשֻׁלָּשׁ לֹא בִמְהֵרָה יִנָּתֵק: טוֹב יֶלֶד מִסְכֵּן
וְחָכָם מִמֶּלֶךְ זָקֵן וּכְסִיל אֲשֶׁר לֹא־יָדַע
לְהִזָּהֵר עוֹד: כִּי־מִבֵּית הָסוּרִים יָצָא לִמְלֹךְ
כִּי גַּם בְּמַלְכוּתוֹ נוֹלַד רָשׁ: רָאִיתִי אֶת־כָּל־
הַחַיִּים הַמְהַלְּכִים תַּחַת הַשָּׁמֶשׁ עִם הַיֶּלֶד
הַשֵּׁנִי אֲשֶׁר יַעֲמֹד תַּחְתָּיו: אֵין־קֵץ לְכָל־
הָעָם לְכֹל אֲשֶׁר־הָיָה לִפְנֵיהֶם גַּם הָאַחֲרוֹנִים
לֹא יִשְׂמְחוּ־בוֹ כִּי־גַם־זֶה הֶבֶל וְרַעְיוֹן רוּחַ:
שְׁמוֹר רגליך [רַגְלְךָ] כַּאֲשֶׁר תֵּלֵךְ אֶל־בֵּית
הָאֱלֹהִים וְקָרוֹב לִשְׁמֹעַ מִתֵּת הַכְּסִילִים זָבַח
ה כִּי־אֵינָם יוֹדְעִים לַעֲשׂוֹת רָע: אַל־תְּבַהֵל
עַל־פִּיךָ וְלִבְּךָ אַל־יְמַהֵר לְהוֹצִיא דָבָר לִפְנֵי
הָאֱלֹהִים כִּי הָאֱלֹהִים בַּשָּׁמַיִם וְאַתָּה עַל־
הָאָרֶץ עַל־כֵּן יִהְיוּ דְבָרֶיךָ מְעַטִּים: כִּי בָּא
הַחֲלוֹם בְּרֹב עִנְיָן וְקוֹל כְּסִיל בְּרֹב דְּבָרִים:
כַּאֲשֶׁר תִּדֹּר נֶדֶר לֵאלֹהִים אַל־תְּאַחֵר
לְשַׁלְּמוֹ כִּי אֵין חֵפֶץ בַּכְּסִילִים אֵת אֲשֶׁר־תִּדֹּר
שַׁלֵּם: טוֹב אֲשֶׁר לֹא־תִדֹּר מִשֶּׁתִּדּוֹר וְלֹא
תְשַׁלֵּם: אַל־תִּתֵּן אֶת־פִּיךָ לַחֲטִיא אֶת־
בְּשָׂרֶךָ וְאַל־תֹּאמַר לִפְנֵי הַמַּלְאָךְ כִּי שְׁגָגָה
הִיא לָמָּה יִקְצֹף הָאֱלֹהִים עַל־קוֹלֶךָ וְחִבֵּל
אֶת־מַעֲשֵׂה יָדֶיךָ: כִּי בְרֹב חֲלֹמוֹת וַהֲבָלִים
וּדְבָרִים הַרְבֵּה כִּי אֶת־הָאֱלֹהִים יְרָא: אִם־
עֹשֶׁק רָשׁ וְגֵזֶל מִשְׁפָּט וָצֶדֶק תִּרְאֶה בַמְּדִינָה
אַל־תִּתְמַהּ עַל־הַחֵפֶץ כִּי גָבֹהַּ מֵעַל גָּבֹהַּ
שֹׁמֵר וּגְבֹהִים עֲלֵיהֶם: וְיִתְרוֹן אֶרֶץ בַּכֹּל
הִיא [הוּא] מֶלֶךְ לְשָׂדֶה נֶעֱבָד: אֹהֵב כֶּסֶף
לֹא־יִשְׂבַּע כֶּסֶף וּמִי־אֹהֵב בֶּהָמוֹן לֹא תְבוּאָה
גַּם־זֶה הָבֶל: בִּרְבוֹת הַטּוֹבָה רַבּוּ אוֹכְלֶיהָ
וּמַה־כִּשְׁרוֹן לִבְעָלֶיהָ כִּי אִם־ראית [רְאוּת]
עֵינָיו: מְתוּקָה שְׁנַת הָעֹבֵד אִם־מְעַט וְאִם־
הַרְבֵּה יֹאכֵל וְהַשָּׂבָע לֶעָשִׁיר אֵינֶנּוּ מַנִּיחַ לוֹ
לִישׁוֹן: יֵשׁ רָעָה חוֹלָה רָאִיתִי תַּחַת הַשָּׁמֶשׁ
עֹשֶׁר שָׁמוּר לִבְעָלָיו לְרָעָתוֹ: וְאָבַד הָעֹשֶׁר
הַהוּא בְּעִנְיַן רָע וְהוֹלִיד בֵּן וְאֵין בְּיָדוֹ
מְאוּמָה: כַּאֲשֶׁר יָצָא מִבֶּטֶן אִמּוֹ עָרוֹם יָשׁוּב
לָלֶכֶת כְּשֶׁבָּא וּמְאוּמָה לֹא־יִשָּׂא בַעֲמָלוֹ
שֶׁיֹּלֵךְ בְּיָדוֹ: וְגַם־זֹה רָעָה חוֹלָה כָּל־עֻמַּת
שֶׁבָּא כֵּן יֵלֵךְ וּמַה־יִּתְרוֹן לוֹ שֶׁיַּעֲמֹל לָרוּחַ:
גַּם כָּל־יָמָיו בַּחֹשֶׁךְ יֹאכֵל וְכָעַס הַרְבֵּה וְחָלְיוֹ
וָקָצֶף: הִנֵּה אֲשֶׁר־רָאִיתִי אָנִי טוֹב אֲשֶׁר־יָפֶה
לֶאֱכוֹל וְלִשְׁתּוֹת וְלִרְאוֹת טוֹבָה בְּכָל־עֲמָלוֹ ׀
שֶׁיַּעֲמֹל תַּחַת־הַשֶּׁמֶשׁ מִסְפַּר יְמֵי־חַיָּו
אֲשֶׁר־נָתַן־לוֹ הָאֱלֹהִים כִּי־הוּא חֶלְקוֹ: גַּם
כָּל־הָאָדָם אֲשֶׁר נָתַן־לוֹ הָאֱלֹהִים עֹשֶׁר
וּנְכָסִים וְהִשְׁלִיטוֹ לֶאֱכֹל מִמֶּנּוּ וְלָשֵׂאת אֶת־
חֶלְקוֹ וְלִשְׂמֹחַ בַּעֲמָלוֹ זֹה מַתַּת אֱלֹהִים
הִיא: כִּי לֹא הַרְבֵּה יִזְכֹּר אֶת־יְמֵי חַיָּיו כִּי
ו הָאֱלֹהִים מַעֲנֶה בְּשִׂמְחַת לִבּוֹ: יֵשׁ רָעָה אֲשֶׁר
רָאִיתִי תַּחַת הַשָּׁמֶשׁ וְרַבָּה הִיא עַל־הָאָדָם:
אִישׁ אֲשֶׁר יִתֶּן־לוֹ הָאֱלֹהִים עֹשֶׁר וּנְכָסִים
וְכָבוֹד וְאֵינֶנּוּ חָסֵר לְנַפְשׁוֹ ׀ מִכֹּל אֲשֶׁר־
יִתְאַוֶּה וְלֹא־יַשְׁלִיטֶנּוּ הָאֱלֹהִים לֶאֱכֹל מִמֶּנּוּ
כִּי אִישׁ נָכְרִי יֹאכְלֶנּוּ זֶה הֶבֶל וָחֳלִי רָע הוּא:
אִם־יוֹלִיד אִישׁ מֵאָה וְשָׁנִים רַבּוֹת יִחְיֶה
וְרַב ׀ שֶׁיִּהְיוּ יְמֵי־שָׁנָיו וְנַפְשׁוֹ לֹא־תִשְׂבַּע
מִן־הַטּוֹבָה וְגַם־קְבוּרָה לֹא־הָיְתָה לּוֹ אָמַרְתִּי
טוֹב מִמֶּנּוּ הַנָּפֶל: כִּי־בַהֶבֶל בָּא וּבַחֹשֶׁךְ יֵלֵךְ
וּבַחֹשֶׁךְ שְׁמוֹ יְכֻסֶּה: גַּם־שֶׁמֶשׁ לֹא־רָאָה וְלֹא
יָדָע נַחַת לָזֶה מִזֶּה: וְאִלּוּ חָיָה אֶלֶף שָׁנִים
פַּעֲמַיִם וְטוֹבָה לֹא רָאָה הֲלֹא אֶל־מָקוֹם
אֶחָד הַכֹּל הוֹלֵךְ: כָּל־עֲמַל הָאָדָם לְפִיהוּ
וְגַם־הַנֶּפֶשׁ לֹא תִמָּלֵא: כִּי מַה־יּוֹתֵר לֶחָכָם
מִן־הַכְּסִיל מַה־לֶּעָנִי יוֹדֵעַ לַהֲלֹךְ נֶגֶד הַחַיִּים:
טוֹב מַרְאֵה עֵינַיִם מֵהֲלָךְ־נָפֶשׁ גַּם־זֶה הֶבֶל
וּרְעוּת רוּחַ: מַה־שֶּׁהָיָה כְּבָר נִקְרָא שְׁמוֹ
וְנוֹדָע אֲשֶׁר־הוּא אָדָם וְלֹא־יוּכַל לָדִין עִם
שהתקיף [שֶׁתַּקִּיף] מִמֶּנּוּ: כִּי יֵשׁ־דְּבָרִים
הַרְבֵּה מַרְבִּים הָבֶל מַה־יֹּתֵר לָאָדָם: כִּי מִי־
יוֹדֵעַ מַה־טּוֹב לָאָדָם בַּחַיִּים מִסְפַּר יְמֵי־חַיֵּי
הֶבְלוֹ וְיַעֲשֵׂם כַּצֵּל אֲשֶׁר מִי־יַגִּיד לָאָדָם

ז מַה־יִּהְיֶה אַחֲרָיו תַּחַת הַשָּׁמֶשׁ: טוֹב שֵׁם
מִשֶּׁמֶן טוֹב וְיוֹם הַמָּוֶת מִיּוֹם הִוָּלְדוֹ: טוֹב
לָלֶכֶת אֶל־בֵּית־אֵבֶל מִלֶּכֶת אֶל־בֵּית מִשְׁתֶּה
בַּאֲשֶׁר הוּא סוֹף כָּל־הָאָדָם וְהַחַי יִתֵּן אֶל־
לִבּוֹ: טוֹב כַּעַס מִשְּׂחוֹק כִּי־בְרֹעַ פָּנִים יִיטַב
לֵב: לֵב חֲכָמִים בְּבֵית אֵבֶל וְלֵב כְּסִילִים
בְּבֵית שִׂמְחָה: טוֹב לִשְׁמֹעַ גַּעֲרַת חָכָם
מֵאִישׁ שֹׁמֵעַ שִׁיר כְּסִילִים: כִּי כְקוֹל הַסִּירִים
תַּחַת הַסִּיר כֵּן שְׂחֹק הַכְּסִיל וְגַם־זֶה הָבֶל:
כִּי הָעֹשֶׁק יְהוֹלֵל חָכָם וִיאַבֵּד אֶת־לֵב מַתָּנָה:
טוֹב אַחֲרִית דָּבָר מֵרֵאשִׁיתוֹ טוֹב אֶרֶךְ־רוּחַ
מִגְּבַהּ רוּחַ: אַל־תְּבַהֵל בְּרוּחֲךָ לִכְעוֹס כִּי
כַעַס בְּחֵיק כְּסִילִים יָנוּחַ: אַל־תֹּאמַר מֶה
הָיָה שֶׁהַיָּמִים הָרִאשֹׁנִים הָיוּ טוֹבִים מֵאֵלֶּה
כִּי לֹא מֵחָכְמָה שָׁאַלְתָּ עַל־זֶה: טוֹבָה חָכְמָה
עִם־נַחֲלָה וְיֹתֵר לְרֹאֵי הַשָּׁמֶשׁ: כִּי בְּצֵל
הַחָכְמָה בְּצֵל הַכָּסֶף וְיִתְרוֹן דַּעַת הַחָכְמָה
תְּחַיֶּה בְעָלֶיהָ: רְאֵה אֶת־מַעֲשֵׂה הָאֱלֹהִים
כִּי מִי יוּכַל לְתַקֵּן אֵת אֲשֶׁר עִוְּתוֹ: בְּיוֹם
טוֹבָה הֱיֵה בְטוֹב וּבְיוֹם רָעָה רְאֵה גַּם אֶת־
זֶה לְעֻמַּת־זֶה עָשָׂה הָאֱלֹהִים עַל־דִּבְרַת
שֶׁלֹּא יִמְצָא הָאָדָם אַחֲרָיו מְאוּמָה: אֶת־
הַכֹּל רָאִיתִי בִּימֵי הֶבְלִי יֵשׁ צַדִּיק אֹבֵד בְּצִדְקוֹ
וְיֵשׁ רָשָׁע מַאֲרִיךְ בְּרָעָתוֹ: אַל־תְּהִי צַדִּיק
הַרְבֵּה וְאַל־תִּתְחַכַּם יוֹתֵר לָמָּה תִּשּׁוֹמֵם:
אַל־תִּרְשַׁע הַרְבֵּה וְאַל־תְּהִי סָכָל לָמָּה תָמוּת
בְּלֹא עִתֶּךָ: טוֹב אֲשֶׁר תֶּאֱחֹז בָּזֶה וְגַם־מִזֶּה
אַל־תַּנַּח אֶת־יָדֶךָ כִּי־יְרֵא אֱלֹהִים יֵצֵא אֶת־
כֻּלָּם: הַחָכְמָה תָּעֹז לֶחָכָם מֵעֲשָׂרָה שַׁלִּיטִים
אֲשֶׁר הָיוּ בָּעִיר: כִּי אָדָם אֵין צַדִּיק בָּאָרֶץ
אֲשֶׁר יַעֲשֶׂה־טּוֹב וְלֹא יֶחֱטָא: גַּם לְכָל־
הַדְּבָרִים אֲשֶׁר יְדַבֵּרוּ אַל־תִּתֵּן לִבֶּךָ אֲשֶׁר
לֹא־תִשְׁמַע אֶת־עַבְדְּךָ מְקַלְלֶךָ: כִּי גַּם־
פְּעָמִים רַבּוֹת יָדַע לִבֶּךָ אֲשֶׁר גַּם־אַתְּ קִלַּלְתָּ
אֲחֵרִים: כָּל־זֹה נִסִּיתִי בַחָכְמָה אָמַרְתִּי
אֶחְכָּמָה וְהִיא רְחוֹקָה מִמֶּנִּי: רָחוֹק מַה־
שֶּׁהָיָה וְעָמֹק ׀ עָמֹק מִי יִמְצָאֶנּוּ: סַבּוֹתִי אֲנִי
וְלִבִּי לָדַעַת וְלָתוּר וּבַקֵּשׁ חָכְמָה וְחֶשְׁבּוֹן
וְלָדַעַת רֶשַׁע כֶּסֶל וְהַסִּכְלוּת הוֹלֵלוֹת:
וּמוֹצֶא אֲנִי מַר מִמָּוֶת אֶת־הָאִשָּׁה אֲשֶׁר־
הִיא מְצוֹדִים וַחֲרָמִים לִבָּהּ אֲסוּרִים יָדֶיהָ
טוֹב לִפְנֵי הָאֱלֹהִים יִמָּלֵט מִמֶּנָּה וְחוֹטֵא
יִלָּכֶד בָּהּ: רְאֵה זֶה מָצָאתִי אָמְרָה קֹהֶלֶת
אַחַת לְאַחַת לִמְצֹא חֶשְׁבּוֹן: אֲשֶׁר עוֹד־
בִּקְשָׁה נַפְשִׁי וְלֹא מָצָאתִי אָדָם אֶחָד מֵאֶלֶף
מָצָאתִי וְאִשָּׁה בְכָל־אֵלֶּה לֹא מָצָאתִי: לְבַד
רְאֵה־זֶה מָצָאתִי אֲשֶׁר עָשָׂה הָאֱלֹהִים אֶת־
הָאָדָם יָשָׁר וְהֵמָּה בִקְשׁוּ חִשְּׁבֹנוֹת רַבִּים:
ח מִי כְּהֶחָכָם וּמִי יוֹדֵעַ פֵּשֶׁר דָּבָר חָכְמַת אָדָם
תָּאִיר פָּנָיו וְעֹז פָּנָיו יְשֻׁנֶּא: אֲנִי פִּי־מֶלֶךְ
שְׁמוֹר וְעַל דִּבְרַת שְׁבוּעַת אֱלֹהִים: אַל־
תִּבָּהֵל מִפָּנָיו תֵּלֵךְ אַל־תַּעֲמֹד בְּדָבָר רָע כִּי
כָּל־אֲשֶׁר יַחְפֹּץ יַעֲשֶׂה: בַּאֲשֶׁר דְּבַר־מֶלֶךְ
שִׁלְטוֹן וּמִי יֹאמַר־לוֹ מַה־תַּעֲשֶׂה: שׁוֹמֵר
מִצְוָה לֹא יֵדַע דָּבָר רָע וְעֵת וּמִשְׁפָּט יֵדַע
לֵב חָכָם: כִּי לְכָל־חֵפֶץ יֵשׁ עֵת וּמִשְׁפָּט
כִּי־רָעַת הָאָדָם רַבָּה עָלָיו: כִּי־אֵינֶנּוּ יֹדֵעַ
מַה־שֶּׁיִּהְיֶה כִּי כַּאֲשֶׁר יִהְיֶה מִי יַגִּיד לוֹ: אֵין
אָדָם שַׁלִּיט בָּרוּחַ לִכְלוֹא אֶת־הָרוּחַ וְאֵין
שִׁלְטוֹן בְּיוֹם הַמָּוֶת וְאֵין מִשְׁלַחַת בַּמִּלְחָמָה
וְלֹא־יְמַלֵּט רֶשַׁע אֶת־בְּעָלָיו: אֶת־כָּל־זֶה
רָאִיתִי וְנָתוֹן אֶת־לִבִּי לְכָל־מַעֲשֶׂה אֲשֶׁר
נַעֲשָׂה תַּחַת הַשָּׁמֶשׁ עֵת אֲשֶׁר שָׁלַט הָאָדָם
בְּאָדָם לְרַע לוֹ: וּבְכֵן רָאִיתִי רְשָׁעִים קְבֻרִים
וָבָאוּ וּמִמְּקוֹם קָדוֹשׁ יְהַלֵּכוּ וְיִשְׁתַּכְּחוּ בָעִיר
אֲשֶׁר כֵּן־עָשׂוּ גַּם־זֶה הָבֶל: אֲשֶׁר אֵין־נַעֲשָׂה
פִתְגָם מַעֲשֵׂה הָרָעָה מְהֵרָה עַל־כֵּן מָלֵא לֵב
בְּנֵי־הָאָדָם בָּהֶם לַעֲשׂוֹת רָע: אֲשֶׁר חֹטֶא
עֹשֶׂה רָע מְאַת וּמַאֲרִיךְ לוֹ כִּי גַּם־יוֹדֵעַ אָנִי
אֲשֶׁר יִהְיֶה־טּוֹב לְיִרְאֵי הָאֱלֹהִים אֲשֶׁר יִירְאוּ
מִלְּפָנָיו: וְטוֹב לֹא־יִהְיֶה לָרָשָׁע וְלֹא־יַאֲרִיךְ
יָמִים כַּצֵּל אֲשֶׁר אֵינֶנּוּ יָרֵא מִלִּפְנֵי אֱלֹהִים:

יֵשׁ־הֶבֶל אֲשֶׁר נַעֲשָׂה עַל־הָאָרֶץ אֲשֶׁר ׀
יֵשׁ צַדִּיקִים אֲשֶׁר מַגִּיעַ אֲלֵהֶם כְּמַעֲשֵׂה
הָרְשָׁעִים וְיֵשׁ רְשָׁעִים שֶׁמַּגִּיעַ אֲלֵהֶם
כְּמַעֲשֵׂה הַצַּדִּיקִים אָמַרְתִּי שֶׁגַּם־זֶה הָבֶל׃
וְשִׁבַּחְתִּי אֲנִי אֶת־הַשִּׂמְחָה אֲשֶׁר אֵין־טוֹב
לָאָדָם תַּחַת הַשֶּׁמֶשׁ כִּי אִם־לֶאֱכֹל וְלִשְׁתּוֹת
וְלִשְׂמוֹחַ וְהוּא יִלְוֶנּוּ בַעֲמָלוֹ יְמֵי חַיָּיו אֲשֶׁר־
נָתַן־לוֹ הָאֱלֹהִים תַּחַת הַשָּׁמֶשׁ׃ כַּאֲשֶׁר
נָתַתִּי אֶת־לִבִּי לָדַעַת חָכְמָה וְלִרְאוֹת אֶת־
הָעִנְיָן אֲשֶׁר נַעֲשָׂה עַל־הָאָרֶץ כִּי גַם בַּיּוֹם
וּבַלַּיְלָה שֵׁנָה בְּעֵינָיו אֵינֶנּוּ רֹאֶה׃ וְרָאִיתִי
אֶת־כָּל־מַעֲשֵׂה הָאֱלֹהִים כִּי לֹא יוּכַל הָאָדָם
לִמְצוֹא אֶת־הַמַּעֲשֶׂה אֲשֶׁר נַעֲשָׂה תַחַת־
הַשֶּׁמֶשׁ בְּשֶׁל אֲשֶׁר יַעֲמֹל הָאָדָם לְבַקֵּשׁ וְלֹא
יִמְצָא וְגַם אִם־יֹאמַר הֶחָכָם לָדַעַת לֹא יוּכַל
ט לִמְצֹא׃ כִּי אֶת־כָּל־זֶה נָתַתִּי אֶל־לִבִּי וְלָבוּר
אֶת־כָּל־זֶה אֲשֶׁר הַצַּדִּיקִים וְהַחֲכָמִים
וַעֲבָדֵיהֶם בְּיַד הָאֱלֹהִים גַּם־אַהֲבָה גַם־
שִׂנְאָה אֵין יוֹדֵעַ הָאָדָם הַכֹּל לִפְנֵיהֶם׃ הַכֹּל
כַּאֲשֶׁר לַכֹּל מִקְרֶה אֶחָד לַצַּדִּיק וְלָרָשָׁע
לַטּוֹב וְלַטָּהוֹר וְלַטָּמֵא וְלַזֹּבֵחַ וְלַאֲשֶׁר אֵינֶנּוּ
זֹבֵחַ כַּטּוֹב כַּחֹטֶא הַנִּשְׁבָּע כַּאֲשֶׁר שְׁבוּעָה
יָרֵא׃ זֶה ׀ רָע בְּכֹל אֲשֶׁר־נַעֲשָׂה תַּחַת הַשֶּׁמֶשׁ
כִּי־מִקְרֶה אֶחָד לַכֹּל וְגַם לֵב בְּנֵי־הָאָדָם
מָלֵא־רָע וְהוֹלֵלוֹת בִּלְבָבָם בְּחַיֵּיהֶם וְאַחֲרָיו
אֶל־הַמֵּתִים׃ כִּי־מִי אֲשֶׁר יבחר [יְחֻבַּר] אֶל
כָּל־הַחַיִּים יֵשׁ בִּטָּחוֹן כִּי־לְכֶלֶב חַי הוּא טוֹב
מִן־הָאַרְיֵה הַמֵּת׃ כִּי הַחַיִּים יוֹדְעִים שֶׁיָּמֻתוּ
וְהַמֵּתִים אֵינָם יוֹדְעִים מְאוּמָה וְאֵין־עוֹד
לָהֶם שָׂכָר כִּי נִשְׁכַּח זִכְרָם׃ גַּם אַהֲבָתָם
גַּם־שִׂנְאָתָם גַּם־קִנְאָתָם כְּבָר אָבָדָה וְחֵלֶק
אֵין־לָהֶם עוֹד לְעוֹלָם בְּכֹל אֲשֶׁר־נַעֲשָׂה
תַּחַת הַשָּׁמֶשׁ׃ לֵךְ אֱכֹל בְּשִׂמְחָה לַחְמֶךָ
וּשֲׁתֵה בְלֶב־טוֹב יֵינֶךָ כִּי כְבָר רָצָה הָאֱלֹהִים
אֶת־מַעֲשֶׂיךָ׃ בְּכָל־עֵת יִהְיוּ בְגָדֶיךָ לְבָנִים
וְשֶׁמֶן עַל־רֹאשְׁךָ אַל־יֶחְסָר׃ רְאֵה חַיִּים עִם־
אִשָּׁה אֲשֶׁר־אָהַבְתָּ כָּל־יְמֵי חַיֵּי הֶבְלֶךָ אֲשֶׁר
נָתַן־לְךָ תַּחַת הַשֶּׁמֶשׁ כֹּל יְמֵי הֶבְלֶךָ כִּי הוּא
חֶלְקְךָ בַּחַיִּים וּבַעֲמָלְךָ אֲשֶׁר־אַתָּה עָמֵל
תַּחַת הַשָּׁמֶשׁ׃ כֹּל אֲשֶׁר תִּמְצָא יָדְךָ לַעֲשׂוֹת
בְּכֹחֲךָ עֲשֵׂה כִּי אֵין מַעֲשֶׂה וְחֶשְׁבּוֹן וְדַעַת
וְחָכְמָה בִּשְׁאוֹל אֲשֶׁר אַתָּה הֹלֵךְ שָׁמָּה׃
שַׁבְתִּי וְרָאֹה תַחַת־הַשֶּׁמֶשׁ כִּי לֹא לַקַּלִּים
הַמֵּרוֹץ וְלֹא לַגִּבּוֹרִים הַמִּלְחָמָה וְגַם לֹא
לַחֲכָמִים לֶחֶם וְגַם לֹא לַנְּבֹנִים עֹשֶׁר וְגַם
לֹא לַיֹּדְעִים חֵן כִּי־עֵת וָפֶגַע יִקְרֶה אֶת־
כֻּלָּם׃ כִּי גַּם לֹא־יֵדַע הָאָדָם אֶת־עִתּוֹ כַּדָּגִים
שֶׁנֶּאֱחָזִים בִּמְצוֹדָה רָעָה וְכַצִּפֳּרִים הָאֲחֻזוֹת
בַּפָּח כָּהֵם יוּקָשִׁים בְּנֵי הָאָדָם לְעֵת רָעָה
כְּשֶׁתִּפּוֹל עֲלֵיהֶם פִּתְאֹם׃ גַּם־זֹה רָאִיתִי
חָכְמָה תַּחַת הַשָּׁמֶשׁ וּגְדוֹלָה הִיא אֵלָי׃ עִיר
קְטַנָּה וַאֲנָשִׁים בָּהּ מְעָט וּבָא־אֵלֶיהָ מֶלֶךְ
גָּדוֹל וְסָבַב אֹתָהּ וּבָנָה עָלֶיהָ מְצוֹדִים
גְּדֹלִים׃ וּמָצָא בָהּ אִישׁ מִסְכֵּן חָכָם וּמִלַּט־
הוּא אֶת־הָעִיר בְּחָכְמָתוֹ וְאָדָם לֹא זָכַר
אֶת־הָאִישׁ הַמִּסְכֵּן הַהוּא׃ וְאָמַרְתִּי אָנִי
טוֹבָה חָכְמָה מִגְּבוּרָה וְחָכְמַת הַמִּסְכֵּן בְּזוּיָה
וּדְבָרָיו אֵינָם נִשְׁמָעִים׃ דִּבְרֵי חֲכָמִים בְּנַחַת
נִשְׁמָעִים מִזַּעֲקַת מוֹשֵׁל בַּכְּסִילִים׃ טוֹבָה
חָכְמָה מִכְּלֵי קְרָב וְחוֹטֶא אֶחָד יְאַבֵּד טוֹבָה
י הַרְבֵּה׃ זְבוּבֵי מָוֶת יַבְאִישׁ יַבִּיעַ שֶׁמֶן רוֹקֵחַ
יָקָר מֵחָכְמָה מִכָּבוֹד סִכְלוּת מְעָט׃ לֵב חָכָם
לִימִינוֹ וְלֵב כְּסִיל לִשְׂמֹאלוֹ׃ וְגַם־בַּדֶּרֶךְ
כשהסכל [כְּשֶׁסָּכָל] הֹלֵךְ לִבּוֹ חָסֵר וְאָמַר
לַכֹּל סָכָל הוּא׃ אִם־רוּחַ הַמּוֹשֵׁל תַּעֲלֶה
עָלֶיךָ מְקוֹמְךָ אַל־תַּנַּח כִּי מַרְפֵּא יַנִּיחַ
חֲטָאִים גְּדוֹלִים׃ יֵשׁ רָעָה רָאִיתִי תַּחַת
הַשָּׁמֶשׁ כִּשְׁגָגָה שֶׁיֹּצָא מִלִּפְנֵי הַשַּׁלִּיט׃ נִתַּן
הַסֶּכֶל בַּמְּרוֹמִים רַבִּים וַעֲשִׁירִים בַּשֵּׁפֶל
יֵשֵׁבוּ׃ רָאִיתִי עֲבָדִים עַל־סוּסִים וְשָׂרִים
הֹלְכִים כַּעֲבָדִים עַל־הָאָרֶץ׃ חֹפֵר גּוּמָּץ בּוֹ
יִפּוֹל וּפֹרֵץ גָּדֵר יִשְּׁכֶנּוּ נָחָשׁ׃ מַסִּיעַ אֲבָנִים

יְעַצֵּב בָּהֶם בּוֹקֵעַ עֵצִים יִסָּכֶן בָּם: אִם־קֵהָה
הַבַּרְזֶל וְהוּא לֹא־פָנִים קִלְקַל וַחֲיָלִים יְגַבֵּר
וְיִתְרוֹן הַכְשֵׁיר חָכְמָה: אִם־יִשֹּׁךְ הַנָּחָשׁ
בְּלוֹא־לָחַשׁ וְאֵין יִתְרוֹן לְבַעַל הַלָּשׁוֹן: דִּבְרֵי
פִי־חָכָם חֵן וְשִׂפְתוֹת כְּסִיל תְּבַלְּעֶנּוּ: תְּחִלַּת
דִּבְרֵי־פִיהוּ סִכְלוּת וְאַחֲרִית פִּיהוּ הוֹלֵלוּת
רָעָה: וְהַסָּכָל יַרְבֶּה דְבָרִים לֹא־יֵדַע הָאָדָם
מַה־שֶּׁיִּהְיֶה וַאֲשֶׁר יִהְיֶה מֵאַחֲרָיו מִי יַגִּיד
לוֹ: עֲמַל הַכְּסִילִים תְּיַגְּעֶנּוּ אֲשֶׁר לֹא־יָדַע
לָלֶכֶת אֶל־עִיר: אִי־לָךְ אֶרֶץ שֶׁמַּלְכֵּךְ נָעַר
וְשָׂרַיִךְ בַּבֹּקֶר יֹאכֵלוּ: אַשְׁרֵיךְ אֶרֶץ שֶׁמַּלְכֵּךְ
בֶּן־חוֹרִים וְשָׂרַיִךְ בָּעֵת יֹאכֵלוּ בִּגְבוּרָה וְלֹא
בַשְּׁתִי: בַּעֲצַלְתַּיִם יִמַּךְ הַמְּקָרֶה וּבְשִׁפְלוּת
יָדַיִם יִדְלֹף הַבָּיִת: לִשְׂחוֹק עֹשִׂים לֶחֶם וְיַיִן
יְשַׂמַּח חַיִּים וְהַכֶּסֶף יַעֲנֶה אֶת־הַכֹּל: גַּם
בְּמַדָּעֲךָ מֶלֶךְ אַל־תְּקַלֵּל וּבְחַדְרֵי מִשְׁכָּבְךָ
אַל־תְּקַלֵּל עָשִׁיר כִּי עוֹף הַשָּׁמַיִם יוֹלִיךְ אֶת־
הַקּוֹל וּבַעַל הכנפים [כְּנָפַיִם] יַגֵּיד דָּבָר:
יא שַׁלַּח לַחְמְךָ עַל־פְּנֵי הַמָּיִם כִּי־בְרֹב הַיָּמִים
תִּמְצָאֶנּוּ: תֶּן־חֵלֶק לְשִׁבְעָה וְגַם לִשְׁמוֹנָה
כִּי לֹא תֵדַע מַה־יִּהְיֶה רָעָה עַל־הָאָרֶץ: אִם־
יִמָּלְאוּ הֶעָבִים גֶּשֶׁם עַל־הָאָרֶץ יָרִיקוּ וְאִם־
יִפּוֹל עֵץ בַּדָּרוֹם וְאִם בַּצָּפוֹן מְקוֹם שֶׁיִּפּוֹל
הָעֵץ שָׁם יְהוּא: שֹׁמֵר רוּחַ לֹא יִזְרָע וְרֹאֶה
בֶעָבִים לֹא יִקְצוֹר: כַּאֲשֶׁר אֵינְךָ יוֹדֵעַ מַה־
דֶּרֶךְ הָרוּחַ כַּעֲצָמִים בְּבֶטֶן הַמְּלֵאָה כָּכָה לֹא
תֵדַע אֶת־מַעֲשֵׂה הָאֱלֹהִים אֲשֶׁר יַעֲשֶׂה
אֶת־הַכֹּל: בַּבֹּקֶר זְרַע אֶת־זַרְעֶךָ וְלָעֶרֶב אַל־
תַּנַּח יָדֶךָ כִּי אֵינְךָ יוֹדֵעַ אֵי זֶה יִכְשַׁר הֲזֶה
אוֹ־זֶה וְאִם־שְׁנֵיהֶם כְּאֶחָד טוֹבִים: וּמָתוֹק
הָאוֹר וְטוֹב לַעֵינַיִם לִרְאוֹת אֶת־הַשָּׁמֶשׁ: כִּי
אִם־שָׁנִים הַרְבֵּה יִחְיֶה הָאָדָם בְּכֻלָּם יִשְׂמָח
וְיִזְכֹּר אֶת־יְמֵי הַחֹשֶׁךְ כִּי־הַרְבֵּה יִהְיוּ כָּל־
שֶׁבָּא הָבֶל: שְׂמַח בָּחוּר בְּיַלְדוּתֶךָ וִיטִיבְךָ
לִבְּךָ בִּימֵי בְחוּרוֹתֶךָ וְהַלֵּךְ בְּדַרְכֵי לִבְּךָ
ובמראי [וּבְמַרְאֵה] עֵינֶיךָ וְדָע כִּי עַל־כָּל־
אֵלֶּה יְבִיאֲךָ הָאֱלֹהִים בַּמִּשְׁפָּט: וְהָסֵר כַּעַס
מִלִּבֶּךָ וְהַעֲבֵר רָעָה מִבְּשָׂרֶךָ כִּי־הַיַּלְדוּת
יב וְהַשַּׁחֲרוּת הָבֶל: וּזְכֹר אֶת־בּוֹרְאֶיךָ בִּימֵי
בְּחוּרֹתֶיךָ עַד אֲשֶׁר לֹא־יָבֹאוּ יְמֵי הָרָעָה
וְהִגִּיעוּ שָׁנִים אֲשֶׁר תֹּאמַר אֵין־לִי בָהֶם
חֵפֶץ: עַד אֲשֶׁר לֹא־תֶחְשַׁךְ הַשֶּׁמֶשׁ וְהָאוֹר
וְהַיָּרֵחַ וְהַכּוֹכָבִים וְשָׁבוּ הֶעָבִים אַחַר הַגָּשֶׁם:
בַּיּוֹם שֶׁיָּזֻעוּ שֹׁמְרֵי הַבַּיִת וְהִתְעַוְּתוּ אַנְשֵׁי
הֶחָיִל וּבָטְלוּ הַטֹּחֲנוֹת כִּי מִעֵטוּ וְחָשְׁכוּ
הָרֹאוֹת בָּאֲרֻבּוֹת: וְסֻגְּרוּ דְלָתַיִם בַּשּׁוּק בִּשְׁפַל
קוֹל הַטַּחֲנָה וְיָקוּם לְקוֹל הַצִּפּוֹר וְיִשַּׁחוּ
כָּל־בְּנוֹת הַשִּׁיר: גַּם מִגָּבֹהַּ יִרָאוּ וְחַתְחַתִּים
בַּדֶּרֶךְ וְיָנֵאץ הַשָּׁקֵד וְיִסְתַּבֵּל הֶחָגָב וְתָפֵר
הָאֲבִיּוֹנָה כִּי־הֹלֵךְ הָאָדָם אֶל־בֵּית עוֹלָמוֹ
וְסָבְבוּ בַשּׁוּק הַסֹּפְדִים: עַד אֲשֶׁר לֹא־
ירחק [יֵרָתֵק] חֶבֶל הַכֶּסֶף וְתָרֻץ גֻּלַּת הַזָּהָב
וְתִשָּׁבֶר כַּד עַל־הַמַּבּוּעַ וְנָרֹץ הַגַּלְגַּל אֶל־
הַבּוֹר: וְיָשֹׁב הֶעָפָר עַל־הָאָרֶץ כְּשֶׁהָיָה
וְהָרוּחַ תָּשׁוּב אֶל־הָאֱלֹהִים אֲשֶׁר נְתָנָהּ:
הֲבֵל הֲבָלִים אָמַר הַקּוֹהֶלֶת הַכֹּל הָבֶל: וְיֹתֵר
שֶׁהָיָה קֹהֶלֶת חָכָם עוֹד לִמַּד־דַּעַת אֶת־
הָעָם וְאִזֵּן וְחִקֵּר תִּקֵּן מְשָׁלִים הַרְבֵּה: בִּקֵּשׁ
קֹהֶלֶת לִמְצֹא דִּבְרֵי־חֵפֶץ וְכָתוּב יֹשֶׁר דִּבְרֵי
אֱמֶת: דִּבְרֵי חֲכָמִים כַּדָּרְבֹנוֹת וּכְמַשְׂמְרוֹת
נְטוּעִים בַּעֲלֵי אֲסֻפּוֹת נִתְּנוּ מֵרֹעֶה אֶחָד:
וְיֹתֵר מֵהֵמָּה בְּנִי הִזָּהֵר עֲשׂוֹת סְפָרִים הַרְבֵּה
אֵין קֵץ וְלַהַג הַרְבֵּה יְגִעַת בָּשָׂר: סוֹף דָּבָר
הַכֹּל נִשְׁמָע אֶת־הָאֱלֹהִים יְרָא וְאֶת־מִצְוֺתָיו
שְׁמוֹר כִּי־זֶה כָּל־הָאָדָם: כִּי אֶת־כָּל־מַעֲשֶׂה
הָאֱלֹהִים יָבִא בְמִשְׁפָּט עַל כָּל־נֶעְלָם אִם־
טוֹב וְאִם־רָע:

סוף דבר הכל נשמע,
את האלהים ירא ואת מצותיו שמור,
כי זה כל האדם

ESTHER / אסתר

אסתר is read twice on פורים, once in the evening and again in the morning. The blessings recited before and after the reading appear on page 954.

Various passages in מגילת אסתר are read by the congregation, then repeated by the reader. These passages are marked by arrows.

א וַיְהִי בִּימֵי אֲחַשְׁוֵרוֹשׁ הוּא אֲחַשְׁוֵרוֹשׁ הַמֹּלֵךְ
מֵהֹדּוּ וְעַד־כּוּשׁ שֶׁבַע וְעֶשְׂרִים וּמֵאָה
מְדִינָה: בַּיָּמִים הָהֵם כְּשֶׁבֶת ׀ הַמֶּלֶךְ
אֲחַשְׁוֵרוֹשׁ עַל כִּסֵּא מַלְכוּתוֹ אֲשֶׁר
בְּשׁוּשַׁן הַבִּירָה: בִּשְׁנַת שָׁלוֹשׁ לְמָלְכוֹ עָשָׂה
מִשְׁתֶּה לְכָל־שָׂרָיו וַעֲבָדָיו חֵיל ׀ פָּרַס וּמָדַי
הַפַּרְתְּמִים וְשָׂרֵי הַמְּדִינוֹת לְפָנָיו: בְּהַרְאֹתוֹ
אֶת־עֹשֶׁר כְּבוֹד מַלְכוּתוֹ וְאֶת־יְקָר תִּפְאֶרֶת
גְּדוּלָּתוֹ יָמִים רַבִּים שְׁמוֹנִים וּמְאַת יוֹם:
וּבִמְלוֹאת ׀ הַיָּמִים הָאֵלֶּה עָשָׂה הַמֶּלֶךְ לְכָל־
הָעָם הַנִּמְצְאִים בְּשׁוּשַׁן הַבִּירָה לְמִגָּדוֹל
וְעַד־קָטָן מִשְׁתֶּה שִׁבְעַת יָמִים בַּחֲצַר גִּנַּת
בִּיתַן הַמֶּלֶךְ: חוּר ׀ כַּרְפַּס וּתְכֵלֶת אָחוּז
בְּחַבְלֵי־בוּץ וְאַרְגָּמָן עַל־גְּלִילֵי כֶסֶף וְעַמּוּדֵי
שֵׁשׁ מִטּוֹת ׀ זָהָב וָכֶסֶף עַל רִצְפַת בַּהַט־
וָשֵׁשׁ וְדַר וְסֹחָרֶת: וְהַשְׁקוֹת בִּכְלֵי זָהָב
וְכֵלִים מִכֵּלִים שׁוֹנִים וְיֵין מַלְכוּת רָב כְּיַד
הַמֶּלֶךְ: וְהַשְּׁתִיָּה כַדָּת אֵין אֹנֵס כִּי־כֵן ׀ יִסַּד
הַמֶּלֶךְ עַל כָּל־רַב בֵּיתוֹ לַעֲשׂוֹת כִּרְצוֹן אִישׁ־
וָאִישׁ: גַּם וַשְׁתִּי הַמַּלְכָּה עָשְׂתָה מִשְׁתֵּה
נָשִׁים בֵּית הַמַּלְכוּת אֲשֶׁר לַמֶּלֶךְ אֲחַשְׁוֵרוֹשׁ:
בַּיּוֹם הַשְּׁבִיעִי כְּטוֹב לֵב־הַמֶּלֶךְ בַּיָּיִן אָמַר
לִמְהוּמָן בִּזְּתָא חַרְבוֹנָא בִּגְתָא וַאֲבַגְתָא זֵתַר
וְכַרְכַּס שִׁבְעַת הַסָּרִיסִים הַמְשָׁרְתִים אֶת־
פְּנֵי הַמֶּלֶךְ אֲחַשְׁוֵרוֹשׁ: לְהָבִיא אֶת־וַשְׁתִּי
הַמַּלְכָּה לִפְנֵי הַמֶּלֶךְ בְּכֶתֶר מַלְכוּת לְהַרְאוֹת
הָעַמִּים וְהַשָּׂרִים אֶת־יָפְיָהּ כִּי־טוֹבַת מַרְאֶה
הִיא: וַתְּמָאֵן הַמַּלְכָּה וַשְׁתִּי לָבוֹא בִּדְבַר
הַמֶּלֶךְ אֲשֶׁר בְּיַד הַסָּרִיסִים וַיִּקְצֹף הַמֶּלֶךְ מְאֹד
וַחֲמָתוֹ בָּעֲרָה בוֹ: וַיֹּאמֶר הַמֶּלֶךְ לַחֲכָמִים
יֹדְעֵי הָעִתִּים כִּי־כֵן דְּבַר הַמֶּלֶךְ לִפְנֵי כָּל־
יֹדְעֵי דָּת וָדִין: וְהַקָּרֹב אֵלָיו כַּרְשְׁנָא שֵׁתָר
אַדְמָתָא תַרְשִׁישׁ מֶרֶס מַרְסְנָא מְמוּכָן שִׁבְעַת
שָׂרֵי ׀ פָּרַס וּמָדַי רֹאֵי פְּנֵי הַמֶּלֶךְ הַיֹּשְׁבִים
רִאשֹׁנָה בַּמַּלְכוּת: כְּדָת מַה־לַּעֲשׂוֹת בַּמַּלְכָּה
וַשְׁתִּי עַל ׀ אֲשֶׁר לֹא־עָשְׂתָה אֶת־מַאֲמַר
הַמֶּלֶךְ אֲחַשְׁוֵרוֹשׁ בְּיַד הַסָּרִיסִים: וַיֹּאמֶר
מומכן [מְמוּכָן] לִפְנֵי הַמֶּלֶךְ וְהַשָּׂרִים לֹא
עַל־הַמֶּלֶךְ לְבַדּוֹ עָוְתָה וַשְׁתִּי הַמַּלְכָּה כִּי
עַל־כָּל־הַשָּׂרִים וְעַל־כָּל־הָעַמִּים אֲשֶׁר
בְּכָל־מְדִינוֹת הַמֶּלֶךְ אֲחַשְׁוֵרוֹשׁ: כִּי־יֵצֵא
דְבַר־הַמַּלְכָּה עַל־כָּל־הַנָּשִׁים לְהַבְזוֹת
בַּעְלֵיהֶן בְּעֵינֵיהֶן בְּאָמְרָם הַמֶּלֶךְ אֲחַשְׁוֵרוֹשׁ
אָמַר לְהָבִיא אֶת־וַשְׁתִּי הַמַּלְכָּה לְפָנָיו וְלֹא־
בָאָה: וְהַיּוֹם הַזֶּה תֹּאמַרְנָה ׀ שָׂרוֹת פָּרַס־
וּמָדַי אֲשֶׁר שָׁמְעוּ אֶת־דְּבַר הַמַּלְכָּה לְכֹל
שָׂרֵי הַמֶּלֶךְ וּכְדַי בִּזָּיוֹן וָקָצֶף: אִם־עַל־
הַמֶּלֶךְ טוֹב יֵצֵא דְבַר־מַלְכוּת מִלְּפָנָיו וְיִכָּתֵב
בְּדָתֵי פָרַס־וּמָדַי וְלֹא יַעֲבוֹר אֲשֶׁר לֹא־תָבוֹא
וַשְׁתִּי לִפְנֵי הַמֶּלֶךְ אֲחַשְׁוֵרוֹשׁ וּמַלְכוּתָהּ יִתֵּן
הַמֶּלֶךְ לִרְעוּתָהּ הַטּוֹבָה מִמֶּנָּה: וְנִשְׁמַע
פִּתְגָם הַמֶּלֶךְ אֲשֶׁר־יַעֲשֶׂה בְּכָל־מַלְכוּתוֹ כִּי
רַבָּה הִיא וְכָל־הַנָּשִׁים יִתְּנוּ יְקָר לְבַעְלֵיהֶן
לְמִגָּדוֹל וְעַד־קָטָן: וַיִּיטַב הַדָּבָר בְּעֵינֵי הַמֶּלֶךְ
וְהַשָּׂרִים וַיַּעַשׂ הַמֶּלֶךְ כִּדְבַר מְמוּכָן: וַיִּשְׁלַח
סְפָרִים אֶל־כָּל־מְדִינוֹת הַמֶּלֶךְ אֶל־מְדִינָה
וּמְדִינָה כִּכְתָבָהּ וְאֶל־עַם וָעָם כִּלְשׁוֹנוֹ לִהְיוֹת
כָּל־אִישׁ שֹׂרֵר בְּבֵיתוֹ וּמְדַבֵּר כִּלְשׁוֹן עַמּוֹ:
ב אַחַר הַדְּבָרִים הָאֵלֶּה כְּשֹׁךְ חֲמַת הַמֶּלֶךְ
אֲחַשְׁוֵרוֹשׁ זָכַר אֶת־וַשְׁתִּי וְאֵת אֲשֶׁר־עָשָׂתָה
וְאֵת אֲשֶׁר־נִגְזַר עָלֶיהָ: וַיֹּאמְרוּ נַעֲרֵי־הַמֶּלֶךְ
מְשָׁרְתָיו יְבַקְשׁוּ לַמֶּלֶךְ נְעָרוֹת בְּתוּלוֹת
טוֹבוֹת מַרְאֶה: וְיַפְקֵד הַמֶּלֶךְ פְּקִידִים בְּכָל־

מְדִינוֹת מַלְכוּתוֹ וְיִקְבְּצוּ אֶת־כָּל־נַעֲרָה־
בְתוּלָה טוֹבַת מַרְאֶה אֶל־שׁוּשַׁן הַבִּירָה
אֶל־בֵּית הַנָּשִׁים אֶל־יַד הֵגֶא סְרִיס הַמֶּלֶךְ
שֹׁמֵר הַנָּשִׁים וְנָתוֹן תַּמְרוּקֵיהֶן: וְהַנַּעֲרָה אֲשֶׁר
תִּיטַב בְּעֵינֵי הַמֶּלֶךְ תִּמְלֹךְ תַּחַת וַשְׁתִּי וַיִּיטַב
הַדָּבָר בְּעֵינֵי הַמֶּלֶךְ וַיַּעַשׂ כֵּן: אִישׁ יְהוּדִי
הָיָה בְּשׁוּשַׁן הַבִּירָה וּשְׁמוֹ מָרְדֳּכַי בֶּן יָאִיר
בֶּן־שִׁמְעִי בֶּן־קִישׁ אִישׁ יְמִינִי: אֲשֶׁר הָגְלָה
מִירוּשָׁלַיִם עִם־הַגֹּלָה אֲשֶׁר הָגְלְתָה עִם
יְכָנְיָה מֶלֶךְ־יְהוּדָה אֲשֶׁר הֶגְלָה נְבוּכַדְנֶצַּר
מֶלֶךְ בָּבֶל: וַיְהִי אֹמֵן אֶת־הֲדַסָּה הִיא אֶסְתֵּר
בַּת־דֹּדוֹ כִּי אֵין לָהּ אָב וָאֵם וְהַנַּעֲרָה יְפַת־
תֹּאַר וְטוֹבַת מַרְאֶה וּבְמוֹת אָבִיהָ וְאִמָּהּ
לְקָחָהּ מָרְדֳּכַי לוֹ לְבַת: וַיְהִי בְּהִשָּׁמַע דְּבַר־
הַמֶּלֶךְ וְדָתוֹ וּבְהִקָּבֵץ נְעָרוֹת רַבּוֹת אֶל־
שׁוּשַׁן הַבִּירָה אֶל־יַד הֵגָי וַתִּלָּקַח אֶסְתֵּר
אֶל־בֵּית הַמֶּלֶךְ אֶל־יַד הֵגַי שֹׁמֵר הַנָּשִׁים:
וַתִּיטַב הַנַּעֲרָה בְעֵינָיו וַתִּשָּׂא חֶסֶד לְפָנָיו
וַיְבַהֵל אֶת־תַּמְרוּקֶיהָ וְאֶת־מָנוֹתֶהָ לָתֵת
לָהּ וְאֵת שֶׁבַע הַנְּעָרוֹת הָרְאֻיוֹת לָתֶת־לָהּ
מִבֵּית הַמֶּלֶךְ וַיְשַׁנֶּהָ וְאֶת־נַעֲרוֹתֶיהָ לְטוֹב
בֵּית הַנָּשִׁים: לֹא־הִגִּידָה אֶסְתֵּר אֶת־עַמָּהּ
וְאֶת־מוֹלַדְתָּהּ כִּי מָרְדֳּכַי צִוָּה עָלֶיהָ אֲשֶׁר
לֹא־תַגִּיד: וּבְכָל־יוֹם וָיוֹם מָרְדֳּכַי מִתְהַלֵּךְ
לִפְנֵי חֲצַר בֵּית־הַנָּשִׁים לָדַעַת אֶת־שְׁלוֹם
אֶסְתֵּר וּמַה־יֵּעָשֶׂה בָּהּ: וּבְהַגִּיעַ תֹּר נַעֲרָה
וְנַעֲרָה לָבוֹא ׀ אֶל־הַמֶּלֶךְ אֲחַשְׁוֵרוֹשׁ מִקֵּץ
הֱיוֹת לָהּ כְּדָת הַנָּשִׁים שְׁנֵים עָשָׂר חֹדֶשׁ כִּי
כֵּן יִמְלְאוּ יְמֵי מְרוּקֵיהֶן שִׁשָּׁה חֳדָשִׁים בְּשֶׁמֶן
הַמֹּר וְשִׁשָּׁה חֳדָשִׁים בַּבְּשָׂמִים וּבְתַמְרוּקֵי
הַנָּשִׁים: וּבָזֶה הַנַּעֲרָה בָּאָה אֶל־הַמֶּלֶךְ אֵת
כָּל־אֲשֶׁר תֹּאמַר יִנָּתֵן לָהּ לָבוֹא עִמָּהּ מִבֵּית
הַנָּשִׁים עַד־בֵּית הַמֶּלֶךְ: בָּעֶרֶב ׀ הִיא בָאָה
וּבַבֹּקֶר הִיא שָׁבָה אֶל־בֵּית הַנָּשִׁים שֵׁנִי אֶל־
יַד שַׁעַשְׁגַז סְרִיס הַמֶּלֶךְ שֹׁמֵר הַפִּילַגְשִׁים
לֹא־תָבוֹא עוֹד אֶל־הַמֶּלֶךְ כִּי אִם־חָפֵץ בָּהּ
הַמֶּלֶךְ וְנִקְרְאָה בְשֵׁם: וּבְהַגִּיעַ תֹּר־אֶסְתֵּר
בַּת־אֲבִיחַיִל ׀ דֹּד מָרְדֳּכַי אֲשֶׁר לָקַח־לוֹ לְבַת
לָבוֹא אֶל־הַמֶּלֶךְ לֹא בִקְשָׁה דָּבָר כִּי אִם
אֶת־אֲשֶׁר יֹאמַר הֵגַי סְרִיס־הַמֶּלֶךְ שֹׁמֵר
הַנָּשִׁים וַתְּהִי אֶסְתֵּר נֹשֵׂאת חֵן בְּעֵינֵי כָּל־
רֹאֶיהָ: וַתִּלָּקַח אֶסְתֵּר אֶל־הַמֶּלֶךְ אֲחַשְׁוֵרוֹשׁ
אֶל־בֵּית מַלְכוּתוֹ בַּחֹדֶשׁ הָעֲשִׂירִי הוּא־
חֹדֶשׁ טֵבֵת בִּשְׁנַת־שֶׁבַע לְמַלְכוּתוֹ: וַיֶּאֱהַב
הַמֶּלֶךְ אֶת־אֶסְתֵּר מִכָּל־הַנָּשִׁים וַתִּשָּׂא־חֵן
וָחֶסֶד לְפָנָיו מִכָּל־הַבְּתוּלֹת וַיָּשֶׂם כֶּתֶר־
מַלְכוּת בְּרֹאשָׁהּ וַיַּמְלִיכֶהָ תַּחַת וַשְׁתִּי: וַיַּעַשׂ
הַמֶּלֶךְ מִשְׁתֶּה גָדוֹל לְכָל־שָׂרָיו וַעֲבָדָיו אֵת
מִשְׁתֵּה אֶסְתֵּר וַהֲנָחָה לַמְּדִינוֹת עָשָׂה וַיִּתֵּן
מַשְׂאֵת כְּיַד הַמֶּלֶךְ: וּבְהִקָּבֵץ בְּתוּלוֹת שֵׁנִית
וּמָרְדֳּכַי יֹשֵׁב בְּשַׁעַר־הַמֶּלֶךְ: אֵין אֶסְתֵּר
מַגֶּדֶת מוֹלַדְתָּהּ וְאֶת־עַמָּהּ כַּאֲשֶׁר צִוָּה עָלֶיהָ
מָרְדֳּכָי וְאֶת־מַאֲמַר מָרְדֳּכַי אֶסְתֵּר עֹשָׂה
כַּאֲשֶׁר הָיְתָה בְאָמְנָה אִתּוֹ: בַּיָּמִים הָהֵם
וּמָרְדֳּכַי יֹשֵׁב בְּשַׁעַר־הַמֶּלֶךְ קָצַף בִּגְתָן וָתֶרֶשׁ
שְׁנֵי־סָרִיסֵי הַמֶּלֶךְ מִשֹּׁמְרֵי הַסַּף וַיְבַקְשׁוּ
לִשְׁלֹחַ יָד בַּמֶּלֶךְ אֲחַשְׁוֵרֹשׁ: וַיִּוָּדַע הַדָּבָר
לְמָרְדֳּכַי וַיַּגֵּד לְאֶסְתֵּר הַמַּלְכָּה וַתֹּאמֶר
אֶסְתֵּר לַמֶּלֶךְ בְּשֵׁם מָרְדֳּכָי: וַיְבֻקַּשׁ הַדָּבָר
וַיִּמָּצֵא וַיִּתָּלוּ שְׁנֵיהֶם עַל־עֵץ וַיִּכָּתֵב בְּסֵפֶר
דִּבְרֵי הַיָּמִים לִפְנֵי הַמֶּלֶךְ: אַחַר ׀ הַדְּבָרִים ג
הָאֵלֶּה גִּדַּל הַמֶּלֶךְ אֲחַשְׁוֵרוֹשׁ אֶת־הָמָן
בֶּן־הַמְּדָתָא הָאֲגָגִי וַיְנַשְּׂאֵהוּ וַיָּשֶׂם אֶת־
כִּסְאוֹ מֵעַל כָּל־הַשָּׂרִים אֲשֶׁר אִתּוֹ: וְכָל־
עַבְדֵי הַמֶּלֶךְ אֲשֶׁר־בְּשַׁעַר הַמֶּלֶךְ כֹּרְעִים
וּמִשְׁתַּחֲוִים לְהָמָן כִּי־כֵן צִוָּה־לוֹ הַמֶּלֶךְ
וּמָרְדֳּכַי לֹא יִכְרַע וְלֹא יִשְׁתַּחֲוֶה: וַיֹּאמְרוּ
עַבְדֵי הַמֶּלֶךְ אֲשֶׁר־בְּשַׁעַר הַמֶּלֶךְ לְמָרְדֳּכָי
מַדּוּעַ אַתָּה עוֹבֵר אֵת מִצְוַת הַמֶּלֶךְ: וַיְהִי
באמרם [כְּאָמְרָם] אֵלָיו יוֹם וָיוֹם וְלֹא שָׁמַע

אֲלֵיהֶם וַיַּגִּידוּ לְהָמָן לִרְאוֹת הֲיַעַמְדוּ דִּבְרֵי
מָרְדֳּכַי כִּי־הִגִּיד לָהֶם אֲשֶׁר־הוּא יְהוּדִי: וַיַּרְא
הָמָן כִּי־אֵין מָרְדֳּכַי כֹּרֵעַ וּמִשְׁתַּחֲוֶה לוֹ
וַיִּמָּלֵא הָמָן חֵמָה: וַיִּבֶז בְּעֵינָיו לִשְׁלֹחַ יָד
בְּמָרְדֳּכַי לְבַדּוֹ כִּי־הִגִּידוּ לוֹ אֶת־עַם מָרְדֳּכָי
וַיְבַקֵּשׁ הָמָן לְהַשְׁמִיד אֶת־כָּל־הַיְּהוּדִים
אֲשֶׁר בְּכָל־מַלְכוּת אֲחַשְׁוֵרוֹשׁ עַם מָרְדֳּכָי:
בַּחֹדֶשׁ הָרִאשׁוֹן הוּא־חֹדֶשׁ נִיסָן בִּשְׁנַת
שְׁתֵּים עֶשְׂרֵה לַמֶּלֶךְ אֲחַשְׁוֵרוֹשׁ הִפִּיל פּוּר
הוּא הַגּוֹרָל לִפְנֵי הָמָן מִיּוֹם | לְיוֹם וּמֵחֹדֶשׁ
לְחֹדֶשׁ שְׁנֵים־עָשָׂר הוּא־חֹדֶשׁ אֲדָר: וַיֹּאמֶר
הָמָן לַמֶּלֶךְ אֲחַשְׁוֵרוֹשׁ יֶשְׁנוֹ עַם־אֶחָד מְפֻזָּר
וּמְפֹרָד בֵּין הָעַמִּים בְּכֹל מְדִינוֹת מַלְכוּתֶךָ
וְדָתֵיהֶם שֹׁנוֹת מִכָּל־עָם וְאֶת־דָּתֵי הַמֶּלֶךְ
אֵינָם עֹשִׂים וְלַמֶּלֶךְ אֵין־שֹׁוֶה לְהַנִּיחָם: אִם־
עַל־הַמֶּלֶךְ טוֹב יִכָּתֵב לְאַבְּדָם וַעֲשֶׂרֶת
אֲלָפִים כִּכַּר־כֶּסֶף אֶשְׁקוֹל עַל־יְדֵי עֹשֵׂי
הַמְּלָאכָה לְהָבִיא אֶל־גִּנְזֵי הַמֶּלֶךְ: וַיָּסַר
הַמֶּלֶךְ אֶת־טַבַּעְתּוֹ מֵעַל יָדוֹ וַיִּתְּנָהּ לְהָמָן
בֶּן־הַמְּדָתָא הָאֲגָגִי צֹרֵר הַיְּהוּדִים: וַיֹּאמֶר
הַמֶּלֶךְ לְהָמָן הַכֶּסֶף נָתוּן לָךְ וְהָעָם לַעֲשׂוֹת
בּוֹ כַּטּוֹב בְּעֵינֶיךָ: וַיִּקָּרְאוּ סֹפְרֵי הַמֶּלֶךְ
בַּחֹדֶשׁ הָרִאשׁוֹן בִּשְׁלוֹשָׁה עָשָׂר יוֹם בּוֹ וַיִּכָּתֵב
כְּכָל־אֲשֶׁר־צִוָּה הָמָן אֶל אֲחַשְׁדַּרְפְּנֵי־הַמֶּלֶךְ
וְאֶל־הַפַּחוֹת אֲשֶׁר | עַל־מְדִינָה וּמְדִינָה
וְאֶל־שָׂרֵי עַם וָעָם מְדִינָה וּמְדִינָה כִּכְתָבָהּ
וְעַם וָעָם כִּלְשׁוֹנוֹ בְּשֵׁם הַמֶּלֶךְ אֲחַשְׁוֵרֹשׁ
נִכְתָּב וְנֶחְתָּם בְּטַבַּעַת הַמֶּלֶךְ: וְנִשְׁלוֹחַ
סְפָרִים בְּיַד הָרָצִים אֶל־כָּל־מְדִינוֹת הַמֶּלֶךְ
לְהַשְׁמִיד לַהֲרֹג וּלְאַבֵּד אֶת־כָּל־הַיְּהוּדִים
מִנַּעַר וְעַד־זָקֵן טַף וְנָשִׁים בְּיוֹם אֶחָד
בִּשְׁלוֹשָׁה עָשָׂר לְחֹדֶשׁ שְׁנֵים־עָשָׂר הוּא־
חֹדֶשׁ אֲדָר וּשְׁלָלָם לָבוֹז: פַּתְשֶׁגֶן הַכְּתָב
לְהִנָּתֵן דָּת בְּכָל־מְדִינָה וּמְדִינָה גָּלוּי לְכָל־
הָעַמִּים לִהְיוֹת עֲתִדִים לַיּוֹם הַזֶּה: הָרָצִים
יָצְאוּ דְחוּפִים בִּדְבַר הַמֶּלֶךְ וְהַדָּת נִתְּנָה
בְּשׁוּשַׁן הַבִּירָה וְהַמֶּלֶךְ וְהָמָן יָשְׁבוּ לִשְׁתּוֹת
ד וְהָעִיר שׁוּשָׁן נָבוֹכָה: וּמָרְדֳּכַי יָדַע אֶת־כָּל־
אֲשֶׁר נַעֲשָׂה וַיִּקְרַע מָרְדֳּכַי אֶת־בְּגָדָיו
וַיִּלְבַּשׁ שַׂק וָאֵפֶר וַיֵּצֵא בְּתוֹךְ הָעִיר וַיִּזְעַק
זְעָקָה גְדוֹלָה וּמָרָה: וַיָּבוֹא עַד לִפְנֵי שַׁעַר־
הַמֶּלֶךְ כִּי אֵין לָבוֹא אֶל־שַׁעַר הַמֶּלֶךְ
בִּלְבוּשׁ שָׂק: וּבְכָל־מְדִינָה וּמְדִינָה מְקוֹם
אֲשֶׁר דְּבַר־הַמֶּלֶךְ וְדָתוֹ מַגִּיעַ אֵבֶל גָּדוֹל
לַיְּהוּדִים וְצוֹם וּבְכִי וּמִסְפֵּד שַׂק וָאֵפֶר יֻצַּע
לָרַבִּים: ותבואינה [וַתָּבוֹאנָה] נַעֲרוֹת אֶסְתֵּר
וְסָרִיסֶיהָ וַיַּגִּידוּ לָהּ וַתִּתְחַלְחַל הַמַּלְכָּה מְאֹד
וַתִּשְׁלַח בְּגָדִים לְהַלְבִּישׁ אֶת־מָרְדֳּכַי וּלְהָסִיר
שַׂקּוֹ מֵעָלָיו וְלֹא קִבֵּל: וַתִּקְרָא אֶסְתֵּר לַהֲתָךְ
מִסָּרִיסֵי הַמֶּלֶךְ אֲשֶׁר הֶעֱמִיד לְפָנֶיהָ וַתְּצַוֵּהוּ
עַל־מָרְדֳּכָי לָדַעַת מַה־זֶּה וְעַל־מַה־זֶּה: וַיֵּצֵא
הֲתָךְ אֶל־מָרְדֳּכָי אֶל־רְחוֹב הָעִיר אֲשֶׁר לִפְנֵי
שַׁעַר־הַמֶּלֶךְ: וַיַּגֶּד־לוֹ מָרְדֳּכַי אֵת כָּל־אֲשֶׁר
קָרָהוּ וְאֵת | פָּרָשַׁת הַכֶּסֶף אֲשֶׁר אָמַר הָמָן
לִשְׁקוֹל עַל־גִּנְזֵי הַמֶּלֶךְ ביהודיים [בַּיְּהוּדִים]
לְאַבְּדָם: וְאֶת־פַּתְשֶׁגֶן כְּתָב־הַדָּת אֲשֶׁר־נִתַּן
בְּשׁוּשָׁן לְהַשְׁמִידָם נָתַן לוֹ לְהַרְאוֹת אֶת־
אֶסְתֵּר וּלְהַגִּיד לָהּ וּלְצַוּוֹת עָלֶיהָ לָבוֹא אֶל־
הַמֶּלֶךְ לְהִתְחַנֶּן־לוֹ וּלְבַקֵּשׁ מִלְּפָנָיו עַל־עַמָּהּ:
וַיָּבוֹא הֲתָךְ וַיַּגֵּד לְאֶסְתֵּר אֵת דִּבְרֵי מָרְדֳּכָי:
וַתֹּאמֶר אֶסְתֵּר לַהֲתָךְ וַתְּצַוֵּהוּ אֶל־מָרְדֳּכָי:
כָּל־עַבְדֵי הַמֶּלֶךְ וְעַם מְדִינוֹת הַמֶּלֶךְ יֹדְעִים
אֲשֶׁר כָּל־אִישׁ וְאִשָּׁה אֲשֶׁר־יָבוֹא אֶל־הַמֶּלֶךְ
אֶל־הֶחָצֵר הַפְּנִימִית אֲשֶׁר לֹא־יִקָּרֵא אַחַת
דָּתוֹ לְהָמִית לְבַד מֵאֲשֶׁר יוֹשִׁיט־לוֹ הַמֶּלֶךְ
אֶת־שַׁרְבִיט הַזָּהָב וְחָיָה וַאֲנִי לֹא נִקְרֵאתִי
לָבוֹא אֶל־הַמֶּלֶךְ זֶה שְׁלוֹשִׁים יוֹם: וַיַּגִּידוּ
לְמָרְדֳּכָי אֵת דִּבְרֵי אֶסְתֵּר: וַיֹּאמֶר מָרְדֳּכַי
לְהָשִׁיב אֶל־אֶסְתֵּר אַל־תְּדַמִּי בְנַפְשֵׁךְ
לְהִמָּלֵט בֵּית־הַמֶּלֶךְ מִכָּל־הַיְּהוּדִים: כִּי אִם־

הַחֲרֵשׁ תַּחֲרִישִׁי בָּעֵת הַזֹּאת רֶוַח וְהַצָּלָה
יַעֲמוֹד לַיְּהוּדִים מִמָּקוֹם אַחֵר וְאַתְּ וּבֵית־
אָבִיךְ תֹּאבֵדוּ וּמִי יוֹדֵעַ אִם־לְעֵת כָּזֹאת
הִגַּעַתְּ לַמַּלְכוּת׃ וַתֹּאמֶר אֶסְתֵּר לְהָשִׁיב אֶל־
מָרְדֳּכָי׃ לֵךְ כְּנוֹס אֶת־כָּל־הַיְּהוּדִים הַנִּמְצְאִים
בְּשׁוּשָׁן וְצוּמוּ עָלַי וְאַל־תֹּאכְלוּ וְאַל־תִּשְׁתּוּ
שְׁלֹשֶׁת יָמִים לַיְלָה וָיוֹם גַּם־אֲנִי וְנַעֲרֹתַי
אָצוּם כֵּן וּבְכֵן אָבוֹא אֶל־הַמֶּלֶךְ אֲשֶׁר לֹא־
כַדָּת וְכַאֲשֶׁר אָבַדְתִּי אָבָדְתִּי׃ וַיַּעֲבֹר מָרְדֳּכָי
וַיַּעַשׂ כְּכֹל אֲשֶׁר־צִוְּתָה עָלָיו אֶסְתֵּר׃ וַיְהִי ׀ ה
בַּיּוֹם הַשְּׁלִישִׁי וַתִּלְבַּשׁ אֶסְתֵּר מַלְכוּת וַתַּעֲמֹד
בַּחֲצַר בֵּית־הַמֶּלֶךְ הַפְּנִימִית נֹכַח בֵּית הַמֶּלֶךְ
וְהַמֶּלֶךְ יוֹשֵׁב עַל־כִּסֵּא מַלְכוּתוֹ בְּבֵית
הַמַּלְכוּת נֹכַח פֶּתַח הַבָּיִת׃ וַיְהִי כִרְאוֹת
הַמֶּלֶךְ אֶת־אֶסְתֵּר הַמַּלְכָּה עֹמֶדֶת בֶּחָצֵר
נָשְׂאָה חֵן בְּעֵינָיו וַיּוֹשֶׁט הַמֶּלֶךְ לְאֶסְתֵּר
אֶת־שַׁרְבִיט הַזָּהָב אֲשֶׁר בְּיָדוֹ וַתִּקְרַב אֶסְתֵּר
וַתִּגַּע בְּרֹאשׁ הַשַּׁרְבִיט׃ וַיֹּאמֶר לָהּ הַמֶּלֶךְ
מַה־לָּךְ אֶסְתֵּר הַמַּלְכָּה וּמַה־בַּקָּשָׁתֵךְ עַד־
חֲצִי הַמַּלְכוּת וְיִנָּתֵן לָךְ׃ וַתֹּאמֶר אֶסְתֵּר
אִם־עַל־הַמֶּלֶךְ טוֹב יָבוֹא הַמֶּלֶךְ וְהָמָן הַיּוֹם
אֶל־הַמִּשְׁתֶּה אֲשֶׁר־עָשִׂיתִי לוֹ׃ וַיֹּאמֶר הַמֶּלֶךְ
מַהֲרוּ אֶת־הָמָן לַעֲשׂוֹת אֶת־דְּבַר אֶסְתֵּר
וַיָּבֹא הַמֶּלֶךְ וְהָמָן אֶל־הַמִּשְׁתֶּה אֲשֶׁר־
עָשְׂתָה אֶסְתֵּר׃ וַיֹּאמֶר הַמֶּלֶךְ לְאֶסְתֵּר
בְּמִשְׁתֵּה הַיַּיִן מַה־שְּׁאֵלָתֵךְ וְיִנָּתֵן לָךְ וּמַה־
בַּקָּשָׁתֵךְ עַד־חֲצִי הַמַּלְכוּת וְתֵעָשׂ׃ וַתַּעַן
אֶסְתֵּר וַתֹּאמַר שְׁאֵלָתִי וּבַקָּשָׁתִי׃ אִם־
מָצָאתִי חֵן בְּעֵינֵי הַמֶּלֶךְ וְאִם־עַל־הַמֶּלֶךְ
טוֹב לָתֵת אֶת־שְׁאֵלָתִי וְלַעֲשׂוֹת אֶת־
בַּקָּשָׁתִי יָבוֹא הַמֶּלֶךְ וְהָמָן אֶל־הַמִּשְׁתֶּה
אֲשֶׁר אֶעֱשֶׂה לָהֶם וּמָחָר אֶעֱשֶׂה כִּדְבַר
הַמֶּלֶךְ׃ וַיֵּצֵא הָמָן בַּיּוֹם הַהוּא שָׂמֵחַ וְטוֹב
לֵב וְכִרְאוֹת הָמָן אֶת־מָרְדֳּכַי בְּשַׁעַר הַמֶּלֶךְ
וְלֹא־קָם וְלֹא־זָע מִמֶּנּוּ וַיִּמָּלֵא הָמָן עַל־
מָרְדֳּכַי חֵמָה׃ וַיִּתְאַפַּק הָמָן וַיָּבוֹא אֶל־בֵּיתוֹ
וַיִּשְׁלַח וַיָּבֵא אֶת־אֹהֲבָיו וְאֶת־זֶרֶשׁ אִשְׁתּוֹ׃
וַיְסַפֵּר לָהֶם הָמָן אֶת־כְּבוֹד עָשְׁרוֹ וְרֹב בָּנָיו
וְאֵת כָּל־אֲשֶׁר גִּדְּלוֹ הַמֶּלֶךְ וְאֵת אֲשֶׁר נִשְּׂאוֹ
עַל־הַשָּׂרִים וְעַבְדֵי הַמֶּלֶךְ׃ וַיֹּאמֶר הָמָן אַף
לֹא־הֵבִיאָה אֶסְתֵּר הַמַּלְכָּה עִם־הַמֶּלֶךְ אֶל־
הַמִּשְׁתֶּה אֲשֶׁר־עָשָׂתָה כִּי אִם־אוֹתִי וְגַם־
לְמָחָר אֲנִי קָרוּא־לָהּ עִם־הַמֶּלֶךְ׃ וְכָל־זֶה
אֵינֶנּוּ שֹׁוֶה לִי בְּכָל־עֵת אֲשֶׁר אֲנִי רֹאֶה אֶת־
מָרְדֳּכַי הַיְּהוּדִי יוֹשֵׁב בְּשַׁעַר הַמֶּלֶךְ׃ וַתֹּאמֶר
לוֹ זֶרֶשׁ אִשְׁתּוֹ וְכָל־אֹהֲבָיו יַעֲשׂוּ־עֵץ גָּבֹהַּ
חֲמִשִּׁים אַמָּה וּבַבֹּקֶר ׀ אֱמֹר לַמֶּלֶךְ וְיִתְלוּ
אֶת־מָרְדֳּכַי עָלָיו וּבֹא עִם־הַמֶּלֶךְ אֶל־
הַמִּשְׁתֶּה שָׂמֵחַ וַיִּיטַב הַדָּבָר לִפְנֵי הָמָן וַיַּעַשׂ
ו הָעֵץ׃ בַּלַּיְלָה הַהוּא נָדְדָה שְׁנַת הַמֶּלֶךְ וַיֹּאמֶר
לְהָבִיא אֶת־סֵפֶר הַזִּכְרֹנוֹת דִּבְרֵי הַיָּמִים וַיִּהְיוּ
נִקְרָאִים לִפְנֵי הַמֶּלֶךְ׃ וַיִּמָּצֵא כָתוּב אֲשֶׁר
הִגִּיד מָרְדֳּכַי עַל־בִּגְתָנָא וָתֶרֶשׁ שְׁנֵי סָרִיסֵי
הַמֶּלֶךְ מִשֹּׁמְרֵי הַסַּף אֲשֶׁר בִּקְשׁוּ לִשְׁלֹחַ יָד
בַּמֶּלֶךְ אֲחַשְׁוֵרוֹשׁ׃ וַיֹּאמֶר הַמֶּלֶךְ מַה־נַּעֲשָׂה
יְקָר וּגְדוּלָּה לְמָרְדֳּכַי עַל־זֶה וַיֹּאמְרוּ נַעֲרֵי
הַמֶּלֶךְ מְשָׁרְתָיו לֹא־נַעֲשָׂה עִמּוֹ דָּבָר׃ וַיֹּאמֶר
הַמֶּלֶךְ מִי בֶחָצֵר וְהָמָן בָּא לַחֲצַר בֵּית־הַמֶּלֶךְ
הַחִיצוֹנָה לֵאמֹר לַמֶּלֶךְ לִתְלוֹת אֶת־מָרְדֳּכַי
עַל־הָעֵץ אֲשֶׁר־הֵכִין לוֹ׃ וַיֹּאמְרוּ נַעֲרֵי הַמֶּלֶךְ
אֵלָיו הִנֵּה הָמָן עֹמֵד בֶּחָצֵר וַיֹּאמֶר הַמֶּלֶךְ
יָבוֹא׃ וַיָּבוֹא הָמָן וַיֹּאמֶר לוֹ הַמֶּלֶךְ מַה־
לַעֲשׂוֹת בָּאִישׁ אֲשֶׁר הַמֶּלֶךְ חָפֵץ בִּיקָרוֹ
וַיֹּאמֶר הָמָן בְּלִבּוֹ לְמִי יַחְפֹּץ הַמֶּלֶךְ לַעֲשׂוֹת
יְקָר יוֹתֵר מִמֶּנִּי׃ וַיֹּאמֶר הָמָן אֶל־הַמֶּלֶךְ אִישׁ
אֲשֶׁר הַמֶּלֶךְ חָפֵץ בִּיקָרוֹ׃ יָבִיאוּ לְבוּשׁ
מַלְכוּת אֲשֶׁר לָבַשׁ־בּוֹ הַמֶּלֶךְ וְסוּס אֲשֶׁר
רָכַב עָלָיו הַמֶּלֶךְ וַאֲשֶׁר נִתַּן כֶּתֶר מַלְכוּת
בְּרֹאשׁוֹ׃ וְנָתוֹן הַלְּבוּשׁ וְהַסּוּס עַל־יַד־אִישׁ
מִשָּׂרֵי הַמֶּלֶךְ הַפַּרְתְּמִים וְהִלְבִּשׁוּ אֶת־הָאִישׁ

אֲשֶׁר הַמֶּלֶךְ חָפֵץ בִּיקָרוֹ וְהִרְכִּיבֻהוּ עַל־
הַסּוּס בִּרְחוֹב הָעִיר וְקָרְאוּ לְפָנָיו כָּכָה יֵעָשֶׂה
לָאִישׁ אֲשֶׁר הַמֶּלֶךְ חָפֵץ בִּיקָרוֹ: וַיֹּאמֶר הַמֶּלֶךְ
לְהָמָן מַהֵר קַח אֶת־הַלְּבוּשׁ וְאֶת־הַסּוּס
כַּאֲשֶׁר דִּבַּרְתָּ וַעֲשֵׂה־כֵן לְמָרְדֳּכַי הַיְּהוּדִי
הַיּוֹשֵׁב בְּשַׁעַר הַמֶּלֶךְ אַל־תַּפֵּל דָּבָר מִכֹּל
אֲשֶׁר דִּבַּרְתָּ: וַיִּקַּח הָמָן אֶת־הַלְּבוּשׁ וְאֶת־
הַסּוּס וַיַּלְבֵּשׁ אֶת־מָרְדֳּכָי וַיַּרְכִּיבֵהוּ בִּרְחוֹב
הָעִיר וַיִּקְרָא לְפָנָיו כָּכָה יֵעָשֶׂה לָאִישׁ אֲשֶׁר
הַמֶּלֶךְ חָפֵץ בִּיקָרוֹ: וַיָּשָׁב מָרְדֳּכַי אֶל־שַׁעַר
הַמֶּלֶךְ וְהָמָן נִדְחַף אֶל־בֵּיתוֹ אָבֵל וַחֲפוּי
רֹאשׁ: וַיְסַפֵּר הָמָן לְזֶרֶשׁ אִשְׁתּוֹ וּלְכָל־אֹהֲבָיו
אֵת כָּל־אֲשֶׁר קָרָהוּ וַיֹּאמְרוּ לוֹ חֲכָמָיו וְזֶרֶשׁ
אִשְׁתּוֹ אִם מִזֶּרַע הַיְּהוּדִים מָרְדֳּכַי אֲשֶׁר
הַחִלּוֹתָ לִנְפֹּל לְפָנָיו לֹא־תוּכַל לוֹ כִּי־נָפוֹל
תִּפּוֹל לְפָנָיו: עוֹדָם מְדַבְּרִים עִמּוֹ וְסָרִיסֵי
הַמֶּלֶךְ הִגִּיעוּ וַיַּבְהִלוּ לְהָבִיא אֶת־הָמָן אֶל־
ז הַמִּשְׁתֶּה אֲשֶׁר־עָשְׂתָה אֶסְתֵּר: וַיָּבֹא הַמֶּלֶךְ
וְהָמָן לִשְׁתּוֹת עִם־אֶסְתֵּר הַמַּלְכָּה: וַיֹּאמֶר
הַמֶּלֶךְ לְאֶסְתֵּר גַּם בַּיּוֹם הַשֵּׁנִי בְּמִשְׁתֵּה הַיַּיִן
מַה־שְּׁאֵלָתֵךְ אֶסְתֵּר הַמַּלְכָּה וְתִנָּתֵן לָךְ וּמַה־
בַּקָּשָׁתֵךְ עַד־חֲצִי הַמַּלְכוּת וְתֵעָשׂ: וַתַּעַן
אֶסְתֵּר הַמַּלְכָּה וַתֹּאמַר אִם־מָצָאתִי חֵן
בְּעֵינֶיךָ הַמֶּלֶךְ וְאִם־עַל־הַמֶּלֶךְ טוֹב תִּנָּתֶן־
לִי נַפְשִׁי בִּשְׁאֵלָתִי וְעַמִּי בְּבַקָּשָׁתִי: כִּי
נִמְכַּרְנוּ אֲנִי וְעַמִּי לְהַשְׁמִיד לַהֲרוֹג וּלְאַבֵּד
וְאִלּוּ לַעֲבָדִים וְלִשְׁפָחוֹת נִמְכַּרְנוּ הֶחֱרַשְׁתִּי
כִּי אֵין הַצָּר שֹׁוֶה בְּנֵזֶק הַמֶּלֶךְ: וַיֹּאמֶר הַמֶּלֶךְ
אֲחַשְׁוֵרוֹשׁ וַיֹּאמֶר לְאֶסְתֵּר הַמַּלְכָּה מִי הוּא
זֶה וְאֵי־זֶה הוּא אֲשֶׁר־מְלָאוֹ לִבּוֹ לַעֲשׂוֹת
כֵּן: וַתֹּאמֶר אֶסְתֵּר אִישׁ צַר וְאוֹיֵב הָמָן הָרָע
הַזֶּה וְהָמָן נִבְעַת מִלִּפְנֵי הַמֶּלֶךְ וְהַמַּלְכָּה:
וְהַמֶּלֶךְ קָם בַּחֲמָתוֹ מִמִּשְׁתֵּה הַיַּיִן אֶל־גִּנַּת
הַבִּיתָן וְהָמָן עָמַד לְבַקֵּשׁ עַל־נַפְשׁוֹ מֵאֶסְתֵּר
הַמַּלְכָּה כִּי רָאָה כִּי־כָלְתָה אֵלָיו הָרָעָה
מֵאֵת הַמֶּלֶךְ: וְהַמֶּלֶךְ שָׁב מִגִּנַּת הַבִּיתָן אֶל־
בֵּית ׀ מִשְׁתֵּה הַיַּיִן וְהָמָן נֹפֵל עַל־הַמִּטָּה
אֲשֶׁר אֶסְתֵּר עָלֶיהָ וַיֹּאמֶר הַמֶּלֶךְ הֲגַם
לִכְבּוֹשׁ אֶת־הַמַּלְכָּה עִמִּי בַּבָּיִת הַדָּבָר יָצָא
מִפִּי הַמֶּלֶךְ וּפְנֵי הָמָן חָפוּ: וַיֹּאמֶר חַרְבוֹנָה
אֶחָד מִן־הַסָּרִיסִים לִפְנֵי הַמֶּלֶךְ גַּם הִנֵּה־
הָעֵץ אֲשֶׁר־עָשָׂה הָמָן לְמָרְדֳּכַי אֲשֶׁר דִּבֶּר־
טוֹב עַל־הַמֶּלֶךְ עֹמֵד בְּבֵית הָמָן גָּבֹהַּ חֲמִשִּׁים
אַמָּה וַיֹּאמֶר הַמֶּלֶךְ תְּלֻהוּ עָלָיו: וַיִּתְלוּ אֶת־
הָמָן עַל־הָעֵץ אֲשֶׁר־הֵכִין לְמָרְדֳּכָי וַחֲמַת
ח הַמֶּלֶךְ שָׁכָכָה: בַּיּוֹם הַהוּא נָתַן הַמֶּלֶךְ
אֲחַשְׁוֵרוֹשׁ לְאֶסְתֵּר הַמַּלְכָּה אֶת־בֵּית הָמָן
צֹרֵר היהודיים [הַיְּהוּדִים] וּמָרְדֳּכַי בָּא לִפְנֵי
הַמֶּלֶךְ כִּי־הִגִּידָה אֶסְתֵּר מַה הוּא־לָהּ: וַיָּסַר
הַמֶּלֶךְ אֶת־טַבַּעְתּוֹ אֲשֶׁר הֶעֱבִיר מֵהָמָן
וַיִּתְּנָהּ לְמָרְדֳּכָי וַתָּשֶׂם אֶסְתֵּר אֶת־מָרְדֳּכַי
עַל־בֵּית הָמָן: וַתּוֹסֶף אֶסְתֵּר וַתְּדַבֵּר לִפְנֵי
הַמֶּלֶךְ וַתִּפֹּל לִפְנֵי רַגְלָיו וַתֵּבְךְּ וַתִּתְחַנֶּן־
לוֹ לְהַעֲבִיר אֶת־רָעַת הָמָן הָאֲגָגִי וְאֵת
מַחֲשַׁבְתּוֹ אֲשֶׁר חָשַׁב עַל־הַיְּהוּדִים: וַיּוֹשֶׁט
הַמֶּלֶךְ לְאֶסְתֵּר אֵת שַׁרְבִט הַזָּהָב וַתָּקָם
אֶסְתֵּר וַתַּעֲמֹד לִפְנֵי הַמֶּלֶךְ: וַתֹּאמֶר אִם־
עַל־הַמֶּלֶךְ טוֹב וְאִם־מָצָאתִי חֵן לְפָנָיו וְכָשֵׁר
הַדָּבָר לִפְנֵי הַמֶּלֶךְ וְטוֹבָה אֲנִי בְּעֵינָיו יִכָּתֵב
לְהָשִׁיב אֶת־הַסְּפָרִים מַחֲשֶׁבֶת הָמָן בֶּן־
הַמְּדָתָא הָאֲגָגִי אֲשֶׁר כָּתַב לְאַבֵּד אֶת־
הַיְּהוּדִים אֲשֶׁר בְּכָל־מְדִינוֹת הַמֶּלֶךְ: כִּי
אֵיכָכָה אוּכַל וְרָאִיתִי בָּרָעָה אֲשֶׁר־יִמְצָא
אֶת־עַמִּי וְאֵיכָכָה אוּכַל וְרָאִיתִי בְּאָבְדַן
מוֹלַדְתִּי: וַיֹּאמֶר הַמֶּלֶךְ אֲחַשְׁוֵרֹשׁ לְאֶסְתֵּר
הַמַּלְכָּה וּלְמָרְדֳּכַי הַיְּהוּדִי הִנֵּה בֵית־הָמָן
נָתַתִּי לְאֶסְתֵּר וְאֹתוֹ תָּלוּ עַל־הָעֵץ עַל אֲשֶׁר־
שָׁלַח יָדוֹ ביהודיים [בַּיְּהוּדִים]: וְאַתֶּם כִּתְבוּ
עַל־הַיְּהוּדִים כַּטּוֹב בְּעֵינֵיכֶם בְּשֵׁם הַמֶּלֶךְ
וְחִתְמוּ בְּטַבַּעַת הַמֶּלֶךְ כִּי־כְתָב אֲשֶׁר־נִכְתָּב

בשם־המלך ונחתום בטבעת המלך אין
להשיב: ויקראו ספרי־המלך בעת־ההיא
בחדש השלישי הוא־חדש סיון בשלושה
ועשרים בו ויכתב ככל־אשר־צוה מרדכי
אל־היהודים ואל האחשדרפנים והפחות
ושרי המדינות אשר | מהדו ועד־כוש שבע
ועשרים ומאה מדינה מדינה ומדינה
ככתבה ועם ועם כלשנו ואל־היהודים
ככתבם וכלשונם: ויכתב בשם המלך
אחשורש ויחתם בטבעת המלך וישלח
ספרים ביד הרצים בסוסים רכבי הרכש
האחשתרנים בני הרמכים: אשר נתן המלך
ליהודים | אשר | בכל־עיר ועיר להקהל
ולעמד על־נפשם להשמיד ולהרג ולאבד
את־כל־חיל עם ומדינה הצרים אתם טף
ונשים ושללם לבוז: ביום אחד בכל־
מדינות המלך אחשורוש בשלושה עשר
לחדש שנים־עשר הוא־חדש אדר: פתשגן
הכתב להנתן דת בכל־מדינה ומדינה גלוי
לכל־העמים ולהיות היהודיים [היהודים]
עתודים [עתידים] ליום הזה להנקם
מאיביהם: הרצים רכבי הרכש האחשתרנים
יצאו מבהלים ודחופים בדבר המלך והדת
נתנה בשושן הבירה: ומרדכי יצא | מלפני
המלך בלבוש מלכות תכלת וחור ועטרת
זהב גדולה ותכריך בוץ וארגמן והעיר
שושן צהלה ושמחה: ליהודים היתה
אורה ושמחה וששן ויקר: ובכל־מדינה
ומדינה ובכל־עיר ועיר מקום אשר דבר־
המלך ודתו מגיע שמחה וששון ליהודים
משתה ויום טוב ורבים מעמי הארץ
מתיהדים כי־נפל פחד־היהודים עליהם:
ט ובשנים עשר חדש הוא־חדש אדר בשלושה
עשר יום בו אשר הגיע דבר־המלך ודתו
להעשות ביום אשר שברו איבי היהודים
לשלוט בהם ונהפוך הוא אשר ישלטו
היהודים המה בשנאיהם: נקהלו היהודים
בעריהם בכל־מדינות המלך אחשורוש
לשלח יד במבקשי רעתם ואיש לא־עמד
לפניהם כי־נפל פחדם על־כל־העמים:
וכל־שרי המדינות והאחשדרפנים והפחות
ועשי המלאכה אשר למלך מנשאים את־
היהודים כי־נפל פחד־מרדכי עליהם: כי־
גדול מרדכי בבית המלך ושמעו הולך בכל־
המדינות כי־האיש מרדכי הולך וגדול: ויכו
היהודים בכל־איביהם מכת־חרב והרג
ואבדן ויעשו בשנאיהם כרצונם: ובשושן
הבירה הרגו היהודים ואבד חמש מאות
איש: ואת |
פרשנדתא ואת |
דלפון ואת |
אספתא: ואת |
פורתא ואת |
אדליא ואת |
ארידתא: ואת |
פרמשתא ואת |
אריסי ואת |
ארידי ואת |
ויזתא: עשרת
בני המן בן־המדתא צרר היהודים הרגו
ובבזה לא שלחו את־ידם: ביום ההוא בא
מספר ההרוגים בשושן הבירה לפני המלך:
ויאמר המלך לאסתר המלכה בשושן
הבירה הרגו היהודים ואבד חמש מאות
איש ואת עשרת בני־המן בשאר מדינות
המלך מה עשו ומה־שאלתך וינתן לך
ומה־בקשתך עוד ותעש: ותאמר אסתר
אם־על־המלך טוב ינתן גם־מחר ליהודים
אשר בשושן לעשות כדת היום ואת עשרת
בני־המן יתלו על־העץ: ויאמר המלך

לְהֵעָשׂוֹת כֵּן וַתִּנָּתֵן דָּת בְּשׁוּשָׁן וְאֵת עֲשֶׂרֶת
בְּנֵי־הָמָן תָּלוּ: וַיִּקָּהֲלוּ היהודיים [הַיְּהוּדִים]
אֲשֶׁר־בְּשׁוּשָׁן גַּם בְּיוֹם אַרְבָּעָה עָשָׂר לְחֹדֶשׁ
אֲדָר וַיַּהַרְגוּ בְשׁוּשָׁן שְׁלֹשׁ מֵאוֹת אִישׁ וּבַבִּזָּה
לֹא שָׁלְחוּ אֶת־יָדָם: וּשְׁאָר הַיְּהוּדִים אֲשֶׁר
בִּמְדִינוֹת הַמֶּלֶךְ נִקְהֲלוּ ׀ וְעָמֹד עַל־נַפְשָׁם
וְנוֹחַ מֵאֹיְבֵיהֶם וְהָרוֹג בְּשֹׂנְאֵיהֶם חֲמִשָּׁה
וְשִׁבְעִים אָלֶף וּבַבִּזָּה לֹא שָׁלְחוּ אֶת־
יָדָם: בְּיוֹם־שְׁלוֹשָׁה עָשָׂר לְחֹדֶשׁ אֲדָר וְנוֹחַ
בְּאַרְבָּעָה עָשָׂר בּוֹ וְעָשֹׂה אֹתוֹ יוֹם מִשְׁתֶּה
וְשִׂמְחָה: והיהודיים [וְהַיְּהוּדִים] אֲשֶׁר־
בְּשׁוּשָׁן נִקְהֲלוּ בִּשְׁלוֹשָׁה עָשָׂר בּוֹ וּבְאַרְבָּעָה
עָשָׂר בּוֹ וְנוֹחַ בַּחֲמִשָּׁה עָשָׂר בּוֹ וְעָשֹׂה אֹתוֹ
יוֹם מִשְׁתֶּה וְשִׂמְחָה: עַל־כֵּן הַיְּהוּדִים
הפרוזים [הַפְּרָזִים] הַיֹּשְׁבִים בְּעָרֵי הַפְּרָזוֹת
עֹשִׂים אֵת יוֹם אַרְבָּעָה עָשָׂר לְחֹדֶשׁ אֲדָר
שִׂמְחָה וּמִשְׁתֶּה וְיוֹם טוֹב וּמִשְׁלֹחַ מָנוֹת
אִישׁ לְרֵעֵהוּ: וַיִּכְתֹּב מָרְדֳּכַי אֶת־הַדְּבָרִים
הָאֵלֶּה וַיִּשְׁלַח סְפָרִים אֶל־כָּל־הַיְּהוּדִים
אֲשֶׁר בְּכָל־מְדִינוֹת הַמֶּלֶךְ אֲחַשְׁוֵרוֹשׁ
הַקְּרוֹבִים וְהָרְחוֹקִים: לְקַיֵּם עֲלֵיהֶם לִהְיוֹת
עֹשִׂים אֵת יוֹם אַרְבָּעָה עָשָׂר לְחֹדֶשׁ אֲדָר
וְאֵת יוֹם־חֲמִשָּׁה עָשָׂר בּוֹ בְּכָל־שָׁנָה וְשָׁנָה:
כַּיָּמִים אֲשֶׁר־נָחוּ בָהֶם הַיְּהוּדִים מֵאֹיְבֵיהֶם
וְהַחֹדֶשׁ אֲשֶׁר נֶהְפַּךְ לָהֶם מִיָּגוֹן לְשִׂמְחָה
וּמֵאֵבֶל לְיוֹם טוֹב לַעֲשׂוֹת אוֹתָם יְמֵי מִשְׁתֶּה
וְשִׂמְחָה וּמִשְׁלֹחַ מָנוֹת אִישׁ לְרֵעֵהוּ וּמַתָּנוֹת
לָאֶבְיֹנִים: וְקִבֵּל הַיְּהוּדִים אֵת אֲשֶׁר־הֵחֵלּוּ
לַעֲשׂוֹת וְאֵת אֲשֶׁר־כָּתַב מָרְדֳּכַי אֲלֵיהֶם: כִּי
הָמָן בֶּן־הַמְּדָתָא הָאֲגָגִי צֹרֵר כָּל־הַיְּהוּדִים
חָשַׁב עַל־הַיְּהוּדִים לְאַבְּדָם וְהִפִּל פּוּר הוּא
הַגּוֹרָל לְהֻמָּם וּלְאַבְּדָם: וּבְבֹאָהּ לִפְנֵי הַמֶּלֶךְ
אָמַר עִם־הַסֵּפֶר יָשׁוּב מַחֲשַׁבְתּוֹ הָרָעָה
אֲשֶׁר־חָשַׁב עַל־הַיְּהוּדִים עַל־רֹאשׁוֹ וְתָלוּ
אֹתוֹ וְאֶת־בָּנָיו עַל־הָעֵץ: עַל־כֵּן קָרְאוּ
לַיָּמִים הָאֵלֶּה פוּרִים עַל־שֵׁם הַפּוּר עַל־
כֵּן עַל־כָּל־דִּבְרֵי הָאִגֶּרֶת הַזֹּאת וּמָה־רָאוּ
עַל־כָּכָה וּמָה הִגִּיעַ אֲלֵיהֶם: קִיְּמוּ וְקִבְּלֻ
הַיְּהוּדִים ׀ עֲלֵיהֶם ׀ וְעַל־זַרְעָם וְעַל כָּל־
הַנִּלְוִים עֲלֵיהֶם וְלֹא יַעֲבוֹר לִהְיוֹת עֹשִׂים
אֶת־שְׁנֵי הַיָּמִים הָאֵלֶּה כִּכְתָבָם וְכִזְמַנָּם
בְּכָל־שָׁנָה וְשָׁנָה: וְהַיָּמִים הָאֵלֶּה נִזְכָּרִים
וְנַעֲשִׂים בְּכָל־דּוֹר וָדוֹר מִשְׁפָּחָה וּמִשְׁפָּחָה
מְדִינָה וּמְדִינָה וְעִיר וָעִיר וִימֵי הַפּוּרִים
הָאֵלֶּה לֹא יַעַבְרוּ מִתּוֹךְ הַיְּהוּדִים וְזִכְרָם
לֹא־יָסוּף מִזַּרְעָם: וַתִּכְתֹּב אֶסְתֵּר הַמַּלְכָּה
בַת־אֲבִיחַיִל וּמָרְדֳּכַי הַיְּהוּדִי אֶת־כָּל־
תֹּקֶף לְקַיֵּם אֵת אִגֶּרֶת הַפֻּרִים הַזֹּאת
הַשֵּׁנִית: וַיִּשְׁלַח סְפָרִים אֶל־כָּל־הַיְּהוּדִים
אֶל־שֶׁבַע וְעֶשְׂרִים וּמֵאָה מְדִינָה מַלְכוּת
אֲחַשְׁוֵרוֹשׁ דִּבְרֵי שָׁלוֹם וֶאֱמֶת: לְקַיֵּם אֶת־
יְמֵי הַפֻּרִים הָאֵלֶּה בִּזְמַנֵּיהֶם כַּאֲשֶׁר קִיַּם
עֲלֵיהֶם מָרְדֳּכַי הַיְּהוּדִי וְאֶסְתֵּר הַמַּלְכָּה
וְכַאֲשֶׁר קִיְּמוּ עַל־נַפְשָׁם וְעַל־זַרְעָם דִּבְרֵי
הַצּוֹמוֹת וְזַעֲקָתָם: וּמַאֲמַר אֶסְתֵּר קִיַּם דִּבְרֵי
י הַפֻּרִים הָאֵלֶּה וְנִכְתָּב בַּסֵּפֶר: וַיָּשֶׂם הַמֶּלֶךְ
אחשרש [אֲחַשְׁוֵרוֹשׁ] ׀ מַס עַל־הָאָרֶץ
וְאִיֵּי הַיָּם: וְכָל־מַעֲשֵׂה תָקְפּוֹ וּגְבוּרָתוֹ
וּפָרָשַׁת גְּדֻלַּת מָרְדֳּכַי אֲשֶׁר גִּדְּלוֹ הַמֶּלֶךְ
הֲלוֹא־הֵם כְּתוּבִים עַל־סֵפֶר דִּבְרֵי הַיָּמִים
לְמַלְכֵי מָדַי וּפָרָס: • כִּי ׀ מָרְדֳּכַי הַיְּהוּדִי
מִשְׁנֶה לַמֶּלֶךְ אֲחַשְׁוֵרוֹשׁ וְגָדוֹל לַיְּהוּדִים
וְרָצוּי לְרֹב אֶחָיו דֹּרֵשׁ טוֹב לְעַמּוֹ וְדֹבֵר שָׁלוֹם
לְכָל־זַרְעוֹ: •

The service continues on page 954.

THE BOOK OF PSALMS / ספר תהלים

SELECTED PSALMS TO BE RECITED IN TIMES OF SPECIAL NEED

CATEGORY	CIRCUMSTANCE OR NEED	PSALM
Personal petitions for relief from:	Depression	6, 13
	Illness and suffering (R. Shlomo Zalman Auerbach ruled that when reciting publicly psalms for the sick, one should start by announcing the name of the sick person, so that everyone will have that person in mind.)	20, 6, 9, 13, 16, 17, 18, 22, 23, 28, 30, 31, 33, 37, 38, 39, 41, 49, 55, ,56, 69, 86, 88, 89, 90, 91, 102, 103, 104, 107, 116, 118, 142, 143, 148.
	Personal misfortune/tragedy	16, 40
	Shame	13, 71
	Slander	120
	Influence of the wicked	141
	Violent men	141
	Guilt and sin	51, 130
Personal petitions for blessing:	Abundance and economic success	67, 144
	Heavenly guidance	139
	Leaving an inheritance	17
	Long life	71, 102
	Piety	16
	In adverse judicial situations	35
	Spiritual and general success	19, 51, 90, 102
	Childbirth	113
	Children's well-being	8, 113, 128
	A wedding or a Brit Mila	128

THE RECITAL OF SELECTED PSALMS IN TIMES OF SPECIAL NEED

The book of Psalms includes compositions by eleven authors, most prominently King David, spanning over one thousand years. According to one view, King David was responsible for their final form (*Bava Batra* 16b), while another view attributes that to Ezra (*Shir HaShirim Raba* 2:4). While the psalms were composed at a particular time and place, the Tanakh intentionally blurred the precise circumstances surrounding the composition of most psalms, so as to make them suitable for the many different needs of countless worshipers throughout the generations (*Daat Mikra*). Some psalms express themselves in the singular, while others do so in the plural. However, regardless of their form, the psalms evoke, and thus apply to, both personal and communal needs. In the words of our sages, when David arranged the psalms, he intended them both as his private prayers, as well as those of all of Israel (*Midrash Tehillim* 24).

Nowadays, it is not uncommon for people to pray for their present needs by meditation on and saying prayers that were written long ago. Such reuse of previously composed prayers was already commonplace during the prophetic era. People would seek out a psalm that contained a verse or an overarching theme that reflected their concerns. They

CATEGORY	CIRCUMSTANCE OR NEED	PSALM
Personal thanks-giving for:	Gifts of God's creation	8, 19, 93
	Salvation from sickness or danger	30, 116
Personal expressions of faith or reflection:	Adoration of God	8, 33
	Allegiance to God	71
	Faith in the face of death	16, 23
	Hope in God	13
	Longing for God	42
	God's knowledge of all	139
	Repentance	32, 40, 51, 130
	Trust in God	16, 91
	Praise of the faithful	33
	Praise of righteousness	128
	Human frailty	90
	When seeing the Temple Mount	24, 137, 120–134,
	When visiting graves (of the pious)	16, 91
	When visiting holy places, such as synagogues, near Temple Mount	84
Communal petitions under duress:	For redemption	42, 102
	General encouragement	121, 125
	General prayer for salvation	22, 102
	General prayer that prayer be heard	40, 102
	Against enemies of our people	20, 35, 83, 142–144
	For communal love	12
	National salvation	44, 67, 69, 80, 94, 104, 115, 126
	For Jerusalem	48, 102, 122, 125
Thanksgiving:	General thanksgiving	100, 107, 111, 113, 135, 136
	Thanksgiving for redemption	98, 118, 126
	Thanksgiving for return to Zion and prayer for its well-being	85
	Thanksgiving for justice/redemption	113–115
	Inauguration of a Sefer Torah or synagogue	24

would use such psalms and prayers to express their profound feelings, yearnings, and pleas, as we still do today. For example, Hannah's song (I *Samuel* 2:1–10), through which she expressed her gratitude to God for giving birth to a long-awaited child, is replete with military themes, which is quite surprising. However, it may have been part of a pre-existing psalm written by an even earlier prophet, and Hannah may have chosen it on account of the phrase (ibid. v. 5), "The barren has borne seven" (R. Elchanan Samet). Likewise,

תפילה לפני אמירת תהלים

יְהִי רָצוֹן מִלְּפָנֶיךָ, יהוה אֱלֹהֵינוּ וֵאלֹהֵי אֲבוֹתֵינוּ, הַבּוֹחֵר בְּדָוִד עַבְדּוֹ וּבְזַרְעוֹ
אַחֲרָיו, וְהַבּוֹחֵר בְּשִׁירוֹת וְתִשְׁבָּחוֹת, שֶׁתֵּפֶן בְּרַחֲמִים אֶל קְרִיאַת
מִזְמוֹרֵי תְהִלִּים שֶׁאֶקְרָא כְּאִלּוּ אֲמָרָם דָּוִד הַמֶּלֶךְ עָלָיו הַשָּׁלוֹם בְּעַצְמוֹ,
זְכוּתוֹ תָּגֵן עָלֵינוּ. וְתַעֲמָד לָנוּ זְכוּת פְּסוּקֵי תְהִלִּים וּזְכוּת תֵּבוֹתֵיהֶם
וְאוֹתִיּוֹתֵיהֶם וּנְקֻדּוֹתֵיהֶם וְטַעֲמֵיהֶם וְהַשֵּׁמוֹת הַיּוֹצְאִים מֵהֶם מֵרָאשֵׁי
תֵבוֹת וּמִסּוֹפֵי תֵבוֹת, לְכַפֵּר פְּשָׁעֵינוּ וַעֲוֹנוֹתֵינוּ וְחַטֹּאתֵינוּ, וּלְזַמֵּר עָרִיצִים
וּלְהַכְרִית כָּל הַחוֹחִים וְהַקּוֹצִים הַסּוֹבְבִים אֶת הַשּׁוֹשַׁנָּה הָעֶלְיוֹנָה, וּלְחַבֵּר
אֵשֶׁת נְעוּרִים עִם דּוֹדָהּ בְּאַהֲבָה וְאַחֲוָה וְרֵעוּת. וּמִשָּׁם יִמָּשֵׁךְ לָנוּ שֶׁפַע
לְנֶפֶשׁ רוּחַ וּנְשָׁמָה, לְטַהֲרֵנוּ מֵעֲוֹנוֹתֵינוּ וְלִסְלֹחַ חַטֹּאתֵינוּ וּלְכַפֵּר פְּשָׁעֵינוּ.
כְּמוֹ שֶׁסָּלַחְתָּ לְדָוִד שֶׁאָמַר מִזְמוֹרִים אֵלּוּ לְפָנֶיךָ, כְּמוֹ שֶׁנֶּאֱמַר, גַּם־יהוה שמואל ב׳ יב
הֶעֱבִיר חַטָּאתְךָ לֹא תָמוּת: וְאַל תִּקָּחֵנוּ מֵהָעוֹלָם הַזֶּה קֹדֶם זְמַנֵּנוּ עַד
מְלֹאת שְׁנוֹתֵינוּ, בְּאֹפֶן שֶׁנּוּכַל לְתַקֵּן אֶת אֲשֶׁר שִׁחַתְנוּ. וּזְכוּת דָּוִד הַמֶּלֶךְ
עָלָיו הַשָּׁלוֹם תָּגֵן עָלֵינוּ וּבַעֲדֵנוּ, שֶׁתַּאֲרִיךְ אַפְּךָ עַד שׁוּבֵנוּ אֵלֶיךָ בִּתְשׁוּבָה
שְׁלֵמָה לְפָנֶיךָ. וּמֵאוֹצַר מַתְּנַת חִנָּם חָנֵּנוּ, כְּדִכְתִיב, וְחַנֹּתִי אֶת־אֲשֶׁר אָחֹן שמות לג
וְרִחַמְתִּי אֶת־אֲשֶׁר אֲרַחֵם: וּכְשֵׁם שֶׁאָנוּ אוֹמְרִים לְפָנֶיךָ שִׁירָה בָּעוֹלָם הַזֶּה,
כָּךְ נִזְכֶּה לוֹמַר לְפָנֶיךָ, יהוה אֱלֹהֵינוּ, שִׁיר וּשְׁבָחָה לָעוֹלָם הַבָּא. וְעַל יְדֵי
אֲמִירַת תְּהִלִּים, תִּתְעוֹרֵר חֲבַצֶּלֶת הַשָּׁרוֹן וְלָשִׁיר בְּקוֹל נָעִים בְּגִילַת וְרַנֵּן,
כְּבוֹד הַלְּבָנוֹן נִתַּן לָהּ, הוֹד וְהָדָר בְּבֵית אֱלֹהֵינוּ בִּמְהֵרָה בְיָמֵינוּ, אָמֵן סֶלָה.

לְכוּ נְרַנְּנָה לַיהוה, נָרִיעָה לְצוּר יִשְׁעֵנוּ: נְקַדְּמָה פָנָיו בְּתוֹדָה, בִּזְמִרוֹת תהלים צה
נָרִיעַ לוֹ: כִּי אֵל גָּדוֹל יהוה, וּמֶלֶךְ גָּדוֹל עַל־כָּל־אֱלֹהִים:

Many are accustomed to recite תהלים *on an ongoing basis, following various patterns. To that end the one hundred and fifty psalms have traditionally been grouped in various ways, i.e., into five books, into seven sections (one for each day of the week), and into thirty segments (one for each day of the month). These divisions are indicated in the pages that follow.*

The תפילה *following the recitation of* תהלים *is on page 1328.*
For a list of psalms and prayers said on behalf of the sick, see the table on the previous page.

Joshua's victory song, "Then spoke Joshua to God on the day when God delivered up the Amorites before the children of Israel; and he said in the sight of Israel: "Sun, stand thou still upon Gibeon: and thou, Moon, in the Valley of Ayalon" (Joshua 10:12), was very possibly adapted from an earlier song about Moses' victory over the Amalekites (R. Y. Etshalom).

Throughout the generations such classic prayers have continued to resonate, helping the Jew express the full spectrum of feelings.

There are differing approaches to the

PRAYER BEFORE RECITING TEHILLIM

יְהִי רָצוֹן MAY IT BE Your will, Lord, our God and the God of our fathers, Who chose His servant David and his descendants after him, and Who chose songs and praises, that You turn with compassion to the psalms I will say, as if King David, of blessed memory, may his merit protect us, had said them himself. May the merit of the verses of the psalms, and the merit of the words and their letters and their vowels and their cantillations, and the holy Names formed from their initial and final letters, stand in our favor, to bring atonement for our transgressions, iniquities, and sins. May they cut down ruthless men and slash away all the thorns and briars surrounding the celestial rose. May they cause the bride of youth to unite with her beloved in love, brotherhood, and companionship. And from that union may we draw abundance for our spirit, breath, and soul, to purify us of our iniquities, to gain forgiveness for our sins and atone for our transgressions, just as
1 Sam. 12 you forgave David, who recited these very same psalms before You, as it says: "The Lord has also forgiven your sin; you shall not die." Do not take us from this world before our time, before completion of our years, in a way that allows us to repair that which we have destroyed. May the merit of King David, of blessed memory, protect and shield us, so that You will be patient with us until we can return to You with complete and prefect repentance. Be gracious to us from Your treasury
Ex. 33 of undeserved grace, as it is written: "I shall show favor when I choose to show favor, and I shall be compassionate when I choose to be compassionate." And just as we sing to You in this world, may we merit, Lord, our God, to sing songs and praises to You in the World to Come. Through saying the psalms may the Rose of Sharon awaken, to sing in a lovely voice, with joy and ecstasy. May the glory of the Lebanon be given her, splendor and majesty in the House of God, speedily, in our days. Amen, Selah.

Ps. 95 **לְכוּ נְרַנְּנָה** COME, let us sing to the Lord, let us shout joyfully to the Rock of our salvation. Let us come before Him with thanksgiving, let us raise our voice in song. For the Lord is a great God, and a great King above all gods.

Many are accustomed to recite Tehillim on an ongoing basis, following various patterns. To that end the one hundred and fifty psalms have traditionally been grouped in various ways, i.e., into five books, into seven sections (one for each day of the week,) and into thirty segments (one for each day of the month). These divisions are indicated in the pages that follow.

The prayer following the recitation of the Psalms is on page 1329.
For a list of psalms and prayers said on behalf of the sick, see the table on the previous page.

---

selection of specific psalms for particular circumstances. Sometimes it is a Midrashic insight on a verse or word in the psalm that evokes the association. At other times it is an explicit phrase in the psalm that does so.

In the table above, we have chosen to pay particular attention to the themes found in the psalms particularly appropriate for expressing the prayers, petitions, and thanksgiving in our hearts (R. Aharon Lichtenstein).

ספר תהלים

ספר ראשון

*א אַשְׁרֵי־הָאִישׁ אֲשֶׁר | לֹא הָלַךְ בַּעֲצַת רְשָׁעִים וּבְדֶרֶךְ חַטָּאִים לֹא עָמָד
וּבְמוֹשַׁב לֵצִים לֹא יָשָׁב: כִּי אִם בְּתוֹרַת יהוה חֶפְצוֹ וּבְתוֹרָתוֹ יֶהְגֶּה
יוֹמָם וָלָיְלָה: וְהָיָה כְּעֵץ שָׁתוּל עַל־פַּלְגֵי מָיִם אֲשֶׁר פִּרְיוֹ | יִתֵּן בְּעִתּוֹ
וְעָלֵהוּ לֹא־יִבּוֹל וְכֹל אֲשֶׁר־יַעֲשֶׂה יַצְלִיחַ: לֹא־כֵן הָרְשָׁעִים כִּי אִם־כַּמֹּץ
אֲשֶׁר־תִּדְּפֶנּוּ רוּחַ: עַל־כֵּן | לֹא־יָקֻמוּ רְשָׁעִים בַּמִּשְׁפָּט וְחַטָּאִים בַּעֲדַת
צַדִּיקִים: כִּי־יוֹדֵעַ יהוה דֶּרֶךְ צַדִּיקִים וְדֶרֶךְ רְשָׁעִים תֹּאבֵד:

ב לָמָּה רָגְשׁוּ גוֹיִם וּלְאֻמִּים יֶהְגּוּ־רִיק: יִתְיַצְּבוּ | מַלְכֵי־אֶרֶץ וְרוֹזְנִים נוֹסְדוּ־
יָחַד עַל־יהוה וְעַל־מְשִׁיחוֹ: נְנַתְּקָה אֶת־מוֹסְרוֹתֵימוֹ וְנַשְׁלִיכָה מִמֶּנּוּ
עֲבֹתֵימוֹ: יוֹשֵׁב בַּשָּׁמַיִם יִשְׂחָק אֲדֹנָי יִלְעַג־לָמוֹ: אָז יְדַבֵּר אֵלֵימוֹ בְאַפּוֹ
וּבַחֲרוֹנוֹ יְבַהֲלֵמוֹ: וַאֲנִי נָסַכְתִּי מַלְכִּי עַל־צִיּוֹן הַר־קָדְשִׁי: אֲסַפְּרָה אֶל
חֹק יהוה אָמַר אֵלַי בְּנִי אַתָּה אֲנִי הַיּוֹם יְלִדְתִּיךָ: שְׁאַל מִמֶּנִּי וְאֶתְּנָה
גוֹיִם נַחֲלָתֶךָ וַאֲחֻזָּתְךָ אַפְסֵי־אָרֶץ: תְּרֹעֵם בְּשֵׁבֶט בַּרְזֶל כִּכְלִי יוֹצֵר
תְּנַפְּצֵם: וְעַתָּה מְלָכִים הַשְׂכִּילוּ הִוָּסְרוּ שֹׁפְטֵי אָרֶץ: עִבְדוּ אֶת־יהוה
בְּיִרְאָה וְגִילוּ בִּרְעָדָה: נַשְּׁקוּ־בַר פֶּן־יֶאֱנַף | וְתֹאבְדוּ דֶרֶךְ כִּי־יִבְעַר כִּמְעַט
אַפּוֹ אַשְׁרֵי כָּל־חוֹסֵי בוֹ:

ג מִזְמוֹר לְדָוִד בְּבָרְחוֹ מִפְּנֵי | אַבְשָׁלוֹם בְּנוֹ: יהוה מָה־רַבּוּ צָרָי רַבִּים
קָמִים עָלָי: רַבִּים אֹמְרִים לְנַפְשִׁי אֵין יְשׁוּעָתָה לּוֹ בֵאלֹהִים סֶלָה: וְאַתָּה
יהוה מָגֵן בַּעֲדִי כְּבוֹדִי וּמֵרִים רֹאשִׁי: קוֹלִי אֶל־יהוה אֶקְרָא וַיַּעֲנֵנִי מֵהַר
קָדְשׁוֹ סֶלָה: אֲנִי שָׁכַבְתִּי וָאִישָׁנָה הֱקִיצוֹתִי כִּי יהוה יִסְמְכֵנִי: לֹא־אִירָא
מֵרִבְבוֹת עָם אֲשֶׁר סָבִיב שָׁתוּ עָלָי: קוּמָה יהוה | הוֹשִׁיעֵנִי אֱלֹהַי כִּי־
הִכִּיתָ אֶת־כָּל־אֹיְבַי לֶחִי שִׁנֵּי רְשָׁעִים שִׁבַּרְתָּ: לַיהוה הַיְשׁוּעָה עַל־
עַמְּךָ בִרְכָתֶךָ סֶּלָה:

ד לַמְנַצֵּחַ בִּנְגִינוֹת מִזְמוֹר לְדָוִד: בְּקָרְאִי עֲנֵנִי | אֱלֹהֵי צִדְקִי בַּצָּר הִרְחַבְתָּ
לִּי חָנֵּנִי וּשְׁמַע תְּפִלָּתִי: בְּנֵי־אִישׁ עַד־מֶה כְבוֹדִי לִכְלִמָּה תֶּאֱהָבוּן רִיק
תְּבַקְשׁוּ כָזָב סֶלָה: וּדְעוּ כִּי־הִפְלָה יהוה חָסִיד לוֹ יהוה יִשְׁמַע בְּקָרְאִי
אֵלָיו: רִגְזוּ וְאַל־תֶּחֱטָאוּ אִמְרוּ בִלְבַבְכֶם עַל־מִשְׁכַּבְכֶם וְדֹמּוּ סֶלָה: זִבְחוּ

---

*א לחודש / ליום הראשון

THE BOOK OF PSALMS

BOOK ONE

*1 HAPPY is the man who does not walk in the counsel of the wicked, and does not stand
in the way of sinners, and does not sit in the seat of the scornful. But his desire is in
the law of the Lord, and he meditates on His law day and night. And he shall be like a
tree planted by streams of water, which gives its fruit in its season, and its leaf does not
wither, and all that it produces prospers. Not so are the wicked, but they are like the
chaff that the wind drives away. Therefore the wicked will not stand at the judgment,
nor sinners in the congregation of the righteous. For the Lord knows the way of the
righteous, but the way of the wicked will perish.

2 WHY do the nations shout, and the peoples plan in vain? The kings of the earth
assemble, and the rulers take counsel together, against the Lord and against His
anointed: "Let us break their bonds, and let us cast off their cords from us." He Who
dwells in heaven will laugh. The Lord will deride them. Then He will speak to them in
His wrath, and in His anger, He will throw them into confusion. "But I have appointed
My king upon Zion, My holy mountain." I will speak on behalf of the pronouncement.
The Lord has said to me: "You are My son; I today have begotten you. Ask Me and
I will give you the nations for your inheritance, and the ends of the earth for your
possession." You will break them with a rod of iron. Like a potter's vessel you will
smash them into pieces. And now, O kings, be wise. Take instruction, O judges of
the earth. Serve the Lord with fear, and rejoice with trembling. Kiss purity, lest He
be angry and you lose your way, for His anger will quickly be kindled. Happy are all
who seek refuge in Him.

3 A PSALM of David when he fled from before Absalom his son. The Lord, how many
are they that trouble me! Many are they that rise up against me. Many are they that
say of my soul: There is no deliverance for him in God. Selah. But You, Lord, are
a shield for me, my glory and the raiser of my head. With my voice, I call on unto
the Lord, and He answers me from His holy mountain. Selah. I lay down and I
slept. I awakened, for the Lord would sustain me. I am not afraid of ten thousands
of people, who have arrayed themselves against me round about. Rise up, Lord.
Save me, O my God. Smite all my enemies on the cheek bone. Smash the teeth
of the wicked. Deliverance is the Lord's. May Your blessing be upon Your people.
Selah.

4 TO THE DIRECTOR of music for instruments. A psalm of David. Answer me when I
call, O my God of righteousness. Enlarge me in my distress. Be gracious unto me and
hear my prayer. O sons of man, how long will my glory be shame? How long will you
love vanity, will you seek falsehood? Selah. But know that the Lord has set apart the
pious man for Himself. The Lord will hear when I call unto Him. Tremble and do not
sin. Commune with your heart upon your bed and be silent. Selah. Offer righteous
sacrifices and trust in the Lord. Many say: "O that someone would show us good!" Lift

*1st DAY of the month / SUNDAY

זִבְחֵי־צֶדֶק וּבִטְחוּ אֶל־יְהוָה: רַבִּים אֹמְרִים מִֽי־יַרְאֵנוּ טוֹב נְֽסָה־עָלֵינוּ
אוֹר פָּנֶיךָ יְהוָה: נָתַתָּה שִׂמְחָה בְלִבִּי מֵעֵת דְּגָנָם וְתִירוֹשָׁם רָבּוּ: בְּשָׁלוֹם
יַחְדָּו אֶשְׁכְּבָה וְאִישָׁן כִּֽי־אַתָּה יְהוָה לְבָדָד לָבֶטַח תּוֹשִׁיבֵנִי:
ה לַמְנַצֵּחַ אֶל־הַנְּחִילוֹת מִזְמוֹר לְדָוִד: אֲמָרַי הַאֲזִינָה ׀ יְהוָה בִּינָה הֲגִיגִי:
הַקְשִׁיבָה ׀ לְקוֹל שַׁוְעִי מַלְכִּי וֵאלֹהָי כִּֽי־אֵלֶיךָ אֶתְפַּלָּל: יְהוָה בֹּקֶר תִּשְׁמַע
קוֹלִי בֹּקֶר אֶעֱרָךְ־לְךָ וַאֲצַפֶּה: כִּי ׀ לֹא אֵל־חָפֵץ רֶשַׁע ׀ אָתָּה לֹא יְגֻרְךָ רָע:
לֹא־יִתְיַצְּבוּ הוֹלְלִים לְנֶגֶד עֵינֶיךָ שָׂנֵאתָ כָּל־פֹּעֲלֵי אָוֶן: תְּאַבֵּד דֹּבְרֵי כָזָב
אִישׁ־דָּמִים וּמִרְמָה יְתָעֵב ׀ יְהוָה: וַאֲנִי בְּרֹב חַסְדְּךָ אָבוֹא בֵיתֶךָ אֶשְׁתַּחֲוֶה
אֶל־הֵיכַל־קָדְשְׁךָ בְּיִרְאָתֶךָ: יְהוָה ׀ נְחֵנִי בְצִדְקָתֶךָ לְמַעַן שׁוֹרְרָי הושר הַיְשַׁר
לְפָנַי דַּרְכֶּךָ: כִּי אֵין בְּפִיהוּ נְכוֹנָה קִרְבָּם הַוּוֹת קֶבֶר־פָּתוּחַ גְּרוֹנָם לְשׁוֹנָם
יַחֲלִיקוּן: הַאֲשִׁימֵם ׀ אֱלֹהִים יִפְּלוּ מִמֹּעֲצוֹתֵיהֶם בְּרֹב פִּשְׁעֵיהֶם הַדִּיחֵמוֹ
כִּי מָרוּ בָךְ: וְיִשְׂמְחוּ כָל־חוֹסֵי בָךְ לְעוֹלָם יְרַנֵּנוּ וְתָסֵךְ עָלֵימוֹ וְיַעְלְצוּ בְךָ
אֹהֲבֵי שְׁמֶךָ: כִּי־אַתָּה תְּבָרֵךְ צַדִּיק יְהוָה כַּצִּנָּה רָצוֹן תַּעְטְרֶנּוּ:
ו לַמְנַצֵּחַ בִּנְגִינוֹת עַל־הַשְּׁמִינִית מִזְמוֹר לְדָוִד: יְהוָה אַל־בְּאַפְּךָ תוֹכִיחֵנִי
וְאַל־בַּחֲמָתְךָ תְיַסְּרֵנִי: חָנֵּנִי יְהוָה כִּי אֻמְלַל אָנִי רְפָאֵנִי יְהוָה כִּי נִבְהֲלוּ
עֲצָמָי: וְנַפְשִׁי נִבְהֲלָה מְאֹד וְאַתְּ יְהוָה עַד־מָתָי: שׁוּבָה יְהוָה חַלְּצָה
נַפְשִׁי הוֹשִׁיעֵנִי לְמַעַן חַסְדֶּךָ: כִּי אֵין בַּמָּוֶת זִכְרֶךָ בִּשְׁאוֹל מִי יוֹדֶה־לָּךְ:
יָגַעְתִּי ׀ בְּאַנְחָתִי אַשְׂחֶה בְכָל־לַיְלָה מִטָּתִי בְּדִמְעָתִי עַרְשִׂי אַמְסֶה:
עָשְׁשָׁה מִכַּעַס עֵינִי עָתְקָה בְּכָל־צוֹרְרָי: סוּרוּ מִמֶּנִּי כָּל־פֹּעֲלֵי אָוֶן כִּי־
שָׁמַע יְהוָה קוֹל בִּכְיִי: שָׁמַע יְהוָה תְּחִנָּתִי יְהוָה תְּפִלָּתִי יִקָּח: יֵבֹשׁוּ ׀
וְיִבָּהֲלוּ מְאֹד כָּל־אֹיְבָי יָשֻׁבוּ יֵבֹשׁוּ רָגַע:
ז שִׁגָּיוֹן לְדָוִד אֲשֶׁר־שָׁר לַיהוָה עַל־דִּבְרֵי־כוּשׁ בֶּן־יְמִינִי: יְהוָה אֱלֹהַי בְּךָ
חָסִיתִי הוֹשִׁיעֵנִי מִכָּל־רֹדְפַי וְהַצִּילֵנִי: פֶּן־יִטְרֹף כְּאַרְיֵה נַפְשִׁי פֹּרֵק וְאֵין
מַצִּיל: יְהוָה אֱלֹהַי אִם־עָשִׂיתִי זֹאת אִם־יֶשׁ־עָוֶל בְּכַפָּי: אִם־גָּמַלְתִּי
שׁוֹלְמִי רָע וָאֲחַלְּצָה צוֹרְרִי רֵיקָם: יִרַדֹּף אוֹיֵב ׀ נַפְשִׁי וְיַשֵּׂג וְיִרְמֹס לָאָרֶץ
חַיָּי וּכְבוֹדִי ׀ לֶעָפָר יַשְׁכֵּן סֶלָה: קוּמָה יְהוָה ׀ בְּאַפֶּךָ הִנָּשֵׂא בְּעַבְרוֹת צוֹרְרָי
וְעוּרָה אֵלַי מִשְׁפָּט צִוִּיתָ: וַעֲדַת לְאֻמִּים תְּסוֹבְבֶךָּ וְעָלֶיהָ לַמָּרוֹם שׁוּבָה:
יְהוָה יָדִין עַמִּים שָׁפְטֵנִי יְהוָה כְּצִדְקִי וּכְתֻמִּי עָלָי: יִגְמָר־נָא רַע ׀ רְשָׁעִים

up upon us the light of Your countenance, Lord. You have put joy in my heart more than theirs at the time when their corn and their wine increase. In peace, I both lie down and sleep, for You, Lord, make me dwell alone in safety.

5 TO THE DIRECTOR of music, *el-HaNeḥilot.* A psalm of David. Give ear to my words,
Lord. Consider my meditation. Hearken to the voice of my cry, my King and my God, for to You will I pray. Lord, in the morning You hear my voice. In the morning, I direct my prayer to You and wait expectantly. For You are not a God Who has pleasure in wickedness. Evil will not dwell with You. The boastful will not stand in Your sight. You hate all workers of iniquity. You destroy those who speak falsehood. The Lord abhors the bloody and deceitful man. But as for me, I will come into Your house in the abundance of Your loving-kindness. I will bow down toward Your holy Temple in the fear of You. Lord, lead me in Your righteousness because of my enemies. Make Your way straight before me. For there is no sincerity in his mouth. Their internal organs are malice. Their throat is an open grave. They flatter with their tongue. Condemn them, O God. Let them fall by their counsels. Cast them out for the multitude of their transgressions, for they have rebelled against You. But let all who put their trust in You rejoice. Let them shout for joy forever, and may You defend them. And let those who love Your name be joyful in You. For You, Lord, will bless the righteous. You will encircle him with favor as with a shield.

6 TO THE DIRECTOR of music for instruments *al-HaSheminit.* A psalm of David. Lord,
do not punish in Your anger, and do not chastise me in Your wrath. Favor me, Lord, for I am broken. Heal me, Lord, for my limbs are dismayed. And my soul is greatly dismayed, but You, Lord, how long? Turn, Lord, rescue my soul. Save me for the sake of Your loving-kindness. For in death there is no remembrance of You. In the underworld, who will give You thanks? I have become weary with my sighing. Every night I make my bed swim. I melt my couch with my tears. My eye is dimmed because of grief. It has become old because of all my adversaries. Depart from me, all you workers of iniquity, for the Lord has heard the voice of my weeping. The Lord has heard my supplication. The Lord will accept my prayer. May all my enemies be frustrated and greatly dismayed. May they turn back, may they be suddenly frustrated.

7 A *SHIGGAYON* of David, which he sang to the Lord concerning the words of Cush the
Benjaminite. Lord my God, in You I trust. Save me from all those who pursue me, and deliver me, Lest he tear my soul like a lion, and rend it in pieces while there is none to deliver. Lord my God, if I have done this, if there is iniquity in my hands, If I have requited with evil him who did me good, or stripped my adversary without cause, Then let the enemy pursue my soul and overtake it, and let him tread my life down to the earth, and let him lay my honor in the dust. Selah. Arise, Lord, in Your anger, raise Yourself up in the wrath provoked by my adversaries, and arouse for me the judgment that You have decreed. Then the congregation of peoples will surround You, and over it return You on high. The Lord will judge the peoples. Judge me, Lord, according to my righteousness

וּתְכוֹנֵן צַדִּיק וּבֹחֵן לִבּוֹת וּכְלָיוֹת אֱלֹהִים צַדִּיק׃ מָגִנִּי עַל־אֱלֹהִים מוֹשִׁיעַ
יִשְׁרֵי־לֵב׃ אֱלֹהִים שׁוֹפֵט צַדִּיק וְאֵל זֹעֵם בְּכָל־יוֹם׃ אִם־לֹא יָשׁוּב חַרְבּוֹ
יִלְטוֹשׁ קַשְׁתּוֹ דָרַךְ וַיְכוֹנְנֶהָ׃ וְלוֹ הֵכִין כְּלֵי־מָוֶת חִצָּיו לְדֹלְקִים יִפְעָל׃
הִנֵּה יְחַבֶּל־אָוֶן וְהָרָה עָמָל וְיָלַד שָׁקֶר׃ בּוֹר כָּרָה וַיַּחְפְּרֵהוּ וַיִּפֹּל בְּשַׁחַת
יִפְעָל׃ יָשׁוּב עֲמָלוֹ בְרֹאשׁוֹ וְעַל קָדְקֳדוֹ חֲמָסוֹ יֵרֵד׃ אוֹדֶה יְהוָה כְּצִדְקוֹ
וַאֲזַמְּרָה שֵׁם־יְהוָה עֶלְיוֹן׃
ח לַמְנַצֵּחַ עַל־הַגִּתִּית מִזְמוֹר לְדָוִד׃ יְהוָה אֲדֹנֵינוּ מָה־אַדִּיר שִׁמְךָ בְּכָל־
הָאָרֶץ אֲשֶׁר־תְּנָה הוֹדְךָ עַל־הַשָּׁמָיִם׃ מִפִּי עוֹלְלִים ׀ וְיֹנְקִים יִסַּדְתָּ
עֹז לְמַעַן צוֹרְרֶיךָ לְהַשְׁבִּית אוֹיֵב וּמִתְנַקֵּם׃ כִּי־אֶרְאֶה שָׁמֶיךָ מַעֲשֵׂה
אֶצְבְּעֹתֶיךָ יָרֵחַ וְכוֹכָבִים אֲשֶׁר כּוֹנָנְתָּה׃ מָה־אֱנוֹשׁ כִּי־תִזְכְּרֶנּוּ וּבֶן־
אָדָם כִּי תִפְקְדֶנּוּ׃ וַתְּחַסְּרֵהוּ מְּעַט מֵאֱלֹהִים וְכָבוֹד וְהָדָר תְּעַטְּרֵהוּ׃
תַּמְשִׁילֵהוּ בְּמַעֲשֵׂי יָדֶיךָ כֹּל שַׁתָּה תַחַת־רַגְלָיו׃ צֹנֶה וַאֲלָפִים כֻּלָּם וְגַם
בַּהֲמוֹת שָׂדָי׃ צִפּוֹר שָׁמַיִם וּדְגֵי הַיָּם עֹבֵר אָרְחוֹת יַמִּים׃ יְהוָה אֲדֹנֵינוּ
מָה־אַדִּיר שִׁמְךָ בְּכָל־הָאָרֶץ׃
ט לַמְנַצֵּחַ עַל־מוּת לַבֵּן מִזְמוֹר לְדָוִד׃ אוֹדֶה יְהוָה בְּכָל־לִבִּי אֲסַפְּרָה
כָּל־נִפְלְאוֹתֶיךָ׃ אֶשְׂמְחָה וְאֶעֶלְצָה בָךְ אֲזַמְּרָה שִׁמְךָ עֶלְיוֹן׃ בְּשׁוּב־
אוֹיְבַי אָחוֹר יִכָּשְׁלוּ וְיֹאבְדוּ מִפָּנֶיךָ׃ כִּי־עָשִׂיתָ מִשְׁפָּטִי וְדִינִי יָשַׁבְתָּ
לְכִסֵּא שׁוֹפֵט צֶדֶק׃ גָּעַרְתָּ גוֹיִם אִבַּדְתָּ רָשָׁע שְׁמָם מָחִיתָ לְעוֹלָם וָעֶד׃
הָאוֹיֵב ׀ תַּמּוּ חֳרָבוֹת לָנֶצַח וְעָרִים נָתַשְׁתָּ אָבַד זִכְרָם הֵמָּה׃ וַיהוָה
לְעוֹלָם יֵשֵׁב כּוֹנֵן לַמִּשְׁפָּט כִּסְאוֹ׃ וְהוּא יִשְׁפֹּט־תֵּבֵל בְּצֶדֶק יָדִין לְאֻמִּים
בְּמֵישָׁרִים׃ וִיהִי יְהוָה מִשְׂגָּב לַדָּךְ מִשְׂגָּב לְעִתּוֹת בַּצָּרָה׃ וְיִבְטְחוּ בְךָ
יוֹדְעֵי שְׁמֶךָ כִּי לֹא־עָזַבְתָּ דֹרְשֶׁיךָ יְהוָה׃ זַמְּרוּ לַיהוָה יֹשֵׁב צִיּוֹן הַגִּידוּ
עֲנָוִים בָעַמִּים עֲלִילוֹתָיו׃ כִּי־דֹרֵשׁ דָּמִים אוֹתָם זָכָר לֹא־שָׁכַח צַעֲקַת עניים׃
חָנְנֵנִי יְהוָה רְאֵה עָנְיִי מִשֹּׂנְאָי מְרוֹמְמִי מִשַּׁעֲרֵי־מָוֶת׃ לְמַעַן אֲסַפְּרָה
כָּל־תְּהִלָּתֶיךָ בְּשַׁעֲרֵי בַת־צִיּוֹן אָגִילָה בִּישׁוּעָתֶךָ׃ טָבְעוּ גוֹיִם בְּשַׁחַת
עָשׂוּ בְּרֶשֶׁת־זוּ טָמָנוּ נִלְכְּדָה רַגְלָם׃ נוֹדַע ׀ יְהוָה מִשְׁפָּט עָשָׂה בְּפֹעַל
כַּפָּיו נוֹקֵשׁ רָשָׁע הִגָּיוֹן סֶלָה׃ יָשׁוּבוּ רְשָׁעִים לִשְׁאוֹלָה כָּל־גּוֹיִם שְׁכֵחֵי
עֲנִיִּים אֱלֹהִים׃ כִּי לֹא לָנֶצַח יִשָּׁכַח אֶבְיוֹן תִּקְוַת ענוים תֹּאבַד לָעַד׃ קוּמָה

and according to my integrity that is in me. Let evil put an end to the wicked, but may
You establish the righteous, for You try hearts and reins, O righteous God. My defense is
in God, Who saves the upright in heart. God judges the righteous, and God rages every
day. If he does not repent, and he sharpens his sword, bends his bow, and makes it ready,
Then for himself he will have prepared in the instruments of death, he will have made his
arrows into blazing missiles. Behold, he conceives iniquity, and he carries mischief, and
he brings forth falsehood. He has dug a pit and hollowed it, and he has fallen into the pit
that he has made. His mischief will return upon his own head, and his crime will come
down upon his own pate. I will thank the Lord in accordance with His righteousness,
and I will sing praise to the name of the Lord Most High.
8 TO THE DIRECTOR of music *al-HaGittit.* A psalm of David. Lord, our Lord, how
majestic is Your name in all the earth, Whose splendor is set upon the heavens! Out
of the mouth of babes and sucklings You have founded a song of praise against Your
adversaries, to put an end to the enemy and the avenger. When I behold Your heavens,
the work of Your fingers, the moon and the stars that You have established, What is
man that You remember him, and the son of man that You are mindful of him? But
You have made him but little lower than the divine, and You have crowned him with
honor and glory. You have given him dominion over the works of Your hands. You
have laid all things under his feet. Sheep and oxen, all of them, and also the beasts of
the field. The fowl of the sky, and the fish of the sea; he passes through the paths of
the sea. Lord, our Lord, how majestic is Your name in all the earth!
9 TO THE DIRECTOR of music *al-mut laben.* A psalm of David. I thank the Lord with all
my heart. I will relate all Your wondrous works. I will rejoice in exulting You. I will sing
praise to Your name, O Most High, When my enemies turn back, when they stumble
and perish from before You, For You have executed my judgment and my cause. You
have sat upon the throne, O judge of righteousness. You have rebuked nations. You have
destroyed the wicked. You have erased their name forever and ever. As for the enemy,
its cities have come to an end and become perpetual ruins, and You have destroyed
the cities, their memorial is gone. But the Lord will sit for ever. He has established
His throne for judgment. And He will judge the world in righteousness. He will judge
the peoples in uprightness. And the Lord will be a refuge for the oppressed, a refuge
in times of trouble. And those who know Your name will trust in You, for You, Lord,
have not abandoned those who seek You. Sing praises to the Lord Who dwells in Zion,
declare His works among the peoples. For He Who avenges blood has remembered it.
He has not forgotten the cry of the oppressed. Be gracious unto me, Lord. Look upon
my affliction from those who hate me, You Who lift me up from the gates of death,
So that I may relate all Your praise in the gates of the daughter of Zion. I will rejoice
in Your salvation. The nations have drowned in the pit that they made. In the net that
they concealed their own foot has been caught. The Lord has become known through
the judgment that He executed. The wicked is snared in the work of his own hands.
Higgayon. Selah. May the wicked turn toward the underworld, all the nations that forget

יהוה אַל־יָעֹז אֱנוֹשׁ יִשָּׁפְטוּ גוֹיִם עַל־פָּנֶיךָ׃ שִׁיתָה יהוה ׀ מוֹרָה לָהֶם
יֵדְעוּ גוֹיִם אֱנוֹשׁ הֵמָּה סֶּלָה׃
*י לָמָה יהוה תַּעֲמֹד בְּרָחוֹק תַּעְלִים לְעִתּוֹת בַּצָּרָה׃ בְּגַאֲוַת רָשָׁע יִדְלַק
עָנִי יִתָּפְשׂוּ ׀ בִּמְזִמּוֹת זוּ חָשָׁבוּ׃ כִּי־הִלֵּל רָשָׁע עַל־תַּאֲוַת נַפְשׁוֹ וּבֹצֵעַ
בֵּרֵךְ נִאֵץ ׀ יהוה׃ רָשָׁע כְּגֹבַהּ אַפּוֹ בַּל־יִדְרֹשׁ אֵין אֱלֹהִים כָּל־מְזִמּוֹתָיו׃
יָחִילוּ דְרָכָו ׀ בְּכָל־עֵת מָרוֹם מִשְׁפָּטֶיךָ מִנֶּגְדּוֹ כָּל־צוֹרְרָיו יָפִיחַ בָּהֶם׃
אָמַר בְּלִבּוֹ בַּל־אֶמּוֹט לְדֹר וָדֹר אֲשֶׁר לֹא־בְרָע׃ אָלָה ׀ פִּיהוּ מָלֵא וּמִרְמוֹת
וָתֹךְ תַּחַת לְשׁוֹנוֹ עָמָל וָאָוֶן׃ יֵשֵׁב ׀ בְּמַאְרַב חֲצֵרִים בַּמִּסְתָּרִים יַהֲרֹג נָקִי
עֵינָיו לְחֵלְכָה יִצְפֹּנוּ׃ יֶאֱרֹב בַּמִּסְתָּר ׀ כְּאַרְיֵה בְסֻכֹּה יֶאֱרֹב לַחֲטוֹף עָנִי
יִדְכֶּה חֵל כָּאִים יַחְטֹף עָנִי בְּמָשְׁכוֹ בְרִשְׁתּוֹ׃ ודכה יָשֹׁחַ וְנָפַל בַּעֲצוּמָיו חלכאים׃ אָמַר
בְּלִבּוֹ שָׁכַח אֵל הִסְתִּיר פָּנָיו בַּל־רָאָה לָנֶצַח׃ קוּמָה יהוה אֵל נְשָׂא יָדֶךָ
עֲנָוִים אַל־תִּשְׁכַּח עניים׃ עַל־מֶה ׀ נִאֵץ רָשָׁע ׀ אֱלֹהִים אָמַר בְּלִבּוֹ לֹא תִדְרֹשׁ׃
רָאִתָה כִּי־אַתָּה ׀ עָמָל וָכַעַס ׀ תַּבִּיט לָתֵת בְּיָדֶךָ עָלֶיךָ יַעֲזֹב חֵלְכָה יָתוֹם
אַתָּה ׀ הָיִיתָ עוֹזֵר׃ שְׁבֹר זְרוֹעַ רָשָׁע וָרָע תִּדְרוֹשׁ־רִשְׁעוֹ בַל־תִּמְצָא׃
יהוה מֶלֶךְ עוֹלָם וָעֶד אָבְדוּ גוֹיִם מֵאַרְצוֹ׃ תַּאֲוַת עֲנָוִים שָׁמַעְתָּ יהוה
תָּכִין לִבָּם תַּקְשִׁיב אָזְנֶךָ׃ לִשְׁפֹּט יָתוֹם וָדָךְ בַּל־יוֹסִיף עוֹד לַעֲרֹץ אֱנוֹשׁ
מִן־הָאָרֶץ׃
נוּדִי יא לַמְנַצֵּחַ לְדָוִד בַּיהוה ׀ חָסִיתִי אֵיךְ תֹּאמְרוּ לְנַפְשִׁי נודו הַרְכֶם צִפּוֹר׃
כִּי הִנֵּה הָרְשָׁעִים יִדְרְכוּן קֶשֶׁת כּוֹנְנוּ חִצָּם עַל־יֶתֶר לִירוֹת בְּמוֹ־אֹפֶל
לְיִשְׁרֵי־לֵב׃ כִּי הַשָּׁתוֹת יֵהָרֵסוּן צַדִּיק מַה־פָּעָל׃ יהוה ׀ בְּהֵיכַל קָדְשׁוֹ
יהוה בַּשָּׁמַיִם כִּסְאוֹ עֵינָיו יֶחֱזוּ עַפְעַפָּיו יִבְחֲנוּ בְּנֵי אָדָם׃ יהוה צַדִּיק
יִבְחָן וְרָשָׁע וְאֹהֵב חָמָס שָׂנְאָה נַפְשׁוֹ׃ יַמְטֵר עַל־רְשָׁעִים פַּחִים אֵשׁ
וְגָפְרִית וְרוּחַ זִלְעָפוֹת מְנָת כּוֹסָם׃ כִּי־צַדִּיק יהוה צְדָקוֹת אָהֵב יָשָׁר
יֶחֱזוּ פָנֵימוֹ׃
יב לַמְנַצֵּחַ עַל־הַשְּׁמִינִית מִזְמוֹר לְדָוִד׃ הוֹשִׁיעָה יהוה כִּי־גָמַר חָסִיד כִּי־
פַסּוּ אֱמוּנִים מִבְּנֵי אָדָם׃ שָׁוְא ׀ יְדַבְּרוּ אִישׁ אֶת־רֵעֵהוּ שְׂפַת חֲלָקוֹת
בְּלֵב וָלֵב יְדַבֵּרוּ׃ יַכְרֵת יהוה כָּל־שִׂפְתֵי חֲלָקוֹת לָשׁוֹן מְדַבֶּרֶת גְּדֹלוֹת׃
אֲשֶׁר אָמְרוּ ׀ לִלְשֹׁנֵנוּ נַגְבִּיר שְׂפָתֵינוּ אִתָּנוּ מִי אָדוֹן לָנוּ׃ מִשֹּׁד עֲנִיִּים

*ב לחודש

God. For may the needy not always be forgotten, and may the hope of the oppressed not perish forever. Arise, Lord, let man not prevail. Let the nations be judged before You. Set fear over them, Lord. The nations will know that they are but men. Selah.

*10 WHY, Lord, do You stand far off? Why do You hide Yourself in times of trouble? The wicked in his pride hotly pursues the poor. They are caught in the plots that they have conceived. For the wicked boasts about his heart's desire, and the robber congratulates himself; he vilifies the Lord. The wicked in the height of his countenance does not seek God. All his thoughts are: "There is no God." His ways are always successful. Your judgments on high are far from him. As for all his adversaries, he snorts at them. He says in his heart: "I shall not fall; for all generations I shall not be in adversity." His mouth is full of cursing and deceits and violence. Under his tongue there is suffering and iniquity. He sits in ambush in the villages. In the secret places he slays the innocent. His eyes lurk for the helpless. He lies in wait in a secret place like a lion in his den. He lies in wait to catch the poor. He catches the poor when he draws him into his net. He lowers himself and crouches, and he falls with his might on the property of the helpless. He said in his heart: "God has forgotten, He hides His face, He does not see forever." Arise, O Lord. O God, lift up Your hand. Do not forget the oppressed. Why does the wicked vilify God? He says in his heart: "You will not avenge." You have seen. Truly You behold suffering and grief to requite with Your hand. The helpless to rely upon You. You are the helper of the fatherless. Break the arm of the wicked. And as for the evil man, avenge his wickedness until You find it no more. The Lord is King forever and ever. The nations have perished from His land. Lord, hear the desire of the humble. Prepare their heart, let Your ear hear. To judge the fatherless and the oppressed, so that he is no longer afraid of the man of the earth.

11 TO THE DIRECTOR of music, of David. In the Lord, I seek refuge. How can you say to my soul: Wander your mountain like a bird? For behold, the wicked bend the bow, they have made their arrow ready on the bowstring, to shoot in the dark at the upright in heart. For the foundations are destroyed. What can the righteous do? The Lord is in His holy Temple, The Lord's throne is in heaven. His eyes behold, His eyelids examine, the children of man. The Lord examines the righteous, but the wicked and him who loves violence His soul hates. He rains coals on the wicked; fire and brimstone and a raging wind are the portion of their cup. For the Lord is righteous, He loves righteous deeds, His face beholds the upright.

12 TO THE DIRECTOR of music on the *Sheminit.* A psalm of David. Help, O Lord, for the pious man is gone, for the faithful have vanished from among the children of man. They speak falsehood everyone with his fellow. They speak with a flattering lip and with a double heart. May the Lord cut off all flattering lips, the tongue that speaks proud words, who have said: "With our tongue we will grow mighty. Our lips are with

---

*2nd DAY of the month

מֵאֶנְקַת אֶבְיוֹנִים עַתָּה אָקוּם יֹאמַר יהוה אָשִׁית בְּיֵשַׁע יָפִיחַ לוֹ: אִמֲרוֹת
יהוה אֲמָרוֹת טְהֹרוֹת כֶּסֶף צָרוּף בַּעֲלִיל לָאָרֶץ מְזֻקָּק שִׁבְעָתָיִם: אַתָּה־
יהוה תִּשְׁמְרֵם תִּצְּרֶנּוּ ׀ מִן־הַדּוֹר זוּ לְעוֹלָם: סָבִיב רְשָׁעִים יִתְהַלָּכוּן
כְּרֻם זֻלּוּת לִבְנֵי אָדָם:

יג לַמְנַצֵּחַ מִזְמוֹר לְדָוִד: עַד־אָנָה יהוה תִּשְׁכָּחֵנִי נֶצַח עַד־אָנָה ׀ תַּסְתִּיר
אֶת־פָּנֶיךָ מִמֶּנִּי: עַד־אָנָה אָשִׁית עֵצוֹת בְּנַפְשִׁי יָגוֹן בִּלְבָבִי יוֹמָם עַד־
אָנָה ׀ יָרוּם אֹיְבִי עָלָי: הַבִּיטָה עֲנֵנִי יהוה אֱלֹהָי הָאִירָה עֵינַי פֶּן־אִישַׁן
הַמָּוֶת: פֶּן־יֹאמַר אֹיְבִי יְכָלְתִּיו צָרַי יָגִילוּ כִּי אֶמּוֹט: וַאֲנִי ׀ בְּחַסְדְּךָ בָטַחְתִּי
יָגֵל לִבִּי בִּישׁוּעָתֶךָ אָשִׁירָה לַיהוה כִּי גָמַל עָלָי:

יד לַמְנַצֵּחַ לְדָוִד אָמַר נָבָל בְּלִבּוֹ אֵין אֱלֹהִים הִשְׁחִיתוּ הִתְעִיבוּ עֲלִילָה אֵין
עֹשֵׂה־טוֹב: יהוה מִשָּׁמַיִם הִשְׁקִיף עַל־בְּנֵי־אָדָם לִרְאוֹת הֲיֵשׁ מַשְׂכִּיל
דֹּרֵשׁ אֶת־אֱלֹהִים: הַכֹּל סָר יַחְדָּו נֶאֱלָחוּ אֵין עֹשֵׂה־טוֹב אֵין גַּם־אֶחָד:
הֲלֹא יָדְעוּ כָּל־פֹּעֲלֵי אָוֶן אֹכְלֵי עַמִּי אָכְלוּ לֶחֶם יהוה לֹא קָרָאוּ: שָׁם ׀
פָּחֲדוּ פָחַד כִּי־אֱלֹהִים בְּדוֹר צַדִּיק: עֲצַת־עָנִי תָבִישׁוּ כִּי יהוה מַחְסֵהוּ:
מִי יִתֵּן מִצִּיּוֹן יְשׁוּעַת יִשְׂרָאֵל בְּשׁוּב יהוה שְׁבוּת עַמּוֹ יָגֵל יַעֲקֹב יִשְׂמַח
יִשְׂרָאֵל:

טו מִזְמוֹר לְדָוִד יהוה מִי־יָגוּר בְּאָהֳלֶךָ מִי־יִשְׁכֹּן בְּהַר קָדְשֶׁךָ: הוֹלֵךְ תָּמִים
וּפֹעֵל צֶדֶק וְדֹבֵר אֱמֶת בִּלְבָבוֹ: לֹא־רָגַל ׀ עַל־לְשֹׁנוֹ לֹא־עָשָׂה לְרֵעֵהוּ
רָעָה וְחֶרְפָּה לֹא־נָשָׂא עַל־קְרֹבוֹ: נִבְזֶה ׀ בְּעֵינָיו נִמְאָס וְאֶת־יִרְאֵי יהוה
יְכַבֵּד נִשְׁבַּע לְהָרַע וְלֹא יָמִר: כַּסְפּוֹ ׀ לֹא־נָתַן בְּנֶשֶׁךְ וְשֹׁחַד עַל־נָקִי לֹא־
לָקָח עֹשֵׂה אֵלֶּה לֹא יִמּוֹט לְעוֹלָם:

טז מִכְתָּם לְדָוִד שָׁמְרֵנִי אֵל כִּי־חָסִיתִי בָךְ: אָמַרְתְּ לַיהוה אֲדֹנָי אַתָּה טוֹבָתִי
בַּל־עָלֶיךָ: לִקְדוֹשִׁים אֲשֶׁר־בָּאָרֶץ הֵמָּה וְאַדִּירֵי כָּל־חֶפְצִי־בָם: יִרְבּוּ
עַצְּבוֹתָם אַחֵר מָהָרוּ בַּל־אַסִּיךְ נִסְכֵּיהֶם מִדָּם וּבַל־אֶשָּׂא אֶת־שְׁמוֹתָם
עַל־שְׂפָתָי: יהוה מְנָת־חֶלְקִי וְכוֹסִי אַתָּה תּוֹמִיךְ גּוֹרָלִי: חֲבָלִים נָפְלוּ־לִי
בַּנְּעִמִים אַף־נַחֲלָת שָׁפְרָה עָלָי: אֲבָרֵךְ אֶת־יהוה אֲשֶׁר יְעָצָנִי אַף־לֵילוֹת
יִסְּרוּנִי כִלְיוֹתָי: שִׁוִּיתִי יהוה לְנֶגְדִּי תָמִיד כִּי מִימִינִי בַּל־אֶמּוֹט: לָכֵן ׀
שָׂמַח לִבִּי וַיָּגֶל כְּבוֹדִי אַף־בְּשָׂרִי יִשְׁכֹּן לָבֶטַח: כִּי ׀ לֹא־תַעֲזֹב נַפְשִׁי

us. Who is lord over us?" Because of the plunder of the poor, because of the sighing
of the needy, may the Lord say: "Now I will arise." "I will fight for their safety," may
He breathe because of it. The words of the Lord are pure words, like refined silver
bright to the world, purified twice seven times. You, O Lord, will keep them. You will
preserve him from eternity to eternity. May the wicked walk round about, when the
downtrodden among the children of man arise.

13 TO THE DIRECTOR of music. A psalm of David. How long, O Lord, will You forget me
forever? How long will You hide Your face from me? How long will I put ideas into
my soul, will grief be in my heart by day? How long will my enemy triumph over me?
Look, and answer me, O Lord, my God. Lighten my eyes, lest I sleep the sleep of death,
lest my enemy say: "I have prevailed against him," and my adversaries rejoice at my fall.
But as for me, I trust in Your loving-kindness. May my heart rejoice in Your salvation.
I will sing to the Lord, because He has dealt bountifully with me.

14 TO THE DIRECTOR of music, of David. The fool says in his heart: "There is no God."
They have acted corruptly, they have practiced abominations. There is none that does
good. The Lord looks down from Heaven upon the children of man to see if there is a
man of understanding who seeks out God. They have all gone astray, they all together
become corrupt. There is none that does good, not even one. Do not all the workers
of iniquity know? Those who ate my people as they would eat bread, they did not
call upon the Lord. There they were in great fear, for God is in the congregation of
the righteous. You will be shamed by your counsel regarding the poor, because the
Lord is his refuge. O that the salvation of Israel will come from his Zion! When the
Lord brings back the return of His people, Jacob will rejoice, Israel will be glad.

15 A PSALM of David. O Lord, who may live in Your tent? Who may dwell in Your holy
mountain? He who walks uprightly, and acts righteously, and speaks truth in his heart.
He who has not spread gossip with his tongue, has not done evil to his fellow, and
has not brought shame upon his friend. In his eyes the vile person is despised, but he
honors those who fear the Lord. He swears to his detriment, and does not change. He
has not given his money on interest, and has not taken a bribe against the innocent.
He who does these things shall never fall.

16 A *MIKHTAM* of David. Preserve me, O God, for I seek refuge in You. You have said to
the Lord: "You are the Lord. My good is from none but You." To the holy that are
in the land, and the mighty in whom is all my desire: "Let their idols multiply, those
who cling to another god. I will not offer their libations of blood, nor will I take their
names upon my lips." The Lord is the portion of my inheritance and of my cup. You
maintain my lot. Portions have fallen to me in pleasant places, and my inheritance is
pleasing to me. I bless the Lord Who has given me counsel. Even at night my kidneys
admonish me. I have set the Lord always before me. Indeed He is at my right hand, so
that I will not stumble. Therefore my heart is glad, and my honor rejoices. My flesh,
too, dwells in safety. For You will not abandon my soul to the underworld. You will

חֲסִידְךָ לִשְׁאוֹל לֹא־תִתֵּן חסידיך לִרְאוֹת שָׁחַת: תּוֹדִיעֵנִי אֹרַח חַיִּים שֹׂבַע
שְׂמָחוֹת אֶת־פָּנֶיךָ נְעִמוֹת בִּימִינְךָ נֶצַח:
יז תְּפִלָּה לְדָוִד שִׁמְעָה יהוה ׀ צֶדֶק הַקְשִׁיבָה רִנָּתִי הַאֲזִינָה תְפִלָּתִי בְּלֹא
שִׂפְתֵי מִרְמָה: מִלְּפָנֶיךָ מִשְׁפָּטִי יֵצֵא עֵינֶיךָ תֶּחֱזֶינָה מֵישָׁרִים: בָּחַנְתָּ לִבִּי ׀
פָּקַדְתָּ לַּיְלָה צְרַפְתַּנִי בַל־תִּמְצָא זַמֹּתִי בַּל־יַעֲבָר־פִּי: לִפְעֻלּוֹת אָדָם
בִּדְבַר שְׂפָתֶיךָ אֲנִי שָׁמַרְתִּי אָרְחוֹת פָּרִיץ: תָּמֹךְ אֲשֻׁרַי בְּמַעְגְּלוֹתֶיךָ בַּל־
נָמוֹטּוּ פְעָמָי: אֲנִי־קְרָאתִיךָ כִי־תַעֲנֵנִי אֵל הַט־אָזְנְךָ לִי שְׁמַע אִמְרָתִי:
הַפְלֵה חֲסָדֶיךָ מוֹשִׁיעַ חוֹסִים מִמִּתְקוֹמְמִים בִּימִינֶךָ: שָׁמְרֵנִי כְּאִישׁוֹן
בַּת־עָיִן בְּצֵל כְּנָפֶיךָ תַּסְתִּירֵנִי: מִפְּנֵי רְשָׁעִים זוּ שַׁדּוּנִי אֹיְבַי בְּנֶפֶשׁ
סְבָבוּנוּ יַקִּיפוּ עָלָי: חֶלְבָּמוֹ סָּגְרוּ פִּימוֹ דִּבְּרוּ בְגֵאוּת: אַשֻּׁרֵנוּ עַתָּה סבבוני
עֵינֵיהֶם יָשִׁיתוּ לִנְטוֹת בָּאָרֶץ: דִּמְיֹנוֹ כְּאַרְיֵה יִכְסוֹף לִטְרֹף וְכִכְפִיר יֹשֵׁב
בְּמִסְתָּרִים: קוּמָה יהוה קַדְּמָה פָנָיו הַכְרִיעֵהוּ פַּלְּטָה נַפְשִׁי מֵרָשָׁע
וּצְפוּנְךָ חַרְבֶּךָ: מִמְתִים יָדְךָ ׀ יהוה מִמְתִים מֵחֶלֶד חֶלְקָם בַּחַיִּים וצפינך תְּמַלֵּא
בִטְנָם יִשְׂבְּעוּ בָנִים וְהִנִּיחוּ יִתְרָם לְעוֹלְלֵיהֶם: אֲנִי בְּצֶדֶק אֶחֱזֶה פָנֶיךָ
אֶשְׂבְּעָה בְהָקִיץ תְּמוּנָתֶךָ:
*יח לַמְנַצֵּחַ לְעֶבֶד יהוה לְדָוִד אֲשֶׁר דִּבֶּר ׀ לַיהוה אֶת־דִּבְרֵי הַשִּׁירָה הַזֹּאת
בְּיוֹם ׀ הִצִּיל־יהוה אוֹתוֹ מִכַּף כָּל־אֹיְבָיו וּמִיַּד שָׁאוּל: וַיֹּאמַר אֶרְחָמְךָ
יהוה חִזְקִי: יהוה ׀ סַלְעִי וּמְצוּדָתִי וּמְפַלְטִי אֵלִי צוּרִי אֶחֱסֶה־בּוֹ מָגִנִּי
וְקֶרֶן־יִשְׁעִי מִשְׂגַּבִּי: מְהֻלָּל אֶקְרָא יהוה וּמִן־אֹיְבַי אִוָּשֵׁעַ: אֲפָפוּנִי חֶבְלֵי־
מָוֶת וְנַחֲלֵי בְלִיַּעַל יְבַעֲתוּנִי: חֶבְלֵי שְׁאוֹל סְבָבוּנִי קִדְּמוּנִי מוֹקְשֵׁי מָוֶת:
בַּצַּר־לִי ׀ אֶקְרָא יהוה וְאֶל־אֱלֹהַי אֲשַׁוֵּעַ יִשְׁמַע מֵהֵיכָלוֹ קוֹלִי וְשַׁוְעָתִי
לְפָנָיו ׀ תָּבוֹא בְאָזְנָיו: וַתִּגְעַשׁ וַתִּרְעַשׁ ׀ הָאָרֶץ וּמוֹסְדֵי הָרִים יִרְגָּזוּ
וַיִּתְגָּעֲשׁוּ כִּי־חָרָה לוֹ: עָלָה עָשָׁן ׀ בְּאַפּוֹ וְאֵשׁ־מִפִּיו תֹּאכֵל גֶּחָלִים בָּעֲרוּ
מִמֶּנּוּ: וַיֵּט שָׁמַיִם וַיֵּרַד וַעֲרָפֶל תַּחַת רַגְלָיו: וַיִּרְכַּב עַל־כְּרוּב וַיָּעֹף וַיֵּדֶא
עַל־כַּנְפֵי־רוּחַ: יָשֶׁת חֹשֶׁךְ ׀ סִתְרוֹ סְבִיבוֹתָיו סֻכָּתוֹ חֶשְׁכַת־מַיִם עָבֵי
שְׁחָקִים: מִנֹּגַהּ נֶגְדּוֹ עָבָיו עָבְרוּ בָּרָד וְגַחֲלֵי־אֵשׁ: וַיַּרְעֵם בַּשָּׁמַיִם ׀ יהוה
וְעֶלְיוֹן יִתֵּן קֹלוֹ בָּרָד וְגַחֲלֵי־אֵשׁ: וַיִּשְׁלַח חִצָּיו וַיְפִיצֵם וּבְרָקִים רָב
וַיְהֻמֵּם: וַיֵּרָאוּ ׀ אֲפִיקֵי מַיִם וַיִּגָּלוּ מוֹסְדוֹת תֵּבֵל מִגַּעֲרָתְךָ יהוה מִנִּשְׁמַת

*ג לחודש

not allow Your pious one to see the pit. You will make known to me the path of life.
In Your presence is fullness of joy. At Your right hand are pleasures forevermore.
17 A PRAYER of David. Hear righteousness, O Lord. Hearken to my cry. Listen to my
prayer which is not from lips of deceit. Let my judgment go out from before You. Your
eyes look on equitably. You have tried my heart. You have punished it in the night.
You have purified me until You found no more. I have silenced myself so that nothing
will pass my mouth about the acts of man by the word of Your lips. I have walked the
paths of the violent. I have held my steps fast to Your paths. My feet have not slipped.
I call out to You that You answer me, O God. Incline Your ear to me, and hear my
speech. Show the wonder of Your loving-kindnesses, You Who save with Your right
hand from their enemies those who seek refuge in You. Protect me as the apple of the
eye. Hide me in the shadow of Your wings from the wicked who have robbed me. My
deadly enemies encompass me. They have enclosed themselves in their own fat. They
speak arrogantly with their mouth. They follow our steps, now they surround us. They
set their eyes so that they are directed to the earth. He is like a lion that longs to tear
in pieces, and like a young lion lurking in secret places. Arise, O Lord, confront him,
bring him down. Save my soul from the wicked, who is Your sword. Among the people
at Your hand, O Lord, among the people of the living world whose portion is among
the living, and whose belly You fill with Your treasure, with which the children will be
satisfied, and they will leave their abundance to their babes. As for me, I will behold
Your face in righteousness. I will be satisfied, when awake, with Your likeness.
*18 TO THE DIRECTOR of music, of David, the servant of the Lord, who spoke to the Lord
the words of this song on the day that the Lord delivered him from the hand of all his
enemies and from the hand of Saul. And he said: I will love You, O Lord, my support.
The Lord is my rock, and my hiding-place, and my savior. My God, my rock, in Whom
I find shelter. My shield, and the horn of my salvation, my refuge. I call the Lord the
praised one, and I am saved from my enemies. The pains of death encircled me, and
the floods of destruction alarmed me. The pains of the underworld encompassed me.
The snares of death confronted me. In my distress, I called upon the Lord, and I cried to
my God. He heard my voice from His sanctuary, and my cry came before Him into His
ears. Then the earth shook and quaked, and the foundations of the mountains trembled.
And they were shaken because He was angry. Smoke went up from His nostrils, and fire
out of His mouth devoured. Coals were kindled from Him. And He bent the heavens
and descended, and heavy cloud was under His feet. And He rode upon a cherub and
flew. And He flew swiftly on the wings of the wind. He has made the darkness His secret
place, His tabernacle around Him, darkness of waters, thick clouds of the skies. From
the brightness that was before Him hail and coals of fire passed through His clouds. And
the Lord thundered in the heavens, and the Most High lifted up His voice, hail and coals
of fire. And He sent out His arrows and scattered them, and He shot bolts of lightning
and confounded them. Then channels of water were seen, and the foundations of the
world were exposed at Your rebuke, O Lord, at the blast of the breath of Your nostrils.

---

*3rd DAY of the month

רֽוּחַ אַפֶּֽךָ׃ יִשְׁלַח מִמָּרוֹם יִקָּחֵנִי יַמְשֵׁנִי מִמַּיִם רַבִּים׃ יַצִּילֵנִי מֵאֹיְבִי עָז
וּמִשֹּׂנְאַי כִּֽי־אָמְצוּ מִמֶּֽנִּי׃ יְקַדְּמוּנִי בְיוֹם־אֵידִי וַֽיְהִי־יְהוָה לְמִשְׁעָן לִֽי׃
וַיּוֹצִיאֵנִי לַמֶּרְחָב יְחַלְּצֵנִי כִּי חָפֵץ בִּֽי׃ יִגְמְלֵנִי יְהוָה כְּצִדְקִי כְּבֹר יָדַי יָשִׁיב
לִֽי׃ כִּֽי־שָׁמַרְתִּי דַּרְכֵי יְהוָה וְלֹא־רָשַׁעְתִּי מֵאֱלֹהָֽי׃ כִּי כׇל־מִשְׁפָּטָיו לְנֶגְדִּי
וְחֻקֹּתָיו לֹא־אָסִיר מֶֽנִּי׃ וָאֱהִי תָמִים עִמּוֹ וָאֶשְׁתַּמֵּר מֵעֲוֺנִֽי׃ וַיָּֽשֶׁב־יְהוָה
לִי כְצִדְקִי כְּבֹר יָדַי לְנֶגֶד עֵינָֽיו׃ עִם־חָסִיד תִּתְחַסָּד עִם־גְּבַר תָּמִים
תִּתַּמָּֽם׃ עִם־נָבָר תִּתְבָּרָר וְעִם־עִקֵּשׁ תִּתְפַּתָּֽל׃ כִּֽי־אַתָּה עַם־עָנִי תוֹשִׁיעַ
וְעֵינַיִם רָמוֹת תַּשְׁפִּֽיל׃ כִּֽי־אַתָּה תָּאִיר נֵרִי יְהוָה אֱלֹהַי יַגִּיהַּ חׇשְׁכִּֽי׃ כִּֽי־
בְךָ אָרֻץ גְּדוּד וּבֵֽאלֹהַי אֲדַלֶּג־שֽׁוּר׃ הָאֵל תָּמִים דַּרְכּוֹ אִמְרַת־יְהוָה
צְרוּפָה מָגֵן הוּא לְכֹל ׀ הַחֹסִים בּֽוֹ׃ כִּי מִי אֱלוֹהַּ מִבַּלְעֲדֵי יְהוָה וּמִי צוּר
זוּלָתִי אֱלֹהֵֽינוּ׃ הָאֵל הַמְאַזְּרֵנִי חָיִל וַיִּתֵּן תָּמִים דַּרְכִּֽי׃ מְשַׁוֶּה רַגְלַי
כָּֽאַיָּלוֹת וְעַל בָּמֹתַי יַעֲמִידֵֽנִי׃ מְלַמֵּד יָדַי לַמִּלְחָמָה וְנִחֲתָה קֶֽשֶׁת־נְחוּשָׁה
זְרוֹעֹתָֽי׃ וַתִּתֶּן־לִי מָגֵן יִשְׁעֶךָ וִֽימִינְךָ תִסְעָדֵנִי וְעַנְוַתְךָ תַרְבֵּֽנִי׃ תַּרְחִיב
צַעֲדִי תַחְתָּי וְלֹא מָעֲדוּ קַרְסֻלָּֽי׃ אֶרְדּוֹף אוֹיְבַי וְאַשִּׂיגֵם וְלֹא־אָשׁוּב
עַד־כַּלּוֹתָֽם׃ אֶמְחָצֵם וְלֹא־יֻכְלוּ קוּם יִפְּלוּ תַּחַת רַגְלָֽי׃ וַתְּאַזְּרֵנִי חַיִל
לַמִּלְחָמָה תַּכְרִיעַ קָמַי תַּחְתָּֽי׃ וְאֹיְבַי נָתַתָּה לִּי עֹרֶף וּמְשַׂנְאַי אַצְמִיתֵֽם׃
יְשַׁוְּעוּ וְאֵין־מוֹשִׁיעַ עַל־יְהוָה וְלֹא עָנָֽם׃ וְאֶשְׁחָקֵם כְּעָפָר עַל־פְּנֵי־רוּחַ
כְּטִיט חוּצוֹת אֲרִיקֵֽם׃ תְּפַלְּטֵנִי מֵרִיבֵי עָם תְּשִׂימֵנִי לְרֹאשׁ גּוֹיִם עַם
לֹא־יָדַעְתִּי יַעַבְדֽוּנִי׃ לְשֵׁמַע אֹזֶן יִשָּׁמְעוּ לִי בְּנֵי־נֵכָר יְכַחֲשׁוּ־לִֽי׃ בְּנֵי־נֵכָר
יִבֹּלוּ וְיַחְרְגוּ מִֽמִּסְגְּרוֹתֵיהֶֽם׃ חַי־יְהוָה וּבָרוּךְ צוּרִי וְיָרוּם אֱלוֹהֵי יִשְׁעִֽי׃
הָאֵל הַנּוֹתֵן נְקָמוֹת לִי וַיַּדְבֵּר עַמִּים תַּחְתָּֽי׃ מְפַלְּטִי מֵאֹיְבָי אַף מִן־קָמַי
תְּרוֹמְמֵנִי מֵאִישׁ חָמָס תַּצִּילֵֽנִי׃ עַל־כֵּן ׀ אוֹדְךָ בַגּוֹיִם ׀ יְהוָה וּלְשִׁמְךָ
אֲזַמֵּֽרָה׃ מַגְדִּל יְשׁוּעוֹת מַלְכּוֹ וְעֹשֶׂה חֶסֶד ׀ לִמְשִׁיחוֹ לְדָוִד וּלְזַרְעוֹ
עַד־עוֹלָֽם׃

יט לַמְנַצֵּחַ מִזְמוֹר לְדָוִֽד׃ הַשָּׁמַיִם מְסַפְּרִים כְּבוֹד־אֵל וּמַעֲשֵׂה יָדָיו מַגִּיד
הָרָקִֽיעַ׃ יוֹם לְיוֹם יַבִּיעַ אֹמֶר וְלַיְלָה לְּלַיְלָה יְחַוֶּה־דָּֽעַת׃ אֵין־אֹמֶר
וְאֵין דְּבָרִים בְּלִי נִשְׁמָע קוֹלָֽם׃ בְּכׇל־הָאָרֶץ ׀ יָצָא קַוָּם וּבִקְצֵה תֵבֵל
מִלֵּיהֶם לַשֶּׁמֶשׁ שָֽׂם־אֹהֶל בָּהֶֽם׃ וְהוּא כְּחָתָן יֹצֵא מֵחֻפָּתוֹ יָשִׂישׂ כְּגִבּוֹר

He sent from on high, He took me, He drew me out of many waters. He delivered me from my fierce enemy, and from those who hated me, though they are mightier than I. They confronted me on the day of my calamity, but the Lord became a support to me. And He brought me forth into a wide space. He rescued me because He delights in me. The Lord has rewarded me according to my righteousness. According to the purity of my hands has He recompensed me. For I have kept the ways of the Lord, and I have not acted wickedly in parting from my God. For all His ordinances are before me, and I do not put away His statutes from me. And I have been perfect with Him, and I have kept myself from my iniquity. Therefore the Lord has recompensed me according to my righteousness, according to the cleanness of my hands before His eyes. With the pious you show Yourself pious. With the upright man You show Yourself upright. With the pure You show Yourself pure, and with the crooked You show Yourself subtle. Indeed, You save an afflicted people, and You humble haughty eyes. Indeed, You light my candle. The Lord my God lightens my darkness. Indeed, with You I run upon a troop, and with my God I leap over a wall. As for God, His way is perfect, the word of the Lord is tried. He is a shield for all those who seek refuge in Him. For who is God apart from the Lord? And who is a rock except our God? It is God Who girds me with strength, and He makes my way perfect. He makes my feet like those of hinds, and He sets me upon my heights. He trains my hands for war, and the bronze bow in my arms shoots. And You have given me the shield of Your salvation, and Your right hand supports me, and Your cry makes me great. You have enlarged my stride under me, and my feet have not slipped. I have pursued my enemies and I have overtaken them, and I did not turn back until I had destroyed them. I crushed them so that they could not rise. They fell under my feet. And You have girded me with strength for war. You have brought down under me those Who rose up against me. And You have made my enemies turn their backs to me, and I have destroyed those Who hate me. They cried, but there was none to save them, to the Lord, but He did not answer them. And I crumbled them like dust before the wind. I poured them out like the mud in the streets. You have delivered me from the conflicts of the people. You have made me the head of nations. Peoples that I have not known serve me. Upon hearing with their ears, they obey me. The sons of the stranger feign obedience to me. The sons of the stranger fade away, and they tremble because of their chains. The Lord lives, and blessed is my rock, and let the God of my salvation be exalted, the God Who avenges me, and has subdued peoples under me. He delivers me from my enemies, and You lift me up above those who rise up against me. You save me from the violent man. Therefore I will thank You among the nations, O Lord, and I will sing praise to Your name. He gives great salvations to His king, and He shows loving-kindness to His anointed, to David and to his seed forevermore.

19 TO THE DIRECTOR of music. A psalm of David. The heavens declare the glory of God,
and the firmament proclaims His handiwork. Day to day utters speech, and night to
night expresses knowledge. There is no speech, nor are there words. Their voice is
not heard. Their call goes out through all the earth, and their words to the end of the
world. In them He has set a tent for the sun. And it is like a bridegroom coming out

לָרוּץ אֹרַח: מִקְצֵה הַשָּׁמַיִם ׀ מוֹצָאוֹ וּתְקוּפָתוֹ עַל־קְצוֹתָם וְאֵין נִסְתָּר
מֵחַמָּתוֹ: תּוֹרַת יהוה תְּמִימָה מְשִׁיבַת נָפֶשׁ עֵדוּת יהוה נֶאֱמָנָה מַחְכִּימַת
פֶּתִי: פִּקּוּדֵי יהוה יְשָׁרִים מְשַׂמְּחֵי־לֵב מִצְוַת יהוה בָּרָה מְאִירַת עֵינָיִם:
יִרְאַת יהוה ׀ טְהוֹרָה עוֹמֶדֶת לָעַד מִשְׁפְּטֵי־יהוה אֱמֶת צָדְקוּ יַחְדָּו:
הַנֶּחֱמָדִים מִזָּהָב וּמִפַּז רָב וּמְתוּקִים מִדְּבַשׁ וְנֹפֶת צוּפִים: גַּם־עַבְדְּךָ
נִזְהָר בָּהֶם בְּשָׁמְרָם עֵקֶב רָב: שְׁגִיאוֹת מִי־יָבִין מִנִּסְתָּרוֹת נַקֵּנִי: גַּם
מִזֵּדִים ׀ חֲשֹׂךְ עַבְדֶּךָ אַל־יִמְשְׁלוּ־בִי אָז אֵיתָם וְנִקֵּיתִי מִפֶּשַׁע רָב: יִהְיוּ
לְרָצוֹן ׀ אִמְרֵי־פִי וְהֶגְיוֹן לִבִּי לְפָנֶיךָ יהוה צוּרִי וְגֹאֲלִי:

כ לַמְנַצֵּחַ מִזְמוֹר לְדָוִד: יַעַנְךָ יהוה בְּיוֹם צָרָה יְשַׂגֶּבְךָ שֵׁם ׀ אֱלֹהֵי יַעֲקֹב:
יִשְׁלַח־עֶזְרְךָ מִקֹּדֶשׁ וּמִצִּיּוֹן יִסְעָדֶךָּ: יִזְכֹּר כָּל־מִנְחֹתֶךָ וְעוֹלָתְךָ
יְדַשְּׁנֶה סֶלָה: יִתֶּן־לְךָ כִלְבָבֶךָ וְכָל־עֲצָתְךָ יְמַלֵּא: נְרַנְּנָה ׀ בִּישׁוּעָתֶךָ
וּבְשֵׁם־אֱלֹהֵינוּ נִדְגֹּל יְמַלֵּא יהוה כָּל־מִשְׁאֲלוֹתֶיךָ: עַתָּה יָדַעְתִּי כִּי
הוֹשִׁיעַ ׀ יהוה מְשִׁיחוֹ יַעֲנֵהוּ מִשְּׁמֵי קָדְשׁוֹ בִּגְבוּרוֹת יֵשַׁע יְמִינוֹ: אֵלֶּה
בָרֶכֶב וְאֵלֶּה בַסּוּסִים וַאֲנַחְנוּ ׀ בְּשֵׁם־יהוה אֱלֹהֵינוּ נַזְכִּיר: הֵמָּה כָּרְעוּ
וְנָפָלוּ וַאֲנַחְנוּ קַּמְנוּ וַנִּתְעוֹדָד: יהוה הוֹשִׁיעָה הַמֶּלֶךְ יַעֲנֵנוּ בְיוֹם־
קָרְאֵנוּ:

יָגֵל כא לַמְנַצֵּחַ מִזְמוֹר לְדָוִד: יהוה בְּעָזְּךָ יִשְׂמַח־מֶלֶךְ וּבִישׁוּעָתְךָ מַה־יגיל
מְאֹד: תַּאֲוַת לִבּוֹ נָתַתָּה לּוֹ וַאֲרֶשֶׁת שְׂפָתָיו בַּל־מָנַעְתָּ סֶּלָה: כִּי־
תְקַדְּמֶנּוּ בִּרְכוֹת טוֹב תָּשִׁית לְרֹאשׁוֹ עֲטֶרֶת פָּז: חַיִּים ׀ שָׁאַל מִמְּךָ
נָתַתָּה לּוֹ אֹרֶךְ יָמִים עוֹלָם וָעֶד: גָּדוֹל כְּבוֹדוֹ בִּישׁוּעָתֶךָ הוֹד וְהָדָר תְּשַׁוֶּה
עָלָיו: כִּי־תְשִׁיתֵהוּ בְרָכוֹת לָעַד תְּחַדֵּהוּ בְשִׂמְחָה אֶת־פָּנֶיךָ: כִּי־הַמֶּלֶךְ
בֹּטֵחַ בַּיהוה וּבְחֶסֶד עֶלְיוֹן בַּל־יִמּוֹט: תִּמְצָא יָדְךָ לְכָל־אֹיְבֶיךָ יְמִינְךָ
תִּמְצָא שֹׂנְאֶיךָ: תְּשִׁיתֵמוֹ ׀ כְּתַנּוּר אֵשׁ לְעֵת פָּנֶיךָ יהוה בְּאַפּוֹ יְבַלְּעֵם
וְתֹאכְלֵם אֵשׁ: פִּרְיָמוֹ מֵאֶרֶץ תְּאַבֵּד וְזַרְעָם מִבְּנֵי אָדָם: כִּי־נָטוּ עָלֶיךָ
רָעָה חָשְׁבוּ מְזִמָּה בַּל־יוּכָלוּ: כִּי תְּשִׁיתֵמוֹ שֶׁכֶם בְּמֵיתָרֶיךָ תְּכוֹנֵן עַל־
פְּנֵיהֶם: רוּמָה יהוה בְעֻזֶּךָ נָשִׁירָה וּנְזַמְּרָה גְּבוּרָתֶךָ:

כב לַמְנַצֵּחַ עַל־אַיֶּלֶת הַשַּׁחַר מִזְמוֹר לְדָוִד: אֵלִי אֵלִי לָמָה עֲזַבְתָּנִי רָחוֹק
מִישׁוּעָתִי דִּבְרֵי שַׁאֲגָתִי: אֱלֹהַי אֶקְרָא יוֹמָם וְלֹא תַעֲנֶה וְלַיְלָה וְלֹא־

of his chamber. It rejoices like a mighty man running along a path. Its going forth is
from the end of the heaven, and its circuit is to its ends, and nothing is hidden from
its heat. The law of the Lord is perfect, restoring the soul. The testimony of the Lord
is faithful, making the simple wise. The statutes of the Lord are upright, rejoicing the
heart. The commandments of the Lord are pure, enlightening the eyes. The fear of
the Lord is pure, standing forever. The judgments of the Lord are true: they are all
righteous. How much more desirable they are than much gold and fine gold, and they
are sweeter than honey and the honeycomb. Indeed, Your servant is careful about
them. In the keeping of them there is great reward. Who can discern errors? Cleanse
me from hidden transgressions. Also keep Your servant from willing sinners. Let them
not rule over me. Then I shall be faultless, and let me be clean of many transgressions.
May the words of my mouth and the meditation of my heart be acceptable before You,
O Lord, my Rock and my Redeemer.

20 TO THE DIRECTOR of music. A psalm of David. May the Lord answer you in the
day of trouble. May the name of the God of Jacob exalt you. May He send you help
from the sanctuary, and may He support you from Zion. May He remember all your
offerings, and may He accept the ashes of your burnt-offerings. Selah. May He grant
to you according to your heart, and may He fulfill all your counsel. May we shout
for joy in your salvation, and may we gather in the name of our God. May the Lord
fulfill all your petitions. Now I know that the Lord will deliver His anointed one. He
will answer him from His sanctuary in heaven, with the mighty acts of His right hand
which delivers. Some trust in chariots, and some in horses, but we will proclaim the
name of the Lord our God. They have knelt down and fallen, but we have risen and
overcome. Lord, save! The King will answer us on the day that we call.

21 TO THE DIRECTOR of music. A psalm of David. O Lord, the king rejoices in Your
strength, and how greatly he exults in Your salvation. You have given him his heart's
desire, and You have not withheld the request of his lips. Selah. For You meet him with
blessings of goodness. You set a crown of gold on his head. He asked life of you, and
You have given it to him, length of days forever and ever. His glory is great through
Your salvation. You lay upon him majesty and splendor. For You make him most
blessed forever. You make him exceedingly glad with Your countenance. Indeed, the
king trusts in the Lord, and through the love of the Most High he shall not be moved.
Your hand will find all your enemies. Your right hand will find those who hate you. You
will make them like a fiery furnace in the time of your anger. The Lord will swallow
them up in His wrath, and fire will devour them. You will destroy their fruit from the
earth, and their seed from among the children of men. For they intended evil against
you. They imagined a device that they cannot carry out. Indeed, you will make them
turn their back. With your bowstrings you will aim against their face. Be exalted, O
Lord, in Your strength. Let us sing and praise Your might.

22 TO THE DIRECTOR of music, on *ayelet hashaḥar*. A psalm of David. My God, my God,
why have You forsaken me? Why are You far from my salvation, from the words of my

דּוּמִיָּה לִי׃ וְאַתָּה קָדוֹשׁ יוֹשֵׁב תְּהִלּוֹת יִשְׂרָאֵל׃ בְּךָ בָּטְחוּ אֲבֹתֵינוּ בָּטְחוּ
וַתְּפַלְּטֵמוֹ׃ אֵלֶיךָ זָעֲקוּ וְנִמְלָטוּ בְּךָ בָטְחוּ וְלֹא־בוֹשׁוּ׃ וְאָנֹכִי תוֹלַעַת
וְלֹא־אִישׁ חֶרְפַּת אָדָם וּבְזוּי עָם׃ כָּל־רֹאַי יַלְעִגוּ לִי יַפְטִירוּ בְשָׂפָה יָנִיעוּ
רֹאשׁ׃ גֹּל אֶל־יהוה יְפַלְּטֵהוּ יַצִּילֵהוּ כִּי חָפֵץ בּוֹ׃ כִּי־אַתָּה גֹחִי מִבָּטֶן
מַבְטִיחִי עַל־שְׁדֵי אִמִּי׃ עָלֶיךָ הָשְׁלַכְתִּי מֵרָחֶם מִבֶּטֶן אִמִּי אֵלִי אָתָּה׃
אַל־תִּרְחַק מִמֶּנִּי כִּי־צָרָה קְרוֹבָה כִּי־אֵין עוֹזֵר׃ סְבָבוּנִי פָּרִים רַבִּים
אַבִּירֵי בָשָׁן כִּתְּרוּנִי׃ פָּצוּ עָלַי פִּיהֶם אַרְיֵה טֹרֵף וְשֹׁאֵג׃ כַּמַּיִם נִשְׁפַּכְתִּי
וְהִתְפָּרְדוּ כָּל־עַצְמוֹתָי הָיָה לִבִּי כַּדּוֹנָג נָמֵס בְּתוֹךְ מֵעָי׃ יָבֵשׁ כַּחֶרֶשׂ ׀
כֹּחִי וּלְשׁוֹנִי מֻדְבָּק מַלְקוֹחָי וְלַעֲפַר־מָוֶת תִּשְׁפְּתֵנִי׃ כִּי סְבָבוּנִי כְּלָבִים
עֲדַת מְרֵעִים הִקִּיפוּנִי כָּאֲרִי יָדַי וְרַגְלָי׃ אֲסַפֵּר כָּל־עַצְמוֹתָי הֵמָּה יַבִּיטוּ
יִרְאוּ־בִי׃ יְחַלְּקוּ בְגָדַי לָהֶם וְעַל־לְבוּשִׁי יַפִּילוּ גוֹרָל׃ וְאַתָּה יהוה אַל־
תִּרְחָק אֱיָלוּתִי לְעֶזְרָתִי חוּשָׁה׃ הַצִּילָה מֵחֶרֶב נַפְשִׁי מִיַּד־כֶּלֶב יְחִידָתִי׃
הוֹשִׁיעֵנִי מִפִּי אַרְיֵה וּמִקַּרְנֵי רֵמִים עֲנִיתָנִי׃ אֲסַפְּרָה שִׁמְךָ לְאֶחָי בְּתוֹךְ
קָהָל אֲהַלְלֶךָּ׃ יִרְאֵי יהוה ׀ הַלְלוּהוּ כָּל־זֶרַע יַעֲקֹב כַּבְּדוּהוּ וְגוּרוּ מִמֶּנּוּ
כָּל־זֶרַע יִשְׂרָאֵל׃ כִּי לֹא־בָזָה וְלֹא שִׁקַּץ עֱנוּת עָנִי וְלֹא־הִסְתִּיר פָּנָיו
מִמֶּנּוּ וּבְשַׁוְּעוֹ אֵלָיו שָׁמֵעַ׃ מֵאִתְּךָ תְהִלָּתִי בְּקָהָל רָב נְדָרַי אֲשַׁלֵּם נֶגֶד
יְרֵאָיו׃ יֹאכְלוּ עֲנָוִים ׀ וְיִשְׂבָּעוּ יְהַלְלוּ יהוה דֹּרְשָׁיו יְחִי לְבַבְכֶם לָעַד׃
יִזְכְּרוּ ׀ וְיָשֻׁבוּ אֶל־יהוה כָּל־אַפְסֵי־אָרֶץ וְיִשְׁתַּחֲווּ לְפָנֶיךָ כָּל־מִשְׁפְּחוֹת
גּוֹיִם׃ כִּי לַיהוה הַמְּלוּכָה וּמֹשֵׁל בַּגּוֹיִם׃ אָכְלוּ וַיִּשְׁתַּחֲווּ ׀ כָּל־דִּשְׁנֵי־אֶרֶץ
לְפָנָיו יִכְרְעוּ כָּל־יוֹרְדֵי עָפָר וְנַפְשׁוֹ לֹא חִיָּה׃ זֶרַע יַעַבְדֶנּוּ יְסֻפַּר לַאדֹנָי
לַדּוֹר׃ יָבֹאוּ וְיַגִּידוּ צִדְקָתוֹ לְעַם נוֹלָד כִּי עָשָׂה׃

*כג מִזְמוֹר לְדָוִד יהוה רֹעִי לֹא אֶחְסָר׃ בִּנְאוֹת דֶּשֶׁא יַרְבִּיצֵנִי עַל־מֵי מְנֻחוֹת
יְנַהֲלֵנִי׃ נַפְשִׁי יְשׁוֹבֵב יַנְחֵנִי בְמַעְגְּלֵי־צֶדֶק לְמַעַן שְׁמוֹ׃ גַּם כִּי־אֵלֵךְ בְּגֵיא
צַלְמָוֶת לֹא־אִירָא רָע כִּי־אַתָּה עִמָּדִי שִׁבְטְךָ וּמִשְׁעַנְתֶּךָ הֵמָּה יְנַחֲמֻנִי׃
תַּעֲרֹךְ לְפָנַי ׀ שֻׁלְחָן נֶגֶד צֹרְרָי דִּשַּׁנְתָּ בַשֶּׁמֶן רֹאשִׁי כּוֹסִי רְוָיָה׃ אַךְ ׀ טוֹב
וָחֶסֶד יִרְדְּפוּנִי כָּל־יְמֵי חַיָּי וְשַׁבְתִּי בְּבֵית־יהוה לְאֹרֶךְ יָמִים׃

כד לְדָוִד מִזְמוֹר לַיהוה הָאָרֶץ וּמְלוֹאָהּ תֵּבֵל וְיֹשְׁבֵי בָהּ׃ כִּי־הוּא עַל־יַמִּים
יְסָדָהּ וְעַל־נְהָרוֹת יְכוֹנְנֶהָ׃ מִי־יַעֲלֶה בְהַר־יהוה וּמִי־יָקוּם בִּמְקוֹם קָדְשׁוֹ׃

*ד לחודש

cry? My God, I call by day, but You do not answer, and at night, and I have no repose. But
You are holy. You sit among the praises of Israel. Our fathers trusted in You. They trusted,
and You delivered them. They cried out to You and escaped. They trusted in You, and
were not disappointed. But I am a worm and not a man, a reproach of man, and despised
by the people. All who see me put me to scorn. They open wide their lips, they shake
their head: "Trust in the Lord. Let Him deliver him, let Him save him, for He delights
in him." Indeed, You are He Who took me out of the womb. You protected me when I
was upon my mother's breasts. I was cast upon You from the womb. You were my God
from my mother's belly. Do not be far from me, for trouble is near, for there is none to
help. Many bulls have encompassed me. Strong bulls of Bashan have encircled me. They
have opened wide their mouths against me, like a lion that rends as it roars. I have been
poured out like water, and all my limbs have been loosened at the joints. My heart has
become like wax, it has melted in the midst of my bowels. My strength is dried up like a
potsherd, and my tongue cleaves to my jaws, and You set me down in the dust of death.
Indeed, dogs have encompassed me, a band of evil-doers has encircled me, my hands
and my feet, like a lion. I count all my bones. They look and stare at me. They divide my
garments among themselves, and they cast lots for my clothing. But You, O Lord, be
not far off. O my strength, hasten to my assistance. Deliver my soul from the sword, my
life from the dog. Save me from the lion's mouth, and answer me from the horns of the
wild oxen. I will declare Your name to my brethren. In the midst of the congregation
I will praise You. You who fear the Lord, praise Him. All you the seed of Jacob, glorify
Him. And fear Him, all you the seed of Israel. For He has not despised nor abhorred the
prayer of the afflicted. And He has not hidden His face from him, but when he cried out
to Him, He heard. My praise is from You. In the great congregation I will pay my vows
in the presence of those who fear Him. The humble will eat and be satisfied. Those who
seek Him will praise the Lord. May your heart live forever! All the ends of the earth
will remember and return to the Lord, and all the families of the nations will bow down
before You. For the kingdom is the Lord's, and He is the ruler over the nations. All the
fat ones of the earth will eat and bow down. All those who go down to the dust and he
who cannot keep his soul alive will kneel before Him. Among the seed of those who
serve Him, it shall be told of the Lord to the next generation. They will come and tell of
His righteousness to a people that will be born, that He has done it.

*23 A PSALM of David. The Lord is my shepherd. I lack for nothing. He makes me lie down
in green pastures. He leads me beside still waters. He restores my soul. He leads me in
the paths of righteousness for His name's sake. Even when I walk in a valley of darkness,
I do not fear evil, for You are with me. Your rod and Your staff, they comfort me. You
prepare a table before me in the presence of my enemies. You have anointed my head
with oil. My cup runs over. Only goodness and loving-kindness will follow me all the
days of my life, and I will dwell in tranquility in the house of the Lord forever.

24 OF DAVID. A psalm. The earth is the Lord's and the fullness thereof, the world and
those who dwell in it. For He has founded it upon the seas, and has established it upon

*4th DAY of the month

נַפְשִׁי נְקִ֥י כַפַּ֗יִם וּֽבַר־לֵ֫בָ֥ב אֲשֶׁ֤ר לֹא־נָשָׂ֣א לַשָּׁ֣וְא נפשו וְלֹ֖א נִשְׁבַּ֣ע לְמִרְמָֽה׃
יִשָּׂ֣א בְ֭רָכָה מֵאֵ֣ת יהוה וּ֝צְדָקָ֗ה מֵאֱלֹהֵ֥י יִשְׁעֽוֹ׃ זֶ֭ה דּ֣וֹר דֹּרְשָׁ֑ו מְבַקְשֵׁ֨י
פָנֶ֖יךָ יַעֲקֹ֣ב סֶֽלָה׃ שְׂא֤וּ שְׁעָרִ֨ים ׀ רָֽאשֵׁיכֶ֗ם וְֽ֭הִנָּֽשְׂאוּ פִּתְחֵ֣י עוֹלָ֑ם וְ֝יָב֗וֹא
מֶ֣לֶךְ הַכָּבֽוֹד׃ מִ֥י זֶה֮ מֶ֤לֶךְ הַכָּ֫ב֥וֹד יהוה עִזּ֣וּז וְגִבּ֑וֹר יהוה גִּבּ֥וֹר מִלְחָמָֽה׃
שְׂא֤וּ שְׁעָרִ֨ים ׀ רָֽאשֵׁיכֶ֗ם וּ֭שְׂאוּ פִּתְחֵ֣י עוֹלָ֑ם וְ֝יָבֹ֗א מֶ֣לֶךְ הַכָּבֽוֹד׃ מִ֤י ה֥וּא
זֶה֮ מֶ֤לֶךְ הַכָּ֫ב֥וֹד יהוה צְבָא֑וֹת ה֤וּא מֶ֖לֶךְ הַכָּב֣וֹד סֶֽלָה׃
כה לְדָוִ֡ד אֵלֶ֥יךָ יהוה נַפְשִׁ֥י אֶשָּֽׂא׃ אֱֽלֹהַ֗י בְּךָ֣ בָ֭טַחְתִּי אַל־אֵב֑וֹשָׁה אַל־יַעַלְצ֖וּ
אֹיְבַ֣י לִֽי׃ גַּ֣ם כׇּל־קֹ֭וֶיךָ לֹ֣א יֵבֹ֑שׁוּ יֵ֝בֹ֗שׁוּ הַבּוֹגְדִ֥ים רֵיקָֽם׃ דְּרָכֶ֣יךָ יהוה
הוֹדִיעֵ֑נִי אֹ֖רְחוֹתֶ֣יךָ לַמְּדֵֽנִי׃ הַדְרִ֘יכֵ֤נִי בַאֲמִתֶּ֨ךָ ׀ וְֽלַמְּדֵ֗נִי כִּֽי־אַ֭תָּה אֱלֹהֵ֣י
יִשְׁעִ֑י אוֹתְךָ֥ קִ֝וִּ֗יתִי כׇּל־הַיּֽוֹם׃ זְכֹר־רַחֲמֶ֣יךָ יהוה וַחֲסָדֶ֑יךָ כִּ֖י מֵעוֹלָ֣ם הֵֽמָּה׃
חַטֹּ֤אות נְעוּרַ֨י ׀ וּפְשָׁעַ֗י אַל־תִּ֫זְכֹּ֥ר כְּחַסְדְּךָ֥ זְכׇר־לִי־אַתָּ֑ה לְמַ֖עַן טוּבְךָ֣
יהוה׃ טוֹב־וְיָשָׁ֥ר יהוה עַל־כֵּ֤ן יוֹרֶ֖ה חַטָּאִ֣ים בַּדָּֽרֶךְ׃ יַדְרֵ֣ךְ עֲ֭נָוִים בַּמִּשְׁפָּ֑ט
וִֽילַמֵּ֖ד עֲנָוִ֣ים דַּרְכּֽוֹ׃ כׇּל־אׇרְח֣וֹת יהוה חֶ֣סֶד וֶֽאֱמֶ֑ת לְנֹצְרֵ֥י בְ֝רִית֗וֹ וְעֵדֹתָֽיו׃
לְמַֽעַן־שִׁמְךָ֥ יהוה וְֽסָלַחְתָּ֥ לַ֝עֲוֺנִ֗י כִּ֣י רַב־הֽוּא׃ מִי־זֶ֣ה הָ֭אִישׁ יְרֵ֣א יהוה
י֝וֹרֶ֗נּוּ בְּדֶ֣רֶךְ יִבְחָֽר׃ נַ֭פְשׁוֹ בְּט֣וֹב תָּלִ֑ין וְ֝זַרְע֗וֹ יִ֣ירַשׁ אָֽרֶץ׃ ס֣וֹד יהוה לִירֵאָ֑יו
וּ֝בְרִית֗וֹ לְהוֹדִיעָֽם׃ עֵינַ֣י תָּ֭מִיד אֶל־יהוה כִּ֤י הֽוּא־יוֹצִ֖יא מֵרֶ֣שֶׁת רַגְלָֽי׃ פְּנֵה־
אֵלַ֥י וְחׇנֵּ֑נִי כִּֽי־יָחִ֖יד וְעָנִ֣י אָֽנִי׃ צָר֣וֹת לְבָבִ֣י הִרְחִ֑יבוּ מִ֝מְּצ֥וּקוֹתַ֗י הוֹצִיאֵֽנִי׃
רְאֵ֣ה עׇ֭נְיִי וַעֲמָלִ֑י וְ֝שָׂ֗א לְכׇל־חַטֹּאותָֽי׃ רְאֵֽה־אוֹיְבַ֥י כִּי־רָ֑בּוּ וְשִׂנְאַ֖ת חָמָ֣ס
שְׂנֵאֽוּנִי׃ שׇׁמְרָ֣ה נַ֭פְשִׁי וְהַצִּילֵ֑נִי אַל־אֵ֝ב֗וֹשׁ כִּֽי־חָסִ֥יתִי בָֽךְ׃ תֹּם־וָיֹ֥שֶׁר
יִצְּר֑וּנִי כִּ֝֗י קִוִּיתִֽיךָ׃ פְּדֵ֣ה אֱ֭לֹהִים אֶת־יִשְׂרָאֵ֑ל מִ֝כֹּ֗ל צָֽרוֹתָיו׃
כו לְדָוִ֨ד ׀ שׇׁפְטֵ֤נִי יהוה כִּֽי־אֲ֭נִי בְּתֻמִּ֣י הָלַ֑כְתִּי וּבַיהוה בָּ֝טַ֗חְתִּי לֹ֣א אֶמְעָֽד׃
צָרְפָה בְּחָנֵ֣נִי יהוה וְנַסֵּ֑נִי צרופה כִלְיוֹתַ֣י וְלִבִּֽי׃ כִּֽי־חַ֭סְדְּךָ לְנֶ֣גֶד עֵינָ֑י וְ֝הִתְהַלַּ֗כְתִּי
בַּאֲמִתֶּֽךָ׃ לֹֽא־יָ֭שַׁבְתִּי עִם־מְתֵי־שָׁ֑וְא וְעִ֥ם נַ֝עֲלָמִ֗ים לֹ֣א אָבֽוֹא׃ שָׂ֭נֵאתִי
קְהַ֣ל מְרֵעִ֑ים וְעִם־רְ֝שָׁעִ֗ים לֹ֣א אֵשֵֽׁב׃ אֶרְחַ֣ץ בְּנִקָּי֣וֹן כַּפָּ֑י וַאֲסֹבְבָ֖ה אֶת־
מִזְבַּחֲךָ֣ יהוה׃ לַ֭שְׁמִעַ בְּק֣וֹל תּוֹדָ֑ה וּ֝לְסַפֵּ֗ר כׇּל־נִפְלְאוֹתֶֽיךָ׃ יהוה אָ֭הַבְתִּי
מְע֣וֹן בֵּיתֶ֑ךָ וּ֝מְק֗וֹם מִשְׁכַּ֥ן כְּבוֹדֶֽךָ׃ אַל־תֶּאֱסֹ֣ף עִם־חַטָּאִ֣ים נַפְשִׁ֑י וְעִם־
אַנְשֵׁ֖י דָמִ֣ים חַיָּֽי׃ אֲשֶׁר־בִּידֵיהֶ֥ם זִמָּ֑ה וִֽ֝ימִינָ֗ם מָ֣לְאָה שֹּֽׁחַד׃ וַאֲנִ֗י בְּתֻמִּ֣י
אֵלֵ֑ךְ פְּדֵ֥נִי וְחׇנֵּֽנִי׃ רַ֭גְלִי עָמְדָ֣ה בְמִישׁ֑וֹר בְּ֝מַקְהֵלִ֗ים אֲבָרֵ֥ךְ יהוה׃

the floods. Who shall ascend the mountain of the Lord, and who shall stand in His
holy place? He who has clean hands and a pure heart, who has not sworn in vain "by
my soul," and has not sworn deceitfully, He shall receive the blessing from the Lord,
and righteousness from the God of his salvation. This is the company of those who
seek Him, who seek Your face, Jacob. Selah. Lift up your heads, O gates, and be lifted
up, O everlasting doors, so that the King of glory may come in. Who is this King of
glory? The Lord strong and mighty, the Lord mighty in battle. Lift up your heads, O
gates, and lift them up, O everlasting doors, so that the King of glory may come in.
Who is He, this King of glory? The Lord of hosts, He is the King of glory. Selah.

25 OF DAVID. To You, O Lord, I lift up my soul. My God, in You I trust. Let me not to be
disappointed. Let my enemies not rejoice over me. Moreover, let none of those who
wait for You be disappointed. Let those who betray without cause be disappointed.
Make me know Your ways, O Lord. Teach me Your paths. Guide me in Your truth,
and teach me, for You are the God of my salvation. For You do I wait all the day.
Remember Your mercy, O Lord, and Your loving-kindnesses, which are of old. Do
not remember the sins of my youth and my transgressions. According to Your loving-
kindness may You remember me, for Your goodness' sake, O Lord. Good and upright
is the Lord, therefore He instructs sinners in the way. He guides the humble in justice,
and He teaches the humble His way. All the paths of the Lord are loving-kindness and
truth to those who keep His covenant and His testimonies. For Your name's sake, O
Lord, please pardon my iniquity, which is great. How great is the man who fears the
Lord! He instructs him in the way that He chooses. His soul will abide in prosperity,
and his seed will inherit the earth. The closeness of the Lord is with those who fear
Him, and He reveals His covenant to them. My eyes are ever toward the Lord, for He
will take my feet out of the net. Turn to me and favor me, for I am alone and oppressed.
Troubles have enlarged my hearts. O take me out of my distresses. See my affliction
and my suffering, and forgive all my sins. See my enemies, for they are many, and
they hate me with a wicked hatred. Please keep my soul and save me. Let me not be
disappointed, for I put my trust in You. Let integrity and uprightness preserve me, for
I wait for You. Redeem Israel, O God, from all his troubles.

26 OF DAVID. Judge me, O Lord, for I have walked in my integrity, and I have trusted in the
Lord. I will not stumble. Examine me, O Lord, and test me. Try my reins and my heart.
For Your loving-kindness is before my eyes, and I have walked in Your truth. I do not
sit with men of falsehood, and I do not go in with dissemblers. I hate the congregation
of evildoers, and I do not sit with the wicked. I wash my hands in innocence, and I will
march round Your altar, O Lord, That I may proclaim with the voice of thanksgiving,
and tell of all Your wondrous works. O Lord, I love the habitation of Your house, and
the place where Your glory dwells. Do not gather my soul with sinners, nor my life
with the men of blood, In whose hands is mischief, and their right hand is full of bribes.
But as for me, I will walk in my integrity. Redeem me and be gracious to me. My foot
stands on an even place. In the congregations I bless the Lord.

כז לְדָוִד ׀ יְהוָה ׀ אוֹרִי וְיִשְׁעִי מִמִּי אִירָא יְהוָה מָעוֹז־חַיַּי מִמִּי אֶפְחָד׃ בִּקְרֹב
עָלַי ׀ מְרֵעִים לֶאֱכֹל אֶת־בְּשָׂרִי צָרַי וְאֹיְבַי לִי הֵמָּה כָשְׁלוּ וְנָפָלוּ׃ אִם־
תַּחֲנֶה עָלַי ׀ מַחֲנֶה לֹא־יִירָא לִבִּי אִם־תָּקוּם עָלַי מִלְחָמָה בְּזֹאת אֲנִי
בוֹטֵחַ׃ אַחַת ׀ שָׁאַלְתִּי מֵאֵת־יְהוָה אוֹתָהּ אֲבַקֵּשׁ שִׁבְתִּי בְּבֵית־יְהוָה
כָּל־יְמֵי חַיַּי לַחֲזוֹת בְּנֹעַם־יְהוָה וּלְבַקֵּר בְּהֵיכָלוֹ׃ כִּי יִצְפְּנֵנִי ׀ בְּסֻכֹּה בְּיוֹם
רָעָה יַסְתִּרֵנִי בְּסֵתֶר אָהֳלוֹ בְּצוּר יְרוֹמְמֵנִי׃ וְעַתָּה יָרוּם רֹאשִׁי עַל אֹיְבַי
סְבִיבוֹתַי וְאֶזְבְּחָה בְאָהֳלוֹ זִבְחֵי תְרוּעָה אָשִׁירָה וַאֲזַמְּרָה לַיהוָה׃ שְׁמַע־
יְהוָה קוֹלִי אֶקְרָא וְחָנֵּנִי וַעֲנֵנִי׃ לְךָ ׀ אָמַר לִבִּי בַּקְּשׁוּ פָנָי אֶת־פָּנֶיךָ יְהוָה
אֲבַקֵּשׁ׃ אַל־תַּסְתֵּר פָּנֶיךָ ׀ מִמֶּנִּי אַל תַּט־בְּאַף עַבְדֶּךָ עֶזְרָתִי הָיִיתָ אַל־
תִּטְּשֵׁנִי וְאַל־תַּעַזְבֵנִי אֱלֹהֵי יִשְׁעִי׃ כִּי־אָבִי וְאִמִּי עֲזָבוּנִי וַיהוָה יַאַסְפֵנִי׃
הוֹרֵנִי יְהוָה דַּרְכֶּךָ וּנְחֵנִי בְּאֹרַח מִישׁוֹר לְמַעַן שׁוֹרְרָי׃ אַל־תִּתְּנֵנִי בְּנֶפֶשׁ
צָרָי כִּי קָמוּ־בִי עֵדֵי־שֶׁקֶר וִיפֵחַ חָמָס׃ לוּלֵא הֶאֱמַנְתִּי לִרְאוֹת בְּטוּב־
יְהוָה בְּאֶרֶץ חַיִּים׃ קַוֵּה אֶל־יְהוָה חֲזַק וְיַאֲמֵץ לִבֶּךָ וְקַוֵּה אֶל־יְהוָה׃

כח לְדָוִד אֵלֶיךָ יְהוָה ׀ אֶקְרָא צוּרִי אַל־תֶּחֱרַשׁ מִמֶּנִּי פֶּן־תֶּחֱשֶׁה מִמֶּנִּי
וְנִמְשַׁלְתִּי עִם־יוֹרְדֵי בוֹר׃ שְׁמַע קוֹל תַּחֲנוּנַי בְּשַׁוְּעִי אֵלֶיךָ בְּנָשְׂאִי יָדַי
אֶל־דְּבִיר קָדְשֶׁךָ׃ אַל־תִּמְשְׁכֵנִי עִם־רְשָׁעִים וְעִם־פֹּעֲלֵי אָוֶן דֹּבְרֵי שָׁלוֹם
עִם־רֵעֵיהֶם וְרָעָה בִּלְבָבָם׃ תֶּן־לָהֶם כְּפָעֳלָם וּכְרֹעַ מַעַלְלֵיהֶם כְּמַעֲשֵׂה
יְדֵיהֶם תֵּן לָהֶם הָשֵׁב גְּמוּלָם לָהֶם׃ כִּי לֹא יָבִינוּ אֶל־פְּעֻלֹּת יְהוָה וְאֶל־
מַעֲשֵׂה יָדָיו יֶהֶרְסֵם וְלֹא יִבְנֵם׃ בָּרוּךְ יְהוָה כִּי־שָׁמַע קוֹל תַּחֲנוּנָי׃ יְהוָה ׀
עֻזִּי וּמָגִנִּי בּוֹ בָטַח לִבִּי וְנֶעֱזָרְתִּי וַיַּעֲלֹז לִבִּי וּמִשִּׁירִי אֲהוֹדֶנּוּ׃ יְהוָה עֹז־
לָמוֹ וּמָעוֹז יְשׁוּעוֹת מְשִׁיחוֹ הוּא׃ הוֹשִׁיעָה ׀ אֶת־עַמֶּךָ וּבָרֵךְ אֶת־נַחֲלָתֶךָ
וּרְעֵם וְנַשְּׂאֵם עַד־הָעוֹלָם׃

*כט מִזְמוֹר לְדָוִד הָבוּ לַיהוָה בְּנֵי אֵלִים הָבוּ לַיהוָה כָּבוֹד וָעֹז׃ הָבוּ לַיהוָה
כְּבוֹד שְׁמוֹ הִשְׁתַּחֲווּ לַיהוָה בְּהַדְרַת־קֹדֶשׁ׃ קוֹל יְהוָה עַל־הַמָּיִם אֵל־
הַכָּבוֹד הִרְעִים יְהוָה עַל־מַיִם רַבִּים׃ קוֹל־יְהוָה בַּכֹּחַ קוֹל יְהוָה בֶּהָדָר׃
קוֹל יְהוָה שֹׁבֵר אֲרָזִים וַיְשַׁבֵּר יְהוָה אֶת־אַרְזֵי הַלְּבָנוֹן׃ וַיַּרְקִידֵם כְּמוֹ־עֵגֶל
לְבָנוֹן וְשִׂרְיוֹן כְּמוֹ בֶן־רְאֵמִים׃ קוֹל־יְהוָה חֹצֵב לַהֲבוֹת אֵשׁ׃ קוֹל יְהוָה
יָחִיל מִדְבָּר יָחִיל יְהוָה מִדְבַּר קָדֵשׁ׃ קוֹל יְהוָה ׀ יְחוֹלֵל אַיָּלוֹת וַיֶּחֱשֹׂף

*ה לחודש

27 OF DAVID. The Lord is my light and my salvation. Whom shall I fear? The Lord is
the refuge of my life. Whom shall I dread? When the evildoers came close to me to
eat my flesh, those who were to me my adversaries and my enemies, it was they who
stumbled and fell. If a host should encamp against me, my heart will not fear. If a war
should rise against me, in this I trust. One thing have I asked of the Lord, that will I
seek: That I may dwell in the house of the Lord all the days of my life, to behold the
beauty of the Lord, and to contemplate His Temple, That He will hide me in His
tabernacle on the day of evil, He will hide me in the shelter of His tent, He will lift me
up upon a rock. And now my head will be lifted up above my enemies round about
me, and I will offer in His tent sacrifices accompanied by the sound of trumpets. I
will sing, and I will sing praises to the Lord. Hear, O Lord, my voice when I call, and
show me favor and answer me. Of You my heart has said: Seek My face. Your face, O
Lord, will I seek. Do not hide Your face from me. Do not turn Your servant away in
anger. You have been my help, do not abandon me and do not forsake me, O God
of my salvation. For my father and my mother have forsaken me, but the Lord will
gather me in. Teach me Your way, O Lord, and lead me on an even path, because of
my enemies. Do not deliver me to the desire of my enemies, for false witnesses have
risen up against me, and a wicked witness. Were it not that I believed I would see the
goodness of the Lord in the land of the living. Wait for the Lord, be strong and let
your heart be encouraged, and wait for the Lord.

28 OF DAVID. To You, O Lord, I call. My Rock, be not deaf to me, lest You remain idle
regarding me, and I become like those who go down into the pit. Hear the sound
of my supplications, when I cry out to You, when I lift up my hands to Your holiest
sanctuary. Draw me not away with the wicked, and with the workers of iniquity, who
speak peace with their neighbors, but evil is in their heart. Give them according to
their deeds, and according to the evil of their practices. Give them according to the
work of their hands. Render to them what they deserve, Because they do not pay heed
to the deeds of the Lord and to the work of His hands. May He destroy them and not
build them up. Blessed is the Lord, for He has heard the sound of my supplications.
The Lord is my strength and my shield. My heart trusted in Him and I was helped,
and my heart rejoiced, and with my song I will thank Him. The Lord is their strength,
and He is a refuge of salvation for His anointed. Save Your people and bless Your
inheritance, and tend them and carry them forever.

*29 A PSALM of David. Ascribe to the Lord, O you divine beings, ascribe to the Lord glory
and strength. Ascribe to the Lord the glory of His name. Bow down to the Lord in
the splendor of holiness. The voice of the Lord is upon the waters. The God of glory
thunders. The Lord is upon many waters. The voice of the Lord is powerful. The voice
of the Lord is majestic. The voice of the Lord breaks cedars, and the Lord breaks the
cedars of Lebanon. And He makes them skip like a calf, Lebanon and Sirion like a
young wild ox. The voice of the Lord hews out flames of fire. The voice of the Lord
shakes the wilderness. The Lord shakes the wilderness of Kadesh. The voice of the

*5th DAY of the month

יְעָר֗וֹת וּבְהֵיכָל֑וֹ כֻּ֝לּ֗וֹ אֹמֵ֥ר כָּבֽוֹד׃ יְ֭הוָה לַמַּבּ֣וּל יָשָׁ֑ב וַיֵּ֥שֶׁב יְ֝הוָ֗ה מֶ֣לֶךְ
לְעוֹלָֽם׃ יְֽהוָ֗ה עֹ֭ז לְעַמּ֣וֹ יִתֵּ֑ן יְהוָ֓ה ׀ יְבָרֵ֖ךְ אֶת־עַמּ֣וֹ בַשָּׁלֽוֹם׃
ל* מִזְמ֡וֹר שִׁיר־חֲנֻכַּ֖ת הַבַּ֣יִת לְדָוִֽד׃ אֲרוֹמִמְךָ֣ יְ֭הוָה כִּ֣י דִלִּיתָ֑נִי וְלֹא־
שִׂמַּ֖חְתָּ אֹיְבַ֣י לִֽי׃ יְהוָ֥ה אֱלֹהָ֑י שִׁוַּ֥עְתִּי אֵ֝לֶ֗יךָ וַתִּרְפָּאֵֽנִי׃ יְֽהוָ֗ה הֶֽעֱלִ֣יתָ
מִיָּרְדִי־ מִן־שְׁא֣וֹל נַפְשִׁ֑י חִ֝יִּיתַ֗נִי מיורדי־בֽוֹר׃ זַמְּר֣וּ לַיהוָ֣ה חֲסִידָ֑יו וְ֝הוֹד֗וּ לְזֵ֣כֶר
קָדְשֽׁוֹ׃ כִּ֤י רֶ֨גַע ׀ בְּאַפּוֹ֮ חַיִּ֪ים בִּרְצ֫וֹנ֥וֹ בָּ֭עֶרֶב יָלִ֥ין בֶּ֗כִי וְלַבֹּ֥קֶר רִנָּֽה׃ וַ֭אֲנִי
אָמַ֣רְתִּי בְשַׁלְוִ֑י בַּל־אֶמּ֥וֹט לְעוֹלָֽם׃ יְֽהוָ֗ה בִּרְצוֹנְךָ֮ הֶעֱמַ֪דְתָּה לְֽהַרְרִ֫י עֹ֥ז
הִסְתַּ֥רְתָּ פָנֶ֗יךָ הָיִ֥יתִי נִבְהָֽל׃ אֵלֶ֣יךָ יְהוָ֣ה אֶקְרָ֑א וְאֶל־אֲ֝דֹנָ֗י אֶתְחַנָּֽן׃
מַה־בֶּ֥צַע בְּדָמִי֮ בְּרִדְתִּ֪י אֶ֫ל שָׁ֥חַת הֲיוֹדְךָ֥ עָפָ֑ר הֲיַגִּ֥יד אֲמִתֶּֽךָ׃ שְׁמַע־
יְהוָ֥ה וְחָנֵּ֑נִי יְ֝הוָ֗ה הֱֽיֵה־עֹזֵ֥ר לִֽי׃ הָפַ֣כְתָּ מִסְפְּדִי֮ לְמָח֪וֹל לִ֥י פִּתַּ֥חְתָּ שַׂקִּ֑י
וַתְּאַזְּרֵ֥נִי שִׂמְחָֽה׃ לְמַ֤עַן ׀ יְזַמֶּרְךָ֣ כָ֭בוֹד וְלֹ֣א יִדֹּ֑ם יְהוָ֥ה אֱ֝לֹהַ֗י לְעוֹלָ֥ם
אוֹדֶֽךָּ׃
לא לַמְנַצֵּ֗חַ מִזְמ֥וֹר לְדָוִֽד׃ בְּךָ֣ יְהוָ֣ה חָ֭סִיתִי אַל־אֵב֣וֹשָׁה לְעוֹלָ֑ם בְּצִדְקָתְךָ֥
פַלְּטֵֽנִי׃ הַטֵּ֤ה אֵלַ֨י ׀ אָזְנְךָ֮ מְהֵרָ֪ה הַצִּ֫ילֵ֥נִי הֱיֵ֤ה לִ֨י ׀ לְֽצוּר־מָ֭עוֹז לְבֵ֥ית
מְ֝צוּד֗וֹת לְהוֹשִׁיעֵֽנִי׃ כִּֽי־סַלְעִ֣י וּמְצוּדָתִ֣י אָ֑תָּה וּלְמַ֥עַן שִׁ֝מְךָ֗ תַּ֜נְחֵ֗נִי
וּֽתְנַהֲלֵֽנִי׃ תּֽוֹצִיאֵ֗נִי מֵרֶ֣שֶׁת ז֭וּ טָ֣מְנוּ לִ֑י כִּ֝י־אַתָּ֗ה מָעוּזִּֽי׃ בְּיָדְךָ֮ אַפְקִ֪יד
ר֫וּחִ֥י פָּדִ֖יתָה אוֹתִ֥י יְהוָ֗ה אֵ֣ל אֱמֶֽת׃ שָׂנֵ֗אתִי הַשֹּׁמְרִ֥ים הַבְלֵי־שָׁ֑וְא וַ֝אֲנִ֗י
אֶל־יְהוָ֥ה בָּטָֽחְתִּי׃ אָ֥גִ֥ילָה וְאֶשְׂמְחָ֗ה בְּחַ֫סְדֶּ֥ךָ אֲשֶׁ֣ר רָ֭אִיתָ אֶת־עָנְיִ֑י
יָ֝דַ֗עְתָּ בְּצָר֥וֹת נַפְשִֽׁי׃ וְלֹ֣א הִ֭סְגַּרְתַּנִי בְּיַד־אוֹיֵ֑ב הֶֽעֱמַ֖דְתָּ בַמֶּרְחָ֣ב רַגְלָֽי׃
חָנֵּ֤נִי יְהוָ֗ה כִּ֥י צַ֫ר לִ֥י עָשְׁשָׁ֖ה בְכַ֥עַס עֵ֝ינִ֗י נַפְשִׁ֥י וּבִטְנִֽי׃ כִּ֤י כָל֨וּ בְיָג֡וֹן חַיַּ֗י
וּשְׁנוֹתַ֗י בַּאֲנָ֫חָ֥ה כָּשַׁ֣ל בַּעֲוֺנִ֣י כֹחִ֑י וַעֲצָמַ֥י עָשֵֽׁשׁוּ׃ מִכָּל־צֹרְרַ֨י הָיִ֪יתִי חֶרְפָּ֡ה
וְלִשְׁכֵנַ֨י ׀ מְאֹ֡ד וּפַ֬חַד לִמְיֻדָּעָ֗י רֹאַ֣י בַּח֣וּץ נָדְד֣וּ מִמֶּֽנִּי׃ נִ֭שְׁכַּחְתִּי כְּמֵ֣ת מִלֵּ֑ב
הָ֝יִ֗יתִי כִּכְלִ֥י אֹבֵֽד׃ כִּ֤י שָׁמַ֨עְתִּי ׀ דִּבַּ֥ת רַבִּים֮ מָג֪וֹר מִסָּ֫בִ֥יב בְּהִוָּסְדָ֣ם יַ֣חַד
עָלַ֑י לָקַ֖חַת נַפְשִׁ֣י זָמָֽמוּ׃ וַאֲנִ֤י ׀ עָלֶ֣יךָ בָטַ֣חְתִּי יְהוָ֑ה אָ֝מַ֗רְתִּי אֱלֹהַ֥י אָֽתָּה׃
בְּיָדְךָ֥ עִתֹּתָ֑י הַצִּ֥ילֵ֥נִי מִיַּד־א֝וֹיְבַ֗י וּֽמֵרֹדְפָֽי׃ הָאִ֣ירָה פָ֭נֶיךָ עַל־עַבְדֶּ֑ךָ הוֹשִׁיעֵ֥נִי
בְחַסְדֶּֽךָ׃ יְֽהוָ֗ה אַל־אֵ֭בוֹשָׁה כִּ֣י קְרָאתִ֑יךָ יֵבֹ֥שׁוּ רְ֝שָׁעִ֗ים יִדְּמ֥וּ לִשְׁאֽוֹל׃
תֵּ֥אָלַ֗מְנָה שִׂפְתֵ֫י שָׁ֥קֶר הַדֹּבְר֖וֹת עַל־צַדִּ֥יק עָתָ֗ק בְּגַאֲוָ֥ה וָבֽוּז׃ מָ֤ה רַֽב
טוּבְךָ֮ אֲשֶׁר־צָפַ֪נְתָּ לִּ֫ירֵאֶ֥יךָ פָּ֭עַלְתָּ לַחֹסִ֣ים בָּ֑ךְ נֶ֝֗גֶד בְּנֵ֥י אָדָֽם׃ תַּסְתִּירֵ֤ם ׀

*ליום השני

Lord causes the hinds to tremble, and strips the forests bare, and in His Temple all
say: Glory. The Lord sat for a flood, but the Lord sits as King forever. The Lord will
give strength to His people. The Lord will bless His people with peace.

*30 A PSALM. A song at the dedication of the house. Of David. I will extol You, O Lord, for
You have lifted me up, and You have not made my enemies rejoice over me. O Lord,
my God, I cried out to You, and You healed me. O Lord, You brought me up from the
underworld. You kept me alive, that I should not go down into the pit. Sing praise to
the Lord, O you His pious ones, and give thanks to the remembrance of His holiness.
For He remains a moment in His anger, a lifetime in His favor. In the evening one
goes to sleep weeping, but in the morning there is joy. But I said in my prosperity: I
will never stumble. O Lord, by Your favor You made my mountain stand strong. You
hid Your face, and I was dismayed. I cried to You, O Lord, and to the Lord I made
supplication. What profit is there in my blood, when I go down into the pit? Shall the
dust give thanks to You? Shall it declare Your truth? Hear, O Lord, and be gracious
to me. O Lord, be my helper. You turned for me my mourning into dancing. You
loosened my sackcloth and girded me with gladness. Therefore glory will sing praise
to You, and will not be silent. O Lord, my God, I will give thanks to You forever.

31 TO THE DIRECTOR of music. A psalm of David. In You, O Lord, do I seek refuge. Let
me never be disappointed. Deliver me in Your righteousness. Incline Your ear to me.
Deliver me speedily. Be for me a fortified rock, a fortress to save me. For You are my
rock and my fortress. Therefore for Your name's sake lead me and guide me. Take
me out of the net that they have hidden for me, for You are my stronghold. Into Your
hand I entrust my spirit. Redeem me, O Lord, God of truth. I hate those who put
their hope in false vanities, but as for me I trust in the Lord. I am glad and I rejoice
in Your loving-kindness; for You had looked upon my affliction, You have known
the troubles of my soul. And You have not delivered me into the hand of the enemy.
You have set my feet in a broad place. Be gracious unto me, for I am in distress. My
eye, my throat, and my belly have become darkened because of affliction. For my
life has been spent in grief, and my years in sighs. My strength has failed because of
my iniquity, and my bones have become black. I have become the scorn of all my
adversaries, and especially of my neighbors, and a dread to my acquaintances. Those
who see me in the marketplace flee from me. I am forgotten as a dead man from the
heart. I have become like a discarded vessel. Indeed, I have heard the slander of many,
fear roundabout. When they all gathered against me, they plotted to take my life. But
I trust in You, O Lord. I said, You are my God. My times are in Your hand. Deliver
me from the hand of my enemies and from those who pursue me. Make Your face
shine upon Your servant. Deliver me in Your loving kindness. O Lord, let me not to
be disappointed that I have called upon You. Let the wicked be disappointed, let them
be silent in the underworld. Let the lying lips be silenced, which speak insolent words,
arrogantly and contemptuously, against the righteous. How great is Your goodness
that You have stored away for those who fear You, that You have performed for those

---

*MONDAY

בְּסֵתֶר פָּנֶיךָ מֵרֻכְסֵי אִישׁ תִּצְפְּנֵם בְּסֻכָּה מֵרִיב לְשֹׁנוֹת: בָּרוּךְ יְהוָה כִּי
הִפְלִיא חַסְדּוֹ לִי בְּעִיר מָצוֹר: וַאֲנִי ׀ אָמַרְתִּי בְחָפְזִי נִגְרַזְתִּי מִנֶּגֶד עֵינֶיךָ
אָכֵן שָׁמַעְתָּ קוֹל תַּחֲנוּנַי בְּשַׁוְּעִי אֵלֶיךָ: אֶֽהֱבוּ אֶת־יְהוָה כָּל־חֲסִידָיו
אֱמוּנִים נֹצֵר יְהוָה וּמְשַׁלֵּם עַל־יֶתֶר עֹשֵׂה גַאֲוָה: חִזְקוּ וְיַאֲמֵץ לְבַבְכֶם
כָּל־הַֽמְיַחֲלִים לַיהוָה:

לב לְדָוִד מַשְׂכִּיל אַשְׁרֵי נְשׂוּי־פֶּשַׁע כְּסוּי חֲטָאָה: אַשְׁרֵי־אָדָם לֹא יַחְשֹׁב
יְהוָה לוֹ עָוֺן וְאֵין בְּרוּחוֹ רְמִיָּה: כִּי־הֶחֱרַשְׁתִּי בָּלוּ עֲצָמָי בְּשַׁאֲגָתִי כָּל־
הַיּוֹם: כִּי ׀ יוֹמָם וָלַיְלָה תִּכְבַּד עָלַי יָדֶךָ נֶהְפַּךְ לְשַׁדִּי בְּחַרְבֹנֵי קַיִץ סֶלָה:
חַטָּאתִי אוֹדִיעֲךָ וַעֲוֺנִי לֹא־כִסִּיתִי אָמַרְתִּי אוֹדֶה עֲלֵי פְשָׁעַי לַיהוָה
וְאַתָּה נָשָׂאתָ עֲוֺן חַטָּאתִי סֶלָה: עַל־זֹאת יִתְפַּלֵּל כָּל־חָסִיד ׀ אֵלֶיךָ
לְעֵת מְצֹא רַק לְשֵׁטֶף מַיִם רַבִּים אֵלָיו לֹא יַגִּיעוּ: אַתָּה ׀ סֵתֶר לִי מִצַּר
תִּצְּרֵנִי רָנֵּי פַלֵּט תְּסוֹבְבֵנִי סֶלָה: אַשְׂכִּילְךָ ׀ וְאוֹרְךָ בְּדֶרֶךְ־זוּ תֵלֵךְ אִיעֲצָה
עָלֶיךָ עֵינִי: אַל־תִּהְיוּ ׀ כְּסוּס כְּפֶרֶד אֵין הָבִין בְּמֶתֶג־וָרֶסֶן עֶדְיוֹ לִבְלוֹם
בַּל קְרֹב אֵלֶיךָ: רַבִּים מַכְאוֹבִים לָרָשָׁע וְהַבּוֹטֵחַ בַּיהוָה חֶסֶד יְסוֹבְבֶנּוּ:
שִׂמְחוּ בַיהוָה וְגִילוּ צַדִּיקִים וְהַרְנִינוּ כָּל־יִשְׁרֵי־לֵב:

לג רַנְּנוּ צַדִּיקִים בַּיהוָה לַיְשָׁרִים נָאוָה תְהִלָּה: הוֹדוּ לַיהוָה בְּכִנּוֹר בְּנֵבֶל
עָשׂוֹר זַמְּרוּ־לוֹ: שִׁירוּ־לוֹ שִׁיר חָדָשׁ הֵיטִיבוּ נַגֵּן בִּתְרוּעָה: כִּי־יָשָׁר דְּבַר־
יְהוָה וְכָל־מַעֲשֵׂהוּ בֶּאֱמוּנָה: אֹהֵב צְדָקָה וּמִשְׁפָּט חֶסֶד יְהוָה מָלְאָה
הָאָרֶץ: בִּדְבַר יְהוָה שָׁמַיִם נַעֲשׂוּ וּבְרוּחַ פִּיו כָּל־צְבָאָם: כֹּנֵס כַּנֵּד מֵי
הַיָּם נֹתֵן בְּאוֹצָרוֹת תְּהוֹמוֹת: יִירְאוּ מֵיְהוָה כָּל־הָאָרֶץ מִמֶּנּוּ יָגוּרוּ כָּל־
יֹשְׁבֵי תֵבֵל: כִּי הוּא אָמַר וַיֶּהִי הוּא־צִוָּה וַיַּעֲמֹד: יְהוָה הֵפִיר עֲצַת־גּוֹיִם
הֵנִיא מַחְשְׁבוֹת עַמִּים: עֲצַת יְהוָה לְעוֹלָם תַּעֲמֹד מַחְשְׁבוֹת לִבּוֹ לְדֹר
וָדֹר: אַשְׁרֵי הַגּוֹי אֲשֶׁר־יְהוָה אֱלֹהָיו הָעָם ׀ בָּחַר לְנַחֲלָה לוֹ: מִשָּׁמַיִם
הִבִּיט יְהוָה רָאָה אֶת־כָּל־בְּנֵי הָאָדָם: מִמְּכוֹן־שִׁבְתּוֹ הִשְׁגִּיחַ אֶל כָּל־
יֹשְׁבֵי הָאָרֶץ: הַיֹּצֵר יַחַד לִבָּם הַמֵּבִין אֶל־כָּל־מַעֲשֵׂיהֶם: אֵין־הַמֶּלֶךְ
נוֹשָׁע בְּרָב־חָיִל גִּבּוֹר לֹא־יִנָּצֵל בְּרָב־כֹּחַ: שֶׁקֶר הַסּוּס לִתְשׁוּעָה וּבְרֹב
חֵילוֹ לֹא יְמַלֵּט: הִנֵּה עֵין יְהוָה אֶל־יְרֵאָיו לַמְיַחֲלִים לְחַסְדּוֹ: לְהַצִּיל
מִמָּוֶת נַפְשָׁם וּלְחַיּוֹתָם בָּרָעָב: נַפְשֵׁנוּ חִכְּתָה לַיהוָה עֶזְרֵנוּ וּמָגִנֵּנוּ הוּא:

who seek refuge in You, in the sight of the sons of man! You hide them in the secret
place of Your presence from the plots of men. You conceal them in a hiding-place
from the strife of tongues. Blessed is the Lord, for He has shown me His marvelous
loving-kindness in a besieged city. For I had said in my dread: I am cut off from before
Your eyes. Nevertheless, You heard the voice of my supplications when I cried to
You. Love the Lord, all you His pious ones. The Lord preserves the faithful, and He
plentifully repays him who acts haughtily. Be strong and let your heart be brave, all
you who hope for the Lord.

32 OF DAVID. A *maskil.* Happy is he whose transgression is forgiven, whose sin is covered.
Happy is the man to whom the Lord does not impute iniquity, and in whose spirit
there is no guile. When I kept silent, my bones wasted away, and I cried out all day
long. For day and night Your hand is heavy upon me. My marrow is dried up because
of the burning heat of summer. Selah. I acknowledge my sin to You, and I did not hide
my iniquity. I said: I will confess my transgressions to the Lord. And You forgave the
iniquity of my sin. Selah. For this everyone who is pious shall pray to You regarding
the time that it finds him, only that when the great waters flood, they will not come
near him. You are my hiding-place. You will protect me from the enemy. You will
surround me with songs of deliverance. Selah. I will grant you success, and I will show
you the way that you shall go. I will guide you with my eye. Be not like a horse or a
mule that has no understanding. With bit and bridle, its ornaments, it is held back.
May it not come near to you. Many are the pains of the wicked, but he who trusts in
the Lord – He will surround him with loving-kindness. Rejoice in the Lord and be
glad, O you righteous, and sing for joy, all you who are upright in heart.

33 REJOICE in the Lord, O you righteous. Praise is seemly for the upright. Give thanks to
the Lord with a lyre. Sing praises to Him with a harp of ten strings. Sing Him a new
song. Play skillfully with a loud sound. For the word of the Lord is upright, and all His
work is done in faithfulness. He loves righteousness and judgment. The earth is full
of the loving-kindness of the Lord. By the word of the Lord were the heavens made,
and by the breath of His mouth all their host. He gathers the waters of the sea as a
heap. He lays the great waters in storehouses. Let all the earth be in fear of the Lord.
Let all the inhabitants of the world stand in awe of Him. For He spoke, and it was. He
commanded, and it stood. The Lord confounds the plan of the nations. He makes
the thoughts of the people of no effect. The plan of the Lord will stand forever, the
thoughts of His heart for all generations. Happy is the nation whose God is the Lord,
the people whom He has chosen for His own inheritance. The Lord looks down from
heaven. He sees all the sons of man. From the place of His habitation He gazes upon
all the inhabitants of the earth. It is He Who creates all their hearts, Who discerns all
their deeds. A king is not saved by a great host. A mighty man is not delivered by great
strength. A horse is a vain thing for safety, and it will not save with its great strength.
Behold, the eye of the Lord is on those who fear Him, on those who hope for His
loving-kindness, To deliver their soul from death, and to keep them alive in famine.

כִּי־בוֹ יִשְׂמַח לִבֵּנוּ כִּי בְשֵׁם קׇדְשׁוֹ בָטָחְנוּ׃ יְהִי־חַסְדְּךָ יהוה עָלֵינוּ כַּאֲשֶׁר
יִחַלְנוּ לָךְ׃
לד לְדָוִד בְּשַׁנּוֹתוֹ אֶת־טַעְמוֹ לִפְנֵי אֲבִימֶלֶךְ וַיְגָרְשֵׁהוּ וַיֵּלַךְ׃ אֲבָרְכָה אֶת־
יהוה בְּכׇל־עֵת תָּמִיד תְּהִלָּתוֹ בְּפִי׃ בַּיהוה תִּתְהַלֵּל נַפְשִׁי יִשְׁמְעוּ עֲנָוִים
וְיִשְׂמָחוּ׃ גַּדְּלוּ לַיהוה אִתִּי וּנְרוֹמְמָה שְׁמוֹ יַחְדָּו׃ דָּרַשְׁתִּי אֶת־יהוה וְעָנָנִי
וּמִכׇּל־מְגוּרוֹתַי הִצִּילָנִי׃ הִבִּיטוּ אֵלָיו וְנָהָרוּ וּפְנֵיהֶם אַל־יֶחְפָּרוּ׃ זֶה עָנִי
קָרָא וַיהוה שָׁמֵעַ וּמִכׇּל־צָרוֹתָיו הוֹשִׁיעוֹ׃ חֹנֶה מַלְאַךְ־יהוה סָבִיב לִירֵאָיו
וַיְחַלְּצֵם׃ טַעֲמוּ וּרְאוּ כִּי־טוֹב יהוה אַשְׁרֵי הַגֶּבֶר יֶחֱסֶה־בּוֹ׃ יְראוּ אֶת־
יהוה קְדֹשָׁיו כִּי־אֵין מַחְסוֹר לִירֵאָיו׃ כְּפִירִים רָשׁוּ וְרָעֵבוּ וְדֹרְשֵׁי יהוה
לֹא־יַחְסְרוּ כׇל־טוֹב׃ לְכוּ־בָנִים שִׁמְעוּ־לִי יִרְאַת יהוה אֲלַמֶּדְכֶם׃ מִי־
הָאִישׁ הֶחָפֵץ חַיִּים אֹהֵב יָמִים לִרְאוֹת טוֹב׃ נְצֹר לְשׁוֹנְךָ מֵרָע וּשְׂפָתֶיךָ
מִדַּבֵּר מִרְמָה׃ סוּר מֵרָע וַעֲשֵׂה־טוֹב בַּקֵּשׁ שָׁלוֹם וְרׇדְפֵהוּ׃ עֵינֵי יהוה
אֶל־צַדִּיקִים וְאׇזְנָיו אֶל־שַׁוְעָתָם׃ פְּנֵי יהוה בְּעֹשֵׂי רָע לְהַכְרִית מֵאֶרֶץ
זִכְרָם׃ צָעֲקוּ וַיהוה שָׁמֵעַ וּמִכׇּל־צָרוֹתָם הִצִּילָם׃ קָרוֹב יהוה לְנִשְׁבְּרֵי־לֵב
וְאֶת־דַּכְּאֵי־רוּחַ יוֹשִׁיעַ׃ רַבּוֹת רָעוֹת צַדִּיק וּמִכֻּלָּם יַצִּילֶנּוּ יהוה׃ שֹׁמֵר
כׇּל־עַצְמוֹתָיו אַחַת מֵהֵנָּה לֹא נִשְׁבָּרָה׃ תְּמוֹתֵת רָשָׁע רָעָה וְשֹׂנְאֵי צַדִּיק
יֶאְשָׁמוּ׃ פּוֹדֶה יהוה נֶפֶשׁ עֲבָדָיו וְלֹא יֶאְשְׁמוּ כׇּל־הַחֹסִים בּוֹ׃
*לה לְדָוִד ׀ רִיבָה יהוה אֶת־יְרִיבַי לְחַם אֶת־לֹחֲמָי׃ הַחֲזֵק מָגֵן וְצִנָּה וְקוּמָה
בְּעֶזְרָתִי׃ וְהָרֵק חֲנִית וּסְגֹר לִקְרַאת רֹדְפָי אֱמֹר לְנַפְשִׁי יְשֻׁעָתֵךְ אָנִי׃
יֵבֹשׁוּ וְיִכָּלְמוּ מְבַקְשֵׁי נַפְשִׁי יִסֹּגוּ אָחוֹר וְיַחְפְּרוּ חֹשְׁבֵי רָעָתִי׃ יִהְיוּ כְּמֹץ
לִפְנֵי־רוּחַ וּמַלְאַךְ יהוה דּוֹחֶה׃ יְהִי־דַרְכָּם חֹשֶׁךְ וַחֲלַקְלַקֹּת וּמַלְאַךְ יהוה
רֹדְפָם׃ כִּי־חִנָּם טָמְנוּ־לִי שַׁחַת רִשְׁתָּם חִנָּם חָפְרוּ לְנַפְשִׁי׃ תְּבוֹאֵהוּ
שׁוֹאָה לֹא־יֵדָע וְרִשְׁתּוֹ אֲשֶׁר־טָמַן תִּלְכְּדוֹ בְּשׁוֹאָה יִפׇּל־בָּהּ׃ וְנַפְשִׁי תָּגִיל
בַּיהוה תָּשִׂישׂ בִּישׁוּעָתוֹ׃ כׇּל עַצְמוֹתַי ׀ תֹּאמַרְנָה יהוה מִי כָמוֹךָ מַצִּיל
עָנִי מֵחָזָק מִמֶּנּוּ וְעָנִי וְאֶבְיוֹן מִגֹּזְלוֹ׃ יְקוּמוּן עֵדֵי חָמָס אֲשֶׁר לֹא־יָדַעְתִּי
יִשְׁאָלוּנִי׃ יְשַׁלְּמוּנִי רָעָה תַּחַת טוֹבָה שְׁכוֹל לְנַפְשִׁי׃ וַאֲנִי ׀ בַּחֲלוֹתָם
לְבוּשִׁי שָׂק עִנֵּיתִי בַצּוֹם נַפְשִׁי וּתְפִלָּתִי עַל־חֵיקִי תָשׁוּב׃ כְּרֵעַ־כְּאָח לִי
הִתְהַלָּכְתִּי כַּאֲבֶל־אֵם קֹדֵר שַׁחוֹתִי׃ וּבְצַלְעִי שָׂמְחוּ וְנֶאֱסָפוּ נֶאֶסְפוּ עָלַי

*ו לחודש

Our soul waits for the Lord. He is our help and our shield. Indeed, in Him does our
heart rejoice. Indeed, in His holy name we trust. May Your loving-kindness, O Lord,
be upon us, as we hope for You.

34 OF DAVID, when he feigned madness before Abimelech, who drove him away, and
he departed. I will bless the Lord at all times. His praise is always in my mouth. My
soul glories in the Lord. But the humble hear and rejoice. Magnify the Lord with me,
and let us exalt His name together. I sought the Lord and He answered me, and He
delivered me from all my fears. They looked to Him, and were radiant. Let their faces
not be abashed. Behold, a poor man cries and the Lord hears, and He saves him from
all his troubles. The angel of the Lord encamps around those who fear Him, and he
rescues them. Taste and see that the Lord is good. Happy is the man who seeks refuge
in Him. Fear the Lord, you His holy ones, for those who fear Him have no lack. The
young lions are poor and hungry, but those who seek the Lord will not lack any good
thing. Come, children, listen to me. I will teach you to fear the Lord. The man who
desires life, who loves days to see good, Guard your tongue from evil, and your lips
from speaking deceit. Turn away from evil, and do good. Seek peace, and pursue it.
The eyes of the Lord are toward the righteous, and His ears are open to their cry. The
face of the Lord is against those who do evil, to cut off the remembrance of them from
the earth. They cry, and the Lord hears, and He delivers them from all their troubles.
The Lord is near to those with a broken heart, and He saves those of contrite spirit.
Many are the afflictions of the righteous, but the Lord delivers him from them all. He
keeps all his bones. Not one of them is broken. Evil will kill the wicked, and those
who hate the righteous will be held guilty. The Lord redeems the soul of His servant,
and none of those who seek refuge in Him will be held guilty.

*35 OF DAVID. Contend, O Lord, with those who contend against me. Fight against those
who fight against me. Take hold of buckler and shield, and rise up in my help. And
draw spear and battle-axe against those who pursue me. Say to my soul: "I am your
salvation." Let those who seek my soul be put to shame and be disgraced. Let those
who plan my harm be turned back and be ashamed. Let them be as chaff before
the wind, and that the angel of the Lord thrust them away. Let their way be dark
and slippery, and let the angel of the Lord pursue them. For without cause they
have hidden their net for me in a pit, without cause they have dug for my soul. Let
destruction come upon him unawares, and let the net that he hid catch him. Then let
him fall in it to destruction. But my soul will be joyful in the Lord. They will rejoice
in His salvation. All my bones will say: O Lord, who is like You, who delivers the
oppressed from him who is stronger than him, and the poor and the needy from him
who robs him? False witnesses rise up. They ask me things I do not know. They repay
me evil for good, bereavement for my soul. But as for me, when they were sick, my
clothing was sackcloth, I afflicted my soul with fasting, and my prayer would return
to my bosom. I went about as for a friend or a brother, I bowed down darkly like
one who mourns for his mother. But when I stumbled, they rejoiced and gathered

---

*6th DAY of the month

נֵכִים וְלֹא יָדַעְתִּי קָרְעוּ וְלֹא־דָמּוּ׃ בְּחַנְפֵי לַעֲגֵי מָעוֹג חָרֹק עָלַי שִׁנֵּימוֹ׃
אֲדֹנָי כַּמָּה תִּרְאֶה הָשִׁיבָה נַפְשִׁי מִשֹּׁאֵיהֶם מִכְּפִירִים יְחִידָתִי׃ אוֹדְךָ
בְּקָהָל רָב בְּעַם עָצוּם אֲהַלְלֶךָּ׃ אַל־יִשְׂמְחוּ־לִי אֹיְבַי שֶׁקֶר שֹׂנְאַי חִנָּם
יִקְרְצוּ־עָיִן׃ כִּי לֹא שָׁלוֹם יְדַבֵּרוּ וְעַל רִגְעֵי־אֶרֶץ דִּבְרֵי מִרְמוֹת יַחֲשֹׁבוּן׃
וַיַּרְחִיבוּ עָלַי פִּיהֶם אָמְרוּ הֶאָח ׀ הֶאָח רָאֲתָה עֵינֵינוּ׃ רָאִיתָה יהוה אַל־
תֶּחֱרַשׁ אֲדֹנָי אַל־תִּרְחַק מִמֶּנִּי׃ הָעִירָה וְהָקִיצָה לְמִשְׁפָּטִי אֱלֹהַי וַאדֹנָי
לְרִיבִי׃ שָׁפְטֵנִי כְצִדְקְךָ יהוה אֱלֹהָי וְאַל־יִשְׂמְחוּ־לִי׃ אַל־יֹאמְרוּ בְלִבָּם
הֶאָח נַפְשֵׁנוּ אַל־יֹאמְרוּ בִּלַּעֲנוּהוּ׃ יֵבֹשׁוּ וְיַחְפְּרוּ ׀ יַחְדָּו שְׂמֵחֵי רָעָתִי
יִלְבְּשׁוּ־בֹשֶׁת וּכְלִמָּה הַמַּגְדִּילִים עָלָי׃ יָרֹנּוּ וְיִשְׂמְחוּ חֲפֵצֵי צִדְקִי וְיֹאמְרוּ
תָמִיד יִגְדַּל יהוה הֶחָפֵץ שְׁלוֹם עַבְדּוֹ׃ וּלְשׁוֹנִי תֶּהְגֶּה צִדְקֶךָ כָּל־הַיּוֹם
תְּהִלָּתֶךָ׃

לו לַמְנַצֵּחַ ׀ לְעֶבֶד־יהוה לְדָוִד׃ נְאֻם־פֶּשַׁע לָרָשָׁע בְּקֶרֶב לִבִּי אֵין־פַּחַד
אֱלֹהִים לְנֶגֶד עֵינָיו׃ כִּי־הֶחֱלִיק אֵלָיו בְּעֵינָיו לִמְצֹא עֲוֺנוֹ לִשְׂנֹא׃ דִּבְרֵי־
פִיו אָוֶן וּמִרְמָה חָדַל לְהַשְׂכִּיל לְהֵיטִיב׃ אָוֶן ׀ יַחְשֹׁב עַל־מִשְׁכָּבוֹ יִתְיַצֵּב
עַל־דֶּרֶךְ לֹא־טוֹב רָע לֹא יִמְאָס׃ יהוה בְּהַשָּׁמַיִם חַסְדֶּךָ אֱמוּנָתְךָ עַד־
שְׁחָקִים׃ צִדְקָתְךָ ׀ כְּהַרְרֵי־אֵל מִשְׁפָּטֶךָ תְּהוֹם רַבָּה אָדָם וּבְהֵמָה
תוֹשִׁיעַ ׀ יהוה׃ מַה־יָּקָר חַסְדְּךָ אֱלֹהִים וּבְנֵי אָדָם בְּצֵל כְּנָפֶיךָ יֶחֱסָיוּן׃
יִרְוְיֻן מִדֶּשֶׁן בֵּיתֶךָ וְנַחַל עֲדָנֶיךָ תַשְׁקֵם׃ כִּי־עִמְּךָ מְקוֹר חַיִּים בְּאוֹרְךָ
נִרְאֶה־אוֹר׃ מְשֹׁךְ חַסְדְּךָ לְיֹדְעֶיךָ וְצִדְקָתְךָ לְיִשְׁרֵי־לֵב׃ אַל־תְּבוֹאֵנִי
רֶגֶל גַּאֲוָה וְיַד־רְשָׁעִים אַל־תְּנִדֵנִי׃ שָׁם נָפְלוּ פֹּעֲלֵי אָוֶן דֹּחוּ וְלֹא־יָכְלוּ
קוּם׃

לז לְדָוִד ׀ אַל־תִּתְחַר בַּמְּרֵעִים אַל־תְּקַנֵּא בְּעֹשֵׂי עַוְלָה׃ כִּי כֶחָצִיר מְהֵרָה
יִמָּלוּ וּכְיֶרֶק דֶּשֶׁא יִבּוֹלוּן׃ בְּטַח בַּיהוה וַעֲשֵׂה־טוֹב שְׁכָן־אֶרֶץ וּרְעֵה
אֱמוּנָה׃ וְהִתְעַנַּג עַל־יהוה וְיִתֶּן־לְךָ מִשְׁאֲלֹת לִבֶּךָ׃ גּוֹל עַל־יהוה דַּרְכֶּךָ
וּבְטַח עָלָיו וְהוּא יַעֲשֶׂה׃ וְהוֹצִיא כָאוֹר צִדְקֶךָ וּמִשְׁפָּטֶךָ כַּצָּהֳרָיִם׃ דּוֹם ׀
לַיהוה וְהִתְחוֹלֵל לוֹ אַל־תִּתְחַר בְּמַצְלִיחַ דַּרְכּוֹ בְּאִישׁ עֹשֶׂה מְזִמּוֹת׃
הֶרֶף מֵאַף וַעֲזֹב חֵמָה אַל־תִּתְחַר אַךְ־לְהָרֵעַ׃ כִּי־מְרֵעִים יִכָּרֵתוּן וְקֹוֵי
יהוה הֵמָּה יִירְשׁוּ־אָרֶץ׃ וְעוֹד מְעַט וְאֵין רָשָׁע וְהִתְבּוֹנַנְתָּ עַל־מְקוֹמוֹ

together. The wicked whom I did not know gathered around me. They opened their
mouths wide and did not remain silent. As hypocrites, mockers for cake, they grind
their teeth against me. O Lord, how long will You look on? Rescue my soul from their
destructions, my life from the young lions. I will thank You in a great congregation.
I will praise You among a vast crowd. Let not those who are wrongfully my enemies
rejoice over me, and let not those who hate me without cause wink an eye. For they
do not speak peace, and against those who are quiet in the land they contemplate
deceitful words. They have opened their mouths wide against me and said: "Aha, aha.
Our eye has seen it." You have seen it, O Lord, be not silent. O Lord, be not far from
me. Rouse Yourself and wake up for my judgment, my God and Lord, to my cause.
Judge me according to Your righteousness, O Lord my God, and let them not rejoice
over me. Let them not say in their hearts: "Aha, we are fortunate." Let them not say:
"We have swallowed him up." Let all those who rejoice in my trouble be disappointed
and confounded. Let those who speak grandly against me be clothed in shame and
disgrace. Let those who desire my vindication shout for joy and be glad, and let them
always say: "Let the Lord be great, Who desires the welfare of His servant." And my
tongue will speak of Your righteousness and of Your praise all the day.

36 TO THE DIRECTOR of music, of the servant of the Lord, of David. The speech of
transgression to the wicked is within my heart. There is no fear of God before his eyes.
For it has led him to flatter with his eyes, to uncover his fellow's iniquity so that he
may be hated. The words in his mouth are iniquity and deceit. He has failed to be wise,
to do good. He thinks of iniquity on his bed. He takes his stand on a path that is not
good. He does not reject evil. O Lord, your loving-kindness is in the heavens. Your
faithfulness reaches the skies. Your righteousness is like the mighty mountains, Your
judgments reach the great deep. O Lord, You deliver both man and beast. How dear
is Your loving-kindness, O God, and the children of man seek refuge in the shadow
of Your wings. They are satisfied by the fatness of Your house, and You make them
drink the river of Your pleasures. For with You is the fountain of life. In Your light we
see light. Draw Your loving-kindness to those who know You, and Your righteousness
to the upright in heart. Let the foot of pride not come against me, and let the hand of
the wicked not move me. There let the workers of iniquity fall. May they be pushed
down so that they cannot rise.

37 OF DAVID. Do not vex yourself on account of evildoers. Do not be envious of the
workers of iniquity. For they will quickly wither like the grass, and will dry up like the
green herb. Trust in the Lord and do good, so that you may dwell in the land and always
sustain yourself. Take delight also in the Lord, and He will give you the desires of your
heart. Point your way to the Lord, and trust in Him that He will bring it to pass. And He
will bring forth your righteousness as the light, and your judgment like a noonday. Wait
in silence for the Lord, and hope for Him. Do not vex yourself on account of him who
prospers in his way, on account of the man who performs wicked devices. Cease from
anger and forsake wrath. Do not vex yourself on account of him who only does evil. For

וְאֵינֶנּוּ׃ וַעֲנָוִים יִירְשׁוּ־אָרֶץ וְהִתְעַנְּגוּ עַל־רֹב שָׁלוֹם׃ זֹמֵם רָשָׁע לַצַּדִּיק
וְחֹרֵק עָלָיו שִׁנָּיו׃ אֲדֹנָי יִשְׂחַק־לוֹ כִּי־רָאָה כִּי־יָבֹא יוֹמוֹ׃ חֶרֶב ׀ פָּתְחוּ
רְשָׁעִים וְדָרְכוּ קַשְׁתָּם לְהַפִּיל עָנִי וְאֶבְיוֹן לִטְבוֹחַ יִשְׁרֵי־דָרֶךְ׃ חַרְבָּם
תָּבוֹא בְלִבָּם וְקַשְּׁתוֹתָם תִּשָּׁבַרְנָה׃ טוֹב־מְעַט לַצַּדִּיק מֵהֲמוֹן רְשָׁעִים
רַבִּים׃ כִּי זְרוֹעוֹת רְשָׁעִים תִּשָּׁבַרְנָה וְסוֹמֵךְ צַדִּיקִים יהוה׃ יוֹדֵעַ יהוה
יְמֵי תְמִימִם וְנַחֲלָתָם לְעוֹלָם תִּהְיֶה׃ לֹא־יֵבֹשׁוּ בְּעֵת רָעָה וּבִימֵי רְעָבוֹן
יִשְׂבָּעוּ׃ כִּי רְשָׁעִים ׀ יֹאבֵדוּ וְאֹיְבֵי יהוה כִּיקַר כָּרִים כָּלוּ בֶעָשָׁן כָּלוּ׃ לֹוֶה
רָשָׁע וְלֹא יְשַׁלֵּם וְצַדִּיק חוֹנֵן וְנוֹתֵן׃ כִּי מְבֹרָכָיו יִירְשׁוּ אָרֶץ וּמְקֻלָּלָיו
יִכָּרֵתוּ׃ מֵיהוה מִצְעֲדֵי־גֶבֶר כּוֹנָנוּ וְדַרְכּוֹ יֶחְפָּץ׃ כִּי־יִפֹּל לֹא־יוּטָל כִּי־
יהוה סוֹמֵךְ יָדוֹ׃ נַעַר ׀ הָיִיתִי גַּם־זָקַנְתִּי וְלֹא־רָאִיתִי צַדִּיק נֶעֱזָב וְזַרְעוֹ
מְבַקֶּשׁ־לָחֶם׃ כָּל־הַיּוֹם חוֹנֵן וּמַלְוֶה וְזַרְעוֹ לִבְרָכָה׃ סוּר מֵרָע וַעֲשֵׂה־
טוֹב וּשְׁכֹן לְעוֹלָם׃ כִּי יהוה ׀ אֹהֵב מִשְׁפָּט וְלֹא־יַעֲזֹב אֶת־חֲסִידָיו
לְעוֹלָם נִשְׁמָרוּ וְזֶרַע רְשָׁעִים נִכְרָת׃ צַדִּיקִים יִירְשׁוּ־אָרֶץ וְיִשְׁכְּנוּ לָעַד
עָלֶיהָ׃ פִּי־צַדִּיק יֶהְגֶּה חָכְמָה וּלְשׁוֹנוֹ תְּדַבֵּר מִשְׁפָּט׃ תּוֹרַת אֱלֹהָיו
בְּלִבּוֹ לֹא תִמְעַד אֲשֻׁרָיו׃ צוֹפֶה רָשָׁע לַצַּדִּיק וּמְבַקֵּשׁ לַהֲמִיתוֹ׃ יהוה
לֹא־יַעַזְבֶנּוּ בְיָדוֹ וְלֹא יַרְשִׁיעֶנּוּ בְּהִשָּׁפְטוֹ׃ קַוֵּה אֶל־יהוה ׀ וּשְׁמֹר דַּרְכּוֹ
וִירוֹמִמְךָ לָרֶשֶׁת אָרֶץ בְּהִכָּרֵת רְשָׁעִים תִּרְאֶה׃ רָאִיתִי רָשָׁע עָרִיץ
וּמִתְעָרֶה כְּאֶזְרָח רַעֲנָן׃ וַיַּעֲבֹר וְהִנֵּה אֵינֶנּוּ וָאֲבַקְשֵׁהוּ וְלֹא נִמְצָא׃
שְׁמָר־תָּם וּרְאֵה יָשָׁר כִּי־אַחֲרִית לְאִישׁ שָׁלוֹם׃ וּפֹשְׁעִים נִשְׁמְדוּ
יַחְדָּו אַחֲרִית רְשָׁעִים נִכְרָתָה׃ וּתְשׁוּעַת צַדִּיקִים מֵיהוה מָעוּזָּם
בְּעֵת צָרָה׃ וַיַּעְזְרֵם יהוה וַיְפַלְּטֵם יְפַלְּטֵם מֵרְשָׁעִים וְיוֹשִׁיעֵם כִּי־
חָסוּ בוֹ׃

לח מִזְמוֹר לְדָוִד לְהַזְכִּיר׃ יהוה אַל־בְּקֶצְפְּךָ תוֹכִיחֵנִי וּבַחֲמָתְךָ תְיַסְּרֵנִי׃
כִּי־חִצֶּיךָ נִחֲתוּ בִי וַתִּנְחַת עָלַי יָדֶךָ׃ אֵין־מְתֹם בִּבְשָׂרִי מִפְּנֵי זַעְמֶךָ אֵין־
שָׁלוֹם בַּעֲצָמַי מִפְּנֵי חַטָּאתִי׃ כִּי עֲוֺנֹתַי עָבְרוּ רֹאשִׁי כְּמַשָּׂא כָבֵד יִכְבְּדוּ
מִמֶּנִּי׃ הִבְאִישׁוּ נָמַקּוּ חַבּוּרֹתָי מִפְּנֵי אִוַּלְתִּי׃ נַעֲוֵיתִי שַׁחֹתִי עַד־מְאֹד
כָּל־הַיּוֹם קֹדֵר הִלָּכְתִּי׃ כִּי־כְסָלַי מָלְאוּ נִקְלֶה וְאֵין מְתֹם בִּבְשָׂרִי׃ נְפוּגֹתִי
וְנִדְכֵּיתִי עַד־מְאֹד שָׁאַגְתִּי מִנַּהֲמַת לִבִּי׃ אֲדֹנָי נֶגְדְּךָ כָל־תַּאֲוָתִי וְאַנְחָתִי

the evildoers will be cut off. But those who wait for the Lord, they will inherit the earth. Behold, in a little while the wicked will be no more, and you will look well at his place, but he will not be there, but the meek will inherit the earth, and will delight themselves in the abundance of peace. The wicked man plots against the righteous, and grinds his teeth against him. The Lord will laugh at him, for He sees that his day is coming. The wicked have drawn the sword, and have bent their bow, to cast down the poor and the needy, to slaughter those of upright ways. Their sword will enter their own heart, and their bows will be broken. The little that the righteous man has is better than the wealth of many wicked men. For the arms of the wicked will be broken, but the Lord supports the righteous. The Lord knows the days of the innocent, and their inheritance will be forever. They will not be disappointed in the evil time, and in the days of famine they will be satisfied. Surely the wicked will perish, and the enemies of the Lord like the splendor of the pastures. They will be consumed in the smoke, consumed. The wicked borrows but does not pay back, but the righteous gives with grace. For those who are blessed by Him will inherit the earth, but those who are cursed by Him will be cut off. The steps of man are established by the Lord, and He wills his way. If he falls, he will not be cast down, for the Lord supports his hand. I was a young man and I have also grown old, but I have not seen a righteous man forsaken and his seed begging bread. All day, he lends compassionately, and his seed is blessed. Turn away from evil and do good, and dwell forever. For the Lord loves justice, and does not forsake His pious ones. They are preserved forever, but the seed of the wicked will be cut off. The righteous will inherit the earth, and will dwell on it forever. The mouth of the righteous utters wisdom, and his tongue speaks justice. The law of his God is in his heart. His steps will not falter. The wicked man watches for the righteous, and seeks to kill him. The Lord will not leave him in his hand, and will not let him be condemned when he is judged. Wait for the Lord and keep His way, and He will raise you up to inherit the earth. When the wicked are cut off, you will see it. I have seen the wicked man inspiring fear, and taking root like a green tree in its native soil. It merely passed, and behold he was no more; I sought him, but he was not to be found. Preserve innocence and behold uprightness, for there is a future for the man of peace. But all the transgressors are destroyed. The future of the wicked is cut off. But the salvation of the righteous is from the Lord. He is their refuge in time of trouble. And the Lord helps them and saves them. He saves them from the wicked and delivers them, for they take refuge in Him.

38 A PSALM of David, for remembrance. O Lord, do not rebuke me in Your wrath, and do not chastise me in Your anger. For Your arrows have fallen upon me, and Your hand has come down upon me. There is no healthy spot in my flesh because of Your anger. There is no peace in my bones because of my sin. For my iniquities have covered my head. Like a heavy burden they are too heavy for me. My wounds stink and fester because of my foolishness. I have been contorted, I have been greatly bowed. All day I walk darkly. Indeed, my loins are filled with agitation, and there is no healthy spot in my flesh. I am weakened and most broken. I cry out because of the roaring of my heart.

מִמְּךָ לֹא־נִסְתָּרָה: לִבִּי סְחַרְחַר עֲזָבַנִי כֹחִי וְאוֹר־עֵינַי גַּם־הֵם אֵין אִתִּי:
אֹהֲבַי ׀ וְרֵעַי מִנֶּגֶד נִגְעִי יַעֲמֹדוּ וּקְרוֹבַי מֵרָחֹק עָמָדוּ: וַיְנַקְשׁוּ ׀ מְבַקְשֵׁי
נַפְשִׁי וְדֹרְשֵׁי רָעָתִי דִּבְּרוּ הַוּוֹת וּמִרְמוֹת כָּל־הַיּוֹם יֶהְגּוּ: וַאֲנִי כְחֵרֵשׁ לֹא
אֶשְׁמָע וּכְאִלֵּם לֹא יִפְתַּח־פִּיו: וָאֱהִי כְּאִישׁ אֲשֶׁר לֹא־שֹׁמֵעַ וְאֵין בְּפִיו
תּוֹכָחוֹת: כִּי־לְךָ יהוה הוֹחָלְתִּי אַתָּה תַעֲנֶה אֲדֹנָי אֱלֹהָי: כִּי־אָמַרְתִּי
פֶּן־יִשְׂמְחוּ־לִי בְּמוֹט רַגְלִי עָלַי הִגְדִּילוּ: כִּי־אֲנִי לְצֶלַע נָכוֹן וּמַכְאוֹבִי נֶגְדִּי
תָמִיד: כִּי־עֲוֺנִי אַגִּיד אֶדְאַג מֵחַטָּאתִי: וְאֹיְבַי חַיִּים עָצֵמוּ וְרַבּוּ שֹׂנְאַי
שָׁקֶר: וּמְשַׁלְּמֵי רָעָה תַּחַת טוֹבָה יִשְׂטְנוּנִי תַּחַת רדופי־טוֹב: אַל־תַּעַזְבֵנִי רְדְפִי־
יהוה אֱלֹהַי אַל־תִּרְחַק מִמֶּנִּי: חוּשָׁה לְעֶזְרָתִי אֲדֹנָי תְּשׁוּעָתִי:

*לט לַמְנַצֵּחַ לידיתון מִזְמוֹר לְדָוִד: אָמַרְתִּי אֶשְׁמְרָה דְרָכַי מֵחֲטוֹא בִלְשׁוֹנִי לִידוּתוּן
אֶשְׁמְרָה־לְפִי מַחְסוֹם בְּעֹד רָשָׁע לְנֶגְדִּי: נֶאֱלַמְתִּי דוּמִיָּה הֶחֱשֵׁיתִי מִטּוֹב
וּכְאֵבִי נֶעְכָּר: חַם־לִבִּי ׀ בְּקִרְבִּי בַּהֲגִיגִי תִבְעַר־אֵשׁ דִּבַּרְתִּי בִּלְשׁוֹנִי:
הוֹדִיעֵנִי יהוה ׀ קִצִּי וּמִדַּת יָמַי מַה־הִיא אֵדְעָה מֶה־חָדֵל אָנִי: הִנֵּה
טְפָחוֹת ׀ נָתַתָּה יָמַי וְחֶלְדִּי כְאַיִן נֶגְדֶּךָ אַךְ־כָּל־הֶבֶל כָּל־אָדָם נִצָּב סֶלָה:
אַךְ־בְּצֶלֶם ׀ יִתְהַלֶּךְ־אִישׁ אַךְ־הֶבֶל יֶהֱמָיוּן יִצְבֹּר וְלֹא־יֵדַע מִי־אֹסְפָם:
וְעַתָּה מַה־קִּוִּיתִי אֲדֹנָי תּוֹחַלְתִּי לְךָ הִיא: מִכָּל־פְּשָׁעַי הַצִּילֵנִי חֶרְפַּת
נָבָל אַל־תְּשִׂימֵנִי: נֶאֱלַמְתִּי לֹא אֶפְתַּח־פִּי כִּי אַתָּה עָשִׂיתָ: הָסֵר מֵעָלַי
נִגְעֶךָ מִתִּגְרַת יָדְךָ אֲנִי כָלִיתִי: בְּתוֹכָחוֹת עַל־עָוֺן ׀ יִסַּרְתָּ אִישׁ וַתֶּמֶס
כָּעָשׁ חֲמוּדוֹ אַךְ הֶבֶל כָּל־אָדָם סֶלָה: שִׁמְעָה תְפִלָּתִי ׀ יהוה וְשַׁוְעָתִי ׀
הַאֲזִינָה אֶל־דִּמְעָתִי אַל־תֶּחֱרַשׁ כִּי גֵר אָנֹכִי עִמָּךְ תּוֹשָׁב כְּכָל־אֲבוֹתָי:
הָשַׁע מִמֶּנִּי וְאַבְלִיגָה בְּטֶרֶם אֵלֵךְ וְאֵינֶנִּי:

מ לַמְנַצֵּחַ לְדָוִד מִזְמוֹר: קַוֹּה קִוִּיתִי יהוה וַיֵּט אֵלַי וַיִּשְׁמַע שַׁוְעָתִי: וַיַּעֲלֵנִי ׀
מִבּוֹר שָׁאוֹן מִטִּיט הַיָּוֵן וַיָּקֶם עַל־סֶלַע רַגְלַי כּוֹנֵן אֲשֻׁרָי: וַיִּתֵּן בְּפִי ׀ שִׁיר
חָדָשׁ תְּהִלָּה לֵאלֹהֵינוּ יִרְאוּ רַבִּים וְיִירָאוּ וְיִבְטְחוּ בַּיהוה: אַשְׁרֵי־הַגֶּבֶר
אֲשֶׁר־שָׂם יהוה מִבְטַחוֹ וְלֹא־פָנָה אֶל־רְהָבִים וְשָׂטֵי כָזָב: רַבּוֹת עָשִׂיתָ ׀
אַתָּה ׀ יהוה אֱלֹהַי נִפְלְאֹתֶיךָ וּמַחְשְׁבֹתֶיךָ אֵלֵינוּ אֵין ׀ עֲרֹךְ אֵלֶיךָ אַגִּידָה
וַאֲדַבֵּרָה עָצְמוּ מִסַּפֵּר: זֶבַח וּמִנְחָה ׀ לֹא־חָפַצְתָּ אָזְנַיִם כָּרִיתָ לִּי עוֹלָה
וַחֲטָאָה לֹא שָׁאָלְתָּ: אָז אָמַרְתִּי הִנֵּה־בָאתִי בִּמְגִלַּת־סֵפֶר כָּתוּב עָלָי:

---

*ז לחודש

O Lord, all my desire is before You, and my sighing is not hidden from You. My heart flutters. My strength has left me. And the light of my eyes - it, too, is not with me. My friends and my companions stand aloof from my plague, and my kinsmen stand far off. And those who seek my life devise plots against me, and those who seek my hurt speak malice, and they utter deceits all the day. But I, like a deaf man, do not hear, and I am like a dumb man who does not open his mouth. I have become like a man who does not hear and in whose mouth there are no arguments. For I hope for you, O Lord. You will answer, O Lord, my God. For I said: Lest they rejoice over me. When my foot slips, they magnify themselves over me. For I am ready to stumble, and my pain is always before me. For I declare my iniquity. I worry on account of my sin. And the enemies of my life are many, and those who wrongfully hate me are very numerous. And those who repay evil for good hate me for pursuing good. Do not for forsake me, O Lord. O my God, do be not far off from me. Hasten to my aid, O Lord, my salvation.

*39 TO THE DIRECTOR of music. For *Yedutun*. A psalm of David. I said: I will guard my
ways from sinning with my tongue. I will guard my mouth with a muzzle so long as
the wicked man is before me. I became dumb with silence, I was quiet about the good,
and my pain disfigured me. My heart was hot within me. In my voice a fire burned.
I spoke with my tongue. O Lord, inform me of my end, and what is the measure of
my days. Let me know when I will cease to be. Behold, You have made my days like
handbreadths, and my age is as nothing before You. Indeed, it is certain that every
man is every vanity. Selah. Surely man walks as a mere semblance. Surely they clamor
in vain. Man piles heaps, but does not know who will gather them. And now, for
what to do I wait, O Lord? My hope is for You. Save me from all my transgressions.
Do not make me the reproach of the base man. I am dumb, I do not open my mouth,
for You did it. Remove Your stroke from me. I am consumed by the hostility of Your
hand. With rebukes You chasten man for iniquity, and like a moth You melt his beauty
away. Surely every man is vanity. Selah. Hear my prayer, O Lord, and hearken to my
cry. Do not remain silent to my tears, for I am a stranger with You, a sojourner, like
all my fathers. Turn away from me, and I will regain strength, before I go and am no
more.

40 TO THE DIRECTOR of music. A psalm of David. I greatly hoped for the Lord, and He
turned to me and heard my cry. And He brought me up out of the pit of rushing water,
out of the deep mire, and He set my feet on a rock. He strengthened my steps. And
He has put a new song into my mouth, praise to our God. Many will see and fear,
and they will trust in the Lord. Happy is the man who has made the Lord his trust,
and has not turned to the arrogant, or to those who stray to lies. You have done
many things, O Lord my God, Your wondrous works and Your thoughts toward us.
There is none to be compared to You, I declare and proclaim. They are too many
to be told. You do not desire a sacrifice or a meal-offering. You have opened my
ears. You do not ask for a burnt-offering or a sin-offering. Then I said: Behold, I
have come with the scroll of the book written for me. I desire to do Your will, O

*7th DAY of the month

לַעֲשׂוֹת־רְצוֹנְךָ אֱלֹהַי חָפָצְתִּי וְתוֹרָתְךָ בְּתוֹךְ מֵעָי: בִּשַּׂרְתִּי צֶדֶק ׀ בְּקָהָל
רָב הִנֵּה שְׂפָתַי לֹא אֶכְלָא יהוה אַתָּה יָדָעְתָּ: צִדְקָתְךָ לֹא־כִסִּיתִי ׀ בְּתוֹךְ
לִבִּי אֱמוּנָתְךָ וּתְשׁוּעָתְךָ אָמָרְתִּי לֹא־כִחַדְתִּי חַסְדְּךָ וַאֲמִתְּךָ לְקָהָל
רָב: אַתָּה יהוה לֹא־תִכְלָא רַחֲמֶיךָ מִמֶּנִּי חַסְדְּךָ וַאֲמִתְּךָ תָּמִיד יִצְּרוּנִי:
כִּי אָפְפוּ־עָלַי ׀ רָעוֹת עַד־אֵין מִסְפָּר הִשִּׂיגוּנִי עֲוֺנֹתַי וְלֹא־יָכֹלְתִּי לִרְאוֹת
עָצְמוּ מִשַּׂעֲרוֹת רֹאשִׁי וְלִבִּי עֲזָבָנִי: רְצֵה יהוה לְהַצִּילֵנִי יהוה לְעֶזְרָתִי
חוּשָׁה: יֵבֹשׁוּ וְיַחְפְּרוּ ׀ יַחַד מְבַקְשֵׁי נַפְשִׁי לִסְפּוֹתָהּ יִסֹּגוּ אָחוֹר וְיִכָּלְמוּ
חֲפֵצֵי רָעָתִי: יָשֹׁמּוּ עַל־עֵקֶב בָּשְׁתָּם הָאֹמְרִים לִי הֶאָח ׀ הֶאָח: יָשִׂישׂוּ
וְיִשְׂמְחוּ ׀ בְּךָ כָּל־מְבַקְשֶׁיךָ יֹאמְרוּ תָמִיד יִגְדַּל יהוה אֹהֲבֵי תְּשׁוּעָתֶךָ:
וַאֲנִי ׀ עָנִי וְאֶבְיוֹן אֲדֹנָי יַחֲשָׁב לִי עֶזְרָתִי וּמְפַלְטִי אַתָּה אֱלֹהַי אַל־
תְּאַחַר:
מא לַמְנַצֵּחַ מִזְמוֹר לְדָוִד: אַשְׁרֵי מַשְׂכִּיל אֶל־דָּל בְּיוֹם רָעָה יְמַלְּטֵהוּ יהוה:
וְאֻשַּׁר יהוה ׀ יִשְׁמְרֵהוּ וִיחַיֵּהוּ יאשר בָּאָרֶץ וְאַל־תִּתְּנֵהוּ בְּנֶפֶשׁ אֹיְבָיו: יהוה
יִסְעָדֶנּוּ עַל־עֶרֶשׂ דְּוָי כָּל־מִשְׁכָּבוֹ הָפַכְתָּ בְחָלְיוֹ: אֲנִי־אָמַרְתִּי יהוה חָנֵּנִי
רְפָאָה נַפְשִׁי כִּי־חָטָאתִי לָךְ: אוֹיְבַי יֹאמְרוּ רַע לִי מָתַי יָמוּת וְאָבַד שְׁמוֹ:
וְאִם־בָּא לִרְאוֹת ׀ שָׁוְא יְדַבֵּר לִבּוֹ יִקְבָּץ־אָוֶן לוֹ יֵצֵא לַחוּץ יְדַבֵּר: יַחַד
עָלַי יִתְלַחֲשׁוּ כָּל־שֹׂנְאָי עָלַי ׀ יַחְשְׁבוּ רָעָה לִי: דְּבַר־בְּלִיַּעַל יָצוּק בּוֹ
וַאֲשֶׁר שָׁכַב לֹא־יוֹסִיף לָקוּם: גַּם־אִישׁ שְׁלוֹמִי ׀ אֲשֶׁר־בָּטַחְתִּי בוֹ אוֹכֵל
לַחְמִי הִגְדִּיל עָלַי עָקֵב: וְאַתָּה יהוה חָנֵּנִי וַהֲקִימֵנִי וַאֲשַׁלְּמָה לָהֶם:
בְּזֹאת יָדַעְתִּי כִּי־חָפַצְתָּ בִּי כִּי לֹא־יָרִיעַ אֹיְבִי עָלָי: וַאֲנִי בְּתֻמִּי תָּמַכְתָּ
בִּי וַתַּצִּיבֵנִי לְפָנֶיךָ לְעוֹלָם: בָּרוּךְ יהוה ׀ אֱלֹהֵי יִשְׂרָאֵל מֵהָעוֹלָם וְעַד־
הָעוֹלָם אָמֵן ׀ וְאָמֵן:

ספר שני

מב לַמְנַצֵּחַ מַשְׂכִּיל לִבְנֵי־קֹרַח: כְּאַיָּל תַּעֲרֹג עַל־אֲפִיקֵי־מָיִם כֵּן נַפְשִׁי תַעֲרֹג
אֵלֶיךָ אֱלֹהִים: צָמְאָה נַפְשִׁי ׀ לֵאלֹהִים לְאֵל חָי מָתַי אָבוֹא וְאֵרָאֶה
פְּנֵי אֱלֹהִים: הָיְתָה־לִּי דִמְעָתִי לֶחֶם יוֹמָם וָלָיְלָה בֶּאֱמֹר אֵלַי כָּל־הַיּוֹם
אַיֵּה אֱלֹהֶיךָ: אֵלֶּה אֶזְכְּרָה ׀ וְאֶשְׁפְּכָה עָלַי ׀ נַפְשִׁי כִּי אֶעֱבֹר ׀ בַּסָּךְ אֶדַּדֵּם
עַד־בֵּית אֱלֹהִים בְּקוֹל־רִנָּה וְתוֹדָה הָמוֹן חוֹגֵג: מַה־תִּשְׁתּוֹחֲחִי ׀ נַפְשִׁי

my God, and Your law is in my inward parts. I have preached righteousness in the great congregation. Behold, I do not restrain my lips. O Lord, You know. I have not concealed Your righteousness within my heart. I have declared Your faithfulness and Your salvation. I have not hidden Your loving-kindness and Your truth from the great congregation. You, O Lord, withhold not Your mercies from me. May Your loving-kindness and Your truth always preserve me. For innumerable evils have encompassed me. My iniquities have overtaken me, and I am unable to see. They are more numerous than the hairs of my head, and my heart has forsaken me. May it be Your will, O Lord, to save me. O Lord, hasten to my help. Let all who seek after my soul to destroy it be ashamed and confounded. Let those who wish me evil be turned backward and put to shame. Let those who say about me. Aha, Aha, tremble on their heels in their shame. Let all who seek You rejoice and be glad in You. Let those who love Your salvation always say, May the Lord be magnified. But I am poor and needy. Let the Lord think of me. You are my help and my deliverer, O my God, tarry not.

41 TO THE DIRECTOR of music. A psalm of David. Happy is he who considers the sick.
The Lord will deliver him on the day of evil. The Lord will protect him and will keep him alive, and he will take steps on the earth. But do not deliver him to the desire of his enemies. The Lord will support him upon the bed of sickness. You turned over his entire bed in his illness. I said: O Lord, be gracious to me. Heal my soul, for I have sinned against You. My enemies speak evil of me: When will he die and his name perish? And if one comes to see, he speaks falsehood. His heart gathers wickedness to itself. When he goes out, he tells it. All who hate me whisper against me. Against me they think evil about me. Something deadly has been poured into him, and he who lay down will not rise again. Even the man who sought my peace, in whom I trusted, who ate my bread, has stamped upon me with his heel. But You, O Lord, be gracious to me and raise me up, and I will pay them back. By this I know that You favor me, that my enemy will not exult over me. But as for me, on account of my integrity You have upheld me, and You have set me before You forever. Blessed is the Lord, the God of Israel, from everlasting to everlasting. Amen and amen.

BOOK TWO

42 TO THE DIRECTOR of music. A *maskil* for the sons of Korah. As a hind craves for
streams of water, my soul craves for You, O God. My soul thirsts for God, for the living God. When will I come and appear before God? My tears have been my bread day and night, for they say to me all day, Where is your God? I remember these things, and I pour out my soul within me, how I was wont to pass in covered wagons and I would walk with them to the house of God, with the voice of joy and thanksgiving, a crowd celebrating a holiday. Why are you cast down, O my soul, and why do you moan within me? Hope for God, for I will still thank Him for

וְתֶהֱמִי עָלָי הוֹחִלִי לֵאלֹהִים כִּי־עוֹד אוֹדֶנּוּ יְשׁוּעוֹת פָּנָיו: אֱלֹהַי עָלַי נַפְשִׁי
תִשְׁתּוֹחָח עַל־כֵּן אֶזְכׇּרְךָ מֵאֶרֶץ יַרְדֵּן וְחֶרְמוֹנִים מֵהַר מִצְעָר: תְּהוֹם־אֶל־
תְּהוֹם קוֹרֵא לְקוֹל צִנּוֹרֶיךָ כׇּל־מִשְׁבָּרֶיךָ וְגַלֶּיךָ עָלַי עָבָרוּ: יוֹמָם ׀ יְצַוֶּה
יהוה ׀ חַסְדּוֹ וּבַלַּיְלָה שִׁירֹה עִמִּי תְּפִלָּה לְאֵל חַיָּי: אוֹמְרָה ׀ לְאֵל סַלְעִי
לָמָה שְׁכַחְתָּנִי לָמָּה־קֹדֵר אֵלֵךְ בְּלַחַץ אוֹיֵב: בְּרֶצַח ׀ בְּעַצְמוֹתַי חֵרְפוּנִי
צוֹרְרָי בְּאׇמְרָם אֵלַי כׇּל־הַיּוֹם אַיֵּה אֱלֹהֶיךָ: מַה־תִּשְׁתּוֹחֲחִי ׀ נַפְשִׁי וּמַה־
תֶּהֱמִי עָלָי הוֹחִילִי לֵאלֹהִים כִּי־עוֹד אוֹדֶנּוּ יְשׁוּעֹת פָּנַי וֵאלֹהָי:

מג שׇׁפְטֵנִי אֱלֹהִים ׀ וְרִיבָה רִיבִי מִגּוֹי לֹא־חָסִיד מֵאִישׁ־מִרְמָה וְעַוְלָה
תְפַלְּטֵנִי: כִּי־אַתָּה ׀ אֱלֹהֵי מָעוּזִּי לָמָה זְנַחְתָּנִי לָמָּה־קֹדֵר אֶתְהַלֵּךְ
בְּלַחַץ אוֹיֵב: שְׁלַח־אוֹרְךָ וַאֲמִתְּךָ הֵמָּה יַנְחוּנִי יְבִיאוּנִי אֶל־הַר־קׇדְשְׁךָ
וְאֶל־מִשְׁכְּנוֹתֶיךָ: וְאָבוֹאָה ׀ אֶל־מִזְבַּח אֱלֹהִים אֶל־אֵל שִׂמְחַת גִּילִי
וְאוֹדְךָ בְכִנּוֹר אֱלֹהִים אֱלֹהָי: מַה־תִּשְׁתּוֹחֲחִי ׀ נַפְשִׁי וּמַה־תֶּהֱמִי עָלָי
הוֹחִילִי לֵאלֹהִים כִּי־עוֹד אוֹדֶנּוּ יְשׁוּעֹת פָּנַי וֵאלֹהָי:

*מד לַמְנַצֵּחַ לִבְנֵי־קֹרַח מַשְׂכִּיל: אֱלֹהִים ׀ בְּאׇזְנֵינוּ שָׁמַעְנוּ אֲבוֹתֵינוּ סִפְּרוּ־לָנוּ
פֹּעַל־פָּעַלְתָּ בִימֵיהֶם בִּימֵי קֶדֶם: אַתָּה ׀ יָדְךָ גּוֹיִם הוֹרַשְׁתָּ וַתִּטָּעֵם תָּרַע
לְאֻמִּים וַתְּשַׁלְּחֵם: כִּי לֹא בְחַרְבָּם יָרְשׁוּ אָרֶץ וּזְרוֹעָם לֹא־הוֹשִׁיעָה לָּמוֹ
כִּי־יְמִינְךָ וּזְרוֹעֲךָ וְאוֹר פָּנֶיךָ כִּי רְצִיתָם: אַתָּה־הוּא מַלְכִּי אֱלֹהִים צַוֵּה
יְשׁוּעוֹת יַעֲקֹב: בְּךָ צָרֵינוּ נְנַגֵּחַ בְּשִׁמְךָ נָבוּס קָמֵינוּ: כִּי לֹא בְקַשְׁתִּי אֶבְטָח
וְחַרְבִּי לֹא תוֹשִׁיעֵנִי: כִּי הוֹשַׁעְתָּנוּ מִצָּרֵינוּ וּמְשַׂנְאֵינוּ הֱבִישׁוֹתָ: בֵּאלֹהִים
הִלַּלְנוּ כׇל־הַיּוֹם וְשִׁמְךָ ׀ לְעוֹלָם נוֹדֶה סֶלָה: אַף־זָנַחְתָּ וַתַּכְלִימֵנוּ
וְלֹא־תֵצֵא בְּצִבְאוֹתֵינוּ: תְּשִׁיבֵנוּ אָחוֹר מִנִּי־צָר וּמְשַׂנְאֵינוּ שָׁסוּ לָמוֹ:
תִּתְּנֵנוּ כְּצֹאן מַאֲכָל וּבַגּוֹיִם זֵרִיתָנוּ: תִּמְכֹּר־עַמְּךָ בְלֹא־הוֹן וְלֹא־רִבִּיתָ
בִּמְחִירֵיהֶם: תְּשִׂימֵנוּ חֶרְפָּה לִשְׁכֵנֵינוּ לַעַג וָקֶלֶס לִסְבִיבוֹתֵינוּ: תְּשִׂימֵנוּ
מָשָׁל בַּגּוֹיִם מְנוֹד־רֹאשׁ בַּל־אֻמִּים: כׇּל־הַיּוֹם כְּלִמָּתִי נֶגְדִּי וּבֹשֶׁת פָּנַי
כִּסָּתְנִי: מִקּוֹל מְחָרֵף וּמְגַדֵּף מִפְּנֵי אוֹיֵב וּמִתְנַקֵּם: כׇּל־זֹאת בָּאַתְנוּ וְלֹא
שְׁכַחֲנוּךָ וְלֹא־שִׁקַּרְנוּ בִּבְרִיתֶךָ: לֹא־נָסוֹג אָחוֹר לִבֵּנוּ וַתֵּט אֲשֻׁרֵינוּ מִנִּי
אׇרְחֶךָ: כִּי דִכִּיתָנוּ בִּמְקוֹם תַּנִּים וַתְּכַס עָלֵינוּ בְצַלְמָוֶת: אִם־שָׁכַחְנוּ
שֵׁם אֱלֹהֵינוּ וַנִּפְרֹשׂ כַּפֵּינוּ לְאֵל זָר: הֲלֹא אֱלֹהִים יַחֲקׇר־זֹאת כִּי־הוּא

*ת לחודש

the salvations of His countenance. My God, my soul is cast down within me, for I remember You from the land of the Jordan and the hills of Hermon, from the mount of Mizar. Torrent calls to torrent, to the sound of Your channels. All Your waves and Your billows pass over me. By day the Lord would command His loving-kindness, and at night His song was with me, a prayer to the God of my life. I say to God my rock, Why have You forgotten in me? Why do I walk darkly under the oppression of the enemy? With a shattering in my bones, my adversaries taunt me, for they say to me all the day, Where is your God? Why are you cast down, O my soul, and why do you moan within me? Hope for God, for I will still thank Him, the salvations of my countenance and my God.

43 JUDGE ME, O God, and plead my cause against ungodly men. Deliver me from deceitful and unjust people. Indeed, You are the God Who is my stronghold. Why have You abandoned me? Why do I walk darkly under the oppression of the enemy? Send Your light and Your truth. Let them lead me. Let them bring me to Your holy mountain and to Your dwelling-place. And I will go to the altar of God, to the God of my delight and joy, and I will thank You with the lyre, O God my God. Why are you cast down, O my soul, and why do you moan within me? Hope for God, for I will still thank Him, the salvations is of my countenance and my God.

*44 TO THE DIRECTOR of music, for the sons of Korah, a *maskil*. O God, we have heard with our ears, our fathers have told us, of the deed You did in their days, in days of old. You with Your hand drove out the nations, and planted them. You broke the peoples and cast them out. For they did not take possession of the land by their own sword, and their own arm did not save them, but Your right hand and Your arm, and the light of Your countenance, for You blessed them. You alone are my king, O God. Command salvations for Jacob. Through You we have smitten our enemies. Through Your name we have trampled on those who rose up against us. Indeed, I did not trust in my bow, and my sword did not save me. But You have saved us from our enemies, and You have put to shame those who hate us. We praise God all the day, and we thank Your name forever. Selah. But You have abandoned us and put us to shame, and You do not go out with our armies. You have made us turn back from the enemy, and those who hate us have plundered us for themselves. You have given us like sheep to be eaten, and You have scattered us among the nations. You have sold Your people for no sum, and You have not set their prices high. You have made us a reproach to our neighbors, a scorn and a derision to those round about us. You have made us a byword among the nations, a shaking of the head among the peoples. All the day my humiliation is before me, and shame covers my face. From the voice of him who taunts and blasphemes, from the enemy and the avenger. All this has come upon us, yet we have not forgotten You, nor have we been false to Your covenant. Our heart has not turned back, nor have our steps turned from Your way, Though You have broken us in the place of jackals, and You have covered us with darkness. I swear that we have not forgotten the name of our God, nor have we stretched out our hands to a strange god. Surely God has

*8th DAY of the month

יֹדֵעַ תַּעֲלֻמוֹת לֵב: כִּי־עָלֶיךָ הֹרַגְנוּ כָל־הַיּוֹם נֶחְשַׁבְנוּ כְּצֹאן טִבְחָה:
עוּרָה ׀ לָמָּה תִישַׁן ׀ אֲדֹנָי הָקִיצָה אַל־תִּזְנַח לָנֶצַח: לָמָּה־פָנֶיךָ תַסְתִּיר
תִּשְׁכַּח עָנְיֵנוּ וְלַחֲצֵנוּ: כִּי שָׁחָה לֶעָפָר נַפְשֵׁנוּ דָּבְקָה לָאָרֶץ בִּטְנֵנוּ: קוּמָה
עֶזְרָתָה לָּנוּ וּפְדֵנוּ לְמַעַן חַסְדֶּךָ:

מה לַמְנַצֵּחַ עַל־שֹׁשַׁנִּים לִבְנֵי־קֹרַח מַשְׂכִּיל שִׁיר יְדִידֹת: רָחַשׁ לִבִּי ׀ דָּבָר
טוֹב אֹמֵר אָנִי מַעֲשַׂי לְמֶלֶךְ לְשׁוֹנִי עֵט ׀ סוֹפֵר מָהִיר: יָפְיָפִיתָ מִבְּנֵי אָדָם
הוּצַק חֵן בְּשְׂפְתוֹתֶיךָ עַל־כֵּן בֵּרַכְךָ אֱלֹהִים לְעוֹלָם: חֲגוֹר־חַרְבְּךָ עַל־
יָרֵךְ גִּבּוֹר הוֹדְךָ וַהֲדָרֶךָ: וַהֲדָרְךָ ׀ צְלַח רְכַב עַל־דְּבַר־אֱמֶת וְעַנְוָה־צֶדֶק
וְתוֹרְךָ נוֹרָאוֹת יְמִינֶךָ: חִצֶּיךָ שְׁנוּנִים עַמִּים תַּחְתֶּיךָ יִפְּלוּ בְּלֵב אוֹיְבֵי
הַמֶּלֶךְ: כִּסְאֲךָ אֱלֹהִים עוֹלָם וָעֶד שֵׁבֶט מִישֹׁר שֵׁבֶט מַלְכוּתֶךָ: אָהַבְתָּ
צֶּדֶק וַתִּשְׂנָא רֶשַׁע עַל־כֵּן ׀ מְשָׁחֲךָ אֱלֹהִים אֱלֹהֶיךָ שֶׁמֶן שָׂשׂוֹן מֵחֲבֵרֶךָ:
מֹר־וַאֲהָלוֹת קְצִיעוֹת כָּל־בִּגְדֹתֶיךָ מִן־הֵיכְלֵי שֵׁן מִנִּי שִׂמְּחוּךָ: בְּנוֹת
מְלָכִים בְּיִקְּרוֹתֶיךָ נִצְּבָה שֵׁגַל לִימִינְךָ בְּכֶתֶם אוֹפִיר: שִׁמְעִי־בַת וּרְאִי
וְהַטִּי אָזְנֵךְ וְשִׁכְחִי עַמֵּךְ וּבֵית אָבִיךְ: וְיִתְאָו הַמֶּלֶךְ יָפְיֵךְ כִּי־הוּא אֲדֹנַיִךְ
וְהִשְׁתַּחֲוִי־לוֹ: וּבַת־צֹר ׀ בְּמִנְחָה פָּנַיִךְ יְחַלּוּ עֲשִׁירֵי עָם: כָּל־כְּבוּדָּה בַת־
מֶלֶךְ פְּנִימָה מִמִּשְׁבְּצוֹת זָהָב לְבוּשָׁהּ: לִרְקָמוֹת תּוּבַל לַמֶּלֶךְ בְּתוּלוֹת
אַחֲרֶיהָ רֵעוֹתֶיהָ מוּבָאוֹת לָךְ: תּוּבַלְנָה בִּשְׂמָחֹת וָגִיל תְּבֹאֶינָה בְּהֵיכַל
מֶלֶךְ: תַּחַת אֲבֹתֶיךָ יִהְיוּ בָנֶיךָ תְּשִׁיתֵמוֹ לְשָׂרִים בְּכָל־הָאָרֶץ: אַזְכִּירָה
שִׁמְךָ בְּכָל־דֹּר וָדֹר עַל־כֵּן עַמִּים יְהוֹדֻךָ לְעֹלָם וָעֶד:

מו לַמְנַצֵּחַ לִבְנֵי־קֹרַח עַל־עֲלָמוֹת שִׁיר: אֱלֹהִים לָנוּ מַחֲסֶה וָעֹז עֶזְרָה בְצָרוֹת
נִמְצָא מְאֹד: עַל־כֵּן לֹא־נִירָא בְּהָמִיר אָרֶץ וּבְמוֹט הָרִים בְּלֵב יַמִּים:
יֶהֱמוּ יֶחְמְרוּ מֵימָיו יִרְעֲשׁוּ־הָרִים בְּגַאֲוָתוֹ סֶלָה: נָהָר פְּלָגָיו יְשַׂמְּחוּ עִיר
אֱלֹהִים קְדֹשׁ מִשְׁכְּנֵי עֶלְיוֹן: אֱלֹהִים בְּקִרְבָּהּ בַּל־תִּמּוֹט יַעְזְרֶהָ אֱלֹהִים
לִפְנוֹת בֹּקֶר: הָמוּ גוֹיִם מָטוּ מַמְלָכוֹת נָתַן בְּקוֹלוֹ תָּמוּג אָרֶץ: יְהוָה
צְבָאוֹת עִמָּנוּ מִשְׂגָּב לָנוּ אֱלֹהֵי יַעֲקֹב סֶלָה: לְכוּ־חֲזוּ מִפְעֲלוֹת יְהוָה
אֲשֶׁר־שָׂם שַׁמּוֹת בָּאָרֶץ: מַשְׁבִּית מִלְחָמוֹת עַד־קְצֵה הָאָרֶץ קֶשֶׁת יְשַׁבֵּר
וְקִצֵּץ חֲנִית עֲגָלוֹת יִשְׂרֹף בָּאֵשׁ: הַרְפּוּ וּדְעוּ כִּי־אָנֹכִי אֱלֹהִים אָרוּם בַּגּוֹיִם
אָרוּם בָּאָרֶץ: יְהוָה צְבָאוֹת עִמָּנוּ מִשְׂגָּב לָנוּ אֱלֹהֵי יַעֲקֹב סֶלָה:

searched this out, for He knows the secrets of the heart. Indeed, for Your sake we are
being killed all the day, we are regarded as sheep for the slaughter. Awake, why do
you sleep, O Lord? Arise, do not abandon us forever. Why do You hide Your face?
Why do You forget our affliction and oppression? For our soul is bowed down to the
dust, our belly cleaves to the ground. Arise and help us, and redeem us for the sake
of Your loving-kindness.

45 TO THE DIRECTOR of music, al-*shoshanim*. A *maskil* for the sons of Korah. A song of
love. My heart is astir with a goodly matter. I will relate my composition for a king. My
tongue is the pen of a ready scribe. You are more handsome than all men, grace was
poured into your lips. Therefore God has blessed you forever. Gird your sword upon
your thigh, O mighty warrior, your glory and your majesty. And in your majesty ride
prosperously in the matter of truth and modesty and righteousness, and your right
hand will teach you awesome things. Your arrows are sharp -- peoples will fall beneath
you -- piercing the heart of the king's enemies. Your throne, of God, is forever and
ever. The scepter of Your kingdom is the scepter of equity. You love righteousness and
hate wickedness. Therefore God, your God, has anointed you with the oil of gladness
from among your fellows. Myrrh and aloes and cassia exude from all your garments.
Out of ivory palaces flutes have made you glad. The daughters of kings are among
your dear women. At your right hand stands the queen in gold of Ophir. Hear, O
daughter, and see, and incline your ear, and forget your own people, and the house of
your father. And the king will desire your beauty, for he is your lord, and bow down to
him. And the rich among the people of Tyre entreat your favor with gifts. The king's
daughter goes inside with all her baggage. Among her garments are those embroidered
with gold. She is brought to the embroidered curtains, to the king. After her, the
virgins, her companions, are brought to her. They are brought with gladness and
rejoicing. They enter the palace of the king. May your sons be in place of your fathers.
May you make them princes throughout the land. May I cause your name to be
remembered in all generations. Therefore the peoples will give thanks to you forever
and ever.

46 TO THE DIRECTOR of music. For the sons of Korah. A song for *alamot*. God is
our refuge and strength. We find great help in trouble. Therefore we do not fear
when the earth is upturned, and when the mountains collapse into the heart
of the sea, If its waters roar and foam, if the mountains quake with its swelling.
Selah. The river, its streams make the city of God glad, the holy dwelling-place of
the Most High. God is in its midst, it shall not fall. God helps it toward morning.
Nations roared, kingdoms fell. He sent forth His voice, the earth melted. The
Lord of hosts is with us. The God of Jacob is our refuge. Selah. Come, behold the works
of the Lord, Who has made desolations on the earth. He causes wars to cease to the end
of the earth. He breaks the bows and He cuts the spears. He burns the chariots in the
fire. Let them be, and know that I am God. I am exalted among the nations, I am exalted
on the earth. The Lord of hosts is with us. The God of Jacob is our refuge. Selah.

מז לַמְנַצֵּחַ לִבְנֵי־קֹרַח מִזְמוֹר׃ כָּל־הָעַמִּים תִּקְעוּ־כָף הָרִיעוּ לֵאלֹהִים
בְּקוֹל רִנָּה׃ כִּי־יהוה עֶלְיוֹן נוֹרָא מֶלֶךְ גָּדוֹל עַל־כָּל־הָאָרֶץ׃ יַדְבֵּר עַמִּים
תַּחְתֵּינוּ וּלְאֻמִּים תַּחַת רַגְלֵינוּ׃ יִבְחַר־לָנוּ אֶת־נַחֲלָתֵנוּ אֶת גְּאוֹן יַעֲקֹב
אֲשֶׁר־אָהֵב סֶלָה׃ עָלָה אֱלֹהִים בִּתְרוּעָה יהוה בְּקוֹל שׁוֹפָר׃ זַמְּרוּ אֱלֹהִים
זַמֵּרוּ זַמְּרוּ לְמַלְכֵּנוּ זַמֵּרוּ׃ כִּי מֶלֶךְ כָּל־הָאָרֶץ אֱלֹהִים זַמְּרוּ מַשְׂכִּיל׃ מָלַךְ
אֱלֹהִים עַל־גּוֹיִם אֱלֹהִים יָשַׁב ׀ עַל־כִּסֵּא קָדְשׁוֹ׃ נְדִיבֵי עַמִּים ׀ נֶאֱסָפוּ
עַם אֱלֹהֵי אַבְרָהָם כִּי לֵאלֹהִים מָגִנֵּי־אֶרֶץ מְאֹד נַעֲלָה׃

מח שִׁיר מִזְמוֹר לִבְנֵי־קֹרַח׃ גָּדוֹל יהוה וּמְהֻלָּל מְאֹד בְּעִיר אֱלֹהֵינוּ הַר־קָדְשׁוֹ׃
יְפֵה נוֹף מְשׂוֹשׂ כָּל־הָאָרֶץ הַר־צִיּוֹן יַרְכְּתֵי צָפוֹן קִרְיַת מֶלֶךְ רָב׃ אֱלֹהִים
בְּאַרְמְנוֹתֶיהָ נוֹדַע לְמִשְׂגָּב׃ כִּי־הִנֵּה הַמְּלָכִים נוֹעֲדוּ עָבְרוּ יַחְדָּו׃ הֵמָּה
רָאוּ כֵּן תָּמָהוּ נִבְהֲלוּ נֶחְפָּזוּ׃ רְעָדָה אֲחָזָתַם שָׁם חִיל כַּיּוֹלֵדָה׃ בְּרוּחַ
קָדִים תְּשַׁבֵּר אֳנִיּוֹת תַּרְשִׁישׁ׃ כַּאֲשֶׁר שָׁמַעְנוּ ׀ כֵּן רָאִינוּ בְּעִיר־יהוה
צְבָאוֹת בְּעִיר אֱלֹהֵינוּ אֱלֹהִים יְכוֹנְנֶהָ עַד־עוֹלָם סֶלָה׃ דִּמִּינוּ אֱלֹהִים
חַסְדֶּךָ בְּקֶרֶב הֵיכָלֶךָ׃ כְּשִׁמְךָ ׀ אֱלֹהִים כֵּן תְּהִלָּתְךָ עַל־קַצְוֵי־אֶרֶץ צֶדֶק
מָלְאָה יְמִינֶךָ׃ יִשְׂמַח ׀ הַר־צִיּוֹן תָּגֵלְנָה בְּנוֹת יְהוּדָה לְמַעַן מִשְׁפָּטֶיךָ׃
סֹבּוּ צִיּוֹן וְהַקִּיפוּהָ סִפְרוּ מִגְדָּלֶיהָ׃ שִׁיתוּ לִבְּכֶם ׀ לְחֵילָה פַּסְּגוּ אַרְמְנוֹתֶיהָ
לְמַעַן תְּסַפְּרוּ לְדוֹר אַחֲרוֹן׃ כִּי זֶה ׀ אֱלֹהִים אֱלֹהֵינוּ עוֹלָם וָעֶד הוּא
יְנַהֲגֵנוּ עַל־מוּת׃

מט* לַמְנַצֵּחַ לִבְנֵי־קֹרַח מִזְמוֹר׃ שִׁמְעוּ־זֹאת כָּל־הָעַמִּים הַאֲזִינוּ כָּל־יֹשְׁבֵי
חָלֶד׃ גַּם־בְּנֵי אָדָם גַּם־בְּנֵי־אִישׁ יַחַד עָשִׁיר וְאֶבְיוֹן׃ פִּי יְדַבֵּר חָכְמוֹת
וְהָגוּת לִבִּי תְבוּנוֹת׃ אַטֶּה לְמָשָׁל אָזְנִי אֶפְתַּח בְּכִנּוֹר חִידָתִי׃ לָמָּה אִירָא
בִּימֵי רָע עֲוֺן עֲקֵבַי יְסוּבֵּנִי׃ הַבֹּטְחִים עַל־חֵילָם וּבְרֹב עָשְׁרָם יִתְהַלָּלוּ׃
אָח לֹא־פָדֹה יִפְדֶּה אִישׁ לֹא־יִתֵּן לֵאלֹהִים כָּפְרוֹ׃ וְיֵקַר פִּדְיוֹן נַפְשָׁם
וְחָדַל לְעוֹלָם׃ וִיחִי־עוֹד לָנֶצַח לֹא יִרְאֶה הַשָּׁחַת׃ כִּי יִרְאֶה ׀ חֲכָמִים
יָמוּתוּ יַחַד כְּסִיל וָבַעַר יֹאבֵדוּ וְעָזְבוּ לַאֲחֵרִים חֵילָם׃ קִרְבָּם בָּתֵּימוֹ ׀
לְעוֹלָם מִשְׁכְּנֹתָם לְדֹר וָדֹר קָרְאוּ בִשְׁמוֹתָם עֲלֵי אֲדָמוֹת׃ וְאָדָם בִּיקָר
בַּל־יָלִין נִמְשַׁל כַּבְּהֵמוֹת נִדְמוּ׃ זֶה דַרְכָּם כֵּסֶל לָמוֹ וְאַחֲרֵיהֶם ׀ בְּפִיהֶם
יִרְצוּ סֶלָה׃ כַּצֹּאן ׀ לִשְׁאוֹל שַׁתּוּ מָוֶת יִרְעֵם וַיִּרְדּוּ בָם יְשָׁרִים ׀ לַבֹּקֶר

*ט לחודש

47 TO THE DIRECTOR of music. For the sons of Korah. A psalm. All peoples, clap your
hands. Shout to God with a voice of joy. For the Lord is most high and awesome.
He is a great king over all the earth. He subdues peoples under us, and nations
under our feet. He chooses our inheritance for us, the heights of Jacob that He
loves. Selah. God has gone up with a shout, the Lord with the sound of a shofar.
Sing praise to God, sing praise. Sing praise to our king, sing praise. For God is the
king of all the earth. Sing a *maskil* song. God has become king over the nations. God
has sat on His holy throne. The princes of the peoples have gathered together, the
people of the God of Abraham, for the shields of the earth belong to God, He is
greatly exalted.

48 A SONG. A psalm for the sons of Korah. The Lord is great and exceedingly praised
in the city of our God, His holy mountain. Beautiful in height, the joy of the whole
earth, Mount Zion, the sides of the north, the city of a great king. In her palaces
God is known as her fortress. For, behold, the kings were assembled, they passed
together. They saw and they were astounded. They were frightened and they became
confused. Trembling took hold of them there, anguish like a woman in travail, Like
an east wind that breaks the ships of Tarshish. As we have heard, so have we seen
in the city of the Lord of hosts, in the city of our God. God establishes it forever.
Selah. We think, O God, about Your loving-kindness in the midst of Your temple.
Like Your name, O God, so is Your praise to the ends of the earth. Your right hand
is full of righteousness. Mount Zion should rejoice, the daughters of Judah should
be glad, on account of Your judgments. Walk around Zion and encircle her. Count
her towers. Consider her rampart, pass through her palaces, so that you may tell
it to the next generation. For such is God, our God, forever and ever. He leads
us *al-mut*.

*49 TO THE DIRECTOR of music. A psalm for the sons of Korah. Hear this, all the peoples.
Listen, all the inhabitants of the world, Both the sons of the low and the sons of the
high, all the rich and the poor. My mouth will speak wisdom, and the meditation of
my heart will be understanding. I will incline my ear to the spirit of the poem. I will
propound my riddle with the lyre. Why should I fear in the days of evil, when iniquity
encompasses my heels? Those who trust in their wealth, and who boast about the
multitude of their riches. No man can redeem his brother, nor give to God his ransom.
And even if they pay dearly for the redemption of their soul, it will be unattained
forever. Will he still live forever? Will he not see the pit? When he sees that wise men
die, that all fools and boors perish, and leave their wealth to others. Inwardly their
houses will stand for ever, their dwelling-places for all generations. Those on earth
call them by their names. But man does not lie in honor. He is like the beasts that
perish. This is their way. It is folly for them. And their posterity praise them with their
mouths. Selah. Like sheep they descend to the underworld. Death is their shepherd,
and the upright strike them in the morning. And their image goes from its dwelling
to the horrors of the underworld. But God will redeem my soul from the hand of the

---

*9th DAY of the month

וְצוּרָם וצירם לְבַלּוֹת שְׁאוֹל מִזְּבֻל לוֹ: אַךְ־אֱלֹהִים יִפְדֶּה נַפְשִׁי מִיַּד שְׁאוֹל כִּי
יִקָּחֵנִי סֶלָה: אַל־תִּירָא כִּי־יַעֲשִׁר אִישׁ כִּי־יִרְבֶּה כְּבוֹד בֵּיתוֹ: כִּי לֹא
בְמוֹתוֹ יִקַּח הַכֹּל לֹא־יֵרֵד אַחֲרָיו כְּבוֹדוֹ: כִּי־נַפְשׁוֹ בְּחַיָּיו יְבָרֵךְ וְיוֹדֻךָ
כִּי־תֵיטִיב לָךְ: תָּבוֹא עַד־דּוֹר אֲבוֹתָיו עַד־נֵצַח לֹא יִרְאוּ־אוֹר: אָדָם
בִּיקָר וְלֹא יָבִין נִמְשַׁל כַּבְּהֵמוֹת נִדְמוּ:

נ מִזְמוֹר לְאָסָף אֵל ׀ אֱלֹהִים יהוה דִּבֶּר וַיִּקְרָא־אָרֶץ מִמִּזְרַח־שֶׁמֶשׁ עַד־
מְבֹאוֹ: מִצִּיּוֹן מִכְלַל־יֹפִי אֱלֹהִים הוֹפִיעַ: יָבֹא אֱלֹהֵינוּ וְאַל־יֶחֱרַשׁ אֵשׁ־
לְפָנָיו תֹּאכֵל וּסְבִיבָיו נִשְׂעֲרָה מְאֹד: יִקְרָא אֶל־הַשָּׁמַיִם מֵעָל וְאֶל־הָאָרֶץ
לָדִין עַמּוֹ: אִסְפוּ־לִי חֲסִידָי כֹּרְתֵי בְרִיתִי עֲלֵי־זָבַח: וַיַּגִּידוּ שָׁמַיִם צִדְקוֹ
כִּי־אֱלֹהִים ׀ שֹׁפֵט הוּא סֶלָה: שִׁמְעָה עַמִּי ׀ וַאֲדַבֵּרָה יִשְׂרָאֵל וְאָעִידָה
בָּךְ אֱלֹהִים אֱלֹהֶיךָ אָנֹכִי: לֹא עַל־זְבָחֶיךָ אוֹכִיחֶךָ וְעוֹלֹתֶיךָ לְנֶגְדִּי תָמִיד:
לֹא־אֶקַּח מִבֵּיתְךָ פָר מִמִּכְלְאֹתֶיךָ עַתּוּדִים: כִּי־לִי כָל־חַיְתוֹ־יָעַר בְּהֵמוֹת
בְּהַרְרֵי־אָלֶף: יָדַעְתִּי כָּל־עוֹף הָרִים וְזִיז שָׂדַי עִמָּדִי: אִם־אֶרְעַב לֹא־אֹמַר
לָךְ כִּי־לִי תֵבֵל וּמְלֹאָהּ: הַאוֹכַל בְּשַׂר אַבִּירִים וְדַם עַתּוּדִים אֶשְׁתֶּה:
זְבַח לֵאלֹהִים תּוֹדָה וְשַׁלֵּם לְעֶלְיוֹן נְדָרֶיךָ: וּקְרָאֵנִי בְּיוֹם צָרָה אֲחַלֶּצְךָ
וּתְכַבְּדֵנִי: וְלָרָשָׁע ׀ אָמַר אֱלֹהִים מַה־לְּךָ לְסַפֵּר חֻקָּי וַתִּשָּׂא בְרִיתִי עֲלֵי־
פִיךָ: וְאַתָּה שָׂנֵאתָ מוּסָר וַתַּשְׁלֵךְ דְּבָרַי אַחֲרֶיךָ: אִם־רָאִיתָ גַנָּב וַתִּרֶץ
עִמּוֹ וְעִם מְנָאֲפִים חֶלְקֶךָ: פִּיךָ שָׁלַחְתָּ בְרָעָה וּלְשׁוֹנְךָ תַּצְמִיד מִרְמָה:
תֵּשֵׁב בְּאָחִיךָ תְדַבֵּר בְּבֶן־אִמְּךָ תִּתֶּן־דֹּפִי: אֵלֶּה עָשִׂיתָ ׀ וְהֶחֱרַשְׁתִּי
דִּמִּיתָ הֱיוֹת־אֶהְיֶה כָמוֹךָ אוֹכִיחֲךָ וְאֶעֶרְכָה לְעֵינֶיךָ: בִּינוּ־נָא זֹאת
שֹׁכְחֵי אֱלוֹהַּ פֶּן־אֶטְרֹף וְאֵין מַצִּיל: זֹבֵחַ תּוֹדָה יְכַבְּדָנְנִי וְשָׂם דֶּרֶךְ אַרְאֶנּוּ
בְּיֵשַׁע אֱלֹהִים:

*נא לַמְנַצֵּחַ מִזְמוֹר לְדָוִד: בְּבוֹא־אֵלָיו נָתָן הַנָּבִיא כַּאֲשֶׁר־בָּא אֶל־בַּת־שָׁבַע:
הֶרֶב חָנֵּנִי אֱלֹהִים כְּחַסְדֶּךָ כְּרֹב רַחֲמֶיךָ מְחֵה פְשָׁעָי: הרבה כַּבְּסֵנִי מֵעֲוֺנִי
וּמֵחַטָּאתִי טַהֲרֵנִי: כִּי־פְשָׁעַי אֲנִי אֵדָע וְחַטָּאתִי נֶגְדִּי תָמִיד: לְךָ לְבַדְּךָ ׀
חָטָאתִי וְהָרַע בְּעֵינֶיךָ עָשִׂיתִי לְמַעַן תִּצְדַּק בְּדָבְרֶךָ תִּזְכֶּה בְשָׁפְטֶךָ:
הֵן־בְּעָווֹן חוֹלָלְתִּי וּבְחֵטְא יֶחֱמַתְנִי אִמִּי: הֵן־אֱמֶת חָפַצְתָּ בַטֻּחוֹת
וּבְסָתֻם חָכְמָה תוֹדִיעֵנִי: תְּחַטְּאֵנִי בְאֵזוֹב וְאֶטְהָר תְּכַבְּסֵנִי וּמִשֶּׁלֶג

*ליום השלישי

underworld, for He will take me. Selah. Do not stand in awe when a man becomes
rich, when the glory of his house becomes great. For when he dies he will not take
anything. His glory will not descend after him. For while he is alive he should bless his
soul, and they will praise you if you do well to yourself. It will go to the generation of
his fathers. They will never see light. A man who is in honor but does not understand
is like the beasts that perish.

50 A PSALM of Asaph. The mighty one, God, the Lord, has spoken, and has called the
earth from the rising of the sun to its going down. From Zion, the perfection of
beauty, God has shone forth. May our God come, and may He not remain silent. A
fire consumes before Him, and it is very tempestuous around Him. He calls to the
heavens above, and to the earth, that He may judge His people. Gather My pious ones
to Me, those who have made a covenant with Me upon a sacrifice. The heavens have
declared His righteousness, for He is a God Who judges. Selah. Hear, O My people,
and I will speak. O Israel, and I will admonish you. I am God, your God. Not about
your sacrifices will I reproach you, nor are your burnt-offerings always before Me. I
will not take a bullock from your house, nor he-goats from your folds. For every beast
of the forest is Mine, and the cattle upon thousands of hills. I know all the birds of
the mountains, and the birds of the fields are with Me. If I am hungry, I will not tell
you, for the world and its fullness is Mine. Do I eat the flesh of bulls, and do I drink
the blood of he-goats? Offer to God a thanksgiving-offering, and pay your vows to
the Most High. And call upon Me in the day of trouble. I will deliver you, and you
will honor Me. But to the wicked man God says: What right have you to declare
My statutes, or that you should raise My covenant upon your mouth? For you hate
instruction, and you cast My words behind you. When you see a thief, you wish to
be with him, and your portion is with adulterers. You let your mouth loose for evil,
and deceit cleaves to your tongue. You sit and speak against your brother. You slander
your mother's son. You have done these things, and shall I remain silent? You imagine
that I am like you. I will reproach you, and I will set the matter before your eyes. Now
consider this, you who forget God, lest I tear you in pieces and there is none to deliver.
Whoever offers a thanksgiving-offering honors Me, and whoever sets his path rightly,
I will show him the salvation of God.

*51 TO THE DIRECTOR of music. A psalm of David, When Nathan the prophet came to
him, after he had gone in to Bath-sheba. Be gracious to me, O God, in accordance
with Your loving-kindness. In accordance with the multitude of Your mercies, erase
my transgressions. Wash me thoroughly from my iniquity, and cleanse me from my
sin. For I acknowledge my transgressions, and my sin is always before me. Against
You, You alone, have I sinned, and I have done what is evil in Your eyes, so that You
are justified in Your sentence and righteous in Your judgment. Behold, I was born in
iniquity, and my mother conceived me in sin. Behold, You desire truth in the inward
parts, and in the hidden part You teach me wisdom. Purify me with hyssop, and I
will be clean. Wash me, and I will be whiter than snow. Let me hear joy and gladness.

---

*TUESDAY

אַלְבִּין: תַּשְׁמִיעֵנִי שָׂשׂוֹן וְשִׂמְחָה תָּגֵלְנָה עֲצָמוֹת דִּכִּיתָ: הַסְתֵּר פָּנֶיךָ
מֵחֲטָאָי וְכָל־עֲוֺנֹתַי מְחֵה: לֵב טָהוֹר בְּרָא־לִי אֱלֹהִים וְרוּחַ נָכוֹן חַדֵּשׁ
בְּקִרְבִּי: אַל־תַּשְׁלִיכֵנִי מִלְּפָנֶיךָ וְרוּחַ קָדְשְׁךָ אַל־תִּקַּח מִמֶּנִּי: הָשִׁיבָה לִּי
שְׂשׂוֹן יִשְׁעֶךָ וְרוּחַ נְדִיבָה תִסְמְכֵנִי: אֲלַמְּדָה פֹשְׁעִים דְּרָכֶיךָ וְחַטָּאִים
אֵלֶיךָ יָשׁוּבוּ: הַצִּילֵנִי מִדָּמִים ׀ אֱלֹהִים אֱלֹהֵי תְּשׁוּעָתִי תְּרַנֵּן לְשׁוֹנִי
צִדְקָתֶךָ: אֲדֹנָי שְׂפָתַי תִּפְתָּח וּפִי יַגִּיד תְּהִלָּתֶךָ: כִּי ׀ לֹא־תַחְפֹּץ זֶבַח
וְאֶתֵּנָה עוֹלָה לֹא תִרְצֶה: זִבְחֵי אֱלֹהִים רוּחַ נִשְׁבָּרָה לֵב־נִשְׁבָּר וְנִדְכֶּה
אֱלֹהִים לֹא תִבְזֶה: הֵיטִיבָה בִרְצוֹנְךָ אֶת־צִיּוֹן תִּבְנֶה חוֹמוֹת יְרוּשָׁלָםִ:
אָז תַּחְפֹּץ זִבְחֵי־צֶדֶק עוֹלָה וְכָלִיל אָז יַעֲלוּ עַל־מִזְבַּחֲךָ פָרִים:

נב לַמְנַצֵּחַ מַשְׂכִּיל לְדָוִד: בְּבוֹא ׀ דּוֹאֵג הָאֲדֹמִי וַיַּגֵּד לְשָׁאוּל וַיֹּאמֶר לוֹ בָּא
דָוִד אֶל־בֵּית אֲחִימֶלֶךְ: מַה־תִּתְהַלֵּל בְּרָעָה הַגִּבּוֹר חֶסֶד אֵל כָּל־הַיּוֹם:
הַוּוֹת תַּחְשֹׁב לְשׁוֹנֶךָ כְּתַעַר מְלֻטָּשׁ עֹשֵׂה רְמִיָּה: אָהַבְתָּ רָּע מִטּוֹב שֶׁקֶר ׀
מִדַּבֵּר צֶדֶק סֶלָה: אָהַבְתָּ כָל־דִּבְרֵי־בָלַע לְשׁוֹן מִרְמָה: גַּם־אֵל יִתָּצְךָ
לָנֶצַח יַחְתְּךָ וְיִסָּחֲךָ מֵאֹהֶל וְשֵׁרֶשְׁךָ מֵאֶרֶץ חַיִּים סֶלָה: וְיִרְאוּ צַדִּיקִים
וְיִירָאוּ וְעָלָיו יִשְׂחָקוּ: הִנֵּה הַגֶּבֶר לֹא יָשִׂים אֱלֹהִים מָעוּזּוֹ וַיִּבְטַח בְּרֹב
עָשְׁרוֹ יָעֹז בְּהַוָּתוֹ: וַאֲנִי ׀ כְּזַיִת רַעֲנָן בְּבֵית אֱלֹהִים בָּטַחְתִּי בְחֶסֶד־
אֱלֹהִים עוֹלָם וָעֶד: אוֹדְךָ לְעוֹלָם כִּי עָשִׂיתָ וַאֲקַוֶּה שִׁמְךָ כִי־טוֹב נֶגֶד
חֲסִידֶיךָ:

נג לַמְנַצֵּחַ עַל־מָחֲלַת מַשְׂכִּיל לְדָוִד: אָמַר נָבָל בְּלִבּוֹ אֵין אֱלֹהִים הִשְׁחִיתוּ
וְהִתְעִיבוּ עָוֶל אֵין עֹשֵׂה־טוֹב: אֱלֹהִים מִשָּׁמַיִם הִשְׁקִיף עַל־בְּנֵי־אָדָם
לִרְאוֹת הֲיֵשׁ מַשְׂכִּיל דֹּרֵשׁ אֶת־אֱלֹהִים: כֻּלּוֹ סָג יַחְדָּו נֶאֱלָחוּ אֵין עֹשֵׂה־
טוֹב אֵין גַּם־אֶחָד: הֲלֹא יָדְעוּ פֹּעֲלֵי אָוֶן אֹכְלֵי עַמִּי אָכְלוּ לֶחֶם אֱלֹהִים
לֹא קָרָאוּ: שָׁם ׀ פָּחֲדוּ־פַחַד לֹא־הָיָה פָחַד כִּי־אֱלֹהִים פִּזַּר עַצְמוֹת
חֹנָךְ הֱבִשֹׁתָה כִּי־אֱלֹהִים מְאָסָם: מִי יִתֵּן מִצִּיּוֹן יְשֻׁעוֹת יִשְׂרָאֵל בְּשׁוּב
אֱלֹהִים שְׁבוּת עַמּוֹ יָגֵל יַעֲקֹב יִשְׂמַח יִשְׂרָאֵל:

נד לַמְנַצֵּחַ בִּנְגִינֹת מַשְׂכִּיל לְדָוִד: בְּבוֹא הַזִּיפִים וַיֹּאמְרוּ לְשָׁאוּל הֲלֹא דָוִד
מִסְתַּתֵּר עִמָּנוּ: אֱלֹהִים בְּשִׁמְךָ הוֹשִׁיעֵנִי וּבִגְבוּרָתְךָ תְדִינֵנִי: אֱלֹהִים
שְׁמַע תְּפִלָּתִי הַאֲזִינָה לְאִמְרֵי־פִי: כִּי זָרִים ׀ קָמוּ עָלַי וְעָרִיצִים בִּקְשׁוּ

Let the bones that You have broken rejoice. Hide Your face from my sins, and erase all my iniquities. Create for me a pure heart, O God, and renew a steadfast spirit within me. Do not cast me out from before You, and do not take Your holy spirit from me. Restore to me the joy of Your salvation, and may a willing spirit uphold me. I will teach transgressors Your ways, and sinners will return to You. Deliver me from blood, O God, my God of salvation. My tongue will sing Your righteousness. O my Master, open my lips, and my mouth will relate Your praise. For You do not desire that I give You a sacrifice. You do not want a burnt-offering. Sacrifices to God are a broken spirit. A broken and shattered heart, O God, You do not despise. Beautify Zion with Your favor. Build the walls of Jerusalem. Then You will desire righteous sacrifices, burnt-offering and whole burnt-offering. Then they will offer bullocks on Your altar.

52 TO THE DIRECTOR of music. A *maskil* of David, When Doeg the Edomite came and
told Saul, and said to him, David has come to the house of Ahimelech. Why do you boast of your evil, O mighty man, of the loving-kindness of God all day long? You devise malice with your tongue, like a sharpened razor, O worker of deceit. You love evil more than good, and lying more than speaking righteousness. Selah. You love all devouring words, a deceitful tongue. Likewise God will destroy you forever. He will break you and pluck you from your tent, and He will uproot you from the land of the living. Selah. And the righteous will see and fear, and they will laugh at him. Behold, this is the man who does not make God his strength, but trusts in the abundance of his wealth, and seeks a stronghold in his riches. But I am like a green olive tree in the house of God. I trust in the loving-kindness of God forever and ever. I will thank You forever for what You have done, and I will put my trust in Your name, for it is good, before Your pious ones.

53 TO THE DIRECTOR of music on *maḥalat*. A *maskil* of David. The fool says in his heart:
"There is no God." They have acted corruptly and they have practiced abominations. There is none that does good. God looks down from heaven upon the children of man to see if there is a man of understanding who seeks out God. Every one of them is dross. All of them have become corrupt. There is none that does good, not even one. Do not do the workers of iniquity know? Those who ate my people as they would eat bread, they did not call upon God. There they were in great fear, but there was no fear, for God scattered the bones of your camp. You have been put to shame, for God has despised them. O that He may send from Zion salvations to Israel! When God brings back the return of His people, may Jacob rejoice, may Israel be glad.

54 TO THE DIRECTOR of music for instruments. A *maskil* of David, When the Ziphites
came and said to Saul, "Surely David is hiding himself with us." Save me, O God, by Your name, and take up my cause by Your strength. O God, hear my prayer. Give ear to the words of my mouth. For enemies have risen up against me, and violent men

נַפְשִׁי לֹא שָׂמוּ אֱלֹהִים לְנֶגְדָּם סֶלָה: הִנֵּה אֱלֹהִים עֹזֵר לִי אֲדֹנָי בְּסֹמְכֵי
יָשִׁיב נַפְשִׁי: יָשׁוּב הָרַע לְשֹׁרְרָי בַּאֲמִתְּךָ הַצְמִיתֵם: בִּנְדָבָה אֶזְבְּחָה־לָּךְ אוֹדֶה
שִּׁמְךָ יהוה כִּי־טוֹב: כִּי מִכָּל־צָרָה הִצִּילָנִי וּבְאֹיְבַי רָאֲתָה עֵינִי:
*נה לַמְנַצֵּחַ בִּנְגִינֹת מַשְׂכִּיל לְדָוִד: הַאֲזִינָה אֱלֹהִים תְּפִלָּתִי וְאַל־תִּתְעַלַּם
מִתְּחִנָּתִי: הַקְשִׁיבָה לִּי וַעֲנֵנִי אָרִיד בְּשִׂיחִי וְאָהִימָה: מִקּוֹל אוֹיֵב מִפְּנֵי
עָקַת רָשָׁע כִּי־יָמִיטוּ עָלַי אָוֶן וּבְאַף יִשְׂטְמוּנִי: לִבִּי יָחִיל בְּקִרְבִּי וְאֵימוֹת
מָוֶת נָפְלוּ עָלָי: יִרְאָה וָרַעַד יָבֹא בִי וַתְּכַסֵּנִי פַּלָּצוּת: וָאֹמַר מִי־יִתֶּן־לִּי
אֵבֶר כַּיּוֹנָה אָעוּפָה וְאֶשְׁכֹּנָה: הִנֵּה אַרְחִיק נְדֹד אָלִין בַּמִּדְבָּר סֶלָה:
אָחִישָׁה מִפְלָט לִי מֵרוּחַ סֹעָה מִסָּעַר: בַּלַּע אֲדֹנָי פַּלַּג לְשׁוֹנָם כִּי־רָאִיתִי
חָמָס וְרִיב בָּעִיר: יוֹמָם וָלַיְלָה יְסוֹבְבֻהָ עַל־חוֹמֹתֶיהָ וְאָוֶן וְעָמָל בְּקִרְבָּהּ:
הַוּוֹת בְּקִרְבָּהּ וְלֹא־יָמִישׁ מֵרְחֹבָהּ תֹּךְ וּמִרְמָה: כִּי לֹא־אוֹיֵב יְחָרְפֵנִי
וְאֶשָּׂא לֹא־מְשַׂנְאִי עָלַי הִגְדִּיל וְאֶסָּתֵר מִמֶּנּוּ: וְאַתָּה אֱנוֹשׁ כְּעֶרְכִּי אַלּוּפִי
יַשִּׁיא מָוֶת וּמְיֻדָּעִי: אֲשֶׁר יַחְדָּו נַמְתִּיק סוֹד בְּבֵית אֱלֹהִים נְהַלֵּךְ בְּרָגֶשׁ: ישימות ׀
עָלֵימוֹ יֵרְדוּ שְׁאוֹל חַיִּים כִּי־רָעוֹת בִּמְגוּרָם בְּקִרְבָּם: אֲנִי אֶל־אֱלֹהִים
אֶקְרָא וַיהוה יוֹשִׁיעֵנִי: עֶרֶב וָבֹקֶר וְצָהֳרַיִם אָשִׂיחָה וְאֶהֱמֶה וַיִּשְׁמַע
קוֹלִי: פָּדָה בְשָׁלוֹם נַפְשִׁי מִקֲּרָב־לִי כִּי־בְרַבִּים הָיוּ עִמָּדִי: יִשְׁמַע ׀ אֵל ׀
וְיַעֲנֵם וְיֹשֵׁב קֶדֶם סֶלָה אֲשֶׁר אֵין חֲלִיפוֹת לָמוֹ וְלֹא יָרְאוּ אֱלֹהִים: שָׁלַח
יָדָיו בִּשְׁלֹמָיו חִלֵּל בְּרִיתוֹ: חָלְקוּ ׀ מַחְמָאֹת פִּיו וּקְרָב־לִבּוֹ רַכּוּ דְבָרָיו
מִשֶּׁמֶן וְהֵמָּה פְתִחוֹת: הַשְׁלֵךְ עַל־יהוה ׀ יְהָבְךָ וְהוּא יְכַלְכְּלֶךָ לֹא־יִתֵּן
לְעוֹלָם מוֹט לַצַּדִּיק: וְאַתָּה אֱלֹהִים ׀ תּוֹרִדֵם לִבְאֵר שַׁחַת אַנְשֵׁי דָמִים
וּמִרְמָה לֹא־יֶחֱצוּ יְמֵיהֶם וַאֲנִי אֶבְטַח־בָּךְ:
נו לַמְנַצֵּחַ ׀ עַל־יוֹנַת אֵלֶם רְחֹקִים לְדָוִד מִכְתָּם בֶּאֱחֹז אוֹתוֹ פְלִשְׁתִּים
בְּגַת: חָנֵּנִי אֱלֹהִים כִּי־שְׁאָפַנִי אֱנוֹשׁ כָּל־הַיּוֹם לֹחֵם יִלְחָצֵנִי: שָׁאֲפוּ
שׁוֹרְרַי כָּל־הַיּוֹם כִּי־רַבִּים לֹחֲמִים לִי מָרוֹם: יוֹם אִירָא אֲנִי אֵלֶיךָ אֶבְטָח:
בֵּאלֹהִים אֲהַלֵּל דְּבָרוֹ בֵּאלֹהִים בָּטַחְתִּי לֹא אִירָא מַה־יַּעֲשֶׂה בָשָׂר לִי:
יִצְפֹּנוּ כָּל־הַיּוֹם דְּבָרַי יְעַצֵּבוּ עָלַי כָּל־מַחְשְׁבֹתָם לָרָע: יָגוּרוּ ׀ יצפינו הֵמָּה
עֲקֵבַי יִשְׁמֹרוּ כַּאֲשֶׁר קִוּוּ נַפְשִׁי: עַל־אָוֶן פַּלֶּט־לָמוֹ בְּאַף עַמִּים ׀ הוֹרֵד
אֱלֹהִים: נֹדִי סָפַרְתָּה אָתָּה שִׂימָה דִמְעָתִי בְנֹאדֶךָ הֲלֹא בְּסִפְרָתֶךָ: אָז ׀

*י לחודש

seek my soul. They have not set God before them. Selah. Behold, God is my helper.
The Lord is among those who support my soul. He will repay evil to my enemies.
Destroy them through Your truth. I will sacrifice freely to You. I will give thanks to
Your name, O Lord, for it is good. For He has delivered me from all my trouble, and
allowed my eyes to gaze upon my enemies.

*55 TO THE DIRECTOR of music for instruments. A *maskil* of David. Listen to my prayer,
O God, and do not hide Yourself from my supplication. Hearken to me and answer
me. I sob in my complaint and I cry out, Because of the sound of my enemy, because
of the pressure of the wicked. For they cause destruction to befall me, and in wrath
they hate me. My heart trembles within me, and the terrors of death have befallen me.
Fear and trembling have entered within me, and shuddering has covered me. And I
said, Oh that I had wings like a dove! Then I would fly away and find rest. Behold, I
would wander far off. I would abide in the wilderness. Selah. I would hasten to find
a refuge for myself from the stormy wind and from the tempest. Destroy, O Lord,
and divide their tongue. For I have seen violence and strife in the city. Day and night
they go about it upon its walls, and crime and wickedness are in its midst. Malice is
in its midst, and falsehood and deceit do not depart its open place. Indeed, it is not
an enemy who abuses me, for then I would bear it. It is not someone who hated me,
who continues to mock me, for then I would hide myself from him. But it is you, a
man like me, my familiar friend and my companion. We kept sweet company together.
We walked in the house of God in the crowd. May God incite death upon them. May
they go down alive into the underworld. For wickedness is in their dwelling-place
and in their midst. As for me, I call upon God, and the Lord will save me. Evening,
morning, and noon, I pray and cry out, and He will hear my voice. Deliver my soul
in peace so that he does not come near me. Indeed, His wonders were many with me.
May God hear and humble them, He Who is enthroned from of old. Selah. May they
have no heirs, for they are not God-fearing. He has put forth his hands against those at
peace with him. He has broken his covenant. The words of his mouth were smoother
than butter, but battle was in his heart. His words were softer than oil, but they were
woundingly sharp. Cast your burden upon the Lord, and He will sustain you. He will
never let the righteous be moved. But You, O God, will bring them down into the
deep pit. Bloody and deceitful men, may they not live out half their days. But I will
trust in You.

56 TO THE DIRECTOR of music, *al-Yonat elem reḥokim*. A *mikhtam* of David, when the
Philistines seized him in Gath. Be gracious unto me, O God, for man tramples upon
me. The foeman constantly oppresses me. My enemies trample me constantly. Indeed,
many fight against me and gain the upper hand. On the day that I fear I trust in You.
I praise God's word. In God I put my trust. I do not fear. What can flesh do to me?
Words about me constantly make me sad. All their thoughts are against me for evil.
They sit and lie in wait, they mark my steps, as they wait for my soul. For their sin
uproot them. In Your anger cast down the peoples, O God. You have counted my

*10th DAY of the month

יָשׁוּבוּ אוֹיְבַי אָחוֹר בְּיוֹם אֶקְרָא זֶה־יָדַעְתִּי כִּי־אֱלֹהִים לִי׃ בֵּאלֹהִים
אֲהַלֵּל דָּבָר בַּיהוָה אֲהַלֵּל דָּבָר׃ בֵּאלֹהִים בָּטַחְתִּי לֹא אִירָא מַה־יַּעֲשֶׂה
אָדָם לִי׃ עָלַי אֱלֹהִים נְדָרֶיךָ אֲשַׁלֵּם תּוֹדֹת לָךְ׃ כִּי הִצַּלְתָּ נַפְשִׁי מִמָּוֶת
הֲלֹא רַגְלַי מִדֶּחִי לְהִתְהַלֵּךְ לִפְנֵי אֱלֹהִים בְּאוֹר הַחַיִּים׃
נז לַמְנַצֵּחַ אַל־תַּשְׁחֵת לְדָוִד מִכְתָּם בְּבָרְחוֹ מִפְּנֵי־שָׁאוּל בַּמְּעָרָה׃ חָנֵּנִי
אֱלֹהִים ׀ חָנֵּנִי כִּי בְךָ חָסָיָה נַפְשִׁי וּבְצֵל־כְּנָפֶיךָ אֶחְסֶה עַד יַעֲבֹר הַוּוֹת׃
אֶקְרָא לֵאלֹהִים עֶלְיוֹן לָאֵל גֹּמֵר עָלָי׃ יִשְׁלַח מִשָּׁמַיִם ׀ וְיוֹשִׁיעֵנִי חֵרֵף
שֹׁאֲפִי סֶלָה יִשְׁלַח אֱלֹהִים חַסְדּוֹ וַאֲמִתּוֹ׃ נַפְשִׁי ׀ בְּתוֹךְ לְבָאִם אֶשְׁכְּבָה
לֹהֲטִים בְּנֵי־אָדָם שִׁנֵּיהֶם חֲנִית וְחִצִּים וּלְשׁוֹנָם חֶרֶב חַדָּה׃ רוּמָה עַל־
הַשָּׁמַיִם אֱלֹהִים עַל כָּל־הָאָרֶץ כְּבוֹדֶךָ׃ רֶשֶׁת ׀ הֵכִינוּ לִפְעָמַי כָּפַף נַפְשִׁי
כָּרוּ לְפָנַי שִׁיחָה נָפְלוּ בְתוֹכָהּ סֶלָה׃ נָכוֹן לִבִּי אֱלֹהִים נָכוֹן לִבִּי אָשִׁירָה
וַאֲזַמֵּרָה׃ עוּרָה כְבוֹדִי עוּרָה הַנֵּבֶל וְכִנּוֹר אָעִירָה שָּׁחַר׃ אוֹדְךָ בָעַמִּים ׀
אֲדֹנָי אֲזַמֶּרְךָ בַּלְאֻמִּים׃ כִּי־גָדֹל עַד־שָׁמַיִם חַסְדֶּךָ וְעַד־שְׁחָקִים אֲמִתֶּךָ׃
רוּמָה עַל־שָׁמַיִם אֱלֹהִים עַל כָּל־הָאָרֶץ כְּבוֹדֶךָ׃
נח לַמְנַצֵּחַ אַל־תַּשְׁחֵת לְדָוִד מִכְתָּם׃ הַאֻמְנָם אֵלֶם צֶדֶק תְּדַבֵּרוּן מֵישָׁרִים
תִּשְׁפְּטוּ בְּנֵי אָדָם׃ אַף־בְּלֵב עוֹלֹת תִּפְעָלוּן בָּאָרֶץ חֲמַס יְדֵיכֶם תְּפַלֵּסוּן׃
זֹרוּ רְשָׁעִים מֵרָחֶם תָּעוּ מִבֶּטֶן דֹּבְרֵי כָזָב׃ חֲמַת־לָמוֹ כִּדְמוּת חֲמַת־נָחָשׁ
כְּמוֹ־פֶתֶן חֵרֵשׁ יַאְטֵם אָזְנוֹ׃ אֲשֶׁר לֹא־יִשְׁמַע לְקוֹל מְלַחֲשִׁים חוֹבֵר
חֲבָרִים מְחֻכָּם׃ אֱלֹהִים הֲרָס־שִׁנֵּימוֹ בְּפִימוֹ מַלְתְּעוֹת כְּפִירִים נְתֹץ ׀ יְהוָה׃
יִמָּאֲסוּ כְמוֹ־מַיִם יִתְהַלְּכוּ־לָמוֹ יִדְרֹךְ חִצָּו כְּמוֹ יִתְמֹלָלוּ׃ כְּמוֹ שַׁבְּלוּל
תֶּמֶס יַהֲלֹךְ נֵפֶל אֵשֶׁת בַּל־חָזוּ שָׁמֶשׁ׃ בְּטֶרֶם יָבִינוּ סִּירֹתֵיכֶם אָטָד כְּמוֹ־
חַי כְּמוֹ־חָרוֹן יִשְׂעָרֶנּוּ׃ יִשְׂמַח צַדִּיק כִּי־חָזָה נָקָם פְּעָמָיו יִרְחַץ בְּדַם
הָרָשָׁע׃ וְיֹאמַר אָדָם אַךְ־פְּרִי לַצַּדִּיק אַךְ יֵשׁ־אֱלֹהִים שֹׁפְטִים בָּאָרֶץ׃
נט לַמְנַצֵּחַ אַל־תַּשְׁחֵת לְדָוִד מִכְתָּם בִּשְׁלֹחַ שָׁאוּל וַיִּשְׁמְרוּ אֶת־הַבַּיִת
לַהֲמִיתוֹ׃ הַצִּילֵנִי מֵאֹיְבַי ׀ אֱלֹהָי מִמִּתְקוֹמְמַי תְּשַׂגְּבֵנִי׃ הַצִּילֵנִי מִפֹּעֲלֵי
אָוֶן וּמֵאַנְשֵׁי דָמִים הוֹשִׁיעֵנִי׃ כִּי הִנֵּה אָרְבוּ לְנַפְשִׁי יָגוּרוּ עָלַי עַזִּים לֹא־
פִשְׁעִי וְלֹא־חַטָּאתִי יְהוָה׃ בְּלִי־עָוֺן יְרוּצוּן וְיִכּוֹנָנוּ עוּרָה לִקְרָאתִי וּרְאֵה׃
וְאַתָּה יְהוָה־אֱלֹהִים ׀ צְבָאוֹת אֱלֹהֵי יִשְׂרָאֵל הָקִיצָה לִפְקֹד כָּל־הַגּוֹיִם

wanderings. Please put my tears in Your bottle, indeed count them. Then my enemies will retreat on the day that I call. This I know – that God is for me. I will praise the word of God. I will praise the word of the Lord. In God I put my trust. I do not fear. What can man do to me? Your vows are upon me, O God. I will pay You thanksgiving-offerings. For you have delivered my soul from death, indeed my feet from stumbling, that I may walk before God in the light of the living!

57 TO THE DIRECTOR of music, *al-tashḥet*. A *mikhtam* of David, when he fled from Saul in the cave. Be gracious unto me, O God, be gracious unto me, for my soul seeks refuge in You. And in the shadow of Your wings let me seek refuge, until calamities are past. I call to God Most High, to God Who completes my wish on my behalf. May He send from heaven and save me. May He disgrace my enemy. Selah. May God send His loving-kindness and His truth. My soul is among lions, I lie down among flaming coals, the sons of men, whose teeth are spears and arrows, and whose tongue is a sharp sword. Be exalted above the heavens, O God. Let Your glory be above all the earth. They prepared a trap for my feet. He bent down my soul. They dug a pit before me, they fell into it. Selah. My heart is steadfast, O God, my heart is steadfast. I sing and I chant. Awake, my honor! Awake, harp and lyre! I awaken the dawn. I thank You, O Lord, among the peoples. I sing to You among the nations. For Your loving-kindness is great unto the heavens, and Your truth to the skies. Be exalted above the heavens, O God. Let Your glory be above all the earth.

58 TO THE DIRECTOR of music, al-*tashḥet*. A *mikhtam* of David. Is it indeed true that you speak righteousness? Do you judge the sons of man uprightly? Indeed, at heart you work wickedness. Your hands weigh out violence in the land. The wicked were strangers from the womb, the liars strayed from birth. Their venom is like the venom of a serpent. They are like the deaf adder that stops its ears, That does not listen to the voice of charmers, to the wise performer of sorceries. O God, shatter their teeth in their mouth. Smash the teeth of the lions, O Lord. Let them melt away like waters that pass away. When he draws his arrows, let them crumble. Like the snail that melts away, like the downfall of moles, that do not see the sun. Before your thorns ripen like a bramble, while it is still fresh, something like an angry storm will sweep it away. The righteous man will rejoice when he sees the vengeance. He will wash his feet in the blood of the wicked. And a man will say: "Indeed there is fruit for the righteous. Indeed there is a God Who judges on the earth."

59 TO THE DIRECTOR of music, *al-tashḥet*. A *mikhtam* of David, when Saul sent, and they watched the house to kill him. Deliver me from my enemies, O my God. Make me safe from those who rise up against me. Deliver me from workers of iniquity, and save me from men of blood. For behold, they lie in wait for my soul. Fierce men gather against me, not for my transgression, nor for my sin, O Lord. For no iniquity of mine they run and prepare themselves. Hasten to me and observe. But You, Lord God of Hosts, the God of Israel, wake up to punish all the nations. Do not be gracious

אַל־תָּחֹן כׇּל־בֹּגְדֵי אָוֶן סֶלָה׃ יָשׁוּבוּ לָעֶרֶב יֶהֱמוּ כַכָּלֶב וִיסוֹבְבוּ עִיר׃
הִנֵּה ׀ יַבִּיעוּן בְּפִיהֶם חֲרָבוֹת בְּשִׂפְתוֹתֵיהֶם כִּי־מִי שֹׁמֵעַ׃ וְאַתָּה יְהוָה
תִּשְׂחַק־לָמוֹ תִּלְעַג לְכׇל־גּוֹיִם׃ עֻזּוֹ אֵלֶיךָ אֶשְׁמֹרָה כִּי־אֱלֹהִים מִשְׂגַּבִּי׃
אֱלֹהֵי חסדו יְקַדְּמֵנִי אֱלֹהִים יַרְאֵנִי בְשֹׁרְרָי׃ אַל־תַּהַרְגֵם ׀ פֶּן־יִשְׁכְּחוּ חַסְדִּי
עַמִּי הֲנִיעֵמוֹ בְחֵילְךָ וְהוֹרִידֵמוֹ מָגִנֵּנוּ אֲדֹנָי׃ חַטַּאת־פִּימוֹ דְּבַר־שְׂפָתֵימוֹ
וְיִלָּכְדוּ בִגְאוֹנָם וּמֵאָלָה וּמִכַּחַשׁ יְסַפֵּרוּ׃ כַּלֵּה בְחֵמָה כַּלֵּה וְאֵינֵמוֹ וְיֵדְעוּ
כִּי־אֱלֹהִים מֹשֵׁל בְּיַעֲקֹב לְאַפְסֵי הָאָרֶץ סֶלָה׃ וְיָשֻׁבוּ לָעֶרֶב יֶהֱמוּ כַכָּלֶב
וִיסוֹבְבוּ עִיר׃ הֵמָּה ינועון לֶאֱכֹל אִם־לֹא יִשְׂבְּעוּ וַיָּלִינוּ׃ וַאֲנִי ׀ אָשִׁיר יְנִיעוּן
עֻזֶּךָ וַאֲרַנֵּן לַבֹּקֶר חַסְדֶּךָ כִּי־הָיִיתָ מִשְׂגָּב לִי וּמָנוֹס בְּיוֹם צַר־לִי׃ עֻזִּי
אֵלֶיךָ אֲזַמֵּרָה כִּי־אֱלֹהִים מִשְׂגַּבִּי אֱלֹהֵי חַסְדִּי׃
לַמְנַצֵּחַ עַל־שׁוּשַׁן עֵדוּת מִכְתָּם לְדָוִד לְלַמֵּד׃ בְּהַצּוֹתוֹ ׀ אֶת אֲרַם נַהֲרַיִם ס*
וְאֶת־אֲרַם צוֹבָה וַיָּשׇׁב יוֹאָב וַיַּךְ אֶת־אֱדוֹם בְּגֵיא־מֶלַח שְׁנֵים עָשָׂר
אָלֶף׃ אֱלֹהִים זְנַחְתָּנוּ פְרַצְתָּנוּ אָנַפְתָּ תְּשׁוֹבֵב לָנוּ׃ הִרְעַשְׁתָּה אֶרֶץ
פְּצַמְתָּהּ רְפָה שְׁבָרֶיהָ כִי־מָטָה׃ הִרְאִיתָ עַמְּךָ קָשָׁה הִשְׁקִיתָנוּ יַיִן
תַּרְעֵלָה׃ נָתַתָּה לִּירֵאֶיךָ נֵּס לְהִתְנוֹסֵס מִפְּנֵי קֹשֶׁט סֶלָה׃ לְמַעַן יֵחָלְצוּן
יְדִידֶיךָ הוֹשִׁיעָה יְמִינְךָ ועננו׃ אֱלֹהִים ׀ דִּבֶּר בְּקׇדְשׁוֹ אֶעְלֹזָה אֲחַלְּקָה וַעֲנֵנִי
שְׁכֶם וְעֵמֶק סֻכּוֹת אֲמַדֵּד׃ לִי גִלְעָד ׀ וְלִי מְנַשֶּׁה וְאֶפְרַיִם מָעוֹז רֹאשִׁי
יְהוּדָה מְחֹקְקִי׃ מוֹאָב ׀ סִיר רַחְצִי עַל־אֱדוֹם אַשְׁלִיךְ נַעֲלִי עָלַי פְּלֶשֶׁת
הִתְרוֹעָעִי׃ מִי יֹבִלֵנִי עִיר מָצוֹר מִי נָחַנִי עַד־אֱדוֹם׃ הֲלֹא־אַתָּה אֱלֹהִים
זְנַחְתָּנוּ וְלֹא־תֵצֵא אֱלֹהִים בְּצִבְאוֹתֵינוּ׃ הָבָה־לָּנוּ עֶזְרָת מִצָּר וְשָׁוְא
תְּשׁוּעַת אָדָם׃ בֵּאלֹהִים נַעֲשֶׂה־חָיִל וְהוּא יָבוּס צָרֵינוּ׃
לַמְנַצֵּחַ ׀ עַל־נְגִינַת לְדָוִד׃ שִׁמְעָה אֱלֹהִים רִנָּתִי הַקְשִׁיבָה תְּפִלָּתִי׃ מִקְצֵה סא
הָאָרֶץ ׀ אֵלֶיךָ אֶקְרָא בַּעֲטֹף לִבִּי בְּצוּר־יָרוּם מִמֶּנִּי תַנְחֵנִי׃ כִּי־הָיִיתָ מַחְסֶה
לִי מִגְדַּל־עֹז מִפְּנֵי אוֹיֵב׃ אָגוּרָה בְאׇהׇלְךָ עוֹלָמִים אֶחֱסֶה בְסֵתֶר כְּנָפֶיךָ
סֶּלָה׃ כִּי־אַתָּה אֱלֹהִים שָׁמַעְתָּ לִנְדָרָי נָתַתָּ יְרֻשַּׁת יִרְאֵי שְׁמֶךָ׃ יָמִים
עַל־יְמֵי־מֶלֶךְ תּוֹסִיף שְׁנוֹתָיו כְּמוֹ־דֹר וָדֹר׃ יֵשֵׁב עוֹלָם לִפְנֵי אֱלֹהִים חֶסֶד
וֶאֱמֶת מַן יִנְצְרֻהוּ׃ כֵּן אֲזַמְּרָה שִׁמְךָ לָעַד לְשַׁלְּמִי נְדָרַי יוֹם ׀ יוֹם׃
לַמְנַצֵּחַ עַל־יְדוּתוּן מִזְמוֹר לְדָוִד׃ אַךְ אֶל־אֱלֹהִים דּוּמִיָּה נַפְשִׁי מִמֶּנּוּ סב

---

*יא לחודש

to any wicked traitors. Selah. They return in the evening. They howl like a dog and go round the city. Behold, they utter sounds with their mouths. Swords are in their lips: "For who is listening?" But You, O Lord, will laugh at them. You will mock all the nations. Against his might I wait for You, for You, O God, are my fortress. The God of my loving-kindness will come to meet me. God will let me see the downfall of my enemies. Do not slay them, lest my people forget. Scatter them by Your power and bring them down, O Lord our shield. The sin of their mouth and the word of their lips! They will be taken for their pride, and for the oaths and lies they speak. Consume them in wrath, consume them, that they may be no more. Let them know that God rules in Jacob to the ends of the earth. Selah. They will return in the evening. They will howl like a dog and go round the city. They will wander up and down for food, if they do not have their fill and sleep. But I will sing of Your might, and I will sing aloud of Your loving-kindness in the morning, for You have been my defense and a refuge in the day of my distress. O my strength, to You will I sing that God is my fortress, the God of my loving-kindness.

*60 TO THE DIRECTOR of music, *al-shushan edut*. A *mikhtam* of David, to teach. When he strove with Aram-naharaim and with Aram-zobah, and Joab returned and smote twelve thousand of Edom in the Valley of Salt. O God, You have abandoned us, You have smitten us, You have been angry. O give us rest! You have made the earth shake. You have split it open. Heal its fragments, for it has fallen. You have shown Your people hardship. You have made us drink poisonous wine. You have left those who fear You a flying banner before the bows. Selah. That Your loved ones may be delivered, save with Your right hand, and answer me. God has spoken in His holiness. I will rejoice. I will divide Shechem and I will measure out the valley of Succoth. Gilead is mine and Manasseh is mine. And Ephraim is the strength of my head. Judah is my scepter. Moab is my washpot. I will cast my shoe over Edom. Philistia, shout with joy because of me! Who brought me to the city under siege? Who led me to Edom? Surely You have abandoned us, O God, and You do not go forth, O God, with our hosts. Give us help against the foe, for vain is the salvation of man. Through God we will do valiantly. And He will defeat our enemies.

61 TO THE DIRECTOR of music, on strings, of David. Hear, O God, my cry. Attend to my prayer. From the end of the earth, I call to You, when my heart faints. Lead me onto the rock that towers over me. Please be my protector, a strong tower before the enemy. Let me dwell in Your tent forever. Let me seek refuge in the shadow of Your wings. Selah. O You, God, hear my vows. Give those who fear Your name their heritage. Add days to the days of the king. May his years be as many generations. May he be enthroned before God forever. Appoint loving-kindness and truth to preserve him. So will I sing to Your name forever, that I may fulfill my vows day by day.

62 TO THE DIRECTOR of music, *al-Yedutun*. A psalm of David. Toward God alone is my

*11th DAY of the month

יְשׁוּעָתִי: אַךְ־הוּא צוּרִי וִישׁוּעָתִי מִשְׂגַּבִּי לֹא־אֶמּוֹט רַבָּה: עַד־אָנָה ׀
תְּהוֹתְתוּ עַל־אִישׁ תְּרָצְּחוּ כֻלְּכֶם כְּקִיר נָטוּי גָּדֵר הַדְּחוּיָה: אַךְ מִשְּׂאֵתוֹ ׀
יָעֲצוּ לְהַדִּיחַ יִרְצוּ כָזָב בְּפִיו יְבָרֵכוּ וּבְקִרְבָּם יְקַלְלוּ־סֶלָה: אַךְ לֵאלֹהִים
דּוֹמִּי נַפְשִׁי כִּי־מִמֶּנּוּ תִּקְוָתִי: אַךְ־הוּא צוּרִי וִישׁוּעָתִי מִשְׂגַּבִּי לֹא אֶמּוֹט:
עַל־אֱלֹהִים יִשְׁעִי וּכְבוֹדִי צוּר־עֻזִּי מַחְסִי בֵּאלֹהִים: בִּטְחוּ בוֹ בְכָל־עֵת ׀
עָם שִׁפְכוּ־לְפָנָיו לְבַבְכֶם אֱלֹהִים מַחֲסֶה־לָּנוּ סֶלָה: אַךְ ׀ הֶבֶל בְּנֵי־אָדָם
כָּזָב בְּנֵי אִישׁ בְּמֹאזְנַיִם לַעֲלוֹת הֵמָּה מֵהֶבֶל יָחַד: אַל־תִּבְטְחוּ בְעֹשֶׁק
וּבְגָזֵל אַל־תֶּהְבָּלוּ חַיִל ׀ כִּי־יָנוּב אַל־תָּשִׁיתוּ לֵב: אַחַת ׀ דִּבֶּר אֱלֹהִים
שְׁתַּיִם־זוּ שָׁמָעְתִּי כִּי עֹז לֵאלֹהִים: וּלְךָ־אֲדֹנָי חָסֶד כִּי־אַתָּה תְשַׁלֵּם
לְאִישׁ כְּמַעֲשֵׂהוּ:

סג מִזְמוֹר לְדָוִד בִּהְיוֹתוֹ בְּמִדְבַּר יְהוּדָה: אֱלֹהִים ׀ אֵלִי אַתָּה אֲשַׁחֲרֶךָּ
צָמְאָה לְךָ ׀ נַפְשִׁי כָּמַהּ לְךָ בְשָׂרִי בְּאֶרֶץ־צִיָּה וְעָיֵף בְּלִי־מָיִם: כֵּן בַּקֹּדֶשׁ
חֲזִיתִךָ לִרְאוֹת עֻזְּךָ וּכְבוֹדֶךָ: כִּי־טוֹב חַסְדְּךָ מֵחַיִּים שְׂפָתַי יְשַׁבְּחוּנְךָ:
כֵּן אֲבָרֶכְךָ בְחַיָּי בְּשִׁמְךָ אֶשָּׂא כַפָּי: כְּמוֹ חֵלֶב וָדֶשֶׁן תִּשְׂבַּע נַפְשִׁי וְשִׂפְתֵי
רְנָנוֹת יְהַלֶּל־פִּי: אִם־זְכַרְתִּיךָ עַל־יְצוּעָי בְּאַשְׁמֻרוֹת אֶהְגֶּה־בָּךְ: כִּי־הָיִיתָ
עֶזְרָתָה לִּי וּבְצֵל כְּנָפֶיךָ אֲרַנֵּן: דָּבְקָה נַפְשִׁי אַחֲרֶיךָ בִּי תָּמְכָה יְמִינֶךָ:
וְהֵמָּה לְשׁוֹאָה יְבַקְשׁוּ נַפְשִׁי יָבֹאוּ בְּתַחְתִּיּוֹת הָאָרֶץ: יַגִּירֻהוּ עַל־יְדֵי־
חָרֶב מְנָת שֻׁעָלִים יִהְיוּ: וְהַמֶּלֶךְ יִשְׂמַח בֵּאלֹהִים יִתְהַלֵּל כָּל־הַנִּשְׁבָּע
בּוֹ כִּי יִסָּכֵר פִּי דוֹבְרֵי־שָׁקֶר:

סד לַמְנַצֵּחַ מִזְמוֹר לְדָוִד: שְׁמַע־אֱלֹהִים קוֹלִי בְשִׂיחִי מִפַּחַד אוֹיֵב תִּצֹּר
חַיָּי: תַּסְתִּירֵנִי מִסּוֹד מְרֵעִים מֵרִגְשַׁת פֹּעֲלֵי אָוֶן: אֲשֶׁר שָׁנְנוּ כַחֶרֶב לְשׁוֹנָם
דָּרְכוּ חִצָּם דָּבָר מָר: לִירוֹת בַּמִּסְתָּרִים תָּם פִּתְאֹם יֹרֻהוּ וְלֹא יִירָאוּ:
יְחַזְּקוּ־לָמוֹ ׀ דָּבָר רָע יְסַפְּרוּ לִטְמוֹן מוֹקְשִׁים אָמְרוּ מִי יִרְאֶה־לָּמוֹ:
יַחְפְּשׂוּ־עוֹלֹת תַּמְנוּ חֵפֶשׂ מְחֻפָּשׂ וְקֶרֶב אִישׁ וְלֵב עָמֹק: וַיֹּרֵם אֱלֹהִים
חֵץ פִּתְאוֹם הָיוּ מַכּוֹתָם: וַיַּכְשִׁילֻהוּ עָלֵימוֹ לְשׁוֹנָם יִתְנֹדְדוּ כָּל־רֹאֵה בָם:
וַיִּירְאוּ כָּל־אָדָם וַיַּגִּידוּ פֹּעַל אֱלֹהִים וּמַעֲשֵׂהוּ הִשְׂכִּילוּ: יִשְׂמַח צַדִּיק
בַּיהוה וְחָסָה בוֹ וְיִתְהַלְלוּ כָּל־יִשְׁרֵי־לֵב:

סה לַמְנַצֵּחַ מִזְמוֹר לְדָוִד שִׁיר: לְךָ דֻמִיָּה תְהִלָּה אֱלֹהִים בְּצִיּוֹן וּלְךָ יְשֻׁלַּם־

soul quiet. From Him comes my salvation. He alone is my rock and my salvation. He is my fortress. I shall surely not collapse. How long will you attack a man? You all murder, like a leaning wall, a tottering fence. Only after raising him up do they plot to cast him down. They delight in lies. With their mouth they bless, but inwardly they curse. Selah. Toward God alone be quiet, my soul. For my hope is from Him. He alone is my rock and my salvation. He is my fortress. I shall not collapse. In God is my deliverance and my glory. The rock of my strength, my refuge is in God. Trust in Him at all times, O people. Pour out your heart before him. God is a refuge for us. Selah. The children of man are but vapor. The children of man are a lie. Together in the balance, they rise up lighter than vapor. Trust not in extortion, and do not be deceived by robbery. If wealth increases, set not your heart upon it. God has spoken once. Twice I have heard that power is God's. And Yours, O Lord, is loving-kindness, for You repay every man according to his deeds.

63 A PSALM of David, when he was in the Judean desert. O God, You are my God. I seek You. My soul thirsts for You, my flesh yearns for You, in a dry land and exhausted, without water. So do I behold You in the sanctuary, to see Your power and Your glory. For Your loving-kindness is better than life, my lips praise You. So will I bless You while I live. In Your name will I lift up my hands, As if my soul is satiated with marrow and fatness, and with lips full of song my mouth will praise You. Indeed, I remember You upon my bedclothes. I meditate on You in the night watches, That You have been my help, and I sing in the shadow of Your wings. My soul follows closely after You. Your right hand supports me. But those who seek to destroy my soul will come to the lower regions of the earth. They will pour it out by the sword. They will be the portion of foxes. But the king will rejoice in God. May all who swear by Him be glorious. For the mouth of those who speak falsehood will be stopped.

64 TO THE DIRECTOR of music. A psalm of David. Hear, O God, my voice in my complaint. Preserve my life from the terror of the enemy. Hide me from the assembly of the wicked, from the throng of evildoers, who have whetted their tongue like a sword, who have pulled their arrows anointed with a bitter potion, to shoot in secret at the innocent man. Suddenly they shoot at him, and they fear not. They intensify for themselves the evil thing. They tell of concealing snares. They say: Who will see them? They search for iniquities. We have completed a diligent search, a man's inner parts, and in the depths of the heart. But God shot at them. Their injuries were a sudden arrow. They tripped up their tongue over themselves. All who look upon them will shake. And all men were afraid, and they recounted the work of God, and they understood His deeds. The righteous man will rejoice in the Lord and will take refuge in Him, and all the upright in heart will glory.

65 TO THE DIRECTOR of music. A psalm of David. A song. Praise awaits You, O God in Zion, and to You shall the vow be fulfilled. O You Who hear prayer! Unto You shall all

נֶדֶר: שֹׁמֵעַ תְּפִלָּה עָדֶיךָ כָּל־בָּשָׂר יָבֹאוּ: דִּבְרֵי עֲוֺנֹת גָּבְרוּ מֶנִּי פְּשָׁעֵינוּ
אַתָּה תְכַפְּרֵם: אַשְׁרֵי | תִּבְחַר וּתְקָרֵב יִשְׁכֹּן חֲצֵרֶיךָ נִשְׂבְּעָה בְּטוּב בֵּיתֶךָ
קְדֹשׁ הֵיכָלֶךָ: נוֹרָאוֹת | בְּצֶדֶק תַּעֲנֵנוּ אֱלֹהֵי יִשְׁעֵנוּ מִבְטָח כָּל־קַצְוֵי־אֶרֶץ
וְיָם רְחֹקִים: מֵכִין הָרִים בְּכֹחוֹ נֶאְזָר בִּגְבוּרָה: מַשְׁבִּיחַ | שְׁאוֹן יַמִּים שְׁאוֹן
גַּלֵּיהֶם וַהֲמוֹן לְאֻמִּים: וַיִּירְאוּ | יֹשְׁבֵי קְצָוֺת מֵאוֹתֹתֶיךָ מוֹצָאֵי־בֹקֶר וָעֶרֶב
תַּרְנִין: פָּקַדְתָּ הָאָרֶץ | וַתְּשֹׁקְקֶהָ רַבַּת תַּעְשְׁרֶנָּה פֶּלֶג אֱלֹהִים מָלֵא מָיִם
תָּכִין דְּגָנָם כִּי־כֵן תְּכִינֶהָ: תְּלָמֶיהָ רַוֵּה נַחֵת גְּדוּדֶהָ בִּרְבִיבִים תְּמֹגְגֶנָּה
צִמְחָהּ תְּבָרֵךְ: עִטַּרְתָּ שְׁנַת טוֹבָתֶךָ וּמַעְגָּלֶיךָ יִרְעֲפוּן דָּשֶׁן: יִרְעֲפוּ נְאוֹת
מִדְבָּר וְגִיל גְּבָעוֹת תַּחְגֹּרְנָה: לָבְשׁוּ כָרִים | הַצֹּאן וַעֲמָקִים יַעַטְפוּ־בָר
יִתְרוֹעֲעוּ אַף־יָשִׁירוּ:

*סו לַמְנַצֵּחַ שִׁיר מִזְמוֹר הָרִיעוּ לֵאלֹהִים כָּל־הָאָרֶץ: זַמְּרוּ כְבוֹד־שְׁמוֹ שִׂימוּ
כָבוֹד תְּהִלָּתוֹ: אִמְרוּ לֵאלֹהִים מַה־נּוֹרָא מַעֲשֶׂיךָ בְּרֹב עֻזְּךָ יְכַחֲשׁוּ־לְךָ
אֹיְבֶיךָ: כָּל־הָאָרֶץ | יִשְׁתַּחֲווּ לְךָ וִיזַמְּרוּ־לָךְ יְזַמְּרוּ שִׁמְךָ סֶלָה: לְכוּ וּרְאוּ
מִפְעֲלוֹת אֱלֹהִים נוֹרָא עֲלִילָה עַל־בְּנֵי אָדָם: הָפַךְ יָם | לְיַבָּשָׁה בַּנָּהָר
יַעַבְרוּ בְרָגֶל שָׁם נִשְׂמְחָה־בּוֹ: מֹשֵׁל בִּגְבוּרָתוֹ | עוֹלָם עֵינָיו בַּגּוֹיִם תִּצְפֶּינָה
יָרוּמוּ הַסּוֹרְרִים | אַל־ירימו לָמוֹ סֶלָה: בָּרְכוּ עַמִּים | אֱלֹהֵינוּ וְהַשְׁמִיעוּ קוֹל
תְּהִלָּתוֹ: הַשָּׂם נַפְשֵׁנוּ בַּחַיִּים וְלֹא־נָתַן לַמּוֹט רַגְלֵנוּ: כִּי־בְחַנְתָּנוּ אֱלֹהִים
צְרַפְתָּנוּ כִּצְרָף־כָּסֶף: הֲבֵאתָנוּ בַמְּצוּדָה שַׂמְתָּ מוּעָקָה בְמָתְנֵינוּ: הִרְכַּבְתָּ
אֱנוֹשׁ לְרֹאשֵׁנוּ בָּאנוּ־בָאֵשׁ וּבַמַּיִם וַתּוֹצִיאֵנוּ לָרְוָיָה: אָבוֹא בֵיתְךָ בְעוֹלוֹת
אֲשַׁלֵּם לְךָ נְדָרָי: אֲשֶׁר־פָּצוּ שְׂפָתָי וְדִבֶּר־פִּי בַּצַּר־לִי: עֹלוֹת מֵחִים
אַעֲלֶה־לָּךְ עִם־קְטֹרֶת אֵילִים אֶעֱשֶׂה בָקָר עִם־עַתּוּדִים סֶלָה: לְכוּ־
שִׁמְעוּ וַאֲסַפְּרָה כָּל־יִרְאֵי אֱלֹהִים אֲשֶׁר עָשָׂה לְנַפְשִׁי: אֵלָיו פִּי־קָרָאתִי
וְרוֹמַם תַּחַת לְשׁוֹנִי: אָוֶן אִם־רָאִיתִי בְלִבִּי לֹא יִשְׁמַע | אֲדֹנָי: אָכֵן שָׁמַע
אֱלֹהִים הִקְשִׁיב בְּקוֹל תְּפִלָּתִי: בָּרוּךְ אֱלֹהִים אֲשֶׁר לֹא־הֵסִיר תְּפִלָּתִי
וְחַסְדּוֹ מֵאִתִּי:

סז לַמְנַצֵּחַ בִּנְגִינֹת מִזְמוֹר שִׁיר: אֱלֹהִים יְחָנֵּנוּ וִיבָרְכֵנוּ יָאֵר פָּנָיו אִתָּנוּ סֶלָה:
לָדַעַת בָּאָרֶץ דַּרְכֶּךָ בְּכָל־גּוֹיִם יְשׁוּעָתֶךָ: יוֹדוּךָ עַמִּים | אֱלֹהִים יוֹדוּךָ
עַמִּים כֻּלָּם: יִשְׂמְחוּ וִירַנְּנוּ לְאֻמִּים כִּי־תִשְׁפֹּט עַמִּים מִישֹׁר וּלְאֻמִּים |

*יב לחודש

flesh come. Tales of iniquities are too strong for me. As for our transgressions, please pardon them. Happy is he whom You choose and bring near, that he may dwell in Your courts. May we be satisfied with the goodness of Your house, Your holy temple. Answer us in righteousness with awesome things, O God of our salvation, the trust of all the faraway ends of the earth and of the sea. Who establishes the mountains by His strength, while He is girded with power. Who stills the roar of the seas, the roar of their waves, and the tumult of the peoples. And those who dwell in the most distant places are afraid of Your signs. You cause the passages of the morning and evening to rejoice. You have visited the earth and caused it to overflow. You have greatly enriched it, a river of God, full of water. You have made ready their grain, for thus have You prepared it. Drench its furrows, bring down its mounds. Make it melt away with showers and bless its vegetation. You have crowned the year of Your goodness, and Your paths drip fatness. The desert pastures drip, and the hills are girded with rejoicing. The meadows are clothed with flocks, and the valleys are wrapped in ears of grain. They shout for joy and sing.

*66 TO THE DIRECTOR of music. A song. A psalm. Shout for joy to God, all the earth. Sing the glory of His name. Give honor to His praise. Say to God: How awesome are Your deeds! In the greatness of your power Your enemies feign obedience to You. All the earth will bow down to You and sing to You. They will sing Your name. Selah. Come and see the works of God. He is awesome in deed toward the children of man. He turned the sea into dry land. They went through the river on foot. There we rejoiced in Him. He rules by His power forever. His eyes watch the nations. Let not the rebellious be exalted. Selah. Bless our God, O you peoples, and make heard the voice of His praise. Who has put our soul among the living, and has not given over our foot to stumble. For You have tested us, O God. You have refined us a silver is refined. You have brought us into the net. You have laid distress upon our loins. You have caused men to ride on our heads. We went through fire and water, but You brought us out to a place of rest. I will come into Your house with burnt-offerings. I will fulfill my vows to You, That my lips uttered and my mouth spoke, when I was in distress. I will offer unto You burnt-offerings of fatlings, with the incense of rams. I will offer bullocks with he-goats. Selah. Come and hear, all you who fear God, and I will relate what He has done for my soul. I cried it to Him with my mouth, and He was extolled with my tongue. If I have seen wickedness in my heart, may the Lord not hear. Indeed, God has heard. He has listened to the sound of my prayer. Blessed be God, Who has not taken away my prayer and His loving-kindness from me.

67 TO THE DIRECTOR of music for instruments. A psalm. A song. May God be gracious to us and bless us. May He cause His face to shine upon us. Selah. That Your way may become known upon the earth, Your salvation among all nations. The peoples will praise You, O God. All the peoples will praise You. The nations will rejoice and sing. For You judge the peoples equitably and govern the nations upon the earth.

---

*12th DAY of the month

בָּאָרֶץ תַּנְחֵם סֶלָה׃ יוֹדוּךָ עַמִּים ׀ אֱלֹהִים יוֹדוּךָ עַמִּים כֻּלָּם׃ אֶרֶץ נָתְנָה
יְבוּלָהּ יְבָרְכֵנוּ אֱלֹהִים אֱלֹהֵינוּ׃ יְבָרְכֵנוּ אֱלֹהִים וְיִירְאוּ אוֹתוֹ כָּל־אַפְסֵי־
אָרֶץ׃

סח לַמְנַצֵּחַ לְדָוִד מִזְמוֹר שִׁיר׃ יָקוּם אֱלֹהִים יָפוּצוּ אוֹיְבָיו וְיָנוּסוּ מְשַׂנְאָיו
מִפָּנָיו׃ כְּהִנְדֹּף עָשָׁן תִּנְדֹּף כְּהִמֵּס דּוֹנַג מִפְּנֵי־אֵשׁ יֹאבְדוּ רְשָׁעִים מִפְּנֵי
אֱלֹהִים׃ וְצַדִּיקִים יִשְׂמְחוּ יַעַלְצוּ לִפְנֵי אֱלֹהִים וְיָשִׂישׂוּ בְשִׂמְחָה׃ שִׁירוּ ׀
לֵאלֹהִים זַמְּרוּ שְׁמוֹ סֹלּוּ לָרֹכֵב בָּעֲרָבוֹת בְּיָהּ שְׁמוֹ וְעִלְזוּ לְפָנָיו׃ אֲבִי
יְתוֹמִים וְדַיַּן אַלְמָנוֹת אֱלֹהִים בִּמְעוֹן קָדְשׁוֹ׃ אֱלֹהִים ׀ מוֹשִׁיב יְחִידִים ׀
בַּיְתָה מוֹצִיא אֲסִירִים בַּכּוֹשָׁרוֹת אַךְ סוֹרְרִים שָׁכְנוּ צְחִיחָה׃ אֱלֹהִים
בְּצֵאתְךָ לִפְנֵי עַמֶּךָ בְּצַעְדְּךָ בִישִׁימוֹן סֶלָה׃ אֶרֶץ רָעָשָׁה ׀ אַף־שָׁמַיִם נָטְפוּ
מִפְּנֵי אֱלֹהִים זֶה סִינַי מִפְּנֵי אֱלֹהִים אֱלֹהֵי יִשְׂרָאֵל׃ גֶּשֶׁם נְדָבוֹת תָּנִיף
אֱלֹהִים נַחֲלָתְךָ וְנִלְאָה אַתָּה כוֹנַנְתָּהּ׃ חַיָּתְךָ יָשְׁבוּ־בָהּ תָּכִין בְּטוֹבָתְךָ
לֶעָנִי אֱלֹהִים׃ אֲדֹנָי יִתֶּן־אֹמֶר הַמְבַשְּׂרוֹת צָבָא רָב׃ מַלְכֵי צְבָאוֹת יִדֹּדוּן
יִדֹּדוּן וּנְוַת־בַּיִת תְּחַלֵּק שָׁלָל׃ אִם־תִּשְׁכְּבוּן בֵּין שְׁפַתָּיִם כַּנְפֵי יוֹנָה נֶחְפָּה
בַכֶּסֶף וְאֶבְרוֹתֶיהָ בִּירַקְרַק חָרוּץ׃ בְּפָרֵשׂ שַׁדַּי מְלָכִים בָּהּ תַּשְׁלֵג בְּצַלְמוֹן׃
הַר־אֱלֹהִים הַר־בָּשָׁן הַר גַּבְנֻנִּים הַר־בָּשָׁן׃ לָמָּה ׀ תְּרַצְּדוּן הָרִים גַּבְנֻנִּים
הָהָר חָמַד אֱלֹהִים לְשִׁבְתּוֹ אַף־יהוה יִשְׁכֹּן לָנֶצַח׃ רֶכֶב אֱלֹהִים רִבֹּתַיִם
אַלְפֵי שִׁנְאָן אֲדֹנָי בָם סִינַי בַּקֹּדֶשׁ׃ עָלִיתָ לַמָּרוֹם ׀ שָׁבִיתָ שֶּׁבִי לָקַחְתָּ
מַתָּנוֹת בָּאָדָם וְאַף סוֹרְרִים לִשְׁכֹּן ׀ יָהּ אֱלֹהִים׃ בָּרוּךְ אֲדֹנָי יוֹם ׀ יוֹם
יַעֲמָס־לָנוּ הָאֵל יְשׁוּעָתֵנוּ סֶלָה׃ הָאֵל ׀ לָנוּ אֵל לְמוֹשָׁעוֹת וְלֵיהוִה אֲדֹנָי
לַמָּוֶת תּוֹצָאוֹת׃ אַךְ־אֱלֹהִים יִמְחַץ רֹאשׁ אֹיְבָיו קָדְקֹד שֵׂעָר מִתְהַלֵּךְ
בַּאֲשָׁמָיו׃ אָמַר אֲדֹנָי מִבָּשָׁן אָשִׁיב אָשִׁיב מִמְּצֻלוֹת יָם׃ לְמַעַן ׀ תִּמְחַץ
רַגְלְךָ בְּדָם לְשׁוֹן כְּלָבֶיךָ מֵאֹיְבִים מִנֵּהוּ׃ רָאוּ הֲלִיכוֹתֶיךָ אֱלֹהִים הֲלִיכוֹת
אֵלִי מַלְכִּי בַקֹּדֶשׁ׃ קִדְּמוּ שָׁרִים אַחַר נֹגְנִים בְּתוֹךְ עֲלָמוֹת תּוֹפֵפוֹת׃
בְּמַקְהֵלוֹת בָּרְכוּ אֱלֹהִים אֲדֹנָי מִמְּקוֹר יִשְׂרָאֵל׃ שָׁם בִּנְיָמִן ׀ צָעִיר רֹדֵם
שָׂרֵי יְהוּדָה רִגְמָתָם שָׂרֵי זְבֻלוּן שָׂרֵי נַפְתָּלִי׃ צִוָּה אֱלֹהֶיךָ עֻזֶּךָ עוּזָּה
אֱלֹהִים זוּ פָּעַלְתָּ לָּנוּ׃ מֵהֵיכָלֶךָ עַל־יְרוּשָׁלָם לְךָ יוֹבִילוּ מְלָכִים שָׁי׃ גְּעַר
חַיַּת קָנֶה עֲדַת אַבִּירִים ׀ בְּעֶגְלֵי עַמִּים מִתְרַפֵּס בְּרַצֵּי־כָסֶף בִּזַּר עַמִּים

Selah. The peoples will praise You, O God. All the peoples will praise You. The earth has yielded its produce. God, our God, will bless us. God will bless us, and all the ends of the earth will fear Him.

68 TO THE DIRECTOR of music. Of David. A psalm. A song. Let God arise. Let His enemies be scattered. And let those who hate Him flee from before Him. As smoke is dispersed, so disperse them. As wax melts before fire, so let the wicked perish before God. But let the righteous be glad, let them rejoice before God, and let them joyfully exult. Sing to God. Sing praise to His name. Raise your voice to Him Who rides upon the clouds by His name, *YaH*, and rejoice before Him. The Father of orphans and the Judge of widows is God in His holy habitation. God seats the lonely at home. He brings out prisoners with joy. But the rebellious dwell in a parched land. O God, when You went out before Your people, when You marched through the wilderness, Selah, The earth shook and the headings dripped because of God. Behold, Sinai, because of God, the God of Israel. You scattered a plentiful rain, O God. When Your inheritance languished, You set it up. Your community dwells in it. In Your goodness, O God, You prepare it for the poor. The Lord has given His word. Those who bear the tidings are a great army. Kings of armies flee, they flee, and you shall divide as spoils their household goods. So will you lie among the sheepfolds, with the wings of a dove overlaid with silver, and her pinions with yellow gold. When the Almighty scattered kings in it, it snowed in darkness. Mount Bashan is a mountain of God. Mount Bashan is a mountain of many peaks. Why do you quake, you many-peaked mountains? Because of the mountain that God has desired for His abode. The Lord will surely dwell there forever. The chariots of God are myriads upon myriads, thousands upon thousands. The Lord is among them, Sinai is in holiness. You ascended on high. You took captives. You took gifts from men. The rebellious also, that *YaH* God might dwell there. Blessed is my Master day by day. The God of our salvation will load us generously. Selah. God is to us a God of salvation, and God the Lord can rescue from death. God will surely crush the heads of His enemies, the hairy crown of him who walks in his trespasses. The Lord said: I will bring back from Bashan, I will bring back from the depths of the sea, So that your foot wades in blood. The tongue of your dogs will take its portion from your enemies. They have seen Your processions, O God, the processions of my God, my King, in holiness. The singers go first, afterward the musicians, among girls beating drums. Bless God in congregations, the Lord from the source of Israel. There is Benjamin, the youngest, ruling them, the princes of Judah in their throng, the princes of Zebulun, the princes of Naphtali. Your God has commanded your strength. Be strong, O God, You Who have acted for us. Because of Your sanctuary overlooking Jerusalem, kings will bring You gifts. Rebuke the beasts of the reeds, the company of bulls, the calves of peoples, him who tramples and crushes for money. He has dispersed the peoples who desire battle. Chariots will come from Egypt. Cush will quickly stretch out its hands to God. Sing to God,

קְרָבוֹת יֶחְפָּצוּ: יֶאֱתָיוּ חַשְׁמַנִּים מִנִּי מִצְרָיִם כּוּשׁ תָּרִיץ יָדָיו לֵאלֹהִים:
מַמְלְכוֹת הָאָרֶץ שִׁירוּ לֵאלֹהִים זַמְּרוּ אֲדֹנָי סֶלָה: לָרֹכֵב בִּשְׁמֵי שְׁמֵי־
קֶדֶם הֵן יִתֵּן בְּקוֹלוֹ קוֹל עֹז: תְּנוּ עֹז לֵאלֹהִים עַל־יִשְׂרָאֵל גַּאֲוָתוֹ וְעֻזּוֹ
בַּשְּׁחָקִים: נוֹרָא אֱלֹהִים ׀ מִמִּקְדָּשֶׁיךָ אֵל יִשְׂרָאֵל הוּא נֹתֵן ׀ עֹז וְתַעֲצֻמוֹת
לָעָם בָּרוּךְ אֱלֹהִים:

*סט לַמְנַצֵּחַ עַל־שׁוֹשַׁנִּים לְדָוִד: הוֹשִׁיעֵנִי אֱלֹהִים כִּי בָאוּ מַיִם עַד־נָפֶשׁ:
טָבַעְתִּי ׀ בִּיוֵן מְצוּלָה וְאֵין מָעֳמָד בָּאתִי בְמַעֲמַקֵּי־מַיִם וְשִׁבֹּלֶת שְׁטָפָתְנִי:
יָגַעְתִּי בְקָרְאִי נִחַר גְּרוֹנִי כָּלוּ עֵינַי מְיַחֵל לֵאלֹהָי: רַבּוּ ׀ מִשַּׂעֲרוֹת רֹאשִׁי
שֹׂנְאַי חִנָּם עָצְמוּ מַצְמִיתַי אֹיְבַי שֶׁקֶר אֲשֶׁר לֹא־גָזַלְתִּי אָז אָשִׁיב: אֱלֹהִים
אַתָּה יָדַעְתָּ לְאִוַּלְתִּי וְאַשְׁמוֹתַי מִמְּךָ לֹא־נִכְחָדוּ: אַל־יֵבֹשׁוּ בִי ׀ קֹוֶיךָ אֲדֹנָי
יהוה צְבָאוֹת אַל־יִכָּלְמוּ בִי מְבַקְשֶׁיךָ אֱלֹהֵי יִשְׂרָאֵל: כִּי־עָלֶיךָ נָשָׂאתִי
חֶרְפָּה כִּסְּתָה כְלִמָּה פָנָי: מוּזָר הָיִיתִי לְאֶחָי וְנָכְרִי לִבְנֵי אִמִּי: כִּי־קִנְאַת
בֵּיתְךָ אֲכָלָתְנִי וְחֶרְפּוֹת חוֹרְפֶיךָ נָפְלוּ עָלָי: וָאֶבְכֶּה בַצּוֹם נַפְשִׁי וַתְּהִי
לַחֲרָפוֹת לִי: וָאֶתְּנָה לְבוּשִׁי שָׂק וָאֱהִי לָהֶם לְמָשָׁל: יָשִׂיחוּ בִי יֹשְׁבֵי שָׁעַר
וּנְגִינוֹת שׁוֹתֵי שֵׁכָר: וַאֲנִי תְפִלָּתִי־לְךָ ׀ יהוה עֵת רָצוֹן אֱלֹהִים בְּרָב־חַסְדֶּךָ
עֲנֵנִי בֶּאֱמֶת יִשְׁעֶךָ: הַצִּילֵנִי מִטִּיט וְאַל־אֶטְבָּעָה אִנָּצְלָה מִשֹּׂנְאַי
וּמִמַּעֲמַקֵּי־מָיִם: אַל־תִּשְׁטְפֵנִי ׀ שִׁבֹּלֶת מַיִם וְאַל־תִּבְלָעֵנִי מְצוּלָה וְאַל־
תֶּאְטַר־עָלַי בְּאֵר פִּיהָ: עֲנֵנִי יהוה כִּי־טוֹב חַסְדֶּךָ כְּרֹב רַחֲמֶיךָ פְּנֵה אֵלָי:
וְאַל־תַּסְתֵּר פָּנֶיךָ מֵעַבְדֶּךָ כִּי־צַר־לִי מַהֵר עֲנֵנִי: קָרְבָה אֶל־נַפְשִׁי גְאָלָהּ
לְמַעַן אֹיְבַי פְּדֵנִי: אַתָּה יָדַעְתָּ חֶרְפָּתִי וּבָשְׁתִּי וּכְלִמָּתִי נֶגְדְּךָ כָּל־צוֹרְרָי:
חֶרְפָּה ׀ שָׁבְרָה לִבִּי וָאָנוּשָׁה וָאֲקַוֶּה לָנוּד וָאַיִן וְלַמְנַחֲמִים וְלֹא מָצָאתִי:
וַיִּתְּנוּ בְּבָרוּתִי רֹאשׁ וְלִצְמָאִי יַשְׁקוּנִי חֹמֶץ: יְהִי־שֻׁלְחָנָם לִפְנֵיהֶם לְפָח
וְלִשְׁלוֹמִים לְמוֹקֵשׁ: תֶּחְשַׁכְנָה עֵינֵיהֶם מֵרְאוֹת וּמָתְנֵיהֶם תָּמִיד הַמְעַד:
שְׁפָךְ־עֲלֵיהֶם זַעְמֶךָ וַחֲרוֹן אַפְּךָ יַשִּׂיגֵם: תְּהִי־טִירָתָם נְשַׁמָּה בְּאָהֳלֵיהֶם
אַל־יְהִי יֹשֵׁב: כִּי־אַתָּה אֲשֶׁר־הִכִּיתָ רָדָפוּ וְאֶל־מַכְאוֹב חֲלָלֶיךָ יְסַפֵּרוּ:
תְּנָה־עָוֺן עַל־עֲוֺנָם וְאַל־יָבֹאוּ בְּצִדְקָתֶךָ: יִמָּחוּ מִסֵּפֶר חַיִּים וְעִם צַדִּיקִים
אַל־יִכָּתֵבוּ: וַאֲנִי עָנִי וְכוֹאֵב יְשׁוּעָתְךָ אֱלֹהִים תְּשַׂגְּבֵנִי: אֲהַלְלָה שֵׁם־
אֱלֹהִים בְּשִׁיר וַאֲגַדְּלֶנּוּ בְתוֹדָה: וְתִיטַב לַיהוה מִשּׁוֹר פָּר מַקְרִן מַפְרִיס:

*יג לחודש

you kingdoms of the earth. Sing praises to the Lord. Selah. To Him Who rides upon the heavens of heavens of old. Behold, He sends forth His voice, a mighty voice. Give God a melody. His majesty is over Israel, and His strength is in the skies. O God, You are awesome from Your Temple. The God of Israel, He gives strength and might to the people. Blessed be God.

*69 TO THE DIRECTOR of music, *al-shoshanim*. Of David. Save me, O God, for the waters have come to my neck. I have sunk into deep mire, where there is no standing. I have come into deep waters, and the flood overwhelms me. I am weary with my crying out, my throat is dry, my eyes fail while I wait for my God. Those who hate me for no reason are more numerous than the hairs of my head. Those who would destroy me are many, who are wrongfully my enemies. What I did not steal, I must then restore. O God, You know my folly, and my sins are not hidden from You. Let those who trust in You, Lord God of hosts, not be ashamed for my sake. Let those who seek You, O God of Israel, not be humiliated for my sake, For on Your account I have borne taunting, humiliation has covered my face. I have become a stranger to my brothers, and an alien to my mother's sons, Because the zeal for Your house has consumed me, and the taunts of those who taunt You have fallen upon me. And I weep with fasting over my soul, and that becomes a taunt for me. And I make sackcloth my garment, and I have become a proverb to them. Those who sit at the gate talk of me, and I am the song of those who drink wine. But I pray to You, O Lord, for a time of favor. O God, in the greatness of Your loving-kindness, answer me, in the truth of Your salvation. Deliver me from the mire, and do not let me sink. Let me be delivered from those who hate me, and from the deep waters. Let floodwaters not overwhelm me, and let deep waters not swallow me up, and let the pit not close its mouth upon me. Answer me, O Lord, for Your loving-kindness is good. Turn toward me in accordance with Your abundant mercy. And do not hide Your face from Your servant. Since I am in distress, answer me speedily. Draw near to my soul and redeem it. Because of my enemies, ransom me. You know my taunting, and my shame, and my humiliation. All of my adversaries are before You. Insult has broken my heart, and I have fallen sick. I hoped for someone to console me, but there was none, and for comforters, but I found none. But they put poison in my food, and for my thirst they gave me vinegar to drink. Let their table be a snare before them, and let the table set up for peace be a trap. Let their eyes be darkened, so that they cannot see, and make their loins constantly tremble. Pour out Your wrath upon them, and let Your burning anger overtake them. Let their encampment be desolate. Let none dwell in their tents. For they pursue those whom You have smitten, and they tell of the pain of those whom You have wounded. Add iniquity to their iniquity, and let them not be admitted to Your vindication. Let them be erased from the book of the living, and let them not be written with the righteous. But I am afflicted and in pain. Your salvation, O God, will protect me. I will praise the name of God with song, and I will magnify Him with thanksgiving. And it will please the Lord more than an ox and a bull that has horns

*13th DAY of the month

רָאוּ עֲנָוִים יִשְׂמָחוּ דֹּרְשֵׁי אֱלֹהִים וִיחִי לְבַבְכֶם׃ כִּי־שֹׁמֵעַ אֶל־אֶבְיוֹנִים
יְהוָה וְאֶת־אֲסִירָיו לֹא בָזָה׃ יְהַלְלוּהוּ שָׁמַיִם וָאָרֶץ יַמִּים וְכָל־רֹמֵשׂ בָּם׃
כִּי אֱלֹהִים ׀ יוֹשִׁיעַ צִיּוֹן וְיִבְנֶה עָרֵי יְהוּדָה וְיָשְׁבוּ שָׁם וִירֵשׁוּהָ׃ וְזֶרַע
עֲבָדָיו יִנְחָלוּהָ וְאֹהֲבֵי שְׁמוֹ יִשְׁכְּנוּ־בָהּ׃

ע לַמְנַצֵּחַ לְדָוִד לְהַזְכִּיר׃ אֱלֹהִים לְהַצִּילֵנִי יְהוָה לְעֶזְרָתִי חוּשָׁה׃ יֵבֹשׁוּ
וְיַחְפְּרוּ מְבַקְשֵׁי נַפְשִׁי יִסֹּגוּ אָחוֹר וְיִכָּלְמוּ חֲפֵצֵי רָעָתִי׃ יָשׁוּבוּ עַל־עֵקֶב
בָּשְׁתָּם הָאֹמְרִים הֶאָח ׀ הֶאָח׃ יָשִׂישׂוּ וְיִשְׂמְחוּ ׀ בְּךָ כָּל־מְבַקְשֶׁיךָ וְיֹאמְרוּ
תָמִיד יִגְדַּל אֱלֹהִים אֹהֲבֵי יְשׁוּעָתֶךָ׃ וַאֲנִי ׀ עָנִי וְאֶבְיוֹן אֱלֹהִים חוּשָׁה לִּי
עֶזְרִי וּמְפַלְטִי אַתָּה יְהוָה אַל־תְּאַחַר׃

עא בְּךָ־יְהוָה חָסִיתִי אַל־אֵבוֹשָׁה לְעוֹלָם׃ בְּצִדְקָתְךָ תַּצִּילֵנִי וּתְפַלְּטֵנִי הַטֵּה־
אֵלַי אָזְנְךָ וְהוֹשִׁיעֵנִי׃ הֱיֵה לִי ׀ לְצוּר מָעוֹן לָבוֹא תָּמִיד צִוִּיתָ לְהוֹשִׁיעֵנִי
כִּי־סַלְעִי וּמְצוּדָתִי אָתָּה׃ אֱלֹהַי פַּלְּטֵנִי מִיַּד רָשָׁע מִכַּף מְעַוֵּל וְחוֹמֵץ׃
כִּי־אַתָּה תִקְוָתִי אֲדֹנָי יֱהוִה מִבְטַחִי מִנְּעוּרָי׃ עָלֶיךָ ׀ נִסְמַכְתִּי מִבֶּטֶן
מִמְּעֵי אִמִּי אַתָּה גוֹזִי בְּךָ תְהִלָּתִי תָמִיד׃ כְּמוֹפֵת הָיִיתִי לְרַבִּים וְאַתָּה
מַחֲסִי־עֹז׃ יִמָּלֵא פִי תְּהִלָּתֶךָ כָּל־הַיּוֹם תִּפְאַרְתֶּךָ׃ אַל־תַּשְׁלִיכֵנִי לְעֵת
זִקְנָה כִּכְלוֹת כֹּחִי אַל־תַּעַזְבֵנִי׃ כִּי־אָמְרוּ אוֹיְבַי לִי וְשֹׁמְרֵי נַפְשִׁי נוֹעֲצוּ
יַחְדָּו׃ לֵאמֹר אֱלֹהִים עֲזָבוֹ רִדְפוּ וְתִפְשׂוּהוּ כִּי־אֵין מַצִּיל׃ אֱלֹהִים אַל־
תִּרְחַק מִמֶּנִּי אֱלֹהַי לְעֶזְרָתִי חישה׃ יֵבֹשׁוּ יִכְלוּ שֹׂטְנֵי נַפְשִׁי יַעֲטוּ חֶרְפָּה חוּשָׁה
וּכְלִמָּה מְבַקְשֵׁי רָעָתִי׃ וַאֲנִי תָּמִיד אֲיַחֵל וְהוֹסַפְתִּי עַל־כָּל־תְּהִלָּתֶךָ׃ פִּי ׀
יְסַפֵּר צִדְקָתֶךָ כָּל־הַיּוֹם תְּשׁוּעָתֶךָ כִּי לֹא יָדַעְתִּי סְפֹרוֹת׃ אָבוֹא בִּגְבֻרוֹת
אֲדֹנָי יֱהוִה אַזְכִּיר צִדְקָתְךָ לְבַדֶּךָ׃ אֱלֹהִים לִמַּדְתַּנִי מִנְּעוּרָי וְעַד־הֵנָּה
אַגִּיד נִפְלְאוֹתֶיךָ׃ וְגַם עַד־זִקְנָה ׀ וְשֵׂיבָה אֱלֹהִים אַל־תַּעַזְבֵנִי עַד־אַגִּיד
זְרוֹעֲךָ לְדוֹר לְכָל־יָבוֹא גְּבוּרָתֶךָ׃ וְצִדְקָתְךָ אֱלֹהִים עַד־מָרוֹם אֲשֶׁר־עָשִׂיתָ
גְדֹלוֹת אֱלֹהִים מִי כָמוֹךָ׃ אֲשֶׁר הראיתנו ׀ צָרוֹת רַבּוֹת וְרָעוֹת תָּשׁוּב הִרְאִיתַנִי
תחיינו וּמִתְּהֹמוֹת הָאָרֶץ תָּשׁוּב תעלנו׃ תֶּרֶב ׀ גְּדֻלָּתִי וְתִסֹּב תְּנַחֲמֵנִי׃ תְּחַיֵּנִי תַּעֲלֵנִי
גַּם־אֲנִי ׀ אוֹדְךָ בִכְלִי־נֶבֶל אֲמִתְּךָ אֱלֹהָי אֲזַמְּרָה לְךָ בְכִנּוֹר קְדוֹשׁ יִשְׂרָאֵל׃
תְּרַנֵּנָּה שְׂפָתַי כִּי אֲזַמְּרָה־לָּךְ וְנַפְשִׁי אֲשֶׁר פָּדִיתָ׃ גַּם־לְשׁוֹנִי כָּל־הַיּוֹם
תֶּהְגֶּה צִדְקָתֶךָ כִּי־בֹשׁוּ כִּי־חָפְרוּ מְבַקְשֵׁי רָעָתִי׃

and hooves. The humble have seen and they will rejoice. You who seek God, let your
heart revive. For the Lord hearkens to the poor, and He does not despise His afflicted.
The heavens and the earth will praise Him, the seas, and everything that moves in
them. For God will deliver Zion, and He will build the cities of Judah. And they will
dwell there, and they will possess it. And the seed of His servants will inherit it, and
those who love His name will dwell in it.

70 TO THE DIRECTOR of music, of David, for remembrance. O God, hasten to deliver
me. O Lord, hasten to help me. Let those who seek my soul be disappointed and
confounded. Let those who desire my harm and be turned backward and put to
confusion. Let those who say, Aha, aha, go back on the heel of their shame. Let all
those who seek You rejoice and be glad in You, and let those who love Your salvation
always say, Let God be magnified. But I am poor and needy. O God, hasten to me.
You are my help and my rescuer. O Lord, do not delay.

71 IN YOU, O Lord, do I trust. May I never be disappointed. Deliver me and rescue me
in Your righteousness. Incline Your ear to me and save me. Be a strong habitation
for me that I may enter. You have always commanded that I be saved, for You are my
rock and my fortress. O my God, rescue me from the hand of the wicked, from the
hand of the evildoer and the robber. For You are my hope. The Lord God has been
my trust from my youth. I have leaned upon you from the womb. You brought me
out of my mother's bowels. My praise is always of You. I have been as an example to
many, and You have been my strong refuge. Let my mouth be filled with Your praise
and with Your glory all the day. Do not cast me off in time of old age. Do not forsake
me when my strength fails. For my enemies have spoken about me, and those who
watch for my soul have taken counsel together, Saying, God has forsaken him. Pursue
and catch him, for there is none to deliver him. O God, be not far from me. My God,
hasten to help me. Let those who hate my soul be disappointed and consumed. Let
those who seek my harm be covered with reproach and humiliation. But I will always
hope, and I will add to all Your praise. My mouth will tell of Your righteousness and
of Your salvation all the day, for I do not know how to count them. I will come with
the mighty deeds of the Lord God. I will make mention of Your righteousness, Yours
alone. O God, You have taught me from my youth, and until now I declare Your
wondrous deeds. And also until ripe old age, O God, do not forsake me, until I had
declared Your strength to the coming generation, and Your power to all who are to
come, And Your righteousness, O God, reaches the high heavens. O God, You Who
have done great things, who is like You? You Who have shown me many grievous
troubles, You returned and restored me to life, and You returned and brought me up
from the depths of the earth. You increased my greatness, and You turned to comfort
me. I too will thank You with the harp for Your loyalty, O my God. I will play for You
on the lyre, O holy One of Israel. My lips will sing when I play for You, and my soul
that You have redeemed. My tongue shall also tell of Your righteousness all the day,
for those who seek my harm are disappointed and confounded.

*עב לִשְׁלֹמֹה ׀ אֱלֹהִים מִשְׁפָּטֶיךָ לְמֶלֶךְ תֵּן וְצִדְקָתְךָ לְבֶן־מֶלֶךְ: יָדִין עַמְּךָ
בְצֶדֶק וַעֲנִיֶּיךָ בְמִשְׁפָּט: יִשְׂאוּ הָרִים שָׁלוֹם לָעָם וּגְבָעוֹת בִּצְדָקָה: יִשְׁפֹּט ׀
עֲנִיֵּי־עָם יוֹשִׁיעַ לִבְנֵי אֶבְיוֹן וִידַכֵּא עוֹשֵׁק: יִירָאוּךָ עִם־שָׁמֶשׁ וְלִפְנֵי יָרֵחַ
דּוֹר דּוֹרִים: יֵרֵד כְּמָטָר עַל־גֵּז כִּרְבִיבִים זַרְזִיף אָרֶץ: יִפְרַח־בְּיָמָיו צַדִּיק
וְרֹב שָׁלוֹם עַד־בְּלִי יָרֵחַ: וְיֵרְדְּ מִיָּם עַד־יָם וּמִנָּהָר עַד־אַפְסֵי־אָרֶץ: לְפָנָיו
יִכְרְעוּ צִיִּים וְאֹיְבָיו עָפָר יְלַחֵכוּ: מַלְכֵי תַרְשִׁישׁ וְאִיִּים מִנְחָה יָשִׁיבוּ מַלְכֵי
שְׁבָא וּסְבָא אֶשְׁכָּר יַקְרִיבוּ: וְיִשְׁתַּחֲווּ־לוֹ כָל־מְלָכִים כָּל־גּוֹיִם יַעַבְדוּהוּ:
כִּי־יַצִּיל אֶבְיוֹן מְשַׁוֵּעַ וְעָנִי וְאֵין־עֹזֵר לוֹ: יָחֹס עַל־דַּל וְאֶבְיוֹן וְנַפְשׁוֹת
אֶבְיוֹנִים יוֹשִׁיעַ: מִתּוֹךְ וּמֵחָמָס יִגְאַל נַפְשָׁם וְיֵיקַר דָּמָם בְּעֵינָיו: וִיחִי
וְיִתֶּן־לוֹ מִזְּהַב שְׁבָא וְיִתְפַּלֵּל בַּעֲדוֹ תָמִיד כָּל־הַיּוֹם יְבָרֲכֶנְהוּ: יְהִי פִסַּת־
בַּר ׀ בָּאָרֶץ בְּרֹאשׁ הָרִים יִרְעַשׁ כַּלְּבָנוֹן פִּרְיוֹ וְיָצִיצוּ מֵעִיר כְּעֵשֶׂב הָאָרֶץ:
ינּוֹן יְהִי שְׁמוֹ ׀ לְעוֹלָם לִפְנֵי־שֶׁמֶשׁ ינין שְׁמוֹ וְיִתְבָּרְכוּ בוֹ כָּל־גּוֹיִם יְאַשְּׁרוּהוּ:
בָּרוּךְ ׀ יהוה אֱלֹהִים אֱלֹהֵי יִשְׂרָאֵל עֹשֵׂה נִפְלָאוֹת לְבַדּוֹ: וּבָרוּךְ ׀ שֵׁם
כְּבוֹדוֹ לְעוֹלָם וְיִמָּלֵא כְבוֹדוֹ אֶת־כֹּל הָאָרֶץ אָמֵן ׀ וְאָמֵן: כָּלּוּ תְפִלּוֹת
דָּוִד בֶּן־יִשָׁי:

ספר שלישי

**עג מִזְמוֹר לְאָסָף אַךְ טוֹב לְיִשְׂרָאֵל אֱלֹהִים לְבָרֵי לֵבָב: וַאֲנִי כִּמְעַט נטוי
נָטָיו
שֻׁפְּכוּ רַגְלָי כְּאַיִן שפכה אֲשֻׁרָי: כִּי־קִנֵּאתִי בַּהוֹלְלִים שְׁלוֹם רְשָׁעִים אֶרְאֶה:
כִּי אֵין חַרְצֻבּוֹת לְמוֹתָם וּבָרִיא אוּלָם: בַּעֲמַל אֱנוֹשׁ אֵינֵמוֹ וְעִם־אָדָם
לֹא יְנֻגָּעוּ: לָכֵן עֲנָקַתְמוֹ גַאֲוָה יַעֲטָף־שִׁית חָמָס לָמוֹ: יָצָא מֵחֵלֶב עֵינֵמוֹ
עָבְרוּ מַשְׂכִּיּוֹת לֵבָב: יָמִיקוּ ׀ וִידַבְּרוּ בְרָע עֹשֶׁק מִמָּרוֹם יְדַבֵּרוּ: שַׁתּוּ
יָשׁוּב בַשָּׁמַיִם פִּיהֶם וּלְשׁוֹנָם תִּהֲלַךְ בָּאָרֶץ: לָכֵן ׀ ישיב עַמּוֹ הֲלֹם וּמֵי מָלֵא
יִמָּצוּ לָמוֹ: וְאָמְרוּ אֵיכָה יָדַע־אֵל וְיֵשׁ דֵּעָה בְעֶלְיוֹן: הִנֵּה־אֵלֶּה רְשָׁעִים
וְשַׁלְוֵי עוֹלָם הִשְׂגּוּ־חָיִל: אַךְ־רִיק זִכִּיתִי לְבָבִי וָאֶרְחַץ בְּנִקָּיוֹן כַּפָּי: וָאֱהִי
נָגוּעַ כָּל־הַיּוֹם וְתוֹכַחְתִּי לַבְּקָרִים: אִם־אָמַרְתִּי אֲסַפְּרָה כְמוֹ הִנֵּה דוֹר
הוּא בָּנֶיךָ בָגָדְתִּי: וָאֲחַשְּׁבָה לָדַעַת זֹאת עָמָל היא בְעֵינָי: עַד־אָבוֹא אֶל־
מִקְדְּשֵׁי־אֵל אָבִינָה לְאַחֲרִיתָם: אַךְ בַּחֲלָקוֹת תָּשִׁית לָמוֹ הִפַּלְתָּם
לְמַשּׁוּאוֹת: אֵיךְ הָיוּ לְשַׁמָּה כְרָגַע סָפוּ תַמּוּ מִן־בַּלָּהוֹת: כַּחֲלוֹם מֵהָקִיץ

*יד לחודש **ליום הרביעי

*72 FOR SOLOMON. O God, give the king Your judgments, and Your righteousness to the son of the king. May he judge Your people with righteousness, and Your poor with justice. May the mountains raise up peace to the people, and the hills with righteousness. May he judge the poor of the people. May he save the needy and break the oppressor. May they fear You with the sun, and before the moon throughout the generations. May it come down like rain upon the grass, like showers that water the earth. May the righteous flourish in his days, and may there be an abundance of peace until the moon is no more. And may he rule from sea to sea, and from the river to the ends of the earth. May the desert dwellers bow down before him, and may his enemies lick the dust. May the kings of Tarshish and of the islands bring presents. May the kings of Sheba and Seba offer gifts. And may all kings bow down before him. May all nations serve him. For he saves the needy who cries, and the poor who has no helper. He protects the poor and needy, and saves the souls of the needy. He redeems their lives from deceit and violence, and precious is their blood in his eyes. And so that he may live, he gives him of the gold of Sheba, and he will always pray for him, all the day he will bless him. May there be an abundance of corn in the land and on the tops of the mountains. May his fruit trees rustle like Lebanon, and may they flourish in the city like the grass of the earth. May his name endure forever. May his name continue as long as the sun, and may all nations bless themselves by him and praise him. Blessed is the Lord God, the God of Israel, Who does wondrous things alone. And blessed is His glorious name forever, and may the whole earth be filled with His glory. Amen and Amen. The prayers of David the son of Jesse are ended.

BOOK THREE

**73 A PSALM of Asaph. Indeed, the Lord is good to Israel, to those of a pure heart. But as for me, my feet almost failed, my steps nearly collapsed. For I was envious of the arrogant, I saw the prosperity of the wicked, That there are no chains to their death, and their belly is fat. They have no share in the trouble of men, and they are not plagued like other men. Therefore pride is their necklace, their arrogance covers their buttocks. Their eyes stand out because of their fat, it flows out of the chambers of their hearts. They deride, and they wickedly speak oppression, they speak haughtily. They set their mouth in the heavens, and their tongue struts across the earth. Therefore His people return here, and abundant waters flow for them. And they say, How does God know, and is there knowledge in the Most High? Behold, these are the wicked, and forever at ease they increase in strength. Surely in vain have I cleansed my heart, and washed my hands so that they will be clean. For all the day I have been stricken, and my chastisement is renewed in the mornings. If I had said, I will speak thus, I would surely have betrayed a generation of Your children. So I pondered in order to understand this. It was toil in my eyes. Until I came to the sanctuaries of God, then I understood their end. Indeed, You benefit them with guile. You cast them down into destruction. How they are brought into desolation in a moment! They are utterly

---

*14th DAY of the month **WEDNESDAY

אֲדֹנָ֗י בָּעִ֤יר ׀ צַלְמָ֬ם תִּבְזֶֽה׃ כִּ֭י יִתְחַמֵּ֣ץ לְבָבִ֑י וְ֝כִלְיוֹתַ֗י אֶשְׁתּוֹנָֽן׃ וַאֲנִי־בַ֭עַר
וְלֹ֣א אֵדָ֑ע בְּ֝הֵמ֗וֹת הָיִ֥יתִי עִמָּֽךְ׃ וַאֲנִ֣י תָמִ֣יד עִמָּ֑ךְ אָ֝חַ֗זְתָּ בְּיַד־יְמִינִֽי׃
בַּעֲצָתְךָ֥ תַנְחֵ֑נִי וְ֝אַחַ֗ר כָּב֥וֹד תִּקָּחֵֽנִי׃ מִי־לִ֥י בַשָּׁמָ֑יִם וְ֝עִמְּךָ֗ לֹא־חָפַ֥צְתִּי
בָאָֽרֶץ׃ כָּלָ֣ה שְׁאֵרִי֮ וּלְבָבִ֪י צוּר־לְבָבִ֥י וְחֶלְקִ֗י אֱלֹהִ֥ים לְעוֹלָֽם׃ כִּֽי־הִנֵּ֣ה
רְחֵקֶ֣יךָ יֹאבֵ֑דוּ הִ֝צְמַ֗תָּה כָּל־זוֹנֶ֥ה מִמֶּֽךָּ׃ וַאֲנִ֤י ׀ קִֽרֲבַ֥ת אֱלֹהִ֗ים לִ֫י ט֥וֹב
שַׁ֤תִּי ׀ בַּאדֹנָ֣י יֱהֹוִ֣ה מַחְסִ֑י לְ֝סַפֵּ֗ר כָּל־מַלְאֲכוֹתֶֽיךָ׃

עד מַשְׂכִּ֗יל לְאָ֫סָ֥ף לָמָ֣ה אֱ֭לֹהִים זָנַ֣חְתָּ לָנֶ֑צַח יֶעְשַׁ֥ן אַ֝פְּךָ֗ בְּצֹ֣אן מַרְעִיתֶֽךָ׃
זְכֹ֤ר עֲדָתְךָ֨ ׀ קָנִ֬יתָ קֶּ֗דֶם גָּאַ֣לְתָּ שֵׁ֣בֶט נַחֲלָתֶ֑ךָ הַר־צִ֝יּ֗וֹן זֶ֤ה ׀ שָׁ֘כַ֥נְתָּ בּֽוֹ׃
הָרִ֣ימָה פְ֭עָמֶיךָ לְמַשֻּׁא֣וֹת נֶ֑צַח כָּל־הֵרַ֖ע אוֹיֵ֣ב בַּקֹּֽדֶשׁ׃ שָׁאֲג֣וּ צֹ֭רְרֶיךָ
בְּקֶ֣רֶב מוֹעֲדֶ֑ךָ שָׂ֖מוּ אוֹתֹתָ֣ם אֹתֽוֹת׃ יִ֭וָּדַע כְּמֵבִ֣יא לְמָ֑עְלָה בִּֽסֲבָךְ־עֵ֝֗ץ
קַרְדֻּמּֽוֹת׃ וְעַתָּ֗ה פִּתּוּחֶ֥יהָ יָּ֑חַד בְּכַשִּׁ֥יל וְ֝כֵילַפֹּ֗ת יַהֲלֹמֽוּן׃ שִׁלְח֣וּ בָ֭אֵשׁ
מִקְדָּשֶׁ֑ךָ לָ֝אָ֗רֶץ חִלְּל֥וּ מִשְׁכַּן־שְׁמֶֽךָ׃ אָמְר֣וּ בְ֭לִבָּם נִינָ֣ם יָ֑חַד שָׂרְפ֖וּ כָל־
מוֹעֲדֵי־אֵ֣ל בָּאָֽרֶץ׃ אוֹתֹתֵ֗ינוּ לֹ֥א רָאִ֗ינוּ אֵֽין־ע֥וֹד נָבִ֑יא וְלֹֽא־אִ֝תָּ֗נוּ יֹדֵ֥עַ
עַד־מָֽה׃ עַד־מָתַ֣י אֱ֭לֹהִים יְחָ֣רֶף צָ֑ר יְנָאֵ֖ץ אוֹיֵ֖ב שִׁמְךָ֣ לָנֶֽצַח׃ לָ֤מָּה תָשִׁ֣יב
חֵיקְךָ יָ֭דְךָ וִֽימִינֶ֑ךָ מִקֶּ֖רֶב חוקךָ כַלֵּֽה׃ וֵֽאלֹהִ֗ים מַלְכִּ֥י מִקֶּ֑דֶם פֹּעֵ֥ל יְ֝שׁוּע֗וֹת
בְּקֶ֣רֶב הָאָֽרֶץ׃ אַתָּ֤ה פוֹרַ֣רְתָּ בְעָזְּךָ֣ יָ֑ם שִׁבַּ֖רְתָּ רָאשֵׁ֥י תַ֝נִּינִ֗ים עַל־הַמָּֽיִם׃
אַתָּ֣ה רִ֭צַּצְתָּ רָאשֵׁ֣י לִוְיָתָ֑ן תִּ֝תְּנֶ֗נּוּ מַ֝אֲכָ֗ל לְעָ֣ם לְצִיִּֽים׃ אַתָּ֣ה בָ֭קַעְתָּ מַעְיָ֣ן
וָנָ֑חַל אַתָּ֥ה ה֝וֹבַ֗שְׁתָּ נַהֲר֥וֹת אֵיתָֽן׃ לְךָ֣ י֭וֹם אַף־לְךָ֣ לָ֑יְלָה אַתָּ֥ה הֲ֝כִינ֗וֹתָ
מָא֥וֹר וָשָֽׁמֶשׁ׃ אַתָּ֣ה הִ֭צַּבְתָּ כָּל־גְּבוּל֣וֹת אָ֑רֶץ קַ֥יִץ וָ֝חֹ֗רֶף אַתָּ֥ה יְצַרְתָּֽם׃
זְכָר־זֹ֗את אוֹיֵ֣ב חֵרֵ֣ף ׀ יְהֹוָ֑ה וְעַ֥ם נָ֝בָ֗ל נִֽאֲצ֥וּ שְׁמֶֽךָ׃ אַל־תִּתֵּ֣ן לְ֭חַיַּת נֶ֣פֶשׁ
תּוֹרֶ֑ךָ חַיַּ֥ת עֲ֝נִיֶּ֗יךָ אַל־תִּשְׁכַּ֥ח לָנֶֽצַח׃ הַבֵּ֥ט לַבְּרִ֑ית כִּ֥י מָלְא֥וּ מַחֲשַׁכֵּי־אֶ֝֗רֶץ
נְא֣וֹת חָמָֽס׃ אַל־יָשֹׁ֣ב דַּ֣ךְ נִכְלָ֑ם עָנִ֥י וְ֝אֶבְי֗וֹן יְהַֽלְל֥וּ שְׁמֶֽךָ׃ קוּמָ֣ה אֱ֭לֹהִים
רִיבָ֣ה רִיבֶ֑ךָ זְכֹ֥ר חֶרְפָּתְךָ֥ מִנִּי־נָ֝בָ֗ל כָּל־הַיּֽוֹם׃ אַל־תִּשְׁכַּ֗ח ק֥וֹל צֹרְרֶ֑יךָ
שְׁא֥וֹן קָ֝מֶ֗יךָ עֹלֶ֥ה תָמִֽיד׃

עה לַמְנַצֵּ֥חַ אַל־תַּשְׁחֵ֑ת מִזְמ֖וֹר לְאָסָ֣ף שִֽׁיר׃ הוֹדִ֤ינוּ לְּךָ֨ ׀ אֱֽלֹהִ֗ים ה֭וֹדִינוּ
וְקָר֣וֹב שְׁמֶ֑ךָ סִ֝פְּר֗וּ נִפְלְאוֹתֶֽיךָ׃ כִּ֭י אֶקַּ֣ח מוֹעֵ֑ד אֲ֝נִ֗י מֵישָׁרִ֥ים אֶשְׁפֹּֽט׃
נְמֹגִ֣ים אֶ֭רֶץ וְכָל־יֹשְׁבֶ֑יהָ אָ֝נֹכִ֗י תִכַּ֥נְתִּי עַמּוּדֶ֗יהָ סֶּֽלָה׃ אָמַ֣רְתִּי לַ֭הוֹלְלִים
אַל־תָּהֹ֑לּוּ וְ֝לָרְשָׁעִ֗ים אַל־תָּרִ֥ימוּ קָֽרֶן׃ אַל־תָּרִ֣ימוּ לַמָּר֣וֹם קַרְנְכֶ֑ם תְּדַבְּר֖וּ

consumed with terrors. As a dream when one awakes, O Lord, in wakefulness You despise their image. Indeed, my heart was embittered, and I was pricked in my kidneys. And I was a fool who does not understand, I was like a beast before You. But I was always with You, You held my right hand. You guided me with Your counsel, and You led me after Your glory. Whom have I in heaven? And besides You there is nothing upon earth that I desire. My flesh and my heart fail. God is the rock of my heart and my portion forever. Indeed, behold, those who are far from You perish. You destroy all those who stray from You. But as for me, the nearness of God is good for me. I have placed my trust in God the Lord, that I may relate all Your works.

74 A *MASKIL* of Asaph. Why, O God, have You cast us off forever? Why does Your anger
smoke against the sheep of Your pasture? Remember Your congregation whom You
acquired of old, the tribe of Your inheritance whom You have redeemed, Mount
Zion in which You have dwelled. Lift up Your feet to the perpetual desolations. The
enemy has destroyed everything in the sanctuary! Your enemies roared in the midst
of Your meeting place. They set up their signs for signs. Let it be known how they
swung their axes upward in a thicket of trees. And behold, they broke down all her
gates with hatchet and hammers. They burned Your sanctuary with fire. They defiled
the dwelling place of Your name to the ground. They said in their heart, We will
destroy them all. They burned all the meeting places of God in the land. We do not
see our signs, there is no longer a prophet, nor is there among us one who knows
anything. How long, O God, will the adversary insult, will the enemy blaspheme
Your name forever? Why do You withdraw Your right hand? Send it forth from Your
bosom! But You, O God, were my king of old, Who performed acts of salvation in
the midst of the earth. You tore the sea with Your strength. You broke the heads of
the sea monsters in the waters. You crushed the heads of Leviathan. You gave him
for food to the community of the creatures of the sea. You split open springs and
streams. You dried up mighty rivers. The day is Yours, the night also is Yours. You
established the light and the sun. You set all the borders of the earth. You made
summer and winter. Remember this, O Lord, when the enemy insults, that a base
people have blasphemed Your name. Do not deliver the life of Your turtledove to the
wild beast. Do not forget the life of Your poor forever. Look upon your covenant, for
the dark places of the earth are filled with habitations of violence. Let the oppressed
not return disappointed. The poor and the needy will praise Your name. Arise, O
God, plead Your cause. Remember how the base have insulted You all the day. Do
not forget the voice of Your enemies, the tumult of those who rise up against You
which continually increases.

75 TO THE DIRECTOR of the music, *al-tashḥet*. A psalm of Asaph. A song. We give thanks
to You, O God. We give thanks, for Your name is near. Men tell of Your wondrous
works. Indeed, I will set a time, I will judge uprightly. The earth and all its inhabitants
melt away. I established its pillars. Selah. I say to the arrogant: Do not act arrogantly,
and to the wicked: Do not lift up the horn. Do not lift your horn on high, do not speak

בְּצַוָּאר עָתָק: כִּי לֹא מִמּוֹצָא וּמִמַּעֲרָב וְלֹא מִמִּדְבַּר הָרִים: כִּי־אֱלֹהִים
שֹׁפֵט זֶה יַשְׁפִּיל וְזֶה יָרִים: כִּי כוֹס בְּיַד־יהוה וְיַיִן חָמַר ׀ מָלֵא מֶסֶךְ וַיַּגֵּר
מִזֶּה אַךְ־שְׁמָרֶיהָ יִמְצוּ יִשְׁתּוּ כֹּל רִשְׁעֵי־אָרֶץ: וַאֲנִי אַגִּיד לְעֹלָם אֲזַמְּרָה
לֵאלֹהֵי יַעֲקֹב: וְכָל־קַרְנֵי רְשָׁעִים אֲגַדֵּעַ תְּרוֹמַמְנָה קַרְנוֹת צַדִּיק:

עו לַמְנַצֵּחַ בִּנְגִינֹת מִזְמוֹר לְאָסָף שִׁיר: נוֹדָע בִּיהוּדָה אֱלֹהִים בְּיִשְׂרָאֵל
גָּדוֹל שְׁמוֹ: וַיְהִי בְשָׁלֵם סֻכּוֹ וּמְעוֹנָתוֹ בְצִיּוֹן: שָׁמָּה שִׁבַּר רִשְׁפֵי־קָשֶׁת
מָגֵן וְחֶרֶב וּמִלְחָמָה סֶלָה: נָאוֹר אַתָּה אַדִּיר מֵהַרְרֵי־טָרֶף: אֶשְׁתּוֹלְלוּ ׀
אַבִּירֵי לֵב נָמוּ שְׁנָתָם וְלֹא־מָצְאוּ כָל־אַנְשֵׁי־חַיִל יְדֵיהֶם: מִגַּעֲרָתְךָ אֱלֹהֵי
יַעֲקֹב נִרְדָּם וְרֶכֶב וָסוּס: אַתָּה ׀ נוֹרָא אַתָּה וּמִי־יַעֲמֹד לְפָנֶיךָ מֵאָז אַפֶּךָ:
מִשָּׁמַיִם הִשְׁמַעְתָּ דִּין אֶרֶץ יָרְאָה וְשָׁקָטָה: בְּקוּם־לַמִּשְׁפָּט אֱלֹהִים
לְהוֹשִׁיעַ כָּל־עַנְוֵי־אֶרֶץ סֶלָה: כִּי־חֲמַת אָדָם תּוֹדֶךָּ שְׁאֵרִית חֵמֹת תַּחְגֹּר:
נִדְרוּ וְשַׁלְּמוּ לַיהוה אֱלֹהֵיכֶם כָּל־סְבִיבָיו יוֹבִילוּ שַׁי לַמּוֹרָא: יִבְצֹר רוּחַ
נְגִידִים נוֹרָא לְמַלְכֵי־אָרֶץ:

*עז יְדוּתוּן לַמְנַצֵּחַ עַל־ידיתון לְאָסָף מִזְמוֹר: קוֹלִי אֶל־אֱלֹהִים וְאֶצְעָקָה קוֹלִי
אֶל־אֱלֹהִים וְהַאֲזִין אֵלָי: בְּיוֹם צָרָתִי אֲדֹנָי דָּרָשְׁתִּי יָדִי ׀ לַיְלָה נִגְּרָה וְלֹא
תָפוּג מֵאֲנָה הִנָּחֵם נַפְשִׁי: אֶזְכְּרָה אֱלֹהִים וְאֶהֱמָיָה אָשִׂיחָה ׀ וְתִתְעַטֵּף
רוּחִי סֶלָה: אָחַזְתָּ שְׁמֻרוֹת עֵינָי נִפְעַמְתִּי וְלֹא אֲדַבֵּר: חִשַּׁבְתִּי יָמִים
מִקֶּדֶם שְׁנוֹת עוֹלָמִים: אֶזְכְּרָה נְגִינָתִי בַּלָּיְלָה עִם־לְבָבִי אָשִׂיחָה וַיְחַפֵּשׂ
רוּחִי: הַלְעוֹלָמִים יִזְנַח ׀ אֲדֹנָי וְלֹא־יֹסִיף לִרְצוֹת עוֹד: הֶאָפֵס לָנֶצַח
חַסְדּוֹ גָּמַר אֹמֶר לְדֹר וָדֹר: הֲשָׁכַח חַנּוֹת אֵל אִם־קָפַץ בְּאַף רַחֲמָיו סֶלָה:
אֶזְכּוֹר וָאֹמַר חַלּוֹתִי הִיא שְׁנוֹת יְמִין עֶלְיוֹן: אזכיר מַעַלְלֵי־יָהּ כִּי־אֶזְכְּרָה מִקֶּדֶם
פִּלְאֶךָ: וְהָגִיתִי בְכָל־פָּעֳלֶךָ וּבַעֲלִילוֹתֶיךָ אָשִׂיחָה: אֱלֹהִים בַּקֹּדֶשׁ דַּרְכֶּךָ
מִי־אֵל גָּדוֹל כֵּאלֹהִים: אַתָּה הָאֵל עֹשֵׂה פֶלֶא הוֹדַעְתָּ בָעַמִּים עֻזֶּךָ:
גָּאַלְתָּ בִּזְרוֹעַ עַמֶּךָ בְּנֵי־יַעֲקֹב וְיוֹסֵף סֶלָה: רָאוּךָ מַּיִם ׀ אֱלֹהִים רָאוּךָ
מַּיִם יָחִילוּ אַף יִרְגְּזוּ תְהֹמוֹת: זֹרְמוּ מַיִם ׀ עָבוֹת קוֹל נָתְנוּ שְׁחָקִים
אַף־חֲצָצֶיךָ יִתְהַלָּכוּ: קוֹל רַעַמְךָ ׀ בַּגַּלְגַּל הֵאִירוּ בְרָקִים תֵּבֵל רָגְזָה
וּשְׁבִילְךָ וַתִּרְעַשׁ הָאָרֶץ: בַּיָּם דַּרְכֶּךָ ושביליך בְּמַיִם רַבִּים וְעִקְּבוֹתֶיךָ לֹא נֹדָעוּ:
נָחִיתָ כַצֹּאן עַמֶּךָ בְּיַד־מֹשֶׁה וְאַהֲרֹן:

*טו לחודש

arrogance with neck upstretched. For success comes neither from the east, nor from the west, nor from the mountain pastures. But God is the judge. He casts one down and lifts one up. Indeed, in the hand of the Lord there is a cup with foaming wine, full of a poisonous mixture, and He pours from this. But all the wicked of the earth will drain and drink its dregs. But I will declare forever, I will sing praises to the God of Jacob. And I will cut off all the horns of the wicked. The horns of the righteous will be exalted.

76 TO THE DIRECTOR of music for instruments. A psalm of Asaph. A song. God is known in Judah. His name is great in Israel. His tabernacle is in Salem, and His dwelling place is in Zion. There He broke the arrows of the bow, the shield, and the sword, and the battle. Selah. You, O mighty one, are the destroyer from the mountains of prey. The stout-hearted were bereft of courage, they slept their sleep, and none of the men of valor found their hands. At Your rebuke, O God of Jacob, both chariot and horse fell silent. You, even You, are to be feared, and who can stand before You? Your anger is from of old. You caused judgment to be heard from heaven. The earth feared and was still, When God rose for judgment, to save all the humble of the earth. Selah. Surely the wrath of man will submit to You. You will gird Yourself with the remainder of wrath. Vow and pay to the Lord your God. From all about Him let them bring presents to Him Who imposes fear. He will cut off the spirit of the rulers. He is awesome to the kings of the earth.

*77 TO THE DIRECTOR of music, *al-Yedutun*. A psalm of Asaph. My voice is to God and I cry out. My voice is to God, that He may hear me. In the day of my trouble I seek the Lord. My hand drips at night and does not rest. My soul refuses to be comforted. I remember God and I moan. I plead and my spirit faints. Selah. You hold fast my eyelids. I am so astonished that I cannot speak. I have pondered the days of old, the years of ancient times. I remember my song at night. I commune with my heart and my spirit searches. Will the Lord forsake us forever? And will He be favorable no more? Has His loving-kindness gone forever? Has His word finished for all generations? Has God forgotten grace? Has He in anger shut up His mercies? Selah. And I said, This is my prayer: Let the right hand of the Most High act again. I will recall the deeds of God, for I remember from of old Your wonders, And I have meditated on all Your work, and I have talked about Your doings. O God, Your way is in holiness. Who is so great a god as our God? You are the God Who performs wonders. You have made Your strength known among the peoples. You have redeemed Your people with Your arm, the sons of Jacob and Joseph. Selah. The waters saw You, O God. The waters saw You and they were afraid, and the deep waters trembled. The clouds poured out water, the skies sent out a sound. Your arrows, too, went out. The voice of Your thunder was in the whirlwind; the lightnings illuminated the world. The earth trembled and shook. Your way was in the sea, and Your path in the mighty waters, and Your footsteps were not known. You led Your people like a flock by the hand of Moses and Aaron.

---

*15th DAY of the month

עח מַשְׂכִּיל לְאָסָף הַאֲזִינָה עַמִּי תּוֹרָתִי הַטּוּ אָזְנְכֶם לְאִמְרֵי־פִי׃ אֶפְתְּחָה
בְמָשָׁל פִּי אַבִּיעָה חִידוֹת מִנִּי־קֶדֶם׃ אֲשֶׁר שָׁמַעְנוּ וַנֵּדָעֵם וַאֲבוֹתֵינוּ
סִפְּרוּ־לָנוּ׃ לֹא נְכַחֵד ׀ מִבְּנֵיהֶם לְדוֹר אַחֲרוֹן מְסַפְּרִים תְּהִלּוֹת יְהוָה
וֶעֱזוּזוֹ וְנִפְלְאוֹתָיו אֲשֶׁר עָשָׂה׃ וַיָּקֶם עֵדוּת ׀ בְּיַעֲקֹב וְתוֹרָה שָׂם בְּיִשְׂרָאֵל
אֲשֶׁר צִוָּה אֶת־אֲבוֹתֵינוּ לְהוֹדִיעָם לִבְנֵיהֶם׃ לְמַעַן יֵדְעוּ ׀ דּוֹר אַחֲרוֹן
בָּנִים יִוָּלֵדוּ יָקֻמוּ וִיסַפְּרוּ לִבְנֵיהֶם׃ וְיָשִׂימוּ בֵאלֹהִים כִּסְלָם וְלֹא יִשְׁכְּחוּ
מַעַלְלֵי־אֵל וּמִצְוֹתָיו יִנְצֹרוּ׃ וְלֹא יִהְיוּ ׀ כַּאֲבוֹתָם דּוֹר סוֹרֵר וּמֹרֶה דּוֹר
לֹא־הֵכִין לִבּוֹ וְלֹא־נֶאֶמְנָה אֶת־אֵל רוּחוֹ׃ בְּנֵי־אֶפְרַיִם נוֹשְׁקֵי רוֹמֵי־
קָשֶׁת הָפְכוּ בְּיוֹם קְרָב׃ לֹא שָׁמְרוּ בְּרִית אֱלֹהִים וּבְתוֹרָתוֹ מֵאֲנוּ לָלֶכֶת׃
וַיִּשְׁכְּחוּ עֲלִילוֹתָיו וְנִפְלְאוֹתָיו אֲשֶׁר הֶרְאָם׃ נֶגֶד אֲבוֹתָם עָשָׂה פֶלֶא
בְּאֶרֶץ מִצְרַיִם שְׂדֵה־צֹעַן׃ בָּקַע יָם וַיַּעֲבִירֵם וַיַּצֶּב־מַיִם כְּמוֹ־נֵד׃ וַיַּנְחֵם
בֶּעָנָן יוֹמָם וְכָל־הַלַּיְלָה בְּאוֹר אֵשׁ׃ יְבַקַּע צֻרִים בַּמִּדְבָּר וַיַּשְׁקְ כִּתְהֹמוֹת
רַבָּה׃ וַיּוֹצִא נוֹזְלִים מִסָּלַע וַיּוֹרֶד כַּנְּהָרוֹת מָיִם׃ וַיּוֹסִיפוּ עוֹד לַחֲטֹא־לוֹ
לַמְרוֹת עֶלְיוֹן בַּצִּיָּה׃ וַיְנַסּוּ־אֵל בִּלְבָבָם לִשְׁאָל־אֹכֶל לְנַפְשָׁם׃ וַיְדַבְּרוּ
בֵּאלֹהִים אָמְרוּ הֲיוּכַל אֵל לַעֲרֹךְ שֻׁלְחָן בַּמִּדְבָּר׃ הֵן הִכָּה־צוּר ׀ וַיָּזוּבוּ
מַיִם וּנְחָלִים יִשְׁטֹפוּ הֲגַם־לֶחֶם יוּכַל תֵּת אִם־יָכִין שְׁאֵר לְעַמּוֹ׃ לָכֵן ׀
שָׁמַע יְהוָה וַיִּתְעַבָּר וְאֵשׁ נִשְּׂקָה בְיַעֲקֹב וְגַם־אַף עָלָה בְיִשְׂרָאֵל׃ כִּי לֹא
הֶאֱמִינוּ בֵּאלֹהִים וְלֹא בָטְחוּ בִּישׁוּעָתוֹ׃ וַיְצַו שְׁחָקִים מִמָּעַל וְדַלְתֵי
שָׁמַיִם פָּתָח׃ וַיַּמְטֵר עֲלֵיהֶם מָן לֶאֱכֹל וּדְגַן־שָׁמַיִם נָתַן לָמוֹ׃ לֶחֶם
אַבִּירִים אָכַל אִישׁ צֵידָה שָׁלַח לָהֶם לָשֹׂבַע׃ יַסַּע קָדִים בַּשָּׁמָיִם וַיְנַהֵג
בְּעֻזּוֹ תֵימָן׃ וַיַּמְטֵר עֲלֵיהֶם כֶּעָפָר שְׁאֵר וּכְחוֹל יַמִּים עוֹף כָּנָף׃ וַיַּפֵּל
בְּקֶרֶב מַחֲנֵהוּ סָבִיב לְמִשְׁכְּנֹתָיו׃ וַיֹּאכְלוּ וַיִּשְׂבְּעוּ מְאֹד וְתַאֲוָתָם יָבִא
לָהֶם׃ לֹא־זָרוּ מִתַּאֲוָתָם עוֹד אָכְלָם בְּפִיהֶם׃ וְאַף אֱלֹהִים ׀ עָלָה בָהֶם
וַיַּהֲרֹג בְּמִשְׁמַנֵּיהֶם וּבַחוּרֵי יִשְׂרָאֵל הִכְרִיעַ׃ בְּכָל־זֹאת חָטְאוּ־עוֹד וְלֹא
הֶאֱמִינוּ בְּנִפְלְאוֹתָיו׃ וַיְכַל־בַּהֶבֶל יְמֵיהֶם וּשְׁנוֹתָם בַּבֶּהָלָה׃ אִם־הֲרָגָם
וּדְרָשׁוּהוּ וְשָׁבוּ וְשִׁחֲרוּ־אֵל׃ וַיִּזְכְּרוּ כִּי־אֱלֹהִים צוּרָם וְאֵל עֶלְיוֹן גֹּאֲלָם׃
וַיְפַתּוּהוּ בְּפִיהֶם וּבִלְשׁוֹנָם יְכַזְּבוּ־לוֹ׃ וְלִבָּם לֹא־נָכוֹן עִמּוֹ וְלֹא נֶאֶמְנוּ
בִּבְרִיתוֹ׃ וְהוּא רַחוּם ׀ יְכַפֵּר עָוֺן וְלֹא־יַשְׁחִית וְהִרְבָּה לְהָשִׁיב אַפּוֹ

78 A *MASKIL* of Asaph. Give ear, O my people, to my teaching. Incline your ear to the words
of my mouth. I will open my mouth with a parable. I will utter riddles concerning ancient
times, Which we have heard and known, and our fathers have told us. We will not hide
them from their children, to the next generation. We will relate the praises of the Lord,
and His strength, and His wondrous works that He has done. And He has established
a testimony in Jacob, and He has fixed a law in Israel, which He commanded our fathers,
that they should make them known to their children, That the next generation might
know them, the children who would be born, who would arise, and who would relate
them to their children. And they would set their trust in God, and they would not
forget the deeds of God, but would keep His commandments. And they would not be
like their fathers, a deviant and rebellious generation, a generation that did not direct
its heart aright, and whose spirit was not steadfast with God. The children of Ephraim,
armed with and shooting bows, turned back on the day of battle. They did not keep the
covenant of God, and they refused to walk in His law. And they forgot His deeds, and
His wonders that He had shown them. He did marvelous things in the sight of their
fathers, in the land of Egypt, in the field of Zoan. He parted the sea, and He caused
them to pass through, and He made the waters stand like a heap. And He led them
with a cloud during the day, and all the night with a light of fire. He split rocks in the
wilderness, and He gave them to drink as out of great springs. And He brought streams
out on the rock, and He made water run down like rivers. But they continued to sin
against Him, to rebel against the Most High in the wilderness. And they tried God in
their heart, asking for food for themselves. And they spoke against God. They said, Can
God arrange a table in the wilderness? Behold, He smote the rock, and waters poured
out, and streams flowed. Can He give bread also? Can He prepare meat for His people?
Therefore the Lord heard and was angry, and a fire was kindled against Jacob, and anger
went up against Israel, Because they did not believe in God, and they did not trust in
His salvation. But He commanded the skies above, and He opened the doors of heaven.
And He rained down manna upon them to eat, and He gave them the corn of heaven.
Man ate the bread of angels. He sent them food to the full. He drove the east wind in
the sky, and by His power He brought the south wind. And He rained down meat upon
them like the dust, and winged birds like the sand of the sea. And He let them fall in
the midst of their camp, round about their dwelling places. And they ate, and they were
very well satisfied, and He brought them their desire. They were not yet estranged from
their desire, their food was still in their mouths, And the anger of God came upon them,
and He slew the fat among them, and He cast down the young men of Israel. With all
this, they sinned more, and they did not believe in His wondrous works. He ended their
days with emptiness, and their years with dread. When He slew them, they sought Him,
and they returned and inquired after God. And they remembered that God was their
rock, and God on high their redeemer. But they flattered Him with their mouths, and
they lied to Him with their tongues. But their heart was not steadfast with Him, and
they were not faithful to His covenant. But He, the compassionate one, forgave iniquity,

וְלֹא־יָעִיר כָּל־חֲמָתוֹ: וַיִּזְכֹּר כִּי־בָשָׂר הֵמָּה רוּחַ הוֹלֵךְ וְלֹא יָשׁוּב: כַּמָּה
יַמְרוּהוּ בַמִּדְבָּר יַעֲצִיבוּהוּ בִּישִׁימוֹן: וַיָּשׁוּבוּ וַיְנַסּוּ אֵל וּקְדוֹשׁ יִשְׂרָאֵל
הִתְווּ: לֹא־זָכְרוּ אֶת־יָדוֹ יוֹם אֲשֶׁר־פָּדָם מִנִּי־צָר: אֲשֶׁר־שָׂם בְּמִצְרַיִם
אֹתוֹתָיו וּמוֹפְתָיו בִּשְׂדֵה־צֹעַן: וַיַּהֲפֹךְ לְדָם יְאֹרֵיהֶם וְנֹזְלֵיהֶם בַּל־יִשְׁתָּיוּן:
יְשַׁלַּח בָּהֶם עָרֹב וַיֹּאכְלֵם וּצְפַרְדֵּעַ וַתַּשְׁחִיתֵם: וַיִּתֵּן לֶחָסִיל יְבוּלָם
וִיגִיעָם לָאַרְבֶּה: יַהֲרֹג בַּבָּרָד גַּפְנָם וְשִׁקְמוֹתָם בַּחֲנָמַל: וַיַּסְגֵּר לַבָּרָד
בְּעִירָם וּמִקְנֵיהֶם לָרְשָׁפִים: יְשַׁלַּח־בָּם ׀ חֲרוֹן אַפּוֹ עֶבְרָה וָזַעַם וְצָרָה
מִשְׁלַחַת מַלְאֲכֵי רָעִים: יְפַלֵּס נָתִיב לְאַפּוֹ לֹא־חָשַׂךְ מִמָּוֶת נַפְשָׁם
וְחַיָּתָם לַדֶּבֶר הִסְגִּיר: וַיַּךְ כָּל־בְּכוֹר בְּמִצְרָיִם רֵאשִׁית אוֹנִים בְּאָהֳלֵי־
חָם: וַיַּסַּע כַּצֹּאן עַמּוֹ וַיְנַהֲגֵם כַּעֵדֶר בַּמִּדְבָּר: וַיַּנְחֵם לָבֶטַח וְלֹא פָחָדוּ
וְאֶת־אוֹיְבֵיהֶם כִּסָּה הַיָּם: וַיְבִיאֵם אֶל־גְּבוּל קָדְשׁוֹ הַר־זֶה קָנְתָה
יְמִינוֹ: וַיְגָרֶשׁ מִפְּנֵיהֶם ׀ גּוֹיִם וַיַּפִּילֵם בְּחֶבֶל נַחֲלָה וַיַּשְׁכֵּן בְּאָהֳלֵיהֶם
שִׁבְטֵי יִשְׂרָאֵל: וַיְנַסּוּ וַיַּמְרוּ אֶת־אֱלֹהִים עֶלְיוֹן וְעֵדוֹתָיו לֹא שָׁמָרוּ:
וַיִּסֹּגוּ וַיִּבְגְּדוּ כַּאֲבוֹתָם נֶהְפְּכוּ כְּקֶשֶׁת רְמִיָּה: וַיַּכְעִיסוּהוּ בְּבָמוֹתָם
וּבִפְסִילֵיהֶם יַקְנִיאוּהוּ: שָׁמַע אֱלֹהִים וַיִּתְעַבָּר וַיִּמְאַס מְאֹד בְּיִשְׂרָאֵל:
וַיִּטֹּשׁ מִשְׁכַּן שִׁלוֹ אֹהֶל שִׁכֵּן בָּאָדָם: וַיִּתֵּן לַשְּׁבִי עֻזּוֹ וְתִפְאַרְתּוֹ בְיַד־צָר:
וַיַּסְגֵּר לַחֶרֶב עַמּוֹ וּבְנַחֲלָתוֹ הִתְעַבָּר: בַּחוּרָיו אָכְלָה־אֵשׁ וּבְתוּלֹתָיו
לֹא הוּלָּלוּ: כֹּהֲנָיו בַּחֶרֶב נָפָלוּ וְאַלְמְנֹתָיו לֹא תִבְכֶּינָה: וַיִּקַץ כְּיָשֵׁן ׀ אֲדֹנָי
כְּגִבּוֹר מִתְרוֹנֵן מִיָּיִן: וַיַּךְ־צָרָיו אָחוֹר חֶרְפַּת עוֹלָם נָתַן לָמוֹ: וַיִּמְאַס
בְּאֹהֶל יוֹסֵף וּבְשֵׁבֶט אֶפְרַיִם לֹא בָחָר: וַיִּבְחַר אֶת־שֵׁבֶט יְהוּדָה אֶת־
הַר צִיּוֹן אֲשֶׁר אָהֵב: וַיִּבֶן כְּמוֹ־רָמִים מִקְדָּשׁוֹ כְּאֶרֶץ יְסָדָהּ לְעוֹלָם:
וַיִּבְחַר בְּדָוִד עַבְדּוֹ וַיִּקָּחֵהוּ מִמִּכְלְאֹת צֹאן: מֵאַחַר עָלוֹת הֱבִיאוֹ לִרְעוֹת
בְּיַעֲקֹב עַמּוֹ וּבְיִשְׂרָאֵל נַחֲלָתוֹ: וַיִּרְעֵם כְּתֹם לְבָבוֹ וּבִתְבוּנוֹת כַּפָּיו
יַנְחֵם:

*עט מִזְמוֹר לְאָסָף אֱלֹהִים בָּאוּ גוֹיִם ׀ בְּנַחֲלָתֶךָ טִמְּאוּ אֶת־הֵיכַל קָדְשֶׁךָ שָׂמוּ
אֶת־יְרוּשָׁלַםִ לְעִיִּים: נָתְנוּ אֶת־נִבְלַת עֲבָדֶיךָ מַאֲכָל לְעוֹף הַשָּׁמָיִם
בְּשַׂר חֲסִידֶיךָ לְחַיְתוֹ־אָרֶץ: שָׁפְכוּ דָמָם ׀ כַּמַּיִם סְבִיבוֹת יְרוּשָׁלָםִ וְאֵין
קוֹבֵר: הָיִינוּ חֶרְפָּה לִשְׁכֵנֵינוּ לַעַג וָקֶלֶס לִסְבִיבוֹתֵינוּ: עַד־מָה יְהוָה

*טז לחודש

and did not destroy them, and He often turned away His anger and did not stir up all His wrath. And He remembered that they were flesh, a wind that passes and does not return. How often did they rebel against Him in the wilderness, did they grieve Him in the desert! And they turned back and tested God, and they pained the Holy One of Israel. They did not remember His hand, nor the day when the He delivered them from the enemy. When He wrought His signs in Egypt, and His wonders in the field of Zoan. And He turned their canals into blood, and they could not drink their waters. He sent beasts among them which devoured them, and frogs which destroyed them. And He gave their produce to the locusts, and their labor to the locusts. He destroyed their grapevines with hail, and their sycamore trees with frost. And He gave over their cattle to the hail, and their flocks to the thunderbolts. He sent upon them His burning anger, wrath, indignation, and trouble, an embassy of messengers of evil. He leveled a path for His anger. He did not spare their soil from death, and He gave over their life to pestilence. And He smote every firstborn in Egypt, the first of their strength in the tents of Ham. And He led His people like sheep, and He guided them in the wilderness like a flock. And He led them safely, and they did not fear, and the sea covered their enemies. And He brought them to His holy border, to the mountain that His right hand had established. And He cast out the nations from before them, and He apportioned them as an inheritance, and He made the tribes of Israel dwell in their tents. But they tested and rebelled against the most high God, and they did not keep His testimonies. But they turned back and they acted treacherously like their fathers. They turned like a deceitful bow. And they made Him angry with their high places, and they made Him jealous with their idols. God heard and became angry, and He greatly abhorred Israel. And He forsook the tabernacle of Shiloh, the tent where He made His dwelling among men. And He gave His strength into captivity, and His glory into the hand of the enemy. And He gave His people over to the sword, and He was angry with His inheritance. Fire consumed their young men, and their virgins had no wedding song. Their priests fell by the sword, and their widows did not weep. Then the Lord awoke as if out of sleep, like a warrior who shouts by reason of wine. And He smote His enemies backward. He put upon them an everlasting reproach. And He abhorred the tent of Joseph, and He did not choose the tribe of Ephraim. But He chose the tribe of Judah, Mount Zion that He loved. And He built His Temple like the high heavens, like the earth that He has established forever. And He chose David His servant, and He took him from the sheepfolds. From following the ewes that give suck He brought him to be a shepherd of Jacob His people and of Israel His inheritance. And he tended them according to the integrity of his heart, and he let them by this skillfulness of his hands.

*79 A PSALM of Asaph. O God, nations have come into Your inheritance. They have defiled Your holy sanctuary, they have laid Jerusalem into heaps. They have given the dead bodies of Your servants as food to the birds of the heavens, the flesh of Your pious ones to the beasts of the earth. They have shed their blood like water round about Jerusalem, and there was none to bury them. We have become a reproach to

*16th DAY of the month

תֶּאֱנַף לָנֶצַח תִּבְעַר כְּמוֹ־אֵשׁ קִנְאָתֶךָ: שְׁפֹךְ חֲמָתְךָ ׀ אֶל־הַגּוֹיִם אֲשֶׁר
לֹא־יְדָעוּךָ וְעַל מַמְלָכוֹת אֲשֶׁר בְּשִׁמְךָ לֹא קָרָאוּ: כִּי אָכַל אֶת־יַעֲקֹב
וְאֶת־נָוֵהוּ הֵשַׁמּוּ: אַל־תִּזְכָּר־לָנוּ עֲוֺנֹת רִאשֹׁנִים מַהֵר יְקַדְּמוּנוּ רַחֲמֶיךָ
כִּי דַלּוֹנוּ מְאֹד: עָזְרֵנוּ ׀ אֱלֹהֵי יִשְׁעֵנוּ עַל־דְּבַר כְּבוֹד־שְׁמֶךָ וְהַצִּילֵנוּ וְכַפֵּר
עַל־חַטֹּאתֵינוּ לְמַעַן שְׁמֶךָ: לָמָּה ׀ יֹאמְרוּ הַגּוֹיִם אַיֵּה אֱלֹהֵיהֶם יִוָּדַע
בַּגּוֹיִם בגיים לְעֵינֵינוּ נִקְמַת דַּם־עֲבָדֶיךָ הַשָּׁפוּךְ: תָּבוֹא לְפָנֶיךָ אֶנְקַת אָסִיר
כְּגֹדֶל זְרוֹעֲךָ הוֹתֵר בְּנֵי תְמוּתָה: וְהָשֵׁב לִשְׁכֵנֵינוּ שִׁבְעָתַיִם אֶל־חֵיקָם
חֶרְפָּתָם אֲשֶׁר חֵרְפוּךָ אֲדֹנָי: וַאֲנַחְנוּ עַמְּךָ ׀ וְצֹאן מַרְעִיתֶךָ נוֹדֶה לְּךָ
לְעוֹלָם לְדֹר וָדֹר נְסַפֵּר תְּהִלָּתֶךָ:

פ לַמְנַצֵּחַ אֶל־שֹׁשַׁנִּים עֵדוּת לְאָסָף מִזְמוֹר: רֹעֵה יִשְׂרָאֵל ׀ הַאֲזִינָה נֹהֵג
כַּצֹּאן יוֹסֵף יֹשֵׁב הַכְּרוּבִים הוֹפִיעָה: לִפְנֵי אֶפְרַיִם ׀ וּבִנְיָמִן וּמְנַשֶּׁה
עוֹרְרָה אֶת־גְּבוּרָתֶךָ וּלְכָה לִישֻׁעָתָה לָּנוּ: אֱלֹהִים הֲשִׁיבֵנוּ וְהָאֵר פָּנֶיךָ
וְנִוָּשֵׁעָה: יהוה אֱלֹהִים צְבָאוֹת עַד־מָתַי עָשַׁנְתָּ בִּתְפִלַּת עַמֶּךָ: הֶאֱכַלְתָּם
לֶחֶם דִּמְעָה וַתַּשְׁקֵמוֹ בִּדְמָעוֹת שָׁלִישׁ: תְּשִׂימֵנוּ מָדוֹן לִשְׁכֵנֵינוּ וְאֹיְבֵינוּ
יִלְעֲגוּ־לָמוֹ: אֱלֹהִים צְבָאוֹת הֲשִׁיבֵנוּ וְהָאֵר פָּנֶיךָ וְנִוָּשֵׁעָה: גֶּפֶן מִמִּצְרַיִם
תַּסִּיעַ תְּגָרֵשׁ גּוֹיִם וַתִּטָּעֶהָ: פִּנִּיתָ לְפָנֶיהָ וַתַּשְׁרֵשׁ שָׁרָשֶׁיהָ וַתְּמַלֵּא־אָרֶץ:
כָּסּוּ הָרִים צִלָּהּ וַעֲנָפֶיהָ אַרְזֵי־אֵל: תְּשַׁלַּח קְצִירֶהָ עַד־יָם וְאֶל־נָהָר
יוֹנְקוֹתֶיהָ: לָמָּה פָּרַצְתָּ גְדֵרֶיהָ וְאָרוּהָ כָּל־עֹבְרֵי דָרֶךְ: יְכַרְסְמֶנָּה חֲזִיר
מִיָּעַר וְזִיז שָׂדַי יִרְעֶנָּה: אֱלֹהִים צְבָאוֹת שׁוּב נָא הַבֵּט מִשָּׁמַיִם וּרְאֵה
וּפְקֹד גֶּפֶן זֹאת: וְכַנָּה אֲשֶׁר־נָטְעָה יְמִינֶךָ וְעַל־בֵּן אִמַּצְתָּה לָּךְ: שְׂרֻפָה
בָאֵשׁ כְּסוּחָה מִגַּעֲרַת פָּנֶיךָ יֹאבֵדוּ: תְּהִי־יָדְךָ עַל־אִישׁ יְמִינֶךָ עַל־בֶּן־
אָדָם אִמַּצְתָּ לָּךְ: וְלֹא־נָסוֹג מִמֶּךָּ תְּחַיֵּנוּ וּבְשִׁמְךָ נִקְרָא: יהוה אֱלֹהִים
צְבָאוֹת הֲשִׁיבֵנוּ הָאֵר פָּנֶיךָ וְנִוָּשֵׁעָה:

פא לַמְנַצֵּחַ ׀ עַל־הַגִּתִּית לְאָסָף: הַרְנִינוּ לֵאלֹהִים עוּזֵּנוּ הָרִיעוּ לֵאלֹהֵי יַעֲקֹב:
שְׂאוּ־זִמְרָה וּתְנוּ־תֹף כִּנּוֹר נָעִים עִם־נָבֶל: תִּקְעוּ בַחֹדֶשׁ שׁוֹפָר בַּכֵּסֶה
לְיוֹם חַגֵּנוּ: כִּי חֹק לְיִשְׂרָאֵל הוּא מִשְׁפָּט לֵאלֹהֵי יַעֲקֹב: עֵדוּת ׀ בִּיהוֹסֵף
שָׂמוֹ בְּצֵאתוֹ עַל־אֶרֶץ מִצְרָיִם שְׂפַת לֹא־יָדַעְתִּי אֶשְׁמָע: הֲסִירוֹתִי
מִסֵּבֶל שִׁכְמוֹ כַּפָּיו מִדּוּד תַּעֲבֹרְנָה: בַּצָּרָה קָרָאתָ וָאֲחַלְּצֶךָּ אֶעֶנְךָ

our neighbors, a scorn a derision to those round about us. How long, O Lord, will You be angry? Forever? How long will Your vengeance burn like fire? Pour out Your wrath upon the nation that do not know You, and upon the kingdoms that do not call upon Your name. For they have devoured Jacob, and they have laid waste his dwelling place. Do not remember against us former iniquities. Let Your mercies quickly go ahead of us, for we are brought very low. Help us, O God of our salvation, because of the glory of Your name, and deliver us and pardon our sins for Your name's sake. Why should the nations say, Where is their God? Let the avenging of the shed blood of Your servants be known to the nations before our eyes. Let the groaning of the prisoners come before You. According to the greatness of Your power, preserve those condemned to die. And repay our neighbors sevenfold into their bosom their insult, with which they have insulted You, O Lord. But we, Your people and the sheep of Your pasture, will thank You forever. We will relate Your praise for all generations.

80 TO THE DIRECTOR of music, *el-shoshanim. Edut.* A psalm of Asaph. O shepherd of
Israel, listen, You Who tend Joseph like sheep. You Who dwell upon the cherubs, shine forth. Before Ephraim, and Benjamin, and Manasseh, stir up Your might, and come to save us. O God, restore us, and cause Your face to shine, and we will be saved. O Lord, God of hosts, how long will You angrily reject the prayer of Your people? You feed them bread of tears, and You give them to drink a cup mixed with tears. You have made us a strife to our neighbors, and our enemies mock them. O God of hosts, restore us, and cause Your face to shine, and we will be saved. You brought a vine out of Egypt. You drove out nations and planted it. You cleared room before it, and it took deep root and filled the land. The hills were covered with its shadow, and the lofty cedars with its boughs. It sent out its boughs to the sea, and its branches to the river. Why have You breached its fences, and all who pass by the way pluck its fruits? The boar of the wood ravages it, and the wild bird devours it. O God of hosts, please return. Look down from heaven and see, and be mindful of its vine, And the sapling that Your right hand planted, and the branch that You attached strongly to Yourself. It is burned with fire, it is cut down. Let them perish at the rebuke of Your face. Let Your hand be upon the man of Your right hand, upon the man whom You have attached strongly to Yourself. He has not turned back from You. Let us live, for we call upon Your name. O Lord, God of hosts, restore us. Cause Your face to shine, and we will be saved.

81 TO THE DIRECTOR of music *al-HaGittit,* of Asaph. Sing for joy to God our strength.
Make a joyful noise for the God of Jacob. Raise a song, sound the timbrel, the sweet lyre and the harp. Sound a shofar on the new moon, on the day of covering for our feast day. For this is a statute for Israel, an ordinance of the God of Jacob. He ordained this in Joseph for a testimony, when He went out over the land of Egypt. I hear a language that I did not know: I removed his shoulder from the burden. His hands were freed from the basket. You called in trouble and I rescued you. I answered you

בְּסֵתֶר רַעַם אֶבְחׇנְךָ עַל־מֵי מְרִיבָה סֶלָה: שְׁמַע עַמִּי וְאָעִידָה בָּךְ
יִשְׂרָאֵל אִם־תִּשְׁמַע־לִי: לֹא־יִהְיֶה בְךָ אֵל זָר וְלֹא תִשְׁתַּחֲוֶה לְאֵל נֵכָר:
אָנֹכִי ׀ יהוה אֱלֹהֶיךָ הַמַּעַלְךָ מֵאֶרֶץ מִצְרָיִם הַרְחֶב־פִּיךָ וַאֲמַלְאֵהוּ: וְלֹא־
שָׁמַע עַמִּי לְקוֹלִי וְיִשְׂרָאֵל לֹא־אָבָה לִי: וָאֲשַׁלְּחֵהוּ בִּשְׁרִירוּת לִבָּם יֵלְכוּ
בְּמוֹעֲצוֹתֵיהֶם: לוּ עַמִּי שֹׁמֵעַ לִי יִשְׂרָאֵל בִּדְרָכַי יְהַלֵּכוּ: כִּמְעַט אוֹיְבֵיהֶם
אַכְנִיעַ וְעַל־צָרֵיהֶם אָשִׁיב יָדִי: מְשַׂנְאֵי יהוה יְכַחֲשׁוּ־לוֹ וִיהִי עִתָּם
לְעוֹלָם: וַיַּאֲכִילֵהוּ מֵחֵלֶב חִטָּה וּמִצּוּר דְּבַשׁ אַשְׂבִּיעֶךָ:

פב מִזְמוֹר לְאָסָף אֱלֹהִים נִצָּב בַּעֲדַת־אֵל בְּקֶרֶב אֱלֹהִים יִשְׁפֹּט: עַד־מָתַי
תִּשְׁפְּטוּ־עָוֶל וּפְנֵי רְשָׁעִים תִּשְׂאוּ־סֶלָה: שִׁפְטוּ־דַל וְיָתוֹם עָנִי וָרָשׁ
הַצְדִּיקוּ: פַּלְּטוּ־דַל וְאֶבְיוֹן מִיַּד רְשָׁעִים הַצִּילוּ: לֹא יָדְעוּ ׀ וְלֹא יָבִינוּ
בַּחֲשֵׁכָה יִתְהַלָּכוּ יִמּוֹטוּ כׇּל־מוֹסְדֵי אָרֶץ: אֲנִי־אָמַרְתִּי אֱלֹהִים אַתֶּם
וּבְנֵי עֶלְיוֹן כֻּלְּכֶם: אָכֵן כְּאָדָם תְּמוּתוּן וּכְאַחַד הַשָּׂרִים תִּפֹּלוּ: קוּמָה
אֱלֹהִים שׇׁפְטָה הָאָרֶץ כִּי־אַתָּה תִנְחַל בְּכׇל־הַגּוֹיִם:

*פג שִׁיר מִזְמוֹר לְאָסָף: אֱלֹהִים אַל־דֳּמִי־לָךְ אַל־תֶּחֱרַשׁ וְאַל־תִּשְׁקֹט אֵל:
כִּי־הִנֵּה אוֹיְבֶיךָ יֶהֱמָיוּן וּמְשַׂנְאֶיךָ נָשְׂאוּ רֹאשׁ: עַל־עַמְּךָ יַעֲרִימוּ סוֹד
וְיִתְיָעֲצוּ עַל־צְפוּנֶיךָ: אָמְרוּ לְכוּ וְנַכְחִידֵם מִגּוֹי וְלֹא־יִזָּכֵר שֵׁם־יִשְׂרָאֵל
עוֹד: כִּי נוֹעֲצוּ לֵב יַחְדָּו עָלֶיךָ בְּרִית יִכְרֹתוּ: אׇהֳלֵי אֱדוֹם וְיִשְׁמְעֵאלִים
מוֹאָב וְהַגְרִים: גְּבָל וְעַמּוֹן וַעֲמָלֵק פְּלֶשֶׁת עִם־יֹשְׁבֵי צוֹר: גַּם־אַשּׁוּר
נִלְוָה עִמָּם הָיוּ זְרוֹעַ לִבְנֵי־לוֹט סֶלָה: עֲשֵׂה־לָהֶם כְּמִדְיָן כְּסִיסְרָא כְיָבִין
בְּנַחַל קִישׁוֹן: נִשְׁמְדוּ בְעֵין־דֹּאר הָיוּ דֹּמֶן לָאֲדָמָה: שִׁיתֵמוֹ נְדִיבֵמוֹ
כְּעֹרֵב וְכִזְאֵב וּכְזֶבַח וּכְצַלְמֻנָּע כׇּל־נְסִיכֵמוֹ: אֲשֶׁר אָמְרוּ נִירְשָׁה לָּנוּ אֵת
נְאוֹת אֱלֹהִים: אֱלֹהַי שִׁיתֵמוֹ כַגַּלְגַּל כְּקַשׁ לִפְנֵי־רוּחַ: כְּאֵשׁ תִּבְעַר־יָעַר
וּכְלֶהָבָה תְּלַהֵט הָרִים: כֵּן תִּרְדְּפֵם בְּסַעֲרֶךָ וּבְסוּפָתְךָ תְבַהֲלֵם: מַלֵּא
פְנֵיהֶם קָלוֹן וִיבַקְשׁוּ שִׁמְךָ יהוה: יֵבֹשׁוּ וְיִבָּהֲלוּ עֲדֵי־עַד וְיַחְפְּרוּ וְיֹאבֵדוּ:
וְיֵדְעוּ כִּי־אַתָּה שִׁמְךָ יהוה לְבַדֶּךָ עֶלְיוֹן עַל־כׇּל־הָאָרֶץ:

פד לַמְנַצֵּחַ עַל־הַגִּתִּית לִבְנֵי־קֹרַח מִזְמוֹר: מַה־יְּדִידוֹת מִשְׁכְּנוֹתֶיךָ יהוה
צְבָאוֹת: נִכְסְפָה וְגַם־כָּלְתָה ׀ נַפְשִׁי לְחַצְרוֹת יהוה לִבִּי וּבְשָׂרִי יְרַנְּנוּ אֶל
אֵל־חָי: גַּם־צִפּוֹר ׀ מָצְאָה בַיִת וּדְרוֹר ׀ קֵן לָהּ אֲשֶׁר־שָׁתָה אֶפְרֹחֶיהָ

*יז לחודש

with thunder in the secret place. I tested you at the waters of Meribah. Selah. Hear,
My people, and I will testify against you, O Israel, if you will hearken to Me. There
shall be no strange god among you, and you shall not worship any foreign deity. I am
the Lord your God Who brought you up from the land of Egypt. Open your mouth
wide, and I will fill it. But My people did not hearken to My voice, and Israel did not
desire Me. So I let them go after the stubbornness of their heart. Let them follow their
own counsels! Oh that My people had hearkened to Me, that Israel had walked in My
ways! I would have subdued their enemies in a moment and turned My hand against
their adversaries. The haters of the Lord feign obedience to Him, and their time of
punishment will last forever. But He will feed him from the finest of the wheat, and
from the rock I will satisfy you with honey.

82 A PSALM of Asaph. God is standing in the congregation of God. He will judge in the
midst of judges. How long will you judge unjustly and favor the wicked? Selah. Judge
the poor and the fatherless. Judge fairly the afflicted and the needy. Deliver the poor
and the destitute. Save them from the hand of the wicked. They do not know and
they do not understand. They walk in darkness. All the foundations of the earth will
collapse. I said: "You are angels, and all of you are sons of the Most High. Nevertheless
you will die like a man, and you will fall like one of the princes." Arise, O God! Judge
the earth. For You possess all the nations.

*83 A SONG. A psalm of Asaph. O God, do not keep silence, do not hold Your peace, and
do not be still, O God. For behold, Your enemies make a tumult and those who
hate You lift up their head. They take cunning counsel against Your people, and they
consult together against Your hidden ones. They have said: "Come, let us destroy them
from among the nations, so that the name of Israel may be remembered no more."
Indeed, they had decided with one heart. They forge a covenant against You: The
tents of Edom and the Yishmaelites, Moab and the Hagarenes, Gebal, and Ammon,
and Amalek, Philistia with the inhabitants of Tyre. Assyria, too, has joined with them.
They lend assistance to the children of Lot. Selah. Do to them as to Midian, as to Sisera
and Jabin at the brook of Kishon. They were destroyed at En-dor. They became dung
for the earth. Make their princes like Oreb and Zeeb, and all their chiefs like Zebah
and Zalmunna. Who said: "Let us take into our possession the habitations of God."
O my God, make them like the thistle, like stubble before the wind. As fire burns a
forest, and as a flame sets mountains on fire, So pursue them with Your tempest, and
terrify them with Your storm. Fill their faces with shame, so that they may seek Your
name, O Lord. Let them be mortified and terrified forever, and let them be put to
shame and destroyed. So that men may know that You, Whose name is the Lord, are
alone, that You are the most high over all the earth.

84 TO THE DIRECTOR of music al-HaGittit. A psalm for the sons of Korah. How lovely
is Your dwelling place, O Lord of hosts! My soul longs and indeed pines for the
courtyard of the Lord. My heart and my flesh cry out for the living God. Even the
bird has found a home, and the sparrow a nest for herself, where she has placed her

---

*17th DAY of the month

אֶת־מִזְבְּחוֹתֶיךָ יהוה צְבָאוֹת מַלְכִּי וֵאלֹהָי: אַשְׁרֵי יוֹשְׁבֵי בֵיתֶךָ עוֹד
יְהַלְלוּךָ סֶּלָה: אַשְׁרֵי אָדָם עוֹז־לוֹ בָךְ מְסִלּוֹת בִּלְבָבָם: עֹבְרֵי | בְּעֵמֶק
הַבָּכָא מַעְיָן יְשִׁיתוּהוּ גַּם־בְּרָכוֹת יַעְטֶה מוֹרֶה: יֵלְכוּ מֵחַיִל אֶל־חָיִל
יֵרָאֶה אֶל־אֱלֹהִים בְּצִיּוֹן: יהוה אֱלֹהִים צְבָאוֹת שִׁמְעָה תְפִלָּתִי הַאֲזִינָה
אֱלֹהֵי יַעֲקֹב סֶלָה: מָגִנֵּנוּ רְאֵה אֱלֹהִים וְהַבֵּט פְּנֵי מְשִׁיחֶךָ: כִּי טוֹב־יוֹם
בַּחֲצֵרֶיךָ מֵאָלֶף בָּחַרְתִּי הִסְתּוֹפֵף בְּבֵית אֱלֹהַי מִדּוּר בְּאָהֳלֵי־רֶשַׁע: כִּי
שֶׁמֶשׁ | וּמָגֵן יהוה אֱלֹהִים חֵן וְכָבוֹד יִתֵּן יהוה לֹא יִמְנַע־טוֹב לַהֹלְכִים
בְּתָמִים: יהוה צְבָאוֹת אַשְׁרֵי אָדָם בֹּטֵחַ בָּךְ:

שְׁבִית פה לַמְנַצֵּחַ לִבְנֵי־קֹרַח מִזְמוֹר: רָצִיתָ יהוה אַרְצֶךָ שַׁבְתָּ שְׁבוּת יַעֲקֹב: נָשָׂאתָ
עֲוֺן עַמֶּךָ כִּסִּיתָ כָל־חַטָּאתָם סֶלָה: אָסַפְתָּ כָל־עֶבְרָתֶךָ הֱשִׁיבוֹתָ מֵחֲרוֹן
אַפֶּךָ: שׁוּבֵנוּ אֱלֹהֵי יִשְׁעֵנוּ וְהָפֵר כַּעַסְךָ עִמָּנוּ: הַלְעוֹלָם תֶּאֱנַף־בָּנוּ
תִּמְשֹׁךְ אַפְּךָ לְדֹר וָדֹר: הֲלֹא־אַתָּה תָּשׁוּב תְּחַיֵּנוּ וְעַמְּךָ יִשְׂמְחוּ־בָךְ:
הַרְאֵנוּ יהוה חַסְדֶּךָ וְיֶשְׁעֲךָ תִּתֶּן־לָנוּ: אֶשְׁמְעָה מַה־יְדַבֵּר הָאֵל | יהוה
כִּי | יְדַבֵּר שָׁלוֹם אֶל־עַמּוֹ וְאֶל־חֲסִידָיו וְאַל־יָשׁוּבוּ לְכִסְלָה: אַךְ קָרוֹב
לִירֵאָיו יִשְׁעוֹ לִשְׁכֹּן כָּבוֹד בְּאַרְצֵנוּ: חֶסֶד־וֶאֱמֶת נִפְגָּשׁוּ צֶדֶק וְשָׁלוֹם
נָשָׁקוּ: אֱמֶת מֵאֶרֶץ תִּצְמָח וְצֶדֶק מִשָּׁמַיִם נִשְׁקָף: גַּם־יהוה יִתֵּן הַטּוֹב
וְאַרְצֵנוּ תִּתֵּן יְבוּלָהּ: צֶדֶק לְפָנָיו יְהַלֵּךְ וְיָשֵׂם לְדֶרֶךְ פְּעָמָיו:

פו תְּפִלָּה לְדָוִד הַטֵּה־יהוה אָזְנְךָ עֲנֵנִי כִּי־עָנִי וְאֶבְיוֹן אָנִי: שָׁמְרָה נַפְשִׁי
כִּי־חָסִיד אָנִי הוֹשַׁע עַבְדְּךָ אַתָּה אֱלֹהַי הַבּוֹטֵחַ אֵלֶיךָ: חָנֵּנִי אֲדֹנָי כִּי־
אֵלֶיךָ אֶקְרָא כָּל־הַיּוֹם: שַׂמֵּחַ נֶפֶשׁ עַבְדֶּךָ כִּי־אֵלֶיךָ אֲדֹנָי נַפְשִׁי אֶשָּׂא:
כִּי־אַתָּה אֲדֹנָי טוֹב וְסַלָּח וְרַב־חֶסֶד לְכָל־קֹרְאֶיךָ: הַאֲזִינָה יהוה תְּפִלָּתִי
וְהַקְשִׁיבָה בְּקוֹל תַּחֲנוּנוֹתָי: בְּיוֹם צָרָתִי אֶקְרָאֶךָּ כִּי תַעֲנֵנִי: אֵין־כָּמוֹךָ
בָאֱלֹהִים | אֲדֹנָי וְאֵין כְּמַעֲשֶׂיךָ: כָּל־גּוֹיִם | אֲשֶׁר עָשִׂיתָ יָבוֹאוּ | וְיִשְׁתַּחֲווּ
לְפָנֶיךָ אֲדֹנָי וִיכַבְּדוּ לִשְׁמֶךָ: כִּי־גָדוֹל אַתָּה וְעֹשֵׂה נִפְלָאוֹת אַתָּה אֱלֹהִים
לְבַדֶּךָ: הוֹרֵנִי יהוה | דַּרְכֶּךָ אֲהַלֵּךְ בַּאֲמִתֶּךָ יַחֵד לְבָבִי לְיִרְאָה שְׁמֶךָ:
אוֹדְךָ | אֲדֹנָי אֱלֹהַי בְּכָל־לְבָבִי וַאֲכַבְּדָה שִׁמְךָ לְעוֹלָם: כִּי־חַסְדְּךָ גָּדוֹל
עָלָי וְהִצַּלְתָּ נַפְשִׁי מִשְּׁאוֹל תַּחְתִּיָּה: אֱלֹהִים | זֵדִים קָמוּ־עָלַי וַעֲדַת
עָרִיצִים בִּקְשׁוּ נַפְשִׁי וְלֹא שָׂמוּךָ לְנֶגְדָּם: וְאַתָּה אֲדֹנָי אֵל־רַחוּם וְחַנּוּן

young. Your altars, O Lord of hosts, my King and my God. Happy are those who
dwell in Your house. They will forever praise You. Selah. Happy is the man whose
strength is in You, in whose heart are the highways. Who, passing through the valley
of Baca, turn it into a spring. The early rain will also cover the pools. They go from
rampart to rampart. Each one of them appears before God in Zion. O Lord God of
hosts, hear my prayer. Give ear, O God of Jacob. Selah. Behold our shield, O God,
and look upon the face of Your anointed. Indeed, a day in Your court is better than
a thousand. I prefer to be at the threshold in the house of My God, than to dwell in
the tents of wickedness. Indeed, the Lord God is a sun and a shield. The Lord gives
grace and honor. He does not withhold the good from those who walk uprightly. O
Lord of hosts, happy is the man who trusts in You.

85 TO THE DIRECTOR of music. A psalm for the sons of Korah. O Lord, You had been
favorable to Your land. You have brought back the return of Jacob. You have removed
the iniquity of Your people. You have covered all their sins. Selah. You have hidden
away all Your wrath. You have turned back from the fierceness of Your anger. Restore
us, O God of our salvation, and cease Your anger toward us. Will You be angry with us
forever? Will You prolong Your anger to all generations? You will surely revive us again,
and Your people will rejoice in You. Show us Your loving-kindness, O Lord, and grant
us Your salvation. I will hear what God the Lord will speak, for He will speak peace to
His people and to His allies. But let them not turn back to folly. Surely His salvation
is near to those who fear Him, so that glory may dwell in our land. Loving-kindness
and truth will meet. Righteousness and peace will join together. Truth will spring
from the earth, and righteousness will be seen in the heavens. Likewise, the Lord
will give what is good, and our land will yield its increase. Righteousness goes before
Him and sets His steps on the way.

86 A PRAYER of David. Incline Your ear, O Lord, and answer me, for I am oppressed and
degraded. Preserve my soul, for I am Your ally. O You, my God, save Your servant
who trusts in You. Be gracious to me, O Lord, for I cry to You all the day. Make the
soul of Your servant rejoice, for to You, O Lord, I lift up my soul. Indeed, You, my
Master, are good and forgiving, and of bountiful loving-kindness to all who call upon
You. Give ear, O Lord, to my prayer, and hearken to the sound of my supplications.
On the day of my trouble I call upon You, that You will answer me. There is none
like You among the powers, O Lord, and there are none like Your deeds. All nations
whom You have made will come and prostrate themselves before You, O Lord, and
they will glorify Your name. Indeed, You are great and You do wondrous things. You
are God alone. Teach me Your way, O Lord. I will walk in Your truth. Make my heart
one to fear Your name. I will thank You, O Lord my God, with all my heart, and I
will glorify Your name forever. That Your loving-kindness has been great toward me,
and You have delivered my soul from the lowest underworld. O God, cruel enemies
rise up against me, and an assembly of violent men seek my soul and do not set You
before them. But You, O Lord, are a merciful and gracious God, slow to anger and

אֶרֶךְ אַפַּיִם וְרַב־חֶסֶד וֶאֱמֶת׃ פְּנֵה אֵלַי וְחָנֵּנִי תְּנָה־עֻזְּךָ לְעַבְדֶּךָ וְהוֹשִׁיעָה
לְבֶן־אֲמָתֶךָ׃ עֲשֵׂה־עִמִּי אוֹת לְטוֹבָה וְיִרְאוּ שֹׂנְאַי וְיֵבֹשׁוּ כִּי־אַתָּה יהוה
עֲזַרְתַּנִי וְנִחַמְתָּנִי׃

פז לִבְנֵי־קֹרַח מִזְמוֹר שִׁיר יְסוּדָתוֹ בְּהַרְרֵי־קֹדֶשׁ׃ אֹהֵב יהוה שַׁעֲרֵי צִיּוֹן
מִכֹּל מִשְׁכְּנוֹת יַעֲקֹב׃ נִכְבָּדוֹת מְדֻבָּר בָּךְ עִיר הָאֱלֹהִים סֶלָה׃ אַזְכִּיר ׀
רַהַב וּבָבֶל לְיֹדְעָי הִנֵּה פְלֶשֶׁת וְצוֹר עִם־כּוּשׁ זֶה יֻלַּד־שָׁם׃ וּלְצִיּוֹן ׀ יֵאָמַר
אִישׁ וְאִישׁ יֻלַּד־בָּהּ וְהוּא יְכוֹנְנֶהָ עֶלְיוֹן׃ יהוה יִסְפֹּר בִּכְתוֹב עַמִּים זֶה
יֻלַּד־שָׁם סֶלָה׃ וְשָׁרִים כְּחֹלְלִים כָּל־מַעְיָנַי בָּךְ׃

*פח שִׁיר מִזְמוֹר לִבְנֵי קֹרַח לַמְנַצֵּחַ עַל־מָחֲלַת לְעַנּוֹת מַשְׂכִּיל לְהֵימָן
הָאֶזְרָחִי׃ יהוה אֱלֹהֵי יְשׁוּעָתִי יוֹם־צָעַקְתִּי בַלַּיְלָה נֶגְדֶּךָ׃ תָּבוֹא לְפָנֶיךָ
תְּפִלָּתִי הַטֵּה־אָזְנְךָ לְרִנָּתִי׃ כִּי־שָׂבְעָה בְרָעוֹת נַפְשִׁי וְחַיַּי לִשְׁאוֹל הִגִּיעוּ׃
נֶחְשַׁבְתִּי עִם־יוֹרְדֵי בוֹר הָיִיתִי כְּגֶבֶר אֵין־אֱיָל׃ בַּמֵּתִים חָפְשִׁי כְּמוֹ
חֲלָלִים ׀ שֹׁכְבֵי קֶבֶר אֲשֶׁר לֹא זְכַרְתָּם עוֹד וְהֵמָּה מִיָּדְךָ נִגְזָרוּ׃ שַׁתַּנִי
בְּבוֹר תַּחְתִּיּוֹת בְּמַחֲשַׁכִּים בִּמְצֹלוֹת׃ עָלַי סָמְכָה חֲמָתֶךָ וְכָל־מִשְׁבָּרֶיךָ
עִנִּיתָ סֶּלָה׃ הִרְחַקְתָּ מְיֻדָּעַי מִמֶּנִּי שַׁתַּנִי תוֹעֵבוֹת לָמוֹ כָּלֻא וְלֹא אֵצֵא׃
עֵינִי דָאֲבָה מִנִּי עֹנִי קְרָאתִיךָ יהוה בְּכָל־יוֹם שִׁטַּחְתִּי אֵלֶיךָ כַפָּי׃ הֲלַמֵּתִים
תַּעֲשֶׂה־פֶּלֶא אִם־רְפָאִים יָקוּמוּ ׀ יוֹדוּךָ סֶּלָה׃ הַיְסֻפַּר בַּקֶּבֶר חַסְדֶּךָ
אֱמוּנָתְךָ בָּאֲבַדּוֹן׃ הֲיִוָּדַע בַּחֹשֶׁךְ פִּלְאֶךָ וְצִדְקָתְךָ בְּאֶרֶץ נְשִׁיָּה׃ וַאֲנִי ׀
אֵלֶיךָ יהוה שִׁוַּעְתִּי וּבַבֹּקֶר תְּפִלָּתִי תְקַדְּמֶךָּ׃ לָמָה יהוה תִּזְנַח נַפְשִׁי
תַּסְתִּיר פָּנֶיךָ מִמֶּנִּי׃ עָנִי אֲנִי וְגֹוֵעַ מִנֹּעַר נָשָׂאתִי אֵמֶיךָ אָפוּנָה׃ עָלַי עָבְרוּ
חֲרוֹנֶיךָ בִּעוּתֶיךָ צִמְּתוּתֻנִי׃ סַבּוּנִי כַמַּיִם כָּל־הַיּוֹם הִקִּיפוּ עָלַי יָחַד׃
הִרְחַקְתָּ מִמֶּנִּי אֹהֵב וָרֵעַ מְיֻדָּעַי מַחְשָׁךְ׃

פט מַשְׂכִּיל לְאֵיתָן הָאֶזְרָחִי׃ חַסְדֵי יהוה עוֹלָם אָשִׁירָה לְדֹר וָדֹר ׀ אוֹדִיעַ
אֱמוּנָתְךָ בְּפִי׃ כִּי־אָמַרְתִּי עוֹלָם חֶסֶד יִבָּנֶה שָׁמַיִם ׀ תָּכִן אֱמוּנָתְךָ בָהֶם׃
כָּרַתִּי בְרִית לִבְחִירִי נִשְׁבַּעְתִּי לְדָוִד עַבְדִּי׃ עַד־עוֹלָם אָכִין זַרְעֶךָ וּבָנִיתִי
לְדֹר־וָדוֹר כִּסְאֲךָ סֶלָה׃ וְיוֹדוּ שָׁמַיִם פִּלְאֲךָ יהוה אַף־אֱמוּנָתְךָ בִּקְהַל
קְדֹשִׁים׃ כִּי מִי בַשַּׁחַק יַעֲרֹךְ לַיהוה יִדְמֶה לַיהוה בִּבְנֵי אֵלִים׃ אֵל
נַעֲרָץ בְּסוֹד־קְדֹשִׁים רַבָּה וְנוֹרָא עַל־כָּל־סְבִיבָיו׃ יהוה ׀ אֱלֹהֵי צְבָאוֹת

*יח לחודש

bountiful and loving-kindness and truth. Turn to me and be gracious to me. Give
Your strength to Your servant, and save the son of Your handmaid. Show me a sign
for good so that those who hate me may see it and be disappointed, because You, O
Lord, have helped me and comforted me.

87 FOR THE SONS of Korah. A psalm. A song. His foundation is in the holy mountains.
The Lord loves the gates of Zion more than all the dwelling places of Jacob. Glorious
things are spoken of you, O city of God. Selah. I remind those who know me of Rahab
and Babylon. Behold! Philistia and Tyre with Ethiopia. This one was born there. But
of Zion it is said: "Every man was born in it," and the Highest Himself establishes it.
The Lord will record, when He registers the peoples: "This one was born there." Selah.
Behold, they are both singing and dancing: "All my springs are in you."

*88 A SONG. A psalm for the sons of Korah. To the director of music on *maḥalat*, to sing.
A *maskil* of Heman the Ezrahite. O Lord God of my salvation, by day and by night
I cry before You. May my prayer come before You. Incline Your ear to my song. For
my soul is sated with evil, and my life draws near to the underworld. I am reckoned
with those who go down into the pit. I am like a man without strength. Free among
the dead, like the slain who lie in the grave, whom You remember no more, and
they are cut off from Your hand. You have laid me in the lowest pit, in darkness, in
the depths. Your wrath has lain hard upon me, and You have afflicted me with all
Your waves. Selah. You have put my close friends far away from me. You have made
me an abomination to them. I am imprisoned and I cannot come out. My eye hurts
by reason of affliction. O Lord, I call upon You constantly. I stretch out my hand to
You. Do You perform wonders for the dead? Do the shades arise and give thanks to
You? Selah. Is Your loving-kindness reported in the grave, or Your faithfulness in the
underworld? Are Your wonders known in the dark, and Your righteousness in the land
of forgetfulness? But I cry to You, O Lord, and in the morning my prayer greets You.
Why, O Lord, do You cast off my soul, do You hide Your face from me? I am afflicted
and close to death from my youth. I suffer Your terrors, I am wasting away. Your fierce
wrath has passed over me. Your terrors have caught me off. They surround me all the
day like water, they all encompass me. You have put friend and companion far for me.
My close friends are in darkness.

89 A *MASKIL* of Ethan the Ezrahite. I will sing of the loving-kindness of the Lord forever.
To all generations, I will make known Your faithfulness with my mouth. Indeed, I have
said that loving-kindness will be built forever, that You have established Your faithfulness
in the heavens. I am making a covenant with My chosen one. I am swearing to David My
servant. I will establish your seed forever, and I will build your throne for all generations.
Selah. And the heavens praise Your wonders, O Lord, Your faithfulness, too, in the
assembly of the holy ones. Indeed, who in the skies can be compared to the Lord? Who
is like the Lord among the divine beings? God is dreaded in the council of the many
holy ones, and He is revered by all those around Him. The Lord God of hosts, who is
mighty like You, O Lord, and Your faithfulness round about You? You rule over the

---

*18th DAY of the month

מִי־כָמוֹךָ חֲסִין ׀ יָהּ וֶאֱמוּנָתְךָ סְבִיבוֹתֶיךָ׃ אַתָּה מוֹשֵׁל בְּגֵאוּת הַיָּם
בְּשׂוֹא גַלָּיו אַתָּה תְשַׁבְּחֵם׃ אַתָּה דִכִּאתָ כֶחָלָל רָהַב בִּזְרוֹעַ עֻזְּךָ פִּזַּרְתָּ
אוֹיְבֶיךָ׃ לְךָ שָׁמַיִם אַף־לְךָ אָרֶץ תֵּבֵל וּמְלֹאָהּ אַתָּה יְסַדְתָּם׃ צָפוֹן
וְיָמִין אַתָּה בְרָאתָם תָּבוֹר וְחֶרְמוֹן בְּשִׁמְךָ יְרַנֵּנוּ׃ לְךָ זְרוֹעַ עִם־גְּבוּרָה
תָּעֹז יָדְךָ תָּרוּם יְמִינֶךָ׃ צֶדֶק וּמִשְׁפָּט מְכוֹן כִּסְאֶךָ חֶסֶד וֶאֱמֶת יְקַדְּמוּ
פָנֶיךָ׃ אַשְׁרֵי הָעָם יוֹדְעֵי תְרוּעָה יהוה בְּאוֹר־פָּנֶיךָ יְהַלֵּכוּן׃ בְּשִׁמְךָ
יְגִילוּן כָּל־הַיּוֹם וּבְצִדְקָתְךָ יָרוּמוּ׃ כִּי־תִפְאֶרֶת עֻזָּמוֹ אָתָּה וּבִרְצוֹנְךָ
תרים קַרְנֵנוּ׃ כִּי לַיהוה מָגִנֵּנוּ וְלִקְדוֹשׁ יִשְׂרָאֵל מַלְכֵּנוּ׃ אָז דִּבַּרְתָּ בְחָזוֹן תָּרוּם
לַחֲסִידֶיךָ וַתֹּאמֶר שִׁוִּיתִי עֵזֶר עַל־גִּבּוֹר הֲרִימוֹתִי בָחוּר מֵעָם׃ מָצָאתִי
דָּוִד עַבְדִּי בְּשֶׁמֶן קָדְשִׁי מְשַׁחְתִּיו׃ אֲשֶׁר יָדִי תִּכּוֹן עִמּוֹ אַף־זְרוֹעִי
תְאַמְּצֶנּוּ׃ לֹא־יַשִּׁא אוֹיֵב בּוֹ וּבֶן־עַוְלָה לֹא יְעַנֶּנּוּ׃ וְכַתּוֹתִי מִפָּנָיו צָרָיו
וּמְשַׂנְאָיו אֶגּוֹף׃ וֶאֱמוּנָתִי וְחַסְדִּי עִמּוֹ וּבִשְׁמִי תָּרוּם קַרְנוֹ׃ וְשַׂמְתִּי
בַיָּם יָדוֹ וּבַנְּהָרוֹת יְמִינוֹ׃ הוּא יִקְרָאֵנִי אָבִי אָתָּה אֵלִי וְצוּר יְשׁוּעָתִי׃
אַף־אָנִי בְּכוֹר אֶתְּנֵהוּ עֶלְיוֹן לְמַלְכֵי־אָרֶץ׃ לְעוֹלָם אשמור־לוֹ חַסְדִּי אֶשְׁמָר־
וּבְרִיתִי נֶאֱמֶנֶת לוֹ׃ וְשַׂמְתִּי לָעַד זַרְעוֹ וְכִסְאוֹ כִּימֵי שָׁמָיִם׃ אִם־יַעַזְבוּ
בָנָיו תּוֹרָתִי וּבְמִשְׁפָּטַי לֹא יֵלֵכוּן׃ אִם־חֻקֹּתַי יְחַלֵּלוּ וּמִצְוֺתַי לֹא יִשְׁמֹרוּ׃
וּפָקַדְתִּי בְשֵׁבֶט פִּשְׁעָם וּבִנְגָעִים עֲוֺנָם׃ וְחַסְדִּי לֹא־אָפִיר מֵעִמּוֹ וְלֹא
אֲשַׁקֵּר בֶּאֱמוּנָתִי׃ לֹא־אֲחַלֵּל בְּרִיתִי וּמוֹצָא שְׂפָתַי לֹא אֲשַׁנֶּה׃ אַחַת
נִשְׁבַּעְתִּי בְקָדְשִׁי אִם־לְדָוִד אֲכַזֵּב׃ זַרְעוֹ לְעוֹלָם יִהְיֶה וְכִסְאוֹ כַשֶּׁמֶשׁ
נֶגְדִּי׃ כְּיָרֵחַ יִכּוֹן עוֹלָם וְעֵד בַּשַּׁחַק נֶאֱמָן סֶלָה׃ וְאַתָּה זָנַחְתָּ וַתִּמְאָס
הִתְעַבַּרְתָּ עִם־מְשִׁיחֶךָ׃ נֵאַרְתָּה בְּרִית עַבְדֶּךָ חִלַּלְתָּ לָאָרֶץ נִזְרוֹ׃ פָּרַצְתָּ
כָל־גְּדֵרֹתָיו שַׂמְתָּ מִבְצָרָיו מְחִתָּה׃ שַׁסֻּהוּ כָּל־עֹבְרֵי דָרֶךְ הָיָה חֶרְפָּה
לִשְׁכֵנָיו׃ הֲרִימוֹתָ יְמִין צָרָיו הִשְׂמַחְתָּ כָּל־אוֹיְבָיו׃ אַף־תָּשִׁיב צוּר חַרְבּוֹ
וְלֹא הֲקֵמֹתוֹ בַּמִּלְחָמָה׃ הִשְׁבַּתָּ מִטְּהָרוֹ וְכִסְאוֹ לָאָרֶץ מִגַּרְתָּה׃ הִקְצַרְתָּ
יְמֵי עֲלוּמָיו הֶעֱטִיתָ עָלָיו בּוּשָׁה סֶלָה׃ עַד־מָה יהוה תִּסָּתֵר לָנֶצַח תִּבְעַר
כְּמוֹ־אֵשׁ חֲמָתֶךָ׃ זְכָר־אֲנִי מֶה־חָלֶד עַל־מַה־שָּׁוְא בָּרָאתָ כָל־בְּנֵי־אָדָם׃
מִי גֶבֶר יִחְיֶה וְלֹא יִרְאֶה־מָּוֶת יְמַלֵּט נַפְשׁוֹ מִיַּד־שְׁאוֹל סֶלָה׃ אַיֵּה ׀ חֲסָדֶיךָ
הָרִאשֹׁנִים ׀ אֲדֹנָי נִשְׁבַּעְתָּ לְדָוִד בֶּאֱמוּנָתֶךָ׃ זְכֹר אֲדֹנָי חֶרְפַּת עֲבָדֶיךָ

swelling of the sea. When its waves rise up, You still them. You have crushed Rahab like one slain. With Your strong arm You have scattered Your enemies. The heavens are Yours; the earth, too, is Yours. The world and the fullness thereof, You have founded them. The north and the south, You have created them. Tabor and Hermon rejoice in Your name. You have an arm and might. Your hand is strong, Your right hand is high. Righteousness and judgment are the base of Your throne. Loving-kindness and truth go before You. Happy is the people that know the joyful shouts. O Lord, they walk in the light of Your countenance. In Your name, they rejoice all the day, and through Your righteousness they are exalted. Indeed, You are the glory of their strength, and by Your will our stature is exalted. Indeed, we call the Lord our shield, and the Holy One of Israel our King. Then You spoke in a vision of Your allies, and You said: I have laid victory upon one who is mighty. I have exalted a chosen one from the people. I have found David My servant. With My holy oil I have anointed him, that My hand will be ready with him. My arm, too, will strengthen him. The enemy will not destroy him, nor will the son of wickedness afflict him. And I will crush his foes out of his sight, and I will strike down those who hate him. But My faithfulness and My loving-kindness will be with him, and through My name his stature will be exalted. And I will set his hand on the sea, and his right hand on the rivers. He will call Me: "You are my Father, my God, and the Rock of my salvation." I, too, will make him firstborn, supreme over the kings of the earth. I will keep My loving-kindness with him forever, and My covenant will be faithful to him. And I will make his seed endure forever, and his throne as the days of the heavens. If his children forsake My Torah and they do not walk in My judgments, if they profane My statutes and they do not keep My commandments, then I will punish their transgression with the rod, and their iniquity with plagues. But I will not annul My loving-kindness from him, and I will not be false to My faithfulness. I will not profane My covenant, and I will not alter that which has issued from My lips. I have sworn one thing by My holiness, that I will not lie to David. His seed will exist forever, and his throne will be like the sun before Me. It will endure forever like the moon, and the witness in the sky will be steadfast. Selah. But You have cast off and rejected him. You have been angry with Your anointed. You have renounced the covenant of Your servant. You have profaned his crown to the ground. You have broken down all his fences. You have brought his strongholds to ruin. All who pass by the way plunder him. He has become a taunt to his neighbors. You have exalted the right hand of his adversaries. You have made all his enemies rejoice. You have also turned back the edge of his sword, and You have not raised him up in battle. You have caused his brightness to cease, and You have cast his throne to the ground. You have shortened the days of his youth. You have covered him in shame. Selah. Until then, O Lord, will You hide Yourself totally, will Your wrath burn like fire? Remember how short my lifetime is. For what falseness have You created all the sons of men? Who is the man who will live and not see death, who will deliver his soul from the hand of the underworld? Selah. Where are Your former loving-kindnesses, O Lord, which You swore to David in Your faithfulness? Consider, O

שְׂאֵתִי בְחֵיקִי כׇּל־רַבִּים עַמִּים׃ אֲשֶׁר חֵרְפוּ אוֹיְבֶיךָ ׀ יהוה אֲשֶׁר חֵרְפוּ
עִקְּבוֹת מְשִׁיחֶךָ׃ בָּרוּךְ יהוה לְעוֹלָם אָמֵן ׀ וְאָמֵן׃

ספר רביעי

צ* תְּפִלָּה לְמֹשֶׁה אִישׁ־הָאֱלֹהִים אֲדֹנָי מָעוֹן אַתָּה הָיִיתָ לָּנוּ בְּדֹר וָדֹר׃
בְּטֶרֶם ׀ הָרִים יֻלָּדוּ וַתְּחוֹלֵל אֶרֶץ וְתֵבֵל וּמֵעוֹלָם עַד־עוֹלָם אַתָּה אֵל׃
תָּשֵׁב אֱנוֹשׁ עַד־דַּכָּא וַתֹּאמֶר שׁוּבוּ בְנֵי־אָדָם׃ כִּי אֶלֶף שָׁנִים בְּעֵינֶיךָ
כְּיוֹם אֶתְמוֹל כִּי יַעֲבֹר וְאַשְׁמוּרָה בַלָּיְלָה׃ זְרַמְתָּם שֵׁנָה יִהְיוּ בַּבֹּקֶר
כֶּחָצִיר יַחֲלֹף׃ בַּבֹּקֶר יָצִיץ וְחָלָף לָעֶרֶב יְמוֹלֵל וְיָבֵשׁ׃ כִּי־כָלִינוּ בְאַפֶּךָ
וּבַחֲמָתְךָ נִבְהָלְנוּ׃ שַׁתָּ עֲוֺנֹתֵינוּ לְנֶגְדֶּךָ עֲלֻמֵנוּ לִמְאוֹר פָּנֶיךָ׃ כִּי כׇל־
יָמֵינוּ פָּנוּ בְעֶבְרָתֶךָ כִּלִּינוּ שָׁנֵינוּ כְמוֹ־הֶגֶה׃ יְמֵי־שְׁנוֹתֵינוּ בָהֶם שִׁבְעִים
שָׁנָה וְאִם בִּגְבוּרֹת ׀ שְׁמוֹנִים שָׁנָה וְרׇהְבָּם עָמָל וָאָוֶן כִּי־גָז חִישׁ
וַנָּעֻפָה׃ מִי־יוֹדֵעַ עֹז אַפֶּךָ וּכְיִרְאָתְךָ עֶבְרָתֶךָ׃ לִמְנוֹת יָמֵינוּ כֵּן הוֹדַע
וְנָבִא לְבַב חׇכְמָה׃ שׁוּבָה יהוה עַד־מָתָי וְהִנָּחֵם עַל־עֲבָדֶיךָ׃ שַׂבְּעֵנוּ
בַבֹּקֶר חַסְדֶּךָ וּנְרַנְּנָה וְנִשְׂמְחָה בְּכׇל־יָמֵינוּ׃ שַׂמְּחֵנוּ כִּימוֹת עִנִּיתָנוּ
שְׁנוֹת רָאִינוּ רָעָה׃ יֵרָאֶה אֶל־עֲבָדֶיךָ פׇעֳלֶךָ וַהֲדָרְךָ עַל־בְּנֵיהֶם׃ וִיהִי ׀
נֹעַם אֲדֹנָי אֱלֹהֵינוּ עָלֵינוּ וּמַעֲשֵׂה יָדֵינוּ כּוֹנְנָה עָלֵינוּ וּמַעֲשֵׂה יָדֵינוּ
כּוֹנְנֵהוּ׃

צא יֹשֵׁב בְּסֵתֶר עֶלְיוֹן בְּצֵל שַׁדַּי יִתְלוֹנָן׃ אֹמַר לַיהוה מַחְסִי וּמְצוּדָתִי אֱלֹהַי
אֶבְטַח־בּוֹ׃ כִּי הוּא יַצִּילְךָ מִפַּח יָקוּשׁ מִדֶּבֶר הַוּוֹת׃ בְּאֶבְרָתוֹ ׀ יָסֶךְ
לָךְ וְתַחַת־כְּנָפָיו תֶּחְסֶה צִנָּה וְסֹחֵרָה אֲמִתּוֹ׃ לֹא־תִירָא מִפַּחַד לָיְלָה
מֵחֵץ יָעוּף יוֹמָם׃ מִדֶּבֶר בָּאֹפֶל יַהֲלֹךְ מִקֶּטֶב יָשׁוּד צׇהֳרָיִם׃ יִפֹּל מִצִּדְּךָ ׀
אֶלֶף וּרְבָבָה מִימִינֶךָ אֵלֶיךָ לֹא יִגָּשׁ׃ רַק בְּעֵינֶיךָ תַבִּיט וְשִׁלֻּמַת רְשָׁעִים
תִּרְאֶה׃ כִּי־אַתָּה יהוה מַחְסִי עֶלְיוֹן שַׂמְתָּ מְעוֹנֶךָ׃ לֹא־תְאֻנֶּה אֵלֶיךָ
רָעָה וְנֶגַע לֹא־יִקְרַב בְּאׇהֳלֶךָ׃ כִּי מַלְאָכָיו יְצַוֶּה־לָּךְ לִשְׁמׇרְךָ בְּכׇל־דְּרָכֶיךָ׃
עַל־כַּפַּיִם יִשָּׂאוּנְךָ פֶּן־תִּגֹּף בָּאֶבֶן רַגְלֶךָ׃ עַל־שַׁחַל וָפֶתֶן תִּדְרֹךְ תִּרְמֹס
כְּפִיר וְתַנִּין׃ כִּי בִי חָשַׁק וַאֲפַלְּטֵהוּ אֲשַׂגְּבֵהוּ כִּי־יָדַע שְׁמִי׃ יִקְרָאֵנִי ׀
וְאֶעֱנֵהוּ עִמּוֹ־אָנֹכִי בְצָרָה אֲחַלְּצֵהוּ וַאֲכַבְּדֵהוּ׃ אֹרֶךְ יָמִים אַשְׂבִּיעֵהוּ
וְאַרְאֵהוּ בִּישׁוּעָתִי׃

*יט לחודש / ליום החמישי

Lord, the insult of Your servants, what I bear in my bosom of all the many peoples, With which Your enemies have insulted, O Lord, with which they have insulted the footsteps of Your anointed. Blessed is the Lord forever. Amen and Amen.

BOOK FOUR

*90 A PRAYER of Moses, the man of God. O Lord, You have been our shelter in all
generations. Before the mountains were born and You had formed the earth and the
world, even from everlasting to everlasting, You are God. You turn man back to dust
and You say, "Return, you children of man." Indeed, a thousand years in Your sight
are like yesterday when it is past, and like a watch in the night. You engulf them, they
are like sleepers. In the morning they are like the short-lived grass. In the morning it
flowers and fades, in the evening it withers and dries. Indeed, we are consumed by
Your anger, and through Your wrath we die. You set our iniquities before You, our
secrets in the light of Your countenance. Indeed, all our days pass away in Your wrath,
we consume our years like a sound. The days of our years are seventy, or even by
reason of strength eighty years, but their pride is trouble and wretchedness, for it soars
in haste, and we fly away. Who knows the power of Your anger, and that Your wrath
is in accordance with Your fear? Teach us to number our days correctly. And may
we get a heart of wisdom. Return, O Lord! How long? And relent concerning Your
servants. Satisfy us in the morning with Your loving-kindness, and let us rejoice and
be glad all our days. Make us glad according to the days in which You have afflicted
us, the years in which we have seen evil. Let Your work be seen by Your servants, and
Your glory through their children. And let the pleasantness of my Master our God
be upon us, and establish the work of our hands upon us, and establish it, the work
of our hands.

91 HE WHO DWELLS in the secret place of the Most High abides in the shadow of the
Almighty. I say to the Lord, my refuge and my fortress, my God, I trust in Him. Indeed,
He will deliver you from the baited trap, from the deadly pestilence. He will cover
you with His pinions, and under His wings you will find refuge. His truth will be your
shield and buckler. You will not be afraid of the terror by night, of the arrow that flies
by day, of the pestilence that walks in the darkness, of the destruction that wastes
at noonday. A thousand will fall at your side and ten thousand at your right hand. It
will not come near to you. Only with your eyes will you behold, and you will see the
destruction of the wicked. Indeed, You, O Lord, are my refuge. You have made the
Most High Your habitation. No evil will befall you, and plague will not come near
to your tent. Indeed, He will give His angels charge over you, to keep you in all your
ways. They will bear you up on their hands, lest you dash your foot against a stone.
You will tread upon the lion and the adder. You will trample the young lion and the
crocodile underfoot. Because he has clung to Me, I will deliver him. I will make him
safe, because he has known My name. When he calls upon Me, I answer him. I am
with him in trouble. I deliver him and I will honor him. I will satisfy him with long
life, and I will show him of My salvation.

*19th DAY of the month / THURSDAY

צב מִזְמוֹר שִׁיר לְיוֹם הַשַּׁבָּת: טוֹב לְהֹדוֹת לַיהוָה וּלְזַמֵּר לְשִׁמְךָ עֶלְיוֹן: לְהַגִּיד
בַּבֹּקֶר חַסְדֶּךָ וֶאֱמוּנָתְךָ בַּלֵּילוֹת: עֲלֵי־עָשׂוֹר וַעֲלֵי־נָבֶל עֲלֵי הִגָּיוֹן בְּכִנּוֹר:
כִּי שִׂמַּחְתַּנִי יהוה בְּפָעֳלֶךָ בְּמַעֲשֵׂי יָדֶיךָ אֲרַנֵּן: מַה־גָּדְלוּ מַעֲשֶׂיךָ יְהוָה
מְאֹד עָמְקוּ מַחְשְׁבֹתֶיךָ: אִישׁ־בַּעַר לֹא יֵדָע וּכְסִיל לֹא־יָבִין אֶת־זֹאת:
בִּפְרֹחַ רְשָׁעִים | כְּמוֹ עֵשֶׂב וַיָּצִיצוּ כָּל־פֹּעֲלֵי אָוֶן לְהִשָּׁמְדָם עֲדֵי־עַד:
וְאַתָּה מָרוֹם לְעֹלָם יהוה: כִּי הִנֵּה אֹיְבֶיךָ יהוה כִּי־הִנֵּה אֹיְבֶיךָ יֹאבֵדוּ
יִתְפָּרְדוּ כָּל־פֹּעֲלֵי אָוֶן: וַתָּרֶם כִּרְאֵים קַרְנִי בַּלֹּתִי בְּשֶׁמֶן רַעֲנָן: וַתַּבֵּט
עֵינִי בְּשׁוּרָי בַּקָּמִים עָלַי מְרֵעִים תִּשְׁמַעְנָה אָזְנָי: צַדִּיק כַּתָּמָר יִפְרָח
כְּאֶרֶז בַּלְּבָנוֹן יִשְׂגֶּה: שְׁתוּלִים בְּבֵית יהוה בְּחַצְרוֹת אֱלֹהֵינוּ יַפְרִיחוּ:
עוֹד יְנוּבוּן בְּשֵׂיבָה דְּשֵׁנִים וְרַעֲנַנִּים יִהְיוּ: לְהַגִּיד כִּי־יָשָׁר יהוה צוּרִי
עַוְלָתָה וְלֹא־עלתה בּוֹ:
צג יהוה מָלָךְ גֵּאוּת לָבֵשׁ לָבֵשׁ יהוה עֹז הִתְאַזָּר אַף־תִּכּוֹן תֵּבֵל בַּל־תִּמּוֹט:
נָכוֹן כִּסְאֲךָ מֵאָז מֵעוֹלָם אָתָּה: נָשְׂאוּ נְהָרוֹת | יהוה נָשְׂאוּ נְהָרוֹת קוֹלָם
יִשְׂאוּ נְהָרוֹת דָּכְיָם: מִקֹּלוֹת | מַיִם רַבִּים אַדִּירִים מִשְׁבְּרֵי־יָם אַדִּיר
בַּמָּרוֹם יהוה: עֵדֹתֶיךָ | נֶאֶמְנוּ מְאֹד לְבֵיתְךָ נַאֲוָה־קֹדֶשׁ יהוה לְאֹרֶךְ
יָמִים:
צד אֵל־נְקָמוֹת יהוה אֵל נְקָמוֹת הוֹפִיעַ: הִנָּשֵׂא שֹׁפֵט הָאָרֶץ הָשֵׁב גְּמוּל
עַל־גֵּאִים: עַד־מָתַי רְשָׁעִים | יהוה עַד־מָתַי רְשָׁעִים יַעֲלֹזוּ: יַבִּיעוּ
יְדַבְּרוּ עָתָק יִתְאַמְּרוּ כָּל־פֹּעֲלֵי אָוֶן: עַמְּךָ יהוה יְדַכְּאוּ וְנַחֲלָתְךָ יְעַנּוּ:
אַלְמָנָה וְגֵר יַהֲרֹגוּ וִיתוֹמִים יְרַצֵּחוּ: וַיֹּאמְרוּ לֹא יִרְאֶה־יָּהּ וְלֹא־יָבִין
אֱלֹהֵי יַעֲקֹב: בִּינוּ בֹּעֲרִים בָּעָם וּכְסִילִים מָתַי תַּשְׂכִּילוּ: הֲנֹטַע אֹזֶן הֲלֹא
יִשְׁמָע אִם־יֹצֵר עַיִן הֲלֹא יַבִּיט: הֲיֹסֵר גּוֹיִם הֲלֹא יוֹכִיחַ הַמְלַמֵּד אָדָם
דָּעַת: יהוה יֹדֵעַ מַחְשְׁבוֹת אָדָם כִּי־הֵמָּה הָבֶל: אַשְׁרֵי הַגֶּבֶר אֲשֶׁר־
תְּיַסְּרֶנּוּ יָּהּ וּמִתּוֹרָתְךָ תְלַמְּדֶנּוּ: לְהַשְׁקִיט לוֹ מִימֵי רָע עַד יִכָּרֶה לָרָשָׁע
שָׁחַת: כִּי | לֹא־יִטֹּשׁ יהוה עַמּוֹ וְנַחֲלָתוֹ לֹא יַעֲזֹב: כִּי־עַד־צֶדֶק יָשׁוּב
מִשְׁפָּט וְאַחֲרָיו כָּל־יִשְׁרֵי־לֵב: מִי־יָקוּם לִי עִם־מְרֵעִים מִי־יִתְיַצֵּב לִי
עִם־פֹּעֲלֵי אָוֶן: לוּלֵי יהוה עֶזְרָתָה לִּי כִּמְעַט | שָׁכְנָה דוּמָה נַפְשִׁי: אִם־
אָמַרְתִּי מָטָה רַגְלִי חַסְדְּךָ יהוה יִסְעָדֵנִי: בְּרֹב שַׂרְעַפַּי בְּקִרְבִּי תַּנְחוּמֶיךָ

92 A PSALM. A song for the Sabbath day. It is good to give thanks to the Lord, and to sing praise to Your name, O Most High, to relate Your loving-kindness in the morning and Your faithfulness in the nights. Upon an instrument of ten strings and upon the harp, to the melody of the lyre. For You, O Lord, make me glad through Your work. I rejoice in the works of Your hands. How great are Your works, O Lord! Your thoughts are very deep. A brutish man does not know, and a fool does not understand this. When the wicked spring forth, they are like grass, and when all the workers of iniquity flourish, it is only that they may be destroyed forever. But You, O Lord, are most high forever. Indeed, behold Your enemies, O Lord! Indeed, behold, Your enemies are perishing. All the workers of iniquity are being scattered. But You have exalted my horn like that of a wild ox. I have anointed myself with fresh oil. My eye has seen the downfall of my enemies, and my ears have heard the doom of the wicked who rise against me. The righteous man flourishes like the palm tree. He grows like a cedar in Lebanon. They are planted in the house of the Lord. They will flourish in the courts of our God. They will still bring forth fruit in old age. They will be fat and flourishing. To declare that the Lord is upright, that He is my Rock, and there is no unrighteousness in Him.

93 THE LORD reigns, He is clothed in majesty, the Lord is clothed, He has girded Himself with strength. The world, too, is established so that it cannot be moved. You throne is established from of old. You are from everlasting. The floodwaters have lifted up, O Lord, the floodwaters have lifted up their voice, the floodwaters have lifted up their pounding. Mightier than the voices of great, mighty waters, breakers of the sea, is the Lord on high. Your testimonies are very true, in Your house, Your holy habitation, O Lord, for length of days.

94 GOD of vengeance, O Lord, God of vengeance, reveal Yourself. Rise up, O Judge of the earth, render to the proud their recompense. How long will the wicked, O Lord, how long will the wicked rejoice? They utter and speak arrogance. All the workers of iniquity speak conceit. They oppress Your people, O Lords, and they afflict Your inheritance. They slay the widow and the stranger, and they murder the fatherless. And they say: the Lord does not see and the God of Jacob does not discern. Understand, you brutes among the people. And you fools, when will you become wise? He Who planted the ear, will He not hear? He Who formed the eye, will He not see? He Who instructs nations, will He not rebuke? It is He Who teaches man knowledge. The Lord knows the thoughts of man, for they are vanity. Happy is the man whom You chasten, O Lord, and whom You teach from Your law, To quiet him from evil days, until the pit is dug for the wicked. For the Lord will not abandon His people, and He will not forsake His inheritance. For judgment will return to righteousness, and all the upright in heart will follow it. Who rose up for me against the evildoers? Who stood up for me against the workers of iniquity? If the Lord had not been my help, my soul would actually have dwelt in the underworld. Whenever I said, My foot slips, Your loving-kindness, O Lord, would support me. When my thoughts within me were many, Your consolations would occupy my soul. Will the seat of wickedness join to

יְשַׁעַשְׁעוּ נַפְשִׁי: הַיְחָבְרְךָ כִּסֵּא הַוּוֹת יֹצֵר עָמָל עֲלֵי־חֹק: יָגוֹדּוּ עַל־נֶפֶשׁ
צַדִּיק וְדָם נָקִי יַרְשִׁיעוּ: וַיְהִי יְהוָה לִי לְמִשְׂגָּב וֵאלֹהַי לְצוּר מַחְסִי: וַיָּשֶׁב
עֲלֵיהֶם ׀ אֶת־אוֹנָם וּבְרָעָתָם יַצְמִיתֵם יַצְמִיתֵם יְהוָה אֱלֹהֵינוּ:

צה לְכוּ נְרַנְּנָה לַיהוָה נָרִיעָה לְצוּר יִשְׁעֵנוּ: נְקַדְּמָה פָנָיו בְּתוֹדָה בִּזְמִרוֹת
נָרִיעַ לוֹ: כִּי אֵל גָּדוֹל יְהוָה וּמֶלֶךְ גָּדוֹל עַל־כָּל־אֱלֹהִים: אֲשֶׁר בְּיָדוֹ
מֶחְקְרֵי־אָרֶץ וְתוֹעֲפוֹת הָרִים לוֹ: אֲשֶׁר־לוֹ הַיָּם וְהוּא עָשָׂהוּ וְיַבֶּשֶׁת יָדָיו
יָצָרוּ: בֹּאוּ נִשְׁתַּחֲוֶה וְנִכְרָעָה נִבְרְכָה לִפְנֵי־יְהוָה עֹשֵׂנוּ: כִּי הוּא אֱלֹהֵינוּ
וַאֲנַחְנוּ ׀ עַם מַרְעִיתוֹ וְצֹאן יָדוֹ הַיּוֹם אִם־בְּקֹלוֹ תִשְׁמָעוּ: אַל־תַּקְשׁוּ
לְבַבְכֶם כִּמְרִיבָה כְּיוֹם מַסָּה בַּמִּדְבָּר: אֲשֶׁר נִסּוּנִי אֲבוֹתֵיכֶם בְּחָנוּנִי גַּם־
רָאוּ פָעֳלִי: אַרְבָּעִים שָׁנָה ׀ אָקוּט בְּדוֹר וָאֹמַר עַם תֹּעֵי לֵבָב הֵם וְהֵם
לֹא־יָדְעוּ דְרָכָי: אֲשֶׁר־נִשְׁבַּעְתִּי בְאַפִּי אִם־יְבֹאוּן אֶל־מְנוּחָתִי:

צו שִׁירוּ לַיהוָה שִׁיר חָדָשׁ שִׁירוּ לַיהוָה כָּל־הָאָרֶץ: שִׁירוּ לַיהוָה בָּרְכוּ שְׁמוֹ
בַּשְּׂרוּ מִיּוֹם־לְיוֹם יְשׁוּעָתוֹ: סַפְּרוּ בַגּוֹיִם כְּבוֹדוֹ בְּכָל־הָעַמִּים נִפְלְאוֹתָיו:
כִּי גָדוֹל יְהוָה וּמְהֻלָּל מְאֹד נוֹרָא הוּא עַל־כָּל־אֱלֹהִים: כִּי ׀ כָּל־אֱלֹהֵי
הָעַמִּים אֱלִילִים וַיהוָה שָׁמַיִם עָשָׂה: הוֹד־וְהָדָר לְפָנָיו עֹז וְתִפְאֶרֶת
בְּמִקְדָּשׁוֹ: הָבוּ לַיהוָה מִשְׁפְּחוֹת עַמִּים הָבוּ לַיהוָה כָּבוֹד וָעֹז: הָבוּ לַיהוָה
כְּבוֹד שְׁמוֹ שְׂאוּ־מִנְחָה וּבֹאוּ לְחַצְרוֹתָיו: הִשְׁתַּחֲווּ לַיהוָה בְּהַדְרַת־קֹדֶשׁ
חִילוּ מִפָּנָיו כָּל־הָאָרֶץ: אִמְרוּ בַגּוֹיִם ׀ יְהוָה מָלָךְ אַף־תִּכּוֹן תֵּבֵל בַּל־
תִּמּוֹט יָדִין עַמִּים בְּמֵישָׁרִים: יִשְׂמְחוּ הַשָּׁמַיִם וְתָגֵל הָאָרֶץ יִרְעַם הַיָּם
וּמְלֹאוֹ: יַעֲלֹז שָׂדַי וְכָל־אֲשֶׁר־בּוֹ אָז יְרַנְּנוּ כָּל־עֲצֵי־יָעַר: לִפְנֵי יְהוָה ׀ כִּי
בָא כִּי בָא לִשְׁפֹּט הָאָרֶץ יִשְׁפֹּט־תֵּבֵל בְּצֶדֶק וְעַמִּים בֶּאֱמוּנָתוֹ:

*צז יְהוָה מָלָךְ תָּגֵל הָאָרֶץ יִשְׂמְחוּ אִיִּים רַבִּים: עָנָן וַעֲרָפֶל סְבִיבָיו צֶדֶק
וּמִשְׁפָּט מְכוֹן כִּסְאוֹ: אֵשׁ לְפָנָיו תֵּלֵךְ וּתְלַהֵט סָבִיב צָרָיו: הֵאִירוּ בְרָקָיו
תֵּבֵל רָאֲתָה וַתָּחֵל הָאָרֶץ: הָרִים כַּדּוֹנַג נָמַסּוּ מִלִּפְנֵי יְהוָה מִלִּפְנֵי אֲדוֹן
כָּל־הָאָרֶץ: הִגִּידוּ הַשָּׁמַיִם צִדְקוֹ וְרָאוּ כָל־הָעַמִּים כְּבוֹדוֹ: יֵבֹשׁוּ ׀ כָּל־
עֹבְדֵי פֶסֶל הַמִּתְהַלְלִים בָּאֱלִילִים הִשְׁתַּחֲווּ־לוֹ כָּל־אֱלֹהִים: שָׁמְעָה
וַתִּשְׂמַח ׀ צִיּוֹן וַתָּגֵלְנָה בְּנוֹת יְהוּדָה לְמַעַן מִשְׁפָּטֶיךָ יְהוָה: כִּי־אַתָּה
יְהוָה עֶלְיוֹן עַל־כָּל־הָאָרֶץ מְאֹד נַעֲלֵיתָ עַל־כָּל־אֱלֹהִים: אֹהֲבֵי יְהוָה

*כ לחודש

You? Will he who performs mischief based on the law? They had gathered bands against the soul of the righteous, and they have condemned innocent blood. But the Lord has been my fortress, and my God has been the rock of my refuge. And He has brought upon them their own iniquity, and He has cut them off because of their wickedness, the Lord our God has cut them off.

95 COME, let us sing to the Lord, let us shout joyfully to the Rock of our salvation. Let
us come before Him with thanksgiving, let us raise our voice in song. For the Lord is a great God, and a great King above all gods, in Whose hand are the deep places of the earth, and the mountain peaks belong to Him. To Whom the sea belongs, and He made it, and His hands formed the dry land. Come, let us bow down and bend the knee, let us kneel before the Lord our Maker. For He is our God, and we are the people of His pasture and the flock of His hand. O that today you would hearken to His voice. Do not harden your heart as at Meribah, as on the day of Massah in the wilderness, When your fathers tried Me, tested Me, although they saw My deeds. Forty years, I loathed that generation, and I said, They are a people who stray in their heart, and they do not know My ways. Therefore, I swore in My anger that they would not enter My resting place.

96 SING a new song to the Lord. Sing to the Lord, all the earth. Sing to the Lord, bless
His name, announce His salvation from day to day. Declare His glory among the nations, His wonders among all the peoples. That the Lord is great and greatly to be praised. He is to be feared above all gods. For all the gods of the peoples are idols, but the Lord made the heavens. Splendor and majesty are before Him, strength and glory are in His sanctuary. Give the Lord, O you families of the peoples, give the Lord glory and strength. Give the Lord of the glory due to His name; bring an offering, and enter His courts. Bow down before the Lord in the splendor of holiness; tremble before Him, all the earth. Say among the nations that the Lord reigns; the world, too, is established so that it shall not be moved. He will judge the people with equity. Let the heavens rejoice, and let the earth be glad. Let the sea roar, and its fullness. Let the field be joyful, and all that is in it. Then let all the trees of the forest sing, Before the Lord Who is coming, for He is coming to judge the earth. He will judge the world in righteousness, and the peoples in His faithfulness.

*97 THE LORD is King, may the earth rejoice. May the many islands be happy. Cloud
and mist are about Him. Justice and law are the foundation of His throne. Fire walks before Him, and it burns His enemies on every side. His lightnings illuminate the world. The earth sees and shudders. The mountains melt like wax before the Lord, before the Lord of all the earth. The heavens proclaim His righteousness, and all the peoples see His glory. Let all those who worship statues be ashamed, those who exult in false gods. All gods bow down to Him. Zion has heard and is glad, and the daughters of Judah rejoice, on account of Your judgments, O Lord. Indeed, You, O Lord, are high above all the earth. You are exalted far above all gods. Those who love the Lord, hate evil. He preserves the souls of His pious ones. He saves them from

*20th DAY of the month

שֹׂנְאוּ רָע שֹׁמֵר נַפְשׁוֹת חֲסִידָיו מִיַּד רְשָׁעִים יַצִּילֵם׃ אוֹר זָרֻעַ לַצַּדִּיק
וּֽלְיִשְׁרֵי־לֵב שִׂמְחָה׃ שִׂמְחוּ צַדִּיקִים בַּיהוָה וְהוֹדוּ לְזֵכֶר קָדְשׁוֹ׃
צח מִזְמוֹר שִׁירוּ לַיהוָה ׀ שִׁיר חָדָשׁ כִּי־נִפְלָאוֹת עָשָׂה הוֹשִׁיעָה־לּוֹ יְמִינוֹ
וּזְרוֹעַ קָדְשׁוֹ׃ הוֹדִיעַ יהוה יְשׁוּעָתוֹ לְעֵינֵי הַגּוֹיִם גִּלָּה צִדְקָתוֹ׃ זָכַר חַסְדּוֹ ׀
וֶאֱמוּנָתוֹ לְבֵית יִשְׂרָאֵל רָאוּ כָל־אַפְסֵי־אָרֶץ אֵת יְשׁוּעַת אֱלֹהֵינוּ׃ הָרִיעוּ
לַיהוָה כָּל־הָאָרֶץ פִּצְחוּ וְרַנְּנוּ וְזַמֵּרוּ׃ זַמְּרוּ לַיהוָה בְּכִנּוֹר בְּכִנּוֹר וְקוֹל
זִמְרָה׃ בַּחֲצֹצְרוֹת וְקוֹל שׁוֹפָר הָרִיעוּ לִפְנֵי ׀ הַמֶּלֶךְ יהוה׃ יִרְעַם הַיָּם
וּמְלֹאוֹ תֵּבֵל וְיֹשְׁבֵי בָהּ׃ נְהָרוֹת יִמְחֲאוּ־כָף יַחַד הָרִים יְרַנֵּנוּ׃ לִפְנֵי־יהוה
כִּי בָא לִשְׁפֹּט הָאָרֶץ יִשְׁפֹּט־תֵּבֵל בְּצֶדֶק וְעַמִּים בְּמֵישָׁרִים׃
צט יהוה מָלָךְ יִרְגְּזוּ עַמִּים יֹשֵׁב כְּרוּבִים תָּנוּט הָאָרֶץ׃ יהוה בְּצִיּוֹן גָּדוֹל וְרָם
הוּא עַל־כָּל־הָעַמִּים׃ יוֹדוּ שִׁמְךָ גָּדוֹל וְנוֹרָא קָדוֹשׁ הוּא׃ וְעֹז מֶלֶךְ מִשְׁפָּט
אָהֵב אַתָּה כּוֹנַנְתָּ מֵישָׁרִים מִשְׁפָּט וּצְדָקָה בְּיַעֲקֹב ׀ אַתָּה עָשִׂיתָ׃ רוֹמְמוּ
יהוה אֱלֹהֵינוּ וְהִשְׁתַּחֲווּ לַהֲדֹם רַגְלָיו קָדוֹשׁ הוּא׃ מֹשֶׁה וְאַהֲרֹן ׀ בְּכֹהֲנָיו
וּשְׁמוּאֵל בְּקֹרְאֵי שְׁמוֹ קֹרְאִים אֶל־יהוה וְהוּא יַעֲנֵם׃ בְּעַמּוּד עָנָן יְדַבֵּר
אֲלֵיהֶם שָׁמְרוּ עֵדֹתָיו וְחֹק נָתַן־לָמוֹ׃ יהוה אֱלֹהֵינוּ אַתָּה עֲנִיתָם אֵל
נֹשֵׂא הָיִיתָ לָהֶם וְנֹקֵם עַל־עֲלִילוֹתָם׃ רוֹמְמוּ יהוה אֱלֹהֵינוּ וְהִשְׁתַּחֲווּ
לְהַר קָדְשׁוֹ כִּי־קָדוֹשׁ יהוה אֱלֹהֵינוּ׃
ק מִזְמוֹר לְתוֹדָה הָרִיעוּ לַיהוָה כָּל־הָאָרֶץ׃ עִבְדוּ אֶת־יהוה בְּשִׂמְחָה בֹּאוּ
וְלוֹ לְפָנָיו בִּרְנָנָה׃ דְּעוּ כִּי־יהוה הוּא אֱלֹהִים הוּא עָשָׂנוּ וְלֹא אֲנַחְנוּ עַמּוֹ
וְצֹאן מַרְעִיתוֹ׃ בֹּאוּ שְׁעָרָיו ׀ בְּתוֹדָה חֲצֵרֹתָיו בִּתְהִלָּה הוֹדוּ לוֹ בָּרְכוּ
שְׁמוֹ׃ כִּי־טוֹב יהוה לְעוֹלָם חַסְדּוֹ וְעַד־דֹּר וָדֹר אֱמוּנָתוֹ׃
קא לְדָוִד מִזְמוֹר חֶסֶד־וּמִשְׁפָּט אָשִׁירָה לְךָ יהוה אֲזַמֵּרָה׃ אַשְׂכִּילָה ׀ בְּדֶרֶךְ
תָּמִים מָתַי תָּבוֹא אֵלָי אֶתְהַלֵּךְ בְּתָם־לְבָבִי בְּקֶרֶב בֵּיתִי׃ לֹא־אָשִׁית ׀
לְנֶגֶד עֵינַי דְּבַר־בְּלִיָּעַל עֲשֹׂה־סֵטִים שָׂנֵאתִי לֹא יִדְבַּק בִּי׃ לֵבָב עִקֵּשׁ
מְלָשְׁנִי יָסוּר מִמֶּנִּי רָע לֹא אֵדָע׃ מלושני בַסֵּתֶר ׀ רֵעֵהוּ אוֹתוֹ אַצְמִית גְּבַהּ־
עֵינַיִם וּרְחַב לֵבָב אֹתוֹ לֹא אוּכָל׃ עֵינַי ׀ בְּנֶאֶמְנֵי־אֶרֶץ לָשֶׁבֶת עִמָּדִי
הֹלֵךְ בְּדֶרֶךְ תָּמִים הוּא יְשָׁרְתֵנִי׃ לֹא־יֵשֵׁב ׀ בְּקֶרֶב בֵּיתִי עֹשֵׂה רְמִיָּה דֹּבֵר
שְׁקָרִים לֹא־יִכּוֹן לְנֶגֶד עֵינָי׃ לַבְּקָרִים אַצְמִית כָּל־רִשְׁעֵי־אָרֶץ לְהַכְרִית
מֵעִיר־יהוה כָּל־פֹּעֲלֵי אָוֶן׃

the hand of the wicked. Light is sown for the righteous, and gladness for the upright in heart. Rejoice, O righteous, in the Lord, and give thanks to the memory of His holiness.

98 A PSALM. Sing to the Lord a new song, for He has done marvels. His right hand and His holy arm have gained Him the victory. The Lord has made known His salvation. He has revealed His righteousness in the sight of the nations. He has remembered His loving-kindness in His faithfulness to the house of Israel. All the ends of the earth have seen the salvation of our God. Make a joyful noise to the Lord, all the earth. Make a loud noise, and sing, and sing praise. Sing praise to the Lord with the lyre, with the lyre and the sound of song. With trumpets and the sound of a shofar, make a joyful noise before the Lord, the King. May the sea roar and the fullness of it, the world and those who dwell in it. May the rivers clap hands. May the mountains sing for joy together, Before the Lord Who is coming to judge the earth. He will judge the world in righteousness, and the peoples with equity.

99 THE LORD is King, let the peoples tremble. He is enthroned upon the cherubim, let the earth move. The Lord is great in Zion, and He is high above all the peoples. Let them praise Your name, O great and awesome One. He is holy. And the strength of the King loves justice. You have established equity, You have performed justice and righteousness in Jacob. Exalt the Lord our God, and bow down before His footstool. He is holy. Moses and Aaron were among His priests, and Samuel was among those who would call upon His name. They would call upon the Lord, and He would answer them. He would speak to them in a pillar of cloud. They kept His testimonies and the statute that He gave them. O Lord our God, You answered them. You were a favoring God to them, and You took vengeance for the wicked deeds performed against them. Exalt the Lord our God, and bow down before His holy mountain. Indeed, the Lord our God is holy.

100 A PSALM of thanksgiving. Make a joyful noise to the Lord, all the earth. Serve the Lord with gladness, come before Him with singing. Know that the Lord is God. He made us, and we belong to Him. We are His people, and the sheep of His pasture. Enter His gates with thanksgiving, His courtyards with praise. Give thanks to Him, and bless His name. For the Lord is good, His loving-kindness is forever, and His faithfulness is for all generations.

101 A PSALM of David. I will sing of loving-kindness and justice. To You, O Lord, will I sing. I contemplate the way of the upright. When will You come to me? I walk within my house in the integrity of my heart. I do not set before my eyes a thing of evil. I hate the commission of sins. It does not cleave to me. I remove from myself a perverse heart. I know no evil. He who secretly slanders his neighbor, him I cut off. He who has elevated eyes and a wide heart, him I do not suffer. My eyes are upon the most faithful of the land, that they may dwell with me. He who walks in the way of the upright, he will serve me. He who works in deceit shall not dwell within my house. He who speaks lies shall not remain before my eyes. Every morning I cut off all the wicked of the land, to destroy all the evildoers from the city of the Lord.

קב תְּפִלָּה לְעָנִי כִֽי־יַעֲטֹף וְלִפְנֵי יהוה יִשְׁפֹּךְ שִׂיחוֹ: יהוה שִׁמְעָה תְפִלָּתִי
וְשַׁוְעָתִי אֵלֶיךָ תָבוֹא: אַל־תַּסְתֵּר פָּנֶיךָ ׀ מִמֶּנִּי בְּיוֹם צַר לִי הַטֵּה־אֵלַי
אָזְנֶךָ בְּיוֹם אֶקְרָא מַהֵר עֲנֵנִי: כִּֽי־כָלוּ בְעָשָׁן יָמָי וְעַצְמוֹתַי כְּמוֹקֵד נִחָֽרוּ:
הוּכָּה כָעֵשֶׂב וַיִּבַשׁ לִבִּי כִּֽי־שָׁכַחְתִּי מֵאֲכֹל לַחְמִי: מִקּוֹל אַנְחָתִי דָּבְקָה
עַצְמִי לִבְשָׂרִי: דָּמִיתִי לִקְאַת מִדְבָּר הָיִיתִי כְּכוֹס חֳרָבוֹת: שָׁקַדְתִּי וָאֶהְיֶה
כְּצִפּוֹר בּוֹדֵד עַל־גָּג: כָּל־הַיּוֹם חֵרְפוּנִי אוֹיְבָי מְהוֹלָלַי בִּי נִשְׁבָּעוּ: כִּֽי־אֵפֶר
כַּלֶּחֶם אָכָלְתִּי וְשִׁקֻּוַי בִּבְכִי מָסָכְתִּי: מִפְּנֵי־זַעַמְךָ וְקִצְפֶּךָ כִּי נְשָׂאתַנִי
וַתַּשְׁלִיכֵנִי: יָמַי כְּצֵל נָטוּי וַאֲנִי כָּעֵשֶׂב אִיבָשׁ: וְאַתָּה יהוה לְעוֹלָם תֵּשֵׁב
וְזִכְרְךָ לְדֹר וָדֹר: אַתָּה תָקוּם תְּרַחֵם צִיּוֹן כִּֽי־עֵת לְחֶנְנָהּ כִּֽי־בָא מוֹעֵד:
כִּֽי־רָצוּ עֲבָדֶיךָ אֶת־אֲבָנֶיהָ וְאֶת־עֲפָרָהּ יְחֹנֵנוּ: וְיִֽירְאוּ גוֹיִם אֶת־שֵׁם יהוה
וְכָל־מַלְכֵי הָאָרֶץ אֶת־כְּבוֹדֶךָ: כִּֽי־בָנָה יהוה צִיּוֹן נִרְאָה בִּכְבוֹדוֹ: פָּנָה
אֶל־תְּפִלַּת הָעַרְעָר וְלֹֽא־בָזָה אֶת־תְּפִלָּתָם: תִּכָּתֶב זֹאת לְדוֹר אַחֲרוֹן
וְעַם נִבְרָא יְהַלֶּל־יָהּ: כִּֽי־הִשְׁקִיף מִמְּרוֹם קָדְשׁוֹ יהוה מִשָּׁמַיִם ׀ אֶל־אֶרֶץ
הִבִּיט: לִשְׁמֹעַ אֶנְקַת אָסִיר לְפַתֵּחַ בְּנֵי תְמוּתָה: לְסַפֵּר בְּצִיּוֹן שֵׁם יהוה
וּתְהִלָּתוֹ בִּירוּשָׁלִָם: בְּהִקָּבֵץ עַמִּים יַחְדָּו וּמַמְלָכוֹת לַעֲבֹד אֶת־יהוה:
כֹּחִי עִנָּה בַדֶּרֶךְ כחו קִצַּר יָמָי: אֹמַר אֵלִי אַל־תַּעֲלֵנִי בַּחֲצִי יָמָי בְּדוֹר דּוֹרִים
שְׁנוֹתֶיךָ: לְפָנִים הָאָרֶץ יָסַדְתָּ וּמַעֲשֵׂה יָדֶיךָ שָׁמָיִם: הֵמָּה ׀ יֹאבֵדוּ וְאַתָּה
תַעֲמֹד וְכֻלָּם כַּבֶּגֶד יִבְלוּ כַּלְּבוּשׁ תַּחֲלִיפֵם וְיַחֲלֹפוּ: וְאַתָּה־הוּא וּשְׁנוֹתֶיךָ
לֹא יִתָּמּוּ: בְּנֵי־עֲבָדֶיךָ יִשְׁכּוֹנוּ וְזַרְעָם לְפָנֶיךָ יִכּוֹן:

קג לְדָוִד ׀ בָּרְכִי נַפְשִׁי אֶת־יהוה וְכָל־קְרָבַי אֶת־שֵׁם קָדְשׁוֹ: בָּרְכִי נַפְשִׁי
אֶת־יהוה וְאַל־תִּשְׁכְּחִי כָּל־גְּמוּלָיו: הַסֹּלֵחַ לְכָל־עֲוֺנֵכִי הָרֹפֵא לְכָל־
תַּחֲלוּאָיְכִי: הַגּוֹאֵל מִשַּׁחַת חַיָּיְכִי הַמְעַטְּרֵכִי חֶסֶד וְרַחֲמִים: הַמַּשְׂבִּיעַ
בַּטּוֹב עֶדְיֵךְ תִּתְחַדֵּשׁ כַּנֶּשֶׁר נְעוּרָיְכִי: עֹשֵׂה צְדָקוֹת יהוה וּמִשְׁפָּטִים
לְכָל־עֲשׁוּקִים: יוֹדִיעַ דְּרָכָיו לְמֹשֶׁה לִבְנֵי יִשְׂרָאֵל עֲלִילוֹתָיו: רַחוּם
וְחַנּוּן יהוה אֶרֶךְ אַפַּיִם וְרַב־חָסֶד: לֹֽא־לָנֶצַח יָרִיב וְלֹא לְעוֹלָם יִטּוֹר:
לֹא כַחֲטָאֵינוּ עָשָׂה לָנוּ וְלֹא כַעֲוֺנֹתֵינוּ גָּמַל עָלֵינוּ: כִּי כִגְבֹהַּ שָׁמַיִם
עַל־הָאָרֶץ גָּבַר חַסְדּוֹ עַל־יְרֵאָיו: כִּרְחֹק מִזְרָח מִמַּעֲרָב הִרְחִיק מִמֶּנּוּ
אֶת־פְּשָׁעֵינוּ: כְּרַחֵם אָב עַל־בָּנִים רִחַם יהוה עַל־יְרֵאָיו: כִּי־הוּא יָדַע

102 A PRAYER of the afflicted, when he is faint, and he pours out his complaints before the
Lord. O Lord, please hear my prayer, and let my cry reach You. Do not hide Your face
from me on the day that I am in trouble. Incline Your ear to me. On the day that I call
answer me speedily. For my days have gone in smoke, and my bones have dried up like
a burning mass. My heart has been smitten like grass and has withered, so that I forget
to eat my bread. Because of the sound of my groaning, my bones cleave to my flesh.
I am like a little owl of the wilderness, I am like an owl of the waste places. I remain
awake, and I am like a lonely bird upon the roof. All of the day my enemies insult
me, those who do me ill swear by me. Indeed, I eat ashes like bread, and I mingle my
drinks with weeping, Because of Your anger and Your wrath, for You have raised me
up and cast me down. My days are like a cast shadow, and I will wither like the grass.
But You, O Lord, exist forever, and Your remembrance endures for all generations.
Please arise and have mercy on Zion, for it is time to favor her, for the set time has
come. For Your servants hold her stones dear, and they cherish her dust. And may the
nations fear the name of the Lord, and all the kings of the earth Your glory. For the
Lord has built up Zion, He has appeared in His glory. He had heeded the prayer of the
tamarisk, and He has not despised their prayer. Let this be written for the generation
to come, so that a people yet to be created shall praise the Lord, That He has looked
down from the heights of His sanctuary. The Lord has beheld the earth from heaven,
To hear the groaning of the prisoner, to free those sentenced to death, So that men
may declare in Zion the name of the Lord, and His praise in Jerusalem, When peoples
are gathered together, and kingdoms, to serve the Lord. He has weakened my strength
on the way, He has shortened my days. I say, My God, do not take me away in the
midst of my days. Your years last to all generations. Of old You founded the earth, and
the heavens are the work of Your hands. They shall perish, but You shall endure, and
all of them shall wear out like a garment. You change them like a cloak, and they pass
away. But You remain the same, and Your years shall have no end. May the children
of Your servants dwell, and may their seed be established before You.

103 OF DAVID. Bless the Lord, O my soul, and all that is within me, bless His holy name.
Bless the Lord, O my soul, and do not forget any of His benefits, Who forgives all
your iniquities, Who heals all your illnesses, Who redeems your life from the pit,
Who encircles you with loving-kindness and mercy, Who satisfies your body with
good, your youth is renewed like the eagle's. The Lord performs righteous deeds,
and judgments for all who are oppressed. He made His ways known to Moses, His
acts to the children of Israel. The Lord is merciful and gracious, slow to anger and
abundant in loving-kindness. He does not always remain angry, and He does not
bear a grudge forever. He has not dealt with us according to our sins, and He has
not repaid us according to our iniquities. But as heaven is high above the earth, so
is His loving-kindness great toward those who fear Him. As far as east is from west,
so far has He removed our transgressions from us. As a father has mercy upon his
children, so does the Lord have mercy upon those who fear Him. Indeed, He knows

יִצְרֵנוּ זָכוּר כִּי־עָפָר אֲנָחְנוּ: אֱנוֹשׁ כֶּחָצִיר יָמָיו כְּצִיץ הַשָּׂדֶה כֵּן יָצִיץ:
כִּי רוּחַ עָבְרָה־בּוֹ וְאֵינֶנּוּ וְלֹא־יַכִּירֶנּוּ עוֹד מְקוֹמוֹ: וְחֶסֶד יהוה | מֵעוֹלָם
וְעַד־עוֹלָם עַל־יְרֵאָיו וְצִדְקָתוֹ לִבְנֵי בָנִים: לְשֹׁמְרֵי בְרִיתוֹ וּלְזֹכְרֵי פִקֻּדָיו
לַעֲשׂוֹתָם: יהוה בַּשָּׁמַיִם הֵכִין כִּסְאוֹ וּמַלְכוּתוֹ בַּכֹּל מָשָׁלָה: בָּרְכוּ יהוה
מַלְאָכָיו גִּבֹּרֵי כֹחַ עֹשֵׂי דְבָרוֹ לִשְׁמֹעַ בְּקוֹל דְּבָרוֹ: בָּרְכוּ יהוה כָּל־צְבָאָיו
מְשָׁרְתָיו עֹשֵׂי רְצוֹנוֹ: בָּרְכוּ יהוה | כָּל־מַעֲשָׂיו בְּכָל־מְקֹמוֹת מֶמְשַׁלְתּוֹ
בָּרְכִי נַפְשִׁי אֶת־יהוה:

*קד
בָּרְכִי נַפְשִׁי אֶת־יְהוָה יְהוָה אֱלֹהַי גָּדַלְתָּ מְּאֹד הוֹד וְהָדָר לָבָשְׁתָּ: עֹטֶה־
אוֹר כַּשַּׂלְמָה נוֹטֶה שָׁמַיִם כַּיְרִיעָה: הַמְקָרֶה בַמַּיִם עֲלִיּוֹתָיו הַשָּׂם־עָבִים
רְכוּבוֹ הַמְהַלֵּךְ עַל־כַּנְפֵי־רוּחַ: עֹשֶׂה מַלְאָכָיו רוּחוֹת מְשָׁרְתָיו אֵשׁ לֹהֵט:
יָסַד־אֶרֶץ עַל־מְכוֹנֶיהָ בַּל־תִּמּוֹט עוֹלָם וָעֶד: תְּהוֹם כַּלְּבוּשׁ כִּסִּיתוֹ
עַל־הָרִים יַעַמְדוּ־מָיִם: מִן־גַּעֲרָתְךָ יְנוּסוּן מִן־קוֹל רַעַמְךָ יֵחָפֵזוּן: יַעֲלוּ
הָרִים יֵרְדוּ בְקָעוֹת אֶל־מְקוֹם זֶה | יָסַדְתָּ לָהֶם: גְּבוּל־שַׂמְתָּ בַּל־יַעֲבֹרוּן
בַּל־יְשׁוּבוּן לְכַסּוֹת הָאָרֶץ: הַמְשַׁלֵּחַ מַעְיָנִים בַּנְּחָלִים בֵּין הָרִים יְהַלֵּכוּן:
יַשְׁקוּ כָּל־חַיְתוֹ שָׂדָי יִשְׁבְּרוּ פְרָאִים צְמָאָם: עֲלֵיהֶם עוֹף־הַשָּׁמַיִם יִשְׁכּוֹן
מִבֵּין עֳפָאיִם יִתְּנוּ־קוֹל: מַשְׁקֶה הָרִים מֵעֲלִיּוֹתָיו מִפְּרִי מַעֲשֶׂיךָ תִּשְׂבַּע
הָאָרֶץ: מַצְמִיחַ חָצִיר | לַבְּהֵמָה וְעֵשֶׂב לַעֲבֹדַת הָאָדָם לְהוֹצִיא לֶחֶם
מִן־הָאָרֶץ: וְיַיִן | יְשַׂמַּח לְבַב־אֱנוֹשׁ לְהַצְהִיל פָּנִים מִשָּׁמֶן וְלֶחֶם לְבַב־
אֱנוֹשׁ יִסְעָד: יִשְׂבְּעוּ עֲצֵי יהוה אַרְזֵי לְבָנוֹן אֲשֶׁר נָטָע: אֲשֶׁר־שָׁם צִפֳּרִים
יְקַנֵּנוּ חֲסִידָה בְּרוֹשִׁים בֵּיתָהּ: הָרִים הַגְּבֹהִים לַיְּעֵלִים סְלָעִים מַחְסֶה
לַשְׁפַנִּים: עָשָׂה יָרֵחַ לְמוֹעֲדִים שֶׁמֶשׁ יָדַע מְבוֹאוֹ: תָּשֶׁת־חֹשֶׁךְ וִיהִי לָיְלָה
בּוֹ־תִרְמֹשׂ כָּל־חַיְתוֹ־יָעַר: הַכְּפִירִים שֹׁאֲגִים לַטָּרֶף וּלְבַקֵּשׁ מֵאֵל אָכְלָם:
תִּזְרַח הַשֶּׁמֶשׁ יֵאָסֵפוּן וְאֶל־מְעוֹנֹתָם יִרְבָּצוּן: יֵצֵא אָדָם לְפָעֳלוֹ וְלַעֲבֹדָתוֹ
עֲדֵי־עָרֶב: מָה־רַבּוּ מַעֲשֶׂיךָ | יהוה כֻּלָּם בְּחָכְמָה עָשִׂיתָ מָלְאָה הָאָרֶץ
קִנְיָנֶךָ: זֶה | הַיָּם גָּדוֹל וּרְחַב יָדַיִם שָׁם־רֶמֶשׂ וְאֵין מִסְפָּר חַיּוֹת קְטַנּוֹת
עִם־גְּדֹלוֹת: שָׁם אֳנִיּוֹת יְהַלֵּכוּן לִוְיָתָן זֶה־יָצַרְתָּ לְשַׂחֶק־בּוֹ: כֻּלָּם אֵלֶיךָ
יְשַׂבֵּרוּן לָתֵת אָכְלָם בְּעִתּוֹ: תִּתֵּן לָהֶם יִלְקֹטוּן תִּפְתַּח יָדְךָ יִשְׂבְּעוּן טוֹב:
תַּסְתִּיר פָּנֶיךָ יִבָּהֵלוּן תֹּסֵף רוּחָם יִגְוָעוּן וְאֶל־עֲפָרָם יְשׁוּבוּן: תְּשַׁלַּח

---

*כא לחודש

our desires, He remembers that we are dust. As for man, his days are as grass. As a flower of the field, so does he bloom. For the wind passes over it and it is gone, and its place knows it no more. But the loving-kindness of the Lord is from everlasting to everlasting upon those who fear Him, and His rewards to children's children, to those who keep His covenant, and to those who remember His commandments and do them. The Lord has established His throne in the heavens, and His kingdom rules over everything. Bless the Lord, you His angels, you mighty ones who perform His bidding, who hearken to the voice of His word. Bless the Lord, all you His hosts, you His ministers, who do His will. Bless the Lord, all His works in all the places of His dominion. Bless the Lord, O my soul.

*104 BLESS O Lord, O my soul. O Lord, my God, You are very great. You are clothed with splendor and majesty. He covers Himself with light as a garment. He spreads the heavens like a curtain. Who roofs His chambers with water, Who makes the clouds His chariot, Who walks upon the wings of the wind. He makes His angels winds, His ministers flaming fire. He established the earth on its foundations, so that it should never collapse. You covered it with great waters as with a garment. The water stood above the mountains. At Your rebuke they fled. At the sound of Your thunder they hastened away. They went up the mountains, they went down the valleys, to the place that You prepared for them. You set a boundary that they could not pass over, that they would not return to cover the earth. He sends the springs into the streams. They go between the mountains. They water every beast of the field. The wild asses quench their thirst. Beside them dwell the birds of the sky. From among the branches they give voice. He waters the mountains from His upper chambers. The earth is satisfied with the fruit of Your works. He causes the grass to grow for the cattle, and plants for the service of man, and He brings forth food from the earth. And wine gladdens the heart of man, to brighten his face with oil, and bread sustains the heart of man. The trees of the Lord are satisfied, the cedars of Lebanon that He planted, Where the birds make their nests. As for the stork, the cypress trees are her house. The high hills are for the wild goats, the rocks are a refuge for the badgers. He made the moon for the seasons. The sun knows its setting place. You put down darkness, and it is night, when all the forest beasts creep out. The young lions roar for their prey, and seek their food from God. The sun rises, they gather together, and lie within their dens. Man goes forth to his work, and to his labor until evening. How great are Your works, O Lord! You have made them all in wisdom. The earth is full of Your creatures. Behold, the great and wide sea, where creeping things are innumerable, small beasts and big ones. There go the ships, the leviathan that You made to play with. All of them wait upon You, to give them their food in its season. You give them, they gather it. You open Your hand, they are filled with good. You hide Your face, they are terrified. You take away their breath, they die and return to their dust. You send forth Your breath, they are created, and You renew the face of the earth. May the glory of the Lord be forever,

---

*21st DAY of the month

רוּחֲךָ יִבָּרֵאוּן וּתְחַדֵּשׁ פְּנֵי אֲדָמָה: יְהִי כְבוֹד יהוה לְעוֹלָם יִשְׂמַח יהוה
בְּמַעֲשָׂיו: הַמַּבִּיט לָאָרֶץ וַתִּרְעָד יִגַּע בֶּהָרִים וְיֶעֱשָׁנוּ: אָשִׁירָה לַיהוָה
בְּחַיָּי אֲזַמְּרָה לֵאלֹהַי בְּעוֹדִי: יֶעֱרַב עָלָיו שִׂיחִי אָנֹכִי אֶשְׂמַח בַּיהוָה:
יִתַּמּוּ חַטָּאִים ׀ מִן־הָאָרֶץ וּרְשָׁעִים ׀ עוֹד אֵינָם בָּרְכִי נַפְשִׁי אֶת־יהוה
הַלְלוּיָהּ:

קה הוֹדוּ לַיהוה קִרְאוּ בִּשְׁמוֹ הוֹדִיעוּ בָעַמִּים עֲלִילוֹתָיו: שִׁירוּ־לוֹ זַמְּרוּ־לוֹ
שִׂיחוּ בְּכָל־נִפְלְאוֹתָיו: הִתְהַלְלוּ בְּשֵׁם קָדְשׁוֹ יִשְׂמַח לֵב ׀ מְבַקְשֵׁי יהוה:
דִּרְשׁוּ יהוה וְעֻזּוֹ בַּקְּשׁוּ פָנָיו תָּמִיד: זִכְרוּ נִפְלְאוֹתָיו אֲשֶׁר־עָשָׂה מֹפְתָיו
וּמִשְׁפְּטֵי־פִיו: זֶרַע אַבְרָהָם עַבְדּוֹ בְּנֵי יַעֲקֹב בְּחִירָיו: הוּא יהוה אֱלֹהֵינוּ
בְּכָל־הָאָרֶץ מִשְׁפָּטָיו: זָכַר לְעוֹלָם בְּרִיתוֹ דָּבָר צִוָּה לְאֶלֶף דּוֹר: אֲשֶׁר
כָּרַת אֶת־אַבְרָהָם וּשְׁבוּעָתוֹ לְיִשְׂחָק: וַיַּעֲמִידֶהָ לְיַעֲקֹב לְחֹק לְיִשְׂרָאֵל
בְּרִית עוֹלָם: לֵאמֹר לְךָ אֶתֵּן אֶת־אֶרֶץ־כְּנָעַן חֶבֶל נַחֲלַתְכֶם: בִּהְיוֹתָם
מְתֵי מִסְפָּר כִּמְעַט וְגָרִים בָּהּ: וַיִּתְהַלְּכוּ מִגּוֹי אֶל־גּוֹי מִמַּמְלָכָה אֶל־עַם
אַחֵר: לֹא־הִנִּיחַ אָדָם לְעָשְׁקָם וַיּוֹכַח עֲלֵיהֶם מְלָכִים: אַל־תִּגְּעוּ בִמְשִׁיחָי
וְלִנְבִיאַי אַל־תָּרֵעוּ: וַיִּקְרָא רָעָב עַל־הָאָרֶץ כָּל־מַטֵּה־לֶחֶם שָׁבָר: שָׁלַח
רַגְלוֹ לִפְנֵיהֶם אִישׁ לְעֶבֶד נִמְכַּר יוֹסֵף: עִנּוּ בַכֶּבֶל רגליו בַּרְזֶל בָּאָה נַפְשׁוֹ: עַד־
עֵת בֹּא־דְבָרוֹ אִמְרַת יהוה צְרָפָתְהוּ: שָׁלַח מֶלֶךְ וַיַּתִּירֵהוּ מֹשֵׁל עַמִּים
וַיְפַתְּחֵהוּ: שָׂמוֹ אָדוֹן לְבֵיתוֹ וּמֹשֵׁל בְּכָל־קִנְיָנוֹ: לֶאְסֹר שָׂרָיו בְּנַפְשׁוֹ
וּזְקֵנָיו יְחַכֵּם: וַיָּבֹא יִשְׂרָאֵל מִצְרָיִם וְיַעֲקֹב גָּר בְּאֶרֶץ־חָם: וַיֶּפֶר אֶת־עַמּוֹ
מְאֹד וַיַּעֲצִמֵהוּ מִצָּרָיו: הָפַךְ לִבָּם לִשְׂנֹא עַמּוֹ לְהִתְנַכֵּל בַּעֲבָדָיו: שָׁלַח
מֹשֶׁה עַבְדּוֹ אַהֲרֹן אֲשֶׁר בָּחַר־בּוֹ: שָׂמוּ־בָם דִּבְרֵי אֹתוֹתָיו וּמֹפְתִים בְּאֶרֶץ
דְּבָרוֹ חָם: שָׁלַח חֹשֶׁךְ וַיַּחְשִׁךְ וְלֹא־מָרוּ אֶת־דבריו: הָפַךְ אֶת־מֵימֵיהֶם לְדָם
וַיָּמֶת אֶת־דְּגָתָם: שָׁרַץ אַרְצָם צְפַרְדְּעִים בְּחַדְרֵי מַלְכֵיהֶם: אָמַר וַיָּבֹא
עָרֹב כִּנִּים בְּכָל־גְּבוּלָם: נָתַן גִּשְׁמֵיהֶם בָּרָד אֵשׁ לֶהָבוֹת בְּאַרְצָם: וַיַּךְ
גַּפְנָם וּתְאֵנָתָם וַיְשַׁבֵּר עֵץ גְּבוּלָם: אָמַר וַיָּבֹא אַרְבֶּה וְיֶלֶק וְאֵין מִסְפָּר:
וַיֹּאכַל כָּל־עֵשֶׂב בְּאַרְצָם וַיֹּאכַל פְּרִי אַדְמָתָם: וַיַּךְ כָּל־בְּכוֹר בְּאַרְצָם
רֵאשִׁית לְכָל־אוֹנָם: וַיּוֹצִיאֵם בְּכֶסֶף וְזָהָב וְאֵין בִּשְׁבָטָיו כּוֹשֵׁל: שָׂמַח
מִצְרַיִם בְּצֵאתָם כִּי־נָפַל פַּחְדָּם עֲלֵיהֶם: פָּרַשׂ עָנָן לְמָסָךְ וְאֵשׁ לְהָאִיר

may the Lord rejoice in His works. He looks upon the earth, and it trembles. He touches the hills, and they smoke. I will sing to the Lord while I live. I will sing praises to my God while I exist. My meditation will be sweet to Him. I will rejoice in the Lord. May the sinners be removed from the earth, and may the wicked be no more. Bless the Lord, O my soul. Praise the Lord.

105 GIVE THANKS to the Lord, call upon His name, make known His deeds among the
peoples. Sing to Him, sing praises to Him, talk of all His wondrous works. Glory in His holy name. Let the heart of those who seek the Lord rejoice. Seek the Lord and His strength, seek His face continually. Remember His wondrous works that He has done, His marvels, and the judgments of His mouth, O seed of Abraham, His servants, O children of Jacob, His chosen ones. He is the Lord our God. His judgments are over all the earth. He has remembered His covenant forever, the word that He has commanded to a thousand generations, which He made with Abraham, and His oath to Isaac, and He confirmed it to Jacob as a law, to Israel as an everlasting covenant. Saying, To you will I give the land of Canaan, the lot of your inheritance. When they were few in number, like those of little account, and sojourners there, And when they went from one nation to another, from one kingdom to another people, He did not allow any man to oppress them, and He rebuked kings for their sakes: Do not touch My anointed ones, and do My prophets no harm. And He called a famine upon the land, He broke every staff of bread. He had sent a man before them, Joseph was sold for a servant. They hurt his leg with fetters, his neck was set in iron. Until the time that His word came to pass, the word of the Lord tested him. He sent the king to set him loose, the ruler of peoples to let him go free. He made him lord of his house, and ruler of all his substance, To bind his princes at his pleasure, and he would teach his elders. Thus Israel came to Egypt, and Jacob sojourned in the land of Ham. And He increased His people greatly, and He made them more numerous than their enemies. He turned their hearts to hate His people, to deal craftily with His servants. He sent Moses His servant, and Aaron whom He had chosen. They brought upon them the things that were His signs, and His wonders in the land of Ham. He sent darkness to make it dark, and they did not rebel against His word. He turned their waters into blood, and He slew their fish. He made frogs swarm in their land, in the chambers of their kings. He spoke, and wild beasts came, and lice in all their borders. He turned their rain into hail, flaming fire in their land. It smote their grapevines and their fig trees, and smashed the trees of their country. He spoke, and locusts came, and locusts without number. And they ate every plant in their land, and they ate the fruit of their ground. And He smote every firstborn in their land, the first of all their strength. And He brought them forth with silver and gold, and there was not one among His tribes who stumbled. Egypt was glad when they departed, for the fear of them had fallen upon them. He spread a cloud for a covering, and fire to give light in the night. They asked, and He brought quails, and He satisfied them with bread from heaven. He opened the rock

לָיְלָה: שָׁאַל וַיָּבֵא שְׂלָו וְלֶחֶם שָׁמַיִם יַשְׂבִּיעֵם: פָּתַח צוּר וַיָּזוּבוּ מָיִם
הָלְכוּ בַּצִּיּוֹת נָהָר: כִּי־זָכַר אֶת־דְּבַר קָדְשׁוֹ אֶת־אַבְרָהָם עַבְדּוֹ: וַיּוֹצִא
עַמּוֹ בְשָׂשׂוֹן בְּרִנָּה אֶת־בְּחִירָיו: וַיִּתֵּן לָהֶם אַרְצוֹת גּוֹיִם וַעֲמַל לְאֻמִּים
יִירָשׁוּ: בַּעֲבוּר ׀ יִשְׁמְרוּ חֻקָּיו וְתוֹרֹתָיו יִנְצֹרוּ הַלְלוּיָהּ:
*קו הַלְלוּיָהּ ׀ הוֹדוּ לַיהוָה כִּי־טוֹב כִּי לְעוֹלָם חַסְדּוֹ: מִי יְמַלֵּל גְּבוּרוֹת יהוָה
יַשְׁמִיעַ כָּל־תְּהִלָּתוֹ: אַשְׁרֵי שֹׁמְרֵי מִשְׁפָּט עֹשֵׂה צְדָקָה בְכָל־עֵת: זָכְרֵנִי
יהוה בִּרְצוֹן עַמֶּךָ פָּקְדֵנִי בִּישׁוּעָתֶךָ: לִרְאוֹת ׀ בְּטוֹבַת בְּחִירֶיךָ לִשְׂמֹחַ
בְּשִׂמְחַת גּוֹיֶךָ לְהִתְהַלֵּל עִם־נַחֲלָתֶךָ: חָטָאנוּ עִם־אֲבוֹתֵינוּ הֶעֱוִינוּ
הִרְשָׁעְנוּ: אֲבוֹתֵינוּ בְמִצְרַיִם ׀ לֹא־הִשְׂכִּילוּ נִפְלְאוֹתֶיךָ לֹא זָכְרוּ אֶת־רֹב
חֲסָדֶיךָ וַיַּמְרוּ עַל־יָם בְּיַם־סוּף: וַיּוֹשִׁיעֵם לְמַעַן שְׁמוֹ לְהוֹדִיעַ אֶת־
גְּבוּרָתוֹ: וַיִּגְעַר בְּיַם־סוּף וַיֶּחֱרָב וַיּוֹלִיכֵם בַּתְּהֹמוֹת כַּמִּדְבָּר: וַיּוֹשִׁיעֵם
מִיַּד שׂוֹנֵא וַיִּגְאָלֵם מִיַּד אוֹיֵב: וַיְכַסּוּ־מַיִם צָרֵיהֶם אֶחָד מֵהֶם לֹא נוֹתָר:
וַיַּאֲמִינוּ בִדְבָרָיו יָשִׁירוּ תְּהִלָּתוֹ: מִהֲרוּ שָׁכְחוּ מַעֲשָׂיו לֹא־חִכּוּ לַעֲצָתוֹ:
וַיִּתְאַוּוּ תַאֲוָה בַּמִּדְבָּר וַיְנַסּוּ־אֵל בִּישִׁימוֹן: וַיִּתֵּן לָהֶם שֶׁאֱלָתָם וַיְשַׁלַּח
רָזוֹן בְּנַפְשָׁם: וַיְקַנְאוּ לְמֹשֶׁה בַּמַּחֲנֶה לְאַהֲרֹן קְדוֹשׁ יהוה: תִּפְתַּח־
אֶרֶץ וַתִּבְלַע דָּתָן וַתְּכַס עַל־עֲדַת אֲבִירָם: וַתִּבְעַר־אֵשׁ בַּעֲדָתָם לֶהָבָה
תְּלַהֵט רְשָׁעִים: יַעֲשׂוּ־עֵגֶל בְּחֹרֵב וַיִּשְׁתַּחֲווּ לְמַסֵּכָה: וַיָּמִירוּ אֶת־כְּבוֹדָם
בְּתַבְנִית שׁוֹר אֹכֵל עֵשֶׂב: שָׁכְחוּ אֵל מוֹשִׁיעָם עֹשֶׂה גְדֹלוֹת בְּמִצְרָיִם:
נִפְלָאוֹת בְּאֶרֶץ חָם נוֹרָאוֹת עַל־יַם־סוּף: וַיֹּאמֶר לְהַשְׁמִידָם לוּלֵי
מֹשֶׁה בְחִירוֹ עָמַד בַּפֶּרֶץ לְפָנָיו לְהָשִׁיב חֲמָתוֹ מֵהַשְׁחִית: וַיִּמְאֲסוּ
בְּאֶרֶץ חֶמְדָּה לֹא־הֶאֱמִינוּ לִדְבָרוֹ: וַיֵּרָגְנוּ בְאָהֳלֵיהֶם לֹא שָׁמְעוּ בְּקוֹל
יהוה: וַיִּשָּׂא יָדוֹ לָהֶם לְהַפִּיל אוֹתָם בַּמִּדְבָּר: וּלְהַפִּיל זַרְעָם בַּגּוֹיִם
וּלְזָרוֹתָם בָּאֲרָצוֹת: וַיִּצָּמְדוּ לְבַעַל פְּעוֹר וַיֹּאכְלוּ זִבְחֵי מֵתִים: וַיַּכְעִיסוּ
בְּמַעַלְלֵיהֶם וַתִּפְרָץ־בָּם מַגֵּפָה: וַיַּעֲמֹד פִּינְחָס וַיְפַלֵּל וַתֵּעָצַר הַמַּגֵּפָה:
וַתֵּחָשֶׁב לוֹ לִצְדָקָה לְדֹר וָדֹר עַד־עוֹלָם: וַיַּקְצִיפוּ עַל־מֵי מְרִיבָה וַיֵּרַע
לְמֹשֶׁה בַּעֲבוּרָם: כִּי־הִמְרוּ אֶת־רוּחוֹ וַיְבַטֵּא בִּשְׂפָתָיו: לֹא־הִשְׁמִידוּ
אֶת־הָעַמִּים אֲשֶׁר אָמַר יהוה לָהֶם: וַיִּתְעָרְבוּ בַגּוֹיִם וַיִּלְמְדוּ מַעֲשֵׂיהֶם:
וַיַּעַבְדוּ אֶת־עֲצַבֵּיהֶם וַיִּהְיוּ לָהֶם לְמוֹקֵשׁ: וַיִּזְבְּחוּ אֶת־בְּנֵיהֶם וְאֶת־

*כב לחודש

and water poured out. It ran in the dry places like a river. For He remembered His holy word, and Abraham His servant. And He brought out His people with joy, His chosen ones with gladness. And He gave them the lands of the nations, and they took possession of the property of the peoples, That they might keep His statutes and observe His laws. Praise the Lord.

*106 PRAISE the Lord! Give thanks to the Lord, for He is good, for His loving-kindness is forever. Who can relate the mighty deeds of the Lord? Who can express all His praise? Happy are those who maintain justice, is he who does righteousness at all times. Remember me, O Lord, when You favor Your people. Include me in Your salvation, That I may see the good of Your chosen ones, that I may rejoice in the gladness of Your nation, that I may glory with Your inheritance. We have sinned with our fathers, we have committed iniquity, we have acted wickedly. Our fathers in Egypt did not reflect on Your wondrous works, they did not remember the multitude of Your deeds of loving-kindness, and they rebelled against You at the sea, regarding the Sea of Reeds. But He saved them for the sake of His name, to make known His mighty power. And He rebuked the Sea of Reeds, and it dried up, and He led them through the great waters as through the wilderness. And He delivered them from the hand of him who hated them, and He redeemed them from the hand of the enemy. And the waters covered their adversaries, not one of them was left. Therefore they believed His words, they sang His praise. They were quick to forget His deeds, they did not wait for His counsel. And they lusted exceedingly in the wilderness, and they tried God in the desert. And He gave them their request, but He sent leanness into their bodies. And they were jealous of Moses in the camp, of Aaron the Lord's holy one. The earth opened and swallowed Dathan, and it covered the company of Abiram. And a fire was kindled in their company, the flame burned up the wicked. They made a calf in Horeb, and they bowed down to a molten image. And they exchanged their glory for the likeness of an ox that eats grass. They forgot God their savior, Who had done great things in Egypt, wonders in the land of Ham, terrible deeds on the Sea of Reeds. And He thought to destroy them, had not Moses, His chosen one, stood in the breach before Him, to prevent His wrath from destroying them. And they despised the delightful land, they did not believe His word. They murmured in their tents, they did not hearken to the voice of the Lord. So He lifted up His hand against them to cast them down in the wilderness, And to cast out their seed among the nations, and to scatter them in the lands. And they joined themselves to Baal-Peor, and they ate the sacrifices of the dead. And they provoked anger with their deeds, and a plague struck them. Then Phineas stood up and executed judgment, and the plague was stayed. And that was counted to him as a virtue to all generations forever. And they aroused anger at the waters of Meribah, so that it went ill for Moses on their account. For they angered His spirit, and He pronounced with His lips. They did not destroy the nations, concerning whom the Lord had commanded them. But they were mingled among the nations, and they learned their works. And they served their idols, which became a snare for them. And they sacrificed their sons and their daughters to

*22nd DAY of the month

בְּנוֹתֵיהֶם לַשֵּׁדִים: וַיִּשְׁפְּכוּ דָם נָקִי דַּם־בְּנֵיהֶם וּבְנוֹתֵיהֶם אֲשֶׁר זִבְּחוּ
לַעֲצַבֵּי כְנָעַן וַתֶּחֱנַף הָאָרֶץ בַּדָּמִים: וַיִּטְמְאוּ בְמַעֲשֵׂיהֶם וַיִּזְנוּ
בְּמַעַלְלֵיהֶם: וַיִּחַר־אַף יהוה בְּעַמּוֹ וַיְתָעֵב אֶת־נַחֲלָתוֹ: וַיִּתְּנֵם בְּיַד־גּוֹיִם
וַיִּמְשְׁלוּ בָהֶם שֹׂנְאֵיהֶם: וַיִּלְחָצוּם אוֹיְבֵיהֶם וַיִּכָּנְעוּ תַּחַת יָדָם: פְּעָמִים
רַבּוֹת יַצִּילֵם וְהֵמָּה יַמְרוּ בַעֲצָתָם וַיָּמֹכּוּ בַּעֲוֺנָם: וַיַּרְא בַּצַּר לָהֶם בְּשָׁמְעוֹ
אֶת־רִנָּתָם: וַיִּזְכֹּר לָהֶם בְּרִיתוֹ וַיִּנָּחֵם כְּרֹב חֲסָדָו: וַיִּתֵּן אוֹתָם לְרַחֲמִים
לִפְנֵי כָּל־שׁוֹבֵיהֶם: הוֹשִׁיעֵנוּ ׀ יהוה אֱלֹהֵינוּ וְקַבְּצֵנוּ מִן־הַגּוֹיִם לְהֹדוֹת
לְשֵׁם קָדְשֶׁךָ לְהִשְׁתַּבֵּחַ בִּתְהִלָּתֶךָ: בָּרוּךְ יהוה ׀ אֱלֹהֵי יִשְׂרָאֵל מִן־הָעוֹלָם ׀
וְעַד הָעוֹלָם וְאָמַר כָּל־הָעָם אָמֵן הַלְלוּיָהּ:

ספר חמישי

קז* הֹדוּ לַיהוה כִּי־טוֹב כִּי לְעוֹלָם חַסְדּוֹ: יֹאמְרוּ גְּאוּלֵי יהוה אֲשֶׁר גְּאָלָם
מִיַּד־צָר: וּמֵאֲרָצוֹת קִבְּצָם מִמִּזְרָח וּמִמַּעֲרָב מִצָּפוֹן וּמִיָּם: תָּעוּ בַמִּדְבָּר
בִּישִׁימוֹן דָּרֶךְ עִיר מוֹשָׁב לֹא מָצָאוּ: רְעֵבִים גַּם־צְמֵאִים נַפְשָׁם בָּהֶם
תִּתְעַטָּף: וַיִּצְעֲקוּ אֶל־יהוה בַּצַּר לָהֶם מִמְּצוּקוֹתֵיהֶם יַצִּילֵם: וַיַּדְרִיכֵם
בְּדֶרֶךְ יְשָׁרָה לָלֶכֶת אֶל־עִיר מוֹשָׁב: יוֹדוּ לַיהוה חַסְדּוֹ וְנִפְלְאוֹתָיו לִבְנֵי
אָדָם: כִּי־הִשְׂבִּיעַ נֶפֶשׁ שֹׁקֵקָה וְנֶפֶשׁ רְעֵבָה מִלֵּא־טוֹב: יֹשְׁבֵי חֹשֶׁךְ
וְצַלְמָוֶת אֲסִירֵי עֳנִי וּבַרְזֶל: כִּי־הִמְרוּ אִמְרֵי־אֵל וַעֲצַת עֶלְיוֹן נָאָצוּ:
וַיַּכְנַע בֶּעָמָל לִבָּם כָּשְׁלוּ וְאֵין עֹזֵר: וַיִּזְעֲקוּ אֶל־יהוה בַּצַּר לָהֶם
מִמְּצֻקוֹתֵיהֶם יוֹשִׁיעֵם: יוֹצִיאֵם מֵחֹשֶׁךְ וְצַלְמָוֶת וּמוֹסְרוֹתֵיהֶם יְנַתֵּק:
יוֹדוּ לַיהוה חַסְדּוֹ וְנִפְלְאוֹתָיו לִבְנֵי אָדָם: כִּי־שִׁבַּר דַּלְתוֹת נְחֹשֶׁת וּבְרִיחֵי
בַרְזֶל גִּדֵּעַ: אֱוִלִים מִדֶּרֶךְ פִּשְׁעָם וּמֵעֲוֺנֹתֵיהֶם יִתְעַנּוּ: כָּל־אֹכֶל תְּתַעֵב
נַפְשָׁם וַיַּגִּיעוּ עַד־שַׁעֲרֵי מָוֶת: וַיִּזְעֲקוּ אֶל־יהוה בַּצַּר לָהֶם מִמְּצֻקוֹתֵיהֶם
יוֹשִׁיעֵם: יִשְׁלַח דְּבָרוֹ וְיִרְפָּאֵם וִימַלֵּט מִשְּׁחִיתוֹתָם: יוֹדוּ לַיהוה
חַסְדּוֹ וְנִפְלְאוֹתָיו לִבְנֵי אָדָם: וְיִזְבְּחוּ זִבְחֵי תוֹדָה וִיסַפְּרוּ מַעֲשָׂיו
בְּרִנָּה: ׆ יוֹרְדֵי הַיָּם בָּאֳנִיּוֹת עֹשֵׂי מְלָאכָה בְּמַיִם רַבִּים: ׆ הֵמָּה
רָאוּ מַעֲשֵׂי יהוה וְנִפְלְאוֹתָיו בִּמְצוּלָה: ׆ וַיֹּאמֶר וַיַּעֲמֵד רוּחַ סְעָרָה
וַתְּרוֹמֵם גַּלָּיו: ׆ יַעֲלוּ שָׁמַיִם יֵרְדוּ תְהוֹמוֹת נַפְשָׁם בְּרָעָה
תִתְמוֹגָג: ׆ יָחוֹגּוּ וְיָנוּעוּ כַּשִּׁכּוֹר וְכָל־חָכְמָתָם תִּתְבַּלָּע: ׆ וַיִּצְעֲקוּ

*ליום השישי

spirits. And they shed innocent blood, the blood of their sons and their daughters whom they sacrificed to the idols of Canaan, and the land became defiled with blood. And they were made impure by their own works, and they went astray by their doings. And the wrath of the Lord was kindled against His people, and He abhorred His inheritance. So He delivered them into the hand of the nations, and those who hated them ruled over them. And their enemies oppressed them, and they were subjected under their hand. Many times He delivered them, but they rebelled in their counsel, and they were brought low through their iniquity. But He saw their affliction, when He heard their cry. And He remembered for them His covenant, and He relented according to the abundance of His loving-kindness. And He caused them to be pitied by all their captors. Save us, O Lord our God, and gather us from among the nations, to give thanks to Your holy name, to triumph in Your praise. Blessed be the Lord God of Israel from everlasting to everlasting, and let all the people say Amen. Praise the Lord!

BOOK FIVE

*107 GIVE THANKS to the Lord, for He is good, for His loving-kindness is forever. Let the redeemed of the Lord say this, whom He has redeemed from the hand of distress, And whom He has gathered from the lands, from the east, and from the west, from the north, and from the south. They lost themselves in the wilderness, their way in the desert. They did not find a city of habitation. Hungry and thirsty, their spirit fainted within them. Then they cried to the Lord in their distress, and He delivered them from their troubles. And He led them on the straight path, to go to a city of habitation. Let them praise the Lord for His loving-kindness, and for His wondrous works to the children of man, That He has satisfied the thirsty soul, and He has filled the hungry soul with good. Those who sat in darkness and the shadow of death, bound in affliction and iron, Because they had rebelled against the words of God, and derided the counsel of the Most High. So He brought down their heart with affliction, they fell down and there was none to help. Then they cried to the Lord in their distress, and He saved them from their troubles. He brought them out from darkness and the shadow of death, and He broke their bonds asunder. Let them praise the Lord for His loving-kindness, and for His wondrous works to the children of man, That He has broken the gates of brass, and He has cut the bars of iron asunder. The foolish who can be recognized by their way of sin, and who are afflicted on account of their iniquities, Whose soul abhors all food, and who have come near the gates of death, Then they cried to the Lord in their distress, and He saved them from their troubles. He sent His word and healed them, and He rescued them from their destructions. Let them praise the Lord for His loving-kindness, and for His wondrous works to the children of man, And let them sacrifice sacrifices of thanksgiving, and let them declare His works with rejoicing. Those who go down to the sea in ships, who do work in great waters, They have seen the works of the Lord, and His wonders in the deep. For He commanded and raised a stormy wind, and it lifted up its waves. They rose up to the sky, they went down to the depths, their soul trembled because of the trouble. They reeled and staggered

---

*FRIDAY

אֶל־יְהוָה בַּצַּר לָהֶם וּמִמְּצֽוּקֹתֵיהֶם יוֹצִיאֵם׃ יָקֵם סְעָרָה לִדְמָמָה
וַיֶּחֱשׁוּ גַּלֵּיהֶם׃ וַיִּשְׂמְחוּ כִי־יִשְׁתֹּקוּ וַיַּנְחֵם אֶל־מְחוֹז חֶפְצָם׃ יוֹדוּ
לַיהוָה חַסְדּוֹ וְנִפְלְאוֹתָיו לִבְנֵי אָדָם׃ וִירוֹמְמוּהוּ בִּקְהַל־עָם וּבְמוֹשַׁב
זְקֵנִים יְהַלְלוּהוּ׃ יָשֵׂם נְהָרוֹת לְמִדְבָּר וּמֹצָאֵי מַיִם לְצִמָּאוֹן׃ אֶרֶץ פְּרִי
לִמְלֵחָה מֵרָעַת יֹשְׁבֵי בָהּ׃ יָשֵׂם מִדְבָּר לַאֲגַם־מַיִם וְאֶרֶץ צִיָּה לְמֹצָאֵי
מָיִם׃ וַיּוֹשֶׁב שָׁם רְעֵבִים וַיְכוֹנְנוּ עִיר מוֹשָׁב׃ וַיִּזְרְעוּ שָׂדוֹת וַיִּטְּעוּ כְרָמִים
וַיַּעֲשׂוּ פְּרִי תְבוּאָה׃ וַיְבָרְכֵם וַיִּרְבּוּ מְאֹד וּבְהֶמְתָּם לֹא יַמְעִיט׃ וַיִּמְעֲטוּ
וַיָּשֹׁחוּ מֵעֹצֶר רָעָה וְיָגוֹן׃ ׆ שֹׁפֵךְ בּוּז עַל־נְדִיבִים וַיַּתְעֵם בְּתֹהוּ
לֹא־דָרֶךְ׃ וַיְשַׂגֵּב אֶבְיוֹן מֵעוֹנִי וַיָּשֶׂם כַּצֹּאן מִשְׁפָּחוֹת׃ יִרְאוּ יְשָׁרִים
וְיִשְׂמָחוּ וְכָל־עַוְלָה קָפְצָה פִּיהָ׃ מִי־חָכָם וְיִשְׁמָר־אֵלֶּה וְיִתְבּוֹנְנוּ חַסְדֵי
יְהוָה׃

*קח שִׁיר מִזְמוֹר לְדָוִד׃ נָכוֹן לִבִּי אֱלֹהִים אָשִׁירָה וַאֲזַמְּרָה אַף־כְּבוֹדִי׃ עוּרָה
הַנֵּבֶל וְכִנּוֹר אָעִירָה שָּׁחַר׃ אוֹדְךָ בָעַמִּים ׀ יְהוָה וַאֲזַמֶּרְךָ בַּלְאֻמִּים׃ כִּי־
גָדוֹל מֵעַל־שָׁמַיִם חַסְדֶּךָ וְעַד־שְׁחָקִים אֲמִתֶּךָ׃ רוּמָה עַל־שָׁמַיִם אֱלֹהִים
וַעֲנֵנִי וְעַל כָּל־הָאָרֶץ כְּבוֹדֶךָ׃ לְמַעַן יֵחָלְצוּן יְדִידֶיךָ הוֹשִׁיעָה יְמִינְךָ ועננו׃
אֱלֹהִים ׀ דִּבֶּר בְּקָדְשׁוֹ אֶעְלֹזָה אֲחַלְּקָה שְׁכֶם וְעֵמֶק סֻכּוֹת אֲמַדֵּד׃ לִי
גִלְעָד ׀ לִי מְנַשֶּׁה וְאֶפְרַיִם מָעוֹז רֹאשִׁי יְהוּדָה מְחֹקְקִי׃ מוֹאָב ׀ סִיר רַחְצִי
עַל־אֱדוֹם אַשְׁלִיךְ נַעֲלִי עֲלֵי־פְלֶשֶׁת אֶתְרוֹעָע׃ מִי יֹבִלֵנִי עִיר מִבְצָר מִי
נָחַנִי עַד־אֱדוֹם׃ הֲלֹא־אֱלֹהִים זְנַחְתָּנוּ וְלֹא־תֵצֵא אֱלֹהִים בְּצִבְאֹתֵינוּ׃
הָבָה־לָּנוּ עֶזְרָת מִצָּר וְשָׁוְא תְּשׁוּעַת אָדָם׃ בֵּאלֹהִים נַעֲשֶׂה־חָיִל וְהוּא
יָבוּס צָרֵינוּ׃

קט לַמְנַצֵּחַ לְדָוִד מִזְמוֹר אֱלֹהֵי תְהִלָּתִי אַל־תֶּחֱרַשׁ׃ כִּי פִי רָשָׁע וּפִי־מִרְמָה
עָלַי פָּתָחוּ דִּבְּרוּ אִתִּי לְשׁוֹן שָׁקֶר׃ וְדִבְרֵי שִׂנְאָה סְבָבוּנִי וַיִּלָּחֲמוּנִי
חִנָּם׃ תַּחַת־אַהֲבָתִי יִשְׂטְנוּנִי וַאֲנִי תְפִלָּה׃ וַיָּשִׂימוּ עָלַי רָעָה תַּחַת
טוֹבָה וְשִׂנְאָה תַּחַת אַהֲבָתִי׃ הַפְקֵד עָלָיו רָשָׁע וְשָׂטָן יַעֲמֹד עַל־יְמִינוֹ׃
בְּהִשָּׁפְטוֹ יֵצֵא רָשָׁע וּתְפִלָּתוֹ תִּהְיֶה לַחֲטָאָה׃ יִהְיוּ־יָמָיו מְעַטִּים
פְּקֻדָּתוֹ יִקַּח אַחֵר׃ יִהְיוּ־בָנָיו יְתוֹמִים וְאִשְׁתּוֹ אַלְמָנָה׃ וְנוֹעַ יָנוּעוּ בָנָיו
וְשִׁאֲלוּ וְדָרְשׁוּ מֵחָרְבוֹתֵיהֶם׃ יְנַקֵּשׁ נוֹשֶׁה לְכָל־אֲשֶׁר־לוֹ וְיָבֹזּוּ זָרִים

*כג לחודש

like a drunkard, and all their skill disappeared. Then they cried to the Lord in their
distress, and He brought them out from their troubles. He made the storm a calm,
and their waves became still. And they were glad because they became quiet, and He
guided them to their desired harbor. Let them praise the Lord for His loving-kindness,
and for His wondrous works to the children of men, And let them exalt Him in the
congregation of the people, and let them praise Him in the assembly of the elders. He
turned rivers into wilderness, and springs of water into dry ground, A fruitful land
into desolation, because of the wickedness of those who dwelled therein. He turned
wilderness into a pool of water, and dry ground into springs of water. And He settled
the hungry there, and they established a city of habitation. And they sowed the fields
and planted vineyards, and they yielded fruits of increase. And He blessed them, and
they multiplied greatly, and He did not diminish their cattle. But they were diminished
and brought low by the dominion of evil and sorrow. He pours contempt upon nobles,
and He makes them wander in the wilderness where there is no way. But He has set the
needy on high from poverty, and He has made their families like a flock. The upright
see this and rejoice, and all iniquity shuts its mouth. Whoever is wise must keep these
things, and let them contemplate the acts of loving-kindness of the Lord.

*108 A SONG. A psalm of David. My heart is steadfast, O God. I and my glory will sing and
will sing praises. Awake, O harp and lyre. I waken them at dawn. I thank You, O Lord,
among the peoples, and I will sing praises to You among the nations. For Your loving-
kindness is great above the heavens, and Your truth reaches to the skies. Be exalted
above the heavens, O God, and let Your glory be above all the earth, That Your loved
ones may be delivered, save with Your right hand, and answer me. God has spoken in
His Holiness, I will rejoice. I will divide Shechem, and I will measure out the valley of
Succoth. Gilead is mine, Manasseh is mine, and Ephraim is the strength of my head,
and Judah is my scepter. Moab is my washpot, I will cast my shoe over Edom, over
Philistia will I cry in triumph. Who brought me to the fortified cities? Who led me
to Edom? Surely, O God, You have abandoned us, and You do not go forth, O God,
with our hosts. Give us help against the foe, for vain is the salvation of man. Through
God we will do valiantly, and He will defeat our enemies.

109 TO THE DIRECTOR of music. A psalm of David. O God of my praise, do not be silent.
For the mouth of the wicked and the mouth of deceit have opened against me. They
have spoken to me with a lying tongue. And they have encompassed me with words of
hate, and they have fought against me without cause. In return for my love they have
denounced me, and I was prayer. And they have repaid me evil for good, and hatred in
return for my love. Set a wicked man over him, and let an adversary stand at his right
hand. When he is judged, let him be found guilty, and let his prayer be considered a
sin. Let his days be few. Let another take his office. Let his children be orphans, and his
wife a widow. And let his children be vagabonds and beg, and let them seek aid from
their desolation. Let the creditor seize everything that he has, and let strangers despoil
his property. Let there be none who extends loving-kindness to him, and let there be

*23rd DAY of the month

יְגִיעוֹ: אַל־יְהִי־לוֹ מֹשֵׁךְ חָסֶד וְאַל־יְהִי חוֹנֵן לִיתוֹמָיו: יְהִי־אַחֲרִיתוֹ
לְהַכְרִית בְּדוֹר אַחֵר יִמַּח שְׁמָם: יִזָּכֵר ׀ עֲוֺן אֲבֹתָיו אֶל־יהוה וְחַטַּאת
אִמּוֹ אַל־תִּמָּח: יִהְיוּ נֶגֶד־יהוה תָּמִיד וְיַכְרֵת מֵאֶרֶץ זִכְרָם: יַעַן אֲשֶׁר ׀
לֹא זָכַר עֲשׂוֹת חָסֶד וַיִּרְדֹּף אִישׁ־עָנִי וְאֶבְיוֹן וְנִכְאֵה לֵבָב לְמוֹתֵת: וַיֶּאֱהַב
קְלָלָה וַתְּבוֹאֵהוּ וְלֹא־חָפֵץ בִּבְרָכָה וַתִּרְחַק מִמֶּנּוּ: וַיִּלְבַּשׁ קְלָלָה כְּמַדּוֹ
וַתָּבֹא כַמַּיִם בְּקִרְבּוֹ וְכַשֶּׁמֶן בְּעַצְמוֹתָיו: תְּהִי־לוֹ כְּבֶגֶד יַעְטֶה וּלְמֵזַח
תָּמִיד יַחְגְּרֶהָ: זֹאת ׀ פְּעֻלַּת שֹׂטְנַי מֵאֵת יהוה וְהַדֹּבְרִים רָע עַל־נַפְשִׁי:
וְאַתָּה ׀ יֱהוִה אֲדֹנָי עֲשֵׂה־אִתִּי לְמַעַן שְׁמֶךָ כִּי־טוֹב חַסְדְּךָ הַצִּילֵנִי:
כִּי־עָנִי וְאֶבְיוֹן אָנֹכִי וְלִבִּי חָלַל בְּקִרְבִּי: כְּצֵל כִּנְטוֹתוֹ נֶהֱלָכְתִּי נִנְעַרְתִּי
כָּאַרְבֶּה: בִּרְכַּי כָּשְׁלוּ מִצּוֹם וּבְשָׂרִי כָּחַשׁ מִשָּׁמֶן: וַאֲנִי ׀ הָיִיתִי חֶרְפָּה
לָהֶם יִרְאוּנִי יְנִיעוּן רֹאשָׁם: עָזְרֵנִי יהוה אֱלֹהָי הוֹשִׁיעֵנִי כְחַסְדֶּךָ: וְיֵדְעוּ
כִּי־יָדְךָ זֹּאת אַתָּה יהוה עֲשִׂיתָהּ: יְקַלְלוּ־הֵמָּה וְאַתָּה תְבָרֵךְ קָמוּ ׀ וַיֵּבֹשׁוּ
וְעַבְדְּךָ יִשְׂמָח: יִלְבְּשׁוּ שׂוֹטְנַי כְּלִמָּה וְיַעֲטוּ כַמְעִיל בָּשְׁתָּם: אוֹדֶה יהוה
מְאֹד בְּפִי וּבְתוֹךְ רַבִּים אֲהַלְלֶנּוּ: כִּי־יַעֲמֹד לִימִין אֶבְיוֹן לְהוֹשִׁיעַ מִשֹּׁפְטֵי
נַפְשׁוֹ:

קי לְדָוִד מִזְמוֹר נְאֻם יהוה ׀ לַאדֹנִי שֵׁב לִימִינִי עַד־אָשִׁית אֹיְבֶיךָ הֲדֹם
לְרַגְלֶיךָ: מַטֵּה עֻזְּךָ יִשְׁלַח יהוה מִצִּיּוֹן רְדֵה בְּקֶרֶב אֹיְבֶיךָ: עַמְּךָ נְדָבֹת
בְּיוֹם חֵילֶךָ בְּהַדְרֵי־קֹדֶשׁ מֵרֶחֶם מִשְׁחָר לְךָ טַל יַלְדֻתֶיךָ: נִשְׁבַּע יהוה ׀
וְלֹא יִנָּחֵם אַתָּה־כֹהֵן לְעוֹלָם עַל־דִּבְרָתִי מַלְכִּי־צֶדֶק: אֲדֹנָי עַל־יְמִינְךָ
מָחַץ בְּיוֹם־אַפּוֹ מְלָכִים: יָדִין בַּגּוֹיִם מָלֵא גְוִיּוֹת מָחַץ רֹאשׁ עַל־אֶרֶץ
רַבָּה: מִנַּחַל בַּדֶּרֶךְ יִשְׁתֶּה עַל־כֵּן יָרִים רֹאשׁ:

קיא הַלְלוּיָהּ ׀ אוֹדֶה יהוה בְּכָל־לֵבָב בְּסוֹד יְשָׁרִים וְעֵדָה: גְּדֹלִים מַעֲשֵׂי יהוה
דְּרוּשִׁים לְכָל־חֶפְצֵיהֶם: הוֹד־וְהָדָר פָּעֳלוֹ וְצִדְקָתוֹ עֹמֶדֶת לָעַד: זֵכֶר עָשָׂה
לְנִפְלְאֹתָיו חַנּוּן וְרַחוּם יהוה: טֶרֶף נָתַן לִירֵאָיו יִזְכֹּר לְעוֹלָם בְּרִיתוֹ: כֹּחַ
מַעֲשָׂיו הִגִּיד לְעַמּוֹ לָתֵת לָהֶם נַחֲלַת גּוֹיִם: מַעֲשֵׂי יָדָיו אֱמֶת וּמִשְׁפָּט
נֶאֱמָנִים כָּל־פִּקּוּדָיו: סְמוּכִים לָעַד לְעוֹלָם עֲשׂוּיִם בֶּאֱמֶת וְיָשָׁר: פְּדוּת ׀
שָׁלַח לְעַמּוֹ צִוָּה־לְעוֹלָם בְּרִיתוֹ קָדוֹשׁ וְנוֹרָא שְׁמוֹ: רֵאשִׁית חָכְמָה ׀
יִרְאַת יהוה שֵׂכֶל טוֹב לְכָל־עֹשֵׂיהֶם תְּהִלָּתוֹ עֹמֶדֶת לָעַד:

none who favors his orphans. Let his prosperity be cut off, in the following generation let their name be blotted out. May the iniquity of his fathers be remembered by the Lord, and may the sin of his mother not be blotted out. May they be before the Lord continually and may He cut off their memory from the earth. Because he did not remember to practice loving-kindness, but pursued the poor and needy man, and the broken-hearted to kill him. And he loved the curse, so let it come upon him, and he did not delight in the blessing, so let it be far from him. And he clothed himself in the curse like his garment. And it came into his bowels like water, and like oil into his bones. Let it be for him like a garment he puts on, and let him wear it continually as a girdle. May this be my adversaries' reward from the Lord, and of those who speak evil against my soul. But You, O God, are the Lord. Act with me for Your name's sake. Because Your loving-kindness is good, deliver me. For I am poor and needy, and my heart is broken within me. I walk like a cast shadow. I am carried away like the locust. My knees totter from fasting, and my flesh has become lean of fatness. And I have become a reproach to them. When they see me, they shake their heads. Help me, O Lord, my God. Save me according to Your loving-kindness. And they will know that this is Your hand, that You, O Lord, did this. Let them curse, but may You bless. When they arise, let them be ashamed, and let Your servant rejoice. Let my adversaries be clothed in shame, and let them cover themselves with their disgrace, as with a cloak. I will greatly thank the Lord with my mouth, and among the multitude I will praise Him, That He stands at the right hand of the needy, to save him from those who condemn his soul.

110 OF DAVID. A psalm. This is the word of the Lord to my master: Sit at My right hand, until I make your enemies your footstool. The Lord will send your mighty scepter from Zion. Rule in the midst of your enemies. Your people will offer themselves on the day of your army, in the majesty of holiness, beloved from the womb. You have the dew of your youth. The Lord has sworn and He will not change His mind. You shall be a priest forever, after the manner of Melchizedek. The Lord is at your right hand. He crushed kings on the day of His wrath. He will judge among the nations, full of bodies. He will crush heads over a great region. He will drink from the brook on the way. Therefore he will lift up his head.

111 PRAISE the Lord! I will thank the Lord with all my heart, in the assembly of the upright and in the congregation. The works of the Lord are great. They are available to all who delight in them. His work is glory and splendor, and His righteousness endures forever. He has made a remembrance for His wonderful works. The Lord is gracious and merciful. He gives food to those who fear Him. He remembers His covenant forever. He declared to His people the power of His works, when He gave them the heritage of the nations. The works of His hands are truth and justice. All His decrees are true. They stand fast forever and ever. They are made in truth and uprightness. He sends redemption to His people. He has commanded His covenant forever. Holy and revered is His name. The fear of the Lord is the beginning of wisdom, good prosperity for all who do them. His praise endures forever.

קיב הַֽלְלוּיָהּ ׀ אַשְׁרֵי־אִישׁ יָרֵא אֶת־יְהוָה בְּמִצְוֺתָיו חָפֵץ מְאֹד: גִּבּוֹר בָּאָרֶץ
יִהְיֶה זַרְעוֹ דּוֹר יְשָׁרִים יְבֹרָךְ: הוֹן־וָעֹשֶׁר בְּבֵיתוֹ וְצִדְקָתוֹ עֹמֶדֶת לָעַד:
זָרַח בַּחֹשֶׁךְ אוֹר לַיְשָׁרִים חַנּוּן וְרַחוּם וְצַדִּיק: טוֹב־אִישׁ חוֹנֵן וּמַלְוֶה
יְכַלְכֵּל דְּבָרָיו בְּמִשְׁפָּט: כִּי־לְעוֹלָם לֹא־יִמּוֹט לְזֵכֶר עוֹלָם יִהְיֶה צַדִּיק:
מִשְּׁמוּעָה רָעָה לֹא יִירָא נָכוֹן לִבּוֹ בָּטֻחַ בַּיהוָה: סָמוּךְ לִבּוֹ לֹא יִירָא עַד
אֲשֶׁר־יִרְאֶה בְצָרָיו: פִּזַּר ׀ נָתַן לָאֶבְיוֹנִים צִדְקָתוֹ עֹמֶדֶת לָעַד קַרְנוֹ תָּרוּם
בְּכָבוֹד: רָשָׁע יִרְאֶה ׀ וְכָעָס שִׁנָּיו יַחֲרֹק וְנָמָס תַּאֲוַת רְשָׁעִים תֹּאבֵד:

*קיג הַלְלוּיָהּ ׀ הַלְלוּ עַבְדֵי יְהוָה הַלְלוּ אֶת־שֵׁם יְהוָה: יְהִי שֵׁם יְהוָה מְבֹרָךְ
מֵעַתָּה וְעַד־עוֹלָם: מִמִּזְרַח־שֶׁמֶשׁ עַד־מְבוֹאוֹ מְהֻלָּל שֵׁם יְהוָה: רָם
עַל־כָּל־גּוֹיִם ׀ יְהוָה עַל הַשָּׁמַיִם כְּבוֹדוֹ: מִי כַּיהוָה אֱלֹהֵינוּ הַמַּגְבִּיהִי
לָשָׁבֶת: הַמַּשְׁפִּילִי לִרְאוֹת בַּשָּׁמַיִם וּבָאָרֶץ: מְקִימִי מֵעָפָר דָּל מֵאַשְׁפֹּת
יָרִים אֶבְיוֹן: לְהוֹשִׁיבִי עִם־נְדִיבִים עִם נְדִיבֵי עַמּוֹ: מוֹשִׁיבִי ׀ עֲקֶרֶת הַבַּיִת
אֵם־הַבָּנִים שְׂמֵחָה הַלְלוּיָהּ:

קיד בְּצֵאת יִשְׂרָאֵל מִמִּצְרָיִם בֵּית יַעֲקֹב מֵעַם לֹעֵז: הָיְתָה יְהוּדָה לְקָדְשׁוֹ
יִשְׂרָאֵל מַמְשְׁלוֹתָיו: הַיָּם רָאָה וַיָּנֹס הַיַּרְדֵּן יִסֹּב לְאָחוֹר: הֶהָרִים רָקְדוּ
כְאֵילִים גְּבָעוֹת כִּבְנֵי־צֹאן: מַה־לְּךָ הַיָּם כִּי תָנוּס הַיַּרְדֵּן תִּסֹּב לְאָחוֹר:
הֶהָרִים תִּרְקְדוּ כְאֵילִים גְּבָעוֹת כִּבְנֵי־צֹאן: מִלִּפְנֵי אָדוֹן חוּלִי אָרֶץ מִלִּפְנֵי
אֱלוֹהַּ יַעֲקֹב: הַהֹפְכִי הַצּוּר אֲגַם־מָיִם חַלָּמִישׁ לְמַעְיְנוֹ־מָיִם:

קטו לֹא לָנוּ יְהוָה לֹא לָנוּ כִּי־לְשִׁמְךָ תֵּן כָּבוֹד עַל־חַסְדְּךָ עַל־אֲמִתֶּךָ: לָמָּה
יֹאמְרוּ הַגּוֹיִם אַיֵּה־נָא אֱלֹהֵיהֶם: וֵאלֹהֵינוּ בַשָּׁמָיִם כֹּל אֲשֶׁר־חָפֵץ עָשָׂה:
עֲצַבֵּיהֶם כֶּסֶף וְזָהָב מַעֲשֵׂה יְדֵי אָדָם: פֶּה־לָהֶם וְלֹא יְדַבֵּרוּ עֵינַיִם לָהֶם
וְלֹא יִרְאוּ: אָזְנַיִם לָהֶם וְלֹא יִשְׁמָעוּ אַף לָהֶם וְלֹא יְרִיחוּן: יְדֵיהֶם ׀ וְלֹא
יְמִישׁוּן רַגְלֵיהֶם וְלֹא יְהַלֵּכוּ לֹא־יֶהְגּוּ בִּגְרוֹנָם: כְּמוֹהֶם יִהְיוּ עֹשֵׂיהֶם כֹּל
אֲשֶׁר־בֹּטֵחַ בָּהֶם: יִשְׂרָאֵל בְּטַח בַּיהוָה עֶזְרָם וּמָגִנָּם הוּא: בֵּית אַהֲרֹן
בִּטְחוּ בַיהוָה עֶזְרָם וּמָגִנָּם הוּא: יִרְאֵי יְהוָה בִּטְחוּ בַיהוָה עֶזְרָם וּמָגִנָּם
הוּא: יְהוָה זְכָרָנוּ יְבָרֵךְ יְבָרֵךְ אֶת־בֵּית יִשְׂרָאֵל יְבָרֵךְ אֶת־בֵּית אַהֲרֹן:
יְבָרֵךְ יִרְאֵי יְהוָה הַקְּטַנִּים עִם־הַגְּדֹלִים: יֹסֵף יְהוָה עֲלֵיכֶם עֲלֵיכֶם וְעַל־
בְּנֵיכֶם: בְּרוּכִים אַתֶּם לַיהוָה עֹשֵׂה שָׁמַיִם וָאָרֶץ: הַשָּׁמַיִם שָׁמַיִם לַיהוָה

*כד לחודש

112 PRAISE the Lord! Happy is the man who fears the Lord, who delights greatly in His
commandments. His seed will be mighty upon the earth. The generation of the
upright will be blessed. Wealth and riches are in his house, and his righteousness
endures forever. Light shines in the darkness for the upright, the gracious, and
the merciful, and the righteous. Good is the man who gives freely and lends, and
who conducts his affairs justly. Surely he will never stumble. The righteous will be
in everlasting remembrance. He is not afraid of evil tidings. His heart is steadfast,
trusting in the Lord. His heart is supported, he is not afraid, until he sees his enemies.
He gives freely to the needy. His righteousness endures forever. His horn will be
exalted with honor. The wicked man will see it and be angry. He will grind his teeth
and melt away. The hope of the wicked will come to naught.

*113 PRAISE the Lord. Praise, you servants of the Lord. Praise the name of the Lord.
Blessed be the name of the Lord from now and forevermore. From the rising of the
sun to its going down the Lord's name is praised. The Lord is high above all nations.
His glory is above the heavens. Who is like the Lord our God, Who dwells on high,
Who looks down low upon the heavens and upon the earth? He raises the poor from
the dust, from the dunghill He lifts the needy, to seat him with princes, with the
princes of his people. He seats the barren woman in her house as the joyful mother
of children. Praise the Lord.

114 WHEN ISRAEL went out of Egypt, the house of Jacob from a people of a foreign
language, Judah became His sanctuary, Israel His dominion. The sea saw and fled,
the Jordan turned backward. The mountains skipped like rams, the hills like lambs.
What has happened to you, O sea, that you flee? O Jordan, that you turn backward?
You mountains, that you skip like rams? You hills, like lambs? Tremble, O earth, at
the presence of the Lord, at the presence of the God of Jacob, Who turned the rock
into a pool of water, the flint into a fountain of water.

115 NOT TO US, O Lord, not to us, but to Your name give glory, for Your loving-kindness
and for Your truth. Why should the nations say: "Where, pray, is their God?" But
our God is in the heavens. All that He wishes He does. Their idols are silver and
gold, the work of man's hands. They have a mouth but they do not speak; they have
eyes but they do not see. They have ears but they do not hear; they have a nose
but they do not smell. They have hands but they do not touch; they have legs but
they do not walk; they do not emit sound with their throat. They that make them
shall be like them, everyone who trusts in them. Israel, trust in the Lord. He is their
help and their shield. House of Aaron, trust in the Lord. He is their help and their
shield. You who fear the Lord, trust in the Lord. He is their help and their shield.
The Lord has remembered us, He will bless us. He will bless the house of Israel;
He will bless the house of Aaron. He will bless those who fear the Lord, the small
together with the great. The Lord will make you increase, you and your children.
May you be blessed of the Lord, the Maker of heaven and earth. The heavens are
the heavens of the Lord, but He has given the earth to the children of man. The

*24th DAY of the month

וְהָאָרֶץ נָתַן לִבְנֵי־אָדָם׃ לֹא הַמֵּתִים יְהַלְלוּ־יָהּ וְלֹא כׇּל־יֹרְדֵי דוּמָה׃
וַאֲנַחְנוּ ׀ נְבָרֵךְ יָהּ מֵעַתָּה וְעַד־עוֹלָם הַלְלוּיָהּ׃

קטז אָהַבְתִּי כִּי־יִשְׁמַע ׀ יהוה אֶת־קוֹלִי תַּחֲנוּנָי׃ כִּי־הִטָּה אׇזְנוֹ לִי וּבְיָמַי
אֶקְרָא׃ אֲפָפוּנִי ׀ חֶבְלֵי־מָוֶת וּמְצָרֵי שְׁאוֹל מְצָאוּנִי צָרָה וְיָגוֹן אֶמְצָא׃
וּבְשֵׁם־יהוה אֶקְרָא אָנָּה יהוה מַלְּטָה נַפְשִׁי׃ חַנּוּן יהוה וְצַדִּיק וֵאלֹהֵינוּ
מְרַחֵם׃ שֹׁמֵר פְּתָאיִם יהוה דַּלּוֹתִי וְלִי יְהוֹשִׁיעַ׃ שׁוּבִי נַפְשִׁי לִמְנוּחָיְכִי
כִּי־יהוה גָּמַל עָלָיְכִי׃ כִּי חִלַּצְתָּ נַפְשִׁי מִמָּוֶת אֶת־עֵינִי מִן־דִּמְעָה אֶת־
רַגְלִי מִדֶּחִי׃ אֶתְהַלֵּךְ לִפְנֵי יהוה בְּאַרְצוֹת הַחַיִּים׃ הֶאֱמַנְתִּי כִּי אֲדַבֵּר
אֲנִי עָנִיתִי מְאֹד׃ אֲנִי אָמַרְתִּי בְחׇפְזִי כׇּל־הָאָדָם כֹּזֵב׃ מָה־אָשִׁיב לַיהוה
כׇּל־תַּגְמוּלוֹהִי עָלָי׃ כּוֹס־יְשׁוּעוֹת אֶשָּׂא וּבְשֵׁם יהוה אֶקְרָא׃ נְדָרַי לַיהוה
אֲשַׁלֵּם נֶגְדָה־נָּא לְכׇל־עַמּוֹ׃ יָקָר בְּעֵינֵי יהוה הַמָּוְתָה לַחֲסִידָיו׃ אָנָּה
יהוה כִּי־אֲנִי עַבְדֶּךָ אֲנִי־עַבְדְּךָ בֶּן־אֲמָתֶךָ פִּתַּחְתָּ לְמוֹסֵרָי׃ לְךָ־אֶזְבַּח
זֶבַח תּוֹדָה וּבְשֵׁם יהוה אֶקְרָא׃ נְדָרַי לַיהוה אֲשַׁלֵּם נֶגְדָה־נָּא לְכׇל־עַמּוֹ׃
בְּחַצְרוֹת ׀ בֵּית יהוה בְּתוֹכֵכִי יְרוּשָׁלָ͏ִם הַלְלוּיָהּ׃

קיז הַלְלוּ אֶת־יהוה כׇּל־גּוֹיִם שַׁבְּחוּהוּ כׇּל־הָאֻמִּים׃ כִּי גָבַר עָלֵינוּ ׀ חַסְדּוֹ
וֶאֱמֶת־יהוה לְעוֹלָם הַלְלוּיָהּ׃

קיח הוֹדוּ לַיהוה כִּי־טוֹב כִּי לְעוֹלָם חַסְדּוֹ׃ יֹאמַר־נָא יִשְׂרָאֵל כִּי לְעוֹלָם
חַסְדּוֹ׃ יֹאמְרוּ־נָא בֵית־אַהֲרֹן כִּי לְעוֹלָם חַסְדּוֹ׃ יֹאמְרוּ־נָא יִרְאֵי יהוה
כִּי לְעוֹלָם חַסְדּוֹ׃ מִן־הַמֵּצַר קָרָאתִי יָּהּ עָנָנִי בַמֶּרְחָב יָהּ׃ יהוה לִי לֹא
אִירָא מַה־יַּעֲשֶׂה לִי אָדָם׃ יהוה לִי בְּעֹזְרָי וַאֲנִי אֶרְאֶה בְשֹׂנְאָי׃ טוֹב
לַחֲסוֹת בַּיהוה מִבְּטֹחַ בָּאָדָם׃ טוֹב לַחֲסוֹת בַּיהוה מִבְּטֹחַ בִּנְדִיבִים׃
כׇּל־גּוֹיִם סְבָבוּנִי בְּשֵׁם יהוה כִּי אֲמִילַם׃ סַבּוּנִי גַם־סְבָבוּנִי בְּשֵׁם יהוה
כִּי אֲמִילַם׃ סַבּוּנִי כִדְבֹרִים דֹּעֲכוּ כְּאֵשׁ קוֹצִים בְּשֵׁם יהוה כִּי אֲמִילַם׃
דַּחֹה דְחִיתַנִי לִנְפֹּל וַיהוה עֲזָרָנִי׃ עׇזִּי וְזִמְרָת יָהּ וַיְהִי־לִי לִישׁוּעָה׃ קוֹל ׀
רִנָּה וִישׁוּעָה בְּאׇהֳלֵי צַדִּיקִים יְמִין יהוה עֹשָׂה חָיִל׃ יְמִין יהוה רוֹמֵמָה
יְמִין יהוה עֹשָׂה חָיִל׃ לֹא אָמוּת כִּי־אֶחְיֶה וַאֲסַפֵּר מַעֲשֵׂי יָהּ׃ יַסֹּר
יִסְּרַנִּי יָּהּ וְלַמָּוֶת לֹא נְתָנָנִי׃ פִּתְחוּ־לִי שַׁעֲרֵי־צֶדֶק אָבֹא־בָם אוֹדֶה
יָהּ׃ זֶה־הַשַּׁעַר לַיהוה צַדִּיקִים יָבֹאוּ בוֹ׃ אוֹדְךָ כִּי עֲנִיתָנִי וַתְּהִי־לִי

dead do not praise the Lord, nor all who go down into silence. But we will bless
the Lord from now and forevermore. Praise the Lord.

116 I LOVE that the Lord has heard my voice, my supplications, that He has inclined His
ear to me, and all my days I will call. The pangs of death encompassed me, and the
straits of the underworld beset me. I found trouble and sorrow. But I called upon the
name of the Lord: "I beseech You, O Lord, deliver my soul." Gracious is the Lord and
righteous, and our God is merciful. The Lord preserves the simple. I was brought low
and He saved me. Return to your rest, O my soul, for the Lord has dealt bountifully
with you. Indeed, You have delivered my soul from death, my eyes from tears, my
feet from stumbling. I will walk before the Lord in the lands of the living. I believed
even when I said: "I have been greatly afflicted." I said in my haste: "The whole of
man is delusive." What can I render to the Lord for all His benefits toward me? I lift
up the cup of salvation, and I call upon the name of the Lord. I pay my vows to the
Lord in the presence of all His people. Precious in the eyes of the Lord is the death
of His pious ones. I beseech You, O Lord, for I am Your servant. I am Your servant,
the son of Your handmaid. You have loosened my bonds. I offer to You a sacrifice of
thanksgiving, and I call upon the name of the Lord. I pay my vows to the Lord in the
presence of all His people, in the courtyards of the house of the Lord, in your midst,
O Jerusalem. Praise the Lord.

117 PRAISE the Lord, all nations. Laud Him, all the peoples. For His loving-kindness is
mighty toward us, and the truth of the Lord is forever. Praise the Lord.

118 GIVE THANKS to the Lord, for He is good, for His loving-kindness is forever. Let Israel
now say, for His loving-kindness is forever. Let the house of Aaron now say, for His
loving-kindness is forever. Let those who fear the Lord now say, for His loving-kindness is forever. From distress I called upon the Lord. The Lord answered me
with enlargement. The Lord is for me, I will not fear. What can man do to me? The
Lord is for me among my helpers, and I will see the downfall of those who hate me.
It is better to seek refuge in the Lord than to trust in man. It is better to seek refuge
in the Lord than to trust in princes. All nations encompassed me. In the name of the
Lord I surely destroyed them. They encompassed me, yes, they encompassed me.
In the name of the Lord I surely destroyed them. They encompassed me like bees.
They crackled like the fire of thorns. In the name of the Lord I surely destroyed them.
You harshly pushed me to fall, but the Lord helped me. The Lord is my strength and
my song, and He has become my salvation. The voice of rejoicing and salvation is in
the tents of the righteous. The right hand of the Lord does valiantly. The right hand
of the Lord is exalted. The right hand of the Lord does valiantly. I did not die but
I lived, and I declare the deeds of the Lord. The Lord made me suffer severely, but
He did not give me over to death. Open to me the gates of righteousness. Let me
enter them and I will thank the Lord. This is the gate of the Lord. Let the righteous
enter it. I give thanks to You, for You have answered me, and You have become my
salvation. The stone that the builders rejected has become the chief cornerstone.

לִישׁוּעָה: אֶבֶן מָאֲסוּ הַבּוֹנִים הָיְתָה לְרֹאשׁ פִּנָּה: מֵאֵת יהוה הָיְתָה
זֹּאת הִיא נִפְלָאת בְּעֵינֵינוּ: זֶה־הַיּוֹם עָשָׂה יהוה נָגִילָה וְנִשְׂמְחָה בוֹ:
אָנָּא יהוה הוֹשִׁיעָה נָּא אָנָּא יהוה הַצְלִיחָה נָּא: בָּרוּךְ הַבָּא בְּשֵׁם יהוה
בֵּרַכְנוּכֶם מִבֵּית יהוה: אֵל ׀ יהוה וַיָּאֶר לָנוּ אִסְרוּ־חַג בַּעֲבֹתִים עַד־
קַרְנוֹת הַמִּזְבֵּחַ: אֵלִי אַתָּה וְאוֹדֶךָּ אֱלֹהַי אֲרוֹמְמֶךָּ: הוֹדוּ לַיהוה כִּי־טוֹב
כִּי לְעוֹלָם חַסְדּוֹ:

קיט* אַשְׁרֵי תְמִימֵי־דָרֶךְ הַהֹלְכִים בְּתוֹרַת יהוה: אַשְׁרֵי נֹצְרֵי עֵדֹתָיו בְּכָל־לֵב
יִדְרְשׁוּהוּ: אַף לֹא־פָעֲלוּ עַוְלָה בִּדְרָכָיו הָלָכוּ: אַתָּה צִוִּיתָה פִקֻּדֶיךָ לִשְׁמֹר
מְאֹד: אַחֲלַי יִכֹּנוּ דְרָכָי לִשְׁמֹר חֻקֶּיךָ: אָז לֹא־אֵבוֹשׁ בְּהַבִּיטִי אֶל־כָּל־
מִצְוֹתֶיךָ: אוֹדְךָ בְּיֹשֶׁר לֵבָב בְּלָמְדִי מִשְׁפְּטֵי צִדְקֶךָ: אֶת־חֻקֶּיךָ אֶשְׁמֹר
אַל־תַּעַזְבֵנִי עַד־מְאֹד:

בַּמֶּה יְזַכֶּה־נַּעַר אֶת־אָרְחוֹ לִשְׁמֹר כִּדְבָרֶךָ: בְּכָל־לִבִּי דְרַשְׁתִּיךָ אַל־תַּשְׁגֵּנִי
מִמִּצְוֹתֶיךָ: בְּלִבִּי צָפַנְתִּי אִמְרָתֶךָ לְמַעַן לֹא אֶחֱטָא־לָךְ: בָּרוּךְ אַתָּה יהוה
לַמְּדֵנִי חֻקֶּיךָ: בִּשְׂפָתַי סִפַּרְתִּי כֹּל מִשְׁפְּטֵי־פִיךָ: בְּדֶרֶךְ עֵדְוֹתֶיךָ שַׂשְׂתִּי
כְּעַל כָּל־הוֹן: בְּפִקֻּדֶיךָ אָשִׂיחָה וְאַבִּיטָה אֹרְחֹתֶיךָ: בְּחֻקֹּתֶיךָ אֶשְׁתַּעֲשָׁע
לֹא אֶשְׁכַּח דְּבָרֶךָ:

גְּמֹל עַל־עַבְדְּךָ אֶחְיֶה וְאֶשְׁמְרָה דְבָרֶךָ: גַּל־עֵינַי וְאַבִּיטָה נִפְלָאוֹת
מִתּוֹרָתֶךָ: גֵּר אָנֹכִי בָאָרֶץ אַל־תַּסְתֵּר מִמֶּנִּי מִצְוֹתֶיךָ: גָּרְסָה נַפְשִׁי לְתַאֲבָה
אֶל־מִשְׁפָּטֶיךָ בְכָל־עֵת: גָּעַרְתָּ זֵדִים אֲרוּרִים הַשֹּׁגִים מִמִּצְוֹתֶיךָ: גַּל מֵעָלַי
חֶרְפָּה וָבוּז כִּי עֵדֹתֶיךָ נָצָרְתִּי: גַּם יָשְׁבוּ שָׂרִים בִּי נִדְבָּרוּ עַבְדְּךָ יָשִׂיחַ
בְּחֻקֶּיךָ: גַּם־עֵדֹתֶיךָ שַׁעֲשֻׁעָי אַנְשֵׁי עֲצָתִי:

דָּבְקָה לֶעָפָר נַפְשִׁי חַיֵּנִי כִּדְבָרֶךָ: דְּרָכַי סִפַּרְתִּי וַתַּעֲנֵנִי לַמְּדֵנִי חֻקֶּיךָ:
דֶּרֶךְ־פִּקּוּדֶיךָ הֲבִינֵנִי וְאָשִׂיחָה בְּנִפְלְאוֹתֶיךָ: דָּלְפָה נַפְשִׁי מִתּוּגָה
קַיְּמֵנִי כִּדְבָרֶךָ: דֶּרֶךְ־שֶׁקֶר הָסֵר מִמֶּנִּי וְתוֹרָתְךָ חָנֵּנִי: דֶּרֶךְ־אֱמוּנָה בָחָרְתִּי
מִשְׁפָּטֶיךָ שִׁוִּיתִי: דָּבַקְתִּי בְעֵדְוֹתֶיךָ יהוה אַל־תְּבִישֵׁנִי: דֶּרֶךְ־מִצְוֹתֶיךָ
אָרוּץ כִּי תַרְחִיב לִבִּי:

הוֹרֵנִי יהוה דֶּרֶךְ חֻקֶּיךָ וְאֶצְּרֶנָּה עֵקֶב: הֲבִינֵנִי וְאֶצְּרָה תוֹרָתֶךָ וְאֶשְׁמְרֶנָּה
בְכָל־לֵב: הַדְרִיכֵנִי בִּנְתִיב מִצְוֹתֶיךָ כִּי־בוֹ חָפָצְתִּי: הַט־לִבִּי אֶל־עֵדְוֹתֶיךָ

*כה לחודש

This was from the Lord; it is marvelous in our eyes. This is the day on which the Lord has acted. Let us be glad and rejoice in Him. We beseech You, O Lord, please save us. We beseech You, O Lord, please give us success. Blessed in the name of the Lord is he who comes. We bless you from the house of the Lord. God is the Lord and He has given us light. Tie the sacrifice with cords to the horns of the altar. You are my God and I give You thanks. You are my God, and I exalt You. Give thanks to the Lord, for He is good, for His loving-kindness is forever.

*119 HAPPY are those whose way is straight, who follow the law of the Lord. Happy are those who keep His testimonies. They seek Him with all their heart. They also do no iniquity. They walk in His ways. You have commanded that Your precepts be kept diligently. O that my ways may be fixed to keep Your statutes! Then I will not be ashamed when I look upon all Your commandments. I thank You in uprightness of heart, when I learn Your righteous judgments. I keep Your statutes. Do not utterly forsake me.

How should a young man keep his way pure? By guarding it according to Your word. With all my heart I seek You. Let me not unwittingly violate Your commandments. I hide Your word in my heart, so that I will not sin against You. Blessed are You, O Lord. Teach me Your statutes. With my lips I declare all the judgments of Your mouth. I rejoice in the way of Your testimonies, as in all riches. I meditate upon Your precepts, and I look upon Your ways. I delight in Your statutes. I do not forget Your word.

Deal bountifully with Your servant and let me live, that I may keep Your word. Open my eyes, that I may behold the hidden things in Your law. I am a stranger on the earth. Do not hide Your commandments from me. My soul is broken by longing for Your judgments at all times. You have rebuked the wicked that they will be cursed, those who wander from Your commandments. Remove insult and contempt from me, for I keep Your testimonies. Even when the princes sit and speak about me, Your servant meditates upon Your statutes. Indeed, Your testimonies are my delights, the men who counsel me.

My soul cleaves to the dust. Let me live according to Your word. I used to relate my ways, and You would answer me. Teach me Your statutes. Make me understand the way of Your precepts, and let me meditate upon Your wonders. My soul melts away from sadness. Strengthen me according to Your word. Remove from me the way of falsehood, and graciously bestow Your law upon me. I have chosen the way of truth. I have laid Your judgments before me. I cleave to Your testimonies, O Lord, do not put me to shame. I will run in the way of Your commandments, if You enlarge my heart.

Teach me, O Lord, the way of Your statutes, and I will keep it in my steps. Make me understand, and I will keep Your law, and I will observe it with all my heart. Guide me in the path of Your commandments, for in it I wish to go. Incline my heart to Your testimonies, and not to money. Turn my eyes away from seeing falsehood.

---

*25th DAY of the month

וְאַל אֶל־בָּצַע: הַעֲבֵר עֵינַי מֵרְאוֹת שָׁוְא בִּדְרָכֶךָ חַיֵּנִי: הָקֵם לְעַבְדְּךָ
אִמְרָתֶךָ אֲשֶׁר לְיִרְאָתֶךָ: הַעֲבֵר חֶרְפָּתִי אֲשֶׁר יָגֹרְתִּי כִּי מִשְׁפָּטֶיךָ טוֹבִים:
הִנֵּה תָּאַבְתִּי לְפִקֻּדֶיךָ בְּצִדְקָתְךָ חַיֵּנִי:

וִיבֹאֻנִי חֲסָדֶךָ יְהוָה תְּשׁוּעָתְךָ כְּאִמְרָתֶךָ: וְאֶעֱנֶה חֹרְפִי דָבָר כִּי־
בָטַחְתִּי בִּדְבָרֶךָ: וְאַל־תַּצֵּל מִפִּי דְבַר־אֱמֶת עַד־מְאֹד כִּי לְמִשְׁפָּטֶךָ
יִחָלְתִּי: וְאֶשְׁמְרָה תוֹרָתְךָ תָמִיד לְעוֹלָם וָעֶד: וְאֶתְהַלְּכָה בָרְחָבָה כִּי
פִקֻּדֶיךָ דָרָשְׁתִּי: וַאֲדַבְּרָה בְעֵדֹתֶיךָ נֶגֶד מְלָכִים וְלֹא אֵבוֹשׁ: וְאֶשְׁתַּעֲשַׁע
בְּמִצְוֹתֶיךָ אֲשֶׁר אָהָבְתִּי: וְאֶשָּׂא־כַפַּי אֶל־מִצְוֹתֶיךָ אֲשֶׁר אָהָבְתִּי וְאָשִׂיחָה
בְחֻקֶּיךָ:

זְכָר־דָּבָר לְעַבְדֶּךָ עַל אֲשֶׁר יִחַלְתָּנִי: זֹאת נֶחָמָתִי בְעָנְיִי כִּי אִמְרָתְךָ
חִיָּתְנִי: זֵדִים הֱלִיצֻנִי עַד־מְאֹד מִתּוֹרָתְךָ לֹא נָטִיתִי: זָכַרְתִּי מִשְׁפָּטֶיךָ
מֵעוֹלָם ׀ יְהוָה וָאֶתְנֶחָם: זַלְעָפָה אֲחָזַתְנִי מֵרְשָׁעִים עֹזְבֵי תּוֹרָתֶךָ: זְמִרוֹת
הָיוּ־לִי חֻקֶּיךָ בְּבֵית מְגוּרָי: זָכַרְתִּי בַלַּיְלָה שִׁמְךָ יְהוָה וָאֶשְׁמְרָה תּוֹרָתֶךָ:
זֹאת הָיְתָה־לִּי כִּי פִקֻּדֶיךָ נָצָרְתִּי:

חֶלְקִי יְהוָה אָמַרְתִּי לִשְׁמֹר דְּבָרֶיךָ: חִלִּיתִי פָנֶיךָ בְכָל־לֵב חָנֵּנִי כְּאִמְרָתֶךָ:
חִשַּׁבְתִּי דְרָכָי וָאָשִׁיבָה רַגְלַי אֶל־עֵדֹתֶיךָ: חַשְׁתִּי וְלֹא הִתְמַהְמָהְתִּי לִשְׁמֹר
מִצְוֹתֶיךָ: חֶבְלֵי רְשָׁעִים עִוְּדֻנִי תּוֹרָתְךָ לֹא שָׁכָחְתִּי: חֲצוֹת־לַיְלָה אָקוּם
לְהוֹדוֹת לָךְ עַל מִשְׁפְּטֵי צִדְקֶךָ: חָבֵר אָנִי לְכָל־אֲשֶׁר יְרֵאוּךָ וּלְשֹׁמְרֵי
פִּקּוּדֶיךָ: חַסְדְּךָ יְהוָה מָלְאָה הָאָרֶץ חֻקֶּיךָ לַמְּדֵנִי:

טוֹב עָשִׂיתָ עִם־עַבְדְּךָ יְהוָה כִּדְבָרֶךָ: טוּב טַעַם וָדַעַת לַמְּדֵנִי כִּי בְמִצְוֹתֶיךָ
הֶאֱמָנְתִּי: טֶרֶם אֶעֱנֶה אֲנִי שֹׁגֵג וְעַתָּה אִמְרָתְךָ שָׁמָרְתִּי: טוֹב־אַתָּה
וּמֵטִיב לַמְּדֵנִי חֻקֶּיךָ: טָפְלוּ עָלַי שֶׁקֶר זֵדִים אֲנִי בְּכָל־לֵב ׀ אֶצֹּר פִּקּוּדֶיךָ:
טָפַשׁ כַּחֵלֶב לִבָּם אֲנִי תּוֹרָתְךָ שִׁעֲשָׁעְתִּי: טוֹב־לִי כִי־עֻנֵּיתִי לְמַעַן אֶלְמַד
חֻקֶּיךָ: טוֹב־לִי תוֹרַת־פִּיךָ מֵאַלְפֵי זָהָב וָכָסֶף:

יָדֶיךָ עָשׂוּנִי וַיְכוֹנְנוּנִי הֲבִינֵנִי וְאֶלְמְדָה מִצְוֹתֶיךָ: יְרֵאֶיךָ יִרְאוּנִי וְיִשְׂמָחוּ
כִּי לִדְבָרְךָ יִחָלְתִּי: יָדַעְתִּי יְהוָה כִּי־צֶדֶק מִשְׁפָּטֶיךָ וֶאֱמוּנָה עִנִּיתָנִי: יְהִי־
נָא חַסְדְּךָ לְנַחֲמֵנִי כְּאִמְרָתְךָ לְעַבְדֶּךָ: יְבֹאוּנִי רַחֲמֶיךָ וְאֶחְיֶה כִּי־תוֹרָתְךָ
שַׁעֲשֻׁעָי: יֵבֹשׁוּ זֵדִים כִּי־שֶׁקֶר עִוְּתוּנִי אֲנִי אָשִׂיחַ בְּפִקּוּדֶיךָ: יָשׁוּבוּ לִי
יְרֵאֶיךָ וידעו עֵדֹתֶיךָ: יְהִי־לִבִּי תָמִים בְּחֻקֶּיךָ לְמַעַן לֹא אֵבוֹשׁ: וְיֹדְעֵי

Make me live in Your ways. Fulfill for Your servant Your word, which concerns the fear of You. Turn away my reproach which I fear, for Your judgments are good. Behold, I yearn for Your precepts. Make me live in Your righteousness.

And may Your acts of loving-kindness come upon me, O Lord, Your salvation according to Your word. And may I be able to answer him who insults me, for I trust in Your word. And do not set the word of truth utterly far from my mouth, for I hope for Your judgment. And may I keep Your law continually forever and ever. And may I walk about freely, for I seek Your precepts. And may I speak of Your testimonies before kings, and may I not be ashamed. And may I delight in Your commandments, which I love. And may I lift up my hands to Your commandments, which I love, and may I meditate upon Your statutes.

Remember for Your servant the word by which You have given me hope. This is my comfort in my affliction, for Your word gives me life. Evil people have ridiculed me greatly. I have not deviated from Your law. I remember Your judgments of old, O Lord, and I am comforted. Trembling takes hold of me because of the wicked, those who have forsaken Your law. Your statutes are as songs for me in the house where I dwell. I remember Your name, O Lord, in the night, and I keep Your law. This is mine -- that I keep Your precepts.

The Lord is my portion, I said, to keep Your words. I pray before You with all my heart. Be gracious to me in accordance with Your word. I consider my ways, and I turn my feet to Your testimonies. I make haste and I do not delay to keep Your commandments. The cords of the wicked have surrounded me. I have not forgotten Your law. At midnight I rise to thank You for Your righteous judgments. I am a companion of all those who fear You, and of those who keep Your precepts. The land, O Lord, is filled with Your loving-kindness. Teach me Your statutes.

You have dealt well with Your servant, O Lord, according to Your word. Teach me good sense and wise conduct, for I believe in Your commandments. Before I studied I sinned unintentionally, but now I keep Your word. You are good and cause others to be good. Teach me Your statutes. The wicked plaster falsehood upon me, but I keep Your precepts with all my heart. Their heart has become gross like fat, but I delight in Your law. It is good for me that I have been afflicted, so that I might learn Your statutes. The law of Your mouth is better for me than thousands of pieces of gold and silver.

Your hands have made me and established me. Make me understand that I may learn Your commandments. May those who fear You see me and rejoice, for I hope for Your word. I know, O Lord, that Your judgments are righteous, and You have rightly afflicted me. May Your loving-kindness comfort me, in accordance with Your word to Your servant. May Your mercies come upon me, that I may live, for Your law is my delight. May the wicked be ashamed, for they deal perversely with me with a lie, but I will meditate upon Your precepts. May those who fear You return to me, and those who know Your testimonies. May my heart be whole with Your statutes, so that I will not be ashamed.

כָּלְתָה לִתְשׁוּעָתְךָ נַפְשִׁי לִדְבָרְךָ יִחָלְתִּי: כָּלוּ עֵינַי לְאִמְרָתֶךָ לֵאמֹר מָתַי
תְּנַחֲמֵנִי: כִּי־הָיִיתִי כְּנֹאד בְּקִיטוֹר חֻקֶּיךָ לֹא שָׁכָחְתִּי: כַּמָּה יְמֵי־עַבְדֶּךָ
מָתַי תַּעֲשֶׂה בְרֹדְפַי מִשְׁפָּט: כָּרוּ־לִי זֵדִים שִׁיחוֹת אֲשֶׁר לֹא כְתוֹרָתֶךָ:
כָּל־מִצְוֺתֶיךָ אֱמוּנָה שֶׁקֶר רְדָפוּנִי עָזְרֵנִי: כִּמְעַט כִּלּוּנִי בָאָרֶץ וַאֲנִי לֹא־
עָזַבְתִּי פִקֻּדֶיךָ: כְּחַסְדְּךָ חַיֵּנִי וְאֶשְׁמְרָה עֵדוּת פִּיךָ:
לְעוֹלָם יְהֹוָה דְּבָרְךָ נִצָּב בַּשָּׁמָיִם: לְדֹר וָדֹר אֱמוּנָתֶךָ כּוֹנַנְתָּ אֶרֶץ וַתַּעֲמֹד:
לְמִשְׁפָּטֶיךָ עָמְדוּ הַיּוֹם כִּי הַכֹּל עֲבָדֶיךָ: לוּלֵי תוֹרָתְךָ שַׁעֲשֻׁעָי אָז אָבַדְתִּי
בְעָנְיִי: לְעוֹלָם לֹא־אֶשְׁכַּח פִּקּוּדֶיךָ כִּי־בָם חִיִּיתָנִי: לְךָ־אֲנִי הוֹשִׁיעֵנִי כִּי
פִקּוּדֶיךָ דָרָשְׁתִּי: לִי קִוּוּ רְשָׁעִים לְאַבְּדֵנִי עֵדֹתֶיךָ אֶתְבּוֹנָן: לְכָל־תִּכְלָה
רָאִיתִי קֵץ רְחָבָה מִצְוָתְךָ מְאֹד:

*מָה־אָהַבְתִּי תוֹרָתֶךָ כָּל־הַיּוֹם הִיא שִׂיחָתִי: מֵאֹיְבַי תְּחַכְּמֵנִי מִצְוֺתֶךָ כִּי
לְעוֹלָם הִיא־לִי: מִכָּל־מְלַמְּדַי הִשְׂכַּלְתִּי כִּי עֵדְוֺתֶיךָ שִׂיחָה לִי: מִזְּקֵנִים
אֶתְבּוֹנָן כִּי פִקּוּדֶיךָ נָצָרְתִּי: מִכָּל־אֹרַח רָע כָּלִאתִי רַגְלָי לְמַעַן אֶשְׁמֹר
דְּבָרֶךָ: מִמִּשְׁפָּטֶיךָ לֹא־סָרְתִּי כִּי־אַתָּה הוֹרֵתָנִי: מַה־נִּמְלְצוּ לְחִכִּי אִמְרָתֶךָ
מִדְּבַשׁ לְפִי: מִפִּקּוּדֶיךָ אֶתְבּוֹנָן עַל־כֵּן שָׂנֵאתִי ׀ כָּל־אֹרַח שָׁקֶר:

נֵר־לְרַגְלִי דְבָרֶךָ וְאוֹר לִנְתִיבָתִי: נִשְׁבַּעְתִּי וָאֲקַיֵּמָה לִשְׁמֹר מִשְׁפְּטֵי צִדְקֶךָ:
נַעֲנֵיתִי עַד־מְאֹד יְהֹוָה חַיֵּנִי כִדְבָרֶךָ: נִדְבוֹת פִּי רְצֵה־נָא יְהֹוָה וּמִשְׁפָּטֶיךָ
לַמְּדֵנִי: נַפְשִׁי בְכַפִּי תָמִיד וְתוֹרָתְךָ לֹא שָׁכָחְתִּי: נָתְנוּ רְשָׁעִים פַּח לִי
וּמִפִּקּוּדֶיךָ לֹא תָעִיתִי: נָחַלְתִּי עֵדְוֺתֶיךָ לְעוֹלָם כִּי־שְׂשׂוֹן לִבִּי הֵמָּה:
נָטִיתִי לִבִּי לַעֲשׂוֹת חֻקֶּיךָ לְעוֹלָם עֵקֶב:

סֵעֲפִים שָׂנֵאתִי וְתוֹרָתְךָ אָהָבְתִּי: סִתְרִי וּמָגִנִּי אָתָּה לִדְבָרְךָ יִחָלְתִּי:
סוּרוּ מִמֶּנִּי מְרֵעִים וְאֶצְּרָה מִצְוֺת אֱלֹהָי: סָמְכֵנִי כְאִמְרָתְךָ וְאֶחְיֶה וְאַל־
תְּבִישֵׁנִי מִשִּׂבְרִי: סְעָדֵנִי וְאִוָּשֵׁעָה וְאֶשְׁעָה בְחֻקֶּיךָ תָמִיד: סָלִיתָ כָּל־
שׁוֹגִים מֵחֻקֶּיךָ כִּי־שֶׁקֶר תַּרְמִיתָם: סִגִים הִשְׁבַּתָּ כָל־רִשְׁעֵי־אָרֶץ לָכֵן
אָהַבְתִּי עֵדֹתֶיךָ: סָמַר מִפַּחְדְּךָ בְשָׂרִי וּמִמִּשְׁפָּטֶיךָ יָרֵאתִי:

עָשִׂיתִי מִשְׁפָּט וָצֶדֶק בַּל־תַּנִּיחֵנִי לְעֹשְׁקָי: עֲרֹב עַבְדְּךָ לְטוֹב אַל־יַעַשְׁקֻנִי
זֵדִים: עֵינַי כָּלוּ לִישׁוּעָתֶךָ וּלְאִמְרַת צִדְקֶךָ: עֲשֵׂה עִם־עַבְדְּךָ כְחַסְדֶּךָ
וְחֻקֶּיךָ לַמְּדֵנִי: עַבְדְּךָ־אָנִי הֲבִינֵנִי וְאֵדְעָה עֵדֹתֶיךָ: עֵת לַעֲשׂוֹת לַיהֹוָה

*כו לחודש

My soul pines for Your salvation. I hope for Your word. My eyes long for Your word, saying, When will You comfort me? Even though I have become like a wineskin in smoke, I have not forgotten Your statutes. How many are the days of Your servant? When will You execute judgment on those who persecute me? The wicked have dug pits for me, which is not in accordance with Your law. All Your commandments are truth. They persecute me with lies. Please help me. They have almost consumed me on the earth, but I have not forsaken Your precepts. In accordance with Your loving-kindness, let me live, and I will keep the testimony of Your mouth.

Forever, O Lord, Your word stands firm in the heavens. Your faithfulness is for all generations. You established the earth, and it stands. They stand every day for Your judgments, for all are Your servants. If Your law had not been my delight, then I would have perished in my affliction. I will never forget Your precepts, for with them You have given me life. I am Yours, save me, for I seek Your precepts. The wicked plot against me to destroy me, but I contemplate Your testimonies. I have seen an end to every matter, but Your commandment is exceedingly broad.

*O how I love Your law. It is my meditation all the day. Your commandments make me wiser than my enemies, for it is forever with me. I gain wisdom from all who teach me, for Your testimonies are my meditation. I gain understanding from the elders, for I keep Your precepts. I restrain my feet from every evil way, so that I may keep Your word. I do not turn aside from Your judgments, for it is You Who have taught me. O how sweet is Your word to my palate, sweeter than honey to my mouth. Through Your precepts I gain understanding, therefore I hate every false way.

Your word is a lamp to my feet, and a light to my path. I have sworn and I fulfill, to keep Your righteous judgments. I have been exceedingly afflicted, O Lord, make me live in accordance with Your word. Please accept, O Lord, the freewill-offerings of my mouth, and teach me Your judgments. My soul is always in my hand, but I do not forget Your law. The wicked have laid a snare for me, but I have not strayed from Your precepts. I have taken Your testimonies as a heritage forever, for they are the joy of my heart. I incline my heart to perform Your statutes forever and ever.

I hate perverse thoughts, but I love Your law. You are my hiding place and my shield. I hope for Your word. Turn away from me, you evildoers, so that I may keep the commandments of my God. Support me in accordance with Your word so that I may live, and let me not be disappointed of my hope. Help me and let me be saved, and I will gaze upon Your statutes continually. You have crushed all those who stray from Your statutes, for their deceit is vain. You have destroyed all the wicked of the earth like dross, therefore I love Your testimonies. My flesh bristled for fear of You, and I am afraid of Your judgments.

I do justice and righteousness. Do not leave me to my oppressors. Be surety for Your servant for good. Do not let the wicked oppress me. My eyes yearn for Your salvation and for Your righteous word. Deal with Your servant in accordance with Your loving-kindness, and teach me Your statutes. I am Your servant, give me understanding, and

---

*26th DAY of the month

הֵפֵרוּ תּוֹרָתֶךָ׃ עַל־כֵּן אָהַבְתִּי מִצְוֺתֶיךָ מִזָּהָב וּמִפָּז׃ עַל־כֵּן ׀ כׇּל־פִּקּוּדֵי
כֹל יִשָּׁרְתִּי כׇּל־אֹרַח שֶׁקֶר שָׂנֵאתִי׃

פְּלָאוֹת עֵדְוֺתֶיךָ עַל־כֵּן נְצָרָתַם נַפְשִׁי׃ פֵּתַח־דְּבָרֶיךָ יָאִיר מֵבִין פְּתָיִים׃
פִּי־פָעַרְתִּי וָאֶשְׁאָפָה כִּי לְמִצְוֺתֶיךָ יָאָבְתִּי׃ פְּנֵה־אֵלַי וְחׇנֵּנִי כְּמִשְׁפָּט
לְאֹהֲבֵי שְׁמֶךָ׃ פְּעָמַי הָכֵן בְּאִמְרָתֶךָ וְאַל־תַּשְׁלֶט־בִּי כׇל־אָוֶן׃ פְּדֵנִי
מֵעֹשֶׁק אָדָם וְאֶשְׁמְרָה פִּקּוּדֶיךָ׃ פָּנֶיךָ הָאֵר בְּעַבְדֶּךָ וְלַמְּדֵנִי אֶת־חֻקֶּיךָ׃
פַּלְגֵי־מַיִם יָרְדוּ עֵינָי עַל לֹא־שָׁמְרוּ תוֹרָתֶךָ׃

צַדִּיק אַתָּה יְהֹוָה וְיָשָׁר מִשְׁפָּטֶיךָ׃ צִוִּיתָ צֶדֶק עֵדֹתֶיךָ וֶאֱמוּנָה מְאֹד׃
צִמְּתַתְנִי קִנְאָתִי כִּי־שָׁכְחוּ דְבָרֶיךָ צָרָי׃ צְרוּפָה אִמְרָתְךָ מְאֹד וְעַבְדְּךָ
אֲהֵבָהּ׃ צָעִיר אָנֹכִי וְנִבְזֶה פִּקֻּדֶיךָ לֹא שָׁכָחְתִּי׃ צִדְקָתְךָ צֶדֶק לְעוֹלָם
וְתוֹרָתְךָ אֱמֶת׃ צַר־וּמָצוֹק מְצָאוּנִי מִצְוֺתֶיךָ שַׁעֲשֻׁעָי׃ צֶדֶק עֵדְוֺתֶיךָ
לְעוֹלָם הֲבִינֵנִי וְאֶחְיֶה׃

קָרָאתִי בְכׇל־לֵב עֲנֵנִי יְהֹוָה חֻקֶּיךָ אֶצֹּרָה׃ קְרָאתִיךָ הוֹשִׁיעֵנִי וְאֶשְׁמְרָה
לִדְבָרְךָ עֵדֹתֶיךָ׃ קִדַּמְתִּי בַנֶּשֶׁף וָאֲשַׁוֵּעָה לדבריך יִחָלְתִּי׃ קִדְּמוּ עֵינַי אַשְׁמֻרוֹת
לָשִׂיחַ בְּאִמְרָתֶךָ׃ קוֹלִי שִׁמְעָה כְחַסְדֶּךָ יְהֹוָה כְּמִשְׁפָּטֶךָ חַיֵּנִי׃ קָרְבוּ רֹדְפֵי
זִמָּה מִתּוֹרָתְךָ רָחָקוּ׃ קָרוֹב אַתָּה יְהֹוָה וְכׇל־מִצְוֺתֶיךָ אֱמֶת׃ קֶדֶם יָדַעְתִּי
מֵעֵדֹתֶיךָ כִּי לְעוֹלָם יְסַדְתָּם׃

רְאֵה־עׇנְיִי וְחַלְּצֵנִי כִּי־תוֹרָתְךָ לֹא שָׁכָחְתִּי׃ רִיבָה רִיבִי וּגְאָלֵנִי לְאִמְרָתְךָ
חַיֵּנִי׃ רָחוֹק מֵרְשָׁעִים יְשׁוּעָה כִּי־חֻקֶּיךָ לֹא דָרָשׁוּ׃ רַחֲמֶיךָ רַבִּים ׀ יְהֹוָה
כְּמִשְׁפָּטֶיךָ חַיֵּנִי׃ רַבִּים רֹדְפַי וְצָרָי מֵעֵדְוֺתֶיךָ לֹא נָטִיתִי׃ רָאִיתִי בֹגְדִים
וָאֶתְקוֹטָטָה אֲשֶׁר אִמְרָתְךָ לֹא שָׁמָרוּ׃ רְאֵה כִּי־פִקּוּדֶיךָ אָהָבְתִּי יְהֹוָה
כְּחַסְדְּךָ חַיֵּנִי׃ רֹאשׁ־דְּבָרְךָ אֱמֶת וּלְעוֹלָם כׇּל־מִשְׁפַּט צִדְקֶךָ׃

וּמִדְּבָרְךָ שָׂרִים רְדָפוּנִי חִנָּם ומדבריך פָּחַד לִבִּי׃ שָׂשׂ אָנֹכִי עַל־אִמְרָתֶךָ כְּמוֹצֵא
שָׁלָל רָב׃ שֶׁקֶר שָׂנֵאתִי וַאֲתַעֵבָה תּוֹרָתְךָ אָהָבְתִּי׃ שֶׁבַע בַּיּוֹם הִלַּלְתִּיךָ
עַל מִשְׁפְּטֵי צִדְקֶךָ׃ שָׁלוֹם רָב לְאֹהֲבֵי תוֹרָתֶךָ וְאֵין־לָמוֹ מִכְשׁוֹל׃ שִׂבַּרְתִּי
לִישׁוּעָתְךָ יְהֹוָה וּמִצְוֺתֶיךָ עָשִׂיתִי׃ שָׁמְרָה נַפְשִׁי עֵדֹתֶיךָ וָאֹהֲבֵם מְאֹד׃
שָׁמַרְתִּי פִקּוּדֶיךָ וְעֵדֹתֶיךָ כִּי כׇל־דְּרָכַי נֶגְדֶּךָ׃

תִּקְרַב רִנָּתִי לְפָנֶיךָ יְהֹוָה כִּדְבָרְךָ הֲבִינֵנִי׃ תָּבוֹא תְּחִנָּתִי לְפָנֶיךָ כְּאִמְרָתְךָ

let me know Your testimonies. It is time to act for the Lord. They have violated Your law. Indeed, I love Your commandments more than gold and more than fine gold. Indeed, all Your precepts I declare right, every false way I hate.

Your testimonies are wonderful, therefore my soul keeps them. May the opening of Your words give light, You Who give understanding to the simple. I open my mouth and I gasp, because I long for Your commandments. Turn to me and be gracious unto me, as is Your way regarding those who love Your name. Direct my steps with Your word, and do not let iniquity have dominion over me. Deliver me from the oppression of man, so that I may keep Your precepts. Cause Your face to shine upon Your servant, and teach me Your statutes. My eyes shed rivers of water for those who do not keep Your law.

You are righteous, O Lord, and upright in Your judgments. You have commanded righteousness in Your testimonies, and great faithfulness. My zeal consumes me, because my adversaries have forgotten Your words. Your word is very pure, therefore Your servant loves it. I am young and despised, yet I do not forget Your precepts. Your righteousness is an everlasting righteousness, and Your law is truth. Trouble and anguish have found me, yet Your commandments are my delights. Your testimonies are righteous forever. Give me understanding and I will live. I cry with all my heart, answer me, O Lord, may I keep Your statutes.

I cry to You, save me, and let me keep Your testimonies. I rise before dawn and cry out. I hope for Your word. My eyes forestall the night watches, to meditate upon Your word. Hear my voice in accordance with Your loving-kindness, O Lord, make me live in accordance with Your judgment. Those who pursue wickedness draw near. They are far from Your law. You are near, O Lord, and all Your commandments are truth. I know about Your testimonies of old, that You have established them forever.

Behold my affliction and save me, for I do not forget Your law. Plead my cause and redeem me. Give me life for the sake of Your word. Remove the wicked far from salvation, for they have not sought Your statutes. Your mercies are many, O Lord. Let me live in accordance with Your judgments. My persecutors and my enemies are many, yet I have not deviated from Your testimonies. I see transgressors and I abhor them, for they do not keep Your word. See how I love Your precepts, O Lord, make me live in accordance with Your loving-kindness. The beginning of Your word is truth, and every one of Your righteous judgments is forever.

Princes persecute me without cause, but my heart fears Your word. I rejoice at Your word, like one who finds great spoil. I hate and abhor falsehood, but I love Your law. Seven times a day I praise You for Your righteous judgments. Those who love Your law have great peace, and they have no stumbling-block. I hope for Your salvation, O Lord, and I perform Your commandments. My soul keeps Your testimonies, and I love them greatly. I keep Your precepts and Your testimonies, for all my ways are before You. May my cry come near to You, O Lord.

Give me understanding according to Your word. May my supplication come before

הַצִּילֵנִי: תַּבַּעְנָה שְׂפָתַי תְּהִלָּה כִּי תְלַמְּדֵנִי חֻקֶּיךָ: תַּעַן לְשׁוֹנִי אִמְרָתֶךָ
כִּי כָל־מִצְוֺתֶיךָ צֶּדֶק: תְּהִי־יָדְךָ לְעָזְרֵנִי כִּי פִקּוּדֶיךָ בָחָרְתִּי: תָּאַבְתִּי
לִישׁוּעָתְךָ יהוה וְתוֹרָתְךָ שַׁעֲשֻׁעָי: תְּחִי־נַפְשִׁי וּתְהַלְלֶךָּ וּמִשְׁפָּטֶךָ יַעְזְרֻנִי:
תָּעִיתִי כְּשֶׂה אֹבֵד בַּקֵּשׁ עַבְדֶּךָ כִּי מִצְוֺתֶיךָ לֹא שָׁכָחְתִּי:

*קכ שִׁיר הַמַּעֲלוֹת אֶל־יהוה בַּצָּרָתָה לִּי קָרָאתִי וַיַּעֲנֵנִי: יהוה הַצִּילָה נַפְשִׁי
מִשְּׂפַת־שֶׁקֶר מִלָּשׁוֹן רְמִיָּה: מַה־יִּתֵּן לְךָ וּמַה־יֹּסִיף לָךְ לָשׁוֹן רְמִיָּה: חִצֵּי
גִבּוֹר שְׁנוּנִים עִם גַּחֲלֵי רְתָמִים: אוֹיָה־לִי כִּי־גַרְתִּי מֶשֶׁךְ שָׁכַנְתִּי עִם־
אָהֳלֵי קֵדָר: רַבַּת שָׁכְנָה־לָּהּ נַפְשִׁי עִם שׂוֹנֵא שָׁלוֹם: אֲנִי־שָׁלוֹם וְכִי
אֲדַבֵּר הֵמָּה לַמִּלְחָמָה:

קכא שִׁיר לַמַּעֲלוֹת אֶשָּׂא עֵינַי אֶל־הֶהָרִים מֵאַיִן יָבֹא עֶזְרִי: עֶזְרִי מֵעִם יהוה
עֹשֵׂה שָׁמַיִם וָאָרֶץ: אַל־יִתֵּן לַמּוֹט רַגְלֶךָ אַל־יָנוּם שֹׁמְרֶךָ: הִנֵּה לֹא־יָנוּם
וְלֹא יִישָׁן שׁוֹמֵר יִשְׂרָאֵל: יהוה שֹׁמְרֶךָ יהוה צִלְּךָ עַל־יַד יְמִינֶךָ: יוֹמָם
הַשֶּׁמֶשׁ לֹא־יַכֶּכָּה וְיָרֵחַ בַּלָּיְלָה: יהוה יִשְׁמָרְךָ מִכָּל־רָע יִשְׁמֹר אֶת־נַפְשֶׁךָ:
יהוה יִשְׁמָר־צֵאתְךָ וּבוֹאֶךָ מֵעַתָּה וְעַד־עוֹלָם:

קכב שִׁיר הַמַּעֲלוֹת לְדָוִד שָׂמַחְתִּי בְּאֹמְרִים לִי בֵּית יהוה נֵלֵךְ: עֹמְדוֹת הָיוּ
רַגְלֵינוּ בִּשְׁעָרַיִךְ יְרוּשָׁלָםִ: יְרוּשָׁלַםִ הַבְּנוּיָה כְּעִיר שֶׁחֻבְּרָה־לָּהּ יַחְדָּו:
שֶׁשָּׁם עָלוּ שְׁבָטִים שִׁבְטֵי־יָהּ עֵדוּת לְיִשְׂרָאֵל לְהֹדוֹת לְשֵׁם יהוה: כִּי
שָׁמָּה ׀ יָשְׁבוּ כִסְאוֹת לְמִשְׁפָּט כִּסְאוֹת לְבֵית דָּוִד: שַׁאֲלוּ שְׁלוֹם יְרוּשָׁלָםִ
יִשְׁלָיוּ אֹהֲבָיִךְ: יְהִי־שָׁלוֹם בְּחֵילֵךְ שַׁלְוָה בְּאַרְמְנוֹתָיִךְ: לְמַעַן אַחַי וְרֵעָי
אֲדַבְּרָה־נָּא שָׁלוֹם בָּךְ: לְמַעַן בֵּית־יהוה אֱלֹהֵינוּ אֲבַקְשָׁה טוֹב לָךְ:

קכג שִׁיר הַמַּעֲלוֹת אֵלֶיךָ נָשָׂאתִי אֶת־עֵינַי הַיֹּשְׁבִי בַּשָּׁמָיִם: הִנֵּה כְעֵינֵי עֲבָדִים
אֶל־יַד אֲדוֹנֵיהֶם כְּעֵינֵי שִׁפְחָה אֶל־יַד גְּבִרְתָּהּ כֵּן עֵינֵינוּ אֶל־יהוה אֱלֹהֵינוּ
עַד שֶׁיְּחָנֵּנוּ: חָנֵּנוּ יהוה חָנֵּנוּ כִּי־רַב שָׂבַעְנוּ בוּז: רַבַּת שָׂבְעָה־לָּהּ נַפְשֵׁנוּ
הַלַּעַג הַשַּׁאֲנַנִּים הַבּוּז לִגְאֵיוֹנִים: לִגְאֵי יוֹנִים

קכד שִׁיר הַמַּעֲלוֹת לְדָוִד לוּלֵי יהוה שֶׁהָיָה לָנוּ יֹאמַר־נָא יִשְׂרָאֵל: לוּלֵי
יהוה שֶׁהָיָה לָנוּ בְּקוּם עָלֵינוּ אָדָם: אֲזַי חַיִּים בְּלָעוּנוּ בַּחֲרוֹת אַפָּם
בָּנוּ: אֲזַי הַמַּיִם שְׁטָפוּנוּ נַחְלָה עָבַר עַל־נַפְשֵׁנוּ: אֲזַי עָבַר עַל־נַפְשֵׁנוּ
הַמַּיִם הַזֵּידוֹנִים: בָּרוּךְ יהוה שֶׁלֹּא נְתָנָנוּ טֶרֶף לְשִׁנֵּיהֶם: נַפְשֵׁנוּ כְּצִפּוֹר

*כז לחודש / ליום השבת

You. Deliver me according to Your word. May my lips utter praise, when You teach
me Your statutes. May my tongue proclaim Your word, for all Your commandments
are righteousness. May Your hand be of help to me, for I have chosen Your precepts.
I long for Your salvation, O Lord, and Your law is my delight. May my soul live and
praise You, and may Your judgments help me. I go astray like a lost sheep. Seek out
Your servant, for I do not forget Your commandments. –

*120 A SONG of Ascents. In my distress I call upon the Lord that He may answer me. O
Lord, deliver my soul from lying lips, from a deceitful tongue. What will He give to
you and what will He add to you, O deceitful tongue? Sharp arrows of the mighty,
with coals of broom. Woe is me, that I sojourn with Meshech, that I dwell among the
tents of Kedar! My soul has long dwelt with him who hates peace. I am for peace; but
when I speak, they are for war.

121 A SONG for Ascents. I lift up my eyes to the hills. From where will my help come? My
help is from the Lord, the Maker of heaven and earth. May He not suffer your foot
to slip. May He Who guards you not slumber. Behold, He Who guards Israel neither
slumbers nor sleeps. The Lord is your guardian. The Lord is your shade upon your
right hand. The sun will not smite you by day, nor the moon by night. The Lord will
guard you from all evil. He will guard your soul. The Lord will guard your going out
and your coming in from now and forever.

122 A SONG of Ascents of David. I was glad when they said to me: We are going to the
house of the Lord. Our feet were standing within your gates, O Jerusalem. Jerusalem
that is built. It is like a city that is united together. For the tribes went up there, the
tribes of the Lord, a testimony to Israel, to give thanks to the name of the Lord. For
there they sat on thrones for judgment, the thrones of the house of David. Pray for
the peace of Jerusalem. May they prosper who love you. May peace be within your
walls, prosperity within your palaces. For my brothers' and companions' sakes may
I now say: "Peace be within you." For the sake of the house of the Lord our God, I
will seek your good.

123 A SONG of Ascents. To You I lift up my eyes, O You Who dwell in the heavens. Behold,
as the eyes of servants to the hand of their masters, as the eyes of a maidservant to
the hand of her mistress, so are our eyes to the Lord our God until He is gracious
unto us. Be gracious unto us, O Lord, be gracious unto us, for we have suffered our
fill of contempt. Our soul has suffered its fill of the scorn of those who are at ease, of
the contempt of the proud.

124 A SONG of Ascents of David. Were it not for the Lord Who was with us, let Israel say,
Were it not for the Lord Who was with us, when people rose against us. Then they
would have swallowed us alive, in their burning fury against us. Then the waters would
have flooded us. The torrent would have passed over our soul. Then over our soul
the treacherous waters would have passed. Blessed is the Lord, Who did not make
us prey to their teeth. Our soul is like a bird escaped from the snare of the hunters.

---

*27th DAY of the month / SHABBAT

נִמְלְטָה מִפַּח יוֹקְשִׁים הַפַּח נִשְׁבָּר וַאֲנַחְנוּ נִמְלָטְנוּ׃ עֶזְרֵנוּ בְּשֵׁם יְהֹוָה
עֹשֵׂה שָׁמַיִם וָאָרֶץ׃

קכה שִׁיר הַמַּעֲלוֹת הַבֹּטְחִים בַּיהֹוָה כְּהַר־צִיּוֹן לֹא־יִמּוֹט לְעוֹלָם יֵשֵׁב׃
יְרוּשָׁלִַם הָרִים סָבִיב לָהּ וַיהוָה סָבִיב לְעַמּוֹ מֵעַתָּה וְעַד־עוֹלָם׃ כִּי לֹא
יָנוּחַ שֵׁבֶט הָרֶשַׁע עַל גּוֹרַל הַצַּדִּיקִים לְמַעַן לֹא־יִשְׁלְחוּ הַצַּדִּיקִים ׀
בְּעַוְלָתָה יְדֵיהֶם׃ הֵיטִיבָה יְהוָה לַטּוֹבִים וְלִישָׁרִים בְּלִבּוֹתָם׃ וְהַמַּטִּים
עֲקַלְקַלּוֹתָם יוֹלִיכֵם יְהוָה אֶת־פֹּעֲלֵי הָאָוֶן שָׁלוֹם עַל־יִשְׂרָאֵל׃

קכו שִׁיר הַמַּעֲלוֹת בְּשׁוּב יְהוָה אֶת־שִׁיבַת צִיּוֹן הָיִינוּ כְּחֹלְמִים׃ אָז יִמָּלֵא
שְׂחוֹק פִּינוּ וּלְשׁוֹנֵנוּ רִנָּה אָז יֹאמְרוּ בַגּוֹיִם הִגְדִּיל יְהוָה לַעֲשׂוֹת עִם־אֵלֶּה׃
שְׁבִיתֵנוּ הִגְדִּיל יְהוָה לַעֲשׂוֹת עִמָּנוּ הָיִינוּ שְׂמֵחִים׃ שׁוּבָה יְהוָה אֶת־שבותנו
כַּאֲפִיקִים בַּנֶּגֶב׃ הַזֹּרְעִים בְּדִמְעָה בְּרִנָּה יִקְצֹרוּ׃ הָלוֹךְ יֵלֵךְ ׀ וּבָכֹה נֹשֵׂא
מֶשֶׁךְ־הַזָּרַע בֹּא־יָבֹא בְרִנָּה נֹשֵׂא אֲלֻמֹּתָיו׃

קכז שִׁיר הַמַּעֲלוֹת לִשְׁלֹמֹה אִם־יְהוָה ׀ לֹא־יִבְנֶה בַיִת שָׁוְא עָמְלוּ בוֹנָיו בּוֹ
אִם־יְהוָה לֹא־יִשְׁמָר־עִיר שָׁוְא ׀ שָׁקַד שׁוֹמֵר׃ שָׁוְא לָכֶם ׀ מַשְׁכִּימֵי קוּם
מְאַחֲרֵי־שֶׁבֶת אֹכְלֵי לֶחֶם הָעֲצָבִים כֵּן יִתֵּן לִידִידוֹ שֵׁנָא׃ הִנֵּה נַחֲלַת
יְהוָה בָּנִים שָׂכָר פְּרִי הַבָּטֶן׃ כְּחִצִּים בְּיַד־גִּבּוֹר כֵּן בְּנֵי הַנְּעוּרִים׃ אַשְׁרֵי
הַגֶּבֶר אֲשֶׁר מִלֵּא אֶת־אַשְׁפָּתוֹ מֵהֶם לֹא־יֵבֹשׁוּ כִּי־יְדַבְּרוּ אֶת־אוֹיְבִים
בַּשָּׁעַר׃

קכח שִׁיר הַמַּעֲלוֹת אַשְׁרֵי כָּל־יְרֵא יְהוָה הַהֹלֵךְ בִּדְרָכָיו׃ יְגִיעַ כַּפֶּיךָ כִּי תֹאכֵל
אַשְׁרֶיךָ וְטוֹב לָךְ׃ אֶשְׁתְּךָ ׀ כְּגֶפֶן פֹּרִיָּה בְּיַרְכְּתֵי בֵיתֶךָ בָּנֶיךָ כִּשְׁתִלֵי זֵיתִים
סָבִיב לְשֻׁלְחָנֶךָ׃ הִנֵּה כִי־כֵן יְבֹרַךְ גָּבֶר יְרֵא יְהוָה׃ יְבָרֶכְךָ יְהוָה מִצִּיּוֹן וּרְאֵה
בְּטוּב יְרוּשָׁלָםִ כֹּל יְמֵי חַיֶּיךָ׃ וּרְאֵה־בָנִים לְבָנֶיךָ שָׁלוֹם עַל־יִשְׂרָאֵל׃

קכט שִׁיר הַמַּעֲלוֹת רַבַּת צְרָרוּנִי מִנְּעוּרָי יֹאמַר־נָא יִשְׂרָאֵל׃ רַבַּת צְרָרוּנִי
לְמַעֲנִיתָם מִנְּעוּרָי גַּם לֹא־יָכְלוּ לִי׃ עַל־גַּבִּי חָרְשׁוּ חֹרְשִׁים הֶאֱרִיכוּ למענותם׃ יְהוָה
צַדִּיק קִצֵּץ עֲבוֹת רְשָׁעִים׃ יֵבֹשׁוּ וְיִסֹּגוּ אָחוֹר כֹּל שֹׂנְאֵי צִיּוֹן׃ יִהְיוּ כַּחֲצִיר
גַּגּוֹת שֶׁקַּדְמַת שָׁלַף יָבֵשׁ׃ שֶׁלֹּא מִלֵּא כַפּוֹ קוֹצֵר וְחִצְנוֹ מְעַמֵּר׃ וְלֹא
אָמְרוּ ׀ הָעֹבְרִים בִּרְכַּת־יְהוָה אֲלֵיכֶם בֵּרַכְנוּ אֶתְכֶם בְּשֵׁם יְהוָה׃

קל שִׁיר הַמַּעֲלוֹת מִמַּעֲמַקִּים קְרָאתִיךָ יְהוָה׃ אֲדֹנָי שִׁמְעָה בְקוֹלִי תִּהְיֶינָה

The snare broke, and we escaped. Our help is in the name of the Lord, the Maker of
heaven and earth.
125 A SONG of Ascents. Those who trust in the Lord are like Mount Zion, which will not
be moved and will abide forever. Jerusalem, mountains surround it, and the Lord
surrounds His people from now and forever. Indeed, the rod of wickedness will not
rest upon the lot of the righteous, so that the righteous will not put forth their hands
unto iniquity. Do good, O Lord, to the good, and to the upright in their hearts. But
as for those who turn aside their crooked ways, may the Lord carry away the workers
of iniquity. Peace be upon Israel.
126 A SONG of Ascents. When the Lord brought back the return of Zion, we were like
those who dream. Then our mouth was filled with laughter and our tongue with joy.
Then they said among the nations: "the Lord did great things for these." The Lord
did great things for us. We were glad. Bring back our return, O Lord, like the streams
in the south. Those that sow in tears will reap in joy. May he who goes out weeping,
bearing the sack of seed, come home in joy, bearing his sheaves.
127 A SONG of Ascents of Solomon. If the Lord does not build a house, those that built
it have labored on it in vain. If the Lord does not guard the city, the watchman has
persevered in vain. It is vain for you who rise early, who sit late, who eat the bread
of toil, truly He gives His loved one sleep. Behold, children are an inheritance of
the Lord, the fruit of the womb is a reward. Like arrows in the hand of a mighty
man, so are the sons of one's youth. Happy is the man who has filled his quiver
with them. They will not be put to shame, when they speak with the enemies in the
gate.
128 A SONG of Ascents. Happy is everyone who fears the Lord, who walks in His ways. If
you eat the labor of your hands, you will be happy and it will be well with you. Your
wife will be like a fruitful vine in the innermost parts of your house, your children
like olive plants around your table. Behold, truly the man who fears the Lord will be
blessed. May the Lord bless you from Zion, and may you see the good of Jerusalem
all the days of your life. And may you see your children's children. Peace be upon
Israel.
129 A SONG of Ascents. They have greatly afflicted me from my youth, let Israel now
say. They have greatly afflicted me from my youth, yet they have not prevailed over
me. The plowers have plowed upon my back, they have made their furrow long.
The Lord is righteous, He has cut apart the cord of the wicked. Let all who hate
Zion be confounded and turned back. Let them be as the grass of the rooftops,
which has withered before it is cut down, with which the reaper has not filled his
hand, nor the binder of sheaves the fold of his garment. And the passers-by have
not said: The blessing of the Lord be upon you. We bless you in the name of the
Lord.
130 A SONG of Ascents. From the depths I call out to You, O Lord. My Master, hear

אָזְנֶיךָ קַשֻּׁבוֹת לְקוֹל תַּחֲנוּנָי: אִם־עֲוֺנוֹת תִּשְׁמָר־יָהּ אֲדֹנָי מִי יַעֲמֹד: כִּי־
עִמְּךָ הַסְּלִיחָה לְמַעַן תִּוָּרֵא: קִוִּיתִי יהוה קִוְּתָה נַפְשִׁי וְלִדְבָרוֹ הוֹחָלְתִּי:
נַפְשִׁי לַאדֹנָי מִשֹּׁמְרִים לַבֹּקֶר שֹׁמְרִים לַבֹּקֶר: יַחֵל יִשְׂרָאֵל אֶל־יהוה
כִּי־עִם־יהוה הַחֶסֶד וְהַרְבֵּה עִמּוֹ פְדוּת: וְהוּא יִפְדֶּה אֶת־יִשְׂרָאֵל מִכֹּל
עֲוֺנוֹתָיו:

קלא שִׁיר הַמַּעֲלוֹת לְדָוִד יהוה ׀ לֹא־גָבַהּ לִבִּי וְלֹא־רָמוּ עֵינַי וְלֹא־הִלַּכְתִּי ׀
בִּגְדֹלוֹת וּבְנִפְלָאוֹת מִמֶּנִּי: אִם־לֹא שִׁוִּיתִי ׀ וְדוֹמַמְתִּי נַפְשִׁי כְּגָמֻל עֲלֵי
אִמּוֹ כַּגָּמֻל עָלַי נַפְשִׁי: יַחֵל יִשְׂרָאֵל אֶל־יהוה מֵעַתָּה וְעַד־עוֹלָם:

קלב שִׁיר הַמַּעֲלוֹת זְכוֹר־יהוה לְדָוִד אֵת כָּל־עֻנּוֹתוֹ: אֲשֶׁר נִשְׁבַּע לַיהוה נָדַר
לַאֲבִיר יַעֲקֹב: אִם־אָבֹא בְּאֹהֶל בֵּיתִי אִם־אֶעֱלֶה עַל־עֶרֶשׂ יְצוּעָי: אִם־
אֶתֵּן שְׁנָת לְעֵינָי לְעַפְעַפַּי תְּנוּמָה: עַד־אֶמְצָא מָקוֹם לַיהוה מִשְׁכָּנוֹת
לַאֲבִיר יַעֲקֹב: הִנֵּה־שְׁמַעֲנוּהָ בְאֶפְרָתָה מְצָאנוּהָ בִּשְׂדֵי־יָעַר: נָבוֹאָה
לְמִשְׁכְּנוֹתָיו נִשְׁתַּחֲוֶה לַהֲדֹם רַגְלָיו: קוּמָה יהוה לִמְנוּחָתֶךָ אַתָּה וַאֲרוֹן
עֻזֶּךָ: כֹּהֲנֶיךָ יִלְבְּשׁוּ־צֶדֶק וַחֲסִידֶיךָ יְרַנֵּנוּ: בַּעֲבוּר דָּוִד עַבְדֶּךָ אַל־תָּשֵׁב
פְּנֵי מְשִׁיחֶךָ: נִשְׁבַּע־יהוה ׀ לְדָוִד אֱמֶת לֹא־יָשׁוּב מִמֶּנָּה מִפְּרִי בִטְנְךָ
אָשִׁית לְכִסֵּא־לָךְ: אִם־יִשְׁמְרוּ בָנֶיךָ ׀ בְּרִיתִי וְעֵדֹתִי זוֹ אֲלַמְּדֵם גַּם־
בְּנֵיהֶם עֲדֵי־עַד יֵשְׁבוּ לְכִסֵּא־לָךְ: כִּי־בָחַר יהוה בְּצִיּוֹן אִוָּהּ לְמוֹשָׁב לוֹ:
זֹאת־מְנוּחָתִי עֲדֵי־עַד פֹּה אֵשֵׁב כִּי אִוִּתִיהָ: צֵידָהּ בָּרֵךְ אֲבָרֵךְ אֶבְיוֹנֶיהָ
אַשְׂבִּיעַ לָחֶם: וְכֹהֲנֶיהָ אַלְבִּישׁ יֶשַׁע וַחֲסִידֶיהָ רַנֵּן יְרַנֵּנוּ: שָׁם אַצְמִיחַ קֶרֶן
לְדָוִד עָרַכְתִּי נֵר לִמְשִׁיחִי: אוֹיְבָיו אַלְבִּישׁ בֹּשֶׁת וְעָלָיו יָצִיץ נִזְרוֹ:

קלג שִׁיר הַמַּעֲלוֹת לְדָוִד הִנֵּה מַה־טּוֹב וּמַה־נָּעִים שֶׁבֶת אַחִים גַּם־יָחַד:
כַּשֶּׁמֶן הַטּוֹב ׀ עַל־הָרֹאשׁ יֹרֵד עַל־הַזָּקָן זְקַן־אַהֲרֹן שֶׁיֹּרֵד עַל־פִּי מִדּוֹתָיו:
כְּטַל־חֶרְמוֹן שֶׁיֹּרֵד עַל־הַרְרֵי צִיּוֹן כִּי שָׁם ׀ צִוָּה יהוה אֶת־הַבְּרָכָה חַיִּים
עַד־הָעוֹלָם:

קלד שִׁיר הַמַּעֲלוֹת הִנֵּה ׀ בָּרְכוּ אֶת־יהוה כָּל־עַבְדֵי יהוה הָעֹמְדִים בְּבֵית־
יהוה בַּלֵּילוֹת: שְׂאוּ־יְדֵכֶם קֹדֶשׁ וּבָרְכוּ אֶת־יהוה: יְבָרֶכְךָ יהוה מִצִּיּוֹן
עֹשֵׂה שָׁמַיִם וָאָרֶץ:

*קלה הַלְלוּיָהּ ׀ הַלְלוּ אֶת־שֵׁם יהוה הַלְלוּ עַבְדֵי יהוה: שֶׁעֹמְדִים בְּבֵית יהוה

---

*כח לחודש

my voice. Let Your ears be attentive to the sound of my supplications. If You, Lord,
pay heed to iniquities, who, my Master, will stand? Indeed, forgiveness is with You,
so that You may be feared. I wait for the Lord, my soul waits, and I hope for His
word. My soul waits for my Master, among those who watch for the morning, who
watch for the morning. Israel, hope for the Lord, for with the Lord is loving-kindness,
and with Him is abundant redemption. And He will redeem Israel from all his
iniquities.

131 A SONG of Ascents of David. O Lord, my heart is not haughty, nor are my eyes
lofty. And I do not occupy myself with great things, or with things beyond my
power. Surely I compose and still my soul, like a weaned child beside its mother:
my soul is to me like a weaned child. Israel, hope for the Lord, from now and
forever.

132 A SONG of Ascents. O Lord, remember for David all his affliction, What he swore
to the Lord, what he vowed to the mighty One of Jacob: I will not come under
the roof of my house, nor will I mount my bed, I will not give sleep to my eyes, or
slumber to my eyelids, Until I find a place for the Lord, a habitation for the mighty
One of Jacob. Behold, we heard it in Ephratah, we found it in Sedei-Ya'ar. Let us
come into His dwelling places, let us bow down to His footstool. Arise, O Lord, to
Your resting place, You and the Ark of Your strength. May Your priests be clothed
in righteousness, and may Your pious ones shout for joy. For the sake of David Your
servant, do not turn away the face of Your anointed. The Lord has sworn to David,
in truth, He will not turn back from it: From the fruit of your body I will place
upon your throne. If your children will keep My covenant and My testimony that
I will teach them, then their children will sit on your throne forevermore. Indeed,
the Lord has chosen Zion, He had desired it for His habitation: This is My resting
place forever. Here I will dwell, for I desire it. I will abundantly bless her food. I
will satisfy her poor with bread. And I will clothe her priests with salvation, and her
pious ones will surely shout for joy. There will I make the horn of David flourish, I
prepare a lamp for My anointed. I will clothe his enemies with shame, but on him
will his crown shine.

133 A SONG of Ascents of David. Behold, how good and how pleasant it is for brothers
to sit together. Like the good oil upon the head that descends upon the beard, the
beard of Aaron, that descends over the border of his garments. So the dew of Hermon
that descends upon the mountains of Zion. For there the Lord has commanded the
blessing, life forevermore.

134 A SONG of Ascents. Behold, bless the Lord, all you servants of the Lord, who stand
in the house of the Lord in the nights. Raise your hands to the sanctuary, and
bless the Lord. May the Lord, the Maker of heaven and earth, bless you from
Zion.

*135 PRAISE the Lord. Praise the name of the Lord, praise, you servants of the Lord, who

---

*28th DAY of the month

בְּחַצְרוֹת בֵּית אֱלֹהֵינוּ: הַֽלְלוּיָהּ כִּי־טוֹב יהוה זַמְּרוּ לִשְׁמוֹ כִּי נָעִים:
כִּֽי־יַעֲקֹב בָּחַר לוֹ יָהּ יִשְׂרָאֵל לִסְגֻלָּתוֹ: כִּי אֲנִי יָדַעְתִּי כִּֽי־גָדוֹל יהוה
וַאֲדֹנֵינוּ מִכׇּל־אֱלֹהִים: כֹּל אֲשֶׁר־חָפֵץ יהוה עָשָׂה בַּשָּׁמַיִם וּבָאָרֶץ בַּיַּמִּים
וְכׇל־תְּהֹמוֹת: מַעֲלֶה נְשִׂאִים מִקְצֵה הָאָרֶץ בְּרָקִים לַמָּטָר עָשָׂה מֽוֹצֵא־
רוּחַ מֵאוֹצְרוֹתָיו: שֶׁהִכָּה בְּכוֹרֵי מִצְרָיִם מֵאָדָם עַד־בְּהֵמָה: שָׁלַח ׀ אֹתוֹת
וּמֹפְתִים בְּתוֹכֵכִי מִצְרָיִם בְּפַרְעֹה וּבְכׇל־עֲבָדָיו: שֶׁהִכָּה גּוֹיִם רַבִּים וְהָרַג
מְלָכִים עֲצוּמִים: לְסִיחוֹן ׀ מֶלֶךְ הָאֱמֹרִי וּלְעוֹג מֶלֶךְ הַבָּשָׁן וּלְכֹל מַמְלְכוֹת
כְּנָעַן: וְנָתַן אַרְצָם נַחֲלָה נַחֲלָה לְיִשְׂרָאֵל עַמּוֹ: יהוה שִׁמְךָ לְעוֹלָם יהוה
זִכְרְךָ לְדֹר־וָדֹר: כִּֽי־יָדִין יהוה עַמּוֹ וְעַל־עֲבָדָיו יִתְנֶחָם: עֲצַבֵּי הַגּוֹיִם
כֶּסֶף וְזָהָב מַעֲשֵׂה יְדֵי אָדָם: פֶּֽה־לָהֶם וְלֹא יְדַבֵּרוּ עֵינַיִם לָהֶם וְלֹא יִרְאוּ:
אׇזְנַיִם לָהֶם וְלֹא יַאֲזִינוּ אַף אֵין־יֶשׁ־רוּחַ בְּפִיהֶם: כְּמוֹהֶם יִהְיוּ עֹשֵׂיהֶם
כֹּל אֲשֶׁר־בֹּטֵחַ בָּהֶם: בֵּית יִשְׂרָאֵל בָּרְכוּ אֶת־יהוה בֵּית אַהֲרֹן בָּרְכוּ
אֶת־יהוה: בֵּית הַלֵּוִי בָּרְכוּ אֶת־יהוה יִרְאֵי יהוה בָּרְכוּ אֶת־יהוה: בָּרוּךְ
יהוה ׀ מִצִּיּוֹן שֹׁכֵן יְרוּשָׁלָ͏ִם הַֽלְלוּיָהּ:

קלו הוֹדוּ לַיהוה כִּי־טוֹב כִּי לְעוֹלָם חַסְדּוֹ: הוֹדוּ לֵאלֹהֵי הָאֱלֹהִים כִּי לְעוֹלָם
חַסְדּוֹ: הוֹדוּ לַאֲדֹנֵי הָאֲדֹנִים כִּי לְעוֹלָם חַסְדּוֹ: לְעֹשֵׂה נִפְלָאוֹת גְּדֹלוֹת
לְבַדּוֹ כִּי לְעוֹלָם חַסְדּוֹ: לְעֹשֵׂה הַשָּׁמַיִם בִּתְבוּנָה כִּי לְעוֹלָם חַסְדּוֹ:
לְרֹקַע הָאָרֶץ עַל־הַמָּיִם כִּי לְעוֹלָם חַסְדּוֹ: לְעֹשֵׂה אוֹרִים גְּדֹלִים כִּי
לְעוֹלָם חַסְדּוֹ: אֶת־הַשֶּׁמֶשׁ לְמֶמְשֶׁלֶת בַּיּוֹם כִּי לְעוֹלָם חַסְדּוֹ: אֶת־
הַיָּרֵחַ וְכוֹכָבִים לְמֶמְשְׁלוֹת בַּלָּיְלָה כִּי לְעוֹלָם חַסְדּוֹ: לְמַכֵּה מִצְרַיִם
בִּבְכוֹרֵיהֶם כִּי לְעוֹלָם חַסְדּוֹ: וַיּוֹצֵא יִשְׂרָאֵל מִתּוֹכָם כִּי לְעוֹלָם חַסְדּוֹ:
בְּיָד חֲזָקָה וּבִזְרוֹעַ נְטוּיָה כִּי לְעוֹלָם חַסְדּוֹ: לְגֹזֵר יַם־סוּף לִגְזָרִים כִּי
לְעוֹלָם חַסְדּוֹ: וְהֶעֱבִיר יִשְׂרָאֵל בְּתוֹכוֹ כִּי לְעוֹלָם חַסְדּוֹ: וְנִעֵר פַּרְעֹה
וְחֵילוֹ בְיַם־סוּף כִּי לְעוֹלָם חַסְדּוֹ: לְמוֹלִיךְ עַמּוֹ בַּמִּדְבָּר כִּי לְעוֹלָם חַסְדּוֹ:
לְמַכֵּה מְלָכִים גְּדֹלִים כִּי לְעוֹלָם חַסְדּוֹ: וַיַּהֲרֹג מְלָכִים אַדִּירִים כִּי לְעוֹלָם
חַסְדּוֹ: לְסִיחוֹן מֶלֶךְ הָאֱמֹרִי כִּי לְעוֹלָם חַסְדּוֹ: וּלְעוֹג מֶלֶךְ הַבָּשָׁן כִּי
לְעוֹלָם חַסְדּוֹ: וְנָתַן אַרְצָם לְנַחֲלָה כִּי לְעוֹלָם חַסְדּוֹ: נַחֲלָה לְיִשְׂרָאֵל
עַבְדּוֹ כִּי לְעוֹלָם חַסְדּוֹ: שֶׁבְּשִׁפְלֵנוּ זָכַר לָנוּ כִּי לְעוֹלָם חַסְדּוֹ: וַיִּפְרְקֵנוּ

stand in the house of the Lord, in the courtyards of the house of our God. Praise the Lord, for the Lord is good. Sing praises to His name, for it is pleasant. For the Lord has chosen Jacob for Himself, Israel for His special possession. Indeed, I know that the Lord is great, and that our Lord is greater than all gods. Whatever the Lord wishes He does, in the heavens and on the earth, in the seas and all the deep places. He causes clouds to rise from the end of the earth. He makes lightnings with the rain. He brings wind out of His treasure-houses. It was He Who smote the firstborn of Egypt, both of man and of beast, Who sent signs and wonders into the midst of Egypt, upon Pharaoh and upon all his servants, Who smote great nations, and slew mighty kings, Sihon King of the Amorites, and Og King of Bashan, and all the kingdoms of Canaan, and Who gave their land as a heritage, a heritage to Israel His people. O Lord, Your name is forever. O Lord, Your renown is for all generations. Indeed, the Lord will judge His people, and He will relent concerning His servants. The idols of the nations are silver and gold, the work of man's hands. They have a mouth but they do not speak, they have eyes but they do not see. They have ears but they do not hear, and there is even no breath in their mouths. Those who make them will become like them, everyone who trusts in them. O house of Israel, bless the Lord. O house of Aaron, bless the Lord. O house of Levi, bless the Lord. You who fear the Lord, bless the Lord. Blessed is the Lord from Zion, He Who dwells in Jerusalem. Praise the Lord.

136 GIVE THANKS to the Lord, for He is good, for His loving-kindness is forever. Give thanks to the God of gods, for His loving-kindness is forever. Give thanks to the Lord of lords, for His loving-kindness is forever. To Him Who alone performs great wonders, for His loving-kindness is forever. To Him Who made the heavens with understanding, for His loving-kindness is forever. To Him Who stretched out the earth over the water, for His loving-kindness is forever. To Him Who made great lights, for His loving-kindness is forever. The sun as ruler over the day, for His loving-kindness is forever. The moon and the stars as rulers over the night, for His loving-kindness is forever. To Him Who smote Egypt in their firstborn, for His loving-kindness is forever. And brought Israel out from among them, for His loving-kindness is forever. With a strong hand and with an outstretched arm, for His loving-kindness is forever. To Him Who divided the Sea of Reeds into halves, for His loving-kindness is forever. And brought Israel through its midst, for His loving-kindness is forever. And cast Pharaoh and his host into the Sea of Reeds, for His loving-kindness is forever. To Him Who led His people through the wilderness, for His loving-kindness is forever. To Him Who smote great kings, for His loving-kindness is forever. And slew mighty kings, for His loving-kindness is forever. Sihon King of the Amorites, for His loving-kindness is forever. And Og King of Bashan, for His loving-kindness is forever. And gave their land as an inheritance, for His loving-kindness is forever. An inheritance to Israel His servant, for His loving-kindness is forever. Who remembered us in our degradation, for His loving-kindness is forever. And delivered us from our enemies, for His loving-kindness is forever. Who gives

מִצָּרֵינוּ כִּי לְעוֹלָם חַסְדּוֹ׃ נֹתֵן לֶחֶם לְכׇל־בָּשָׂר כִּי לְעוֹלָם חַסְדּוֹ׃ הוֹדוּ
לְאֵל הַשָּׁמָיִם כִּי לְעוֹלָם חַסְדּוֹ׃

קלז עַל־נַהֲרוֹת ׀ בָּבֶל שָׁם יָשַׁבְנוּ גַּם־בָּכִינוּ בְּזׇכְרֵנוּ אֶת־צִיּוֹן׃ עַל־עֲרָבִים
בְּתוֹכָהּ תָּלִינוּ כִּנֹּרוֹתֵינוּ׃ כִּי שָׁם ׀ שְׁאֵלוּנוּ שׁוֹבֵינוּ דִּבְרֵי־שִׁיר וְתוֹלָלֵינוּ
שִׂמְחָה שִׁירוּ לָנוּ מִשִּׁיר צִיּוֹן׃ אֵיךְ נָשִׁיר אֶת־שִׁיר־יהוה עַל אַדְמַת
נֵכָר׃ אִם־אֶשְׁכָּחֵךְ יְרוּשָׁלָ͏ִם תִּשְׁכַּח יְמִינִי׃ תִּדְבַּק לְשׁוֹנִי ׀ לְחִכִּי אִם־לֹא
אֶזְכְּרֵכִי אִם־לֹא אַעֲלֶה אֶת־יְרוּשָׁלַ͏ִם עַל רֹאשׁ שִׂמְחָתִי׃ זְכֹר יהוה ׀ לִבְנֵי
אֱדוֹם אֵת יוֹם יְרוּשָׁלָ͏ִם הָאֹמְרִים עָרוּ ׀ עָרוּ עַד הַיְסוֹד בָּהּ׃ בַּת־בָּבֶל
הַשְּׁדוּדָה אַשְׁרֵי שֶׁיְשַׁלֶּם־לָךְ אֶת־גְּמוּלֵךְ שֶׁגָּמַלְתְּ לָנוּ׃ אַשְׁרֵי ׀ שֶׁיֹּאחֵז
וְנִפֵּץ אֶת־עֹלָלַיִךְ אֶל־הַסָּלַע׃

קלח לְדָוִד ׀ אוֹדְךָ בְכׇל־לִבִּי נֶגֶד אֱלֹהִים אֲזַמְּרֶךָּ׃ אֶשְׁתַּחֲוֶה אֶל־הֵיכַל קׇדְשְׁךָ
וְאוֹדֶה אֶת־שְׁמֶךָ עַל־חַסְדְּךָ וְעַל־אֲמִתֶּךָ כִּי־הִגְדַּלְתָּ עַל־כׇּל־שִׁמְךָ
אִמְרָתֶךָ׃ בְּיוֹם קָרָאתִי וַתַּעֲנֵנִי תַּרְהִבֵנִי בְנַפְשִׁי עֹז׃ יוֹדוּךָ יהוה כׇּל־
מַלְכֵי־אָרֶץ כִּי שָׁמְעוּ אִמְרֵי־פִיךָ׃ וְיָשִׁירוּ בְּדַרְכֵי יהוה כִּי־גָדוֹל כְּבוֹד
יהוה׃ כִּי־רָם יהוה וְשָׁפָל יִרְאֶה וְגָבֹהַּ מִמֶּרְחָק יְיֵדָע׃ אִם־אֵלֵךְ ׀ בְּקֶרֶב
צָרָה תְּחַיֵּנִי עַל אַף אֹיְבַי תִּשְׁלַח יָדֶךָ וְתוֹשִׁיעֵנִי יְמִינֶךָ׃ יהוה יִגְמֹר בַּעֲדִי
יהוה חַסְדְּךָ לְעוֹלָם מַעֲשֵׂי יָדֶיךָ אַל־תֶּרֶף׃

קלט לַמְנַצֵּחַ לְדָוִד מִזְמוֹר יהוה חֲקַרְתַּנִי וַתֵּדָע׃ אַתָּה יָדַעְתָּ שִׁבְתִּי וְקוּמִי
בַּנְתָּה לְרֵעִי מֵרָחוֹק׃ אׇרְחִי וְרִבְעִי זֵרִיתָ וְכׇל־דְּרָכַי הִסְכַּנְתָּה׃ כִּי אֵין מִלָּה
בִּלְשׁוֹנִי הֵן יהוה יָדַעְתָּ כֻלָּהּ׃ אָחוֹר וָקֶדֶם צַרְתָּנִי וַתָּשֶׁת עָלַי כַּפֶּכָה׃
פְּלִיאָה פלאיה דַעַת מִמֶּנִּי נִשְׂגְּבָה לֹא־אוּכַל לָהּ׃ אָנָה אֵלֵךְ מֵרוּחֶךָ וְאָנָה
מִפָּנֶיךָ אֶבְרָח׃ אִם־אֶסַּק שָׁמַיִם שָׁם אָתָּה וְאַצִּיעָה שְּׁאוֹל הִנֶּךָּ׃ אֶשָּׂא
כַנְפֵי־שָׁחַר אֶשְׁכְּנָה בְּאַחֲרִית יָם׃ גַּם־שָׁם יָדְךָ תַנְחֵנִי וְתֹאחֲזֵנִי יְמִינֶךָ׃
וָאֹמַר אַךְ־חֹשֶׁךְ יְשׁוּפֵנִי וְלַיְלָה אוֹר בַּעֲדֵנִי׃ גַּם־חֹשֶׁךְ לֹא־יַחְשִׁיךְ מִמֶּךָ
וְלַיְלָה כַּיּוֹם יָאִיר כַּחֲשֵׁיכָה כָּאוֹרָה׃ כִּי־אַתָּה קָנִיתָ כִלְיֹתָי תְּסֻכֵּנִי בְּבֶטֶן
אִמִּי׃ אוֹדְךָ עַל כִּי נוֹרָאוֹת נִפְלֵיתִי נִפְלָאִים מַעֲשֶׂיךָ וְנַפְשִׁי יֹדַעַת מְאֹד׃
לֹא־נִכְחַד עׇצְמִי מִמֶּךָּ אֲשֶׁר־עֻשֵּׂיתִי בַסֵּתֶר רֻקַּמְתִּי בְּתַחְתִּיּוֹת אָרֶץ׃
וְלוֹ גׇּלְמִי ׀ רָאוּ עֵינֶיךָ וְעַל־סִפְרְךָ כֻּלָּם יִכָּתֵבוּ יָמִים יֻצָּרוּ ולא אֶחָד בָּהֶם׃ וְלִי

bread to all flesh, for His loving-kindness is forever. Give thanks to the God of the heavens, for His loving-kindness is forever.

137 BY THE RIVERS of Babylon, there we sat and wept, as we remembered Zion. On the
willows in its midst we hung our lyres. For there our captors required of us words of song, and our mockers music, Sing to us of the songs of Zion. How shall we sing the Lord's song in a foreign land? If I forget you, O Jerusalem, may my right hand forget. May my tongue cleave to the roof of my mouth, if I do not make mention of you, if I do not raise Jerusalem to the head of my joy. Remember, O Lord, against the children of Edom the day of Jerusalem, those who said, Raze it, raze it, to its very foundations. O daughter of Babylon, marked for devastation, happy is he who will repay you your recompense for what you have done to us. Happy is he who will seize and dash your infants against the rock.

138 OF DAVID. I thank You with my whole heart. Before the gods I sing to You. I bow
down toward Your holy Temple, and I thank Your name for Your loving-kindness and for Your truth, that You have magnified Your word above all Your name. On the day that I called out, You answered me. You invigorated me with strength in my soul. All the kings of the earth thank You, O Lord, for they have heard the words of Your mouth. And they sing of the ways of the Lord, for great is the honor of the Lord. For the Lord is high, but He sees the lowly, and He is lofty, but He knows from afar. If I walk in the midst of trouble, You will keep me alive. Against the anger of my enemies You will send Your hand, and Your right hand will save me. The Lord will finish on my behalf. O Lord, Your loving-kindness is forever. Do not forsake the works of Your hands.

139 TO THE DIRECTOR of music. A psalm of David. O Lord, You examine me, and You
know me. You know my sitting down and my rising up. You understand my thoughts from afar. You measure my path and my resting-place, and You oversee all my ways. When no word is yet on my tongue, behold, O Lord, You know it all. You enclose me behind and before, and You lay Your hand upon me. Such knowledge is too wonderful for me. It is high, I cannot attain it. Where can I go from Your spirit? And where can I flee from Your presence? If I ascend to heaven, there You are, and if I make the underworld my bed, behold, You are there. If I am borne to the wings of the east, if I dwell at the end of the west, Even there Your hand will guide me, and Your right hand will grasp me. And I said: Only darkness will cover me, and night the light from me. Even darkness is not dark for You, and night shines like day. Darkness is like light. Indeed, You formed my kidneys, You wove me in my mother's womb. I thank You, that I am made with awesome wonders. Wonderful are Your works, and my soul knows this well. My essence is not hidden from You, that I was formed in secret, I was wrought in the lowest parts of the earth. Your eyes saw my unshaped flesh, and all of them were written in Your book, the days when they were to be fashioned, when there was not one of them. As for me, how precious are your thoughts, O God! How great are their principles! If I count them, they are more

מַה־יָּקְרוּ רֵעֶיךָ אֵל מֶה עָצְמוּ רָאשֵׁיהֶם: אֶסְפְּרֵם מֵחוֹל יִרְבּוּן הֱקִיצֹתִי
וְעוֹדִי עִמָּךְ: אִם־תִּקְטֹל אֱלוֹהַּ | רָשָׁע וְאַנְשֵׁי דָמִים סוּרוּ מֶנִּי: אֲשֶׁר יֹמְרוּךָ
לִמְזִמָּה נָשׂוּא לַשָּׁוְא עָרֶיךָ: הֲלוֹא־מְשַׂנְאֶיךָ יהוה | אֶשְׂנָא וּבִתְקוֹמְמֶיךָ
אֶתְקוֹטָט: תַּכְלִית שִׂנְאָה שְׂנֵאתִים לְאוֹיְבִים הָיוּ לִי: חָקְרֵנִי אֵל וְדַע לְבָבִי
בְּחָנֵנִי וְדַע שַׂרְעַפָּי: וּרְאֵה אִם־דֶּרֶךְ־עֹצֶב בִּי וּנְחֵנִי בְּדֶרֶךְ עוֹלָם:
*קמ לַמְנַצֵּחַ מִזְמוֹר לְדָוִד: חַלְּצֵנִי יהוה מֵאָדָם רָע מֵאִישׁ חֲמָסִים תִּנְצְרֵנִי:
אֲשֶׁר חָשְׁבוּ רָעוֹת בְּלֵב כָּל־יוֹם יָגוּרוּ מִלְחָמוֹת: שָׁנְנוּ לְשׁוֹנָם כְּמוֹ־נָחָשׁ
חֲמַת עַכְשׁוּב תַּחַת שְׂפָתֵימוֹ סֶלָה: שָׁמְרֵנִי יהוה | מִידֵי רָשָׁע מֵאִישׁ
חֲמָסִים תִּנְצְרֵנִי אֲשֶׁר חָשְׁבוּ לִדְחוֹת פְּעָמָי: טָמְנוּ־גֵאִים | פַּח לִי וַחֲבָלִים
פָּרְשׂוּ רֶשֶׁת לְיַד־מַעְגָּל מֹקְשִׁים שָׁתוּ־לִי סֶלָה: אָמַרְתִּי לַיהוה אֵלִי אָתָּה
הַאֲזִינָה יהוה קוֹל תַּחֲנוּנָי: יֱהֹוִה אֲדֹנָי עֹז יְשׁוּעָתִי סַכֹּתָה לְרֹאשִׁי
בְּיוֹם נָשֶׁק: אַל־תִּתֵּן יהוה מַאֲוַיֵּי רָשָׁע זְמָמוֹ אַל־תָּפֵק יָרוּמוּ סֶלָה:
יְכַסֵּמוֹ רֹאשׁ מְסִבָּי עֲמַל שְׂפָתֵימוֹ יכסומו: ימיטו עֲלֵיהֶם גֶּחָלִים בָּאֵשׁ יַפִּלֵם
יִמּוֹטוּ בְּמַהֲמֹרוֹת בַּל־יָקוּמוּ: אִישׁ לָשׁוֹן בַּל־יִכּוֹן בָּאָרֶץ אִישׁ־חָמָס רָע יְצוּדֶנּוּ
לְמַדְחֵפֹת: יָדַעְתָּ כִּי־יַעֲשֶׂה יהוה דִּין עָנִי מִשְׁפַּט אֶבְיֹנִים: אַךְ צַדִּיקִים
יוֹדוּ לִשְׁמֶךָ יֵשְׁבוּ יְשָׁרִים אֶת־פָּנֶיךָ:
קמא מִזְמוֹר לְדָוִד יהוה קְרָאתִיךָ חוּשָׁה לִּי הַאֲזִינָה קוֹלִי בְּקָרְאִי־לָךְ: תִּכּוֹן
תְּפִלָּתִי קְטֹרֶת לְפָנֶיךָ מַשְׂאַת כַּפַּי מִנְחַת־עָרֶב: שִׁיתָה יהוה שָׁמְרָה לְפִי
נִצְּרָה עַל־דַּל שְׂפָתָי: אַל־תַּט־לִבִּי | לְדָבָר | רָע לְהִתְעוֹלֵל עֲלִלוֹת | בְּרֶשַׁע
אֶת־אִישִׁים פֹּעֲלֵי־אָוֶן וּבַל־אֶלְחַם בְּמַנְעַמֵּיהֶם: יֶהֶלְמֵנִי צַדִּיק | חֶסֶד
וְיוֹכִיחֵנִי שֶׁמֶן רֹאשׁ אַל־יָנִי רֹאשִׁי כִּי־עוֹד וּתְפִלָּתִי בְּרָעוֹתֵיהֶם: נִשְׁמְטוּ
בִידֵי־סֶלַע שֹׁפְטֵיהֶם וְשָׁמְעוּ אֲמָרַי כִּי נָעֵמוּ: כְּמוֹ פֹלֵחַ וּבֹקֵעַ בָּאָרֶץ
נִפְזְרוּ עֲצָמֵינוּ לְפִי שְׁאוֹל: כִּי אֵלֶיךָ | יֱהֹוִה אֲדֹנָי עֵינָי בְּכָה חָסִיתִי אַל־
תְּעַר נַפְשִׁי: שָׁמְרֵנִי מִידֵי פַח יָקְשׁוּ לִי וּמֹקְשׁוֹת פֹּעֲלֵי אָוֶן: יִפְּלוּ בְמַכְמֹרָיו
רְשָׁעִים יַחַד אָנֹכִי עַד־אֶעֱבוֹר:
קמב מַשְׂכִּיל לְדָוִד בִּהְיוֹתוֹ בַמְּעָרָה תְפִלָּה: קוֹלִי אֶל־יהוה אֶזְעָק קוֹלִי אֶל־
יהוה אֶתְחַנָּן: אֶשְׁפֹּךְ לְפָנָיו שִׂיחִי צָרָתִי לְפָנָיו אַגִּיד: בְּהִתְעַטֵּף עָלַי |
רוּחִי וְאַתָּה יָדַעְתָּ נְתִיבָתִי בְּאֹרַח־זוּ אֲהַלֵּךְ טָמְנוּ פַח לִי: הַבֵּיט יָמִין |

*כט לחודש

numerous than sand. When I am awake, I am still with you. O that you would slay the wicked, O God! And depart from me, you men of blood! Who speak of You with intrigue, Your enemies who take You in vain. Surely, O Lord, I hate those who hate You, and I strive against those who rise up against You. With the utmost hate do I hate them, they are enemies. Probe me, O God, and know my heart, test me and know my thoughts. And see if there is any wicked way in me, and guide me in the everlasting way.

*140 TO THE DIRECTOR of music. A psalm of David. Rescue me, O Lord, from evil men, protect me from violent men, Who devise mischief in their heart, every day they foment wars. They have sharpened their tongues like a serpent, a spider's venom is under their lips. Selah. Guard me, O Lord, from the hands of the wicked, protect me from violent men, who devise to trip my feet. The proud have laid a snare for me. They have spread cords and a net along the way. They have set traps for me. Selah. I say to the Lord: You are my God. Hear, O Lord, the voice of my supplications. O God, O Lord, the strength of my salvation, You cover my head on the day of battle. Do not grant, O Lord, the desires of the wicked. Do not further his wicked scheme. Let them be exalted. Selah. As for the heads of those who encompass me, let the evil work of their lips cover them. May burning coals fall upon them, may He cast them into the fire, into pits, so that they do not rise. May the man of the tongue not be established on the earth. As for the man of evil violence, they will hunt him and repel him. I know that the Lord will execute the cause of the afflicted, the right of the poor. But the righteous will give thanks to Your name. The upright will dwell in Your presence.

141 A PSALM of David. O Lord, I cry to You. Make haste to me. Hear my voice when I cry to You. May my prayer be set before You like incense, the lifting of my hands like the evening sacrifice. Set a guard, O Lord, to my mouth, a lock on the door of my lips. Do not incline my heart to any evil thing, to perform wicked deeds with men who work iniquity, and may I not eat of their delicacies. May the righteous man strike me with loving-kindness, and may he rebuke me. May the oil on my head not cause my head to incline. But may my prayer be forever against their evil ways. Their judges fell upon the hands of rocks, though they heard my words that are pleasant. As when one cuts and breaks up the earth, so are our bones strewn at the mouth of the underworld. Indeed, my eyes are toward You, O God O Lord. In You do I trust, do not pour away my life. Keep me from the snare that they have laid for me, and the traps of the workers of iniquity. May the wicked fall into their own nets. May I alone pass.

142 A *MASKIL* of David, when he was in the cave. A prayer. With my voice, I cry to the Lord. With my voice I entreat the Lord. I pour out my prayer before Him, I declare my trouble before Him. When my spirit faints within me – but You know my path. In the way that I walk they have hidden a snare for me. Look to my right and see that

*29th DAY of the month

וּרְאֵה וְאֵין־לִי מַכִּיר אָבַד מָנוֹס מִמֶּנִּי אֵין דּוֹרֵשׁ לְנַפְשִׁי: זָעַקְתִּי אֵלֶיךָ
יְהוָה אָמַרְתִּי אַתָּה מַחְסִי חֶלְקִי בְּאֶרֶץ הַחַיִּים: הַקְשִׁיבָה ׀ אֶל־רִנָּתִי
כִּי־דַלּוֹתִי מְאֹד הַצִּילֵנִי מֵרֹדְפַי כִּי אָמְצוּ מִמֶּנִּי: הוֹצִיאָה מִמַּסְגֵּר ׀ נַפְשִׁי
לְהוֹדוֹת אֶת־שְׁמֶךָ בִּי יַכְתִּרוּ צַדִּיקִים כִּי תִגְמֹל עָלָי:
קמג מִזְמוֹר לְדָוִד יְהוָה ׀ שְׁמַע תְּפִלָּתִי הַאֲזִינָה אֶל־תַּחֲנוּנַי בֶּאֱמֻנָתְךָ עֲנֵנִי
בְּצִדְקָתֶךָ: וְאַל־תָּבוֹא בְמִשְׁפָּט אֶת־עַבְדֶּךָ כִּי לֹא־יִצְדַּק לְפָנֶיךָ כָל־
חָי: כִּי רָדַף אוֹיֵב ׀ נַפְשִׁי דִּכָּא לָאָרֶץ חַיָּתִי הוֹשִׁיבַנִי בְמַחֲשַׁכִּים כְּמֵתֵי
עוֹלָם: וַתִּתְעַטֵּף עָלַי רוּחִי בְּתוֹכִי יִשְׁתּוֹמֵם לִבִּי: זָכַרְתִּי יָמִים ׀ מִקֶּדֶם
הָגִיתִי בְכָל־פָּעֳלֶךָ בְּמַעֲשֵׂה יָדֶיךָ אֲשׂוֹחֵחַ: פֵּרַשְׂתִּי יָדַי אֵלֶיךָ נַפְשִׁי ׀
כְּאֶרֶץ־עֲיֵפָה לְךָ סֶלָה: מַהֵר עֲנֵנִי ׀ יְהוָה כָּלְתָה רוּחִי אַל־תַּסְתֵּר פָּנֶיךָ
מִמֶּנִּי וְנִמְשַׁלְתִּי עִם־יֹרְדֵי בוֹר: הַשְׁמִיעֵנִי בַבֹּקֶר ׀ חַסְדֶּךָ כִּי־בְךָ בָטָחְתִּי
הוֹדִיעֵנִי דֶּרֶךְ־זוּ אֵלֵךְ כִּי־אֵלֶיךָ נָשָׂאתִי נַפְשִׁי: הַצִּילֵנִי מֵאֹיְבַי ׀ יְהוָה
אֵלֶיךָ כִסִּתִי: לַמְּדֵנִי ׀ לַעֲשׂוֹת רְצוֹנֶךָ כִּי־אַתָּה אֱלוֹהָי רוּחֲךָ טוֹבָה תַּנְחֵנִי
בְּאֶרֶץ מִישׁוֹר: לְמַעַן־שִׁמְךָ יְהוָה תְּחַיֵּנִי בְּצִדְקָתְךָ ׀ תּוֹצִיא מִצָּרָה נַפְשִׁי:
וּבְחַסְדְּךָ תַּצְמִית אֹיְבָי וְהַאֲבַדְתָּ כָּל־צֹרְרֵי נַפְשִׁי כִּי אֲנִי עַבְדֶּךָ:
קמד לְדָוִד ׀ בָּרוּךְ יְהוָה ׀ צוּרִי הַמְלַמֵּד יָדַי לַקְרָב אֶצְבְּעוֹתַי לַמִּלְחָמָה: חַסְדִּי
וּמְצוּדָתִי מִשְׂגַּבִּי וּמְפַלְטִי לִי מָגִנִּי וּבוֹ חָסִיתִי הָרוֹדֵד עַמִּי תַחְתָּי: יְהוָה
מָה־אָדָם וַתֵּדָעֵהוּ בֶּן־אֱנוֹשׁ וַתְּחַשְּׁבֵהוּ: אָדָם לַהֶבֶל דָּמָה יָמָיו כְּצֵל
עוֹבֵר: יְהוָה הַט־שָׁמֶיךָ וְתֵרֵד גַּע בֶּהָרִים וְיֶעֱשָׁנוּ: בְּרוֹק בָּרָק וּתְפִיצֵם
שְׁלַח חִצֶּיךָ וּתְהֻמֵּם: שְׁלַח יָדֶיךָ מִמָּרוֹם פְּצֵנִי וְהַצִּילֵנִי מִמַּיִם רַבִּים מִיַּד
בְּנֵי נֵכָר: אֲשֶׁר פִּיהֶם דִּבֶּר־שָׁוְא וִימִינָם יְמִין שָׁקֶר: אֱלֹהִים שִׁיר חָדָשׁ
אָשִׁירָה לָּךְ בְּנֵבֶל עָשׂוֹר אֲזַמְּרָה־לָּךְ: הַנּוֹתֵן תְּשׁוּעָה לַמְּלָכִים הַפּוֹצֶה
אֶת־דָּוִד עַבְדּוֹ מֵחֶרֶב רָעָה: פְּצֵנִי וְהַצִּילֵנִי מִיַּד בְּנֵי־נֵכָר אֲשֶׁר פִּיהֶם
דִּבֶּר־שָׁוְא וִימִינָם יְמִין שָׁקֶר: אֲשֶׁר בָּנֵינוּ ׀ כִּנְטִעִים מְגֻדָּלִים בִּנְעוּרֵיהֶם
בְּנוֹתֵינוּ כְזָוִיֹּת מְחֻטָּבוֹת תַּבְנִית הֵיכָל: מְזָוֵינוּ מְלֵאִים מְפִיקִים מִזַּן אֶל
זַן צֹאונֵנוּ מַאֲלִיפוֹת מְרֻבָּבוֹת בְּחוּצוֹתֵינוּ: אַלּוּפֵינוּ מְסֻבָּלִים אֵין פֶּרֶץ
וְאֵין יוֹצֵאת וְאֵין צְוָחָה בִּרְחֹבֹתֵינוּ: אַשְׁרֵי הָעָם שֶׁכָּכָה לּוֹ אַשְׁרֵי הָעָם
שֶׁיהוָה אֱלֹהָיו:

there is no man who helps me, I have nowhere to flee, no one cares for me. I cry to You, O Lord. I say, You are my refuge, my portion in the land of the living. Listen to my prayer, for I have been brought very low. Deliver me from my persecutors, for they are stronger than I. Bring me out of prison to thank Your name. For me the righteous will make circles, for You have dealt bountifully with me.

143 A PSALM of David. O Lord, hear my prayer, give ear to my supplications. In Your fidelity answer me, in Your righteousness. And do not enter into judgment with Your servant, for no living being will be justified before You. For the enemy has persecuted my soul, he has oppressed my life to the ground. He has set me in darkness like those who are eternally dead. Therefore my spirit faints within me, inside me my heart is astonished. I remember the days of old, I meditate on all Your works. I conversed about the work of Your hands. I stretch out my hands to You. My soul is like a land thirsty for You. Selah. Be quick and answer me, O Lord, my spirit pines. Do not hide Your face from me, lest I be like those to descend into the pit. Let me hear Your loving-kindness in the morning, for in You do I trust. Let me know the path on which I should walk, for to You do I lift up my soul. Deliver me from my enemies, O Lord, in my trust in You I cover myself. Teach me to do Your will, for You are my God. Let Your spirit, which is good, lead me on level land. For Your name's sake, O Lord, let me live. In Your righteousness remove my soul from trouble. And in Your loving-kindness cut off my enemies, and destroy all those who hate my soul, for I am Your servant.

144 OF DAVID. Blessed be the Lord, my rock, Who teaches my hands for battle, my fingers for war. My gracious One, and my fortress, my high tower, and my deliverer, my shield, and the One in Whom I find shelter, Who subdues people under me. O Lord, what is man, that You know him, the son of man, that You consider him! Man is like a breath. His days are like a passing shadow. O Lord, bow Your heavens and come down. Touch the mountains so that they smoke. Fire lightning and scatter them. Send Your arrows and destroy them. Send Your hands from on high. Rescue me and deliver me from many waters, from the hand of strangers, whose mouth speaks deceit, and whose right hand is a right hand of falsehood. O God, I will sing a new song to You, upon a ten-string harp I will sing praises to You. He Who gives salvation to kings, Who rescues David, His servant, from the evil sword, Rescue me and deliver me from the hand of strangers, whose mouth speaks deceit, and whose right hand is a right hand of falsehood. So that our sons will be like saplings raised in their youth, our daughters like cornerstones, carved in the fashion of a palace. Our storehouses are full, supplying all kinds of produce, our sheep bring forth thousands, tens of thousands in our markets. Our rams are stout. There is no breach and there is no leaving, and there is no outcry in our streets. Happy is the people that has this. Happy is the people whose God is the Lord.

*קמה תְּהִלָּה לְדָוִד אֲרוֹמִמְךָ אֱלוֹהַי הַמֶּלֶךְ וַאֲבָרְכָה שִׁמְךָ לְעוֹלָם וָעֶד: בְּכָל־
יוֹם אֲבָרְכֶךָּ וַאֲהַלְלָה שִׁמְךָ לְעוֹלָם וָעֶד: גָּדוֹל יהוה וּמְהֻלָּל מְאֹד וְלִגְדֻלָּתוֹ
אֵין חֵקֶר: דּוֹר לְדוֹר יְשַׁבַּח מַעֲשֶׂיךָ וּגְבוּרֹתֶיךָ יַגִּידוּ: הֲדַר כְּבוֹד הוֹדֶךָ
וְדִבְרֵי נִפְלְאֹתֶיךָ אָשִׂיחָה: וֶעֱזוּז נוֹרְאֹתֶיךָ יֹאמֵרוּ וגדלותיך אֲסַפְּרֶנָּה: וּגְדוּלָּתְךָ
זֵכֶר רַב־טוּבְךָ יַבִּיעוּ וְצִדְקָתְךָ יְרַנֵּנוּ: חַנּוּן וְרַחוּם יהוה אֶרֶךְ אַפַּיִם וּגְדָל־
חָסֶד: טוֹב־יהוה לַכֹּל וְרַחֲמָיו עַל־כָּל־מַעֲשָׂיו: יוֹדוּךָ יהוה כָּל־מַעֲשֶׂיךָ
וַחֲסִידֶיךָ יְבָרְכוּכָה: כְּבוֹד מַלְכוּתְךָ יֹאמֵרוּ וּגְבוּרָתְךָ יְדַבֵּרוּ: לְהוֹדִיעַ ׀
לִבְנֵי הָאָדָם גְּבוּרֹתָיו וּכְבוֹד הֲדַר מַלְכוּתוֹ: מַלְכוּתְךָ מַלְכוּת כָּל־עֹלָמִים
וּמֶמְשַׁלְתְּךָ בְּכָל־דּוֹר וָדֹר: סוֹמֵךְ יהוה לְכָל־הַנֹּפְלִים וְזוֹקֵף לְכָל־
הַכְּפוּפִים: עֵינֵי־כֹל אֵלֶיךָ יְשַׂבֵּרוּ וְאַתָּה נוֹתֵן־לָהֶם אֶת־אָכְלָם בְּעִתּוֹ:
פּוֹתֵחַ אֶת־יָדֶךָ וּמַשְׂבִּיעַ לְכָל־חַי רָצוֹן: צַדִּיק יהוה בְּכָל־דְּרָכָיו וְחָסִיד
בְּכָל־מַעֲשָׂיו: קָרוֹב יהוה לְכָל־קֹרְאָיו לְכֹל אֲשֶׁר יִקְרָאֻהוּ בֶאֱמֶת: רְצוֹן־
יְרֵאָיו יַעֲשֶׂה וְאֶת־שַׁוְעָתָם יִשְׁמַע וְיוֹשִׁיעֵם: שׁוֹמֵר יהוה אֶת־כָּל־אֹהֲבָיו
וְאֵת כָּל־הָרְשָׁעִים יַשְׁמִיד: תְּהִלַּת יהוה יְדַבֶּר פִּי וִיבָרֵךְ כָּל־בָּשָׂר שֵׁם
קָדְשׁוֹ לְעוֹלָם וָעֶד:

קמו הַלְלוּיָהּ הַלְלִי נַפְשִׁי אֶת־יהוה: אֲהַלְלָה יהוה בְּחַיָּי אֲזַמְּרָה לֵאלֹהַי
בְּעוֹדִי: אַל־תִּבְטְחוּ בִנְדִיבִים בְּבֶן־אָדָם ׀ שֶׁאֵין לוֹ תְשׁוּעָה: תֵּצֵא רוּחוֹ
יָשֻׁב לְאַדְמָתוֹ בַּיּוֹם הַהוּא אָבְדוּ עֶשְׁתֹּנֹתָיו: אַשְׁרֵי שֶׁאֵל יַעֲקֹב בְּעֶזְרוֹ
שִׂבְרוֹ עַל־יהוה אֱלֹהָיו: עֹשֶׂה ׀ שָׁמַיִם וָאָרֶץ אֶת־הַיָּם וְאֶת־כָּל־אֲשֶׁר־
בָּם הַשֹּׁמֵר אֱמֶת לְעוֹלָם: עֹשֶׂה מִשְׁפָּט ׀ לָעֲשׁוּקִים נֹתֵן לֶחֶם לָרְעֵבִים
יהוה מַתִּיר אֲסוּרִים: יהוה ׀ פֹּקֵחַ עִוְרִים יהוה זֹקֵף כְּפוּפִים יהוה אֹהֵב
צַדִּיקִים: יהוה ׀ שֹׁמֵר אֶת־גֵּרִים יָתוֹם וְאַלְמָנָה יְעוֹדֵד וְדֶרֶךְ רְשָׁעִים
יְעַוֵּת: יִמְלֹךְ יהוה ׀ לְעוֹלָם אֱלֹהַיִךְ צִיּוֹן לְדֹר וָדֹר הַלְלוּיָהּ:

קמז הַלְלוּיָהּ ׀ כִּי־טוֹב זַמְּרָה אֱלֹהֵינוּ כִּי־נָעִים נָאוָה תְהִלָּה: בּוֹנֵה יְרוּשָׁלִַם
יהוה נִדְחֵי יִשְׂרָאֵל יְכַנֵּס: הָרֹפֵא לִשְׁבוּרֵי לֵב וּמְחַבֵּשׁ לְעַצְּבוֹתָם: מוֹנֶה
מִסְפָּר לַכּוֹכָבִים לְכֻלָּם שֵׁמוֹת יִקְרָא: גָּדוֹל אֲדוֹנֵינוּ וְרַב־כֹּחַ לִתְבוּנָתוֹ
אֵין מִסְפָּר: מְעוֹדֵד עֲנָוִים יהוה מַשְׁפִּיל רְשָׁעִים עֲדֵי־אָרֶץ: עֱנוּ לַיהוה
בְּתוֹדָה זַמְּרוּ לֵאלֹהֵינוּ בְכִנּוֹר: הַמְכַסֶּה שָׁמַיִם ׀ בְּעָבִים הַמֵּכִין לָאָרֶץ

*ל לחודש

*145 A PRAISE of David. I exalt You, my God, the king, and I will bless Your name forever and ever. Every day I will bless You, and I will praise Your name forever and ever. Great is the Lord, and very praiseworthy, and His greatness is boundless. One generation lauds Your works to another, and they declare Your mighty deeds. I speak of the splendid glory of Your majesty and of Your wondrous works, And they speak of the might of Your awesome deeds, and I declare Your greatness. They express the renown of Your great goodness, and sing of Your righteousness. Gracious and merciful is the Lord, slow to anger and great in loving-kindness. The Lord is good to all, and His mercies are upon all His works. All Your works thank You, O Lord, and Your pious ones bless You. They describe the glory of Your kingdom, and speak of Your might, To make known to the sons of man His mighty deeds, and the glorious splendor of His kingdom. Your kingdom is a kingdom for all times, and Your dominion is for every generation. The Lord supports all who fall and raises up all who are bowed down. The eyes of all await You, and You give them their food in its time. You open Your hand, and You satisfy the desire of every living thing. The Lord is righteous in all His ways and kind in all His works. The Lord is near to all who address Him, to all who address Him in truth. He does the will of those who fear Him, and He hears their cry and saves them. The Lord preserves all who love Him, but all the wicked He destroys. May my mouth speak the praise of the Lord, and may all flesh bless His holy name forever and ever.

146 PRAISE the Lord. Praise the Lord, O my soul. I will praise the Lord while I live. I will sing praises to my God while I exist. Do not put your trust in princes, in a son of man in whom there is no help. His breath will leave, he will return to his earth. On that day his thoughts will perish. Happy is he who has the God of Jacob as his helper, whose hope is in the Lord his God, Who makes heaven and earth, the sea, and all that is in them, Who keeps truth forever, Who executes judgment for the oppressed, Who gives bread to the hungry, the Lord sets the prisoners free. The Lord opens the eyes of the blind, the Lord raises up those who are bowed down, the Lord loves the righteous. The Lord preserves the strangers, He strengthens the fatherless and the widow, and He makes crooked the way of the wicked. The Lord will reign forever, your God, O Zion, to all generations. Praise the Lord.

147 PRAISE the Lord. Indeed, it is good to sing to our God. Indeed, it is pleasant. Praise is seemly. The Lord is the builder of Jerusalem. He gathers the outcasts of Israel. He heals the broken-hearted, and binds their wounds. He counts the number of the stars. He calls them all by names. Great is the Lord, and of great power. His understanding has no measure. The Lord lifts up the humble. He casts the wicked down to the ground. Sing to the Lord with thanksgiving, play the lyre to our God, Who covers heaven with clouds, Who prepares rain for the earth, Who makes

*30th DAY of the month

מְטָר הַמַּצְמִיחַ הָרִים חָצִיר׃ נוֹתֵן לִבְהֵמָה לַחְמָהּ לִבְנֵי עֹרֵב אֲשֶׁר יִקְרָאוּ׃
לֹא בִגְבוּרַת הַסּוּס יֶחְפָּץ לֹא־בְשׁוֹקֵי הָאִישׁ יִרְצֶה׃ רוֹצֶה יהוה אֶת־יְרֵאָיו
אֶת־הַמְיַחֲלִים לְחַסְדּוֹ׃ שַׁבְּחִי יְרוּשָׁלַםִ אֶת־יהוה הַלְלִי אֱלֹהַיִךְ צִיּוֹן׃
כִּי־חִזַּק בְּרִיחֵי שְׁעָרָיִךְ בֵּרַךְ בָּנַיִךְ בְּקִרְבֵּךְ׃ הַשָּׂם־גְּבוּלֵךְ שָׁלוֹם חֵלֶב חִטִּים
יַשְׂבִּיעֵךְ׃ הַשֹּׁלֵחַ אִמְרָתוֹ אָרֶץ עַד־מְהֵרָה יָרוּץ דְּבָרוֹ׃ הַנֹּתֵן שֶׁלֶג כַּצָּמֶר
כְּפוֹר כָּאֵפֶר יְפַזֵּר׃ מַשְׁלִיךְ קַרְחוֹ כְפִתִּים לִפְנֵי קָרָתוֹ מִי יַעֲמֹד׃ יִשְׁלַח
דְּבָרוֹ וְיַמְסֵם יַשֵּׁב רוּחוֹ יִזְּלוּ־מָיִם׃ מַגִּיד דְּבָרָו לְיַעֲקֹב חֻקָּיו וּמִשְׁפָּטָיו
לְיִשְׂרָאֵל׃ לֹא עָשָׂה כֵן ׀ לְכָל־גּוֹי וּמִשְׁפָּטִים בַּל־יְדָעוּם הַלְלוּיָהּ׃

קמח הַלְלוּיָהּ ׀ הַלְלוּ אֶת־יהוה מִן־הַשָּׁמַיִם הַלְלוּהוּ בַּמְּרוֹמִים׃ הַלְלוּהוּ כָל־
מַלְאָכָיו הַלְלוּהוּ כָּל־צְבָאָו׃ הַלְלוּהוּ שֶׁמֶשׁ וְיָרֵחַ הַלְלוּהוּ כָּל־כּוֹכְבֵי
אוֹר׃ הַלְלוּהוּ שְׁמֵי הַשָּׁמָיִם וְהַמַּיִם אֲשֶׁר ׀ מֵעַל הַשָּׁמָיִם׃ יְהַלְלוּ אֶת־שֵׁם
יהוה כִּי הוּא צִוָּה וְנִבְרָאוּ׃ וַיַּעֲמִידֵם לָעַד לְעוֹלָם חָק־נָתַן וְלֹא יַעֲבוֹר׃
הַלְלוּ אֶת־יהוה מִן־הָאָרֶץ תַּנִּינִים וְכָל־תְּהֹמוֹת׃ אֵשׁ וּבָרָד שֶׁלֶג וְקִיטוֹר
רוּחַ סְעָרָה עֹשָׂה דְבָרוֹ׃ הֶהָרִים וְכָל־גְּבָעוֹת עֵץ פְּרִי וְכָל־אֲרָזִים׃ הַחַיָּה
וְכָל־בְּהֵמָה רֶמֶשׂ וְצִפּוֹר כָּנָף׃ מַלְכֵי־אֶרֶץ וְכָל־לְאֻמִּים שָׂרִים וְכָל־שֹׁפְטֵי
אָרֶץ׃ בַּחוּרִים וְגַם־בְּתוּלוֹת זְקֵנִים עִם־נְעָרִים׃ יְהַלְלוּ ׀ אֶת־שֵׁם יהוה
כִּי־נִשְׂגָּב שְׁמוֹ לְבַדּוֹ הוֹדוֹ עַל־אֶרֶץ וְשָׁמָיִם׃ וַיָּרֶם קֶרֶן ׀ לְעַמּוֹ תְּהִלָּה
לְכָל־חֲסִידָיו לִבְנֵי יִשְׂרָאֵל עַם קְרֹבוֹ הַלְלוּיָהּ׃

קמט הַלְלוּיָהּ ׀ שִׁירוּ לַיהוה שִׁיר חָדָשׁ תְּהִלָּתוֹ בִּקְהַל חֲסִידִים׃ יִשְׂמַח יִשְׂרָאֵל
בְּעֹשָׂיו בְּנֵי־צִיּוֹן יָגִילוּ בְמַלְכָּם׃ יְהַלְלוּ שְׁמוֹ בְמָחוֹל בְּתֹף וְכִנּוֹר יְזַמְּרוּ־
לוֹ׃ כִּי־רוֹצֶה יהוה בְּעַמּוֹ יְפָאֵר עֲנָוִים בִּישׁוּעָה׃ יַעְלְזוּ חֲסִידִים בְּכָבוֹד
יְרַנְּנוּ עַל־מִשְׁכְּבוֹתָם׃ רוֹמְמוֹת אֵל בִּגְרוֹנָם וְחֶרֶב פִּיפִיּוֹת בְּיָדָם׃ לַעֲשׂוֹת
נְקָמָה בַּגּוֹיִם תּוֹכֵחוֹת בַּלְאֻמִּים׃ לֶאְסֹר מַלְכֵיהֶם בְּזִקִּים וְנִכְבְּדֵיהֶם
בְּכַבְלֵי בַרְזֶל׃ לַעֲשׂוֹת בָּהֶם ׀ מִשְׁפָּט כָּתוּב הָדָר הוּא לְכָל־חֲסִידָיו
הַלְלוּיָהּ׃

קנ הַלְלוּיָהּ ׀ הַלְלוּ־אֵל בְּקָדְשׁוֹ הַלְלוּהוּ בִּרְקִיעַ עֻזּוֹ׃ הַלְלוּהוּ בִגְבוּרֹתָיו
הַלְלוּהוּ כְּרֹב גֻּדְלוֹ׃ הַלְלוּהוּ בְּתֵקַע שׁוֹפָר הַלְלוּהוּ בְּנֵבֶל וְכִנּוֹר׃ הַלְלוּהוּ
בְּתֹף וּמָחוֹל הַלְלוּהוּ בְּמִנִּים וְעוּגָב׃ הַלְלוּהוּ בְצִלְצְלֵי־שָׁמַע הַלְלוּהוּ
בְּצִלְצְלֵי תְרוּעָה׃ כֹּל הַנְּשָׁמָה תְּהַלֵּל יָהּ הַלְלוּיָהּ׃

grass grow upon the mountains. He gives to the beast its food, to the ravens that cry. He does not desire the strength of the horse. He does not want the thighs of man. The Lord wants those who fear Him, those who hope for His loving-kindness. Praise the Lord, O Jerusalem. Extol your God, O Zion. For He has strengthened the bars of your gates, He has blessed your sons in your midst. He places peace in your border. He satisfies you with the finest of wheat. He sends His command to the earth. His word runs very swiftly. He gives snow like wool. He scatters frost like ashes. He casts His ice like crumbs. Who can stand before His cold? He sends His word and melts them. He makes His wind blow, and the waters flow. He proclaimed His words to Jacob, His statutes and judgments to Israel. He has not done so for any other nation, and as for judgments, they do not know them. Praise the Lord.

148 PRAISE the Lord. Praise the Lord from the heavens, praise Him in the heights.
Praise Him, all you His angels. Praise Him, all you His hosts. Praise Him, sun and
moon. Praise Him, all you stars of light. Praise Him, heavens of the heavens, and
the waters that are above the heavens. Let them praise the name of the Lord, that
He commanded and they were created. And He established them forever and ever.
He gave a command and it will not be annulled. Praise the Lord from the earth, O
sea creatures and all depths. Fire and hail, snow and vapors, stormy wind fulfilling
His word. The mountains and all hills, fruit trees and all cedars. Beasts and all cattle,
creeping things, and winged birds. Kings of the earth and all peoples, princes, and
all judges of the earth. Both young men and virgins, old men and boys. Let them
praise the name of the Lord, that His name alone is exalted. His glory is over the
earth and the heavens. And He has raised the horn of His people, praise for all His
pious ones, for the children of Israel, the people near to Him. Praise the Lord.

149 PRAISE the Lord. Sing to the Lord a new song, His praise in the congregation of
the pious. Let Israel rejoice in Him Who made him. Let the children of Zion be
joyful in their King. Let them praise His name in dance. Let them play to Him on
the timbrel and the lyre, That the Lord takes pleasure in His people, He honors
the oppressed with salvation. Let the pious be joyful in glory, let them sing upon
their beds. The praises of God are in their throat, and a two-edged sword in their
hand, to execute vengeance upon the nations, chastisements upon the peoples,
To bind their kings with chains, and their nobles with fetters of iron, to execute
upon them the written judgment. He is an honor to all His pious ones. Praise
the Lord.

150 PRAISE the Lord. Praise God for His sanctity, praise Him for His power in the
firmament. Praise Him for His mighty acts, praise Him in accordance with His
exceeding greatness. Praise Him with the sounding of the shofar, praise Him with
the harp and lyre. Praise Him with the timbrel and the dance, praise Him with flutes
and the pipe. Praise Him with sounding cymbals, praise Him with loud clashing
cymbals. Let everything that has breath praise the Lord. Praise the Lord.

תפילה אחר אמירת תהלים

After reciting תהלים *it is customary to say:*

מִי יִתֵּן מִצִּיּוֹן יְשׁוּעַת יִשְׂרָאֵל, בְּשׁוּב יהוה שְׁבוּת עַמּוֹ, יָגֵל יַעֲקֹב, יִשְׂמַח תהלים יד
יִשְׂרָאֵל: וּתְשׁוּעַת צַדִּיקִים מֵיהוה, מָעוּזָּם בְּעֵת צָרָה: וַיַּעְזְרֵם תהלים לז
יהוה וַיְפַלְּטֵם, יְפַלְּטֵם מֵרְשָׁעִים וְיוֹשִׁיעֵם, כִּי־חָסוּ בוֹ:

יְהִי רָצוֹן מִלְּפָנֶיךָ יהוה אֱלֹהֵינוּ וֵאלֹהֵי אֲבוֹתֵינוּ, בִּזְכוּת

After one of the five books of תהלים:

סֵפֶר רִאשׁוֹן / שֵׁנִי / שְׁלִישִׁי / רְבִיעִי / חֲמִישִׁי / שֶׁבַּתְּהִלִּים
שֶׁקָּרֵאנוּ לְפָנֶיךָ שֶׁהוּא כְּנֶגֶד סֵפֶר בְּרֵאשִׁית / שְׁמוֹת / וַיִּקְרָא /
בְּמִדְבַּר / דְּבָרִים / בִּזְכוּת מִזְמוֹרָיו וּבִזְכוּת פְּסוּקָיו וּבִזְכוּת
תֵּבוֹתָיו וּבִזְכוּת שְׁמוֹתֶיךָ הַקְּדוֹשִׁים וְהַטְּהוֹרִים הַיּוֹצְאִים מִמֶּנּוּ,

After less than an entire book:

מִזְמוֹרֵי תְּהִלִּים שֶׁקָּרֵאנוּ לְפָנֶיךָ, וּבִזְכוּת פְּסוּקֵיהֶם וּבִזְכוּת
תֵּבוֹתֵיהֶם וּבִזְכוּת שְׁמוֹתֶיךָ הַקְּדוֹשִׁים וְהַטְּהוֹרִים הַיּוֹצְאִים
מֵהֶם,

On weekdays add (on שבת *continue on the next page):*

שֶׁתְּכַפֵּר לָנוּ עַל כָּל חַטֹּאתֵינוּ, וְתִמְחַל לָנוּ עַל כָּל עֲוֹנוֹתֵינוּ, וְתִסְלַח לָנוּ
עַל כָּל פְּשָׁעֵינוּ, שֶׁחָטֶאנוּ וְשֶׁעָוִינוּ וְשֶׁפָּשַׁעְנוּ לְפָנֶיךָ, וְתַחֲזִירֵנוּ בִּתְשׁוּבָה
שְׁלֵמָה לְפָנֶיךָ, וְתַדְרִיכֵנוּ לַעֲבוֹדָתֶךָ, וְתִפְתַּח לִבֵּנוּ בְּתַלְמוּד תּוֹרָתֶךָ, וְתִשְׁלַח
רְפוּאָה שְׁלֵמָה לְחוֹלֵי עַמְּךָ (לְחוֹלֶה/לְחוֹלָה [פלוני/ת בֶּן/בַּת פלונית]), וְתִקְרָא
לִשְׁבוּיִם דְּרוֹר, וְלַאֲסוּרִים פְּקַח־קוֹחַ: וּלְכָל הוֹלְכֵי דְרָכִים וְעוֹבְרֵי יַמִּים ישעיה סא
וּנְהָרוֹת מֵעַמְּךָ יִשְׂרָאֵל תַּצִּילֵם מִכָּל צַעַר וָנֶזֶק, וְתַגִּיעֵם לִמְחוֹז חֶפְצָם
לְחַיִּים וּלְשָׁלוֹם. וְתִפְקֹד לְכָל חֲשׂוּכֵי בָנִים בְּזֶרַע שֶׁל קַיָּמָא לַעֲבוֹדָתֶךָ
וּלְיִרְאָתֶךָ, וְעֻבָּרוֹת שֶׁל עַמְּךָ בֵּית יִשְׂרָאֵל תַּצִּילֵן שֶׁלֹּא תַפֵּלְנָה וַלְדוֹתֵיהֶן,
וְהַיּוֹשְׁבוֹת עַל הַמַּשְׁבֵּר בְּרַחֲמֶיךָ הָרַבִּים תַּצִּילֵן מִכָּל רָע, וְאֶל הַמֵּינִיקוֹת
תַּשְׁפִּיעַ שֶׁלֹּא יֶחְסַר חָלָב מִדַּדֵּיהֶן. וְאַל יִמְשֹׁל אַסְכָּרָה וְשֵׁדִין וְכָל פְּגָעִים
וּמַרְעִין בִּישִׁין בְּכָל יַלְדֵי עַמְּךָ בֵּית יִשְׂרָאֵל, וּתְגַדְּלֵם לְתוֹרָתֶךָ לִלְמֹד תּוֹרָה
לִשְׁמָהּ, וְתַצִּילֵם מֵעַיִן הָרָע וּמִדֶּבֶר וּמִמַּגֵּפָה וּמִשָּׂטָן וּמִיֵּצֶר הָרָע. וּתְבַטֵּל
מֵעָלֵינוּ וּמִכָּל עַמְּךָ בֵּית יִשְׂרָאֵל בְּכָל מָקוֹם שֶׁהֵם כָּל גְּזֵרוֹת קָשׁוֹת וְרָעוֹת.

PRAYER AFTER RECITING TEHILLIM

After reciting the Psalms it is customary to say:

Ps. 14 מִי יִתֵּן O THAT THE SALVATION of Israel will come from Zion! When the Lord
Ps. 37 brings back the return of His people, Jacob will rejoice, Israel will be glad. But the salvation of the righteous is from the Lord. He is their refuge in time of trouble. And the Lord helps them and saves them. He saves them from the wicked and delivers them, for they take refuge in Him.

יְהִי רָצוֹן MAY IT BE Your will, Lord, our God and the God of our fathers, in the merit of the

After one of the five books of Tehillim:

First / Second / Third / Fourth / Fifth book of Psalms that we have said, which corresponds to the Book of Genesis / Exodus / Leviticus / Numbers / Deuteronomy. In the merit of its psalms, and in the merit of its verses and in the merit of its words, and in the merit of Your holy and pure Names that emerge from them,

After less than an entire book:

psalms that we have said, and in the merit of its verses and in the merit of its words, and in the merit of Your holy and pure Names that emerge from them,

On weekdays add (on Shabbat continue on the next page):

that You grant us atonement for all our transgressions, pardon all our iniquities, and forgive all our sins, which we have transgressed, committed, and sinned before You. Return us in complete and perfect repentance. Guide us in Your service and open our hearts to the study of Your Torah. Send a full recovery to those in your nation who are sick (and for the sick person, *name* son/daughter
Is. 61 of *mother's name*). Proclaim liberty for captives and freedom for prisoners. Save all those of Your nation, Israel, who are traveling on land and sea and river, from pain and injury, and bring them to their destination alive and well. Remember all those who are childless, and grant them healthy children to serve and fear You. Protect the pregnant women of Your nation, Israel, so that they do no miscarry; and in Your great compassion guard those giving birth from all evil. Let nursing mothers not lack for milk in their breasts. May diphtheria, all forms of evil spirits, and all afflictions and evil occurrences have no power over the children of Your people, the family of Israel. Raise them to Your Torah – to learn Torah for its own sake – and protect them from the evil eye, from infectious disease, from contagion, from Satan, and from the evil inclination. Nullify all harsh and evil decrees from us and from all of Your nation, the family

וְתַטֶּה לֵב הַמַּלְכוּת עָלֵינוּ לְטוֹבָה, וְתִגְזֹר עָלֵינוּ גְּזֵרוֹת טוֹבוֹת, וְתִשְׁלַח בְּרָכָה וְהַצְלָחָה בְּכָל מַעֲשֵׂה יָדֵינוּ. וְהָכֵן פַּרְנָסָתֵנוּ מִיָּדְךָ הָרְחָבָה וְהַמְּלֵאָה, וְלֹא יִצְטָרְכוּ עַמְּךָ יִשְׂרָאֵל זֶה לָזֶה וְלֹא לְעַם אַחֵר, וְתֵן לְכָל אִישׁ וָאִישׁ דֵּי פַרְנָסָתוֹ וּלְכָל גְּוִיָּה וּגְוִיָּה דֵּי מַחְסוֹרָהּ וּתְמַהֵר וְתָחִישׁ לְגָאֳלֵנוּ, וְתִבְנֶה בֵּית מִקְדָּשֵׁנוּ וְתִפְאַרְתֵּנוּ. (*If a מנין is present add:* וּבִזְכוּת שְׁלֹשׁ עֶשְׂרֵה מִדּוֹתֶיךָ

שמות לד שֶׁל רַחֲמִים הַכְּתוּבוֹת בְּתוֹרָתֶךָ, כְּמוֹ שֶׁנֶּאֱמַר: יהוה, יהוה, אֵל רַחוּם וְחַנּוּן, אֶרֶךְ אַפַּיִם וְרַב־חֶסֶד וֶאֱמֶת: נֹצֵר חֶסֶד לָאֲלָפִים, נֹשֵׂא עָוֹן וָפֶשַׁע

תהלים עט וְחַטָּאָה, וְנַקֵּה: שֶׁאֵינָן חוֹזְרוֹת רֵיקָם מִלְּפָנֶיךָ). עָזְרֵנוּ אֱלֹהֵי יִשְׁעֵנוּ עַל־

תהלים עט דְּבַר כְּבוֹד־שְׁמֶךָ, וְהַצִּילֵנוּ וְכַפֵּר עַל־חַטֹּאתֵינוּ לְמַעַן שְׁמֶךָ: בָּרוּךְ יהוה לְעוֹלָם אָמֵן וְאָמֵן:

On שבת add:

שֶׁתְּהֵא נֶחְשֶׁבֶת לָנוּ אֲמִירַת מִזְמוֹרֵי תְהִלִּים אֵלּוּ כְּאִלּוּ אֲמָרָם דָּוִד מֶלֶךְ יִשְׂרָאֵל בְּעַצְמוֹ, זְכוּתוֹ יָגֵן עָלֵינוּ, וְיַעֲמָד לָנוּ לְחַבֵּר אֵשֶׁת נְעוּרִים עִם דּוֹדָהּ, בְּאַהֲבָה וְאַחֲוָה וְרֵעוּת, וּמִשָּׁם יִמָּשֵׁךְ לָנוּ שֶׁפַע לְנֶפֶשׁ רוּחַ וּנְשָׁמָה. וּכְשֵׁם שֶׁאֲנַחְנוּ אוֹמְרִים שִׁירִים בָּעוֹלָם הַזֶּה, כָּךְ נִזְכֶּה לוֹמַר לְפָנֶיךָ יהוה אֱלֹהֵינוּ וֵאלֹהֵי אֲבוֹתֵינוּ, שִׁיר וּשְׁבָחָה לָעוֹלָם הַבָּא. וְעַל יְדֵי אֲמִירַת תְּהִלִּים תִּתְעוֹרֵר חֲבַצֶּלֶת הַשָּׁרוֹן לָשִׁיר בְּקוֹל נָעִים

ישעיה לה גִּילַת וְרַנֵּן, כְּבוֹד הַלְּבָנוֹן נִתַּן־לָהּ הוֹד וְהָדָר בְּבֵית אֱלֹהֵינוּ, בִּמְהֵרָה בְיָמֵינוּ, אָמֵן סֶלָה.

תפילה בעד החולה

After reciting psalms for those who are sick (appropriate psalms for this purpose are listed on page 1190), the following prayers are recited.

שמות לד [**יהוה** יהוה, אֵל רַחוּם וְחַנּוּן, אֶרֶךְ אַפַּיִם וְרַב־חֶסֶד וֶאֱמֶת: נֹצֵר חֶסֶד

דברי הימים א׳ כט לָאֲלָפִים, נֹשֵׂא עָוֹן וָפֶשַׁע וְחַטָּאָה, וְנַקֵּה:] לְךָ יהוה הַגְּדֻלָּה וְהַגְּבוּרָה וְהַתִּפְאֶרֶת וְהַנֵּצַח וְהַהוֹד, כִּי־כֹל בַּשָּׁמַיִם וּבָאָרֶץ, לְךָ יהוה הַמַּמְלָכָה וְהַמִּתְנַשֵּׂא לְכֹל לְרֹאשׁ: וְאַתָּה בְּיָדְךָ נֶפֶשׁ כָּל חָי וְרוּחַ כָּל בְּשַׂר אִישׁ, וּבְיָדְךָ כֹּחַ וּגְבוּרָה לְגַדֵּל וּלְחַזֵּק וּלְרַפְּאוֹת אֱנוֹשׁ עַד דַּכָּא עַד דִּכְדּוּכָהּ שֶׁל נֶפֶשׁ, וְלֹא יִפָּלֵא מִמְּךָ כָּל דָּבָר, וּבְיָדְךָ נֶפֶשׁ כָּל

of Israel, wherever they are. Give the rulers a benevolent heart toward us, so that they decree favorable laws upon us. Grant blessing and success upon all our handiwork. Prepare our livelihood from Your open and generous hand, and may Your people, Israel, not be forced to rely on one another, nor on any other nation. Give every person an ample livelihood, and grant everyone whatever he lacks. Hurry, speedily, to redeem us and build our splendid Temple. (*If a minyan is present add:* In the merit of the Thirteen Attributes of Mercy recorded in Your
Ex. 34 Torah, as it says: The Lord, the Lord, compassionate and gracious God, slow
to anger and great in mercy and truth, keeping loving-kindness for thousands,
forgiving iniquity, transgression, and sin, and offering absolution – which do
Ps. 79 not return unanswered from before You). Help us, God of our salvation, for
the sake of Your name's glory. Save us and atone for our transgressions for the
Ps. 79 sake of Your name. Blessed is the Lord forever, Amen and Amen.

On Shabbat add:

that our recitation of these psalms be considered as if they had been said by King David himself, may he rest in peace, and may his merit protect us. May it stand in our favor to unite the Bride of Youth with her beloved, in love, brotherhood and companionship. And from that unification may we draw abundance to our spirit, breath, and soul. And just as we sing before You in this world, let us merit, Lord, our God and the God of our fathers, to sing and to praise You in the World to Come. Through the recitation of psalms arouse
Is. 35 the Rose of Sharon to sing with a pleasant voice, with joy and ecstasy. May the
glory of Lebanon be given to her, splendor and majesty in the House of our God, speedily and in our days – Amen, Selah.

PRAYER FOR THE SICK

After reciting psalms for those who are sick (appropriate psalms for this purpose are listed on page 1190), the following prayers are recited.

Ex. 34 [יהוה THE LORD, the Lord, compassionate and gracious God, slow to
anger and great in mercy and truth, keeping loving-kindness for thousands,
I Chr. 29 forgiving iniquity, transgression, and sin, and offering absolution]. Yours,
Lord, are greatness, power, glory, victory, and majesty. Indeed, everything that is in the heavens and on earth. Yours, Lord, is the dominion, and You are supreme over all. The soul of every living thing is in Your hands, and the spirit of all mankind. Your hand holds the strength and the power to make great, to strengthen, and to cure every man, even he who is crushed, crushed to the very depths of his soul. Nothing is unknown to You, and the soul of every living thing is in Your hand. Therefore may it be Your will, trustworthy

חַי. לָכֵן יְהִי רָצוֹן מִלְּפָנֶיךָ, הָאֵל הַנֶּאֱמָן אַב הָרַחֲמִים, הָרוֹפֵא לְכָל
תַּחֲלוּאֵי עַמּוֹ יִשְׂרָאֵל הַקְּרוֹבִים עַד שַׁעֲרֵי מָוֶת, וְהַמְחַבֵּשׁ מָזוֹר
וּתְעָלָה לִידִידָיו, וְהַגּוֹאֵל מִשַּׁחַת חֲסִידָיו, וְהַמַּצִּיל מִמָּוֶת נֶפֶשׁ מְרוּדָיו,
אַתָּה רוֹפֵא נֶאֱמָן תִּשְׁלַח מַרְפֵּא וַאֲרוּכָה וּתְעָלָה בְּרֹב חֶסֶד וַחֲנִינָה
וְחֶמְלָה

For a male:

לְנֶפֶשׁ (פלוני בֶּן פלונית) לְרוּחוֹ וְנַפְשׁוֹ הָאֻמְלָלָה וְלֹא תֵרֵד נַפְשׁוֹ
שְׁאוֹלָה, וְהִמָּלֵא רַחֲמִים עָלָיו לְהַחֲלִים וּלְרַפְּאוֹת וּלְהַחֲזִיק
וּלְהַחֲלִיף וּלְהַחֲיוֹת אוֹתוֹ כִּרְצוֹן כָּל קְרוֹבָיו וְאֹהֲבָיו, וְיֵרָאוּ לְפָנֶיךָ
זְכֻיּוֹתָיו וְצִדְקוֹתָיו, וְתַשְׁלִיךְ בִּמְצֻלוֹת יָם כָּל־חַטֹּאתָיו, וְיִכְבְּשׁוּ מיכה ז
רַחֲמֶיךָ אֶת כַּעַסְךָ מֵעָלָיו, וְתִשְׁלַח לוֹ רְפוּאָה שְׁלֵמָה, רְפוּאַת
הַנֶּפֶשׁ וּרְפוּאַת הַגּוּף, וּתְחַדֵּשׁ כַּנֶּשֶׁר נְעוּרָיו וְתִשְׁלַח לוֹ

For a female:

לְנֶפֶשׁ (פלונית בַּת פלונית) לְרוּחָהּ וְנַפְשָׁהּ הָאֻמְלָלָה וְלֹא תֵרֵד נַפְשָׁהּ
שְׁאוֹלָה, וְהִמָּלֵא רַחֲמִים עָלֶיהָ לְהַחֲלִים וּלְרַפְּאוֹת וּלְהַחֲזִיק
וּלְהַחֲלִיף וּלְהַחֲיוֹת אוֹתָהּ כִּרְצוֹן כָּל קְרוֹבֶיהָ וְאֹהֲבֶיהָ וְיֵרָאוּ
לְפָנֶיךָ זְכֻיּוֹתֶיהָ וְצִדְקוֹתֶיהָ וְתַשְׁלִיךְ בִּמְצֻלוֹת יָם כָּל חַטֹּאתֶיהָ: מיכה ז
וְיִכְבְּשׁוּ רַחֲמֶיךָ אֶת כַּעַסְךָ מֵעָלֶיהָ וְתִשְׁלַח לָהּ רְפוּאָה שְׁלֵמָה,
רְפוּאַת הַנֶּפֶשׁ וּרְפוּאַת הַגּוּף, וּתְחַדֵּשׁ כַּנֶּשֶׁר נְעוּרֶיהָ וְתִשְׁלַח
לָהּ

וּלְכָל חוֹלֵי יִשְׂרָאֵל מַרְפֵּא אֲרוּכָה, מַרְפֵּא בְּרָכָה, מַרְפֵּא תְּרוּפָה
וּתְעָלָה, מַרְפֵּא חֲנִינָה וְחֶמְלָה, מַרְפֵּא יְדוּעִים וּגְלוּיִים, מַרְפֵּא רַחֲמִים
וְשָׁלוֹם וְחַיִּים, מַרְפֵּא אֹרֶךְ יָמִים וְשָׁנִים טוֹבוֹת, וִיקֻיַּם בּוֹ/בָּהּ וּבְכָל
חוֹלֵי יִשְׂרָאֵל מִקְרָא שֶׁכָּתוּב עַל יְדֵי מֹשֶׁה עַבְדְּךָ נֶאֱמַן בֵּיתֶךָ: וַיֹּאמֶר, שמות טו
אִם־שָׁמוֹעַ תִּשְׁמַע לְקוֹל יהוה אֱלֹהֶיךָ, וְהַיָּשָׁר בְּעֵינָיו תַּעֲשֶׂה וְהַאֲזַנְתָּ
לְמִצְוֹתָיו וְשָׁמַרְתָּ כָּל־חֻקָּיו, כָּל־הַמַּחֲלָה אֲשֶׁר־שַׂמְתִּי בְמִצְרַיִם,
לֹא־אָשִׂים עָלֶיךָ, כִּי אֲנִי יהוה רֹפְאֶךָ: וַעֲבַדְתֶּם אֵת יהוה אֱלֹהֵיכֶם, שמות כג

God, merciful Father, Healer of all illnesses of Your people, Israel, even those near the very gates of death; the One Who anoints His beloved ones with healing preparations, and Who redeems His devout ones from the pit of destruction, and Who delivers the souls of His servants from death – You, trustworthy Healer – please send healing, cure and remedy, with abundant kindness, graciousness, and compassion

For a male:

to (*name*) son of (*mother's name*). Restore his unfortunate spirit and soul, so that he should not descend to the grave. May You be filled with compassion upon him to restore him to health, to cure, strengthen and invigorate him as all of his relatives and friends wish. May all his
Mic. 7 merits and charitable deeds appear before You and may You cast into the depths of the sea all of his sins. May Your mercy overcome Your anger against him, and may You send him a complete recovery. Renew his youth like the eagle's; send him and all sick people a lasting cure, a gracious and compassionate cure, a merciful cure, with peace and life and lengthy days and years. May there be fulfilled for him

For a female:

to (*name*) daughter of (*mother's name*). Restore her unfortunate spirit and soul, so that she should not descend to the grave. May You be filled with compassion upon her to restore her to health, to cure, strengthen and invigorate her as all of her relatives and friends wish.
Mic. 7 May all her merits and charitable deeds appear before You and may You cast into the depths of the sea all of her sins. May Your mercy overcome Your anger against her, and may You send her a complete recovery. Renew her youth like the eagle's; send her and all sick people a lasting cure, a gracious and compassionate cure, a merciful cure, with peace and life and lengthy days and years. May there be fulfilled for her

and for all the sick people of Israel the verse written by Your servant Moses,
Ex. 15 the most trustworthy of Your House: And he [Moses] said: If you diligently listen to the voice of the Lord, your God, and you do what is fair in His eyes, and you give ear to His commandments and you observe all His statutes – any sickness that I have brought upon Egypt I will not bring upon you, for I am the
Ex. 23 Lord, your healer. And you shall serve the Lord, your God, and He shall bless your food and your water, and I shall remove sickness from among you. None shall miscarry nor be barren in your land; I will fill out the number of your
Deut. 7 days. And the Lord will remove from you all sickness, and He will not place

וּבֵרַךְ אֶת־לַחְמְךָ וְאֶת־מֵימֶיךָ, וַהֲסִרֹתִי מַחֲלָה מִקִּרְבֶּךָ: לֹא תִהְיֶה
מְשַׁכֵּלָה וַעֲקָרָה בְּאַרְצֶךָ, אֶת־מִסְפַּר יָמֶיךָ אֲמַלֵּא: וְהֵסִיר יהוה מִמְּךָ דברים ז
כָּל־חֹלִי, וְכָל־מַדְוֵי מִצְרַיִם הָרָעִים אֲשֶׁר יָדַעְתָּ, לֹא יְשִׂימָם בָּךְ, וּנְתָנָם
בְּכָל־שֹׂנְאֶיךָ: וְעַל יְדֵי עֲבָדֶיךָ הַנְּבִיאִים כָּתוּב לֵאמֹר: וַאֲכַלְתֶּם אָכוֹל יואל ב
וְשָׂבוֹעַ, וְהִלַּלְתֶּם אֶת־שֵׁם יהוה אֱלֹהֵיכֶם אֲשֶׁר־עָשָׂה עִמָּכֶם לְהַפְלִיא,
וְלֹא־יֵבֹשׁוּ עַמִּי לְעוֹלָם: דְּרָכָיו רָאִיתִי, וְאֶרְפָּאֵהוּ וְאַנְחֵהוּ וַאֲשַׁלֵּם ישעיה נז
נִחֻמִים לוֹ וְלַאֲבֵלָיו: בּוֹרֵא נִיב שְׂפָתָיִם, שָׁלוֹם שָׁלוֹם לָרָחוֹק וְלַקָּרוֹב,
אָמַר יהוה, וּרְפָאתִיו: וְזָרְחָה לָכֶם יִרְאֵי שְׁמִי שֶׁמֶשׁ צְדָקָה וּמַרְפֵּא מלאכי ג
בִּכְנָפֶיהָ: אָז יִבָּקַע כַּשַּׁחַר אוֹרֶךָ, וַאֲרֻכָתְךָ מְהֵרָה תִצְמָח: רְפָאֵנוּ יהוה ישעיה נח
וְנֵרָפֵא, הוֹשִׁיעֵנוּ וְנִוָּשֵׁעָה, כִּי תְהִלָּתֵנוּ אָתָּה. וְהַעֲלֵה רְפוּאָה שְׁלֵמָה
לְכָל מַכּוֹת עַמְּךָ יִשְׂרָאֵל,

For a male:

וּבִפְרָט (פלוני בֶּן פלונית) רְפוּאָה שְׁלֵמָה לרמ"ח אֵבָרָיו וּשְׁסָ"ה גִּידָיו
לְרַפְּאוֹת אוֹתוֹ כְּחִזְקִיָּהוּ מֶלֶךְ יְהוּדָה מֵחָלְיוֹ וּכְמִרְיָם הַנְּבִיאָה
מִצָּרַעְתָּהּ. בְּשֵׁם הַשֵּׁמוֹת הַקְּדוֹשִׁים שֶׁל שְׁלֹשׁ עֶשְׂרֵה מִדּוֹתֶיךָ,
אֵל נָא רְפָא נָא (פלוני בֶּן פלונית) לְהָקִים אוֹתוֹ מֵחָלְיוֹ זֶה וּלְהַאֲרִיךְ
עוֹד יְמֵי חַיָּיו, חַיִּים שֶׁל רַחֲמִים, חַיִּים שֶׁל בְּרִיאוּת, חַיִּים שֶׁל
שָׁלוֹם, חַיִּים שֶׁל בְּרָכָה, כְּדִכְתִיב: כִּי אֹרֶךְ יָמִים וּשְׁנוֹת חַיִּים משלי ג
וְשָׁלוֹם יוֹסִיפוּ לָךְ: אָמֵן סֶלָה.

For a female:

וּבִפְרָט (פלונית בַּת פלונית) רְפוּאָה שְׁלֵמָה לְאֵבָרֶיהָ וְגִידֶיהָ לְרַפְּאוֹת
אוֹתָהּ כְּחִזְקִיָּהוּ מֶלֶךְ יְהוּדָה מֵחָלְיוֹ וּכְמִרְיָם הַנְּבִיאָה
מִצָּרַעְתָּהּ. בְּשֵׁם הַשֵּׁמוֹת הַקְּדוֹשִׁים שֶׁל שְׁלֹשׁ עֶשְׂרֵה מִדּוֹתֶיךָ,
אֵל נָא רְפָא נָא (פלונית בַּת פלונית) לְהָקִים אוֹתָהּ מֵחָלְיָהּ זֶה
וּלְהַאֲרִיךְ עוֹד יְמֵי חַיֶּיהָ חַיִּים שֶׁל רַחֲמִים, חַיִּים שֶׁל בְּרִיאוּת,
חַיִּים שֶׁל שָׁלוֹם, חַיִּים שֶׁל בְּרָכָה, כְּדִכְתִיב: כִּי אֹרֶךְ יָמִים משלי ג
וּשְׁנוֹת חַיִּים וְשָׁלוֹם יוֹסִיפוּ לָךְ: אָמֵן סֶלָה.

upon you any of the evil diseases of Egypt, of which you know, but He will
bring them upon all your enemies. And through Your servants, the prophets,
Joel 2 the following is written: And you shall eat in plenty and be satisfied and you
will praise the name of the Lord your God Who treated you wondrously, and
Is. 57 My people shall never be ashamed. I have seen his ways and I will heal him; I
will guide him and bestow consolations upon him and upon his mourners. I
will create a new expression of the lips: "Peace, peace, to thousands, who are
Mal. 3 far and near," says the Lord. "And I will heal him." For you who fear My name,
Is. 58 there will shine a sun of righteousness, with healing in its wings. Then your
light shall burst out like the dawn and your health shall sprout speedily. Heal
us, Lord – then we will be healed; save us – then we will be saved, for You are
our praise. Bring complete recovery for all the ailments of Your people, the
family of Israel,

For a male:

and particularly to (*name*) son of (*mother's name*), a complete recovery to his two hundred and forty-eight organs and his three hundred and sixty-five sinews. Cure him like Hezekiah, King of Judah, from his sickness, and like Miriam the prophetess from her leprosy. Employ the sacred names that emanate from the verses containing Your Thirteen Attributes of Divine Mercy. Please, God heal (*name*) son of (*mother's name*) and raise him from his sickbed. Grant lengthy days and years to him, so that he may serve You with love and fear. And grant him a life of mercy, a life of health, a life of peace, a life of blessing, as it is
Prov. 3 written: For length of days and years of life and peace, shall they add to you. Amen, Selah.

For a female:

and particularly to (*name*) daughter of (*mother's name*), a complete recovery to all her organs and sinews. Cure her like Hezekiah, King of Judah, from her sickness, and like Miriam the prophetess from her leprosy. Employ the sacred names that emanate from the verses containing Your Thirteen Attributes of Divine Mercy. Please, God heal (*name*) daughter of (*mother's name*) and raise her from her sickbed. Grant lengthy days and years to her, so that she may serve You with love and fear. And grant her a life of mercy, a life of health, a life of peace, a
Prov. 3 life of blessing, as it is written: For length of days and years of life and peace, shall they add to you. Amen, Selah.

תפילות נוספות

Regarding these preparatory and supplementary prayers, see commentary on page 765.

עטיפת טלית

Some add this prayer when putting on the טלית:

לְשֵׁם יִחוּד קֻדְשָׁא בְּרִיךְ הוּא וּשְׁכִינְתֵּהּ, בִּדְחִילוּ וּרְחִימוּ לְיַחֵד שֵׁם י״ה בו״ה בְּיִחוּדָא שְׁלִים בְּשֵׁם כָּל יִשְׂרָאֵל.

הֲרֵינִי מִתְעַטֵּף גּוּפִי בְּצִיצִת, כֵּן תִּתְעַטֵּף נִשְׁמָתִי וּרְמַ״ח אֵבָרַי וּשְׁסָ״ה גִידַי בְּאוֹר הַצִּיצִת הָעוֹלֶה תַרְיַ״ג. וּכְשֵׁם שֶׁאֲנִי מִתְכַּסֶּה בְּטַלִּית בָּעוֹלָם הַזֶּה, כָּךְ אֶזְכֶּה לַחֲלוּקָא דְרַבָּנָן וּלְטַלִּית נָאָה לָעוֹלָם הַבָּא בְּגַן עֵדֶן. וְעַל יְדֵי מִצְוַת צִיצִת תִּנָּצֵל נַפְשִׁי וְרוּחִי וְנִשְׁמָתִי וּתְפִלָּתִי מִן הַחִיצוֹנִים. וְהַטַּלִּית יִפְרֹשׂ כְּנָפָיו עֲלֵיהֶם וְיַצִּילֵם כְּנֶשֶׁר יָעִיר קִנּוֹ, עַל גּוֹזָלָיו יְרַחֵף. וּתְהֵא חֲשׁוּבָה מִצְוַת צִיצִת לִפְנֵי הַקָּדוֹשׁ בָּרוּךְ הוּא כְּאִלּוּ קִיַּמְתִּיהָ בְּכָל פְּרָטֶיהָ וְדִקְדּוּקֶיהָ וְכַוָּנוֹתֶיהָ וְתַרְיַ״ג מִצְוֹת הַתְּלוּיִם בָּהּ. אָמֵן סֶלָה.

הנחת תפילין

Some say the following meditation before putting on the תפילין*.*

לְשֵׁם יִחוּד קֻדְשָׁא בְּרִיךְ הוּא וּשְׁכִינְתֵּהּ בִּדְחִילוּ וּרְחִימוּ, לְיַחֵד שֵׁם י״ה בו״ה בְּיִחוּדָא שְׁלִים בְּשֵׁם כָּל יִשְׂרָאֵל.

הִנְנִי מְכַוֵּן בְּהַנָּחַת תְּפִלִּין לְקַיֵּם מִצְוַת בּוֹרְאִי, שֶׁצִּוָּנוּ לְהָנִיחַ תְּפִלִּין,
כַּכָּתוּב בְּתוֹרָתוֹ: וּקְשַׁרְתָּם לְאוֹת עַל־יָדֶךָ, וְהָיוּ לְטֹטָפֹת בֵּין עֵינֶיךָ: וְהֵן אַרְבַּע דברים ו
פָּרָשִׁיּוֹת אֵלּוּ, שְׁמַע, וְהָיָה אִם שָׁמֹעַ, קַדֶּשׁ לִי, וְהָיָה כִּי יְבִאֲךָ, שֶׁיֵּשׁ בָּהֶם יִחוּדוֹ וְאַחְדוּתוֹ יִתְבָּרַךְ שְׁמוֹ בָּעוֹלָם, וְשֶׁנִּזְכֹּר נִסִּים וְנִפְלָאוֹת שֶׁעָשָׂה עִמָּנוּ בְּהוֹצִיאוֹ אוֹתָנוּ מִמִּצְרַיִם, וַאֲשֶׁר לוֹ הַכֹּחַ וְהַמֶּמְשָׁלָה בָּעֶלְיוֹנִים וּבַתַּחְתּוֹנִים לַעֲשׂוֹת בָּהֶם כִּרְצוֹנוֹ. וְצִוָּנוּ לְהָנִיחַ עַל הַיָּד לְזִכְרוֹן זְרוֹעַ הַנְּטוּיָה, וְשֶׁהִיא נֶגֶד הַלֵּב, לְשַׁעְבֵּד בָּזֶה תַּאֲוֹת וּמַחְשְׁבוֹת לִבֵּנוּ לַעֲבוֹדָתוֹ יִתְבָּרַךְ שְׁמוֹ. וְעַל הָרֹאשׁ נֶגֶד הַמֹּחַ, שֶׁהַנְּשָׁמָה שֶׁבְּמֹחִי עִם שְׁאָר חוּשַׁי וְכֹחוֹתַי כֻּלָּם יִהְיוּ מְשֻׁעְבָּדִים לַעֲבוֹדָתוֹ, יִתְבָּרַךְ שְׁמוֹ. וּמִשֶּׁפַע מִצְוַת תְּפִלִּין יִתְמַשֵּׁךְ עָלַי לִהְיוֹת לִי חַיִּים אֲרוּכִים וְשֶׁפַע קֹדֶשׁ וּמַחֲשָׁבוֹת קְדוֹשׁוֹת בְּלִי הִרְהוּר חֵטְא וְעָוֹן כְּלָל, וְשֶׁלֹּא יְפַתֵּנוּ וְלֹא יִתְגָּרֶה בָּנוּ יֵצֶר הָרָע, וְיַנִּיחֵנוּ לַעֲבֹד אֶת יהוה כַּאֲשֶׁר עִם לְבָבֵנוּ.

ADDITIONAL PRAYERS

Regarding these preparatory and supplementary prayers, see commentary on page 765.

TALLIT

Some add this prayer when putting on the Tallit:

לְשֵׁם FOR THE SAKE of the unification of the Holy One, blessed is He, and His Divine Presence, in reverence and love, to unify the name *Yod-Heh* with *Vav-Heh* in perfect unity in the name of all Israel.

I AM READY to wrap my body in *tzitzit*. So, too, may my soul, my two hundred and forty-eight organs and my three hundred and sixty-five sinews be wrapped in the light of the *tzitzit*, the numerical value of which is six hundred and thirteen. And just as I cover myself with a tallit in this world, so may I merit the rabbinical garb and a beautiful tallit in the World to Come, in the Garden of Eden. Through the commandment of *tzitzit* may my life force, spirit, soul, and prayer be rescued from the external forces. May the tallit spread its wings over them and rescue them like an eagle awaking its nest, fluttering over its young. May the commandment of *tzitzit* be worthy before the Holy One, blessed is He, as if I Had fulfilled it in all its details, implications, and intentions, as well as the 613 commandments that are dependent upon it. Amen, Selah.

PUTTING ON TEFILLIN

Some say the following meditation before putting on the Tefillin.

לְשֵׁם FOR THE SAKE of the unification of the Holy One, blessed is He, and His Divine Presence, in reverence and love, to unify the name *Yod-Heh* with *Vav-Heh* in perfect unity in the name of all Israel.

BY PUTTING on *tefillin* I intend to fulfill the commandment of my Creator, Who has
Deut. 6 commanded us to put on *tefillin*, as is written in His Torah: "Bind them as a sign upon your arm and let them be *tefillin* between your eyes." These four passages [contained in the *tefillin*] – [1] "*Shema*" (Deuteronomy 6:4–9); [2] "And it will come to pass, if you will listen (Deuteronomy 11:13–21); [3] "Sanctify" (Exodus 13:1-10); and [4] "And it will come to pass when He shall bring you" (Exodus 13:11–16) – contain His Oneness and Unity, may His Name be blessed, in the universe; so that we will recall the miracles and wonders that He did for us when He removed us from Egypt; and that He has the strength and dominion over those above and those below to do with them as He wishes. He has commanded us to put [*tefillin*] upon the arm to recall the "outstretched arm" [of the Exodus], and that it be opposite the heart to subjugate the desires and thoughts of our heart to His service, may His Name be blessed; and [to put *tefillin*] upon the head opposite the brain, so that the soul that is in my brain, together with my other senses and potentials, will all be subjugated to His service, may His name be blessed. May some of the spiritual influence of the commandment of *tefillin* be extended upon me so that I have a long life, a flow of holiness, and holy thoughts, without even an inkling of sin or iniquity; and that the Evil Inclination will not seduce us nor incite against us, and that it permit us to serve the Lord as is our hearts' desire.

וִיהִי רָצוֹן מִלְּפָנֶיךָ, יהוה אֱלֹהֵינוּ וֵאלֹהֵי אֲבוֹתֵינוּ, שֶׁתְּהֵא חֲשׁוּבָה מִצְוַת הֲנָחַת תְּפִלִּין לִפְנֵי הַקָּדוֹשׁ בָּרוּךְ הוּא, כְּאִלּוּ קִיַּמְתִּיהָ בְּכָל פְּרָטֶיהָ וְדִקְדּוּקֶיהָ וְכַוָּנוֹתֶיהָ וְתַרְיַ״ג מִצְוֹת הַתְּלוּיוֹת בָּהּ, אָמֵן סֶלָה.

פסוקי דזמרה

Some say the following meditation before פסוקי דזמרה:

הֲרֵינִי מְזַמֵּן אֶת פִּי לְהוֹדוֹת וּלְהַלֵּל וּלְשַׁבֵּחַ אֶת בּוֹרְאִי, לְשֵׁם יִחוּד קֻדְשָׁא בְּרִיךְ הוּא וּשְׁכִינְתֵּהּ עַל יְדֵי הַהוּא טָמִיר וְנֶעְלָם בְּשֵׁם כָּל יִשְׂרָאֵל.

ספירת העומר

Some say the following meditation before ספירת העומר:

לְשֵׁם יִחוּד קֻדְשָׁא בְּרִיךְ הוּא וּשְׁכִינְתֵּהּ בִּדְחִילוּ וּרְחִימוּ, לְיַחֵד שֵׁם י״ה בו״ה בְּיִחוּדָא שְׁלִים בְּשֵׁם כָּל יִשְׂרָאֵל.

הִנְנִי מוּכָן וּמְזֻמָּן לְקַיֵּם מִצְוַת עֲשֵׂה שֶׁל סְפִירַת הָעֹמֶר. כְּמוֹ שֶׁכָּתוּב
ויקרא כג בַּתּוֹרָה, וּסְפַרְתֶּם לָכֶם מִמָּחֳרַת הַשַּׁבָּת, מִיּוֹם הֲבִיאֲכֶם אֶת־עֹמֶר
הַתְּנוּפָה, שֶׁבַע שַׁבָּתוֹת תְּמִימֹת תִּהְיֶינָה: עַד מִמָּחֳרַת הַשַּׁבָּת הַשְּׁבִיעִת
תהלים צ תִּסְפְּרוּ חֲמִשִּׁים יוֹם, וְהִקְרַבְתֶּם מִנְחָה חֲדָשָׁה לַיהוה: וִיהִי נֹעַם אֲדֹנָי
אֱלֹהֵינוּ עָלֵינוּ, וּמַעֲשֵׂה יָדֵינוּ כּוֹנְנָה עָלֵינוּ, וּמַעֲשֵׂה יָדֵינוּ כּוֹנְנֵהוּ:

נטילת לולב

Some say the following before reciting the blessing over the לולב:

יְהִי רָצוֹן מִלְּפָנֶיךָ יהוה אֱלֹהַי וֵאלֹהֵי אֲבוֹתַי, בִּפְרִי עֵץ הָדָר וְכַפֹּת תְּמָרִים וַעֲנַף עֵץ עָבוֹת וְעַרְבֵי נַחַל, אוֹתִיּוֹת שִׁמְךָ הַמְיֻחָד תְּקָרֵב אֶחָד אֶל אֶחָד וְהָיוּ לַאֲחָדִים בְּיָדִי, וְלֵידַע אֵיךְ שִׁמְךָ נִקְרָא עָלַי וְיִירְאוּ מִגֶּשֶׁת אֵלָי. וּבְנַעֲנוּעִי אוֹתָם תַּשְׁפִּיעַ שֶׁפַע בְּרָכוֹת מִדַּעַת עֶלְיוֹן לִנְוֵה אַפִּרְיוֹן לִמְכוֹן בֵּית אֱלֹהֵינוּ, וּתְהֵא חֲשׁוּבָה לְפָנֶיךָ מִצְוַת אַרְבָּעָה מִינִים אֵלּוּ כְּאִלּוּ קִיַּמְתִּיהָ בְּכָל פְּרָטוֹתֶיהָ וְשָׁרָשֶׁיהָ וְתַרְיַ״ג מִצְוֹת הַתְּלוּיוֹת בָּהּ, כִּי כַוָּנָתִי לְיַחֲדָא שְׁמָא דְקֻדְשָׁא בְּרִיךְ הוּא וּשְׁכִינְתֵּהּ בִּדְחִילוּ וּרְחִימוּ, לְיַחֵד
תהלים פט שֵׁם י״ה בו״ה בְּיִחוּדָא שְׁלִים בְּשֵׁם כָּל יִשְׂרָאֵל, אָמֵן. בָּרוּךְ יהוה לְעוֹלָם,
אָמֵן וְאָמֵן:

MAY IT BE Your will, Lord, our God and the God of our fathers, that the commandment of putting on *tefillin* be considered as worthy before the Holy One, blessed is He, as if I had fulfilled it in all its details, implications, and intentions, as well as the six hundred and thirteen commandments that are dependent upon it. Amen, Selah.

PESUKEI DEZIMRA

Some say the following meditation before Pesukei DeZimra:

הֲרֵינִי I HEREBY prepare my lips to thank, glorify, and praise my Creator, for the sake of the unification of the Holy One, blessed is He, and His Divine Presence, through He Who is hidden and inscrutable, in the name of all Israel.

COUNTING OF THE OMER

Some say the following meditation before the Counting of the Omer:

לְשֵׁם FOR THE SAKE of the unification of the Holy One, blessed is He, and His Divine Presence, in reverence and love, to unify the name *Yod-Heh* with Vav-Heh in perfect unity, in the name of all Israel.

הִנְנִי I AM NOW READY and prepared to fulfill the commandment of counting the
Lev. 23 Omer, as prescribed in the Torah: "And you shall count, from the morrow after the
day of rest, starting on the day that you bring the sheaf (omer) of the wave-offering,
seven complete weeks. Until the morrow of the seventh week you shall have counted
Ps. 90 fifty days. And then you shall offer a new meal-offering to the Lord." And let the
pleasantness of my Master our God be upon us, and establish the work of our hands
upon us, and establish it, the work of our hands.

BLESSINGS OVER THE LULAV

Some say the following before reciting the blessing over the lulav:

יְהִי רָצוֹן MAY IT BE Your will, Lord, my God, God of my fathers, that as I think of the very letters of Your unifying name I may bring together the fourfold fruit of the goodly citron tree, palm branch, thick leaved myrtle boughs and willows of the brook, so that they shall be as one in my hand. May I feel that Your name protects me and no evil shall come close to me. As I wave these before You, may the fullness of Your blessing be poured out from on high on the abode of the Tabernacle, on the site of the Temple. May my fulfillment of Your command of taking the fourfold citron, palm branch, myrtle, and willow, be considered by You as if I had fulfilled this command in all its details and roots, and all the 613 commandments dependent on it. For my spiritual intent in taking them is together with all Israel to proclaim with awe and love the all-embracing unity of the sacred name of You, the Holy One,
Ps. 89 blessed is He, and His Divine Presence among us. Amen. Blessed is the Lord forever.
Amen and Amen.

אושפיזין

On entering the סוכה:

הֲרֵינִי מוּכָן וּמְזֻמָּן לְקַיֵּם מִצְוַת סֻכָּה, כַּאֲשֶׁר צִוַּנִי הַבּוֹרֵא יִתְבָּרַךְ שְׁמוֹ:
בַּסֻּכֹּת תֵּשְׁבוּ שִׁבְעַת יָמִים, כָּל־הָאֶזְרָח בְּיִשְׂרָאֵל יֵשְׁבוּ בַּסֻּכֹּת: ויקרא כג
לְמַעַן יֵדְעוּ דֹרֹתֵיכֶם, כִּי בַסֻּכּוֹת הוֹשַׁבְתִּי אֶת־בְּנֵי יִשְׂרָאֵל, בְּהוֹצִיאִי אוֹתָם מֵאֶרֶץ מִצְרָיִם:

תֵּיבוּ תֵּיבוּ אֻשְׁפִּיזִין עִלָּאִין, תֵּיבוּ תֵּיבוּ אֻשְׁפִּיזִין קַדִּישִׁין, תֵּיבוּ תֵּיבוּ
אֻשְׁפִּיזִין דִּמְהֵימְנוּתָא. זַכָּאָה חֻלְקְהוֹן דְּיִשְׂרָאֵל, דִּכְתִיב: כִּי חֵלֶק יהוה דברים לב
עַמּוֹ, יַעֲקֹב חֶבֶל נַחֲלָתוֹ:

יְהִי רָצוֹן מִלְּפָנֶיךָ יהוה אֱלֹהַי וֵאלֹהֵי אֲבוֹתַי, שֶׁתַּשְׁרֶה שְׁכִינָתְךָ בֵּינֵינוּ, וְתִפְרֹשׂ עָלֵינוּ סֻכַּת שְׁלוֹמֶךָ, בִּזְכוּת מִצְוַת סֻכָּה שֶׁאֲנַחְנוּ מְקַיְּמִין לְיַחֲדָא שְׁמָא דְקֻדְשָׁא בְּרִיךְ הוּא וּשְׁכִינְתֵּהּ בִּדְחִילוּ וּרְחִימוּ, לְיַחֲדָא שֵׁם י״ה בו״ה בְּיִחוּדָא שְׁלִים בְּשֵׁם כָּל יִשְׂרָאֵל, וּלְהַקִּיף אוֹתָהּ מִזִּיו כְּבוֹדְךָ הַקָּדוֹשׁ וְהַטָּהוֹר, נָטוּי עַל רָאשֵׁיהֶם מִלְמַעְלָה כְּנֶשֶׁר יָעִיר קִנּוֹ, וּמִשָּׁם יַשְׁפִּיעַ שֶׁפַע הַחַיִּים לְעַבְדְּךָ (פלוני בֶּן פלונית אֲמָתֶךָ). וּבִזְכוּת צֵאתִי מִבֵּיתִי הַחוּצָה וְדֶרֶךְ מִצְוֹתֶיךָ אָרוּצָה, יֵחָשֵׁב לִי זֹאת כְּאִלּוּ הִרְחַקְתִּי נְדוֹד, וְהֶרֶב כַּבְּסֵנִי מֵעֲוֹנִי וּמֵחַטָּאתִי טַהֲרֵנִי, וּמֵאֻשְׁפִּיזִין עִלָּאִין אֻשְׁפִּיזִין דִּמְהֵימְנוּתָא תִּהְיֶינָה אָזְנֶיךָ קַשֻּׁבוֹת רַב בְּרָכוֹת (וְלָרְעֵבִים גַּם צְמֵאִים תֶּן לַחְמָם וּמֵימָם הַנֶּאֱמָנִים), וְתִתֶּן לִי זְכוּת לָשֶׁבֶת וְלַחֲסוֹת בְּסֵתֶר צֵל כְּנָפֶיךָ בְּעֵת פְּטִירָתִי מִן הָעוֹלָם, וְלַחֲסוֹת מִזֶּרֶם וּמִמָּטָר, כִּי תַמְטִיר עַל רְשָׁעִים פַּחִים. וּתְהֵא חֲשׁוּבָה מִצְוַת סֻכָּה זוֹ שֶׁאֲנִי מְקַיֵּם, כְּאִלּוּ קִיַּמְתִּיהָ בְּכָל פְּרָטֶיהָ וְדִקְדּוּקֶיהָ וּתְנָאֶיהָ וְכָל מִצְוֹת הַתְּלוּיוֹת בָּהּ. וְתֵיטִיב לָנוּ הַחֲתִימָה, וּתְזַכֵּנוּ לֵישֵׁב יָמִים
רַבִּים עַל הָאֲדָמָה אַדְמַת קֹדֶשׁ, בַּעֲבוֹדָתְךָ וּבְיִרְאָתֶךָ. בָּרוּךְ יהוה לְעוֹלָם תהלים פט
אָמֵן וְאָמֵן:

רִבּוֹן כָּל הָעוֹלָמִים יְהִי רָצוֹן מִלְּפָנֶיךָ, שֶׁתְּהֵא חֲשׁוּבָה לְפָנֶיךָ מִצְוַת יְשִׁיבַת סֻכָּה זוֹ, כְּאִלּוּ קִיַּמְתִּיהָ בְּכָל פְּרָטֶיהָ וְדִקְדּוּקֶיהָ, וְתרי״ג מִצְוֹת הַתְּלוּיוֹת בָּהּ, וּכְאִלּוּ כִּוַּנְתִּי בְּכָל הַכַּוָּנוֹת שֶׁכִּוְּנוּ אַנְשֵׁי כְנֶסֶת הַגְּדוֹלָה.

USHPIZIN

On entering the sukka:

הֲרֵינִי I AM NOW spiritually ready and prepared to fulfill the command of dwelling in a
Lev. 23 sukka as the Creator, blessed be His name, commanded me to do in the words, "You shall dwell in booths seven days, all that are Israelite born shall dwell in the booths, in order that your generations may know that I made the children of Israel dwell in booths when I brought them out from the land of Egypt."

TAKE YOUR PLACE, take your place, exalted guests. Take your place, take your place, hallowed guests. Take your place, take your place, faithful guests; take your place under the protection of the Holy One, blessed is He. A holy privilege is this our lot
Deut. 32 and the lot of Israel, for it is written that "the portion of the Lord is His people, Jacob the lot of His inheritance."

יְהִי רָצוֹן IT IS our precious privilege in carrying out this command to glorify the sacred name of Your hallowed unity and Your indwelling presence among us and among all Israel. And let the pleasantness of the Lord our God be upon us, and establish the work of our hands upon us, and establish it, the work of our hands. May it be Your will, Lord my God and God of my fathers, that You set Your Divine Presence among us and spread over us Your tabernacle of peace – in the merit of this commandment of dwelling in the sukka that we are fulfilling – to unify the name of the Holy One, blessed is He, and His Divine Presence, in fear and love, to unify the name *Yod-Heh* with *Vav-Heh* in perfect unity in the name of all Israel, and surrounding us with the radiance of Your glory, holy and pure, spread above our heads from above like an eagle stirring up its nest. And from there may You pour an abundance of life upon Your servant (*name*) son of (*mother's name*) Your maidservant. In the merit of leaving my house to go outside, running in the way of Your commandments, may I be considered as if I had wandered far. Cleanse me thoroughly from my iniquity and purify me from my sin. From the exalted guests, the guests in faith, may Your ears attend to much blessing. (To the hungry and thirsty grant unfailing food and drink.) Grant me the privilege of sitting and taking refuge under the shadow of Your wings when I take leave of this world, taking refuge from stream and rain when You rain fiery coals on the wicked. May this commandment of sukka that I am fulfilling be considered by You as if I had fulfilled it in all its specifics, details and conditions, as well as all the commandments dependent on it. May the sealing of our fate be for good, and grant us the merit of living for many years on the soil of the Holy Land, serving You and
Ps. 89 revering You. Blessed is the Lord forever, Amen and Amen.

RULER OF ALL WORLDS, may it be Your will that this commandment of dwelling in the sukka be considered before You as if I had fulfilled it in all its specifics and details as well as all the commandments dependent on it, and as though I intended all those intentions which the Men of the Great Assembly intended upon it.

יהי רצון לברכה השלישית של הכהנים

יְהִי רָצוֹן מִלְּפָנֶיךָ, יהוה אֱלֹהַי וֵאלֹהֵי אֲבוֹתַי, שֶׁתַּעֲשֶׂה לְמַעַן קְדֻשַּׁת חֲסָדֶיךָ וְגֹדֶל רַחֲמֶיךָ הַפְּשׁוּטִים, וּלְמַעַן טָהֳרַת שִׁמְךָ הַגָּדוֹל הַגִּבּוֹר וְהַנּוֹרָא, בֶּן עֶשְׂרִים וּשְׁתַּיִם אוֹתִיּוֹת הַיּוֹצֵא מִפְּסוּקִים שֶׁל בִּרְכַּת כֹּהֲנִים הָאֲמוּרָה מִפִּי אַהֲרֹן וּבָנָיו עַם קְדוֹשֶׁךָ, שֶׁתִּהְיֶה קָרוֹב לִי בְּקָרְאִי לָךְ, וְתִשְׁמַע תְּפִלָּתִי נַאֲקָתִי וְאֶנְקָתִי תָּמִיד, כְּשֵׁם שֶׁשָּׁמַעְתָּ אֶנְקַת יַעֲקֹב תְּמִימֶךָ הַנִּקְרָא אִישׁ תָּם. וְתִתֶּן לִי וּלְכָל נַפְשׁוֹת בֵּיתִי מְזוֹנוֹתֵינוּ וּפַרְנָסָתֵנוּ בְּרֶוַח וְלֹא בְצִמְצוּם, בְּהֶתֵּר וְלֹא בְאִסּוּר, בְּנַחַת וְלֹא בְצַעַר, מִתַּחַת יָדְךָ הָרְחָבָה, כְּשֵׁם שֶׁנָּתַתָּ פִּסַּת לֶחֶם לֶאֱכֹל וּבֶגֶד לִלְבֹּשׁ לְיַעֲקֹב אָבִינוּ הַנִּקְרָא אִישׁ תָּם. וְתִתְּנֵנוּ לְאַהֲבָה, לְחֵן וּלְחֶסֶד וּלְרַחֲמִים בְּעֵינֶיךָ וּבְעֵינֵי כָל רוֹאֵינוּ, וְיִהְיוּ דְבָרַי נִשְׁמָעִים לַעֲבוֹדָתֶךָ, כְּשֵׁם שֶׁנָּתַתָּ אֶת יוֹסֵף צַדִּיקֶךָ בְּשָׁעָה שֶׁהִלְבִּישׁוֹ אָבִיו כְּתֹנֶת פַּסִּים לְחֵן וּלְחֶסֶד וּלְרַחֲמִים בְּעֵינֶיךָ וּבְעֵינֵי כָל רוֹאָיו. וְתַעֲשֶׂה עִמִּי נִפְלָאוֹת וְנִסִּים, וּלְטוֹבָה אוֹת, וְתַצְלִיחֵנִי בִּדְרָכַי, וְתֵן בְּלִבִּי בִּינָה לְהָבִין וּלְהַשְׂכִּיל וּלְקַיֵּם אֶת כָּל דִּבְרֵי תַלְמוּד תּוֹרָתֶךָ וְסוֹדוֹתֶיהָ, וְתַצִּילֵנִי מִשְּׁגִיאוֹת, וּתְטַהֵר רַעְיוֹנַי וְלִבִּי לַעֲבוֹדָתֶךָ, וְתַאֲרִיךְ יָמַי (וִימֵי אָבִי וְאִמִּי / וְאִשְׁתִּי / וּבַעְלִי / וּבָנַי וּבְנוֹתַי) בְּטוֹב וּבִנְעִימוּת, בְּרֹב עֹז וְשָׁלוֹם, אָמֵן סֶלָה.

ידיד נפש

יְדִיד נֶפֶשׁ, אָב הָרַחֲמָן, מְשֹׁךְ עַבְדְּךָ אֶל רְצוֹנֶךָ,
יָרוּץ עַבְדְּךָ כְּמוֹ אַיָּל, יִשְׁתַּחֲוֶה מוּל הֲדָרֶךָ,
כִּי יֶעֱרַב לוֹ יְדִידוּתָךְ, מִנֹּפֶת צוּף וְכָל טָעַם.

הָדוּר, נָאֶה, זִיו הָעוֹלָם, נַפְשִׁי חוֹלַת אַהֲבָתָךְ, אָנָּא,
אֵל נָא, רְפָא נָא לָהּ, בְּהַרְאוֹת לָהּ נֹעַם זִיוָךְ,
אָז תִּתְחַזֵּק וְתִתְרַפֵּא, וְהָיְתָה לָךְ שִׁפְחַת עוֹלָם.

וָתִיק, יֶהֱמוּ רַחֲמֶיךָ, וְחוּס נָא עַל בֵּן אוֹהֲבָךְ,
כִּי זֶה כַּמָּה נִכְסֹף נִכְסַף לִרְאוֹת בְּתִפְאֶרֶת עֻזָּךְ,
אָנָּא, אֵלִי, מַחְמַד לִבִּי, חוּשָׁה נָּא, וְאַל תִּתְעַלָּם.

הִגָּלֵה נָא וּפְרֹשׂ, חָבִיב, עָלַי אֶת סֻכַּת שְׁלוֹמָךְ,
תָּאִיר אֶרֶץ מִכְּבוֹדָךְ, נָגִילָה וְנִשְׂמְחָה בָּךְ.
מַהֵר, אָהוּב, כִּי בָא מוֹעֵד, וְחָנֵּנִי כִּימֵי עוֹלָם.

YEHI RATZON FOR THE THIRD BLESSING OF THE KOHANIM

יְהִי MAY IT BE Your will, Lord my God and God of my fathers, that You act for the sake of the simple holiness of Your loving-kindness and the greatness of Your compassion, and for the purity of Your great, mighty and awesome name of twenty-two letters derived from the verses of the priestly blessing spoken by Aaron and his sons, Your holy people. May You be close to me when I call to You. May You always hear my prayer, plea and cry as You did the cry of Jacob Your perfect one who was called "a plain man." May You grant me and all the members of my household our food and sustenance, generously not meagerly, honestly not otherwise, with satisfaction not pain, from Your generous hand, just as You gave a portion of bread to eat and clothes to wear to Jacob our father who was called "a plain man." May we find love, grace, kindness and compassion in Your sight and in the eyes of all who see us. May my words in service to You be heard, as You granted Joseph Your righteous one, at the time when his father dressed him in a cloak of fine wool, that he find grace, kindness and compassion in Your sight and in the eyes of all who saw him. May You do wonders and miracles with me, and a sign for good. Grant me success in my ways, and set in my heart comprehension that I may understand, discern and fulfill all the words of Your Torah's teachings and mysteries. Save me from errors and purify my thoughts and my heart to serve You and be in awe of You. Prolong my days (*add, as applicable:* and those of my father, mother, wife, husband, son/s, and daughter/s) in goodness and pleasantness, with much strength and peace. Amen, Selah.

YEDID NEFESH

יְדִיד נֶפֶשׁ BELOVED of the soul, Father of compassion, draw Your servant close to Your will.
Like a deer will Your servant run and fall prostrate before Your beauty.
To him Your love is sweeter than honey from the comb, than any taste.

GLORIOUS, beautiful, radiance of the world, my soul is sick with love for You.
Please, God, heal her now by showing her Your tender radiance.
Then she will recover her strength and be healed, Be Your servant for eternity.

ANCIENT of Days, let Your mercy be aroused; please have pity on Your beloved child.
How long have I yearned to see the glory of Your strength.
Please, my God, my heart's desire – hasten; do not hide Yourself.

REVEAL Yourself, beloved, and spread over me the tabernacle of Your peace.
Let the earth shine with Your glory, let us be overjoyed and rejoice in You.
Hurry, beloved, for the appointed time has come, and be gracious to me as in the times of old.

RABBIS' KADDISH

Mourner: YITGADAL VE-YITKADASH shemeh raba, be-alema di vera khir'uteh. Ve-yamlikh malkhuteh, be-ḥayyeikhon, uv-yomeikhon, uv-ḥayyei de-khol beit Yisrael, ba-agala uvi-zman kariv, ve-imru Amen. (*Cong:* Amen)

All: Yeheh shemeh raba mevarakh le'alam ul-alemei alemaya.

Mourner: Yitbarakh ve-yishtabaḥ ve-yitpa'ar ve-yitromam ve-yitnaseh ve-yit-hadar ve-yit'aleh ve-yit-hallal shemeh dekudsha, berikh hu, le-ela min kol birkhata / *Between Rosh HaShana & Yom Kippur:* Le-ela (u)le-ela mi-kol birkhata/ve-shirata, tushbeḥata ve-neḥemata, da-amiran be-alema, ve-imru, Amen. (*Cong:* Amen)

Al Yisrael, ve-al rabanan, ve-al talmideihon, ve-al kol talmidei talmideihon, ve-al kol man de-asekin be-oraita di be-atra ha-dein ve-di be-khol atar va-atar, yeheh lehon ul-khon shelama raba, ḥina ve-ḥisda, ve-raḥamei, ve-ḥayyei arikhei, um-zonei re-viḥei, u-furkana min kodam avuhon di vish-maya, ve-imru Amen. (*Cong:* Amen)

Yeheh shelama raba min shemaya ve-ḥayyim, aleinu ve-al kol Yisrael, ve-imru Amen. (*Cong:* Amen)

Bow, take three steps back, as if taking leave of the Divine Presence, then bow, first left, then right, then center, while saying:

Oseh shalom/*Between Rosh HaShana & Yom Kippur:* ha-shalom/ bim-romav, hu ya'aseh shalom aleinu, ve-al kol Yisrael, ve-imru Amen. (*Cong:* Amen)

MOURNER'S KADDISH

Mourner: YITGADAL VE-YITKADASH shemeh raba, be-alema di vera khir'uteh. Ve-yamlikh malkhuteh, be-ḥayyeikhon, uv-yomeikhon, uv-ḥayyei de-khol beit Yisrael, ba-agala uvi-zman kariv, ve-imru Amen. (*Cong:* Amen)

All: Yeheh shemeh raba mevarakh le'alam ul-alemei alemaya.

Mourner: Yitbarakh ve-yishtabaḥ ve-yitpa'ar ve-yitromam ve-yitnaseh ve-yit-hadar ve-yit'aleh ve-yit-hallal shemeh dekudsha, berikh hu, le-ela min kol birkhata / *Between Rosh HaShana & Yom Kippur:* Le-ela (u)le-ela mi-kol birkhata/ve-shirata, tushbeḥata ve-neḥemata, da-amiran be-alema, ve-imru, Amen. (*Cong:* Amen)

Yeheh shelama raba min shemaya ve-ḥayyim, aleinu ve-al kol Yisrael, ve-imru Amen. (*Cong:* Amen)

Bow, take three steps back, as if taking leave of the Divine Presence, then bow, first left, then right, then center, while saying:

Oseh shalom/*Between Rosh HaShana & Yom Kippur:* ha-shalom/ bim-romav, hu ya'aseh shalom aleinu, ve-al kol Yisrael, ve-imru Amen. (*Cong:* Amen)

PAGINATION TABLE

	PRAYER	RCA ARTSCROLL SIDDUR	THIS SIDDUR
Weekday Mornings	Birkhot HaShaḥar	18	20
	Principles of R. Yishmael	48	48
	Mizmor Shir Ḥanukkat HaBayit	54	54
	Daily Taḥanun (Monday & Thursday)	124	144
	Daily Taḥanun (not Monday & Thursday)	132	152
	Removing Torah from the Ark	138	158
	Second Ashrei	150	172
Weekday Minḥa/Ma'ariv	Minḥa	232	256
	Ma'ariv	256	290
Shabbat/Yom Tov Evening	Yedid Nefesh	590	358
	Kabbalat Shabbat	308	360
	Barekhu	330	384
	Vayekhulu	346	404
	Kiddush	348	426
	Adon Olam/Yigdal	12	414
Shabbat/Yom Tov Morning	Mizmor Shir Ḥanukkat HaBayit	368	444
	Shokhen Ad	404	484
	Shema	414	498
	Shaḥarit Amida	420	506
	Removing Torah from the Ark	432	524
	Misheberakh LeḤolim	442	534
	Birkat HaGomel	444	542
	Prayers for Tzahal/Armed Forces	444	540
	Yekum Purkan	448	550
	Prayers for USA/ Israel	450	554
	Birkat HaḤodesh	452	558
	Av HaRaḥamim	454	560
	Ashrei	456	562
	Musaf Amida	462	568
	Ein Kelokeinu	476	586
	Aleinu	480	594
	Anim Zemirot	484	598
	Adon Olam / Yigdal	12	414
Shabbat/Yom Tov Minḥa/Ma'ariv	Ashrei	502	626
	Amida	514	640
	Tzidkatekha	524	652
	Aleinu	526	654
	Pirkei Avot	544	674
	Ma'ariv	266	730
	Vihi No'am	594	732
	Kiddush Levana	612	750
	Havdala	618	756
Rosh Ḥodesh/ Yom Tov	Hallel	632	766
	Amida for Rosh Ḥodesh Musaf	644	780
	Kiddush for Yom Tov	656	794
	Amida for Yom Tov	660	810
	Musaf for Yom Tov	674	828
	Birkat Kohanim	692	852
	Tefillat Tal	702	862
	Tefillat Geshem	704	866

סידור עבודת הלב

איזו היא
עבודה
שבלב
הוי אומר
זו תפלה

THE RABBINICAL COUNCIL OF AMERICA

ESSAY SECTION

RABBI BASIL HERRING
Editor-in-Chief

Essays On Prayer:
Selected Aspects of its History, Halakha, and Kavana

EDITOR'S INTRODUCTION

Throughout this Siddur one can find rabbinic, halakhic, historical, philosophical, and ethical perspectives on the texts and services that constitute our prayers. Yet, there are aspects of prayer that demand a more detailed and expansive analysis and understanding than is possible in a brief paragraph or two of instruction or commentary.

For this reason, the following essay section features in-depth presentations and analyses of various prayer-related topics, some of which are specifically related to one or another of the prayers or texts in the Siddur. The goal, as throughout the Siddur, is to facilitate an ever more knowledgable, inspired, and satisfying prayer experience, that also adheres faithfully to the traditional texts, practices, laws, and customs that constitute Jewish prayer.

The essays are divided into three groups:

- Historical analyses and background to several services found in the *Sha'ar Yisrael* section of the Siddur that commemorate the Holocaust and celebrate events relating to the State of Israel.
- In-depth halakhic presentations of the laws of proper *Nusaḥ* and *Nigunim*; of *Keriat HaTorah*; and of interpersonal behavior in public prayer – all of which are essential aspects of correct public prayer.
- Multiple inspirational and educational essays on the subject of *Kavana* (prayer with proper intent and concentration). These essays include discussions of the centrality of *Kavana*, what to focus on when reciting core prayers and blessings, how to beneficially approach and prepare for meaningful prayer experiences, and what are effective practices and thought-modalities for both men and women to transform simple words and mechanical actions into truly special spiritual experiences.

Careful readers will note that some of the essays found here that have appeared in earlier publications do not always conform to the stylistic practices found elsewhere in the Siddur. In those instances we have chosen for various reasons to retain the author's original language and stylistic preferences.

In presenting these essays it is our hope that readers will be inspired to find an ever-deeper and more meaningful connection to the multifaceted jewel that is the Siddur and its texts, connecting us as they do to our inner selves, to each other, and ultimately to the *Ribono shel Olam*, the Master of the Universe.

Finally, and in this very context of connecting with God by means of our prayers, I would point out that the cover of the Siddur appropriately illustrates the same idea: that is, the elongated *lamed* that reaches from the word *she'ba'lev* (that is in the heart) at the bottom, ascending through the sphere to penetrate the higher realm of heaven, succinctly reflects the power of our prayers, when suffused with *kavana*, to connect us with our Father in heaven. ◆

ESSAYS ON PRAYER

SELECTED ASPECTS OF ITS HISTORY, HALAKHA, AND KAVANA

SHA'AR YISRAEL

HISTORICAL AND HALAKHIC BACKGROUND

Commemorating the Holocaust:
A Historical and Halakhic Review
R. JACOB J. SCHACTER
E7

Prayer on Israel's Days of Remembrance and Celebration
PROF. DAVID BERGER
E12

SHA'AR HAHALAKHA

Nusaḥ and *Nigunim* in *Tefilla*
R. GEDALIA DOV SCHWARTZ
E15

Lesser-Known Laws of Torah Reading
R. HERSHEL SCHACHTER
E17

Prayer and Interpersonal Halakha
R. DANIEL FELDMAN
E33

SHA'AR HAKAVANA

ON THE NATURE AND IMPORTANCE OF *KAVANA* IN PRAYER

Why Prayer Requires a Fixed Place and Fixed Texts
R. YECHIEL YAAKOV WEINBERG
E48

The Efficacy of Prayer
R. AHARON LICHTENSTEIN
E49

Fundamentals of Prayer
R. YEHUDAH AMITAL
E53

The Ultimate Goal of Our Prayers
R. CHAIM YAAKOV GOLDVICHT
E64

Praying with *Kavana*: Ḥasidic Perspectives
R. NORMAN LAMM
E66

Berakhot – The Gateway to Prayer
R. PINCHAS PELI
E70

Understanding the Term *Tefilla*
R. HESHIE BILLET
E77

THE KAVANA OF SPECIFIC PRAYERS

The Correct *Kavana* When Reciting the *Shema* and Its Blessings According to R. Joseph B. Soloveitchik
R. BASIL HERRING
E80

The Shabbat Prayers as Explained by R. Joseph B. Soloveitchik
R. ATON HOLZER
E88

Introduction to *Yigdal* and the *Ani Ma'amin* Principles
PROF. DAVID SHATZ
E93

Sacrifices and Prayer: Past, Present, and Future
R. SHALOM CARMY
E95

Achieving *Kavana*: Praying from the Heart
RABBANIT ROOKIE BILLET
E97

A More Meaningful Prayer Experience
R. DAVID MESCHELOFF
E105

Commemorating the Holocaust: A Historical and Halakhic Review

R. Jacob J. Schacter

Toward the end of November, 1942, word reached the *Yishuv* in Israel for the first time about the full magnitude of the destruction of European Jewry that was, by then, well under way. In response to this terrible news, R. Yitzḥak Isaac HaLevi Herzog, Ashkenazi Chief Rabbi of Israel since 1937, announced that December 2, 1942/23 Kislev 5703 would be a day of fasting and prayer (*"yom tzom gadol ve'evel kaved kelali"*). Indeed, on that day, a massive crowd of thousands, including several hundred rabbis led by the revered Rebbe of Gur, gathered first in the Ḥurva Synagogue in Jerusalem's Old City and then at the Kotel. They heard sounds of the shofar and recited prayers including verses from the book of Lamentations and selections from the *kinot* (elegies) recited on the Fast of the Ninth of Av.

It was around this time that R. Herzog paid a visit to R. Yitzhak Ze'ev HaLevi Soloveitchik (known also as "Reb Velvel," "the Griz," and "the Brisker Rav"), son of the legendary R. Hayyim Soloveitchik of Brisk and formidable Torah scholar in his own right, who had recently escaped from Europe and settled in Jerusalem. R. Herzog inquired whether R. Soloveitchik would support the establishment of such a "day of mourning (*yom evel*)" for the tragedy and destruction that was underway in Europe. R. Soloveitchik opposed R. Herzog's initiative, basing his objection on a passage in one of the *kinot* recited on Tisha B'Av dealing with the destruction wrought by Crusades at the end of the eleventh century. The author of this *kina*, entitled "*Mi yiten roshi mayim,*" describes the devastation of the German communities of Speyer, Worms and Mainz and, although explicitly noting that they were destroyed during the months of Iyar and Sivan, goes on to state that the appropriate time to commemorate these tragic events is on Tisha B'Av. "Since one may not add a time [to commemorate] destruction and conflagration... therefore today [i.e., Tisha B'Av] I will raise my cries of woe (*Ve-khi ein lehosif mo'ed shever vetavera… taḥat ken hayom livyati a'orara*)." One cannot institute new days of commemoration for tragedies that followed the destruction of the Temples. There is one day in the Jewish calendar designated to commemorate Jewish tragedy and that day is Tisha B'Av. Mourning for – and commemoration of – all subsequent Jewish tragedies are to take place on that date and on that date alone, wrote the author of this *kina*. Some

eight hundred and fifty years later, R. Soloveitchik applied the principle delineated here in the context of the Crusades to the situation he was facing in 1942. On the basis of this statement he concluded that establishing a special – even temporary – day of mourning for the growing number of Jews being exterminated in Europe would be inappropriate and contrary to Jewish tradition.

Indeed, this principle expressed – and, to the best of my knowledge, first formulated – by the Brisker Rav proved to be a very influential one in later generations, particularly in the context of Holocaust commemoration. After the war, the question moved from establishing a one-time *ad hoc* fast day for the destruction of European Jewry to establishing a ritually mandated fast day – and even just a day of commemoration which would lack any mandated normative ritual behavior – as a way of permanently remembering the unprecedented tragedy that had taken place. In opposing this practice, R. Joseph B. Soloveitchik, R. Moses Feinstein, R. Menaḥem M. Kasher and others cited and applied this *kina* already written in the twelfth century: "We do not add times (of mourning) for destruction and conflagration."

But there is an alternative model, one widely accepted in modern times, that also brings us back to the twelfth century. In the early spring of 1171, a Jew by the name of Isaac the son of Elazar was watering his horse along the banks of the Loire River as it was coursing through the town of Blois in north-central France. It was dusk and the edge of an animal skin that he was carrying slipped out and was visible under his cloak. At the same time, a Christian servant also came to the river to water his horse, but when that horse saw the whiteness of the protruding hide in the hazy darkness, it became frightened. The Christian immediately went to his master and reported that at the bank of the Loire River he had just seen a Jew disposing of the corpse of a Christian child. This charge was taken seriously and, less than three months later, on the twentieth of the month of Sivan 1171, some thirty-one or thirty-three Jews (the sources have conflicting numbers) were burned in Blois as a punishment for this allegedly grievous act.

In the aftermath of the catastrophe, R. Ephraim of Bonn noted in his *Sefer Zekhira* that a fast on that day was mandated by none other than the great twelfth-century Tosafist and communal leader, Rabbeinu Tam, and that it was actually accepted as such by all the Jewish communities in France, England and the Rhineland. It has been argued, and mostly accepted, by scholars that R. Ephraim of Bonn was mistaken; that, in fact, Rabbeinu Tam never did

establish a new fast day on this date. But, regardless, R. Ephraim of Bonn, and later generations who took him at his word, assumed that he did. Nowhere is there evident any impulse to subsume commemoration of the Blois episode under that of the Temple's destruction; nowhere is there any assumption that "we do not add times (of mourning) for destruction and conflagration." A new catastrophe occurs and a new fast day is established, separate from and irrelevant to the Fast of the Ninth of Av.

Almost five hundred years later, from the second half of 1648 through 1649, Bogdan Chmielnicki and his followers attacked dozens of Jewish communities in Eastern Europe and killed thousands of Jews. In 1650 there was a respite, and the super-communal organization in charge of governing the Jewish community, the *Va'ad Arba Arazot*, wanted to commemorate the catastrophe. R. Nathan Nata Hannover wrote in his *Yeven Mezula*, the best-known work describing the massacres, that the decision was made to choose as a fast day the date on which they began, which, as he had already informed his readers, was in the city of Niemirów on the twentieth of Sivan.

Once again, a fast day on the twentieth of Sivan. This time there is no doubt that an entirely new day of fasting was established. Absent now for sure is any interest in subsuming the commemoration of this catastrophe under the commemoration of the destruction of the Temple; absent now for sure is the self-evident assumption of "we do not add times (of mourning) for destruction and conflagration." A new calamity occurs and a new fast day is established, separate from and irrelevant to the Fast of the Ninth of Av.

This Fast of the Twentieth of Sivan played a central role in support of the arguments made by those in favor of the establishment of a special date for commemoration of the Holocaust. In a responsum written a few months before the end of the war, R. Herzog cited the existence of this fast as a precedent in support of establishing even a separate fast day to commemorate the Holocaust, and it was also cited as the only historical precedent for the establishment of a national Yom HaShoah commemoration in Israel in the first speech delivered on this topic from the podium of the Knesset in 1951. In both cases, the Fast of the Twentieth of Sivan was adduced as a precedent for the establishment of a day of commemoration for the Holocaust separate from the Ninth of Av, although it was not suggested that the commemoration take place necessarily on that date. And, indeed, different dates were suggested

for this purpose. The Chief Rabbinate of Israel designated the fast day of Asara beTevet as *Yom haKaddish haKelali*, the day to be set aside annually for the recital of *Kaddish* by all those who did not know the date of the murder of their loved ones, and the Knesset designated the twenty-seventh of Nisan as Yom HaShoah vehaGevura.

The debate as to whether or not Holocaust commemoration should be subsumed under Tisha B'Av or should merit its own independent day continues into the twenty-first century, and there are strong feelings on either side of this issue. Many rationales were – and continue to be – offered by segments of the traditional community in opposition to the establishment of Yom HaShoah as a separate day of commemoration for the Holocaust. Among the most significant of them are the following:

1. Like the Crusades discussed in the *kina* entitled, "*Mi yiten roshi mayim*" cited above, the Holocaust is not a unique event requiring its own separate day of commemoration. It is, rather, to be seen as one more horrible tragedy to be plotted along the continuum of other tragedies that befell the Jewish people throughout history. Although, indeed, more severe than the others, it is part of the same category of tragedies that includes the destruction of both Temples, the Ten Martyrs, the Crusades, and all other Jewish tragedies which are to be commemorated on Tisha B'Av.
2. It is inappropriate to commemorate the Holocaust in Nisan, the month of redemption ("*Ḥodesh haGe'ula*"), during which time the recital of *Taḥanun*, fasting, and eulogies are prohibited.
3. Yom HaShoah is nothing more than the invention of the secular Zionist Knesset, and since when do secularists – and anti-religious ones at that – have any religious authority to establish a day, or anything for that matter, of even the slightest religious significance.
4. The official name of this day, Yom HaShoah vehaGevura, as well as its close proximity to the anniversary of the Warsaw Ghetto Uprising preceding it, is offensive because it privileges armed resistance over more spiritual forms of heroism. Genuine Jewish heroism entails living a life of morality, optimism, and hope and maintaining a will to live with human decency in the face of the most unspeakable bestiality: lining up for hours to have one minute with a pair of *tefillin*, smuggling a *shofar* into concentration camps, sharing

half a piece of bread with a starving barracks-mate, and more. These are examples of *real* Jewish heroism.

5. Finally, the form of commemoration mandated by Israeli law is alien to Jewish tradition. Secular ceremonies like halting public and private transportation to listen to a two-minute siren, a moment of silence, lowering the flag to half-mast, and sad music are simply imitations of non-Jewish practices ("vapid ceremonies and vain rituals drawn from heathen idolatry") and not appropriate and are, anyway, ineffective.

Yet, there are those like R. Yeḥiel Yaakov Weinberg who have supported the establishment of a separate day of commemoration for the Holocaust. He wrote: "In my mind it is appropriate to establish a separate day of mourning and memory (*ra'ui likboa yom evel vezikhron meyuḥad*) in memory of the rabbis and sanctified ones of Israel who were killed, butchered and burned for the sanctification of the Name, and to mention the souls of these sanctified ones on this day." And there are many synagogues and communities who do commemorate the Holocaust on the day designated as Yom HaShoah.

The liturgy we propose (page 1024) consists of Torah study and memorial prayers and, hence, is appropriate regardless of where one stands on this fundamental question. Indeed, this liturgy is appropriate for any day of the year except, ironically, for Tisha B'Av, since it features the type of Torah study prohibited on that day of national mourning.

With this service, we aim to bring merit to the souls of the deceased and to implore the Holy One, blessed is He, always to remember both the individuals and the holy communities who were murdered and destroyed in the conflagration that consumed six million of our people. *Hashem yinkom damam.*[1] ◆

1. For more on the issues and sources presented here, including references to all the opinions cited here, see Jacob J. Schacter, "Holocaust Commemoration and *Tish'a be-Av*: The Debate Over *'Yom ha-Sho'a,'" Tradition* 41:2 (2008):164–97; "Remembering The Temple: Commemoration and Catastrophe in Ashkenazi Culture," in Steven Fine, ed., *The Temple of Jerusalem: From Moses to the Messiah* (Brill, 2011), 275–301.

Prayer on Israel's Days of Remembrance and Celebration

Prof. David Berger

The religious significance of the State of Israel has stimulated theological reflections, ideological divisions, and halakhic debates across the full spectrum of Orthodox Jewry. The discourse about this issue is of sufficient prominence and centrality that a non-Jewish historian of American religion posed a striking question one Yom HaAtzma'ut morning. "Tell me," he said, "What are the differences of opinion about what you say in the synagogue today?"

The Zionist movement was dominated by secular Jews, many of whom saw their mission as the "normalization" of the Jewish people through a process that included the abandonment of religion as it had been practiced through the years of exile. This secular, even anti-religious ideology was one important factor in leading many rabbinic leaders to oppose the new movement, and their opposition was reinforced by the conviction that the return of the Jewish people to their land is a messianic event that must be initiated by God alone.

At the same time, some of the forerunners of the movement were Orthodox thinkers, exemplified by R. Zvi Hirsch Kalischer, who saw the settlement of the land as a means by which human initiative could arouse a divine response inaugurating the messianic age. With the birth of political Zionism, the Mizrachi movement emerged, which deemphasized the messianic dimension and concentrated instead on the *mitzva* of living in Israel and the opportunity to observe commandments tied to the land, not to speak of the concerns that it shared with secular Zionists regarding the need for a homeland that would provide a refuge from anti-Semitism.

As the *Yishuv* grew, with formerly arid land beginning to bloom, with the revival of Hebrew as a spoken language, and with the efflorescence of Jewish cultural expression, many believing Jews, inspired by the teachings of Rav Kook, could not help but attribute messianic significance to the events unfolding before their eyes. Had not the sages taught us that there is no more manifest sign of the end of days (*ketz meguleh*) than the restored fecundity of the Land of Israel?

The conviction that Jews were living during the period called "the beginning of redemption" (*Atḥalta diGe'ula*) was both severely challenged and paradoxically reinforced by the horrors of the Holocaust. The Divine Presence was obscured during those terrible years, and yet many Jews found hope in the concept of the "birth pangs of the Messiah" that had led one Talmudic rabbi to say that he wants the Messiah to come but does not want to be present to see his arrival.

And then, in the wake of unspeakable catastrophe, a Jewish State was proclaimed. The return of a significant portion of the Land of Israel to Jewish sovereignty after two millennia was manifestly an event of staggering importance in Jewish history. It is a daunting, nearly insuperable challenge to formulate a theory of providence within the framework of traditional Judaism that perceives this as anything other than a manifestation of divine grace. In 1948, even some rabbinic opponents of Zionism allowed themselves some expression of this sentiment, seeing the State as an opportunity that God has extended to the Jewish people. The distinguished authors of the newly composed Prayer for the Welfare of the State described it as "the beginning of the flowering of our redemption," but even those religious Zionists who were uneasy with a confident affirmation that they were seeing the early stage of a guaranteed messianic process considered it self-evident that this monumental expression of divine favor must be marked by celebration and thanksgiving.

Thus, Yom HaAtzma'ut was born. For secular Jews, it is a national holiday; for religious Jews, it is more than that. A dizzying variety of positions regarding the proper liturgy developed: *Hallel* or no *Hallel*? *Hallel* with a blessing or without a blessing? *Hallel* at night or only during the day? Reciting Shabbat and holiday psalms in the morning prayer? Reading a *Haftara*? However these questions were to be resolved, the significance of the day for anyone who identified as a Zionist was not in question.

For all its celebratory character, Yom HaAtzma'ut is preceded by a day of profound sadness. A religiously meaningful connection between the tragedy of the Holocaust and the establishment of the State remains a theological conundrum, but the relevance of the tears of families whose children, spouses, and parents gave their lives to establish and preserve the State is beyond question. It is Yom HaZikaron that makes Yom HaAtzma'ut possible.

Nineteen years after the first Yom HaAtzma'ut, the Jewish people witnessed

another providential moment. After weeks of acute fear, Israel not only succeeded in staving off an existential threat; it found itself in control of all the historic Land of Israel west of the Jordan, including the Old City of Jerusalem with its Wall and its Temple Mount that had served as the focus of Jewish laments and dreams through the millennia. In the years that followed, the consequences of these events have been far more complicated than they appeared in the first flush of victory, but no religious Zionist – and almost no committed Jew – can be indifferent to the restoration to Jewish control of the city whose name evokes sentiments that animate the very core of Jewish identity. Thus, Yom HaAtzma'ut was joined by Yom Yerushalayim.

Judaism has long lived with the creative tension between reliance on divine providence and the necessity of human initiative. With respect to the yearning for Zion, non-Zionist Orthodoxy stressed the former while secular Zionists unavoidably saw the latter as the only option. In addressing this issue, Religious Zionism pursued the path that believing Jews endorsed in almost all other contexts: Human initiative is indispensable, but so is recognition of the role of God in determining its failure or success. Yom HaZikaron, Yom HaAtzma'ut and Yom Yerushalayim celebrate heroic human self-sacrifice and simultaneously express humble, joyful gratitude to the true Protector and ultimate Redeemer of Israel. ◆

Nusaḥ and Nigunim in Tefilla

R. Gedalia Dov Schwartz

The word *nusaḥ* is not only confined to the rendition of a particular text or a form of worship, such as *Nusaḥ Ashkenaz* or *Nusaḥ Sepharad*, but also to the specific tunes of *Tefilla*, of worship. Just as there is a *mesora*, a tradition regarding ritual customs and regarding sacred texts, there is one of particular chants and melodies for worship. Consequently, when the halakhic authorities discuss the various regional rites of *tefilla*, e.g., *Ashkenaz* or *Sepharad*, they include directives regarding maintaining the traditional *nigunim* too: *One must not change from the custom of the city even in regard to the melodies and piyutim that are recited there* (Maharil, cited by Rema, *OḤ* 619:1). Any changes that might cause *bilbul da'at hakahal*, confusion in the congregation, would be unacceptable.

Melodies that are identified with any kind of foreign, non-Jewish worship would automatically fail the test of not causing *bilbul da'at hakahal*, and are prohibited by many authorities (*Darkhei Teshuva*, *YD* 142:27, citing several sources).

Even a tune that is recognizable as belonging to a prevailing non-Jewish culture, although not connected to any non-Jewish worship, is unacceptable. Use of such tunes is considered improper, especially in the synagogue, based on the Talmud's criticism of the apostate Elisha ben Abuya or "Aḥer" for constantly singing Greek tunes, even when not in the synagogue. The introduction of melodies that are clearly part of prevailing pop culture into our *tefillot* is all the more objectionable and would erode or eliminate the proper intent and musical significance of *shir*, of *nigunim*, and *nusaḥ* – i.e., the manner in which we make our offerings of prayer.

When the Torah (Gen. 43:11) quotes the patriarch Jacob speaking to his sons, "קחו מזמרת הארץ Take from the best of the land," the Hebrew word used here for "best" is the uncommon *zimrat*. R. Naḥman of Breslov found in it a reference to the traditional *nigunim*, expounding the verse as follows: You, the tribal founders, take with you the *zimra* – meaning the *nigun* of the Land of Israel, the special tunes of the Jewish people (*Likutei Maharan Tinyana*).

Even when making use of permitted melodies, one should do so in a

manner that avoids repetition of the words of the *Tefilla* where that is not permitted. This is because repetition of words in the *Tefilla,* in the *Amida,* and other places where interruption is not permitted, is itself considered an interruption (*hefsek*) (*Iggerot Moshe, OḤ* II, §22). R. Joseph B. Soloveitchik (*HaDarom,* Elul 5754 p. 27) opposed the repetition of words during the blessings of the *Shema*, the Leader's repetition of the *Amida*, during *Hallel*, or in reciting any biblical verse during *Tefilla*. ◆

Lesser-Known Laws of Torah Reading[1]

R. Hershel Schachter

A. HOTZA'A AND HAKHNASA

It is preferable to remove the *Sefer Torah* from the *Aron HaKodesh* before the congregation recites *Berikh Shemeh.*[2]

On Yamim Tovim when we recite God's Thirteen Attributes of Mercy – the *Yud-Gimmel Midot HaRaḥamim*, it is proper to begin softly each time from the beginning of the verse, *"Vaya'avor Hashem al panav vayikra"* (Ex. 34:6) before saying aloud *"Hashem Hashem."* This way one avoids the prohibition of saying only a fragment of a verse (*kol pesuka d'lo paskei Moshe anan lo paskinan – Megilla* 22a).[3]

At the time of *hotza'a* we recite the verse *Vayehi binso'a* (Num. 10:35) and during *hakhnasa* we recite *Uvenuḥo yomar* (Num. 10:36). The *Humash* records these *pesukim* in reference to the traveling of the *Aron HaKodesh* in the wilderness. Accordingly, R. Ḥayyim Volozhiner prescribes that during *Hagbaha* after saying *"VeZot HaTorah... lifnei Bnei Yisrael,"* we should recite the verse *"Al pi Hashem yaḥanu... al pi Hashem beyad Moshe"* (Num. 9:23) which also deals with that same topic.[4]

---

1. This article originally appeared in the *Journal of Jewish Music and Liturgy*, Vol. 7 (1984–1985) published by the Cantorial Council of America. It was revised and expanded in *Chemdas HaRav: Insights of HaRav Yosef Dov HaLevi Soloveitchik ztz"l into the Laws of Kerias Hatorah* (YBH of Passaic, March 2014), compiled by R. Michoel Zylberman, and is reprinted here with permission.
2. *Iggerot Moshe* (*Oraḥ Ḥayyim* Vol. 4, p.129).
3. *Sha'arei Efraim* (10:5) and *Pitḥei She'arim* (note 9 on the bottom of *Sha'arei Efraim*). One might perhaps suggest an additional reason for beginning with *Vaya'avor* etc. Tosafot (*Rosh HaShana* 17b s.v. *shelash*) present two views as to whether the Thirteen Attributes begin with *Hashem Hashem* or whether we should punctuate the *pasuk* as *Vaya'avor Hashem al panav, vayikra Hashem* (and God declared): *Hashem El Raḥum veḤanun* etc. According to the latter opinion, the first *Hashem* is not the beginning of the listing of the Thirteen Attributes. According to that view, if one were to recite *Hashem Hashem* etc., the first mention of God's name would constitute a violation of mentioning God's name in vain. Perhaps it is for this reason that some *poskim* recommend starting from *Vaya'avor* to avoid getting involved in this controversy.
4. *Sha'arei Raḥamim* (10:15 on the bottom of *Sha'arei Efraim*).

B. PRIOR TO READING THE TORAH

It is not permissible to roll the *Sefer* to the proper place in such a way as to keep the *tzibbur* waiting. The *Gabbaim* must *shtel* (find the place in) the *Sefer* in advance of *Keriat HaTorah*.[5]

One may not *shtel* the *Sefer* on the first day of Yom Tov for the second day, or on Shabbat for Yom Tov. Regarding preparing the *Sefer* on Yom Tov for *leining* on Shabbat, there are three opinions. Some forbid it even if one has made an *eiruv tavshilin*; others only allow it in the event that an *eiruv tavshilin* was made; and R. Akiva Eiger, whose view is generally accepted, permits it even if one has not made an *eiruv tavshilin*.[6]

Out of respect for the *Sefer Torah*, one may not touch the *klaf* with his bare hands. When the parchment must be handled, the common practice is that one holds it with a *tallit* separating his hands from the *klaf*.[7] This prohibition applies to *Nevi'im* and *Ketuvim* as well, when they are written on *klaf*. Regarding *Nakh*, however, unlike Torah, if one has properly washed *Netillat Yadayim* beforehand (without a *berakha*), he may hold the *klaf* with his bare hands. This is especially relevant on Purim. *Megillot* generally have no wooden handles, and one must wash his hands in advance to be allowed to handle the *klaf*.[8]

As an additional sign of respect, one may not turn his back to the *Sefer Torah* unless it is in a different room or at least a different *reshut* (domain). The *Aron HaKodesh* constitutes a separate domain in this regard, since it is at least four by four *tefaḥim*, and ten *tefaḥim* tall.[9] There is a dispute among the *poskim* as to whether a table of the above dimensions constitutes a separate domain, and, consequently, whether one may turn his back to the *Shulḥan* when the

---

5. *Yoma* (70a). If by error the *Sefer Torah* removed from the *Aron HaKodesh* was not the one that was prepared for that day's reading, the proper practice is that the *tzibbur* be *moḥel* on its *kavod* and have the *Sefer* rolled to the proper place, rather than return it to the *Aron* and remove the *Sefer* that was rolled to the proper place (see *Iggerot Moshe, Oraḥ Ḥayyim* 2:37).
6. *Sha'arei Teshuva* (*Oraḥ Ḥayyim* 667) and *Ḥidushei R. Akiva Eiger* there.
7. *Megilla* (32a) and *Mishna Berura* (147:2).
8. *Shulḥan Arukh, Oraḥ Ḥayyim* (147:1) and *Mishna Berura* (147:4).
9. *Yoreh De'a* (282:1), Taz and *Arukh HaShulḥan*, *Sha'arei Ḥayyim* (notes on *Sha'arei Efraim* 10:19).

Torah is resting upon it.[10] Some opinions go so far as to say that a person with his back to the *Sefer Torah* cannot fulfill his obligation of participating in *Keriat HaTorah* when the Torah is read.[11]

C. THE KOHEN ALIYA

When there is no Kohen present, there is no need to call a Levi first.[12] One opinion even forbids calling a Levi.[13]

Our custom is to never, under normal circumstances, give a Kohen or a Levi any *aliya* after the first two, except for *Aḥaron* or *Maftir*. On Simḥat Torah or when a great need arises, we allow the Kohen or the Levi to receive an *aliya* after the basic number of required *aliyot* has been completed (five on Yom Tov or seven on Shabbat). When the need is even greater, we would allow the Kohen to receive the fourth *aliya*. It is, however, important to make sure that each time a Kohen gets an *aliya* he is followed by a Levi and a Yisrael (except of course, when the Kohen is called to *Aḥaron* or *Maftir*).[14]

Opinions differ as to whether it is at all possible to call a Yisrael instead of a Kohen when a Kohen is present. Some authorities categorically forbid such procedure, even when no Levi is present and the Kohen involved will receive two *aliyot*.[15]

R. Moshe Feinstein permits the Kohen to forgo his *aliya* under certain circumstances.[16]

On a biblical level the Kohen may indeed forgo the privilege of receiving the first *aliya*. The sages of the Mishna, however, instituted a rabbinic edict, insisting that the Kohen always accept his *aliya*, lest he defer to some people and not to others, causing discord among members of the

10. See *Pri Megadim Mishbetzot Zahav* (*Oraḥ Ḥayyim* 150: 2) *Pardes Mordechai* (Williger), p. 134.
11. R. Soloveitchik based on Tosafot (*Sota* 39a s.v. *kivan*). *Nefesh HaRav* pp. 139–140.
12. *Gittin* (59b) and Rashi (s.v. *nitparda haḥavila*) and Rema *Oraḥ Ḥayyim* (135:6).
13. R. Soloveitchik used to insist on following this opinion. *Nefesh HaRav* p. 130.
14. See Rema (*Oraḥ Ḥayyim* 135:10) and *Mishna Berura* (135:36–37).
15. *Shu"t Maharam Shick* (*Oraḥ Ḥayyim* 61).
16. *Iggerot Moshe* (*Oraḥ Ḥayyim* 2:34 and 3:20). See, however, *Mishna Berura* (135:9) quoting *Pri Megadim* and *Arukh HaShulḥan* (135:10) who assume that nowadays the *minhag* is to never allow the Kohen to forgo the first *aliya*.

shul. According to the Talmud, this edict was only enacted with respect to Shabbat and Yom Tov, when shul attendance, and hence potential friction, were greatest.

The edict never applied to weekdays, and the Kohen retained his right to defer. Tosafot, however, comment, that in their day, weekday *minyanim* were as well attended as those of Shabbat and Yom Tov, and therefore a Kohen should not be permitted to defer even during the week.[17]

In our own day, unfortunately, we have regressed to the situation at the time of the Gemara, with our *minyanim* being significantly smaller during the week than on Shabbat. Consequently, the *Iggerot Moshe* rules the Kohen may once again forgo his *aliya*, provided the three conditions are met: (a) the Kohen must be sincerely willing to relinquish his *aliya*, as opposed to merely having the *Gabbai* call out a perfunctory *bemeḥilat HaKohen*; (b) the Kohen should step out of shul until after the beginning of the *berakhot*; and (c) this should be done only on weekdays – never on Shabbat or Yom Tov.[18]

Even for those who never permit the Kohen to be *moḥel*, two exceptions exist: On a public fast day, if the Kohen is not fasting, and cannot, therefore, be accorded an *aliya* according to our custom, he is sent out of shul while his *aliya* is assigned to a non-Kohen. Likewise if the Kohen is in the middle of *Shema* or *Shemoneh Esreh* and may not take an *aliya*, a non-Kohen may be called up even without sending out the Kohen.[19]

D. CALLING TO THE TORAH – HOW AND HOW MANY

It is improper to call *Ya'amod Kohen*, or *Ya'amod Ḥamishi*. The correct way to call the *oleh* is by mentioning his name: *Ya'amod Ploni ben Ploni*.[20] In some

17. *Gittin* (59b) and Tosafot (s.v. *aval*).
18. See *Edut LeYisrael*, by R. Yosef Eliyahu Henkin, p. 164, who offers a suggestion regarding why in many communities they were not so careful about the Kohen *aliya*. This was reprinted in the *Shu"t Gevurot Eliyahu* (*Oraḥ Ḥayyim* p. 84).
19. Rema (*Oraḥ Ḥayyim* 135:5), and *Mishna Berura* (135:18).
20. *Shu"t Avnei Nezer, Ḥoshen Mishpat* 103. See also *Sha'arei Raḥamim* (19) and *Sha'arei Ḥayyim* (20) to *Sha'arei Efraim* (1:26). See also *Sha'arei Raḥamim* (21), that several *poskim* were very insistent on not calling one up to the Torah with the title *Morenu* unless the *oleh* was actually one who taught Torah publicly. *Mipninei HaRav* p. 43. See *Sha'arei Raḥamim* (25).

communities, however, an exception is made regarding *Shevi'i*, when the *Gabbai* simply calls out *Ya'amod Shevi'i*.[21]

The common practice is to allow *hosafot* (additional *aliyot*) only on Shabbat, but not on Yom Kippur or other festivals (with the exception of Simḥat Torah). Even when Yom Kippur falls on Shabbat, we do not allow *hosafot*.[22] When other Yamim Tovim occur on Shabbat, we allow *hosafot*. Still, there are communities where the practice is not to allow *hosafot* even then.[23] Some recommend that no *hosafot* be allowed when we read two *parashot*.[24]

Some authorities rule that today, when the practice is to have one *Ba'al Keria* reading on behalf of all the *olim*, it is no longer permissible to add *hosafot*. This view is not generally accepted; however, in some communities there were rabbinic enactments (*takkanot*) not to allow more than three *hosafot*, so that the total of all the *aliyot* (aside from *Maftir*) would not exceed ten.[25]

E. DINIM OF THE OLEH

It is forbidden to refuse an *aliya*. Likewise, one may not refuse the honors of *hotza'a* and *hakhnasa*, *Hagbaha* and *Gelila*.[26]

---

21. See *Mishna Berura* (141:21) who notes that some communities do not call up *Maftir* by name.
22. Rema (*Oraḥ Ḥayyim* 282:1) and *Mishna Berura* (282:6).
23. *Mishna Berura* (ibid). R. Soloveitchik mentioned that the *minhag* of many communities in Lithuania was to not allow any *hosafot* even when Yom Tov occurred on a Shabbat. The rationale behind this apparently was that a Yom Tov *leining* does not lend itself to *hosafot*, while a Shabbat *leining* did lend itself to *hosafot*. Therefore, on Simḥat Torah, when the *Keria* consists of *Parashat VeZot HaBerakha*, rather than a Yom Tov *Keria*, we do allow *hosafot*. See *Shiurei HaRav: Keriat HaTorah* (TorahWeb), p. 139.
24. R. Soloveitchik in the name of his father, R. Moshe Soloveichik. *Nefesh HaRav* p. 139.
25. See *Binyan Shlomo* by the *Vilna Dayan* (1:20), and *Edut LeYisrael*, p. 164. See also note 11 of *Sha'arei Ḥayyim* to chapter 7 of the *Sha'arei Efraim*.
26. *Berakhot* (55a) quoted by *Mishna Berura* (139:1). R. Soloveitchik related that his grandfather, R. Ḥayyim Brisker, was of the opinion that one holding a *Sefer Torah* may not give it away to someone else, unless that other person needs it, and asks for it. On Simḥat Torah evening R. Ḥayyim, as rabbi of the town, would be honored with the first *hakafa*. At the end of the *hakafa*, he would not volunteer on his own to give away the Torah he was holding to someone else; and the *ba'alei-batim* did not have the nerve to ask him for his *Sefer* for the next *hakafa*. It often occurred that R. Ḥayyim would be holding the *Sefer* he was given for the first *hakafa* until the end of all the *hakafot*. See *Nefesh HaRav*

The *Meḥaber* rules that one who is called to the Torah should approach and ascend the *bima* using the shortest route from his seat. If both possible routes are approximately equidistant, the *oleh* should ascend from the right side. The Vilna Gaon, however, disagrees, prescribing the use of the right side in all instances.[27]

It was a widespread custom in Europe that both the *oleh* and the *Ba'al Keria* would practice *atifa*, i.e., they would wear a special head covering. Such *atifa* can be accomplished by wearing the *tallit* over one's head, or by wearing a hat, or a special higher *yarmulke*.[28]

The *Tannaim* were concerned that when the *olim* recite the *berakhot* before their *aliyot*, the listeners might mistakenly think that the *berakhot* were actually written in the *Sefer Torah*. For this reason, according to *Tosafot*, the *oleh* should open the *Sefer* to see where his *aliya* will begin, and then close it to recite the opening *berakha*.[29] Other authorities maintain that the *oleh* should not close the *Sefer Torah* before reciting the preceding *berakha*. Instead, to demonstrate that he is not reading from the *Sefer*, some recommend that he close his eyes or turn slightly to his left.[30] No such debate exists with regard to the *berakha* after the *aliya*, for it is agreed that the *oleh* must close the *Sefer Torah*, and only then may he recite the concluding *berakha*.[31]

Although there is an opinion which forbids holding on to even the wooden

---

p. 222. See *Iggerot Moshe* (*Oraḥ Ḥayyim* 1:38) that it is improper to have a special chair upon which to put the *Sefer* after completing the *Gelila*. See, however, the end of that *teshuva*, that according to some commentaries this practice existed in the days of the Talmud.

27. *Shulḥan Arukh, Oraḥ Ḥayyim* (141:7). The Gra in note 14 writes that this has no source anywhere, neither in *Tosefta* nor in the Talmud. See also *Birkat Eliyahu* (commentary on *Biur HaGra*), who quotes that the Ḥatam Sofer had the same practice as the Gra.

28. See *Mishna Berura* (91:6, 12 and 183:11) and *Yeḥave Da'at* (R. Ovadia Yosef), vol. 4, no. 1. See also *Sha'arei Efraim* (3:18) who writes that one should perform *atifa* with a *tallit* even for Shabbat *Minḥa*.

29. See *Megilla* (32a) and Tosafot (s.v. *golelo*), *Mishna Berura* (139:17) and *Biur Halakha* (139 s.v. *vero'eh*). R. Soloveitchik's practice was not to close the *Sefer* while reciting the *berakha* before the *aliya*. He recalled that many great rabbis in Europe had this practice as well.

30. See Rema to *Oraḥ Ḥayyim* (139:4) and *Mishna Berura* (139:19). The *Mishna Berura* prefers closing one's eyes to turning away from the *Sefer*.

31. Tosafot mentioned above in note 29.

handles, or *Atzei Ḥayyim*, of a *Sefer Torah* with bare hands,[32] this view has not been accepted by the *poskim*. Should one choose to personally adopt the stringent view and hold the *Atzei Ḥayyim* only with a *tallit*, he may do so only in an inconspicuous fashion.[33]

In Talmudic times, one who got an *aliya* would have to read his own section of the *Keria*. Today, in order not to embarrass those who cannot *lein* properly, we have instituted the practice of having a *Ba'al Keria* who reads the portion on behalf of all those who get *aliyot*. It is proper, however, for each *oleh* to read softly along with the *Ba'al Keria* from the *Sefer Torah*. Nevertheless, one who is blind, or otherwise unable to read along with the *Ba'al Keria*, may still be called to the Torah. The *Mishna Berura* stipulates, though, that such a person should not be called to *Parashat Zakhor* or *Parashat Para*.[34]

Some are of the opinion that the only time we now permit the individual getting an *aliya* to read his section is for the *Tokheḥa*, when the *Ba'al Keria* himself takes the *aliya*, without being called up by name.[35]

It is improper to follow the custom of some communities, whereby no one

---

32. *Magen Avraham* introductory note to *Oraḥ Ḥayyim* 147
33. *Mishna Berura* (147:2) quoting from *Shu"t Noda BiYehuda* (*Oraḥ Ḥayyim* 8).
34. Tosafot *Megilla* (21b s.v. *Tanna*), *Mishna Berura* (139:13) and *Sha'ar HaTziyun* (139:66). Regarding the *oleh*'s reading along with the *Ba'al Keria* see *Shulḥan Arukh, Oraḥ Ḥayyim* (141:2) that it is preferable that he read in a whisper, such that even he should not be able to hear himself read. However, if he should read so loud that he should be able to hear himself read, this would also be acceptable. See *Mishna Berura* (141:13).
35. R. Soloveitchik was opposed to the common practice of having a Bar Mitzva boy read the entire *Parasha* including his own *aliya*. He felt that this constituted a violation of the *minhag* not to allow anyone to *lein* his own *aliya*. From the Rema (*Oraḥ Ḥayyim* 139:3) this would not seem to have been the *minhag* in his times. *Shulḥan Arukh, Even HaEzer* (34:1) records a similar *minhag* to not allow any *ḥatan* to recite *Birkat Erusin* for himself, in order not to embarrass the *ḥatanim* who were not able to recite the *berakhot* on their own. This is why the rabbi recites the *berakhot* for all couples. Nevertheless, if the rabbi is single, when he gets married, the *poskim* allow him to recite *Birkat Erusin* for himself. The situation of the *Ba'al Keria* receiving an *aliya* and reading for himself seems parallel to the rabbi reciting *Birkat Erusin* at his own wedding. See Rema (*Oraḥ Ḥayyim* 139:3) that we do not call up the *Ba'al Keria* by name since he is standing there already. According to this custom of the Rema, when a Bar Mitzva boy is reading the *Parasha* and is honored with *Maftir*, we do not "call him up" by name, but he merely recites the *berakhot* over his *aliya*. Regarding the *Tokheḥa* see *Magen Avraham* (*Oraḥ Ḥayyim* 428:8).

recited the *berakhot* on the *aliya* of the *Tokheḥa*. The *Ba'al Keria* should recite the appropriate *berakhot* before and after reading the section of the *Tokheḥa*.[36]

Many *poskim* rule that one who receives the last *aliya* in a *Sefer* should not say "*ḥazak ḥazak*" along with the congregation, for this would constitute a *hefsek* between the reading and the *berakha* following it.[37]

F. LAWS OF THE BA'AL KERIA

Many *Ba'alei Keria* pause briefly after the *oleh* has recited the *berakha*, before beginning to read. They then say amen aloud, and proceed with the *Keria*. This practice is improper, because one must respond with amen immediately following the conclusion of the *berakha* to which it relates. We refer to an amen recited before the conclusion of the last syllable of its *berakha* as an amen *ḥatufa* – a hastily grabbed amen, and one recited after a pause following its *berakha* as an amen *yetoma* – an orphaned amen, bereft of the *berakha* over which it was recited.[38]

The *Ba'al Keria* must regulate his reading according to the various subdivisions of the Torah's text. Only by doing so does he fulfill the requirement of reading the Torah *kikhtava*, precisely as it is written. This requirement includes the following *dinim*.

The *Ba'al Keria* may not pause in the middle of a verse, reading it as if it were two verses. Likewise, he may not read two verses together, without pausing, as if they were a single verse.[39]

He must pause between reading two *parshiyot* (paragraphs) in the Torah even longer than between two verses, and the pause for a *petuḥa* (an open space in the Torah which extends until the end of the line) must be longer than that of a *setuma* (an enclosed space of nine-letters length within a line).[40]

Kikhtava applies as well to certain poetic sections of the *Ḥumash*. The

---

36. *Iggerot Moshe* (*Oraḥ Ḥayyim* 2:35).
37. See *Shulḥan HaKeria* to *Oraḥ Ḥayyim* (end of 139) and *Mishneh Halakhot* (7:22). The *Luaḥ* printed by Kollel Chabad of Jerusalem records the Lubavitcher *minhag* that allows the *oleh* to recite "*ḥazak ḥazak*" along with the *tzibbur*, presuming that it does not constitute a *hefsek*.
38. *Shulḥan Arukh* (*Oraḥ Ḥayyim* 124:8).
39. *Megilla* (22a). R. Soloveitchik explained that reading two *pesukim* together as if they were one would be a violation of the same principle. See *Nefesh HaRav* p. 141.
40. See *Mekor Ḥayyim* (by the author of *Ḥavat Ya'ir*) to *Oraḥ Ḥayyim* (61:14) concerning

Talmud states that the *Shira* of *Ha'azinu* should be broken up into *aliyot* just as it was divided into weekly portions for the song of the Levi'im in the *Beit HaMikdash*.[41] While the acronym denoting the beginning of these *aliyot* is acknowledged to be HaZIV LaKH, views differ as to exactly which verses the acronym refers. The *Mishna Berura* advises that Ashkenazim and Sephardim should each follow their own separate customs, and not be misled by *Ḥumashim* used in Ashkenazic shuls that were printed with the *aliyot* according to the Sephardic *minhag*.[42]

The Rema rules that these stops govern only the Shabbat morning reading, while other *poskim* feel that we must adhere to them on Monday, Thursday, and Shabbat *Minḥa* as well.[43]

Along these lines, *kikhtava* also governs the reading of *Shirat HaYam* and prohibits us from breaking up the *Shira* into more than one *aliya*.[44]

In addition, the forty-two *masa'ot* ("Journeys") of the Jews in the wilderness, as recorded in *Parashat Masei*, must be read together, according to the *Magen Avraham*, disregarding the erroneous stop for *Sheni* recorded in most *Ḥumashim*.[45] Some are careful not to break up the *masa'ot* even on Monday and Thursday mornings and at Shabbat *Minḥa*.[46]

---

pausing slightly at an *etnaḥta* in the middle of a *pasuk*. See also *Shulḥan HaKeria* (*Oraḥ Ḥayyim* 141:8) regarding the same point.

41. *Rosh HaShana* (31a).
42. *Mishna Berura* (*Oraḥ Ḥayyim* (428:5) and *Sha'ar HaTziyun* (428:7). See *Shu"t Devar Avraham* (1:36) who has an amazing original opinion regarding this *halakha* that does not seem to follow the understanding of the nature of this *halakha* as we have presented it. Our understanding is based on the *shiurim* of R. Soloveitchik.
43. *Shulḥan Arukh* (*Oraḥ Ḥayyim* 428:5), *Pri Ḥadash* and *Shiyarei Knesset Hagedola* there. R. Soloveitchik did not follow the view of the Rema, based on his understanding of the nature of this *halakha*, and held that if the *Shirat Ha'azinu* is broken up improperly this would constitute a *keria shelo kikhtava*. *Nefesh HaRav* pp. 140–141. See above pp. 23–25.
44. Abudarham. See *Sha'arei Efraim* (7:25) and *Sha'arei Raḥamim* (7:27); *Ta'anugei Yisrael* vol. I, no. 37.
45. *Magen Avraham* (428:8) in the name of *Tzror Hamor* and quoted by *Mishna Berura* (428:21); *Sha"arei Raḥamim* to *Sha'arei Efraim* (7:26). See comment of *Rashash* to *Menaḥot* (30a) regarding the exact calculation of the forty-two sojourns. When we read *Parashat Masei* alone, the first *aliya* should end where the printed *Ḥumashim* say *Sheni*. The second *aliya* can then end after Numbers 33:53.
46. According to *Hayom Yom*, the *minhag* of Lubavitch is to be careful about this point even

The *Ba'al Keria* must be careful to read every word from inside the *Sefer*, and not recite any part of the *Keria* from memory. Even when there is a *keri ukhetiv*, and we do not read the word as it is written, the *Ba'al Keria* must still read from the *Sefer*. Only when the word to be read is not written in the text at all (*keri velo ketiv*), or when the *mesora* substitutes an entirely different pronunciation, may the *Ba'al Keria* recite a word by heart.[47]

It is preferable for the entire *Keria* to be read properly, with the correct pronunciation of each word, and the correct tune for each *trop*. In fact, Rambam maintains that even for a slight error in *trop*, the *Ba'al Keria* must repeat the reading. The accepted ruling is, however, that one need repeat the reading only for an error in pronunciation that alters the meaning of the word.[48]

If the *Ba'al Keria* made a mistake in the middle of a verse, there are three opinions as to whether he must reread the entire verse correctly from the beginning, only reread from the corrected word onward, or begin to read from the beginning of the phrase in which he made the mistake. The third view, that of the Ba'al HaTanya, is the most commonly followed.[49]

Therefore, whenever there is a doubt as to how to properly read part of a verse (as, for example, in *Parashat Zakhor – timḥeh et zekher Amalek*, or *zeikher Amalek* (*Devarim* 25:19), in *Megillat Esther – Ve'ish lo amad bifneihem* or *lifneihem* (9:2), *laharog ule'abed* or *velaharog ule'abed* (8:11), the common practice is that the *Ba'al Keria* reads that phrase over again, with its variant reading, without necessarily reading the entire verse twice.[50]

There is a common misconception that in the event that the *Ba'al Keria* made an error, and has already read God's name in the verse, he should first complete the reading of the verse, and then reread it correctly. The *poskim* write explicitly that such an approach is highly illogical. Rather, the *Ba'al Keria*

---

on Monday and Thursday mornings. This was also the practice of R. Soloveitchik. See *Nefesh HaRav* p. 141.

47. *Iggerot Moshe* (*Oraḥ Ḥayyim* Vol. 4, p. 41).

48. R. Soloveitchik in the name of his grandfather, R. Ḥayyim Soloveichik based on Rambam (*Hilkhot Tefilla* 12:6); *Shulḥan Arukh*, (*Oraḥ Ḥayyim* 142:1), and *Mishna Berura* (142:4).

49. See *Tosafot Anshei Shem* to Mishna *Berakhot* (2:3).

50. R. Soloveitchik.

should stop immediately upon realizing his mistake, and reread the verse correctly, starting from the phrase containing the error.[51]

Optimally, it is not proper to divide the *Parasha* among several *Ba'alei Keria*, with each reading only a part.[52] This regulation is even more important with regard to the reading of the *Megilla*. Some opinions maintain that listeners do not fulfill their obligation even *bedi'eved* if they hear the *Megilla* read by more than one person.[53]

When the *Ba'al Keria* himself is honored with an *aliya*, the *Gabbai* does not call *ya'amod Ploni ben Ploni*. He merely recites the *Mi Sheberakh* following the *aliya* just completed, whereupon the *Ba'al Keria* continues with *Barekhu*.[54]

It is customary to read the *Tokheḥa* softly. Nonetheless, the *Ba'al Keria* should be careful to read loudly enough to ensure that every person in shul hears every word.[55]

According to R. Moshe Feinstein, it is improper for the *Ba'al Keria* to keep a *Ḥumash* next to him to refer to, even though he will read afterward from the *Sefer Torah*.[56]

The *Ba'al Keria* should not touch the Torah text with the tip of his pointer, even for the purpose of keeping the place, lest he contribute to the wear and tear, and eventual fading of the letters. For the same reason, the *oleh* should not touch the actual words with his *tallit* before beginning his *aliya*.[57]

G. KADDISH

Some are of the opinion that the *Kaddish* recited after *Keriat HaTorah* does not especially "belong" to the *Ba'al Keria*. Anyone who is a *ḥiyuv* (one who

51. *Ḥayyei Adam*. See *Sha'arei Raḥamim* to *Sha'arei Efraim* (3:18).
52. *Sha'arei Efraim* (3:6).
53. *Magen Avraham* (692:2). See *Sha'arei Teshuva* (692:2) and *Mishna Berura* (692:2).
54. See above note 35.
55. *Pri Ḥadash* (428:7).
56. *Iggerot Moshe* (*Oraḥ Ḥayyim* 3:19).
57. *Sha'arei Raḥamim* (4:4); *Edut LeYisrael*, p. 159.

is obligated to say *Kaddish* that day) may insist on reciting this *Kaddish*.[58] R. Soloveitchik disagreed with these authorities.[59]

The *Kaddish* following *Keriat HaTorah* should be recited immediately after the final *berakha* of the last *oleh* without any interruption. If the *oleh* wishes to recite *Birkat HaGomel* he should do so following the *Kaddish*.[60]

At *Minḥa* on Shabbat afternoon, when the *Kaddish* following the reading is not recited until right before the *Amida*, some *poskim* rule that it is not proper to say any additional chapters of *Tehillim* (such as *Mizmor Shir leYom haShabbat* or *Halleluya Odeh Hashem beKhol Levav*) during *Gelila*, for this would constitute a *hefsek*.[61]

There is a minority opinion among the *poskim* that the *Kaddish* after *Uvenuḥo Yomar* and before *Musaf* is not the introduction to the *Musaf Tefilla*, but rather the conclusion of the verses that preceded it. Therefore, when the Leader chants the *Hineni* prayer, or if the rabbi delivers a sermon before *Musaf*, the Leader should repeat softly a minimum of three verses before reciting the *Kaddish* aloud.[62]

H. MI SHEBERAKH

While one recites a *Mi Sheberakh* it is proper to cover the *Sefer Torah* with a special cover, or *mentile*. The *mentile* should not be placed over the *Sefer* until after the *oleh* has completed the *berakha* following his *aliya*.[63]

When one recites a *Mi Sheberakh*, it is improper to say *ba'avur shePloni mevarekh otam*. Instead, one should pledge a gift to charity, and insert *ba'avur shePloni yiten tzedaka ba'avuram*.[64]

---

58. The *Mateh Efraim* (*Dinei Kaddish* 3:1) rules that if an *avel* receives *Shlishi* during the week or the last *aliya* on Shabbat, he is entitled to recite the *Ḥatzi Kaddish* following *Keriat HaTorah*. He also quotes (*Elef HaMagen* note 3) some authorities who hold that the *avel* may recite that *Kaddish* even if he did not receive an *aliya*, as the *Kaddish* after *Keriat HaTorah* need not be recited by the *Ba'al Keria*.
59. *Mipninei HaRav* p. 45 in the name of R. Yitzchak Cohen.
60. R. Soloveitchik as cited in *Divrei HaRav* p. 152.
61. See *Pitḥei She'arim* to *Sha'arei Efraim* (10:46) and *Sha'arei Raḥamim* (end of note 57).
62. See *Shu"t Maharam Shick*, (*Oraḥ Ḥayyim* 126; *Mishna Berura* (25:59), and *Ot Ḥayyim VeShalom* (there) by Munkatcher Rebbe; *Matteh Efraim* (591:38).
63. See *Oraḥ Ḥayyim* (139:5) and *Sha'arei Efraim* (421).
64. *Edut LeYisrael*, p. 164 (reprinted in *Shu"t Gevurot Eliyahu, Oraḥ Ḥayyim* p. 84).

I. DINIM OF HAGBAHA AND GELILA

The one who lifts the *Sefer Torah* for *Hagbaha* should open it wide enough to show the congregation at least three columns. He should first show the open *Sefer Torah* to those on his right and then to those on his left.[65]

The one honored with rolling up the Torah (the *Golel*) should arrange to have the connecting stitch showing in the center.[66] It is a common practice that one set the *Bereshit* side of the Torah above the *Devarim* side.[67]

He should bind the Torah with its special belt (or *gartel*) on the upper half of the *Sefer*. In doing so, he should not start the tying between the *Magbiha* and the Torah, pulling the *gartel* and the Torah towards himself to complete the tying on his side. This might cause the Torah to slip and fall, God forbid. Instead, he should begin on his side, extending the *gartel* around the Torah and always pulling towards the *Magbiha*, ultimately completing the tying between the *Magbiha* and the *Sefer*.[68]

On Shabbat or Yom Tov, it is not proper to tie even a bow which will last for more than twenty-four hours. In the event that this *Sefer* will not be used again within the next twenty-four hours, the *Golel* should wind the *gartel* around several times, and then tuck it in so that it will hold together without any knot or bow.[69]

J. MORE THAN ONE PARASHA – MORE THAN ONE SEFER

When the *Keria* consists of two *Parashot*, the common practice is to read half of the basic seven obligatory *aliyot* from each *Parasha*, with *Revi'i* connecting the two *Parashot*. This rule may be overlooked when there is a need to include more than three and a half *aliyot* in the first *Parasha*.[70]

If the majority of the *minyan* missed *Keriat HaTorah* one Shabbat, they

---

R. Soloveitchik was also very adamant about not saying "*mevarekh otam*" (*Nefesh HaRav* p. 143).

65. *Shulḥan Arukh, Oraḥ Ḥayyim* (134:2); *Massekhet Soferim* (14:14), quoted by *Sha'arei Efraim* (10:13).

66. See above.

67. *Sha'arei Efraim* (10:17).

68. *Sha'arei Ḥayyim* (10:21) and Rema to (*Oraḥ Ḥayyim* 147:4). See *Mishna Berura* (147:17) where he explains why this is not commonly practiced today.

69. See *Sha'arei Raḥamim* (no. 18) and *Sha'arei Ḥayyim* (no. 22) to *Sha'arei Efraim* ch. 10.

70. See note 22 above and *Sha'arei Raḥamim* (to 7:21).

should read both *Parashot* in shul the next Shabbat, in the same manner as they would read two *Parashot* that are *meḥubarim*.[71]

On a day when we read from two *Sifrei Torah*, the second Torah should be placed on the *Shulḥan* next to the first before the *Kaddish* is recited.[72] On a day when we read from three *Sifrei Torah*, we recite the *Kaddish* after reading from the second. The third *Sefer* should be placed on the *Shulḥan* next to the second *Sefer* before reciting the *Kaddish*. It is generally assumed that the first *Sefer* need not be returned to the *Shulḥan* before the *Kaddish*.[73]

K. THE HAFTARA

In the event that the *Haftara* is not being read from a parchment (*klaf*), some authorities maintain that one can only fulfill his obligation by reading along with the *Ba'al Maftir*. According to these *poskim*, if nine people have not recited the *Haftara* along with the *Ba'al Maftir*, the *mitzva* of *Keriat haHaftara* has not been fulfilled.[74]

According to the *Iggerot Moshe*, it is not permissible for one to stand for the *Keria* in a shul where the custom is to sit. Other *poskim* dispute this point.[75]

L. LESSER-KNOWN PRONUNCIATIONS AND PRACTICES

1. In *Shirat HaYam*, the *Ba'al Keria* should pause between *bemayim* and *adirim* (Ex. 15:10).[76] Additionally, the *Ba'al Keria* should use the special tune for *Shirat HaYam* for the first occurrence of the phrase *vehamayim lahem ḥoma miyminam umismolam* (14:22) but not the second (14:29).[77]

---

71. Rema (*Oraḥ Ḥayyim* 135:2). See *Pitḥei She'arim* (7:10). See *Shiurei HaRav* (TorahWeb) pp. 141–143.
72. *Mishna Berura* (147:27).
73. Ibid.
74. *Sha'arei Ḥayyim* (9:11). See also *Nefesh HaRav* p. 161.
75. *Oraḥ Ḥayyim*, (4:22) and *Devar Yehoshua* (Ehrenberg) vol. 2, end of no. 15.
76. *Mishna Berura* (51:17).
77. R. Mendy Gopin in the name of R. Soloveitchik. *Ba'al HaTurim* notes that in the second instance the word *ḥoma* is missing a *vav*. This is a reference to the *ḥema*, the anger, of *HaKadosh Barukh Hu*, which was aroused by the presence of *pesel Mikha* at *Yam Suf* (see *Sanhedrin* 103b). Because of this negative reference it is inappropriate to use the special tune.

2. In *Parashat Ki Tisa*, the *Ba'al Keria* should pause between *vayikra beshem* and *Ado-nai* (Ex. 34:5).[78] He should also be careful to pause between *venakeh* and *lo yenakeh*, in the Thirteen Attributes of Mercy (34:7).[79]
3. In *Parashat Beha'alotekha*, the *aliya* of *Ḥamishi* should conclude at *vehayita lanu la'enayim* (10:31) and not, as is printed in the *Ḥumashim*, at *benas'am min hamaḥaneh* (10:34).[80]
4. In *Shira Ha'azinu*, the correct pronunciation is *Eloah* rather than *Eloha* (Deut. 32:17).[81]
5. In the *Haftara* of *Parashat Lekh Lekha*, according to the Radak, the correct pronunciation is *vekoyei Hashem yaḥalifu ko'aḥ* (Is. 4:31).
6. In the *Haftara* of Shabbat Rosh Ḥodesh, the correct reading is *miziz kevoda* (Is. 66:11).[82]
7. When Rosh Ḥodesh Av occurs on Shabbat, most authorities rule that we read *Shimu*, the second of the three *Haftarot* of *puranuta*. Some communities do, however, have the custom of reciting the *Haftara* of *Hashamayim Kisi*, as on any other Shabbat Rosh Ḥodesh.[83]
8. According to many customs, the *Haftara* of *Shabbat Shuva* consists of verses from three prophets: Hoshea, Micha and Yoel. The Gemara stipulates however, that one must arrange such various verses in the order in which they appear in Tanakh (Hoshea first, then Yoel, and finally Micha).[84]

---

78. *Mishna Berura* (58:4).
79. R. Soloveitchik. See *Nefesh HaRav* p. 290.
80. This is in the *minhag* in Belz (*Luaḥ Temidim KeSidram*). Rema (138:2) writes that every *aliya* should begin and conclude with a positive matter. The stop in the printed *Ḥumashim* corresponds to the *puranut*, the negative matter, referenced in *Shabbat* 116a.
81. The same applies to the pronunciation of the same word in *Hallel* (Ps. 114:7) and in *Nishmat*.
82. See *Minḥat Shai*.
83. See Rema, *Dagul Merevava*, Gra, and *Mishna Berura* to *Oraḥ Ḥayyim* (425:1). *Sha'arei Efraim* (9:22) records that the *minhag* was like the Rema to recite *Hashamayim Kisi*. See also *Ta'anugei Yisrael* (5741), no. 44.
84. *Sha'arei Efraim* (9:28). See however note 9 there in *Sha'arei Ḥayyim*, where he explains the widespread practice to recite the *pesukim* out of order. See *Iggerot Moshe* (*Oraḥ Ḥayyim* 1:174) that there is no need to conclude the *Haftara* with *pesukim* from both Yoel and Micha. In the event that the *Haftara* is read from a *klaf*, one should read from

9. In the *Haftara* of the first day of Shavuot, the two names of Hashem are read *Elokim Ado-nai* (Hab. 3:19).[85]
10. The paragraph of *berakhot* following the *Haftara* which ends *emet vatzedek* is not the end of the *berakha* and the congregation should not answer amen. The reason *ne'eman* is written as a separate paragraph is that the *minhag* used to be for the congregation to say this part along with the *Ba'al Maftir* until the words *lo yashuv rekam*.[86]
11. According to R. Soloveitchik, one should pause between *midvarekha aḥor* and *lo yashuv rekam*.[87]
12. According to the *Ba'al HaTanya*, the word *veraḥaman* should be deleted from the concluding line, with the amended version reading: *Ki Kel Melekh Ne'eman Ata*. [88] ◆

Hoshea and conclude with Yoel; if the *Haftara* is read from a printed *Ḥumash*, one should read from Hoshea and conclude with Micha.

Regarding the closing two *pesukim* of the *Haftara* of *Parashat Mishpatim*, see note by R. David Feinstein in *LeTorah VeHora'a*, vol. 3, p. 20, in the name of his father, R. Moshe Feinstein. The last two *pesukim* of chapter 35 of Jeremiah should be substituted in place of the last two *pesukim* of chapter 33, so that the reading will not be out of order.

85. Care should be taken to pronounce God's name properly: *Ah-do-noi* is the correct (Ashkenazi) pronunciation, as opposed to *Ahdi-noi*, or other common distortions. See *Geonei Polin Ha'aḥaronim*, Aaron Sorasky (5743), p. 265.
86. *Tosafot* (*Pesaḥim* 104b s.v. *ḥutz*). See *Mipninei HaRav* p. 85.
87. The meaning of the phrase *midvarekha aḥor* is "Your words of the past." See note at the end of *Torah Temima Ḥumashim* regarding this phrase. See *Nefesh HaRav* pp. 161–2.
88. See *Sha'ar Hakolel* (25:3). This was the practice of R. Soloveitchik as well. *Nefesh HaRav* p. 162. R. Soloveitchik also recited in the *berakha* of *Raḥem*.

Prayer and Interpersonal Halakha

R. Daniel Feldman

I. PRAYER AND THE MITZVA OF LOVING ONE'S FELLOW

The time of *tefilla* is one of focus on the relationship with God; nonetheless, it is crucial that the relationship between man and his fellow be strengthened and emphasized at this time as well. Recognizing this requirement, the famous Kabbalist R. Yitzḥak Ashkenazi (Arizal) recommended that prior to praying, one express the acceptance upon one's self of particular attention to the commandment of "Love your neighbor as yourself."[1] Some have suggested that this idea manifests itself as the one praying having in mind any other individual who may have similar needs and supplications, and thus including these others in his prayers.[2]

As others have noted,[3] this "acceptance" is strengthened by immediate action, such as issuing forgiveness to all who have caused pain to the one praying, and resolving to treat these individuals and others not only according to strict justice but with an attitude of *lifnim mishurat hadin*.

Similarly, the *Shulḥan Arukh*[4] recommends giving *tzedaka* before prayer, to thus realize the verse,[5] "I, in righteousness (*tzedek*) will behold Your face."[6] However, it should be noted, as R. Shlomo Zalman Auerbach maintained,[7] that it is inappropriate for collectors to circulate in the synagogue and request *tzedaka* during davening itself, particularly during the points of the service when it is forbidden to interrupt. Nonetheless, if one is approached at this time, it is permissible to silently hand over a donation, and it is preferable to prepare

1. *Sefer Sha'ar HaMitzvot*, quoted in *Magen Avraham, Oraḥ Ḥayyim* 46:1. See also *Maḥatzit HaShekel*; R. Asher Anshel Katz, *Shemen Rosh*, vol. 2, p. 569; R. David Ariav, *LeRe'akha Kamokha*, (II, p. 181, *Nir LeDavid*, # 268); R. Yeshayah Braver, *Shome'a Tefilla*, I, 13:5; and R. Ovadia Yosef, *Anaf Etz Avot* to *Pirkei Avot*, 5:16.
2. See R. Yoḥanan Segal Vosner, *Responsa Ḥayyei HaLevi*, II, 19:3. Compare as well *Derashot Ḥatam Sofer*, III, p. 77.
3. Note, for example, R. Yonatan Eibshutz, *Ya'arot Devash*, II, p. 77.
4. *Oraḥ Ḥayyim* 92:10. See also R. Yitzḥak Zilberstein, *Ḥashukei Ḥemed, Berakhot* p. 85.
5. Psalms 17:15.
6. See *Taz*, 92:4.
7. *Halikhot Shlomo, Tefilla* 7:4.

the money prior so as to minimize any distraction. (Although some *poskim* do maintain that one is exempt from giving *tzedaka* during prayer itself, due to the rule of *"osek bemitzva patur min hamitzva."*)[8]

II. EXTENDING GREETINGS BEFORE PRAYER

Extending a greeting to a human being before praying to God in the morning[9] is considered inappropriate.[10] This behavior is criticized primarily when one goes to the house of another to offer greetings, an overt act of homage, before prayers.[11] The nature of this issue is explicit in Rashi's language:[12] "When one is supposed to be involved in the honor of heaven, it is forbidden to become involved in the honor of humans." As such, incidental greetings and common courtesy would not be included in this prohibition.

In addition, another element exists to this prohibition, that of avoiding the danger of forgetting to pray altogether. To address this issue, the Ra'avad[13] advocates utilization of alternative types of greetings, to serve as a reminder that prayer still awaits.[14] The length of time devoted to the greeting may also be a factor.[15]

This topic must be carefully analyzed, for, as R. Shmuel Baruch Ohayoun observes,[16] one who is unnecessarily stringent in this area may violate either

8. This question may hinge on an issue debated by halakhic authorities, some of whom have maintained that this principle does not exempt one from interpersonal obligations.
9. Whether this law is relevant to the afternoon and evening prayers as well is the topic of an analysis by R. Ephraim Greenblatt (*Rivevot Efraim* 1:63); he concludes that it is applicable only to the mornings.
10. *Berakhot* 14a; *Tur* and *Shulḥan Arukh, Oraḥ Ḥayyim* 89. See R. Ya'akov Reisher, *Responsa Shevut Ya'akov* 2:22; R. Yeḥezkel Landau, *Tziyun LeNefesh Ḥaya* to *Berakhot*; R. Betzalel Stern, *Responsa BeTzel HaḤokhma* 5:71 and 73; and R. Aharon Rosenfeld, *Responsa Minḥat Aharon* 1:19.
11. Ibid.; so, too, leniencies exist depending on the nature of the greeting used; note also *Pri Megadim, Mishna Berura*, and *Kaf HaḤayyim, Oraḥ Ḥayyim* 89l; *Orḥot Ḥayyim* 89:8; *Da'at Torah, Oraḥ Ḥayyim* 89:2; *Eliya Raba, Oraḥ Ḥayyim* 66:2, citing *Tashbetz* 246; and *Responsa Teshuvot VeHanhagot* 1:71.
12. *Berakhot*, ibid., s.v. *Ḥadlu Lakhem min HaAdam*.
13. Cited in *Ḥidushei HaRashba, Berakhot*, ibid.
14. See also *Pri Megadim, Oraḥ Ḥayyim* 89 and *Orḥot Ḥayyim*.
15. See *Ḥidushei HaRitva* to *Berakhot*. See also R. Mordechai Willig, *Am Mordechai* 10.
16. *Responsa Halikhot SheBa* 1.

the Talmudic prohibition of rejecting a greeting or the positive obligation of initiating a greeting.

INTERRUPTING KERIAT SHEMA TO GREET OTHERS

Nonetheless, once prayer has begun, various personal considerations do allow interruptions for the sake of greetings, at least during the recitation of *Keriat Shema* and its surrounding blessings.[17] These factors differ in weight and, consequently, in the nature of interruption that is allowed, as far as the point in the prayer service and whether the greeting is an initiation or a response.[18] The first such recognized consideration is *yira*, normally translated as "fear," which allows greetings even in the middle of the *Shema*. Rashi interprets this factor as fear for one's life; others disagree, noting such a concern would permit any violation and merit no special mention here. As such, the Rosh translates the term as the halakhic *mora*, or "awe," accorded to parents and *rabbanim*.[19] R. Yoel Sirkes[20] argues, noting that such awe is generally passive in nature, and upholds the position of Rashi, which is shared by Rambam. The Meiri modifies it slightly to mean fear for any kind of harm. The other consideration is *kavod*, "honor," which justifies interrupting between blessings; Rashi understands this as referring to a dignified individual, while Rambam[21] applies it to halakhic recipients of *kavod*, such as parents.[22] At some points in the recitation, greetings may be extended or returned only within these categories; at others, greetings may be exchanged with "any person." The details of these rules are codified in *Shulḥan Arukh*.[23]

Despite these dispensations, the *Mishna Berura*[24] notes that current

---

17. *Berakhot* 13a. See R. Ya'akov of Karlin, *Responsa Mishkenot Ya'akov, Oraḥ Ḥayyim* 83. As to whether these interruptions are permitted or actually obligated, see at length, R. Avraham Yitzḥak HaKohen Kook, *Tov Ro'i to Berakhot*. See also R. Yekutiel Yehudah Rosenberger, *Responsa Torat Yekutiel, Mahadura Kama, Oraḥ Ḥayyim* 46, and R. Eliyahu Ragoler, *Responsa Yad Eliyahu* 1:13 and 3:3.
18. The *Tosafot* (*Bava Kama* 73b, s.v. *Ki*) suggest that avoiding the "theft" inherent in returning a greeting is a fundamental motivation behind rabbinical sanction of these interruptions.
19. See also *Ḥidushei HaRashba* and *Tur, Oraḥ Ḥayyim* 65.
20. *Bayit Ḥadash* to *Tur*.
21. See *Kesef Mishneh, Hilkhot Keriat Shema* 2:15.
22. See *Eliya Raba* 66:1.
23. *Oraḥ Ḥayyim* 88.
24. *Mishna Berura*, 66:2.

synagogue norms and understandings generally obviate the need to interrupt prayer for greetings. However, it is important to ascertain that this is indeed the case in each instance, as this law is not a leniency, but rather reflects the obligations and priorities involved in extending greetings and honor to other people. R. Joseph B. Soloveitchik[25] explained this *halakha* as emanating from the lesson of Avraham, who interrupted a visit from God Himself in order to welcome guests. This action was a reflection of Avraham's awareness that respecting human dignity in this way was one of God's priorities and thus consistent with His will. As such, *Keriat Shema,* the acceptance of God's commandments, is an appropriate time to incorporate interpersonal responsibilities as well.

III. CONFLICTS BETWEEN HOSPITALITY AND PRAYING WITH A MINYAN

Despite the value and importance of praying with a *minyan,* there are times when other obligations present a conflict. One possible example of this is the *mitzva* of hosting guests (*hakhnasat orḥim*). R. Shlomo Zalman Auerbach[26] ruled, based on the statement of the Talmud[27] that "*hakhnasat orḥim* is greater than receiving the Divine Presence," that if one is hosting guests, and they will be uncomfortable being left alone, and no other family member can attend to their needs, that one should forgo communal prayer in favor of the *mitzva* of hospitality.

PRAYER ON AN AIRPLANE

Praying with a *minyan* on an airplane is fraught with difficulties, in that it often disturbs other passengers, wakes up people who are sleeping, interferes with the flight attendants, and causes a *ḥillul Hashem.* As such, *poskim* have ruled that it is preferable to pray without a *minyan,* and also to remain seated when doing so, if that is indicated by the circumstances.[28]

---

25. As quoted by R. Herschel Schachter, *MiPeninei HaRav* p. 271.
26. *Halikhot Shelomo*, ch. 5, in *Devar Halakha*, 25, and *Orḥot Halakha*, 52. See also R. Yitzḥak Zilberstein, *Responsa Avnei Choshen* III, 438–439.
27. *Shabbat* 127a.
28. See *Responsa Iggerot Moshe OḤ* IV, 20; *Halikhot Shlomo, Tefilla* p. 95; R. Shlomo Wahrman, *She'erit Yosef*, VII, 3; and R. Herschel Schachter's essay at http://www.torahweb.org/torah/special/2010/rsch_airplanes.html.

MAKING UP PRAYERS MISSED BECAUSE OF ATTENDING TO COMMUNAL NEEDS

One who is involved in a *mitzva* is exempt from interrupting and performing a second *mitzva* that presents itself. As such, one who is involved with *tzorkhei tzibbur*, such as answering an emergency medical call, is exempt from prayer. A question arises, however, as to whether one who misses a *Tefilla* is required to make it up with an extra *Shemoneh Esreh* after the following *Tefilla (tashlumin)*. The question apparently hinges on the following issue: is it understood that the individual is prevented from praying for valid reasons, and thus would be given an opportunity to make up the prayer;[29] or, rather, is it understood that the prior *mitzva* involvement literally exempts the individual from prayer completely, and thus no makeup is even necessary.[30] As the issue is disputed, the recommended practice is unclear. As such, it might be assumed that there is no obligation to make up the prayer (*Safek deRabbanan LeHakel*), while one may volunteer an optional additional prayer (*nedava*).[31]

IV. PRAYING OUT LOUD

One area that requires balancing one's own *Tefilla* needs with those of others pertains to the volume of one's prayers. The Talmud[32] rules that one should not pray out loud, noting that doing so could imply a lack of faith in a God Who can hear all prayers. After noting that one may need to raise one's voice in order to properly focus attention on the prayer and achieve the requisite *kavana*, the conclusion is that it is nonetheless inappropriate to do so in a public setting, as it will detract from the focus of others who are praying as well.

This ruling is codified in the *Shulḥan Arukh*,[33] while the Rema adds that it is permissible to pray loudly within one's house if doing so will be beneficial to the members of the household, in that it will teach them the text of the prayers. While some maintain the prohibition of loud prayer applies only to the *Shemoneh Esreh*,[34] others extended this even to *Pesukei DeZimra*.[35] There

---

29. *Taz, Yoreh De'ah* 341:5.
30. *Drisha*, cited in *Taz*. See also *Magen Avraham, Oraḥ Ḥayyim* 93, and *Mishna Berura* 93:4.
31. See R. Chanoch Padwa, *Responsa Ḥeshev HaEfod*, II, 46.
32. *Berakhot* 31a.
33. *Oraḥ Ḥayyim* 101:2.
34. See *Kaf HaḤayyim* 101:12.
35. See *Mishna Berura* 101:7.

are some opinions that the prayer on Rosh HaShana and Yom Kippur is an exception to this rule,[36] and one may pray aloud on those days, within reason; however, even this dispensation applies only to the established text, and not to personal prayers that one might add.[37]

PRAYING *SHEMONEH ESREH* IN A PLACE OR AT A TIME WHEN OTHERS ARE PREVENTED FROM WALKING PAST

The *Halakha* prohibits walking within four *amot* of one who is praying the *Shemoneh Esreh*. In one sense, this *halakha* reflects sensitivity to the one who is praying, and the need to not interfere with his concentration by walking in front of him. (In addition, there is also the concern of invading the space that is at that time graced by the presence of the *Shekhina*.)

However, sensitivity need also be extended to those who are not currently at prayer and would be affected by this *halakha*. As such, it is important for the one praying to be aware of the potential difficulty caused by choice of location, particularly if one will be praying either longer than others or at a time and/or place not dedicated for prayer, and to decide accordingly on a considerate place to stand when praying.[38] If one does pray in an area that is used as a public passageway and is not set aside for prayer, some *poskim* maintain that it is permissible for others to walk in front of him.[39] Similarly, even within a synagogue, *poskim* allow one to pass in front of a praying individual if this is the only way to perform a communal *mitzva*, ruling the needs of the public outweigh the needs of the individual.[40]

---

36. See *Shulḥan Arukh* 101:3 and Rema, and *Mishna Berura* #11.
37. See *Ḥashukei Ḥemed, Berakhot* p. 192.
38. See the discussion in R. Moshe Sternbuch, *Responsa Teshuvot VeHanhagot*, I, 75. See also R. Yitzḥak Ya'akov Fox, *Halikhot Bein Adam LeḤaveiro*, introduction, sec. 8, fn 11 and 12.
39. See R. Betzalel Stern, *Responsa BeTzeil HaḤokhma*, VI, 30. R. Stern maintains, in disagreement with his questioner, that this license would only apply outside of a synagogue, and not within a synagogue, even if one is praying in a passageway rather than in the section devoted to prayer. R. Sternbuch maintains that the question may hinge on the reason for the prohibition: if the concern is disturbing the one at prayer, the latter may not be entitled to such consideration if he has appropriated a public space. If the concern is interfering with the *Shekhina*, this consideration may be irrelevant.
40. See *Teshuvot VeHanhagot*, ibid., citing *Responsa Yad Eliyahu*, 6.

AWAKENING A SLEEPING PERSON FOR PRAYER

The prohibition against disturbing the sleep of another is branded with the stigma of theft (*gezel sheina*).[41] Thus, the question arises as whether one may awaken another who is at risk of oversleeping and missing the appointed times for prayer.

Many *poskim*[42] are reluctant to allow this except in cases of clear biblical obligation (such as *Keriat Shema*), unless there is prior indication or a reliable assumption that awakening the sleeping individual would be in consonance with his wishes.

R. Shimon Sofer[43] considers an act of greater premeditation: altering another's alarm clock in order to create a situation in which he will wake up earlier for prayer. This also involves issues of dishonesty, and R. Sofer's conclusion is to recommend against this course of action.[44]

Poskim are stricter in requiring the awakening of those who fall asleep wearing *tefillin*, which is independently forbidden.[45]

USING OTHER'S PROPERTY FOR PRAYER

In general, using an item without an owner's permission is considered theft, and it is not permissible to perform *mitzvot* through theft.[46] However, if one needs to borrow a *siddur* or *tefillin* belonging to another who is not present to give permission, it can sometimes be presumed that "one is agreeable

---

41. See *Responsa Keren LeDavid*, 18.
42. See, for example, R. Moshe Sternbuch, *Responsa Teshuvot VeHanhagot* II, 50; R. Aharon Rosenfeld *Responsa Minḥat Aharon*, vol. 3, *Oraḥ Ḥayyim* 180. (His discussion focuses on a person who has fallen asleep accidentally and thus has the status of being a transgressor against his will – "*onus*.")
43. *Responsa Hitorerut Teshuva, Oraḥ Ḥayyim* 36.
44. On dishonesty in *mitzvot*, see R. Ya'akov Yichizkiyahu Fish, *Titen Emet LeYa'akov, Responsa* 4.
45. See R. Raphael Evers, *Responsa VeShav VeRafa* 1:2, and see also R. Yochanan Segal Vosner, *Responsa Ḥayyei HaLevi* 3:45:13.
46. As to whether or not the use of someone else's *siddur* without permission would disqualify the prayer, see *Sefer Ḥasidim*, 772 with commentary *Brit Olam* of the *Ḥida*; R. Yekutiel Yehuda Halberstam, *Responsa Divrei Yatziv*, *OḤ* 84; and R. Yitzḥak Zilberstein, *VeHa'arev Na*, pp. 415–416. R. Zilberstein also discusses whether any disqualification attaches in a situation of theft of a less tangible nature, e.g., theft of time (he considers the question of the effectiveness of a *minyan* formed at the unnecessary expense of keeping nonparticipants waiting).

to having a *mitzva* performed with his property (*niḥa lei dilitavad mitzva bimamonei*)."[47]

Based on that principle, one may use another's *mitzva* article[48] if all of the following conditions are present: (a) the owner has not expressed his refusal to allow his property to be used, and it is not possible to get his explicit permission at the moment;[49] (b) care is taken not to damage or depreciate the property in any way;[50] (c) the item is found accessible in a public space;[51] (d) the item is not moved to a different location; (e) this is done only occasionally, and not regularly.[52]

Whether one uses the property of another individual or communal property, in both cases a priority is to return the item in its original condition to its original location. In the case of communal property, this is required as well out of consideration for others who would look to use the item.[53]

FIGHTING AND ARGUING OVER SYNAGOGUE HONORS AND LEADERSHIP OF THE SERVICE

Often, synagogues are the scene of conflict, when members clash over the opportunity for a *kibbud* or other type of participation in the service. While the combatants may consider their dispute to be "for the sake of heaven," this is categorically rejected in a sweeping statement by the *Magen Avraham*.[54] The Rema, discussing the laws governing communal prayer, rules that no individual may lead the congregation against the will of the members.[55] In this context, the *Magen Avraham* writes, "One is not to quarrel over any *mitzva*." His source for this

---

47. *Bekhorot* 18b, etc.
48. *Shulḥan Arukh, Oraḥ Ḥayyim* 14:4.
49. See *Mishna Berura* 14:13. See also *Responsa Iggerot Moshe OḤ* V, 20, who asserts that it can be presumed that one who leaves his *tallit* in synagogue is willing to allow others to use it, as he knows that this will be the assumption of those who find it there.
50. For this reason, the Rema (14:4) forbids taking books, under the assumption that all usage depreciates them. By contrast, others feel that a *tallit* is more of a personal item subject to the owner's likely refusal to lend; see *Responsa Tzitz Eliezer*, XII, 7.
51. See *Arukh HaShulḥan* 14:12.
52. See *Mishna Berura* ibid. On this issue in general, see *Halikhot Bein Adam LeḤavero*, introduction, sec. 5.
53. See *VeEin Lamo Mikhshol*, III, pp. 33–34 and R. Yisrael Ya'akov Kanievsky, *Kreina Delgrita* I, p. 78.
54. *Oraḥ Ḥayyim* 53:26.
55. *Oraḥ Ḥayyim* 53:22, citing the *Responsa Binyamin Ze'ev* 183.

principle is a Talmudic statement concerning Kohanim looking to partake in the consumption of the limited *Leḥem HaPanim*: "*Vehatznu'im moshkhim et yedeihem* – and the modest ones [i.e., the refined ones] would draw back their hands."[56]

The *Maḥatzit HaShekel* questions the *Magen Avraham*'s extrapolation from this passage to all *mitzvot*,[57] but concedes, however, that any occasion falling short of a complete *mitzva* certainly cannot justify quarrelling. He further restricts his objection by suggesting that if a quarrel is inevitable, and not merely possible, he would concede to the *Magen Avraham* that even an actual *mitzva* does not warrant such engagement.[58] Many authorities rise to defend the *Magen Avraham* against even the modified limitations of the *Maḥatzit HaShekel*.[59] Further, R. Ya'akov Ariel[60] notes that the *Magen Avraham*'s words are not referring to a situation where the religious needs will go unfulfilled; rather, his position is addressed toward those who would fight over their own opportunity to be the one to perform the *mitzva*. In any event, the margin of disagreement is minor; the *Magen Avraham*'s admonition against quarrelling over *mitzvot* is applicable, even according to his detractors, to anything short of a complete, genuine *mitzva* obligation, and perhaps even then if a quarrel is a definite outcome.[61]

Thus, the very introduction of an environment of combativeness into the arena of spiritual behavior is anathema to the halakhic spirit. This is certainly true when it comes to communal activities in which the individual hopes his

56. See also *Be'er Heitev* and R. Gedalya Felder, *Gilyonei Yeshurun, Yoma* 39a.
57. See also R. Eliezer Zusman Sofer's glosses to R. Yaakov Alfandari's *Responsa Mutzal MeEish* 51, and R. Meshulam Roth's *Responsa Kol Mevaser* 2:28.
58. A similar objection is noted by the *Ḥatam Sofer, Hagahot to Shulḥan Arukh, Oraḥ Ḥayyim* 53, as well as *Responsa Oraḥ Ḥayyim* 49 and *Kovetz Teshuvot* 3.
59. See R. Shimon Greenfeld, *Responsa Maharshag* 3:16 and R. Shlomo Reizner, *Ginzei Ḥayyim, Oraḥ Ḥayyim* 53:9. R. Yitzḥak Motchen, in the journal *Otzerot Yerushalayim* 34:542 also supports the *Magen Avraham*'s position. See also *Likutei He'arot* to *Responsa Ḥatam Sofer, Oraḥ Ḥayyim* 49, for a detailed explanation of the *mitzvot* relevant to eating sanctified foods, and the relevance of this analysis to this Talmudic passage.
60. *Responsa BeOhela Shel Torah*, vol. 1, 4:5. R. Ariel points out that this distinction is also in the *Mishna Berura* (53:5).
61. R. Ovadia Yosef (*Responsa Yabia Omer*, vol. 7, *Oraḥ Ḥayyim* 23:4) quotes the *Magen Avraham* without noting any dissent, instead recording the approving citation of his words in the *Knesset HaGedola* (#153) and by R. Chaim Yosef David Azulai in *Emet LeYa'akov* (*Mitzvot Sefer Torah* 3) and *LeDavid Emet* (2:3).

heightened participation will reap additional merit for him; in these instances the loss engendered by the belligerence will easily outweigh any benefit. R. Ovadia Yosef expresses this directly, advising a family fractured by dissension on the issue of a proper memorial for a beloved relative, writing that the soul of the deceased will profit much more from harmony among his family than from any specific gesture marred by dispute.[62] Further, R. Moshe Dov Wolner[63] observes that these concepts are found in the Talmud in relation to the consumption of sanctified foods, an area of *Halakha* that specifically mandates dignity in its details. This translates itself most particularly to the parallel topic of leading in prayer, which is often the source of much debate on the communal level.

Rambam enters these concerns into his halakhic codification, specifically in his treatment of the edible gifts to which Kohanim are entitled. "A Kohen should not grab the gifts," he writes,[64] "nor should he ask for them verbally; rather, if he is given them with dignity, he should take them. And when there are many people in the slaughterhouse, the modest draw back their hands, while the gluttons take." The reserved manner appropriate for Kohanim is emblematic of the proper conduct in all things, and certainly in prayer.[65]

CORRECTING BA'ALEI KERIA

A sensitive area of balance in a synagogue setting is the question of correcting those who are reading the Torah for the congregation. While it is important that the Torah be read precisely and accurately, there exists a serious concern that correcting the reader in an insensitive manner may cause him embarrassment, and thus constitute a serious transgression.[66] In order to minimize compromising either side of this equation, the following practices should be enacted: (a) care should be taken to appoint readers who are fluent, conscientious, and adequately prepared; (b) a single individual should be tasked with

62. See similarly R. Avigdor Neventzahl, *Siḥot LeSefer Bemidbar*, p. 288.
63. *Responsa Ḥemdat Tzvi* 2:3.
64. *Mishneh Torah, Hilkhot Bikkurim* 9:22.
65. For an interpretation more specific to the laws of gifts of the Kohanim, see R. Yechiel Michel Charlop's *Torat Ḥof Yamim*.
66. Reflecting this tension, the *Tur, Oraḥ Ḥayyim* 142, records a dispute among the *Rishonim* as to how this situation should be handled.

the responsibility of correcting mistakes, and this individual should be standing close to the Torah and thus able to correct in a discreet manner; (c) the one correcting should be knowledgable in the laws of what constitutes a mistake requiring correction, thus assuring that he will not interrupt in an incorrect or unnecessary manner.[67]

DELAYING THE CONGREGATION THROUGH PROLONGED PERSONAL PRAYER

A recurring principle in the laws of the synagogue is the need to avoid unnecessary burdening of the congregation, primarily through delays of the service when a good portion of the congregation will be forced to stand idle. As such, when the congregation is awaiting the beginning of the repetition of the *Shemoneh Esreh*, there is the concern that there will be a significant lag between the point at which most of the congregation completes their silent prayer and the *Shaliaḥ Tzibbur* beginning. While the pace of prayer need not be dictated by the fastest *Shemoneh Esreh* of the congregation, those individuals who might cause a delay at this point should be mindful to not overburden the congregation by praying significantly longer that the average member.[68] These individuals might include (a) the *Shaliaḥ Tzibbur* himself; (b) the rabbi, or any person for whom the *Shaliaḥ Tzibbur* waits before starting; (c) one who is part of an exact *minyan* of ten, and thus must be ready to answer before the *Shaliaḥ Tzibbur* can start the repetition.[69]

TALKING DURING PRAYERS, AND OBJECTING

One who talks during the prayer service, particularly during those points when one is forbidden to interrupt, is committing a transgression between man and God while at the same time grievously offending his fellow congregants. This is so, both because of the physical obstruction to prayer and decorum, and because of the spiritual impact on the communal unit, whose prayer Is correspondingly flawed. As such, it is the right and the obligation of the other congregants to object to this behavior. Nonetheless, care and sensitivity

67. See, at length, R. Moshe Rosenberg, "Correcting the *Ba'al Koreh*: Punctilious Performance vs. Public Embarrassment," in the *Journal of Halacha and Contemporary Society*, LVIII, pp. 5–44.
68. See *Berakhot* 31a and Rambam, *Hilkhot Tefilla* 6:2.
69. See *Halikhot Bein Adam LeḤaveiro*, introduction, sec. 7.

should be taken so that the objection be conveyed in a way that is effective and appropriate in light of the responsibilities of interpersonal interaction.[70]

RESPECT TOWARD WHAT OTHERS ARE DOING IN SYNAGOGUE

It is important to show respect for what the congregation is doing, even if one would not otherwise be participating. For example, this is one reason cited why one should bow with the congregation and join in in the recitation of *Aleinu,* or of *Ashrei,* even if one is not currently praying.[71] Conversely, R. Joseph B. Soloveitchik explained the practice of those with living parents leaving the synagogue during *Yizkor,* as it would not be respectful to be present during that recitation without participating.[72]

SENSITIVITY TO A VISITOR SITTING IN ONE'S *MAKOM KAVUA*

It is appropriate for one to establish a set place within the synagogue where one regularly prays (*Makom Kavua*),[73] which is considered a significant enhancement to one's prayer. Nonetheless, if one comes to synagogue and sees that a guest has inadvertently taken one's seat, hospitality and sensitivity to the guest's embarrassment should take priority, and one should sit elsewhere rather than offend the visitor. This is the case even if one's concentration will be significantly diminished by sitting in a different seat. The best practice is for the synagogue to have officials who are charged with the task of welcoming visitors and guiding them to open seats, so as to avoid conflict.[74]

KISSING A CRYING CHILD IN THE SYNAGOGUE

In general, there is a prohibition against kissing one's children while in

---

70. See *Responsa Ateret Moshe* 1, 72, and *Ḥashukei Ḥemed, Berakhot* pp. 124–125. For a discussion of the precise parameters of the obligation to object to talkers during prayer, and the balance of that obligation with the prohibition of embarrassing others, see the journal *Torat HaAdam LeAdam*, VI, pp. 214–219.
71. *Mishna Berura* 65:9; see also *Responsa Ohr LeTziyon*, II, p. 78 and *VeEin Lamo Mikhshol*, III, pp. 31–32.
72. See *Nefesh HaRav* p. 153, and *Maḥzor Mesoret HaRav, Hanhagot HaRav* #78, based on *Berakhot* 20b.
73. *Shulḥan Arukh, Oraḥ Ḥayyim* 90:19, based on *Berakhot* 7b.
74. See the discussion in R. Yitzḥak Zilberstein, *Aleinu LeShabe'aḥ*, II, p. 583, responsum 10.

synagogue, in order to establish that no love is equal to that of God.[75] However, if a child is hurt or otherwise distressed, to kiss the child in order to soothe is not included in this prohibition.[76]

INTERPERSONAL REQUIREMENTS FOR PARTICIPATING IN BIRKAT KOHANIM

It should be noted that Kohanim who take part in blessing the congregation have additional responsibilities regarding their interpersonal attitudes, at least in theory. The *Magen Avraham*[77] states, based on the *Zohar*, that a Kohen who does not have a loving relationship with the congregation may not participate in the blessing, as reflected in the fact that the Kohanim are required to first recite a *berakha* on the *mitzva* of blessing the people "*BeAhava,*" or "with love."[78] In practice, however, this is not investigated.[79]

A further, related issue concerns the Talmudic equation of humiliating others to homicide. R. Natan Gestetner, in his responsa,[80] considers an issue relevant to evaluating the comparison. A Kohen who has killed someone is prohibited from partaking in the *Birkat Kohanim*.[81] Would a Kohen who embarrasses others be similarly excluded? R. Gestetner proceeds to analyze the issue, noting the debated question of martyrdom to avoid shaming others. He concludes leniently, citing a supporting implication in the *Responsa Ralbaḥ*,[82] finding the comparison to be less than total. He concurrently advances a technical argument, proving that even were the severity of humiliation equivalent to (or worse than, as he notes in the name of the *Penei Yehoshua*) homicide, this Kohen would nonetheless not be excluded; the category is limited to

75. *Shulḥan Arukh, Oraḥ Ḥayyim* 98:1.
76. See R. Yitzḥak Zilberstein, *Aleinu LeShabe'aḥ*, II, p. 578, responsum 5, and R. Herschel Schachter, cited in R. Moshe Schapiro, *Ketonet Yosef*, p. 632.
77. *Oraḥ Ḥayyim* 128:18.
78. See also R. Sholom Rivkin, in the journal *HaDarom*, XL, pp. 45–46.
79. See *Responsa Da'at Sofer, OḤ* 13.
80. *Responsa LeHorot Natan* VIII, 2.
81. *Berakhot* 32b, and *Shulḥan Arukh, Oraḥ Ḥayyim* 128:35. See, at length, R. Yitzḥak Fishberg, *Nesiat Kapayim*, pp. 186–194.
82. Number 117, referred to in the *Magen Avraham, Oraḥ Ḥayyim* 128:153. The Ralbaḥ considers the instance of a Kohen, guilty of many offenses, repeatedly humiliating others among them. However, in evaluating his status for the purposes of *Birkat Kohanim*, he does not take the embarrassments into account.

physical murder, as indicated by Talmud, citing the verse, "your hands are filled with blood."[83] The identical conclusion is reached in a responsum by R. Shmuel Wosner.[84] Nonetheless, R. Baruch Weiss, in an independent analysis of the issue in his book-length treatment of the laws of *Birkat Kohanim*,[85] reaches a stringent conclusion and forbids such a Kohen from partaking in the blessing.

DONATIONS TO THE SYNAGOGUE

In general, a commitment, or a *neder,* toward charitable purposes is treated more stringently than other commitments. Reflections of this stringency include the possibility that the commitment may be binding even if it is not verbalized; the inability to reverse one's intent even within the *tokh kedei dibbur* period of a few seconds; and general restrictions and limitations on having the *neder* nullified. It is likely that commitments of donations to the synagogue are of a similar nature and should be taken very seriously.[86]

An additional consideration is relevant to the pledges made during the *Mi Sheberakh* recited during *Keriat HaTorah.* While there is some debate as to whether these constitute actual *nedarim,*[87] there is an additional aspect to these statements that was emphasized by R. Soloveitchik. The Talmud[88] is critical of *"iyun tefilla,"* which, in the view of some *Rishonim,*[89] refers to the idea of one who prays and feels unwarranted confidence that his prayers will be answered. Accordingly, R. Soloveitchik felt that it was inappropriate for the

83. Isaiah 1:15, brought in *Berakhot* 32b; see *Tosafot, Yevamot* 7a, s.v. *SheNe'amar*, who explain that hands used for murder cannot then be effective in prayer. Although a similar conclusion might be reached as to the appropriateness of a mouth that has embarrassed another being used to pronounce the prayer, this is nonetheless not explicitly within the text.
84. *Responsa Shevet HaLevi*, VIII, 172.
85. *Birkhot Horai* 23:12:9.
86. See the discussions of the various sides of these issues in R. Ya'akov Yeshaya Bloi, *Tzedaka uMishpat*, ch. 4, 4–5 and in footnotes.
87. See *Responsa Maharsham* I, *maftehot* to *YD* 76 (#201); *Responsa Erekh Shai YD* 203; *Responsa Shevet HaLevi* IV, 125; *Responsa Dovev Meisharim* I, 87. See also *Tzedaka uMishpat*, ibid, n. 12.
88. *Rosh HaShana* 16b.
89. See *Tosafot*, ibid.

Mi Sheberakhs to attribute their efficacy to the fact of the prayer itself (*ba'avur shekol hakahal mitpalelim ba'avuro,* etc.) but rather a pledge of *tzedaka* must be made (and, presumably, honored) for the *Mi Sheberakh* to be appropriate.[90]

MAINTAINING AN ATMOSPHERE OF SHALOM IN THE SYNAGOGUE

In light of all of the above, it is considered crucial and fundamental that the atmosphere of the synagogue be one of *shalom*. The Radbaz[91] points out that in choosing a synagogue, and a seat within the synagogue, the ability to get along with the surrounding congregants must be taken seriously into account.[92] He even goes as far as to consider, although prefacing with an apprehensive *lulei demistafina,* "were that I were not afraid," that praying at home without a *minyan* is preferable to joining one that will lead to an experience of disharmony. R. Yehoshua Tzvi Michel Shapiro[93] endorses the overall concept, while disagreeing with the last detail; he infers that this is also the position of R. Yonatan Eibshutz[94] and assumes that the Radbaz, too, would agree for practical purposes. What is indisputable, however, is that every effort and priority must be placed upon ensuring that the synagogue is a place of respect, mutual concern, sensitivity, love, and harmony. ◆

90. As quoted by R. Herschel Schachter, *Nefesh HaRav* p. 143.
91. *Responsa Radbaz* III, 472.
92. See also R. Betzalel Stern, *Responsa BeTzeil HaḤokhma* IV, 19:7, citing *Mesader Ḥilukim VeShitot* 53.
93. *Kuntres Imrot Tehorot*, ch. 12.
94. Comments printed in *Sefer Halakha Aḥarona* and *Kuntres Hara'ayot in Sefer HaPardes*, p. 8b.

Why Prayer Requires a Fixed Place and Fixed Texts

R. Yechiel Yaakov Weinberg

> The Beraita states: Abba Binyamin said: "Prayer is only answered if it is said in a synagogue, as it says: לשמוע אל הרינה ואל התפילה, 'To hear the song and the prayer' (II Kings 8:28). That is, where there is *song* there is *prayer*." Rashi says: In a synagogue the congregation sings God's praises with sweet and harmonious sounds. (*Berakhot* 6a)

In this statement the sages sought to strengthen the connection between set prayer and the location of prayer. They understood that prayer requires permanence and regularity, whether as regards prayer texts or having a fixed place in the synagogue where one regularly prays.

Even in earlier times there were those who opposed the notion that prayer requires such continuity. They said, "Prayer is best when it emerges spontaneously from a person's heart, flowing from pure emotion," for they claimed that it is impossible to have *kavana* or feel spiritually uplifted when surrounded by large numbers of people. They advocated withdrawal from other people so as to experience solitude when praying, and they also favored the freedom to formulate one's own prayer in order to express the deepest outpourings and truest longings of the soul.

But the sages understood what the end result of leaving prayer up to every individual would be, and what would happen were prayer only a matter of individual choice, without a fixed structure or place. People would slowly feel more and more "liberated" from any need to pray whatsoever, and ultimately all prayer would cease, together with any genuine religious sensibility.

For this reason they insisted on maintaining the fixed nature of prayer, to ensure its continuity, and to facilitate its real purpose, which is to be an educational vehicle that teaches us how to serve God. Thus fixed prayer stimulates and prepares the individual for approaching his or her Creator.

From such permanence and structure in prayer we can experience spiritual elevation and a prayerful state of mind. Regularity in the form and place of prayer is thus the means by which a person can maintain and enhance a prayerful state of mind. ◆

The Efficacy of Prayer

R. Aharon Lichtenstein

When we ask ourselves about the efficacy of prayer, we are speaking, in the first sense, about the efficacy of *bakasha* (petition): Are we granted what we request? Idealists, ranging from the mystics to Kant, have expressed opposition to the entire enterprise of *bakasha*, claiming it is selfish and egocentric. This position, however, is not characteristic of Judaism. We neither countenance nor encourage a sense of human independence, the feeling that we could somehow manage on our own. Indeed, we do not think that there is anything idealistic or self-sacrificing in thinking we can fend for ourselves.

It is an open question whether or not the essence of religion relates to the sense of dependence, as Schleiermacher stated and as the Maharal, *lehavdil*, suggested before him; perhaps other elements are the quintessence of Judaism. But the sense of dependence and the recognition of human need, and the subsequent turning to the *Ribbono shel Olam* for succor and sustenance, are certainly critical. According to the sages (*Berakhot* 10a–b), this is the import of the verses that speak of Hezekiah's illness (II Kings 20, Is. 38) – when one is in need, one should turn to the *Ribbono shel Olam* with *bakasha*.

However, *tefilla* can be considered efficacious regardless of whether there is a positive response to the request that is presented. *Tefilla* is listed among the three elements about which we declare on the High Holy Days that they revoke the evil decree: *teshuva, tefilla,* and *tzedaka*. What is common to all three is that they can be effective by making one into a better person, a better *oved* or *ovedet Hashem* (servant of God), thereby nullifying the previously issued decree. Accordingly, not only *bakasha*, but also the prayer of *shevaḥ* (praise) and the prayer of *hoda'a* (thanksgiving) are certainly part of *avodat Hashem*, and they too can lead to the desired result.

Thus, we confront the question of the efficacy of *bakasha* on two planes. First, is our request answered? Second, are we worthy, or worthier, of its being

---

This essay was adapted by R. Reuven Ziegler, R. Dov Karoll, and Meira Mintz from an address delivered on December 7, 2003.

answered by dint of the fact that we have turned to the *Ribbono shel Olam* and acknowledged His control "like a servant before his Master," thereby giving expression to the quality of our relationship with Him? Every time one prays properly, whether one says so explicitly or not, implicit in the *tefilla* is the declaration, "*Ana avda deKudsha berikh Hu* – I am a servant of the Holy One, blessed is He." This is the essence of *avodat Hashem*, service of God. The Maharal properly noted that this *avoda* is related to servitude, the sense of subservience to the *Ribbono shel Olam* that is the essence of religious life; "*Avadai hem* – They are My servants" (Lev. 25:42, 55).

Thus, a *ma'amin* believes that his prayers are efficacious in some way even if the particular request he makes is not granted. R. Soloveitchik often emphasized that *tefilla* is essentially an experience of standing before the King. During the *Amida* in particular, one does not send a missive to the *Ribbono shel Olam*, but rather stands before Him, like a servant before his Master. Even the great *mitzva* of *Keriat Shema* does not entail the awe and trembling that accompany the *Amida*, when one stands before the King Himself. This is the reason, according to Rashi (*Berakhot* 25a), that while minimal clothing is sufficient for the recitation of the *Shema*, it does not suffice for the *Amida*. For the *Amida*, one must conduct himself as one standing before royalty, while for Keriat Shema, one is not talking before the King, but rather making a statement about Him. There are numerous *halakhot* regarding how one must prepare oneself prior to *tefilla* to create the proper environment for one's interaction with God, based on the principle of "*Hikkon likrat Elokekha Yisrael* – Prepare to meet your God, Israel" (Amos 4:12; see *Shabbat* 10a).

Thus, *tefilla* is a stance, a position, a presentation, and a communication. It entails seeking and attaining some measure of contact with the *Ribbono shel Olam*. That contact is not simply an opportunity to present what we need. Rather, the very contact with the *Ribbono shel Olam* is itself meaningful and purgative; it brings one to heights of experience and of personality that are otherwise beyond one's reach. Anyone who has had the experience of contact with a great person knows that a sense of greatness rubs off through that contact. That sense is infinitesimal compared to what is produced through contact with the *Ribbono shel Olam*!

Thus, a prayer for a particular response that fails to achieve that goal is not wasted or ineffective. There is merit and significance to the very turning to

the *Ribbono shel Olam*, a deepening and intensification of one's sense of His Presence. Prayer can be effective by ennobling and uplifting the one praying, by making him or her a better person and a better *oved/et Hashem*. In that respect, *tefilla* is efficacious even when, for whatever reasons, the *Ribbono shel Olam* chooses not to respond to our prayers in the way we had hoped.

But there is another level of efficacy as well. The verse tells us, "*Tov laḥasot baHashem mibeto'aḥ ba'adam* – It is better to seek refuge in the Lord than to trust in man" (Ps. 118:8). In what sense is this good? From a certain perspective, it is *tov* because it produces results. We believe that the possibility that our prayers will produce results is indeed there, and we turn, humbly and with an outstretched hand, imploring that we be given what we need. There is also, as stated above, a sense of "*tov laḥasot*" that is not simply prudential and pragmatic, but rather spiritual and ennobling. Finally, there is a third sense of "*tov laḥasot*" that straddles the line between the pragmatic and the idealistic.

One of the seven *Haftarot* of consolation begins with the prophet speaking in God's name, "*Anokhi, Anokhi Hu menaḥemkhem* – I, even I, am your comforter" (Is. 51:12). The *Midrash* (*Yalkut Shimoni, Isaiah*, 474) expands upon this verse, explaining that there are times when no human comfort is available, even that of a mother or father – only *Anokhi, Anokhi Hu menaḥemkhem*. That sense of comfort derives in part from the sheer presence of the *Ribbono shel Olam*; it need not be verbalized by Him or by the human. People in need of comfort can be consoled through an embrace; often, in fact, such a gesture is more significant, more genuine, and more profound to a mourner than any statement that could be articulated in words. A hug is an expression of commiseration, of participation in pain, of empathy at its deepest level.

"*Tov laḥasot baHashem*" – there is goodness that results from the sheer presence of the *Ribbono shel Olam*. In our moments of greatest trial and need, in our hours of greatest crisis, His presence is comforting, to the same extent that it is humbling. In times of pain, prayer reminds us that our tower of strength is there, the Source of being, the Source of all good and all value and all worth. Much has been lost, yet we still have the *Ribbono shel Olam* – and that in and of itself is a source of sustenance and comfort. There is efficacy to prayer on a psychological level, above and beyond its practical and spiritual effects.

We are comforted when we turn to the *Ribbono shel Olam* in times of crisis,

but He also sometimes turns to us to offer comfort, as it were. The *Midrashim* describe that when we cry when tragedy strikes, the *Ribbono shel Olam* cries with us, *kivyakhol*. When we transcend the anthropomorphic component of this description, we are left with the sense that our pain is not only our own; it is shared at the ultimate level by *Malkhut Shamayim*, by God Himself. "*Ke'ish asher imo tinaḥmenu, ken Anokhi anaḥemkhem* – As a man is comforted by his mother, so shall I comfort you" (Is. 66:13). When a mother comforts her child who has suffered a terrible tragedy, she does not stand there dispassionately; her presence is comforting because she cries along with her child. The *Ribbono shel Olam* similarly comforts us with His "tears."

"*Tov lahasot baHashem*" is a pillar of our faith and of our very existence. In that respect, *tefilla* is certainly efficacious – if we understand the ultimate purpose of prayer in all its fullness. ◆

Fundamentals of Prayer

R. Yehuda Amital

I. THE MERIT OF PRAYER

In Isaiah's prophecy, God declares: "I shall make them rejoice in My house of prayer" (56:7). Indeed, man, who was created in the image of God, enjoys an enormous privilege in that God has made it possible for him to pray. Humanity would look different – more sad, more dejected – were it not for this privilege which has been bestowed upon us.

But can a person come before the Creator of the universe, the "great and mighty and awesome God," with his personal, seemingly petty, requests? At first glance, it would seem that this type of petition is out of place.

The Gemara teaches:

> In every place that you find God's greatness, you also find His humility. This idea is found in the Torah and reiterated in the Prophets and again in the Writings.
>
> It is written in the Torah (Deut. 10:17), "For the Lord your God is the God of gods, and Lord of lords, the great and mighty and awesome God Who shows no favor and takes no bribe." The next verse continues, "He does justice to the orphan and the widow, and loves the stranger, providing him food and clothing." [What an enormous gap separates the concept of the "great and mighty and awesome God" from He Who "loves the stranger, providing him food and clothing"!]
>
> In the Prophets it says (Is. 57:15), "For so says the high and lofty One, Who inhabits eternity and Whose name is holy: I dwell in a high and holy place, yet also with he who is of low and humble spirit, to revive the spirit of the humble, and to revive the heart of the lowly."
>
> And in the Writings it says (Ps. 68:5–6), "Praise He Who rides upon the clouds...and rejoice before Him. Father of orphans and champion of widows, God is in His holy dwelling place." (*Megilla* 31a)

This essay appeared in his book *Jewish Values in a Changing World* (Jersey City: Ktav, 2005), 117–129. It was adapted by Aviad Hacohen from an oral discourse and was translated from Hebrew by Kaeren Fish with Reuven Ziegler.

God's greatness is of a scale where the difference between the sun and moon and food and clothing is obliterated. This is a philosophical response, perhaps one which satisfies our theological hesitations, but it falls short of providing an existential answer. From an existential point of view the problem remains: Can I turn to God with my small, personal problems?

In truth, God has inculcated in man the feeling that not only is he able to pray, but that God "hears the prayer of every mouth," that He listens to every prayer and every type of request, in whatever form it comes.

King David declared, "I pour out my complaint before Him; I lay my trouble before Him" (Ps. 142:3). How comforting it is for a person to be able to pour out his troubles before God! A world which has lost its faith in God seeks alternatives: psychologists, doctors, social workers – anyone who will listen. A person should be eternally grateful for the possibility of pouring out his heart to God: "I cry aloud to the Lord; I appeal to the Lord for mercy" (Ps. 142:2).

There is a level still higher than this: "My words will be sweet to Him; I shall rejoice in the Lord" (Ps. 104:34). In the midst of man's deliberations as to whether he is able existentially to turn to God, he receives the good tidings: "My words will be sweet to Him." My prayer finds favor in His eyes. Were it not for the existence of this verse, we wouldn't dream of suggesting such an idea. Like a mother who enjoys listening to the babbling of her infant, so – as it were – God enjoys listening to our prayers.

Can there be any greater joy than this? Someone is hearing us; someone is ready to listen. Sometimes we pass a beggar in the street and give him a few coins, and he thanks us over and over again. We do not stop to listen to him, but he continues nevertheless, feeling a need to thank us. Sometimes a person confides in a close friend and pours out all his sorrows, while thinking to himself, "Why am I muddling his thoughts with my problems; why am I wasting his time?"

But in the case of our prayers to God, "My words will be sweet to Him; I shall rejoice in the Lord." God turns to man, as it were, and says, "I am waiting and eager to hear you."

II. CONNECTION TO GOD

Yet another dimension is included in prayer, and that is the constant contact

with God. The "Holy Jew" of Peshiskhe once questioned the severity of the snake's curse in the Garden of Eden, "You shall eat dust all the days of your life" (Gen. 3:14). What is so bad about that? He is assured of food every day, at every hour, continually! The curse, he explained, was that the snake now had no need of contact with God.

The Gemara (*Yevamot* 64a) says, "The Matriarchs were barren only because God desired their prayers." Sometimes God may send us troubles because He desires to hear our voice: "For your voice is sweet and your appearance lovely" (Song. 2:14).

The Torah recounts the story of Isaac blessing his sons (Gen. 27). Jacob is blessed with the words, "May God give you of the dew of heaven and the fatness of the earth, abundance of new grain and wine," while Esau is blessed as follows: "Behold, your dwelling shall enjoy the fatness of the earth, and of the dew of heaven above." What is the difference between them? The *Midrash* (*Bereshit Raba* 66:3) explains: "[Jacob's blessing starts,] 'May God give you' – i.e., may He give, and give again." Esau, on the other hand, need have no worries. He has an "insurance policy." Jacob has to turn to God for the fulfillment of every wish, great or small. That which is taken for granted by Esau is something for which Jacob will have to ask.

Let me share with you a conversation I had with the director of a large retirement home in Miami. The residents' children all lived far away – for example, in New York, Washington, or Chicago. There were three categories of children. Some sent a check every month to their parents. Sometimes the son or daughter would include a short note, sometimes not even that. In any event, the parent knew that the child remembered him every month. Others sent the monthly check straight to the retirement-home office. It didn't go to the parent, but at least they remembered their parents every month. The third type, explained the director, made use of a standing bank order, such that the money was sent each month by a teller at the bank without the child having any idea as to whether his parent was even still alive. Everything was conducted automatically.

This was the difference between Jacob and Esau. God told Jacob, "You have to ask every time. You'll receive nothing without asking." Esau, on the other hand, enjoyed the benefits of a "standing bank order."

We are not speaking here of a trivial connection, but rather of a close relationship. We address God in the second person: "Blessed are *You*, Lord..."

The wording of blessings actually switches at midpoint from second to third person. The Rashba explains (Responsa 5:52) that this is in order to teach us that on the one hand, God is hidden and removed from us, while on the other hand, He is near and addressable in the second person – "You."

III. THE POWER OF PRAYER

The possibility of change always exists; we are able to build a new world. Nothing is ever "sealed." Trouble, distress, illness – everything can be changed. God hears every prayer. The Gemara teaches:

> R. Ḥama bar Ḥanina said: If a person sees that he prayed and was not answered, let him pray again, as it is written (Ps. 27:14), "Look to God; be strong and of good courage, and look to God." (*Berakhot* 32b)

It is specifically prayer which shows us the way toward this strength. As the Gemara teaches, further on:

> R. Elazar said: Prayer is greater than good deeds, for no one was greater in his performance of good deeds than Moses our teacher, and even so he was only answered because of his prayer, as it is written (Deut. 3:26): "Do not say anything else to Me," and immediately thereafter he is told, "Ascend to the top of the mountain." (*Ibid.*)

Man has to know that everything is possible, that he is capable of achieving something with his prayer, and that his words are reaching ears, as it were, that are waiting to hear his prayer. Recently, I met someone who told me something that moved me very deeply. Many years ago, at a time when he had no children, he had come to me for help. I brought his case to one of the most famous doctors in New York, but the answer I received was, "There's nothing that can be done. He can't have children." But the same person who gave me this answer added, "Let him plead for God's mercy." Ten years – maybe more – have passed since then, and recently he told me that his wife is pregnant. Indeed, nothing is "sealed" before the gates of prayer. "Let him pray – and let him pray again."

IV. PRAYER AS AN EXPRESSION OF ONE'S PERSONALITY

The Psalmist says, "*Ani tefilla*" (109:4), which can be translated, "I am prayer."

Tefilla is expressed in the personality of the individual. If you wish to know something of a person's character – watch him at prayer.

The *Midrash* (*Bereshit Raba* 60:15) comments on the verse, "And Rebecca lifted her eyes and she saw Isaac, and she fell from the camel" (Gen. 24:64), as follows: "She saw that his arm was outstretched in prayer, and she said, 'This must be a great man.'" Having observed him at prayer (v. 63, "And Isaac went out to meditate in the field"), she realized his greatness.

The first thing that prayer requires is openness – openness toward oneself. Sometimes people think, "So-and-so isn't open toward others." But many people are closed even toward themselves. Everyone – parents, teachers, rabbis – asks his children or students, "How are you doing?" and the standard response is, "Fine." You can't talk to them or engage them. They are closed not only toward others, but also to themselves. They cannot look inwards. In order to "open up" in front of God, a person first has to "open up" to himself. He should not be satisfied with merely reciting the prayers that appear in the siddur; he should add petitions of his own – even if only in his heart.

We start our recitation of the *Amida* with the words, "O my Master, open my lips, and my mouth will relate Your praise" (Ps. 51:17). According to many authorities (see *Biur Halakha*, 111, s.v. *Ḥozer ve'omer*), this is an integral part of *tefilla* itself. "Open my lips" – in other words, open my heart. I feel "closed"; my heart refuses to disclose itself.

King David said, "I meditate (pray) with *my heart*" (Ps. 77:7). A person's ability to "meditate" with his heart is an art which reveals much about him. A person has to be capable of holding an honest dialogue with himself, in complete privacy. Only thereafter can he attain the level described by the Psalmist, "I pour out my complaint before Him; I lay my trouble before Him" (142:3).

Man is separated from animal by his ability to pray. "You separated man from the start, and allowed him to stand before You" (from the High Holy Day prayers). The Mishna (*Bava Kama* 1:1) teaches: "There are four primary types of damages: the ox and the pit, the *maveh* and the fire." According to one opinion, the "*maveh*" refers to man. When compiling the Mishna, R. Yehuda HaNasi was faced with a problem: it would not have been seemly for the Mishna to read, "There are four primary types of damages: the ox and the pit, the man and the

fire." Therefore man is not mentioned by name, but rather by means of one of the most accurate descriptions of him – "*maveh*," from a root referring to prayer (as in the verse [Is. 21:12], "*Im tiv'ayun be'ayu* – If you should pray, pray"). Only one creature among all of creation is able to pray – namely, man. Indeed, could there be a more beautiful description of man that sets him apart from the beasts of the field? He is not called, "the one who studies" or "the thinker," but rather "the one who prays." This gives us some idea of the importance of the concept of prayer.

Another foundation of prayer is the sense of deficiency. The Gemara in *Megilla* (15b) asks, "What made Esther invite Haman [to the feast]?" One of the answers given is a quotation from Proverbs (25:21): "If your enemy is hungry, feed him bread." A person who is hungry is always alert, while someone who is satisfied after a meal tends to become drowsy. Esther hoped to cause Haman to fall asleep, to blunt his alertness. Therefore, she sought to satisfy him.

Human nature is such that a person always feels that he is "lacking," that something is causing him pain, and therefore he is defined as a being who prays and supplicates. He engages not only in prayer of praise and thanksgiving, but also in petition.

Prayer can be an experience which nourishes a person for many subsequent years. In his commentary to the siddur, *Olat Re'iya* (*Inyanei Tefilla*, 6), R. Kook wrote: "Prayer – for us and for the entire world – is an absolute necessity. It is also the most sublime of pleasures." It is both a necessity and a pleasure! The first contact that the great R. Yaakov Moshe Charlap, of blessed memory, had with R. Kook, his teacher whom he loved with all his soul, was when he stayed once in Jaffa and heard R. Kook reciting *Birkat Kohanim* (the priestly blessing). That was enough for him. At that moment, he attached himself to R. Kook forever.

A similar event occurred to another one of R. Kook's prominent disciples, R. David HaKohen, known later as "the *Nazir*." In his introduction to R. Kook's *Orot HaKodesh*, he describes his first meeting with R. Kook in Switzerland:

> I came to him, and found him immersed in [studying] *halakha* with his son. A conversation arose about Greek wisdom and its literature, which did not yet satisfy one who knew it from its primary sources. I stayed and slept at their house.

> I lay upon my bed, yet my heart was not still; the fate of my life hung in the balance. Early in the morning, I heard the sound of pacing, and of the morning blessings and the prayer of the *Akeda* being recited in song and sublime melody, from the highest heavens, recalling the love of our forebears. I listened, and I changed and became a different man. After the prayer, I hastened to write a letter, informing my correspondent that I had found more than I had hoped for – I had found a master.

V. FOREIGN THOUGHTS

However, there are many impediments to prayer. One of the main problems is that of "foreign thoughts," of wandering attention during prayer. We have already mentioned the saying of R. Menachem Mendel of Vitebsk, a student of the Maggid of Mezeritch, that when a person stands in prayer and wishes to climb to heights which are beyond his grasp, they throw him down by means of foreign thoughts, which become entangled with his prayers (*Peri HaAretz*, letter 22). This means that when one's prayer is artificial, alien thoughts will enter his mind. In a heart-to-heart conversation, in a genuine exchange, there are no foreign thoughts. When one person talks directly to another, his mind does not wander. When a person climbs to "heights which are beyond his grasp," when his prayer doesn't flow naturally from him, then he is attacked by foreign thoughts.

There are those who invest an enormous amount of energy in bodily movements during prayer, convinced that they will thereby drive away foreign thoughts. True, one is permitted to sway slightly during prayer (*Mishna Berura* 48:5), but some people think that in order to arouse profound *kavana* one has to sway mightily. Yet, clearly, physical movement alone lacks the power to solve a spiritual problem. When King David said, "I pour out my complaint before Him," he was not referring to jumping and moaning, but rather to flowing and natural prayer.

The Gemara recounts the following story:

> When R. Eliezer fell ill, his students came to visit him. They said, "Rebbe – teach us a way to conduct ourselves, that we may thereby merit eternal life."
>
> He answered, "Be careful with the honor of your friends...and when you

> pray – know in front of Whom you are standing. By means of this, you will merit eternal life." (*Berakhot* 28b)

Is this supposed to be some kind of great revelation? If a person didn't know in front of Whom he was standing, surely he wouldn't pray at all! But R. Eliezer emphasized, "Know..." – don't be satisfied simply with *kavana*, for that can be artificial and external. "Know in front of Whom you are standing" – then, out of that "knowledge," your prayer will be natural.

"The early righteous ones used to tarry an hour before prayer in order to direct their hearts toward their Father in heaven" (Mishna *Berakhot* 5:1). They tarried not because they needed to direct their hearts more, but to attain the knowledge of Whom they were standing in front of, so that their hearts would be directed automatically. Rambam likewise teaches in his *Hilkhot Tefilla* (4:16): "What is *kavana*? A person must clear his heart of all thoughts and see himself as if he is standing before the Divine Presence." One cannot rid oneself of foreign thoughts in an incidental manner, as if brushing them off. There is only one solution: to stand (and see oneself as standing) before the Holy One, blessed is He.

We adopt the advice of the "early righteous ones" in our recitation of *Pesukei DeZimra*, the first section of the morning prayer service, consisting of psalms and praises. Rambam (*Hil. Tefilla* 9:1) writes that communal prayer begins only with *Kaddish* and *Barekhu*. He defines *Pesukei DeZimra*, from *Barukh She'amar* until *Yishtabaḥ*, as a custom praised by the sages (*Hil. Tefilla* 7:12). Before commencing prayer, we sing God's praises, telling of His wonders, mercies, and greatness, so that we will sense before Whom we are coming to stand. Generally, it is easier to speak of Torah, fear of heaven, *mitzva* observance, etc., than it is to address oneself directly to God. This is the root of our custom of opening prayer with the recitation of *Pesukei DeZimra*.

It is a mistake to think that by physical means, using energetic body movements, one can free oneself of foreign thoughts and keep them at bay. This is merely a *segula*, a mystical remedy of the type described by the Ba'al Shem Tov. Once his students came to him and asked whether it was permissible for them to approach a famous *tzaddik*, well-known for the *segulot* which he handed out to his followers. The Ba'al Shem Tov replied, "If you want to go to him, then

go." They persisted and asked for a sign that would help them know whether he was a true *tzaddik*, and not a charlatan. The Ba'al Shem Tov replied, "I will give you a sign. This *tzaddik* gives *segulot* for every type of illness and trouble. Ask him for a *segula* for foreign thoughts in prayer. If he offers you one, then you can be sure he is a charlatan."

Various prayer books contain biblical verses whose recital supposedly acts as a "*segula* against foreign thoughts." Is it really *segulot* that we need?

There is another method, which appears far removed from us, but which is in fact "very close to us, in our mouths and in our hearts, to do it." *Ḥasidut* teaches that when a particular issue is disturbing a person, he has to "elevate" his foreign thoughts. This kabbalistic concept means the following, in practical terms: You must translate the problem which occupies your thoughts into the language of prayer. Whether you are thinking about business or family or anything else, God is certainly able to help you in solving the problem. Don't banish this "foreign thought" from your mind; on the contrary – keep it with you, and turn that very thought into a prayer.

VI. THE VALUE OF ROTE PRAYER

With all the importance of the experiential dimension of prayer, we certainly should not ignore or belittle the importance of "dry," uninspired prayer. Sometimes a person is not on the level which allows him to sense the experiential dimension of prayer. Yet there is value even to "dry" prayers devoid of the vitality of a lofty experience.

A student once came to me with a complaint. Throughout the month of Elul, his prayer had been full of emotion, yet now, the day before Rosh HaShana, the "spring had dried up," everything was dry. What was he to do? I told him, "Turn to God and say to Him, 'Master of the universe, this is what there is. I can't do any more than this.'"

In the Temple, there were both "great" sacrifices – bulls, goats, and sheep – as well as the humble *minḥa*, the grain-offering of the poor: "whatever his hand can attain" (Lev. 14:30). Both are desirable to God. "One with more and the other with less; [it matters not,] so long as his heart is directed toward heaven" (*Berakhot* 5b).

VII. INDIVIDUAL AND COMMUNAL PRAYER

The beginning of *Parashat Ki Tavo* discusses the pilgrim's recitation over the *bikkurim* (first fruits) upon bringing them to Jerusalem:

> And it shall come to pass, when you come to the land which the Lord your God has given you as an inheritance...that you shall take of the first of all the fruit of the earth which you shall gather from the land which the Lord your God has given you...and you shall come to the priest who will be in those days, and you shall say to him: "I declare this day before the Lord your God that I have come to the land which God promised to our forefathers to give us." (Deuteronomy 26:1–3)

The *Midrash Tanḥuma* adds (beginning of *Ki Tavo*):

> Moses gazed with the holy spirit and saw that the Temple was destined to be destroyed, and that the *bikkurim* would cease. He therefore instituted [a law] for Israel that they should pray three times each day, because prayer is more beloved to God than any good deeds and any sacrifices.

What do *bikkurim* have to do with prayer? Rightfully, a person standing before God, with the first fruits of his land in his hands, should thank Him and say: "You have given me the strength to work the fields this year; please give me the strength to do the same during the coming year." But this is not the prayer that the bearer of the first fruits is commanded to recite. Instead, the Torah commands him:

> And you shall speak and declare before the Lord your God: "A wandering Aramean was my father, and he went down to Egypt, and lived there with a few, and became a great nation there – great, mighty, and numerous. The Egyptians were evil toward us, and tortured us, and gave us hard labor. We cried to the Lord God of our fathers, and the Lord heard our voice, and saw our suffering, and our labor, and our oppression. The Lord brought us out of Egypt with a mighty hand, and with an outstretched arm, and with great terror, and with signs, and with wonders. He brought us to this place, and gave us this land, a land flowing with milk and honey. Now, behold, I have brought the first fruits of the land which You, O God, have given me." You shall set it before the Lord your God, and you shall prostrate yourself before the Lord your God. (Deuteronomy 26:5–10)

The Torah is concerned lest a person who is busy with his vineyard and his field, his vine and his fig tree, come to forget the nation of Israel, God forbid. All his desires will be subordinated to his own progress and to material acquisitions, directed toward the construction of his house and his estate. "What car shall I buy? What type of house shall I build?" The Torah therefore commands us: Go up to Jerusalem. Forget your private concerns for a while. Concern yourself with the nation, with its history and its fate. At the end, don't forget to thank, praise, and glorify God for that which He has given you. All of these issues – the history of *Am Yisrael*, the Exodus from Egypt – are also part of you: "which You ... have given *me*."

The same problem exists when the Jews are in exile. A multitude of existential troubles and concerns occupy the individual in his effort toward his personal survival. And what is to become of *Am Yisrael*? Therefore, Moses instituted that Jews should pray three times each day. *Tefilla* is not limited to the individual's problems and troubles. *Tefilla* directs itself toward the community, toward *Am Yisrael* as a whole. "Cause the offspring of David, Your servant, to flourish"; "Restore our judges as of old, and our counselors as at first"; "Rebuild Jerusalem"; "May our eyes behold Your return to Zion in compassion."

Moreover, *tefilla* expresses our complete dependence on God. Were it not for Him, we wouldn't be holding these first fruits. Without God, a person has neither knowledge nor repentance, neither redemption nor healing, neither "restoration of judges" nor "dew and rain for a blessing," neither the rebuilding of Jerusalem nor the blessing of peace. Everything depends on God's will.

Prayer is the source of faith, and its foundation. Through prayer, man expresses his complete dependence on God. *Tefilla* strengthens our faith. •

The Ultimate Goal of Our Prayers

R. Chaim Yaakov Goldvicht

We need to understand why, at the end of every *Amida*, we say "May it be Your will, Lord our God and God of our ancestors, that the Temple be rebuilt speedily in our days *and may You grant our portion in Your Torah*." What does the first request have to do with the second one?

It says in the *Midrash:*

> "Let them take for Me a portion." Is there any purchase in which the seller is sold with it? God said to Israel: "I sold you My Torah. As it were, I was sold with it" as it says, "Let them take for Me a portion." This is comparable to a king who had an only daughter. One of the kings came and took her as a wife. He wanted to go back to his country and to take his wife with him. The king said to him: "The daughter that I gave to you, is my only one. To separate from her, I cannot. To tell you not to take her with you I also cannot, as she is your wife. Rather, do me this favor: wherever you go, set aside a small room for me so that I can live with you, because I cannot leave my daughter." So, too, God said to Israel: "I gave you the Torah. To separate from it, etc. Rather, wherever you go, make a place for Me that I may dwell in it," as it says, "They shall make a Sanctuary for Me, so that I may dwell among them." (*Shemot Raba* 33:1)

The analogy in this parable is difficult to understand. We do not find that the Jewish people sought to distance themselves from God in a way that He needed to ask them to find a little room for Him to live in, as we find in the metaphor, where the husband wanted to take the king's daughter away.

In the blessings of *Parashat Beḥukotai*, it says, "I will place My Sanctuary among you; and My Spirit will not reject you. I will walk among you, I will be God unto you and you will be a people unto Me" (Lev. 26:11–12). Why do these verses repeat the promise "I will place My Sanctuary among you" and "I will walk among you"? The meaning of the first phrase is clear, that God's presence will dwell in the sanctuary, but what does the second phrase add?

R. Ovadia Seforno explains that if we think that the ultimate goal of our prayers that the Temple be rebuilt is so that God will dwell there amongst us through

---

R. Chaim Yaakov Goldvicht was the founding and long-serving Rosh Yeshiva of Yeshivat Kerem B'Yavneh. This shiur was transcribed by R. S. Y. Lau, and translated by R. Meir Orlian.

His presence there, in the Temple, we are mistaken. This is only the beginning of the process, but the culmination of this ideal is that His presence will accompany us everywhere we go, without the intermediary medium of the Temple: "In my heart I will build a tabernacle." This is alluded to in these verses, implying that the result of "I will place My tabernacle among you," is only "I will not reject you." However, when we merit, "I will walk among you," then the larger promise of "I will be God unto you," will be fulfilled. Not only will the rejection of the Jewish nation be annulled, there will also be great closeness of God to the nation. But this will happen only through, "If you will follow My decrees" – that is, when you will toil in My Torah, i.e., by your complete dedication to Torah and *mitzvot*.

This is well explained based on what was cited from Seforno. At the Revelation of Mount Sinai, the people merited the greatest spiritual elevation, and corrected the sin of Adam in Eden. At that time the all-encompassing presence of "I will walk amongst you" dwelt upon them, without the medium of the Tabernacle. However, after they sinned with the Golden Calf, they lost their elevated status, and were no longer worthy of this height. From that point on they needed the tabernacle, so that the Divine Presence could draw closer to them from between the poles of the Holy Ark, to dwell in their midst. Thus they were commanded at that point, "They shall make a Sanctuary for Me."

Therefore, when the Torah was revealed God gave His daughter, the Torah, to the Jewish people in marriage, so to speak, and He did not need a small room to live in, because He would always be present, just as He was at Mount Sinai. However, after Israel worshiped the Golden Calf, they were exiled from God's table. This is the time that the parable alludes to, when the son-in-law sought to go back to his land, and at that point there was a need for a solution to keep God close at all times. Thus God requested "Make a little room for Me, so that I should live with you," so that the Divine Presence would be able to dwell, so to speak, between the cherubim of the *Mishkan*.

This in turn explains why we say at the end of every *Amida*, "[May] the Temple be rebuilt...and may You grant our portion in Your Torah," – it does not suffice that the Divine Presence simply dwells in the tabernacle, what we really ask for is that "I will walk amongst you" be fulfilled. This will occur only if we embrace our share in Torah, and thus we ask: "Grant our portion in Your Torah," i.e., may we, through achieving our portion in Your Torah, achieve the level in which the Divine Presence will be present in the heart of each one of us, even beyond the confines of the future Temple.◆

Praying with Kavana: Hasidic Perspectives

R. Norman Lamm

Of the many aspects of religious life, none is as intimate as the service of God as manifested in the act of prayer; yet nothing in man's private spiritual life is so enmeshed in the public realm. Many have lived without devoting themselves to contemplation of the deeper religious mysteries, but every observant Jew daily brings himself to God in prayer. Hence it is not surprising that prayer, more than any other area of Jewish existence, exhibits the interplay of theoretical probing and practical implications. The specific contributions of Hasidic thought on prayer are rooted in its mystical, kabbalistic orientation and its stress on mental purity and emotional intensity.

The question of focus or attention (*kavana*) is central to the "service of the heart" that is prayer. Proper intention is a halakhic requisite of prayer. Hasidic masters were aware that prayer was threatened by the crisis of the individual frustrated in his desire to summon the proper *kavana*. How to channel one's thoughts during prayer also raises the general problem of *maḥashavot zarot* ("alien [i.e., unwelcome] thoughts"), generally referring to sexual thoughts. The desire for sustained attention also inspired specific Hasidic practices, on which more below.

But what is the content of the *kavana* that is to be attained? The halakhic backbone of prayer is petition. For many religious persons, however, petition seems fatally tinged with selfish desire and with the presumption that man can somehow wheedle God into conforming to his wishes. While some Hasidic teachers deal with the philosophical problem – how man can change God's will – much attention was devoted to elaborating a kabbalistic theory that "elevated" the idea of petition. According to this view, the *Shekhina* suffers cosmic exile, in sympathy with man's own suffering. The purpose of prayer is not to realize the petitioner's goals, but to redeem the *Shekhina*. One prays, then, not for his own sake, but for the sake of God, as it were. This redefinition of the element of petition is shared by *mitnagdic* kabbalists like R. Ḥayyim of Volozhin.

Kabbalistic theory occasionally influences both the general mood and the specific thoughts that accompany prayer. Thus, R. Dov Baer, son of R. Shneur Zalman, the founder of Chabad Hasidism, painstakingly mapped the terrain

---

This article is taken from his volume, *The Religious Thought of Hasidism: Text and Commentary.*

of contemplative and ecstatic prayer. Contemplation (*hitbonenut*) involves meditation on God's presence in the world and the detailed structure of the *sefirot* and their interrelationships, while genuine ecstasy (*hitpa'alut*) grows out of this rigorous meditation. An approach of this kind restricts the emotional spontaneity we customarily associate with the Hasidic world, and was far from being universally adopted. A striking contrast is evident in the approach of R. Naḥman of Breslov, for whom prayer is a virtual conversation between man and his Maker.

Another kabbalistic notion with broad implications for the halakhic and social standing of Hasidism is presented by the special *kavanot* associated with R. Isaac Luria, "the Holy Ari." These mystical "intentions" attached to the text of the liturgy shifted the emphasis from the manifest content of the prayer to the kabbalistic "secrets" encoded therein. As the *kavanot* were introduced into a modified version of the Sephardic prayer book, adopting them required the Eastern European Jew to relinquish the Ashkenazic text of his fathers, and this change of custom added a halakhic difficulty to the innovation. In fact, the new text was used privately by several renowned non-Hasidic rabbis, including R. Moshe Sofer (the *Ḥatam Sofer*) of Pressburg (following his teacher, R. Nathan Adler), who objected, nonetheless, to its acceptance by laymen.

Hasidic thinkers were impelled to endorse the popular employment of the Lurianic text. To justify the deviation from the inherited communal practice, they argued that the tradition of each group of Jews was authoritatively ordained as the unique channel to God for that group; the Lurianic version, however, remains supreme and was never rejected by the elite. But what right have simple Jews to use *kavanot* that they do not understand? To this, R. Elimelech of Lizhensk answered that the average man need not dwell upon the mysteries of the text, and indeed it would be presumptuous of him to do so; his *kavanot* are taken care of, so to speak, through his faith in the *tzaddik*.

It may be instructive to compare this characteristic approach with that of R. Ḥayyim of Volozhin. R. Ḥayyim insists that prayer should concentrate on the simple meaning of the words, using the authoritative text, and eschewing any other thoughts. What of the esoteric reasons hidden in the recesses of the text? Since we cannot penetrate the full meaning intended by the Men of the Great Assembly, who fixed the text, we must remain faithful to their conception. Note that the function of Talmudic authority in R. Ḥayyim's framework is similar to

that of the *tzaddik* in R. Elimelech's scheme, namely, to enable the common man to pray simply, without worrying about the deeper *kavanot*.

The propensity of Hasidism to encourage the recitation of esoteric formulas also came to the fore in the controversy of *leshem yiḥud*. This phrase serves as a preface to the performance of a *mitzva*, expressing the desire to unite *Kudsha Berikh Hu*, the *sefira* of *Tiferet* (symbolically identified as masculine), with the *Shekhina* (the *sefira* of *Malkhut*, regarded as feminine). In a famous responsum, the eminent Talmudist R. Ezekiel Landau of Prague criticizes the popularization of this practice. He does not see the need for elaborate formulations of *kavana* in general, and is particularly concerned that a worshiper preoccupied with striving to articulate secret intentions risks falling into erroneous ones instead.

Distinct from the mystical affiliations of Hasidim at prayer that divided them from other Jews, the emotional intensity fostered by the movement also tended to confirm their social apartness. In addition to the cultivation of melody as an element in worship, Hasidic prayer was marked by dramatic gestures. While physical demonstrativeness in prayer has a respectable Talmudic pedigree, Hasidic behavior often called forth the satire of opponents, and sometimes internal criticism as well. A parable attributed to the Besht will make the point. A drowning man gesticulates wildly because he is trying to save himself; similarly, an individual for whom prayer is a matter of life and death will make violent gestures while praying. Neither action should arouse scorn in the spectator.

The scheduling of prayer presented a more serious halakhic and social cause of dissension. Because of the emphasis on proper intention, Hasidim habitually recited the set prayers after the time mandated by *halakha* had elapsed, for such intention cannot be summoned up instantly; it requires deliberate and often time-consuming effort. Their elaborate preparations for prayer included resort to tobacco in order to bring about the right frame of mind, seemingly immoderate attention to physical purity, immersion in the *mikveh*, and so forth. Beyond the apparent halakhic transgression, laxity with respect to the set times for prayer unavoidably led Hasidim to worship separately from their non-Hasidic brethren. Especially in a period when the specter of Sabbatean heresy had not been banished, the establishment of separate *minyanim* could not fail to reinforce suspicions. Thus, for example, when R. Yaakov Yosef turned to Hasidism, his final rupture with his community is said to have resulted from his instituting his own prayer services.

Once they began to pray, Hasidim were also known for the length of their worship. This was a natural consequence of the emphasis on wholehearted intention and emotional involvement, though there were noteworthy exceptions, such as R. Menaḥem Mendel of Kotzk, who completed his prayers rapidly precisely because he upheld the highest standards of concentration. For their adversaries, the very duration of their devotions was a mark against the Hasidim, for it seemed to reverse the hierarchy which placed the study of Torah above prayer. Hasidic thinkers, in fact, often argued for the merit of prayer as a central institution of religious existence.

As pointed out by the late Professor Jacob Katz, the Hasidic approach to the institution of prayer liberates the spiritual life, in effect, from the tyranny of the clock, be it halakhic or economic: "The rational use of time, that is, its division and fullest exploitation for practical purposes and for the realization of religious values, was basically impaired by making a virtue out of waiting hours until the opportune moment arrived for communion with God." Whether one approves of this mode of structuring time or not, it ought to be recognized that much in the Hasidic outlook is fundamentally out of harmony with what we call modernity, characterized by the Weberian concept of rationality.

A STORY:

Once the Ba'al Shem Tov and his disciples were on a journey. In a forest along the way, they chanced upon an abandoned synagogue and decided to pray *Minḥa* there. The disciples opened the door and invited their master to be the first to enter. Just as he was about the step into the synagogue, the holy Ba'al Shem Tov stopped and would not cross the threshold. The Hasidim were perplexed but reluctant to question their master. But after a while, when the sun began to set and it would soon be too late for *Minḥa*, they summoned up the courage to ask why he would not enter the synagogue. The Ba'al Shem Tov replied, "I can't go in because it is so crowded; there is no room for us." The Hasidim were astounded, because the synagogue was empty. Taking note of their confusion, he explained: "A prayer, when uttered sincerely and wholeheartedly, always sprouts wings and soars upward to the Throne of Glory of the Creator Himself. But I feel that the people who once prayed here had no *kavana*. Their prayers had no wings and collapsed and fell upon one another, so that the synagogue is now densely packed with dead, wingless prayers – and there is no room for us." ◆

Berakhot – The Gateway to Prayer

R. Pinchas Peli

Berakhot were instituted by the rabbis as a means for directing man into the presence of God at all times, thus providing for the continuous preservation of contact with the Creator. *Berakhot* have, however, a second function. They enable man to descend from the heights of his abiding attachment to God in order to live in this material, human world. But there is an apparent contradiction. It is written, "The heavens are the heavens of the Lord" (Ps. 115:16), so that man cleaves to God and to His heavens. Yet in the same verse it is also written, "But He has given the earth to the children of man" (*ibid.*) How is man to accept this gift of God – to live in the world and enjoy its bounty – while remaining attached to God in heaven? The answer is given by the *berakha*, through whose power man enters the world below without detaching himself from the world above. Just as through the *berakha* he leaves the spiritual for the material world, so through the selfsame *berakha* does he return and enter the upper world of the spirit while still abiding within the lower, human, material world. *Berakhot* are formulated at one and the same time in both the second and third persons ("Blessed are You...through Whose word everything came to be"). These two facets are like the two ends of a bridge that traverse a surging river. With a *berakha*, man may descend into the depths of materialism but he can also be elevated to the heights of absolute spirituality.

If there is a view that man should spend the whole of his life in prayer ("Would that man would pray the whole day long!" – *Berakhot* 33b) then it is the *berakhot* which preserve the state of prayer between one formal prayer service and the next:

> Our rabbis have taught: It is forbidden for a man to enjoy anything of this world without a *berakha*, and if anyone enjoys anything of this world without a *berakha*, he commits sacrilege. What is his remedy? He should consult a wise man. What will a wise man do for him? He has already committed the offense! Said Raba: What it means is that he should consult a wise man beforehand, so that he should teach him *berakhot* and he should not

---

This essay has been excerpted and slightly edited from an article that appeared in *Tradition* 14:2 (Fall, 1973). Footnotes have been omitted. Those who wish to read the full article in its original form can do so by visiting www.traditiononline.org.

> commit sacrilege. R. Yehuda said in the name of Shmuel: To enjoy anything in this world without a *berakha* is like making personal use of things consecrated to heaven, since it says [Ps. 24:1], "The earth is the Lord's and the fullness thereof," and it is also written [115:16], "The heavens are the heavens of the Lord but He has given the earth to the children of man!" There is no contradiction: in the one case (the former) it is before a *berakha* has been recited; in the other case after. (*Berakhot* 35a)

At first glance there seems to be a contradiction between the two views of the world expressed in the biblical verses, but the contradiction is reconciled by the *berakha*, which brings heaven and earth nearer and effaces the distances between them.

If anyone enjoys anything of this world without a *berakha* he commits sacrilege. The world is holy. The world belongs to the Lord. The Creator has not forsaken His world, for otherwise the world would not exist at all. The Lord continues to create His world unceasingly. If anyone enjoys anything without a *berakha*, i.e., diverts his mind from the abiding reality of God in each of the manifestations of the universe and of life, he commits sacrilege. A pledge was delivered to his care and he knew not how to maintain it. He who commits sacrilege is worse than a thief or robber. The latter are suspect from the beginning of the dishonest deeds they perform, while he who commits sacrilege is at first presumed to be honest and faithful. The holy things of heaven were entrusted to him and only later did it become clear that he had betrayed His trust. Therefore, he committed sacrilege.

Judaism is not opposed to enjoyment. On the contrary, "Man will have to render account and be brought to judgment for all he saw with his eyes and did not partake of" (Yerushalmi, end of *Kiddushin*). When this enjoyment, however, becomes the most important thing and devours the whole person, making him forget his essential nature and dulling his soul – this is sacrilege. It is treachery to the sacred things of heaven, to the community of Israel, and to his own self.

There is a Talmudic discussion which attempts to discover biblical sources for the rule that man is duty bound to say *berakhot* over his enjoyments. Proof is brought from a variety of biblical verses, each of which is found not to be quite satisfactory. Finally, the Talmud concludes the argument in an unusual manner: "The fact is that it is a reasonable supposition that it is forbidden for a man to enjoy anything of this world without saying a *berakha*" (*Berakhot* 35a).

It is a reasonable supposition; it is self-evident to him who knows his place in the world and senses the mystery of the universe in which he is placed. Such a person walks in the world of the Holy One with exceptional care, his eyes open, his ears alerted. He walks as if in a mysterious sanctuary, fearful for each step, trembling over every stride. Before deriving any enjoyment in the world, he meditates on Him Who planted him in it. Man does not need to search for Him in distant and exalted worlds but sees Him everywhere so that he can even address Him as "You." Rav, interpreting the verse, "I have set the Lord always before me" (Ps. 16:18), stated that when man utters a *berakha* he must say, "*Barukh Ata Hashem*" (*Midrash Tehillim* 16). Man does not need special warnings and profound learning to know that he ought to utter *berakhot* and request permission before having enjoyment of the world. For him it is a "supposition" that is self-evident. R. Akiva said, "A man is forbidden to taste anything before saying a *berakha* over it" (*Berakhot, ibid.*). The *berakha* puts a different perspective on the enjoyment, for without it, the enjoyment is a misappropriation.

To quote another text:

> R. Ḥanina b. Papa said: To enjoy this world without a *berakha* is like robbing the Holy One, blessed is He, and the community of Israel. For it says [Prov. 28:24], "Who robs his father or his mother and says, 'It is no transgression' is the companion of a destroyer," and "father" is none other than the Holy One, blessed is He, as it says [Deut. 32:6], "Is He not your Father that has begotten you?" And "mother" is none other than the community of Israel, as it says [Prov. 1:8], "Hear, my son, the instruction of your father, and forsake not the teaching of your mother." What is the meaning of "the companion of a destroyer?" R. Ḥanina b. Papa answers: He is the companion of Jeroboam, son of Nebat, who destroyed Israel's (faith in) their Father in heaven. (*Berakhot* 35b)

The basic idea of the *berakha* and its reasoning are already found in the Torah:

> And you shall eat and you shall be satisfied, and you shall bless the Lord... Beware lest you forget the Lord your God...and say in your heart: "My power and the might of my hand has gotten me this wealth." But you shall remember the Lord your God, for it is He Who gives you power to get wealth. (Deuteronomy 8:10)

The sages, however, clothed the idea with sinews and flesh. They arranged

the *berakhot* in accordance with categories and topics, each type having its own *berakha*. They also prescribed which *berakhot* are appropriate at a meal, which *berakha* should be said first, and which *berakha* should be said when a full meal is not being taken. Thus a man is obliged to reflect before each of his actions and turn his attention to the *berakha* he must utter before he acts. This is to prevent *berakhot* from becoming mere force of habit. *Berakhot* were preparation and training for prayer. If prayer uplifts a man and elevates him to the highest peaks, then the *berakha* brings heaven down to earth into the personal sphere of every man. Wherever he goes and whatever he does the *berakha* reminds man that even when he is upon the earth the heavens are close by. Just as it is forbidden to eat bread without a *berakha* so it is forbidden to say the *berakha* "Who brings forth bread from the earth" without eating bread. This is not merely saying an unnecessary *berakha* but also taking the name of the Lord in vain. The *berakha* is directed to the Lord, but it becomes attached to an object or a physical act. The *berakha* and its object become a single unity. The *berakha* elevates the piece of bread over which it is recited above its single material existence, imparting to the bread a spiritual object.

"The way to prayer extends during moments of wonder and amazement." Such moments are not isolated and fortuitous. Should you so wish it, they can encompass the life of a man. As soon as a man awakes from his sleep he senses that "the great King is protecting him," and says: "Blessed are You, Lord, Who restores souls to the dead." When he hears the cock crowing, he says: "Blessed are You, Lord, Who gave the heart understanding to help us distinguish between day and night." When he opens his eyes, he says: "Blessed are You, Lord, Who opens the eyes of the blind." When he stretches himself and sits up, he says: "Blessed are You, Lord, Who executes judgment for the oppressed." When he dresses, he says: "Blessed are You, Lord, Who clothes the naked." When he draws himself up, he says: "Blessed are You, Lord, Who raises up those who are bowed down." When he steps onto the ground, he says: "Blessed are You, Lord, Who stretches forth the earth over the waters." When he commences to walk, he says: "Blessed are You, Lord, Who guides man's steps." When he ties his shoes, he says: "Blessed are You, Lord, Who provides for my every need." When he fastens his girdle, he says: "Blessed are You, Lord, Who girds Israel with might." When he spreads a kerchief over his head, he says: "Blessed are You, Lord, Who crowns Israel with glory." When he wraps himself with the fringed garments, he says: "Blessed are You, Lord, Who has sanctified us with His commandments

and has commanded us to wrap ourselves with *tzitzit*." When he puts the *tefillin* on his arm, he says: "Blessed are You, Lord, Who has sanctified us with His commandments, and has commanded us about the commandment of *tefillin*." When he washes his hands he says: "Blessed are You, Lord, Who has sanctified us with His commandments and commanded us to wash our hands." When he washes his face, he says: "Blessed are You, Lord, Who removes sleep from my eyes and slumber from my eyelids."

At every turn made by a man a *berakha* awaits. He who blesses everything recognizes the existence and the presence of God. In everything he sees the Creator Who has not severed His connection with His creation. "All those *berakhot* point to the renewal daily of the acts of Creation."

The experience of the *berakha* is the important thing; the formula was only coined as an external framework to preserve the inner content:

> R. Meir says: Even if on seeing the bread, he said, "Blessed is He Who created this bread; how beautiful is this bread" – this is its *berakha*. Even if on seeing figs, he said, "Blessed is He Who created those figs; how beautiful they are" – this is their *berakha*. (*Tosefta, Berakhot* 4:4–5)

Although the *halakha* does not follow R. Meir, his concept is undisputed.

As noted above, the morning blessings were originally formulated in response to observed and experienced phenomena. However, over the course of the centuries, the rabbis instituted that these *berakhot* be recited in the synagogue. But even after the fixing of the text and the arrangement in the synagogue had displaced the connection of the *berakha* with extemporized devotion, there still remained a definite method of preserving the spiritual tension demanded by the *berakha*. The number of *berakhot* that a person must say daily was established at one hundred, according to a Tannaitic tradition. Hence opportunity remained for spiritual alertness and persisted devotion in order to obtain the required number. The ruling stressing the number of *berakhot* induces a state of permanent alertness, eyes wide open to look, ears alerted to hear, and even nostrils quivering to smell a pleasant smell. It did not permit a person to accept the manifestations of nature with indifference. He who sees the Mediterranean Sea after an interval of at least thirty days is obliged to say a *berakha*. For thunder and for lightning, he must say a *berakha*. For a friend not seen in thirty days, he must say a *berakha*. On seeing kings and scholars, he must say a *berakha*. Man must be continually steeped in a

state of watchfulness and instantaneous response. In other words, he must always be alive to his surroundings so that he is on the threshold of prayer all the time. For it is by this means that the living person reacts to Him Who gives life to all the living.

The *halakha* requires a person to say a *berakha* when he tastes, hears, sees, or smells. Whoever is not doing one of these is not bound to say a *berakha*. Though he is bound to attain a hundred *berakhot*, it is not the number which is important but the intention of each of the *berakhot*. "Whoever says a *berakha* which is not necessary transgresses the command of 'You shall not take (God's name in vain).'" "Some complain against those who are pious and complete the hundred *berakhot* each day through guile by eating fruits without bread" (*Berakhot* 33a). The number of *berakhot* is important, but more important are the *berakhot* themselves; one hundred *berakhot* are one hundred invitations to one hundred spiritual experiences, one hundred occurrences. The duty to say a *berakha*, and its classification into categories and forms, occurs only after something has transpired in the person. One of the chapters of tractate *Berakhot* that deals with the laws of *berakhot* commences with the words: "If one sees a place where miracles have been wrought for Israel, he should say 'Blessed are You Who wrought miracles for our ancestors in this place.'" A person can pass by a place a hundred and one times and see nothing. The duty to say a *berakha* arises only "if one sees." To anyone who does not see by himself it comes as a reminder of his duty that *he ought to see*. But only then, when he does see, is he bound to bless.

The duty to recite the *berakha* and all the admonitions connected therewith call upon man to be continuously amazed before the wonders of the Creator, and to perceive Him in everything, small and great. Whenever a man moves to do anything – to derive benefit from the world, to eat, to drink, to live in the lap of nature – immediately rushing to meet him is the duty to say the *berakha* instituted by the halakhic sages, commanding: "Mortal man, open up your eyes and see; do not move through the world like one blind; alert your brain and think; do not pass through the world like a robot." The duty to say the *berakha* restrains man in each of his actions, telling him to pause and ask himself a number of questions. The *berakha* itself is not simply an answer to questions; it is a conclusion. You stand amazed, wondering Who has created all these. You do not understand how the simplest things in the world act, just as you don't understand how the complex ones act. You wish to know: how, what, who? The answer thereto is: "By Whose word all things exist." The

berakha takes you beyond the borderline between the known and the mysterious. You are now within, standing face-to-face, opposite that which is "beyond the mysterious" and He, King of the universe and of the unknown – but also the "Blessed" One; He reveals Himself to you wherever you turn, like a pool whose water flows from the unknown into the open. Here is He Who made Creation, Who imparts of His wisdom to them that revere Him, Who creates the fruit of the tree and brings forth bread from the earth, Who causes this drop of water to descend and gives you life, preserving you to see it. In brief, here is He "by Whose word all things exist."

As for you, mortal man, when you attain this sensation as you look at the world surrounding you – then you are to pray. But when you pray, do not pray before some "third person," before the "that" Who made all this. When you achieve this feeling and knowledge that "by His word all things exist," and apart from Him there is nothing in the world, then you are also to feel and know that just as you are now standing before Him, so He is standing before you. The moment you are aware of "*barukh*," you may continue and murmur, "You" – and He, by Whose word all things exist, has become "You," to Whom you utter a prayer. Your *berakha* is more than a process of thought and a movement of the lips; it is "an occurrence transpiring between man and God in the presence of God."

Thus the *berakhot* serve as a gateway through which we enter into prayer. There can be no acceptance of the yoke of the kingdom of heaven contained in reading the *Shema* without the *berakha* before it and after it, and there is no *Amida* prayer without its *berakhot*. In all our supplications for knowledge and healing, and for blessing and for salvation, and for our other human needs, we come first to the recognition of "Blessed are You, Lord," gracious Giver of knowledge, Who delights in repentance, Who heals the sick of His people Israel, Who blesses the years, etc.

The development of prayer can best be summed up as follows: from man to the world, through the *berakha*, which makes us arrive at the correct view and time perception of our inner world and of the world about us as part of the regenerating world of God. Through the power of the *berakha* all common things become holy; all those things which at first sight seem explicable become wonders. On having this vision and feeling we say "*barukh*," and thereby proclaim the entry into the material and human world of Him Who is the source of all these and gives life to them all. From this recognition of "*barukh*" the way is open to prayer itself, to the intimate saying of "You." ◆

Understanding the Term Tefilla

R. Heshie Billet

The siddur is the formalized text of the required conversation with God which our tradition calls *tefilla*, prayer. But the siddur is not limited to what is simply required. Within the siddur itself at designated places there is room for subjective texts inserted by the user. In addition there is room to pray to God using a personal formulation. Furthermore the text of the siddur allows itself to be interpreted differently by each individual through the medium we call *kavana*.

In a sense the subjective human element of choosing or needing to pray coexists in Jewish tradition with the objective requirement to pray. Rambam (*Hil. Tefilla* 1:1), sees prayer as an objective mandated daily obligation. Prayer is not a response to a spontaneous need, but rather the duty of a servant to the Master. In a sense we say to God, "I pray to You because You have commanded me to serve You." But Ramban, in his commentary on Rambam's *Sefer HaMitzvot* (*Mitzvat Aseh* 5), sees prayer as a spontaneous reaction to an urgent need in a pressing time, *be'et tzara*. From this perspective, when we pray we declare to God, "I am praying to You because I want to and need to pray to You." This too, may explain the different models for daily prayer cited by the Talmud (*Berakhot* 26b). One view is that the patriarchs instituted the morning, afternoon, and evening prayers. Clearly Abraham, Isaac, and Jacob were responding spontaneously to satisfy a need, or impulse, to relate to God, each in his own way, at a particular moment. It was an opportunity for each patriarch to say to God, "I want to pray because I need You." The other view is that the daily prayers were instituted to parallel the two daily sacrifices and the evening altar procedures in the Temple. The sacrifice ritual in the Temple was called *avoda*, which followed formalized procedures with standardized rules. And prayer is called *avoda shebalev*, i.e., "service of the heart." From this perspective prayer is a formal statement, an obligatory act that declares, "I serve You not only through my actions but through the thoughts in my heart and the words on my lips."

However even the formal objective aspect of prayer gives license to human creativity in prayer. This comes about through what we call *kavana*. R. Ḥayyim Soloveitchik in his *Ḥiddushei HaGraḥ* (*Hil. Tefilla* 4:1) explains that there are three kinds of *kavana*. The first refers to how we understand the words. This includes giving personal meaning to the words of prayer. For example, when

we pray for health, wisdom, or good fortune, each person may have a unique personal circumstance or reality in mind. Reuven's petition for sustenance may be different from Shimon's even though they are saying the exact same words. The second type of *kavana* is when we keep in mind when praying that we are standing before the King. Each of us may experience a different emotion in internalizing such a scenario. And finally *kavana* can refer to being aware that when we pray, we are fulfilling the formal commandment to pray.

The Hebrew word for prayer is *tefilla*. What is the connotation of the term? On the most basic grammatical level it is a conjugation (in the so-called *Ḥasrei peh nun* form) of the root *nun, feh, lamed – nafal*, which refers to the act of falling. When finite man stands before Almighty, Omniscient, Eternal God, he is humbled and bows and falls before Him. In this sense, prayer is a humble act of acknowledgment of the vulnerability of the human condition and our need to communicate with God. Even if we do not prostrate ourselves physically, we do so metaphysically.

Another possibility is that *tefilla* is the reflexive form of the Hebrew root *peh, lamed, lamed*, i.e., *palal*, which (according to R. Samson Raphael Hirsch) refers to the act of judging. For instance, Jacob says to Joseph at their reunion after twenty-two years of absence and silence, "In my evaluation of circumstances, I never thought (*lo pilalti*) that I would see you again" (Gen. 48:11). So too the Psalmist in Psalm 106:30 uses the term *vayefalel* to describe Pinḥas' act of judging Zimri ben Salu and Kozbi bat Tzur, and the resultant action he undertook. So too, says R. Hirsch, when we pray, we engage in self-judgment (hence the reflexive form *lehitpalel*, i.e., to do a self-evaluation), and consider "Who am I, where do I stand vis-à-vis man and God, and where am I heading?" In this sense prayer is the opportunity to audit ourselves as we engage in a conversation with God.

A third interpretation (suggested by R. Shlomo Riskin) is that *tefilla* is derived from the *root peh, lamed, heh*, i.e., *palah*, which refers to an act that separates one thing from another. For instance, during the plague of hail God separated, "*vehifla*" (Ex. 9:4), between the cattle of the Jews and the cattle of the Egyptians. Used in this sense, the term conveys that when we pray we ought to disengage from the distractions of the world, separating ourselves from our activities, to engage in a private conversation with God, standing existentially alone, absorbed in this unique dialogue.

Finally, *tefilla* might be from the root *peh, taf, lamed*, i.e., *patal*, one meaning of which is to wrestle. But by metathesis (i.e., rearranging the letters) *peh, taf, lamed* is the equivalent of *taf, peh, lamed*, i.e., to pray (the same way that *keves* and *kesev* both refer to sheep, while *simla* and *salma* both refer to a garment). R. Soloveitchik explained that struggle is an integral element of prayer. For instance, Rachel called the first child Jacob had from her maidservant Bilhah, Naftali, because: *naftulei Elokim niftalti* (Gen. 30:8). Onkelos explains the term as referring to the gratitude she felt for being victorious in prayer, in her struggle with her sister, Leah. It means that she prayed to God concerning her perceived competition with her sister to bear sons for Jacob and God answered her prayer. Ibn Ezra interprets *naftulei* not as referring to prayer per se, but rather to the struggle between Rachel and Leah, i.e., with the birth of Naftali, Rachel "won" a round in the "match." R. Soloveitchik viewed these interpretations of Ibn Ezra and Onkelos as being essentially in harmony. They both convey a sense of struggle and overcoming a difficult situation. Accordingly, *tefilla* conveys that sometimes prayer entails a struggle, so to speak, with God. Biblical examples include Abraham's prayer/struggle with God on behalf of Sodom, and Moses' prayer/struggle with God after the sin of the Golden Calf. As long as we know our place and speak respectfully, we may, at times, struggle with God in prayer.

No wonder the Mishna in *Berakhot* (5:1) tells us that "early pious ones" used to wait an hour before praying. If you respect something, you prepare for it. If we understand the humble nature of the experience of prayer when we evaluate ourselves, separate ourselves, and even at times struggle as we pray to God, then we can understand that preparation for prayer is a necessary prerequisite. ◆

The Correct Kavana When Reciting the Shema and Its Blessings, According to R. Joseph B. Soloveitchik

R. Basil Herring

Rav Soloveitchik analyzed the *Shema* and its associated blessings on numerous occasions, and at length. While much of his attention was devoted to the many purely halakhic aspects of the *Shema* he also focused on the proper *kavana*, or intent, required when reciting the words of this prayer that is so pivotal to the religious life of the Jew. What, according to the Rav, should one be thinking when fulfilling the obligation to recite the *Shema* twice a day?

YIḤUD HASHEM (THE UNITY OF GOD)

It is certainly true that when proclaiming the words: *Shema Yisrael Hashem Elokeinu Hashem Eḥad* (Deut. 6:4) one should bear in mind the simple meaning of the words, i.e., "Hear, O Israel, the Lord is our God, the Lord is One."

Yet the rabbinic tradition has always understood that the plain words point to much more than their literal translation might connote.

To start with, the Rav accepted Rambam's view (as is done throughout this Siddur) that when we say that God is "One" we are not merely making a quantitative statement (i.e., that God is One and not many), but a qualitative one – that is, that God is One of a kind, unique, incomparable, and different from every other being. Hence this opening verse of the *Shema* really declares God's uniqueness.

But for the Rav it is important to understand the implications that follow from recognizing God's uniqueness.

KABBALAT OL MALKHUT SHAMAYIM (THE AFFIRMATION OF GOD'S SOVEREIGNTY)

The sages taught that in reciting the *Shema*, one must affirm *kabbalat ol malkhut Shamayim*, i.e., one's personal submission to the yoke of the kingdom of heaven (*Berakhot* 13b, 14b). What exactly does this phrase mean? What is the "kingdom of heaven"? Why is it a "yoke"? What is involved in submitting to, or accepting, that yoke? Are the words simply a broad declaration of faith regarding God (for instance that He exists, that He is unique), or do they constitute a commitment to specific actions?

In the essay that forms the introduction to this Siddur, the Rav explains in striking poetic terms that the opening verses of the *Shema* refer to how God's will is manifested in our cosmos in two dimensions:

1. In the physical dimension of His creation God's will directs and controls every object, phenomenon, and event. Except for those events which are the result of human choices, everything that transpires in the natural order is willed by Him. From the cosmic and earth shattering, to the microscopic and seemingly inconsequential – it is all an expression of His will. Put simply, whatever happens in the natural world occurs because that is what God has willed to happen, almost always by means of natural processes which themselves are expressions of God's will, but also (even if very rarely) by God's direct miraculous intervention. How do we encounter this aspect of God's will? By observing and studying nature in all of its forms. To do this we do not need to be scientists or intellectuals. We need simply to be sensitive observers of God's world in its daily rhythms, and thereby to sense God's hand in all that transpires around us in the natural order.
2. The same will of God expresses itself in a second way, not in the world of nature, but in human affairs. Because we are uniquely granted the ability to choose between alternatives, God's will does not control our choices. Rather, He asks us to choose to act in accordance with what He desires. God's wishes, or commandments, are found in the Torah and its *mitzvot*, as revealed to Moses our teacher and the Jewish people at Sinai. Unlike God's will that is manifested in nature, God's will in Revelation is not general and implicit, but specific and explicit. These details were preserved and elaborated upon by the rabbinic *mesora* (tradition) in subsequent generations.

Thus, whenever we say the opening words of the *Shema* we must have in mind both dimensions of God's will, and their implications for us. On the one hand we must consciously reaffirm that everything that occurs naturally in the physical world is absolutely governed by God's will. On the other hand we commit ourselves to faithfully uphold and adhere to the will of God that is embodied in the Torah, in its commandments, and in its system of laws known collectively as the *Halakha*.[1]

1. While the Rav does not say so explicitly, these two aspects of God's will might also account for the unusual formulation of the verse "Hear, O Israel, the Lord is our God,

Both affirmations together constitute *kabbalat ol malkhut Shamayim*, i.e., with these principles in mind we accept that God's will governs the natural world, and that as Jews (i.e., "Israel" in the verse) we must submit to God's will as found in the Torah and its accompanying *mesora*.[2]

BOTH COMFORT AND CHALLENGE

These words of the *Shema* thus lead to two conflicting emotions.

On the one hand there is a sense of tranquility and inner peace when we recognize God's all-powerful will and its complete governance of the events of the natural world. Once we affirm that even if we cannot always understand God's will and His ways, whatever happens is what He has decreed, we are in some measure comforted and reassured. And indeed, as the Rav explains (see *Reshimot Shiurim* to *Berakhot*, pp. 141–142), that is how the sages understood the ensuing verse of the *Shema* that commands us to love God *uvekhol me'odekha*, saying "this refers to every measure (*midda*) that He metes out to you, whether good or bad" (*Sifri* 32, as quoted by Rashi to this verse). Hence an *onen* (a mourner in the period prior to burial of a loved one), who is otherwise exempt from *mitzvot*, must nonetheless recite the *Shema*, because in reciting this phrase the *onen* is fulfilling his or her singular obligation of *tzidduk*

the Lord is One." Should it not have more simply and unambiguously affirmed God's Oneness by saying *Shema Yisrael Hashem Elokeinu Eḥad* ("Hear, O Israel, the Lord our God is One")? In light of the Rav's analysis we can suggest that the verse is proclaiming that as Jews we must affirm ("*Shema Yisrael*") that the divine will that was revealed in the Torah to our people by God ("*Hashem*," i.e., the name of God known by our people via Revelation), and the divine will that is found throughout nature ("*Elokeinu*," i.e., the name of God that appears in the beginning of Genesis as the Creator and Master of nature), are two expressions of one and the same divine will, because the Lord Himself is One and indivisible ("*Hashem Eḥad*").

2. Implicit in the Rav's analysis is the conviction that there cannot be an inherent conflict between nature and the Torah. Once we understand that both are expressions of God's will, albeit experienced in separate dimensions, they cannot contradict each other, but must be seen as two sides of the same coin, united in a higher truth. The scientific study of nature properly done can ultimately only buttress the truths of the Torah, while the proper study of Torah can only cast deeper light on the workings of God's will in nature. And by the appropriate study of Torah in all its facets, while living in accordance with the Torah and its *mitzvot*, the Jew can live in accordance with nature in the most profound sense.

hadin, by which one unconditionally accepts the death as having occurred in accordance with God's will.

But on the other hand, the very idea that we must bear the weight of living under the discipline of the Torah's commandments leads to stress and anxiety. To live with such constant responsibilities demands self-discipline, sacrifice, and sometimes loneliness. It means recognizing that while in the natural order God's will controls everything, in our own moral and spiritual lives we are fully responsible for any failure to live up to His commandments. Such feelings are only heightened by the preceding words of the same verse that (as understood by the *Sifri*, quoted by Rashi) direct us to harness our every instinct, whether good or bad (*bekhol levavekha, bishnei yitzrekha*), in submitting to God's will, even if it is necessary to sacrifice our lives to that end (*uvekhol nafshekha, shehu notel et nafshekha*).

Such is the mental and emotional duality embedded in the opening verses of the *Shema*. On the one hand they confer clarity and comfort – but on the other they lead to anxiety and resolve. Both must be kept in mind and balanced as we recite the *Shema*.

BARUKH SHEM KEVOD MALKHUTO LE'OLAM VA'ED (BLESSED IS THE NAME OF HIS GLORIOUS KINGDOM FOREVER AND EVER)

Why do we insert this blessing of God's name when the Torah itself, which is the source of the entire paragraph, does not contain it? The Gemara (*Pesaḥim* 56a) accounts for this insertion by recounting the deathbed exchange between Jacob and his sons, in which they assured him of their faithfulness by declaring *Shema…eḥad*, and he gratefully responded *Barukh... va'ed*. According to this Gemara we insert *Barukh…va'ed* in imitation of Jacob's declaration. But, the Rav asks, is this not an improper interruption (*hefsek*) in the obligation to recite the *Shema* as it appears in Deuteronomy?

To answer this question (see *Reshimot* pp. 316–322) the Rav referred to the Vilna Gaon, who said that in reciting *Shema…eḥad* one should concentrate on the principle of God's eternity. For the grammatical root of the name of God (spelled *Yud, Heh, Vav, Heh*, and usually referred to as *Shem Havaya*), as it appears twice in the verse, connotes God's eternal existence, encompassing all of the past, present, and future. And even though the name is not pronounced as it is written, but rather as *Adonai* (which connotes God as

Master of the universe), it is the written connotation (i.e., God the Eternal One) that one should keep in mind when reciting this verse. For this reason, having proclaimed God's name, we bless it – just as was done by the people when they heard this name proclaimed in the Temple. Hence we say *Barukh...va'ed*.[3]

Consequently, as explained by the Rav, there are two separate obligations: one (learned from Moses our teacher) is to recite the *Shema* as it appears in the Torah, and the second (learned from our forefather Jacob) is to respond to this invocation of God's name by blessing it silently (so as to avoid a misleading impression that the blessing is part of the Torah's *Shema* text itself).

That said, it is also true that the *Barukh...va'ed* proclamation is essential to accepting the heavenly yoke. For this reason various authorities, including the *Shulḥan Arukh* and the Rema, insist that without saying it one has not fulfilled the obligation to recite the *Shema*. Why is this so? One explanation is that of the Vilna Gaon and the *Beit Yosef*, that without it one's saying of *Shema... eḥad* is no more than *sippur devarim be'alma*, i.e., "a mere recitation" of what Moses wrote in the Torah, or at most a quote of what Jews declare when they affirm God's uniqueness. By proclaiming *Barukh...va'ed*, reciting the *Shema* becomes a personal declaration of submission to God's will. That is, "I hereby bless the name of His glorious kingdom which must be blessed for all time." Hence reciting it affirms acceptance of the yoke of heaven.

THE THREE ENSUING PARAGRAPHS OF THE *SHEMA*

It is not only the *Shema...eḥad* and *Barukh...va'ed* that affirm the heavenly yoke. In fact all three paragraphs of the *Shema* do so as well. The Rav explained (see *Shiurim LeZekher Aba Mari* 1:20–24) that while it is true that if we recite only the first verse (*Shema...eḥad*) with proper *kavana* we have discharged our obligation to recite the *Shema*, that is only because we accept the view of R. Meir in *Berakhot* 13a that *Shema...eḥad* itself echoes the various affirmations that constitute acceptance of the heavenly yoke found in the three paragraphs of the *Shema*. Thus optimally one should recite all three paragraphs, each of which focuses on a different aspect of acceptance of the heavenly yoke.

---

3. It is noteworthy that the blessing concludes with the phrase *le'olam va'ed* ("forever and ever"), i.e., the name that connotes that the Eternal God should be blessed throughout all eternity.

What are the additional aspects found in the three paragraphs of the *Shema*? The Rav quotes Rambam (*Hil. Keriat Shema* 1:2) that "We first recite the *Shema* and its first paragraph because they contain the uniqueness of God, the love of God, and the study of God, which constitute the great pillar upon which everything depends, and thereafter we recite the second paragraph which includes the obligation to uphold all the other commandments." In other words:

1. In the first paragraph, the term *ve'ahavta* ("you shall love") instructs us that we must submit to God's will by loving Him unconditionally, and *veshinantam/vedibarta bam* ("you shall teach them/speak of them") teaches that we must submit to His will by studying and teaching Torah.
2. In the second paragraph, *shamoa tishme'u el mitzvotai* ("you will listen diligently to My commandments") instructs us that we must submit to God's will by upholding the *mitzvot* of the Torah.
3. In the third paragraph, *hotzeti etkhem me'Eretz Mitzrayim lihyot lakhem le'Elokim* ("I brought you out of the land of Egypt to be your God") instructs us that we must submit to God's will insofar as He freed us from subservience to Pharaoh and Egypt so that we should serve God alone as our King and Ruler.

While Rambam in the above ruling does not explicitly reference the third paragraph of the *Shema*, it is significant that he (unlike other authorities) never mentions a particular obligation to mention the Exodus on a daily basis. The Rav explains that for Rambam the obligation to remember the Exodus from Egypt every day is part of the daily affirmation of *kabbalat ol malkhut Shamayim*, to which it is intimately connected.[4]

Thus in reciting these three paragraphs we must keep in mind these various obligations that result in complete submission to God's will and the heavenly yoke.

4. One might say that this paragraph provides a political dimension to the acceptance of divine sovereignty, i.e., we affirm that our ultimate political allegiance is to God alone. While we certainly owe allegiance to properly constituted human rulers and governments, it is true only to the extent to which their laws are in accordance with God's will.

THE THREE BLESSINGS SURROUNDING KERIAT SHEMA

On various occasions the Rav pointed out how these major themes of the *Shema* are echoed and amplified by the three *berakhot* (and their associated texts) that precede and follow the *Shema*, whether during *Shaḥarit* or *Ma'ariv*. By reciting these blessings we prepare for, and recapitulate, the thoughts that should be uppermost in our minds when we recite the *Shema* itself. Thus:

1. The first blessing spells out in detail the many ways in which God uniquely sustains the cosmos – as a result of which His creatures affirm His sovereignty and bless Him. Thus at *Shaḥarit* the angels are described as *kulam mekabelim aleihem ol malkhut Shamayim* ("All accept upon themselves the yoke of the heavenly kingdom" when they recognize the many ways that He governs His creation), while the *Ma'ariv* equivalent proclaims *tamid yimlokh aleinu le'olam va'ed* ("Who will always rule over us, forever and ever"), reflecting the first lines of the *Shema*.
2. The second blessing focuses primarily on our renewed commitment to study God's Torah, and observe its commandments. Thus at *Shaḥarit* we say *ha'er eineinu beToratekha vedabek libenu bemitzvotekha* ("Open our eyes through Your Torah, so that our hearts can cleave to Your commandments"), and at *Ma'ariv* we proclaim *nismaḥ bedivrei Toratekha uvmitzvotekha le'olam va'ed* ("We shall rejoice in the words of Your Torah and Your commandments forever and ever").[5]
3. In the third blessing (following the third paragraph of the *Shema*) we accept the yoke of heaven (in *Shaḥarit* we say *malkhuto ve'emunato la'ad kayamet*, "His sovereignty and faithfulness endure forever," while in *Ma'ariv* we say *malkenu hago'alenu mikaf kol he'aritzim*, "our King Who saves us from the hand of all oppressors") by virtue of His having freed us from Egyptian servitude. Thus it describes at length not just the Exodus from Egypt, but most significantly how at the Sea of Reeds, Israel submitted to God's sovereignty, which was the model for all time.

---

5. One should also note how the conclusion of the second blessing in both the morning and at night refers to God's love for the people of Israel. In so doing, it ever so subtly teaches us that it is His unconditional love for us that makes it possible, and indeed necessary, for us to love Him unconditionally in return, as in *ve'ahavta et Hashem Elokekha*, "You shall love the Lord your God."

In these ways, the entire section of the siddur from *Barekhu* till the *Amida* constitutes an affirmation not just of faith in the God Who created and governs the entire cosmos, but of a renewed commitment to live in accordance with God's will, as it was revealed in the Torah and preserved in the rabbinic *mesora* throughout the generations.

It is this faith, and these commitments, that we must keep in mind, according to R. Soloveitchik, when we recite the *Shema* and its accompanying blessings with full *kavana*. ◆

The Shabbat Prayers as Explained by R. Joseph B. Soloveitchik

R. Aton Holzer

According to R. Soloveitchik, there are two separate, but related, aspects of the laws and the prayers of Shabbat.

The first aspect relates to the technical *halakhot* that embody the commandments and prohibitions regarding actions that we are permitted or forbidden to do on that day. The second, broader, aspect relates to the spiritual awareness and affirmation that the entire cosmos was created, is sustained, and will be perfected in due course, at God's command. This aspect also affirms and testifies to the special covenant between God and the Jewish people in the realization of that cosmic drama. When the Jew observes both aspects of Shabbat, he and the Jewish people are sanctified.

The dynamics of this sanctification process through history can be seen by a careful analysis of Shabbat prayers, as they progress from the beginning to the end of Shabbat.

FRIDAY EVENING

אַתָּה קִדַּשְׁתָּ אֶת יוֹם הַשְּׁבִיעִי לִשְׁמֶךָ, תַּכְלִית מַעֲשֵׂה שָׁמַיִם וָאָרֶץ.

> You sanctified the seventh day for the sake of Your name, the culmination of the creation of heaven and earth.

This prayer describes Shabbat as celebrating the completion of God's act of creation of the cosmos. It is therefore a holy day because it attests to the majesty and power of the Creator of the universe. While some of the daily prayers address God as Creator, they do so in the context of an ongoing process of creation. Shabbat prayers are unique in their focus upon the achievement of completion of this process. (Other Shabbat prayers also reflect the completion of God's creation, such as *Kel Adon*, which speaks of the complete cosmological order, as does the psalm of the day, Psalm 92, whose opening verses

---

This essay derives from R. Soloveitchik's *Shiurim LeZekher Aba Mari*, vol. 2, pp. 127–130; 146–150; 79. All page numbers refer to that work unless otherwise noted.

praise God upon beholding His completed world which manifests divine glory.)

SHABBAT MORNING

The morning *Amida* addresses not merely the revelation at Sinai, as Franz Rosenzweig had suggested, but the sanctification of the Jewish people via the Shabbat covenant at Sinai. God "used" the already sacred Shabbat, sanctified by dint of its attestation to God's majesty, to confer sanctity upon the Jewish people.[1] As such, its observance serves as both the basis and sign of the Sinaitic covenant.[2] This explains the relevance of "וְשָׁמְרוּ בְנֵי־יִשְׂרָאֵל אֶת־הַשַּׁבָּת לַעֲשׂוֹת אֶת־הַשַּׁבָּת לְדֹרֹתָם, בְּרִית עוֹלָם – And the Children of Israel shall keep Shabbat, observing Shabbat throughout their generations as an everlasting covenant" – which stresses the function of Shabbat observance as the sign of the covenant. This sanctification process began with the initial command of Shabbat observance at Marah, where Israel encamped prior to reaching Sinai, and only culminated at Sinai. For this reason, the relevant scriptural citation in our liturgy is not the fourth commandment, but *Veshameru* (Ex. 31:16–17). The

1. For R. Soloveitchik, the mechanics of the sanctification of the Jewish people is explored most fully in the *Kedusha* liturgy. In particular, the stanza of "*Mimkomkha* – from Your place" in the *Kedusha* of Shabbat *Shaḥarit* expresses that "In Jewish thought, the key principle of divine providence is cleaving unto God, of desolate reality – the sense of divine hiddenness – grasping the living, eternal reality. Man must strive to become an abode for the *Shekhina* by means of *halakha*, by attaching to God within the framework of real life. Though the essence of the state of cleaving to God is found in the prophecies regarding the end of days, it begins to be realized in this divided world, in the actual life of man, though flawed; thus, when ten Jews sit and study Torah together and complete their study, one stands up and proclaims the *Kaddish*, the vision of the redemption of the *Shekhina* and man's cleaving to his Creator; the group that studies Torah is bringing about the vision's gradual realization" (*And From There You Shall Seek*).
2. R. Soloveitchik taught that there are two determinants of Jewish nationhood. There is the Covenant of Fate, *brit goral*, the experience of Jewish loneliness, of shared suffering and responsibility, giving rise to the consciousness of the need for *Ḥesed* (loving-kindness), that was born of the enslavement in Egypt. At Sinai, a second covenant was introduced, the Covenant of Destiny, *brit yiud*; at Sinai, the Jewish people embarked upon a life with direction, the quest for self-transcendence, in which *ḥesed* and brotherhood spring not from a shared sense of isolation but from a sense of fellowship in a filial relationship with God (*Kol Dodi Dofek*).

Veshameru verse, as well as the *Velo netato* ("And You did not give it...") passage that follows it, that reference the unique relationship between Shabbat and the Jewish people, encapsulate the process of sanctification far better than would a citation from the Ten Commandments, which fails to impart this dimension.

Similarly, the text of the Shabbat *Kiddush* incorporates two themes, that of the completion of creation, זִכָּרוֹן לְמַעֲשֵׂה בְרֵאשִׁית, which reflects the intrinsic sanctity of the day, and that of the chosenness of the Jewish people – כִּי בָנוּ בָחַרְתָּ וְאוֹתָנוּ קִדַּשְׁתָּ מִכָּל הָעַמִּים, "For You have chosen us and sanctified us from among all peoples," which derives from the sanctity of Shabbat day.

A further stage in the historical drama of sanctity becomes evident later on Shabbat morning. Unlike the festivals, whose establishment depends upon the Jewish people, the core sanctity of Shabbat derives from God, not the Jewish people. However, the day is not sanctified by God alone; it is imparted additional sanctity by the Jewish people. The sanctity that the Jewish people, sanctified by the sanctity of Shabbat itself, impart reciprocally to Shabbat comes to expression in the *Amida* of *Musaf*. Like *Kiddush*, the *Musaf* offering is a feature of all days sanctified by the Jewish people;[3] it derives not from the primordial sanctity of Shabbat from creation, but is of a piece with the sanctity of the festivals, which is derived from the sanctity of the Jewish people. In the *Musaf Amida*, the focus is not Marah, but Sinai, because this is

3. R. Soloveitchik explained that the *Musaf* prayer is qualitatively distinct, in a manner which reflects its theme – the communal imparting of sanctity. The blessing of *Retzeh* requests of God to accept our prayers as a sacrifice, and thus serves to transform the spoken *Amida* into a Temple offering. The last section of the *Amida*, beginning with *Retzeh*, represents the element of prayer instituted to parallel the sacrificial order, and recasts the foregoing private prayer, mere "speech," into a sacrificial offering (cf. *Berakhot* 26b). Generally, the prayers do not specifically reference the offerings, so that private prayers, by default, may be rendered as "individual offerings" by the *Retzeh* section. In the presence of a *minyan* and a Torah scroll, the same prayer binds to those of the entire nation, and serves as a communal offering. However, since the *Musaf* service specifically references the *Musaf* offering, the blessing of *Retzeh* can transform it only into a communal offering. (Thus, donative *Musaf* prayers are impossible, and there is no remedial prayer if *Musaf* was forgotten.) As such, *Musaf* stands unique as a prayer service that is communal and unitive at its very core (*Shiurim LeZekher Aba Mari*).

where we were first commanded regarding the festivals – days whose sanctity derives from that of the Jewish people. Thus Sinai is where derivative sanctity was first expounded: אָז מִסִּינַי נִצְטַוּוּ עָלֶיהָ... לְהַקְרִיב בָּהּ קָרְבַּן מוּסַף שַׁבָּת כָּרָאוּי, "Then, at Sinai, they were commanded regarding it... to offer on it the additional Shabbat sacrifice, properly". It is further extended, reflexively, to Shabbat itself.

SHABBAT AFTERNOON

The Levites in the Temple would sing three independent songs reflecting three aspects of the sanctity of Shabbat, and indeed there is yet another: the *Amida* of *Minḥa* represents praise for God stemming from a third sanctity associated with the day – not merely that imbued by God at creation, nor that infused by the sanctification on the part of the Jewish people, but that drawn directly from the eschatological "Shabbat" of Messianic times, of which Shabbat is a foretaste. This is the essence of "אַתָּה אֶחָד וְשִׁמְךָ אֶחָד – You are One and Your Name is One". Apparently, the culmination of the sanctification process envisions the entire world enveloped in sanctity, drawing from the sanctity of the Jewish people.

A hint to this theme may be found in the coda to the Shabbat verses of praise, *Nishmat kol ḥai*, "The soul of every living being," which moves beyond the national redemption of the Jewish people described in the Song at the Sea to address the redemption of all of mankind, of every living soul, even of the cosmos. Indeed, R. Soloveitchik notes[4] that *Nishmat* teaches that the Jew is not satisfied with his redemption unless all the world is redeemed with him – the Jewish experience is all-embracing, sympathetic to all.

With *Minḥa*, the historical drama is complete. *Kedusha* has emerged from its divine source to permeate all of Creation, by means of the eternal partners in the historical drama of sanctity: Shabbat and the Jewish people.

SUMMARY

For R. Soloveitchik Shabbat embodies holiness, but it also recapitulates the history and destiny of holiness, from the Shabbat of creation to the end of time: what R. Soloveitchik calls the "mystery of creation":

---

4. *Days of Deliverance*, p. 77.

The idea of Shabbat, its interpretation, is clear to everyone and does not require elucidation. We know that Shabbat means rest; hence one-seventh of man's life is spent in comfort, in rest, free from the worries and care to which both great and small are subject. The Shabbat also perpetuates and forever confirms the very sublime idea, namely, faith in the divine act of creation (Rambam, *Guide* 3:43).

Rambam here offers two possible aspects from which the Shabbat may be viewed. One is based upon divine benevolence which, in this instance, allots man a full measure of happiness for one-seventh of his life span. The other, which is borrowed from the Scriptures and which Rambam adopted in the Code, is of symbolic strain: the Shabbat symbolizes the act of creation. The first yields a purely pragmatic interpretation; the goal of the Shabbat is hedonic, and the means leading to its realization belong to a religious technical discipline. Thus the Shabbat idea is dispossessed of its breadth and warmth. The metaphysical sweep is checked and the religious ardor is cooled. Yet, the second interpretation, envisaging the Shabbat as the incarnation of the mystery of creation, penetrates infinity itself. It discovers in dead matter and mechanical motion the fingerprints of a Creator and the contours of a conscious creation. The covenant-idea and the incomprehensible God–man contact emerge in full refulgence… (*Halakhic Mind*, 97–98). ◆

Introduction to Yigdal and to the Ani Ma'amin Principles

Prof. David Shatz

The poem *Yigdal* (page 18), as well as the *Ani Ma'amin* which appears after *Shaḥarit* (page 206), are both modeled after a famous list of principles formulated by Rambam. Scholars generally attribute *Yigdal* to Daniel ben Yehuda HaKohen of Rome, who lived around the year 1300. The authorship of the *Ani Ma'amin* is unknown.

Rambam's list appears in his commentary to the Mishna, at the end of his lengthy introduction to his commentary to "*Perek Ḥelek*," the tenth chapter of Tractate *Sanhedrin*. *Perek Ḥelek* begins with the words, "All of Israel have a share (*ḥelek*) in the World to Come (*Olam HaBa*)." The Mishna, however, then names three exceptions. Building on the Mishna's assertion that denying certain beliefs excludes one from a share in the World to Come, Rambam formulates thirteen principles of Judaism, the *Yud-Gimmel Ikkarim*. *Yigdal* presents each *ikkar* in one line of poetry. The *Ani Ma'amin*'s prose wordings of the *Ikkarim* are generally shorter than their counterparts in the introduction to *Perek Ḥelek*, as they lack the philosophical elaboration provided in the latter work.

Why did Rambam compose his list? The most natural answer is that he wanted to provide all Jews with the beliefs necessary to attain *Olam HaBa*. Additional explanations have been proposed, however. One element emerges in a letter in which Rambam explains why he wrote his monumental legal code, *Mishneh Torah*. He declares: "I am most zealous for the Lord God of Israel, when I see before me a nation that does not have a comprehensive book [of laws] in the true sense, nor true and accurate [theological] opinions" (following the translation of Prof. Isadore Twersky *z"l*). As Prof. Twersky puts it, speaking of *Mishneh Torah* as a whole, "He felt the urgent need not only for a book of statutes and rulings but also for the standardization and systematization of the '*halakhot* of belief'" (*Introduction to the Code of Maimonides* [*Mishneh Torah*] [New Haven, CT: Yale University Press, 1981], p. 77). Indeed, Rambam begins *Mishneh Torah* with a rigorous presentation of beliefs, and much other material throughout his writings establishes the importance of correct beliefs. Beliefs and halakhic observance, furthermore, must go together. Although the quotations above pertain to *Mishneh Torah*, one surmises that Rambam's stress on the importance of belief helped inspire the earlier list in his commentary to the Mishna.

The structure of the principles has been construed in various ways, but the most straightforward description is this: The principles deal first with God (1–5), then with revelation (6–9), and finally (10–13) with God's relationship with the world, present and future, highlighting reward and punishment. Some of the beliefs (such as the belief that God is incorporeal, i.e., lacking a body, and the belief in divine unity) Maimonides argues for elsewhere on philosophical grounds. Other beliefs, such as the guaranteed arrival of the Messiah and resurrection of the dead, are known by means of biblical and rabbinic texts.

Later authors, such as R. Shimon ben Tzemaḥ Duran (*Tashbetz*), R. Ḥasdai Crescas, R. Joseph Albo, R. Yitzḥak Arama (*Akeidat Yitzḥak*) and R. Isaac Abarbanel, as well as lesser figures, differed with Maimonides as to which beliefs of Judaism should count as *ikkarim* and which, by contrast, are true beliefs but not *ikkarim*. Several of the later authorities subsumed the specific principles of Maimonides under larger rubrics, and there was disagreement over the purpose of determining *ikkarim*. Abarbanel, (*Rosh Amana*, ch. 23) argues, contrary to that work's earlier chapters, that all beliefs in Judaism have equal status, since all are obligatory, and so none should be singled out as special principles.

In *Mishneh Torah* (*Hil. Teshuva*, ch. 3) Rambam identifies twenty-four categories of people who have no share in the World to Come. These include various types of heretics. The forms of heresy encompass those who deny the principles listed in the introduction to *Ḥelek*, with one exception: *Ikkar* 11, reward and punishment, is not mentioned in the *Hilkhot Teshuva* listing. However, the eighth *Ikkar* is expanded to produce two categories: one who denies the divine origin of the Torah, and one who denies the Oral Law's authority as the authentic interpretation of the Written Law. Thus, the number of beliefs of which denial deprives one of a share in the World to Come remains at thirteen. There are differences between the structure, order and wordings of the respective lists in *Mishneh Torah* and the introduction to *Ḥelek*.

The absence of a belief from the list of *Ikkarim* does not imply lack of high importance. Thus, Rambam calls free will "a great principle (**עיקר גדול**) and a pillar of Torah and *mitzva* (**עמוד התורה והמצווה**)" (*Hil. Teshuva* 5:3) – but it is not on his list of Thirteen Principles. Commentators have sought to explain this anomaly.

While some differences have persisted regarding the precise parameters of Maimonides' principles, their essential content has been accepted (by Orthodox Jewry) as the classic formulation of the core beliefs of Judaism. •

Sacrifices and Prayer: Past, Present, and Future

R. Shalom Carmy

God is sovereign. We are to serve Him with "all our heart and all our soul and all our might." The institution of sacrifice enacts God's sovereignty. Regarding the *Olah*, Ramban explains that in offering an animal on the altar, it is as if the individual were offering up his own body on the altar. Both the individual and the community bring sacrifices to atone for sin. Sacrifices are integral to the everyday Temple service. They are even brought at times of joy and thanksgiving, as *Shelamim* and *Toda*, when we are invited to partake of the offering, supping, as it were, at the divine table.

With the destruction of the *Mikdash*, the offering of animals is replaced with the study and recitation of the laws of sacrifice. That is why the morning prayers are prefaced with the Mishna of *Eizehu Mekoman*. That is why every *Amida* culminates in the plea that God accept the burnt-offerings of Israel and restore the *Mikdash*.

Some modern people are displeased with this feature of Judaism. Unfamiliarity breeds discomfort – it is hard to request sincerely what is difficult to imagine. If words atone as well as actions, why not abandon physical sacrifices, replete with disturbing reminders of flesh, blood, mortality and suffering? For many modern people, the elementary experience of God's sovereignty and the human being's absolute commitment are alien. Hence Jewish theological liberalism, like liberal, secularized, Christianity, tends to stress what God does for us, rather than what He summons us to do in His service. With this reversal comes the downplaying of concrete, particular reality. Like the concrete Jewish connection to the land of Israel, like belief in bodily resurrection, like the very singularity of the Jewish people, the enactment of physical sacrifice reminds us of what many are desperate to forget.

Some take comfort in Rambam's theory that sacrifices, like verbal prayer, accommodate human frailty, allowing concrete expression of intellectual truths that most people are unable to fully internalize in purely abstract form, and that the sacrificial cult served, in the past, to counter the vivid imagery associated with ancient paganism. Having presumably transcended the bonds of bodily existence, one might dispense with the physical sacrifices prescribed by the halakha. Rambam himself subsumed the sacrifices in the eternal

Torah. Easy preference for intellectual gestures over concrete performance invariably arises and ends in the replacement of real existence with empty abstraction.

Jewish mystics have dreamed of a world where all nature, human and non-human, is reconciled in an eschatological vision of universal harmony. In such a universe, hinted at in the writings of R. Kook, the human act of sacrifice will no longer exploit the animal world, perhaps because the animals will embrace their role in the service of God, perhaps because the voluntary sacrifices in the Messianic age will come entirely from grain.

Prayer is not only an expression of what we want of God, but also our education in what we ought to want of Him. The king in R. Yehuda HaLevi's *Kuzari* reduced the rabbi to shameful contrition when he observed that Jewish prayers to return to Israel, lacking apposite actions, meant no more than the mimicry of the parrot. We do not always bring to our prayer the desire to serve God with "all our heart and all our soul and all our might," nor do we enjoy being reminded of what that may entail, in all its concrete particularity. May the words we offer up, however half-heartedly, ripen into readiness, and may that readiness transform our lives. ◆

Achieving Kavana: Praying from the Heart

Rabbanit Rookie Billet

An in-depth inquiry into prayer necessarily reflects many fundamental assumptions and attitudes, relating not only to prayer, but also to our pursuit of a relationship with God. This essay is both subjective and objective; it reflects my perspective as a Jewish person and as a Jewish woman, and is the result of a personal quest to understand prayer, as well as the journey of a teacher to assist students who struggle with the prayer experience.

Some difficult questions with which to grapple follow: Is prayer for man or for God? Why are we obligated to pray? Shouldn't prayer stem from an inner yearning or personal need, rather than an obligation imposed on us by the Ultimate Being to Whom we address these prayers? What is the essence of prayer? What exactly are we trying to accomplish when we pray? Is it appropriate to pray spontaneously for trivial things (such as success on the sports field or finding a good parking space), or should prayer always follow a set form and content, addressing larger, communal or global needs like world peace, healing the sick, or rain in its time? Why must I pray regularly, even when I'm distracted or not inspired, and my *tefilla* may be rote and mindless? What is the difference between praying alone and praying in public in the synagogue? Must I use the language of the siddur, even if I don't understand it, or may I use my own words to speak from the heart and thus to truly communicate from my innermost being? What should I do when I feel that I've prayed with fervor, intention, and *kavana*, yet the things I asked for were not forthcoming? Are there concrete steps I can take to make my prayer more meaningful and personally fulfilling?

It is challenging to confront many of these problems for two reasons: First, in Judaism, as in most intellectual endeavors, the questions are often stronger than the answers. Second, insofar as truly meaningful prayer is an intensely personal experience, answers that work for some may not be helpful for others. And yet despite these challenges, numerous answers or at least approaches have been formulated in our rabbinic tradition over the ages. What follows here builds on what is found in that tradition.

WHO IS PRAYER FOR?

Prayer must be for man's benefit, and not "for God's sake," because God is

Shalem, complete and perfect, and hence lacks for nothing. If God does not need our prayers, then, why should we pray? Prayer is man's way of connecting to God, of affirming several times each and every day that we believe in God's existence, in His continuing power to influence the world at large and our own personal lives in particular. When we pray we affirm our conviction that we can indeed influence God not just for ourselves but on behalf of others for whom we pray as well. Prayer enables us to communicate with the Master of the universe three times every day, and for as many unstructured, spontaneous times as we desire, any day, any time, and any place. "When we learn, God talks to us; when we pray, we talk to God." And whatever else our prayers accomplish, talking to God in heartfelt prayer raises our lives to a higher and more profound level.

PRAYER AS COMMUNICATION WITH THE DIVINE

It is important to note that our rabbis differ on the exact nature of the *mitzva* of *tefilla*. Most prominently, Rambam tells us that when the Torah speaks of "service of the heart," it is referring to the obligation to pray to God daily. Rambam further explains that while the Torah's obligation is simply to pray, the rabbinic tradition provides the particulars of the *mitzva*: how often, when, and the basic structure and laws of specific prayers.

But beyond prayer as a fulfillment of a formal obligation, whether biblical or rabbinic, prayer must be seen as essential to building a personal relationship with the Master of the universe. This can happen in various ways:

1. The Yom Kippur liturgy portrays the relationship of man and God using various powerful metaphors. "We are Your children and You are our Father." "We are Your people and You are our King." "We are Your vineyard and You are our Vintner." "We are Your servants and You are our Master." All of these relationships demand communication, whether we are personally motivated to communicate or not.
2. The Talmud teaches that there are two explanations for how our prayers were established. The first is that our prayers were instituted as a replacement for the daily sacrifices in the Temple, after the Temple was destroyed. The second explains that our prayers actually derive from each of the patriarchs, Abraham, Isaac, and Jacob, each of whom was responsible for establishing one of the daily prayers. Putting these two explanations together,

> it could be said that they are both valid explanations, but refer to different aspects of our prayers. Prayer as a substitute for sacrifice is the source of the public communal prayer experience, while prayer based on the patriarchal precedent reflects our deeply personal communication with God. The fact that the Torah reports that Abraham arose early (to pray *Shaḥarit*), Isaac went out to "communicate" in the field before evening (to pray *Minḥa*), and Jacob petitioned God in a particular place (to pray *Ma'ariv*), suggests that prayer fulfills a deep personal need, as modeled for us by our forefathers. Forging such a relationship with God requires work, cultivation, and nurturing, involving love and care, day after day. This is how our prayers transcend rote words or empty gestures, to become personal spiritual adventures in communicating with the *Ribbono shel Olam* on the most intimate level.

Seen in this light, the question of women's obligation to prayer is not "do they have to or are they exempt." Certainly there are halakhic opinions that are lenient when it comes to a woman's obligation to pray, especially when childcare or family responsibilities make urgent demands upon her time. The question rather is why would a woman want to deprive herself of such uplifting opportunities for cultivating a meaningful relationship with the Almighty, sharing her deepest yearnings with God, encountering the Divine in the everyday details of her life, experienced as a woman, a *bat Torah*, a daughter or sister, mother or grandmother, or for that matter as a communal role model for other women? A woman who wishes to be a full participant in Jewish life will want to take complete advantage of the opportunity to pray at every stage of her life, to address her Creator on a daily basis as a confident but humble human being, fashioned in God's image and blessed with a woman's *ḥokhma* (wisdom) and special *bina* (understanding).

THE STRUCTURE OF PRAYER

Prayer clearly consists of praise for the Almighty, petitions for our needs and expression of heartfelt gratitude. Prayer recalls our national history; it quotes from many of our classic biblical and rabbinic texts; it takes the form of prose, poetry, and song; it rejoices and it mourns; it is expressed in the voice of the individual and the collective voice of the community, in many places and over hundreds of generations. Is there a common thread to all of this?

R. Elimelech bar Shaul, author of the series *Mitzva VaLev*, suggests that the

essence of prayer is *kirva Elokit*, closeness to God, which is best achieved not through expressions of thanks or praise, but through petitioning for our needs. We approach God more consistently and diligently when we feel vulnerable or in need of help, support, or a way out of our solitude. Very often our prayers are most meaningful and memorable when they come at a time of profound anxiety: when a family member is ill, when there is turbulence on our airplane, on Yom Kippur when we sense that our lives are on the line, or when we hear an intruder breaking an upstairs window in our home.

PRAYING REGULARLY OR ONLY WHEN INSPIRED?

Can we ever create a masterpiece if we never engage in artistic efforts? Can we ever play a piano concerto brilliantly if we never practice? Can we ever write a great novel if we never put pen to paper? By the same measure, can we ever pray effectively and authentically if we allow our internal prayer mechanisms and capacities to rust and atrophy? If we are to have moments when we truly connect to God and feel that our supplications reach the divine throne, we must pray on a regular basis, even if all too often our prayers seem to us to be rushed or mindless. Regular prayer ingrains the words and melodies of *tefilla* indelibly in the heart and mind. A person who articulates the prayers carefully on a daily basis will surely be able to communicate with God at a time of crisis or elation, without being deprived of the essential tools that regular *tefilla* imprints in our minds and hearts.

PRAYING ALONE OR PRAYING WITH THE TZIBBUR?

Men are obligated to pray with a *minyan betzibbur* (nine other males similarly obligated). As mentioned earlier, *halakha* exempts women from the obligation to pray with a *minyan*, even during those times in their lives when they are not involved in child-raising responsibilities. While many women express their gratitude for this exemption and cherish the opportunity to pray alone, or at home, at their own pace, beyond the pressures of the *minyan*, there are many reasons that women should value praying in the synagogue, especially on Shabbat and Yom Tov. In the synagogue, a woman may derive inspiration in the company of others who pray fervently and with *kavana*. In the synagogue, the time for prayer is set aside and consecrated, whereas in our homes, household responsibilities can all too easily beckon to us silently but forcefully from an adjacent room.

And then there is the benefit of *tefilla betzibbur*, public prayer. R. Elimelech bar Shaul draws a parallel to a symphony orchestra, in which each instrument brings its own voice, rhythm, tenor, and intensity. The sounds made by each instrument by itself are certainly beautiful, but the harmony achieved by the blending of the entire symphony orchestra is vastly more moving and complete. A soloist may be brilliant, but when the soloist is accompanied by a symphony orchestra, the music is beyond beautiful – it can be sublime. Similarly, in the *tzibbur*, each *mitpalel* comes with his or her own personality. One brings love, another awe. One brings depth, another the merits of the Holocaust survivor. Still another offers the pain of the childless, or of the homeless or the jobless; another reflects the challenge of a single parent or of profound loneliness. One contributes the magical passion of the *ba'al teshuva*, while another brings the lifelong dedication of the *talmid ḥakham*. The combined voices of the entire congregation come together, reinforcing and supporting each other in their shared search for the Divine. Only with the *tzibbur* can this melding of voices and feelings reach a crescendo. Only in the *tzibbur* can we participate in *devarim shebikedusha* such as the public Torah Reading, the *Kaddish*, and the *Kedusha*.

Today's lifestyles make it easier for women with young children to attend the synagogue. For communities that have one, the Shabbat or Yom Tov *hashkama* (early morning) *minyan* allows a husband and wife to attend services at different times so as to share childcare responsibilities accordingly. Many synagogues conduct prayer groups for youth while their parents attend services. Shadow programs for children with disabilities make it possible for their parents to attend services as well.

THE LANGUAGE OF THE SIDDUR OR OUR OWN WORDS?

As we have seen, prayer is a *mitzva shebalev*, a commandment that must be fulfilled with heartfelt conviction, not just with a rote recitation of fixed words. Yet our sages insist that our prayers cannot abandon the prescribed texts that *halakha* requires. How do we achieve both goals – inner devotion, and following prescribed words and actions with set rules and regulations? When Rambam recounts the development of prayer and the siddur, he explains that when our ancestors were exiled, many tried to compose their own Hebrew prayers but were hampered by their inability to speak fluent Hebrew. For this reason Ezra established the daily *Amida* so every Jew could pray with

confidence in clear, appropriate language. To what can we compare this? To when we feel inarticulate in expressing our love or appreciation for a friend or a loved one, and turn to the true and tried sonnets or words of others, be it the poetry of Elizabeth Barrett Browning ("How do I Love Thee: Let Me Count the Ways"), or even the simple words of a preprinted card, to evoke and express our innermost thoughts with elegance and precision. So too, in addressing the King of kings, ancient words and phrases that have withstood the test of time surely fulfill the same purpose. Given our own inadequacies in finding the right words to pour out our hearts in praise, petition, or thanks to the infinite Creator of the cosmos, should we not avail ourselves of the words of our masters of spiritual expression?

This does not mean that we should not also express our innermost thoughts in our own simple, sincere words that come directly from the heart and from the pain of the struggling soul. We need both. We need the sublime words of King David's Psalms accompanied by the compositions of the sages of the Great Assembly that lie at the heart of the siddur. And we also need the additional personal expressions of the heart that the siddur allows for in paragraphs such as *Shema Kolenu* and *Refa'enu*. Or when we cover our eyes as we stand before the Shabbat candles, when we immerse in the *mikveh*, when we stand at the graves of our parents, or at the *Kotel*, or at *Kever Raḥel*. And, closer to home, when we open our hearts to God, to feel His presence, feel His love and strength enveloping us, as we stand in our kitchen or our yard, gaze at the seashore, or watch our peacefully sleeping children. At times such as these we can and should reach out to Him with our very own words.

WHEN WE DON'T GET WHAT WE PRAY FOR

Often we are disappointed when we pray long and hard for something, be it the recovery of a loved one, a suitable life-partner for someone who is lonely, a child for the childless, consolation for the bereaved, or any other legitimate hope or dream, but our prayers are not answered. How should we feel? May we express our pain or even despair in the absence of a positive response? Is anger an appropriate reaction? There are no simple or even satisfying answers for these intense theological questions, which even people of deep faith ask. And yet, certain things need to be kept in mind. Perhaps when we don't get what we pray for, it's not that God isn't listening; perhaps His answer is "No,"

for reasons that we can never understand. In the *Amida* we identify God as *Shome'a tefilla*, (He Who hears prayers) not as *Oneh latefilla* (He Who answers prayers). Perhaps we are praying for something that is not good for us, and God in His infinite wisdom knows that. That is how some sages understand the *Birkat HaḤodesh* prayer "*sheyimal'u mishalot libenu letova* – Our hearts' requests will be fulfilled *for the good*!" Sometimes God's response can come about slowly, or partially, in spite of our impatience. There are situations where the good things come over time – how many times have we heard someone who lost her job describe her despair, only to have her dream job come along in due course? On occasion, we don't get all that we hope for, but we need to appreciate what we did receive.

Consider the following example: I remember a time that I served as assistant principal to a principal who was taken ill with cancer. The students and I prayed for his recovery every single day for a year and a half. When he passed away, I confided to his widow that I was not prepared to face the students who would surely ask me why God had "rejected" their *tefillot*. Without missing a beat, she comforted me and said I should tell them that on the last day of his life, he was fully conscious. Each of his children and grandchildren came to his bedside to say they loved him and to say goodbye. He said *Viduy* with his rav. He had the strength to charge his children with continuing the ethical values and Jewish traditions they had grown up with in their parents' home. When his time came, he slipped away peacefully in his sleep. "Tell the students that if that's not having your prayers answered," she concluded, "I don't know what is."

Sometimes, perhaps, we need to draw the conclusion that we have to pray "better," that we have to improve our technique, pray more frequently or more fervently, lead the services, raise our voices higher, spend more time in prayer, petition more passionately, or give charity before prayer.

CONCRETE STEPS TO FIND MORE INSPIRATION FROM PRAYER

We each must seek to find our unique way to make our *tefilla* experience more personal and inspirational. These might include: Choosing a siddur that works for you. Choose one with a better translation, or an interlinear translation, or an inspirational commentary. When using the siddur during the week, make your own notes in pencil in the margin of your siddur. Think of something that uplifts you that relates to a particular paragraph in the service. Study the prayers

when you are not praying so you can better understand the words when you do pray. Like the Hasidim of old, prepare for engagement with God with study, with introspection, with an uplifting story, with a beautiful *nigun*. Dress as if you are going to meet royalty. Wash your hands. Close your eyes; visualize yourself as an integral and everlasting part of the Jewish people. Concentrate on the One before Whom you stand. Set goals to reach even higher levels of intensity in prayer. Make yourself vulnerable: imagine yourself yet again in the fragile situation in which you did feel moved to pray powerfully. When praying with others, see your prayer not only as a commandment between man and God, but also as an interpersonal *mitzva*, since our sincerity at prayer can contribute to a better ambience for everyone else's *tefilla* and inspire others as well. Make a careful list of all the people in your life and community who need God's help and concentrate on their needs when you pray. Many women find particular meaning in praying *Kabbalat Shabbat* with their daughters if they are not going to the synagogue on Friday nights. Make your *tefilla* time sacred and do not relinquish it no matter how pressed you are for time. Feel as if the welfare of the entire community depends on your passionate prayer. Take pride in your ability to balance the humility required to acknowledge our dependence on God with the confidence required to address Him directly and personally, with a deep understanding of the myriad needs and complex solutions required to help us mortals confront the challenges of everyday life in an ever-more challenging world.

CONCLUSION

Prayer then, is a multifaceted halakhic event as well as a very personal, challenging religious experience. It is objective and subjective, both bounded by parameters and flexible at the same time. R. Soloveitchik once observed that the *Beit Knesset* (synagogue) is the home of the collective prayers of *Knesset Yisrael* (the Jewish people of all times). Perhaps that is precisely what the prayer experience is – a blending of the thought and experience of the timeless efforts of the Jewish people to communicate with God, and an opportunity for Him to hear the harmony of the voices of His children. ◆

A More Meaningful Prayer Experience

R. David Mescheloff

The words of the prayers that are in this Siddur have been likened to a body. Your thoughts and feelings, your faith and belief, your sincere communications with God, are the soul that infuses that body with life.

Here are seven suggestions for enhancing your prayer experience with this Siddur:

1. As your soul gives life to your body, so it is your thoughts and feelings, your faith and belief, which give life and human significance to your words of prayer. Without them prayer has, at best, limited significance, and hardly fulfills any Jewish duty. So take your time, do not feel pressed "to keep up" with the Leader or the congregation. A little – with heartfelt meaning – is better than a lot without meaning. The halakhic instructions spell out the points at which you must join the congregation in prayer, and what you may have to skip in order to do so.
2. Our belonging to the Jewish people is a major component of our personal identities. Virtually all of our prayers are couched in the plural, for we pray not only for our own welfare, but for that of each and every one of our people and for our people as a whole. Moreover, praying is not only an intensely personal act; rather, whenever we pray the fixed prayers in this Siddur, many thousands of other Jews are praying the same prayers at the same time in our time zone, while many thousands of others are praying the other fixed prayers that are appropriate in their time zones. Our sages compared the Jewish people to a vast choir singing God's praises and serving Him together, using the same words, each in his or her own individual voice. Indeed, at any given time three different group voices rise from around planet Earth in prayer to God – *Ma'ariv, Shaḥarit*, and *Minḥa*. All choir members are called upon to put their full spirit into the words being sung, and every voice is needed to make the choir's service complete.
3. As you pray, ask yourself how what you are saying relates to your own personal needs, and to the needs of our people. Rambam noted that the central blessings of the weekday *Amida* comprise requests relating to all the fundamental spiritual and material needs of an individual, and to all the

fundamental spiritual and material needs of our people. By way of example – for our spiritual health we need the intelligence to distinguish right from wrong (חוֹנֵן הַדָּעַת), we need to know that we can correct our mistakes and that God wants and enables us to do so (הָרוֹצֶה בִּתְשׁוּבָה), and we need to earn forgiveness (חַנּוּן הַמַּרְבֶּה לִסְלֹחַ), so that we can move on to better lives. We need health (רוֹפֵא חוֹלֵי עַמּוֹ יִשְׂרָאֵל) and to earn a livelihood (מְבָרֵךְ הַשָּׁנִים). We long for the complete ingathering of our exiles (מְקַבֵּץ נִדְחֵי עַמּוֹ יִשְׂרָאֵל) and the rebuilding of the material, political, and spiritual infrastructure of Jerusalem (בּוֹנֵה יְרוּשָׁלָיִם). And so one may relate real life to all of our prayers.

4. Ours is an era of mass communication, but also of improved awareness of effective individual communication. Prayer is, *inter alia*, a form of individual communication with God. Thus when we pray we ought to speak freely, openly, and honestly – and keep our inner spiritual ears attuned to God's myriad answers as He speaks to each of us through the daily events of our individual lives.
5. Prayer should not be a burden. To the contrary, approach prayer with the full awareness of the many challenges on your shoulders, realizing that by sharing them with God you will find your burden lightened.
6. שִׁוִּיתִי ה׳ לְנֶגְדִּי תָמִיד – Keep in mind as you pray that you are standing before God, Whose complex relationship with each individual and with our people as a whole is an intensely personal one.
7. Finally, a practical tip: study the translation and commentaries *before* praying, in preparation for praying, preferably in the quiet of your own home, by coming to the synagogue early to prepare yourself for prayer, or in study with your local rabbi. Praying and studying are two very different experiences, and each deserves its own special time and place. Do feel free, however, to use the aid of the translation as well as the commentary to enhance your prayer when necessary.

May *the words of our mouths and the meditations of our hearts* be acceptable before You, Lord, our Rock and our Redeemer! ◆

PAGINATION TABLE

Over the course of decades, many have become accustomed to the pagination system found in the earlier RCA Siddur. For such users, we here provide a listing of corresponding page numbers (see facing page) for the more commonly referenced prayers, as found in both versions of the RCA Siddur.